the Southern Living® GARDEN BOOK

Edited by Steve Bender,
Senior Writer, *Southern Living*

Oxmoor
House®

Southern Living® Garden Book
Editor: Steve Bender
Managing Editors: Pamela Cornelison, Fiona Gilsenan
Senior Editor: Tom Wilhite
Art Director, Design and Production Director: Alice Rogers
Consulting Art Directors: Cynthia Cooper, Melissa Clark
Consulting Editors: Bob Doyle, John R. Dunmire, Philip Edinger,
    Suzanne Normand Eyre, Marianne Lipanovich, Janet H. Sanchez
Writers: Susan Lang, Lance Walheim
Researchers: Lisa Cericola, Susan M. Guthrie
Photography Editor: Kimberly Parsons
Production Director: Lory Day
Chief Copy Editor: Rebecca LaBrum
Copy Editors: Pamela Evans, Christine Miklas, Libby Monteith
Proofreaders: Mary Roybal (principal), Alicia Eckley, Lura Dymond,
    Terry Nagel, Michelle Pollace, Elissa Rabellino, David Sweet
Computer Production: Linda M. Bouchard (principal),
    Elaine Holland, Janie Farn, Joan Olson, Janis Reed,
    Maureen Spuhler, David Van Ness
Indexer: Erin Hartshorn, The Well-Chosen Word
Botanical Illustrators: Jenny Speckels (principal), Mimi Osborne,
    Erin O'Toole
Map Design and Cartography: Reineck & Reineck, San Francisco
Icon Design: Elisa Tanaka

Southern Living®
Editor: John Alex Floyd, Jr.
Executive Editor: Derick Belden
Garden Editor: Gene B. Bussell
Associate Garden Editors: Ellen Ruoff Riley, Charlie Thigpen
Assistant Garden Editor: Edwin Marty
Photographers: Jean M. Allsopp, Ralph Anderson, Van Chaplin,
    Tina Cornett, Sylvia Martin, Allen Rokach
Photo Services Director: Ann Nathews
Photo Librarian: Tracy Duncan
Photo Services: Amanda Abbett, Ginny P. Allen, Greg Cosby,
    Lisa Trial, Roseanna Whiteside
Editorial Assistant: Lynne Long

10 9 8 7 6 5 4 3 2
First printing January 2004

Copyright © by Oxmoor House, Inc.
Book Division of Southern Progress Corporation
P.O. Box 2463, Birmingham, Alabama 35201

Southern Living® is a federally registered trademark
    of Southern Living, Inc.

Hardcover Edition:
Library of Congress Catalog Control Number 2003110194
ISBN: 0-376-03909-1
Softcover Edition
Library of Congress Catalog Control Number 2003110194
ISBN: 0-376-03910-8

Cover photograph: Black-eyed Susans, Ralph Anderson
Title page photograph: Camellias, Van Chaplin
Copyright page photograph: Hollyhocks and hydrangeas,
    Van Chaplin

Welcome

"The chief knowledge that a man gets from reading books," wrote H.L. Mencken, "is the knowledge that very few of them are worth reading." All modesty aside, the *Southern Living Garden Book* is one of them. We've literally packed it from cover to cover with the very latest information useful to both beginning and experienced gardeners alike.

Try these numbers on for size—we've added 2,000 more plants, bringing the grand total of plant listings to more than 7,000. We've added scores of beautiful photographs to both the "Southern Plant Encyclopedia" and "A Practical Guide to Gardening." Thousands of plants described here carry both a *Southern Living* Climate Zone rating and an American Horticultural Society Heat Zone rating. And I'm pleased to say that every plant illustration is now in living color.

This new *Southern Living Garden Book* may be bigger and better, but its core remains the same. Written and researched by Southerners for Southerners, it's the most comprehensive book on Southern gardening around. Thanks to the many talented people whose photographs and wisdom grace these pages. And thanks to you, our loyal readers, who make putting together a book like this one truly a labor of love.

Steve Bender
Editor

CONTENTS

Gardening for the New Century

A Lively Look Ahead

"It's tough to make predictions," Yogi Berra once said, "especially about the future." That's certainly true when it comes to Southern gardening. For more than two centuries, the South has prided itself on being a region apart—a place steeped in tradition, molded by family, and governed by seemingly limitless horizons. While those values remain, the way we live is changing.

We no longer farm, by and large. We commute. We get down on our knees only in prayer. Spare time is harder to find than a snowball in the Amazon. Mayberry just opened a technology park.

Far left: 'Watermelon Red' crepe myrtles
Above: Picking sunflowers

We are, by and large, a far-flung, fast-moving and affluent people now, and they call us, not the South, but the Sunbelt. But here is the truth: Look into a Southern heart and there at its core, in the secret place where we have our beings, you will find the roots of home.

—Anne Rivers Siddons

Above: Hedge trimmers are the artist's tool at Pearl Fryar's topiary garden in Bishopville, South Carolina.

Right: Palms, ferns, and water create a tropical oasis for Deborah Balter in Coconut Grove, Florida.

Given this, you might think that traditional Southern gardens are doomed to follow the friendly milkman into oblivion. But fear not. Southerners will keep what works, as we always have, but tweak the recipe to accommodate the brave new world of the 21st century. Whether we're happy with the results will ultimately depend on the priorities we establish today. As the Cheshire Cat reminded Alice when asked which way she ought to go, "That depends a good deal on where you want to get to."

Yuccas adorn the Pickens homestead in Columbus, Texas.

*My special cause, the one that alerts my interest and quickens
my pace of life, is to preserve the wildflowers and native plants that
define the regions of our land.*
— Lady Bird Johnson

They are to this day the sure image of the South:
grand old homes graced by glorious gardens.
—Charlie Thigpen

Mrs. Gertrude Gibson McGehee's family homestead in Verbena, Alabama.

New Trends, New Directions

One fact of life current and future generations of Southern gardeners will deal with is downsizing. Gone are the days of toiling alongside the family in the boundless vegetable garden out back. Chalk it up to lack of time, year-round fresh produce at the supermarket, or the advent of universal air-conditioning. Birmingham author John Logue ruefully recalls his childhood garden in Pine Apple, Alabama: "My father's idea of a modest garden was 1 acre. I remember it as a long day's journey into night."

Above: Glimpsing the future—growing vegetables and flowers in a small space. Right: Proud of the past—Drew Collier still tends a 12-acre garden in Cleveland, Alabama.

No matter where there is a garden, its essence lies in one simple, satisfying combination—here is a person, and here is the earth.

—Charles McNair

No occupation is so delightful to me as the culture of the earth, and no culture comparable to that of the garden.
— Thomas Jefferson

Gardens may be getting smaller, but they're using more water, primarily because of our love affair with lawns. Scarcely a house can be built in the South now without an in-ground lawn sprinkler system that comes on daily, rain or shine. Unfortunately, water supplies aren't keeping up with demand; a day of reckoning is fast approaching. We can avoid a crisis by choosing plants that tolerate drought, by mulching planting beds, by making lawns smaller, and by watering only when plants really need it. As Mark Twain put it, "Water, taken in moderation, cannot hurt anybody."

A more thoughtful approach might also be applied to pesticides. Generations have grown up thinking of these products as medicines for the garden. And indeed they were. So efficiently did they dispatch mosquitoes, aphids, beetles, caterpillars, mildew, leaf spots, and dandelions that, as with water, we started using them by reflex. We didn't read the labels. We sprayed first and asked questions later. The results are legions of resistant pests as well as a host of potential health problems for people.

Today's gardeners want pesticides that are both safe and family friendly. Some look to "organic" ones made from naturally occurring, biodegradable chemicals that originate in plants. Others tout biological controls, such as beneficial insects, that restore nature's system of checks and balances. This concept of working with the environment is not exactly new. The French author Voltaire expressed it more than 200 years ago. "The art of medicine," he wrote, "consists of amusing the patient while nature cures the disease."

Left: Agarita, autumn sage, purple fountain grass, and candlestick tree thrive with little water in this Austin, Texas garden.

'Golden Russet' apple

Purple coneflower

Blackberry

*Live oak allee, Seaside Farms,
Mt. Pleasant, South Carolina*

The special charm of a Southern spring is its earliness;
it is as long drawn out as it is sweet.

—Elizabeth Lawrence

Above: Dwarf crested irises

Left: Family cemetery, Newnan, Georgia

Below: Art Tucker garden, Camden, Delaware

Opposite page: 'George Lindley Taber' azalea

Gardens with Personality

Years ago, when the gardening world thought that all significant horticulture halted just north of the Mason-Dixon Line, hot, cheery, assertive colors were deemed tacky and bohemian. Cool, tranquil colors showed true sophistication. But as times passed and our choices of plants grew, Southern gardeners had an amazing epiphany: pink + lavender + white = boring. Radiant scarlets, oranges, and yellows made our gardens ring.

Pam Baggett of Singing Springs Nursery in Cedar Grove, North Carolina agrees. "We've gotten over wanting our gardens to look soft and silver like British gardens," she concludes. "People are injecting more personality into their gardens."

For proof, just visit the Bishopville, South Carolina garden of Pearl Fryar, whose 3-acres of topiary showcases hundreds of evergreen and deciduous plants pruned into fanciful forms. "Most plants I have are the same as you'd find in any garden in Bishopville," he says. "The difference is, I believed in my art and went one step further."

So did Leon ("Doctor Dirt") Goldsberry of Edwards, Mississippi. His swept yard cottage garden teems with sunflowers, cosmos, four o'clocks, dahlias, and angel's trumpets. Some folks dismiss his yard as a jungle, but he takes such criticism in stride. Leon observes, "Suburbia is so artificial—everything's in rows. But I like to be an individual. Society ladies will say, 'Oooh, you can't mix those colors,' And I'll say, 'Says who?'"

Of course, a free-form cottage garden isn't for everybody. Many of us desire a more structured approach, in which fences, gates, walks, and evergreens form the "bones" of the garden, framing views and shaping different spaces. Careful planning invariably leads to a happier result. Good design is a hallmark of the gardens that appear in *Southern Living*.

Top: Mexican flame vine; middle: A bounty of cut flowers; left: 'Heritage' rose

Leon ("Doctor Dirt") Goldsberry on the Mississippi Delta shares mustard seedlings and much more from his garden.

In the beginning, God put us in a garden. That is where we all come from.

—Leon Goldsberry

*Peg and Truman Moore garden
Charleston, South Carolina*

The Good News Remains

Times may change, but the fundamental things we love about living and gardening here do not. Our mild climate, for example, constantly draws us outdoors. "It's a joy to have things growing and blooming all year-round," says Charleston, South Carolina gardener Peg Moore. "You don't have to endure nine months of nothing, like you do up North." Moreover, our position at a crossroads between cold weather and tropical regions means we can grow an extremely varied palette of plants, from California poppies to Canadian hemlocks to Florida flame azaleas.

Southerners will always instinctively view plants as an ideal way of connecting with people. No one understands this better than octogenarian Margaret Moseley, as she gazes upon the many shared plants that grace her garden in Decatur, Georgia. "I think I can name every friend I have just by looking out there," she says.

Margaret Moseley in her Decatur, Georgia garden

My garden is like a fruitcake. If you stick a shovel in, you hit a lot of things.

—Margaret Sanders

Angel's trumpet

Orchid tree

Hardy begonia

Cross vine

Kay Bullitt garden, Louisville, K

Far left: Black-eyed Susans; middle left: hosta; middle right: daylily; far right: Mexican bush sage

Bob and Mary Anne Pickens sense this too. At their restored homestead in Columbus, Texas, they treasure the snowflakes, narcissus, oxblood lilies, and grape hyacinths planted by her grandmother decades ago. The yucca that blooms in their front yard each year descends from a plant featured in a painting of the original garden done in 1863.

Gardening in the South is, and will always be, an optimistic enterprise. No failure will ever be permanent, so long as faith, curiosity, and the love of nature endure. Carter Giltinan, a gardener in Charleston, West Virginia, expresses it beautifully. "The garden," she says, "is full of hope in the morning—and so am I."

Far left: Plumleaf azalea; middle left: bluebonnets; middle right: windmill palm; far right: 'Okame' flowering cherry

"If you wait until the wind and the weather are just right, you will never plant anything and never harvest anything."

—Ancient proverb

The South's
Climate Zones

Anyone who says, "If you don't like the weather, wait ten minutes and it'll change," isn't talking about the South. Southern weather isn't fickle; it's stubborn as a mule. When it's hot, it stays hot. And when it turns cold and rainy, you'd better get used to it.

Our land is one of climatic extremes: withering heat, merciless drought, unrelenting downpours, paralyzing ice storms, and restless wind. This doesn't mean we don't have our share of good weather—we do. But gardening here can be challenging. To succeed requires the necessary resources, and no resource is more important than a good climate zone map.

Knowing what climate zone you live in can help answer everyday questions: When can I set out tomato plants? Why won't my hydrangea bloom? Should I plant Kentucky bluegrass or St. Augustine? Is passion vine hardy here?

READING THE MAPS

Southern Living divides the South into five broad climate zones: Upper South (US), Middle South (MS), Lower South (LS), Coastal South (CS), and Tropical South (TS). The boundaries of these zones correspond to those of the recently updated United States Department of Agriculture (USDA) Plant Hardiness Zone Map. The Upper South is in USDA Zone 6, the Middle South in Zone 7, the Lower South in Zone 8, the Coastal South in Zone 9, and the Tropical South in Zone 10. You'll find our *Southern Living* map on pages 30–31.

It's important to note that because the USDA map reflects minimum yearly temperatures, it functions solely as a cold-hardiness map. In the South, however, heat is as much a limiting factor as cold. Therefore, when we give a plant a *Southern Living* climate zone rating, we take into account both summer heat and winter cold. For example, if we recommend astilbe as a permanent plant for your area, we mean that it will not only survive your winters but also endure your summers, and that it will perform satisfactorily for you. We won't recommend astilbe for the Coastal or Tropical South, because although it takes

winters there, in summer it melts faster than ice sculptures on a cruise ship.

To help you pinpoint the climate zone in which you garden, we've greatly enlarged the map that regularly appears in *Southern Living*. We've also added many more details, such as major cities, rivers, and interstate highways. Once you've identified your climate zone, be sure to check our zone ratings in the Plant Encyclopedia listings to verify that a particular plant will grow well in your area.

Because heat takes such a toll on plants in the South, this book features an extra tool to help you fine-tune your choices— the American Horticultural Society (AHS) Plant Heat Zone Map. This map, found on pages 32–33, divides the United States into 12 zones. Heat zones are based on the average number of days in the year that high temperatures reach or exceed 86 degrees F, the point at which plants suffer heat stress. Most plant listings in our encyclopedia show both the *Southern Living* rating and the heat zone rating. You'll notice that the heat zone rating has two numbers. The first indicates the warmest zone in which the plant will thrive, the second the coolest zone in which it will bloom or bear fruit.

Keep in mind that the AHS heat zone system is still a work in progress. We've adjusted some of the ratings slightly to better reflect our experience of Southern gardening. Heat zone ratings for two categories of plants—tropicals and cool-season annuals—may seem confusing at first, so let us explain.

Most tropical plants have a heat zone rating of 12–10. Does this mean they will grow only in southern Florida and southern Texas? No; it simply means that these are the only places gardeners can grow them outdoors year-round. However, many tropicals (such as philodendron) make fine houseplants for anyone. If that's the case, their rating might read "H 12–10; or houseplant." Other tropicals (such as tree ferns) are typically grown in pots that are taken outdoors during summer and brought indoors for the winter in cold-winter areas. In this case, the rating might be "H 12–10; or grow in pot."

Cool-season annuals and vegetables (such as pansy and cabbage) may be rated as 7–1, 6–1, or 5–1. This doesn't mean they grow only in the Upper South, but rather that it's the only zone where these plants will survive summer heat. Gardeners in warmer zones can grow them in cooler weather by planting in fall or winter.

STILL NO PROMISES

Despite all these up-to-date maps and data, we can't promise that a particular plant will grow for you. Many factors other than heat and cold determine a plant's ultimate fate—factors such as elevation, soil pH, topography, prevailing winds, sun exposure, humidity, nearby structures, and proximity to water. Taken together, these produce a multitude of microclimates too small to show on a map. This is why the *Southern Living* map has only five zones. We purposely made it simple to use and

understand. Consider it a guideline, rather than a guarantee.

As any veteran gardener will attest, all the scientific data in the world are no substitute for your own real-life experiences and those of your neighbors. If you wonder whether a particular species will thrive in your garden, first consult the two maps here. Then ask neighbors, friends, garden club members, and local garden centers what they think.

No matter how accomplished a gardener you become, some favorite plants will inevitably die. Don't be bitter. Plenty of other great plants await your discovery, providing the chance to plant something even better, bigger, or even more beautiful. In the words of Henry Mitchell—the late, great garden columnist for the Washington Post—"If hard experience shows you that for some reason you cannot grow good lilies, peonies, lilacs, or irises, then concentrate on flowers that do well for you."

The Southern Zones

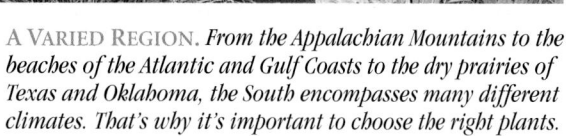

A VARIED REGION. *From the Appalachian Mountains to the beaches of the Atlantic and Gulf Coasts to the dry prairies of Texas and Oklahoma, the South encompasses many different climates. That's why it's important to choose the right plants.*

The Southern Living
Climate Zones

IOWA

NEBRASKA

COLORADO

Denver

70

70

70

70

KANSAS

35

135

Wichita

Missouri River

Kansas City

70

7

MISS

13

44

Springfield

44

Arkansas River

25

Rio Grande River

Santa Fe

40

25

Albuquerque

40

NEW MEXICO

25

Roswell

Alamogordo

10

10

MEXICO

Rio Grande River

El Paso

10

20

Odessa

Davis
Mountains

Lower
South

Upper
South

TEXAS

Amarillo

40

Middle
South

27

Lubbock

Wichita
Falls

287

Abilene

Midland

20

OKLAHOMA

40

Oklahoma
City

44

35

Lake
Texoma

Tulsa

44

40

Fort
Smith

Ouachita
Mountains

Boste
Moun

Arkansas River

Ouachita
Mountains

ARKA

30

Fort
Worth

Dallas

30

20

Shreveport

20

167

49

84

35

45

Lower
South

Waco

10

Davis
Mountains

10

TEXAS

45

Austin

Lake
Charles

Co
So

LOU

Houston

10

Gulf of
Mexico

San
Antonio

35

37

Rio Grande R.

Coastal
South

Corpus
Christi

Tropical
South

Brownsville

10

45

Average Annual Minimum Temperature

Temperature (°F)	Zone Color
-20 to -1	Upper South
0 to 10	Middle South
11 to 20	Lower South
21 to 30	Coastal South
31 to 40	Tropical South

ILLINOIS

INDIANA

OHIO

PENNSYLVANIA

- Pittsburgh
Philadelphia
- Wilmington

Wheeling
Columbus
Indianapolis
Cincinnati

WEST VIRGINIA

Appalachian Mountains

Cumberland
Frederick
Baltimore
Washington, D.C.
Alexandria

DELAWARE

Delaware Bay
Dover

MARYLAND

Chesapeake Bay

Charleston

Charlottesville
Richmond

VIRGINIA

Lynchburg

Virginia Beach

Cape Girardeau

Louisville
Lexington

KENTUCKY

Upper South

Appalachian Mountains

Middle South

Lower South

Greenville

Bowling Green

Paducah

Winston-Salem
Durham
Greensboro
Raleigh

NORTH CAROLINA

Nashville
Knoxville
Asheville

Charlotte

TENNESSEE

Middle South

Appalachian Mountains

Spartanburg
Greenville

Wilmington

Memphis
Huntsville

Chattanooga

Blue Ridge Mountains

Columbia

SOUTH CAROLINA

Florence

Tupelo

Gadsden

Atlanta

Augusta

Charleston

MISSISSIPPI

Columbus

Birmingham
Anniston
Tuscaloosa

Macon

Savannah

ALABAMA

Columbus

GEORGIA

Coastal South

Atlantic Ocean

Jackson
Meridian

Montgomery

Lower South

Albany

Okefenokee Swamp

Hattiesburg

Dothan

Jacksonville

Baton Rouge
Biloxi
Mobile

Pensacola

Tallahassee

Lake Maurepas
Lake Pontchartrain
Lake Borgne

New Orleans

Mississippi R. The Delta

Gainesville

Lake George

Daytona Beach

Coastal South

Orlando

Tampa

FLORIDA

Gulf of Mexico

Fort Myers

Lake Okeechobee

Sanibel Island

Miami

Tropical South

The Everglades

Florida Keys

Key West

0   50   100   150 Miles

The American Horticultural Society
Plant Heat Zone Map

IOWA

NEBRASKA

COLORADO

Arkansas River

KANSAS

Missouri River

Kansas City (70)

(7)

MISS

(13)

Wichita

Springfield (44)

(35)

TEXAS

OKLAHOMA

Tulsa (44)

Amarillo (40)

(40)

Oklahoma City

(40)

Fort Smith

Arkansas River

NEW MEXICO

(27)

(44)

(35)

Ouachita Mountains

Bost Mour

Ouachita Mountains

ARKA

Lubbock

Wichita Falls

(287)

Lake Texoma

(30)

Fort Worth

Dallas

(30)

Abilene

(20)

(20)

(20)

Shreveport

(20)

(167)

El Paso

(35)

(45)

(49) (84)

Midland

(20)

Odessa

Waco

TEXAS

Davis Mountains

(10)

(10)

(45)

Lake Charles

(10)

Austin

Houston

(10)

LOU

(10)

San Antonio

(45)

(35)

MEXICO

(37)

Corpus Christi

Rio Grande R.

Gulf of Mexico

Brownsville

Zone Color	Average Number of Days per Year Above 86°F
1	Less than 1
2	1-7
3	8-14
4	15-30
5	31-45
6	46-60
7	61-90
8	91-120
9	121-150
10	151-180
11	181-210
12	211 or more

Rio Grande River

(10)

INDIANA

OHIO

PENNSYLVANIA

ILLINOIS

• Pittsburgh

Philadelphia

76   83   • Wilmington

70   Wheeling   70   81   95   Delaware
                          70   Bay
68   Cumberland   Frederick   Baltimore   Dover

• Columbus   WEST   Appalachian   66   • Alexandria   DELAWARE
70   VIRGINIA   Mountains   29   Washington, D.C.   MARYLAND
75   71   81
Indianapolis   74   • Cincinnati   77   79   • Charleston   64   • Charlottesville   Chesapeake
                                        Richmond   Bay
71   75   64   • Lexington   81   VIRGINIA   64   Virginia
• Louisville   77   VIRGINIA   360   Beach
                Lynchburg   95
KENTUCKY   Appalachian   85
65   Mountains   77
                        Winston-   29
• Bowling   75   Salem   40   • Durham
Green   81   181   Greensboro   • Raleigh   Greenville
                                NORTH
24   • Nashville   Knoxville   Asheville   40   77   85   CAROLINA
TENNESSEE   40   26   • Charlotte   40
65   24   • Chattanooga   Appalachian   Spartanburg
                        Mountains   Greenville   77   • Wilmington
                        Blue   385   95
• Memphis   78   • Tupelo   Ridge   Columbia   20   • Florence
                        Mountains   SOUTH
40   45   • Huntsville   26   CAROLINA
78   59   515   20
Tupelo   65   • Gadsden   20   Augusta
MISSISSIPPI   78   • Atlanta   20
Columbus   Birmingham   Anniston   85   95   • Charleston
20   65   185   75   • Macon
59   Tuscaloosa   85   • Columbus
ALABAMA   16   • Savannah
Jackson   Meridian   Montgomery   GEORGIA
49   59   Albany   95   Atlantic
Hattiesburg   65   Dothan   75   Ocean
45   Okefenokee
49   Mobile   10   Swamp
Biloxi   10   • Pensacola   10   Tallahassee   10   • Jacksonville
                                75   301
                                        95
Lake   12   Gainesville   27   Lake   Daytona
Maurepas Lake   George   Beach
Pontchartrain   4
New   Lake   75   27   • Orlando
Orleans   Borgne   4
Mississippi R. The   Tampa   FLORIDA
Delta   75
                                27   95
                                Fort   Lake Okeechobee
                                Myers   80   80
                                Sanibel   27   95
                                Island   75
                                        • Miami
Gulf of   The
Mexico   Everglades

0   50   100   150 Miles   Florida
                                Keys
                Key West

33

The Upper South

The Upper South experiences the longest winters and shortest summers in our region. But summers are still hot and sticky. Some sample record highs are 108 in Lexington, Kentucky, 107 in Charlottesville, and 115 in St. Louis. Fortunately, such sizzling temperatures seldom last long. Summer nights usually drop into the 60s, a necessity for the many cool-weather plants that grow here. Winter lows range from 0 to minus 10 degrees, but severe freezes have pushed the mercury as low as minus 16 degrees in Charleston, West Virginia, and minus 29 degrees in Springfield, Missouri. The last frost occurs anywhere from mid-April to the first 10 days of May.

Plants that need cool nights and long periods of winter chill do well here. Cold winters bring constraints, however. Frozen soil means that dahlias, cannas, glads, and other summer-flowering bulbs must be dug up in fall and stored over winter. Crepe myrtles, camellias, and figs may not be cold-hardy in all areas.

FLOWER POWER. *The Blue Ridge Mountains provide a dramatic background for this outstanding display of black-eyed Susans, purple coneflowers, Russian sage, butterfly weed, Sedum 'Vera Jameson', and moor grass. Warm summer days and cool nights extend the floral show.*

10 GREAT PLANTS FOR THE UPPER SOUTH: astilbe, Colorado blue spruce, delphinium, highbush blueberry, Japanese pachysandra, Japanese yew *(Taxus)*, lilac, rhododendron, sugar maple, and white pine

'Trude Webster' rhododendron

ABOVE: 'Ostrich Plume' astilbe
RIGHT: Eastern white pine

'Sara Bernhardt' peony

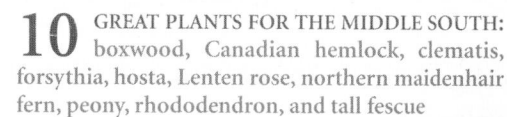

10 GREAT PLANTS FOR THE MIDDLE SOUTH: boxwood, Canadian hemlock, clematis, forsythia, hosta, Lenten rose, northern maidenhair fern, peony, rhododendron, and tall fescue

TOP: 'Blue Angel' hosta
ABOVE: 'Henryi' clematis

The Middle South

The Middle South forms a transition zone between warm-weather and cool-weather growing zones. Here you often encounter plants from the Northeast, the Midwest, and the Northwest growing alongside Southern natives.

Summers are hot and, in most places, humid, though nights cool off in the mountains. Winter lows typically range from 0 to 10 degrees F, but Lubbock has shivered through minus 16 degrees and Nashville has survived a low of minus 17. The last spring frost generally occurs in the last two weeks of April.

AMAZING GRACE. *A weeping katsura tree* (Cercidiphyllum japonicum) *and a red Japanese maple frame a spectacular pond garden in the Middle South. The area's moderate climate permits such winning combinations of both warm-weather and cool-weather plants.*

The Lower South

Spring comes early to the Lower South. Daffodils, flowering quince, and winter daphne open their buds in February. Flowering dogwood, Yoshino cherry, and eastern redbud put on a dazzling show in March. Summer is hot and sultry. Though summer droughts are common, torrential downpours more than make up the difference—Birmingham and Jackson both receive about 55 inches of rain a year. Winter lows usually range from 10 to 20 degrees F, but occasionally plummet below zero. Snow is rare, but ice storms are not. The last spring frost generally occurs in the first two weeks of April.

Lilacs and rhododendrons often flop here, but cannas, glads, dahlias, and elephant's ears usually overwinter in the ground. The Lower South marks the northern limit for many mild-weather plants such as Lady Banks's rose, holly fern, Indian hawthorn, and windmill palm. Tulips and hyacinths may need refrigeration in order to bloom well.

'Galaxy' Magnolia

'Cherokee Chief' flowering dogwood, hostas

THE ENDLESS SUMMER. *Plants that need lots of heat and a long growing season find things to their liking in the Lower South. Once things warm up in April and May, they stay nice and steamy into October. The folks here are used to it, and so are their gardens.*

10 GREAT PLANTS FOR THE LOWER SOUTH: azalea, camellia, crepe myrtle, daffodil, daylily, dogwood, hydrangea, Southern magnolia, watermelon, and zoysia grass

Watermelon

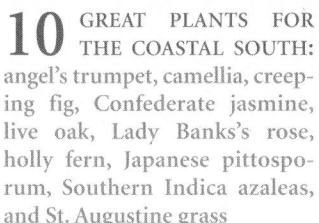

10 GREAT PLANTS FOR THE COASTAL SOUTH: angel's trumpet, camellia, creeping fig, Confederate jasmine, live oak, Lady Banks's rose, holly fern, Japanese pittosporum, Southern Indica azaleas, and St. Augustine grass

LEFT: Lady Banks's rose
ABOVE: Angel's trumpet

A garden by the sea

Two large bodies of water—the Atlantic Ocean and the Gulf of Mexico—rule the Coastal South. Their close proximity ensures that winters are mild and brief but summers long and humid. Winter lows can drop to 17 to 25 degrees F at the northern end of this zone and 25 to 32 degrees at the southern end. The last spring frost usually comes in the second or third week in March. Spring commences in January, when the oriental magnolias and common camellias bloom.

The Coastal South

The luxurious growth associated with the Old South is promoted by high rainfall. Mobile receives the highest annual rainfall of any city in the continental United States—64 inches a year.

GARDENS BY THE SEA. *Long, humid summers and short, mild winters characterize the Coastal South. The moderating influence of the Atlantic Ocean and Gulf of Mexico reduce extremes of temperature. Subtropical plants abound, such as oleander, bougainvillea, gingers, palms, and loquat. Citrus trees grow in the lower end of the range. Of course, every few years a freeze comes through and lays waste to these and other tender plants. But gardens here recover so quickly that the damage is soon forgotten. Winter is a great time for gardening in this region—cool-weather flowers and vegetables absolutely thrive during the cooler months.*

The Tropical South is its own gardening world. It rarely feels frost—in fact, the lowest temperature on record for Miami is 30 degrees F. Annual rainfall averages about 26 inches in Brownsville,

The Tropical South

Texas, and more than twice that across the lower Florida peninsula. Whereas most of the South deals with dry summers and wet winters, a large portion of the Tropical South reverses that pattern.

All sorts of lush, exotic plants with strikingly colorful blooms and foliage flourish. To outsiders, this region can seem like a paradise. But the lack of winter chill comes at a price. Apples, azaleas, forsythia, hosta, hydrangeas, and many other temperate plants fail here.

A SPECIAL PLACE. *In a region where cold is a stranger, the gardens grow lush and exotic. That's just how it is in the Tropical South, home to tree ferns, mango trees, cycads, palms, bird-of-paradise, bromeliads, and passion vines. Gardening here is truly a year-round experience, with something in bloom every month.*

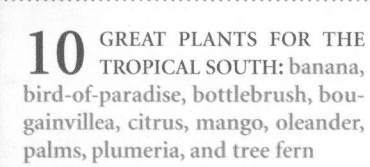

10 GREAT PLANTS FOR THE TROPICAL SOUTH: banana, bird-of-paradise, bottlebrush, bougainvillea, citrus, mango, oleander, palms, plumeria, and tree fern

Bird-of-paradise

Mucho mangos

Kumquat

A Guide to
Plant Selection

The thousands of plants described in the A to Z Plant Encyclopedia *(beginning on page 145) include an infinitely varied assortment of sizes, shapes, textures, and colors. The pleasure of choosing from such abundance is available to anyone with a sense of adventure and a bit of earth. But such a choice can sometimes be bewildering. The lists of plants that follow, used with the Plant Encyclopedia, will help you to select the right plants— whether you are looking to achieve a special effect with flowers or foliage, tackling a difficult landscape situation, or starting out with the basics.*

Bougainvillea and nasturtium

Sun

☼ Grows best with unobstructed sunlight all day long or almost all day—you can overlook an hour or so of shade at the beginning or end of a summer day

◐ Needs partial shade—that is, shade for half the day or for at least 3 hours during the hottest part of the day

● Prefers little or no direct sunlight—for example, it does best on the north side of a house or beneath a broad, dense tree

Water

○ Needs no supplemental watering once it is established—usually 1 or 2 years after planting

◔ Thrives with less than regular moisture—moderate amounts for some plants, little for those with more drought tolerance

◐ Performs well with regular moisture

◕ Takes more than regular moisture—includes plants needing constantly moist soil, bog plants, and aquatic plants

Climate

A plant's climate adaptability is shown after the symbol ✎. The letters US, MS, LS, CS, and TS refer to the *Southern Living* Climate Zones (✎). For more information on these climate zones, and on the American Horticultural Society (AHS) heat zones, see pages 28–38.

Color

Basic Landscaping

Special Situations

Snapdragon
Antirrhinum majus

Annuals
for Seasonal Color

Flowering annuals provide quick, nonstop color and come in a nearly boundless variety of colors, shapes, and sizes. Yes, most die after one growing season, but that gives you the chance to try something new. Cool-season annuals prefer cool weather, blossoming in spring and fall (and, in mild climates, winter). Warm-season annuals hate frost but love the heat, generally blooming from late spring to fall. Plants marked with the symbol ✷ are actually tender perennials that may live from year to year in mild-winter areas.

Carefree spires of larkspur (*Consolida ajacis*) bloom in spring.

California poppy
Eschscholzia californica

Delphinium

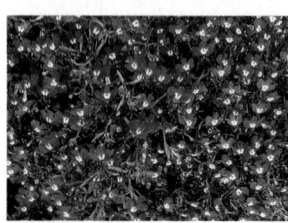

Edging lobelia
Lobelia erinus

Flowering cabbage

COOL-SEASON ANNUALS

Calendula
☼ ◑ ◐ ✎ ALL
Calendula officinalis — p. 216

California poppy
☼ ◯ ◐ ◑ ✎ ALL
Eschscholzia californica — p. 302

Delphinium
☼ ◐ ✎ VARY
— p. 281

Edging lobelia
◐ ◑ ◐ ◑ ◐ ✎ ALL
Lobelia erinus — p. 396

English daisy ✷
☼ ◐ ◐ ✎ US, MS, LS, TS
Bellis perennis — p. 198

English wallflower
☼ ◐ ◯ ◐ ◑ ✎ VARY
Erysimum cheiri — p. 300

Flowering cabbage and kale
☼ ◐ ◐ ✎ ALL
— p. 214

Forget-me-not
◐ ◐ ✎ US, MS, LS
Myosotis sylvatica — p. 425

Foxglove
◐ ◐ ◐ ✎ US, MS, LS, CS
Digitalis — p. 287

Larkspur
☼ ◐ ◑ ✎ ALL
Consolida ajacis — p. 258

Lupine
☼ ◯ ◐ ◑ ✎ VARY
Lupinus — p. 398

Monkey flower
◐ ◐ ✎ ALL
Mimulus × hybridus — p. 419

Pansy, viola, violet
☼ ◐ ◐ ◑ ✎ VARY
Viola — p. 587

Poppy (some)
☼ ◐ ◑ ✎ VARY
Papaver — p. 445

Primrose (many)
◐ ◐ ✎ VARY
Primula — p. 491

Snapdragon
☼ ◐ ✎ ALL
Antirrhinum majus — p. 169

Stock
☼ ◐ ◐ ✎ ALL
Matthiola incana — p. 415

Sweet William ✷
☼ ◐ ◐ ✎ ALL
Dianthus barbatus — p. 283

Twinspur
☼ ◐ ◐ ✎ VARY
Diascia — p. 284

WARM-SEASON ANNUALS

Amethyst flower ✷
◐ ◐ ✎ ALL
Browallia — p. 209

Angelonia ✷
☼ ◐ ✎ LS, CS, TS
Angelonia angustifolia — p. 167

Annual phlox
☼ ◐ ✎ ALL
Phlox drummondii — p. 469

Bachelor's button
☼ ◐ ✎ ALL
Centaurea cyanus — p. 234

Bat-faced cuphea ✷
☼ ◐ ◐ ✎ CS, TS, OR ANNUAL
Cuphea llavea — p. 272

Lupine
Lupinus, Russell hybrid

Bat-faced cuphea
Cuphea llavea

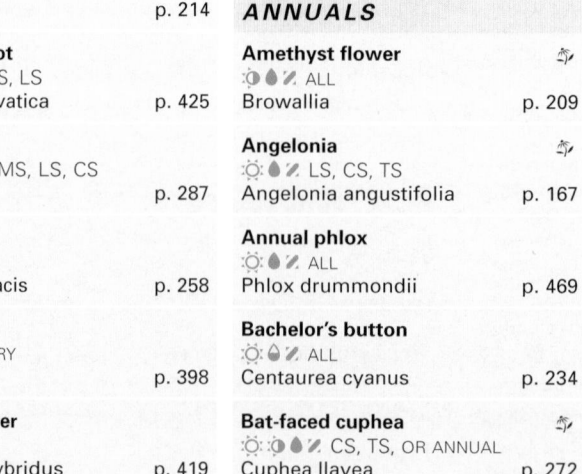

Stock
Matthiola incana

For growing symbol explanations, please see page 39.

Coleus
Coleus × hybridus

Flowering tobacco
Nicotiana sylvestris

Globe amaranth
Gomphrena globosa

Impatiens

Begonia
ALL
p. 196

Blue daze
ALL
Evolvulus glomeratus   p. 307

Calliopsis
ALL
Coreopsis tinctoria   p. 260

Cockscomb
ALL
Celosia argentea   p. 233

Coleus
ALL
Coleus × hybridus   p. 256

Copper leaf
ALL
Acalypha wilkesiana   p. 148

Corn cockle
ALL
Agrostemma githago   p. 157

Cosmos, common
ALL
Cosmos bipinnatus   p. 265

Fanflower
ALL
Scaevola aemula   p. 537

Floss flower
ALL
Ageratum houstonianum   p. 156

Flowering tobacco
ALL
Nicotiana   p. 431

Geranium
ALL
Pelargonium   p. 458

Globe amaranth
ALL
Gomphrena   p. 326

Heliotrope, common
ALL
Heliotropium arborescens   p. 341

Impatiens
ALL
p. 358

Indian blanket
ALL
Gaillardia pulchella   p. 318

Lantana
ALL
p. 382

Lisianthus
ALL
Eustoma grandiflorum   p. 307

Madagascar periwinkle
ALL
Catharanthus roseus   p. 231

Mexican sunflower
ALL
Tithonia rotundifolia   p. 573

Million bells
ALL
Calibrachoa   p. 216

Money plant
US, MS, LS, CS
Lunaria annua   p. 398

Moss rose
ALL
Portulaca grandiflora   p. 489

Nasturtium
ALL
Tropaeolum majus   p. 577

Ornamental pepper
ALL
p. 462

Perilla
ALL
Perilla frutescens   p. 463

Petunia
ALL
Petunia × hybrida   p. 465

Pink (some)
US, MS, LS, CS
Dianthus   p. 283

Silk flower
ALL
Abelmoschus moschatus   p. 146

Spider flower
ALL
Cleome hasslerana   p. 252

Star Daisy
ALL
Melampodium paludosum   p. 416

Strawflower
ALL
Helichrysum bracteatum   p. 339

Sunflower, common
ALL
Helianthus annuus   p. 339

Swan River daisy
ALL
Brachyscome iberidifolia   p. 207

Sweet alyssum
ALL
Lobularia maritima   p. 396

Verbena (some)
VARY
p. 583

Wishbone flower
ALL
Torenia fournieri   p. 575

Zinnia
ALL
p. 595

Monkey flower
Mimulus × hybridus

Million bells
Calibrachoa

Nasturtium
Tropaeolum majus

Silk flower
Abelmoschus moschatus

Spider flower
Cleome hasslerana

Zinnia
Zinnia elegans

For climate zone explanations, please see pages 28–38.

Coral bells
Heuchera
× brizoides

Showy Perennials
for Beds and Borders

I t's sometimes said that a perennial is any plant that, had it survived, could have come back year after year. Fortunately, most
perennials are tougher than this, offering us decades of dazzling
flowers and foliage. Among their ranks you'll find an astonishing
array of choices, literally something for everyone. Perennials range
in size and shape from small mounds to giant towers, and there
are choices for every imaginable garden spot. Try out some new
plants this year. It's one of the things that makes gardening fun.

Geum, alliums, delphiniums, and verbascum.

Alstroemeria

New England aster
Aster novae-angliae

Balloon flower
Platycodon grandiflorus

Bee balm
Monarda didyma

Aconite
☼ ☼ ◑ ▲ ◔ ✂ US, MS
Aconitum   p. 152

Agastache
☼ ☼ ◑ ✂ VARY
                            p. 155

Alpinia
☼ ◑ ▲ ✂ VARY
                            p. 162

Alstroemeria
☼ ◑ ▲ ◔ ✂ MS, LS, CS
                            p. 162

Anthemis
☼ ◑ ▲ ✂ VARY
                            p. 168

Anthurium
☼ ◑ ▲ ✂ TS
                            p. 169

Asclepias
☼ ◑ ▲ ▲ ◔ ✂ VARY
                            p. 184

Aster
☼ ◑ ▲ ▲ ✂ US, MS, LS
                            p. 186

Baby's breath
☼ ◑ ▲ ✂ US, MS, LS, CS
Gypsophila paniculata   p. 335

Balloon flower
☼ ☼ ◑ ▲ ✂ US, MS, LS, CS
Platycodon grandiflorus   p. 479

Beard tongue
☼ ◑ ◑ ▲ ▲ ✂ VARY
Penstemon (many)   p. 461

Bear's breech
☼ ☼ ◑ ▲ ▲ ▲ ✂ US, MS, LS, CS
Acanthus mollis   p. 148

Bee balm
☼ ◑ ◑ ▲ ▲ ✂ US, MS, LS
Monarda didyma   p. 421

Bellflower
☼ ☼ ◑ ▲ ▲ ✂ US, MS, LS
Campanula   p. 223

Bergenia
☼ ◑ ▲ ▲ ✂ US, MS, LS
                            p. 199

Betony
☼ ◑ ▲ ✂ US, MS, LS
Stachys officinalis   p. 554

Bird of Paradise
☼ ☼ ◑ ▲ ✂ CS, TS
Strelitzia reginae   p. 559

Blanket flower
☼ ◔ ▲ ✂ ALL
Gaillardia × grandiflora   p. 318

Blazing star
☼ ◑ ▲ ✂ US, MS, LS, CS
Liatris   p. 389

Bleeding heart, common
◑ ▲ ✂ US, MS, LS, CS
Dicentra spectabilis   p. 285

Bluestar
☼ ☼ ◑ ▲ ▲ ✂ US, MS, LS, CS   p. 165
Amsonia tabernaemontana

Bowman's root
☼ ◑ ▲ ✂ US, MS, LS
Gillenia trifoliata   p. 324

Bush daisy
☼ ☼ ◔ ▲ ▲ ✂ CS, TS
Euryops pectinatus   p. 307

Butterfly weed
☼ ◑ ▲ ◔ ✂ US, MS, LS, CS
Asclepias tuberosa   p. 184

Candy lily
☼ ☼ ◑ ▲ ✂ ALL
× Pardancanda norrisii   p. 447

Cardinal flower
◑ ● ▲ ◔ ✂ US, MS, LS, CS
Lobelia cardinalis   p. 396

Beard tongue
Penstemon

Peach-leafed bluebell
Campanula persicifolia

Bleeding heart, common
Dicentra spectabilis

For growing symbol explanations, please see page 39.

Celandine poppy
☼ ◐ ● ◖ ✂ US, MS, LS
Stylophorum diphyllum   p. 560

Checkerbloom
☼ ● ◖ ✂ US, MS
Sidalcea   p. 544

Chilean avens
☼ ◐ ● ◖ ✂ US, MS
Geum chiloense   p. 323

Chinese foxglove
◐ ● ◖ ✂ MS, LS, CS
Rehmannia elata   p. 505

Chrysanthemum
☼ ● ◖ ✂ VARY
                              p. 243

Cinquefoil
☼ ◐ ● ◖ ✂ VARY
Potentilla   p. 490

Columbine
☼ ◐ ● ◖ ✂ VARY
Aquilegia   p. 176

Coneflower
☼ ◐ ● ◖ ✂ US, MS, LS, CS
Rudbeckia   p. 526

Coral bells
◐ ● ◖ ✂ US, MS, LS
Heuchera   p. 344

Coreopsis
☼ ◐ ○ ● ● ◖ ✂ US, MS, LS, CS
                              p. 260

Cranesbill
☼ ◐ ● ◖ ✂ US, MS, LS
Geranium   p. 322

Crinum
☼ ◐ ● ● ◐ ◖ ✂ VARY
                              p. 269

Crocosmia
☼ ◐ ● ◖ ✂ US, MS, LS, CS
                              p. 270

Cupid's dart
☼ ◐ ● ✂ US, MS, LS
Catananche caerulea   p. 231

Dancing girl ginger
◐ ● ✂ CS, TS
Globba   p. 325

Daylily
☼ ◐ ● ◖ ✂ ALL
Hemerocallis   p. 342

Delphinium
☼ ● ◖ ✂ VARY
                              p. 281

Dicliptera
☼ ◐ ○ ● ● ◖ ✂ VARY
                              p. 286

Euphorbia
☼ ◐ ● ● ● ● ◐ ◖ ✂ VARY
                              p. 305

Evergreen candytuft
☼ ● ◖ ✂ US, MS, LS
Iberis sempervirens   p. 355

False indigo
☼ ● ◖ ✂ US, MS, LS, CS
Baptisia   p. 194

False spiraea
☼ ◐ ● ◖ ✂ US, MS
Astilbe   p. 187

False sunflower
☼ ◐ ● ◖ ✂ US, MS, LS, CS
Heliopsis helianthoides   p. 340

Fanflower
☼ ● ● ◖ ✂ CS, TS OR ANNUAL
Scaevola aemula   p. 537

Filipendula
◐ ● ● ◖ ✂ US, MS, LS
                              p. 313

Firecracker plant
☼ ◐ ● ● ◖ ✂ CS, TS
Russelia equisetiformis   p. 527

Fortnight lily
☼ ◐ ● ● ◖ ✂ LS, CS, TS
Dietes iridioides   p. 287

Fountain grass
☼ ◐ ● ● ◖ ✂ VARY
Pennisetum   p. 460

Four o'clock
☼ ◐ ● ◖ ✂ ALL
Mirabilis jalapa   p. 420

Foxtail lily
☼ ● ◖ ✂ US, MS, LS
Eremurus   p. 299

Gas plant
☼ ◐ ● ● ◐ ◖ ✂ US, MS, LS
Dictamnus albus   p. 286

Gaura
☼ ● ✂ US, MS, LS, CS
Gaura lindheimeri   p. 320

Geranium
☼ ◐ ● ● ◖ ✂ CS, TS OR ANNUAL
Pelargonium   p. 458

Gerbera daisy
☼ ◐ ● ✂ ALL
Gerbera jamesonii   p. 323

Ginger lily
☼ ◐ ● ● ✂ VARY
Hedychium   p. 338

Globe centaurea
☼ ◐ ● ✂ US, MS, LS
Centaurea macrocephala   p. 234

Globeflower
☼ ◐ ● ● ◖ ✂ US, MS
Trollius   p. 577

Globe mallow
☼ ○ ✂ VARY
Sphaeraclea   p. 551

Columbine
Aquilegia McKana Giants

Crocosmia

Dancing girl ginger
Globba

Coneflower
Rudbeckia

Purple fountain grass
Pennisetum setaceum 'Rubrum'

Fortnight lily
Dietes iridioides

Four o'clock
Mirabilis jalapa

Globeflower
Trollius

Delphinium

For climate zone explanations, please see pages 28–38. ▶

Gooseneck loosestrife
Lysimachia clethroides

Hollyhock
Alcea rosea

Bearded iris

Japanese anemone
Anemone × hybrida 'Prinz Heinrich'

Jerusalem sage
Phlomis fruticosa

Globe thistle
US, MS, LS, CS
Echinops · p. 293

Goat's beard
VARY
Aruncus · p. 183

Golden aster
US, MS, LS, CS
Chrysopsis · p. 245

Golden marguerite
US, MS, LS
Anthemis tinctoria · p. 168

Golden ray
US, MS, LS
Ligularia · p. 389

Goldenrod
US, MS, LS, CS
Solidago and Solidaster · p. 548/549

Gooseneck loosestrife
US, MS, LS
Lysimachia clethroides · p. 400

Greek yarrow
US, MS, LS
Achillea ageratifolia · p. 151

Hellebore
VARY
Helleborus · p. 341

Hesperaloe
MS, LS, CS, TS
· p. 344

× Heucherella
US, MS, LS
· p. 345

Hollyhock
US, MS, LS, CS
Alcea rosea · p. 158

Incarvillea
VARY
· p. 359

Iris
VARY
· p. 362

Jacob's ladder
US, MS, LS
Polemonium caeruleum · p. 486

Japanese anemone
US, MS, LS
Anemone × hybrida · p. 166

Jerusalem sage
US, MS, LS
Phlomis fruticosa · p. 468

Joe-Pye weed
US, MS, LS, CS
Eupatorium purpureum · p. 305

Lady bells
US, MS
Adenophora · p. 153

Lavender (shrubby perennial)
VARY
Lavandula · p. 384

Lily
US, MS, LS, CS
Lilium · p. 391

Lily-of-the-Nile
VARY
Agapanthus · p. 154

Lion's tail
VARY
Leonotis · p. 386

Live-forever sedum
US, MS, LS, CS
Sedum telephium · p. 541

Lobster-claw
TS
Heliconia · p. 340

Lupine
VARY
Lupinus · p. 398

Meadow rue
VARY
Thalictrum · p. 568

Mexican hat
US, MS, LS, CS
Ratibida columnifera · p. 505

Mount Atlas daisy
US, MS, LS
Anacyclus depressus · p. 165

Muhly grass
MS, LS, CS, TS
Muhlenbergia · p. 423

Mullein
US, MS, LS
Verbascum · p. 583

Nepeta
VARY
· p. 429

Nerine
LS, CS, TS
· p. 430

Nodding ladies' tresses
US, MS, LS, CS
Spiranthes cernua odorata · p. 552

Obedient plant
US, MS, LS, CS
Physostegia virginiana · p. 472

Pampas grass
MS, LS, CS, TS
Cortaderia selloana · p. 264

Pearly everlasting
US, MS, LS
Anaphalis · p. 165

Peony
US, MS, LS
Paeonia (herbaceous) · p. 442

Regal lily
Lilium regale

Showy evening primrose
Oenothera speciosa

Mullein
Verbascum

Obedient plant
Physostegia virginiana

For growing symbol explanations, please see page 39.

Peony
Paeonia

Blue phlox
Phlox divericata

Red-hot poker
Kniphofia uvaria

Russian sage
Perovskia atriplicifolia

Perennial blue flax
US, MS, LS
Linum perenne — p. 394

Perennial hibiscus
ALL
Hibiscus moscheutos — p. 345

Phlox
VARY
— p. 469

Pincushion flower
ALL
Scabiosa — p. 537

Pink
US, MS, LS, CS
Dianthus — p. 283

Plaintain lily
US, MS, LS
Hosta — p. 348

Plume poppy
US, MS, LS
Macleaya cordata — p. 401

Porterweed
TS
Stachytarpheta — p. 554

Prickly poppy
ALL
Argemone — p. 180

Primrose
VARY
Primula — p. 491

Purple coneflower
US, MS, LS, CS
Echinacea purpurea — p. 293

Red-hot poker
US, MS, LS, CS
Kniphofia uvaria — p. 377

Rose campion
US, MS, LS
Lychnis coronaria — p. 399

Royal catchfly
US, MS, LS, CS
Silene regia — p. 545

Russian sage
US, MS, LS, CS
Perovskia atriplicifolia — p. 463

Sage
VARY
Salvia (many) — p. 530

Sea holly
US, MS, LS, CS
Eryngium amethystinum — p. 300

Sedge (some)
US, MS, LS, CS
Carex — p. 226

Showy evening primrose
ALL
Oenothera speciosa — p. 434

Showy sedum
US, MS, LS, CS
Sedum spectabile — p. 541

Silphium
US, MS, LS, CS
— p. 545

Sneezeweed
US, MS, LS, CS
Helenium autumnale — p. 338

Snow-in-summer
US, MS, LS
Cerastium tomentosum — p. 235

Southern star
CS, TS
Tweedia caerulea — p. 581

Speedwell
US, MS, LS
Veronica — p. 584

Spiderwort
US, MS, LS, CS
Tradescantia virginiana — p. 576

Spiral flag
CS, TS
Costus — p. 266

Statice
VARY
Limonium — p. 393

Stokesia
ALL
Stokesia laevis — p. 557

Thrift, common
US, MS, LS, CS
Armeria maritima — p. 181

Toadflax
US, MS, LS, CS
Linaria — p. 393

Toad lily
US, MS, LS, CS
Tricyrtis — p. 576

Valerian
US, MS, LS
Centranthus ruber — p. 234

Verbena bonariensis
MS, LS, CS, TS
— p. 583

Wand loosestrife
US, MS, LS
Lythrum virgatum — p. 401

White turtlehead
US, MS, LS, CS
Chelone glabra — p. 239

Yarrow
US, MS, LS
Achillea — p. 151

Yellow waxbells
US, MS, LS
Kirengeshoma palmata — p. 376

Sneezeweed
Helenium autumnale

Speedwell
Veronica

Valerian
Centranthus ruber

Yarrow, common
Achillea millefolium

Spiderwort
Tradescantia virginiana

For climate zone explanations, please see pages 28–38.

Bulbs
and Bulblike Plants

Paperwhite daffodils *(Narcissus)*

Because bulbs are often dormant during the most desolate weather, they can survive with little care. That's why many have become heirloom plants, dug and passed along from generation to generation. Some—tulips, hyacinths, and crocuses—need months of winter cold to bloom well. Others can thrill without the chill. Bulbs (and corms, tubers, and rhizomes) may flower for only a few weeks each year, but multiplied by scores of blossoms over a lifetime, they make the garden rich with flowers.

Crocus

Fancy-leafed caladium
Caladium bicolor 'White Queen'

Crinum

Daffodil
Narcissus 'Peeping Tom'

AUTUMN-PLANTED BULBS

Atamasco lily
☼ ◑ ☄ MS, LS, CS, TS
Zephyranthes atamasco   p. 594

Aztec lily
☼ ◑ ☄ LS, CS, TS
Sprekelia formosissima   p. 553

Baboon flower
☼ ◐ ◑ ☄ LS, CS, TS
Babiana   p. 190

Blackberry lily
☼ ◑ ◐ ☄ US, MS, LS, CS
Belamcanda chinensis   p. 198

Black calla
☼ ◐ ◑ ◑ ☄ CS, TS
Arum palaestinum   p. 182

Blue flag
☼ ◐ ◑ ◐ ☄ US, MS, LS, CS
Iris versicolor   p. 365

Brimeura amethystina
☼ ◑ ☄ US, MS, LS, CS
    p. 208

Brodiaea
☼ ◐ ☄ VARY
    p. 208

Camass
☼ ◐ ◑ ◐ ☄ US, MS, LS, CS
Camassia   p. 219

Crested iris
◐ ◑ ☄ US, MS, LS, CS
Iris cristata   p. 365

Crinum
☼ ◐ ◑ ◐ ◐ ◑ ☄ VARY
    p. 269

Crocus
☼ ◐ ◑ ☄ US, MS, LS
    p. 270

Daffodil
☼ ◐ ◑ ◑ ☄ US, MS, LS, CS
Narcissus   p. 426

Dog-tooth violet
◐ ◑ ◑ ☄ US, MS, LS
Erythronium dens-canis   p. 301

English bluebell
◐ ◑ ◐ ☄ US, MS
Hyacinthoides non-scripta   p. 351

Eucharist lily
◑ ◐ ☄ TS OR INDOORS
Eucharis × grandiflora   p. 303

Fancy-leafed caladium
◐ ◑ ◐ ◐ ◑ ☄ TS
Caladium bicolor   p. 214

Foxtail lily
☼ ◑ ◐ ☄ US, MS, LS
Eremurus   p. 299

Freesia
☼ ◐ ◑ ◐ ☄ CS, TS
    p. 317

Fritillary
◐ ◑ ◐ ☄ US MS LS
Fritillaria   p. 317

Glory-of-the-snow
☼ ◐ ◑ ◐ ☄ US, MS
Chionodoxa   p. 242

Grape hyacinth
☼ ◐ ◑ ◐ ☄ US, MS, LS
Muscari   p. 424

Greek anemone
◐ ◑ ◐ ◑ ☄ US, MS, LS
Anemone blanda   p. 166

Hidden lily
◐ ◑ ☄ LS, CS, TS
Curcuma petiolata   p. 273

Hyacinth, common
☼ ◐ ◑ ◐ ◑ ☄ VARY
Hyacinthus orientalis   p. 351

Freesia

Grape hyacinth
Muscari

Greek anemone
Anemone blanda

For growing symbol explanations, please see page 39.

Oriental lily
Lilium 'Acapulco'

Squill
Scilla

Lily-of-the-Valley
Convallaria majalis

Hymenocallis
☀ ◐ ● ◖ ✂ VARY
p. 353

Ixiolirion tataricum
☀ ◖ ● US, MS, LS, CS
p. 366

Jack-in-the-pulpit
◑ ● ● ✂ US, MS, LS, CS
Arisaema triphyllum p. 180

Lily
☀ ◑ ● ◖ ✂ US, MS, LS, CS
Lilium p. 391

Lily-of-the-Nile
☀ ◑ ● ○○○ ◖ ✂ VARY
Agapanthus p. 154

Lily-of-the-Valley
◑ ● ● ◖ ✂ US, MS, LS
Convallaria majalis p. 258

Ornamental allium
☀ ◑ ● ◖ ✂ VARY
Allium p. 159

Oxalis
☀ ◑ ● ◖ ✂ ALL
Oxalis rubra p. 441

Oxblood lily
☀ ◑ ● ✂ MS, LS, CS
Rhodophiala bifida p. 513

Parrot lily
● ◑ ● ◖ ✂ MS, LS, CS
Alstroemeria psittacina p. 162

Persian ranunculus
☀ ◑ ● ✂ LS, CS, TS
Ranunculus asiaticus p. 503

Pineapple lily
☀ ◑ ● ◖ ✂ LS, CS, TS
Eucomis p. 303

Pregnant onion
☀ ◑ ● ◖ ◖ ✂ TS p. 439
Ornithogalum longibracteatum

Rain lily
☀ ● ◖ ✂ VARY
Zephyranthes p. 594

Snowdrop
☀ ◑ ● ◖ ◖ ✂ US, MS, LS
Galanthus p. 318

Snowflake
☀ ◑ ● ◖ ✂ VARY
Leucojum p. 388

Southern spider lily
☀ ◑ ● ◖ ◖ ✂ MS LS CS
Hymenocallis caroliniana p. 354

Spanish bluebell
☀ ◑ ● ◖ ◖ ✂ US, MS, LS, CS
Hyacinthoides hispanica p. 351

Spring star flower
☀ ◑ ● ◖ ✂ US, MS, LS, CS
Ipheion uniflorum p. 360

Squill
☀ ◑ ● ◖ ✂ US, MS, LS
Scilla p. 359

Star of Bethlehem
☀ ◑ ● ◖ ◖ ✂ US, MS, LS, CS
Ornithogalum umbellatum p. 439

Star of Persia
☀ ◑ ● ◖ ✂ US, MS, LS
Allium christophii p. 159

Sternbergia lutea
☀ ◑ ● ✂ US, MS, LS
p. 556

Summer hyacinth
☀ ◑ ● ◖ ✂ LS, CS, TS
Galtonia candicans p. 319

Triteleia
☀ ◑ ◖ ✂ US, MS, LS, CS
p. 577

Tulip
☀ ◑ ● ◖ ✂ ALL
Tulipa p. 578

Virginia bluebells
◑ ● ● ◖ ✂ US, MS, LS
Mertensia pulmonarioides p. 417

Winter aconite
☀ ◑ ● ◖ ✂ US, MS
Eranthis hyemalis p. 298

Yellow star grass
☀ ◑ ● ◖ ✂ US, MS, LS, CS
Hypoxis hirsuta p. 355

SPRING-PLANTED BULBS

Abyssinian sword lily
☀ ● ◖ ✂ MS, LS, CS
Gladiolus callianthus p. 324

Achimenes
◑ ● ◖ ✂ CS, TS
p. 151

African corn lily
☀ ◑ ● ◖ ✂ LS, CS, TS
Ixia p. 366

× Amarcrinum memoria-corsii
☀ ◑ ● ◖ ✂ LS, CS, TS
p. 163

Amaryllis
☀ ◑ ● ◖ ✂ LS, CS, TS
Hippeastrum p. 347

Bolivian sunset
◑ ● ◖ ✂ CS TS OR INDOORS
Gloxinia sylvatica p. 326

Calla
☀ ◑ ● ◖ ✂ CS, TS
Zantedeschia p. 593

Candy lily
☀ ◑ ● ◖ ✂ ALL
× Pardancanda norrisii p. 447

Snowdrop
Galanthus

Sternbergia
Sternbergia lutea

Lady tulip
Tulipa clusiana

Tulip and hyacinth bulbs

Golden calla
Zantedeschia elliottiana

For climate zone explanations, please see pages 28–38. ▶

47

Chinese ground orchid
Bletilla striata

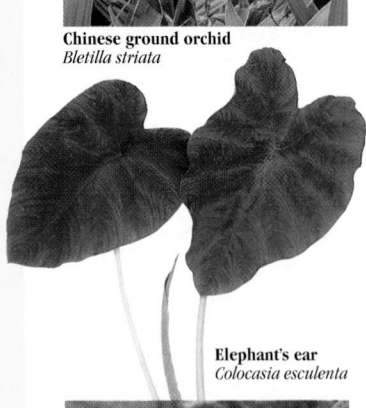

Elephant's ear
Colocasia esculenta

Dahlia

Magic lily
Lycoris squamigera

Rain lily
Habranthus

Canna
☼ ⚫💧 LS, CS, TS
p. 224

Chinese ground orchid
⚫💧 US, MS, LS, CS
Bletilla striata   p. 203

Crinum
☼ ⚫💧💧💧💧 VARY
p. 269

Crimson flag
☼ ⚫💧💧 LS, CS, TS
Schizostylis coccinea   p. 538

Crocosmia
☼ ⚫💧 US, MS, LS, CS
p. 270

Curcuma
☼ ⚫💧 LS, CS, TS
p. 273

Dahlia
☼ ⚫💧 US, MS, LS
p. 276

Elephant's ear
⚫💧💧💧 LS, CS, TS
Colocasia esculenta   p. 257

Giant alocasia
⚫💧💧💧 CS, TS
Alocasia macrorrhiza   p. 160

Ginger lily
☼ ⚫💧💧 VARY
Hedychium   p. 338

Gladiolus
☼ ⚫💧 MS, LS, CS
p. 324

Glory lily
☼ ⚫💧💧💧 TS   p. 326
Gloriosa superba 'Rothschildiana'

Homeria collina
☼ ⚫💧 CS, TS
p. 347

Jerusalem artichoke
☼ ⚫💧 US MS LS CS
Helianthus tuberosus   p. 339

Lily
☼ ⚫💧💧 US, MS, LS, CS
Lilium, Asiatic hybrids   p. 391

Magic lily
☼ ⚫💧 US, MS, LS, CS
Lycoris squamigera   p. 400

Nerine
☼ ⚫💧 LS, CS, TS
p. 430

Rain lily
☼ ⚫💧 LS, CS, TS
Habranthus   p. 335

Society garlic
☼ ⚫💧 LS, CS, TS
Tulbaghia violacea   p. 578

Spider lily
☼ ⚫💧 ALL
Lycoris   p. 400

Trout lily
⚫💧💧 US, MS, LS, CS
Erythronium americanum   p. 301

Tuberose
☼ ⚫💧 MS, LS, CS, TS
Polianthes tuberosa   p. 486

Tuberous begonia
⚫💧💧 US OR ANNUAL
Begonia   p. 197

Voodoo lily
⚫💧💧 VARY
Amorphophallus   p. 164

Walking iris
☼ ⚫💧 CS, TS
Neomarica gracilis   p. 429

Amaryllis
☼ ⚫💧 LS, CS, TS
Hippeastrum   p. 347

Belladonna lily
☼ ◊💧 LS, CS, TS
Amaryllis belladonna   p. 163

Crocus (fall-flowering)
☼ ⚫💧 US, MS, LS
p. 270

Cyclamen (except florists' types)
☼ ⚫💧 VARY
p. 274

Meadow saffron
☼ ⚫◊💧 US, MS, LS
Colchicum   p. 256

Clivia
⚫💧💧 TS
Clivia miniata   p. 254

Daylily
☼ ⚫💧 ALL
Hemerocallis   p. 342

Fortnight lily
☼ ⚫◊💧 LS, CS, TS
Dietes   p. 287

Montbretia
☼ ⚫💧 US, MS, LS, CS
Crocosmia crocosmiiflora p. 270

St. Joseph's lily
☼ ⚫💧 LS CS TS
Hippeastrum × johnsonii   p. 347

Yellow flag
☼ ⚫💧💧 US, MS, LS, CS
Iris pseudacorus   p. 364

Tuberose
Polianthes tuberosa

Daylily
Hemerocallis

Meadow saffron
Colchicum

Clivia
Clivia miniata

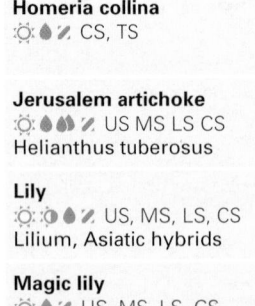

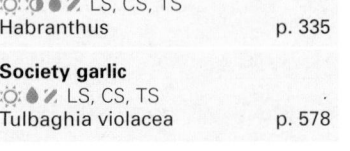

Amaryllis
Hippeastrum

For growing symbol explanations, please see page 39.

Azalea
Rhododendron

Landscape Plants
with Showy Flowers

French hydrangea
Hydrangea macrophylla

Just because trees, shrubs, vines, and ground covers form the garden's "backbone" doesn't mean it can't be a colorful back-bone. Many of these plants put on a show every bit as striking as that of annuals and perennials. To help you plan multiple seasons of bloom, we've arranged this list according to the season in which the different plants flower.

Empress tree
Paulownia tomentosa

Flowering peach
Prunus persica

Beach plum
Prunus maritima

Flowering dogwood
Cornus florida

SPRING
Trees

Black locus
☼ ○ ◐ ◊ ✂ US, MS, LS, CS
Robinia pseudoacacia .... p. 516

Bottlebrush
☼ ◐ ◊ ✂ VARY
Callistemon .... p. 217

Bradford pear
☼ ◐ ◊ ✂ US, MS, LS, CS
Pyrus calleryana 'Bradford' ... p. 499

Buttercup tree
☼ ◊ ✂ TS
Cochlospermum vitifolium ...... p. 255

Catalpa
☼ ◑ ◐ ◊ ✂ US, MS, LS, CS
.... p. 230

Dove tree
◑ ◊ ✂ US, MS, LS
Davidia involucrata .... p. 280

Empress tree
☼ ◑ ◐ ◊ ✂ US, MS, LS
Paulownia tomentosa .... p. 450

Epaulette tree
☼ ◊ ✂ US, MS, LS
Pterostyrax hispida .... p. 496

Flowering cherry, peach, plum
☼ ◐ ◊ ✂ VARY
Prunus (many) .... p. 493

Flowering crabapple
☼ ◐ ◊ ✂ VARY
Malus .... p. 409

Flowering dogwood
☼ ◑ ◊ ✂ US, MS, LS, CS
Cornus florida .... p. 262

Fringe tree
☼ ◑ ◐ ◊ ✂ US, MS, LS, CS
Chionanthus virginicus .... p. 241

Goldenchain tree
◑ ◐ ◊ ◊ ✂ US, MS
Laburnum .... p. 379

Hawthorn
☼ ◐ ✂ VARY
Crataegus .... p. 268

Jacaranda
☼ ◐ ✂ TS
Jacaranda mimosifolia .... p. 367

Juneberry
☼ ◑ ◐ ◊ ✂ VARY
Amelanchier .... p. 164

Kousa dogwood
☼ ◑ ◐ ◊ ✂ US, MS, LS
Cornus kousa .... p. 263

Magnolia (most deciduous)
☼ ◑ ◊ ✂ VARY
.... p. 402

Orchid tree
☼ ◐ ◊ ✂ TS
Bauhinia .... p. 194

Redbud
☼ ◑ ○ ◐ ◊ ✂ VARY
Cercis .... p. 236

Red horsechestnut
☼ ◑ ◐ ◊ ✂ US, MS, LS
Aesculus × carnea .... p. 154

Silk-cotton tree
☼ ◐ ◊ ✂ TS
Ceiba pentandra .... p. 232

Silver bell
☼ ◑ ◐ ◊ ✂ US, MS, LS
Halesia .... p. 336

Snowbell
☼ ◑ ◐ ◊ ✂ VARY
Styrax .... p. 560

SPRING
Shrubs

Acacia (most)
☼ ○ ✂ VARY
.... p. 147

Azalea and rhododendron
☼ ◐ ◐ ◊ ✂ VARY
Rhododendron .... p. 507

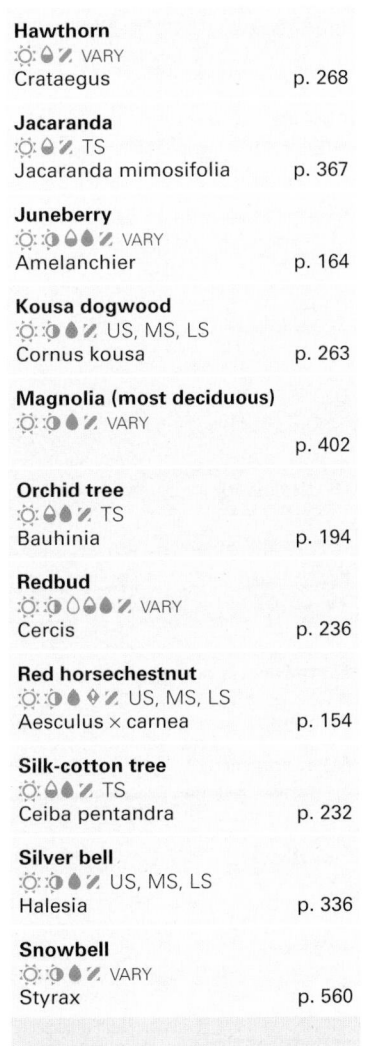

Orchid tree
Bauhinia

Red horsechestnut
Aesculus × carnea

Snowbell
Styrax

Rhododendron

For climate zone explanations, please see pages 28–38.

Beauty bush
Kolkwitzia amabilis

Bush daisy
Euryops pectinatus 'Viridis'

Chinese fringe tree
Chionanthus retusus

Red flowering currant
Ribes sanguineum

Daphne

Banana shrub
☼ ◐ ◑ ◗ ⚊ LS, CS, TS
Michelia figo   p. 418

Beauty bush
☼ ◐ ◑ ◗ ⚊ US, MS, LS
Kolkwitzia amabilis   p. 378

Black jetbead
☼ ◐ ◑ ◗ ◇ ⚊ US, MS, LS
Rhodotypos scandens   p. 513

Bramble
☼ ◐ ◑ ◗ ⚊ VARY
Rubus   p. 526

Broom
☼ ◇ ◗ ◗ ⚊ US, MS, LS
Genista   p. 321

Bush daisy
☼ ◐ ◇ ◗ ⚊ CS, TS OR ANNUAL
Euryops pectinatus   p. 307

Camellia, common
◐ ◑ ◗ ⚊ US, MS, LS, CS
Camellia japonica   p. 221

Chinese fringe tree
☼ ◐ ◑ ◗ ⚊ US, MS, LS, CS
Chionanthus retusus   p. 241

Daphne
☼ ◑ ◗ ◇ ⚊ VARY
                                      p. 278

Deutzia
☼ ◐ ◑ ◗ ⚊ US, MS, LS
                                      p. 282

Dwarf flowering almond
☼ ◐ ◑ ◗ ⚊ US, MS, LS
Prunus glandulosa   p. 494

Enkianthus
☼ ◐ ◑ ◗ ◐ ⚊ US, MS, LS
                                      p. 296

Firethorn
☼ ◑ ◗ ⚊ VARY
Pyracantha   p. 498

Flowering currant
☼ ◐ ◑ ◗ ⚊ VARY
Ribes   p. 515

Forsythia
☼ ◑ ◗ ⚊ US, MS, LS
                                      p. 315

Fothergilla
☼ ◐ ◑ ◗ ⚊ US, MS, LS
                                      p. 315

Fragrant abelia
☼ ◐ ◑ ◗ ⚊ US, MS, LS, CS
Abelia mosanensis   p. 146

Grevillea
☼ ◐ ◇ ◑ ◗ ⚊ VARY
                                      p. 333

Hardy orange
☼ ◑ ◗ ◇ ⚊ US, MS, LS, CS
Poncirus trifoliata   p. 488

Honeysuckle
☼ ◐ ◑ ◗ ◇ ⚊ VARY
Lonicera   p. 397

Horsechestnut
☼ ◐ ◑ ◗ ◇ ⚊ VARY
Aesculus   p. 154

Indian hawthorn
☼ ◐ ◑ ◗ ◇ ⚊ LS, CS
Rhaphiolepis indica   p. 505

Japanese kerria
◐ ◑ ◗ ◇ ⚊ US, MS, LS, CS
Kerria japonica   p. 376

Jasmine
☼ ◐ ◑ ◗ ◇ ⚊ VARY
Jasminum (some)   p. 367

Leucothoe
◐ ◑ ◗ ◇ ◇ ⚊ VARY
                                      p. 388

Lilac
☼ ◑ ◗ ◇ ⚊ VARY
Syringa   p. 563

Mahonia
☼ ◐ ◑ ● ◗ ◇ ◇ ⚊ VARY
                                      p. 408

Mexican orange
☼ ◐ ◑ ◗ ⚊ LS, CS, TS
Choisya ternata   p. 242

Mountain laurel
☼ ◐ ◑ ◗ ◇ ⚊ US, MS, LS, CS
Kalmia latifolia   p. 375

Myrtle
☼ ◐ ◇ ◗ ⚊ CS
Myrtus communis   p. 425

New Zealand tea tree
☼ ◇ ◗ ⚊ CS, TS
Leptospermum scoparium   p. 387

Pearl bush
☼ ◐ ◑ ◇ ⚊ US, MS, LS
Exochorda   p. 308

Peony
☼ ◐ ◑ ◗ ⚊ US, MS, LS
Paeonia   p. 442

Photinia
☼ ◐ ◑ ◗ ⚊ VARY
                                      p. 471

Pieris
◐ ◑ ◗ ◇ ⚊ US, MS
                                      p. 473

Rose
☼ ◐ ◑ ◗ ⚊ ALL
Rosa   p. 516

Sweet mock orange
☼ ◐ ◑ ◗ ⚊ US, MS, LS, CS
Philadelphus coronarius   p. 467

Texas mountain laurel
☼ ◐ ◑ ◗ ◇ ⚊ LS, CS
Sophora secundiflora   p. 549

Indian hawthorn
Rhaphiolepis indica

Japanese kerria
Kerria japonica

Lilac
Syringa vulgaris

Peony
Paeonia

For growing symbol explanations, please see page 39.

COLOR

Sweet mock orange
Philadelphus coronarius

Texas mountain laurel
Sophora secundiflora

Viburnum

Yellow bells
Tecoma stans

Clematis 'Nelly Moser'

Viburnum (some)
☼ ◑ ● ◑ ⚡ VARY
p. 585

Virginia sweetspire
☼ ● ◑ ⚡ US, MS, LS, CS
Itea virginica   p. 366

Weigela florida
☼ ● ◑ ⚡ US, MS, LS
p. 590

White forsythia
☼ ◑ ● ◑ ⚡ US, MS, LS
Abeliophyllum distichum   p. 146

Wild lilac
☼ ◊ ⚡ US, MS, LS, CS
Ceanothus   p. 232

Yellow bells
☼ ◑ ● ◑ ⚡ CS, TS
Tecoma stans   p. 567

SPRING
Ground Covers and Vines

Bougainvillea
☼ ● ◑ ⚡ CS, TS
p. 205

Carolina jessamine
☼ ◑ ● ◑ ◑ ● ◑ ⚡ MS, LS, CS
Gelsemium sempervirens   p. 321

Carpet bugleweed
☼ ◑ ● ◑ ⚡ US, MS, LS
Ajuga reptans   p. 157

Cat's claw
☼ ◑ ● ◑ ⚡ LS, CS, TS
Macfadyena unguis-cati   p. 401

Cheddar pink
☼ ● ◑ ⚡ US, MS, LS, CS
Dianthus gratianopolitanus   p. 284

Cherokee rose
☼ ◑ ● ⚡ LS, CS, TS
Rosa laevigata   p. 523

Cinquefoil
☼ ◑ ● ◑ ⚡ VARY
Potentilla (some)   p. 490

Clematis
☼ ● ⚡ VARY
p. 250

Golden globes
☼ ◑ ● ◑ ⚡ MS, LS, CS
Lysimachia congestiflora   p. 400

Lady Banks's rose
☼ ◑ ● ⚡ LS, CS, TS
Rosa banksiae   p. 523

Mazus
☼ ◑ ● ◑ ⚡ US, MS, LS
Mazus reptans   p. 415

Moss pink
☼ ◑ ● ⚡ US, MS, LS
Phlox subulata   p. 469

Periwinkle
◑ ● ◑ ◑ ⚡ VARY
Vinca   p. 587

Trumpet honeysuckle
☼ ◑ ● ◑ ⚡ US, MS, LS, CS
Lonicera sempervirens   p. 397

Wisteria
☼ ◊ ● ⚡ US, MS, LS, CS
p. 590

SUMMER
Trees

Cassia
☼ ◊ ◊ ● ⚡ TS
p. 229

Catalpa
☼ ◑ ● ◑ ⚡ US, MS, LS, CS
p. 230

Chitalpa
☼ ◊ ● ⚡ MS, LS, CS
× Chitalpa tashkentensis   p. 242

Coral tree
☼ ● ◑ ⚡ VARY
Erythrina (some)   p. 301

Crepe myrtle
☼ ● ⚡ US, MS, LS, CS
Lagerstroemia indica   p. 379

Desert willow
☼ ◊ ● ⚡ MS, LS, CS
Chilopsis linearis   p. 240

Franklin tree
☼ ● ◑ ⚡ US, MS, LS, CS
Franklinia alatamaha   p. 316

Goldenrain tree
☼ ● ◑ ⚡ US, MS, LS, CS
Koelreuteria paniculata   p. 378

Harlequin glorybower
◑ ● ◑ ⚡ MS, LS, CS, TS
Clerodendrum trichotomum   p. 253

Japanese pagoda tree
☼ ◑ ● ◑ ⚡ US, MS, LS
Sophora japonica   p. 549

Jerusalem thorn
☼ ◊ ◊ ● ⚡ CS, TS
Parkinsonia aculeata   p. 447

Lilac chaste tree
☼ ● ◑ ⚡ ALL
Vitex agnus-castus   p. 588

Loblolly bay
☼ ◑ ● ◑ ⚡ MS, LS, CS, TS
Gordonia lasianthus   p. 327

Pomegranate
☼ ● ⚡ MS, LS, CS
p. 488

Purple trumpet tree
☼ ◑ ● ⚡ TS
Tabebuia impetiginosa   p. 564

Trumpet honeysuckle
Lonicera sempervirens

Wisteria

Cassia

Chitalpa
× Chitalpa tashkentensis

Purple trumpet tree
Tabebuia impetiginosa

For climate zone explanations, please see pages 28–38. ▶

Royal poinciana
☼ ◐ ◖ ✂ TS
Delonix regia — p. 281

Cinquefoil
☼ ◐ ◖ ✂ VARY
Potentilla — p. 490

Royal poinciana
Delonix regia

Southern magnolia
☼ ◐ ◖ ✂ US, MS, LS, CS
Magnolia grandiflora — p. 404

Coral plant
☼ ◐ ◖ ◖ ✂ TS
Jatropha multifida — p. 368

Stewartia
☼ ◐ ◖ ✂ VARY
— p. 556

Fairy duster
☼ ◖ ◖ ✂ CS, TS
Calliandra eriophylla — p. 217

Butterfly bush
Buddleia

Sweet bay
☼ ◐ ◖ ◖ ✂ US, MS, LS, CS
Magnolia virginiana — p. 408

Firecracker plant
☼ ◐ ◖ ◖ ✂ CS, TS
Russelia equisetiformis — p. 527

Southern magnolia
Magnolia grandiflora

Yellow poinciana
☼ ◐ ◖ ✂ TS
Peltophorum pterocarpum — p. 460

Flame of the woods
☼ ◐ ◖ ✂ TS
Ixora coccinea — p. 367

SUMMER
Shrubs and Perennials

Flowering maple
☼ ◐ ◖ ◖ ✂ CS, TS
Abutilon — p. 147

Abelia
☼ ◐ ◖ ✂ VARY
— p. 146

Frangipani
☼ ◐ ◖ ◖ ✂ TS
Plumeria — p. 484

Cape plumbago
Plumbago auriculata

Adina
☼ ◐ ◖ ◖ ✂ US, MS, LS, CS
Adina rubella — p. 153

Fuchsia
☼ ◐ ◖ ✂ VARY
— p. 317

Angel's trumpet
☼ ◐ ◖ ◖ ✂ LS, CS, TS
Brugmansia — p. 209

Gardenia, common
☼ ◐ ◖ ✂ LS, CS, TS
Gardenia jasminoides — p. 319

Bear's breech
☼ ◐ ◖ ◖ ◖ ✂ US, MS, LS, CS
Acanthus — p. 148

Glorybower
☼ ◐ ◖ ✂ TS
Clerodendrum — p. 252

Blue mist
☼ ◖ ✂ US, MS, LS, CS
Caryopteris × clandonensis — p. 229

Hibiscus
☼ ◐ ◖ ✂ VARY
— p. 345

Angel's trumpet
Brugmansia versicolor 'Ecuador Pink'

Bottlebrush buckeye
☼ ◐ ◖ ◖ ✂ US, MS, LS, CS
Aesculus parviflora — p. 154

Hydrangea
☼ ◐ ◖ ✂ VARY
— p. 352

Bouvardia
☼ ◖ ◖ ✂ CS, TS
— p. 207

Indigo bush
☼ ◖ ✂ US, MS, LS, CS
Amorpha fruticosa — p. 164

Brazilian plume flower
☼ ◖ ◖ ◖ ✂ CS, TS
Justicia carnea — p. 373

Jasmine
☼ ◐ ◖ ◖ ✂ VARY
Jasminum (some) — p. 367

Chilean cestrum
Cestrum parqui

Brunfelsia
☼ ◐ ◖ ◖ ✂ CS, TS
— p. 210

Mexican abelia
☼ ◐ ◖ ✂ LS, CS
Abelia floribunda — p. 146

Butterfly bush
☼ ◐ ◖ ◖ ✂ VARY
Buddleia — p. 211

Oleander
☼ ◖ ◖ ◖ ◖ ✂ LS, CS, TS
Nerium oleander — p. 431

Bottlebrush buckeye
Aesculus parviflora

Cape plumbago
☼ ◐ ◖ ◖ ◖ ✂ CS, TS
Plumbago auriculata — p. 481

Ornamental pomegranate
☼ ◖ ◖ ✂ LS, CS, TS
Punica granatum — p. 498

Cat's whiskers
☼ ◖ ◖ ✂ TS
Orthosiphon aristatus — p. 439

Pentas
☼ ◖ ✂ US, MS, LS, CS, TS
Pentas lanceolata — p. 461

Cestrum
◐ ◖ ◖ ✂ TS
— p. 237

Peregrina
☼ ◐ ◖ ◖ ✂ TS
Jatropha integerrima — p. 368

Blue mist
Caryopteris × clandonensis

Oakleaf hydrangea
Hydrangea quercifolia

For growing symbol explanations, please see page 39.

Pentas
Pentas lanceolata

Chestnut rose
Rosa roxburghii

Mexican bush sage
Salvia leucantha

Baby's breath spiraea
Spiraea thunbergii

Tree mallow
Lavatera thuringiaca 'Barnsley'

Plumleaf azalea
US, MS, LS, CS
Rhododendron prunifolium   p. 513

Princess flower
TS
Tibouchina urvilleana   p. 572

Rose
ALL
Rosa   p. 516

Rose of Sharon
US, MS, LS, CS
Hibiscus syriacus   p. 346

Sage (several)
VARY
Salvia   p. 530

St. Johnswort
VARY
Hypericum   p. 354

Senna
VARY
                                  p. 542

Spiraea (some)
VARY
                                  p. 552

Summersweet
US, MS, LS, CS
Clethra alnifolia   p. 253

Sundrops
US, MS, LS
Calylophus   p. 219

Texas ranger
LS, CS, TS
Leucophyllum frutescens   p. 388

Tree mallow
VARY
Lavatera   p. 386

Yellow bird of paradise
CS, TS
Caesalpinia gilliesii   p. 214

Yellow shrimp plant
CS, TS
Pachystachys lutea   p. 442

SUMMER
Ground Covers, Vines

Allamanda
TS OR ANNUAL
Allamanda cathartica   p. 159

Aristolochia (some)
VARY
                                  p. 180

Black-eyed Susan vine
CS, TS
Thunbergia alata   p. 570

Bleeding heart vine
TS
Clerodendrum thomsoniae   p. 253

Blue pea vine
TS OR ANNUAL
Clitoria ternatea   p. 254

Bower vine
CS, TS
Pandorea jasminoides   p. 445

Clematis (some)
VARY
                                  p. 250

Confederate jasmine
LS, CS, TS
Trachelospermum jasminoides   p. 575

Coral vine
LS, CS, TS
Antigonon leptopus   p. 169

Creeping liriope
ALL
Liriope spicata   p. 395

Crossvine
US, MS, LS, CS
Bignonia capreolata   p. 201

Cypress vine
ALL
Ipomoea quamoclit   p. 361

Distictis
VARY
                                  p. 289

Dwarf plumbago
US, MS, LS, CS
Ceratostigma plumbaginoides   p. 235

Firecracker vine
TS OR ANNUAL
Ipomoea lobata   p. 361

Glory lily
TS
Gloriosa superba 'Rothschildiana' p. 326

Honeysuckle
VARY
Lonicera   p. 397

Hyacinth bean
LS, CS, TS
Dolichos lablab   p. 289

Jasmine
VARY
Jasminum (some)   p. 367

Lantana, common
LS, CS, TS OR ANNUALS
Lantana camara   p. 382

Mandevilla
VARY
                                  p. 412

Manettia
LS, CS, TS
                                  p. 413

Moonflower
ALL
Ipomoea alba   p. 360

Princess flower
Tibouchina urvilleana

Coral vine
Antigonon leptopus

Gold flame honeysuckle
Lonicera × heckrottii

Mandevilla

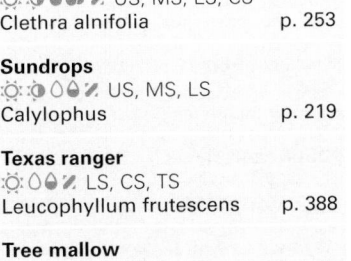

For climate zone explanations, please see pages 28–38.

COLOR

Rangoon creeper
Quisqualis indica

Rose, climbing
Rosa 'Cl. Cécile Brunner'

Snail vine
Vigna caracalla

King's mantle
Thunbergia erecta

Verbena

Morning glory, common
☼ ⬤⬤⬤✂ ALL
Ipomoea purpurea   p. 361

Passion vine
☼ ◐⬤⬤✂ VARY
Passiflora   p. 449

Pink trumpet vine
☼ ◐⬤⬤✂ CS, TS
Podranea ricasoliana   p. 485

Purple allamanda
☼⬤◈✂ TS OR ANNUAL
Allamanda blanchetii   p. 159

Rangoon creeper
☼ ◐⬤✂ TS
Quisqualis indica   p. 502

Rose (many climbers)
☼ ◐⬤✂ ALL
Rosa   p. 516

Snail vine
☼ ⬤✂ TS
Vigna caracalla   p. 587

Thunbergia
☼ ◐⬤✂ TS
                                p. 570

Trumpet creeper
☼ ◐⬤⬤✂ VARY
Campsis   p. 224

Verbena
☼ ⬤✂ VARY
                                p. 583

AUTUMN

AUTUMN
Trees and Shrubs

Angel's trumpet
☼ ◐⬤◈✂ LS, CS, TS
Brugmansia   p. 209

Autumn flowering cherry
☼ ⬤✂ US, MS, LS   p. 493
Prunus × subhirtella 'Autumnalis'

Butterfly bush
☼ ◐⬤⬤✂ VARY
Buddleia   p. 211

Caesalpinia
☼ ◐⬤◈✂ VARY
                                p. 214

Cat's whiskers
☼ ⬤⬤✂ TS
Orthosiphon aristatus   p. 439

Floss silk tree
☼ ⬤✂ TS
Chorisia   p. 242

Fuchsia
☼ ⬤✂ VARY
                                p. 317

Hibiscus (some)
☼ ⬤✂ VARY
                                p. 345

Hong Kong orchid tree
☼ ⬤⬤✂ TS
Bauhinia × blakeana   p. 194

Mexican bird of paradise
☼ ◐⬤◈✂ TS
Caesalpinia mexicana   p. 214

Mexican bush sage
☼ ⬤✂ LS, CS, TS
Salvia leucantha   p. 531

Peregrina
◐⬤⬤◈✂ TS
Jatropha integerrima   p. 368

Pink wild petunia
☼ ◐⬤⬤✂ CS, TS
Ruellia macrantha   p. 527

Princess flower
☼ ◐⬤✂ TS
Tibouchina urvilleana   p. 572

Rose (some)
☼ ◐⬤✂ ALL
Rosa   p. 516

Sasanqua camellia
☼ ◐⬤⬤✂ US, MS, LS, CS
Camellia sasanqua   p. 222

Shower-of-gold
☼ ◐⬤✂ CS, TS
Galphimia glauca   p. 319

Shrub bush clover
☼ ◐⬤⬤✂ US, MS, LS
Lespedeza thunbergii   p. 387

'Tardiva' hydrangea
☼ ◐⬤✂ US, MS, LS, CS
Hydrangea paniculata   p. 352

Witch hazel, common
☼ ◐⬤✂ US, MS, LS, CS
Hamamelis virginiana   p. 336

Yellow bells
☼ ◐⬤⬤✂ CS, TS
Tecoma stans   p. 567

AUTUMN
Vines, Perennials

Allamanda
☼⬤◈✂ TS OR AS ANNUAL
Allamanda cathartica   p. 159

Bleeding heart vine
◐⬤✂ TS
Clerodendrum thomsoniae   p. 253

Cape honeysuckle
☼ ◐⬤✂ CS, TS
Tecoma capensis   p. 567

Flame vine
☼ ◐⬤✂ CS, TS
Pyrostegia venusta   p. 499

Chinese abelia
Abelia chinensis

Hibiscus

Shower-of-gold
Galphimia glauca

Shrub bush clover
Lespedeza thunbergii

For growing symbol explanations, please see page 39.

Potato vine
Solanum jasminoides

Sweet autumn clematis
Clematis terniflora

Cornelian cherry
Cornus mas

Japanese flowering apricot
Prunus mume

Yulan magnolia
Magnolia denudata

Glorybower
☼ ◐ ● ✿ TS
Clerodendrum (many)   p. 252

Honeysuckle
☼ ◐ ● ● ✿ VARY
Lonicera (some)   p. 397

Mandevilla (some)
☼ ◐ ● ✿ VARY
                             p. 412

Potato vine
☼ ◐ ● ● ● ✿ CS, TS
Solanum jasminoides   p. 547

Rose (some climbers)
☼ ◐ ● ✿ ALL
Rosa   p. 516

Silver lace vine
☼ ◐ ● ● US, MS, LS
Fallopia baldschuanica   p. 309

Sneezeweed
☼ ● ● ✿ US, MS, LS, CS
Helenium autumnale   p. 338

Sweet autumn clematis
☼ ● ✿ US, MS, LS, CS
Clematis terniflora   p. 252

Thunbergia
☼ ◐ ● ✿ TS
                             p. 570

Virgin's bower
☼ ● ✿ US, MS, LS
Clematis virginiana   p. 252

WINTER
Trees

African tulip tree
☼ ● ✿ TS
Spathodea campanulata   p. 551

Bailey acacia
☼ ◐ ✿ CS, TS
Acacia baileyana   p. 147

Cascalote
☼ ◐ ● ● ● ✿ TS
Caesalpinia cacalaco   p. 214

Cornelian cherry
☼ ◐ ● ✿ US, MS, LS
Cornus mas   p. 263

Flowering cherry
☼ ● ● ✿ US, MS, LS, CS
Prunus 'Okame'   p. 493

Japanese flowering apricot
☼ ◐ ● ✿ US, MS, LS, CS
Prunus mume   p. 495

Purple orchid tree
☼ ● ● ✿ TS
Bauhinia variegata   p. 194

Red maple
☼ ◐ ● ● ✿ US, MS, LS, CS
Acer rubrum   p. 150

Yulan magnolia
☼ ◐ ● US, MS, LS, CS
Magnolia denudata   p. 403

WINTER
Shrubs

Camellia (many)
◐ ● ● ✿ US, MS, LS, CS
                             p. 220

Flowering quince
☼ ● ● ✿ US, MS, LS, CS
Chaenomeles   p. 237

Heath
☼ ◐ ● ✿ VARY
Erica   p. 299

Leatherleaf mahonia
☼ ● ● ✿ US, MS, LS, CS
Mahonia bealei   p. 409

Stachyurus praecox
☼ ● ● ✿ US, MS, LS
                             p. 555

Winter daphne
◐ ◐ ● ● ✿ MS, LS
Daphne odora   p. 279

Winter hazel
☼ ◐ ● ✿ US, MS, LS
Corylopsis   p. 265

Winter honeysuckle
☼ ● ● ● ✿ US, MS, LS
Lonicera fragrantissima   p. 397

Wintersweet
☼ ◐ ● ✿ US, MS, LS, CS
Chimonanthus praecox   p. 241

Witch hazel
☼ ◐ ● ● ✿ US, MS, LS
Hamamelis (most)   p. 336

WINTER
Ground Cover and Vines

Carolina jessamine
☼ ◐ ◐ ● ● ● ✿ ✿ MS, LS, CS
Gelsemium sempervirens   p. 321

Flame vine
☼ ◐ ● ✿ CS, TS
Pyrostegia venusta   p. 499

Lenten rose
◐ ● ● ● ✿ US, MS, LS
Helleborus orientalis   p. 341

Pink jasmine
☼ ◐ ● ✿ LS, CS, TS
Jasminum polyanthum   p. 368

Red clerodendrom
☼ ● ✿ TS
Clerodendrum splendens   p. 253

Winter jasmine
☼ ◐ ● ● ✿ US, MS, LS, CS
Jasminum nudiflorum   p. 368

Camellia

Flowering cherry
Prunus 'Okame'

Flowering quince
Chaenomeles 'Cameo'

Wintersweet
Chimonanthus praecox

Winter jasmine
Jasminum nudiflorum

For climate zone explanations, please see pages 28–38.

Flowers
for Cutting

A garden isn't meant to be enjoyed outdoors only. You can cut many different kinds of flowers and bring them indoors. The ones you see here generally last about a week in water. Many of them, indicated by the symbol ⚘, are easy to dry for permanent arrangements. Annuals and biennials must be planted every year; perennials and most bulbs provide flowers year after year. Shrubs are another good source of cut flowers, and some even respond obligingly to cutting by blooming again and again.

Freshly picked common camellias.

Butterfly bush
Buddleia

French hydrangea
Hydrangea macrophylla

Rose
Rosa 'Leander'

Larkspur
Consolida ajacis

SHRUBS

Butterfly bush
☼ ◐ ◖ ◆ ⚘ VARY
Buddleia   p. 211

Camellia
☼ ◐ ◆ ⚘ US, MS, LS, CS
                                p. 220

Gardenia
☼ ◐ ◆ ⚘ VARY
                                p. 319

Hydrangea   ⚘
◐ ◆ ⚘ VARY
                                p. 352

Japanese kerria   ⚘
◐ ◐ ◆ ⚘ US, MS, LS, CS
Kerria japonica   p. 376

Lavender   ⚘
☼ ◆ ⚘ VARY
Lavandula   p. 384

Lilac
☼ ◐ ◆ ⚘ VARY
Syringa   p. 563

Rose
☼ ◐ ◆ ⚘ ALL
Rosa   p. 516

Spiraea
☼ ◐ ◆ ⚘ VARY
                                p. 552

ANNUALS

Angelonia angustifolia
☼ ◆ ⚘ LS, CS, TS
                                p. 167

Annual phlox
☼ ◆ ⚘ ALL
Phlox drummondii   p. 469

Bachelor's button   ⚘
☼ ◐ ◆ ⚘ ALL
Centaurea cyanus   p. 234

Bells-of-Ireland   ⚘
☼ ◐ ◆ ⚘ ALL
Moluccella laevis   p. 421

Calendula
☼ ◐ ◆ ⚘ ALL
Calendula officinalis   p. 216

Chinese lantern plant   ⚘
☼ ◐ ◆ ⚘ US, MS, LS
Physalis alkekengi   p. 471

Cockscomb   ⚘
☼ ◐ ◆ ⚘ ALL
Celosia argentea   p. 233

Corn cockle
☼ ◐ ◆ ⚘ ALL
Agrostemma githago   p. 157

Cosmos, common   ⚘
☼ ◐ ◆ ⚘ ALL
Cosmos bipinnatus   p. 265

Globe amaranth   ⚘
☼ ◐ ◆ ⚘ ALL
Gomphrena globosa   p. 326

Gypsophila elegans   ⚘
☼ ◐ ◆ ⚘ ALL
                                p. 335

Larkspur   ⚘
☼ ◐ ◆ ⚘ ALL
Consolida ajacis   p. 258

Lisianthus
☼ ◐ ◐ ◆ ⚘ ALL
Eustoma grandiflorum   p. 307

Love-in-a-mist   ⚘
☼ ◐ ◐ ◆ ⚘ ALL
Nigella damascena   p. 432

Mexican sunflower   ⚘
☼ ◐ ◆ ⚘ ALL
Tithonia rotundifolia   p. 573

Bachelor's button
Centaurea cyanus

Larkspur
Consolida ajacis

Money plant
Lunaria annua

For growing symbol explanations, please see page 39.

Money plant 〰
☼ ◐ ◊ ◊◊◊ ◢ US, MS, LS, CS
Lunaria annua   p. 398

Pincushion flower 〰
☼ ◊◊◢ ALL
Scabiosa atropurpurea   p. 537

Safflower 〰
☼ ◊◢ ALL
Carthamus tinctorius   p. 228

Snapdragon
☼ ◊◢ ALL
Antirrhinum majus   p. 169

Spider flower
☼ ◊◊◢ ALL
Cleome hasslerana   p. 252

Statice 〰
☼ ◊◢ ALL
Limonium sinuatum   p. 393

Stock
☼ ◐ ◊◢ ALL
Matthiola   p. 415

Strawflower 〰
☼ ◊◢ ALL
Helichrysum bracteatum   p. 339

Sunflower, common 〰
☼ ◊◊◊ ◢ ALL
Helianthus annuus   p. 339

Sweet pea
☼ ◊◊◊ ◢ ALL
Lathyrus odoratus   p. 383

Zinnia 〰
☼ ◊◢ ALL
                                p. 595

PERENNIALS, BULBS

Alstroemeria
◐ ◊ ◊ ◢ MS, LS, CS
                                p. 162

Angel's trumpet
☼ ◐ ◊ ◊ ◊ ◢ LS, CS, TS
Brugmansia   p. 209

Artemisia 'Powis Castle' 〰
☼ ◐◊◢ US, MS, LS
                                p. 182

Aster 〰
☼ ◊◊◢ US, MS, LS
                                p. 186

Baby's breath 〰
☼ ◊◢ US, MS, LS, CS
Gypsophila paniculata   p. 335

Balloon flower
☼ ◐ ◊◢ US, MS, LS, CS
Platycodon grandiflorus   p. 479

Beard tongue
☼ ◐ ◊◊◢ VARY
Penstemon   p. 461

Bird of paradise
☼ ◐ ◊◢ VARY
Strelitzia   p. 559

Black-eyed Susan
☼ ◊◊◢ ALL
Rudbeckia hirta   p. 526

Blazing star
☼ ◊◊◢ US, MS, LS, CS
Liatris   p. 389

Bush strawflower 〰
☼ ◊◢ TS OR ANNUAL
Bracteantha bracteata   p. 207

Calla
☼ ◐ ◊◢ CS, TS
Zantedeschia   p. 593

Candy lily
☼ ◊◊◢ ALL
× Pardancanda norrisii   p. 447

Centaurea (most)
☼ ◊◢ VARY
                                p. 234

China aster 〰
☼ ◊◢ ALL
Callistephus chinensis   p. 218

Chrysanthemum (some) 〰
☼ ◊◢ VARY
                                p. 243

Columbine meadow rue
◊ ◊◢ US, MS, LS
Thalictrum aquilegifolium   p. 568

Coneflower
☼ ◊◊◢ US, MS, LS, CS
Rudbeckia   p. 526

Coreopsis (most)
☼ ◊ ◊◊◊◊ ◢ US, MS, LS, CS
                                p. 260

Crinum
☼ ◐ ◊◊◊ ◊ ◢ VARY
                                p. 269

Daffodil
☼ ◐ ◊◢ US, MS, LS, CS
Narcissus   p. 426

Dahlia 〰
☼ ◐ ◊◢ US, MS, LS
                                p. 276

Delphinium
☼ ◊◢ VARY
                                p. 281

False sunflower 〰
☼ ◊◊◊ ◢ US, MS, LS, CS
Heliopsis helianthoides   p. 340

Fountain grass 〰
☼ ◐ ◊◊◊ ◢ VARY
Pennisetum   p. 460

Fritillary
◐ ◊◢ US, MS, LS
Fritillaria   p. 317

Spider flower
Cleome hasslerana

Alstroemeria

Strawflower
Helichrysum bracteatum

Crinum

Dahlia

Delphinium

Checkered lily (Fritillary)
Fritillaria meleagris

For climate zone explanations, please see pages 28–38. ▶

Gerbera daisy
Gerbera jamesonii

Ginger lily, common
Hedychium coronarium

Hollyhock
Alcea rosea

Japanese anemone
Anemone × hybrida 'Honorine Jobert'

Gaillardia × grandiflora
☼ ◑◐☀ ALL
p. 318

Gas plant
☼ ◐ ◑◐◑ ☀☀ US, MS, LS
Dictamnus albus   p. 286

Gerbera daisy
☼ ◐ ◑◐☀ ALL
Gerbera jamesonii   p. 323

Geum
☼ ◐ ◑◐☀ US, MS
p. 323

Ginger lily, common
☼ ◐ ◑◐☀ MS, LS, CS, TS
Hedychium coronarium   p. 338

Gladiolus
☼ ◑◐☀ MS, LS, CS
p. 324

Globe mallow
☼ ◑◐ ☀ VARY
Sphaeralcea   p. 551

Globe thistle   ⸭
☼ ◑◐☀ US, MS, LS, CS
Echinops   p. 293

Golden aster   ⸭
☼ ◐ ◑◐☀ US, MS, LS, CS
Chrysopsis   p. 245

Goldenrod   ⸭
☼ ◐ ◑◐☀ US, MS, LS, CS
Solidago and Solidaster p. 548, 549

Greek yarrow   ⸭
☼ ◐ ◑◐☀ US, MS, LS
Achillea ageratifolia   p. 151

Hollyhock
☼ ◐ ◑◐☀ US, MS, LS, CS
Alcea   p. 158

Iris
☼ ◐ ◑◐◑◐◑ ☀ VARY
p. 362

Japanese anemone
◐ ◑◐◑☀ US, MS, LS
Anemone × hybrida   p. 166

Lily
☼ ◐ ◑◐☀ US, MS, LS, CS
Lilium   p. 391

Ornamental allium
☼ ◐ ◑◐☀ VARY
Allium   p. 159

Pampas grass   ⸭
☼ ◐◑◐◑◐◑ ☀ MS, LS, CS, TS
Cortaderia selloana   p. 264

Pearly everlasting   ⸭
◐ ◑◐◑◐☀ US, MS, LS
Anaphalis   p. 165

Pentas
☼ ◑◐☀ ALL
Pentas lanceolata   p. 461

Peony
☼ ◐ ◑◐☀ US, MS, LS
Paeonia   p. 442

Persian ranunculus
☼ ◑◐☀ LS, CS, TS
Ranunculus asiaticus   p. 503

Phlomis
☼ ◐◑◐☀ VARY
p. 468

Pincushion flower   ⸭
☼ ◐ ◑◐☀ ALL
Scabiosa (some)   p. 537

Pink
☼ ◑◐☀ US, MS, LS, CS
Dianthus (many)   p. 283

Purple coneflower   ⸭
☼ ◑◐☀ US, MS, LS, CS
Echinacea purpurea   p. 293

Reed grass   ⸭
☼ ◐ ◑◐☀ US, MS, LS, CS
Calamagrostis   p. 215

Ruby grass   ⸭
☼ ◑◐☀ TS OR ANNUAL
Rhynchelytrum nervinglume p. 515

Seashore mallow
☼ ◑◐◑ ☀ ALL
Kosteletzkya virginica   p. 378

Speedwell
☼ ◑◐☀ US, MS, LS
Veronica spicata   p. 584

Spike blazing star   ⸭
☼ ◑◐☀ US, MS, LS, CS
Liatris spicata   p. 389

Star of Bethlehem
☼ ◐ ◑◐◑☀ LS, CS, TS
Ornithogalum arabicum   p. 438

Statice   ⸭
☼ ◑☀ VARY
Limonium (most)   p. 393

Stokesia   ⸭
☼ ◑☀ US, MS, LS, CS
Stokesia laevis   p. 557

Summer phlox
☼ ◐ ◑◐☀ US, MS, LS, CS
Phlox paniculata   p. 469

Sunflower   ⸭
☼ ◑◐◑ ☀ VARY
Helianthus (most)   p. 339

Tulip
☼ ◐ ◑◐☀ ALL
Tulipa   p. 578

Verbena bonariensis   ⸭
☼ ◑◐☀ MS, LS, CS, TS OR ANNUAL
p. 583

Viola, violet, pansy
☼ ◐ ◑◐☀ VARY
Viola   p. 587

Giant allium
Allium giganteum

Pansy
Viola

Pearly everlasting
Anaphalis margaritacea

Speedwell
Veronica spicata

For growing symbol explanations, please see page 39.

Peony
Paeonia

Chinese pink
Dianthus chinensis

Fragrant
Flowering Plants

A garden's fragrance can be as unforgettable as its appearance; the scent of a particular flower can evoke memories of past times and places. You can use fragrant plants in a variety of ways. En masse, they create a bathed-in-scent garden; set out in just a few spots, they provide a mystery perfume from who-knows-where. Plant them in containers to scent a deck or patio; locate them beneath a window to let fragrance waft indoors.

Yoshino flowering cherry
Prunus × yedoensis

Harlequin glorybower
Clerodendrum trichotomum

Jerusalem thorn
Parkinsonia aculeata

Yulan magnolia
Magnolia denudata

TREES

Black locust
☼ ◌◊◖◗⚡ US, MS, LS, CS
Robinia pseudoacacia   p. 516

Citrus
☼ ◖◗⚡ CS, TS
                              p. 247

Flowering cherry, apricot
☼ ◖◗⚡ VARY
Prunus (some)   p. 493

Flowering crabapple
☼ ◖◗⚡ VARY
Malus (some)   p. 409

Fragrant snowbell
☼ ◑◖◗⚡ US, MS, LS
Styrax obassia   p. 560

Fringe tree
☼ ◖◗⚡ US, MS, LS, CS
Chionanthus virginicus   p. 241

Harlequin glorybower
◑◖⚡ MS, LS, CS, TS
Clerodendrum trichotomum p. 253

Jerusalem thorn
☼ ◌◊◖◗⚡ CS, TS
Parkinsonia aculeata   p. 447

Magnolia (many)
☼ ◑◖◗⚡ VARY
                              p. 402

Russian olive
☼ ◑◌◊◖◗⚡ US, MS
Elaeagnus angustifolia   p. 295

Sweet acacia
☼ ◊⚡ LS, CS, TS
Acacia farnesiana   p. 147

Texas mountain laurel
☼ ◑◌◊◖⚡ LS, CS
Sophora secundiflora   p. 549

Yellow wood
☼ ◖⚡ US, MS, LS
Cladrastis kentukea   p. 250

SHRUBS

Acacia (several)
☼ ◊⚡ VARY
                              p. 147

Adina rubella
☼ ◑◖◗⚡ US, MS, LS, CS
                              p. 153

Alabama azalea
◑◖◗⚡ MS, LS
Rhododendron alabamense   p. 512

Angel's trumpet
☼ ◑◖◗⚡ LS, CS, TS
Brugmansia   p. 209

Anise tree
◑●◑◖◗⚡ MS, LS, CS
Illicium   p. 358

Banana shrub
☼ ◑◖⚡ LS, CS, TS
Michelia figo   p. 418

Bouvardia longiflora 'Albatross'
◑◖⚡ CS, TS
                              p. 207

Broom
☼ ◖⚡ US, MS, LS
Cytisus   p. 276

Cashmere bouquet
◑◖⚡ LS, CS, TS
Clerodendrum bungei   p. 252

Cestrum (some)
◑◖◗⚡ TS
                              p. 237

Daphne (many)
◑◖◗⚡ VARY
                              p. 278

Elaeagnus
☼ ◑◌◊◖⚡ VARY
                              p. 295

Fothergilla
☼ ◑◖⚡ US, MS, LS
                              p. 315

Texas mountain laurel
Sophora secundiflora

Angel's trumpet
Brugmansia

Burkwood daphne
Daphne × burkwoodii

For climate zone explanations, please see pages 28–38.   ▶

Gardenia, common
Gardenia jasminoides 'Radicans'

Frangipani
Plumeria

Cut-leaf lilac
Syringa × laciniata

Mock orange
Philadelphus

Florida flame azalea
Rhododendron austrinum

Rose
Rosa 'Charmian'

Fragrant snowball
☼ ◐ ♦ ⚡ US, MS, LS
Viburnum × carlcephalum   p. 585

Frangipani
☼ ◐ ◐ ♦ ⚡ TS
Plumeria   p. 484

Gardenia
☼ ◐ ♦ ⚡ VARY
        p. 319

Hardy orange
☼ ◐ ♦ ♦ ⚡ US, MS, LS, CS
Poncirus trifoliata   p. 488

Japanese pittosporum
☼ ◐ ♦ ♦ ⚡ LS, CS, TS
Pittosporum tobira   p. 478

Japanese skimmia
◐ ♦ ♦ ⚡ US, MS, LS
Skimmia japonica   p. 546

Korean spice viburnum
☼ ◐ ♦ ⚡ US, MS, LS
Viburnum carlesii   p. 585

Lavender
☼ ♦ ⚡ VARY
Lavandula   p. 384

Leatherleaf mahonia
☼ ◐ ♦ ⚡ US, MS, LS, CS
Mahonia bealei   p. 409

Lilac
☼ ◐ ♦ ⚡ VARY
Syringa (many)   p. 563

Mexican orange
☼ ◐ ♦ ♦ ⚡ LS, CS, TS
Choisya ternata   p. 242

Mock orange
☼ ◐ ♦ ♦ ⚡ VARY
Philadelphus (most)   p. 467

Natal plum
☼ ◐ ◐ ♦ ♦ ⚡ CS, TS
Carissa macrocarpa   p. 227

Orange jessamine
◐ ♦ ⚡ TS
Murraya paniculata   p. 423

Osmanthus (most)
☼ ◐ ◐ ♦ ♦ ⚡ VARY
        p. 439

Rhaphiolepis 'Majestic Beauty'
☼ ◐ ◐ ♦ ♦ ⚡ LS, CS
        p. 506

Rhododendron, azalea
◐ ♦ ♦ ♦ ⚡ VARY
Rhododendron (some)   p. 507

Rose
☼ ◐ ♦ ⚡ ALL
Rosa (most)   p. 516

Summersweet
☼ ◐ ◐ ♦ ♦ ⚡ US, MS, LS, CS
Clethra alnifolia   p. 253

Sweet box
◐ ◐ ♦ ♦ ⚡ US, LS, MS, CS
Sarcococca   p. 535

Sweetshrub, common
☼ ◐ ◐ ♦ ⚡ US, MS, LS, CS
Calycanthus floridus   p. 219

Sweetspire
☼ ◐ ♦ ⚡ VARY
Itea   p. 366

White forsythia
☼ ◐ ♦ ⚡ US, MS, LS
Abeliophyllum distichum   p. 146

Winter hazel
☼ ◐ ♦ ⚡ US, MS, LS
Corylopsis   p. 265

Winter honeysuckle
☼ ◐ ♦ ⚡ US, MS, LS
Lonicera fragrantissima   p. 397

Wintersweet
☼ ◐ ♦ ⚡ US, MS, LS, CS
Chimonanthus praecox   p. 241

Witch hazel
☼ ◐ ♦ ⚡ US, MS, LS
Hamamelis   p. 336

VINES

Armand clematis
☼ ◐ ♦ ⚡ LS, CS
Clematis armandii   p. 251

Carolina jessamine
☼ ◐ ◐ ♦ ♦ ♦ ⚡ MS, LS, CS
Gelsemium sempervirens   p. 321

Chilean jasmine
☼ ◐ ♦ ⚡ CS, TS
Mandevilla laxa   p. 413

Confederate jasmine
☼ ◐ ◐ ♦ ♦ ⚡ LS, CS, TS   p. 575
Trachelospermum jasminoides

Herald's trumpet
☼ ◐ ♦ ⚡ TS
Beaumontia grandiflora   p. 196

Japanese honeysuckle
☼ ◐ ♦ ♦ ⚡ ALL
Lonicera japonica   p. 397

Jasmine
☼ ◐ ♦ ♦ ⚡ VARY
Jasminum   p. 367

Madagascar jasmine
◐ ♦ ⚡ TS OR INDOORS
Stephanotis floribunda   p. 555

Moonflower
☼ ♦ ♦ ⚡ ALL
Ipomoea alba   p. 360

Passion vine
☼ ◐ ♦ ♦ ⚡ TS
Passiflora × alatocaerulea   p. 449

Summersweet
Clethra alnifolia

Sweetshrub, common
Calycanthus floridus 'Athens'

Winter hazel
Corylopsis

Chinese witch hazel
Hamamelis mollis

Passion vine
Passiflora × alatocaerulea

For growing symbol explanations, please see page 39.

Sweet autumn clematis
Clematis terniflora

Sweet pea
Lathyrus odoratus

English wallflower
Erysimum cheiri

Flowering tobacco
Nicotiana sylvestris

Fragrant plantain lily
Hosta plantaginea

Sweet autumn clematis
☼ ◐ ◑ ☇ US, MS, LS, CS
Clematis terniflora   p. 252

Sweet pea
☼ ◐ ☇ ALL
Lathyrus odoratus   p. 383

Vanilla trumpet vine
☼ ◑ ◐ ☇ TS
Distictis laxiflora   p. 289

Wax flower
☼ ◐ ◑ ☇ TS
Hoya carnosa   p. 350

Wisteria
☼ ◑ ◐ ☇ US, MS, LS, CS
                                   p. 590

PERENNIALS, ANNUALS, BULBS

Angel's trumpet
☼ ◑ ◐ ☇ VARY
Datura   p. 280

Blue corydalis
◑ ◐ ☇ US, MS, LS
Corydalis flexuosa   p. 264

Calanthe
◑ ◐ ◑ ☇ MS, LS, CS
                                   p. 215

Chocolate cosmos
☼ ◐ ◑ ☇ MS, LS, CS
Cosmos atrosanguineus   p. 265

Crinum
☼ ◑ ◐ ◐◑ ◐ ☇ VARY
                                   p. 269

Crocus
☼ ◑ ◐ ◑ ☇ US, MS, LS
Crocus chrysanthus   p. 270

Daffodil
☼ ◑ ◐ ◑ ☇ US, MS, LS, CS
Narcissus (many)   p. 426

Dendrobium (some)
◑ ◐ ☇ TS OR INDOORS
                                   p. 282

English bluebell
◑ ◐ ◑ ☇ US, MS
Hyacinthoides non-scripta   p. 351

English primrose
◑ ◐ ☇ US, MS, LS
Primula vulgaris (some)   p. 491

English wallflower
☼ ◑ ◐◑◐◑ ☇ US, MS
Erysimum cheiri   p. 300

Flowering tobacco
☼ ◑ ◐ ◑ ☇ ALL
Nicotiana sylvestris   p. 432

Four o'clock
☼ ◐ ◑ ☇ ALL
Mirabilis jalapa   p. 420

Fragrant plantain lily
◑ ◐ ◑ ☇ US, MS, LS, CS
Hosta plantaginea   p. 349

Freesia
☼ ◑ ◐ ◑ ☇ CS, TS
                                   p. 317

Ginger lily
☼ ◑ ◐◑ ☇ VARY
Hedychium   p. 338

Heliotrope, common
☼ ◑ ◐ ◑ ☇ TS OR ANNUAL
Heliotropium arborescens   p. 341

Hyacinth
☼ ◑ ◐ ◑ ☇ VARY
Hyacinthus   p. 351

Hymenocallis
☼ ◑ ◐ ◑ ☇ VARY
                                   p. 353

Indian lotus
☼ ◑ ◐◑ ☇ ALL
Nelumbo nucifera   p. 428

Iris, bearded (many)
☼ ◑ ◐ ☇ US, MS, LS, CS
                                   p. 362

Lady bells
☼ ◑ ◐◑ ☇ US, MS
Adenophora   p. 153

Lemon daylily
☼ ◑ ◐ ☇ ALL   p. 343
Hemerocallis lilioasphodelus

Lily
☼ ◑ ◐ ☇ US, MS, LS, CS
Lilium (many)   p. 391

Lily-of-the-valley
◑ ◐◑ ◐ ☇ US, MS, LS
Convallaria majalis   p. 258

Peony
☼ ◑ ◐ ☇ US, MS, LS
Paeonia (many)   p. 442

Petunia
☼ ◑ ◐ ☇ ALL
Petunia × hybrida   p. 465

Pink
☼ ◑ ◐ ☇ US, MS, LS, CS
Dianthus (many)   p. 283

Stock
☼ ◑ ◐ ☇ ALL
Matthiola   p. 415

Summer hyacinth
☼ ◑ ◐ ☇ LS, CS, TS
Galtonia candicans   p. 319

Summer phlox
☼ ◑ ◐ ☇ US, MS, LS, CS
Phlox paniculata   p. 469

Tuberose
☼ ◐ ☇ MS, LS, CS, TS
Polianthes tuberosa   p. 486

Hymenocallis 'Sulphur Queen'

Hyacinth, common
Hyacinthus orientalis

Stock
Matthiola incana

Cheddar pink
Dianthus gratianopolitanus 'Bath's Pink'

Indian lotus
Nelumbo nucifera

For climate zone explanations, please see pages 28–38.

Colorful Fruits and Berries

Nandina
Nandina domestica

If you judge a plant solely on the merits of its flowers, you may be doing it a great injustice. Many plants sport showy fruits and berries, principally in fall and winter, when the garden is often devoid of bright color. Bring in some of the cheery fruits as bouquets. Not only do these fruits catch your eye, but they often attract hungry birds as well. If you'd like to join them for a snack, look for plants with the symbol 🍐 next to their name. This tells you that people can eat the fruit, too, either fresh or in jams and jellies.

Deciduous possumhaw *(Ilex decidua)* keeps its berries through the winter.

Flowering crabapple
Malus 'Red Jewel'

Harlequin glorybower
Clerodendrum trichotomum

Hawthorn
Crataegus

European mountain ash
Sorbus aucuparia

TREES

Citrus 🍐
☀️●💧✂️ CS, TS
p. 247

Dogwood
☀️●◑💧✂️ VARY
Cornus (several)   p. 262

Eastern red cedar
☀️●◑◐💧✂️ ALL
Juniperus virginiana   p. 373

Flowering crabapple 🍐
☀️●💧✂️ VARY
Malus   p. 409

Harlequin glorybower
●💧✂️ MS, LS, CS, TS
Clerodendrum trichotomum   p. 253

Hawthorn
☀️●💧✂️ VARY
Crataegus   p. 268

Holly
☀️●◑💧✂️ VARY
Ilex (many)   p. 356

Juneberry 🍐
☀️●◑◐💧✂️ US, MS, LS, CS
Amelanchier arborea   p. 164

Koelreuteria
☀️●💧✂️ VARY
p. 378

Korean evodia
☀️●💧✂️ US, MS, LS
Tetradium daniellii   p. 567

Loquat 🍐
☀️◑◐◑●💧✂️ LS, CS, TS
Eriobotrya japonica   p. 300

Lychee 🍐
☀️●✂️ CS, TS
p. 399

Mountain ash
☀️●◑●✂️ VARY
Sorbus   p. 549

Persimmon 🍐
☀️●◑✂️ VARY
p. 464

Sea grape 🍐
☀️●✂️ TS
Coccoloba uvifera   p. 255

Southern magnolia
☀️●◑✂️ US, MS, LS, CS
Magnolia grandiflora   p. 404

SHRUBS

Alexandrian laurel
●◑◑✂️ MS, LS, CS
Danae racemosa   p. 278

American elderberry 🍐
☀️●◑✂️ US, MS, LS, CS
Sambucus canadensis   p. 533

Bayberry
☀️●✂️ US, MS
Myrica pensylvanica   p. 425

Bearberry
☀️●◐◑●✂️ US, MS
Arctostaphylos uva-ursi   p. 178

Beautyberry
☀️●◑●✂️ US, MS, LS
Callicarpa   p. 217

Blueberry 🍐
☀️●◑◐◑●◑✂️ VARY
Vaccinium   p. 582

Chinese photinia
☀️●◑●✂️ US, MS, LS, CS
Photinia serratifolia   p. 471

Chokeberry
☀️●◑◐●◑✂️ VARY
Aronia   p. 181

Persimmon
Diospyros

Southern magnolia
Magnolia grandiflora

American elderberry
Sambucus canadensis

Bearberry
Arctostaphylos uva-ursi
'Wood's Compact'

For growing symbol explanations, please see page 39.

Blueberry 'Coville'

Teton pyracantha (Firethorn)
Pyracantha 'Teton'

Japanese aucuba
Aucuba japonica 'Variegata'

Japanese barberry
Berberis thunbergii

Cotoneaster
:☼: ○ ● ● ◢ VARY
p. 266

Elaeagnus (several)
:☼: ○ ◐ ○ ● ● ◢ VARY
p. 295

Eugenia
:☼: ● ● ◢ VARY
p. 304

Euonymus
:☼: ○ ● ● ● ◢ VARY
p. 304

Firethorn
:☼: ● ◢ VARY
Pyracantha
p. 498

Flowering currant
:☼: ○ ● ● ◢ VARY
Ribes
p. 515

Golden dewdrop
:☼: ○ ● ● ◢ TS
Duranta erecta
p. 292

Holly
:☼: ○ ● ◢ VARY
Ilex (many)
p. 356

Honeysuckle
:☼: ○ ● ● ◢ VARY
Lonicera (most shrubby types)
p. 397

Japanese aucuba
:☼: ● ● ● ◢ ALL
Aucuba japonica
p. 189

Japanese barberry
:☼: ● ● ● ◢ US, MS, LS
Berberis thunbergii
p. 199

Japanese skimmia
:● ● ● ◢ US, MS, LS
Skimmia japonica
p. 546

Jerusalem cherry
:☼: ○ ● ◢ ◢ CS, TS
Solanum pseudocapsicum
p. 548

Mahonia
:☼: ● ● ○ ● ◢ VARY
p. 408

Marlberry
:☼: ● ● ● ◢ VARY
Ardisia
p. 179

Nandina
:☼: ● ● ● ● ◢ US, MS, LS, CS
Nandina domestica
p. 425

Natal plum
:☼: ○ ○ ● ● ◢ CS, TS
Carissa macrocarpa
p. 227

Oriental photinia
:☼: ● ● ◢ US, MS, LS
Photinia villosa
p. 471

Ornamental pomegranate (some)
:☼: ● ● ◢ MS, LS, CS, TS
Punica granatum
p. 498

Prickly pear
:☼: ○ ◢ VARY
Opuntia (several)
p. 436

Rose
:☼: ● ◢ ALL
Rosa (especially rugosas) p. 516, 524

Sapphireberry
:☼: ● ◢ US, MS, LS
Symplocos paniculata
p. 562

Sea buckthorn
:☼: ● ● ◢ US, MS
Hippophae rhamnoides
p. 347

Spicebush
:☼: ● ● ◢ US, MS, LS
Lindera benzoin
p. 393

Staghorn sumac
:☼: ○ ● ◢ US, MS, LS
Rhus typhina
p. 514

Turk's cap
:● ● ○ ● ● ◢ LS, CS, TS
Malvaviscus arboreus drummondii
p. 412

Viburnum (many)
:☼: ● ◢ VARY
p. 585

Yew
:☼: ● ● ● ● ◢ ◢ US, MS
Taxus
p. 566

PERENNIALS AND VINES

American bittersweet
:☼: ● ◢ US, MS, LS
Celastrus scandens
p. 233

Blackberry lily
:☼: ● ● ◢ US, MS, LS, CS
Belamcanda
p. 198

Gladwin iris
:● ● ○ ● ● ◢ US, MS, LS, CS
Iris foetidissima
p. 364

Honeysuckle
:☼: ● ● ● ◢ VARY
Lonicera (some)
p. 397

Italian arum
:● ● ● ● ◢ ◢ US, MS, LS, CS
Arum italicum
p. 182

Jack-in-the-pulpit
:● ● ● ◢ US, MS, LS, CS
Arisaema triphyllum
p. 180

Lily of China
:● ● ● ◢ MS, CS
Rohdea japonica
p. 516

Partridgeberry
:● ● ● ● ◢ US, MS, LS
Mitchella repens
p. 421

Porcelain berry
:☼: ● ● ● ● ◢ US, MS, LS, CS p. 165
Ampelopsis brevipedunculata

Japanese ardisia (Marlberry)
Ardesia japonica

Red chokeberry
Aronia arbutifolia

Rose
Rosa

American bittersweet
Celastrus scandens

Porcelain berry
Ampelopsis brevipedunculata

For climate zone explanations, please see pages 28–38.

Plants with
Colorful Foliage

The pale color of this urn is a perfect foil to the deep red burst of barberry behind it.

Not all garden color comes from flowers and fruit. The plants listed below offer long-term accents in the form of colored leaves: gray or silver; bronze, red, or purple; yellow or gold; blue; and even multiple hues. Variegated leaves can feature stripes, spots, zigzags or just a slender edging drawn in a contrasting color. Place them where they'll enliven the greens of other garden plants, combine them in dramatic partnerships, or highlight them as eye-catching focal points.

Fancy-leafed caladium
Caladium bicolor 'Florida Elise'

Agave

GRAY, SILVER
Trees and Shrubs

Agave
☼ ◐ ◊ ◊ ◊ ⚡ CS, TS
    p. 156

Aloe
☼ ◐ ◊ ◊ ◊ ◊ ⚡ TS
    p. 161

Arizona cypress
☼ ◊ ◊ ⚡ MS, LS, CS
Cupressus arizonica glabra p. 272

Bush germander
☼ ◊ ⚡ US, MS, LS, CS
Teucrium fruticans p. 568

Eucalyptus (many)
☼ ◊ ⚡ VARY
    p. 302

Feijoa, Pineapple guava
☼ ◐ ⚡ LS, CS, TS
Feijoa sellowiana p. 310

Juniper
☼ ◊ ◊ ◊ ◊ ⚡ VARY
Juniperus (many) p. 370

Lavender
☼ ◐ ⚡ VARY
Lavandula (most) p. 384

Lavender cotton
☼ ◊ ◊ ⚡ US, MS, LS, CS p. 534
Santolina chamaecyparissus

Red yucca
☼ ◊ ◊ ◊ ◊ ⚡ ALL
Hesperaloe parviflora p. 344

Rockrose
☼ ◊ ⚡ LS, CS
Cistus p. 247

Russian olive
☼ ◐ ◊ ◊ ◊ ⚡ US, MS
Elaeagnus angustifolia p. 295

Plectranthus argentatus
☼ ◐ ◊ ⚡ TS OR INDOORS
    p. 480

Sunrose
☼ ◊ ⚡ US, MS p. 338
Helianthemum nummularium (some)

Texas ranger
☼ ◊ ◊ ⚡ LS, CS, TS
Leucophyllum (most) p. 388

Thorny elaeagnus
☼ ◐ ◊ ◊ ◊ ◊ ⚡ US, MS, LS, CS
Elaeagnus pungens p. 295

GRAY, SILVER
Perennials

Artemisia (many)
☼ ◊ ◊ ⚡ VARY
    p. 181

'Berggarten' common sage
☼ ◐ ⚡ ALL
Salvia officinalis p. 532

'Bowles Mauve' wallflower
☼ ◐ ◊ ◊ ◊ ⚡ US, MS, LS, CS
Erysimum p. 300

Dusty miller
☼ ◐ ⚡ LS, CS, TS
Centaurea cineraria p. 234

Dusty miller
☼ ◊ ◊ ⚡ MS, LS, CS
Senecio cineraria p. 542

Echeveria (many)
☼ ◐ ◊ ⚡ VARY
    p. 292

Germander sage
☼ ◊ ◊ ⚡ LS, CS, TS
Salvia chamaedryoides p. 530

Globe thistle
☼ ◐ ⚡ US, MS, LS, CS
Echinops p. 293

Juniper
Juniperus scopulorum 'Wichita Blue'

Red yucca
Hesperaloe parviflora

Echeveria

Arizona cypress
Cupressus arizonica glabra

Bush germander
Teucrium fruticans

Silver dollar tree
Eucalyptus cinerea

Germander sage
Salvia chamaedryoides

For growing symbol explanations, please see page 39.

Lavender cotton
Santolina chamaecyparissus

Rose campion
Lychnis coronaria

Silver sage
Salvia argentea

Woolly thyme
Thymus pseudolanuginosus

Horehound
☼ ◖◖❍ ✂ ALL
Marrubium vulgare   p. 414

Jerusalem sage
☼ ◐ ◖◖❍ ✂ US, MS, LS
Phlomis fruticosa   p. 468

Lamb's ears
☼ ◐ ◖◖❍ ✂ US, MS, LS
Stachys byzantina   p. 554

Licorice plant
☼ ◖◖ ✂ TS OR ANNUAL
Helichrysum petiolare   p. 340

Mountain mint
☼ ◐ ◖◖❍ ✂ US, MS, LS
Pycnanthemum incanum   p. 498

Pink
☼ ◖◖❍ ✂ US, MS, LS, CS
Dianthus (many)   p. 283

Red-hot poker
☼ ◐ ◖◖❍ ✂ VARY
Kniphofia (some)   p. 377

Rose campion
☼ ◐ ◖◖ ✂ US, MS, LS
Lychnis coronaria   p. 399

Russian sage
☼ ◖◖❍ ✂ US, MS, LS, CS
Perovskia atriplicifolia   p. 463

Silver sage
☼ ◖◖ ✂ US, MS, LS, CS
Salvia argentea   p. 530

Snow-in-summer
☼ ◐ ◖◖❍ ✂ US, MS, LS
Cerastium tomentosum   p. 235

Thyme
☼ ◐ ◖◖ ✂ VARY
Thymus (several)   p. 571

Yarrow
☼ ◖◖❍ ✂ US, MS, LS
Achillea (many)   p. 151

BRONZE, RED, PURPLE
Trees and Shrubs

Bronze dracaena
☼ ◖◖ ✂ CS, TS OR INDOORS   p. 259
Cordyline australis 'Atropurpurea'

Bronze loquat
☼ ◐ ◖◖◖❍ ✂ CS, TS
Eriobotrya deflexa   p. 300

Caribbean copper plant
☼ ◖◖ ◖ ✂ CS, TS
Euphorbia cotinifolia   p. 306

'Crimson King' Norway maple
☼ ◐ ◖◖◖ ✂ US, MS
Acer platanoides   p. 149

European beech
☼ ◐ ◖◖ ✂ US, MS
Fagus sylvatica (some)   p. 308

European filbert
☼ ◐ ◖◖ ✂ US, MS, LS   p. 265
Corylus avellana 'Fusco-rubra'

Flowering crabapple
☼ ◖◖ ✂ VARY
Malus (some)   p. 409

'Forest Pansy' Eastern redbud
◐ ◖◖ ✂ US, MS, LS, CS
Cercis canadensis   p. 236

Japanese barberry
☼ ◐ ◖◖ ✂ US, MS, LS, CS
Berberis thunbergii (several) p. 199

Japanese maple
☼ ◐ ◖◖❍ ✂ US, MS, LS, CS
Acer palmatum (some)   p. 149

Purple-leaf sand cherry
☼ ◖◖ ✂ US, MS
Prunus × cistena   p. 494

Smoke tree
☼ ◖◖ ✂ US, MS, LS
Cotinus coggygria (some)   p. 266

Thundercloud plum
☼ ◖◖ ✂ US, MS, LS   p. 494
Prunus cerasifera 'Thundercloud'

BRONZE, RED, PURPLE
Perennials

Anthriscus sylvestris 'Ravenswing'
☼ ◖◖ ✂ US, MS
            p. 169

Bergenia (some)
◐ ◖◖ ✂ US, MS, LS
            p. 199

'Black Magic' elephant's ear
◐ ◖◖◖ ◖ ✂ VARY OR INDOORS
Alocasia   p. 160

Bronze fennel
☼ ◖◖ ✂ US, MS, LS, CS   p. 314
Foeniculum vulgare 'Purpurascens'

Canna (some)
☼ ◖◖ ✂ LS, CS, TS
            p. 224

Carpet bugleweed
☼ ◐ ◖◖◖ ✂ US, MS, LS
Ajuga (several)   p. 157

Coleus
☼ ◐ ◖◖◖◖ ✂ TS OR ANNUAL
Coleus × hybridus   p. 256

Coral bells
◐ ◖◖ ✂ US, MS, LS   p. 345
Heuchera micrantha 'Palace Purple'

Earth star
◐ ◖◖ ✂ TS OR INDOORS
Cryptanthus zonatus   p. 271

'Fanal' false spiraea
☼ ◐ ◖◖ ✂ US, MS
Astilbe × arendsii 'Fanal'   p. 187

Caribbean copper plant
Euphorbia cotinifolia

'Forest Pansy' Eastern redbud
Cercis canadensis

Coral bells
Heuchera micrantha 'Palace Purple'

Thundercloud plum
Prunus cerasifera 'Thundercloud'

Canna

For climate zone explanations, please see pages 28–38. ▶

Japanese blood grass
☼ ◑ ◐ ◊ ◒ US, MS, LS, CS
Imperata cylindrica 'Rubra'   p. 359

Japanese blood grass
Imperata cylindrica 'Rubra'

New Zealand flax
Phormium tenax 'Purpureum'

Purple fountain grass
Pennisetum setaceum 'Rubrum'

American Arborvitae
Thuja occidentalis

Blue mist
Caryopteris × clandonensis

Knotweed
☼ ◑ ◐ ◊ ◒ VARY
Persicaria (some)   p. 463

Lobelia (some)
☼ ◐ ● ◐ ◊ ◊ ◔ ◒ VARY
    p. 396

New Zealand flax
☼ ◑ ◯ ◐ ◊ ◊ ◒ LS, CS, TS
Phormium tenax (several)   p. 470

'Pele's Smoke' sugar cane
☼ ◐ ◒ CS, TS
Saccharum officinarum   p. 528

Pilea
☼ ◐ ● ◐ ◒ TS OR INDOORS
    p. 473

Purple fountain grass
☼ ◑ ◯ ◐ ◊ ◒ CS, TS OR ANNUAL   p. 460
Pennisetum setaceum 'Rubrum'

Purple velvet plant
☼ ◐ ◒ LS, CS, TS OR INDOORS
Gynura aurantiaca   p. 334

Red ivy
☼ ◐ ◒ TS OR ANNUAL
Hemigraphis alternata   p. 343

Sweet potato vine
☼ ◐ ◒ LS, CS, TS
Ipomoea batatas (some)   p. 361

Wood spurge
☼ ◑ ● ◐ ◊ ◒ US, MS, LS, CS   p. 305
Euphorbia amygdaloides 'Purpurea'

YELLOW, GOLD
Trees and Shrubs

Arborvitae
☼ ◑ ◐ ◊ ◒ VARY
Thuja (some)   p. 569

Blue mist 'Worcester Gold'
☼ ◐ ◒ US, MS, LS, CS
Caryopteris × clandonensis   p. 229

Box honeysuckle
☼ ◐ ◊ ◒ US, MS, LS, CS
Lonicera nitida 'Baggesen's Gold'   p. 397

'Castlewellan' Leyland cypress
☼ ◐ ◊ ◒ US, MS, LS, CS
× Cupressocyparis leylandii   p. 272

English yew
☼ ◐ ● ◐ ◊ ◔ ◒ US, MS
Taxus baccata (several)   p. 566

European cranberry bush
☼ ◐ ◊ ◒ US, MS, LS
Viburnum opulus 'Aureum'   p. 586

Frisia black locust
☼ ◯ ◊ ◔ ◒ US, MS, LS, CS
Robina pseudoacacia   p. 516

Golden fullmoon maple
☼ ◐ ◊ ◒ US   p. 150
Acer shirasawanum 'Aureum'

Golden Hinoki false cypress
☼ ◐ ◊ ◒ US, MS, LS   p. 237
Chamaecyparis obtusa 'Crippsii'

Italian cypress 'Swane's Golden'
☼ ◑ ◯ ◐ ◊ ◒ MS, LS, CS
Cupressus sempervirens   p. 273

Japanese aucuba
☼ ◐ ● ◐ ◊ ◒ ALL
Aucuba japonica (many)   p. 189

Japanese barberry
☼ ◑ ◐ ◊ ◊ ◒ US, MS, LS
Berberis thunbergii (some)   p. 199

Juniper
☼ ◐ ◯ ◊ ◊ ◒ VARY
Juniperus (several)   p. 370

Spiraea japonica (several)
☼ ◑ ◐ ◊ ◒ US, MS, LS
    p. 552

'Sunburst' honey locust
☼ ◐ ◊ ◒ US, MS
Gleditsia triacanthos   p. 325

'Sundance' Mexican orange
☼ ◐ ◒ LS, CS, TS
Choisya ternata   p. 242

Vicary golden privet
☼ ◑ ◐ ◊ ◔ ◒ US, MS, LS, CS
Ligustrum 'Vickryi'   p. 390

YELLOW, GOLD
Perennials

Bleeding heart, common
☼ ◐ ● ◐ ◒ US, MS, LS, CS
Dicentra spectabilis (some)   p. 285

Bowles' golden grass
☼ ◐ ◊ ◔ ◒ US, MS, LS
Milium effusum 'Aureum'   p. 419

Feverfew 'Aureum'
☼ ◑ ◐ ◊ ◒ US, MS, LS, CS
Chrysanthemum parthenium   p. 245

Golden moneywort
◐ ◊ ◊ ◒ US, MS, LS   p. 401
Lysimachia nummularia 'Aurea'

Japanese forest grass
☼ ◐ ● ◐ ◒ US, MS, LS
Hakonechloa macra 'Aureola'   p. 335

Japanese sweet flag
☼ ◐ ◊ ◒ US, MS, LS, CS
Acorus gramineus 'Ogon'   p. 152

'Limelight' licorice plant
☼ ◐ ◊ ◒ TS OR ANNUAL
Helichrysum petiolare   p. 340

Oregano
☼ ◐ ◯ ◊ ◒ VARY
Origanum (several)   p. 437

English yew
Taxus baccata 'Aurea'

Golden Hinoki false cypress
Chamaecyparis obtusa 'Crippsii'

Bleeding heart, common
Dicentra spectabilis

Feverfew
Chrysanthemum parthenium 'Aureum'

Licorice plant
Helichrysum petiolare 'Limelight'

For growing symbol explanations, please see page 39.

Plantain lily
Hosta

Bowles' golden sedge
Carex elata 'Aurea' ('Bowles' Golden')

Bougainvillea
Bougainvillea 'Hawaii'

China fir
Cunninghamia lanceolata 'Glauca'

Colorado blue spruce
Picea pungens

Switch grass
Panicum virgatum 'Heavy Metal'

Plantain lily
☼ ◑ ● ▲ ✂ US, MS, LS
Hosta (several)   p. 348

Sedge
☼ ☼ ◑ ▲▲▲▲ ✂ US, MS, LS, CS
Carex (several)   p. 226

Thyme
☼ ◑ ● ✂ VARY
Thymus (several)   p. 571

BLUE
Trees, Shrubs and Perennials

Atlas cedar
☼ ● ✂ US, MS, LS
Cedrus atlantica 'Glauca'   p. 232

Blue fescue
☼ ◑ ● ▲ ✂ US, MS
Festuca glauca   p. 311

Blue lyme grass
☼ ☼ ◑▲▲ ✂ US, MS, LS, CS
Leymus arenarius   p. 389

China fir
☼ ● ✂ MS, LS, CS   p. 272
Cunninghamia lanceolata 'Glauca'

Colorado blue spruce
☼ ◑ ▲▲ ✂ US, MS, LS
Picea pungens (some)   p. 472

Eucalyptus (some)
☼ ◑ ✂ VARY
                               p. 302

Plantain lily
☼ ◑ ● ▲ ✂ US, MS, LS
Hosta (several)   p. 348

Rue
☼ ● ▲ ✂ US, MS, LS, CS
Ruta graveolens   p. 527

Switch grass
☼ ◑ ▲▲▲▲ ✂ US, MS, LS
Panicum virgatum (some)   p. 445

VARIEGATED
Trees, Shrubs, Vines

Actinidia kolomikta
☼ ☼ ◑ ✂ US, MS, LS
                               p. 152

Bougainvillea (some)
☼ ◑ ▲ ✂ CS, TS
                               p. 205

Caricature plant
☼ ◑ ✂ TS OR INDOORS
Graptophyllum pictum   p. 328

Confederate jasmine 'Variegatum'
☼ ◑ ● ▲ ✂ LS, CS, TS   p. 575
Trachelospermum jasminoides

Drooping leucothoe 'Rainbow'
☼ ◑ ● ▲ ◑ ✂ US, MS
Leucothoe fontanesiana   p. 388

Euonymus (some)
☼ ◑ ● ▲ ✂ VARY
                               p. 304

Farfugium japonicum (some)
◑ ● ▲ ✂ MS, LS, CS, TS OR INDOORS
                               p. 309

Fiveleaf aralia 'Variegatus'
☼ ◑ ● ▲▲▲ ✂ US, MS, LS
Eleutherococcus sieboldianus p. 295

Flowering dogwood
☼ ◑ ● ✂ US, MS, LS, CS
Cornus florida (several)   p. 262

Flowering maple
☼ ◑ ● ▲ ✂ CS, TS
Abutilon (some)   p. 147

French hydrangea
◑ ● ✂ US, MS, LS, CS   p. 352
Hydrangea macrophylla (several)

Golden elaeagnus
☼ ◑ ● ▲▲ ✂ US, MS, LS, CS p. 295
Elaeagnus pungens 'Maculata'

Holly
☼ ◑ ● ✂ VARY
Ilex (several)   p. 356

Holly osmanthus
☼ ◑ ● ▲▲ ✂ US, MS, LS, CS p. 439
Osmanthus heterophyllus 'Goshiki'

Ivy
☼ ◑ ● ▲ ✂ VARY
Hedera (some)   p. 337

Japanese andromeda
◑ ● ◑ ✂ US, MS
Pieris japonica 'Variegata'   p. 473

Japanese aucuba
◑ ● ▲ ✂ ALL
Aucuba japonica (several)   p. 189

Japanese pittosporum
☼ ◑ ● ▲ ✂ LS, CS, TS
Pittosporum tobira (several)   p. 478

Juniper
☼ ☼ ◑ ▲ ● ✂ VARY
Juniperus (several)   p. 370

Laurustinus
☼ ◑ ● ✂ CS   p. 586
Viburnum tinus 'Bewley's Variegated'

Mosaic Swedish ivy
◑ ● ✂ TS OR INDOORS
Plectranthus oertendahlii   p. 480

Myrtle
☼ ◑ ● ▲ ✂ CS
Myrtus communis (some)   p. 425

Orange-eye butterfly bush
☼ ◑ ● ▲ ✂ US, MS, LS, CS
Buddleia davidii 'Harlequin'   p. 211

Rock cotoneaster
☼ ◑ ▲ ● ✂ US, MS, LS
Cotoneaster horizontalis 'Variegatus'   p. 267

English holly
Ilex aquifolium 'Aurea Marginata'

Wintercreeper euonymus
Euonymus fortunei

English ivy
Hedera helix

Japanese aucuba
Aucuba japonica 'Variegata'

Japanese pittosporum
Pittosporum tobira 'Variegatum'

Juniper
Juniperus horizontalis

For climate zone explanations, please see pages 28–38.

Golden elaeagnus
Elaeagnus pungens 'Maculata'

Weigela
Weigela 'Variegata'

Winter daphne
Daphne odora 'Aureomarginala'

Bishop's weed
Aegopodium podagraria 'Variegata'

Carpet bugleweed
Ajuga reptans

Snow bush
☼ ◐ ◗ ✿ TS OR INDOORS
Breynia nivosa   p. 208

Trailing lantana
☼ ◐ ✿ LS, CS, TS OR ANNUAL
Lantana montevidensis   p. 382

Tricolor beech
☼ ◐ ◗ ✿ US, MS
Fagus sylvatica   p. 308

Variegated box elder
☼ ☼ ◐ ◗ ✿ US, MS
Acer negundo 'Variegatum'   p. 149

Variegated Chinese privet
☼ ◐ ◗ ✿ MS, LS, CS, TS   p. 390
Ligustrum sinense 'Variegatum'

Variegated winter daphne
☼ ◐ ◗ ✿ MS, LS   p. 279
Daphne odora 'Aureomarginata'

Weigela hybrid 'Variegata'
☼ ☼ ◐ ◗ ✿ US, MS, LS
                                          p. 590

VARIEGATED
Perennials

Big blue liriope
☼ ☼ ◐ ◗ ✿ ALL
Liriope muscari (some)   p. 395

Bishop's weed
☼ ☼ ◐ ◗ ✿ US, MS, LS   p. 154
Aegopodium podagraria 'Variegatum'

Bulbous oat grass
☼ ☼ ◐ ✿ US, MS, LS
Arrhenatherum   p. 181

Calathea
☼ ◐ ✿ TS OR INDOORS
                                          p. 216

Calla
☼ ◐ ◗ ✿ CS, TS
Zantedeschia   p. 593

Carpet bugleweed
☼ ◐ ◗ ● ✿ US, MS, LS
Ajuga reptans (some)   p. 157

Century plant
☼ ☼ ◐ ◊ ◊ ✿ CS, TS
Agave attenuata   p 156

Coleus
☼ ☼ ◐ ◗ ◐ ● ✿ TS OR ANNUAL
Coleus × hybridus   p. 256

Coral bells
☼ ◐ ◗ ✿ US, MS, LS
Heuchera (some)   p. 344

Cranesbill
☼ ☼ ◐ ◗ ✿ US, MS, LS
Geranium (many)   p. 322

Dead nettle
☼ ◐ ● ◗ ✿ US, MS, LS
Lamium (many)   p. 382

Obedient plant
☼ ☼ ◐ ◗ ✿ US, MS, LS, CS   p. 472
Physostegia virginiana 'Variegata'

Fancy-leafed caladium
☼ ◐ ● ◗ ◊ ✿ TS
Caladium bicolor   p. 214

Gaura (some)
☼ ◐ ◗ ✿ US, MS, LS, CS
Gaura lindheimeri   p. 320

Geranium
☼ ☼ ◐ ◗ ◗ ✿ CS, TS OR ANNUAL
Pelargonium (several)   p. 458

Impatiens, New Guinea hybrids
☼ ☼ ◐ ● ◗ ✿ TS OR ANNUAL
                                          p. 359

Japanese pachysandra
☼ ◐ ● ◗ ✿ US, MS, LS   p. 442
Pachysandra terminalis 'Variegata'

Japanese painted fern
☼ ◐ ● ◗ ◐ ✿ US, MS, LS   p. 188
Athyrium niponicum 'Pictum'

Japanese silver grass
☼ ☼ ◐ ◗ ◗ ✿ US, MS, LS
Miscanthus sinensis (several) p. 420

Lungwort
☼ ◐ ● ◗ ✿ US, MS, LS
Pulmonaria (several)   p. 497

Maranta
☼ ◐ ● ● ✿ VARY
                                          p. 414

New Zealand flax
☼ ☼ ◐ ◊ ◐ ◗ ✿ LS, CS, TS
Phormium tenax (many)   p. 470

Periwinkle
☼ ◐ ● ◐ ◗ ✿ VARY
Vinca (some)   p. 587

Plantain lily
☼ ◐ ● ◗ ✿ US, MS, LS
Hosta (several)   p. 348

Plectranthus (some)
☼ ◐ ◗ ✿ TS OR INDOORS
                                          p. 480

Sedge
☼ ☼ ◐ ● ◐ ◗ ✿ US, MS, LS, CS
Carex (several)   p. 226

Society garlic
☼ ◐ ◗ ✿ LS, CS, TS
Tulbaghia violacea (some)   p. 578

Solomon's seal
☼ ◐ ● ◗ ✿ US, MS, LS
Polygonatum   p. 486

Tricolor common sage
☼ ☼ ◐ ◗ ✿ ALL
Salvia officinalis   p. 532

Yucca (some)
☼ ◊ ◐ ◗ ✿ VARY
                                          p 592

Spotted dead nettle
Lamium maculatum

Geranium
Pelargonium × hortorum 'Golden Ears'

New Zealand flax
Phormium tenax

Plantain lily
Hosta

Tricolor common sage
Salvia officinalis 'Tricolor'

For growing symbol explanations, please see page 39.

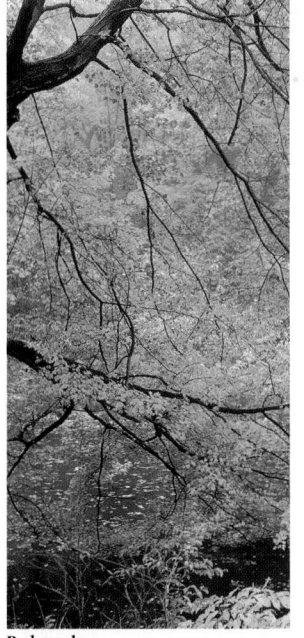
Red maple
Acer rubrum

Autumn Foliage Color

Boston ivy
Parthenocissus tricuspidata

I n most places, autumn brings the year's most pleasant weather. Just as welcome is the foliage show that accompanies it — reds, oranges, yellows, burgundies, pinks, and parchment browns. The show is brightest in the Upper and Middle South, where autumns are cooler and fewer pines and cedars dot the countryside. Fall color is hit-or-miss in the Lower South; in the Coastal and Tropical South, it's mostly a theory. But when conditions are right, the following plants take center stage. Because leaf color often varies within a species, shop for plants when they're in color, or buy reliable named selections.

American beech
Fagus grandifolia

Black gum
Nyssa sylvatica

Bald cypress
Taxodium distichum

TREES

American beech
☼ ☼ ◑ ◐ ◐ ☇ US, MS, LS, CS
Fagus grandifolia   p. 308

Ash
☼ ◐ ◑ ◐ ◐ ☇ VARY
Fraxinus   p. 316

Bald cypress
☼ ◑ ◐ ◐ ◐ ☇ US, MS, LS, CS
Taxodium distichum   p. 566

Birch
☼ ◐ ◑ ☇ VARY
Betula   p. 200

Black cherry
☼ ◑ ◐ ☇ US, MS, LS, CS
Prunus serotina   p. 495

Black gum
☼ ◐ ◑ ◐ ◐ ☇ US, MS, LS, CS
Nyssa sylvatica   p. 433

Black locust
☼ ◐ ◑ ◐ ◐ ☇ US, MS, LS, CS
Robinia pseudoacacia   p. 516

Callery pear
☼ ◐ ◑ ◐ ☇ US, MS, LS, CS
Pyrus calleryana   p. 499

Carolina silverbell
☼ ◑ ◐ ◐ ☇ US, MS, LS
Halesia carolina   p. 336

Chinese parasol tree
☼ ◑ ◐ ◐ ☇ MS, LS, CS, TS
Firmiana simplex   p. 314

Chinese pistache
☼ ◐ ◑ ◐ ☇ US, MS, LS, CS
Pistacia chinensis   p. 478

Chinese quince
☼ ◑ ◐ ☇ US, MS, LS
Pseudocydonia sinensis   p. 495

Chinese tallow
☼ ◐ ◑ ◐ ☇ LS, CS, TS
Sapium sebiferum   p. 535

Crepe myrtle
☼ ◑ ◐ ☇ US, MS, LS, CS
Lagerstroemia indica   p. 379

Dawn redwood
☼ ◑ ◐ ☇ US, MS, LS, CS
Metasequoia glyptostroboides   p. 418

Fig
☼ ◑ ◐ ☇ MS, LS, CS, TS
          p. 313

Flowering crabapple
☼ ◐ ◑ ◐ ☇ VARY
Malus   p. 409

Flowering dogwood
☼ ☼ ◑ ◐ ☇ US, MS, LS, CS
Cornus florida   p. 262

Franklin tree
☼ ☼ ◑ ◐ ☇ US, MS, LS, CS
Franklinia alatamaha   p. 316

Fringe tree
☼ ◐ ◑ ◐ ◐ ☇ US, MS, LS, CS
Chionanthus virginicus   p. 241

Goldenrain tree
☼ ◐ ◑ ◐ ☇ US, MS, LS, CS
Koelreuteria paniculata   p. 378

Hackberry
☼ ☼ ◑ ◐ ☇ US, MS, LS, CS
Celtis   p. 233

Hawthorn
☼ ◑ ◐ ☇ VARY
Crataegus (some)   p. 268

Honey locust
☼ ◐ ◑ ◐ ☇ US, MS, LS
Gleditsia triacanthos   p. 325

Ironwood
☼ ☼ ◑ ◐ ◐ ☇ US, MS, LS, CS
Carpinus caroliniana   p. 227

Chinese pistache
Pistacia chinensis

Crepe myrtle
Lagerstroemia indica

Fringe tree
Chionanthus virginicus

For climate zone explanations, please see pages 28–38. ▶

Japanese maple
Acer palmatum

Sugar maple
Acer saccharum

Persimmon
Diospyros

Quaking aspen
Populus tremuloides

Sassafras
Sassafras albidum

Juneberry
☼ ◐ ● ● ✂ US, MS, LS, CS
Amelanchier arborea   p. 164

Katsura tree
☼ ◐ ● ✂ US, MS, LS
Cercidiphyllum japonicum   p. 235

Kentucky coffee tree
☼ ● ✂ US, MS, LS
Gymnocladus dioica   p. 334

Larch
☼ ● ✂ VARY
Larix   p. 383

Linden
☼ ● ✂ VARY
Tilia   p. 572

Maidenhair tree
☼ ● ● ✂ US, MS, LS, CS
Ginkgo biloba   p. 324

Maple
☼ ◐ ● ● ✂ VARY
Acer (many)   p. 148

Mountain ash
☼ ◐ ● ● ✂ VARY
Sorbus   p. 549

Oak
☼ ● ✂ VARY
Quercus (deciduous)   p. 500

Ohio buckeye
☼ ◐ ● ◆ ✂ US, MS
Aesculus glabra   p. 154

Osage orange
☼ ◯ ● ● ✂ US, MS, LS
Maclura pomifera   p. 401

Pawpaw
☼ ● ✂ US, MS, LS, CS
          p. 450

Persimmon
☼ ● ● ✂ VARY
          p. 464

Quaking aspen
☼ ● ● ✂ US, MS
Populus tremuloides   p. 489

Redbud
☼ ◐ ◯ ● ● ✂ VARY
Cercis   p. 236

Sassafras
☼ ● ✂ US, MS, LS, CS
Sassafras albidum   p. 536

Sawleaf zelkova
☼ ● ● ✂ US, MS, LS
Zelkova serrata   p. 594

Shagbark hickory
☼ ● ● ✂ US, MS, LS, CS
Carya ovata   p. 228

Sourwood
☼ ● ● ✂ US, MS, LS, CS
Oxydendrum arboreum   p. 441

Southern wild crab
☼ ◐ ● ● ✂ US, MS, LS
Malus angustifolia   p. 410

Stewartia
☼ ● ✂ VARY
          p. 556

Sweet gum, American
☼ ◐ ● ● ✂ US, MS, LS, CS
Liquidambar styraciflua   p. 394

Tulip poplar
☼ ● ✂ US, MS, LS, CS
Liriodendron tulipifera   p. 395

Willow
☼ ● ● ✂ US, MS, LS
Salix   p. 529

Yellow wood
☼ ● ✂ US, MS, LS
Cladrastis kentukea   p. 250

Yoshino flowering cherry
☼ ● ● ✂ US, MS, LS
Prunus × yedoensis   p. 493

Yulan magnolia
☼ ◐ ● ● ✂ US, MS, LS, CS
Magnolia denudata   p. 403

SHRUBS

Azalea (deciduous)
◐ ● ● ◐ ◆ ✂ VARY
Rhododendron   p. 507

Beautyberry
☼ ◐ ● ● ✂ US, MS, LS
Callicarpa   p. 217

Blueberry
☼ ● ✂ VARY
          p. 203

Bottlebrush buckeye
☼ ◐ ● ◆ ✂ US, MS, LS, CS
Aesculus parviflora   p. 154

Chokeberry
☼ ◐ ● ● ● ✂ VARY
Aronia   p. 181

Cotoneaster (most deciduous)
☼ ◯ ● ● ✂ VARY
          p. 266

Disanthus cercidifolius
☼ ● ✂ US, MS, LS
          p. 289

Farkleberry
☼ ◐ ● ✂ MS, LS, CS
Vaccinium arboreum   p. 582

Flame grass
☼ ◐ ● ● ● ✂ US MS LS   p. 420
Miscanthus sinensis 'Purpurascens'

Fothergilla
☼ ● ✂ US, MS, LS
          p. 315

American sweet gum
Liquidambar styraciflua

Sourwood
Oxydendrum arboreum

Azalea, deciduous
Rhododendron

Chokeberry
Aronia

For growing symbol explanations, please see page 39.

Japanese barberry
Berberis thunbergii

Nandina
Nandina domestica

Oakleaf hydrangea
Hydrangea quercifolia

Shadblow serviceberry
Amelanchier canadensis

Spicebush
Lindera benzoin

Heart's-a-bustin'
☼ ◑ ● ◐ ◊ ✂ US, MS, LS, CS
Euonymus americanus   p. 304

Hercules' club
☼ ◑ ● ◐ ✂ US, MS, LS, CS
Aralia spinosa   p. 177

Japanese barberry
☼ ◑ ● ◐ ✂ US, MS, LS
Berberis thunbergii   p. 199

Japanese kerria
☼ ◑ ● ◐ ✂ US, MS, LS, CS
Kerria japonica   p. 376

Mahonia
☼ ◑ ● ◐ ◊ ◊ ✂ VARY
                             p. 408

'Miss Kim' lilac
☼ ◑ ◐ ✂ US, MS, LS
Syringa patula 'Miss Kim'   p. 563

Nandina
☼ ◑ ● ◐ ◐ ✂ US, MS, LS, CS
Nandina domestica   p. 425

Oakleaf hydrangea
◑ ● ✂ US, MS, LS, CS
Hydrangea quercifolia   p. 353

Oriental photinia
☼ ● ◐ ✂ US, MS, LS
Photinia villosa   p. 471

Persian parrotia
☼ ◑ ● ◐ ✂ US, MS, LS
Parrotia persica   p. 447

Pomegranate
☼ ● ◐ ✂ MS, LS, CS
                             p. 488

Redvein enkianthus
☼ ◑ ● ◐ ◐ ✂ US, MS, LS
Enkianthus campanulatus   p. 296

Rose
☼ ◑ ◐ ✂ ALL
Rosa (some)   p. 516

Shadblow serviceberry
☼ ● ◐ ✂ US, MS, LS
Amelanchier canadensis   p. 164

Smoke tree
☼ ◑ ◐ ✂ US, MS, LS
Cotinus   p. 266

Spicebush
☼ ◑ ● ◐ ✂ US, MS, LS
Lindera benzoin   p. 393

Star magnolia
☼ ◑ ● ◐ ✂ US, MS, LS, CS
Magnolia stellata   p. 407

Sumac
☼ ● ◐ ◐ ✂ VARY
Rhus   p. 514

Summersweet
☼ ◑ ● ◐ ◐ ✂ US, MS, LS, CS
Clethra alnifolia   p. 253

Sweetshrub, common
☼ ◑ ● ◐ ◊ ✂ US, MS, LS, CS
Calycanthus floridus   p. 219

Sweetbells
◑ ● ◐ ◊ ✂ US, MS, LS, CS
Leucothoe racemosa   p. 389

Titi
☼ ◑ ● ◐ ◐ ✂ ALL
Cyrilla racemiflora   p. 276

Van Houtte spiraea
☼ ◑ ● ◐ ✂ US, MS, LS
Spiraea × vanhouttei   p. 552

Viburnum (many)
☼ ◑ ● ◐ ✂ VARY
                             p. 585

Virginia sweetspire
☼ ● ◐ ✂ US, MS, LS, CS
Itea virginica   p. 366

Winged euonymus
☼ ◑ ● ◐ ◐ ✂ US, MS, LS
Euonymus alatus   p. 304

Winterberry
☼ ◑ ● ◐ ◐ ✂ US, MS, LS, CS
Ilex verticillata   p. 358

Witch hazel, common
☼ ◑ ● ◐ ✂ US, MS, LS, CS
Hamamelis virginiana   p. 336

VINES, PERENNIALS

Bittersweet
☼ ◑ ◐ ✂ US, MS, LS
Celastrus   p. 233

Boston ivy
☼ ◑ ● ◐ ◐ ✂ US, MS, LS
Parthenocissus tricuspidata p. 448

Bowman's root
☼ ● ◐ ✂ US MS LS
Gillenia trifoliata   p. 324

Dwarf plumbago
☼ ● ◐ ✂ US MS LS CS   p. 235
Ceratostigma plumbaginoides

Grape
☼ ◐ ◐ ✂ VARY
                             p. 328

Hubricht's bluestar
☼ ◑ ● ◐ ◐ ✂ US MS LS CS
Amsonia hubrichtii   p. 165

Royal fern
☼ ◑ ● ◐ ✂ ALL
Osmunda regalis   p. 440

Virginia creeper
☼ ◑ ● ◐ ✂ US, MS, LS, CS
Parthenocissus quinquefolia p. 448

Wisteria
☼ ◑ ◐ ✂ US, MS, LS, CS
                             p. 590

Sumac
Rhus

Doublefile viburnum
Viburnum plicatum 'Marresii'

Summersweet
Clethra alnifolia

Smoke tree
Cotinus coggygria

Virginia creeper
Parthenocissus quinquefolia

For climate zone explanations, please see pages 28–38.   ▶

Deciduous Plants
for Winter Interest

Persimmon

Most Southerners prefer evergreens for their long season of color. Still, deciduous plants offer a special beauty, especially in gardens in the Upper South, where winters can be long. Peeling bark, contorted limbs, and winter fruit cause us to reflect on the subtleties of gardening, those quiet details that make every day outdoors a learning adventure.

Yellowtwig dogwood
Cornus sericea 'Flaviramea'

American beech
Fagus grandifolia

American beech
☼ ◐ ● ◑ ◑ ✂ US, MS, LS, CS
Fagus grandifolia   p. 308

Birch
☼ ◑ ◑ ✂ VARY
Betula (most)   p. 200

Black walnut
☼ ◑ ✂ US, MS, LS, CS
Juglans nigra   p. 369

Chinese elm
☼ ◑ ✂ US, MS, LS, CS
Ulmus parvifolia   p. 581

Coral bark maple
☼ ◐ ◑ ◑ ✂ US, MS, LS, CS   p. 149
Acer palmatum 'Sango Kaku'

Corkscrew willow
☼ ◑ ◑ ✂ US, MS, LS
Salix matsudana 'Tortuosa'   p. 530

Crepe myrtle
☼ ◑ ✂ US, MS, LS, CS
Lagerstroemia indica   p. 379

Flowering dogwood
☼ ◑ ✂ US, MS, LS, CS
Cornus florida   p. 262

Harry Lauder's walking stick
☼ ◐ ◑ ✂ US, MS, LS
Corylus avellana 'Contorta'   p. 265

Heart's-a-bustin'
◐ ● ◑ ◑ ✂ US, MS, LS, CS
Euonymus americanus   p. 304

Ironwood
☼ ◐ ● ◑ ◑ ✂ US, MS, LS, CS
Carpinus caroliniana   p. 227

Japanese flowering cherry
☼ ◑ ◑ ✂ VARY
Prunus serrulata   p. 493

Japanese kerria
◐ ◑ ◑ ✂ US, MS, LS, CS
Kerria japonica   p. 376

Japanese tree lilac
☼ ◑ ✂ US, MS
Syringa reticulata   p. 564

Kentucky coffee tree
☼ ◑ ✂ US, MS, LS
Gymnocladus dioica   p. 334

Lacebark pine
☼ ○ ◑ ✂ US, MS
Pinus bungeana   p. 475

Maidenhair tree
☼ ◑ ◑ ✂ US, MS, LS, CS
Ginkgo biloba   p. 324

Oakleaf hydrangea
◐ ◑ ✂ US, MS, LS, CS
Hydrangea quercifolia   p. 353

Paperbark maple
☼ ◐ ◑ ◑ ✂ US, MS
Acer griseum   p. 149

Persimmon
☼ ◑ ◑ ✂ VARY
                                     p. 464

Redtwig, yellowtwig dogwood
☼ ◐ ◑ ● ◑ ◑ ✂ US, MS
Cornus   p. 262

Saucer magnolia
☼ ◑ ◑ ✂ US, MS, LS, CS
Magnolia × soulangeana   p. 406

Shagbark hickory
☼ ◑ ◑ ✂ US, MS, LS, CS
Carya ovata   p. 228

Stewartia
◐ ◑ ✂ VARY
                                     p. 556

Sycamore
☼ ◑ ✂ VARY
Platanus   p. 479

White oak
☼ ◑ ✂ US, MS, LS, CS
Quercus alba   p. 500

Winged euonymus
☼ ◐ ● ◑ ◑ ✂ US, MS, LS
Euonymus alatus   p. 304

Winterberry
☼ ◐ ◑ ◑ ✂ US, MS, LS, CS
Ilex verticillata   p. 358

Chinese elm
Ulmus parvifolia

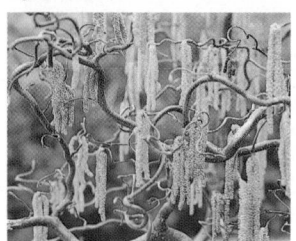

Crepe myrtle
Lagerstroemia indica

Redtwig dogwood
Cornus sericea

Japanese stewartia
Stewartia pseudocamellia

Sycamore
Platanus

Winterberry
Ilex verticillata

Harry Lauder's walking stick
Corylus avellana 'Contorta'

For growing symbol explanations, please see page 39.

Trees

Magnolia

No decision affects your garden more than the numbers and types of trees you plant. So save yourself a lot of time, money, and trouble by selecting trees that are long-lived, strong-wooded, and not pestered by insects and diseases. Lawn trees should cast light, filtered shade and be deep rooted. Trees that shade decks, patios, and parking areas shouldn't drop messy fruits. Always consider a tree's mature size. Here, small trees grow up to 30 feet tall and wide; medium trees grow 30 to 60 feet; and large trees grow more than 60 feet—but mature sizes vary somewhat across the South.

Flowering dogwood
Cornus florida

Crepe myrtle
Lagerstroemia indica

Franklin tree
Franklinia alatamaha

English hawthorn
Crataegus laevigata

SMALL TREES
Deciduous

Amur maple
☼ ◐ ◊ ◖ ✂ US, MS, LS
Acer tataricum ginnala   p. 151

Brazilian orchid tree
☼ ◐ ◊ ◖ ✂ CS, TS
Bauhinia forficata   p. 194

Carolina silver bell
☼ ◐ ◊ ✂ US, MS, LS
Halesia carolina   p. 336

Crepe myrtle
☼ ◊ ◖ ✂ US, MS, LS, CS
Lagerstroemia indica   p. 379

Cry-baby tree
☼ ◊ ◖ ✂ LS, CS, TS
Erythrina crista-galli   p. 301

Desert willow
☼ ◊ ◖ ✂ MS, LS, CS
Chilopsis linearis   p. 240

Flowering crabapple
☼ ◖ ✂ VARY
Malus   p. 409

Flowering dogwood
☼ ◖ ◖ ✂ US, MS, LS, CS
Cornus florida   p. 262

Franklin tree
☼ ◐ ◖ ◖ ✂ US, MS, LS, CS
Franklinia alatamaha   p. 316

Fringe tree
☼ ◐ ◖ ◖ ✂ US, MS, LS, CS
Chionanthus   p. 241

Harlequin glorybower
◐ ◖ ✂ MS, LS, CS, TS
Clerodendrum trichotomum p. 253

Hawthorn
☼ ◖ ✂ VARY
Crataegus   p. 268

Hong Kong orchid tree
☼ ◖ ◖ ✂ TS
Bauhinia × blakeana   p. 194

Hop hornbeam
☼ ◐ ◖ ◖ ✂ US, MS, LS, CS
Ostrya   p. 440

Japanese flowering apricot
☼ ◐ ◖ ◖ ✂ US, MS, LS, CS
Prunus mume   p. 495

Japanese maple
☼ ◐ ◖ ◖ ✂ US, MS, LS, CS
Acer palmatum   p. 149

Japanese stewartia
◐ ◖ ✂ US, MS
Stewartia pseudocamellia   p. 556

Jerusalem thorn
☼ ◊ ◖ ◖ ✂ CS, TS
Parkinsonia aculeata   p. 447

Jujube
☼ ◖ ◖ ✂ US, MS, LS, CS
          p. 370

Juneberry
☼ ◐ ◖ ◖ ✂ US, MS, LS, CS
Amelanchier arborea   p. 164

Kousa dogwood
☼ ◐ ◖ ◖ ✂ US, MS, LS
Cornus kousa   p. 263

Lilac chaste tree
☼ ◖ ◖ ✂ US, MS, LS, CS
Vitex agnus-castus   p. 588

Mountain ash
☼ ◐ ◖ ◖ ✂ VARY
Sorbus   p. 549

Paperbark maple
☼ ◐ ◖ ◖ ✂ US, MS
Acer griseum   p. 149

Persian parrotia
☼ ◐ ◖ ◖ ✂ US, MS, LS
Parrotia persica   p. 447

Persimmon (Japanese)
☼ ◖ ◖ ✂ MS, LS, CS
          p. 464

Purple orchid tree
☼ ◖ ◖ ✂ TS
Bauhinia variegata   p. 194

Japanese maple
Acer palmatum

Kousa dogwood
Cornus kousa

Lilac chaste tree
Vitex agnus-castus

Paperpark maple
Acer griseum

For climate zone explanations, please see pages 28–38.   ▶

Redbud
☼ ◑ ◊ ◊ ◊ ❚ VARY
Cercis p. 236

Silky stewartia
☼ ◑ ◊ ❚ MS, LS, CS
Stewartia malacodendron p. 556

Smoke tree
☼ ◑ ❚ US, MS, LS
Cotinus coggygria p. 266

Sourwood
☼ ◑ ◊ ◊ ❚ US, MS, LS, CS
Oxydendrum arboreum p. 441

Star magnolia
☼ ◑ ◊ ◊ ❚ US, MS, LS, CS
Magnolia stellata p. 407

Snowbell
☼ ◑ ◊ ◊ ❚ VARY
Styrax p. 560

Sweet acacia
☼ ◊ ❚ LS, CS, TS
Acacia farnesiana p. 147

Titi
☼ ◑ ◊ ◊ ◊ ❚ ALL
Cyrilla racemiflora p. 276

Trident maple
☼ ◑ ◊ ◊ ❚ US, MS, LS
Acer buergerianum p. 148

Trumpet tree
☼ ◑ ◊ ❚ TS
Tabebuia p. 564

Yellow wood
☼ ◊ ❚ US, MS, LS
Cladrastis kentukea p. 250

SMALL TREES
Evergreen

Bottlebrush
☼ ◊ ◊ ❚ VARY
Callistemon p. 217

Buckwheat tree
☼ ◊ ◊ ❚ LS, CS
Cliftonia monophylla p. 254

Citrus
☼ ◊ ❚ CS, TS
 p. 247

Dracaena
☼ ◑ ◊ ❚ TS
 p. 290

Fern pine
☼ ◑ ◊ ❚ TS
Podocarpus gracilior p. 485

Giant dracaena
☼ ◊ ◊ ❚ CS, TS
Cordyline australis p. 259

Giant thevetia
☼ ◊ ◊ ❚ TS
Thevetia thevetioides p. 569

Glossy privet
☼ ◑ ◊ ◊ ◊ ❚ LS, CS, TS
Ligustrum lucidum p. 390

Gold medallion tree
☼ ◊ ◊ ❚ TS
Cassia leptophylla p. 229

Hawaiian tree fern
◊ ◊ ❚ TS
Cibotium p. 246

'Little Gem' Southern magnolia
☼ ◊ ◊ ❚ US, MS, LS, CS
Magnolia grandiflora p. 404

Loquat
☼ ◑ ◊ ◊ ◊ ❚ LS, CS, TS
Eriobotrya japonica p. 300

Mango
☼ ◊ ◊ ❚ TS
 p. 413

Plum yew
☼ ◑ ◊ ◊ ❚ VARY
Cephalotaxus p. 235

Sea grape
☼ ◊ ❚ TS
Coccoloba p. 255

Silver dollar tree
☼ ◊ ❚ LS, CS, TS
Eucalyptus cinerea p. 303

Sweet bay
☼ ◑ ◊ ❚ US, MS, LS, CS
Magnolia virginiana p. 408

Sweet olive
◊ ◊ ◊ ◊ ❚ LS, CS, TS
Osmanthus fragrans p. 439

Texas mountain laurel
☼ ◑ ◊ ◊ ❚ LS, CS
Sophora secundiflora p. 549

Wax myrtle
☼ ◊ ◊ ❚ MS, LS, CS, TS
Myrica cerifera p. 425

MEDIUM TREES
Deciduous

Birch
☼ ◊ ◊ ◊ ❚ VARY
Betula p. 200

Buttercup tree
☼ ◊ ❚ TS
Cochlospermum vitifolium p. 255

Callery pear
☼ ◊ ◊ ❚ US, MS, LS, CS
Pyrus calleryana p. 499

Chestnut
☼ ◊ ❚ US, MS, LS
 p. 240

Chinaberry
☼ ◊ ◊ ❚ MS, LS, CS, TS
Melia azedarach p. 416

Smoke tree
Cotinus coggygria

Orange tree
Citrus

Giant dracaena
Cordyline australis

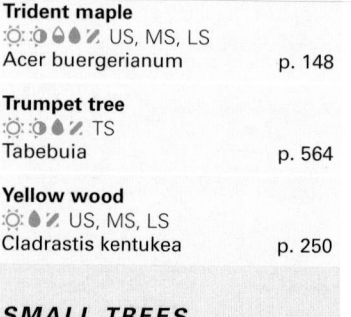

Redbud
Cercis

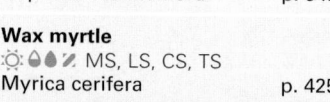

Glossy privet
Ligustrum lucidum

Star magnolia
Magnolia stellata

Silver dollar tree
Eucalyptus cinerea

Texas mountain laurel
Sophora secundiflora

Chinese elm
Ulmus parvifolia

For growing symbol explanations, please see page 39.

Goldenchain tree
Laburnum

Honey locust
Gleditsia triacanthos inermis 'Sunburst'

Jacaranda
Jacaranda mimosifolia

Saucer magnolia
Magnolia soulangiana

Chinese elm
☼ ● ◑ ✺ US, MS, LS, CS
Ulmus parvifolia p. 581

Chinese pistache
☼ ◑ ◐ ◑ ✺ US, MS, LS, CS
Pistacia chinensis p. 478

Chinese tallow
☼ ● ◐ ◑ ◊ ✺ LS, CS, TS
Sapium sebiferum p. 535

Chitalpa
☼ ◑ ◐ ◑ ✺ MS, LS, CS
× Chitalpa tashkentensis p. 242

Dove tree
◑ ● ✺ US, MS, LS
Davidia involucrata p. 280

Floss silk tree
☼ ◑ ✺ TS
Chorisia p. 242

Goldenchain tree
◑ ● ◐ ● ◊ ✺ US, MS
Laburnum p. 379

Hardy rubber tree
☼ ● ◑ ✺ US, MS
Eucommia ulmoides p. 303

Honey locust
☼ ● ◑ ✺ US, MS, LS
Gleditsia triacanthos p. 325

Ironwood
☼ ● ◐ ● ◑ ✺ US, MS, LS, CS
Carpinus caroliniana p. 227

Jacaranda
☼ ● ✺ TS
Jacaranda mimosifolia p. 367

Japanese pagoda tree
☼ ◑ ● ✺ US, MS, LS
Sophora japonica p. 549

Katsura tree
☼ ◑ ● ✺ US, MS, LS
Cercidiphyllum japonicum p. 235

Koelreuteria
☼ ● ◑ ✺ VARY
p. 378

Korean evodia
☼ ● ◑ ✺ US, MS, LS
Tetradium daniellii p. 567

Little-leaf linden
☼ ● ✺ US, MS
Tilia cordata p. 572

Magnolia (some)
☼ ● ◑ ● ✺ VARY
p. 402

Mesquite
☼ ◊ ✺ MS, LS, CS, TS
Prosopis glandulosa p. 492

Sassafras
☼ ◑ ● ✺ US, MS, LS, CS
Sassafras albidum p. 536

Shower of gold
☼ ◑ ◐ ✺ TS
Cassia fistula p. 229

Texas persimmon
☼ ◑ ◊ ✺ MS, LS, CS, TS
Diospyros texana p. 289

Willow
☼ ● ◐ ● ✺ US, MS, LS
Salix p. 529

Yoshino flowering cherry
☼ ● ◑ ✺ US, MS, LS
Prunus × yedoensis p. 493

MEDIUM TREES
Evergreen

Arborvitae
☼ ◑ ● ◑ ✺ VARY
Thuja p. 569

Bailey acacia
☼ ◊ ✺ CS, TS
Acacia baileyana p. 147

Chilean wine palm
☼ ◑ ◐ ✺ LS, CS, TS
Jubaea chilensis p. 369

Eastern red cedar
☼ ◑ ◐ ◑ ✺ ALL
Juniperus virginiana p. 373

Eucalyptus (several)
☼ ◊ ✺ VARY
p. 302

Hinoki false cypress
◑ ● ✺ US, MS, LS
Chamaecyparis obtusa p. 237

Holly (many)
☼ ◑ ● ✺ VARY
Ilex p. 356

Loblolly bay
☼ ◑ ● ◑ ✺ MS, LS, CS, TS
Gordonia lasianthus p. 327

Lychee
☼ ● ✺ CS, TS
p. 399

Queen palm
☼ ● ✺ CS, TS
Syagrus romanzoffiana p. 562

Southern sweet bay
☼ ◑ ● ✺ MS, LS, CS, TS
Magnolia virginiana australis p. 408

Windmill palm
☼ ◑ ● ◐ ✺ LS, CS, TS
Trachycarpus fortunei p. 575

LARGE TREES
Deciduous

American beech
☼ ◑ ● ◑ ✺ US, MS, LS, CS
Fagus grandifolia p. 308

Sassafras
Sassafras albidum

Hinoki false cypress
Chamaecyparis obtusa

Eastern red cedar
Juniperus virginiana

Windmill palm
Trachycarpus fortunei

For climate zone explanations, please see pages 28–38.

American beech
Fagus grandifolia

Catalpa, common
Catalpa bignonioides

Sweet gum
Liquidambar

Dawn redwood
Metasequoia glyptostroboides

American sycamore
☼ ◑ ✂ US, MS, LS, CS
Platanus occidentalis   p. 479

Ash (white and green)
☼ ◑ ✂ US, MS, LS, CS
Fraxinus   p. 316

Bald cypress
☼ ○ ◐ ◑ ◐ ✂ US, MS, LS, CS
Taxodium distichum   p. 566

Black gum
☼ ◑ ◐ ◑ ◐ ✂ US, MS, LS, CS
Nyssa sylvatica   p. 433

Black locust
☼ ○ ◐ ◑ ◐ ✂ US, MS, LS, CS
Robinia pseudoacacia   p. 516

Catalpa
☼ ◑ ○ ◐ ◑ ✂ US, MS, LS, CS
            p. 230

Dawn redwood
☼ ◐ ◑ ✂ US, MS, LS, CS   p. 418
Metasequoia glyptostroboides

Hackberry
☼ ◑ ◐ ✂ US, MS, LS, CS
Celtis   p. 233

Kentucky coffee tree
☼ ◐ ✂ US, MS, LS
Gymnocladus dioica   p. 334

London plane tree
☼ ◐ ✂ US, MS, LS
Platanus × acerifolia   p. 479

Maidenhair tree
☼ ◐ ◑ ✂ US, MS, LS, CS
Ginkgo biloba   p. 324

Norway maple
☼ ◑ ○ ◐ ◑ ✂ US, MS
Acer platanoides   p. 149

Oak (many)
☼ ◐ ✂ VARY
Quercus   p. 500

Pecan
☼ ◐ ✂ US, MS, LS, CS
            p. 456

Red maple
☼ ◑ ○ ◐ ◑ ✂ US, MS, LS, CS
Acer rubrum   p. 150

River birch
☼ ◐ ◑ ✂ US, MS, LS, CS
Betula nigra   p. 200

Sawleaf zelkova
☼ ◐ ◑ ✂ US, MS, LS
Zelkova serrata   p. 594

Shagbark hickory
☼ ◐ ◑ ✂ US, MS, LS, CS
Carya ovata   p. 228

Silk-cotton tree
☼ ◐ ◑ ✂ TS
Ceiba pentandra   p. 232

Sugar maple
☼ ◑ ○ ◐ ◑ ✂ US, MS, LS
Acer saccharum   p. 150

Sweet gum
☼ ◐ ◑ ✂ VARY
Liquidambar   p. 394

Tulip poplar
☼ ◐ ✂ US, MS, LS, CS
Liriodendron tulipifera   p. 395

LARGE TREES
Evergreen

Cabbage palm
☼ ◑ ◐ ✂ LS, CS, TS
Sabal palmetto   p. 528

Camphor tree
☼ ◑ ○ ◐ ◑ ✂ LS, CS, TS
Cinnamomum camphora   p. 246

Canadian hemlock
☼ ◑ ◐ ✂ US, MS, LS
Tsuga canadensis   p. 578

Cedar
☼ ◐ ✂ VARY
Cedrus   p. 232

Cypress
☼ ○ ◐ ✂ VARY
Cupressus   p. 272

Date palm
☼ ◐ ✂ CS, TS
Phoenix   p. 469

Incense cedar
☼ ◑ ○ ◐ ◑ ✂ US, MS, LS
Calocedrus decurrens   p. 218

Japanese cryptomeria
☼ ◐ ◑ ✂ US, MS, LS
Cryptomeria japonica   p. 271

Laurel oak
☼ ◐ ◑ ✂ MS, LS, CS, TS
Quercus laurifolia   p. 501

Live oak
☼ ◐ ✂ LS, CS, TS
Quercus virginiana   p. 502

Pines (most)
☼ ○ ◐ ✂ VARY
Pinus   p. 474

Royal palm
☼ ◐ ✂ TS
Roystonea   p. 525

Southern magnolia
☼ ◑ ◐ ✂ US, MS, LS, CS
Magnolia grandiflora   p. 404

Spruce
☼ ◑ ◐ ◑ ✂ US, MS
Picea   p. 472

White cedar
☼ ◑ ◐ ✂ US, MS, LS, CS
Chamaecyparis thyoides   p. 238

Cabbage palm
Sabal palmetto

Camphor tree
Cinnamomum camphora

Blue Atlas cedar
Cedrus atlantica 'Glauca'

Live oak
Quercus virginiana

For growing symbol explanations, please see page 39.

Rose
Rosa

Plants for
Hedges and Screens

W hen Robert Frost wrote, "Good fences make good neighbors," he might have added, "and so do hedges and screens." Shrubs and trees with dense foliage from top to bottom can block unwanted views, create privacy, edge a walk or path, lessen the effects of noise and wind, and provide a pleasant background for flowering plants. Some shrubs and trees, indicated by the symbol ♦♦♦, can be sheared into formal hedges.

Lemon bottlebrush
Callistemon citrinus

Flowering quince
Chaenomeles

Bay
Laurus nobilis 'Saratoga'

Hawthorn
Crataegus

Japanese barberry
Berberis thunbergii

DECIDUOUS

Bayberry
☼ ◐ ❀ ✿ US, MS
Myrica pensylvanica   p. 425

Beauty bush
☼ ◐ ❀ ✿ US, MS, LS
Kolkwitzia amabilis   p. 378

Callery pear
☼ ◐ ❀ ✿ US, MS, LS, CS
Pyrus calleryana   p. 499

Doublefile viburnum
☼ ◐ ❀ ✿ US, MS, LS   p. 586
Viburnum plicatum tomentosum

English oak
☼ ❀ ✿ US, MS, LS
Quercus robur   p. 501

European beech   ♦♦♦
☼ ◐ ❀ ✿ US, MS
Fagus sylvatica   p. 308

European hornbeam   ♦♦♦
☼ ◐ ❀ ✿ US, MS, LS
Carpinus betulus   p. 227

Fiveleaf aralia   ♦♦♦
☼ ◐ ❀ ◐ ◐ ❀ ◐ ✿ US, MS, LS p. 295
Eleutherococcus sieboldianus

Flowering quince   ♦♦♦
☼ ❀ ✿ US, MS, LS, CS
Chaenomeles   p. 237

Hardy orange   ♦♦♦
☼ ❀ ✿ US, MS, LS, CS
Poncirus trifoliata   p. 488

Hawthorn
☼ ❀ ✿ VARY
Crataegus   p. 268

Hedge maple   ♦♦♦
☼ ◐ ◐ ❀ ✿ US, MS, LS
Acer campestre   p. 149

Japanese barberry   ♦♦♦
☼ ◐ ❀ ✿ US, MS, LS
Berberis thunbergii   p. 199

Osage orange
☼ ◐ ◐ ❀ ✿ US, MS, LS
Maclura pomifera   p. 401

'PJM' rhododendron   ♦♦♦
☼ ◐ ❀ ◐ ✿ US, MS, LS
                                      p. 509

Rose
☼ ◐ ❀ ✿ ALL
Rosa (shrub)   p. 516

Russian olive
☼ ◐ ◐ ◐ ❀ ✿ US, MS
Elaeagnus angustifolia   p. 295

Spiraea
☼ ◐ ❀ ✿ VARY
                                      p. 552

Weigela
☼ ◐ ❀ ✿ US, MS, LS
Weigela florida   p. 590

Winged euonymus (some)   ♦♦♦
☼ ◐ ❀ ◐ ❀ ✿ US, MS, LS
Euonymus alatus   p. 304

Winter honeysuckle   ♦♦♦
☼ ◐ ◐ ❀ ✿ US, MS, LS
Lonicera fragrantissima   p. 397

EVERGREEN

Arborvitae   ♦♦♦
☼ ◐ ❀ ◐ ✿ VARY
Thuja   p. 569

Bamboo
☼ ◐ ◐ ◐ ❀ ✿ VARY
                                      p. 190

Banana shrub
☼ ◐ ❀ ✿ LS, CS, TS
Michelia figo   p. 418

Barberry (some)   ♦♦♦
☼ ◐ ❀ ✿ VARY
Berberis   p. 198

Bay   ♦♦♦
☼ ◐ ❀ ✿ LS, CS, TS
Laurus nobilis   p. 384

Spiraea
Spiraea japonica 'Goldflame'

Weigela
Weigela florida

Winged euonymus
Euonymus alatus

Bamboo

For climate zone explanations, please see pages 28–38. ▶

EASY LANDSCAPING

Boxwood
Buxus

Sasanqua camellia
Camellia sasanqua

Chinese fringe
Loropetalum chinense

English holly
Ilex aquifolium 'Argentea Marginata'

Japanese black pine
Pinus thunbergii

Boxwood ♦♦♦
☼ ☼ ◐ ♦ ✂ VARY
Buxus — p. 213

Camellia
☼ ◐ ♦ ✂ US, MS, LS, CS
— p. 220

Canadian hemlock ♦♦♦
☼ ☼ ◐ ♦ ✂ US, MS, LS
Tsuga canadensis — p. 578

Cape honeysuckle
☼ ☼ ◐ ♦ ✂ CS, TS
Tecoma capensis — p. 567

Carolina cherry laurel ♦♦♦
☼ ◐ ◐ ♦ ✂ US, MS, LS, CS
Prunus caroliniana — p. 492

Chinese fringe
☼ ☼ ◐ ♦ ✂ MS, LS, CS
Loropetalum chinense — p. 398

Chinese hibiscus
☼ ♦ ✂ CS, TS
Hibiscus rosa-sinensis — p. 346

Colorado blue spruce
☼ ☼ ◐ ◐ ◐ ✂ US, MS, LS
Picea pungens — p. 472

Elaeagnus (some) ♦♦♦
☼ ☼ ◐ ◐ ◐ ✂ VARY
— p. 295

Feijoa, Pineapple guava
☼ ◐ ♦ ✂ LS, CS, TS
— p. 310

Firethorn ♦♦♦
☼ ◐ ♦ ✂ VARY
Pyracantha — p. 498

Gardenia, common
☼ ☼ ◐ ♦ ✂ LS, CS, TS
Gardenia jasminoides — p. 319

Germander ♦♦♦
☼ ☼ ◐ ♦ ✂ US, MS, LS, CS
Teucrium chamaedrys — p. 568

Glossy abelia ♦♦♦
☼ ☼ ◐ ♦ ✂ US, MS, LS, CS
Abelia × grandiflora — p. 146

Holly ♦♦♦
☼ ☼ ◐ ♦ ✂ VARY
Ilex — p. 356

Indian hawthorn ♦♦♦
☼ ☼ ◐ ◐ ◐ ✂ LS, CS
Rhaphiolepis indica — p. 505

Italian cypress
☼ ◐ ◐ ✂ MS, LS, CS
Cupressus sempervirens — p. 273

Japanese anise
☼ ● ◐ ◐ ♦ ✂ MS, LS, CS
Illicium anisatum — p. 358

Japanese aucuba
☼ ◐ ◐ ◐ ♦ ✂ ALL
Aucuba japonica — p. 189

Japanese black pine
☼ ◐ ♦ ♦ ✂ US, MS, LS, CS
Pinus thunbergii — p. 477

Japanese cleyera ♦♦♦
☼ ☼ ◐ ♦ ✂ MS, LS, CS, TS
Ternstroemia gymnanthera — p. 567

Japanese pittosporum ♦♦♦
☼ ☼ ◐ ◐ ♦ ✂ LS, CS, TS
Pittosporum tobira — p. 478

Juniper ♦♦♦
☼ ☼ ◐ ◐ ◐ ♦ ✂ VARY
Juniperus (shrub, columnar) — p. 370

Lemon bottlebrush ♦♦♦
☼ ◐ ♦ ✂ LS, CS, TS
Callistemon citrinus — p. 218

Leyland cypress ♦♦♦
☼ ◐ ♦ ✂ US, MS, LS, CS
× Cupressocyparis leylandii — p. 272

Nandina
☼ ☼ ◐ ◐ ♦ ✂ US, MS, LS, CS
Nandina domestica — p. 425

Natal plum ♦♦♦
☼ ☼ ◐ ◐ ◐ ♦ ✂ CS, TS
Carissa macrocarpa — p. 227

Oleander
☼ ☼ ◐ ◐ ♦ ◐ ✂ LS, CS, TS
Nerium oleander — p. 431

Orange jessamine
☼ ◐ ♦ ✂ TS
Murraya paniculata — p. 423

Osmanthus (several) ♦♦♦
☼ ☼ ◐ ◐ ◐ ♦ ✂ VARY
— p. 439

Podocarpus ♦♦♦
☼ ☼ ◐ ♦ ✂ VARY
— p. 485

Privet (some)
☼ ☼ ◐ ♦ ◐ ✂ VARY
Ligustrum — p. 390

Texas ranger
☼ ☼ ◐ ◐ ✂ LS, CS, TS
Leucophyllum frutescens — p. 388

Viburnum (several)
☼ ☼ ◐ ♦ ✂ VARY
— p. 585

Wax myrtle ♦♦♦
☼ ☼ ◐ ♦ ✂ MS, LS, CS, TS
Myrica cerifera — p. 425

White pine
☼ ☼ ◐ ♦ ✂ US, MS
Pinus strobus — p. 476

Yellow bells
☼ ☼ ◐ ♦ ✂ CS, TS
Tecoma stans — p. 567

Yew ♦♦♦
☼ ☼ ◐ ◐ ◐ ♦ ✂ US, MS
Taxus — p. 566

Leyland cypress
× Cupressocyparis leylandii

Oleander
Nerium oleander

Holly osmanthus
Osmanthus heterophyllus 'Goshiki'

Privet
Ligustrum

Leatherleaf viburnum
Viburnum rhytidophyllum

For growing symbol explanations, please see page 39.

Trumpet honeysuckle
Lonicera sempervirens

Vines
and Vinelike Plants

Vines are the garden's most flexible members. Unlike trees and shrubs, which have fairly rigid stems, the stems of most vines can be guided to grow where you want them. You can train them to grow upward or outward on a flat, vertical surface; up and around a tree trunk; or up and over an arbor. Many perform alternative duty as a ground cover. Some vines climb with tendrils, some use aerial roots, and some employ suction-cuplike holdfasts. Some simply laze about; they only climb if tied to a support. On the following chart, the symbol ❋ indicates vines with showy flowers.

Bower vine
Pandorea jasminoides

Armand clematis
Clematis armandii

Bougainvillea

Cape honeysuckle
Tecoma capensis

Fiveleaf akebia
Akebia quinata

Cape honeysuckle
Tecoma capensis

EVERGREEN

Allamanda ❋
☼ ◑ ♦ ✂ TS OR ANNUAL
p. 159

Armand clematis ❋
☼ ◑ ✂ LS, CS
Clematis armandii   p. 251

Bleeding heart vine ❋
☼ ◑ ◑ ✂ TS
Clerodendrum thomsoniae   p. 253

Blue pea vine ❋
☼ ☼ ◑ ◑ ✂ TS OR ANNUAL
Clitoria ternatea   p. 254

Boston Ivy
☼ ☼ ◑ ◑ ✂ US, MS, LS
Parthenocissus tricuspidata   p. 448

Bougainvillea ❋
☼ ◑ ◑ ✂ CS, TS
p. 205

Cape honeysuckle ❋
☼ ☼ ◑ ◑ ✂ CS, TS
Tecoma capensis   p. 567

Carolina jessamine ❋
☼ ☼ ◑ ◑ ◑ ✂ MS, LS, CS
Gelsemium sempervirens   p. 321

Cat's claw ❋
☼ ☼ ◑ ✂ LS, CS, TS
Macfadyena unguis-cati   p. 401

Confederate jasmine ❋
☼ ☼ ◑ ◑ ✂ LS, CS, TS   p. 575
Trachelospermum jasminoides

Creeping fig ❋
☼ ☼ ◑ ◑ ◑ ✂ LS, CS, TS OR INDOORS
Ficus pumila   p. 312

Crossvine ❋
☼ ☼ ◑ ◑ ✂ US, MS, LS, CS
Bignonia capreolata   p. 201

Cup-of-gold vine ❋
☼ ◑ ◑ ✂ TS
Solandra maxima   p. 547

× Fatshedera lizei
☼ ◑ ◑ ◑ ✂ LS, CS, TS
p. 309

Fiveleaf akebia ❋
☼ ☼ ◑ ◑ ✂ US, MS, LS, CS
Akebia quinata   p. 158

Flame vine ❋
☼ ☼ ◑ ✂ CS, TS
Pyrostegia venusta   p. 499

Grape ivy
☼ ◑ ◑ ◑ ✂ TS OR INDOORS
Cissus rhombifolia   p. 246

Herald's trumpet ❋
☼ ☼ ◑ ✂ TS
Beaumontia grandiflora   p. 196

Honeysuckle ❋
☼ ☼ ◑ ◑ ◑ ✂ VARY
Lonicera (some)   p. 397

Ivy
☼ ☼ ◑ ◑ ◑ ◑ ✂ VARY
Hedera   p. 337

Jackson vine
☼ ☼ ◑ ◑ ◑ ◑ ✂ MS, LS, CS
Smilax smallii   p. 547

Jasmine ❋
☼ ☼ ◑ ◑ ✂ VARY
Jasminum (several)   p. 367

Madagascar jasmine ❋
◑ ◑ ✂ TS, OR INDOORS
Stephanotis floribunda   p. 555

Mandevilla (several) ❋
☼ ☼ ◑ ✂ TS
p. 412

Mexican flame vine ❋
☼ ☼ ◑ ✂ CS, TS
Senecio confusus   p. 542

Carolina jessamine
Gelsemium sempervirens

Crossvine
Bignonia capreolata

Madagascar jasmine
Stephanotis floribunda

Mandevilla 'Alice du Pont'

For climate zone explanations, please see pages 28–38.   ▶

Passion vine
Passiflora

Queen's wreath
Petrea volubilis

*Clematis,
large-flowered
hybrid*

Sky flower
Thunbergia grandiflora

Violet trumpet vine
Clytostoma callistegioides

Night-blooming jasmine ☀
☼ ● ● ▲ ✂ TS
Cestrum nocturnum   p. 237

Pandorea ☀
☼ ● ● ▲ ✂ CS, TS
    p. 445

Passion vine (most) ☀
☼ ☼ ● ● ▲ ✂ VARY
Passiflora   p. 449

Pink trumpet vine ☀
☼ ● ● ▲ ✂ CS, TS
Podranea ricasoliana   p. 485

Potato vine ☀
☼ ☼ ● ● ▲ ● ✂ CS, TS
Solanum jasminoides   p. 547

Queen's wreath ☀
☼ ● ✂ TS
Petrea volubilis   p. 465

Sky flower ☀
☼ ☼ ● ✂ TS
Thunbergia grandiflora   p. 570

Tater vine ☀
☼ ☼ ● ● ▲ ✂ CS, TS
Dioscorea bulbifera   p. 288

Violet trumpet vine ☀
☼ ● ● ▲ ✂ CS, TS
Clytostoma callistegioides   p. 255

Wintercreeper euonymus
☼ ● ● ● ▲ ✂ US, MS, LS, CS
Euonymus fortunei   p. 304

DECIDUOUS

Bittersweet
☼ ● ✂ US, MS, LS
Celastrus   p. 233

Chilean jasmine ☀
☼ ☼ ● ✂ CS, TS
Mandevilla laxa   p. 413

Clematis (most) ☀
☼ ● ✂ VARY
    p. 250

Climbing hydrangea
☼ ● ✂ US, MS, LS   p. 352
Hydrangea anomala petiolaris

Coral vine ☀
☼ ● ● ▲ ✂ LS, CS, TS
Antigonon leptopus   p. 169

Costa Rican nightshade ☀
☼ ● ● ● ▲ ✂ TS
Solanum wendlandii   p. 548

Dutchman's pipe ☀
☼ ☼ ● ● ● ● ▲ ✂ VARY
Aristolochia (several)   p. 180

Grape ☀
☼ ● ✂ VARY
    p. 328

Japanese hydrangea vine
☼ ● ✂ US, MS, LS   p. 538
Schizophragma hydrangeoides

Kiwi vine ☀
☼ ☼ ● ● ▲ ✂ US, MS, LS
Actinidia kolomikta   p. 152

Porcelain berry
☼ ☼ ● ● ● ▲ ✂ US, MS, LS, CS
Ampelopsis brevipedunculata p. 165

Rangoon creeper ☀
☼ ☼ ● ✂ TS
Quisqualis indica   p. 502

Rose ☀
☼ ☼ ● ✂ ALL
Rosa (climbers)   p. 516

Silver lace vine ☀
☼ ○ ● ● ▲ ✂ US, MS, LS
Fallopia baldshuanica   p. 309

Trumpet creeper, common ☀
☼ ☼ ● ● ▲ ✂ US, MS, LS, CS
Campsis radicans   p. 224

Virginia creeper
☼ ☼ ● ● ▲ ✂ US, MS, LS, CS
Parthenocissus quinquefolia p. 448

Wisteria ☀
☼ ○ ● ● ✂ US, MS, LS, CS
    p. 590

ANNUAL

Bean, scarlet runner ☀
☼ ● ● ✂ ALL
    p. 195

Black-eyed Susan vine
☼ ☼ ● ● ✂ CS, TS
Thunbergia alata   p. 570

Cup-and-saucer vine ☀
☼ ● ✂ ALL
Cobaea scandens   p. 255

Firecracker vine ☀
☼ ● ● ✂ ALL
Ipomoea lobata   p. 361

Hyacinth bean ☀
☼ ● ✂ LS, CS, TS
Dolichos lablab   p. 289

Moonflower ☀
☼ ● ● ✂ ALL
Ipomoea alba   p. 360

Morning glory (several) ☀
☼ ● ● ✂ VARY
Ipomoea   p. 360

Nasturtium ☀
☼ ☼ ● ● ✂ ALL
Tropaeolum majus   p. 577

Sweet pea ☀
☼ ● ● ▲ ✂ ALL
Lathyrus odoratus   p. 383

Grape 'Swenson Red'

Porcelain berry
Ampelopsis brevipedunculata

American wisteria
Wisteria frutescens

Morning glory
Ipomoea tricolor

Nasturtium
Tropaeolum majus

For growing symbol explanations, please see page 39.

Dwarf mondo grass
Ophiopogon japonicus 'Nana'

Baby's tears
Soleirolia soleirolii

Bergenia

Carpet bugleweed
Ajuga reptans

Catmint
Nepeta × *faassenii*

Plants for
Ground Cover

Periwinkle, common
Vinca minor 'La Grave'

While a lawn can be the best ground cover, not every garden is suited to turf. Some sites are too shady, others too steep. Sometimes you just don't feel like mowing. Consider the following plants as options. These low-growing plants shelter the soil, prevent erosion, and may also have striking flowers, foliage, or berries. Some spread by underground runners or root as they grow. Others sprawl over the soil. The symbol ♔ indicates ground covers with showy flowers.

Artemisia (several)
☼◐◓◑◢ VARY
p. 181

Asian star jasmine
☼◐◓◑◢ LS, CS, TS
Trachelospermum asiaticum   p. 575

Baby's tears
☼◑●◓◑◢ CS, TS
Soleirolia soleirolii   p. 548

Bamboo (dwarf types)
☼◑◐◓◑◢ VARY
p. 190

Bergenia ♔
☼◑●◓◢ US, MS, LS
p. 199

Bishop's weed
☼◑●◓◢ US, MS, LS
Aegopodium podagraria   p. 154

Blue fescue
☼◑◐◓◢ US, MS
Festuca glauca   p. 311

Canada wild ginger
◑●◓◑◢ US, MS, LS
Asarum canadense   p. 183

Carpet bugleweed ♔
☼◑●◓◢ US, MS, LS
Ajuga reptans   p. 157

Catmint ♔
☼◑●◓◑◢ US, MS, LS, CS
Nepeta × faassenii   p. 429

Cinquefoil ♔
☼◑◐◓◢ VARY
Potentilla (several)   p. 490

Cotoneaster (some)
☼◑◐◓◢ VARY
p. 266

Creeping buttercup ♔
☼◑●◓◢ US, MS, LS   p. 503
Ranunculus repens pleniflorus

Creeping Jenny
●◐◓◢ US, MS, LS
Lysimachia nummularia   p. 401

Cumberland rosemary ♔
☼◑◢ MS, LS, CS
Conradina verticillata   p. 258

Dwarf-eared coreopsis ♔
☼◑◢ US, MS, LS, CS
Coreopsis auriculata 'Nana'   p. 260

Dwarf plumbago ♔
☼◑◐◓◢ US, MS, LS, CS   p. 235
Ceratostigma plumbaginoides

Epimedium ♔
◑●◓◢ US, MS, LS
p. 296

Evergreen candytuft ♔
☼◑◢ US, MS, LS
Iberis sempervirens   p. 355

Galax
◑●◓◢ US, MS, LS
Galax urceolata   p. 318

Germander
☼◑◢ US, MS, LS, CS
Teucrium chamaedrys   p. 568

Golden globes ♔
☼◑●◓◢ MS, LS, CS
Lysimachia congestiflora   p. 400

Golden star ♔
◑◢ US, MS, LS, CS
Chrysogonum virginianum   p. 245

Grape ivy
◑●◓◢ TS
Cissus rhombifolia   p. 246

Holly fern
◑●◓◢ LS, CS, TS
Cyrtomium falcatum   p. 276

Houttuynia cordata
☼◑●◓◑◢ ALL
p. 350

Ice plant ♔
☼◑◓◢ CS, TS
Drosanthemum   p. 291

Ivy
☼◑●◓◢ VARY
Hedera   p. 337

Dwarf-eared coreopsis
Coreopsis auriculata 'Nana'

Dwarf plumbago
Ceratostigma plumbaginoides

Epimedium

Golden star
Chrysogonum virginianum

For climate zone explanations, please see pages 28–38. ▶

Juniper
Juniperus horizontalis 'Prince of Wales'

Lamb's ears
Stachys byzantina

Lady's-mantle
Alchemilla mollis

Lenten rose
Helleborus orientalis

Lungwort
Pulmonaria

Japanese ardisia
☼ ● ◗ ◢ ✓ LS, CS
Ardisia japonica — p. 179

Japanese pachysandra
● ◗ ◢ ✓ US, MS, LS
Pachysandra terminalis — p. 442

Jasmine (some) ♛
☼ ☼ ● ◗ ◢ ✓ VARY
Jasminum — p. 367

Juniper
☼ ☼ ○ ◗ ◢ ✓ VARY
Juniperus (low-growing) — p. 370

Knotweed
☼ ● ◗ ◢ ✓ VARY
Persicaria — p. 463

Lady's-mantle
☼ ● ◗ ◢ ✓ US, MS, LS
Alchemilla mollis — p. 158

Lamb's ears
☼ ☼ ● ◗ ✓ US, MS, LS
Stachys byzantina — p. 554

Lavender cotton ♛
☼ ○ ◗ ✓ US, MS, LS, CS
Santolina chamaecyparissus — p. 534

Lenten rose ♛
☼ ● ◗ ◢ ✓ US, MS, LS
Helleborus orientalis — p. 341

Lily-of-the-valley ♛
☼ ● ◗ ◢ ✓ US, MS, LS
Convallaria majalis — p. 258

Lungwort ♛
☼ ● ◗ ✓ US, MS, LS
Pulmonaria (several) — p. 497

Mazus reptans ♛
☼ ☼ ● ◗ ✓ US, MS, LS — p. 415

Memorial rose ♛
☼ ● ◗ ◢ ✓ US, MS, LS, CS
Rosa wichuraiana — p. 524

Mondo grass
☼ ● ◗ ◗ ◢ ✓ MS, LS, CS, TS
Ophiopogon japonicus — p. 436

Monkey grass (several) ♛
☼ ● ◗ ✓ VARY
Liriope — p. 395

Moss pink ♛
☼ ☼ ◗ ✓ US, MS, LS
Phlox subulata — p. 469

Oregano
☼ ○ ◗ ✓ VARY
Origanum (several) — p. 437

Ornamental strawberry ♛
☼ ☼ ● ◗ ✓ US, MS, LS, CS
Fragaria hybrids — p. 315

Partridgeberry
● ◗ ◗ ◢ ✓ US, MS, LS, CS
Mitchella repens — p. 421

Periwinkle ♛
☼ ● ◗ ◢ ✓ VARY
Vinca — p. 587

Pussy toes
☼ ● ◗ ◢ ✓ US, MS, LS
Antennaria dioica — p. 168

Rockcress ♛
☼ ● ◗ ✓ US, MS, LS
Arabis — p. 177

Rock soapwort ♛
☼ ● ◗ ✓ US, MS
Saponaria ocymoides — p. 535

Rosemary ♛
☼ ○ ◗ ✓ US, MS, LS, CS
Rosmarinus officinalis (low) — p. 524

St. Johnswort ♛
☼ ☼ ○ ◗ ◢ ✓ VARY
Hypericum (low-growing) — p. 354

Sedge
☼ ☼ ● ◗ ◗ ◢ ✓ US, MS, LS, CS
Carex (several) — p. 226

Snow-in-summer ♛
☼ ☼ ● ◗ ✓ US, MS, LS
Cerastium tomentosum — p. 235

Spotted dead nettle ♛
☼ ● ◗ ✓ US, MS, LS
Lamium maculatum — p. 382

Sprenger asparagus
☼ ● ◗ ✓ CS, TS
Asparagus densiflorus 'Sprengeri' — p. 185

Stonecrop (many) ♛
☼ ☼ ○ ◗ ◢ ✓ US, MS, LS
Sedum — p. 540

Strawberry geranium ♛
☼ ● ◗ ◢ ✓ MS, LS, CS
Saxifraga stolonifera — p. 537

Sweet box
☼ ● ◗ ◢ ✓ US, MS, LS, CS
Sarcococca hookeriana humilis — p. 535

Sweet flag
☼ ● ◗ ◢ ✓ US, MS, LS, CS
Acorus — p. 152

Sweet woodruff
☼ ● ◗ ◗ ◢ ✓ US, MS, LS
Galium odoratum — p. 318

Thrift, common ♛
☼ ○ ◗ ✓ US, MS, LS, CS
Armeria maritima — p. 181

Thyme
☼ ○ ◗ ✓ VARY
Thymus — p. 571

Wedelia trilobata ♛
☼ ● ◗ ✓ CS, TS — p. 590

Wintercreeper euonymus (some)
☼ ● ◗ ● ◢ ✓ US, MS, LS, CS
Euonymus fortunei — p. 304

Pussy toes
Antennaria dioica

Rock soapwort
Saponaria ocymoides

Wall rockcress
Arabis caucasica

Aaron's beard (St. Johnswort)
Hypericum calycinum

Stonecrop
Sedum spathulifolium 'Cape Blanco'

For growing symbol explanations, please see page 39.

Oleander and myrtle (*Nerium oleander* and *myrtus communis*)

Evergreen Plants

Southerners think that a plant that never loses its leaves is a very good thing. Whether it is broad-leafed or needle-leafed, an evergreen helps to define the garden's spaces and give it structure year-round. Many evergreens also contribute colorful flowers, foliage, and berries. Keep in mind, however, that it's often difficult to grow grass and other plants beneath large evergreens.

Lime
Citrus 'Bearss'

Anise tree
Illicium

BROAD-LEAFED TREES AND SHRUBS

African tulip tree
☼ ◐ ❋ TS
Spathodea campanulata   p. 551

Anise tree
☼ ◐ ◑ ◐ ❋ MS, LS, CS
Illicium   p. 358

Alexandrian laurel
◐ ◐ ◐ ❋ MS, LS, CS
Danae racemosa   p. 278

Bamboo (many)
NEEDS, ZONES VARY
                               p. 190

Banana shrub
☼ ◐ ◐ ❋ LS, CS, TS
Michelia figo   p. 418

Barberry
☼ ☼ ◐ ◐ ❋ VARY
Berberis   p. 198

Boxwood
☼ ☼ ◐ ❋ VARY
Buxus   p. 213

Bailey acacia
☼ ◐ ❋ CS, TS
Acacia baileyana   p. 147

Camellia
☼ ◐ ◐ ❋ US, MS, LS, CS
                               p. 220

Carolina cherry laurel
☼ ◐ ◐ ❋ US, MS, LS, CS
Prunus caroliniana   p. 492

Cestrum
☼ ◐ ◐ ❋ TS
                               p. 237

Chinese fringe
☼ ◐ ◐ ◐ ❋ MS, LS, CS
Loropetalum chinense   p. 398

Citrus
☼ ◐ ❋ CS, TS
                               p. 247

Coastal leucothoe
◐ ◐ ◐ ◐ ❋ US, MS, LS
Leucothoe axillaris   p. 388

Feijoa, pineapple guava
☼ ◐ ❋ LS, CS, TS
Feijoa   p. 310

Firethorn
☼ ◐ ❋ VARY
Pyracantha   p. 498

Florida leucothoe
◐ ◐ ◐ ◐ ❋ MS, LS, CS
Agarista populifolia   p. 155

Gardenia
☼ ◐ ◐ ❋ VARY
                               p. 319

Germander
☼ ◐ ❋ US, MS, LS, CS
Teucrium chamaedrys   p. 568

Glossy abelia
☼ ◐ ◐ ❋ US, MS, LS, CS
Abelia × grandiflora   p. 146

Golden dewdrop
☼ ◐ ❋ TS
Duranta erecta   p. 292

Heath
☼ ☼ ◐ ◐ ❋ VARY
Erica   p. 299

Holly
☼ ☼ ◐ ❋ VARY
Ilex (most)   p. 356

Indian hawthorn
☼ ◐ ◐ ◐ ◐ ❋ LS, CS
Rhaphiolepis indica   p. 505

Ixora
☼ ◐ ◐ ❋ TS
                               p. 366

Glossy privet
☼ ◐ ◐ ◐ ❋ LS, CS, TS
Ligustrum lucidum   p. 390

Japanese andromeda
◐ ◐ ◐ ❋ US, MS
Pieris japonica   p. 473

Barberry
Berberis thunbergii 'Rose Glow'

Sasanqua camellia
Camellia sasanqua

Bamboo (label under img_3/4 area)

Glossy abelia
Abelia × grandiflora

Firethorn
Pyracantha

Heath
Erica carnea 'Springwood Pink'

American holly
Ilex opaca

For climate zone explanations, please see pages 28–38.

Japanese cleyera
Ternstroemia gymnanthera

Japanese pittosporum
Pittosporum tobira

Mahonia

Rhododendron 'Trude Webster'

Sago palm
Cycas revoluta

Japanese aucuba
☼ ◐ ● ◊ ◊ ⚡ ALL
Aucuba japonica   p. 189

Japanese cleyera
☼ ◐ ◊ ⚡ MS, LS, CS, TS
Ternstroemia gymnanthera   p. 567

Japanese fatsia
☼ ◐ ● ◊ ⚡ LS, CS, TS
Fatsia japonica   p. 310

Japanese pittosporum
☼ ◐ ● ◊ ● ⚡ LS, CS, TS
Pittosporum tobira   p. 478

Lady Banks's rose
☼ ◐ ◊ ● ⚡ LS, CS, TS
Rosa banksiae   p. 523

Loquat
☼ ◐ ◊ ◊ ● ◊ ⚡ VARY
Eriobotrya japonica   p. 300

Mahonia
NEEDS, ZONES VARY
                                         p. 408

Mexican orange
☼ ◐ ◊ ● ⚡ LS, CS, TS
Choisya ternata   p. 242

Mountain laurel
☼ ◐ ◊ ● ◊ ⚡ US, MS, LS, CS
Kalmia latifolia   p. 375

Myrtle
☼ ◐ ◊ ● ◊ ⚡ CS
Myrtus communis   p. 425

Nandina
☼ ◐ ● ◊ ● ◊ ⚡ US, MS, LS, CS
Nandina domestica   p. 425

Natal plum
☼ ◐ ◊ ● ◊ ● ⚡ CS, TS
Carissa macrocarpa   p. 227

Oak (some)
☼ ● ◊ ⚡ VARY
Quercus   p. 500

Oleander, common
☼ ◐ ◊ ◊ ● ◊ ⚡ LS, CS, TS
Nerium oleander   p. 431

Osmanthus
☼ ◐ ◊ ◊ ● ◊ ⚡ VARY
                                         p. 439

Palms (some)
NEEDS, ZONES VARY
                                         p. 444

Persea
NEEDS, ZONES VARY
                                         p. 463

Rhododendron and azalea
☼ ◐ ● ◊ ● ◊ ◊ ⚡ VARY
Rhododendron (some)   p. 507

Snow bush
☼ ◐ ◊ ● ⚡ TS
Breynia nivosa   p. 208

Sotol
☼ ◐ ◊ ◊ ● ⚡ VARY
Dasylirion   p. 279

Southern magnolia
☼ ◐ ◊ ● ⚡ US, MS, LS, CS
Magnolia grandiflora   p. 404

Sweet bay
☼ ◐ ◊ ● ◊ ● ⚡ US, MS, LS, CS
Magnolia virginiana   p. 408

Texas mountain laurel
☼ ◐ ◊ ● ◊ ⚡ LS, CS
Sophora secundiflora   p. 549

Texas ranger
☼ ◐ ◊ ● ⚡ LS, CS
Leucophyllum frutescens   p. 388

Thorny elaeagnus
☼ ◐ ◊ ● ◊ ⚡ US, MS, LS, CS
Elaeagnus pungens   p. 295

Wax myrtle
☼ ◐ ● ◊ ● ⚡ MS, LS, CS, TS
Myrica cerifera   p. 425

Winter daphne
☼ ◐ ◊ ● ⚡ MS, LS
Daphne odora   p. 279

Wintergreen
☼ ◐ ● ⚡ US, MS
Gaultheria procumbens   p. 320

NEEDLE-LEAFED TREES AND SHRUBS

American arborvitae
☼ ◐ ◊ ● ◊ ● ⚡ US, MS
Thuja occidentalis   p. 569

Canadian hemlock
☼ ◐ ◊ ● ⚡ US, MS, LS
Tsuga canadensis   p. 578

Cedar
☼ ◊ ● ⚡ VARY
Cedrus   p. 232

Cypress
☼ ◐ ◊ ● ⚡ VARY
Cupressus   p. 272

Douglas fir
☼ ◐ ◊ ● ◊ ● ⚡ US, MS
Pseudotsuga menziesii   p. 496

Eastern red cedar
☼ ◐ ◊ ◊ ● ◊ ● ⚡ ALL
Juniperus virginiana   p. 373

Fir
☼ ◐ ◊ ● ◊ ● ⚡ VARY
Abies   p. 146

Incense cedar
☼ ◐ ◊ ● ◊ ⚡ US, MS, LS
Calocedrus decurrens   p. 218

Japanese cryptomeria
☼ ◐ ● ◊ ● ⚡ US, MS, LS
Cryptomeria japonica   p. 271

Southern magnolia
Magnolia grandiflora

Texas mountain laurel
Sophora secundiflora

Winter daphne
Daphne odora

Wintergreen
Gaultheria procumbens

Canadian hemlock
Tsuga canadensis

For growing symbol explanations, please see page 39.

White pine
Pinus strobus

Spruce
Picea pungens

Japanese pachysandra
Pachysandra terminalis

Carpet bugleweed
Ajuga reptans

Rock cotoneaster
Cotoneaster horizontalis

Evergreen candytuft
Iberis sempervirens

Juniper
☼ ◐ ◌ ◌ ◑ ⚡ VARY
Juniperus (many) p. 370

Leyland cypress
☼ ◐ ◑ ⚡ US, MS, LS, CS
× Cupressocyparis leylandii p. 272

Pine
☼ ◐ ◑ ⚡ VARY
Pinus (many) p. 474

Plum yew
☼ ◐ ◐ ◑ ⚡ VARY
Cephalotaxus p. 235

Spruce
☼ ◐ ◐ ◑ ⚡ US, MS
Picea p. 472

White cedar
☼ ◐ ◐ ◑ ⚡ US, MS, LS, CS
Chamaecyparis thyoides p. 238

Yew
☼ ◐ ◐ ◌ ◑ ◊ ⚡ US, MS
Taxus p. 566

GROUND COVERS

Asian star jasmine
☼ ◐ ◐ ◑ ⚡ LS, CS, TS
Trachelospermum asiaticum p. 575

Carpet bugleweed
☼ ◐ ◐ ◑ ⚡ US, MS, LS
Ajuga reptans p. 157

Cotoneaster (several)
☼ ◌ ◐ ◑ ⚡ VARY
  p. 266

Evergreen candytuft
☼ ◐ ◑ ⚡ US, MS, LS
Iberis sempervirens p. 355

Hellebore
◐ ◐ ◐ ◑ ◊ ⚡ MS, LS
Helleborus lividus p. 341

Ivy
☼ ◐ ◐ ◐ ◑ ⚡ VARY
Hedera p. 337

Japanese ardisia
◐ ◐ ◑ ⚡ LS, CS
Ardisia japonica p. 179

Japanese pachysandra
◐ ◐ ◑ ⚡ US, MS, LS
Pachysandra terminalis p. 442

Mazus
☼ ◐ ◐ ◑ ⚡ US, MS, LS
Mazus reptans p. 415

Mondo grass
◐ ◐ ◐ ◑ ⚡ MS, LS, CS, TS
Ophiopogon japonicus p. 436

Monkey grass
◐ ◐ ◑ ⚡ VARY
Liriope p. 395

Periwinkle
◐ ◐ ◐ ◑ ⚡ VARY
Vinca p. 587

Wintercreeper euonymus
☼ ◐ ◐ ◐ ◑ ⚡ US, MS, LS, CS
Euonymus fortunei p. 304

VINES

Allamanda
☼ ◐ ◑ ⚡ TS
Allamanda cathartica p. 159

Armand clematis
☼ ◐ ◑ ⚡ LS, CS
Clematis armandii p. 251

Cape honeysuckle
☼ ◐ ◐ ◑ ⚡ CS, TS
Tecoma capensis p. 567

Carolina jessamine
☼ ◐ ◌ ◌ ◑ ◊ ⚡ MS, LS, CS
Gelsemium sempervirens p. 321

Confederate jasmine
☼ ◐ ◐ ◑ ⚡ LS, CS, TS p. 575
Trachelospermum jasminoides

Creeping fig
☼ ◐ ◐ ◑ ⚡ LS, CS, TS
Ficus pumila p. 312

Crossvine
☼ ◐ ◐ ◑ ⚡ US, MS, LS, CS
Bignonia capreolata p. 201

Cup-of-gold vine
☼ ◐ ⚡ TS
Solandra maxima p. 547

Evergreen wisteria
☼ ◐ ◑ ⚡ LS, CS, TS
Millettia reticulata p. 419

Fiveleaf akebia
☼ ◐ ◐ ◑ ⚡ US, MS, LS, CS
Akebia quinata p. 158

Flame vine
☼ ◐ ◐ ◑ ⚡ CS, TS
Pyrostegia venusta p. 499

Jackson vine
☼ ◐ ◌ ◌ ◐ ◑ ⚡ MS, LS, CS
Smilax smallii p. 547

Jasmine
☼ ◐ ◐ ◑ ⚡ VARY
Jasminum (some) p. 367

Passion vine
☼ ◐ ◐ ◑ ⚡ VARY
Passiflora (most) p. 449

Potato vine
☼ ◐ ◌ ◐ ◑ ◊ ⚡ CS, TS
Solanum jasminoides p. 547

Violet trumpet vine
☼ ◐ ◐ ◑ ⚡ CS, TS
Clytostoma callistegioides p. 255

Carolina jessamine
Gelsemium sempervirens

Confederate jasmine
Trachelospermum jasminoides

Fiveleaf akebia
Akebia quinata

Showy jasmine
Jasminum floridum

Wintercreeper euonymus
Euonymus fortunei

For climate zone explanations, please see pages 28–38.

Ferns
for Foliage Interest

When you think of ferns, you conjure up beautiful foliage. But this diverse group of plants ranges from forest-floor creepers to majestic tree ferns right out of *Jurassic Park*. Some are deciduous; others are evergreen. Some form clumps, others spread by rhizomes, and one fern listed here climbs. Most prefer shade and moist, fertile soil. Use them in solid sweeps or in combination with other shade lovers in formal or naturalized areas. Many ferns, particularly evergreen types, also make superb houseplants.

Southern shield fern
Thelypteris kunthii

Bird's nest fern
Asplenium nidus

Australian tree fern
Cyathea cooperi

Brake
Pteris

Chain fern
Woodwardia

Cinnamon fern
Osmunda cinnamomea

Asplenium (several)
VARY
p. 186

Australian tree fern
TS
Cyathea cooperi   p. 273

Autumn fern
US, MS, LS, CS
Dryopteris erythrosora   p. 292

Blunt-lobed woodsia
US, MS, LS, CS
Woodsia obtusa   p. 591

Brake
TS OR INDOORS
Pteris   p. 496

Chain fern
US, MS, LS, CS
Woodwardia   p. 591

Christmas fern
US, MS, LS, CS
Polystichum acrostichoides   p. 487

Cinnamon fern
ALL
Osmunda cinnamomea   p. 440

Cliff-brake
VARY OR INDOORS
Pellaea   p. 460

Ebony spleenwort
US MS LS CS
Asplenium platyneuron   p. 186

Hay-scented fern
US, MS
Dennstaedtia punctilobula   p. 282

Holly fern
LS, CS, TS
Cyrtomium falcatum   p. 276

Japanese climbing fern
LS, CS, TS OR INDOORS
Lygodium japonicum   p. 400

Japanese painted fern
US, MS, LS   p. 188
Athyrium niponicum 'Pictum'

Lady fern
US, MS, LS
Athyrium filix-femina   p. 188

Maidenhair fern
VARY
Adiantum   p. 153

Marginal shield fern
US, MS, LS
Dryopteris marginalis   p. 292

Ostrich fern
US, MS
Matteuccia struthiopteris   p. 415

Royal fern
ALL
Osmunda regalis   p. 440

Sensitive fern
US, MS, LS, CS
Onoclea sensibilis   p. 436

Southern shield fern
MS, LS, CS
Thelypteris kunthii   p. 569

Staghorn fern
TS
Platycerium   p. 479

Sword fern
TS OR INDOORS
Nephrolepis   p. 430

Tasmanian tree fern
TS
Dicksonia antarctica   p. 285

Tassel fern
US MS LS CS
Polystichum polyblepharum   p. 487

Variegated holly fern
US, MS, LS, CS
Arachniodes simplicior   p. 177

Japanese painted fern
Athyrium niponicum 'Pictum'

Royal fern
Osmunda regalis

Staghorn fern
Platycerium bifurcatum

Tasmanian tree fern
Dicksonia antarctica

For growing symbol explanations, please see page 39.

Gulf muhly
Muhlenbergia filipes

Golden bamboo
Phyllostachys aurea

Bowles' golden grass
Milium effusum 'Aureum'

Chinese pennisetum
Pennisetum alopecuroides

Lemon grass
Cymbopogon citratus

Grasses and Grasslike Plants

I f you only think of grass as something you mow, it's time you discovered ornamental grasses. The beauty of these denizens of prairie, marsh, seashore, and forest lies in their graceful, fountainlike foliage and remarkable floral displays. As a group, ornamental grasses are easy to grow, free from pests, and simple to divide. Some, such as sea oats, palm grass, and silver grass, readily self-sow.

Bowles' golden sedge
Carex elata 'Aurea'

Bamboos
(Many kinds) VARY — p. 190

Blue fescue
US, MS
Festuca glauca — p. 311

Blue lyme grass
US, MS, LS, CS
Leymus arenarius — p. 389

Blue oat grass
US, MS, LS, CS
Helictotrichon sempervirens — p. 340

Bluestem
US, MS, LS, CS
Andropogon — p. 166

Bowles' golden grass
US, MS, LS
Milium effusum 'Aureum' — p. 419

Feather reed grass
US, MS, LS, CS
Calamagrostis × acutiflora — p. 215

Fountain grass
VARY
Pennisetum — p. 460

Giant reed
ALL
Arundo donax — p. 183

Hair grass
US, MS, LS
Deschampsia — p. 282

Japanese blood grass
US, MS, LS, CS
Imperata cylindrica 'Rubra' — p. 359

Lemon grass
TS OR ANNUAL
Cymbopogon citratus — p. 275

Mexican feather grass
MS, LS, CS, TS
Nassella tenuissima — p. 428

Moor grass
US, MS, LS
Molinia caerulea — p. 421

Muhly grass
MS, LS, CS, TS
Muhlenbergia — p. 423

Natal ruby grass
TS OR ANNUAL
Rhynchelytrum — p. 515

New Zealand flax
LS, CS, TS
Phormium tenax — p. 470

Palm grass
CS, TS
Setaria palmifolia — p. 543

Pampas grass
MS, LS, CS, TS
Cortaderia selloana — p. 264

Prairie dropseed
US, MS, LS, CS
Sporobolus heterolepis — p. 553

Rattlesnake grass
ALL
Briza maxima — p. 208

Ravenna grass
ALL
Saccharum ravennae — p. 528

Ribbon grass
US, MS, LS, CS
Phalaris arundinacea picta — p. 467

Sea oats
US, MS, LS, CS
Chasmanthium latifolium — p. 238

Sedge
US, MS, LS, CS
Carex — p. 226

Silver grass
US, MS, LS, CS
Miscanthus — p. 420

Sweet flag
US, MS, LS, CS
Acorus — p. 152

Switch grass
US, MS, LS
Panicum virgatum — p. 445

Mexican feather grass
Nassella tenuissima

Pampas grass
Cortaderia selloana 'Pumila'

Silver grass
Miscanthus

Leather leaf sedge
Carex buchananii

For climate zone explanations, please see pages 28–38.

Vegetables and Fruits

This homegrown bounty includes radishes and carrots.

Considering the bounty of fresh produce that's available year-round at the grocery store, why would anyone grow their own? Actually, there are plenty of reasons. Fresh garden vegetables and fruits taste better, and if you grow them organically you won't have to worry about pesticides. You can also grow uncommon varieties not found in supermarkets. Moreover, many edible plants make fine ornamentals—kale, chard, lettuce, persimmons, blueberries, and figs are good examples.

'Sierra' and 'Rosy' Lettuce

Cucumber

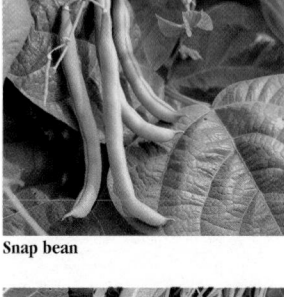
Avocado

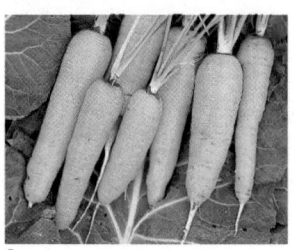
Snap bean

Carrot

Eggplants

Jicama

Kohlrabi

VEGETABLES

Asparagus ☼ ● % US, MS, LS	p. 184
Corn ☼ ● % ALL	p. 260
Avocado ☼ ● % CS, TS	p. 189
Cucumber ☼ ● % ALL	p. 271
Bean ☼ ● % ALL	p. 195
Eggplant ☼ ● % ALL	p. 294
Beet ☼ ● % ALL	p. 196
Garlic ☼ ● % ALL	p. 319
Bitter melon ☼ ● % ALL	p. 202
Gourd ☼ ● % ALL	p. 327
Broccoli ☼ ● % ALL	p. 208
Horseradish ☼ ● % US, MS, LS	p. 348
Brussels sprouts ☼ ● % ALL	p. 210
Jerusalem artichoke ☼ ● ● ● % US, MS, LS, CS Helianthus tuberosus	p. 339
Cardoon ☼ ● % LS, CS	p. 226
Jicama ☼ ● ● ◑ % LS, CS, TS	p. 369
Carrot ☼ ● % ALL	p. 228
Kohlrabi ☼ ● % ALL	p. 378
Cauliflower ☼ ● % ALL	p. 231
Leek ☼ ◑ ● % ALL	p. 386
Celery ☼ ● ● ● % ALL	p. 233
Okra ☼ ● % ALL	p. 434
Chayote ☼ ● % CS, TS	p. 238
Onion ☼ ● % ALL	p. 435
	Parsnip ☼ ● % US, MS	p. 448

For growing symbol explanations, please see page 39.

Virginia peanut

Southern pea

Tomatoes

Pea (shelling, snap, or snow)
☼ ◐ ✂ ALL
p. 451

Peanut
☼ ◐ ✂ ALL
p. 455

Pepper
☼ ◐ ✂ ALL
p. 462

Potato
☼ ◐ ◊ ✂ ALL
p. 489

Pumpkin
☼ ◐ ✂ ALL
p. 497

Radish
☼ ◑ ◐ ✂ ALL
p. 503

Rhubarb
☼ ◑ ◐ ◊ ✂ US, MS, LS
p. 514

Shallot
☼ ◐ ✂ ALL
p. 544

Southern pea
☼ ◐ ✂ ALL
p. 550

Squash, summer or winter
☼ ◐ ✂ ALL
p. 553

Sweet potato
☼ ◐ ✂ US, MS, LS
p. 561

Tomatillo
☼ ◐ ✂ ALL
p. 573

Tomato
☼ ◐ ✂ ALL
p. 573

Turnip and rutabaga
☼ ◐ ✂ ALL
p. 580

Zucchini (summer squash)
☼ ◐ ✂ ALL
p. 553

LEAFY VEGETABLES

Asian greens
☼ ◑ ◐ ✂ ALL
p. 184

Cabbage
☼ ◑ ◐ ✂ ALL
p. 213

Chicory and radicchio
☼ ◐ ✂ US, MS, LS
p. 240

Chinese cabbage
☼ ◐ ✂ ALL
p. 241

Cress, garden
☼ ◑ ◐ ◐ ✂ ALL
p. 269

Dandelion
☼ ◐ ✂ US, MS, LS, CS
p. 278

Fennel, common
☼ ◐ ✂ VARY
p. 314

Garden burnet
☼ ◑ ◐ ✂ US, MS, LS, CS
Sanguisorba minor
p. 534

Kale and collards
☼ ◑ ◐ ✂ ALL
p. 375

Lettuce
☼ ◐ ✂ ALL
p. 387

Mustard
☼ ◐ ✂ ALL
p. 424

Rocket
☼ ◐ ✂ ALL
Arugula
p. 182

Spinach
☼ ◐ ✂ VARY
p. 551

Swiss chard
☼ ◐ ✂ ALL
p. 561

Turnip greens
☼ ◐ ✂ ALL
p. 580

FRUIT

Apple
☼ ◐ ✂ VARY
p. 170

Apricot
☼ ◐ ✂ US
p. 171

Banana
☼ ◐◐ ✂ VARY
p. 191

Blackberry
☼ ◐ ✂ US, MS, LS, CS
p. 202

Blueberry
☼ ◐ ✂ VARY
p. 203

Carambola
☼ ◐ ✂ TS
p. 226

Asian greens

Radicchio

Kale

Swiss chard

Blackberry

For climate zone explanations, please see pages 28–38. ▶

Citrus
(Calamondin)

Mandarin orange
Citrus

Muscadine grape

Natal plum
Carissa macrocarpa

Persimmon

Cherry
☼ ◗ ✂ VARY
p. 239

Citrus
☼ ◗ ✂ CS, TS
p. 247

Crabapple
☼ ◗ ✂ US, MS, LS
p. 267

Date palm
☼ ◗ ✂ CS, TS
Phoenix   p. 469

Elderberry, American
☼ ◒ ◗ ✂ US, MS, LS, CS
Sambucus canadensis   p. 533

Fig
☼ ◗ ✂ MS, LS, CS, TS
p. 313

Grape and muscadine
☼ ◗ ✂ VARY
p. 328

Guava
☼ ◒ ◗ ✂ VARY
p. 333

Jujube
☼ ◒ ◗ ✂ US, MS, LS, CS
p. 370

Juneberry
☼ ◒ ◯ ◗ ✂ VARY
Amelanchier   p. 164

Kiwi
☼ ◒ ◗ ✂ VARY
p. 376

Lychee
☼ ◗ ✂ CS, TS
p. 399

Mango
☼ ◗ ◆ ✂ TS
p. 413

Mayhaw
☼ ◒ ◗ ✂ MS, LS, CS
Crataegus opaca   p. 268

Melon, cantaloupe, and honeydew
☼ ◗ ✂ ALL
p. 417

Natal plum
☼ ◒ ◯ ◗ ◆ ✂ CS, TS
Carissa macrocarpa   p. 227

Papaya
☼ ◗ ✂ TS
p. 446

Passion fruit
☼ ◗ ✂ TS
p. 449

Pawpaw
☼ ◒ ◗ ✂ US, MS, LS, CS
p. 450

Peach and nectarine
☼ ◗ ✂ VARY
p. 451

Pear, Asian and European
☼ ◗ ✂ VARY
p. 455, 456

Persimmon
☼ ◒ ◗ ✂ VARY
p. 464

Pineapple
☼ ◒ ◗ ✂ TS
p. 474

Plum (including prune)
☼ ◒ ◗ ✂ VARY
p. 481

Pomegranate
☼ ◗ ✂ MS, LS, CS
p. 488

Quince
☼ ◗ ✂ US, MS, LS
p. 502

Raspberry
☼ ◗ ✂ US, MS
p. 503

Strawberry
☼ ◗ ✂ ALL
p. 557

Watermelon
☼ ◗ ✂ ALL
p. 589

NUTS

Almond
☼ ◗ ✂ US, MS
p. 160

Chestnut
☼ ◗ ✂ US, MS, LS
p. 240

Coconut palm
☼ ◒ ◗ ✂ TS
Cocos nucifera   p. 256

Filbert
☼ ◒ ◗ ✂ US, MS, LS
Corylus   p. 265

Hickory or pecan
☼ ◗ ✂ US, MS, LS, CS
Carya   p. 228

Pecan
☼ ◗ ✂ US, MS, LS, CS
p. 456

Pistachio
☼ ◗ ◯ ◗ ✂ CS, TS
Pistacia vera   p. 478

Walnut
☼ ◗ ✂ VARY
Juglans   p. 369

'Stanley' Plum

'Wonderful' Pomegranate

Quince

Raspberry

'Chandler' Strawberry

Almond

For growing symbol explanations, please see page 39.

Herbs are both colorful and culinary.

Herbs
for Southern Gardens

The great thing about herbs is that they don't need much space. Most tolerate cramped roots and do just fine in a pot or a small kitchen garden. But two things they do demand are lots of sun and well-drained soil. In addition to their culinary uses, many herbs make excellent ornamentals. For instance, thymes make wonderful ground covers, bay can be clipped into a hedge or topiary, and germander is the standard edging used in formal parterres.

Basil
Ocimum basilicum 'Dark Opal'

Chamomile
Chamaemelum nobile

Dill
Anethum graveolens

Common fennel and chives
Foeniculum vulgare, Allium schoenoprasum

Tricolor sage
Salvia officinalis 'Tricolor'

Basil
☼ ◑ ✱ ALL
Ocimum basilicum   p. 433

Bay
☼ ◐ ◑ ✱ LS, CS, TS
Laurus nobilis   p. 384

Borage
☼ ◐ ◑ ✱ ALL
Borago officinalis   p. 205

Caraway
☼ ◑ ✱ US, MS, LS
Carum carvi   p. 228

Chamomile
☼ ◑ ✱ US, MS, LS, CS
Chamaemelum nobile   p. 238

Chervil
◑ ◑ ✱ ALL
Anthriscus cerefolium   p. 169

Chives
☼ ◑ ◑ ✱ ALL
Allium schoenoprasum   p. 160

Comfrey
☼ ◑ ◑ ◐ ✱ US, MS, LS, CS
Symphytum officinale   p. 562

Coriander
☼ ◑ ◑ ✱ ALL
Coriandrum sativum   p. 260

Dill
☼ ◑ ✱ ALL
Anethum graveolens   p. 167

Fennel, common
☼ ◑ ✱ VARY
Foeniculum vulgare   p. 314

French tarragon
☼ ◐ ◑ ✱ US, MS
Artemisia dracunculus   p. 182

Lavender
☼ ◑ ✱ VARY
Lavandula   p. 384

Lemon balm
☼ ◑ ◑ ✱ ALL
Melissa officinalis   p. 416

Lemon grass
☼ ◑ ✱ TS OR ANNUAL
Cymbopogon citratus   p. 275

Lovage
☼ ◑ ◑ ✱ US, MS, LS
Levisticum officinale   p. 389

Mexican mint marigold
☼ ◐ ◑ ✱ MS, LS, CS, TS
Tagetes lucida   p. 565

Mint
☼ ◑ ◑ ✱ US, MS, LS, CS
Mentha   p. 417

Oregano
☼ ◐ ◑ ✱ US, MS, LS, CS
Origanum vulgare   p. 438

Paraguayan sweet herb
☼ ◑ ✱ TS
Stevia rebaudiana   p. 556

Parsley
☼ ◑ ◑ ✱ ALL
Petroselinum crispum   p. 465

Pineapple sage
☼ ◑ ✱ CS, TS
Salvia elegans   p. 531

Rosemary
☼ ◐ ◑ ✱ ALL
Rosmarinus officinalis   p. 524

Sage, common
☼ ◑ ✱ ALL
Salvia officinalis   p. 532

Savory, summer
☼ ◑ ✱ ALL
Satureja hortensis   p. 537

Savory, winter
☼ ◑ ✱ US, MS, LS, CS
Satureja montana   p. 537

Sweet marjoram
☼ ◑ ✱ CS, TS
Origanum marjorana   p. 438

Thyme, common
☼ ◑ ◑ ✱ US, MS, LS, CS
Thymus vulgaris   p. 571

Lavender
Lavandula

Lovage
Levisticum officinale

Oregano
Origanum vulgare

Rosemary
Rosmarinus officinalis

For climate zone explanations, please see pages 28–38.

Plants That Attract
Butterflies

utterflies are nature's music on the wing. They add movement, color, and fleeting moments of wonder to a garden. Encourage them to stay a while by providing host plants for larvae (caterpillars) and nectar-bearing flowers for adults. Most welcoming areas are sunny, sheltered meadows and borders with butterfly-friendly features such as leaf litter, rock crevices, water, and even a few weeds. Never use pesticides in butterfly gardens, unless you can target a specific pest without harming your fluttering friends.

A butterfly feast of orange coreopsis, yarrow, zinnia, fountain grass, and butterfly bush.

Columbine
Aquilegia

Butterfly weed
Asclepias tuberosa

Fringed bleeding heart
Dicentra exima

Hollyhock
Alcea rosea

Joe-Pye weed
Eupatorium purpureum

HOST PLANTS
Annuals, Perennials

Aster
US, MS, LS
p. 186

Beard tongue
VARY
Penstemon p. 461

Bleeding heart
VARY
Dicentra p. 285

Bluestem
US, MS, LS, CS
Andropogon p. 166

Butterfly weed
US, MS, LS, CS
Asclepias tuberosa p. 184

Chilean avens
US, MS
Geum chiloense p. 323

Dill
ALL
Anethum graveolens p. 167

Fennel, common
VARY
Foeniculum vulgare p. 314

Foxglove, common
US, MS, LS, CS
Digitalis purpurea p. 287

Hollyhock
US, MS, LS, CS
Alcea rosea p. 158

Joe-Pye weed
US, MS, LS, CS
Eupatorium purpureum p. 305

Lupine
VARY
Lupinus p. 398

Nasturtium
ALL
Tropaeolum majus p. 577

Parsley
ALL
Petroselinum crispum p. 465

Rue
US, MS, LS, CS
Ruta graveolens p. 527

Snapdragon
ALL
Antirrhinum majus p. 169

Speedwell
VARY
Veronica p. 584

Spider flower
ALL
Cleome hasslerana p. 252

Sunflower
VARY
Helianthus p. 339

Swamp milkweed
US, MS, LS, CS
Asclepias incarnata p. 184

Sweet white violet
US, MS, LS
Viola blanda p. 587

HOST PLANTS
Shrubs, Vines

Cape plumbago
CS, TS
Plumbago auriculata p. 481

Dutchman's pipe
VARY
Aristolochia (several) p. 180

Hibiscus
VARY
p. 345

Cape plumbago
Plumbago auriculata

Parsley
Petroselinum crispum

Spider flower
Cleome hasslerana 'Rose Queen'

Swamp sunflower
Helianthus angustifolius

For growing symbol explanations, please see page 39.

Mallow
☼ ◑ ◐ ◑ ✂ US, MS, LS
Malva   p. 412

Passion vine
☼ ◑ ◐ ◐ ✂ VARY
Passiflora   p. 449

Pentas
☼ ◐ ✂ ALL
Pentas lanceolata   p. 461

Rose
☼ ◐ ◐ ✂ ALL
Rosa   p. 516

Senna
☼ ◑ ◐ ◐ ✂ VARY
                                         p. 542

Spicebush
☼ ◐ ✂ US, MS, LS
Lindera benzoin   p. 393

Spiraea
☼ ◑ ◐ ◐ ✂ VARY
                                         p. 552

Viburnum
☼ ◑ ◐ ✂ VARY
                                         p. 585

Wisteria
☼ ◑ ◐ ✂ US, MS, LS, CS
                                         p. 590

HOST PLANTS
Trees

Ash
☼ ◑ ◐ ◐ ◐ ✂ VARY
Fraxinus   p. 316

Birch
☼ ◑ ◐ ◐ ✂ VARY
Betula   p. 200

Cherry, peach, plum
☼ ◐ ◐ ✂ VARY
Prunus   p. 492

Citrus
☼ ◐ ✂ CS, TS
                                         p. 247

Dogwood
☼ ◑ ◐ ✂ VARY
Cornus   p. 262

Flowering crabapple
☼ ◐ ◐ ✂ VARY
Malus   p. 409

Hackberry
☼ ◑ ◐ ◐ ✂ US, MS, LS, CS
Celtis   p. 233

Hawthorn
☼ ◐ ✂ VARY
Crataegus   p. 268

Honey locust
☼ ◐ ◐ ✂ US, MS, LS
Gleditsia triacanthos   p. 325

Horsechestnut
☼ ◑ ◐ ◐ ◑ ✂ VARY
Aesculus   p. 154

Oak
☼ ◐ ✂ VARY
Quercus   p. 500

Pawpaw
☼ ◑ ◐ ◐ ✂ US, MS, LS, CS
                                         p. 450

Pine
☼ ◐ ◑ ✂ VARY
Pinus   p. 474

Red bay
☼ ◑ ◐ ◐ ◐ ✂ MS, LS, CS, TS
Persea borbonia   p. 463

Sassafras
☼ ◐ ✂ US, MS, LS, CS
Sassafras albidum   p. 536

Sweet bay
☼ ◑ ◐ ◐ ◐ ✂ US, MS, LS, CS
Magnolia virginiana   p. 408

Sycamore
☼ ◐ ✂ VARY
Platanus   p. 479

Tulip poplar
☼ ◐ ✂ US, MS, LS, CS
Liriodendron tulipifera   p. 395

Willow
☼ ◐ ◐ ✂ US, MS, LS
Salix   p. 529

NECTAR PLANTS
Annuals, Perennials, Grasses

Aster
☼ ◑ ◐ ✂ US, MS, LS
                                         p. 186

Beard tongue
☼ ◑ ◐ ◐ ✂ VARY
Penstemon   p. 461

Bee balm
☼ ◑ ◐ ◐ ◐ ✂ US, MS, LS
Monarda didyma   p. 421

Black-eyed Susan
☼ ◐ ◐ ✂ ALL
Rudbeckia hirta   p. 526

Blanket flower
☼ ◐ ◐ ✂ ALL
Gaillardia   p. 318

Blazing star
☼ ◐ ◐ ✂ US, MS, LS, CS
Liatris   p. 389

Borage
☼ ◑ ◐ ◐ ✂ ALL
Borago officinalis   p. 205

Butterfly weed
☼ ◑ ◐ ✂ US, MS, LS, CS
Asclepias tuberosa   p. 184

Rose of Sharon
Hibiscus syriacus

Rose
Rosa

Flowering crabapple
Malus 'Liset'

Bridal wreath
Spiraea prunifolia 'Plena'

Single weeping cherry
Prunus × subhirtella 'Pendula'

Bee balm
Monarda didyma

Japanese black pine
Pinus thunbergii

Blanket flower
Gaillardia × grandiflora 'Goblin'

Borage
Borago officinalis

For climate zone explanations, please see pages 28–38.   ▶

False spiraea
Astilbe × arendsii 'Fanal'

Globe thistle
Echinops

Impatiens

Catmint
Nepeta × faassenii

Cosmos, common
Cosmos bipinnatus

Candytuft
☼ ◐ ◑ ✂ VARY
Iberis   p. 355

Cardinal flower
☼ ◐ ● ◐ ✦ ✂ US, MS, LS, CS
Lobelia cardinalis   p. 396

Catmint
☼ ◐ ● ◐ ✂ US, MS, LS, CS
Nepeta × faassenii   p. 429

Columbine
☼ ◐ ● ◑ ✂ VARY
Aquilegia   p. 176

Coreopsis
☼ ◐ ● ● ● ✂ US, MS, LS, CS
                                                p. 260

Cosmos
☼ ● ✂ ALL
                                                p. 265

Cupid's dart
☼ ● ✂ US, MS, LS
Catananche caerulea   p. 231

Dame's rocket
☼ ◐ ● ✂ ALL
Hesperis matronalis   p. 344

Dwarf plumbago
☼ ◐ ● ● ✂ US, MS, LS, CS   p. 235
Ceratostigma plumbaginoides

English wallflower
☼ ◐ ● ● ✂ US, MS OR ANNUAL
Erysimum cheiri   p. 300

False spiraea
☼ ◐ ● ● ✂ US, MS
Astilbe   p. 187

Globe amaranth
☼ ◐ ● ● ✂ ALL
Gomphrena   p. 326

Globe thistle
☼ ● ✂ US, MS, LS, CS
Echinops   p. 293

Goldenrod
☼ ◐ ● ✂ US, MS, LS, CS
Solidago and Solidaster   p. 548/549

Impatiens
☼ ◐ ● ● ✦ ✂ ALL
                                                p. 358

Ironweed
☼ ◐ ● ● ● ✂ US, MS, LS
Vernonia noveboracensis   p. 584

Joe-Pye weed
☼ ◐ ● ✂ US, MS, LS, CS
Eupatorium purpureum   p. 305

Lantana
☼ ● ✦ ✂ LS, CS, TS OR ANNUAL
                                                p. 382

Lily
☼ ◐ ● ✂ US, MS, LS, CS
Lilium   p. 391

Lily-of-the-Nile
☼ ◐ ○ ◐ ● ✂ VARY
Agapanthus   p. 154

Marigold
☼ ● ✂ VARY
Tagetes   p. 564

Mexican sunflower
☼ ◐ ● ✂ ALL
Tithonia rotundifolia   p. 573

Oregano
☼ ○ ◐ ✂ US, MS, LS, CS
Origanum vulgare   p. 438

Pentas
☼ ● ✂ ALL
Pentas lanceolata   p. 461

Phlox
☼ ◐ ● ✂ VARY
                                                p. 469

Pincushion flower
☼ ● ✂ ALL
Scabiosa   p. 537

Pink
☼ ● ● ✂ US, MS, LS, CS
Dianthus   p. 283

Primrose
☼ ◐ ● ● ✂ VARY
Primula   p. 491

Purple coneflower
☼ ● ✂ US, MS, LS, CS
Echinacea purpurea   p. 293

Queen Anne's lace
☼ ● ✂ US, MS, LS, CS
Daucus carota carota   p. 280

Ranunculus
☼ ◐ ● ● ✂ VARY
                                                p. 503

Sage
☼ ● ✂ VARY
Salvia   p. 530

Sea holly
☼ ● ✂ US, MS, LS, CS
Eryngium   p. 300

Shasta daisy
☼ ◐ ● ✂ US, MS, LS, CS
Chrysanthemum maximum   p. 243

Showy sedum
☼ ● ✂ US, MS, LS, CS
Sedum spectabile   p. 541

Snapdragon
☼ ● ✂ ALL
Antirrhinum majus   p. 169

Spider flower
☼ ● ● ✂ ALL
Cleome hasslerana   p. 252

Stonecrop
☼ ◐ ○ ● ✂ US, MS, LS
Sedum (tall)   p. 540

Asiatic hybrid lily
Lilium

Mexican sunflower
Tithonia rotundifolia 'Goldfinger'

Phlox

Pincushion flower
Scabiosa columbaria 'Pink Mist'

Purple coneflower
Echinacea purpurea

Persian ranunculus
Ranunculus asiaticus 'La Belle Salmon'

For growing symbol explanations, please see page 39.

Verbena
Verbena bonariensis

Yarrow
Achillea

Azalea
Rhododendron

Butterfly bush
Buddleia 'Lochinch'

Rabbiteye blueberry
Vaccinium ashei

Sweet alyssum
☼ ◐ ◐ ✄ ALL
Lobularia maritima   p. 396

Thrift, common
☼ ◐○◐ ✄ US, MS, LS, CS
Armeria maritima   p. 181

Turtlehead
☼ ◐ ◐ ✄ US, MS, LS, CS
Chelone   p. 239

Valerian
☼ ◐ ○○◐ ✄ US, MS, LS
Centranthus ruber   p. 234

Verbena
☼ ◐ ◐ ✄ MS, LS, CS, TS
Verbena bonariensis   p. 583

Wand loosestrife
☼ ◐ ◐ ✄ US, MS, LS
Lythrum virgatum   p. 401

Wild ageratum
☼ ◐ ◐ ✄ ALL
Eupatorium coelestinum   p. 305

Yarrow
☼ ◐ ○◐ ✄ US, MS, LS
Achillea   p. 151

NECTAR PLANTS
Shrubs and Trees

American elderberry
☼ ◐ ◐ ✄ US, MS, LS, CS
Sambucus canadensis   p. 533

Apple
☼ ◐ ✄ VARY
    p. 170

Azalea
☼ ○ ◐◐ ◑ ✄ VARY
Rhododendron   p. 507

Bluebeard, common
☼ ◐ ◐ ✄ US, MS, LS
Caryopteris incana   p. 229

Blueberry
☼ ◐ ● ○◐◐◐ ✄ VARY
Vaccinium   p. 582

Butterfly bush
☼ ◐ ◐◐ ✄ VARY
Buddleia   p. 211

Buttonbush
☼ ◐ ◐◐ ✄ ALL
Cephalanthus occidentalis   p. 234

Cape plumbago
☼ ◐ ○◐◐ ✄ CS, TS
Plumbago auriculata   p. 481

Chaste tree
☼ ◐ ◐ ✄ VARY
Vitex   p. 588

Cherry, peach, plum
☼ ◐ ◐ ✄ VARY
Prunus   p. 492

Chinese hibiscus
☼ ◐ ● ✄ CS, TS
Hibiscus rosa-sinensis   p. 346

Cinquefoil
☼ ◐ ◐ ✄ VARY
Potentilla   p. 490

Citrus
☼ ◐ ● ✄ CS, TS
    p. 247

Glossy abelia
☼ ◐ ◐ ✄ US, MS, LS, CS
Abelia x grandiflora   p. 146

Glossy privet
☼ ◐ ◐ ◐ ✄ LS, CS, TS
Ligustrum lucidum   p. 390

Hercules' club
☼ ◐ ○◐◐ ✄ US, MS, LS, CS
Aralia spinosa   p. 177

Honeysuckle
☼ ◐ ◐◐ ✄ VARY
Lonicera   p. 397

Lavender
☼ ◐ ● ✄ VARY
Lavandula   p. 384

Lilac
☼ ◐ ◐ ✄ VARY
Syringa   p. 563

Mahonia
☼ ◑ ● ○○◐ ✄ VARY
    p. 408

Mimosa
☼ ◐ ◐ ✄ US, MS, LS, CS
Albizia julibrissin   p. 158

Mock orange
☼ ◐ ◐ ✄ VARY   p. 467
Philadelphus (single-flowering)

New Jersey tea
☼ ○ ✄ US, MS, LS, CS
Ceanothus americanus   p. 232

Palmetto
☼ ◑ ◐ ✄ VARY
Sabal   p. 528

Rhododendron
◐ ◐◐ ◑ ✄ VARY
    p. 507

Rosemary
☼ ○◐ ✄ US, MS, LS, CS
Rosmarinus officinalis   p. 524

Spiraea
☼ ◐ ◐◐ ✄ VARY
    p. 552

Summersweet
☼ ◐ ◐◐ ✄ US, MS, LS, CS
Clethra alnifolia   p. 253

Viburnum
☼ ◐ ◐ ✄ VARY
    p. 585

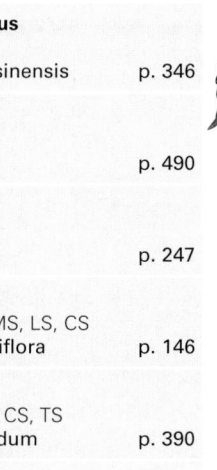

Chinese hibiscus
Hibiscus rosa-sinensis

Chaste tree
Vitex

Glossy privet
Ligustrum lucidum

Lilac, common
Syringa vulgaris

Summersweet
Clethra alnifolia

Chinese snowball
Viburnum macrocephalum

For climate zone explanations, please see pages 28–38.

Plants That Attract
Songbirds and Hummingbirds

B irds and blossoms seem to go together. Spying a cardinal, goldfinch, or bluebird sitting in a nearby tree can be as exciting as spotting a new rose in bloom. Attracting birds to your garden isn't hard—just provide water, dense plants for nesting and shelter, and food in the form of berries, seeds, and nectar. (But remember to put a bell on your cat's collar.)

A hummingbird samples a delphinium on the wing.

Montbretia
Crocosmia crocosmiiflora

(left column photos)

American bittersweet
Celastrus scandens

American elderberry
Sambucus canadensis

Purple beautyberry
Callicarpa dichotoma

Chokeberry
Aronia

SONGBIRDS
Vines, Shrubs

American bittersweet
☼ ◑ ✀ US, MS, LS
Celastrus scandens   p. 233

American elderberry
☼ ◑ ◆ ✀ US, MS, LS, CS
Sambucus canadensis   p. 533

Bayberry
☼ ◆ ✀ US, MS
Myrica pensylvanica   p. 425

Beautyberry
☼ ◑ ◐ ◆ ✀ US, MS, LS
Callicarpa   p. 217

Blueberry
☼ ◑ ● ◐◐◆ ✀ VARY
Vaccinium   p. 582

Boston ivy
☼ ◑ ◆ ✀ US, MS, LS
Parthenocissus tricuspidata   p. 448

Carolina buckthorn
☼ ◑ ◆ ✀ US, MS, LS, CS
Rhamnus caroliniana   p. 505

Chinaberry
☼ ◑ ◆ ✀ MS, LS, CS, TS
Melia azedarach   p. 416

Chokeberry
☼ ◑ ◐◆◐ ✀ VARY
Aronia   p. 181

Coralberry
☼ ◑◆ ✀ US, MS
Symphoricarpos orbiculatus p. 562

Cotoneaster
☼ ◑ ◐◆ ✀ VARY
          p. 266

Darwin barberry
☼ ◑ ◐◆ ✀ MS, LS, CS
Berberis darwinii   p. 198

Elaeagnus
☼ ◑ ◐◐◆ ✀ VARY
          p. 295

Euonymus
☼ ◑ ◐ ◐◆ ✀ VARY
          p. 304

Firethorn
☼ ◆ ✀ VARY
Pyracantha   p. 498

Grape
☼ ◆ ✀ VARY
          p. 328

Holly
☼ ◑ ◆ ✀ VARY
Ilex   p. 356

Honeysuckle
☼ ◑ ◐◆ ✀ VARY
Lonicera   p. 397

Mahonia
☼ ◑ ◐ ◐◐◆ ✀ VARY
          p. 408

Photinia
☼ ◑ ◆ ✀ VARY
          p. 471

Privet
☼ ◑ ◐ ◆ ✀ VARY
Ligustrum   p. 390

Rose (some)
☼ ◑ ◆ ✀ ALL
Rosa   p. 516

Spicebush
☼ ◑ ◆ ✀ US, MS, LS
Lindera benzoin   p. 393

Sumac
☼ ◑ ◆ ✀ VARY
Rhus   p. 514

Viburnum (deciduous)
☼ ◑ ◆ ✀ VARY
          p. 585

Cranberry cotoneaster
Cotoneaster apiculatus

Firethorn
Pyracantha 'Teton'

Japanese holly
Ilex crenata

Mahonia

For growing symbol explanations, please see page 39.

Yaupon
☼ ◐ ♦ ♦ ✂ MS, LS, CS, TS
Ilex vomitoria   p. 358

SONGBIRDS
Trees

American beech
☼ ◐ ♦ ♦ ✂ US, MS, LS, CS
Fagus grandifolia   p. 308

American sweet gum
☼ ◐ ♦ ♦ ✂ US, MS, LS, CS
Liquidambar styraciflua   p. 394

Arborvitae
☼ ◐ ♦ ♦ ✂ VARY
Thuja   p. 568

Birch
☼ ♦ ♦ ✂ VARY
Betula   p. 200

Black gum
☼ ◐ ♦ ♦ ✂ US, MS, LS, CS
Nyssa sylvatica   p. 433

Cabbage palm
☼ ◐ ♦ ✂ LS, CS, TS
Sabal palmetto   p. 528

Dogwood
☼ ◐ ♦ ✂ VARY
Cornus   p. 262

Eastern red cedar
☼ ◐ ◊ ♦ ♦ ✂ ALL
Juniperus virginiana   p. 373

Flowering crabapple
☼ ♦ ♦ ✂ VARY
Malus   p. 409

Glossy privet
☼ ◐ ♦ ♦ ✂ LS, CS, TS
Ligustrum lucidum   p. 390

Hackberry, common
☼ ◐ ♦ ✂ US, MS, LS, CS
Celtis occidentalis   p. 234

Hawthorn
☼ ♦ ✂ VARY
Crataegus   p. 268

Hemlock
☼ ◐ ♦ ✂ VARY
Tsuga   p. 578

Holly
☼ ◐ ♦ ✂ VARY
Ilex   p. 356

Juneberry
☼ ◐ ♦ ♦ ✂ VARY
Amelanchier   p. 164

Loquat
☼ ◐ ♦ ◊ ♦ ♦ ✂ VARY
Eriobotrya   p. 300

Magnolia
☼ ◐ ♦ ✂ VARY
                                  p. 402

Maple
☼ ◐ ♦ ♦ ✂ VARY
Acer   p. 148

Mountain ash
☼ ◐ ♦ ♦ ✂ VARY
Sorbus   p. 549

Mulberry
☼ ♦ ✂ VARY
Morus   p. 422

Oak
☼ ♦ ✂ VARY
Quercus   p. 500

Persimmon
☼ ♦ ♦ ✂ VARY
                                  p. 464

Pine
☼ ◊ ♦ ♦ ✂ VARY
Pinus   p. 474

Sassafras
☼ ♦ ✂ US, MS, LS, CS
Sassafras albidum   p. 536

Spruce
☼ ◐ ♦ ♦ ✂ US, MS, LS
Picea   p. 472

Wax myrtle
☼ ♦ ♦ ✂ MS, LS, CS, TS
Myrica cerifera   p. 425

HUMMINGBIRDS
Annuals, Perennials, Bulbs

Aloe
☼ ◐ ◊ ◊ ♦ ✂ TS
                                  p. 161

Alstroemeria
♦ ♦ ♦ ✂ MS, LS, CS
                                  p. 162

Beard tongue
☼ ◐ ♦ ♦ ✂ VARY
Penstemon   p. 461

Bee balm
☼ ◐ ♦ ♦ ✂ US, MS, LS
Monarda didyma   p. 421

Bird of paradise
☼ ◐ ♦ ✂ CS, TS
Strelitzia reginae   p. 559

Butterfly weed
☼ ◐ ♦ ✂ US, MS, LS, CS
Asclepias tuberosa   p. 184

Canna
☼ ♦ ✂ LS, CS, TS
                                  p. 224

Cape fuchsia
☼ ◐ ♦ ✂ US, MS, LS
Phygelius capensis   p. 471

Cardinal flower
♦ ◐ ♦ ◊ ♦ ✂ US, MS, LS, CS
Lobelia cardinalis   p. 396

Spicebush
Lindera benzoin

Yaupon
Ilex vomitoria

Black gum
Nyssa sylvatica

Hawthorn
Crataegus

Juneberry
Amelanchier arborea

Oak
Quercus

Bird of paradise
Strelitzia reginae

Canna

Butterfly weed
Asclepias tuberosa

For climate zone explanations, please see pages 28–34. ▶

Columbine
☼ ☽ ◐ ◑ ✂ VARY
Aquilegia   p. 176

Coral bells
☼ ○ ◐ ◑ ✂ US, MS, LS
Heuchera sanguinea   p. 345

Cotoneaster
☼ ○ ◐ ◑ ✂ VARY
                             p. 266

Delphinium
☼ ◐ ✂ VARY
                             p. 281

Dicliptera
☼ ☽ ○ ◐ ◑ ✂ VARY
                             p. 286

Firecracker plant
☼ ○ ◐ ◑ ✂ CS, TS
Russelia equisetiformis   p. 527

Firecracker vine
☼ ◐ ◑ ✂ TS
Ipomoea lobata   p. 361

Firecracker vine
☼ ☽ ◐ ◑ ✂ LS, CS, TS
Manettia cordifolia   p. 413

Flowering maple
☼ ☽ ◐ ◑ ✂ CS, TS
Abutilon   p. 147

Four o'clock
☼ ◐ ◑ ✂ ALL
Mirabilis jalapa   p. 420

Foxglove
☽ ◐ ◑ ✂ US, MS, LS, CS
Digitalis   p. 287

Fuchsia
☽ ◐ ✂ VARY
                             p. 317

Geranium
☼ ☽ ○ ◐ ◑ ✂ CS, TS
Pelargonium   p. 458

Ginger lily
☼ ◐ ◑ ✂ VARY
Hedychium   p. 338

Gladiolus
☼ ◐ ◑ ✂ MS, LS, CS
                             p. 324

Hen and chicks
☼ ☽ ◐ ◑ ✂ CS, TS
Echeveria (several)   p. 292

Hollyhock
☼ ☽ ◐ ✂ US, MS, LS, CS
Alcea rosea   p. 158

Impatiens
☼ ☽ ○ ◐ ◑ ✂ ALL
                             p. 358

Indian paintbrush
☼ ☽ ◐ ✂ ALL
Castilleja indivisa   p. 230

Iris
☼ ☽ ● ◐ ◑ ◐ ◑ ✂ VARY
                             p. 362

Jatropha
◐ ◑ ◐ ✂ TS
                             p. 368

Montbretia
☼ ☽ ◐ ◑ ✂ US, MS, LS, CS
Crocosmia crocosmiiflora   p. 270

Pentas
☼ ◐ ✂ ALL
Pentas lanceolata   p. 461

Phlox
☼ ☽ ◐ ✂ VARY
                             p. 469

Porterweed
☼ ◐ ◑ ✂ TS
Stachytarpheta   p. 554

Red-hot poker
☼ ☽ ◐ ◑ ✂ US, MS, LS, CS
Kniphofia uvaria   p. 377

Red yucca
☼ ○ ◐ ✂ ALL
Hesperaloe parviflora   p. 344

Rose campion
☼ ☽ ◐ ✂ US, MS, LS
Lychnis coronaria   p. 399

Sage (many)
☼ ◐ ✂ VARY
Salvia   p. 530

Snapdragon
☼ ◐ ✂ ALL
Antirrhinum majus   p. 169

Speedwell
☼ ○ ◐ ◑ ✂ US, MS, LS
Veronica   p. 584

Spider flower
☼ ◐ ◑ ✂ ALL
Cleome hasslerana   p. 252

Texas tuberose
☼ ☽ ○ ◐ ◑ ✂ MS, LS, CS
Manfreda maculosa   p. 413

Zinnia
☼ ◐ ✂ ALL
                             p. 595

HUMMINGBIRDS
Vines

Bean, scarlet runner
☼ ◐ ✂ ALL
                             p. 195

Cape honeysuckle
☼ ☽ ◐ ✂ CS, TS
Tecoma capensis   p. 567

Cypress vine
☼ ◐ ◑ ✂ ALL
Ipomoea quamoclit   p. 361

Delphinium

Geranium
Pelargonium

Firecracker plant
Russelia equisetiformis

Four o'clock
Mirabilis jalapa

Ginger lily, common
Hedychium coronarium

Red yucca
Hesperaloe parviflora

Pineapple sage
Salvia elegans

Scarlet runner bean

For growing symbol explanations, please see page 39.

Passion vine
Passiflora × alatocaerulea

Flowering quince
Chaenomeles

Bearberry
Arctostaphylos uva-ursi

Cape honeysuckle
Tecoma capensis

'Canberra Gem' grevillea

Flame vine
☼ ◗ ◆ ⚡ CS, TS
Pyrostegia venusta — p. 499

Morning glory, common
☼ ◗ ◆ ⚡ ALL
Ipomoea purpurea — p. 361

Passion vine
☼ ◗ ◆ ◗ ⚡ VARY
Passiflora — p. 449

Trumpet creeper
☼ ◗ ◆ ◗ ⚡ VARY
Campsis — p. 224

HUMMINGBIRDS
Shrubs, Trees, Groundcovers

Acacia
☼ ◗ ◗ ⚡ VARY — p. 147

American elderberry
☼ ◗ ◆ ◗ ⚡ US, MS, LS, CS
Sambucus canadensis — p. 533

Bearberry
☼ ◗ ◗ ◆ ◗ ⚡ US, MS
Arctostaphylos uva-ursi — p. 178

Beauty bush
☼ ◗ ◆ ⚡ US, MS, LS
Kolkwitzia amabilis — p. 378

Bird of paradise
☼ ◗ ◆ ⚡ CS, TS
Strelitzia reginae — p. 559

Bottlebrush
☼ ◆ ◗ ⚡ VARY
Callistemon — p. 217

Butterfly bush
☼ ◗ ◆ ◗ ⚡ VARY
Buddleia — p. 211

Cape honeysuckle
☼ ◗ ◗ ⚡ CS, TS
Tecoma capensis — p. 567

Cestrum
◗ ◆ ◗ ◆ ⚡ TS — p. 237

Citrus
☼ ◆ ◗ ⚡ CS, TS — p. 247

Coral tree
☼ ◆ ◗ ⚡ TS
Erythrina — p. 301

Desert willow
☼ ◗ ◆ ◗ ⚡ MS, LS, CS
Chilopsis linearis — p. 240

Eucalyptus
☼ ◗ ◗ ⚡ VARY — p. 302

Feijoa, Pineapple guava
☼ ◆ ◗ ⚡ LS, CS, TS
Feijoa sellowiana — p. 310

Firebush
☼ ◆ ◗ ⚡ CS, TS
Hamelia patens — p. 336

Flowering quince
☼ ◗ ◆ ◗ ⚡ US, MS, LS, CS
Chaenomeles — p. 237

Glossy abelia
☼ ◗ ◆ ◗ ⚡ US, MS, LS, CS
Abelia × grandiflora — p. 146

Grevillea
☼ ◗ ◗ ◆ ◗ ⚡ VARY — p. 333

Hibiscus
☼ ◆ ⚡ VARY — p. 345

Honeysuckle
☼ ◗ ◆ ◗ ⚡ VARY
Lonicera — p. 397

Horsechestnut
☼ ◗ ◆ ◗ ◆ ⚡ VARY
Aesculus — p. 154

Lavender (many)
☼ ◆ ◗ ⚡ VARY
Lavandula — p. 384

Lilac
☼ ◆ ◗ ⚡ VARY
Syringa — p. 563

Mimosa
☼ ◆ ◗ ⚡ US, MS, LS, CS
Albizia julibrissin — p. 158

Orchid tree
☼ ◆ ◗ ⚡ TS
Bauhinia — p. 194

Pink powder puff
☼ ◆ ◗ ⚡ CS, TS
Calliandra haematocephala — p. 217

Red clerodendrum
☼ ◆ ◗ ⚡ TS
Clerodendrum splendens — p. 253

Texas ranger
☼ ◗ ◗ ◆ ◗ ⚡ LS, CS, TS
Leucophyllum frutescens — p. 388

Trailing lantana
☼ ◆ ◗ ⚡ LS, CS, TS
Lantana montevidensis — p. 382

Weigela
☼ ◗ ◆ ◗ ⚡ US, MS, LS
Weigela florida — p. 590

Yellow bird of paradise
☼ ◗ ◗ ◆ ◗ ⚡ CS, TS
Caesalpinia gilliesii — p. 214

Yellow justicia
☼ ◗ ◆ ◗ ⚡ CS, TS
Justicia aurea — p. 373

Yellow shrimp plant
☼ ◗ ◆ ◗ ⚡ CS, TS
Pachystachys lutea — p. 442

Red horsechestnut
Aesculus × carnea

Lavender
Lavandula

Mimosa
Albizia julibrissin

Yellow justicia
Justicia aurea

Trumpet creeper, common
Campsis radicans

For climate zone explanations, please see pages 28–34.

Hybrid fuchsia
Fuchsia × hybrida

Plants for
Hanging Baskets
and Window Boxes

The charm of a garden in the air—whether it is suspended or perched—derives from the choice of plants. You need a full and colorful show with foliage that is lax enough to soften the edges of the arrangement. Here's a selection of proven aerial artists, drawn from a variety of annuals, perennials, and woody plants. Mix and match between them to create your own seasonal effects.

A basket filled with double-flowered impatiens, sweet alyssum, and ornamental asparagus.

Coleus
Coleus × hybridus

Dwarf cup flower
Nierembergia caerulea

Dwarf morning glory
Convolvulus tricolor

ANNUALS

Amethyst flower
☼ ◑ ● ✄ ALL
Browallia p. 209

Angelonia angustifolia
☼ ● ✄ LS, CS, TS
 p. 167

Bacopa
☼ ◑ ● ✄ ALL
Sutera cordata p. 561

Black-eyed Susan vine
☼ ◑ ● ✄ ALL
Thunbergia alata p. 570

Blue daze
☼ ◑ ● ● ✄ ALL
Evolvulus glomeratus p. 307

Calendula
☼ ◑ ● ✄ ALL
Calendula officinalis p. 216

Coleus
☼ ◑ ● ● ● ✄ ALL
Coleus × hybridus p. 256

Creeping zinnia
☼ ◑ ● ✄ ALL
Sanvitalia procumbens p. 534

Dwarf cup flower
☼ ◑ ● ✄ ALL
Nierembergia caerulea p. 432

Dwarf morning glory
☼ ◑ ● ✄ ALL
Convolvulus tricolor p. 259

Edging lobelia
☼ ● ● ● ✄ ✄ ALL
Lobelia erinus p. 396

English daisy
☼ ◑ ● ✄ US, MS, LS, TS
Bellis perennis p. 198

Floss flower
☼ ◑ ● ✄ ALL
Ageratum houstonianum p. 156

Flowering cabbage and kale
☼ ◑ ● ✄ ALL
 p. 214

Flowering tobacco
☼ ◑ ● ● ✄ ALL
Nicotiana alata p. 431

Forget-me-not
● ● ✄ US, MS, LS
Myosotis sylvatica p. 425

Garden verbena
☼ ● ● ✄ ALL
Verbena × hybrida p. 583

Geranium, common
☼ ◑ ● ● ● ✄ ALL
Pelargonium hortorum p. 459

Globe amaranth
☼ ◑ ● ✄ ALL
Gomphrena p. 326

Hyacinth bean
☼ ● ✄ LS, CS, TS
Dolichos lablab p. 289

Impatiens (many)
☼ ◑ ● ● ✄ ALL
 p. 358

Ivy geranium
☼ ◑ ● ● ✄ ALL
Pelargonium peltatum p. 459

Million bells
☼ ◑ ● ✄ ALL
Calibrachoa p. 216

Monkey flower
☼ ● ✄ ALL
Mimulus × hybridus p. 419

Morning glory
☼ ● ● ✄ ALL
Ipomoea tricolor p. 361

Hyacinth bean
Dolichos lablab

Ivy geranium
Pelargonium peltatum

Monkey flower
Mimulus × hybridus

Moss rose
Portulaca grandiflora

For growing symbol explanations, please see page 39.

Moss rose
☼ ◐●●✄ ALL
Portulaca grandiflora   p. 489

Nasturtium
☼ ◑●●✄ ALL
Tropaeolum majus   p. 577

Narrow-leaf zinnia
☼ ●✄ ALL
Zinnia angustifolia   p. 595

Persian shield
☼●●✄ ALL
Strobilanthes dyeranus   p. 559

Persian violet
◑●●●✄ ALL OR INDOORS
Exacum affine   p. 307

Petunia
☼ ●●✄ ALL
Petunia × hybrida   p. 465

Polka-dot plant
☼◑●●✄ ALL OR INDOORS
Hypoestes phyllostachya   p. 355

Snapdragon
☼◑●✄ ALL
Antirrhinum majus   p. 169

Stock
☼◑●●✄ ALL
Matthiola incana   p. 415

Swan river daisy
☼●✄ ALL
Brachyscome iberidifolia   p. 207

Sweet alyssum
☼◑●●✄ ALL
Lobularia maritima   p. 396

Sweet pea
☼◑●●●✄ ALL
Lathyrus odoratus   p. 383

Sweet potato vine
☼●●●✄ LS, CS, TS OR INDOORS
Ipomoea batatus   p. 361

Tickseed
☼●●●✄ VARY
Bidens   p. 201

Tuberous begonia
◑●●✄ ALL
          p. 197

Viola, Violet, Pansy
☼◑●●●✄ VARY
Viola   p. 587

Wishbone flower
◑●●✄ ALL
Torenia fournieri   p. 575

PERENNIALS, BULBS

Achimenes
◑●●●✄ CS, TS OR INDOORS
          p. 151

Basket-of-gold
☼◑●●✄ US, MS, LS, CS
Aurinia saxatilis   p. 189

Billbergia
◑●●✄ ALL
          p. 201

Cactus
☼◑●○●●✄ VARY
Cactaceae (many)   p. 214

Coral bells
☼●●●✄ US, MS, LS
Heuchera   p. 344

Crassula
☼◑○✄ TS
          p. 268

Creeping Jenny
☼◑●●●✄ US, MS, LS
Lysimachia nummularia   p. 401

Dendrobium
◑●●✄ TS OR INDOORS
          p. 282

Donkey tail
☼◑○●✄ TS OR INDOORS
Sedum morganianum   p. 540

Dusty miller
☼◑○●✄ MS, LS, CS
Senecio cineraria   p. 542

Echeveria
☼◑○●✄ VARY
          p. 292

Evergreen candytuft
☼◑●✄ US, MS, LS
Iberis sempervirens   p. 355

Fancy-leafed caladium
◑●●●●◑✄ ALL
Caladium bicolor   p. 214

Flame violet
●●●✄ TS OR INDOORS
Episcia   p. 297

Fleabane
☼◑◑●✄ VARY
Erigeron   p. 299

Freesia
☼◑●✄ CS, TS OR INDOORS
          p. 317

Gazania daisy
☼◑●●✄ ALL
Gazania   p. 320

Greater periwinkle
☼◑●●●✄ MS, LS, CS
Vinca major   p. 587

Heliotrope, common
◑●●✄ TS OR ANNUAL
Heliotropium arborescens   p. 341

Hyacinth
☼◑◑●◑✄ VARY
Hyacinthus   p. 351

Billbergia

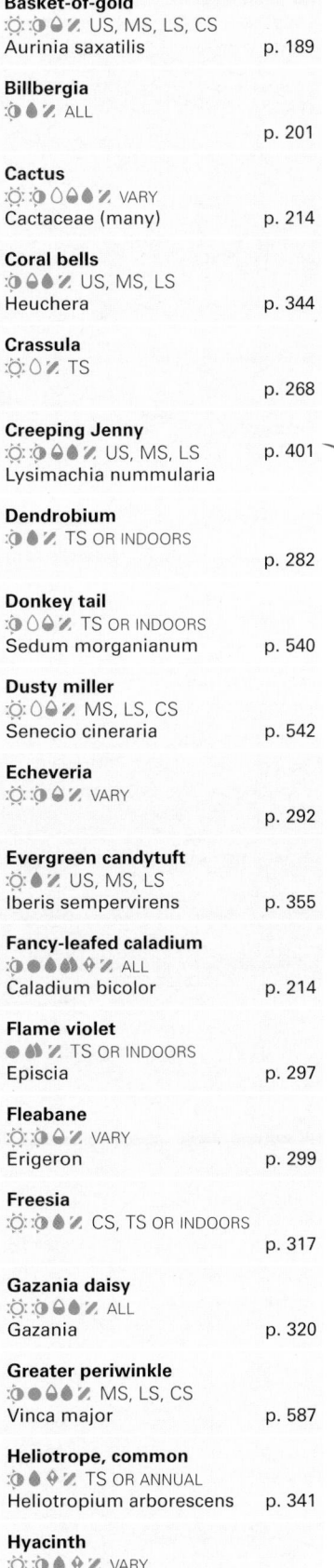

Gazania daisy
Gazania

Heliotrope, common
Heliotropium arborescens 'Black Beauty'

Creeping Jenny
Lysimachia nummularia 'Aurea'

Donkey tail
Sedum morganianum

Nasturtium
Tropaeolum majus

Tuberous begonia

Viola
Viola × wittrockiana

For climate zone explanations, please see pages 28–38.

Jewel orchid
Ludisia discolor

Kalanchoe

Licorice plant
Helichrysum petiolare 'Limelight'

Himalayan maidenhair
Adiantum venustum

Meyers asparagus
Asparagus densiflorus 'Meyers'

Spotted dead nettle
Lamium maculatum 'Beacon Silver'

Ice plant
☼ ◐◊◊ ✂ ALL   p. 418
Mesembryanthemum crystallinum

Japanese felt fern
◐ ◢ ✂ CS, TS
Pyrrosia lingua   p. 499

Japanese forest grass
◐ ● ◢ ✂ US, MS, LS
Hakonechloa macra   p. 335

Jewel orchid
☼ ◢ ✂ TS OR INDOORS
Ludisia discolor   p. 398

Kalanchoe
☼ ☼ ◐ ◢◢ ✂ TS OR INDOORS
                                p. 374

Lantana
☼ ◢◊◢ ✂ LS, CS, TS OR ANNUAL
                                p. 382

Licorice plant
☼ ◢ ✂ TS OR ANNUAL
Helichrysum petiolare   p. 340

Maidenhair fern
☼ ● ◢◊ ✂ VARY
Adiantum   p. 153

Neomarica
☼ ☼ ◢ ✂ ALL
                                p. 429

Oregano
☼ ◊◢ ✂ VARY
Origanum   p. 437

Ornamental asparagus
☼ ◢ ✂ CS, TS OR INDOORS
                                p. 185

Ornamental strawberry
☼ ☼ ◢ ✂ US, MS, LS, CS
Fragaria hybrids   p. 315

Plectranthus (some)
☼ ◢ ✂ TS OR INDOORS
                                p. 480

Pocketbook plant
☼ ◢ ◢ ✂ ALL
Calceolaria   p. 216

Primrose (some)
☼ ◢ ✂ VARY
Primula   p. 491

Red ivy
☼ ◢ ✂ TS OR ANNUAL
Hemigraphis alternata   p. 343

Sedum sieboldii
☼ ◊◊ ✂ US, MS, LS
                                p. 541

Spider plant
☼ ◢ ✂ TS OR INDOORS
Chlorophytum comosum   p. 242

Spotted dead nettle
☼ ◢ ◢ ✂ US, MS, LS
Lamium maculatum   p. 382

Staghorn fern
☼ ◢ ✂ CS, TS
Platycerium bifurcatum   p. 479

Strawberry geranium
☼ ◢ ◢ ✂ MS, LS, CS OR INDOORS
Saxifraga stolonifera   p. 537

Sweet flag
☼ ◢ ◢ ✂ US, MS, LS, CS
Acorus   p. 152

Threadleaf coreopsis
☼ ◊◢ ✂ US, MS, LS, CS
Coreopsis verticillata   p. 260

Tulip
☼ ☼ ◢ ✂ ALL
Tulipa   p. 578

Twinspur
☼ ☼ ◢ ◢ ✂ VARY
Diascia   p. 284

Velvet plant
☼ ☼ ◢ ✂ LS, CS, TS OR INDOORS
Gynura   p. 334

Wandering jew
☼ ☼ ◢ ◢◢ ✂ CS, TS OR INDOORS
Tradescantia fluminensis   p. 576

SHRUBS, WOODY VINES

Boxwood (dwarf forms)
☼ ☼ ◢ ✂ VARY
Buxus   p. 213

Creeping rosemary
☼ ◊◢ ✂ ALL   p. 525
Rosmarinus officinalis 'Prostratus'

Dwarf Japanese garden juniper
☼ ☼ ◊◊◢ ✂ US, MS, LS, CS p. 371
Juniperus procumbens 'Nana'

English ivy
☼ ☼ ◢ ◢ ◢ ✂ ALL
Hedera helix   p. 337

Flowering maple
☼ ☼ ◢ ◢ ✂ ALL
Abutilon   p. 147

Hybrid fuchsia
☼ ◢ ✂ US OR ANNUAL
Fuchsia × hybrida   p. 317

Japanese ardisia
☼ ☼ ◢ ◢ ✂ LS, CS
Ardisia japonica   p. 179

Jasmine
☼ ☼ ◢ ◢ ✂ VARY
Jasminium   p. 367

Myrtle (dwarf forms)
☼ ☼ ◊◊ ◢ ✂ CS
Myrtus communis   p. 425

Pentas
☼ ◢ ✂ ALL
Pentas lanceolata   p. 461

Staghorn fern
Platycerium bifurcatum

Threadleaf coreopsis
Coreopsis verticillata

Tulip
Tulipa saxatilis 'Lilac Wonder'

Flowering maple
Abutilon megapotamicum

English ivy
Hedera helix
'Needlepoint'

For growing symbol explanations, please see page 39.

Trees and Shrubs
for Containers

A nnuals, perennials, herbs, and even vegetables are standard choices for container gardening. But many larger, woody plants can be equally versatile. Perhaps you want a tall accent for the patio; maybe you long to grow a favorite camellia but have no ground available for planting. Or it may be that you have your heart set on a lemon tree, but your winters are too chilly. The trees and shrubs that follow adapt well to life in larger containers.

Chinese hibiscus
Hibiscus rosa-sinensis

Edible fig

Lemon
Citrus

Japanese maple
Acer palmatum

Possumhaw
Ilex decidua

Bay
Laurus nobilis

TREES

Apple (dwarf)
☼ ◐ ✿ VARY
p. 171

Broadleaf podocarpus
☼ ◐ ◐ ✿ CS, TS
Podocarpus nagi   p. 485

Chinese redbud
☼ ◐ ✿ US, MS, LS
Cercis chinensis   p. 236

Citrus
☼ ◐ ✿ ALL
p. 248

Edible fig
☼ ◐ ✿ ALL
p. 313

Japanese maple
☼ ◐ ◐ ◐ ✿ US, MS, LS, CS
Acer palmatum   p. 149

Juniper
☼ ◐ ◐ ◐ ◐ ✿ VARY
Juniperus (upright types) p. 370

Magnolia grandiflora 'Little Gem'
☼ ◐ ◐ ✿ US, MS, LS, CS
p. 404

Possumhaw
☼ ◐ ◐ ✿ US, MS, LS, CS
Ilex decidua   p. 357

Texas mountain laurel
☼ ◐ ◐ ◐ ✿ LS, CS
Sophora secundiflora   p. 549

Windmill palm
☼ ◐ ◐ ◐ ◐ ✿ LS, CS, TS OR INDOORS
Trachycarpus fortunei   p. 575

SHRUBS

Abelia
☼ ◐ ◐ ✿ VARY
p. 146

Agave
☼ ◐ ◐ ◐ ✿ CS, TS
p. 156

Aloe
☼ ◐ ◐ ◐ ✿ TS
p. 161

Angel's trumpet
☼ ◐ ◐ ◐ ✿ LS, CS, TS
Brugmansia   p. 209

Azalea
◐ ◐ ◐ ◐ ✿ VARY
Rhododendron   p. 510

Bamboos
☼ ◐ ◐ ◐ ◐ ✿ VARY
(Many kinds)   p. 190

Banana
☼ ◐ ◐ ◐ ✿ ALL
Musa   p. 423

Banana shrub
☼ ◐ ◐ ✿ LS, CS, TS
Michelia figo   p. 418

Bay
☼ ◐ ◐ ✿ ALL
Laurus nobilis   p. 384

Bougainvillea (shrubby selections)
☼ ◐ ◐ ✿ ALL
p. 205

Boxwood
☼ ◐ ◐ ◐ ✿ VARY
Buxus   p. 213

Bronze loquat
☼ ◐ ◐ ◐ ◐ ✿ CS, TS
Eriobotrya deflexa   p. 300

Brunfelsia
☼ ◐ ◐ ◐ ◐ ✿ ALL
p. 210

Camellia
◐ ◐ ◐ ◐ ✿ US, MS, LS, CS
p. 220

Chinese fringe
☼ ◐ ◐ ◐ ◐ ✿ MS, LS, CS
Loropetalum chinense   p. 398

Angel's trumpet
Brugmansia

Bamboo

Abyssinian banana
Ensete ventricosum

Bronze loquat
Eriobotrya deflexa

For climate zone explanations, please see pages 28–34. ▶

Flowering maple
Abutilon

Gardenia, common
Gardenia jasminoides

*Berberis
thunbergii
'Atropurpurea'*

Japanese barberry
Berberis thunbergii

Japanese fatsia
Fatsia japonica

Japanese pittosporum
Pittosporum tobira

Chinese hibiscus
☼ ◑ ♦ ⁒ CS, TS
Hibiscus rosa-sinensis   p. 346

Crepe myrtle
☼ ◑ ♦ ⁒ US, MS, LS, CS   p. 379
Lagerstroemia indica (dwarf forms)

Dwarf Alberta spruce
☼ ◑ ◐ ♦ ♦ ⁒ US, MS   p. 472
Picea glauca 'Conica'

Dwarf Japanese garden juniper
☼ ◑ ◐ ◐ ♦ ♦ ⁒ US, MS, LS, CS   p. 371
Juniperus procumbens 'Nana'

False aralia
☼ ◑ ♦ ⁒ TS OR INDOORS
Schefflera elegantissima   p. 538

Florida leucothoe
◑ ● ♦ ♦ ⁒ MS, LS, CS
Agarista populifolia   p. 155

Flowering maple
☼ ◑ ♦ ♦ ⁒ CS, TS
Abutilon   p. 147

Frangipani
☼ ◑ ♦ ♦ ⁒ ALL
Plumeria   p. 484

French hydrangea
◑ ♦ ⁒ US, MS, LS, CS   p. 352
Hydrangea macrophylla

Gardenia
☼ ◑ ♦ ⁒ VARY
          p. 319

Harry Lauder's walking stick
☼ ◑ ♦ ⁒ US, MS, LS
Corylus avellana 'Contorta'   p. 265

Holly (many)
☼ ◑ ♦ ⁒ VARY
Ilex   p. 356

Indian hawthorne
☼ ◑ ◐ ♦ ♦ ⁒ LS, CS
Rhaphiolepis   p. 505

Japanese aucuba
◑ ● ◐ ♦ ⁒ ALL
Aucuba japonica   p. 189

Japanese barberry
☼ ◑ ◐ ♦ ⁒ US, MS, LS
Berberis thunbergii   p. 199

Japanese fatsia
◑ ● ♦ ⁒ LS, CS, TS OR INDOORS
Fatsia japonica   p. 310

Japanese pittosporum
☼ ◑ ● ♦ ♦ ⁒ LS, CS, TS
Pittosporum tobira   p. 478

Japanese privet
☼ ◑ ♦ ♦ ⁒ MS, LS, CS, TS
Ligustrum japonicum   p. 390

Japanese skimmia
◑ ● ♦ ⁒ US, MS, LS
Skimmia japonica   p. 546

Lantana
☼ ◑ ♦ ♦ ⁒ ALL
          p. 382

Lavender
☼ ◑ ♦ ⁒ VARY
Lavandula   p. 384

Mahonia (most)
☼ ◑ ● ◐ ◐ ♦ ⁒ VARY
          p. 408

Mexican orange
☼ ◑ ◐ ♦ ⁒ LS, CS, TS
Choisya ternata   p. 242

Mountain laurel
☼ ◑ ● ♦ ♦ ⁒ US, MS, LS, CS
Kalmia latifolia   p. 375

Nandina
☼ ◑ ● ♦ ♦ ⁒ US, MS, LS, CS
Nandina domestica   p. 425

New Zealand flax
☼ ◑ ◐ ◐ ♦ ⁒ ALL
Phormium tenax   p. 470

New Zealand tea tree
☼ ◐ ◐ ⁒ CS, TS
Leptospermum scoparium   p. 387

Oleander
☼ ◐ ◐ ◐ ♦ ⁒ ALL
Nerium oleander   p. 431

Pieris
◑ ● ♦ ♦ ⁒ US, MS
          p. 473

Sago palm
◑ ● ♦ ⁒ CS, TS OR INDOORS
Cycas revoluta   p. 274

Shrimp plant
☼ ◑ ◐ ♦ ⁒ CS, TS
Justicia brandegeeana   p. 373

Slender deutzia
☼ ◑ ● ♦ ♦ ⁒ US, MS, LS
Deutzia gracilis   p. 283

Snow bush
☼ ◑ ● ♦ ⁒ TS OR INDOORS
Breynia nivosa   p. 208

Solanum rantonnetii
☼ ◑ ◐ ♦ ♦ ⁒ TS
          p. 548

Southern yew
☼ ◑ ● ♦ ⁒ LS, CS, TS
Podocarpus macrophyllus   p. 485

Strawberry tree
☼ ◑ ◐ ◐ ♦ ⁒ MS, LS, CS   p. 178
Arbutus unedo (smaller selections)

Winter daphne
◑ ● ♦ ⁒ MS, LS
Daphne odora   p. 279

Yew
☼ ◑ ● ◐ ♦ ♦ ⁒ US, MS
Taxus   p. 566

Oleander
Nerium oleander

Lantana, common
Lantana camara

Leatherleaf mahonia
Mahonia bealei

New Zealand flax
Phormium tenax

Strawberry tree
Arbutus unedo 'Compacta'

For growing symbol explanations, please see page 39.

Palms underplanted with peace lilies
(*Spathiphyllum*)

Plants for Tropical Effects

You don't have to fly to Hawaii or Grand Bahama to enjoy the lushness of the tropics. Garden centers carry a surprising number of tropical and tropical-looking plants that offer spectacular blooms and foliage. Some are perfectly winter hardy, while others won't take frost. But you needn't say good-bye to your tropical friends in November. Many can be easily overwintered indoors.

Coral tree
Erythrina

Banana
Musa acuminata

TREES

Abyssinian banana
☼ ◑ ● ⚡ LS, CS, TS
Ensete ventricosum   p. 296

Australian tree fern
◑ ● ⚡ TS
Cyathea cooperi   p. 273

Banana
☼ ◑ ● ⚡ CS, TS
Musa   p. 423

Bottlebrush
☼ ◑ ● ● ⚡ VARY
Callistemon   p. 217

Carambola
☼ ● ⚡ TS
                            p. 226

Catalpa
☼ ◑ ● ● ⚡ US, MS, LS, CS
                            p. 230

Chinese parasol tree
☼ ◑ ● ⚡ MS, LS, CS, TS
Firmiana simplex   p. 314

Coral tree
☼ ◑ ● ⚡ TS
Erythrina   p. 301

Empress tree
☼ ◑ ● ● ⚡ US, MS, LS
Paulownia tomentosa   p. 450

Fiddleleaf fig
☼ ◑ ● ⚡ TS OR INDOORS
Ficus lyrata   p. 312

Fig, edible
☼ ● ⚡ MS, LS, CS, TS
                            p. 313

Guava
☼ ◑ ● ⚡ VARY
                            p. 333

Hawaiian tree fern
◑ ● ⚡ TS
Cibotium glaucum   p. 246

Hercules' club
☼ ◑ ● ● ⚡ US, MS, LS, CS
Aralia spinosa   p. 177

Mexican grass tree
☼ ◑ ● ⚡ CS, TS
Nolina longifolia   p. 432

Mimosa
☼ ◑ ● ⚡ US, MS, LS, CS
Albizia julibrissin   p. 158

Orchid tree
☼ ● ● ⚡ TS
Bauhinia   p. 194

Palms
☼ ◑ ● ● ● ⚡ VARY
(Many kinds)   p. 444

Papaya
☼ ● ⚡ TS
                            p. 446

Silk-cotton tree
☼ ● ● ⚡ TS
Ceiba pentandra   p. 232

Tasmanian tree fern
◑ ● ● ⚡ TS
Dicksonia antarctica   p. 285

Traveler's tree
☼ ● ⚡ TS
Ravenala madagascariensis   p. 505

Trumpet tree
☼ ◑ ● ⚡ TS
Tabebuia   p. 564

VINES

Allamanda
☼ ● ● ◑ ⚡ TS
Allamanda   p. 159

Bougainvillea
☼ ● ● ⚡ CS, TS
                            p. 205

California dutchman's pipe
◑ ● ● ⚡ LS, CS, TS
Aristolochia californica   p. 180

Cry-baby tree
Erythrina crista-galli

Australian tree fern
Cyathea cooperi

Empress tree
Paulownia tomentosa

Orchid tree
Bauhinia

Pygmy date palm
Phoenix roebelenii

Tasmanian tree fern
Dicksonia antarctica

For climate zone explanations, please see pages 28–38. ▶

Cup-of-gold vine
Solandra maxima

Passion vine
Passiflora × alatocaerulea

Bamboo
Pleioblastus

Copper leaf
Acalypha wilkesiana

Cup-of-gold vine
☼ ◑ ✿ TS
Solandra maxima   p. 547

× Fatshedera lizei
☼ ◐ ◑ ✿ LS, CS, TS
                                   p. 309

Firecracker vine
☼ ◐ ◑ ✿ LS, CS, TS
Manettia cordifolia   p. 413

Flame vine
☼ ◐ ◑ ✿ CS, TS
Pyrostegia venusta   p. 499

Glorybower
☼ ◐ ◑ ✿ TS
Clerodendrum   p. 252

Herald's trumpet
☼ ◐ ◑ ✿ TS
Beaumontia grandiflora   p. 196

Jasmine
☼ ◐ ○ ◐ ◑ ✿ VARY
Jasminum   p. 367

Mandevilla
☼ ◐ ◑ ✿ VARY
                                   p. 412

Pandorea
◐ ◑ ◑ ✿ CS, TS
                                   p. 445

Passion vine
☼ ◐ ○ ◑ ◑ ✿ VARY
Passiflora   p. 449

Rangoon creeper
☼ ◐ ◑ ✿ TS
Quisqualis indica   p. 502

Split-leaf philodendron
◐ ◑ ◑ ✿ TS OR INDOORS
Monstera deliciosa   p. 422

Trumpet creeper
☼ ◐ ○ ◑ ◑ ✿ VARY
Campsis   p. 224

SHRUBS

Angel's trumpet
☼ ◐ ○ ◑ ◑ ✿ LS, CS, TS
Brugmansia   p. 209

Bamboo
☼ ◐ ○ ◑ ◑ ✿ VARY
                                   p. 190

Beschorneria
☼ ◐ ◑ ◑ ✿ VARY
                                   p. 200

Caesalpinia
☼ ○ ◑ ◑ ✿ VARY
                                   p. 214

Caribbean copper plant
☼ ◑ ◑ ✿ CS, TS
Euphorbia cotinifolia   p. 306

Chinese hibiscus
☼ ◑ ◑ ✿ CS, TS
Hibiscus rosa-sinensis   p. 346

Copper leaf
☼ ◐ ◑ ◑ ✿ TS OR INDOORS
Acalypha wilkesiana   p. 148

Feijoa, Pineapple guava
☼ ◑ ◑ ✿ LS, CS, TS
                                   p. 310

Ficus auriculata
☼ ◑ ◑ ✿ TS
                                   p. 311

Firespike
☼ ◐ ◑ ✿ CS, TS
Odontonema strictum   p. 434

Flowering maple
☼ ◐ ◑ ◑ ✿ CS, TS
Abutilon   p. 147

Frangipani
☼ ◐ ○ ◑ ◑ ✿ TS
Plumeria   p. 484

Grevillea
☼ ◐ ○ ◑ ◑ ✿ VARY
                                   p. 333

Japanese fatsia
◐ ◑ ◑ ✿ LS, CS, TS OR INDOORS
Fatsia japonica   p. 310

New Zealand flax
☼ ◐ ○ ◑ ◑ ✿ LS, CS, TS
Phormium tenax   p. 470

Princess flower
☼ ◐ ◑ ◑ ✿ TS
Tibouchina urvilleana   p. 572

Rice paper plant
☼ ◐ ◑ ◑ ✿ LS, CS, TS
Tetrapanax papyriferus   p. 568

Sago palm
◐ ◑ ◑ ◑ ✿ CS, TS OR INDOORS
Cycas revoluta   p. 274

Shower-of-gold
☼ ◐ ◑ ✿ CS, TS
Galphimia glauca   p. 319

Yellow bells
☼ ◐ ◑ ✿ CS, TS
Tecoma stans   p. 567

Yellow shrimp plant
☼ ◐ ◑ ✿ CS, TS
Pachystachys lutea   p. 442

PERENNIALS

Alpinia
◐ ◑ ◑ ✿ VARY
                                   p. 162

Angelica
◐ ◑ ◑ ✿ US, MS, LS, CS
                                   p. 167

Flowering maple
Abutilon pictum 'Thompsonii'

Frangipani
Plumeria

Princess flower
Tibouchina urvilleana

Yellow bells
Tecoma stans

Yellow shrimp plant
Pachystachys lutea

For growing symbol explanations, please see page 39.

Bird of paradise
Strelitzia reginae

Calla, common
Zantedeschia aethiopica

Parlor palm
Chamaedorea elegans

Ginger lily
Hedychium

Anthurium hookeri
☼ ◐ ✦ ✂ TS OR INDOORS
p. 169

Bear's breech
☼ ☼ ◐ ● ✦ ✂ US, MS, LS, CS
Acanthus mollis   p. 148

Billbergia
☼ ◐ ✦ ✂ TS
p. 201

Bird of Paradise
☼ ☼ ◐ ✦ ✂ VARY
Strelitzia   p. 559

Calathea
◐ ✦ ✂ TS OR INDOORS
p. 216

Calla, common
☼ ◐ ✦ ✂ CS, TS
Zantedeschia aethiopica   p. 593

Canna
☼ ◐ ✦ ✂ LS, CS, TS
p. 224

Caricature plant
☼ ◐ ✦ ✂ TS OR INDOORS
Graptophyllum pictum   p. 328

Cast-iron plant
◐ ● ✦ ✂ LS, CS, TS OR INDOORS
Aspidistra elatior   p. 186

Cestrum
☼ ◐ ✦ ✂ TS
p. 237

Chamaedorea
◐ ● ✦ ✂ TS
p. 238

Clivia
◐ ● ✦ ✂ TS
Clivia miniata   p. 254

Crinum
☼ ☼ ◐ ● ✦ ✂ ✂ VARY
p. 269

Dancing girl ginger
☼ ◐ ● ✂ CS, TS
Globba   p. 325

Dendrobium
◐ ● ✦ ✂ TS OR INDOORS
p. 282

Elephant's ear
◐ ● ✦ ✂ LS, CS, TS
Colocasia esculenta   p. 257

Fancy-leafed caladium
◐ ● ● ✦ ✂ TS
Caladium bicolor   p. 214

Ginger, common
◐ ● ● ✂ LS, CS, TS
Zingiber officinale   p. 595

Ginger lily
☼ ☼ ◐ ● ✂ VARY
Hedychium   p. 338

Gunnera
☼ ◐ ● ✂ MS, LS, CS, TS
p. 334

Hidden lily
◐ ● ✂ LS, CS, TS
Curcuma petiolata   p. 273

Japanese coltsfoot
◐ ● ● ✂ US, MS, LS, CS
Petasites japonicus   p. 464

Jatropha
◐ ● ● ✦ ✂ TS
p. 368

Joseph's coat
☼ ◐ ● ✂ TS OR ANNUAL
Alternanthera dentata   p. 163

Lobster-claw
☼ ◐ ● ✂ TS
Heliconia   p. 340

Orchid cactus
◐ ● ✂ TS OR INDOORS
Epiphyllum   p. 297

Papyrus
☼ ◐ ● ● ✂ CS, TS
Cyperus papyrus   p. 275

Peace lily
◐ ● ● ● ✂ TS OR INDOORS
Spathiphyllum   p. 550

Philodendron
☼ ◐ ● ● ✂ VARY OR INDOORS
p. 467

Pineapple lily
☼ ◐ ● ✂ LS, CS, TS OR INDOORS
Eucomis   p. 303

Shell ginger
◐ ● ● ✂ LS, CS, TS
Alpinia zerumbet   p. 162

Shooting stars
◐ ● ✂ TS   p. 495
Pseuderanthemum laxiflorum

Spiral flag
◐ ● ● ✂ CS, TS
Costus   p. 266

Staghorn fern
◐ ● ✂ TS
Platycerium   p. 479

Udo
☼ ◐ ● ● ✂ US, MS, LS
Aralia cordata   p. 177

Velvet plant
☼ ◐ ● ✂ LS, CS, TS OR INDOORS
Gynura   p. 334

Voodoo lily
◐ ● ✂ VARY
Amorphophallus   p. 164

Xanthosoma
◐ ● ✂ TS OR INDOORS
p. 592

Canna 'Pretoria'

Lobster-claw
Heliconia

Shell ginger
Alpinia zerumbet

Xanthosoma sagittifolium

For climate zone explanations, please see pages 28–38.

SPECIAL SITUATIONS

Plants for
Coastal Gardens

Life is no walk on the beach for plants near the coast. They endure constant wind, salt-laden air, and poor, sandy soil. Fortunately, many plants thrive under such conditions. Grouping these plants helps them meet the challenge. And some, indicated by the symbol ♕, are suitable for planting right on the dunes.

The cabbage palm *(Sabal palmetto)* matches the stature of a coastal home.

Confederate jasmine
Trachelospermum jasminoides

Beach plum
Prunus maritima

Japanese cryptomeria
Cryptomeria japonica

New Zealand tea tree
Leptospermum scoparium

TREES

American arborvitae
☼ ◐ ◖◗ ⚡ US, MS
Thuja occidentalis — p. 569

American holly
☼ ◐ ◗ ⚡ ALL
Ilex opaca — p. 357

Beach plum
☼ ◖◗ ⚡ US, MS
Prunus maritima — p. 495

Beefwood ♕
☼ ○◖◗ ⚡ TS
Casuarina — p. 230

Chinese elm
☼ ◐ ◗ ⚡ US, MS, LS, CS
Ulmus parvifolia — p. 581

Dahoon
☼ ◐ ● ◖◗ ⚡ MS, LS, CS, TS
Ilex cassine — p. 356

Eastern red cedar
☼ ◐ ○◖◗ ⚡ ALL
Juniperus virginiana — p. 373

Japanese black pine
☼ ◖◗ ⚡ US, MS, LS, CS
Pinus thunbergii — p. 477

Japanese cryptomeria
☼ ◐ ○◖◗ ⚡ US, MS, LS
Cryptomeria japonica — p. 271

Jerusalem thorn
☼ ○◖◗ ⚡ CS, TS
Parkinsonia aculeata — p. 447

Live oak
☼ ◖◗ ⚡ LS, CS, TS
Quercus virginiana — p. 502

Marlberry
☼ ◐ ○◗ ⚡ TS
Ardisia paniculata — p. 179

New Zealand tea tree
☼ ○◗ ⚡ CS, TS
Leptospermum scoparium — p. 387

Norfolk Island pine
☼ ◖◗ ⚡ TS
Araucaria heterophylla — p. 178

Palms (most)
☼ ◐ ● ○◖◗◖◗ ⚡ VARY
(Many kinds) — p. 444

Sand pine
☼ ○◖◗ ⚡ LS, CS, TS
Pinus clausa — p. 475

Sawara false cypress
☼ ◐ ◗ ⚡ US, MS, LS
Chamaecyparis pisifera — p. 237

Sea grape ♕
☼ ◖◗ ⚡ TS
Coccoloba uvifera — p. 255

Slash pine
☼ ○◖◗ ⚡ LS, CS, TS
Pinus elliottii — p. 475

Southern magnolia
☼ ◐ ◖◗ ⚡ US, MS, LS, CS
Magnolia grandiflora — p. 404

Southern red cedar ♕
☼ ◐ ○◖◗ ⚡ LS, CS, TS
Juniperus silicicola — p. 373

Tamarisk
☼ ○◖◗ ⚡ VARY
Tamarix — p. 565

Yaupon
☼ ◐ ◗ ⚡ MS, LS, CS, TS
Ilex vomitoria — p. 358

SHRUBS

Arrowwood
☼ ◐ ◖◗ ⚡ US, MS, LS, CS
Viburnum dentatum — p. 585

Broom
☼ ◖◗ ⚡ US, MS, LS
Cytisus — p. 276

Century plant ♕
☼ ◐ ○◖◗ ⚡ CS, TS
Agave americana — p. 156

Southern magnolia
Magnolia grandiflora

Canary Island date palm
Phoenix canariensis

Sea grape
Coccoloba uvifera

For growing symbol explanations, please see page 39.

Century plant
Agave americana

Brightbead cotoneaster
Cotoneaster lacteus

Japanese pittosporum
Pittosporum tobira

Hollywood juniper
Juniperus chinensis 'Kaizuka'

Oleander
Nerium oleander

Coontie ♛
☼ ◐ ● ⚡ CS, TS
Zamia pumila — p. 593

Cotoneaster
☼ ◑ ○ ◐ ● ⚡ VARY
— p. 266

Croton
☼ ◑ ● ◐ ● ◑ ⚡ TS
Codiaeum variegatum pictum p. 256

Dwarf palmetto ♛
☼ ◑ ● ⚡ MS, LS, CS, TS
Sabal minor — p. 528

Dwarf yaupon
☼ ◑ ● ⚡ MS, LS, CS, TS
Ilex vomitoria 'Stokes' — p. 358

Feijoa, Pineapple guava
☼ ● ⚡ LS, CS, TS
— p. 310

Flame of the woods
☼ ◑ ● ⚡ TS
Ixora coccinea — p. 367

Indian hawthorn ♛
☼ ◑ ● ◐ ○ ● ⚡ LS, CS
Rhaphiolepis indica — p. 505

Inkberry
☼ ◑ ● ◐ ⚡ ALL
Ilex glabra — p. 357

Japanese ardisia
◑ ● ◐ ⚡ LS, CS
Ardisia japonica — p. 179

Japanese barberry
☼ ● ◐ ● ⚡ US, MS, LS
Berberis thunbergii — p. 199

Japanese fatsia
◑ ● ◐ ⚡ LS, CS, TS
Fatsia japonica — p. 310

Japanese pittosporum ♛
☼ ◑ ● ◐ ⚡ LS, CS, TS
Pittosporum tobira — p. 478

Juniper
☼ ◑ ● ○ ◐ ● ⚡ VARY
Juniperus — p. 370

Lavender
☼ ● ⚡ VARY
Lavandula — p. 384

Mound-lily yucca
☼ ◑ ● ⚡ US, MS, LS, CS
Yucca gloriosa — p. 592

Myrtle
☼ ◑ ● ○ ● ⚡ CS
Myrtus communis — p. 425

Natal plum ♛
☼ ◑ ● ◐ ○ ● ⚡ CS, TS
Carissa macrocarpa — p. 227

Oleander
☼ ◑ ○ ◐ ● ◑ ⚡ LS, CS, TS
Nerium oleander — p. 431

Pampas grass
☼ ◑ ○ ◐ ● ◑ ● ⚡ MS, LS, CS, TS
Cortaderia selloana — p. 264

Red chokeberry
☼ ◑ ● ◐ ● ● ⚡ US, MS, LS, CS
Aronia arbutifolia — p. 181

Redtwig dogwood
☼ ◑ ● ⚡ US, MS
Cornus sericea — p. 263

Rockrose
☼ ◑ ● ⚡ LS, CS
Cistus — p. 247

Rose of Sharon
☼ ◑ ○ ◐ ● ⚡ US, MS, LS, CS
Hibiscus syriacus — p. 346

Rosemary
☼ ◑ ○ ● ⚡ ALL
Rosmarinus officinalis — p. 524

Rugosa rose
☼ ◑ ● ⚡ US, MS, LS, CS
Rosa rugosa — p. 524

Sea buckthorn ♛
☼ ◑ ● ⚡ US, MS
Hippophae rhamnoides — p. 347

Seashore mallow
☼ ● ◐ ⚡ ALL
Kosteletzkya virginica — p. 378

Southern yew
☼ ◑ ● ⚡ LS, CS, TS
Podocarpus macrophyllus — p. 485

Sumac
☼ ◑ ● ⚡ VARY
Rhus — p. 514

Tree aloe
☼ ◑ ● ○ ◐ ● ◑ ⚡ TS
Aloe arborescens — p. 161

Wax myrtle
☼ ● ◐ ⚡ MS, LS, CS, TS
Myrica cerifera — p. 425

VINES, GROUND COVERS

Allamanda
☼ ● ◐ ◑ ⚡ TS
Allamanda cathartica — p. 159

Beach morning glory ♛
☼ ● ◐ ⚡ CS, TS
Ipomoea pes-caprae — p. 361

Bittersweet
☼ ● ⚡ US, MS, LS
Celastrus — p. 233

Cape honeysuckle
☼ ◑ ● ⚡ CS, TS
Tecoma capensis — p. 567

Confederate jasmine
☼ ◑ ● ◐ ⚡ LS, CS, TS — p. 575
Trachelospermum jasminoides

Red chokeberry
Aronia arbutifolia

Redtwig dogwood
Cornus sericea

Rugosa rose
Rosa rugosa

Sumac
Rhus

Allamanda
Allamanda cathartica

For climate zone explanations, please see pages 28–34.

Trumpet creeper, common
Campsis radicans

Wedelia
Wedelia trilobata

Cape plumbago
Plumbago auriculata

Daylily
Hemerocallis

Grand crinum
Crinum asiaticum

Silver lace vine
☼ ◌ ⚡ US, MS, LS
Fallopia baldschuanica   p. 309

Trumpet creeper, common
☼ ◑ ◌ ◔ ⚡ US, MS, LS, CS
Campsis radicans   p. 224

Virginia creeper
☼ ◑ ◌ ◔ ⚡ US, MS, LS, CS
Parthenocissus quinquefolia p. 448

Wedelia   ♔
☼ ◑ ◔ ⚡ CS, TS
Wedelia trilobata   p. 590

PERENNIALS, BULBS

Alpine sea holly
☼ ◔ ⚡ US, MS, LS, CS
Eryngium alpinum   p. 300

Artemisia (most)
☼ ◌ ◔ ⚡ VARY
          p. 181

Blue wild indigo
☼ ◌ ⚡ US, MS, LS, CS
Baptisia australis   p. 194

Bush daisy
☼ ◌ ◔ ◑ ⚡ CS, TS OR ANNUAL
Euryops pectinatus   p. 307

Cape plumbago
☼ ◑ ◌ ◔ ◑ ⚡ CS, TS
Plumbago auriculata   p. 481

Chinese pennisetum
☼ ◑ ◌ ◔ ⚡ US, MS, LS, CS
Pennisetum alopecuroides   p. 460

Crinum
☼ ◑ ◌ ◑ ◔ ⚡ ⚡ VARY
          p. 269

Daylily
☼ ◑ ◌ ◔ ⚡ ALL
Hemerocallis   p. 342

Dusty miller
☼ ◌ ◔ ⚡ MS, LS, CS
Senecio cineraria   p. 542

Euphorbia (most)
☼ ◑ ◌ ◔ ⚡ VARY
          p. 305

Evergreen candytuft
☼ ◔ ⚡ US, MS, LS
Iberis sempervirens   p. 355

Fernleaf yarrow
☼ ◌ ◔ ⚡ US, MS, LS
Achillea filipendulina   p. 151

Fleabane
☼ ◑ ◔ ◌ ⚡ VARY
Erigeron   p. 299

Geranium
☼ ◑ ◌ ◔ ◑ ⚡ CS, TS OR ANNUALS
Pelargonium   p. 458

Ice plant
☼ ◔ ◌ ◑ ⚡ CS, TS
Carpobrotus   p. 227

Ice plant
☼ ◑ ◌ ◔ ◑ ⚡ US, MS, LS, CS
Delosperma   p. 281

Indian blanket   ♔
☼ ◌ ◔ ⚡ ALL
Gaillardia pulchella   p. 318

Jerusalem sage
☼ ◑ ◌ ◔ ◑ ⚡ US, MS, LS
Phlomis fruticosa   p. 468

Lamb's ears
☼ ◑ ◌ ◔ ⚡ US, MS, LS
Stachys byzantina   p. 554

Lantana
☼ ◔ ◑ ⚡ LS, CS, TS
          p. 382

Lily-of-the-Nile
☼ ◑ ◌ ◔ ◑ ⚡ LS, CS, TS
Agapanthus africanus   p. 154

Lobster-claw
☼ ◑ ◔ ◑ ⚡ TS
Heliconia   p. 340

Opuntia
☼ ◔ ⚡ VARY
          p. 436

Perennial hibiscus
☼ ◔ ◑ ⚡ ALL
Hibiscus moscheutos   p. 345

Pine cone ginger
◌ ◔ ◑ ◑ ⚡ LS, CS, TS
Zingiber zerumbet   p. 595

Red-hot poker
☼ ◑ ◌ ◔ ◑ ⚡ US, MS, LS, CS
Kniphofia uvaria   p. 377

Sandwort
☼ ◌ ◔ ◑ ⚡ US, MS, LS
Arenaria montana   p. 179

Santolina
☼ ◌ ◔ ◑ ⚡ US, MS, LS, CS
          p. 534

Sea oats
☼ ◑ ◌ ◔ ⚡ US, MS, LS, CS
Chasmanthium latifolium   p. 238

Snow-in-summer
☼ ◑ ◌ ◔ ◑ ⚡ US, MS, LS
Cerastium tomentosum   p. 235

Spanish bayonet   ♔
☼ ◔ ◑ ⚡ LS, CS, TS
Yucca aloifolia   p. 592

Statice
☼ ◔ ⚡ TS
Limonium perezii   p. 393

Stonecrop
☼ ◑ ◌ ◔ ◑ ⚡ US, MS, LS
Sedum   p. 540

Purple ice plant
Delosperma cooperi

Indian blanket
Gaillardia pulchella

Lobster-claw
Heliconia

Red-hot poker
Kniphofia uvaria

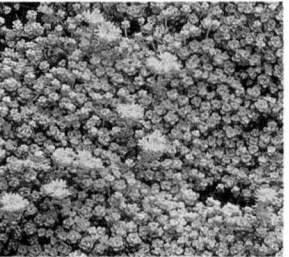

Stonecrop
Sedum spathulifolium 'Cape Blanco'

For growing symbol explanations, please see page 39.

Plants for
Rock Gardens

Gypsophila repens

Rosemary
Rosmarinus 'Prostratus'

Germander
Teucrium

Heath
Erica

The premier rock garden plants include dwarf trees, shrubs and miniature bulbs, along with creeping perennials and herbs that form low tufts or mats of foliage. Favorites in all these categories are listed below. For greatest success, tailor your choice of plants to the climate where you live, and group them together according to their light and water needs.

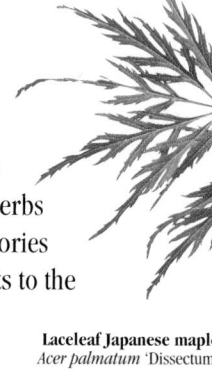

Laceleaf Japanese maple
Acer palmatum 'Dissectum'

TREES AND SHRUBS

Aaron's beard
☼ ☼ ◐ ● ◗ ✄ US, MS, LS
Hypericum calycinum .... p. 354

Azalea Satsuki hybrids
◐ ● ♠ ◗ ✄ MS, LS, CS
Rhododendron .... p. 511

Barberry
☼ ◐ ● ◗ ✄ VARY
Berberis (dwarf forms) .... p. 198

Bog rosemary
◐ ♠ ✄ US
Andromeda polifolia .... p. 166

Broom (several)
☼ ◐ ◐ ◗ ✄ US, MS, LS
Genista (dwarf forms) .... p. 321

Canadian hemlock
☼ ☼ ◐ ◗ ✄ US, MS, LS .... p. 578
Tsuga canadensis (dwarf forms)

Cotoneaster (dwarf forms)
☼ ◐ ◐ ● ◗ ✄ VARY
.... p. 266

Dwarf jasmine
☼ ☼ ◐ ◐ ◗ ✄ LS, CS, TS
Jasminum parkeri .... p. 368

Germander
☼ ◐ ◗ ✄ US, MS, LS, CS
Teucrium (low-growing) .... p. 568

Heath
☼ ◐ ● ◗ ✄ VARY
Erica (dwarf forms) .... p. 299

Hinoki false cypress
◐ ● ◗ ✄ US, MS, LS .... p. 237
Chamaecyparis obtusa (dwarf forms)

Indian hawthorn
☼ ☼ ◐ ◐ ● ◗ ✄ LS, CS .... p. 505
Rhaphiolepis indica (dwarf forms)

Japanese andromeda
◐ ● ♠ ◗ ✄ US, MS
Pieris japonica (dwarf forms) p. 473

Japanese barberry
☼ ☼ ◐ ● ◗ ✄ US, MS, LS
Berberis thunbergii (smaller) p. 199

Japanese holly (several)
☼ ☼ ◐ ◗ ✄ US, MS, LS
Ilex crenata (dwarf forms) .... p. 357

Japanese maple
☼ ☼ ◐ ● ◗ ✄ US, MS, LS, CS .... p. 149
Acer palmatum (dwarf forms)

Juniper (many)
☼ ◐ ◐ ● ◗ ✄ VARY
Juniperus (smallest) .... p. 370

Lavender
☼ ● ◗ ✄ VARY
Lavandula .... p. 384

Pine
☼ ◐ ◐ ◗ ✄ VARY
Pinus (dwarf forms) .... p. 474

Rhododendron (dwarf types)
◐ ● ♠ ◗ ✄ VARY
.... p. 507

Rockrose (some)
☼ ◐ ◗ ✄ LS, CS
Cistus .... p. 247

Rose daphne
◐ ◗ ♠ ◗ ✄ US, MS
Daphne cneorum .... p. 278

Rosemary
☼ ◐ ◐ ◗ ✄ ALL
Rosmarinus officinalis .... p. 524

Slender deutzia
☼ ☼ ◐ ● ◗ ✄ US, MS, LS
Deutzia gracilis 'Nikko' .... p. 283

Spiraea (summer flowering)
☼ ☼ ◐ ● ◗ ✄ VARY
.... p. 552

Spruce
☼ ◐ ◐ ● ◗ ✄ US, MS
Picea (dwarf forms) .... p. 472

Sunrose
☼ ◐ ● ◗ ✄ US, MS .... p. 338
Helianthemum nummularium

Mugho pine
Pinus mugo mugo

Rose daphne
Daphne cneorum

Colorado blue spruce
Picea pungens

Sunrose
Helianthemum nummularium

Dwarf white pine
Pinus strobus Nana Group

For climate zone explanations, please see pages 28–38. ▶

Basket-of-gold
Aurinia saxatilis

Blue-eyed grass, Western
Sisyrinchium bellum

Blue star creeper
Pratia pedunculata

Cinquefoil
Potentilla

Coral bells
Heuchera micrantha 'Palace Purple'

Sweet box
☼ ◐ ◖ ◔ ◇ ✂ US, MS, LS, CS
Sarcococca   p. 535

Wintergreen
◔ ◆ ✂ US, MS   p. 320
Gaultheria procumbens 'Macrocarpa'

PERENNIALS AND BULBS

Agave
☼ ◔ ◇ ◔ ✂ CS, TS
                                              p. 156

Alpine aster
☼ ◆ ◔ ✂ US, MS
Aster alpinus   p. 186

Baby's breath (several)
☼ ◆ ✂ US, MS, LS, CS   p. 335
Gypsophila paniculata (several)

Basket-of-gold
☼ ◔ ◆ ✂ US, MS, LS, CS
Aurinia saxatilis   p. 189

Beard tongue
☼ ◔ ◆ ◔ ✂ VARY
Penstemon (subshrubs)   p. 461

Blue-eyed grass, Western
☼ ◔ ◆ ◔ ✂ MS, LS
Sisyrinchium bellum   p. 546

Blue fescue
☼ ◔ ◇ ◔ ✂ US, MS
Festuca glauca   p. 311

Blue star creeper
◔ ◆ ✂ US, MS, LS
Pratia pedunculata   p. 491

Carpet bugleweed
☼ ◔ ◆ ● ✂ US, MS, LS
Ajuga reptans   p. 157

Catmint
☼ ◔ ◆ ◔ ✂ US, MS, LS, CS
Nepeta × faassenii   p. 429

Chamomile
☼ ◔ ◆ ✂ US, MS, LS, CS
Chamaemelum nobile   p. 238

Cheddar pink
☼ ◆ ◆ ✂ US MS LS CS
Dianthus gratianopolitanus   p. 284

Cinquefoil (most)
◔ ◆ ◆ ✂ VARY
Potentilla   p. 490

Columbine
☼ ◔ ◆ ✂ VARY
Aquilegia (dwarf forms)   p. 176

Coral bells
◔ ◆ ◔ ✂ US, MS, LS
Heuchera   p. 344

Cranesbill
☼ ◔ ◆ ✂ US, MS, LS
Geranium (smallest)   p. 322

Crassula (several)
☼ ◔ ◇ ✂ TS
                                              p. 268

Creeping Jacob's ladder
◔ ◆ ◆ ✂ US, MS, LS
Polemonium reptans   p. 486

Crocus
☼ ◔ ◆ ◆ ✂ US, MS, LS
                                              p. 270

Cyclamen (except C. persicum)
☼ ◔ ◆ ◆ ✂ VARY
                                              p. 274

Daffodil
☼ ◔ ◆ ✂ US, MS, LS, CS
Narcissus (small)   p. 426

Dwarf-eared coreopsis
☼ ◔ ◆ ✂ US, MS, LS, CS
Coreopsis auriculata 'Nana'   p. 260

Dwarf plumbago
☼ ◔ ◆ ◔ ✂ US, MS, LS, CS   p. 235
Ceratostigma plumbaginoides

Echeveria (many)
☼ ◔ ◆ ◔ ✂ VARY
                                              p. 292

Ferns
◔ ◆ ● ◆ ◔ ✂ VARY
(Many kinds)   p. 310

Flax
☼ ◆ ✂ VARY
Linum   p. 394

Fleabane
☼ ◔ ◆ ◔ ✂ VARY
Erigeron (smallest)   p. 299

Freesia
☼ ◔ ◆ ◔ ✂ CS, TS
                                              p. 317

Gentian
◔ ◆ ● ◆ ✂ US, MS, LS
Gentiana   p. 321

Glory-of-the-snow
☼ ◔ ◆ ◔ ✂ US, MS
Chionodoxa   p. 242

Grape hyacinth
☼ ◔ ◆ ◔ ✂ US, MS, LS
Muscari   p. 424

Green carpet
☼ ◔ ◆ ● ◔ ✂ LS, CS, TS
Herniaria glabra   p. 344

Gypsophila cerastioides
☼ ◆ ✂ US, MS, LS
                                              p. 335

Houseleek
☼ ◔ ◇ ◆ ◔ ✂ US, MS, LS, CS
Sempervivum   p. 542

Ice plant
☼ ◔ ◇ ◆ ◔ ✂ US, MS, LS, CS
Delosperma   p. 281

Crocus

Echeveria

Carpet bugleweed
Ajuga reptans

Fleabane
Erigeron

Bottle gentian
Gentiana andrewsii

For growing symbol explanations, please see page 39.

Grape hyacinth
Muscari armeniacum

Mazus
Mazus reptans

Ornamental strawberry
Fragaria chiloensis

White rain lily
Zephyranthes candida

Rock soapwort
Saponaria ocymoides

Iris (smallest)
☼ ☼ ● ● ◑ ◐ ◐ ⁄ VARY
p. 362

Lady's-mantle
☼ ● ◐ ◑ ⁄ VARY
Alchemilla p. 158

Lavender cotton
☼ ◌ ◐ ⁄ US, MS, LS, CS
Santolina chamaecyparissus p. 534

Lenten rose
☼ ● ● ◐ ◑ ⁄ US, MS, LS
Helleborus orientalis p. 341

'Little Bunny' fountain grass
☼ ◌ ◐ ◑ ⁄ US, MS, LS, CS
Pennisetum alopecuroides p. 460

Liverwort
☼ ● ◐ ◑ ⁄ US, MS, LS, CS
Hepatica p. 343

Mazus reptans
☼ ◌ ● ◐ ◑ ⁄ US, MS, LS
p. 415

Mondo grass
☼ ● ● ◐ ◑ ⁄ MS, LS, CS, TS
Ophiopogon japonicus p. 436

Oregano
☼ ◌ ◐ ⁄ VARY
Origanum (low-growing) p. 437

Ornamental allium
☼ ◌ ◐ ⁄ VARY
Allium (smallest) p. 159

Ornamental strawberry
☼ ◌ ◐ ⁄ US, MS, LS, CS
Fragaria hybrids p. 315

Oxalis
☼ ◌ ◐ ⁄ VARY
p. 441

Phlox (trailing or creeping)
☼ ◌ ◐ ⁄ VARY
p. 469

Pink
☼ ◌ ◐ ◑ ⁄ US, MS, LS, CS
Dianthus (smallest) p. 283

Plantain lily
☼ ● ◐ ◑ ⁄ US MS LS
Hosta (dwarf forms) p. 348

Primrose (most)
☼ ◌ ◑ ⁄ VARY
Primula p. 491

Pussy toes
☼ ◌ ◐ ◑ ⁄ US, MS, LS
Antennaria dioica p. 168

Rain lily
☼ ◐ ◑ ⁄ VARY
Zephyranthes p. 594

Rockcress
☼ ◐ ⁄ US, MS, LS
Arabis p. 177

Rock soapwort
☼ ◐ ◑ ⁄ US, MS
Saponaria ocymoides p. 535

Sandwort
☼ ◌ ◐ ◑ ⁄ US, MS, LS
Arenaria montana p. 179

Sedge
☼ ☼ ◌ ◐ ◑ ● ⁄ US, MS, LS, CS
Carex p. 226

Senecio (some)
☼ ☼ ● ◌ ◐ ◑ ● ⁄ VARY
p. 542

Snowflake
☼ ☼ ◐ ◑ ⁄ VARY
Leucojum p. 388

Snow-in-summer
☼ ◌ ◐ ◑ ⁄ US, MS, LS
Cerastium tomentosum p. 235

Speedwell
☼ ◌ ◐ ◑ ⁄ US, MS, LS
Veronica (mat-forming) p. 584

Spring star flower
☼ ◌ ◐ ◑ ⁄ US, MS, LS, CS
Ipheion uniflorum p. 360

Spurge
☼ ☼ ◐ ◑ ⁄ US, MS, LS, CS
Euphorbia myrsinites p. 306

Squill
☼ ◌ ◐ ◑ ⁄ US, MS, LS
Scilla p. 539

Sternbergia lutea
☼ ◐ ◑ ⁄ US, MS, LS
p. 556

Stonecrop (many)
☼ ◌ ◐ ◑ ⁄ US, MS, LS
Sedum p. 540

Strawberry geranium
☼ ● ◐ ◑ ⁄ MS, LS, CS
Saxifraga stolonifera p. 537

Sweet flag
☼ ◐ ● ◑ ⁄ US, MS, LS, CS
Acorus p. 152

Thrift
☼ ◌ ◐ ◑ ⁄ VARY
Armeria p. 181

Thyme
☼ ◌ ◐ ◑ ⁄ VARY
Thymus p. 571

Tulip
☼ ◌ ◐ ◑ ⁄ US, MS OR ANNUAL
Tulipa (species only) p. 578

Tussock bellflower
☼ ◌ ◐ ◑ ⁄ US, MS, LS
Campanula carpatica p. 224

Wild ginger
☼ ● ◐ ◑ ● ◑ VARY
Asarum p. 183

Freesia

Sedge
Carex morrowii

Spurge
Euphorbia myrsinites

Thrift, common
Armeria maritima

Tulip
Tulipa saxatilis

For climate zone explanations, please see pages 28–38. ▶

Houseplants

W hen it's mild and sunny outside, there's no better place than the garden. But gardens can also grow indoors. Houseplants give us color and fragrance with their blooms, and texture and mass with their foliage. Large ones can balance a room or anchor a corner just like a piece of furniture. Houseplants also humidify dry winter air, and some even absorb air pollutants. But in the end, what makes growing houseplants so rewarding is that it satisfies our desire to see beautiful plants even when it's cold and dreary outside.

Potted geraniums liven up a table.

Polka-dot plant
Hypoestes phyllostachya

Aechmea (Bromeliad)

FLOWERING

Aechmea (Bromeliad)
☼ ◑ ● ✂ TS
Aechmea   p. 153

African violet
◑ ● ●
Saintpaulia   p. 529

Amaryllis
☼ ◑ ● ◑ ✂ LS, CS, TS
Hippeastrum   p. 347

Anthurium
◑ ● ◑ ✂ TS OR INDOORS
                               p. 169

Begonia (many)
◑ ● ✂ TS
                               p. 196

Bleeding heart vine
☼ ◑ ● ◑ ✂ TS
Clerodendrum thomsoniae   p. 253

Cattleya orchids
☼ ◑ ● ✂ TS OR INDOORS
                               p. 231

Christmas cactus
☼ ◑ ● ✂ TS
Schlumbergera × buckleyi   p. 539

Clivia
◑ ● ● ✂ TS
Clivia miniata   p. 254

Coral plant
☼ ◑ ● ● ◑ ✂ CS, TS
Russelia sarmentosa   p. 527

Coryphantha vivipara
☼ ◑ ● ◑ ✂ US, MS, LS, CS
                               p. 265

Crinum (some)
☼ ◑ ● ● ◑ ◑ ✂ VARY
                               p. 269

Cymbidium orchids
◑ ● ✂ ALL
                               p. 274

Dendrobium orchids
◑ ● ✂ TS
                               p. 282

Desert rose
☼ ◑ ● ◑ ✂ TS
Adenium obesum   p. 152

Devil's backbone
☼ ◑ ● ◑ ● ✂ TS   p. 458
Pedilanthus tithymaloides smallii

Earth star
☼ ◑ ● ◑ ✂ TS
Cryptanthus zonatus   p. 271

Easter cactus
☼ ◑ ● ✂ TS
Rhipsalidopsis gaertneri   p. 506

Echeveria (some)
☼ ◑ ◑ ● ✂ VARY
                               p. 292

Eucharist lily
● ✂ TS
Eucharis × grandiflora   p. 303

Flame violet
● ● ◑ ✂ TS
Episcia   p. 297

Florists' cyclamen
☼ ◑ ● ●
Cyclamen persicum   p. 274

Gardenia, common
☼ ◑ ● ◑ ✂ LS, CS, TS
Gardenia jasminoides   p. 319

Geranium
☼ ◑ ● ◑ ✂ CS, TS
Pelargonium (many)   p. 458

Ginger lily
☼ ◑ ● ◑ ● ✂ VARY
Hedychium   p. 338

Gloxinia
☼ ◑ ● ◑
Sinningia speciosa   p. 545

Hedgehog cactus
☼ ◑ ● ◑ ✂ VARY
Echinocereus   p. 293

Florists' cyclamen
Cyclamen persicum

Desert rose
Adenium obesum

Bleeding heart vine
Clerodendrum thomsoniae

Clivia
Clivia miniata

Gloxinia
Sinningia speciosa

For growing symbol explanations, please see page 39.

Hybrid fuchsia
☼ ◐ ❋ US
Fuchsia × hybrida   p. 317

Lobster-claw
☼ ◐ ● ❋ TS
Heliconia   p. 340

Kalanchoe (most)
☼ ◐ ● ❋ TS
                            p. 374

Moth orchid
◐ ● ❋ TS
Phalaenopsis   p. 466

Nun's orchid
◐ ● ❋ CS, TS
Phaius tankervilliae   p. 466

Oncidium orchids
☼ ◐ ● ❋ TS
                            p. 435

Peace lily
◐ ● ● ● ❋ TS
Spathiphyllum   p. 550

Persian violet
◐ ● ●
Exacum affine   p. 307

Peruvian old man cactus
☼ ◐ ○ ● ❋ TS
Espostoa lanata   p. 302

Poinsettia
☼ ◐ ● ❋ CS, TS
Euphorbia pulcherrima   p. 306

Strawberry geranium
◐ ● ● ● ❋ MS, LS, CS
Saxifraga stolonifera   p. 537

Vriesea
◐ ● ❋ TS
                            p. 589

Walking iris
☼ ◐ ● ❋ CS, TS
Neomarica gracilis   p. 429

Wax flower
◐ ● ● ❋ TS
Hoya carnosa   p. 350

Yucca (some)
☼ ◐ ○ ● ● ❋ VARY
                            p. 592

FOLIAGE

African mask
◐ ● ● ● ◗ ❋ TS
Alocasia x amazonica   p. 160

Aglaonema
◐ ● ❋ TS
                            p. 156

Arrowhead vine
◐ ● ❋ TS
Syngonium   p. 562

Asparagus, ornamental
◐ ● ❋ CS, TS
Asparagus densiflorus   p. 185

Baby rubber plant
◐ ●
Peperomia obtusifolia   p. 462

Bamboo (several)
NEEDS, ZONES VARY
                            p. 190

Bear's foot fern
◐ ● ❋ TS
Humata tyermannii   p. 350

Bloodleaf
☼ ◐ ● ❋ TS
Iresine   p. 361

Brake
◐ ● ● ❋ TS
Pteris   p. 496

Bunny ears
☼ ◐ ○ ❋ TS
Opuntia microdasys   p. 437

Burmese fishtail palm
☼ ◐ ● ◗ ❋ TS
Caryota mitis   p. 229

Burro tail
◐ ○ ○ ❋ TS
Sedum morganianum   p. 540

Caricature plant
◐ ● ❋ TS
Graptophyllum pictum   p. 328

Cast-iron plant
◐ ● ● ● ❋ LS, CS, TS
Aspidistra elatior   p. 186

China doll
☼ ◐ ● ● ❋ TS
Radermachera sinica   p. 502

Coffee
◐ ● ● ❋ TS
Coffea arabica   p. 256

Coleus
☼ ◐ ● ● ● ● ❋ TS
Coleus x hybridus   p. 256

Coontie
◐ ● ❋ CS, TS
Zamia pumila   p. 593

Corn plant
☼ ◐ ● ❋ TS
Dracaena fragrans   p. 290

Croton
☼ ◐ ● ● ● ❋ TS   p. 256
Codiaeum variegatum pictum

Davallia
◐ ● ● ❋ TS
                            p. 280

Dumb cane
☼ ◐ ● ● ◗ ❋ TS
Dieffenbachia   p. 286

Hybrid fuchsia
Fuchsia ×hybrida

Moth orchid
Phalaenopsis

Vriesea

Aglaonema 'Silver Queen'

Bloodleaf
Iresine lindenii

China doll
Radermachera sinica

Croton
Codiaeum variegatum pictum

For climate zone explanations, please see pages 28–38. ▶

Paradise palm
Howea forsteriana

Dumb cane
Dieffenbachia

Nerve plant
Fittonia verschaffeltii

Pilea

Eternal flame
☼ ◑ ✿ % TS
Calathea crocata — p. 216

Giant yucca
☼ ◑ ✿ % CS, TS
Yucca elephantipes — p. 592

Jade plant
☼ ◌ % TS
Crassula ovata — p. 268

Japanese felt fern
☼ ◑ % CS, TS
Pyrrosia lingua — p. 499

Jewel orchid
◑ ✿ % TS OR INDOORS
Ludisia discolor — p. 398

Lady palm
☼ ◑ ✿ % CS, TS
Rhapis excelsa — p. 506

Madagascar dragon tree
☼ ◌ ✿ % TS
Dracaena marginata — p. 290

Madagascar palm
☼ ◌ ✿ % TS
Pachypodium lamerei — p. 441

Milkbush
☼ ◑ ◌ ✿ % TS
Euphorbia tirucalli — p. 307

Moses-in-the-cradle
☼ ◌ ◑ ✿ % TS
Tradescantia spathacea — p. 576

Neoregelia
☼ ◔ ✿ % TS — p. 429

Nerve plant
◑ ✿ % TS
Fittonia verschaffeltii — p. 314

Norfolk Island pine
☼ ◑ ✿ % TS
Araucaria heterophylla — p. 178

Paradise palm
☼ ◑ ✿ % TS
Howea forsteriana — p. 350

Parlor palm
☼ ◑ ◑ ✿ % TS
Chamaedorea elegans — p. 238

Peacock plant
☼ ◑ ✿ % TS
Calathea makoyana — p. 216

Philodendron (many)
☼ ◌ ◑ ◑ ✿ % VARY — p. 467

Pilea (many)
☼ ◑ ◑ ✿ % TS — p. 473

Polka-dot plant
☼ ◌ ◑ ✿ % ALL
Hypoestes phyllostachya — p. 355

Polypody fern
☼ ◑ ◑ ✿ % VARY
Polypodium — p. 487

Ponytail palm
☼ ◑ ✿ % TS
Beaucarnea recurvata — p. 195

Prayer plant
☼ ◑ ◑ ✿ % TS
Maranta leuconeura — p. 414

Rattlesnake plant
☼ ◑ ✿ % TS
Calathea lancifolia — p. 216

Rex begonia
☼ ◑ ✿ % TS — p. 197

Roundleaf fern
☼ ◑ ✿ % TS
Pellaea rotundifolia — p. 460

Rubber plant
☼ ◑ ◑ ✿ % TS
Ficus elastica — p. 312

Sansevieria
☼ ◌ ◑ — p. 534

Satin pothos
☼ ◑ ◑ ✿ % TS
Scindapsus pictus — p. 539

Schefflera
☼ ◌ ◑ ✿ % TS — p. 538

Split-leaf philodendron
☼ ◑ ✿ % TS
Monstera deliciosa — p. 422

Swedish ivy
☼ ◑ ✿ % TS
Plectranthus verticillatus — p. 480

Sword fern
☼ ◑ ◑ ✿ % TS
Nephrolepis exaltata — p. 430

Tillandsia
☼ ◌ ◑ ◑ ✿ % TS — p. 572

Venus's fly trap
☼ ◑ ◑ % MS, LS
Dionaea muscipula — p. 288

Wandering jew
☼ ◌ ◑ ◑ ◑ ✿ % CS, TS
Tradescantia fluminensis — p. 576

Weeping fig
☼ ◌ ◑ ✿ % TS
Ficus benjamina — p. 311

Xanthosoma
☼ ◑ ✿ % TS — p. 592

Zebra plant
☼ ◑ ✿ % TS
Calathea zebrina — p. 216

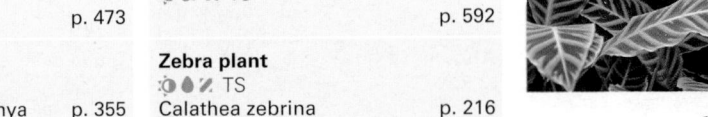

Satin pothos
Scindapsus pictus

Tillandsia

Rubber plant
Ficus elastica

Venus's fly trap
Dionaea muscipula

Zebra plant
Calathea zebrina

For growing symbol explanations, please see page 39.

Southern Natives

Bluebonnets and Indian paintbrush

A sk a roomful of gardeners if they like native plants and you'll probably see a lot of raised hands. No wonder—plants indigenous to a region like the South give it a special sense of place. Moreover, native plants are usually less susceptible to pests than introduced ones and are well attuned to the vagaries of local weather. But remember—the South is a big, big place. Just because a plant is native to the Southeast doesn't mean it will thrive in the Southwest. Check the Encyclopedia for each plant listed here to see if it's a good choice for your area.

Cardinal flower
Lobelia cardinalis

American beech
Fagus grandifolia

Bald cypress
Taxodium distichum

Eastern red cedar
Juniperus virginiana

Fringe tree
Chionanthus virginicus

TREES

American beech
☼ ◐ ◑ ◐ ⚡ US, MS, LS, CS
Fagus grandifolia   p. 308

American holly
☼ ◐ ◑ ⚡ ALL
Ilex opaca   p. 357

American sweet gum
☼ ◐ ◑ ⚡ US, MS, LS, CS
Liquidambar styraciflua   p. 394

American sycamore
☼ ◑ ⚡ US, MS, LS, CS
Platanus occidentalis   p. 479

Ash
☼ ◐ ◑ ◑ ⚡ VARY
Fraxinus (most)   p. 316

Bald cypress
☼ ◐ ◑ ◑ ⚡ US, MS, LS, CS
Taxodium distichum   p. 566

Black gum
☼ ◐ ◑ ◑ ⚡ US, MS, LS, CS
Nyssa sylvatica   p. 433

Cabbage palm
☼ ◐ ◑ ⚡ LS, CS, TS
Sabal palmetto   p. 528

Canadian hemlock
☼ ◐ ◑ ⚡ US, MS, LS
Tsuga canadensis   p. 578

Carolina silver bell
☼ ◐ ◑ ⚡ US, MS, LS
Halesia carolina   p. 336

Eastern red cedar
☼ ◐ ◑ ◐ ◑ ⚡ ALL
Juniperus virginiana   p. 373

Eastern redbud
☼ ◐ ◑ ⚡ US, MS, LS, CS
Cercis canadensis   p. 236

Flowering dogwood
☼ ◐ ◑ ⚡ US, MS, LS, CS
Cornus florida   p. 262

Fringe tree
☼ ◐ ◑ ⚡ US, MS, LS, CS
Chionanthus virginicus   p. 241

Ironwood
☼ ◐ ◑ ◑ ⚡ US, MS, LS, CS
Carpinus caroliniana   p. 227

Juneberry
☼ ◐ ◑ ◑ ⚡ US, MS, LS, CS
Amelanchier arborea   p. 164

Live oak
☼ ◑ ◑ ⚡ LS, CS, TS
Quercus virginiana   p. 502

Loblolly bay
☼ ◐ ◑ ◑ ◑ ⚡ MS, LS, CS, TS
Gordonia lasianthus   p. 327

Loblolly pine
☼ ◐ ◑ ⚡ US, MS, LS, CS
Pinus taeda   p. 477

Longleaf pine
☼ ◐ ◑ ⚡ MS, LS, CS, TS
Pinus palustris   p. 476

Mesquite
☼ ◐ ⚡ MS, LS, CS, TS
Prosopis glandulosa   p. 492

Pecan
☼ ◑ ⚡ US, MS, LS, CS
Carya illinoensis   p. 456

Red buckeye
◐ ◑ ◑ ⚡ US, MS, LS, CS
Aesculus pavia   p. 154

Red maple
☼ ◐ ◑ ◑ ⚡ US, MS, LS, CS
Acer rubrum   p. 150

Red oak
☼ ◑ ⚡ US, MS, LS
Quercus rubra   p. 501

Live oak
Quercus virginiana

Red maple
Acer rubrum

River birch
Betula nigra

For climate zone explanations, please see pages 28–38. ▶

Southern magnolia
Magnolia grandiflora

Sugar maple
Acer saccharum

Sweet bay
Magnolia virginiana

Tulip poplar
Liriodendron tulipifera

Bottlebrush buckeye
Aesculus parviflora

River birch
☼ ◑ ◆ ◆ ◀ US, MS, LS, CS
Betula nigra   p. 200

Sassafras
☼ ◆ ◀ US, MS, LS, CS
Sassafras albidum   p. 536

Shumard red oak
☼ ◐ ◆ ◆ ◀ US, MS, LS, CS
Quercus shumardii   p. 502

Sourwood
☼ ◐ ◆ ◀ US, MS, LS, CS
Oxydendrum arboreum   p. 441

Southern magnolia
☼ ◐ ◆ ◀ US, MS, LS, CS
Magnolia grandiflora   p. 404

Sugar maple
☼ ◐ ◆ ◆ ◀ US, MS, LS
Acer saccharum   p. 150

Sweet bay
☼ ◐ ◆ ◀ US, MS, LS, CS
Magnolia virginiana   p. 408

Texas persimmon
☼ ◐ ◯ ◀ MS, LS, CS, TS
Diospyros texana   p. 289

Tulip poplar
☼ ◆ ◀ US, MS, LS, CS
Liriodendron tulipifera   p. 395

Virginia pine
☼ ◯ ◆ ◀ US, MS, LS
Pinus virginiana   p. 477

Western soapberry
☼ ◯ ◆ ◀ US, MS, LS, CS
Sapindus drummondii   p. 535

White oak
☼ ◆ ◀ US, MS, LS, CS
Quercus alba   p. 500

Willow oak
☼ ◆ ◀ US, MS, LS, CS
Quercus phellos   p. 501

Yellow wood
☼ ◆ ◀ US, MS, LS
Cladrastis kentukea   p. 250

SHRUBS

American beautyberry
☼ ◐ ◆ ◆ ◀ ALL
Callicarpa americana   p. 217

Bayberry
☼ ◆ ◀ US, MS
Myrica pensylvanica   p. 425

Bottlebrush buckeye
☼ ◐ ◆ ◆ ◀ US, MS, LS, CS
Aesculus parviflora   p. 154

Bush honeysuckle
☼ ◐ ◆ ◀ US, MS, LS
Diervilla   p. 286

Buttonbush
☼ ◐ ◆ ◆ ◀ ALL
Cephalanthus occidentalis   p. 234

Conradina
☼ ◆ ◀ MS, LS, CS
                                p. 258

Coontie
☼ ◆ ◀ CS, TS OR INDOORS
Zamia pumila   p. 593

Florida flame azalea
◐ ◯ ◆ ◆ ◆ ◀ MS, LS, CS
Rhododendron austrinum   p. 512

Heart's-a-bustin'
☼ ◐ ◆ ◆ ◀ US, MS, LS, CS
Euonymus americanus   p. 304

Hop tree
☼ ◐ ◆ ◀ US, MS, LS, CS
Ptelea trifoliata   p. 496

Indigo bush
☼ ◆ ◀ US, MS, LS, CS
Amorpha fruticosa   p. 164

Inkberry
☼ ◐ ◆ ◀ ALL
Ilex glabra   p. 357

Mountain laurel
☼ ◐ ◆ ◆ ◀ US, MS, LS, CS
Kalmia latifolia   p. 375

Oakleaf hydrangea
◐ ◆ ◀ US, MS, LS, CS
Hydrangea quercifolia   p. 353

Piedmont azalea
☼ ◐ ◆ ◆ ◆ ◆ ◀ US, MS, LS, CS
Rhododendron canescens   p. 512

Pinxterbloom azalea
◐ ◆ ◆ ◆ ◀ US, MS, LS
Rhododendron periclymenoides   p. 344

Plumleaf azalea
◐ ◆ ◆ ◆ ◀ US, MS, LS, CS
Rhododendron prunifolium   p. 513

Possumhaw
☼ ◐ ◆ ◀ US, MS, LS, CS
Ilex decidua   p. 357

Red chokeberry
☼ ◐ ◆ ◆ ◆ ◀ US, MS, LS, CS
Aronia arbutifolia   p. 181

Sotol
☼ ◐ ◯ ◆ ◀ VARY
Dasylirion   p. 279

Staghorn sumac
☼ ◯ ◆ ◀ US, MS, LS
Rhus typhina   p. 514

Summersweet
☼ ◐ ◆ ◆ ◀ US, MS, LS, CS
Clethra alnifolia   p. 253

Texas ranger
☼ ◯ ◆ ◀ LS, CS, TS
Leucophyllum frutescens   p. 388

Heart's-a-bustin'
Euonymus americanus

Mountain laurel
Kalmia latifolia

Possumhaw
Ilex decidua

Summersweet
Clethra alnifolia

For growing symbol explanations, please see page 39.

Witch hazel, common
Hamamelis virginiana

Blazing star
Liatris

Bloodroot
Sanguinaria canadensis

Butterfly weed
Asclepias tuberosa

Virginia sweetspire
☼ ◐ ◢ ⁒ US, MS, LS, CS
Itea virginica   p. 366

Wax myrtle
☼ ◐ ◢ ◢ ⁒ MS, LS, CS, TS
Myrica cerifera   p. 425

Witch hazel, common
☼ ◐ ◢ ◢ ⁒ US, MS, LS, CS
Hamamelis virginiana   p. 336

Yaupon
☼ ◐ ◢ ◢ ⁒ MS, LS, CS, TS
Ilex vomitoria   p. 358

PERENNIALS AND ANNUALS

American maidenhair fern
◐ ● ◢ ◢ ⁒ US, MS
Adiantum pedatum   p. 153

Blazing star
☼ ◐ ◢ ⁒ US, MS, LS, CS
Liatris   p. 389

Bloodroot
◐ ● ◢ ◢ ◢ ⁒ US, MS, LS
Sanguinaria canadensis   p. 533

Blue phlox
◐ ◢ ⁒ US, MS, LS, CS
Phlox divaricata   p. 469

Bluebonnet
☼ ◌ ◢ ⁒ MS, LS, CS
Lupinus havardii   p. 399

Bluestar
☼ ◐ ◌ ◢ ◢ ⁒ US, MS, LS, CS
Amsonia tabernaemontana   p. 165

Bluestem
☼ ◐ ◌ ◢ ◢ ◢ ◢ ⁒ US, MS, LS, CS
Andropogon   p. 166

Bowles' golden grass
◐ ◢ ◢ ◢ ⁒ US, MS, LS
Milium effusum 'Aureum'   p. 419

Bowman's root
◐ ◢ ◢ ⁒ US, MS, LS
Gillenia trifoliata   p. 324

Butterfly pea
☼ ◐ ◌ ◢ ◢ ⁒ ALL
Clitoria mariana   p. 254

Butterfly weed
☼ ◐ ◌ ◢ ⁒ US, MS, LS, CS
Asclepias tuberosa   p. 184

Calliopsis
☼ ◌ ◢ ⁒ ALL
Coreopsis tinctoria   p. 260

Cardinal flower
◐ ● ◌ ◢ ◢ ◢ ⁒ US, MS, LS, CS
Lobelia cardinalis   p. 396

Carolina bush pea
☼ ◐ ◢ ⁒ US, MS, LS
Thermopsis villosa   p. 569

Clinton lily
● ◢ ⁒ US, MS
Clintonia umbellulata   p. 254

Clustered goldflower
☼ ◌ ◢ ⁒ US, MS, LS, CS
Tetraneuris scaposa   p. 568

Coneflower
☼ ◐ ◢ ⁒ VARY
Echinacea   p. 293

Coryphantha vivipara
☼ ◌ ◢ ⁒ US, MS, LS, CS OR INDOORS
                                        p. 265

Dahlberg daisy
☼ ◌ ◢ ⁒ CS, TS OR ANNUAL
Thymophylla tenuiloba   p. 571

Dropseed
☼ ◌ ◢ ⁒ US, MS, LS, CS
Sporobolus   p. 553

Erect dayflower
☼ ◌ ◢ ⁒ ALL
Commelina erecta   p. 258

False indigo
☼ ◌ ◢ ⁒ US, MS, LS, CS
Baptisia   p. 194

Foamflower
◐ ● ◢ ⁒ US, MS, LS
Tiarella   p. 571

Galax
◐ ● ◢ ⁒ US, MS, LS
Galax urceolata   p. 318

Gaura
☼ ◌ ◢ ⁒ US, MS, LS, CS
Gaura lindheimeri   p. 320

Golden columbine
☼ ◐ ◢ ⁒ US, MS
Aquilegia chrysantha   p. 176

Goldenrod
☼ ◐ ◢ ⁒ US, MS, LS, CS
Solidago   p. 548

Golden star
◐ ◢ ⁒ US, MS, LS, CS
Chryosogonum virginianum   p. 245

Hardy begonia
◐ ◢ ⁒ ALL
Begonia grandis   p. 197

Indian blanket
☼ ◌ ◢ ⁒ ALL
Gaillardia pulchella   p. 318

Indian paintbrush
☼ ◐ ◢ ⁒ ALL
Castilleja indivisa   p. 230

Indian pink
◐ ◢ ⁒ US, MS, LS, CS
Spigelia marilandica   p. 551

Joe-Pye weed
☼ ◐ ◢ ◢ ⁒ US, MS, LS, CS
Eupatorium purpureum   p. 305

Golden columbine
Aquilegia chrysantha

Purple coneflower
Echinacea purpurea

Goldenrod
Solidago

Hardy begonia
Begonia grandis

For climate zone explanations, please see pages 28–38.

SPECIAL SITUATIONS

119

Lousiana iris

Sundrops
Calylophus

Venus's flytrap
Dionaea muscipula

Virginia bluebells
Mertensia pulmonarioides

Wake robin
Trillium

Louisiana iris
☼ ◐ ♦ ✂ US, MS, LS, CS
p. 364

Mayapple
☼ ◐ ◑ ♦ ◊ ✂ US, MS, LS, CS
Podophyllum peltatum p. 485

Mountain mint
☼ ◑ ◐◊ ✂ US, MS, LS
Pycnanthemum incanum p. 498

New England aster
☼ ♦ ◑ ✂ US, MS, LS
Aster novae-angliae p. 187

Prairie sage
☼ ♦ ✂ ALL
Salvia azurea grandiflora p. 530

Red yucca
☼ ◑ ◐◊ ✂ ALL
Hesperaloe parviflora p. 344

Royal catchfly
☼ ◐◊✂ US, MS, LS, CS
Silene regia p. 545

Sea oats
☼ ◑ ♦ ✂ US, MS, LS, CS
Chasmanthium latifolium p. 238

Seashore mallow
☼ ♦ ◑ ✂ ALL
Kosteletzkya virginica p. 378

Silphium
☼ ◑ ♦ ◑ ✂ US, MS, LS, CS
p. 545

Southern maidenhair
◑ ● ◑ ✂ LS, CS, TS
Adiantum capillus-veneris p. 153

Sundrops
☼ ◑ ◐◊ ✂ US, MS, LS
Calylophus p. 219

Swamp milkweed
☼ ♦ ◑ ◊ ✂ US, MS, LS, CS
Ascelpias incarnata p. 184

Texas yellow star
☼ ◊ ✂ ALL
Lindheimera texana p. 394

Twinleaf
◑ ● ◐ ✂ US, MS
Jeffersonia diphylla p. 368

Venus's flytrap
☼ ♦ ◑ ✂ MS, LS OR HOUSEPLANT
Dionaea muscipula p. 288

Virginia bluebells
◑ ● ◐ ✂ US, MS, LS
Mertensia pulmonarioides p. 417

Wake robin
◑ ● ◑ ♦ US, MS, LS
Trillium p. 577

Wild columbine
☼ ◑ ♦ ◑ ✂ US, MS, LS
Aquilegia canadensis p. 176

Wild ginger
☼ ● ♦ ◑ ✂ VARY
Asarum (some) p. 183

Wine cups
☼ ◊◊✂ US, MS, LS, CS
Callirhoe involucrata p. 217

VINES

Carolina jessamine
☼ ◑ ◐ ♦ ◑ ✂ MS, LS, CS
Gelsemium sempervirens p. 321

Climbing hydrangea
☼ ● ◑ ♦ ◑ ✂ US, MS, LS, CS
Decumaria barbara p. 280

Crossvine
☼ ◑ ♦ ◑ ✂ US, MS, LS, CS
Bignonia capreolata p. 201

Jackson vine
☼ ◑ ◐◊ ✂ MS, LS, CS
Smilax smallii p. 547

Jujube
☼ ◑ ◐ ✂ US, MS, LS, CS
p. 370

Maypop
☼ ◑ ♦ ◑ ✂ US, MS, LS, CS
Passiflora incarnata p. 449

Trumpet creeper, common
☼ ◑ ♦ ◑ ✂ US, MS, LS, CS
Campsis radicans p. 224

Trumpet honeysuckle
☼ ◑ ♦ ◑ ✂ US, MS, LS, CS
Lonicera sempervirens p. 397

Virginia creeper
☼ ◑ ● ♦ ◑ ✂ US, MS, LS, CS
Parthenocissus quinquefolia p. 448

FRUITS

American persimmon
☼ ♦ ◑ ✂ US, MS, LS, CS
p. 464

Blackberry
☼ ♦ ✂ US, MS, LS, CS
p. 202

Blueberry
☼ ♦ ✂ VARY
Vaccinium (some) p. 203

Mayhaw
☼ ◑ ♦ ✂ MS, LS, CS
Crataegus opaca p. 268

Muscadine grape
☼ ♦ ✂ VARY
p. 331

Pawpaw
☼ ◑ ♦ ✂ US, MS, LS, CS
p. 450

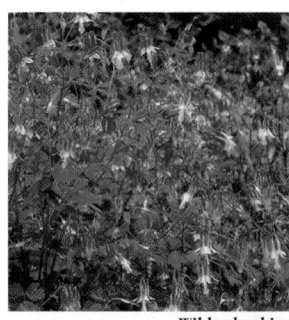

Wild columbine
Aquilegia canadensis

Trumpet creeper
Campsis radicans

Trumpet honeysuckle
Lonicera sempervirens 'Sulphurea'

Blackberry

Pawpaw

For growing symbol explanations, please see page 39.

Foxglove
Digitalis

Southern Heritage Plants

Certain plants can define a region. They shape its character, infiltrate its culture, influence its aesthetics, and even affect its industry. Daily life wouldn't be the same without them. This chart represents a thin slice of the pie of the cherished Southern plants we grew up with, handed down, and expect to see in our beds and borders today. When you encounter one in either a fancy garden or a simple swept yard, you know you're in the South.

Sweet pea
Lathyrus odoratus

Bee balm
Monarda didyma

Coleus
Coleus × hybridus 'India Frills'

Coleus

Four o'clock
Mirabilis jalapa

ANNUALS, PERENNIALS

African violet
HOUSEPLANTS
Saintpaulia — p. 529

Bee balm
US, MS, LS
Monarda didyma — p. 421

Big blue liriope
ALL
Liriope muscari — p. 395

Bird of paradise
CS, TS
Strelitzia reginae — p. 559

Blackberry lily
US, MS, LS, CS
Belamcanda chinensis — p. 198

Canna
LS, CS, TS
— p. 224

Carpet bugleweed
US, MS, LS
Ajuga reptans — p. 157

Chinese ground orchid
US, MS, LS, CS
Bletilla striata — p. 203

Coleus
TS OR ANNUAL
Coleus × hybridus — p. 256

Cosmos, common
ALL
Cosmos bipinnatus — p. 265

Dame's rocket
ALL
Hesperis matronalis — p. 344

Fortnight lily
LS, CS, TS
Dietes iridioides — p. 287

Four o'clock
ALL
Mirabilis jalapa — p. 420

Foxglove, common
US, MS, LS, CS
Digitalis purpurea — p. 287

Giant reed
ALL
Arundo donax — p. 183

Ginger lily, common
MS, LS, CS, TS
Hedychium coronarium — p. 338

Hen and chickens
US, MS, LS, CS
Sempervivum tectorum — p. 542

Horsetail
ALL
Equisetum hyemale — p. 297

Jewels-of-Opar
CS, TS
Talinum paniculatum — p. 565

Larkspur
ALL
Consolida ambigua — p. 258

Lemon daylily
ALL
Hemerocallis lilioasphodelus — p. 343

Lenten rose
US, MS, LS
Helleborus orientalis — p. 341

Mondo grass
MS, LS, CS, TS
Ophiopogon japonicus — p. 436

Money plant
US, MS, LS, CS
Lunaria annua — p. 398

Moses-in-the-cradle
TS
Tradescantia spathecea — p. 576

Moss pink
US, MS, LS
Phlox subulata — p. 469

Night-blooming cereus
TS
Hylocereus undatus — p. 353

Ginger lily, common
Hedychium coronarium

Larkspur
Consolida ambigua

Money plant
Lunaria annua

Mondo grass
Ophiopogon japonicus

For climate zone explanations, please see pages 28–38. ▶

Ribbon grass
Phalaris arundinacea picta

Spanish moss
Tillandsia usneoides

Spider flower
Cleome hasslerana

Summer phlox
Phlox paniculata

Snake plant
Sansevieria trifasciata
'Laurentii'

Opium poppy
☼ ◐ ♦♦ ✂ ALL
Papaver somniferum   p. 446

Orange daylily
☼ ◑ ◐ ♦ ✂ ALL
Hemerocallis fulva   p. 342

Pampas grass
☼ ○ ◐♦♦♦ ✂ MS, LS, CS, TS
Cortaderia selloana   p. 264

Parrot lily
◐ ♦ ♦ ✂ MS, LS, CS
Alstroemaria psittacina   p. 162

Peony 'Festiva Maxima'
☼ ◑ ◐ ♦ ✂ US, MS, LS
Paeonia   p. 443

Perennial hibiscus
☼ ◐ ♦ ✂ ALL
Hibiscus moscheutos   p. 345

Perilla
☼ ◑ ◐ ♦ ✂ ALL
Perilla frutescens   p. 463

Purple heart
☼ ◑ ◐ ♦ ✂ MS, LS, CS, TS   p. 576
Tradescantia pallida 'Purple Heart'

Ribbon grass
☼ ◑ ◐ ♦ ✂ US, MS, LS, CS
Phalaris arundinacea picta   p. 467

Snake plant
☼ ◑ ◐ ♦ ✂ TS OR HOUSEPLANT
Sansevieria trifasciata   p. 534

Soapwort
☼ ◐ ♦ ✂ US, MS, LS, CS
Saponaria officinalis   p. 535

Spanish moss
◑ ◐ ♦♦♦ ✂ LS, CS, TS
Tillandsia usneoides   p. 573

Spider flower
☼ ◐♦ ✂ ALL
Cleome hasslerana   p. 252

Spiderwort
☼ ◑ ◐ ♦♦♦ ✂ US, MS, LS, CS
Tradescantia virginiana   p. 576

Strawberry geranium
◑ ◐ ♦ ✂ MS, LS, CS
Saxifraga stolonifera   p. 537

Summer phlox
☼ ◑ ◐ ♦ ✂ US, MS, LS, CS
Phlox paniculata   p. 469

Sundrops
☼ ◑ ○ ◐♦ ✂ US, MS, LS, CS
Oenothera fruticosa   p. 434

Sweet William
☼ ◑ ◐ ♦♦ ✂ ALL
Dianthus barbatus   p. 283

Texas bluebonnet
☼ ○◐♦ ✂ MS, LS, CS
Lupinus texensis   p. 399

Texas star
☼ ◐♦♦ ✂ MS, LS, CS, TS
Hibiscus coccineus   p. 345

Tuberose
☼ ◐ ♦ ✂ MS, LS, CS, TS
Polianthes tuberosa   p. 486

Walking iris
☼ ◑ ◐ ♦ ✂ CS, TS
Neomarica gracilis   p. 429

Willowleaf Mexican petunia
☼ ◑ ◐ ♦ ♦ ✂ ALL
Ruellia brittoniana   p. 526

Zebra grass
☼ ◑ ◐ ♦ ✂ US, MS, LS, CS   p. 421
Miscanthus sinensis 'Zebrinus'

Zinnia, common
☼ ◐ ♦ ✂ ALL
Zinnia elegans   p. 595

BULBS & BULB-LIKE PLANTS

Crinum
☼ ◑ ◐ ♦♦♦ ♦ ✂ VARY
          p. 269

Daffodil
☼ ◑ ◐ ♦ ✂ US, MS, LS, CS
Narcissus   p. 426

Elephant's ear
◐♦ ♦ ✂ LS, CS, TS
Colocasia esculenta   p. 257

Grape hyacinth
☼ ◑ ◐ ♦ ✂ US, MS, LS
Muscari botryoides   p. 424

Hardy gladiolus
☼ ◐ ♦ ✂ MS, LS, CS   p. 324
Gladiolus communis byzantinum

Iris
☼ ◑ ◐ ○♦♦♦ ✂ VARY
          p. 362

Lily-of-the-Nile
☼ ◑ ○◐♦ ✂ LS, CS, TS
Agapanthus africanus   p. 154

Lily-of-the-valley
◐♦♦ ♦ ✂ US, MS, LS
Convallaria majalis   p. 258

Magic lily
☼ ◐ ✂ US, MS, LS, CS
Lycoris squamigera   p. 400

Montbretia
☼ ◐ ♦ ✂ US, MS, LS, CS
Crocosmia crocosmiiflora   p. 270

Pink wood sorrel
☼ ◑ ◐ ♦ ✂ MS, LS, CS, TS
Oxalis crassipes   p. 441

Pregnant onion
☼ ◑ ◐ ♦♦ ✂ TS   p. 439
Ornithogalum longibracteatum

Zinnia, common
Zinnia elegans

Daffodil
Narcissus cyclamineus

Bearded iris

Magic lily
Lycoris squamigera

Rain lily
Zephyranthes

St. Joseph's lily
Hippeastrum johnsonnii

Beauty bush
Kolkwitzia amabilis 'Pink Cloud'

Camellia
Camellia japonica

Flowering quince
Chaenomeles

Rain lily
☼ ◐ ✿ VARY
Zephyranthes   p. 594

Saint Joseph's lily
☼ ☼ ◐ ✿ LS, CS, TS
Hippeastrum × johnsonii   p. 347

Society garlic
☼ ◐ ✿ LS, CS, TS
Tulbaghia violacea   p. 578

Spider lily
☼ ☼ ◐ ✿ ALL
Lycoris radiata   p. 400

Spring star flower
☼ ☼ ◐ ✿ US, MS, LS, CS
Ipheion uniflorum   p. 360

Star of Bethlehem
☼ ☼ ◐ ◐ ✿ US, MS, LS, CS
Ornithogalum umbellatum   p. 438

Summer snowflake
☼ ☼ ◐ ✿ US, MS, LS, CS
Leucojum aestivum   p. 388

SHRUBS

American beautyberry
☼ ☼ ◐ ◐ ✿ ALL
Callicarpa americana   p. 217

Angel's trumpet
☼ ☼ ◐ ◐ ✿ LS, CS, TS
Brugmansia   p. 209

Baby's breath spiraea
☼ ☼ ◐ ◐ ✿ US, MS, LS
Spiraea thunbergii   p. 552

Banana shrub
☼ ☼ ◐ ✿ LS, CS, TS
Michelia figo   p. 418

Beauty bush
☼ ☼ ◐ ✿ US, MS, LS
Kolkwitzia amabilis   p. 378

Border forsythia
☼ ◐ ◐ ✿ US, MS, LS
Forsythia × intermedia   p. 315

Bridal wreath spiraea
☼ ☼ ◐ ◐ ✿ US, MS, LS
Spiraea prunifolia   p. 552

Butcher's broom
◐ ● ◐ ◐ ◐ ✿ MS, LS, CS, TS
Ruscus   p. 527

Camellia, common
◐ ◐ ◐ ✿ US, MS, LS, CS
Camellia japonica   p. 221

China rose
☼ ☼ ◐ ✿ ALL
Rosa chinensis   p. 522

Chinese hibiscus
☼ ◐ ✿ CS, TS
Hibiscus rosa-sinensis   p. 346

Confederate rose
☼ ◐ ✿ LS, CS, TS
Hibiscus mutabilis   p. 346

Coontie
☼ ◐ ✿ CS, TS
Zamia pumila   p. 593

Flowering quince
☼ ◐ ◐ ✿ US, MS, LS, CS
Chaenomeles   p. 237

French hydrangea
◐ ◐ ✿ US, MS, LS, CS
Hydrangea macrophylla   p. 352

Fuzzy deutzia
☼ ☼ ◐ ◐ ✿ US, MS, LS
Deutzia scabra   p. 283

Harison's yellow rose
☼ ☼ ◐ ✿ US, MS, LS
Rosa × harisonii   p. 523

Japanese kerria
◐ ◐ ◐ ✿ US, MS, LS, CS
Kerria japonica   p. 376

Lady Banks's rose
☼ ☼ ◐ ✿ LS, CS, TS
Rosa banksiae   p. 523

Lantana, common
☼ ◐ ◐ ✿ LS, CS, TS OR ANNUAL
Lantana camara   p. 382

Lemon verbena
☼ ◐ ✿ LS, CS, TS OR INDOORS
Aloysia triphylla   p. 161

Nandina
☼ ☼ ◐ ◐ ◐ ✿ US, MS, LS, CS
Nandina domestica   p. 425

Noisette rose
☼ ☼ ◐ ✿ ALL
Rosa   p. 522

Oleander
☼ ◐ ◐ ◐ ◐ ✿ LS, CS, TS
Nerium oleander   p. 431

Orange-eye butterfly bush
☼ ☼ ◐ ◐ ✿ US, MS, LS, CS
Buddleia davidii   p. 211

Pomegranate
☼ ◐ ✿ MS, LS, CS
                                p. 488

Prickly pear
☼ ◐ ◊ ✿ ALL
Opuntia compressa   p. 436

Rice paper plant
☼ ☼ ◐ ✿ LS, CS, TS
Tetrapanax papyriferus   p. 568

Rose of Sharon
☼ ◐ ◐ ◐ ◐ ✿ US, MS, LS, CS
Hibiscus syriacus   p. 346

Sago palm
◐ ◐ ✿ CS, TS
Cycas revoluta   p. 274

Japanese kerria
Kerria japonica

Society gardlic
Tulbaghia violacea

Prickly pear
Opuntia humifusa

Sago palm
Cycas revoluta

For climate zone explanations, please see pages 28–38. ▶

123

Weigela
Weigela florida

Catalpa, common
Catalpa bignonioides

Crabapple
Malus

Mimosa
Albizia julibrissin

Southern magnolia
Magnolia grandiflora

Sweet mock orange
☼ ☽ ◖ ◗ ✿ US, MS, LS, CS
Philadelphus coronarius   p. 467

Sweetshrub, common
☼ ☽ ◖ ● ◗ ✿ US, MS, LS, CS
Calycanthus floridus   p. 219

Van Houtte spiraea
☼ ☽ ◖ ◗ ✿ US, MS, LS
Spiraea × vanhouttei   p. 552

Weigela
☼ ☽ ◖ ✿ US, MS, LS
Weigela florida   p. 590

TREES

Cabbage palm
☼ ☽ ◗ ✿ LS, CS, TS
Sabal palmetto   p. 528

Catalpa, common
☼ ☽ ◖ ◗ ✿ US, MS, LS, CS
Catalpa bignonioides   p. 230

Chinaberry
☼ ◗ ◆ ✿ MS, LS, CS, TS
Melia azedarach   p. 416

Chinese parasol tree
☼ ☽ ◗ ✿ MS, LS, CS, TS
Firmiana simplex   p. 314

Chinese tallow
☼ ◖ ◗ ◆ ✿ LS, CS, TS
Sapium sebiferum   p. 535

Crepe myrtle
☼ ◗ ✿ US, MS, LS, CS
Lagerstroemia indica   p. 379

Empress tree
☼ ☽ ◗ ◖ ✿ US, MS, LS
Paulownia tomentosa   p. 450

Flowering crabapple
☼ ◖ ◗ ✿ VARY
Malus   p. 409

Fringe tree
☼ ☽ ◗ ◖ ✿ US, MS, LS, CS
Chionanthus virginicus   p. 241

Lilac chaste tree
☼ ◖ ◗ ✿ US, MS, LS, CS
Vitex agnus-castus   p. 588

Live oak
☼ ◗ ✿ LS, CS, TS
Quercus virginiana   p. 502

Mimosa
☼ ☽ ◗ ✿ US, MS, LS, CS
Albizia julibrissin   p. 158

Pecan
☼ ◗ ✿ US, MS, LS, CS
                                           p. 456

Southern magnolia
☼ ☽ ◗ ✿ US, MS, LS, CS
Magnolia grandiflora   p. 404

Texas mountain laurel
☼ ☽ ◗ ◗ ✿ LS, CS
Sophora secundiflora   p. 549

VINES

Bougainvillea
☼ ◖ ◗ ✿ CS, TS
                                           p. 205

Cape plumbago
☼ ☽ ◖ ◖ ◗ ✿ CS, TS
Plumbago auriculata   p. 481

Carolina jessamine
☼ ☽ ◗ ◖ ◗ ✿ MS, LS, CS
Gelsemium sempervirens   p. 321

Cherokee rose
☼ ◖ ◗ ✿ LS, CS, TS
Rosa laevigata   p. 523

Chinese wisteria
☼ ☽ ◖ ✿ US, MS, LS, CS
Wisteria sinensis   p. 591

Confederate jasmine
☼ ☽ ◖ ◗ ✿ LS, CS, TS   p. 575
Trachelospermum jasminoides

Coral vine
☼ ◖ ◗ ✿ LS, CS, TS
Antigonon leptopus   p. 169

Creeping fig
☼ ☽ ◗ ◖ ✿ LS, CS, TS
Ficus pumila   p. 312

Crossvine
☼ ☽ ◖ ◗ ✿ US, MS, LS, CS
Bignonia capreolata   p. 201

Gourd
☼ ◖ ✿ ALL
                                           p. 327

Heart-leaf philodendron
☼ ☽ ◗ ◖ ◗ ✿ HOUSEPLANTS   p. 468
Philodendron scandens oxycardium

Japanese honeysuckle
☼ ☽ ◖ ✿ ALL
Lonicera japonica   p. 397

Kudzu
☼ ◖ ✿ MS, LS, CS, TS
Pueraria lobata   p. 497

Maypop
☼ ☽ ◗ ◖ ✿ ALL
Passiflora incarnata   p. 449

Moonflower
◖ ◗ ✿ ALL
Ipomoea alba   p. 360

Sweet pea
☼ ◖ ◖ ✿ ALL
Lathyrus odoratus   p. 383

Trumpet honeysuckle
☼ ☽ ◗ ◖ ✿ US, MS, LS, CS
Lonicera sempervirens   p. 397

Texas mountain laurel
Sophora secundiflora

Carolina jessamine
Gelsemium sempervirens

Chinese wisteria
Wisteria sinensis

Trumpet honeysuckle
Lonicera sempervirens

For growing symbol explanations, please see page 39.

Wood fern, hostas, and other shade lovers

Plants That
Tolerate Shade

A lot of folks think of shade as a problem. But actually, shade presents a great opportunity to use a wide range of plants that offer stunning flowers, fruits, or foliage in the absence of bright sun. And because fewer weeds plague shady gardens, these leafy retreats usually need less maintenance. The lists below contain trees, shrubs, ground covers, vines, perennials, bulbs, and annuals that prefer or accept some degree of shade. The symbol ✳ indicates plants having showy flowers.

Siebold plantain lily
Hosta sieboldiana

TREES

American beech
☀ ☽ ◐ ◑ ⚡ US, MS, LS, CS
Fagus grandifolia   p. 308

Black gum
☀ ☽ ◐ ◑ ⚡ US, MS, LS, CS
Nyssa sylvatica   p. 433

Dove tree   ✳
☽ ◐ ⚡ US, MS, LS
Davidia involucrata   p. 280

Dwarf palmetto
☀ ☽ ◐ ⚡ MS, LS, CS, TS
Sabal minor   p. 528

Eastern redbud   ✳
☀ ☽ ◐ ⚡ US, MS, LS, CS
Cercis canadensis   p. 236

False aralia
☀ ☽ ◐ ⚡ TS
Schefflera elegantissima   p. 538

Flowering dogwood   ✳
☀ ☽ ◐ ⚡ US, MS, LS, CS
Cornus florida   p. 262

Franklin tree   ✳
☀ ☽ ◐ ⚡ US, MS, LS, CS
Franklinia alatamaha   p. 316

Fringe tree   ✳
☀ ☽ ◐ ◑ ⚡ US, MS, LS, CS
Chionanthus virginicus   p. 241

Hemlock
☀ ☽ ◐ ⚡ VARY
Tsuga   p. 578

Holly
☀ ☽ ◐ ⚡ VARY
Ilex   p. 356

Ironwood
☀ ☽ ◐ ◑ ⚡ US, MS, LS, CS
Carpinus caroliniana   p. 227

Japanese maple
☀ ☽ ◐ ◑ ⚡ US, MS, LS, CS
Acer palmatum   p. 149

Juneberry   ✳
☀ ☽ ◐ ◑ ⚡ VARY
Amelanchier   p. 164

Katsura tree
☀ ☽ ◐ ◑ ⚡ US, MS, LS
Cercidiphyllum japonicum   p. 235

Mountain ash   ✳
☀ ☽ ◐ ◑ ⚡ VARY
Sorbus   p. 549

Palms (some)
☀ ☽ ◐ ◐ ◑ ⚡ VARY
(Many kinds)   p. 444

Pawpaw   ✳
☽ ◐ ◑ ⚡ US, MS, LS, CS
Asimina triloba   p. 450

Podocarpus
☀ ☽ ◐ ◑ ⚡ VARY
                                     p. 485

Sassafras
☀ ☽ ◐ ◑ ⚡ US, MS, LS, CS
Sassafras albidum   p. 536

Silver bell   ✳
☀ ☽ ◐ ◑ ⚡ US, MS, LS
Halesia   p. 336

Snowbell   ✳
☀ ☽ ◐ ◑ ⚡ VARY
Styrax   p. 560

Sourwood   ✳
☀ ☽ ◐ ◑ ⚡ US, MS, LS, CS
Oxydendrum arboreum   p. 441

Stewartia   ✳
☽ ◐ ◑ ⚡ VARY
                                     p. 556

Sweet bay   ✳
☀ ☽ ◐ ◑ ⚡ US, MS, LS, CS
Magnolia virginiana   p. 408

Dove tree
Davidia involucrata

Dwarf palmetto
Sabal minor

False aralia
Schefflera elegantissima

Canadian hemlock
Tsuga canadensis

Juneberry
Amelanchier

Sassafras
Sassafras albidum

Snowbell
Styrax

For climate zone explanations, please see pages 28–38.   ▶

Tasmanian tree fern
Dicksonia antarctica

Florida flame azalea
Rhododendron austrinum

Chinese fringe
Loropetalum chinense

Winter daphne
Daphne odora 'Aureomarginata'

Gardenia, common
Gardenia jasminoides

Tasmanian tree fern
☼ ● ▲ ✂ TS
Dicksonia antarctica   p. 285

Trumpet tree   ✻
☼ ☼ ● ▲ ✂ TS
Tabebuia   p. 564

SHRUBS

Alexandrian laurel
☼ ● ▲ ✂ MS, LS, CS
Danae racemosa   p. 278

Anise tree
☼ ● ▲ ◊ ✂ MS, LS, CS
Illicium   p. 358

Azalea, native   ✻
☼ ☼ ● ▲◊ ◊ ✂ VARY
Rhododendron   p. 512

Banana shrub   ✻
☼ ☼ ● ▲ ✂ LS, CS, TS
Michelia figo   p. 418

Bottlebrush buckeye   ✻
☼ ☼ ● ▲ ◊ ✂ US, MS, LS, CS
Aesculus parviflora   p. 154

Boxwood
☼ ☼ ● ▲ ✂ VARY
Buxus   p. 213

Bramble   ✻
☼ ☼ ● ▲ ✂ VARY
Rubus   p. 526

Butcher's broom
☼ ● ▲ ◊ ▲ ✂ MS, LS, CS, TS
Ruscus aculeatus   p. 527

Camellia (most)   ✻
☼ ● ▲ ✂ US, MS, LS, CS
                              p. 220

Chinese fringe   ✻
☼ ☼ ● ▲ ✂ MS, LS, CS
Loropetalum chinense   p. 398

Daphne   ✻
☼ ● ▲ ◊ ✂ VARY
                              p. 278

Farkleberry
☼ ☼ ● ▲ ✂ MS, LS, CS
Vaccinium arboreum   p. 582

Fiveleaf aralia
☼ ● ▲ ◊ ▲◊ ✂ US, MS, LS   p. 295
Eleutherococcus sieboldianus

Fothergilla   ✻
☼ ● ▲ ✂ US, MS, LS
                              p. 315

Gardenia, common   ✻
☼ ☼ ● ▲ ✂ LS, CS, TS
Gardenia jasminoides   p. 319

Holly
☼ ☼ ● ▲ ✂ VARY
Ilex   p. 356

Hop tree
☼ ☼ ● ▲ ✂ US, MS, LS, CS
Ptelea trifoliata   p. 496

Hybrid fuchsia   ✻
☼ ● ▲ ✂ US OR ANNUAL
Fuchsia × hybrida   p. 317

Hydrangea   ✻
☼ ● ▲ ✂ VARY
                              p. 352

Japanese aucuba
☼ ● ▲ ◊ ✂ ALL
Aucuba japonica   p. 189

Japanese cleyera
☼ ☼ ● ▲ ✂ MS, LS, CS, TS
Ternstroemia gymnanthera   p. 567

Japanese fatsia
☼ ● ▲ ◊ ✂ LS, CS, TS
Fatsia japonica   p. 310

Japanese kerria   ✻
☼ ☼ ● ▲ ✂ US, MS, LS, CS
Kerria japonica   p. 376

Japanese pittosporum   ✻
☼ ☼ ● ▲ ✂ LS, CS, TS
Pittosporum tobira   p. 478

Japanese skimmia   ✻
☼ ● ▲ ✂ US
Skimmia japonica   p. 546

Lady palm
☼ ● ▲ ✂ CS, TS
Rhapis   p. 506

Leucothoe   ✻
☼ ● ▲ ◊ ◊ ✂ VARY
                              p. 388

Mahonia   ✻
☼ ☼ ● ○ ▲ ◊ ✂ VARY
                              p. 408

Mountain laurel   ✻
☼ ☼ ● ▲ ◊ ✂ US, MS, LS, CS
Kalmia latifolia   p. 375

Nandina
☼ ☼ ● ▲ ●◊ ✂ US, MS, LS, CS
Nandina domestica   p. 425

Osmanthus
☼ ☼ ● ◊ ▲ ✂ VARY
                              p. 439

Philodendron
☼ ☼ ● ▲ ✂ VARY OR INDOORS
                              p. 467

Pieris   ✻
☼ ● ▲ ◊ ✂ US, MS
                              p. 473

Redvein enkianthus   ✻
☼ ☼ ● ▲ ◊ ✂ US, MS, LS
Enkianthus campanulatus   p. 296

Sago palm
☼ ● ▲ ◊ ✂ CS, TS
Cycas revoluta   p. 274

French hydrangea
Hydrangea macrophylla

Japanese skimmia
Skimmia japonica

Mountain laurel
Kalmia latifolia

Holly osmanthus
Osmanthus heterophyllus

Mountain pieris
Pieris floribunda

For growing symbol explanations, please see page 39.

Summersweet
Clethra alnifolia

Doublefile viburnum
Viburnum plicatum tomentosum

Bishop's weed
Aegododium podagraria 'Variegatum'

Carolina jessamine
Gelsemium sempervirens

Creeping buttercup
Ranunculus repens pleniflorus

Snowberry, common
US, MS
Symphoricarpos albus   p. 562

Spicebush
US, MS, LS
Lindera benzoin   p. 393

Summersweet   ✳
US, MS, LS, CS
Clethra alnifolia   p. 253

Sweet box
US, MS, LS, CS
Sarcococca   p. 535

Viburnum   ✳
VARY
          p. 585

Witch hazel   ✳
US, MS, LS
Hamamelis   p. 336

Yesterday-today-and-tomorrow ✳
CS, TS
Brunfelsia pauciflora   p. 210

Yew
US, MS
Taxus   p. 566

GROUND COVERS, VINES

Actinidia kolomikta
US, MS, LS
          p. 152

Bamboo (some)
LS, CS, TS
          p. 190

Bishop's weed
US, MS, LS
Aegopodium podagraria   p. 154

Boston ivy
US, MS, LS
Parthenocissus tricuspidata   p. 448

Carolina jessamine   ✳
MS, LS, CS
Gelsemium sempervirens   p. 321

Carpet bugleweed   ✳
US, MS, LS
Ajuga reptans   p. 157

Confederate jasmine   ✳
LS, CS, TS   p. 575
Trachelospermum jasminoides

Creeping buttercup   ✳
US, MS, LS   p. 503
Ranunculus repens pleniflorus

Creeping fig
LS, CS, TS
Ficus pumila   p. 312

English ivy
ALL
Hedera helix   p. 337

✕ **Fatshedera lizei**
LS, CS, TS
          p. 309

Fiveleaf akebia
US, MS, LS, CS
Akebia quinata   p. 158

Forget-me-not   ✳
US, MS, LS
Myosotis sylvatica   p. 425

Grape ivy
TS
Cissus rhombifolia   p. 246

Hellebore   ✳
VARY
Helleborus   p. 341

Houttuynia cordata
ALL
          p. 350

Japanese ardisia
LS, CS
Ardisia japonica   p. 179

Japanese pachysandra   ✳
US, MS, LS
Pachysandra terminalis   p. 442

Lily-of-the-valley   ✳
US, MS, LS
Convallaria majalis   p. 258

Mazus reptans   ✳
US, MS, LS
          p. 415

Mondo grass
MS, LS, CS, TS
Ophiopogon japonicus   p. 436

Monkey grass
VARY
Liriope   p. 395

Partridgeberry
US, MS, LS, CS
Mitchella repens   p. 421

Periwinkle   ✳
VARY
Vinca   p. 587

Split-leaf philodendron
TS
Monstera deliciosa   p. 422

Spotted dead nettle   ✳
US, MS, LS
Lamium maculatum   p. 382

Sweet woodruff   ✳
US, MS, LS
Galium odoratum   p. 318

Virginia creeper
US, MS, LS, CS
Parthenocissus quinquefolia p. 448

Wintercreeper euonymus
US, MS, LS, CS
Euonymus fortunei   p. 304

Forget-me-not
Myosotis sylvatica

Lenten rose
Helleborus orientalis

Periwinkle
Vinca

Virginia creeper
Parthenocissus quinquefolia

For climate zone explanations, please see pages 28–38. ▶

False spiraea
Astilbe

Bergenia

Brunnera
Brunnera macrophylla

Chinese foxglove
Rehmannia elata

American alum root (Coral bells)
Heuchera americana 'Pewter Veil'

PERENNIALS, BULBS, ANNUALS

Aconite ✳
☼ ◔ ◗ ◆ ✎ US, MS
Aconitum   p. 152

African violet ✳
◔ ◗ ◆ ✎ INDOORS
Saintpaulia   p. 529

Anemone ✳
☼ ◔ ◗ ◆ ◆ ✎ US, MS, LS
                                p. 166

Arum
☼ ◔ ◗ ◆ ✎ VARY
                                p. 182

Bear's breech ✳
☼ ◔ ◗ ◆ ◆ ✎ US, MS, LS, CS
Acanthus mollis   p. 148

Begonia ✳
☼ ◔ ◗ ✎ TS OR ANNUAL
                                p. 196

Bergenia ✳
☼ ◔ ◗ ✎ US, MS, LS
                                p. 199

Black snakeroot ✳
☼ ◗ ✎ US, MS, LS, CS
Cimicifuga racemosa   p. 246

Bleeding heart ✳
☼ ◔ ◗ ✎ VARY
Dicentra (most)   p. 285

Bloodroot ✳
☼ ◔ ◗ ◆ ◆ ✎ US, MS, LS
Sanguinaria canadensis   p. 533

Bowles' golden grass ✳
☼ ◆ ◆ ✎ US, MS, LS
Milium effusum 'Aureum'   p. 419

Brunnera ✳
☼ ◗ ◆ ✎ US, MS
Brunnera macrophylla   p. 210

Calanthe ✳
☼ ◔ ◗ ✎ MS, LS, CS
                                p. 215

Cape primrose ✳
☼ ◔ ◗ ◆ ✎ TS OR INDOORS
Streptocarpus   p. 559

Cardinal flower ✳
☼ ◔ ◗ ◆ ◆ ✎ US, MS, LS, CS
Lobelia cardinalis   p. 396

Cast-iron plant
☼ ◔ ◗ ◆ ◆ ✎ LS, CS, TS
Aspidistra   p. 185

Celandine poppy
☼ ◔ ◗ ✎ US, MS, LS
Stylophorum diphyllum   p. 560

Chinese foxglove ✳
☼ ◗ ✎ MS, LS, CS
Rehmannia elata   p. 505

Clivia ✳
☼ ◔ ◗ ◆ ✎ TS
Clivia miniata   p. 254

Columbine ✳
☼ ◔ ◗ ✎ VARY
Aquilegia   p. 176

Coral bells ✳
☼ ◔ ◗ ◆ ✎ US, MS, LS
Heuchera   p. 344

Corydalis ✳
☼ ◗ ✎ US, MS, LS
                                p. 264

Cranesbill ✳
☼ ◗ ✎ US, MS, LS
Geranium   p. 322

Crested iris ✳
☼ ◔ ◗ ✎ US, MS, LS, CS
Iris cristata   p. 365

Cyclamen ✳
☼ ◔ ◗ ✎ VARY
                                p. 274

Elephant's ear
☼ ◗ ◆ ◆ ✎ LS, CS, TS
Colocasia esculenta   p. 257

Epimedium
☼ ◔ ◗ ◆ ✎ US, MS, LS
                                p. 296

Erythronium ✳
☼ ◔ ◗ ✎ VARY
                                p. 301

False solomon's seal ✳
☼ ◗ ✎ US, MS, LS
Smilacina racemosa   p. 546

False spiraea ✳
☼ ◔ ◗ ✎ US, MS
Astilbe   p. 187

Fancy-leafed caladium
☼ ◗ ◆ ◆ ✎ ✎ TS
Caladium bicolor   p. 214

Ferns
NEEDS, ✎ VARY
(Many kinds)   p. 310

Filipendula ✳
☼ ◔ ◗ ◆ ✎ US, MS, LS
                                p. 313

Foamflower ✳
☼ ◗ ✎ US, MS, LS
Tiarella   p. 571

Foxglove ✳
☼ ◗ ◆ ✎ US, MS, LS, CS
Digitalis   p. 287

Galax
☼ ◗ ◆ ✎ US, MS, LS
Galax urceolata   p. 318

Ginger lily ✳
☼ ◔ ◗ ◆ ✎ VARY
Hedychium   p. 338

Yellow corydalis
Corydalis lutea

Columbine
Aquilegia McKana Giants strain

Crested iris
Iris cristata

Japanese painted fern
Athyrium niponicum 'Pictum'

Foxglove, common
Digitalis purpurea

For growing symbol explanations, please see page 39.

Creeping Jacob's ladder
Polemonium reptans

Japanese primrose
Primula japonica

Lady's-mantle
Alchemilla mollis

Oxalis

Plantain lily
Hosta 'Sun Power'

Globeflower ❋
☼ ◑ ◍ ◖ ⚡ US, MS
Trollius   p. 577

Goat's beard ❋
☼ ◑ ◖ ⚡ VARY
Aruncus   p. 183

Golden ray ❋
◑ ● ◖ ◍ ⚡ US, MS, LS
Ligularia   p. 389

Golden seal
◑ ● ◖ ⚡ US, MS
Hydrastis canadensis   p. 353

Golden star ❋
◑ ◖ ⚡ US, MS, LS, CS
Chrysogonum virginianum   p. 245

Greater celandine ❋
◑ ● ◖ ◍ ⚡ US, MS, LS
Chelidonium majus   p. 239

Impatiens ❋
☼ ◑ ● ◖ ⚡ ALL
                                 p. 358

Jack-in-the-pulpit ❋
◑ ● ◖ ⚡ US, MS, LS, CS
Arisaema   p. 180

Jacob's ladder ❋
◑ ● ◖ ⚡ US, MS, LS
Polemonium   p. 486

Japanese coltsfoot ❋
◑ ● ◍ ◖ ⚡ US, MS, LS, CS
Petasites japonicus   p. 464

Japanese forest grass ❋
◑ ● ◖ ⚡ US, MS, LS
Hakonechloa macra   p. 335

Japanese primrose ❋
◑ ● ◖ ⚡ US, MS, LS
Primula japonica   p. 491

Lady's-mantle ❋
◑ ● ◖ ⚡ US, MS, LS
Alchemilla mollis   p. 158

Liverwort ❋
◑ ● ◖ ⚡ US, MS, LS, CS
Hepatica   p. 343

Lobelia ❋
◑ ● ◍ ◖ ◗ ⚡ VARY
                                 p. 396

Lungwort ❋
◑ ● ◖ ⚡ US, MS, LS
Pulmonaria   p. 497

Mayapple ❋
◑ ● ◍ ◖ ◗ ⚡ US, MS, LS, CS
Podophyllum peltatum   p. 485

Meadow rue ❋
◑ ◖ ⚡ VARY
Thalictrum   p. 568

Neoregelia
◑ ◖ ⚡ TS OR INDOORS
                                 p. 429

Oxalis ❋
☼ ◑ ◖ ⚡ VARY
                                 p. 441

Palm grass
☼ ◑ ● ◖ ⚡ CS, TS
Setaria palmifolia   p. 543

Partridgeberry
◑ ● ◍ ◖ ⚡ US, MS, LS, CS
Mitchella repens   p. 421

Peace lily
◑ ● ◍ ◖ ⚡ TS OR INDOORS
Spathiphyllum   p. 550

Peacock ginger
● ◖ ⚡ CS, TS
Kaempferia   p. 374

Piggyback plant
◑ ● ◍ ◖ ⚡ TS OR INDOORS
Tolmiea menziesii   p. 573

Plantain lily
◑ ● ◖ ⚡ US, MS, LS
Hosta   p. 348

Sea oats
☼ ◑ ● ◖ ⚡ US, MS, LS, CS
Chasmanthium latifolium   p. 238

Sedge
☼ ◑ ● ◍ ◍ ◖ ⚡ US, MS, LS, CS
Carex   p. 226

Solomon's seal
◑ ● ◖ ⚡ US, MS, LS
Polygonatum   p. 486

Strawberry geranium ❋
◑ ● ◖ ⚡ MS, LS, CS OR INDOORS
Saxifraga stolonifera   p. 537

Sweet flag
◑ ● ◖ ⚡ US, MS, LS, CS
Acorus   p. 152

Toad lily ❋
◑ ● ◍ ◍ ◖ ⚡ US, MS, LS, CS
Tricyrtis   p. 576

Tradescantia ❋
☼ ◑ ● ◍ ◍ ◍ ◖ ⚡ VARY
                                 p. 576

Twinleaf
◑ ● ◖ ⚡ US, MS
Jeffersonia diphylla   p. 368

Viola ❋
☼ ◑ ● ◖ ⚡ VARY
Viola   p. 587

Virginia bluebells ❋
◑ ● ◖ ⚡ US, MS, LS
Mertensia pulmonarioides   p. 417

Wake robin ❋
◑ ● ◖ ⚡ US, MS, LS
Trillium   p. 577

Wild ginger ❋
◑ ● ◍ ◖ ⚡ VARY
Asarum   p. 183

Sea oats
Chasmanthium latifolium

Bowles' golden sedge
Carex elata 'Aurea'

Toad lily
Tricyrtis hirta

Viola

Wake robin
Trillium

For climate zone explanations, please see pages 28–38.

Plants That Tolerate
Drought

Bougainvillea

Unthirsty purple coneflower, dusty miller, and mullein

W ith water conservation fast becoming a front-page issue in the South, it only makes sense to try to include in your garden plants that sip, rather than guzzle. Fortunately, many plants, once established, grow just fine with infrequent watering. Here are some proven performers. The symbol ✳ indicates plants that have showy flowers.

Baily acacia
Acacia bailyana

Lilac chaste tree
Vitex agnus-castus

Chitalpa
Chitalpa tashkentensis

Eastern redbud
Cercis canadensis

TREES

Acacia ✳
☼ ◐ ⁑ VARY
p. 147

Ash ✳
☼ ◐ ◖ ⁑ VARY
Fraxinus (most) p. 316

Beefwood
☼ ◐ ◖ ⁑ TS
Casuarina p. 230

Caddo maple
☼ ◐ ◖ ⁑ US, MS, LS
Acer saccharum 'Caddo' p. 150

Caesalpinia ✳
☼ ◐ ◖ ⁑ VARY
p. 214

Cedar
☼ ◖ ⁑ VARY
Cedrus p. 232

Chaste tree ✳
☼ ◖ ⁑ US, MS, LS, CS
Vitex p. 588

Chinese elm
☼ ◖ ⁑ US, MS, LS, CS
Ulmus parvifolia p. 581

Chinese pistache
☼ ◖ ⁑ US, MS, LS, CS
Pistacia chinensis p. 478

Chitalpa ✳
☼ ◐ ⁑ MS, LS, CS
× Chitalpa tashkentensis p. 242

Crepe myrtle ✳
☼ ◖ ⁑ US, MS, LS, CS
Lagerstroemia indica p. 379

Desert willow ✳
☼ ◐ ⁑ MS, LS, CS
Chilopsis linearis p. 240

Eastern redbud ✳
☼ ◐ ◖ ⁑ US, MS, LS, CS
Cercis canadensis p. 236

Eastern red cedar
☼ ◐ ◐ ◖ ⁑ ALL
Juniperus virginiana p. 373

Gold medallion tree ✳
☼ ◐ ⁑ TS
Cassia leptophylla p. 229

Golden ball lead tree ✳
☼ ◐ ◖ ⁑ MS, LS, CS
Leucaena retusa p. 388

Goldenrain tree ✳
☼ ◐ ◖ ⁑ US, MS, LS, CS
Koelreuteria paniculata p. 378

Hackberry
☼ ◐ ◖ ⁑ US, MS, LS, CS
Celtis p. 233

Italian cypress
☼ ◖ ⁑ MS, LS, CS
Cupressus sempervirens p. 273

Japanese pagoda tree ✳
☼ ◐ ◖ ◖ ⁑ US, MS, LS
Sophora japonica p. 549

Jerusalem thorn ✳
☼ ◐ ◐ ◖ ⁑ CS, TS
Parkinsonia aculeata p. 447

Kentucky coffee tree
☼ ◖ ⁑ US, MS, LS
Gymnocladus dioica p. 334

Locust ✳
☼ ◐ ◖ ◖ ⁑ US, MS, LS
Robinia p. 515

Maidenhair tree
☼ ◐ ◖ ⁑ US, MS, LS, CS
Ginkgo biloba p. 324

Mesquite
☼ ◐ ⁑ MS, LS, CS, TS
Prosopis glandulosa p. 492

Oak
☼ ◖ ⁑ VARY
Quercus (some) p. 500

Pine
☼ ◐ ⁑ VARY
Pinus (many) p. 474

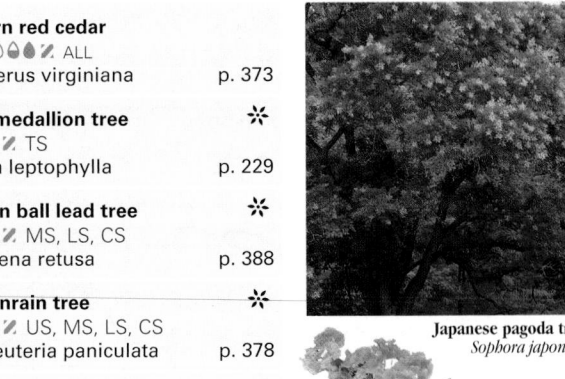

Japanese pagoda tree
Sophora japonica

Crepe myrtle
Lagerstroemia indica

Idaho locust
Robinia × ambigua 'Idaho'

Jerusalem thorn
Parkinsonia aculeata

For growing symbol explanations, please see page 39.

Agave

Aloe

Blue mist
Caryopteris × clandonensis

Broom
Cytisus

Russian olive
☼ ◗ ○◖◗◘✺ US, MS
Elaeagnus angustifolia   p. 295

Strawberry tree
☼ ◗ ○◖◗◘✺ MS, LS, CS
Arbutus unedo   p. 178

Sumac
☼ ○◖◗◘✺ VARY
Rhus   p. 514

Texas persimmon
☼ ◗ ○◗✺ MS, LS, CS, TS
Diospyros texana   p. 289

Windmill palm
☼ ◗ ◖◗◘✺ LS, CS, TS
Trachycarpus fortunei   p. 575

SHRUBS AND SHRUBLIKE

Agave   ✳
☼ ◗ ○◖◗✺ CS, TS
                                p. 156

Aloe   ✳
☼ ◗ ○◖◗◘✺ TS
                                p. 161

Barberry
☼ ◖◗◘✺ VARY
Berberis   p. 198

Bay
☼ ◗ ○◗✺ LS, CS, TS
Laurus nobilis   p. 384

Blue mist   ✳
☼ ◖◗✺ US, MS, LS, CS
Caryopteris × clandonensis   p. 229

Broom   ✳
☼ ◖◗✺ US, MS, LS
Cytisus   p. 276

Bush daisy   ✳
○◖◗◘✺ CS, TS
Euryops pectinatus   p. 307

Butterfly bush   ✳
☼ ◗ ◖◗◘✺ VARY
Buddleia   p. 211

Cape plumbago   ✳
☼ ◗ ○◖◗◘✺ CS, TS
Plumbago auriculata   p. 481

Carolina buckthorn
☼ ◗ ○◗✺ US, MS, LS, CS
Rhamnus caroliniana   p. 505

Cereus peruvianus   ✳
☼ ◗ ○◖◗✺ CS, TS OR INDOORS
                                p. 236

Chinese photinia   ✳
☼ ◗ ◖◗✺ US, MS, LS, CS
Photinia serratifolia   p. 471

Cotoneaster
☼ ◗ ○◖◗◘✺ VARY
                                p. 266

Elaeagnus (some)
☼ ◗ ○◖◗◘✺ VARY
                                p. 295

Feijoa, pineapple guava   ✳
☼ ◗ ◖✺ LS, CS, TS
                                p. 310

Firethorn   ✳
☼ ◗ ◖✺ VARY
Pyracantha   p. 498

Flowering quince   ✳
☼ ◗ ◖◗✺ US, MS, LS, CS
Chaenomeles   p. 237

Germander
☼ ◗ ◖✺ US, MS, LS, CS
Teucrium chamaedrys   p. 568

Grevillea   ✳
☼ ◗ ○◖◗✺ VARY
                                p. 333

Holly
☼ ◗ ◖✺ VARY
Ilex   p. 356

Indian hawthorn   ✳
☼ ◗ ○◖◗◘✺ LS, CS
Rhaphiolepis indica   p. 505

Japanese fatsia
◗ ◖◗✺ LS, CS, TS
Fatsia japonica   p. 310

Japanese pittosporum
☼ ◗ ◖◗✺ LS, CS, TS
Pittosporum tobira   p. 478

Juniper
☼ ◗ ○◖◗✺ VARY
Juniperus (some)   p. 370

Lemon bottlebrush   ✳
☼ ◗ ◖✺ LS, CS, TS
Callistemon citrinus   p. 218

Mahonia (most)   ✳
☼ ◗ ◖ ○◖◗◘✺ VARY
                                p. 408

Mediterranean fan palm
☼ ◗ ○◖◗✺ LS, CS, TS
Chamaerops humilis   p. 238

Myrtle
☼ ◗ ○◖✺ CS
Myrtus communis   p. 425

Nandina
☼ ◗ ◖ ○◖◗◘✺ US, MS, LS, CS
Nandina domestica   p. 425

Needle palm
☼ ◗ ◖ ● ◖◗◘✺ ALL
Rhapidophyllum hystrix   p. 506

New Zealand tea tree   ✳
☼ ○◖✺ CS, TS
Leptospermum scoparium   p. 387

Oleander   ✳
☼ ○◖◗◘ ◗✺ LS, CS, TS
Nerium oleander   p. 431

Butterfly bush
Buddleia

Strawberry tree
Arbutus unedo

Japanese fatsia
Fatsia japonica

Myrtle
Myrtus communis

New Zealand tea tree
Leptospermum scoparium

PROBLEM SOLVERS

For climate zone explanations, please see pages 28–38.   ▶

Pomegranate
Punica granatum

Rockrose
Cistus

Rose of Sharon
Hibiscus syriacus

Rugosa rose
Rosa rugosa

Smoke tree
Cotinus coggygria

Pearl bush ✳
☼ ◖◗◗▨ US, MS, LS
Exochorda p. 308

Pomegranate ✳
☼ ◗▨ MS, LS, CS
p. 488

Prickly pear cactus ✳
☼ ◊▨ VARY
Opuntia p. 436

Rockrose ✳
☼ ◊▨ LS, CS
Cistus p. 247

Rose of Sharon ✳
☼ ◊◗◗▨ US, MS, LS, CS
Hibiscus syriacus p. 346

Rosemary ✳
☼ ◊◗▨ ALL
Rosmarinus officinalis p. 524

Rugosa rose ✳
☼ ◗◗◗▨ US, MS, LS, CS
Rosa rugosa p. 524

Sago palm
☼ ◗▨ CS, TS
Cycas revoluta p. 274

Senna (some) ✳
☼ ☼ ◗◗▨ VARY
p. 542

Screw bean
☼ ◊▨ MS, LS, CS, TS
Prosopis pubescens p. 492

Smoke tree ✳
☼ ◗▨ US, MS, LS
Cotinus p. 266

Sotol
☼ ☼ ◊◗▨ VARY
Dasylirion p. 279

Sumac
☼ ◊◗▨ VARY
Rhus p. 514

Texas ranger ✳
☼ ◊◗▨ LS, CS, TS
Leucophyllum frutescens p. 388

Woadwaxen
☼ ◗▨ US, MS, LS
Genista p. 321

Yellow bells ✳
☼ ◗◗▨ CS, TS
Tecoma stans p. 567

VINES AND GROUNDCOVERS

Beach morning glory ✳
☼ ◗◗▨ CS, TS
Ipomoea pes-caprae p. 361

Bittersweet
☼ ◗◗▨ US, MS, LS
Celastrus p. 233

Boston ivy
☼ ☼ ◗◗▨ US, MS, LS
Parthenocissus tricuspidata p. 448

Bougainvillea ✳
☼ ◗◗◗▨ CS, TS
p. 205

Carolina jessamine ✳
☼ ☼ ◗◗◗◗▨ MS, LS, CS
Gelsemium sempervirens p. 321

Coral vine ✳
☼ ◗◗▨ LS, CS, TS
Antigonon leptopus p. 169

Crossvine ✳
☼ ☼ ◗◗◗▨ US, MS, LS, CS
Bignonia capreolata p. 201

Drosanthemum ✳
☼ ◊◗▨ CS, TS
p. 291

Ice plant ✳
☼ ◊◗▨ CS, TS
Carpobrotus p. 227

Ice plant ✳
☼ ☼ ◊◗◗▨ US, MS, LS, CS
Delosperma p. 281

Lady Banks's rose ✳
☼ ☼ ◗◗▨ LS, CS, TS
Rosa banksiae p. 523

Lamb's ears ✳
☼ ◗◗▨ US, MS, LS
Stachys byzantina p. 554

Pink trumpet vine ✳
☼ ◗◗◗▨ CS, TS
Podranea ricasoliana p. 485

Porcelain berry
☼ ☼ ◗◗◗▨ US, MS, LS, CS p. 165
Ampelopsis brevipedunculata

Potato vine ✳
☼ ◗◗◗◗▨ CS, TS
Solanum jasminoides p. 547

Silver lace vine ✳
☼ ◗▨ US, MS, LS
Fallopia baldschuanica p. 309

Snow-in-summer ✳
☼ ☼ ◗◗◗▨ US, MS, LS
Cerastium tomentosum p. 235

Sweet autumn clematis ✳
☼ ◗▨ US, MS, LS, CS
Clematis terniflora p. 252

Trumpet creeper, common ✳
☼ ◗◗▨ US, MS, LS, CS
Campsis radicans p. 224

Virginia creeper
☼ ◗◗◗▨ US, MS, LS, CS
Parthenocissus quinquefolia p. 448

Wisteria ✳
☼ ◊◗▨ US, MS, LS, CS
p. 590

Bougainvillea

Coral vine
Antignon leptopus

Potato vine
Solanum jasminoides

Trumpet creeper, common
Campsis radicans

For growing symbol explanations, please see page 39.

Coreopsis
Coreopsis grandiflora
'Early Sunrise'

Blazing star
Liatris spicata 'Kobold'

Blue fescue
Festuca glauca

Copper canyon daisy
Tagetes lemmonii

EVERGREEN SHRUBS, PERENNIALS, BULBS, ANNUALS

African daisy ☀
☀ ◖ ⚡ ALL
Arctotis   p. 179

Apache plume ☀
☀ ◗ ⚡ ALL
Fallugia paradoxa   p. 309

Artemisia
☀ ◗ ◖ ⚡ VARY
                                  p. 181

Baby's breath ☀
☀ ◖ ⚡ US, MS, LS, CS
Gypsophila paniculata   p. 335

Bear grass ☀
☀ ◗ ◖ ⚡ LS, CS, TS
Nolinia erumpens   p. 432

Beard tongue ☀
☀ ◗ ◖ ◖ ⚡ VARY
Penstemon   p. 461

Black-eyed Susan ☀
☀ ◖ ◖ ⚡ ALL
Rudbeckia hirta   p. 526

Blackfoot daisy ☀
☀ ◖ ⚡ ALL
Melampodium leucanthum   p. 416

Blanket flower ☀
☀ ◗ ◖ ⚡ ALL
Gaillardia   p. 318

Blazing star ☀
☀ ◖ ◖ ⚡ US, MS, LS, CS
Liatris   p. 389

Blue fescue ☀
☀ ◗ ◖ ◖ ⚡ US, MS
Festuca glauca   p. 311

Blue grama grass ☀
☀ ◗ ⚡ ALL
Bouteloua gracilis   p. 206

Broom sedge ☀
☀ ◗ ◖ ◗ ⚡ US, MS, LS, CS
Andropogon virginicus   p. 166

Bouvardia ☀
◗ ◖ ◖ ⚡ CS, TS
                                  p. 207

Brodiaea ☀
☀ ◗ ⚡ VARY
                                  p. 208

Bulbine frutescens ☀
☀ ◗ ◖ ◖ ◖ ⚡ CS, TS
                                  p. 212

Butterfly weed ☀
☀ ◗ ◖ ◖ ⚡ US, MS, LS, CS
Asclepias tuberosa   p. 184

California poppy ☀
☀ ◗ ◖ ◖ ⚡ ALL
Eschscholzia californica   p. 302

Cockscomb ☀
☀ ◗ ◖ ⚡ ALL
Celosia argentea   p. 233

Copper canyon daisy ☀
☀ ◖ ◖ ⚡ LS, CS
Tagetes lemmonii   p. 565

Coreopsis ☀
☀ ◗ ◖ ◖ ◖ ◖ ⚡ US, MS, LS, CS
                                  p. 260

Coryphantha vivipara ☀
☀ ◖ ◖ ⚡ US, MS, LS, CS
                                  p. 265

Crassula ☀
☀ ◗ ⚡ TS
                                  p. 268

Daylily ☀
☀ ◗ ◖ ◖ ⚡ ALL
Hemerocallis   p. 342

Dicliptera ☀
☀ ◗ ◗ ◖ ◖ ⚡ VARY
                                  p. 286

Dusty miller ☀
☀ ◗ ◖ ⚡ MS LS CS OR ANNUAL
Senecio cineraria   p. 542

Echeveria (most) ☀
☀ ◖ ◖ ⚡ VARY
                                  p. 292

Euphorbia (most) ☀
☀ ◗ ◗ ● ◖ ◖ ◗ ⚡ VARY
                                  p. 305

False indigo ☀
☀ ◖ ⚡ US, MS, LS, CS
Baptisia   p. 194

False sunflower ☀
☀ ◗ ◖ ◖ ⚡ US, MS, LS, CS
Heliopsis helianthoides   p. 340

Feather grass ☀
☀ ◖ ◖ ⚡ US, MS, LS, CS
Stipa   p. 557

Fortnight lily ☀
☀ ◗ ◖ ◖ ⚡ LS, CS, TS
Dietes   p. 287

Fountain grass ☀
☀ ◗ ◖ ◖ ⚡ CS, TS
Pennisetum setaceum   p. 460

Gaura ☀
☀ ◖ ⚡ US, MS, LS, CS
Gaura lindheimeri   p. 320

Gazania daisy ☀
☀ ◗ ◖ ◖ ⚡ ALL
Gazania   p. 320

Geranium ☀
☀ ◗ ◖ ◖ ⚡ CS, TS
Pelargonium   p. 458

Globe amaranth ☀
☀ ◗ ◖ ⚡ ALL
Gomphrena globosa   p. 326

Daylily
Hemerocallis

False sunflower
Heliopsis helianthoides

Feather grass
Stipa gigantea

Gaura
Gaura lindheimeri

Globe amaranth
Gomphrena globosa

For climate zone explanations, please see pages 28–38. ▶

Iris, bearded

Jerusalem sage
Phlomis fruticosa

Lion's tail
Leonotis leonorus

Madagascar periwinkle
Catharanthus roseus

Lily-of-the-Nile
Agapanthus
'Peter Pan'

Globe mallow ☀
☀ ◐ ◊ ⚡ VARY
Sphaeralcea   p. 551

Golden aster ☀
☀ ◐ ◆ ◊ ⚡ US, MS, LS, CS
Chrysopsis   p. 245

Hedgehog cactus ☀
☀ ◐ ◊ ⚡ VARY
Echinocereus   p. 293

Hummingbird mint ☀
☀ ◆ ◊ ⚡ VARY
Agastache   p. 155

Iris, bearded ☀
☀ ◐ ◆ ◊ ⚡ US, MS, LS, CS
                              p. 362

Jerusalem sage ☀
☀ ◐ ◊ ◆ ⚡ US, MS, LS
Phlomis fruticosa   p. 468

Lantana ☀
☀ ◆ ◊ ⚡ LS, CS, TS
                              p. 382

Lavender ☀
☀ ◆ ◊ ⚡ VARY
Lavandula   p. 384

Lavender cotton ☀
☀ ◊ ◆ ⚡ US, MS, LS, CS
Santolina chamaecyparissus p. 534

Lily-of-the-Nile ☀
☀ ◐ ◊ ◆ ◊ ⚡ VARY
Agapanthus   p. 154

Lion's tail ☀
☀ ◊ ⚡ CS, TS
Leonotis leonorus   p. 386

Madagascar periwinkle ☀
☀ ◆ ◊ ⚡ ALL
Catharanthus roseus   p. 231

Mexican sunflower ☀
☀ ◆ ⚡ ALL
Tithonia rotundifolia   p. 573

Mount Atlas daisy ☀
☀ ◊ ◆ ⚡ US, MS, LS
Anacyclus depressus   p. 165

Mullein ☀
☀ ◆ ⚡ US, MS, LS
Verbascum   p. 583

Orange justicia ☀
☀ ◊ ⚡ LS, CS, TS
Justicia leonardii   p. 374

Prickly poppy ☀
☀ ◊ ⚡ ALL
Argemone   p. 180

Purple coneflower ☀
☀ ◆ ◊ ⚡ US, MS, LS, CS
Echinacea purpurea   p. 293

Red-hot poker ☀
☀ ◐ ◊ ◆ ◊ ⚡ VARY
Kniphofia   p. 377

Red yucca ☀
☀ ◐ ◊ ◆ ◊ ⚡ MS, LS, CS, TS
Hesperaloe parviflora   p. 344

Ruby grass ☀
☀ ◆ ◊ ◆ ⚡ TS
Rhynchelytrum nerviglume   p. 515

Ruellia ☀
☀ ◐ ◆ ◊ ⚡ ALL
                              p. 526

Russian sage ☀
☀ ◐ ◊ ◆ ⚡ US, MS, LS, CS
Perovskia atriplicifolia   p. 463

Sage ☀
☀ ◆ ◊ ⚡ VARY
Salvia (most)   p. 530

Silphium ☀
☀ ◐ ◊ ◆ ◊ ⚡ US, MS, LS, CS
                              p. 545

Silver grass ☀
☀ ◐ ◊ ◆ ◊ ⚡ US, MS, LS, CS
Miscanthus   p. 420

Stonecrop ☀
☀ ◐ ◊ ◆ ⚡ US, MS, LS
Sedum (many)   p. 540

Sundrops ☀
☀ ◐ ◊ ◆ ⚡ US, MS, LS
Calylophus   p. 219

Thrift ☀
☀ ◆ ◊ ⚡ VARY
Armeria   p. 181

Valerian ☀
☀ ◐ ◊ ◆ ◊ ⚡ US, MS, LS
Centranthus ruber   p. 234

Verbena (most) ☀
☀ ◆ ⚡ VARY
                              p. 583

Wild ageratum ☀
☀ ◐ ◊ ◆ ◆ ◊ ⚡ ALL
Eupatorium coelestinum   p. 305

Wild foxglove ☀
☀ ◐ ◊ ◆ ◊ ⚡ US, MS, LS, CS
Penstemon cobaea   p. 461

Wine cups ☀
☀ ◊ ◆ ◊ ⚡ US, MS, LS, CS
Callirhoe   p. 217

Yarrow ☀
☀ ◊ ◆ ⚡ US, MS, LS
Achillea   p. 151

Yellow coneflower ☀
☀ ◊ ◆ ⚡ US, MS, LS, CS
Rudbeckia fulgida   p. 526

Yucca (most) ☀
☀ ◊ ◆ ◊ ⚡ VARY
                              p. 592

Zinnia ☀
☀ ◆ ⚡ ALL
                              p. 395

Mexican sunflower
Tithonia rotundifolia

Mullein
Verbascum

Ruby grass
Rhynchelytrum nerviglume

Valerian
Centranthus ruber 'Pink Crystals'

Wild foxglove
Penstemon cobaea

For growing symbol explanations, please see page 39.

Siberian iris and pentas

Plants for
Damp Soil

Swamps and marshes may be heaven to alligators, but most garden plants have a devil of a time growing there. Well-drained soil is what they want, but providing it can be a labor of Job. Fortunately, a myriad of attractive plants flourish in heavy, soggy, oxygen-poor soils. And some, indicated by the symbol ☖, will grow with their roots totally submerged.

Texas star
Hibiscus coccineus

Bald cypress
Taxodium distichum

Laurel oak
Quercus laurifolia

Sweet bay
Magnolia virginiana

Swamp white oak
Quercus bicolor

TREES

American sweet gum
☼ ◗ ◖ ✂ US, MS, LS, CS
Liquidambar styraciflua p. 394

American sycamore
☼ ◖ ✂ US, MS, LS, CS
Platanus occidentalis p. 479

Bald cypress ☖
☼ ◗◖◗ ✂ US, MS, LS, CS
Taxodium distichum p. 566

Box elder
☼ ◖ ◗◖ ✂ US, MS, LS, CS
Acer negundo p. 149

Dahoon
☼ ◖ ◗◖ ✂ MS, LS, CS
Ilex cassine p. 356

Loblolly bay
☼ ◖ ◗◖ ✂ MS, LS, CS, TS
Gordonia lasianthus p. 327

Magnolia (some)
☼ ◖ ◗ ✂ VARY
  p. 402

Pond cypress ☖
☼ ◗◖◗ ✂ US, MS, LS, CS
Taxodium ascendens p. 566

Possumhaw
☼ ◖ ◗ ✂ US, MS, LS, CS
Ilex decidua p. 357

Red maple
☼ ◖ ◗◖ ✂ US, MS, LS, CS
Acer rubrum p. 150

River birch
☼ ◖ ◗◖ ✂ US, MS, LS, CS
Betula nigra p. 200

Sugarberry
☼ ◖ ◗ ✂ US, MS, LS, CS
Celtis laevigata p. 234

Swamp white oak
☼ ◗◖◗ ✂ US, MS, LS
Quercus bicolor p. 500

Water oak
☼ ◗◖◗ ✂ US, MS, LS, CS
Quercus nigra p. 501

Water tupelo ☖
☼ ◖ ◗◖ ✂ US, MS, LS, CS
Nyssa aquatica p. 433

Weeping willow
☼ ◗◖◗ ✂ US, MS, LS
Salix babylonica p. 529

White cedar
☼ ◖ ◗ ✂ US, MS, LS, CS
Chamaecyparis thyoides p. 238

SHRUBS

American elderberry
☼ ◖ ◗ ✂ US, MS, LS, CS
Sambucus canadensis p. 533

American arborvitae
☼ ◖ ◗◖ ✂ US, MS
Thuja occidentalis p. 569

Bamboo (many)
☼ ◖ ◗◖ ✂ VARY
  p. 190

Bayberry
☼ ◗ ✂ US, MS
Myrica pensylvanica p. 425

Bog rosemary
◖ ◗◖ ✂ US
Andromeda polifolia p. 166

Bramble
☼ ◖ ◗◖ ✂ VARY
Rubus p. 526

Buttonbush ☖
☼ ◖ ◗◖ ✂ ALL
Cephalanthus occidentalis p. 234

Dwarf palmetto
☼ ◖ ◗◖◗ ✂ MS, LS, CS, TS
Sabal minor p. 528

Florida anise
◖ ◗◖ ✂ MS, LS, CS
Illicium floridanum p. 358

Weeping willow
Salix babylonica

Bamboo

Creeping bramble
Rubus pentalobus

Florida anise
Illicium floridanum

For climate zone explanations, please see pages 28–38. ▶

Sweetshrub, common
Calycanthus floridus

Virginia sweetspire
Itea virginica

Aconite
Aconitum

Bloodroot
Sanguinaria canadensis

Florida leucothoe
MS, LS, CS
Agarista populifolia   p. 155

Inkberry
ALL
Ilex glabra   p. 357

Leucothoe
NEEDS, VARY
          p. 388

Red chokeberry
US, MS, LS, CS
Aronia arbutifolia   p. 181

Redtwig dogwood
US, MS
Cornus sericea   p. 263

Sea buckthorn
US, MS
Hippophae rhamnoides   p. 347

Spicebush
US, MS, LS
Lindera   p. 393

Summersweet
US, MS, LS, CS
Clethra alnifolia   p. 253

Sweetshrub, common
US, MS, LS, CS
Calycanthus floridus   p. 219

Turk's-cap
LS, CS, TS
Malvaviscus arboreus   p. 412

Virginia sweetspire
US, MS, LS, CS
Itea virginica   p. 366

Wax myrtle
MS, LS, CS, TS
Myrica cerifera   p. 425

Winterberry
US, MS, LS, CS
Ilex verticillata   p. 358

PERENNIALS, ANNUALS, BULBS

Aconite
US, MS
Aconitum   p. 152

Bee balm
US, MS, LS
Monarda didyma   p. 421

Black snakeroot
US, MS, LS, CS
Cimicifuga racemosa   p. 246

Bloodroot
US, MS, LS
Sanguinaria canadensis   p. 533

Blue cardinal flower
US, MS, LS
Lobelia siphilitica   p. 396

Bluets
US, MS, LS
Houstonia caerulea   p. 350

Braken
ALL
Pteridium aquilinum   p. 496

Calla
CS, TS
Zantedeschia   p. 593

Canna
LS, CS, TS
          p. 224

Cardinal flower
US, MS, LS, CS
Lobelia cardinalis   p. 396

Cinnamon fern
ALL
Osmunda cinnamomea   p. 440

Crinum
VARY
          p. 269

Crimson flag
LS, CS, TS
Schizostylis coccinea   p. 538

Daylily
ALL
Hemerocallis   p. 342

Elephant's ear
VARY
Alocasia   p. 160

False spiraea
US, MS
Astilbe   p. 187

Farfugium japonicum
MS, LS, CS, TS OR INDOORS
          p. 309

Filipendula
US, MS, LS
          p. 313

Forget-me-not
US, MS, LS
Myosotis scorpioides   p. 425

Gentian
US, MS, LS
Gentiana   p. 321

Ginger lily
VARY
Hedychium   p. 338

Globeflower
US, MS
Trollius   p. 577

Goat's beard
US, MS
Aruncus dioicus   p. 183

Golden ray
US, MS, LS
Ligularia   p. 389

Cinnamon fern
Osmunda cinnamomea

Elephant's ear
Alocasia

Chinese astilbe
Astilbe chinensis
'Pumila'

Goat's beard
Aruncus dioicus

For growing symbol explanations, please see page 39.

Golden ray
Ligularia

Greater celandine
Chelidonium majus

Horsetail
Equisetum hyemale

Yellow flag
Iris pseudoacorus

Gooseneck loosestrife
☼ ◐ ◖◖ ✂ US, MS, LS
Lysimachia clethroides   p. 400

Greater celandine
◑ ◐ ◖◖ ◊✂ US, MS, LS
Chelidonium majus   p. 239

Gunnera
☼ ◐ ◖◖ ✂ MS, LS, CS, TS
                                p. 334

Horsetail   ♛
☼ ◐ ◖◖ ✂ ALL
Equisetum hyemale   p. 297

Houttuynia cordata   ♛
☼ ◑ ◐ ◖◖◖ ✂ ALL
                                p. 350

Iris (several)   ♛
☼ ◐ ◖◖◖◖ ◖ ✂ VARY
                                p. 362

Ironweed
☼ ◑ ◐ ◖◖◖◖ ✂ US, MS, LS
Vernonia noveboracensis   p. 584

Jack-in-the-pulpit
◑ ◐ ◖◖ ✂ US, MS, LS, CS
Arisaema   p. 180

Japanese coltsfoot
◑ ◐ ◖◖ ✂ US, MS, LS, CS
Petasites japonicus   p. 464

Japanese primrose
◑ ◐ ◖◖ ✂ US, MS, LS
Primula japonica   p. 491

Joe-Pye weed
☼ ◑ ◐ ◖◖ ✂ US, MS, LS, CS
Eupatorium purpureum   p. 305

Lady fern
◑ ◐ ◖◖◖ ✂ US, MS, LS
Athyrium filix-femina   p. 188

Marsh marigold   ♛
☼ ◑ ◐ ◖◖ ◊✂ US, MS, LS
Caltha palustris   p. 219

Marsh fern
◑ ◐ ◖◖ ✂ US, MS, LS
Thelypteris palustris   p. 569

Mint
☼ ◑ ◐ ◖ ✂ US, MS, LS, CS
Mentha   p. 417

Moor grass
☼ ◑ ◐ ◖◖ ✂ US, MS, LS
Molinia caerulea   p. 421

New England aster
☼ ◑ ◐ ◖◖ ✂ US, MS, LS
Aster novae-angliae   p. 187

Papyrus   ♛
☼ ◑ ◐ ◖◖ ✂ CS, TS
Cyperus papyrus   p. 275

Pentas
☼ ◐ ◖ ✂ ALL
Pentas lanceolata   p. 461

Perennial hibiscus
☼ ◐ ◖ ✂ ALL
Hibiscus moscheutos   p. 345

Pitcher plant
☼ ◐ ◖ ✂ US, MS, LS, CS
Sarracenia   p. 536

Royal fern   ♛
☼ ◑ ◐ ◖◖ ✂ ALL
Osmunda regalis   p. 440

Rush
☼ ◑ ◐ ◖◖ ✂ US, MS, LS, CS
Juncus   p. 370

Sea oats
☼ ◑ ◐ ◖ ✂ US, MS, LS, CS
Chasmanthium latifolium   p. 238

Sedge (some)
☼ ◑ ◐ ◖◖◖◖ ✂ US, MS, LS, CS
Carex   p. 226

Sensitive fern
☼ ◑ ◐ ◖◖◖◖ ✂ US, MS, LS, CS
Onoclea sensibilis   p. 436

Shortia
◑ ◐ ◖◖◖ ✂ US, MS
                                p. 544

Spiderwort
☼ ◑ ◐ ◖◖◖◖ ✂ US, MS, LS, CS
Tradescantia virginiana   p. 576

Swamp milkweed   ♛
☼ ◐ ◖◖◖ ✂ US, MS, LS, CS
Asclepias incarnata   p. 184

Swamp sunflower
☼ ◐ ◖◖◖ ✂ US, MS, LS, CS
Helianthus angustifolius   p. 339

Sweet flag
◑ ◐ ◖◖ ✂ US, MS, LS, CS
Acorus   p. 152

Sweet woodruff
◑ ◐ ◖◖◖ ✂ US, MS, LS
Galium odoratum   p. 318

Texas star   ♛
☼ ◐ ◖◖◖ ✂ MS, LS, CS, TS
Hibiscus coccineus   p. 345

Toad lily
◑ ◐ ◖◖◖ ✂ US, MS, LS, CS
Tricyrtis   p. 576

Wand loosestrife   ♛
☼ ◐ ◖ ✂ US, MS, LS
Lythrum virgatum   p. 401

White trillium
◑ ◐ ◖ ✂ US, MS, LS
Trillium grandiflorum   p. 577

White turtlehead
☼ ◑ ◐ ◖◖ ✂ US, MS, LS, CS
Chelone glabra   p. 239

Xanthosoma
◑ ◐ ◖ ✂ TS OR INDOORS
                                p. 592

Pitcher plant
Sarracenia

Bowles' golden grass (Sedge)
Carex elata 'Aurea'

Spiderwort
Tradescantia virginiana

Japanese sweet flag
Acorus gramineus

White trillium
Trillium grandiflorum

For climate zone explanations, please see pages 28–38.

Deer-resistant Plants

Appearances to the contrary, deer can be discriminating diners. Some plants are particular favorites; others are more or less left alone. If you live in deer country, it's far simpler to fill the garden with less-favored plants than to protect the more choice morsels. But a word of warning: Although deer generally ignore the plants listed below, their preferences vary in different areas, from year to year, and even from season to season. So don't blame us if Bambi occasionally chomps a plant on this list.

Lupine
Lupinus,
Russell hybrid

Arizona cypress
Cupressus arizonica

Crepe myrtle
Lagerstroemia indica

Golden Hinoki false cypress
Chamaecyparis obtusa 'Crippsii'

Feather reed grass
Calamagrostis × acutiflora 'Karl Foerster'

Saucer magnolia
Magnolia × soulangeana

Mediterranean fan palm
Chamaerops humilis

Japanese black pine
Pinus thunbergii

TREES

Acacia
☼ ◐ ✂ VARY
p. 147

American beech
☼ ◐ ◕ ◕ ✂ US, MS, LS, CS
Fagus grandiflora — p. 308

Ash
☼ ◐ ◕ ◕ ✂ VARY
Fraxinus — p. 316

Bald cypress
☼ ◕ ◕ ◕ ✂ US, MS, LS, CS
Taxodium distichum — p. 566

Bottlebrush
☼ ◕ ◕ ✂ VARY
Callistemon — p. 217

Cedar
☼ ◕ ✂ VARY
Cedrus — p. 232

Crepe myrtle
☼ ◕ ◕ ✂ US, MS, LS, CS
Lagerstroemia — p. 379

Cypress
☼ ◐ ◕ ✂ VARY
Cupressus — p. 272

Eucalyptus
☼ ◐ ✂ VARY
p. 302

False cypress
☼ ◐ ◕ ✂ US, MS, LS
Chamaecyparis — p. 237

Fig, edible
☼ ◕ ✂ MS, LS, CS, TS
p. 313

Fir
☼ ◐ ◕ ◕ ✂ VARY
Abies — p. 146

Flowering dogwood
☼ ◐ ◕ ✂ US, MS, LS, CS
Cornus florida — p. 262

Gold medallion tree
☼ ◐ ◕ ◕ ✂ TS
Cassia leptophylla — p. 229

Japanese maple
☼ ◐ ◕ ◕ ✂ US, MS, LS, CS
Acer palmatum — p. 149

Live oak
☼ ◕ ◕ ✂ LS, CS, TS
Quercus virginiana — p. 502

Loquat
☼ ◐ ◐ ◕ ◕ ✂ VARY
Eriobotrya — p. 300

Magnolia
☼ ◐ ◕ ✂ VARY
p. 402

Orchid tree
☼ ◕ ◕ ✂ TS
Bauhinia — p. 194

Pine
☼ ◐ ◕ ✂ VARY
Pinus — p. 474

Palms (many)
NEEDS, ZONES VARY
p. 444

Podocarpus
☼ ◐ ◕ ✂ VARY
p. 485

Spruce
☼ ◐ ◕ ◕ ✂ US, MS
Picea — p. 472

Texas mountain laurel
☼ ◐ ◕ ◕ ◕ ✂ LS, CS
Sophora secundiflora — p. 549

Texas persimmon
☼ ◐ ◕ ◕ ✂ MS, LS, CS, TS
Diospyros texana — p. 289

For growing symbol explanations, please see page 39.

Daphne

Flowering quince
Chaenomeles

Eastern red cedar
Juniperus virginiana

Japanese kerria
Kerria japonica

SHRUBS

Abelia
☼ ◐ ◐ ✿ VARY
p. 146

Angels trumpet
☼ ◐ ◐ ◈ ✿ LS, CS, TS
Brugmansia p. 209

Banana shrub
☼ ◐ ◐ ✿ LS, CS, TS
Michelia figo p. 418

Bamboo
☼ ◐ ○◐◐ ✿ VARY
p. 190

Barberry
☼ ◐ ◐◐ ✿ VARY
Berberis p. 198

Bird of Paradise
☼ ◐ ◐ ✿ VARY
Strelitzia reginae p. 559

Butterfly bush
☼ ◐ ◐ ◐ ✿ VARY
Buddleia p. 211

Boxwood
☼ ◐ ◐ ✿ VARY
Buxus p. 213

Cape plumbago
☼ ◐ ○◐◐ ✿ VARY
Plumbago auriculata p. 481

Cotoneaster
☼ ○◐◐ ✿ VARY
p. 266

Daphne
◐ ◐ ◈ ✿ VARY
p. 278

Elaeagnus
☼ ◐ ○◐◐ ✿ VARY
p. 295

Feijoa, pineapple guava
☼ ◐ ✿ LS, CS, TS
p. 310

Flowering quince
☼ ◐ ◐ ✿ US, MS, LS, CS
Chaenomeles p. 237

Heath
☼ ◐ ◐ ✿ VARY
Erica p. 299

Holly
☼ ◐ ◐ ✿ VARY
Ilex p. 356

Ixora
☼ ◐ ◐ ✿ TS
p. 366

Juniper
☼ ◐ ○◐◐ ✿ VARY
Juniperus p. 370

Japanese kerria
◐ ◐◐ ✿ US, MS, LS, CS
Kerria japonica p. 376

Lantana species
☼ ◐ ◐ ✿ LS, CS, TS
p. 382

Leatherleaf mahonia
☼ ◐ ◐ ✿ US, MS, LS, CS
Mahonia bealei p. 409

Nandina
☼ ◐ ◐◐ ◐ ✿ US, MS, LS, CS
p. 425

Natal plum
☼ ◐ ○◐◐ ✿ CS, TS
Carissa macrocarpa p. 227

Oleander
☼ ○◐◐ ◈ ✿ LS, CS, TS
Nerium oleander p. 431

Pomegranate
☼ ◐ ✿ MS, LS, CS
p. 488

Privet
☼ ◐ ◐ ◈ ✿ VARY
Ligustrum p. 390

Rockrose
☼ ◐ ✿ LS, CS
Cistus p. 247

Southern Indica azalea
◐ ◐◐◐ ◈ ✿ MS, LS, CS
Rhododendron p. 511

Sweet olive
☼ ◐ ◐◐◐ ✿ LS, CS, TS
Osmanthus fragrans p. 439

Ti
◐ ◐◐◐ ✿ TS
Cordyline fruticosa p. 259

Tree aloe
☼ ◐ ○◐◈ ✿ TS
Aloe arborescens p. 161

Viburnum
☼ ◐ ◐ ✿ VARY
p. 585

Wax myrtle
☼ ◐ ◐ ✿ MS, LS, CS, TS
Myrica cerifera p. 425

Wild lilac
☼ ○ ✿ US, MS, LS, CS
Ceanothus p. 232

ANNUALS, BULBS, PERENNIALS

Agave
☼ ◐ ○◐ ✿ CS, TS
p. 156

African daisy
☼ ◐ ✿ ALL
Dimorphotheca p. 288

Oleander
Nerium oleander

Privet
Ligustrum japonicum 'Texanum'

Rockrose
Cistus

Tea viburnum
Viburnum setigerum

Tree aloe
Aloe arborescens

For climate zone explanations, please see pages 28–38. ▷

Artemisia

Bear's breech
Acanthus mollis

California poppy
Eschscholzia californica

Cape plumbago
Plumbago auriculata

Coreopsis

Angelonia angustifolia
☼ ♦ ✿ ✁ LS, CS, TS
p. 167

Angel's trumpet
☼ ♦ ✿ ✁ VARY
Datura p. 280

Artemisia
☼ ○ ♦ ✁ VARY
p. 181

Aster
☼ ♦ ♦ ✁ US, MS, LS
p. 186

Beard tongue
☼ ♦ ○ ♦ ✁ VARY
Penstemon p. 461

Bear's breech
☼ ◐ ○ ♦ ♦ ✁ US, MS, LS, CS
Acanthus mollis p. 148

Begonia, tuberous
◐ ♦ ✁ TS OR ANNUAL
p. 197

Bleeding heart
◐ ♦ ♦ ✁ VARY
Dicentra p. 285

Blue-eyed grass
☼ ♦ ♦ ♦ ♦ ✁ VARY
Sisyrinchium p. 546

Calendula
☼ ♦ ✁ ALL
Calendula officinalis p. 216

California poppy
☼ ○ ♦ ♦ ✁ ALL
Eschscholzia californica p. 302

Calla lily
☼ ◐ ♦ ✁ CS, TS
Zantedeschia p. 593

Coneflower
☼ ♦ ♦ ✁ VARY
Echinacea p. 293

Coreopsis
☼ ○ ♦ ♦ ◑ ✁ US, MS, LS, CS
p. 260

Cranesbill
☼ ◐ ♦ ♦ ✁ US, MS, LS
Geranium p. 322

Crinum
☼ ◐ ♦ ♦ ♦ ✁ VARY
p. 269

Daffodil
☼ ◐ ♦ ♦ ✁ US, MS, LS, CS
Narcissus p. 426

Dahlia
☼ ◐ ♦ ✁ US, MS, LS
p. 276

Dusty miller
☼ ◐ ♦ ✁ MS, LS, CS
Senecio cineraria p. 542

Euphorbia
☼ ◐ ♦ ○ ♦ ♦ ✁ VARY
p. 305

Feather grass
☼ ♦ ✁ US, MS, LS, CS
Stipa p. 557

Fescue
☼ ◐ ♦ ♦ ✁ US, MS
Festuca p. 311

Fleabane
☼ ◐ ♦ ✁ VARY
Erigeron p. 299

Floss flower
☼ ◐ ♦ ✁ ALL
Ageratum houstonianum p. 156

Fountain grass
☼ ◐ ♦ ♦ ✁ VARY
Pennisetum p. 460

Ginger lily
☼ ◐ ♦ ♦ ✁ VARY
Hedychium p. 338

Gloriosa daisy
☼ ♦ ♦ ✁ ALL
Rudbeckia hirta p. 526

Hellebore
◐ ♦ ♦ ♦ ♦ ✁ VARY
Helleborus p. 341

Lamb's ears
☼ ◐ ♦ ♦ ✁ US, MS, LS
Stachys byzantina p. 554

Lily-of-the-Nile
☼ ◐ ○ ♦ ♦ ✁ VARY
Agapanthus p. 154

Lobster-claw
☼ ◐ ♦ ♦ ✁ TS
Heliconia p. 340

Lupine
☼ ○ ♦ ♦ ✁ VARY
Lupinus p. 398

Madagascar periwinkle
☼ ◐ ♦ ✁ ALL
Catharanthus roseus p. 231

Maidenhair fern
◐ ♦ ◐ ♦ ✁ VARY
Adiantum p. 153

Mexican mint marigold
☼ ♦ ✁ MS, LS, CS, TS
Tagetes lucida p. 565

Mondo grass
◐ ♦ ♦ ○ ✁ MS, LS, CS, TS
Ophiopogon japonicus p. 436

Montbretia
☼ ◐ ♦ ✁ US, MS, LS, CS
Crocosmia × crocosmiiflora p. 270

Opuntia (cactus)
☼ ○ ✁ VARY
p. 436

Daffodil
Narcissus

Floss flower
Ageratum houstonianum

Gloriosa daisy
Rudbeckia hirta

Hellebore
Helleborus

Southern maidenhair fern
Adiantum capillus-veneris

For growing symbol explanations, please see page 39.

Madagascar periwinkle
Catharanthus roseus

Shirley poppy
Papaver rhoeas

Whorled clary (sage)
Salvia verticillata

Santolina
Santolina

Silver grass
Miscanthus

Oregano
☼ ◐ ◌ ◖ ◗ ⚡ VARY
Origanum   p. 437

Pampas grass
☼ ◌ ◖ ◗ ◖ ◗ ⚡ MS, LS, CS, TS
Cortaderia selloana   p. 264

Peace lily
☼ ◐ ◖ ◗ ◖ ◗ ⚡ TS
Spathiphyllum   p. 550

Petunia × hybrida
☼ ◗ ◖ ◗ ⚡ ALL
                                      p. 465

Philodendron
☼ ◑ ◐ ◖ ◗ ⚡ VARY
                                      p. 467

Polystichum (ferns)
◑ ◐ ◖ ◗ ⚡ VARY
                                      p. 487

Poppy
☼ ◗ ◖ ◗ ⚡ VARY
Papaver   p. 445

Reed grass
☼ ◑ ◗ ◖ ◗ ⚡ US, MS, LS, CS
Calamagroslis   p. 215

Rosemary
☼ ◌ ◗ ◖ ◗ ⚡ ALL
Rosmarinus officinalis   p. 524

Sage
☼ ◖ ◗ ⚡ VARY
Salvia   p. 530

Santolina
☼ ◌ ◗ ◖ ◗ ⚡ US, MS, LS, CS
                                      p. 534

Sedge
☼ ◑ ◌ ◖ ◗ ◖ ◗ ⚡ US, MS, LS, CS
Carex   p. 226

Shasta daisy
☼ ◑ ◖ ◗ ⚡ US, MS, LS, CS
Chrysanthemum maximum   p. 243

Silver grass
☼ ◌ ◗ ◖ ◗ ⚡ US, MS, LS, CS
Miscanthus   p. 420

Snapdragon
☼ ◖ ◗ ⚡ ALL
Antirrhinum majus   p. 169

Snow-in-summer
☼ ◑ ◖ ◗ ◖ ◗ ⚡ US, MS, LS
Cerastium tomentosum   p. 235

Society garlic
☼ ◖ ◗ ⚡ LS, CS, TS
Tulbaghia violacea   p. 578

Sweet violet
◑ ◖ ◗ ⚡ US, MS, LS
Viola odorata   p. 588

Sword fern
◑ ◖ ◗ ⚡ TS
Nephrolepis   p. 430

Wake robin
◑ ◖ ◗ ⚡ US, MS, LS
Trillium   p. 577

Thyme
☼ ◑ ◗ ◖ ◗ ⚡ VARY
Thymus   p. 571

Turk's cap
☼ ◑ ◌ ◖ ◗ ◖ ◗ ⚡ LS, CS, TS   p. 412
Malvaviscus arboreus drummondii

Valerian
☼ ◑ ◌ ◗ ◖ ◗ ⚡ US, MS, LS
Centranthus ruber   p. 234

Wallflower
☼ ◑ ◌ ◗ ◖ ◗ ⚡ VARY
Erysimum   p. 300

Wandering jew
◑ ◖ ◗ ⚡ TS
Tradescantia zebrina   p. 576

Yarrow
☼ ◌ ◗ ⚡ US, MS, LS
Achillea   p. 151

Yucca
☼ ◌ ◗ ◖ ◗ ⚡ VARY
                                      p. 592

VINES

Allamanda
☼ ◖ ◗ ♦ ⚡ TS OR ANNUALS
                                      p. 159

Bougainvillea
☼ ◗ ◖ ◗ ⚡ CS, TS
                                      p. 205

Carolina jassamine
☼ ◑ ◗ ◖ ◗ ⚡ MS, LS, CS
Gelsemium sepervirens   p. 321

Crossvine
☼ ◑ ◗ ◖ ◗ ⚡ US, MS, LS, CS
Bignonia capreolata   p. 201

English ivy
☼ ◑ ◗ ◖ ◗ ◖ ◗ ⚡ ALL
Hedera helix   p. 337

Jackson vine
☼ ◑ ◌ ◖ ◗ ⚡ MS, LS, CS
Smilax smallii   p. 547

Jasmine
☼ ◑ ◗ ◖ ◗ ⚡ VARY
Jasminium   p. 367

Star jasmine
☼ ◗ ◖ ◗ ⚡ LS, CS, TS   p. 575
Trachelospermum

Trumpet creeper
☼ ◗ ◖ ◗ ⚡ VARY
Campsis   p. 224

Wisteria
☼ ◌ ◗ ◖ ◗ ⚡ US, MS, LS, CS
                                      p. 590

Thyme
Thymus vulgaris 'Silver Posie'

Wallflower
Erysimum 'Bowles Mauve'

Common yarrow
Achillea millefolium

English ivy
Hedera helix

Chinese wisteria
Wisteria sinensis 'Alba'

For climate zone explanations, please see pages 28–38.

Carefree Plants

For many gardeners today, time is of the essence. We can't spare an hour or three to fuss over plants that need constant watering, fertilizing, and spraying for insects and diseases. The following plants make life easier. Most tolerate different soils and seldom fall victim to serious pests. So plant them, relax, and enjoy.

Also known as swamp iris, Louisiana iris thrive in damp conditions.

Sedum 'Autumn Joy'

Bald cypress
Taxodium distichum

Maidenhair tree
Ginkgo biloba

Eastern red cedar
Juniperus virginiana

TREES

Bald cypress
☼ ◑◑◑◑◐ ✕ US, MS, LS, CS
Taxodium distichum   p. 566

Cabbage palm
☼ ☼ ◐◑ ✕ LS, CS, TS
Sabal palmetto   p. 528

Chaste tree
☼ ◐◑ ✕ ALL
Vitex   p. 588

Chinaberry
☼ ◐◑ ✕ MS, LS, CS, TS
Melia azedarach   p. 416

Chinese elm
☼ ◐ ✕ US, MS, LS, CS
Ulmus parvifolia   p. 581

Chinese pistache
☼ ○◐◑ ✕ US, MS, LS, CS
Pistacia chinensis   p. 478

Eastern red cedar
☼ ○◐◑◑ ✕ ALL
Juniperus virginiana   p. 373

Goldenrain tree
☼ ◑◐◑ ✕ US, MS, LS, CS
Koelreuteria paniculata   p. 378

Japanese pagoda tree
☼ ◐◑◐ ✕ US, MS, LS
Sophora japonica   p. 549

Lemon bottlebrush
☼ ◐◑◐ ✕ LS, CS, TS
Callistemon citrinus   p. 218

Longleaf pine
☼ ○◑ ✕ MS, LS, CS, TS
Pinus palustris   p. 476

Maidenhair tree
☼ ◑◐◑ ✕ US, MS, LS, CS
Ginkgo biloba (male)   p. 324

Mesquite
☼ ○◑ ✕ MS, LS, CS, TS
Prosopis glandulosa   p. 492

Mexican buckeye
☼ ○◑○◐◑◐ ◑✕ MS, LS, CS
Ungnadia speciosa   p. 581

Oak (many)
☼ ◑◐ ✕ VARY
Quercus   p. 500

Pawpaw
☼ ◑◐ ✕ US, MS, LS, CS
                            p. 450

Redbud
☼ ☼ ○◑◑◐◑ ✕ VARY
Cercis   p. 236

Trumpet tree
☼ ☼ ◑◐ ✕ TS
Tabebuia   p. 564

Windmill palm
☼ ☼ ◐◑◐ ✕ LS, CS, TS
Trachycarpus fortunei   p. 575

SHRUBS

Beautyberry
☼ ☼ ◐◑◐ ✕ US, MS, LS
Callicarpa   p. 217

Beauty bush
☼ ◐◑◐ ✕ US, MS, LS
Kolkwitzia amabilis   p. 378

Border forsythia
☼ ◐◑◐ ✕ US, MS, LS
Forsythia × intermedia   p. 315

Butterfly bush
☼ ☼ ○◐◑◐ ✕ VARY
Buddleia   p. 211

Firethorn
☼ ◐◑ ✕ VARY
Pyracantha   p. 498

Flowering quince
☼ ◐◑◐ ✕ US, MS, LS, CS
Chaenomeles   p. 237

Fuzzy deutzia
☼ ☼ ○◐◑◐◑ ✕ US, MS, LS
Deutzia scabra   p. 283

Live oak
Quercus virginiana

Redbud
Cercis

Beautyberry
Callicarpa

Border forsythia
Forsythia × intermedia

For growing symbol explanations, please see page 39.

Chinese holly
Ilex cornuta

Oakleaf hydrangea
Hydrangea quercifolia

Sweet mock orange
Philadelphus coronarius

Wax myrtle
Myrica cerifera

Holly
☼ ◖ ◗ ✂ VARY
Ilex   p. 356

Japanese cleyera
☼ ◖ ◗ ✂ MS, LS, CS, TS
Ternstroemia gymnanthera   p. 567

Juniper
☼ ◐ ◖ ◖ ◗ ✂ VARY
Juniperus   p. 370

Oakleaf hydrangea
◐ ◗ ✂ US, MS, LS, CS
Hydrangea quercifolia   p. 353

Oleander
☼ ◖ ◖ ◗ ◗ ✂ LS, CS, TS
Nerium oleander   p. 431

Rosemary
☼ ◖ ◗ ✂ ALL
Rosmarinus officinalis   p. 524

Rose of Sharon
☼ ◗ ✂ US, MS, LS, CS
Hibiscus syriacus   p. 346

Sea grape
☼ ◗ ✂ TS
Coccoloba   p. 255

Spiraea
☼ ◐ ◗ ◗ ✂ VARY
                                        p. 552

Sumac
☼ ◖ ◗ ✂ VARY
Rhus   p. 514

Sweet mock orange
☼ ◐ ◗ ◗ ✂ US, MS, LS, CS
Philadelphus coronarius   p. 467

Sweetshrub, common
☼ ◗ ◖ ◗ ✂ US, MS. LS
Calycanthus floridus   p. 219

Thorny elaeagnus
☼ ◐ ◖ ◖ ◗ ✂ US, MS, LS, CS
Elaeagnus pungens   p. 295

Titi
☼ ◐ ◗ ◗ ✂ ALL
Cyrilla racemiflora   p. 276

Viburnum
☼ ◐ ◗ ✂ VARY
                                        p. 585

Virginia sweetspire
☼ ◗ ✂ US, MS. LS, CS
Itea virginica   p. 366

Wax myrtle
☼ ◗ ✂ MS, LS, CS, TS
Myrica cerifera   p. 425

Weigela
☼ ◐ ◗ ✂ US, MS, LS
                                        p. 590

Winter honeysuckle
☼ ◐ ◗ ◗ ✂ US, MS, LS
Lonicera fragrantissima   p. 397

Winter jasmine
☼ ◐ ◗ ◗ ✂ US, MS, LS, CS
Jasminum nudiflorum   p. 368

Witch hazel
☼ ◐ ◗ ✂ US, MS, LS
Hamamelis   p. 336

GROUND COVERS AND VINES

Boston ivy
☼ ◐ ◗ ◗ ✂ US, MS, LS
Parthenocissus tricuspidata   p. 448

Bougainvillea
☼ ◗ ✂ CS, TS
                                        p. 205

Cape honeysuckle
☼ ◐ ◖ ◗ ✂ CS, TS
Tecoma capensis   p. 567

Carolina jessamine
☼ ◐ ◖ ◖ ◖ ◗ ✂ MS, LS, CS
Gelsemium sempervirens   p. 321

Coral vine
☼ ◗ ✂ LS, CS, TS
Antigonon leptopus   p. 169

Creeping fig
☼ ◐ ◗ ◗ ✂ LS, CS, TS
Ficus pumila   p. 312

Crossvine
☼ ◗ ◗ ✂ US, MS, LS, CS
Bignonia capreolata   p. 201

Fiveleaf akebia
☼ ◐ ◗ ◗ ✂ US, MS, LS, CS
Akebia quinata   p. 158

Ivy
☼ ◐ ◗ ◖ ◗ ✂ VARY
Hedera   p. 337

Jackson vine
☼ ◐ ◖ ◖ ◗ ✂ MS, LS, CS
Smilax smallii   p. 547

Mondo grass
◐ ◖ ◗ ◗ ✂ MS, LS, CS, TS
Ophiopogon japonicus   p. 436

Monkey grass
◐ ◗ ◗ ✂ VARY
Liriope   p. 395

Morning glory
☼ ◗ ◗ ✂ VARY
Ipomoea   p. 360

Silver lace vine
☼ ◗ ◗ ✂ US, MS, LS
Fallopia baldschuanica   p. 309

Star jasmine
☼ ◐ ◗ ◗ ✂ LS, CS, TS
Trachelospermum   p. 575

Sweet autumn clematis
☼ ◐ ◗ ✂ US, MS, LS, CS
Clematis terniflora   p. 252

Winter jasmine
Jasminum nudiflorum

Coral vine
Antigonon leptopus

Creeping fig
Ficus pumila

English ivy
Hedera helix

Morning glory
Ipomoea

For climate zone explanations, please see pages 28–38.

143

Blue star
Amsonia tabernaemontana

Four o'clock
Mirabilis jalapa

Gaura
Gaura lindheimeri

Japanese silver grass
Miscanthus sinensis

Trumpet creeper, common
☼ ☽ ◗ ◖ ✹ ⊘ US, MS, LS, CS
Campsis radicans   p. 224

Trumpet honeysuckle
☼ ◗ ◖ ✹ ⊘ US, MS, LS, CS
Lonicera sempervirens   p. 397

Wedelia
☼ ☽ ◗ ✹ ⊘ CS, TS
Wedelia trilobata   p. 590

PERENNIALS

Blackberry lily
☼ ◗ ✹ ⊘ US, MS, LS, CS
Belamcanda   p. 198

Bluestar
☼ ☽ ◗ ◖ ✹ ⊘ US, MS, LS, CS
Amsonia tabernaemontana   p. 165

Butterfly weed
☼ ◗ ✹ ⊘ US, MS, LS, CS
Asclepias tuberosa   p. 184

Coneflower
☼ ◗ ◖ ✹ ⊘ VARY
Rudbeckia   p. 526

Crinum
☼ ☽ ◗ ◖ ◗ ✹ ⊘ VARY
    p. 269

Daffodil
☼ ☽ ◗ ✹ ⊘ US, MS, LS, CS
Narcissus   p. 426

Daylily
☼ ☽ ◗ ◖ ✹ ⊘ VARY
Hemerocallis   p. 342

Fernleaf yarrow
☼ ◗ ◖ ✹ ⊘ US, MS, LS
Achillea filipendulina   p. 151

Fortnight lily
☼ ☽ ◗ ◖ ✹ ⊘ LS, CS, TS
Dietes vegeta   p. 287

Four o'clock
☼ ◗ ◗ ✹ ⊘ ALL
Mirabilis jalapa   p. 420

Gaura
☼ ☽ ◗ ✹ ⊘ US, MS, LS, CS
Gaura lindheimeri   p. 320

Ginger lily, common
☼ ☽ ◗ ◗ ✹ ⊘ MS, LS, CS, TS
Hedychium coronarium   p. 338

Goldenrod
☼ ☽ ◗ ◖ ✹ ⊘ US, MS, LS, CS
Solidago   p. 548

Hen and chickens
☼ ☽ ◗ ◖ ✹ ⊘ US, MS, LS, CS
Sempervivum tectorum   p. 542

Iris (some)
NEEDS, ZONES VARY
    p. 362

Japanese silver grass
☼ ☽ ◗ ◖ ✹ ⊘ US, MS, LS, CS
Miscanthus sinensis   p. 420

Mexican bush sage
☼ ☽ ◗ ◖ ✹ ⊘ LS, CS, TS
Salvia leucantha   p. 531

Montbretia
☼ ◗ ◖ ✹ ⊘ US, MS, LS, CS
Crocosmia crocosmiiflora   p. 270

Parrot lily
☼ ◗ ◗ ◖ ✹ ⊘ MS, LS, CS
Alstroemeria psittacina   p. 162

Prickly pear cactus
☼ ◗ ⊘ VARY
Opuntia   p. 436

Purple coneflower
☼ ◗ ◖ ✹ ⊘ US, MS, LS, CS
Echinacea purpurea   p. 293

Purple heart
☼ ☽ ◗ ✹ ⊘ MS, LS, CS, TS   p. 576
Tradescantia pallida 'Purpurea'

Queen Anne's lace
☼ ◗ ✹ ⊘ US, MS, LS, CS
Daucus carota carota   p. 280

Russian sage
☼ ◗ ◖ ✹ ⊘ US, MS, LS, CS
Perovskia artriplicifolia   p. 463

Southern shield fern
◗ ◗ ◖ ◗ ✹ ⊘ MS, LS, CS
Thelypteris kunthii   p. 569

Spider lily
☼ ☽ ◗ ◖ ✹ ⊘ ALL
Lycoris radiata   p. 400

Stokesia
☼ ☽ ◗ ✹ ⊘ US, MS, LS, CS
Stokesia laevis   p. 557

Stonecrop
☼ ☽ ◗ ◗ ◖ ✹ ⊘ US, MS, LS
Sedum   p. 540

Texas star
☼ ◗ ✹ ⊘ MS, LS, CS, TS
Hibiscus coccineus   p. 345

Threadleaf coreopsis
☼ ☽ ◗ ◖ ✹ ⊘ US, MS, LS, CS
Coreopsis verticillata   p. 260

Turk's cap
☼ ◗ ◗ ◗ ◖ ✹ ⊘ LS, CS, TS   p. 412
Malvaviscus arboreus drummondii

Wild ageratum
☼ ☽ ◗ ◗ ✹ ⊘ ALL
Eupatorium coelestinum   p. 305

Wine cups
☼ ☽ ◗ ◖ ✹ ⊘ US, MS, LS, CS
Callirhoe   p. 217

Yucca
NEEDS, ZONES VARY
    p. 592

Montbretia
Crocosmia 'Lucifer'

Queen Anne's lace
Daucus carota carota

Southern shield fern
Thelypteris kunthii

Stokesia
Stokesia laevis

Stonecrop
Sedum spathulifolium 'Cape Blanco'

For growing symbol explanations, please see page 39.

Southern Plant
Encyclopedia

T his encyclopedia describes more than 7,000 plants—everything from trees, perennials, and annuals to vegetables, herbs, and houseplants. Many of these plants are available at garden centers. Acquiring others may involve leafing through mail-order catalogs (see pages 681–688 for a listing of suppliers) or engaging in some friendly horse-trading with neighbors.

Rhododendron
'George Lindley Taber'

Herbs and ornamental plants are listed alphabetically by botanical name, such as *Ocimum basilicum* (basil) and *Quercus* (oak). Fruits, nuts, and vegetables, such as apple, pecan, and cabbage, are listed by common name. You'll find both botanical and common names in the index in the back of this book, as well as cross-listings of many common names throughout the encyclopedia.

A sample entry is shown at right below. The botanical name (genus and species) comes first. Alternate botanical names (former ones still commonly used or new ones that aren't widely known) are shown in parentheses. Next come the plant's common name or names, followed by the plant family to which it belongs. The next four lines tell you the type of plant and how to grow it. An additional line notes any toxic properties.

Climate

⚆ Refers to the *Southern Living* climate zones where the plant grows best. For example, "⚆ US, MS, LS" means that it is best suited to the Upper, Middle, and Lower South. Numerous factors, including cold, coastal influences, soil type, topography, and humidity, are taken into account in this zoning. Many plants also carry an American Horticultural Society heat-zone rating (indicated by the symbol H), telling you how much summer heat a plant will tolerate and/or how much heat it requires to flower or fruit properly. Heat zones range from 12 (warmest) to 1 (coolest). For more on climate and heat zones, see pages 28–38.

Exposure

☼ Grows best with full sunlight all or almost all day; you can overlook an hour of shade at the start or end of a summer day

◑ Needs partial shade—shade for half the day or for at least 3 hours during the hottest part of the day

● Prefers little or no direct sunlight—for example, does best on the north side of a house or beneath a broad, densely foliaged tree

Some listings have qualifications. For example, "☼ ◑ Partial shade in Tropical South" means the plant must have part shade in Zone TS but succeeds in sun or part shade elsewhere.

Watering

○ Indicates unthirsty plants; some thrive in drought conditions once established, while others need a little water

◖ Thrives with moderate—less than regular—moisture; this may mean soaking every 2 or 3 weeks

◗ Needs regular moisture—soil shouldn't become too dry

◗◗ Requires ample moisture—includes plants needing constantly moist soil, such as bog and aquatic plants

Many plants show a range of moisture needs. For instance, "◗ ◗◗" means the plant can take regular moisture or wetter conditions.

Toxicity

◊ Plant or some of its parts are known to have toxic or irritant properties

The drawings accompanying the entries illustrate one or more members of a genus; photos are also included for many popular plants. Be sure to read individual descriptions, however, as not all members look alike. The descriptions contain approximate plant heights and widths. Often a range is given; the same plant may grow larger where summers are long and winters short, but stay smaller in a short-summer, long-winter climate. Bloom times have been averaged; flowering may begin earlier or last longer in mild-winter climates. Details about growing—such as pruning, soil requirements, and pests to watch for—are also included in these entries.

CHELIDONIUM majus
GREATER CELANDINE
Papaveraceae
PERENNIAL OR BIENNIAL
⚆ US, MS, LS H 8–4
☼◑ ● PARTIAL TO FULL SHADE
◗ REGULAR WATER
◊ SAP IS IRRITATING TO THE SKIN

Chelidonium majus

A

AARON'S BEARD. See HYPERICUM calycinum

ABELIA

Caprifoliaceae

EVERGREEN, SEMIEVERGREEN, DECIDUOUS SHRUBS

✿ ZONES VARY BY SPECIES

☼ ◖ BEST IN SUN, TOLERATE SOME SHADE,
EXCEPT AS NOTED

● REGULAR WATER

Abelia × grandiflora

U sually seen in older gardens, abelia is one of those "grandma shrubs" that deserves much wider usage. Its graceful, arching branches are densely set with oval, glossy, ½- to 1½-in.-long leaves that emerge a handsome bronze and then turn green. Tubular or bell-shaped blossoms cluster among the leaves or at ends of branches, typically from spring until fall. Though small, they put on a good show. Butterflies like the flowers.

To retain abelia's naturally graceful shape, use hand pruners to cut a few of the main stems to the ground each winter or early spring. This produces more of the vigorous, arching stems that create the plant's pleasing form. Do not shear.

Include abelias in shrub borders or use them as foundation plantings or informal hedges and screens. Low-growing kinds make nice bank and ground covers. *A. chinensis* is showy enough in flower to be used as a specimen plant, either in the garden or in a large container.

A. chinensis. CHINESE ABELIA. Deciduous. Zones US, MS, LS; 12–6. Chinese native growing to 4–5 ft. tall and wide, with fragrant, pink-tinted white flowers.

A. 'Edward Goucher'. Evergreen to semievergreen. Zones US, MS, LS, CS. Resembles *A. ×grandiflora* but is less hardy, lacier, and more compact (to 3–5 ft. tall and wide). Bears small lilac-pink flowers with orange throats.

A. floribunda. MEXICAN ABELIA. Evergreen. Zones LS (protected), CS; 12–8. Native to Mexico. Usually 3–6 ft. tall; sometimes up to 10 ft. tall and 12 ft. wide. Arching, reddish, downy or hairy stems. Pendulous reddish purple flowers appear singly or in clusters. Heaviest bloom is in summer, with sporadic bloom during rest of year. Needs partial shade in hottest climates. Severely damaged at 20°F.

A. ×grandiflora. GLOSSY ABELIA. Evergreen to semievergreen. Zones US, MS, LS, CS; 9–6. This cross between two Chinese species is the best known and most popular of the abelias. To 8 ft. or taller, spreading to 5 ft. or wider. Flowers white or faintly tinged pink. Leaves may take on bronzy tints in fall. Loses most of its leaves at 15°F. Freezes to the ground at 0°F but usually recovers to bloom the same year, making a graceful border plant 10–15 in. high. The following are among the selections grown.

'Francis Mason'. Compact (to 3–4 ft. high and wide) and densely branched, with pink flowers and yellow-variegated leaves.

'Prostrata'. Low grower (1½–2 ft. high, spreading 4–5 ft. wide) useful as ground cover, bank planting, foreground shrub.

'Sherwoodii'. Dense, compact, refined growth to 3–4 ft. tall, 5 ft. wide.

'Sunrise'. Densely branched, with gold-edged green leaves that turn red and purple in fall. To 3–6 ft. tall and wide.

A. mosanensis. FRAGRANT ABELIA. Deciduous. Zones US, MS, LS, CS. Korean native to 5–6 ft. high and wide. Rich pink buds opening to sweet-scented white flowers. Blooms in late spring, early summer. Foliage turns orange red in autumn.

ABELIA-LEAF. See ABELIOPHYLLUM distichum

FOR INFORMATION ON YOUR CLIMATE ZONES
PLEASE SEE PAGES 28–38

ABELIOPHYLLUM distichum

WHITE FORSYTHIA, ABELIA-LEAF

Oleaceae

DECIDUOUS SHRUB

✿ US, MS, LS ⊢ 9–1

☼ ◖ BEST IN SUN, TOLERATES SOME SHADE

● REGULAR WATER

Abeliophyllum distichum

T his attractive but rarely planted shrub from Korea resembles its cousin, border forsythia *(Forsythia ×intermedia)*, in habit, flower shape, and time of bloom—but its blossoms are white rather than yellow. Reaches 3–4 ft. tall and wide; good-looking bluish green leaves are 1–2 in. long. From mid- to late winter, young pink blossoms along the dark brown branches open to very fragrant white flowers, sometimes tinged with pink. 'Roseum' is a pink-flowering selection. As with border forsythia, the cut branches are easy to force into early bloom indoors. To rejuvenate older shrubs, cut a few of the thicker branches to the ground in spring, after the bloom season has ended.

ABELMOSCHUS

Malvaceae

PERENNIALS GROWN AS ANNUALS

✿ US, MS, LS, CS, TS

☼ FULL SUN

● REGULAR WATER

Abelmoschus moschatus

I n bloom, these Asian natives are reminiscent of tropical hibiscus and okra, to which they are related. (In fact, okra—*A. esculentus*—belongs to the same genus; for information, see Okra.) Deeply cut leaves and large, showy flowers are their hallmarks. Commonly grown as annuals, they thrive in high heat, humidity, and good, fertile soil.

A. manihot (Hibiscus manihot). Heat zones 12–7. To 6 ft. or taller, 2–3 ft. wide. Large, coarse leaves and 3- to 5-in., cream to deep yellow flowers with maroon central blotch. Cooked leaves are edible.

A. moschatus (Hibiscus moschatus). SILK FLOWER. Heat zones 12–1. Bushy plant about 1½ ft. high and wide, with deep green leaves. Five-petaled, 3- to 4½-in., cherry red or deep pink blooms. Can be grown as a houseplant in 6-in. pot; set on a windowsill in bright light.

ABIES

FIR

Pinaceae

EVERGREEN TREES

✿ ZONES VARY BY SPECIES

☼ ◖ FULL SUN OR LIGHT SHADE

● ● MODERATE TO REGULAR WATER

Abies concolor

F irs are handsome, erect, symmetrical trees with branches in regularly spaced whorls. Needles are short (mostly in the 1- to 2-in. range) and closely set along the branches; they're often banded white on the undersides. Attractive cones of most types grow 2–5 in. long.

Many people confuse firs with spruces *(Picea)*, but the two are easily distinguished. Fir needles are typically soft and pull cleanly from the stem; spruce needles have sharp points and pull off with a piece of stalk. Also, fir cones stand upright, while spruce cones hang down.

With the exception of the Appalachian region, the South is generally a difficult environment for firs. They dislike summer heat and drought and heavy, poorly drained soils. Success depends on having rich, deep, well-drained soil, providing light shade in the afternoon, and replenishing mulch regularly to keep roots moist and cool. Firs are popular Christmas trees, both live and cut.

A. balsamea. BALSAM FIR. Zones US; 6–1. Native to Northeast. Pyramidal tree to 50 ft. tall and 20 ft. wide; ½- to 1-in.-long, dark green needles. Legendary fragrance makes it a favorite for Christmas trees, wreaths. Use dwarf 'Nana' in rock gardens, containers.

A. concolor. WHITE FIR. Zones US, MS; 7–1. Native to mountain regions of West and Southwest but tolerates hot, humid summers better than most firs. Grows 50–70 ft. tall and 15 ft. wide in gardens. Bluish green, 1- to 2-in.-long needles. 'Candicans' is bluish white.

A. firma. JAPANESE FIR, MOMI FIR. Zones US, MS, LS, CS; 9–6. Native to Japan. Broadly pyramidal to 40–50 ft. tall and about half as wide, with branches held slightly above horizontal. Needles are 1–1½ in. long, dark green above, lighter beneath; unlike needles of other firs, they are very sharp at the tips. Can tolerate hot, moist climates.

A. fraseri. FRASER FIR, SOUTHERN FIR. Zones US; 7–1. Native to higher, cooler elevations of the Appalachian Mountains. Attractive pyramidal tree resembling *A. balsamea* in both looks and fragrance. Widely grown as a Christmas tree where summers are not too hot.

A. homolepis. NIKKO FIR. Zones US, MS; 6–4. Native to Japan. Broad, dense, rather formal-looking fir to 80 ft. tall and 20 ft. wide. Dark green, ½- to 1-in. needles are densely arranged and point toward ends of branches. Adapted to warm, moist regions. 'Prostrata' is a low, spreading form that reaches 5–10 ft. tall and wide in 10 years.

A. procera (A. nobilis). NOBLE FIR. Zones US; 6–4. Native to the Northwest. Narrow, graceful tree to 100 ft. or more, spreading to 25 ft. wide. Blue-green, 1- to 1½-in. needles; short, stiff branches. Cones are 6–10 in. long, 3 in. wide; each cone scale has a long, slender, pointed bract.

ABUTILON

FLOWERING MAPLE, CHINESE LANTERN

Malvaceae

EVERGREEN SHRUBS

CS, TS H 12–8; OR GROW IN POTS

PARTIAL SHADE IN HOTTEST CLIMATES

MODERATE TO REGULAR WATER

Abutilon hybrid

Long a favorite in Florida gardens, flowering maples continue to win new fans in other regions of the South. This group of semitropical shrubs grows quickly and produces attractive blooms nearly continuously in warm weather. Provide moist, fertile, well-drained soil; watch out for whiteflies and scale insects. Excellent in containers on porch, deck, or patio; in cold-winter areas, bring inside to a sunny window before frost. Easily propagated from cuttings taken from current season's growth. Do not overfeed with nitrogen or you'll get lots of leaves and few flowers.

A. hybrids. Also grown as annuals in colder climates. The best-known flowering maples. Upright, arching growth to 4–10 ft. tall, with equal spread. Broad, maplelike leaves can reach 8 in. across; drooping, bell-like, 2- to 3-in. flowers come in white, yellow, pink, or red. The following are all good choices.

'Bartley Schwartz'. Arching and weeping, with nearly constant production of orange-yellow, drooping blossoms. Good hanging basket plant or standard.

'Boule de Neige'. Large, vigorous, upright plant with white flowers.

'Clementine'. Compact. Red-orange bells over a long season.

'Crimson Belle'. Deep red blossoms.

'Dwarf Red'. Compact and free branching, with orange-red flowers.

'Kentish Belle'. Trailing habit; yellow-orange flowers.

'Linda Vista Peach'. Orange petals protrude from deep pink calyxes.

'Little Imp'. Narrow yellow flowers with red calyxes. Compact plant with arching habit.

'Marion Stewart'. Upright growing plant producing orange flowers with attractive red veins.

'Mobile Pink'. Upright, compact growth. Large, wide-open flowers in pale pink with deeper pink veining.

'Moonchimes'. Yellow flowers on a compact plant.

A. megapotamicum. Vine-shrub from Brazil. Vigorous growth to 10 ft. and as wide, with arrowlike, 1½- to 3-in.-long leaves. Red-and-yellow, 1½-in. flowers resembling tiny lanterns gaily decorate the long, rangy branches in spring and summer. Pinch branch tips to control size, force bushier growth. More graceful in detail than in entirety but can be trained to an interesting pattern. Usually best as loose, informal espalier. Good hanging basket plant. 'Marianne' has better, more intense flower color; 'Variegatum' has leaves mottled with yellow; 'Victory' is compact and floriferous, with small deep yellow flowers.

A. pictum 'Thompsonii'. A selection of a Brazilian species. Erect grower reaches 12 ft. tall and 5–12 ft. wide; foliage is strikingly variegated with creamy yellow. Blooms almost continuously, bearing pale orange bells veined with red.

A. vitifolium (Corynabutilon vitifolium). From Chile. To 15 ft. tall, 8 ft. wide. Gray-green, maplelike leaves to 6 in. or longer. In summer, lilac-blue to white flowers are borne singly or in clusters on long stalks. Needs high humidity.

ABYSSINIAN BANANA. See ENSETE ventricosum

ABYSSINIAN SWORD LILY. See GLADIOLUS callianthus

ACACIA

Fabaceae (Leguminosae)

EVERGREEN AND DECIDUOUS SHRUBS OR TREES

ZONES VARY BY SPECIES

FULL SUN

LITTLE OR NO WATER

Acacia baileyana

Prized for their feathery foliage and showy blooms, acacia species hail from such warm-weather climes as Central and South America, Australia, Mexico, and the American Southwest. In the South, they are typically shrubs or small trees, most commonly grown in Florida and Texas. They are relatively short lived (20 to 30 years), but grow quickly, suffer from few pests, and tolerate poor and dry soils. Requires excellent drainage.

A. baileyana. BAILEY ACACIA (often called mimosa as a cut flower). Evergreen. Zones CS, TS; 12–8. Most widely planted acacia and among the hardiest to cold. Often grown as a multitrunked plant 20–30 ft. high, 20–40 ft. wide. Feathery, finely cut, blue-gray leaves. Starts blooming when young; profuse, fragrant yellow flowers early in the year. Thornless.

'Purpurea'. PURPLE-LEAF ACACIA. Same as *A. baileyana* except for purple new growth.

A. berlandieri. GUAJILLO. Deciduous. Zones CS, TS; 12–8. Southwestern native planted as a shrub, hedge, or small tree. Thornless growth to about 15 ft. high and wide. Fernlike foliage. Fragrant white flowers, rich in nectar, bloom winter to spring.

A. farnesiana. SWEET ACACIA, HUISACHE. Deciduous. Zones LS, CS, TS; 12–8. To 20 ft. high and 15–25 ft. wide, with feathery foliage and thorny branches. Fragrant deep yellow blossoms are borne nearly year-round. In the Lower South, however, cold winters may reduce bloom; and flowers may freeze in a cold snap in any area. Garden centers often sell the more cold-tolerant *A. smallii* under this name.

A. schaffneri. Deciduous. Zones CS, TS; 12–8. To about 18 ft. tall and a bit wider, with curving branches like green tentacles and finely divided leaves hiding short thorns. Perfumed yellow balls in spring.

A. wrightii. WRIGHT ACACIA. Deciduous. Zones LS, CS, TS. Cold-hardy acacia native to Texas; survives winter as far north as Dallas–Fort Worth. Usually grows to 6–10 ft. tall and wide, occasionally to 20 ft. Pale yellow flowers bloom in spring on 2-in. spikes. Delicate foliage sometimes persists through winter. Thorns on branches have sharp hooks. Does best in dry, well-drained soil. Not well adapted to the Southeast.

ACALYPHA

Euphorbiaceae

EVERGREEN SHRUBS

TS H 12–10; OR HOUSEPLANTS

FULL SUN; BRIGHT LIGHT

REGULAR WATER

Acalypha hispida

All three species described here are native to Southeast Asia and the Pacific Islands. Beyond their hardiness range, they can be grown indoors; species *A. wilkesiana* and *A. pendula* can be used as annuals in cold-winter areas. All bloom intermittently during the warm months and all must have good drainage. Pinch young plants regularly to encourage bushy growth. Feed houseplants monthly in summer; reduce watering in winter.

A. hispida. CHENILLE PLANT. Can grow to a bulky 10 ft. tall and 6 ft. wide. Heavy, rich green leaves to 8 in. wide. Flowers come in hanging, 1½-ft.-long clusters that look similar to tassels of crimson chenille. Produces heaviest bloom in early summer, with scattered bloom all year. Thrives in semitropical and tropical climates. This shrub can also be grown in a greenhouse or enclosed patio or, with heavy pruning, indoors.

A. pendula. FIRETAIL. Resembles *A. hispida* in flower form, but plant is much smaller; shorter tassels droop from trailing branches. Good in hanging basket.

A. wilkesiana (A. tricolor). COPPER LEAF. Foliage more colorful than many flowers. Often used as an annual, substituting for flowers from late summer to frost. Leaves to 8 in. long, in color combinations including bronzy green mottled with red and purple; red with crimson and bronze; and green edged with crimson and stippled with orange and red. In a warm, sheltered spot it can grow as a shrub to 6 ft. or taller, nearly as wide. Outdoor potted plants should be kept slightly dry through winter.

Selections worth trying include the following.

'Cypress Elf'. Sold under various names, including *A.* 'Mardi Gras' and *A. godseffiana* 'Heterophylla'. Reaches just 1½–2 ft. high and wide. Narrow, wavy-edged, weeping leaves to 2 in. long are reddish brown with coral margins.

'Macafeeana'. Vigorous plant grows 3–4 ft. high and almost as wide in a single season; tops out at 12–15 ft. in frost-free areas. Giant (to 1-ft.-long) heart-shaped leaves in red and bronze tones.

'Obovata'. To 5 ft. tall and about as wide. Oval, 4- to 6-in.-long, slightly weeping leaves are chocolate brown with hot pink edges.

Acanthaceae. The acanthus family consists of herbs and shrubs, generally from warm or tropical areas. Many have showy flowers or foliage. Examples are bear's breech (*Acanthus*), zebra plant (*Aphelandra*), and *Thunbergia.*

ACANTHOPANAX sieboldianus. See ELEUTHEROCOCCUS sieboldianus

ACANTHUS

BEAR'S BREECH

Acanthaceae

PERENNIALS

US, MS, LS, CS

SUN OR SHADE

MODERATE TO REGULAR WATER

Acanthus mollis

There is nothing subtle about these plants: bold and coarse textured, they make a grand statement in any garden. Native to southern Europe and the Mediterranean, they feature large, deeply lobed, sometimes spiny leaves in clumps to about 3 ft. wide. The flowers that appear in late spring or summer are a sight to behold— tall spikes of hooded whitish, rose, or purple blossoms beneath green or purplish bracts.

These tough plants have spreading roots and can be invasive in rich soil, so give them plenty of room or confine their roots with a barrier at least 8 in. deep. Extended drought causes the leaves to yellow and wither in summer; deep watering or rain results in a flush of fresh foliage. Plants do fine in shade gardens, where their foliage and flowers combine well with hostas and ferns. They also thrive in drier, sunny spots, in the company of daylilies (*Hemerocallis*), bearded irises, and ornamental grasses. Good drainage is important.

A. balcanicus (A. hungaricus). Heat zones 9–5. Somewhat smaller than *A. mollis*, with more finely cut and toothed leaves.

A. mollis. Heat zones 12–6. Most commonly grown species. To 4–5 ft. high in bloom. Spineless leaves to 2 ft. long are deeply lobed and cut. 'Latifolius' has larger leaves and is hardier.

A. spinosus. Heat zones 9–6. Similar to *A. mollis* in size, but leaves are more finely cut and armed with long spines. Foliage is silvery on the true species. Hybrids have bright green leaves and are known as the Spinosissimus Group.

A. 'Summer Beauty'. Heat zones 12–6. Thought to be a hybrid between *A. mollis* and *A. spinosus.* It's similar to *A. mollis*, but it has more finely cut foliage and is better suited to hot, humid summers.

ACCA sellowiana. See FEIJOA

ACER

MAPLE

Aceraceae

DECIDUOUS TREES AND SHRUBS

ZONES VARY BY SPECIES

FULL SUN OR PARTIAL SHADE, EXCEPT AS NOTED

MODERATE TO REGULAR WATER

Acer palmatum

As a group, only oaks rival maples for usefulness in the garden—and there's hardly a place in the South where some kind of maple won't grow. The major limiting factors are extended summer heat or drought and lack of winter cold. Maples come in many shapes and sizes; among them, you'll find large and midsize shade trees, small specimen trees, and dwarf, weeping kinds the size of a shrub. What really sets these trees apart, though, is their spectacular autumn foliage in warm shades of red, orange, and yellow. Color can be quite variable, especially among seedling trees, so shop while the trees are showing their fall color.

Most maples do better when the soil stays moist, though just about all prefer well-drained soil. (*A. rubrum* is an exception, doing fine in boggy soil.) Large maples can be difficult to garden beneath; in addition to casting dense shade, they grow shallow roots that compete with other plants for water and nutrients. The roots can also crack and lift pavement and invade water and sewer lines.

Medium to large maples need little pruning. On smaller types, prune to accentuate the natural form. Avoid pruning in late winter or early spring, as cuts will "bleed" sap. Prune in summer or early winter instead.

A. barbatum (A. floridanum). SOUTHERN SUGAR MAPLE, FLORIDA MAPLE. Deciduous tree. Zones MS, LS, CS; 9–1. Native from Virginia south to Florida and west to Oklahoma and Texas. Grows to 25–30 ft. tall and as wide. Usually turns the same rich yellow and occasionally red in autumn as *A. saccharum*, but it is smaller in stature and has smaller leaves, paler bark, and a more open habit. It is also better adapted to the low, wet Coastal Plains of the South. Found in forest understory alongside streams.

A. buergerianum. TRIDENT MAPLE. Deciduous tree. Zones US, MS, LS; 8–1. Native to China and Japan. Grows to 20–25 ft. high and about as wide. Roundish crown of 3-in.-wide, glossy green, three-lobed leaves that are paler green beneath. Fall color usually red, sometimes orange or yellow. Attractive, flaking bark on older wood. Low, spreading growth; stake and prune to make it branch high. A decorative, useful patio tree and favorite bonsai subject.

A. campestre. HEDGE MAPLE. Deciduous tree. Zones US, MS, LS; 8–1. Native to Europe, western Asia. Slow growing to 70 ft., seldom over 30 ft. tall and wide in cultivation. Forms an especially dense, compact, rounded head. Leaves 2–4 in. wide, with three to five lobes, dull green above, downy beneath; turn yellow in fall. 'Queen Elizabeth' has glossier foliage, more erect habit.

A. capillipes. SNAKEBARK MAPLE. Deciduous tree. Zones US, MS; 7–2. Native to Japan. Moderate growth rate to 30 ft. tall and wide. Young branches are red; with age, they become brown with white stripes. Shallowly three-lobed leaves are 3–5 in. long; red when new, retain red leafstalks and midribs at maturity, turn scarlet in fall. In warmer climates, does better in partial shade.

A. ginnala. See A. tataricum ginnala

A. griseum. PAPERBARK MAPLE. Deciduous tree. Zones US, MS; 8–1. Native to China. Grows to 25 ft. or higher; may be half to equally as wide as tall. In winter it makes a striking picture with bare branches angling out and up from main trunk and reddish bark peeling away in paper-thin sheets. Late to leaf out in spring. Leaves are divided into three coarsely toothed, 1½- to 2½-in.-long leaflets, dark green above, silvery below. Inconspicuous red flowers in spring develop into showy winged seeds. Foliage turns brilliant red in fall.

A. japonicum. FULLMOON MAPLE. Deciduous shrub or tree. Zones US, MS; 7–1. Native to Japan. To 20–30 ft. high, with equal or greater spread. Nearly round, 2- to 5-in.-long leaves cut into 7 to 11 lobes. Give regular moisture, part shade in warm regions.

'Aconitifolium', fernleaf fullmoon maple, is a slow-growing, small selection (to just 10–12 ft. tall and wide) with deeply cut leaves (almost to the leafstalk); each lobe is also cut and toothed. Fine fall color where adapted; nice specimen tree. For the tree often sold as golden fullmoon maple, see *A. shirasawanum* 'Aureum'.

A. leucoderme (A. saccharum leucoderme). CHALKBARK MAPLE. Deciduous tree. Zones US, MS, LS, CS; 9–1. Native from North Carolina south to Florida and west to Texas and Oklahoma. Multitrunked tree to 30 ft. tall and almost as wide, with brilliant yellow, orange, and red fall color. Quite similar to *A. barbatum,* but grows faster; prefers drier, upland sites; and tolerates limy soils. Its leaves are green on the underside, while those of *A. barbatum* are gray green beneath.

A. macrophyllum. BIGLEAF MAPLE. Deciduous tree. Zones US, MS; 8–2. Native to stream banks and moist canyons, southern Alaska to foothills of California. Dense shade tree 30–75 ft. tall, 30–50 ft. wide—too big for a small garden or a street tree. Three- to five-lobed leaves are 6–15 in. wide, sometimes bigger on young, vigorous sapling growth; leaves turn from medium green to yellow in fall. Small, greenish yellow

Acer macrophyllum

spring flowers are followed by tawny winged seeds hanging in long, chain-like clusters.

A. negundo. BOX ELDER. Deciduous tree. Zones US, MS, LS, CS; 9–1. Native to most of U.S. The plain species is a weed tree of many faults—it seeds readily, hosts box elder bugs, suckers badly, and is subject to breakage. Fast growing to 60 ft. (usually less) and as wide or wider. Leaves divided into three to nine oval, 2- to 5-in.-long leaflets with toothed margins; yellow in fall. Several selections improve on the species.

'Flamingo'. White and pink leaf markings. Does require some shade in warmer areas.

'Sensation'. Zones US, MS. Slower growth (to 30 ft. tall, 25 ft. wide) and better branch structure than the species. Doesn't sucker. Good deep pink fall color.

'Variegatum'. VARIEGATED BOX ELDER. Zones US, MS. Not as large or weedy as the species. Leaf color—a combination of green and creamy white—makes this selection a standout. Prune out growth that reverts to green. Large, pendent clusters of white fruit are spectacular.

A. nigrum. BLACK MAPLE. Deciduous tree. Zones US, MS, LS; 8–1. Native to eastern North America. Similar to *A. saccharum* but more resistant to heat and drought. Light green leaves turn yellow in fall. 'Green-column' can reach 65 ft. tall, 25 ft. wide.

A. palmatum. JAPANESE MAPLE. Deciduous shrub or tree. Zones US, MS, LS, CS; 9–2. Native to Japan and Korea. Slow growing to 20 ft., with equal or greater spread; normally many stemmed. Airiest and most delicate of all maples. Leaves 2–4 in. long, deeply cut into five to nine toothed lobes. All-year interest—young spring growth is glowing red; summer's leaves are soft green; fall foliage is scarlet, orange, or yellow. In winter, slender leafless branches in greens and reds provide interest. Japanese maples tend to grow in flat, horizontal planes, so pruning to accentuate this growth habit is easy. Plants fare best in filtered shade, though full sun can be satisfactory in Upper and Middle South.

Grafted garden forms are popular, but common seedlings have uncommon grace and usefulness. They are more rugged, faster growing, and more drought tolerant than named forms; they also tolerate more sun and wind. Grafted forms are usually smaller, more weeping and spreading in form, brighter in foliage color, and more finely cut in leaf. The following list includes the best known of the numerous selections available.

'Atropurpureum'. RED JAPANESE MAPLE. Purplish or bronze to bronzy green leaves, brighter in sun. Color tends to fade in summer heat.

'Bloodgood'. Vigorous, upright growth to 15 ft. Foliage is deep red in spring and summer, scarlet in fall. Blackish red bark. Holds red color in summer.

'Bonfire'. Orange-pink spring and fall foliage; twisted trunk, short branches, drooping branchlets.

'Burgundy Lace'. Has purplish leaves that are more deeply cut than those of 'Atropurpureum'; bright green branchlets. Leaves turn a bronzy green in summer.

'Butterfly'. Small (to 7-ft.) shrub with small bluish green leaves edged in white. Cut out growth that reverts to plain green. Needs some shade.

'Crimson Queen'. Shrubby, 9-ft. mound. Finely cut reddish leaves turn bronze in summer, then scarlet in fall.

'Dissectum' ('Dissectum Viridis'). LACELEAF JAPANESE MAPLE. Small grower to 6 ft. high, 12 ft. wide, with drooping branches, green bark. Pale green, finely divided leaves turn gold in autumn.

'Ever Red' ('Dissectum Atropurpureum'). A 7-ft. mound with weeping branches. Finely divided, purple-tinged, lacy foliage turns bronzy green in summer, crimson in fall.

'Filiferum Purpureum'. Mounding shrub to 10 ft., with threadlike leaf segments opening dark red and aging to bronzy green.

'Garnet'. Similar to 'Crimson Queen' and 'Ever Red'; somewhat more vigorous grower.

'Hogyoku'. Upright growth to 15 ft. Sturdy and easy to grow in most situations. Green leaves turn a deep yellow-orange pumpkin color in fall.

'Ornatum' ('Dissectum Atropurpureum'). RED LACELEAF JAPANESE MAPLE. Like 'Dissectum' but with red leaves turning brighter red in fall.

'Osakazuki'. Large leaves (to 5 in. wide) turn from a rich green in summer to brilliant crimson in fall. Often considered the Japanese maple with the best fall color. Grows upright, becomes wider with age; eventually makes a 20- to 25-ft. round-topped tree. Sun, heat, and drought tolerant.

'Oshio Beni'. Like 'Atropurpureum' but more vigorous; has long, arching branches.

'Sango Kaku' ('Senkaki'). CORAL BARK MAPLE. Vigorous, upright growth to 20 ft. Yellow fall foliage. Twigs, branches are a striking coral red in winter.

'Tamukeyama'. Leaves open deep crimson red in spring and turn quickly to dark purple red; color holds well through summer, even in high heat and humidity. Scarlet fall color. Leaves less lacy than those of 'Crimson Queen', branches more cascading.

'Waterfall'. Very similar to 'Dissectum'. Branches cascade. Leaves deeply divided, fernlike, flowing and elegant. Brilliant yellow and gold fall color. Takes full sun quite well.

A. platanoides. NORWAY MAPLE. Deciduous tree. Zones US, MS; 7–1. Native to Europe, western Asia. Broad-crowned, densely foliaged tree to 50–60 ft. tall, from two-thirds as wide to equally as wide as high. Leaves five lobed, 3–5 in. wide, deep green above, paler beneath; turn yellow in fall. Showy clusters of small, greenish yellow flowers in early spring. Very adaptable, tolerating many soil and environmental conditions. Seldom browsed by deer. Once a widely recommended street tree but now less popular because of voracious roots, self-sown seedlings, and aphid-caused honeydew drip and sooty mold. Here are some of the better selections (purple-leafed forms perform poorly in alkaline soils unless soil is conditioned).

'Cavalier'. Compact, round headed, to 30 ft.

'Cleveland' and 'Cleveland II'. Shapely, compact, well-formed trees about 50 ft. tall, 40 ft. wide. Excellent golden yellow fall color.

'Columnare'. Slower growing, narrower form than the species (about 20 ft. wide).

'Crimson King'. Maroon-purple foliage from spring through fall. Slower growing than the species.

'Deborah'. Like 'Schwedler' but faster growing, straighter.

'Drummondii'. Leaves are edged with silvery white; unusual and striking. Prefers afternoon shade.

'Faassen's Black'. Pyramidal in shape, with dark purple leaves. Grows 40–50 ft. tall and wide.

'Globosum'. Slow growing with dense, round crown; eventually reaches 15–20 ft. high.

'Green Lace'. Finely cut, dark green leaves; moderate growth rate to 40 ft.

'Jade Glen'. Vigorous, straight-growing form with bright yellow fall color. Grows 40–50 ft. tall and wide.

'Parkway'. A broader tree than 'Columnare' (about 25 ft. wide), with a dense canopy.

'Royal Red'. A good red- or purple-leafed form. Similar to selection 'Crimson King'.

'Schwedler' ('Schwedleri'). Purplish red leaves in spring turn to dark bronzy green by summer, gold in autumn.

'Summershade'. Fast-growing, upright, heat-resistant selection. Poor fall color.

A. pseudoplatanus. SYCAMORE MAPLE. Deciduous tree. Zones US; 7–1. Native to Europe, western Asia. Moderate growth to 40 ft. or taller, and two-thirds as wide to equally as wide as tall. Leaves 3–5 in. wide, five lobed, thick, prominently veined, dark green above, pale below. No particular fall color. 'Atropurpureum' ('Spaethii') has leaves that are rich purple underneath.

A. rubrum. RED MAPLE, SWAMP MAPLE. Deciduous tree. Zones US, MS, LS, CS; 10–1. Native to low, wet areas in eastern North America. Fairly fast growth to 60 ft. or taller and 40 ft. or wider. Faster growing than *A. platanoides* or *A. saccharum*. Red twigs, branchlets, and buds; quite showy flowers in late winter. Dull red seeds. Leaves 2–4 in. long, with three to five lobes, shiny green above, pale beneath; brilliant scarlet fall color

Acer rubrum

in frosty areas. Often among the first trees to color up in fall. Tolerates most soils. Not at its best in urban areas. Selected forms include the following.

'Autumn Flame'. Rounded form, 60 ft., excellent early red fall color.

'Autumn Radiance'. Broad oval form, 50 ft., orange-red fall color.

'Bowhall'. Narrow (15 ft. wide), cone shaped, with orange-red color in fall.

'Brandywine.' Seedless male clone. Hybrid of 'October Glory' and 'Autumn Flame'. Moderately columnar; grows about half as wide as tall. Bright red color holds for at least 2 weeks in fall.

'Columnare'. Broadly columnar; 70 ft. tall, 20 ft. wide.

'October Glory'. Round-headed tree; last to turn color in fall. Good scarlet fall color even in the Lower South. Reaches 50–60 ft.

'Red Sunset'. Upright, vigorous, fast growing to 50–60 ft. Early orange-red fall color.

'Scarlet Sentinel'. Hybrid between *A. rubrum* and *A. saccharinum*. Broadly columnar, fast-growing form; 50 ft. tall and half as wide. Yellow-orange fall color.

WHAT JAPANESE MAPLES NEED

LIGHT: Dappled sun is best. Too much shade may lessen intensity of fall color or turn red-leafed selections green.

EXPOSURE: Protect plants from strong winds and hot afternoon sun. Do not plant near pavement.

SOIL: Make sure it is moist, fertile, and well drained.

WATER: These shallow-rooted plants are susceptible to drought. Water during dry spells to prevent wilting and leaf scorch.

PRUNING: Require very little pruning; do it in summer or early winter.

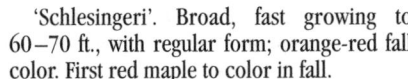

Acer palmatum 'Sango Kaku'

'Schlesingeri'. Broad, fast growing to 60–70 ft., with regular form; orange-red fall color. First red maple to color in fall.

'Shade King'. Very fast grower to 50 ft. tall, 40 ft. wide. Pale green foliage turns bright red in fall.

'Tilford'. Nearly globe-shaped crown if grown in the open; pyramidal when crowded. To 40 ft. Fall color varies from yellow to red.

A. saccharinum. SILVER MAPLE. Deciduous tree. Zones US, MS, LS, CS; 9–1. Native of eastern North America. Grows rapidly to 40–100 ft. with equal spread. Open form, with semipendulous branches; casts fairly open shade. Silvery gray bark peels in long strips on old trees. Leaves 3–6 in. wide, five lobed, light green above, silvery beneath. Fall color is usually a poor yellow green. Aggressive roots are hard on sidewalks, sewers.

You pay a penalty for the advantage of fast growth: weak wood and narrow crotch angles make this tree break easily. Unusually susceptible to aphids and cottony scale. Suffers from chlorosis in alkaline soils. Many rate it the least desirable of maples, but nonetheless it is often planted for fast growth and graceful habit. Seldom browsed by deer.

'Silver Queen'. More upright form than the species, seedless. Bright gold fall color.

'Wieri' ('Laciniatum'). WIER MAPLE, CUTLEAF SILVER MAPLE. Similar to species, but leaves are much more finely cut; provides open shade.

A. saccharum. SUGAR MAPLE. Deciduous tree. Zones US, MS, LS; 8–1. Native to eastern North America. The source of maple sugar in the Northeast, this tree is renowned for spectacular fall color in the Upper South. Moderate growth to 60 ft. or more, with stout branches and upright oval to rounded canopy to about 40 ft. wide. Leaves 3–6 in. wide, with three to five lobes, green above, pale below. Brilliant autumn foliage ranges from yellow and orange to deep red and scarlet. Intolerant of road salt; also not suited to humid heat of the Lower South (though some selections succeed there).

Smaller than the species is *A. s. grandidentatum* (*A. grandidentatum*), big-tooth maple, which grows as a shrub or 20- to 30-ft. tree. Three- to five-lobed leaves with large, blunt teeth turn brilliant yellow, orange, or rose red in fall. In nature, this species grows in canyons and on stream banks; in gardens, it requires well-drained soil on the dry side. Good choice for the Southwest.

Other selections are closer to the species in stature; commonly available choices include the following.

'Arrowhead'. Erect pyramid to 60 ft. tall and 30 ft. wide, with yellow to orange leaves in fall.

'Bonfire'. Spreading tree to 50 ft. tall, 40 ft. wide. Poor fall color.

'Caddo'. CADDO MAPLE. Not a single selection, but a distinct group of heat- and drought-tolerant sugar maples native to Oklahoma. To 50 ft. More tolerant of alkaline soils than eastern maples. Yellow and orange fall color. Good for the Southwest.

'Commemoration'. Heavy leaf texture; yellow, orange, and red fall color. Faster growing than the species; tolerates heat and drought.

'Green Mountain'. Tolerant of heat and drought; autumn leaves are yellow to orange to reddish orange. To 70 ft. Fall color better in Upper South.

'Legacy'. Fast growing, drought tolerant, multihued in fall; best selection for the Lower South. To 50 ft.

'Monumentale' ('Temple's Upright'). Narrow, erect form to 60 ft. tall, 15 ft. wide. Yellow-orange fall leaves.

'Seneca Chief'. Narrow form, orange to yellow fall color. To 20 ft. wide.

A. shirasawanum 'Aureum' (*A. japonicum* 'Aureum'). GOLDEN FULLMOON MAPLE. Deciduous shrub or tree. Zones US; 7–3. Japanese native; grows to 20 ft. tall and wide. Leaves open pale gold in spring and remain pale chartreuse all summer. Partial shade.

A. tataricum. TATARIAN MAPLE. Deciduous shrub or tree. Zones US, MS; 7–1. Native to southeastern Europe, western Asia. Reaches 20–25 ft. high and wide. Tooth-edged leaves (lobed on young plants) are 2–3½ in. long. Showy red-winged seeds appear in summer. Yellow to reddish brown fall color. Leaves of 'Rubrum' turn deep red in fall.

A. t. ginnala. AMUR MAPLE. Zones US, MS, LS; 8–1. Native to Manchuria, northern China, Japan. Toothed leaves are three lobed, even on mature plants. Clusters of small, fragrant, yellowish flowers bloom in early spring; these are followed by handsome winged seeds in bright red. Striking red fall color. 'Flame', 15–20 ft. high and wide, has especially fiery foliage in autumn.

A. truncatum. PURPLEBLOW MAPLE. Deciduous tree. Zones US, MS, LS; 8–1. Native to China. Grows fairly rapidly to 25 ft., with equal or slightly smaller spread. Like a small *A. platanoides* with more deeply lobed leaves to 4 in. wide. Leaves emerge purplish red, mature to green by summer, and turn yellow to orange-toned in fall. Good lawn or patio tree.

Aceraceae. The maple family consists of deciduous, rarely evergreen, trees and shrubs with paired opposite leaves and paired, winged seeds.

ACHILLEA

YARROW

Asteraceae (Compositae)

PERENNIALS

🗡 US, MS, LS

☼ FULL SUN

◐ ◑ LITTLE TO MODERATE WATER

Achillea tomentosa

Mainstays of the summer perennial border, yarrows offer showy blooms and finely cut, aromatic foliage. Their flat-topped flower clusters are excellent for drying. Though often considered carefree, they do require excellent drainage, especially in high-rainfall, high-humidity areas; planting in heavy clay usually results in rot. Once established, they thrive in drought and heat. Seldom browsed by deer. Cut back plants after they finish blooming. Divide and replant clumps every 3 years in late winter.

A. ageratifolia (*A. serbica*). GREEK YARROW. Heat zones 9–1. Native to Balkan region. Low, foot-wide mats of silvery leaves, toothed or nearly smooth edged. White, ½- to 1-in.-wide flower clusters are carried on stems 4–10 in. tall.

A. clavennae. SILVERY YARROW. Heat zones 8–1. Native to Europe. Silvery gray, silky leaves, lobed somewhat like chrysanthemum leaves, form mats about 8 in. wide. Loose, flat-topped clusters of ½- to ¾-in.-wide, ivory white flower heads on 5- to 10-in. stems. Often sold as *A. argentea.*

A. filipendulina. FERNLEAF YARROW. Heat zones 9–1. From the Caucasus. Tall, erect plants 4–5 ft. high and to 3 ft. wide, with deep green, fernlike leaves. Bright yellow flower heads in large, flat-topped clusters. Dried or fresh, they are good for flower arrangements. Several selections are available. 'Gold Plate' has flower clusters up to 6 in. wide; hybrid 'Coronation Gold', to about 3 ft. high, also has large flower clusters.

A. millefolium. COMMON YARROW, MILFOIL. Heat zones 9–1. Native to Europe, western Asia. Erect plant with narrow green or grayish green leaves and flat-topped white flower clusters on 3-ft. stems. Spreads by underground runners. Many selections are available. 'The Beacon' ('Fanal') and 'Rosea' are bright rose pink; 'Cerise Queen' is deeper pink, 'Lavender Beauty' lavender pink, 'Weser River' rose pink fading to tan, and 'Salmon Beauty' ('Lachsschönheit') salmon pink. 'Hoffnung' is pale yellow; 'Fire King', 'Fireland', and 'Paprika' all are red (with yellow center) aging to coppery red.

Seed-grown garden strains include Summer Pastels and Debutante, with flowers ranging from white and cream to yellow and red, and Galaxy, with deeper colors. Summer Shades has both pastel and deeper colors.

A. 'Moonshine'. Heat zones 8–1. Resembles *A. × taygetea*, but grows somewhat taller (to 2 ft. high) and bears deeper yellow flowers.

A. ptarmica. Heat zones 8–1. From Europe, Asia. Erect plant to 2 ft. high and wide. Narrow leaves with finely toothed edges. White flower heads in rather open, flattish clusters. 'The Pearl' has double flowers.

A. ×taygetea. Heat zones 8–1. Native to the eastern Mediterranean. Grows to 1½ ft. high and wide. Gray-green, divided leaves 3–4 in. long. Dense clusters of flower heads open bright yellow, then fade to soft primrose yellow—excellent contrast in yellow shades until it's time to shear off old stalks. Good cut flowers.

A. tomentosa. WOOLLY YARROW. Heat zones 8–1. From Europe, western Asia. Makes a flat, spreading mat (to about 1½ ft. wide) of fernlike, gray-green, hairy leaves. Golden flower heads in flat clusters top 6- to 10-in. stems. 'Primrose Beauty' has pale yellow flowers; 'King George' has cream blooms. A good edging and a neat ground cover for small areas; used in rock gardens. Shear off dead flowers to leave an attractive gray-green mat.

ACHIMENES

Gesneriaceae

PERENNIALS FROM RHIZOMES

🗡 CS, TS, EXCEPT AS NOTED; IN CONTAINERS OUTDOORS; OR HOUSEPLANTS OR IN GREENHOUSE

◐ ● PARTIAL TO FULL SHADE; BRIGHT LIGHT

● REGULAR WATER

Achimenes

Native to tropical America. Related to African violet (*Saintpaulia*) and gloxinia (*Sinningia*). Plants 1–2 ft. high, some trailing. Slender stems; roundish, crisp, bright to dark green, hairy leaves. Blooms from summer to autumn, bearing flaring, tubular, 1- to 3-in.-wide flowers in pink, orange, blue, lavender, orchid, or purple.

Sometimes grown in beds as ground cover in Coastal and Tropical South, but more commonly used in containers, either outdoors (protected from direct sun and wind) in window box, on porch or patio, under lath; or indoors (in bright light) or in greenhouse. Plant rhizomes in March or April, placing them ½–1 in. deep in moist peat moss and sand. Keep in light shade at 60°F. When plants are 3 in. high, set 6 to 12 of them in 6- to 7-in. fern pot or hanging basket, in potting mix of equal parts peat moss, perlite, and leaf mold. In fall, dig rhizomes and let dry. Store in cool, dry place over winter; repot in spring.

'Purple King' is unusually hardy and suited to Zones MS, LS, CS, TS. Can be brought back from 0°F. Grows to 6 in. tall. Flowers deep purple, 2 in. across, on trailing stems. Breaks dormancy late, not appearing until late May. Blooms intermittently throughout summer.

ACOELORRHAPHE wrightii (Paurotis wrightii)

PAUROTIS PALM, CAPE SABLE PALM

Arecaceae (Palmae)

PALM

🗡 TS ⊞ 12–10; OR HOUSEPLANT

☼ ◐ FULL SUN OR PARTIAL SHADE; BRIGHT LIGHT

● ●● REGULAR TO AMPLE WATER

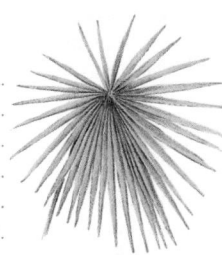

Acoelorrhaphe wrightii

Beautiful clumping fan palm; native to the Florida Everglades and West Indies. One of its common names, paurotis palm, refers to its former botanical name, *Paurotis wrightii*. Forms a cluster of slender trunks topped by tufts of fan-shaped, 2- to 3-ft.-wide fronds, green above and silvery beneath. Leafstalks are armed with sharp spines. In Florida, it reaches 30 ft. tall and 20 ft. wide, but it grows considerably smaller in South Texas, where it's somewhat difficult to establish. Hardy to 20°F. Does best in moist, fertile soil but will tolerate many types; good beach plant, as it takes sandy soil and salt spray. Manageable size and attractive shape make this plant a favorite with homeowners and garden designers.

ACONITUM

ACONITE, MONKSHOOD

Ranunculaceae

PERENNIALS

🌿 US, MS ⊢ 7–3, EXCEPT AS NOTED

☼ ◐ FULL SUN OR PARTIAL SHADE

💧 REGULAR WATER

☠ ALL PARTS ARE POISONOUS IF INGESTED

Aconitum napellus

Not easy plants to grow in most of the South, as they dislike extended summer heat, drought, and mild winters. Sow seeds in moist, fertile, well-drained soil in late summer or autumn for flowers the following year. Seedlings started in spring may take a year to bloom. Aconite combines effectively with hosta, ferns, meadow rue *(Thalictrum)*, and astilbe in lightly shaded gardens; it can also substitute for delphinium in shade. Plants are seldom browsed by deer.

A. carmichaelii (A. fischeri). Native to central China. Densely foliaged plant 2–4 ft. high, nearly as wide. Leathery dark green leaves are lobed and coarsely toothed. Blooms from late summer into fall; deep purple-blue flowers form dense, branching clusters 4–8 in. long. 'Wilsonii' grows 6–8 ft. high and 1–2 ft. wide, has more open flower clusters 10–18 in. long.

A. napellus. GARDEN MONKSHOOD. Native to Europe. Upright, leafy plants 2–5 ft. high, up to 1 ft. wide. Leaves 2–5 in. wide, divided into narrow lobes. Spikelike clusters of typically blue or violet flowers in late summer.

A. selections and hybrids. The following grow to about 3½ ft. tall, 1 ft. wide. Leaves are deeply cut.

'Bressingham Spire'. Upright plant with deep violet blossom spikes from midsummer to early fall. Glossy dark green leaves.

'Eleonara'. White flowers edged in bluish purple; early summer bloom. Glossy deep green leaves.

'Stainless Steel'. Heat zones 7–5. Steel blue flowers in loosely branched spikes bloom in midsummer. Dark grayish green leaves.

ACORUS

SWEET FLAG

Araceae

PERENNIALS

🌿 US, MS, LS, CS

◐ LIGHT SHADE

💧 AMPLE WATER

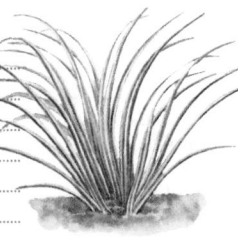

Acorus gramineus
'Variegatus'

Sweet flags look like small ornamental grasses, but they're actually related to calla *(Zantedeschia)*. Grown for highly attractive foliage. Use in damp borders, at pond edges, or in shallow water. Propagate by dividing clumps in spring or fall.

A. calamus. SWEET FLAG. Heat zones 12–3. Native to the Northern Hemisphere. Sword-shaped leaves resembling those of bearded iris are 1½ in. wide, 4–5 ft. long, growing in a clump about 2 ft. wide. Foliage is fragrant when bruised, as are the thick rhizomes. 'Variegatus' has very showy white-edged leaves. Dies to the ground in winter.

A. gramineus. JAPANESE SWEET FLAG. Heat zones 12–2. Native to Japan, China. A trouble-free plant that prefers moist, fertile soil, either boggy or well drained. Fans of narrow, 6- to 12-in.-long semievergreen leaves rise from the ends of slowly creeping rhizomes; the plant eventually forms a rounded clump. Excellent for massing, combining with coarser-leafed plants, or growing in containers. 'Ogon' is especially showy, with arching golden yellow leaves to 10 in. long; it looks great beside dark green, burgundy, or purplish foliage. 'Variegatus' has white-striped green leaves; leaves of 'Licorice' are 1½ ft. long, with fragrance and flavor of licorice. Dwarf 'Pusillus', just 3–5 in. high, spreads very slowly and is useful between stepping-stones or tucked into niches in a rock garden.

ACTAEA

BANEBERRY

Ranunculaceae

PERENNIALS

🌿 US ⊢ 7–1

◐ ● PARTIAL TO FULL SHADE

💧 REGULAR WATER

☠ ALL PARTS ARE POISONOUS IF INGESTED

Actaea rubra

Very desirable woodland plants native to the eastern U.S. and grown chiefly for their showy berries. To 2½ ft. tall and not quite as wide, with gracefully divided leaves somewhat like those of astilbe or goat's beard *(Aruncus)*. Small white springtime blossoms give rise to clusters of ornamental (but highly toxic) fruit. To thrive, these plants need moist, rich, acid, well-drained, woodsy soil and coolness around their roots. In the South, they do best in the mountainous regions of West Virginia, Virginia, North Carolina, and Tennessee.

A. alba (A. pachypoda). WHITE BANEBERRY, DOLL'S EYES. Plant produces showy ¼-in. berries that are white with a dark spot at the tip; berry stalks are swollen and red.

A. rubra. RED BANEBERRY. Similar to *A. alba*, but berries are scarlet, somewhat larger, and borne on slender stems.

ACTINIDIA kolomikta

Actinidiaceae

DECIDUOUS VINE

🌿 US, MS, LS ⊢ 12–1

☼ ◐ FULL SUN OR PARTIAL SHADE

💧 💧 MODERATE TO REGULAR WATER

Actinidia kolomikta

Most kiwi vines are valued for delicious fruit, but this eastern Asian species is grown for its flamboyant foliage. Grows rapidly to 15 ft. or more, producing a marvelous mass of 3- to 5-in.-long leaves with elongated heart shape: some in solid green, others white-splashed green, others green variegated in pink to red. Female selections produce small fruits, but males (which are nonfruiting) typically have better leaf color. Color is best in cool weather and—in warmer regions—in partial shade. Small, fragrant white flowers appear in early summer. Plants climb by twining; provide sturdy support and train new stems into place. Thin growth in late dormant season.

For information on growing kiwi vines for their fruit, see Kiwi.

ADENIUM obesum

Apocynaceae

SUCCULENT SHRUB

🌿 TS ⊢ 12–10; OR HOUSEPLANT

☼ FULL SUN; BRIGHT INDIRECT LIGHT

💧 REGULAR WATER

☠ MILKY SAP IS POISONOUS IF INGESTED

Adenium obesum

Called desert rose or desert azalea in its native tropical eastern Africa, this odd-looking plant has twisted trunks that emerge from a bulbous, swollen rootstock resembling a giant onion. Leafless for long stretches during dry periods, it redeems itself periodically throughout the growing season with gray-green, 4-in.-long leaves and clusters of deep pink, saucer-shaped, 2-in. flowers.

Desert rose will grow outdoors in south Florida and the southernmost parts of Texas, sometimes reaching 9 ft. tall—but it remains primarily a collector's plant, typically topping out at about 5 ft. tall and 3 ft. wide. Because it won't tolerate frost or take less-than-perfect drainage, it's best grown in a pot and moved to a bright, heated room for the winter.

ADENOPHORA

LADY BELLS

Campanulaceae (Lobeliaceae)

PERENNIALS

US, MS

FULL SUN OR PARTIAL SHADE

MODERATE TO REGULAR WATER

Adenophora liliifolia

These showy perennials bear fragrant, bell-shaped flowers on their upper stems. Uncommon in the South and difficult to find at nurseries, they prefer moist, fertile, well-drained soil. Once established, they resent being moved.

A. bulleyana. Heat zones 8–1. From western China. Grows to 3 ft. tall, 1 ft. wide. Pale blue bells in autumn.

A. confusa. Heat zones 7–1. From western China. To 3 ft. tall, 2 ft. wide. Dark blue flowers in summer.

A. liliifolia. Heat zones 7–1. Native from central Europe to Siberia. To 1½ ft. high, 1 ft. wide. Pale blue or white flowers in midsummer.

ADIANTUM

MAIDENHAIR FERN

Polypodiaceae

FERNS

ZONES VARY BY SPECIES

PARTIAL TO FULL SHADE

AMPLE WATER

Adiantum pedatum

It would be hard to imagine daintier, more graceful ferns than the maidenhairs. Most hail from the tropics, but some originate in North America. Dark, thin, wiry stems hold delicate, finely cut fronds. In most types, the individual leaflets are bright green and fan shaped.

Maidenhairs typically need rich organic soil, steady moisture, and shade. Tender species are useful as houseplants; provide bright filtered or indirect light and apply a general-purpose liquid houseplant fertilizer diluted to half strength once a month in spring and summer.

A. capillus-veneris. SOUTHERN MAIDENHAIR. Zones LS, CS, TS; 12–8. Native to North America. To 1½ ft. tall and 16 in. wide; fronds twice divided but not forked. Easy to grow. Best in slightly alkaline soil.

A. hispidulum. ROSY MAIDENHAIR. Zones TS; 12–1. Native to tropics of Asia, Africa. To 1 ft. tall and wide. Young fronds rosy brown, turning medium green, shaped somewhat like those of *A. pedatum*. Good indoor or greenhouse plant.

A. pedatum. AMERICAN MAIDENHAIR FERN, NORTHERN MAIDENHAIR. Zones US, MS; 8–1. Native to North America. Fronds fork to make a fingerlike pattern atop slender, 1- to 2½-ft. stems; clumps grow about as wide as high. General effect is airy and fresh. Excellent in containers or shaded beds.

A. peruvianum. SILVER DOLLAR MAIDENHAIR. Zones CS, TS; 12–1. Native to Peru. To 1½ ft. or more tall and about as wide. Leaflets quite large, to 2 in. wide. Good choice for indoors or in greenhouse.

A. raddianum (A. cuneatum, A. decorum). Zones TS; 12–10. Native to Brazil. Fronds cut three or four times, 15–18 in. long. There are many named types, differing in texture and compactness. Grow in pots; move outdoors to a sheltered, shaded patio in summer. Selections commonly sold are 'Fritz-Luthii', 'Gracillimum' (most finely cut), and 'Pacific Maid'. Good indoors or in greenhouse.

A. tenerum. Zones TS; 12–9. Native to New World tropics. Grows about 2 ft. tall, 3 ft. wide. Long, broad fronds arch gracefully, are finely divided into many deeply cut segments ½–¾ in. wide. 'Wrightii' is similar or identical. In cooler areas, can be grown indoors or in greenhouse.

A. venustum. HIMALAYAN MAIDENHAIR. Zones CS, TS; 8–3. Chinese native to 8 in. high. Young fronds are bright bronzy pink, maturing to medium green. Grows slowly but forms a 3-ft.-wide clump in 5 to 10 years.

ADINA rubella

Rubiaceae

DECIDUOUS SHRUB

US, MS, LS, CS

FULL SUN OR PARTIAL SHADE

MODERATE TO REGULAR WATER

Adina rubella

This Chinese native looks much like our native buttonbush *(Cephalanthus)*, but it's showier. Fragrant pink flowers that look like little pincushions appear atop the plant from late spring to late summer. The glossy, bronzy green leaves, similar to those of abelia, persist into late fall. Grows 6–10 ft. tall and wide and needs fertile, well-drained soil. No serious pests or diseases.

AECHMEA

Bromeliaceae

PERENNIALS

TS 12–10; OR HOUSEPLANTS

PARTIAL SHADE; BRIGHT LIGHT

UNIQUE WATER NEEDS AND METHODS

Aechmea fasciata

Most Southerners grow these exotic bromeliads as houseplants, but they can also be grown outdoors in light shade in pots, hanging baskets, or even the ground. Just be ready to bring them indoors before a frost. Indoors or out, they require moist, fast-draining soil. Contrary to popular belief, it's not a good idea to keep the central cup of plants grown indoors filled with water; this often causes rot. Instead, water the soil around the plant. Let the soil surface go dry to the touch between waterings; mist the foliage of indoor plants frequently. Soft leaf tips indicate overwatering; hard tips indicate underwatering.

A. chantinii. Upright or urnlike rosettes of 1- to 3-ft.-long leaves in green to gray green or olive green are banded with silver or darker green. Tall flower clusters have orange, pink, or red bracts, yellow-and-red flowers. Fruit is white or blue.

A. fasciata. Funnel-shaped rosette of handsome gray-green leaves cross-banded with silvery white. From the center grows a cluster of rosy pink flower bracts enclosing pale blue flowers that change to deep rose. The selection 'Silver King' has unusually silvery leaves; 'Marginata' has leaves edged with creamy white bands.

A. fulgens. Green leaves dusted with gray, 12–16 in. long, 2–3 in. wide. Flower cluster usually above the leaves; red, blue, or blue-violet blossoms. *A. f. discolor* has brownish red or violet-red leaves, usually faintly striped.

A. hybrids. The following are among the most commonly grown hybrid bromeliads.

'Foster's Favorite'. Bright wine red, lacquered-looking leaves about 1 ft. long grow in a fountainlike rosette. Drooping, spikelike flower clusters are coral red and blue.

'Royal Wine'. Forms open rosette of somewhat leathery, glossy light green leaves that are burgundy red beneath. Drooping clusters of orange-and-blue flowers.

A. pectinata. Stiff rosettes up to 3 ft. wide; leaves to 3 in. wide, strongly marked pink or red at bloom time. Flowers are whitish and green.

A. weilbachii. Shiny leaves to 2 ft. long, green or suffused with red tones, in rosettes 2–3 ft. wide. Dull red, 1½-ft. flower stalk has orange-red berries tipped with lilac.

FOR INFORMATION ON SELECTING PLANTS

PLEASE SEE PAGES 39–144

AEGOPODIUM podagraria

BISHOP'S WEED, GOUT WEED

Apiaceae (Umbelliferae)

PERENNIAL

US, MS, LS ┣ 9–1

SUN OR SHADE

MODERATE WATER

Aegopodium podagraria
'Variegatum'

Keep an eye on this one. Native to Europe and western Asia, it's a rampant ground cover that has established a beachhead in much of the South. It spreads indefinitely by creeping roots and is especially aggressive in rich soil. Confine it behind a concrete, stone, or metal barrier set 8–12 in. deep into the soil. Light green leaves, each with three leaflets, form a dense mass to 6 in. high; flat-topped clusters of white flowers rise above the foliage in summer. Mowing two or three times a year keeps the planting neat. Remove faded flowers promptly to prevent unwanted seedlings. Clumps of bishop's weed are easy to dig and divide, making it a popular passalong plant.

'Variegatum' is the selection most often seen, with white-edged leaflets that create a luminous effect in shade (pull up any plants that revert to solid green).

AESCULUS

HORSECHESTNUT, BUCKEYE

Hippocastanaceae

DECIDUOUS TREES OR SHRUBS

ZONES VARY BY SPECIES

FULL SUN OR LIGHT SHADE

REGULAR WATER

SEEDS OF ALL ARE SLIGHTLY TOXIC IF INGESTED

Aesculus ×carnea

Noted for leaflets arranged like the fingers of a hand, these trees sport long, showy, typically upright clusters of flowers atop their branches in springtime. Some develop good fall color. Leathery capsules release glossy dark brown, chestnutlike seeds (buckeyes) in autumn. Prune established horsechestnuts only to remove dead, damaged, or awkward-looking branches. Summer leaf scorch is common when the plants are grown in poor, dry soil; severe cases result in defoliation.

A. 'Autumn Splendor'. Zones US, MS. Very attractive, cold-hardy hybrid. To 35–40 ft. tall and nearly as wide. Glossy dark green leaves with five (rarely seven) leaflets turn brilliant maroon in autumn and are resistant to leaf scorch. Yellow flowers, each with an orange-red blotch, are borne in clusters to 8 in. long. Best with some shade.

A. ×carnea. RED HORSECHESTNUT. Zones US, MS, LS; 8–2. Hybrid between *A. hippocastanum* and *A. pavia*. To 40 ft. high and 30 ft. wide—smaller than *A. hippocastanum*, better fit for small gardens. Round headed with large, dark green leaves, each divided into five leaflets; casts dense shade. Bears hundreds of 8-in.-long plumes of soft pink to red flowers. 'Briotii' has rosy crimson flowers; 'O'Neill Red' has bright red blooms.

A. flava (A. octandra). YELLOW BUCKEYE, SWEET BUCKEYE. Zones US, MS, LS; 8–1. Native to the American South. Most majestic of the North American native species: handsome, round-crowned tree to 90 ft. tall and 50 ft. wide, with dark green leaves divided into five to seven finely toothed, 5- to 8-in.-long leaflets. Yellow flowers form on erect panicles; less showy than those of *A. hippocastanum*. Smooth brown bark. Orange fall foliage.

A. glabra. OHIO BUCKEYE. Zones US, MS; 7–1. From the central and eastern U.S. Low-branching tree with dense, rounded form; to 40 ft. or possibly taller, to 30 ft. wide. Early to leaf out. Foliage is bright green when new, matures to dark green, turns yellow to orange in fall. Greenish yellow flowers in 4- to 7-in. clusters. Prickly seed capsules enclose shiny brown buckeyes.

A. g. arguta (A. arguta). TEXAS BUCKEYE. Zones US, MS, LS. Native to southern U.S. Attractive small tree to 15–20 ft. or taller, 12–15 ft. wide. Leaves divided into seven to nine narrow, pointed, 3- to 5-in.-long leaflets. Pale yellow flowers in late spring. Weight of fruit may bend branches in fall.

A. hippocastanum. COMMON HORSECHESTNUT. Zones US, MS; 8–1. Native to Europe. To 60 ft. tall, 40 ft. wide. Bulky and densely foliaged; gives heavy shade. Leaves divided into five to seven toothed, 4- to 10-in.-long leaflets. Spectacular flower show: ivory blooms with pink markings in 1-ft. plumes. Invasive roots can break up sidewalks. 'Baumannii' has double flowers, sets no seed.

A. parviflora. BOTTLEBRUSH BUCKEYE. Zones US, MS, LS, CS; 9–1. Native to southeastern U.S. Shrub to 12–15 ft. tall and wide, spreading by suckers, with dark green leaves divided into five to seven 3- to 8-in.-long leaflets. Very showy white flower clusters (8–12 in. tall, 2–4 in. wide). Bright yellow fall foliage. Good choice for massing, shrub borders, or specimen or understory planting. *A. p. serotina* 'Rogers' has 1½- to 2½-ft.-long flower clusters that are drooping rather than upright.

A. pavia. RED BUCKEYE. Zones US, MS, LS, CS; 9–2. Native to eastern U.S. Bulky shrub or tree grows to 12–20 ft. tall and as wide, with irregular rounded crown. Glossy deep green leaves with five to seven 3- to 6-in.-long leaflets. Bears narrow, erect 10-in. clusters of bright red or orange-red (rarely yellow) flowers. Does best in light shade. Good choice for warm, humid climates.

AFRICAN CORN LILY. See IXIA

AFRICAN DAISY. See ARCTOTIS, DIMORPHOTHECA, OSTEOSPERMUM

AFRICAN VIOLET. See SAINTPAULIA

AGAPANTHUS

LILY-OF-THE-NILE

Amaryllidaceae

PERENNIALS

ZONES VARY BY SPECIES

FULL SUN OR PARTIAL SHADE

LITTLE TO REGULAR WATER

Agapanthus orientalis

All of these South African natives form handsome, fountainlike clumps of strap-shaped leaves that are evergreen in some species and selections, deciduous in others. In summer, the clumps send up bare stems ending in spherical clusters of funnel-shaped flowers, each cluster like a burst of blue or white fireworks. Some nursery plants are labeled only as "blue" or "white"; if you want a particular shade of blue, choose plants in bloom.

Prosper in full sun or light shade. Evergreen types tend to be less hardy, and (despite their description) they may become briefly deciduous in cold weather. Best in loamy soil but will grow in heavy soils. Thrive with regular water, but established plants in the ground year-round can grow and bloom without irrigation during prolonged dry periods in most areas. Mulch for winter protection in Middle and Lower South.

For mass plantings, space plants 1–1½ ft. apart (use the tighter spacing for smaller varieties). Divide infrequently; every 6 years or so is usually sufficient. These are superb container plants. Good near pools. Seldom browsed by deer, but need protection from snails and slugs.

Names of species have been much confused over the years, largely because the plants hybridize so easily. It has even been suggested that all agapanthus are merely forms of one species.

A. africanus. Evergreen. Zones LS, CS, TS; 12–8. Shorter, narrower leaves than those of *A. orientalis;* shorter flower stalks (to 1½ ft. high) with fewer flowers (20 to 50 per cluster). Blossoms are deep blue. Often sold as *A. umbellatus.*

A. campanulatus. Deciduous. Zones US, MS, LS, CS, TS; 12–6. To 3 ft. high, with drooping dark blue flowers. 'Albus' is white flowered.

A. inapertus. Deciduous. Zones MS, LS, CS, TS; 12–7. As tall as *A. orientalis* and nearly as many-flowered, but its deep blue blossoms are in drooping clusters.

A. orientalis (A. praecox orientalis). Evergreen. Zones CS, TS; 12–7. The most commonly planted species. Broad, arching leaves in big clumps. Stems to 4–5 ft. tall bear up to 100 blue flowers. There are white ('Albus'), double ('Flore Pleno'), and light to fairly dark blue selections, as well as some with striped leaves. Often sold as *A. africanus, A. umbellatus.*

A. selections and hybrids. Zones MS, LS, CS, TS. Types sold by selection or hybrid name include the following. All are evergreen, except as noted.

'Blue Baby'. Deciduous. Pale blue blossoms on 1½-ft. stems.

'Elaine.' Large clusters of nodding bluish purple blossoms borne on 4-ft.-tall stems.

'Ellamae'. Big clusters of large dark blue flowers on stems to 5 ft. tall.

'Fragrant Glen'. Sweet-scented, many-petaled lilac-blue flowers on stems to more than 3 ft. tall. Slightly bluish foliage.

Headbourne Hybrids. Deciduous. Flowers in this group come in a range of blues and in white on 2½-ft.-tall stems above fairly narrow, rather upright foliage.

'Henryi'. Resembles 'Peter Pan' but has white flowers.

'Midknight Blue'. To 3–4 ft. tall, with deepest blue flowers.

'Mood Indigo'. Deciduous. Hybrid involving *A. inapertus,* with deep violet blooms on 3- to 4-ft. stems.

'Peter Pan'. Outstanding free-blooming dwarf selection. Foot-high foliage mass and blue flowers on 1½-ft. stems.

'Queen Anne'. Foliage clump to 1½ ft. high; blue blossoms on stems to 2 ft.

'Rancho White'. Foliage clump grows 1–1½ ft. high; broad leaves. Flower stalks 1½–2 ft. tall carry heavy clusters of white flowers. This selection is also known as 'Dwarf White' and 'Rancho'. 'Peter Pan Albus' is similar or identical.

'Snowstorm'. To 2½ ft. tall, with snow white flowers.

'Storm Cloud'. Deciduous in cooler part of range. Developed from deciduous 'Mood Indigo' and an evergreen agapanthus; has deep blue-violet blossoms on 4-ft. stems.

'Streamline'. Dwarf form to just 1½ ft. high, with grassy leaves and grayish blue blooms.

'Tinkerbell'. Grows to 2 ft. tall, with light blue flowers and white-striped leaves.

AGARISTA populifolia (Leucothoe populifolia)

FLORIDA LEUCOTHOE

Ericaceae

EVERGREEN SHRUB

✺ MS, LS, CS ⵎ 9–7

☼ ● PARTIAL TO FULL SHADE

◐ ◕ REGULAR TO AMPLE WATER

Agarista populifolia

Attractive arching evergreen shrub native to South Carolina and south to Florida. Grows to 8–12 ft. tall and wide. Oval leaves to 4 in. long are glossy rich green. Cream-colored flowers, borne in early summer, are fragrant but not showy. This plant has an open, multistemmed form that makes it an excellent addition to the woodland garden; it likes shade and moist, acid soil. Good companion for azaleas, rhododendrons, mountain laurel *(Kalmia),* and ferns. Prune out old branches periodically to retain the handsome open habit.

FOR GROWING SYMBOL EXPLANATIONS
PLEASE SEE PAGE 145

AGASTACHE

Lamiaceae (Labiatae)

PERENNIALS

✺ ZONES VARY BY SPECIES

☼ ◗ FULL SUN OR PARTIAL SHADE

◔ MODERATE WATER

Agastache foeniculum

Summer-blooming perennials with aromatic foliage and whorls of pink, purple, blue, red, or orange flowers in spikelike clusters. All rebloom if deadheaded. Favorites with hummingbirds and butterflies. Species from Mexico and the Southwest need excellent drainage, especially in wet-winter areas.

A. aurantiaca. ORANGE HUMMINGBIRD MINT. Zones MS, LS, CS, TS; 12–7. Native to northern Mexico. To 2½ ft. tall, 2 ft. wide; pink flowers fade to orange. Can be grown as an annual. 'Apricot Sprite' grows 1½ ft. tall.

A. barberi. Zones US, MS, LS, CS, TS; 11–6. From Arizona, New Mexico. To 2 ft. tall and wide, with reddish purple flowers.

A. breviflora. Zones US, MS, LS; 12–1. From Arizona, New Mexico, northern Mexico. To 2 ft. tall, 1½ ft. across; purplish red blossoms.

A. cana. TEXAS HUMMINGBIRD MINT. Zones US, MS, LS, CS, TS; 12–1. Native to Texas, New Mexico. To 2–3 ft. tall, 1½ ft. across. Blooms heavily, bearing reddish pink flowers that smell like bubble gum. A seed-grown selection, 'Heather Queen', blooms the first year if sown early.

A. foeniculum. ANISE HYSSOP. Zones US, MS, LS, CS; 9–6. From north-central North America. Erect, narrow plant to 3 ft. tall and 2 ft. wide, with dense clusters of lilac-blue flowers. Its anise- or licorice-scented leaves make a pleasant tea. Useful and attractive in perennial borders and herb gardens. More tolerant of winter cold and wet than other species.

A. hybrids. Zones US, MS, LS, CS. The following are among the many fine hybrids sold.

'Apricot Sunrise'. To 2½ ft. tall, 2 ft. wide. Deep orange flowers fade to apricot on opening.

'Blue Fortune'. To 3 ft. tall, 1½ ft. wide, with powder blue flower spikes.

'Firebird'. To 1½–2 ft. tall, 1½ ft. wide; coppery orange-red blooms.

'Summer Breeze'. To 3 ft. tall, 2 ft. wide. Large lavender-pink flowers; dark gray-green leaves.

'Tangerine Dreams'. Forms a compact, 1½- to 2-ft.-wide clump; orange flowers, larger and deeper in color than those of 'Apricot Sunrise', are carried atop many 2- to 3-ft. stems.

'Tutti Frutti'. To 3–4 ft. tall, 1–2 ft. wide, with purplish red blooms set off nicely by gray-green foliage.

A. mexicana. GIANT MEXICAN LEMON HYSSOP. Zones CS, TS; 12–9. Rangy Mexican native to 2–3 ft. (possibly to 5 ft.) tall and 1 ft. wide. Bears masses of pink flowers, starting in spring and continuing until late fall. Lemon-scented leaves can be used in tea and as a flavoring.

A. rugosa. KOREAN HUMMINGBIRD MINT. Zones US, MS, LS, CS; 12–5. Native to Korea. To 5 ft. tall, 2 ft. wide. Licorice-scented foliage is glossy green with a purple tinge. Flowers are purplish blue. Like *A. foeniculum,* tolerates wet winters. 'Honeybee Blue' and 'Honeybee White' are compact growers 2–2½ ft. high. The species and its selections will bloom the first year from seed sown early.

A. rupestris. LICORICE MINT, SUNSET HYSSOP. Zones US, MS, LS, CS; 9–5. From southern Arizona, northern Mexico. To 1½–2½ ft. tall and 1½ ft. wide, with threadlike gray-green leaves and spikes of orange flowers with lavender calyxes. Exceptionally fragrant foliage, with a scent that reminds some of licorice, others of root beer. Outstanding garden performance.

Agastache rupestris

Agavaceae. The agave family contains rosette-forming, sometimes treelike plants that generally come from dry regions. All bear spikelike flower clusters; leaves often contain tough fibers.

A

AGAVE

Agavaceae

SUCCULENT PERENNIALS

CS, TS ♦ 12–7, EXCEPT AS NOTED

FULL SUN OR PARTIAL SHADE, EXCEPT AS NOTED

LITTLE TO MODERATE WATER, EXCEPT AS NOTED

Agave havardiana

Superb as accents, focal points, or in combination with plants of contrasting texture, agaves command attention with their large, fleshy, straplike leaves and tall, unearthly-looking blossom spikes. Flowering is sporadic, however, and may not occur for years. The original plant dies after it blooms, leaving offshoots that make new plants.

Like all succulents, agaves tolerate drought but demand excellent drainage. They grow well in containers and are not browsed by deer. Most are tender, but some species withstand freezing weather. Wet soil in winter decreases hardiness.

A. americana. CENTURY PLANT. From Mexico. Blue-green leaves to 6 ft. long, with hooked spines along the edges and a wicked spine at the tip. Be sure you really want one before planting it; its spines and bulk make it formidable to remove. After 10 years or more, plant produces a branched, 15- to 40-ft. flower stalk bearing yellowish green flowers. There are several selections with yellow- or white-striped leaves. The subspecies *A. a. protoamericana* is hardy in the Middle and Lower South; does well in coastal gardens.

A. attenuata. CENTURY PLANT. Native to mountains of Jalisco, Mexico. Leaves 2½ ft. long, soft green or gray green, fleshy, somewhat translucent, without spines. Makes clumps to 5 ft. across; older plants develop a stout trunk to 5 ft. tall. Greenish yellow flowers are set densely on arching spikes to 12–14 ft. long. Will take poor soil but does best in rich soil with regular water. Protect from frost and hot sun. Statuesque container plant. Good plant for coastal gardens.

A. celsii. From the cloud forests of Mexico; tolerates more humidity than other agaves. Bright green leaves with small, neat teeth form a rosette to 2½ ft. high and wide. Spreads by offsets to form small colonies. Blossom stalk to 5 ft. tall bears yellowish green to purplish flowers. Provide regular summer water. Needs afternoon shade in hottest areas.

A. chrysantha (A. palmeri chrysantha). Native to Arizona. Dense rosette to 3 ft. high, 5 ft. wide. Gray-green leaves have hooked spines along the edges and a sharp spine at the tip. Golden yellow flowers are borne on short branches along upper part of a stalk that reaches 12–20 ft. tall.

A. colorata. Heat zones 12–10. From Mexico. Rosette of broad, flat, spiny-edged, bluish leaves grows slowly to 3 ft. high and wide. Each leaf is tipped with a wickedly sharp 2-in. spine; cut back these spines if you plant this species near a walkway. Reddish orange to yellow flowers on a stalk to 10 ft. tall. Takes heat and cold well.

A. filifera. Heat zones 12–10. Mexican native. Rosettes are less than 2 ft. wide; leaves are narrow, dark green, lined with white, and edged with long white threads.

A. havardiana. Zones US, MS, LS, CS, TS. Cold-hardy native of West Texas and New Mexico. Silvery gray leaves form a sturdy rosette to 3 ft. high and wide. Spines along leaf edges and at tips. Greenish yellow flowers with a reddish tinge are borne on a stalk to 12 ft. tall. Produces the occasional offset but is not really a spreader.

A. lophantha. Zones MS, LS, CS, TS. From Mexico. To 2 ft. high, 4 ft. wide; may spread by offsets to form colonies. Glossy sword-shaped leaves are dark green with a lighter green stripe (most noticeable in spring and early summer) running down the center. Leaf edges and tips are very spiny. Pale green blossoms on a 6- to 10ft.-tall stalk.

A. parryi. Two similar varieties native to Arizona—*A. p. parryi* (Zones US, MS, LS, CS, TS) and *A. p. huachucensis* (Zones MS, LS, CS, TS)—produce rosettes resembling giant artichokes 1½–2 ft. high, 2–2½ ft. wide. Both spread by offsets; both have thick blue-green leaves tipped with long spines. *A. p. parryi* is quite cold hardy, and its leaves and spines are smaller than those of *A. p. huachucensis*. When plants are about 20 years old, they

produce yellow flowers on a stalk to 15 ft. Both grow well in containers, thrive in partial shade.

A. parviflora. Heat zones 12–10. Native from southeastern Arizona into Mexico. One of the smallest agaves, producing a rosette 6 in. high, 9 in. wide; spreads by offsets. Dark green leaves with white markings; pale yellow flowers on a stalk to about 3 ft. or a little taller.

A. salmiana. From Mexico. Rosette to 3–4 ft. high and wide, spreading by offsets. Broad dark green leaves have smooth edges and spiny tips. Blossom stalk grows 15–25 ft. tall; red buds open to greenish yellow flowers. Dramatic plant for large landscapes.

A. victoriae-reginae. Mexican species, forming clumps only a foot or so across. The many stiff, thick leaves are 6 in. long, 2 in. wide, dark green with narrow white lines. Slow growing; will stand in pot or ground 20 years before flowering. Blossoms are greenish, borne on tall stalks.

AGERATINA altissima. See EUPATORIUM rugosum

AGERATUM houstonianum

FLOSS FLOWER

Asteraceae (Compositae)

ANNUAL

US, MS, LS, CS, TS ♦ 12–1

FULL SUN OR PARTIAL SHADE

REGULAR WATER

Ageratum houstonianum

Reliable favorite for summer and fall color in borders and containers. Native to Central America, West Indies. Hairy, soft green leaves are roundish, usually heart shaped at the base. Tiny, tassel-like flowers in blue, white, or pink come in dense clusters that resemble powder puffs. Most floss flowers form foot-wide clumps, but heights vary. Dwarf kinds (4–6 in. high) with blue flowers include 'Blue Blazer', 'Blue Danube' ('Blue Puffs'), 'Blue Surf', and 'Royal Delft'. Taller (9- to 12-in.) types include 'Blue Mink' and 'North Sea'. Good selections in other colors are 'Pink Powder-puffs' and white-blossomed 'Summer Snow', both 9 in. high.

Best in rich, moist soil. Easy to transplant even when in bloom. Low growers make excellent edgings or pattern plantings with other annuals of similar size. Taller types provide good cut flowers. Seldom browsed by deer.

AGLAONEMA

Araceae

PERENNIALS

TS ♦ 12–10; OR HOUSEPLANTS

PARTIAL SHADE; CAN TAKE VERY LOW LIGHT

REGULAR WATER

Aglaonema 'Silver King'

Grown for their highly ornamental foliage, these tropical plants are made for the shade. In most areas, they're grown strictly indoors, prized for their ability to flourish in low light. In fact, *A. modestum*, the most popular species, will thrive in an interior room lit only by a fluorescent light. In the Tropical South, aglaonemas can be used outdoors in shady plantings.

Potted plants need rich, well-drained soil mix. Let soil go slightly dry between waterings; in spring and summer, fertilize every other week with general-purpose houseplant fertilizer. Plants growing in dim light will require less frequent watering and feeding. Mealybugs are the most common pests.

A. commutatum. Grows to 2 ft. tall and wide. Deep green leaves to 6 in. long, 2 in. across, with pale green markings on veins. Flowers followed by inch-long clusters of yellow to red berries. *A. c. maculatum*, with many irregular gray-green stripes on leaves, is the most common.

'Pseudobracteatum', 1–2 ft. tall, has white leafstalks and deep green leaves marked with pale green and creamy yellow. 'Treubii' has narrow bluish green leaves heavily marked with silvery gray.

A. costatum. Slow-growing plant to 2½ ft. tall and wide, with leaves to 8 in. long, 4 in. wide. Leaves are bright green, with white spots and a broad white stripe along the midrib. 'Foxii' is similar or identical.

A. crispum (A. roebelenii). PAINTED DROP-TONGUE. Robust plant to 4 ft. tall and broad. Leathery leaves to 10 in. long, 5 in. wide, dark green with pale green markings. Sometimes sold as *A.* 'Pewter'.

A. modestum. CHINESE EVERGREEN. A tough-as-nails, easily grown plant, in time forming substantial clumps with several stems 2–3 ft. high. Shiny dark green leaves grow to 1½ ft. long and 5 in. wide. Often sold as *A. simplex.*

A. 'Silver King' and **'Silver Queen'.** Both grow to 2 ft. high and wide and are heavy producers of narrow dark green leaves strongly marked with silver. Leaves of 'Silver King' can reach about 1 ft. long and 4 in. wide; those of 'Silver Queen' are a little smaller.

AGROSTEMMA githago

CORN COCKLE

Caryophyllaceae

ANNUAL

☘ US, MS, LS, CS, TS **H** 9–1

☼ FULL SUN

💧 MODERATE WATER

⬥ SEEDS ARE POISONOUS IF INGESTED

Agrostemma githago

This attractive weed of roadside and grain field is a Mediterranean species that has naturalized in North America. Several selections offered are superior plants; they're 2–3 ft. tall and 1 ft. wide, wispy but sturdy. (Like the species, they will self-sow.) Blooms are 2–3 in. wide, on 6- to 12-in. stems; make good cut flowers. 'Milas' has deep purplish pink blossoms lined and spotted with deep purple and centered with a white eye; 'Purple Queen' bears deeper purple-pink blooms; 'Ocean Pearl' has white flowers with black flecks. Sow seeds in spring or early summer for summer and fall bloom (or in fall for winter-to-spring bloom in mild-winter climates). Mass at rear of border, among shrubs, or in front of fence or hedge. Self-sown seedlings tend to revert to the plain species (with dark pink flowers) over time.

AILANTHUS altissima

TREE-OF-HEAVEN

Simaroubaceae

DECIDUOUS TREE

☘ US, MS, LS **H** 8–1

☼ FULL SUN

◐ 💧 💧 LITTLE OR NO WATER TO REGULAR WATER

Ailanthus altissima

If any tree could be termed a "garbage tree," this is it. Native to China, it has spread by seed over much of the South. Because it tolerates drought, pollution, wind, and terrible soil (not to mention verbal abuse), it comes up everywhere—alleys, yards, parking lots, roadsides, even cracks in the pavement. Often seen on city streets, thriving where all other trees have failed. Grows very fast to 50 ft. tall and wide. The leaves reach 1–3 ft. long and are divided into many leaflets; they resemble sumac *(Rhus)* foliage. Male trees bear malodorous green flowers; females produce inconspicuous blooms that give rise to showy clusters of reddish winged seedpods. Branches release a sickening smell when cut or broken. Whoever named this plant "tree-of-heaven" had a dim view of the afterlife.

AIR PLANT. See KALANCHOE pinnata

AIR POTATO. See DIOSCOREA bulbifera

Aizoaceae. This family of succulent plants includes all the ice plants.

AJANIA pacifica. See CHRYSANTHEMUM pacificum

AJUGA

CARPET BUGLEWEED, AJUGA

Lamiaceae (Labiatae)

PERENNIALS

☘ US, MS, LS **H** 9–1

☼ ◐ ● SUN OR SHADE

💧 REGULAR WATER

Ajuga reptans

These low-growing ground covers and rock garden plants from Europe offer both handsome foliage and showy flowers; both leaves and blossoms come in several different colors. Bloom runs from spring through early summer. Most types spread quickly to form mats. Easy to divide at any time of year. Good drainage is essential to avoid crown rot. Plants are not browsed by deer.

A. 'Chocolate Chip'. See A. reptans 'Valfredda'

A. genevensis. Rock garden plant 5–14 in. high, 1½ ft. wide; does not spread by runners. Grayish, hairy stems and coarse-toothed leaves to 3 in. long. Blue flowers in spikes; rose and white forms are also sold.

A. pyramidalis. Erect plant 2–10 in. high, 1½–2 ft. wide; does not spread by runners. Stems have long grayish hairs, are set with many roundish, 1½- to 4-in.-long leaves. Violet-blue flowers are not obvious among the large leaves. 'Metallica Crispa' has reddish brown leaves with a metallic glint.

A. reptans. The most popular form. Spreads rapidly by runners, making a mat of dark green leaves in the basic species. Each oval to tongue-shaped leaf is 2–3 in. wide in full sun, to 4 in. wide in shade; entire foliage mass tops out at around 4 in. high. Blue flowers in 6-in. spikes. Plant 1 ft. apart in spring or early fall. Subject to root rots and fungal diseases where drainage or air circulation is poor. Mow or trim off old flower spikes.

Many selections are available, and some are sold under several names. The following are among the better choices; all have blue flowers unless otherwise noted. Selections with bronzy or metallic-looking leaves keep their color best in sun.

'Alba'. White-blooming form.

'Burgundy Lace' ('Burgundy Glow'). Reddish purple foliage variegated with white and pink.

'Catlin's Giant'. Large, bronzy green leaves; flower spikes to 8 in. tall.

'Giant Bronze'. Deep metallic bronze leaves are larger than those of the species. To 6 in. high in sun, 9 in. in shade.

'Giant Green'. Like 'Giant Bronze' but with bright green leaves.

'Jungle Bronze'. Clumps of large, rounded, wavy-edged, bronze-toned leaves; flower spikes to 8–10 in. high.

'Jungle Green'. Large-leafed form with green foliage. Less mounded than 'Jungle Bronze'.

'Multicolor'. Leaves are green blended with white and pinkish purple.

'Purpurea' ('Atropurpurea'). Bronze-tinted green leaves.

'Rosea'. Pink blossoms.

'Valfredda'. Also sold as 'Chocolate Chip'. This dwarf form grows just 2–3 in. high but spreads 2–3 ft. wide. Narrow leaves (only ½ in. wide) come in attractive shades of plum and brown. Flower spikes stand about 3 in. high.

'Variegata'. Leaves edged and splotched with creamy yellow.

FOR INFORMATION ON YOUR CLIMATE ZONES
PLEASE SEE PAGES 28–38

A

AKEBIA quinata

FIVELEAF AKEBIA

Lardizabalaceae

SEMIEVERGREEN TO DECIDUOUS VINE

US, MS, LS, CS 9–1

SUN OR SHADE

REGULAR WATER

Akebia quinata

If you're one of those impatient people who think "The Minute Waltz" is 30 seconds too long, you'll love fiveleaf akebia. Native to Japan, China, and Korea, it covers large areas with impressive speed. Leaves are 1½–3 in. long, each with five oblong leaflets that are notched at the tips. New leaves are tinged purple, then mature to bluish green. Blossoms in early spring, bearing fragrant, rosy purple to chocolate-purple flowers in hanging clusters to 5 in. long; they're mostly hidden by leaves and are not terribly showy. 'Alba' and 'Shirobana' have white flowers; those of 'Rosea' are lavender. 'Variegata' has light pink flowers and leaves splashed with creamy white. Edible fruit, only occasionally produced, resembles a thick purplish sausage 2–4 in. long.

Like wisteria, akebia climbs by twining and will climb as tall as its support. It can easily grow 20 ft. in a year, but its stems don't crush lattice or wood or metal supports the way those of wisteria do. Good for quick coverage of arbors, chain-link fences, or large walls (if given support for its stems). Can also be used to frame a doorway, though it will require pruning almost weekly to keep it in bounds. From the Lower South on down, the vine is mostly evergreen. May be deciduous in the Upper and Middle South. Should it ever grow bare at the bottom, just cut it to the ground; it will spring back up in the wink of an eye.

A. trifoliata, threeleaf akebia, is similar to *A. quinata*, but each leaf has three leaflets. It's also less vigorous and less common. 'Deep Purple' boasts blackish purple, extremely fragrant flowers.

ALABAMA AZALEA. See RHODODENDRON alabamense

ALABAMA SNOW-WREATH. See NEVIUSIA alabamensis

ALABAMA WILD GINGER. See ASARUM speciosum

ALBIZIA julibrissin

MIMOSA

Fabaceae (Leguminosae)

DECIDUOUS TREES

US, MS, LS, CS 9–6

FULL SUN OR PARTIAL SHADE

REGULAR WATER

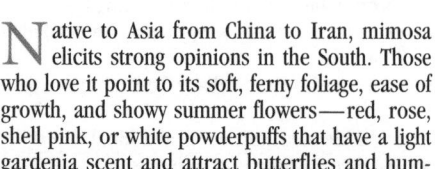

Albizia julibrissin

Native to Asia from China to Iran, mimosa elicits strong opinions in the South. Those who love it point to its soft, ferny foliage, ease of growth, and showy summer flowers—red, rose, shell pink, or white powderpuffs that have a light gardenia scent and attract butterflies and hummingbirds. What's more, these proponents would say, the plant's branching structure makes it a good climbing tree for children. Those who hate mimosa, however, emphasize its susceptibility to webworms and wilt diseases; its weak, brittle branches and invasive roots; its knack for reseeding all over creation; its terribly unattractive appearance in winter; and its relatively short life span.

Mimosa grows rapidly to 40 ft. tall with a wider spread. It tolerates drought, pollution, wind, salt spray, and alkaline soil. Most nurseries don't sell it, but seedlings are easy to find. 'Rosea' has rich pink flowers and is considered more cold hardy than the species. 'Flame' has rosy red flowers; 'California Red' boasts red blossoms.

ALCEA (Althaea)

HOLLYHOCK

Malvaceae

BIENNIALS OR SHORT-LIVED PERENNIALS

US, MS, LS, CS

PARTIAL SHADE IN HOTTEST CLIMATES

REGULAR WATER

Alcea rosea

Hollyhocks are cultivated for their big, colorful, funnel-shaped summer flowers. Need rich, well-drained soil. Attractive to butterflies, bees.

A. rosea. HOLLYHOCK. Heat zones 10–3. This old-fashioned favorite from the Mediterranean region has its place against a fence or wall or at the back of a border. Old single types can reach 9 ft. tall; newer strains and selections are shorter. Big, rough, roundish heart-shaped leaves, more or less lobed, form a clump to about 3 ft. wide. Upper parts of stems are hairy. Flowers are 3–6 in. wide, carried on spikes; they may be single, semidouble, or double in colors including white, pink, rose, red, purple, creamy yellow, apricot. Chater's Double is a fine perennial strain; 6-ft. spires have 5- to 6-in.-wide flowers. So-called annual strains (biennials treated as annuals) that bloom the first year from seed include 5- to 6-ft.-tall Summer Carnival, double 4-in. flowers; and 2½-ft.-tall Majorette, 3- to 4-in. blossoms.

Sow seeds in ground in late summer for next season's bloom; sow annual strains in early spring for bloom that summer. After flowers fade, cut stalks just above the ground; continue to feed and water plants to encourage late summer or early fall rebloom. Destroy any rust-infected leaves as soon as disease appears. Watch for slugs, snails.

A. rugosa. RUSSIAN HOLLYHOCK. Heat zones 9–3. From southern Russia, Ukraine. Similar to old single forms of *A. rosea*, but the stems are hairy top to bottom and the leaves are deeply lobed. Tall spikes of showy, butter yellow blossoms. Disease resistant.

ALCHEMILLA

LADY'S-MANTLE

Rosaceae

PERENNIALS

ZONES VARY BY SPECIES

PARTIAL TO FULL SHADE

REGULAR WATER

Alchemilla mollis

Rounded, pale green, lobed leaves have a silvery look; after rain or watering, they hold beads of water on their surfaces. Summer flowers are yellowish green, individually inconspicuous but borne in attractive large, branched clusters. For edgings in shady places, as ground cover, as contrast to brighter flowers.

A. alpina. Zones US, MS; 8–1. Native to northern Europe, Greenland. Mat-forming plant creeping by runners, with flowering stems 6–8 in. tall. Leaves 2 in. wide, divided into five to seven leaflets.

A. ellenbeckii. Zones US; 7–5. Native to mountains of East Africa. Attractive small-scale ground cover to about 2 in. high, with creeping, rooting stems and leaves less than 1 in. wide.

A. erythropoda. Zones US, MS; 7–1. Native to mountains of Balkans, Turkey. Resembles *A. glaucescens* but has more deeply lobed leaves and red-tinted flowering stems.

A. glaucescens (A. pubescens). Zones US, MS; 7–1. Native to Europe. Dense grower, wide spreading in time. Nearly round leaves with seven to nine lobes. Flowering stems to 8 in. high.

A. mollis. Zones US, MS, LS; 7–1. Native to Asia Minor. The most commonly planted lady's-mantle. Clump-forming plant to 2 ft. or taller, 2½ ft. wide. Nearly circular, scallop-edged leaves to 6 in. across. Self-sows.

A. pectinata. Zones MS, LS. Native to Mexico. Miniature, creeping ground cover with inch-wide leaves.

ALEURITES fordii

TUNG-OIL TREE

Euphorbiaceae

DECIDUOUS TREE

✔ LS, CS, TS ❊ 12–9

☼ ◑ FULL SUN OR PARTIAL SHADE

● REGULAR WATER

✧ ALL PARTS ARE POISONOUS IF INGESTED

Aleurites fordii

This plant gets its common name from the oil in its seeds, which is used as a drying agent in paints and varnishes—and was also used to lubricate jet engines in World War II. Native to central Asia, the tree grows quickly to 15–20 ft. tall and wide, with broadly rounded form. Dark green leaves to 6 in. across turn orange and red in fall. Small, tubular, pinkish white flowers with darker markings appear in early spring. These are followed in autumn by large (2- to 3-in.-wide) nuts that change from green to reddish to brownish black as they mature. All plant parts are toxic, but the nuts are especially poisonous; they can be lethal if eaten.

Tung-oil tree self-sows prolifically and is naturalized throughout much of the Lower and Coastal South. It is seldom grown as an ornamental, since the nuts make a mess when they fall.

ALEXANDER PALM. See PTYCHOSPERMA elegans

ALEXANDRA PALM. See ARCHONTOPHOENIX alexandrae

ALEXANDRIAN LAUREL. See DANAE racemosa

ALGERIAN IVY. See HEDERA canariensis

ALLAMANDA

Apocynaceae

EVERGREEN VINES OR SHRUBS

✔ TS ❊ 12–7; ANYWHERE AS ANNUALS OR INDOOR/OUTDOOR PLANTS

☼ FULL SUN

● REGULAR WATER

✧ ALL PARTS ARE POISONOUS IF INGESTED

Allamanda cathartica

These handsome plants from tropical South and Central America tolerate very little frost and require considerable heat for proper growth and bloom; warm nights as well as warm days seem necessary. Trumpet-shaped flowers (borne nearly year-round) and foliage are both imposing. Permanent outdoor plants only in the mildest climates. Elsewhere, grow as summer-blooming potted plants; keep indoors during cold weather.

A. blanchetii (A. violacea). PURPLE ALLAMANDA. Shrubby or with a few vining stems; usually grows 6–10 ft. tall and wide. Somewhat downy leaves up to 5 in. long. Rose purple flowers are 4½ in. across. 'Chocolate Cherry' and 'Chocolate Swirl' have pinkish purple flowers with purple-brown throats.

A. cathartica. ALLAMANDA, GOLDEN TRUMPET. Can grow to great heights (over 50 ft.) as a vine; it can clamber through trees but must be tied to other supports. Often pinched back to grow as a large freestanding shrub. Leaves are glossy, leathery, 4–6 in. long. Yellow trumpets are 5 in. wide, 3 in. long. 'Flore Pleno' bears double flowers. 'Hendersonii' bears exceptionally attractive orange-yellow blooms.

A. schottii (A. neriifolia). BUSH ALLAMANDA. Shrubby growth to 5 ft. high and wide; produces occasional climbing stems. Flowers are 3 in. wide, tinted orange or reddish.

FOR INFORMATION ON SELECTING PLANTS
PLEASE SEE PAGES 39–144

ALLEGHENY CHINKAPIN. See CHESTNUT

ALLEGHENY SPURGE. See PACHYSANDRA procumbens

ALLIUM

ORNAMENTAL ALLIUM

Liliaceae

PERENNIALS FROM BULBS

✔ ZONES VARY BY SPECIES

☼ ◑ FULL SUN OR PARTIAL SHADE

● REGULAR WATER DURING GROWTH AND BLOOM

Allium giganteum

About 500 species, all from the Northern Hemisphere. Relatives of the edible onion, peerless as cut flowers (fresh or dried), useful in borders; smaller kinds are effective in rock gardens. Most ornamental alliums are hardy, sun loving, easy to grow; they thrive in deep, rich, sandy loam. Plant bulbs in fall. Lift and divide only after they become crowded.

Leaves of most alliums are narrow and upright, varying in form from grassy to strap shaped; they often begin to die back before flowering starts. Small flowers come in roundish, compact or loose clusters at ends of leafless stems that range in height from 6 in. to 5 ft. tall or more. Some are delightfully fragrant; those with onion odor must be bruised or cut to give it off. Various species provide flowers from late spring through summer, in white and shades of pink, rose, violet, red, blue, yellow. All alliums die to the ground after bloom, even in mild climates. Seldom browsed by deer.

A. aflatunense. Zones US, MS, LS; 8–1. Blooms in late spring, bearing tennis ball–size clusters of lilac flowers on stems 2½–5 ft. tall. Resembles *A. giganteum* but with smaller flower clusters.

A. atropurpureum. Zones US, MS, LS; 8–1. Stems to 2½ ft. tall carry 2-in. clusters of dark purple to nearly black flowers in late spring.

A. caeruleum (A. azureum). BLUE ALLIUM. Zones US, MS, LS; 10–1. Cornflower blue flowers in dense, round, 2-in. clusters on 1- to 1½-ft. stems. Late spring bloom.

A. carinatum pulchellum (A. pulchellum). Zones US, MS, LS; 9–6. Loose, pendent, 2½-in. clusters of reddish purple flowers on 1- to 2-ft. stems. Blooms in summer.

A. cepa. See Onion

A. christophii (A. albopilosum). STAR OF PERSIA. Zones US, MS, LS; 9–5. Distinctive. Very large clusters (6–12 in. across) of starlike, lavender to deep lilac flowers with metallic sheen. Late spring bloom. Stems are 12–15 in. tall. Leaves to 1½ ft. long, white and hairy beneath. Dried flower cluster looks like an elegant holiday ornament.

A. giganteum. GIANT ALLIUM. Zones US, MS, LS; 9–5. Spectacular softball-size clusters of bright lilac flowers on stems to 3–5 ft. or taller. Late spring bloom. Leaves 1½ ft. long, 2 in. wide.

A. karataviense. TURKESTAN ALLIUM. Zones US, MS, LS; 9–5. Dense, round, 2- to 3-in. flower clusters in midspring, in colors from pinkish to beige to reddish lilac. Broad, flat, recurved leaves, 2–5 in. across.

A. moly. GOLDEN GARLIC. Zones US, MS, LS; 9–1. Stems 9–18 in. tall bear open clusters of flowers in bright, shining yellow. Late spring bloom.

A. neapolitanum. Zones US, MS, LS, CS; 9–1. Spreading, 2-in. clusters of large, fragrant, white flowers on 1-ft. stems bloom in midspring. Leaves 1 in. wide. 'Grandiflorum' is larger, blooms earlier. A form of 'Grandiflorum' listed as 'Cowanii' is considered superior. Grown commercially as cut flowers.

A. oreophilum (A. ostrowskianum). Zones US, MS, LS, CS; 9–1. Loose, 1½-in. clusters of rose-colored flowers on 8- to 12-in. stems in late spring; two or three gray-green leaves. Good for rock gardens, cutting.

A. porrum. See Leek

A. rosenbachianum. Zones US, MS, LS; 10–1. Baseball-size clusters of rosy purple blossoms with contrasting white stamens in late spring.

A. sativum. See Garlic

▶

A

A. schoenoprasum. CHIVES. Zones US, MS, LS, CS, TS; 12–1. Leaves are grasslike in general appearance but round and hollow in cross section. Clumps may reach 2 ft. tall but are usually shorter. Cloverlike, rosy purple spring flowers are carried in clusters atop thin stems. Plant is pretty enough to use as edging in sunny or lightly shaded flower border or herb garden. Does best in moist, fairly rich soil. May be increased by divisions or grown from seed. Evergreen (or nearly so) in mild regions; goes dormant where winters are cold, but small divisions may be potted in rich soil and grown on kitchen windowsill. Chop or snip leaves; use as garnish or add to salads, cream cheese, cottage cheese, or cooked dishes for delicate onionlike flavor. For garlic chives, see *A. tuberosum*.

A. scorodoprasum. See Garlic

A. sphaerocephalum. DRUMSTICKS, ROUND-HEADED GARLIC. Zones US, MS, LS, CS; 8–1. Tight, dense, spherical, inch-wide red-purple flower clusters on 2-ft. stems in early to midsummer. Spreads freely.

A. tuberosum. GARLIC CHIVES. Zones US, MS, LS, CS; 9–1. Spreads by tuberous rootstocks and by seeds. Plant grows in clumps of gray-green, flat leaves ¼ in. wide, up to 1 ft. long. Many 1- to 1½-ft.-tall stalks bear 2-in. clusters of white flowers in summer. Flowers are violet scented and excellent for fresh or dry arrangements. Leaves have mild garlic flavor, are useful in salads and cooked dishes.

Allium tuberosum

ALLOPLECTUS nummularia. See NEMATANTHUS gregarius

ALLSPICE, CAROLINA. See CALYCANTHUS floridus

ALMOND

Rosaceae

DECIDUOUS TREE

🌿 US, MS 🌡 8–6

☼ FULL SUN

💧 MODERATE WATER

Almond

In most parts of the South, growing almonds is no joy. Though closely related to the peach, the almond (*Prunus dulcis*) is considerably fussier about its requirements. Nuts develop properly only in regions with long, hot, dry summers, like those in the plant's native Asia Minor and North Africa, and late spring frosts can spell the end for a developing crop. For these reasons, almost all commercially grown almonds come from Southern California. Some selections, however, can succeed in Texas, Oklahoma, and southwestern Missouri.

An almond tree grows 20–30 ft. high; it's upright when young, then becomes more rounded with age. Pale pink or white flowers appear in early spring. Fruit looks like a flattened, undersized green peach. In autumn, the pit splits to reveal the nut inside, which is the almond.

Almonds thrive in deep, fertile, well-drained soil. Some selections are self-fruitful, while others require pollination by another selection. Planting a late-blooming selection gives you a better chance at a crop. Almonds suffer from most of the same pests that afflict peaches and nectarines.

'All-in-One'. Semidwarf tree blooms at same time as 'Mission'. Medium to large, sweet, soft-shelled nuts. Self-fruitful. Best selection for home gardens.

'Butte'. Semihard-shelled nut, slightly smaller than 'Mission'. Very productive tree. Late bloomer, flowering just before 'Mission'. Pollinate with 'All-in-One' or 'Mission'.

'Hall' ('Hall's Hardy'). Hard-shelled, bitter, small nut of low quality. Pink bloom comes late, an advantage in late-frost regions. Tree may actually be a peach-almond hybrid. Partially self-fruitful but better with 'Mission' as pollenizer.

'Mission' ('Texas'). Small, semihard-shelled nut. Regular, heavy producer. Late bloomer; one of the safest for cold-winter, late-frost areas. Pollinate with 'Hall' or 'All-in-One'.

ALMOND, FLOWERING. See PRUNUS triloba

ALOCASIA

ELEPHANT'S EAR

Araceae

PERENNIALS

🌿 ZONES VARY BY SPECIES; OR HOUSEPLANTS

☼ PARTIAL SHADE; BRIGHT INDIRECT LIGHT

💧 💧 REGULAR TO AMPLE WATER

☘ SAP IS POISONOUS IF INGESTED

Alocasia macrorrhiza

Splendid plants prized for their lush, bold, tropical-looking foliage, these Asian natives are riding a wave of new-found popularity. Many fancy-leafed selections have been introduced recently, and more are sure to follow. Can be grown indoors in bright light or outdoors in filtered sunlight. Give them moist, well-drained soil containing lots of organic matter; provide shelter from wind so leaves don't get tattered. Useful in garden beds and containers. Most are tender to frost.

A. × amazonica. AFRICAN MASK. Zones TS; 12–8. Leathery, deep bronzy green leaves to 16 in. long have wavy edges, heavy white main veins. Plants may grow as tall as 4 ft. and about half as wide. This species is the one most commonly available as a houseplant.

A. cucullata. CHINESE TARO, CHINESE APE. Zones LS, CS, TS; 12–7. Slow-growing, clumping evergreen plant to 2 ft. high. Grown for shiny, deep green, pointed leaves to 15 in. long, 1 ft. wide. Usually massed as a ground cover; plant 1½–2 ft. apart. Requires moist, rich, well-drained soil and protection from wind. Excellent container plant.

A. macrorrhiza. GIANT ALOCASIA, GIANT TARO. Zones CS, TS; 12–7. Evergreen at 29°F; loses leaves at lower temperatures but comes back in spring if frosts are not too severe. Medium to dark green, arrow-shaped leaves grow to 2 ft. or longer on stalks to 5 ft. tall, form a dome-shaped plant 4 ft. across; may grow as large as 12 ft. tall, 10 ft. wide in Tropical South. Tiny flowers on spike surrounded by greenish white bract. Flowers are followed by reddish fruit, giving spike the look of corn on the cob. The foliage of 'Variegata' is blotched with creamy white, gray green, or darker green.

A. odora. Zones LS, CS, TS; 12–7. Similar to *A. macrorrhiza* but hardier. Fragrant flowers.

A. plumbea. Zones CS, TS; 12–7. This Indonesian species resembles *A. macrorrhiza* but isn't quite as hardy and bears fragrant flowers. Selections with colorful leaves include 'Metallica', with a purple luster; dark green to black 'Nigra'; and red-tinted 'Rubra'.

A. 'Portodora'. Zones LS, CS, TS; 12–7. This hybrid elephant's ear looks much like *A. macrorrhiza* but reaches 8 ft. tall, with giant (4-ft.) wavy, scalloped leaves on purple stems.

A. sanderiana. Zones TS; 12–8. Grows to 6 ft. tall and wide. Arrow-shaped, deeply lobed leaves about 12–16 in. long, metallic dark purplish green with silver veining on surface.

A. wentii. Zones LS, CS, TS; 12–7. This is an especially hardy species, surviving 10°F. Grows in a tight clump. Can reach 4 ft. high and wide, but may not get much bigger than 1½ ft. if grown outdoors in colder part of range. Arrow-shaped leaves to 1 ft. long are bronzy green on top, purplish underneath.

FOR GROWING SYMBOL EXPLANATIONS
PLEASE SEE PAGE 145

ALOE

Liliaceae

SUCCULENT TREES, SHRUBS, AND PERENNIALS

✎ TS 〽 12–9, EXCEPT AS NOTED

☼ ◑ FULL SUN OR LIGHT SHADE, EXCEPT
AS NOTED

◐ ◗ LITTLE TO MODERATE WATER

✦ SAP BENEATH PLANTS' SKIN IS AN IRRITANT

Aloe arborescens

Primarily South African natives, the aloes range from 6-in. miniatures to trees; all form clumps of fleshy, pointed leaves and bear branched or unbranched clusters of orange, yellow, cream, or red flowers. Some species bloom nearly every month, but the biggest show comes from midwinter through summer. Leaves may be green or gray green, often strikingly banded or streaked with contrasting colors. Showy and easy to grow in well-drained soil in reasonably frost-free areas; need little water but can take more. Most tolerate salt spray and are good beach plants. Seldom browsed by deer.

Where winters are too cold for all-year outdoor culture, grow aloes in pots and shelter from frosts. Most kinds make outstanding container plants. Highly valued as ornamentals, in the ground or in pots. The aloes listed here are only a few of the many kinds. Sizes given apply to plants grown outdoors in the ground.

A. arborescens. TREE ALOE. Grows about 10 ft. tall, 6 ft. wide, though older clumps may reach 18 ft. Branching stems carry big clumps of gray-green, spiny-edged leaves. Winter flowers in long, spiky clusters, bright vermilion to clear yellow. Withstands salt spray. Tolerates shade. Foliage damaged at 29°F, but plants have survived 17°F.

A. aristata. Dwarf for pots, edging, and ground covers; just 8–12 in. tall and about as wide. Rosettes are packed with 4-in.-long, ¾-in.-wide leaves ending in whiplike threads. Produces orange-red winter flowers in 1- to 1½-ft.-tall clusters.

A. bainesii. Slow-growing tree to 20–30 ft. or taller, with heavy, forking trunk and branches. Rosettes of 2- to 3-ft. leaves; spikes of rose pink flowers in winter on 1½- to 2-ft. stalks. Used for stately, sculptural pattern in landscape. Tender to frost.

A. barbadensis. See A. vera

A. 'Blue Elf'. Dwarf hybrid with 6-in. rosettes of tooth-edged blue-green foliage. Eventually forms a dense mound 1–2 ft. high and wide. Has never been known to flower. Similar or identical to 'Walmsley's Blue'.

A. brevifolia. Heat zones 12–3. Low, spreading clumps of blunt, thick, gray-green, spiny-edged leaves 3 in. long. Clusters of red flowers on 20-in. stalks, intermittent all year.

A. ciliaris. Climbing, sprawling form with pencil-thick stems to 10 ft. long. Small, thick, soft green leaves. Long-stalked, 3- to 6-in. flower clusters with 20 to 30 green- or yellow-tipped scarlet flowers; intermittent bloom all year. Takes a bit more shade than other species listed here.

A. distans. JEWELED ALOE. Running, rooting, branching stems make clumps of 6-in., fleshy blue-green leaves with scattered whitish spots and white teeth along edges. Forked flower stems, 1½–2 ft. tall, carry clusters of red flowers in winter.

A. ferox. BITTER ALOE. Treelike aloe with a large single trunk rising 6–10 ft. high (after 10 years). Trunk is topped by a single crown of gray-green, spiny, red-toothed leaves 3–4 ft. long and 6–8 in. wide. Each branched inflorescence holds hundreds of bright scarlet or orange blossoms in late winter or early spring.

A. marlothii. Large, treelike aloe with a stout trunk to 12 ft. tall, topped by a single dense foliage rosette. Leaves are green or grayish, 3–4 ft. long and up to 8 in. wide, often spined on both surfaces and margins. Old dried leaves persist on trunk. Winter flower clusters branch horizontally, holding many spikes in yellow, orange, or (rarely) red or bicolors.

A. nobilis. Dark green leaves edged with small hooked teeth grow in rosettes to 1 ft. wide and high. Clustered orange-red flowers on 2-ft. stalks in early summer. Good in pots—takes limited root space.

A. saponaria. SOAP ALOE. Short-stemmed rosettes a foot or more wide feature broad, white-spotted green leaves to 8 in. long. Multibranched, 1½- to 2½-ft. flower stalks rise in summer, topped with tight heads of nodding blossoms in scarlet, red orange, salmon pink, or yellow. Sends out suckers to form dense, expanding colonies. Dig and separate when plants become too crowded. 'Yellow Form' corresponds to *A. s. fixburgeana*. Among forms with shrimp pink flowers, the most widely grown is old hybrid 'Commutata'.

Aloe saponaria

A. × spinosissima. Heat zones 12–3. Dense, compact, multibranched shrub, expanding slowly to 4–6 ft. high and wide. Leaf surfaces are not as spiny as the species name *spinosissima* would suggest. Unbranched, 1½-ft.-tall flower stalks bear coral red blossoms from late winter to early spring.

A. striata. CORAL ALOE. Broad, spineless leaves to 20 in. long are gray green with a narrow pinkish red edge. They grow in rosettes 2 ft. wide on short trunk. Brilliant coral pink to orange flowers in branched clusters, midwinter into spring. Handsome, tailored-looking plant.

A. striatula. HARDY ALOE. Zones LS, CS, TS. Scrambling shrub has glossy green leaves, each edged with a thin white margin and minute teeth; distinctly striped leaf bases surround the stem. Multiple stems form a dense mound 5–6 ft. tall and to 15 ft. across, but plant may be kept much more compact with occasional hard pruning. Single spikes of flowers in scarlet, orange, or yellow rise 6–18 in. above the foliage in summer.

A. tenuior. Dense, much-branched, climbing or scrambling shrub to 2–4 ft. tall. Lax stems to 10 ft. long (often horizontal) are tipped with rosettes of 6-in.-long, 1-in.-wide leaves edged with tiny white teeth. In late spring, 6- to 12-in. unbranched spikes of tiny, cylindrical yellow (sometimes red) flowers are held horizontally above the mound. Best given support of a fence or rocks or trained up a palm trunk.

A. variegata. PARTRIDGE-BREAST ALOE, TIGER ALOE. Foot-high, tight rosette of fleshy, triangular, dark green, 5-in.-long leaves strikingly banded and edged with white. Loose clusters of pink to dull red flowers, intermittent all year.

A. vera (A. barbadensis). MEDICINAL ALOE, BARBADOS ALOE. Heat zones 12–3. Rosettes of narrow, fleshy, upright leaves 1–2 ft. long. Yellow flowers in dense spike atop 3-ft. stalk, spring and summer. Favorite folk medicine plant used to treat burns, bites, inflammation, and a host of other ills. Needs a moderate amount of water to look good.

ALOYSIA

Verbenaceae

DECIDUOUS OR SEMIEVERGREEN SHRUBS

✎ LS, CS, TS 〽 12–8; OR GROW IN POTS

☼ FULL SUN

◗ REGULAR WATER

Aloysia triphylla

With their tiny flowers and leggy stems, these aromatic shrubs from the warmer parts of the Americas aren't grown for their looks; they're valued for their blossoms and scented leaves, which can be used for seasoning or to flavor iced drinks and teas. Like most herbs, they require good drainage.

A. triphylla (Lippia citriodora). LEMON VERBENA. May succeed outdoors north of its usual range if grown against a warm wall; otherwise, it can be grown as a houseplant.

Legginess is the natural state of this plant; it's the herb that grew like a gangling shrub in grandmother's garden. When you read of "the scent of verbena" in novels of the antebellum South, this is the plant being described. Prized for its shiny, aromatic foliage, which fills the air with a citruslike fragrance.

Grows to 6 ft. or taller, sprawling to 6 ft. wide; narrow leaves to 3 in. long are arranged in whorls of three or four along the branches. Bears open

A

clusters of very small lilac or whitish flowers in summer. By pinch-pruning, you can shape the plant to create an interesting tracery against a wall. Or let it grow among lower plants to hide its gangly look. Needs well-drained soil.

A. wrightii. OREGANILLO, MEXICAN OREGANO. Native to desert mountains from California to Texas and northern Mexico. Dense grower to 5 ft. high and wide, with numerous small stems and small (½-in.) leaves. From spring through fall, produces very sweet-scented white flowers that can be used as a flavoring or for tea. Performs best when it gets lots of heat. Good in natural landscape, herb garden, as informal hedge.

Often confused with *A. lycioides,* a larger plant (to 8 ft. tall and 6 ft. wide) bearing blossoms that have a more vanilla-like fragrance and are sometimes tinged with purple. Plants sold under either name may be one or the other—but both are outstanding ornamentals. Both make excellent honey. *A. lycioides* is the Mexican oregano of commerce.

FRAGRANCE AND FLAVOR. *Lemon verbena leaves add a lemon flavor to teas and iced drinks; they can also be dried for potpourri. When making apple jelly, try placing a large fresh leaf in the bottom of each jar. For all flavoring purposes, pluck fresh-looking leaves from the tops of the stems.* ❖

ALPINIA

Zingiberaceae

PERENNIALS

⚹ ZONES VARY BY SPECIES

◑ LIGHT SHADE

💧 AMPLE WATER

Alpinia zerumbet

These striking, upright-growing semitropical perennials offer exotic blooms and lush foliage. Most form clumps half to fully as wide as they are tall. Evergreen in the Tropical South, they are root-hardy to about 15°F. They often need to settle in for 2 years after planting before they start to bloom; the clusters of ½- to 2½-in. blossoms typically appear in summer. Give moist, fertile, well-drained soil and a wind-sheltered location. Each year, cut back to the ground all canes that have finished flowering.

A. aquatica. Zones LS, CS, TS; 12–8. From China. To 7 ft. tall, with small pink flowers. Among the few gingers that will grow in water. Planted at the edge of a pond, it will eventually creep in.

A. coerulea. Zones CS, TS; 12–10. From Australia. To 6 ft. tall. Dark green leaves with red undersides; small white blossoms with purple stamens. Deep blue berries follow the flowers.

A. formosana. Zones MS, LS, CS, TS; 12–10. Cold-hardy (to 10°F) species from Taiwan, southern Japan. To 4–5 ft. high. Green leaves sport white veining that looks like pinstripes. Small, creamy white flowers are marked with red and yellow.

A. henryi. SWEET DRAGON. Zones CS, TS; 12–10. Reaching 6–9 ft. tall, this Chinese native blooms in spring, bearing cream-colored blossoms that are marked with dark red lines and give off a honeylike perfume. Performs well as a houseplant.

A. katsumadai. Zones LS, CS, TS; 12–9. From Japan. To 4–5 ft. high, with dark green, wavy-edged leaves. Yellow flowers in upright clusters.

A. purpurata. RED GINGER. Zones TS; 12–10. To 9–12 ft. tall, 2–3 ft. wide. Brilliant inflorescences of red bracts and small white flowers.

A. vittata (A. sanderae). VARIEGATED GINGER. Zones TS; 12–10. Native to Solomon Islands. To 3–4 ft. tall, with white-striped leaves. Rarely blooms. A good container plant.

A. zerumbet (A. nutans, A. speciosa). SHELL GINGER, SHELL FLOWER. Zones LS, CS, TS; 12–9. Native to Polynesia and tropical Asia. Grandest of gingers, best all-year appearance. To 8–9 ft. tall. Shiny leaves with distinct parallel veins; maroon leafstalks at maturity. Waxy white or pinkish, shell-like, fragrant flowers marked red, purple, or brown in pendent clusters on arching stems. 'Variegata' has green leaves with yellow bands.

ALSOPHILA australis, A. cooperi. See CYATHEA cooperi

ALSTROEMERIA

Liliaceae

PERENNIALS FROM TUBEROUS ROOTS

⚹ MS, LS, CS H 9–7, EXCEPT AS NOTED

◑ PARTIAL SHADE, EXCEPT AS NOTED

💧 REGULAR WATER DURING GROWTH AND BLOOM

◊ CAN CAUSE DERMATITIS IN ALLERGIC PEOPLE

Alstroemeria aurea

There's a good reason why most Southerners see these flashy perennials only at the florist's: they're difficult to grow in regions with hot, rainy, humid summers and heavy clay soil. They may put on a good show for a while, but they seldom last for more than a year or two. *A. psittacina* and a couple of new hybrids are exceptions.

The fanciest alstroemerias, often used for cut flowers, are hybrids. The deciduous Dr. Salter's Hybrids feature beautiful flowers in red, orange, peach, shrimp, salmon, and near-white; all are flecked and striped with deeper colors. They produce leafy shoots 2–5 ft. tall in late winter and early spring. As these shoots begin to turn brown, the flowering stems arise, with blooms appearing in early to midsummer. If allowed to set seed, plants will self-sow. They go dormant after blooming. Sow seeds in fall, winter, or early spring.

Evergreen hybrids include such series as Cordu, Inca, Meyer, and Premier. They vary in height and come in many colors—mostly in the pink-purple-red range, with petals marked with dark flecks. They're usually sold by color, so buy them in bloom.

A. aurea (A. aurantiaca). YELLOW ALSTROEMERIA. Heat zones 10–7. Deciduous species to 3–4 ft. tall, with many leafy flowering stems. Yellow, orange, or orange-red blooms are flecked and striped in darker colors. 'Orange King' offers outstanding cut flowers—large, long-lasting, dark-spotted bright orange blossoms reminiscent of tiger lilies.

A. 'Freedom.' New introduction from the University of Connecticut sports peachy red blossoms adorned with yellowish white blotches and carmine specks. Grows 2½ ft. tall and forms clumps to about 1 ft. wide. Surprisingly tolerant of Southern growing conditions.

A. psittacina. PARROT LILY. The best alstroemeria for the South, and a true conversation piece. Evergreen in mildest areas; elsewhere, mounds of dark green leaves emerge from the ground in winter. Flowering stalks, separate from the foliage, sprout in summer and rise as tall as 2½ ft. Odd-looking red-and-green flowers are marked with purple blotches. Prefers growing in all-day shade; spreads steadily and can be invasive in good soil. Usually obtained as a passalong plant. 'Variegata' has striking white-edged leaves.

A. 'Sweet Laura'. Like 'Freedom', this one was introduced by the University of Connecticut. Mildly fragrant golden flowers sport orange petal tips and cinnamon flecks. Grows 2½ ft. tall; spreads slowly by underground stems. Tolerates summer heat well.

ALTERNANTHERA

JOSEPH'S COAT

Amaranthaceae

PERENNIALS OFTEN TREATED AS ANNUALS

⚹ TS; ANYWHERE AS ANNUAL; H 12–1

☀ FULL SUN

💧 MODERATE WATER

Alternanthera ficoidea 'Magnifica'

These foliage plants grab attention, whether used in large sweeps, in combination with other plants, or in containers. Wonderfully gaudy foliage looks something like that of coleus. Prefer moist, fertile, well-drained soil; easy to root from cuttings. Native from Mexico to Argentina. Thrive in heat.

A. dentata. Upright grower to 1–3 ft. tall and 1–2 ft. wide, with broadly lance-shaped dark green leaves to 3½ in. long and 2 in. wide. Blooms in late fall and winter, bearing small greenish white flowers that resemble clover blossoms and are held erect on the stems. 'Rubiginosa' has burgundy stems and leaves. 'Tricolor' offers burgundy foliage edged in deep pink; its new leaves include some green.

A. ficoidea. Sprawling or upright grower ranging from 6 to 20 in. tall, with elliptic to oval or rounded leaves to about 1 in. long. 'Aurea Nana' is a low grower with yellow-splotched foliage; 'Bettzickiana' has spoon-shaped leaves with red and yellow markings. 'Magnifica' is a red-bronze dwarf. 'Parrot Feather' and 'Versicolor' have broad green leaves with yellow markings and pink veins. In 'Sessilis Alba', leaves are pure white on the upper part of the plant, green closer to the ground.

A. polygonoides. Sprawling plant with reddish brown, elliptical to oval leaves to 1 in. long. Grows to 4 in. tall and 15 in. wide.

ALTHAEA. See ALCEA

ALUMINUM PLANT. See PILEA cadierei

ALUM ROOT. See HEUCHERA

ALYSSUM

Brassicaceae (Cruciferae)

PERENNIALS

🗡 US, MS, LS

☀ ◐ FULL SUN OR LIGHT SHADE

💧 MODERATE WATER

Alyssum montanum

Mostly native to Mediterranean region. Mounding plants or shrublets that brighten spring borders and rock gardens with their cheerful bloom. They thrive in poor, rocky soil as long as it is well drained.

A. montanum. Heat zones 9–1. To 8 in. high, 1½ ft. wide; leaves are gray and hairy (more so on underside). Fragrant yellow flowers in dense, short clusters.

A. saxatile. See Aurinia saxatilis

A. wulfenianum. Heat zones 9–6. Prostrate and trailing to about 1½ ft. wide, with fleshy, silvery leaves and sheets of pale yellow flowers.

ALYSSUM, SWEET. See LOBULARIA maritima

AMARACUS dictamnus. See ORIGANUM dictamnus

Amaranthaceae. The amaranth family consists largely of herbaceous plants, many of them weedy. The small flowers are dry and papery but can be effective when massed.

AMARANTHUS

AMARANTH

Amaranthaceae

ANNUALS

🗡 US, MS, LS, CS, TS

☀ ◐ FULL SUN OR PARTIAL SHADE

💧 REGULAR WATER

Amaranthus caudatus

Coarse, sometimes weedy plants; a few ornamental kinds are grown for colorful foliage or flowers. Sow seed in early summer; soil temperature must be above 70°F for germination. When young and tender, leaves and stems of many species (even some of the weedy ones) can be cooked like spinach, taking its place in hot weather. Blooms late summer and fall. In some species, seeds look like sesame seeds; they are high in protein and can be used as a grain.

A. caudatus. LOVE-LIES-BLEEDING, TASSEL FLOWER. Heat zones 12–1. Sturdy, branching plant 3–8 ft. high, 1½–3 ft. wide; leaves 2–10 in. long, ½–4 in. wide. Red flowers in drooping, tassel-like clusters. A curiosity rather than a pretty plant. One of the amaranths that produce grain.

A. hypochondriacus (A. hybridus erythrostachys). PRINCE'S FEATHER. Heat zones 12–5. To 5 ft. high, 2 ft. wide, with leaves 1–6 in. long, ½–3 in. wide, usually reddish. Red or brownish red flowers in many-branched clusters. Some strains are grown as a spinach substitute or for grain.

A. tricolor. JOSEPH'S COAT. Heat zones 12–5. Branching plant 1–4 ft. high, 1–1½ ft. wide. Leaves 2½–6 in. long, 2–4 in. wide, blotched in shades of red and green. 'Early Splendor', 'Flaming Fountain', and 'Molten Fire' bear masses of yellow to scarlet foliage at tops of main stems and principal branches. Green-leafed strains are used as a spinach substitute under the name "tampala."

× AMARCRINUM memoria-corsii 'Fred Howard' (× Crinodonna corsii 'Fred Howard')

Amaryllidaceae

PERENNIAL FROM BULB

🗡 LS, CS, TS ⊮ 12–8

☀ ◐ FULL SUN OR PARTIAL SHADE

💧 REGULAR WATER

× Amarcrinum memoria-corsii 'Fred Howard'

This bigeneric hybrid of *Crinum moorei* and belladonna lily (*Amaryllis belladonna*) was developed by California plantsman Fred Howard. Much more dependable in the South than belladonna lily, it features 2-ft. blossom stalks, each of which carries six to ten buds. In midsummer, these open into waxy, fragrant, white-throated pink flowers, each 2½–4 in. across. Successive stalks emerge and bloom until frost. Strap-shaped glossy green leaves to 1½ ft. long provide a pleasing backdrop for the blossoms. The plant is nearly evergreen in mild winters and prefers lean, sandy soil. It's not bothered by rodents or deer.

Plant bulbs in spring or late summer, setting them barely below the soil surface and spacing them 2–4 ft. apart. Also a good container plant.

AMARYLLIS belladonna (Brunsvigia rosea)

BELLADONNA LILY, NAKED LADY

Amaryllidaceae

PERENNIAL FROM BULB

🗡 LS, CS, TS ⊮ 12–7

☀ FULL SUN

◌ NO IRRIGATION NEEDED

☠ ALL PARTS ARE POISONOUS IF INGESTED

Amaryllis belladonna

Native to South Africa, this beautiful bulb likes warm, dry summers; summer rains make it hard to grow in most of the South. Bold, straplike leaves form a fountainlike clump about 1 ft. high, 2 ft. wide in fall and winter; the foliage dies down completely in late spring or early summer. About 6 weeks later, leafless stalks rise from bare earth to a height of 2–3 ft.; each is topped by a cluster of 4 to 12 fragrant, trumpet-shaped, rosy pink flowers. Grows in almost any well-drained soil; gets all the moisture it needs from rainfall. Plant bulbs immediately after the bloom period ends, setting them a foot apart and just below the soil surface. They may be injured if winter temperatures drop below 20°F; otherwise, they are very long lived.

AMAZON VINE. See STIGMAPHYLLON

AMELANCHIER

JUNEBERRY, SHADBLOW, SERVICEBERRY

Rosaceae

DECIDUOUS SHRUBS OR SMALL TREES

🌿 ZONES VARY BY SPECIES

☀️ ◐ FULL SUN OR PARTIAL SHADE

💧 ◐ MODERATE TO REGULAR WATER

Amelanchier laevis

Deserving of much wider use in the landscape, these graceful, airy trees and shrubs provide year-round interest. Drooping clusters of white or pinkish flowers, showy but short lived, appear in early spring, just before or during leaf-out. They are followed in early summer by delicious blueberry-flavored fruits that are excellent for use in pies and jams—if you can beat the birds to them. New spring foliage is purplish; it turns green by summer, then red, orange, or yellow in fall.

Excellent in woodland gardens, these plants all grow about twice as high as wide. They are easy to garden under due to their noninvasive roots and the light shade they cast. Try planting them against a dark background to better show off the flowers, foliage, and form. All need some winter chill. Rust and fireblight sometimes appear but are seldom serious. Some folks call serviceberries "sarvistrees."

A. alnifolia. SASKATOON. Zones US; 6–1. Native to western Canada and mountainous parts of the western U.S. To 20 ft. tall, spreading by rhizomes. 'Regent', 4–6 ft. tall, bears heavy crop of fruit in early summer. Red-and-yellow fall foliage.

A. arborea. JUNEBERRY. Zones US, MS, LS, CS; 9–1. Native to eastern and southern U.S. Narrow tree. Similar to *A. canadensis* but is sometimes taller, more often forms a nice round-headed tree, and has larger, pendulous, loose racemes of white flowers that bloom as the leaves unfold. Delicious dark red-purple fruit.

A. canadensis. SHADBLOW SERVICEBERRY. Zones US, MS, LS; 8–1. Narrowish, to 25 ft. tall, with short, erect flower clusters. Plants offered under this name may actually belong to other species. Often suckering and multitrunked.

A. ×grandiflora. APPLE SERVICEBERRY. Zones US, MS, LS, CS; 9–1. Hybrid between *A. arborea* and *A. laevis*. Named selections may be sold under any of the three names. Most grow to 25 ft. tall, with drooping clusters of white flowers opening from pinkish buds. Outstanding selections include the following.

'Autumn Brilliance'. Strong stems stand up well to winter storms. Bluegreen leaves turn orange red in fall.

'Cole's Selection'. Orange-red autumn color.

'Forest Prince'. Robust selection with especially handsome dark green foliage that turns orange red in autumn.

'Princess Diana'. Orange-red fall color.

'Prince William'. Shrubby selection to 10 ft. high; orange red in fall.

'Robin Hill'. Pink buds open to white flowers. Red to yellow fall leaf color.

A. laevis. ALLEGHENY SERVICEBERRY. Zones US, MS, LS; 9–1. Native to eastern North America. Narrow shrub or small tree to 40 ft., with nodding or drooping, 4-in., white flower clusters. Leaves are bronzy purple when new, dark green in summer, yellow to red in autumn. Small blackpurple fruit is very sweet.

A. ×lamarckii. Zones US, MS, LS; 9–1. Probably a hybrid derived from the species *A. laevis*. Plant may reach 30 ft. tall. Leaves emerge bronze, mature to dark green, and take on shades of orange to red in autumn. Young stems and leaves are coated with silky white hairs. Bears purplish black fruit.

AMERICAN ELDERBERRY. See SAMBUCUS canadensis

AMERICAN SWEET GUM. See LIQUIDAMBAR styraciflua

AMETHYST FLOWER. See BROWALLIA

AMORPHA

Fabaceae (Leguminosae)

DECIDUOUS SHRUBS

🌿 US, MS, LS, CS ⊩ 8–1

☀️ FULL SUN

💧 MODERATE WATER, EXCEPT AS NOTED

Amorpha fruticosa

Shrubs with leaves divided featherwise into many leaflets. Spikelike, 3- to 6-in.-long clusters of blue or purple, single-petaled flowers typically bloom in early summer. In cold weather, plants may die back nearly to the ground; in warmer areas, they should be cut back severely to prevent lankiness. Tough and undemanding, withstanding heat and wind.

A. canescens. LEAD PLANT. Native to the High Plains from Canada to Texas. About 3 ft. tall and wide, with silvery, downy foliage.

A. fruticosa. INDIGO BUSH, FALSE INDIGO. Native to eastern U.S. Lanky grower reaches 10–15 ft. tall and wide, with light green foliage. Needs hard pruning in winter or early spring to maintain some degree of compactness.

A. texana (A. roemeriana). INDIGO BUSH. Native to the Texas Hill Country. Grows to 3–9 ft. high and 3–5 ft. wide, with silvery, downy leaves and spring bloom. This shrub is quite drought tolerant, requiring little supplemental water.

AMORPHOPHALLUS

VOODOO LILY

Araceae

PERENNIALS FROM TUBERS

🌿 ZONES VARY BY SPECIES

◐ ● PART SUN TO SHADE

💧 REGULAR WATER

Amorphophallus konjac

Plants don't get much stranger than the voodoo lilies. This large group of aroids, mostly from Asia, grows from huge underground cormlike tubers, some weighing up to 100 pounds. In summer, each produces a single inflorescence that looks like a giant calla *(Zantedeschia)*: a large, hoodlike bract called a spathe surrounds a central spike- or finger-shaped spadix. The fragrance this emits is unforgettable—the breath of the Devil—but it lasts only for about a day. The carrion stench attracts flies, which are the plant's chief pollinators.

After flowering, voodoo lilies rest for about a month before producing a single giant (to 3-ft.-wide) leaf, which lasts for the rest of the summer. Plants need moist, woodsy, well-drained soil. Set the tubers 4 in. deep in late winter or early spring; apply fertilizer monthly for best results. Often grown in pots or tubs; also good for naturalized areas and woodland gardens where neighbors aren't too close.

A. bulbifer. Zones LS, CS, TS; 12–8. To 3 ft. high. Stem mottled in various shades of green produces a 1½-ft. spathe—blotched with pink on the outside, red on the inside—surrounding a cream-colored spadix. The flower is followed by a segmented leaf that produces bulbils in its forks by the end of summer; these can be removed and planted.

A. kiusianus. Zones MS, LS, CS, TS; 10–8. To 3 ft. high. Stem speckled with green and white is topped with a 6-in. spathe spotted in the same manner; a dark purple, 8-in. spadix protrudes from the spathe. The leafstalk that follows is topped by an umbrella-like leaf composed of numerous leaflets.

A. konjac. Zones US, MS, LS, CS, TS; 12–7. To 6 ft. tall. Purple-spotted stem holds a similarly mottled 3-ft. spathe from which protrudes a dark purple spadix. Leafstalk holds an umbrella-like, deeply lobed leaf. Increases by offsets underground, eventually forming a big clump.

A. paeonifolius. Zones MS, LS, CS, TS; 10–7. Grows to 8 ft. tall. A green-marbled stalk that shades to purple at the top carries a ruffled,

1½-ft.-wide, purple-and-green spathe spotted with white. The spathe holds a large, protruding purple spadix that looks like a bulbous knob—or, as some say, a brain. Leaf is divided into many leaflets and carried atop a green-marbled stalk.

AMPELOPSIS brevipedunculata

PORCELAIN BERRY

Vitaceae

DECIDUOUS VINE

✕ US, MS, LS, CS ♨ 8–2

☀ ◑ ● SUN OR SHADE

◔ ◕ MODERATE TO REGULAR WATER

Ampelopsis brevipedunculata

This Asian native is the Dr. Jekyll and Mr. Hyde of ornamental vines. On the one hand, it produces an absolutely stunning display of colorful fruit: clusters of small, grapelike berries that change from greenish ivory to yellowish to metallic blue in late summer and fall, often with several colors present at the same time. On the other hand, it can be extremely invasive. Its rampant stems, clinging by tendrils, can easily grow 15 ft. in a year, and birds eat the fruit and spread the seeds all over. Plant it only where you can contain it; don't let it escape to woods or natural areas. Handsome dark green leaves to 5 in. across turn red in fall; unfortunately, they are often damaged by Japanese beetles.

In the garden, give porcelain berry the strong support of an arbor, trellis, or wall. 'Elegans' has leaves variegated in white and pink; selection is less vigorous than the species and makes a splendid choice for a hanging basket or container.

Boston ivy and Virginia creeper, both formerly included in the genus *Ampelopsis,* are now considered members of *Parthenocissus* because, unlike *Ampelopsis,* both have disks at the end of their tendrils.

AMSONIA

BLUESTAR

Apocynaceae

PERENNIALS

✕ US, MS, LS, CS

☀ ◑ FULL SUN OR LIGHT SHADE

◔ ◕ MODERATE TO REGULAR WATER

Amsonia tabernaemontana

These elegant milkweed relatives are native to the South. Plants grow 2–3 ft. high and wide, with narrow leaves and erect stems crowned by clusters of small, star-shaped blue flowers in late spring. They are among the best perennials for fall color—foliage turns bright yellow in autumn. All are tough plants that succeed in ordinary soil. They tolerate some drought and suffer from few pests. Deer don't eat them.

A. ciliata. NARROWLEAF BLUESTAR. Heat zones 9–6. From southeastern U.S. Leaves narrower than those of *A. tabernaemontana,* wider than those of *A. hubrichtii.* Rich blue flowers; good fall leaf color.

A. hubrichtii. HUBRICHT'S BLUESTAR. Heat zones 9–3. Soft leaves are very narrow, almost needlelike. Discovered in Arkansas in 1942 by Leslie Hubricht and considered by many to be the finest of bluestars. It forms a clump to 3 ft. tall and wide; blossoms are sky blue. Fall foliage is an exceptionally bright, clear gold.

A. illustris. SHINING BLUESTAR. Heat zones 9–3. Native to Texas, Oklahoma, Arkansas, Missouri, and Kansas. Leathery, shiny, willowlike leaves; pale blue blossoms.

A. ludoviciana. LOUISIANA BLUESTAR. Heat zones 9–1. Rare bluestar native to Louisiana, Mississippi, Alabama, and Georgia. Backs of leaves are coated with a soft felt. Light blue flowers.

A. rigida. STIFF BLUESTAR. Heat zones 9–1. Compact species native to Florida and Georgia. Grows 1½–2 ft. high. Light blue flowers are held atop firm stems. Both leaves and stems are smoky purple when new.

A. tabernaemontana. BLUESTAR. Heat zones 9–1. Native to the Southeast, this is the species most commonly available commercially. It has dull dark green, willowlike leaves and slate blue flowers. Two selections with deep blue blossoms are 'Blue Ice', a compact grower to 15 in. tall and 2 ft. wide, and 'Louisiana Dwarf', to 1½ ft. tall and 2 ft. wide. 'Purple' has showy purple blooms.

AMUR CHOKECHERRY. See PRUNUS maackii

AMUR MAPLE. See ACER tataricum ginnala

ANACACHO ORCHID TREE. See BAUHINIA lunaroides

ANACAHUITA. See CORDIA boissieri

Anacardiaceae. The cashew family includes evergreen or deciduous trees, shrubs, and vines with small, unshowy, but often profuse flowers. Attractive foliage is colorful in fall; fruits are sometimes showy or edible. Many of these plants have poisonous or irritating sap. Mango and poison oak (*Toxicodendron*) indicate the diversity of the family.

ANACYCLUS depressus (A. pyrethrum depressus)

MOUNT ATLAS DAISY

Asteraceae (Compositae)

PERENNIAL

✕ US, MS, LS ♨ 8–5

☀ FULL SUN

◔ ◕ LITTLE TO MODERATE WATER

Anacyclus depressus

Native to North Africa, Spain. Slowly forms a dense, spreading mat somewhat like that of chamomile (*Chamaemelum*). Grayish, finely divided leaves. Single daisylike summer flowers to 2 in. across, with yellow center disks and white rays (red on reverse side). Good in sunny, dry, hot rock gardens. May freeze in severe winters or rot in cold, wet, heavy soil. Dislikes humidity.

ANAPHALIS

PEARLY EVERLASTING

Asteraceae (Compositae)

PERENNIALS

✕ US, MS, LS

◑ ● PARTIAL OR FULL SHADE

◔ ◕ MODERATE TO REGULAR WATER

Anaphalis triplinervis

Furry gray foliage is the outstanding characteristic of the pearly everlastings. Most are heat-tolerant, mounding plants with erect, branching stems carrying attractive (though not showy) clusters of papery-textured daisies that may be cut in summer for use in dried arrangements. Since they withstand lower light than most other gray-leafed plants, they're ideal for brightening semishady borders. Not fussy about soil but need reasonably good drainage. Seldom browsed by deer.

A. margaritacea. Heat zones 8–1. From many northern climates of the world. To 2–3 ft. high and wide. Leaves, to 6 in. long, are green above, white and woolly undersides. Pearly white flowers have yellow centers. *A. m. yedoensis* has smaller leaves and brown-tinted flowers; it is less cold hardy than the species.

A. triplinervis. Heat zones 8–3. Species from the Himalayas. Slightly smaller in overall size than *A. margaritacea,* with similar flowers but somewhat smaller, silvery leaves.

A

ANDROMEDA floribunda. See PIERIS floribunda

ANDROMEDA polifolia

BOG ROSEMARY

Ericaceae

EVERGREEN SHRUB

☒ US ⌶ 6–1

◐ LIGHT SHADE

💧 AMPLE WATER

Andromeda polifolia

Mounding shrub to 1–1½ ft. high and 2–3 ft. wide; native to northern climates in North America, Europe, Asia. Narrow, leathery leaves ½–2 in. long, dark green above, blue gray beneath. Urn-shaped, nodding spring flowers are white to pink, carried in clusters of up to eight at top of stems.

This little shrub requires strongly acid soil and protection from hot sun; intolerance of summer heat and drought limits its use in the South. It's a connoisseur's plant for rock garden, pot culture, or streamside or bog garden. Selections include 'Grandiflora', a dwarf with blue-green leaves and large, creamy, pink-shaded flowers; 'Nana', very compact and vigorous, with nearly round pink flowers; and 'Blue Ice', with powder blue foliage and profuse soft pink blooms.

ANDROPOGON

BLUESTEM

Poaceae (Gramineae)

PERENNIAL GRASSES

☒ US, MS, LS, CS ⌶ 8–1

☼ ◐ FULL SUN OR LIGHT SHADE

◌ ◖ ● ◕ WATER NEEDS VARY BY SPECIES

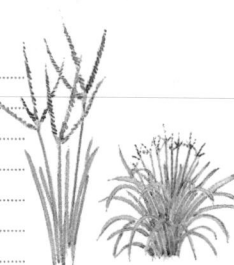
Andropogon gerardii

Once found in most of the continental U.S., these slender-leafed, upright, clumping native grasses formed a predominant part of old tall- and short-grass prairies. Big bluestem made waves of rippling green, sometimes nearly twice as tall as the settlers. Plant in drifts or masses, for erosion control, as airy vertical accents in flower or shrub borders, or in a natural garden with sunflowers *(Helianthus)*, goldenrod *(Solidago)*, and coreopsis. Be sure to divide clumps every few years when centers start to die; discard the center and replant vigorous young clumps from the edge. Every year, shear dried stems to base before new growth begins in spring.

A. gerardii. BIG BLUESTEM, TURKEYFOOT. Plant has variable growth to 3–7 ft., sometimes reaching to 10 ft. in moist, warm soil. Clumps can spread up to 3 ft. wide. Often tall enough to make a screen or dramatic specimen in large perennial borders. Thin blades are blue green or silvery in summer, bronze red in fall. In late summer, smoky purple flower spikes form at stem end in sets of three, like the toes of a turkey foot; these are followed in autumn by purple seed heads. Prefers moisture throughout the growing season; though it takes drought, it grows much less vigorously in dry conditions. Tolerates a wide range of soils, including clay soils and acid or alkaline soils.

A. glomeratus. BUSHY BLUESTEM, BUSHY BROOM SEDGE. Native to marshy areas in coastal eastern U.S. To 4–6 ft. tall, 2–3 ft. wide. Leaves are bluish green; bushy white flower plumes appear in late summer or early fall. Foliage and blossoms turn coppery orange with autumn's chill; the first heavy frost usually turns the flower plumes into billowing clouds of color that last well into winter. Regular to ample water.

A. virginicus. BROOM SEDGE. Grows to 3–4 ft. tall when in flower and usually less than 1 ft. across. Leaves are light green in summer, changing to a showy orange in fall. Produces silvery white blossom spikes that appear in autumn. Tolerates poor, dry, clay, or rocky soil. Often colonizes abandoned farm fields, roadsides, and disturbed areas such as construction sites. Little water.

ANEMONE

ANEMONE, WINDFLOWER

Ranunculaceae

PERENNIALS

☒ US, MS, LS

☼ ◐ ● EXPOSURE NEEDS VARY BY SPECIES

💧 REGULAR WATER

☣ ALL PARTS ARE POISONOUS IF INGESTED

Anemone blanda
'White Splendor'

A rich and varied group of plants ranging in size from alpine rock garden miniatures to tall Japanese anemones grown in borders; bloom extends from very early spring to fall, depending on species. Seldom browsed by deer.

Most of the anemones described below have fibrous roots or creeping rhizomes or rootstocks, but *A. blanda* and *A. coronaria* are grown from tubers requiring special attention. Set out *A. blanda* in fall; where winter temperatures drop below −10°F, apply a thick mulch after first hard frost. Plant *A. coronaria* in fall where it is hardy in the ground; in cooler regions, plant in early spring. In warmer climates, some gardeners soak tubers for a few hours before planting.

Plant tubers scarred side up (look for depressed scar left by base of last year's stem), setting them 1–2 in. deep and 8–12 in. apart in rich, light, well-drained loam. Or start in flats of damp sand; set out in garden when stems are a few inches tall. Keep soil moist during growth and bloom. Protect from birds until leaves toughen. In high-rainfall areas, excess moisture induces rot. Tuberous types best treated as annuals in much of the South, since they tend to be short lived where summers are rainy or winters are warm; *A. blanda*, in particular, needs distinct winter chill for good performance. Tuberous anemones make good container plants.

A. blanda. GREEK ANEMONE, GREEK WINDFLOWER. Heat zones 8–1. Native to southeastern Europe. Tubers produce a spreading mat of finely divided, softly hairy leaves (clumps are wider spreading in colder climates). In spring, each 2- to 8-in. stem bears one sky blue flower, 1–1½ in. across. Often confused with *A. apennina*, which has more pointed leaf segments. Selections with 2-in. flowers on 10- to 12-in. plants include 'Blue Star', 'Pink Star', 'White Splendor', and purplish red 'Radar'. All work well as underplantings for tulips, as ground cover drifts under deciduous shrubs and trees, and naturalized in short grass. Soak tubers in water for several hours before planting. Partial shade.

A. coronaria. POPPY-FLOWERED ANEMONE. Heat zones 12–8. Native to the Mediterranean; grows from a tuber. Species rarely planted; has been replaced by showy large-flowered hybrids for cutting and for spectacular spring color in borders or mass plantings. Blooms are 1½–2½ in. across, borne singly on 6- to 18-in. stems above finely divided leaves; come in shades of red and blue, as well as white. Among the most popular strains available are De Caen (single flowers) and St. Brigid (semidouble to double). Full sun or partial shade.

A. ×hybrida (A. japonica, A. hupehensis japonica). JAPANESE ANEMONE. Heat zones 8–4. Long-lived, fibrous-rooted perennial indispensable for fall flower color. Graceful, branching stems 2–4 ft. high rise from clump of dark green, three- to five-lobed leaves covered with soft hairs. Single or semidouble flowers in white, silvery pink, or rose. Slow to establish, but once started it spreads readily if roots are not disturbed. Space plants 2 ft. apart. May need staking. Mulch in fall

Anemone ×hybrida

where winters are severe. Increase by divisions in fall or early spring or by root cuttings in spring. Effective in clumps in front of tall shrubbery or under high-branching trees. Partial shade.

Many named selections of Japanese anemone are available, including the following.

'Honorine Jobert'. Single white flowers on 2- to 3-ft. stems; blooms reliably in Lower South.

'Königin Charlotte' ('Queen Charlotte'). Pink single flowers bloom on 3-ft. stems.

'Margarete' ('Lady Gilmour'). Semidouble or double rose pink flowers, 2- to 3-ft. stems.

'Prinz Heinrich'. Rosy red semidouble flowers on 1½- to 2-ft. stems.

'September Charm'. Single flowers in silvery pink on 2-ft. stems.

'Whirlwind'. Large, semidouble white flowers on 3-ft. stems.

A. nemorosa. WOOD ANEMONE. Heat zones 8–1. European native to 1 ft. high, with creeping rhizomes, deeply cut leaves, and inch-wide white (rarely pinkish or blue) spring flowers held above the foliage. Spreads slowly to make an attractive woodland ground cover. Many named selections exist; 'Allenii' has large blue flowers, and there are double forms. Partial or full shade.

A. pulsatilla. See Pulsatilla vulgaris

A. quinquefolia. Heat zones 8–1. American native. Attractive woodland ground cover like *A. nemorosa;* inch-wide white flowers in spring. *A. q. oregana* is similar but may have blue or pink blooms. Partial shade.

A. sylvestris. SNOWDROP ANEMONE. Heat zones 9–1. European native grows to 1½ ft. tall from a creeping rootstock. Fragrant, 1½- to 3-in., yellow-centered white flowers in spring, followed by cottony seed heads. Plant spreads readily in damp, wooded locations. 'Grandiflora' has larger blossoms; 'Flore Pleno' is double flowered. Partial or full shade.

A. tomentosa. GRAPELEAF ANEMONE. Heat zones 9–3. Vigorous, fibrous-rooted Tibetan native often sold as *A. vitifolia* 'Robustissima'. Foliage resembles grape leaves, grows in a spreading clump that gives rise to branching, 3½-ft.-high stems bearing single pink flowers in late summer, early fall. Allow 3 ft. between plants. Partial shade.

ANEMONELLA thalictroides

RUE ANEMONE

Ranunculaceae

PERENNIAL

☀ US, MS, LS H 8–1

◑ ● PARTIAL OR FULL SHADE

💧 REGULAR WATER

Anemonella thalictroides

Delicate woodland plant native to eastern North America. To 9 in. high and up to 1 ft. wide, with finely divided leaves resembling those of meadow rue *(Thalictrum)*. Loose clusters of inch-wide white (usually) or pink flowers appear in early spring. Attractive for close-up viewing. Selection known as either 'Rosea Plena' or 'Schoaff's Double Pink' has long-lasting, fully double pink flowers like tiny roses.

ANETHUM graveolens

DILL

Apiaceae (Umbelliferae)

ANNUAL

☀ US, MS, LS, CS, TS H 12–1

☀ FULL SUN

💧 REGULAR WATER

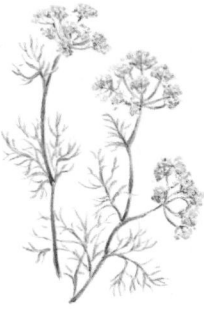

Anethum graveolens

Aromatic herb to 3–4 ft. tall. Soft, feathery leaves; umbrella-like, 6-in.-wide clusters of small yellow flowers. The seeds and leaves have a pungent fragrance. Sow seed where the plants are to be grown; for a constant supply, sow several times during spring and summer (germinates and grows better in spring than in summer). Thin seedlings to about 1½ ft. apart. An easy way to grow it in a casual garden is to let a few plants go to seed. Seedlings appear here and there at odd times and can be pulled and chopped for use as seasoning. Use seeds in pickling and vinegar; use fresh or dried leaves in cooked dishes, salads, sauces, as garnish. Caterpillars of swallowtail butterflies often feed on the foliage.

ANGELICA

ANGELICA

Apiaceae (Umbelliferae)

BIENNIALS

☀ US, MS, LS, CS H 9–1

◑ ● PARTIAL TO FULL SHADE

💧 REGULAR WATER

Angelica archangelica

Tropical-looking carrot relatives with divided and toothed, yellow-green leaves 2–3 ft. long. In early summer, the plant sends up a thick, hollow stem to 6 ft. tall topped by a 4-ft.-wide, umbrella-shaped cluster of small flowers. Dramatic in a woodland garden. Grow in moist, rich soil. Propagate from seeds as soon as they ripen in fall. Because plants are taprooted and don't transplant well, sow seed in place. To prolong plant's life for a few years, cut out the flowering stem as soon as it forms.

A. archangelica. Native to northern Europe and western Asia. Green stem topped by greenish yellow flowers. Leaves are a nice addition to salads; the leafstalks can be cooked and eaten like asparagus. Both leafstalks and hollow flower stems can be candied and used to decorate pastries. Seeds are used commercially in flavoring spirits, candies, and cakes.

A. atropurpurea. PURPLESTEM ANGELICA. Native from Newfoundland to Delaware and west to Minnesota. Purple stem capped by greenish white blossoms. This species was used by Native Americans to soothe an upset stomach.

ANGELICA TREE. See ARALIA elata

ANGELONIA angustifolia

Scrophulariaceae

PERENNIAL OFTEN TREATED AS ANNUAL

☀ LS, CS, TS H 12–7

☀ FULL SUN

💧 REGULAR WATER

Angelonia angustifolia 'Hilo Princess'

Native to tropics of the Americas, angelonia is perennial in Florida but grown as an annual in most other places. It looks a bit like a shorter delphinium, but it blooms all summer and loves the heat. Showy spikes of blue, purple, pink, or white blossoms appear atop plants that grow 1–1½ ft. tall and about 1 ft. wide. Periodic deadheading keeps the flowers coming. Excellent both as a bedding plant and in containers; provides long-lasting cut flowers. Easy to grow in moist, well-drained soil; not bothered by pests. Deer don't usually eat it.

Many hybrids are offered. 'Alba' has white flowers; 'Blue Pacific' has blue-and-white blooms, 'Pink' pastel pink ones. Purple-flowered 'Hilo Princess' is bushy and very floriferous. The AngelMist series features a variety of colors, including plum, lavender, and white; some flowers are marked with white, pink, or purple. In the Carita series, stems branch at the base, giving the plant a full look; blossoms are deep pink, lavender, purple, or white.

ANGEL'S HAIR. See ARTEMISIA schmidtiana

ANGEL'S TEARS. See NARCISSUS triandrus

ANGEL'S TRUMPET. See BRUGMANSIA, DATURA

ANGELWING JASMINE. See JASMINUM laurifolium nitidum

ANISACANTHUS

DESERT HONEYSUCKLE

Acanthaceae

EVERGREEN AND DECIDUOUS SHRUBS

✂ LS, CS, TS

☼ ◐ EXPOSURE NEEDS VARY BY SPECIES

◐ MODERATE WATER

Anisacanthus thurberi

These heat-loving shrubs have nectar-filled tubular flowers with two lobes above the mouth, three on the lower lip. Highly favored by hummingbirds and butterflies. Fairly drought tolerant. For best growth and bloom, water deeply every 2 to 3 weeks in summer.

A. quadrifidus wrightii (A. wrightii). Heat zones 10–9. Deciduous. Native to southeastern Texas, northeastern Mexico. To 3 ft. tall, 4 ft. wide, with dark green leaves 2 in. long and 1 in. wide. Spikes of 2-in.-long, brilliant red-orange flowers from early summer to fall. Rabbits love new shoots; protect with wire cage until a woody structure is established. For compact shape and prolific bloom, cut back by one-half to two-thirds before new spring growth commences. Full sun or light shade. 'Mexican Flame' is a superior selection grown from cuttings.

A. thurberi. CHUPAROSA. Heat zones 12–9. Mostly evergreen. Native to northern Mexico and to canyons and washes of the Sonoran Desert of southern Arizona and New Mexico. In mild-winter areas grows to 4 ft. tall (or more) and about as wide, with stout branches. Best appearance when treated as a perennial, cut to ground before new spring growth begins. Much valued for its spikes of 1½-in.-long, yellow-orange flowers held above light green leaves 1½–2 in. long, ½ in. wide. Blooms most prolifically in spring, with occasional blossoms in summer and fall. Full sun. Plants with red or orange-red flowers sold under this name may actually be *Justicia spicigera*.

ANISE. See PIMPINELLA anisum

ANISE HYSSOP. See AGASTACHE foeniculum

ANISE TREE. See ILLICIUM

Annonaceae. The annona family consists primarily of tropical trees and shrubs; many of the plants have edible fruit. A familiar example is pawpaw (*Asimina triloba*).

ANNUAL BLUEGRASS. See POA annua

ANNUAL MALLOW. See LAVATERA trimestris

ANREDERA cordifolia (Boussingaultia baselloides)

MADEIRA VINE

Basellaceae

PERENNIAL VINE

✂ CS, TS ⊞ 12–9; OR DIG AND STORE

☼ FULL SUN

◐ MODERATE WATER

Anredera cordifolia

Native to South America. Old-fashioned plant useful for summer screening of decks or other sitting areas. Heart-shaped green leaves 1–3 in. long; fragrant white flowers in foot-long spikes in late summer, fall. Climbs by twining; may reach 20 ft. in one season. Small tubers form where leaves join stems. Can run rampant in the Coastal and Tropical South. In areas farther north, dig in fall and store tubers over winter.

ANTENNARIA dioica

PUSSY TOES

Asteraceae (Compositae)

PERENNIAL

✂ US, MS, LS ⊞ 9–4

☼ FULL SUN

◐◐ MODERATE TO REGULAR WATER

Antennaria dioica

Native to Europe, North America. Forms inch-high mats of woolly foliage and slowly spreads among rocks, between paving stones, or at front of border. Furry puffs of flowers are pinkish white in the basic species, deep pink in 'Rubra', and rose pink in 'Rosea'. Extremely hardy to cold; will withstand some light foot traffic.

ANTHEMIS

Asteraceae (Compositae)

PERENNIALS

✂ ZONES VARY BY SPECIES

☼ FULL SUN

◐◐ MODERATE TO REGULAR WATER

Anthemis tinctoria
'E. C. Buxton'

Some species are weedy, but those listed here (from southern Europe and Turkey) are garden plants with long-lasting daisylike or buttonlike flowers. Many-segmented leaves are aromatic, especially when bruised. Provide good drainage.

A. carpatica (A. cretica carpatica). Zones US, MS, LS, CS; 8–1. Forms low, 2-ft.-wide mounds of green to gray-green foliage. Stems about 6 in. high rise from foliage clumps in spring and summer, bearing 1½-in. white daisies with yellow centers.

A. marschalliana (A. biebersteiniana). Zones US, MS, LS; 9–6. Rounded plant 1 ft. tall and wide, with finely cut, fernlike, silvery leaves and 1-in., brilliant yellow daisylike blooms in summer.

A. nobilis. See Chamaemelum nobile

A. punctata cupaniana. Zones US, MS, LS, CS; 9–6. Mound of silvery foliage 1 ft. tall and at least as wide, topped by 2½-in., long-lasting white daisies in summer.

A. tinctoria. GOLDEN MARGUERITE. Zones US, MS, LS; 8–3. Erect, shrubby plant to 2–3 ft. tall and wide, with angular stems, light green leaves, and golden yellow, 2-in. daisies in summer and early fall. Good cut flower. Cut back lightly after first flush of bloom to keep flowers coming. Short lived; start new plants from stem cuttings in spring or divide clumps in spring or fall. Selections include 'Beauty of Grallagh', with flowers in golden orange; 'E. C. Buxton', white with yellow centers; 'Kelwayi', golden yellow; and 'Moonlight', pale yellow.

ANTHRISCUS

Apiaceae (Umbelliferae)

ANNUALS AND PERENNIALS OR BIENNIALS

✂ ZONES VARY BY SPECIES

☼ ◐ EXPOSURE NEEDS VARY BY SPECIES

◐ REGULAR WATER

Anthriscus cerefolium

Native to Europe, North Africa, and Asia. Though both of these plants produce many umbrella-shaped clusters of tiny flowers, they are valued for their fernlike foliage. In the first species, the leaves are used in cooking; in the second, the foliage brings deep, striking color to the perennial border.

A. cerefolium. CHERVIL. Annual. Zones US, MS, LS, CS, TS; 6–1. Low foliage mounds about a foot wide; 1- to 2-ft. flower stems topped with white blossoms in summer. The leaves have a parsleylike flavor with overtones of anise; use like parsley, fresh or dried. Sow seeds in place in early spring (in cold-winter areas) or in fall (where winters are mild). In the following years, volunteer seedlings will keep you supplied with new plants. Goes to seed quickly in hot weather; keep flower clusters cut to encourage leafy growth. Partial shade.

A. sylvestris 'Ravenswing'. Perennial or biennial. Zones US, MS; 6–1. Very attractive purple-black foliage in clump 1½ ft. high, 2½ ft. wide. In late spring or early summer, flowering stems to 3 ft. tall bear white blossoms with purplish pink bracts. Deadhead for best appearance and to prevent self-sowing. Full sun or light shade.

ANTHURIUM

Araceae

PERENNIALS

☘ TS H 12–10; OR HOUSEPLANTS

☼ PARTIAL SHADE; BRIGHT INDIRECT LIGHT

💧 REGULAR WATER

Anthurium andraeanum

Native to tropical American rain forests. Exotic plants with handsome dark green leaves and lustrous flower bracts. Bloom best in moderate shade. Among species listed here, all but *A. hookeri* are usually grown as potted plants, even in tropical climates.

Anthuriums make unusual indoor plants. As such, they are no more difficult to grow than some orchids. The higher the humidity, the better. Leaves lose shiny texture and may die if humidity drops below 50 percent for more than a few days. Keep pots on trays of moist gravel, in bathroom, or under polyethylene cover. Sponge or spray leaves several times daily. For good bloom, locate by window with good light but no direct sun. Generally grow best in 80–90°F temperature range but will get along at normal house temperature. Growth stops below 65°F, and plant is damaged below 50°F. Protect from drafts. Pot in coarse, porous mix of leaf mold, sandy soil, and shredded osmunda. Give light feeding every 4 weeks.

A. andraeanum. FLAMING ANTHURIUM. Dark green, oblong leaves to 1 ft. long and 6 in. wide, heart shaped at base. Spreading, heart-shaped flower bracts in shades of red, rose, pink, or white shine as though lacquered. Bracts reach 6 in. long, surround yellow, callalike flower spike. Bloom more or less continuously—plant may have from four to six flowers during the year. Flowers last 6 weeks on plant, 4 weeks after cutting.

A. crystallinum. Leaves to 1½ ft. long, 1 ft. wide, deep green with striking white veining. Unexciting flowers with small, narrow, greenish bracts. Many similar anthuriums exist in the florist trade; plants offered as *A. crystallinum* may be *A. clarinervium, A. magnificum,* or some other species.

A. hookeri. Grown in the tropical landscape for handsome foot-wide "nest" of leaves that can reach 8 in. long. Excellent as an accent in a wind-sheltered garden or as a potted specimen. Indoors or out, needs high humidity. Grow in well-aerated, rich, moist soil; feed regularly.

A. scandens. Climbing or trailing plant to 2 ft., with 3-in.-long, tapered oval leaves. Small, fragrant, greenish flowers; translucent lilac berries.

A. scherzerianum. Slow-growing, compact plant to 2 ft. Dark green leaves 8 in. long, 2 in. wide. Broad, 3-in.-long bracts in deep red varying to rose, salmon, white. Yellow, spirally coiled flower spikes.

FOR INFORMATION ON YOUR CLIMATE ZONES
PLEASE SEE PAGES 28–38

ANTIGONON leptopus

CORAL VINE, QUEEN'S WREATH, ROSA DE MONTANA

Polygonaceae

EVERGREEN OR DECIDUOUS VINE

☘ LS, CS, TS H 12–8

☼ FULL SUN

💧 LITTLE TO REGULAR WATER

Antigonon leptopus

This classic vine of the Deep South is actually native to Mexico and thrives in sweltering summer weather. A rampant grower that climbs by tendrils, it can easily cover 20 ft. in a year. Its handsome, bright green, heart- or arrow-shaped leaves reach 3–5 in. long. From summer to fall, bears a profusion of coral pink flowers in airy, arching sprays to 6 in. or longer; a vine in full bloom is a magnificent sight. Selections include white 'Album', deep reddish pink 'Baja Red', and near-red 'Rubrum'. Seedlings of these selections vary in flower color.

Coral vine grows from a large tuber and is evergreen in the Tropical South. In regions where winter temperatures drop below 25°F, the plant often dies back to the ground, then resprouts in spring. Mulching in autumn helps to protect the roots during winter in the Lower South. In the Upper and Middle South, treat coral vine as an annual, saving the seeds for next year's plants.

Coral vine is a common sight in Florida, Louisiana, the Gulf Coast, and parts of Central and Southeast Texas. Use it to shade a patio, porch, or terrace, or let its blossoms and foliage adorn fences, walls, railings, and balconies.

ANTIRRHINUM majus

SNAPDRAGON

Scrophulariaceae

PERENNIAL TREATED AS ANNUAL

☘ US, MS, LS, CS, TS H 9–1

☼ FULL SUN

💧 REGULAR WATER

Antirrhinum majus

Among the best flowers for sunny borders and cutting, reaching greatest perfection in spring and early summer. In the Lower, Coastal, and Tropical South, will bloom in winter and spring. Individual flower of basic snapdragon has five lobes, which are divided into unequal upper and lower "jaws"; slight pinch at sides of flower will make the dragon open its jaws. Later developments include double flowers; the bell-shaped kind, with round, open flowers; and the azalea-shaped bloom, which is a double bell flower. All are available in many colors. Plants range from 6 in. across for smallest types to 2 ft. wide for the tallest.

Tall and intermediate forms are splendid vertical accents in beds and borders with delphinium, iris, daylily *(Hemerocallis)*, peach-leafed bluebell *(Campanula persicifolia)*, and foxglove *(Digitalis)*. Dwarf kinds are quite effective as edgings and in rock gardens, in raised beds, and in containers.

Snapping snapdragons in tall (2½- to 3-ft.) range include Rocket and Topper strains (single flowers) and Double Supreme strain. Intermediates (12–20 in.) are Cinderella, Coronette, Liberty, Minaret, Sprite, and Tahiti, and the selection 'Princess White with Purple Eye'. Dwarfs (6–8 in.) include Dwarf Bedding Floral Carpet, Kim, Kolibri, and Royal Carpet.

Bell-flowered strains include Bright Butterflies and Wedding Bells (both 2½ ft.); Little Darling and Liberty Bell (both 15 in.); and Pixie (6–8 in.). Among azalea-flowered strains are Madame Butterfly (2½ ft.) and Sweetheart (1 ft.).

Sow seed in flats from late summer to early spring for later transplanting; or buy started plants at a garden center. Set out plants in early fall in

A

the Lower, Coastal, and Tropical South, spring in the Upper and Middle South. If snapdragons set out in early fall reach bud stage before night temperatures drop below 50°F, they will start blooming in winter in mild areas and continue until weather gets hot.

Snapdragons—like lawn grasses, roses, and hollyhocks (*Alcea*)—can fall victim to rust, a sometimes persistent fungal disease (see "A Practical Guide to Gardening," page 604). To avoid or minimize the problem, start with rust-resistant selections and plant in area with good air circulation. Keep plants well watered, but avoid overhead watering (or do it only in the morning or on sunny days). Feed regularly. If the disease does persist, change planting locations from one year to the next—or select a different annual.

APACHE PLUME. See FALLUGIA paradoxa

APHELANDRA squarrosa

ZEBRA PLANT

Acanthaceae

EVERGREEN SHRUB

⚡ TS **H** 12–10; OR HOUSEPLANT

◑ SOME SHADE; BRIGHT INDIRECT LIGHT

💧 REGULAR WATER

Aphelandra squarrosa

There's little doubt how zebra plant got its name. Its large (8- to 12-in.-long), blackish green leaves are adorned with striking white stripes along the veins and midribs. As a bonus, the plant blooms for about 6 weeks in fall, when small yellow blossoms peek out from showy, waxy yellow bracts. 'Louisae' is the most common selection, but selections 'Apollo' and 'Dania' are more compact and have more striking venation.

For most Southerners, this native of Mexico and South America is an indoor plant. It prefers filtered sun from a south or west window. Too much sunlight burns the foliage; too little results in leggy growth and small leaves. Let the soil surface dry slightly between waterings, but don't let the plant wilt. Feed with a water-soluble houseplant fertilizer every 2 weeks from spring until fall. Cut back leggy stems after bloom to encourage branching and create a bushier plant.

Gardeners in south Florida can grow zebra plant outdoors, where it blooms in summer and fall. Give it dappled shade and well-drained soil. If an unexpected freeze injures the top, cut the plant to the ground; it will resprout.

Apiaceae. This family, also known as Umbelliferae, comprises nearly 3,000 plants, most of them annuals and perennials. All have flowers in umbels—flat- or round-topped clusters whose individual flower stems all originate at a single point. Many are vegetables (carrot, parsnip, celery) or aromatic herbs (parsley, coriander, dill). Others are grown for ornament, such as Queen Anne's lace (*Daucus carota carota*), sea holly (*Eryngium*), and blue lace flower (*Trachymene*).

Apocynaceae. The dogbane family contains shrubs, trees, and vines with milky, often poisonous sap. Flowers are often showy and fragrant, as in *Plumeria* and oleander (*Nerium*).

Aponogetonaceae. Only *Aponogeton* genus is of gardening importance in this small family of aquatic plants.

FOR INFORMATION ON SELECTING PLANTS
PLEASE SEE PAGES 39–144

APONOGETON distachyus

CAPE PONDWEED, WATER HAWTHORN

Aponogetonaceae

AQUATIC PLANT

⚡ US, MS, LS, CS, TS **H** 12–5

☼ ◑ FULL SUN OR PARTIAL SHADE

💧 LIVES IN WATER

Aponogeton distachyus

Native to South Africa. Suitable for small water gardens. Like miniature water lily (*Nymphaea*), it produces floating leaves from a submerged tuber. Leaves are long and narrow; ⅓-in.-long white, fragrant flowers stand above water in double-branched clusters. In hot-summer climates, blooms in cool weather and is dormant in hottest weather; where winters are cold, blooms in summer and is dormant in winter. Same culture as water lily.

APPLE

Rosaceae

DECIDUOUS FRUIT TREES

⚡ ZONES VARY BY SELECTION

☼ FULL SUN

💧 REGULAR WATER DURING FRUIT DEVELOPMENT

▶ SEE CHART PAGE 172

Apple

Johnny Appleseed wasn't a Southerner, but the seed he spread took root in much of the South. Our most widely adapted fruit tree, the apple thrives in home gardens and orchards from central Florida all the way north to Canada. The apple blossom is the state flower of Arkansas.

Depending on the selection, apples ripen anywhere from June to early November. To grow and fruit properly, most selections require between 900 and 1,200 "chill hours" (hours of temperatures at 45°F or below) each winter. If you live in the Coastal South, be sure you select types with a low chill requirement, such as 'Anna' or 'Dorsett Golden'. Apples won't grow in the Tropical South.

Not all selections require cross-pollination with a different selection to produce fruit, but most do—so unless you already have apples or crabapples growing nearby, you'll need at least two different selections to get fruit. Be aware that some apples, called triploids ('Stayman' is a good example), produce sterile pollen and will not pollinate themselves or other trees. If you're planting only two trees and a triploid is one of them, make sure the other is self-fruitful—'Golden Delicious', 'Golden Russet', or 'Grimes Golden', for example. That way, each will bear fruit.

A standard apple tree grows 20–25 ft. tall and wide. If space is at a premium, consider planting dwarf or semidwarf trees. These take up much less room and give you more fruit per square foot. You can even buy a standard or dwarf tree with four or five different selections grafted onto it.

In choosing selections, don't limit yourself to the ones you can buy at the grocery store. Remember, most are there because they ship well without bruising and look pretty. ('Delicious' is a perfect example—you could fire it from a cannon and it wouldn't bruise, but the taste is rather bland compared to that of some other selections.) Instead, consider how you'll be using the fruit and how much work you want to put into the tree. Want a good all-around tree that's easy to grow? Try 'Golden Delicious'. A good fresh-eating apple? Bite into a 'Fuji', 'Ginger Gold', 'Grimes Golden', 'Liberty', or 'Stayman'. For a good baking apple, try 'Rome Beauty', 'Pound Sweet', 'Jonathan', or 'Jonagold'. If you'd prefer a tree that you'll seldom have to spray, plant 'Freedom' or 'Liberty'.

Apple trees are longer lived and easier to grow than most fruit trees, but they still require regular care. Though they'll tolerate heavy clay and even rocky soil, they prefer deep, fertile, well-drained soil. They typically need regular applications of nitrogen; amount and frequency depend on soil. Check with your Cooperative Extension Office for fertilizing information.

To avoid frost damage in spring, plant on slopes rather than in low spots. Supplemental watering during summer dry spells produces juicier fruit. Apples often bear fruit in clusters of three or four; if you let all of them ripen, they'll all be small. Thinning the clusters to one or two in spring results in bigger, juicier fruit.

The main insect pests are apple maggot, codling moth, and plum curculio, all of which infest the fruit. Pheromone traps, *Bacillus thuringiensis (Bt)*, or horticultural oil may be enough to thwart these pests in most areas, but proper timing of controls is critical. Synthetic insecticides such as malathion or carbaryl (Sevin) provide longer-lasting control, but be aware that applying carbaryl just after fruit set may cause the young apples to drop. It can also increase problems with mites.

Diseases cause problems more commonly than insects do. Typical diseases include apple scab, which causes hard, corky spots on fruit; cedar-apple rust, which produces orange spots on leaves and fruit; and fireblight, which blackens and kills young twigs and leaves. To avoid these problems, consider planting disease-resistant selections. Applying proper fungicides, as well as dormant oil in winter, can also aid in control. For more information, consult the *Southern Living Garden Problem Solver*.

Dwarf, semidwarf, and spur apples. Dwarf apples (5–8 ft. tall and wide) are good choices if you have limited space or want to grow several types of apples in the space a standard tree would take. Dwarfs bear at a younger age than standard apples, but they have shallow roots and need the support of a post, fence, wall, or sturdy trellis to withstand wind and heavy rain. They also need well-drained soil and extra care in feeding and watering. Genetic dwarf apples, such as 'Garden Delicious', are naturally small and stay that way; even grafting them onto a standard (non-dwarfing) rootstock would not produce a standard-size tree.

Semidwarf trees are larger than dwarfs but smaller than standard trees. They're the best choice for most people, producing a bigger crop than dwarfs in a relatively short period of time.

Spur apples are natural or genetically engineered semidwarfs about two-thirds the size of standard apple trees. Their fruiting spurs—short branches that grow from wood 2 years old and older—form earlier than those of nonspur types (within 2 to 3 years of planting) and grow closer together on shorter branches, giving more apples per foot of branch. Unfortunately, relatively few spur-type apple selections are readily available. Those you may be able to find include 'Redchief Red Delicious', 'Cumberland Spur Red Delicious', and 'Starkspur Golden Delicious'.

Garden centers and mail-order nurseries won't generally specify the name of the dwarfing or semidwarfing rootstock they use on the tree they sell you. There are many different rootstocks, however, and not all perform well in the South. If you have a choice, select M9, M26, or P22 rootstocks for dwarf trees. For semidwarfs, select MM106 or M7A (MM106 produces a tree about 12–15 ft. tall and wide; M7A produces a tree about 8–12 ft. tall and wide). Combining a spur apple with a dwarfing rootstock isn't a good idea; the resulting tree is puny and bears small crops. Combining a spur apple with a semidwarfing rootstock, however, is okay.

Training and pruning apple trees. For most home use, plant dwarf or semidwarf trees for ease in maintenance and harvest. Even commercial growers favor these smaller trees, since closer spacing permits more trees to the acre and a heavier crop. Preferred style is pyramidal or modified leader, in which widely angled branches are encouraged to grow in spiral placement around the trunk. Don't worry about fruit production the first 2 or 3 years—prune to develop strong, evenly spaced scaffold branches. Keep narrow-angled crotches from developing; don't let side branches outgrow the leader, or secondary branches outgrow the primary branches.

To prune mature trees (do it late in the dormant season), remove weak, dead, or poorly placed branches and twigs, especially those growing toward the center of the tree (bearing is heaviest when some sun can reach

---

WHAT APPLES NEED

WINTER CHILL: Most selections demand 900 to 1,200 hours of temperatures at or below 45°F. In mild-winter areas, look for low-chill selections (100 to 400 hours).

FULL SUN: Plenty of sunshine is essential for a good crop—so don't crowd an apple tree into a partially shaded site. To plant more than one selection in a small space, choose dwarf or multiple-selection trees.

WATERING: When fruit is developing, make up for any lack of rainfall with periodic deep soakings.

POLLINATION: Although some selections are self-pollinating, most need cross-pollination with another selection to bear fruit.

'Spitzenberg'

---

the middle). Also remove any suckers from the base and any water sprouts (unbranched shoots that grow straight up from the main limbs). Removing such growth will encourage development of strong new wood with new fruiting spurs (on apples, spurs may produce for up to 20 years but they tend to weaken after about 3 years) and discourage mildew. If you have inherited an old tree, selective thinning of branches will accomplish the same goal.

Dwarf trees can be grown as espaliers tied to wood or wire frames, fences, or other supports. The technique requires manipulating the branches to the desired pattern and pruning out excess growth.

For ornamental relatives, see *Malus*.

IN-CIDER TRADING. *You might think that the colonists who brought apples to the South from Europe raised them for their tasty fruit, but you'd be wrong. In fact, most early apple orchards were primarily planted for cider. Why? Because drinking water was often polluted, whereas the acidity and alcohol in hard cider killed bacteria—and gave the settlers a beverage that was safe to drink. The desire for cider led to the dissemination of many classic heirloom apples, including 'Ashmead's Kernel', 'Grimes Golden', 'Limbertwig', and 'Roxbury Russet'.* ❖

APRICOT

Rosaceae

DECIDUOUS FRUIT TREES

US

FULL SUN

REGULAR WATER DURING FRUIT DEVELOPMENT

Apricot

There's a good reason why most Southerners see apricots only in cans and jars. These tasty stone fruits fall victim to a host of insects and diseases here and seldom live for long. What's more, they bloom so early in the South—often in late winter—that sudden frosts kill the blooms, precluding a crop. Complicating matters is their need for distinct winter chill to set flower buds. The parts of the South most favorable for growing apricots include West Virginia, western Maryland, the Blue Ridge Mountains of Virginia, northern Kentucky, southern Missouri, and western North Carolina. If you do decide to try them, it's always a good idea to plant late-blooming selections, which are less likely to sustain frost damage.

▶ page 176

APPLE

NAME	ZONES	RIPENING DATE	FRUIT	COMMENTS
'Adina'	LS, CS; 9–1	Midseason	Large, round, fragrant, dark red. Firm, sweet, creamy white flesh with cinnamon overtones	Needs very little winter chill. Use 'Anna', 'Dorsett Golden', 'Ein Shemer' as pollenizer
'Anna'	LS, CS; 9–1	Early. Sometimes a light second crop later in the season	Large. Pale green blushed red. Crisp, sweet, slightly tangy	Begins producing at a young age. Needs very little winter chill. Good annual bearer. Use 'Dorsett Golden' as pollenizer
'Arkansas Black'	US, MS, LS; 8–1	Late	Medium size. Dark, deep red. Hard-crisp. Excellent keeper; best flavor after storage for 2 months. Good for cooking, fresh eating	Born 1870 in Benton County, Arkansas. 'Arkansas Black Spur' is spurred variation
'Ashmead's Kernel'	US, MS; 8–1	Late	Medium size. Red-orange blush over rough yellow-green skin. Crisp, juicy, aromatic. Good keeper; best flavor after a few months' storage. A favorite for cider	Good disease resistance. Originated in Gloucester, England, around 1700
'Black Twig'	US, MS, LS; 8–1	Late	Large to medium. Green to yellow flushed with red. Tart, fine-grained flesh. Good for fresh eating, cooking, and cider. Good keeper; best flavor develops in storage	Good disease resistance. Originated near Fayetteville, Tennessee, in the early 1800s
'Braeburn'	US, MS, LS; 8–1	Late	Medium size. Orange-red blush over yellow ground. Crisp, sweet-tart; stores well	From New Zealand. Thin fruit to prevent bearing in alternate years. Susceptible to mites
'Calville Blanc d'Hiver'	US, MS; 8–1	Late	Medium to large. Light green spotted with red; flattish shape. Good for cider or vinegar	Susceptible to cedar-apple rust, powdery mildew, and scab. Bears at a young age. Grown in France since 1627
'Carolina Red June'	US, MS, LS; 8–1	Early	Pale yellow flushed with purplish red. Juicy, aromatic. Good for fresh eating, pies, cider	Originated in North Carolina. Not a good keeper, but ripens fruit over a long period. Heavy bearer. Thin crop for bigger fruit
'Carter's Blue'	MS, LS; 8–1	Midseason	Medium to large, with a roundish oblong shape. Greenish yellow skin with unique bluish purple bloom. Crisp, yellowish white flesh with a sweet-tart flavor	Discovered by Colonel Carter in Mt. Meigs, Alabama, around 1840
'Cortland'	US, MS; 8–1	Early midseason	Large. Dark bluish red skin streaked with yellow. Excellent all-purpose fruit; does not turn brown when sliced	Vigorous; bears at a young age. Produces annually. Holds fruit better than 'McIntosh'. Excellent pollenizer
'Delicious' ('Red Delicious')	US, MS, LS; 8–1	Midseason to late	Medium to large; easily recognized by pointed blossom end with five knobs. Color and shape vary with strain and climate; best where days are warm and sunny, nights cool. Older, striped kinds have better flavor than highly colored commercial strains	'Crimson Spur', 'Cumberland Spur Red Delicious', and 'Redchief' are popular home selections. All types susceptible to scab
'Dorsett Golden'	LS, CS; 9–1	Early	Medium to large. Yellow or greenish yellow; sweet flavor. Good for eating fresh or cooking. Keeps a few weeks	Seedling of 'Golden Delicious' from Bermuda. Needs very little winter chill. Good pollenizer for 'Adina', 'Anna', and 'Ein Shemer'
'Earlycrisp'	US, MS; 8–1	Early	Medium size. Smooth, almost translucent, greenish yellow skin with a pinkish red blush. Fruit has a sweet-tart flavor. Good fresh or for cooking	One of the better early apples
'Ein Shemer'	LS, CS; 9–1	Early	Medium size. Yellow to greenish yellow. Juicy, crisp, mildly tangy	Needs very little winter chill. Pollinates 'Adina', 'Anna', and 'Dorsett Golden'
'Empire'	US, MS, LS; 8–1	Late midseason	Small to medium, roundish, dark red. Creamy white flesh is juicy, crisp, mildly tart. Good keeper	Cross between 'McIntosh' and 'Delicious'. Semispur growth habit. Good tree structure. Susceptible to spring frost damage

APPLE

NAME	ZONES	RIPENING DATE	FRUIT	COMMENTS
'Enterprise'	US, MS, LS; 8–1	Late	Medium-size, firm fruit with red blush. Sweet-tart flavor. Keeps well; good cooking apple	Disease resistant; subject to preharvest fruit drop
'Freedom'	US, MS, LS, CS; 8–1	Midseason	Medium to large. Round red fruit. Good for fresh eating and cooking. Sweet-tart flavor	Disease resistant. Excellent pollenizer for 'Liberty', another disease-resistant selection
'Fuji'	US, MS, LS; 8–1	Late	Medium to large. Yellow-green ground with red stripes; firm, very sweet, excellent flavor. Stores exceptionally well	Tends to bear heavy crops in alternate years. A cross between 'Rall's Janet' and 'Delicious' made in Japan in 1939
'Gala'	US, MS, LS; 8–1	Early to midseason	Medium size. Beautiful red-on-yellow color. Highly aromatic, firm, crisp, juicy, sweet yellow flesh. Loses flavor in storage	From New Zealand. Vigorous, heavy bearer with long, supple branches that break easily; may need support. Susceptible to fireblight
'Garden Delicious'	US, MS; 8–1	Midseason	Medium to large; golden green with red blush	Genetic dwarf growing 5–8 ft. tall and wide
'Ginger Gold'	US, MS, LS; 8–1	Early midseason	Medium to large. Yellow, firm, crisp; mild flavor. Resembles 'Golden Delicious'. Good keeper; also good for cooking, eating fresh	One of the better early yellow apples. Ripens over 2–3 weeks. Susceptible to mildew. Resistant to sunburn. Chance seedling from the orchard of Ginger Harvey in Livingston, Virginia
'Golden Delicious' ('Yellow Delicious')	US, MS, LS; 8–1	Late midseason	Medium to large. Clear yellow, may develop skin russeting in some areas. Similar in shape to 'Delicious', with less prominent knobs. Highly aromatic, crisp. Excellent for eating fresh, cooking, cider	Not related to 'Red Delicious'; different flavor, habit. Self-fruitful. Long bloom season, heavy pollen production make it a good pollenizer. Various strains available. Spur types include 'Goldspur', 'Starkspur Golden Delicious', 'Yellospur'
'Golden Russet'	US, MS, LS; 8–1	Late	Medium size. Greenish yellow to gold, marked with russet. Fine-grained yellow flesh. Excellent for cider, fresh eating, and cooking	Vigorous; resistant to scab but susceptible to rust and fireblight. Self-fruitful. Good pollenizer for other selections
'Gold Rush'	US, MS, LS; 8–1	Late	Medium size. Yellow, often with russeting. Best after storage. Good for pies, fresh eating	Immune to scab; good resistance to mildew; some resistance to fireblight
'Granny Smith'	US, MS, LS, CS; 8–1	Early midseason	Large. Bright to yellowish green; firm and tart. Good quality. Stores well; good for pies, sauce	Australian favorite before it came to U.S. Resistant to rust. Good pollenizer
'Grimes Golden'	US, MS, LS; 8–1	Midseason	Medium size. Round, golden. Crisp, spicy-sweet yellow flesh. Good for fresh eating, cider, desserts. Stores moderately well	Bears young. Discovered in West Virginia by Thomas Grimes around 1804. Self-fruitful. Good pollenizer for other selections
'Horse'	US, MS, LS; 8–1	Early midseason	Greenish yellow, blushed pink. Tart flavor. Excellent for jelly, vinegar, or cooking	Slow to bear. Allow to ripen fully for good flavor. Probably originated in North Carolina
'Jonagold'	US, MS, LS; 8–1	Midseason	Large. Heavy red striping over yellow ground. Firm and juicy; fine, mildly tart flavor. Frequent taste-test favorite. Good cooking apple	Productive medium-size tree. Heavy bearer. Pollen-sterile; won't pollinate others. Not pollinated by 'Golden Delicious'
'Jonathan'	US, MS, LS; 8–1	Midseason	Small to medium, roundish oblong. High-colored red. Juicy, moderately tart, crackling crisp, sprightly. All-purpose apple, good keeper	Subject to mildew, somewhat resistant to scab
'Kinnaird's Choice'	US, MS, LS; 8–1	Early midseason	Smooth-skinned fruit is yellow flushed with red, deep red in sun. Crisp white flesh. Good for fresh eating, cider	Old favorite in north Georgia. Originated in Franklin, Tennessee. Will bear heavily one year and lightly the next unless crop is thinned
'Liberty'	US, MS; 8–1	Late midseason	Medium size. Heavy red blush. Crisp flesh with fine, sweet-tart flavor; dessert quality	Productive annual bearer. One of the better disease-resistant selections. Immune to scab; resists cedar-apple rust, fireblight

APPLE

NAME	ZONES	RIPENING DATE	FRUIT	COMMENTS
'Limbertwig'	US, MS, LS; 8–1	Late	Medium size. Greenish yellow flushed red. Hard yellow flesh. Excellent for cider. Good keeper	An old Southern favorite with many regional forms
'Lodi'	US, MS, LS; 8–1	Very early	Large. Green to greenish yellow. Crisp, tart; good for pies, sauce. Not a good keeper	Vigorous tree, heavy bearer
'Magnum Bonum'	US, MS, LS; 8–1	Midseason	Greenish yellow heavily streaked with red. Crisp, juicy, aromatic flesh. Excellent for fresh eating; stores well	North Carolina heirloom originating in Davidson County about 1828. Bears at early age
'McIntosh'	US; 6–1	Midseason	Medium to large. Bright red, nearly round. Snowy white, tender flesh. Excellent, tart flavor	Very susceptible to scab and preharvest drop. Not a good choice for most of the South; doesn't like long, hot summers
'Mollie's Delicious'	US, MS, LS; 8–1	Midseason	Large, light yellow blushed red. Light yellow flesh is aromatic, juicy, sweet	Bears at a young age. Well adapted to Southeast. Susceptible to fireblight
'Mutsu' ('Crispin')	US, MS, LS, CS; 8–1	Late	Very large. Greenish yellow to yellow blushed red. Cream-colored, very crisp flesh with sweet-tart flavor. Excellent dessert or cooking apple with long storage life	Exceptionally large and vigorous tree. Pollen-sterile; won't pollinate other selections. Resists mildew
'Newtown Pippin' ('Albemarle Pippin')	US, MS, LS; 8–1	Late	Large. Greenish yellow or clear yellow. Crisp, firm, juicy, slightly tart. Good all-purpose apple. Excellent keeper. Flavor improves in storage	Large, vigorous tree. Self-fruitful. Originated in Newtown, Long Island, early 1700s
'Ozark Gold'	US, MS, LS; 8–1	Midseason	Medium to large yellow fruit with pointed blossom end. So-so flavor	Bears young. Spreading habit. Similar to 'Golden Delicious' but ripens 2–3 weeks earlier. Disease resistant
'Paulared'	US; 8–1	Early	Large, red skinned, mild flavored. One of the better early apples	Good branch structure. Has some resistance to scab
'Pink Pearl'	US, MS, LS; 8–1	Early	Medium size. Pale green skin, often blushed red. Sweet-tart, pinkish flesh. Makes colorful sauce	Very attractive in bloom; has deeper pink blossoms than most other selections
'Pound Sweet' ('Pumpkin Sweet')	US, MS; 8–1	Midseason	Very large golden fruit. Crisp and sweet. Excellent fresh or baked	Vigorous grower. Originated in Manchester, Connecticut, around 1834
'Pristine'	US, MS, LS; 8–1	Early	Medium size. Bright yellow. Mildly tart white flesh. Good for fresh eating, baking, sauce	Immune to scab; resistant to cedar-apple rust; some resistance to mildew and fireblight
'Rall's Janet' ('Ralls')	US, MS; 8–1	Late	Small to medium. Greenish yellow, streaked with red. Crisp white flesh, good for fresh eating. Keeps well	Late to bloom; good in areas with late frosts. Probably originated in Amherst County, Virginia, on farm of Caleb Ralls
'Redfree'	US, MS, LS; 8–1	Early	Medium size. Glossy red. Firm, crisp flesh with good flavor	Heavy bearer. Very disease resistant
'Rome Beauty' ('Red Rome')	US, MS, LS; 8–1	Late	Large, round, smooth red apple with greenish white flesh. Outstanding baking apple, good for cider, only fair for eating fresh	Bears at an early age. Self-fruitful. Several regional strains; Law strain is self-fruitful
'Roxbury Russet'	US, MS, LS; 8–1	Late	Large green fruit with brown russeting. Firm, sweet, yellowish flesh. Good for eating and cooking; superior for cider. Good keeper	Blooms late. Resistant to scab and mildew. Oldest named American apple, originating in Roxbury, Massachusetts, in early 1600s
'Scarlett O'Hara'	US, MS, LS; 8–1	Midseason	Medium size. Red blush over yellow background. Mild, slightly spicy, crisp, juicy. Stores well	Immune to scab and cedar-apple rust. Resistant to mildew but susceptible to fireblight

APPLE

NAME	ZONES	RIPENING DATE	FRUIT	COMMENTS
'Spitzenberg' ('Esopus Spitzenberg')	US, MS; 8–1	Midseason	Medium to large. Red-dotted yellow. Crisp, fine grained, tangy, spicy. Eat fresh; it is not a good keeper	Old favorite; best in Upper South. Subject to fireblight, mildew
'Stayman' (often called 'Winesap')	US, MS, LS; 8–1	Late	'Stayman' (a 'Winesap' cross) is large, greenish yellow with red stripes. Fine grained, firm, aromatic, with "winy" flavor. Good for fresh eating, applesauce, cider, baking. Good keeper	Pollinate with 'Golden Delicious', 'Grimes Golden', 'Lodi', 'Golden Russet'. Bears at a young age. Pollen-sterile; won't pollinate other selections. Fruit subject to cracking in wet weather
'TropicSweet'	LS, CS; 9–1	Early	Medium to large. Green skin blushed with red. Very sweet	Low-chill type from Florida. Similar to 'Anna' but sweeter. 'Anna', 'Dorsett Golden' are pollenizers
'Williams' Pride'	US, MS, LS; 8–1	Early	Medium-size, dark red fruit with spicy-sweet flavor. One of the better early red apples	Immune to scab; resistant to fireblight; susceptible to mildew
'Winter Banana'	US, MS, LS; 8–1	Late midseason	Large, attractive, pink-blushed yellow fruit with waxy finish. Tender, aromatic; good keeper	Good pollenizer. Ripe fruit has banana-like aroma
'Winter Pearmain'	US, MS; 8–5	Midseason	Medium to large. Pale greenish yellow skin with pink blush. Excellent flavor; tender, fine-grained flesh. Good keeper	All-purpose apple
'Yates' ('Jates')	US, MS, LS, CS; 8–5	Late	Small, aromatic fruit; bright red with yellow spots. Spicy flavor, best after a frost. Keeps well	Originated in Georgia in 1813. Heavy bearer, vigorous grower. Good pollenizer for other selections
'York Imperial'	US, MS; 8–1	Late	Medium to large. Yellow or green flushed pink. Firm, juicy, yellowish flesh. Great for cooking, baking. Best flavor if kept till Christmas	One of the best old-time selections for winter keeping. Discovered around 1830 by Mr. Johnson in York, Pennsylvania

TOP: 'Fuji'
BOTTOM: 'McIntosh'

TOP: 'Mutsu'
BOTTOM: 'Pink Pearl'

A

Apricot trees *(Prunus armeniaca)* bear fruit on spurs that form on the previous year's growth; these spurs remain productive for about 4 years. Many apricot selections are self-fruitful, but some require a pollenizer. Fruit ripens in late spring and summer. To get a good harvest of large apricots, thin the crop in midspring, leaving 2 to 4 in. between fruits. Apricot trees need only moderate pruning: the goals are to remove old, exhausted spurs and conserve enough new growth (which will produce spurs) for a satisfactory quantity of fruit. Consult your Cooperative Extension Office about a preventive spray program to control diseases and insects.

Growing about 15 ft. high and wide, apricots make nice-size ornamental trees; they're also well suited to espalier. Thin-textured, roundish leaves to 3 in. long are reddish when new, then mature to bright green; attractive flowers are pink or white.

Recommended selections include the following; all are self-fruitful.

'Harcot'. Heat zones 9–5. Sweet and juicy medium-size orange fruit with red blush. Blooms late; ripens early.

'Harglow'. Heat zones 9–5. Medium-size orange fruit with red blush; firm, sweet, tasty. Disease resistant. Blooms late; ripens early.

'Moorpark.' Heat zones 8–5. Very large fruit with fine flavor. Good for fresh eating, drying, or dessert; poor for canning. Ripens midseason.

'Tilton'. Heat zones 8–5. Medium-size golden fruit with firm flesh; excellent for fresh eating, freezing, canning, drying. Blooms late. Ripens midseason.

WHAT APRICOTS NEED

CLIMATE: Ideal climate provides chilly winters, freedom from late frosts, and fairly warm, dry springs.

POLLINATION: Most types are self-fruitful; some need pollen from another apricot selection.

PRUNING: Moderation is the key. The goals are to remove old, exhausted spurs and to conserve enough new growth to produce adequate new fruiting spurs.

DISEASE PREVENTION: Several rounds of preventive sprays may keep some problems at bay.

'Harcot'

Aquifoliaceae. The holly family contains evergreen trees and shrubs with berrylike fruit. *Ilex* (holly) is the only important genus.

AQUILEGIA

COLUMBINE

Ranunculaceae

PERENNIALS

🗡 ZONES VARY BY SPECIES

☼ ◐ FULL SUN OR LIGHT SHADE

💧 REGULAR WATER

Lacy foliage and beautifully presented flowers in exquisite pastels, deeper shades, and white give columbines a fairylike, woodland-glen quality. Plants are erect and range in size from 2 in. to 4 ft. high, depending on individual species or hybrid. Divided leaves similar to maidenhair fern *(Adiantum)* may be fresh green, blue green, or gray green. Slender, branching stems carry erect or nodding flowers to 3 in. across, often with sepals and petals in contrasting colors; they usually

Aquilegia McKana Giant

have backward-projecting, nectar-bearing spurs. Some columbines have large flowers and very long spurs; these have an airier look than short-spurred and spurless kinds. Double-flowered types lack the delicacy of the single-flowered sort, but they make a bolder color mass. Blossoms typically appear in spring and early summer.

Columbines are not fussy about soil as long as it is well drained. On all, cut back old stems for second crop of flowers. All kinds attract hummingbirds. Deer tend to leave them alone. Most are not long lived and will need to be replaced every 3 or 4 years. Allow the spent flowers to form seed capsules to ensure a crop of volunteer seedlings. If you're growing hybrids, the seedlings won't necessarily duplicate the parent plants, but seedlings from species (if grown isolated from other columbines) should closely resemble the originals. Leaf miners are a potential pest, especially on hybrids.

A. alpina. ALPINE COLUMBINE. Zones US, MS; 7–1. Native to the Alps. Grows 1–2 ft. tall, 1 ft. wide. Nodding, bright blue flowers to 2 in. across, with curved spurs to 1 in. long. Good rock garden plant.

A. caerulea. ROCKY MOUNTAIN COLUMBINE. Zones US, MS; 7–1. Native to the Rocky Mountains. To 1½–3 ft. high, 2 ft. wide. Erect blue-and-white flowers, 2 in. or more across, with straight or spreading spurs to 2 in. long. An important parent of many long-spurred hybrids.

A. canadensis. WILD COLUMBINE. Zones US, MS, LS; 8–1. Native to much of eastern and central North America. Grows 1–2 ft. tall (occasionally taller) and about 1 ft. wide. Red-and-yellow, 1½-in., nodding flowers have slightly curved, 1-in. spurs. Red color may wash out to pink in areas with warm night temperatures. Less susceptible to leaf miners than most columbines. 'Corbett' *(A. c. flavescens)* has creamy yellow flowers.

A. chrysantha. GOLDEN COLUMBINE, GOLDEN-SPURRED COLUMBINE. Zones US, MS; 8–1. Native to Arizona, New Mexico, and adjacent Mexico. One of showiest species. Large, many-branched plant to 3–4 ft. tall, 1–2 ft. wide. Undersides of leaflets densely covered with soft hairs. Upright, clear yellow, 1½- to 3-in. flowers with slender, hooked spurs 2–2½ in. long.

A. flabellata. FAN COLUMBINE. Zones US, MS, LS; 9–1. Native to Japan. Stocky plant 8 in.–1½ ft. high, 1 ft. wide, with nodding, 1½-in., two-tone flowers of lilac blue and creamy white. Hooked spurs to 1 in. long. Differs from most other columbines in having thicker, darker leaves, often with overlapping segments. *A. f. minor* is a very dwarf form (just 4 in. high). Good rock garden plant.

A. hinckleyana. HINCKLEY'S COLUMBINE. Zones US, MS, LS. Native to Big Bend country of Texas. To 1½–2 ft. high and wide, with long-spurred flowers in chartreuse yellow. Blue-gray foliage stays handsome in summer, and leaf miners aren't a big problem.

A. hybrids. Zones US, MS, LS. Derived from several species. Preferred tall hybrid strains include graceful, long-spurred McKana Giants and double-flowering Spring Song (both to 3 ft. tall, 2 ft. wide). Nora Barlow Mixed, reaching 2–2½ ft. high and 2 ft. wide, has double flowers in a wide range of colors (the original 'Nora Barlow' has reddish pink blooms with white margins). Lower-growing strains include Biedermeier and Dragonfly (1 ft. high and wide); long-spurred Music (1½ ft. high and wide); and single to double, upward-facing Fairyland (15 in. high and wide).

A. longissima. LONGSPUR COLUMBINE. Zones US, MS, LS, CS; 9–1. Native to Southwest Texas, southern Arizona, and northern Mexico. Grows 2½–3 ft. tall and about 1½–2 ft. wide. This species is quite similar to *A. chrysantha.* Numerous erect, pale yellow blossoms with very narrow, drooping, 4- to 6-in.-long spurs.

A. saximontana. Zones US, MS; 7–1. Native to the Rocky Mountains. In effect, a miniature *A. caerulea,* just 4–8 in. high and wide.

A. sibirica. Zones US, MS, LS; 8–1. Native of Siberia. Grows to 2 ft. tall and wide, with short-spurred, 1½-in., blue to dark purplish red flowers on leafless stalks.

A. vulgaris. EUROPEAN COLUMBINE. Zones US, MS, LS; 8–1. Native to western, central, and southern Europe; naturalized in eastern U.S. Grows 1–2½ ft. tall, 1 ft. wide. Nodding blue or violet flowers to 2 in. across; short, knobby spurs about ¾ in. long. Many selections and hybrids offer single to fully double blooms, either short spurred or spurless. Plants in the Vervaeneana Woodside Variegated Mixed group are 2–2½ ft. tall and 2 ft. wide, with variegated leaves and various flower colors.

ARABIS

ROCKCRESS

Brassicaceae (Cruciferae)

PERENNIALS

🌿 US, MS, LS ⵜ 8-1, EXCEPT AS NOTED

☼ FULL SUN

💧 MODERATE WATER

Arabis caucasica

Low-growing, spreading plants for edgings, rock gardens, ground covers, pattern plantings. All kinds have attractive year-round foliage and clusters of small white, pink, or rose purple flowers in spring. Seldom browsed by deer. Give good drainage.

A. alpina. MOUNTAIN ROCKCRESS. Native to mountain elevations of Europe. Low, tufted, rough-hairy plant 4–10 in. high, 2 ft. wide. Produces white flowers in dense, short clusters. Selection 'Rosea' bears pink flowers; 'Variegata' has yellow-edged green leaves. Plants sold as *A. alpina* are often really *A. caucasica*.

A. caucasica (A. albida). WALL ROCKCRESS. Native from Mediterranean region to Iran. This plant is a dependable old favorite. Forms mat of gray-green leaves to 6 in. high, 1½ ft. wide. White flowers almost cover plant during bloom season. Excellent ground cover and base planting for spring-flowering bulbs such as daffodils and 'Paper White' narcissus. Provide some shade in hot climates. 'Variegata' has gray leaves with creamy white margins; 'Flore Plena' is double flowered; 'Rosabella' and 'Pink Charm' bear pink blooms.

A. procurrens. WHITE ROCKCRESS. Zones US, MS. Native to southeastern Europe. Creeping plant with 1½-in. leaves and white flowers clustered on 4- to 12-in. stems. Over time, spreads widely.

A. ×sturii. Heat zones 8–5. Dense, fist-size cushions of small bright green leaves eventually grow into small mats bearing clusters of white flowers on 2- to 3-in. stems. Some consider this species among the finest rock garden plants.

Araceae. The arum family contains plants ranging from tuberous or rhizomatous perennials to shrubby or climbing tropical foliage plants. Leaves are often highly ornamental; while variable in shape, they tend to be arrow-like. Inconspicuous flowers cluster tightly on a club-shaped spadix within an often showy leaflike bract (spathe). Examples are *Anthurium*, voodoo lily (*Amorphophallus*), calla (*Zantedeschia*), and *Philodendron*. Sap of many is highly irritating to the mouth and throat.

ARACHNIODES simplicior 'Variegata'

VARIEGATED HOLLY FERN

Dryopteridaceae

FERN

🌿 US, MS, LS, CS

◐ ● PARTIAL OR FULL SHADE

💧💧 REGULAR TO AMPLE WATER

Arachniodes simplicior 'Variegata'

Native to Japan and China, this beautiful fern features shiny dark green fronds, erect and deeply cut, with a yellow stripe down the center of each segment. It forms a clump 10–18 in. tall and twice as wide. Evergreen in the Lower and Coastal South; deciduous in the Middle and Upper South, where it emerges late in spring. Naturalized in some parts of the Southeast. Showy addition to the shade garden.

FOR INFORMATION ON SELECTING PLANTS
PLEASE SEE PAGES 39–144

ARALIA

Araliaceae

DECIDUOUS SHRUB-TREES

🌿 ZONES VARY BY SPECIES

☼ ◐ FULL SUN OR PARTIAL SHADE

💧 MODERATE TO REGULAR WATER

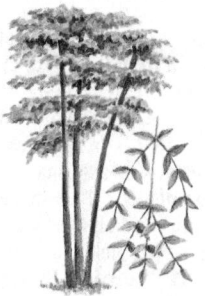

Aralia elata

Most are striking bold-leafed plants that may eventually grow to 25–30 ft. tall under ideal conditions. Not for small gardens. Often shrublike and multistemmed (because of suckering habit), especially in colder areas, where they may grow just 10 ft. high. Clumps range from one-half to almost as wide as they are tall. Branches are nearly vertical or slightly spreading, usually very spiny. Huge leaves, clustered at ends of branches and divided into many leaflets, look quite exotic. White midsummer flowers, small but in such large, branched clusters that they are showy, are followed by berrylike purplish fruit that is enjoyed by birds.

Grow in well-drained soil. Not good near swimming pools because of spines; even leafstalks are sometimes prickly. Wind can burn the foliage, so provide a sheltered location. Need minimal pruning; dig out suckers to limit spread of clump.

A. cordata. UDO. Zones US, MS, LS; 9–6. From Japan. To 6 ft. tall, half as wide. This species doesn't have spines; forms an attractive foliage mass of oval, unevenly toothed leaflets 2–6 in. long. In Asia, the young spring shoots are blanched and eaten.

A. elata (A. chinensis). ANGELICA TREE. Zones US, MS, LS; 8–1. Native to Asia. Only moderately spiny. Leaves 2–3 ft. long, divided into toothed, stalkless, 2- to 6-in.-long leaflets. 'Variegata' has leaflets strikingly bordered with creamy white.

A. elegantissima. See Schefflera elegantissima

A. papyrifera. See Tetrapanax papyriferus

A. sieboldii. See Fatsia japonica

A. spinosa. HERCULES' CLUB, DEVIL'S WALKING STICK. Zones US, MS, LS, CS; 9–1. Native to eastern U.S. Puts up several spiny, usually unbranched stems, each of them crowned by 2- to 6-ft.-long leaves. This is one of the most tropical-looking genuinely hardy plants. Has a coarse appearance in winter.

Araliaceae. The aralia family of herbaceous and woody plants is marked by leaves that are divided fanwise into leaflets or veined in a pattern like the fingers of a hand. Individually tiny flowers come in small, round heads or in larger compound clusters. Examples are ivy (*Hedera*), Japanese fatsia (*Fatsia japonica*), and *Schefflera*.

ARAUCARIA

Araucariaceae

EVERGREEN TREES

🌿 ZONES VARY BY SPECIES

☼ FULL SUN

💧 REGULAR WATER

Araucaria araucana

These distinctive conifers are commonly seen in Florida gardens, but some are hardy enough to grow outdoors farther north. Most species bear stiff, closely overlapping leaves in dark to bright green. They accept a wide range of soils, but good drainage is a must. They thrive in containers for several years.

These trees' striking form may tempt you to plant them in a small garden, but don't make that mistake. Not only do they take up a huge amount of space, but as they age they bear spiny cones that can weigh up to 15 pounds. If one falls on your head from the top of the tree, you'll wander aimlessly for years—should you survive the initial impact.

A. araucana (A. imbricata). MONKEY PUZZLE TREE. Zones MS, LS, CS, TS; 12–6. A source of wonderment to all who see it, this Chilean native features evenly spaced tiers of heavy, spreading branches and ropelike branchlets. Tree huggers beware—its dark green leaves are armed with needlelike points. Slow growing when young, it eventually grows to 70–90 ft. tall and 30 ft. wide.

A. bidwillii. BUNYA-BUNYA. Zones CS, TS; 12–8. Native to Australia. Moderate growth to 80 ft. tall, 60 ft. wide. Broadly rounded crown casts dense shade. Juvenile leaves are glossy, lance-shaped, 1–2 in. long, arranged in two rows; mature leaves are oval, ½ in. long, rather woody, spirally arranged and overlapping along the branches. Sometimes used as a lawn tree in large yards; grows well in large containers. Very tough, very tolerant of low light; makes an unusual houseplant.

A. heterophylla (A. excelsa). NORFOLK ISLAND PINE. Zones TS; 12–9. Native to Norfolk Island, near Australia. Grown outdoors in central and south Florida, where it may reach 80–100 ft. tall and 60 ft. wide. Elsewhere in the South, it's a popular houseplant, prized for its symmetrical shape, evenly spaced whorls of branches, and soft, lush, rich green foliage.

Araucaria heterophylla

In December, people often bedeck Norfolk Island pines with ribbons, ornaments, and twinkle-lights and turn them into indoor Christmas trees. If you want them to last for long indoors, pay attention to their care. Make sure they receive bright light, either natural or artificial; they do well near a south- or west-facing window. Let the soil go slightly dry on the surface between waterings, but don't let it dry out completely—if it does, the lower tiers of branches will die one by one and won't be replaced. Apply a general-purpose liquid houseplant fertilizer twice monthly in spring and summer, monthly in fall and winter. Eventually, your tree will grow tall enough to touch the ceiling—but don't try to give it to a botanical garden. They already have plenty.

Araucariaceae. Coniferous trees with symmetrical branching habit and leaves that vary from needlelike to broad and leathery. *Araucaria* is the only representative in this book.

ARBORVITAE. See THUJA

ARBUTUS

Ericaceae
EVERGREEN TREES OR SHRUBS
✂ MS, LS, CS
☼ ◑ EXPOSURE NEEDS VARY BY SPECIES
◇ ◐ ● LITTLE TO REGULAR WATER

All types have ornamental bark, clusters of little urn-shaped flowers, decorative (and edible) fruit, and handsome foliage. Provide good drainage, especially if plant receives regular water. Best in low-humidity, low-rainfall areas such as West Texas.

Arbutus unedo

A. unedo. STRAWBERRY TREE. Heat zones 9–6. Native to southern Europe, Ireland. Slow to moderate growth to 8–35 ft. tall and wide; tends to be a small shrub in Southeast. Trunk and branches have red-brown, shredding bark, become twisted and gnarled in age. Dark green, red-stemmed leaves 2–3 in. long. Small, white or greenish white flowers; red-and-yellow, ¾-in. fruits resemble strawberries but are mealy and bland tasting. Clusters of flowers and fruit often appear simultaneously in fall and winter. Selections include 'Elfin King', a dwarf form (not over 5 ft.

tall at 10 years old) that flowers and fruits nearly continuously; 'Compacta', seldom exceeding 10 ft.; and 'Oktoberfest', a 6- to 8-ft. form with deep pink flowers. Give species and selections sun or part shade.

A. xalapensis (A. texana). TEXAS MADRONE. Heat zones 10–5. Native to Texas, New Mexico, Mexico to Guatemala. Striking multitrunked small tree to 20–30 ft. tall and wide, with handsome deep green leaves, clusters of small white or pale pink flowers in spring, raspberry-like fruit in fall. Extremely showy bark changes in color through the year, from cream (when young) to pink and then to brown before it peels, revealing new bark beneath. Requires careful attention to get established. Provide light shade; water consistently for several years but never allow soil to become waterlogged. Grows well in chalky soil.

ARCHONTOPHOENIX

Arecaceae (Palmae)
PALMS
✂ TS; OR GROW IN POTS
☼ ◑ FULL SUN OR PART SHADE; BRIGHT INDIRECT LIGHT
◐ ● MODERATE TO REGULAR WATER

Handsome, slender palms native to the rain forests of eastern Australia. Both species described here feature a single narrow trunk and may reach 50 ft. or taller, with a 10- to 15-ft. spread. Their compact, formal shape makes them good lawn and street trees; they tolerate shade and can grow for many years beneath taller trees. Feathery fronds, green above and gray green beneath, may reach 8–10 ft. long on mature trees. Old fronds shed cleanly, leaving attractive rings on the trunk. Easy to grow in containers, indoors or out. Large specimens are difficult to transplant.

Archontophoenix cunninghamiana

A. alexandrae. ALEXANDRA PALM. Heat zones 12–10. Widely planted in south Florida. Very tender to cold; young trees won't take frost. Trunk is swollen at the base. In summer, clusters of tiny white flowers form beneath the crown. Sometimes confused with *A. cunninghamiana* at nurseries.

A. cunninghamiana (Seaforthia elegans). KING PALM. Heat zones 12–9. A better, hardier archontophoenix for many Florida gardens. Mature plants may take brief periods of 28°F. Frond leaflets are broader than those of *A. alexandrae*, trunk is less swollen at base. Flowers are lilac.

ARCTANTHEMUM arcticum. See CHRYSANTHEMUM arcticum

ARCTOSTAPHYLOS uva-ursi

BEARBERRY, KINNIKINNICK
Ericaceae
EVERGREEN SHRUB
✂ US, MS ⊩ 6–1
☼ ◑ FULL SUN OR LIGHT SHADE
◇ ◐ LITTLE TO MODERATE WATER

Arctostaphylos uva-ursi

Considered one of the prettiest and most serviceable ground covers, bearberry is most commonly seen in the northern U.S. It will, however, grow as far south as Virginia, Tennessee, Kentucky, and parts of the Carolinas. Spreading widely and rooting as it goes, this creeper forms a mat about 6 in. high, 15 ft. wide. Glossy, leathery, ¾- to 1½-in., typically bright green leaves turn red or purplish in cold weather. Urn-shaped white or pinkish flowers bloom in summer; these are followed by bright red fruits that last into winter. Given good drainage, bearberry tolerates most soils. Start with containerized plants, since established ones are difficult to transplant. Mulch heavily between young plants to suppress weeds until branches provide cover. Regular pruning isn't necessary. Do not fertilize. The following selections provide uniform appearance in large plantings.

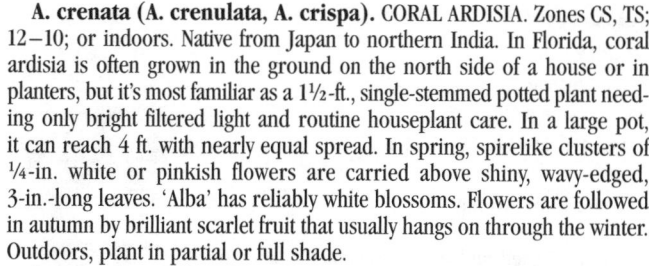
'Alaska'. Flat grower with small, round, dark green leaves.

'Massachusetts'. Small leafed, flat growing. Abundant pinkish white flowers and plentiful fruit.

'Point Reyes'. Dark green leaves closely set along branches. More tolerant of heat and drought than 'Radiant'.

'Radiant'. Leaves lighter green and more widely spaced than those of 'Point Reyes'. Heavy crop of large fruit in fall, lasting into winter (but sometimes fails to fruit if pollinating insects are not active at bloom time).

'Vancouver Jade'. Flat growing like 'Alaska' and 'Massachusetts', but not as wide spreading as those two selections. Jade green leaves turn bronzy red in winter.

'Wood's Compact'. Compact grower with red branches densely clad in dark green leaves. Pink flowers.

'Wood's Red'. Reliable crop of large berries. Small dark green leaves turn reddish in cold weather.

ARCTOTIS

AFRICAN DAISY

Asteraceae (Compositae)

ANNUALS AND PERENNIALS, USUALLY TREATED AS ANNUALS

✿ US, MS, LS, CS, TS H 10–1

☼ FULL SUN

💧 MODERATE WATER

Arctotis hybrid

This is just one of several plants referred to as "African daisy." Gardeners and even seed companies and nurseries often confuse them, so let's set the record straight. *Arctotis* species hail from South Africa and have lobed leaves that are rough, hairy, or woolly; their blossoms usually sport a contrasting ring of color around a central eye. *Dimorphotheca* species have smooth green foliage; their ringless flowers either are white or fall into the yellow-salmon-orange range. Woody, shrubby white-and-blue African daisies and the trailing types used as ground cover belong to the genus *Osteospermum*.

Seedlings begin blooming about 3 months after germination. They're grown as summer annuals in most of the South but may be used for winter color in Florida and South Texas. The blossoms make good cut flowers, even though they close at night. Plants reseed readily.

A. hirsuta. Masses of 3-in., black-centered, bright orange (or, occasionally, lemon yellow) blossoms on a plant to 1–1½ ft. tall and wide.

A. hybrids. Most *Arctotis* sold in garden centers are hybrids that grow 1–1½ ft. tall and wide. The 3-in. flowers come in white, pink, purplish, cream, yellow, and orange—usually with a dark ring around a nearly black central eye. Hybrids will self-sow, but the seedlings they produce tend to revert to orange.

A. venusta (A. stoechadifolia, Venidium fastuosum). Bushy growth to 2 ft. tall and 1½ ft. wide, with slightly hairy gray-green leaves. Silvery blue, 3-in.-wide daisies have a yellow ring surrounding a deep blue eye. Tolerates poor, sandy soil. In the selection 'Zulu Prince,' inner rings of yellow and purple encircle a black center.

ARDISIA

MARLBERRY

Myrsinaceae

EVERGREEN SHRUBS

✿ ZONES VARY BY SPECIES

☼ ◑ ● EXPOSURE NEEDS VARY BY SPECIES

💧 REGULAR WATER, EXCEPT AS NOTED

Ardisia japonica

Of the 150 species of evergreen shrubs in this genus, only the following three are commonly grown. All are valued both for attractive foliage and for their beadlike fruits.

A. crenata (A. crenulata, A. crispa). CORAL ARDISIA. Zones CS, TS; 12–10; or indoors. Native from Japan to northern India. In Florida, coral ardisia is often grown in the ground on the north side of a house or in planters, but it's most familiar as a 1½-ft., single-stemmed potted plant needing only bright filtered light and routine houseplant care. In a large pot, it can reach 4 ft. with nearly equal spread. In spring, spirelike clusters of ¼-in. white or pinkish flowers are carried above shiny, wavy-edged, 3-in.-long leaves. 'Alba' has reliably white blossoms. Flowers are followed in autumn by brilliant scarlet fruit that usually hangs on through the winter. Outdoors, plant in partial or full shade.

A. japonica. JAPANESE ARDISIA. Zones LS, CS; 9–1. From Japan and China. Prostrate shrub spreads by rhizomes to produce a succession of upright branches that are 5–12 in. high. A high-quality ground cover in partial or full shade. Leathery bright green leaves to 4 in. long are clustered at the branch tips. White, ¼-in. flowers in clusters of two to six appear in fall; these are followed by small, round, bright red fruits that last into winter. 'Chirimen' is an especially cold-hardy selection and may survive even in the Middle South. Selections with colorful foliage include 'Amanogawa', with particularly bright red berries and green leaves centered in gold; and 'Hakuokan', bearing green leaves heavily variegated with white on the edges.

A. paniculata. MARLBERRY. Zones TS; 12–10. Slender shrub or small tree to 20–25 ft. high, 10–12 ft. wide. Native to south Florida. Coarse, lance-shaped, dark green leaves to 6 in. long; fragrant, ¼-in., purple-marked white flowers at intervals for much of the year. Small, glossy black fruits. Excellent for coastal gardens; takes salt spray and flourishes in sun or light shade. Tolerates clay and alkaline soils. Needs less water than the above two species.

Arecaceae. It's difficult to generalize about any plant family as large and widespread as palms. Generally speaking, they have single, unbranched trunks of considerable height; some grow in clusters, though, and some are dwarf or stemless. The leaves are usually divided into many leaflets, either like ribs of a fan (fan palms) or like a feather, with many parallel leaflets growing outward from a long central stem (feather palms). Some palms have undivided leaves, however. This family was formerly called Palmae. See also Palms.

ARECA lutescens. See CHRYSALIDOCARPUS lutescens

ARECASTRUM romanzoffianum. See SYAGRUS romanzoffianum

ARENARIA montana

SANDWORT

Caryophyllaceae

PERENNIAL

✿ US, MS, LS H 9–6

◑ PARTIAL SHADE

💧💧 MODERATE TO REGULAR WATER

Arenaria montana

Native to the mountains of southwestern Europe, this evergreen plant carpets the ground with mats of mosslike foliage 2–4 in. high. Weak stems to 1 ft. long are set with grayish green, ½- to ¾-in.-long leaves that are usually coated with soft hairs. In late spring and summer, the plant is covered by a profusion of inch-wide white flowers. Needs well-drained soil. Good for trailing over sunny rocks or tumbling over a low wall; ideal for rock gardens or for planting between stepping-stones. For the plant sometimes sold as *A. verna (A. v. caespitosa)*, see *Sagina subulata*.

FOR INFORMATION ON YOUR CLIMATE ZONES
PLEASE SEE PAGES 28–38

A

ARGEMONE

PRICKLY POPPY

Papaveraceae

ANNUALS OR BIENNIALS

US, MS, LS, CS, TS H 12–6

FULL SUN

LITTLE OR NO WATER

Argemone mexicana

Prickly-leafed and prickly-stemmed plants to 3 ft. tall, 1½ ft. wide, with large, showy poppies that bloom mainly in summer. Easy to grow from seed sown in place or in pots (transplant gently). Will reseed and colonize. Provide good drainage. Seed specialists may offer additional species.

A. mexicana. MEXICAN POPPY. Annual. Native to West Indies and probably Central America and Florida. Yellow to orange, 1½- to 2½-in. flowers. 'Yellow Lustre' grows 1½–2 ft. tall, has lemony orange blooms.

A. polyanthemos (A. intermedia). Annual or biennial. Western native with white, 2½- to 4-in. flowers.

ARGYRANTHEMUM frutescens. See CHRYSANTHEMUM frutescens

ARISAEMA

JACK-IN-THE-PULPIT, COBRA LILY

Araceae

PERENNIALS FROM TUBERS

US, MS, LS, CS

PARTIAL OR FULL SHADE

REGULAR WATER DURING GROWTH AND BLOOM

Arisaema sikokianum

Curious rather than beautiful relatives of calla (*Zantedeschia*), attractive both to children and to fanciers of the unusual. Flowers are tiny, crowded on a club-shaped spadix surrounded by an overarching, typically green or dull purple spathe (flower bract) that is often striped in a contrasting color. In late spring, tubers send up one to three leaves, each divided into three or more leaflets. Inflorescences appear on a separate stalk in spring or early summer. As the flowers fade, the spathe withers and the spadix forms orange to red seeds.

These are woodland plants, appreciative of organic material in the soil. Plant in fall, setting tubers 1 ft. apart, 2 in. deep. Plants die to the ground in winter; don't let dormant tubers dry out completely. Species other than those listed below may appear from time to time in specialists' catalogs.

A. fargesii. Heat zones 10–5. From China. To 1½ ft. high. Between a pair of big, three-part leaves sits a burgundy red spathe striped with white; the spathe tip curves over and ends in what looks like a mass of red threads. A dark red spadix peeks from the spathe.

A. kishidae 'Silver Pattern'. Heat zones 9–5. Selection of a little-known Japanese species. To 2 ft. high. Each leafstalk bears two leaves consisting of seven to nine leaflets marked with a central silver band. The spathe is brownish purple, with a hooded extension curving out to one side. A thin, light brown spadix is barely visible.

A. ringens. Heat zones 9–6. From China, Japan, Korea. To 2 ft. high. Inflorescence sits on short stalk between two large, three-part leaves. The spathe is striped purple and white; its tip curls and flares to show off a glossy purple interior. A white spadix is almost hidden by the spathe.

A. serratum 'Silver Center'. Heat zones 9–5. Selection of a Japanese species. To 3 ft. high. Each of the two leaves is divided into 7 to 13 leaflets marked down the middle with a silver streak. A thin stem rises slightly above the foliage, bearing a narrow, purple- and white-streaked spathe with a tip that drapes downward. The spadix is yellow green.

A. sikokianum. Heat zones 9–3. From Japan. To 20 in. tall, with 6-in. leaflets. A 4- to 12-in. stalk supports a 6-in. spathe that is erect rather than arching. Spathe is purplish brown on the outside, yellowish white within; pure white spadix is thicker and rounded at the tip.

A. speciosum. Heat zones 9–7. Himalayan native. A single leaf grows to 2 ft., with 8- to 16-in.-long leaflets on a stalk marbled with dark purple. Spathe is blackish purple outside, whitish within, up to 8 in. long; spadix has a long, whiplike tip that can reach 2½ ft. in length.

A. tortuosum. Heat zones 9–7. Himalayan native. Can reach 4 ft. tall. Leaves have many narrow leaflets. Green or purple spathe to 6 in. long; spadix protrudes from spathe, then curves upward for several inches.

A. triphyllum. JACK-IN-THE-PULPIT. Heat zones 9–1. From eastern North America; the common Jack-in-the-pulpit familiar to Easterners. Grows to 2 ft. tall. Both spathe and spadix are green or purple; spathe is striped in white or green.

ARISTOLOCHIA

Aristolochiaceae

DECIDUOUS AND EVERGREEN VINES

ZONES VARY BY SPECIES

EXPOSURE NEEDS VARY BY SPECIES

REGULAR TO AMPLE WATER

Aristolochia littoralis

Twining vines noted for curiously shaped flowers in rather somber colors; the flowers resemble curved pipes with flared bowls or birds with bent necks. Vigorous growers; thin out unwanted growth in late dormant season or wait until after bloom. If plant is too thick and tangled for selective thinning, cut it to the ground before spring growth begins.

A. californica. CALIFORNIA DUTCHMAN'S PIPE. Deciduous. Zones LS, CS, TS; 9–5. Native to Coast Ranges and Sierra Nevada foothills of Northern California. Will cover an 8- by 12-ft. screen with some training or climb by long, thin shoots 10–16 ft. into any nearby tree without harming it. Flower display comes before leaf-out in late winter or early spring; pendulous, 1-in.-long blooms are cream colored with red-purple veins. Bright green, heart-shaped leaves to 5 in. long. Interesting and useful where many less hardy vines would freeze. Sometimes used as a ground cover. Grows from seed. Accepts any soil; needs partial shade.

A. gigantea. GIANT DUTCHMAN'S PIPE. Evergreen. Zones TS; 12–10. From Panama and Brazil. To 30 ft. Triangular to heart-shaped dark green leaves can reach 4 in. long. Blooms in summer, bearing flowers to 1 ft. long and half as wide; blossoms are burgundy with creamy white netting and a golden throat. *A. g.* 'Brasiliensis' (*A. brasiliensis*) has flowers to 10 in. long and 7 in. wide, in an intricate netted pattern of white and brown. Sun or partial shade.

A. grandiflora. PELICAN FLOWER. Evergreen. Zones TS; 12–10. From Central America and the West Indies. Vigorous grower to 30 ft. or more. Deep green, heart-shaped leaves to 10 in. long. Roundish flowers to 8 in. across bloom in late summer; they are white with burgundy red veining, a red center, and a slender, foot-long, dangling "tail" (an extension of the blossom's lower lip). Flowers are smelly, so be careful where you plant this one. Give partial shade.

A. littoralis (A. elegans). CALICO FLOWER. Evergreen. Zones TS; 12–10; or indoors. Native to Brazil. Grows 15–25 ft. high. Wiry, slender stems; heart-shaped leaves 3 in. long. Blooms in summer; whitish buds shaped like little pelicans open to 3-in.-wide, heart-shaped flowers of deep purple veined in creamy white. Needs rich soil, partial shade.

A. macrophylla (A. durior). DUTCHMAN'S PIPE. Deciduous. Zones US, MS, LS, CS; 8–4; short lived in warm-winter areas. From eastern U.S. Easily grown from seed. Large (6- to 14-in.-long), kidney-shaped deep green leaves are carried in shinglelike pattern to form a dense cloak on a trellis; the vine will cover a 15- by 20-ft. area in a single season and is a longtime favorite for screening porches. Blooms in late spring, early summer. Flowers are almost hidden by leaves; each is a yellowish green, 3-in., curved tube flaring into three brownish purple lobes about 1 in.

wide. Thrives in full sun to heavy shade. Give average to good soil and ample water for fastest growth, largest leaves. Will not stand strong winds.

A. peruviana. Evergreen. Zones TS; 8–4. From South America. Rare but worth the search. Grows upright to 1–2 ft., with medium green, heart-shaped leaves to 3 in. long. Cup-shaped blooms about 1 in. long and ¾ in. wide may bloom in spring, summer, or fall; they are golden yellow with red edge markings on the inside, mottled chocolate brown on the outside. Performs well in low light; fine on shaded patio in warmest areas. Interesting houseplant or indoor/outdoor plant.

Aristolochiaceae. This family includes *Aristolochia* and wild ginger *(Asarum)*. All its members display odd-shaped flowers in subdued colors.

ARMERIA

THRIFT, SEA PINK

Plumbaginaceae

PERENNIALS

ZONES VARY BY SPECIES

FULL SUN

LITTLE TO MODERATE WATER

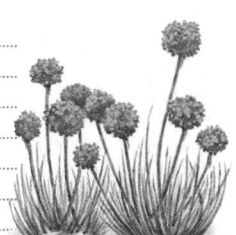
Armeria maritima

Narrow, stiff, evergreen leaves grow in compact tufts or basal rosettes; small white, pink, rose, or red flowers are carried in dense, globular heads. Main bloom period is spring to early summer, but shearing off faded flowers may prolong flowering. Sturdy, dependable plants for edging walks or borders and for tidy mounds in rock gardens or raised beds. Attractive in containers.

Good drainage is essential and permits regular watering, but safest tactic is to water moderately in dry climates, sparingly in moister regions. Tolerate seaside conditions, infertile soil. Seldom browsed by deer. Clumps spread slowly and need dividing only when bare centers show.

A. alliacea. Zones US, MS, LS; 8–5. From southern Europe. Plants grow 2–6 in. high and 20 in. wide, produce 8- to 16-in. blossom stalks with bright pink flowers. 'Leucantha' has white blooms.

A. girardii (A. juncea, A. setacea). Zones LS, CS; 8–4. From southern France. Narrow, needlelike foliage in dense mounds to 10–12 in. high and wide. Lavender-pink flowers.

A. juniperifolia (A. caespitosa). Zones US, MS, LS; 8–4. From Spain. Stiff, needle-shaped leaves ½ in. long form low, extremely compact rosettes about 6 in. across. Rose pink or white flowers are carried on 2-in. stems. This little mountain native is very touchy about drainage; apply a mulch of fine gravel around plants to prevent basal stem rot, especially in summer.

A. maritima (A. vulgaris, Statice armeria). COMMON THRIFT. Zones US, MS, LS, CS; 9–1. Native to Europe, North America. Tufted mounds spread to 1 ft.; leaves are 6 in. long. White to rose pink flowers in tight clusters atop 6- to 10-in. stalks. Bloom is profuse in spring (goes on almost all year in mildest climates). 'Bloodstone' has rose red flowers, 'Cotton Tail' white blooms. 'Rubrifolia', with purplish red foliage and rosy pink blossoms, provides color for much of the year.

ARONIA

CHOKEBERRY

Rosaceae

DECIDUOUS SHRUBS

ZONES VARY BY SPECIES

FULL SUN OR LIGHT SHADE

MODERATE TO AMPLE WATER

Aronia arbutifolia

Native to southern Canada and the eastern U.S., these are tough, undemanding shrubs useful as fillers or background plantings. They tolerate a wide variety of soils and can thrive on much or just moderate

water. All tend to spread by suckering but are somewhat leggy (good for planting beneath). Small white or pinkish flowers appear in late spring and are followed by showy fruits that last well into winter. Fall foliage is brightly colored.

A. arbutifolia. RED CHOKEBERRY. Zones US, MS, LS, CS; 9–1. Clumping shrub to 6–8 ft. tall and about half as wide, with many erect stems bearing shiny foliage that is rich green above, paler beneath. Fruits are clustered, ¼ in. wide, brilliant red, long lasting. Fall foliage is also bright red, and plants tend to color early. 'Brilliant' ('Brilliantissima') is a selected form with exceptionally fine fall color.

A. melanocarpa. BLACK CHOKEBERRY. Zones US, MS, LS; 8–1. Lower growing than *A. arbutifolia*, to just 3–5 ft. tall, rarely taller; spreads to about 10 ft. Foliage turns purple red in fall. Shiny black, ½-in. fruits.

ARRHENATHERUM elatius bulbosum 'Variegatum'

BULBOUS OAT GRASS

Poaceae (Gramineae)

PERENNIAL GRASS

US, MS, LS 8–5

FULL SUN OR PARTIAL SHADE

REGULAR WATER

Arrhenatherum elatius bulbosum 'Variegatum'

Attractive European grass with narrow leaves boldly edged and striped in white; forms a graceful clump 1 ft. high and wide. Good looking in a perennial border or large rock garden; useful for brightening dark places under trees or big shrubs. Flowering stems in summer double the plant's height. Goes dormant in summer in hot climates; does best in cool weather. If it flops over in heat, shear for fresh growth in fall. Bulbous structures at stem bases root on contact with soil to produce new plants; clumps may need curtailing. Divide and replant as needed.

ARROWROOT. See MARANTA arundinacea

ARTEMISIA

Asteraceae (Compositae)

PERENNIALS AND EVERGREEN SHRUBS

ZONES VARY BY SPECIES

FULL SUN

LITTLE TO MODERATE WATER

Artemisia abrotanum

Chiefly valued for their ornamental foliage, artemisias offer lacy leaf patterns and aromatic, silvery gray or white leaves. Most of the plants described here have woody stems; however, *A. dracunculus, A. lactiflora, A. ludoviciana albula,* and *A. stellerana* are herbaceous. Most need excellent drainage. Not the best choice for high-rainfall areas, particularly along the Gulf Coast and in Florida. Plants are seldom browsed by deer.

Most artemisias are excellent in mixed borders, where their white or silvery leaves soften harsh reds and oranges and blend with blues, lavenders, pinks. Flowers are usually insignificant. Divide plants in spring or autumn.

A. abrotanum. SOUTHERNWOOD, OLD MAN. Woody perennial. Zones US, MS, LS, CS; 8–5. To 3–5 ft. tall and wide. Native to southern Europe. Beautiful green, feathery, lemon-scented foliage; yellowish white flowers. Use in shrub border for its fragrant foliage. Hang sprigs in closets to discourage moths. Burn a few leaves in the kitchen to kill cooking odors.

A. absinthium. COMMON WORMWOOD. Woody perennial. Zones US, MS, LS, CS; 10–4. To 2–4 ft. tall, 2 ft. wide. Native to Europe, temperate Asia. Silvery gray, finely divided leaves with a pungent odor; tiny yellow flowers. Prune for better shape. Divide every 3 years. Use as background

A

shrub; makes a good gray feature in a flower border, looks particularly fine with delphiniums. 'Lambrook Silver' is a 1½-ft.-tall form with silvery white, especially finely cut leaves.

A. arborescens. Evergreen shrub or woody perennial. Zones CS; 9–5. Highly attractive. Mediterranean native to 3 ft. or a little taller, 2 ft. wide, with silvery white, very finely cut leaves.

A. caucasica. SILVER SPREADER. Evergreen shrublet. Zones US, MS, LS; 9–1. Caucasus native grows just 3–6 in. tall, spreading to 2 ft. wide. Silky foliage in silvery green; small yellow flowers. Use as bank or ground cover; plant 1–2 ft. apart. Needs good drainage. Takes extremes of heat and cold.

A. dracunculus. FRENCH TARRAGON, TRUE TARRAGON. Perennial. Zones US, MS; 7–1. Native to central and eastern Europe and southern Russia. To 1–2 ft.; spreads slowly by creeping rhizomes. Shiny dark green, narrow, very aromatic leaves; greenish white flowers in branched clusters. Attractive container plant. Cut sprigs in early summer to use for seasoning vinegar. Use fresh or dried leaves to season salads, cooked dishes. Divide every 3 or 4 years. Propagate by divisions or cuttings; plants grown from seed are not true culinary tarragon. Not for warmer areas; Mexican mint marigold (*Tagetes lucida*) is a good substitute.

A. 'Huntington'. Woody perennial. Zones US, MS, LS; 12–8. To 3 ft. tall and 4 ft. wide, with spreading stems covered by a thick dome of very silvery foliage. Resembles *A.* 'Powis Castle' but has bigger, softer leaves.

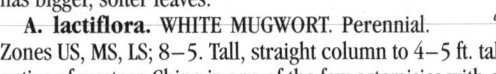

Artemisia dracunculus

A. lactiflora. WHITE MUGWORT. Perennial. Zones US, MS, LS; 8–5. Tall, straight column to 4–5 ft. tall, 2 ft. wide. This native of western China is one of the few artemisias with attractive flowers: in late summer, it bears creamy white blooms in branching, 1½-ft. sprays. Dark green leaves with broad, tooth-edged lobes. 'Guizhou' has purple stems but is otherwise similar to the species.

A. ludoviciana albula (A. albula). SILVER KING ARTEMISIA. Perennial. Zones US, MS, LS, CS; 12–8. Native to Southwest deserts, adjacent areas of Mexico. Bushy growth to 2–3½ ft. tall, 2 ft. wide, with slender, spreading branches and silvery white, 2-in. leaves. The lower leaves have three to five lobes; the upper ones are narrow and unlobed. Cut foliage is useful in arrangements. Two popular selections are 'Silver Queen', a compact form that grows to 1½–2½ ft. tall with larger foliage; and 'Valerie Finnis', which reaches 2 ft. and has even broader silver leaves that are slightly lobed toward the tips.

A. pontica. ROMAN WORMWOOD. Evergreen shrub or woody perennial. Zones US, LS, MS, CS; 8–1. Native to southeastern and central Europe; naturalized in eastern North America. Grows 2–4 ft. tall and spreads by rhizomes; makes a good ground cover if given ample room. Silvery gray, feathery leaves can be used in sachets. Heads of nodding, whitish yellow flowers are carried in long, open, branched clusters.

A. 'Powis Castle'. Woody perennial. Zones US, MS, LS; 9–6. A probable parent of this hybrid is *A. absinthium*. Hybrid grows in a silvery, lacy mound to 3 ft. tall and 6 ft. wide. Unlike most artemisias, does not "melt" during hot, humid summers; retains dense shape and is not invasive. Don't prune in fall; instead, wait to cut back until new growth begins to sprout near crown in spring.

A. schmidtiana. ANGEL'S HAIR. Woody perennial. Zones US, MS, LS; 8–3. Japanese native forms a 2-ft.-high, 1-ft.-wide dome of silvery white, woolly, finely cut leaves. Selection 'Silver Mound' is 1 ft. high. 'Silverado' is somewhat more open and upright than the species; tolerates heat and humidity well.

A. stellerana. BEACH WORMWOOD, OLD WOMAN, DUSTY MILLER. Perennial. Zones US, MS, LS; 8–1. Native to northeastern Asia; naturalized in eastern North America. Dense, silvery gray plant to 2½ ft. tall and 3 ft. wide, with lobed leaves 1–4 in. long. Hardier than *Senecio cineraria* (another dusty miller) and often used in its place in colder climates. Yellow flowers in spikelike clusters. 'Silver Brocade' is a superior, dense-growing selection.

ARTILLERY PLANT. See PILEA microphylla

ARUGULA

ROCKET, ROQUETTE

Brassicaceae (Cruciferae)

COOL-SEASON ANNUAL

✿ US, MS, LS, CS, TS ⊩ 7–1

☀ FULL SUN

💧 REGULAR WATER

Arugula

Arugula isn't the name of a corrupt Roman emperor. It's a gourmet green grown for its 1- to 4-in.-long leaves, which look like small mustard leaves and lend a nutty, somewhat peppery zing to salads.

Arugula grows best in cool weather. In Florida and South Texas, sow seed in fall and winter; elsewhere, sow in early spring or early fall. Thin seedlings to about 6 in. apart. Tender young leaves have the best flavor; older ones often taste too sharp. Eventually, the plants will shoot up to 3 ft. tall and bloom; at this point, pull them up and throw them away, as their flavor will be too pungent. Watch out for cabbage butterflies—their caterpillars find arugula just as tasty as cabbage.

ARUM

Araceae

PERENNIALS FROM TUBERS

✿ ZONES VARY BY SPECIES

◐ ● PARTIAL OR FULL SHADE

💧 REGULAR WATER DURING GROWTH AND BLOOM

☠ SAP IS AN IRRITANT IF INGESTED

Arum italicum 'Pictum'

Tubers give rise to attractively veined, arrow-shaped leaves in fall or winter. Short stalks bear curious callalike blooms featuring a leaflike bract (spathe) that half encloses a thick, fleshy spike (spadix) set with tiny flowers. These blossoms are followed by dense clusters of typically bright red fruit that look like little ears of corn and persist after leaves have died to the ground. Use in shady flower borders.

Plant tubers during late summer or in early autumn (toward the end of their dormancy), setting them 8–12 in. apart and about 2 in. deep. Dormant plantings accept summer water but don't need it. *A. palaestinum* and *A. pictum* are sometimes used as houseplants in colder climates.

A. italicum. ITALIAN ARUM. Zones US, MS, LS, CS; 9–3. Native to southern and western Europe. Foot-long leaves on leafstalks of equal length appear in fall or early winter. Very short stems carry white or greenish white (sometimes purple-spotted) flowers in spring and early summer; the fruits that follow are orange red. Spathe first stands erect, then folds over and conceals short yellow spadix. Leaves die to ground after bloom. In favorable situations, naturalizes by volunteer seedlings. Selection 'Pictum' has white-veined leaves and makes an extremely attractive winter carpet.

A. palaestinum. BLACK CALLA. Zones CS, TS; 9–1. Native to Israel. Leaves emerge in winter; to about 8 in. long, on 1-ft. leafstalks. Spathe is 8 in. long, green outside; opens outward and curls back at tip to reveal purple interior and black spadix. Blooms in spring and early summer; then leaves die back.

A. pictum. Zones LS, TS; 9–6. Native to western Mediterranean. May be called black calla, like *A. palaestinum*—but unlike that species, it has an 8-in. violet spathe with a white base that encloses a dark purple spadix. Flowers appear in fall—sometimes with emerging foliage, sometimes before. Light green leaves with white veins reach 10 in. long and are borne on equally long leafstalks. Foliage dies to ground in hot weather.

ARUNCUS

GOAT'S BEARD

Rosaceae

PERENNIALS

ZONES VARY BY SPECIES

FULL SUN IN COOLER REGIONS ONLY

REGULAR WATER

Aruncus dioicus

These perennials resemble astilbe, with slowly spreading clumps of finely divided leaves topped in summer by branching plumes of tiny white or cream flowers. Good in perennial borders or at edge of woodland.

A. aethusifolius. Zones US, MS, LS; 8–1. Native to Korea. Deep green, finely divided leaves make a mound about 1 ft. tall and wide. White flower plumes reach 16 in. high. Useful in rock garden, as edging, for small-scale ground cover.

A. dioicus (A. sylvester). Zones US, MS; 7–1. Native to Eurasia and to southeastern and south-central Alaska. Grows to 6 (sometimes 7) ft. tall, 4 ft. wide, with foamy plumes of white flowers in 20-in., much-branched clusters. 'Kneiffii' is half the size of the species, with more finely divided leaves. 'Child of Two Worlds' ('Zweiweltenkind'), which is sometimes sold as *A. chinensis,* grows to 5 ft. tall, with gracefully drooping flower clusters.

ARUNDO donax

GIANT REED

Poaceae (Gramineae)

PERENNIAL GRASS

US, MS, LS, CS, TS   12–1

FULL SUN

REGULAR TO AMPLE WATER

Arundo donax

One of the tallest grasses, often seen in rural gardens throughout the South. A real conversation piece, thanks to strong, woody stems that can tower to 20 ft. or more. Useful as a windbreak, screen, or vertical accent. In most areas, it dies to the ground in winter but regrows quickly in spring. Flat leaves grow to 2 ft. long and 3 in. wide. In summer, the plant is crowned by greenish or purplish blooms in showy panicles that grow up to 2 ft. long.

Spreads quickly by thick rhizomes and can be invasive in moist soil, a quality that has made it a classic passalong plant (it is easy to dig and divide in spring or fall). Seeds can also travel far and wide on the wind, increasing the plant's chances of spreading—so be careful where you plant it, and don't let it escape to the wild. Cut withered stems to the ground in winter; they make good plant stakes.

'Versicolor' ('Variegata') flaunts leaves with creamy or yellowish stripes. It grows about half as tall as the species and is less likely to bloom (but can be invasive nonetheless).

ASARUM

WILD GINGER

Aristolochiaceae

PERENNIALS

ZONES VARY BY SPECIES

PARTIAL OR FULL SHADE

REGULAR TO AMPLE WATER

Asarum shuttleworthii 'Carolina Silver'

Roots and leaves of the wild gingers have a scent somewhat like that of culinary ginger *(Zingiber),* but they are not used as seasoning. Low, creeping plants bearing roundish or heart-shaped leaves, they make very attractive woodland ground covers. Their flowers are curious rather than showy, almost hidden among the leaves; they are small (usually less than 2 in. wide) and oddly shaped, with three spreading, leathery lobes that may be brownish, purplish, or greenish. Of the many species that exist, only a few are available to gardeners. Asiatic species with fancy variegated leaves, now grown as connoisseurs' plants in Japan, may eventually make their way here.

A. arifolium. HEARTLEAF, ARROWLEAF GINGER. Zones US, MS, LS, CS; 9–3. Native from Virginia south to Florida and Alabama. Tough, easy-to-grow evergreen wild ginger with glossy green (sometimes silver-mottled) leaves to 5 in. long. Flowers are reddish brown. Spreads slowly to form 1½-ft.-wide clumps.

A. campaniforme. Zones LS, CS; 9–8. From China. Evergreen, deep green leaves grow to 6 in. long and 4 in. wide. Brownish purple flowers are white inside, with a purple ring partway down. Plant is sometimes called kiwi ginger because the inside of the flower resembles a slice of kiwi fruit.

A. canadense. CANADA WILD GINGER. Zones US, MS, LS; 8–1. Native to eastern North America. Deciduous, kidney-shaped, dark green leaves to 4 in. long, 6 in. wide. Flowers are purplish brown. The hardiest species.

A. caudatum. Zones US, MS, LS; 8–1. Native to the West Coast. Evergreen in warmest areas of the zones where it will grow. Heart-shaped leaves are 2–7 in. long and wide. Reddish brown flowers have lobes elongated into tails. Where adapted, a valuable, quick-growing ground cover for shady places.

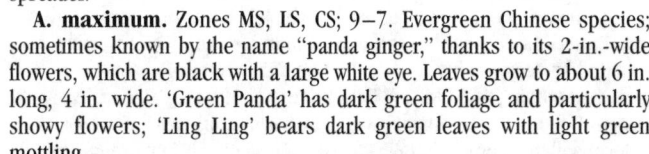

Asarum caudatum

A. europaeum. EUROPEAN WILD GINGER. Zones US, MS, LS; 8–1. Native to Europe. Evergreen, shiny, kidney-shaped, dark green leaves 2–3 in. long and wide. Small brown flowers. Slow spreader.

A. maximum. Zones MS, LS, CS; 9–7. Evergreen Chinese species; sometimes known by the name "panda ginger," thanks to its 2-in.-wide flowers, which are black with a large white eye. Leaves grow to about 6 in. long, 4 in. wide. 'Green Panda' has dark green foliage and particularly showy flowers; 'Ling Ling' bears dark green leaves with light green mottling.

A. shuttleworthii. MOTTLED WILD GINGER. Zones US, MS, LS, CS; 9–1. Native to the Appalachians. Evergreen, 4-in., heart-shaped or roundish leaves, usually variegated with silvery markings. Brown flowers with red spots. Slow growing. 'Callaway' spreads more quickly and has extremely handsome, mottled foliage. The foliage of 'Carolina Silver' is attractively marked with silvery cream. 'Velvet Queen' has silver-mottled leaves and double-size blossoms.

A. speciosum. ALABAMA WILD GINGER. Zones US, MS, LS, CS; 9–1. This Alabama native is a favorite and the showiest of the North American wild ginger species. The plant features large, evergreen, variably mottled leaves and bold black-and-cream flowers. Selection 'Buxom Beauty' is bigger than the species overall: its silver-marbled leaves grow to 10 in. long, and its flowers are about 2 in. across. Like 'Buxom Beauty', 'Woodlander's Select' also has silver-marked leaves, but they reach just 6 in. long; its flowers are about 1½ in. across.

A. splendens. Zones US, MS, LS, CS; 9–6. Easy-to-grow Chinese native. Evergreen leaves in dark green heavily mottled with silver are heart shaped with an elongated tip; may reach 7 in. long, 3 in. wide. Large (2-in.-wide) dark purple flowers. Grows quite vigorously in loose, rich soil, forming large colonies.

A. virginicum virginicum 'Silver Splash'. Zones US, MS, LS, CS; 9–5. Selection of a southeastern U.S. native, with round, evergreen, 2-in. leaves in green boldly marked with silver. Relatively small flowers are reddish brown.

Asclepiadaceae. Best-known family members are the milkweeds *(Asclepias),* but other garden plants also belong to this group, among them many succulents and some perennials and vines, including *Stephanotis.*

ASCLEPIAS

Asclepiadaceae

PERENNIALS

⚡ ZONES VARY BY SPECIES

☼ FULL SUN

◑ ● ●● WATER NEEDS VARY BY SPECIES

⚠ ALL PARTS OF MANY SPECIES ARE POISONOUS
IF INGESTED

Though classified as milkweeds (so named for their milky sap), the plants listed here are anything but weeds—they're showy, easy-to-grow garden plants. All bloom in summer, typically bearing many small, starlike flowers in broad, flattened clusters at branch tips. After the flowers fade, silky seeds burst from inflated seedpods and float through the air like dandelion seeds. Among the best plants for attracting butterflies—particularly monarchs, whose caterpillars feast on the foliage.

Asclepias tuberosa

A. curassavica. BLOOD FLOWER. Zones CS, TS; Zones US, MS, LS, CS, TS as annual; 12–6. Native to South America. Woody-based plant with stiff stems and narrow, 6-in. leaves; grows 3 ft. tall, 2 ft. wide. Clusters of vivid red flowers. 'Silky Gold' is similar but bears bright yellow to yellow-orange blooms. Moderate water.

A. humistrata. SANDHILL MILKWEED. Zones MS, LS, CS; 12–7. Herbaceous perennial native to the southeastern U.S. Attractive gray-green leaves with distinct purple veins are widely spaced along 1½- to 2-ft. stems that lean over to form a spreading plant. White flowers may be tinged with lavender. Regular water.

A. incarnata. SWAMP MILKWEED. Zones US, MS, LS, CS; 9–2. Native to eastern U.S. Herbaceous perennial to 2–4 ft. tall, 2 ft. wide. Narrow, pointed leaves to 6 in. long; ball-shaped clusters of pinkish purple flowers. 'Ice Ballet' has pure white blooms. 'Soulmate' has white flowers surrounded by deep red bracts. Regular to ample water.

A. tuberosa. BUTTERFLY WEED. Zones US, MS, LS, CS; 9–2. Native to eastern U.S. From a perennial root, many herbaceous stems rise every year to form a clump about 3 ft. tall, 1 ft. wide. Clusters of bright orange flowers attract swarms of butterflies. Gay Butterflies strain features yellow, red, orange, pink, or bicolored blossoms; selection 'Hello Yellow' has bright yellow blooms. All make long-lasting cut flowers. Provide good drainage, moderate water.

ASH. See FRAXINUS

ASH, MOUNTAIN. See SORBUS

ASIAN GREENS

Brassicaceae (Cruciferae)

COOL-SEASON ANNUALS

⚡ US, MS, LS, CS, TS ⫶ 7–1

☼ ◐ FULL SUN OR LIGHT SHADE

● REGULAR WATER

Chinese Mustard Greens

The annual vegetables in this large group are the mainstays of stir-fry dishes and excellent in salads. Asian greens are primarily quick-maturing cool-season crops that are planted at the same time as other cool-season vegetables: late winter to early spring for spring-to-summer harvest, late summer to early fall for fall and winter harvest.

Many Asian greens, especially the mustards, are attractive foliage plants that make a colorful addition to the vegetable garden and also look good mixed with flowering annuals and spring bulbs.

Listed here are some of the most common Asian greens; specialty seed catalogs may carry additional kinds. For planting depth and row spacing, follow the instructions on the seed packet.

Broadleaf mustard (dai gai choy). Large green leaves with a pungent, somewhat bitter, mustardlike flavor that gets stronger as the plant matures. Hot weather or inadequate moisture also increases pungency. Best used in soup to tone down the sharp flavor.

Thin or transplant seedlings to 10 in. apart. Harvest plants when they are loose headed and 10–14 in. high, about 65 days after sowing.

Chinese broccoli (gai lohn). Similar in flavor and texture to standard broccoli, but with a slight pungency like that of mustard. Thin or transplant seedlings to 10 in. apart. Harvest central stalk and side shoots when stalk is 8–10 in. tall or when flower buds just begin to form, usually about 70 days after sowing.

Chinese mustard greens (gai choy). Milder member of the mustard family. Thin or transplant seedlings to 10 in. apart. Harvest the first greens when the plants are 2 in. high; continue harvesting until leaves turn tough or bitter. It usually takes 45 days after sowing for plants to reach mature height of 6–8 in.

Chinese white cabbage (bok choy, pac choi). One of the more familiar Asian greens. Tender-crisp, sweet, very mild; good alone, with meat, in soups and stir-fries. Many selections are sold. Tat-soi is similar but more compact.

Thin or transplant seedlings to 6–12 in. apart. Plants are ready to harvest approximately 50 days after sowing seed, when they are loose headed and 10–12 in. tall.

Flowering cabbage (yao choy, choy sum, ching sow sum). Tender, delicate, broccoli-type vegetable. Thin or transplant seedlings to about 6 in. apart. Harvest about 60 days after sowing, when 8–12 in. high.

Mizuna. Mild-flavored, leafy vegetable with finely cut, frilly, white-stemmed leaves. Great in salads. Thin or transplant seedlings to 8–10 in. apart. Start cutting leaves when plants are a few inches tall, or wait until they are mature (8–10 in. high)—about 40 days after sowing.

ASIMINA triloba. See PAWPAW

ASPARAGUS, EDIBLE

Liliaceae

PERENNIAL

⚡ US, MS, LS ⫶ 8–1

☼ FULL SUN

● REGULAR WATER

Asparagus

One of the most permanent and dependable of home garden vegetables. Plants take 2 to 3 years to come into full production but then furnish delicious spears every spring for 10 to 15 years or more. They take up considerable space but do so in grand manner: plants are tall, feathery, graceful, highly ornamental. Use along a sunny fence or as background for flowers or vegetables.

Seeds grow into strong young plants in one season (sow in spring), but roots are far more widely used. Set out seedlings or roots (not wilted, no smaller than an adult's hand) in fall or winter, or in early spring in Upper South. Make trenches 1 ft. wide and 8–10 in. deep; space them 4–6 ft. apart. Heap loose soil enriched with composted manure at bottom of trenches and soak well. Space plants 1 ft. apart, setting them so that tops are 6–8 in. below top of trench. Spread roots out evenly. Cover with 2 in. of soil and water again.

As young plants grow, gradually fill in trench, taking care not to cover growing tips. Soak deeply whenever soil begins to dry out at root depth. Don't harvest spears the first year; object is to build a big root mass. When plants turn brown in late fall or early winter, cut stems to ground.

The following spring you can cut your first spears; cut only for 4 to 6 weeks, or until appearance of thin spears indicates that roots are nearing exhaustion. Then permit plants to grow. Cultivate, feed, and irrigate heavily. The third year you should be able to cut spears for 8 to 10 weeks. Spears are ready to cut when they are 5–8 in. long. Thrust knife down at

45° angle to soil; flat cutting may injure adjacent developing spears. If asparagus beetles appear during cutting season, hand-pick them, knock them off the plant with water jets, or spray with malathion, carefully noting label precautions (see "A Practical Guide to Gardening," page 623).

Asparagus seed and roots are sold as "traditional" ('Martha Washington' and others) and "all-male." All-male types include 'UC 157', 'Jersey Giant', and 'Jersey Knight' (the best male for Southern growers). Male hybrids typically produce more and larger spears, because they don't have to put energy into seed production. Such selections still produce an occasional female plant.

'Purple Passion' is an unusual selection that produces deep burgundy spears with a sweet, nutty flavor (the spears turn green when cooked).

HOW TO BLANCH ASPARAGUS. *Fresh white asparagus is a delicacy. It's not a special kind of asparagus; blanching makes it white. To blanch asparagus, do this: in early spring, before spears emerge, mound soil 8 in. high over a row of asparagus. Then, when tips emerge from the mounded soil, push a long-handled knife into the base of the mound to cut each spear well below the surface. Pull cut shoots out by the tips; level mound after the harvest season is over.* ❖

ASPARAGUS, ORNAMENTAL

Liliaceae

PERENNIALS, SHRUBS, OR VINES

CS, TS; H 12–10; OR HOUSEPLANTS

PARTIAL SHADE; BRIGHT FILTERED LIGHT

REGULAR WATER

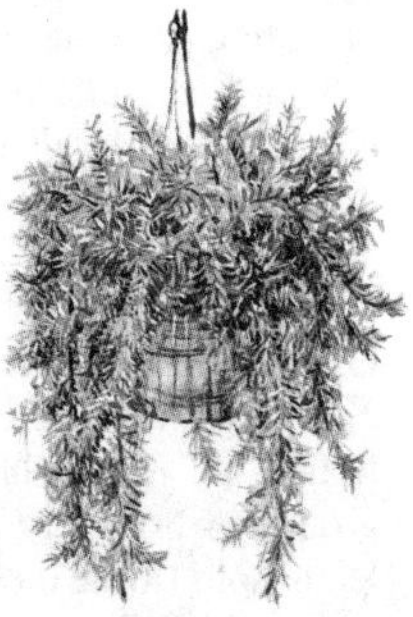

Asparagus densiflorus 'Sprengeri'

There are about 150 kinds of asparagus besides the edible one—all are members of the lily family. Those described here are native to South Africa. Best known is asparagus fern *(A. setaceus),* which is not a true fern. Although valued mostly for handsome foliage of unusual textural quality, some of the ornamental species have small but fragrant flowers and colorful berries. Green foliage sprays are made up of what look like leaves. Needlelike or broader, these are actually short branches called cladodes. The true leaves are inconspicuous dry scales.

Most ornamental asparagus look greenest in partial shade. Leaves yellow in dense shade. Plant in well-drained soil amended with peat moss or ground bark. Thanks to their fleshy roots, plants can go for some time without water, but they grow better when watered regularly. Feed in spring with complete fertilizer. Trim out old shoots to make room for new growth. Ornamental asparagus will survive light frosts but may be killed to ground by severe cold. After frost, plants often come back from roots.

A. asparagoides. SMILAX ASPARAGUS. Much-branched vine with spineless stems to 20 ft. or more. Often seen in older gardens. Leaves to 1 in. long, sharp pointed, stiffish, glossy grass green. Small, fragrant white flowers in spring followed by blue berries. Birds feed on berries, drop seeds that sprout at random about the garden. (Plant also self-sows readily.) Fleshy tuberous roots are nearly immortal, surviving long drought, then sprouting when rains come. Foliage sprays are prized for table decoration. If it doesn't get much water, plant dies back in summer, revives with fall rains. Becomes a tangled mass unless trained. 'Myrtifolius', commonly called baby smilax, is a more graceful form with smaller leaves.

A. crispus. BASKET ASPARAGUS. Airy, graceful plant for hanging baskets. Drooping, zigzag stems have bright green, three-angled leaves in whorls of three. Often sold as *A. scandens* 'Deflexus'.

A. densiflorus. The species is less commonly grown than its forms; the following are the two most popular. Plants are seldom browsed by deer.

'Myers'. MYERS ASPARAGUS. Several to many stiffly upright stems to 2 ft. or more, densely clothed with needlelike deep green leaves that give the plant a fluffy look. Forms a 3- to 4-ft.-wide clump. Good in containers. A little less hardy than 'Sprengeri'. May be sold as *A. meyeri* or *A. myersii.*

'Sprengeri'. SPRENGER ASPARAGUS. Arching or drooping stems 3–6 ft. long. Shiny, bright green, needlelike leaves, 1 in. long, in bundles. Bright red berries. Popular for hanging baskets or containers, indoors and out. Train on trellis; climbs by means of small hooked prickles. Used as billowy ground cover where temperatures stay above 24°F. Grows in ordinary or even poor soil. Will tolerate dryness of indoors. Sometimes sold as *A. sprengeri.* Form sold as 'Sprengeri Compacta' or *A. sarmentosus* 'Compacta' is denser, with shorter stems.

A. falcatus. SICKLE-THORN ASPARAGUS. Leaves are 2–3 in. long and very narrow, resembling flattened pine needles; they are borne in clusters of three to five at ends of branches. Tiny, fragrant white flowers in loose clusters are followed by brown berries. The plant derives its common name from curved thorns along its stems, which it uses to clamber rapidly as high as 40 ft. in its native area (in gardens, it usually reaches about 10 ft.). Makes an excellent foliage mass to cover fence or wall or provide shade for pergola or lathhouse.

A. meyeri, A. myersii. See A. densiflorus 'Myers'

A. officinalis. See Asparagus, edible

A. retrofractus (A. macowanii). Erect, shrubby, slightly climbing, very tender. Slender silvery gray stems grow slowly to 8–10 ft. high. Threadlike, inch-long leaves, in fluffy, rich green tufts. Clusters of small white flowers. Handsome in containers; useful in flower arrangements. Cut foliage lasts about 10 days out of water, several weeks in water.

A. scandens. BASKET ASPARAGUS. Slender, branching vine climbing to 6 ft. Deep green, needlelike leaves on zigzag, drooping stems. Tiny greenish white flowers; scarlet berries.

A. setaceus (A. plumosus). ASPARAGUS FERN. Sometimes called by the name "emerald feather." Branching, woody vine climbs by wiry, spiny stems to 10–20 ft. Tiny threadlike leaves form feathery dark green sprays that resemble fern fronds. Tiny white flowers; purple-black berries. Dense, fine-textured foliage mass useful as screen against walls, fences. Florists use foliage as filler in bouquets; it holds up better than delicate ferns. Dwarf 'Nanus' is good in containers. 'Pyramidalis' has upswept, windblown look, is less vigorous than the species.

A. sprengeri. See A. densiflorus 'Sprengeri'

ASPEN. See POPULUS

ASPERULA odorata. See GALIUM odoratum

ASPIDISTRA

CAST-IRON PLANT

Liliaceae

PERENNIALS

LS, CS, TS; OR HOUSEPLANTS

PARTIAL OR FULL SHADE; BRIGHT TO DIM LIGHT

MODERATE TO REGULAR WATER

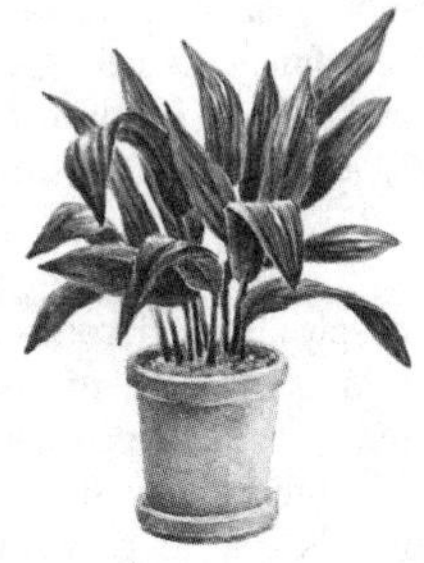

Aspidistra elatior

Cast-iron plants were made for brown-thumb gardeners. Sturdy, long-lived, and nearly bulletproof, these evergreen perennials typically form rather open clumps; they tolerate very low light and almost total neglect. Although they don't require well-drained soil enriched with organic matter, they'll be very happy if they get it—and if you really want to pamper them, fertilize them occasionally in spring and summer. They make excellent houseplants if placed where they'll get light (4–5 ft. from a sunny, south-facing window, for example). Let the soil surface go dry between waterings. From the Lower South on down, cast-iron plants are also good for deeply shaded areas around the house where few other plants will grow—under a deck, for example. Bright, hot sunlight will burn their leaves.

A. caespitosa 'Jade Ribbons'. Heat zones 10–7. Selection of a Chinese species. Forms a tight clump; looks a lot like a daylily *(Hemerocallis)* plant. Shiny dark green leaves are 2 ft. long, ½ in. wide. ▸

A. 'China Star'. Heat zones 10–8. Fast-spreading dwarf collected in the Qing Cheng San Mountains of China. The leaves reach 8–10 in. long and just 2¼ in. wide; they are attractively speckled with yellow.

A. elatior. Heat zones 12–4. Native to Japan and China. The most common cast-iron plant, with upright, arching leaves sporting distinctive parallel veins from base to tip. Leaf blades are 1–2½ ft. long and 4–5 in. wide, carried on grooved, 6- to 8-in.-long leafstalks. In spring, bears inconspicuous brownish flowers. Selections include the following.

'Akebono'. Leaves to 2½ ft. long flaunt a narrow white streak down the center.

'Asahi'. Deep green leaves reach 20 in. long. As the season progresses, the top third of each leaf turns white. Color holds all winter.

'Okame'. Green leaves to 20 in. long, dramatically marked with irregular longitudinal white stripes.

'Variegata'. Rich green leaves are marked from base to tip with streaks of white. Loses variegation if planted in soil that's too rich.

A. linearifolia 'Leopard'. Heat zones 10–8. A bizarre clump-forming selection of a Chinese species; looks like a cross between cast-iron plant and mother-in-law's tongue *(Sansevieria)*. Deep green, yellow-speckled leaves are held erect; they grow about 2½ ft. long but just ½ in. wide.

ASPIDIUM capense. See RUMOHRA adiantiformis

ASPLENIUM

Polypodiaceae

FERNS

ZONES VARY BY SPECIES

PARTIAL TO FULL SHADE

REGULAR TO AMPLE WATER

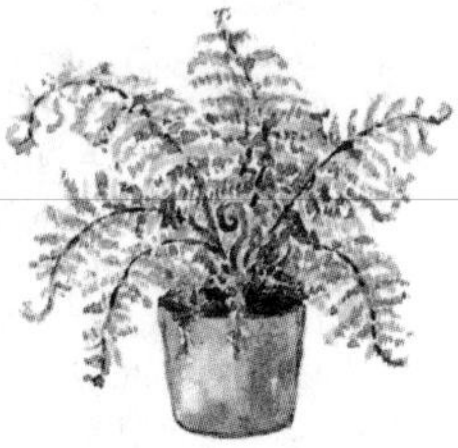

Asplenium bulbiferum

Widespread and variable group of rhizomatous ferns, once called spleenwort for their purported medicinal value. These evergreen species resemble one another only in botanical details and in their need for shade and liberal watering. Unlike many other ferns, they need a rest period from late fall to early spring when grown indoors; during that time, reduce watering and withhold fertilizer. Indoor plants like bright filtered light; a spot in an east-facing window is ideal.

A. bulbiferum. MOTHER FERN. Zones TS; 12–8; or indoors. From New Zealand. Evergreen or semievergreen. To 4 ft. tall and wide. Graceful, very finely cut light green fronds produce plantlets that can be removed and planted. Hardy to 26°F.

A. ebenoides (Asplenosorus ebenoides). SCOTT'S SPLEENWORT, DRAGON TAIL FERN. Zones US, MS, LS, CS; 9–1. Hybrid of *A. platyneuron* and *A. rhizophyllum*. Small evergreen fern of variable appearance, with deeply indented fronds to 6–12 in. long. Good in rock garden.

A. nidus (A. nidus-avis). BIRD'S NEST FERN. Zones TS; 12–3; or indoors. Evergreen native of Old World tropics. Striking foliage: showy, apple green, undivided fronds 4 ft. long by 8 in. wide, growing upright in a cluster to about 3 ft. wide. Tender; if grown in pots, keep indoors in winter, move to shady patio in summer.

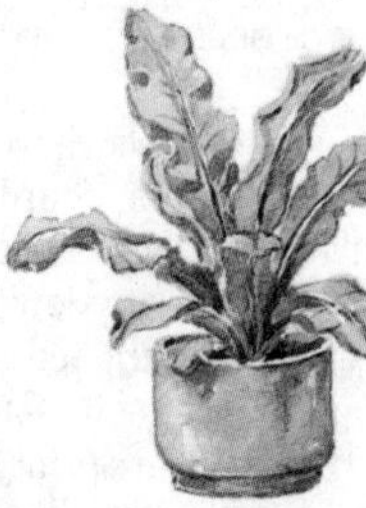

Asplenium nidus

A. platyneuron. EBONY SPLEENWORT. Zones US, MS, LS, CS; 9–1. Native to eastern U.S. Evergreen; 1½ ft. tall and about as wide. Erect, once-divided, dark green fronds have blackish brown midribs.

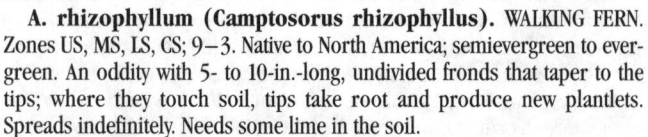

A. rhizophyllum (Camptosorus rhizophyllus). WALKING FERN. Zones US, MS, LS, CS; 9–3. Native to North America; semievergreen to evergreen. An oddity with 5- to 10-in.-long, undivided fronds that taper to the tips; where they touch soil, tips take root and produce new plantlets. Spreads indefinitely. Needs some lime in the soil.

A. scolopendrium (Phyllitis scolopendrium). HART'S TONGUE FERN. Zones US, MS, LS; 8–6. Native to Europe (rare native in eastern U.S.). Strap-shaped, evergreen, 9- to 18-in.-long fronds form a clump about 2 ft. wide. Dwarf, crested, puckered, and forked kinds are collector's items. Plant in humusy soil; add limestone chips if soil is acid. Good woodland plant, fine companion for rhododendrons and azaleas; also makes an excellent potted plant.

A. trichomanes. MAIDENHAIR SPLEENWORT. Zones US, MS, LS; 8–3. Native to much of the Northern Hemisphere. Delicate evergreen fern with narrow, bright green, 4- to 8-in.-long fronds; forms a clump to 8 in. wide. Leaflets are only ½ in. long, round or nearly so. Likes lime. Attractive in shady rock garden or on a wall where it can be seen close up.

ASTER

Asteraceae (Compositae)

PERENNIALS

US, MS, LS H 8–1, EXCEPT AS NOTED

FULL SUN, EXCEPT AS NOTED

MODERATE TO REGULAR WATER, EXCEPT AS NOTED

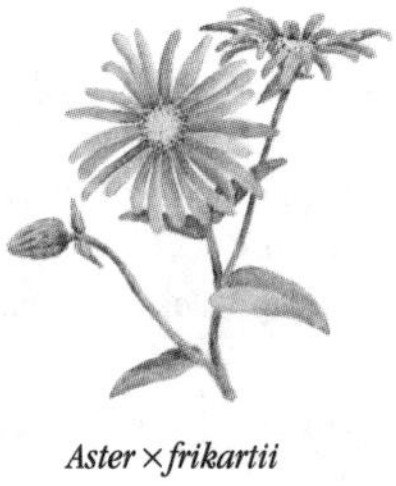

Aster × frikartii

There are more than 600 species of true asters, ranging from alpine kinds forming compact, 6-in. mounds to open-branching plants 6 ft. tall. Flowers come in white or shades of blue, red, pink, lavender, or purple, mostly with yellow centers; they bloom in late summer to early fall, except as noted. Taller asters are invaluable for abundant color in large borders or among shrubs. Large sprays are effective in arrangements. Compact dwarf or cushion types make tidy edgings, mounds of color in rock gardens, good container plants. For the common annual or China aster sold at nurseries, see *Callistephus chinensis*.

True asters are adapted to most soils, but growth is most luxuriant in fertile soil. Few problems except for mildew on leaves in late fall. Strong-growing hybrids have invasive roots; they can regrow from small fragments left in soil. Divide these yearly in late fall or early spring. Replant vigorous young divisions from outside of clump; discard old center. Divide smaller, tufted, less vigorously growing kinds every 2 years.

A. alpinus. ALPINE ASTER. Zones US, MS. Native to Alps, Pyrenees. Mounding plant to 1 ft. high, 1½ ft. wide. Leaves ½–5 in. long, mostly in basal tuft. Several stems grow from the leafy clump, each with one violet-blue flower 1½–2 in. across. Late spring to early summer bloom. Best in cold-winter areas. White and pink forms are uncommon.

A. amellus. ITALIAN ASTER. Native to Europe, western Asia. Sturdy, hairy plant grows about 2 ft. tall, 1½ ft. wide. Branching stems bear yellow-centered violet flowers 2 in. across.

A. carolinianus. CLIMBING ASTER. Zones MS, LS, CS. Native from North Carolina to Florida. Unusual climber, reaching 10–20 ft. if given support. Grayish green leaves; inch-wide autumn flowers in pink aging to purplish blue. Does best in fertile soil with ample moisture.

A. cordifolius. BLUE WOOD ASTER. Native to eastern North America. To 6 ft. tall, 3 ft. wide, with loose, branching clusters of inch-wide lavender flowers. Sun or light shade. 'Little Carlow', to 2 ft. high, bears a profusion of violet-blue flowers.

A. divaricatus. WHITE WOOD ASTER. Native to eastern North America. To 3 ft. tall and wide, with a strong horizontal branching pattern and a generous show of ½-in. flowers in white aging to pink. Thrives in shade.

A. ericoides. HEATH ASTER. Native to eastern North America. To 3 ft. tall and 1 ft. wide, with narrow leaves and strong horizontal branching. Profuse ½-in. blooms in white, pink, or blue. Plants sold as *A. e.* 'Monte Cassino' may actually belong to *A. pringlei*.

A. × frikartii. FRIKART ASTER. One of the finest, most useful and widely adapted perennials. Hybrid between *A. amellus* and *A. thomsonii*, a hairy-leafed, lilac-flowered, 3-ft.-tall species native to the Himalayas. Dark green leaves; abundant clear lavender to violet-blue single flowers about 2½ in. across. Open growth to 2 ft. high and wide. Blooms early summer to fall—almost all year in mild-winter areas if spent flowers are removed regularly. May be short lived. 'Wonder of Staffa' and 'Mönch' are favorites, with blossoms in lavender blue. 'Flora's Delight', to 1½ ft. high, has gray-green foliage and abundant pale lilac flowers with large yellow centers.

A. fruticosus. See Felicia fruticosa

A. laevis. SMOOTH ASTER. Native to eastern North America. Grows to 3½ ft. tall, 1½ ft. wide, with smooth, mildew-free foliage and clustered 1-in. flower heads of deep purplish blue. 'Bluebird' is a superior selection to 4–5 ft. tall.

Aster ×frikartii 'Wonder of Staffa' *Aster novi-belgii* 'Professor Anton Kippenburg' *Aster novae-angliae* 'Alma Potschke'

A. lateriflorus. CALICO ASTER. North American native. Species grows to 4 ft. tall, 1 ft. wide. Garden selections are shorter (to 2 ft.), with profuse branching, tiny leaves and a haze of ½-in., purplish pink flowers. Foliage turns a coppery purplish red in early fall. 'Prince' has blackish purple stems and leaves; its blooms are white with a red center. 'Lady in Black' is a bolder version of 'Prince', with the same dark foliage and masses of tiny, red-centered white flowers; it grows 3–4 ft. tall. 'Coombe Fishacre' is a hybrid developed from *A. lateriflorus;* it produces tiny pink flowers with red centers on a plant to 2–3 ft. tall.

A. novae-angliae. NEW ENGLAND ASTER. Native from Vermont to Alabama, west to North Dakota, Wyoming, and New Mexico. Stout-stemmed plant to 3–5 ft. tall and nearly as wide, with hairy leaves to 5 in. long. Flowers are 2 in. wide; they are violet blue in the basic form, with selections in other blue shades, white, pink, nearly red, and deep purple. All are very tolerant of wet soils and will reseed. Two longtime favorite selections are good garden plants: 'Alma Potschke' produces salmon pink single blooms on 3-ft. stems from late summer to early fall; 'Harrington's Pink' produces clear pink single flowers over a long autumn season on 3- to 4-ft. stems. Another good selection is 'Purple Dome', which reaches just 1½ ft. tall and has brilliant purple blooms.

A. novi-belgii. NEW YORK ASTER, MICHAELMAS DAISY. Native to eastern North America. To 4 ft. tall and 3 ft. wide, with full clusters of bright blue-violet flowers. Similar to *A. novae-angliae* but with smooth leaves. Hundreds of selections are available, varying in height from less than a foot to over 4 ft.; flower colors include white, cream, blue, lavender, purple, rose, and pink. Among the many choices are 'Persian Rose' (rose pink) and semidouble 'Professor Anton Kippenburg' (lavender blue), both under 1 ft. high and 1½ ft. wide. Robust 'Climax' bears large sprays of single medium blue blossoms on stems to 6 ft. high.

A. oblongifolius. AROMATIC ASTER. From the central U.S. Grows 2 ft. tall and wide, with light blue-violet, 1-in. flowers that last into late fall, unperturbed by heavy frosts. Pale green leaves are aromatic when crushed. Prefers a dry, open site; tolerates harsh conditions, including heat, cold, poor or alkaline soil, and strong winds. Selection 'October Skies' produces rich sky blue flowers; 'Raydon's Favorite' bears bluish purple ones. 'Fanny', growing 3–4 ft. tall, has grayish green leaves and masses of bright purple blossoms.

A. patens. LATE PURPLE ASTER. Heat zones 9–1. From the eastern and southeastern U.S. To 3 ft. tall, 1½–2 ft. wide. Prolific show of bright violet-blue, 1-in. flowers. Tolerates drought and partial shade.

A. pringlei. Eastern U.S. native known in cultivation through its selection 'Monte Cassino', a familiar florists' cut flower. Grows to 5 ft. tall and 1½ ft. wide; tall, narrow stems have many short side branches set with starry, white, ¾-in. flowers. This plant is often sold as *A. ericoides* 'Monte Cassino'.

A. sibiricus. SIBERIAN ASTER. Zone US. From northern parts of North America and Eurasia. To 16 in. high and as broad, with 9-in.-long basal leaves, purplish stems, and ¾-in. purple flowers borne singly or a few to the cluster.

A. tataricus. TATARIAN ASTER. Heat zones 9–1. Native to Siberia, China, Japan. Not for small gardens, this giant grows to 5–7 ft. tall and 3 ft. wide, with 2-ft.-long leaves and sheaves of inch-wide blue flowers in flat clusters in fall. Can be invasive. Takes sun or shade.

A. tongolensis (A. subcaeruleus, A. yunnanensis). EAST INDIES ASTER. From China, Himalayas. Dark green leaves in basal tufts; clumps grow

to 1½ ft. high and 1 ft. wide. Each stem bears a single lavender-blue, orange-centered, 2½-in. flower in late spring to early summer. 'Napsbury' has dark blue blooms. 'Wartburg Star' forms a dense mound and has violet-blue flowers.

A. Wood's Series. 'Wood's Light Blue' is a bushy plant with dark green leaves. It grows 1–1½ ft. high, 1½–2 ft. wide, but it can be severely cut back in early summer and will still flower well at only 6 in. high, bearing an abundance of medium blue, 1-in. blossoms late in the season. 'Wood's Purple', to barely 1 ft. high and wide, has deep purple blooms.

Asteraceae. The sunflower or daisy family, one of the largest plant families, is characterized by flowers borne in tight clusters (heads). In the most familiar form, these heads contain two types of flowers—small, tightly clustered disk flowers in the center of the head and larger, strap-shaped ray flowers around the edge. The sunflower *(Helianthus)* is a familiar example. The family was formerly called Compositae.

ASTILBE

FALSE SPIRAEA, MEADOW SWEET

Saxifragaceae

PERENNIALS

⚡ US, MS ⊞ 8–2

☼ ◑ FULL SUN OR PARTIAL SHADE, EXCEPT AS NOTED

💧 REGULAR WATER

Astilbe ×arendsii

These graceful plants combine showy flowers and handsome, fernlike foliage. Small blossoms in white, pink, peach, rose, red, or purple appear in airy, feathery plumes held by thin, wiry stems ranging in length from 6 in. to 3 ft. or more. Most grow 2–3 ft. wide.

Astilbes are the mainstay of shady borders in the Upper and Middle South, but can take some sun in the Upper South if given plenty of water. Combine with columbine *(Aquilegia)*, meadow rue *(Thalictrum)*, hosta, and epimedium in shady borders, or with peonies *(Paeonia)*, delphinium, and irises in sunnier spots. Effective at the edge of ponds, along shady paths, in mass plantings, and in pots. Seldom browsed by deer.

All astilbes need moist, well-drained soil with ample organic matter. Cut off faded flower stems. Divide clumps every 4 to 5 years in autumn or in early spring.

Growing astilbes in the Lower South is challenging, to say the least. Give them rich, well-drained soil, full shade, and plenty of water. If they dry out in summer, the party's over.

A. ×arendsii. Most astilbes sold belong to this hybrid group or are sold as such. Parentage is complex, but plants often have *A. japonica, A. chinensis,* and/or *A. thunbergii* in their ancestry. The plants differ chiefly in minor botanical details. Here are some of the many selections in use. Bloom times run from late spring for the early types to late summer for the late-flowering sorts.

'Amethyst'. Late. Lavender, 3–4 ft.
'Bonn'. Early. Medium pink, 1½–2 ft.
'Bremen'. Midseason. Dark rose, 1½–2 ft.
'Bressingham Beauty'. Late midseason. Drooping pink clusters, 3 ft.
'Bridal Veil'. Midseason to late. Full white plumes, 3 ft.
'Deutschland'. Early. White, 1½ ft.
'Erica'. Midseason. Slender pink plumes, 2½–3 ft.
'Fanal'. Early. Blood red flowers, bronzy foliage, 1½–2½ ft.
'Hyacinth'. Midseason. Purplish pink, 2–3 ft.
'Koblenz'. Early to midseason. Bright red, 1½–2½ ft.

'Ostrich Plume' ('Straussenfeder'). Midseason to late. Drooping pink clusters, 3–3½ ft.

'Peach Blossom'. Midseason. Light salmon pink, 2 ft.

'Red Sentinel'. Midseason. Bright red, 2½ ft.

'Rheinland'. Early. Deep pink, 2–2½ ft.

'White Gloria'. Early to midseason. Creamy white, 2 ft.

A. chinensis. CHINESE ASTILBE. Resembles the *A.* ×*arendsii* hybrids but generally blooms in late summer, grows taller, and tolerates dryness a little better. Varieties and selections include the following.

A. c. davidii. Late blooming, with dense, narrow, pink plumes 3 ft. tall. Pink-flowered 'Finale' grows only 18–20 in. tall.

'Pumila'. Dwarf form with low mats of leaves topped by lilac-pink flower clusters that rise 12–15 in. high.

A. c. taquetii 'Superba'. Bright pinkish purple flowers in spikelike clusters 4–5 ft. tall. 'Purple Candles' is deeper purple, slightly shorter.

'Visions'. Upright-growing dwarf to 15 in. high, with raspberry pink plumes above bronzy green leaves. Blooms a little earlier than other *A. chinensis* selections.

A. simplicifolia. JAPANESE ASTILBE. Grows to 16 in., with leaves merely cut or lobed instead of divided into leaflets. Known for its selections. Summer-blooming 'Sprite', the best known, is a low, compact plant with abundant pink, drooping, 1-ft. spires above bronze-tinted foliage. 'Hennie Graefland' is similar but grows a few inches taller and blooms somewhat earlier.

A. taquetii 'Superba'. See A. chinensis taquetii 'Superba'

ASTILBOIDES tabularis (Rodgersia tabularis)

Saxifragaceae

PERENNIAL

✗ US, MS ‖ 7–4

◑ PARTIAL SHADE

◉ AMPLE WATER

Astilboides tabularis

Large plant from China and Korea, with imposing (2-ft.-wide), nearly round leaves attached at the centers to 3-ft.-long stems. Small white flowers in large clusters appear in summer on stalks to 5 ft. high. Plants spread slowly from thick, creeping rhizomes; count on at least a 3-ft. spread. Needs plenty of water; leaves wilt quickly in hot, dry weather. Striking plant for woodland or pond-side garden. Good substitute for hostas where slugs and snails cause problems.

ASTRANTIA

MASTERWORT

Apiaceae (Umbelliferae)

PERENNIALS

✗ US, MS, LS

☀◑ FULL SUN OR PARTIAL SHADE

◉ REGULAR WATER

Astrantia major

Flowering stems rise from leafy clumps in summer, bearing dense, tight clusters of blossoms surrounded by papery bracts. Flower heads look something like pincushions; they make attractive, long-lasting cut flowers and can also be dried for winter arrangements. Useful plants for woodland or cottage gardens—native to alpine woods and meadows of Europe. Spread by underground runners. Die back in winter, even in mild climates. Need good drainage.

A. carniolica. Heat zones 7–1. To 1½ ft. tall and wide, with finely divided leaves. Bracts are shorter than in other species. 'Rubra' has dark red flowers with silvery accents.

A. major. Heat zones 8–1. Grows to 3 ft. high, 1–2 ft. wide, with inch-wide clusters of white-and-green or white-and-pink blossoms. Good selections with colorful blooms include deep red 'Hadspen Blood'; 'Lars', with deep pink blooms opening from maroon buds; 'Rainbow', featuring a range of colors, from white through light pink to rose; and 'Ruby Wedding', with rosy red flowers on ruby stems. Selection *A. m. involucrata* 'Shaggy' ('Margery Fish') is a white-flowered form with elongated, green-tipped bracts.

A. maxima. Heat zones 8–1. Similar to *A. major* but grows just 2 ft. high and bears pink flowers.

ATAMASCO LILY. See ZEPHYRANTHUS atamasco

ATHYRIUM

Polypodiaceae

FERNS

✗ US, MS, LS

◐ ● PARTIAL OR FULL SHADE, EXCEPT AS NOTED

◉ ◉ REGULAR TO AMPLE WATER

Prized since Victorian times for their beautiful foliage, these ferns are very easy to grow. All species described here prefer rich, moist, well-drained soil containing lots of organic matter. They do not tolerate extended summer drought or heavy root competition from trees. Fronds of most types turn brown after repeated frosts; leave the dead foliage on the plants through winter to provide mulch and to shelter the delicate fronds as they emerge in spring. Propagate by dividing clumps in early spring.

Athyrium filix-femina

A. filix-femina. LADY FERN. Heat zones 9–1. Native to much of North America. Grows to 4 ft. or taller, 2–3 ft. wide. Rootstock rises up on older plants to make short trunk. Vertical effect; narrow at bottom, spreading at top. Thin, finely divided fronds. Vigorous; can be invasive. Tolerates full sun in constantly moist soil. Specialists stock many selections with oddly cut and feathered fronds. In 'Frizelliae' (about 8 in. high, 1 ft. wide), frond leaflets are reduced to balls; fronds look like strings of beads. 'Vernoniae Cristatum' (to 2½ ft. high and wide) has crested and feathered fronds.

A. hybrids. Heat zones 9–1. Crosses between *A. filix-femina* and *A. niponicum* 'Pictum', combining characteristics of each. These plants are vigorous and easy to grow.

'Branford Beauty'. Upright growth to 2 ft. high, 2½ ft. wide, with silvery gray fronds and red stalks.

'Ghost'. Rigidly upright to 2–3 ft. high, 1½ ft. wide, with pale silvery gray fronds. A standout in deep shade.

A. niponicum (A. goeringianum). JAPANESE PAINTED FERN. Heat zones 8–1. Arching fronds grow to 1½ ft. long, making a tight, slowly spreading clump 1 ft. high, 1½ ft. wide. Known for its colorful selections. In 'Pictum', fronds are purplish at base, then lavender, then silvery greenish gray toward the tip. 'Silver Falls' has long, arching, silver-and-green fronds with purplish red veins; foliage of 'Ursula's Red' is silver flushed with wine red.

A. otophorum. ENGLISH PAINTED FERN. Heat zones 8–2. Actually a native of the Orient. Resembles *A. niponicum* in size and habit; dark green fronds have a reddish or purple midrib.

A. pycnocarpon (Diplazium pycnocarpon). GLADE FERN, SILVERY SPLEENWORT. Heat zones 8–2. From eastern North America. Attractive rosette-forming deciduous fern with once-divided fronds to 4 ft. long. New spring fronds are silvery light green; they turn darker in summer, then russet before dying back. Tolerates full sun in constantly moist soil.

ATLANTIC PIGEON WINGS. See CLITORIA mariana

ATLANTIC ST. JOHNSWORT. See HYPERICUM reductum

ATLAS CEDAR. See CEDRUS atlantica

AUCUBA japonica

JAPANESE AUCUBA

Cornaceae

EVERGREEN SHRUB

⚡ US, MS, LS, CS, TS

◐ ● PARTIAL OR FULL SHADE

◓ ● MODERATE TO REGULAR WATER

Aucuba japonica
'Variegata'

Native from the Himalayas to Japan. Seedlings vary in leaf form and variegation; many selections are offered. Standard green-leafed aucuba grows at a moderate rate to 6–10 ft. (sometimes to 15 ft.) high and almost as wide; can be kept lower by pruning. Buxom shrub, densely clothed with polished-looking, tooth-edged, dark green leaves 3–8 in. long, 1½–3 in. wide.

Minute dark maroon flowers in earliest spring are followed by clusters of bright red, ¾-in. berries in fall and winter. Both sexes must be planted to ensure fruit. 'Rozannie', however, is self-fruitful, producing a heavy crop of berries without a pollenizer.

Other green-leafed selections include 'Lance Leaf', with smooth-edged, lance-shaped leaves (male); 'Longifolia' ('Salicifolia'), narrow willowlike foliage (female); 'Nana', dwarf to about 3 ft. (female); 'Serratifolia', long leaves with coarsely toothed edges (female).

Variegated selections (usually slower growing) include 'Crotonifolia', leaves heavily splashed with white and gold (male); 'Fructu Albo', white-variegated leaves and pale pinkish buff berries (female); 'Picturata' ('Aureo-maculata'), leaves centered with golden yellow, edged with dark green dotted yellow (female); 'Sulphur', green leaves with broad yellow edge (female). 'Variegata', often called gold dust plant, is the best-known aucuba. It has dark green leaves spotted with yellow; plants may be male or female. 'Mr. Goldstrike' (male) has heavier gold splashings.

Japanese aucuba is tolerant of a wide range of soils but will grow and look better if poor or heavy soils are improved. Requires shade from hot sun, accepts deep shade. Grows well in low light under trees, competes successfully with tree roots. Tolerates sea air. Gets mealybug and mites. Prune to control height or form by cutting back to a leaf joint.

All aucuba selections make choice container plants for shady patio or in the house. Use variegated forms to lighten up dark corners. Plants combine effectively with ferns, hydrangeas.

AURICULA. See PRIMULA auricula

AURINIA saxatilis (Alyssum saxatile)

BASKET-OF-GOLD

Brassicaceae (Cruciferae)

PERENNIAL

⚡ US, MS, LS, CS H 9–5

◔ ◑ FULL SUN OR LIGHT SHADE

◓ MODERATE WATER

Aurinia saxatilis

Mustard relative native to mountains of central and southern Europe, Turkey. Gray, 2- to 5-in.-long leaves form a spreading evergreen mound 8–12 in. high. Dense clusters of tiny golden yellow flowers cover the plant in spring and early summer. Use as foreground plant in borders, in rock gardens, atop walls; plant about 1½ ft. apart. Poor soils or moderately fertile ones suit the plant perfectly—as long as drainage is good. Shear lightly (don't cut back stems by more than half) right after bloom. Generally hardy but may be killed in extremely cold winters. Short lived in hot, humid climates. Self-sows readily.

Selections include 'Citrina' ('Lutea'), with pale yellow flowers; 'Compacta', a dwarf; 'Plena' ('Flore Pleno'), double flowered; 'Silver Queen', compact grower with pale yellow flowers; 'Sunnyborder Apricot', with apricot-shaded flowers; 'Dudley Neville', similar in flower color to 'Sunnyborder Apricot' but with white-variegated leaves; and dwarf forms 'Goldkugel' ('Gold Ball'), 6 in. high, and 'Tom Thumb', 3 in. high.

AUSTRALIAN FAN PALM. See LIVISTONA australis

AUSTRALIAN TREE FERN. See CYATHEA cooperi

AUSTRIAN BRIER. See ROSA foetida

AUTUMN CROCUS. See COLCHICUM, CROCUS sativus

AUTUMN FERN. See DRYOPTERIS erythrosora

AUTUMN OLIVE. See ELAEAGNUS umbellata

AUTUMN SAGE. See SALVIA greggii

AVENS. See GEUM

AVOCADO

Lauraceae

EVERGREEN TREE

⚡ CS (MILDER PARTS), TS H 12–10

◔ FULL SUN

◓ REGULAR WATER

Avocado

Delicious and popular tropical fruit, native to Mexico and to Central and South America. Three races of avocado *(Persea americana)* are grown, and numerous hybrids among them exist. In Florida, the Mexican (the hardiest, often surviving to 18°F) is grown in the colder parts of central Florida, while the Guatemalan (hardy to 21–25°F) and the West Indian (the most tropical type, often perishing at temperatures below 25°F) and their hybrids are cultivated southward. Mexican race seedlings are often grown in home gardens across South Texas. For this plant's ornamental relatives, see *Persea*.

Plants bloom in late winter, and pollination is complex. Most types will produce some fruit if grown alone, but production is heavier when two or more selections are planted. Fruit ripens from summer into winter, depending on selection. Guatemalan and West Indian fruits differ from Mexican in generally being larger and having a lower oil content.

All avocado trees require good drainage; constantly wet soil encourages fatal root rot. Tree is shallow rooted; do not cultivate deeply. In the absence of rainfall, irrigate lightly and frequently enough to keep soil moist but not wet. A mulch is helpful; the tree's own fallen leaves can provide this. Scab disease can be a problem in Florida; choose resistant selections. Cercospora leaf spot and anthracnose are also serious problems there. Anthracnose is a secondary pathogen, usually taking advantage of injury or another disease, such as leaf spot, to gain entry. Both problems can be prevented by applying appropriate fungicides and handling the fruit carefully.

When planting an avocado tree in the landscape, consider that most selections will eventually grow quite large (to 40 ft.), produce dense shade, and shed leaves all year. Growth is quite rapid, but plants may be shaped by pinching terminal shoots. Avocado takes well to container culture, and selections in marginal climates can be moved to a protected location during cold spells.

Florida selections include hardy 'Brogdon', 'Gainesville', 'Mexicola', and 'Tonnage' (all moderately scab resistant); somewhat less hardy 'Booth', 'Hall', 'Monroe' (all moderately scab resistant), and 'Choquette' (very scab resistant); and least hardy 'Pollock', 'Ruehle', 'Simmonds', and 'Waldin' (all very scab resistant). Two hardy types that set good crops without cross-pollination are the commercial selections 'Lula' (susceptible to scab) and 'Taylor' (very scab resistant).

In Texas, 'Lula' is grown commercially in the lower Rio Grande Valley. Most avocado trees in home gardens are selections developed from Mexican race seedlings that survived cold winters. For the selections that grow best in your area, check with a local garden center.

AXONOPUS affinis

CARPET GRASS

Poaceae (Gramineae)

PERENNIAL LAWN GRASS

🖊 CS, TS ▮ 12–8

☀ FULL SUN

💧 REGULAR WATER

Axonopus affinis

This is a lawn grass of last resort, grown chiefly in areas of Florida where wet, acid soil makes it difficult to grow other grasses. Does not tolerate drought, alkaline soil, or salt spray. Produces numerous tall, unsightly seed heads. Needs mowing every 10 to 14 days to 1–2 in. to stay attractive. Susceptible to nematodes and brown patch. Turns brown with first cold spell in fall and greens up slowly in spring. Start from seeds or sprigs. Feed each spring with a complete controlled-release fertilizer, such as 16-4-8.

AZALEA. See RHODODENDRON

AZTEC LILY. See SPREKELIA formosissima

BABIANA

BABOON FLOWER

Iridaceae

PERENNIALS FROM CORMS

🖊 LS, CS, TS ▮ 12–10; OR DIG AND STORE

☀ FULL SUN OR LIGHT SHADE

💧 REGULAR WATER DURING GROWTH AND BLOOM

Babiana stricta

From Africa. Plants bear spikes of freesialike flowers in blue, lavender, purple, or red. Each flowering stem bears six or more 2-in.-wide blooms in mid- to late spring. Ribbed, hairy leaves grow in fans. Plant corms 4–6 in. deep, 6 in. apart—as edging, in a rock garden, or in pots. In the Lower, Coastal, and Tropical South, plant out in fall; in the Upper and Middle South, plant in spring; lift and store corms in fall. Where corms can overwinter in ground, leave them in place; they'll multiply and bloom more profusely each year. Plants get their common name from the fact that baboons like to eat the corms—so don't plant them if baboons are a problem in your neighborhood.

B. rubrocyanea. Ruby-throated royal blue blossoms on 6-in. stems.

B. stricta. Flowers in royal blue, purple, lavender, white, or blue-and-white appear on stems to 1 ft. tall.

BABY BLUE EYES. See NEMOPHILA menziesii

BABY'S BREATH. See GYPSOPHILA paniculata

BABY SNAPDRAGON. See LINARIA maroccana

BABY'S TEARS. See SOLEIROLIA soleirolii

BACCHARIS halimifolia

SALTBUSH, GROUNDSEL BUSH

Asteraceae (Compositae)

DECIDUOUS TO SEMIEVERGREEN SHRUB

🖊 US, MS, LS, CS ▮ 9–1

☀ FULL SUN

💧 LITTLE TO MODERATE WATER

Baccharis halimifolia

Saltbush has so much going for it, it's a mystery why it remains largely unknown to Southern gardeners. This upright, multistemmed shrub grows 6–10 ft. tall and wide

and features handsome leaves in soft gray green. What really sets it apart are the fluffy white seed heads that cover it in fall—though it's actually gone to seed, the plant looks as if it's in bloom. It's tough and resilient, needing only a sunny spot. It tolerates poor, clay, and rocky soil, as well as drought, wind, and salt spray. Excellent in naturalized areas or at the beach. Cut seed heads look great in arrangements. 'Orient Point' forms a mound 5–6 ft. tall and wide and features seed heads that are red at the base, creating a bicolor effect. 'White Caps' grows upright to 10 ft. and has especially showy seed heads.

BACHELOR'S BUTTON. See CENTAUREA cyanus

BAGAUAK. See CLERODENDRUM quadriloculare

BALLOON FLOWER. See PLATYCODON grandiflorus

BAMBOO

Poaceae (Gramineae)

GIANT GRASSES

🖊 SEE CHART FOR HARDINESS, HEAT TOLERANCE

☀ FULL SUN OR PARTIAL SHADE

💧 LITTLE TO REGULAR WATER

▶ SEE CHART PAGE 192

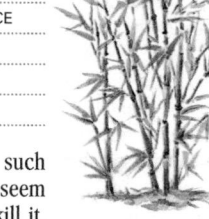
Bambusa multiplex

Among Southerners, few plants elicit such strong emotions as bamboo: people seem either to love it or to want desperately to kill it. Though some bamboos grow as tall as trees, all are actually giant grasses. They consist of large, woody stems (culms) divided into sections (internodes) by obvious joints (nodes). Bamboos spread by underground stems (rhizomes) that are jointed and carry buds. The manner in which the rhizomes grow explains the difference between running and clump bamboos.

In the running bamboos (*Arundinaria, Phyllostachys, Pleioblastus, Pseudosasa, Sasa,* and *Semiarundinaria),* underground stems grow rapidly to varying distances from the parent plant before sending up new vertical shoots. These bamboos eventually form large patches or groves unless spread is curbed. They are generally fairly hardy plants from temperate regions in China and Japan, and they are tolerant of a wide variety of soils.

In clump bamboos (*Bambusa, Fargesia),* underground stems grow only a short distance before sending up new stems. These form clumps that slowly expand around the edges. Most are tropical or subtropical.

See chart for hardiness. Figures indicate temperatures at which leaf damage occurs; stems and rhizomes may be considerably hardier.

Planting and growing. Plant container-grown bamboos at any time of year. Best time to propagate from existing clumps is just before growth begins in spring; divide hardy kinds in March or early April, tropical ones in May or early June. (Transplanting at other times is possible, but risk of losing divisions is high in summer heat or winter chill and wet soil.) Cut or saw out divisions with roots and at least three connected culms. If divisions are large, cut back tops to balance loss of roots and rhizomes. Foliage may wilt or wither, but culms will send out new leaves.

Rhizome cutting is another means of propagation. In clump bamboos, the cutting consists of the rooted base of a culm; in running bamboos, it is a foot-long length of rhizome with roots and buds. Plant in rich soil mix with ample organic material added.

Culms of all bamboos have already attained their maximum diameter when they poke through ground; in mature plants, they usually reach their maximum height within a month. Many do become increasingly leafy in subsequent years, but not taller. Plants are evergreen, but there is considerable dropping of older leaves; old plantings develop a nearly weedproof mulch of dead leaves. Individual culms live for several years but eventually die and should be cut out.

Care and feeding. Mature bamboos grow phenomenally fast during their brief growth period—culms of giant types may increase in length by several feet a day. Don't expect such quick growth the first year after transplanting, though. Giant timber bamboo (*Phyllostachys bambusoides*), for example, needs 3 to 5 years to build up a rhizome system capable of supporting culms that grow several feet a day; aboveground growth during a plant's early years will be much less impressive. To get fast growth and great size, water frequently and feed once a month with high-nitrogen or lawn fertilizer; to restrict size and spread, water and feed less. Once established, plants tolerate considerable drought, but rhizomes will not spread into dry soil (or into water). The accompanying chart lists two heights for each bamboo. "Controlled height" means average height under dry conditions with little feeding, or with rhizome spread controlled by barriers. "Uncontrolled height" refers to plants growing under optimum conditions and without any confinement.

In the case of bamboo, disregard the rule of never buying root-bound plants. The more crowded the plant is in the container, the faster it will grow when planted. Both running and clump types grow well when roots are confined. To keep running bamboo from running too far, contain it with 2- to 3-ft.-deep barriers made from strips of galvanized sheet metal, 30-mil plastic, or poured concrete; or plant in long flue tiles or large plastic plant containers with the bottoms cut out.

Should you find yourself with unwanted bamboo, you can use several methods to get rid of it. Digging it out with mattock and spade is the surest tactic, though sometimes difficult. Rhizomes are generally not deep, but they may be widespread. Remove them all or regrowth will occur. Starve out roots by cutting off all shoots before they exceed 2 ft. in height; repeat as needed—probably many times over the course of a year. Contact herbicide sprays that kill leaves have the same effect as removing culms. You can also cut off culms, then cut gashes in the stumps and paint them with full-strength glyphosate (Roundup); repeated treatments may be necessary.

Scale, mealybugs, and aphids are occasionally found on bamboo but seldom do any harm; if they excrete honeydew in bothersome amounts, spray with insecticidal soap or summer oil.

Growth habits. The chart classifies each bamboo by habit of growth, which, of course, determines its use in the garden. In **Group I** are the dwarf or low-growing ground cover types. These can be used for erosion control or, in small clumps (carefully confined in a long section of flue tile), in a border or rock garden. **Group II** includes clump bamboos with a fountainlike habit of growth. These have widest use in landscaping. They require no more space than the average strong-growing shrub. Clipped, they make hedges or screens that won't spread much into surrounding soil. Unclipped, they create informal screens or grow singly to show off their graceful form.

Bamboos in **Group III** are running bamboos of moderate size and more or less vertical growth. Curb them and use as screens, hedges, or alone. **Group IV** includes the giant bamboos. Use running kinds for groves or for oriental effects on a grand scale. Clump kinds have a tropical look, especially if they are used with broad-leafed tropical plants. All may be thinned and clipped to show off the culms. Thin clumps or groves by cutting out old or dead culms at the base.

Phyllostachys aurea

Some smaller bamboos bloom on some of their stalks every year and continue to grow. Some bloom partially, at erratic intervals. Some have never been known to bloom. Others bloom heavily, set seed, and die. Giant timber bamboo (*Phyllostachys bambusoides*) and other species of *Phyllostachys* bloom at rare intervals of 30 to 60 years, produce flowers for a long period, and become enfeebled. They may recover slowly or die.

Bamboos are not recommended for year-round indoor culture, but container-grown plants can spend extended periods indoors in cool, bright rooms. You can revive plants by taking them outdoors, but it is important to avoid sudden changes in temperature and light.

BAMBOO MUHLY. See MUHLENBERGIA dumosa

BAMBOO PALM. See CHAMAEDOREA erumpens

BAMBUSA. See BAMBOO

BANANA

Musaceae

PERENNIAL

FOR ZONES, SEE TEXT

FULL SUN

AMPLE WATER

Banana

Popular symbols of the tropics, lush banana "trees" are not trees at all, but gigantic herbaceous perennials that grow from corms (or pseudobulbs). Thick, fleshy stalks (pseudostems) emerge from the large corms and can increase in height anywhere from 1 to 30 ft. in a year, depending on the selection and location. Each stalk carries spectacular broad, 5- to 9-ft.-long leaves. Each also produces a single flower cluster, which develops fruit; the stalk dies after fruiting, and new stalks then grow from the corm.

Fruiting bananas are often grouped botanically under *Musa acuminata*. To produce a crop, these plants generally need 10 to 15 months of frost-free conditions and a long, warm growing season. They fruit best in the Coastal and Tropical South, but old, established plants growing in protected spots in the Lower South occasionally bear fruit. Drooping clusters of orange-yellow flowers appear in spring, followed by bunches of bananas. The fruit usually ripens by late summer or fall—but whenever you see that the bananas at the top of the bunch have begun to turn yellow, cut off the whole bunch and let it ripen at room temperature. If left on the plant, the fruit will split and rot. Banana sap permanently stains fabric, so wear old clothes when harvesting or pruning.

Each plant can produce as many as ten suckers, eventually forming a sizable clump. If you want large, high-quality fruit, let just one or two stalks per clump grow; prune out all others as they emerge. After the stalks have bloomed, allow replacement stalks to begin developing for next year's crop. After cutting the bunches of bananas, remove any stalks that have fruited.

Certain types of bananas are grown strictly as ornamentals (see *Ensete ventricosum* and *Musa*), but even fruiting types make bold and striking garden plants. Use them for tropical accents near pools, in sitting areas, at the back of a border, or in large containers. Strong winds tatter the leaves, but some selections have wind-resistant foliage.

Bananas need moist, fertile, well-drained soil and lots of sun. Feed liberally in spring. They will reliably survive winter outdoors in the Coastal and Tropical South; in the Lower South, spread a generous layer of mulch around the plant's base in fall to insulate the corm. Gardeners in the Middle and Upper South can save a banana plant from year to year by cutting off and discarding the top (leafy part) of the plant in fall, then digging up the stalk and corm and storing them for the winter in a cool, dark place such as a basement or garage. No watering is required during the dormant period. Replant after all danger of frost is past. Heat zone range is 12–6.

Dwarf selections are the best bets for most home gardens. They mature at about 7–15 ft. high and usually ripen fruit 70 to 100 days after blooming. Recommended selections include the following.

'Dwarf Brazilian'. To 8 ft. tall. Excellent fruit. Wind-resistant foliage.

'Dwarf Cavendish'. The most popular dwarf banana, growing only 5 ft. tall. Sweet fruit. Excellent in containers.

'Dwarf Orinoco'. Grows just 5–6 ft. high, yet produces fruit clusters weighing up to 40 pounds. Good cold tolerance and wind resistance.

'Goldfinger'. Grows 12–14 ft. tall. Cold tolerant and disease resistant. Reliable producer of very tasty fruit. ▶ page 194

BAMBOO

For explanation of height, see pages 190–191; for Roman numerals I, II, III, and IV, see page 191. Hardiness is temperature at which leaf damage occurs.

NAME	ALSO SOLD AS	ZONES	CONTROLLED (UNCONTROLLED) HEIGHT	GROUP AND GROWTH HABIT	CULM DIAMETER	COMMENTS (FORM, CHARACTERISTICS, USES)
Arundinaria amabilis TONKIN CANE, TEASTICK BAMBOO		LS, CS, TS; hardy to 10°F; 9–5	20–25 ft. (50 ft.)	III. Running	2½ in.	Erect, thick-walled culms with small nodes. Beautiful, useful for wood
Bambusa multiplex	*B. glaucescens*	CS, TS; hardy to 15°F; 12–6	8–10 ft. (15–25 ft.)	II. Clump	1½ in.	Branches from base to top. Dense growth. Good for hedges, screens
B. m. 'Alphonse Karr' ALPHONSE KARR BAMBOO		CS, TS; hardy to 15°F; 12–6	8–10 ft. (15–35 ft.)	II. Clump	½–1 in.	Similar to species, but culms are brilliantly striped green on yellow. New culms are pinkish and green
B. m. 'Golden Goddess' GOLDEN GODDESS BAMBOO		CS, TS; hardy to 15°F; 10–6	6–8 ft. (6–10 ft.)	II. Clump	½ in.	Golden-stemmed form with graceful, dense, arching growth. Good container or screen plant. Give tops room to spread
B. m. 'Silverstripe' SILVERSTRIPE HEDGE BAMBOO		LS, CS, TS; hardy to 11°F; 12–6	20–35 ft. (45 ft.)	IV. Clump	1½ in.	Leaves and occasional culms striped in white
B. oldhamii OLDHAM BAMBOO, CLUMPING GIANT TIMBER BAMBOO	*Sinocalamus oldhamii*	CS, TS; hardy to 15°F; 12–8	15–25 ft. (20–55 ft.)	IV. Clump	4 in.	Densely foliaged, erect clumps make it good plant for big, dense screens. Or use single plant as imposing vertical mass
Fargesia murielae UMBRELLA BAMBOO	*Sinarundinaria murielae*	US, MS, LS, CS; hardy to –20°F; 9–1	6–8 ft. (to 15 ft.)	II. Clump	¾ in.	One of two hardiest bamboos listed here. Light, airy, narrow clump, arching and drooping at top. Needs shade to look best. Rare
F. nitida FOUNTAIN BAMBOO	*Sinarundinaria nitida*	US, MS, LS, CS; hardy to 0°F; 10–5	6–8 ft. (15–20 ft.)	II. Clump	¾ in.	Airy, graceful, narrow clump, arching and drooping at top. Greenish purple culms mature to deep purplish black. Needs shade to look its best. Rare
Phyllostachys aurea GOLDEN BAMBOO		US, MS, LS, CS, TS; hardy to 0°F; 12–4	6–10 ft. (10–20 ft.)	III. Running	2 in.	Erect, stiff culms, usually with crowded joints at base—good identifying mark. Dense foliage; makes a good screen or hedge. Can take much drought but looks better with regular water. Good for containers
P. aureosulcata YELLOW GROOVE BAMBOO		US, MS, LS, CS; hardy to –20°F; 12–1	12–15 ft. (15–25 ft.)	III. Running	1½ in.	Like more slender, more open *P. aurea*. Young culms green with pronounced yellowish groove. One of two hardiest bamboos listed here
P. bambusoides GIANT TIMBER BAMBOO, JAPANESE TIMBER BAMBOO	*P. reticulata*	MS, LS, CS, TS; hardy to near 0°F; 10–4	15–35 ft. (25–45 ft.)	IV. Running	6 in.	Once the most common of large, hardy timber bamboos. Most perished during blooming period in 1960s–70s. New plants from seed are available. Makes beautiful groves if lowest branches are trimmed off
P. b. 'Castillon'	*P. castillonis*	MS, LS, CS, TS; hardy to near 0°F; 10–4	10–15 ft. (15–20 ft.)	III. Running	2 in.	Yellow culms show green stripe above each branch cluster. Rare
P. flexuosa ZIGZAG BAMBOO		US, MS, LS, CS, TS; hardy to –8°F; 12–1	8–12 ft. (20–30 ft.)	III. Running	2¾ in.	Named for zigzag habit of some of the culms. Foliage bright green when young, yellow brown to nearly black with age

BAMBOO

For explanation of height, see pages 190–191; for Roman numerals I, II, III, and IV, see page 191. Hardiness is temperature at which leaf damage occurs.

NAME	ALSO SOLD AS	ZONES	CONTROLLED (UNCONTROLLED) HEIGHT	GROUP AND GROWTH HABIT	CULM DIAMETER	COMMENTS (FORM, CHARACTERISTICS, USES)
P. nigra BLACK BAMBOO		MS, CS, LS, TS; hardy to near 0°F; 12–4	4–8 ft. (10–15 ft.)	III. Running	1½ in.	New culms green, turning black in second year (rarely olive green dotted black). Best in afternoon shade
P. n. 'Henon' HENON BAMBOO		MS, CS, LS, TS; hardy to near 0°F; 12–4	50 ft. (to 54 ft.)	III. Running	3½ in.	Much larger than *P. nigra*. Whitish green culms don't blacken with age; rough to the touch
Pleioblastus argenteostriatus		LS, CS, TS; hardy to 10°F; 12–7	2–3 ft. (3–4 ft.)	I. Running	¼ in.	Good light-colored ground cover for shade. Cut back every year. White stripes on leaves
P. pygmaeus PYGMY BAMBOO	*Sasa pygmaea*	MS, CS, LS, TS; hardy to near 0°F; 10–5	½–1 ft. (1–1½ ft.)	I. Running	⅛ in.	Aggressive spreader. Good for erosion control and for holding banks. Mow every few years to keep it attractive
P. variegatus DWARF WHITESTRIPE BAMBOO	*Sasa variegata, S. fortunei*	US, MS, LS, CS, TS; hardy to –10°F; 12–4	1–2 ft. (2–3 ft.)	I. Running	¼ in.	Fast spreader; curb rhizomes. Use in tubs or as deep ground cover
Pseudosasa japonica ARROW BAMBOO	*Arundinaria japonica*	US, MS, LS, CS, TS; hardy to 0°F; 12–3	6–10 ft. (10–18 ft.)	III. Running	¾ in.	Stiffly erect culms; one branch at each joint. Large leaves with long, pointed tails. Rampant thick hedge; slower in Upper South, making dense clumps
Sasa palmata PALMATE BAMBOO	Sometimes sold as *S. senanensis*	US, MS, LS, CS, TS; hardy to –5°F; 12–5	4–5 ft. (8–12 ft.)	III. Running	⅜ in.	Broad, handsome leaves (to 15 in. long by 4 in. wide) spread fingerlike from stem and branch tips. Rampant spreader
S. veitchii KUMA BAMBOO GRASS		MS, LS, CS, TS; hardy to near 0°F; 10–6	2–3 ft. (2–3 ft.)	I. Running	¼ in.	Rampant spreader with large (7- by 1-in.) dark green leaves that turn whitish buff around the edges in autumn. Appropriate in Japanese-style gardens if curbed
Semiarundinaria fastuosa NARIHIRA BAMBOO		US, MS, LS, CS, TS; hardy to –4°F; 9–5	8–10 ft. (12–25 ft.)	III. Running	1¼ in.	Rigidly upright growth. Slow spreader; easily kept to a clump. Makes a good tall, narrow, dense hedge or windbreak

Phyllostachys nigra

TOP: *Sasa veitchii*
BOTTOM: *Phyllostachys bambusoides*

Bambusa multiplex 'Golden Goddess'

TOP: *Sasa palmata*
BOTTOM: *Pleioblastus pygmaeus*

B

'Grand Nain'. To 6−8 ft. tall. The "Chiquita" banana from Central America. Bears up to 50 pounds of fruit per year. Wind-resistant foliage.

'Ice Cream' ('Blue Java'). Fruit tastes like vanilla custard. Grows 12 ft. tall.

'Mysore'. Sturdy plant, 14−16 ft. tall. Produces large bunches of sweet, thin-skinned fruit.

'Rajapuri'. Cold-hardy selection from India that fruits reliably in Lower South. Sweet fruit. Grows 8 ft. tall, with stout trunk and extra-large leaves.

BANANA SHRUB. See MICHELIA figo

BANEBERRY. See ACTAEA

BANYAN TREE. See FICUS

BAPTISIA

FALSE INDIGO, WILD INDIGO

Fabaceae (Leguminosae)

PERENNIALS

⚡ US, MS, LS, CS

☼ FULL SUN

💧 MODERATE WATER

Baptisia australis

Native to eastern and midwestern U.S. The false indigos somewhat resemble lupines (*Lupinus*), but they have deep taproots that enable them to survive difficult conditions. They are long-lived plants that become large clumps with many stems and bloom spikes. They resent transplanting once established. Bluish green leaves are divided into three leaflets. Flower spikes to 1 ft. long top the plants in late spring or early summer. Flowers resemble small sweet peas and are followed by inflated seedpods; both flowers and pods are interesting in arrangements. Remove spent flowers to encourage repeat bloom.

B. alba. WHITE FALSE INDIGO. Heat zones 9−2. To 3 ft. tall and wide; clusters of white flowers. Attractive smoky gray stems.

B. australis. BLUE WILD INDIGO. Heat zones 9−1. Grows 3−6 ft. tall, 4 ft. wide; flowers are indigo blue. 'Purple Smoke', a hybrid between this species and *B. alba*, reaches 4½ ft. tall and has violet flowers with dark purple centers.

B. 'Carolina Moonlight'. Hybrid between *B. alba* and *B. sphaerocarpa*. To 4−4½ ft. high, 3−4 ft. wide. Profuse clusters of soft yellow flowers. Foliage turns silvery blue in summer heat.

B. leucophaea (B. bracteata leucophaea). PLAINS WILD INDIGO. Heat zones 9−5. To 1−1½ ft. high, 2−2½ ft. wide. Creamy white to pale yellow flowers are held nearly horizontally on arching stems. Especially attractive where it can be viewed from below—planted on a hillside or spilling over a wall, for example.

B. minor (B. australis minor). Heat zones 9−1. Similar to *B. australis* but about half the size, with correspondingly smaller leaves; also comes into bloom earlier.

B. pendula. Heat zones 8−5. To 3−3½ ft. tall, 2−2½ ft. wide. Bushy plant with upright clusters of white flowers followed by drooping black seedpods.

B. sphaerocarpa. YELLOW WILD INDIGO. Heat zones 9−5. To 2−3 ft. tall and wide, with clear yellow blossoms.

BARBERRY. See BERBERIS

BASIL. See OCIMUM basilicum

BASKET FLOWER. See CENTAUREA americana, HYMENOCALLIS narcissiflora

BASKET-OF-GOLD. See AURINIA saxatilis

BASSIA scoparia. See KOCHIA scoparia

BASSWOOD. See TILIA americana

BAUHINIA

ORCHID TREE

Fabaceae (Leguminosae)

EVERGREEN, SEMIEVERGREEN, DECIDUOUS TREES AND SHRUBS

⚡ TS **H** 12−10, EXCEPT AS NOTED

☼ FULL SUN, EXCEPT AS NOTED

💧 MODERATE TO REGULAR WATER

Bauhinia × blakeana

These flamboyant flowering plants have a very special place in central and southern Florida. Common to all garden bauhinias are twin "leaves," actually twin lobes. Not fussy about soil as long as it is reasonably well drained. Not browsed by deer.

B. ×blakeana. HONG KONG ORCHID TREE. Partially deciduous tree. Native to southern China. The showiest and most coveted bauhinia; also the least cold hardy. Grows to 20 ft. high and wide; umbrella-type habit. Flowers are much larger (5½−6 in. wide) than those of other bauhinias and appear in late fall to spring. They are shaped like some orchids; colors range from cranberry maroon through purple and rose to orchid pink, often in the same blossom. Gray-green leaves tend to drop off around bloom time, but the tree does not lose all of its foliage.

B. forficata (B. candicans). BRAZILIAN ORCHID TREE. Evergreen to deciduous large shrub or tree. Zones CS, TS. Native to Brazil. From spring through summer, bears narrow-petaled, creamy white flowers to 3 in. wide. Deep green leaves with lobes that are more pointed than those of other species. Grows to 20 ft. tall and broad, often with twisted, leaning trunk, picturesque angled branches. Short, sharp thorns at branch joints. Good canopy for patio. In the Tropical South, give some afternoon shade; when unshaded, blooms tend to shrivel during the day.

B. galpinii (B. punctata). RED BAUHINIA. Evergreen to semievergreen shrub. Native to tropical and southern Africa. Brick red to orange, 2½- to 3-in. flowers, as spectacular as those of bougainvillea, spring to fall. Sprawling, half-climbing plant to about 10 ft. tall, spreading to 15 ft. Best as espalier on warm wall. With hard pruning, can make splendid flowering bonsai for large pot or box.

B. lunarioides (B. congesta). ANACACHO ORCHID TREE. Evergreen to semievergreen shrub or tree. Zones CS, TS. Native from southwestern Texas into northeastern Mexico. To 8−12 ft. high, 4−5 ft. wide, with rounded, very small leaves (½ to ¾ in. long). White- and pink-flowering forms are available. Begins bloom in early spring and repeats many times over spring and summer. Open structured in afternoon shade; bushier in full sun.

B. macranthera. SIERRA ORCHID TREE. Evergreen to semievergreen shrub. Zones CS, TS. From eastern Mexico. Grows 8 ft. high and 12 ft. wide; blooms intermittently from spring through autumn, bearing small, exotic-looking flowers that combine tones of lavender and purple. Attractive glossy green leaves.

B. monandra. BUTTERFLY FLOWER, JERUSALEM DATE. Deciduous shrub or small tree. Heat zones 12−9. Native to tropical Asia. Similar to *B. variegata* but 20 ft. tall and wide. Clusters of 4- to 5-in.-wide, pale pink to magenta blossoms, streaked or spotted with purple, come in clusters at ends of branches. Typically flowers in summer, but in Florida bloom time may run from spring through late fall.

B. variegata (B. purpurea). PURPLE ORCHID TREE. Partially to wholly deciduous large shrub or tree. Native to India, China. The most frequently planted species. Hardy to 22°F. Spectacular street tree where spring is reliably and steadily warm. Wonderful show of light pink to orchid purple, broad-petaled, 2- to 3-in.-wide flowers, usually blooming January to April. Light green, broad-lobed leaves generally drop in midwinter. Produces huge crop of messy-looking beans after blooming. Trim beans off if you wish—trimming brings new growth earlier. Inclined to grow as shrub with many stems. Staked and pruned, becomes attractive tree to 25−30 ft. tall and wide. 'Candida' is the same, but with white flowers.

BAY. See LAURUS nobilis

BAYBERRY. See MYRICA pensylvanica

BEACH WORMWOOD. See ARTEMISIA stellerana

BEAN

Fabaceae (Leguminosae)

ANNUALS AND PERENNIALS GROWN AS ANNUALS

✄ US, MS, LS, CS, TS

☼ FULL SUN

💧 REGULAR WATER

Scarlet Runner Bean

Gardeners can choose from many types of beans, the most common of which are described below. These are New World plants belonging to the genus *Phaseolus*. Most are frost-sensitive heat lovers, easy to grow from seed. With all, moisten soil thoroughly before planting, then do not water again until seedlings have emerged. Once growth starts, keep soil moist. Feed after plants are in active growth and again when pods start to form. Control aphids, cucumber beetles, spider mites, and whiteflies if any of these pests cause problems in your garden.

For information on black-eyed peas and other popular Southern "peas," see Southern Pea.

Dry bean. Heat zones 12–1. Grow as you would bush form of snap bean (see below). Leave pods on bush until they dry or begin to shatter; then thresh beans from pods, dry, and store to soak and cook later. 'Pinto', 'Red Kidney', and 'White Marrowfat' belong to this group.

Some types are particularly delicious when harvested at the green shelling stage and cooked like green limas. These include the flageolet bean (a French favorite) and 'French Horticultural Bean', also known as 'October Bean'. Heirloom selections such as 'Aztec Dwarf White', 'Mitla White', and 'New Mexico Appaloosa' were grown by Native Americans of the Southwest and are very well adapted to that region.

Lima bean. Heat zones 12–6. Like snap beans (which they resemble), lima beans come in either bush or vine (pole) form. They develop more slowly than snap beans—bush types need 65 to 75 days from planting to harvest, pole kinds 78 to 95 days—and do not produce as reliably in extremely hot weather. Must be shelled before cooking, a tedious chore but worth it if you like fresh limas. Grow like snap beans (see below).

Scarlet runner bean. Heat zones 12–1. Perennial twining vine (hardy in Coastal and Tropical South) commonly grown as annual. Showy and ornamental, with slender clusters of vivid scarlet flowers and bright green leaves divided into three roundish, 3- to 5-in.-long leaflets. Use it to cover fences, arbors, outbuildings; it provides quick shade on porches. Pink- and white-flowered selections exist.

Flowers are followed by flattened, very dark green pods that are edible and tasty when young but toughen as they reach full size. Beans from older pods can be shelled and cooked like green limas. Grow as you would snap beans (see below).

Snap bean (string bean, green bean). Heat zones 12–1. The most widely planted bean type. Tender, fleshy pods, not stringy; may be green, yellow (wax beans), or purple (these turn green when cooked). Plants grow as self-supporting bushes (bush beans) or as climbing vines (pole beans). Bush types bear earlier, but vining sorts are more productive. Plants resemble scarlet runner bean, but their white or purple flowers are not as showy.

Sow seeds as soon as soil is warm. Heavy seed leaves must push through soil, so be sure that it is reasonably loose and open. Plant seeds of bush

Snap Bean

types 1 in. deep and 1–3 in. apart, allowing 2–3 ft. between rows. Pole beans can be managed in a number of ways. Set three or four 8-ft. stakes in the ground and tie together at top in tepee fashion; or set single poles 3–4 ft. apart and sow six or eight beans around each, thinning to three or four strongest seedlings; or insert poles 1–2 ft. apart in rows and sow seeds as you would bush beans; or sow along sunny wall, fence, or trellis and train vines on web of light string supported by wire or heavy twine. Pods are ready in 50 to 70 days, depending on selection. Pick every 3 to 5 days; if pods mature, plants will stop bearing.

Soybean. Heat zones 10–1. Newcomers to most home gardens, soybeans are an excellent source of protein. Shelled from short, plump, fuzzy pods, the seeds are called "green vegetable soybeans" when harvested green and eaten raw; they are sold in grocery stores as *edamame*. These are also delicious cooked; prepare them as you would green shelling or lima beans. Dried ground soybeans are used in the preparation of substitutes for flour, nuts, meat, and even milk.

Soybeans grow well in the warm, humid climates of the South and Midwest, forming a bush about the size of a lima bean bush. Treat the seeds with soybean inoculant prior to planting; then plant them 1 in. deep, 4–6 in. apart, in rows spaced 2½ ft. apart. Harvest when the seeds have reached full size but the pods are still green. Before shelling, pour boiling water over the pods to soften them. 'Butterbean' and 'Shironomai' are best eaten fresh, either raw or cooked; 'Envy' is good fresh or dried.

BEARBERRY. See ARCTOSTAPHYLOS uva-ursi

BEARD TONGUE. See PENSTEMON

BEAR'S BREECH. See ACANTHUS

BEAR'S FOOT FERN. See HUMATA tyermannii

BEAUCARNEA recurvata (Nolina recurvata)

PONYTAIL PALM, BOTTLE PALM

Agavaceae

EVERGREEN SHRUB OR TREE

✄ TS ⯈ 12–10; OR HOUSEPLANT

☼ FULL SUN; BRIGHT LIGHT

💧 MODERATE WATER

Beaucarnea recurvata

Despite its common name, this Mexican native isn't a palm, but a relative of yucca and agave. Lush, pendulous, bright green leaves sprout from a woody trunk held above a greatly swollen base that the plant uses to store water. Young plants resemble big onions sitting atop the soil (with just a bit of the base below ground); older ones can reach 15 ft. tall and about half as wide, with leaves to 3 ft. or longer. Very old plants may develop several branching trunks and produce large clusters of tiny creamy white flowers in summer.

Ponytail palms won't tolerate extended cold, so they're indoor plants outside of central and south Florida. Indoors, they need at least 4 hours of sun per day; a south- or west-facing window is a good spot. Make sure the soil is fast draining, and let it go dry between thorough soakings. Overwatering results in soft spots on the plant's base. Feed with a general-purpose liquid houseplant fertilizer every other week in spring and summer, once a month in fall and winter. Use horticultural oil or insecticidal soap to control scale insects and mealybugs (take plants outdoors to spray them). Prune the woody stem just above a leaf to encourage branching. When repotting, set the plant at the same depth at which it was growing; do not cover the woody base with soil.

Outdoors, plants make striking specimens in the ground or in large containers; they are not browsed by deer. A mature plant can endure 18°F for brief periods—but young plants in pots will quickly freeze to death at even a few degrees higher than this, so bring them indoors when necessary.

B

BEAUMONTIA grandiflora

HERALD'S TRUMPET, EASTER LILY VINE

Apocynaceae

EVERGREEN VINE

✂ TS ⊞ 12–10

☼ ◑ FULL SUN OR PARTIAL SHADE

◗ REGULAR WATER

Beaumontia grandiflora

From the Himalayas. Rampant vine with arching, twining branches; climbs as high as 30 ft. and spreads just as wide. Large (6- to 9-in.), oval to roundish dark green leaves, smooth and shiny above, slightly downy beneath, give lush tropical look. From spring through summer, bears fragrant, trumpet-shaped, 5-in.-long, green-veined white blossoms that look like Easter lilies (*Lilium longiflorum*).

Does best in well-drained soil enriched with organic matter; regular feeding produces most lavish display of foliage and flowers. Prune after bloom to shape or limit size; flowers are produced on wood 2 years old or older, so keep a good proportion of old wood. Hardy to 28°F. Frost kills the vine to the ground, but it usually comes back from the roots. Use as big espalier on warm, wind-sheltered wall or train along eaves of house; sturdy supports are essential, since growth is heavy. Good choice for planting near swimming pools.

BEAUTYBERRY. See CALLICARPA

BEAUTY BUSH. See KOLKWITZIA amabilis

BEE BALM. See MONARDA didyma

BEECH. See FAGUS

BEEFWOOD. See CASUARINA

BEET

Chenopodiaceae

BIENNIAL GROWN AS COOL-SEASON ANNUAL

✂ US, MS, LS, CS, TS ⊞ 7–1

☼ FULL SUN

◗ REGULAR WATER

Beet

European native, known botanically as *Beta vulgaris*. Beets are grown mainly for their edible roots, but many Southerners also enjoy the tender, fresh greens, which can be cooked or eaten raw in salads. Beets are relatively pest free and make a good crop for small gardens, because they produce a lot in a limited space.

For best flavor and texture, beets need to grow in the cool weather of spring and fall; they become tough and woody in hot weather. Early spring or late summer is the time to sow in most areas, but in the Coastal and Tropical South, you can grow beets as a winter crop. Most selections take around 50 days from sowing to harvest.

For spring crops, begin sowing seeds 2 to 4 weeks before the last spring frost; making three sowings spaced 2 to 3 weeks apart will give you a steady supply of roots and greens. For fall and winter crops, make three successive sowings 2 to 3 weeks apart, beginning in late summer.

Seeds germinate slowly; soaking them in water overnight before planting will speed the process. Before planting, work into the soil ½ cup of 10-10-10 fertilizer for every 10 ft. of row (or bed). Scatter the seeds over a 15-in.-wide bed, or sow in single rows spaced 1 ft. apart. Cover seeds with ½–1 in. of soil and water gently. When seedlings are about an inch tall, thin them to 2–4 in. apart. Early thinning is important, because crowded plants develop small, tough roots. Four to 6 weeks after planting, sprinkle ½ cup of 10-10-10 fertilizer per 10 ft. of row or bed around the plants. To ensure tender roots, keep soil evenly moist throughout the season.

WHAT BEETS NEED

CLIMATE: In much of the South, seed is best sown in early spring or late summer.

SOIL: Fertile, even textured (no clumps or rocks), and well drained.

WATER: Consistent, even moisture produces the most tender roots.

GERMINATION: For a quicker start, soak seeds in water overnight before planting.

TIME TO HARVEST: Allow about 50 days from sowing until roots are ready to dig.

'Chioggia'

Beet greens can be harvested when they are 6 in. tall. Snap off the outer leaves, but don't disturb the inner ones; more leaves will grow for future harvests. If you plan to harvest greens regularly, plant beets for this purpose alone, as continual harvesting of greens makes for small roots. Pull roots when they're 1–3 in. wide; larger ones may be tough. In the Upper South, pull roots before the soil freezes in winter.

Types with round red roots include old favorites 'Detroit Dark Red' and 'Crosby's Egyptian' as well as newer selections such as 'Red Ace', 'Sangria', and 'Kleine Bol'. 'Bull's Blood' and 'Lutz Green Leaf' are grown both for roots and for particularly tasty greens. Novelties include 'Cylindra' and 'Formanova' (long, cylindrical roots), 'Chioggia' (rings of red and white), and 'Golden' (yellow roots).

BEGONIA

Begoniaceae

PERENNIALS

✂ TS; OR TREAT AS ANNUALS ⊞ 12–1, EXCEPT AS NOTED; OR INDOORS; OR DIG AND STORE

◑ FILTERED SUNLIGHT; BRIGHT INDIRECT LIGHT

◗ REGULAR WATER, EXCEPT AS NOTED

Tuberous Begonia

Tender perennials, sometimes shrubby, grown for textured, multicolored foliage and for flowers—sometimes saucer size, sometimes much smaller and borne in lacy clusters. Outdoors, most grow well in pots, in the ground, or in hanging baskets in filtered shade with rich, porous, fast-draining soil; consistent but light feeding; and enough water to keep soil moist but not soggy. Most thrive as indoor plants, in greenhouse, or under lath. Some prefer terrarium conditions. Almost all require at least moderate humidity. (In dry-summer areas or indoors during winter, set pots in saucers filled with wet pebbles.)

Most begonias are easy to propagate from leaf, stem, or rhizome cuttings. They also grow from dust-fine seed. Of the many hundreds of species and selections, relatively few are sold widely.

Begonia enthusiasts group or classify the different kinds generally by growth habit, which coincidentally groups them by their care needs.

Cane-type begonias. They get their name from their stems, which are tall and woody, with prominent bamboolike joints. The group includes so-called angel-wing begonias, named for their folded, often spotted or splotched leaves, which resemble wings.

Cane-type begonias have multiple stems, some reaching 5 ft. or more under the right conditions. Most bear profuse large clusters of white, pink, orange, or red flowers from early spring through autumn. Some are everblooming. When roots fill 4-in. pots, plants can be moved to larger containers or planted in the ground. Position plants where they will get plenty of light, some sun, and no wind. They may require staking. Protect them from heavy frosts. Old canes that have grown barren should be pruned to two leaf joints in early spring to stimulate new growth.

'Bubbles'. Spotted foliage; pink flowers with apple-blossom fragrance.

'Honeysuckle'. Plain green foliage and fragrant pink flowers.

'Irene Nuss'. Dark red-and-green leaves and huge, drooping clusters of coral pink flowers.

Dragonwing begonias. A new hybrid between angel-wing (cane-type) and semperflorens begonias. Shiny green leaves form a foliage mass 1–1½ ft. high and 10–12 in. wide; bright red flowers bloom from spring until frost. Excellent as bedding plants and in containers. Do best with morning sun and light afternoon shade; tend to burn in hot afternoon sun. In shade, plants have a more open habit and bloom less generously.

Hardy begonias. Several begonias are hardy throughout the South, but *B. grandis* (called hardy begonia and sometimes offered as *B. evansiana* or *B. grandis evansiana*) is the best known. It grows from a tuber and reaches 2–3 ft. tall and wide, its branching red stems set with large, smooth coppery green leaves with red undersides. Pink or white summer flowers are borne in drooping clusters. The plant multiplies readily by bulbils produced in leaf axils; it dies down after a frost. Likes moist, woodsy soil and light shade. Excellent companion for ferns, hostas, and hellebores. 'Heron's Pirouette' features exceptionally large clusters of hot pink flowers.

B. sinensis has much smaller leaves on a lower-growing plant (to 1 ft. tall and wide). It blooms from summer to fall. The species has pink flowers; 'Shaanxi White' bears pure white blooms.

B. sutherlandii is hardy from the Middle South southward and grows 1 ft. tall, with wider spread; its weeping form makes it a good choice for hanging baskets and containers. Tooth-edged bright green leaves have red veins and margins. Clusters of creamy orange to bright tangerine blossoms appear in midsummer.

Hiemalis begonias. Heat zones 9–3. Usually sold as Rieger begonias. Bushy, compact, to 10–12 in. tall and wide. Profuse bloomers and outstanding outdoor or indoor plants. Flowers average about 2 in. across and appear over a long season that includes winter. On well-grown plants, green leaves and stems are all but invisible beneath a blanket of bloom. Give indoor plants plenty of light in winter. In summer, keep out of hot noonday sun. Water thoroughly when top inch of soil is dry. Don't mist leaves. Plants may get rangy, an indication of approaching dormancy; if they do, cut stems to 4-in. stubs.

Multiflora begonias. Heat zones 7–1. Bushy, compact plants grow to 1–1½ ft. tall and wide. Abundant summer and fall blooms in carmine, scarlet, orange, yellow, apricot, salmon, pink. Includes the Nonstop strain. All multifloras are essentially small-flowered, profuse-blooming tuberous begonias; for care, see Tuberous begonias.

Rex begonias. With their bold, multicolored leaves, these probably have the most striking foliage of all begonias. They grow 6–14 in. tall and wide. While many named selections are grown by collectors, easier-to-find unnamed seedling plants are almost as decorative. The leaves grow from a rhizome.

Give rex begonias bright light through a window, and water only when top inch of soil is dry. They also need high humidity (at least 50 percent) to do their best. In dry climates or indoors in winter, provide moisture in the air by misting plants with a spray bottle, placing pots on wet pebbles in a tray, or keeping plants in a greenhouse. When the rhizome grows too far past edge of pot for your taste, either repot into slightly larger container or cut off rhizome end inside pot edge. Old rhizome will branch and grow new leaves. Make rhizome cuttings of the piece you remove and root in mixture of half peat moss, half perlite.

'Bowkit'. Leaves are reddish beneath, green striped with gold and brown above.

'Fireworks'. Quilted-looking leaves are edged in metallic purple that shades inward to a bright band of white around a dark central starburst.

Rex Begonia 'Fireworks'

'Merry Christmas' ('Ruhrtal'). Large central swirl of bright red is surrounded by white-speckled green; leaf edges are deep green.

'Venetian Red'. Deep red leaves with charcoal black veins have a velvety appearance.

Rhizomatous begonias. Like rex begonias, these grow from a rhizome. Although some have handsome flowers, they are grown primarily for foliage, which varies in color and texture among species and selections. The group includes so-called star begonias, named for their leaf shape. Rhizomatous begonias perform well as houseplants. Plant them in wide, shallow pots. Give them bright light through a window, and water only when the top inch or so of soil is dry. They flower from winter through summer, the season varying among specific plants. White to pink flowers appear in clusters on erect stems above the foliage. Rhizomes will grow over edge of pot, eventually forming a ball-shaped plant; if you wish, cut rhizomes back to pot. (For care of rhizomes, see Rex begonias, this page.)

B. masoniana. IRON CROSS BEGONIA. Large puckered leaves; known for chocolate brown pattern resembling Maltese cross on green background. Flowers are insignificant.

Semperflorens begonias. Also known as fibrous, bedding, or wax begonias. Dwarf (6- to 8-in.) and taller (10- to 12-in.) strains are grown in garden beds or containers as annuals; they bloom from spring through fall, producing lots of small flowers in a white through red range. Foliage can be green, red, bronze, or variegated. In mild climates, plants can overwinter and live for years. They thrive in full sun in the Upper South; prefer filtered shade elsewhere, but dark-foliaged kinds will take sun if well watered.

Shrublike begonias. This large class is marked by multiple stems that are soft and green rather than bamboolike as in the cane-type group. Grown for both foliage and flowers. Leaves are very interesting. Some are heavily textured, others grow white or red "hairs," and still others develop a soft, feltlike coating. Most begonias in this group grow upright and bushy, but others are less erect and make suitable subjects for hanging baskets. Flowers in shades of pink, red, white, and peach can come any time, depending on species or selection. Care consists of repotting into larger containers as the plants outgrow their pots. Some shrublike begonias can get very large—as tall as 8 ft. They require ample moisture, but let soil begin to dry on surface between waterings. Prune to shape; pinch tips to encourage branching.

'Digswelliana'. Grows 2–3 ft. high, with glossy, 2- to 4-in.-long leaves. Clusters of red flowers appear almost continuously from spring until fall.

B. foliosa. Twiggy plant densely foliaged with inch-long leaves; has a fernlike look. Stems arch or droop to 3 ft. Everblooming in mild weather, bearing small flowers in white or red shades. 'Miniata' has rose pink to rose red blossoms.

'Richmondensis'. Over 2 ft. tall, with arching stems and shiny, crisp, deep green leaves with red undersides. Blooms almost year-round, with vivid pink to crimson flowers opening from darker buds. Big, sturdy, tolerant of sun and wind.

Trailing or climbing begonias. These have stems that trail or climb, depending on how you train them. They are suited to hanging basket culture or planting in the ground where well protected. Growing conditions are similar to those for tuberous begonias, though trailing types are not lifted. Sporadic bloom during warm weather.

B. solananthera. Glossy light green leaves; fragrant white flowers with red centers.

Tuberous begonias. These magnificent large-flowered hybrids grow from tubers. They range from plants with saucer-size blooms and a few upright stems to multistemmed hanging basket types covered with small flowers. Except for some rare kinds, they bloom in summer and fall, in almost every color except blue.

Strains are sold as hanging or upright. The former bloom more profusely; the latter have larger flowers. Colors are white, red, pink, yellow, and peach; shapes are frilly (carnation), formal double (camellia), and tight-centered (rose). Some flower forms have petal edges in contrasting

B

colors (picotee). Popular strains are Double Trumpet (improved rose form), Prima Donna (improved camellia form), and Hanging Sensation (camellia form).

Grow tuberous begonias in filtered shade, such as under lath or in the open with eastern exposure. Tuberous begonias are best in the Upper South; not suited to areas of extreme heat. In autumn, when leaves begin to yellow and wilt, reduce watering. When stems have fallen off the plants, lift tubers and shake off dirt; then dry tubers in sun for 3 days and store in a cool, dry place, such as a garage, until spring. When little pink growth buds appear, plant the tubers once again. You can also buy tubers from garden centers in spring.

BELAMCANDA

BLACKBERRY LILY

Iridaceae

PERENNIALS FROM RHIZOMES

US, MS, LS, CS

FULL SUN OR PARTIAL SHADE

REGULAR WATER DURING GROWTH AND BLOOM

Belamcanda chinensis

Like their iris relatives, these plants form clumps of sword-shaped leaves in fanlike sheaves from slowly creeping rhizomes. Flowers appear on zigzag stems in summer; each blossom lasts only a day, but new ones keep opening for weeks. As blooms fade, rounded seed capsules develop; they split open to expose shiny black seeds that look like blackberries (hence the plant's common name). Cut seed-bearing stems for unique dried arrangements. Plant is effective in clumps in border. Plant rhizomes in porous soil, 1 in. deep and 1 ft. apart.

B. chinensis. Heat zones 9–5. Stems grow 3–4 ft. high, bearing sprays of 1½-in. flowers in yellowish orange dotted with red. 'Freckle Face' grows to 12–15 in. high; has slightly larger flowers with distinct red spots.

B. flabellata 'Hello Yellow'. Heat zones 9–3. Dwarf blackberry lily growing under 2 ft. high. Yellow flowers.

BELLADONNA LILY. See AMARYLLIS belladonna

BELLFLOWER. See CAMPANULA

BELLIS perennis

ENGLISH DAISY

Asteraceae (Compositae)

PERENNIAL OFTEN TREATED AS ANNUAL

US, MS, LS, TS ⊩ 8–1

LIGHT SHADE IN HOTTEST CLIMATES

REGULAR WATER

Bellis perennis

Native to Europe and Mediterranean region. The original English daisies are the kind you sometimes see growing in lawns in winter. Plump, fully double ones sold in garden centers are horticultural selections. Dark green leaves 1–2 in. long form rosettes to 8 in. wide. Pink, rose, red, or white double flowers bloom on 3- to 6-in. stems in spring and early summer. Edging or bedding plant; effective with bulbs. In the South, usually a cool-weather annual planted in fall, then allowed to overwinter; blooms in winter or spring.

BELLS-OF-IRELAND. See MOLUCCELLA laevis

BELLWORT. See UVULARIA

BELOPERONE guttata. See JUSTICIA brandegeeana

BENJAMIN FIG. See FICUS benjamina

Berberidaceae. The barberry family contains shrubs and herbaceous perennials. Barberry *(Berberis)* and heavenly bamboo *(Nandina)* are typical of the former; *Epimedium* and *Jeffersonia* are among the latter.

BERBERIS

BARBERRY

Berberidaceae

EVERGREEN, SEMIEVERGREEN, DECIDUOUS SHRUBS

ZONES VARY BY SPECIES

FULL SUN OR LIGHT SHADE

MODERATE TO REGULAR WATER

Berberis darwinii

These dense, spiny-stemmed plants, especially the deciduous species, tolerate climate and soil extremes. They require no more than ordinary garden care and are not browsed by deer. Each year, thin out oldest wood and prune as needed to shape—late in the dormant season for deciduous kinds, after bloom for evergreen and semievergreen types. Barberries make fine hedges. Species grown for their foliage can be sheared, but those grown for their spring flowers and the fruit that follows are best pruned informally, because they bloom on the preceding year's growth. To rejuvenate overgrown or neglected plants, cut them to within a foot of the ground before new spring growth begins. Flowers are yellow unless otherwise noted.

B. buxifolia. MAGELLAN BARBERRY. Evergreen. Zones US, MS; 8–6. Hardy to 0°F. Native to Chile and Argentina. Rather rigid and upright, to 6 ft. tall and as wide. Leathery, 1-in. leaves. Orange-yellow flowers; dark purple berries, one or two at each leaf cluster. Dwarf 'Nana' ('Pygmaea') grows to 1½ ft. high, 2 ft. wide; makes a good hedge or rock garden plant.

B. ×chenaultii (B. ×hybrido-gagnepainii). CHENAULT BARBERRY. Evergreen. Zones US, MS, LS; 9–7. Hardy to 0°F. Slow growing to 4 ft. tall and 5 ft. wide, with arching branches. Dark green, spiny-toothed leaves 1–1½ in. long. Bluish black berries. Barrier hedge, foreground planting.

B. darwinii. DARWIN BARBERRY. Evergreen. Zones MS, LS, CS; 9–7. Hardy to 10°F. Very showy barberry from Chile. Fountainlike growth to 5–10 ft. tall, 4–7 ft. wide. Crisp, dark green, hollylike, 1-in. leaves. Orange-yellow flowers are borne so thickly along branches that foliage is hard to see; these are followed by profuse dark blue berries, popular with birds. Spreads by underground runners to form a thicket.

B. ×gladwynensis 'William Penn'. Evergreen; drops some leaves at 0 to 10°F. Zones US, MS, LS, CS; 9–4. Resembles *B. julianae* in general effect but has broader, glossier leaves and is faster growing, with denser growth. Reaches 4 ft. tall and wide. Good floral display.

B. ×irwinii. See B. ×stenophylla 'Irwinii'

B. julianae. WINTERGREEN BARBERRY. Evergreen to semievergreen. Zones US, MS, LS, CS; 9–4. Hardy to 0°F, but foliage is damaged by severe winter cold. Chinese native. Dense, upright, to 6 ft. tall and wide; angled branches. Spiny-toothed, dark green, leathery leaves to 3 in. long; reddish fall color. Blue-black berries. One of the spiniest barberries; good as barrier hedge.

B. koreana. KOREAN BARBERRY. Deciduous. Zones US, MS. Hardy to −35°F. Korean native grows erect to 4–6 ft. and not quite as wide. Densely foliaged in medium to dark green, 1–3-in. leaves that turn purple in fall. Fragrant flowers in drooping, 3- to 4-in. clusters. Bright red fruit.

B. linearifolia 'Orange King'. Evergreen. Zones US, MS, LS; 9–6. Hardy to 0 to 10°F. This selection of a Chilean species has an open growth habit to 5 ft. tall and wide, with narrow, glossy, 2-in. leaves. Short clusters of deep orange flowers; bluish black fruit.

B. ×mentorensis. MENTOR BARBERRY. Evergreen to deciduous. Zones US, MS, LS; 8–5. Hardy to −20°F but loses some or all leaves below 0°F. Compact growth to 7 ft. tall and wide. Dark green, 1-in. leaves turn a beautiful red in fall where winters are cold. Berries are dull dark red but are rarely seen. Easy to maintain as a hedge. Tolerates hot, dry weather.

B. ×stenophylla. ROSEMARY BARBERRY. Evergreen. Zones US, MS, LS; 9–6. Hardy to 0°F. Narrow, ½- to 1-in.-long leaves with rolled-in edges and spiny tip. Species is 10 ft. tall, 15 ft. wide, but selections are more commonly grown. 'Corallina Compacta', called coral barberry, reaches 1½ ft. high and wide and bears nodding clusters of bright orange flowers and bluish black fruit; effective in rock garden or as foreground plant. 'Irwinii', to 4–5 ft. tall and wide, resembles a compact-growing *B. darwinii*.

B. swaseyi. TEXAS BARBERRY. Evergreen or semievergreen. Zones MS, LS. Native to South-Central Texas. Very thorny shrub grows slowly to 3–5 ft. tall and wide. Light green-gray leaves turn pale purple and red in fall. Very fragrant golden yellow flowers; small amber to red berries. Thrives in limy soil.

B. thunbergii. JAPANESE BARBERRY. Deciduous. Zones US, MS, LS; 8–5. Hardy to −20°F. Graceful habit with slender, arching, spiny branches; if not sheared, usually reaches 4–6 ft. tall with equal spread. Densely covered with roundish, ½- to 1½-in.-long leaves that are deep green above, paler beneath; leaves turn yellow, orange, and red before they fall. Beadlike bright red berries stud branches in fall and through winter. Use as hedge, barrier planting, or specimen shrub. The following are among the many attractive selections grown for vivid foliage.

'Atropurpurea'. RED-LEAF JAPANESE BARBERRY. Plants sold as such vary in plant size and foliage color (from bronzy red to purple red). They must have sun to develop red color (which they will hold all summer).

'Aurea'. Bright golden yellow foliage. Best color in full sun (though it can't take it in Coastal South), but plant will tolerate light shade. Slow growing to 2½–3 ft. tall and wide.

'Cherry Bomb'. Resembles 'Crimson Pygmy' but is taller (to 4 ft.), with larger leaves and more open growth.

'Crimson Pygmy' ('Atropurpurea Nana'). Selected miniature form, generally less than 1½ ft. high and 2½ ft. wide at 10 years old. Leaves are bright red when new, maturing to bronzy blood red. Must have sun to develop color.

'Golden Nugget'. Dwarf selection reaching 1–1½ ft. tall and wide. Golden leaves may be tinged orange.

'Golden Ring'. Purple leaves with a thin, green or golden green border.

'Helmond Pillar'. Purple-leafed form to 4–5 ft. tall, 2 ft. wide.

'Kobold'. Extra-dwarf bright green selection. Like 'Crimson Pygmy' in habit but fuller and rounder.

'Rose Glow'. To 4–6 ft. tall and wide. New foliage marbled bronzy red and pinkish white, deepening to rose and bronze with age. For best color, plant in full sun or lightest shade.

'Sparkle'. To 5 ft. tall and 6 ft. wide, with rich green foliage that turns vivid yellow, orange, and red in fall.

B. verruculosa. WARTY BARBERRY. Evergreen. Zones US, MS, LS; 9–4. Hardy to 0°F. Native to China. Neat, tailored looking. Will reach 4–5 ft. tall and wide but can be kept to 1½ ft. Perky, 1-in.-long leaves are glossy dark green above, whitish beneath. In fall and winter, the odd red leaf develops as a highlight here and there. Black berries with a purplish bloom. Very choice and effective on banks, in front of leggy rhododendrons or azaleas, in foreground of shrub border.

B. wilsoniae. WILSON BARBERRY. Deciduous to semievergreen. Zones US, MS, LS; 9–4. Hardy to 5°F. Native to China. To 6 ft. tall and wide, but it can be held to 3–4 ft. Light green, roundish, ½- to 1-in. leaves give the plant a fine-textured look. Beautiful coral to salmon red berries. Makes a handsome barrier hedge.

BERGENIA

Saxifragaceae

PERENNIALS

✿ US, MS, LS **H** 8–1

☼ ● PARTIAL OR FULL SHADE

◐ REGULAR WATER, EXCEPT AS NOTED

Bergenia cordifolia

Native to the Himalayas and the mountains of China. Thick rootstocks produce rosettes of large, ornamental, glossy green leaves that are evergreen except in the coldest areas; foliage of many types blushes red in cool weather. Thick, leafless, 1- to 1½-ft.-tall stalks bear graceful, nodding clusters of small white, pink, or rose flowers shaped like funnels or bells;

blossoms are typically ½–1 in. across. Bergenias lend a strong, substantial textural quality to borders and plantings under trees; also make a bold-patterned ground cover. Effective with ferns, hostas, hellebores; good as foreground planting for aucubas, rhododendrons, Japanese yew (*Taxus cuspidata*).

Bergenias do well in part shade in the Upper and Middle South, full shade in Lower South. Plant about 1½ ft. apart. Cut back yearly to prevent legginess. Divide crowded clumps and replant vigorous divisions in late winter or early spring.

B. 'Appleblossom'. Hybrid developed from *B. emeiensis*. Reddish stems hold large (1½-in.-wide) light pink blossoms in spring.

B. ciliata (B. ligulata). HAIRY BERGENIA. Choicest, most elegant. To 1 ft. Lustrous light green leaves to 1 ft. across, smooth on edges but fringed with soft hairs; young leaves bronzy. White, rose, or purplish flowers bloom in late spring, summer. Slightly tender; leaves burn in severe frost. Plants sold under this name may be garden hybrids.

B. cordifolia. HEARTLEAF BERGENIA. Leaves, to 1 ft. across, are glossy, roundish, heart shaped at base, with wavy, toothed edges. In spring, rose or lilac flowers appear in pendulous clusters partially hidden by leaves. Plant grows to 20 in. Endures neglect, poor soil, and cold, but responds to good soil, regular watering, feeding, and grooming. 'Morning Red' ('Morgenrote') has bronzy-toned leaves, dark red flowers. 'Perfecta' (*B.* 'Perfect') has rosy red flowers and glossy, rounded green leaves flushed dark red when mature.

B. emeiensis. CHINESE BERGENIA. Forms a rosette about 10 in. high. Blooms over a long period in spring, bearing large white or pinkish blossoms—shaped more like daisies than funnels or bells—on stalks to 1 ft. tall. Foliage doesn't color up like that of other bergenias, but the striking flowers more than make up for it. Heat tolerant. Can take a wide range of soil and moisture conditions. Used in creating vigorous, long-flowering hybrids.

BERLANDIERA

Asteraceae (Compositae)

PERENNIALS

✿ ZONES VARY BY SPECIES; ANYWHERE AS ANNUALS

☼ ◑ EXPOSURE NEEDS VARY BY SPECIES

◐ ● WATER NEEDS VARY BY SPECIES

Berlandiera lyrata

Tough and undemanding, these plants decorate the meadows of their native Southwest with cheerful yellow daisies. They're also easy to grow outside their native range, thriving in most soils as long as they have good drainage. Sow seed in fall; or set out small plants in spring.

B. lyrata. CHOCOLATE DAISY, CHOCOLATE FLOWER. Zones LS, CS, TS. The luscious fragrance of chocolate permeates the morning air wherever this daisy blooms. Rounded, somewhat coarse-foliaged plant reaches 1½–3 ft. high and wide. Blooms in spring and summer, sometimes into fall, bearing light yellow daisies with a maroon-and-green center. Native Americans used the flower heads to flavor foods. Butterflies can't resist the blossoms, which dry well for use in winter bouquets. Give moderate water; plant in full sun.

B. texana. GREEN EYES. Zones US, MS, LS, CS, TS; 9–7. Named for the green center of its yellow blossoms. Grows 1–4 ft. tall; blooms profusely in spring, then again in summer and autumn. Gets by on moderate water but responds well to regular watering and fertilizing. Full sun or dappled shade.

BERMUDA, BERMUDA GRASS. See CYNODON dactylon

FOR INFORMATION ON SELECTING PLANTS

PLEASE SEE PAGES 39–144

B

BESCHORNERIA

Agavaceae

PERENNIALS

ZONES VARY BY SPECIES

PARTIAL SHADE IN HOTTEST CLIMATES

MODERATE TO REGULAR WATER

Beschorneria yuccoides

Native to Mexico, these striking plants combine handsome, lance-shaped dark green leaves with showy, tubular summer flowers. They are related to yuccas and agaves, but they have spineless leaves and need a bit more water and shade than their cousins. They prefer fertile, well-drained soil, though they will tolerate short periods of drought. Excellent as specimen plants, in lightly shaded borders, or in containers.

B. decosteriana. Zones LS, CS, TS. Grows 4 ft. tall and wide, with waxy blue-green leaves and a tall red flower stalk bearing green-and-red blossoms. 'Ding Dong', a hybrid between this species and *B. septentrionalis,* has a reddish, 7-ft.-tall flower stalk topped by bell-shaped red-and-green blossoms.

B. septentrionalis. Zones MS, LS, CS, TS; 12–7. To 3 ft. tall and wide. Lush, pendulous green leaves to about 2 ft. long; fuchsia red flowers atop a glossy red spike. Needs light shade in the Coastal and Tropical South. Tolerates considerable moisture if soil is well drained.

B. yuccoides. Zones CS, TS. The most widely available species. Clump slowly grows 3–4 ft. tall and wide; narrow gray-green leaves can reach 2 ft. long. Flowers in early summer, when a thick, branching, coral pink, 3- to 6-ft. stalk is topped by pendulous yellowish green blooms with red bracts.

BETA vulgaris. See BEET

BETHLEHEM LUNGWORT. See PULMONARIA saccharata

BETULA

BIRCH

Betulaceae

DECIDUOUS TREES

ZONES VARY BY SPECIES

FULL SUN

REGULAR TO AMPLE WATER

Betula pendula

No tree has more beautiful bark than a white-barked birch—the tree that comes to mind when most people think of birches. Trouble is, these trees are often difficult to keep alive in most of the South. Native to mountain regions, where summers are cooler and winters long, they tend to struggle when faced with the hot summers common to our region. And they often succumb to a serious pest: the bronze birch borer, which causes them to die slowly from the top down.

Fortunately, a number of birches that resemble white-barked birches do succeed here; they too have a graceful habit, thin bark that peels in sheets, and small, finely toothed leaves that turn glowing yellow in fall. After the leaves drop, the trees' delicate limbs, handsome bark, and small, conelike fruits provide a striking winter display.

Birches need a steady supply of moisture at all times; drought in summer can cause leaf drop. All fall victim to aphids that drip honeydew; for this reason, they should never be planted near a porch, patio, or parking area. Prune in summer, as trees will bleed sap if pruned in winter. Susceptibility to heat and the bronze birch borer limits most birches to the Upper South and the Appalachians; exceptions are *B. maximowicziana,* *B. nigra,* and *B. platyphylla japonica.*

B. lenta. SWEET BIRCH, CHERRY BIRCH. Zones US; 7–2. Native to eastern U.S. Seldom sold. An attractive tree with shiny reddish to blackish brown bark; grows to 40–50 ft. tall, up to 40 ft. wide. Leaves to 4 in. long; turn rich yellow in fall. Many country children have sampled the bark of this tree, which has a sweet wintergreen flavor and was once routinely used to make a tasty soft drink known as birch beer.

B. maximowicziana. MONARCH BIRCH. Zones US, MS; 8–6. Native to Japan. Fast growing; open growth when young. Can reach 80–100 ft. tall, 40 ft. wide. Flaking, orange-brown bark eventually turns gray or white. Leaves up to 6 in. long. Plants sold under this name are not always the true species.

B. nigra. RIVER BIRCH, RED BIRCH. Zones US, MS, LS, CS; 9–1. Native to eastern U.S. Very fast growth in first years; eventually reaches 50–90 ft. tall, 40–60 ft. wide. Trunk often forks near ground, but tree can be trained to a single stem. Young bark is apricot to pinkish, very smooth, and shiny; on older trees, bark flakes and curls in cinnamon brown to blackish sheets. Diamond-shaped leaves, 1–3 in. long, are bright glossy green above, silvery below. 'Heritage' has darker leaves and tan-and-apricot bark; keeps apricot color longer than the species. These are the best birches for hot, humid climates; they drop leaves in hot, dry weather. Tolerate poor drainage.

WHAT BIRCHES NEED

CLIMATE: With notable exceptions, they prefer the relatively cool summers and long winters of the Upper South. Not a good choice for urban areas.

SOIL: Moist, fertile, slightly acid; most species prefer good drainage.

MOISTURE: Most trees do not tolerate drought; water freely during summer dry spells.

PRUNING: Prune in summer to remove weak, damaged, or dead branches.

Betula papyrifera

B. papyrifera. PAPER BIRCH, CANOE BIRCH. Zones US; 7–1. Native to northern part of North America. Similar to *B. pendula* but taller (to 100 ft. tall, half as wide), less weeping, with a stouter trunk that is creamy white. Bark peels off in papery layers. Leaves are larger (to 4 in. long), sparser. Excellent fall color. More resistant to bronze birch borer than *B. pendula.* 'Snowy' is a cold-hardy selection with especially handsome white bark; it is said to be particularly resistant to borers and grows quickly when young

B. pendula. EUROPEAN WHITE BIRCH. Zones US; 7–1. Native from Europe to Asia Minor. Delicate and lacy. Upright branching with weeping side branches. Average mature tree is 30–40 ft. high and half as wide. Bark on twigs and young branches is golden brown; as tree matures, bark on trunk and main limbs becomes white, marked with black clefts. Oldest bark (at base of tree) is blackish gray. Rich green, glossy leaves to 2½ in. long, diamond shaped with slender, tapered point. Often sold as weeping birch, although trees vary somewhat in habit and young trees show little inclination to weep. Very susceptible to bronze birch borer. The following are some of the selections offered.

'Crimson Frost'. Apparently a hybrid between *B. pendula* and an Asian birch, with burgundy leaf color that persists all summer. Somewhat resistant to borers.

'Dalecarlica' ('Laciniata'). CUTLEAF WEEPING BIRCH. Graceful, open tree with deeply cut leaves, strongly weeping branches. Weeping forms are more affected by dry, hot weather than is the species; foliage will show stress by late summer.

'Fastigiata' (*B. alba* 'Fastigiata'). PYRAMIDAL WHITE BIRCH. Branches upright; habit somewhat like Lombardy poplar (*Populus nigra* 'Italica'). Excellent screening tree.

'Purple Rain'. A purple-leafed selection like 'Purpurea', but it holds its color all summer.

'Purpurea' (*B. alba* 'Purpurea'). PURPLE BIRCH. Purple-black twigs. Foliage is rich purple maroon when new, fading to purplish green in summer; looks striking against white bark.

'Youngii'. YOUNG'S WEEPING BIRCH. Slender branches hang straight down. Resembles weeping forms of mulberry (*Morus*) but is more graceful. Decorative tree. Trunk must be staked to desired height. Same climate limitations as those of 'Dalecarlica'.

B. platyphylla japonica. JAPANESE WHITE BIRCH. Zones US, MS, LS; 7–4. Native to Japan. Fast growth to 40–50 ft. tall, about half as wide; open habit. Glossy green leaves to 3 in. long; white bark. 'Whitespire' is a narrowly pyramidal, heat-tolerant selection resistant to bronze birch borer.

Betulaceae. The birch family includes deciduous trees and shrubs with inconspicuous flowers in tight clusters (catkins). Representatives are alder (*Alnus*), birch (*Betula*), filbert (*Corylus*), and hornbeam (*Carpinus*).

BIDENS

TICKSEED
Asteraceae (Compositae)
ANNUALS AND PERENNIALS
ZONES VARY BY SPECIES
FULL SUN
REGULAR TO AMPLE WATER

Bidens ferulifolia

These wildflowers are also known as beggar-ticks and stick-tights—references to their barbed seeds, which stick to the clothing or fur of anything that brushes by, allowing the plants to spread by hitchhiking. Many types of tickseed exist; most are out-and-out weeds, but a few offer showy flowers and make fine additions to the border. They prefer full sun and fertile soil that is always moist, be it boggy or well drained. Seeds planted in spring or summer sprout and grow quickly. Once you plant them, you'll have them forever, as they reseed profusely. Seedlings are nice to share, though, and it's easy to pull out those you don't want.

B. aristosa. Annual. Zones US, MS, LS, CS, TS; 12–1. North American prairie native grows 4–5 ft. tall and 2 ft. wide. Strongly dissected, toothed leaves resemble those of marigold (*Tagetes*). Masses of showy, daisylike yellow flowers to 2 in. wide appear in summer and fall, carried atop the foliage.

B. coronata. Annual. Zones US, MS, LS, CS, TS; 12–1. From bogs and meadows of North America. To 5 ft. tall, 2 ft. wide. Blooms in late summer, bearing golden yellow, daisylike blooms to 3 in. across. Foliage is more deeply dissected than that of *B. aristosa*.

B. ferulifolia. Perennial. Zones CS, TS; 12–1; anywhere as annual. Native to southern U.S., Mexico, Guatemala. The species grows to 3 ft. tall and wide, but the forms most commonly seen are trailing. Bright green leaves are divided into threadlike segments. Flower heads are bright golden yellow, an inch or so wide, with fewer ray flowers than most daisies and a light honey fragrance. Plants bloom almost continuously during mild weather. Extremely heat tolerant. Can be aggressive, clambering into or sprawling over their neighbors; when this happens, cut plants back (they will recover quickly).

Sold under a wide variety of names. Seed-grown kinds include 'Golden Eye', 10–12 in. tall and broad, and 'Golden Goddess', 1½–2 ft. high and wide, with larger (2½-in.) flowers. 'Goldie', 'Goldmarie', and 'Peter's Gold Carpet' are cutting-grown plants similar in size to 'Golden Eye'.

BIG BLUESTEM. See ANDROPOGON gerardii

BIGNONIA capreolata

CROSSVINE
Bignoniaceae
EVERGREEN OR SEMIEVERGREEN VINE
US (MILDER PARTS), MS, LS, CS ⊩ 9–6
FULL SUN OR LIGHT SHADE
MODERATE TO REGULAR WATER

Bignonia capreolata

Native to the South and southern Midwest. Climbs rapidly to 30 ft. or more by tendrils and holdfast disks; useful for covering fences, masonry walls. Shiny dark green leaves consist of two 2- to 6-in. leaflets and a branching tendril. Leaves turn purplish in winter, will fall off in frigid weather. Clustered, 2-in., trumpet-shaped flowers, typically brownish red or brownish orange, in spring. 'Atrosanguinea' has reddish purple blooms and longer, narrower leaves than the species. 'Dragon Lady' bears red flowers with bright orange throats; blossoms of 'Jekyll' are orange outside, yellow within. Stunning 'Tangerine Beauty' blooms profusely, producing tangerine red blossoms with yellow throats.

Bignoniaceae. The bignonia family includes vines (mostly), trees, shrubs, and (rarely) perennials or annuals—all with trumpet-shaped, often two-lipped flowers. The family gets its name from the genus *Bignonia*, which once included most of the trumpet vines; most of these have now been reclassified, but they are often still sold as *Bignonia*. Listed below are the older names, followed by the new.

Bignonia australis. See Pandorea pandorana
B. cherere. See Distictis buccinatoria
B. chinensis. See Campsis grandiflora
B. jasminoides. See Pandorea jasminoides
B. radicans. See Campsis radicans
B. speciosa. See Clytostoma callistegioides
B. tweediana. See Macfadyena unguis-cati
B. venusta. See Pyrostegia venusta
B. violacea. See Clytostoma callistegioides

BILLBERGIA

Bromeliaceae
PERENNIALS
TS ⊩ 12–10; OR GROW IN POTS
FILTERED SUN; BRIGHT INDIRECT LIGHT
REGULAR WATER

Billbergia nutans

These pineapple relatives are native to Brazil and other parts of the tropics, where they grow as epiphytes on trees. Basal rosettes of stiff, spiny-toothed evergreen leaves produce drooping clusters of showy bracts and tubular flowers. Usually grown in containers for display indoors or on patios. In south Florida, however, they are often planted under trees as an easy ground cover, used in borders, or grown on limbs of trees or bark slabs, with roots wrapped in sphagnum moss and leaf mold. They make excellent cut flowers.

Need regular moisture during active growth in warm weather; reduce water as weather cools and growth slows. Plants usually hold water in the funnel-like center of the leaf rosette, which acts as a reservoir. Grow in well-drained soil; or pot in a light, porous mixture of sand, ground bark, and leaf mold. Give houseplants warmth and lots of light; mist foliage frequently. To get more plants, cut off suckers from base of plant and pot them up. Specialists in bromeliads list dozens of selections.

B. nutans. QUEEN'S TEARS. Most commonly grown. Narrow (½-in.-wide), spiny green leaves to 1½ ft. long. Rosy red bracts in 6- to 12-in. spikes; drooping flowers with green petals edged deep blue. Vigorous. Makes offsets freely; easy to grow and propagate.   ▸

B. pyramidalis. Leaves to 3 ft. long, 2½ in. wide, with spiny-toothed margins. Dense flowers spikes to 4 in. long; bright red bracts, red petals tipped in violet.

B. sanderiana. Leathery, spiny-toothed, white-dotted leaves grow to 1 ft. long, 2½ in. wide. Produces loose, nodding, 10-in.-long flower clusters with rose-colored bracts, blue-tipped sepals, and blue petals that are yellowish green at the base.

BIRCH. See BETULA

BIRD OF PARADISE. See CAESALPINIA, STRELITZIA

BIRD OF PARADISE, FALSE. See HELICONIA brasiliensis

BIRD'S FOOT FERN. See PELLAEA mucronata

BIRD'S NEST FERN. See ASPLENIUM nidus

BISHOP'S HAT. See EPIMEDIUM grandiflorum

BISHOP'S WEED. See AEGOPODIUM podagraria

BITTER MELON

Cucurbitaceae

ANNUAL VINE

✂ US, MS, LS, CS, TS ⫶ 12–6

☼ FULL SUN

💧 REGULAR WATER

Bitter Melon

Also called balsam pear or bitter cucumber, bitter melon is classified botanically as *Momordica charantia*. Widespread in tropics, naturalized in southeastern U.S. Sprawls or climbs by tendrils to 16 ft. Deeply lobed leaves; yellow to white, 1-in.-wide flowers with fringed petals. Fruit, to 8 in. long, is cylindrical with tapered ends, ridged and warty, bright yellow when ripe, splitting to show scarlet seeds. Immature fruit is cherished in Asian cooking despite its bitter flavor. Ripe fruit is showy, sometimes used in arrangements. Sow seed when soil warms, feed generously, and provide a trellis or other support.

BITTERSWEET. See CELASTRUS

BLACKBERRY

Rosaceae

BERRY-PRODUCING VINES

✂ US, MS, LS, CS ⫶ 8–1, EXCEPT AS NOTED

☼ FULL SUN

💧 REGULAR WATER

Blackberry

Blackberries grow in areas of the South where summers are not too dry and winters not too harsh. They thrive along the eastern coast, as well as in the cool-night areas of the Appalachians, Ozarks, and Blue Ridge Mountains.

Upright types tend to be hardy and stiff caned; they usually grow 4–6 ft. high. Trailing kinds, known as dewberries or boysenberries, are more lax plants that need support. Crosses between upright and trailing types are termed semierect. Canes of most blackberries are covered with sharp thorns.

All types bear fruit in summer. The fruit clusters of trailing plants ripen earlier and are smaller and more open than those of erect or semierect types. For good crops, all blackberries need full sun; deep, well-drained soil; and regular water throughout the growing season. The fruit makes excellent pies, fine jams and jellies, tangy syrups, and even good wines.

Blackberries are subject to many pests and diseases, including scale, borers, anthracnose, leaf spot, powdery mildew, rust, and cane blight; for best success, start with healthy plants from a reputable supplier. Also look for disease-resistant selections. Blackberries are also susceptible to verticillium wilt, so don't locate them where potatoes, tomatoes, eggplants, or peppers have grown in the preceding 3 years. To control red-berry mites, spider mites, and whiteflies, apply a dormant spray containing lime sulfur once in winter, then again as buds are about to break.

Rosette (also called double blossom) is a serious fungal disease of blackberries in the South. New growth and blossoms of infected plants are deformed, and fruit fails to set. Most selections are susceptible, though 'Navaho' and 'Gem' have shown some resistance. Good sanitation is the best control. Cut back infected plants to 1 ft. immediately after harvest; burn or discard prunings. Keep plantings weed free. Wild blackberries can spread the disease, so be sure to plant well away from them.

Blackberries are usually planted in late winter to early spring. Set new bare-root plants an inch deeper than they grew at the garden center, their crowns covered with an inch of soil. Plant container-grown plants so that the top of the root ball is even with the soil surface.

In general, blackberries will grow in the Upper, Middle, Lower, and Coastal South. They are best located on slight slopes. Northern exposures help keep them dormant until spring freezes are past. Don't put plants where they will be in standing water during the dormant season.

Although blackberry roots are perennial, the canes are biennial; they develop and grow one year, flower and fruit the second, then die. Erect types can be tied to wire, though they don't need support. First-year canes can be pruned back a little in midsummer to encourage side branches; the lateral branches can then be cut to 1 ft. long in early spring.

Trailing and semierect types should be allowed to grow unrestricted the first year, then trained onto some kind of trellis in their second year. Train year-old canes fanwise onto the trellis; after harvest, cut to the ground all canes that have fruited. The canes of the current season—those growing beneath the trellis—should now be trained onto it; thin to desired number of canes and prune these to 6–8 ft., spreading them fanwise on trellis. Canes of semierect types often become more upright as plants mature.

The following are some of the top blackberry selections.

'Apache'. Erect, thornless canes bear a large crop of large, late-ripening berries with fine flavor. Good vigor and hardiness.

'Arapaho'. Heat zones 9–1. Erect, thornless. Large, firm berries ripen 3 weeks before 'Navaho'. Disease resistant. Will grow in north Florida.

'Black Satin'. Semierect, thornless, vigorous. Shiny black, very tart fruit. Does best in Upper South.

'Boysen' and 'Thornless Boysen'. Most commonly grown trailing types. Large, reddish berries with sweet-tart flavor, delightful aroma.

'Brazos'. Erect. Productive, disease resistant, with large, fairly firm, tart fruit. Good for mild-winter areas such as Texas, Florida, Gulf Coast states.

'Cherokee'. Erect, thorny. Firm berries with excellent flavor. Resists anthracnose. Heat tolerant. Good for Gulf Coast, north Florida.

'Chester'. Semierect, thornless, heavy bearing, and resistant to cane blight. Very cold tolerant.

'Cheyenne'. Erect. Vigorous and moderately thorny. Large, firm fruit with very good flavor. Excellent for freezing. Resistant to rust.

'Chickasaw'. Erect, thorny canes. Very productive. Large fruit.

'Choctaw'. Erect. Ripens early, producing berries with excellent flavor and very small seeds. Heat tolerant.

'Darrow'. Erect. A heavy bearer, with large berries ripening over a long season. Reliable in Virginia.

'Dirksen'. Semierect, thornless selection with large, sweet, glossy black berries. Resistant to anthracnose, leaf spot, and mildew. Good selection for Delaware, Maryland, and Virginia.

'Flordagrand'. Heat zones 9–1. Vigorous, thorny evergreen canes are somewhat trailing. Large, tasty berries. Well adapted to hot, humid summers and mild winters. Plant with 'Oklawaha' for best pollination.

'Gem'. Trailing, thorny canes. Excellent berries. Resists rosette.

'Hull'. Erect. Heavy bearing, with large, glossy black fruit that holds up well in heat.

'Illini Hardy'. Erect, very thorny. Cold hardy. Introduced by University of Illinois. Good in southern Midwest.

'Kiowa'. Developed by the University of Arkansas. Erect, vigorous, very thorny. Extra-large fruit matures over a long season. Performs well in areas where 'Shawnee' succeeds. Resistant to rust.

'Navaho'. Heat zones 9–1. Erect, thornless. Firm, sweet fruit that ripens late. Resistant to diseases (including rosette). Heat tolerant. Will grow in north Florida.

'Oklawaha'. Heat zones 9–1. Trailing. Vigorous, partially evergreen to evergreen. Developed for Florida and other areas with hot, humid summers and mild winters. Large, good-tasting berries. Best production when planted near 'Flordagrand' for pollination.

'Rosborough'. Erect. Resembles 'Brazos', but fruit is smaller, sweeter, ripens earlier. Heat tolerant. Good choice for Texas.

'Shawnee'. Erect. Heavy crop ripens late, over a long period. Large, glossy, sweet black berries.

'Thornfree'. Semierect, thornless canes bearing large crop of tart berries. Productive from Maryland south to North Carolina and west to Arkansas.

'Triple Crown'. Semierect; late. An improved 'Chester' type with large, very flavorful berries. Vigorous canes.

BLACKBERRY LILY. See BELAMCANDA

BLACK CALLA. See ARUM palaestinum

BLACK-EYED SUSAN. See RUDBECKIA hirta

BLACK-EYED SUSAN VINE. See THUNBERGIA alata

BLACK GUM. See NYSSA sylvatica

BLACK SNAKEROOT. See CIMICIFUGA racemosa

BLANKET FLOWER. See GAILLARDIA

BLAZING STAR. See LIATRIS

BLEEDING HEART. See DICENTRA

BLEEDING HEART VINE. See CLERODENDRUM thomsoniae

BLETILLA striata (B. hyacinthina)

CHINESE GROUND ORCHID, HARDY ORCHID

Orchidaceae

TERRESTRIAL ORCHID

✂ US, MS, LS, CS H 9–5

☼ FILTERED SUN OR PARTIAL SHADE

💧 REGULAR WATER DURING GROWTH AND BLOOM

Bletilla striata

Native to China and Japan. Each 1- to 1½-ft. stem carries up to 12 pinkish purple, 2-in. blossoms resembling cattleyas. Bloom lasts for about 6 weeks in late spring or early summer. Medium to yellowish green leaves, three to six to a plant, remain attractive into early fall. 'Alba' is a white-flowered form. 'First Kiss' has white-edged leaves and small white blossoms flushed purple on the lip. *B. s. albostriata* bears light pink blossoms above leaves striped in green and white.

Grow in pots or in ground. Plant pseudobulbs anytime during dormancy (late fall to early spring), 1 ft. apart, with tops 1 in. below soil surface. Plant in humus-rich, well-drained soil; mulch if temperatures will drop below 20°F. Protect from slugs and snails when leaves emerge. Taper off watering when foliage begins to yellow in fall; discontinue when leaves have died back. Plant forms large clumps that can be divided in early spring, before growth starts. (It blooms better, however, when crowded.)

BLOOD FLOWER. See ASCLEPIAS curassavica

BLOODLEAF. See IRESINE herbstii

BLUEBEARD. See CARYOPTERIS

BLUEBELL. See HYACINTHOIDES, SCILLA

BLUEBERRY

Ericaceae

DECIDUOUS SHRUB

✂ ZONES VARY BY TYPE

☼ FULL SUN

💧 REGULAR WATER

Blueberry

Native to eastern North America, blueberries thrive in soil conditions that suit rhododendrons and azaleas, to which they are related. Plants require sun and moist, well-drained acid soil (pH 4.5–5.5). Where soil pH isn't acidic enough, create proper conditions by adding sulfur and sphagnum peat moss; or grow plants in containers filled with acidic potting mix.

Most blueberries grown for fruit are also handsome plants suitable for hedges or shrub borders. Dark green or blue-green leaves to 3 in. long change to red, orange, or yellow combinations in autumn. Spring flowers are small, white or pinkish, urn shaped. Summer fruit is very decorative. Set plants about 3 ft. apart for an informal hedge; as individual shrubs, space them at least 4–5 ft. apart.

Blueberries are available bare-root or in containers. Plant in late winter to early spring. Position crown so that it is ½ in. above the ground. Grow at least two kinds for better pollination, resulting in larger berries and bigger yields per plant. For a long harvest season, choose types that ripen at different times. Blueberries have fine roots near the soil surface; keep them moist but don't subject them to standing water. A 4- to 6-in.-thick mulch of pine straw, ground bark, or the like will protect roots and help conserve soil moisture. Don't cultivate around the plants.

Plants often produce so many fruit buds that berries are undersized and growth of plants slows down. Pruning will prevent overbearing. Keep first-year plants from bearing by stripping off flowers; on older plants, cut back ends of twigs until fruit buds are widely spaced. Or simply remove some of oldest branches each year. Also get rid of all weak shoots. Netting will keep birds from getting the berries before you do.

In home gardens, blueberries don't usually suffer from serious pests or diseases requiring regular controls. One exception is blueberry stem blight, caused by the fungus *Botryosphaeria dothidea*, which can be a severe problem for all blueberries in the Southeast. The disease enters plants through wounds in the bark and causes rapid death of some or many stems, which drop their leaves and turn dark brown to black. Young plants may be killed outright. There is no chemical control; prompt pruning of infected stems back to healthy wood is the best way to limit the disease. Stop fertilizing after July to reduce succulent new growth, which is more vulnerable to infection. Avoid the selections 'Bluechip' and 'Bounty', which are very susceptible.

The following are some of the major types of blueberries grown. (For ornamental relatives, see *Vaccinium*.)

Northern highbush blueberries. Heat zones 7–1. Selections of *Vaccinium corymbosum*, these are the blueberries that are usually found in grocery stores. They're the best tasting, but because they dislike mild winters and extended summer heat, they are recommended for only the Upper and Middle South. Most grow upright to 6 ft. or more; a few are rather spreading and top out at under 5 ft. Most ripen their berries between June and August.

'Berkeley'. Midseason. Open, spreading, tall. Large light blue berries.

'Bluecrop'. Midseason. Attractive tall, erect shrub. Large berries with excellent flavor.

'Bluejay'. Early midseason. Very vigorous, tall plant. Large crop of medium-size, mild-flavored fruit that holds well on the bush.

'Coville'. Late. Very attractive tall, open, spreading shrub with unusually large leaves. Long clusters of very large light blue berries.

'Darrow'. Late. Vigorous, upright grower. Very large berries, up to the size of a quarter. Heavy producer.

'Duke'. Early. Upright plant. Firm, large fruit. Heavy producer. ▶

B

WHAT BLUEBERRIES NEED

CLIMATE: Rabbiteye and Southern highbush types take extended heat better than Northern highbush kinds. Choose the type best suited to your region.

SOIL: Fertile, well drained, quite acid (pH 4.5–5.5), containing lots of organic matter.

MOISTURE: Keep soil moist, especially while plants are fruiting.

MULCHING: A 4- to 6-in.-deep layer of mulch placed around the plants will cool the soil, conserve moisture, and discourage weeds.

POLLINATION: For the best crops, plant two or more selections.

'Bluecrop'

'Earliblue'. Early. Tall and erect, with large, heavy-textured leaves. Large berries of excellent flavor.

'Elliott'. Late. Tall and upright plant; medium to large berries with excellent flavor.

'Herbert'. Late. Vigorous, open, spreading plant. Berries are among the largest and best flavored.

'Patriot'. Midseason. Large, firm, tasty berries. Consistently high yields.

Southern highbush blueberries. These relatively new selections are hybrids of *Vaccinium corymbosum*, *V. ashei*, and *V. darrowi*. They combine the Northern highbush fruit quality with the rabbiteye tolerance for heat and mild winters, and they ripen up to a month earlier than rabbiteye blueberries do. They generally can be grown in the Middle, Lower, and Coastal South and have performed well in southern Georgia and the Florida Panhandle. Heat zones 9–1. Most reach 4–6 ft. tall. Form varies from upright to spreading. Recommended selections include the following.

'Blue Ridge'. Midseason. Small, dense shrub. Large, high-quality fruit. Performs best in Middle South.

'Georgiagem'. Early. Large and upright. Medium-size fruit with excellent flavor. Does well in Middle and Lower South.

'Jubilee'. Midseason. Upright, vigorous. Medium-size, good-quality fruit.

'Magnolia'. Midseason. Vigorous, spreading plant. Medium-size fruit of fine quality.

'Misty'. Early. Large shrub. Heavy producer of sky blue, medium-size berries of excellent quality. 'Sharpblue' is best pollenizer.

'O'Neal'. Early. Medium-size bush with spreading habit. Large light blue fruit of excellent quality. Best-tasting Southern highbush selection (but susceptible to stem canker).

'Sharpblue'. Early. Large, fast-growing shrub. Large light blue berries with sweet-tart flavor.

'Summit'. Midseason to late. Semiupright plant; large, excellent-quality berries.

'Sunshine Blue'. Midseason. Compact, reaching only 3 ft. tall; makes an attractive landscape plant. Large light blue berries with tangy flavor. Self-fertile. Tolerates a higher soil pH than other blueberries.

Rabbiteye blueberries. Zones MS, LS, CS; 9–7. Like Southern highbush blueberries, these selections of the Southeast native *Vaccinium ashei* are adapted to hot, humid summers and mild winters. They are often taller and wider than highbush plants and ripen their large light blue berries from May into August, depending on location and selection. Can be grown as far south as Ocala, Florida. Fruit is not generally as tasty as that of highbush types, although it's still quite good. Foliage has good fall color. The following list includes some of the most flavorful selections.

'Austin'. Early. Upright, productive. Large berries with good flavor.

'Baldwin'. Late. Vigorous, upright, and productive. Dark blue, medium-size berries with good flavor. Holds well on the bush.

'Beckyblue'. Early. Tall, upright bush with medium to large berries of excellent quality.

'Brightwell'. Midseason. Tolerant of spring freezes. Large, sweet, light blue berries.

'Briteblue'. Late. Open, spreading form. Large light blue berries with fair flavor.

'Centurion'. Late, after 'Tifblue'. Vigorous, upright, and productive. Dark blue, medium to large fruit with good flavor.

'Chaucer'. Late. Vigorous, tall, and spreading. Medium to large berries with fair to good flavor. Blooms early; not for colder areas.

'Choice'. Late. Vigorous, tall, and productive plant. Dark blue, small to medium-size berries of good quality. Blooms early; not for colder areas.

'Climax'. Early. Upright and spreading. Good pollenizer. Medium-size dark blue berries.

'Delite'. Midseason to late. Medium-large light blue fruit. Excellent flavor. Blooms in very early spring; flowers may be killed in areas with late freezes in spring.

'Powderblue'. Midseason. Vigorous, tall, and productive. Large powder blue berries of excellent quality. Resists cracking after rain.

'Premier'. Early. Large light blue fruit.

'Tifblue'. Midseason to late. Vigorous, upright. Good commercial selection. Firm light blue berries with excellent flavor (tart until completely ripe). The most cold-hardy rabbiteye.

'Woodward'. Early. Shorter, more spreading than other rabbiteyes. Rather soft light blue berries, tart until fully ripe.

BLUEBONNET. See LUPINUS

BLUE BUTTONS. See KNAUTIA arvensis

BLUE CURLS. See PHACELIA congesta

BLUE DAWN FLOWER. See IPOMOEA indica

BLUE DAZE. See EVOLVULUS glomeratus

BLUE-EYED GRASS. See SISYRINCHIUM bellum

BLUE-EYED MARY. See OMPHALODES verna

BLUE FESCUE. See FESTUCA glauca

BLUE FLAG. See IRIS versicolor

BLUE GINGER. See DICHORISANDRA thyrsiflora

BLUE GRAMA GRASS. See BOUTELOUA gracilis

BLUEGRASS. See POA

BLUE LACE FLOWER. See TRACHYMENE coerulea

BLUE LYME GRASS. See LEYMUS arenarius

BLUE MIST. See CARYOPTERIS ×clandonensis

BLUE PEA VINE. See CLITORIA ternatea

BLUE SAGE. See ERANTHEMUM pulchellum

BLUE SPIRAEA. See CARYOPTERIS incana

BLUESTAR. See AMSONIA

BLUE STAR CREEPER. See PRATIA pedunculata

BLUESTEM. See ANDROPOGON

BLUETS. See HOUSTONIA caerulea

BLUNT-NOSE FRANGIPANI. See PLUMERIA obtusa

BOCCONIA cordata. See MACLEAYA cordata

BOG ROSEMARY. See ANDROMEDA polifolia

BOK CHOY. See ASIAN GREENS

BOLIVIAN SUNSET. See GLOXINIA sylvatica

BOLTONIA

FALSE ASTER

Asteraceae (Compositae)

PERENNIALS

US, MS, LS, CS

FULL SUN OR LIGHT SHADE

REGULAR WATER

Boltonia asteroides

These tall asters are much loved for the masses of showy blooms they bear in late summer and fall. They like moist, fertile soil containing lots of organic matter and will tolerate very damp soil. Good for the back of the border.

B. asteroides. FALSE ASTER. Heat zones 9–1. Native to eastern U.S. Tall stems bear broad, mounded clusters of yellow-centered white, pink, or pale to deeper purple flowers about ¾ in. across; blossoms resemble Michaelmas daisies *(Aster novi-belgii)*. Plant grows to 6 ft. or taller and about 3 ft. wide; may need support to keep from flopping over after rain or overhead watering. 'Pink Beauty' has pink flowers. 'Snowbank' is a more compact (to 5 ft. tall) and upright selection than the species, with larger flowers in pure white.

B. decurrens. WINGED FALSE ASTER. Heat zones 8–3. Rarely seen species with larger, more numerous leaves and showier blooms than *B. asteroides*—huge masses of inch-wide white flowers with yellow centers. May reach 7 ft. tall and about 3 ft. wide. Listed as a threatened species; its only remaining wild populations are in its native range of Illinois and Missouri. Buy plants only from reputable nurseries that start their plants from seed.

Bombacaceae. This tropical family of trees and shrubs contains a popular genus grown in mild-winter areas: *Chorisia*, both species of which have showy flowers.

Boraginaceae. The borage family consists of annuals and perennials (rarely shrubs or trees), most of which have small flowers in coiled clusters that straighten as bloom progresses. Forget-me-not *(Myosotis)* is a familiar example.

BORAGO officinalis

BORAGE

Boraginaceae

ANNUAL

US, MS, LS, CS, TS

FULL SUN OR PARTIAL SHADE

MODERATE WATER

Borago officinalis

Native European herb forms a rounded clump 2–3 ft. high, 1½–2 ft. wide. Bristly gray-green leaves to 4–6 in. long are edible, with a cucumber-like flavor, but many people grow the plant simply for its summer flowers: pretty, star-shaped, inch-wide blue blossoms that nod in leafy clusters from branched stems.

Tolerates poor soil. Reseeds itself, but deep taproot makes transplanting difficult. In most of the South, the best way to start borage is to sow seeds in place in spring, after the danger of frost is past. In the Coastal and Tropical South, sow in fall and grow as a fall-into-spring crop. Use small, tender leaves in salads, pickle them, or cook them as you would greens. Cut flowers are attractive in arrangements and can also be used as a decorative garnish.

BOSTON FERN. See NEPHROLEPIS exaltata 'Bostoniensis'

BOSTON IVY. See PARTHENOCISSUS tricuspidata

BO-TREE. See FICUS religiosa

BOTTLEBRUSH. See CALLISTEMON

BOTTLE PALM. See BEAUCARNEA recurvata

BOUGAINVILLEA

Nyctaginaceae

EVERGREEN SHRUBBY VINES

CS, TS 12–10; OR GROW IN POTS

FULL SUN

MODERATE TO REGULAR WATER

Bougainvillea 'San Diego Red'

For sheer spectacle and exuberance, no flowering vines surpass bougainvilleas. Native to Central and South America, they're common in Florida, South Texas, and along the Gulf and south Atlantic coasts. And with the advent of low-growing, shrubby types that can be bought in full bloom and grown in containers, more Southerners can enjoy these plants than ever before. Established vines withstand light frosts, but plan to take the plants indoors to a sunny window for the winter if you live where temperatures drop below 20°F.

Bougainvillea's vibrant colors come not from its small, inconspicuous true flowers, but from the three large bracts that surround them. Heaviest bloom comes during the cooler months of spring and fall and, in Florida, in winter. Both single- and double-flowering kinds are sold; double sorts can look messy, as they hold faded blooms for a long time.

These vines are fast, vigorous growers, reaching 15–30 ft., depending on the selection. Stiff stems are armed with long, needlelike thorns and are moderately to densely clothed in medium green, 2½-in., heart-shaped leaves. Bougainvilleas are superb trained against walls or on sturdy fences, trellises, or arbors. They have no means of attachment (though their thorns help them scramble through shrubs and trees), so you must tie stems to the support while the vine is young.

Plant in a sunny spot in spring, after the last frost. Provide well-drained, slightly acid soil; alkaline soil can cause chlorosis (yellow leaves with green veins). Fertilize in spring and summer. Water regularly while plants are actively growing; then ease off in midsummer to promote better flowering in fall. Don't be afraid to prune to shape or rejuvenate the plant. Heavy pruning is best done after the blooming period. Nip back long stems during the growing season to produce more flowering wood. Shrubby forms and heavily pruned plants make good self-supporting container plants for terrace or patio. Without support and with occasional corrective pruning, bougainvillea becomes a broad, sprawling shrub; a bank or ground cover; or an attractive choice for hanging baskets. ▶

WHAT BOUGAINVILLEAS NEED

CAREFUL PLANTING: Roots do not knit soil together in a firm root ball, and they are highly sensitive to disturbance. To minimize shock when planting, cut off container bottom; then set both plant and container in planting hole. Slide container up over the plant, filling in with soil as you go. Don't worry about damaging upper part of plant as you do so; stems are pliant, with little horizontal growth.

STRONG SUPPORT: Fasten shoots to a sturdy support so they won't whip in wind. Strong gusts can shred leaves against sharp thorns along stems.

NUTRIENTS: Fertilize when growing season begins and again in early summer.

MOISTURE: Water regularly in spring, moderately during bloom period.

Bougainvillea 'Orange King'

TOP: *Bougainvillea* 'Barbara Karst'
BOTTOM: *Bougainvillea* 'Rosenka'

TOP: *Bougainvillea* 'California Gold'
BOTTOM: *Bougainvillea* 'Mary Palmer's Enchantment'

TOP: *Bougainvillea* 'Hawaii'
BOTTOM: *Bougainvillea* 'Camarillo Festival'

TOP: *Bougainvillea* 'Oo-La-La'
BOTTOM: *Bougainvillea* 'Texas Dawn'

All of the following are tall-growing vines unless otherwise noted. Most are hybrids produced from *B. glabra* and *B. spectabilis* (from Brazil) and *B. peruviana* (from Colombia and Peru).

'Afterglow'. Heavy bloomer with yellow-orange blossoms. Open growth, sparse foliage.

'Barbara Karst'. Bright red in sun, bluish crimson in shade; blooms young and for a long period. Vigorous growth. Fast comeback after frost. A popular selection.

'Betty Hendry' ('Indian Maid'). Basically red but with touches of yellow and purple. Blooms young and for a long period.

'Brilliant Variegated'. Spreading, mounding shrub. Leaves variegated with gray green and silver. Brick red bracts. Often used in hanging baskets, containers.

'California Gold' ('Sunset'). Deep golden yellow. Blooms young.

'Camarillo Festival'. Hot pink to coral to gold blend.

'Cherry Blossom'. Double-flowered rose pink, with centers of white to pale green.

'Crimson Jewel'. Vigorous, shrubby, sprawling plant. Good in containers, as shrub, or as sunny bank cover. Lower growth, better color than 'Temple Fire'. Heavy bloom, long season.

'Don Mario'. Large and vigorous vine with huge clusters of deep purple-red blooms.

'Hawaii' ('Raspberry Ice'). Shrubby, mounding, spreading. Leaves have golden yellow margins. Red-tinged new leaves; cherry red bracts. Good hanging basket plant. Regardless of its tropical name, it's one of the hardiest.

'Isabel Greensmith'. Bracts variously described as orange, red orange, or red with yellow tinting.

'Jamaica White'. White bracts veined in light green. Blooms young. Moderately vigorous.

'James Walker'. Big reddish purple bracts on big vine.

'La Jolla'. Bright red bracts; compact, shrubby habit. Good shrub or container plant.

'Lavender Queen'. An improved *B. spectabilis*, with bigger bracts, heavier bloom.

'Manila Red'. Double magenta red; blossoms are carried in heavy clusters.

'Mary Palmer's Enchantment'. Bracts are pure white. Quite vigorous, very large-growing vine.

'Mrs. Butt' ('Crimson Lake'). Old-fashioned type with good crimson color. Needs lots of heat for bloom. Moderately vigorous.

'Oo-La-La'. Vibrant magenta red. Compact, trailing form to 1½ ft. tall, 6–8 ft. wide; good for hanging baskets. Blooms over a long season.

'Orange King'. Bronzy orange. Open growth. Needs long summer; won't take frost.

'Pink Tiara'. Abundant pale pink to rose bracts over a long season.

'Purple Queen'. Deep purple bracts; compact grower. Can reach 15 ft. with support; as a trailer, it grows 1½ ft. tall, 6–8 ft. wide.

'Rosea'. Large rose red bracts on large vine.

'Rosenka'. Can be held to shrub proportions if the occasional wild shoot is pruned out. Gold bracts age to pink.

'San Diego Red' ('San Diego', 'Scarlett O'Hara'). One of the best, with large deep green leaves that hold well in mild winters and deep red bracts over a long season. Vigorous, hardy, and high climbing. Can be trained to tree form by staking and pruning.

'Singapore Pink'. Bright pink. Shrubby and compact; can easily be kept to 3–4 ft. high and wide. Thornless.

'Singapore White'. White bloomer. Shrubby, compact plant; can be held to 3–4 ft. high and wide. Thornless.

'Southern Rose'. Lavender rose to pink.

B. spectabilis (*B. brasiliensis*). Hardy and vigorous. Blooms well in cool summers. Purple bracts.

'Tahitian Dawn'. Big vine with gold bracts aging to rosy purple.

'Tahitian Maid'. Double-flowered blush pink.

'Temple Fire'. Shrublike growth to 4 ft. high, 6 ft. wide. Partially deciduous. Bronze red.

'Texas Dawn'. Choice, vigorous plant. Purplish pink bracts form large sprays of color.

'Torch Glow'. An oddity: an erect, multistemmed plant to 6 ft. Needs no support. Reddish pink bracts grow close to the stems and are partially hidden by foliage.

'White Madonna'. Pure white.

BOUNCING BET. See SAPONARIA officinalis

BOUTELOUA gracilis

BLUE GRAMA GRASS, MOSQUITO GRASS

Poaceae (Gramineae)

PERENNIAL GRASS

⚡ US, MS, LS, CS, TS ☀ 9–5

☼ FULL SUN

◊ LITTLE WATER

Bouteloua gracilis

Native to dry grasslands of North America. Clumping growth to 1½–2 ft. high and 1 ft. wide, with very narrow semievergreen leaves and, in summer, 1½-in.-long, dark red to purple flower spikes. Spikes are held at a right angle to the slender stems and have the look of hovering mosquitoes. If mowed at 1½ in., blue grama grass makes a fair lawn requiring little maintenance or water; also used for pasture grass. Tolerates the sunny, arid, alkaline conditions of Central and West Texas and western Oklahoma. Sow seed at 1 pound per 1,000 sq. ft. Not for high-rainfall areas.

BOUVARDIA

Rubiaceae

EVERGREEN SHRUBS

✿ CS, TS ❋ 12–10

◑ PARTIAL SHADE

◊ ◉ WATER NEEDS VARY BY SPECIES

Bouvardia longiflora
'Albatross'

These plants are valued for their showy clusters of tubular flowers; their growth habit is loose, often straggling. One type has fragrant blossoms, but it is also the most tender and looks poorest after flowers are gone. The unscented red-flowered species are hardier, easier to grow. All appreciate well-drained soil, midday shade. To encourage compact growth, prune hard annually after bloom.

B. glaberrima. Native to mountain canyons in southern Arizona, New Mexico. To 3 ft. tall and wide. Shrubby, but top growth dies back in cold weather. Smooth green leaves 1–3 in. long. Clustered 1-in., red (rarely pink or white), unscented flowers. Little water.

B. longiflora 'Albatross' (B. humboldtii 'Albatross'). Selection of a Mexican species. Jasmine-scented, 3-in., snow white flowers appear at almost any time; excellent in bouquets. Plant is 2–3 ft. high and 2 ft. wide, with paired 2-in. leaves. Pinch out stem tips to make bushier. If soil is poor, grow in tubs or raised beds in rich, fast-draining soil mix. 'Stephanie' is more compact and floriferous. Regular water.

B. ternifolia (B. jacquinii). Native to Texas, Mexico. To 3 ft. tall, 2½–3 ft. wide; 2-in. leaves in whorls of three or four. Produces unscented, inch-long, red flowers in loose clusters at branch ends in summer and early autumn. Forms are available with pink, rose, or coral blossoms. Little water.

BOWER VINE. See PANDOREA jasminoides

BOWLES' GOLDEN GRASS. See MILIUM effusum 'Aureum'

BOWMAN'S ROOT. See GILLENIA trifoliata

BOX, BOXWOOD. See BUXUS

BOX ELDER. See ACER negundo

BOX HONEYSUCKLE. See LONICERA nitida

BOYSENBERRY. See BLACKBERRY

BRACHYSCOME iberidifolia

SWAN RIVER DAISY

Asteraceae (Compositae)

ANNUAL

✿ US, MS, LS, CS, TS ❋ 12–1

◔ FULL SUN

◉ REGULAR WATER

Brachyscome iberidifolia

Neat, charming Australian daisy bears a profusion of 1-in. blue, pink, or white flowers in spring and summer. The plant has finely divided leaves and forms a mound about 1 ft. tall, 1½ ft. across. Useful at the front of a border, in pots, in rock gardens. Sow seeds where plants are to grow—in fall in Florida, in spring elsewhere. 'Blue Star' has blue flowers with unique tubular petals. 'Blue Splendor' features different shades of blue, and central disk varies in color, too—it may be yellow or black.

BRACKEN. See PTERIDIUM aquilinum

BRACTEANTHA bracteata
(Helichrysum bracteatum)

BUSH STRAWFLOWER

Asteraceae (Compositae)

SHRUBBY PERENNIAL

✿ TS ❋ 12–10; ANYWHERE AS ANNUAL

◔ FULL SUN

◉ REGULAR WATER

Bracteantha bracteata

Australian native. Formerly considered an atypical example of annual strawflower *(Helichrysum bracteatum)*, this plant has now been given a genus of its own. Flowers, held well above the foliage, resemble strawflowers in having many rows of papery bracts; narrow leaves are gray green. 'Diamond Head' grows 8 in. high and 1½ ft. wide, with 1½-in., golden yellow flowers. 'Dargan Hill Monarch' is larger overall at 2½ ft. tall and 3–6 ft. wide; leaves to 6 in. long and golden yellow flowers to 3½ in. across. 'Cockatoo' is similar but has light yellow blossoms. Plants in the Florabella series form sturdy, 1- to 1½-ft. mounds with blossoms in pink, white, lemon yellow, or particularly rich golden tones. Newer Sundaze series includes selections with golden yellow, bronzy gold, lemon yellow, pink, or white blossoms on plants 10–14 in. high and wide. Flowers of all types may be dried for arrangements. Needs good drainage.

BRAHEA (Erythea)

Arecaceae (Palmae)

PALMS

✿ ZONES VARY BY SPECIES

◔ FULL SUN

◊ LITTLE OR NO WATER

Brahea armata

These fan palms from Mexico resemble washingtonias but are shorter growing and less cold hardy. Fanlike leaves reach 3–6 ft. across. All of the species listed here can tolerate drought.

B. armata. BLUE FAN PALM. Zones CS, TS; 12–10. Hardy to 15°F. Grows slowly to 40 ft. tall, with top spreading to 15–20 ft. Leaves are a silvery blue in color, almost white. Creamy flowers in summer. Takes heat and wind.

B. brandegeei. SAN JOSE HESPER PALM. Zones TS; 12–10. Hardy to 26°F. Slow grower with slender, flexible trunk. Reaches 40 ft. tall and 15 ft. wide. Light gray-green foliage. Trunk sheds oldest leaves.

B. dulcis. MEXICAN CLIFF PALM. Zones TS; 12–10. Hardy to 25°F. To 20 ft. high, 8 ft. wide. Trunk may be solitary or suckering, foliage green or silvery blue. Fronds are smaller and more delicate than those of most fan palms. Tough and drought resistant; often grows right out of rocky cliff sides in its native range.

BRAKE. See PTERIS

BRAMBLE. See RUBUS

BRASSAIA actinophylla. See SCHEFFLERA actinophylla

Brassicaceae. The mustard, or cress, family contains many food plants and ornamentals as well as a number of weeds. Shared characteristic of all is a four-petaled, cross-shaped flower. Familiar members include the cabbage group, radish, turnip, stock *(Matthiola)*, and sweet alyssum *(Lobularia)*. This family was formerly called Cruciferae.

BRAZILIAN FLAME BUSH. See CALLIANDRA tweedii

BRAZILIAN ORCHID TREE. See BAUHINIA forficata

BRAZILIAN PLUME FLOWER. See JUSTICIA carnea

BRAZILIAN SKY FLOWER. See DURANTA stenostachya

B

BREYNIA nivosa (B. disticha)

SNOW BUSH

Euphorbiaceae

EVERGREEN SHRUB

✍ TS ⛅ 12–10; OR HOUSEPLANT

☼ ◐ FULL SUN OR LIGHT SHADE; BRIGHT INDIRECT LIGHT

💧 REGULAR WATER

Breynia nivosa
'Roseopicta'

Native to Melanesia. Delicate, open growth to 3–4 ft. tall and wide, with gracefully arching branches in zigzag pattern. Thin, roundish leaves are rich green variegated with white; they are held nearly opposite each other along the branches. Flowers insignificant. Can naturalize in humid tropical or subtropical regions. Selection 'Roseopicta', sweet pea bush or calico plant, has leaves that are mottled red, pink, white, and green. Colorful plant, though prone to mites in dry indoor air.

BRIMEURA amethystina (Hyacinthus amethystinus)

Liliaceae

PERENNIAL FROM BULB

✍ US, MS, LS, CS ⛅ 9–5

☼ FULL SUN

💧 REGULAR WATER DURING GROWTH AND BLOOM

Brimeura amethystina

European native for naturalizing or for rock gardens. In bulb and leaf, resembles a small hyacinth, but 10-in. spikes of bright blue, pendent flowers in spring to summer look like bluebells (*Hyacinthoides*). 'Alba' is a white-flowering form. Plant in mid- to late fall (before ground freezes), 2 in. deep and 3 in. apart. Keep soil moist after planting; continue to water regularly until foliage yellows after bloom. Needs no moisture during dormancy.

BRIZA maxima

RATTLESNAKE GRASS, QUAKING GRASS

Poaceae (Gramineae)

ANNUAL GRASS

✍ US, MS, LS, CS, TS ⛅ 12–1

☼ FULL SUN

◌ NO IRRIGATION NEEDED

Briza maxima

Native to Mediterranean region. Delicate, graceful ornamental grass; attractive in fresh or dried arrangements. Grows 1–2 ft. high. Leaves are ¼ in. wide, to 6 in. long. Clusters of nodding, seed-bearing spikelets (like rattlesnake rattles), ½ in. long (or longer), papery and straw colored when dry, dangle on threadlike stems. Scatter seed where plants are to grow; thin seedlings to 1 ft. apart. *B. media* is similar but perennial.

BROCCOLI

Brassicaceae (Cruciferae)

BIENNIAL GROWN AS COOL-SEASON ANNUAL

✍ US, MS, LS, CS, TS ⛅ 6–1

☼ FULL SUN

💧 REGULAR WATER

Thought to be a Mediterranean native, broccoli grows 2–3 ft. tall, with a branching habit. Many Southerners grow two crops each year—one in spring and one in fall. To produce the mammoth heads you admire in seed catalogs or

Broccoli

the grocery store, you'd need longer periods of cool weather than we have over most of the South, but you can realistically expect heads to grow to 4–8 in. across.

To get a jump on the growing season, always start broccoli from transplants (you can buy them at the garden center or grow your own from seed in cell-packs). Broccoli doesn't grow well after warm weather arrives in spring, and a hard freeze in fall will kill it. For a spring crop, set out seedlings 4 weeks before the last frost; for a fall crop, plant in late summer or early fall. In the Coastal South, plant between September and March; in the Tropical South, plant between September and January.

For spring planting, choose early-maturing types, so the heads will form before hot weather arrives. Try 'Early Emerald' (50 days between transplanting and harvest), 'Green Comet' (55 days), 'Green Duke' (55 days), 'Green Goliath' (55 days), 'Packman' (57 days), and 'Premium Crop' (58 days). All of these are also good for fall planting. In the Coastal and Tropical South, late-maturing 'Waltham 29' (80 days) is another good selection for fall planting.

Set transplants 1–1½ ft. apart in rows 2–3 ft. apart. Feed with water-soluble 20-20-20 fertilizer. Three weeks after planting, sprinkle ½ cup of 10-10-10 fertilizer per 10 ft. of row around plants. Water regularly to maintain steady, rapid growth. Harvest when the hundreds of tiny flower buds that form the head are still green and tightly closed; a head showing yellow flowers is past its prime. Cut the stem 5–6 in. below the head.

In addition to the main head, broccoli forms small (about 1-in.-wide) flower clusters or side shoots along the stem. These are usually ready to harvest 2 to 3 weeks after you cut the central head—but if the weather gets too warm, they'll quickly bloom. Production of side shoots is usually more dependable in fall. Selections noted for extended production of side shoots include 'Green Comet', 'Packman', and 'Waltham 29'.

A number of pests plague broccoli; they are usually more troublesome in spring than in fall. To prevent a buildup of soil-borne pests, plant in a different site each year. Club root is a serious fungal pest in acid soils; apply lime, if necessary, to raise the pH to at least 6.5. Floating row covers do a good job of controlling insects such as cabbage loopers, cabbageworms, cutworms, and root maggots. You can also control cutworms and root maggots by ringing the base of the plant with a collar made from cardboard. *Bacillus thuringiensis* (*Bt*; sold as Dipel) applied according to label directions controls cabbageworms and loopers.

COOL HEADS PREVAIL. *Broccoli and its cole family relatives Brussels sprouts, cabbage, and cauliflower form and keep their heads (tight florets or thick rosettes of leaves) in cool weather (55–70°F); their flavor is often improved by light frosts. When planting, keep in mind that they need fertile, well-drained soil that is kept evenly moist throughout the growing season. Common traits and needs are not all they share; the pests and soil-borne diseases that favor broccoli also favor its cousins. To control them, change planting locations annually and follow the advice given in the encyclopedia entries.* ❖

BRODIAEA

Liliaceae

PERENNIALS FROM CORMS

✍ ZONES VARY BY SPECIES

☼ FULL SUN

◌ NO IRRIGATION NEEDED

Brodiaea elegans

Many of these plants are native to the Pacific Coast, where they bloom in sunny fields and meadows in spring and early summer. Leaves are sparse and grasslike; a cluster of funnel-shaped or tubular, ½- to 2-in.-long flowers tops the stem during bloom. Good cut flowers. After blooming, the plants die to the ground. In nature, these plants are often found in adobe soil, in areas where it rains heavily in winter and early spring and corms completely dry out in summer. They appreciate similar conditions in gardens, as demonstrated by their fondness for the Texas Hill Country. If you cannot keep corms dry in summer, plant in sandy or gritty soil to lessen the chance of rot. Plant corms 2–3 in. deep and 2–4 in. apart. In cold-winter areas, grow in containers or mulch to protect from freezing and thawing.

Brodiaea includes many plants now listed under different botanical species names. The cross-references below will guide you to appropriate entries under *Triteleia*.

B. coronaria (B. grandiflora). HARVEST BRODIAEA. Zones LS, CS; 10–8. Clusters of dark blue, inch-long flowers on 6- to 10-in. stems.

B. elegans. HARVEST BRODIAEA. Zones US, MS, LS, CS, TS; 12–6. Similar to *B. coronaria*, but taller (to 16 in.). Often listed as *B. grandiflora* or *B. coronaria*.

B. laxa. See Triteleia laxa

B. minor. Zones US, MS, LS, CS; 10–8. Dark blue flowers on stems 3–4 in. long (rarely up to 1 ft. long).

B. 'Queen Fabiola'. See Triteleia laxa 'Queen Fabiola'

B. tubergenii. See Triteleia tubergenii

Bromeliaceae. This is the bromelia, or pineapple, family; all its members are called bromeliads. Most are stemless perennials with clustered leaves and showy flowers in unbranched or branched clusters. Leaves of many kinds are handsomely marked, and the flower clusters gain beauty from colorful bracts. Pineapple is the best-known example; other well-known bromeliads are *Aechmea, Billbergia, Cryptanthus,* and *Vriesia*.

Bromeliads are considered choice houseplants in most areas of the South. Kinds most often grown indoors are, in their native homes, epiphytes: plants that perch on trees or rocks and gain their sustenance from rain and from whatever leaf mold gathers around their roots. These plants often have cupped leaf bases that hold water between rains. In the mildest regions of the South, many of these epiphytic plants grow well outdoors in sheltered places.

BRONZE LOQUAT. See ERIOBOTRYA deflexa

BROOM. See CYTISUS, GENISTA

BROOM SEDGE. See ANDROPOGON virginicus

BROUSSONETIA papyrifera

PAPER MULBERRY

Moraceae

DECIDUOUS TREE

✿ US, MS, LS, CS, TS ◫ 10–6

☼ FULL SUN

◐ ◖ ● LITTLE TO REGULAR WATER

Broussonetia papyrifera

Native to China and Japan. Common name comes from inner bark, used for making paper and Polynesian tapa cloth. Has been sold as *Morus papyrifera*. Quite valuable as a shade tree where soil and climate limit choices. Tolerates heat, drought, strong winds, city pollution, and stony, sterile, or alkaline soils.

Moderate to fast growth to 50 ft., with dense, broad crown reaching 40 ft. across. Often considerably smaller and more shrublike in gardens. Suckering, weedy habit can be problem in rainy climates and highly cultivated gardens. Good in rough bank plantings. Smooth gray bark can become ridged and furrowed with age, creating handsome old specimens. Heart-shaped, sometimes lobed, 4- to 8-in. leaves are green and rough textured on the upper surface, gray and velvety underneath; edges are toothed. Blooms in spring. Flowers on male trees are catkins; on female trees, rounded flower heads are followed by red fruits if a male tree is growing nearby.

BROWALLIA

AMETHYST FLOWER

Solanaceae

ANNUALS AND PERENNIALS

✿ US, MS, LS, CS, TS

◐ PARTIAL SHADE

● REGULAR WATER

Browallia speciosa
'Marine Bells'

Choice plants for connoisseurs of blue flowers. Bear one-sided clusters of lobelia-like blooms in brilliant blue, violet, or white; blue and violet flowers are striking because of contrasting white eye or throat. Bloom profusely in warm shade or filtered sunlight. Graceful in hanging baskets or pots. Fine cut flowers. Sow seeds in early spring for summer bloom, in fall for winter color in warmest-winter areas or indoors. You can lift plants in fall, cut back, and pot; new growth will produce flowers through winter in warm spots. Usually sold as seeds.

B. americana (B. elata). Annual. Heat zones 8–1. Branching, 1–2 ft. high and wide; roundish leaves. Violet or blue flowers ½ in. long, ½ in. across, borne among leaves. Dwarf compact selection 'Sapphire' blooms profusely, bearing dark blue blossoms with a white eye.

B. speciosa. Tender perennial usually grown as annual. Heat zones 12–1. Sprawling, to 1–2 ft. high, nearly a foot wide. Flowers dark purple above, pale lilac beneath, 1½–2 in. across. 'Blue Bells Improved', with lavender-blue blooms, grows 10 in. tall, needs no pinching to make it branch. 'Marine Bells' has deep indigo blossoms, 'Silver Bells' white flowers.

BROWN-EYED SUSAN. See RUDBECKIA triloba

BRUGMANSIA

ANGEL'S TRUMPET

Solanaceae

EVERGREEN TO SEMIEVERGREEN SHRUBS

✿ LS (PROTECTED), CS, TS ◫ 12–8;
  OR GROW IN POTS

☼ ◐ FULL SUN OR LIGHT SHADE

● REGULAR WATER

☠ ALL PARTS ARE POISONOUS IF INGESTED

Brugmansia ×candida

Thanks to the tropical look of their oversize leaves and huge, exotic blossoms, brugmansias are soaring in popularity. Related to jimsonweeds, these South American natives are often confused with plants in the genus *Datura*—but brugmansias are large, woody shrubs with typically pendent flowers and bean-shaped seedpods; daturas are lower growing and herbaceous, with upward-pointing flowers and swollen, spiny seedpods. Most brugmansias bloom in summer and autumn. For *Datura*, see page 280.

Brugmansias prefer moist, fertile, well-drained soil that contains plenty of organic matter. Boggy soil results in gradual dieback and eventual death. A site providing morning sun and light afternoon shade is ideal. During active growth in spring and summer, water freely and feed every 2 weeks with a balanced water-soluble fertilizer. In fall and winter, reduce watering and cease feeding. Brugmansias are winter hardy in the Coastal and Tropical South. In the Lower South, heavy mulching in late fall is necessary. In the Upper and Middle South, treat them as annuals or grow them in containers that you take indoors for winter. Potted plants can spend winters indoors with low light and little water. Prune only after flowering.

B. arborea. Plants sold under this name are often either *B. ×candida* or *B. ×insignis*. The true *B. arborea* has smaller flowers than the plant commonly in cultivation.

B. ×candida. Fast growing to 10–12 ft. tall and wide; dull green leaves to 1 ft. long. Sweet-scented, 8- to 12-in.-long, cream to white trumpets hang straight down from the branches. 'Double White' has creamy white double blossoms, distinctly grayish green foliage. ▶

B

B. 'Charles Grimaldi'. Vigorous California hybrid between *B. ×insignis* 'Frosty Pink' and another selection. Fast growing to 10–12 ft. tall and 10 ft. wide. Huge (15-in.), golden yellow to golden orange, powerfully fragrant trumpets cover the plant during the bloom season.

B. 'Cypress Gardens'. Grows 5–10 ft. tall and not quite as wide. Blooms heavily even when small, producing 6- to 8-in. white blossoms that age to light pink; they hang straight down from the branches and are fragrant at night and in the morning. Excellent in containers.

B. ×insignis. To 10–12 ft. tall and wide. Flowers are large, flaring trumpets that are held at an angle rather than pointing straight down; they have a spicy-sweet fragrance and come in white, pink, yellow, and orange. Size ranges from 8 to 14 in. long, depending on selection. 'Frosty Pink' has salmon pink blooms; 'Jamaica Yellow' has light yellow flowers. 'Jean Pasco' has golden yellow flowers with a lighter yellow throat and a red-orange tinge at the edges. 'Orange' has rich golden yellow blooms. 'Betty Marshall' bears white blossoms on a compact plant 6–8 ft. high.

B. 'Peaches and Cream'. To 5 ft. tall and wide. Flowers over a long spring-into-fall season, producing richly perfumed, light peachy pink blossoms to 8 in. long that open from buds striped in white and green. Blooms profusely, even in small containers. Leaves are dark green, splashed with light green and edged in white and pale yellow.

B. suaveolens. Plants offered as this species are usually *B. ×insignis*.

B. 'Sunset' (B. ×candida 'Variegata'). To 5 ft. tall and wide. Big (to 1-ft.), fragrant blossoms in a light golden peach color appear in late summer. Green leaves are attractively edged in white.

B. versicolor. The most treelike species, to 15 ft. tall and wide. Huge (15-in.) flowers are a peachy apricot color; they hang straight down from the branches, covering the plant during bloom time. Blossoms are sweetly fragrant at night and in the morning. Pink- and white-flowered selections are also sold.

'Ecuador Pink' has especially fragrant pink trumpets up to 1½ ft. long, with distinctively curled edges. It blooms over a long season, from spring to fall.

BRUNFELSIA

Solanaceae

EVERGREEN TO SEMIEVERGREEN SHRUBS OR SMALL TREES

🌱 CS, TS ⊬ 12–10; OR GROW IN POTS

☼ ◗ FULL SUN OR PARTIAL SHADE

💧 REGULAR WATER

✿ ALL PARTS ARE POISONOUS IF INGESTED

Brunfelsia pauciflora 'Floribunda'

These natives of the American tropics feature clusters of showy flowers during the warmer months. The blossoms are tubular, opening out to flat, round, five-petaled disks; blooms of some species are fragrant, while those of others change color as they age. These are handsome plants that deserve the extra attention they need: grow them in rich, well-drained, slightly acid soil, and give regular feedings throughout the growing season. In alkaline soils, they will develop chlorosis (yellow leaves with green veins). Prune in spring to remove straggly growth and to shape the plants. In central and south Florida, use in large containers, as specimens, or in shrub borders. Elsewhere, grow in a pot that can be brought indoors to a sunny window for the winter.

B. americana. LADY-OF-THE-NIGHT. Large shrub or small tree to 15 ft. tall and 10 ft. wide; grows even larger in south Florida. Elliptical, 2- to 5-in.-long leaves are medium to dark green. White, 3-in. summer flowers are fragrant at night.

B. australis. MORNING-NOON-AND-NIGHT. Large shrub to 12 ft. tall and wide. Elliptical dark green leaves, 1½–5 in. long. Blooms from spring through fall, bearing sweet-scented, 1½-in.-wide flowers that open rich purple, then fade through lavender shades to white.

B. jamaicensis. To 8 ft. tall and wide. Endangered species from the Blue Mountains of Jamaica. Dark green leaves to 4 in. long; ruffled, white to cream flowers to 1½ in. across, fragrant at night. Blooms from spring to fall.

B. pauciflora (B. calycina). YESTERDAY-TODAY-AND-TOMORROW. The best known of the brunfelsias, this species gets its common name from clustered spring-to-summer flowers that quickly change from purple to lavender to white as they age; often, all three colors are present on a single plant. Oval to lance-shaped leaves reach 3–6 in. long. Recommended selections include the following three.

Brunfelsia pauciflora 'Floribunda'

'Floribunda'. Flowers to 2 in. wide are borne profusely all over the plant. Oval leaves are dark green above, pale green below, 3–4 in. long. Plant may exceed 10 ft. in height, but it can be held to 3–4 ft. by pruning. Has a rather spreading habit, with several stems from the base; width is nearly equal to height.

'Floribunda Compacta'. Two-thirds the size of the more widely planted 'Floribunda', with slightly smaller flowers but even more profuse bloom.

'Macrantha' ('Magnifica'). Least hardy of the brunfelsias listed here, suitable for planting outdoors only in south Florida. Differs from 'Floribunda' in having fewer but larger flowers, 2–4 in. across. Also has a more slender habit and bigger leaves (to 8 in. long).

B. pilosa. To 4 ft. tall and wide. Leaves 1½–3 in. long, purple when new, age to green. Deep purple, mostly solitary flowers 1½ in. across have a white ring at mouth; flowers gradually age to white. Summer bloom.

BRUNNERA macrophylla

BRUNNERA, SIBERIAN BUGLOSS

Boraginaceae

PERENNIAL

🌱 US, MS ⊬ 7–1

☼ ◗ PARTIAL TO FULL SHADE

💧 REGULAR WATER

Brunnera macrophylla

Eastern European woodland plant to 1½ ft. tall, 2 ft. wide. Heart-shaped dark green leaves, 3–4 in. wide; airy clusters of tiny, yellow-centered, clear blue flowers reminiscent of forget-me-nots (*Myosotis*). Blooms in spring—often into summer, especially in shade. Variegated-leaf selections, excellent for brightening shady areas, include 'Hadspen Cream', with foliage broadly edged in creamy white; 'Jack Frost', silver leaves with green margins and veins; and 'Langtrees', with silver-spotted foliage.

Brunnera is useful as an informal ground cover under high-branching deciduous trees; among spring-flowering shrubs such as forsythia, deciduous magnolias; and as filler between newly planted evergreen shrubs. Freely self-sows once established. Seeds you plant may not germinate easily (try freezing them before sowing). Needs well-drained, moisture-retentive soil. Increase by dividing clumps in fall.

BRUNSVIGIA rosea. See AMARYLLIS belladonna

BRUSSELS SPROUTS

Brassicaceae (Cruciferae)

BIENNIAL GROWN AS COOL-SEASON ANNUAL

🌱 US, MS, LS, CS, TS ⊬ 6–1

☼ FULL SUN

💧 REGULAR WATER

Brussels Sprouts

Raising Brussels sprouts in the South can be challenging—like their relatives broccoli, cabbage, and cauliflower, they need a long, cool growing season to produce firm, tasty, sizable sprouts. But it's well worth the effort, as each plant produces as many as 100 sprouts over a period of 6 to 8 weeks. You can grow both spring and fall crops, but fall crops are much more dependable here. In Florida and the Coastal South, plant in fall for a winter crop.

Always start with transplants. You can buy these from garden centers or sow seed yourself in cell-packs. For a spring crop, set out transplants 4 weeks before the last frost. For fall and winter harvests in the Upper, Middle, and Lower South, set them out 10 to 14 weeks before the first fall frost; in Florida and the Coastal South, plant in October. Space transplants 1½–2 ft. apart in rows about 2½ ft. apart. Feed at planting time with a water-soluble 20-20-20 fertilizer. Water regularly to keep soil evenly moist. Three to 4 weeks after planting, sprinkle ½ cup of 10-10-10 fertilizer per 10 ft. of row around plants; repeat 3 to 4 weeks later.

Sprouts develop progressively from the bottom of the plant toward the top, appearing first as tiny buds within the leaf axils. Removing the terminal growth tip when the plants are 15–20 in. tall makes the sprouts grow larger and mature more quickly; this is a particularly useful technique for spring crops. Harvest sprouts when they're about 1 in. wide. Brussels sprouts can survive occasional hard frosts (the chill even sweetens their flavor), but temperatures below 26°F may kill them. Recommended selections include 'Jade Cross Hybrid', 'Long Island Improved', 'Prince Marvel', and 'Valiant', all of which mature in about 90 days.

To prevent a buildup of soil-borne pests, plant Brussels sprouts in a different site each year. Club root is a serious fungal pest in acid soils; apply lime, if necessary, to raise the pH to at least 6.5. Floating row covers do a good job of controlling insects such as cabbage loopers, cabbageworms, cutworms, and root maggots. You can also control cutworms and root maggots by ringing the base of the plant with a collar made from cardboard. *Bacillus thuringiensis* (*Bt;* sold as Dipel) applied according to label directions controls cabbageworms and loopers.

BUCHLOE dactyloides

BUFFALO GRASS

Poaceae (Gramineae)

PERENNIAL GRASS

✓ US, MS, LS, CS, TS H 12–2

☼ FULL SUN

◌ LITTLE WATER

Buchloe dactyloides

Native from central Montana south to Arizona, this grass makes a relatively low-maintenance lawn that takes hard wear and looks fairly good with very little irrigation during dry periods. Green from late spring to the first hard frosts; then straw colored through winter. Not well adapted to Florida or Gulf Coast. Buffalo grass is at its best when allowed to grow tall but needs mowing three times a year to form a good thick turf. Cut it short (to about 1 in.) in late winter or very early spring; then cut it to 2 in. in mid-June and again to 2 in. in early fall. Between mowings, it will grow to 4–6 in.

Sodded lawns look best, but seed and plugs are less expensive. Sow seed at the rate of 2 pounds per 1,000 sq. ft. In absence of rain, soak soil occasionally to a depth of 1 ft. while grass is getting started. Slow to sprout and fill in. Plant 4-in.-wide plugs 3–4 ft. apart in prepared soil in spring; cover should be complete in two seasons. Once established, buffalo grass spreads rapidly, even invasively, by surface runners.

Selections include the following.

'Bison'. Very cold hardy. Produces seed heads. Summer color and thickness not as good as '609' or 'Prairie'. Available as seed.

'Prairie'. Spreads more aggressively than '609', but summer color is not quite as good. Produces a thick turf without seed heads. Available as sod or plugs.

'609'. Lovely blue-green summer color. Makes a thick lawn with no seed heads. Available as sod or plugs.

'Stampede'. Dense-growing semidwarf to about 4 in. high. Attractive green color. Available only as sod.

'Texoka'. Produces lots of seed heads. Inferior quality for home-lawn use; much better suited to roadsides and industrial parks. An old selection, available as seed.

'Top Gun'. Superior to 'Bison' in appearance and thickness. Produces seed heads. Available as seed.

BUCKEYE. See AESCULUS

BUCKTHORN, CAROLINA. See RHAMNUS caroliniana

BUCKWHEAT TREE. See CLIFTONIA monophylla

BUDDLEIA

BUTTERFLY BUSH

Buddleiaceae

EVERGREEN, SEMIEVERGREEN, OR DECIDUOUS SHRUBS

✓ ZONES VARY BY SPECIES

☼ ◐ FULL SUN OR LIGHT SHADE

◗ ◗ MODERATE TO REGULAR WATER

Buddleia davidii

Colorful spring or summer flowers, sweet fragrance, attractiveness to butterflies, and easy care make these shrubs extremely popular. The vast majority sold are selections of *B. davidii*, but many other species are highly ornamental and deserve their fair share of attention. All types prefer sun and fertile, moist, well-drained soil. Not browsed by deer. Removing spent flowers extends bloom.

B. alternifolia. FOUNTAIN BUTTERFLY BUSH. Deciduous. Zones US, MS, LS, CS; 10–1. Native to China. Shrub can reach 12 ft. or taller and equally as wide, with arching, willowlike branches rather thinly clothed with 1- to 4-in.-long leaves, dark dullish green above, gray and hairy beneath. Blooms in spring from the previous year's growth; produces profuse small clusters of mildly fragrant, lilac purple flowers that create sweeping wands of color. Tolerates many soils; does very well in poor, dry gravel. Prune after bloom: remove some of oldest wood down to within a few inches of ground. Or train up into small single- or multiple-trunked tree. So trained, it somewhat resembles a small weeping willow. 'Argentea' has silvery gray foliage.

B. crispa. Deciduous. Zones MS, LS; 9–7. Native to Himalayas. To 6–10 ft. tall and wide, with silvery gray foliage and 4-in. clusters of fragrant lilac flowers with orange or white throats. Peak bloom comes in late summer. For heaviest bloom and to keep plant neat, cut back nearly to ground in late winter.

B. davidii. ORANGE-EYE BUTTERFLY BUSH, SUMMER LILAC. Deciduous or semievergreen. Zones US, MS, LS, CS; 9–1. Native to China, Japan. Fast, rank growth each spring and summer to 5, 6, or even 10 ft. tall and wide. Leaves tapering, 4–12 in. long, dark green above, white and felted beneath. In midsummer, branch ends adorned with small, fragrant flowers in dense, arching, spikelike, slender clusters from 6 to 12 in. or longer. This species and its selections require little more than good drainage and enough water to maintain growth. Cut back plants heavily in late winter to early spring to promote strong new growth for good flowering. In Upper South, plants may freeze to the ground but will regrow each year from the roots. Here are a few of the many selections available; heat zones 9–2, except as noted.

'Black Knight'. Darkest flowers, very deep purple, in 4- to 6-in. spikes. Small leaves. Grows to 6–7 ft.

'Bonnie'. Light lavender blooms in spikes 8–12 in. long. To 10 ft.

'Charming'. Lots of large lavender-pink flowers in spikes 6–8 in. long. To 7 ft. tall and 10 ft. across.

'Dartmoor'. Strongly fragrant purple flowers in 6- to 8-in., branching spikes with a very full look. To 6 ft.

'Ellen's Blue'. Deep, intense true blue flowers in 6- to 10-in. spikes. Deep green to gray-green leaves. To 4–6 ft. tall and wide.

'Empire Blue'. Violet-blue flowers in spikes to 1 ft. long. Silvery green foliage. Vigorous, upright growth to 10–12 ft.

'Harlequin'. Cream variegation on leaves. Reddish purple flowers in 6- to 8-in. spikes. Slower growing. To 7–8 ft.

'Nanho Alba'. To 4–6 ft., with white flowers in 8- to 10-in. spikes. Full, dense form. Small, narrow, silvery leaves.

▶

B

'Nanho Blue'. Profuse blue blooms in 4- to 6-in. spikes on a 4- to 6-ft. plant. Small, narrow silvery leaves.

'Nanho Purple'. Dark violet flowers in 4- to 6-in. spikes; small, narrow silvery leaves. Plant grows to 4–6 ft.

'Opera'. Bright pink to fuchsia-colored spikes 10–12 in. long. Bushy plant to 5–7 ft.

'Orchid Beauty'. Clusters of lilac to purple flowers up to 20 in. long. To 5–8 ft.

'Pink Delight'. Spikes of clear pink flowers to 1 ft. long. Silvery foliage. To 6–8 ft.

'Potters Purple'. Violet flower spikes to 10 in. long. Vigorous, upright. To 7 ft. tall.

'Purple Prince'. Very fragrant violet flowers in spikes 6–14 in. long. Upright growth to 6 ft.

'Raspberry Wine'. Large clusters (to 8 in. long) of ruffled rosy violet flowers with a golden eye. To 6–8 ft.

'White Profusion'. The best white selection. To 6–8 ft., with many 8- to 12-in. flower spikes produced over a long period. A magnet for butterflies.

B. fallowiana alba. Deciduous or semievergreen. Zones US, MS, LS; 9–7. Native to China. Similar to *B.* 'Lochinch' but has long panicles of white blossoms and felty-textured gray leaves. Reaches 5 ft. tall and somewhat wider. Blooms in late summer. Prune as for *B. davidii.*

B. globosa. ORANGE BUTTERFLY BUSH. Evergreen to semievergreen. Zones LS, CS; 9–7. Chilean native grows to 10–15 ft. tall and wide. Blooms in late spring or early summer, bearing fragrant orange-yellow flowers that are tightly bunched into ¾-in. balls; these in turn are carried in narrow, spikelike, 6- to 8-in. clusters. This species blooms on the previous year's wood; prune as for *B. alternifolia.*

B. lindleyana. WEEPING MARY. Semievergreen. Zones MS, LS, CS; 9–7. Native to China but sometimes found growing wild in the southeastern U.S. Graceful, open growth to 6–12 ft. tall, not quite as wide. Purplish violet flowers appear in late summer and fall, carried in nodding clusters that may reach 2 ft. long. Deep green, semiglossy foliage; cinnamon-colored, shedding bark. Try removing lower limbs to allow for understory plantings. Blooms on new growth; prune as for *B. davidii.*

Buddleia globosa

B. 'Lochinch'. Deciduous. Zones US, MS, LS, CS; 9–6. A hybrid between *B. davidii* and *B. fallowiana.* To 5–6 ft. tall. Displays woolly white new growth and branching, foot-long clusters of intensely fragrant lilac blossoms with an orange eye. Produces summer flowers on current year's growth, so prune as for *B. davidii.* Excellent flowers and foliage.

B. marrubiifolia. WOOLLY BUTTERFLY BUSH. Deciduous. Zones CS, TS; 9–6. Native to Southwest Texas and northern Mexico. Densely foliaged shrub to 5 ft. tall and broad, with soft, silvery, woolly foliage and small, ball-shaped orange flower clusters in spring and summer. Prune after bloom.

B. pikei 'Hever' ('Hever Castle'). Deciduous. Zones US, MS, LS, CS; 12–6. Hybrid between *B. alternifolia* and a Himalayan species. Resembles a smaller *B. alternifolia,* with fragrant, orange-centered lilac flowers in mid- to late spring. Gray-green leaves. Prune as for *B. alternifolia.*

B. weyeriana 'Sungold'. Deciduous. Zones MS, LS, CS; 9–2. Hybrid between *B. davidii* and *B. globosa.* Resembles latter parent but is probably hardier (and is deciduous), with orange-yellow flower clusters that are somewhat less globular. To 8–10 ft. tall and wide. Blooms on old wood, so cut back after flowering as for *B. alternifolia.* (In coldest part of range, however, it freezes to the ground and so blooms on new wood.)

BUFFALO GRASS. See BUCHLOE dactyloides

BUGBANE. See CIMICIFUGA

BULBINE frutescens
(B. caulescens)
Liliaceae
SUCCULENT SHRUBBY PERENNIAL

☑ CS, TS Ⓗ 12–10

☼ ◑ PARTIAL SHADE IN TROPICAL SOUTH

◐ ◓ ● LITTLE TO REGULAR WATER

Bulbine frutescens

Native to South Africa. Branching, barely woody stems sprawl to make clump 1 ft. high, 2–3 ft. wide. Leaves are fleshy, bright green, and shaped like slender, pointed pencils. Blooms through most of the year, producing spikelike, 6- to 12-in. clusters of tubular, bright yellow flowers resembling those of aloe or red-hot poker (*Kniphofia*). 'Hallmark' has orange flowers with fuzzy yellow stamens; it is more compact, less heat tolerant than species.

Useful as ground or bank cover in dry, well-drained soil. Don't locate the species or its selections where they will be stepped on; leaves are slippery when crushed.

BUNCHBERRY. See CORNUS canadensis

BUNNY EARS. See OPUNTIA microdasys

BUNYA-BUNYA. See ARAUCARIA bidwillii

BURMESE PLUMBAGO. See CERATOSTIGMA griffithii

BURRO TAIL. See SEDUM morganianum

BUSH DAISY. See EURYOPS pectinatus

BUSH HONEYSUCKLE. See DIERVILLA

BUSH STRAWFLOWER. See BRACTEANTHA bracteata

BUTCHER'S BROOM. See RUSCUS

BUTIA capitata
PINDO PALM, JELLY PALM
Arecaceae (Palmae)
PALM

☑ CS, TS Ⓗ 12–9

☼ ◑ FULL SUN OR LIGHT SHADE

● REGULAR WATER

Butia capitata

Native to Brazil, Uruguay, Argentina. Very hardy (to 15°F), slow-growing palm to 10–20 ft. tall, with a crown of feathery, gray-green, arching leaves spreading 10–15 ft. wide. Heavy trunk is patterned with stubs of old leaves; tree is more attractive if stubs are all trimmed to the same length. Long spikes of small flowers are followed in summer by showy clusters of yellow to red edible fruits that can be used to make jelly.

BUTTERCUP TREE. See COCHLOSPERMUM vitifolium

BUTTERFLY BUSH. See BUDDLEIA

BUTTERFLY FLOWER. See BAUHINIA monandra

BUTTERFLY PEA. See CLITORIA mariana

BUTTERFLY WEED. See ASCLEPIAS tuberosa

BUTTERNUT. See JUGLANS cinerea

BUTTONBUSH. See CEPHALANTHUS occidentalis

Buxaceae. The boxwood family comprises principally evergreen shrubs with inconspicuous flowers (fragrant in *Sarcococca*). Other members include boxwood (*Buxus*) and *Pachysandra*.

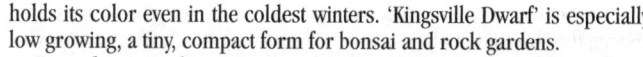

BUXUS

BOXWOOD, BOX

Buxaceae

EVERGREEN SHRUBS

ZONES VARY BY SPECIES

FULL SUN OR LIGHT SHADE

REGULAR WATER

Buxus microphylla japonica

True garden aristocrats, boxwoods may well be the world's oldest cultivated ornamental plants: they were grown as hedges in ancient Egypt and decorated the gardens of wealthy Romans during the reign of Caesar Augustus. Today, they are still widely used as hedges, as well as in formal foundation plantings and as edgings for walkways and planting beds.

Boxwoods have small (just ¼- to 1-in.), lance-shaped to roundish leaves. All are easy to grow where they are adapted, provided they receive good drainage and a modicum of care. If they're grown in loose, fertile soil that contains plenty of organic matter, fertilizing is seldom necessary. They tolerate pruning well, but unless you are training a formal hedge, use hand pruners (rather than hedge shears) to maintain the plants' natural, billowy form. Each year, clean out dead leaves and other debris that has accumulated in the center of the plant. Susceptibility to nematodes limits the use of boxwoods in Florida.

B. Green Series. Zones US, MS, LS, CS. Group of Canadian hybrids derived from *B. microphylla koreana* and *B. sempervirens.* Hardy to between −2°F and −30°F. All feature handsome, rich green foliage and a naturally attractive shape; need very little pruning.

'Green Gem'. Heat zones 9–6. Slowly forms a mound 3–4 ft. high and wide. Some bronzing of foliage in winter cold.

'Green Mountain'. Heat zones 9–5. Forms a dense cone to 5 ft. high, 3 ft. wide. Leaves hold their color all year. Developed as an alternative to dwarf Alberta spruce (*Picea glauca* 'Conica').

'Green Velvet'. Heat zones 9–3. Rounded habit to 3–4 ft. tall and wide. Good green color through winter.

B. microphylla. LITTLELEAF BOXWOOD. Zones US, MS, LS, CS; 9–6. Hardy to 10°F. Slow-growing species from Japan reaches 3–4 ft. tall and wide. Rarely planted; the following varieties and selections are much more common.

'Compacta'. Small, dense form with tiny dark green leaves. Extremely slow growing; 50-year-old plants may reach just 1 ft. tall.

B. m. japonica. JAPANESE BOXWOOD. Zones US, MS, LS, CS; 9–5. Faster growing and taller than the species, to 6 ft. tall and wide. Well suited to the Coastal South; tolerates heat, humidity, and nematodes better than most boxwoods. Round-tipped leaves, ⅓–1 in. long. Foliage may take on a bronzy cast in cold winters. Often used as a clipped hedge in Gulf Coast areas. 'Green Beauty' is a compact form with glossy deep green leaves; it

holds its color even in the coldest winters. 'Kingsville Dwarf' is especially low growing, a tiny, compact form for bonsai and rock gardens.

B. m. koreana (*B. sinica insularis*). KOREAN BOXWOOD. Zones US, MS, LS, CS; 9–5. Hardy to −25°F. Slower growing and lower than *B. m. japonica,* with smaller leaves. Good choice for severe winters of the Upper South. 'Winter Gem' retains its deep green foliage color through winter.

B. sempervirens. COMMON BOXWOOD, AMERICAN BOXWOOD. Zones US, MS, LS; 8–5. Native to southern Europe, North Africa, western Asia. Hardy to −10°F. Densely foliaged shrub is virtually indispensable in formal garden settings. Slowly grows to 15–20 ft. tall and wide. Dark green, oval leaves. Can be used in foundation plantings, for hedges, or pruned into a small tree. Control leaf miner by spraying with dimethoate (Cygon) in May, following label directions. To prevent common diseases of canker and root rot, avoid planting in low, wet areas.

Of the many selections available, the following are most common.

'Graham Blandy'. Narrow, columnar; to 7–9 ft. tall and 1 ft. wide.

'Newport Blue'. Dense, low grower (to 1½ ft. tall, 3 ft. wide) with bluish green foliage.

'Suffruticosa'. EDGING BOXWOOD, ENGLISH BOXWOOD. Dense, compact, very slow growing; takes many years to reach 3 ft. Often used for edging in formal garden settings.

'Vardar Valley'. Becomes a flat-topped mound, 2–3 ft. tall, nearly twice as wide. Dark blue-green foliage. Discovered in the Vardar Valley of Macedonia. Hardy to about −15°F.

CABBAGE

Brassicaceae (Cruciferae)

BIENNIAL GROWN AS COOL-SEASON ANNUAL

US, MS, LS, CS, TS H 7–1

TOLERATES LIGHT SHADE IN HOT CLIMATES

REGULAR WATER

Cabbage

You can grow an amazing variety of cabbages. Besides the familiar round, light green sorts, you can find types with flat, rounded, or pointed heads in colors ranging from white to dark green to red. Leaves may be packed loosely or tightly; Savoy types have crinkly leaves. Given such an array of choices, gardeners may decide to grow cabbage simply for the opportunity to try something different every year. (For Chinese cabbages, see Asian Greens and Chinese Cabbages; for ornamental relatives, see Cabbage and Kale, Flowering.)

Few vegetable crops can match cabbage in total return per square foot of garden space. To avoid overproduction, set out a few plants every week or two, or plant both early and late kinds. Time your plantings so that heads will form either before or after the hot summer months. In most parts of the South, you can plant both spring and fall crops. For a spring crop, set out transplants 4 to 6 weeks before the last frost. For a fall crop (which may be preferable, because cabbage pests are less numerous then), set out transplants in mid- to late summer, 8 to 14 weeks before the first frost. Gardeners in Florida can plant in fall for a winter crop.

Buy seedlings at garden centers or start your own transplants from seed. Sow seeds about 6 weeks prior to planting-out time. When the seedlings have several sets of leaves, transplant them to rich, moist soil, spacing plants 1½–2 ft. apart in rows 2½ ft. apart. Cabbage plants are heavy feeders, so be sure to give them a water-soluble 20-20-20 fertilizer weekly for 3 weeks after setting out. Then sprinkle ½ cup of 10-10-10 fertilizer per 10 ft. of row around plants; repeat 3 weeks later. Don't fertilize after heads begin forming—excess nitrogen can cause them to split. Overwatering at this stage can do the same. Apply a mulch between plants to keep down weeds, cool the soil, and reduce extremes of soil moisture. Harvest heads anytime after they are firm and solid. Light frosts don't hurt cabbage, but be sure to harvest and store before hard freezes arrive.

To prevent a buildup of soil-borne pests, plant cabbage in a different site each year. Club root is a serious fungal pest in acid soils; apply lime, if necessary, to raise the pH to at least 6.5. Floating row covers do a good job of controlling insects such as cabbage loopers, cabbageworms, cutworms,

---

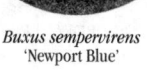

Buxus sempervirens 'Newport Blue'

C

and root maggots. You can also control cutworms and root maggots by ringing the base of the plant with a collar made from cardboard. *Bacillus thuringiensis* (*Bt*; sold as Dipel) applied according to label directions controls cabbageworms and loopers.

Recommended selections of regular, green-leafed cabbage include 'Dynamo' (70 days from setting out plants until harvest, compact plants, good for small gardens), 'Early Flat Dutch' (85 days, heat tolerant), 'Early Jersey Wakefield' (65 days, frost resistant), 'Emerald Cross' (63 days, easy to grow), 'Megaton' (88 days, 15-pound heads), and 'Stonehead' (60 days, solid heads). For red-leafed cabbage, try 'Red Acre' (76 days, compact plants), 'Red Express' (63 days, compact plants), and 'Super Red 80' (78 days, heat tolerant). Recommended Savoy selections include 'Chieftain Savoy' (83 days, tolerates frost and heat), 'Colorosa' (100 days, red leaves), and 'Savoy Express' (55 days, compact plants).

CABBAGE AND KALE, FLOWERING

Brassicaceae (Cruciferae)

BIENNIALS GROWN AS COOL-SEASON ANNUALS

US, MS, LS, CS, TS

BEST IN SUN, TOLERATE SOME SHADE

REGULAR WATER

Flowering Cabbage

Flowering cabbage and flowering kale are grown for their very ornamental, highly colored leaf rosettes, which look like giant, deep blue-green peonies marbled and edged with white, cream, rose, or purple. Kale differs from cabbage in that its head is slightly looser and its leaf edges are more heavily fringed. Both are spectacular in the cool-season garden. They appreciate the same soil, care, and timing as conventional cabbage. Plant 15–18 in. apart in open-ground beds, singly in 8-in. pots, or several to a large container. Colors are strongest after first frosts touch plants. A single rosette cut and placed on a spike holder in a bowl makes a striking harvest arrangement. Foliage is edible raw or cooked and is highly decorative as a salad garnish. For the edible flowering cabbage typically used in Chinese cooking, see Asian Greens.

CABBAGE PALM. See SABAL palmetto

Cactaceae. The cactus family contains a huge number of succulent plants (see also Succulents). Generally leafless, they have stems modified into cylinders, pads, or joints that store water in times of drought. Thick skin reduces evaporation, and most species have spines for protection against browsing animals. Flowers are usually large and brightly colored; fruit may also be colorful and is sometimes edible.

Almost all are native to the Americas—from Canada to Argentina, from sea level into high mountains, from deserts to tropical rain forests.

Cacti range in height from a few inches to 50 ft. tall. Smaller species are grown in pots or, if sufficiently hardy, in rock gardens. Many are easy-care, showy house- or greenhouse plants. Large landscaping types require full sun, well-drained soil. Water newly planted cacti very little; roots are subject to rot before they begin active growth. In 4 to 6 weeks, when new roots are active, water thoroughly; then let soil dry before watering again. Reduce watering in fall to allow plants to go dormant. Feed monthly in spring and summer. For some larger kinds appropriate for garden use, see *Cereus peruvianus, Echinocereus, Espostoa lanata, Opuntia.*

Smaller cacti for pot or rock garden culture usually have interesting forms, brightly colored flowers. Feed and water plants well during warm weather; taper off on fertilizer to encourage winter dormancy. Use fast-draining planting mix. See *Coryphantha vivipara.*

Showiest in flower are tropical cacti that grow as epiphytes on trees or rocks. These need rich soil with much humus, frequent fertilizing and watering, partial shade, and frost protection. In all but the mildest climates, grow in lathhouse or greenhouse, or handle as outdoor/indoor plants. See *Epiphyllum, Rhipsalidopsis, Schlumbergera.*

CADAGA. See EUCALYPTUS torelliana

CAESALPINIA (Poinciana)

Fabaceae (Leguminosae)

EVERGREEN AND DECIDUOUS SHRUBS AND TREES

ZONES VARY BY SPECIES

FULL SUN

LITTLE TO MODERATE WATER

PODS AND SEEDS ARE POISONOUS IF INGESTED

Caesalpinia gilliesii

Ferny-leafed plants grown for their branch-end clusters of colorful blossoms featuring (except *C. platyloba*) protruding stamens. Flowers attract hummingbirds. Plants grow quickly and easily in hot, sunny locations if given light, well-drained soil and infrequent, deep watering. Prune before first flush of spring growth to remove any dead or damaged wood and wayward branches; remove lower limbs for treelike shape in shrubby species.

C. cacalaco. CASCALOTE. Evergreen tree. Zones TS; 12–9. Mexican native grows slowly to 20 ft. tall and wide, with thorny branches and bright green foliage, coarser than that of *C. pulcherrima.* Very showy, large yellow flowers carried well above branches in winter.

C. gilliesii (Poinciana gilliesii). YELLOW BIRD OF PARADISE. Evergreen to deciduous shrub or tree; drops leaves in cold winters. Zones CS, TS; 12–8. From South America. Tough, fast growing to 10 ft. tall, 8 ft. wide, with finely cut foliage and open, angular branch structure. Blooms all summer, producing clusters of yellow flowers adorned with bright red stamens.

C. mexicana. MEXICAN BIRD OF PARADISE. Evergreen shrub or tree. Zones TS; 12–9. Moderately fast growth to 10–12 ft. tall and wide; can be maintained at 6–8 ft. with pruning. Leaves are coarser than those of species *C. pulcherrima.* Blooms throughout year except in coldest months, bearing 6-in. clusters of lemon yellow flowers.

C. platyloba. CURLY PAELA. Evergreen tree. Zones TS; 12–10. From Mexico. To 20 ft. tall and wide. Narrow, elongated clusters of tiny yellow flowers in spring lack the long, protruding stamens of other caesalpinias. Best feature is airy appearance due to open branching habit and relatively few leaflets. Leaves turn rust red in fall.

C. pulcherrima (Poinciana pulcherrima). RED BIRD OF PARADISE, DWARF POINCIANA. Deciduous shrub; may be evergreen in mild winters. Zones TS; 12–9. Native to tropical America. Fast, dense growth to 10 ft. tall and wide; useful for quick screening. Dark green leaves with many ¾-in. leaflets. Blooms throughout warm weather, bearing clusters of orange or red flowers with red stamens. 'Cream Puff' has cream-colored flowers and chartreuse leaves; 'Phoenix Bird' bears bright yellow blooms.

Plants freeze to ground in colder part of range but rebound quickly in spring. In milder climates, you can cut them to ground in early spring to make a more compact shrub.

CAJEPUT TREE. See MELALEUCA quinquenervia

CALADIUM bicolor

FANCY-LEAFED CALADIUM

Araceae

PERENNIAL FROM TUBER

TS 12–4; OR DIG AND STORE; OR GROW IN POTS

SOME SELECTIONS TOLERATE SOME SUN

REGULAR TO AMPLE WATER

SAP CAN CAUSE SWELLING IN MOUTH, THROAT

Caladium bicolor

With the exception of impatiens, no plants are more popular than caladiums for brightening shady spots in Southern gardens. These tropical American natives are grown not for their flowers, but for their marvelous foliage: large (to 1½-ft.), long-stalked, arrow-shaped, almost translucent leaves colored in bands and blotches of red, rose, pink, white, silver, bronze, and green. Caladiums are excellent both as bedding plants and in containers.

Most selections sold at garden centers are fancy-leafed types, typically reaching 2 ft. (occasionally to 4 ft.) tall and wide. Popular choices include 'Aaron' (white with green edges), 'Candidum' (white with green veins), 'Fanny Munson' (pink with crimson veins), and 'Freida Hemple' (red with green border). These and other older selections need shade, but newer ones have thicker leaves that tolerate some sun; examples include 'Fire Chief' (red with green border), 'Pink Beauty' (pink with green speckles and edges),'Rosebud' (pink with green border), 'Red Flash' (green with red center and veins), and 'White Queen' (white with red veins).

Hybridizing has produced three new classes of caladiums: strap leaf, lance leaf, and dwarf. The selections noted here all tolerate some sun.

Strap-leaf caladiums produce large bunches of leaves and stay under a foot in height; they're useful as edging or in mass plantings. Recommended selections include 'Florida Cardinal' (burgundy with green edges), 'Florida Sweetheart' (rose with green edges), 'Pink Gem' (pink with red veins and green edges), and 'Red Frill' (red with green edges). *Lance-leaf* caladiums also grow about a foot tall, but their leaves have a lance-shaped point and ruffled edges. Try 'Lance Wharton' (pink with red veins and green edges), 'Pink Symphony' (mottled pink), and 'White Wing' (pure white with green edges). *Dwarf* caladiums have small leaves but grow about as tall as fancy-leafed types. Two of the best are 'Gingerland' (white with pink speckles and green edges) and 'Miss Muffet' (lime green with burgundy spots).

Caladiums need rich soil, high humidity, and heat. They won't tolerate soil cooler than 60°F and are likely to rot if planted too early in spring. Gardeners wanting to get a jump on the season can start caladiums indoors in pots, then transplant them to the garden. In the Tropical South, the tubers can remain in the ground all year; elsewhere, dig and store them in fall, or grow the plants in pots and bring them indoors for winter.

To grow in the ground, plant tubers in spring when daytime temperatures are consistently in the 70s. Place them knobby side up, tops level with the soil surface; space about 1 ft. apart. Keep well watered and feed lightly with water-soluble fertilizer during the growing season. When foliage begins to look ratty in late summer or fall, cut it back. Where freezes are likely, dig tubers and remove most of the soil from them; then dry them for several days in a shaded, dry location and store in dry peat moss at 50–60°F until planting time in spring.

To grow in pots, start tubers indoors in late winter or outdoors in spring. Plant tubers 2 in. deep in well-drained potting mix to which you've added controlled-release fertilizer; space just an inch apart for the best display. Water thoroughly.

CALAMAGROSTIS

REED GRASS

Poaceae (Gramineae)

PERENNIAL GRASSES

✎ US, MS, LS, CS ❚ 9–5

☼ ◐ FULL SUN OR PARTIAL SHADE

💧 REGULAR WATER

Calamagrostis ×acutiflora 'Karl Foerster'

Among the most effective and handsome of ornamental grasses, the reed grasses feature feathery flower plumes that fade from purple-tinted green to yellow to buff. Flowers persist into fall and can be used for fresh or dried arrangements. Cut clumps almost to the ground in late winter, before new growth begins. These clumping Eurasian natives bloom well in the Upper and Middle South, less well in the Coastal South. Need moist, well-drained soil.

C. ×acutiflora. FEATHER REED GRASS. Known mainly in the following evergreen to semievergreen selections. 'Karl Foerster' ('Stricta'), with narrow bright green leaves, forms an erect, somewhat arching clump 2–3 ft. tall and somewhat broader. Upright flowering stems increase the height to

5–6 ft. when they first appear in summer. 'Overdam', to 3 ft. tall, is similar but has variegated leaves. Its young foliage is striped and edged with yellow; as the leaves mature, the yellow ages to white highlighted with pink. Purplish pink tassels bloom in mid- to late summer. Prefers light afternoon shade.

C. brachytricha. REED GRASS. Deciduous. Upright, arching clump to 1½–2½ ft. tall, 2 ft. wide. Broad, rosy purple flower spikes resembling foxtails increase plant height to 4 ft. in late summer or early fall.

CALAMINTHA

CALAMINT

Lamiaceae (Labiatae)

PERENNIALS

✎ US, MS, LS, CS

☼ ◐ FULL SUN OR LIGHT SHADE

💧 MODERATE WATER

Calamintha grandiflora

Perennials in the mint family with pleasant-scented foliage and pretty, two-lipped flowers in clusters. Herb fanciers brew tea from the leaves. Plants need well-drained soil.

C. grandiflora. LARGE-FLOWERED CALAMINT. Heat zones 9–3. Native from Mediterranean region to Iran. Creeping rhizomes produce a clump to 2 ft. tall and wide, with slender stems and 1½-in. pink flowers in summer. Better with some shade.

C. nepeta (C. nepetoides). LESSER CALAMINT. Heat zones 9–5. Native from Mediterranean region to Great Britain. To 1½ ft. high, 2½ ft. wide. Many tough, slender stems grow outward, then erect. Upper portion of the plant carries a profusion of ½-in. pale lilac to white flowers in late summer and fall.

CALAMONDIN. See CITRUS, Sour-Acid Mandarin

CALANTHE

Orchidaceae

TERRESTRIAL ORCHIDS

✎ MS, LS, CS

◐ ● PARTIAL TO FULL SHADE

💧 REGULAR WATER

Calanthe reflexa

Orchids are reputed to be difficult, but the following hardy terrestrial types from Japan are easy to grow if given moist, woodsy, well-drained soil and partial to full shade. Lush leaves of most types have an attractively pleated look. Their sensational blooms often bear a clovelike scent. Plants are often late to emerge in spring.

C. discolor. Evergreen or semievergreen. Heat zones 9–6. Dark green, heavily pleated leaves are 6–12 in. long, 2 in. wide and form a clump to 1 ft. across. In midspring, small, fragrant mahogany flowers with a white or pale pink lower lip appear on 1- to 1½-ft.-tall stalks. *C. d. sieboldii* (*C. sieboldii*, *C. striata sieboldii*) features profuse blooms in clear yellow. The Takane hybrids have yellow flowers marked with brown, gold, white, and red.

C. Kozu hybrids. These hybrids between *C. discolor* and *C. izu-insularis* are largely evergreen. Heat zones 9–7. Dark green leaves, 4–6 in. long and 1–2 in. wide, form a foliage clump to about 8 in. tall and wide. In spring, foot-tall flower spikes are covered in clove-scented flowers; blossoms come in red, pink, white, and yellow, in both solid colors and bicolor combinations.

C. reflexa. Evergreen. Heat zones 9–7. Narrow, pleated leaves to 6–8 in. long, about 1½ in. wide form a clump to 1 ft. tall, 15 in. wide. Unlike most other species, this one blooms in mid- to late summer, when lightly fragrant lavender-and-white flowers appear on 1½-ft.-tall spikes.

CALATHEA

Marantaceae

PERENNIALS

⚘ TS ⊩ 12–10; OR HOUSEPLANT

◐ PARTIAL SHADE; BRIGHT INDIRECT LIGHT

💧 REGULAR WATER

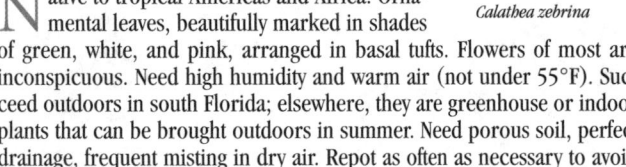

Calathea zebrina

Native to tropical Americas and Africa. Ornamental leaves, beautifully marked in shades of green, white, and pink, arranged in basal tufts. Flowers of most are inconspicuous. Need high humidity and warm air (not under 55°F). Succeed outdoors in south Florida; elsewhere, they are greenhouse or indoor plants that can be brought outdoors in summer. Need porous soil, perfect drainage, frequent misting in dry air. Repot as often as necessary to avoid root-bound condition. Calatheas are often mistakenly called marantas.

C. crocata. ETERNAL FLAME. Grows to 10 in. high, 1 ft. wide. Leaves to 6 in. long, 1–1½ in. wide, dark green above, purple beneath. Spikes 2 in. long, consisting of bright orange flower bracts that look like little torches. Clump has several shoots; each shoot dies after blooming, but new ones appear to keep up the show. Variable performance as houseplant; subject to mites in low humidity. Does better in greenhouse.

C. lancifolia (C. insignis). RATTLESNAKE PLANT. To 1½–2½ ft. tall, 2 ft. wide. Narrow, wavy-edged, 1- to 1½-ft. leaves are yellow green banded with deep olive green.

C. louisae. To 3 ft. tall, 1½ ft. wide. Foot-long dark green leaves heavily feathered with gray green along midrib.

C. majestica (C. ornata). Sturdy plant can reach 6 ft. tall and 3 ft. wide. Leaves 2–3 ft. long, rich green above, purplish red beneath. Juvenile leaves usually pink striped between veins; intermediate foliage striped white. 'Roseo-lineata' has pink and white stripes at an angle to midrib.

C. makoyana. PEACOCK PLANT. Showy plant to 2–4 ft. high and wide. Leaves have areas of olive green or cream above, pink blotches beneath. Silver featherings on rest of upper surface, corresponding cream-colored areas underneath.

C. zebrina. ZEBRA PLANT. Compact plant to 1–3 ft. high, 1–2 ft. wide. Elliptic leaves reach 1–2 ft. long, almost half as wide. Upper surfaces are velvety green with alternating bars of pale yellow green and olive green extending outward from midrib; undersides are purplish red.

CALCEOLARIA

POCKETBOOK PLANT

Scrophulariaceae

PERENNIALS GROWN AS ANNUALS

⚘ US, MS, LS, CS, TS ⊩ 6–1; OR HOUSEPLANT

◐ ● PARTIAL TO FULL SHADE; BRIGHT INDIRECT LIGHT

💧 REGULAR WATER

Calceolaria

Unusual, puffed-up flowers resembling inch-long pocketbooks give calceolarias their common name. The blooms may be bright yellow, red, or orange and are often marked with spots. Commonly available types are hybrids belonging to the Herbeohybrida group; most reach 9–15 in. high and 6–12 in. wide.

Hailing from the mountains of South America, these are short-lived plants that won't take sustained temperatures higher than 65°F. They can be grown from seed, but most people buy plants in bloom from a florist or greenhouse in winter. Pocketbook plants are largely grown as short-term indoor plants, though they are sometimes bedded out for late winter color in the Coastal South. For best results indoors, place near a north- or east-facing window, away from heating vents or other heat sources. Keep at 50–60°F to prolong the flowering period. The soil should be moist but never soggy; no fertilizing is necessary. When the blooms fade, discard the plant.

CALENDULA officinalis

CALENDULA, POT MARIGOLD

Asteraceae (Compositae)

COOL-SEASON ANNUAL

⚘ US, MS, LS, CS, TS ⊩ 6–1

☀ FULL SUN

💧 MODERATE WATER

Calendula officinalis

This Mediterranean native is a popular source of sure, easy color in the cooler months—from late fall through spring in the Lower, Coastal, and Tropical South; from spring to early summer in the Upper and Middle South. Daisylike double blossoms, 2½–4½ in. wide, come not only in the familiar orange and bright yellow, but also in more subtle shades of apricot, cream, and soft yellow. The plant is somewhat branching, reaching 1–2 ft. high, 1–1½ ft. wide. Leaves are long and narrow, with rounded ends; they are aromatic and slightly sticky. Plants are not browsed by deer.

Calendulas are effective for masses of bright, warm color in borders, along drives, or in containers; they make long-lasting cut flowers. In the past, the leaves and flowers went into vegetable stews—hence the common name "pot marigold," a reference to the plant's culinary use as a "pot herb." The vivid petals are still popular today for the tangy flavor they bring to salads and cooked dishes; if simmered with rice, they lend a saffron color to the grain.

Sow seed in place in the garden or in flats—in late summer or early fall in mild-winter areas, in spring elsewhere. Or buy seedlings at garden centers. Plant adapts well to most soils if drainage is fast. Remove spent flowers to prolong bloom.

Dwarf strains (12–15 in.) include Bon Bon (earliest), Dwarf Gem, and Fiesta (Fiesta Gitana). Taller (1½–2 ft.) are Kablouna (pompon centers with looser edges), Pacific Beauty, and Radio (quilled, "cactus"-type blooms).

CALIBRACHOA

MILLION BELLS

Solanaceae

PERENNIAL OFTEN GROWN AS ANNUAL

⚘ US, MS, LS, CS, TS ⊩ 12–1

☀ ◐ FULL SUN OR LIGHT SHADE

💧 REGULAR WATER

Calibrachoa

Million bells look like miniature forms of petunia, to which they are related—but they differ from petunias in having smaller flowers (to 1 in. across); wiry, slender stems; and tiny, closely set leaves. The strong, wiry stems make the plants less subject to breakage than petunias, and tobacco budworms (which often attack petunias) seem uninterested in the foliage and flowers.

Calibrachoa is native to Brazil, but garden forms result from hybridization. The common name "million bells" is actually a brand name created by a grower, but it's now popularly applied to all plants of this type.

Habit may be either trailing or mounding. Blossoms appear from spring to frost and come in a wide range of colors, including white, pink, cherry, rose, salmon, terra-cotta, yellow, violet, and blue. Once the flowers fade, they drop cleanly from the plant. Where frosts are light or nonexistent, million bells behave like short-lived perennials. Good for winter color in Florida and South Texas. Superb performers in hanging baskets, window boxes, and mixed containers; less successful as bedding plants, particularly where the soil is heavy and summers are wet and humid.

CALICO FLOWER. See ARISTOLOCHIA littoralis

CALICO PLANT. See BREYNIA nivosa 'Roseopicta'

CALIFORNIA FAN PALM. See WASHINGTONIA filifera

CALIFORNIA POPPY. See ESCHSCHOLZIA californica

CALLA. See ZANTEDESCHIA

CALLIANDRA

Fabaceae (Leguminosae)

EVERGREEN AND DECIDUOUS SHRUBS

⚘ CS, TS ⩩ 12–10; OR GROW IN POTS

☼ FULL SUN, EXCEPT AS NOTED

◐ ◑ ◕ WATER NEEDS VARY BY SPECIES

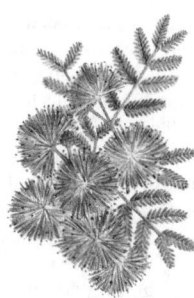
Calliandra tweedii

Grown as landscape plants in the Coastal and Tropical South and in greenhouses elsewhere, these plants sport feathery foliage and blossoms that look like powder puffs. The showy parts of the flowers are actually long, silky stamens. Prune out any dead, damaged, or unwanted growth immediately following bloom.

C. eriophylla. FAIRY DUSTER, FALSE MESQUITE. Deciduous. Native from Southern California east to Texas and south into Baja California. Open growth to 3 ft. tall, 4–5 ft. wide. Leaves finely divided into tiny leaflets. Flower clusters show pink to white stamens in fluffy balls to 1½ in. across in late winter or early spring. No irrigation needed, but flowers and leaves (plant is summer-deciduous) will last longer with some summer water.

C. grandiflora. GIANT FAIRY DUSTER. Evergreen. Native to eastern Mexico and Central America. To 5 ft. tall, 3 ft. wide. Red, 3-in. puffballs in clusters to 15 in. long at branch ends. Attractive, glossy dark green foliage. Little to moderate water.

C. haematocephala (C. inaequilatera). PINK POWDER PUFF, RED POWDER PUFF. Evergreen. Native to Bolivia. Grows fast to 10 ft. or more, with equal spread. Among the most popular large flowering shrubs in central Florida. Its beauty has carried it into areas harsher than those to which it is adapted; it will grow in the Coastal South if given special protection of overhang or warm, sunny wall. In form, it's a natural espalier. Foliage not as feathery as that of *C. tweedii;* leaflets longer, broader, and darker—glossy copper when new, turning to dark metallic green. Big puffs (2–3 in. across) of silky, watermelon pink stamens are produced in fall and winter. There is a rare white-flowered form. Needs light soil and regular water.

C. tweedii. TRINIDAD FLAME BUSH, BRAZILIAN FLAME BUSH. Evergreen. Native from Brazil to Uruguay. Best in the Tropical South. Freezes back but recovers in the Coastal South. To 6–8 ft. tall, 5–8 ft. wide, with graceful, picturesque structure. Fernlike leaves, divided into many tiny leaflets, scarcely hide branches. Aside from a rest period in early winter, blooms all year, bearing 2- to 3-in., bright crimson pompons at branch ends. Not fussy about soil. Takes regular to little water. Prune to thin and to retain interesting branch pattern. Often sold as *C. guildingii.*

CALLICARPA

BEAUTYBERRY

Verbenaceae

DECIDUOUS SHRUBS

⚘ US, MS, LS, EXCEPT AS NOTED

☼ ◐ FULL SUN OR LIGHT SHADE

◑ ◕ MODERATE TO REGULAR WATER

Callicarpa bodinieri

Graceful, arching shrubs grown for showy fruit. Small lilac or pink flowers in summer are followed by tight clusters of little, round violet to purple fruits that last into winter. Effective in woodland gardens or massed in borders. Bloom and fruit occur on current season's growth, so prune in late winter: remove a third of oldest stems or lop whole plant low to ground. Plants may freeze to ground in Upper South, but they come back from roots.

C. americana. AMERICAN BEAUTYBERRY. Zones US, MS, LS, CS, TS; 11–1. Native to eastern U.S. To 6 ft. tall, 5 ft. wide. Leaves to 6 in. long turn purplish in fall. Biggest, coarsest foliage of the species listed here.

C. bodinieri. BODINIER BEAUTYBERRY. Heat zones 8–1. Native to China. Grows to 6 ft. or more and nearly as wide, with willowlike leaves that turn pink or orange to purple in fall. 'Profusion' is a heavy bearer.

C. dichotoma. PURPLE BEAUTYBERRY. Heat zones 8–5. Native to China, Korea, Japan. The best, most refined-looking species for the home garden. About 4 ft. tall and slightly wider, with slender branches that sweep the ground. Resembles a smaller, finer-textured *C. bodinieri.* 'Issai' bears abundant purple fruits; 'Early Amethyst' ripens its bright purple berries earlier than the species and other selections. *C. d. albifructus*, 8–3, has white fruit.

C. japonica. JAPANESE BEAUTYBERRY. Heat zones 9–3. Native to China, Taiwan, Japan. To 5 ft. tall and wide, with deep reddish purple fall foliage. 'Leucocarpa' bears white fruit.

CALLIOPSIS. See COREOPSIS tinctoria

CALLIRHOE

WINE CUPS, POPPY MALLOW

Malvaceae

PERENNIALS

⚘ US, MS, LS, CS ⩩ 9–1

☼ FULL SUN

◐ ◕ LITTLE TO MODERATE WATER

Callirhoe involucrata

Few perennials can match the eye-popping show of wine cups in full bloom. Native to the American Southwest and Midwest, they grow from fleshy roots to become wide-spreading mats of foliage; the leaves are deeply cut, resembling those of some scented geraniums. A profusion of cup-shaped flowers smothers the plant during hot weather. As long as they have good drainage, wine cups will tolerate infertile soil, intense heat. Use them at front of border and on slopes.

C. alcaeoides. Native from Illinois to Nebraska, south to Tennessee and Texas. Whitish (often pink-tinged) flowers to 2½ in. across are held on slender, 5- to 20-in. stems; plant spreads 1–3 ft. wide. 'Logan Calhoun' is an improved selection with sparkling white blossoms; it grows 8–12 in. high, sprawling 3–4 ft. wide.

C. involucrata. Native from Missouri to Wyoming and south to Texas. To 6 in. tall and 2–3 ft. wide. Produces purplish red flowers are 2 in. across. *C. i. tenuissima*, from the mountains of Mexico, 9–1, has light purple flowers and more deeply cut foliage than the species.

C. papaver. WOODLAND POPPY MALLOW. From northern Florida to Texas, north to Georgia and Arkansas. Resembles *C. involucrata* but has deep magenta blossoms on stems 5–12 in. long.

CALLISTEMON

BOTTLEBRUSH

Myrtaceae

EVERGREEN SHRUBS OR TREES

⚘ ZONES VARY BY SPECIES

☼ FULL SUN

◐ ◕ MODERATE TO REGULAR WATER

Callistemon citrinus

Fast-growing plants with colorful flowers carried in dense spikes or round clusters that consist mainly of long, bristlelike stamens—hence the common name "bottlebrush." Attractive to hummingbirds. Flowers are followed by woody capsules that can last for years and may resemble rows of beads pressed into bark.

Some bottlebrushes are naturally dense and compact (making good informal hedges); others are sparse and open (can be pruned up to become small trees). Those with pliant branches can be grown as informal espaliers. Very little routine pruning is needed—just remove any weak or dead branches after bloom or before spring growth. Don't cut into bare wood beyond leaves; if you do, plant may not send out new growth. ▸

Generally found in moist ground in their native Australia, bottlebrushes can withstand waterlogged soil. Normally tolerant of saline or alkaline soils but sometimes suffer from chlorosis (yellow leaves with green veins). Often severely damaged at 20°F.

C. citrinus (C. lanceolatus). LEMON BOTTLEBRUSH. Zones LS, CS, TS; 12−9. Shrub or tree. Most commonly grown bottlebrush; most tolerant of heat, cold, and poor soils. Massive shrub to 10−15 ft. tall and wide, but with staking and pruning in youth easily trained into narrowish, round-headed, 20- to 25-ft. tree. Nurseries offer it as a shrub, espalier, or tree. Narrow, 3-in.-long leaves are coppery when new, maturing to vivid green. Bruised leaves smell lemony. Bright red, 6-in.-long brushes appear in waves throughout the year.

Variable plant when grown from seed. Cutting-grown selections with good flower size and color include 'Improved' and 'Splendens'. 'Compacta' makes a 4-ft. mound with smaller spikes. 'Violaceus' ('Jeffersii'), about 6 ft. tall and 4 ft. wide, has stiffer branches, narrower, shorter leaves, and reddish purple flowers fading to lavender. 'Mauve Mist' is the same but can reach 10 ft. 'Perth Pink', 10 ft. tall, has pink flower clusters.

C. rigidus. STIFF BOTTLEBRUSH. Zones LS, CS, TS; 12−9. Rigid, sparse shrub or small tree to 20 ft. with 10-ft. spread. Sharp-pointed, gray-green (sometimes purplish) leaves to 6 in. long. Spring and summer red flower brushes are 2½−4½ in. long. Produces prominent seed capsules. Least graceful of the bottlebrushes. 'Clemson Hardy' ('Clemson') is a compact form (2−3 ft. tall and wide) with bright red flowers; it succeeds in Zones US, MS, LS, CS, TS and has withstood −8°F.

C. salignus. WHITE BOTTLEBRUSH. Zones TS; 12−10. Shrub or tree to 20−25 ft. tall, 10−15 ft. wide. Dense crown of foliage. Bright pink to copper new growth. Willowlike leaves 2−3 in. long. Pale yellow to cream-colored flowers appear in 1½- to 3-in. clusters in spring, early summer. Train as small shade tree or plant 4−5 ft. apart as hedge.

C. sieberi. ALPINE BOTTLEBRUSH. Zones MS, LS, CS, TS; 12−7. Shrub. To 3−6 ft. tall and wide, with a somewhat upright habit. Small (to 1½-in.-long) dark green leaves densely cover the branches. Cream to yellow flowers in 1½- to 6-in.-long brushes bloom from late spring to midsummer.

C. viminalis. WEEPING BOTTLEBRUSH. Zones CS, TS; 12−9. Shrub or small tree with pendulous branches. Fast growing to 20−30 ft. tall, with 15-ft. spread. Narrow, light green, 6-in.-long leaves. Bright red, 4- to 8-in.-long brushes from late spring into summer; scattered bloom rest of year. Not for windy, dry areas. As a tree, needs staking, thinning to prevent tangled, top-heavy growth. Leaves tend to grow toward ends of long, hanging branches.

'Little John' is a superior dwarf form to 3 ft. tall and wide, with dense growth and blood red flowers in fall, winter, and spring. 'Captain Cook' is dense, rounded, to 6 ft. tall and wide; good for border, hedge, or screen. 'McCaskillii' has denser habit than others, is more vigorous (to 20 ft. tall), and has better flower color and form.

Callistemon viminalis

C. 'Woodlanders' Hardy'. Zones US, MS, LS, CS, TS. Shrub. Similar to *C. sieberi* but with bright red flowers. Hardy to −8°F.

CALLISTEPHUS chinensis

CHINA ASTER

Asteraceae (Compositae)

ANNUAL

US, MS, LS, CS, TS ⚑ 9–1

☼ FULL SUN

💧 REGULAR WATER

Callistephus chinensis

This Chinese native is a splendid cut flower and an effective bedding plant when well grown and free of disease. Plants range from 8 in. to 3 ft. high, 10−18 in. wide. Some kinds are branching; others (developed mainly for florists) have strong stems and no side shoots. Leaves are deeply toothed or lobed.

Bloom comes in summer. Many different flower forms: quilled, curled, incurved, ribbonlike, or with interlaced rays; some have crested centers. Selections are classified as peony flowered, pompon, anemone flowered, and ostrich feather. Colors range from white to pastel pink, rose pink, lavender, lavender blue, violet, purple, crimson, wine, and scarlet.

Plant in rich, loamy or sandy soil. After danger of frost is past, sow seed in place or set out plants started in flats. Keep growth steady; sudden checks in growth are harmful. Subject to aster yellows, a viral disease carried by leafhoppers. Discard infected plants; control leafhoppers. All but wilt-resistant types are subject to aster wilt or stem rot, caused by a parasitic fungus that lives in soil and is transmitted through roots into plants. Over-watering produces an ideal environment for diseases, especially in heavy or poorly drained soil. Never plant in the same location in successive years.

CALLUNA vulgaris

SCOTCH HEATHER

Ericaceae

EVERGREEN SHRUB

US ⚑ 7–5

☼ FULL SUN

💧 REGULAR WATER

Calluna vulgaris

This, the true Scotch heather, is native to Europe and Asia Minor. It bears tiny, needle-like dark green leaves and spikes of rosy pink, bell-shaped flowers. Garden types (far more common than the species) range from dwarf ground cover and rock garden sorts only a couple of inches high to plants reaching 3 ft. tall. Blossom colors include white, pale to deep pink, lavender, and purple. Most selections flower in mid- to late summer; a few continue on into late fall. Handsome foliage—pale and deeper greens, chartreuse, yellow, gray, or russet—often changes color in winter.

Unfortunately, despite its obvious appeal, Scotch heather is difficult to grow in the South. This attractive plant does best where conditions are neither too hot nor too cold, too dry nor too wet, and it must be grown in strongly acid, sandy or peaty, well-drained soil that is low in nutrients. You can amend the soil with organic matter, but don't apply fertilizer. Avoid cultivating near the plant, as this may damage shallow feeder roots. Mulch thoroughly to keep the soil cool and retain its moisture. Water during summer droughts. To prune, shear off faded flowers and branch tips immediately after bloom (for types blooming into late fall, delay pruning until late winter).

Hundreds of selections are available from specialty nurseries. Try them if you're adventurous, but keep in mind that unless you live in the Upper South or high up in the Appalachians, Scotch heather will probably be short lived in your garden. It is not browsed by deer.

CALOCEDRUS decurrens
(Libocedrus decurrens)

INCENSE CEDAR

Cupressaceae

EVERGREEN TREE

US, MS, LS ⚑ 8–1

☼ ◑ FULL SUN OR LIGHT SHADE

◖ 💧 NO IRRIGATION TO MODERATE WATER

Calocedrus decurrens

You wouldn't think that a conifer native to Oregon and California would tolerate the heat and humidity of the South. But incense cedar does. It has been grown successfully from one end of the South to the other—from Stillwater, Oklahoma, to Athens, Georgia.

Growing 75–90 ft. tall and only 10–15 ft. wide, this symmetrical tree forms a dense, narrow, pyramidal crown. It features flat sprays of rich green foliage and handsome reddish brown bark. Small yellowish to reddish brown cones resembling duckbills ripen in autumn. The foliage is aromatic when crushed, hence the tree's common name.

Although it's slow growing at first, incense cedar may grow 2 ft. per year when established. It takes blazing summer heat and poor soil in stride. Makes an excellent tall screen, windbreak, or specimen for spacious lawns. No pruning required.

CALONYCTION aculeatum. See IPOMOEA alba

CALTHA palustris

MARSH MARIGOLD

Ranunculaceae

PERENNIAL

US, MS, LS 8–1

SUN OR SHADE

AMPLE WATER

ANY PART CAN CAUSE INFLAMMATION, PAIN IF INGESTED

Caltha palustris

Native to Eurasia—and from Newfoundland to Alaska, south to North Carolina and Tennessee. Vigorous, lushly foliaged plant, well adapted to life at the edges of pools, ponds, streams, and other moist locations. Given sufficient water, it can also be grown in borders; it looks good with bog irises and moisture-loving ferns. Reaches 2 ft. tall and wide; rounded, 2- to 7-in.-wide, glossy green leaves are heart shaped at the base, give an almost tropical effect. Clusters of cheery yellow flowers to 2 in. across bloom in spring; a double-flowered form is available. Increase by divisions or sow seed in boggy soil.

Calycanthaceae. The calycanthus family contains shrubs with paired opposite leaves and flowers that somewhat resemble small water lilies—each bloom has an indefinite number of segments not easily defined as petals or sepals. *Calycanthus* and wintersweet (*Chimonanthus praecox*) are typical representatives.

CALYCANTHUS

Calycanthaceae

DECIDUOUS SHRUBS

US, MS, LS, CS

SUN OR SHADE

REGULAR WATER

SEEDS CAN PRODUCE CONVULSIONS IF INGESTED

Calycanthus occidentalis

Deciduous shrubs, represented here by two U.S. natives. Both of these are bulky plants with lush foliage and flowers valued for their fragrance and form.

C. floridus. COMMON SWEETSHRUB, CAROLINA ALLSPICE. Heat zones 9–1. Native from Virginia to Florida. Suckering, fast-spreading, stiffly branched plant to 6–10 ft. tall and as wide or wider. Leaves are oval, to 5 in., glossy dark green above, grayish green beneath; turn yellow in fall. Plant blooms most heavily in April and May, and then sporadically to July. Reddish brown, 2-in.-wide flowers, often with heady strawberry fragrance, are carried at ends of leafy branchlets. Blooms are followed by brownish, pear-shaped capsules that are very fragrant when crushed.

Plant in shrub border or around outdoor living space where the flowers' fragrance can be appreciated. Aroma varies, so buy when plants are in bloom. 'Athens' has yellow flowers and an outstanding fragrance reminiscent of cantaloupe.

C. occidentalis. SPICE BUSH. Heat zones 9–6. Native to California. Grows to 4–12 ft. high and wide. Bright green leaves are 2–6 in. long and 1–2 in. wide, yellow in autumn. Reddish brown flowers to 2 in. across resemble small water lilies. Blossoms appear from April to August, depending on climate and exposure. Both flowers and bruised leaves have the pleasing fragrance of an old wine barrel. Shrub can be trained into a multistemmed small tree but is most useful as a background shrub or medium to tall screen. Easily grown from seed.

CALYLOPHUS

SUNDROPS

Onagraceae

PERENNIALS

US, MS, LS 8–1

FULL SUN OR LIGHT SHADE

LITTLE TO MODERATE WATER

Calylophus hartwegii

Found across the Southwest, these showy perennials share the same common name as some of their close relatives (and look-alikes) in the genus *Oenothera*. Bloom over a long season, from spring into late fall, bearing bright yellow, four-petaled flowers that open at sunset and remain open for most of the next day. Plants go dormant in winter and may be sheared just before spring growth begins. They spread by rhizomes and can take over a garden bed if unrestrained by a physical barrier, such as metal edging sunk 6 in. deep into the ground. Good for summer color in rock gardens or on rocky slopes; make nice filler plants in mixed borders. Like lots of heat and excellent drainage.

C. drummondianus. To 1½ ft. high, 2 ft. wide, with narrow, tooth-edged, somewhat drooping leaves and inch-wide flowers. This species blooms for a longer period than *C. hartwegii* in spring, but it does not rebloom as well in fall. 'Texas Gold' is a clumping, noninvasive form with particularly bright yellow flowers.

C. hartwegii. To 1 ft. high, 2 ft. across, with inch-wide flowers; those of 'Sierra Sundrop' are larger. *C. h. lavandulifolius* (*C. lavandulifolius*) has narrow gray leaves. Excellent in hot, dry locations and when mixed with desert perennials.

C. serrulatus. Prairie wildflower found from Saskatchewan to Texas. To 1½ ft. high and wide, with ¾-in. flowers.

CAMASSIA

CAMASS

Liliaceae

PERENNIALS FROM BULBS

US, MS, LS, CS 9–1

FULL SUN OR LIGHT SHADE

AMPLE WATER DURING GROWTH AND BLOOM

Camassia quamash

Starlike, slender-petaled blossoms are carried on spikes in late spring, early summer; grasslike basal leaves dry quickly after bloom. Plant in consistently moist, fairly heavy soil, where bulbs can remain undisturbed for many years. Set bulbs 4 in. deep, 6 in. apart. To avoid premature sprouting, plant after weather cools in fall.

C. cusickii. Dense clusters of pale blue flowers are borne on stems that grow to 3 ft. tall.

C. leichtlinii. Large, handsome clusters of blue to creamy white flowers on stems to 4 ft. tall. Selections include 'Alba' (*C. l. leichtlinii*), white with bluish tinge, and 'Semiplena', with creamy white semidouble blooms. *C. l. suksdorfii* (often sold as *C. l.* 'Coerulea') has blue to deep blue-violet flowers. This subspecies' selection 'Blue Danube' is deep blue.

C. quamash (C. esculenta). Loose clusters of blue flowers on 1- to 2-ft. stems. Flowers of 'Orion' are deeper blue, those of 'San Juan Form' deeper still. 'Blue Melody' has dark blue flowers and cream-striped foliage.

CAMELLIA

Theaceae

EVERGREEN SHRUBS OR TREES

US (MILDER PARTS, PROTECTED), MS, LS, CS
H 10–7

LIGHT SHADE

MODERATE TO REGULAR WATER

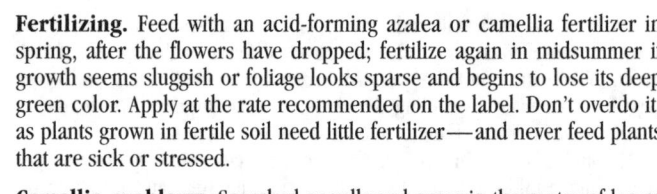

Camellia × hiemalis

The South is the heart of camellia country. Indeed, common camellia (*Camellia japonica*) is Alabama's state flower. Although it seems these beautiful plants must have been born here, in truth they hail from eastern and southern Asia. More than 3,000 named kinds of camellias exist, in a remarkable range of colors, forms, and sizes; they are not browsed by deer.

If you live in the Upper or Tropical South and have problems growing camellias, take heart: you can now enjoy hybrids that flourish in the extremes of weather found in both regions. See "Hardy hybrids" and "Heat-tolerant camellias" (page 223).

The following pages offer a brief discussion of camellias' cultural requirements and describe some lesser-known species as well as old favorites and new selections. The plant descriptions also include cultural needs unique to individual species and selections.

Establishing new plants. Spring or fall planting is fine for most areas. Spring is better in the Upper South, where the root system needs time to get established before onset of cold weather. Mulch thoroughly to keep the roots cool and the soil moist. Regular watering is critical during the first year. Water thoroughly to moisten the entire root ball; then let the top of the root ball go slightly dry before the next watering.

WHAT CAMELLIAS NEED

SOIL: Give them well-drained soil rich in organic material. Never plant so trunk base is below soil line, and never let soil cover base. Keep roots cool with a 2-in.-thick mulch (kept away from base).

WATERING: Though camellias appreciate regular water (as long as drainage is good), established older plants can survive—even thrive—on fairly little supplemental moisture.

FERTILIZING: Feed with a commercial acid plant food, being sure not to overfertilize plants.

SHELTER: Protect plants from strong, hot sun and drying winds.

PRUNING: Some judicious pruning right after flowering or during summer and fall will improve plant appearance and next year's flower display.

Camellia sasanqua 'Cleopatra'; Semidouble

Exposure and watering. In general, camellias grow and bloom better in partial shade, with shelter from hot afternoon sun. This is especially true for young plants, which thrive under the shade of tall trees or when grown on the north side of a house. As they grow larger and their thick canopy of leaves shades and cools their roots, they gradually will accept more sun. Shade provided in winter reduces cold damage in the Upper South.

Established plants (over 3 years old, vigorous, and shading their own roots) get by with little supplemental water. If you do water them, make sure the soil is well drained. Shelter them from strong winds, particularly in the Upper South or near the coast. They do not tolerate salt spray.

Fertilizing. Feed with an acid-forming azalea or camellia fertilizer in spring, after the flowers have dropped; fertilize again in midsummer if growth seems sluggish or foliage looks sparse and begins to lose its deep green color. Apply at the rate recommended on the label. Don't overdo it, as plants grown in fertile soil need little fertilizer—and never feed plants that are sick or stressed.

Camellia problems. Scorched or yellowed areas in the center of leaves usually indicate sunburn. Burned leaf edges, excessive leaf drop, or corky leaf spots generally point to overfertilizing. Chlorosis (yellow leaves with green veins) results from planting in neutral or alkaline soil; to correct, feed plant with chelated iron and amend soil with sphagnum peat moss and/or garden sulfur to adjust the pH.

Tea scale is a common pest. These pests look like tiny brown or white specks on leaf undersides; sooty mold grows on the honeydew they secrete. Infested leaves turn yellow and drop. To treat tea scale, apply horticultural oil or a systemic insecticide such as acephate (Orthene) or dimethoate (Cygon), following label directions.

Two fungal diseases are common. Camellia petal blight causes flowers to turn brown rapidly, then drop. Sanitation is the best control: pick up and destroy all fallen blossoms as well as infected ones still on the plant. Remove and discard any existing mulch, then replace it with a 4- to 5-in. layer of fresh mulch. Camellia leaf gall causes leaves to become distorted, pale, thick, and fleshy; they gradually turn white, then brown, then drop from the plant. The best control is to pick off and destroy affected leaves before they turn white.

Bud drop is a frequent complaint. To some extent, this is natural for camellias (many set more buds than they can open), but it also may be caused by overwatering, summer drought, or sudden freezes.

For more detailed information on camellia problems, see the *Southern Living Garden Problem Solver.*

Pruning. Prune after blooming has ended. Remove dead or weak wood; thin out growth when it is so dense that flowers have no room to open properly. Shorten lower branches to encourage upright growth; cut back top growth to make lanky shrubs bushier. When pruning, cut just above a scar that marks the end of the previous year's growth (often a slightly thickened, somewhat rough area where bark texture and color change slightly). Making your cuts just above this point usually forces three or four dominant buds into growth.

Camellias in containers. Camellias are outstanding container plants, whether you grow them outdoors on a terrace or indoors in a cool greenhouse. As a general rule, plant gallon-size camellias in 12- to 14-in.-diameter containers, 5-gallon ones in 16- to 18-in. containers. Fill the container with a potting mix containing 50 percent or more organic material. Make sure the container has a generous drainage hole.

Flower forms. The American Camellia Society defines six basic camellia flower forms; these are illustrated by the photographs on the facing page.
Single. One row (a single layer) of up to eight petals surrounding a conspicuous cluster of stamens.
Semidouble. Two or more rows (layers) of regular, irregular, or loose petals surrounding a conspicuous cluster of stamens.
Anemone form. One or more rows (layers) of petals, flat or undulating, surrounding a central mound of intermingled petaloids (petal-like structures) and stamens.
Peony form. Mounded to nearly ball-shaped flower consisting of petals in no regular arrangement, forming a sort of powder-puff effect. In loose peony form, blossoms contain loose petals (some irregular) intermingled with stamens. In full peony form, flowers are a tighter mass of petals, petaloids, and stamens, or petals and petaloids with no stamens visible.
Rose-form double. Multiple layers of regularly overlapping (imbricated) petals revealing a central cluster of stamens when flowers are fully open.
Formal double. Flowers consisting of multiple layers of overlapping petals, never showing stamens even when fully open.
C. ×hiemalis. Formerly considered a separate species, this group of hybrids involving *C. sasanqua* is noted for bushy, compact growth habit.

Often called "dwarf sasanquas"; many are low growing and spreading, although some are tall and upright. Examples include the following; all have 2- to 2½-in. blossoms.

'Bonanza'. Upright, strong grower, 3–10 ft. tall and 3–6 ft. wide. Red flowers of loose peony form.

'Chansonette'. Vigorous, spreading growth to 6 ft. high, 8 ft. wide. Large, bright pink formal double flowers with frilled petals.

'Kanjiro'. Upright plant to 8–10 ft. tall and wide. Single to semidouble blossoms in rose pink edged with red.

'Shishi-Gashira'. One of the most useful and ornamental shrubs. Low growing (3 ft. high and 6 ft. wide), with arching branches that in time pile up tier on tier to make a compact, dark green, glossy-leafed plant. Leaves rather small for camellia, giving medium-fine foliage texture. Flowers are rose red, semidouble to double, 2–2½ in. wide, heavily borne over long season—October through March in a good year. Full sun or shade.

'Showa-No-Sakae'. To 3 ft. high, 6–8 ft. wide. Faster growing, more open than 'Shishi-Gashira'; willowy, arching branches. Semidouble to double flowers of soft pink, occasionally marked with white. Try this as an espalier.

'Showa Supreme'. Very similar to 'Showa-No-Sakae' but has somewhat larger flowers of peony form.

'Sparkling Burgundy'. Upright, slow grower to 5–10 ft. tall and 3–6 ft. wide, with narrow leaves and ruby red peony-form flowers.

C. japonica. COMMON CAMELLIA. This is the plant most gardeners have in mind when they speak of camellias. Naturally a large shrub or small tree but variable in size, growth rate, and habit. Hundred-year-old plants reach 20 ft. high and equally wide, and even larger specimens exist. However, most gardeners can consider japonicas to be shrubs 6–12 ft. high and wide. Many are lower growing.

The following list describes japonica selections that are favorites among Southern gardeners. Included here are a number of old standbys whose beauty belies their age. Some of them are among the oldest camellias still in commerce, having been brought to Europe and the U.S. from China and Japan in the 19th century or even earlier (these venerable camellias are noted by date of introduction in the text).

The list specifies season of bloom as early, midseason, or late. In the Coastal South, early is November and December; midseason is January and February; late is March. In the Lower South, early is December and January; midseason is February and March; late is March and April. In the Middle South, early is February; midseason is March and April; late is April and May. In the Upper South, early is March; midseason is April; late is May. Flower size is also noted for each selection. Very large blooms are over 5 in. wide; large, 4–5 in.; medium-large, 3½–4 in.; medium, 3–3½ in.; small, 2½–3 in.; and miniature, 2½ in. or less. Those described as "hardy" will survive temperatures as low as 0–5°F. Some in the following list take the heat even in the Tropical South (see page 223).

'Adolphe Audusson' (1877). Midseason. Very large, dark red semi-double flowers, heavily borne on a medium-size, symmetrical, vigorous shrub. Hardy. 'Adolphe Audusson Variegated' is identical, but its blossoms are heavily marbled with white on red.

'Alba Plena' (1792). Early. Brought from China over two centuries ago and still a favorite. Large, white formal double. Slow, bushy growth. Early

bloom is a disadvantage in cold or rainy areas; protect blossoms from rain and wind.

'Berenice Boddy'. Midseason. Medium, light pink semidouble blooms with deeper shading. Vigorous, upright growth. One of the hardiest.

'Carter's Sunburst'. Early to late. Large to very large flowers, semidouble to peony form to formal double, in pale pink striped with deeper pink. Medium-size, compact plant.

'C. M. Wilson'. Early to midseason. Sport of 'Elegans' and identical to it except for its pale pink flower color. 'C. M. Wilson Variegated' has white petal markings; many plants sold as 'C. M. Wilson' are actually the variegated form.

'Covina' (1888). Midseason to late. Semidouble to rose-form double, rose red, medium-size flowers on a compact plant. Highly sun tolerant.

'Daikagura' (1891). Early to late. Large, rose red peony-form blooms on a dense, upright bush. Very long bloom season. 'Daikagura Variegated' is similar but has rose red blossoms marbled in white.

'Debutante'. Early to midseason. Medium-large, light pink peony-form flowers. Profuse bloomer. Vigorous upright growth. Takes some sun.

'Elegans' ('Chandler'); also sold as 'Francine' ('Chandleri Elegans Pink') (1831). Early to midseason. The founder of a large and growing family of sports. The original plant is slow growing and spreading, bearing large anemone-form blossoms in rose pink; center petaloids are often marked with white. More frequently grown is 'Elegans Variegated', identical except for white variegation on all petals; it is often known simply as 'Chandleri Elegans'. 'Elegans Supreme' is like 'Elegans' with the addition of deep serrations on petal edges. 'Elegans Champagne' is a white sport of 'Elegans Supreme' with creamy central petaloids. 'Elegans Splendor' has white-margined pale pink petals with fringed edges. For other sports in the 'Elegans' family, see 'C. M. Wilson', 'Shiro Chan'.

'Gigantea'. Midseason. Enormous, semidouble red blooms marbled with white. Vigorous plant.

'Glen 40' ('Coquetii'). Midseason to late. Large, deep red formal double. One of the best red camellia blooms for corsages. Slow, compact, upright growth. Plant is handsome even out of bloom. Hardy; very good container plant.

'Governor Mouton'. Midseason. Upright. Medium, semidouble or loose peony-form flowers are red marked with white. Hardy.

'Guilio Nuccio'. Midseason. Considered by many to be the world's finest camellia. Coral rose, very large semidouble flowers of unusual depth and substance have inner petals fluted in "rabbit ear" effect. Vigorous, upright growth. Forms with variegated, fringed blossoms are available.

'Herme' ('Jordan's Pride') (1875). Midseason. Medium-large, pink semidouble flowers irregularly bordered in white and streaked with deeper pink. Sometimes bears solid pink blooms on certain branches. Free blooming and dependable.

'Kramer's Supreme'. Midseason. Full peony-form, very large flowers in deep, clear red. Some people can detect a faint fragrance. Compact, upright, unusually vigorous. Takes some sun.

'Kumasaka' (1896). Midseason to late. Medium-large, rose pink rose-form double to peony-form flowers. Vigorous, compact, upright growth and remarkably heavy flower production make it a choice landscape plant. Hardy. Takes morning sun.

▶

Camellia Flower Forms

| *Camellia sasanqua* 'Apple Blossom'; Single | *Camellia japonica* 'C. M. Wilson'; Anemone Form | *Camellia japonica* 'Alba Plena'; Formal Double | *Camellia japonica* 'Mathotiana'; Rose-form Double | *Camellia japonica* 'Debutante'; Peony Form | *Camellia sasanqua* 'Cleopatra'; Semidouble |

'Lady Clare' ('Akashigita'). Early and midseason. Dense, rounded, vigorous. Large, semidouble deep pink blooms. Hardy.

'Lady Vansittart'. Midseason to late. Moderate growth; upright form. Medium, semidouble white flowers are streaked to varying degrees in shades of rosy red, giving the look of several different flower colors on a single plant. Hardy.

'Magnoliiflora' (1886). Midseason. Medium, pale pink semidouble flowers are borne profusely, make good cut flowers. Medium-size plant with compact yet spreading form. Hardy.

'Mathotiana' (1840s). Midseason to late. Very large rose-form double to formal double blooms in deep crimson, sometimes showing a purplish cast. Vigorous, upright grower. Tolerates cold and stands up well in hot-summer regions.

'Mrs. Charles Cobb'. Midseason to late. Large, deep red semidouble to peony-form flowers. Free blooming. Compact plant with dense foliage; best in warmer areas.

'Nuccio's Gem'. Midseason. Medium to large, white, perfectly formed formal double. Strong-growing, full, upright plant.

'Nuccio's Jewel'. Midseason to late. Large flowers in loose to full peony form are white with pink petal edges.

'Nuccio's Pearl'. Midseason. Full formal double, medium blossoms are white with a rim of deep pink outer petals.

'Paulette Goddard'. Midseason. Vigorous and upright. Medium, semidouble or loose peony-form blossoms in deep red. Quite hardy and tough.

'Pink Perfection' ('Otome'). Early to late. Erect to spreading. Small, pale pink formal double flowers. Hardy.

'Prince Eugene Napoleon' ('Pope Pius IX') (1859). Midseason. Cherry red, medium-large formal double. Medium-size, compact, upright plant.

'Professor Charles S. Sargent' ('Professor Sargent'). Midseason. Compact and upright. Medium-size, dark red anemone-form flowers with ruffled petals in the center. Hardy.

'Purity' (1887). Late. White, medium flowers, rose-form double to formal double, usually showing a few stamens. Vigorous, upright plant. Late bloom means it often escapes rain damage.

'Red Giant'. Midseason. Large, red peony-form flowers. Upright grower.

'Rev. John C. Drayton'. Late. Moderate grower. Medium, semidouble bright carmine rose blossoms. Hardy.

'R. L. Wheeler'. Late. Very large, rose red, semidouble flowers. Hardy.

'Shiro Chan'. Early to midseason. A sport of 'C. M. Wilson' with identical habit and flower form. Blossoms may open palest pink, fading to white blushed with pink at petal bases. 'Snow Chan' is a pure white sport.

'Silver Waves'. Early to midseason. Large, white semidouble blooms with wavy petal edges.

'Swan Lake'. Midseason to late. Very large white flowers with formal double to peony form. Vigorous, upright growth.

'Tiffany'. Midseason to late. Very large blossoms in warm pink; rose-form double to loose, irregular semidouble. Vigorous, upright shrub.

'Tom Knudsen'. Early to midseason. Medium to large blooms in dark red with deeper red veining. Formal double to peony form to rose-form double.

'Ville de Nantes'. Midseason to late. Large semidouble flowers have white-blotched deep red petals with fringed edges. Bushy, slow-growing plant. 'Lady Kay' is a sport with full peony form.

'Wildfire'. Early to midseason. Medium, orange-red semidouble flowers on a vigorous, upright plant.

C. oleifera. TEA-OIL CAMELLIA. Large shrub or small tree to 20 ft. tall and 12 ft. wide, with glossy dark green leaves and fragrant, 2-in. white flowers in fall. Specific name *oleifera* means "oil bearing"; oil extracted from the large seeds has been used in China for cooking or as a hair conditioner. Possibly the hardiest of all the camellias. A parent of hardy hybrids (see listing page 223).

C. reticulata. NETVEIN CAMELLIA. Some of the biggest and most spectacular camellia flowers occur in this species, and as likely as not they appear on some of the lankiest and least graceful of camellia plants.

Camellia reticulata

Plants differ somewhat according to selection, but generally speaking they are rather gaunt, open shrubs that eventually become trees of considerable size—possibly 35–50 ft. tall. In gardens, consider them 10-ft.-tall shrubs, 8 ft. wide. Leaves are also variable but tend to be dull green, leathery, and strongly net veined.

Culture is similar to that of other camellias, except that these plants seem intolerant of heavy pruning. This, with their natural lankiness and size, makes them difficult to place in the garden. They are at their best in light shade of old oaks, where they should stand alone with plenty of room to develop. They look good in containers while young but are not handsome there out of bloom. Develop better form and heavier foliage in open ground. These camellias are less hardy than *C. japonica* (not recommended for the Upper or Middle South). In Lower South, grow in containers so you can move them into winter protection, or plant beneath an overhang or near a wall.

Best-known kinds have large (4- to 6-in.) semidouble flowers with deeply fluted and curled inner petals. These inner petals give great depth to the flower. All bloom from late winter to early spring. The following are the best choices for garden use.

'Buddha'. Very large rose pink flowers; inner petals unusually erect and wavy. Gaunt and open; grows fast.

'Butterfly Wings'. Rose pink, loose semidouble flower of great size (reported as large as 9 in. across), with broad, wavy petals. Open, rather narrow plant.

'Captain Rawes'. Reddish rose pink semidouble flowers of large size. Vigorous bushy plant with good foliage. Hardiest of reticulatas.

'Chang's Temple'. True selection bears large, open-centered, deep rose flowers, with notched, fluted center petals. 'Cornelian' is sometimes sold as 'Chang's Temple'.

'Cornelian'. Large, deep, loose peony-form flowers with wavy petals; rosy pink to red, heavily variegated with white. Vigorous plant with big leaves that are usually marked with white. This plant is often sold as 'Chang's Temple' or as 'Lion Head'. (The true 'Lion Head' is not found in American gardens.)

'Crimson Robe'. Very large, bright red semidouble flowers. Firm-textured, wavy petals. Vigorous plant of better appearance than most other reticulatas.

'Purple Gown'. Large, purplish red peony-form to formal double flowers. Compact plant with best growth habit and foliage in the group.

'Shot Silk'. Large, loose semidouble flowers of brilliant pink with iridescent finish that sparkles in sunlight. Fast, rather open growth.

'Tali Queen'. Very large, deep reddish pink flowers of loose semidouble form with heavily crinkled petals. Plant form and foliage are very good. This selection is often sold as 'Noble Pearl'; true 'Noble Pearl' is not available in the U.S.

C. sasanqua. SASANQUA CAMELLIA. Though often dismissed as "those other camellias" by Southerners smitten with the huge blooms of *C. japonica,* sasanqua camellias deserve better. True, their flowers are smaller, but the plants offer many advantages over common camellias. They tolerate more sun, more heat, and a wider range of soils, and their looser habit and smaller leaves make them easier to incorporate into a landscape. In form, they vary from upright and treelike to bushy and spreading; heights range from 6 to 15 ft. Glossy dark green leaves are 1½–3½ in. long, about a third as wide. The plants bloom heavily from late summer through autumn and into winter, depending on the selection, bearing single, semidouble, or double flowers that are sometimes lightly fragrant. Blossoms typically come in pink or white, but there are also some reds. Individual blooms last only a short time, but they're so numerous that the show goes on for months.

Established sasanqua camellias tolerate drought, but those growing in full sun need more water. They make excellent espaliers, tall screens, informal hedges, and bonsai specimens, as they accept frequent pruning. Upright selections can be pruned into standards (single trunks). Sasanquas are not as hardy to cold as common camellias; gardeners in the Upper South should plant them in spots protected from winter wind and sun or grow them in cool greenhouses.

'Apple Blossom'. Medium single white flowers blushed with pink, from pink buds. Spreading plant.

'Cleopatra'. Large, rose pink semidouble flowers with narrow, curving petals. Growth is erect, fairly compact. Takes clipping well. Very hardy.

'Crimson King'. Large, rich red single blossoms. Vigorous, upright, open growth.

'Hana Jiman'. Large semidouble flowers, white with pink edges. Fast and open growth; good espalier.

'Jean May'. Large double blossoms in shell pink. Compact, upright grower with exceptionally glossy foliage.

'Mine-No-Yuki' ('White Doves'). Large white flowers of full peony form. Spreading, willowy growth; effective espalier.

'Momozono-Nishiki'. Large semidouble flowers are rose, shaded white. Twisted petals.

'Narumi-gata'. Large, cupped single flowers, white tinged pink.

'Setsugekka'. Large, white semidouble flowers with fluted petals. Blossoms have considerable substance; cut sprays hold well in water. Upright and rather bushy shrub.

'Tanya'. Small single flowers in deep rose pink. Tolerates much sun. Low-growing, spreading plant. Good ground cover.

C. sinensis (Thea sinensis). TEA PLANT. Dense, rounded shrub is grown in Asia as the commercial source of tea, but in the South it is an ornamental. Reaches 15 ft. tall and wide, with leathery dark green leaves to 5 in. long. Blooms in fall, bearing scented white flowers to 1½ in. wide. Takes well to pruning; can be trimmed into a hedge. 'Blushing Maiden' bears nodding pink flowers; 'Teabreeze' offers fragrant white blooms.

C. ×vernalis. A group of sasanqua hybrids noted for later bloom (all flower in late fall and winter), denser growth, shinier foliage, and firmer-textured flowers. Most reach about 9 ft. tall and 6 ft. wide. They take the same care as sasanquas and are often sold as such.

'Dawn'. Small, single to semidouble white flowers blushed pink. Dense, upright shrub of unusual hardiness.

'Hiryu'. Small, deep red, rose-form double blooms on a dense, upright plant. 'Hiryu Nishiki' has white markings on flowers.

'Star Above Star'. Medium semidouble flowers in white shading to lavender pink. Upright and bushy; may reach 10–20 ft. tall and wide.

'Yuletide'. Profusion of small, brilliant red single flowers on a dense, upright, compact plant. Blooms in late December.

Hybrid camellias. Several categories of hybrids, described here, have been produced.

Medium-flowered hybrids. The first wave of hybridizing involved *C. japonica* and *C. saluenensis*. The resulting hybrids, most of them medium to large shrubs, are of generally good garden form, with foliage like that of *C. japonica* and abundant flowers. See *C. japonica* for explanations of bloom season and flower-size terminology.

'Coral Delight'. Midseason. Large, coral pink semidouble flowers form garlands along the branches. Slow grower.

'Donation'. Midseason. Large semidouble flowers in orchid pink are borne all along stems. Vigorous, upright, compact plant with slightly pendulous branches; blooms young and heavily. Quite resistant to cold and sun. Appreciates a little shade in hot, dry areas. There is a form with variegated flowers.

'E. G. Waterhouse'. Midseason to late. Formal double of excellent form. Light pink, medium flowers heavily produced on vigorous, upright shrub.

'Fragrant Pink'. Midseason. An exception in that it is a cross between *C. j. rusticana* (*C. rusticana*) and *C. lutchuensis*. Loose peony-form flowers on spreading bush. Flowers are small, deep pink, very fragrant.

'Freedom Bell'. Midseason. Small to medium, semidouble, bell-shaped blooms of dark red open beneath branches.

'J. C. Williams'. Early to late. Single, cup-shaped, medium flowers of purplish pink over very long season. Vigorous, upright shrub with rather pendulous branches.

'Jury's Yellow'. Early to late. Medium anemone-form blooms with ivory white outer petals, creamy yellow central petaloids. Compact, upright.

'Taylor's Perfection'. Midseason. Profuse show of large, light pink semidouble flowers.

Large-flowered hybrids. A second wave of hybridizing, involving *C. japonica*, *C. reticulata*, and *C. sasanqua*, produced plants with more spectacular blossoms than the medium-flowered hybrids. See *C. japonica* for explanations of bloom season and flower-size terminology.

'Dr. Clifford Parks'. Midseason. Very large blossoms in a rich, orange-toned red are semidouble to loose peony form to anemone form. Vigorous, upright plant.

'Flower Girl'. Early to midseason. Large to very large, semidouble to peony-form flowers of bright pink. Vigorous, upright growth. Profuse flowering and small leaves come from its sasanqua parent, big flowers from its reticulata ancestor.

'Francie L.'. Midseason to late. Very large semidouble flowers with wavy petals. Deep rose pink.

'Valentine Day'. Midseason to late. Large to very large, salmon pink formal double flowers. Fast, upright grower.

'Valley Knudsen'. Midseason to late. Large to very large, deep orchid pink blooms, semidouble to loose peony form. Compact, upright growth.

Hardy hybrids. Dr. William Ackerman of the National Arboretum in Washington, D.C., and Dr. Clifford Parks of the University of North Carolina, Chapel Hill, bred a number of species, notably the hardy *C. oleifera*, to produce hardy camellias. These hybrids withstand temperatures as low as −15°F with little or no damage provided they have some shelter from winter sun and wind. They bear 3½- to 4-in. flowers in October and November. Selections include 'Polar Ice' and 'Snow Flurry', with white anemone-form blossoms; 'Winter's Charm', pink peony form; 'Winter's Dream', semidouble pink blooms; 'Winter's Fire', with semidouble to peony-form, hot pink flowers in midwinter; 'Winter's Star', lavender-pink single blooms; 'Winter's Waterlily', white formal double.

'Pink Icicle', with shell pink peony-form flowers, was selected from *C. japonica* and blooms in early spring. Also selected from *C. japonica* is the April series of hardy camellias, named for the time they typically bloom in the cooler, northern part of their range. Included are 'April Blush', shell pink semidouble; 'April Dawn', formal double, variegated pink and white; 'April Remembered', cream to pink shaded, semidouble; 'April Rose', rose red formal double; 'April Snow', white rose-form double; and 'April Tryst', bright red anemone form.

HEAT-TOLERANT CAMELLIAS. *Most camellias get flambéed in the Tropical South, but these japonicas perform well as far south as Fort Myers and West Palm Beach in Florida: 'Alba Plena', 'Debutante', 'Gigantea', 'Lady Clare', 'Mathotiana', 'Professor Charles S. Sargent', and 'Red Giant'. You can even try them in Miami, though you'll have to grow them in pots because of the alkaline soil there.* ❖

CAMPANULA

BELLFLOWER

Campanulaceae (Lobeliaceae)

PERENNIALS

US, MS, LS

FULL SUN IN COOLER CLIMATES ONLY

MODERATE TO REGULAR WATER

Campanula persicifolia
'Telham Beauty'

Vast and varied group (nearly 300 species) encompassing trailers, creeping or tufted miniatures, and erect kinds 1–6 ft. tall. Native throughout the Northern Hemisphere; species described here are perennials mostly from southern Europe, Turkey, the Caucasus, and northern Asia. Flowers are generally bell shaped, but some are star shaped, cup shaped, or round and flat. Usually blue, lavender, violet, purple, or white; some pink.

Uses are as varied as the plants. Gemlike miniatures deserve special settings—close-up situations in rock gardens, niches in dry walls, raised beds, containers. Trailing kinds are ideal for hanging pots or baskets, wall crevices; vigorous, spreading growers serve well as ground covers. Upright growers are valuable in borders, for cutting, occasionally in containers.

In general, campanulas grow better in good, well-drained soil and the cooler climates of the Upper and Middle South. Most species are fairly easy to grow from seed sown in flats in spring or early summer, then transplanted to the garden in fall for bloom the following year; also may be increased by cuttings or divisions. Divide clumps in fall—typically every 3 or 4 years, though some may need yearly division.

C. carpatica (C. turbinata). TUSSOCK BELLFLOWER. Heat zones 7–1. Forms compact, leafy tufts with branching, spreading stems. About 8 in. tall but may reach 1–1½ ft. Smooth, bright green, wavy, toothed leaves, 1–1½ in. long. Single blue or white flowers to 1–2 in. across are upward facing, bell or cup shaped. Blooms in late spring. Use in rock gardens, borders, edging. Not browsed by deer. 'Blue Chips' and 'White Chips' are good dwarf selections that are easily grown from seed; they are sometimes sold as 'Blue Clips', 'White Clips'. 'China Doll' is a 6-in.-high selection with pale lavender-blue flowers.

C. glomerata. CLUSTERED BELLFLOWER. Heat zones 8–1. Upright, with erect side branches to 1–2 ft. Leaves are broad and somewhat hairy, 2–4 in. long; basal leaves are wavy edged, stem leaves toothed. Narrow, bell-shaped, 1-in.-long, blue-violet flowers are tightly clustered at stem tops. Summer bloom. Plant in shaded borders. Seed-grown strains Superba and Alba are deepest purple and white, respectively. 'Joan Elliott' is deep violet blue. 'Caroline' is lavender.

C. lactiflora. MILKY BELLFLOWER. Heat zones 7–5. Erect, branching plant to 3½–5 ft. tall. Oblong, toothed leaves, 2–3 in. long. Broadly bell-shaped to star-shaped, 1-in.-long, white to pale blue flowers in drooping clusters at ends of branches. Summer bloom. Plant in back of borders in sun or partial shade. Endures even dry shade and is long lived. 'Loddon Anna' has pale pink flowers.

C. persicifolia. PEACH-LEAFED BLUEBELL. Heat zones 8–1. Graceful, strong-growing plant with bright green foliage. Narrow basal leaves, 4–8 in. long, form a low clump to 1½ ft. wide. Slender, erect, leafy stems rise 2–3 ft. high in summer, in loose spires of open, cup-shaped, inch-wide blossoms of blue, pink, or white. Choice plants for borders. Easy to grow from seed sown in late spring. Longtime favorite 'Telham Beauty' has 3-in. blue flowers. 'Blue Gardenia' and 'White Pearl' have double flowers. 'Chettle Charm' has creamy white flowers edged with lavender.

C. takesimana 'Elizabeth'. Heat zones 8–5. Selection of a Korean species. Forms a flat basal rosette, then spreads rapidly by underground runners. Flower stems to 2 ft. high bear long (2-in.), pendent bells of deep rosy red with lighter edges. Rounded, tooth-edged dark green leaves are 4–5 in. across, narrower on upper stems. Too invasive for mixed borders; plant it where it can roam freely.

Campanulaceae. The campanula, or bellflower, family contains perennials and biennials, typically with bell-, star-, or saucer-shaped flowers in shades of blue to purple, lilac, and white. This family includes plants formerly grouped under Lobeliaceae.

CAMPHOR TREE. See CINNAMOMUM camphora

CAMPSIS

TRUMPET CREEPER, TRUMPET VINE
Bignoniaceae
SEMIEVERGREEN TO DECIDUOUS VINES
✎ ZONES VARY BY SPECIES
☼ ◐ FULL SUN OR PARTIAL SHADE
◐ ● MODERATE TO REGULAR WATER

Campsis radicans 'Flamenco'

V igorous climbers used for large-scale effects, quick summer screens. All bear radiant, orange-toned blossoms shaped like flaring trumpets, in clusters at branch tips, midsummer to fall.

Glossy leaves are divided into 2½-in., ovate leaflets. Stems have aerial rootlets, cling to wood, brick, stucco, and other surfaces. Unless pruned and tied to supporting surface, old plants can become top-heavy and pull away. Each dormant season, shorten some branches and thin others. Pinch back shoot tips in summer to keep plants bushy. Plants spread by suckering roots; pull any that appear. If older plants become unmanageable, cut to ground before spring growth begins and train a few strong new stems.

C. grandiflora (Bignonia chinensis). CHINESE TRUMPET CREEPER. Zones MS, LS, CS; 9–7. Not as vigorous, large, or hardy as the American native *C. radicans*, but flowers are slightly larger and redder. Each leaf has up to nine leaflets. Grows to 30 ft. under ideal conditions. 'Morning Charm' has peach-colored flowers.

C. radicans (Bignonia radicans). COMMON TRUMPET CREEPER. Zones US, MS, LS, CS; 9–3. Native to eastern U.S. Each leaf has up to 11 leaflets. Flowers are 3-in.-long orange tubes with scarlet lobes flaring to 2 in. wide. Grows fast to 40 ft. or more, bursting with health and vigor. 'Flamenco' features red trumpets with orange centers. 'Flava' has yellow blossoms and somewhat lighter green leaves.

C. ×tagliabuana. Zones US, MS, LS, CS; 9–5. Hybrid between above two species. 'Mme Galen', best-known selection, has salmon red flowers. 'Crimson Trumpet' bears pure red blooms.

CANDLESTICK SENNA. See SENNA alata

CANDY LILY. See ×PARDANCANDA norrissii

CANDYTUFT. See IBERIS

CANE PALM. See CHRYSALIDOCARPUS lutescens

CANNA

Cannaceae
PERENNIALS FROM RHIZOMES
✎ LS, CS, TS ⌶ 12–4; OR DIG AND STORE
☼ FULL SUN
● REGULAR WATER DURING GROWTH AND BLOOM

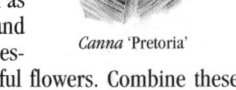

Canna 'Pretoria'

T here's nothing timid about cannas. Native to the southeastern region of the U.S. as well as to subtropical and tropical parts of Central and South America, they loudly proclaim their presence with large, bold leaves and wildly colorful flowers. Combine these striking good looks with ease of culture, and you understand why cannas are ubiquitous throughout the South.

In summer and fall, flower stalks (typically 3–6 ft. tall) bear blossoms to 3 in. across, in shades of red, orange, yellow, salmon, coral, pink, and cream; both solids and bicolors are available. Lance-shaped, 1- to 4-ft.-long leaves resemble banana foliage. Green and bronze are the typical leaf colors, but many newer selections feature shockingly bright striped and variegated foliage in all sorts of riotous combinations. Deep-colored foliage typically fades somewhat in hot sun.

Cannas are most effective when planted as masses of a single color against a solid background. Their leaves combine well with finer-textured foliage, such as that of daylilies (*Hemerocallis*) and lantana. Use taller kinds at the back of borders; compact sorts make good container plants.

Plant rhizomes in spring, after the danger of frost is past. Set them 2–4 in. deep and 1–2 ft. apart. Cannas like lots of moisture (they'll even grow in standing water), but the soil doesn't need to be boggy, just moist. They're heavy feeders and prefer rich soil containing lots of organic matter, such as composted manure and chopped leaves. If you see ragged, stunted foliage and canna leaf roller (see below) is not the problem, the plants are hungry; give them weekly feedings of water-soluble 20-20-20 fertilizer until they perk up. They grow best with full sun and high heat, forming lush, spreading colonies. Cut each flower stalk to the ground after it finishes blooming; new stalks will appear and continue to grow into early fall. In the Lower, Coastal, and Tropical South, cannas can overwinter in the ground; elsewhere, lift the rhizomes in fall and store over winter. Divide clumps every 3 or 4 years, making sure each piece of rhizome includes a bud or "eye."

Canna leaf roller is a common pest, mainly attacking hybrids. This caterpillar rolls up the leaves and feeds inside them; infested foliage looks ragged and is full of holes. Sanitation is the best solution. Cut off and destroy infested leaves as soon as you notice them and, in late fall, cut all plants to the ground and destroy all leaves and stems to prevent the pest from overwintering. Applying a fertilizer containing the systemic insecticide disulfoton (Di-Syston) during the growing season may also be effective. Disulfoton is found in some rose- and shrub-care products.

C. flaccida. SWAMP CANNA, SOUTHERN MARSH CANNA. Native to swamps and riverbanks from South Carolina to Florida. Grows 4 ft. tall, 3 ft. wide, with green leaves reaching 2 ft. long and 6 in. wide. Bright yellow, 3-in.-wide flowers.

C. hybrids. The vast majority of cannas grown are hybrids grouped under *Canna × generalis.* They feature larger flowers than their parent species and often have strikingly ornate foliage. Most are good subjects for the back of the border. Give them plenty of room, as nearly all spread quickly. Recommended selections include the following.

'Australia'. To 4–5 ft. tall. Glossy, burgundy black foliage holds color in summer heat. Bright red flowers.

'Black Knight'. To 5–6 ft. tall, with blackish bronze foliage and velvety deep red flowers.

'City of Portland'. To 4 ft. tall. Vigorous, bushy plant. Broad green leaves; showy rosy pink to salmon flowers.

'Cleopatra'. To 4 ft. tall. Green leaves and stalks are marked with large purple blotches. Flowers arising from purple tissue are red; those coming from green tissue are yellow. The bicolored foliage tends to revert to plain green; cut out solid green stalks to prevent reversion.

'Constitution'. Grows 5 ft. tall. Narrow grayish purple leaves with burgundy edges; pale coral pink flowers. Slower spreader than most cannas.

'Declaration'. To 3½ ft. tall. Bright red flowers held above gray-green leaves with burgundy margins.

'Durban'. To 4 ft. tall. Strikingly variegated foliage features yellow veins against a reddish purple background. Large scarlet flowers. Slow spreader.

'Minerva'. To 4 ft. tall. Leaves are striped green and white; large yellow flowers open from red buds.

'President'. To 4 ft. Masses of large scarlet blooms top glossy green foliage.

'Pretoria' ('Bengal Tiger'). To 6 ft. tall. Dramatic-looking foliage features green and yellow stripes and maroon edges; glows brilliantly when backlit. Bright orange flowers.

'Red King Humbert'. To 4 ft. Reddish bronze foliage; large orange-scarlet to red flowers.

'Tropicanna' ('Phaison'). To 6 ft. The most shockingly gaudy foliage imaginable—purple leaves striped with yellow and red. Backlit leaves glow as if ablaze; bright orange flowers complete the fiery picture. Very susceptible to canna leaf roller. Feed frequently to keep foliage looking its best.

'Tropicanna Gold'. To 4–5 ft. Orange-yellow flowers speckled with dark orange. Leaves striped in green and gold.

'Wyoming'. To 4 ft. Bronzy purple foliage and bright orange blooms.

'Yellow King Humbert'. To 5 ft. Green leaves; large bright yellow flowers splashed with spots of crimson.

C. indica. INDIAN-SHOT. Native to the tropical Americas; naturalized in the Southeast. To 4 ft. tall, 1½ ft. wide. Green leaves 1½ ft. long, 8 in. wide. Bright red, 3-in. flowers. The hard, round seeds were used as shot by early colonists.

C. musifolia. BANANA CANNA. Grows 12 ft. tall. Huge canna that resembles a banana tree. Large green leaves—to 2 ft. long and half as wide—have burgundy red margins and stalks. Small red flowers are sparsely produced. Great as a tropical-looking accent.

Canna 'City of Portland'

WHAT CANNAS NEED

EXPOSURE: They thrive in heat and bright sunshine.

SOIL: Work in lots of organic matter before planting. Provide regular moisture during growth and bloom. Cannas tolerate wet soil and will grow with roots in water.

PRUNING: As each stem finishes flowering, cut it to the ground. New stems will grow throughout summer and early autumn.

DIVIDING: In mild climates where cannas can remain in the ground, clumps become overcrowded every 3 or 4 years. Dig in early spring, cut the rhizomes apart, let them dry for 24 hours, and replant.

PESTS: Canna leaf roller is a serious pest in the South. Cut off and destroy infested foliage. You can also control with systemic insecticides.

Canna 'Wyoming'

C. warscewiczii. Native to Mexico. To 6 ft. tall, 3 ft. wide. Big burgundy leaves, 2 ft. long and 1 ft. wide, on very dark stems. Small, tubular red flowers, attractive to hummingbirds, are carried in spikes held high above the foliage; spent blossoms drop cleanly from the spike. Not susceptible to canna leaf roller.

Low-growing cannas. Standard-size cannas take up a lot of room—but fortunately, you can find many low-growing hybrids that are better suited to containers and small gardens. 'Striped Beauty' ('Bangkok Yellow'), to 2–3 ft. tall, has striped foliage and flowers: leaves are striped in green and white, and red-throated yellow flowers are marked with white stripes. 'Pink Sunburst', to 3 ft. tall, has green- and white-striped leaves with a reddish cast; its large flowers are salmon pink. Cannas in the Pfitzer's series are green-leafed plants 2–2½ ft. tall, with coral, crimson, primrose yellow, or salmon pink flowers. Tropical series plants grow 2½ ft. tall, have green leaves and rose, red, or salmon flowers. They're easy to grow from seed, blooming 90 days after sowing. The shortest of all cannas—to just 1½ ft. high—belong to the Seven Dwarfs series; they have green leaves and sport flowers in the full range of typical canna colors.

CANOE BIRCH. See BETULA papyrifera

CANTALOUPE. See MELON

CAPE FUCHSIA. See PHYGELIUS

CAPE HONEYSUCKLE. See TECOMA capensis

CAPE MARIGOLD. See DIMORPHOTHECA

CAPE PONDWEED. See APONOGETON distachyus

CAPE PRIMROSE. See STREPTOCARPUS

CAPE SABLE PALM. See ACOELORRHAPHE wrightii

Capparidaceae. A familiar member of the caper family is spider flower (*Cleome basslerana*).

Caprifoliaceae. The honeysuckle family of shrubs and vines contains many ornamentals in addition to honeysuckle (*Lonicera*); among them are *Abelia*, *Viburnum*, and *Weigela*.

FOR INFORMATION ON YOUR CLIMATE ZONES
PLEASE SEE PAGES 28–38

CARAMBOLA

CARAMBOLA, STARFRUIT

Oxalidaceae

EVERGREEN TREE

✀ TS **H** 12–10

☼ FULL SUN

◖ REGULAR WATER

Carambola

Carambola (known botanically as *Averrhoa carambola*) is a rising star in the world of tropical fruit. It's reliably hardy only in south Florida, but its unique yellow fruits are popular in supermarkets throughout the South: peeling isn't necessary, and the flavorful slices can be added to fruit salads, floated in bowls of punch, or enjoyed as a dessert.

Native to Sri Lanka and Southeast Asia, carambola is a slow-growing evergreen tree with a short trunk and a broad, rounded canopy, reaching 25–30 ft. tall and wide at maturity. Leaves are arranged spirally on the branches; they are medium green, 6–10 in. long, each with 5 to 11 ovate leaflets. Clusters of fragrant pink to lavender flowers appear in several flushes throughout the year; they are followed by ovate, waxy-skinned, juicy yellow fruits, 4–6 in. long, with five prominent longitudinal ribs. Cutting the fruit crosswise produces star-shaped slices. Some compare the flavor to mild citrus, while others call it a blend of pineapple, apple, and citrus. Overall, it may be sweet or rather sour; named selections are usually sweet. Some selections are self-fertile, while others need cross-pollination with another selection to bear fruit.

Carambola

Although carambola briefly tolerates temperatures as low as 27°F, it really is best planted in frost-free locations. The soil should be well drained and moderately acid (pH 5.5–6.5); chlorosis (yellow leaves with green veins) often occurs in alkaline soil. Fertile soil containing lots of organic matter results in faster growth and more fruit. The tree is quite susceptible to drought, so water it regularly during dry periods, even in winter. Fertilize two or three times a year during periods of active growth with an appropriate fruit-tree fertilizer. Full sun is a must. Pruning is rarely necessary, and pests are seldom serious.

Carambola is popular as a small shade tree in south Florida. Careful siting is necessary, however, because grass will not grow beneath the dense canopy.

Recommended selections include these four.

'Arkin'. Bright yellow to yellow-orange fruit, 4–5 in. long; firm and very sweet, with few seeds. Keeps well. Self-fertile but bears better with a pollenizer.

'Fwang Tung'. Pale yellow, 5- to 6-in.-long fruit is firm and very sweet, with few seeds. Needs a pollenizer.

'Golden Star'. Originated in Homestead, Florida, in the 1940s. Golden yellow fruit with very waxy skin; 5–6 in. long, crisp and mildly sweet. Self-fertile.

'Sri Kembanqan' ('Sri Kembangan'). Firm, bright yellow-orange, 5- to 6-in.-long fruit with few seeds. Rich, sweet flavor; excellent dessert quality. Needs a pollenizer.

CARAWAY. See CARUM carvi

CARDBOARD PALM. See ZAMIA furfuracea

CARDINAL CLIMBER. See IPOMOEA quamoclit

CARDINAL FLOWER. See LOBELIA cardinalis

CARDINAL'S-GUARD. See PACHYSTACHYS coccinea

FOR INFORMATION ON SELECTING PLANTS
PLEASE SEE PAGES 39–144

CARDOON

Asteraceae (Compositae)

PERENNIAL

✀ LS, CS **H** 10–1

☼ FULL SUN

◖ REGULAR WATER

Cardoon

Native to the Mediterranean and related to the artichoke, cardoon (*Cynara cardunculus*) has culinary uses but is principally grown for its striking, unusual foliage and interesting form. It reaches 5 ft. tall and 4 ft. wide, with coarse, spiny gray-green leaves that look striking in combination with finer-textured plants. In summer, it flaunts purple flowers resembling large thistle blossoms; these can be cut and dried for arrangements. Cardoon naturalizes in the Lower and Coastal South and can become a weed.

Leafstalks are edible. To prepare them for harvest, blanch them by gathering leaves together, tying them up, and wrapping them with paper to exclude light. Do this in late summer or early fall, 4 to 5 weeks before harvesting. To cook, cut the heavy leaf midribs into 3- to 4-in. lengths. Boil until almost tender; then sauté; or boil till tender and serve with butter or a sauce.

CAREX

SEDGE

Cyperaceae

PERENNIALS

✀ US, MS, LS, CS

☼ ◗ SOME SHADE IN HOTTEST CLIMATES

◖ ◖ ◖ WATER NEEDS VARY BY SPECIES

Carex buchananii

Gardeners may think of the sedges as ornamental grasses, but in fact they belong to an entirely different plant family. Found worldwide, they form clumping tufts of gracefully arching, grasslike foliage. The long, narrow evergreen leaves are often striped or oddly colored. Flowers are generally insignificant. Use sedges in borders, containers, rock gardens, and water gardens. Although they are commonly recommended for moist soils, many will grow in relatively dry soils.

C. buchananii. LEATHER LEAF SEDGE. Heat zones 9–5. From New Zealand. Curly-tipped, arching, 2- to 3-ft.-long blades make striking reddish bronze clumps 2–2½ ft. wide. Use with gray foliage or with deep greens. Moderate water.

C. comans. NEW ZEALAND HAIR SEDGE. Heat zones 9–7. Dense, fine-textured clumps of narrow, silvery green foliage. Leaves are usually 1 ft. long but may reach 6 ft.; on slopes, they look like flowing water. 'Bronze' is similar but has coppery brown leaves. Green-leafed selection sold as 'Frosted Curls' ('Frosty Curls') is usually a selection of another sedge, *C. albula*. Moderate water.

C. conica 'Snowline' ('Marginata'). Heat zones 9–1. Variegated selection of a species native to Japan and Korea. To 2 ft. wide and a little over a foot high, with white-margined dark green leaves. Regular water.

C. dolichostachya 'Kaga-nishiki' ('Gold Fountains'). Heat zones 9–5. Variegated selection of a Japanese species. To 1–2 ft. high and wide. Forms an elegant clump of medium green leaves edged in gold. Somewhat drought tolerant but does best with moderate to regular water.

C. elata 'Aurea' ('Bowles' Golden'). Heat zones 9–3. Selection of a European native. Clump to 2½ ft. high, 1½ ft. wide, with leaves that emerge bright yellow in spring and hold some color until late summer. Needs ample moisture; will grow in standing water.

C. flacca (C. glauca). BLUE SEDGE. Heat zones 9–5. From Europe. Creeping perennial with blue-gray, grasslike foliage that ranges from 6 in. to 2 ft. tall and wide. Evergreen only in mildest climates. Tolerant of many soils and irrigation schemes. Not invasive; spreads slowly and can be clipped like a lawn. Endures light foot traffic, moderate shade, competition with tree roots. Moderate to regular water.

C. morrowii. Heat zones 9–5. Green-leafed Japanese species known for its variegated forms. All take regular water.

'Variegata' is a name given to many selections with white leaf edges. Forms a clump 1 ft. high, 1½ ft. wide, with fairly coarse (½-in.-wide) leaves. 'Goldband' ('Aurea-variegata') is similar but has creamy yellow leaf margins. Both of these make good edging plants; individual clumps look great among rocks. 'Ice Dance' has more prominent white leaf borders than 'Variegata' and a spreading habit; it forms a carpet 2–3 ft. wide. Although it increases by rhizomes, it's not invasive. 'Silver Sceptre' has white-edged leaves about ¼ in. wide. It is somewhat spreading but does not cover ground as fast as 'Ice Dance'.

Fine-textured, very narrow (⅛-in.) leaves, dark green with a white center, give *C. m. temnolepis* 'Silk Tassel' its delicate, airy look. It spreads about 2 ft. wide.

C. muskingumensis. PALM SEDGE. Heat zones 8–1. From North America. The basic species, to 2 ft. tall and spreading widely by rhizomes, has tapered green leaves radiating from lax stems, creating the effect of small, feathery palms. 'Little Midge', to 10 in. high, is miniature in all its parts. Leaves of 'Oehme' are solid green when new, but they quickly develop yellow margins. Regular water.

CARICA. See PAPAYA

CARICATURE PLANT. See GRAPTOPHYLLUM pictum

CARISSA macrocarpa

NATAL PLUM

Apocynaceae

EVERGREEN SHRUB

🌿 CS (PROTECTED), TS 🌡 12–9; OR GROW IN POT

☀️ ◐ ● BEST IN SUN, TOLERATES SOME SHADE; BRIGHT LIGHT

◌ ◍ LITTLE TO REGULAR WATER

Carissa macrocarpa

One of Florida's most versatile landscape plants, Natal plum is valued for both its ornamental qualities and its tasty fruit. Vigorous, fast-growing, rounded shrub to 10 ft. tall and wide, with oval, leathery, rich green leaves to 3 in. long. Native to South Africa; prefers the frost-free climes of south Florida but will grow as far north as Orlando with few problems. It blooms throughout the year, bearing star-shaped, five-petaled white flowers that are nearly as fragrant as those of Confederate jasmine (*Trachelospermum jasminoides*) but larger (to 2 in. across). Oval, fleshy red or purple fruits, 1–1½ in. long, follow the flowers; blossoms and fruit at various stages of ripeness often appear together. The fruit has a cranberrylike flavor and can be eaten fresh or used in jelly, sauce, or pie; be sure it is ripe before you harvest it.

Natal plum is easy to grow in most soils. It's one of the very best plants for the beach, as it tolerates salt spray, wind, and sandy soil. Accepts heavy pruning and makes a superior hedge. Sharp spines along its branches discourage trespassers, so it works well as a barrier plant—but don't plant it near walkways, pools, or steps, where the spines might prove hazardous. In bright light, it can be grown as a houseplant. Not browsed by deer.

'Boxwood Beauty'. Exceptionally compact, thornless growth to 2 ft. high and as wide. Has deep green leaves like those of a large-leafed boxwood (*Buxus*). Good for hedging and shaping.

'Fancy'. More upright growth than species, with unusually large fruit.

'Green Carpet'. Low grower to 1–1½ ft. high, spreading to 4 ft. or wider. Smaller leaves than those of species. Excellent ground cover.

'Horizontalis'. To 1½–2 ft. high, spreading, trailing. Dense foliage.

'Minima'. Slow growth to 1–1½ ft. high, about 2 ft. wide. Tiny leaves and flowers.

'Prostrata'. Vigorous spreader to 2 ft. high; good ground cover. Prune out any upright growth. Can be trained as espalier.

'Ruby Point'. Red-foliaged selection that holds its color well. Grows more upright than species.

'Tomlinson'. Thornless. Compact, slow growth to 2–2½ ft. high and about 3 ft. wide. Good in large container or as a foundation plant.

'Tuttle' ('Nana Compacta Tuttlei'). Compact, dense growth to 2–3 ft. high, 3–5 ft. wide. Heavy production of flowers and fruit. Effective as a ground cover.

CARNATION. See DIANTHUS caryophyllus

CAROLINA ALLSPICE. See CALYCANTHUS floridus

CAROLINA JESSAMINE. See GELSEMIUM sempervirens

CAROLINA LAUREL CHERRY. See PRUNUS caroliniana

CAROLINA MOONSEED. See COCCULUS carolinus

CARPET BUGLEWEED. See AJUGA

CARPET GRASS. See AXONOPUS affinis

CARPINUS

HORNBEAM

Betulaceae

DECIDUOUS TREES

🌿 ZONES VARY BY SPECIES

☀️ ◐ ● EXPOSURE NEEDS VARY BY SPECIES

◍ REGULAR WATER

Carpinus betulus

These are well-behaved, long-lived, relatively small shade trees; make fine street or lawn trees. Growth rate is slow to moderate. Very hard, tough wood. Dark green, sawtooth-edged leaves color up agreeably in the Upper and Middle South, hang on late in season. Fruits (small, hard nutlets in leaflike bracts) are carried in attractive drooping clusters to 5 in. long. Mature trees need little or no pruning.

C. betulus. EUROPEAN HORNBEAM. Zones US, MS, LS; 8–1. Native from Europe to Iran. Excellent landscape tree to 40 ft. tall. Dense pyramidal form, eventually becoming as broad as tall, with drooping outer branches. Handsome, furrowed gray bark like that of *C. caroliniana*. Leaves seldom marred by insects or disease, 2–5 in. long, turn yellow or dark red in autumn. Best in full sun but tolerates light shade. 'Fastigiata' is the selection commonly sold; tree develops an oval-vase shape with age.

C. caroliniana. IRONWOOD. Zones US, MS, LS, CS; 9–1. Native from Nova Scotia to Minnesota, southward to Texas and Florida. Also known as blue beech and musclewood in its native range, where it is often found at forest edges or as an understory plant along rivers and streams. Those common names refer to the tree's trunk, which is blue gray and smooth, with undulations that look like muscles flexing beneath the surface. Grows to 25–30 ft. tall and wide, with round head; can be grown as single- or multitrunked tree. Leaves, 1–3 in. long, turn mottled yellow and red in fall; they drop before those of *C. betulus*. Ironwood does well in a range of exposures from full sun to heavy shade. Best in natural gardens.

CARPOBROTUS

ICE PLANT

Aizoaceae

SUCCULENT WOODY-BASED PERENNIALS

🌿 CS, TS 🌡 12–10

☀️ FULL SUN

◌ ◍ LITTLE TO MODERATE WATER

Carpobrotus chilensis

Trailing plants with coarse, succulent leaves and showy summer flowers; in the South, they are primarily seen in central and south Florida and in South and Southwest Texas. Their acceptance of salt spray and sandy soil makes them superior candidates for oceanfront planting as a

C

ground or bank cover. They also do well in containers. Full sun and good drainage are essential. Plant about 1½ ft. apart.

C. chilensis (Mesembryanthemum aequilaterale). Probably from South Africa; naturalized along West Coast in U.S. Straight, three-sided, fleshy leaves are 2 in. long. Lightly fragrant, rosy purple flowers.

C. edulis (Mesembryanthemum edule). HOTTENTOT FIG. From South Africa. Curved, 4- to 5-in.-long leaves; pale yellow to rose flowers. Fruit is edible but not particularly tasty.

CARRION FLOWER. See STAPELIA

CARROT

Apiaceae (Umbelliferae)

BIENNIAL GROWN AS COOL-SEASON ANNUAL

⚡ US, MS, LS, CS, TS H 12–1

☼ FULL SUN

💧 REGULAR WATER

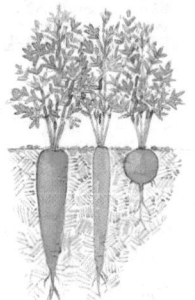

Carrot

Native to Afghanistan, carrots are known botanically as *Daucus carota sativus*. The key to success in growing them is loose, deep soil: carrots reach smooth perfection only in light soils free of stones and clods. If you have heavy clay or rocky soil, plant in raised beds or choose short-growing kinds. Carrots are a good spring crop and even better for fall; their flavor sweetens as the weather cools. You can leave roots in the ground until a hard freeze, pulling them as desired. In the Coastal and Tropical South, grow them as a winter crop.

For spring harvests, sow seeds about 6 weeks before the last frost. To extend your harvest, make two or three small, consecutive plantings 10 days apart. For a fall crop, sow in midsummer in the Upper and Middle South, in August or September in the Lower South. For winter crops in the Coastal and Tropical South, sow in November or December.

Before planting, work into the soil ½ cup of 10-10-10 fertilizer per 10 ft. of row. Cover with no more than ¼ in. of soil. If your soil tends to crust over when dry, cover the seeds with sand, milled peat moss, or potting mix instead of soil. Seeds may take 1 to 3 weeks to germinate. Keep soil evenly moist. When seedlings are 2 in. tall, thin them to 2–4 in. apart. (You can steam these tiny carrots in butter or chop the entire miniature plant, tops and all, for a fresh addition to tossed salads.) Cover root tops with soil to keep them from turning green, which results in bitterness. Most types are ready to harvest 60 to 70 days from sowing.

Plant the right selection for your type of soil. Long grocery-store kinds, such as 'Scarlet Nantes', require loose, sandy soil at least 1 ft. deep. For shallower, heavier soils that contain some clay, try blunt-nosed, half-long selections such as 'Caroline', 'Danvers Half Long', 'Nelson', 'Royal Chantenay', and 'Sweet Sunshine' (a yellow carrot). Other selections include the short and round 'Thumbelina' and miniatures such as 'Little Finger' and 'Short 'n Sweet'.

CARTHAMUS tinctorius

SAFFLOWER, FALSE SAFFRON

Asteraceae (Compositae)

ANNUAL

⚡ US, MS, LS, CS, TS H 12–1

☼ FULL SUN

💧 MODERATE WATER

Carthamus tinctorius

This thistle relative (probably an Asian native) is ornamental as well as useful: it is grown commercially for the oil extracted from its seeds. To 3 ft. tall, 1–1½ ft. wide, with erect, spiny-leafed stems. In summer, bears orange-yellow flower heads above leafy

bracts; inner bracts are spiny. Durable cut flower, fresh or dried. An ornamental spine-free form is also available. Dried safflower blossoms have been used for seasoning in place of true saffron, which they somewhat resemble in color and flavor. Sow seeds in place in spring, after danger of frost is past.

CARUM carvi

CARAWAY

Apiaceae (Umbelliferae)

BIENNIAL

⚡ US, MS, LS H 8–1

☼ FULL SUN

💧 REGULAR WATER

Carum carvi

Native to Asia Minor. Caraway is prized for its edible seeds, used in flavoring pickles, vegetables, and breads. In the first year after planting, carrotlike leaves grow from a taproot, forming a mound 1–2 ft. high. In the second spring, umbrella-like clusters of white flowers rise above the foliage and set seed; after the seeds ripen in midsummer, the plant dies.

Start seeds in a garden bed in fall or early spring; be sure soil is well drained. Thin seedlings to 1½ ft. apart. Harvest the seed heads after they have turned brown, then dry them in paper bags until you can shake the seeds loose.

CARYA

HICKORY

Juglandaceae

DECIDUOUS TREES

⚡ US, MS, LS, CS

☼ FULL SUN

💧💧 MODERATE TO REGULAR WATER, EXCEPT AS NOTED

Carya glabra

Large trees with leaves divided featherwise into leaflets. Inconspicuous flowers are followed by nuts enclosed in husks that usually break away at maturity. Trees are too large for smaller yards but are attractive where space is available. All develop deep taproots, so they should be planted while young and not moved later.

C. glabra. PIGNUT HICKORY. Heat zones 8–1. Native to southern and eastern U.S. Grows to 50–60 ft., sometimes 100 ft., with a canopy nearly as broad. Leaves, 8–10 in. long, with five to nine leaflets, are retained into late fall and turn a beautiful orange, brown, and yellow, even in the Lower South. Smooth bark. Nuts are bitter.

C. illinoensis. See Pecan

C. laciniosa. SHELLBARK HICKORY. Heat zones 9–4. Native from New York to Iowa, south to Tennessee and Oklahoma; found in lowlands that are periodically flooded. Similar to *C. ovata* but smaller. Grows slowly to 60–80 ft. tall, 40–60 ft. wide. Leaves usually divided into seven leaflets. Largest of hickory nuts; sweet, hard shelled. Regular to ample water.

C. ovata. SHAGBARK HICKORY. Heat zones 8–1. Native to eastern U.S. Typically grows to 60–100 ft. tall and 30–40 ft. wide. Most conspicuous feature is the gray, shaggy bark, with large plates curving out and away from the trunk. The hard-shelled nuts are sweet. Leaves typically have five leaflets; autumn foliage is an attractive bright yellow. Wood is proverbially tough and hard.

Caryophyllaceae. This is the pink family, including many garden annuals and perennials as well as a few weeds. Leaves are borne in opposite pairs at joints that are often swollen; leaves are often joined together at their bases. Pinks and carnations (*Dianthus*) are typical representatives, along with snow-in-summer (*Cerastium tomentosum*) and *Lychnis*.

CARYOPTERIS

BLUEBEARD
Verbenaceae
DECIDUOUS SHRUBS
☀ ZONES VARY BY SPECIES
☼ FULL SUN
💧 MODERATE WATER

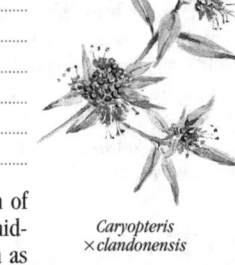

*Caryopteris
×clandonensis*

Asian natives valued for their contribution of cool blue color to flower borders from mid-summer to frost. Erect form. Generally grown as woody-based perennials—if plants don't freeze back in winter, cut them nearly to ground before spring growth flush to ensure a good base for the new season's growth. Bear dense, stalked clusters of small flowers on cur-rent season's growth; trim after each wave of bloom to encourage repeat flowering. Provide good drainage, since plants can rot in wet soil. Not browsed by deer.

C. ×clandonensis. BLUE MIST. Zones US, MS, LS, CS; 9–1. Low-growing mound (to 2 ft. tall and wide) of narrow, 3-in.-long, gray-green leaves. Clusters of small flowers top upper parts of stems. The original selection, 'Arthur J. Simmonds', is still the hardiest and most reliable; it has bright blue blossoms and gray-green leaves with silvery undersides. 'Azure' and 'Heavenly Blue' bear deep blue blossoms; 'Dark Knight' and 'Longwood Blue', also with deep blue blooms, have silvery foliage. 'Worcester Gold' has yellow leaves and lavender-blue flowers. 'First Choice', with profuse dark purple blossoms, blooms over a longer period than other selections.

C. incana (C. mastacanthus). COMMON BLUEBEARD, BLUE SPI-RAEA. Zones US, MS, LS; 9–1. Taller than *C. ×clandonensis,* with looser, more open growth to 3–4 ft. tall, 5 ft. wide. Lavender-blue flowers appear in leaf joints.

CARYOTA

FISHTAIL PALM
Arecaceae (Palmae)
PALMS
☀ TS H 12–10; OR GROW IN POTS
☼ ◑ SUN OR PART SHADE; BRIGHT INDIRECT LIGHT
💧 REGULAR WATER
⚠ CRYSTALS ON FRUIT CAN IRRITATE SKIN

Caryota ochlandra

Feather palms (see *Arecaceae*) with huge, finely divided leaves; leaflets flattened and split at tips like fish tails. Tender. Native to South-east Asia, where they grow in full sun. Not browsed by deer. In pots indoors, place them near a southern or western window. Let the soil surface go dry to the touch between waterings. Avoid handling fruit with bare hands; invis-ible crystals on its skin can cause severe itching and burning.

C. mitis. BURMESE FISHTAIL PALM. Slow grower to 10–40 ft. tall, spreading to 10–20 ft. Basal offshoots eventually form clustered trunks. Light green foliage.

C. ochlandra. CANTON FISHTAIL PALM. May reach 25 ft. tall and spread half as wide. Medium dark green leaves. Hardiest of the caryotas; has survived to 26°F.

C. urens. WINE PALM. Single-stemmed palm to 100 ft. tall and 30 ft. wide in Asia, to 20 ft. tall and 8 ft. wide in Tropical South with careful protec-tion. If temperatures go below 32°F, it's certain to die. Dark green leaves.

CASCADE PALM. See CHAMAEDOREA cataractum

CASCALOTE. See CAESALPINIA cacalaco

CASHMERE BOUQUET. See CLERODENDRUM bungei

CASSIA

Fabaceae (Leguminosae)
EVERGREEN, SEMIEVERGREEN, DECIDUOUS TREES
☀ TS H 12–10
☼ FULL SUN
◐ ◑ ◕ WATER NEEDS VARY BY SPECIES

Cassia ×nealiae

The genus *Cassia* once included many yellow-flowered trees and shrubs now reclassified as *Senna* (see that entry), though some are still sold under their old names. These cassias are showy flowering trees that brighten landscapes in the warmest climates—not just with yellow blossoms but also with pink, cerise, and white ones. Flowering times are approximate, since plants may bloom at any time or bloom intermittently over a long period. Most have long seedpods that can present a litter problem. Grow in well-drained soil. Plants are best pruned when young (to develop a strong framework) and as needed after flower-ing is finished.

C. excelsa. CROWN OF GOLD TREE. Partially evergreen. Native to Argentina. Grows fast to 25–30 ft. high and wide. Leaves are divided into 10 to 20 pairs of inch-long leaflets; large bright yellow flowers in 12- to 16-in.-long clusters bloom in late summer and early fall. Prune hard after flowering. Moderate water.

C. fistula. SHOWER OF GOLD, GOLDEN SHOWER. Deciduous or partially evergreen. From India. To 30–40 ft. high and 35 ft. wide, with 2-ft. leaves divided into four to eight pairs of 3- to 6-in.-long leaflets. Summer flowers are bright yellow, in drooping, nearly 2-ft.-long clusters of 50 or more. Prune hard after bloom. Extremely showy. Good drought tolerance.

Cassia fistula

C. grandis. PINK SHOWER, CORAL SHOWER. Deciduous. From tropical America. Fast growing to 20–50 ft. tall and 30 ft. wide. Abundant coral pink flowers in 7-in.-long clusters in early spring. Leaves divided into 8 to 20 pairs of 2½-in. leaflets, pink when young. Use for color accent or as shade, street, or park tree. Somewhat drought tolerant but blooms best with regular water.

C. javanica. PINK AND WHITE SHOWER. Deciduous. From Indonesia. To 30–35 ft. high and 25 ft. wide, with irregular habit. Masses of light pink flowers in clusters to 4 in. or longer appear along branches from spring to fall, peaking in early summer. Leaves divided into 5 to 15 pairs of oval, 1- to 2-in.-long leaflets. Useful as color accent or shade, street, or park tree. Good wind tolerance; moderate drought and salt tolerance. Best with moderate water.

C. leptophylla. GOLD MEDALLION TREE. Nearly evergreen. Native to Brazil. Shapeliest and most graceful of the cassias. Grows fast to 20–25 ft. tall, 30 ft. wide, with an open-headed, low-spreading structure; tends to weep. Shape to a single trunk; otherwise, plant becomes very sprawling. Leaves have up to 12 pairs of narrow, 1½- to 2½-in. leaflets; deep yellow flowers are borne in 6- to 8-in. clusters in July and August, with scattered bloom later. Prune hard after bloom. Little to moderate water.

C. ×nealiae. RAINBOW SHOWER. Semievergreen to deciduous. A sterile hybrid between *C. fistula* and *C. javanica,* originating in Hawaii. Moderately fast grower to 30–40 ft. high and 35 ft. wide. Dark green foliage. Thrives in any well-drained soil. Withstands drought well but has only moderate wind tolerance and poor salt tolerance.

Several named selections are available in a range of flower colors from pale yellow through golden yellow to orange and cerise—the "rainbow" of the common name. Some may produce occasional seedpods.

'Lunalilo Yellow'. Flowers open a bright yellow orange, then age to bright yellow. Late spring to fall bloom.

'Nii Gold'. A sport of 'Wilhelmina Tenney'. Blooms anytime from spring to fall; deep gold buds open to blooms that age to strong yellow. ▶

'Queen's Hospital White'. Flowers open pale yellow, fade rapidly to very light yellow to white. Blooms in spring to late summer.

Selection 'Wilhelmina Tenney' produces spectacular blossom clusters from spring to fall. Petal exteriors are deep cerise aging to paler shades; interiors are yellow.

CASTANEA. See CHESTNUT

CASTILLEJA

INDIAN PAINTBRUSH

Scrophulariaceae

ANNUALS, BIENNIALS, PERENNIALS

✄ US, MS, LS, CS, TS

☼ ◑ FULL SUN OR PARTIAL SHADE

◒ WATER DURING DRY SEASON

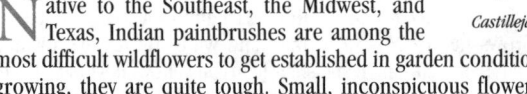

Castilleja indivisa

Native to the Southeast, the Midwest, and Texas, Indian paintbrushes are among the most difficult wildflowers to get established in garden conditions, but once growing, they are quite tough. Small, inconspicuous flowers appear in spring among showy fan-shaped bracts that range in color from pink and purple to yellow, orange, and flame red. Sow seeds thickly among plants such as grasses or perennials, because during germination these wildflowers may draw nourishment from the roots of other plants.

C. indivisa. INDIAN PAINTBRUSH. Annual or biennial. Heat zones 12–9. Native to southeastern Oklahoma, eastern Texas, and the Coastal Plains. Plant varies from 6 to 16 in. tall, with a width of 6 in. Orange to red, 3- to 8-in.-long flower spikes bloom through spring.

C. purpurea. PURPLE PAINTBRUSH. Perennial. Heat zones 9–3. Native to the Midwest and Texas. To 9 in. tall, 6 in. wide. Flowers vary widely in color; they may be purple, but are just as often pink, red, or yellow. Also known as lemon paintbrush. Blooms in late spring.

CAST-IRON PLANT. See ASPIDISTRA

CASTOR ARALIA. See KALOPANAX septemlobus

CASTOR BEAN. See RICINUS communis

CASUARINA

BEEFWOOD, SHE-OAK

Casuarinaceae

EVERGREEN TREES

✄ TS

☼ FULL SUN

◔ ◒ LITTLE TO REGULAR WATER

Casuarina equisetifolia

Native primarily to Australia, these trees prove that you can get too much of a good thing. Because they tolerate challenging conditions, such as poor soil, salt spray, wind, and heat, Floridians happily planted them as windbreaks and at the beach to stabilize dunes. Unfortunately, the trees quickly spread by seeds and suckers, invading new locations and forming solid stands. Their heavy root mats quickly eliminate competing species. If you want to plant casuarina, exercise great caution.

Trees have long, thin, jointed green branchlets that resemble pine needles; true leaves are inconspicuous. They bear small, conelike fruits.

C. cunninghamiana. RIVER SHE-OAK. Largest species—to 70 ft. tall, 30 ft. wide—and also the finest in texture. Branches are dark green. Spreads mainly by seed, infrequently by suckers. Naturalized in the southwestern and southeastern coastal areas of Florida as far north as Tampa and Titusville. Accepts wet or dry soil.

C. equisetifolia. AUSTRALIAN PINE, HORSETAIL TREE. Fast grower to 60 ft. tall, 20 ft. wide. Pendulous gray-green branches resemble horsetail (*Equisetum hyemale*). Often found along beaches in southern Florida. Sometimes used as a clipped hedge. Thrives in dry soil as well as in moist conditions (as long as drainage is good). Spreads mainly by winged seeds.

C. glauca. To 50 ft. tall, 20 ft. wide. Suckers aggressively to form dense stands; common along roadways and fence lines. Looks something like *C. cunninghamiana*. Takes wet or dry soil. Hardiest to cold of the species listed here (survives 30°F).

CATALPA

Bignoniaceae

DECIDUOUS TREES

✄ US, MS, LS, CS

☼ ◑ FULL SUN OR LIGHT SHADE

◔ ◒ MODERATE TO REGULAR WATER

Catalpa speciosa

Catalpas are among the few truly deciduous trees that can compete in flower and leaf with subtropical species. They bloom in late spring and summer, bearing large, upright clusters of trumpet-shaped, 2-in.-wide flowers in pure white, striped and marked with yellow and soft brown; flowers are held above large, bold, heart-shaped leaves. Long, bean-shaped seed capsules, sometimes called Indian beans, follow the blossoms.

Unusually well adapted to extremes of heat and cold; take any type of soil. Where winds are strong, plant in lee of taller trees or buildings to protect leaves from damage. Some gardeners object to litter of fallen flowers in summer and seed capsules in autumn. Plants need shaping while young; they seldom develop a well-established dominant shoot on their own. Shorten side branches as tree grows. When branching begins at desired height, remove lower branches.

For the tree sometimes called desert catalpa, see *Chilopsis linearis*. Another tree sometimes mistakenly called catalpa is the very similar *Paulownia tomentosa* (empress tree), with lavender flowers. *Paulownia* shows flower buds in winter; catalpa does not.

C. bignonioides. COMMON CATALPA, INDIAN BEAN. Heat zones 9–5. Native to southeastern U.S. Grows to 30–50 ft. according to climate or soil, with somewhat smaller spread. Leaves are 5–8 in. long, often in whorls, and give off an odd odor when crushed. Subject to chlorosis (yellow leaves with green veins) in alkaline soil. Yellow leaves of 'Aurea' are showiest in the Upper South. 'Purpurea' has dark purple new growth that later turns green.

'Nana'. UMBRELLA CATALPA. A dense globe form usually grafted high on *C. bignonioides*. Almost always sold as *C. bungei*. It never blooms. Usually about 6 ft. high, 5 ft. wide.

C. bungei. See C. bignonioides 'Nana'

C. ×erubescens 'Purpurea'. Heat zones 9–5. Selection of a hybrid between *C. bignonioides* and *C. ovata*; resembles *C. bignonioides*. Leaves (to 10–16 in. long) and branchlets are deep blackish purple when young, maturing to purplish green in summer.

C. fargesii. Heat zones 9–5. From China. Open habit to 60 ft. high and wide; notable mainly for clusters of rosy purple, 1½-in. flowers. Leaves are 3–6 in. long.

C. ovata. CHINESE CATALPA. Heat zones 8–1. To 30 ft. tall and wide, with 4- to 10-in.-long leaves and yellowish white flowers.

C. speciosa. NORTHERN CATALPA. Heat zones 8–1. Native to central and southern Midwest. Round headed; 40–70 ft. tall, 20–40 ft. wide. Leaves 6–12 in. long. Fewer flowers per cluster than for *C. bignonioides*. Early training and pruning will give tall trunk and umbrella-shaped crown.

Catalpa speciosa

CATANANCHE caerulea

CUPID'S DART

Asteraceae (Compositae)

PERENNIAL

✿ US, MS, LS ╟ 8–1

☼ FULL SUN

💧 MODERATE WATER

Catananche caerulea

Wispy, free-flowering plant from Europe, good for summer borders and fresh or dried arrangements. Gray-green, grassy leaves form a clump to 1 ft. high and wide. Lavender-blue, 2-in. flower heads, reminiscent of cornflowers *(Centaurea cyanus)* and surrounded by strawlike, shining bracts, appear atop leafless stems to 2 ft. high. Remove faded flowers to prolong bloom. Selections include white 'Alba', cornflower blue 'Blue Giant', and deep blue-violet 'Major'. Plants will flower first year from seed sown in early spring. Rather short lived, but volunteer seedlings usually provide replacements.

CATHARANTHUS roseus (Vinca rosea)

MADAGASCAR PERIWINKLE

Apocynaceae

PERENNIAL USUALLY GROWN AS ANNUAL

✿ US, MS, LS, CS, TS ╟ 12–1

☼ ◐ FULL SUN OR PARTIAL SHADE

💧 MODERATE WATER

Catharanthus roseus

Native to Madagascar, India, and tropical Asia, Madagascar periwinkle blooms continuously in hot weather, thriving in both humid and dry heat. Bushy plant grows 1–1½ ft. high and wide, with upright stems clothed in glossy green leaves and adorned with phloxlike, 1½-in. flowers in pure white, pink, rose, or white with a rose or red eye. Bloom goes on all summer, but by autumn the plant gets leggy and flowering is spotty. Survives winter in central and south Florida, where it has escaped cultivation and naturalized. Self-sows readily, especially in sandy or gritty soil.

Recent breeding has produced plants with larger blossoms in a wider range of colors, including vibrant shades of red, lavender, and purple. Flowers of some new types sport overlapping petals, giving them a fuller, more rounded look. Pacifica and Cooler series are compact, 12- to 15-in. plants with large (2-in.) flowers. The Tropicana series features blooms in shades of pink and coral on foot-tall plants. The Stardust series bears orchid, pink, or raspberry red flowers centered with a white starburst.

Variations in form among Madagascar periwinkles include shorter and more compact types and those with trailing habits. The Little series grows 8–10 in. high; the Carpet series grows 4–8 in. tall, creeping to 1½ ft. wide. Plants in the Mediterranean series grow 5–6 in. high and can spread 2½ ft. wide; they're useful as a seasonal ground cover or in hanging baskets. Blossom colors include apricot, pink, rose, lilac, and white.

All types bloom the first season from seed sown early indoors or in a greenhouse or cold frame, but most people buy transplants at garden centers. Unfortunately, the newer hybrids seem more susceptible than their predecessors to wilt and rot diseases caused by planting in heavy, wet soil. Be sure to plant in loose, fast-draining soil, and take care not to crowd plants.

Madagascar periwinkle was formerly known botanically as *Vinca rosea*, and many people still call it by the name "vinca."

CATMINT. See NEPETA faassenii

CATNIP. See NEPETA cataria

CAT'S CLAW. See MACFADYENA unguis-cati

CAT'S WHISKERS. See ORTHOSIPHON aristatus

CATTLEYA

Orchidaceae

EPIPHYTIC ORCHIDS

✿ TS ╟ 12–5; OR HOUSEPLANTS

◐ LIGHT SHADE; BRIGHT INDIRECT LIGHT

💧 REGULAR WATER

Cattleya

Native to tropical America. Among the most popular and best-known orchids, with showy flowers that are used for corsages.

Species, varieties, and hybrids are too numerous to list here. All have pseudobulbs 1–3 in. thick, bearing leathery leaves and a stem topped with one to four or more flowers. Plants range in size from a few inches tall to 2 ft. or more. Commercial growers offer choices with flowers in many shades of lavender and purple, as well as white-blossomed kinds and semialbas (white blossoms with colored lip). Also available are novelties in yellow, orange, red, green, and bronze; many of these are crosses between cattleyas and other orchids.

Cattleyas are widely grown outdoors year-round in the Tropical South, either in containers or naturalized on trees. Elsewhere, they are indoor plants that can be brought outdoors during warm weather. They grow best in a greenhouse where temperature, humidity, and light can be readily controlled. However, they also can be grown successfully as houseplants if the following needs are satisfied: (1) warm temperatures (55–60°F at night, 65–80°F or higher during the day); (2) relatively high humidity (50 to 60 percent or more); (3) bright indirect light with protection from hot midday sun. Leaves should be light green and erect; if light is too low, they turn dark green and new growth becomes soft. See also Orchidaceae.

CAULIFLOWER

Brassicaceae (Cruciferae)

BIENNIAL GROWN AS COOL-SEASON ANNUAL

✿ US, MS, LS, CS, TS ╟ 6–1

☼ FULL SUN

💧 REGULAR WATER

Cauliflower

Cauliflower is related to broccoli and cabbage (all members of genus *Brassica*) and has similar cultural needs, but it is less tolerant of heat and harder to grow. Time plantings so plants mature either well before or well after summer heat; early-maturing or heat-tolerant types are your best bets. 'Snow Crown' (50 days from setting out plants until harvest) is the standard early cauliflower. Heat-tolerant kinds include 'Ravella Hybrid' (70 days) and 'Amazing' (75 days). Romanesco types have cone-shaped heads of lime green florets with fine flavor; 'Shannon' (70 days) and 'Tower' (78 days) are examples. For interesting color, plant purple-headed 'Violet Queen' (54 days; turns green when cooked).

Start with small plants; set them 1½–2 ft. apart in rows spaced 3 ft. apart. Keep plants actively growing, as any check during transplanting or later growth is likely to cause premature setting of undersized heads. At planting, feed with water-soluble 20-20-20 fertilizer; 3 weeks after planting, sprinkle ½ cup of 10-10-10 fertilizer per 10 ft. of row around plants. When heads first appear, tie up the large leaves around them to keep them white. On self-blanching types, leaves curl over heads without assistance. Harvest heads as soon as they reach full size. Most kinds are ready 50 to 100 days after transplanting; overwintering types may take 6 months.

To prevent a buildup of soil-borne pests, plant cauliflower in a different site each year. Club root is a serious fungal pest in acid soils; apply lime, if necessary, to raise the pH to at least 6.5. Floating row covers do a good job of controlling insects such as cabbage loopers, cabbageworms, cutworms, and root maggots. You can also control cutworms and root maggots by ringing the base of the plant with a collar made from cardboard. *Bacillus thuringiensis* (Bt; sold as Dipel) applied according to label directions controls cabbageworms and loopers.

C

CEANOTHUS

WILD LILAC

Rhamnaceae

EVERGREEN SHRUBS

✿ US, MS, LS, CS

☼ FULL SUN

◯ LITTLE OR NO WATER

As a group, these are some of the prettiest flowering shrubs around, with blooms ranging from white through all shades of blue to deep violet. Unfortunately, most fail miserably in the heavy soils and rainy, humid climates of the South. A few notable exceptions are listed below. Give them excellent drainage and full sun. They rarely suffer pest damage.

C. americanus. NEW JERSEY TEA. Heat zones 8–1. Native from Canada south to South Carolina and west to Texas. Compact, rounded shrub 3–4 ft. tall and wide, with slender, upright branches. Ovate, 2- to 3-in.-long, dark green leaves may turn yellow in fall. White, 1- to 2-in.-long flower clusters appear atop the plant in spring and early summer. Colonists reputedly brewed a tea substitute from the leaves during the boycott of British tea prior to the American Revolution.

C. × delilianus. FRENCH HYBRID CEANOTHUS. Heat zones 10–7. Result of a cross between *C. americanus* and a blue-flowered Mexican species; has oval dark green leaves to 3 in. long and 5-in. clusters of gorgeous blue flowers. 'Gloire de Versailles', to 10 ft. high and wide, is the best-known selection; it blooms in late summer or fall.

C. × pallidus. Heat zones 10–7. Result of a cross between a close relative of *C. americanus* and *C. × delilianus.* Grows to form a broad, 2- to 3-ft.-high mound. Shiny, oval to oblong green leaves are 1–2 in. long. Bears dense clusters of pink flowers in summer. 'Marie Simon' bears soft pink blossoms, 'Ceres' lilac-pink blooms. 'Plenus' has pink buds that open to double white flowers.

Ceanothus × delilianus
'Gloire de Versailles'

CEDAR. See CEDRUS

CEDAR, INCENSE. See CALOCEDRUS decurrens

CEDAR, WESTERN RED. See THUJA plicata

CEDAR OF LEBANON. See CEDRUS libani

CEDRUS

CEDAR

Pinaceae

EVERGREEN TREES

✿ ZONES VARY BY SPECIES

☼ FULL SUN

◯ MODERATE WATER

These conifers, the true cedars, are stately specimen trees that look best when given plenty of room. Needles are borne in tufted clusters. Cone scales, like those of firs (*Abies*), fall from tree, leaving a spiky core behind. Male catkins produce prodigious amounts of pollen that may cover you with yellow dust on a windy day. Plant in deep, well-drained soil. All species are deep rooted and drought tolerant once established.

C. atlantica (C. libani atlantica). ATLAS CEDAR. Zones US, MS, LS; 9–6. From North Africa. Slow to moderate growth to 60 ft. or more. Open and angular in youth; branches usually get too long and heavy on young trees unless tips are pinched or cut back. Growth naturally less open with age. Less spreading than other true cedars, but still needs a 30-ft. circle. Needles are bluish green, less than 1 in. long.

Selections include 'Aurea', needles with yellowish tint; 'Glauca', silvery blue; 'Glauca Pendula', weeping form with blue needles; 'Pendula', verti-

Cedrus atlantica

cally drooping branches. Untrained, spreading, informally branching plants are sold as "rustics." All types stand up well to hot, humid weather.

C. deodara. DEODAR CEDAR. Zones MS, LS, CS, protected sites in US; 9–6. Native to the Himalayas. Fast growing to 80 ft., with 40-ft. spread at ground level; planted in a small lawn, it soon overpowers the area. Lower branches sweep down to ground, then upward. Upper branches openly spaced, graceful. Nodding tip identifies it in skyline. Has a softer, lighter texture than other cedars. To control this tree's spread, cut new growth of side branches halfway back in late spring. Such pruning also makes tree more dense.

Although deodars sold by garden centers are very similar in form, many variations occur in a group of seedlings—from scarecrowlike forms to compact, low shrubs. Needles, to 2 in. long, may be green or have a blue, gray, or yellow cast. Seed-grown 'Shalimar', an extra-hardy selection that has survived to −15°F, has good blue-green color and is the best choice for the Upper South. The following three variations are propagated by cuttings or grafting: 'Aurea', with yellow new foliage turning golden green in summer; 'Descanso Dwarf' ('Compacta'), a slow-growing form reaching 15 ft. in 20 years; and 'Pendula' ('Prostrata'), which grows flat on the ground or will drape over rocks or walls. Deodar cedar can be pruned to grow as a spreading low or high shrub. Annual pruning in late spring will keep it to the shape you want. This is the best species for hot, humid climates.

C. libani. CEDAR OF LEBANON. Zones US, MS, LS; 9–3. Native to Asia Minor. To 80 ft., but slow—to 15 ft. in 15 years. Variable in habit. Usually a dense, narrow pyramid in youth. Spreads picturesquely as it matures to become a majestic skyline tree with long horizontal branches and irregular crown. Needles, less than 1 in. long, are brightest green of any cedar on young trees; on old trees, they are dark gray green. Rather scarce and expensive because of time it requires to reach marketable size. Routine garden care. No pruning needed. 'Sargentii' ('Pendula Sargentii') grows even more slowly, has a short trunk and crowded, pendulous branches; choice container or rock garden plant. 'Pendula' is a weeping form.

C. l. stenocoma. Hardiest of the cedars; has survived −24°F. More stiffly branched than the species, with good green color.

Cedrus deodara

CEIBA pentandra

SILK-COTTON TREE, KAPOK TREE

Bombacaceae

DECIDUOUS TREE

✿ TS H 12–10

☼ FULL SUN

◖◖ MODERATE TO REGULAR WATER

From the tropics of Africa, America, and Southeast Asia. Easily recognized by its huge, spiny, buttressed trunk, this majestic deciduous tree is hardy only in south Florida. Given good soil and moderate to regular moisture, it grows rapidly to 60–70 ft. tall and 15–40 ft. wide. Leaves are medium green, to 6 in. long, each with five to seven leaflets. The tree blooms before leaf-out, bearing cup-shaped, ½-in. flowers in white, pink, or yellow. The flowers are followed by woody seed capsules containing a cottonlike substance—the kapok of commerce (used as a stuffing for pillows and lifejackets).

Silk-cotton tree makes a fine street tree or large shade tree. It needs plenty of room, though: its trunk can grow to 9 ft. wide, with buttresses extending out to 15 ft. or more.

Ceiba pentandra

Celastraceae. This family of evergreen and deciduous woody plants has undistinguished flowers, but fruit is often brightly colored. Bittersweet (*Celastrus*) and *Euonymus* are examples.

CELASTRUS

BITTERSWEET

Celastraceae

DECIDUOUS VINES

US, MS, LS 8–1

FULL SUN

REGULAR WATER

Celastrus scandens

Grown principally for clusters of handsome summer fruit—yellow to orange capsules that split open to display brilliant red seeds inside. Birds seem uninterested in the fruit, so the display extends into winter. Branches bearing fruit are much prized for indoor arrangements. To produce fruit, you will need to plant a male and a female plant close to each other; self-fertile forms of *C. orbiculatus* are available.

Bittersweets are vigorous, twining vines with ropelike branches; they need support. They will become a tangled mass of intertwining branches unless pruned constantly. Cut out fruiting branches in winter; pinch out tips of vigorous branches in summer.

C. orbiculatus. ORIENTAL BITTERSWEET. From Japan. To 30–40 ft. Roundish, toothed, medium green leaves to 4 in. Fruit on short side shoots is partially obscured until leaves drop. Foliage may turn an attractive yellow in fall. A very aggressive grower that has escaped gardens and become a weed in the Upper South.

C. rosthornianus (C. loeseneri). LOESENER BITTERSWEET. Native to central and western China. Grows to 20 ft. Dark green, oval leaves to 5 in. long. Heavy crops of fruit. Like *C. orbiculatus* but not as rampant.

C. scandens. AMERICAN BITTERSWEET. Native to eastern U.S. To 20 ft., or even higher if plant has something to grow on. If allowed to climb shrubs or small trees, it can kill them by girdling the stems. Very light green, oval, toothed leaves to 4 in. Fruit is borne in scattered dense clusters that are held above leaves; it looks showy even before foliage falls.

CELERY

Apiaceae (Umbelliferae)

BIENNIAL GROWN AS ANNUAL

US, MS, LS, CS, TS 8–1

FULL SUN

REGULAR TO AMPLE WATER

Celery

Celery (*Apium graveolens dulce*) is native to Europe and Asia and is grown commercially in muck fields in Florida. It's difficult to grow in home gardens, because it needs more moisture and fertilizer than most other vegetables. The keys to success in the South are very rich, organic soil and an unfailing, plentiful water supply. Homegrown celery doesn't taste much different from that sold in markets, so grow it only if you enjoy a challenge.

Transplants are hard to find, so be prepared to start plants from seed. For a spring crop, sow seeds indoors 10 to 12 weeks before the last frost; then set out young plants 4 weeks before the last frost. For a fall crop, sow in summer, timing so that you can set out transplants 10 to 12 weeks before the first autumn frost. Work lots of composted manure and other organic material into the soil before planting. Space seedlings 7 in. apart in rows 2 ft. apart; plant them so that the crown is level with the soil. Keep soil constantly moist. Side-dress rows every 4 weeks with ½ cup of 10-10-10 fertilizer per 10 ft. of row. To whiten stalks (thought to make them less stringy), place a bottomless milk or orange juice carton over each plant to keep out sunlight, but don't cover the leaves. Available selections include 'Tango Hybrid' (85 days from sowing to harvest), 'Utah 52-70' (98 days), and 'Ventura' (80 days).

FOR GROWING SYMBOL EXPLANATIONS
PLEASE SEE PAGE 145

CELOSIA

COCKSCOMB, CHINESE WOOLFLOWER

Amaranthaceae

ANNUALS

US, MS, LS, CS, TS 12–1

FULL SUN

MODERATE WATER

Celosia argentea

Richly colored tropical plants, some with flower clusters in bizarre shapes. In cut arrangements, celosias are attractive with other flowers, but in gardens they are most effective by themselves. Dry cut blooms for winter bouquets. Sow seed in place in late spring or early summer, or set out started plants. Plants will bloom by summer.

C. argentea. COCKSCOMB. Two kinds of cockscombs are derived from this species, which has silvery white flowers and narrow leaves to 2 in. or longer. One group, the plume cockscombs (often sold as *C.* 'Plumosa'), has plumy flower clusters. Some of these (sometimes sold as Chinese woolflower or *C.* 'Childsii') have flower clusters that look like tangled masses of yarn. Flowers come in brilliant shades of pink, orange red, gold, crimson. You can get forms that grow 2½–3 ft. high and 1½ ft. wide. Dwarf, more compact selections grow about 1 ft. high and half as wide; they bear heavily branched plumes.

The other celosia group is the crested cockscombs (often sold as *C.* 'Cristata'). These have velvety, fan-shaped flower clusters, often much contorted and fluted. Flowers are yellow, orange, crimson, purple, or red. Tall kinds grow to 3 ft. tall and 1½ ft. wide, dwarf selections to 10 in. high and 6 in. wide.

C. spicata. WHEAT CELOSIA. Plant is covered in small silvery pink and purple spikes; it looks like a tall wild grass with elegant flowers. Ideal for a natural planting or rock garden and good for drying. Reseeds readily. Reaches 3½ ft. high, just 6 in. wide. Selections include 'Flamingo Feather' (soft pink to white), 'Flamingo Purple' (purple spikes and dark reddish green leaves), and 'Pink Candle' (rose pink spikes).

BRAINY BLOOMS. *No need to reach for the Ginkgo biloba to boost your horticultural brain power. Just sow a few seeds of one of the South's most gaudy passalong plants—the crested cockscomb,* Celosia argentea. *(See page 21. That's red crested cockscomb behind Dr. Dirt.) It's great for cutting and drying and comes in a variety of colors. Best of all, its convoluted flower clusters look just like brains!* ❖

CELTIS

HACKBERRY

Ulmaceae

DECIDUOUS TREES

US, MS, LS, CS 9–1

FULL SUN OR PARTIAL SHADE

MODERATE WATER

Celtis occidentalis

Related to elms (*Ulmus*) and similar to them in most details, but smaller. All have virtue of deep rooting; old trees in narrow planting strips expand in trunk diameter and nearly fill strips without surface roots or any sign of heaving the sidewalk or curb. Good choice for street or lawn tree, even near buildings or paving. Canopy casts moderate shade in spring and summer; leaves turn yellow in fall. Mature trees have picturesque gray bark with corky warts and ridges. Small, berry-like fruit attracts birds.

Hackberry is exceptionally tough, taking strong winds (stake young trees until well established), dry heat, and dry, alkaline soils. Bare-root plants, especially in larger sizes, sometimes fail to leaf out. Buy in containers or try for small bare-root trees with big root systems. ▶

C. laevigata. SUGARBERRY, SUGAR HACKBERRY. Native to southern Midwest and South. Grows to 60 ft. or taller and equally wide, with rounded crown. Similar to *C. occidentalis* but resistant to witches'-broom (ugly clusters of dwarfed twigs). This species is a desirable street or park tree.

C. occidentalis. COMMON HACKBERRY. Native from the Rocky Mountains to the Atlantic, north to Quebec and south to Alabama. Grows to form a rounded crown 50 ft. high or more and nearly as wide. Branches are spreading and sometimes pendulous. Oval light green leaves are 2–5 in. long, finely toothed on edges. Leafs out fairly late. Withstands urban pollution. Widely used in plains and prairie states, since it endures adverse conditions, including extreme cold, wind, soggy soil. Sometimes disfigured by witches'-broom. 'Prairie Pride' has handsome glossy leaves and a uniform habit; it is resistant to witches'-broom.

CENTAUREA

Asteraceae (Compositae)

ANNUALS AND PERENNIALS

ZONES VARY BY SPECIES

FULL SUN

MODERATE WATER, EXCEPT AS NOTED

Centaurea cineraria

Out of some 500 species, only a dozen or so are widely cultivated. Of these, annuals are grown mainly for cut flowers; perennial kinds are used principally for soft, silvery foliage. All are relatively easy to grow. For best performance, add lime to acid soils. In most cases, plan to sow seeds of annuals or set out plants of perennial kinds in spring (or in fall, in mild-winter areas).

C. americana. BASKET FLOWER. Annual. Zones US, MS, LS, CS, TS; 9–1. Native to central and southwestern U.S. Grows to 5–6 ft. high, 3 ft. wide, with rather rough, oval leaves to 4 in. long. Blooms in summer; flower heads to 4 in. wide are rose pink, paler toward center. Good in arrangements, fresh or dried.

C. cineraria (C. candidissima). DUSTY MILLER. Perennial in Zones LS, CS, TS; annual anywhere; 12–1. (This common name applies to many plants with whitish to silvery white foliage.) From Italy. Compact plant grows to 1 ft. wide, 1 ft. or taller. Velvety white, 3- to 6-in. leaves, mostly in basal clump, are strap shaped, with broad, roundish lobes. Solitary 1-in. flower heads (purple, occasionally yellow) in summer. Trim back after flowering. Attracts bees.

C. cyanus. BACHELOR'S BUTTON, CORNFLOWER. Annual. Zones US, MS, LS, CS, TS; 12–1. Native to northern temperate regions. Grows 1–2½ ft. tall and less than a foot wide; will send out branches if given sufficient space. Narrow gray-green leaves are 2–3 in. long; spring to midsummer flowers are 1–1½ in. wide, in blue, pink, rose, wine red, white. Blue forms are traditional favorites for boutonnieres. Bushy, compact 'Jubilee Gem' reaches just 1 ft. high, has deep blue blooms; Polka Dot strain has all the typical cornflower colors on 16-in. plants. Sow seed in late summer or fall.

C. dealbata. PERSIAN CORNFLOWER. Perennial. Zones US, MS, LS; 9–1. Native to the Caucasus. Forms an upright, bushy clump 2–3 ft. tall and about as wide. Deeply cut leaves to 8 in. long are deep green above, silvery beneath. In midsummer, leafy stems bear thistlelike pink blossoms to 1½ in. across; they make long-lasting cut flowers. May require staking, especially if grown in rich soil. 'Steenbergii' is a compact selection just 1–2 ft. tall, with 2-in. blooms in rich carmine pink.

C. gymnocarpa. DUSTY MILLER. Perennial. Zones LS, CS, TS; 10–1. Italian native; considered to be a form of *C. cineraria*. To 1–3 ft. tall, 1 ft. wide. Feltlike white leaves up to 8 in. long resemble those of *C. cineraria*, but they are more finely divided. Blooms in summer, when purple flower heads appear in twos or threes at ends of leafy branches. Trim plants after bloom. Very drought tolerant.

C. hypoleuca 'John Coutts'. Perennial. Zones US, MS, LS; 9–1. Variety of a species from Asia Minor. Looks something like *C. montana* but has more deeply lobed leaves and deep rose flower heads. Sometimes offered as a selection of *C. dealbata*.

C. macrocephala. GLOBE CENTAUREA. Perennial. Zones US, MS, LS; 7–1. From the Caucasus. Leafy plant with coarse leaves 6–8 in. long; reaches 3–4 ft. tall, 2 ft. wide, with 2-in. clusters of yellow summer flowers tightly enclosed at the base by overlapping papery, shiny brown bracts. Flower heads resemble thistles. Use in fresh or dried arrangements.

C. montana. Perennial. Zones US, MS, LS; 9–1. Native to the mountains of central Europe. Forms clumps to 1½ ft. tall and wide, with grayish green, broadly lance-shaped, 5- to 7-in.-long leaves. Flowers resembling ragged, 3-in. blue cornflowers top the stems in late spring to midsummer. Divide every other year. This is a cool-season plant and is less vigorous in warmer climates. Regular water.

C. moschata (Amberboa moschata). SWEET SULTAN. Annual. Zones US, MS, LS, CS, TS; 12–7. From Asia Minor. Erect plant, branching at base; grows to 2 ft. tall, 10 in. wide. Imperialis strain reaches 3 ft. high. Deeply toothed green leaves to 4 in. long. Thistlelike, 2-in. flower heads with a musky fragrance bloom from spring to fall—mostly in shades of lilac through rose, but sometimes in white or yellow. Splendid cut flower. Sow seed directly on soil in spring or set out as transplants. Needs lots of heat.

CENTIPEDE GRASS. See EREMOCHLOA ophiuroides

CENTRANTHUS ruber
(Valeriana rubra)

VALERIAN, JUPITER'S BEARD

Valerianaceae

PERENNIAL

US, MS, LS H 8–5

FULL SUN OR PARTIAL SHADE

LITTLE TO MODERATE WATER

Centranthus ruber

Trouble-free plant from the Mediterranean. Self-sows prolifically, thanks to small dandelion-like parachutes on seeds. Forms a bushy clump to 3 ft. high and wide, with upright stems bearing 4-in.-long bluish green leaves. Dusty crimson or rose pink flowers about ½ in. long in dense terminal clusters bloom in late spring, early summer. 'Albus' is white.

Valerian puts on a long, showy display in difficult situations: it grows in poor, dry soil and accepts almost any condition except damp shade. Cut off old flowering stems to shape plant, prolong bloom, and prevent seeding.

CENTURY PLANT. See AGAVE americana, A. attenuata

CEPHALANTHUS
occidentalis

BUTTONBUSH, BUTTON WILLOW

Rubiaceae

DECIDUOUS SHRUB OR TREE

US, MS, LS, CS, TS H 11–5

FULL SUN OR LIGHT SHADE

REGULAR TO AMPLE WATER

Cephalanthus occidentalis

Remarkable for wide distribution—eastern Canada to Florida, Minnesota south through Oklahoma and west to California, with outposts in Cuba, Mexico, and Asia. Grows from 3 to 15 ft. or taller and equally wide, with rounded, rather open habit and bright green, 2- to 6-in.-long leaves in pairs or whorls. Leafs out late in spring. Creamy white, slender-tubed flowers crowded in rounded, 1- to 1½-in.-wide heads in late summer. Blooms have projecting stigmas that give the flower clusters the appearance of a pincushion. Blossoms attract butterflies. Useful for naturalizing in wet areas. *C. o. californicus* is very similar.

CEPHALOTAXUS

PLUM YEW
Cephalotaxaceae
EVERGREEN SHRUBS OR TREES
⚡ ZONES VARY BY SPECIES
☀ ◐ ● SUN OR SHADE
💧 MODERATE WATER

Cephalotaxus harringtonia

Still unknown to most Southerners, the plum yews give hope to gardeners in the Lower and Coastal South who love the look of traditional yew *(Taxus)* but whose climates are too hot to grow it. These slow-growing evergreens from Asia have long bright green needles and, on female plants, produce small green or brown fruits that resemble plums. They accept almost any well-drained soil; do best in partial to full shade but will tolerate sun. And whereas deer will gnaw most *Taxus* species to the ground, they turn up their noses at plum yews.

C. fortunei. FORTUNE'S PLUM YEW. Zones MS, LS, CS; 9–3. Large shrub or small tree to 10–15 ft. tall and wide, with soft, medium green needles up to 3½ in. long. Reddish brown bark peels off in large pieces. 'Prostrate Spreader' is a low-growing, spreading form.

C. harringtonia. JAPANESE PLUM YEW. Zones US, MS, LS, CS; 9–3. Spreading shrub or small tree with bright green, 1- to 2½-in.-long needles. Can grow 10–15 ft. tall and wide, but named selections are smaller and more compact. 'Duke Gardens' grows 3–4 ft. tall and wide and has survived −24°F; 'Fastigiata' ('Stricta') is a broadly columnar form that can reach 10 ft. tall, 6–8 ft. wide. 'Korean Gold' has golden new foliage, columnar habit. 'Prostrata' is the name given to plants propagated from side branches; these do not form a central leader and remain 2–3 ft. tall, spreading somewhat wider. Japanese plum yew tolerates much pruning and will resprout even if you cut back into older wood. Makes an excellent substitute for shrub-type junipers *(Juniperus)* and hollies *(Ilex)*.

C. sinensis. CHINESE YEW. Zones MS, LS, CS; 9–6. Plant somewhat resembles *C. harringtonia* but with needles that are blackish green above and silvery to bluish green beneath.

CERASTIUM tomentosum

SNOW-IN-SUMMER
Caryophyllaceae
PERENNIAL
⚡ US, MS, LS H 7–1
☀ ◐ LIGHT SHADE IN HOTTEST CLIMATES
💧 💧 MODERATE TO REGULAR WATER

Cerastium tomentosum

Vigorous, low-growing European native forms spreading, dense, tufty mats of silvery gray leaves to ¾ in. long. Impressive masses of snowy white, ½- to ¾-in.-wide blossoms appear in early summer. Plant grows 6–8 in. high, spreads 2–3 ft. in a year.

Plant as ground cover on slopes or level ground, as bulb cover, in rock gardens, as edging for paths, and between stepping-stones. Particularly attractive against darker-colored backgrounds. Avoid extensive planting in prominent situations, however, since plant is not long lived.

In warmest areas of range, provide some shade. Tolerates any type of soil as long as the drainage is good; heavy, wet soil or standing water causes root rot. Set divisions or plants 1–1½ ft. apart; or sow seed. Fertilize two or three times a year to speed growth. Shear off faded flowers. Plants may look a bit shabby in winter but revive rapidly in spring. Divide in autumn or early spring.

FOR INFORMATION ON YOUR CLIMATE ZONES
PLEASE SEE PAGES 28–38

CERATOSTIGMA

PLUMBAGO
Plumbaginaceae
EVERGREEN AND DECIDUOUS SHRUBS AND PERENNIALS
⚡ ZONES VARY BY SPECIES
☀ ◐ FULL SUN OR PARTIAL SHADE
💧 💧 MODERATE TO REGULAR WATER

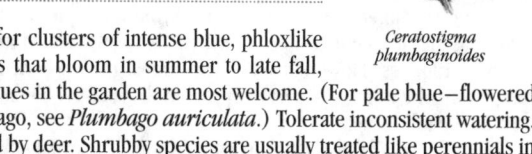

Ceratostigma plumbaginoides

Valued for clusters of intense blue, phloxlike flowers that bloom in summer to late fall, when cool hues in the garden are most welcome. (For pale blue–flowered Cape plumbago, see *Plumbago auriculata*.) Tolerate inconsistent watering. Not browsed by deer. Shrubby species are usually treated like perennials in colder zones; cut them back after bloom and mulch heavily.

C. griffithii. BURMESE PLUMBAGO. Evergreen shrub. Zones CS, TS; 9–4. Himalayan native. Resembles *C. willmottianum* but has rounder leaves and more compact, somewhat lower growth (to 2½–3 ft. high and wide). Also blooms somewhat later. Growth often nipped back by frost.

C. plumbaginoides (Plumbago larpentae). DWARF PLUMBAGO. Perennial. Zones US, MS, LS, CS; 9–4. Native to China. Wiry-stemmed ground cover 6–12 in. high. Bronzy green to dark green, 3-in.-long leaves turn reddish brown with frosts. Most effective in early or midautumn, when blue flowers contrast with red fall foliage. In loose soil and where growing season is long, spreads rapidly by underground stems, eventually covering large areas; plant 1–1½ ft. apart for quick cover.

Dwarf plumbago is semievergreen only in the mildest-winter areas; best to cut back after bloom. Dies back elsewhere; leafs out late in spring. When plants show signs of aging, remove old crowns and replace with rooted stems.

C. willmottianum. CHINESE PLUMBAGO. Deciduous shrub. Zones US, MS, LS, CS; 9–6. Grows as airy mass of wiry stems 2–4 ft. high and wide. Deep green, 2-in.-long leaves are somewhat diamond shaped, with tapering tips; turn yellow or red and drop quickly after frost.

CERATOZAMIA mexicana

Zamiaceae
CYCAD
⚡ TS H 12–10
☀ PARTIAL SHADE
💧 💧 MODERATE TO REGULAR WATER

Ceratozamia mexicana

From Mexico. Related to sago palm *(Cycas revoluta)* and similar to it in appearance and very slow growth. Trunk usually 1 ft. high (4–6 ft. in great age) and 1 ft. thick. Leaves are carried in a whorl at top of trunk; they are 3–6 ft. long, divided featherwise into 15 to 20 pairs of foot-long, inch-wide leaflets. Striking in container or protected place in open ground. Protect from frosts.

CERCIDIPHYLLUM japonicum

KATSURA TREE
Cercidiphyllaceae
DECIDUOUS TREE
⚡ US, MS, LS H 8–1
☀ ◐ FULL SUN OR LIGHT SHADE
💧 REGULAR WATER

Native to China, Japan. A specimen tree of many virtues if given regular moisture (especially during youth) and shelter from intense sun and wind. Light, dainty branch and

Cercidiphyllum japonicum

leaf pattern. Foliage, always fresh looking, changes color during the growing season: it is reddish purple when new, maturing to bluish green in summer, then turning yellow to apricot in autumn. To enhance fall color, water less frequently in late summer. Trees grown in acid soil will have the best color. Foliage of some katsura trees smells like burnt sugar on warm autumn days when leaves are falling.

Katsura trees are rather slow growing, eventually reaching 40 ft. or more. They have a pyramidal form when young; growth may remain upright or become more spreading (to as wide as tree is tall) with maturity. Some specimens have a single trunk, but multiple trunks are more common. Nearly round, 2- to 4-in. leaves are neatly spaced in pairs along arching branches. Flowers are inconspicuous. Brown bark is somewhat shaggy on old trees. No serious pest or disease problems. Selections include the following:

'Heronswood Globe'. Dense, rounded dwarf that eventually tops out at about 15 ft. high and wide; it grows about 6 ft. in 8 years. Good for smaller gardens.

'Pendula' ('Amazing Grace'). To 15–25 ft. high and usually somewhat wider than tall, with pendulous branches arranged in tiers. Attractive orange-yellow fall color.

'Pendulum' (*C. j. pendulum*). WEEPING KATSURA. To 20 ft. high, 25 ft. wide, with weeping branches. Slower growing than 'Pendula'.

'Red Fox'. Resembles the species, but young leaves are an especially rich purplish red; they mature to dark purplish green and hold their dark color all summer.

CERCIS

REDBUD

Fabaceae (Leguminosae)

DECIDUOUS SHRUBS OR TREES

ZONES VARY BY SPECIES

FULL SUN OR LIGHT SHADE, EXCEPT AS NOTED

WATER NEEDS VARY BY SPECIES

Cercis canadensis

Adaptable and dependable, redbuds include some of our most charming native trees. In early spring, before leaf-out, a profusion of small, sweet pea–shaped, lavender-pink to rosy purple flowers appears on twigs, branches, and even the main trunk. Blossoms are followed by clusters of flat, beanlike pods that persist into winter and give rise to numerous seedlings around the tree. Handsome, broad, rounded or heart-shaped leaves may change to bright yellow in fall, but fall color is inconsistent.

Redbuds make fine lawn trees, look great in groupings, and have their place in shrub borders and even foundation plantings. In winter, the dark, leafless branches form an attractive silhouette, especially effective against a light-colored wall. Larger types make nice small shade trees for patios and courtyards. And you can't miss when using redbuds in naturalized settings, such as at the edge of a woodland. Do any pruning in the dormant season or after bloom.

C. canadensis. EASTERN REDBUD. Zones US, MS, LS, CS; 9–2. Native to eastern U.S. The fastest growing and largest (to 25–35 ft. tall) of the redbuds, and the most apt to take tree form. Round headed but with horizontally tiered branches in age. Leaves are rich green, 3–6 in. long, with pointed tips. Flowers are small (½ in. long), rosy pink or lavender. Needs some winter chill to flower profusely. Regular water.

Eastern redbud is valuable for bridging the color gap between the early-flowering fruit trees (flowering peach, flowering plum) and the crabapples and late-flowering dogwoods and cherries. Effective as a specimen or understory tree.

Available selections include the following:

'Alba'. White blossoms.

'Appalachian Red' ('Appalachia'). Flowers are deep pink—not a true red but close to it.

'Covey'. Dwarf weeping selection with unusual zigzagging, twisting branches. Lavender flowers; leaves slightly larger than those of the species. Original plant was only 4½ ft. high, 7 ft. wide at 40 years old.

'Flame'. Double pink blooms.

'Forest Pansy'. Foliage emerges a gaudy purple in spring, then gradually changes to burgundy-toned green as summer heat increases. Rosy purple flowers. Nice color accent; benefits from afternoon shade in summer.

'Rubye Atkinson'. Pure pink flowers.

'Silver Cloud'. Leaves marbled with white.

'Tennessee Pink'. True pink flowers.

Among the deserving subspecies available are these two:

C. c. mexicana (*C. mexicana*). Heat zones 9–3. From many areas of Mexico. Most typical form is single trunked, to 15 ft. with leathery blue-green leaves and pinkish purple flowers. Moderate to regular water.

C. c. texensis. (*C. reniformis*). Zones US, MS, LS, CS; 9–4. Native to Texas, Oklahoma, and Mexico. To 15–25 ft. high and wide. Takes moderate to regular water. 'Oklahoma' has deep purple buds opening to rosy purple flowers; 'Texas White' bears pure white blossoms. Both have thick, leathery dark green leaves.

C. chinensis. CHINESE REDBUD. Zones US, MS, LS; 9–3. Native to China, Japan. Seen mostly as light, open shrub to 10–12 ft. tall, 10 ft. wide. Flower clusters are 3–5 in. long, deep rose, almost rosy purple. Leaves (to 5 in. long) are sometimes glossier and brighter green than those of *C. canadensis,* with a transparent line around the edge. 'Avondale' is a superior form with profuse deep purple flowers. Full sun; regular water.

C. occidentalis. WESTERN REDBUD. Zones US, MS, LS; 9–7. Native to California, Arizona, Utah. Shrub or small tree to 10–18 in. tall and wide; typically multitrunked. Provides all-year interest, with a profusion of ½-in. magenta flowers in spring; handsome, 3-in. blue-green leaves and newly forming magenta seedpods in summer; light yellow or red fall foliage; and picturesque bare branches adorned with reddish brown seedpods in winter. Best floral display comes in areas with some winter chill. Little to moderate water; excellent for seldom-watered banks.

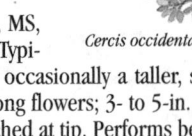

Cercis occidentalis

C. siliquastrum. JUDAS TREE. Zones US, MS, LS; 9–3. Native to Europe and western Asia. Typically a shrubby plant to 25 ft. tall and wide, occasionally a taller, slender tree with single trunk. Purplish rose, ½-in.-long flowers; 3- to 5-in. leaves, deeply heart shaped at base, rounded or notched at tip. Performs best with some winter chill. Moderate to regular water.

CEREUS peruvianus
(C. uruguayanus)

Cactaceae

CACTUS

CS, TS **H** 12–10; OR GROW IN POT

BEST IN SUN, TOLERATES SOME SHADE

MODERATE TO REGULAR WATER

Native to South America. Tall, treelike cactus, branching from base; stems are ribbed and set with scattered spines. Can form "bushes" to 10 ft. tall with eventual spread of 15 ft. Striking bluish green color, especially when young. Large white flowers—6–7 in. long, 5 in. across—open at night in late spring. Big, egg-shaped red fruits split open when fully ripe to reveal white pulp and black seeds. Striking outline; effective in ground or in large containers. Protect from hard frosts. Tolerates much drought, but better appearance with regular water and fertilizer during hot, dry months. Propagate by large cuttings (2–6 ft. long) any time of year. 'Monstrosus' is smaller and slower growing than the species, with ribs irregularly broken up into knobs and crests.

Cereus peruvianus 'Monstrosus'

CESTRUM

Solanaceae

EVERGREEN SHRUBS

TS 12–8, EXCEPT AS NOTED

PARTIAL SHADE, EXCEPT AS NOTED

REGULAR WATER

FRUIT AND SAP ARE POISONOUS IF INGESTED

Cestrum elegans

All are native to the tropical Americas. Those in cultivation have clusters of tubular, inch-long flowers attractive to hummingbirds; the showy fruit that follows can also attract birds. Plants grow fast and are inclined to be rangy and top-heavy unless regularly pruned. Best in warm, sheltered spot. Add organic soil amendments before planting. Feed generously. Nip back as needed to maintain compact form; cut back severely after flowering or fruiting.

C. aurantiacum. ORANGE CESTRUM. Native to Guatemala. Rare and handsome. To 8 ft. tall and wide. Brilliant show of clustered orange-yellow flowers in late spring and summer, followed by white berries. Deep green, oval, 4-in. leaves.

C. elegans (C. purpureum). RED CESTRUM. Native to Mexico. Shrub or semiclimber to 10 ft. or more in height and spread, with arching branches and deep green, 4-in. leaves. Plant produces masses of purplish red flowers in spring and summer; these are followed by red berries. Good choice for espalier. 'Smithii' has pink flowers.

C. fasciculatum. Heat zones 10–9. A native of Mexico. Similar to *C. elegans* but larger in all its parts.

C. 'Newellii'. Zones CS, TS; 12–9. May be a hybrid of *C. fasciculatum* and *C. elegans;* resembles the former but has bright crimson flowers. Some plants listed as *C.* 'Newellii' may in fact be *C. fasciculatum.*

C. nocturnum. NIGHT-BLOOMING JASMINE. Heat zones 12–9. Native to West Indies. To 12 ft. tall and wide, with 4- to 8-in.-long leaves and clusters of creamy white summer flowers followed by white berries. Blossoms powerfully fragrant at night—too much so for some people. Full sun.

C. parqui. CHILEAN CESTRUM, WILLOW-LEAFED JESSAMINE. Zones CS, TS. Native to Chile. To 6–10 ft. tall and wide, with many branches from base. Densely clothed in willowlike, 3- to 6-in.-long leaves. Greenish yellow summer flowers in clusters. Dark violet-brown berries. Not as attractive as other species in form, flowers, or fruit, but its perfume is potent. Leaves blacken in light frost. Best used where winter appearance is unimportant. In Coastal South, protect roots with mulch, treat as perennial.

CHAENOMELES

FLOWERING QUINCE

Rosaceae

DECIDUOUS SHRUBS

US, MS, LS, CS 9–2

FULL SUN

MODERATE TO REGULAR WATER

Chaenomeles 'Apple Blossom'

These are among the first shrubs to bloom each year. As early as January, you can bring a budded stem indoors, place it in water in a sunny window, and watch it burst into flower. Blossoms are 1½–2½ in. across, single to semidouble or double, in a wide range of colors. Leaves are red tinged when young, then mature to shiny green. Most types are thorny, take pruning well, and make excellent barriers and hedges. Not browsed by deer.

Flowering quince is easy to grow and practically indestructible; its only requirements are sun and well-drained soil. Even if leaf spot (a common disease in humid areas) defoliates the plant by midsummer, the next year's bloom won't be reduced. Prune to shape the plant or reduce its size—either immediately after bloom or during the flowering season (you can use cut branches in bloom for indoor arrangements). Lack of winter chill may lead to sparse bloom in the Coastal South.

Some selections bear small (2- to 4-in.), hard, delightfully fragrant fruits. Although not as tasty as that of common quince (*Cydonia oblonga;* see Quince), the fruit contains lots of pectin, making it good for jelly or preserves. If your flowering quince fails to bear, it probably needs cross-pollination with another selection.

The following list of garden hybrids gives height and flower color. Tall types reach 6 ft. or taller, low types 2–3 ft. Most are broader than tall.

'Apple Blossom'. Tall. White blossoms with pink tones. Good for fruit.
'Cameo'. Low, compact. Double blooms in apricot pink. Good for fruit.
'Contorta'. Low. White to pink; twisted branches. Good as bonsai.
'Corallina' ('Coral Glow'). Tall. Reddish orange.
'Coral Sea'. Tall. Large, coral pink.
'Enchantress'. Tall. Large, shell pink.
'Falconnet Charlet'. Tall, thornless. Double salmon pink flowers.
'Hollandia'. Tall. Large red flowers; reblooms in fall.
'Jet Trail'. Low. Pure white.
'Low-n-White'. Low, spreading. White.
'Minerva'. Low, spreading. Cherry red.
'Nivalis'. Tall. Large, pure white. Good for fruit.
'Orange Delight' ('Maulei'). Low, spreading. Orange to orange red.
'Pink Beauty'. Tall. Purplish pink.
'Pink Lady'. Low. Rose pink blooms from deeper-colored buds.
'Red Ruffles'. Tall, almost thornless. Large, ruffled red blooms.
'Rowallane'. Low. Darkest red.
'Snow'. Tall. Large, pure white.
'Stanford Red'. Low, almost thornless. Tomato red. Good for fruit.
'Super Red'. Tall, upright. Large, bright red.
'Texas Scarlet'. Low. Tomato red. Good for fruit.
'Toyo Nishiki'. Tall. Pink, white, pink-and-white, red all on same branch. Good for fruit.

CHAIN FERN. See WOODWARDIA

CHAMAECYPARIS

FALSE CYPRESS

Cupressaceae

EVERGREEN SHRUBS AND TREES

US, MS, LS 8–3, EXCEPT AS NOTED

FULL SUN OR PARTIAL SHADE, EXCEPT AS NOTED

REGULAR WATER

Chamaecyparis obtusa 'Nana Gracilis'

False cypress is sometimes mistaken for arborvitae (*Thuja*), but the leaves of false cypress have white lines on the undersides, while those of arborvitae are entirely green. Most false cypresses have two distinct types of leaves: juvenile and mature. Juvenile leaves (short, needlelike, soft but often prickly) appear on young plants and some new growth of larger trees. Mature foliage consists of tiny, scalelike, overlapping leaves. Cones are small and round.

All of the many selections sold are forms of three species—one from the eastern U.S. and two from Japan. Many closely resemble one another and are often mislabeled. Dwarf and variegated kinds are available, providing a rich source of plants for bonsai and rock gardens. All need good drainage and protection from wind.

C. obtusa. HINOKI FALSE CYPRESS. There are dozens of golden, dwarf, and fern-leafed forms of this Japanese native, but a few are the most important ones in landscaping. 'Crippsii' is a golden-leafed form to 50 ft. high and 25 ft. wide; the strongest yellow color is mainly at the end of foliage sprays. 'Gracilis', slender hinoki cypress, is a slender, upright tree to 20 ft. with nodding branch tips. 'Nana Gracilis' is a miniature of the former reaching just 4 ft. tall. Bright yellow–foliaged 'Nana Lutea', ideal plant for bonsai, reaches just 1 ft. high and 10 in. wide. It needs protection from full sun.

C. pisifera. SAWARA FALSE CYPRESS. Japanese native to 20–30 ft., rarely seen except in its garden forms. Selections include 'Cyano-Viridis'

('Boulevard'), a slow-growing, dense bush to 6–8 ft. high and wide, with silvery blue-green foliage; 'Filifera', to 8 ft., with drooping, threadlike branchlets; and 'Filifera Aurea', with similar branchlets in yellow.

C. thyoides. WHITE CEDAR. Zones US, MS, LS, CS; 9–1. Eastern U.S. timber tree to 75 ft. tall; columnar form. Found in wet sites in the wild. Garden forms include 'Andelyensis', dense, columnar gray-green shrub to 10 ft., turning bronze in cold weather; and 'Heather Bun', broader than 'Andelyensis', turning intense plum purple in winter.

CHAMAEDOREA

Arecaceae (Palmae)

PALMS

☀ TS ⊩ 12–10, EXCEPT AS NOTED; OR GROW IN POTS

◑ ● PARTIAL OR FULL SHADE; BRIGHT INDIRECT LIGHT

● REGULAR WATER

Chamaedorea elegans

Generally small, slow-growing, feather-type palms from the rain forests of Mexico and Central and South America. Some have single trunks, others clustered trunks; leaves are variable in shape. Perfect for a large container on a shaded patio.

C. cataractarum. CASCADE PALM. From southern Mexico. Forms a dense clump to 6 ft. tall, 9 ft. wide. Dark green, arching, feathery leaves to 3 ft. or longer. Does best in a moist, partially shaded location with protection from drying winds. Good as informal hedge, screen, border, or understory plant. Hardy to 24°F.

C. costaricana. From Costa Rica. If well fed and liberally watered, develops fairly quickly into bamboolike clumps 8–10 ft. tall and wide. Lacy, feathery leaves 3–4 ft. long. Good potted palm.

C. elegans (Neanthe bella). PARLOR PALM. Native to Mexico and Guatemala. The best indoor chamaedorea, tolerating crowded roots, poor light. Single stemmed; grows very slowly to an eventual 3–4 ft. tall and nearly as wide. Feathery, lush green leaves to 2 ft. long. Douse the tops of potted plants with water occasionally. Feed regularly. Groom by removing old leafstalks. Repot every 2 or 3 years, carefully washing off old soil and replacing it with good potting mix. Plant three or more in a container for most effective display.

C. erumpens. BAMBOO PALM. Heat zones 12–7. From British Honduras and Guatemala. To 4–14 ft. tall, 3–6 ft. wide. Produces a clump of slender, bright green, bamboolike canes bearing deep green leaves. New stems keep forming at the base of the plant, so it never looks sparse. Handsome, fine-textured accent for indoors or out.

C. tenella. Native to Mexico. Single-trunked palm to 3–4 ft. tall and wide. Dark bluish green leaves to 8 in. long, 2–3 in. wide have a distinctive look: they are undivided except for a deep cleft at the tip.

C. tepejilote. PACAYA PALM. Native from Mexico to Colombia. Single trunk ringed with swollen joints like those of bamboo. Moderate growth to 10 ft. or taller and about 8 ft. wide. Velvety green, feathery leaves reach 4 ft. long. Hardy to 28°F.

CHAMAEMELUM nobile (Anthemis nobilis)

CHAMOMILE

Asteraceae (Compositae)

PERENNIAL OFTEN GROWN AS ANNUAL

☀ US, MS, LS, CS ⊩ 9–6

◑ ● FULL SUN OR PARTIAL SHADE

● MODERATE WATER

Chamaemelum nobile

Soft-textured, spreading mat of bright light green, finely cut, aromatic leaves. Reaches 3–12 in. high. Blooms in summer, sometimes continuing into fall. Blossoms of the most commonly grown form look like small yellow buttons, while those of other types resemble little daisies. Useful

between stepping-stones or as a low edging along path. 'Treneague' is a nonflowering selection; 'Flore Pleno' has double daisylike flowers.

Fragrant, sweet chamomile tea comes from the dried flowers of *Matricaria recutita (M. chamomilla).*

CHAMAEROPS humilis

MEDITERRANEAN FAN PALM

Arecaceae (Palmae)

PALM

☀ LS, CS, TS ⊩ 12–8 OR GROW IN POT

◒ ◑ FULL SUN OR PARTIAL SHADE

◔ ● MODERATE TO REGULAR WATER

Chamaerops humilis

From the western Mediterranean. One of the hardiest palms; survives temperatures as low as 10°F. Clumps slowly develop from offshoots, curving to height of 20 ft.; may also reach 20 ft. wide. Growth is extremely slow in northern part of range. Green to bluish green leaves on spiny leafstalks. Use in containers, mass under trees, grow as impenetrable hedge. Tolerates poor soil, strong winds.

CHAMOMILE, FALSE. See MATRICARIA recutita

CHARD. See SWISS CHARD

CHASMANTHIUM latifolium (Uniola latifolia)

SEA OATS, BAMBOO GRASS

Poaceae (Gramineae)

PERENNIAL GRASS

☀ US, MS, LS, CS ⊩ 9–5

◒ ◑ FULL SUN OR LIGHT SHADE

● REGULAR WATER

Chasmanthium latifolium

Ornamental grass from moist woodlands of eastern U.S. Broad, bamboolike leaves form 2-ft.-wide clump topped in midsummer by arching, 2- to 5-ft. flowering stems carrying showers of silvery green spikelets that resemble flattened clusters of oats (or flattened armadillos). These turn copper in fall, look good through winter; they dry to a greenish straw color and are attractive in dried arrangements. Clumps widen slowly and are not aggressive. Leaves turn brown in winter, when plants should be cut back almost to ground. Divide clumps when they become crowded and flowering diminishes. Stake if flowering stems sprawl too far. Self-sows extensively and can become invasive. To control spread, remove seed heads before they mature.

CHASTE TREE. See VITEX

CHAYOTE

Cucurbitaceae

PERENNIAL VINE OFTEN GROWN AS ANNUAL

☀ CS, TS; ANYWHERE AS ANNUAL

◒ FULL SUN

● REGULAR WATER

Chayote

Known botanically as *Sechium edule*, this native of the tropical Americas belongs to the same family as squash and resembles a squash vine, but its flowers are inconspicuous. Grown for edible fruit: 3–8 in. long, green or yellow green, irregularly oval, grooved, with a large edible seed surrounded by solid flesh. Flavor like that of summer squash. Eat young fruit

C

raw or cooked; boil or bake mature fruit. Large, fleshy tuberous roots can also be eaten—though you cannot, of course, grow the plant as a perennial and consume its roots as well. Also known as mirliton or christophine.

Needs rich soil. Climbs by tendrils; provide fence or trellis. In areas where fruit is sold in stores, buy in fall and allow to sprout in cupboard; then plant whole fruit edgewise and slanted, with sprouted end at lowest point, narrow end exposed. If shoot is long, cut it back to 1–2 in. Plant two or more vines to ensure pollination. In the Coastal and Tropical South, plant sprouted fruit in ground in late winter; in colder areas, pot in a 5-gallon container and store in a dark, cool spot until frost danger is past. Plant can produce a 20- to 30-ft. vine in first year, reach 40–50 ft. in second. Top dies down in frost. Bloom starts with shorter days in fall; fruit is ripe within a month. A plant can bear 200 or more fruits.

CHECKERBERRY. See GAULTHERIA procumbens

CHECKERED LILY. See FRITILLARIA meleagris

CHEIRANTHUS cheiri. See ERYSIMUM cheiri

CHELIDONIUM majus

GREATER CELANDINE

Papaveraceae

PERENNIAL OR BIENNIAL

☀ US, MS, LS ◫ 8–4

☼ ● PARTIAL TO FULL SHADE

● REGULAR WATER

◊ SAP IS IRRITATING TO THE SKIN

Chelidonium majus

Native to Europe. Grows to 2–3 ft. tall and 10 in. wide, with several erect stems rising from the rootstock. Smooth bright green leaves, 4–10 in. long, are attractively cut and lobed. Profuse yellow to orange-yellow flowers to 1 in. wide; summer bloom. Self-sows freely and naturalizes (sometimes too well; may become invasive). Double-flowered 'Flore Pleno' also seeds itself freely. Both forms are best in wild gardens. Juice from the stems is said to get rid of warts.

CHELONE

TURTLEHEAD

Scrophulariaceae

PERENNIAL

☀ US, MS, LS, CS ◫ 9–3, EXCEPT AS NOTED

☼ ◐ FULL SUN OR LIGHT SHADE

◊◊ AMPLE WATER

Chelone lyonii

Leafy, clump-forming perennials related to penstemon. All are native to the eastern U.S. and grow in damp places in sun or light shade. Frequently used in bog gardens. All bloom in late summer and autumn. Common name comes from the oddly formed flowers—inch-long, puffy, and two lipped, with a fancied resemblance to a turtle's head. Useful for cut flowers, shade gardens, wild gardens.

C. glabra. WHITE TURTLEHEAD. Heat zones 9–1. Grows 2–3 ft. tall (occasionally much taller), 1½ ft. wide. Medium green leaves to 8 in. long; white or palest pink flowers. 'Black Ace', with white blossoms, typically grows 3–4 ft. tall but can reach 6 ft. Its leaves emerge deep green with an almost black cast, then usually lighten to green by late summer.

C. lyonii. PINK TURTLEHEAD. Reaches 3–4 ft. tall, 2 ft. wide. Dark green, 4- to 6-in.-long leaves; rose pink flowers. 'Hot Lips' has red stems and reddish purple flowers with a spot of white at the base.

C. obliqua. ROSE TURTLEHEAD. Grows to 2–2½ ft. tall, 1 ft. wide. Dark green leaves to 8 in. long; deep pink blossoms. Latest bloomer among the species listed here.

CHENILLE PLANT. See ACALYPHA hispida

Chenopodiaceae. The goosefoot family contains many annuals and perennials (some of them weeds) and a few shrubs. Flowers are inconspicuous. Many will tolerate salty or alkaline soil, and some (notably beet and spinach) are useful food plants.

CHERRY

Rosaceae

DECIDUOUS FRUIT TREES

☀ ZONES VARY BY TYPE

☼ FULL SUN

● REGULAR WATER

Cherry

If George Washington indeed chopped down a cherry tree, it was probably because he was miffed about not getting any fruit. Fruiting cherries, both sweet and sour types, make attractive trees for the home garden, but getting a decent crop is a challenge in the South. For strictly ornamental cherries, see *Prunus*.

Sweet cherries. Best grown in the Upper South, preferably in the Appalachian and Blue Ridge Mountains. Heat zones 8–1. Most common market type. Their high chilling requirement (many hours needed below 45°F) makes them poorly adapted to most of the South. They can't take extreme summer heat or intense winter cold, and freezes and heavy spring rains can damage crop. Trees reach 20–35 ft. tall and broad in some selections.

Two trees are usually needed to produce fruit, and the second tree must be chosen with care. No combination of these will produce fruit: 'Bing', 'Lambert', 'Royal Ann'. However, the following selections will pollinate these and any other cherry: 'Black Tartarian', 'Hedelfingen', 'Stella', and 'Van'. 'Lapins' and 'Stella' are self-fertile (a lone tree will bear).

Fruiting spurs are long lived and do not need to be renewed by pruning. Prune trees only to maintain good structure and shape. Fruit appears in late spring to early summer. Use netting to keep birds from eating the crop. For control of brown rot and blossom blight, apply a copper spray just as leaves fall in autumn, then a fungicide when first blooms appear and weekly during bloom. Resume fungicide program about 2 weeks before harvest. Dormant oil spray will control various pests, including scale insects and mites. Good selections include the following.

'Bing'. Top quality. Large, dark red, meaty fruit of fine flavor. Midseason.

'Black Tartarian'. Fruit smaller than 'Bing', purplish black, firm and sweet. Early.

'Hedelfingen'. Medium-large black cherry. Ripens with 'Van', but fruit colors before maturity, needs early protection from birds. Productive tree begins bearing fruit when young.

'Lambert'. Large, firm black fruit. Flavor more sprightly than 'Bing'. Late.

'Lapins'. Resembles 'Bing' but is self-fruitful. Early to midseason.

'Royal Ann' ('Napoleon'). Large, spreading tree; very productive. Tender, crisp, light yellow fruit with pink blush. Sprightly flavor. Midseason.

'Stella'. Dark fruit like 'Lambert'; ripens a few days later. Self-fertile and good pollenizer for other cherries.

'Van'. Heavy-bearing tree. Shiny black fruit, firmer and slightly smaller than 'Bing'. Ripens slightly earlier than or at the same time as 'Bing'.

Sour cherries. Also known as pie cherries. More widely adapted than sweet cherries; succeed along the Atlantic Coast and farther north and south than sweet cherries do. In home gardens and orchards, grow in Upper and Middle South in well-drained soil. Heat zones 8–1.

Sour cherry trees are smaller than sweet cherry trees—to about 20 ft. tall, with spreading habit. They are self-fertile. There are far fewer types of sour cherries than sweet ones.

'Early Richmond'. Highly recommended. Like 'Montmorency'. Early.

'English Morello'. Dark red, somewhat tart fruit with red juice. Late.

'Meteor'. Fruit like 'Montmorency' but on a smaller tree. Late. ▶

'Montmorency'. Highly recommended. Small, bright red, soft, juicy fruit with a sweet-tart flavor. Midseason to late.

'North Star'. Fruit has red to dark red skin and sour yellow flesh. Small, very hardy tree. Midseason.

CHERRY, FLOWERING. See PRUNUS

CHERRY OF THE RIO GRANDE. See EUGENIA aggregata

CHERRY PLUM. See PRUNUS cerasifera

CHERVIL. See ANTHRISCUS cerefolium

CHESTNUT

Fagaceae

DECIDUOUS TREES OR SHRUBS

US, MS, LS

FULL SUN

MODERATE WATER

Chinese Chestnut

The American chestnut *(Castanea dentata)* has become nearly extinct in its native range as a result of chestnut blight, but other species and hybrids that resist the disease are available. They make wonderful, dense shade trees where there is space to accommodate them and where their litter and rank-smelling pollen won't be too obtrusive. All have handsome dark to bright green foliage. Small, creamy white flowers in long (8- to 10-in.), slim catkins make quite a display in summer. The large edible nuts are enclosed in prickly burs. Nuts fall to the ground when ripe. Gather daily, remove from burs, and dry in the sun (in shade, in hot climates). Plant two or more trees to ensure cross-pollination and a substantial crop; single trees bear lightly or not at all. Give occasional deep irrigation.

Hybrid chestnuts. Heat zones 8–1. Two types of hybrid chestnuts are available. The first group comprises offspring of American and Chinese chestnuts *(C. dentata* and *C. mollissima),* with characteristics intermediate between the two (American chestnut is—or was—a tall, broad timber tree with small but very sweet nuts). Included here are the blight-resistant Dunstan hybrids, 'Alachua', 'Carolina', 'Carpenter', 'Heritage', 'Revival', and 'Willamette'. The second group is made up mostly of crosses between Japanese chestnut *(C. crenata)* and European chestnut *(C. sativa).* Trees usually grow 40–60 ft. tall and wide and do not tolerate alkaline soils. Selections include 'Colossal', 'Nevada' (small-nutted type; proven pollenizer for 'Colossal'), 'Schrader', and 'Skioka'.

Chestnut

European chestnut. Heat zones 7–5. Native to southern Europe, North Africa, western Asia; botanical name is *C. sativa.* Larger, broader than *C. mollissima:* can reach 100 ft. tall with greater spread, but typically grows 40–60 ft. high in gardens. Leaves 4–9 in. long, with sharply toothed edges. Large nuts of excellent quality—the nuts usually sold in markets.

Chinese chestnut. Heat zones 8–1. Native to China, Korea; known botanically as *C. mollissima.* To 35–40 ft. tall, with a rounded crown that may spread to 20–25 ft. Leaves 3–7 in. long, with coarsely toothed edges. Most nursery trees are grown from seed, not cuttings; hence, nuts are variable but generally of good quality. Intolerant of alkaline soil. Recommended selections include 'AU-Cropper', 'AU-Homestead', 'AU-Leader', 'Black Beauty', 'Crane', 'Meiling', and 'Nanking'.

Allegheny chinkapin. Heat zones 9–5. This eastern U. S. native is known botanically as *C. pumila.* Usually a 6- to 10-ft.-tall shrub, but it can reach 20–25 ft. Leaves are dark green above, fuzzy white underneath, 3–6 in. long, with sharply toothed edges. Nuts are sweet. Good in natural plantings and for attracting wildlife.

CHICORY and RADICCHIO

Asteraceae (Compositae)

PERENNIALS

US, MS, LS H 8–1

FULL SUN

REGULAR WATER

Chicory

Botanically known as *Cichorium intybus.* Native to Mediterranean region; wild form grows as perennial roadside weed 2–4 ft. tall in much of the South and is recognized by its pretty sky blue flowers. Different chicories are grown for three purposes: for salad greens (small-rooted types); for roots to make a coffee substitute (large-rooted types); and for Belgian or French endive ('Witloof' chicory). To grow 'Witloof', sow seeds in spring or early summer; plants will mature by fall. In winter, trim the greens to an inch of stem; then dig the roots, bury them diagonally in moist sand, and set in dark, cool room until pale, tender new growth has been forced. (For the standard salad green called endive, see Endive.)

Radicchio is the name given to red-leafed chicories grown for salads. 'Rossa de Verona' ('Rouge de Verone'), 'Red Treviso', and 'Rossana' are good selections. Radicchio makes lettucelike heads that color to a deep rosy red as weather grows cold in fall or winter; its slight bitterness lessens as color deepens. Best sown in mid- to late summer to mature in cool fall months, though the selection 'Giulio' can be sown in spring to harvest in summer. Sow green-leafed chicory beginning in early spring (and up to early summer where that season is not too hot); in areas with mild winters, you can also plant in mid- to late summer for fall and winter harvest. Sow both green and red types ¼–½ in. deep; thin seedlings to 6–12 in. apart. Before planting, work into the soil ½ cup of 10-10-10 fertilizer per 10 ft. of row.

CHILEAN JASMINE. See MANDEVILLA laxa

CHILEAN WINE PALM. See JUBAEA chilensis

CHILOPSIS linearis

DESERT WILLOW, DESERT CATALPA

Bignoniaceae

DECIDUOUS SHRUB OR TREE

MS, LS, CS H 9–7

FULL SUN

LITTLE TO MODERATE WATER

Chilopsis linearis

Native to desert washes and streambeds below 5,000 ft. from California to Texas, south into Mexico. To 15–30 ft. tall, 10–20 ft. wide; grows fast at first (as much as 3 ft. in a season), then slows. With age, develops shaggy bark and twisting trunks. Narrow, willow-type leaves grow to 2–5 in. long. From spring to fall, produces fragrant, trumpet-shaped blossoms with crimped lobes, resembling those of catalpa or small cattleya orchids; flowers attract hummingbirds. Flower color varies among seedlings; blossoms may be reddish purple, lavender, rose, pink, or white, often marked with purple and gold. Nurseries select for good color, large size, ruffled form. Gallon-size plants can bloom first year. Plant drops leaves early; holds a heavy crop of catalpa-like seedpods through winter and can look messy. Thin growth to enhance picturesque shape. Does best in dry, limy soil. Not for humid, high-rainfall areas.

'Burgundy' ('Burgundy Lace'). Deep purplish red flowers.

'Dark Storm'. Lower lip of flower is deep wine red, upper one lavender; lips are usually curved inward. Slow grower to 12–15 ft. high and wide.

'Hope'. White flowers with a pale yellow throat. Wispy, open growth.

'Lois Adams'. Profuse two-tone blooms in pale lavender and magenta; no seedpods. Compact, upright growth.

'Lucretia Hamilton'. Dark purple flowers in large clusters. To 15–18 ft. high and wide.

'Regal'. Combination of lavender and wine red like that of 'Dark Storm', but display is better, since blooms are flat faced and open throated.

'Rio Salado'. Large, ruffled, deep burgundy flowers. Vigorous growth.

'Warren Jones'. Large, ruffled blossoms in pure, unshaded pink with paler throat. Holds its leaves longer; evergreen in Coastal South.

CHIMONANTHUS praecox (C. fragrans, Meratia praecox)

WINTERSWEET

Calycanthaceae

DECIDUOUS SHRUB

US, MS, LS, CS 9–6

FULL SUN OR PARTIAL SHADE

MODERATE WATER

Chimonanthus praecox

Native to China and Japan. Winter-blooming shrub with wonderfully spicy-scented blossoms. Needs some winter cold. Tall, open-structured plant grows slowly to 10–15 ft. high and 6–8 ft. wide, with many basal stems. Flowers appear on leafless branches in late winter to early spring, depending on climate. Blossoms are 1 in. wide, with pale yellow outer sepals and smaller, chocolate-colored inner sepals. Tapered leaves are rough to the touch, medium green, 3–6 in. long and half that wide; turn yellow green in fall. 'Grandiflorus' has larger (1¾-in.) blossoms than the basic species, but they are not as fragrant. 'Luteus' has clear yellow flowers.

In the Upper South, plant in a sheltered site to prevent frost damage. In all areas, locate plant where its winter fragrance can be enjoyed, such as near an entrance or path or under a bedroom window. Keep plant lower by cutting back after bloom; shape as a small tree by removing excess basal stems; rejuvenate a leggy plant by trimming to within a foot of the ground in spring. Needs good drainage.

CHINA ASTER. See CALLISTEPHUS chinensis

CHINABERRY. See MELIA azedarach

CHINA FIR. See CUNNINGHAMIA lanceolata

CHINESE BUTTONBUSH. See ADINA rubella

CHINESE CABBAGE

Brassicaceae (Cruciferae)

BIENNIAL GROWN AS COOL-SEASON ANNUAL

US, MS, LS, CS, TS 7–1

FULL SUN

REGULAR WATER

Chinese Cabbage

Makes a head somewhat looser than that of usual cabbage; sometimes called celery cabbage. Raw or cooked, it has a more delicate flavor than cabbage. There are two kinds: pe-tsai, with tall, narrow heads; and wong bok, with short, broad heads. Pe-tsai types are 'Michihli' (76 days to maturity) and 'Greenwich' (50 days); wong-bok types are 'Minuet' (48 days) and 'Rubicon' (52 days). Prone to bolt in hot weather if planted in spring; makes a better fall or winter crop. In colder-winter areas, plant seeds in ground in July; in milder climates, plant in August or September. Sow seeds thinly in rows 2–2½ ft. apart; thin plants to 1½–2 ft. apart.

To prevent a buildup of soil-borne pests, plant in a different site each year. Club root is a serious fungal pest in acid soils; apply lime, if necessary, to raise the pH to at least 6.5. Floating row covers do a good job of controlling insects such as cabbage loopers, cabbageworms, cutworms,

and root maggots. You can also control cutworms and root maggots by ringing the base of the plant with a collar made from cardboard. *Bacillus thuringiensis* (*Bt;* sold as Dipel) applied according to label directions controls cabbageworms and loopers.

CHINESE ELM. See ULMUS parvifolia

CHINESE EVERGREEN. See AGLAONEMA modestum

CHINESE FLAME TREE. See KOELREUTERIA bipinnata

CHINESE FRINGE. See LOROPETALUM chinense

CHINESE GOOSEBERRY VINE. See KIWI

CHINESE GROUND ORCHID. See BLETILLA striata

CHINESE LANTERN. See ABUTILON

CHINESE LANTERN PLANT. See PHYSALIS alkekengi

CHINESE PARASOL TREE. See FIRMIANA simplex

CHINESE PLUMBAGO. See CERATOSTIGMA willmottianum

CHINESE REDBUD. See CERCIS chinensis

CHINESE SCHOLAR TREE. See SOPHORA japonica

CHINESE SWEET GUM. See LIQUIDAMBAR formosana

CHINESE TALLOW. See SAPIUM sebiferum

CHINESE TARO. See ALOCASIA cucullata

CHINESE YELLOW BANANA. See MUSELLA lasiocarpa

CHIONANTHUS

FRINGE TREE

Oleaceae

DECIDUOUS SHRUBS OR TREES

US, MS, LS, CS

FULL SUN OR PARTIAL SHADE

MODERATE TO REGULAR WATER

Chionanthus retusus

Spectacular flowering plants requiring some winter chill. Common name refers to narrow, fringelike white petals on flowers that are borne in impressive, ample, lacy clusters. Male and female plants are separate; males have larger flowers. If both plants are present, females produce clusters of small, dark, olivelike fruit that is favored by birds. Broad leaves turn bright to deep yellow in fall. Give good drainage. Minimal pruning needed.

C. retusus. CHINESE FRINGE TREE. Heat zones 9–3. From China. To about 20 ft. tall, not quite as wide spreading as *C. virginicus.* Usually seen as a big multistemmed shrub but can be trained as a small tree. Leaves 2–4 in. long. Pure white, fragrant blossoms in clusters to 4 in. long appear in late spring or early summer, 2 to 3 weeks before *C. virginicus* comes into flower. A magnificent plant when in bloom, something like a tremendous white lilac (*Syringa*). Handsome gray-brown bark (sometimes golden on young stems) provides winter interest.

C. virginicus. FRINGE TREE, GRANCY GRAY-BEARD. Heat zones 9–1. Native to southeastern U.S. Leaves and flower clusters often twice as big as those of *C. retusus;* blooms appear a few weeks later. Lightly fragrant, greenish white flowers. Can reach 30 ft. tall, but in gardens usually grows 12–20 ft. high with equal spread. Habit varies from

Chionanthus virginicus

very shrubby and open to more treelike. Grows more slowly in the Upper South, where young plants can be used as shrubs for a number of years. In that zone, it's one of the last deciduous plants to leaf out in spring.

CHIONODOXA

GLORY-OF-THE-SNOW

Liliaceae

PERENNIALS FROM BULBS

✿ US, MS ⧗ 8–1

☼ ◐ FULL SUN DURING BLOOM,
LIGHT SHADE AFTER

💧 REGULAR WATER DURING GROWTH AND BLOOM

Chionodoxa luciliae

Charming little bulbous plants native to alpine meadows of Crete, Cyprus, and Turkey. They are among the first flowers to bloom in spring; each bulb produces a stem to 6 in. high, with six-pointed, starlike blossoms in blue, white, or pink spaced along upper part. Straight, narrow leaves are a little shorter than flower stem. In fall, plant bulbs in rich, well-drained soil, setting them 2–3 in. deep and 3 in. apart. When bloom quality declines, dig and divide clumps in early fall. Plantings may also increase from self-seeding. Ideal beneath deciduous trees.

C. luciliae. Most commonly grown species; often confused with other species. Stems typically bear one to four 1½-in., violet-blue blooms. 'Gigantea' has larger leaves and larger blossoms; 'Alba' has white flowers larger than those of the species; 'Pink Giant' and 'Rosea' bear pink blooms.

C. sardensis. Inch-wide violet-blue flowers with a very small white eye, carried 4 to 12 to a stem.

✕ CHITALPA tashkentensis

Bignoniaceae

DECIDUOUS TREE

✿ MS, LS, CS ⧗ 10–5

☼ FULL SUN

◌💧 LITTLE TO MODERATE WATER

✕ Chitalpa tashkentensis

Fast growing to 20–30 ft. and as wide, this tree combines the larger flowers of its *Catalpa bignonioides* parent with the desert toughness and flower color of *Chilopsis linearis*, its other parent. Leaves are 4–5 in. long, an inch wide. Blooms from late spring to fall, bearing clusters of frilly, trumpet-shaped flowers in pink, white, or lavender. 'Pink Dawn' has pink flowers, 'Morning Cloud' white ones. Like catalpa, unusually tolerant of heat, cold, and various soils; even better suited than catalpa to dry, limy soil. Litter is not a problem, as flowers dry on tree and no seedpods are formed. Tolerates wind.

CHIVES. See ALLIUM schoenoprasum

CHLOROPHYTUM

Liliaceae

PERENNIALS

✿ TS ⧗ 12–10; OR HOUSEPLANTS

◐ PARTIAL SHADE; BRIGHT INDIRECT LIGHT

💧 REGULAR WATER

Chlorophytum comosum

Frost-tender lily relatives form clumps of attractive evergreen foliage and bear small white flowers in long clusters. In most areas, they are grown indoors.

C. bichetii. West African native grows slowly to 8–10 in. high, 1½ ft. across. Dark green leaves with white stripes, shorter and broader than those of *C. comosum*, gracefully recurved. Flowers carried on 8-in. stalks. Does not produce runners.

C. comosum (C. capense). SPIDER PLANT. From South Africa. Forms 1- to 3-ft.-high clumps of soft, curving leaves like long, broad grass blades. Both 'Variegatum' and 'Vittatum' have white-striped leaves. Flowers about ½ in. long, in loose, leafy-tipped spikes held above foliage. Greatest attraction: miniature duplicates of mother plant, complete with root, at end of curved stems (as with offsets of strawberry plants). These can be cut off and potted individually.

Spider plant is a good choice for hanging baskets. To use as ground cover, set 2 ft. apart in diamond pattern; plants will fill in the area in that same year.

CHOCOLATE DAISY, CHOCOLATE FLOWER. See BERLANDIERA lyrata

CHOISYA ternata

MEXICAN ORANGE

Rutaceae

EVERGREEN SHRUB

✿ LS, CS, TS ⧗ 10–8

☼ ◐ LIGHT SHADE IN ZONE TS

💧 MODERATE WATER

Choisya ternata

Mexican native hardy to 15°F. Fast growing to 6–8 ft. high and wide. Lustrous, rich green leaves are held toward ends of branches; each leaf is divided into a fan of three leaflets to 3 in. long. Fans give shrub a dense, massive look—but with highlights and shadows. Clusters of fragrant white flowers, somewhat like small orange blossoms, open in late winter or early spring and bloom continuously for a couple of months, then intermittently through summer. Appealing to bees. Sometimes called mock orange. Foliage of 'Sundance' is yellow when young, gradually turning green.

Attractive informal hedge or screen. During growing season, thin out older branches in plant's center to force leafy new interior growth. Cut freely for decoration when in bloom. Touchy about soil conditions—difficult to grow in alkaline soils or where water is high in salts. Under such conditions, amend soil as for azaleas (*Rhododendron*). Prone to root rot and crown rot if drainage is poor. Subject to damage from sucking insects and mites. Not browsed by deer.

CHOKEBERRY. See ARONIA

CHOKECHERRY. See PRUNUS virginiana

CHORISIA

FLOSS SILK TREE, SILK FLOSS TREE

Bombacaceae

EVERGREEN TO BRIEFLY DECIDUOUS TREES

✿ TS ⧗ 12–10

☼ FULL SUN

💧 MODERATE WATER

Chorisia speciosa

Native to South America. Heavy trunk is studded with thick spines; it is green in youth, turns gray with age. Leaves divided into 5-in.-long leaflets like fingers of a hand; they drop during autumn flowering or whenever temperatures fall below 27°F. Large, showy flowers somewhat resemble narrow-petaled hibiscus blooms. Fast drainage and controlled watering are keys to success. Water established trees about once a month during the growing season; ease off in late summer to encourage more flowers. Need little pruning except to remove wayward or dead growth.

C. insignis. WHITE FLOSS SILK TREE. To 50 ft. tall and wide. White to pale yellow, 5- to 6-in. flowers. Blooms from fall into winter; stopped by frost.

C. speciosa. Grows 3–5 ft. a year for first few years, then more slowly to an eventual 30–50 ft. tall and wide. Blooms in fall, bearing pink, purplish rose, or burgundy flowers to 4 in. or more across. Grafted selections include 'Los Angeles Beautiful', with wine red flowers, and 'Majestic Beauty', a thornless selection bearing rich pink blooms.

CHRISTMAS CACTUS. See SCHLUMBERGERA ×buckleyi

CHRISTMAS FERN. See POLYSTICHUM acrostichoides

CHRISTMAS ROSE. See HELLEBORUS niger

CHRYSALIDOCARPUS
lutescens (Areca lutescens)

ARECA PALM, CANE PALM

Arecaceae (Palmae)

PALM

⚡ TS ◫ 12–10; OR HOUSEPLANT

☼ ◑ ● SUN OR SHADE; BRIGHT LIGHT

💧 REGULAR WATER

Chrysalidocarpus lutescens

From Madagascar. Clumping feather palm grows slowly to 10–15 ft. or even taller, spreading to at least 8 ft. wide. Graceful plant with smooth trunks and yellowish green leaves. Can take dense shade; intolerant of salt. Used in foundation plantings and as a patio plant in the Tropical South; elsewhere, grow indoors. Tricky to maintain indoors, but a lovely palm. Prone to spider mites as a houseplant.

CHRYSANTHEMUM

Asteraceae (Compositae)

PERENNIALS AND ANNUALS

⚡ ZONES VARY BY SPECIES

☼ FULL SUN, EXCEPT AS NOTED

💧 REGULAR WATER, EXCEPT AS NOTED

Chrysanthemum ×morifolium

Heaven help us when taxonomists get bored. In the name of botanical purity, they start changing all the familiar names, thoroughly confusing everyone. That's what happened with good old chrysanthemums, which were suddenly split into *Leucanthemum, Dendranthema,* and other arcane classifications, only to be returned to their original names a few years later.

About 160 species of chrysanthemums exist, mostly native to China, Japan, and Europe. Florists' chrysanthemum *(C. ×morifolium)* is the most familiar. In the following descriptions, original botanical names are given first, followed by "new and improved" names in parentheses. None of these plants is browsed by deer.

C. arcticum (Arctanthemum arcticum). ARCTIC CHRYSANTHEMUM. Perennial. Zones US; 5–1. Native to Alaska. Very hardy fall bloomer. Forms a foot-wide clump of spoon-shaped, leathery, usually three-lobed leaves 1–3 in. long. Stems 6–12 in. high bear white or pinkish, 1- to 2-in. flowers. The species is primarily a rock garden plant. Taller-growing hybrids reach 16–20 in. and are best in mixed borders.

C. balsamita (Tanacetum balsamita). COSTMARY. Perennial. Zones US, MS, LS, CS; 9–6. Native from Europe to central Asia. Weedy, rhizomatous plant grown for its sweet-scented foliage (used in salads and sachets) rather than its tiny daisies. Leggy stems reach 3 ft. high; if these are cut back, the gray-green, finely scallop-margined basal leaves can make a nice edging for an herb garden. Divide clumps and reset divisions in late summer or fall.

C. coccineum (Pyrethrum roseum, Tanacetum coccineum). PAINTED DAISY, PYRETHRUM. Perennial. Zones US, MS, LS; 9–5. Native to Iran and the Caucasus. Bushy plant to 2–3 ft. high, 1½ ft. wide, with bright green, very finely divided leaves and single, daisylike, long-stemmed flowers to 3 in. across in pink, red, or white. Also available in double and anemone-flowered forms. Starts blooming in April, May, or June; if cut back, blooms again in late summer. Excellent for cutting, borders. Divide clumps or sow seeds in spring. Double forms may not come true from seed; they may revert to single flowers.

C. frutescens (Argyranthemum frutescens). MARGUERITE, PARIS DAISY. Short-lived shrubby perennial in Zones CS, TS; grown as summer annual elsewhere; 12–1. Canary Island native has bright green, coarsely divided leaves and abundant daisies 1½–2½ in. across in white, yellow, or pink. Plant reaches about 2½ ft. tall and wide. 'Pink Lady' and 'White Lady' produce buttonlike flower heads; 'Silver Leaf' has gray-green leaves and masses of very small white flowers. 'Snow White', double anemone type, has pure white flowers, more restrained growth habit. Dwarf selections also available. All types are splendid in containers and for quick effects in borders, mass displays in new gardens. For continued bloom, prune lightly at frequent intervals. In Coastal and Tropical South, do not prune severely, since plants seldom produce new growth from hardened wood; replace every 2 to 3 years.

Chrysanthemum frutescens

C. leucanthemum (Leucanthemum vulgare). OX-EYE DAISY, COMMON DAISY. Perennial. Zones US, MS, LS, CS; 9–6. European native naturalized in many places. To 2 ft. high, 1 ft. wide, with bright green foliage and yellow-centered, 1- to 2-in. daisies from late spring through fall. 'May Queen' begins blooming in early spring. Spreads by rhizomes and seeds.

C. maximum (C. ×superbum, Leucanthemum maximum, L. ×superbum). SHASTA DAISY. Perennial. Zones US, MS, LS, CS; 9–1. Summer and fall bloomer. Original 2- to 4-ft.-tall Shasta daisy, with coarse, leathery leaves and gold-centered, white flower heads 2–4 in. across, has been largely superseded by types with larger, better-formed, longer-blooming flowers. These are available in single, double, quilled, and shaggy-flowered forms. All are white, but two show a touch of yellow. Some bloom from May to October. Shasta daisies are splendid in borders and cut arrangements.

Some of the selections available in garden centers include: 'Esther Read', most popular double white, long bloom; 'Marconi', large, frilly double; 'Aglaya', similar to 'Marconi', long blooming season; 'Wirral Supreme', double white with short white central petals; 'Alaska', big, old-fashioned single; 'Horace Read', 4-in.-wide dahlialike flower; 'Majestic', large, yellow-centered single flower; 'Thomas Killin' ('T. E. Killin'), 6-in.-wide (largest) yellow-centered double flower. 'Becky', a tall single selection with sturdy stems, is a popular Southern passalong plant known by several names, including "July daisy," "Ryan's daisy," and "Becky's daisy."

▶

WHAT FLORISTS' MUMS NEED

SOIL: Dig organic matter and a complete fertilizer into good, well-drained garden soil a few weeks before planting.

PLANTING: Set out young pot plants, rooted cuttings, or vigorous single-stem divisions in early spring. When dividing clumps, take divisions from outside; discard the woody centers.

FERTILIZING: Feed plants in ground two or three times during the growing season. Make last application with low-nitrogen fertilizer not less than 2 weeks before bloom.

PINCHING: Frequent pinching produces sturdy plants with big flowers. Begin at planting time by removing plant tip. Lateral shoots will form; select one to four shoots for continued growth. Keep pinching all summer, nipping top pair of leaves on every shoot that reaches 5 in. long. For huge blooms (on large-flowered sorts), disbud (remove all flower buds except one or two per cluster).

'Yellow Quill'; Spoon

Florists' Chrysanthemum Flower Forms

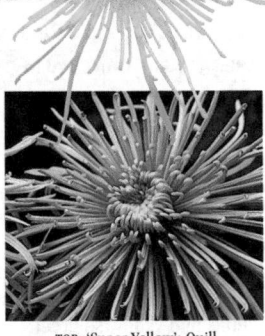

TOP: 'Firewheel'; Spoon
BOTTOM: 'Apricot'; Single

TOP: 'Kelvin Mandarin'; Pompon
BOTTOM: 'Fireflash'; Decorative

TOP: 'Penny Lane'; Anemone Form
BOTTOM: 'Crimson Tide'; Irregular Incurve

TOP: 'Dorridge King'; Reflex
BOTTOM: 'Pink Miss Olympia';
Laciniated

TOP: 'Super Yellow'; Quill
BOTTOM: 'Virginia'; Spider

'Cobham's Gold' has distinctive flowers in a yellow-tinted off-white shade. 'Canarybird', another yellow-toned selection, is a dwarf with attractive dark green foliage.

Most popular selections for cut flowers are 'Esther Read', 'Majestic', 'Aglaya', and 'Thomas Killin'.

Shasta daisies are easy to grow from seed. Catalogs offer many strains, including Diener's Strain (double) and Roggli Super Giant (single). 'Marconi' (double), also available in seed, nearly always blooms double. 'Silver Princess' ('Little Princess', 'Little Miss Muffet') is a 12- to 15-in. dwarf single. 'Snow Lady' (single), an All-America winner, 10–12 in. tall, begins to bloom in 5 months from seed, then blooms nearly continuously.

Set out divisions of Shasta daisies in fall or early spring; set out container-grown plants any time. These plants thrive in fairly rich, moist, well-drained soil. Prefer sun but do well in partial shade in Lower and Coastal South; double-flowered kinds hold up better in very light shade in all zones. Divide clumps every 2 or 3 years in early spring (or in fall, in Lower and Coastal). Shasta daisies are generally easy to grow but have a few problems. Gall disease causes the crown to split into many weak, poorly rooted growing points that soon die. Dig out and dispose of afflicted plants; don't replant Shasta daisies in the same spot.

C. × morifolium (Dendranthema × grandiflorum). FLORISTS' CHRYSANTHEMUM. Perennial. Zones US, MS, LS, CS; 9–1. The most useful of all autumn-blooming perennials for borders, containers, and cutting— and the most versatile and varied of all chrysanthemum species, available in many flower forms, colors, plant and flower sizes, and growth habits. Colors include white, yellow, red, pink, orange, bronze, purple, and lavender, as well as multicolors. Following are flower forms as designated by chrysanthemum hobbyists.

Anemone. One or more rows of rays with large raised center disk or cushion. Center disk may be same color as rays or different.

Brush. Narrow, rolled rays give brush or soft cactus dahlia effect.

Decorative. Long, broad rays overlap like shingles to form a full flower.

Incurve. Big double flowers with broad rays curving upward and inward.

Irregular incurve. Like above, but with looser, more softly curving rays.

Laciniated. Fully double, with rays fringed and cut at tips in carnation effect.

Pompon. Globular, neat, compact flowers with flat, fluted, or quilled rays. Usually small, they can reach 5 in. if buds are thinned to one or two per cluster.

Quill. Long, narrow, rolled rays; like spider but less droopy.

Reflex. Big double flowers with rays that curl in, out, and sideways, creating a shaggy effect.

Semidouble. Somewhat like single or daisy, but with two, three, or four rows of rays around a yellow center.

Single or daisy. Single row of rays around a yellow center. May be large or small, with broad or narrow rays.

Spider. Long, curling, tubular rays ending in fishhook curved tips.

Spoon. Tubular rays flatten at tip to make little disks, sometimes in colors that contrast with body of flower.

MY FAVORITE MUMS. *Bred and tested at the University of Minnesota, a group of cold-hardy interspecific hybrids sold as My Favorite Perennial Mums has performed well in Southern gardens. The plants form uniform, bushy mounds to 2½ ft. high and up to 4 ft. across, needing no staking, and they bloom profusely over a 4- to 5-week period. Unlike other florists' mums, they're self-branching and don't need regular pinching; just cut back to 2 in. in late winter or early spring. Selections include 'Autumn Red', 'Coral', Twilight Pink', 'White', and 'Yellow Quill'.* ❖

Garden culture. It's easy to grow florists' chrysanthemums, not so easy to grow prize-winning ones. The latter need more water, feeding, pinching, pruning, grooming, and pest control than most perennials.

Plant in well-drained garden soil improved with organic matter and a complete fertilizer dug in 2 to 3 weeks before planting. In the Lower and Coastal South, provide shade from afternoon sun. Don't plant near large trees or hedges with invasive roots.

Set out young plants in early spring. Water deeply at intervals determined by your soil structure—frequently in porous soils, less often in heavy soils. Too little water causes woody stems and loss of lower leaves; overwatering causes leaves to yellow, then blacken and drop. Feed plants in ground two or three times during the growing season; make last application with low-nitrogen fertilizer not less than 2 weeks before bloom. Aphids are the only notable pest in all areas.

Sturdy plants and big flowers are result of frequent pinching; see "What Florists' Mums Need," previous page. Stake plants to keep them upright. (My Favorite Mums are an exception; they do not require pinching and staking.)

Take cuttings from early to late spring (up until May for some types), or when shoots are 3–4 in. long. As new shoots develop, you can make additional cuttings of them.

Pot culture. Pot rooted cuttings any time from February to April, using porous, fibrous, moisture-holding planting mix. Move plants to larger pots as growth requires—don't let them become root-bound. Pinch as directed in "What Florists' Mums Need"; stake as required. Plants need water daily in warm weather, every other day in cool conditions. Feed with liquid fertilizer every 7 to 10 days until buds show color.

Care after bloom. Sometimes mums are fooled by cool weather and short days into blooming in spring. After they flower, cut them back to within 8 in. of the ground; they'll bloom again in fall. (However, any mum that blooms prematurely in late summer isn't going to bloom again that year, even if you do cut it back.) After fall bloom, cut plants back to 8 in.; where soils are heavy and likely to remain wet in winter, dig clumps with soil intact and set them on top of the ground in an inconspicuous place. Cover with sand or sawdust, if you wish.

C. multicaule (Coleostephus myconis). Annual. Zones US, MS, LS, CS, TS; 9–6. Native to southern Europe. Blooms in spring, when broad-rayed, buttery yellow daisies 2½ in. wide rise above 6- to 8-in.-wide mats of bright green, fleshy foliage. Blooms best in cool weather; plants usually sold in fall, winter, or early spring. 'Moonlight' has lemon yellow flowers.

C. nipponicum (Nipponanthemum nipponicum). NIPPON DAISY. Perennial. Zones US, MS, LS, CS; 10–6. Japanese native resembling a large (up to 3-ft.-tall, 2-ft.-wide), rounded, shrubby Shasta daisy with a dense mass of nearly succulent bright green leaves. White, 2-in. daisies on long stems bloom in fall. In Lower and Coastal South, you may cut back after flowering; in Upper and Middle South, wait until strong new growth shows in spring, then cut back partway.

C. pacificum (Ajania pacifica, Pyrethrum marginatum, Dendranthema pacificum). GOLD AND SILVER CHRYSANTHEMUM. Perennial. Zones US, MS, LS, CS; 9–3. Semitrailing and semishrubby perennial from Japan; to 1 ft. tall, 3 ft. wide. Stems densely clad in lobed, dark green leaves with woolly white undersides that show at leaf edges. Broad clusters of yellow, ¾-in. flowers appear in fall; lacking rays, they resemble brass buttons. 'Pink Ice' is pale pink with short rays. Use as bank or ground cover or at front of perennial border. In Lower and Coastal South, you may cut back after bloom to keep compact form; in Upper and Middle South, wait until strong new growth appears in spring, then cut back partway.

C. paludosum (Leucanthemum paludosum). SWAMP CHRYSANTHEMUM. Annual, sometimes living over for a second bloom season. Zones US, MS, LS, CS, TS; 9–6. In summer, this western Mediterranean native bears white daisies 1–1½ in. wide on 8- to 10-in. stems above dark green, deeply toothed leaves. Flowers look like miniature Shasta daisies.

C. parthenium (Tanacetum parthenium). FEVERFEW. Perennial. Zones US, MS, LS, CS; 9–1. Native to southern Europe. Once favored in Victorian gardens. Compact, leafy, aggressive; foliage has a strong odor that some find offensive. Named selections range from 1 to 3 ft. tall, with 1-in. blossoms. 'Golden Ball' has bright yellow flower heads and no rays; 'Silver Ball' is completely double with only the white rays showing. In 'Aureum', often sold in flats as 'Golden Feather', chartreuse-colored foliage is the principal attraction. Sow seeds in spring for bloom by midsummer; or plant from divisions in fall or spring. Can also be grown from cuttings. Full sun or light shade. Self-sows prolifically.

C. ×rubellum (Dendranthema zawadskii). Perennial. Zones US, MS, LS, CS; 9–1. To 2–2½ ft. high and wide, with finely cut leaves and 2- to 3-in. daisies over a long season beginning in late summer. 'Clara Curtis' has soft pink flowers; 'Mary Stoker' has blooms of soft yellow touched with apricot.

C. serotinum (C. uliginosum, Leucanthemella serotina). GIANT DAISY. Perennial. Zones US, MS, LS, CS; 9–6. From central Europe. Grows 5–6 ft. tall, 3 ft. wide, producing sheaves of 3-in., yellow-eyed white daisies in late summer. Useful for late flowers in back of perennial border. Can tolerate damp soil better than most daisies.

C. weyrichii (Dendranthema weyrichii). Perennial. Zones US, MS. From Japan. Rock garden plant with finely cut leaves; forms a mat to 1–1½ ft. high and 1 ft. wide. Single, 2-in., white to pink daisies with yellow centers appear just above foliage in fall. 'Pink Bomb' has rosy pink rays, 'White Bomb' creamy white ones.

DEAR OLD MUMS. *Concerned that your mums will suffer from neglect? Not to worry. Choose from these old-fashioned florists' chrysanthemums—all longtime favorites that have survived at old homesites without a gardener in sight. Most have an open, casual look and bloom later than their modern counterparts. Try these: 'Ryan's Pink', 1½–2 ft., soft pink; 'Emperor of China', to 4 ft., silvery rose pink flowers and red-flushed foliage; 'Hillside Sheffield' ('Sheffield Pink'), 2½–3 ft., clear pink; 'Mrs. Hathaway', 2½ ft., yellow; 'Single Apricot Korean', 2–3 ft., pale apricot; 'Venus', 2–3 ft., pale pink to white; 'Virginia's Sunshine', 2 ft., soft yellow flowers as late as November.* ❖

CHRYSOGONUM virginianum

GOLDEN STAR, GREEN AND GOLD

Asteraceae (Compositae)

PERENNIAL

US, MS, LS, CS   9–2

PARTIAL SHADE

REGULAR WATER

Chrysogonum virginianum

Native to eastern U.S. Useful and attractive native plant for ground cover or foreground planting. Grows 8 in. tall and spreads freely by underground rhizomes. Bright green, toothed leaves, 1–3 in. long, make a good background for the bright yellow flower heads. Blossoms have five rays, resemble stars more than daisies. Bloom is heavy in spring and fall, sporadic through summer months. For quick ground cover, plant 1 ft. apart in rich soil high in organic matter. 'Allen Bush' is an excellent selection with dark green leaves. 'Eco Lacquered Spider' has long runners (to 3 ft.) that radiate from the center of the plant like spider legs.

C. v. australe is a more prostrate form with shorter stems. Its flowers aren't as showy as those of the species, and it spreads by aboveground stolons or runners (much as strawberry plants do) rather than rhizomes.

CHRYSOPSIS (Heterotheca)

GOLDEN ASTER

Asteraceae (Compositae)

PERENNIALS

US, MS, LS, CS

FULL SUN

REGULAR TO MODERATE WATER

Chrysopsis villosa

These tough, showy, little-known perennials native to the eastern U.S. deserve wider use. They tolerate heat, drought, humidity, and poor soil and have no serious pests. Daisylike yellow blooms decorate the plants for many weeks in late summer and fall. Give them good drainage and plenty of sun. Dig and divide crowded clumps in early spring.

C. falcata (Pityopsis falcata). Heat zones 9–7. Grows to about 1 ft. high, 1 ft. wide. Small (¾-in.) flowers appear on branched stems above a rosette of broadly linear leaves to 3½ in. long.

C. mariana (Heterotheca mariana). MARYLAND GOLDEN ASTER. Heat zones 9–2. Grows to 2 ft. or possibly 3 ft. high, 1½ ft. wide, with large (9-in.) basal leaves, smaller stem leaves, and tight clusters of 1½-in. flowers.

C. villosa (Heterotheca villosa). GOLDEN ASTER. Heat zones 9–2. Taller than *C. mariana* (to 4–5 ft. tall, 2 ft. wide), with smaller, more scattered flowers. Blooms for a long time; excellent cut flower. Good to combine with ironweed, fall asters, and blue salvia. 'Golden Sunshine' is a compact form to about 3 ft. tall, with large (2-in.) golden flowers.

CHUPAROSA. See ANISACANTHUS thurberi

CIBOTIUM

HAWAIIAN TREE FERN

Dicksoniaceae

TREE FERN

🗡 TS; OR GROW IN POTS

◐ PARTIAL SHADE

💧 REGULAR WATER

Cibotium glaucum

Evergreen ferns, superb for creating tropical effects. A solitary brown trunk—the upper portion of which is thickly covered with silky hairs—supports arching, intricately divided, feathery-looking fronds. Provide reasonably fertile, well-drained soil and shelter from strong winds. Prune to remove old or injured fronds. The two Hawaiian natives listed here are hardy to 30°F; beyond their hardiness range, they can be grown in a large greenhouse or sunroom in bright light.

C. chamissoi. To 6 ft., possibly 20 ft. tall, with crown spreading about 10 ft. wide. Yellow-green fronds.

C. glaucum. Very slow growth to 20 ft. tall, with crown to 15 ft. wide. Leathery, gray-green to bluish fronds with waxy undersides.

CICHORIUM intybus. See CHICORY and RADICCHIO

CIDER GUM. See EUCALYPTUS gunnii

CIGAR PLANT. See CUPHEA ignea

CILANTRO. See CORIANDRUM sativum

CIMICIFUGA (Actaea)

BUGBANE

Ranunculaceae

PERENNIALS

🗡 US, MS, LS, CS

◐ PARTIAL SHADE

💧 REGULAR WATER

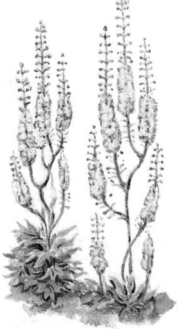

Cimicifuga racemosa

Stately, upright, slim spikes of small white flowers like elongated bottlebrushes rise from clumps of shiny dark green leaves divided into many deeply toothed, 1½- to 3-in. leaflets; overall effect is delicate and airy. The various species bloom midsummer to fall; dried seed clusters are used in flower arrangements. All are handsome among large ferns in woodland gardens; tallest types are also good back-of-border plants. Best in rich, well-drained soil. Will take considerable sun if given adequate moisture. Need some winter chill for best bloom. Clumps can remain undisturbed for many years. In cold-winter areas, divide in early spring before growth starts; in Lower and Coastal South, divide in fall.

C. japonica. JAPANESE BUGBANE. Heat zones 8–1. Native to Japan. White autumn flowers on purplish black, leafless stalks. In bloom, plant is 3–4 ft. tall, 2 ft. wide. Variety *C. j. acerina* has white flowers opening from pink buds.

C. racemosa. BLACK SNAKEROOT, COHOSH BUGBANE. Heat zones 9–1. Native to eastern North America. Leafy clump to 3–4 ft. tall, 3 ft. wide. Flowering stalks are typically branched and carry dense spikes of white flowers that increase plant height to 7 ft. Blooms between midsummer and early fall.

C. simplex. KAMCHATKA BUGBANE. Heat zones 9–1. Native to Siberia and Japan. Foliage clump to 2 ft. tall and wide, with 3- to 4-ft. flower stalks in fall. 'Atropurpurea' has purplish leaves and pink-tinted flower buds on 5-ft. stems. 'Brunette' and 'Hillside Black Beauty' have even darker foliage and pinkish flowers. 'Prichard's Giant' (*C. ramosa*) has foliage clumps to 4 ft. tall and wide; erect stems to 7 ft. high carry foot-long, narrow spikes of white flowers.

CINERARIA. See SENECIO ×hybridus

CINNAMOMUM camphora

CAMPHOR TREE

Lauraceae

EVERGREEN TREE

🗡 LS, CS, TS 🌡 10–8

☼ ◐ FULL SUN OR LIGHT SHADE

◔ ◑ ● LITTLE TO REGULAR WATER

Cinnamomum camphora

Native to China, Japan. Grows slowly to 50 ft. or taller, 60 ft. wide. Typically a strong-structured tree with heavy trunk and heavy, upright, spreading limbs. Beautiful in rain, when trunk looks black. Aromatic, 2½- to 5-in.-long leaves smell like camphor when crushed. New foliage in early spring is pink, red, or bronze; matures to shiny yellow green. Inconspicuous but fragrant yellow flowers bloom profusely in late spring, followed by small blackish fruits.

Drops leaves quite heavily in early spring; flowers, fruits, and twigs drop later. Plant where litter will not be a problem. Competitive roots also make this tree a poor choice near garden beds and paved areas; roots may invade sewer and drainage lines as well.

Camphor tree is subject to verticillium wilt. Symptoms are wilting and dying of twigs, branches, center of tree, or entire tree; wood in twigs or branches shows brownish discoloration. Most susceptible after wet winters or if planted in poorly drained soil. No cure is known, though trees often outgrow the problem. To treat, cut out damaged branches. Apply nitrogen fertilizer and water it in well.

CINNAMON FERN. See OSMUNDA cinnamomea

CINQUEFOIL. See POTENTILLA

CISSUS rhombifolia

GRAPE IVY

Vitaceae

EVERGREEN VINE

🗡 TS 🌡 12–10; OR HOUSEPLANT

◐ ● PARTIAL TO FULL SHADE; BRIGHT LIGHT

💧 REGULAR WATER

Cissus rhombifolia

Native to South America, grape ivy is one of those long-established, dependable indoor plants that practically everyone grows at one time or another. Handsome dark green leaves have attractive bronze overtones due to reddish hairs on the leaf undersides. Each leaf is divided into three diamond-shaped, 1- to 4-in.-long leaflets with sharply toothed edges; leaves look like miniature grape leaves in overall outline, hence the common name. Tendrils twine around any support provided. Propagate by taking stem cuttings in spring and summer. 'Mandaiana' is more upright and compact than the species, with larger, more substantial leaflets. 'Ellen Danica' is another more compact selection, with darker green, less lustrous leaves than the species; its leaflets are shallowly lobed, like an oak leaf.

Indoors, grape ivy is ideal for hanging baskets. Situate it in bright light but not in direct, hot sun. Let soil go slightly dry between waterings. In the Tropical South, you can grow grape ivy outdoors; train it on a wall, pergola, or trellis, or use as ground cover for shaded areas.

Cistaceae. Members of the rockrose family grown in the South are evergreen shrubs with flowers that look something like single roses—small in sunrose (*Helianthemum*), large in rockrose (*Cistus*). Individual flowers are short lived but appear over a long season.

CISTUS

ROCKROSE

Cistaceae

EVERGREEN SHRUBS

LS, CS

FULL SUN

LITTLE OR NO WATER

Cistus ×purpureus

These Mediterranean natives are carefree shrubs that grow well in limy soils and perform beautifully in dry-summer areas such as Southwest Texas, blooming profusely for a month or more in spring or early summer. They need no fertilizer and very little water; if they will be watered, be sure to provide excellent drainage. Periodically prune out a few of the old stems to keep plants looking neat; tip-pinch young plants to make them bushy.

C. ladanifer (C. ladaniferus maculatus). CRIMSON-SPOT ROCKROSE. Heat zones 10–7. Compact to 3–5 ft. high with equal spread. Fragrant leaves to 4 in. long are dark green above, lighter beneath; 3-in.-wide flowers are white with a dark crimson spot at each petal base. 'Cordoba' is a choice selection, 'Albiflorus' an unspotted form. *C. l. latifolius (C. palhinhae)* is a lower grower (to 2 ft.) but has larger blooms (3–4 in. across). Hybrids include 'Maculatus', to 6 ft. tall, 4–5 ft. wide; 'Blanche', to 8–12 ft. high, 6–8 ft. wide, with 4-in. white flowers; and 'Frank Birch', to 6–8 ft. tall and wide, also with pure white, 4-in. blossoms.

C. laurifolius. LAUREL ROCKROSE. Heat zones 10–8. Stiff, erect growth to 4–6 ft. high and wide. Dark green, 5-in. leaves with pale undersides. White, 2- to 2½-in. flowers, in long-stalked clusters of three or more. 'Bennett's White' has 3- to 4-in. flowers with wavy, crepe paper–textured petals around a large cluster of yellow stamens. Good hedge or background shrub for dry areas.

C. ×purpureus. ORCHID ROCKROSE. Heat zones 10–8. Compact grower to 4 ft. tall and wide. Leaves 1–2 in. long, dark green above, gray and hairy beneath. Reddish purple, 3-in. flowers with red spot at base of each petal.

C. ×skanbergii. Heat zones 12–9. Low, broad bush to 3 ft. tall and 8 ft. wide. Gray-green, 2-in. leaves; pure pink, 1-in. flowers in great profusion.

CITRON. See CITRUS

CITRUS

Rutaceae

EVERGREEN TREES AND SHRUBS

CS, TS H 12–10 FOR MOST, POSSIBLY LS FOR HARDIER TYPES, EXCEPT AS NOTED; OR GROW IN POTS

FULL SUN; BRIGHT LIGHT

REGULAR WATER

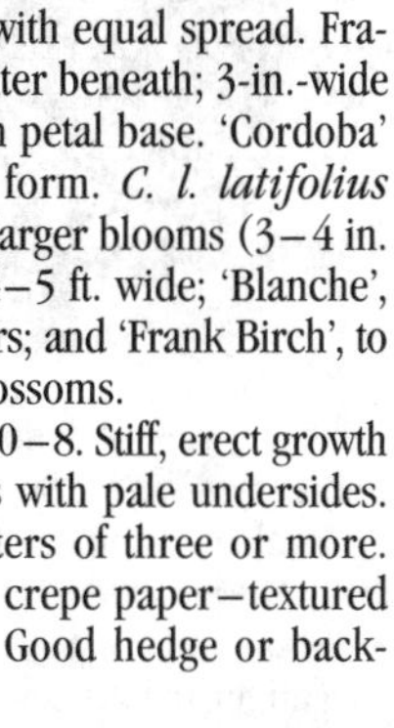

Orange

Citrus plants offer year-round attractive form and glossy deep green foliage. They also produce fragrant flowers and brightly colored, decorative fruit in season. If you want quality fruit, your choice of plants will largely depend on the amount of winter cold in your area.

Hardiness. Citrus plants of one type or another are grown outdoors year-round in the Tropical South and mildest parts of the Coastal South. Lemons and limes are most sensitive to freezes. Sweet oranges, grapefruit, and most mandarins and their hybrids are intermediate. Kumquats, satsuma mandarins, and calamondins are cold resistant, withstanding temperatures in the high teens. Hardy citrus (see page 250) is available to gardeners just beyond the citrus belt.

Other factors affecting a tree's cold tolerance include preconditioning to cold (it will have more endurance if exposed to cold slowly and if first freeze comes late), type of rootstock, and location in garden (planting on the south side of the house is preferred). Prolonged exposure to freezing weather is more damaging than a brief plunge in temperature. All citrus fruit is damaged at several degrees below freezing, so if you live in a freeze-prone area, choose early-ripening types.

Anatomy. Almost all commercially grown citrus trees are grafted, consisting of two parts: scion (upper part of tree producing desirable fruit) and rootstock (lower few inches of trunk and the roots). These are joined at the bud union. Grafted trees begin bearing fruit in just a few years, contrasted with 10 to 15 years for seedling trees. Most kinds produce a single crop in fall or winter, but everbearing types (lemons, limes, calamondins) can produce throughout the year, though they fruit most heavily in spring. Plants don't go completely dormant, but their growth does slow in winter. Citrus fruit ripens only on the tree.

Tree size depends on the category of citrus and on the selection within that category. Standard trees (the norm in Florida, Texas, and along the Gulf Coast) grow full size—typically 20–30 ft. tall and wide. Dwarf trees are grafted onto a rootstock that reduces the size of the tree but not that of the fruit; they are sold through mail-order suppliers (these cannot ship to commercial citrus-producing states) and at some nurseries in Florida.

Drainage. Fast drainage is essential. In poorly drained soils or in areas with heavy rainfall or a high water table, plant above soil level in raised beds or on a soil mound. To speed up drainage in average soil and improve water retention in sandy soil, dig in a 4- to 6-in. layer of organic matter (such as garden compost or aged sawdust) to a depth of 1 ft.

Watering. Citrus trees need moist soil, but never standing water. They require moisture all year, but their demand for it is highest during active growth (usually from late winter or early spring through summer), and they *must* have plenty of water when fruit is developing. Irrigate when top few inches of soil are dry but rest of root zone is still slightly moist. To check soil moisture, simply stick your finger in the soil; or use a moisture meter.

Fertilizing. In general, use a balanced, relatively low-nitrogen fertilizer, such as 6-6-6, 8-8-8, or 10-10-10. If possible, choose a fertilizer containing slow-release nitrogen. Where soil tests reveal a deficiency in certain minor nutrients, particularly magnesium, zinc, manganese, or iron, make sure the fertilizer contains them. (A popular fruit tree fertilizer in south Florida is 8-4-9-3, the last number representing magnesium.) Be careful not to overfertilize citrus plants growing in alkaline soils. Apply a total of 1 pound of fertilizer per inch of trunk diameter per year, dividing that amount into four equal portions to be applied every 2 months during the 8 months of most active growth. Sprinkle fertilizer over soil surface under entire tree canopy, keeping it 2 in. away from trunk; then water it in.

Pests and diseases. Most problems are minor or can be solved by improving growing conditions. Treat citrus leaf miner, mites, and scale insects with horticultural oil spray; treat greasy spot with either oil spray or copper fungicide spray (and remove fallen leaves to keep the disease from spreading). Unlike deciduous fruit trees such as apples and peaches, however, citrus trees do not need regular spraying. For more information on problems common in your area and the best controls for them, check with your Cooperative Extension Office or local garden centers.

One serious problem is citrus canker, a highly contagious bacterial disease that first appeared in Miami-Dade County, Florida, in 1995. Since then, it has spread to 15 counties in south Florida, threatening that state's multibillion-dollar citrus industry. The pathogen affects all types of citrus. Leaves develop brown spots with a yellow halo; infected trees usually don't die, but they eventually lose vigor and may stop producing. Their fruit cannot legally be sold fresh, though it can be used for juice. There is no chemical control for the disease. To stop its spread, the Florida Department of Agriculture and Consumer Services prohibits the movement of citrus trees into or out of certain areas. For more information, see "A Practical Guide to Gardening" (page 603); also check with your Cooperative Extension Office for county-specific recommendations.

Pruning. Commercial trees are allowed to carry branches right to ground; production is heaviest on lower branches. Growers prune only to remove

C

twiggy growth and weak branches or, in young plants, to nip back wild growth and balance the plant. You can prune garden trees to shape as desired; espalier is traditional. Lemons are often planted close and pruned as hedges, as are sour oranges. Many citrus plants are thorny, so wear gloves and a long-sleeved shirt when picking fruit or pruning. In freeze-prone areas, don't prune in fall or winter.

Citrus in containers. Use containers at least 1½ ft. in diameter, though calamondin can stay in an 8- to 10-in. pot for years. Plant in light, well-drained soil mix. Daily watering may be necessary in hot weather. Use a slow-release fertilizer to keep nutrients from washing out with each watering.

Potted citrus plants can stay outdoors most or all year in mild-winter climates, but they should be moved to a protected area if a freeze is predicted. In the Upper, Middle, and Lower South, shelter plants in winter. A cool greenhouse is best, but a basement area or garage with good bright light is satisfactory.

Citrus as houseplants. There is no guarantee of flowering or fruiting indoors, but the plants are still appealing. 'Improved Meyer' and 'Ponderosa' lemons, 'Bearss' lime, kumquats, calamondins, and 'Rangpur' sour-acid mandarin are the most likely to produce good fruit. Locate no more than 6 ft. from a sunny window, away from radiators or other heat sources. Ideal humidity level is 50 percent. Increase air moisture by misting tree; also ring tree with pebble-filled trays of water. Water sparingly in winter.

SWEET ORANGE

Heat zones 12–10. Dense globes to about 25 ft. tall. Fruit usually stores on the tree for a few months. The orange blossom is Florida's state flower.

'Cara Cara'. First rosy-fleshed navel, bearing at about same time as 'Washington'. Red flesh in Florida.

'Hamlin'. Nearly seedless juice orange. Matures early, fall into winter. Best in South Texas, Florida.

'Jaffa' ('Shamouti'). Midseason (ripens winter into spring), nearly seedless eating orange from Israel. Grown in South Texas.

'Marrs'. Low-acid fruit with few seeds, ripening fall into winter. Grows well in South Texas.

'Parson Brown'. Early-ripening, small, seedy juice orange. Best in Florida.

'Pineapple'. Leading midseason orange in Florida; also grown in South Texas. Fairly seedy but excellent for juicing. Fruit tends to drop from tree after ripening.

'Valencia'. This is the premier juice orange. Widely adapted, bearing nearly seedless fruit in midwinter and spring. 'Delta' and 'Midknight' are seedless selections ripening a little earlier. If grown in Florida, 'Rohde Red' has more highly colored flesh than 'Valencia'.

'Washington'. Original navel selection from which the other navels developed. Seedless eating orange ripens early, fall into winter. In Texas and Florida, local selections sold simply as "navel" have better flavor.

Blood oranges. These are characterized by red pigmentation in flesh, juice, and (to a lesser degree) rind. Flavor has raspberry overtones. Need chilly nights during ripening. Main kinds grown are 'Moro', 'Sanguinelli', and 'Tarocco'.

MANDARIN

Heat zones 11–8. Small to medium-size trees (10–20 ft. tall and wide) bearing juicy, loose-skinned, and often slightly flattened-looking fruit; most produce in winter. Selections with red-orange peel are usually called tangerines. Many mandarins tend to bear heavily in alternate years.

WHAT CITRUS NEED

CLIMATE: Most kinds of citrus flourish in areas with warm to hot summers and mild winters.

SOIL: Citrus trees are quite tolerant, as long as the soil is well drained.

WATERING: Be consistent; don't let the soil dry out completely or get soggy.

FERTILIZING: Keep the nitrogen coming—citrus demands a fairly large amount of this nutrient every year. Apply micronutrients—iron, zinc, and magnesium.

RIPENING: All citrus fruits ripen only on the tree. Don't go by rind color; taste fruit to determine its ripeness.

'Valencia' Sweet Orange

'Clementine' (Algerian tangerine). Sweet, variably seedy flesh. Ripens early (from fall into winter), holds well on tree. Light crop without a pollenizer. Good for Texas Gulf Coast.

'Dancy'. Small, seedy fruit is traditional Christmas "tangerine"; ripens late fall into winter. Needs high heat; best in Florida. Also grows in hot, dry regions. Alternate bearer.

'Encore'. Ripens very late (spring into summer) and holds on tree until fall. Sweet-tart, seedy fruit. Alternate bearer. Good for South Texas.

'Fremont'. Ripens from late fall into winter; seedy, richly sweet fruit. Alternate bearer. Does well along Upper Gulf Coast.

'Honey'. Seedy, very sweet fruit from winter into spring. Different from 'Murcott' tangor (see "Mandarin hybrids," below), which is marketed as "Honey tangerine." Alternate bearer. Does well in South Texas, Gulf Coast.

'Mediterranean' ('Willow Leaf'). Springtime crop of sweet, aromatic, very juicy fruit gets puffy soon after ripening. Needs high heat. Alternate bearer. Good for South Texas, Gulf Coast.

'Pixie'. Late selection with seedless, mild, sweet fruit. Alternate bearer. Recommended for South Texas.

'Ponkan' (Chinese honey mandarin). Early crop of seedy, very sweet fruit. Alternate bearer. Good for South Texas, Gulf Coast, Florida.

Satsuma. Group of mandarins with mild, sweet fruit that ripens early (beginning in fall). Succeeds in areas too cold for most citrus; mature trees can withstand 15°F. Ripe fruit deteriorates quickly on tree but keeps well in cool storage. Selections include 'Dobashi Beni', 'Kimbrough', 'Okitsu Wase', and 'Owari'. Does well in South Texas, Gulf Coast, north Florida.

'Wilking'. Midseason selection with rich, distinctive flavor. Juicy fruit holds fairly well on tree. Alternate bearer. Recommended for South Texas.

MULTIPLE-SELECTION CITRUS PLANTS. *The garden center offerings go by such names as cocktail citrus, salad citrus, and citrus medley. On these plants, which bear more than one kind of fruit, multiple selections (usually two or three) have been budded onto one stem. Such plants save space, but you must continually cut back the vigorous growers (limes, lemons, grapefruit) so the weaker ones (oranges, mandarins) can survive.* ❖

MANDARIN HYBRIDS

These hybrids generally perform best in hot weather. Many were developed in Florida, where they produce outstanding crops.

Tangelo. Hybrid between mandarin and grapefruit. Best with a pollenizer like 'Dancy' or 'Clementine' (both mandarins) or another tangelo. In winter, 'Minneola' bears bright orange-red fruit (often with a noticeable "neck") with rich, tart flavor and some seeds. 'Orlando' produces mild, sweet, fairly seedy fruit about a month earlier than 'Minneola'.

Tangor. Hybrid between mandarin and sweet orange. Especially well adapted to sweet orange–growing areas of Florida. 'Murcott' is an alternate bearer with very sweet, seedy, yellowish orange fruit winter into spring; it's marketed under the name "Honey tangerine." 'Ortanique' has sweet, juicy, variably seedy fruit ripening spring to summer. 'Temple' bears a winter-to-spring crop of sweet to tart, seedy fruit; needs high heat and is more cold sensitive than other tangors.

Other mandarin hybrids include the following.

'Ambersweet'. Result of crossing a hybrid of 'Clementine' mandarin and 'Orlando' tangelo with a midseason orange. Juicy fruit, borne fall to winter, is classified as an orange by fresh fruit marketers. Very seedy when grown near another selection.

Citrus Types

TOP: 'Minneola' Tangelo
BOTTOM: 'Sanguinelli' Blood Orange

TOP: 'Oroblanco' Grapefruit
BOTTOM: Calamondin

TOP: 'Nagami' Kumquat
BOTTOM: 'Valencia' Sweet Orange

TOP: 'Bearss' Lime
BOTTOM: 'Dancy' Mandarin

TOP: 'Etrog' Citron
BOTTOM: 'Improved Meyer' Lemon

'Fairchild'. Hybrid of 'Clementine' mandarin and 'Orlando' tangelo. Juicy, sweet fruit in winter. Bigger crop with a pollenizer.

'Fallglo'. Somewhat cold sensitive, like its 'Temple' tangor parent. Juicy, tart, very seedy fruit ripens in fall.

'Lee'. Hybrid between 'Clementine' and an unknown pollen parent. Fairly seedy fruit matures fall to winter. Has best flavor if grown in Florida.

'Nova'. Cross between 'Clementine' mandarin and 'Orlando' tangelo. Juicy, richly sweet fruit fall to winter. Needs a pollenizer.

'Osceola'. Hybrid of 'Clementine' mandarin and 'Orlando' tangelo. Medium-size, seedy fruit ripens in November. Best flavor in Florida. Pollinate with 'Lee' or 'Orlando'.

'Page'. Parents are 'Clementine' mandarin and 'Minneola' tangelo. Many small, juicy, sweet fruits fall into winter. Few seeds, even with a pollenizer to improve fruit set.

'Robinson'. Hybrid between 'Clementine' mandarin and 'Orlando' tangelo. Very sweet fruit in fall. Quite seedy with a pollenizer. Best flavor if grown in Florida.

'Sunburst'. Cross between 'Robinson' and 'Osceola'. Big, sweet redorange fruit in late fall. Nearly seedless without a pollenizer. Best flavor in Florida.

'Wekiwa' (pink tangelo, 'Lavender Gem'). A cross between a tangelo and a grapefruit: looks like a small grapefruit but is eaten like a mandarin. Juicy, mild, sweet flesh is purplish rose in hot climates. Ripens late fall into winter.

SOUR-ACID MANDARIN
Both of the following bear throughout the year in mild-winter climates; they also fruit well indoors.

Calamondin. A mandarin-kumquat hybrid with fruit like a very small orange but a sweet, edible rind. Juicy, tart flesh has some seeds. Variegated form is especially ornamental.

'Rangpur'. Often called Rangpur lime, though it's not a lime and doesn't taste like one. Fruit looks and peels like a mandarin. Less acid than lemon; a good base for punches and mixed drinks. 'Otaheite' (Tahiti orange) is an acidless form sold as a houseplant.

GRAPEFRUIT
Trees to about 30 ft. tall and wide. Best in Florida and South Texas. Heat zones 12–10.

'Duncan'. Oldest known grapefruit selection in Florida and the one from which all the others developed. Extremely seedy white flesh with better flavor than modern seedless types. Good for juice.

'Flame'. Red flesh similar to that of 'Star Ruby', slight rind blush, and few to no seeds. Now widely planted in Florida.

'Marsh' ('Marsh Seedless'). Main white-fleshed commercial kind. Seedless offspring of 'Duncan'. A pigmented form, 'Pink Marsh' ('Thompson'), tends to lose its pink tones as the season progresses.

'Melogold'. Grapefruit-pummelo hybrid. Seedless white flesh is sweeter than fruit of its sister selection 'Oroblanco'; tree tolerates slightly more cold than 'Oroblanco'.

'Oroblanco'. Grapefruit-pummelo hybrid. Fruit containing few to no seeds has a thicker rind and more sweet-tart flavor than 'Melogold'.

'Ray Ruby' and 'Henderson'. Almost identical seedless types that have good rind blush and flesh pigmentation.

'Redblush' ('Ruby', 'Ruby Red'). Seedless, red-tinted flesh. Red internal color fades to pink, then buff by end of season.

'Rio Red'. Seedless type with good rind blush and flesh nearly as red as that of 'Star Ruby'. More dependable producer than 'Star Ruby'.

'Star Ruby'. Seedless selection with the reddest color. Tree is subject to cold damage, erratic bearing, and other growing problems.

Grapefruit

LEMON
Low heat requirement; will even produce indoors. Most grow 20–25 ft. tall and wide.

'Bearss'. Selection of a Sicilian lemon grown in Florida; no relation to 'Bearss' lime. Fruit similar to 'Eureka'. Some fruit all year, but main crop comes in fall and winter.

'Eureka'. Familiar lemon sold in grocery stores. Some fruit all year in mild climates. Big, vigorous, nearly thornless tree. Prune regularly to maintain tree shape and make fruit easily accessible for harvest.

'Improved Meyer'. Hybrid between lemon and sweet orange or mandarin. More cold tolerant than true lemon. Bears yellow-orange, juicy fruit with few seeds throughout the year. Can grow to 15 ft. tall but is usually considerably shorter.

'Lisbon'. Fruit is similar to 'Eureka' (and is also sold in markets), but tree is bigger, thornier, and more cold tolerant. 'Lisbon Seedless' is the same, but without seeds. These are the best lemons for hot, dry areas. Bear some fruit all year in mild climates. Prune regularly to maintain tree shape and make fruit easily accessible for harvest.

'Ponderosa' ('American Wonder'). Thorny lemon-citron hybrid, naturally dwarf. Seedy, thick-skinned, moderately juicy fruits weighing up to

C

2 pounds apiece. Some fruit all year. More susceptible to cold than true lemon. Thrives indoors.

'Variegated Pink' ('Pink Lemonade'). Sport of 'Eureka' with green-and-white leaves and green stripes on immature fruit. Light pink flesh doesn't need heat to develop color. Grows to about 8 ft. tall.

LIME

There's a lime for just about every area of the citrus belt warm enough for sweet oranges. Limes outperform lemons in Florida.

'Bearss' ('Persian', 'Tahiti'). Commonly grown in Florida. To 15–20 ft. tall and wide (half that size on dwarf rootstock). Thorny and inclined to drop many leaves in winter; quite angular and open when young but forms a dense, round crown when mature. The seedless fruit is almost the size of a lemon; it is green when immature, light yellow when ripe. Main crop comes from winter to late spring, though some fruit ripens all year. Needs less heat for fruiting and tolerates more cold than 'Mexican'.

'Kieffer'. Leaves are used in Thai and Cambodian cooking, as is bumpy, sour fruit. Ripens in spring.

'Mexican' ('Key', West Indian lime, bartender's lime). Very thorny plant to about 15 ft. high and wide, bearing small, rounded, intensely flavored fruit all year. 'Mexican Thornless' is the same, minus the spines. Plants need high heat and are very cold sensitive.

'Palestine Sweet'. Shrubby plant to 15–20 ft. tall and wide, with acidless fruit resembling that of 'Bearss' and used in Middle Eastern, Indian, and Latin American cooking. Ripens fall or winter.

KUMQUAT

Shrubby plants 6–15 ft. or taller (and about as wide as high) bear yellow to reddish orange fruits that look like tiny oranges. Eat whole and unpeeled—spongy rind is sweet, pulp is tangy. Best in areas with warm to hot summers and chilly nights during fall or winter, when fruit is ripening. Hardy to at least 12°F.

'Marumi'. Slightly thorny plant with round fruit. Peel is sweeter than that of 'Nagami', but slightly seedy flesh is more acidic.

'Meiwa'. Round fruit is sweeter, juicier, and less seedy than other forms. Considered the best kumquat for eating fresh. Nearly thornless.

'Nagami'. Main commercial type. Oval-shaped, slightly seedy fruit. The hotter the summer, the more abundant and sweeter the fruit. Thornless.

KUMQUAT HYBRIDS

These were the results of early experiments by the citrus industry to produce cold-tolerant kinds of citrus. Fruit has never been a commercial success, but it's good for home gardens. Plants tend to be fairly small even as standards; on dwarfing rootstocks, they reach only 3–6 ft.

Limequat. These hybrids of 'Mexican' lime and kumquat are more cold tolerant and need less heat than their lime parent. Good lime substitutes; edible rind like kumquat parent. Some fruit all year, but main crop comes from fall to spring. 'Eustis' bears fruit shaped like a big olive. 'Tavares' has elongated oval fruit on a more compact, better-looking plant than 'Eustis'.

Orangequat. Most commonly grown is 'Nippon', a cross between 'Meiwa' kumquat and satsuma mandarin. It is cold tolerant and has a fairly low heat requirement. Small, round, deep orange fruit with sweet, spongy rind and slightly acidic flesh. Sweeter than kumquat when eaten whole. Ripens winter and spring, but holds on the tree for months.

CITRON

Citron was the first type of citrus cultivated. Plant is small, thorny, irregular in shape; grown for its big, fragrant, unusual fruit. Very sensitive to cold.

'Buddha's Hand'. Fruit is divided into "fingers" that contain all rind and no pulp. Bears some fruit all year round. This plant has absolutely no tolerance for frost.

'Etrog'. Fruit resembles a big, warty-skinned lemon with dry pulp; the peel is sometimes candied. Used in Jewish Feast of the Tabernacles.

HARDY CITRUS

For areas beyond citrus belt. Most are good choices for Lower and Coastal South; some can be grown in chillier areas. Hardiness figures apply to established plants conditioned to cold by the time freezes arrive.

'Changsha' mandarin. Can reach 15–20 ft. high and wide. Fruit is similar to satsuma mandarin but not as tasty. Ripens from fall into winter. Sometimes grown in regions of Texas, Gulf Coast, and Southwest too cold for regular mandarin selections. Hardy to about 5°F.

Citrange. Hybrid between sweet orange and hardy orange. To 15–20 ft. tall and wide. 'Morton' has fruit like slightly tart sweet orange. 'US-119' is newer and sweeter. Ripens late fall. Hardy to 5–10°F.

Hardy orange. See *Poncirus trifoliata*, page 488.

'Thomasville'. Hybrid between citrange and kumquat. Reaches 15 ft. tall and wide. Small, nearly seedless fruit used as lime substitute if picked soon after ripening in fall. Left on tree, may become sweet enough to eat fresh. Hardy to about 0°F.

CLADRASTIS kentukea (C. lutea)

YELLOW WOOD	
Fabaceae (Leguminosae)	
DECIDUOUS TREE	
US, MS, LS **H** 9–1	
FULL SUN	
REGULAR WATER	

Cladrastis kentukea

Native to Kentucky, Tennessee, and North Carolina. Slow-growing tree to 30–50 ft. tall, with broad, rounded head half as wide as tree is high. Leaves are 8–12 in. long, divided into many (usually 7 to 11) oval leaflets resembling those of English walnut (see *Juglans regia*). Foliage is yellowish green when new, turning bright green in summer and brilliant yellow in fall. Bark is gray in maturity; the common name "yellow wood" refers to the color of the freshly cut heartwood.

May not flower until 10 years old and may skip bloom some years, but the late spring display is spectacular when it comes: clusters of fragrant, wisteria-like white flowers to 14 in. long. 'Perkin's Pink' and 'Rosea' are pink-flowering forms. Blooms are followed by flat, 3- to 4-in.-long seedpods. Attractive as terrace, patio, or lawn tree even if it never blooms. Deep rooted, so you can grow other plants beneath it. Tolerates alkaline soils; withstands some drought.

Prune when young to shorten side branches or correct narrow, weak branch crotches susceptible to breakage in storms. Usually low branching; you can remove lower branches entirely when tree is at desired height. Prune in summer, since cuts made in winter or spring bleed profusely.

CLEMATIS

Ranunculaceae	
DECIDUOUS AND EVERGREEN VINES AND PERENNIALS	
ZONES VARY BY SPECIES	
ROOTS COOL, TOP IN SUN	
REGULAR WATER, EXCEPT AS NOTED	

Clematis armandii

Most of the 200-odd species are deciduous vines; the evergreen *C. armandii* and a few interesting freestanding or sprawling perennials are exceptions. Flowers are attractive in all kinds, spectacular in many. The clustered true flowers are tiny and inconspicuous; the showy part consists of petal-like sepals that surround them. Blossoms are followed by fluffy clusters of seeds with tails, often quite effective in flower arrangements. Leaves of vining kinds are dark green, usually divided into leaflets; leafstalks twist and curl to hold plant to its support.

Clematis are not demanding, but their few specific requirements should be met. Plant vining types next to trellis, tree trunk, or open framework to give stems support for twining. Provide rich, loose, fast-draining soil; add generous quantities of organic matter such as decomposed ground bark. Add lime only where soil tests indicate calcium deficiency.

To provide cool area for roots, spread mulch or place a large flat rock over soil; or plant shallow-rooted ground cover over the root area; or plant in shade of low shrubs (with noncompetitive roots). Install the support at planting time and tie up stems at once. Stems are fragile and easily broken, so protect them with wire netting if child or dog traffic is heavy. Clematis need constant moisture and nutrients to make their great rush of growth; apply a complete liquid fertilizer monthly during the growing season.

When planting a deciduous vine, cut stems to 6–12 in. from ground or to two or three pairs of growth buds, whichever is lower. Late in next dormant season, cut back first year's growth to two or three pairs of buds; train shoots emerging that second spring. Don't prune evergreen vines at first; just start training shoots after planting.

Subsequent yearly pruning sounds complicated, but it need not be—plants are forgiving and will quickly repair mistakes. Do remember that dormant wood can look dead. Watch for healthy buds at leaf bases and preserve them. The basic objective is to get the greatest number of flowers on the shapeliest plant.

The type of pruning you do depends on when your plants flower. If you don't know what kind you have, watch them for a year to see when they bloom; then prune accordingly.

Spring-blooming clematis (their blooms may start in winter in mild-winter climates) flower only on stems produced the previous year. After bloom, cut back shoots that have flowered to about half their length; thin out weak and tangled stems.

Summer- or fall-blooming clematis bloom only at ends of new stems produced in spring. Cut back to 1–2½ ft. in late fall after bloom is over or in early spring as buds swell.

Twice-flowering clematis bloom on last year's stems in spring, then on the current year's shoots in summer or fall. In late fall or early spring, prune lightly to thin out excess shoots or untangle stems. After spring flowers fade, prune more heavily so that new shoots will develop for second round of flowers.

Cut flowers are choice for indoors (float in bowl). Burn cut stems with match to make flowers last longer. Unless otherwise specified, flowers are 4–6 in. across.

C. alpina. ALPINE CLEMATIS. Deciduous vine. Zones US, MS, LS; 9–6. European native. To 8–12 ft., with dangling, 1½- to 3-in.-wide flowers borne singly on long stalks in spring. Flowers may be blue, white, purple, pink, or red, depending on selection; they have four spreading, pointed, petal-like sepals and an inner, smaller cup of modified stamens. 'Willy' has pale pink blooms, 'Helsingborg' dark blue flowers; 'Pamela Jackman' is lavender blue.

C. armandii. ARMAND CLEMATIS, EVERGREEN CLEMATIS. Zones LS, CS; 9–7. Native to China. Fast-growing vine to 20–35 ft. Leaves divided into three glossy dark green, 3- to 5-in.-long leaflets; they droop downward, creating a strongly textured look. Glistening white, 2½-in., fragrant flowers in large, branched clusters in spring. 'Hendersonii Rubra' is a pink-flowered form.

Leaves burn badly at tips in areas where soil or water contains excess salts. Train along substantial frames such as sturdy fence tops or roof gables; or allow to climb tall trees. Makes privacy screen if not allowed to become bare at base. Slow to start but races when established. Needs relentless pruning after flowering to prevent tangling and buildup of dead thatch on inner parts of vine. Keep and tie up stems you want; cut out all others. Frequent pinching will hold foliage to eye level.

C. × cartmanii 'Avalanche'. Evergreen shrubby vine. Zones MS, LS, CS; 9–1. Vigorous hybrid with dark green, deeply cut leaves. Blooms profusely in spring, bearing panicles of 2- to 3-in. white flowers with yellow stamens. Prune after bloom is over.

C. chrysocoma. GOLD WOOL CLEMATIS. Deciduous vine. Zones LS, CS; 9–6. Native to western China. Grows to 6–8 ft. or more in height; fairly open. Young branches, leaves, and flower stalks covered with yellow down. Clusters of long-stalked, 2-in.-wide, pink-shaded white blossoms on old wood in spring; later flowers follow from new wood. Will take considerable shade.

C. 'Durandii' (C. integrifolia 'Durandii'). Perennial. Zones US, MS, LS; 9–1. Hybrid between *C. integrifolia* and *C. × jackmanii*. Sprawling,

nonclimbing plant with simple, undivided leaves; 4-in., deep blue flowers with white anthers in summer. Use it to weave through shrubs or sturdy perennials. It can be staked or tied to a support to reach 4–6 ft. high, 3 ft. wide.

C. florida 'Sieboldii' ('Bicolor'). Deciduous vine. Zones US, MS, LS; 9–6. Selection of an Asian species. To 8–12 ft. Not as rugged as other clematis vines, but summer flowers are striking: 3–4 in. across, creamy white with a central puff of purple petal-like stamens. 'Alba' ('Alba Plena') is similar but has a creamy to greenish white central puff.

C. 'Hendersonii' (C. integrifolia 'Hendersonii'). Perennial. Zones US, MS, LS; 9–1. Hybrid between *C. integrifolia* and *C. viticella*. A nonclimbing plant somewhat like *C.* 'Durandii' but with smaller violet flowers.

C. heracleifolia davidiana (C. davidiana). Woody-based perennial. Zones US, MS, LS; 8–1. Native to China. To 4 ft. high, 3 ft. wide. Deep green leaves divided into three broad, oval, 3- to 6-in. leaflets. Dense clusters of 1-in.-long, tubular, medium to deep blue, fragrant flowers in summer. Use in perennial or shrub border.

C. integrifolia. Woody-based perennial. Zones US, MS, LS; 8–1. Native to Europe and Asia. To 3 ft. tall, 2 ft. wide, with dark green, undivided, 2- to 4-in.-long leaves and nodding, urn-shaped, 1½-in. blue flowers in summer. Provide twigs for the plant to sprawl over. For two popular hybrids often sold as selections of this species, see *C.* 'Durandii' and *C.* 'Hendersonii'.

C. × jackmanii. Deciduous vines. Zones US, MS, LS; 9–1; plants freeze to the ground in severe winters. Series of hybrids between forms of *C. lanuginosa* and *C. viticella*. All are vigorous and grow rapidly to 10 ft. or more in one season. The best known of the older large-flowered hybrids, sold simply as *C. × jackmanii*, is a profuse bloomer bearing 4- to 5-in., rich purple blossoms with four sepals; it flowers from early summer through fall, with heaviest bloom coming early in season. Newer hybrids have larger flowers with more sepals, but none blooms as lavishly. 'Comtesse de Bouchaud' has silvery rose pink flowers; 'Mme Edouard André' bears purplish red blossoms. 'Jackmanii Superba' ('Jackmanii Purpureus Superba') has broader segments that open a deeper purple, fading as they age. (For more on large-flowered hybrid clematis, see next page.)

C. lanuginosa. Deciduous vine. Zones US, MS, LS; 9–1. Chinese species is best known as a parent of many of the large-flowered hybrids. Its selection 'Candida' has breathtaking 8-in.-wide white blooms on a vigorous but small (6- to 10-ft.) vine. Blooms in spring, again in summer.

C. × lawsoniana. Deciduous vine. Zones US, MS, LS; 9–1. Thought to be a hybrid of *C. lanuginosa* and another species. To 6–10 ft., with 6- to 9-in., rosy purple, dark-veined flowers in summer. Its best-known form is 'Henryi', which bears 8-in. white flowers with dark stamens.

C. macropetala. DOWNY CLEMATIS. Deciduous vine. Zones US, MS, LS; 9–6. Native to China, Siberia. Variable in size; may reach 6–10 ft. Lavender to powder blue flowers to 4 in. across appear in early spring; they look double, resembling a ballerina's tutu. Blooms are followed by bronzy pink seed clusters with silvery tails—very showy. 'Blue Bird' has soft blue flowers, 'Markham Pink' lavender-pink blossoms.

C. montana. ANEMONE CLEMATIS. Deciduous vine. Zones US, MS, LS; 9–6. Native to Himalayas, China. Vigorous grower to 20–30 ft. Massive early spring display of 2- to 2½-in., anemone-like flowers that open white, then turn pink. 'Elizabeth' has pale pink flowers and bronzy foliage that matures to green; 'Grandiflora' produces 3-in. white flowers. *C. m. rubens* has crimson new leaves maturing to bronzy green; the fragrant flowers are pink to rose red. Among its selections are 'Odorata', notable for fragrance, and 'Tetrarose', known for bronze foliage and 3-in., thick-textured floral segments.

Clematis montana rubens

C. paniculata. See C. terniflora

C. recta. Perennial. Zones US, MS, LS; 8–1. From central and southern Europe. To 3–6 ft. tall and wide, with dark green, divided leaves and clouds of starlike, inch-wide, white flowers with fragrance of vanilla; blooms from midsummer to early fall. Some forms have purple foliage that gradually fades to green. Give support to keep plants from flopping over onto their neighbors. ▶

C. tangutica. GOLDEN CLEMATIS. Deciduous vine. Zones US, MS, LS; 9–6. Native to Mongolia, northern China. To 10–15 ft., with finely divided gray-green leaves. Nodding, lantern-shaped bright yellow flowers, 2–4 in. across, in great profusion from midsummer into fall. Blossoms are followed by handsome, silvery, mop-headed seed clusters.

C. terniflora (C. dioscoreifolia). SWEET AUTUMN CLEMATIS. Deciduous vine. Zones US, MS, LS, CS; 9–1. Native to Japan. Tall and vigorous (some would say rampant), producing billowy masses of 1-in.-wide, fragrant, creamy white flowers in late summer, fall. Glossy leaves divided into three to five oval, 1- to 2½-in.-long leaflets. Good privacy screen, arbor cover. Self-sows readily; can become a pest. Often erroneously sold as *C. paniculata,* a little-grown species from New Zealand.

C. texensis. SCARLET CLEMATIS. Deciduous vine. Zones US, MS, LS; 9–1. Native to Texas. Fast growing to 6–10 ft. Dense bluish green foliage; bright scarlet, urn-shaped flowers to 1 in. long from early summer until frost. More tolerant of dry soils than most clematis. 'Duchess of Albany', a hybrid of this species with a large-flowered clematis, has upward-facing, cup-shaped, 2-in. deep pink flowers with pointed segments.

C. virginiana. VIRGIN'S BOWER. Deciduous vine. Zones US, MS, LS; 9–1. Native to moist lowlands of eastern North America as far south as Georgia. To 12–20 ft. Bright green foliage; profuse show of sweetly fragrant, 1¼-in. white blossoms in 3- to 6-in.-long clusters in late summer, fall. Will bloom in a fair amount of shade. Best in a native garden, where it can be allowed to scramble casually over the ground, through shrubs, or along a sturdy fence. Self-seeding and suckering can make it invasive.

C. viticella. Deciduous vine. Zones US, MS, LS; 9–1. Native to southern Europe, western Asia. To 12–15 ft. Purple or rose purple, 2-in. blooms in summer. Selections include 'Mme Julia Correvon', with rosy red flowers, and 'Polish Spirit', bearing deep purple-blue blooms with a red center.

Large-flowered hybrid clematis. Zones US, MS, LS, CS. Although well over a hundred selections of large-flowered hybrid clematis are being grown today, your local nursery is not likely to offer more than a dozen of the old favorites. Mail-order catalogs remain the best source for collectors seeking the newest. Flowers on some of these may reach 10 in. across.

Following is a list of old favorites and newer selections.

White. 'Henryi' is the classic white choice. 'Marie Boisselot' ('Mme Le Coultre'), with large, round, flat flowers, and 'Gillian Blades' (huge, star-shaped blooms) are newer. Also worth mentioning in this group is long-time favorite *C. lanuginosa* 'Candida'.

Pink. 'Comtesse de Bouchaud', a longtime popular pink, has these rivals: 'Charissima' (veined pink with deeper bars); 'Hagley Hybrid' ('Pink Chiffon'), shell pink with pointed sepals; and 'Lincoln Star' (pink with paler pink edges).

Red. Red clematis have deep purplish red flowers that are best displayed where the sun can shine through them, as on the top of a fence. 'Mme Edouard André', 'Ernest Markham', and 'Red Cardinal' are standards. 'Ville de Lyon' has full, rounded, velvety flowers; 'Niobe' has the darkest red blossoms of all.

Blue. Medium blue 'Ramona' is always popular. Other selections include 'Edomurasaki' (deep blue), 'General Sikorski' (huge, with faint red bar), 'Lady Betty Balfour' (dark blue), 'Mrs. Cholmondeley' (big, soft lavender blue), 'Piccadilly' (purplish blue), 'Prince Philip' (huge purplish blue with ruffled edges), and 'Will Goodwin' (lavender to sky blue).

Purple. Classic *C. ×jackmanii* is the most popular. Others include 'Gipsy Queen' (deepest purple), 'Mrs. N. Thompson' (deep bluish purple with red bar), and 'Richard Pennell' (rosy purple).

Bicolor. 'Nelly Moser' (purplish pink with reddish center bar) is deservedly one of the most popular clematis. 'Carnaby' (white with a red bar) and 'Dr. Ruppel' (pink with red bar) are newer, splashier.

Double. Fully double, roselike blooms in early summer on old wood are usually followed later by single or semidouble flowers on new wood. Selections include silvery blue 'Belle of Woking', white 'Duchess of Edinburgh', deep blue 'Mrs. P. T. James', lavender 'Teshio'. 'Vyvyan Pennell' has deep blue flowers centered in lavender blue; 'Arctic Queen' bears fully double white flowers on both old and new wood.

CLEOME hasslerana (C. spinosa)

SPIDER FLOWER

Capparidaceae

ANNUAL

US, MS, LS, CS, TS H 12–1

FULL SUN

MODERATE TO REGULAR WATER

Cleome hasslerana

Shrubby, branching South American native topped in summer and fall with many open, fluffy clusters of pink or white flowers with extremely long, protruding stamens. Slender seed capsules follow the blossoms. Stems usually have short, strong spines; lower leaves are divided, upper ones undivided. Leaves and stems feel clammy to the touch; they have a strong but not unpleasant smell.

Plant grows 4–6 ft. tall, 4–5 ft. wide; especially vigorous in warm, dry inland areas. Grow in background, as summer hedge, against walls or fences, in large containers; or—since plants self-sow to a fault—naturalize in fringe areas of garden. Flowers and dry seed capsules are useful in arrangements.

Sow seeds in place in spring; they sprout rapidly in warm soil. A number of selections can be grown from seed. In most cases color is indicated by the selection's name: 'Cherry Queen', 'Mauve Queen', 'Pink Queen', 'Purple Queen', 'Rose Queen', 'Ruby Queen'. 'Helen Campbell' is snow white. 'Sparkler Blush' is a bushy dwarf hybrid to 3–4 ft. tall, loaded with pink flowers at bloom time.

CLERODENDRUM

GLORYBOWER

Verbenaceae

EVERGREEN AND DECIDUOUS SHRUBS AND VINES

TS H 12–10, EXCEPT AS NOTED

EXPOSURE NEEDS VARY BY SPECIES

REGULAR WATER

Clerodendrum bungei

Diverse group of plants grown for big clusters of showy, brightly colored flowers that are fragrant in some species. Bloom comes on current season's growth. Provide support for climbing species. Grow in well-drained soil. Good greenhouse plants in areas that are beyond their hardiness limits.

C. buchananii fallax (C. speciosissimum). JAVA GLORYBOWER. Evergreen shrub. From Indonesia. Erect growth to 12 ft. tall and 6 ft. wide. Plant produces brilliant scarlet flowers throughout much of the year. Densely hairy, heart-shaped leaves grow to 1 ft. long. Suitable shrub for mass plantings, hedges, or colorful screens; it also makes a good container plant. You can prune to improve appearance and shape as needed. Full sun or partial shade.

C. bungei (C. foetidum). CASHMERE BOUQUET. Evergreen shrub. Zones LS, CS, TS; 12–8. Native to China. Plant grows rapidly to 6 ft. tall and wide; spreads rapidly by suckers, eventually forming a thicket if not restrained. Big (to 1-ft.), coarse, broadly oval leaves with toothed edges are dark green above, with rust-colored fuzz beneath. Leaves release a sickening odor when bruised or crushed. Loose clusters of delightfully fragrant rosy red flowers in summer, sometimes into fall. Plant where its appearance (except during bloom time) is not important. Prune severely in spring and pinch back throughout the growing season to make a compact, 2- to 3-ft. shrub. Deer resistant. Partial shade.

C. chinense pleniflorum (C. fragrans pleniflorum). Evergreen to semievergreen shrub. Zones CS, TS; 10–8. Native to southern China. A coarse-looking plant that grows to 5–8 ft. tall, spreading freely by root suckers unless controlled or confined. Its 10-in. leaves resemble those of *C. bungei* but are not malodorous when bruised or crushed. (This species may also be called cashmere bouquet, a name more often applied to *C. bungei*.) Pale pink double flowers with a sweet, clean fragrance are carried in broad clusters resembling those of florists' hydrangea. Partial shade.

C. myricoides 'Ugandense'. Evergreen shrub. Heat zones 12–3. Native to tropical Africa. Grows to 10 ft. tall and about half as wide. Glossy dark green leaves to 4 in. long. Each five-petaled blossom has one violet-blue petal and four pale blue ones; pistil and stamens arch outward and upward. Partial shade.

C. quadriloculare. BAGAUAK. Evergreen shrub. From the Philippines. To 15 ft. tall, spreading by root suckers. Has an upright habit; can be trained to tree form. Clusters of fragrant pink flowers in fall and spring enhance the deep purple of the leaf undersides. Use as color accent, hedge, screen, or tubbed specimen for the lanai. Protect from harsh winds. Prune to shape. Full sun.

C. × speciosum. CLERODENDRUM VINE. Evergreen shrubby vine. Hybrid between *C. splendens* and *C. thomsoniae*. A vine of fairly rapid growth to 30 ft. Glossy, oval dark green leaves to 7 in. long. Blooms in winter and spring, bearing clusters of bicolored blooms with a dull pink or red calyx surrounding a short tube in deep crimson shaded with violet. Calyxes hang on. Full sun.

C. splendens. RED CLERODENDRUM, FLAMING GLORYBOWER. Evergreen vine. From tropical Africa. Climbs rapidly to 30 ft. Rich green, glossy leaves to 7 in. long. Large clusters of brilliant red flowers bloom profusely during winter. Protect from strong winds. Best in sun on vertical supports such as a fence or trellis, and can be trained along eaves.

C. thomsoniae (C. balfouri). BLEEDING HEART VINE. Evergreen vine. Heat zones 12–1. Native to West Africa. Restrained and mannerly growth to no more than 12 ft. Distinctly ribbed, oval, shiny dark green leaves, 4–7 in. long. Blooms from summer to fall, bearing flattish, 5-in. clusters of up to 20 flowers. White calyxes reminiscent of paper lanterns surround scarlet flowers, displaying a striking two-tone contrast. Use it on sheltered patio walls or arbor posts. Grows well in large containers; move it to a frost-free shelter in winter. Partial shade.

C. trichotomum. HARLEQUIN GLORYBOWER. Deciduous shrub. Zones MS, LS, CS, TS; 11–7. Native to Japan. Reaches 10–15 ft. tall and wide, with many stems growing from base; can also be trained as a small tree. Soft, hairy, oval dark green leaves to 5 in. long. Fragrant blossoms—each a white tube almost twice as long as the prominent, fleshy, scarlet calyx surrounding it—come in late summer. Calyxes hang on and contrast pleasingly with metallic-looking turquoise or blue-green fruit. Give this shrub plenty of room to spread at top; add plants underneath it to hide its legginess. 'Carnival' and 'Variegata' have leaves broadly edged in creamy white. *C. t. fargesii*, from China, is somewhat hardier and smaller; it has smooth leaves and green calyxes that turn pink. Partial shade.

CLETHRA

Clethraceae
DECIDUOUS SHRUBS
⚡ ZONES VARY BY SPECIES
☼ ◑ BEST IN PARTIAL SHADE BUT ADAPTABLE
💧 💧 REGULAR TO AMPLE WATER

Clethra alnifolia
'Pink Spires'

These attractive shrubs are grown for the small, five-lobed, sweet-scented white or pink flowers that cluster at branch tips in mid- to late summer. Tolerate many soils but do best in moist, organic, slightly acid, well-drained soil. Prefer partial shade but can adapt successfully to less light as well as to full sun, though they need some shade where

summers are very hot. Remove some old wood from base annually before spring growth begins. Not browsed by deer.

C. acuminata. CINNAMON CLETHRA. Zones US, MS, LS; 8–3. Native to mountain areas of Virginia, Georgia, and Alabama. Grows to 8–12 ft. (rarely 20 ft.) tall and wide. Habit is open, even gaunt, so that polished-looking bark in various shades of cinnamon, tan, and reddish brown is displayed beautifully. Fragrant white flowers in 3- to 6-in. spires. Oblong, 3- to 6-in.-long leaves are dark green in summer, then turn golden yellow in autumn.

C. alnifolia. SUMMERSWEET, SWEET PEPPERBUSH. Zones US, MS, LS, CS; 9–1. Eastern U.S. native to 4–10 ft. tall and wide, spreading slowly by suckers. Thin, strong branches form a vertical pattern. Tooth-edged, dark green, 3- to 4-in. leaves appear late in spring, turn golden yellow to brownish in fall. At bloom time, each branch tip carries several 4- to 6-in.-long spires of tiny, gleaming white flowers with a spicy perfume.

Selections include the following; most grow about as wide as tall.

'Anne Bidwell'. To 4–6 ft., with extra-large flower clusters late in the season.

'Compacta'. Dwarf, shrubby form to just 2½–3½ ft. tall.

'Creel's Calico'. To 4 ft.; foliage irregularly variegated in cream.

'Hummingbird'. Reaches 2½–3½ ft. tall and spreads by suckers to form large colonies.

'Pink Spires'. To 4 ft., with deep pink blooms.

'Rosea'. To 6–10 ft. Pale pink flowers.

'Ruby Lace'. To 5 ft., with deep pink blossoms.

'Ruby Spice'. To 6–8 ft.; dark rosy pink blooms. Wonderful for borders, shade plantings. Spreads by suckers to make a broad clump. Tolerates coastal conditions.

'September Beauty'. Late bloomer; reaches 4–6 ft.

'Sixteen Candles'. Similar to 'Hummingbird', but flower spikes are held upright like candles on a birthday cake.

'White Dove'. Compact, profusely blooming dwarf reaching 2–3 ft.

C. barbinervis. JAPANESE CLETHRA. Zones US, MS, LS; 8–6. Slow-growing plant reaches 15–18 ft. tall and about one-half to two-thirds as wide; has attractive, peeling, glossy gray to brown bark when mature. Produces drooping, 4- to 6-in. clusters of fragrant, bell-shaped white flowers. Oval, pointed, sharply toothed, dark green leaves turn bright yellow in fall. 'Variegata' has leaves attractively splashed with golden yellow.

CLEYERA japonica
(Eurya ochnacea)

Theaceae
EVERGREEN SHRUB
⚡ MS, LS, CS, TS ⎈ 12–7
◑ PARTIAL SHADE
💧 💧 MODERATE TO REGULAR WATER

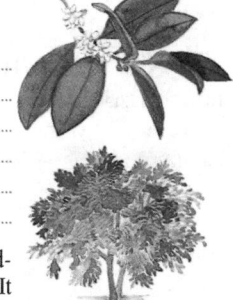

Cleyera japonica

Native to Japan and southeast Asia. Handsome foliage shrub related to camellia. It is quite similar in character to *Ternstroemia gymnanthera*, with which it is often confused. Grows at moderate rate to 15 ft. tall and wide, with graceful, arching branches. New leaves are a beautiful deep brownish red. Mature leaves, 3–6 in. long, are glossy dark green with reddish midrib. Plant produces small clusters of fragrant, creamy white flowers in summer, followed by small, puffy dark red berries that last throughout winter. Flowers and berries are attractive but not showy. Foliage of 'Tricolor' (*C. fortunei*) is variegated in yellow and rose.

FOR INFORMATION ON SELECTING PLANTS
PLEASE SEE PAGES 39–144

CLIANTHUS formosus

DESERT PEA

Fabaceae (Leguminosae)

ANNUAL OR SHORT-LIVED PERENNIAL

✎ CS, TS AS PERENNIAL; ANYWHERE AS ANNUAL; H 12–1

☼ FULL SUN

💧 MODERATE WATER

Clianthus formosus

Native to Australia, this sprawling plant grows 1–4 ft. tall and wide. Downy gray-green leaves to 7 in. long, each with 10 to 12 leaflets to 1 in. long. Intriguing beak-shaped, 3-in. scarlet blooms appear continuously in warm weather; each has a shiny black spot resembling an eye. Thrives in hot sun and well-drained soil; tolerates some drought. Protect from strong winds. 'Desert Dragon' is a compact form only 12–14 in. tall.

CLIFF-BRAKE. See PELLAEA

CLIFF DATE PALM. See PHOENIX rupicola

CLIFTONIA monophylla

BUCKWHEAT TREE

Cyrillaceae

EVERGREEN SHRUB OR TREE

✎ LS, CS H 10–8

☼ FULL SUN

💧💧 REGULAR TO AMPLE WATER

Cliftonia monophylla

Outstanding multitrunked shrub or small tree native to swamps and moist forests of the Southeast. Grows upright to 10–20 ft. tall, half as wide. Leaves are glossy, dark green, leathery, 2–3 in. long. Spreads by suckers to form thickets along streams. Best used in a naturalized area. Clusters of small, fragrant pinkish white flowers bloom in early spring and attract bees and butterflies. Tiny egg-shaped fruits appear in fall. Prefers acid soil with lots of organic matter. 'Berry Pink' is a pink-flowered selection.

CLIMBING LILY. See GLORIOSA superba 'Rothschildiana'

CLINTONIA umbellulata

CLINTON LILY

Liliaceae

PERENNIAL

✎ US, MS H 7–1

💧 FULL SHADE

💧 REGULAR WATER

Clintonia umbellulata

This lovely and little-known wildflower, native to the upland forests of the Appalachians, is a veritable gem. It gently spreads across the forest floor to form lush mats of deep green, oblong leaves (to 10 in. long and 3 in. wide) that are every bit as attractive as those of lily-of-the-valley (*Convallaria majalis*). In late spring, rounded clusters of ½-in., fragrant white blossoms (sometimes speckled with purple) appear atop leafless stalks rising 8–18 in. high. Distinctive round, black berries follow the flowers. Plant dies down in winter.

Clinton lily needs moist, well-drained, slightly acid soil that contains lots of organic matter. Mulch around it every spring to keep the roots cool and moist. Water during summer drought. Ideal at the foot of tall trees and shrubs in naturalized areas and woodland gardens. Good companions include rhododendron, mountain laurel (*Kalmia*), mayapple (*Podophyllum peltatum*), Christmas fern (*Polystichum acrostichoides*), trillium, and wild ginger (*Asarum*).

CLINTON LILY. See CLINTONIA umbellulata

CLITORIA

Fabaceae (Leguminosae)

PERENNIALS, ONE GROWN AS ANNUAL

✎ ZONES VARY BY SPECIES

☼ ☽ EXPOSURE NEEDS VARY BY SPECIES

💧💧 WATER NEEDS VARY BY SPECIES

Clitoria ternatea

This genus includes many and varied species of perennials, vines, and shrubs, but all have the distinctive flowers and foliage of the pea family. Of the two listed here, one is a popular twining vine, the other a native wildflower.

C. mariana. BUTTERFLY PEA, ATLANTIC PIGEON WINGS. Zones US, MS, LS, CS, TS; 12–7. Native to the dry woods, sand hills, and scrub of the eastern U.S. (from New Jersey to Florida), west to Texas and Mexico. Upright and spreading, sometimes twining, thin-stemmed plant that may reach 3 ft. tall. Leaves with three ovate leaflets to 2 in. long; lavender flowers to 2 in. long, 1½ in. wide in early summer. Dies to ground in winter. Best with moderate to regular water and full sun but tolerates some drought and light shade. Good for naturalized areas.

C. ternatea. BLUE PEA VINE. Perennial in Zones TS; 12–10; annual elsewhere. Native to tropical Americas and Asia. A fast-growing, twining vine to 10 ft.; often used to decorate trellises and posts. Blooms continuously in warm weather, bearing deep blue, white-eyed flowers to 2 in. long and 1 in. wide. Leaves consist of five to nine leaflets, each up to 2 in. long. Plant in well-drained soil; give full sun and regular water. Easy to start from seed (soak seed for 3 to 4 hours before sowing). Can bloom as soon as 6 weeks after sowing.

CLIVIA miniata

Amaryllidaceae

PERENNIAL FROM TUBEROUS ROOTS

✎ TS H 12–10; OR GROW IN POT

☽ ● PARTIAL TO FULL SHADE; BRIGHT INDIRECT LIGHT

💧 REGULAR WATER

Clivia miniata

Native to South Africa, this evergreen member of the amaryllis family offers both spectacular flowers and handsome foliage. It makes an exceptional and long-lived potted plant for indoors or out. In the Tropical South, where it is hardy, it's also a great addition to the mixed border. Blooms dependably in shade.

Large clusters of brilliant orange, funnel-shaped blossoms are carried atop 2-ft. stalks that rise above dense clumps of strap-shaped dark green leaves to 1½ ft. long; attractive red berries follow the flowers. Blossoms may appear in winter, but bloom mainly comes in spring and lasts for weeks. French and Belgian hybrids have extra-wide leaves and yellow to deep orange-red blooms on thick, rigid stalks. Solomone Hybrids have pale to deep yellow flowers. 'Flame' is an exceptionally brilliant orange red.

Clivias like bright light—but don't expose them to direct, hot sun, which will burn and yellow the foliage. Plants with crowded roots bloom better, so resist the urge to repot or divide. You can keep potted plants outdoors from spring to fall, but bring them indoors for winter; they are badly damaged by freezing temperatures. Indoors, they do best near an east-facing window. From spring to autumn, fertilize every other week with a general-purpose liquid houseplant fertilizer; water when the soil surface becomes dry. In winter, let the soil dry to a depth of 1 in. between waterings and do not feed. Cool temperatures (50–60°F) will encourage bud set. Outdoors, set plants 1½–2 ft. apart in fertile, moist, well-drained soil.

CLOVE PINK. See DIANTHUS caryophyllus

CLYTOSTOMA callistegioides

VIOLET TRUMPET VINE

Bignoniaceae

EVERGREEN VINE

✂ CS, TS ⊩ 12–9

☼ ◑ FULL SUN OR PARTIAL SHADE

◐ ● MODERATE TO REGULAR WATER

Clytostoma callistegioides

Formerly *Bignonia violacea*, *B. speciosa*. Strong-growing vine from Argentina and Brazil will clamber over anything by tendrils; needs support on walls. Leaves are 3–4 in. long, divided into two glossy, dark green leaflets with wavy margins. Extended terminal shoots hang down to create a curtainlike effect. Blooms from late spring to fall, bearing trumpet-shaped blossoms in sprays at ends of shoots; flowers are violet, lavender, or pale purple, 3 in. long and nearly as wide at the open end. Tops hardy to 20°F, roots to 10°F. Excellent vine for areas of Florida too cold for more tender bignonia relatives such as pandorea. Remove unwanted long runners and spent flower sprays. Prune in late winter to discipline growth.

COBAEA scandens

CUP-AND-SAUCER VINE

Polemoniaceae

PERENNIAL VINE USUALLY GROWN AS ANNUAL

✂ US, MS, LS, CS, TS ⊩ 12–1

☼ FULL SUN

● REGULAR WATER

Cobaea scandens

Native to Mexico. Extremely vigorous growth to 25 ft. in a single season. Bell-shaped, summer-to-fall flowers are first greenish, then violet or rose purple; there is also a white-flowered form. The common name describes the flower form: a 2-in.-long cup of petals sits in large, saucerlike green calyx. Leaves are divided into two or three pairs of oval, 4-in. leaflets; a curling tendril at the end of each leaf enables the vine to climb rough surfaces without support. 'Key Lime' has pale green flowers. Blossoms of 'Royal Plum' emerge light green, then mature to rich deep purple with a white-streaked throat and chartreuse anthers.

The hard-coated seeds may rot if sown outdoors in cool weather. Start indoors in 4-in. pots; notch seeds with a knife and press them edgewise into moistened potting mix, barely covering them. Keep moist but not wet; transplant to warm, sunny location when weather warms up. Protect from wind. Blooms first year from seed. In the Tropical South and milder parts of the Coastal South, the vine lives from year to year, eventually reaching more than 40 ft. in length and blooming heavily from spring to fall.

COCCOLOBA

SEA GRAPE

Polygonaceae

EVERGREEN SHRUBS OR TREES

✂ TS

☼ FULL SUN

◐ MODERATE WATER

Coccoloba uvifera

The quintessential seaside plants: tolerant of wind, sand, and salt, though tender to frost. Useful for windbreaks. Thick, often picturesquely twisted trunk and branches. New leaves reddish or coppery, mature ones glossy green with reddish veins. Small white flowers are followed by clusters of greenish fruits that turn purple when ripe; they can be made into jelly. Shape plant by pruning just before new growth emerges. Small plants in containers can be used for bonsai.

C. diversifolia (**C. laurifolia**). PIGEON PLUM. Heat zones 12–10. Native to southern Florida and the Caribbean. Can reach 30 ft. high and wide. Similar to *C. uvifera* but with shorter flower clusters, smaller fruits, and 2- to 4-in. oval leaves.

C. uvifera. SEA GRAPE. Heat zones 12–9. From the tropical Americas. Can grow to 30 ft. high and wide but is usually kept much smaller. Nearly round leaves to 8 in. wide. Fragrant flowers in foot-long clusters; fruits ¾ in. wide. Will grow right on the dunes.

COCCULUS

Menispermaceae

DECIDUOUS AND EVERGREEN VINES AND SHRUBS

✂ ZONES VARY BY SPECIES

☼ ◑ FULL SUN OR PARTIAL SHADE

● REGULAR WATER

Cocculus laurifolius

Woody vines and vinelike shrubs that are easy to grow in moist soil. Flowers are not prominent, but foliage is a lovely glossy green.

C. carolinus. CAROLINA MOONSEED. Woody deciduous or evergreen vine. Zones MS, LS, CS; 9–5. Deciduous in Middle South; evergreen in Lower and Coastal South. Native from Florida to Virginia and west to Texas. Grows rapidly to 10–12 ft., climbing by tendrils; needs support. Oval, pointed, medium green leaves reach 4 in. long. Blooms in spring, with greenish white flowers in 3- to 5-in.-long clusters; blossoms are not as showy as the glossy bright red berries that appear in late summer and fall. Gets its common name from its crescent-shaped seeds. Tolerates most soils, including alkaline ones.

C. laurifolius. WILD OLIVE. Evergreen shrub. Zones CS, TS; 12–7. Native to the Himalayas. Usually multistemmed, with arching, spreading growth; shiny, leathery oblong leaves to 6 in., with three strongly marked veins running from base to tip. Grows slowly at first, then moderately rapidly to 25 ft. (or more) tall and wide; can be kept smaller by pruning. Long, willowy branches are as easily led and trained as vines; fastened to a trellis, they make an effective screen. Can also be trained as an espalier. Staked and trained as a tree, the plant takes on an umbrella shape.

COCHLOSPERMUM vitifolium

BUTTERCUP TREE

Cochlospermaceae

DECIDUOUS TREE

✂ TS

☼ FULL SUN

● REGULAR WATER DURING GROWTH AND BLOOM

Cochlospermum vitifolium

This is one of those flowering trees that make visitors to Florida insanely jealous. Native to Mexico and Central and South America, it grows to 40 ft. tall and about half as wide, often with a leaning trunk. Broadly star-shaped leaves can reach 1 ft. across; brilliant yellow, 4-in. blossoms appear in terminal clusters in spring, often before the leaves emerge. There is a double-flowered form. Velvety green seedpods to 3 in. long are filled with tiny, fluffy seeds. Buttercup tree makes a nice street, lawn, or small shade tree. It likes moist, well-drained soil and has no serious pests. Do not water leafless trees in winter; they are dormant then and will rot if they get much water.

COCKSCOMB. See CELOSIA

COCKSPUR CORAL TREE. See ERYTHRINA crista-galli

COCKSPUR THORN. See CRATAEGUS crus-galli

COCONUT PALM. See COCOS nucifera

COCOS nucifera

COCONUT PALM

Arecaceae (Palmae)

PALM

✍ TS **H** 12–10; OR GROW IN POT

☼ FULL SUN

💧 MODERATE WATER

Cocos nucifera

The coconut palm is both an economically valuable plant and a handsome ornamental, but it is hardy only in south Florida. Can grow to 80 ft. or more but is usually much shorter, with a leaning or curving trunk and a crown of feathery, 20-ft. fronds. Flowers are not notable, but the fruit is the coconut of commerce. Sprouted coconuts are seen fairly often in large pots or tubs; such plants are attractive until they grow too large. Grows best near the shore. Landscape use is limited by the risk that falling coconuts pose to passersby and by a potentially fatal plant disease, lethal yellows. For home gardens, dwarf forms such as 10-ft. 'Nino' are the wisest choice.

CODIAEUM variegatum pictum

CROTON

Euphorbiaceae

EVERGREEN SHRUB

✍ TS **H** 12–10; OR HOUSEPLANT

☼ ◑ ● SOME FORMS TAKE SUN, OTHERS SHADE; BRIGHT LIGHT

💧💧 REGULAR TO AMPLE WATER

Codiaeum variegatum pictum

Native to the tropics. Can reach 6 ft. or more (and as wide) outdoors in Tropical South; indoors, usually seen as single-stemmed plant, 6–24 in. tall. Grown principally for its showy large, leathery, glossy leaves, which may be green, yellow, red, purple, bronze, pink, or almost any combination of these colors. Leaves may be oval, lance shaped, or very narrow; edges may be straight or lobed. Dozens of named forms combine these differing features.

Outdoor exposure depends on the selection. It needs bright light and regular misting indoors; does well in a warm, humid greenhouse, provided you control spider mites, mealybugs, and thrips. Can be brought outdoors at warm times of the year. Repeated contact with croton leaves can cause a skin rash in some people.

COFFEA arabica

COFFEE

Rubiaceae

EVERGREEN SHRUB

✍ TS **H** 12–10; OR HOUSEPLANT

◑ ● SOME SHADE; BRIGHT INDIRECT LIGHT

💧 REGULAR WATER

Coffea arabica

Native to East Africa. The coffee tree of commerce can be grown as a specimen or in shrub borders in the Tropical South; elsewhere, it's a handsome container plant for patios or large, well-lit rooms. Upright shrub to 15 ft., with evenly spaced tiers of branches clothed in shiny, dark green, oval leaves to 6 in. long. Small (¾-in.), fragrant white flowers are clustered near leaf bases. These are followed by ½-in. fruits—green when they first appear, then turning purple or red. Each fruit contains two seeds—coffee beans. Grow in rich, well-drained soil and mist frequently. In spring and summer, feed with a complete water-soluble fertilizer every other week. Protect from frosts.

COIX lacryma-jobi

JOB'S TEARS

Poaceae (Gramineae)

ANNUAL GRASS

✍ CS, TS; ANYWHERE AS ANNUAL; **H** 12–1

☼ FULL SUN OR PARTIAL SHADE

💧 REGULAR WATER

Coix lacryma-jobi

A curiosity from Southeast Asia, grown for its ornamental beadlike seeds. Leaves are to 1½ in. wide and 2 ft. long, growing in loose, sprawling clumps up to 1½ ft. across. Smooth, prominently jointed stems to 6 ft. long bear separate male and female flower spikelets in autumn. Outside coverings of female flowers harden as seeds ripen, turning to shiny, ¼- to ½-in. "beads" in pearly white, gray, or violet; these can be strung like actual beads. For use in dried arrangements, cut stems before seeds dry and shatter.

Sow seeds in place in early to midspring. Plants need heat and a long growing season to flower. In cold-winter zones, start seeds indoors and set out plants after danger of frost is past.

COLCHICUM

MEADOW SAFFRON, AUTUMN CROCUS

Liliaceae

PERENNIALS FROM CORMS

✍ US, MS, LS **H** 9–1; OR GROW IN POT

☼ FULL SUN; BRIGHT INDIRECT LIGHT

💧 REGULAR WATER DURING GROWTH AND BLOOM

☣ ALL PARTS ARE POISONOUS IF INGESTED

Colchicum

Native to Mediterranean regions. Many species. Plants are sometimes called autumn crocus, but they are not true crocuses. Shining, brown-skinned, thick-scaled corms send up clusters of long-tubed, flaring flowers to 4 in. across in late summer, whether corms are sitting in dish on windowsill or planted in soil. Colors include rosy purple, lavender, pink, and white. If grown in ground, broad leaves to 6–12 in. long show in spring, last for a few months, and then die long before flower cluster rises from ground. Best planted where they need not be disturbed more often than every 3 years or so. Corms are sold during brief dormant period in July and August. Best selections are 'The Giant', single lavender, and 'Waterlily', double violet. Plant 3–4 in. deep and 6–8 in. apart. To plant in bowls, set upright on 1–2 in. of pebbles or in special fiber sold for this purpose; fill bowl with water to base of corms.

COLEUS ×hybridus (Solenostemon scutellarioides)

COLEUS

Lamiaceae (Labiatae)

PERENNIALS USUALLY GROWN AS ANNUALS

✍ TS; ANYWHERE AS ANNUAL; **H** 12–1; OR HOUSEPLANT

☼ ◑ ● SOME FORMS TAKE SUN, OTHERS SHADE; BRIGHT INDIRECT LIGHT

💧💧 REGULAR TO AMPLE WATER

Coleus ×hybridus

Coleus hybrids were all the rage when they were first introduced into Europe from Java in the 1700s—and their popularity has remained high. The dizzying array of electrifying colors and foliage shapes enthralled the Victorians, and more than 100 years later, these seed-grown, shade-loving plants are still the most widely sold types. Useful for adding color to beds, in window boxes, and in pots used indoors or out. They need constantly moist, fertile, well-drained soil and should be fed every other week

Coleus Hybrids

'Black Magic'　　　'Kiwi Fern'　　　'Ducksfoot Red'　　　'Alabama Sunset'　　　'Ducksfoot Yellow'　　　'The Line'

from spring to fall with a general-purpose water-soluble fertilizer. Pinch out flower spikes as soon as they appear (they are not attractive, and, if allowed to develop, they'll cause plants to look leggy and untidy).

Don't plant too early in spring—all coleus hate the cold. They're winter-hardy only in south Florida and south Texas. (Cuttings root quickly in water, though, so gardeners in cold-winter areas can save prized selections from year to year.) Large-leafed strains, such as Giant Exhibition and Oriental Splendor, grow 1½–2 ft. tall and wide, with leaves 3–6 in. long; dwarf strains, such as Fairway, Carefree, and Wizard, grow 8–12 in. tall and wide, with 1- to 1½-in. leaves.

Newer, more sun-tolerant types, collectively referred to as "sun coleus," have now arrived on the scene. As their name implies, these plants (which are propagated by cuttings rather than from seed) thrive in sun or light shade. They're tougher, larger, more vigorous, and tidier than seed-grown types, and they offer an incredible array of growth habits, colors, and leaf shapes. They range from tiny-leafed ground-cover types to large-foliaged sorts with the size and form of small shrubs. The following listing describes just a few of the hundreds of selections; you will find them in mail-order nursery catalogs and, increasingly, in garden and home centers. With the exception of their light requirements, care for them as you would for seed-grown coleus. They grow about as wide as tall, except as noted.

'Alabama Sunset'. Large cranberry pink leaves with gold centers. Grows to 3–4 ft., with shrublike form.

'Amazon'. Ruffled, puckered chartreuse leaves with a metallic sheen. To 3 ft.

'Aurora'. Broad, luminescent leaves of cream, pink, and green with soft pink undersides. To 2 ft.

'Black Magic'. Upright grower to 1½–2 ft. tall and not quite as wide, with dark purple leaves edged in lime green.

'Buttercream'. Strongly ruffled leaves of soft cream edged in medium green. A little over 2 ft.

'Dark Heart'. Trailing type to 1 ft. tall, 1½–2 ft. wide. Small, rounded wine red leaves edged in bright green.

'Ducksfoot Red'. Trailing type with small maroon leaves that resemble a duck's foot. To 2 ft. tall and a little wider. 'Ducksfoot Yellow' is similar in size and form.

'Gay's Delight'. Chartreuse to yellow, slightly cupped leaves sport dramatic dark purple veins. Upright grower to 2 ft.

'Glen Lake'. Pointed green leaves with yellow centers, purple-pink veins and edges, and purple stems. To 1½ ft.

'India Frills'. Tough, sprawling ground cover type to 1 ft. tall and 2 ft. wide. Small, deeply cut leaves in soft red with sharply contrasting yellow and green edges.

'Indo Five'. Low-growing form with broad, scalloped leaves in red, rose, purple, chocolate, and green. Dark purple stems. Grows to 1½ ft. tall, 2½ ft. wide.

'Inky Fingers'. Rounded, deeply lobed bright green leaves with dark purple centers. To 2 ft. tall, 1½ ft. wide.

'Kiwi Fern'. Low-growing form with deeply cut burgundy leaves edged in gold and green. May reach 1½ ft.

'Mardi Gras'. Bushy plant with foliage splashed in red, green, and yellow. To 1½ ft.

'Orange King'. Exquisite selection features broad, orange-tinged golden leaves with reddish purple undersides and purple stems. To 2 ft. tall and 1½ ft. wide.

'Saturn'. Maroon leaves with contrasting edges and centers of guacamole green. To 1½ ft.

'Solar Sunrise' ('Alabama Sunrise'). Large, scallop-edged leaves combine flashes of burgundy, rose, pink, cream, and green. Grows to a shrubby 3–4 ft.

'The Line'. Narrow, pointed leaves in soft yellow with a prominent purple midvein. To 1½ ft.

COLLARDS. See KALE AND COLLARDS

COLOCASIA esculenta

ELEPHANT'S EAR, TARO

Araceae

PERENNIAL FROM TUBER

🗡 LS, CS, TS ⊪ 12–4; OR DIG AND STORE; OR GROW IN POTS

🌓 BEST IN WARM, FILTERED SHADE

💧 AMPLE WATER

⚠ ALL PARTS MAY CAUSE INDIGESTION IF INGESTED RAW; CONTACT WITH SAP MAY IRRITATE SKIN

Colocasia esculenta

Every garden needs its share of bold foliage, and no foliage is bolder than that of elephant's ear. Most Southerners are familiar with the common green-leafed variety of this tropical Asian plant, but many new and exciting forms are making their way to the marketplace. Growing from large tubers, these perennials attain enormous size—some reach 8 ft. or taller—with leathery, heart-shaped leaves that may reach 2½ by 3 ft. Flowers resemble giant callas (*Zantedeschia*) but seldom appear. Some elephant's ears form a single clump; others spread.

Choose a planting spot protected from strong wind, which tears leaves. Plant in soil enriched with lots of organic matter, and be sure to provide plenty of moisture (plants thrive in boggy conditions or even standing water). Set tubers about 2 in. deep and 1–1½ ft. apart. Plants grow rapidly in hot, rainy weather, especially when given light applications of fertilizer monthly during growth. Tubers are hardy in the Lower, Coastal, and Tropical South; tops die to the ground with the first frost, then reappear in spring. Elsewhere, dig tubers in fall and store them over winter.

Elephant's ears are effective with tree ferns and other large-leafed tropical plants; they're also good in pots or when massed to create a quick—if temporary—screen. Try combining dark-foliaged selections with yellow- or green-leafed plants.

'Black Magic'. Spectacular purplish black leaves with purplish red stems. Forms a 5-ft. clump. Great color accent for containers or the back of the border. Hardy to 0°F.

'Chicago Harlequin'. Large green leaves blotched with lighter green. Stems to 5 ft. long are adorned with unusual cream and light green vertical bands. Spreads rapidly in moist soil.

▶

'Fontanesii.' Purplish black stems rise to 7 ft.; each carries a huge (3-ft.) green leaf with a shiny violet cast. Yellow, papaya-scented flowers to 1 ft. long appear in late summer. Clump forming.

'Illustris'. Charcoal black, 8-in. leaves with glowing green veins. Grows to 3 ft. tall, 4 ft. wide; spreads slowly in heavy soil, more quickly in loose, rich, wet soil. Good in containers. Hardy to 0°F.

'Ruffles'. Green, 3-ft. leaves with ruffled edges. Forms a 6-ft. clump.

COLUMBINE. See AQUILEGIA

COMFREY. See SYMPHYTUM officinale

COMMELINA

DAYFLOWER

Commelinaceae

PERENNIALS

✿ US, MS, LS, CS, TS H 10–7

☼ ◐ ● EXPOSURE NEEDS VARY BY SPECIES

◔ ● WATER NEEDS VARY BY SPECIES

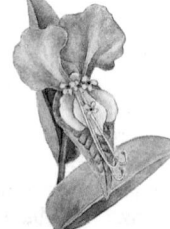

Commelina communis

Large group of plants featuring jointed stems, lance-shaped leaves, and showy, three-petaled blue flowers. Individual blossoms stay open only for a day. Good casual ground covers. Often confused with spiderwort (*Tradescantia virginiana*), a plant from the same family.

C. communis. COMMON DAYFLOWER. From eastern Asia; naturalized in eastern U.S. Forms a widely spreading mat of fleshy, succulent stems that root where the nodes touch ground; also reseeds readily, so can be weedy. Grows 12–15 in. tall, with medium green leaves to 4 in. long. Blooms from late spring until fall. Vivid blue, ½-in. flowers; the two upper petals are much larger and more deeply colored than the lower one. Thrives in moist, shady areas. Stems thrown on ground or compost pile often root in place.

C. erecta. ERECT DAYFLOWER. Southern wildflower with upright, 1½- to 3-ft. stems loosely clothed in dark green, narrow leaves 4–6 in. long. Spring to fall, bears ½- to ¾-in.-wide blooms with blue upper petals, white lower one. Best in dry, sunny areas with well-drained soil.

C. virginica. VIRGINIA DAYFLOWER. Native to the South. Grows 3–4 ft. tall, with lance-shaped leaves to 8 in. long. Inch-wide flowers with petals of nearly equal size. Blooms from summer into fall. Thrives in moist, shady areas.

Commelinaceae. The spiderwort family is composed of herbaceous perennials that are often fleshy, mostly tropical or subtropical. Wandering Jew (*Tradescantia albiflora*) and spiderwort (*Tradescantia virginiana*) are familiar examples. Flowers generally have three rounded petals.

Compositae. See Asteraceae

CONFEDERATE JASMINE. See TRACHELOSPERMUM jasminoides

CONFEDERATE ROSE. See HIBISCUS mutabilis

CONRADINA

Lamiaceae (Labiatae)

EVERGREEN SHRUBS

✿ MS, LS, CS

☼ FULL SUN

● REGULAR WATER

Conradina verticillata

Freely branching shrubs that root from trailing branches to make a small-scale ground cover. To 1–1½ ft. high, spreading to 3 ft. or more. Needlelike leaves like those of rosemary (*Rosmarinus*) have a minty scent. Small flowers in spring or early summer. Thrive in lean, sandy soils.

C. canescens. SCRUB ROSEMARY, SANDHILL ROSEMARY. Heat zones 11–7. Native to sandy pinelands of the Gulf Coast. Gray foliage; pale lavender flowers.

C. verticillata. CUMBERLAND ROSEMARY. Heat zones 10–6. Native to sandy riverbanks of eastern Tennessee and Kentucky. Dark green foliage; lavender-pink blossoms. 'Snowflake' has pure white flowers.

CONSOLIDA ajacis (C. ambigua)

LARKSPUR

Ranunculaceae

ANNUAL

✿ US, MS, LS, CS, TS H 12–1

☼ FULL SUN

● REGULAR WATER

◆ ALL PARTS, ESPECIALLY SEEDS, ARE POISONOUS IF INGESTED

Consolida ajacis

The colorful spires of larkspur punctuate many a Southerner's garden in spring. Unlike their regal cousins, the delphiniums, these natives of southern Europe flourish in the hot Southern climate. They die after flowering but reseed so readily that they might as well be perennials. The blooms attract butterflies and make superb cut flowers. Larkspurs look great in combination with Shirley poppies (*Papaver rhoeas*).

Plants grow 1–5 ft. tall, about 1 ft. wide. Flowers (double on most types) are up to 1½ in. wide, borne on vertical spikes above deeply cut, almost fernlike leaves; blossom colors include blue, lilac, purple, pink, rose, salmon, and white. Improved strains branch at the base, producing several flower spikes per stalk. Giant Imperial strain bears 4- to 5-ft.-tall stalks of double, densely packed blossoms; Regal strain features thick spikes of large flowers similar to delphiniums, grows 4–5 ft. tall. Super Imperial strain produces cone-shaped spikes to 1½ ft. tall. Heat-tolerant Steeplechase strain, 4–5 ft. tall, bears the largest flowers of all.

Of course, some folks prefer the simpler, "unimproved" larkspurs of their childhoods. Heirloom types include the following.

'Blue Bell'. Soft lilac-blue flowers on 3-ft. spikes. All-America Selections winner in 1934.

'Blue Cloud'. Airy, branching plant producing 3-ft. spikes of deep blue to purple blossoms.

'Earl Grey'. Erect, 3- to 4-ft. spikes of double blooms in a silvery mauve.

'White King'. Double white blossoms on sturdy, 3-ft. stalks. All-America Selections winner in 1937.

Plant seeds in fall where plants are to grow; sow them on bare soil and barely scratch in (do not mulch over them). For greatest impact, sow in large clusters or sweeps. After flowers fade, allow seeds to drop naturally for a casual look; or collect and store them for fall sowing.

CONVALLARIA majalis

LILY-OF-THE-VALLEY

Liliaceae

PERENNIAL FROM RHIZOME

✿ US, MS, LS H 8–1

◑ ● PARTIAL TO FULL SHADE

● REGULAR WATER

◆ ALL PARTS ARE POISONOUS IF INGESTED

Convallaria majalis

Graceful, creeping, 6- to 8-in.-high ground cover blooms in spring, sending up arching stems that bear small, nodding, delightfully sweet-scented, waxy white bells along one side. The flowers last only 2 to 3 weeks, but broad, bold, glossy green deciduous leaves are attractive throughout growing season. Bright red berries may appear in autumn; they, like the rest of the plant, are poisonous.

Selections include 'Aureo-variegata', with yellow-striped leaves; 'Fortin's Giant', to 12–15 in. high, with extra-large blooms; 'Prolificans', a double-flowered form; and *C. m. rosea,* with light pink blooms. All are charming in woodland gardens; use as carpet between camellias, rhododendrons, pieris, or under deciduous trees or high-branching, not-too-dense evergreens. Best in Upper and Middle South. In Lower South, needs full shade and moist, rich soil that does not dry out. Can become invasive where well adapted.

Plant clumps or single rhizomes (commonly called pips) in fall before the soil freezes. Give rich soil with ample humus. Set 1½ in. deep; space clumps 1–2 ft. apart, single pips 4–5 in. apart. Spread 1-in. layer of leaf mold, peat moss, or ground bark over bed each year in fall.

Large, prechilled pips are available in December and January and can be potted for bloom indoors in bright light. After bloom, plunge pots in ground in cool, shaded area. When dormant, remove plants from pots and plant in garden; or wash soil off pips, place in plastic bags, and store in vegetable bin of refrigerator until time to repot in December or January.

Convolvulaceae. The morning glory family contains climbing or trailing plants, usually with funnel-shaped flowers. Morning glories (*Convolvulus* and *Ipomoea*) are typical examples.

CONVOLVULUS tricolor

DWARF MORNING GLORY

Convolvulaceae

ANNUAL

✿ US, MS, LS, CS, TS ⊞ 12–1

☼ ☼ BEST IN SUN, TOLERATES SOME SHADE

◐ MODERATE WATER

Convolvulus tricolor

Thanks to its brightly colored, funnel-shaped flowers, this old-fashioned European native is often confused with morning glory (*Ipomoea tricolor),* a twining vine of the tropics. Dwarf morning glory, however, doesn't climb—and its flowers stay open all day, unlike those of its familiar relative. A traditional (if somewhat forgotten) bedding plant, it is excellent for massing, edging, hanging baskets, or containers. Forms a bushy, slightly trailing mound to 12–16 in. high and 2 ft. wide, with narrow dark green leaves to 1½ in. long. Blooms profusely in summer, covering itself with striking, 1- to 2-in.-wide flowers in royal blue, red, pink, or white, all with a yellow-and-white starburst pattern in the throat. Plants in the Ensign series are compact and free blooming.

Nick the hard seeds with a knife and soak them in water overnight before sowing. Plant in fall in central and south Florida; elsewhere, plant in spring after the soil has warmed.

COPPER LEAF. See ACALYPHA wilkesiana

CORAL BEAN, CORAL TREE. See ERYTHRINA

CORAL BELLS. See HEUCHERA sanguinea

CORALBERRY. See SYMPHORICARPOS orbiculatus

CORAL VINE. See ANTIGONON leptopus

CORDIA

Boraginaceae

EVERGREEN SHRUBS OR TREES

✿ CS, TS ⊞ 12–10

☼ FULL SUN

◐ ◐ ◐ WATER NEEDS VARY BY SPECIES

Cordia boissieri

Members of the forget-me-not family, these are shrubs or trees of tropical or subtropical origin with showy flowers and rough-surfaced, almost sandpapery

leaves. Species grown in the U.S. include Southwestern and tropical natives. The two listed here do best in the lower Rio Grande Valley and along the Texas coast from Corpus Christi to Brownsville.

C. boissieri. TEXAS OLIVE, ANACAHUITA. Native to New Mexico, Texas, Mexico. Grayish green, oval leaves to 3 in. long; clusters of white, 2½-in.-wide flowers with yellow throats. Begins flowering in midspring and continues over a long season; may bloom again in autumn. Naturally reaches 8–10 ft. high and 6–8 ft. wide, but can be pruned low (3–5 ft.); can also be trained as small tree. Regular moisture until established; thereafter, give little to moderate water.

Cordia boissieri

C. sebestena. GEIGER TREE. Native to the West Indies. Usually 10–15 ft. (possibly 25 ft.) tall and wide, with dark green leaves 9–12 in. long and half as wide. Brilliant orange-red summer flowers, to 2 in. wide, come in large clusters. Regular water.

CORDYLINE

Agavaceae

EVERGREEN PALMLIKE SHRUBS OR TREES

✿ ZONES VARY BY SPECIES; OR HOUSEPLANT

☼ ☼ ● EXPOSURE NEEDS VARY BY SPECIES; BRIGHT INDIRECT LIGHT

◐ ◐ ◐ WATER NEEDS VARY BY SPECIES

Cordyline australis

These woody plants with swordlike leaves are related to yuccas and agaves, but they have lusher foliage and need more water. Good next to swimming pools. Often sold as *Dracaena;* for true *Dracaena,* see that entry.

C. australis (Dracaena australis). GIANT DRACAENA. Zones CS, TS; 12–7. From New Zealand. Hardiest of cordylines, to 15°F. In youth, forms a fountain of 3-ft.-long leaves. Upper leaves are erect; lower ones arch and droop. In maturity, a tree to 20–30 ft. high, 6–12 ft. wide, branching high on trunk, rather stiff looking. Small, fragrant, creamy white flowers appear in long, branched clusters to 3 ft. long in late spring. For a more graceful plant, cut back when young to force multiple trunks. Grows fastest in soil deep enough for big, carrotlike root. Used for tropical effects, with boulders and gravel for desert look, near seashore. Full sun. Moderate to regular water.

Colorful forms include 'Atropurpurea', known as bronze dracaena, with bronzy red leaves; 'Pink Stripe', bronze with pink margins; 'Red Sensation' and 'Red Star', purplish red; and 'Sundance', green with a pink midrib.

C. fruticosa (C. terminalis). TI. Zones TS; 12–7. From tropical Southeast Asia. Many named forms with red, yellow, or variegated leaves. White, foot-long flower clusters. Plants are usually started from "logs"—sections of stem that you root. Lay short lengths in mixture of peat moss and sand, covering about one-half their diameter. Keep moist. When shoots grow out and root, cut them off and plant them. Outdoors, ti grows 6–8 ft. tall, 3–8 ft. wide in frost-free areas where it receives ample water and soil stays warm; accepts considerable shade. Indoors, it takes ordinary houseplant care; tolerates low light.

C. stricta. AUSTRALIAN DRACAENA. Zones TS; 12–7. Australian native; hardy to 26°F. Slender, erect stems to 2 ft. long, clustered at base or branching low. Leaves are 2 ft. long, dark green with hint of purple. Fragrant lavender flowers in branched clusters to 2 ft. long, very decorative in spring. To 15 ft. tall and 6 ft. wide but can be kept lower by cutting tall canes to ground; new canes replace them. Long cuttings stuck in ground will root quickly. Fine container plant indoors or out; good for tropical effect in sunrooms or side gardens. Needs some shade. Regular water.

FOR GROWING SYMBOL EXPLANATIONS
PLEASE SEE PAGE 145

COREOPSIS

Asteraceae (Compositae)

PERENNIALS AND ANNUALS

US, MS, LS, CS | 9–1, EXCEPT AS NOTED

FULL SUN, EXCEPT AS NOTED

WATER NEEDS VARY BY SPECIES

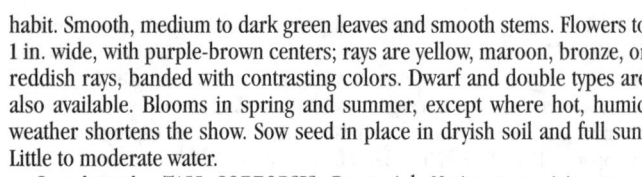

Coreopsis grandiflora

Easily grown members of sunflower family, yielding a profusion of yellow, orange, maroon, or reddish flowers over a long bloom season. Easy to propagate—annuals from seed sown in place or in pots, perennials from seed or division of root crown. Tend to self-sow; seeds attract birds. Not browsed by deer.

C. auriculata 'Nana'. DWARF-EARED COREOPSIS. Perennial. Selection of a species native to the southeastern U.S. Forms a 5- to 6-in.-high mat of medium green, 2- to 5-in.-long leaves; under ideal conditions, spreads by stolons to form a 2-ft.-wide clump in a year. Bright orange-yellow, 1- to 2½-in.-wide flowers rise well above the foliage; bloom is heaviest in spring, but flowers keep on coming over a long season if you deadhead regularly. Best used in front of taller plants, in borders, or as edging. Moderate water.

C. grandiflora. BIGFLOWER COREOPSIS. Perennial. From the central and southeastern U.S. Narrow dark green leaves with three to five lobes form a foliage clump 1–2 ft. high, spreading to 3 ft. wide. Bright yellow, 2½- to 3-in.-wide flowers bloom all summer on long, slender stems high above foliage. 'Sunburst' has large semidouble flowers; it blooms the first year from seed sown early in spring, then spreads by self-sowing. 'Early Sunrise' is similar but may begin blooming in late spring. 'Flying Saucers' is a nearly sterile selection with flat, single, 2-in. yellow flowers over a long period; 'Sunray' is a dense, compact selection with double and semidouble flowers. All are tough enough for roadside planting. Moderate water.

C. helianthoides. SWAMP TICKSEED. Perennial. Zones MS, LS, CS, TS. Native to swampy woods from North Carolina to Florida. To 2½ ft. high, spreading at least as wide. Shiny deep green leaves; small, dark-centered yellow-orange blossoms in late summer and fall. Will take regular moisture or boggy conditions.

C. integrifolia. CHIPOLA RIVER TICKSEED. Perennial. Zones MS, LS, CS; 9–5. Native to riverbanks and floodplains in South Carolina, Georgia, and northwestern Florida. To 1–2½ ft. high; spreads slowly by rhizomes. Dark green, heart-shaped leaves. Blooms over a long period in late summer and fall, bearing small flowers in bright yellow orange with a dark center. Thrives in damp or even boggy sites but tolerates drier soil.

C. lanceolata. LANCE COREOPSIS. Perennial from the central and southern U.S. To 1–2 ft. high, 1–1½ ft. wide. Narrow, somewhat hairy, medium green leaves, mostly in a tuft near plant's base; some leaves on lower stem have a few lobes. Yellow, 1½- to 2-in. flowers on pale green stems bloom from spring to summer, make excellent cut flowers. When well established, plant persists year after year. Moderate water.

C. 'Limerock Ruby'. Perennial. Zones US, MS, LS. Hybrid to 20 in. tall, 2½ ft. wide; forms a clump of fine-textured foliage similar to that of *C. verticillata*. Ruby red flowers to 1 in. across appear from late spring through summer. Moderate water.

C. rosea. ROSE COREOPSIS. Perennial. Zones US, MS, LS; 8–1. Native from Nova Scotia to Delaware. Fine-textured plant with bright green foliage; grows 1½–2 ft. tall, 1 ft. wide, with 1-in.-wide, yellow-centered pink flowers from summer to fall. 'Sweet Dreams' has threadlike leaves and masses of big white flowers with a raspberry-colored ring surrounding a golden eye. Shorter lived than other species. Prefers moist soil.

C. 'Tequila Sunrise'. Perennial. To 1½ ft. high, 1 ft. wide. Narrow olive green leaves are irregularly variegated with cream and yellow, supplemented by touches of pinkish red in spring and deeper red in fall. Golden yellow, 1½-in. flowers with deep orange-red centers bloom continuously in summer. Self-sows but is not invasive. Moderate water.

C. tinctoria. CALLIOPSIS, ANNUAL COREOPSIS. Annual. Zones US, MS, LS, CS, TS; 12–1. Native to much of North America. Slender, upright, wiry-stemmed plant 1½–3 ft. tall, 1–1½ ft. wide; much like cosmos in growth habit. Smooth, medium to dark green leaves and smooth stems. Flowers to 1 in. wide, with purple-brown centers; rays are yellow, maroon, bronze, or reddish rays, banded with contrasting colors. Dwarf and double types are also available. Blooms in spring and summer, except where hot, humid weather shortens the show. Sow seed in place in dryish soil and full sun. Little to moderate water.

C. tripteris. TALL COREOPSIS. Perennial. Native to prairies, open woods, and roadsides from Ontario south to Georgia, Mississippi, and Louisiana. To 5–7 ft. tall, 4 ft. wide. Shiny dark green, three-leafleted leaves. Blooms from midsummer into fall, carrying many 2-in., brown-eyed, butter yellow flowers on branching stems. Both foliage and flowers are anise scented. Use at the back of a border or in a wildflower or butterfly garden. Prefers moist soil and some shade.

C. verticillata. THREADLEAF COREOPSIS. Perennial. Native from Maryland to Florida, west to Arkansas. To 2½–3 ft. tall, half as broad; many erect or slightly leaning stems carry many whorls of medium green, finely divided, very narrow leaves. At stem tips are 2-in. bright yellow daisies, freely borne over a long summer and autumn season. One of the most tolerant of drought and neglect. 'Moonbeam', to 1½–2 ft. tall, has pale yellow blooms; 'Zagreb', to 1 ft., bears golden yellow flowers. Divide in fall or spring every third year to maintain vigor. Little to moderate water.

COIFING COREOPSIS. *Early in the season, you can keep coreopsis blooming by using pruning shears to remove spent flowers. By midsummer, though, dead blooms may outnumber the new ones. If that's the case, switch to hedge trimmers and give the plant a quick all-over "crew cut." You'll get fresh growth and lots more flowers.* ❖

CORIANDRUM sativum

CORIANDER, CILANTRO

Apiaceae (Umbelliferae)

ANNUAL

US, MS, LS, CS, TS | 10–1

LIGHT SHADE IN HOTTEST CLIMATES

REGULAR WATER

Coriandrum sativum

Mediterranean native grows 1–1½ ft. high, 9 in. wide. Delicate, fernlike foliage; flat clusters of pinkish white flowers in summer. Both fresh leaves and seeds are widely used as seasoning. Leaves (usually called cilantro) are popular in salads, salsa, and many cooked dishes; crush the aromatic seeds for use in sausage, beans, stews, baked goods. Start from seed (including coriander seed sold in grocery stores) in early spring after all danger of frost is past; in Florida and south Texas, plant in fall. Sow in place in good, well-drained soil; plant is taprooted and transplants poorly. Grows quickly, self-sows.

CORN

Poaceae (Gramineae)

ANNUAL

US, MS, LS, CS, TS | 12–1

FULL SUN

REGULAR WATER

Sweet Corn

Nothing beats the taste of sweet corn picked fresh from the garden. Trouble is, corn takes considerable space to produce a decent crop, so it's better suited to large country gardens than to small suburban plots. Another potential drawback is that once sweet corn is picked, its sugar changes to starch nearly as fast as you can run the ears inside to a pot of boiling water. Still, many folks yearn for traditional kinds of sweet corn, such as 'Early Sunglow' (yellow, 62 days from planting to harvest), 'Golden Queen' (yellow, 92 days), 'Merit' (yellow,

WHAT SWEET CORN NEEDS

CLIMATE: Ideal planting time is spring, well after last frost and when soil warms to at least 65°F. Requires warm temperatures throughout the growing season.

WATER: Consistent and regular; most critical as tassels form.

SPACING: Thin seedlings to 1 ft. apart. Planting in blocks at least five rows deep helps ensure pollination of silks.

FERTILIZER: Work a balanced fertilizer into the soil at planting time. Add a controlled-release fertilizer around plants at 8 in. tall, then again at 18 in. high.

HARVEST: On the average, ears take 80 to 90 days to mature from seed.

Supersweet 'Honey 'N' Pearl'

80 days), and the all-time favorite 'Silver Queen' (white, 92 days). For information on new hybrids that stay sweet much longer after they're picked, see "Improved sweet corn" (below).

Corn is a warm-weather crop, so don't rush planting in spring: seeds planted in soil cooler than 65°F will simply rot. Plant at least 2 weeks after the last frost in loose, fertile, well-drained soil. If you plant just a few long, single rows, you won't get much corn, because pollen must be transferred from the tassels (held atop the plants) to the silks (held lower down). A stiff wind can send pollen flying far beyond its mark, so you should always plant in blocks of at least five rows deep.

Before planting, work into the soil 1 cup of 10-10-10 or 10-14-10 fertilizer per 10 ft. of row. Plant seeds 1 in. deep (¾ in. deep for supersweet types), in rows spaced 2–3 ft. apart. When seedlings are 6 in. tall, thin them to 1 ft. apart. To extend the harvest, make three or four more plantings at 2-week intervals—or plant early, midseason, and late selections.

Corn has a hefty appetite. Fertilize plants when they're 8 in. tall and again when they've reached 18 in.; each time, apply ½ cup of controlled-release 10-14-10 fertilizer per 10 ft. of row. Regular watering is critical, too, especially when tassels are being formed. Drought-stressed plants produce puny ears with missing kernels. Most types are capable of producing two or more ears per stalk. However, rows planted less than 2 ft. apart generally yield one ear per stalk.

Check your crop when the ears are plump and the silks have withered; corn is usually ready for harvest 3 weeks after the silks first appear. To test, pull back the husks and try popping a kernel with your thumbnail. It should squirt milky juice; watery juice means that corn isn't ready to eat.

Corn earworm is the principal insect pest. There is no simple control. Most gardeners expect some ears to show worm damage at the silk ends, and they just cut off those ends. The prevention (it's tedious) goes like this: 3 to 7 days after silks appear, use a medicine dropper to put two drops of mineral oil just inside the tip of each ear. As an alternative, plant selections with tight husks that discourage earworms; these include 'Country Gentleman', 'Hickory King', and 'Texas Honey June'.

Improved sweet corn. There are two basic classes. The first, called sugary enhanced corn, is about as sweet as or slightly sweeter than regular sweet corn, but the "se" gene slows the conversion of sugar to starch. Among the top sugary enhanced selections are 'Breeder's Choice' (yellow, 73 days), 'Bodacious' (yellow, 75 days), 'Trinity' (bicolor, 70 days), and 'Ambrosia' (bicolor, 75 days).

The second class, known as supersweet corn, contains twice as much sugar as regular sweet corn. It's sometimes called "sh2" corn, because the gene responsible for the added sweetness also causes dry kernels to look shrunken. Supersweet corn stays sweet for days after picking, as long as

you refrigerate it promptly. Recommended selections include 'How Sweet It Is' (white, 80 days), 'Honey 'N' Pearl' (bicolor, 76 days), 'Early Xtra-Sweet' (yellow, 71 days), 'Illini Xtra-Sweet' (yellow, 85 days), and 'Florida Staysweet' (yellow, 87 days).

It's perfectly fine to plant sugary enhanced types near regular sweet corn—but don't let supersweet types cross-pollinate with other sweet corn (either regular or sugary enhanced), or the kernels of both will be tough and starchy. Isolate supersweets from other types either by distance (at least 200 ft. away) or by time (stagger plantings so that different types don't tassel at the same time).

Heirloom sweet corn. Unlike hybrid corn, heirloom types are open-pollinated, which means they come true from seed. 'Golden Bantam' (yellow, 78 days) was introduced in 1902 and is still the best choice for small spaces, as its stalks reach only 5–6 ft.; ripened ears must be rushed to the cooking pot to taste sweet. 'Stowell's Evergreen' (white, 98 days), introduced in 1856, remains in the milky stage a long time and is well adapted to the Upper South. 'Country Gentleman' (white, 93 days), introduced in 1891, is a shoepeg corn (with small kernels that are not arranged in rows) with an extended milky stage. 'Texas Honey June' (white, 97 days) has a sweet flavor reminiscent of honey.

Dent corn. Starchy dent corns (named for the dent in the seed's crown) are well adapted to the Southeast and Midwest; many are heirloom types, dating back to the mid-1800s. They are primarily used for roasting and for making cornmeal and hominy. 'Blue Clarage' (90 days) features solid blue ears (one ear per stalk) and has a higher sugar content than most dents; in the milky stage, it can be eaten fresh. 'Hickory King' (white, 85 days) produces two ears per stalk and is the best for hominy. Drought-tolerant 'Tennessee Red Cob' (120 days) bears red cobs with white kernels, two ears per stalk. It is excellent for cornmeal, and the cob makes an attractive pipe.

Baby corn. Contrary to popular belief, baby corn isn't a miniature variety—it's just corn harvested very early, when the ears are only a few inches long. The tender ears may be pickled or used fresh in salads or Asian cuisine. Plant seeds 1–2 in. apart; thin seedlings to 4 in. apart. Harvest shortly after the first silks appear, which may be only a few weeks after sowing. 'Bonus' (yellow, 32 days) produces 3-in. ears that are ready to pick when the plant is only 1½ ft. tall.

Ornamental corn. Some kinds of corn are grown for the beauty of their shelled ears rather than for eating. Calico, Indian, Squaw, and Rainbow are some names given to strains with intensely colored kernels—red, brown, blue, gray, black, bright yellow, or mixed colors. 'Indian Summer' has brightly colored, edible kernels. Grow ornamental corn well away from sweet corn; mix of pollen can affect the latter's flavor. For ornamental display, grow like sweet corn, but let ears ripen fully; silks will be withered, husks will turn straw color, and kernels will be firm. Cut ear from plant, including 1½ in. of stalk below ear; pull back husks (leave attached to ears) and dry thoroughly.

Ornamental Corn

Zea mays japonica includes several kinds of corn grown for ornamental foliage. One occasionally sold is 'Gracilis', a dwarf form with bright green leaves striped white.

Popcorn. Grow and harvest just like ornamental corn. When ears are thoroughly dry, rub kernels off cobs and store in a dry place. White, red, and yellow kinds of popcorn look like other types of corn.

Strawberry popcorn, grown either for its ornamental value or for popping, has stubby, fat, strawberry-like ears packed with red kernels.

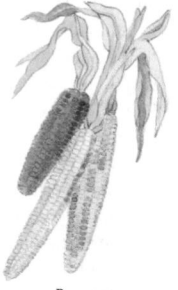

Popcorn

C

Cornaceae. The dogwood family consists of trees and shrubs with clustered inconspicuous flowers (sometimes surrounded by showy bracts) and berrylike fruit. *Aucuba* and dogwood (*Cornus*) are examples.

CORN COCKLE. See AGROSTEMMA githago

CORNELIAN CHERRY. See CORNUS mas

CORNFLOWER. See CENTAUREA cyanus

CORN PLANT. See DRACAENA fragrans

CORNUS

DOGWOOD

Cornaceae

DECIDUOUS SHRUBS AND TREES AND A PERENNIAL

🌡 ZONES VARY BY SPECIES

☼ ◑ FULL SUN OR LIGHT SHADE, EXCEPT AS NOTED

💧 REGULAR WATER, EXCEPT AS NOTED

Cornus florida
'Rubra'

For many Southerners, there's only one dogwood: flowering dogwood (*Cornus florida*), widely considered the region's finest ornamental tree. But many types of dogwood exist, from good-sized, single-trunked trees to small, multistemmed, stoloniferous shrubs; there's even a ground-covering perennial dogwood. Some are spectacular in bloom, others barely noticeable. Some sport dazzling fall foliage; others don't. And even dogwoods lacking showy flowers or foliage have their strong points. Some flaunt colorful bark; others produce attractive fruits that feed birds and other wildlife.

What appear to be flower petals in many dogwoods are in fact bracts—petal-like modified leaves. These surround the inconspicuous true flowers.

C. alba. TATARIAN DOGWOOD. Shrub. Zones US; 7–1. Native to Siberia, northern China, Korea. In cold-winter areas, the bare, blood red twigs are colorful against the snow. Upright to about 10 ft. high; wide spreading, eventually producing a thicket of many stems. Branches densely clothed with leaves 2½–5 in. long, to 2½ in. wide, deep rich green above, lighter beneath; turn red in fall. Small, fragrant, creamy white flowers in 1- to 2-in.-wide, flattish clusters in spring. Small whitish fruits.

Selections include the following. In all, new wood is brightest; cut back in spring to force new growth.

'Argenteomarginata' (*C.* 'Elegantissima'). Showy green-and-white leaves on red stems.

'Bud's Yellow'. Bright yellow stems. Disease resistance makes it a good substitute for *C. sericea* 'Flaviramea'.

'Gouchaltii'. Leaves have yellow borders suffused with pink.

'Sibirica'. SIBERIAN DOGWOOD. Less rampant than the species, growing to 7 ft. tall, 5 ft. wide. Coral red branches in winter.

C. alternifolia. PAGODA DOGWOOD. Shrub or small tree. Zones US, MS; 8–1. From eastern North America. Multitrunked, to 20 ft. high and wide. Strong horizontal branching pattern makes attractive winter silhouette. Light green leaves to 5 in. long turn red in fall. Small clusters of creamy spring flowers are not showy. Small but handsome blue-black fruits follow the flowers. Foliage of 'Argentea' has white markings.

C. canadensis. BUNCHBERRY. Perennial. Zones US; 6–1. Native from southern Greenland to northern areas of North America. Ground cover 6–9 in. high, found in the wild under trees by lakes and streams. Creeping rootstocks send up stems topped by whorls of oval or roundish, 1- to 2-in.-long, deep green leaves that turn yellow in fall, die down in winter. In late spring or early summer, plants bear small, compact clusters of tiny flowers surrounded by (usually) four oval, ½- to ¾-in., pure white bracts. Clusters of small, shiny red fruits follow in late summer.

Best performance in full shade in cool, mountain climates, in acid soil with generous amounts of organic matter. Set out small plants from pots

about 1 ft. apart. Small rooted pieces gathered from the woods may not establish easily. Excellent with rhododendrons, ferns, trilliums, lilies.

C. drummondii. ROUGH-LEAF DOGWOOD. Shrub or small tree. Zones US, MS, LS, CS; 8–1. Native from Texas to Virginia and north to Ontario. To 15–20 ft. tall, spreading to 12 ft. Shrubby and rugged, quite unlike elegant *C. florida;* likely to form a thicket, though it can be trained to make a small tree. Grows quickly. Soft, furry olive green leaves 1½–3½ in. long hang a little limply from branches. Blooms briefly in early spring, bearing white blossoms (true flowers, not bracts) in clusters to 3 in. across. Planted mostly for its striking orange, red, and purple fall foliage and its adaptability—takes rocky limestone soils, clay, wetlands, drought, full sun or full shade. A beautiful addition to a natural garden; good understory plant in the deep shade of tall trees.

C. florida. FLOWERING DOGWOOD. Tree. Zones US, MS, LS, CS; 9–5. Native to eastern U.S., from New England to central Florida. Has been called the most beautiful native tree of North America. Blossom is the state flower of North Carolina and Virginia. May reach 40 ft. high and wide, but 20–30 ft. more common. Low branching, with a fairly horizontal branch pattern, upturned branch tips; makes beautiful winter silhouette. Old trees are broadly pyramidal but rather flat topped. Blooms profusely in midspring before leaves expand, almost covering itself with small flower clusters surrounded by four roundish, inch-wide bracts with notched tips. White is the usual color in the wild, but named selections (see below) also offer bracts in pink shades to nearly red. Only the white-bracted sorts seem to succeed in Florida, however. Oval leaves, 2–6 in. long, 2½ in. wide, are bright green above, lighter beneath; they turn glowing red and crimson before they drop. Clusters of small, oval, scarlet fruits last into winter or until birds eat them.

Flowering dogwood grows fine in full sun if planted in deep, fertile soil that retains moisture. In shallow, dry, or rocky soil, it often leaf-scorches badly in summer droughts. Succeeds most reliably as an understory tree where it receives light shade; in heavy shade, it will not bloom. Not browsed by deer.

Unfortunately, an anthracnose fungus has been infecting and destroying these trees throughout their range. Trees growing at high elevations and in shade are more susceptible. Dieback symptoms show up first in lower branches and can spread to whole tree. Borers often attack trunks and limbs of stressed trees. *C. florida* has been bred with *C. kousa* to produce more disease-resistant hybrids; see *C.* × *rutgersensis.*

'Appalachian Spring'. White bracts; attractive foliage. Resists anthracnose.

'Barton'. Large white bracts, profuse even when tree is young.

WHAT FLOWERING DOGWOOD NEEDS

EXPOSURE: Most take full sun or light shade. Excellent lawn, patio, or understory tree; not recommended for planting near pavement.

SOIL: Moist, acid, well drained, with lots of organic matter.

WATERING: Shallow-rooted tree is susceptible to summer drought. Water deeply during dry spells to prevent scorched leaves, but do not wet foliage.

MULCHING: Apply a thick layer of mulch beneath tree to cool soil, conserve moisture. Keep mulch a few inches away from trunk.

PRUNING: Seldom necessary except to remove weak or crossed branches; prune immediately after bloom.

Cornus florida

Cornus kousa

Cornus florida
'Pluribracteata'

Cornus ×rutgersensis
'Constellation'

Cornus kousa
'Satomi'

Cornus sericea

Cornus sericea
'Flaviramea'

'Cherokee Brave'. Red bracts with white centers. Resists mildew.

'Cherokee Chief'. Deep rosy red bracts, paler at base.

'Cherokee Daybreak'. Variegated green-and-white leaves turn pink and red in fall. White bracts.

'Cherokee Princess'. Unusually heavy display of white blooms.

'Cherokee Sunset'. Variegated green-and-yellow leaves turn red purple in fall. Reddish bracts. Resistant to anthracnose.

'Cloud Nine'. Blooms young and heavily. Tolerates heat and lack of winter chill better than other selections. White bracts.

'Junior Miss'. Deep pink bracts, paler at center. Resists anthracnose.

'Pendula'. Drooping branches give it a weeping look. White bracts.

'Pink Flame'. Green-and-cream leaves deepen to dark green and red with maturity. Pink bracts.

'Pluribracteata'. Two sets of white bracts (some large, many tiny aborted ones) give appearance of double flowers.

'Pygmy'. White-flowered dwarf; blooms at 2 ft. tall. Only 12 ft. tall after 20 years.

'Rainbow'. Leaves strongly marked bright yellow on green. Heavy bloomer with large white bracts.

'Royal Red'. Big deep red bracts. Leaves are red when young, turn red again in fall.

'Rubra'. Longtime favorite for its pink or rose bracts.

'Spring Grove'. Extra-large bracts; often bears two or three flower buds at branch tips.

'Sweetwater Red'. Dark red bracts. Reddish young leaves; good red-purple fall foliage.

'Welchii'. TRICOLOR DOGWOOD. Selection best known for its beautiful 4-in.-long leaves. Variegated in creamy white, pink, deep rose, and green throughout spring and summer, they turn deep rose to almost red in fall. Inconspicuous pinkish to white bracts are not profuse. Best with some shade.

C. kousa. KOUSA DOGWOOD. Shrub or small tree. Zones US, MS, LS; 8–5. Native to Japan and Korea. Later blooming (late spring or early summer) than other flowering dogwoods. Can be big multistemmed shrub or (with training) small tree to 20 ft. tall and wide (or even larger). Delicate limb structure and spreading, dense horizontal growth habit. Lustrous medium green leaves, 4 in. long, have rusty brown hairs at base of veins on undersurface. Yellow or scarlet fall color. Handsome peeling bark.

Cornus kousa

Flowers are carried along tops of branches and show above the leaves. Narrow, 2- to 3-in.-long bracts with slender, pointed tips are creamy white, turning pink along edges. In late summer and fall, red fruits like big raspberries hang below branches. This species is less susceptible to diseases than *C. florida* and has been bred with the latter to produce resistant hybrids; see *C. ×rutgersensis*.

C. kousa selections include the following.

'Autumn Rose'. To 20 ft. tall, 25 ft. wide. Leaves are light green when new, pink to red in fall.

C. k. chinensis. CHINESE DOGWOOD. Chinese native to 15–30 ft. tall and wide, with larger leaves and larger bracts than the species.

'Gold Star'. To 12 ft. tall and wide, with yellow-centered green leaves.

'Milky Way'. To 15–20 ft. tall and wide. More floriferous than the species, with pure white bracts.

'National'. To 25–30 ft. tall, 12–15 ft. wide, with bright red fall color. Blooms earlier than the species.

'Satomi'. ('Satomi Red', 'Rosabella'). Reaches 20 ft. tall and wide. Rose red bracts.

'Summer Stars'. To 25 ft. tall, 18 ft. wide, with vase-shaped form. Lavish bloom; later than the species.

C. mas. CORNELIAN CHERRY. Shrub or small tree. Zones US, MS, LS; 8–5. Pest-free dogwood native to southern Europe and Asia. Usually an airy, twiggy shrub but can be trained as a small tree, 15–20 ft. high and wide. Provides a progression of color throughout the year. One of earliest dogwoods to bloom, bearing clustered masses of small, soft yellow blossoms on bare twigs in late winter or early spring. Shiny green, oval, 2- to 4-in.-long leaves turn yellow in fall; some forms turn red. Autumn color is enhanced by clusters of bright scarlet, cherry-size fruits that hang on until birds get them. Fruits are edible and are frequently used in making preserves. In winter, flaking bark mottled in gray and tan provides interest. 'Variegata' features leaves marbled creamy white.

C. officinalis. JAPANESE CORNEL DOGWOOD. Shrub or small tree. Zones US, MS, LS; 8–6. Similar to *C. mas* but blooms slightly earlier and has handsome bark in gray, brown, and orange. Showier in bloom than *C. mas* and a better performer in the Lower South.

C. racemosa. GRAY DOGWOOD. Shrub or small tree. Zones US, MS, LS; 8–3. Native from Minnesota to Maine, south to Nebraska and Georgia. To 10–15 ft. high and wide; will spread even wider, but this can be controlled by removing suckers. Creamy white flowers are held in racemes at branch tips in late spring. Attractive blue-green, 2- to 4-in.-long leaves turn deep purplish red in fall and contrast nicely with white fruits. Adapts to various soils and moisture levels; tolerates air pollution and a good bit of shade.

C. ×rutgersensis. STELLAR DOGWOOD. Tree. Zones US, MS, LS; 8–3. This hybrid between *C. florida* and *C. kousa* has greater disease resistance than *C. florida*. Single-stemmed tree to about 20 ft. tall, 25–30 ft. wide. Bloom time falls between the midspring bloom of *C. florida* and the late spring or early summer bloom of *C. kousa;* bracts are produced with the leaves. 'Stellar Pink' has pink bracts; 'Aurora', 'Galaxy', and 'Ruth Ellen' bear broad white bracts; 'Constellation' and 'Stardust' have narrower white bracts. 'Constellation' has the most upright growth habit; other selections are more rounded. All have brilliant red fall leaves.

C. sanguinea. BLOODTWIG DOGWOOD. Shrub. Zones US, MS; 7–1. Multistemmed growth to 12 ft. high, about 8 ft. wide, with dark green, 1½- to 3-in.-long leaves. Greenish white late spring flowers in 2-in. clusters are followed by black fruits. Big show comes in fall, with dark blood red foliage color, and in winter, when purplish to dark red twigs and branches are on display. Prune back hard in late dormant season to produce new branches and twigs for winter color. 'Midwinter Fire' has brilliant orange-red fall color, red fruits.

C. sericea (C. stolonifera). REDTWIG DOGWOOD, RED-OSIER DOGWOOD. Shrub. Zones US, MS; 7–1. Native to moist places, eastern North America and Northern California to Alaska. Another dogwood with brilliant red fall foliage and bright red winter twigs that look striking against

C

a snowy backdrop. Grows rapidly to 7–9 ft. high; spreads to 12 ft. or wider by creeping underground stems and rooting branches. Leaves oval, to 1½–2½ in. long, fresh deep green. Blooms throughout the summer months, bearing small, creamy white flowers in 2-in.-wide clusters among the leaves; blooms are followed by white or bluish fruits. Canker disease can devastate this shrub.

Cornus sericea

Good space filler in moist ground (good for holding banks); also good planted along property line as a screen. To control spread, use a spade to cut off roots; also trim branches that touch ground. Shade tolerant.

'Alleman's Compact'. To 4–6 ft. tall, with red winter stems.

'Cardinal'. Cherry red stems.

C. s. coloradensis. COLORADO REDTWIG. Native from the Yukon southwest to New Mexico; grows 5–6 ft. high. Brownish red stems. Its selection 'Cheyenne' is redder.

'Flaviramea'. YELLOWTWIG DOGWOOD. Yellow twigs and branches. Very susceptible to disease.

'Isanti'. Compact growth to 5 ft. tall. Bright red stems.

'Silver and Gold'. Yellow branches and cream-edged green leaves.

CORONILLA varia

CROWN VETCH

Fabaceae (Leguminosae)

PERENNIAL

US, MS, LS, CS 9–1

FULL SUN, EXCEPT AS NOTED

MODERATE WATER

Coronilla varia

Weedy European native related to peas, beans, and clovers. Creeping roots and rhizomes make it a tenacious ground cover. Sprawling stems to 2 ft. long are set with leaves divided into 11 to 25 oval, ½- to ¾-in.-long leaflets. Lavender-pink flowers in 1-in. clusters bloom from summer into fall; these are followed by bundles of brown, fingerlike seedpods. Dies to the ground in winter, even in mild climates. Too invasive and rank for flower beds; use it for covering erosion-prone banks and at garden fringes. Mow, feed, and—in absence of rainfall—irrigate in early spring for best appearance. Difficult to eliminate once established. 'Penngift' has a somewhat neater habit and takes sun or shade.

CORTADERIA selloana

PAMPAS GRASS

Poaceae (Gramineae)

PERENNIAL GRASS

MS, LS, CS, TS 12–7

FULL SUN

ANY AMOUNT OF WATER

Cortaderia selloana

If Southerners know one ornamental grass well, this is it. Thanks to its ease of culture, imposing stature, and exceedingly showy plumes, pampas grass has been showcased throughout the Deep South to the point of cliché. Native to Argentina, it grows very fast in good soil in warm climates—from gallon-size transplant to 8-ft. giant in one season. Established clumps can reach 10–12 ft. tall and wide. Each plant forms a fountain of narrow, cascading, medium green, sawtoothed leaves (be careful—they can cut you). Long stalks bearing 1- to 3-ft., white to chamois or pink flower plumes rise above the foliage in late summer. Plants may be either male or female; females have much showier plumes, but unfortunately, few garden centers

sell pampas grass by sex. To ensure that you get a showy specimen, buy a plant in bloom or obtain a division from a known female plant. Or purchase a named selection, like those listed below.

Pampas grass likes heat, sun, and well-drained soil. It tolerates wind, sand, and salt spray, so it's ideal for growing at the beach. To renew ragged-looking clumps, cut them to within a foot or two of the ground in late winter, using shears or hedge trimmers. Regular pampas grass doesn't do well in the colder winters of the Upper South and often fails to bloom there, but a number of cold-hardy selections (noted below) solve that problem.

Use pampas grass as a specimen, vertical accent, or tall screen. Especially effective when massed near water. Most are somewhat taller than wide when not in bloom.

'Andes Silver'. To 7 ft. tall in bloom. Cold-hardy selection with silver flower plumes.

'Patagonia'. To 6 ft. tall in bloom. Leaves have a blue-gray cast; flower plumes are silver. Cold hardy.

'Pumila' ('Ivory Feathers'). Smaller than species and a better fit for most home gardens. Gray-green leaves form a clump to 3 ft. tall, 4 ft. wide; white flower plumes increase the height to 6 ft. Quite cold hardy.

'Rosea' ('Rosa Feder'). To 8 ft. tall in bloom. Silvery white plumes with a pink cast.

'Sun Stripe'. Yellow-striped foliage in clumps to 4 ft. tall, 5 ft. wide. White flower plumes rise to 6 ft. high.

'Sunningdale Silver'. Large, sturdy selection that may reach 10 ft. tall and 8 ft. wide in flower. Huge, fluffy, creamy white plumes.

CORYDALIS

Fumariaceae

PERENNIALS

US, MS, LS

PARTIAL SHADE

REGULAR WATER

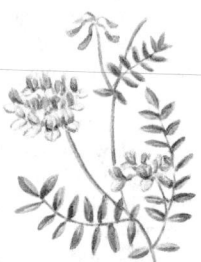
Corydalis lutea

Handsome clumps of dainty divided leaves like those of bleeding heart (*Dicentra*, to which it is closely related) or maidenhair fern (*Adiantum*). Clusters of small, spurred flowers. Plant in rich, moist soil. Effective in rock crevices, in open woodland, near pool or streamside. Divide clumps or sow seed in spring or fall. Plants self-sow. Summer-flowering species may stop flowering during hottest months; keep soil moist to encourage some continued bloom.

C. cheilanthifolius. Heat zones 7–3. Hardy Chinese native to 8–10 in. high and wide. Fernlike green foliage; clusters of yellow, ½-in.-long flowers in spring.

C. elata. Heat zones 8–6. Native to China. Upright grower to 15 in. high, 2–3 ft. wide. Heat-tolerant species that won't go dormant in summer; the best choice for the South. Cobalt blue blossoms are carried above attractive, fleshy green leaves from spring through summer. Tantalizing fragrance has been described as a combination of gardenia and coconut.

C. flexuosa. BLUE CORYDALIS. Heat zones 8–6. From western China. Typically to 1 ft. high, 8 in. wide, but when conditions are favorable, it rapidly spreads more widely by bulblets on the roots. Finely divided blue-green leaves. Spikelike clusters of blue flowers appear in early spring, often continuing into summer. May go dormant in summer, especially in hot climates, but will reappear the following spring. Selections include gentian blue 'Blue Panda', pure sky blue 'China Blue', blue-and-lavender 'Nightshade', and lavender to light blue 'Père David'. 'Purple Leaf', the earliest bloomer, has purplish blue flowers and purple-blotched green leaves.

C. heterocarpa. Heat zones 8–3. Native to Japan. Makes a 3- by 3-ft. blue-green mound. Rich yellow flowers cover the plant in late winter or early spring and continue to bloom intermittently throughout the growing season.

C. lutea. YELLOW CORYDALIS. Heat zones 8–4. Native to southern Europe. Grows to 15 in. tall, 1 ft. wide. Many-stemmed plant with masses of gray-green foliage. Bears golden yellow, ¾-in.-long, short-spurred flowers throughout summer.

C. ophiocarpa. Heat zones 8–4. From the Himalayas. To 1½ ft. tall and wide, 3 ft. tall in flower. Gray-green, feathery evergreen foliage. Blooms in spring, bearing cream-colored flowers with dark red tips.

C. solida. FUMEWORT. Heat zones 7–5. From northern Europe, Asia. Grows from tubers (sometimes available from bulb catalogs). To 10 in. high and 8 in. wide, with gray-green leaves and erect clusters of up to 20 purplish red, inch-long flowers in spring.

CORYLOPSIS

WINTER HAZEL

Hamamelidaceae

DECIDUOUS SHRUBS

US, MS, LS

FULL SUN OR PARTIAL SHADE

REGULAR WATER

Corylopsis spicata

Asian natives valued for sweet-scented, bell-shaped, soft yellow flowers that hang in short, chainlike clusters on bare branches in early spring. Foliage that follows is often tinged pink; it later turns bright green. Toothed, nearly round leaves somewhat resemble those of hazelnut *(Corylus)*; fall color varies from none to poor to a good clear yellow. Rather open structure with attractive, delicate branching pattern. Give same soil conditions as you would rhododendrons. Grow in wind-sheltered location in shrub border or at edge of woodland.

C. glabrescens. FRAGRANT WINTER HAZEL. Heat zones 9–6. Hardiest species. To 8–15 ft. high and wide. Can be trained as a small tree. Flower clusters are 1–1½ in. long.

C. pauciflora. BUTTERCUP WINTER HAZEL. Heat zones 9–1. Dainty habit to 4–6 ft. high and wide. Blossom clusters are 1¼ in. long, each containing two or three blooms.

C. sinensis. Heat zones 9–2. A variable species. The typical form is a spreading shrub to 15 ft. tall and wide, bearing crowded flower spikes to 2 in. long. Variety *C. s. sinensis (C. willmottiae)* has velvety blue-green leaves, hairy leafstalks, and flower clusters to 3 in. long. Its selection 'Spring Purple' has purplish young stems that mature to green. *C. s. calvescens (C. platypetala)* has smooth leaf surfaces and almost hairless leafstalks.

C. spicata. SPIKE WINTER HAZEL. Heat zones 8–5. To 8 ft. high, 10 ft. wide. New growth is purple, maturing to bluish green. Each 1- to 2-in.-long flower cluster holds 6 to 12 blossoms.

CORYLUS

FILBERT, HAZELNUT

Betulaceae

DECIDUOUS SHRUBS AND TREES

US, MS, LS 9–1

FULL SUN OR PARTIAL SHADE

REGULAR WATER, EXCEPT AS NOTED

Corylus avellana
'Fusco-rubra'

Although filberts and hazelnuts are usually thought of as trees grown for their edible nuts, most listed here are grown for their pleasing ornamental value. Plants have separate female and male flowers; female blossoms are inconspicuous, while male ones, appearing in pendent catkins on bare branches in winter or early spring, are showy. Leaves are roundish to oval, with toothed margins.

C. avellana. EUROPEAN FILBERT. Shrub. European native grows to 10–15 ft. high and wide. Ornamental selections are more widely grown than the species; the following two are popular.

'Contorta'. HARRY LAUDER'S WALKING STICK. Rounded growth to 8–10 ft. tall, 12 ft. wide. Grown for fantastically gnarled and twisted

branches and twigs, revealed after its 2- to 2½-in. leaves turn yellow and drop in autumn. Branches are used in flower arrangements. Plants are almost always grafted, so suckers arising from the base below the graft should be removed; they won't have contorted form.

'Fusco-rubra' ('Atropurpurea'). Grows to 10–15 ft. high and wide, with 3- to 4-in., reddish purple leaves.

C. maxima. Shrub or tree. Native to southeastern Europe. One of the species grown for nuts. Suckering shrub to 12–15 ft. high and wide; can be trained as small tree. 'Purpurea', most widely grown ornamental form, has rich dark purple leaves to 6 in. long; male catkins are also heavily tinted purple. In most areas, leaves fade to green by early summer.

CORYNABUTILON vitifolium. See ABUTILON vitifolium

CORYPHANTHA vivipara
(Mammillaria vivipara)

Cactaceae

CACTUS

US, MS, LS, CS 9–6; OR HOUSEPLANT

FULL SUN; BRIGHT SUNNY WINDOW

LITTLE TO REGULAR WATER

Coryphantha vivipara

Native from Alberta to North Texas, west to Arizona, Utah, Nevada, and deserts of California. Has single or clustered globular, 2-in. bodies covered with little knobs bearing white spines. Showy pink to purple flowers to 2 in. long. Wide-spreading plant. One of the hardiest cacti; subspecies native to the coldest areas will take temperatures far below zero. Indoors, cut back on moisture during winter.

COSMOS

Asteraceae (Compositae)

PERENNIALS AND ANNUALS

US, MS, LS, CS, TS 12–1, EXCEPT AS NOTED

FULL SUN

MODERATE WATER

Cosmos bipinnatus

Native to tropical America, mostly Mexico. Showy summer- and fall-blooming plants, open and branching in habit, with bright green, divided leaves and daisy-like flowers in many colors and forms (single, double, crested, frilled). Heights vary from 2½ to 8 ft. Use for mass color in borders or background, or as a filler among shrubs. Useful in arrangements if flowers are cut just after they open and placed immediately in deep, cool water. Sow seed in open ground where plants are to grow; or set out transplants from spring to summer. Plant in not-too-rich soil. Plants self-sow freely, attract birds.

C. atrosanguineus. CHOCOLATE COSMOS. Perennial from tuberous roots. Zones MS, LS, CS. Where winters are colder, dig and store as for dahlias. Grows 2–2½ ft. tall, 1½ ft. wide, with coarsely cut foliage. Blooms in late summer and fall, with deep brownish red, nearly 2-in.-wide flowers with a strong perfume of chocolate (or vanilla). Attractive companion for silvery-foliaged plants. Provide well-drained soil. Winter mulch is prudent in all but mildest regions (where plant tends to be rather short lived).

C. bipinnatus. COMMON COSMOS. Annual. Heights up to 8 ft., widths to 1½–2½ ft. Blossoms are 3–4 in. wide, with tufted yellow centers and rays in white and shades of pink, rose, lavender, purple, or crimson. Among the many types are 3- to 4-ft.-tall 'Candystripe', with white-and-rose flowers; 'Picotee', to 2½ ft. high, white flowers edged red; Sensation strain, 3–6 ft. tall, including 'Dazzler' (crimson) and 'Radiance' (rose with red center); and 'Sea Shells', to 3 ft. tall, grown for quilled ray flowers that look like long, slender cones. Sonata is a dwarf strain 1½–2 ft. high; 'Sweet Dreams' reaches 3 ft. tall and has pale pink to white blossoms with rose centers. Versailles strain, bred for cut flowers, reaches 3½ ft. and bears its blossoms on long, strong stems.

C. sulphureus. YELLOW COSMOS. Annual. To 7 ft. tall, 1½–2½ ft. wide, with yellow-centered, yellow or orange-yellow single flowers. Tends to become weedy looking at end of season. Two 3- to 4-ft.-tall, semidouble-flowering strains are Bright Lights, with 3½-in. flowers in yellow, gold, orange, and orange red; and Klondike strain, with 2-in. flowers ranging from scarlet orange to yellow. Dwarf Klondike or Sunny strain is 1½ ft. tall, bears 1½-in. flowers. Foot-tall semidouble bloomers include Ladybird mix, with 2½-in. scarlet, yellow, and orange flowers; and 'Sunny Red', with orange-red blooms.

COSTMARY. See CHRYSANTHEMUM balsamita

COSTUS

SPIRAL FLAG, GINGER LILY

Zingiberaceae

PERENNIALS

⚡ CS, TS ♨ 12–10, EXCEPT AS NOTED

☼ LIGHT SHADE

💧 AMPLE WATER DURING ACTIVE GROWTH

Costus speciosus

Plants in this genus are related to true gingers (*Zingiber*) and other so-called gingers (*Alpinia, Hedychium*), and like them have fleshy rhizomes and stems bearing large leaves. In *Costus*, the leaves are spirally arranged around the stem. Flowers emerge from a tight, conelike cluster of colored bracts at stem ends in summer and fall.

Plants have sprawling, mounding habit. Native to the tropical forest floor, they prefer light shade but can stand full sun if roots are shaded. Use around foundation or near patio or pool; can also be grown in large pots. Plants are dormant in winter and need little water at that time. Provide a winter mulch.

C. barbatus. RED TOWER GINGER. From Costa Rica. To 6–8 ft. tall, 5 ft. wide. Bright green, 5- to 10-in.-long leaves have downy undersides. Flowering cone is 7–13 in. long, with dark red bracts and 1½-in. yellow flowers; lasts for a long time on the plant. Blossoms attract hummingbirds.

C. curvibracteatus. From Central America. To 2 ft. high and 3 ft. wide. Shiny dark green leaves grow 8–12 in. long. Flowering cone is 2–7 in. long, with 1½-in. reddish orange flowers. Good container plant.

C. cuspidatus (C. igneus). FIERY COSTUS. Native to Brazil. Forms a neat clump to 1½–2 ft. high and wide. Deep green, 4- to 7-in.-long leaves with reddish undersides. Unusual, almost cup-shaped, 3-in. orange flowers, often produced in twos or threes at stem ends. Good potted plant; attractive even when out of bloom.

C. pictus. To 7–8 ft. tall, 5 ft. wide. From Mexico and Costa Rica. Red-spotted stems bear shiny green, narrow leaves 4–9 in. long. Flowering cone to 3 in. long, with green bracts and 2½-in. flowers in yellow striped with red.

C. speciosus. CREPE GINGER, MALAY GINGER. Heat zones 12–9. Native to the East Indies. Clusters of stems grow to 6–8 ft., spreading to 3 ft. Medium green, 5- to 10-in.-long leaves; 5-in.-long flowering cone with green bracts tipped red. Crepe paper–textured white or pink flowers to 4 in. wide emerge from the cone two or three at a time.

C. spiralis. SPIRAL FLAG, SPIRAL GINGER. Heat zones 12–9. From South America. Reaches 4–6 ft. tall, 3–4 ft. wide. Glossy bright green, 8-in. leaves. Flowering cone has orange bracts and pink to red, 1½-in. flowers.

A PRACTICAL GUIDE TO GARDENING
PLEASE SEE PAGES 596–669

COTINUS

SMOKE TREE

Anacardiaceae

DECIDUOUS SHRUBS OR TREES

⚡ US, MS, LS

☼ FULL SUN

💧 MODERATE WATER

Cotinus coggygria
'Royal Purple'

Unusual and colorful shrub-trees creating broad, urn-shaped mass usually as wide as high. Naturally multistemmed but can be trained to a single trunk. Common name derived from dramatic puffs of "smoke" from fading flowers: as the tiny greenish blooms wither, they send out elongated stalks clothed in a profusion of fuzzy lavender-pink hairs. Plants are at their best under stress in poor or rocky soil. In cultivated gardens, give them fast drainage and avoid overly wet conditions. Not browsed by deer.

C. coggygria. SMOKE TREE. Heat zones 9–3. Native from southern Europe to central China. Typically 12–15 ft. high and wide, though it may eventually reach 25 ft. The roundish, 1½- to 3-in. leaves are bluish green in the species, but purple-leafed types are more commonly grown. Leaves of 'Nordine' ('Nordine Red') and 'Purpureus' emerge purple and gradually turn green; 'Notcutt's Variety', 'Royal Purple', and 'Velvet Cloak' hold their purple color through most of the summer. Those with purple foliage have richer purple "smoke puffs" than the species. 'Pink Champagne' is a green-leafed selection with pinkish tan puffs. Leaves of all types change in fall, taking on colors ranging from yellow to orange red.

C. 'Grace'. Heat zones 8–3. Handsome hybrid between *C. coggygria* and *C. obovatus*. To 15 ft. tall and wide, with blue-green foliage shaded purple. Large deep pink puffs. Orange and purple-red fall foliage.

C. obovatus. AMERICAN SMOKE TREE. Heat zones 8–1. From eastern U.S. Small, rounded tree to 20–30 ft. tall and wide; deserves much wider use. Blue-green leaves turn yellow, orange, and reddish purple in fall. Takes alkaline soil; often found growing wild on Edwards Plateau in Texas.

COTONEASTER

Rosaceae

EVERGREEN, SEMIEVERGREEN, DECIDUOUS SHRUBS

⚡ ZONES VARY BY SPECIES

☼ FULL SUN, EXCEPT AS NOTED

💧 LITTLE TO REGULAR WATER

Cotoneaster glaucophyllus

Native to China, the Himalayas, northern India. Plants range from low types used as ground covers to small, stiffly upright shrubs to tall-growing (18-ft.) shrubs of fountainlike form with graceful, arching branches. All grow vigorously and thrive with little or no maintenance, can tolerate poor soil and drought. White or pinkish springtime flowers resemble tiny single roses; though not showy, they are pretty because of their abundance. Berries are typically red or orange red, less than ½ in. across; they appear in fall and winter. Plants are not browsed by deer.

While some medium and tall growers can be sheared, they look best when allowed to maintain their natural fountain shapes. Prune only to enhance graceful arch of branches. Keep medium growers looking young by pruning out some of the oldest wood each year. Prune ground covers to remove dead or awkward branches. Give flat growers room to spread. Don't plant near walk or drive where branch ends will need frequent cutting back.

Cotoneasters are useful shrubs and can be attractive in the proper setting. Some are especially good looking in form and branching pattern (*C. congestus, C. horizontalis*), while others are notable for colorful, long-lasting fruit (*C. apiculatus*). Trailing types are popular as ground cover plants. However, ground cover plantings seldom grow dense enough to keep weeds from coming up. Branches also tend to snag blowing litter.

C. adpressus praecox (C. nanshan). PRAECOX COTONEASTER. Deciduous. Zones US, MS; 8–1. To 1½ ft. tall, 6 ft. wide, with shiny medium green leaves turning maroon red in fall. Profuse large berries in bright red. Bank or ground cover. Tolerates some shade. *C. adpressus* is similar but somewhat smaller.

C. apiculatus. CRANBERRY COTONEASTER. Deciduous. Zones US, MS; 8–1. Best in cold-winter areas. Dense grower to 3 ft. tall, 6 ft. wide. Small, round, medium green leaves turn deep red in fall. Clustered fruits are about the size of large cranberries. Can take some shade. Use as bank cover, hedge, background planting. Tolerates alkaline soil.

C. congestus (C. microphyllus glacialis). PYRENEES COTONE-ASTER. Evergreen. Zones US, MS; 8–7. Slow grower to 3 ft. tall and wide, with dense, downward-curving branches, tiny dark green leaves, and bright red fruit. Use in containers, rock gardens, above walls.

C. dammeri (C. humifusus). BEARBERRY COTONEASTER. Evergreen. Zones US, MS, LS; 8–3. Fast, prostrate growth to 3–6 in. tall, 10 ft. wide. Branches root along ground. Bright, glossy green leaves; bright red fruit. 'Coral Beauty' is 6 in. tall; 'Eichholz', 10–12 in. tall with a scattering of red-orange leaves in fall; 'Lowfast', 1 ft. tall; 'Skogsholmen', 1½ ft. tall. All are good ground covers in sun or partial shade and can drape over walls, cascade down slopes.

C. franchetii. FRANCHET COTONEASTER. Evergreen. Zones MS, LS; 9–7. Arching growth to 10 ft. tall, 6–9 ft. wide. Leaves are grayish green when new, maturing to bright green; undersides are fuzzy. Pink-tinged white flowers in clusters of up to 20 are followed by orange-red berries.

C. glaucophyllus. GRAYLEAF COTONEASTER. Evergreen. Zones US, MS, LS; 8–7. To 6–8 ft. tall and broad, with gracefully arching branches clothed in gray-green foliage. Dense clusters of white flowers are followed by dark red berries. Attractive in shrub beds or as informal hedge.

C. horizontalis. ROCK COTONEASTER. Deciduous. Zones US, MS, LS; 7–3. Can be 2–3 ft. tall, 15 ft. wide, with stiff horizontal branches, many branchlets set in herringbone pattern. Leaves are small, round, bright green; turn orange and red before falling. Out of leaf very briefly. Showy red fruit. Give it room to spread. Fine bank cover or low traffic barrier. 'Variegatus' has leaves edged in white. *C. h. perpusillus* is smaller, more compact than species.

Cotoneaster horizontalis

C. lacteus (C. parneyi). BRIGHTBEAD COTONEASTER. Evergreen. Zones MS, LS, CS; 9–7. Graceful, arching habit to 8 ft. or taller, 10 ft. or wider, with dark green leaves 2 in. long, clustered white flowers, and a heavy crop of long-lasting red fruit in 2- to 3-in. clusters. Best as informal hedge, screen, or espalier. Can be clipped as formal hedge, but form suffers.

C. microphyllus. LITTLELEAF COTONEASTER. Evergreen. Zones US, MS, LS; 8–6. Its horizontal branches trail and root, forming a mass to 6 ft. wide; secondary branches grow erect to 2–3 ft. Small (⅓-in.) dark green leaves with gray undersides; rosy red fruit. *C. m. thymifolius*, thyme rockspray cotoneaster, is a smaller plant (2–3 ft. high and wide); it has even tinier leaves with edges rolled under. Both are effective in rock gardens, on banks.

Cotoneaster lacteus

C. salicifolius. WILLOWLEAF COTONEASTER. Evergreen or semiever-green. Zones US, MS, LS; 8–6. Erect, spreading shrub, 15–18 ft. high and wide, with narrow, dark green, 1- to 3½-in.-long leaves and bright red fruits. Graceful screening or background plant. Better known are trailing forms used as ground covers. Compact, small-leafed 'Emerald Carpet' is 12–15 in. tall, spreading to 8 ft. wide; 'Autumn Fire' ('Herbstfeuer') grows to 2–3 ft. tall and 8 ft. wide. 'Repens' is similar; it is sometimes grafted to another cotoneaster species and grown as a weeping tree.

COTTON. See GOSSYPIUM tomentosum

COTTONWOOD. See POPULUS

COWBERRY. See VACCINIUM vitis-idaea

CRABAPPLE

Rosaceae

DECIDUOUS FRUIT TREES

🌿 US, MS, LS H 8–2

☼ FULL SUN

💧 REGULAR WATER DURING FRUIT DEVELOPMENT

Crabapple

Crabapple is a small, usually tart apple. Many kinds are valued more for their springtime flowers than for their fruit; these are flowering crabapples, described under *Malus*. Among the most popular crabapple selections grown for fruit (used for jelly making and pickling) are 'Tran-scendent', with 2-in., red-cheeked yellow apples that ripen in summer; 'Centennial', with 1½-in., scarlet-and-yellow fruit; and 'Dolgo', with 1½-in. crimson fruit. The red-fruited 'Maypole' is a newer columnar dwarf crabapple. Other crabapples are prized for cider, including 'Virginia Crab' ('Hewe's Crab'), 'Geneva', and 'Giant Russian'. For information about general care, see Apple.

CRAMBE

Brassicaceae (Cruciferae)

PERENNIALS

🌿 US, MS, LS H 9–6

☼ ◐ FULL SUN OR LIGHT SHADE

💧 REGULAR WATER

Crambe cordifolia

Two species of these big, cabbagelike perenni-als are occasionally seen. Both have large, smooth leaves and much-branched clusters of small, honey-scented white flowers. They appreciate rich, well-drained garden soil and require con-siderable space. In the Lower South, provide light afternoon shade.

C. cordifolia. GIANT KALE, HEARTLEAF COLEWORT. From the Cauca-sus. Forms a 3-ft.-wide mound of branching stems bearing dark green, 1-ft.-wide leaves on long stalks. Flowering stem set with smaller leaves can reach 8 ft. tall. Broad, branching flower cluster, up to 5 ft. wide, somewhat resembles a gargantuan baby's breath (*Gypsophila*). Requires a big garden and leaves a big vacancy when summer flowering is finished; plug in annuals to fill the space. Use in big borders to astonish your friends.

C. maritima. SEA KALE. From coastal northern Europe. To 2 ft. tall and wide, with branched, purplish stems carrying blue-gray leaves up to 1 ft. wide. In early summer, sends up a 1- to 2½-ft.-tall stem with flower clusters to 1½ ft. wide. Leafstalks were once widely used as a cooked (steamed) vegetable. Blanch leafstalks as they grow by placing large pots or boxes over them.

CRANESBILL. See GERANIUM

CRASPEDIA globosa

DRUMSTICKS

Asteraceae (Compositae)

PERENNIAL

🌿 TS H 12–9; ANNUAL ANYWHERE

☼ FULL SUN

💧 REGULAR WATER

Craspedia globosa

Odd, attractive, offbeat Australian daisy. Sil-very leaves form 8- to 12-in.-wide clumps, send up 2-ft. stalks, each topped by a 1-in. globe of tiny yellow flowers. Bloom may occur at any time of year. Flowers are useful, fresh or dried, in arrangements.

CRASSULA

Crassulaceae

SUCCULENT PERENNIALS

TS H 12–10, EXCEPT AS NOTED; OR INDOORS

FULL SUN, EXCEPT AS NOTED; BRIGHT LIGHT

LITTLE TO NO WATER

Crassula ovata

This interesting group of succulents, mostly from South Africa, includes many plants with unusual geometric forms. Excellent drainage is a must—be careful not to overwater. Most prefer full sun, but a few tolerate shade. All make excellent houseplants. Gardeners in the Tropical South can use them outdoors in containers, rock gardens, and borders.

C. arborescens. Heat zones 12–1. Shrubby, heavy-branched plant is very similar to jade plant *(C. ovata),* but it's smaller, grows more slowly, and has gray-green, red-edged, red-dotted leaves. Star-shaped summer flowers (usually seen only on old plants) are white aging to pink.

C. falcata (C. perfoliata minor). Grows to 4 ft. high, 2½ ft. wide. Fleshy, gray-green, sickle-shaped, 4-in. leaves are vertically arranged in two rows on stems. Dense clusters of scarlet flowers appear in late summer.

C. lactea. Spreading, semishrubby plant grows to 1–2 ft. tall and 3 ft. wide, with fleshy dark green leaves to 3 in. long. Produces white flowers in 4- to 6-in. clusters during autumn. Will grow in shade, even dense shade. Fine rock garden plant.

C. lycopodioides (C. muscosa). Leafy, branching, erect stems to 1 ft. high and wide, closely packed with tiny green leaves in four rows; effect is that of braided chain or of some strange green coral. Very small, inconspicuous greenish flowers. Easy to grow and useful in miniature and dish gardens.

Crassula falcata

C. ovata (C. argentea). JADE PLANT. Top-notch houseplant, large container plant anywhere; an excellent landscaping shrub in the Tropical South. Sometimes sold as *C. portulacea.* Stout trunk, sturdy limbs even on small plant—and plant will stay small in small container. Can reach 9 ft. in time but is usually shorter; grows about half as wide as tall. Glossy leaves are thick, oblong, fleshy pads with roundish tips, 1–2 in. long; color is bright green, sometimes with red-tinged edges. 'Crosby's Dwarf' is a low, compact grower; variegated kinds are 'Sunset' (yellow tinged red) and 'Tricolor' (green, white, and pinkish). Clusters of pink, star-shaped flowers bloom profusely from fall into spring.

C. pyramidalis. Interesting oddity grows 3–4 in. high and wide; flat, triangular, 1½- to 5-in.-long leaves are closely packed in four rows to give plant a squarish cross section.

C. schmidtii. Mat-forming, spreading plant to 4 in. tall, 1 ft. wide, with slender, rich green leaves to 1½ in. long. Clusters of small dark rose or purplish flowers put on a show in winter and spring. Good choice for pots or rock gardens.

C. tetragona. Upright plants with treelike habit, 1–2 ft. high and a little narrower. Narrow, 1-in.-long leaves. Inconspicuous white flowers. Widely used in dish gardens to suggest miniature pine trees.

Crassulaceae. This large family of usually herbaceous (rarely shrubby) plants is familiar through *Sedum, Sempervivum,* and a host of other popular succulents. Leaves are often in rosettes, as in the familiar hen and chicks *(Echeveria).*

FOR INFORMATION ON YOUR CLIMATE ZONES

PLEASE SEE PAGES 28–38

CRATAEGUS

HAWTHORN

Rosaceae

DECIDUOUS TREES

ZONES VARY BY SPECIES

FULL SUN, EXCEPT AS NOTED

MODERATE WATER

Crataegus laevigata

Members of the rose family, these small to medium-size, multitrunked trees are well known for their pretty, typically white flower clusters, which appear after leaf-out in spring—in fact, the hawthorn blossom is Missouri's state flower. Showy fruits resembling tiny apples appear in summer and autumn and often hang on into winter. The thorny branches need some pruning to thin out twiggy growth. Hawthorns attract bees and birds.

These trees will grow in any soil as long as it is well drained. Better grown under somewhat austere conditions, since good soil, regular water, and fertilizer all promote succulent new growth that is most susceptible to fireblight. The disease makes entire branches die back quickly; cut out blighted branches well below dead part. The rust stage of cedar-apple rust can be a problem wherever eastern red cedar *(Juniperus virginiana)* grows nearby. Aphids and scale are widespread potential pests. Hawthorns are not browsed by deer.

C. crus-galli. COCKSPUR THORN. Zones US, MS; 7–1. Native to eastern U.S. and Canada. Wide-spreading tree to 30 ft. high, 35 ft. across. Stiff thorns to 3 in. long. Smooth, glossy, toothed, 1- to 3-in.-long leaves are dark green, turning orange to red in fall. Dull orange-red fruit. Most successful hawthorn for Oklahoma. *C. c. inermis* ('Crusader') is thornless.

C. laevigata (C. oxyacantha). ENGLISH HAWTHORN. Zones US, MS; 8–3. Native to Europe and North Africa. Moderate growth to 18–25 ft. high, 15–20 ft. wide. Best known through its selections. 'Crimson Cloud' ('Superba') has bright red single flowers with white centers, vivid red fruit. Double-flowered forms (which set little fruit) include 'Double White', 'Double Pink', and 'Paul's Scarlet', with clusters of rose to red flowers. All have 2-in. toothed, lobed leaves lacking good fall color. Trees are prone to leaf spot, which can defoliate them and shorten their life.

C. marshallii (C. apiifolia). PARSLEY HAWTHORN. Zones MS, LS, CS; 9–1. Native to southern U.S. To 10–15 ft. and wide, occasionally to 25 ft. Early spring flowers are dainty white with purple-tipped anthers. Finely cut leaves to 1½ in. long resemble parsley, turn red or yellow in fall. Striking cherry red fruits persist after leaves drop. Tolerates a wide range of soils. Relatively disease free.

C. mollis. DOWNY HAWTHORN. Zones US; 6–1. Native to central North America. Big, broad tree to 30 ft. tall, 35 ft. wide; looks like mature apple tree. Leaves to 4 in. long, lobed, toothed, covered with down. Flowers to 1 in. wide. Red fruit to 1 in. across, also downy; fruit doesn't last on tree as long as that of other species but has value in jelly making.

C. monogyna. SINGLESEED HAWTHORN. Zones US, MS; 7–4. Native to Europe, North Africa, and western Asia. Classic hawthorn of English countryside for hedges, boundary plantings. Best known is upright selection 'Stricta', 30 ft. tall and 8 ft. wide. Lobed leaves to 2 in. long. Small red fruit in clusters, rather difficult to see. Very prone to fireblight, mites, and leaf diseases.

C. opaca. MAYHAW. Zones MS, LS, CS; 9–3. Native to southeastern U.S. Attractive large shrub or small tree famous for its fruits—called mayhaws—which are prized for making jelly. Eventually reaches 20–30 ft. tall and wide. Inch-wide flowers; matte green, lobed, 1- to 2½-in.-long leaves with hairy undersides. Fruits are typically red and ripen in early summer (though in the Lower and Coastal South, bloom may occur as early as January, and fruits may ripen by April or May). In its native range, mayhaw grows in damp ground, but it will tolerate some dryness. If you want to harvest the fruit to make jelly, choose a heavy-yielding selection such as those listed on facing page. The plant is self-fertile, but cross-pollination between two different selections produces heavier crops. Full sun or light shade.

'Big Red'. Red fruits to 1 in. across. Very dependable selection from the Pearl River swamps of Mississippi.

'Elite'. Red fruits to ¾ in. across; all ripen at the same time, rather than over several weeks.

'Golden Farris'. Golden fruits over ½ in. in diameter. Bears heavily and at an early age.

'Goliath'. Dark red fruits almost 1 in. across. Very productive.

'Super Spur'. Heavy crop of ¾-in. red fruit; particularly good for jelly.

'Texas Star'. Red to orange-red fruits to almost 1 in. across.

C. phaenopyrum (C. cordata). WASHINGTON HAWTHORN. Zones US, MS, LS; 8–1. Native to southeastern U.S. Moderate growth to 25 ft. tall, 20 ft. across. Graceful, open limb structure. Glossy leaves 2–3 in. long with three to five sharp-pointed lobes (like some maples). In Upper and Middle South, foliage turns beautiful orange, scarlet, or purplish in fall. Broad flower clusters. Shiny red fruit hangs on well into winter. Not successful in the southern Midwest but a choice hawthorn elsewhere. One of the least prone to fireblight but quite susceptible to rust.

C. pinnatifida. CHINESE HAWTHORN. Zones US, MS; 7–1. Native to northeastern Asia, this tree has been cultivated for its fruit for more than 2,000 years in China, where it is known as *shan-cha*. To 20 ft. high, 10–12 ft. wide. Flowers to ¾ in. across are carried in 3-in. clusters. Leaves are lobed like those of *C. laevigata* but are bigger and thicker; they turn red in fall. Round, purple, 1½-in.-wide fruits have soft, sweet-tart yellow-orange flesh. Eat fresh or use for jellies, preserves, candy.

C. punctata 'Ohio Pioneer' (C. p. inermis). THORNLESS DOTTED HAWTHORN. Zones US; 7–1. Native to eastern and midwestern U.S. Essentially thornless, to 30 ft. high and somewhat wider at maturity. Long-lasting, dark red, ¾-in. fruits.

C. viridis. GREEN HAWTHORN. Zones US, MS; 7–1. Native to southeastern U.S. Moderate growth to 25–30 ft.; broad, spreading crown. Red fruit. 'Winter King' is vase shaped, with silvery stems and showy red fruit that lasts all winter; among the most attractive, trouble-free hawthorns.

CREAM LACE CACTUS. See ECHINOCEREUS reichenbachii

CREEPING BUTTERCUP. See RANUNCULUS repens pleniflorus

CREEPING JENNY. See LYSIMACHIA nummularia

CREEPING ZINNIA. See SANVITALIA procumbens

CREOLE LILY. See CRINUM scabrum

CREOSOTE BUSH. See LARREA tridentata

CREPE GINGER. See COSTUS speciosus

CREPE MYRTLE. See LAGERSTROEMIA indica

CRESS, GARDEN

Brassicaceae (Cruciferae)

ANNUAL

✿ US, MS, LS, CS, TS ▯ 12–1

◐ ◑ FULL SUN OR PARTIAL SHADE

◗ ◖ REGULAR TO AMPLE WATER

Sometimes called pepper grass; tastes like watercress. Easy to grow as long as weather is cool, so sow seed as early in spring as possible.

Garden Cress

Plant in rich, moist soil. Make rows 1 ft. apart; thin plants to 3 in. apart (eat thinnings). Cress matures fast; make successive sowings every 2 weeks up to middle of May. Where frosts are mild, sow through fall and winter. Try growing garden cress in shallow pots in a sunny kitchen window. It sprouts in a few days, can be harvested (with scissors) in 2 to 3 weeks. Or grow it by sprinkling seeds on pads of wet cheesecloth; keep damp until harvest in 2 weeks.

CRINKLED HAIR GRASS. See DESCHAMPSIA flexuosa

CRINUM

Liliaceae

PERENNIALS FROM BULBS

✿ ZONES VARY BY SPECIES; OR GROW IN POTS

◐ ◑ SOME SHADE IN HOTTEST CLIMATES

◗ ◖ REGULAR TO AMPLE WATER

◊ ALL PARTS ARE POISONOUS IF INGESTED

Crinum ×powellii

Among the South's most classic and cherished passalong plants, crinums combine bold, fragrant flowers, imposing foliage, and a bulldog constitution. Seldom seen in newer suburbs, they are now found largely in country gardens, at old home sites, and in cemeteries, where they thrive with little care. Indeed, they tolerate adversity so well that some say no crinum has ever died.

Native to many warm and tropical parts of the world; evergreen in the Tropical South, deciduous elsewhere. Each bulb tapers to an elongated, stemlike neck, from which radiate handsome long, broad, straplike leaves. Rising from the foliage mass are thick stems to 4 ft. or taller, each bearing a cluster of long-stalked, lilylike flowers in white, pink, rose red, or reddish purple. Most are 4–6 in. long; many are highly fragrant. Depending on the type, crinums may flower from spring through late summer; in the Tropical South, some bloom year-round. Can be brought indoors in winter.

Crinum bulbs are hard to find at most garden centers, so specialty and mail-order nurseries may be your best bet. You can also dig and divide bulbs from a friend's garden, but be warned—old, established bulbs are huge, weighing up to 40 pounds. Plant in fall or early spring in fertile, well-drained soil that contains plenty of organic matter. Set bulbs 2–4 ft. apart, with tops of necks even with soil surface. Divide infrequently, as established bulbs resent disturbance and may not bloom the first year after replanting. In the Upper and Middle South, plant in sheltered, sunny sites and mulch heavily in late fall.

C. americanum. SOUTHERN SWAMP CRINUM. Zones LS, CS, TS; 12–8. Native to water edges and swamps in the southeastern U.S. and on the Gulf Coast. Fragrant white flowers on 2-ft. stems appear from spring to late fall. Takes deep shade. Spreads by stolons and likes wet soil.

C. asiaticum. GRAND CRINUM, ST. JOHN'S LILY. Zones CS, TS; 12–8. From Southeast Asia. Large (6- to 8-in.-wide), fragrant, spidery-looking white flowers in clusters of up to 50. 'Purple Leaf' has purplish foliage (color is more vivid when plant is grown in sun). Grows 4–6 ft. tall.

C. bulbispermum (C. longifolium). HARDY CRINUM. Zones US, MS, LS, CS, TS; 12–8. Native to South Africa. Deep pink, fragrant flowers. Long, narrow, twisting gray-green leaves tend to lie on the ground. 'Album' has white flowers; 'Rubrum' has red blooms.

C. erubescens. Zones LS, CS, TS; 11–7. From South America. To 3 ft. high. Broad, shiny green leaves form a clump that spreads by rhizomes. Makes a large colony in moist soil. Reddish stems bear fragrant, spidery-looking white flowers from midsummer until frost.

C. hybrids. Zones LS, CS, TS, except as noted. Those listed below are some of the many fine choices available.

'Bradley'. Zones MS, LS, CS, TS; 10–7. To 2–3 ft. high. Hybrid of Australian origin. Narrow, arching, glossy green leaves. Very fragrant, waxy, open-faced flowers of deep rosy pink with white centers bloom in summer.

'Carnival'. Zones MS, LS, CS, TS; 12–7. Cold-hardy selection with stems to 2½ ft. tall. Flowers in shades of pink and red are marked with white streaks.

'Ellen Bosanquet'. Heat zones 12–8. Broad bright green leaves. Fragrant flowers are deep rose, nearly red. An all-time favorite.

Crinum 'Bradley'

'Emma Jones'. Heat zones 12–8. Taller than the usual, with large, fragrant, ruffled pink flowers. Continuous bloom.

▶

'Hannibal's Dwarf'. Zones MS, LS, CS, TS; 11–7. To 1½ ft. high, with strap-shaped, shiny green leaves. Fragrant deep pink flowers bloom in midsummer, rebloom in early fall. Multiplies quickly to form attractive clumps.

'J.C. Harvey'. Heat zones 11–7. To 2½ ft. tall. Shiny, ribbed green leaves. Blooms in summer, bearing reddish pink buds that open to clear pink, headily fragrant flowers with wide-spreading petals. Each flower stalk bears about six blossoms. Spreads rapidly.

'Milk and Wine'. Heat zones 12–8. Creamy white, fragrant flowers with pink stripes; continuous bloom. "Milk and wine" is also a common name for several similar-looking selections and for *C. scabrum.*

'Mrs. James Hendry'. Zones MS, LS, CS, TS; 12–7. To 2 ft. high, with rigidly upright, shiny green leaves. Very fragrant white blossoms blushed with pinkish lavender appear in early summer.

'Peach Blow'. Heat zones 12–7. Long leaves; pale lavender, spicily fragrant flowers with recurving petals. The classic crinum of the Old South.

'Royal White'. Heat zones 12–8. Narrow, semierect leaves. Very large, fragrant white flowers with rose pink stripes.

'Walter Flory'. Heat zones 10–7. To 4 ft. tall. Lush green foliage. Rich pink, fragrant flowers with a lengthwise burgundy stripe down center of each petal.

C. moorei. LONGNECK CRINUM. Zones MS, LS, CS, TS; 12–7. From South Africa. Large (6- to 8-in.-wide) bulbs with stemlike neck to 1 ft. long or more. Long, thin, wavy-edged bright green leaves. Pinkish red, fragrant, bell-shaped blossoms. Cold hardy.

C. ×powellii. Zones US, MS, LS, CS, TS; 12–7. Resembles its parent *C. moorei* but has fragrant dark rose flowers. 'Album' is a good pure white form, vigorous enough to serve as a tall ground cover in shade. 'Cecil Houdyshel' (Zones MS, LS, CS, TS) has long, tapering leaves and deep rose red blossoms.

C. scabrum (C. zeylanicum). MILK-AND-WINE LILY, CREOLE LILY. Zones LS, CS, TS; 10–8. From tropical Africa. Usually low-growing but may reach 6 ft. tall under ideal conditions. Sweetly fragrant, 3-in., spidery-looking flowers in pure white with a red stripe lengthwise down middle of each petal. Blooms in midsummer, with some rebloom in early fall.

BLOOMS OF MILK AND WINE. *Many folks refer to crinums as milk-and-wine lilies, because numerous forms bear white blossoms with pink, rose, or red stripes. But crinums with solid white, pink, rose, or red flowers are popular, too. According to Texas horticulturist William Welch, crinums were among the earliest ornamental plants to be extensively hybridized. By 1837, nearly 30 hybrids had already been recorded.* ❖

CROCOSMIA

Iridaceae

PERENNIALS FROM CORMS

🗡 US, MS, LS, CS ◧ 9–2

☼ ◑ SOME SHADE IN COASTAL SOUTH

◗ REGULAR WATER DURING GROWTH AND BLOOM

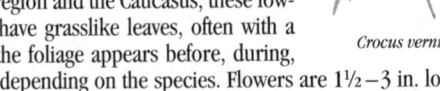

Native to tropical and southern Africa. Formerly called tritonia; related to freesia. Sword-shaped leaves grow in basal clumps; small orange, red, or yellow flowers bloom in summer. Useful for splashes of garden color; good cut flowers. Plant in well-drained, enriched soil, setting corms 2 in. deep, 3 in. apart.

Crocosmia crocosmiiflora

C. crocosmiiflora (Tritonia crocosmiiflora). MONTBRETIA. A favorite for generations, montbretias can still be seen in older gardens, where they have spread freely, bearing orange-crimson, 1½- to 2-in. blossoms on stems 3–4 ft. tall. Leaves are 3 ft. long. Many once-common named forms are making a comeback; colors include yellow, orange, cream, and near-scarlet. Good for naturalizing on slopes or in fringe areas.

C. hybrids. Sturdy plants with branching spikes of showy flowers.

'Bressingham Beacon'. To 3 ft. tall. Brilliant orange buds open to orange-and-yellow flowers. Purple stems.

'Citronella'. To 2 ft. high. Light yellow flowers with a dark eye.

'Emberglow'. To 2½ ft. high. Burnt orange-red flowers with yellow throat.

'Emily McKenzie'. Grows to 2 ft. tall. Orange with red eye.

'Jenny Bloom'. To 2–3 ft. tall. Golden yellow flowers.

'Lucifer'. To 4 ft. tall. Popular selection with bright red blossoms.

'Solfatare'. To 2 ft. tall, with yellow flowers and unusual bronze foliage.

'Star of the East'. To 2½ ft. high. Spreads slowly. Clear orange blooms with burgundy markings and a lighter orange center.

'Venus'. To 2 ft. high. Peachy yellow flowers with maroon-blotched throats. Purple stems.

C. masoniorum. Leaves grow to 2½ ft. long; flaming orange, 1½-in.-wide flowers in dense, one-sided clusters on 2½- to 3-ft. stems. Buds open slowly from base to tip of clusters; old flowers drop cleanly from stems. Cut flowers last about 2 weeks.

Crocosmia masoniorum

CROCUS

Iridaceae

CORMS

🗡 US, MS, LS ◧ 8–1

☼ ◑ FULL SUN OR PARTIAL SHADE

◗ REGULAR WATER DURING GROWTH AND BLOOM

For many gardeners, the appearance of crocuses signals the end of winter. Native to the Mediterranean region and the Caucasus, these low-growing plants have grasslike leaves, often with a silvery midrib; the foliage appears before, during, or after bloom, depending on the species. Flowers are 1½–3 in. long, with flaring or cup-shaped petals; they're available in a wide range of colors.

Crocus vernus

Most crocus bloom in late winter or earliest spring, but some bloom in fall, the flowers rising from bare earth weeks or days after planting. Mass them for best effect. Lovely in rock gardens, between stepping-stones, in containers. Set corms 2–3 in. deep and 3–4 in. apart in light, porous soil. Divide every 3 to 4 years. Don't bother planting crocus if your garden has chipmunks—these rodents will dig up and eat every one. Better in Upper and Middle South. Won't naturalize where winters are warm.

C. ancyrensis. Small golden yellow flowers. Blooms very early.

C. angustifolius (C. susianus). CLOTH OF GOLD CROCUS. Orange-gold, starlike flowers with dark brown center stripe. Starts blooming in January in warmest areas, in March in coldest areas.

C. chrysanthus. Orange yellow, sweet scented. Hybrids and selections range from white through yellow to blue, often marked with deeper color. Spring bloom. 'Blue Pearl' is palest blue; 'Cream Beauty', pale yellow; 'E. P. Bowles', yellow with purple markings; 'Ladykiller', outside purple edged white, inside white feathered purple; 'Princess Beatrix', blue with yellow center; and 'Snow Bunting', pure white.

C. imperati. Bright lilac inside, buff veined purple outside. Early spring.

C. kotschyanus (C. zonatus). Pinkish lavender or lilac flowers in early fall.

C. sativus. SAFFRON CROCUS. Lilac flowers appear in autumn; the orange-red stigma is true saffron. To harvest, pluck stigmas as soon as flowers open, dry them, and store them in vials. Stigmas from a dozen blooms will season a good-size paella or similar dish. To continue good yields of saffron, divide corms as soon as leaves turn brown; replant in fresh or improved soil. Mark planting site so you won't dig up dormant corms.

C. sieberi. Delicate lavender-blue flowers with golden throat. One of the earliest bloomers, with flowers appearing in January and February.

C. speciosus. AUTUMN CROCUS. Showy blue-violet flowers in early fall. Lavender and mauve selections available. Fast increase by seed and division. Showiest autumn-flowering crocus.

C. tommasinianus. Slender buds; star-shaped, silvery lavender-blue flowers, sometimes with dark blotch at tips of petals. Very early—January or February in milder areas.

C. vernus. DUTCH CROCUS. Most vigorous crocus, with blooms in shades of white, yellow, lavender, purple; flowers are often penciled or streaked. Blooms in February and March.

CROTON. See CODIAEUM variegatum pictum

CROWN IMPERIAL. See FRITILLARIA imperialis

CROWN OF GOLD TREE. See CASSIA excelsa

CROWN OF THORNS. See EUPHORBIA milii

CROWN VETCH. See CORONILLA varia

Cruciferae. See Brassicaceae

CRYPTANTHUS zonatus

EARTH STAR

Bromeliaceae

PERENNIAL

✿ TS ╫ 12–10; OR HOUSEPLANT

☽ ● SOME SHADE; BRIGHT INDIRECT LIGHT

● MODERATE WATER

Cryptanthus zonatus

Native to Brazil. Bromeliad grown for showy leaves in spreading, low-growing clusters to 1½ ft. wide, usually less. Leaves are wavy, dark brownish red, banded crosswise with green, brown, or white. Unimportant little white flowers grow among leaves. Pot in equal parts coarse sand, shredded osmunda, and ground bark or peat moss. Makes a fine houseplant; ideal in dish gardens.

C. bivittatus is similar to *C. zonatus* in cultural needs and general appearance, but it has green leaves striped lengthwise in creamy white. Many other striped and banded species and hybrids are available from specialists.

CRYPTOMERIA japonica

JAPANESE CRYPTOMERIA

Taxodiaceae

EVERGREEN TREE

✿ US, MS, LS ╫ 9–4

☽ ☾ FULL SUN OR LIGHT SHADE

◐ ● MODERATE TO REGULAR WATER

Graceful conifer, fast growing (3–4 ft. a year) in youth. Eventually skyline tree to 100 ft. tall, 30 ft. wide at base, with straight, columnar trunk, thin red-brown bark peeling in strips. Slightly pendulous branches are clothed with needlelike leaves ½–1 in. long; foliage is soft bright green to bluish green during the grow-

Cryptomeria japonica

ing season, brownish purple in cold weather. Roundish, red-brown cones ¾–1 in. wide. Trees are sometimes planted in groves for Japanese garden effect; they also make a good tall screen. Not browsed by deer.

'Benjamin Franklin'. Foliage stays green even with exposure to cold or wind. Salt tolerant.

'Black Dragon'. New spring growth is light green; mature foliage is blackish green. Grows only about 5 ft. high and 7 ft. wide in 10 years.

'Elegans'. PLUME CEDAR, PLUME CRYPTOMERIA. Quite unlike species. Feathery, grayish green, soft-textured foliage turns rich coppery red or purplish in winter. Grows slowly into dense pyramid to 20–60 ft. tall, about 20 ft. wide. Trunks on old trees may lean or curve. For effective display, give it space.

'Lobbii Nana' ('Lobbii'). Dwarf selection with very slow, upright growth to 4 ft. high and wide. Dark green foliage.

'Pygmaea' ('Nana'). DWARF CRYPTOMERIA. Bushy dwarf 1½–2 ft. high, 2½ ft. wide. Dark green leaves, twisted branches.

'Vilmoriniana'. Slow-growing dwarf to 1–2 ft. high and wide. Fluffy gray-green foliage turns bronze in late fall and winter. Rock garden or container plant.

'Yoshino'. Resembles the species but is smaller (to 30–40 ft. tall and 20 ft. wide), with bluish green foliage that takes on reddish tones in winter.

CUCUMBER

Cucurbitaceae

ANNUAL VINE

✿ US, MS, LS, CS, TS ╫ 12–2

☽ FULL SUN

● REGULAR WATER

Cucumber

For crisp texture and cool flavor, a freshly harvested homegrown cucumber beats the waxy-coated ones found at the grocery hands down. And it doesn't take many plants to keep a family supplied for most of summer.

Cucumbers won't take cold, so plant them at least 2 weeks after the last frost or when the soil and weather are warm. Plant again in midsummer to extend the harvest into fall. Each vigorous, sprawling vine can cover up to 25 sq. ft.; to save space, grow on a trellis or inside wire cages. Sow seeds at base of support, planting them ½–1 in. deep and 4–6 in. apart. Thin seedlings to 8–12 in. apart. If you prefer to let vines ramble over the ground, sow seeds in small hills spaced 4 ft. apart; sow four to six seeds per hill and thin to the strongest two or three seedlings.

Before planting, work into the soil ½ cup of 10-10-10 fertilizer per 10 ft. of row (or ¼ cup per hill). One week after bloom begins, sprinkle area around plants with this same amount and water in. Repeat 3 weeks later. Don't get discouraged if flowers don't immediately produce young cucumbers: vines bear both male and female flowers, and the male flowers, which don't produce fruit, tend to appear first. Be patient—fruiting female flowers will soon appear. Harvest cucumbers when young and tender. Don't leave any to mature on the vine or the plant will stop producing.

Floating row covers will protect young plants from various pests, including cucumber beetles and flea beetles; remove covers when flowering occurs so that bees can pollinate the flowers. Whiteflies are a potential pest late in the season; hose off plants regularly or hang yellow sticky traps. Misshapen fruit is usually due to uneven watering or poor pollination. Bitter flavor (a common problem) results from stress brought on by drought, inconsistent watering, and excessive heat.

If you don't have the room that regular cucumber vines demand, plant smaller bush types that grow short vines, such as 'Spacemaster' (60 days from sowing to harvest) and 'Salad Bush' (57 days). For mild-flavored, "burpless" cucumbers, try 'Sweet Slice' (62 days) or 'Sweet Success' (54 days, doesn't need pollination). Good slicing cucumbers include 'Ashley' (66 days), 'Fanfare' (63 days), 'General Lee' (66 days), and 'Poinsett' (67 days). For pickles, try 'Bush Pickle' (45 days, short vines), 'County Fair' (48 days), and 'Homemade Pickles' (55 days).

CUCUMBER TREE. See MAGNOLIA acuminata

Cucurbitaceae. The gourd family as seen in Southern gardens consists of annual vines with yellow or white flowers and large, fleshy, seedy fruits—cucumbers, gourds, melons, pumpkins, and squash.

CUNNINGHAMIA lanceolata

CHINA FIR

Taxodiaceae

EVERGREEN TREE

✻ MS, LS, CS ⬛ 9–7

☼ FULL SUN

💧 REGULAR WATER

Native to China. Picturesque conifer with heavy trunk, stout, whorled branches, and drooping branchlets. Stiff, needlelike, sharp-pointed leaves are 1½–2½ in. long, green above, whitish beneath. Brown, 1- to 2-in. cones are interesting but not profuse. Grows at moderate rate to 30 ft. tall with 20-ft. spread. Becomes less attractive as it ages. Prune out dead branchlets. Among palest of needled evergreens in spring and summer; turns red bronze in cold winters. Protect from wind. 'Glauca', which has striking blue-gray foliage, is more widely grown and hardier than the species.

Cunninghamia lanceolata

CUP-AND-SAUCER VINE. See COBAEA scandens

CUP FLOWER. See NIEREMBERGIA

CUPHEA

Lythraceae

EVERGREEN SHRUBS OR WOODY PERENNIALS

✻ CS, TS; ANNUALS ANYWHERE; ⬛ 12–1

☼ ◐ FULL SUN OR PARTIAL SHADE

💧 REGULAR WATER

These natives of Mexico and Central America provide color throughout warm months; use them in small beds, as formal edging for borders, along paths, in containers. Flowers attract hummingbirds. Pinch tips of shoots for compact growth; severely cut back older plants in late fall or early spring. Reliably perennial only in frost-free areas, but may survive light frosts in Coastal South. Easy to grow from cuttings.

Cuphea ignea

C. cyanea. VIOLET CUPHEA. Can reach 6 ft. in its native Mexico, but usually half that tall and wide in home gardens; as an annual, it grows 1–1½ ft. high. Medium to dark green, ovate leaves 2–3 in. long. Each tubular, ¾- to 1¼-in.-long flower is bright pink with a yellow tip and two earlike violet-blue petals.

C. hyssopifolia. HAWAIIAN HEATHER, MEXICAN HEATHER. To 1–2 ft. tall, about 2½ ft. wide. Flexible, leafy branchlets clothed in very narrow, ½- to ¾-in.-long, medium to dark green leaves. Tiny flowers (scarcely half as long as leaves) in pink, purple, or white. 'Itsy Bitsy White' and 'Itsy Bitsy Lilac', both 8 in. high and 1½ ft. wide, are excellent rock garden plants that produce masses of flowers in white and lilac, respectively.

C. ignea. CIGAR PLANT. Leafy, compact plant to 1 ft. or taller, as wide as tall. Narrow dark green leaves, 1–1½ in. long. The flowers explain the "cigar" of the common name: they're tubular, ¾ in. long, bright orange red with white tip and dark ring at end. Flowers of 'Lutea' are a very soft yellow; those of 'Petite Peach' are a light peach.

C. llavea. BAT-FACED CUPHEA. To 2–3 ft. tall, 3 ft. wide. Medium green leaves to 3 in. long. Red-and-purple, 1½-in.-long flowers are said to look like a bat's face. Occasionally spreads by seed in gardens. Though cultivated in the desert, it is not drought tolerant—in nature, it grows along stream banks in Mexico.

C. micropetala. To 4 ft. tall, 3–4 ft. wide. Arching stems, each closely set with narrow, 5-in., medium green leaves and topped by a slender, spikelike cluster of 1½-in., bright red flowers tipped with yellow. Deciduous in cold weather.

C. ×purpurea. Hybrid to 1–1½ ft. high and wide, good for ground covers and hanging baskets. Red flowers to 1¼ in. long; dark green leaves to 3 in. long. 'Firecracker', bearing dark purple flowers with two earlike bright red petals, thrives in Southern heat and humidity.

CUPID'S DART. See CATANANCHE caerulea

CUP-OF-GOLD VINE. See SOLANDRA maxima

Cupressaceae. The cypress family differs from the pine and yew families (Pinaceae, Taxaceae) in having leaves that are usually reduced to scales and in having cones with few scales. Cones may even be berrylike, as in juniper (*Juniperus*).

×CUPRESSOCYPARIS leylandii

LEYLAND CYPRESS

Cupressaceae

EVERGREEN TREE

✻ US, MS, LS, CS ⬛ 9–3

☼ FULL SUN

💧 MODERATE TO REGULAR WATER

×Cupressocyparis leylandii

Hybrid of *Chamaecyparis nootkatensis* and *Cupressus macrocarpa*. Grows very fast (from cuttings to 15–20 ft. in 5 years). Usually reaches 60–70 ft. tall and 8–15 ft. wide in gardens. Most often planted as a quick screen; becoming quite popular as a cut Christmas tree in Lower and Coastal South. Long, slender, upright branches of flattened gray-green foliage sprays give youthful tree a narrow pyramidal form, though it can become open and floppy. Can be pruned into tall (10- to 15-ft.) hedge but will quickly get away from you without regular maintenance. Produces small cones composed of scales. Accepts a wide variety of soil and climate conditions; takes strong wind. In Coastal South, loses stiff, upright habit and is subject to coryneum canker fungus. Bagworms are a potential problem. Popular selections include 'Castlewellan', with golden new growth and narrow, erect habit; 'Emerald Isle', with bright green foliage on plant 20–25 ft. tall and 6–8 ft. wide; and 'Naylor's Blue', bearing grayish blue foliage.

CUPRESSUS

CYPRESS

Cupressaceae

EVERGREEN TREES

✻ ZONES VARY BY SPECIES

☼ FULL SUN

💧 LITTLE TO MODERATE WATER

These conifers have tiny, scalelike leaves, closely set on cordlike branches, and interesting globular, golf ball–size cones made up of shield-shaped scales. For the dry Southwest, choose *C. arizonica* or *C. sempervirens;* these species and their selections thrive in dry, rocky, alkaline soil. In high-rainfall areas, however, they are short lived; *C. lusitanica* is the better choice there. Cypresses are not browsed by deer.

Cupressus arizonica

C. arizonica. ARIZONA CYPRESS. Zones MS, LS, CS; 9–7. To 40 ft. tall, spreading to 20 ft. wide; rough, furrowed bark. Seedlings are variable, with foliage varying from green to blue gray or silvery. *C. a. glabra* (often sold as *C. glabra*) is like the species but has smooth cherry red bark. Other forms include 'Blue Pyramid', a dense blue-gray pyramid to 20–25 ft. tall; 'Carolina Sapphire', to 30 ft., with steely blue-green foliage and broad, symmetrical

C

form; 'Gareei', with silvery blue-green foliage; and 'Pyramidalis', a compact, symmetrical grower. Mass trees for windbreak or screen.

C. lusitanica. MEXICAN CYPRESS. Zones LS, CS; 10–8. Native to northern Florida and Central America. Grows rapidly to 50 ft. tall, 15 ft. wide, with symmetrical, spreading, pendulous branches and beautiful, ferny blue-green foliage. Use as specimen tree or windbreak. Choose plants grown from cuttings of selected blue clones; these are more uniform and bluer in color than plants grown from seed. Likes fertile, well-drained soil.

C. sempervirens. ITALIAN CYPRESS. Zones MS, LS, CS; 9–3. Native to southern Europe, western Asia. Species has horizontal branches and dark green foliage, but variants are more often sold. 'Stricta' ('Fastigiata'), columnar Italian cypress, and 'Glauca', blue Italian cypress (really blue green in color), are classic Mediterranean landscape plants; both are dense, narrow trees to 60 ft. high, 5–10 ft. wide at maturity. 'Swane's Golden', another columnar form, has golden yellow new growth. 'Tiny Tower' is a slow, dense grower that reaches only 8 ft. tall, 2 ft. wide after 10 years.

Cupressus sempervirens
'Stricta'

CURCUMA

Zingiberaceae

PERENNIALS FROM RHIZOMES

 LS, CS, TS H 12–8, EXCEPT AS NOTED

LIGHT SHADE OR MORNING SUN, EXCEPT AS NOTED

REGULAR WATER, EXCEPT AS NOTED

Curcuma alismatifolia

Native to tropical Asia, this group of highly ornamental gingers has both handsome foliage and colorful flowers. Leaves of most are broadly lance shaped, deep green, and attractively pleated. Bloom typically comes in summer, when small blossoms are borne in spikes of colorful bracts; the flower spikes may be hidden beneath the leaves or tower above them.

Most are hardy only in the Coastal and Tropical South, though *C. elata, C. longa* 'Bright White', *C. petiolata*, and *C. rubescens* 'Scarlet Fever' will winter over in the Lower South. They make excellent additions to mixed borders. Plant in spring, setting rhizomes 1 in. deep in moist, well-drained, humus-rich soil. Plants die down in winter and need very little water during dormancy.

C. alismatifolia. SIAM TULIP. Heat zones 10–8. Grows 2 ft. tall, with foliage like small canna leaves. At bloom time (early summer to early fall), flowering stems are topped by clusters of pink, rose, or white bracts that hide tiny flowers; the inflorescence is shaped a bit like a flaring pinecone. Plant 6 in. apart for lush cover. Each blossom spike lasts for several weeks, then is replaced by others as new plants arise from the rhizome. Spectacular as a bedding plant.

C. elata. GIANT PLUME. The tallest species, growing to 6–7 ft. tall and wide. Among the first gingers to bloom in spring, with large (1- to 2-ft.-long) inflorescences appearing before the leaves. Bracts are greenish near the bottom of the spike, bright pink at the top; yellow flowers bloom along its length. Dramatic cut flower. Performs well in full sun or partial shade.

C. gracillima. Notable for selections with colorful, 4-in.-long inflorescences borne above the foliage. 'Burnt Burgundy' has burgundy-colored flower spikes with darker, burnt-looking streaks on the bracts. 'Candy Cane', sensational in mass plantings, has bracts striped in red and creamy white. Both selections grow to 1½–2 ft. tall, 2 ft. wide.

C. longa 'Bright White' (C. domestica 'Bright White'). To 4 ft. tall, 3 ft. wide. Glowing white inflorescence makes an excellent cut flower. The basic species, which bears creamy white flower spikes, is the source of the spice turmeric. Full sun or partial shade.

C. petiolata. HIDDEN LILY, QUEEN LILY. Grows 2–3 ft. high and almost as wide, with very handsome, tropical-looking, 10-in.-long, sheathlike leaves. Rosy purple, 6- to 8-in. bracts are largely hidden by the leaves,

which are thin and may burn in hot afternoon sun and tear in strong winds. Cut back to ground in winter; new foliage will sprout from tuberous roots in spring. In the selection 'Emperor' (to 2 ft. tall and wide), the foliage—gray-green leaves edged in creamy white—is the main attraction; the 6-in. flower spikes are white suffused with shades of pale purple.

C. roscoeana. To 3 ft. high and wide. The 8-in.-long inflorescence consists of orange bracts and bright yellow flowers; good for cutting. One of the latest to bloom, at summer's end and in fall.

C. rubescens 'Scarlet Fever'. To 4–6 ft. high, 4 ft. wide. Blood red stems bear gray-green leaves with a prominent red midrib. Spectacular plant even without the foot-long flowering spikes, which resemble those of *C. elata.* Does well in full sun or partial shade.

C. zedoaria. To 3 ft. high and wide. Dark green leaves have a maroon stripe down the center. Large inflorescence (to 1 ft. long) has bright red bracts and yellow flowers.

CYATHEA cooperi

AUSTRALIAN TREE FERN

Cyatheaceae

TREE FERN

TS H 12–10; OR GROW IN POT

PARTIAL SHADE; BRIGHT LIGHT

REGULAR WATER

Fastest growing of the fairly hardy tree ferns (to 27°F, but with damage to fronds). To an eventual 20 ft. tall, 12 ft. wide. Starts out as a low, wide clump (can spread from 1 ft. to as much as 6 ft. in a year) before growing upward. Broad, bright green, finely cut fronds. Brownish hairs on leafstalks and leaf undersurfaces can irritate skin; wear long sleeves, hat, and neckcloth when grooming plants. Often sold as *Alsophila australis, A. cooperi,* or *Sphaeropteris cooperi.*

Wet down the fronds and trunk on dry days in summer and autumn. Every spring, cover the base with a few inches of organic fertilizer, such as garden compost or aged cow manure. Prune off old fronds—but not until new ones emerge. Where plant is not hardy, grow in large container and bring indoors to your brightest window for winter. Mist fronds and trunk daily; never let soil dry out. Don't feed with liquid fertilizer; instead, feed monthly with a balanced, controlled-release fertilizer, such as 14-14-14.

Cyathea cooperi

Cycadaceae. *Cycas* is the sole genus in this family; closely related plants in the family Zamiaceae are *Ceratozamia, Dioon,* and *Zamia.* Collectively, these plants (all in the order Cycadales) are known as cycads, though the general public may consider them to be types of palms. They are slow-growing evergreen plants with large, firm, palmlike or fernlike leaves and conelike fruit. Most are native to tropical regions, but some are subtropical—and among these, certain ones are hardy enough to grow outdoors in mild-winter climates.

CYCAS

Cycadaceae

CYCADS

ZONES VARY BY SPECIES

PARTIAL SHADE

MODERATE TO REGULAR WATER

Neither ferns nor palms, these evergreen plants are primitive, cone-bearing relatives of conifers, excellent for tropical effects. A rosette of dark green, feathery leaves grows from a central point at the top of a single trunk (sometimes several trunks). Eventually as wide as tall. Female plants bear conspicuous, egg-shaped, red to orange seeds. Plants can be propagated (best done in spring) either from seed or by separating offsets that sprout near the base. ▶

Cycas revoluta

C

C. circinalis. QUEEN SAGO. Zones TS; 12–6. Native to Old World tropics. Beautiful specimen plant to 20 ft. tall, 10–20 ft. wide. Graceful, drooping leaves to 8 ft. long atop unbranching trunk. Protect from frost.

C. revoluta. SAGO PALM. Zones CS (protected), TS; 12–6; or indoors. Hardy to 15°F. Native to Japan. In youth, reaches 2–3 ft. tall and wide and has an airy, lacy, fernlike appearance; with age (grows very slowly to 10 ft.), looks more like a palm. Leaves are 2–3 ft. long (larger on very old plants) and divided into many narrow, leathery segments. Tough, tolerant patio plant; good in foundation or entry planting. Leaf spot disease is a problem in high-rainfall areas. Makes an outstanding houseplant in bright indirect light. Needs only occasional watering (less in winter) and takes many years to outgrow its container.

CYCLAMEN

Primulaceae

PERENNIALS FROM TUBERS

⚘ ZONES VARY BY SPECIES

☼ ◖ FULL SUN OR PARTIAL SHADE

◗ REGULAR WATER

Cyclamen persicum

Native to Europe, Mediterranean region, Asia. Grown for their pretty flowers carried atop attractive clump of roundish to heart-shaped basal leaves that are reddish beneath and often patterned with silver above. Blossoms, 1–3 in. long, resemble shooting stars or butterflies and typically come in white and shades of pink, rose, or red. Most types go through a near-leafless or leafless dormant period at some time during summer.

Large-flowered florists' cyclamen (*C. persicum*) is most often seen as a container-grown gift plant. The other species described here are smaller-flowered, hardier plants better adapted to outdoor culture. Use them in rock gardens, in naturalized clumps under trees, or as carpets under camellias, rhododendrons, and large noninvasive ferns; hardy types also grow well under native oaks. All are good container plants if grown out of direct sun.

All cyclamens grow best in fairly rich, porous soil. Loosen soil to a depth of 1 ft. and mix in coarse sand and lots of organic matter. If soil is acid, also work in some lime, as cyclamens prefer a neutral to slightly alkaline pH. Plant tubers of most types 6–10 in. apart, ½ in. deep. (Florists' cyclamen is an exception: upper half of tuber should protrude above soil level.) Best planting time for tubers is dormant period in summer—except for florists' cyclamen, which is always sold as a potted plant and can be planted out at any time. Top-dress annually with light application of potting soil with complete fertilizer added (being careful not to cover top of florists' cyclamen tubers). Do not cultivate around roots.

Plants grow readily from seed. Small-flowered hardy species take several years to bloom; older strains of florists' cyclamen need 15 to 18 months to mature and bloom from seed, while newer strains can bloom in as little as 7 months. Grown outdoors in open ground, plants often self-sow. To encourage this, mulch around plants with a thin layer of fine gravel. This provides niches where seeds can lodge—and has the added benefit of improving drainage.

When buying any species cyclamen other than *C. persicum,* always check to ascertain that the tubers are commercially grown and not taken from the wild. Look for labels that mention "Holland" or "cultivated."

C. ×atkinsii. Zones US, MS; 9–3. Crimson flowers on 4- to 6-in. stems in winter. Deep green, silver-mottled leaves to 2½ in. across. Selections with pink or white blooms are also sold.

C. cilicium. Zones US, MS; 9–3. Fragrant pale pink flowers with purple blotches on 2- to 6-in. stems, fall into winter. Leaves are ½–2½ in. across, heavily mottled with silver. 'Album' has white blossoms.

C. coum. Zones US, MS, LS; 9–5. Deep crimson rose flowers on 4- to 6-in. stems in winter and early spring. Round deep green leaves reach 1–2½ in. across. Selections with pink or white flowers are available.

C. hederifolium (C. neapolitanum). Zones US, MS, LS; 9–7. Light green, 2- to 6-in. leaves marbled silver and white. Rose pink flowers bloom on 3- to 4-in. stems in late summer, early fall. One of the most vigorous and easiest to grow; very reliable in cold-winter climates. Set tubers a foot apart. A white-flowered selection is available.

C. persicum. FLORISTS' CYCLAMEN. Heat zones 6–1. Mainly grown indoors. Original species has 2-in., fragrant, deep to pale pink or white blooms borne on 6-in. stems. Selective breeding has resulted in large-flowered florists' cyclamen (the old favorites) and newer, smaller strains; with rare exceptions, fragrance has disappeared. Plants typically have heart- or kidney-shaped dark green leaves in the 1- to 5½-in. range, most often with silvery mottling. They bear crimson, red, salmon, purple, pink, or white flowers on 6- to 8-in. stems from late fall to spring. Potted plants can be kept from year to year by withholding water at end of blooming period. Let plants go dormant in summer. Repot in late summer, resume watering, and place in bright light. Make sure top half of tuber is above soil surface.

Dwarf or miniature florists' cyclamens are half- or three-quarter–size replicas of standards. They can bloom in 7 to 8 months from seed. Miniature strains (profuse show of 1½-in. flowers on 6- to 8-in. plants) include Miracle and Laser, both with fragrant blossoms.

C. purpurascens (C. europaeum). Zones US, MS, LS. Distinctly fragrant crimson flowers on 5- to 6-in. stems, late summer or early fall. Nearly evergreen leaves are 3 in. wide, bright green mottled silvery white.

C. repandum. Zones US, MS; 9–7. Bright crimson flowers with long, narrow petals on 5- to 6-in. stems in spring. Tooth-edged, ivy-shaped leaves to 5 in. long are rich green marbled silver.

CYDONIA. See CHAENOMELES

CYDONIA oblonga. See QUINCE

CYMBIDIUM

Orchidaceae

TERRESTRIAL ORCHIDS

⚘ US, MS, LS, CS, TS—SUBJECT TO CONDITIONS BELOW; ☒ 10–8

◖ PARTIAL SHADE

◗ REGULAR WATER

Miniature Cymbidium

Native to high altitudes in Southeast Asia, where rainfall is heavy and nights cool. Very popular because of their relatively easy culture. Except in frost-free areas, grow plants in containers in greenhouse or sunroom, or under overhang or high-branching tree. Long, narrow, grasslike leaves form a sheath around short, stout, oval pseudobulbs. Long-lasting flowers grow on erect or arching spikes, make excellent cut flowers. Standard types usually bloom from February to early May. Bloom season for miniatures starts in September and is usually heaviest from November to January.

For best bloom, give as much light as possible without burning foliage. Plants do well under shade cloth or lath. Leaf color is the guide: plants with yellow-green leaves generally flower best; dark green foliage means too much shade. Cymbidiums should have shade during the flowering period, though; it prolongs bloom life and keeps flowers from fading.

Plants prefer 45–55°F night temperature, rising to as high as 80–90°F during day. They'll stand temperatures as low as 28°F for a short time only, so where there is any danger of harder frosts, take plants inside or protect them with a covering of polyethylene film. Flower spikes are more tender than other plant tissues.

Keep potting medium moist as new growth develops and matures—usually March to September. In winter, water just enough to keep bulbs from shriveling. On hot summer days, mist foliage early in day.

Feed every 10 days to 2 weeks. From January to July, use a complete liquid fertilizer high in nitrogen, such as 30-10-10; from August to December, use a bloom-booster, lower-nitrogen fertilizer, such as 10-30-10.

Transplant potted plants when bulbs fill pots. When dividing plants, keep a minimum of three healthy bulbs (with foliage) in each division. Dust cuts with sulfur or charcoal to discourage rot.

Cymbidium growers typically list only hybrids in their catalogs—large-flowered selections with white, pink, yellow, green, or bronze blooms. Most have a yellow throat and dark red markings on lip. Large-flowered forms produce a dozen or more 4½- to 5-in. flowers per stem. Plants reach 2–3 ft. high. Miniature selections, about a quarter the size of large-flowered forms, are popular for their smaller size and free-blooming qualities.

SOIL MIX FOR CYMBIDIUMS. *If the store where you buy your cymbidiums doesn't offer a packaged cymbidium soil mix, here's a good one you can make: 2 parts composted bark, 2 parts peat moss, 1 part builder's sand. Packaged or homemade, the medium should drain quickly but still retain moisture.* ❖

CYMBOPOGON citratus

LEMON GRASS

Poaceae (Gramineae)

TENDER PERENNIAL

✂ TS; ANNUAL ANYWHERE; H 12–1

☼ FULL SUN

💧 REGULAR WATER

Cymbopogon citratus

From India. All plant parts are strongly lemon scented and are widely used as an ingredient in Southeast Asian cooking. Clumps of inch-wide leaves grow 3–4 ft. tall (or more) and 3 ft. wide. Base of clump, composed of overlapping leaf bases, is nearly bulbous in appearance. Lemon grass is occasionally grown in gardens and looks especially attractive in a large container. It can live over in the mildest-winter regions, but it's safer to pot up a division and keep it indoors or in a greenhouse over winter.

CYNARA. See CARDOON

CYNODON dactylon

BERMUDA GRASS, BERMUDA

Poaceae (Gramineae)

PERENNIAL LAWN GRASS

✂ MS, LS, CS, TS H 12–7

☼ FULL SUN

💧💧 MODERATE TO REGULAR WATER

Cynodon dactylon

Fine-textured subtropical grass that spreads rapidly by surface and underground runners. Tolerates heat; looks good if well maintained. It turns brown in winter; some selections stay green longer than others, and most stay green longer if well fed. Bermuda grass can be overseeded with rye grasses for winter color. Needs full sun and should be cut low; ½–1½ in. is desirable. Needs annual dethatching—removal of matted layer of old stems and stolons beneath the leaves—to look its best.

Common Bermuda is a good lower-maintenance lawn for large areas. Needs feeding in spring and summer, and careful and frequent mowing to remove seed spikes. Plant from hulled seed, plugs, or sod. Will invade flower and shrub beds unless controlled.

Hybrid Bermudas are finer in texture and better in color than the common kind. They crowd out common Bermuda in time but are harder to overseed with rye. They also need more frequent fertilizing, watering, and dethatching. Grow from seed, plugs, sprigs, or sod.

'Floratex'. Keeps green color well into fall and greens up early in spring. Needs less water and fertilizer than most other hybrid Bermudas but produces numerous seed heads. Available only as sod or plugs.

'Tifdwarf'. Extremely low and dense; takes very close mowing. Slower to establish than others—but also slower to spread where it's not wanted.

'Tifgreen'. Fine textured, deep blue green, dense. Few seed spikes; sterile seeds. Takes close mowing; preferred for putting greens.

'Tiflawn'. Medium fine texture, not as dense as 'Tifgreen'. More seed heads than other hybrids but extremely wear resistant.

'Tifway'. Low growing and fine textured, with stiff dark green blades. Dense, wear resistant. Slow to start. Sterile (no seeds).

'Yuma'. Low, dense grower. Tolerates heat, drought, cold.

Cyperaceae. Members of the sedge family superficially resemble grasses, but their stems are usually three-sided and their leaves are arranged in three ranks. They generally grow in wet places. *Carex* and *Cyperus* are examples.

CYPERUS

Cyperaceae

PERENNIALS

✂ ZONES VARY BY SPECIES

☼ ◑ ● SUN OR SHADE

💧 AMPLE WATER

Cyperus papyrus

These African natives are sedges—grasslike plants distinguished from true grasses by three-angled, solid stems and very different flowering parts. Valued for striking form, silhouette, shadow pattern.

Most species grow in rich, moist soil or with roots submerged in water. Keep plants groomed by removing dead or broken stems; divide and replant when the clump becomes too large, saving smaller, outside divisions and discarding the overgrown centers. Beyond their hardiness range, pot up divisions and keep them over the winter as houseplants.

C. albostriatus (C. diffusus). DWARF UMBRELLA PLANT. Zones CS, TS; 12–4. Resembles *C. alternifolius* but tends to be less hardy and shorter (to 20 in.), with broader leaves and lusher, softer appearance. Vigorous, invasive plant; best used in contained space.

C. alternifolius. UMBRELLA PLANT. Zones LS, CS, TS; 12–8. Narrow, firm, spreading leaves arranged like ribs of umbrella at tops of 2- to 4-ft. stems. Flowers in dry greenish brown clusters. Grows in water or moist soil. Effective near pools, in pots or planters, or in dry streambeds or small rock gardens. Self-sows. Can become weedy and take over a small pool. 'Gracilis' ('Nanus') is a dwarf form to 1½ ft. high.

C. papyrus. PAPYRUS. Zones CS, TS; 12–6. Tall, graceful dark green stems 6–10 ft. high, topped with clusters of green, threadlike parts to 1½ ft. long (longer than small leaves at base of cluster). Will grow quickly in 2 in. of water in shallow pool, or can be potted and placed on bricks or inverted pot in deeper water. Protect from strong wind. Also grows well in rich, moist soil out of water. Used by flower arrangers.

C. prolifer (C. isocladus). DWARF PAPYRUS. Zones CS, TS; 12–7. Flowers and long, thin leaves combine to make filmy brown-and-green clusters on slender stems about 1½ ft. high. Use in Asian-style gardens; sink in pots in water gardens where delicate design of slender, leafless stems will not be lost among larger and coarser plants.

CYPRESS. See *Cupressus*. True cypresses are all *Cupressus;* many plants erroneously called cypress are under *Chamaecyparis* and *Taxodium.*

CYPRESS VINE. See IPOMOEA quamoclit

Cypripedium. For tropical and subtropical orchids sold under this name, see *Paphiopedilum.* True cypripediums, the hardy lady's slipper orchids, are rare or endangered in the wild and extremely difficult to maintain in gardens. Most are collected from wild stands and seldom survive.

D

CYRILLA racemiflora

TITI, LEATHERWOOD	
Cyrillaceae	
SHRUB OR SMALL TREE	
☘ US, MS, LS, CS, TS ☀ 9–5	
☼ ◐ FULL SUN OR PART SHADE	
◖ ◗ REGULAR TO AMPLE WATER	

Cyrilla racemiflora

Native from Virginia to Florida and to eastern South America and the West Indies. Beautiful flowering shrub or small tree, 10–15 ft. (sometimes 30 ft.) tall, spreading to 15 ft.; deciduous in Upper South, semievergreen in Middle and Lower South, evergreen elsewhere. Grows naturally at water edges and in damp, low-lying areas. Noted for its twisted, contorted branches. Narrow, glossy dark green, 1½- to 4-in.-long leaves; many of the leaves turn orange, rust, or red in fall. Blooms in early summer, bearing fragrant white flowers in dangling, 4- to 6-in.-long sprays. Tan seeds form in late summer and persist into winter. Needs moist, acid soil that is high in organic matter. Tolerates seasonal standing water. 'Graniteville' is a low-growing, spreading selection with smaller leaves.

CYRTANTHUS elatus (C. purpureus, Vallota speciosa)

SCARBOROUGH LILY	
Amaryllidaceae	
PERENNIAL FROM BULB	
☘ CS, TS ☀ 10–8; OR GROW IN POT	
◐ LIGHT SHADE; BRIGHT LIGHT	
◖ REGULAR WATER	

Cyrtanthus elatus

This South African native looks like a slightly smaller version of the familiar amaryllis (*Hippeastrum*). Good-looking, strap-shaped evergreen leaves grow to 1–2 ft. long. In summer and early autumn, clusters of bright orange-red, funnel-shaped flowers, each 2½–3 in. wide, appear atop 2-ft.-tall stalks. Pink- and white-flowered forms are also available. Will live in the ground year-round in the Coastal and Tropical South; quite tolerant of competition from tree roots. Usually grown in pots, however, since bulbs bloom better when somewhat potbound. Excellent potted plant for the patio or indoors (best with east- or south-facing exposure). Plant in well-drained potting mix in June or July or just after flowering; set bulbs with tips just below soil surface. During active growth, fertilize monthly with a general-purpose liquid houseplant fertilizer. Water regularly during summer and fall, but let soil go slightly dry between waterings during semidormant period in winter and spring.

CYRTOMIUM falcatum

HOLLY FERN	
Polypodiaceae	
FERN	
☘ LS (PROTECTED), CS, TS ☀ 12–8; OR GROW IN POT	
◐ ● PARTIAL OR FULL SHADE	
◖ REGULAR WATER	

Cyrtomium falcatum

From Asia, South Africa, Polynesia. Coarse-textured but handsome evergreen fern to at least 2–3 ft. tall, somewhat wider. Large, leathery, glossy dark green fronds. Beautiful when used as a solid border or massed with other broad-leafed evergreens beneath the canopies of tall trees. Hardy to 14°F. Provide good soil; take care not to plant too deeply. Protect from wind. Can be brought indoors; give bright indirect light. 'Rochfordianum' has fringed leaflets.

CYTISUS

BROOM	
Fabaceae (Leguminosae)	
EVERGREEN AND DECIDUOUS SHRUBS	
☘ US, MS, LS	
☼ FULL SUN	
◖ MODERATE WATER	

Cytisus scoparius 'Burkwoodii'

Tough, showy shrubs for dunes, dry hillsides, and other challenging spots. Sweet pea–shaped flowers are often fragrant. Tolerate wind, seashore conditions, and rocky, infertile soil. Prune after bloom to limit size, lessen production of unsightly seedpods. Not browsed by deer.

C. × praecox. WARMINSTER BROOM. Deciduous. Heat zones 9–4. Compact growth to 3–5 ft. high and 4–6 ft. wide, with many slender stems. Plant resembles a mounding mass of pale yellow to creamy white flowers in spring. Small leaves drop early. Effective as informal screen or hedge, along drives, paths, garden steps. 'Allgold', slightly taller, has bright yellow flowers; 'Hollandia' has pink ones. 'Moonlight', formerly considered a selection of *C. × praecox*, is now thought to be a form of *C. scoparius*.

C. scoparius. SCOTCH BROOM. Evergreen. Heat zones 8–6. Upright-growing mass of wandlike green stems (often leafless or nearly so) may reach 10 ft. Golden yellow, ¾-in. flowers bloom in spring and early summer. Reseeds readily; can be invasive.

Selections exist that are lower growing, more colorful, and much better behaved than *C. scoparius*. Most of these grow 5–8 ft. tall and wide. Choices include 'Burkwoodii', red blossoms touched with yellow; 'Carla', pink and crimson lined white; 'Dorothy Walpole', rose pink and crimson; 'Lena', lemon yellow and red; 'Lilac Time', lilac-pink blooms on a compact plant; 'Lord Lambourne', scarlet and cream; 'Minstead', white flushed deep purple and lilac; 'Moonlight', compact, pale yellow; 'Pomona', orange and apricot; 'St. Mary's', white; 'San Francisco' and 'Stanford', red.

DAFFODIL. See NARCISSUS

DAHLBERG DAISY. See THYMOPHYLLA tenuiloba

DAHLIA

Asteraceae (Compositae)	
PERENNIALS FROM TUBEROUS ROOTS	
☘ US, MS, LS ☀ 9–5	
☼ ◐ LIGHT AFTERNOON SHADE IN LOWER SOUTH	
◖ REGULAR WATER	

Dahlia Hybrid

Native to Mexico and Guatemala. Through centuries of hybridizing and selection, dahlias have become tremendously diversified, available in numerous flower types and flower sizes (from 2 to 12 in. across) and all colors but true blue.

Bush and bedding dahlias range from 1 ft. to over 7 ft. tall. The tall bush forms are useful as summer hedges, screens, and fillers among shrubs; lower kinds give mass color in borders and containers. Modern dahlias, with their strong stems, long-lasting blooms that face outward or upward, and substantial, attractive foliage, are striking cut flowers. Leaves are generally divided into many large, deep green leaflets. Not browsed by deer.

Dahlia flower forms. Dahlia flowers are composite (daisylike) blooms containing many individual flowers called florets. One type of dahlia flower is composed of ray florets (which look like petals) surrounding a central cluster of petal-less disk florets. A second type has ray florets only. The American Dahlia Society has classified dahlias according to the flower forms described on facing page. Blooms range in size from giant (over 10 in.), large (8–10 in.), and medium (6–8 in.) to small (4–6 in.), miniature (2–4 in.), and mignon (under 2 in.).

Dahlia Flower Forms

'Elvira'; Peony Form   'Star Lite'; Cactus Form   'Red Velvet'; Waterlily Form   'Tasagore'; Peony Form   'Corvette'; Anemone Form

'Dizzy'; Single   'Mrs. Santa Claus'; Informal Decorative   'Winnie'; Pompon   'Candy Cane'; Formal Decorative   'Ace of Hearts'; Collarette   'Apache'; Fimbriated

Anemone form. Single or multiple layers of rays surround tubular disk florets that form a "pincushion" center.

Collarette. One layer of long rays and a second, inner layer of shorter ones that form a "collar" around the center of the flower.

Orchid form. A single layer of rays with inrolled margins for two-thirds or more of their length, giving the flower a pinwheel appearance.

Peony form. Central disk florets are surrounded by two or more rows of rays; innermost rays may be curled or twisted.

Single. One layer of rays arranged in a plane around a central cluster of disk florets.

The following flower forms are composed of ray florets only.

Ball. Flower looks spherical, though it's flattish in profile. Rays have inrolled margins for at least half their length.

Cactus form. Ray margins roll downward; tips are pointed. *Straight cactus* rays radiate in all directions from center; may be straight or curved downward, margins rolled for over half their length. *Incurved cactus* rays are similar, but they curve upward. *Semicactus* flowers have broad-based rays with margins rolled along outer half (portion farthest from center); the rays may be straight or curve upward or downward.

Decorative. Full flowers of two types. *Formal decorative* has many overlapping layers of symmetrically arranged, fairly flat rays that tend to curve downward. *Informal decorative* is just as full, but rays are curved, curled, or twisted and are often arranged in a more irregular pattern.

Fimbriated. All rays are split at tips with split portions twisted, giving the flower a fringed look.

Pompon. Similar to ball form, but rays are inrolled along their entire length, giving them a tubular appearance.

Waterlily form. Broad rays curve slightly upward; flower profile is flat to saucer shaped, resembling a waterlily bloom.

Novelty. Any flower form not covered in previous categories.

Planting. Most dahlias are started from tuberous roots planted in spring, after danger of frost is past and soil is warm. Several weeks before planting, dig soil to a foot deep and work in organic matter such as compost or ground bark. Dig deep planting holes, incorporate fertilizer, and insert stakes (for tall selections) as described in "What Most Dahlias Need." Cover roots with 3 in. of soil. Water thoroughly. As shoots grow, gradually fill hole with soil.

Dahlias can be started from seed. For tall types, start seeds early indoors; transplant seedlings into garden beds after frost danger is past. For dwarf dahlias, sow seed in place after soil is warm, or buy and plant started seedlings from the nursery. Dwarf dahlias are usually replaced each year, though they can be lifted and stored.

Thinning, pinching. On tall-growing dahlias, thin out shoots when they're about 6 in. high, leaving only the strongest one or two. When remaining shoots have three sets of leaves, pinch off tops just above the upper set; smaller-flowered dahlias, such as pompons, singles, and dwarfs, need only this first pinching. For the best show of larger-flowered dahlias, pinch again by removing all but terminal flower buds on side shoots.

Plant care. After shoots are aboveground, start watering regularly to a foot deep; continue throughout active growth. Dahlias planted in enriched soil shouldn't need additional food, but if your soil is light or if roots stayed in the ground the previous year, apply a granular low-nitrogen fertilizer when the first flower buds show. Mulch to discourage weeds and to eliminate cultivating, which may injure feeder roots.

Cutting flowers. Pick nearly mature flowers in early morning or evening. Immediately place cut stems in 2–3 in. of hot water; let stand in gradually cooling water for several hours or overnight.

Lifting, storing. In climates where ground freezes in winter, dig and store tuberous roots in fall. In other regions, roots may remain in place as long as drainage is excellent and winter temperatures remain above 20°F. In borderline climates, mulch with 4-in. layer of straw or similar material. Gardeners in most areas, however, prefer to dig the roots annually. ▸

WHAT MOST DAHLIAS NEED

GOOD SOIL: Plants grow best in well-drained soil that is liberally enriched with organic matter.

PLANTING: Dig about 1-ft.-deep planting holes—1½ ft. wide for larger dahlias (over 4 ft. tall), 9–12 in. wide for smaller types. Space roots of larger selections 4–5 ft. apart, those of smaller ones 1–2 ft. apart.

FERTILIZING: At the bottom of the planting hole, incorporate about ¼ cup of granular low-nitrogen fertilizer into the soil. Then add 4 in. of plain soil.

STAKING: When planting a tall selection, drive a 5- to 6-ft. stake into the hole just off center; place the root horizontally in bottom of hole, 2 in. from the stake and with growth bud pointing toward it.

'Deniska'; Novelty

D

To lift the roots, cut stalks to 4 in. above ground after the tops turn yellow or are frosted. Dig a 2-ft.-wide circle around each plant; carefully pry up clump with spading fork, shake off loose soil, and let the clump dry in sun for several hours. From that point, follow either of these methods.

Method 1: Divide clumps immediately after digging in fall. Freshly dug roots are easy to cut, and eyes (growth buds) are easy to recognize at this time. To divide, cut the stalks with a sharp knife, leaving 1 in. of stalk attached to each section; make sure each division has an eye, so it will produce a new plant. Dust cut surfaces with sulfur to prevent rot; bury in dry sand, sawdust, peat moss, or perlite and store over winter in a cool (40–45°F), dark, dry place.

Method 2: Leave clumps intact until spring. Cover them with dry sand, sawdust, peat moss, or perlite and store in cool, dark, dry place as directed above. With Method 2, roots are less likely to shrivel.

About 2 to 4 weeks before planting in spring, separate intact clumps, as described under Method 1. Then place all roots—whether fall- or spring-divided—in moist sand to plump them up and encourage sprouting.

D. imperialis. TREE DAHLIA. Zones LS, CS, TS; hardy in MS, but frost there usually kills flower buds before they open. Multistemmed tree grows each year from permanent roots to a possible 10–20 ft. tall, 4–6 ft. wide. Daisylike, 4- to 8-in.-wide lavender flowers with yellow centers bloom at branch ends in late fall. Leaves divided into many leaflets. Frost kills tops completely; cut back to ground afterward. Annual dieback relegates tree dahlia to tall novelty class; available from specialists. Grow from cuttings taken near stem tops (or from side shoots) in fall; root in containers of moist sand kept in a protected place over winter. Or dig root clump and divide in fall.

DAHOON. See ILEX cassine

DANAE racemosa
ALEXANDRIAN LAUREL

Liliaceae

EVERGREEN SHRUB

✂ MS, LS, CS ꓧ 9–2

◐ ● PARTIAL TO FULL SHADE

● REGULAR WATER

Danae racemosa

Native to northern Iran and Asia Minor. Rare in gardens, this elegant, pest-free shrub deserves much wider use. It grows 2–4 ft. tall and wide, spreading slowly by underground rhizomes. The glossy green, lance-shaped "leaves" along its arching stems are actually modified stems called cladophylls; they reach 4 in. long. Inconspicuous greenish yellow flowers appear in summer, followed by showy red berries at least ¼ in. across that persist into fall and winter. Cut branches are highly prized by flower arrangers. Newly emerging shoots in spring resemble elongating spears of asparagus, to which the plant is closely related.

Alexandrian laurel makes an elegant addition to the shade border. Give it moist, rich, well-drained soil and shield it from direct sun. Propagate by division in spring. Prune away winter-damaged foliage in early spring.

DANCING GIRL GINGER. See GLOBBA

DANDELION

Asteraceae (Compositae)

PERENNIAL

✂ US, MS, LS, CS ꓧ 8–1

☀ FULL SUN

● REGULAR WATER

Dandelion

If the sight of bright yellow dandelions dotting your otherwise perfect lawn drives you to distraction, blame it on the Pilgrims. It was they who reportedly brought the plant to America from its homeland in northern Europe in the early 1600s. Of course, they had good reasons for doing so. The common dandelion (*Taraxacum officinale*) is among the most nutritious and useful of herbs, with a long history of culinary and medicinal use. Its leaves, which can be boiled or eaten fresh, are high in potassium, iron, and vitamins A, C, B1, and B2. The dried and roasted roots make an acceptable coffee substitute, and the fermented flowers produce dandelion wine and beer. Dandelion tonics are a folk-medicine remedy for liver problems. Beekeepers value dandelions as a rich source of nectar and pollen.

This deep-rooted perennial forms a rosette of sharply tooth-edged leaves 6–12 in. long. Their fancied resemblance to a lion's teeth give the plant its common name—"dandelion" is a corruption of the French *dent de lion* ("lion's tooth"). Blossoms appear from late winter through fall, carried atop hollow stems 4–15 in. high; they're followed by the familiar puffball seed heads that children like to blow on, releasing the seeds to fly hither and yon on the wind.

Dandelions are usually quickly dispatched by gardeners armed with broadleaf weed killers, but some folks grow the culinary types (selected for larger, thicker leaves) found in specialty seed catalogs. Culinary selections such as 'Pissenlit' and 'Ameliore' give best yield with full sun and fertile, moist, well-drained soil. Pick only young leaves for salads; old ones can be bitter. Culinary dandelions are just as invasive as the common ones, so be sure to remove and dispose of the seed heads before they mature.

DAPHNE

Thymelaeaceae

EVERGREEN, SEMIEVERGREEN, DECIDUOUS SHRUBS

✂ ZONES VARY BY SPECIES

◑ LIGHT SHADE

● MODERATE WATER, EXCEPT AS NOTED

☣ ALL PARTS, ESPECIALLY FRUITS, ARE POISONOUS IF INGESTED

Daphne odora
'Aureomarginata'

These delightful, well-behaved shrubs merit a place in practically every garden. Having one or more on display earns you instant respect from the gardening cognoscenti. Although some daphnes are easier to grow than others, all require excellent drainage, cool soil (accomplished with mulch and light afternoon shade), occasional watering during summer dry spells, and protection from hot sun and heavy winds. Plants respond well to heavy pruning but rarely need more than an occasional snip to correct their shape—cut back to lateral branches or just above a growth bud. Cut branches can be forced into early bloom indoors in winter. Daphnes are not browsed by deer.

D. ×burkwoodii. BURKWOOD DAPHNE. Evergreen or semievergreen to deciduous. Zones US, MS, LS; 9–2. Erect, compact growth to 3–4 ft. tall and wide, densely foliaged with narrow medium green leaves to 1½ in. long. Abundant small clusters of fragrant flowers (white fading to pink) appear at branch ends in late spring and again in late summer. 'Brigg's Moonlight' has pale yellow leaves with a narrow green border; 'Carol Mackie' has gold-edged green leaves. 'Somerset' is larger (to 4 ft. tall and 6 ft. wide) and produces pink flowers. Use all in shrub borders, at woodland edges, as foundation plantings.

D. cneorum. ROSE DAPHNE, GARLAND DAPHNE. Evergreen. Zones US, MS; 7–5. From mountains of central and southern Europe. Matting and spreading; less than 1 ft. high and 3 ft. wide. Good container plant. Trailing branches covered with narrow, 1-in.-long, dark green leaves. Clusters of fragrant rosy pink flowers appear in spring. Choice rock garden plant. After bloom is through, top-dress with mix of peat moss and sand to keep roots cool and induce additional rooting of trailing stems.

Selections include 'Eximia', lower than the species (to 8 in. high) and with larger flowers; *D. c. pygmaea* 'Alba', 3 in. tall, 1 ft. wide, with white flowers; 'Ruby Glow', with larger, more deeply colored flowers than those of the species and with late-summer rebloom; and 'Variegata', with attractive gold-edged leaves.

D. genkwa. LILAC DAPHNE. Deciduous. Zones US, MS, LS; 9–6. From China. Erect, open growth to 3–4 ft. high and wide. Before leaves expand, clusters of lilac-blue, scentless flowers wreathe branches, making foot-long wands of blossoms. White fruit follows flowers. Oval, medium green, 2-in.-long leaves. Use in rock garden, shrub border.

D. mezereum. FEBRUARY DAPHNE. Deciduous. Zones US, MS; 8–5. From Europe, Caucasus, Siberia. Rather gawky, stiff-twigged, erect growth to 4 ft. tall and 3 ft. wide, with thin, roundish, 2- to 3-in.-long leaves in pale green to gray green. Plant in groups for best appearance. Fragrant reddish purple flowers in short, stalkless clusters are carried along branches in mid- or late winter before leaf-out and continue into spring. May go dormant in summer. Clustered red fruit follows flowers. 'Alba' has white flowers and yellow fruit and is not as rangy as the species.

D. odora. WINTER DAPHNE. Evergreen. Zones MS, LS; 9–7. From China, Japan. So prized for its pervasive floral perfume that it continues to be widely planted despite its unpredictable behavior—it can die despite the most attentive care, or flourish with little attention until you invite all your gardening friends over to admire it, at which point it promptly succumbs without warning, just to show you who's in charge. Very neat, handsome plant, usually to about 4 ft. high (occasionally 8–10 ft. high) and 6 ft. wide. Rather narrow, deep green, 3-in.-long leaves are thick and glossy. Nosegay clusters of charming, intensely fragrant flowers—pink to deep red on outside, with creamy pink throats—appear at branch ends in winter.

The following are among the selections available. 'Alba' has white flowers; terminal growth sometimes distorted by fasciation (convoluted-looking growths resembling cockscombs). 'Leucanthe' is relatively disease resistant, with white-throated pale pink blooms; 'Aureomarginata' ('Marginata'), more widely grown than the species, has yellow-edged leaves.

This species needs much air around its roots, so plant in porous soil (as you would rhododendrons). Always set plant a bit high, so the juncture of roots and stems is 1–2 in. above soil grade. Where soil is heavy and poorly drained, grow in porous, organic soil mixture in raised bed or container. Transplanting is risky, so choose site carefully.

Plant this daphne where it can get at least 3 hours of shade each day around midday. If possible, shade soil around roots with living ground cover. A soil pH of 7.0 is right for it. Feed right after bloom with complete fertilizer (but not with acid plant food).

During dry season, water as infrequently as plant will allow. Little or no water in summer increases flowering next spring and helps prevent death from root rot.

PRUNING DAPHNE. *Most daphnes need little corrective pruning, but feel free to harvest branches of fragrant blooms from* Daphne odora *and other daphnes for indoor display or corsages. When you take the branches, cut back to an outward-facing bud; this will help produce a bushy, spreading plant.* ❖

DARMERA peltata (Peltiphyllum peltatum)

UMBRELLA PLANT, INDIAN RHUBARB

Saxifragaceae

PERENNIAL

⚡ US, MS, LS ⊞ 9–5

☼ PARTIAL SHADE

💧 AMPLE WATER

Darmera peltata

Native to mountains of Northern California and Oregon. Large, round clusters of pink flowers appear on bare stalks to 6 ft. tall in spring. Shield-shaped, 1- to 2-ft.-wide leaves appear later on 2- to 6-ft. stalks. Each plant spreads 4–8 ft. wide. Stout rhizomes to 2 in. thick grow in damp ground or even into streams. A spectacular plant for pond, stream, or damp, cool woodland site.

DASYLIRION

SOTOL

Agavaceae

EVERGREEN SHRUBS

⚡ ZONES VARY BY SPECIES

☼ ◑ FULL SUN OR LIGHT SHADE

◊ 💧 LITTLE OR NO WATER TO MODERATE WATER

Dasylirion wheeleri

Native to the deserts and mountains of the Southwest and Mexico, these yucca relatives tolerate dry, rocky, alkaline soil and considerable drought, though some irrigation will speed growth. They resemble *Nolina*—but unlike those plants, most sotols have sharp prickles along their leaf margins.

Given plenty of room to spread out, sotols make a bold statement in the garden. Their long, narrow leaves—ranging in color from dark green to blue green to silvery—can be upright or drooping. The foliage rosette sits atop a woody base that can, with age, form a treelike trunk. Mature plants may bloom in summer, bearing tiny flowers in tight clusters on a tall, narrow spike. There are male and female plants; you need one of each to obtain seed.

Fast-draining soil is essential. If your soil is heavy, amend it with lots of sand and coarse gravel—or plant in large containers. Spring is the best time for planting. Mulch with gravel rather than organic matter, and keep plants as dry as possible during winter. Promptly remove old, withered leaves at the base for a neater appearance. Pests aren't usually a problem.

D. berlandieri. Zones LS, CS, TS; 12–8. Native to Mexico. Grows 4–6 ft. tall and wide, with slightly arching blue-green leaves to 4 ft. long and 7 in. wide. Male flowers are rust colored; female blossoms are chartreuse. Leaves of 'Delores' curl at the ends. 'Monterrey' features swordlike silvery foliage; 'Zaragoza' sports twisted, strikingly blue leaves.

D. leiophyllum. SMOOTH SOTOL. Zones MS, LS, CS, TS; 12–7. Native to West Texas, New Mexico, and northeastern Mexico. Grows 4–5 ft. tall and wide. Smooth, shiny, green to blue-green leaves are just 1¼ in. wide but over 3 ft. long; margins are lined with stout teeth. Whitish flowers are borne on a spike to 12 ft. or taller. One of the most cold-hardy and drought-tolerant sotols.

D. miquihuanensis. TREE SOTOL. Zones MS, LS, CS, TS; 12–7. Large, fast-growing native of the mountains of northeastern Mexico. Over time, grows 8 ft. tall and 6 ft. wide, with a massive trunk and green leaves that reach 4 ft. long and 2 in. wide. Flowers similar to those of *D. texanum.*

D. quadrangulatum (D. longissimum). MEXICAN GRASS TREE. Zones LS, CS, TS; 12–8. Native to mountains of northeastern Mexico. Forms a fountainlike clump to about 5 ft. high and wide. Dark green, 3-ft.-long leaves are very narrow—less than ½ in. wide—and unlike leaves of other species, they have smooth margins. Trunk grows slowly, extending the plant's height to at least 15 ft. over time. White to cream-colored flowers appear on a 6-ft. spike.

D. texanum. TEXAS SOTOL. Zones LS, CS, TS; 12–8. Native to Texas Hill Country. Stiff, spiny, sharp-edged green leaves, to 2½–3 ft. long and 1½ in. wide, reflect light prettily as they move in the breeze. Plant grows 3 ft. tall and 4 ft. wide; small whitish flowers appear on a spike that may reach 15 ft. high. More tolerant of cold, moisture, and shade than most other sotols.

D. wheeleri. DESERT SPOON, DESERT SOTOL. Zones MS, LS, CS, TS; 12–8. Native to West Texas, Arizona, and northern Mexico. Forms a near-spherical clump 3–5 ft. high, 4–5 ft. wide. Spiky, fairly stiff, bluish gray leaves to 3 ft. long and less than 1 in. wide. Slowly forms a trunk covered with dried, drooping shag of old leaves (if these are not trimmed off as they fade). Base of each leaf broadens where it joins the trunk to form a long-handled "spoon" prized in dried arrangements. Produces white flowers on a 9- to 15-ft.-tall spike; plants occasionally die after flowering.

DATE PALM. See PHOENIX

DATURA

ANGEL'S TRUMPET

Solanaceae

ANNUALS AND PERENNIALS

🗡 ZONES VARY BY SPECIES

☼ FULL SUN

💧 REGULAR WATER

✿ ALL PARTS ARE HIGHLY TOXIC IF INGESTED

Datura metel 'Cornucopia'

Together with *Brugmansia*, this genus forms the showy group of plants known as angel's trumpets. Daturas differ from brugmansias in several ways, however: they are herbaceous rather than shrublike, their flowers are upright rather than pendent, and their seedpods are swollen and spiny rather than beanlike.

Daturas are easy to grow if given fertile, moist, well-drained soil; full sun; and an occasional feeding with a balanced general-purpose houseplant fertilizer. They're easily propagated from seeds, which burst from seed capsules in late summer. Some species reseed rampantly. Where plants aren't winter hardy, store them in a cool greenhouse or unheated garage during cold months.

D. innoxia. DOWNY ANGEL'S TRUMPET. Perennial. Zones LS, CS, TS; 12–1. Bushy plant native to the southwestern U.S. and Mexico. To 3 ft. tall and wide, with oval, pointed, downy leaves to 10 in. long. Showy, lightly fragrant flowers, 6–8 in. long, may be pink, lavender, or white. Good choice for containers. Sometimes listed as *D. inoxia*.

D. 'La Fleur Lilac' ('La Fleur Lilas'). Perennial. Zone TS. Dwarf hybrid involving *D. stramonium* that reaches only 3–4 ft. tall and not quite as wide. Serrated dark green leaves; pale lilac, sweetly fragrant blooms. Small size and compact habit make it ideal for containers.

D. metel. HORN OF PLENTY. Annual. Zones US, MS, LS, CS, TS; 12–1. Native to southern China and India. Grows quickly, reaching 5 ft. tall and 4 ft. wide by late summer. Oval, pointed leaves to 8 in. long; exotic-looking flowers, up to 8 in. long, in white or purple shades. Selections include 'Alba', bearing pure white flowers; 'Aurea', with golden yellow blooms; and 'Caerulea', with blue blossoms. 'Cornucopia' features gorgeous double purple-and-white blossoms. This species self-sows aggressively; seedlings are easily transplanted, making it a favorite passalong plant.

DAUCUS carota carota

QUEEN ANNE'S LACE

Apiaceae (Umbelliferae)

BIENNIAL

🗡 US, MS, LS, CS H 9–1

☼ FULL SUN

💧 MODERATE WATER

Daucus carota carota

Though we think of it as a Southern wild-flower, Queen Anne's lace actually hails from northern Europe and Asia and is a wild form of the carrot (*D. carota sativus*)—but unlike its culinary kin (see Carrot), it forms only a small, inedible root. It compensates for that lack, however, with the lacy, flat-topped white flower clusters that grace fields and meadows in early summer.

Plants grow to about 3 ft. tall. After the flowers fade, old blooms curl up into a cup-shaped clump of seeds resembling a bird's nest. Seeds disperse widely and germinate readily, which explains how the plant has become so widespread. Queen Anne's lace is ideal for naturalized areas and cottage gardens; to add it to your plantings, gently crush a seed cluster in your hand and sprinkle the seeds onto bare soil in late summer. One seed cluster per garden is plenty. Plants thrive in full sun and well-drained soil. Seedlings form tufts of lacy foliage the first year, flower and set seed the second year, then die. Excellent as a cut flower—and if you gather most of the blooms for arrangements, fewer seeds will be formed and spread will be more manageable.

DAVALLIA

Polypodiaceae

FERN

🗡 TS H 12–10; OR HOUSEPLANT

☼ PARTIAL SHADE; BRIGHT INDIRECT LIGHT

💧💧 MODERATE TO REGULAR WATER

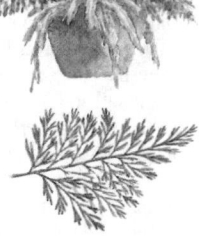

Davallia trichomanoides

These ferns have long, thick, furry rhizomes (like animals' feet) that creep over the soil. They're epiphytes in nature but will make a delicate ground cover in the Tropical South if the soil is well drained. Excellent indoors or out in hanging baskets and pots; use a coarse bark or moss potting mix, and repot when the mix breaks down so the roots don't rot. Feed occasionally with a general-purpose liquid houseplant fertilizer diluted to half strength.

D. fejeensis. RABBIT'S FOOT FERN. Native to Fiji. Graceful, finely cut fronds 1–2½ ft. long. Makes large specimen plant with age. 'Plumosa' is exceptionally lacy and drooping.

D. trichomanoides. SQUIRREL'S FOOT FERN. Native to Southeast Asia. Finely divided fronds to 1 ft. long, 6 in. wide; purplish to burgundy when young, turning to light green, then to medium green. Light reddish brown, very furry rhizomes. Hardier than *D. fejeensis*, to 30°F.

DAVIDIA involucrata

DOVE TREE, HANDKERCHIEF TREE

Nyssaceae

DECIDUOUS TREE

🗡 ZONES US, MS, LS H 8–6

☼ PARTIAL SHADE

💧 REGULAR WATER

Davidia involucrata

Native to China. In gardens, grows 20–40 ft. tall, 12–25 ft. wide, with pyramidal to rounded crown and strong branching pattern. Has clean look in and out of leaf. Roundish to heart-shaped, 3- to 6-in.-long leaves are vivid green. Comes into bloom in spring; general effect is that of white doves resting among green leaves (or handkerchiefs drying on branches). Small, clustered, red-anthered flowers are carried between two large white or creamy white bracts of unequal size (one 6 in. long, the other about 4 in. long). Trees often take 10 years to come into flower, then may bloom more heavily in alternate years. No fall color. Brown fruits about the size of golf balls hang on tree well into winter.

Plant this tree by itself; it should not compete with other flowering trees. Pleasing in front of dark conifers, where vivid green and white stand out.

DAWN REDWOOD. See METASEQUOIA glyptostroboides

DAYLILY. See HEMEROCALLIS

DEAD NETTLE. See LAMIUM

DECUMARIA barbara

CLIMBING HYDRANGEA, WOOD VAMP

Saxifragaceae

DECIDUOUS VINE

🗡 US, MS, LS, CS H 9–6

☼● PARTIAL OR FULL SHADE

💧💧 REGULAR TO AMPLE WATER

Decumaria barbara

Native to wet woodlands and swamps from East Texas to Florida and Virginia. Grows to 30 ft. or more, attaching to walls with aerial rootlets or running loose over the ground. Handsome, oval and pointed glossy green leaves, 2–4 in. long, 1–2 in. wide. Fragrant white or yellowish white flowers in dense clusters 2–4 in. across appear in May or June. Old vines sometimes bear showy urn-shaped fruit. Leaves turn yellow in fall. Best in moist, shady sites and fertile soil but will also grow in fairly dry woods. Takes some direct sun if kept moist. Of the three vines known as climbing hydrangeas—*Hydrangea anomala* and *Schizophragma hydrangeoides* are the others—this is the only Southern native, and it is the least known.

DELONIX regia

ROYAL POINCIANA, FLAMBOYANT

Fabaceae (Leguminosae)

PARTIALLY OR WHOLLY DECIDUOUS TREE

TS

FULL SUN

REGULAR WATER DURING GROWTH AND BLOOM

Delonix regia

From Madagascar. "Flamboyant" is the word to describe poinciana. Its large trusses of 4-in., orange to scarlet flowers with white markings put on a spectacular display in late spring or early summer. Considered by many the most beautiful of the world's flowering trees. Wide-spreading, umbrella-shaped tree of rapid growth to 30 ft. tall and twice as wide. Fernlike leaves, finely cut into many tiny leaflets, give filtered shade. Blooms are followed by 2-ft.-long black seedpods that hang on bare winter branches. Easy to grow but sensitive to cold.

DELOSPERMA

ICE PLANT

Aizoaceae

SUCCULENT PERENNIALS

US, MS, LS, CS, EXCEPT AS NOTED

LIGHT AFTERNOON SHADE IN HOTTEST CLIMATES

LITTLE TO MODERATE WATER

Delosperma cooperi

Along with a few other genera, these low-growing succulents are all known as ice plants. *Delosperma* species, most of which hail from South Africa, are the best ice plants for the South (they do particularly well in the Southwest). They never grow more than a few inches high, but spread to form ground-hugging mats ideal for covering a bank or slope. Daisylike flowers (about 2 in. across) appear above the small, succulent leaves, which may be cylindrical or flattened. Need full sun, good drainage, and just enough water to keep them looking fresh. Mulch with gravel to keep base of plant dry. Withhold water in fall to harden off plants for winter.

D. ashtonii. ASHTON'S ICE PLANT. Zones MS, LS, CS; 10–7. Dark lavender-pink flowers with yellow centers bloom over a long period in summer, held on 4- to 6-in.-tall stalks above gray-green leaves that are broader than those of most other species.

D. congestum 'Gold Nugget'. Heat zones 12–7. Summer into fall, butter yellow blossoms emerge from tight clumps of beadlike dark green leaves. Grows ½ in. tall, up to 9 in. wide. Foliage turns red in winter.

D. cooperi. PURPLE ICE PLANT. Zones MS, LS, CS; 10–7. Purple flowers appear all summer above light blue-green foliage. To 3–5 in. tall, spreading quickly to 2 ft. across. Hardy to 0°F if protected by snow or mulch.

D. floribundum 'Starburst'. Heat zones 9–6. Glowing lilac-pink blooms, each with a central white eye, appear above shiny deep green foliage from summer to fall. Grows 4 in. tall, 10–20 in. wide.

D. nubigenum. HARDY ICE PLANT. Heat zones 9–6. Only 1–2 in. tall, spreading to 3 ft. Cylindrical lime green leaves turn red in winter. Bright yellow flowers, 1–1½ in. wide, are borne in great profusion in late spring. Excellent ground cover. Very cold hardy, surviving to −10°F. 'Basutoland' is an improved form that reaches 2–4 in. tall.

D. sphalmanthoides. TUFTED ICE PLANT. Heat zones 12–10. Tight mat of gray-green foliage grows only ½ in. high and 8 in. wide. Early spring show of pinkish purple flowers.

DELPHINIUM

Ranunculaceae

PERENNIALS, SOME TREATED AS BIENNIALS OR ANNUALS

ZONES VARY BY SPECIES

FULL SUN, EXCEPT AS NOTED

REGULAR WATER, EXCEPT AS NOTED

Delphinium elatum

Often associated with the grand borders of England, stately delphiniums are problematic in most of the South. Those fancy hybrids (such as *D. elatum* hybrids) can't take our long, hot, humid summers and seldom last more than a year or two; in fact, they're best treated as annuals. Native species may be less spectacular than the hybrids, but they are reliably perennial, rising up in the garden year after year.

Bloom typically comes from spring to early summer. Cool blue is the classic—and probably the favorite—color, but delphiniums are also available in white, yellow, pink, lavender, purple, and red. Leaves are lobed and fanlike, variously cut and divided. All delphiniums are effective in borders and make good cut flowers; lower-growing types do well in containers. The blossoms attract birds. For annual delphinium (larkspur), see *Consolida ajacis*.

Delphiniums are easy to grow from seed. In the Middle, Lower, and Coastal South, sow fresh seed in flats or pots filled with potting soil in July or August; set out transplants in October for bloom in late spring and early summer. In the Upper South, sow seed in March or April and set out transplants in June or July for first bloom by September (and more bloom the following spring).

Plants need rich, porous soil and regular feeding. Improve poor or heavy soils by working in lots of organic matter. Add lime to strongly acid soils. Work a handful of superphosphate into the soil around the root ball. Be careful not to bury the plant's root crown.

D. ×belladonna. Zones US, MS; 7–3. To 3–4 ft. tall, 2 ft. wide. Sturdy, bushy plant with deeply cut leaves and short-stemmed, airy flower clusters. Selections include light blue 'Belladonna', dark blue 'Bellamosum', white 'Casa Blanca', and deep turquoise blue 'Cliveden Beauty'. All have 1½- to 2½-in.-wide flowers and are longer lived than tall hybrids listed under *D. elatum*.

D. carolinianum. CAROLINA LARKSPUR. Zones US, MS, LS; 8–3. Native to the Southeast, southern Midwest, Texas. Narrow plant (just 6 in. wide at base) bears erect, 1- to 3-ft. spikes of blue or white flowers. Blooms heavily in spring, then goes dormant in summer. Reseeds readily and tolerates just about any well-drained soil.

D. elatum. CANDLE DELPHINIUM. Zones US; 7–3. Siberian species to 3–6 ft. tall and 2 ft. wide, with small dark or dull purple flowers. Along with *D. cheilanthum* and others, it is a parent of modern tall-growing delphinium strains.

Pacific strain hybrids (also called Giant Pacific, Pacific Hybrids, and Pacific Coast Hybrids) grow to 8 ft. tall. They are available in selected color series; members of these include 'Blue Bird', medium blue; 'Blue Jay', medium to dark blue; 'Galahad', white with white center; 'Percival', white with black center; 'Summer Skies', light blue. Other purple, lavender, pink named selections are sold.

Like Pacific strain but shorter (2–2½ ft. tall) are the Blue Fountains, Blue Springs, and Magic Fountains strains. Even shorter is the Stand Up strain (15–20 in.). These shorter strains seldom require staking.

Other strains have flowers in shades of lilac pink to deep raspberry rose, clear lilac, lavender, royal purple, and darkest violet. Wrexham strain, tall growing with large spikes, was developed in England.

D. exaltatum. TALL LARKSPUR. Zones US, MS, LS; 8–1. Native to moist woods from Pennsylvania and Ohio south to North Carolina and Alabama. Showy true blue flowers appear on spikes 3–6 ft. tall in summer; plants reach 1–2 ft. wide. Best in light shade but blooms even in full shade. Tolerates drought once established.

D. grandiflorum (D. chinense). CHINESE DELPHINIUM, BOUQUET DELPHINIUM. Short-lived perennial treated as biennial or annual. Zones US, MS, LS, CS, TS; 8–1. Native to Siberia and eastern Asia. Bushy, branching, 1 ft. tall or less. Selections include 'Dwarf Blue Mirror', 1 ft., upward-facing deep blue flowers; and 'Tom Thumb', 8 in. tall, pure gentian blue flowers.

D. virescens. WHITE LARKSPUR, PRAIRIE LARKSPUR. Zones US, MS, LS; 9–1. Native to poor, rocky limestone soils from Texas north to Canada. Very slender plant, 1–2 ft. tall. White flowers, with a hint of pale blue, spring to midsummer. Plant in clusters for best effect. Tolerates heat, some shade, and clay and caliche soils. Poisonous to cattle.

DYNAMITE DELPHINIUMS. *If you live in the Upper South, you can set off a burst of delphinium blooms like those you see in English gardens. When new stalks appear in spring, remove all but the strongest two or three, tie to stakes, and apply a bloom-booster fertilizer. After blooms fade, cut stalks nearly to the ground, leaving foliage at the bottom. Fertilize again and you may get a second bloom.* ❖

DENDRANTHEMA. See CHRYSANTHEMUM

DENDROBIUM

Orchidaceae

EPIPHYTIC ORCHIDS

⚡ TS ⋈ 12–10; OR HOUSEPLANT

◑ LIGHT SHADE; BRIGHT LIGHT

💧 REGULAR WATER

Dendrobium nobile

This huge genus (it may include as many as 1,400 species and even more hybrids) ranges from Japan and the Himalayas to Australia and the Pacific islands. Many are grown by orchid fanciers in greenhouses (outdoors in southern Florida). Some have thin, canelike pseudobulbs (see Orchidaceae), others short, fat ones. Only a few of the more widely grown are mentioned here. Culturally, they fall into two classes. Intermediate-climate types are evergreen; they need water throughout the year (somewhat less in winter) and temperatures similar to those required by cattleya orchids. Cool growers drop some or all of their leaves during a period of winter dormancy, at which time they need very little water (only enough to keep pseudobulbs from shrinking) and temperatures suitable for green-leafed paphiopedilums.

Indoors, dendrobiums need at least 6 hours of good sunlight per day; place them directly in front of a southern window. During active growth and bloom, feed monthly with water-soluble 30-10-10 fertilizer.

D. bigibbum phalaenopsis (D. phalaenopsis). Intermediate grower. Native to Australia, New Guinea. Blooms throughout the year, with canes up to 3 ft. tall producing arching spikes that carry as many as ten 3-in. purple flowers. The parent of many hybrids.

D. hybrids. A bewildering number of hybrids have been produced in Hawaii and elsewhere, both for ornamental pot plants and for cut flowers and leis. Most are intermediate growers. Buy plants in bloom to get desired flower color and bloom season.

D. kingianum. Cool grower. Native to Australia. Makes large clumps of 2- to 20-in. pseudobulbs topped by 4-in. leaves. In late winter or early spring, erect spikes to 8 in. long carry a few or up to as many as 20 fragrant, inch-wide flowers in pink, white, or red.

D. nobile. Cool grower. Himalayan native. Canes 12–20 in. tall carry two ranks of 2- to 3½-in. leaves; leaves last for about 2 years. Short inflorescences on leafy and leafless canes carry two to four fragrant, 1½-in., white to purplish pink flowers with a yellow or white zone around a dark purple eye. Blooms almost any time of year. The parent of many colorful hybrids.

D. speciosum. Cool grower. From Australia. Large masses of pseudobulbs (ranging in height from 4 in. to 3 ft.) are topped with leaves that are 1½- to 10-in. long. Blooms in late winter or early spring. Inflorescences are crowded spikes of fragrant, creamy to yellow flowers; they resemble bushy foxtails, can reach 2–2½ ft. long.

DENNSTAEDTIA
punctilobula

HAY-SCENTED FERN

Dennstaedtiaceae

FERN

⚡ US, MS ⋈ 8–1

◑ LIGHT SHADE

💧💧 MODERATE TO REGULAR WATER

Dennstaedtia punctilobula

Native from eastern Canada to the mid-South. Deciduous fern with finely divided yellow-green fronds to 2 ft. tall arising from creeping rhizomes. Plant spreads quickly to make an attractive ground cover. Crushed fronds smell like freshly cut hay. If given adequate water, thrives even in poor, rocky soil. Can form mats that cover rocks. You may see it growing along the roadside or under rail fences in partly shaded areas.

DEODAR CEDAR. See CEDRUS deodara

DESCHAMPSIA

HAIR GRASS

Poaceae (Gramineae)

PERENNIAL GRASSES

⚡ US, MS, LS

◐◑ FULL SUN OR PARTIAL SHADE

💧💧 MODERATE TO REGULAR WATER

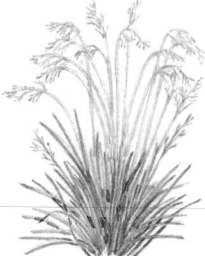

Deschampsia cespitosa

Ornamental clumping grasses with narrow, rough leaves obscured by clouds of yellowish flower panicles in late spring or early summer. Use in mass plantings. Best suited to Upper South. Evergreen in warmer part of range, semievergreen in colder part.

D. cespitosa. TUFTED HAIR GRASS. Heat zones 8–1. Native to much of North America, but most forms are imports from Europe. Dark green foliage. Purple-tinged greenish yellow panicles persist into winter. Fountain-like clumps typically 2–3 ft. high in bloom. 'Bronzeschleier' ('Bronzy Veil') has bronzy yellow blooms. Selections with golden yellow flowers include 'Goldgehange', 'Goldschleier', 'Goldstaub'. *D. c. vivipara* has darkest green foliage; instead of flowers, it produces plantlets that droop to the ground.

D. flexuosa. CRINKLED HAIR GRASS. Heat zones 9–1. Glossy, wiry green leaves in tight clumps 1–2 ft. high. Nodding, purple-tinged flowers mature to a yellowish brown color.

DESERT HONEYSUCKLE. See ANISACANTHUS

DESERT PEA. See CLIANTHUS formosus

DESERT SPOON. See DASYLIRION wheeleri

DESERT WILLOW. See CHILOPSIS linearis

DEUTZIA

Saxifragaceae

DECIDUOUS SHRUBS

⚡ US, MS, LS

◐◑ FULL SUN OR LIGHT SHADE

💧💧 MODERATE TO REGULAR WATER

Deutzia 'Pink-a-Boo'

These shrubs are best used among evergreens, where they can make a show with their small, often fragrant flowers, then blend back in with other greenery later on. Bloom season coincides with that of late spring bulbs such as tulips and Dutch iris. Prune as soon as flowers fade. With low- or medium-growing kinds, cut some of oldest stems to ground every other year. With tall kinds, prune heavily each year after bloom, cutting back wood that has flowered to outward-facing branches.

D. crenata. Heat zones 8−3. Native to Japan. Similar to *D. scabra* but has white flowers. Foliage turns deep purple red in fall. *D. c. nakaiana*, a dwarf form to only 2 ft. tall and 4 ft. wide, has double blossoms.

D. ×elegantissima. Heat zones 8−3. Grows to 6 ft. tall and wide, with pink flowers and dull green, oval, 2- to 3-in.-long leaves. 'Rosealind', to 4−5 ft. tall and wide, has deep rose blooms.

D. gracilis. SLENDER DEUTZIA. Heat zones 8−1. Native to Japan. To 2−4 ft. (possibly 6 ft.) tall, 3−4 ft. wide, with many slender, gracefully arching stems. Clusters of snowy white flowers; broadly lance-shaped, bright green, 2½-in. leaves with finely toothed edges. 'Nikko' grows only 1−2 ft. high, spreading to 5 ft. wide; can be used as a ground cover.

D. hybrids. These include 'Pink-a-Boo', an erect grower to 6−8 ft. tall and 6 ft. wide, with large clusters of pink flowers; and 'Magicien' ('Magician'), similar but with dark red blossoms.

D. ×magnifica. SHOWY DEUTZIA. Heat zones 8−3. An open, multistemmed shrub that grows 6−10 ft. tall and about 6 ft. wide. Blooms profusely; probably the showiest of the deutzias.

D. ×rosea. Heat zones 8−3. To 3−4 ft. tall and wide. Short clusters of pinkish flowers with white interiors; broadly lance-shaped, dark green, 1- to 3-in.-long leaves with finely toothed edges.

D. scabra. FUZZY DEUTZIA. Heat zones 8−3. Native to Japan, China. To 7−10 ft. by 6 ft. Oval, scallop-toothed, 3-in.-long, dull green leaves are roughish to the touch. White or pinkish flowers in narrow, upright clusters. 'Pride of Rochester' has large clusters of small, frilly, double white flowers tinged pink. 'Codsall Pink' ('Godsall Pink') bears double pink blooms. Leaves of 'Variegata' are marked with white.

DEVIL'S SHOESTRING. See NOLINA lindheimeri

DEVIL'S WALKING STICK. See ARALIA spinosa

DEVILWOOD. See OSMANTHUS americanus

DIANTHUS

PINK
Caryophyllaceae
PERENNIALS, BIENNIALS, AND ANNUALS

US, MS, LS, CS, EXCEPT AS NOTED

FULL SUN, EXCEPT AS NOTED

MODERATE TO REGULAR WATER

Dianthus caryophyllus

The pinks include more than 300 species and an extremely large number of hybrids, many with high garden value. Most kinds form attractive evergreen mats or tufts of grasslike green, gray-green, blue-green, or blue-gray leaves. Single, semidouble, or double flowers in white and shades of pink, rose, red, yellow, and orange; many have rich, spicy fragrance. Main bloom period for most is spring into early summer; some kinds rebloom later in season or keep going into fall if faded flowers are removed.

Among dianthus are appealing border favorites such as cottage pink *(D. plumarius)* and sweet William *(D. barbatus)*, highly prized cut flowers such as carnation *(D. caryophyllus)*, and rock garden miniatures. Many excellent named selections not mentioned here are available locally.

All dianthus require well-drained soil. Sow seed of annual or biennial types in flats or directly in garden. Propagate perennial dianthus by cuttings made from tips of growing shoots, by division or layering, or from seed. Perennials are often short lived, especially in Lower, Coastal, and Tropical South, where they are often treated as annuals. Carnations and sweet William are subject to rust and fusarium wilt.

D. ×allwoodii. Perennial. Heat zones 8−1. Group of modern pinks derived from crossing *D. plumarius* and *D. caryophyllus*. Plants vary, but

WHAT PINKS NEED

LIGHT: Full sun, but with some protection from hottest afternoon exposure.

SOIL: Must be light and fast draining. Give carnations, sweet William, and cottage pinks fairly rich soil. Rock garden or alpine types need a gritty medium, with added lime if the soil is acid.

WATERING: Can take moderate to regular watering, depending on the selection.

MULCHING: Organic mulches around the base of plants can cause fungal diseases. Use an inorganic material like gravel instead.

DIVIDING: To invigorate and prolong the life of perennial pinks, divide the clumps every 2 or 3 years. When planting, allow enough space between plants for good air circulation.

Dianthus plumarius 'Dad's Favorite'

most tend to be more compact and more vigorous than their *D. plumarius* parent. They typically grow 10−15 in. high and 2 ft. wide, with gray-green foliage and two 1½- to 2-in. blossoms per stem; they bloom over a long period if deadheaded. One excellent selection is 'Aqua', which bears very fragrant, pure white double flowers on 10- to 12-in. stems. Plants sold as 'Allwoodii Alpinus' are crosses of *D. ×allwoodii* with dwarf species.

D. arenarius. Perennial. Heat zones 9−2. From Europe. Tufted plant to 1½ ft. tall and wide, with narrow, grass green leaves and fringed, inchwide white flowers sometimes marked with purple or green. Powerfully fragrant; can tolerate some shade. 'Snow Flurries' has pure white flowers.

D. barbatus. SWEET WILLIAM. Vigorous biennial often grown as annual. Zones US, MS, LS, CS, TS; 10−1. From southern Europe. Sturdy stems 10−20 in. high; plants reach 1 ft. wide. Leaves are flat, light to dark green, 1½−3 in. long. Dense clusters of white, pink, rose, red, purplish, or bicolored flowers, about ½ in. across, set among leafy bracts; spicily fragrant. Sow seed in late spring for bloom following year, or set out transplants in fall. Double-flowered and dwarf strains are obtainable from seed. Indian Carpet strain is only 6 in. tall. Roundabout and Summer Beauty strains (1 ft.) bloom the first year from seed.

D. caryophyllus. CARNATION, CLOVE PINK. Perennial. Heat zones 10−6. Highly bred Mediterranean species. There are two distinct categories of carnations: florists' and border types. Both have double flowers, bluish green leaves, and branching, leafy stems that often become woody at the base.

Border carnations grow 12−14 in. high and wide; they are bushier and more compact than the florists' type. Flowers 2−2½ in. wide, fragrant, borne in profusion. Effective as shrub border edgings, in mixed flower border, and in containers. Hybrid carnations grown from seed are usually treated as annuals, but they often live over. 'Juliet' makes compact, foot-tall clumps and bears 2½-in. scarlet flowers over a long season; 'Luminette', 2 ft. tall, is similar. 'Pixie', to 1 ft. tall, sports inch-wide, fringed pink blossoms with red centers. Knight series has strong stems, blooms in 5 months from seed; Bambino strain is a little slower to bloom. There is also a strain simply called Hanging Mixed, with pink- or red-flowered plants that sprawl or hang from pot or window box.

When grown commercially, florists' carnations are raised in greenhouses; gardeners in mild-winter areas can grow them outdoors. Plants may reach 4 ft.; they have fragrant, 3-in.-wide flowers in many colors—white, shades of pink and red, orange, purple, yellow; some are variegated. For large flowers, leave only terminal bloom on each stem, pinching out all other buds down to fifth joint, below which new flowering stems will develop. Stake to prevent sprawling. Start with strong cuttings taken from

D

the most vigorous plants of selected named types. Sturdy plants conceal supports, look quite tidy.

D. chinensis. CHINESE PINK, RAINBOW PINK. Biennial or short-lived perennial; most selections grown as annuals. Zones US, MS, LS, CS, TS; 12–1. From China. Erect, 6–30 in. high and 6–10 in. wide; stems branch only at top. Medium green foliage. Stem leaves narrow, 1–3 in. long, ½ in. wide, hairy on margins. Basal leaves are usually gone by flowering time. Flowers about 1 in. across, rose lilac with deeper-colored eye; lack fragrance. Modern strains are compact domes (to 1 ft. tall or less) covered with bright flowers in white, pink, red, and all variations and combinations of those colors. 'Fire Carpet' is a brilliant solid red; 'Snowfire' is white with a red eye. Telstar is an extra-dwarf (6- to 8-in.) strain. Petals are deeply fringed on some, smooth edged on others. Some flowers have intricately marked eyes. Sow directly in ground in spring, in full sun, for summer bloom; or, in mild areas, set out nursery plants in fall for spring bloom. Pick off faded flowers with their bases to prolong bloom. If set out in summer, Telstar will often bloom through the winter in the Lower South.

D. deltoides. MAIDEN PINK. Hardy perennial (even though it blooms in a few weeks from seed). Heat zones 10–1. From Europe and Asia. Flowering stems 8–12 in. high with short leaves; forms a loose dark green mat to 1 ft. wide. Flowers, about ¾ in. across with sharp-toothed petals, are borne at end of forked stems. Colors include white and light or dark rose to purple, spotted with lighter colors. Can tolerate up to a half day of shade. Blooms in summer, sometimes again in fall. Useful, showy ground or bank cover.

Selections include pure white 'Albus', deep red 'Vampire', bright scarlet 'Zing', and rose red 'Zing Rose'. Microchip is a seed mixture including white, reds, and pinks, often with a contrasting eye.

D. gratianopolitanus (D. caesius). CHEDDAR PINK. Perennial. Heat zones 8–1. Neat, compact mound of blue-gray to gray-green foliage on weak, branching stems. Erect, 9- to 12-in.-tall flowering stems produce 1½-in.-wide, very fragrant, typically pink to rose single flowers with toothed petals. Bloom season runs from spring to fall if plants are deadheaded regularly. Effective for ground cover, rock gardens, edging. Performs well in Lower South.

'Bath's Pink'. An old favorite. Blue-green foliage forms a neat mat about 4 in. high and 1 ft. wide, topped by 12- to 15-in. stems bearing single, fringed blossoms in soft pink with a red eye. Blooms profusely in spring, sporadically through summer. Stands up well to summer heat and humidity. Good choice for Lower South.

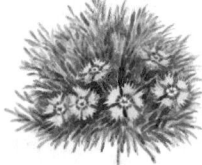

Dianthus gratianopolitanus
'Bath's Pink'

'Firewitch' ('Feuerhexe'). To 8 in. high, eventually spreading to as wide as 3 ft. Narrow blue-green leaves; single magenta flowers. Blooms heavily in early spring, sporadically in summer, and heavily again in fall. Heat tolerant and long flowering. Handsome even when out of bloom; foliage is bluer than that of 'Bath's Pink'. Good choice for Lower South.

'Greystone'. Steel gray leaves. Blooms in early spring, bearing very fragrant, fringed, single white flowers that may be tinged pink in cool weather. To 9 in. high, up to 4 ft. wide. Somewhat like a white-flowered version of 'Bath's Pink'.

'Little Boy Blue'. To 1 ft. high, 2½ ft. wide, with intensely blue-gray leaves and single white flowers dotted with pink.

'Little Joe'. Forms a clump of deep blue-gray foliage 4–6 in. high and about 6 in. across. Crimson single flowers. Especially effective with rock garden campanulas.

'Mountain Mist'. To 1 ft. high and wide. Attractive silvery blue foliage is topped in early spring by pink, fringed, lightly scented blossoms. Similar to 'Bath's Pink' but needs more cold and thus blooms less profusely in the Lower South. Good-looking foliage plant, even in winter.

'Spotty'. Very narrow leaves form a tight gray-green mat 2–3 in. high. Cerise rose flowers heavily spotted with white are carried on 6-in. stems.

'Tiny Rubies'. Makes a low mat of gray-green foliage to 3 in. high, spreading to 4 in. wide. Small, double, ruby red flowers produced on 4-in. stems. Ideal for rock gardens and containers.

D. plumarius. COTTAGE PINK. Perennial. Heat zones 9–1. Charming, almost legendary European species; cultivated for hundreds of years and used in developing many hybrids. Typically has loosely matted gray-green foliage in a clump to 2 ft. wide. Flowering stems grow 10–18 in. tall, bearing spicily fragrant, 1½- to 2-in., single or double flowers with more or less fringed petals. Colors include rose, pink, and white, some with a dark center. Most highly prized are the old laced pinks, with spicy-scented white flowers in which each petal is outlined in red or pink. Blooms in late spring and summer. Indispensable and much-favored edging for borders or for peony or rose beds. Perfect flowers for small arrangements and old-fashioned bouquets.

Choice selections include 'Dad's Favorite', which bears red-edged double white flowers on 10-in. stems; 'Essex Witch', with semidouble rose pink flowers on 5-in. stems; 'Itsaul White', with pure white, vanilla-scented single blooms on 8-in. stems; and 'Musgrave's Pink', a foot-tall classic that is at least 200 years old and bears intensely fragrant, single white blooms with a green eye.

THINK PINKS FOR FRAGRANCE. *Most dianthus offer cheerful colors, striking patterns, and a strong, clovelike scent. Among those best known for fragrance are* D. arenarius, D. caryophyllus *(border types),* D. gratianopolitanus, *and* D. plumarius. ❖

Diapensiaceae. The diapensia family contains a few perennials and tiny shrubs native to northern parts of the globe. Some, such as *Shortia*, are useful in shady gardens or rock gardens.

DIASCIA

TWINSPUR

Scrophulariaceae

PERENNIALS AND COOL-SEASON ANNUALS

ZONES VARY BY SPECIES

PARTIAL SHADE IN HOTTEST CLIMATES

MODERATE TO REGULAR WATER

Diascia barberae

South African natives related to snapdragon (*Antirrhinum*), bearing spikelike clusters of blossoms at stem ends from spring through early summer and often into fall. Flowers are coral to purplish pink, about ¾ in. across, with two prominent spurs on the back; these spurs produce oils attractive to pollinating bees. Leaves of most types are medium green, heart shaped, from ¾ in. to 1½ in. long.

Twinspurs are at their best in rock gardens, borders, and containers. With the exceptions noted, all of the species listed here are perennial, though these perennials may die in winter if planted in heavy, wet soil.

D. barberae. Annual. Zones US, MS, LS, CS, TS; 7–1. Mat-forming plant to 10 in. tall, 20 in. wide, with rose pink blossoms. 'Blackthorn Apricot' bears apricot-colored flowers.

D. fetcaniensis. Zones LS, CS; 9–8. To 10 in. high and 20 in. wide, with rose pink blooms.

D. hybrids. Zones LS, CS. These include 'Emma', an especially cold-hardy selection to 2 ft. tall and 4 ft. wide, with raspberry-colored blossoms; 'Langthorn's Lavender', to 1 ft. tall and wide, bearing lavender flowers; 'Red Start', to 8 in. high and 1 ft. wide, with watermelon red blooms; and 'Ruby Field', to 10 in. high and 2 ft. wide, with salmon pink flowers. A group of newer hybrids from England (all to 7–10 in. high and 1½ ft. wide) includes coral pink 'Coral Belle'; 'Little Charmer', pink with dark red eye; rosy red 'Red Ace'; and deep pink 'Strawberry Sundae'.

The Whisper series is a group of annual hybrids. These compact, heat-resistant plants grow 8–10 in. high, spreading to about 2 ft. wide, and bear long-blooming, pansylike flowers. Selections include 'Apricot', 'Cranberry Red', 'Lavender Pink', and 'Salmon Red'.

D. integerrima. Zones LS, CS; 9–8. To 1½ ft. tall, creeping to 3–4 ft. wide. Narrow leaves to 1 in. long; loose spikes of rich purplish pink flowers. 'Coral Canyon' grows 12–15 in. high and 1½ ft. wide, bears salmon pink blooms.

D. rigescens. Zones MS, LS, CS; 9–7. Sprawling stems form a clump to 1 ft. tall, 2 ft. wide, turn up at ends to display 6- to 8-in. spikes of rich pink flowers. Cut out old stems.

DICENTRA

BLEEDING HEART

Fumariaceae

PERENNIALS

ZONES VARY BY SPECIES

PARTIAL TO FULL SHADE, EXCEPT AS NOTED

REGULAR WATER, EXCEPT AS NOTED

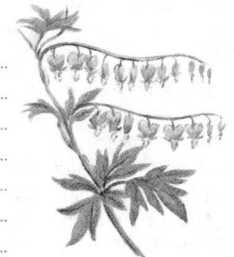

Dicentra spectabilis

Graceful, fernlike foliage. Leafless stems carry dainty, pendent flowers, usually heart shaped and ½ to 1 in. long, in pink, rose, yellow, or white. Combine handsomely with ferns, hostas, astilbes, epimediums, foamflowers *(Tiarella),* hellebores. In general, they need rich, light, moist, porous soil. Never let water stand around roots.

D. canadensis. SQUIRREL CORN. Zones US, MS; 8–1. Native from North Carolina to Missouri, Minnesota, and Canada. Reaches just 6–8 in. tall and wide, growing from small tubers resembling ears of corn. White, perfectly heart-shaped flowers in early spring. Foliage dies back after flowering. Locate in ground cover or other area where shallow-growing tubers will not be disturbed. Prefers slightly alkaline soil.

D. chrysantha. GOLDEN EARDROPS. Zones US, MS, LS; 8–1. Native to inner Coast Ranges and Sierra Nevada foothills of California. Erect plant with stout, hollow stems sparsely clothed in divided blue-gray leaves; grows 4–5 ft. tall, 1½ ft. wide. Golden yellow, short-spurred flowers, held upright in large clusters, bloom in spring and summer. Requires warmth. Unlike many bleeding hearts, this species needs soil that is not too rich; make sure drainage is good. Has a deep taproot and does not need irrigation during the bloom period. Seed is available from wildflower specialists.

D. eximia. FRINGED BLEEDING HEART. Zones US, MS, LS, CS; 9–1. Native to northeastern U.S. Forms tidy clump 1–1½ ft. high and wide. Blue-gray basal leaves are more finely divided than those of *D. formosa.* Big, deep rose pink flowers with short, rounded spurs bloom from mid-spring into summer. Cut back for second growth and occasional repeat bloom. Spreads by self-sowing.

D. formosa. WESTERN BLEEDING HEART. Zones US, MS, LS, CS; 10–1. Native to moist woods along Pacific Coast. To 1½ ft. tall, 3 ft. or wider. Blue-green foliage. Blooms in spring, bearing clusters of pendulous pale or deep rose flowers on reddish stems. Spreads freely by rhizomes and seeding, forming large colonies. 'Zestful' is everblooming, with deep rose flowers. *D. f. oregana* grows to 1 ft. tall, has silvery green leaves and cream-colored flowers that are tipped with purple.

D. hybrids. Zones US, MS, LS. *D. eximia* and *D. formosa* cross freely to yield hybrids, many of which have been named. The following are among the most commonly cultivated; they grow 1–1½ ft. high and 1½–2 ft. across (eventually spreading more widely) and bloom from spring into summer.

'Bacchanal'. Finely cut gray-green leaves and dark red flowers.

'Bountiful'. Dark blue-green foliage and purplish pink to dusky red flowers.

'King of Hearts'. Lacy blue-green leaves and big flowers in deep pink.

'Langtrees'. Silvery green foliage and white flowers shaded pink.

'Luxuriant'. Medium to dark green leaves and red flowers.

D. scandens 'Athens Yellow'. Zones MS, LS, CS; 8–6. Selection of a Himalayan species. Climbing plant reaches to 10 ft., blanketed with bright yellow, inch-long flowers starting in late spring or early summer, then continuing all summer. Yellowish green leaves to 1 ft. long are divided into ovate to lance-shaped leaflets; terminal leaflet reaches out like a tendril.

Vigorous, rapid grower but not invasive. Can be grown as an annual. Needs more sun than other bleeding hearts, but it should be protected from hot afternoon sun.

D. spectabilis. COMMON BLEEDING HEART. Zones US, MS, LS, CS; 9–1. Native to Japan. Old garden favorite; showiest and largest leafed of all bleeding hearts. To 2–3 ft. high, 3 ft. wide; stems are set with soft green leaves. Blooms in late spring, bearing big flowers on one side of arching stems—rose pink, pendulous, heart shaped, with protruding white inner petals. 'Gold Heart' has bright golden leaves that hold their color into summer. 'Alba' ('Pantaloons') is a pure white form.

Plants usually die down to the ground by midsummer. To keep the gap from showing, plant next to perennials that hold their foliage all summer. Prefers light shade.

DICHORISANDRA
thyrsiflora

BLUE GINGER

Commelinaceae

PERENNIAL

TS 12–9; OR GROW IN POTS

LIGHT SHADE; BRIGHT INDIRECT LIGHT

AMPLE WATER

Dichorisandra thyrsiflora

This Brazilian native is not a true ginger but rather a robust and upright-growing relative of wandering Jew *(Tradescantia).* Succulent, unbranched or sparsely branched stems rise from a short, fleshy rhizome and reach 6–8 ft. tall. Deep green, oval, 6- to 12-in.-long, evergreen leaves are spirally arranged around the stem, forming a 3-ft.-wide foliage clump. Deep violet-blue flowers appear in 6-in. spikes at tops of stems throughout the year. Best in moist soil enriched with organic matter. Easy to propagate by cuttings. As a houseplant or in greenhouse, grows 3 ft. tall in an 8-in. pot, taller in a large container.

DICKSONIA

Dicksoniaceae

TREE FERNS

TS; OR GROW IN POTS

PARTIAL TO FULL SHADE

REGULAR WATER

Dicksonia antarctica

These hardy, slow-growing tree ferns from the Southern Hemisphere are easy to transplant and establish. Arguably the most beautiful of the tree ferns, they produce long, lacy, arching fronds. Caring for them isn't difficult. They need high humidity, so wet down the trunks on dry summer and autumn days. Overhead watering is preferred. Give them moist, well-drained soil rich in humus; shield them from drying winds. Every spring, spread a few inches of organic fertilizer, such as garden compost or composted cow manure, around the base. Don't trim off the old fronds until new ones emerge. Beyond hardiness range, grow in containers.

D. antarctica. TASMANIAN TREE FERN. Heat zones 12–10. Native to southeastern Australia, Tasmania. Hardiest of tree ferns; well-established plants tolerate 20°F. Thick, red-brown, fuzzy trunk grows slowly to 15 ft. From top of trunk grow many arching, 3- to 6-ft. fronds; mature fronds are more finely cut than those of Australian tree fern *(Cyathea cooperi).*

D. squarrosa. Heat zones 10–9. Native to New Zealand. Slender, dark trunk grows slowly to 20 ft. tall. Flat crown of 8-ft.-long, stiff, leathery fronds. Much less frequently grown than *D. antarctica.*

FOR INFORMATION ON SELECTING PLANTS

PLEASE SEE PAGES 39–144

Dicksoniaceae. The dicksonia family of tree ferns differs only in minor botanical details from the other tree fern family, Cyatheaceae. One representative is *Dicksonia*.

DICLIPTERA

Acanthaceae

PERENNIALS

⚡ ZONES VARY BY SPECIES

☼ ◑ FULL SUN OR PARTIAL SHADE

◐ ◓ ● WATER NEEDS VARY BY SPECIES

Dicliptera suberecta

These tender, shrublike perennials offer colorful tubular blossoms from spring to fall. They hold up well in heat, but they must have good drainage. Where stems are not killed to the ground by frost, shear to about 6 in. high in late winter.

D. resupinata. Zones CS, TS; root hardy to about 22°F. Native to washes and rocky slopes from southeastern Arizona and southwestern New Mexico south into Mexico. Open growth to 2 ft. tall, 2–3 ft. wide, with branches sparsely foliaged in elongated heart-shaped, inch-long, dark green leaves that take on an attractive purplish cast in cool weather. Slender, rosy purple, ¾-in.-long flowers bloom from late spring to fall. Sometimes reseeds but is not invasive. Little or no water.

D. suberecta (Jacobinia suberecta, Justicia suberecta). Zones LS, CS, TS. Native to Uruguay. Woody-based perennial 2 ft. tall, 1½ ft. wide, with grayish green, softly downy leaves 1½–3 in. long and about half as wide. Summertime clusters of bright orange-red, 1½-in.-long flowers attract hummingbirds. Moderate to regular water.

DICTAMNUS albus

GAS PLANT

Rutaceae

PERENNIAL

⚡ US, MS, LS ⬧ 8–1

☼ ◑ FULL SUN OR LIGHT SHADE

◐ ● MODERATE TO REGULAR WATER

◊ OIL FROM IMMATURE SEED CAPSULES MAY CAUSE AN ALLERGIC SKIN REACTION

Dictamnus albus
'Purpureus'

Native from Europe to northern China. Sturdy, long lived, practically immortal in colder climates, needing little care once established. Forms clumps 2½–4 ft. high, 3 ft. wide. In early summer, produces loose spires of blossoms at branch tips; each flower resembles a wild azalea, with narrow petals and prominent greenish stamens. Pink is the basic color, but nurseries offer lilac-purple 'Purpureus' and white 'Albiflorus'. Seedpods that follow can be left in place for fall interest. Glossy olive green leaves with 9 to 11 leaflets, each 1–3 in. long, are handsome throughout the growing season.

Plant emits a strong lemony scent when rubbed or brushed against. In warm, humid weather, oils from immature seed capsules may briefly ignite if you hold a lighted match immediately beneath a flower cluster—hence the common name "gas plant" (this "ignition test" does not harm plant).

Effective in borders; good cut flower. Divide infrequently, since divisions are difficult to establish and often take 2 or 3 years to bloom well. Propagate from seed sown in fall or spring; or take root cuttings in spring.

DIDISCUS coeruleus. See TRACHYMENE coerulea

FOR GROWING SYMBOL EXPLANATIONS
PLEASE SEE PAGE 145

DIEFFENBACHIA

DUMB CANE

Araceae

PERENNIALS

⚡ TS ⬧ 12–10; OR HOUSEPLANT

☼ ◑ ● SUN OR SHADE; BRIGHT INDIRECT LIGHT

◐ MODERATE WATER

◊ SAP BURNS MOUTH, MAY PARALYZE VOCAL CORDS

Dieffenbachia amoena

From forests of the tropical Americas. Grown for their striking evergreen foliage—in colors varying from dark green to yellow green and chartreuse, with variegations in white or pale cream. In the Tropical South, will grow year-round outdoors, either potted or in the ground as accent plants. Elsewhere, grow them indoors. Young plants generally have single stems, while older ones may develop multiple stems. Taller than wide; those listed here are 1½–2 ft. wide. Mature plants bear flowers resembling odd, narrow callas (*Zantedeschia*).

Give container plants fast-draining potting mix, and be sure to let the mix dry to a depth of at least 1 in. before watering. Feed with half-strength general-purpose liquid houseplant fertilizer bimonthly in spring and summer. Underfed, underwatered plants show amazing endurance, recovering from severe wilting when better conditions come. Repotting is necessary when roots begin pushing plant up out of pot. Once repotted, plants usually send out new basal shoots. Sudden change from low to high light level will burn leaves, but you can move houseplants to a sheltered patio or lanai in summer. If plants get leggy, you can cut them back to 6 in. above the soil line; gangly specimens cut back in this way will usually resprout with multiple stems. Or start new plants by air layering or taking stem cuttings; discard the original, overly leggy plant. Spider mites can be a serious pest indoors, causing discolored leaves; treat with insecticidal soap or horticultural oil (take plants outdoors to spray).

Nomenclature is somewhat confused. Some of the plants described below may be sold as varieties of *D. seguine*, a highly variable species quite similar to *D. maculata*.

D. amoena. To 6 ft. or taller. Broad, dark green, 1½-ft.-long leaves with narrow, slanting white stripes on either side of midrib.

D. × bausei. To 3 ft. or taller. Greenish yellow, 1-ft.-long leaves have deep green blotches and white flecks.

D. 'Exotica'. To 3–4 ft. tall, with 9-in.-long leaves featuring dull green edges and extensive creamy white variegation. Midrib is creamy white.

D. maculata (D. picta). Grows to 6 ft. or taller. Broad, oval green leaves reach 10 in. or longer, have greenish white dots and patches. 'Rudolph Roehrs' has pale chartreuse foliage blotched with ivory and edged with green. Foliage of 'Superba' is thicker and slightly more durable than that of species and is more generously marked with creamy dots and patches.

DIERVILLA

BUSH HONEYSUCKLE

Caprifoliaceae

DECIDUOUS SHRUBS

⚡ US, MS, LS ⬧ 8–1, EXCEPT AS NOTED

☼ ◑ FULL SUN OR PARTIAL SHADE

◐ MODERATE WATER

Diervilla rivularis

This is a small and relatively unknown group of shrubs native to eastern North America. Spreading by suckers, they are suitable for massing or as a ground cover. Oval, pointed leaves make an attractive backdrop for summertime clusters of small yellow flowers that look something like honeysuckle (*Lonicera*) blooms. Tough, hardy, and pest free; cut back in early spring to renew vigor.

D. lonicera. DWARF BUSH HONEYSUCKLE. Native from Canada to North Carolina. Forms a low mound 2–4 ft. tall and wide. Leaves are dark green above, a bit lighter beneath, 2–4 in. long. Sulfur yellow, ½-in.-long flowers appear all summer. 'Copper' produces flushes of copper-colored new foliage throughout the growing season.

D. rivularis. GEORGIA BUSH HONEYSUCKLE. Heat zones 8–3. Native from North Carolina and Tennessee south to Georgia and Alabama. Grows 6 ft. tall and wide. Dark green, fuzzy leaves are 2–3 in. long, turn yellow-red in autumn. Clusters of lemon yellow, inch-long flowers appear in June. 'Summer Stars' is a dwarf selection to 2–3 ft. tall and a bit wider, with profuse trumpetlike flowers in sulfur yellow.

D. sessilifolia. SOUTHERN BUSH HONEYSUCKLE. Same native range as *D. rivularis*. Grows 3–5 ft. high with equal or greater spread. Glossy green leaves to 6 in. long. Sulfur yellow flowers to ½ in. long appear through much of summer. Selection 'Butterfly' features deep yellow blooms and purple autumn foliage.

DIETES

FORTNIGHT LILY, AFRICAN IRIS

Iridaceae

PERENNIALS FROM RHIZOMES

LS (PROTECTED), CS, TS

FULL SUN OR PARTIAL SHADE

MODERATE TO REGULAR WATER

Dietes iridioides

Irislike plants with fans of stiff, narrow evergreen form dense, long-lasting clumps. Flowers rese small Japanese irises consist of three outer and three inner segments; they appear on branched stalks throughout spring, summer, and fall, and sometimes well into winter in mild climates. Bloom bursts seem to occur at 2-week intervals, hence the common name "fortnight lily." Flowers come in solid colors—white, cream, yellow; each of the three outer segments features a small contrasting blotch of orange, yellow, or brown. Each flower lasts only a day (with the exception of *D. grandiflora*), but the supply of flowers on a stem is seemingly endless. Excellent in permanent landscape plantings with pebbles and rocks, shrubs, and other long-lived perennials.

Plant from containers (bare rhizomes are not sold) at any time of year, setting plants 2–3 ft. apart. All types look best with good soil and regular moisture, but once established they will perform satisfactorily even in poor soil or with infrequent or erratic watering. Clumps can remain undisturbed for years; when you need to divide, do so in fall or winter.

D. bicolor. Heat zones 10–8. From South Africa. Stems 2–3 ft. tall. Flowers about 2 in. wide and circular in outline, light yellow with dark brown to maroon blotches. Flower stems last only 1 year.

D. grandiflora (D. iridioides 'Johnsonii'). Heat zones 12–8. From South Africa. In general aspect, this is a somewhat taller, larger version (up to 3–4 ft. tall) of *D. iridioides* and is usually sold as a variety of that species. Other differences include brown markings at the bases of inner segments and, on outer segments, yellow blotches that are actually bearded. Unlike all others, this species has flowers that last for 3 days before folding. Flower stems are perennial; see *D. iridioides* for care.

D. hybrids. Both 'Lemon Drops' and 'Orange Drops' are hybrids of *D. bicolor* and resemble it save for flower color. 'Lemon Drops' is ivory with yellow blotches, 'Orange Drops' ivory with orange blotches. As is true for their other parent, *D. iridioides*, these hybrids' flower stems last more than a year; for care see *D. iridioides*.

D. iridioides (D. vegeta, Moraea iridioides). Heat zones 12–8. From East Africa. Stems to 2½ ft. tall. Waxy white flowers to 3 in. across have yellow-orange blotches and a few orange marks at bases of inner three segments. Three style arms—appendages radiating from flower's center—are usually pale violet. To prolong bloom and prevent self-sowing, break off blossoms individually. Don't cut flower stems (they last for more than a year) until they clearly have stopped producing blooms; then cut back to lower leaf joint near base of stem. For the plant sold as *D. iridioides* 'Johnsonii', see *D. grandiflora*.

DIGITALIS

FOXGLOVE

Scrophulariaceae

PERENNIALS AND BIENNIALS

US, MS, LS, CS

LIGHT SHADE

REGULAR WATER, EXCEPT AS NOTED

ALL PARTS ARE POISONOUS IF INGESTED

Digitalis purpurea

Mainly from Europe, Mediterranean region. Erect plants 2–8 ft. high form low foliage clumps topped by spikes of tubular flowers shaped like fingertips of a glove; colors include purple, yellow, white, pastels. Blossoms attract hummingbirds. Leaves are typically gray green and hairy. Common foxglove (*D. purpurea*) is widely grown for height and color display in shaded gardens, but other, less well-known species are deserving subjects for borders, woodland edges, and larger rock gardens. Most tend to be biennials, but some can be coaxed into a second year of bloom if spent flowers are removed before they set seed.

Foxgloves like moist, rich, well-drained soil. Protect the plants from snails and slugs. (Deer leave them alone.) After the first flush of flowers, cut off the main spike; side shoots will develop and bloom late in the season. In the Lower and Coastal South, treat as annuals; set out new transplants in summer and fall for bloom the next spring or summer. In the Upper and Middle South, set out plants or sow seed in spring for bloom the following year. Plants self-sow freely; blooms of volunteers are often white or light-colored.

D. ferruginea. RUSTY FOXGLOVE. Biennial or short-lived perennial. Heat zones 7–1. To 4 ft. tall, 1½ ft. wide, with stems densely clothed in deeply veined leaves. Long, dense spikes of ¾- to 1¼-in.-long, yellowish flowers netted with rusty red. 'Yellow Herald' ('Gelber Herold') is a good yellow-flowering selection.

D. grandiflora (D. ambigua). YELLOW FOXGLOVE. Biennial or short-lived perennial. Heat zones 8–1. To 3 ft. tall, 1½ ft. wide. Toothed leaves wrap around stem. Flowers are 2–3 in. long, yellowish marked with brown. 'John Innes Tetra' is a choice selection to 20 in. tall, with pale yellow flowers richly netted with gold and brown.

D. laevigata. Perennial. Heat zones 9–3. To 3 ft. high, 1½ ft. wide, with smooth, narrow dark green leaves and inch-long, creamy yellow flowers speckled with purplish brown.

D. lanata. GRECIAN FOXGLOVE. Biennial or short-lived perennial. Heat zones 9–3. To 2 ft. high and 1 ft. wide, with 1¼-in.-long, cream to light tan flowers netted with brown.

D. ×mertonensis. Perennial. Heat zones 8–1. Spikes to 2–3 ft. high, bearing attractive coppery rose, 2½-in.-long blooms above a foot-wide clump of furry leaves. Though a hybrid, it comes true from seed.

D. obscura. NARROW-LEAF FOXGLOVE. Woody-based perennial. Heat zones 7–5. To 1½ ft. tall, 1 ft. wide, with lance-shaped leaves and spikes of drooping brown-and-yellow bells about 1 in. long. Takes well-drained but not rich soil and occasional deep watering.

D. purpurea. COMMON FOXGLOVE. Biennial or short-lived perennial. Heat zones 9–1. Variable, appearing in many garden forms. Bold, erect growth to 4 ft. or taller, with stems rising from clumps of large, rough, woolly light green leaves. Short-stalked stem leaves become smaller toward top of plant; these are the source of digitalis, a much valued but highly poisonous medicinal drug. Pendulous flowers are 2–3 in. long, purple with darker spots on lower, paler lip. Flowers are borne in one-sided, 1- to 2-ft.-long spikes.

Selections include 'Alba', with white flowers spotted brownish red on the lower lip, and 'Apricot Beauty', with pale apricot blossoms. Garden strains include 5-ft.-tall Excelsior, with fuller spikes than species and flowers held more horizontally to show off interior spotting; 3-ft. Foxy, which performs as an annual and blooms in 5 months from seed; 4-ft. Gloxiniiflora, bearing flowers that are larger and open wider than those of species; 3-ft.-high Peloric Mixed, with topmost flower of each spike open or bowl

D

shaped and 3 in. wide; and Shirley, a tall (6-ft.), robust strain with a full range of colors.

D. thapsi. Perennial. Heat zones 8–1. From Spain. To 1 ft. tall and wide, with furry foliage and short spires of drooping purplish pink, 2- to 3-in.-long flowers. Thrives under the same conditions as *D. obscura*. 'Spanish Peaks' is an outstanding selection.

FOXGLOVES—TOWERS OF FLOWERS. *Of all the flowering plants with spirelike blooms, foxgloves are perhaps the easiest to grow. They're great for the back of the border or in a mass all by themselves. In most places, they'll live for 1 or 2 years. To ensure beautiful flowers every spring, set out new transplants each year in early summer or autumn.* ❖

DILL. See ANETHUM graveolens

DIMORPHOTHECA

AFRICAN DAISY, CAPE MARIGOLD

Asteraceae (Compositae)

ANNUALS

🗡 US, MS, LS, CS, TS

☼ FULL SUN

💧 MODERATE WATER

Dimorphotheca sinuata

Cheery, free-blooming South African natives with daisy flowers that close when shaded, during heavy overcast, and at night. Use in broad masses—as ground cover, in borders and parking strips, along rural roadsides, as filler among low shrubs. Broadcast seed where plants are to grow; sow in early spring (or in late fall or winter, in mildest climates). Do best in light soil. For other plants known as African daisy, see *Arctotis* and *Osteospermum*.

D. barberae. See Osteospermum barberae

D. ecklonis. See Osteospermum ecklonis

D. fruticosa. See Osteospermum fruticosum

D. pluvialis (D. annua). Heat zones 12–6. Branched stems 4–16 in. high. Leaves to 3½ in. long, 1 in. wide, coarsely toothed. Yellow-centered, 1- to 2-in.-wide flower heads with rays that are white above, violet or purple beneath. 'Glistening White', a dwarf form with 4-in.-wide flowers, is especially desirable.

D. sinuata (D. aurantiaca). Heat zones 9–1. Best known of annual African daisies. To 4–12 in. high. Narrow, 2- to 3-in.-long leaves with a few teeth or shallow cuts. Flowers 1½ in. wide, with orange-yellow rays that are sometimes deep violet at the base; centers are yellow or dark with flecks of yellow. Hybrids between this species and *D. pluvialis* come in white and shades of yellow and light orange, often with contrasting dark centers.

In north Florida, grow this species as a summer annual. In central and south Florida, it can also be grown as a winter annual, but it's susceptible to soil-borne diseases that make it short-lived there. Not bothered by deer.

DIONAEA muscipula

VENUS'S FLYTRAP

Droseraceae

INSECTIVOROUS PERENNIAL

🗡 MS, LS 🅷 8–6; OR HOUSEPLANT

☼ FULL SUN; BRIGHT LIGHT

💧💧 REGULAR TO AMPLE WATER

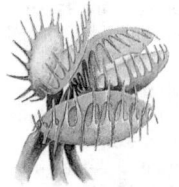

Dionaea muscipula

If ever a plant turned the table on insects, Venus's flytrap is the one. Native to the nutrient-starved bogs of the Carolinas, it forms a low rosette of semievergreen leaves to 5–6 in. long. At the tip of each leaf are

two hinged lobes that form a 1- to 2-in.-long trap, its margins lined with stout bristles and nectar-producing glands. Insects are attracted to the nectar, and when their movement triggers the tiny, sensitive hairs inside the trap, it closes quickly, ensnaring the hapless insect-turned-dinner within the interlocking bristles. The plants use this mechanism to obtain nutrients unavailable in the soil. Tiny white flowers appear in summer. Leaves and traps of the species are green to yellowish green, and traps are often flushed red. Selection 'Akai Ryu' displays bright red stems and carmine red traps.

These carnivorous curiosities are difficult to cultivate under garden conditions. Outdoors, they need full sun and constantly moist, peaty soil that contains few nutrients. They should not be fertilized, and the traps should never be fed with meat or anything else. Indoors, they need bright light, moist soil, and very high humidity; a terrarium containing finely milled sphagnum peat moss should do the trick. Plants go semidormant in winter and appreciate cooler temperatures then.

Unfortunately, Venus's flytraps are collected from the wild by the thousands each year. Most collected plants die, either at the store or shortly after purchase. To avoid depleting wild populations, buy plants only from reputable nurseries that propagate their own plants by seed, division, or tissue culture.

DIOON

Zamiaceae

CYCADS

🗡 TS 🅷 12–10; OR GROW IN POTS

☼ PARTIAL SHADE

💧 REGULAR WATER

Dioon edule

These cycads resemble *Cycas revoluta*, but they are less widely sold, more tender, and even slower growing. Male and female plants are separate. Dioons are excellent choices for tropical effects and as container plants.

D. edule. Very slow growing. Eventually forms cylindrical trunk 6–10 in. wide, 3 ft. high. Spreading, slightly arching, 3- to 5-ft. leaves are made up of many leaflets that may be toothed at the tips or smooth edged. Foliage on young plants is dusty blue green and feathery; that on mature plants is deeper green, shiny, more rigid. Tolerates occasional frost.

D. spinulosum. Slow growth to 12 ft. Leaves reach about 5 ft. long, with up to 100 narrow, spine-toothed, dark green, 6- to 8-in.-long leaflets. Protect plants from frost.

DIOSCOREA bulbifera

TATER VINE, AIR POTATO

Dioscoreaceae

PERENNIAL VINE

🗡 CS, TS 🅷 12–7

☼ ◑ ● SUN OR SHADE

💧 REGULAR WATER

Dioscorea bulbifera

A member of the yam family and native to tropical East Asia, this handsome vine gets its common name from its unusual aerial tubers, which range from 1 to 6 in. wide and have a woody, waffle-patterned surface that gives them the look of rough-textured potatoes—or brownish hand grenades. The plant produces large, glossy, heart-shaped leaves that have a coppery sheen when they unfurl, then mature to rich green. Flowers are inconspicuous but have a pleasing scent.

In the Coastal and Tropical South, tater vine is perennial; tubers fall to the ground and sprout where they land. In colder areas, it dies with the first hard frost, but gardeners there can keep it going by harvesting tubers before frost and storing them over winter. Tubers often sprout by late winter, but they should not be planted outdoors until the ground warms in spring.

Grown on a trellis, tater vine makes a quick, attractive screen for shading a porch. You can also grow it on posts, fences, and arbors. Keep in mind, though, that it grows extremely quickly—nearly as fast as kudzu, up to 20 ft. in a single season. And be very careful where you plant it in the Coastal or Tropical South; it has escaped cultivation and become a serious pest in central and south Florida.

DIOSPYROS texana

TEXAS PERSIMMON

Ebenaceae

DECIDUOUS OR EVERGREEN TREE

🗲 MS, LS, CS, TS 🅷 12–7

☼ ◑ FULL SUN OR PARTIAL SHADE

◊ LITTLE WATER ONCE ESTABLISHED

Diospyros texana

Native to South Texas and Mexico, this tree is grown primarily for its lovely shape and bark. (For persimmons grown mainly for their edible fruit, see Persimmon.) Grows to 30 ft. tall, 10–15 ft. wide, with multiple slender trunks; silvery gray bark peels off in strips. Fragrant, urn-shaped greenish white flowers, attractive to bees, bloom in early spring. Thick-textured, dark green, 1- to 2-in.-long leaves are evergreen in mild-winter climates. Female trees bear small (1- to 2-in.-wide), edible black fruits—but fruit drop is messy, so male trees are often preferred for the garden. In naturalized settings, however, female trees are valuable for the food they supply to birds and other wildlife. Well suited to dry, rocky, alkaline soils. Not a good choice for high-rainfall, high-humidity areas. Not browsed by deer.

DIPLADENIA splendens. See MANDEVILLA splendens

DISANTHUS cercidifolius

Hamamelidaceae

DECIDUOUS SHRUB

🗲 US, MS, LS 🅷 8–1

◑ LIGHT SHADE

◊ REGULAR WATER

Disanthus cercidifolius

Native to Japan. Slender-branched shrub to 10–12 ft. tall and wide, grown for magnificent fall color. Nearly round, smooth, 2- to 4-in.-wide leaves turn from bluish green to shades of deep red with orange tints at the onset of colder weather. Tiny, purplish fall flowers are mildly fragrant. Provide rich soil and protection from wind. No special pruning needed. Plant can be finicky and performs better in the Upper and Middle South. For connoisseurs, not beginners.

DISTICTIS

Bignoniaceae

EVERGREEN VINES

🗲 ZONES VARY BY SPECIES

☼ ◑ FULL SUN OR PARTIAL SHADE

◊ REGULAR WATER

Distictis buccinatoria

These Mexican natives are spectacular vines for milder climates, reaching heights of 20–30 ft. Glossy leaves consist of two leaflets with a central, three-part tendril that plants use for climbing. All bear long-lasting, trumpet-shaped flowers. Plant in good, well-drained soil; provide sturdy support, since growth is dense and heavy. Prune in winter to thin stems, control size.

D. buccinatoria (Bignonia cherere, Phaedranthus buccinatorius). BLOOD-RED TRUMPET VINE. Zones CS, TS; 12–9. Oblong to oval leaflets 2–4 in. long. Clusters of 4-in.-long, yellow-throated flowers in orange red fading to bluish red; blossoms stand out well from vine. Blooms in bursts throughout year when weather warms. Give protected site in hottest climates.

D. laxiflora (D. lactiflora, D. cinerea). VANILLA TRUMPET VINE. Zones TS; 12–10. More restrained than most trumpet vines and requires less pruning. Oblong, 2½-in.-long leaflets. Vanilla-scented, 3½-in.-long trumpets appear in generous clusters throughout warmer months, sometimes giving 8 months of bloom; they are violet at first, fading to lavender and white.

D. 'Rivers'. ROYAL TRUMPET VINE. Zones TS; 12–9. Plants sold under this name are nearly a match for *D. buccinatoria* in vigor and foliage and have flowers of about the same size; blossoms are mauve to purple with a yellow to orange throat. Sometimes labeled *D. riversii*.

Distictis 'Rivers'

DITTANY OF CRETE. See ORIGANUM dictamnus

DIZYGOTHECA elegantissima. See SCHEFFLERA elegantissima

DODECATHEON meadia

SHOOTING STAR

Primulaceae

PERENNIAL

🗲 US, MS, LS 🅷 8–1

◑ PARTIAL SHADE

◊ REGULAR WATER DURING GROWTH AND BLOOM

Dodecatheon meadia

Native to the eastern U.S. Light green, oblong leaves to 10 in. long form a basal rosette nearly a foot across. In early to midspring, leafless stalks rise to 16 in. high, topped by many-flowered clusters of ½- to ¾-in.-long blossoms in white to occasionally pink or purple with quite prominent, downward-pointing yellow stamens. Swept-back petals give blooms the look of small cyclamen flowers. Dies back completely at onset of hot weather. Prefers rich, loose, well-drained soil. Excellent in woodland gardens.

DOG-TOOTH VIOLET. See ERYTHRONIUM dens-canis

DOGWOOD. See CORNUS

DOLICHOS lablab
(Lablab purpureus)

HYACINTH BEAN

Fabaceae (Leguminosae)

PERENNIAL VINE ALSO GROWN AS ANNUAL

🗲 LS, CS, TS 🅷 12–1

☼ FULL SUN

◊ REGULAR WATER

Dolichos lablab

Probably from Asia. Fast-growing, twining vine to 10 ft. Leaves are made up of three broad, oval leaflets to 3–6 in. long. Fragrant, sweet pea–shaped, purple or white flowers appear in late summer or autumn, borne in loose clusters on long stems that stand out from foliage. Blossoms are followed by velvety, bean-like pods to 2½ in. long, in a stunning shade of bright magenta purple. Grow like string beans for quick, dense screening. Provide trellis or other support. Needs good drainage.

DOLL'S EYES. See ACTAEA alba

DORONICUM

LEOPARD'S BANE

Asteraceae (Compositae)

PERENNIALS

US, MS, LS H 8–1

PARTIAL SHADE

REGULAR WATER

Doronicum columnae

Summer is the season for most yellow daisies, but these European natives bear their profuse showy flowers in mid- to late spring. The 1- to 3-in. blooms are carried on long, slender, branching stems that rise from low, dense foliage clumps; make good cut flowers. Dark green, 2½- to 5-in.-long leaves are rounded to heart-shaped, with toothed edges.

Most types die back by midsummer, so they're best used in a strictly spring-flowering scheme or where summer annuals can fill the gap. Combine with white, purple, or lavender tulips and blue violas or forget-me-nots *(Myosotis);* use in front of purple lilacs *(Syringa)* or with hellebores at edge of woodland or shade border. Mark location before plants die back so you don't accidentally disturb them. Provide some moisture during dormancy. Divide clumps every 2 or 3 years in early autumn; young plants bloom best.

D. columnae (D. cordatum). Bright yellow flower heads up to 3 in. across, borne singly on 1- to 2-ft. stems above a foot-wide foliage clump. Usually dies back in summer.

D. 'Miss Mason'. Choice hybrid between *D. columnae* and another species. Bright yellow, 3-in. daisies on a plant to 2½ ft. tall, about 1½ ft. wide. Leaves are a little less toothed, flowers a little bigger than those of *D. columnae;* plants also are less likely to die back in summer.

D. orientale (D. caucasicum). Golden yellow, 1- to 2-in.-wide blossoms are borne singly on 2-ft. stems; clumps may spread to a width of 3 ft. Dies back in summer. 'Finesse' has larger flowers (to 3 in.) on sturdy stems; excellent for cutting. 'Magnificum' is a compact grower to about 20 in. tall.

D. plantagineum. PLANTAIN LEOPARD'S BANE. Larger, coarser-leafed plant than the others, suitable for a wild garden. Each stout, 2½- to 3-ft.-tall stem bears a few golden yellow, 2- to 3-in.-wide flowers. Clumps reach about 1½ ft. wide. Dies back in summer. 'Harpur Crewe' (*D. ×excelsum* 'Harpur Crewe') is a little shorter, with strong-stemmed blooms to 4 in. across that make it one of the best choices for cutting.

DOUBLE REEVES SPIRAEA. See SPIRAEA cantoniensis

DOUGLAS FIR. See PSEUDOTSUGA menziesii

DOVE TREE. See DAVIDIA involucrata

DOXANTHA unguis-cati. See MACFADYENA unguis-cati

DRABA

Brassicaceae (Cruciferae)

PERENNIALS

ZONES VARY BY SPECIES

FULL SUN

REGULAR WATER

Draba aizoides

Some 300 species native to mountainous and subarctic regions of the world. All are low, mat- or cushion-forming plants with tightly clustered, tiny leaves in rosettes and four-petaled yellow (rarely white) flowers in short, spikelike clusters in spring or early summer. All require perfect drainage, dislike soggy soil. Can endure great cold. Use in rock gardens. The following are some of the most commonly planted species.

D. aizoides. Zones US; 6–1. Native to mountains of central and southern Europe. Tufts of tiny dark green rosettes form clumps 2–4 in. across. Bears four to ten or more bright yellow flowers on 4-in. stems.

D. oligosperma. Zones US; 6–1. One of more than a dozen species native to the Rocky Mountain area. Makes silvery mats up to 1 ft. wide topped with loose clusters of yellow flowers carried on 4-in. stems.

D. sibirica (D. repens). Zones US, MS; 7–1. Native to Siberia, Greenland. Trailing stems set with soft green leaves form a 1½-ft.-wide carpet. Profuse show of small yellow flowers on 2- to 4-in. stems.

DRACAENA

Agavaceae

EVERGREEN PALMLIKE TREES

TS H 12–10; OR HOUSEPLANTS

FULL SUN OR PARTIAL SHADE; BRIGHT INDIRECT LIGHT

MODERATE WATER

Dracaena draco

About 40 species of tropical trees and shrubs. Although they're hardy outdoors in the Tropical South, most people grow them indoors. Some varieties and selections display graceful, fountainlike forms with broad, curved, ribbonlike leaves that may be striped with chartreuse or white; others bear stiff, swordlike foliage.

Dracaenas are popular houseplants because they look good even if neglected or grown in low light. Let soil dry to a depth of ½ in. between waterings; overwatering results in leaves that are yellowed or spotted with brown. In spring and summer, feed twice monthly with a general-purpose liquid houseplant fertilizer; don't feed at all in fall and winter. If stems get leggy, cut them back to just above a node; new shoots will sprout. Outdoors, all but *D. draco* need protection from sweeping winds. For other plants often called dracaena, see *Cordyline.*

D. australis. See Cordyline australis

D. deremensis. Native to tropical Africa. Most commonly sold selection is 'Warneckii': erect, slow growing to 15 ft. tall, 3–4 ft. wide, with 2-ft.-long, 2-in.-wide leaves in rich green striped white and gray. 'Bausei' has green leaves with a white center stripe; 'Longii' has a broader white center stripe; 'Janet Craig' has broad dark green leaves. Compact forms of 'Janet Craig' and 'Warneckii' are also available.

D. draco. DRAGON TREE. Native to Canary Islands. Stout trunk with upward-reaching or spreading branches topped by clusters of heavy, sword-shaped, 2-ft.-long leaves. Grows slowly to 20 ft. high and wide. Makes odd but interesting silhouette. Clusters of greenish white flowers form at branch ends. After blossoms drop, stemmy clusters remain; trim them off to keep plant neat.

D. fragrans. CORN PLANT. Native to West Africa. Upright and slow growing, eventually reaching 20 ft. high and 5 ft. wide. Heavy, ribbonlike blue-green leaves grow to 3 ft. long and 4 in. wide. (Typical plant in 8-in. container will bear leaves about 1½ ft. long.) 'Massangeana' has broad yellow stripe in center of each leaf. Other selections with striped foliage are 'Lindenii' and 'Victoriae'.

D. marginata. MADAGASCAR DRAGON TREE. Very easy to grow and one of the most popular species. To 12 ft. tall and 5–6 ft. wide. Slender, erect, smooth gray stems are topped by crowns of narrow, leathery leaves to 2 ft. long, ½ in. wide; stems carry chevron markings where old leaves have fallen. Leaves are deep glossy green with a narrow margin of purplish red. If plant grows too tall, cut off crown and reroot it. New crowns will appear on old stem. 'Tricolor' ('Candy Cane') adds a narrow gold stripe to the green and red of the species.

Dracaena marginata

D. sanderiana. RIBBON PLANT. Native to West Africa. Neat and upright, to a possible 6–10 ft. tall, 2 ft. wide; somewhat resembles a young corn plant. Strap-shaped, 9-in.-long leaves striped with white. Unrooted trunk sections of a green-leafed selection are marketed in gift shops as "lucky bamboo." If their bases are placed in several inches of water, they'll quickly root and sprout foliage. Add a small amount of half-strength general-purpose liquid houseplant fertilizer to the water every couple of months. Change water if it becomes cloudy.

DRACOPIS amplexicaulis (Rudbeckia amplexicaulis)

CLASPING CONEFLOWER

Asteraceae (Compositae)

ANNUAL

🌿 US, MS, LS, CS ✂ 10–1

☼ ◑ FULL SUN OR PARTIAL SHADE

◊ ◖ ● ◗ LITTLE TO AMPLE WATER

Dracopis amplexicaulis

Native from Kansas to Texas and Georgia; closely related to coneflowers *(Echinacea, Rudbeckia)* and Mexican hat *(Ratibida columnifera)*. Slender stems reach 2–3 ft. tall; oval, pointed, medium green leaves clasp the stems. Blooms in late spring, bearing flowers to 2 in. across with a dark brown or purple central cone and yellow rays that are sometimes flushed orange or brown at the base. Tolerates a wide range of soils, including wet, heavy, poorly drained ones. Use in wildflower meadows or naturalized areas; also good in mixed herbaceous borders.

DROPWORT. See FILIPENDULA vulgaris

DROSANTHEMUM

Aizoaceae

SUCCULENT PERENNIALS

🌿 CS, TS ✂ 12–9

☼ FULL SUN

◊ ◖ LITTLE TO MODERATE WATER

Drosanthemum floribundum

The two South African ice plants described here are often mistaken for each other, although they are quite different. In both, leaves are covered by glistening dots that look like tiny ice crystals; both have typical ice plant flowers with many narrow petals, bloom in late spring and early summer, and endure poor soil.

D. floribundum. ROSEA ICE PLANT. Grows to 6 in. tall, but rooting stems trail to considerable length or drape over rocks or walls. Best ice plant for reducing erosion on steep slopes (plant 1½ ft. apart). Pale pink, ¾-in.-wide flowers form sheets of bloom, attract bees.

D. hispidum. To 2 ft. tall, 3 ft. wide; less inclined to stem-root than *D. floribundum.* Showy, 1-in. purple flowers.

DROSERA

SUNDEW

Droceraceae

INSECTIVOROUS PERENNIALS

🌿 US, MS, LS, CS, TS; OR INDOORS

☼ FULL SUN; BRIGHT LIGHT

◖ ● REGULAR TO AMPLE WATER

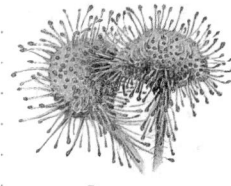

Drosera rotundifolia

These wonderfully bizarre plants inhabit bogs in many parts of the world. Leaves vary from narrow and arching to almost round, but all are covered with small hairs that hold drops of sticky liquid. These hairs trap and digest the insects that land on them, providing the plant with nutrients not found in the soil where it grows. All species bear small, five-petaled flowers.

Care for sundews as you would Venus's flytrap *(Dionaea muscipula);* the two can be grown indoors and make good companions for a terrarium. Outdoors, they thrive in full sun and constantly moist, peaty soil. Be sure to purchase only nursery-propagated plants that are grown from seed, division, or tissue culture; buying wild-collected plants depletes native populations.

D. brevifolia. DWARF SUNDEW. Heat zones 12–7. Native from Virginia south to Florida and west to East Texas. Small, low-growing plant, forming a rosette only 1–2 in. across. Spoon-shaped, ½-in.-long leaves are covered with red hairs. White or pink blossoms about ½ in. wide appear atop 3- to 6-in.-tall stems in summer.

D. capillaris. PINK SUNDEW. Heat zones 12–7. Same native range as *D. brevifolia.* Forms a tight rosette of short-stemmed, rounded, reddish leaves, each ½–1 in. long. Pink, ¼-in.-wide flowers bloom in summer on stems 2–16 in. tall.

D. filiformis. THREADLEAF SUNDEW. Heat zones 10–8. Native to the Coastal Plains from South Carolina to Florida, west to Louisiana. Reddish, threadlike, 4- to 10-in.-long leaves grow upright, unfurling like the fiddlehead of a fern. Blooms in spring, bearing lavender, ⅝-in.-wide blossoms on stems 3–9 in. tall.

D. rotundifolia. ROUND-LEAFED SUNDEW. Heat zones 12–1. Native to bogs throughout North America. Grows 1–3 in. wide, with rounded, ½-in. leaves on thin stems; leaves turn from green to bright red in sun. White to pink flowers, ¼ in. wide, on stems reaching 2–12 in. tall; blooms from summer to early fall. One of the easier sundews to grow.

DRUMSTICKS. See ALLIUM sphaerocephalum, CRASPEDIA globosa

DRYOPTERIS

WOOD FERN

Polypodiaceae

FERNS

🌿 ZONES VARY BY SPECIES

☼ ● PARTIAL TO FULL SHADE

● REGULAR WATER, EXCEPT AS NOTED

Dryopteris dilatata

The more than 100 species in this genus are found in many parts of the world, though only a few are generally offered by garden centers. Use them in shade or woodland gardens, where their fronds contrast nicely with the bolder foliage of other perennials, especially such large-leafed plants as hosta and hydrangea. They prefer rich soil with adequate organic material and moisture—but as a rule they are rather forgiving, making them good choices for beginning gardeners. Some species tolerate drought and less-than-ideal soil. They are seldom bothered by deer or other pests.

D. affinis. SCALY MALE FERN. Semievergreen. Zones US, MS, LS; 8–1. Native to Europe and southwestern Asia. To 3–5 ft. high and wide. Finely cut fronds are chartreuse green with light brown scales when they unfold, dark green later.

D. carthusiana (D. spinulosa). SPINULOSE WOOD FERN, TOOTHED WOOD FERN, SHIELD FERN. Evergreen. Zones US, MS, LS; 8–1. A native of Europe, Asia, and North America. Clumps reach 1 ft. across. Coarsely cut yellowish green fronds to 6–18 in. tall, half as wide, have shaggy black scales on frond stem and lower part of midrib. Tolerates bog conditions.

D. celsa. LOG FERN. Semievergreen. Zones US, MS, LS, CS; 9–1. Native to moist woods and bogs in eastern U.S.; often found growing on rotting logs in the wild, hence the common name. Upright habit to 3–4 ft. high, 1½–2½ ft. wide. Deeply cut, glossy deep green fronds with darker stems and midribs.

D. dilatata. BROAD BUCKLER FERN. Evergreen. Zones US, MS, LS; 8–1. Native to many areas in Northern and Southern Hemispheres. Grows to 1–2 ft. tall, possibly much taller; spreads a little wider than it is high. Finely cut, dark green, widely spreading fronds. ▸

E

D. erythrosora. AUTUMN FERN. Evergreen. Zones US, MS, LS, CS; 9–1. Native to China and Japan. Erect growth in tuft to 2 ft. tall, 1½ ft. wide. One of the few ferns with seasonal color variation. Expanding fronds in spring are an attractive blend of copper, pink, and yellow; they turn green in summer, then rusty brown in autumn. Bright red spore cases are produced on leaf undersides in fall; they become a handsome winter feature. Takes some drought.

Dryopteris erythrosora

D. filix-mas. MALE FERN. Evergreen, sometimes becoming deciduous. Zones US, MS, LS; 8–1. Native to much of Northern Hemisphere. Grows 2–5 ft. tall and wide, with finely cut medium green fronds to 1 ft. wide. 'Linearis Polydactyla' has very narrow leaf divisions with spreading, fingerlike tips.

D. goldiana (D. goldieana). GOLDIE'S WOOD FERN, GIANT WOOD FERN. Evergreen in milder climates, deciduous in colder-winter areas. Zones US, MS; 7–1. Native to North America. Robust grower to 4 ft. tall, half as wide, with arching light green fronds to 1½ ft. wide.

D. marginalis. MARGINAL SHIELD FERN, LEATHER WOOD FERN. Evergreen. Zones US, MS, LS; 8–1. From eastern North America. Grows 2–4 ft. tall and wide. Finely cut, dark blue-green fronds. Takes some drought.

D. wallichiana. WALLICH'S WOOD FERN. Evergreen. Zones US, MS, LS; 8–5. Native to India, China. Stately fern 3–5 ft. high, not quite as wide. Fronds have scaly brown stems, turn from bright golden green to dark green with maturity.

DUMB CANE. See DIEFFENBACHIA

DURANTA

Verbenaceae

EVERGREEN SHRUBS

⚡ TS ▯ 12–10; OR GROW IN POTS

☼ FULL SUN

💧 REGULAR WATER

⚘ D. ERECTA BERRIES ARE POISONOUS IF INGESTED

Duranta erecta

These tender flowering shrubs feature glossy green leaves arranged in pairs or whorls along stems. Attractive blue or white flowers in clusters attract butterflies in summer, are followed by bunches of berrylike yellow fruit. Plants marketed as *D. stenostachya* are often actually *D. erecta*; distinguishing characteristics are described below. Use as quick, tall screen. Thrive in heat. Need continual thinning and pruning to stay under control. Good container plants.

D. erecta (D. repens, D. plumieri). SKY FLOWER, GOLDEN DEWDROP, PIGEON BERRY. Native to southern Florida, West Indies, Mexico to Brazil. Fast growing to 10–25 ft. tall, 6–10 ft. wide. Tends to form multistemmed clumps; branches often drooping and vinelike. Stems may or may not have sharp spines. Oval to roundish leaves are 1–2 in. long, rounded or pointed at tip. Tubular violet-blue flowers flare to less than ½ in. wide; they are followed by waxy yellow berries in clusters 1–6 in. long. 'Alba' has white flowers. 'Golden Edge' has brilliant gold leaves with a streak of dark green down the center; often grown as an annual in areas where it isn't hardy. The golden-leafed 'Aurea' is a drought-tolerant dwarf form reaching only 2 ft. high.

D. stenostachya. BRAZILIAN SKY FLOWER. Native to Brazil. Not as hardy as *D. erecta*; seems to require more heat. Makes neater, more compact shrub than *D. erecta*, growing to about 4–6 ft. tall, 3–5 ft. wide (under ideal conditions, 15 ft. high). Stems do not have spines. Leaves are larger (3–8 in. long) than those of *D. erecta* and taper to a long, slender point. Lavender-blue flowers are also somewhat larger; fruit clusters grow to 1 ft. long.

DUSTY MILLER. This name is given to a number of plants with gray foliage. The dusty miller of one region may be unknown in another. Among the many dusty millers are *Artemisia stellerana*, *Centaurea cineraria*, *C. gymnocarpa*, *Senecio cineraria*, and *S. vira-vira*.

DUTCHMAN'S PIPE. See ARISTOLOCHIA macrophylla

DYER'S GREENWEED. See GENISTA tinctoria

DYER'S WOAD. See ISATIS tinctoria

DYSSODIA. See THYMOPHYLLA

EARTH STAR. See CRYPTANTHUS zonatus

EASTER CACTUS. See RHIPSALIDOPSIS gaertneri

EASTER LILY VINE. See BEAUMONTIA grandiflora

ECHEVERIA

Crassulaceae

SUCCULENT PERENNIALS

⚡ ZONES VARY BY SPECIES

☼ ◐ FULL SUN OR PARTIAL SHADE, EXCEPT AS NOTED

💧 MODERATE WATER, EXCEPT AS NOTED

Echeveria agavoides

Mexican natives that form rosettes of fleshy leaves, often marked or overlaid with deeper colors. Bell-shaped, nodding flowers, usually pink, red, or yellow, in long, slender, sometimes branched clusters. Good in rock gardens. Some make good houseplants if sited in a south- or west-facing window; they benefit from being moved outdoors to a lightly shaded spot during the warm months. Feed houseplants monthly with a general-purpose liquid houseplant fertilizer diluted to half-strength; reduce feeding and watering in winter.

E. agavoides (Urbinia agavoides). MOLDED WAX AGAVE. Zones TS; 12–10. Stiff, fleshy, smooth, sharp-pointed leaves are bright green, marked with deep reddish brown at tips and edges. Rosettes reach 6–8 in. across; flower stalks to 1½ ft. bear small red-and-yellow blooms in spring to early summer.

E. crenulata. Zones TS; 12–10. Short, thick stems hold foliage rosettes to 1½ ft. across. Pale green or white-powdered leaves to 1 ft. long, 6 in. wide, with purplish red, crimped edges. Blooms from early summer until winter; flower stalk rises to 3 ft., topped by clusters of a few yellow-and-red blossoms. Shelter from hottest sun; water freely in warm weather. Makes a striking container plant, indoors or out.

E. elegans. HEN AND CHICKS. Zones CS, TS; 12–9. Tight grayish white rosettes to 4 in. across, spreading freely by offsets. Pink flowers tipped in yellow, in clusters to 8 in. long, bloom from late winter to early spring. Useful for pattern planting, edging, containers. May burn in hot summer sun.

E. hybrids. Zones CS, TS; 12–9. Often grown as houseplants. Generally have large, loose rosettes of big leaves on branched or unbranched stems; leaves are crimped, waved, or wattled, sometimes heavily shaded with red, bronze, or purple. 'Arlie Wright' has large, open rosettes of wavy-edged pinkish leaves; 'Cameo' has big blue-gray leaves, each centered with a large, raised lump in the same color; 'Perle von Nürnberg' features pearly lavender blue foliage. 'Doris Taylor' is a smaller selection with short, close-set leaves densely covered with short white hairs.

E. ×imbricata. HEN AND CHICKS. Zones CS, TS; 12–9. Saucer-shaped gray-green rosettes reach to 4–6 in. across. Clusters of bell-shaped red-orange flowers bloom from late spring to early summer. Spreads freely by offsets.

E. runyonii. Zones LS, CS, TS; 12–8. Blunt-tipped gray-green leaves form an open rosette to 5 in. across. Showy spikes of coral blossoms from late spring to early summer. Likes the dry, chalky, rocky soils of the Southwest.

Echeveria ×imbricata

E. secunda. HEN AND CHICKS. Zones TS; 12–10. Gray-green or blue-green rosettes to 4 in. across; spreads freely by offsets. Egg-shaped red flowers with a yellow interior bloom in late spring or early summer. *E. s. glauca (E. glauca)* has blue-green leaves faintly edged in purple red.

E. setosa. Zones TS; 12–9. Very tender species forms dense rosettes to 4 in. wide; leaves are dark green, densely covered in stiff white hairs. Urn-shaped red flowers tipped in yellow appear in late spring or summer. Good choice for rock gardens, shallow containers; makes an excellent houseplant.

ECHINACEA

CONEFLOWER

Asteraceae (Compositae)

PERENNIALS

✎ ZONES VARY BY SPECIES

☼ FULL SUN

◗ MODERATE TO REGULAR WATER

Echinacea purpurea

These sun-loving perennials form large clumps of long-stemmed, very showy flowers with drooping to horizontal rays and a beehivelike central cone. Bloom over a long period in summer and may continue sporadically until frost; deadheading prolongs bloom. May start blooming in spring in mild-winter climates. If left in place, the bristly seed heads hang on into winter; finches like the seeds.

Use on outskirts of garden or in wide borders with other robust perennials such as Shasta daisy *(Chrysanthemum maximum)*, sunflower *(Helianthus)*, Michaelmas daisy *(Aster novi-belgii)*. Generally do not need staking. Seldom bothered by deer. Perform well in summer heat; good cut flowers. Can self-sow enthusiastically. Clumps spread slowly, become crowded after 3 or 4 years. Fleshy rootstocks can be difficult to separate; divide carefully, making sure each division has a shoot and roots. Or increase plantings by seeding or by transplanting self-sown seedlings.

E. angustifolia. Zones US, MS, LS, CS; 9–1. Native to central U.S. Prairie wildflower to 3–4 ft. high, 2 ft. wide. Flowers to 2 in. wide, with pink to rosy purple rays drooping from a purple-brown cone. Narrow, bristly leaves to 6 in. long.

E. paradoxa. YELLOW CONEFLOWER. Zones US, MS, LS; 9–2. Native to the Ozarks. To 2–3 ft. high, 2 ft. wide. Drooping yellow to orange-yellow rays surround a brown cone; flowers are about 2 in. wide. Smooth, lance-shaped leaves to 8 in. long.

E. purpurea. PURPLE CONEFLOWER. Zones US, MS, LS, CS; 9–1. Native to central and eastern North America. Coarse, stiff plant to 4–5 ft. tall, about 2 ft. wide, with bristly, oblong leaves 3–8 in. long. Blossoms reach 2–3 in. wide, with drooping rosy purple rays and an orange-brown central cone.

'Bright Star'. Rosy pink flowers.

'Cygnet White'. Compact form to about 1½ ft. high; white flowers have horizontal to slightly drooping rays.

'Kim's Knee High'. To 2 ft. high. Clear pink, drooping rays.

'Magnus'. To 3 ft. tall. Flowers may reach 3 in. across, have horizontally spreading rays and a low, dark cone.

'Razzmatazz'. To 2½ ft. tall, with rosy pink double flowers.

'White Lustre'. White rays around an orange-yellow cone.

'White Swan'. Similar to 'White Lustre'.

E. tennesseensis. TENNESSEE CONEFLOWER. Zones US, MS, LS; 9–1. From the southeastern U.S. Similar to *E. purpurea*, but rays are horizontal rather than drooping, and cone is greenish pink. Stems to 1½ ft. tall. Forms a low, casual mound. This beautiful coneflower is rare and endangered in the wild but is being propagated under permit. Available from a few wildflower nurseries.

FOR INFORMATION ON YOUR CLIMATE ZONES
PLEASE SEE PAGES 28–38

ECHINOCEREUS

HEDGEHOG CACTUS

Cactaceae

CACTI

✎ ZONES VARY BY SPECIES

☼ FULL SUN

◗ ◖ LITTLE TO MODERATE WATER

Echinocereus engelmannii

Nearly 50 species of hedgehog cactus are native to the Southwest, including Texas, New Mexico, and Mexico. Some grow at fairly high elevations, where they survive freezing temperatures. All have cylindrical, ribbed stems in clumps; showy flowers in spring to early summer; and fleshy fruit that is edible in some species. Blooms come in red, yellow, purple, pink, or white and have many rows of petals; they typically close at night. Plant in masses for best effect. Excellent choices for dry-land gardens. Give them maximum sun and gritty, well-drained soil.

E. berlandieri. Zones LS, CS, TS; 12–7. Stems 1 in. thick, 1 ft. long; forms a clump 2 ft. wide. Purplish pink, 3-in. flowers with darker throats. Good candidate for a hanging basket.

E. engelmannii. Zones MS, LS, CS, TS; 12–6. Clumps 1–2 ft. tall, 3 ft. wide, with 3- to 4-in.-thick stems. Lavender to deep purplish red flowers are 2–3 in. wide. Inch-long red fruits are edible.

E. enneacanthus. STRAWBERRY CACTUS. Zones CS, TS; 12–10. Stems 1½–4 in. thick, 2½ ft. long. Forms colonies 3 ft. wide. New stems start at or just above the ground and grow sideways, then upright. Goblet-shaped, purplish red, 2- to 3-in. flowers remain open at night. The inch-long, greenish to brownish purple fruits are edible and taste like strawberries.

E. reichenbachii. CREAM LACE CACTUS. Zones TS; 12–10. Each stem is 2 in. thick, 6 in. tall. Plant may have a single stem or as many as a dozen. Large (4-in.) flowers vary from pink to magenta. White, lacy-looking spines.

E. triglochidiatus. CLARET CUP. Zones US, MS, LS, CS; 10–6. Dense clump, up to 3 ft. wide, sometimes with hundreds of 2- to 3-in.-diameter stems to a foot tall. Flowers are 3½ in. wide, orange to red; inch-long fruits (not edible) are pink to red.

E. viridiflorus. Zones US, MS, LS, CS, TS; 12–6. Stems grow to 2 in. thick, 1 ft. long, forming a clump to 2 ft. wide. Slender, 1-in. flowers are yellowish green with a lemon scent; remain nearly closed day and night.

ECHINOPS

GLOBE THISTLE

Asteraceae (Compositae)

PERENNIAL

✎ US, MS, LS, CS ⊩ 9–1

☼ FULL SUN

◗ MODERATE WATER

Echinops exaltatus

Well-behaved, decorative thistle relative for the perennial border. Rugged-looking, erect, rigidly branched plant 2–4 ft. tall and 2 ft. wide, with coarse, prickly, deeply cut gray-green leaves to 1 ft. long. Distinctive flower heads are spherical, about the size of golf balls; they look like pincushions stuck full of tubular, metallic blue pins. Bloom midsummer to late fall.

Plants may be offered as *E. exaltatus, E. humilis, E. ritro,* or possibly *E. sphaerocephalus*. Whatever name you encounter, you're likely to get a plant closely resembling the general description above. 'Taplow Blue' has bright blue blossoms on 3- to 4-ft. stems. 'Veitch's Blue' has darker blue flowers on a plant 2½–3 ft. high.

Grow from divisions in spring or fall, or sow seed in flats or open ground in spring. Provide average, well-drained soil and moderate water. (With enriched soil and regular moisture, may grow too robustly and require staking.) Clump can be left in place, undivided, for many years. Flowers are excellent for dried arrangements; cut them before they open and dry them upside down.

293

EDGEWORTHIA chrysantha (E. papyrifera)

PAPER BUSH

Thymelaeaceae

DECIDUOUS SHRUB

⚏ MS, LS, CS ⊞ 10–6

☼ ◑ FULL SUN OR LIGHT SHADE

💧 REGULAR WATER

Edgeworthia chrysantha

Native to China, this daphne relative is rare enough to stump gardening know-it-alls who think they've seen everything. It's prized in Asia for its bark, which is used to make high-quality paper. Grows 6 ft. tall and wide, with pliable stems produced freely from the base; dark blue-green, 3- to 4-in.-long leaves are clustered at branch tips. Flower buds covered with silky white hairs emerge in late summer; they resemble white blossoms, so after leaves drop in fall, the plant looks like it's already in bloom. Lightly fragrant, pale yellow flowers finally open in late winter. 'Rubra' has red-orange blooms.

Paper bush is a pest-free shrub that prefers light shade and moist, fertile, well-drained soil containing plenty of organic matter. Water during summer droughts. Little pruning required.

EGGPLANT

Solanaceae

ANNUAL

⚏ US, MS, LS, CS, TS ⊞ 12–1

☼ FULL SUN

💧 REGULAR WATER

'Black Beauty'

Few vegetable plants are more beautiful than this Southeast Asian native, known botanically as *Solanum melongena*. Although most people associate eggplant with big purple fruit, the common name comes from a small type with white fruit that does indeed resemble a swan's egg.

The plant grows to a shrubby 2–3 ft. high and wide, with large, lobed leaves that are green with a purplish tinge. Drooping violet flowers shaped like those of potato (a close relative) are 1½ in. across. The glossy-skinned fruits may be blackish purple, purple, pink, green, orange red, white, or bicolored. Fruits are generally oval or rounded and may reach 1 ft. long, depending on type; those that are long and slender are often called Japanese or Ichiban eggplants. An eggplant or two adds striking color to vegetable gardens; single plants make good container subjects.

Plants are quite sensitive to cold, so don't set out in spring until daytime temperatures are in the 70s—about 2 to 6 weeks after the last frost. In Florida and along the Gulf Coast, you can grow plants from seed started indoors 8 to 10 weeks before the last frost. Elsewhere, it's easier to buy transplants. Space transplants 2–3 ft. apart in rows spaced 2–2½ ft. apart. At planting time, feed with liquid 20-20-20 fertilizer. Every 4 to 6 weeks, sprinkle ½ cup of 10-10-10 fertilizer per 10 ft. of row around plants. Control weeds. Eggplant grows rapidly in warm weather and, if cared for properly, will produce over a long season. In warmest climates, you can also plant a second crop for harvest in late summer and fall.

If you enjoy eating tiny whole eggplants, allow the plants to grow and produce naturally. If you want large fruit, pinch out some terminal growth and some blossoms; three to six big fruits per plant will result. To harvest, use a knife or hand pruners to cut fruit from the plant, leaving an inch or so of stem on each fruit. Flea beetles are often a problem on young plants. Grow plants under row covers until they're big enough to tolerate leaf damage. Control aphids and whiteflies. Recommended selections include the following.

'Black Beauty'. Rounded black-purple fruits to 8 in. long. 74 days from transplant to harvest.

'Blue Marble'. Gorgeous, rounded fruits 7–8 in. wide, deep violet with white tops. 62 days.

WHAT EGGPLANT NEEDS

TEMPERATURE: Consistently warm temperatures throughout the growing season. Plants may be killed by even a light frost.

SOIL: Loose, fertile, and well drained.

WATER: To maintain healthy growth, keep soil evenly moist.

STAKING: Stake plants to keep fruit off the ground and to keep branches from breaking under the weight of a heavy crop.

HARVESTING: Pick fruit when it develops color but before it loses shine.

'Rosa Bianca'

'Cloud Nine'. Pure white, oblong fruits; best when harvested at 7 in. long. 75 days.

'Ichiban Hybrid'. Japanese type. Slender, dark purple fruits may reach 10 in. long. Purple foliage. 61 days.

'Louisiana Long Green'. Light green, zucchini-shaped fruits to 7 in. long. Southern heirloom. 100 days.

'Neon'. Deep pink, semicylindrical fruits. Ready to pick when 5–6 in. long. 73 days.

'Pingtung Long'. Japanese type. Slender, pinkish purple fruits up to 1 ft. long. Heavy producer. 50 days.

'Purple Rain'. Egg-shaped fruits to 6 in. long, in a beautiful shade of magenta purple. 66 days.

'Rosa Bianca'. Italian heirloom noted for delicious flavor. Elongated egg–shaped, 4- to 5-in.-long fruits in creamy white with lavender striping. 75 days.

'White Beauty'. Oval white fruits, 7–8 in. across. Very productive in hot, humid areas. 70 to 74 days.

EGLANTINE. See ROSA rubiginosa

EICHHORNIA crassipes

WATER HYACINTH

Pontederiaceae

AQUATIC PLANT

⚏ LS, CS, TS; ANNUAL IN COLDER CLIMATES; ⊞ 12–1

☼ FULL SUN

💧 LOCATE IN PONDS OR POOLS

Native to tropical America. Feathery roots; inflated stems set with floating, nearly circular leaves ½–5 in. wide. Showy, 2-in. flowers, carried many to a spike, are lilac blue; upper petals have a yellow spot in center. Needs warmth to flower profusely. Where it is perennial, it can become an extremely serious, ineradicable pest; do not turn it loose in natural or large bodies of water.

Eichhornia crassipes

Elaeagnaceae. This family contains trees and shrubs with a coating of tiny silvery or brown scales on leaves (and sometimes on flowers) and with small, tart-tasting, single-seeded fruits. Most are tough plants from arid or semiarid climates.

FOR INFORMATION ON SELECTING PLANTS
PLEASE SEE PAGES 39–144

E

ELAEAGNUS

Elaeagnaceae

DECIDUOUS AND EVERGREEN SHRUBS AND TREES

🗡 ZONES VARY BY SPECIES

☼ ◑ FULL SUN OR PARTIAL SHADE

◊ ◓ ● LITTLE TO REGULAR WATER

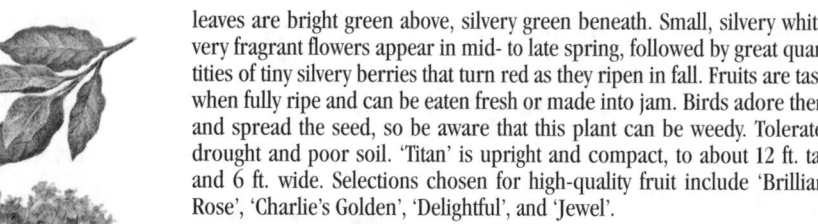

Elaeagnus pungens

These useful screening plants grow fast when young, becoming dense, full, firm, and tough—and they do it with little upkeep. All tolerate seashore conditions, heat, and wind. Established plants will tolerate considerable drought. Resistant to damage by deer.

Evergreen kinds serve a prime role as screening plants and are also useful as natural espaliers, clipped hedges, and high bank covers. Their foliage is distinguished by silvery (sometimes brown) dots on leaves; these reflect sunlight, giving the plants their distinctive sparkle. Both evergreen and deciduous sorts bear insignificant but usually fragrant flowers that are followed by decorative fruit (typically red with silvery flecks).

E. angustifolia. RUSSIAN OLIVE. Deciduous tree. Zones US, MS; 7–1. Native from Europe to Asia. To 20 ft. high and wide, but can be clipped as medium-height hedge. Angular trunk and branches (sometimes thorny) are covered by shredding dark brown bark that is picturesque in winter. Bark contrasts with narrow, willowlike, silvery gray leaves to 2 in. long. Small, very fragrant greenish yellow flowers in early summer are followed by berrylike fruit resembling miniature olives. Can take almost any kind of punishment, including hot summers, bitterly cold winters, drought, poor soil. Doesn't do as well in mild winters or very humid summers. Good background plant, barrier.

E. × ebbingei. Evergreen shrub. Zones MS, LS, CS; 10–6. Hybrid derived from *E. pungens*. More upright (to 10–12 ft. high and wide) than its parent, with thornless branches. Leaves are 2–4 in. long; they are silvery on both sides when young, later dark green above and silvery beneath. Tiny, fragrant, silvery flowers in fall. Red fruit makes good jelly. 'Gilt Edge' has striking yellow leaf margins.

E. multiflora. CHERRY ELAEAGNUS. Deciduous shrub. Zones US, MS; 7–3. From China and Japan. To 6–10 ft. high and wide. Leaves are 1½–2½ in. long, silvery green above, silvery brown below. Small, fragrant spring flowers followed by bright orange-red, ½-in.-long berries on 1-in. stalks; fruit is edible but tart, loved by birds. 'Variegata' has leaves variegated with gold, yellow, and cream; its berries are red.

E. pungens. THORNY ELAEAGNUS, SILVERBERRY. Evergreen shrub. Zones US, MS, LS, CS; 9–4. From Japan. To 6–15 ft. tall and wide, with rather rigid, sprawling, angular habit. Long, naked shoots, some of them 5–6 ft. long, tend to skyrocket off in all directions, creating a Medusa-like appearance. Fortunately, these shoots can be pruned away (flower arrangers prize them) to give the shrub a neater look; it also can be sheared into a nice hedge. Grayish green, wavy-edged, 1- to 3-in.-long leaves have rusty dots that give them a brown tint; spiny branches are also covered with rusty dots. Shrub has an overall olive drab color. Small, fragrant cream-colored blossoms appear in fall; the oval, 2½-in.-long berries that follow are red with silvery dust. Tough container plant in reflected heat and wind. The variegated forms listed below are more widespread than the species and have a brighter, lighter, and often startling look in the landscape; they are less hardy than the species, however, and may suffer damage in the Upper South. Be sure to cut out growth that reverts to green. Effective barrier plantings—growth is dense and twiggy, and spininess is a help, yet plants are not aggressively spiny.

'Fruitlandii'. Large, silvery leaves.

'Maculata'. GOLDEN ELAEAGNUS. Leaves have gold blotch in center.

'Marginata'. SILVER-EDGE ELAEAGNUS. Silvery white leaf margins.

'Variegata'. YELLOW-EDGE ELAEAGNUS. Leaf edges yellowish white.

E. umbellata. AUTUMN OLIVE. Deciduous shrub. Zones US, MS, LS; 8–1. From Himalayas, China, Japan. Spiny-branched plant to 12–18 ft. high and wide, with an open, spreading shape. Elliptical, 2- to 4-in.-long leaves are bright green above, silvery green beneath. Small, silvery white, very fragrant flowers appear in mid- to late spring, followed by great quantities of tiny silvery berries that turn red as they ripen in fall. Fruits are tasty when fully ripe and can be eaten fresh or made into jam. Birds adore them and spread the seed, so be aware that this plant can be weedy. Tolerates drought and poor soil. 'Titan' is upright and compact, to about 12 ft. tall and 6 ft. wide. Selections chosen for high-quality fruit include 'Brilliant Rose', 'Charlie's Golden', 'Delightful', and 'Jewel'.

ELDERBERRY, AMERICAN. See SAMBUCUS canadensis

ELECAMPANE. See INULA helenium

ELEPHANT'S EAR. See ALOCASIA, COLOCASIA esculenta

ELEUTHEROCOCCUS
sieboldianus

FIVELEAF ARALIA

Araliaceae

DECIDUOUS SHRUB

🗡 US, MS, LS ⊩ 8–1

☼ ◑ ● SUN OR SHADE

◊ ◓ ● ◕ ANY AMOUNT OF WATER

Eleutherococcus sieboldianus 'Variegatus'

Native to China, Japan. Grows 8–10 ft. tall and wide; erect, eventually arching stems have short thorns below each leaf. Bright green leaves have five to seven 1- to 2½-in.-long leaflets arranged like fingers on a hand. Small, inconspicuous white flowers are borne in clusters; these are very occasionally followed by clusters of small black berries. This plant's virtues are its somewhat tropical appearance, adaptability (takes rich or poor soil, any exposure, any amount of irrigation), and high tolerance for difficult conditions, including air pollution. 'Variegatus', a 6- to 8-ft. shrub with white-bordered leaflets, is more widely grown than the species. Formerly known as *Acanthopanax sieboldianus*.

ELM. See ULMUS

ELYMUS arenarius. See LEYMUS arenarius

EMPRESS TREE. See PAULOWNIA tomentosa

ENDIVE

Asteraceae (Compositae)

BIENNIAL OR ANNUAL

🗡 US, MS, LS, CS, TS ⊩ 8–1

☼ FULL SUN

● REGULAR WATER

Endive

Mediterranean native known botanically as *Cichorium endivia*. This species includes curly as well as broad-leafed endive (escarole), both of which form rosettes of leaves. Tolerates more heat than lettuce and grows faster in cold weather. Matures in 90 to 95 days from seed.

For a spring crop, sow seeds 2 to 4 weeks before the last frost; for a fall crop, set out transplants in late summer. Space plants 1½ ft. apart in rows 2 ft. apart. Water and fertilize as directed for lettuce (see Lettuce). To harvest, remove the outer leaves; the inner ones keep growing. Or cut the entire plant at the base when the heads are full and leafy. As warm weather approaches, leaves may develop a slightly bitter taste; for a milder flavor, blanch the head before harvest by pulling up the large outer leaves and tying them up at the top (but not when they're wet, as that may cause decay). After a week, the head should be ready to pick. In fall, harvest before the first hard frost. 'Green Curled' is the standard curly endive; 'Broad-leaved Batavian' ('Full Heart Batavian') is a good choice among escaroles. Belgian or French endives are the blanched sprouts of a kind of chicory; see Chicory.

E

ENDYMION. See HYACINTHOIDES

ENGLISH DAISY. See BELLIS perennis

ENGLISH PAINTED FERN. See ATHYRIUM otophorum

ENKIANTHUS

Ericaceae

DECIDUOUS SHRUBS

US, MS, LS

FULL SUN OR PARTIAL SHADE

REGULAR TO AMPLE WATER

Enkianthus campanulatus

Native to Japan. Upright stems with tiers of nearly horizontal branches; plants are narrow in youth, broader in age, but always attractive. Leaves are grouped or crowded near branch ends, turn orange or red in autumn. Clusters of nodding, bell-shaped flowers bloom in spring. Like rhododendrons, these shrubs require moist, well-drained acid soil enriched with plenty of organic matter such as peat moss or ground bark. Prune only to remove dead or broken branches. Plant in location where silhouette, flowers, and fall color can be enjoyed close up. Deer don't care for these plants.

E. campanulatus. REDVEIN ENKIANTHUS. Heat zones 7–3. Slow-growing shrub to 10–20 ft. tall and half as wide. Bluish green, 1½- to 3-in.-long leaves turn brilliant red in fall. In late spring, pendulous clusters of yellow-green, red-veined, ½-in.-long bells hang below leaves. 'Albi-florus' bears white blooms; 'Red Bells' has red flowers and notably deep red fall color. In 'Sikokianus', maroon buds open to dark red flowers with pink streaks. *E. c. palibinii* bears deep red blossoms.

E. cernuus. Heat zones 8–4. Seldom over 10 ft. tall and wide, with bright green, 1- to 2-in.-long leaves. White flowers. Better known than the species is the variety *E. c. rubens,* which has translucent deep red flowers in late spring.

E. perulatus. WHITE ENKIANTHUS. Heat zones 8–4. To 6–8 ft. high and wide. Roundish, medium green, 1- to 2-in.-long leaves; exceptionally good scarlet fall color. Small white flowers open in early spring before leaves emerge.

ENSETE ventricosum
(Musa ensete)

ABYSSINIAN BANANA

Musaceae

PERENNIAL

LS, CS, TS 12–6; OR GROW IN POTS

FULL SUN OR PART SHADE

REGULAR WATER

Ensete ventricosum

African native grown for its lush, tropical-looking foliage. For fruit-bearing banana trees, see Banana. Fast growing to 15–20 ft. high, 10–15 ft. wide. Dark green leaves with stout midribs grow out in arching form from a single vertical stem; each leaf is 10–20 ft. long, 2–4 ft. wide. 'Maurelii' has dark red leafstalks and leaves tinged with red on upper surface, especially along edges. 'Red Stripe' has green leaves with a red midrib. Bloom typically occurs 2 to 5 years after planting, when inconspicuous flowers form within a cylinder of bronzy red bracts at end of stem. Plant dies to roots after flowering; it's possible to grow new plants from the shoots that will sprout from the crown but easier simply to discard the old plant and replace it with a new one from the nursery. Unlike fruiting bananas, Abyssinian banana doesn't form suckers.

Leaves are easily shredded by wind, so plant in a wind-sheltered location. Evergreen only in the Tropical South. Root-hardy in Coastal and Lower South and survives temperatures down to 10°F if mulched heavily in late fall and kept dry. Attractive near swimming pools. Good container subject to grow outdoors in summer, move indoors or into a greenhouse over winter.

EPAULETTE TREE. See PTEROSTYRAX hispidus

EPIMEDIUM

Berberidaceae

PERENNIALS

US, MS, LS

PARTIAL TO FULL SHADE

MODERATE WATER

Epimedium grandiflorum

Low-growing plants that spread by creeping underground stems. Thin, wiry leafstalks hold leathery leaves divided into heart-shaped leaflets 3–4 in. long. Foliage is bronzy pink in spring, green in summer, bronzy in fall. Even in deciduous types, leaves last late into the year. In spring, plants produce loose spikes of small, waxy flowers like tiny columbines (*Aquilegia*) in pink, red, red orange, creamy yellow, or white. The flowers have four petals, which may be spurred or hooded, and eight sepals—four inner ones resembling petals and four (usually small) outer ones.

Use as ground cover under trees or among rhododendrons, azaleas, camellias; good in large rock gardens. Compete well with surface-rooted trees. Prefer partial shade but tolerate heavy shade. Foliage and flowers are long lasting in arrangements. Cut back foliage of semievergreen and deciduous types in late winter before bloom. Divide large clumps in spring or fall by severing tough roots with a sharp spade. Adaptable to containers. Not favored by deer.

E. alpinum. ALPINE EPIMEDIUM. Evergreen. Heat zones 9–3. From southern Europe. Spreads fast; grows 6–9 in. high. Flowers to 1½ in. across, with red inner sepals and yellow petals.

E. ×cantabrigiense. Semievergreen. Heat zones 8–5. To 8–12 in. high, with olive-tinted foliage and ½-in. yellow-and-red flowers.

E. franchetii. Evergreen. Heat zones 9–5. From China. Forms a clump of 5-in. leaves on stems that can reach 2 ft. high. Large, lemon yellow, 1-in. flowers appear over a long period.

E. grandiflorum. BISHOP'S HAT, LONGSPUR EPIMEDIUM. Deciduous. Heat zones 9–3. From China, Korea, Japan. About 1 ft. high. Flowers 1–2 in. across, shaped like a bishop's miter; they have red outer sepals, pale violet inner sepals, white petals with long spurs. Selections have white, pinkish, or violet flowers. 'Rose Queen', bearing crimson flowers with white-tipped spurs, is outstanding. 'White Queen', with silvery white blooms, is another good selection.

E. perralderianum. Evergreen. Heat zones 9–4. From northern Africa. To 1 ft. tall, with shiny leaves and bright yellow, ¾-in. flowers. A hybrid of this species and *E. pinnatum colchicum* is *E. ×perralchicum* 'Frohnleiten', a 1½-ft. plant with large yellow flowers and leaves marked with brown in frosty weather.

E. pinnatum. Nearly evergreen. Heat zones 9–3. From northern Africa. To 12–15 in. high. Flowers are ⅔ in. across and have bright yellow inner sepals and short red spurs. *E. p. colchicum* (often sold as *E. p. elegans*) is larger, has showier flowers.

E. pubescens. Evergreen. Heat zones 9–5. Native to China. Foliage stays attractive year-round; new growth is mottled in crimson. Tiny white flowers with yellow spurs float above the leaves like little stars on 2-ft. stems. Blooms in early spring.

E. ×rubrum. RED EPIMEDIUM. Semievergreen. Heat zones 9–1. A hybrid of *E. alpinum* and *E. grandiflorum*. To 1 ft. high. Flowers, to ¾ in. across, are borne in showy clusters, have bright crimson inner sepals, white or pale yellow slipperlike petals, upward-curving spurs. Among the best selections offered by specialty nurseries are rosy 'Pink Queen', white 'Snow Queen', and 'Sweetheart', with large, sturdy leaves and pinkish flowers sporting creamy white spurs.

E. × versicolor. YELLOW EPIMEDIUM. Semievergreen. Heat zones 9–3. Several hybrids of *E. grandiflorum* and *E. pinnatum* bear this name. Best-known selection is vigorous 'Sulphureum', a 12- to 20-in. plant with clusters of light yellow, ¾-in.-wide flowers and leaves marked with brownish red.

E. × warleyense. Evergreen. Heat zones 9–3. To 1½ ft. high. Light green foliage; clusters of coppery orange-red, ½-in. flowers. Also known as *E.* 'Ellen Wilmott'. 'Orangekönigin' spreads more slowly and has flowers in a softer shade of orange.

E. × youngianum. Deciduous. Heat zones 8–3. Hybrid derived from *E. grandiflorum*; grows to 8–10 in. high, bears ¾-in.-wide flowers in palest pink. Leaves often have wavy margins. The most common selection sold is 'Niveum', with pure white blossoms; 'Yenomoto' is similar but bears larger flowers.

EPIPHYLLUM

ORCHID CACTUS

Cactaceae

CACTI

✂ TS ♨ 12–10; OR HOUSEPLANT

● BEST UNDER LATH IN SUMMER OR UNDER TREES; BRIGHT FILTERED LIGHT

💧 REGULAR WATER IN SUMMER, LITTLE IN WINTER

Epiphyllum hybrid

Growers use the name "epiphyllum" to refer to a wide range of plants—*Epiphyllum* itself and a number of crosses with related plants. All are tropical (not desert) cacti, and most grow on tree branches as epiphytes, like some orchids. Grow epiphyllums indoors or in lathhouse or in shade outdoors. They require rich, quick-draining soil with plenty of sand and leaf mold, peat moss, or ground bark. Cuttings are easy to root in spring or summer. Let the base of the cutting dry for a day or two before potting it up. Overwatering and poor drainage cause bud drop.

In winter, epiphyllums need protection from frost. Most have arching (to 2-ft.-high), trailing stems and look best in hanging pots or baskets. Stems are long, flat, smooth, quite spineless, and usually notched along edges. Spring flowers range from medium size to very large (up to 10 in. across); colors include white, cream, yellow, pink, rose, lavender, scarlet, and orange. Many selections have blends of two or more colors. Feed with low-nitrogen fertilizer before and after bloom.

EPIPREMNUM aureum (Pothos aureus, Scindapsus aureus)

POTHOS, DEVIL'S IVY

Araceae

EVERGREEN VINE

✂ TS ♨ 12–10; OR HOUSEPLANT

☼ ◐ ● SUN OR SHADE; BRIGHT INDIRECT LIGHT

💧 REGULAR WATER

Epipremnum aureum

If you can't grow pothos, you may as well give up gardening. This philodendron relative from the Solomon Islands is one of the toughest houseplants around, tolerating low light, infrequent watering, and nearly total neglect. Oval, leathery, 2- to 4-in.-long leaves are dark green splashed or marbled with cream or yellow. Indoors, pothos is commonly used as a trailing vine for decorating tabletops, window boxes, and plant stands; it never stops growing and eventually follows you from one room to another. Outdoors in the Tropical South, it becomes a big, tropical-looking vine with deeply cut, really large (2- to 2½-ft.-long) leaves. It is capable of climbing the tallest trees. Popular 'Marble Queen' displays white foliage flecked with cream and green.

Pothos tolerates shade but shows better color when grown in sun. Allow the soil to become fairly dry between waterings. Feed every other week in spring and summer and monthly in fall and winter with a general-purpose liquid houseplant fertilizer. Mist occasionally for best appearance. Do not expose plants to temperatures below 50°F. Easily propagated by cuttings (best taken in summer). Mealybugs can be a problem; wipe them off with a cotton swab dipped in alcohol.

EPISCIA

FLAME VIOLET

Gesneriaceae

PERENNIALS

✂ TS; OR HOUSEPLANTS

● FULL SHADE; BRIGHT INDIRECT LIGHT

💧 AMPLE WATER

Episcia 'Kee Wee'

Related to African violets *(Saintpaulia)*, these low-growing natives of tropical America are popular chiefly for their striking foliage: oval, velvety, beautifully colored leaves to 2–5 in. long, 1–3 in. wide. They bloom sporadically throughout the year, bearing tubular, 2-in.-long flowers in shades of red, pink, orange, yellow, lavender, or white. Plants spread by runners that form new plants at their tips, a trait that makes them excellent candidates for hanging baskets or strawberry pots.

Flame violets are among the most cold-sensitive plants in this book. They sulk when the temperature drops to 60°F and die if it dips much below 50°F. Yet they don't like temperatures much above 80°F either. You can take potted plants outdoors to a lightly shaded spot when the temperature is just right, but most people grow them as houseplants. Indoors, they need morning sun to retain their foliage color and compact form, but hot midday or afternoon sun will burn their leaves. You can grow them under fluorescent lights left on at least 12 hours a day. Let the soil go slightly dry between waterings. Use room-temperature water—never cold water. Feed every other week in spring and summer and monthly during fall and winter with a general-purpose liquid houseplant fertilizer diluted to half-strength. Check plants periodically for mealybugs; if you see them, wipe them off with a cotton swab dipped in alcohol.

Many different selections are available, including the following.

'Alice's Aussie'. Foliage in shimmering pink and chocolate brown. Orange-red flowers.

'Chocolate Soldier'. Chocolate brown leaves with silver veins. Orange-red blooms.

'Kee Wee'. Chocolate brown leaves prominently veined in deep pink. Orange-red flowers.

'Metallica'. Olive green leaves with red edges. Bright red flowers.

'Pink Brocade'. Leaves marked in white and brown, with pink edges. Flowers are red orange.

'Pink Panther'. Chocolate brown leaves with central pattern of lime green. Fuchsia pink blooms.

'Silver Sheen'. Crinkled leaves are silver and green, with coppery margins. Deep red flowers.

EQUISETUM hyemale

HORSETAIL

Equisetaceae

PERENNIAL

✂ US, MS, LS, CS, TS ♨ 12–1

☼ ◐ FULL SUN OR PARTIAL SHADE

💧 LOCATE IN MARSHY AREA OR POOL

Equisetum hyemale

Rushlike survivor of Carboniferous Age in Europe, North America. There are several species, but *E. hyemale* is most common. Slender, hollow, 4-ft. stems are bright green, showing a ring of black and ash gray at each joint. Spores are borne in conelike spikes at stem ends. Miniature *E. scirpoides* is similar but only 6–8 in. high. The common name "horsetail" refers to the bushy look produced by the many whorls of slender, jointed green stems that radiate out from joints of main stems on some of the other species.

Although horsetail is effective in some garden situations, especially near water, use it with caution: it is extremely invasive and difficult to get rid of. Best confined to containers. In open ground, be sure to root-prune or dig out unwanted shoots rigorously and constantly.

ERAGROSTIS

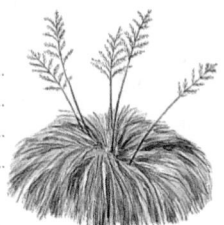

LOVE GRASS

Poaceae (Gramineae)

PERENNIAL GRASSES

ZONES VARY BY SPECIES

FULL SUN TO PARTIAL SHADE

LITTLE TO MODERATE WATER

Eragrostis curvula

Of about 250 species native to many temperate and tropical regions of the world, only a few are cultivated in gardens. These tough, carefree perennials form graceful clumps of fine-textured foliage. Airy floral plumes look like clouds floating above the leaves. Use love grasses as textural accents or as bank or ground covers. They are drought tolerant and need excellent drainage; they thrive in sandy soils. Reseed readily.

E. curvula. WEEPING LOVE GRASS. Zones US, MS, LS, CS, TS; 12–6. From southern Africa and India. Billowing mass of slender, dark green, hairlike leaves reaches 3 ft. tall and wide. Purple-black flower plumes appear in summer, increasing plant height to 4 ft. Foliage turns bronzy red after frost. Evergreen in Florida. Excellent massed; controls erosion.

E. elliottii. ELLIOTT'S LOVE GRASS. Zones MS, LS, CS, TS; 12–7. From Puerto Rico, Virgin Islands, and southeastern U.S. Narrow powder blue leaves form a clump 3 ft. high and wide. Airy tan flower plumes are held above the leaves in spring and persist into fall. Makes a dramatic specimen plant.

E. spectabilis. PURPLE LOVE GRASS. Zones US, MS, LS, CS, TS; 10–5. Native from Maine to Minnesota, south to Florida, Arizona, and Mexico. Light green, narrow leaves form a compact clump to almost 1½ ft. tall and wide. In late summer, plants are covered by wispy clouds of rosy purple blooms that increase the clump's height to 2 ft. Leaves reddish in fall, when flowers have faded to soft brown. Combines well with gray-leafed plants.

E. trichodes. SAND LOVE GRASS. Zones US, MS, LS, CS; 10–5. Native from Illinois to Colorado and Texas. Narrow bright green leaves grow in an upright clump to 1½–2 ft. tall and wide; they turn buff to russet in fall. Delicate bronze to purplish blooms double the plant's height in late summer and last through winter.

ERANTHEMUM pulchellum (E. nervosum)

BLUE SAGE

Acanthaceae

EVERGREEN SHRUB

TS 12–10; OR GROW IN POTS

PARTIAL SHADE

REGULAR WATER

Eranthemum pulchellum

Native to India, blue sage is a large, tender shrub that's prized in central and south Florida and the Rio Grande Valley for its showy flowers of celestial blue. It grows fairly quickly into an open, upright plant about 4–5 ft. high and half as wide. Deep green, prominently veined leaves reach 8 in. long. In winter, spikes of intensely blue, ¾- to 1½-in.-wide blossoms, attractive to butterflies, appear along the branches and at their tips. Blue sage prefers sandy, well-drained soil of moderate fertility; it does not tolerate salt spray. If frost kills branches, cut shrub to the ground; new growth will emerge with the advent of warm weather.

ERANTHIS hyemalis

WINTER ACONITE

Ranunculaceae

PERENNIAL FROM TUBER

US, MS 7–1

FULL SUN DURING BLOOM, PART SHADE DURING REST OF YEAR

REGULAR WATER DURING GROWTH AND BLOOM

Eranthis hyemalis

Native to Europe, Asia. Charming plant that reaches 2–8 in. high, blooming in late winter or early spring. Single yellow flowers resembling buttercups are about 1½ in. wide, with five to nine petal-like sepals; each bloom sits on a single, deeply lobed, bright green leaf that looks like a ruff. Immediately after the flowers bloom, round basal leaves divided into narrow lobes emerge; all traces of the plant have vanished by the time summer arrives. The species *E. cilicica* is similar but blooms later, bears slightly larger flowers, and has bronze-tinted new leaves.

Plant tubers in late summer; if they look dry or shriveled, plump them up in wet sand before planting. Plant 3 in. deep and 4 in. apart, in moist, porous soil. Reduce water in summer but don't let soil dry out completely. Divide clumps infrequently; when doing so, separate into small clumps rather than single tubers.

EREMOCHLOA ophiuroides

CENTIPEDE GRASS

Poaceae (Gramineae)

PERENNIAL LAWN GRASS

LS, CS 12–8

FULL SUN OR LIGHT SHADE

REGULAR TO MODERATE WATER

Eremochloa ophiuroides

Native to southern and central China, centipede grass is sometimes known by the name "poor man's grass," thanks to its ease of establishment and the minimal attention required to keep it going. It thrives in areas with poor, acidic, infertile soil; annual rainfall greater than 40 in.; and mild winter temperatures. A popular lawn grass in the Lower and Coastal South, it's probably the most widely used grass in the Florida Panhandle. People sometimes confuse it with St. Augustine grass (*Stenotaphrum secundatum*), but centipede grass has narrower leaves, is a lighter green in color, and takes longer to green up in spring. It is also more cold hardy and less prone to diseases and insects.

This is one grass you won't spend endless weekends fertilizing. In fact, too much fertilizer will kill it. Apply controlled-release 15-0-15 centipede-grass fertilizer just once per year, in spring or summer, at the rate specified on the package. Note that centipede grass is naturally apple green; extra nitrogen won't deepen the color. Maintain soil pH between 5.0 and 6.0.

Seed at the rate of ¼ to ½ pound per 1,000 sq. ft. Seed takes 2 to 3 weeks to germinate. You can also start centipede grass from plugs or sprigs; also available as sod. Mow at 1–2 in.; if left unmowed, it will reach no more than 3 in., but it will look unkempt when it seeds. Centipede grass is fairly tolerant of drought and shade, but it doesn't stand up to salt spray or heavy wear. Improved selections are available only as sod or plugs. Cold-hardy types include 'Oklawn' and 'Tennessee Hardy', which may be hard to find, and the more widely available 'AU Centennial'. This last selection was released by Auburn University in 1983; it is lower growing and denser than other choices, with shorter seed heads. It is also more cold hardy and tolerates neutral to slightly alkaline soil.

FOR GROWING SYMBOL EXPLANATIONS

PLEASE SEE PAGE 145

EREMURUS

FOXTAIL LILY, DESERT CANDLE

Liliaceae

PERENNIALS FROM TUBEROUS ROOTS

US, MS, LS

FULL SUN

REGULAR WATER DURING GROWTH AND BLOOM

Eremurus himalaicus

Native to western and central Asia, these imposing lily relatives have spirelike flowering stems that look great in bulb catalogs. Unfortunately, they're difficult to grow well in most of the South. They need long, cold winters, which we seldom have—and they require absolutely perfect drainage. When these conditions are met, however, the results are spectacular.

Flower spikes stand 3–9 ft. tall. Spaced closely along the upper third to half of the spike are bell-shaped, 1/4- to 1-in.-wide flowers in white, yellow, pink, or orange. Rosettes of strap-shaped basal leaves appear in early spring, then wither after summer bloom. Magnificent in large borders against a background of dark green foliage, wall, or solid fence. Dramatic in arrangements; cut when lowest flowers on spike have opened.

Handle the thick, brittle roots carefully; they tend to rot when bruised or broken. Plant them in rich, fast-draining soil, setting crown just below surface in mild-winter climates, 4–6 in. deep in colder ones. Space roots 2–4 ft. apart. When leaves die down, mark spot; don't disturb roots. Don't let soil dry out completely during dormancy. Provide winter mulch in coldest areas.

E. himalaicus. Heat zones 8–1. To 4–8 ft. tall, with white flowers. Leaves to 1 1/2 ft. long.

E. × isabellinus. Heat zones 9–1. Likely best known in this group are Shelford Hybrids, 4–5 ft. tall, with blossoms in mixed colors (white, yellow, pink, orange). 'Cleopatra' is a 3- to 6-ft.-tall, orange-and-red selection of the Ruiter Hybrids, a Dutch strain featuring bright, clear flower colors.

E. robustus. Heat zones 8–1. To 6–9 ft. tall, with pink flowers lightly veined in brown. Dense basal rosettes of leaves to 2 ft. long.

E. stenophyllus (E. bungei). Heat zones 8–1. To 3–5 ft. tall, with bright yellow flowers aging to orange brown. Leaves to 1 ft. long.

ERICA

HEATH

Ericaceae

EVERGREEN SHRUBS

ZONES VARY BY SPECIES

PARTIAL SHADE IN SUMMER

REGULAR WATER

Erica carnea
'Springwood White'

Usually associated with the Scottish highlands, heaths are delightful little shrubs. They combine fine-textured, short, needlelike leaves with masses of showy flowers in winter, spring, or summer; blooms may be shaped like tiny bells, urns, or tubes. Flower color ranges from white to pink through lavender to red; foliage colors include bright green, gray green, yellow, orange, and bronze. Heaths are most effective when massed on berms and banks or used as a ground cover. Deer don't bother them.

Heaths do better in the South than their cousins the heathers (*Calluna*), but that doesn't mean they're easy to grow well. They require a sunny spot but need light afternoon shade during the hottest days of summer. The soil should be loose, acidic, and well drained, with plenty of organic matter. Sandy soil amended with sphagnum peat moss or compost is ideal; heavy clay usually proves fatal. Do not fertilize heaths. Shear or cut off faded flower spikes in spring, but don't cut back into leafless wood—if you do, new foliage may not sprout. The most dependable heath for the South is *E. ×darleyensis*.

E. carnea. SPRING HEATH. Zones US, MS; 7–5. From central and southern Europe. Forms a cushionlike mound to 6–10 in. high, 12–20 in. wide. Foliage is green, yellow, orange, or bronze, depending on selection.

In winter or early spring, single or double flowers appear in 2- to 4-in. spikes; bees like them. Among the hundreds of named selections are 'Ruby Glow', with dark green leaves and ruby red flowers; 'Springwood Pink', bright green foliage and pink blossoms; 'Springwood White', light green leaves, white blooms; 'Winter Beauty' ('King George'), dark green leaves and deep pink flowers.

E. ×darleyensis. DARLEY HEATH. Zones US, MS, LS; 8–6. Hybrid involving *E. carnea* and *E. erigena*. Has performed reasonably well in the Southeast. Larger and more shrublike than *E. carnea*; forms an attractive low mound that is broader than tall. Blooms late winter to early spring. 'Darley Dale', 1 ft. tall and 2 ft. wide, has medium green leaves and shell pink flowers that darken to rosy purple. 'George Rendall' reaches 1 ft. tall, 2 ft. wide, has bluish green foliage and purple blooms. 'Ghost Hills', to 2 ft. tall and 2 1/2 ft. wide, has bright green, white-tipped leaves and pink flowers. 'Silberschmelze' ('Molten Silver'), to about 1 ft. tall and 2 1/2–3 ft. wide, has medium green leaves and white blossoms.

E. tetralix. CROSS-LEAFED HEATH. Zones US; 7–1. From western Europe. Grows 1–2 ft. high and about half as wide. Very cold hardy. Blooms midsummer to fall. Selections include 'Afternoon', with gray-green foliage and lilac-pink flowers; 'Alba Mollis', silvery gray foliage and white blooms; and 'Ken Underwood', gray-green leaves and deep salmon flowers.

Ericaceae. The heath family contains shrubs and trees with rounded, bell-shaped, tubular, or irregular flowers, often showy, and fruits that are either capsules or berries. All share a preference, if not always a need, for acid soil with plenty of water and excellent aeration (a few plants from dry-summer climates are exceptions). Many are fine garden plants; azalea and rhododendron (*Rhododendron*), blueberry, heath (*Erica*), and heather (*Calluna*) are examples.

ERIGERON

FLEABANE

Asteraceae (Compositae)

PERENNIALS

ZONES VARY BY SPECIES

FULL SUN OR LIGHT SHADE

MODERATE WATER

Erigeron speciosus

Free-blooming plants with daisylike flowers, the fleabanes are similar to closely related Michaelmas daisy (*Aster novi-belgii*), except that flower heads have threadlike rays in two or more rows rather than broader rays in a single row. White, pink, lavender, or violet flowers, usually with yellow centers, bloom from early summer into fall. Give sandy soil. Cut back after flowering to prolong bloom.

E. karvinskianus. MEXICAN DAISY, SANTA BARBARA DAISY. Zones US, MS, LS; 8–5. Native to Mexico. Graceful, trailing plant 10–20 in. high, 3 ft. wide. Leaves 1 in. long, often toothed at tips. Dainty, 3/4-in.-wide flowers with numerous white or pinkish rays. Use as ground cover in garden beds or large containers, in rock gardens, in hanging baskets, on dry walls. Naturalizes easily; invasive unless controlled. 'Moerheimii' is somewhat more compact than species, with lavender-tinted flowers.

E. 'Prosperity'. Zones US, MS, LS, CS. Compact hybrid with lance-shaped leaves in a rosette to 1 1/2 ft. Clusters of lavender blue, semidouble, 1 1/2-in.-wide flowers are borne on stems to about 1 1/2 ft. tall. Does particularly well in the South; takes heat, humidity, and considerable drought.

E. pulchellus. ROBIN'S PLANTAIN. Zones US, MS, LS; 8–1. Native from Maine to Minnesota, south to Georgia and East Texas. Crinkled, 5-in.-long leaves grow in flat, ground-hugging rosettes that reach 1 1/2 ft. across. Erect stems about 2 ft. tall carry flowers to 1 1/2 in. wide, in blue, pink, or sometimes white. Spreads slowly.

E. speciosus. OREGON FLEABANE. Zones US, MS, LS; 8–1. Native to the Pacific Northwest. Erect, leafy stemmed, 2 ft. high. Flowers 1–1 1/2 in. across, with dark violet or lavender rays.

E

ERIOBOTRYA

LOQUAT

Rosaceae

EVERGREEN TREES OR SHRUBS

ZONES VARY BY SPECIES

FULL SUN OR PARTIAL SHADE

LITTLE TO REGULAR WATER

*Eriobotrya
japonica*

You know you're in the Deep South when you start seeing loquats. Native to China, these handsome evergreens feature large, glossy, prominently veined foliage. Use them for tall screens or as large container subjects; beautiful when espaliered against a fence or wall. Both of the species listed here produce fruit enjoyed by birds, but only that of *E. japonica* is eaten by people. Loquats thrive in fertile, well-drained soil. They accept heavy pruning. Subject to fireblight, especially if given too much fertilizer. Not bothered by deer.

E. deflexa. BRONZE LOQUAT. Zones CS, TS; 12–8. Shrubby but easily trained into small tree form. Leaves are slightly smaller, shinier, and more pointed than those of *E. japonica,* but not as leathery or deeply veined. They emerge bright copper and hold that color for a long time before turning green. Attractive spring show of creamy white flowers in garlands to 4–5 in. long. Good for espaliers (not on hot wall), patio planting, or containers. Fast growing.

E. japonica. LOQUAT. Zones LS, CS, TS; 12–8. Tree is hardy to 20°F; has survived 12°F, but fruit often injured by low temperatures. Grows 15–30 ft. tall, equally broad in sun, slimmer in shade. Leathery, crisp leaves, stoutly veined and netted, 6–12 in. long, 2–4 in. wide; they are glossy deep green above and show rust-colored wool beneath. New branches are woolly; small, dull white flowers, fragrant but not showy, in woolly, 3- to 6-in. clusters in fall. Orange to yellow, 1- to 2-in.-long fruit ripens in winter or spring. Sweet, aromatic, tangy flesh; seeds (usually big) in center.

Plant in well-drained soil. In dry climates, it will thrive with no irrigation once established, but it does better in youth with regular moisture. Mulch over root zone. Prune to shape; if you like the fruit, thin branches somewhat to let light into tree's interior. If tree sets fruit heavily, remove some while it's small to increase the size of remaining fruit and to prevent limb breakage. Fireblight is a danger. If leaves and stems blacken from top downward, prune back 1 ft. or more into healthy wood. Use as lawn tree; train as espalier on fence or trellis but not in reflected heat. Good in container for several years. Cut foliage is good for indoor decorating. Attracts bees. Caribbean fruit fly and anthracnose can cause severe problems in south Florida. Consult your Cooperative Extension Office for controls.

Most trees sold are seedlings; they are good ornamental plants with unpredictable fruit quality. If you definitely want fruit, look for a grafted selection. Early-ripening 'Champagne' has yellow-skinned, white-fleshed, juicy, tart fruit. Midseason 'Gold Nugget' has sweeter orange fruit. Early 'MacBeth' has exceptionally large fruit with yellow skin, creamy flesh. 'Thales' is a late yellow-fleshed selection.

ERYNGIUM

SEA HOLLY, AMETHYST ERYNGIUM

Apiaceae (Umbelliferae)

PERENNIALS

US, MS, LS, CS

FULL SUN

MODERATE WATER, LESS IN WINTER

Eryngium amethystinum

Most are erect, stiff-branched, thistlelike plants that bloom in summer, putting on a show of striking oval, steel blue or amethyst flower heads surrounded by spiny blue bracts. They make long-lasting cut flowers and dry well for winter arrangements. Plants are sparsely clothed in deeply cut dark green leaves with spiny-toothed edges; upper leaves and stems are sometimes blue.

Another group of sea hollies has long, narrow, spiny-edged leaves that are quite similar to those of yucca. One of these, *E. yuccifolium*, is native to the U.S.

Use sea hollies in borders or fringe areas, in deep, well-drained, sandy or gritty soils that are low in fertility. They are taprooted and difficult to divide, so propagate by root cuttings or by sowing seed in place (thin seedlings to 1 ft. apart). Plants often self-sow.

E. alpinum. ALPINE SEA HOLLY. Heat zones 9–2. From southeastern Europe. To 2½ ft. high, 1½ ft. wide, with steel blue, 2-in. flower heads and large, deeply cut blue bracts. Upper leaves and stems are tinged with soft blue to steel blue. 'Blue Star' is a choice selection.

E. amethystinum. Heat zones 8–1. From Italy and the Balkans. To 2½ ft. tall, 1½ ft. wide. Silvery blue stems; rich blue, inch-wide flower heads surrounded by silvery blue, 2-in. bracts.

E. planum. FALSE SEA HOLLY. Heat zones 9–1. From southeastern Europe to central Asia. To 3 ft. high, 1½ ft. wide. Leathery evergreen leaves; freely borne light blue flower heads to ¾ in. across, surrounded by narrow blue-green bracts.

E. variifolium. MOROCCAN SEA HOLLY. Heat zones 9–3. From Morocco. Grows to 16 in. tall and 10 in. wide, with inch-wide, rounded blue-gray flower heads and bluish white bracts. Thistlelike evergreen leaves are heavily veined with white.

E. yuccifolium. RATTLESNAKE MASTER. Heat zones 12–1. Native to eastern and central U.S. Long (to 3-ft.), narrow, spiny-edged leaves in a basal rosette to 2 ft. wide. Erect stems to 3–4 ft. branch toward top and carry 1½-in.-wide white flowers without significant bracts.

SEA HOLLY FLOWERS NEED LONGER STEMS. *Sea holly flowers have such dramatic form and unusual color that they're perfect for arrangements. But their individual flower stems are too short (3–6 in.) to be seen in long-stemmed company. Cut florists' wire as needed, and fasten pieces to the stems with florists' tape. Sea holly flowers are everlasting; their stems don't need to be in water.* ❖

ERYSIMUM

WALLFLOWER

Brassicaceae (Cruciferae)

PERENNIALS AND BIENNIALS, SOME GROWN AS ANNUALS

ZONES VARY BY SPECIES

FULL SUN OR LIGHT SHADE

WATER NEEDS VARY BY SPECIES

*Erysimum
'Bowles Mauve'*

This genus swallowed up *Cheiranthus*, which included the old-fashioned biennial bedding-plant wallflowers and several choice perennials. All have the clustered four-petaled flowers typical of the plants in the brassica (mustard) family, but their habits and uses differ widely.

E. 'Bowles Mauve'. Perennial. Zones US, MS, LS, CS; 10–3. Massed erect stems with narrow gray-green leaves form a plant to 3 ft. tall, 6 ft. wide; each stem is topped by 1½-ft.-long, narrow, spikelike clusters of mauve flowers. Often begins blooming in midwinter, continuing until hot weather begins in May. Plants may be short lived. Moderate to little water. 'Wenlock Beauty', 2 ft. high and wide, has flowers from buff to purple in a single spike.

E. cheiri (Cheiranthus cheiri). ENGLISH WALLFLOWER. Perennial in Zones US, MS, but usually grown as a biennial or an annual; 9–2. Branching, woody-based plants 1–2½ ft. tall, 1–1½ ft. wide, with narrow bright green leaves and broad clusters of showy, delightfully sweet-scented flowers in spring. Blossoms are yellow, cream, orange, red, brown, or burgundy, sometimes shaded or veined with contrasting color. Sow seeds in spring for bloom the following year (some strains flower the first year if seeded early); or set out plants in fall or earliest spring. May self-sow. Regular water. Charity Series includes dwarf plants (12–14 in. tall and not quite as wide) that don't need winter chill to induce flowering; set out in spring for fall bloom. Selections include soft yellow 'Charity Cream', golden yellow 'Charity Yellow', and dusty rose 'Charity Rose'.

E. hieraciifolium (E. alpinum). SIBERIAN WALLFLOWER. Biennial or short-lived perennial in Zones US, MS, CS, frequently treated as an annual; 9–1. Narrow-leafed, branching plants 1–1½ ft. tall, covered with fragrant, rich orange flowers in spring. Sow seeds or set out plants as for *E. cheiri*. Often self-sows. Regular water. 'Moonlight' has bright yellow flowers that open from red buds.

E. kotschyanum. Short-lived perennial in Zones US and MS, often treated as an annual; 8–5. Light green leaves form 6-in. mats from which rise scented, deep yellow flowers on 2-in. stems in spring. Moderate water. Use in rock garden or with other small perennials between paving stones. If plants hump up, cut out central portions, transplant them, and press original plants flat again. Divide clumps in fall.

ERYTHEA. See BRAHEA

ERYTHRINA

CORAL TREE

Fabaceae (Leguminosae)

DECIDUOUS OR NEARLY EVERGREEN TREES AND SHRUBS, SOME GROWN AS PERENNIALS

TS 12–10, EXCEPT AS NOTED

FULL SUN

MODERATE WATER

SEEDS ARE POISONOUS IF INGESTED

These thorny trees and shrubs are prized for their brilliant flowers, in colors ranging from pink through red, orange, and yellow. The flat, beanlike pods that follow contain poisonous seeds. Leaves have three leaflets and usually drop in fall or winter. *E. ×bidwillii, E. crista-galli,* and *E. herbacea* are hardy outside the Tropical South.

Erythrina crista-galli

E. acanthocarpa. TAMBOOKIE THORN. Deciduous shrub. Native to South Africa. To 3 ft. tall (rarely 6 ft.); as wide as tall. Roundish blue-green leaflets to 1½ in. long. Spring flower spikes are 7 in. long, 6 in. wide, with scarlet, yellow-tipped flowers. Thorny plant grows from large, thick tuber-like root. Don't plant it near pavement, which can be lifted by root.

E. americana. Deciduous tree. Native to Mexico; used as street tree in Mexico City. Grows to 25 ft. tall and wide. Resembles *E. coralloides* in both habit and flowers. Leaves are gray green.

E. ×bidwillii. Deciduous shrub. Zones LS, CS, TS; 12–8. To 8 ft., sometimes treelike to 20 ft. or more, wide spreading. Hybrid of *E. crista-galli* and *E. herbacea*. Leaves to 8 in. long. Pure red, 2-ft.-long flower clusters on long, willowy stalks from spring until winter; main show in summer, when display is spectacular. Cut back flowering wood when flowers are spent. Very thorny, so plant away from paths and prune with long-handled shears.

E. coralloides. NAKED CORAL TREE. Deciduous tree. Native to Mexico. To 30 ft. high and as wide, but easily contained by pruning. Fiery red blossoms like fat candles or pinecones bloom at the tips of naked, twisted, black-thorned branches in spring. At end of flowering season, 8- to 10-in. leaves develop; these give shade in summer, then turn yellow in late fall before dropping. Bizarre branch structure when tree is out of leaf is almost as valuable as spring flower display. Sometimes sold as *E. poianthes*.

E. crista-galli. CRY-BABY TREE, COCKSPUR CORAL TREE. Deciduous shrub or small tree 15–20 ft. high and wide in nearly frostless areas; perennial to 4 ft. in colder areas. Zones LS, CS, TS; 12–8. From eastern South America. Leathery leaves 1 ft. long. First flowers form after leaves come in spring—at each branch tip is a big, loose, spikelike cluster of velvety, birdlike blossoms in warm pink to wine red (plants vary). Teardrops of nectar that drip from flowers explain common name "cry-baby tree." There can be as many as three flowering periods, spring through fall. Cut back old flower stems and dead branch ends after each bloom.

E. falcata. Nearly evergreen tree. Native to Brazil and Peru. Grows upright to 30–40 ft. high. Must be in ground several years before it flowers (may take 10 to 12 years). Leaves similar to those of *E. crista-galli*. Rich deep red (occasionally orange-red), sickle-shaped flowers in hanging, spikelike clusters at branch ends in late winter, early spring. Some leaves fall at flowering time.

E. herbacea. CORAL BEAN, CHEROKEE BEAN. Perennial to 6 ft. high in Middle and Lower South; deciduous shrub or small tree to 15 ft. tall in Coastal and Tropical South. Zones MS, LS, CS, TS; 12–7. Grows taller than wide. Bright red, 2-in. blooms appear in 8- to 12-in. spikes from spring until frost. Red seeds that follow the flowers are attractive but extremely poisonous.

E. humeana. NATAL CORAL TREE. Deciduous shrub or tree (sometimes almost evergreen). Native to South Africa. May reach 30 ft. tall and wide but begins to bear bright orange-red flowers when 3 ft. high. Blooms continuously from late summer to late fall, with flowers in long-stalked clusters at branch ends well above foliage (unlike many other types). Dark green leaves. 'Raja' is shrubbier, has leaflets with long, pointed "tails."

E. lysistemon. Deciduous tree. Heat zones 12–9. Native to South Africa. Eventually reaches 25–40 ft. high, spreads 40–60 ft. wide. Light orange (sometimes shrimp-colored) flowers. Time of bloom varies greatly; may bloom intermittently from fall into spring, occasionally in summer. Many handsome black thorns. A magnificent tree of great landscape value. Very sensitive to wet soil. Sometimes erroneously sold as *E. princeps*.

Erythrina humeana

E. variegata. VARIEGATED CORAL TREE. Deciduous tree. Heat zones 12–9. Native to Africa, Asia, Polynesia. To 20–30 ft. tall or much taller, with spreading form. Thick, prickly trunk and branches. Rich green leaves have 3- to 8-in. leaflets. Profuse display of coral red flowers in late winter, early spring. Forms are available with white flowers and variegated leaves.

ERYTHRONIUM

Liliaceae

PERENNIALS FROM BULBS

ZONES VARY BY SPECIES

LIGHT SHADE

REGULAR WATER DURING GROWTH AND BLOOM

Erythronium americanum

Spring-blooming plants with dainty, nodding, lily-shaped flowers to 1–1½ in. across, on stems usually 1 ft. high or less. All have two (rarely three) broad, tongue-shaped, basal leaves that are mottled in many species. All need some subfreezing temperatures. Plant in groups under trees, in rock gardens, beside pools or streams. Set out bulbs in fall, 2–3 in. deep, 4–5 in. apart, in rich, porous soil; plant bulbs as soon as you receive them, and don't let them dry out. May take a few years after planting to begin blooming. Difficult to transplant once established, because bulbs work their way deep into the soil.

E. albidum. WHITE TROUT LILY. Zones US, MS, LS; 9–1. Native from Minnesota to Ontario and south to Texas. White flowers flushed yellow at the base come on stems 6–12 in. tall. Blooms later in spring than most other species. Leaves are soft green, sometimes mottled with silver or brown. Spreads slowly to form colonies.

E. americanum. TROUT LILY. Zones US, MS, LS, CS; 9–1. Native from Minnesota to Nova Scotia and south to Florida. Shiny green leaves mottled brown and purple. Blooms in late spring, at about the same time as *E. albidum;* 3- to 6-in. stems bear pale yellow blossoms sometimes flushed with purple.

E. dens-canis. DOG-TOOTH VIOLET. Zones US, MS, LS; 8–2. European species. Leaves mottled with reddish brown; 6-in. stems bear purple or rose flowers. Specialists can supply named forms with white, pink, rose, and violet blossoms.

ESCHSCHOLZIA

Papaveraceae

ANNUALS

US, MS, LS, CS, TS 12–1

FULL SUN

LITTLE TO REGULAR WATER

Eschscholzia californica

Poppy relatives with upward-facing, four-petaled, typically yellow or orange blooms above finely cut foliage. Individual plants grow about 6 in. wide. Of the several species native to western North America and Mexico, *E. californica* is the most outstanding and the most widely used; it is the state flower of California. All are drought tolerant, but giving them summer water will extend the flowering season.

E. caespitosa. Native to California and southwestern Oregon. Smaller plant than *E. californica*; garden variety 'Sundew', for example, has densely tufted growth to 6 in. high. Plants bear bright yellow, 1-in. flowers. Use for edging, in containers.

E. californica. CALIFORNIA POPPY. Native to California, Oregon. Free branching from base, with slender, 8- to 24-in.-long stems and blue-green, finely divided leaves. Single, satiny-petaled flowers about 2 in. wide; color varies from pale yellow to deep orange. Flowers close at night and on overcast days. In mild climates, it blooms from spring to summer, reseeds freely.

California poppy is not the best choice for important beds viewed close up—unless you trim off dead flowers regularly, plants go to seed and all parts turn straw colored. It can't be surpassed, however, for naturalizing on sunny hillsides, along drives, or in dry fields, vacant lots, parking strips, or country gardens.

Sow seeds in fall where plants are to grow; seedlings don't transplant well. Broadcast on cultivated, well-drained soil; if rain is absent, water to keep ground moist until seeds germinate. For large-scale sowing, use 3 to 4 pounds of seeds per acre. Birds are attracted to the seeds.

There are also garden forms with blooms of yellow, pink, rose, flame orange, red, cream, and white. Sunset strain has single flowers. Strains with semidouble blossoms include Ballerina, with frilled and fluted petals; Mission Bells; and Thai Silk, with bronze-tinted foliage and flowers in the full color range. Among the many California poppy selections are 'Apricot Flambeau', yellow with orange-pink borders; 'Carmine King', a blend of deep pink and white; 'Dalli', orange-red blooms with yellow eye; and 'Inferno', orange scarlet. Names 'Cherry Ripe', 'Milky White', and 'Purple Cap' describe flower color. 'Champagne and Roses' has heavily frilled flowers in rose or light pink. 'Golden Tears' bears single golden yellow blooms on trailing stems to 2 ft. long. Garden forms usually revert to orange or yellow when they reseed.

E. mexicana. Native Arizona to West Texas, southern Utah, Mexico. Very similar to *E. californica* but generally a smaller plant (to 8 in. high) with less finely divided leaves. Sun Shades strain has brilliant orange flowers.

ESPOSTOA lanata

PERUVIAN OLD MAN CACTUS

Cactaceae

CACTUS

TS 12–10; OR HOUSEPLANT

FULL SUN OR LIGHT AFTERNOON SHADE; BRIGHT LIGHT

LITTLE TO MODERATE WATER

Espostoa lanata

From southern Ecuador and Peru. Columnar cactus, branching with age, usually grown as a houseplant. May eventually reach 8 ft. tall and 2 ft. wide, but grows very slowly. Light brown, bristly, ½- to 2-in.-long spines are usually concealed in long white hairs that cover plant. Hair is especially long and dense near the top. Tubular, pink, 2-in.-long flowers appear in spring.

Indoors, place directly in front of southern or western window. In spring and summer, water as soon as soil surface goes dry to the touch. Decrease frequency of watering in fall and winter; water only on sunny days when soil is dry. Feed every other week in spring and summer with a general-purpose liquid houseplant fertilizer diluted to half-strength. Don't feed in fall and winter. Make sure soil drains freely. Outdoors, protect plant from frost.

ETLINGERA elatior (Nicolaia elatior, Phaeomeria speciosa)

TORCH GINGER

Zingiberaceae

PERENNIAL

TS 12–10; OR GROW IN POTS

LIGHT SHADE

REGULAR WATER

Etlingera elatior

From Indonesia. One of the most imposing and spectacular of the flowering gingers, with large clumps of leafy stalks that rise as high as 15 ft. Rich green, lance-shaped leaves are up to 2 ft. long, 6 in. wide. In summer, flower stems grow to 4 ft. tall, each topped by a spectacular, pyramidal inflorescence consisting of clustered, waxy pinkish bracts and a red corolla. Easy to grow in rich, acid soil; ideal location is in the light shade of tall trees. Propagate by division in spring. Very tender to cold. Choice container plant.

EUCALYPTUS

Myrtaceae

EVERGREEN TREES AND SHRUBS

ZONES VARY BY SPECIES

FULL SUN

LITTLE WATER, EXCEPT AS NOTED

Eucalyptus pauciflora niphophila

Prized for their beautiful foliage, these fast-growing plants are also famously drought tolerant. Most are native to Australia. Lack of cold-hardiness limits their use in the South. Sudden freezes or hard winters may kill fairly large trees to the ground or kill them outright. For this reason, some Southerners grow them as annuals or herbaceous perennials for summer color. Still, some species are surprisingly hardy; they are listed here. None is bothered by deer.

Outside of prime eucalyptus territory, you may wish to try your hand at growing the plants if you enjoy experimenting. Plants are easily started from seed; most grow very rapidly, perhaps as much as 10–15 ft. in 1 year. Some are large trees with great skyline value; some are medium to large shrubs or multitrunked trees. Most bear small white or cream flowers that are conspicuous only in masses, while others have colorful, showy blooms. Some have leaves of unusual form, highly valued in floral arrangements. Nearly all have foliage that is aromatic when crushed. Most have two different kinds of leaves; those on young plants or new growth differ markedly from mature foliage.

In Victorian England, some species were grown as summer annuals for bedding out. In borderline climates, such bedded-out plants function today as perennials—tops are killed, but plants resprout vigorously the next year. Sow seeds in spring or summer, in flats or pots of prepared soil or planting mix. Keep flats shaded and water sparingly. As soon as seedlings are 2–3 in. tall, separate them carefully and transplant to pots or other containers. Spray lightly and frequently with quarter-strength general-purpose liquid fertilizer. Plant in open ground or large container when 6–12 in. tall; trees seldom thrive if roots have become pot-bound. Limbs are subject to breakage on larger species, so choose planting site carefully.

The sizes listed for trees below apply to plants grown in mildest areas; plants grown elsewhere are unlikely to reach such heights. Hardiness figures are not absolute. In addition to air temperature, you must take into account the plant's age (generally, the older the hardier), its condition, and the timing of the frost (24°F following several light frosts is not as dangerous as the same low temperature following warm autumn and winter weather). Consider any eucalyptus a risk; occasional deep or prolonged freezes can kill even large trees. If you are committed to growing eucalyptus, don't hasten to remove apparently dead trees; although their appearance may be damaged, they could resprout from trunk or main branches.

E. cinerea. SILVER DOLLAR TREE. Zones LS (protected), CS, TS; grow as annual in Upper South and Middle South; 11–7. Hardy to 10–12°F. Small to medium tree of irregular habit; grows 20–50 ft. tall and nearly as wide. Grown for attractive juvenile foliage, which is popular in floral arrangements: paired gray-green to blue-green, nearly round, 1- to 2-in.-long leaves. Mature leaves are green, narrow, up to 4½ in. long. Unimportant small white flowers. Cut back often to maintain a good supply of young foliage. Recovers from freezes if base of trunk is heavily mulched.

E. gunnii. CIDER GUM. Zones MS (protected), LS, CS, TS; 10–7. Hardy to 5–10°F. Dense form; upright, medium to tall tree—to 30–70 ft. tall, 18–40 ft. wide. One of the fastest-growing eucalypts. Silvery blue-green, oval to roundish young foliage; dark green, narrowly oval, 3- to 5-in.-long mature leaves. Small, creamy white flowers.

E. neglecta. OMEO GUM. Zones MS (protected), LS, CS, TS; 10–7. Hardy to near 0°F. Shrubby, fast-growing, small to medium tree to 20 ft. tall and 12 ft. wide (or larger). Handsome round, blue-green, paired juvenile leaves to about 2 in. long; excellent for cutting. Mature leaves are more oval in shape; they retain the attractive color of the juvenile foliage. Good-looking brown, peeling bark. Unimportant white flowers.

E. pauciflora niphophila (E. niphophila). SNOW GUM. Zones MS (protected), LS, CS, TS; 10–7. Hardy to near 0°F. Small, picturesque tree to 20 ft. tall, with wide-spreading, open habit. Oval, pointed young leaves are gray green, to 2–3 in. long. Lance-shaped, silvery blue adult leaves reach 4 in. long. Smooth, peeling white bark on trunk contrasts handsomely with red branches.

E. torelliana. CADAGA. Zones TS; 12–10. Hardy to 28–30°F. Straight-trunked tree with rounded or spreading form; grows fast to 45–60 ft. tall. Juvenile leaves are 2–4 in. long, broadly oval; mature leaves are dark green, 3–6 in. long, narrower and more pointed. Profuse display of showy white flowers. Regular water. Often grown in south Florida.

EUCALYPTUS IN BOUQUETS. *Though florists sell eucalyptus stems to include in arrangements, foliage you pick yourself is fresher and more fragrant. If you have an E. cinerea, clip young foliage regularly for its gray-green to blue-green, nearly round leaves. The silvery blue young foliage of E. gunnii is another attractive choice.* ❖

EUCHARIS ×grandiflora

EUCHARIST LILY, AMAZON LILY

Amaryllidaceae

PERENNIAL FROM BULB

✿ TS ⫯ 12–10; OR HOUSEPLANT

● FULL SHADE; BRIGHT FILTERED LIGHT

◐ REGULAR WATER DURING GROWTH AND BLOOM

Eucharis ×grandiflora

Native to the Andes of Colombia and Peru, this evergreen plant combines handsome, glossy deep green foliage with showy, sweet-smelling flowers. It forms a cluster of short-stemmed, broadly oval leaves with pointed tips; leaves are about 1 ft. long, and foliage mass reaches 1½–2 ft. high and wide. In late winter or early spring, a leafless stalk rises above the leaves, carrying up to six nodding white flowers that look something like daffodils. Older plants may stay in bloom for 6 weeks.

Eucharist lily is very tender and can be grown in the ground only in south Florida and South Texas, where it should be sited in full shade. Even there, it does better in a pot, as plants bloom more heavily when pot-bound; plant four or five bulbs in a 6-in. pot. Indoors, mist frequently (leaves but not flowers) and give bright filtered light. Let the soil go slightly dry between waterings. Gradually reduce watering in fall and winter, but don't let plants dry out completely. Feed with a general-purpose liquid houseplant fertilizer—every other week in spring and summer, once a month in fall. In winter, cease fertilizing; this encourages formation of flower buds. When new leaves appear, resume regular watering and fertilizing schedule. Check foliage frequently for scale, which is a common pest; treat with horticultural oil.

EUCOMIS

PINEAPPLE LILY

Liliaceae

PERENNIALS FROM BULBS

✿ LS, CS, TS ⫯ 12–8; OR DIG AND STORE; OR HOUSEPLANT

☼ ◐ FULL SUN OR LIGHT SHADE; BRIGHT LIGHT

◐ REGULAR WATER DURING GROWTH AND BLOOM

Eucomis comosa

It's easy to see how these unusual plants from southern Africa got their common name—the summertime spikes of tiny, closely packed, star-shaped blossoms are topped with leaflike bracts resembling those of a pineapple. They make striking cut flowers. Purplish seed capsules follow the flowers, keeping the show going even longer. Leaves are coarse and straplike, emerging from large bulbs to form a basal rosette. Plants go dormant in winter.

Plant bulbs 5 in. deep and 8 in. apart in well-drained, humus-rich soil in fall—or start plants from seed in spring. Bulbs are hardy to about 5°F; where temperatures dip lower, mulch plantings heavily in late fall, or dig and store bulbs over winter. Divide clumps when they become crowded (every 5 or 6 years). Pineapple lilies can also be grown as houseplants beside a bright (south- or west-facing) window; while they are actively growing, give plenty of water and feed monthly with a general-purpose liquid houseplant fertilizer.

E. bicolor. Spikes to 2 ft. tall; green flowers with purple-edged petals. Attractive, wavy-edged light green leaves to 1 ft. long, 3–4 in. wide.

E. comosa (E. punctata). Thick spikes 2–3 ft. tall are set with greenish white flowers tinged pink or purple. Stems are spotted purple at the base. Light green leaves grow to 2 ft. long and are less wavy than those of *E. bicolor.*

E. 'Sparkling Burgundy'. To 1½–2 ft. tall. Foliage emerges deep burgundy, then slowly fades to olive green as weather warms. Flower spikes to 20 in. tall are set with creamy white blossoms tinged pink and purple. Flowers are followed by a new crop of burgundy leaves.

EUCOMMIA ulmoides

HARDY RUBBER TREE

Eucommiaceae

DECIDUOUS TREE

✿ US, MS ⫯ 7–1

☼ FULL SUN

◑ MODERATE TO REGULAR WATER

Eucommia ulmoides

From central China. Rubber can be made from this tree's sap, but the process isn't economically feasible—instead, the plant is grown for its ornamental qualities. Attractive rounded habit; can reach 40–60 ft. tall, with equal or greater spread. Leaves resemble those of elm *(Ulmus)* but are glossier and more leathery. When a leaf is slowly torn in two, sap from the veins congeals into threads of rubber, holding the two halves together. Tolerates a wide variety of soils but requires good drainage. Not troubled by pests.

EUGENIA

Myrtaceae

EVERGREEN SHRUBS OR TREES

ZONES VARY BY SPECIES

FULL SUN OR PARTIAL SHADE

REGULAR WATER

Grown for attractive foliage, white flowers, edible "cherries." Perform best in a moist atmosphere, with rich, well-drained soil and a sheltered location.

Eugenia uniflora

E. aggregata. CHERRY OF THE RIO GRANDE. Zones TS; 12–10. Native to Brazil. To 15 ft. tall and 10 ft. wide, with bark peeling in thin layers. Narrow, elliptical, glossy dark green leaves to 3 in. long. Showy flowers to about 1 in. across. Oval fruit to 1 in. long ripens from orange red to deep purplish red, is said to taste like cherries. Eat fresh or use for jams, jellies.

E. uniflora. SURINAM CHERRY, PITANGA. Zones CS, TS; 12–10. From the tropical Americas. Very slow, open growth to about 15–25 ft. tall and 10–15 ft. wide, though it's commonly seen at 6–8 ft. tall with equal spread. Glossy, copper-tinged green leaves reach 2 in. long, deepen in color to purplish or red in cold weather. Fragrant, showy, ½-in.-wide flowers with prominent stamens. Roundish, inch-wide fruit ripens from yellow to orange to deep red; it is edible when fully ripe. Fruit of seedlings ranges from quite sweet and cherrylike to very sour. 'Lolita' has sweet black fruit that is far superior in flavor to that of seedlings; it's good for jams, jellies. Grafted selections are sometimes available. Good screen. Can be sheared into a hedge, but by doing so you'll sacrifice fruit.

EUONYMUS

Celastraceae

EVERGREEN AND DECIDUOUS SHRUBS AND VINES

ZONES VARY BY SPECIES

EXPOSURE NEEDS VARY BY SPECIES

MODERATE TO REGULAR WATER

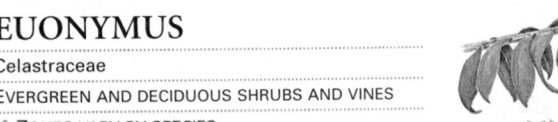

Maybe the reason so many people mistakenly call euonymus "anonymous plants" is that they can be hard to recognize—the ever-

Euonymus alatus

green and deciduous kinds look nothing alike. The colorful seed capsules common to both provide the only obvious hint that they're related. Deciduous types are valued for their brilliant fall leaf color or showy fruit. Evergreen types—which include some of the most cold-hardy broad-leafed evergreens—are employed as hedges, screens, and foundation plants. Foliage is quite variable in shape, but leaves of most are pointed-oval to lance-shaped. Most species tolerate either sun or shade, but deciduous types need sun for good fall color. Scale is a likely problem on any euonymus; treat with horticultural oil.

E. alatus. WINGED EUONYMUS, BURNING BUSH. Deciduous shrub. Zones US, MS, LS; 8–1. Native of China and Japan. Though nursery tags may indicate a much smaller plant, the species can reach 15–20 ft. high and wide. This plant is quite dense, twiggy, and flat topped, with horizontal branching; if lower limbs are removed, it makes an attractive, vase-shaped small tree. Young twigs have flat, corky wings; these disappear on older growth. Fruit is smaller and less profuse than that of *E. europaeus,* but fall color is impressive: the dark green, 3-in.-long leaves turn flaming red (or pink, in shade). Best autumn color comes in Upper and Middle South. 'Compactus', a smaller plant (grows 6–10 ft. high and wide) with smaller corky wings, isn't quite as hardy; 'Rudy Haag', even more compact, grows to 3–5 ft. high and wide.

Species *E. alatus* and its selections take sun or shade. Group them as a screen or plant them singly against dark evergreen plants for the greatest color impact. Compact selections make excellent unclipped hedges or foundation plants.

E. americanus. HEART'S-A-BUSTIN', STRAWBERRY BUSH. Deciduous shrub. Zones US, MS, LS, CS; 9–4. Native to eastern and southern U.S. Many-stemmed, suckering, well-behaved shrub that deserves wider use. To 6 ft. tall and broad, with green stems clothed in medium green, 3-in.-long leaves that turn pale yellowish pink in fall. Showy scarlet fruits about ¾ in. wide open in September and October to reveal purple interiors and bright orange seeds. Stems hold their green color all winter. Tolerates much shade; use in woodland plantings.

E. europaeus. SPINDLE TREE. Deciduous shrub or tree. Zone US. From Europe and western Asia. Eventually grows as tall as 30 ft.; narrow when young, becoming rounded with age. Dark green leaves to 3 in. long; fall color varies from yellowish green to yellow to red. Profuse, ¾-in.-wide fruit is the ornamental feature: four-chambered, pink to red capsules that open to reveal bright orange seeds. 'Aldenham' ('Aldenhamensis') bears large pink capsules on long stems; 'Red Cascade' has rosy red capsules. Full sun or partial shade.

E. fortunei. WINTERCREEPER EUONYMUS. Evergreen vine or shrub. Zones US, MS, LS, CS; 9–4. Native to China. One of best broad-leafed evergreens where temperatures drop below 0°F. Trails or climbs by rootlets. Use prostrate forms to control erosion. Rich dark green, 1- to 2½-in.-long leaves with scallop-toothed edges; round white or pinkish fruits just ¼ in. wide. Mature growth is shrubby and bears fruit; cuttings taken from this shrubby wood produce upright plants. Sun or shade.

The selections of *E. fortunei,* several of which are listed here, are better known than the species itself. Many garden centers still sell them as forms of *E. radicans,* which was once thought to be the species but is now considered to be a botanical variety (see *E. f. radicans*). Use restraint when considering the variegated forms; gaudy foliage can be overpowering.

'Canadale Gold'. Compact growth to 4 ft. high, 3–3½ ft. wide, with light green, yellow-edged leaves.

'Coloratus'. PURPLE-LEAF WINTER CREEPER. To 2 ft. high, 6–8 ft. wide. Same sprawling growth habit as *E. f. radicans* but makes a more even ground cover. Leaves turn dark purple in fall and winter.

'Emerald Gaiety'. To 4–5 ft. high, 3 ft. wide. Dense-growing, erect shrub with deep green leaves edged in white.

'Emerald 'n Gold'. Similar to Emerald Gaiety, but with gold-edged leaves.

'Golden Prince'. To 4 ft. high and wide. New growth tipped gold. Older leaves turn green. Extremely hardy; good hedge plant.

'Green Lane'. To 3–4 ft. high, 4–5 ft. wide, with erect branches, deep green foliage, orange fruit in fall.

'Ivory Jade'. Resembles 'Green Lane' but has creamy white leaf margins that show pink tints in cold weather.

Euonymus fortunei
'Emerald 'n Gold'

E. f. radicans. COMMON WINTER CREEPER. Zones US, MS, LS, CS. A tough, hardy, trailing or vining shrub with dark green, thick-textured, 1-in.-long leaves. Given no support, it's a sprawling, foot-high ground cover. Given a masonry wall to cover, it does the job completely.

'Sunspot'. To 3–6 ft. high and wide; dark green leaves have a central bright yellow spot.

E. japonicus. EVERGREEN EUONYMUS. Evergreen shrub. Zones MS, LS, CS; 9–1. Japanese native grows upright to 8–10 ft. tall and 6 ft. wide, but it's usually held lower by pruning or shearing. Older shrubs are attractive trained as trees, pruned and shaped to show their curving trunks and umbrella-shaped tops. Can be grouped to form a hedge or screen. Very glossy, leathery leaves are deep green, 1–2½ in. long, oval to roundish.

The species and its selections are very tolerant of heat, unfavorable soil, and seacoast conditions, but they're pest prone and susceptible to scale insects, thrips, and spider mites. Plants are notorious for powdery mildew; place in full-sun location with good air circulation.

Variegated forms are most popular; they are among the few shrubs that keep variegation in full sun in hot-summer climates. Their dazzling foliage can be hard to work into landscaping, however, and may become an eyesore. Some confusion may exist in plant labeling of variegated types.

'Aureomarginatus'. GOLDEN EUONYMUS. To 5–10 ft. tall and 3–5 ft. wide. Gaudy, bright golden foliage nearly glows in the dark. Extremely popular; extremely overplanted.

'Aureovariegatus' ('Ovatus Aureus'). GOLDSPOT EUONYMUS. To 10 ft. tall, 6 ft. wide. Leaves have brilliant yellow blotches, green edges.

'Grandifolius'. To 6–8 ft. tall, 4–6 ft. wide. Plants sold under this name have shiny dark green leaves that are larger than those of the species. Compact, well branched; good for shearing into pyramids, globes.

'Microphyllus' (*E. j. microphyllus*). BOX-LEAF EUONYMUS. Compact and small leafed, 1–2 ft. tall and half as wide. Formal looking; usually trimmed as low hedge.

'Microphyllus Variegatus'. Resembles 'Microphyllus' but has white-splashed leaves.

'Silver King'. To 6 ft. tall and about half as wide. Green leaves with silvery white edges.

'Silver Princess'. Like 'Microphyllus Variegatus' but larger (to 3 ft. tall, 2 ft. wide), with larger leaves.

'Silver Queen'. Similar to 'Silver King', but green leaves are edged in creamy white.

E. kiautschovicus (E. patens). SPREADING EUONYMUS. Evergreen shrub. Zones US, MS, LS; 8–1. From China. To 8 ft. high and as wide or wider, with some low branches trailing on the ground and rooting. Light green, relatively thin-textured leaves to 3 in. long; profuse tiny, greenish cream flowers in late summer. Bees and flies swarm the plant when it is in bloom, so it is not a good choice for planting near porches, terraces, or walkways. Flowers are followed by conspicuous pink to reddish fruits with red seeds. Two hybrids make good hedges: 'DuPont', a 4- to 6-ft.-high plant with large dark green leaves; and 'Manhattan', an upright grower to 6–8 ft., with dark, glossy leaves. Scale is a serious problem on all forms. Full sun or partial shade.

EUPATORIUM

Asteraceae (Compositae)

PERENNIALS

US, MS, LS, CS ❘❘ 9–1, EXCEPT AS NOTED

☼ ☼ LIGHT SHADE IN HOTTEST CLIMATES

◑ ◕ ◕ WATER NEEDS VARY BY SPECIES

Eupatorium maculatum 'Gateway'

These are generally large plants with big domes of small flower heads that are rich in nectar and pollen. Blossoms attract butterflies. Most of the species described here are native to meadows of the eastern and central U.S.; popular in perennial borders and naturalistic meadow plantings.

E. cannabinum. HEMP AGRIMONY. Native to Europe. Grows 5–6 ft. tall, 4 ft. wide, with opposite pairs of deeply cut, 5-in.-long leaves and broad clusters of fluffy white, pink, or purple flowers in the summer. 'Album' produces white flowers; 'Plenum', pinkish purple blooms. Ample water.

E. coelestinum (Conoclinium coelestinum). WILD AGERATUM, HARDY AGERATUM. Zones US, MS, LS, CS, TS. Native to the West Indies, and from New Jersey to Missouri, south to Florida and Texas. Reaches 3 ft. tall and 2–3 ft. wide, with freely branching stems set with pairs of toothed, dark green, 4-in. leaves. From summer until frost, bears broad clusters of fluffy blue flowers that exactly resemble those of floss flower (*Ageratum*). Vigorous and freely spreading; invasive in fertile soil. Prefers ample moisture but will not thrive in soggy soil in winter. Late to appear in spring. Selections include 1½- to 2-ft.-tall 'Album', with pure white flowers; 2-ft. 'Cori', bearing exceptionally clear blue blossoms, later blooming than the species; and compact 'Wayside Form', to just 15 in.

E. greggii. GREGG'S MIST FLOWER. Native to Arizona, Texas. Weak-stemmed plant to 1½–2½ ft. tall, 2–3 ft. wide, with clusters of fluffy lavender flowers similar in form to those of floss flower (*Ageratum*). Blooms from spring to fall. Lacy, divided light green leaves are somewhat hairy and usually sparse. Excellent for attracting butterflies. Native to dry, hot, rocky places but prefers some shade in low desert. Drought tolerant but looks best with occasional water. 'Boothill', first found near Tombstone, Arizona, is a choice form.

E. maculatum (E. purpureum maculatum). SPOTTED JOE-PYE WEED. Similar to *E. purpureum* but smaller (to 6 ft. tall, 3 ft. wide at most), with green stems speckled or blotched in purple. Flat-topped clusters of pink, purple, or white flowers bloom from midsummer to early fall. Commonly sold is 'Gateway', to 5 ft. tall, with dusky purplish rose flowers at the tops of purplish stems. Give ample water, rich soil.

E. perfoliatum. BONESET. Grows to 3–5 ft. tall and 2–3 ft. wide. Long (8-in.), narrow, medium green leaves are joined at their bases, so that the stem seems to grow through the leaves. Blooms from late summer to fall, with fluffy white flowers in flat-topped clusters. Attractive in meadow restoration, but poisonous to cattle and thus considered a nuisance by ranchers. Best with regular to ample water but takes considerable drought. In the past, it was thought to have medicinal value, helping to knit broken bones (hence the common name).

E. purpureum. JOE-PYE WEED. Often sold as *E. fistulosum*. Native to damp meadows in the eastern U.S., this imposing plant deserves wider use. Clumps of hollow stems reach 3–9 ft. tall and 1–3 ft. wide. Whorls of medium green, strongly toothed leaves to 1 ft. long; leaves have a vanilla scent when bruised. Dusty rose flowers, which are attractive to butterflies, appear in large, dome-shaped clusters in late summer or early fall. 'Carin' grows 5–7 ft. tall, has dark purple stems topped by silvery pink flowers. Ample water.

E. rugosum (Ageratina altissima). WHITE SNAKEROOT. Zones US, MS, LS; 8–2. To 4 ft. tall, 2 ft. wide. Stems and lance-shaped gray-green leaves to 5 in. long are heavily marked with deep brownish red; 'Chocolate' has especially dark color. Fluffy white flowers in late summer and early fall. Give rich soil, ample water.

EUPHORBIA

Euphorbiaceae

ANNUALS, BIENNIALS, PERENNIALS, AND EVERGREEN AND DECIDUOUS SHRUBS OR TREES

✿ ZONES VARY BY SPECIES

☼ ☼ ● EXPOSURE NEEDS VARY BY SPECIES

◑ MODERATE TO REGULAR WATER, EXCEPT AS NOTED

◈ SAP IS IRRITATING TO SKIN OR POISONOUS WHEN INGESTED IN MANY SPECIES

Euphorbia characias wulfenii

Large genus of about 2,000 species. What is called a "flower" is technically a cyathium, which consists of fused bracts that form a cup around the much-reduced true flowers. Cyathia may appear singly or in clusters. In some cases, as with poinsettia (*E. pulcherrima*), additional bracts below provide most of the color. Fruit is usually a dry capsule that releases seeds explosively, shooting them up to several feet away. Many euphorbias are succulents; these often mimic cacti in appearance and are as diverse in form and size. Only a few succulent types are listed here, but specialists in cacti and succulents can supply scores of species and selections.

All euphorbias have milky white sap that is irritating on contact or toxic if ingested (degree of irritation or toxicity varies, depending on species). Before using cut flowers in arrangements, dip stems in boiling water or hold in a flame for a few seconds to prevent sap bleed.

Give these plants well-drained soil. Deer don't care for them.

E. amygdaloides. WOOD SPURGE. Perennial. Zones US, MS, LS, CS; 9–2. From Europe and Turkey. To 3 ft. tall, 1 ft. wide, with reddish green stems. Evergreen, 1- to 3-in.-long, dark green leaves have red undersides that turn darker red in winter. Greenish yellow flowers in clusters to 8 in. long at stem ends in late winter to early spring. Best in sun but tolerates some shade. 'Purpurea' has heavily purple-tinted foliage, bright green inflorescences.

E. a. robbiae (E. robbieae). MRS. ROBB'S BONNET. Zones MS, LS, CS; 9–6. Shorter than the species, usually under 1 ft. high. Pale lime green flower clusters. Spreads slowly but surely from underground rhizomes. Can thrive in sun (but not hottest afternoon sun) and in deep shade. Regular to little water.

E. biglandulosa. See E. rigida

E. characias. Perennial. Zones MS, LS, CS; 10–7. Mediterranean native. Upright stems crowded with narrow blue-green leaves form a dome-shaped bush 4 ft. high and wide. Chartreuse or lime green flowers in dense, round to cylindrical clusters appear in late winter, early spring. Color holds with only slight fading until seeds ripen; then stalks turn yellow and should be cut out at base, since new shoots have already made growth for next year's flowers. 'Humpty Dumpty' is a shorter (to 2½-ft.-high), vigorous selection. *E. c. wulfenii (E. veneta),* the most commonly grown form, has broader clusters of yellow flowers. All are fairly drought resistant and perform best in full sun.

E. cotinifolia. CARIBBEAN COPPER PLANT. Shrub or tree. Deciduous in Zone CS; evergreen in Zone TS. Heat zones 12–7. From tropical America. Usually a multistemmed shrub 9–10 ft. high and wide, though it can become a small tree to 18 ft. tall if grown in a warm, frost-free spot. Long-stalked leaves to 4 in. long, 3 in. wide, usually borne in threes, are similar to those of smoke tree *(Cotinus);* 'Atropurpurea', the form most commonly grown, has wine red leaves. Loose flower clusters have small white bracts, are not showy. Likes full sun, heat, good drainage; can't take frost.

E. cyparissias. CYPRESS SPURGE. Perennial. Zones US, MS, LS, CS; 9–1. European native forms feathery clump to 8 in. (possibly to 16 in.) high; spreads vigorously by rhizomes, often becoming invasive. Slender, erect stems branch toward tips. Crowded blue-green, needlelike leaves. Terminal clusters of yellow-green flowers appear in late spring to early summer; these may turn orange in poor soils. Plant may go dormant in winter. Full sun or light shade. Little to moderate water. 'Orange Man' has flowers that are brighter yellow than those of basic species; they turn glowing orange as they age.

E. dulcis 'Chameleon'. Perennial. Zones US, MS, LS, CS; 9–1. Forms a mound to 2 ft. high and wide. New spring growth is burgundy, maturing to dark bronzy green. Greenish yellow flower heads with a purplish tint appear at stem ends in early summer. Leaves and bracts turn rich purple in fall. Spreads by self-sowing; comes true from seed. Full sun. Tolerates dry soil.

E. epithymoides. See E. polychroma

E. griffithii. Perennial. Zones US, MS, LS, CS; 9–2. Erect-stemmed Himalayan native to 3 ft. tall and wide; spreads by creeping roots but is not aggressive. Narrow leaves are medium green, tinged with red when they emerge. Reddish orange to red bracts in early summer; those of 'Fireglow' are vivid orange red. Dies back in winter. Full sun or light shade.

E. lathyris. MOLE PLANT, GOPHER PLANT. Biennial. Zones US, MS, LS, CS; 9–3. From Europe, northwest Africa. Legend claims that it repels gophers and moles. Stems have poisonous, caustic milky juice; keep away from skin and especially eyes, as painful burns can result. Juice could conceivably bother a gopher or mole enough to make it beat a hasty retreat. Single-stemmed plant to 5 ft. tall and 1 ft. wide. Stem is densely set with large leaves growing at right angles to the stem and to each other (forming four longitudinal rows along stem). In second summer, produces short-lived cluster of unspectacular yellow flowers at top of stem. Flowers soon go to seed, after which the plant dies. Start from seed; plant will keep going by self-sowing. Sun or shade. Little to regular water.

E. marginata. SNOW-ON-THE-MOUNTAIN. Annual. Zones US, MS, LS, CS, TS; 12–1. From central North America. To 2 ft. high, 1 ft. wide. Oval light green leaves; upper ones are striped and margined white, sometimes even solid white. Summer flowers are variegated in green and white. Good for contrast with bright-colored dahlias, scarlet sage *(Salvia splendens),* zinnias, or with dark-colored plume celosia. Sow seeds in place in spring, in sun or partial shade. Thin to only a few inches apart, since plants are somewhat rangy.

E. milii (E. splendens). CROWN OF THORNS. Woody shrub; evergreen but sparsely leafed. Zones TS; 12–10; or indoor, greenhouse, or summer potted plant. Some frost damage below 28°F. From Madagascar. To 1–4 ft. high, 1½ ft. wide. Stems armed with long, sharp thorns. Roundish, thin light green leaves are usually found only near branch ends. Clustered pairs of bright red bracts put on a show nearly all year. Many selections and hybrids, varying in form, size, and bract color (yellow, orange, pink). Train

on small frame or trellis against a sheltered wall; or grow in container. Salt tolerance makes it an ideal choice for seaside plantings. Grow in porous but not rocky soil, in full sun or light shade. Indoors, give bright light, regular water (less in winter); feed with half-strength general-purpose liquid houseplant fertilizer once a week in spring and summer.

E. myrsinites. SPURGE. Perennial. Zones US, MS, LS, CS; 8–5. Native from southern Europe to central Asia. To 6 in. high, 1 ft. wide. Evergreen plant with stems that trail outward from central crown, then rise toward tips. Stiff, roundish blue-gray leaves set closely in spirals around stems. Flattish clusters of chartreuse to yellow flowers top stem ends in late winter, early spring. Cut out old stems as they turn yellow. Withstands cold, heat, and aridity but is short lived in warm-winter areas. Use in sunny rock garden with succulents and gray-leafed plants.

E. polychroma (E. epithymoides). CUSHION SPURGE. Perennial. Zones US, MS, LS, CS; 9–1. From Europe. Neatly rounded hemisphere to 1½ ft. high, 2 ft. wide, with deep green leaves symmetrically arranged on closely set, hairy stems. From midspring to midsummer, plant is covered with rounded clusters of bright yellow flowers surrounded by whorls of yellow-green bracts. Effect is of a gold mound suffused with green. Displays good fall color (yellow to orange or red) before going dormant. Use in rock gardens, perennial borders. Needs some shade in hottest climates. Short lived but reseeds.

E. pulcherrima. POINSETTIA. Evergreen, semievergreen, or deciduous shrub. Zones CS (protected), TS; 12–10; or indoors. Native to Mexico. Leggy plant to 10 ft. or taller, 6 ft. wide. Coarse leaves grow on stiffly upright canes. Showy part of plant consists of petal-like bracts; true flowers in center are yellowish and inconspicuous. Red single form is the most familiar; less well known are double-bracted red sorts and forms with white, yellowish, pink, or marbled bracts. Plants bloom only when they experience long nights—in winter and into spring. Bracts of paler kinds often last

Euphorbia pulcherrima

until later in spring. Milky sap is not poisonous; most people find it either completely harmless or at most mildly irritating to skin or stomach.

GETTING POTTED POINSETTIAS TO BLOOM. *Plants bloom only when they experience long nights. Starting in October, put them in a closet (no light at all) each night for 14 hours, then move them into light in the morning for a maximum of 10 hours. Continue this procedure for 10 weeks; you can have poinsettia blossoms by Christmas.* ❖

Useful garden plant in well-drained soil and full sun. Where adapted outdoors, needs no special care. Grow as informal hedge in the Tropical South; in the Coastal South, plant against sunny wall, in sheltered corner, under south-facing eaves. Plants grown outdoors in the Coastal South are likely to die down in winter. Thin branches in summer to produce larger bracts; or prune them back at 2-month intervals for bushy growth (but often smaller bracts). To improve red color, feed every 2 weeks with high-nitrogen fertilizer, starting when color begins to show.

Unlike their predecessors, modern poinsettia selections retain their foliage well into spring if given reasonable light. To care for holiday gift plants, keep them in a cool, well-lit room until after the last frost. Avoid sudden temperature changes; keep soil moist, but don't let water stand in pot saucer. When frost danger is past, cut back stems to two buds and set plants out in garden; or keep them in containers in a sunny spot on the patio. Potted plant will probably grow too tall for indoor use the next winter but may survive winter if well sheltered. Start new plants by making late-summer cuttings of stems with four or five eyes (joints).

E. rigida (E. biglandulosa). Perennial. Zones LS, CS, TS; 12–7. Mediterranean native forms a 3- to 5-ft.-wide clump of stems that angle outward, then rise up to 2 ft. high. Fleshy gray-green leaves to 1½ in. long are narrow and pointed, their bases set tightly against stems. Broad, domed flower clusters in late winter or early spring are chartreuse yellow fading to pinkish. After seeds ripen, stems die back and should be removed; new stems take their place. Reseeds in mildest-winter areas, but not enough to become a pest. Showy display plant in borders, rock gardens, containers. Full sun. Tolerates drought.

E. robbiae. See E. amygdaloides robbiae

E. tirucalli. MILKBUSH, PENCILBUSH, PENCIL TREE. Succulent tree or shrub. Zones TS; 12–10; or indoors. From tropical eastern Africa. Grown for striking pattern of silhouette or shadow. Fast growing to possible 30 ft. tall and 6 ft. wide, usually much smaller. Single or multiple trunks support tangle of light green, pencil-thick, succulent branches with tiny leaves present only on actively growing tips. Flowers are unimportant. 'Sticks on Fire' has pale pink to fiery salmon pink stems; new growth has the most intense color in bright light. Both species and selections are very tolerant of seacoast conditions. Full sun. Keep milky sap away from eyes, as it can cause severe damage. As houseplant, thrives in driest atmosphere; needs plenty of light, well-drained potting mix, routine watering and fertilizing.

E. veneta, E. wulfenii. See E. characias

Euphorbiaceae. The euphorbia family contains annuals, biennials, perennials, shrubs, trees, and an enormous number of succulents. Most have milky sap, and many have small, unshowy flowers made decorative by larger (often colorful) bracts or bractlike structures. Poinsettia *(Euphorbia pulcherrima)* is the best-known example.

EURYOPS pectinatus

BUSH DAISY, GRAY-LEAFED EURYOPS

Asteraceae (Compositae)

EVERGREEN SHRUB

CS, TS ╫ 12–9; ANYWHERE AS ANNUAL

FULL SUN

LITTLE TO REGULAR WATER

Native to South Africa, this tender shrub combines handsome foliage with showy, daisylike blooms. It's easy to grow and quite long blooming, making it a natural choice for low-maintenance gardens; it is also good for the back of the border, in containers, or as a low screen. Grows 3–6 ft. high and wide, with gray-green, deeply cut leaves about 2 in. long. Bright yellow, 1½- to 2-in.-wide daisies on 6-in. stems appear nearly continuously in warm weather, though blooming may slow during the dog days of summer. 'Viridis' is identical to the species but has deep green leaves. 'Munchkin' tops out at 3 ft. tall and 4 ft. wide.

Bush daisy thrives in almost any well-drained soil and tolerates buffeting ocean winds. It's winter hardy in the Coastal and Tropical South; in colder areas, grow it as an annual. Pick off old blooms to maintain neat appearance and extend the blooming season; shear lightly to control size.

Euryops pectinatus

EUSTOMA grandiflorum (Lisianthus russellianus)

LISIANTHUS, TULIP GENTIAN, TEXAS BLUEBELL

Gentianaceae

BIENNIAL OR SHORT-LIVED PERENNIAL GROWN AS ANNUAL

US, MS, LS, CS, TS ╫ 12–1

FULL SUN OR LIGHT SHADE

MODERATE TO REGULAR WATER

Eustoma grandiflorum

You won't find many cut flowers better than this one. Native to the High Plains of the western U.S., it was perfected for the garden by hybridizers in Japan. Long-stemmed cut flowers last a week or more in water.

In summer, foot-wide clumps of gray-green foliage send up 1½-ft. stems topped by tulip-shaped, 2- to 3-in. flowers in purplish blue, pink, or white; plants will produce flowers all summer long if all blooms are deadheaded.

Double Eagle and Lion strains have double flowers resembling roses. Heidi strain of F1 hybrids features vigorous plants with long-stemmed blossoms that come in soft yellow as well as the typical colors. 'Forever Blue' is a hybrid with profuse purplish blue blossoms on 1-ft.-high stems; it has a better branching habit than other lisianthus. 'Red Glass' has rose red flowers. Picotee types are also available.

It's easiest to start lisianthus from transplants, but you can also grow it, with much care, from the dust-fine seeds. Sprinkle seeds over surface of potting soil; don't cover them with soil. Soak well, then cover pot with glass or plastic until seeds germinate. At the four-leaf stage (about 2 months), transplant three or four plants into each 6-in. pot. Set out in beds after plants put on some size. Needs good garden soil, good drainage. Apply a balanced liquid fertilizer every 2 or 3 weeks. Use in pots, borders, cutting gardens. May overwinter in the Lower, Coastal, and Tropical South.

EVENING PRIMROSE. See OENOTHERA

EVERGREEN CANDYTUFT. See IBERIS sempervirens

EVERGREEN RED WISTERIA. See MILLETTIA reticulata

EVODIA daniellii. See TETRADIUM daniellii

EVOLVULUS glomeratus

Convolvulaceae

PERENNIAL USUALLY GROWN AS ANNUAL

TS; ANYWHERE AS ANNUAL; ╫ 12–1

FULL SUN OR LIGHT SHADE

MODERATE TO REGULAR WATER

Evolvulus glomeratus 'Blue Daze'

Native to Brazil. Small, trailing morning glory relative with stems to 20 in. long and oval leaves ⅓–1¼ in. long. Half-inch-wide blue flowers bloom in summer; they close in the evening and on dark, cloudy days. Plants most widely offered are labeled 'Blue Daze', 'Hawaiian Blue Eyes', or *E. g. grandiflorus*; or they may simply bear the common name "blue daze." These plants vary somewhat: foliage may be green or gray, blossoms bright blue or powder blue. Stems of all root where they touch the ground, and cuttings root very easily in water or moist soil. Use in hanging baskets, beds, borders.

EXACUM affine

PERSIAN VIOLET

Gentianaceae

ANNUAL OR SHORT-LIVED PERENNIAL GROWN AS ANNUAL

HOUSEPLANT

BRIGHT INDIRECT LIGHT

REGULAR TO AMPLE WATER

Exacum affine

This is the little potted flower you see in the grocery store that looks so pretty you'd swear it was fake. Despite the common name, it comes not from Persia but from Socotra, an island off the Horn of Africa. Sweet-scented, star-shaped blue flowers with yellow stamens are held above inch-long, egg-shaped leaves. A white-flowered form is also available.

Persian violet is not a long-lived plant: you can keep it for 6 to 8 weeks at best, after which you should throw it away. To get the best and longest show, give it bright light (but not hot sun) and pick off faded blooms regularly. Allow the soil surface to become dry to the touch before watering; overwatering will cause the plant to collapse. Make sure the pot drains freely. Thrives in high humidity, such as near the sink or shower. Don't bother to fertilize—the plant won't last long enough to make it worthwhile. Just enjoy the brief beauty it brings indoors at any time of the year.

EXOCHORDA

PEARL BUSH

Rosaceae

DECIDUOUS SHRUBS

US, MS, LS H 9–4

FULL SUN

MODERATE TO REGULAR WATER

Exochorda racemosa

From China. Loose, spikelike clusters of 1½- to 2-in.-wide white flowers open from a profusion of buds resembling pearls. Flowering spans several weeks in early spring, at about the same time the roundish, 1½- to 2-in.-long leaves expand. Foliage and arching growth suggest the related spiraea, but pearl bush's individual blossoms are considerably larger.

These shrubs are showy during spring but undistinguished at other times of year, so choose your site accordingly. Prefer well-drained, acid soil but will grow in neutral or alkaline soil; will take considerable neglect. Pest free. Flowers are formed on previous year's growth, so prune after bloom to control size and form.

E. giraldii. Resembles the more widely grown species *E. racemosa* but is somewhat smaller, with slightly smaller flowers and red tints in leaf veins and flower stalks.

E. × macrantha. Hybrid between *E. racemosa* and another species. The only selection available, 'The Bride', is a compact shrub to about 4 ft. tall and wide. Very showy bloom.

E. racemosa (E. grandiflora). COMMON PEARL BUSH. Loose, open, slender; grows to 10–15 ft. tall and wide, possibly larger. In small gardens, remove lower branches to make small, upright, airy, multistemmed tree. Often found in older gardens in the Middle and Lower South. Reseeds readily, and seedlings are often shared.

Fabaceae. Previously called Leguminosae, the pea family is an enormous group containing annuals, perennials, shrubs, trees, and vines. Many are useful as food (beans, peas), while others furnish timber, medicines, pesticides, and a host of other products. Many are ornamental.

The best-known members of the pea family—sweet pea (*Lathyrus*), for example—have flowers shaped rather like butterflies. Others have a more regular flower shape (*Caesalpinia, Cassia*); still others have tightly clustered flowers that appear to be puffs of stamens, as in acacia and mimosa (*Albizia*). All bear seeds in pods (legumes). Many have on their roots colonies of bacteria that can extract nitrogen from air spaces in the soil and convert it to a form usable by plant roots; clover (*Trifolium*) is a familiar example.

Fagaceae. The beech family contains evergreen and deciduous trees characterized by fruit that is a nut enclosed in either a cup, as in oak (*Quercus*), or a bur, as in beech (*Fagus*) and chestnut (*Castanea*).

FAGUS

BEECH

Fagaceae

DECIDUOUS TREES

ZONES VARY BY SPECIES

FULL SUN OR LIGHT SHADE

MODERATE TO REGULAR WATER

Fagus sylvatica

Beeches are grand trees, capable of growing 90 ft. tall and 60 ft. wide after many years. Their majestic outlines range from rounded to broadly pyramidal, with wide, sweeping lower branches that sometimes touch the ground; some

selections weep attractively. Handsome, smooth gray bark contrasts nicely with glossy dark green foliage. In autumn, leaves turn yellow with green veins, then golden or reddish brown, then fade to tan; these buff-colored leaves hang on through most of winter and are quite beautiful in the winter landscape. A layered, lacy branching pattern and long, pointed leaf buds add to the attractive winter silhouette. Small nuts enclosed in spiny husks attract squirrels, blue jays, and other wildlife.

Beeches aren't the easiest trees to work into a home landscape. They are too large to be appropriate for smaller lots; their thick network of surface roots and the heavy shade they cast make it almost impossible to grow a lawn or other plants beneath them. However, they work well at the edge of a woodland or in naturalized areas. Fancy-leafed or weeping forms of European beech (*F. sylvatica*) are good as specimens or accents. Beeches like deep, fertile, loose, well-drained soil that is neutral to slightly acid. Never park cars or heavy vehicles under a large beech, as this crushes sensitive feeder roots and results in the tree's slow demise. Woolly beech aphids on the undersides of the leaves sometimes cause the foliage to pucker, turn blotchy, and drop, but they are seldom a serious problem.

F. crenata. JAPANESE BEECH. Zones US, MS, LS; 8–1. From Japan. Leaves scallop edged, somewhat smaller than those of other beeches. Reddish brown fall color. Likes some shade, especially when young.

F. grandifolia. AMERICAN BEECH. Zones US, MS, LS, CS; 9–1. A stately tree and a principal component of the vast hardwood forests that once covered much of the eastern U.S. Tolerates shade and makes a good understory tree when young. More tolerant of summer heat than the other two species described here; can be grown farther south. Toothed, 3- to 6-in.-long leaves turn to golden bronze in fall, then to a beautiful parchment tan; they stay on the tree throughout winter. Allow plenty of room for this tree.

F. sylvatica. EUROPEAN BEECH. Zones US, MS; 7–1. Native from central Europe to the Caucasus. Lustrous green leaves to 4 in. long turn russet and bronzy in autumn. Many selections, including the following.

'Asplenifolia'. FERNLEAF BEECH. Large, robust, spreading tree with delicate-looking foliage—narrow leaves, deeply cut or lobed nearly to the midrib.

'Atropunicea'. COPPER BEECH, PURPLE BEECH. Grows to 50–60 ft. high, 35–45 ft. wide. Often sold as 'Purpurea'. Good in containers. Deep reddish or purple leaves. Seedlings are usually bronzy purple, turning bronzy green in summer.

Fagus sylvatica 'Purpurea Pendula'

'Fastigiata'. DAWYCK BEECH. Narrow, upright form like Lombardy poplar (*Populus nigra* 'Italica'); 8 ft. wide when 35 ft. tall. Broader in great age but still narrower than the species.

'Laciniata'. CUTLEAF BEECH. Narrow, deeply cut green leaves.

'Pendula'. WEEPING BEECH. Irregular, spreading form with green leaves and long, weeping branches that reach to the ground and can root where they touch. Without staking to establish vertical trunk, it will grow wide rather than high.

'Purpurea Pendula'. WEEPING COPPER BEECH. Purple-leafed weeping form matures to 10 ft. tall and wide. Splendid container plant.

'Riversii'. Deep purple leaves hold color all summer. Rounded tree to 50 ft. tall and wide.

'Rohanii'. Wavy-edged leaves open dark purple and gradually mature to green. Fall color is reddish to purplish brown.

'Tricolor'. TRICOLOR BEECH. Grows slowly to 24–40 ft., usually less. Green leaves are marked white and edged pink. Foliage burns in hot sun or dry winds. Choice container plant.

'Zlatia'. GOLDEN BEECH. Leaves are yellow when new, then age to yellow green. Subject to sunburn. Good container plant.

A PRACTICAL GUIDE TO GARDENING
PLEASE SEE PAGES 596–669

FAIRY DUSTER. See CALLIANDRA eriophylla

FALLOPIA
Polygonaceae
DECIDUOUS VINES
US, MS, LS
EXPOSURE NEEDS VARY BY SPECIES
LITTLE TO REGULAR WATER

Fallopia baldschuanica

Formerly listed as *Polygonum*, the two plants described here were renamed *Fallopia* (to the confusion of everyone). Both offer showy flowers; both merit vigilance, as they spread by rhizomes and can be highly invasive and difficult to eradicate. Don't plant them near open areas.

F. baldschuanica (Polygonum aubertii). SILVER LACE VINE. Heat zones 9–5. This extremely vigorous vine from Asia can cover a large space in a short time. It typically puts on 10–15 ft. of new growth in a single season and can fully drape an arbor, fence, or gazebo in short order. Glossy dark green leaves are arrowhead shaped, 1½–2 in. long. A frothy mass of fragrant, creamy white flowers, sometimes tinged with pink, smothers the plant in summer and fall. Prune silver lace vine severely to keep it in bounds; you can cut it to the ground in winter and it will resprout in spring and bloom in summer. Adaptable to most well-drained soils; tolerates drought. Full sun.

F. japonica (Polygonum cuspidatum, Reynoutria japonica). JAPANESE KNOTWEED. Heat zones 9–2. From eastern Asia. Tough, vigorous plant with wiry, reddish brown stems that form large clumps to 4–8 ft. tall. Pale green leaves are nearly heart shaped, to 5 in. long. Showy clusters of greenish white flowers appear in leaf axils in late summer and fall. Spreads rampantly by underground runners and is particularly hard to control: shoots have been known to push up through asphalt. Good choice for bank cover or erosion control in difficult areas where little else will grow. Full sun or partial shade. 'Crimson Beauty' bears fiery red flowers on 7- to 8-ft. stems from late summer through fall; it is known to some Southerners by the name "kiss-me-at-the-gate." It's better behaved than the species, forming clumps that are not invasive.

FALLUGIA paradoxa
APACHE PLUME
Rosaceae
SEMIEVERGREEN SHRUB
US, MS, LS, CS, TS H 10–5
FULL SUN
NO IRRIGATION NEEDED

Fallugia paradoxa

Native to mountains of medium and high deserts of California, west Edwards Plateau and Trans-Pecos regions of Texas, and northern Mexico. Grows 4–6 ft. tall, 5 ft. wide, with straw-colored branches and flaky bark. Small, lobed leaves are deep green on top, rusty beneath; carried in clusters. Flowers resembling single white roses just 1½ in. wide bloom in spring, summer. Large, showy clusters of feathery seed heads follow, creating a soft haze through which you can see the shrub's rigid branch pattern; they are greenish at first, then later turn pink or take on a reddish tinge. Needs gritty, well-drained soil. Pruning usually not needed. Reseeds freely, which makes it good for naturalized areas but a problem in formal beds. Not for areas with high rainfall, heavy soil.

FALSE ASTER. See BOLTONIA, KALIMERIS pinnatifida

FALSE BIRD-OF-PARADISE. See HELICONIA

FALSE CYPRESS. See CHAMAECYPARIS

FALSE DRAGONHEAD. See PHYSOSTEGIA virginiana

FALSE HEATHER. See CUPHEA hyssopifolia

FALSE INDIGO. See AMORPHA fruticosa, BAPTISIA

FALSE MESQUITE. See CALLIANDRA eriophylla

FALSE SOLOMON'S SEAL. See SMILACINA racemosa

FALSE SPIRAEA. See ASTILBE, SORBARIA

FALSE SUNFLOWER. See HELIOPSIS helianthoides

FANCY-LEAFED CALADIUM. See CALADIUM bicolor

FAN PALM. See WASHINGTONIA

FARFUGIUM japonicum (Ligularia tussilaginea)
Asteraceae (Compositae)
PERENNIAL
MS, LS, CS, TS H 11–7, EXCEPT AS NOTED; OR HOUSEPLANT
SOME SHADE; BRIGHT INDIRECT LIGHT
AMPLE WATER

Farfugium japonicum 'Aureomaculatum'

From China and Japan. Glossy bright green, 6- to 12-in.-wide leaves on long (1- to 2-ft.) leafstalks form a clump to about 2 ft. tall and wide; leaves are kidney shaped, scalloped, or shallowly lobed. From fall into winter, flower stems rise 1½ to 2 ft. tall, each carrying several yellow, 1½- to 2-in. daisies. The species is not as popular or widely grown as its selections, which include the following.

'Argenteum'. Somewhat smaller leaves than the species, in deep green marbled with gray green and white.

'Aureomaculatum'. Zones US, MS, LS, CS, TS. Thick, leathery leaves are heavily, evenly speckled with yellow. Also called leopard plant.

'Crispatum'. Thick, ruffle-edged gray-green leaves; sometimes called pie crust ligularia.

'Gigantea'. Zones LS, CS, TS. Thick, glossy leaves up to 15 in. across.

'Kagami Jishi'. Combines the ruffled edges of 'Crispatum' with the yellow-spotted foliage of 'Aureomaculatum'.

All are choice container plants for shady beds or entryways. Tops hardy to 20°F. Plants die back to roots at 0°F but put on new growth in spring. Control snails and slugs. Can be grown indoors if placed near a window with bright light.

FARKLEBERRY. See VACCINIUM arboreum

×FATSHEDERA lizei
Araliaceae
EVERGREEN SHRUB, VINE, OR GROUND COVER
LS, CS, TS H 12–8
PARTIAL TO FULL SHADE
REGULAR WATER

×Fatshedera lizei

Hybrid between Japanese fatsia (*Fatsia japonica*) and English ivy (*Hedera helix*), with characteristics of both parents. Highly polished, 4- to 10-in.-wide leaves with three to five pointed lobes look like giant ivy leaves; plant also sends out long, trailing or climbing stems like ivy, though without aerial holdfasts. This hybrid inherited shrubbiness from its Japanese parent, though its habit is more irregular and sprawling. Leaves of 'Variegata' are bordered in white; those of 'Media-Picta' have a central yellow blotch. ▶

Leaves are injured at 15°F, tender new growth at 20–25°F. Seems to suffer more from late frosts than from winter cold. Give it protection from hot, drying winds. Watch out for slugs and snails. Good near swimming pools.

This plant tends to grow in a straight line, but it can be shaped if you work at it. Pinch tip growth to force branching. Two or three times a year, guide and tie stems before they become brittle. If plant gets away from you, cut it back to ground; it will regrow quickly. If you use it as ground cover, cut back vertical growth every 2 or 3 weeks during growing season. Grown as vine or espalier, plants are heavy, so give them strong support. Even a well-grown vine is leafless at base.

FATSIA japonica
(Aralia sieboldii, A. japonica)

JAPANESE FATSIA, JAPANESE ARALIA

Araliaceae

EVERGREEN SHRUB

⚘ LS (PROTECTED), CS, TS ⊞ 12–8; OR HOUSEPLANT

◐ ● PARTIAL TO FULL SHADE; BRIGHT LIGHT

● REGULAR WATER

Fatsia japonica

From Korea, Japan. Tropical-looking, sparsely branched shrub with long-stalked, big, glossy dark green, deeply lobed, fanlike leaves to 16 in. wide. Moderate growth to 5–8 ft. high and wide (rarely more). Many roundish clusters of small, creamy white flowers in fall and winter; these are followed by clusters of small, shiny black berries.

Grows in nearly all soils except soggy ones. Adapted to containers. If leaves are chronically yellow, add iron to soil. During prolonged dry spells, wash occasionally with hose to clean leaves and to lessen insect attack. Control slugs and snails. Established plants sucker freely; keep suckers or remove them with spade. Rejuvenate spindly plants by cutting back hard in early spring. Plants that set fruit often self-sow.

A natural landscaping choice where bold pattern is wanted. Most effective when thinned to show some branch structure. Provides year-round good looks for shaded entryway or patio. Useful near swimming pools. 'Moseri' has a compact habit; 'Variegata' has leaves edged golden yellow to creamy white.

In areas where Japanese fatsia isn't winter hardy, it's a popular indoor plant. It does best with lots of morning sun—but not hot afternoon sun. Allow the soil surface to go dry between waterings, but don't let the plant wilt; reduce watering somewhat in winter. Feed every other week in spring and summer and monthly in fall and winter with a general-purpose liquid houseplant fertilizer. Spider mites are common pests; use insecticidal soap or horticultural oil to control them.

FEATHERED HYACINTH. See MUSCARI comosum 'Monstrosum'

FEATHER GRASS. See STIPA

FEATHER REED GRASS. See CALAMAGROSTIS × acutiflora

FEIJOA, PINEAPPLE GUAVA

Myrtaceae

EVERGREEN SHRUB OR TREE

⚘ LS, CS, TS ⊞ 12–8

☼ FULL SUN

● REGULAR WATER

South American native known botanically as *Feijoa sellowiana* (*Acca sellowiana*). Hardiest of so-called subtropical fruits. Normally a large multistemmed plant; reaches 18–25 ft. with equal spread if not pruned or killed back by

Feijoa

frosts. Can take almost any amount of training or pruning to shape as espalier, screen, hedge, or small tree (late spring is the best time to prune). Oval, 2- to 3-in.-long leaves are glossy green above, silvery white beneath. Blooms in spring, bearing unusual inch-wide flowers with big central tufts of red stamens and four fleshy white petals tinged purplish on inside; blossoms attract bees and birds. Flowers are edible and can be added to fruit salads or used for jams and jellies. Plant is drought tolerant, but give it regular water for best fruiting.

Fruit ripens 4 to 5½ months after flowering in the Tropical South, 5 to 7 months after bloom in Lower and Coastal South. Oval, grayish green, 1- to 4-in.-long fruit has soft, sweet to bland pulp with flavor that is somewhat like pineapple. The best way to harvest is to wait until first fruit drops, then spread a tarp underneath and give the tree a shake. Repeat every few days. Fruit is sometimes sold in markets; it may be labeled "feijoa" or "pineapple guava."

Improved selections 'Beechwood', 'Coolidge', 'Mammoth', 'Nazemetz', and 'Trask' are self-fruitful, although cross-pollination will produce a better crop. Single plants of seedlings or other named selections may need cross-pollination.

FELT PLANT. See KALANCHOE beharensis

FENNEL, COMMON. See FOENICULUM vulgare

FERNLEAF YARROW. See ACHILLEA filipendulina

FERN PINE. See PODOCARPUS gracilior

FERNS. Large group of perennial plants grown for their lovely and interesting foliage. They vary in height from a few inches to 50 ft. or more and are found in all parts of the world; most are forest plants, but some grow in deserts, in open fields, or near the timberline in high mountains. Most have finely cut leaves (fronds). They do not flower but reproduce by spores that form directly on the fronds.

Ferns are divided into several families, according to botanical differences. Such technical differences aside, these plants fall into several groups based on general appearance.

Most spectacular are tree ferns, which display their finely cut fronds atop a treelike stem. These need rich, well-drained soil; moisture; and shade. Most are rather tender to frost, and all suffer in hot, drying winds and low humidity. Frequent watering of tops, trunks, and root area will help pull them through unusually hot or windy weather. For the various kinds of tree ferns, see *Cibotium, Cyathea, Dicksonia*.

Native ferns do not grow as tall as tree ferns, but their fronds are handsome and they can perform a number of landscape jobs. Naturalize them in woodland or wild gardens, or use them to fill shady beds, as ground cover, as interplantings between shrubs, or along a shady house wall. Some ferns native to eastern North America grow well in the South; these take extreme cold and are usually deciduous. For native ferns, see *Adiantum, Asplenium, Athyrium, Dryopteris, Onoclea, Osmunda, Pellaea, Phyllitis, Polypodium, Polystichum, Pteridium, Woodwardia*.

Many ferns from other parts of the world grow well in the South; although some are subjects for house, greenhouse, or (in mildest climates) lathhouse, many others are fairly hardy. Use them as you would native ferns, unless some peculiarity of habit makes it necessary to grow them in baskets or on slabs. Some exotic ferns will be found under *Adiantum, Asplenium, Cyrtomium, Davallia, Humata, Microlepia, Nephrolepis, Pellaea, Platycerium, Polypodium, Polystichum, Pteris, Pyrrosia, Rumobra*.

All ferns look best if groomed. Cut off dead or injured fronds near ground or trunk—but don't cut back the more tender deciduous outdoor ferns until new growth is evident, since old fronds protect growing tips. Native ferns growing outdoors don't need fertilizer, but feed others frequently during growing season, preferably with light applications of organic fertilizer such as blood meal or fish emulsion. Mulch with organic matter such as peat moss occasionally, especially if shallow fibrous roots are exposed by rain or irrigation.

FESTUCA

FESCUE
Poaceae (Gramineae)
PERENNIAL GRASSES
US, MS, EXCEPT AS NOTED
BEST IN SUN, TOLERATE SOME SHADE
MODERATE TO REGULAR WATER

Festuca glauca

Although one species listed here is an ornamental grass, the other fescues listed are mainly grown as lawn grasses for their pleasing texture, quick establishment from seed, shade tolerance, and green winter color. All fescues need good drainage. Resistant to damage by deer.

F. arundinacea (F. elatior). TALL FESCUE. Heat zones 8–1. This clumping, tall-growing grass is native to Europe and northern Asia. In the Upper and Middle South, it is a popular substitute for Kentucky bluegrass and perennial ryegrass in lawns, as it stands up better to heat, wear, and compacted soil. It should not be used as a pasture grass; it is toxic to horses, sheep, cattle, and goats.

People living in the "transition zone" (the lower part of the Middle South and upper part of the Lower South) often grow tall fescue for its green winter color. To keep it attractive in this area, give it afternoon shade, lots of summertime water, and yearly overseeding. Irrigate only when the grass shows signs of thirst (wilting or rolling leaves); then water deeply, wetting the soil to a depth of 3–4 in. Seed new lawns heavily, at the rate of 8 pounds per 1,000 sq. ft. Fertilize once in September and again in March or April with a controlled-release high-nitrogen fertilizer, such as 30-3-8 or 27-3-6. To keep the lawn thick, overseed every fall at the rate of 4 pounds per 1,000 sq. ft. The typical mowing height is 2–3 in., though dwarf types such as 'Bonsai' and 'Duster' can be mowed at 1–2 in. high.

An old, coarse-bladed tall fescue selection, 'Kentucky-31' ('K-31'), is still widely planted because it's inexpensive and readily available, but many fine-bladed selections have appeared on the scene—and these can produce a lawn every bit as attractive as Kentucky bluegrass in color and texture. Choices include 'Bonanza', 'Bonsai', 'Duster', 'Finelawn', 'Houndog', 'Mustang II', 'Rebel II', and 'Virtue'. Blends such as Enviro and Triad combine several different selections for improved resistance to heat, drought, and pests.

F. glauca (F. cinerea, F. ovina glauca). BLUE FESCUE. Heat zones 9–1. From Europe. Ornamental grass grows to 1 ft. high, 10 in. wide. Dense tufts of extremely fine leaves; color varies from blue gray to silvery white. Summer flowers in upright spikes. Tolerates drought and thrives with good drainage and air circulation. Use as edging or ground cover. Effective in rock gardens, between stepping-stones, in containers. 'Elijah Blue' forms an 8-in.-high foliage clump in intense silver blue; it is one of the tougher, longer-lived selections. 'Siskiyou Blue', to 1–2 ft. high, has luminous blue leaves.

F. rubra. RED FESCUE, CREEPING RED FESCUE. Heat zones 7–1. From Europe, North America. Spreads by rhizomes. Principal use is in blends with Kentucky bluegrass or other lawn grasses; also used to overseed Bermuda lawns in winter. Narrow dark green blades, pink seed heads. Not fussy about soil. Tolerates shade better than most grasses but doesn't take heavy traffic. It's a light feeder, too—fertilize once in September with a controlled-release fertilizer such as 20-5-10. Seed new lawns at 3 to 5 pounds per 1,000 sq. ft. Mow at 1½–2½ in.

FETTERBUSH. See LYONIA lucida

FEVERFEW. See CHRYSANTHEMUM parthenium

FOR INFORMATION ON YOUR CLIMATE ZONES
PLEASE SEE PAGES 28–38

FICUS

Moraceae
EVERGREEN AND DECIDUOUS TREES, SHRUBS, VINES
ZONES VARY BY SPECIES
EXPOSURE NEEDS VARY BY SPECIES
REGULAR WATER

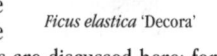

Ficus elastica 'Decora'

The average gardener would never expect to find the commercial edible fig, small-leafed climbing fig, banyan tree, and potted rubber tree under one common heading—but they are classed together because they bear small or large figs (inedible in most species). Ornamental types are discussed here; for sorts grown for tasty fruit, see Fig.

Many ornamental species make good houseplants. Generally, they thrive on rich, steadily moist (not wet) soil; frequent light feedings; and bright, indirect light.

F. auriculata (F. roxburghii). Briefly deciduous shrub or small tree. Zones TS; 12–10. Native to India. To 25 ft. high and wide. Sandpapery-textured, unusually large leaves—broadly oval to round, about 15 in. across. New growth is mahogany red, turning to rich green. Large figs are borne in clusters on trunk and framework branches. Can be shaped into a small tree or espaliered. Beautiful in large container; good near swimming pools. Grow in wind-protected, sunny location.

Ficus auriculata

F. benghalensis. INDIAN BANYAN. Evergreen tree. Zones TS; 12–10. Native to India and Pakistan. Only for large spaces: grows very slowly to an eventual 80 ft. tall and initially as wide, spreading (potentially up to several acres) by accessory trunks developing from aerial roots. Dull green, leathery leaves, rounded at tips, to 8 in. long. Full sun.

F. benjamina. WEEPING FIG, BENJAMIN TREE, BENJAMIN FIG. Evergreen tree. Zones TS; 12–10; or houseplant. From India and Malaysia. Grows to 30 ft. tall, with greater spread. Good shade or specimen tree for larger gardens or parks, since it requires space for its invasive surface root system. Used in large containers as entryway or patio tree; also good as screen, espalier, or clipped hedge. Leathery, 5-in.-long, shiny green leaves densely clothe drooping branches. New plants are easy to start from semihardwood cuttings taken between late spring and early summer. Give a frost-free, wind-protected location in sun or shade.

One of the most popular indoor plants for a place in bright light. Sudden leaf shedding is a common problem, often resulting from plant's being moved to a new location. If shedding begins shortly after a move, be patient; leaves usually grow back. Leaves that fall off while green usually indicate insufficient water; try to keep soil evenly moist. If fallen leaves are yellow, overwatering may be to blame. If shedding is accompanied by a sweet smell and sticky leaves, look for scale insects and control with horticultural oil as needed. For an indoor tree that is similar in size and habit to *F. benjamina* but doesn't drop its foliage, try *F. binnendijkii* 'Alii'. As an indoor plant, weeping fig typically grows slowly to 8–10 ft. tall, not quite as wide. These five are among the most popular selections.

Ficus benjamina

'Exotica'. Like the species but has wavy-edged leaves with long, twisted tips. Often sold simply as *F. benjamina.*

'Indigo'. Open, weeping habit. Thick, glossy leaves are a very dark green when young, maturing to blue black. Some leaves may be slightly variegated with lighter tones. Quite shade tolerant.

'Midnight'. Compact and bushy, with very thick leaves. Foliage is such a deep green that it looks almost blue black. ▶

'Monique'. Upright habit. Elliptical, shiny bright green leaves with ruffled edges. Very resistant to leaf drop.

'Too Little'. Dwarf form that may reach only 3–4 ft. high after many years; densely foliaged with tiny, slightly curled leaves. Ideal for bonsai.

F. binnendijkii (F. maclellandii). Evergreen tree. Zones TS; 12–10; or indoors. Similar to *F. benjamina* but easier to grow indoors, less likely to shed leaves. Dark green, stiff, willowlike leaves reach 7 in. long, less than 1 in. wide. Outdoors, grow in sun or partial shade. Indoors, select a permanent position with good light and no drafts. Let soil go dry between waterings, then soak thoroughly—but don't leave plant standing in water. Dust or rinse leaves with water occasionally. Feed with a general-purpose liquid houseplant fertilizer once in spring and once in fall, more often if plant is in very bright light. Pest problems are rare. If scale or mealybugs appear, spray the former with horticultural oil; wipe off the latter with a cotton swab dipped in alcohol. 'Alii' is an outstanding selection, particularly resistant to leaf drop. 'Amstel King' is similar to the species but has thicker, wider, glossier leaves; when plant is actively growing, leaf tips may be pink or red.

F. carica. See Fig

F. deltoidea (F. diversifolia). MISTLETOE FIG. Evergreen shrub. Zones TS; 12–10; or houseplant. Native to Southeast Asia. Grows very slowly to 8–10 ft. high, about half as wide. Interesting open, twisted branch pattern. Thick, dark green, roundish, 2-in. leaves are sparsely stippled with tan specks on upper surface and a few black dots underneath. Attractive, small greenish to yellow fruit borne continuously. As outdoor plant, most often grown in container on patio. Part shade.

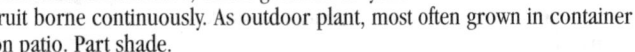

Ficus deltoidea

F. elastica. RUBBER PLANT. Evergreen shrub or tree. Zones TS; 12–10; or houseplant. Native to India and Malaysia. Familiar plant found in almost every florists' shop. It can become a 40-ft. tree in the Tropical South; often seen as a small tree or shrub in shaded "tunnel" garden entrances in cooler part of range. Comes back quickly if killed to ground by frost. Narrow, leathery dark green leaves are 8–12 in. long. New leaves unfold from rosy pink sheaths that soon wither and drop. Partial or full shade.

One of the most foolproof indoor plants; can take less light than most big houseplants. If potted plant becomes too tall and leggy, you can cut off the top and select a side branch to form a new main shoot. Or get a new plant by air layering the top section; when roots form, cut branch section with attached roots and pot it up. The following are among the best selections.

'Abidjan' ('Burgundy'). West African selection made from 'Decora'. New growth, leaf sheaths, and leaf midribs are red. On plants grown in bright light, older leaves are dark maroon.

'Asahi'. Selection from Japan. Similar to 'Doescheri' but with slightly smaller leaves and more extensive creamy yellow variegation.

'Decora' ('Belgica'). The common rubber plant sold for indoor use is usually this selection. Superior to the species because of its broader, glossier leaves. Foliage is bronzy when young.

'Doescheri'. Leaves are marbled in green and gray green, with green margins, creamy yellow midribs, and pink leafstalks.

'Rubra'. New leaves are reddish and retain a red edge as rest of leaf turns green.

'Schrijveriana'. Broad leaves are variegated in green, gray green, creamy yellow, and white. Leafstalks are red.

'Variegata'. Long, narrow leaves variegated in yellow and green. Variegation is interesting when leaves are viewed close up in container—but as an outdoor tree, plant has a sickly look.

F. lyrata (F. pandurata). FIDDLELEAF FIG. Evergreen tree or shrub. Zones TS; 12–10; or houseplant. Native to tropical Africa. Dramatic structural form with prominently veined, fiddle-shaped, huge leaves (to 15 in. long, 10 in. wide) in glossy dark green. In protected outdoor position, can grow to 20 ft. high and as wide, with trunks 6 in. thick. Good near swimming pools. To increase

Ficus lyrata

branching, pinch back when plant is young. Full sun or light shade. Highly effective as a houseplant; give bright light.

F. macrophylla. MORETON BAY FIG. Evergreen tree. Zones TS; 12–10. Native to Australia. Grows to enormous dimensions, eventually reaching 75 ft. tall and 150 ft. wide, with massive buttressed trunk and surface roots. Blunt, oval, leathery leaves, 10 in. long and 4 in. wide, glossy green above, brownish beneath. Rose-colored leaf sheaths appear like candles at branch ends. Inch-long figs are purple spotted with white. Although plant is tender when young, it acquires hardiness with size. Shows damage at 24–26°F. Be sure to give it plenty of room. Full sun.

F. microcarpa (F. retusa). INDIAN LAUREL FIG, CHINESE BANYAN. Evergreen tree. Zones TS; 12–10. Native from Malay peninsula to Borneo. Grows at a moderate rate to 25–30 ft. high, 35–40 ft. wide. Beautiful weeping form, with long, drooping branches thickly clothed with blunt-tipped, 2- to 4-in.-long leaves. Light rose to chartreuse new leaves, produced almost continuously, give pleasing two-tone effect. Plants sold as *F. m. nitida* (a name with no botanical standing) may have the same weeping form as the species or may have upright-growing branches.

Prune at any time of year to shape as desired. Remove lower branches to reveal slim, light gray trunk. Responds well to shearing into formal hedge as low as 5 ft. Where pest free, makes a highly satisfactory tree or tub plant. Unfortunately, subject to thrips damage in some areas; these pests are hard to control, since they quickly curl new leaves (thus protecting themselves from sprays). Afflicted leaves show stippling, then drop. 'Green Gem' has thicker, darker green leaves and is apparently unaffected by thrips. Full sun.

F. pumila (F. repens). CREEPING FIG. Evergreen vine. Zones LS, CS, TS; 12–8; or houseplant. Native to China, Japan, Australia. Has a most unfiglike habit; it is one of the few plants that attaches itself securely to wood, masonry, or even metal in barnacle fashion. Because it is grown on walls and thus protected, it is found in colder climates more often than any other evergreen fig. Grows in sun or shade; not for hot south or west wall. Indoors, provide consistently moist soil and a location in bright filtered or indirect light.

Looks innocent enough in youth, making a delicate tracery of tiny, heart-shaped leaves. Neat little juvenile foliage ultimately develops into big (2- to 4-in.-long), leathery leaves borne on stubby branches that bear large, oblong fruits. In time, stems will envelop a three- or four-story building so completely that it becomes necessary to keep them trimmed away from windows. It's safe to use on house walls if you cut it to the ground every few years; also control by removing fruiting stems from time to time as they form. Roots are invasive. 'Minima' has shorter, narrower leaves than the species. Small, lobed leaves of 'Quercifolia' look like miniature oak leaves. 'Variegata' has standard-size leaves with creamy white markings.

F. religiosa. PEEPUL, BO-TREE. Briefly deciduous tree. Zones TS; 12–10. Native from India to Southeast Asia. May reach 40 ft. high and wide after 25 years or more. Foliage is quite open and delicate, revealing structure of tree at all times. Bark is warm, rich brown. Pale green leaves are thin textured and rather crisp, 4 to 7 in. long, roundish in shape but with a long, tail-like point. They move easily in even the slightest breeze, giving the foliage mass a fluttering look. Leaves drop completely in late spring or early summer—a frightening experience for the gardener who has bought an "evergreen" fig. Full sun.

F. retusa. See F. microcarpa

F. roxburghii. See F. auriculata

F. rubiginosa. RUSTYLEAF FIG. Evergreen tree. Zones TS; 12–10. Native to Australia. A single- or multitrunked, densely foliaged tree to 20–50 ft. tall, with broad crown 30–50 ft. wide. Leaves about 5 in. long, deep green above, generally rust colored and woolly beneath. Plant may develop hanging aerial roots characteristic of many of the evergreen figs that grow in tropical and semitropical environments. A small-leafed form has been sold as *F. microphylla*. Full sun.

F. r. australis is virtually identical to the species but may vary in having leaf undersides with a less pronounced rust color. Its selections 'El Toro' and 'Irvine' have exceptionally dark green leaves; 'Florida' has lighter green leaves. 'Variegata', with leaves mottled green and cream, is sometimes sold as a houseplant.

SUDDEN LEAF-SHEDDING ON A WEEPING FIG? Moving your plant to a new location—even if it's just across the room—can cause it to drop its leaves with alarming speed. But don't give up on it; foliage usually grows back once the plant has adjusted to its new setting. If you haven't moved your plant and it's dropping green leaves, you may not be watering enough. If leaves turn yellow and then fall, you're probably watering too much. Don't site weeping figs in drafty areas or near stoves or heat registers. ❖

FIG

Moraceae

DECIDUOUS FRUIT TREE

🗷 MS, LS, CS, TS ⬩ 12–6; OR GROW IN POTS

☼ FULL SUN

💧 REGULAR WATER

Fig

A traditional favorite fruit tree of the Deep South, edible fig (*Ficus carica*) is a low-branching plant with multiple trunks; it grows fairly rapidly to 15–30 ft. tall and spreads at least as wide. In the Middle South, it may freeze back to the ground during cold winters and act like a big shrub. It's easy to grow in a large container and can also be trained as an espalier.

Heavy, gray-barked, smooth trunks (gnarled in really old trees) are picturesque in silhouette. Bright green, rough-textured leaves with three to five lobes are 4–9 in. long and nearly as wide. Casts dense shade. Winter framework, tropical-looking foliage, strong trunk and branch pattern make fig a top-notch ornamental tree, especially near a patio where it can be illuminated from beneath. Protect container plants in winter. Fruit drop is a problem immediately above deck or paving.

Not particular about soil. In the Middle South, plant figs near a south wall—or train them against one—to benefit from reflected heat. Cut back tops hard at planting. As tree grows, prune lightly each winter: cut out dead wood, crossing branches, and low-hanging branches that interfere with traffic. Pinch back runaway shoots at any time. Avoid deep cultivation, which may damage surface roots. Do not use high-nitrogen fertilizers; they stimulate growth at expense of fruit. If burrowing animals are a problem, plant trees in ample wire baskets. Figs are not usually browsed by deer.

Home garden figs do not need pollinating, and most kinds bear two crops a year. Depending on the selection, the first crop comes in June or July on last year's wood; the second and more important one comes in August to October from current summer's wood. Ripe figs will detach easily when lifted and bent back toward the branch. Keep fruit picked as it ripens; protect from birds if you can. In late fall, pick off any remaining ripe figs and clean up fallen fruit.

Types differ in climate adaptability; most need prolonged high temperatures to bear good fruit, while some thrive in cooler conditions. Selections are noted below. Those with "everbearing" in their name will produce a good crop even if damaged by cold the previous winter.

'Alma'. Very sweet, medium-size fig with golden brown skin and amber to tan flesh.

'Brown Turkey' ('San Pedro', 'Black Spanish'). Adaptable to most fig climates; widely grown in Southeast. Small and cold hardy; good garden tree. Fruit has purplish brown skin, pinkish amber flesh; good for fresh eating.

'Celeste' ('Blue Celeste', 'Celestial'). The most widely grown fig in the Southeast. Cold-hardy plant. Bronzy, violet-tinged skin, rosy amber flesh; good for fresh eating.

'Conadria'. Choice thin-skinned white fig blushed violet; white to red flesh, fine flavor. Takes intense heat without splitting.

'Genoa' ('White Genoa'). Greenish yellow to white skin; strawberry to yellow flesh.

'Green Ischia'. Light green to yellowish green skin, pink flesh. Light and refreshing; good fresh or dried. Plant has low, spreading form.

'Italian Everbearing'. Resembles 'Brown Turkey' but bears somewhat larger fruit with reddish brown skin. Good fresh or dried.

'Kadota' ('White Kadota', 'Florentine'). Tough-skinned yellowish green fruit with rich, sweet amber to yellow flesh. Excellent for canning. Strong grower; needs little pruning. If pruned severely, will bear later, with fewer, larger fruits.

'LSU Everbearing'. Medium-large figs with yellow-green skin and sweet white to amber flesh. Produces fruit from July through fall.

'LSU Gold'. Very large bright yellow fruit with exceptionally sweet amber flesh. Vigorous tree.

'LSU Purple'. Dark purplish-red fruit with light amber to strawberry red flesh. Excellent flavor. Vigorous, upright tree.

'Magnolia' ('Brunswick'). Medium to large figs with reddish brown skin and amber to strawberry-colored flesh. Widely grown in Southeast.

'Mission' ('Black Mission'). Large tree bearing purple-black figs with pink flesh; good fresh or dried. Grown in areas of Southeast.

'Peter's Honey' ('Rutara'). Fruit has greenish yellow skin, amber flesh. Very sweet.

'Texas Everbearing'. Medium to large fig with brownish yellow skin, strawberry-colored flesh.

'White Adriatic'. Medium to large, sweet white figs with yellowish green skin, strawberry pink flesh. Very drought tolerant.

FILIPENDULA

Rosaceae

PERENNIALS

🗷 US, MS, LS ⬩ 8–1

☼ PARTIAL SHADE, EXCEPT AS NOTED

💧💧 REGULAR TO AMPLE WATER, EXCEPT AS NOTED

Filipendula rubra 'Venusta'

Like the related astilbe, these plumes bear tiny flowers above coarsely divided leaves. Most species prefer moist to constantly damp soil. Use in borders, in naturalistic landscapes, beside ponds.

F. purpurea. From Japan. Pink, 3- to 4-ft.-tall plumes rise above maplelike, 5- to 7-in. leaves in clumps to 2 ft. across. Selections include 'Alba' (*F. p. albiflora*), with white plumes 2 ft. tall; 'Elegans', bearing 2-ft.-tall white plumes with red stamens; and 'Nana', with salmon pink plumes 12–15 in. tall.

F. rubra. QUEEN OF THE PRAIRIE. Native to eastern U.S. Given plenty of moisture and rich soil, can reach 8 ft. high in bloom and about half as wide. Bears pink plumes. 'Venusta' has purplish pink flowers and is a little shorter, to 4–6 ft. high.

F. ulmaria. MEADOW SWEET, QUEEN OF THE MEADOW. From Europe, western Asia. To 4–6 ft. high and 2 ft. wide, with 10-in. creamy white plumes. 'Flore Pleno', just 3 ft. tall, has dense plumes of double white flowers; 'Variegata' is similar, but with gold-speckled leaves. 'Aurea' is grown not for flowers but for bright golden leaves; protect from sun.

F. vulgaris (F. hexapetala). DROPWORT. Native to Europe and northern and central Asia. White plumes on 3-ft. stems rise above 10-in., fernlike leaves with 1-in. leaflets; mounds reach 1½ ft. wide. Double-flowered 'Flore Pleno' has heavier-looking plumes. Needs less water than the other species; also prefers full sun in the Upper and Middle South. Thrives in alkaline soils.

FINOCCHIO. See FOENICULUM vulgare azoricum

FIR. See ABIES

FIREBUSH. See HAMELIA patens

FIRECRACKER PLANT. See RUSSELIA equisetiformis

FIRECRACKER VINE. See IPOMOEA lobata, MANETTIA cordifolia

FIRESPIKE. See ODONTONEMA strictum

FIRETAIL. See ACALYPHA pendula

FIRETHORN. See PYRACANTHA

FIRMIANA simplex
(F. platanifolia)

CHINESE PARASOL TREE

Sterculiaceae

DECIDUOUS TREE

✿ MS, LS, CS, TS ☼ 12–6

☼ ◐ FULL SUN OR PARTIAL SHADE

💧 REGULAR WATER

Firmiana simplex

Native to China, Japan. Fast growth to 35–40 ft. tall and half as wide, with unique light gray-green bark. Trunk often is unbranched for 4–5 ft. before dividing into three or more slender, upright, slightly spreading stems that carry lobed, tropical-looking, 1-ft. leaves. Each stem looks as if it could be cut off and carried away as a parasol. Large, loose, upright clusters of greenish white flowers appear at branch ends in early summer. Interesting fruit resembles two opened green pea pods with seeds on margins. Tree goes leafless for a long period in winter—an unusual trait for a tropical-looking tree.

Tolerates all soil types. Does well in courtyards protected from wind. Useful near swimming pools. Large trees are hard to transplant because of deep taproot. Prolific self-seeder; can be a pest.

FISHTAIL PALM. See CARYOTA

FITTONIA verschaffeltii

NERVE PLANT

Acanthaceae

PERENNIAL

✿ TS; OR HOUSEPLANT

● SHADE; BRIGHT INDIRECT LIGHT

💧 REGULAR WATER

Fittonia verschaffeltii

Native to Peru, this evergreen plant gets its common name from the network of rosy red veins that decorate its dark green, 4-in.-long, oval or elliptical leaves. It grows about 4 in. tall and produces long, cascading stems that can spread widely. Bracts containing small flowers appear sporadically, but they detract from the plant's appearance and should be pinched off.

Nerve plant does well in hanging baskets, in terrariums, or as a tabletop houseplant. Indoors, place it near a window where it receives bright light but no direct sun. Keep the soil evenly moist; the plant wilts dramatically if it dries out, and though it recovers quickly if watered promptly, the foliage will be left with unattractive brown spots. Feed every other week in spring and summer and once a month in fall and winter with a general-purpose liquid houseplant fertilizer diluted to half-strength. Frequent misting is beneficial. Stem cuttings taken in summer root easily. Watch out for mealybugs; wipe them off with a cotton swab dipped in alcohol. Outdoors, plant in rich, well-drained soil and keep moist. Do not expose plants to temperatures lower than 55°F.

Several forms of nerve plant are available. *F. v. argyroneura* has silvery white veins on leaves that are somewhat narrower and paler green than those of the species. *F. v. pearcei* has bright pink veins.

FLAG. See IRIS

FLAMBOYANT. See DELONIX regia

FLAMEGOLD. See KOELREUTERIA elegans

FLAME OF THE WOODS. See IXORA coccinea

FLAME VINE. See PYROSTEGIA venusta

FLAX. See LINUM

FLAX, NEW ZEALAND. See PHORMIUM

FLEABANE. See ERIGERON

FLORIDA LEUCOTHOE. See AGARISTA populifolia

FLORIDA MAPLE. See ACER barbatum

FLOSS FLOWER. See AGERATUM houstonianum

FLOSS SILK TREE. See CHORISIA

FLOWERING ALMOND, CHERRY. See PRUNUS

FLOWERING CRABAPPLE. See MALUS

FLOWERING DOGWOOD. See CORNUS florida

FLOWERING MAPLE. See ABUTILON

FLOWERING PEACH, PLUM. See PRUNUS

FLOWERING QUINCE. See CHAENOMELES

FOAMFLOWER. See TIARELLA

FOENICULUM vulgare

COMMON FENNEL

Apiaceae (Umbelliferae)

PERENNIAL, SOMETIMES TREATED AS ANNUAL

✿ ZONES VARY BY TYPE

☼ FULL SUN

💧 MODERATE WATER

Foeniculum vulgare

Two forms of this Mediterranean native are commonly grown. One is a perennial, popular for its licorice-flavored seeds and young leaves; the other is grown as an annual for its edible leaf bases.

The plain species is a perennial (Zones US, MS, LS, CS; 9–1) reaching 3–5 ft. tall, about 1½ ft. wide, with finely cut yellow-green leaves and flat clusters of yellow flowers. Looks much like dill *(Anethum graveolens)* but is coarser in texture. Bronze fennel ('Purpurascens', 'Smokey') grows to 6 ft. tall and has bronzy purple foliage; it is handsome enough to be grown as an ornamental. Sow in light, well-drained soil; thin seedlings to 1 ft. apart. Use seeds to flavor baked goods; use leaves as a garnish for salads, fish. Fennel often grows as a roadside or garden weed; it's attractive until the tops turn brown, and even then birds like the seeds. New stems grow in spring from the perennial root.

F. v. azoricum, called Florence fennel or finocchio, is grown as a summer annual in Zones US, MS, LS, CS, TS; 10–1. Lower growing than the species (to 2 ft.), with larger, thicker leafstalk bases that are used as a vegetable to be eaten cooked or raw.

FEED THEM FENNEL. *Don't reach for the bug killer if you see large, black-and-green caterpillars munching on your fennel plants. These are the larvae of beautiful swallowtail butterflies—so let them have a plant or two. Fennel blossoms' pollen and nectar also feed many beneficial insects, such as lacewings, ladybugs, hover flies, and soldier beetles.* ❖

FORGET-ME-NOT. See MYOSOTIS

FORMOSA LILY. See LILIUM formosanum

FOR INFORMATION ON SELECTING PLANTS
PLEASE SEE PAGES 39–144

FORMOSA FIRETHORN. See PYRACANTHA koidzumii

FORSYTHIA

Oleaceae

DECIDUOUS SHRUBS

✿ US, MS, LS, EXCEPT AS NOTED

☀ FULL SUN, EXCEPT AS NOTED

◑ MODERATE TO REGULAR WATER

Forsythia ×intermedia

Though it's originally from China and Korea, this harbinger of spring has adorned Southern gardens for so long that folks assume it's native. At garden centers, it's often the top-selling flowering deciduous shrub because it's inexpensive, easy to grow, and dependably colorful. From late winter to early spring, countless yellow, ¾- to 1½-in. flowers smother the arching, leafless branches. During the rest of the growing season, the medium green foliage blends well with that of other shrubs. Fall color is inconsistent, but leaves may turn purplish or burgundy.

Forsythia can be used as a clipped hedge, an informal screen, a bank cover, or part of a shrub border. It thrives in most well-drained soils. Somewhat resistant to damage by deer. Rejuvenate after bloom by cutting a third of the oldest canes to the ground in late spring; also remove dead wood and old, woody branches. Prune to preserve graceful, fountainlike form; do not shear into balls or boxes. Cut branches are easy to root—just stick them into moist soil.

F. 'Arnold Dwarf'. Heat zones 8–3. Grows 1½–3 ft. high, to 6 ft. wide. Flowers are sparse and not especially attractive, but plant is a useful, fast-growing ground cover.

F. ×intermedia. BORDER FORSYTHIA. Heat zones 8–3. The most widely grown forsythias are in this hybrid group. Most grow 7–10 ft. tall and have arching branches; smaller selections are also included in the following list.

'Beatrix Farrand'. Upright to 10 ft. tall, 7 ft. wide. Branches thickly set with 2- to 2½-in.-wide flowers in deep yellow marked with orange.

'Fiesta'. Grows 3–4 ft. tall and a little wider. Deep yellow flowers are followed by green-and-yellow variegated leaves that hold their color all summer long.

'Golden Times'. To 6–8 ft. tall and wide. Variegated selection with yellowish green leaves edged in gold; extremely attractive, especially when grown in light shade. Remove any branches that revert to green. Soft yellow flowers.

'Goldtide'. Compact growth to 20 in. tall by 4 ft. wide; profuse bright yellow flowers.

'Goldzauber' ('Gold Charm'). Erect to 6–8 ft. high and not quite as wide, with large flowers in deep yellow.

'Karl Sax'. Resembles 'Beatrix Farrand' but is lower growing, neater, more graceful.

'Lynwood' ('Lynwood Gold'). Stiffly upright to 7 ft., with 4- to 6-ft. spread. Profuse tawny yellow blooms survive spring storms.

'Spectabilis'. Dense, upright, vigorous shrub to 9 ft. tall and 6 ft. wide. Deep yellow blossoms.

'Spring Glory'. To about 6 ft. tall and wide, with a profuse show of pale yellow flowers.

F. ovata. KOREAN FORSYTHIA. Zones US, MS; 7–1. To 4–6 ft., with wider spread. Heavy crop of bright yellow blossoms appears early in the season. Flower buds are hardy to 20°F. 'Tetragold' is lower growing (3–5 ft. high and wide) and has deep yellow blooms.

F. suspensa. WEEPING FORSYTHIA. Heat zones 8–2. Dense, upright growth habit to 8–10 ft. tall, 6–8 ft. wide. Drooping, vinelike branches root where they touch damp soil. Golden yellow flowers. Useful large-scale bank cover. Can be trained as vine; if you support main branches, branchlets will cascade. 'Fortunei' is somewhat more upright, more available in garden centers.

F. viridissima. GREENSTEM FORSYTHIA. Heat zones 8–3. Stiff-looking shrub to 6–10 ft. high and wide with deep green foliage, olive green stems, greenish yellow flowers. 'Bronxensis' is slow-growing dwarf to 16 in. tall, for shrub borders or ground cover. *F. v. koreana (F. koreana)*, to 8 ft., has larger, brighter yellow flowers and attractive purplish fall foliage.

FORSYTHIA, WHITE. See ABELIOPHYLLUM distichum

FORTNIGHT LILY. See DIETES

FOTHERGILLA

Hamamelidaceae

DECIDUOUS SHRUBS

✿ US, MS, LS

☀◑ PARTIAL SHADE IN LOWER SOUTH

◑ REGULAR WATER

Fothergilla major

Native to southeastern U.S. Grown mainly for fall foliage color, but spring bloom is pretty: small, honey-scented white flowers in 1- to 2-in., brushlike clusters on zigzagging stems. Blossoms may appear before or with leaves. Perform best in moist, well-drained, acid soil.

F. gardenii. DWARF FOTHERGILLA. Heat zones 8–1. Typically 2–3 ft. high (though it can grow considerably taller) and as wide or wider, with 1- to 2½-in.-long, dark green leaves. Foliage turns intense yellow to orange to scarlet in autumn, often with all three colors in the same leaf. 'Blue Mist' is a blue-foliaged selection that doesn't color up as well in fall.

F. major (F. monticola). LARGE FOTHERGILLA. Heat zones 8–2. Erect shrub to 9 ft. tall and 6 ft. wide, with roundish, 2- to 4-in.-long leaves turning yellow to orange to purplish red in autumn. 'Mount Airy' is smaller (3–5 ft. high and wide), with abundant bloom, good dark green leaf color, and consistently superb fall color in yellow, orange, and scarlet.

FOUNTAIN GRASS. See PENNISETUM

FOUR O'CLOCK. See MIRABILIS

FOXGLOVE. See DIGITALIS

FOXTAIL LILY. See EREMURUS

FRAGARIA hybrids

ORNAMENTAL STRAWBERRY

Rosaceae

PERENNIALS

✿ US, MS, LS, CS ╟ 10–1

☀◑ AFTERNOON SHADE IN COASTAL SOUTH

◑ REGULAR WATER

Fragaria 'Pink Panda'

The genus *Fragaria* includes all types of strawberry plants; for those types grown strictly for their edible fruit, see Strawberry. The hybrids described here are crosses of wild strawberry with *Potentilla*. They spread widely by trailing runners to form a mat of rich green, glossy leaves. Leaves are made up of three oval, tooth-edged leaflets 1–1½ in. long; colorful inch-wide flowers contrast beautifully with the foliage. Fruits are few and far between—edible but not tasty. Pretty in borders, rock gardens, as edging; excellent in planters, window boxes, and hanging baskets. Grow in sandy or other well-drained soil. 'Pink Panda' grows 4–6 in. tall and bears showy bright pink flowers from spring to fall. 'Lipstick' reaches 6–8 in. high, has rosy red flowers.

FRANGIPANI. See PLUMERIA

FRANKLINIA alatamaha (Gordonia alatamaha)

FRANKLIN TREE

Theaceae

DECIDUOUS TREE

✂ US, MS, LS, CS ⊞ 9–6

☀ ☽ FULL SUN OR PART SHADE

⬤ REGULAR WATER

Franklinia alatamaha

This legendary tree, native to the banks of Georgia's Alatamaha River, mysteriously disappeared from the wild shortly after it was discovered there in 1770 by famed botanist John Bartram. All plants in commerce today can be traced to the ones he collected. Open, airy form; may reach 30 ft., but more typically grows 10–20 ft. high. Tree tends to be fairly slender when grown with a single trunk; when grown as a multi-trunked plant, it is broad spreading. Attractive dark gray bark has faint white vertical striping. Shiny dark green leaves are spoon-shaped to oblong and pointed, 4–6 in. long; they turn orange and red in fall and hang on for a long time before dropping. Fragrant, white, 3-in.-wide, five-petaled flowers centered with clusters of yellow stamens open from round white buds from July to early October, sometimes coinciding with fall foliage color in the Upper South. Blossoms somewhat resemble single camellias—not surprising, since *Franklinia* and *Camellia* belong to the same family. Flowers are followed by small, woody capsules that are split into ten segments, each containing five seeds.

Provide moist, rich, light, acid soil. Good drainage is critical. Not the easiest plant to grow. Susceptible to phytophthora root rot, a fatal soilborne disease, in heavy, wet soils during hot weather. Grows well in light shade but has best bloom and fall color in full sun. Easy to grow from seed, blooming in 6 to 7 years. Highly decorative lawn or accent tree. Use for contrast in azalea or rhododendron plantings.

FRAXINUS

ASH

Oleaceae

DECIDUOUS AND EVERGREEN TREES

✂ ZONES VARY BY SPECIES

☀ FULL SUN

◯ ◗ ⬤ WATER NEEDS VARY BY SPECIES

Fraxinus americana

Fairly fast-growing trees, most of which tolerate hot summers, cold winters, and many kinds of soil, including alkaline sorts. Chiefly used as street, shade, and lawn trees. In most cases, leaves are divided into leaflets. Male and female flowers (generally inconspicuous, in clusters) grow on separate trees in some species, on the same tree in others. In the latter case, flowers are often followed by clusters of single-seeded, winged fruit, often in such abundance that they can be a litter problem. When flowers are on separate trees, you'll get fruit on a female tree only if a male tree grows nearby.

F. americana. WHITE ASH. Deciduous. Zones US, MS, LS, CS; 9–1. From eastern U.S. Reaches 80 ft. or more, with straight trunk and oval-shaped crown to 50 ft. wide. Leaves 8–15 in. long, with five to nine oval, 2- to 6-in.-long leaflets; dark green above, paler beneath. Foliage turns purplish in fall. Male and female flowers on separate trees, but plants sold are generally seedlings, so you don't know what you're getting. If you end up with both male and female trees, you will get a heavy crop of seed; both litter and seedlings can be problems. Give this tree regular water.

Seedless selections include 'Autumn Applause' and 'Autumn Purple', both with exceptionally good, long-lasting purple fall color; 'Champaign County', a dense grower with pale yellow fall color; 'Greenspire', narrow, upright habit, deep orange fall color; 'Rosehill', with bronzy red fall color;

'Royal Purple', upright grower with purple autumn leaves; and 'Skyline', an upright oval with brown and purple fall color.

F. berlandierana. MEXICAN ASH. Deciduous. Zones MS, LS, CS, TS; 12–7. From southern Texas and northeastern Mexico; often found along stream banks. Grows very fast when young, eventually reaching 30–40 ft. tall, with a symmetrical, dense crown (to about 25 ft. across) that provides good shade. Glossy green leaves are made up of three to five leaflets to 4 in. long. Moderate water.

F. cuspidata. FRAGRANT ASH. Deciduous. Zones MS, LS, CS, TS; 12–7. From Texas, Southwest, Mexico. Bushy shrub or small tree, 10–15 ft. tall and broad, sometimes 20 ft. Leaves are divided into seven 2½-in.-long leaflets; turn yellow in fall. Long panicles of white, vanilla-scented flowers cover the tree in mid- or late spring, making a very showy display against a dark background. Tolerant of drought and alkaline soil. Grows fast if watered regularly.

F. greggii. LITTLELEAF ASH, GREGG ASH. Evergreen. Zones MS, LS, CS, TS. Native from Arizona to Texas. To 25 ft. tall and 20 ft. wide, with leaves divided into three to seven ¾-in., leathery bright green leaflets. Useful desert tree. Little water.

F. ornus. FLOWERING ASH, MANNA ASH. Deciduous. Zones US, MS; 7–1; best in Upper South. From southern Europe and Asia Minor. To 30–40 ft., with rounded crown 20–30 ft. wide. Luxuriant foliage mass: 8- to 10-in.-long leaves divided into 7 to 11 oval, medium green, 2-in.-long leaflets with toothed edges. Foliage turns to soft shades of lavender and yellow in fall. In spring, displays quantities of fluffy, branched, 3- to 5-in.-long clusters of showy, fragrant, white to greenish white blossoms. Moderate water.

Fraxinus ornus

F. pennsylvanica (F. lanceolata). GREEN ASH. Deciduous. Zones US, MS, LS, CS; 9–1. Native to eastern U.S. To 50–60 ft. tall, with irregular oval crown 25–30 ft. across. Gray-brown bark; dense, twiggy structure. Bright green leaves 10–12 in. long, divided into five to nine rather narrow, 4- to 6-in.-long leaflets. Inconsistent yellow fall color. For assured fall color, plant a named selection. Male and female flowers on separate trees. Takes wet soil and severe cold, but foliage burns in hot, dry winds. Regular water.

Seedless kinds include 'Emerald', a round-headed tree with glossy deep green leaves and yellow fall color; 'Marshall's Seedless', a seedless male form with lustrous, deep green foliage and good yellow fall color; 'Summit', upright habit, good golden yellow fall color; and 'Urbanite', pyramidal shape and bronze fall color.

F. texensis. TEXAS ASH. Deciduous. Zones MS, LS, CS; 9–1. From Oklahoma and Texas. Round-headed tree to 35–50 ft. tall and wide, fairly fast growing. Leaves have five dark green, 3-in.-long leaflets, which may turn shades of gold, orange, maroon in fall. Particularly suited to rocky limestone soils, but well adapted to regular garden watering and average soil. Usually long lived. Very drought tolerant.

F. velutina. ARIZONA ASH. Deciduous. Zones US, MS, LS, CS; 9–1. Southeastern native. Takes hot, dry conditions and cold to about −10°F. To 30 ft. (possibly 50 ft.) tall. Pyramidal when young; spreading 30–40 ft. wide when mature, with a more open shape. Gray-green leaves are divided into three to five narrow to oval, 3-in.-long leaflets; turn bright yellow in fall. Male and female flowers on separate trees. Regular water.

'Rio Grande' ('Fan-Tex') is most commonly grown in Texas. Its leaflets are larger and darker green than those of the species; they resist windburn.

FRECKLE FACE. See HYPOESTES phyllostachya

FOR GROWING SYMBOL EXPLANATIONS
PLEASE SEE PAGE 145

FREESIA

Iridaceae

CORMS

☘ CS, TS ⊞ 12–9; OR HOUSEPLANTS

☼ ◑ FULL SUN OR PARTIAL SHADE; BRIGHT LIGHT

💧 REGULAR WATER DURING GROWTH AND BLOOM

Freesia hybrids

Native to South Africa. Prized for rich perfume of flowers; white and yellow types tend to be more fragrant than those with blooms in other colors. Slender, branched stems and lowest leaves grow 1–1½ ft. long; stem leaves are shorter. Tubular, 2-in.-long blossoms are borne in one-sided spikes. Older selection 'Alba' has fragrant white or creamy blooms. Newer, larger-flowered types with 1- to 1½-ft. stems are Tecolote and Dutch hybrids, with white, pink, red, lavender, purple, blue, yellow, and orange flowers; you can buy mixed colors or selections named for single colors. Freesias will self-sow if faded flowers are not removed; volunteers tend to revert to cream marked with purple and yellow.

Hardy to 20°F. Plant corms 2 in. deep (pointed end up) and 2 in. apart in fall, in well-drained soil. Plants go dormant after bloom and need no irrigation until growth resumes in fall; they increase rapidly. In Upper, Middle, and Lower South, plant 2 in. deep, 2 in. apart in pots and grow indoors in a sunny window. Keep room temperature as cool as possible at night. Freesias are easily grown from seed sown in July or August; often bloom following spring. Flowering potted freesias grown from chilled and stored corms are available throughout the year.

FRINGE BELLS. See SHORTIA soldanelloides

FRINGE HYACINTH. See MUSCARI comosum

FRINGE TREE. See CHIONANTHUS

FRITILLARIA

FRITILLARY

Liliaceae

PERENNIALS FROM BULBS

☘ US, MS, LS ⊞ 8–2, EXCEPT AS NOTED

◑ LIGHT SHADE, EXCEPT AS NOTED

💧 REGULAR WATER DURING GROWTH AND BLOOM

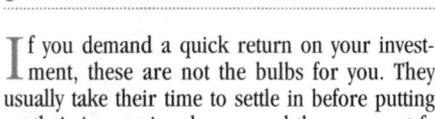

Fritillaria imperialis

If you demand a quick return on your investment, these are not the bulbs for you. They usually take their time to settle in before putting on their impressive show—and they may rest for a year after blooming, too. In spring, unbranched stems ranging from 6 in. to 3 ft. high are topped by bell-shaped, nodding flowers, often unusually colored and mottled. Use in woodland gardens, rock gardens, or borders. In fall, plant bulbs in porous soil with ample humus. Set smaller bulbs 3–4 in. deep and 6 in. apart; set largest ones (*F. imperialis*) 4–5 in. deep, 8–12 in. apart. All appreciate some winter chill and tend to perform poorly where summers are hot and dry. Reduce watering as foliage dies back in summer. Clumps seldom need dividing.

F. imperialis. CROWN IMPERIAL. Native to Europe. Stout stalk to 3 ft. tall, clothed with broad, glossy leaves and crowned by circle of large (2- to 3-in.-long) bells in red, orange, or yellow; a tuft of leaves tops the flowers. Bulb and plant have musky odor that some people find offensive. Can take full sun in Upper South.

F. meleagris. CHECKERED LILY, SNAKESHEAD. Native to damp meadows in Europe, Asia; tolerates occasional flooding. One to three showy, 2-in. bells top each 1- to 1½-ft. stem; blossoms are checkered and veined with reddish brown and purple. Lance-shaped leaves are 3–6 in. long. There is a white-blossomed form.

F. michailovskyi. Heat zones 8–5. From Turkey. To 6 in. high. Each stem bears one to six 1- to 1½-in. bells that are purplish brown at base, bright yellow toward tip.

F. pallidiflora. From northern China, Siberia. Each 2- to 3-ft. stem carries one to six 1¼-in. bells in pale yellow tinted with green.

F. persica 'Adiyaman'. Heat zones 8–6. Selection of a species from western Asia. Stems 2–3 ft. tall carry up to 30 deep plum purple, inch-long flowers on upper half. Foliage is gray green. Plant is hardy and easy to grow, but emerging stems need protection from late frosts. Can take full sun in Upper South.

F. verticillata. Heat zones 8–6. Native to central Asia. Stems 1–2 ft. tall bear one to six flowers in white or yellow speckled with green or purple. Upper leaves have a tendril-like tip.

FUCHSIA

Onagraceae

TENDER SHRUBS, MANY TREATED AS ANNUALS

☘ ZONES VARY

◑ PARTIAL SHADE

💧 REGULAR WATER

Fuchsia × hybrida, Double Type

Native to wet, mountainous areas mainly in the tropical Americas, these colorful shrubs have a hard time in most parts of the South. While they do fine in the Upper South and higher elevations of the Appalachian and Blue Ridge Mountains, they suffer in the hot summers elsewhere in our region.

F. × hybrida. HYBRID FUCHSIA. Zone US (if overwintered indoors); or grow as annual. The vast majority of fuchsias sold in garden centers fall into this group. Hundreds of selections offer a wide array of color combinations. Sepals (top parts that flare back) are always white, pink, or red. Corolla (inside part of flower) may be almost any color in the range of white, blue, violet, purple, pink, red, and shades approaching orange. Plant form varies widely, from erect shrubs 3–6 ft. high to trailing types grown for hanging baskets. You can also buy fuchsias trained as espaliers and standards (single-trunked tree form). Hummingbirds find the flowers irresistible.

Hybrid fuchsias need porous, water-retentive soil containing plenty of organic matter; those in hanging baskets require frequent watering. Give sun in the morning and shade in the afternoon; protect from any wind. To keep blooms coming, feed every other week during growing season with water-soluble 20-20-20 fertilizer. Blooming decreases during hot weather. To overwinter indoors, cut back severely; then place beside a sunny window. Watch out for whiteflies—spray the leaf undersides from time to time with insecticidal soap or horticultural oil just to make sure these pests don't take up residence.

Fuchsia × hybrida, Single Type

F. magellanica. HARDY FUCHSIA. Zones MS, LS, CS; 12–7. A tender shrub that dies down to the ground each winter, then resprouts in spring. Native to Chile and Argentina. Grows 3 ft. tall and wide. Blooms profusely in summer, bearing drooping, 1½-in.-long, red-and-purple flowers. Plant in rich, well-drained soil; mulch heavily in late fall. 'Riccartonii' (*F.* 'Riccartonii') is an especially cold-hardy form.

FUKI. See PETASITES japonicus

Fumariaceae. This family consists of annuals and perennials, usually with irregularly shaped flowers. *Corydalis* and bleeding heart (*Dicentra*) are examples. This family is considered by many to be included in the poppy family (Papaveraceae).

GAILLARDIA

BLANKET FLOWER

Asteraceae (Compositae)

PERENNIALS, ONE GROWN AS ANNUAL

🌿 US, MS, LS, CS, TS **H** 9–1, EXCEPT AS NOTED

☀ FULL SUN

◐ 💧 LITTLE TO MODERATE WATER

Gaillardia ×grandiflora

Native to the South and Midwest, these easy-going summer bloomers feature daisylike flowers in warm colors—yellow, orange, and red. They thrive on neglect, so put away the watering can and fertilizer. They love heat, have no serious pests, and are not fussy about soil (though they must have good drainage). Easy to grow from seed; excellent cut flowers.

G. aristata. BLANKET FLOWER. Perennial. This parent of the hybrid *G. ×grandiflora* has been replaced to a large degree by its offspring, but the wild form is still much used in prairie restoration and wildflower mixes. Grows 2–2½ ft. tall and 2 ft. across, with flower heads up to 4 in. wide. Colors range from yellow to red; most familiar form is red with a jagged yellow border on the ray flowers.

G. ×grandiflora. Perennial. Offspring of *G. pulchella* and *G. aristata*. Grows to 2–4 ft. high, 1½ ft. wide. Somewhat rough, gray-green foliage; single or double flowers to 3–4 in. across. Much variation in flower color: range includes various warm shades of red and yellow with orange or maroon bands. Exceptionally long bloom period for a perennial—from early summer until frost. Plants flower first year from seed. Can be short lived in hottest, most humid areas.

Many strains and selections are available, including dwarf kinds and types with extra-large blossoms. 'Goblin', to 1 ft. tall, is a good compact choice with large deep red flowers bordered in bright yellow; 'Goblin Yellow' is similar but has solid yellow blooms. 'Baby Cole', another red-and-yellow type, grows 7–8 in. tall. Among 2½-ft.-tall choices are deep red 'Burgundy'; pure orange 'Tokajer'; 'Painter's Palette', a seed strain with blooms in burgundy, clear yellow, rosy red with golden tips, and other red-and-gold combinations; and 'Torchlight', with yellow flowers bordered in red. 'Yellow Queen' has clear yellow blossoms with a golden eye and may reach 3 ft. tall.

G. pulchella. INDIAN BLANKET. Short-lived perennial usually treated as an annual. Heat zones 12–1. To 1½–2 ft. high, 1 ft. wide, with soft, hairy leaves and long, whiplike stems carrying 2-in. flowers in red, yellow, gold. Easy to grow; sow seeds in warm soil after danger of frost is past. 'Red Plume' and 'Yellow Plume' are double flowered, with 2-in. blossoms on uniform 12- to 14-in. plants.

GALANTHUS

SNOWDROP

Amaryllidaceae

PERENNIALS FROM BULBS

🌿 US, MS, LS **H** 8–1

☀◐ FULL SUN DURING BLOOM, LIGHT SHADE AFTER

💧 REGULAR WATER

☠ BULBS ARE POISONOUS IF INGESTED

Galanthus nivalis

These natives of Europe and Asia Minor perform best in cold-winter climates. Closely related to and often confused with *Leucojum* (snowflake). These harbingers of spring are among the first bulbs to bloom as winter ends. Nodding, bell-shaped white flowers are borne one per stalk; inner flower segments are infused or marked with green, while larger outer segments are pure white. Plants have two or three strap-shaped basal leaves. Effective in rock gardens or under flowering shrubs, naturalized in woodland settings, or grown in pots. Plant in autumn, setting bulbs 3–4 in. deep and 3 in. apart in moist soil with ample humus. Bulbs prefer year-round moisture. Do not divide often; when division is necessary, do the job right after bloom.

G. 'Atkinsii'. Stems to 8 in. high bear slender, 1½-in.-long blooms. Each inner flower segment has a heart-shaped green mark at the tip. Narrow leaves to 4 in. long.

G. elwesii. GIANT SNOWDROP. Foot-high stems carry 1½-in. flowers; inner segments are heavily infused with green. Blooms a little earlier in spring and is better adapted to mild-winter climates than *G. nivalis*.

G. nivalis. COMMON SNOWDROP. More delicate version of *G. elwesii*. Stems 6–9 in. high bear inch-long flowers, their inner segments marked at tips with a green crescent. 'Flore Pleno' has double blooms.

G. 'S. Arnott' ('Sam Arnott'). To 8 in. high. Rounded blossoms to 1½ in. long have an inverted V-shaped green mark at the tip of each inner flower segment. Leaves 3–6 in. long.

GALAX urceolata (G. aphylla)

GALAX

Diapensiaceae

PERENNIAL

🌿 US, MS, LS **H** 8–4

◑● PARTIAL TO FULL SHADE

💧 REGULAR WATER

Galax urceolata

Native to mountain woodlands from Virginia to Georgia. Often used as a ground cover, although it spreads slowly. The plant's real distinction comes from its evergreen foliage, which is much used in indoor arrangements. The shiny, heart-shaped leaves grow in basal tufts that reach 6–9 in. high; they turn bronzy in fall unless the plant is grown in deep shade. In early summer, flower stems rise to 2½ ft., bearing foxtails of small white flowers at their tips.

Grow in acid soil with plenty of organic material—preferably mulch of leaf mold. Locate under plants that appreciate the same conditions: dogwood *(Cornus),* rhododendron, azalea, pieris. Space 1 ft. apart.

GALEOBDOLON luteum. See LAMIUM galeobdolon

GALIUM odoratum (Asperula odorata)

SWEET WOODRUFF

Rubiaceae

PERENNIAL

🌿 US, MS, LS **H** 8–4

◑● PARTIAL TO FULL SHADE

💧💧 REGULAR TO AMPLE WATER

Galium odoratum

Attractive, low-spreading perennial that brings to mind deep-shaded woods. Slender, square stems 6–12 in. high are encircled every inch or so by whorls of six to eight aromatic, bristle-tipped leaves. Clusters of tiny white flowers show above foliage in late spring and summer. Leaves and stems give off a fragrant, haylike odor when dried; they are used to make May wine.

In the shade garden, sweet woodruff is best used as ground cover or edging. Will spread rapidly in rich soil with abundant moisture—can become a pest if allowed to grow unchecked. Self-sows freely. Increase by division in fall or spring. Give full shade in Lower South.

FOR INFORMATION ON YOUR CLIMATE ZONES

PLEASE SEE PAGES 28–38

GALPHIMIA glauca
(Thryallis glauca)

SHOWER-OF-GOLD, THRYALLIS

Malpighiaceae

EVERGREEN SHRUB

✓ CS, TS ⌇ 12–9; OR GROW IN POTS

☼ FULL SUN

◊ MODERATE WATER

Galphimia glauca

Native to Mexico and Guatemala. Tropical evergreen shrub, 4–6 ft. tall and wide; grows outdoors only in the Coastal and Tropical South. Handsome 2-in., oblong, gray-green leaves; showy, ¾-in. bright yellow flowers in branched clusters, summer and fall. Fertilize from spring through fall. Prune out crowded branches to keep shape open. Brittle stems break easily, so don't plant where people will brush against the foliage. In cooler climates, grow in a pot that you can bring indoors for winter.

GALTONIA candicans

SUMMER HYACINTH

Liliaceae

PERENNIAL FROM BULB

✓ LS, CS, TS ⌇ 10–7

☼◑ LIGHT SHADE IN TROPICAL SOUTH

◊ REGULAR WATER DURING GROWTH AND BLOOM

Galtonia candicans

If you're looking for a way to add punch to your summer border, this bold, little-known bulb from South Africa may be the answer. Stout, 4-ft. spikes of nodding, sweet-scented white flowers rise above clumps of strap-shaped, 2- to 3-ft.-long leaves. The summer show is so grand that a half-dozen bulbs can dominate a border. Hardy to about 10°F. Where winters are colder, dig bulbs in fall and store over winter as you would gladiolus—though summer hyacinth does bloom best when left undisturbed. Plant bulbs 6 in. deep and 1 ft. apart in moist, well-drained soil that contains lots of organic matter.

GARDENIA

Rubiaceae

EVERGREEN SHRUBS

✓ ZONES VARY BY SPECIES

☼◑ FULL SUN OR PARTIAL SHADE

◊ REGULAR WATER

Gardenia jasminoides

No plant expresses the grace of the South better than gardenia. Intensely fragrant white blossoms contrast beautifully with shiny, leathery dark green leaves. Double forms are classic corsage flowers. In borders, gardenias need good drainage and acid soil containing lots of organic matter. Plant them high (like azaleas and rhododendrons) and don't let them be crowded by other plants or competing roots. Mulch plants instead of cultivating; feed every 3 to 4 weeks during the growing season with acid fertilizer, fish emulsion, or blood meal. Prune to remove straggly branches and faded flowers. Control whiteflies, aphids, and other sucking insects with light horticultural oil.

Gardenias do well in large pots on decks and patios; gardeners in cold-winter areas can grow them in cool greenhouses. Unfortunately, they make poor houseplants— they attract mites, mealybugs, and whiteflies.

G. jasminoides (G. augusta). COMMON GARDENIA, CAPE JASMINE. Zones LS, CS, TS, except as noted; 12–8. Native to China, Taiwan, Japan. Glossy bright green leaves and usually double white flowers to 3 in. across. Hardy to about 10°F. Will survive 0°F but is likely to die back to roots.

The many selections are useful in containers or raised beds, as hedges, espaliers, low screens, or single plants.

'Aimee' ('First Love'). Somewhat larger shrub than 'August Beauty', with larger flowers. Spring bloom.

'August Beauty'. Grows 4–6 ft. high and 3–4 ft. wide. Blooms heavily midspring into fall. Large double flowers.

'Chuck Hayes'. Extra-hardy type, possibly as hardy as 'Klein's Hardy'. To 4 ft. high and wide. Double flowers in summer, heavy rebloom in fall.

'Golden Magic'. Reaches 3 ft. tall, 2 ft. wide in 2 to 3 years, eventually larger. Extra-full flowers open white, gradually age to deep golden yellow. Blooms from spring through summer, peaking in midspring.

'Grif's Select'. Compact, 3–4 ft. tall and wide; profuse single flowers in late spring and early summer, red seed capsules in fall. Hardy to about 5°F.

'Kimura Shikazaki' ('Four Seasons'). Compact plant 2–3 ft. tall. Flowers similar to those of 'Veitchii', but slightly less fragrant. Extremely long bloom season—spring to fall.

'Klein's Hardy'. For cold-winter areas; hardy to 0°F. To 2–3 ft. high and wide. Single flowers in summer. Grow in a wind-protected site.

'Miami Supreme'. Grows to 6 ft. tall and wide, with large double flowers (4–6 in. wide) in spring, periodic flowering through summer.

'Mystery'. Best-known selection. Bears 4- to 5-in. double flowers from mid- to late spring or longer. Tends to be rangy and needs pruning to keep it neat. Can reach 6–8 ft. high and wide.

'Radicans' ('Prostrata'). Grows 6–12 in. tall and spreads to 2–3 ft., with small leaves; inch-wide double flowers bloom in summer. Good for small-scale ground cover or pots. Not as cold hardy as the species; not well suited to Middle South. 'Radicans Variegata' ('Prostrata Variegata') has gray-green leaves with white markings.

'Shooting Star'. Upright grower to 6–8 ft. tall and wide, with large leaves and single flowers in late spring and early summer. Hardy to 0°F.

'Veitchii'. Compact, reliable grower to 3½–4½ ft. tall and 6 ft. wide. Blooms prolifically from midspring into fall (and sometimes even during warm winters), bearing fully double 1- to 1½-in. flowers.

'White Gem'. At just 1–2 ft. tall and wide, this selection is useful for edgings, containers, or raised beds, where the fragrance of its single, creamy white summer flowers can be appreciated.

G. thunbergia. STARRY GARDENIA. Zones TS; 12–8. Native to South Africa, this winter bloomer is much less common than *G. jasminoides*, because it is less cold hardy and not as showy. Sometimes grown as an ornamental in south Florida. Primary use is as a rootstock to impart nematode resistance and increased vigor to *G. jasminoides*. Reaches 15 ft. tall and as wide. Dark green leaves to 6 in. long; single, 3- to 4-in., white- to cream-colored flowers with a long tube and typically eight overlapping, petal-like lobes.

GARDENIA'S DEMANDS. *Like a Hollywood star, gardenia is as fussy as it is beautiful. Acid soil and good drainage are just its initial requirements. If you want blooms, you'll also need to provide night temperatures of 50–55°F in winter or spring. Though you can grow gardenia as a houseplant, doing so can be pure torture: mealybugs, mites, and whiteflies love it.* ❖

GARLIC

Liliaceae

PERENNIAL FROM BULB

✓ US, MS, LS, CS, TS ⌇ 12–1

☼ FULL SUN

◊ REGULAR WATER

Garlic

Classified botanically as *Allium sativum*; not known in the wild. For ornamental relatives, see *Allium*. Seed stores and some mail-order seed houses sell disease-free mother bulbs ("sets") for planting—and some gardeners have had good luck planting bulbs from grocery stores. In mild-winter areas, plant in fall for early summer harvest; where winters are cold, plant in early spring. Break up bulbs into cloves and select largest ones. Plant in rich, well-drained soil, setting cloves pointed end up, 1 in. deep, 3–6 in. apart, in rows 15 in. apart. Harvest when leafy tops fall over; lift out with garden fork rather than pulling. Air-dry bulbs, cut off most of tops and roots, and store in cool, well-ventilated place out of sunlight. Giant or elephant garlic (*A. scorodoprasum*) has unusually large (fist-size) bulbs and mild flavor. Grow as for regular garlic, but space 8–12 in. apart.

GAS PLANT. See DICTAMNUS albus

GAULTHERIA procumbens

WINTERGREEN, CHECKERBERRY

Ericaceae

EVERGREEN GROUND COVER

US, MS H 8–1

LIGHT SHADE

REGULAR WATER

Gaultheria procumbens

Native to eastern North America, this handsome, low-growing shrub is the source of oil of wintergreen. Creeping stems send up erect stems to 6 in. high, with oval, 2-in.-long, glossy dark green leaves clustered near their tips. Foliage emits a strong wintergreen odor when bruised, turns reddish in winter. Small, pinkish white summer flowers are followed by scarlet berries. Ideal as ground cover for a partly shaded rock garden or a woodland garden. Space plants 1 ft. apart in acid, well-drained soil containing plenty of organic matter; wintergreen will not survive in clay soil. It performs best in the Upper South and higher elevations of the Appalachian and Blue Ridge Mountains. 'Macrocarpa' is more compact than the species and bears a very heavy crop of berries.

GAURA lindheimeri

Onagraceae

PERENNIAL

US, MS, LS, CS H 9–6

FULL SUN

MODERATE WATER

Gaura lindheimeri

Native to Texas and Louisiana. Airy plant growing to 2¼–4 ft. high, 2–3 ft. wide. Stalkless leaves to 1½–3½ in. long grow directly on stems. Long bloom period (often from late spring into fall). Pink buds closely set on branching spikes open just a few at a time; blossoms are about 1 in. long, white aging to rose. Faded flowers drop cleanly from stems, but seed-bearing spikes should be cut to improve appearance, prevent overly enthusiastic self-sowing, and prolong bloom.

Selected forms include the following.

'Corrie's Gold'. To 2½–3 ft. tall and wide. Leaves edged with gold.

'Crimson Butterflies'. Grows only 1½ ft. high and a little wider, with smaller, more closely spaced leaves and dark pink blossoms. Good in containers.

'Dauphin'. Rigidly upright to 5–7 ft. tall, not quite as wide. Dark pink buds open to pink flowers that quickly turn white.

'Pink Cloud'. Upright plant to 2½ ft. high and 2 ft. wide. Profuse bright pink blooms.

'Siskiyou Pink'. Reaches 2–2½ ft. tall and a little wider. Deep maroon buds open to rose pink flowers. Leaves are mottled with rich maroon.

'Whirling Butterflies'. To 3 ft. tall and wide. White flowers are slightly larger than those of the species.

Needs good drainage. Used widely in most of the South. Performs best in the Southwest, where it is a profusely blooming, long-lived perennial. Taproot makes it very drought tolerant. Clumps never need dividing; for additional plants, allow some of the volunteer seedlings to grow. Plant prefers lean, unfertilized soil; planting in rich soil results in legginess and sparse bloom.

GAYFEATHER. See LIATRIS

GAZANIA

GAZANIA DAISY

Asteraceae (Compositae)

PERENNIALS, SOME GROWN AS ANNUALS

US, MS, LS, CS, TS H 12–3

EXPOSURE NEEDS VARY BY SPECIES

MODERATE TO REGULAR WATER

Gazania hybrid

Native to South Africa. The daisy flowers put on a dazzling display of color during peak bloom in late spring, early summer, and they continue to bloom intermittently throughout the year. Gazanias grow well in almost any well-drained soil. Feed once in spring with slow-acting fertilizer. Divide plants every 3 to 4 years. In the Upper, Middle, and Lower South, carry gazanias through winter by taking cuttings in fall as you would for annual geraniums.

G. hybrids. The two basic types are clumping and trailing; both take full sun. Clumping gazanias (complex hybrids involving a number of species) form a mound of evergreen leaves—dark green above, gray and woolly beneath, often lobed. Flowers are 3–4 in. wide, on 6- to 10-in.-long stems; they open on sunny days, close at night and in cloudy weather. Available in single colors or in a mixture (as plants or seeds) in different hues. Available colors include yellow, orange, white, or rosy pink, with reddish purple petal undersides and (often) dark blossom centers. Among seed-grown kinds are Carnival, with silver leaves and flowers in many colors; Chansonette, an early bloomer with round, medium-size blossoms on compact plants; and Daybreak, with low-growing, spreading plants bearing flowers in orange, bronze, yellow, yellow striped with red, and mixed colors. Harlequin has eyed and banded blooms in many colors. Mini-Star is compact and floriferous; named selections include 'Mini-Star Yellow' and 'Mini-Star Tangerine'. Sundance produces especially large (to 5-in.-wide) striped and banded flowers; Sunshine Giants produce big, multicolored flowers and gray leaves.

Selections of special merit are 'Aztec Queen' (multicolored), 'Burgundy', 'Copper King', and 'Fiesta Red'. All are best used in small-scale plantings, though the last is sturdy enough for large areas. 'Moonglow' is a double-flowered bright yellow of unusual vigor; its blossoms, unlike most, stay open even on overcast, dull days.

Trailing gazanias (derived from *G. rigens leucolaena*, formerly sold as *G. uniflora* or *G. leucolaena*) grow about as tall as clumping ones but spread rapidly by long, trailing stems. Foliage is a handsome silvery gray; flowers are yellow, white, orange, or bronze. Larger-flowered kinds are 'Sunburst' (orange with black eye) and 'Sunglow' (yellow). 'Sunrise Yellow', also in larger-flowered group, has black-eyed yellow blooms; leaves are green. Hybrid trailing plants are superior to older kinds in length of bloom and resistance to dieback. Use trailing gazanias on banks; or grow them at the top of a wall and allow them to trail over. Attractive in hanging baskets.

G. linearis 'Colorado Gold'. Unlike other gazanias, this is a hardy perennial in much of the South. Grows to 4 in. high and 15 in. wide. Strap-shaped leaves are dark green above, woolly white underneath. Bright yellow flowers to 3 in. wide bloom all summer. Self-sows. Full sun or partial shade.

GEIGER TREE. See CORDIA sebestena

GELSEMIUM

JESSAMINE

Loganiaceae

EVERGREEN VINES

⚡ MS, LS, CS ⊞ 9–4

☼ ◐ FULL SUN OR PARTIAL SHADE

◑ ◕ WATER NEEDS VARY BY SPECIES

⬧ ALL PARTS ARE POISONOUS IF INGESTED

Gelsemium sempervirens

These fast-growing, twining vines are beloved for their showy yellow flowers. They'll quickly cover a lamppost, trellis, or arbor, but their thin, twining stems won't damage the support. May be semievergreen in the Middle South. Deer usually leave them alone.

G. rankinii. SWAMP JESSAMINE. Native to swamps from North Carolina to Florida and Louisiana. To 20 ft. Foliage is similar to that of *G. sempervirens*. Bright yellow, scentless, inch-wide flowers bloom in both spring and fall, and they appear sporadically all winter in the Coastal South. Prefers regular to ample water; tolerates boggy soil. 'Winter Purple' offers purple fall and winter foliage.

G. sempervirens. CAROLINA JESSAMINE, YELLOW JESSAMINE. One of the South's most popular native vines and the state flower of South Carolina. Grows quickly to 20 ft. or more. Pairs of light green, shiny, 1- to 4-in.-long leaves clothe long, streamerlike branches. Fragrant, tubular, 1½-in.-long flowers bloom in late winter and early spring. 'Pride of Augusta' ('Plena') has double flowers. 'Woodlander's Light Yellow' has large blooms in creamy yellow.

Prefers fertile soil but adapts to almost any well-drained soil. Needs regular water in youth but is very drought tolerant once established. Blooms better in sun but tolerates partial shade. Often seen scrambling companionably through tree branches in the wild. In gardens, it's a favorite choice for climbing over mailboxes; also excellent for training above doorways and bay windows, along fences and walls. May be used as a ground cover on banks; keep trimmed to 3 ft. high. Sometimes gets too heavy on top and bare around the base; if this happens, cut back severely after bloom.

GENISTA

BROOM, WOADWAXEN

Fabaceae (Leguminosae)

DECIDUOUS AND EVERGREEN SHRUBS

⚡ US, MS, LS

☼ FULL SUN

◔ ◑ LITTLE TO MODERATE WATER

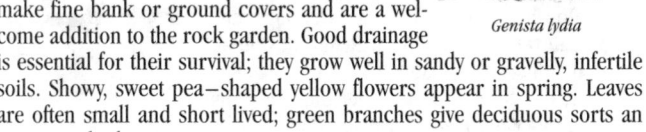

Genista lydia

Related to *Cytisus* but not as well known, these small, low-growing, twiggy shrubs make fine bank or ground covers and are a welcome addition to the rock garden. Good drainage is essential for their survival; they grow well in sandy or gravelly, infertile soils. Showy, sweet pea–shaped yellow flowers appear in spring. Leaves are often small and short lived; green branches give deciduous sorts an evergreen look.

G. lydia. Evergreen; nearly leafless. Heat zones 9–3. Often erroneously sold as *Cytisus lydia*. Grows to 2 ft. tall and 3 ft. wide; makes a good ground cover. Profuse show of blossoms at tips of shoots in late spring. Sets few seeds.

G. pilosa. SILKYLEAF WOADWAXEN. Deciduous. Heat zones 9–3. Fairly fast-growing prostrate shrub, ultimately to 1–1½ ft. tall with 7-ft. spread. Intricately branched gray-green twigs; roundish, ¼- to ½-in.-long leaves. Blooms in spring. 'Vancouver Gold' is a good selection.

G. tinctoria. DYER'S GREENWEED, WOADWAXEN. Deciduous. Heat zones 8–1. To 6 ft. tall and wide, with undivided leaves to 2 in. long. Upright flower spikes in late spring or early summer. 'Royal Gold' is a compact selection 2 ft. tall and wide.

GENTIANA

GENTIAN

Gentianaceae

PERENNIALS

⚡ US, MS, LS

◐ PARTIAL SHADE

◑ ◕ WATER NEEDS VARY BY SPECIES

Gentiana andrewsii

Offering some of the richest blues in the garden, these delightful, refined plants are considered by many to be difficult customers—and some of the rock-garden types are indeed pretty finicky. All of the species listed here, however, are easy to grow if planted in moist, acid soil enriched with plenty of organic matter. They are best suited to the Upper and Middle South and the higher elevations of the Appalachians, Blue Ridge Mountains, and Ozarks, but they can also be grown as far south as Mississippi and Alabama, particularly if planted in a cool, moist part of the garden. Do not disturb plants once they're established.

G. andrewsii. BOTTLE GENTIAN. Heat zones 8–1. A legendary wildflower of the eastern U.S. To 2 ft. tall and less than half as wide, with erect, unbranched stems set with paired dark green, 2- to 3-in.-long leaves. Clusters of 2-in.-long, deep blue flowers appear atop the plant in autumn. Blossoms never open completely, so they have a distinctive bottle shape. Often the last wildflower to bloom in fall. Does well in soil that is constantly moist or even boggy; perfect along the edge of a stream or pond. A white-flowering form is available.

G. asclepiadea. WILLOW GENTIAN. Heat zones 9–6. Native to Europe and western Asia. Forms a clump of arching stems to 2 ft. tall, 1½ ft. wide. Dark green, 2- to 3-in.-long leaves. Blooms in late summer and early fall, with deep blue blossoms appearing singly or in twos or threes in joints of upper leaves; flowers are 1½ in. wide and open into a star shape. Give regular water and well-drained soil. 'Rosea' has pink blooms.

G. clausa. CLOSED GENTIAN. Heat zones 8–1. Native to eastern U.S. Very similar to *G. andrewsii*, but the flowers are slightly larger and have white showing around the edges of the petals. Give same conditions as *G. andrewsii*.

G. saponaria. SOAPWORT GENTIAN. Heat zones 8–1. Native to eastern and midwestern U.S. Slender, erect stems to 2 ft. tall, with medium green, broadly lance-shaped leaves to 3½ in. long. Clusters of light blue, closed, cigar-shaped flowers to 1½ in. long appear in fall. Does well with regular to ample water; best in moist, rich, well-drained soil but tolerates boggy conditions.

G. septemfida. SUMMER GENTIAN. Heat zones 8–6. From Caucasus, Turkey, and Iran to central Asia. Arching or sprawling stems 9–18 in. long form a spreading mass about 8 in. high, 1 ft. wide. Medium green, oval leaves to 1½ in. long. Clusters of 2-in., dark blue flowers in late summer. Easy to grow if given regular water and rich, well-drained soil. Good choice in rock gardens; tolerates a bit more sun than other species listed. *G. s. lagodechiana*, the form commonly sold, is similar but has more widely spaced flowers.

Gentianaceae. The gentian family includes annuals and perennials from many parts of the world. Many plants in this family have blue or purple flowers, including gentian (*Gentiana*), Persian violet (*Exacum*), and lisianthus (*Eustoma*).

Geraniaceae. The cranesbill family of annuals and perennials (the latter sometimes shrubby) includes true geranium as well as *Pelargonium*.

FOR INFORMATION ON SELECTING PLANTS

PLEASE SEE PAGES 39–144

GERANIUM

CRANESBILL
Geraniaceae
PERENNIALS
US, MS, LS
AFTERNOON SHADE
REGULAR WATER

Geranium phaeum
'Samobor'

The common indoor/outdoor plant that most people know as geranium is, botanically, *Pelargonium*. Considered here are true geraniums, which are hardy plants. Many types bloom over a fairly long period, bearing flowers that are attractive, though not as showy as those of *Pelargonium*. Carried singly or in clusters of two or three, flowers have five overlapping petals that look alike. (*Pelargonium* blossoms also have five petals, but two point in one direction, the other three in the opposite direction.) Colors include rose, blue, and purple; a few are pure pink or white. The beaklike fruit that follows the flowers accounts for the common name "cranesbill." Leaves are roundish or kidney shaped, with lobed or deeply cut edges; plants may be upright or trailing. Good in perennial borders; some are useful as small-scale ground covers.

Give afternoon shade. All of the species listed here appreciate moist, well-drained soil. Clumps of most types can be left in place for many years before they decline due to crowding; at that point, divide clumps in early spring. Increase plantings by transplanting rooted portions from a clump's edge. Most types bloom heavily in spring and early summer, then go dormant when the weather gets hot in July and August. The longest bloom period occurs in Upper South and southern Midwest. Resistant to damage by browsing deer.

G. 'Ann Folkard'. Heat zones 9–3. Mounding, billowing plant (1 ft. high, to 5 ft. wide) with chartreuse leaves that age to light green. Saucer-shaped, 1½-in.-wide blossoms are rich magenta purple suffused with pink and blue, centered and veined in black. Blooms from June through August. Effective planted at edge of patio and sprawling onto it.

G. 'Brookside'. Heat zones 8–1. Hybrid developed from *G. pratense*. To 2½ ft. tall and wide, with deeply serrated leaves. Covered in late spring with rich blue, bowl-shaped flowers to 2 in. across. Somewhat similar to *G.* 'Johnson's Blue' but easier to grow.

G. ×cantabrigiense. Heat zones 8–2. Excellent ground cover, 6–8 in. high, spreading slowly but widely. Dark green leaves 1½–2½ in. wide, deeply cut with multiple lobes. 'Cambridge' has bright bluish pink flowers, ¾–1 in. wide. The blooms of 'Biokovo' are white blushed pale pink, and slightly larger.

G. cinereum. Heat zones 9–5. From the Pyrenees. Grows to 6 in. tall, much wider, with deeply cut, soft gray-green leaves. Inch-wide pink flowers with darker veining appear in late spring and summer. 'Ballerina' has lilac-pink flowers with purple veining; blooms over a long summer season. 'Laurence Flatman' has slightly larger flowers of a deeper color. Variety *G. c. subcaulescens* (*G. subcaulescens*) has darker green leaves and deep purplish red flowers with black centers.

Geranium cinereum
'Ballerina'

G. dalmaticum. Heat zones 7–5. From the Balkans. Dwarf (6-in.) plant with glossy, 1½-in., finely cut leaves and bright pink, inch-wide flowers in spring. Spreads slowly to make a 2-ft.-wide mat; useful in rock gardens.

G. endressii. Heat zones 8–5. From southern Europe to southwest Asia. Bushy plant to 1–1½ ft. tall, spreading to 2 ft. across. Leaves are 2–3 in. wide, deeply cut into five lobes. Rose pink flowers to about 1 in. across.

G. himalayense (G. grandiflorum). Heat zones 7–1. Wiry, branching stems form a clump to 1–2 ft. high, spreading wider. Roundish, long-stalked, five-lobed leaves to 1¾ in. across. Clustered, 1½- to 2-in.-wide

flowers are lilac with purple veins and a red-purple eye. 'Plenum' ('Birch Double') has double flowers in a somewhat lighter shade.

G. 'Johnson's Blue'. Heat zones 8–1. Hybrid resembling its *G. himalayense* parent, but with more finely divided leaves and blue-violet, 2-in.-wide flowers.

G. macrorrhizum. Heat zones 8–1. From southern Europe. To 8–10 in. high, spreading by underground rootstocks and fleshy rhizomes that root on soil surface. Inch-wide magenta flowers in spring; fragrant, five- to seven-lobed, 4- to 8-in.-wide leaves that take on attractive tints in autumn. Good ground cover for small areas, though it can overwhelm delicate smaller plants. Selections include deep reddish purple 'Bevan's Variety'; pink 'Spessart'; 'Ingwersen's Variety', with soft bluish pink blossoms over a long season; and 'Album', bearing white flowers with pink sepals and stamens.

G. maculatum. WILD GERANIUM, WILD CRANESBILL. Heat zones 8–1. Native to eastern North America; the only commonly cultivated native cranesbill. To 2 ft. tall and somewhat narrower, with deeply lobed leaves and an abundance of lilac-pink, 1- to 1½-in.-wide flowers in spring. 'Album' has white blooms.

G. ×oxonianum. Heat zones 8–1. Among the superior selections is 'Claridge Druce', which forms a vigorous clump 2–3 ft. tall, 3 ft. wide. Rounded, 3- to 4-in. leaves are deeply cut into broad, toothed lobes. Funnel-shaped, broad-petaled, 1½- to 1¾-in., cool pink flowers with purplish veins bloom late spring to summer. Good large-scale ground cover but can overwhelm adjacent plants. Self-sows profusely; seedlings resemble parent, but blossoms often have narrower petals. 'Wargrave Pink' is similar in habit but a little less vigorous, with glossy warm pink blossoms that resemble those of *G. endressii*.

G. phaeum. MOURNING WIDOW, DUSKY CRANESBILL. Heat zones 8–1. This species is a shade-loving native of southern and central European mountains. Grows to 2 ft. high, 1½ ft. wide. Leaves are basal, 3–4 in. across, shallowly cut into seven to nine tooth-edged lobes, often with brown markings. Bears clusters of dusky purple or maroon, ¾- to 1-in. blossoms in May and June. 'Lily Lovell' has purplish maroon blooms with a white eye. 'Samobor' has maroon flowers and leaves heavily marked with maroon.

G. platypetalum. Heat zones 8–1. From Turkey and the Caucasus. Clump 1½ ft. high and wide with rounded, quilted, 4- to 8-in.-wide leaves, shallowly cut into seven to nine scalloped lobes. Saucer-shaped, 1½- to 1¾-in. flowers with notched petals are deep violet blue with paler center and dark veins. Late spring bloomer.

G. pratense. MEADOW CRANESBILL. Heat zones 8–1. Native from Ireland to Siberia and Japan. Forms a clump 1½–2 ft. tall, 2–3 ft. wide. Hairy, 3- to 6-in. leaves on upright stalks are deeply cut into seven narrow, pointed, divided lobes. Flowers about 1 in. wide, typically blue with reddish veins. Self-sows profusely; cut to ground when flowers fade to prevent seedlings and encourage rebloom. 'Midnight Reiter' has plum-colored foliage that maintains its hue through summer; the flowers are lavender blue. 'Plenum Violaceum' ('Flore Pleno') has fully double, deep

Geranium pratense

violet-blue blossoms. 'Mrs. Kendall Clark' has pale blue flowers with lighter veins. 'Striatum' has white blossoms irregularly splashed, streaked, or spotted with violet blue.

WHICH IS REALLY A GERANIUM? *When gardeners use the word "geranium," they may be talking about ivy geraniums, fancy-leafed types, common geraniums, or scented types—all of which, botanically speaking, are species of the genus Pelargonium. Botanists, however, reserve the name "geranium" for plants in the genus Geranium; these are typically hardy perennials bearing flowers that have five identical-looking overlapping petals. For more about Pelargonium, see that entry.* ❖

G. sanguineum. BLOODY CRANESBILL. Heat zones 8–1. Native from western Europe to the Caucasus and Turkey. Grows 1½ ft. high, with trailing stems spreading to 2 ft. Roundish, 1- to 2½-in.-wide dark green leaves with five to seven lobes; turn blood red in fall. Deep purple to almost crimson flowers, 1½ in. wide, bloom from late spring well into summer. 'Album' is somewhat taller than the species and has white flowers. Other 1- to 1½-ft. selections include 'John Elsley', pink with deeper pink veins; 'Max Frei', reddish purple; 'New Hampshire', deep purple; and 'Vision', reddish purple.

The variety *G. s. striatum* (*G. s.* 'Prostratum', *G. lancastriense*) is a dwarf form—lower and more compact and an excellent choice for rock garden or foreground. It has light pink flowers heavily veined with red (its seedlings may vary somewhat).

G. sylvaticum. Heat zones 8–1. Native from Ireland to Siberia, south to Turkey. To 2½ ft. tall and wide. Leaves are deeply lobed and toothed; inch-wide flowers range in color from bluish to reddish purple.

G. wallichianum. Heat zones 8–1. Native to the Himalayas. Grows to 1 ft. tall and 3 ft. wide, with marbled, wrinkled, tooth-edged leaves. Lilac, 1- to 1½-in. flowers with a white eye. 'Buxton's Variety' has pure blue flowers with a large white eye.

GERBERA jamesonii

GERBERA DAISY, TRANSVAAL DAISY

Asteraceae (Compositae)

PERENNIAL IN COASTAL AND TROPICAL SOUTH; ANNUAL ELSEWHERE

✓ US, MS, LS, CS, TS **H** 12–6

☼ ◐ FULL SUN OR PARTIAL SHADE

◖ REGULAR WATER

Gerbera jamesonii

For stunning, vibrant color, it's hard to beat this South African native. Slim yet sturdy stems, up to 1½ ft. tall, emerge from clumps of tongue-shaped, lobed leaves. The 4- to 5-in. daisies, borne one to a stem, fairly glow in colors of red, orange, coral, pink, yellow, and cream. The basic form features a single ring of petal-like rays surrounding a prominent central disk. Hybrid forms may display two rows of long rays or an outer ring of long rays and an inner ring of short, tufted ones; or they may be fully double with a fluffy look.

Many strains are available, including types with dark centers and dwarfs just 6 in. tall. Where gerberas are perennial, they can bloom at almost any time of year, unless frost kills them to the ground. In this case, they'll sprout from underground stems in spring and begin blooming shortly afterward. Outside the Coastal and Tropical South, they're traditionally treated as annuals, though plants from a very hardy strain called Wolfpack Country, bred at North Carolina State University, will overwinter in the Middle and Lower South and bloom continuously from spring until frost.

Gerberas need excellent drainage; if your soil drains poorly, plant in raised beds. Space about 2 ft. apart, with root crowns at least ½ in. above soil level. Feed monthly with a balanced liquid fertilizer. Pick off old, yellow leaves. Water deeply and let soil become nearly dry before watering again. Divide (in late winter) only when clump is crowded and flowering declines. When cutting flowers for arrangements, slit the bottom inch of stem before placing in water.

Most people start with transplants, but you can also grow gerberas from seed. Seed must be fresh to germinate well. Sow in moist potting soil; keep air temperature at about 70°F. Water carefully. Seed may take several weeks to sprout. Seedlings flower in 4 to 6 months.

GERMAN CATCHFLY. See LYCHNIS viscaria

GERMANDER. See TEUCRIUM

GERMAN STATICE. See GONIOLIMON tataricum

Gesneriaceae. The gesneriads are perennials, usually tropical or subtropical, grown for attractive flowers or foliage. Although a few are rock garden perennials, most are grown as houseplants. African violet (*Saintpaulia*) and gloxinia (*Sinningia*) are examples.

GEUM

AVENS

Rosaceae

PERENNIALS

✓ US, MS

☼ ◐ FULL SUN OR PARTIAL SHADE

◖ REGULAR WATER, EXCEPT AS NOTED

Geum chiloense

This group of plants combines handsome foliage with showy flowers. Double, semidouble, or single blossoms in red, orange, pink, or yellow appear throughout the summer if plants are deadheaded regularly; they make good cut flowers. Leaves of most are divided into many leaflets, often with scalloped or toothed margins. Geums are not suited to extended summer heat. They'll grow in the Middle South, but they prefer the Upper South, at higher elevations of the Appalachians, Blue Ridge Mountains, and Ozarks. Soil should be consistently moist and, except for *G. rivale*, well drained. Start from seed sown in early spring or set out transplants. Divide established plants in fall or spring.

G. chiloense. CHILEAN AVENS. Heat zones 9–3. Best-known species. Native to Chile. Mounding foliage clump to 15 in. high, 2 ft. wide. Leafy, branched flowering stems reach about 2 ft. high, topped by 1½-in.-wide flowers. Selections include semidouble orange 'Dolly North', semidouble orange-scarlet 'Fire Opal', double yellow 'Lady Stratheden', double scarlet 'Mrs. J. Bradshaw', and semidouble soft yellow 'Prinses Juliana' ('Princess Juliana').

G. coccineum. Heat zones 8–5. Native to the Balkans, Asia Minor. To 12–20 in. tall and wide, with coarsely divided foliage and brick red, 1½-in. flowers. Two selections to 1 ft. tall and wide are 'Borisii', with orange-red flowers, and 'Werner Arends', with bright orange blooms. 'Red Wings', to 28 in. tall and wide, has semidouble scarlet flowers.

G. 'Georgenberg'. Heat zones 7–1. Hybrid to 12–15 in. tall and wide, with apricot blossoms about 1½ in. across.

G. rivale. WATER AVENS, INDIAN CHOCOLATE. Heat zones 7–1. Native to North America and Eurasia. Grows to 1 ft. tall and wide, bearing slightly nodding, ivory to pink, ¾-in. flowers. Needs a cool site with boggy soil. Boiled roots of plant yield a liquid that tastes faintly like chocolate. 'Leonard's Variety' has double coppery rose flowers, 'Lionel Cox' light yellow blooms.

G. 'Starker's Magnificum'. Heat zones 9–5. Hybrid to 1½ ft. tall and wide, with double tangerine orange, 1-in. flowers.

G. triflorum. PRAIRIE SMOKE. Heat zones 6–1. Native to the prairies and mountains of North America. Foot-wide, leafy mound produces stems to 20 in. tall, each bearing clusters of nodding maroon flowers to 1½ in. wide. Entire plant is often furry. Seeds have long, upright, feathery gray "tails" resembling wisps of smoke.

GIANT DAISY. See CHRYSANTHEMUM serotinum

GIANT MEXICAN LEMON HYSSOP. See AGASTACHE mexicana

GIANT PLUME. See CURCUMA elata

GIANT REED. See ARUNDO donax

FOR GROWING SYMBOL EXPLANATIONS

PLEASE SEE PAGE 145

GILLENIA trifoliata

BOWMAN'S ROOT, INDIAN PHYSIC

Rosaceae

PERENNIAL

✂ US, MS, LS ⊞ 9–1

◑ PARTIAL SHADE

💧 REGULAR WATER

Gillenia trifoliata

Native to eastern North America, this charming woodland wildflower is found from southern Ontario south to Georgia and Alabama. Grows 2–3 ft. tall and 2 ft. wide, with reddish stems and bronzy green, 2- to 4-in.-long leaves divided into three narrow, toothed leaflets; foliage turns yellow, orange, and red in fall. Panicles of starlike, white or pinkish, 1½-in.-wide flowers seem to float above the leaves in late spring and early summer. Red sepals remain after the petals drop. Bark from the thick root has many uses in traditional medicine. Plant thrives in moist, well-drained soil loaded with organic matter; a good companion for hostas, ferns, foamflower (*Tiarella*), false solomon's seal (*Polygonatum*), blue phlox.

GINGER, COMMON. See ZINGIBER officinale

GINGER, WILD. See ASARUM

GINGER LILY. See COSTUS, HEDYCHIUM

GINKGO biloba

MAIDENHAIR TREE

Ginkgoaceae

DECIDUOUS TREE

✂ US, MS, LS, CS ⊞ 9–3

☼ FULL SUN

◐💧 MODERATE TO REGULAR WATER

Ginkgo biloba

Ancient survivor from prehistoric times (200 million years ago), when it grew worldwide; now native only to two small areas in China. Related to conifers but differs in having broad (1- to 4-in.-wide), fan-shaped leaves rather than needlelike foliage. In shape and veining, leaves resemble leaflets of maidenhair fern, hence the tree's common name. Attractive in any season—especially in fall, when the leathery light green leaves suddenly turn gold (they practically glow when backlit by the sun). Leaves hang on for a time, then drop quickly and cleanly to make a golden carpet where they fall.

Can grow to 70–80 ft. tall, but most mature trees are 50–60 ft. May be gawky in youth, but becomes graceful and well proportioned with age—narrow to spreading or even umbrella shaped. Typical width is no more than one-half to two-thirds height. Usually grows slowly, about 1 ft. a year, but under ideal conditions can grow up to 3 ft. a year. Seeds are considered a delicacy in China and Japan, and an extract made from ginkgo is said to improve brain function, especially memory, by increasing blood flow. Not favored by browsing deer.

Plant male trees (grafted or grown from cuttings of male plants); female trees produce messy, fleshy, ill-smelling fruit in quantity. Named selections listed below are male. Use as street tree or lawn tree. Plant in deep, loose, well-drained soil. Be sure nursery plants are not root-bound. Young growth may be brittle, but wood becomes strong with age. In general, ginkgos are not bothered by insects or diseases, and they're very tolerant of air pollution, heat, and acid or alkaline conditions. Water young trees regularly until they reach about 15 ft. tall, then cut back to occasional irrigation. On young trees, cut back any awkward branches and vertical shoots growing parallel to central leader. Older trees need minimal pruning; just remove weak, broken, or dead branches.

'Akigane'. Large, broadly symmetrical tree with bright yellow fall color. To 50 ft. tall, 30 ft. wide.

'Autumn Gold'. Upright to 50 ft., eventually rather broad and spreading to about 30 ft.

'Fairmount'. Fast-growing, pyramidal form similar to 'Princeton Sentry'. To 60 ft. tall, 30 ft. wide.

'Jade Butterflies'. Vase-shaped, shrubby form growing only about 10 ft. tall in 10 years. Dark green leaves have a deep V-shape cut in the center of the leaf, giving the impression of a butterfly.

'Princeton Sentry'. Erect to 60 ft. high; 25-ft. spread at base, tapering toward top.

'Saratoga'. Similar to 'Autumn Gold', with a distinct central leader. To 40 ft. tall, 30 ft. wide.

'Shangri-La'. Pyramidal shape; to 45 ft. tall, 25 ft. wide.

'Windover Gold'. Resembles 'Shangri-La' in habit and size.

GLADIOLUS

Iridaceae

PERENNIALS FROM CORMS

✂ MS, LS, CS ⊞ 9–1, EXCEPT AS NOTED; OR DIG AND STORE

☼ FULL SUN

💧 REGULAR WATER DURING GROWTH AND BLOOM

Gladiolus callianthus

All have sword-shaped leaves and tubular, often flaring or ruffled blossoms borne in unbranched or branching, usually one-sided spikes. Extremely wide color range. Bloom from spring to fall, depending on kind and time of planting. Superb cut flowers. Good in borders or beds behind mounding plants that cover lower parts of stems, or in large containers with low annuals at base. Thrips are a likely pest.

Plant in rich, sandy soil. Set corms about four times deeper than their height (plant somewhat shallower in heavy soils). Space big corms 6 in. apart, smaller ones 4 in. apart. Corms can generally be left in the ground from year to year in Middle, Lower, and Coastal South. In the Upper South, dig soon after first frost in autumn. Dry corms on a flat surface in a dark, dry area for 2 to 3 weeks; then store over winter in a single layer in flats or ventilated trays in a cool place (40–50°F). In the Tropical South, refrigerate corms for a month before planting, then treat as annuals and discard after plant has finished blooming.

Baby gladiolus. Hybrid race resulting from crossing of several species. (Sometimes referred to as *Gladiolus nanus,* a name of no botanical standing.) Flaring, 2½- to 3¼-in. flowers in short, loose spikes on 1½-ft. stems. Flowers are white, pink, red, or lilac; they may be solid or blotched with contrasting color. When left in the ground, will form large clumps in border or among shrubs. Plant in fall or early spring for late spring bloom.

Butterfly gladiolus. See Primulinus and butterfly hybrids

G. callianthus (Acidanthera bicolor). ABYSSINIAN SWORD LILY. Native to Africa. Stems grow 2–3 ft. tall, bearing two to ten fragrant, creamy white flowers marked chocolate brown on lower segments. Each blossom is 2–3 in. wide and 4–5 in. long. Excellent cut flowers. Plant in spring for bloom in late summer and fall. 'Murielae' is taller, with purple-crimson blotches.

G. communis byzantinus (G. byzantinum). HARDY GLADIOLUS, BYZANTINE GLADIOLUS. Mainly maroon, sometimes reddish or coppery, 1- to 3-in. flowers in groups of 6 to 12 on 2- to 3-ft. stems. Narrower leaves than garden gladiolus. Plant in early spring for summer bloom. An old Southern favorite.

Primulinus and butterfly hybrids. Heat zones 12–7. These summer bloomers derive in

Butterfly Hybrid Gladiolus

part from *G. dalenii* (formerly *G. primulinus*), an African species with hooded (rather than funnel-shaped), primrose yellow flowers. Named selections grow 3–4 ft. tall, each spike carrying up to 18 widely spaced, somewhat hooded blossoms in a wide range of colors. Group known as butterfly gladiolus has 2- to 3-ft. stems bearing more closely spaced flowers; distinct throat markings or blotches of contrasting color give butterfly appearance. Plant in early spring.

Summer-flowering grandiflora hybrids. GARDEN GLADIOLUS. Usually dug and stored even in Zones MS, LS, CS. Commonly grown garden gladiolus are a complex group of hybrids derived by variation and hybridization from several species. These are the best-known gladiolus, with the widest color range—white, cream, buff, yellow, orange, apricot, salmon, red shades, rose, lavender, purple, smoky shades, even green shades. Individual blooms may be as large as 8 in. across. Stems are 4–5 ft. tall.

Grandiflora Hybrid Gladiolus

The newer types of garden gladiolus grow to about 5 ft. tall, have sturdier spikes bearing from 12 to 14 open flowers at one time. They are better garden plants than older types and stand upright without staking. Another group, called miniature gladiolus, grows 3 ft. tall, with spikes of 15 to 20 flowers, each 2½–3 in. wide; useful in garden beds and for cutting.

High-crowned corms, 1½–2 in. wide, are more productive than older, larger corms (2 in. wide or more). After soil has warmed in spring, plant at 1- to 2-week intervals for 4 to 6 weeks for progression of bloom. Corms bloom 65 to 100 days after planting. If soil is poor, mix in complete fertilizer or superphosphate (4 pounds per 100 sq. ft.) before planting; do not place fertilizer in direct contact with corms. Be sure to treat corms with bulb dust (insecticide-fungicide) before planting. When plants have five leaves, apply complete fertilizer 6 in. from plants and water it in thoroughly. For cut flowers, cut spikes when lowest buds begin to open, leaving a minimum of four leaves on plants to build up corms. If thrips cause whitish streaking on leaves, spray foliage with insecticidal soap or horticultural oil.

GLEDITSIA triacanthos

HONEY LOCUST

Fabaceae (Leguminosae)

DECIDUOUS TREE

✇ US, MS, LS 🌢 8–1

☼ FULL SUN

◐ ● MODERATE TO REGULAR WATER

Gleditsia triacanthos

Native to central and eastern North America. Fast growing, especially when young, with upright trunk and spreading, arching branches. To 35–70 ft. tall and 25–35 ft. wide. Bright green, fernlike leaves to 10 in. long are divided into many oval, ¾- to 1½-in.-long leaflets. Late to leaf out; leaves turn yellow and drop early in fall. Inconspicuous flowers are followed by broad, 1- to 1½-ft.-long pods filled with sweetish pulp and hard, roundish seeds.

Foliage casts filtered shade, allowing growth of lawn or other plants beneath. Small leaflets dry up and filter into grass, decreasing raking chores, but pods make a mess in autumn. Trunks and branches are formidably thorny. Honey locusts for the garden, however, are selections of *G. t. inermis*, thornless honey locust, with no thorns and few or no pods.

These trees are not good in narrow area between curb and sidewalk, since roots of old plants will heave paving. Stake until good basic branch pattern is established. Tolerant of acid or alkaline conditions, salt, drought,

cold, heat, wind. Do best in areas with sharply defined winters, hot summers. Prune out any wayward or crossing branches. Susceptible to many pests, several of which are prevalent in humid-summer regions: mimosa webworm (chews leaves), pod gall midge (deforms foliage), honey locust borer (attacks limbs and trunks).

Popular garden selections include the following.

'Halka'. Fast growing; forms sturdy trunk early. Strong horizontal branching pattern; oval shape. To 50 ft.

'Imperial'. Spreading, symmetrical tree to about 35 ft. More densely foliaged than other forms; gives heavier shade.

'Moraine'. MORAINE LOCUST. Best-known selection. Fast-growing (to 50 ft. high), spreading tree with branches angled upward, then outward. Yellow fall color. Subject to wind breakage. Has greater resistance to webworms than do some of the newer selections.

'Rubylace'. Deep red new growth, fading to bronzed green by midsummer. Subject to wind breakage, webworm attack.

'Shademaster'. More upright and faster growing than 'Moraine'—to 24 ft. tall, 16 ft. wide in 6 years.

'Skyline'. Pyramidal and symmetrical, growing to 45 ft. tall. Bright golden fall color.

'Sunburst'. Golden yellow new leaves are showy against deep green background. Summer color is better in Upper and Middle South. Defoliates early in response to temperature changes, drought. Prone to wind breakage. Very susceptible to foliage pests. To 40 ft. tall.

'Trueshade'. To 40 ft. tall, with rounded form. Light green foliage.

GLOBBA

DANCING GIRL GINGER

Zingiberaceae

PERENNIALS

✇ CS, TS 🌢 12–8; OR GROW IN POTS

◑ PARTIAL SHADE; BRIGHT INDIRECT LIGHT

● REGULAR WATER DURING GROWING SEASON

Globba globulifera

These small, delicate-flowered members of the ginger family are native to Southeast Asia. They grow upright to 1–3 ft. tall; leaves are lustrous green sheaths, and graceful, spidery flowers bloom in summer or fall among long, arching sprays of brightly colored bracts. Bulbils are often found inside the bracts and if planted promptly will produce new plants. Space 1½ ft. apart. Easy to grow if fertilized and kept moist during the growing season and fed with a balanced controlled-release fertilizer in early spring and again in midsummer. In cold-winter areas, bring indoors before frost; mist to provide humidity if necessary, and stop watering during the winter to give plant a period of dormancy. Resume watering gradually in spring. Most make good cut flowers.

G. atrosanguinea. Produces 2½-in. panicles of deep red bracts and yellow flowers.

G. globulifera. PURPLE GLOBE GINGER. Has short panicles of purple bracts and yellow flowers.

G. marantina (G. schomburgkii). YELLOW DANCING GIRLS. Produces 3-in. panicles of light green-yellow bracts and yellow flowers with red spots.

G. winitii. Has 6-in. panicles of rosy purple bracts and bright yellow flowers. Particularly delicate and long blooming. 'Mauve Dancing Girl' has lavender purple bracts and golden yellow flowers; panicles may reach 8–10 in. long. Foliage of 'Red Leaf' has maroon undersides. 'White Dragon' has pure white bracts and small yellow flowers.

GLOBE AMARANTH. See GOMPHRENA

FOR INFORMATION ON YOUR CLIMATE ZONES

PLEASE SEE PAGES 28–38

GLOBEFLOWER. See TROLLIUS

GLOBE MALLOW. See SPHAERALCEA

GLOBE THISTLE. See ECHINOPS

GLORIOSA DAISY. See RUDBECKIA hirta

GLORIOSA superba 'Rothschildiana' (G. rothschildiana)

GLORY LILY, CLIMBING LILY

Liliaceae

PERENNIAL FROM TUBER

✿ TS H 12–10; OR DIG AND STORE; OR GROW IN POTS

☼ ◑ LIGHT SHADE IN HOTTEST CLIMATES

● REGULAR WATER DURING GROWTH AND BLOOM

☢ ALL PARTS ARE POISONOUS IF INGESTED

Gloriosa superba 'Rothschildiana'

Lily relative native to tropical Africa and Asia. A tendril at the tip of each tapering, lance-shaped, 5- to 7-in. leaf wraps around any handy support, helping plant climb to 6 ft. In summer, top part of plant bears flashy 4-in. blossoms, each with six recurved, wavy-edged segments in brilliant red banded with yellow.

Can survive outdoors all year in completely frost-free areas, but even there is best grown in pots. For appearance of permanent planting, sink containers into garden bed. Choose pots at least 8 in. in diameter; fill with rich, loose soil mix. Set in tubers horizontally, one to a container, about 4 in. deep. Start indoors or in greenhouse in winter; set out after frosts. Give climbing stems support from trellis, wires, string, or even loose-growing shrubs. Feed with a balanced liquid fertilizer every 3 weeks. Withhold water and fertilizer when leaves begin to yellow and die back in fall. Sever dead stems and move pots to dry, cool spot for winter. In late winter, knock tubers out of containers; repot in fresh soil mix. Or dig tubers from pots in fall and store.

GLORYBOWER. See CLERODENDRUM

GLORY-OF-THE-SNOW. See CHIONODOXA

GLOXINIA. See SINNINGIA speciosa

GLOXINIA sylvatica

BOLIVIAN SUNSET

Gesneriaceae

PERENNIAL FROM RHIZOME

✿ CS, TS H 12–9; OR HOUSEPLANT

◑ PARTIAL SHADE; BRIGHT INDIRECT LIGHT

● MODERATE WATER

Gloxinia sylvatica

Hailing from Bolivia and Peru, this tender beauty is usually grown as a houseplant—though it is hardy enough to grow outdoors in the Coastal and Tropical South. A single stem rises to 1–2 ft., clothed in narrow, pointed dark green leaves to 6 in. long. From late summer into winter, slender stems rise from the upper leaf joints, bearing tubular, nodding flowers about 1 in. long. Blossoms are orange red with a golden interior and seem to glow from within.

Indoors, plant in regular potting mix and water only when soil is dry to the touch. Feed monthly with half-strength general-purpose liquid house-plant fertilizer during active growth. After bloom, stop fertilizing and reduce watering until spring. Outdoors, grow in fairly moist, humus-rich soil in dappled shade or morning sun.

For other plants often called gloxinia, see *Sinningia*.

GOAT'S BEARD. See ARUNCUS

GOLD DUST PLANT. See AUCUBA japonica 'Variegata'

GOLDEN ASTER. See CHRYSOPSIS

GOLDEN BALL LEAD TREE. See LEUCAENA retusa

GOLDEN BRODIAEA. See TRITELEIA ixioides

GOLDENCHAIN TREE. See LABURNUM

GOLDEN DEWDROP. See DURANTA erecta

GOLDEN EARDROPS. See DICENTRA chrysantha

GOLDEN FLEECE. See THYMOPHYLLA tenuiloba

GOLDEN GARLIC. See ALLIUM moly

GOLDEN GLOBES. See LYSIMACHIA congestiflora

GOLDEN MARGUERITE. See ANTHEMIS tinctoria

GOLDENRAIN TREE. See KOELREUTERIA paniculata

GOLDEN RAY. See LIGULARIA

GOLDENROD. See SOLIDAGO

GOLDEN SEAL. See HYDRASTIS canadensis

GOLDEN SHOWER. See CASSIA fistula

GOLDEN STAR. See CHRYSOGONUM virginianum

GOLDEN TRUMPET. See ALLAMANDA cathartica

GOLDEN TRUMPET TREE. See TABEBUIA chrysotricha

GOLDEN WONDER SENNA. See SENNA splendida

GOLD FLOWER. See HYPERICUM ×moserianum

GOLD MEDALLION TREE. See CASSIA leptophylla

GOMPHRENA

GLOBE AMARANTH

Amaranthaceae

ANNUALS AND PERENNIALS GROWN AS ANNUALS

✿ US, MS, LS, CS, TS H 12–1

☼ ◑ FULL SUN OR PARTIAL SHADE

● MODERATE WATER

Gomphrena globosa

Stiffly branching plants to 1–2 ft. tall, 1 ft. wide, covered in summer and fall with rounded, papery, cloverlike flower heads ¾–1 in. wide. These are easy to dry, retaining color and shape for winter arrangements. Narrow, oval leaves are 2–4 in. long. Drought tolerant and easy to grow; rarely bothered by pests, including deer. It's easy to harvest seeds from the faded flowers and save them for planting next year; start indoors or sow in place after soil has warmed in spring.

G. globosa. Annual. From Central America. White, pink, lavender, or purple flower heads on 1- to 2-ft. stems. 'Strawberry Fields' has hot red, ½-in. blossoms on 2-ft. stems. Dwarf selections for use as edging or bed-ding plants include 9-in. 'Buddy' (purple) and 'Cissy' (white). All types can be planted closely in large containers—six to a shallow 10-in. pot—for a long-lasting living bouquet.

G. haageana. Perennial treated as annual. From southern U.S., Mexico. Heads of tightly clustered bright orange bracts resembling inch-wide pinecones are borne on 2-ft. stems. Tiny yellow flowers peek from the bracts. Often sold as 'Haageana Aurea' or orange gomphrena.

FOR INFORMATION ON SELECTING PLANTS
PLEASE SEE PAGES 39–144

GONIOLIMON tataricum
(Limonium tataricum)

GERMAN STATICE

Plumbaginaceae

PERENNIAL

✄ US, MS, LS, CS, TS H 12–1

☼ FULL SUN

◐ MODERATE WATER

Goniolimon tataricum

From southern Russia, Caucasus. Dense clumps of dark green, narrowly oval leaves grow from a woody rootstock. In summer, leafless flower stalks rise to 1½ ft., forking repeatedly to form a broad, domed cluster to 1½ ft. wide. Tiny flowers are light purplish to white. Entire inflorescence can be dried for winter arrangements. Plant withstands both cold and heat. Best where summers are hot and dry.

Goodeniaceae. Members of this small family of perennials and shrubs—principally from the Southern Hemisphere, most notably Australia—have irregularly lipped flowers. A commonly grown example is *Scaevola*.

GOOD LUCK PLANT. See OXALIS tetraphylla

GOOSE PLUM. See PRUNUS americana

GOPHER PLANT. See EUPHORBIA lathyris

GORDONIA lasianthus

LOBLOLLY BAY

Theaceae

EVERGREEN TREE

✄ MS, LS, CS, TS H 12–7

☼◐ FULL SUN OR LIGHT SHADE

◐◐ REGULAR TO AMPLE WATER

Gordonia lasianthus

Native to wet soils ("loblollies") of the Coastal Plain from Virginia to Louisiana. Narrow, erect, rather open-structured tree to 30–40 ft. tall and half as wide, with shiny, oval leaves 4–6 in. long. Attractive flowers up to 2½ in. wide bloom from midspring to midautumn; they look something like single white camellias and are enhanced by a big central brush of yellow stamens. Although wild trees grow in bogs, those in garden conditions need good drainage. They are sometimes transplanted from the wild (with the owner's permission, of course), but these transplants are difficult to grow. Easier to grow are container-grown plants from garden centers.

GOSSYPIUM tomentosum

COTTON

Malvaceae

ANNUAL

✄ US, MS, LS, CS, TS H 12–7

☼ FULL SUN

◐ REGULAR WATER

Gossypium tomentosum

No plant is more cloaked in Southern history and culture than cotton. Among the world's oldest cultivated plants, it was used for cloth making in Mexico as early as 5,000 B.C. Upland cotton, the type grown in the South, is native to Central America and the West Indies. First grown in the American colonies in 1607, it flourished in the South's warm, humid climate—and with Eli Whitney's invention of the cotton gin in 1793, the industry got a dramatic boost, as the new machine removed seeds from the fibers 50 times faster than a person could by hand.

Cotton is a shrubby plant 4–6 ft. tall, about half as wide. It belongs to the mallow family, a fact clearly evidenced by its foliage and flowers. Coarse dark green leaves are usually palmately lobed; attractive summer flowers to 3 in. long are white or yellowish, fading to pinkish purple. Blossoms are followed by prominent, sharp-edged seed capsules or "bolls" filled with seeds and cotton. White cotton is the cotton of commerce, but there are also other colors, including brown, green, yellow, and pink. Heirloom types, such as those noted below, are still grown and spun.

Cotton makes an interesting and historically relevant addition to the garden—and the fluffy bolls never fail to fascinate children. Include a few plants in your vegetable beds; they also make fine additions to a cottage planting. Plants thrive in hottest sites with regular water and well-drained soil. Cut branches of mature cotton are excellent for use in flower arrangements. Two favorite heirloom kinds are 'Erlene's Green', a green cotton from East Texas that turns yellowish green after the fibers are spun and washed, and 'Nankeen', a short-fiber brown cotton that grows well in poor, dry soil and has a long bloom cycle that lasts into fall.

G

GOURD

Cucurbitaceae

ANNUAL VINES

✄ US, MS, LS, CS, TS H 12–1

☼ FULL SUN

◐ REGULAR WATER

Many plants bear gourds. One of the most commonly planted is *Cucurbita pepo ovifera*, a yellow-flowered vine that produces small ornamental gourds in various shapes and sizes, in both solid colors and stripes; many of the

Gourd

little gourds you see in stores likely come from this plant. *Luffa cylindrica* (*L. aegyptiaca*), called loofah, dishcloth gourd, or vegetable sponge gourd, is another yellow-flowered plant; it bears cylindrical, 1- to 2-ft.-long fruits with a fibrous interior that, when dried, may be used as a sponge or cloth for scrubbing or bathing. *Lagenaria siceraria* (*L. vulgaris*), white-flowered gourd, produces fruits from 3 in. to 3 ft. long, in round, crooknecked, coiled, bottle, dumbbell, or spoon shapes. Dipper gourds and birdhouse gourds are favorites from this species.

All gourd vines grow fast and will reach 10–15 ft. Sow seeds when ground is warm; start indoors if growing season is short. In order to develop fruit by frost, gourds need all the summer heat they can get. If you plan to use the gourds for ornamental purposes, give vines the support of wire or a trellis to hold ripening fruits off ground. Set out transplants or thin seedlings to 2 ft. apart. You can harvest gourds when tendrils next to their stems are dead, but it's best to leave them on the vine as long as possible—until the gourds turn yellow or brown. They can even stay on the vine through frosts, but a heavy frost can discolor them. Cut each gourd with some stem attached so you can hang it up to dry slowly in a cool, airy spot. When thoroughly dry, preserve with coating of paste wax, lacquer, or shellac.

HOW TO MAKE A LOOFAH SPONGE. *Harvest the loofah gourds in late summer or fall. Those picked earlier will make softer sponges than ones picked later. Cure the gourds in a dry, warm location until the skin turns brown and papery. Slice off the ends and peel off the skin. Shake out the seeds and store them for planting next year. Soak the fibrous "sponges" in a solution consisting of 1 part bleach and 3 parts water for several hours to brighten their color, then soak for several hours in pure water to remove the bleach. Finally, air-dry the sponges and store in a mesh bag until you're ready to use them.* ❖

GOUT PLANT. See JATROPHA podagrica

GOUT WEED. See AEGOPODIUM podagraria

Gramineae. See Poaceae

GRAPE

Vitaceae

DECIDUOUS VINES

☀ ZONES VARY BY SELECTION

☼ FULL SUN

💧 MODERATE WATER

▶ SEE CHART PAGE 330

Grape

Grapes are valued for fruit, wine, shade, and fall color; they're among the few ornamental vines with bold, textured foliage; colorful edible fruit; and a dominant trunk and branch pattern for winter interest. A single grapevine can produce enough new growth every year to arch over a walk, roof an arbor, form a leafy wall, or provide an umbrella of shade over deck or terrace.

For good-quality fruit, choose a type that fits your climate, train it carefully, and prune it regularly.

There are several basic types of grapes. European grapes *(Vitis vinifera)* have tight skin, a high heat requirement, and cold tolerance to about 0°F. These are the market table grapes, such as 'Thompson Seedless'. The classic wine grapes, such as 'Cabernet', 'Chardonnay', and 'Pinot Noir', are also European in origin. Production of European wine grapes is well established in Texas, Virginia, Maryland, Missouri, and North Carolina.

American grapes are derived from *V. labrusca,* with some influence from other American native species and also often from *V. vinifera.* These are slipskin grapes of the 'Concord' type, which have a moderate summer heat requirement and tolerate temperatures well below 0°F. American grapes are used mainly for jelly, in unfermented grape juice, and as soft-drink flavoring; some wine, usually sweet, is also made from them. Most will not thrive in the Lower and Coastal South; there the grape of choice is the muscadine *(V. rotundifolia),* which bears large fruit in small clusters. Some muscadine selections are self-fertile, while others (females) require cross-pollination. (All other types of grapes are self-pollinating.)

Pierce's disease, caused by a bacterium spread by the sharpshooter insect, is lethal to European grapes and severely limits their cultivation in Florida and the Coastal South. They should not be planted south of a line that runs roughly from Raleigh, North Carolina, west through Atlanta, Birmingham, and Greenwood, Mississippi, to Shreveport, Louisiana. In Texas, Pierce's disease affects only the state's southeastern corner. Most muscadine grapes and some American grapes resist Pierce's disease.

European and American grapes may also suffer from the fungal diseases black rot, which causes fruit to rot on the vine, and downy mildew, resulting in cottony white patches on the leaf undersides and shoot dieback. Control both by applying a fixed-copper fungicide. Muscadines are much less susceptible to these two diseases.

In some areas, a regular spraying program may be necessary to protect vines and fruit from insects and/or diseases. Refer to the *Southern Living Garden Problem Solver* or contact your Cooperative Extension Office for specific instructions. Netting will protect fruit from birds.

Vines need regular applications of fertilizer to remain productive. Specific recommendations vary slightly among different parts of the South, so contact your Cooperative Extension Office to see whether additional nutrients are needed in your area. In general, however, you can begin fertilizing after the newly planted vines have been settled by a drenching rain. Before growth begins, apply ¼ cup of 10-10-10 fertilizer around each plant, keeping the fertilizer at least 6 in. away from the vine. Repeat every 6 weeks until mid-July. Two-year-old vines need double that amount of fertilizer applied at the same 6-week intervals and for the same duration. For mature vines, apply 2½ pounds of 10-10-10 fertilizer per plant in March. If growth is poor, an additional pound of the same fertilizer can be applied in May.

Once established, grapevines grow rampantly. If all you want is a leafy cover for an arbor or a sitting area, you need only train a strong vine up and over its support and thin out tangled growth each year. But most people plant grapes for fruit, even if they want shade as well. For good fruit production, you will need to follow more careful pruning procedures (see illustrations on facing page).

WHAT GRAPES NEED

SOIL: Deep, fertile, well-drained sandy loam is ideal, but plants adapt to many soil types.

AIR CIRCULATION: Free movement of air around plants is important. If you're on hilly terrain, it's better to plant on a slope than in a low-lying basin, where trapped air increases danger from frost and disease.

PRUNING: High-quality crop depends on initial training and dormant-season pruning (see facing page).

HARVESTING: Cut bunches from vines of American and European grapes in late summer or fall, when grapes are sweet and fully colored. Muscadine grapes can also be harvested cluster by cluster or collected in tarps as the crop fully matures.

Muscadine 'Carlos'

Grapes are produced in late summer and fall on stems that develop from 1-year-old wood—stems that formed the previous season. These stems have smooth bark; older ones have rough, shaggy bark. The purpose of pruning is to limit the amount of potential fruiting wood, ensuring that the plant doesn't produce too much fruit and that the fruit it does bear is of good quality.

The two most widely used methods are spur pruning and cane pruning; see chart for recommended pruning method for each selection. Either technique can be used for training grapes on arbors. Whichever method you choose, the initial steps—planting and creating a framework—are the same. Pruning should be done in winter or earliest spring, before the buds swell. (See facing page for planting and pruning details.)

GRAPEFRUIT. See CITRUS

GRAPE HYACINTH. See MUSCARI

GRAPE IVY. See CISSUS rhombifolia

GRAPTOPHYLLUM pictum

CARICATURE PLANT

Acanthaceae

EVERGREEN SHRUB

☀ TS ❄ 12–10; OR INDOORS

☼ LIGHT SHADE; BRIGHT FILTERED LIGHT

💧 REGULAR WATER

Graptophyllum pictum 'Tricolor'

This frost-tender native of New Guinea is prized for its fancy marbled foliage. Reaching 6–8 ft. tall and wide, it features handsome, glossy deep green leaves about 6 in. long and half as broad. Distinctive cream-colored marbling decorates each leaf along the midrib. In summer, purplish red, tubular, 1½-in.-long flowers are borne in short clusters. 'Chocolate' offers leaves mottled burgundy green and bronze, with pinkish cream marbling and deep pink midribs. 'Tricolor' has bright green leaves with white marbling and pink midribs.

In frostless locations, may be used as a landscape plant in light shade; the broad, colorful leaves make a good contrast to ferns. Plant in well-drained soil containing lots of organic matter. Elsewhere, grow in pots that are brought indoors to a bright location during late fall and winter, or grow as houseplants year-round. Keep soil evenly moist and make sure potting mix drains well. Prune lightly or pinch out growing tips to promote bushy growth. Propagate by cuttings. Susceptible to nematodes in Florida.

GRAPE PLANTING AND TRAINING

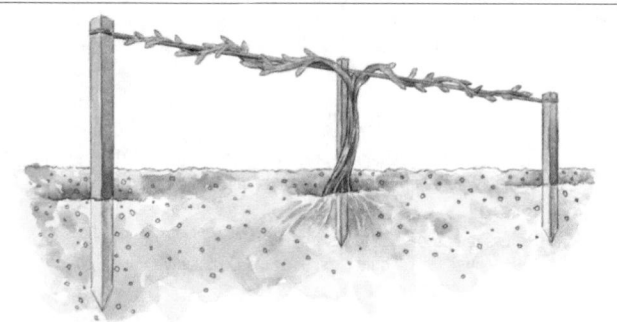

Single-Wire Trellis A single-wire trellis for grapes is easy to build and maintain, and it makes harvesting simple. Set stout posts in the ground 15–20 ft. apart (farther apart for more vigorous grapes, such as muscadines) so that their tops are 5 ft. above the ground. String sturdy galvanized wire across the top posts. Some gardeners may wish to add a second wire at the 2½-ft. level.

Planting Plant grapevine next to support stake at same depth as it grew in the nursery pot. Cut the stem back to two buds.

First Spring Let the vine grow without pruning. The more leaves, the better the root development. Select the strongest shoot and tie it loosely to stake.

First Summer When shoot reaches wire, remove top 4 inches. This forces lateral buds to produce shoots that will form the vine's lateral arms. Train the arms to the wire. Remove all other branches growing from the trunk.

Second Summer Continue training arms along wire. Prune off ends of arms when they reach halfway to the adjacent support post. To prevent girdling, remove any tendrils that wrap around arms.

Second Winter Prune all shoots growing from arms to four buds. Remove any shoots growing from trunk beneath the arms.

Third Summer Allow vine to grow and fruit freely.

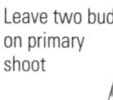

Leave two buds on primary shoot

Remove secondary shoot from each spur

Spur Pruning from Third Winter This type of pruning is done for all muscadine and some American grapes. Remove weak side shoots from the arms. Leave the strongest shoots (spurs) spaced 6–10 in. apart, and cut each to two buds. Each spur will produce two fruit-bearing shoots during the next growing season. During next winter and every winter thereafter, remove the secondary shoot on each spur and cut the primary shoot to two buds. Those buds will develop into stems that bear fruit the following summer.

Cut renewal shoots to two buds

Cane Pruning from Third Winter This type of pruning is done for all European and most American grapes. Cut back each arm to 12 buds; these will produce shoots and fruit the following summer. Then select two strong lateral shoots at the trunk just above or below the arms and cut each to two buds. These renewal shoots will grow canes that will eventually replace the existing arms. During the fourth winter and every winter thereafter, remove the previous year's arms. Select the two strongest canes from the renewal shoots and tie each to the wire as shown; prune each of these canes to 12 buds. These are the next season's fruit-producing arms.

▶

GRAPE

SELECTION	ZONES	SEASON	PRUNING	COMMENTS
AMERICAN AND AMERICAN HYBRID SELECTIONS				
'Buffalo'	US, MS, LS; 9–1	Early	Cane	Seeded black table and juice grape with spicy flavor. Performs well; may bloom again after late frost and bear a crop
'Canadice'	US, MS; 9–1	Early	Spur	Seedless red grape. Very heavy bearing. Cane pruning often recommended, but should be spur pruned, possibly thinned, to prevent overcropping
'Concord'	US, MS, LS; 9–1	Midseason	Cane	Oldest cultivated American grape and the one most commonly used for juice, jelly. Seeded dark blue fruit
'Conquistador'	MS, LS, CS; 9–1	Midseason	Cane	High-quality seeded black grape introduced by the University of Florida. Good for juice, wine, jelly, fresh eating. Resistant to Pierce's disease. American hybrid
'Delaware'	US, MS, LS; 9–1	Early midseason	Cane	Seeded reddish fruit, small but sweet. Good selection for wine, juice, and jelly. American hybrid
'Fredonia'	US, MS, LS; 9–1	Early midseason	Cane	Large, seeded, deep bluish purple grape produced in small clusters. Good for juice, fresh eating
'Golden Muscat'	US, MS, LS; 9–1	Late	Spur	Very large, seeded, yellowish green fruit with citrusy flavor. Not a true muscat. Good for fresh eating, juice, jelly. American hybrid
'Himrod'	US, MS; 9–1	Very early	Cane	Firm, seedless white grape with spicy flavor. For fresh eating, raisins. Very vigorous; well suited to arbors
'Interlaken'	US, MS; 9–1	Very early	Cane or spur	Like 'Himrod' but sweeter, less vigorous, and more productive. Ripens a week earlier
'Lakemont'	US, MS; 9–1	Early midseason	Cane or spur	Seedless white table grape with higher acid content than 'Himrod' or 'Interlaken'; keeps well in cold storage
'Niagara'	US, MS, LS; 9–1	Midseason	Cane	Seedless green to pale yellow grape. Good for juice, jelly, fresh eating. Vigorous and productive
'Reliance'	US, MS, LS; 9–1	Early midseason	Spur	Seedless red grape for fresh eating, juice. May be ready to eat before it colors up. Reliably heavy bearer, very cold hardy. Resistant to black rot, downy mildew

'Canadice', American   'Concord', American   'Lakemont', American   'Reliance', American

GRAPE

SELECTION	ZONES	SEASON	PRUNING	COMMENTS
'Steuben'	US, MS; 9–1	Midseason	Cane	Seeded blue grape with spicy flavor for fresh eating, juice. Very productive. Good resistance to black rot, downy mildew
'Suwanee'	MS, LS, CS; 9–1	Early	Cane	Seeded white grape developed by the University of Florida. Good-flavored fruit for fresh eating and wine. Resistant to Pierce's disease. American hybrid
'Swenson Red'	US, MS; 9–1	Early	Spur	Red or reddish blue grape with excellent strawberry-like flavor, small seeds. Clusters may have distinctive dumbbell shape; vines may take a few years to develop full vigor and yield
'Valiant'	US, MS; 9–1	Early	Cane or spur	Small, seeded blue grape makes good juice. Colors before full sweetness develops; leave on vine awhile. Not very resistant to diseases
'Vanessa'	US, MS; 9–1	Early	Cane	Seedless red grape stands up to rain. Vines tend to have excess vigor
'Venus'	US, MS, LS; 9–1	Early	Cane	Large, seedless blue grape. Flavor can be very good, aromatic. For fresh eating, juice, jelly. Good fall leaf color. Resistant to black rot, downy mildew
EUROPEAN SELECTIONS				
'Centennial'	US, MS, LS; 9–1	Late midseason	Cane	Big clusters of elongated, firm white grapes for fresh eating, raisins. Among the largest of the seedless grapes
'Flame'	US, MS, LS, CS; 9–1	Early	Cane	Seedless red grape with excellent flavor. Takes heat and humidity well
'Thompson Seedless'	US, MS, LS; 9–1	Late midseason	Cane	Big bunches of small, sweet, mild-flavored, greenish amber grapes for fresh eating, raisins, wine. The most common type sold in grocery stores
MUSCADINE SELECTIONS (All are seeded.)				
'Alachua'	MS, LS, CS; 9–1	Early to midseason	Spur	Small, deep purple table or juice grape with very good flavor. Self-fertile
'Black Beauty'	MS, LS, CS; 9–1	Midseason to late	Spur	Large purple grape with excellent flavor. Great for fresh eating. Very vigorous and productive

G

▶

'Swenson Red', American

'Vanessa', American

'Flame', European

'Scuppernong', Muscadine

GRAPE

SELECTION	ZONES	SEASON	PRUNING	COMMENTS
'Carlos'	MS, LS, CS; 9–1	Midseason	Spur	Large clusters of small bronze fruit. Heavy producer. Best bronze muscadine for making wine. Self-fertile
'Cowart'	MS, LS, CS; 9–1	Early to midseason	Spur	Large blue-black table and juice grape. Self-fertile
'Fry'	MS, LS, CS; 9–1	Midseason to late	Spur	Very large clusters of big bronze fruit with excellent flavor. Needs pollenizer. Quite vigorous and productive, but susceptible to black rot. Best for fresh eating. Developed in Georgia
'Golden Isles'	MS, LS, CS; 9–1	Midseason	Spur	Bronze grape for table, wine, juice. Self-fertile
'Higgins'	MS, LS, CS; 9–1	Midseason to late	Spur	Medium to large clusters of huge pinkish to reddish bronze fruit. Needs pollenizer. Cold hardy and very productive. Good for fresh eating but poor for wine. Great type for roadside sales. Developed by the Georgia Experiment Station
'Hunt'	MS, LS, CS; 9–1	Early to midseason	Spur	Large bunches of medium to large black fruit; good yield. Sweet and flavorful. Ripens uniformly. Needs pollenizer. All-purpose grape for wine, juice, jelly
'Ison'	MS, LS, CS; 9–1	Early midseason	Spur	Medium to large purple fruit with excellent flavor. Good for fresh eating. Self-fertile; good pollenizer. Productive
'Jumbo'	MS, LS, CS; 9–1	Midseason to late	Spur	Huge black fruit. Vigorous vines. Heavy producer. Needs pollenizer
'Magnolia'	LS, CS; 9–1	Midseason	Spur	Medium clusters of bronzy, medium to large, sweet fruit. Excellent quality. Self-fertile; vigorous, prolific grower. Superb for wine. Does better in Lower South
'Noble'	MS, LS, CS; 9–1	Early to midseason	Spur	Large clusters of small to medium, bluish black fruits of good quality. Good disease resistance. Quite vigorous and productive. Self-fertile. Excellent for wine, juice, and jelly. Selection developed in North Carolina
'Scuppernong'	MS, LS, CS; 9–1	Midseason	Spur	The classic muscadine, and the one most Southerners know and love. Bronze, speckled grape with distinctive aroma and flavor. Needs pollenizer. Good for fresh eating, wine
'Southland'	MS, LS, CS; 9–1	Midseason	Spur	Medium to large, sweet purple-black fruit. Good quality. Self-fertile. Pest and disease resistant. Excellent for fresh eating, jams, jellies. Better in Lower and Coastal South
'Sterling'	MS, LS, CS; 9–1	Midseason	Spur	Medium-size bronze fruit. Excellent for juice, wine, jelly, fresh eating. Self-fertile. Good pollenizer
'Supreme'	MS, LS, CS; 9–1	Midseason to late	Spur	Large purple grape with excellent flavor; good for fresh eating. Productive
'Sweet Jenny'	MS, LS, CS; 9–1	Early midseason	Spur	Large bronze fruit with excellent flavor. Great for fresh eating
'Triumph'	MS, LS, CS; 9–1	Early midseason	Spur	Reliably heavy crop of bronze to nearly yellow grapes with pineapple flavor. Thin-skinned. For juice, fresh eating, wine. Self-fertile. Good pollenizer for other selections
'Welder'	MS, LS, CS; 9–1	Midseason	Spur	Medium-size bronze fruit; great quality. Vigorous and productive. Good for fresh eating and jelly; superb for wine. Tolerates partial shade. Good for garden and commercial plantings. Disease resistant. Self-fertile. Excellent pollenizer

G

GRASSES. The grasses in this book are either lawn or ornamental plants—except for corn, the only cereal commonly grown in home gardens. They are described under entries headed by their botanical names; to find these, check lists below. (Bamboos, which are grasses, are listed by botanical name under Bamboo.)

Lawn grasses include *Axonopus*, carpet grass; *Bouteloua*, blue grama grass; *Buchloe*, buffalo grass; *Cynodon*, Bermuda grass; *Eremochloa*, centipede grass; *Festuca*, fescue; *Lolium*, ryegrass; *Paspalum*, seashore paspalum; *Poa*, bluegrass; *Stenotaphrum*, St. Augustine grass; *Zoysia*.

Ornamental grasses include *Andropogon*, bluestem, turkeyfoot; *Arrhenatherum*, bulbous oat grass; *Arundo*, giant reed; *Bouteloua*, blue grama grass; *Briza*, rattlesnake grass; *Calamagrostis*, reed grass; *Chasmanthium*, sea oats; *Coix*, Job's tears; *Cortaderia*, pampas grass; *Deschampsia*, hair grass; *Festuca*, fescue; *Hakonechloa*, Japanese forest grass; *Helictotrichon*, blue oat grass; *Imperata*, Japanese blood grass; *Leymus*, blue lyme grass; *Milium*, golden grass; *Miscanthus*, silver grass; *Molinia*, moor grass; *Muhlenbergia*, including bamboo muhly, deer grass; *Nassella*, needle grass; *Panicum*, switch grass; *Pennisetum*, fountain grass; *Phalaris*, ribbon grass; *Rhynchelytrum*, ruby grass; *Schizachyrium*, little bluestem; *Sporobolus*, dropseed; and *Stipa*, feather grass.

GRASS NUT. See TRITELEIA laxa

GREATER CELANDINE. See CHELIDONIUM majus

GRECIAN LAUREL. See LAURUS nobilis

GREEN AND GOLD. See CHRYSOGONUM virginianum

GREEN CARPET. See HERNIARIA glabra

GREEN EYES. See BERLANDIERA texana

GREVILLEA

Proteaceae

EVERGREEN SHRUBS AND TREES

ZONES VARY BY SPECIES

EXPOSURE NEEDS VARY BY SPECIES

WATER NEEDS VARY BY SPECIES

Native to Australia. Many species and hybrids. Plants vary in size and appearance, but generally have fine-textured foliage and long, slender, curved flowers, usually in dense clusters. Provide good drainage. Like other members of the protea family, grevilleas are sensitive to high levels of phosphorus in the soil, so feed lightly and avoid fertilizers with high phosphorus content. Intolerant of salt. Seldom browsed by deer.

Grevillea robusta

G. banksii. BANKS GREVILLEA. Shrub or small tree. Zones TS; 12–10. Often sold as *G. banksii forsteri*. To 9–20 ft. tall and 9–12 ft. wide. Leaves 4–10 in. long, deeply cut into narrow lobes. Erect, 3- to 6-in.-long clusters of dark red flowers appear sporadically all year; bloom is heaviest in late spring. Showy used singly against high wall, near entryway, or grouped with other big shrubs. Freezes at 24°F; takes wind. Full sun. Little to regular water.

G. 'Canberra Gem' ('Canberra'). Shrub. Zones TS; 12–9. Open, graceful growth to 8 ft. tall, 12 ft. wide. Bright green, needlelike, 1-in. leaves. Clusters of red flowers in spring (and intermittently at other times). Has been sold as 'Pink Pearl'. Full sun or partial shade. Little water.

G. 'Noellii'. Shrub. Zones CS, TS; 12–10. To 4 ft. tall, 4–5 ft. wide. Densely clad with narrow, 1-in.-long, glossy medium green leaves. Clusters of pink-and-white flowers bloom in spring. Full sun. Moderate water.

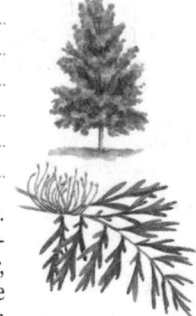

Grevillea 'Noellii'

G. robusta. SILK OAK. Tree. Zones CS, TS; 12–3. Fast growing to 50–60 ft. (rarely to 100 ft.) tall. Symmetrical, pyramidal when young. Old trees are broad topped (30–35 ft. wide), usually with a few heavy, horizontal limbs; picturesque against skyline. Fernlike leaves are golden green to deep green above, silvery beneath. Heavy leaf fall in spring, sporadic leaf drop through rest of year. Large clusters of bright golden orange flowers in early spring. Wood is brittle, easily damaged in high wind. Young trees damaged at 24°F; older ones hardy to 16°F. Use for quick, tall screen, or clip as tall hedge. Full sun. Grows in poor, heavy soils if not overwatered; can take regular water in fast-draining soils.

G. rosmarinifolia. ROSEMARY GREVILLEA. Shrub. Zones TS; 12–9. To 6 ft. tall, nearly as broad. Narrow, 1½-in.-long leaves are dark green on top, silvery beneath; look a bit like those of rosemary (*Rosmarinus*). Red-and-cream flower clusters (rarely pink or white) in fall and winter; scattered bloom in other seasons. Use as clipped or informal hedge in dryish places. Impervious to heat and aridity. A dwarf form, 3 ft. high and 6 ft. wide, bears pink-and-cream flowers in waves throughout the year, most heavily in spring and fall. 'Scarlet Sprite', another dwarf, is similar but bears blooms in bright red and cream. Full sun or partial shade. Little water.

GROUNDSEL BUSH. See BACCHARIS halimifolia

GUAJILLO. See ACACIA berlandieri

GUAVA

Myrtaceae

EVERGREEN SHRUBS OR TREES

ZONES VARY BY SPECIES

FULL SUN OR PARTIAL SHADE

REGULAR WATER

Guava

Native to tropical America, guavas (botanical name *Psidium*) are prized for their tasty fruits. They are resilient plants, easy to grow along the Gulf Coast and in South Texas and Florida; in fact, they have escaped cultivation and become invasive in some areas of Florida. (For pineapple guava, see Feijoa.)

Common or tropical guava. Zones TS; 12–10. Native to southern Mexico and Central America; known botanically as *P. guajava*. Grows into a small tree to 20 ft. tall, with branches close to the ground and a spreading crown to 20 ft. wide. Smooth, reddish brown or mottled green bark peels off in flakes. Dull green, leathery, prominently veined, oblong leaves are 3–7 in. long, 1–2 in. wide. Lightly fragrant white flowers to 1 in. across are borne singly or in clusters; heaviest bloom comes in spring, but flowers appear year-round in south Florida and South Texas. Blossoms quickly shed petals, leaving tufts of white stamens tipped with pale yellow anthers.

Fruit generally ripens in summer and fall, but some selections ripen fruit nearly year-round. Each guava weighs up to a pound and may be round, oval, or pear-shaped. Skin is usually yellow; flesh may be white, yellow, pink, or red and often contains small seeds (fully edible in most selections). Fruit is rich in potassium, vitamin A, and vitamin C—in fact, the fruit of some selections has five times the vitamin C of an orange. Trees are self-fruitful but bear more heavily if cross-pollinated with another selection. Fruit ripens better on the tree but can be picked green and ripened at room temperature; when ready to eat, it emits a sweet, pungent odor and is soft to the touch.

Common guava tolerates most soils but grows best in those with a pH between 5 and 7. Withstands temporary flooding and seasonal drought, but not salt. Responds well to fertilizer: feed monthly during the growing season with 8-4-8 fertilizer, using the amounts specified on the package. For good fruit production in areas with limestone soils, applications of iron chelate or iron sulfate may be necessary. Common pests in Florida include nematode, guava whitefly, Caribbean fruit fly, and guava moth. Consult your local Cooperative Extension Office for best methods of control. Young trees may be killed by frost, but older trees are hardy to about 29°F; if frozen to the ground, they usually resprout and bear fruit within 2 years. Recommended selections include these four:

'Red Indian'. Large, round fruit. Yellow skin with pink blush; sweet red flesh, high in sugar and vitamin C.

'Ruby × Supreme'. Hybrid with small to medium-size, roundish fruit. Greenish yellow skin, pinkish orange flesh. Sweet, delicious flavor. Particularly high in vitamin C.

'Sweet White Indonesian'. Large, round fruit with pale yellow skin and juicy, sweet, delicious white flesh. Very productive.

'White Seedless'. Small to medium-size, roundish fruit. Seedless white flesh with excellent flavor.

Strawberry guava. Zones CS, TS; 12–10. From Brazil; known botanically as *P. cattleianum*. Large shrub or small tree to 15 ft. tall and wide, with smooth, attractive reddish to golden brown bark. Oval, shiny dark green leaves are 2–4 in. long and 1–2 in. wide. Solitary, sweetly fragrant white flowers to 1 in. across appear in spring; these are followed in summer by edible purple or yellow fruits about the size and shape of a golf ball. Flesh is white, with a sweet-tart, resinous flavor. Strawberry guava has become a serious pest in Florida because it reproduces freely by seeds and root suckers and tolerates a wide range of growing conditions. More cold hardy than common guava.

GUERNSEY LILY. See NERINE sarniensis

GULF MUHLY. See MUHLENBERGIA filipes

GUNNERA

Gunneraceae

PERENNIALS

✔ MS, LS, CS, TS

◐ PARTIAL SHADE

💧 AMPLE WATER

Gunnera tinctoria

Big, bold, awe-inspiring South American plants to 8 ft. high and as wide or wider, with giant leaves (4–8 ft. across) on 4- to 6-ft.-long stalks covered in stiff hairs. Leaves are conspicuously veined, with lobed and cut edges. Given space (they need plenty) and the necessary care, these plants can be the ultimate summertime conversation pieces. New sets of leaves grow each spring. In mild-winter areas, old leaves remain green for more than a year. Elsewhere, leaves die back completely in winter. Flower clusters form at base of plants and resemble corncobs to 1½ ft. long. Tiny fruits are red.

Soil must be rich in nutrients and organic material. Feed with a balanced all-purpose fertilizer three times a year, beginning when new growth starts, to keep leaves maximum size. Give overhead sprinkling when humidity is low or drying winds occur. Use plants where they can be focal point in summer—beside a pool or dominating a bed of low, fine-textured ground cover.

G. manicata. Heat zones 12–7. Native to Brazil, Colombia. Leaves carried fairly horizontally. Spinelike hairs on leafstalks and leaf ribs are red. Leaf lobes are flatter than those of *G. tinctoria* and do not have frilled margins.

G. tinctoria (G. chilensis). Heat zones 10–9. From Chile. Most common species. Leaf margins are lobed, toothed, somewhat frilled. Leaves are cupped and flaring, held more vertically than those of *G. manicata*.

FOR GROWING SYMBOL EXPLANATIONS
PLEASE SEE PAGE 145

GYMNOCLADUS dioica

KENTUCKY COFFEE TREE

Fabaceae (Leguminosae)

DECIDUOUS TREE

✔ US, MS, LS H 9–5

☀ FULL SUN

💧 REGULAR WATER

Gymnocladus dioica

Native to eastern U.S. Grows very fast as a sapling but slows once it hits 8–10 ft. Give it plenty of room, since it will ultimately reach 60–100 ft. tall and 45–50 ft. wide. Provides year-round interest, featuring attractive foliage as well as striking branch structure. Leaves are 1½–3 ft. long, divided into many 1- to 3-in. leaflets; they are pinkish when emerging late in spring, deep bluish green by summer. In leaf, the tree casts light shade. Fall color usually not effective, but foliage sometimes turns bright yellow. The relatively few, heavy, contorted branches and stout twigs make the bare tree picturesque in winter.

Male and female plants are separate. Narrow, creamy to greenish white flower panicles at ends of branches in spring are up to 1 ft. long (and fragrant) on female trees, to 4 in. long on males. Blossoms on female trees are followed by flat, 6- to 10-in.-long, reddish brown pods containing hard black seeds. Pods persist through winter. Early settlers roasted the seeds to make a coffee substitute, hence the tree's common name. Grows best in moist, rich, deep soil but adapts to poor soil, drought, city conditions. Can take much heat and cold. Needs minimal pruning.

Gymnocladus dioica

Three male—and therefore seedless—kinds are sometimes offered at garden centers; all have potential for use as street trees. 'Espresso' grows to 50 ft. tall, 30 ft. wide, has an attractive spreading form and vase shape. 'Prairie Titan' may reach 60–70 ft. tall, 30–40 ft wide; it has particularly good-looking foliage. 'Stately Manor' grows in a narrow and upright form, to 50 ft. tall and only 20 ft. wide.

GYNURA

VELVET PLANT

Asteraceae

EVERGREEN PERENNIALS OR SMALL SHRUBS

✔ LS (MILD AREAS), CS, TS
  H 12–10; OR INDOORS

☀◐ EXPOSURE NEEDS VARY BY SPECIES;
  BRIGHT LIGHT

💧 REGULAR WATER

Gynura aurantiaca
'Purple Passion'

These natives of the Old World tropics offer strikingly colorful foliage. Usually grown as houseplants, they also make interesting additions to borders. Thrive in fertile, well-drained soil outdoors.

G. aurantiaca. PURPLE VELVET PLANT. Native to Indonesia. Upright in youth, clambering when mature. Grows 4–5 ft. tall in south Florida but is shorter elsewhere; may spread twice as wide as tall. Deeply toothed leaves, to 8 in. long and 4 in. wide, are heavily cloaked with velvety purple hairs, as are the stems. Leaves emerge bright purple, then mature to deep green. Sometimes blooms in late summer, bearing ¾-in., yellowish orange flowers that take on purple tones with age. 'Purple Passion' ('Sarmentosa') has smaller leaves and is distinctly trailing; excellent for use in hanging baskets.

Outdoors, purple velvet plant grows best in light shade. Indoors, give it bright light from a south- or west-facing window. Let the soil surface

G

become dry to the touch before watering; then water thoroughly. Feed every other week in spring and summer and monthly in fall and winter with a general-purpose liquid houseplant fertilizer. Watch out for mealybugs and dispatch them by dabbing them with a cotton swab dipped in alcohol. Propagate by stem cuttings taken in spring and summer. Cut back old, woody plants to produce fresh, colorful foliage.

G. bicolor. Native to the Moluccas in east Indonesia. Forms a leafy mass to 1–2 ft. tall, 2–3 ft. wide. Coarse, deeply toothed, nearly hairless leaves reach 6 in. long and half as wide; they are chocolate purple with prominent green veins on their upper surface, rich purple beneath. Showy orange-yellow blossoms to ½ in. across are borne on slender, erect stems; they attract butterflies and emit a sweet, pungent odor that some people do not enjoy. Good in combination with finer-textured plants. Outdoors, plant in full sun or partial shade. Indoor culture is same as for *G. aurantiaca.*

GYPSOPHILA

Caryophyllaceae

ANNUALS AND PERENNIALS

✿ ZONES VARY BY SPECIES

☼ FULL SUN

◑ MODERATE WATER

Slender-stemmed, much-branched plants are upright or spreading, ranging from 3 in. to 4 ft. tall. Bloom profusely in summer, covering themselves in clusters of tiny single or double flowers in white, pink, or rose. Leaves (sparse when plants are in bloom) are typically blue green. Use for airy look in borders and bouquets and for contrast with large-flowered, coarse-textured plants. Dwarf kinds are ideal for rock gardens, for trailing from pockets in walls or over tops of dry rock walls.

Gypsophila repens

Add lime to strongly acid soils before planting. Perennial kinds are not always easy to transplant (especially *G. paniculata*, which has deep, carrotlike roots). If possible, do not disturb them often. Protect roots from gophers; protect tender new growth from snails and slugs. To encourage repeat bloom on perennial sorts, cut back flowering stems before seed clusters form. Perennial species are usually short lived in the Coastal and Tropical South; treat as annuals there.

G. cerastioides. Perennial. Zones US, MS, LS; 8–5. Native to the Himalayas. Gray leaves may be spoon shaped or pointed-oval; they form a mat to 3 in. high and twice as broad. Clustered flowers, ½ in. across, vary from pink-veined white to pure pink. Use in rock gardens or between stepping-stones.

G. elegans. Annual. Zones US, MS, LS, CS, TS; 9–1. Native to Asia Minor, the Caucasus, southern Ukraine. Upright grower to 1½ ft. high and wide. Lance-shaped, rather fleshy leaves to 3 in. long. Profuse single white flowers to ½ in. wide or wider; pink and rose forms are also available. Plants live only 5 to 6 weeks; for continuous bloom, sow seed in open ground every 3 to 4 weeks from late spring into summer. Sow in fall and winter in the Tropical South. Excellent cut flower.

G. paniculata. BABY'S BREATH. Perennial. Zones US, MS, LS, CS; 9–1. Native to central Asia, central and eastern Europe. This is the classic filler in bouquets. To 3 ft. or taller and as broad. Slender, sharp-pointed leaves 2½–4 in. long. Single, very tiny white flowers (about ¹⁄₁₆ in. across), hundreds in a spray. 'Bristol Fairy' is an improved, more billowy form to 4 ft. high, covered with double blossoms ¼ in. wide. Florists' favorite is 'Perfecta', which bears even larger flowers (to about ½ in. wide). Dwarf, double-flowered forms include white-blossomed 'Compacta Plena', 1½ ft. high, and pink 'Viette's Dwarf', 12–15 in. high.

G. repens. Perennial. Zones US, MS, LS; 8–1. Alpine native to 6–9 in. high. Trailing stems reach 1½ ft. long and are set with narrow leaves less than 1 in. long; clustered, ½-in. flowers may be pink or white. Selections include 'Alba' (white) and 'Rosea' (pink).

HABRANTHUS

RAIN LILY

Amaryllidaceae

PERENNIALS FROM BULBS

✿ LS (PROTECTED), CS, TS; OR GROW IN POTS

☼ ◑ FULL SUN OR LIGHT SHADE

◑ REGULAR WATER DURING GROWTH AND BLOOM

Habranthus robustus

Native from Texas to Argentina, these bulbous plants sprout and bloom almost immediately following a summer rain (thus their common name). Their grassy foliage and trumpet- to funnel-shaped blossoms closely resemble those of their relatives, *Zephyranthes*. Plant bulbs in spring in well-drained soil, spacing them 3 in. apart, with tips at soil level. Plant in sweeps for best effect. Good plants for the front of borders, in rock gardens, or in naturalized areas. In areas where ground freezes in winter, grow in pots.

H. brachyandrus. Heat zones 12–10. Blooms from early summer to fall. Lavender-pink, 3-in.-long flowers with shades of blackish purple at petal bases are borne one per stem.

H. ×floryi. Heat zones 12–10. Hybrid between *H. brachyandrus* and *H. robustus*. 'Purple Base' is the selection usually offered; it has blue-green foliage and 2- to 3-in.-long, rosy pink flowers with crimson purple throats atop 15-in. stems. Blooms intermittently all summer.

H. robustus. Heat zones 10–7. Blooms midsummer to fall. Flowers—sometimes borne two to each 9-in. stem—are 3 in. long, light pink with green throats and deeper pink veining. 'Russell Manning' is an especially floriferous, large-flowered selection that multiplies quickly.

H. tubispathus (H. andersonii). Heat zones 12–10. Summer bloomer with 1½-in.-long flowers in yellow veined with red. Stems and leaves about 6 in. high. 'Cupreus' is coppery orange; *H. t. texanus*, known as Texas copper lily, has bronzy yellow flowers.

HACKBERRY. See CELTIS

HAIR GRASS. See DESCHAMPSIA

HAKONECHLOA macra

JAPANESE FOREST GRASS, HAKONE GRASS

Poaceae (Gramineae)

PERENNIAL GRASS

✿ US, MS, LS ♓ 9–5

◑ ● PARTIAL TO FULL SHADE

◑ REGULAR WATER

Hakonechloa macra 'Aureola'

This choice perennial from Japan is one of the few ornamental grasses that thrives in shade. Clumps of narrow, gracefully arching leaves grow 1–3 ft. tall; they spread somewhat wider by underground runners but advance slowly and are not invasive. Delicate sprays of flowers among the leaves in mid- to late summer are attractive but not showy. Good candidate for rock gardens, patio containers. Plant in spring, in rich, moist, well-drained soil. The species has solid green leaves that turn coppery orange in fall, but most gardeners plant types with variegated leaves to bring summer color to shade gardens. Try them in combination with evergreens with dark green foliage, such as rhododendron, camellia, Japanese black pine *(Pinus thunbergii),* or green-leafed Japanese aucuba.

'Albostriata' ('Albovariegata'). To 3 ft. high, with leaves striped lengthwise in green and white.

'Aureola'. Most popular form. To 1½ ft. high. Green leaves have longitudinal yellow stripes; in deep shade, the yellow turns to chartreuse. Foliage is sometimes suffused with pink in cool weather. Looks nice next to blue-leafed hostas.

HALESIA

SILVER BELL

Styracaceae

DECIDUOUS TREES

US, MS, LS 8–4, EXCEPT AS NOTED

FULL SUN OR PARTIAL SHADE

REGULAR WATER

Halesia carolina

These elegant and underappreciated trees are native to the Southeast. Bell-shaped white flowers appear in spring, usually just before the leaves emerge. Grow best in rich, well-drained, acid soil. Pretty in woodland gardens. Good substitute for dogwood (*Cornus*) where dogwoods will not grow. Buy container-grown plants, as balled-and-burlapped ones do not transplant easily. Medium green foliage turns yellow in fall.

H. carolina (H. tetraptera). CAROLINA SILVER BELL. Moderate growth to 30–40 ft. tall, 20–35 ft. wide. Clusters of snow white, ½-in. flowers in midspring hang along length of graceful branches. Oval, finely toothed, 2- to 5-in.-long leaves. Four-winged brown fruits hang on almost all winter. Train to a single trunk when young or it will grow as a large shrub. Flowers show off to best advantage when you can look up into tree.

H. diptera. TWO-WINGED SILVER BELL. Zones US, MS, LS, CS. To 20–30 ft. tall and wide, usually multitrunked. Oval leaves, pointed at the tip. Flowers resemble those of *H. carolina*, but they are more deeply lobed and bloom a week or two later, just after leaves emerge. Fruits are similar to those of *H. carolina* but have two rather than four wings. *H. d. magniflora*, the showiest silver bell, has larger flowers and is a more profuse bloomer.

H. monticola. MOUNTAIN SILVER BELL. Heat zones 9–6. Similar to *H. carolina* but larger, eventually to 60–80 ft. tall and at least half as wide. Leaves are also bigger (3–6 in. long), but tree casts only moderate shade. Flowers and fruit are also somewhat larger. 'Rosea' has light pink flowers.

Hamamelidaceae. The witch hazel family contains deciduous (rarely evergreen) trees and shrubs. Some have showy flowers; these include *Fothergilla*, witch hazel (*Hamamelis*), and *Loropetalum*. Many have brilliant fall color, such as sweet gum (*Liquidambar*) and *Parrotia*.

HAMAMELIS

WITCH HAZEL

Hamamelidaceae

DECIDUOUS SHRUBS OR TREES

US, MS, LS, EXCEPT AS NOTED

FULL SUN OR PARTIAL SHADE

REGULAR WATER

Hamamelis mollis

Medium-size to large shrubs, sometimes treelike, usually spreading with angular or zigzag branches. Valued for bright fall foliage and nodding clusters of interesting yellow to red blooms that typically appear in winter. Flowers consist of many narrow, crumpled petals and are said to resemble shredded coconut, eyelashes, or spiders. Most witch hazels are fragrant and bloom over a long period. They appreciate rich, organic soil. Prune only to guide growth, remove suckers, or obtain flowering stems for scented bouquets. In some types, old leaves hang on into winter, obscuring flowers; it may be necessary to strip them by hand.

H. ×intermedia. Heat zones 9–1. Group of winter-blooming hybrids between *H. mollis* and *H. japonica*. Big shrubs (12–15 ft. high and wide). Often grafted; remove any growth originating from below graft. The following selections are among the best.

'Allgold'. Deep yellow flowers with red sepals; yellow fall foliage.

'Arnold Promise'. The best yellow-flowering selection, with bright yellow blossoms. Yellow, orange, and red fall foliage.

'Carmine Red'. Light red flowers; red-orange fall foliage.

'Diane'. Dark red flowers aging to orange red. Red-purple fall foliage.

'Hiltingbury'. Coppery red flowers; orange-yellow fall color.

'Jelena' ('Copper Beauty', 'Orange Beauty'). Coppery orange flowers. Fall foliage in orange, red, and scarlet.

'Magic Fire' ('Fire Charm', 'Feuerzauber'). Flowers in coppery orange blended with red. Fiery red fall foliage.

'Moonlight'. Pale yellow blooms marked red at base; yellow fall foliage.

'Pallida'. Luminous light yellow blossoms; yellow fall foliage.

'Primavera'. Broad-petaled light yellow flowers. Yellow-orange autumn foliage.

'Ruby Glow'. Coppery red flowers; bright red fall foliage.

'Sunburst'. Heavy clusters of radiant yellow, unscented flowers. Yellow fall foliage.

'Westerstede'. Pure yellow-orange flowers. Orange-red fall foliage.

H. japonica. JAPANESE WITCH HAZEL. Heat zones 9–5. From Japan. Much like *H. ×intermedia*, though perhaps somewhat more erect and treelike (to 12–20 ft. tall and broad). Broadly oval, medium to dark green leaves are 2–4 in. long. Fairly small, lightly scented yellow flowers in late winter or earliest spring. Chief draw is fall foliage in shades of red, purple, and yellow. *H. j. flavopurpurascens* has yellow-orange flowers, purple at the base, and reddish yellow fall foliage. *H. j.* 'Arborea' grows 20–25 ft. tall, has yellow blossoms and yellow autumn leaves.

H. mollis. CHINESE WITCH HAZEL. Heat zones 9–1. From China. Moderately slow-growing shrub to 8–10 ft. tall and wide (may reach twice that size after many years). Roundish, 3½- to 6-in.-long leaves are dark green and rough above, gray and felted beneath, turning a good pure yellow in fall. Sweetly fragrant, 1½-in.-wide, rich golden yellow flowers with red-brown sepals bloom on bare stems in winter. Flowering branches excellent for cutting. Selections include 'Coombe Wood', a very heavy bloomer with especially fine fragrance, and 'Early Bright', earliest to bloom.

H. vernalis. OZARK WITCH HAZEL. Heat zones 8–1. Native to central and southern U.S. Multistemmed shrub 6–10 ft. tall, spreading wider. Small, fragrant yellow to orange flowers from winter to spring. Medium to dark green, 2- to 5-in.-long leaves turn bright yellow in fall and hold for several weeks in favorable weather. 'Autumn Embers' has orange blossoms and brilliant red-purple fall foliage. 'Lombart's Weeping' is a 5- to 6-ft. tree with drooping branches. 'Sandra' has unremarkable yellow spring flowers but bears reddish purple new growth and brilliant red fall foliage.

H. virginiana. COMMON WITCH HAZEL. Zones US, MS, LS, CS; 9–1. Native to eastern North America. Sometimes reaches 25 ft. tall but usually grows 10–15 ft. high and wide. Open, spreading, rather straggling habit. Moderately slow growing. Bark is the source of the liniment witch hazel. Roundish leaves are similar to those of *H. mollis*, but they are not gray and felted beneath; turn yellow to orange in fall. Small, fragrant golden yellow blossoms appear in fall but tend to be lost in colored foliage.

HAMELIA patens

FIREBUSH

Rubiaceae

EVERGREEN SHRUB OR TREE

CS, TS

FULL SUN

REGULAR TO AMPLE WATER

Hamelia patens

From southern Florida south to Central and South America. Gardenia and coffee relative grows to 9–10 ft. tall (possibly much taller), 5–6 ft. wide, with whorls of oval, gray-green, 6-in. leaves. Leafstalks and flower stems are red. Clusters of ¾-in., tubular, orange to bright red blooms form at branch tips all summer long; thanks to their shape and color, plant is also known as firecracker shrub. Blooms attract butterflies and hummingbirds. Flowers are followed by small dark red, purple, or black fruits much relished by birds. Likes lots of moisture but needs good drainage. Tolerant of salt, lime.

HEDERA

IVY

Araliaceae

EVERGREEN VINES

ZONES VARY BY SPECIES

SHADE IN LOWER, COASTAL, AND TROPICAL SOUTH

MODERATE TO REGULAR WATER

Hedera helix

Ivy is appreciated by some gardeners for its ability to cover quickly, reviled by others for its invasive tendencies. Spreads horizontally over the ground; also climbs on walls, fences, trellises. Sometimes a single planting does both: wall ivy spreads to become a surrounding ground cover, or vice versa. Climbs almost any vertical surface by aerial rootlets—a factor to consider in planting against surfaces that must be painted. A chain link fence planted with ivy soon becomes a wall of foliage. As a ground cover, it holds the soil, discouraging erosion and slippage on slopes. Roots grow deep and fill soil densely; branches root as they grow, further knitting soil.

Thick, leathery leaves are usually lobed. Mature plants will eventually develop stiff branches that bear round clusters of small greenish flowers followed by black berries. These branches have unlobed leaves; cuttings taken from them will also have unlobed leaves and will produce shrubby rather than vining plants. Such shrubs taken from variegated Algerian ivy (*H. canariensis* 'Variegata') are known by the name "ghost ivy." Plain green *H. helix* 'Arborescens' is another selection of this shrubby type.

Plant ivy in spring or fall. It can be grown from cuttings, but planting from pots is more dependable and gives faster growth. Standard spacing is 1½–2 ft. apart. Amend soil (to depth of 8–12 in. if possible) with organic matter such as ground bark or peat moss. Before planting, thoroughly moisten soil; also make sure transplants' roots are moist and their leaves and stems full of moisture (not wilted). Feed with high-nitrogen fertilizer after planting (for spring-planted ivy) or, for autumn-planted ivy, in first spring after planting. Feed again in midsummer. For best growth, continue to feed every year in early spring and midsummer.

Most ivy ground covers should be trimmed around edges two or three times a year (use hedge shears or a sharp spade). Fence and wall plantings likewise need shearing or trimming two or three times a year. When ground cover builds up higher than you want, mow it with a rugged rotary power mower or cut it back with hedge shears. Do this in spring so ensuing growth will quickly cover bald look.

Many trees and shrubs can grow compatibly in ivy ground cover, but small, soft, or fragile plants will be smothered. Ivy ground covers can be a haven for slugs and snails and can also harbor rodents, especially if the ivy is never cut back.

H. canariensis. ALGERIAN IVY. Zones CS, TS; 12–6. Shiny, rich green leaves 5–8 in. wide, with three to five shallow lobes. Leaves are more widely spaced along stems than those of *H. helix*. Coarse-looking plant; aggressive grower. 'Variegata' ('Gloire de Marengo') has dark leaves marbled with gray green and irregularly margined in creamy white; it does not take extreme heat.

H. colchica. PERSIAN IVY. Zones US, MS, LS, CS, TS; 12–1. Oval to heart-shaped leaves are largest among all ivies: 3–7 in. wide, to 10 in. long. 'Dentata' has slightly toothed leaves; 'Dentata Variegata' is marbled with deep green, gray green, and creamy white. 'Sulphur Heart' ('Paddy's Pride') has central gold variegation.

H. helix. ENGLISH IVY. Zones US, MS, LS, CS, TS; 12–6. Not as vigorous as *H. canariensis*, this ubiquitous species features three- to five-lobed leaves that are dull green with paler veins and reach 2–4 in. long and wide. Tremendous genetic variation has given rise to a dizzying assortment of foliage shapes, sizes, and colors. Ivy fanciers classify the hundreds of selections according to leaf shape, and also by type if unusual. Leaf-shape categories are bird's foot (leaves have long, prominent main lobe), curly (undulated, frilled, or curly leaves), fan (broad leaves with small lobes of roughly equal size), heart-shaped, and ivy (traditional five-lobed leaves). Plants are also grouped as miniature (very small leaves), variegated, or arborescent (shrublike plants with unlobed leaves propagated from mature ivies). Oddity types have unusual growth patterns, odd leaf forms, or both.

English ivies have many uses besides their usual role as ground covers. They are excellent in pots and hanging baskets, trained into intricate patterns on walls, or grown on wire frames to create topiaries. Arborescent forms make superb additions to foundation plantings and shade gardens. Some arborescent ivies are short and mounding, others more upright. All are drought tolerant and care-free—good substitutes for euonymus and cherry laurel (*Prunus laurocerasus*). Resistant to damage by deer. Recommended selections include the following.

'Baltica'. Ivy type. Dark green leaves with whitish veins. Very cold hardy.

'California'. Curly type. Dense grower with dark green leaves.

'California Fan'. Fan type. Broad light green leaves with frilly edges. Perhaps the most beautiful fan ivy.

'Conglomerata'. Oddity type. Upright grower with stiff stems and closely set, curly green leaves.

'Deltoidea'. Heart-shaped type. Dark green leaves. Also known by the name "sweetheart ivy."

'Fluffy Ruffles'. Curly type. Ruffly, nearly circular, medium green leaves resemble pompons.

'Glacier'. Ivy type, variegated. Leaves are patched in blue green and gray green and edged in white.

'Gnome' ('Spetchley'). Bird's-foot type, miniature. Leaves are only ¼–½ in. long, turn from dark green to bronze purple in winter.

'Gold Dust'. Ivy type, variegated. Green leaves with bright gold specks and blotches.

'Gold Heart'. Heart-shaped type, variegated. Irregular gold splash in center of dark green leaf.

'Manda Crested'. Curly type. Light green leaves with long, curly lobes.

'Minima'. Ivy type, miniature. Medium green leaves just ½–1 in. across. Very cold hardy.

'Needlepoint'. Bird's-foot type. Slim, graceful, medium green leaves. Very popular.

'Ritterkreuz'. Bird's-foot type. Dark green, five-lobed leaves with lighter midrib.

'Thorndale' ('Sub-Zero'). Ivy type. Large dark green leaves with veins that turn light green to white in winter. Very cold hardy.

Hedera helix 'Gold Heart'

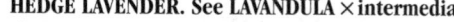

HEDYCHIUM

GINGER LILY

Zingiberaceae

PERENNIALS

🌿 ZONES VARY BY SPECIES

☀️ ◑ FULL SUN OR LIGHT SHADE

💧 AMPLE WATER

Hedychium gardnerianum

Native to India and tropical Asia, these old Southern favorites combine handsome foliage with showy, deliciously fragrant flowers. Rich green, alternate leaves ascend stems growing from stout rhizomes. In late summer or early fall, honeysuckle-scented blossoms in dense spikes open from cones of overlapping bracts at the ends of stalks. Southern specialty growers offer dozens of species and selections in heights from 2 to 9 ft., in colors ranging from white and cream through pink to red—and a host of yellow, orange, and salmon shades.

Ginger lilies need moist, well-drained soil that contains lots of organic matter. Use them in borders or grow in containers. Cutting back old stems after the flowers fade encourages new growth. Plants are evergreen in the Tropical South, deciduous elsewhere. Propagate by division in late fall or early spring.

H. coccineum. RED GINGER LILY. Zones LS, CS, TS; 11–8. To 6–9 ft. tall, with leaves to 20 in. long and 2 in. wide. Particularly showy, bearing orange-scarlet flowers with prominent red stamens on blossom spikes to 10 in. long. 'Disney' ('Orange Brush') has reddish stems and leaf undersides. *H. c. aurantiacum* 'Flaming Torch' produces large spikes of orange flowers that resemble lighted torches.

H. coronarium. COMMON GINGER LILY, WHITE GINGER. Zones MS, LS, CS, TS; 12–7. To 3–7 ft. high, with leaves 8–24 in. long and 2–5 in. wide. White flowers in 6- to 12-in.-long clusters are especially fragrant; good cut flowers.

H. flavum. GOLDEN BUTTERFLY GINGER. Zones LS, CS, TS; 12–8. Old Southern favorite. To 5–7 ft. tall, with oblong leaves 4–20 in. long and 1–4 in. wide. Dense, 6-in. spikes of particularly fragrant, rich yellow-orange flowers with orange spots on the tips.

H. gardnerianum. KAHILI GINGER. Zones LS, CS, TS; 12–8. To 8 ft. high, with leaves 8–18 in. long, 4–6 in. wide. Pure yellow flowers with red stamens are borne in 1½-ft.-long spikes.

H. greenei. Zones MS, LS, CS, TS; 12–7. To 5 ft. tall. Leaves 8–10 in. long, 2 in. wide; orange-red flowers in 5-in. spikes.

H. hasseltii. Zones LS, CS, TS; 12–8. Small plant (to just 2 ft.), with broadly lance-shaped leaves to 1½ ft. long. Spidery-looking white flowers in slender spikes. Seedpods split to reveal pretty red seeds.

H. hybrids. Zones MS, LS, CS, TS; 11–8. These hybrids feature excellent foliage and blossoms; all are worth trying. Leaves are typically large, lance shaped, and rich green.

'Daniel Weeks'. Among the longest-blooming ginger lilies, with stems to 4 ft. tall carrying yellow flowers with a darker gold throat. Grows quickly, making a clump 3–4 ft. wide in its second year.

'Doctor Moy'. Handsome foliage speckled with white. Stalks to 3 ft. tall bear peachy orange blooms with a darker orange throat.

'Elizabeth'. Among the most impressive of the ginger lilies, with towering 9-ft.-tall stems carrying huge reddish orange flowers.

'Golden Butterfly'. Stems 6 ft. tall are topped with bright orange flowers with red stamens.

'Moy Giant'. To 7 ft. tall, featuring large clusters of pale yellow blossoms with a darker yellow throat.

'Pradhan' ('Pradhanii'). To 6 ft. Creamy white blooms with peach-tinged yellow throats and pink stamens.

HEDYOTIS caerulea. See HOUSTONIA caerulea

A PRACTICAL GUIDE TO GARDENING

PLEASE SEE PAGES 596–669

HELENIUM autumnale

SNEEZEWEED, HELEN'S FLOWER

Asteraceae (Compositae)

PERENNIAL

🌿 US, MS, LS, CS **H** 8–1

☀️ FULL SUN

💧 REGULAR WATER

Helenium autumnale

This native perennial should be one of our more popular summer and fall flowers—but when folks hear the common name "sneezeweed," they assume that the plant causes hay fever and grows invasively. In fact, sneezeweed does neither. Numerous leafy stems yield great sheaves of daisylike, typically dark-centered blossoms with yellow, orange, red, or coppery rays (folded back, in many types). Although sneezeweeds are usually listed as selections of *H. autumnale*, most are hybrids.

Trim off faded blooms to encourage more flowers; be sparing with fertilizer. Divide clumps every 2 or 3 years. Sneezeweeds tolerate drought but look better with regular moisture; they must have good drainage, though. Space plants 2 ft. apart.

The following selections are widely available. Tall types reach 4–5 ft. and need staking so are best suited to back of the border. Compact types reach about 3 ft. tall and look great in mixed borders. Both sizes combine well with ornamental grasses.

'Baudirektor Linne'. Tall. Velvety red blooms with a brown center.

'Butterpat'. Tall. Light yellow blossoms with a deeper yellow center.

'Coppelia'. Compact grower. Warm coppery orange petals surround a brown cone.

'Crimson Beauty'. Compact. Dusky deep red, brown-centered flowers.

'Cymbal Star' ('Zimbelstern'). Tall. Gold touched with bronze; brown centers.

'Dunkelpracht' ('Dark Beauty'). Tall. Dark red petals; brown centers.

'Goldkogel'. Compact. Dark-centered yellow blossoms.

'Moerheim Beauty'. Compact. Coppery red petals; brown centers.

'September Gold'. Compact. Bright yellow, brown-centered blooms.

'Sunball' ('Kugelsonne'). Tall. Lemon yellow petals, chartreuse centers.

'Waldtraut'. Tall. Copper-tinged petals surround a dark center.

'Wyndley'. Compact grower. Butter yellow petals around a yellow-brown central disk.

HELIANTHEMUM
nummularium

SUNROSE

Cistaceae

EVERGREEN SHRUBS

🌿 US, MS **H** 8–6

☀️ FULL SUN

💧 MODERATE WATER

Helianthemum nummularium

Commonly sold under this name are a number of forms as well as hybrids between this species and others. They grow about 6–8 in. high and spread to about 3 ft. Leaves are ½–1 in. long; they may be glossy green above and fuzzy gray beneath, or gray on both sides. Plants produce a delightful late spring to early summer display of clustered, inch-wide, single or double flowers in bright or pastel colors—flame red, apricot, orange, yellow, pink, rose, peach, salmon, or white. Each blossom lasts only a day, but new buds continue to open. Shear plants back after they flower to encourage repeat bloom.

Specialists offer many named selections. Especially noteworthy is one sold as *H. apenninum roseum* or as 'Wisley Pink', with comparatively large, pure pink flowers that contrast nicely with the furry gray foliage.

Let sunroses tumble over rocks, set them in niches in dry rock walls, or grow in planters on a sunny terrace. Use them at the seashore (but not on the dunes) or in rock gardens; let them ramble over a gentle slope. If used as ground cover, plant 2–3 ft. apart. In the Upper South, lightly cover plants with branches from evergreens in winter to keep foliage from dehydrating. Plants will be hardier if given not-too-rich soil that is kept on the dry side (good drainage is essential). Object is to encourage hard, nonsucculent growth.

HELIANTHUS

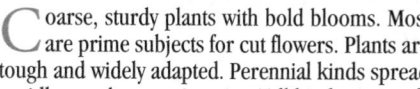

SUNFLOWER

Asteraceae (Compositae)

ANNUALS AND PERENNIALS

ZONES VARY BY SPECIES

FULL SUN

REGULAR TO AMPLE WATER, EXCEPT AS NOTED

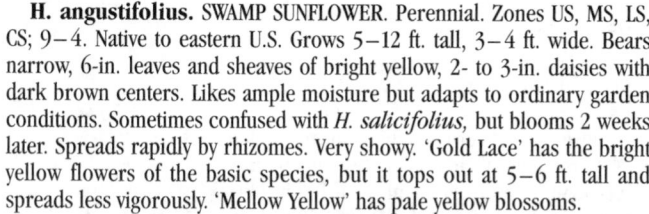

Helianthus annuus

Coarse, sturdy plants with bold blooms. Most are prime subjects for cut flowers. Plants are tough and widely adapted. Perennial kinds spread rapidly, may become invasive. Tall kinds are not for tidy gardens; may need staking. All bloom in summer and fall.

H. angustifolius. SWAMP SUNFLOWER. Perennial. Zones US, MS, LS, CS; 9–4. Native to eastern U.S. Grows 5–12 ft. tall, 3–4 ft. wide. Bears narrow, 6-in. leaves and sheaves of bright yellow, 2- to 3-in. daisies with dark brown centers. Likes ample moisture but adapts to ordinary garden conditions. Sometimes confused with *H. salicifolius,* but blooms 2 weeks later. Spreads rapidly by rhizomes. Very showy. 'Gold Lace' has the bright yellow flowers of the basic species, but it tops out at 5–6 ft. tall and spreads less vigorously. 'Mellow Yellow' has pale yellow blossoms.

H. annuus. COMMON SUNFLOWER. Annual. Zones US, MS, LS, CS, TS; 12–1. The wild ancestor of today's familiar sunflowers is a coarse, hairy plant with 2- to 3-in.-wide flowers, native to much of the central U.S. and southward to Central America. It is the state flower of Kansas and the only plant native to the contiguous 48 states to have become an important agricultural commodity. It has been bred to produce giant plants as well as a host of smaller (but still significant) selections for garden decoration and cut flowers.

Best known among the giant forms are 'Mammoth Russian' and 'Russian Giant'. They grow 10 ft. (possibly 15 ft.) tall and 2 ft. wide, typically producing a single huge head (sometimes over a foot across) consisting of a circle of short yellow rays with a brown central cushion of seeds. Newer selection 'Kong' is similarly towering; 'Sunspot' carries 10-in.-wide flower heads on 2-ft.-high plants. For children, annual sunflowers are easy to grow and bring a sense of great accomplishment. Sow seeds in spring where plants are to grow. Large-flowered kinds need rich, moist soil. People eat the roasted seeds; birds enjoy the raw ones in fall and winter.

Sunflowers for cutting come on compact, branching plants and bear 4- to 8-in.-wide blooms in a rich variety of colors. They fall into two basic categories: pollen-bearing types and pollenless ones. Kinds with pollen include 'Del Sol', early-blooming, yellow, 5 ft. tall; 'Indian Blanket', red with yellow tips, 4–5 ft.; 'Italian White', creamy yellow to near white, 5 ft.; 'Lemon Eclair', light yellow, 4–6 ft.; 'Moonshadow', pale yellow to cream, 4 ft.; Parasol Mix, lemon, orange, red, and bicolor, 4–5 ft.; and 'Ring of Fire', petals dark red at base and golden yellow at tips, 5–6 ft. tall. 'Teddy Bear', only 1½ ft. high, has fully double, 6-in.-wide flowers that look like pompons.

Kinds without pollen, classified as *H. ×hybridus,* have the advantage of not shedding on tabletops. They include Large Flowered Mix, yellow, red, and bronze, 6–10 ft. tall; 'Bright Bandolier', yellow-and-mahogany bicolor, 5–7 ft.; 'Cinnamon Sun', cinnamon bronze, 4–7 ft.; 'Prado Red', deep garnet, 3½–4 ft.; 'Valentine', light yellow, 4–5 ft.; and 'Velvet Queen', combination of bronze, burgundy, chestnut red, and mahogany, 6–8 ft.

H. atrorubens. DARK-EYED SUNFLOWER. Perennial. Zones US, MS, LS, CS; 9–3. Native to southeastern U.S. Grows 5–6 ft. tall, not quite as wide, with coarse, bristly foliage and 2-in. yellow flower heads centered in

dark purple. 'Monarch' has semidouble flowers somewhat resembling the quilled flowers of a cactus-form dahlia.

H. 'Lemon Queen'. Perennial. Zones US, MS, LS, CS; 12–1. Selected from a hybrid of two species native to the U.S., this stately plant grows 6–8 ft. tall, 2–3 ft. wide. Numerous pale yellow, brown-centered, 2-in. flowers appear in late summer. Perfect for back of casual border or in combination with large ornamental grasses. Takes moist or dry soil.

H. maximilianii. MAXIMILIAN SUNFLOWER. Perennial. Zones US, MS, LS, CS; 9–1. Native to central and southwestern U.S. Clumps of 10-ft. stems clothed in narrow, 8- to 10-in. leaves and topped with narrow spires of 3-in. yellow flowers. Spreads to 3 ft. wide.

H. microcephalus. SMALLHEAD SUNFLOWER. Perennial. Zones US, MS, LS, CS; 9–1. Native from New Jersey to Florida. To 3–6 ft. tall, 2–3 ft. wide. Lance-shaped to ovate 3- to 4-in.-long leaves. Clear yellow, 1- to 1½-in. flowers.

H. ×multiflorus. Perennial. Zones US, MS, LS, CS; 9–3. Hybrid between *H. annuus* and a perennial species. To 5 ft. high, 2½–3 ft. wide, with thin, toothed, 3- to 8-in.-long leaves and numerous 3-in.-wide flower heads with yellow centers. Excellent for cutting. Flowers of 'Capenoch Star' are single, lemon yellow with a large central brown disk. Recommended double-flowered types include bright yellow 'Flore Pleno' and golden yellow 'Loddon Gold'.

H. salicifolius (H. orgyalis). WILLOWLEAF SUNFLOWER. Perennial. Zones US, MS, LS, CS; 9–6. Native to the central U.S. Looks somewhat like *H. angustifolius* (the two are sometimes mistaken for each other) but has narrower, more willowy, drooping leaves.

H. tuberosus. JERUSALEM ARTICHOKE. Perennial. Zones US, MS, LS, CS; 9–1. From eastern and central North America. Also grown as a commercial crop; tubers are edible and sold in markets under the name "sunchokes." Grows 6–10 ft. tall, 3 ft. wide, with bright yellow flower

Helianthus tuberosus

heads. Oval leaves 8 in. long. Spreads readily and can become a pest. Best to harvest tubers every year and save out two or three for replanting. If controlled, makes a good, quick temporary screen or hedge.

HELICHRYSUM

Asteraceae (Compositae)

ANNUALS AND PERENNIALS

ZONES VARY BY SPECIES

FULL SUN

MODERATE WATER

Helichrysum petiolare 'Limelight'

Best known are the annual strawflowers (*H. bracteatum* and *H. subulifolium*) used in fresh and dried arrangements. Others, though less familiar, are choice plants for landscape use. Seldom bothered by deer.

H. bracteatum. STRAWFLOWER. Annual. Zones US, MS, LS, CS, TS; 12–1. From Australia. To 2–3 ft. tall, 1 ft. wide, with straplike, 2- to 5-in.-long, medium green leaves. Blooms from summer until frost, bearing many papery, 2½-in. flowers that look like prickly pompons. Colors include yellow, orange, red, pink, and white. Known as "everlasting" because its blossoms last indefinitely when dried. Sow in place in late spring or earliest summer (at same time as zinnias). Dwarf forms are also available.

For shrubby perennial forms (such as 'Cockatoo', 'Dargan Hill Monarch', 'Diamond Head') previously included with annual strawflower, see *Bracteantha bracteata.*

H. italicum (H. angustifolium). CURRY PLANT. Woody-based perennial in Zones LS, CS, TS; can be grown as an annual elsewhere; 12–1. From southern Europe. Spreading, branching plant to 2 ft. high, about as broad, with crowded, narrow, nearly white leaves to 1½ in. long. Leaves emit a strong fragrance of curry powder when bruised or pinched; though they are not used in curry, a few can add a pleasant aroma to a salad or meat dish. Bright yellow, ½-in. flower heads appear in clusters 2 in. across, midsummer to autumn.

H. petiolare. LICORICE PLANT. Perennial in Zones TS; can be grown as annual elsewhere; 12–1. From South Africa. Woody-based plant to 1½–3 ft. high, with trailing stems to 4 ft. long. White, woolly, inch-long leaves; insignificant flowers. Licorice aroma sometimes noticeable—in hot, still weather, for example, or when leaves are dry. 'Limelight' has luminous light chartreuse leaves; 'Variegatum' has foliage with white markings. All kinds are useful for their trailing branches, which will thread through mixed plantings or mix with other plants in large pots or hanging baskets. For the so-called dwarf form, see *Plecostachys serpyllifolia*.

H. subulifolium. Annual. Zones US, MS, LS, CS, TS; 12–1. From western Australia. Mound-shaped plant to 20 in. tall, 10–12 in. wide, with glossy green, 5-in. leaves and bright, shining, orange-yellow summer flowers 1½ in. wide. Excellent for fresh or dried arrangements.

HELICONIA

LOBSTER-CLAW, FALSE BIRD-OF-PARADISE

Heliconiaceae

PERENNIALS

TS H 12–10; OR GROW IN POTS

FULL SUN OR LIGHT SHADE

AMPLE WATER

Heliconia angusta

Few plants combine the colorful and bizarre as well as these natives of tropical America. Members of this large group feature big clusters of showy bracts containing small true flowers. In some, the clusters look like lobster claws; in others, they remind you of bird-of-paradise *(Strelitzia)* blossoms. Bract colors include red, orange, yellow, pink, lavender, and green. Plants form sizable clumps of large leaves and range in size from 3-ft.-tall patio plants (excellent in containers) to giants reaching upwards of 15 ft. Clumps expand with age, so provide sufficient room.

Heliconias prefer fertile, moist, acid soil. Chlorosis (yellow leaves with green veins) is common in alkaline soil. During periods of active growth, give plants plenty of water and feed frequently with a balanced liquid fertilizer. Stems that have flowered should be cut away to make room for new growth. Reduce watering in cool weather. Frost will kill plants to the ground, but they will resprout from rhizomes if the cold spell is short. Where winters are cold for long periods, take potted plants indoors until spring. Smaller types can be easily stored in a garage without water or light; they will turn brown but will green up when taken outdoors once winter is over. Potted plants can bloom any time; those in the ground flower in spring and summer. Deer don't seem to care for them.

Heliconias are excellent cut flowers. To extend the bloom's life, cut off the bottom ½ in. of the stem; then submerge the flowers and foliage in tepid water for an hour prior to display.

H. angusta. To 4–10 ft. tall, with leaves to 3 ft. long. Erect flower clusters to 2½ ft. long. Yellow or orange to vermilion or scarlet bracts; white or yellow-tipped green flowers.

H. bihai (H. humilis). To 6–15 ft. tall, with 2- to 6-ft.-long leaves. Erect blossom clusters 1½–3½ ft. long. Reddish orange bracts with green margins; white to pale green flowers.

H. brasiliensis. To 3–5 ft. tall, with 2½-ft. leaves. Erect clusters of red bracts enfold white or red flowers.

H. caribaea. WILD PLANTAIN. To 6–15 ft. tall, with 5-ft.-long leaves and erect flower clusters to 1½ ft. Bracts are red or yellow, often marked with contrasting colors; flowers are white with green tips.

H. latispatha. Can reach 10 ft. tall, with leaves to 5 ft. long. Erect flower clusters to 1½ ft. tall, with spirally set orange, red, or yellow bracts and green-tipped yellow flowers.

H. pendula. To 6 ft. tall; 2- to 3-ft.-long leaves. Pendulous, 2-ft. inflorescence with spirally arranged red bracts, white flowers. Sometimes sold as *H. collinsiana*.

H. psittacorum. PARROT HELICONIA. Highly variable species; more vigorous than other heliconias. Grows 4–8 ft. tall, with leaves to 20 in. long, blossom clusters to 7 in. long. Bracts spread upward at a 45° angle. They vary in color; may be red, sometimes shading to cream or orange, and are often multicolored. Flowers are yellow, orange, or red, usually tipped in dark green or white. Many named selections are available.

H. rostrata. To 4–6 ft. tall, with 2- to 4-ft.-long leaves. Hanging inflorescences to 1–2 ft. long contain red bracts shading to yellow at the tip; flowers are greenish yellow.

H. schiedeana. Grows to 6–10 ft. tall, with leaves to 5 ft. long. Upright, 1½-ft.-long blossom clusters feature red or orange-red, spiraling bracts that enclose yellow-green flowers.

H. wagneriana. To 6–12 ft. tall, with 4- to 6-ft.-long leaves. Erect flower clusters 6 in.–1½ ft. long. Heavy, overlapping, green-edged bracts are deep pink to pale crimson, shading to cream at base; flowers are white.

HELICTOTRICHON sempervirens
(Avena sempervirens)

BLUE OAT GRASS

Poaceae (Gramineae)

PERENNIAL GRASS

US, MS, LS, CS H 9–1

FULL SUN

REGULAR WATER

Helictotrichon sempervirens

Native to western Mediterranean region. Resembles a giant blue fescue *(Festuca glauca)* but is more graceful, with bright blue-gray, narrow leaves forming a fountainlike clump 2–3 ft. high and wide. In spring, stems to 2 ft. or taller rise above foliage, bearing wispy, straw-colored flower clusters. Grows best in rich, well-drained soil. Attractive in borders or with boulders in rock garden. Pull out occasional withered leaves. Evergreen in mild-winter climates; semievergreen in colder areas. 'Sapphire' has bluer leaves than species.

HELIOPSIS helianthoides
(H. scabra)

FALSE SUNFLOWER

Asteraceae (Compositae)

PERENNIAL

US, MS, LS, CS H 9–1

FULL SUN OR LIGHT SHADE

REGULAR TO MODERATE WATER

Heliopsis helianthoides 'Summer Sun'

This tough, easy-to-grow, long-flowering plant deserves much wider use in gardens. Native from Ontario to the midwestern and southern U.S., it resembles the annual sunflower, *Helianthus annuus*. Forms clumps to 5 ft. high and half as wide, with 6-in., rough-textured, medium green leaves. Bright yellow to orange-yellow flowers, 3 in. wide, appear from June until frost. Good, long-lasting cut flower. Tolerates drought and is seldom bothered by pests. Selections are sometimes offered as varieties of *H. scabra*. The following are some of the best selections.

'Ballerina'. Compact plant to 3 ft. tall, 2 ft. wide. Early bloomer with semidouble yellow flowers.

'Bressingham Doubloon'. Sturdy plant to 4–5 ft. tall, 2–4 ft. wide, with semidouble yellow blooms.

'Goldgefeider' ('Golden Plume'). Double yellow flowers on a plant reaching 3 ft. tall and 2 ft. wide.

'Goldgrünherz' ('Gold Greenheart'). Double golden flowers with unusual green centers. To 3 ft. tall, 2 ft. wide.

'Hohlspiegel'. Deep orange-yellow blooms with concave centers. To 4 ft. tall, 2 ft. wide.

'Karat'. Large single flowers in bright yellow. Grows to 3½ ft. tall and 2 ft. wide.

'Loraine Sunshine'. A conversation piece. White leaves with green veins; single yellow blooms. Compact plant grows just 2½ ft. tall and 1½ ft. wide.

'Summer Sun'. Yellow blooms—some single, some semidouble. To 3 ft. tall, 2 ft. wide.

HELIOTROPE. See HELIOTROPIUM arborescens, VALERIANA officinalis

HELIOTROPIUM
arborescens

COMMON HELIOTROPE

Boraginaceae

PERENNIAL USUALLY TREATED AS ANNUAL

✿ TS; ANYWHERE AS ANNUAL; H 12–1

☼ AFTERNOON SHADE

💧 REGULAR WATER

✿ ALL PARTS ARE POISONOUS IF INGESTED

Heliotropium arborescens

From Peru. This old-fashioned favorite is prized for its showy, vanilla-scented flowers. Although it's most often treated as an annual, it can be grown as a short-lived perennial in the Tropical South. Plants grow 1–1½ ft. tall and wide. Dark green leaves have an overall purplish cast; they are 1–3 in. long, crinkled, and hairy, with sunken veins. Individual flowers, while tiny, are borne in striking clusters, typically 3–4 in. across. Recommended selections include white 'Alba', deep purple 'Black Beauty', and deep violet-blue 'Marine', with blossom clusters up to 10 in. across. The Regal Hybrids sport rose and lavender flowers on the same plant.

In Southern gardens, common heliotrope grows best with morning sun and afternoon shade. Pinch young plants to encourage bushy growth. If growing as a perennial, prune back hard in early spring. Be sure to keep watered during dry spells. Plants can be massed in flower beds; they also look great in window boxes and planters. The sweet-smelling blooms attract butterflies.

HELLEBORUS

HELLEBORE

Ranunculaceae

PERENNIALS

✿ ZONES VARY BY SPECIES

☼◐ FULL OR PARTIAL SHADE

💧💧 WATER NEEDS VARY BY SPECIES

✿ ALL PARTS ARE POISONOUS IF INGESTED

Helleborus argutifolius

Distinctive, long-lived plants that add color to the garden for several months in winter and spring, hellebores are also appreciated for their attractive foliage. Each leaf consists of a long leafstalk ending in large, leathery leaflets grouped together like fingers on an outstretched hand.

All hellebores form tight clumps of many growing points, but species differ in their manner of growth. Some have stems that rise from the ground, with leaves all along their length; stems produce flowers at their tip in their second year, then die to the ground as new stems emerge to replace them. In other species, leaves are not carried on tall stems but arise directly from growing points at ground level; separate (typically leafless) flower stems spring from the same points.

Flowers are usually cup or bell shaped (those of *H. niger* are saucer shaped), either outward facing or drooping; they consist of a ring of petal-like sepals ranging in color from white and green through pink and red to deep purple (rarely yellow). Flowers of all hellebores persist beyond the bloom periods listed below, gradually turning green. Blossoms are attractive in arrangements: after you cut them, slice the bottom inch of the stems lengthwise or seal cut ends by searing over a flame or immersing in boiling water for a few seconds. Then place in cold water. Or simply float flowers in a bowl of water.

Plant in good, well-drained soil amended with plenty of organic matter. Plants prefer soil that is somewhat alkaline but will also grow well in neutral to slightly acid conditions (*H. niger* is an exception; it must have alkaline soil). Feed once or twice a year. Don't disturb hellebores once planted; they resent moving and may take 2 or more years to re-establish. If well sited, however, they may self-sow, and young seedlings can be transplanted in early spring. Offspring may not resemble the parent exactly, but all are attractive. Mass under high-branching trees, on north or east side of walls, or in beds. Not damaged by deer or rodents.

In addition to the following, a half-dozen or more other species are sometimes available. Species here have leafy stems unless otherwise noted.

H. argutifolius (H. corsicus). CORSICAN HELLEBORE. Zones MS, LS; 9–6. From Corsica, Sardinia. Erect or sprawling, to 2–3 ft. tall and wide. Substantial enough to use as a small shrub. Blue-green, 6- to 9-in. leaves divided into three sharply toothed leaflets. Leafy stems carry clusters of 2-in., pale green flowers from winter into spring. More sun tolerant than other hellebores. Moderate water. Two selections with white-marbled leaves are 'Janet Starnes' (which has a touch of pink in the foliage) and 'Pacific Frost'. Seedlings of these plants, sold as Janet Starnes strain and Pacific Frost strain, closely resemble the parents.

H. foetidus. BEAR'S-FOOT HELLEBORE. Zones US, MS, LS; 9–6. From western and central Europe. To 2½ ft. high and wide, the stems clothed with dark green leaves divided into seven to ten narrow, leathery leaflets to 8 in. long. Blooms from winter to spring, bearing clusters of inch-wide light green flowers with purplish red edges. Plant parts are malodorous if crushed or bruised (don't smell bad otherwise). Self-sows freely where adapted. Moderate water. 'Green Giant' is bigger than the basic species, forming a 2½-ft. clump of green foliage that is topped at bloom time with 1-ft.-tall clusters of green bells. 'Piccadilly' has whitish green blossoms and dark green leaves tinged with reddish purple. 'Pontarlier' has toothed green leaves and large clusters of light green, long-lasting flowers. Wester Flisk strain has stems, flower stems, and leafstalks infused with purplish red, with the color extending into leaf bases.

H. hybrids. Zones US, MS, LS; 9–6. Leaves have no obvious stems. Hybrid plants generally resemble principal parent *H. orientalis*, but flower color range has been extended and superior parents selected for seed production. Some are sold under the breeder's name (*H. ×ballardiae*), some as strains (Royal Heritage strain), some merely as color groups (Ballard Red Group; *H. ×hybridus* Purple Group, Pink Group, Picotee Group). Regular water.

H. lividus. Zones MS, LS; 9–7. From Majorca. To 1½ ft. high and twice as wide. Leaves resemble those of *H. argutifolius* but lack noticeable teeth and have purplish undersides and a network of pale veins above. Winter-to-spring flowers are 1¼–2 in. wide, pale green washed with pinkish purple; carried in clusters of up to ten. Moderate water.

H. niger. CHRISTMAS ROSE. Zones US, MS; 8–1. From Europe. Leaves have no obvious stems. Elegant plant to 1 ft. tall, 1½ ft. wide, blooming from December into spring. Lustrous dark green leaves are divided into seven to nine lobes with a few large teeth; they seem to rise directly from the soil. White, 2-in. flowers appear singly or in groups of two or three on a stout stem about the same height as the foliage clump. Blooms turn pinkish with age. Less tolerant of light than other hellebores; needs more definite shade. Needs alkaline soil and regular water. 'White Magic' is a large-flowered selection. Plants of *H. orientalis* are often mislabeled Christmas rose.

H. orientalis. LENTEN ROSE. Zones US, MS, LS; 8–3. From Greece, Turkey, Caucasus. Leaves have no obvious stems. Much like *H. niger* in growth but more tolerant of warm-winter climates. Basal leaves with 5 to 11 sharply toothed leaflets; branched flowering stems to 1 ft. tall, with

Helleborus orientalis

H

leaflike bracts at branching points. Blooms in late winter and spring; flowers are 2–4 in. wide, in colors including white, pink, purplish, cream, and greenish, often spotted with deep purple. Easier to transplant than other hellebores. A widely variable plant, but all forms are attractive. Encourage self-sowing and keep the colors you like. Hybridizes freely with many other species; many nursery plants may be hybrids. Regular water.

H. × sternii. Zones US, MS, LS; 9–6. Hybrid between *H. argutifolius* and *H. lividus,* with bluish green foliage netted with white or cream. Greenish, 1- to 2-in. flowers suffused with pink bloom from winter to spring. Variable from seed. Moderate water.

H. viridis. GREEN HELLEBORE. Zones US, MS, LS; 8–1. To 1½ ft. tall, 1½ ft. wide. Graceful bright green leaves are divided into 7 to 11 leaflets; leafy stems bear 1- to 2-in.-wide flowers in pure green to yellowish green, sometimes with purple on inside. Blooms from winter through late spring. *H. v. occidentalis* has smaller blossoms and larger leaves. Regular water.

HELXINE soleirolii. See SOLEIROLIA soleirolii

HEMEROCALLIS

DAYLILY

Liliaceae

PERENNIALS FROM TUBEROUS ROOTS

US, MS, LS, CS, TS, EXCEPT AS NOTED

PARTIAL SHADE IN HOTTEST CLIMATES

REGULAR WATER

Hemerocallis hybrid

When talk turns to surefire perennials for the South, it doesn't take long for the word "daylily" to come up. Few plants offer so many flowers in so many colors for so little care. Tuberous, somewhat fleshy roots give rise to large clumps of arching, sword-shaped leaves that may be evergreen, semievergreen, or deciduous, depending on type. Deciduous daylilies die down completely in winter and perform best where they get some winter chill. Evergreen kinds maintain their foliage throughout winter, claiming a permanent spot in the garden. Semievergreen daylilies may or may not keep their leaves, depending on where they are grown.

Clusters of flowers resembling lilies appear at the end of generally leafless, wandlike stems that rise well above the foliage. Most daylilies bloom once a year, producing numerous flowers over a 3-week period. Other types bloom off and on all summer. The older orange- and yellow-flowered species have now been largely supplanted by hundreds of newer hybrids in a rainbow of colors; both tall and dwarf types are available. If you want to try species daylilies, you'll probably have to order from a specialty nursery.

Mass daylilies in solid sweeps or mix them into herbaceous borders. Plant them on banks and roadsides or group them near pools and streams. Dwarf types are excellent in rock gardens and containers or as low edging. All daylilies make good cut flowers. Cut stems with well-developed buds; these open on successive days, though each blossom is slightly smaller than the previous one.

Set out bare-root plants in spring or fall. Container-grown daylilies can be planted at any time, provided the ground isn't frozen.

Though normally pest-free, daylilies are now threatened by a serious disease, daylily rust (*Puccinia hemerocallidis*). First identified in Georgia in 2000, this rapidly spreading fungus causes yellow to orange streaks and pustules to form on the leaves. A number of widely planted selections, including 'Stella de Oro' and 'Pardon Me', are highly susceptible. The growing popularity of evergreen daylilies may help spread the disease, because the rust overwinters on live foliage. To control, pick off and burn all infected leaves; then spray at regular intervals with a recommended fungicide according to label directions.

H. altissima. TALL DAYLILY. Deciduous. From China. To 5–6 ft. tall, 3 ft. wide. Blooms in late summer and early autumn; the pale yellow, 4-in.

---

flowers give off a light perfume at night. 'Statuesque', with 5-ft. stems, blooms in mid- to late summer.

H. citrina. Deciduous. Heat zones 9–1. From China. To 3–4 ft. high, 1½–2 ft. wide. Blooms in midsummer, bearing fragrant, narrow-petaled, soft lemon yellow flowers to 3 in. across that open in early evening and last until noon the next day. Leaves are longer and narrower than those of most daylilies.

H. dumortieri. Deciduous. Heat zones 9–1. From Korea, Japan, eastern Russia. To 1½–2 ft. tall, 2 ft. wide. Attractive reddish buds open to 2- to 3-in.-wide, fragrant, lemon yellow flowers streaked with brown on the petal backs. Blooms in midspring.

H. fulva. TAWNY DAYLILY, COMMON ORANGE DAYLILY. Deciduous. Heat zones 12–1. From China or Japan. To 3–5 ft. high and 4 ft. wide; quickly spreads into colonies. Leaves are 2 ft. or longer. Tawny orange-red, 3- to 5-in., unscented flowers in summer. A tough, persistent plant suitable for holding banks; rarely sold but commonly seen in old gardens and along roadsides. Double-flowered 'Kwanso' and 'Flore Pleno' are sometimes seen in the same locales.

H. hybrids. Deciduous, evergreen, and semievergreen. Standard-size hybrids generally grow 2½–4 ft. tall, 2–3 ft. wide; some selections reach 6 ft. high. Dwarf types grow just 1–2 ft. tall and wide. Flowers of standard kinds are 4–8 in. across, those of dwarfs 1½–3½ in. wide. Some have broad petals, others narrow, spidery ones; many have ruffled petal edges. Colors range far beyond the basic yellow, orange, and rusty red to pink, vermilion, buff, apricot, plum or lilac purple, cream, and near-white, often with contrasting eyes or midrib stripes that yield a bicolor effect. Many are sprinkled with tiny iridescent dots known as diamond dust. Selections with semidouble and double flowers are available. Tetraploid types have unusually heavy-textured petals.

Bloom usually begins in midspring, but early and late bloomers are also available. By planting all three types, you can extend the bloom period. Scattered bloom may occur during summer, and reblooming types put on second display in late summer to midautumn. Some selections bloom throughout warm weather. These include 3-ft.-tall Starburst series, which comes in a variety of colors, as well as 2-ft.-high dwarf selections 'Black-eyed Stella' (yellow with red eye), bright yellow 'Happy Returns' and 'Stella de Oro', and red 'Pardon Me'.

New hybrids appear in such numbers that no book can keep up. To get the ones you want, visit daylily specialists, buy plants in bloom at your local nursery, or study catalogs. Look for selections that have won awards from the American Hemerocallis Society. AM stands for Award of Merit, given to ten selections each year. HM means Honorable Mention, awarded to any plant receiving ten votes from the selection committee. SM stands for Stout Medal, the highest award a daylily can receive. Past SM winners include the long-blooming 'Stella de Oro' and the free-blooming yellow tetraploid 'Mary Todd'. An old selection that has maintained its popularity is 'Hyperion', a 4-footer with exceptionally fragrant yellow blooms.

H. lilioasphodelus (H. flava). LEMON DAYLILY. Deciduous. Heat zones 12–2. From China. Reaches to 3 ft. high and wide, with 2-ft.-long leaves and 4-in., fragrant, pure yellow flowers in mid- to late spring. Newer hybrids may be showier, but this species is still cherished for its delightful perfume and early bloom time.

H. minor. GRASS-LEAF DAYLILY. Deciduous. Zones US, MS, LS; 9–3. From eastern Asia. To 2 ft. high and wide, with narrow (¼-in.-wide) leaves. Blooms for a relatively short time in late spring or early summer, when fragrant, bright golden yellow, 4-in. flowers are held just above the foliage.

HEMIGRAPHIS alternata

Hemigraphis alternata

RED IVY

Acanthaceae

PERENNIAL

☈ TS ⌑ 12–10; ANYWHERE AS ANNUAL

◑ PARTIAL SHADE

◕ REGULAR WATER

Native to Indonesia and Malaysia, this creeping tropical vine is grown for its extremely attractive foliage: oval to heart-shaped, silvery green leaves with a reddish purple flush toward the tips and vivid burgundy undersides. Leaves are 1–3 in. long, with toothed edges. Inch-long spikes of small, bell-shaped, rather inconspicuous white flowers appear off and on throughout the growing season.

Where it is winter hardy, red ivy spreads by rooting stems to make a beautiful ground cover about 6 in. tall. Elsewhere, it's a colorful candidate for hanging baskets and mixed planters—or as a seasonal ground cover or edging plant. It needs well-drained soil and protection from afternoon sun. Easy to propagate from cuttings.

HEMLOCK. See TSUGA

HEMP AGRIMONY. See EUPATORIUM cannabinum

HEN AND CHICKENS. See SEMPERVIVUM tectorum

HEN AND CHICKS. See ECHEVERIA

HEPATICA

Hepatica americana

LIVERWORT, HEPATICA

Ranunculaceae

PERENNIALS

☈ US, MS, LS, CS

◑● PARTIAL TO FULL SHADE

◕ REGULAR WATER

Reaching 6–9 in. high and 6 in. wide, these low-growing, evergreen or nearly evergreen woodland plants resemble smaller sorts of anemones (and were formerly considered to be anemones). In herbal medicine, they have been used to treat disorders of the liver, hence the common name. Plants bloom in early spring, bearing flowers with numerous narrow, petal-like sepals arranged around a central mass of yellow stamens. Each bloom rises on its own stalk above the clump of last year's foliage. A new crop of leaves follows bloom.

These are choice plants for woodland gardens and shaded rock gardens. Though little known in North America except among wildflower fanciers, they are popular with plant collectors in Japan, where many selections are cultivated.

H. acutiloba. SHARPLOBE HEPATICA. Heat zones 9–3. Native to eastern and central North America. Leathery, 4-in. leaves are divided into three sharp-pointed lobes. Flowers are lilac and white, ½–1 in. across, on stems to 9 in. high.

H. americana. LIVERWORT. Heat zones 8–1. Native to eastern and central North America. Leathery, 4-in. leaves with three rounded lobes. Flowering stems are usually 6 in. high. Flowers are ½–1 in. wide, typically light blue but sometimes pink or white.

H. nobilis (H. triloba). Heat zones 8–4. Native to Europe. Very similar to *H. americana*. Flowers are usually bluish purple but may be white or pink.

HEPTACODIUM miconioides

Heptacodium miconioides

SEVEN SONS FLOWER

Caprifoliaceae

DECIDUOUS SHRUB OR TREE

☈ US, MS, LS ⌑ 9–4

☀◐ FULL SUN OR LIGHT SHADE

◕ REGULAR WATER

From China. Fountain-shaped shrub to 15–20 ft. tall, 8–10 ft. wide. Large, narrowly heart-shaped leaves are shiny green, deeply veined. Fragrant, creamy white flowers in 6-in.-long clusters at branch ends open over a long bloom season in late summer and fall. Blooms are succeeded by even showier masses of small fruits with bright purplish red calyxes. Common name derives from the number of flowers in each of the clusters forming part of the larger inflorescence. Picturesque even in winter, when bark is on show: thin, pale tan strips peel away to reveal dark brown bark beneath. Not fussy about soil; not bothered by pests or diseases. Can be trained as a single- or multitrunked tree.

HERALD'S TRUMPET. See BEAUMONTIA grandiflora

HERB-OF-GRACE. See RUTA graveolens

HERBS. At some time in history, the plants in this category have been valued for seasoning, medicine, fragrance, or general household use.

Herbs are versatile. Some creep along the ground, making fragrant carpets. Others are shrublike. Many make attractive pot plants—but quite a few do have a weedy look, especially next to ornamental plants. Many are hardy and adaptable. Hot, dry, sunny conditions with poor but well-drained soil are usually considered best, but some herbs thrive in shady, moist locations with light soil rich in humus.

Following are lists of herbs for specific situations and uses.

Kitchen garden. Plant these basic cooking herbs in a sunny raised bed near the kitchen door, in a planter box near the barbecue, or as part of the vegetable garden: sweet basil (*Ocimum basilicum*), chives (*Allium schoenoprasum*), cilantro (*Coriandrum sativum*), dill (*Anethum graveolens*), sweet marjoram (*Origanum majorana*), mint (*Mentha*), oregano (*Origanum vulgare*), parsley (*Petroselinum*), rosemary (*Rosmarinus*), sage (*Salvia officinalis*), savory (*Satureja*), Mexican mint marigold (*Tagetes lucida*), thyme (*Thymus*).

Ground cover for sunny areas. Prostrate rosemary, creeping thyme (*Thymus praecox arcticus*), lemon thyme (*T. citriodorus*), silver thyme (*T. pseudolanuginosus*).

Ground cover for shade. Sweet woodruff (*Galium odoratum*).

Perennial border. Common wormwood (*Artemisia absinthium*), garden burnet (*Sanguisorba minor*), lavender (*Lavandula*), monarda, rosemary, scented geraniums (*Pelargonium*).

Hedges. Formal clipped hedge—santolina, germander (*Teucrium*). Informal hedge—lavender, winter savory (*Satureja montana*).

Herbs for moist areas. Mint, parsley, sweet woodruff.

Herbs for partial shade. Lemon balm (*Melissa officinalis*), parsley, sweet woodruff. ▶

H

Herbs for containers. Crete dittany *(Origanum dictamnus)*, chives, lemon verbena *(Aloysia triphylla)*, sage, pineapple sage *(Salvia elegans)*, summer savory *(Satureja hortensis)*, sweet marjoram, mint, garden burnet.

Potpourris and sachets. Lavender, lemon balm, sweet woodruff, lemon verbena, monarda.

EDIBLE HERB BOUQUETS. *Don't worry about snipping more kitchen herbs than you need. Put the extra cuttings of basil, marjoram, mint, oregano, rosemary, sage, and thyme in a vase of water and use them to decorate the table. They'll remain kitchen-useful as long as they stay perky (often a week or more).* ❖

HERCULES' CLUB. See ARALIA spinosa

HERNIARIA glabra

GREEN CARPET, RUPTURE WORT

Caryophyllaceae

PERENNIAL SOMETIMES TREATED AS ANNUAL

LS, CS, TS H 12–8

SUN OR SHADE

REGULAR WATER

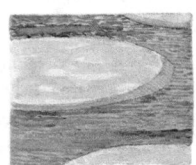

Herniaria glabra

From Eurasia and North Africa, especially the Mediterranean area. Trailing plant 1–3 in. high, with crowded, tiny (less than ¼-in.-long) bright green leaves. Flowers are negligible. Spreads well by rooting stems but won't grow out of control. Use it between stepping-stones, on mounds, among rocks, or between sidewalk and street curb. Plant 1 ft. apart. Endures the occasional footstep but won't take constant traffic. Provide well-drained soil.

HESPERALOE

Agavaceae

PERENNIALS

MS, LS, CS, TS H 12–7, EXCEPT AS NOTED

FULL SUN OR LIGHT SHADE

LITTLE TO MODERATE WATER

Hesperaloe parviflora

Clumps of narrow evergreen leaves with threadlike fringe along edges give rise to tall, branching inflorescences set with many tubular flowers. Foliage clumps resemble yucca or coarse grass. Plants require little maintenance aside from removal of spent flower clusters. Established plants can get by with little summer water, but they look and bloom better with a soaking every 2 weeks or so during warm weather.

H. campanulata. From northern Mexico. Bright green leaves form tight clumps of rosettes to 3 ft. high and wide. In summer, stems to 9 ft. tall bear bell-shaped light pink flowers about 1 in. across. Hardy to 10°F.

H. funifera. From northern Mexico. Clumps to 6 ft. tall, 6–8 ft. wide. Stems to 15 ft. high bear inch-wide, greenish white flowers in late spring or early summer.

H. nocturna. From northern Mexico. Foliage clump 5 ft. tall, 6 ft. wide. In late spring and early summer, blossom spikes, to 12 ft. high, bear many 1-in., night-blooming, slightly fragrant greenish lavender flowers.

H. parviflora. RED YUCCA. Zones US, MS, LS, CS, TS. From Texas and New Mexico. Foliage clumps 3–4 ft. tall and wide produce 5-ft. stalks carrying many rose red to bright red, 1¼-in. flowers from late spring through midsummer, sometimes into early fall. Especially heat tolerant, thriving even in reflected heat. Excellent container plant. A yellow-flowered form is available.

HESPERIS matronalis

DAME'S ROCKET, SWEET ROCKET

Brassicaceae (Cruciferae)

PERENNIAL OR BIENNIAL

US, MS, LS, CS, TS H 12–1

FULL SUN OR LIGHT SHADE

REGULAR WATER

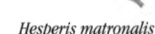

Hesperis matronalis

An old-fashioned favorite for Southern cottage gardens. Freely branched plant grows to 3 ft. tall and as broad, with 4-in., toothed leaves and rounded clusters of ½-in., four-petaled lavender to purple blooms. Flowers resemble those of stock *(Matthiola)* and are fragrant at night. Plant grows readily from seed and often self-sows. Old, woody plants should be replaced by young seedlings. White and double-flowered forms exist but are rare. Rarely damaged by browsing deer.

HETEROTHECA. See CHRYSOPSIS

HEUCHERA

CORAL BELLS, ALUM ROOT

Saxifragaceae

PERENNIALS

US, MS, LS

LIGHT SHADE OR MORNING SUN

MODERATE TO REGULAR WATER

Heuchera sanguinea

Refined, well-behaved plants that offer both attractive bell-shaped blossoms and handsome evergreen foliage. Slender, wiry, 1- to 2½-ft. stems bear loose clusters of nodding flowers that are typically no more than ⅛ in. across. These dainty blooms, which often lack petals, make an interesting and long-lasting addition to arrangements; they also attract hummingbirds. Colors include carmine, crimson, red, coral, rose, pink, greenish, and white. Most bloom in spring and late summer, and some continue into fall. Leaves are roundish, with scalloped edges; many recent introductions are grown more for fancy foliage than flowers.

Use coral bells in combination with other perennials in mixed borders; try them in rock gardens and in sweeping masses. Plant in well-drained soil containing lots of organic matter. Divide clumps every 3 to 4 years in spring or fall. Replant vigorous rooted divisions; discard older, woody portions. Can also be started from seed sown in spring. Watch out for mealybugs, which sometimes infest plants near the base; control with regular applications of insecticidal soap.

H. americana. AMERICAN ALUM ROOT. Heat zones 8–1. From central U.S. Foliage mound 1–2 ft. high and wide. Leaves 1½–4½ in. wide, marbled and veined brown or purple when young, maturing to green mottled with white. Flower stalks to 3 ft. high bear tiny greenish white blossoms in early summer.

The following are selections grown for handsome foliage (a few also have somewhat more attractive flowers than the basic species).

'Amber Waves'. Heavily ruffled leaves emerge golden, then age to burnished orange. Light rose flowers.

'Chocolate Ruffles'. Leaves dark chocolate above, burgundy underneath; burgundy color also shows in the ruffles on leaf edges. Purple blossom spikes and flowers.

'Chocolate Veil'. Chocolate-colored leaves with maroon undersides; top surfaces of leaves are marbled with light purple and silver between veins. Purple flowers tinged lime green.

'Garnet'. Deep red winter foliage; brighter new foliage in spring.

'Lace Ruffles'. Ruffled, scalloped green leaves mottled silvery white.

'Persian Carpet'. Silver leaves with dark purple veins and leaf edges.

'Pewter Moon'. Purple leaves centered with silver.

'Pewter Veil'. Shining silvery leaves; small purple flowers.

'Plum Pudding'. Ruffled leaves are plum purple with silver veins. Thin purple stems bear pink flowers.

'Ring of Fire'. Silvery, purple-veined leaves develop a red rim in fall.

'Ruby Veil'. Large (8-in.), silvery leaves; veins red near leaf base.

'Velvet Night'. Deep bluish purple leaves.

H. × brizoides. Heat zones 8–1. Diverse group of hybrids between *H. sanguinea* and other species. To 1–2½ ft. tall, 1–1½ ft. wide, with spring or summer bloom. Seed-grown strain called Bressingham Hybrids offers flowers in white and shades of pink and red. Selected cutting-grown types include 'Firefly' ('Leuchtkäfer'), with fragrant bells in fiery scarlet; 'Freedom', profuse rosy pink blooms; 'Bressingham White', long-blooming white; 'June Bride', large pure white blossoms; 'Snowstorm', deep reddish pink flowers above white-variegated foliage.

H. micrantha. Heat zones 8–2. Native to California, Washington, Oregon, Idaho. Adapts easily to garden conditions. Long-stalked, roundish, gray-green, 1- to 3-in.-wide leaves are toothed and lobed, hairy on both sides. Late-spring to early-summer flowers are whitish or greenish, about ⅛ in. long, carried in loose clusters on leafy, 2- to 3-ft. stems. Hybrid forms developed from *H. micrantha* are more adaptable than the species. Seed-grown (hence variable) selections include 'Palace Purple', with maplelike, rich brownish or purplish leaves that retain their color year-round if given adequate sunlight; and 'Ruffles', with leaves that are deeply lobed and ruffled around the edges.

Heuchera micrantha
'Palace Purple'

H. sanguinea. CORAL BELLS. Heat zones 8–1. Native to New Mexico and Arizona. Round, 1- to 2-in. leaves with scalloped edges form neat foliage tufts. From spring into summer, slender, wiry, 1- to 2-ft. stems bear open clusters of nodding, bell-shaped, bright red or coral pink flowers. Selections include deep brick red 'Carmen', rosy coral 'Chatterbox', coral pink 'Gaiety', and pure white 'White Cloud'. 'Cherry Splash' and 'Frosty' display red flowers above variegated foliage—the former has white-and-gold variegation, the latter silvery variegation.

H. villosa. HAIRY ALUM ROOT. Heat zones 9–1. Native from Virginia to Georgia and Tennessee. Both foliage and flowers are softly hairy. Toothed-edged green leaves to 5 in. across have triangular lobes, form a mound 1½–2 ft. high and wide. White to pinkish blossoms on stems to 3 ft. tall appear late in the season, near the end of summer. 'Autumn Bride' has lime green leaves and white flowers. 'Purpurea' features deep purple foliage and white blossoms.

× HEUCHERELLA

Saxifragaceae

PERENNIALS

☘ US, MS, LS ❈ 8–5, EXCEPT AS NOTED

◑ LIGHT SHADE

⬤ REGULAR WATER

×*Heucherella alba*
'Bridget Bloom'

These hybrids combine the flowering habit of coral bells (*Heuchera*) with the heart-shaped leaves of foamflower (*Tiarella cordifolia*). Most produce foliage clumps 4–5 in. high and about 1 ft. wide; good in shaded rock gardens or as woodland ground cover. Most bloom in late spring or early summer, with a possible second bloom in fall. Unless otherwise noted, all types described here produce plumes of small pink flowers. Require well-drained, humus-rich soil.

× H. alba 'Bridget Bloom'. Flowering stems to 16 in. high. Blooms from spring to midsummer.

× H. 'Crimson Cloud'. Green leaves with silver veins. Red flowers on stems 1½ ft. high.

× H. 'Dayglow Pink'. Green leaves with chocolate brown veins. Blossoms are densely packed on stems to 1½ ft. tall.

× H. 'Kimono'. Forms a big (up to 3-ft.-wide) foliage clump; green leaves have a wide black stripe down the middle, turn reddish when temperature drops. White flowers on stems to 20 in. high.

× H. 'Pink Frost'. Heat zones 7–1. Plumes rise to 2 ft. Blooms from spring to fall.

× H. 'Quicksilver'. Bronzy foliage with silver highlights. Stems to 1½ ft. high bear profuse, especially large white flowers.

× H. 'Silver Streak'. Green leaves overlaid with purple and silver. Stems to 1½ ft. tall hold white flowers tinged with lavender.

× H. tiarelloides. Sprays of flowers to 1½ ft. high. Blooms from spring to midsummer, often with repeat flowering in autumn.

× H. 'Viking Ship'. Silvery leaves (tinged with purple in spring) have olive green veins. Two-tone pink flowers on 1½- to 2-ft. stems. Especially tolerant of high humidity.

HIBISCUS

Malvaceae

DECIDUOUS AND EVERGREEN SHRUBS, PERENNIALS, AND ANNUALS

☘ ZONES VARY BY SPECIES

☼ FULL SUN, EXCEPT AS NOTED

⬤ REGULAR WATER, EXCEPT AS NOTED

Hibiscus syriacus
'Diana'

Among the showiest flowering plants in Southern gardens, hibiscus typically bear funnel-shaped blossoms—sometimes as big as dinner plates, and often with prominent stamens. The many species offer an astonishing range of flower colors, and most bloom over a long season. Whiteflies and aphids are common pests; insecticidal soap is a good control for both.

H. acetosella (H. eetveldeanus). REDLEAF HIBISCUS. Evergreen shrubby perennial. Zones TS; 12–10; or grow in pot. From central and eastern Africa. Reaches 5 ft. tall and 3 ft. wide. Cultivated more for its foliage than its dark-centered red or yellow flowers. Leaves are up to 1 ft. across; they may be lobed (somewhat like a maple leaf) or unlobed. Color varies from green to deep purplish red. Only the red form is commonly grown; it is often used as a coarse hedge.

H. coccineus. TEXAS STAR. Shrubby perennial. Zones MS, LS, CS, TS; 12–6. Native to coastal swamps of Florida and Georgia. Moderately fast-growing bush to 6 ft. tall and 3 ft. wide, with handsome glossy foliage; very showy scarlet flowers, 3 in. wide, bloom from June to October. Palmate leaves with three to seven lobes look much like those of Japanese maple (*Acer palmatum*). Use as an accent or at the back of a perennial border. Does well in either wet or well-drained soil.

H. militaris. HALBERD-LEAFED ROSE-MALLOW. Shrubby perennial. Zones US, MS, LS, CS, TS; 9–1. Native to marshes and wet woods from Pennsylvania to Minnesota, south to Florida and Texas. If grown in moist soil, quickly attains 8 ft. tall, 3 ft. wide. Dagger-shaped dark green leaves to 6 in. long; pinkish white, 4- to 6-in. flowers from May to October. Tolerates partial shade; takes heavy soils with poor drainage.

H. moscheutos. PERENNIAL HIBISCUS, COMMON ROSE-MALLOW. Perennial. Zones US, MS, LS, CS, TS; 12–1. Native to the southern U.S., and an old Southern favorite. Largest flowers of all hibiscus, some to 1 ft. across, on a plant 6–8 ft. tall and 3 ft. wide. Bloom starts in June, continues until fall. Oval, toothed leaves to 8 in. long are deep green above, whitish beneath. Plants die down in winter. Feed at 6- to 8-week intervals during growing season. Protect from wind.

Seed-grown strains often flower the first year if sown indoors and planted out early. Southern Belle strain grows 4 ft. tall; Disco Belle, Frisbee, and Rio Carnival strains are 2–2½ ft. tall. Flowers are 8–12 in. wide, come in red, pink, rose, or white, often with a red eye.

The many cutting-grown selections and hybrids include the following. Unless otherwise noted, all reach about 4 ft. high. ▶

H

'Anne Arundel'. Blooms to 9 in. across, in clear pink with a red eye.

'Blue River'. Pure white flowers to 10 in. across. Foliage may have a bluish cast.

'Fantasia'. To 2−3 ft. high, with rosy pink, 9-in. flowers with a rosy red center.

'George Riegel'. Pink, ruffly, 10-in. blooms with a red eye.

'Lady Baltimore'. Glowing pink, 6- to 8-in.-wide flowers with a large red center.

'Lord Baltimore'. Deep red, 10-in. blossoms over an exceptionally long period.

'The Clown'. Light pink flowers with red eye; 6−8 in. across.

'Turn of the Century'. Red-centered blooms with bicolor petals of pink and white range from 5 to 10 in. wide.

H. mutabilis. CONFEDERATE ROSE. Deciduous shrub. Zones LS, CS, TS; 12−8. From China. Shrubby or treelike in the Coastal and Tropical South, 15 ft. tall, 8 ft. wide; acts more like a perennial in the Lower South, growing flowering branches from woody base or short trunk. Broad, oval leaves have three to five lobes. In late summer and fall, flowers open from buds that resemble cotton bolls. Blooms are 4−6 in. wide, opening white or pink and changing to deep red by evening. 'Rubrus' has red flowers. Double-flowered forms also exist.

H. rosa-sinensis. CHINESE HIBISCUS, TROPICAL HIBISCUS. Evergreen shrub. Zones CS, TS; provide overhead protection where winter lows frequently drop below 30°F; 12−1. Where temperatures go much lower, grow in containers and shelter indoors over winter; or grow as annual, setting out fresh plants each spring. Also makes a good houseplant that can be brought outdoors during the warm season.

Hibiscus rosa-sinensis

A longtime favorite of Southern gardeners, this is one of the showiest flowering shrubs. Reaches 30 ft. tall and 15−20 ft. wide in its native tropical Asia, but seldom grows over 15 ft. tall in the U.S. Glossy foliage varies somewhat in size and texture depending on selection. Growth habit may be dense and dwarfish or loose and open. Summer flowers are single or double, 4−8 in. wide. Colors range from white through pink to red, from yellow and apricot to orange. Individual flowers last only a day, but the plant blooms continuously.

Requires excellent drainage; if necessary, improve soil or set plants in raised beds or containers. Fertilize monthly (potted plants twice monthly) with a general-purpose liquid fertilizer April to September, then stop fertilizing and let growth harden. For good branch structure, prune poorly shaped young plants when you set them out in spring. To keep a mature plant growing vigorously, prune out about a third of old wood in early spring. Pinching out tips of stems in spring and summer increases flower production. These are some of the selections available:

'Agnes Galt'. Big single pink flowers. Vigorous, hardy plant to 15 ft. Prune to prevent legginess.

'All Aglow'. Tall (10- to 15-ft.) plant has large single flowers with broad, gold-blotched orange petals, pink halo around a white throat.

'Bridal Veil'. Large pure white single flowers last 3 or 4 days. Grows 10−15 ft. tall.

'Bride'. Very large, single, palest blush to white flowers. Slow to moderate growth to open-branched 4 ft.

'Brilliant' ('San Diego Red'). Bright red single flowers in profusion. Tall, vigorous, compact, to 15 ft. Hardy.

'Butterfly'. Small, single bright yellow flowers. Slow, upright growth to 7 ft.

'California Gold'. Heavy yield of single yellow flowers with red centers. Slow to moderate growth to a compact 7 ft.

'Crown of Bohemia'. Double gold flowers; petals shade to carmine orange toward base. Moderate or fast growth to 5 ft. Bushy, upright. Hardy.

'Diamond Head'. Large double flowers in deepest red (nearly black red). Compact growth to 5 ft.

'Ecstasy'. Large, bright red single flowers with striking white variegation. Upright growth to 4 ft.

'Fiesta'. Large single flowers in bright orange centered with a red-edged white eye; petal edges are ruffled. Strong, erect growth to 6−7 ft.

'Full Moon' ('Mrs. James E. Hendry'). Double pure yellow flowers. Moderately vigorous growth to a compact 6 ft.

'Golden Dust'. Bright orange single flowers with yellow-orange centers. Compact, thick-foliaged plant to 4 ft. tall.

'Hula Girl'. Large single flowers in canary yellow with a deep red eye. Compact growth to 6 ft. Flowers stay open several days.

'Itsy Bitsy Peach', 'Itsy Bitsy Pink', and 'Itsy Bitsy Red'. Tall (10- to 15-ft.) plants with small leaves and small single flowers.

'Kate Sessions'. Large single flowers with broad petals; red with a gold tinge on petal undersides. Moderate growth to 10 ft. tall. Upright and open habit.

'Kona'. Ruffled, double pink flowers. Vigorous, upright, bushy growth to 15−20 ft. Prune regularly. 'Kona Improved' produces fuller flowers in a richer pink.

'Kona Princess'. Small, double pink flowers on a 6- to 7-ft. shrub.

'Morning Glory'. Single blush pink flowers changing to warmer pink with white petal tips. Grows 8−10 ft. tall.

'Moy Grande'. Compact grower to 5 ft. tall. Single, brilliant rosy red flowers are huge, to more than 1 ft. across.

'Powder Puff'. Double flowers of creamy white; during cool weather, take on a pink tinge. Grows 8−10 ft. tall.

'President'. Large single blossoms, intense red shading to deep pink in throat. Upright, compact, 6−7 ft. tall.

'Red Dragon' ('Celia'). Small to medium, double, dark red flowers. Upright, compact, 6−8 ft. tall.

'Ross Estey'. Heavy-textured, very large single blooms with broad, overlapping petals of pink shading to coral orange toward tips; last 2 or 3 days on bush. Vigorous. To 8 ft. Very large, ruffled leaves in polished dark green.

'The Path'. Large, ruffled single flowers in bright yellow shading to orange and bright fuchsia pink in the center. Grows 6−8 ft. high.

'Vulcan'. Yellow buds open to large single flowers in red with yellow on the petal backs. Blossoms often last for more than a day. Compact grower to 4−6 ft. high.

'White Wings'. Profuse, narrow-petaled, single white flowers with small red eye. Vigorous, open, upright to 20 ft.; prune to control legginess. A compact form with smaller flowers is available.

H. schizopetalus. FRINGED HIBISCUS, CORAL HIBISCUS. Evergreen shrub in Zone TS; annual elsewhere; 12−1. From tropical east Africa. To 9−15 ft. tall, 6−12 ft. wide, with weeping habit. Blooms almost all year, bearing white, pink, red, or yellow blossoms with fringed petals and an unusually long column of stamens that resembles a bottlebrush. Plants are sometimes kept small and grown in hanging baskets.

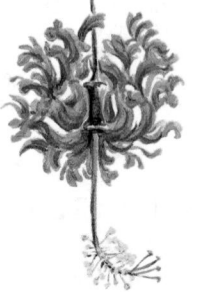

Hibiscus schizopetalus

H. syriacus. ROSE OF SHARON, SHRUB ALTHAEA. Deciduous shrub or small tree. Zones US, MS, LS, CS; 10−3. Native from China to India. To 10−12 ft. tall, 6 ft. wide. Upright and compact when young, spreading and open with age. Easily trained to single trunk with treelike top or as an espalier. Leaves to 4 in. long, often with three coarsely toothed lobes. Leaves come later in spring than those of most other deciduous shrubs; drop in fall without coloring. In summer, resembles a bush covered with hollyhock (*Alcea*) flowers: blossoms are single, semidouble, or double, 2½−3 in. across, some with a contrasting red to purple throat. Single flowers are slightly more effective, opening somewhat wider, but tend to produce many unattractive capsule-type fruits—which tend to produce many unwanted seedlings.

This old-fashioned favorite is easy to grow. Tolerates heat and drought; not fussy about soil as long as it's well-drained. Prune in winter; for bigger blooms, cut back side branches to two buds. Japanese beetles, which eat flowers and leaves, can be serious pests. For small infestations, hand-picking the beetles may be sufficient for control.

For many years, most nurseries sold unnamed plants simply by color. Named selections are now the norm, however, and better forms are coming along all the time. Recommended selections, some of which may be hard to find, include the following.

'Ardens'. Double lilac purple flowers with darker center.

'Blue Bird'. Single blue flowers with small red eye. Considered the best blue form for many years, this selection has now been surpassed by newer introductions.

'Blue Satin'. Flower color is similar to that of 'Blue Bird', but the plant is a much stronger grower.

'Blushing Bride'. Double bright pink blossoms.

'Blush Satin'. Light pink flowers with prominent red eye. Strong grower.

'Boule de Feu'. Double deep violet-pink flowers.

'Freedom'. Double flowers in deep mauve pink. Larger flowers than most doubles. Strong grower with handsome foliage.

'Jeanne d'Arc'. Double flowers of pure white.

'Lavender Chiffon'. Lavender-pink flowers resemble anemone blossoms. Strong grower.

'Pink Giant'. Large rose pink blooms with a red eye and yellow stamens.

'Red Heart'. Single white flowers with a red eye. Strong grower.

'Rose Satin'. Large, ruffle-edged single blooms in clear pink.

'Violet Satin'. Deep reddish violet, single flowers with a dark red center.

'White Chiffon'. Anemone-like pure white flowers.

The U.S. National Arboretum has introduced selections developed by famed plant breeder Don Egolf. These plants are triploids; the extra set of chromosomes results in large blossoms with strong, heavy-textured petals. Because plants are sterile and produce no seed, flowers appear over a long period. Choices include 'Aphrodite', bearing single rose pink flowers with a deep red eye; 'Diana' (the most popular of this group), with single pure white blossoms; 'Helene', single white flowers with a deep red eye; 'Minerva', single, ruffled, lavender blooms with a reddish purple eye.

HICKORY. See CARYA

HIDDEN LILY. See CURCUMA petiolata

HIMALAYAN GLOXINIA. See INCARVILLEA arguta

HIPPEASTRUM

AMARYLLIS

Amaryllidaceae

PERENNIALS FROM BULBS

✿ LS, CS, TS ⊞ 12–8, EXCEPT AS NOTED; OR GROW IN POTS

☼ ◖ FULL SUN OR LIGHT SHADE; BRIGHT LIGHT

◖ REGULAR WATER DURING GROWTH AND BLOOM

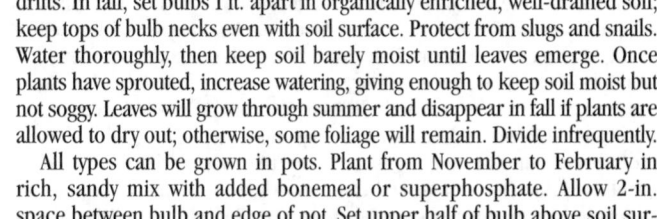

Hippeastrum hybrid

Native to the tropics and subtropics. Many species are useful in hybridizing, but only hybrids are generally available; these are often sold as giant amaryllis or Royal Dutch amaryllis (though many are grown in South Africa or elsewhere). Named selections come in reds, pinks, white, salmon, near-orange; some are variously marked and striped. Two to several flowers, often 8–9 in. across, form on stout, 2-ft. stems. Where plants are grown outdoors, flowers bloom in spring; indoors, they bloom just a few weeks after planting.

Newer forms include double-flowered selections in white (some with red picotee edges), creamy yellow, or pink; miniatures, with 3- to 5-in. flowers topping 12- to 15-in. stems; and an unusual evergreen species, *H. papilio*, with 5-in. greenish white flowers heavily patterned with dark red. Hardy hybrid 'San Antonio Rose' (Zones MS, LS, CS, TS) is a compact grower to 15 in. high; it has reddish veins on the leaf undersides and single flowers in bright rosy red.

H. ×*johnsonii*, Saint Joseph's lily, is an early hybrid popular in old gardens in the South. Its 5-in.-wide trumpet flowers are scarlet with white stripes and emerge in clusters of four to six atop 2-ft. stems; mature bulbs may produce four stems and 24 blooms. Tough and resilient, it blooms well in sun or light shade. *H. reginae*, Mexican lily, another heirloom type, has satiny bright red trumpets with white stars in the throats. Flowers appear in clusters of two, three, or four on 1-ft. stems in summer.

Where hardy in the ground, amaryllis can be planted in large clumps or drifts. In fall, set bulbs 1 ft. apart in organically enriched, well-drained soil; keep tops of bulb necks even with soil surface. Protect from slugs and snails. Water thoroughly, then keep soil barely moist until leaves emerge. Once plants have sprouted, increase watering, giving enough to keep soil moist but not soggy. Leaves will grow through summer and disappear in fall if plants are allowed to dry out; otherwise, some foliage will remain. Divide infrequently.

All types can be grown in pots. Plant from November to February in rich, sandy mix with added bonemeal or superphosphate. Allow 2-in. space between bulb and edge of pot. Set upper half of bulb above soil surface. Firm soil and water it well; then keep barely moist until growth begins. Water regularly during growth and bloom. When flowers fade, cut off stem, keep up watering; feed to encourage leaf growth. When leaves start to yellow, withhold water and let plants dry out. Repot in late fall or early winter.

AMARYLLIS INDOORS? IT'S EASY. *A potted amaryllis bulb can bloom indoors in just a few weeks. Keep it in a warm, dark place until the roots have formed. Then move it to a warm, lightly shaded place where the air is not too dry. Increase watering as leaves form. Feed lightly every 2 weeks during the flowering period.* ❖

HIPPOPHAE rhamnoides

SEA BUCKTHORN

Elaeagnaceae

DECIDUOUS SHRUB OR TREE

✿ US, MS ⊞ 8–1

☼ FULL SUN

◖ ◗ MODERATE TO REGULAR WATER

Hippophae rhamnoides

Native from Europe to Mongolia. Usually seen as an open, mounding shrub 8–10 ft. tall and wide, but it can grow much taller and spread by suckering from the roots. Thorny branches carry narrow (¼-in.-wide), 3-in.-long, silvery green to grayish green leaves. Flowers are inconspicuous, but fruits on female plants are showy—bright orange, round or oval, to ⅓ in. long. Fruit persists on the plant into winter—apparently it is too sour to appeal to birds. High in vitamin C, it can be made into sauces or jam. You need both male and female plants to get fruit. Female 'Sunny' is a heavy producer of fruit. Male 'Romeo' has foliage that looks good all season.

Sea buckthorn tolerates cold, wind, poor soil (as long as it is well drained), and salt spray. Good screen plant for difficult situations, such as the beach.

HOLLY. See ILEX

HOLLY FERN. See ARACHNIODES simplicior, CYRTOMIUM falcatum

HOLLYHOCK. See ALCEA

HOLLYLEAF SWEETSPIRE. See ITEA ilicifolia

HOMERIA collina

Iridaceae

PERENNIAL FROM CORM

✿ CS, TS ⊞ 10–9; OR DIG AND STORE; OR GROW IN POTS

☼ FULL SUN

◖ REGULAR WATER DURING GROWTH AND BLOOM

Homeria collina

Native to South Africa, where it is often found growing on slopes at various elevations from low to high. First comes one floppy, grasslike leaf. It is followed by branching or unbranched, 1½-ft. stems bearing 2½- to 3-in.-wide flowers in soft yellow or muted orange. Soon after bloom, the foliage yellows and dies down. Where this plant is adapted, you can plant corms at any time from fall through winter, setting them 2 in. deep, 3 in. apart; they can be left in the ground and allowed to multiply freely. If they are to receive moisture during their long dormancy, however, soil must be very well drained. If drainage is less than excellent and you can't keep planting area dry, dig after leaves have died down and store over summer; or grow in pots. In areas beyond hardiness range, plant in spring (as soon as soil can be worked) for summer flowers; lift corms in late summer or early fall and store over winter. In areas where the species has escaped gardens and naturalized, it has been found to be toxic to livestock.

HONEY LOCUST. See GLEDITSIA triacanthos

HONEYSUCKLE. See LONICERA

HONG KONG ORCHID TREE. See BAUHINIA ×blakeana

HOP. See HUMULUS

HOP HORNBEAM. See OSTRYA

HOREHOUND. See MARRUBIUM vulgare

HORNBEAM. See CARPINUS

HORN OF PLENTY. See DATURA metel

HORSECHESTNUT. See AESCULUS

HORSERADISH

Brassicaceae (Cruciferae)

PERENNIAL

✍ US, MS, LS **H** 8–1

☼ FULL SUN

💧 REGULAR WATER

Horseradish

B otanically known as *Armoracia rusticana*. Native to southeastern Europe. Large (to about 3-ft.), coarse, weedy-looking plant grown for its large white roots. Does best in rich, moist soils in cooler areas of the Upper and Middle South. Grow it in some sunny, out-of-the-way corner. In late winter or early spring, set root horizontally in a 3- to 4-in.-deep trench and cover with 2 in. of soil. One plant should provide enough horseradish for a family of four. For multiple plants, space 2½–3 ft. apart.

Through fall, winter, and spring, harvest pieces of horseradish roots from the outside of the root clump as you need them—that way you'll have your horseradish fresh and tangy. Scrub and peel the roots, cutting away any dark parts; then grate them. Mix with vinegar, sweet cream, or sour cream—or simply sprinkle directly onto food.

HORSETAIL. See EQUISETUM hyemale

HORSETAIL TREE. See CASUARINA equisetifolia

HOSTA

PLANTAIN LILY

Liliaceae

PERENNIALS

✍ US, MS, LS, EXCEPT AS NOTED

◐ ● PARTIAL OR FULL SHADE

💧 REGULAR WATER

Hosta 'Great Expectations'

T he most popular of all plants for shade, hostas are prized for their marvelous foliage. The thin spikes of blue or white, trumpet-shaped flowers that appear for several weeks in summer are a bonus. There's a

---

tremendous variety in leaf size, shape, and color; to fully appreciate the diversity, you'll need to consult a specialist's catalog or visit a well-stocked garden center. All hostas are native to eastern Asia.

Leaves may be heart shaped, lance shaped, oval, or nearly round, carried at the ends of leafstalks that rise from the ground and radiate from a central point. Leaves overlap to form symmetrical, almost shingled foliage mounds ranging in size from dwarf (as small as 3–4 in.) to giant (as big as 5 ft.). Leaf texture may be smooth, deeply veined, quilted, or puckery; surface may be glossy or dull; edges may be smooth or wavy. Colors range from light to dark green to chartreuse, gray, and blue. There are also combinations of colors, including variegations with white, cream, or yellow.

All hostas go dormant in winter, collapsing to almost nothing. All are splendid companions for ferns and for plants with fernlike foliage, such as bleeding heart *(Dicentra)*. They're also good in containers. In the ground, hostas last for years; clumps expand in size and shade out weeds. Many are susceptible to slug and snail attack.

New selections are entering the scene in ever-increasing numbers. In few other plants, though, have species undergone so many name changes; to be sure you're getting the one you want, buy the plant in full leaf or deal with an expert. Species and selections listed below are just a few of the many available.

H. clausa. Heat zones 9–1. Good ground-cover species. Foliage clump to 10 in. high spreads to 2 ft. by runners. Lance-shaped dark green leaves to 5 in. long. Flower stalks bear deep lavender buds that don't open.

H. crispula. CURLED-LEAF HOSTA. Heat zones 9–2. Oval, 7-in.-long, dark green leaves with irregular white margins, wavy edges, and drooping, curly, pointed tips. Foliage mound to 1½ ft. high, 3 ft. wide. Many lavender flowers early in the season. Plant is sometimes confused with *H. fortunei* 'Albomarginata', which blooms later.

H. decorata (H. 'Thomas Hogg'). Heat zones 9–2. A foot-high mound of oval leaves, 6 in. long, bluntly pointed at tips, dull green with silvery white margins. Reaches 1½ ft. wide. Dark violet flowers bloom early.

H. fortunei. FORTUNE'S PLANTAIN LILY. Heat zones 9–1. May be an ancient hybrid affiliated with *H. sieboldiana*. Variable plant known for its many selections in a wide range of foliage colors. Plants grow to 1–1½ ft. high, up to 3 ft. wide, with oval, foot-long leaves, lilac flowers. Young leaves of 'Albopicta' are yellow with uneven green border; the yellow fades to a greenish shade by summer. Leaves of 'Albomarginata' have an irregular yellow border that fades to white; late bloom. 'Hyacinthina' has large gray-green leaves edged with a fine white line.

H. hybrids. The following list includes some of the best, most widely grown hostas.

Hosta 'Antioch'   *Hosta* 'Frances Williams'   *Hosta* 'Golden Tiara'   *Hosta* 'Piedmont Gold'   *Hosta* 'Royal Standard'   *Hosta sieboldiana* 'Elegans'

'Antioch'. To 1½ ft. tall, 3 ft. wide. Broad green leaves with wide, creamy white margins. Lavender flowers are held well above foliage mound.

'August Moon'. To 20 in. tall, 2½ ft. wide. Spade-shaped, lightly crinkled, bright chartreuse leaves. White flowers.

'Blue Angel'. Heavily veined blue-green leaves 16 in. long, nearly as wide. White flowers over a long bloom period. Enormous mound to 3–4 ft. tall and 4 ft. wide.

'Blue Wedgwood'. To 2 ft. high, 1 ft. wide. Wavy-edged, strongly veined, heart-shaped leaves in 1½-ft. mound. Pale lavender flowers bloom early.

'Chartreuse Wiggles'. Dwarf (6–8 in. high, 10 in. wide), with lance-shaped, wavy-edged, chartreuse-gold leaves. Lavender flowers bloom late.

'Francee'. To 1½–2 ft. tall, 3 ft. wide. Broadly heart-shaped leaves to 6 in. long with striking white edges. Lavender flowers bloom late. Sun tolerant.

'Frances Williams' ('Gold Edge', 'Golden Circles'). Forms a mound to 2½–3 ft. tall and 3 ft. wide. Round, puckered blue-green leaves have a bold, irregular yellow edge. Pale lavender flowers bloom early.

'Ginko Craig'. To 1–1½ ft. tall and wide. Elongated, frosty green leaves with silver margins. Abundant lavender flowers.

'Gold Edger'. To 10–12 in. high, 1½ ft. wide. Heart-shaped, 3-in. leaves in chartreuse gold. Masses of lavender blossoms. One of the most sun tolerant; in fact, it needs some sun for best color.

'Golden Tiara'. To 1 ft. tall, 1½ ft. wide. Heart-shaped leaves are 4 in. long, light green with gold edge. Purple flowers. Sun tolerant.

'Gold Standard'. To 2 ft. tall, 3 ft. wide. Heart-shaped bright golden leaves with a green margin. Pale lavender flowers. Sun tolerant.

'Great Expectations'. To 2 ft. tall, 2½ ft. wide. Leaves sport a creamy yellow center surrounded by a wide blue-green edge. White flowers.

'Hadspen Blue'. Low grower (to 1 ft. tall, spreading to 1½ ft.) with slightly wavy, broadly oval, slug-resistant blue leaves. Many lavender flowers.

'Halcyon'. To 1½ ft. tall, 3 ft. wide. Heart-shaped, heavy-textured blue-gray leaves. Short spikes of rich lilac-blue flowers.

'Honeybells'. To 2½ ft. high, 4 ft. wide. Wavy-edged yellow-green leaves; lightly scented pale lilac flowers.

'Krossa Regal'. Big, leathery, frosty blue leaves arch up and out, making a vase-shaped clump to 3 ft. tall and wide. Slug-resistant foliage. Blooms late, with lavender flower spikes that can reach 5–6 ft. high.

'Patriot'. To 15 in. tall, 3 ft. wide. Resembles 'Francee', but leaves have a wider white border. Lavender blooms.

'Piedmont Gold'. To 2 ft. high, 3 ft. wide. Broadly heart-shaped, heavily veined, slightly wavy-edged, 7-in. leaves of glowing chartreuse gold. White flowers. Sun tolerant.

'Royal Standard'. To 2 ft. high, 3–4 ft. wide. Glossy light green leaves, elongated and undulated. Fragrant white flowers. Sun tolerant.

'Shade Fanfare'. To 1–1½ ft. high, 1½ ft. wide. Leaves are pointed ovals to 7 in. long, green to gold with creamy white margin. Lavender flowers. Very sun tolerant.

'Sum and Substance'. To 3 ft. high, 5 ft. wide. Textured, shiny yellow leaves to 20 in. long. Slug-resistant foliage. Lavender flowers. Very sun tolerant.

'Sun Power'. To 2 ft. high, 3 ft. wide. Ruffled, twisted leaves are chartreuse to golden; retain their color all season. Lavender flowers on 3-ft. stalks. Takes morning sun.

H. lancifolia (H. 'Lancifolia'). NARROW-LEAFED PLANTAIN LILY. Heat zones 9–1. Glossy deep green, 6-in.-long, lance-shaped leaves, the bases tapering into the long stalks. Foot-high foliage mound spreads 2 ft. or more. Pale lavender flowers bloom late.

H. minor. Heat zones 9–2. Small, creeping species forms a clump 5 in. high, 8 in. wide. Heart-shaped leaves about 3 in. across are yellowish green above, lighter green on undersides. Light violet flowers.

H. plantaginea (H. grandiflora, H. subcordata). FRAGRANT PLANTAIN LILY. Zones US, MS, LS, CS; 9–1. Glossy bright green leaves, to 10 in. long, broadly oval with parallel veins and quilted surface. Foliage mound 2 ft. high, 3 ft. wide. Noticeably fragrant, large white flowers bloom late. Heat tolerant. Performs better than other species in Coastal South. 'Aphrodite' is double flowered.

H. pulchella. Heat zones 9–2. Dwarf form makes a clump only 4 in. high and 8 in. wide. Thick, heart-shaped, shiny green leaves to 2 in. long. Bicolored white-and-lavender flowers. There are selections with blue-green or yellow-edged leaves.

H. sieboldiana (H. glauca). SIEBOLD PLANTAIN LILY. Heat zones 9–1. To 2½–3 ft. tall, 4 ft. wide. Blue-green, broadly heart-shaped leaves, 10–15 in. long, heavily veined and puckered. Many slender, pale lilac flower spikes nestle close to foliage mound early in season. Foliage dies back early. 'Elegans' has especially handsome blue-gray leaves that are slug resistant.

H. sieboldii 'Kabitan' (H. 'Kabitan'). Heat zones 9–2. To 8 in. tall, 10 in. wide. Wavy, lance-shaped leaves to 5 in. long, chartreuse to yellow with thin green margins. White flowers.

H. tardiflora. Heat zones 9–2. Small plant (to 1 ft. high, 2 ft. wide), with lance-shaped leaves to 6 in. long. Pale purple flowers bloom very late, are held on spikes the same height as foliage clump.

H. tokudama. Heat zones 9–2. Like *H. sieboldiana*, but smaller (to 1 ft. tall, 2 ft. wide), with a more crepelike texture. Slug-resistant foliage. White flowers. 'Flavocircinalis', with irregular yellow margins, is more sun tolerant than the species.

H. undulata (H. media picta, H. variegata). WAVY-LEAFED PLANTAIN LILY. Heat zones 9–2. Wavy-edged, narrowly oval leaves, 6–8 in. long, in a mound 1½ ft. tall and wide. Typical leaf is green with a creamy white center stripe. Foliage is used in arrangements. Pale lavender flowers. 'Albomarginata' has creamy white margins on leaves. 'Erromena' is a solid green.

H. ventricosa (H. caerulea). BLUE PLANTAIN LILY. Heat zones 9–1. To 2 ft. tall, 3 ft. wide. Named for its violet-blue blooms. Leaves are glossy deep green, broadly heart shaped, prominently veined, to 8 in. long. Leaves of 'Aureomaculata' are yellowish green with a green border. In 'Aureomarginata' ('Variegata'), each leaf is green edged with creamy white.

HOTTENTOT FIG. See CARPOBROTUS edulis

HOUSELEEK. See SEMPERVIVUM

FOR INFORMATION ON YOUR CLIMATE ZONES
PLEASE SEE PAGES 28–38

HOUSTONIA caerulea
(Hedyotis caerulea)

BLUETS, QUAKER LADIES

Rubiaceae

PERENNIAL

✿ US, MS, LS **H** 8–7

◐ LIGHT SHADE

💧 REGULAR WATER

Houstonia caerulea

Creeping perennial that forms low (2- to 3-in.), widely spreading mounds of tiny oval leaves. Flowers appear singly on 2- to 2½-in. stalks in late spring. The ½-in.-wide, four-lobed flowers are pale blue (sometimes white) with a yellow eye. Although small, they are profuse enough to create a charming effect. Use in woodland gardens, around stepping-stones, or as carpet for large potted shrubs like camellia or aucuba. Needs acid soil. In the wild, thrives among mosses in light shade under tall oak trees. Will also grow in sparse lawns.

HOUTTUYNIA cordata

Saururaceae

PERENNIAL

✿ US, MS, LS, CS, TS **H** 12–1

☀ ◐ ● SUN OR SHADE

💧 💧💧 REGULAR TO AMPLE WATER

Houttuynia cordata
'Chameleon'

From China, Japan. Spreading underground stems send up a 9-in.-high blanket of foliage—heart-shaped green leaves to 3 in. long that look very much like those of English ivy *(Hedera helix)*. Foliage emits an odd scent when crushed, reminiscent of orange peel. Inconspicuous clusters of white-bracted flowers like tiny dogwood *(Cornus)* blossoms. Unusual ground cover that disappears completely in winter, even in mild climates. Most commonly grown form is showy 'Chameleon' ('Tricolor', 'Variegata'), with green leaves splashed in cream, pink, yellow, and red; colors are most intense in sun. Attractive in containers.

Can spread aggressively in wet ground and will even thrive with roots in water. For ground cover, plant 1½–2 ft. apart; curb growth with wood, concrete, or metal barrier extending 8–12 in. into the soil. The plant can also spread by seed. Once you bring it into your garden, it may well be with you forever.

HOWEA

Arecaceae (Palmae)

PALMS

✿ TS **H** 12–10; OR HOUSEPLANTS

◐ PARTIAL SHADE; BRIGHT INDIRECT LIGHT

💧 REGULAR WATER

Howea forsteriana

Native to Lord Howe Island in the South Pacific. These slow-growing feather palms are the kentia palms of florists and are usually sold under the name "kentia." With age, leaves drop to show clean green trunk ringed with leaf scars. When using these palms outdoors, plant them beneath another tree to provide cold protection (they are very sensitive to frost) and to shield them from strong winds. Give them well-drained soil high in organic matter. They do not tolerate salt.

Howeas are ideal potted plants—the classic parlor palms. To minimize problems with spider mites, keep the fronds clean and free of dust. Feed with quarter-strength general-purpose liquid houseplant fertilizer monthly from spring through fall.

H. belmoreana. SENTRY PALM. Less common than *H. forsteriana*; also smaller and more compact (to 25 ft. tall, 15 ft. wide), with overarching fronds 6–7 ft. long. Withstands some neglect—capricious watering, drafts, dust.

H. forsteriana. PARADISE PALM, FORSTER'S SENTRY PALM. Faster growing than *H. belmoreana*, to 60 ft. tall and 20 ft. wide. Fronds reach 9 ft. long, have long, drooping leaflets.

HOYA

WAX FLOWER, WAX PLANT

Asclepiadaceae

PERENNIALS

✿ ZONES VARY BY SPECIES; OR HOUSEPLANTS

◐ ● PARTIAL TO FULL SHADE; BRIGHT LIGHT

💧 REGULAR WATER

Hoya carnosa

Tropical plants with thick, waxy evergreen leaves and tight clusters of small, waxy flowers that appear in leaf joints during summer. These plants prefer rich, loose, well-drained soil. When grown as container plants, they bloom best when pot-bound. Do not prune out the short stalks that bear flowers, because new flower clusters will develop on them. Feed with a quarter-strength general-purpose liquid houseplant fertilizer monthly from spring through fall. Specialists list dozens of available species and hybrids, with growth habit varying from vining to shrubby.

H. carnosa. WAX FLOWER, WAX PLANT. Zones TS; 12–8. From India, Burma, southern China. Vining plant grows to 10–20 ft., with green, oval, rigid, 2- to 4-in.-long leaves. Big, round, convex clusters of ½-in., creamy white blossoms, each centered with a five-pointed pink star. Flowers are fragrant, especially at night. Red young leaves give extra color. Attractive trained on a pillar or trellis. Indoors, traditionally trained on wire in a sunny window.

'Variegata' has leaves edged in white suffused with pink; it is not as vigorous or hardy as the plain species. 'Exotica' shows yellow-and-pink variegation. 'Krinkle Kurl' has crinkly leaves closely spaced on short stems; it is often sold as 'Compacta' or as Hindu-rope plant.

H. lanceolata bella. House or greenhouse plant. Native from Himalayas to Burma. Shrubby growth to 1½–3 ft. high and wide, with fleshy green leaves to 1½ in. long and sweetly aromatic clusters of ½-in., purple-centered white flowers. Slender, upright branches droop as they grow older. Best used in hanging basket.

HUISACHE. See ACACIA farnesiana

HUMATA tyermannii

BEAR'S FOOT FERN

Polypodiaceae

FERN

✿ TS **H** 12–10; OR HOUSEPLANT

◐ PARTIAL SHADE; BRIGHT INDIRECT LIGHT

💧 REGULAR WATER

Humata tyermannii

Native to China. This small fern has furry, creeping rhizomes that look something like bear's feet. Fronds 8–10 in. long, very finely cut, rising at intervals from the rhizome. Like squirrel's foot fern *(Davallia trichomanoides)* in appearance and uses, but slower growing.

FOR INFORMATION ON SELECTING PLANTS

PLEASE SEE PAGES 39–144

HUMULUS

HOP

Cannabaceae

PERENNIAL VINES

US, MS, LS, CS | 9–1

FULL SUN

REGULAR WATER

Humulus lupulus

Extremely fast-growing perennial vines are attractive for summer screening on trellises or arbors—and one species yields the hops used in beer. Leaves to 6 in. long are deeply lobed and toothed. Bloom in late summer. Male plants produce flower panicles; females bear blossoms in greenish spikes resembling pinecones. Squarish, hairy stems are set with deeply lobed, toothed leaves to 6 in. long. Stems twine vertically; to get horizontal growth, twine stem tips by hand. Cut stems to ground after frost turns them brown; regrowth comes the following spring.

H. japonicus. JAPANESE HOP. From eastern Asia. To 20–30 ft. Bears ¾-in. female flower spikes. Dark green leaves have five to seven lobes; foliage of 'Variegatus' is marked with white. Sow seeds in place in spring.

H. lupulus. COMMON HOP. From many northern temperate regions of the world. This species produces the traditional flavoring for beer. The hops—female flowers—are soft, flaky, 1- to 2-in., light green cones of bracts and blossoms with a fresh, piny fragrance. Bright green leaves have three to five lobes. Tender top shoots can be cooked as a vegetable. Plants sold in nurseries are typically female; no pollenizer needed. May be offered as potted plants or as dormant roots. The roots should be planted in rich soil in early spring; set just below soil surface with thick end up. Many selections are available, including 'Aureus', which has attractive chartreuse foliage. *H. l. neomexicanus (H. americanus)*, native to the central and southern Rockies, differs from the plain species only in minor botanical details.

HYACINTH BEAN. See DOLICHOS lablab

HYACINTHOIDES

BLUEBELL, WOOD HYACINTH

Liliaceae

PERENNIALS FROM BULBS

ZONES VARY BY SPECIES

FILTERED SUN OR LIGHT SHADE

REGULAR WATER DURING GROWTH AND BLOOM

BULBS MAY CAUSE AN ALLERGIC SKIN REACTION

Hyacinthoides hispanica

These spring-blooming bulbs were once classed in the genus *Scilla* and are still popularly known by that name; some bulb dealers continue to list them as such. They were later reclassified as *Endymion* and now have been renamed *Hyacinthoides*. They resemble hyacinths but are taller, with looser flower clusters and fewer, narrower leaves.

Spanish bluebell *(H. hispanica)* is the preferred choice for most Southern gardens. English bluebell *(H. non-scripta)* definitely prefers colder winters and moderate to cool summers. When grown near each other, the two species sometimes hybridize, producing intermediate forms. Plant bulbs in fall, setting them 3 in. deep in mild climates, as deep as 6 in. where winters are severe. Space about 6 in. apart. Propensity for reseeding makes these good subjects for naturalizing; lovely in informal drifts among tall shrubs, under deciduous trees, among low-growing perennials. Need regular moisture from planting time until foliage dies and at least some moisture in summer. Divide infrequently; when division is needed, do it in fall. Plants thrive in pots, and flowers are good for cutting. Bulbs can cause allergic reactions on contact. Not favored by browsing deer.

H. hispanica (Scilla campanulata, S. hispanica). SPANISH BLUE-BELL. Zones US, MS, LS, CS; 9–1. From Spain, North Africa. Prolific and vigorous, with inch-wide, strap-shaped leaves and sturdy, 20-in. stems bearing 12 or more nodding, unscented bells about ¾ in. long. Blue is the most popular color, 'Excelsior' (deep blue) the most popular selection. There are also white, pink, and rose forms. Leaves can look a trifle ratty before dying back.

H. non-scripta (Scilla non-scripta). ENGLISH BLUEBELL, WOOD HYACINTH. Best in Zones US, MS; 8–1. From western Europe. Fragrant blue flowers are narrower and smaller than those of *H. hispanica*, on 1-ft. stems that nod at the tip and carry their flowers on only one side. Leaves are also narrower—only about ½ in. wide. 'Alba' is white flowered; 'Rosea' has pink blooms.

HYACINTHUS

HYACINTH

Liliaceae

PERENNIALS FROM BULBS

ZONES VARY BY TYPE

FULL SUN OR PARTIAL SHADE

REGULAR WATER DURING GROWTH AND BLOOM

BULBS MAY CAUSE AN ALLERGIC SKIN REACTION

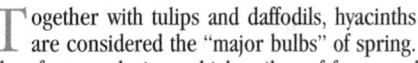

Hyacinthus orientalis

Together with tulips and daffodils, hyacinths are considered the "major bulbs" of spring. They feature glorious, thick spikes of fragrant, bell-shaped flowers that rise from a clump of narrow bright green leaves. Plant from October to December. Two species formerly sold as *Hyacinthus* have been reclassified; remaining is *H. orientalis*, the common hyacinth.

H. amethystinus. See Brimeura amethystina

H. azureus. See Muscari azureum

H. orientalis. COMMON HYACINTH. Grows to 1 ft. tall, with straplike leaves that may be erect or somewhat arching. Blossom spikes are tightly packed with flowers in white, pale blue, or purple blue. Two basic forms are the Dutch and the Roman or French Roman.

Dutch hyacinth, derived from *H. orientalis* by breeding and selection, has large, dense spikes of waxy, bell-like flowers in white, cream, buff, and shades of blue, purple, pink, red, and salmon. Size of flower spike is directly related to size of bulb. Biggest bulbs are desirable for exhibition plants or for potting; next largest size is satisfactory for bedding outside. Small bulbs give smaller, looser clusters with more widely spaced flowers. These are sometimes called miniature hyacinths. As perennials, Dutch hyacinth is best adapted to the Upper and Middle South, but it can be grown as an annual anywhere.

Roman or French Roman hyacinth *(H. o. albulus)* has white, pink, or light blue flowers loosely carried on slender stems, usually several stems to a bulb. Earlier to bloom than Dutch hyacinth; also needs little or no winter chill, making it better adapted to the Lower, Coastal, and Tropical South (where it will grow as a perennial under favorable conditions).

Set larger Dutch hyacinth bulbs 6 in. deep, 5 in. apart; set smaller ones and Roman hyacinth bulbs 4 in. deep, 4–5 in. apart. The bulbs have invisible barbs on the surface that can cause your skin to itch; after handling them, wash hands before touching your face or eyes. Hyacinths are at their best when massed or grouped; if set out in rows, they tend to look too stiff and formal. Try massing a single color beneath a flowering tree or in a border. If you are growing hyacinths as perennials, fertilize just as blossoms fade; then remove spent spikes and continue to water regularly until foliage yellows. Flowers typically are smaller in succeeding years, but they keep the same color and fragrance.

Choice container plants. Pot in porous mix with bulb tip near surface. Then cover containers with thick mulch of sawdust, wood shavings, or peat moss to keep bulbs cool, moist, and shaded until roots are well formed; when tips of shoots show, remove mulch and place pots in full light. You can also grow hyacinths in water in a special hyacinth glass, the bottom filled with pebbles and water. Keep in dark, cool place until rooted; give light when top growth appears, then place in a sunny window when leaves have turned uniformly green.

HYDRANGEA

Hydrangeaceae (Saxifragaceae)

EVERGREEN AND DECIDUOUS SHRUBS AND VINES

⚡ ZONES VARY BY SPECIES

◑ MORNING SUN, LIGHT AFTERNOON SHADE

🌢 REGULAR WATER

Hydrangea macrophylla

Big, bold leaves and large clusters of long-lasting flowers in white, pink, red, or blue. Bloom in late spring or summer. Flower clusters may contain sterile flowers (conspicuous, with large, petal-like sepals) or fertile flowers (small, starry petaled); or they may feature a cluster of small fertile flowers surrounded by ring of big sterile ones (these are called lace-cap hydrangeas). Sterile flowers last for a long time (often holding up for months), gradually fading in color. Hydrangeas are good looking as single plants, massed, or in tubs on the patio. Grow quickly and easily in rich, porous soil.

In some hydrangea selections, blue or pink flower color is affected by soil pH—bluest color is produced in strongly acid soils (below pH 5.5), pink or red in neutral to alkaline soils (pH 7.0 and higher). Florists control flower color of potted hydrangeas by controlling soil mix; blue-flowered florists' plants may show pink blossoms when planted out in less acid soil. Flowers can be made (or kept) blue by applying aluminum sulfate to the soil, kept red (or pink) or made redder by liming the soil or applying superphosphate in quantity. Flower-color treatment is not effective unless started well ahead of bloom.

H. anomala petiolaris (H. petiolaris). CLIMBING HYDRANGEA. Deciduous vine. Zones US, MS, LS; 9–1. From Russia, Korea, Japan. Climbs high (as far as 60 ft.) by clinging aerial rootlets; shrubby and sprawling without support. Green, 2- to 4-in.-long leaves have a rounded heart shape. Mature plants develop short, flowering branches with flat, white, 6- to 10-in.-wide lace-cap flower clusters. Becomes woody with age. Prune out overly vigorous growth only after vine is well established and climbing. Can be rejuvenated by cutting back to framework late in dormant season.

H. arborescens. SMOOTH HYDRANGEA. Deciduous shrub. Zones US, MS, LS, CS; 9–1. Native from New York to Iowa, south to Florida, Louisiana. Upright, dense growth to 10 ft. tall and wide. Oval, grayish green, 4- to 8-in. leaves; white flowers. In basic species, most flowers in a cluster are fertile; the few sterile ones are not plentiful enough for full lace-cap effect. Much showier is 'Annabelle', which produces enormous (to 1-ft.) globular clusters of sterile flowers on a plant about 4 ft. tall and wide. 'Grandiflora' is another 4-footer; its flower clusters are 6 in. across. Prune in late winter. Hard pruning produces bigger flowers.

H. aspera. Deciduous shrub. Zones MS, LS; 9–7. From eastern Asia. Imposing shrub to 10–12 ft. tall, spreading nearly as wide. Dark green, somewhat hairy leaves to 10 in. long, 4 in. wide. Rather flat, 10-in. flower clusters contain purplish white to pink fertile flowers surrounded by 1-in. white, pink, or purple sterile blooms. Prune in late winter. To make a broad, many-stemmed plant, cut back hard for first 3 years; flowering will be delayed, but plant form will be improved.

H. a. sargentiana (H. sargentiana) has broader, more heavily furred leaves. Fertile flowers are light purple; sterile outer ones are pinkish white, about 1½ in. across.

Villosa Group *(H. villosa)* has blue or purple fertile flowers and 1-in.-wide, pale pinkish purple sterile flowers.

H. integrifolia. Evergreen vine. Zones MS, LS, CS; 9–6. From the Philippines, Taiwan. Rambling vine that climbs 25–30 ft. by clinging aerial rootlets. Somewhat similar to *H. anomala petiolaris* but has smaller, lance-shaped leaves and smaller flowers. Stems are red tinged and covered with fine hairs. Prune in winter.

H. macrophylla (H. hortensia, H. opuloides). FRENCH HYDRANGEA, BIGLEAF HYDRANGEA. Deciduous shrub. Zones US, MS, LS, CS; 9–3. From Japan. Symmetrical, rounded habit; grows to 4–8 ft. high (or more) and as wide. Thick, shiny, coarsely toothed leaves to 8 in. long; white, pink, red, or blue flowers in big clusters. Great performer in areas where winters are fairly mild; disappointing where plants freeze to ground every year (they

WHAT HYDRANGEAS NEED

EXPOSURE: For better and more blooms, give plants morning sun and light afternoon shade.

SOIL: Make it rich and well drained. Add plenty of organic material at planting time. Don't forget to mulch.

PRUNING: Make cuts as needed to control form—late in dormant season for types blooming on new growth, after flowering for those blooming on previous year's growth. For biggest flower clusters, reduce number of stems; for numerous medium-size clusters, keep more stems.

Hydrangea serrata 'Preziosa'

may never bloom under these conditions, since flower buds are usually produced on old wood). Protect in colder zones by mounding soil or leaves over base of plants. Prune immediately after bloom.

There are hundreds of named selections, and plants may be sold under many names. Florists' plants are usually French hybrids, shorter (1–3 ft. tall) and larger flowered than old garden types. Dozens of selections are sold; here are some of the best, including a couple of old favorites as well as some newer choices.

'All Summer Beauty'. Unlike most other French hydrangeas, this one produces its dark blue or pinkish flower heads on current season's growth and blooms all summer. Prune late in dormant season.

'Ayesha'. Heads of light purplish pink, cupped flowers (like tiny buttons).

'Blue Wave'. Lace-cap type with light blue to pink sterile flowers and darker fertile ones.

'Buttons 'n Bows'. Grows 3–4 ft. high and wide, bearing deep pink flowers with white-edged petals.

'Domotoi'. Well-known old garden selection, featuring clusters of double pink or blue sterile flowers.

'Endless Summer'. Produces flowers on new growth and blooms all summer. Blossoms are blue or pink, depending on soil pH.

'Glowing Embers'. Dark pink to red sterile flowers in big, round clusters.

'Lanarth White'. Reaches 3–4 ft. high and wide. Lace-cap type with white sterile flowers and pink or blue fertile blooms.

'Lemon Wave'. Rich green leaves edged in yellow; lace-cap flowers in white tinged with pink.

'Mariesii'. Pink or mauve lace-cap blooms.

'Merritt's Supreme'. Rosy red lace-cap flowers. Very showy.

'Nikko Blue'. Large, round blue blossom clusters. Old standby.

'Penny Mac'. Vivid blue flowers in 7-in. clusters. Sets buds on both old and new wood—so even if a late frost kills the buds set in autumn, the plant may still bloom on growth formed the next spring.

'Pia' ('Pink Elf'). Only 1½ ft. high and 2 ft. wide, with deep pink sterile flowers.

'Pink 'n Pretty'. Pink sterile flowers in large clusters.

'Red 'n Pretty'. Red sterile flowers in big clusters.

'Variegata'. Unmistakable old lace-cap form with dark green leaves strongly marked in cream and light green.

H. paniculata. Deciduous shrub or small tree. Zones US, MS, LS, CS; 8–1. Native to Japan and China. Best known for its selections. Among the most widely grown is 'Grandiflora', peegee hydrangea, an upright, coarse-textured plant that can be trained as a 25-ft. tree but performs best as a shrub to 10–15 ft. high, 8 ft. wide. Pointed oval leaves are 5 in. long, turning bronzy in fall. Large (10- to 15-in.-long), upright clusters of mainly fertile flowers are white, slowly fading to pinky bronze.

Other selections include 'Kyushu', with white blooms, and 'Limelight', bearing bright lime green flowers. In 'Pink Diamond', pink buds open to cream-colored flowers that gradually darken to rosy red; all three colors appear together. 'Tardiva' is similar to 'Grandiflora' but blooms later, in early and midautumn. Prune all types in late winter.

H. petiolaris. See H. anomala petiolaris

H. 'Preziosa'. See H. serrata 'Preziosa'

H. quercifolia. OAKLEAF HYDRANGEA. Deciduous shrub. Zones US, MS, LS, CS; 9–1. From southeastern U.S. Broad, rounded shrub to 6 ft. tall and 8 ft. wide, with handsome, deeply lobed, 8-in.-long leaves that resemble those of oaks, turn scarlet or crimson in fall. Elongated clusters of white flowers in late spring and early summer change to pinkish purple as they age; fertile flowers are usually concealed by larger sterile flowers. Foliage of 'Alice' colors a particularly rich red in autumn. 'Harmony' features mostly sterile white flowers that weigh down the branches. 'Semmes Beauty' is a large plant, to 8–12 ft. tall and 12 ft. wide, with upright flower clusters to an impressive 20 in. across. 'Sike's Dwarf' is a white-flowered selection to only 2½ ft. high and 4 ft. wide. 'Snowflake' bears double flowers; as they age, inner sepals stay white, outer ones turn dusty rose. 'Snow Queen' is noted for its profuse, dense, upright flower clusters and rich red fall color. Prune right after bloom. Flower buds and stems may be damaged where temperatures go much below −10°F; in these areas, oakleaf hydrangea is best grown for its handsome foliage.

Hydrangea quercifolia

H. sargentiana. See H. aspera sargentiana

H. seemannii. Evergreen vine. Zones LS, CS; 9–8. From Sierra Madre mountains in Mexico. Vigorous grower to 30 ft.; climbs by clinging aerial roots. Leathery, very shiny, elliptical dark green leaves to 6 in. long. White lace-cap flowers emerge from round, showy buds. Pruning is seldom necessary but may be done after flowers fade.

H. serrata. Deciduous shrub. Zones US, MS. LS, CS; 9–6. From Korea, Japan. Resembles *H. macrophylla*. The species and most selections grow 4–6 ft. tall and wide. 'Blue Billow', however, reaches only 3 ft. tall and wide; its blossoms keep their blue color in most soils. 'Bluebird' is a lace-cap type with pale blue sterile blooms and deep blue fertile flowers. The lace caps of 'Grayswood' consist of bright blue fertile blossoms surrounded by sterile flowers that gradually turn from white to red. 'Miyama-yae-murasaki' ('Purple Tiers') sports soft pink lace caps of double inner flowers surrounded by double sterile blooms. Pink-blossomed 'Pretty Maiden' features unusual lace caps made up of a large cluster of fertile flowers surrounded by very double sterile blooms. 'Preziosa' (*H.* 'Preziosa') has round clusters of white sterile flowers that age to red, blue, or mauve. 'Woodlander' has shell pink lace caps. Prune all immediately after bloom.

H. villosa. See H. aspera Villosa Group

Hydrangeaceae. The hydrangea family includes several woody-stemmed plants formerly listed under Saxifragaceae. *Hydrangea* and mock orange (*Philadelphus*) are examples.

HYDRASTIS canadensis

GOLDEN SEAL

Ranunculaceae

PERENNIAL

✂ US, MS ⌶ 8–4

◐ ● PARTIAL OR FULL SHADE

● REGULAR WATER

Hydrastis canadensis

Native to the eastern U.S., this handsome plant offers bold, luxuriant foliage for woodland and shade gardens. It grows from a thick yellow rootstock, sending up two deeply lobed, maplelike, 8-in.-long leaves that are held 10–12 in. above the ground. In spring, a foot-tall stalk appears, topped by a solitary, short-lived white flower to ½ in. across. The blossom is followed in summer by a large, showy red berry that resembles a raspberry, though it isn't edible.

Golden seal accepts ordinary garden soil but prefers moist soil containing plenty of organic matter. Because the root contains berberine, an antibacterial agent used in herbal medicine, the plant is threatened in the wild due to overcollection. Fortunately, it is easily propagated by seed, and in time specialty nurseries will be able to meet the demands of herbalists and native plant enthusiasts alike.

Hydrophyllaceae. The waterleaf family, largely but not entirely native to North America, includes annuals, perennials, and a few shrubs. *Nemophila* and *Phacelia* are among the few members of this family sometimes grown in gardens.

HYLOCEREUS undatus

NIGHT-BLOOMING CEREUS, QUEEN OF THE NIGHT

Cactaceae

CACTUS

✂ TS ⌶ 12–10; OR GROW IN POT

☀ ◐ FULL SUN OR LIGHT SHADE; BRIGHT INDIRECT LIGHT

◔ ◑ ● LITTLE TO REGULAR WATER

Hylocereus undatus

A plant that is often passed along from friend to friend, parent to child. Of unknown origin, but it is widely grown and naturalized in the tropical Americas. Deep green, three-ribbed, 2-in.-wide stems with short dark spines grow quickly to 15 ft. (possibly to 30 ft.), attaching themselves to a tree trunk, wall, or house by means of strong aerial roots. Without a support, the stems create a large, freestanding mound with a beautiful snaking pattern. Grown primarily for its waxy, fragrant, nocturnal white flowers, which are up to 1 ft. long. Individual flowers last just one night, but plant may bloom all summer. May also produce showy, 4-in.-long red fruits, which are edible and even deliciously sweet. Tolerates salt spray.

Easy to grow outdoors in well-drained soil in Tropical South. Elsewhere, grow in container and bring indoors in winter; keep humidity high and night temperature above 55°F. Fertilize monthly in spring and summer with balanced liquid fertilizer diluted to half-strength. Can survive drought but does best if watered regularly until flowering starts, then sparingly through the summer to encourage flowering.

HYLOTELEPHIUM. See SEDUM

HYMENOCALLIS

Amaryllidaceae

PERENNIALS FROM BULBS

✂ ZONES VARY BY SPECIES; OR DIG AND STORE DECIDUOUS TYPES; OR GROW IN POTS

☀ ◐ FULL SUN OR PARTIAL SHADE

● REGULAR WATER DURING GROWTH AND BLOOM, EXCEPT AS NOTED

☠ BULBS ARE POISONOUS IF INGESTED

Hymenocallis narcissiflora

Clumps of strap-shaped leaves like those of amaryllis. Stems, to 2 ft. tall in most types, bear very fragrant flowers in summer; blooms resemble daffodils in having a center cup, but cup is surrounded by six slender, spidery segments. Deciduous species maintain foliage throughout summer if watered, then die back in fall. Unusual plants for borders or containers. Plant in rich, well-drained soil—in late fall or early winter in frostless areas, after frosts in other areas. Set bulbs with tips 1 in. below surface; space 1 ft. apart. Deciduous sorts can be dug after foliage has yellowed (do not cut off fleshy roots), dried in an inverted position, and stored in open trays in a cool, dark, dry place.

▶

H. caroliniana. SOUTHERN SPIDER LILY. Deciduous. Zones MS, LS, CS; 12–8. Native to swampy woodlands of Georgia, Indiana, and Louisiana. Each bulb produces as many as 12 deep green leaves 1½ ft. long, ½ in. wide. White flowers to 5 in. across appear in spring and summer, in clusters of two to seven. Multiplies rapidly.

H. coronaria. SHOALS SPIDER LILY, CAHABA LILY. Deciduous. Zone LS. Rare species found in a few rocky shoals of rivers in Alabama, Georgia, and South Carolina. Straplike leaves up to 3 ft. long rise above water from bulbs anchored in soil between rocks. Groups of six to nine fragrant white flowers with yellowish centers, to 2 in. across, appear atop 3-ft. stalks from mid-May to early June. Each flower lasts one day. Species endangered by degradation of habitat due to sedimentation; do not collect plants from the wild.

H. eulae (H. galvestonensis). Deciduous. Zones MS, LS, CS; 12–8. Native to Texas and Louisiana. Blue-green foliage appears in late winter, disappears in spring. Flower stems to 20 in. high emerge in midsummer, bearing clusters of six to nine white flowers, each about 5 in. across.

H. latifolia (H. keyensis). SPIDER LILY. Evergreen. Zones CS, TS; 12–8. Native to Florida and the West Indies. Clusters of 6 to 12 white flowers, each consisting of a 3-in. cup outlined by spidery segments to 5 in. long.

H. liriosme. Deciduous. Zones MS, LS, CS; 12–8. Native to Texas, Mississippi. White, exceedingly fragrant flowers to 8 in. across are held in clusters of eight to ten. Likes wet soil.

H. maximiliani. Deciduous. Zones MS, LS, CS; 12–8. From Mexico. Dense clump of slender, glossy green leaves. Each stem bears a cluster of several 6-in. white flowers in early summer.

H. narcissiflora (Ismene calathina). BASKET FLOWER, PERUVIAN DAFFODIL. Deciduous. Zones LS; 12–10. Leaves 1½–2 ft. long, 1–2 in. wide. White, green-striped flowers to 4 in. across are held in clusters of two to five. 'Advance' has pure white flowers, faintly lined with green in throat.

H. 'Sulphur Queen'. Deciduous. Zones LS, CS, TS; 12–9. Primroselike yellow flowers, to 6 in. across, with light yellow, green-striped throats; up to six per cluster. Leaves are much like those of *H. narcissiflora*.

H. 'Tropical Giant'. Deciduous. Zones MS, LS, CS. Reliable old garden hybrid often found on abandoned properties in the South. Excellent foliage plant, its glossy green leaves forming an impressive clump in the boggy conditions it prefers. Blooms in midsummer, bearing small-cupped white flowers to 6 in. across on 2- to 3-ft. stems. Good in containers.

HYMENOXYS. See TETRANEURIS

HYPERICUM

ST. JOHNSWORT

Hypericaceae

EVERGREEN, SEMIEVERGREEN, AND DECIDUOUS SHRUBS OR PERENNIALS

🖊 ZONES VARY BY SPECIES

☼ ◐ PARTIAL SHADE IN LOWER AND COASTAL SOUTH

💧 MODERATE TO REGULAR WATER, EXCEPT AS NOTED

Hypericum calycinum

Large group of shrubs and perennials bearing yellow flowers that resemble single roses with a prominent sunburst of stamens in center. Open, cup-shaped, five-petaled blooms range in color from creamy yellow to gold; flowers may be solitary or in clusters. Neat leaves vary in form and color. Plants are useful for summer flower color and fresh green foliage. Various kinds are used for mass plantings, ground covers, informal hedges, borders. Most types resist deer damage. Perform especially well in mild, moist areas.

H. androsaemum. Semievergreen shrub. Zones US, MS, LS; 8–6. Shade-tolerant native of Europe, western Asia. To 3 ft. tall and wide, with stems arching toward the top. Leaves are medium green above, paler beneath, to 4 in. long and 2 in. wide. Clusters of ¾-in., golden yellow flowers in summer. Blossoms are followed by inedible berrylike fruits that turn from red to purple to black as they age. Useful as tall ground cover at edge of woods, on shaded slopes, in a wild garden.

H. beanii (H. patulum henryi). Evergreen shrub or perennial; more perennial-like in Upper South. Zones US, MS; 7–6. From China. To 4 ft. tall and slightly wider, with light green, oblong leaves on graceful, willowy branches. Flowers brilliant golden yellow, 2 in. across, midsummer into fall. Good for low, untrimmed hedge, mass planting. Shabby in winter.

H. buckleyi. BLUERIDGE ST. JOHNSWORT. Deciduous shrub. Zones US, MS, LS; 8–5. Native to mountains from North Carolina to Georgia. Spreading plant to 1 ft. high; space plants 2 ft. apart for ground cover. Rich green leaves to 1 in. long, rounded at tip. Golden yellow flowers to 1 in. wide bloom in summer.

H. calycinum. AARON'S BEARD, CREEPING ST. JOHNSWORT. Evergreen to semievergreen shrub; tops often killed in cold winters but come back in spring. Zones US, MS, LS; 9–4. From Bulgaria, Turkey. To 1 ft. high, spreading by vigorous underground stems. Short-stalked leaves to 4 in. long are medium green in sun, yellow green in shade. Bright yellow, 3-in.-wide flowers bloom all summer. A tough, dense ground cover that competes successfully with tree roots, takes poor soil. Fast growing; will control erosion on hillsides. May be invasive unless confined. Plant from flats or as rooted stems 1½ ft. apart. Clip or mow tops every 2 or 3 years during dormant season.

H. frondosum. BLUELEAF ST. JOHNSWORT. Deciduous shrub; evergreen in mildest areas. Zones US, MS, LS; 8–4. Native to southeastern U.S. Grows 1–3 ft. tall, with mounding form. Blue-green leaves set off clusters of 1½-in. bright yellow flowers that bloom from midsummer to early autumn. 'Sunburst' forms a tight mound to 3 ft. tall and wide.

H. 'Hidcote' (H. patulum 'Hidcote'). Evergreen to semievergreen shrub. Zones US, MS, LS; 9–6. To 4 ft. tall and 5 ft. wide. Leaves 2–3 in. long. Yellow flowers, 2½–3 in. wide, bloom all summer. Very prone to root rot and wilt in Lower South.

H. kouytchense. Semievergreen shrub. Zones US, MS, LS; 9–6. From China. Twiggy, rounded, to 1½–2 ft. tall, 2–3 ft. wide. Pointed oval, 2-in. leaves. Golden yellow, 2- to 3-in.-wide flowers bloom in summer. Often sold as *H.* 'Sungold'.

H. ×moserianum. GOLD FLOWER. Evergreen subshrub or perennial. Zones MS, LS; 9–7. Mounding plant with arching, reddish stems; reaches 2–3 ft. tall and wide. Leaves are 2 in. long, with blue-green undersides. Blooms in summer and possibly into fall, with golden yellow, 2½-in. flowers borne singly or in clusters of up to five. Cut back in early spring. 'Tricolor' has gray-green leaves edged in pink and white.

Hypericum ×moserianum 'Tricolor'

H. patulum henryi. See *H. beanii*

H. prolificum. SHRUBBY ST. JOHNSWORT. Deciduous shrub. Zones US, MS, LS; 8–5. Native from New Jersey to Georgia. Slow, dense grower to 1–4 ft. high and wide. Narrow, shiny dark green leaves grow 1–3 in. long. Bears 1-in. yellow blossoms late spring to late summer. Attractive in masses.

H. reductum. ATLANTIC ST. JOHNSWORT. Evergreen shrub. Zones MS, LS, CS, TS; 12–7. Native to sandy, scrubby sites from North Carolina to Florida and Alabama. Forms a mat to 1–1½ ft. high, 2–4 ft. wide. Aromatic, needlelike green leaves turn bronzy in winter. Small (to ⅔-in.-wide) yellow flowers bloom in early summer. Once established, needs no supplemental watering.

H. 'Rowallane'. Evergreen to semievergreen shrub. Zones MS, LS; 9–7. Upright, rather straggly growth to 3–6 ft. tall, 3 ft. wide. Bright yellow, 2½- to 3-in.-wide flowers bloom profusely in late summer and fall. Leaves reach 2½–3½ in. long. Remove older branches annually.

H. 'Sungold'. See *H. kouytchense*

FOR GROWING SYMBOL EXPLANATIONS
PLEASE SEE PAGE 145

HYPOESTES phyllostachya (H. sanguinolenta)

POLKA-DOT PLANT, FRECKLE FACE

Acanthaceae

PERENNIAL TREATED AS ANNUAL

🌱 US, MS, LS, CS, TS ⊪ 12–1; OR HOUSEPLANT

☼:◑ FULL SUN OR LIGHT SHADE; BRIGHT LIGHT

💧 REGULAR WATER

*Hypoestes
phyllostachya*

From South Africa. Though this tender plant is actually a perennial, it is almost always grown as a bedding annual or houseplant. Can reach 1–2 ft. tall, about 1 ft. wide. Slender stems bear oval, 2- to 3-in.-long leaves spotted irregularly with pink or white. A selected form known as 'Splash' has larger spots. Tiny, inconspicuous lavender flowers are not always produced. For indoor use, plant in loose, peaty mixture in pots or planters. Feed every 2 weeks with half-strength general-purpose liquid houseplant fertilizer. Pinch tips to make bushy.

Hypoxidaceae. The star grass family consists of a small number of perennial plants growing from corms or rhizomes. Flowers have six equal segments and resemble those of the lily and amaryllis families. Star grass *(Hypoxis)* is one of the commonly seen examples.

HYPOXIS

STAR GRASS

Hypoxidaceae

PERENNIAL

🌱 ZONES VARY BY SPECIES

☼:◑ FULL SUN OR LIGHT SHADE

💧💧 MODERATE TO REGULAR WATER

Hypoxis hirsuta

Pretty woodland plants with narrow to lance-shaped green leaves and small, star-shaped flowers. Need light, well-drained soil; well suited to rock gardens. Plants spread into wide colonies over time, but they're not invasive; dig up offsets to obtain new plants.

H. decumbens. GIANT STAR GRASS. Zones US, MS, LS, CS; 9–1. Native to Mexico. Dense mound of light green, grassy leaves to 8 in. tall, sprawling at least twice as wide. Bright yellow, 1-in. flowers in spring, summer, and fall.

H. hirsuta. YELLOW STAR GRASS. Zones US, MS, LS, CS; 9–4. Native from Maine to Florida and west to Texas. Usually found in dryish, open woodlands, growing in sandy or stony soil. Grassy, somewhat hairy, foot-long leaves rise from a short rhizome. In spring and early summer, a foot-tall stem carries one to seven bright yellow, starlike, inch-wide flowers. A second bloom may follow later.

HYSSOP. See AGASTACHE, HYSSOPUS officinalis

HYSSOPUS officinalis

HYSSOP

Lamiaceae (Labiatae)

PERENNIAL

🌱 US, MS, LS ⊪ 9–6

☼:◑ FULL SUN OR LIGHT SHADE

💧💧 MODERATE TO REGULAR WATER

Hyssopus officinalis

From southern Europe. Compact growth to 1½–2 ft. tall and 3 ft. wide. Narrow, glossy dark green leaves on woody-based stems; foliage has a pungent scent. Profusion of dark blue flower spikes throughout summer and into autumn; not a dramatic show but pleasant looking. Selections with white, pink, or lavender blooms are available.

Start from seed sown in early spring or stem cuttings in late spring or early summer. Once established, it may self-sow. Takes some drought but will thrive with regular moisture if drainage is good. Tolerates trimming as a low hedge or as border for a knot garden. Peppery-tasting leaves are sometimes used in cooking.

IBERIS

CANDYTUFT

Brassicaceae (Cruciferae)

PERENNIALS AND ANNUALS

🌱 ZONES VARY BY SPECIES

☼ FULL SUN

💧 REGULAR WATER

*Iberis
sempervirens*

Free-blooming plants from southern and western Europe with clusters of white, lavender, lilac, pink, rose, purple, carmine, or crimson flowers. Perennial candytufts bloom in spring; can be used as winter annuals in Coastal and Tropical South. Annual species bloom in spring and summer; they are most floriferous when nights are cool. Use all types for borders, cutting; use perennials for edging, rock gardens, small-scale ground covers, containers.

All types need well-drained soil. In early spring (or in fall in mild climates), sow seed of annuals in place or in flats; set transplants 6–9 in. apart. Plant perennials in spring or fall. After they bloom, shear lightly to stimulate new growth.

I. amara. HYACINTH-FLOWERED CANDYTUFT, ROCKET CANDYTUFT. Annual. Zones US, MS, LS, CS, TS; 12–1. To 12–15 in. high and 6 in. wide. Fragrant white flowers in tight, round clusters that elongate into hyacinth-like spikes. Narrow, slightly fuzzy leaves.

I. gibraltarica. Perennial. Zones MS, LS. Like *I. sempervirens* but is less hardy to cold and bears flatter clusters of light pinkish or purplish flowers, sometimes white near center.

I. sempervirens. EVERGREEN CANDYTUFT. Perennial. Zones US, MS, LS; 9–3. Grows 8 in. to 1 ft. or even 1½ ft. high, spreading about as wide. Narrow, shiny dark green leaves look good all year. Pure white flower clusters carried on stems long enough to cut for bouquets.

Several lower-growing, more compact types are available. These selections include 'Alexander's White', 6 in. tall, with fine-textured foliage; 'Kingwood Compact', also 6 in. high; 'Little Gem', 4–6 in. tall; and 'Purity', a wide-spreading selection 6–12 in. high. 'Snowflake', 4–12 in. tall, spreading to 1½–3 ft., has broader, more leathery leaves than the species; it also has larger flowers in larger clusters on shorter stems. It is extremely showy in spring and continues sporadic bloom through summer and fall. 'Snowmantle' is a similar vigorous type.

I. umbellata. GLOBE CANDYTUFT. Annual. Zones US, MS, LS, CS, TS; 12–1. Bushy plant to 12–15 in. high, 9 in. wide. Lance-shaped leaves to 3½ in. long; flowers in pink, rose, carmine, crimson, salmon, lilac, and white. Dwarf strains Dwarf Fairy and Magic Carpet, available in the same colors, grow 6 in. tall.

ICE PLANTS. These low-growing, succulent perennials (and a few annuals) were once conveniently lumped together as *Mesembryanthemum*, but they are now classified under several names. Where hardy, they are among the most useful and colorful of flowering ground covers. In colder climates, grow them as summer bloomers in window boxes or hanging baskets; or treat as houseplants. All take most soils; none will tolerate foot traffic. Feed lightly in fall, again after bloom. The various perennial ice plant genera include *Carpobrotus*, *Delosperma*, and *Drosanthemum*. *Mesembryanthemum*—the original, all-encompassing genus—now contains only annuals of little ornamental value.

ILEX

HOLLY

Aquifoliaceae

EVERGREEN AND DECIDUOUS SHRUBS AND TREES

ZONES VARY BY SPECIES

FULL SUN OR PARTIAL SHADE

REGULAR WATER, EXCEPT AS NOTED

Ilex aquifolium

Few plants are as dependable, versatile, and popular as hollies. More than 400 species and countless hybrids exist—and though a number of deciduous kinds have spectacular winter berries, Southerners generally prefer evergreen types that feature handsome foliage year-round and showy fruit as a bonus. In size, hollies range from foot-high mounds to trees 40–50 ft. tall. Smaller, shrublike plants are useful as foundation plantings and low hedges. Large evergreen hollies make attractive tall screens and hedges, and they're also good in corner plantings or as single specimens in a spacious lawn.

Nearly all holly plants are either male or female, and as a rule both sexes must be present for female plants to set fruit. The selections described here are female unless otherwise noted. A few set fruit without a pollenizer; these are noted too.

Most types prefer rich, moist, slightly acid, well-drained soil, though there are some exceptions (these are noted). All appreciate a layer of mulch to discourage weeds and keep the soil cool and moist. Though hollies will grow in sun or light shade, you'll get denser growth and heavier berry production in full sun. Diseases and insects are seldom serious; scale and leaf miner are the most common pests.

Evergreen hollies accept pruning quite well. Prune in winter to shape, control size, and harvest berry-laden branches for holiday arrangements. Also remove dead, broken, or crossing branches. Hollies that have grown too large or have become misshapen can be restored by severely shortening main branches; new growth will sprout from branch stubs and quickly fill in. Small-leafed hollies can be sheared into formal hedges or used for topiary.

I. ×altaclerensis (I. altaclarensis). ALTACLARA HOLLY. Evergreen shrub or tree. Zones US, MS; 8–1. Hybrid between *I. aquifolium* and a species from western Europe. Large, vigorous plant naturally reaches 60 ft. tall and 40 ft. wide, but it can be trained into a large shrub or small tree to 15–20 ft. high, 10–12 ft. wide. Adapts to most soils, tolerates wind.

'Camelliifolia'. Lustrous, nearly spineless dark green leaves up to 5 in. long. Large berries are dark red.

'James G. Esson'. Dark green, undulating, spiny leaves are a bit smaller than those of 'Camelliifolia'. Glossy red berries.

'Wilsonii'. Spiny, glossy bright green leaves up to 5 in. long. Heavy crop of bright red berries. Makes a nice espalier, screen, or formal clipped hedge. Not as cold hardy as other selections.

I. aquifolium. ENGLISH HOLLY. Evergreen shrub or tree. Zones US, MS; 8–1. Native to Europe, this is the holly of song, legend, and Christmas wreaths. It's a slow-growing plant that can eventually reach 40 ft. tall and 25 ft. wide, though it is usually much smaller in the South. Leaves are 2–4 in. long, highly variable in color, shape, and spininess. Some selections bear fruit without pollination, but the berries so produced are usually small and drop quickly.

English holly is arguably the most ornamental holly, but it's not easy to grow in most of the South. Dislikes high humidity coupled with high temperatures; does not do well with poor drainage, extreme cold, dry winter winds. It has succeeded in ideal locations, but it's chancy. *I.* 'Nellie R. Stevens' is a better choice for achieving a similar effect. Selections of English holly include the following.

'Argentea Marginata'. Dark green leaves with whitish margins.

'Aurea Marginata'. Dark green leaves edged in bright yellow.

'Balkans'. Upright grower with smooth dark green leaves; most cold hardy of the English hollies. Both male and female forms are available.

'Sparkler'. Strong, upright growth to about 12 ft. tall, 8 ft. wide. Heavy crop of glistening red berries at an early age.

'Zero' ('Teufel's Zero'). Upright grower with long, slender, weeping branches. Dark red berries ripen early. Cold hardy.

I. ×aquipernyi. Evergreen shrub or tree. Zones US, MS, LS; 8–1. Hybrid between *I. aquifolium* and *I. pernyi*. Dense, conical plant to 20 ft. tall (or taller), 12 ft. wide. Deep green, spiny leaves to 1½ in. long; red berries.

'Aquipern'. Male form used as a pollenizer.

'Brilliant'. Compact, dense grower. Dependably sets abundant fruit without a pollenizer.

'Carolina Sentinel'. Narrow, columnar form. Very deep green leaves; bright red berries. A good choice for screening in narrow spaces.

'Dorothy Lawton'. Rounded and shrubby, with somewhat round leaves.

'Patricia Varner'. Broad, upright form with dark green foliage and heavy crops of large berries. Fast grower.

'San Jose'. Dense, pyramidal form; reaches 15 ft. tall, 10 ft. wide. Glossy leaves and plenty of bright red berries. Sets fruit without a pollenizer.

I. ×attenuata. Evergreen tree. Zones US, MS, LS, CS; 9–1. Hybrid between *I. opaca* and *I. cassine*. To 12–30 ft. tall and about half as wide, with dense foliage and a conical or pyramidal habit. Light green leaves are sparsely toothed, to 3 in. long. Dark red berries. Fast growing; a popular choice for screening. Selections include these four:

'East Palatka'. Discovered near East Palatka, Florida, in 1927. Abundant bright red berries. More open and less hardy than 'Foster #2'. Young leaves have few spines; mature leaves are often spineless.

'Foster #2'. The most popular and ornamental of several hybrids known by the name "Foster holly." Narrow, conical form. Small, narrow leaves with short spines. Plentiful red berries.

'Hume #2'. Glossy, rounded, nearly spineless leaves. Shiny red berries. Can reach 35 ft. tall.

'Savannah'. Very popular selection prized for fast growth and tremendous crops of bright red berries. Leaves have short spines and look more like traditional holly foliage than do leaves of other *I.* ×*attenuata* selections. Tolerates limy soil.

I. cassine. DAHOON. Large evergreen shrub or small tree. Zones MS, LS, CS, TS; 12–7. Native to swamps and moist lowlands from North Carolina to Florida and Louisiana. Dense, upright habit to 20–30 ft. tall, 8–15 ft. wide. Leathery medium green leaves, 2–4 in. long, toothed only at tips. Heavy crops of small berries in red to reddish orange (sometimes nearly yellow). Grows naturally in wet, acid soils; tolerates mild alkalinity and has some salt tolerance. Regular to ample water.

I. cornuta. CHINESE HOLLY. Evergreen shrub or small tree. Zones US, MS, LS, CS; 9–1. From China and Korea. Very tolerant of heat, drought, alkaline soil. Dense or open form to 10 ft. or more. Leaves typically glossy, leathery, nearly rectangular, 1½–4 in. long, with spines at four corners and at tip. Very large, bright red, long-lasting berries. Selections rather than species usually grown; fruit set, leaf form, and spininess vary. The following selections set fruit without pollination.

Ilex cornuta 'Burfordii'

'Berries Jubilee'. Dome-shaped plant to 6–10 ft., with large leaves and heavy crop of large, bright red berries. Leaves are larger, spinier than those of 'Burfordii'.

'Burfordii'. BURFORD HOLLY. To 20 ft. tall and wide. Leaves nearly spineless, cupped downward. Sets a heavy crop of red fruit (much prized by mockingbirds and cedar waxwings) without a pollenizer. Useful as espalier. Discovered in Atlanta's Westview Cemetery around 1900.

'Carissa'. Dwarf to 3–4 ft. high and 4–6 ft. wide at maturity. Dense grower with small leaves; good for low hedge. No berries. Has been known to revert to 'Rotunda', the plant from which it was developed.

'Dazzler'. Compact, upright growth. Glossy leaves have a few stout spines along wavy margins. Loaded with rich red berries.

'D'Or'. Quite similar to 'Burfordii' but has bright yellow berries.

'Dwarf Burford' ('Burfordii Nana'). Like 'Burfordii' but is somewhat smaller, to about 8 ft. tall and wide. Densely covered with small (1½-in.), light green, nearly spineless leaves. Dark red berries.

'Needlepoint'. Dense, upright, a little larger than 'Dwarf Burford'. Dark green leaves with a single spine at tip; large crops of red berries.

'Rotunda'. DWARF CHINESE HOLLY. Compact grower to 3–4 ft. tall and 6–8 ft. wide at maturity. Usually does not produce berries. A few stout spines and rolled leaf margins between spines make the medium light green leaves nearly rectangular.

'Willowleaf'. WILLOWLEAF HOLLY. Dense spreader to 15 ft. high and wide; makes a good screen. Oblong dark green leaves have smooth margins and a single spine at the tip. Blood red berries.

I. crenata. JAPANESE HOLLY. Evergreen shrub. Zones US, MS, LS; 8–1. From Russia, Japan, Korea. The backbone of many a foundation planting because it's an attractive plant that's hard to kill. Looks more like boxwood (*Buxus*) than holly. Dense, erect, usually 3–4 ft. high, sometimes to 10 ft. Narrow, fine-toothed dark green leaves, ½–¾ in. long; black berries. Extremely hardy and useful where winter cold limits choice of tender evergreens for hedges, edgings. Selections include the following.

'Beehive'. Dense, compact mound to 3–4 ft. tall, 5–6 ft. wide.

'Compacta'. Rounded shrub to 6 ft. tall. Dense habit. Many different plants are sold under this name.

'Convexa'. Compact, rounded shrub to 4–6 ft. high, spreading wider. Leaves are roundish, cupped downward at the edges. Use clipped or unclipped. Many different plants are sold under this name.

'Dwarf Pagoda'. Exceptionally dense, slow-growing plant—to 1 ft. high and wide in 8 years. Leaves are tiny.

'Glory'. Male (fruitless) selection. Small, dense, round form; grows 5 ft. tall, 8 ft. wide. Extremely hardy.

'Helleri'. Dwarf selection to 1 ft. high, 2 ft. wide; larger after many years, to 4 ft. tall and 5 ft. wide. Very sensitive to poor drainage.

'Jersey Pinnacle'. Compact, dense, erect. To eventual 8 ft. tall, 2 ft. wide.

'Piccolo'. Slowly forms a tidy, dense dark green mound 1 ft. high and wide.

'Sky Pencil'. Columnar plant to 6 ft. tall and only 10 in. wide.

'Soft Touch'. Grows 2 ft. tall, 3 ft. wide. Unlike other selections, it has soft, flexible branches.

I. decidua. POSSUMHAW. Deciduous tree. Zones US, MS, LS, CS; 11–1. Native to the Southeast. To 6–10 ft., possibly to 20 ft. Pale gray stems; shiny dark green leaves to 3 in. long. Orange to red berries last into winter or spring. 'Warren's Red', eventually 15–20 ft. tall, bears a heavy crop of large red berries. 'Byers Golden' is a yellow-fruited selection. 'Council Fire' is lower growing, sports orange-red berries. For fruit production, need a male pollenizer such as 'Red Escort' or any male selection of *I. opaca*, such as 'Jersey Knight'.

I. 'Doctor Kassab'. Evergreen shrub or tree. Zones US, MS, LS, CS; 9–1. Hybrid between *I. cornuta* and *I. pernyi*. To 15–20 ft. high and 12–15 ft. wide, with broad, pyramidal form. Beautiful foliage: lustrous dark green, oval, pointed leaves with toothed edges, to 2 in. long. Plenty of bright red berries. Quite cold hardy, surviving −10°F.

I. 'Ebony Magic'. Evergreen shrub. Zones US, MS; 9–1. Hybrid between *I. aquifolium* and another species, most likely *I. rugosa* or *I. × meserveae*. Reaches at least 8–12 ft. tall, 6–8 ft. wide, with upright, pyramidal form. Blackish purple stems and spiny-edged, shiny dark green leaves to 1–2 in. long. Big orange-red berries last through spring. Use 'Ebony Male' as pollenizer.

I. 'Emily Bruner'. Evergreen shrub or tree. Zones MS, LS, CS; 9–7. Chance hybrid between *I. cornuta* 'Burfordii' and *I. latifolia*. Dense, pyramidal grower to 12–20 ft. tall, 10–15 ft. wide. Handsome dark green leaves to 4–5 in. long, with prominently toothed edges. Large red berries. Use male selection *I.* 'James Swann' as pollenizer.

I. glabra. INKBERRY. Evergreen shrub. Zones US, MS, LS, CS, TS; 12–3. Native to eastern North America. To 10 ft. tall and wide, with thick, spineless dark green leaves to 2 in. long (leaves turn olive green in winter). Berries are black. More widely sold than the species is dwarf form 'Compacta'; it reaches 4 ft. high and wide but can be sheared to make a 2-ft. hedge. 'Densa', 'Nordic', and 'Shamrock' are other dwarf forms. Grows in sun or partial shade; prefers acid soil. Tolerates wet soil and salt spray.

I. latifolia. LUSTERLEAF HOLLY. Evergreen tree. Zones MS, LS, CS; 9–6. Native to China, Japan. Slow-growing, stout-branched plant to

20–25 ft. tall, 15 ft. wide. Leaves are 6–8 in. long (largest of all hollies), dull dark green, leathery, fine toothed. Big clusters of large, dull red berries. In youth, resembles Southern magnolia (*Magnolia grandifolia*).

I. 'Lydia Morris'. Evergreen shrub or small tree. Zones US, MS, LS, CS; 9–6. Hybrid between *I. cornuta* 'Burfordii' and *I. pernyi*. Dense, pyramidal habit; reaches 20–25 ft. tall, 15 ft. wide. Very spiny, 1½- to 3-in.-long, lustrous blackish green leaves are held close to stems. Cardinal red berries. Use male selection *I.* 'John Morris' as pollenizer.

I. 'Mary Nell'. Evergreen shrub or small tree. Zones US, MS, LS, CS; 9–6. Complex hybrid involving *I. cornuta* 'Burfordii', *I. latifolia*, and a selection of *I. pernyi*. To 25–30 ft. tall, 15 ft. wide, with pyramidal habit. Very shiny, spiny dark green leaves to 4 in. long; great quantities of bright red berries. Increasingly popular in the Southeast.

I. × meserveae. MESERVE HOLLY. Evergreen shrub. Zones US, MS; 9–1. Apparently the most cold hardy of hollies with the true holly look. Most plants in this category are hybrids between *I. aquifolium* and *I. rugosa*, a cold-tolerant species from northern Japan; they are dense, bushy shrubs 6–7 ft. tall and wide, with purple stems and spiny, glossy blue-green leaves. Among red-berried female selections are 'Blue Angel', 'Blue Girl', and 'Blue Princess'; male pollenizers include 'Blue Boy' and 'Blue Prince'. 'Golden Girl' has yellow berries. Red-fruited 'China Girl' and male pollenizer 'China Boy', both to 10 ft. tall, are crosses of *I. cornuta* and *I. rugosa*. They are slightly hardier and tolerate more summer heat than the Blue series.

I. 'Nellie R. Stevens'. Evergreen shrub or small tree. Zones US, MS, LS, CS; 9–3. Hybrid between *I. aquifolium* and *I. cornuta*. The South's most popular large holly. Dense, fast-growing, conical plant to 15–20 ft. tall, 10 ft. wide. Leathery, glossy dark green leaves are sparsely toothed and reach 3 in. long. Sets fruit without a pollenizer but produces more berries if pollinated by a male selection of *I. cornuta*. A favorite for foundation and corner plantings as well as for tall screens. Probably the best all-around holly for the South.

Ilex 'Nellie R. Stevens'

I. opaca. AMERICAN HOLLY. Evergreen tree. Zones US, MS, LS, CS, TS; 11–1. Native to eastern U.S. Slowly grows to 40–50 ft. tall, 20–40 ft. wide; densely pyramidal when young, then becomes open, irregular, and picturesque with age. Spiny green leaves reach 2–4 in. long, may be glossy or dull; show some bronzing in winter. Red berries. Site in a wind-protected spot. Subject to many pests, with leaf miner being perhaps the most troublesome; to control, spray foliage with dimethoate (Cygon) in spring and summer. Rarely bothered by deer. Hundreds of selections exist, offering great variety. The following are some of the better and more widely available forms.

'Canary'. Large crops of buttercup yellow berries. Light olive green leaves have small spines and do not discolor in winter.

'Dan Fenton'. Forms a compact pyramid to 20 ft. tall and 15 ft. wide. Large dark green leaves have a squarish appearance. Lustrous red berries.

'Jersey Knight'. Male selection with shiny dark green leaves. Selected to pollinate 'Jersey Princess'.

'Jersey Princess'. Lustrous, very dark green leaves hold color throughout winter. Abundant red berries. Very cold hardy. Excellent performer in the Southeast.

'Maryland Dwarf'. Unusual prostrate form grows slowly to 3 ft. high, 6 ft. wide. Large, glossy deep green leaves; red berries.

'Merry Christmas'. Fast-growing, densely branched tree. Glossy deep green leaves have short spines. Profuse bright red berries.

'Miss Helen'. Dense, conical tree with leathery dark green leaves and plenty of egg-shaped dark red berries.

I. pedunculosa. LONGSTALK HOLLY. Evergreen shrub or small tree. Zones US, MS, LS; 9–1. Exceptionally cold hardy for a broad-leafed evergreen. From China, Japan. Grows to 15 ft. or taller; awkward shape when young. Narrow, smooth-edged leaves 1–3 in. long, half as wide. Bright red, ¼-in. berries dangle on 1- to 1½-in.-long stalks in fall.

▶

I. pernyi. PERNY HOLLY. Evergreen tree. Zones US, MS, LS; 9–6. Native to China. Slow growth to 20–30 ft. tall, 10 ft. wide. Glossy, 1- to 2-in.-long leaves, square at base, one to three spines on each side; closely packed against branchlets. Red berries set tightly against stems.

I. 'Robin'. Evergreen shrub or small tree. Zones US, MS, LS, CS; 8–5. Seedling of *I.* 'Mary Nell'. Beautiful, spiny leaves to 3 in. long emerge maroon, then mature to dark green. Abundant red berries. Similar in form and cold hardiness to *I.* 'Nellie R. Stevens' but may grow somewhat taller.

I. 'Sparkleberry'. Deciduous shrub. Zones US, MS, LS, CS; 9–1. Selection of hybrid between *I. verticillata* and *I. serrata*, released by the U.S. National Arboretum. Grows to 6 ft. high and wide; old specimens may reach 12 ft. Tooth-edged dark green leaves to 4 in. long drop in early winter. Sets copious amounts of large, bright red fruits that persist through winter. Probably the showiest deciduous holly of all. Tolerates wet soils. Pollinate with male selections 'Apollo' or 'Raritan Chief'.

I. verticillata. WINTERBERRY. Deciduous shrub. Zones US, MS, LS, CS; 9–1. Native to swamps of eastern North America. Unlike most hollies, this one thrives in boggy soils, but it will succeed in any moist, acid, organic soil. Species and most selections grow 6–10 ft. tall and wide, eventually forming clumps by suckering. Dark green, oval leaves to 3 in. long may turn yellow in autumn. Female plants bear enormous crops of bright red berries that ripen in early fall and last all winter (if the birds don't eat them). Plant one male plant for every six females. Selections include the following.

'Afterglow'. Orange to orange-red berries on a slow-growing, compact, globe-shaped plant.

'Cacapon'. Compact and upright, with glossy, crinkled leaves. Particularly long-lasting berries. Does very well in the Southeast.

'Jim Dandy'. Male form used to pollinate 'Afterglow', 'Cacapon', 'Red Sprite', and 'Shaver'. Grows 3–6 ft. tall, 4–8 ft. wide.

'Red Sprite'. Dwarf form grows to 3–5 ft. high and wide. Large bright red berries—the largest fruit of all winterberries.

'Shaver'. Slow-growing plant with large orange-red berries.

'Southern Gentleman'. Male form used to pollinate 'Cacapon', 'Shaver', 'Winter Red'.

'Winter Red'. Large, rounded form; profuse bright red berries that retain their color into February. Lustrous, good-looking leaves. Considered by many to be the best winterberry. Use male selection 'Southern Gentleman' as pollenizer.

I. vomitoria. YAUPON. Evergreen shrub or small tree. Zones MS, LS, CS, TS; 11–7. Native to the South. Grows in almost any soil—acid or alkaline, wet or dry, rich or poor. Good plant for the beach. Tolerates salt spray. Grows to 15–20 ft. tall, with narrow, inch-long, shallowly toothed dark green leaves. Can be grown as standard or sheared into columnar form; good topiary plant. Tiny scarlet berries are borne in profusion. Resists damage by deer. Popular selections include the following.

'Bordeaux'. To 3–4 ft. high and wide, with lustrous green leaves.

'Gold Top'. Golden new growth. Red fruit.

'Katherine'. Bears a heavy crop of golden yellow fruit.

'Nana'. DWARF YAUPON. Low shrub. Compact grower to 1½ ft. high and twice as wide. Refined, attractive. Inconspicuous berries.

'Pendula'. Weeping branches look best when plant is trained as standard.

'Pride of Houston'. Upright, freely branching. Use as screen or hedge. Bears an abundant crop of berries.

'Stokes' ('Stokes Dwarf', 'Shillings'). Male form. Compact plant with dark green leaves closely set on branches. Smaller than 'Nana'.

'Will Fleming'. Male form with narrow, upright habit. Good for tight spaces.

ENGLISH HOLLY RULES. *Few plants are as rooted in superstition and folklore as holly. In Merrie Olde England, for example, it was vitally important which kind of holly was brought into the house on New Year's Day. If the holly had smooth leaves (called a she-holly), the wife commanded the house for the year. If the holly was prickly (a he-holly), the husband laid down the law.* ❖

ILLICIUM

ANISE TREE

Illiciaceae

EVERGREEN SHRUBS OR TREES

🌱 MS, LS, CS

◐ ● PARTIAL OR FULL SHADE, EXCEPT AS NOTED

💧 AMPLE WATER, EXCEPT AS NOTED

☠ ALL PARTS OF I. ANISATUM ARE POISONOUS IF INGESTED

Illicium anisatum

Little-used but attractive clan of shrubs or small trees noted for both foliage and flowers. Thick, leathery, glossy leaves are anise-scented when crushed; spring flowers have many petal-like segments and are reminiscent of small magnolia blossoms. Fruits that follow are small, one-sided pods arranged in a ring. The star anise of Chinese cookery is the fruit of the tropical tree *I. verum*, apparently not grown in North America. All like rich soil with abundant organic material. Big, bold foliage gives the impression of rhododendrons. Good understory plants for woodland gardens; also useful for screening. Seldom need pruning.

I. anisatum (I. religiosum). JAPANESE ANISE. Heat zones 9–7. Native to Japan, South Korea, Taiwan. To 6–10 ft. (possibly 15 ft.) tall, 6–8 ft. wide; conical growth habit. Oval to lance-shaped, blunt-tipped, glossy leaves to 5 in. long, 2 in. wide. Inch-wide, scentless flowers on short, nodding stalks cluster in leaf axils; they open yellowish green, then fade to creamy white. Much planted in Buddhist cemeteries; cut branches are used to decorate graves. Highly fragrant wood is used for incense. Seeds, wood, and foliage are toxic if ingested.

I. floridanum. FLORIDA ANISE. Heat zones 12–4. Native Florida to Louisiana. Reaches 6–10 ft. or taller, equally wide. Pointed oval leaves 6 in. long and 2 in. wide, with prominent midribs. Waxy, nodding maroon flowers 1–2 in. across on 1½- to 2-in.-long stalks; most people find scent unpleasant. 'Halley's Comet' is more compact, with larger, redder flowers than the species; often blooms into fall. 'Album' is white flowered; 'Variegatum' has maroon purple flowers with subtle green-on-green leaf variegation. 'Woodland Ruby' is a hybrid with ruby pink, 2-in. flowers shaped like starfish; flowering period extends through summer.

I. parviflorum. YELLOW ANISE. Native to Southeast. Grows 15–20 ft. tall, 10–15 ft. wide, with 4-in., oblong olive green leaves and ½-in. yellow-green flowers. Can form small colonies by suckering. More tolerant of sun and dry soil than other anise trees, but equally at home in damp shade.

IMPATIENS

IMPATIENS, SULTANA, BALSAM

Balsaminaceae

PERENNIALS AND ANNUALS

🌱 US, MS, LS, CS, TS ⚘ 12–1, EXCEPT AS NOTED

☀ ◐ ● EXPOSURE NEEDS VARY BY SPECIES

💧 REGULAR WATER

Impatiens walleriana

Of the hundreds of species, only the following are usually seen in gardens. Most of these are annuals or tender perennials treated as annuals; all are valuable for long bloom period (most flower in summer, and a few continue into fall). When lightly touched, ripe seed capsules burst open and scatter seeds.

I. balfourii. Annual. From the Himalayas. To 20 in. high and broad, with 4- to 5-in. leaves and loose clusters of inch-wide, pink-tinted white flowers. Seldom planted but often pops up unannounced. It can become a pest by reseeding, but it is attractive in shady, informal plantings.

I. balsamina. BALSAM. Annual. From Southeast Asia. Erect, branching plant reaches 8–30 in. high and 6–8 in. wide. Sharp-pointed, 1½- to 6-in.-long leaves with deeply toothed edges. Large, spurred flowers are borne among leaves along main stem, branches; they may be solid colored or variegated, in white or shades of pink, rose, lilac, or red. Compact, double camellia–flowered forms are most frequently grown. Sow seeds in flats or pots in early spring; after frost danger is past, set out young plants (or purchased transplants) in full sun (light shade in hottest climates).

I. capensis. JEWEL WEED. Annual. Native to damp, shady sites in Canada and the northern U.S. Grows 2–5 ft. tall, 2 ft. wide. Smooth, toothedged green leaves to 3½ in. long. Spurred, 1-in. orange-yellow flowers with reddish brown splotches; blooms in summer, fall. Partial or full shade. Juice from crushed stems is used to treat dermatitis caused by poison ivy, poison oak.

I. glandulifera (I. roylei). Annual. From the Himalayas. To 3–6 ft. tall, with thick, juicy stems and leaves to 8 in. long. Profuse show of yellow-spotted purple to white flowers. Like a larger *I. balfourii* and just as likely to self-sow all over the place. Light to full shade.

I. holstii. See I. walleriana

I. New Guinea hybrids. Perennials in Zone TS; annuals anywhere. A varied group of striking plants developed from a number of species native to New Guinea, especially *I. hawkeri*. Plants can be upright to spreading; most are 1–2 ft. tall and as wide or wider (though some are smaller, such as 8-in.-high Baby Bonita series). Leaves are typically large, often variegated with cream or red. Flowers usually large (2½ in. wide) though not profuse, held well above foliage; colors include lavender, purple, pink, red, orange, and white. Once considered primarily potted plants, they may also be grown in the open ground; provide ample fertilizer and give somewhat more sun than you would *I. walleriana*.

Impatiens New Guinea Hybrid 'Tango'

Popular strains include Celebration (with 3-in. flowers), Paradise, and Pure Beauty. Most New Guinea hybrids are cutting-grown plants, but Spectra (Firelake) and Java strains can be grown from seed. Spectra offers a mix of flower colors and has leaves variegated with cream or white; bronze-leafed Java is available in single or mixed colors. 'Tango', also seed-grown, has bright orange blooms and bronze-green foliage.

I. omeiana. HARDY IMPATIENS. Perennial. From mountainous areas of China. To 1–1½ ft. high, spreading by runners. Attractive leaves to 1½ in. long are velvety dark green with a whitish stripe down the center. Blooms in early fall, bearing small yellow to apricot flowers that resemble little goldfish. Partial or full shade.

I. repens. YELLOW IMPATIENS. Perennial in Zone TS; usually grown as annual. From India, Sri Lanka. To 8 in. high, 1 ft. wide, with thick reddish stems and kidney-shaped, 1-in. green leaves. Hooded, clear yellow, 1½-in. flowers from summer to fall. Good choice for hanging baskets. Partial shade.

I. sodenii (I. oliveri). POOR MAN'S RHODODENDRON. Perennial in Zone TS; indoor/outdoor plant elsewhere. From eastern tropical Africa. To 4–8 ft. tall, 10 ft. wide, with woody-based stems clothed in whorls of 8-in.-long, glossy dark green leaves. Produces many 2½-in., slender-spurred flowers in lilac, pale lavender, or pinkish shades. Tolerates seacoast conditions. Frosts kill it to ground, but it regrows in spring. Blooms in partial or deep shade; takes sun in cool-summer areas.

I. sultani. See I. walleriana

I. walleriana. IMPATIENS, SULTANA. Perennial in Zone TS; annual anywhere. Includes plants formerly known as *I. holstii* and *I. sultani*. The South's most popular flowers for partial or full shade; will take full sun if watered almost daily. Rapid, vigorous growth; tall types reach 2 ft. high, dwarf kinds 6–12 in. high. Narrow, glossy dark green, 1- to 3-in.-long leaves on juicy pale green stems. Flowers 1–2 in. wide, in all colors but yellow and true blue. All types are useful for many months of bright color. Grow plants from seed or cuttings, or buy them in cell-packs or pots. Space taller types 1 ft. apart, dwarfs 6 in. apart. If plants overgrow, cut them back to 6 in. above ground—it's a tonic. New growth emerges in a few days, and flowers cover it in 2 weeks. Plants often reseed in moist ground.

Among the many strains and selections are the following, all bearing the typical five-petaled blooms.

Accent. To 10 in. high. Strain comes in various individual colors or a mix.

Accent Star. Variation of Accent strain, with white central star extending across the petals.

Bruno. To 10–12 in. Tetraploid strain (double the usual number of chromosomes), with large (2½-in.) flowers on extremely sturdy plants. Available in single or mixed colors.

Butterfly. To 10 in. high. Blossoms show contrasting central patch in butterfly form.

Mosaic. To 12–14 in. Comes in several lilac or rosy shades, all irregularly splashed with white.

Pride. To 10–16 in. Flowers are larger than usual (to 2½ in. across), in single or mixed colors.

Stardust. To 12–14 in. Central white star tapers off into a dusting of white.

Super Elfin. To 8–10 in. Comes in an exceptionally wide range of individual colors and blends of harmonizing hues. One example is 'Blue Pearl', with flowers in an unusual bluish lilac shade.

Swirl. To 10–12 in. Pastel shades with picotee edges of deeper color.

Many novelty strains and selections are available. They include Firefly, dwarf series to 6–8 in. high, with ½-in. flowers in the full range of impatiens colors; Confection, 10–12 in., producing a high percentage of double and semidouble flowers from seed; and 'Victorian Rose', 10–12 in., with frilly rose pink semidouble flowers. Other double impatiens with flowers resembling rosebuds include cutting-grown Fiesta and Tioga strains. The double-flowered types are best used as potted plants, located where flower detail can be observed close up.

IMPERATA cylindrica 'Rubra' ('Red Baron')

JAPANESE BLOOD GRASS

Poaceae (Gramineae)

PERENNIAL GRASS

US, MS, LS, CS 9–1

FULL SUN OR PARTIAL SHADE

REGULAR WATER

Imperata cylindrica 'Rubra'

From Japan. Ornamental grass with erect stems forms a clump 1–2 ft. tall, 1 ft. wide. Striking in borders, especially where sun can shine through blades. Completely dormant in winter. Spreads slowly by underground runners. Rarely, if ever, flowers. Good for textural contrasts; mixes well with perennials that have yellow-green or blue-green foliage. Best in rich, well-drained soil.

INCARVILLEA

Bignoniaceae

PERENNIALS

ZONES VARY BY SPECIES

LIGHT SHADE IN HOTTEST CLIMATES

REGULAR WATER

Incarvillea delavayi

Native to the Himalayas and China, these plants have showy trumpet-shaped flowers similar to those of their trumpet vine relatives (*Bignonia, Campsis,* and the like). Flowers are large for the size of the plant. Many species are coming into cultivation, but only the following two have reached North American gardens in any numbers. Leaves are 2–8 in. long, divided featherwise into leaflets. Plants are deep rooted and need reasonably deep soil and excellent drainage. In Upper South, mulch plants after the soil has frozen (to prevent ground from heaving). Protect from slugs and snails.

I. arguta. HIMALAYAN GLOXINIA. Zones LS, CS; 9–7. Can be treated as annual in colder areas, since it will bloom first year from seed if started in earliest spring. Grows erect to 5 ft. tall and 3 ft. wide, or sprawls to 3 ft. tall and 5 ft. wide; somewhat shrubby at base. Leaves divided into 4 to 12 leaflets, each up to 2 in. long. Blooms in spring and summer; inflorescences have 5 to 20 pink or white, 1½-in.-long flowers. Effective leaning over walls or spilling down slopes. Self-sows but not a pest. ▶

I. delavayi. HARDY GLOXINIA. Zones US, MS, LS; 9–3. To 2 ft. high, 1 ft. wide. Like *I. arguta*, has divided leaves and trumpet-shaped flowers—but in other respects, it is entirely different. Grows from a carrot-shaped perennial root and forms a rosette of foot-long leaves, each divided into many leaflets. The foot-tall flower stalk is topped by 2 to 12 flowers that are 3 in. long and wide, rosy purple outside, yellow and purple within. Blooms in late spring, early summer. Division is difficult.

INCENSE CEDAR. See CALOCEDRUS decurrens

INDIAN BLANKET. See GAILLARDIA pulchella

INDIAN CHOCOLATE. See GEUM rivale

INDIAN HAWTHORN. See RHAPHIOLEPIS indica

INDIAN PAINTBRUSH. See CASTILLEJA

INDIAN PHYSIC. See GILLENIA trifoliata

INDIAN RHUBARB. See DARMERA peltata

INDIAN-SHOT. See CANNA indica

INDIGO BUSH. See AMORPHA, INDIGOFERA

INDIGOFERA

INDIGO BUSH

Fabaceae (Leguminosae)

DECIDUOUS SHRUBS

🗡 US, MS, LS, CS

☼ FULL SUN

💧 REGULAR WATER, EXCEPT AS NOTED

Indigofera kirilowii

Native to northern China, Korea, Japan. Woody-stemmed plants with finely divided, almost ferny foliage and dense clusters of tiny, sweet pea–shaped flowers in spring and summer. Plants can be killed to the ground in a hard winter, but they recover quickly from the roots and bloom on new wood. Even in mild-winter areas, they are more compact and attractive when cut back hard in late dormant season. Provide good drainage.

I. decora. CHINESE INDIGO. Heat zones 9–7. To 1–2½ ft. tall and 3 ft. wide, with arching branches. Narrow, somewhat drooping blossom clusters to 8 in. long hold as many as 40 white blooms suffused with pink.

I. heterantha. HIMALAYAN INDIGO. To 4–8 ft. high and wide, with arching branches. Purplish pink flowers in upright clusters 6–8 in. long. Moderate water.

I. kirilowii. KIRILOW INDIGO. Heat zones 9–5. To 2½–3 ft. tall, 3 ft. wide, with upright shoots and erect, 5-in. clusters of rose pink flowers.

INKBERRY. See ILEX glabra

INULA

Asteraceae

PERENNIALS

🗡 US, MS, LS

☼ ◑ EXPOSURE NEEDS VARY BY SPECIES

💧 💧 WATER NEEDS VARY BY SPECIES

Large group of plants native to Europe and Asia grown for their showy, daisylike yellow flowers. Imposing and erect, they have large basal leaves and progressively smaller leaves higher up on the stems. Medium green, oval, pointed leaves are often hairy or downy. Good for open, casual gardens or against a dark-colored background. Soil should be well drained.

Inula magnifica

I. helenium. ELECAMPANE. Heat zones 9–1. Robust plant to 6 ft. tall, 3 ft. wide, with basal leaves 1½–2 ft. long. Blooms in summer, bearing single or clustered, bright yellow flowers to 3 in. across. Widely naturalized in the U.S. Root is used medicinally for respiratory complaints. Full sun or partial shade. Regular water.

I. magnifica. SUNRAY FLOWER. Heat zones 8–5. About the same size as *I. helenium* but with broader, rougher leaves. Clusters of up to 20 deep yellow, 6-in. flowers appear in late summer. Good plant for the back of the border. Excellent cut flower. Full sun. Regular to ample water; will grow in boggy soil.

IPHEION uniflorum (Brodiaea uniflora, Triteleia uniflora)

SPRING STAR FLOWER

Liliaceae

PERENNIAL FROM BULB

🗡 US, MS, LS, CS ⊩ 9–5

☼ ◑ FULL SUN OR PARTIAL SHADE

💧 REGULAR WATER DURING GROWTH AND BLOOM

Ipheion uniflorum

Spring-blooming Argentine native with wildflower charm. Each bulb produces several slender stems, each bearing a single half-inch blossom with six overlapping petals. Usual color is white tinged with blue, but variants include white 'Album', bright blue 'Rolf Fiedler', and dark blue 'Wisley Blue'. All have narrow, nearly flat, bluish green leaves that smell like onions when bruised.

Use in borders or under deciduous shrubs; or naturalize in woodland areas or among low grasses. In fall, set bulbs 2 in. deep and 2 in. apart. Prefers dry conditions during summer dormancy but will accept water if drainage is good. Divide infrequently—plantings become more attractive over the years as bulbs multiply. Not bothered by rodents.

IPOMOEA

MORNING GLORY

Convolvulaceae

PERENNIAL AND ANNUAL VINES

🗡 ZONES VARY BY SPECIES

☼ FULL SUN

💧 💧 MODERATE TO REGULAR WATER

Ipomoea tricolor
'Heavenly Blue'

Native to tropical and subtropical regions of the world. This genus includes many ornamental twining vines as well as the edible sweet potato (see Sweet Potato); it does not include the weedy plant known as wild morning glory or bindweed (*Convolvulus arvensis*). The plants described here may self-sow, but they do not spread by nearly ineradicable underground runners as wild morning glory does. They tend to have hard seeds; to encourage faster sprouting, nick the coating or soak overnight in water before planting. For annual display, sow seeds in place after frost danger is past; or, for an earlier start, sow seeds indoors, then set out plants 6–8 in. apart. Use morning glory vines on fence or trellis or as ground cover. Or grow in containers; provide stakes or a wire cylinder for support, or let plant cascade. For cut flowers, pick stems with buds in various stages of development and place in deep vase; buds open on consecutive days.

I. alba (Calonyction aculeatum). MOONFLOWER, MOON VINE. Perennial in Tropical South; annual elsewhere. Zones US, MS, LS, CS, TS; 12–1. Fast growing (20–30 ft. in a season), providing quick shade for arbor, trellis, or fence. Luxuriantly clothed in heart-shaped leaves to 8 in. long, closely spaced on stems. Blooms from early summer until fall, showing off fragrant, 6-in., funnel-shaped white blossoms after sundown and into the night (flowers also open on cloudy or dark days).

I. batatas. SWEET POTATO VINE. Perennial from tuberous roots. Zones LS, CS, TS; 12–1; or indoor/outdoor plant. For the edible sort, see Sweet Potato; the following fancy-leafed forms are grown for ornament. Trailing in habit, they have leaves that vary in size from 2 to 4 in. long, range in shape from heart shaped to deeply lobed. 'Ace of Spades' has purple-black, perfectly heart-shaped leaves; those of 'Blackie' are similar in color but are deeply lobed. 'Marguerite' (alternate spellings include 'Margurite' and 'Margarita') and 'Sulfur' have golden green foliage. A selection variously called 'Tricolor' and 'Pink Frost' has green foliage with white and pink variegation. 'Ladyfingers' has medium green leaves divided into long, fingerlike lobes; veins and leafstalks are burgundy red. Sweet Caroline series features deeply toothed leaves available in four colors: green, bright lime green, dark burgundy, and bronze (rust color). All of these selections look great in window boxes and hanging baskets.

I. indica (I. acuminata, I. learii). BLUE DAWN FLOWER. Perennial. Zones CS, TS; 12–9. Vigorous, rapid growth to 15–30 ft. Dark green, 2½- to 7-in. heart-shaped or three-lobed leaves. Clusters of 3- to 4-in., funnel-shaped flowers from spring into fall; blooms open bright blue, then fade to pinkish purple by day's end. Use to cover large bank, wall, or unsightly fence or other structure. Blooms in 1 year from seed; can also be grown from cuttings, divisions, and layering of established plants.

I. lindheimeri. Perennial. Zones LS, CS, TS; 12–1. Native from Texas to New Mexico and Mexico. Deeply cleft leaves; blue flowers to 3½ in. long from spring until fall. Trailing habit, but not invasive. Well suited to dry, chalky soils.

I. lobata (Mina lobata). FIRECRACKER VINE, SPANISH FLAG. Perennial. Zones TS; 12–10; grown as annual elsewhere. Grows quickly to 10–15 ft. Dark green, deeply lobed leaves are 4 in. long. Bloom begins in late summer and continues until frost; flower spikes to 6 in. long are held above the foliage and carry tubular, ½- to ¾-in. blossoms on just one side. Blooms start out red, then fade to orange, yellow, and finally white; 'Citronella' features lemon yellow flowers

Ipomoea lobata

that age to cream and white. Blossoms attract hummingbirds; also make good cut flowers. Plant in fertile, well-drained soil, and provide a post, trellis, or fence for support. Don't overdo the fertilizer or you'll get mostly leaves and few flowers.

I. ×multifida (Quamoclit multifida). CARDINAL CLIMBER. Annual. Zones US, MS, LS, CS, TS; 12–1. To 15 ft. Broad leaves to 4½ in. wide, each divided into 7 to 15 sharp-pointed segments to ½ in. wide. Crimson flowers with a white eye bloom in summer.

I. nil. MORNING GLORY. Annual. Zones US, MS, LS, CS, TS; 12–1. Summer bloomer resembling *I. tricolor,* but with leaves that are often shallowly three-lobed (leaves of *I. tricolor* are unlobed). The large-flowered (to 6-in.-wide) Imperial Japanese strain belongs to this species; other selections include rosy red 'Scarlett O'Hara', odd pinkish tan 'Chocolate', and mixed-color Early Call strain (useful where summers are short).

I. pes-caprae. BEACH MORNING GLORY, RAILROAD VINE. Evergreen perennial. Zones CS, TS; 12–9. Native to Florida. Sprawling vine grows to great length, rooting at leaf joints as it runs. Medium green leaves are fleshy, 1½–4 in. long, notched at the tip, and nearly round to kidney shaped. Pink summer flowers to 2 in. wide. Useful as a ground cover on sandy saltwater beaches.

I. purpurea. COMMON MORNING GLORY. Perennial in Tropical South; annual elsewhere. Zones US, MS, LS, CS, TS; 12–1. Like *I. tricolor* but generally has smaller leaves and flowers. Blooms in summer. Rapid growth to 30–40 ft. Medium green leaves are broadly oval and pointed, three lobed or unlobed. First flowers appear a few weeks after sowing seed; then vine quickly covers itself in 5-in.-wide purple, blue, white, and pink blooms with pale throats, especially showy because of their many colors. Water and fertilize sparingly during summer, to encourage flowers. Reseeds and returns in spring; watch that it doesn't escape and become a nuisance. 'Grandpa Otts' and 'President Tyler' are deep purple with a rosy red star-shaped overlay and white throat; 'Milky Way' is pure white with a maroon star.

I. quamoclit (Quamoclit pennata). CYPRESS VINE. Annual. Zones US, MS, LS, CS, TS; 12–1. To 20 ft., with 2½- to 4-in.-long, dark green leaves finely divided into slender threads. Summer flowers are scarlet (rarely white), 1½-in.-long tubes that flare at mouth into a five-pointed star.

I. tricolor. MORNING GLORY. Annual. Zones US, MS, LS, CS, TS; 12–1. Vigorous growth to 10–15 ft., with large, heart-shaped leaves in light to medium green. Showy, funnel-shaped to bell-like flowers are single or double, in solid colors of blue, lavender, pink, red, or white, often with throats in contrasting colors; some are bicolored or striped. Most types open only in morning, fade in afternoon. Bloom from summer until frost. Among the most popular selections is 'Heavenly Blue', to 15 ft., bearing 4- to 5-in., pure sky blue flowers with yellow throat. 'Tie Dye', to 6–8 ft., bears 6-in.-wide lavender blooms marked with deep purple swirls, stripes, and flecks; its foliage is splashed silvery white. 'Flying Saucers' has 4- to 5-in. white blossoms variably streaked with purplish blue. Dwarf strain with white markings on the leaves (known as Spice Islands or simply as Variegated) grows only 9 in. high and spills to 1 ft. across; flower colors include red, pink, blue, and bicolors.

IPOMOPSIS rubra (Gilia rubra)

STANDING CYPRESS

Polemoniaceae

BIENNIAL OR SHORT-LIVED PERENNIAL

🗡 MS, LS, CS ⌗ 9–5

☼ ◗ FULL SUN OR PARTIAL SHADE

◐ ◖ MODERATE TO REGULAR WATER

Ipomopsis rubra

Native to the South. To 6 ft. tall, 1 ft. wide. Tubular flowers are red outside, yellow marked with red inside. Erect, unbranched stems are clothed in finely divided dark green leaves. Startling in appearance, best massed; individual plants are narrow. Sow seed in spring or early summer for bloom the following summer. Difficult to transplant once established. Adapts to almost any well-drained soil. Attracts hummingbirds.

IRESINE herbstii

BLOODLEAF

Amaranthaceae

PERENNIAL

🗡 TS ⌗ 12–7; OR GROW IN POT

☼ FULL SUN; BRIGHT LIGHT

◐ REGULAR WATER

Iresine herbstii

From Brazil. Tender, upright plant to 1–3 ft. high and wide, grown for attractive leaf color; flowers are inconspicuous. Leaves are 1–2 in. long, oval to round, usually notched at tip. Leaf color may be purplish red with lighter midrib and veins, or green or bronze with yellowish veins. Stems may be green, purple, or red. Pinch plant tips for bushiness. Good in containers. Beyond hardiness range, bring indoors for winter, treat as annual, or grow as houseplant next to a south-facing window. Easy to propagate from cuttings taken in fall and grown for spring and summer display. Similar to *I. herbstii* is *I. lindenii,* bearing deep red leaves with prominent dark or light red veins; they are pointed rather than notched at the tip.

Iridaceae. The large iris family includes many familiar (and unfamiliar) garden bulbs, corms, and fibrous-rooted perennials. Leaves are swordlike or grasslike, often in two opposing rows. Flowers may be simply arranged with six equal segments (as in *Crocus,* for example) or highly irregular in appearance (as in *Iris*).

IRIS

Iridaceae

PERENNIALS FROM BULBS AND RHIZOMES

✔ ● ZONES VARY BY SPECIES OR TYPE

☼ ◑ ● EXPOSURE NEEDS VARY BY SPECIES

◗ ◗ ◗ WATER NEEDS VARY BY SPECIES

Japanese Iris

A large and remarkably diverse group of 200 to 300 species, varying in flower color and form, cultural needs, and blooming periods (although the majority flower in spring or early summer). Leaves are swordlike or grasslike. Flowers (fragrant, in many kinds) are showy and complex in structure. The three inner segments (the standards) are petals; they are usually erect or arching but, in some kinds, may flare to horizontal. The three outer segments (the falls) are petal-like sepals; they are held at various angles, from nearly horizontal to drooping.

Irises grow from bulbs or rhizomes. In floral detail, there are three categories: bearded (each fall bears an adornment resembling a small, fuzzy caterpillar), beardless (each fall is smooth), and crested (each fall bears a comblike ridge instead of a full beard).

Described here are the irises most available in the South. Tall bearded irises (and other bearded classes) are the most widely sold; many new hybrids are cataloged every year. Specialty growers abound. A smaller number offer various beardless classes and some species. Retail nurseries carry bulbous irises for fall planting. Deer don't seem to care for irises.

BULBOUS IRISES

Irises that grow from bulbs have beardless flowers. Bulbs go dormant in summer and can be lifted and stored until planting time in fall.

Dutch and Spanish irises. Zones US, MS, LS; 9–5. The species that parented this group come from Spain, Portugal, Sicily, and northern Africa. (Dutch irises acquired their name because the hybrid group was developed by Dutch bulb growers.) Flowers are borne atop slender stems that rise from rushlike foliage. Standards are narrow and upright; oval to circular falls project downward. Colors include white, mauve, blue, purple, brown, orange, yellow, as well as bicolor combinations—usually with a yellow blotch on falls. Dutch iris flowers reach 3–4 in. across, on stems 1½–2 ft. tall; these are the irises sold by florists. Bloom is early spring in warm-winter regions, late spring in colder ones. Spanish irises are similar but have smaller flowers that bloom about 2 weeks later.

Dutch Iris

Plant bulbs in autumn, setting them 4 in. deep, 3–4 in. apart; give full sun. Bulbs are hardy to about –10°F; in Upper South, apply a mulch in winter. Give regular water during growth and bloom. Bulbs can be left in the ground for several years where summers are dry; elsewhere, they should be lifted. After bloom, let foliage ripen before digging; store bulbs in a cool, dry place for no more than 2 months before replanting. Dutch and Spanish irises are good in containers; plant five bulbs in a 5- to 6-in. pot.

The widely sold 'Wedgwood' is a Dutch hybrid hardy only in the Lower South. It blooms earlier than others (generally coinciding with 'King Alfred' daffodils), bearing large lavender-blue flowers with yellow markings. Bulbs are larger than those of average Dutch hybrid. Vigorous foliage dies down after bloom and is best masked by bushy annuals or perennials that will mature later in the season.

English irises. Zones US, MS; 8–6. The species (*I. latifolia*) from which named selections were made is native to the Pyrenees, where it grows in moist meadows. Early botanists first noticed the iris growing in southern England, where it had been taken by traders. Flowers are similar in structure to Dutch and Spanish irises, but falls are broader and decorated with a hairline stripe of yellow. Colors include bluish purple, wine red, maroon, blue, mauve, white. Bloom comes in early summer. Plant bulbs in fall, 3–4 in. deep, 4 in. apart, in cool, moist, acid soil. Choose a partly shaded location. Because English irises don't need complete dryness after flowering, they can be left in the ground in suitable climates (bulbs are hardy to about –10°F). Or they can be lifted and replanted.

Reticulata irises. Zones US, MS, LS; 8–5. The netted outer covering on the bulbs gives the group its name. These are classic rock garden and container plants, with flowers like small Dutch irises appearing on 6- to 8-in. stems in early spring. Narrow blue-green leaves appear after bloom. Available species include *I. reticulata*, with 2- to 3-in. violet-scented flowers (purple, in the usual forms), and *I. danfordiae*, with bright yellow blooms. Pale blue–flowered species *I. histrio* and large-flowered, blue-and-yellow *I. histrioides* may be carried by some specialists. Far more common are named hybrids such as 'Cantab' (pale blue with orange markings), 'Harmony' (sky blue marked yellow), 'J. S. Dijt' (reddish purple).

Bulbs are hardy to about –10°F and need some subfreezing winter temperatures to thrive. Plant in autumn, in well-drained soil in a sunny location; set bulbs 3–4 in. deep and 3–4 in. apart. Need regular moisture from fall through spring. Soil should be kept dry during summer dormant period; in rainy climates, lift bulbs in summer or grow in pots so you can control moisture. Divide only when vigor and flower quality deteriorate. Watch for slugs and snails.

RHIZOMATOUS IRISES

Irises that grow from rhizomes (thickened, modified stems) may have bearded, beardless, or crested flowers; among this group are the most widely grown types. Leaves are swordlike, overlapping each other to form flat fans of foliage.

Bearded irises. Zones US, MS, LS, CS. The most widely grown irises fall into the bearded group. More than a century of breeding has produced a vast array of beautiful hybrids. All have upright standards and flaring to pendent falls that have characteristic epaulette-like beards. Tall bearded irises are the most familiar of these, but they represent just one subdivision of the entire group.

Dutch Irises

Reticulata Irises

Standard Dwarf Bearded Iris 'Sarah Taylor'

Border Bearded Iris 'Brown Lasso'

A BORING SOLUTION. *Bearded irises often fall victim to iris borers, the wormlike larvae of night-flying moths. The larvae hollow out rhizomes and induce a smelly bacterial rot. To prevent them from attacking your irises, pull off and destroy old brown leaves in fall. In spring, when foliage reaches 5 in. tall, apply dimethoate (Cygon), acephate (Orthene), or pyrethrum according to label directions.*

Bearded irises need good drainage. They'll grow in soils from sandy to claylike—but in clay soils, plant in raised beds or on ridges to assure good drainage, avoid rhizome rot. Plant in September or October, in full sun or light shade. Space rhizomes 1–2 ft. apart; set with tops barely beneath soil surface, spreading roots well. Water to settle soil and start growth. Thereafter, water judiciously until new growth shows plants have rooted; then water regularly until fall rains or frosts arrive. If weather turns hot, shade newly planted rhizomes to prevent sunscald, possible rot.

From the time growth starts in late winter or early spring, water regularly until about 6 weeks after flowers fade; buds for next year's flowers form during postbloom period. During the summer, plants require less water. In heavy soil, it may be sufficient to water plants every other week; in lighter soils, try watering weekly. For best performance, feed plants with commercial bulb fertilizer as growth begins in spring, then again after bloom has finished. In cool, moist springs, leaf spot may disfigure foliage; use appropriate fungicide at first sign of infection. Remove old and dry leaves in fall.

Clumps become overcrowded after 3 or 4 years, and quantity and quality of bloom decrease. Lift and divide crowded clumps at best planting time for your area. Save large rhizomes with healthy leaves; discard old and leafless ones from clump's center. Break rhizomes apart or use a sharp knife to separate. Trim leaves, roots to about 6 in.; let cut ends heal for several hours to a day before replanting. If replanting in the same soil, amend it with organic matter.

Dwarf and median bearded irises. These irises generally have flowers shaped like those of the familiar tall beardeds, but flower size, plant size, and stature are smaller. Median iris is a collective term for the categories standard dwarf, intermediate and border bearded, and miniature tall bearded.

Miniature dwarf bearded irises. Grow to 8 in. tall; flowers large for size of plant. Earliest to bloom of bearded irises (about 6 weeks before main show of tall beardeds). Hardy, need winter chill. Plants multiply quickly. Shallow root systems need regular moisture and periodic feeding.

Standard dwarf bearded irises. Grow 8–15 in. tall. Flowers and plants are larger than miniature dwarfs. Profuse bloom. Perform best with some winter chill.

Intermediate bearded irises. Grow 15–28 in. tall, bear flowers 3–5 in. across. Flower later than dwarfs but 1 to 3 weeks before tall bearded irises. Most are hybrids between standard dwarfs and tall bearded selections and resemble larger standard dwarfs rather than border beardeds. Some give second bloom in fall.

Border bearded irises. Grow 15–28 in. tall—proportionately smaller versions of tall beardeds in the same wide range of colors and patterns. Bloom period is same as for tall bearded.

Miniature tall bearded irises. Grow 15–28 in. high and flower at the same time as tall beardeds. Their small flowers (2–3 in. wide), narrower foliage, and pencil-thin stems give them appearance of tall bearded irises reduced in every proportion. Good for cutting and arrangements—hence their original name, "table irises."

Tall bearded irises. Among choicest perennials for borders, massing, and cutting. Easy to grow. Midspring flowers come on branching stems 2½–4 ft. high. All colors but pure red and green; patterns of two colors or more and blends produce infinite variety. Countless named selections are available. Modern hybrids often have elaborately ruffled, fringed flowers. Available variegated-foliage selections include 'Pallida Variegata' (often cataloged as 'Zebra'), with green leaves striped with cream; and 'Argentea', producing green leaves with white stripes. Both bear smallish blue-lavender flowers on stems to 2 ft. high.

Tall Bearded Iris
'Beverly Sills'

Remontant (reblooming) tall bearded irises flower in spring, again in mid- to late summer or fall, depending on selection and climate. Plants need fertilizer, regular moisture for best performance. Specialists' catalogs offer increasing numbers of remontant tall beardeds.

Beardless irises. Flowers in this group all have smooth, "beardless" falls but otherwise differ considerably in appearance from one type or species to another. Rhizomes have fibrous roots (unlike fleshy roots of bearded types); most prefer or demand more moisture than bearded irises. Many can perform well in crowded clumps but will eventually need division when performance declines. Timing varies; dig and replant quickly, keeping roots moist until planted.

The following four hybrid groups contain the most widely sold beardless irises. Also described are individual species (and their named selections) available from growers of specialty irises and perennials.

Japanese irises. Zones US, MS, LS, CS; 10–1. Derived solely from *I. ensata* (formerly *I. kaempferi*), these irises feature sumptuous blossoms 4–12 in. across on slender stems to 4 ft. high. Flower shape is essentially flat. "Single" types have three broad falls and much-reduced standards, giving triangular flower outline; "double" blossoms have standards marked like the falls and about the same size and shape, resulting in circular flower outline. Colors are purple, violet, pink, rose, red, white—often veined or edged in contrasting shade. Plants have graceful narrow, upright leaves with distinct raised midribs.

Plants need much moisture during growing, flowering period. Both soil and water should be neutral to acid. If soil or water is alkaline, apply aluminum sulfate or iron sulfate (1 ounce to 2 gallons water) several times

Miniature Tall Bearded Iris
'Rosemary's Dream'

Tall Bearded Iris
'Cinderella's Coach'

Tall Bearded Iris
'Too Sweet'

Japanese Iris

during growing season. Plant rhizomes in fall or spring, 2 in. deep and 1½ ft. apart; or plant up to three per 12-in. container. Use in moist borders, at edge of pools or streams, or even in boxes or pots plunged halfway to rim in pond or pool during growing season. Full sun except in hottest areas. Divide about every 3 years, in early fall.

Louisiana irises. Zones US, MS, LS, CS; 9−5. Approximately four species from the lower Mississippi region and Gulf Coast compose this group of so-called swamp irises. Graceful, flattish blossoms on stems 2−5 ft. tall, carried above and among leaves that are long, narrow, and unribbed. The range of flower colors and patterns is extensive—nearly the equal of tall beardeds.

Specialists offer a vast array of named hybrids; some may carry the basic species as well. *I. brevicaulis (I. foliosa)* has blue flowers with flaring segments carried on zigzag stems among the foliage. *I. fulva* has coppery to rusty red (rarely yellow) blossoms with narrow, drooping segments. *I. giganticaerulea* is indeed a "giant blue" (sometimes white) with upright standards and flaring falls; stems to 4 ft. or more, with proportionally large leaves. *I. hexagona* also comes in blue shades with upright standards and flaring falls. *I. × nelsonii,* a natural hybrid population derived from *I. fulva* and *I. giganticaerulea,* resembles the *I. fulva* parent in flower shape and color (but also includes purple and brown tones) and approaches the *I. giganticaerulea* parent in size.

Plants thrive in well-watered, rich garden soil as well as at pond margins; soil and water should be neutral to acid. Locate in light afternoon shade. Plant in late summer; set rhizomes 1 in. deep, 1½−2 ft. apart. Mulch for winter where ground freezes. Divide every 3 to 4 years, in late summer or early fall.

Siberian irises. Zones US, MS, LS; 9−1. The most widely sold members of this group are named hybrids derived from *I. sibirica* and *I. sanguinea* (formerly *I. orientalis*)—species native to Europe, Asia. Clumps of narrow, almost grasslike leaves (deciduous in winter) bear slender stems to 4 ft. high (depending on selection), each bearing two to five blossoms with upright standards and flaring to drooping falls. Colors include white and shades of blue, lavender, purple, wine, pink, and light yellow.

Siberian Iris

Give plants partial or dappled shade, neutral to acid soil. Plant in spring or fall; set rhizomes 1−2 in. deep, 1−2 ft. apart. Water liberally from onset of growth until several weeks after bloom. Divide infrequently—when clumps show hollow centers—in late spring or fall.

Spuria irises. Zones US, MS, LS, CS; 9−5. In flower form, spurias resemble Dutch irises. Older members of this group had primarily yellow or white-and-yellow blossoms; *I. orientalis* (universally known as *I. ochroleuca*) has naturalized in many parts of the South, its 3- to 5-ft. stems bearing white

flowers with yellow blotches on the falls. Dwarf *I. graminea* bears narrow-petaled, fragrant blue-and-maroon blossoms on foot-high stems. Modern hybrids show a great color range: blue, lavender, gray, orchid, tan, bronze, brown, purple, earthy red, and near black—often with a prominent yellow spot on the falls. Flowers are held closely against 3- to 6-ft. stems, rising above handsome clumps of narrow dark green leaves. Flowering starts during latter part of tall bearded bloom and continues for several weeks beyond.

Plant rhizomes in late summer or early fall, in rich, neutral to slightly alkaline soil; set them 1 in. deep, 1½−2 ft. apart. Plants grow well in full sun but will also take light shade for part of the day. They need ample moisture from onset of growth through bloom period but little moisture during summer. Divide clumps (not an easy task) infrequently; do the job in late summer or early fall.

I. albicans. YEMEN IRIS, WHITE FLAG. Zones US, MS, LS. Sterile hybrid originating in the Middle East, where it was often planted in Muslim graveyards. Popular passalong plant in the South, usually seen in older gardens and cemeteries. Sword-shaped leaves to 1½ ft.; white flowers with yellow-and-white beards in very early spring. Easy to grow, needing only good drainage and a spot in full sun or light shade. Moderate to regular water; established plants take drought and neglect.

I. foetidissima. GLADWIN IRIS. Zones US, MS, LS, CS; 9−2. Native to Europe. Glossy evergreen leaves to 2 ft. make handsome foliage clumps. Stems 1½−2 ft. tall bear subtly attractive flowers in blue gray and dull tan; specialists may offer color variants in soft yellow and lavender blue, as well as a form with white-variegated leaves. Real attraction is large seed capsules that open in fall to show numerous round, orange-scarlet seeds; the cut stems with seed capsules are attractive in arrangements. Grow in partial to full shade. Likes moist soil, but established plants tolerate drought. Mulch in fall in Upper South.

I. laevigata. Zones US, MS, LS, CS; 9−1. Native to China, Korea, Japan. Smooth, glossy leaves reach 1½−2½ ft. long, to 1 in. wide. Flower stems grow to about the same height, bearing violet-blue blossoms with upright standards and drooping falls enlivened with yellow central stripes. Bloom period comes after that of tall bearded irises. Named color variants include kinds with white, magenta, and patterned purple-and-white blooms. 'Variegata' sports crested flowers in light blue and leaves with longitudinal white stripes. There are also selections whose standards mimic falls in shape, pattern, and carriage, producing the effect of a double blossom. This is a true bog plant, growing best in constantly moist, acid soil—even in shallow water. Full sun.

I. prismatica. SLENDER BLUE FLAG. Zones US, MS, LS, CS; 9−6. Native to eastern North America. Foliage and flowers suggest a small Siberian iris. Typical form grows about 1 ft. high, bearing dainty purple-and-white blossoms on branching, sinuous stems. A pure white form exists. *I. p. austrina,* native to the southern Appalachians, is a bit taller and coarser, with lilac-blue blossoms. Give plants full sun and moist (but not boggy), acid soil. Rhizomes spread widely, forming loose colonies rather than tight clumps.

I. pseudacorus. YELLOW FLAG. Zones US, MS, LS, CS; 9−3. Native to Europe but now found worldwide in temperate regions; seeds float, aiding

Louisiana Iris 'Inner Beauty'

Iris pseudacorus

Siberian Iris

Spuria Iris 'Barbara's Kiss'

Iris laevigata

plant's dispersal. Impressive foliage plant; under best conditions, upright leaves may reach 5 ft. tall. Flower stems grow 4–7 ft. (depending on culture), bear bright yellow flowers 3–4 in. across. Selected forms offer ivory and lighter yellow flowers, double flowers, variegated foliage, and plants with shorter and taller leaves. Plant in sun to light shade. Needs acid soil and more than average moisture; thrives in shallow water and can become invasive where running water disperses seeds.

Several hybrids are excellent foliage plants with distinctive blossoms. All prefer ample water (but not pond conditions), sun to light shade. 'Holden Clough' perhaps has *I. foetidissima* as its other parent. Flowers, 3–4 in. across, are soft tan heavily netted with maroon veins. Stems grow to 4 ft.; leaves reach 4–5 ft., but tips arch over. Two of its seedlings are similar but larger. 'Phil Edinger' grows to 4½ ft. with arching foliage; 4- to 5-in. flowers are brass colored, heavily veined in brown. 'Roy Davidson' is similar, but flowers are dark yellow with fine brown veining and maroon thumbprint on falls.

I. setosa. Zones US, MS, LS; 8–1. Native to Siberia (extending to Kamchatka), Alaska, eastern Canada, and New England. Leaves are a slightly grayed green, ½–1 in. wide; plants vary from less than 1 ft. to about 2 ft. high, with flower stems taller than leaves. Blooms in late spring and summer, bearing typically blue-purple to red-purple flowers with broadly rounded falls, standards reduced to mere bristles. *I. s. nasuensis* is larger in all parts than species, reaches about 3 ft. high. Garden culture as for Siberian irises: moist, well-drained, neutral to acid soil; partial or dappled shade. Will grow where buffeted by salt-laden ocean spray. Plant in late summer, early fall.

I. unguicularis (I. stylosa). WINTER IRIS. Zones MS, LS, CS; 9–7. Native to Greece, the Near East, northern Africa. Dense clump of narrow dark green leaves. Depending on selection and mildness of winter, flowers appear from November to March. Typical form has violet-tinted blue blossoms elevated on 6- to 9-in. tubes that serve as stems. Named selections vary in flower color (lighter and darker lavender, orchid pink, white) and in coarseness and length of foliage. Plants require neutral to acid soil, heat, and scant water during summer (but will take moderate water if soil is very well drained). In the Middle South, grow against sunny wall or house foundation to increase summer heat and to lessen winter cold. Divide overcrowded clumps in early fall (mild regions) or in late winter after flowering (colder regions). Slugs and snails are attracted to the flowers.

I. versicolor. BLUE FLAG. Zones US, MS, LS, CS; 9–1. Widely distributed North American species, found in bogs and swamps from Mississippi Valley to eastern Canada. Grows 1½–4 ft. tall; narrow leaves are thicker in the center but not ribbed. Shorter-growing forms have upright leaves, but foliage of taller types may recurve gracefully. The typical wild flowers are a light violet blue, but lighter and darker forms exist; a wine red variant has been sold as 'Kermesina'. Named selections include pink 'Rosea' and 'Vernal', as well as others with flowers in violet red. Like *I. pseudacorus,* this species thrives in sun to light shade, in moist, acid soil or shallow water.

Specialty growers offer hybrids between *I. versicolor* and other species such as *I. ensata, I. laevigata,* and *I. virginica*. Violet-flowered 'Gerald Darby', a hybrid with *I. virginica,* has striking wine red stems.

I. virginica. SOUTHERN BLUE FLAG. Zones US, MS, LS, CS; 9–1. Native to Eastern seaboard, from Virginia south and west to Mississippi River and Gulf Coast. Similar to *I. versicolor* in form and flower; distinguishing floral feature is longer standards. Flower colors include light to dark blue, wine red, pink, lavender, and white. A plant sold as 'Giant Blue' is distinctly larger in all parts, approaching *I. pseudacorus* in size. Plant in moist, acid soil or grow in shallow water. In deep ponds, plant in large pots barely submerged beneath the surface. Full sun or light shade.

Crested irises. Though these are botanically placed with beardless irises, they represent a transition between beardless and bearded: each fall bears a narrow, comblike crest where a beard would be in bearded sorts. Slugs and snails are especially attracted to foliage and flowers.

I. cristata. CRESTED IRIS. Zones US, MS, LS, CS; 10–1. From the northeastern U.S. Leaves 4–6 in. long, ½ in. wide; slender greenish rhizomes spread freely. White, lavender, or light blue flowers with golden crests. Give light shade, organically enriched soil, regular water. Divide just after bloom or in fall after leaves die down.

I. tectorum. ROOF IRIS. Zones US, MS, LS, CS; 9–3. Native to Japan, where it is planted on cottage roofs. Foliage fans to 1 ft. tall look like those of bearded irises, but light green leaves are ribbed and glossy. Foliage looks good all summer. Flowers suggest an informal bearded iris with fringed petals and crests in place of beards. Blooms are violet blue with white crests; standards are upright at first, opening to horizontal as flower matures. 'Alba' has white petals with yellow crests. Provide organically enriched soil, light shade, and regular water. Good companion for hostas. Short lived in regions where summers are hot and dry. 'Paltec', a hybrid of *I. tectorum* with a bearded iris, will grow with bearded irises; it reaches about 1 ft. high, with lavender flowers suggesting a bearded iris with beards superimposed on crests.

IRISH MOSS. See SAGINA subulata

IRONWOOD. See OSTRYA virginiana

ISATIS tinctoria

DYER'S WOAD

Brassicaceae (Cruciferae)

SHORT-LIVED PERENNIAL OR BIENNIAL

US, MS, LS, CS **H** 9–1

FULL SUN

MODERATE TO REGULAR WATER

Isatis tinctoria

Known since pre-Christian times as a source for deep blue dye (it is extracted from the foliage), this plant was probably imported into the U.S. by European colonists in the late 17th century. It quickly spread by seed and is now considered a weed in many dry Western states. In the South, however, it's less likely to become weedy and makes a fine addition

Iris virginica 'Contraband Girl'

Iris unguicularis 'Walter Butt'

Iris setosa

Crested Iris *Iris tectorum*

to a mixed herbaceous border. Bluish green, 8-in.-long basal leaves grow in clump from a thick taproot. Flowers usually come in April and May of the second year, when the plant sends up 2- to 4-ft.-tall stems tightly clasped by lance-shaped blue-green leaves with white midveins; blossom stalks branch off near the stem tops, bearing large (up to 1-ft.-wide) clusters of small bright yellow blooms. Deep purplish black seedpods form after the flowers fade. Plant in well-drained soil; space 1½ ft. apart. Rarely bothered by pests or diseases.

ISMENE calathina. See HYMENOCALLIS narcissiflora

ISOTOMA fluviatilis. See PRATIA pedunculata

ITALIAN CYPRESS. See CUPRESSUS sempervirens

ITALIAN JASMINE. See JASMINUM humile

ITEA

SWEETSPIRE
Escalloniaceae
EVERGREEN, SEMIEVERGREEN, DECIDUOUS SHRUBS

🗡 ZONES VARY BY SPECIES
☼ FULL SUN, EXCEPT AS NOTED
💧 REGULAR WATER

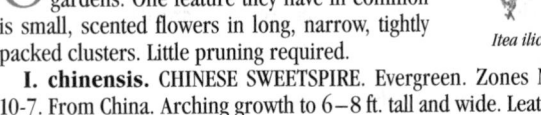

Itea ilicifolia

Only a few of the ten or so species are seen in gardens. One feature they have in common is small, scented flowers in long, narrow, tightly packed clusters. Little pruning required.

I. chinensis. CHINESE SWEETSPIRE. Evergreen. Zones MS, LS, CS; 10–7. From China. Arching growth to 6–8 ft. tall and wide. Leathery, glossy dark green leaves are 3–5 in. long and narrowly oval. Handsome clusters of white flowers in spring.

I. ilicifolia. HOLLYLEAF SWEETSPIRE. Evergreen. Zones CS, TS; 10–6. Native to China. Graceful, arching, open habit to 10–15 ft. tall and 10 ft. wide. Oval, spiny-toothed leaves to 4 in. long; they emerge bronzy red, mature to glossy dark green. Lightly fragrant greenish white flowers in nodding or drooping clusters to 1 ft. long in autumn; blooms sparsely where winters are mild. Not striking, but a graceful plant of distinction. Attractive near water or espaliered against a wall. Needs partial shade.

I. japonica 'Beppu'. Semievergreen. Zones MS, LS, CS; 10–7. Selection of a Japanese species. Dwarf shrub to 2½ ft. tall, spreading widely by suckers. Leaves and flowers resemble those of *I. virginica*, under which name this shrub is often mistakenly sold. Foliage turns reddish purple in autumn.

I. virginica. VIRGINIA SWEETSPIRE. Deciduous. Zones US, MS, LS, CS; 10–1. Native to eastern U.S. To 3–10 ft. tall. Where well adapted, spreads by suckers to form large patches. Narrow, oval, 4-in.-long, dark green leaves turn purplish or bright red in fall, hang on the plant for a long time—possibly all winter. Fragrant, creamy white summer flowers in erect clusters to 6 in. long. 'Henry's Garnet', a superior selection, grows 3–4 ft. tall, 4–6 ft. wide, has brilliant purplish red fall foliage. 'Little Henry' is a more compact selection, reaching just 2 ft. high. 'Longspire' has flower clusters to 7 in. long. 'Sarah Eve' has pink-tinged blossoms. 'Saturnalia' features autumn foliage of orange, purple, and wine red.

ITHURIEL'S SPEAR. See TRITELEIA laxa

IVY. See HEDERA

IXIA

AFRICAN CORN LILY
Iridaceae
PERENNIALS FROM CORMS

🗡 LS, CS, TS **H** 10–5; OR DIG AND STORE
☼ FULL SUN
💧 REGULAR WATER DURING GROWTH AND BLOOM

Ixia maculata hybrid

Clump of narrow, almost grasslike leaves sends up wiry, 18- to 20-in. stems topped by short spikes of 2-in. flowers in late spring. Each six-petaled blossom opens out nearly flat in full sun but remains cup shaped or closed on overcast days. Colors include cream, yellow, red, orange, and pink, typically with dark centers. Most ixias sold are hybrids of the South African species *I. maculata*. They aren't usually browsed by deer.

Grow ixias in well-drained soil. They prefer slightly alkaline conditions, so add lime to acid soil at planting time. Space corms about 3 in. apart. Where winter temperatures typically remain above 20°F, plant in early fall and set corms 2 in. deep; where lows dip to 10°F, plant in late fall, set corms 4 in. deep, and cover the planting with mulch. In areas where winter temperatures fall below 10°F, delay planting until spring (set corms 2 in. deep); you will get flowers in early summer.

Let soil go dry when foliage yellows after bloom. Where corms won't be subject to rainfall or irrigation during dormant period, they can be left undisturbed until the planting becomes crowded or flowering declines. When this occurs, dig corms in summer and store as for gladiolus until recommended planting time in your area. Where corms will receive summer moisture, dig and store them after foliage dies back; or treat as annuals. Potted corms (planted close together and about 1 in. deep) can be stored in pots of dry soil.

IXIOLIRION tataricum (I. montanum)

Amaryllidaceae
PERENNIAL FROM BULB

🗡 US, MS, LS, CS **H** 10–6
☼ FULL SUN
💧 MODERATE WATER DURING GROWTH AND BLOOM

Ixiolirion tataricum

Native to central Asia. Wiry, 12- to 16-in. stems rise from a clump of narrow gray-green leaves, bearing loose clusters of 1½-in. flowers in late spring. Each blue-violet blossom has six narrow petals marked with a darker central line. Foliage dies down in summer, not to reappear until the following spring. Bulbs tolerate moderate summer moisture but don't need any.

Plant in fall, setting bulbs 3 in. deep, 3 in. apart. Bulbs can remain in place for many years—though good drainage is essential to keep them from rotting. Dig and divide clumps in fall when they become crowded.

IXORA

Rubiaceae
EVERGREEN SHRUBS

🗡 TS **H** 12–10; OR GROW IN POTS
☼ ◐ FULL SUN OR LIGHT SHADE
💧 REGULAR WATER

Ixora coccinea

Large group of tropical evergreen shrubs with handsome foliage, showy clusters of flowers. They take salt air and prefer fertile, well-drained, acid soil; plants suffer from chlorosis (yellow leaves with green veins) in alkaline soil. Subject to a host of insects and diseases; difficult to keep healthy without constant vigilance. Not usually browsed by deer.

I. casei (I. duffii). MALAY IXORA. Native to Caroline Islands. To 3–10 ft. tall, 5 ft. wide. Slender, oblong leaves are somewhat leathery, 6–12 in. long, 2½ in. wide. Large flower clusters, sometimes up to 10 in. across; blossoms open deep red, then fade to crimson. 'Super King' is an excellent, long-blooming selection.

I. coccinea. FLAME OF THE WOODS, JUNGLE FLAME. Native to India. Most commonly grown ixora, with many selections featuring blossoms in shades of red, orange, pink, yellow. Grows 7–8 ft. high and 6 ft. wide but is usually kept smaller by occasional tip pinching or pruning. Whorled leaves are glossy and leathery, 2–4 in. long and about half as wide. Flowers are 2 in. long and appear in large, dense clusters at branch tips throughout the warm months of the year. Dies back after a freeze but recovers. Favorite decorative hedge or show plant in southern Florida; greenhouse plant in most of the country.

JACARANDA mimosifolia

Bignoniaceae
DECIDUOUS OR SEMIEVERGREEN TREE
✿ TS **H** 12–10
☼ FULL SUN
◐ MODERATE WATER

Jacaranda mimosifolia

Native to Brazil, Bolivia, and Argentina, this is surely one of the world's prettiest flowering trees. Quickly grows to 45–60 ft. tall and 25–40 ft. wide, with rounded, spreading form. Large, bright green, much-divided leaves up to 20 in. long are soft and fernlike, resembling those of mimosa (*Albizia julibrissin*), hence the species name *mimosifolia*. Leaves drop in late winter. New leaves may emerge quickly or branches may remain bare until tree comes into bloom, usually in mid- to late spring. Tubular, 2-in.-long, blue or lavender-blue blossoms with white throats appear in many 8-in.-long clusters. Flat, mahogany-colored seedpods look great in arrangements but are messy on the ground. 'Alba', a white-flowered selection, is sometimes offered; it has lusher foliage and sparser blooms.

Jacaranda is fairly hardy after it matures a bit; young plants are injured below 25°F but often come back from a hard freeze to make multistemmed, bushy plants. Prefers sandy, well-drained, moderately fertile soil. Not salt tolerant—often fails to flower in the path of ocean winds. Makes a nice lawn, shade, or street tree. Stake young plants and prune out wayward branches to produce a single, sturdy trunk. Once established, needs little pruning.

JACK-IN-THE-PULPIT. See ARISAEMA

JACOBEAN LILY. See SPREKELIA formosissima

JACOBINIA carnea. See JUSTICIA carnea

JACOBINIA suberecta. See DICLIPTERA suberecta

JACOB'S LADDER. See POLEMONIUM

JADE PLANT. See CRASSULA ovata

JAPANESE BLOOD GRASS. See IMPERATA cylindrica 'Rubra'

JAPANESE CLIMBING FERN. See LYGODIUM japonicum

JAPANESE COLTSFOOT. See PETASITES japonicus

JAPANESE FATSIA, JAPANESE ARALIA. See FATSIA japonica

JAPANESE FELT FERN. See PYRROSIA lingua

JAPANESE FLOWERING APRICOT. See PRUNUS mume

JAPANESE LACE FERN. See POLYSTICHUM polyblepharum

JAPANESE PAGODA TREE. See SOPHORA japonica

JAPANESE SNOWBALL. See VIBURNUM plicatum plicatum

JAPANESE SNOWBELL, JAPANESE SNOWDROP TREE. See STYRAX japonicus

JAPANESE SPURGE. See PACHYSANDRA terminalis

JASMINUM

JASMINE
Oleaceae
EVERGREEN, SEMIEVERGREEN, DECIDUOUS SHRUBS AND VINES
✿ ZONES VARY BY SPECIES
☼ ◐ FULL SUN OR LIGHT SHADE
◐ ◐ MODERATE TO REGULAR WATER

Jasminum laurifolium nitidum

Think of fragrance, and jasmine is one of the first plants that comes to mind. Yet not all jasmines are fragrant; and despite its common name, the intensely sweet Confederate jasmine is not a true jasmine at all, but a member of the genus *Trachelospermum*. Growth habits of jasmines range from vining to vining-shrubby to decidedly shrubby. True vining types climb by twining stems. Vining shrubs do not twine, but rather put out long, slender, lax stems that must be tied into place if the plants are to function as vines. Otherwise, they'll flop over to make green haystacks of foliage. To grow these plants as shrubs, shorten any shoots that become too long. Only one of the species listed here, *J. parkeri*, is a true shrub; its dwarf size suits it to rock gardens.

Jasmines grow more rapidly in fertile, well-drained soil and bloom more profusely in sunny sites, but all adapt quite well to less-than-perfect conditions. When plants become tangled or untidy, cut them back heavily just before spring growth begins. Pinch and prune as needed throughout the year to control growth.

J. angulare. SOUTH AFRICAN JASMINE. Evergreen vining shrub. Zones CS, TS; 12–9. From South Africa. Vigorous grower with stems 10–20 ft. long. Rich green leaves are divided into three leaflets. White summer flowers over 1 in. wide are borne in groups of three; some folks detect a subtly sweet scent, others no fragrance at all.

J. floridum. SHOWY JASMINE. Evergreen or semievergreen vining shrub. Zones LS, CS, TS; 10–4. From China. To 5 ft. high. Dark green leaves divided into three (rarely five) small (½- to 1½-in.-long) leaflets. Clusters of golden yellow, ½- to ¾-in., scentless flowers bloom primarily from spring into fall.

J. gracillimum. PINWHEEL JASMINE. Evergreen vining shrub. Zones TS; 12–10. From Borneo. Similar to *J. multiflorum* but with darker green leaves.

J. humile. ITALIAN JASMINE. Evergreen vining shrub. Zones CS, TS; 12–9. From the Mideast, Myanmar, and China. Erect, willowy shoots reach 20 ft., arch to make 10-ft. mound. Light green leaves with three to seven 2-in.-long leaflets. Clusters of ½-in., fragrant bright yellow flowers all summer. Can be clipped into a hedge. 'Revolutum' has larger flowers (to 1 in. wide) and larger, darker green leaves than the species.

J. laurifolium nitidum (J. nitidum). SHINING JASMINE, ANGEL-WING JASMINE. Evergreen or semievergreen vine. Zones TS; 12–7. From Admiralty Islands in the southwest Pacific. Requires long, warm growing season to bloom satisfactorily. Not reliably hardy below 25°F. Moderate growth to 10–20 ft. Undivided glossy green leaves to 2 in. long. Very fragrant flowers shaped like 1-in. pinwheels open from purplish buds in late spring and summer. Flowers are white inside, purplish outside, borne in clusters of three. Can be used as ground cover or container plant. Often sold as *J. magnificum*.

J. leratii. PRIVET-LEAFED JASMINE. Evergreen vine. Zones TS; 12–10. From New Caledonia. To 15 ft., with glossy dark green leaves to 2 in. long that resemble those of privet (*Ligustrum*). Slightly fragrant white flowers in spring.

J. magnificum. See J. laurifolium nitidum

J. mesnyi (J. primulinum). PRIMROSE JAS-
MINE. Evergreen vining shrub. Zones LS, CS, TS;
12–8. From China. Willowy, arching branches
6–10 ft. long. Dark green leaves with three lance-
shaped, 2- to 3-in. leaflets. Bright lemon yellow,
unscented flowers to 2 in. across are semidouble
or double, produced singly rather than in clusters. Main bloom in winter or spring; may flower
sporadically at other times. Needs space. Best tied
up at desired height and permitted to spill down in
waterfall fashion. Use to cover pergola, bank, or
large wall; or clip as 3-ft.-high hedge. In any form,
may need occasional severe pruning to avoid
brush pile look.

Jasminum mesnyi

J. multiflorum. DOWNY JASMINE. Evergreen vining shrub. Zones CS,
TS; 12–9. From India. Leaves (to 2 in. long) and stems have a downy coating, producing an overall gray-green effect. Clustered white flowers in early
spring; not strongly scented.

J. nudiflorum. WINTER JASMINE. Deciduous vining shrub. Zones US,
MS, LS, CS; 9–6. From China. If unsupported, reaches 4 ft. or higher and
7 ft. wide; if trained on a trellis or wall, can grow to 15 ft. Slender, willowy
green stems stand out in winter landscape. Unscented, bright yellow, 1-in.
flowers appear in winter or early spring, before handsome, glossy green,
three-leafleted leaves unfurl. Good bank cover; spreads by rooting where
stems touch soil. Attractive planted at the top of retaining walls, with
branches cascading over side. Can also be trained like *J. mesnyi* (tie plant
at desired height and let branches spill down like a waterfall).

J. officinale. COMMON WHITE JASMINE, POET'S JASMINE. Semievergreen or deciduous vine. Zones LS (protected), CS, TS; 12–9. From
Himalayas, Caucasus. To 30 ft. Very fragrant white flowers to 1 in. across;
blooms throughout summer and into fall. Rich green leaves have five to
nine leaflets, each to 2½ in. long.

J. o. affine (J. grandiflorum). SPANISH JASMINE. Zones CS, TS; 12–9.
Main difference from basic species is size—this form climbs only to 15 ft.
but bears larger (1½-in.) blooms.

J. parkeri. DWARF JASMINE. Evergreen shrub. Zones LS (protected),
CS, TS; 12–7. From India. Dwarf, twiggy, tufted shrub to 1 ft. high, 1½–2 ft.
wide. Bright green, ½- to 1-in.-long leaves with three to five tiny leaflets.
Small, scentless yellow flowers borne profusely in spring. Good choice in
rock garden or as container plant.

J. polyanthum. PINK JASMINE. Evergreen vine. Zones LS (protected),
CS, TS; 11–8. From China. Fast-climbing, strong-growing vine to 20 ft.
Bright to dark green leaves are slightly paler on undersides, have five to
seven 1- to 3-in.-long leaflets. Highly fragrant, ¾-in. blossoms are white
inside, rose colored outside, borne in dense clusters. Blooms in late winter
and spring; sporadic flowers rest of year. Can be used as ground cover;
sometimes grown in large containers or hanging baskets. 'Variegatum' has
leaves with pale yellow margins.

J. primulinum. See J. mesnyi

J. sambac. ARABIAN JASMINE. Evergreen vining shrub. Zones CS, TS;
12–9. Thought to be native to tropical Asia. To 6–10 ft. Undivided glossy
green leaves to 3 in. long. Blooms in summer, bearing clusters of powerfully fragrant, ¾- to 1-in. white flowers. 'Grand Duke of Tuscany' has
double blooms. 'Maid of Orleans' has single blossoms and a compact,
shrubby form; it is well suited to containers. In Asia, leaves of this species
are used in jasmine tea.

J. ×stephanense. Evergreen to deciduous vine. Zones LS, CS, TS;
12–8. To 15–20 ft., with dull green foliage. Evergreen in Tropical South,
semievergreen to deciduous elsewhere. Leaves may be undivided and
about 2 in. long or divided into five 2-in.-long leaflets. Pale pink, ½-in.,
fragrant flowers, carried in clusters of five or more, appear in late spring
and summer.

J. volubile. WAX JASMINE. Evergreen shrub or vine. Zones TS; 12–10.
Native to Australia. To 10–15 ft., with glossy, undivided dark green leaves
about 2 in. long. Small, fragrant white flowers appear intermittently
throughout the year.

JATROPHA

Euphorbiaceae

EVERGREEN AND DECIDUOUS SHRUBS AND TREES

✂ TS; OR GROW IN POTS

☼ LIGHT SHADE; BRIGHT LIGHT

💧 MODERATE TO REGULAR WATER

❖ VARIOUS PLANT PARTS ARE EXTREMELY
POISONOUS IF INGESTED

Jatropha integerrima

Large group of tropical and subtropical plants related to poinsettia
(*Euphorbia pulcherrima*), with milky latex or clear juice in the
stems. The most commonly grown species are popular for their large,
deeply lobed, typically heart-shaped leaves, which provide tropical effects
in the garden. Need well-drained soil; not salt tolerant.

Indoors, site in bright light, but don't expose to direct hot sun. In spring
and summer, water moderately and feed monthly with a general-purpose
liquid houseplant fertilizer. Leave plants unwatered in fall and winter.

J. curcas. PHYSIC NUT. Evergreen shrub or small tree. Heat zones
12–10. Native to the tropical Americas. Reaches 8–15 ft. tall and wide.
Easy to grow; cuttings from mature stems are sometimes set out in the
ground, watered, and left to make a hedge. Deep green leaves are heart
shaped, to 1 ft. long and 7 in. wide, on 4- to 6-in. stalks. Inconspicuous
yellowish green flowers appear in spring. Oval, 1½-in.-long nuts contain
poisonous seeds. Leaves and stems of this species are also poisonous.

J. integerrima. PEREGRINA. Heat zones 12–9. Evergreen shrub or
small tree. Native to Cuba and the West Indies. Can reach 20 ft. tall, 15 ft.
wide, but usually attains just half that size in gardens. Grow as a multitrunked shrub or prune into tree shape. Good in a container or as a patio
tree. Glossy, pointed leaves to 5 in. long emerge bronzy red, then age to
dark green with brownish undersides. Bright scarlet to coral flowers about
an inch across bloom in clusters at branch tips most of the year; they
attract hummingbirds and butterflies. Berries and sap are poisonous.
'Compacta' grows about half as large as the species.

J. multifida. CORAL PLANT. Evergreen shrub or small tree. From Mexico, Brazil, West Indies. To 20 ft. tall, 12 ft. wide. Leaves 1 ft. across, white
on undersides; almost circular but deeply divided into 7 to 11 narrow
lobes. Scarlet, ¼-in. flowers on red stems bloom in summer; they are followed by oval fruits to 1 in. long. All plant parts are poisonous.

J. podagrica. GOUT PLANT. Deciduous shrub. From Central America,
West Indies. Grows to 1½–5 ft. tall, about 1 ft. wide. Named for its
swollen, gouty-looking trunk. Three- to five-lobed leaves reach 10 in.
across, have white undersides. Coral red flowers about ½ in. wide appear
from winter through summer. Berries and sap are poisonous.

JEFFERSONIA diphylla

TWINLEAF

Berberidaceae

PERENNIAL

✂ ZONES US, MS ⊢ 7–5

☼ ● PARTIAL TO FULL SHADE

💧 MODERATE WATER

Jeffersonia diphylla

Native from Maryland and Virginia south to Georgia and Alabama.
Named for Thomas Jefferson. Pretty, cup-shaped, white flowers, an
inch across, appear briefly in spring among new leaves. At bloom time,
plant is no more than 8 in. high; once flowers fade, leaves develop into
handsome mounds 1½ ft. high and about half as wide. Foliage is unusual:
each 5- to 6-in.-wide leaf looks like a shield split into two parts. Leaves
emerge purplish gray, then mature to light green.

Grow in rich, preferably limy soil amended with organic matter. Lovely
in a woodland garden with ferns, primroses (*Primula*), trilliums, and
bloodroot (*Sanguinaria canadensis*). Cover dormant plants with a humus-
rich mulch. Keep soil evenly moist; watch out for slugs and snails.

JELLY PALM. See BUTIA capitata

JERUSALEM ARTICHOKE. See HELIANTHUS tuberosus

JERUSALEM CHERRY. See SOLANUM pseudocapsicum

JERUSALEM DATE. See BAUHINIA monandra

JERUSALEM SAGE. See PHLOMIS fruticosa

JERUSALEM THORN. See PARKINSONIA aculeata

JESSAMINE. See GELSEMIUM

JEWEL MINT OF CORSICA. See MENTHA requienii

JEWEL ORCHID. See LUDISIA discolor

JEWEL WEED. See IMPATIENS capensis

JICAMA

Fabaceae (Leguminosae)

ANNUAL VINE

✄ LS, CS, TS ♦ 12–8

☼ FULL SUN

💧 AMPLE WATER

☕ SEEDS ARE POISONOUS IF INGESTED

Jicama

Known botanically as *Pachyrhizus erosus*, this tropical American native is grown for its edible taproot, which resembles a large brown turnip and tastes something like a water chestnut. Twining or scrambling vines (to 14 ft. high) are attractive, with luxuriant deep green foliage and pretty flower clusters. Leaves have three leaflets, each the size of a hand; upright spikes of sweet pea–shaped purple or violet blossoms appear in late summer. Flowers should be pinched out to encourage maximum root production, but you can allow seed for next year's crop to form on one or two plants. Needs a long, warm growing season and rich soil. Train on a trellis or grow on the ground as a trailing mound. Sow seeds after danger of frost is past, 1–1½ in. deep and 6–12 in. apart, in rows 3–4 ft. apart. Feed once or twice in early or midsummer with a high-nitrogen fertilizer. The edible roots will form as days begin to grow shorter; harvest them before the first frost. Each vine produces a single 1- to 6-pound taproot.

JOB'S TEARS. See COIX lacryma-jobi

JOE-PYE WEED. See EUPATORIUM purpureum, E. maculatum

JOHNNY-JUMP-UP. See VIOLA tricolor

JONQUIL. See NARCISSUS

JOSEPH'S COAT. See ALTERNANTHERA, AMARANTHUS tricolor

JUBAEA chilensis

CHILEAN WINE PALM

Arecaceae (Palmae)

PALM

✄ LS (PROTECTED), CS, TS ♦ 12–8

☼ FULL SUN

◊💧 LITTLE TO MODERATE WATER

Jubaea chilensis

From Chile. Slow-growing, single-stemmed palm to 50–60 ft. tall, 25 ft. wide. Trunk is massive—up to 3 ft. thick—and patterned with the scars of old leaf bases. Feather-type leaves; insignificant flowers. Hardy for a palm (to 12°F). Water moderately in youth; established plants are very drought tolerant.

JUDAS TREE. See CERCIS siliquastrum

Juglandaceae. The walnut family consists of nut-bearing trees with leaves divided into many paired leaflets. Pecan and hickory (*Carya*) and walnut (*Juglans*) are examples.

JUGLANS

WALNUT

Juglandaceae

DECIDUOUS TREES

✄ ZONES VARY BY SPECIES

☼ FULL SUN

💧 REGULAR WATER

Juglans nigra

Large, spreading trees suitable for big properties. All produce oval or round, edible nuts in fleshy husks. Nuts of native species have a wild flavor; those of English walnut (*J. regia*) are the ones sold commercially. These trees have shallow, competitive root systems (a chemical released by the roots, fallen leaves, and nuts of black walnut trees can kill other plants), and their pollen can cause an allergic reaction. They tend to be out of leaf for a long time and can be messy when in leaf. Worth growing if you like the nuts or need large trees that thrive in adverse conditions.

J. cinerea. BUTTERNUT. Zones US, MS; 8–1. Native from New Brunswick to Georgia, west to Arkansas and North Dakota. To 50–60 ft. (even 100 ft.) tall, with broad, spreading canopy 40–50 ft. across. Resembles *J. nigra* but is smaller, with 11 to 19 leaflets per leaf and fewer nuts, which are oval or elongated rather than round. Flavor is good, but shells are thick and hard to crack. Tolerates alkaline soil.

J. microcarpa. RIVER WALNUT. Zones US, MS, LS, CS, TS; 9–6. Native to Oklahoma, Texas, New Mexico, and northwest Mexico. Grows to about 20 ft. (rarely 30 ft.) tall and wide; often multistemmed and more shrubby than treelike. Dark green leaves have 15 to 23 leaflets, each about 3 in. long. Small (¾-in.) nuts are mostly eaten by wildlife. Thrives in dry, rocky, limy soil.

J. nigra. BLACK WALNUT. Zones US, MS, LS, CS; 9–1. Native from Massachusetts to Florida, west to Texas and Minnesota. A huge tree that can reach 150 ft. high, though it's usually closer to 50–75 ft. tall and wide in gardens. High-branched, oval- to round-headed habit. Furrowed blackish brown bark. Leaves have 11 to 23 dark green leaflets, each 2½–5 in. long. Nuts are 1–1½ in. across, with a rich, distinctive flavor and very thick, hard shells (some types, such as 'Thomas Myers' and 'Surprise', are easier to crack than others). Wood is highly prized for furniture, cabinets.

J. regia. ENGLISH WALNUT, PERSIAN WALNUT, CARPATHIAN WALNUT. Zones US, MS, LS; 8–1. Native to southwest Asia, southeastern Europe. To 60 ft. high, with equal spread. Fast growing, especially when young. Trunk and heavy, horizontal or upward-angled branches are covered with smooth gray bark. Leaves are medium to dark green, with five to seven (occasionally more) 3- to 6-in.-long leaflets. Roundish nuts to 2 in. long, with ridged shells and sweet, rich flavor. Husks open in fall, dropping nuts to the ground; to hasten drop, knock nuts from tree. Gather fallen nuts immediately, remove any adhering husks, and dry in a single layer in airy shade until kernels are brittle (crack a nut open to test); then store.

THE UNGRATEFUL DEAD. *Some plants don't appreciate being sited under or even near a black walnut tree, and for good reason: it may mean a different kind of "black death" for them. To limit competition from other plants for sunlight, water, and nutrients, black walnuts (Juglans nigra) release a toxin called juglone into the soil. Susceptible plants are stunted or killed. To avoid this sinister plague, choose plants that tolerate juglone or plant susceptible ones far from the root zones of these trees. Sure-to-expire plants include tomato, potato, eggplant, cucumber, pepper, azalea, cotoneaster, and rhododendron. Juglone-tolerant plants include chrysanthemum, crocus, maple, red cedar, and viburnum.* ❖

J

JUJUBE

Rhamnaceae

DECIDUOUS SMALL TREE

🌿 US, MS, LS, CS ⌇ 9–6

☀️ ◑ BEST IN SUN, TOLERATES SOME SHADE

💧 MODERATE WATER

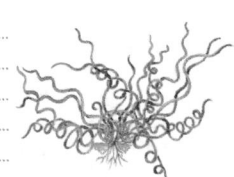

Jujube

ative to temperate regions of Asia and known botanically as *Ziziphus jujuba*. Slow to moderate growth to 15–20 ft. (possibly 30 ft.) tall and 10–15 ft. wide. Spiny, gnarled, somewhat pendulous branches. Glossy bright green, 1- to 2-in.-long leaves with three prominent veins; good yellow fall color. Clusters of small yellowish flowers appear in late spring or summer.

Round to oval fruit with a central pit matures in fall; it can be eaten fresh from the tree or dried. Harvest the fruit for fresh eating when it begins to turn from yellow green to reddish brown; it has a crisp texture and tastes like a sweet apple. If allowed to turn completely brown and become mushy, fruit is better for drying. The dried fruits look and taste like dates. The two most common cultivated selections are 'Lang', with 1½- to 2-in., elongated fruit, and 'Li', bearing 2-in., round fruit with a very small pit. 'Lang' needs 'Li' as pollenizer; 'Li' is more productive with 'Lang' nearby, though it will produce some fruit if planted alone.

Jujube is a decorative tree but a tough one, too. It withstands drought and heat; it takes saline and alkaline soils (but grows better in good garden soil). Thrives in lawns, though suckering from roots can be a problem in moist soil. Prune in winter to shape, encourage weeping habit, or reduce size.

JUNCUS

RUSH

Juncaceae

PERENNIALS

🌿 US, MS, LS, CS, EXCEPT AS NOTED

☀️ ◑ FULL SUN OR LIGHT SHADE

💧 AMPLE WATER

Juncus effusus 'Spiralis'

ushes somewhat resemble grasses, with leaflike, cylindrical stems and tiny, inconspicuous flowers clustered near stem tips. Some have a rigid, upright habit; stems of others are twisted into spirals. Specialists usually suggest planting them with grasses or aquatic plants at the edge of a pond or stream, in water, or among stones and pebbles.

J. decipiens 'Curly-wurly'. Grows 6 in. tall and twice as wide, with tightly coiled, slender, glossy bright green stems that radiate in all directions. Best in wet soils or submerged up to 1 in. deep. Established clumps spread slowly by creeping roots.

J. effusus. SOFT RUSH. Heat zones 9–1. Native to many temperate regions of the world. To 2½ ft. high and wide. Medium green stems are erect, arching somewhat toward tips. Stems turn brown with frost. 'Spiralis' has stems that coil in spirals.

J. inflexus. HARD RUSH. Native to many parts of the world. Upright blue-gray stems form a clump to 2½ ft. tall, 2 ft. wide. 'Afro' grows to 1–1½ ft. tall and 2 ft. wide; coiled stems give it the look of a blue-gray *J. effusus* 'Spiralis'. 'Lovesick Blues' forms a striking 3-ft. mound of steely blue stems.

J. patens. CALIFORNIA GRAY RUSH. Zones MS, LS, CS; 10–7. Native to California and Oregon. To 2 ft. high and wide, with stiffly upright green or gray-green stems. Tolerates more heat and drought than *J. effusus* but thrives best in moist soil or even shallow water. Gray-green 'Carman's Gray' and blue-gray 'Elk Blue' are good selections.

JUNGLE FLAME. See IXORA coccinea

JUNIPERUS

JUNIPER

Cupressaceae

EVERGREEN SHRUBS AND TREES

🌿 ZONES VARY BY SPECIES

☀️ ◑ FULL SUN OR LIGHT SHADE;
SEE CARE BOX BELOW

💧 LITTLE TO REGULAR WATER;
SEE CARE BOX BELOW

▶ SEE CHART

Juniperus chinensis 'Kaizuka'

anging from low ground covers to large trees, these widely grown evergreen plants are conifers, though they produce fleshy, berry-like fruits instead of woody cones. Foliage may consist of small, prickly needles (juvenile foliage) or tiny overlapping scales (mature foliage); or the same plant may show both types. Foliage colors include various shades of green as well as silvery blue, gray, and creamy yellow.

In the chart opposite, junipers are grouped by form: ground covers, shrubs, columnar types, and trees. Look for the general size and shape that will serve your purpose in the landscape, so that you won't later be forced to lop off branches to make the juniper fit the spot. Be aware, however, that many of the shrub junipers can become small trees in time.

The ground cover group includes plants from a few inches to a few feet high; the lower sorts are particularly useful in rock gardens. In the first few years after planting, a mulch will help keep soil cool and suppress weeds as the junipers fill in.

Shrub types range from low to quite tall. Shapes include mounding, gracefully spreading, irregularly twisted, and spirelike. In the chart, the latter type of shrubs—the columnar sort—is listed separately, since these narrow, upright plants perform a distinct function in the landscape. They're excellent accents and perfect for tight spots where you want some height, offering you a wider range of choices than other plants do. Tree junipers (grown more rarely than shrubs) are valued for picturesque habit. Their height and form vary greatly, depending on growing conditions; plants are lower and shrubbier in poor soil and arid climates, much larger if given good soil and more moisture. Many of the larger junipers serve well as screens or windbreaks in cold-winter areas.

Though junipers are extremely tolerant of various soil types, you can expect root rot if the soil is waterlogged (plants will turn yellow and collapse). Avoid planting junipers so close to lawn sprinklers that their roots stay wet. Deer don't usually browse junipers, but the plants are subject to

▶ page 373

WHAT JUNIPERS NEED

EXPOSURE: Junipers grow best in full sun. Most will tolerate light shade, but foliage thins and disease problems increase.

SOIL: They will grow in virtually any soil—light to heavy, acid to alkaline—as long as drainage is good.

WATERING: Plants in lighter soils should have moderate to regular water, while those in heavier soils will do well on little to moderate water. Wherever drainage is slow, be careful to avoid overwatering—when junipers fail, the cause is usually too much moisture.

PRUNING: Very little trimming is needed if you choose a plant of the right size and shape to fill the allotted space.

Juniperus chinensis 'Gold Coast'

J

JUNIPERUS

NAME	ZONES	SIZE, HABIT	COMMENTS
GROUND COVERS			
Juniperus chinensis 'San Jose' SAN JOSE JUNIPER	US, MS, LS, CS; 9–1	To 2 ft. by 6 ft. or more. Prostrate, dense, spreading	Dark sage green, with both needle and scale foliage. Heavy trunked; slow growing
J. c. sargentii SARGENT CHINESE JUNIPER	US, MS, LS, CS; 9–1	To 2 ft. by 10 ft. Ground hugging, spreading	Feathery gray-green or green foliage. Classic bonsai plant. Selections include blue-green 'Glauca', bright green 'Viridis'
J. conferta SHORE JUNIPER	US, MS, LS, CS; 9–1	To 1 ft. by 6–8 ft. Prostrate, creeping	Bright green, soft needles. Excellent for seashore. Takes sandy soil, salt spray. 'Blue Pacific' is denser, bluer, more heat tolerant. 'Emerald Sea' is bright green
J. davurica 'Parsonii' PARSON'S JUNIPER	US, MS, LS, CS; 9–1	To 1½ ft. by 8 ft. or more. Spreading	Rich sprays of dark green needles on long, slender branches. One of best junipers for the Southeast
J. horizontalis 'Bar Harbor' BAR HARBOR CREEPING JUNIPER	US, MS, LS, CS; 9–1	To 1 ft. by 10 ft. Ground hugging, creeping	Fast growing. Feathery blue-gray foliage turns plum purple in winter. Tolerates salt spray
J. h. 'Icee Blue'	US, MS, LS, CS; 9–1	To 4 in. by 6–8 ft. Very flat, creeping	A marked improvement over *J. h.* 'Wiltonii'; intense silvery blue and denser foliage
J. h. 'Plumosa' ANDORRA CREEPING JUNIPER	US, MS, LS, CS; 9–1	To 1½ ft. by 10 ft. Creeping	Plumy foliage is gray green in summer, plum purple in winter. Flat branches, upright branchlets
J. h. 'Prince of Wales'	US, MS, LS, CS; 9–1	To 8 in. by 8–10 ft. Creeping	Medium green foliage turns purplish in fall
J. h. 'Wiltonii' BLUE RUG CREEPING JUNIPER	US, MS, LS, CS; 9–1	To 4 in. by 8–10 ft. Very flat, creeping	Silver blue. Long, trailing branches set with dense, short branchlets. Like *J. h.* 'Bar Harbor' but tighter; rarely shows limbs
J. h. 'Yukon Belle'	US, MS, LS; 9–1	To 6 in. by 6–8 ft. Creeping	Silvery blue foliage. Extremely cold hardy
J. procumbens JAPANESE GARDEN JUNIPER	US, MS, LS, CS; 9–1	To 2 ft. by 12–20 ft.	Feathery yet substantial blue-green foliage on strong branches
J. p. 'Nana' DWARF JAPANESE GARDEN JUNIPER	US, MS, LS, CS; 9–1	To 1 ft. by 4–6 ft. Curved branches spreading in all directions	Shorter needles, slower growth than *J. procumbens*. Can be staked into upright, picturesque shrub. Good in containers
J. sabina 'Broadmoor'	US, MS; 8–1	To 2–3 ft. by 10 ft. Dense, mounding, spreading	Soft bright green foliage
J. s. 'Buffalo'	US, MS; 8–1	8–12 in. by 8 ft.	Soft, feathery bright green foliage
J. s. 'Tamariscifolia' TAMARIX JUNIPER, TAM	US, MS; 8–1	To 1½ ft. by 10–20 ft. Symmetrically spreading	Dense blue-green foliage. Widely used
J. scopulorum 'Blue Creeper'	US, MS; 7–1	To 2 ft. by 6–8 ft. Spreading	Bright blue-green foliage

Juniperus chinensis 'San Jose'   *Juniperus conferta*   *Juniperus horizontalis* 'Wiltonii'   *Juniperus sabina* 'Buffalo'   *Juniperus sabina* 'Tamariscifolia'

JUNIPERUS

NAME	ZONES	SIZE, HABIT	COMMENTS
SHRUBS			
J. chinensis 'Armstrongii' (J. × pfitzeriana 'Armstrongii') ARMSTRONG JUNIPER	US, MS, LS, CS; 9–1	To 4 ft. by 4 ft. Upright, dense	Lacy medium green foliage
J. c. 'Gold Coast' (J. × pfitzeriana 'Gold Coast') GOLD COAST JUNIPER	US, MS, LS, CS; 9–1	To 3 ft. by 5 ft. Compact	Soft, lacy, golden yellow foliage
J. c. 'Hetzii' HETZ CHINESE JUNIPER	US, MS, LS, CS; 9–1	To 15 ft. by 15 ft. Inverted pyramid	Blue-gray foliage. Branches spread outward and upward at 45° angle. Fast growing in youth. Needs lots of room
J. c. 'Kaizuka' ('Torulosa') HOLLYWOOD JUNIPER	US, MS, LS, CS; 9–1	To 20 ft. by 10 ft. Irregular, upright	Rich green foliage with soft texture. Branches have outlandish, twisted appearance. Give it plenty of room. Good in large containers. Tolerates salt spray
J. c. 'Mint Julep' (J. × pfitzeriana 'Mint Julep')	US, MS, LS, CS; 9–1	4–6 ft. by 6 ft. Vase shaped	Mint green foliage, arching branches. Very handsome
J. c. 'Pfitzeriana' PFITZER JUNIPER	US, MS, LS, CS; 9–1	5–6 ft. by 15–20 ft. Arching	Feathery gray-green, sharp-needled foliage
J. c. 'Pfitzeriana Aurea' GOLDEN PFITZER JUNIPER	US, MS, LS, CS; 9–1	3–4 ft. by 8–10 ft. Arching	Greenish gray foliage; current season's growth golden yellow
J. c. 'Pfitzeriana Glauca' BLUE PFITZER JUNIPER	US, MS, LS, CS; 9–1	5–6 ft. by 10–15 ft. Arching	Silvery blue foliage
J. squamata 'Blue Star' BLUE STAR JUNIPER	US, MS; 8–1	To 3 ft. by 5 ft. Mounding	Squat, dense plant with silvery blue, sharp-pointed needles
COLUMNAR TYPES			
J. chinensis 'Blue Point'	US, MS, LS, CS; 9–1	To 12 ft. by 8 ft. Broadly columnar	Dense blue-green foliage (both scale and needle)
J. c. 'Robusta Green'	US, MS, LS, CS; 9–1	To 12–18 ft. by 5–7 ft. Irregular column	Brilliant green, dense foliage
J. c. 'Spartan'	US, MS, LS, CS; 9–3	To 20 ft. by 3–4 ft. Pyramid or column	Rich green, dense foliage. Fast-growing, very handsome plant
J. scopulorum 'Blue Heaven' ('Blue Haven')	US, MS; 7–1	To 20 ft. by 6 ft. Neatly pyramidal	Foliage remains bright blue all year
J. s. 'Gray Gleam'	US, MS; 7–2	To 15 ft. by 5–7 ft. Symmetrical column	Gray-blue foliage. Slow grower. Tidy, formal-looking plant

Juniperus scopulorum 'Blue Creeper'

Juniperus chinensis 'Hetzii'

Juniperus chinensis 'Pfitzeriana'

Juniperus chinensis 'Robusta Green'

Juniperus virginiana

JUNIPERUS

NAME	ZONES	SIZE, HABIT	COMMENTS
J. scopulorum 'Pathfinder'	US, MS; 7–1	To 25 ft. by 12 ft. Upright pyramid	Gray-blue foliage; looser than 'Gray Gleam'
J. s. 'Skyrocket'	US, MS; 7–1	10–15 ft. tall, 1–2 ft. wide. Narrowest spire	Blue-gray foliage. Good vertical accent
J. s. 'Wichita Blue'	US, MS; 7–2	To 18 ft. by 6 ft. Broad pyramid	Bright blue foliage; very striking
TREES			
J. ashei OZARK WHITE CEDAR, ASHE JUNIPER	US, MS, LS, CS; 9–4	To 20 ft. by 20 ft. Irregular or spherical crown	Trunk often divides near base. Gray-green foliage; shredding gray bark. Female plants bear blue, ¼- to ½-in. berries with a waxy sheen. Likes dry, chalky soil. Immune to cedar-apple rust. Pollen of male plants can trigger allergies
J. scopulorum 'Tolleson's Blue Weeping' ('Repandens')	US, MS; 7–1	To 20 ft. by 10 ft. Weeping form	Gracefully drooping branches clothed in silvery blue-green foliage. Interesting accent or container specimen
J. silicicola SOUTHERN RED CEDAR	LS, CS, TS; 12–4	To 30 ft. by 20 ft. Conical	Very similar to *J. virginiana*, though often more open and wide spreading. Grows in sand; frequently planted in rows and used as windbreak. Tolerates seaside conditions
J. virginiana EASTERN RED CEDAR	US, MS, LS, CS, TS; 11–1	40–50 ft. or more by 15–30 ft. Conical	Picturesque tree with dark green foliage that turns bronze in cold weather. Tolerates drought, poor soil; thrives in limy soil. Many selections sold. Aromatic foliage, wood

a number of pests and diseases. Among the most serious are bagworms (foliage is stripped); blight (twig and branch dieback); twig borers (browning and dying branch tips); cedar-apple rust (disease alternating between junipers and apple trees; causes twig dieback); juniper scale (no new growth, yellowed foliage); juniper webworm (webbing together and browning of foliage). To confirm a problem or decide on control measures, consult your Cooperative Extension Office or local garden center.

JUPITER'S BEARD. See **CENTRANTHUS ruber**

JUSTICIA

Acanthaceae

PERENNIALS AND EVERGREEN AND DECIDUOUS SHRUBS

ZONES VARY BY SPECIES

EXPOSURE NEEDS VARY BY SPECIES

WATER NEEDS VARY BY SPECIES

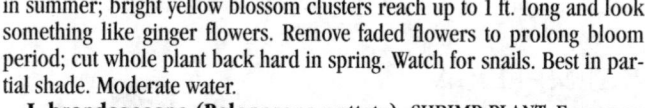

Justicia brandegeeana

Group of plants grown chiefly for their tubular, tightly clustered flowers—or, in the case of *J. brandegeeana,* for showy spikes of bracts. Blossoms of all species attract hummingbirds. Leaves are paired, opposite each other on the stems.

J. americana. AMERICAN WATER-WILLOW. Perennial. Zones US, MS, LS, CS, TS; 12–1. Aquatic species native to eastern half of U.S. Upright, 15-in. stems are clothed in willowlike deep green leaves with a white midrib. Small, white to pale violet flowers with splashy purple markings appear atop stems from early summer into fall. Spreads by creeping rhizomes to form large colonies. Plant at edge of pond for a natural look; grows best in shallow water or very moist soil. Full sun.

J. aurea. YELLOW JUSTICIA, BRAZILIAN PLUME. Evergreen shrub. Zones CS, TS; 12–6. From Mexico and Central America. To 6–10 ft. tall and 6–8 ft. wide, with dark green leaves to 1 ft. long, half as wide. Blooms in summer; bright yellow blossom clusters reach up to 1 ft. long and look something like ginger flowers. Remove faded flowers to prolong bloom period; cut whole plant back hard in spring. Watch for snails. Best in partial shade. Moderate water.

J. brandegeeana (Beloperone guttata). SHRIMP PLANT. Evergreen shrub. Zones CS, TS; elsewhere as annual or indoor/outdoor plant; 12–1. Native to Mexico. To 3–4 ft. high and wide. Apple green, oval to elliptic leaves to 2½ in. long. Tubular white flowers spotted with purple are enclosed in overlapping coppery bronze bracts to form compact, drooping, jointed-looking spikes 3 in. long (eventually lengthening to 6–7 in.). Spike formation somewhat resembles a large shrimp. Blooms mainly from spring to fall, sporadically rest of year. 'Chartreuse' has chartreuse yellow bracts that sunburn more easily than the coppery kind.

Good in pots and for close-up planting near terraces, patios, entryways. To shape, pinch young plants continuously until compact mound of foliage is obtained, then let bloom. To encourage bushiness, cut back stems when bracts turn black. Leaves often drop in cold weather or if soil is too wet or dry. Give moderate water (less in winter) and feed with a balanced liquid fertilizer monthly during active growth. Takes full sun, but bracts and foliage fade unless plant is grown in partial shade. Give at least half-day shade in hottest climates.

J. carnea (Jacobinia carnea). BRAZILIAN PLUME FLOWER. Evergreen shrub. Zones CS (protected), TS; elsewhere as annual or indoor/outdoor plant; 12–1. From South America. Erect, soft-wooded shrub to 4–6 ft. high, 2½–3 ft. wide. Medium green, prominently veined leaves to 10 in. long. Dense, 6-in.-long clusters of pink to crimson, tubular, 2-in. flowers from midsummer to fall. 'Huntington Form' is a more compact plant (3–4 ft. high) with deeper pink flowers and leaves that are bronze colored on lower surfaces. Cut back plants in early spring to encourage strong new growth. Upper portions of branches freeze at 29°F. Give partial or full shade, rich soil, regular to ample water.

Justicia carnea

J. leonardii. ORANGE JUSTICIA. Evergreen shrub. Zones LS, CS, TS; 12–6. Exotic-looking Mexican native reaching 3 ft. tall and wide, with gray-green stems and velvety dark green leaves to 6 in. long. Small clusters of reddish orange, 1½-in. flowers appear at branch tips and along stems off and on through warm months. Full sun. Little water.

J. runyonii. RUNYON'S WATER-WILLOW. Perennial. Zones CS, TS; 12–6. From Texas and northern Mexico. Rare. To 2–3 ft. tall, with stems sparsely clothed in soft, narrow leaves that may turn from green to deep maroon when temperatures drop. Small purple flowers with white markings are held above foliage in fall. Cut back hard in winter. Full sun. Needs regular water.

J. suberecta. See Dicliptera suberecta

KADSURA japonica

JAPANESE KADSURA

Schisandraceae

EVERGREEN VINE

◿ MS, LS, CS ◪ 9–1

◔ PARTIAL TO FULL SHADE

◖ REGULAR WATER

Kadsura japonica

This elegant twining vine from Japan and Korea is seldom seen in Southern gardens, but discriminating gardeners may wish to track it down. It reaches 12–15 ft. and does so in well-behaved fashion—it won't strangle nearby trees or shrubs. Handsome, glossy dark green leaves are oval and pointed, 2–4 in. long and 1–2 in. wide. Small, yellowish white flowers bloom from summer to autumn; these are followed by pretty red berries to 1¼ in. across on female plants. Vines of both sexes must be present for fruit to be produced. Needs fertile, well-drained soil. Easy to propagate from cuttings. 'Alba' has white fruits. 'Chirimen' has leaves marbled with creamy white; 'Fukurin' offers striking foliage edged in cream and yellow.

KAEMPFERIA

PEACOCK GINGER

Zingiberaceae

PERENNIALS

◿ CS, TS ◪ 12–9; OR GROW IN POTS

● FULL SHADE; BRIGHT INDIRECT LIGHT

◖◗ AMPLE WATER DURING GROWING SEASON

Kaempferia pulchra mansonii

Native to tropical Asia, these small, shade-loving plants grow outdoors only in humid, very warm climates. Flowers (sometimes fragrant) resemble small orchids or African violets (*Saintpaulia*) but have just three petals, one of which is a deeply lobed "lip." Foliage is usually more decorative than the flowers; leaves of many species have iridescent veining and feathery zoning, giving them the look of a peacock's tail. Leaves of most species lie horizontally, making a low (1- to 6-in.-tall), strikingly textured ground cover during the growing season. In winter, foliage dies back and plant becomes dormant. Reduce watering in fall; stop watering altogether in winter; resume watering in spring. Plants grow easily in moist soil with lots of organic matter. Some spread by rhizomes. Tuberous types can be divided.

In the Upper, Middle, and Lower South, grow in containers and overwinter indoors. Keep nighttime temperature above 60°F. During growing season, air and soil must be moist and daytime temperatures high; plants will thrive in temperatures over 90°F.

K. atrovirens. PEACOCK PLANT. Oval, 4- to 6-in.-long leaves are deep green and bronze with iridescent veining, green-purple undersides. Flowers are white with violet lip, bloom spring to summer. Plant is about 1 ft. wide and spreads by rhizomes.

K. galanga. Rounded, shiny green leaves to 6 in. long. Fragrant white flowers with purple spots on lip bloom in spikes of up to 12. Plant is tuberous and spreads to about 1 ft. wide.

K. gilbertii. VARIEGATED PEACOCK LILY. Narrow, pointed bright green leaves, 4–7 in. long and 1–2 in. wide, with white margins and stripes, gray undersides. White flowers with violet lip bloom from late spring into summer. Reaches 9 in. wide and spreads by rhizomes.

K. pulchra. Broad, oval leaves to 7 in. long are dark green and bronze, marked with silvery veining; undersides are pale green. Lilac flowers with a white eye bloom from summer to early fall. Plant grows about 1 ft. wide, spreading by rhizomes. *K. p. mansonii* has iridescent leaves that are deeply veined, nearly pleated looking; it is about 2 in. taller than the species and blooms continuously from spring to fall.

K. roscoeana. PEACOCK LILY. Similar to *K. pulchra,* but leaf undersides are reddish and flowers are white. Spreads by rhizomes.

K. rotunda. Narrow leaves to 1 ft. long are carried erect, making this a much taller plant than other species. Leaves are purplish beneath, show a featherlike pattern of dark and pale green on top surface. Fragrant white flowers with purple lip bloom before leaves appear. Tuberous plant to 1½ ft. wide.

KAHILI GINGER. See HEDYCHIUM gardnerianum

KALANCHOE

Crassulaceae

SUCCULENT PERENNIALS

◿ TS ◪ 12–8; OR HOUSEPLANT

☼ ◐ FULL SUN OR PARTIAL SHADE; BRIGHT LIGHT

◖◗ MODERATE TO REGULAR WATER

Kalanchoe blossfeldiana

From Old World tropics. Kalanchoes have fleshy, typically green leaves and bell-shaped flowers; they are used principally as houseplants but can be grown outdoors year-round where winters are mild and frost free. Site indoor plants in a south-facing window and let them go fairly dry between waterings. Feed with a general-purpose liquid houseplant fertilizer monthly from spring until fall. Reduce watering in winter, but don't let soil dry out so much that leaves wither.

K. beharensis. FELT PLANT. Very narrow plant; grows to 4–5 ft. (possibly even 10 ft.) tall, just 1–2 ft. wide. Stems are typically unbranched, carrying thick, triangular to lance-shaped leaves—usually six to eight pairs of them—at the tips. Leaves are 4–8 in. long and half as wide, strikingly waved and crimped at the edges and covered with a dense, feltlike coating of white to brown hairs. Flowers are unimportant. Hybrids between this and other species differ in leaf size, color, and degree of felting and scalloping. Impressive in big rock gardens and raised beds.

K. blossfeldiana. KALANCHOE. To 1½ ft. tall and wide. Shiny dark green, smooth-edged or slightly lobed leaves thinly bordered in red; 2½ in. long, 1–1½ in. wide. Small bright red flowers come in big clusters held above the leaves. Hybrids and named selections come in regular or dwarf (6-in.) sizes and in different flower colors, including yellow, orange, salmon. 'Pumila' and 'Tetra Vulcan' are choice dwarf seed-grown selections. Blooms in winter and early spring. Popular houseplant for the winter holidays (often sold in supermarkets then).

K. daigremontiana. MOTHER-OF-THOUSANDS, MATERNITY PLANT. Upright, single-stemmed plant 1½–3 ft. tall, 1 ft. wide. Leaves to 6–8 in. long, 1½ in. wide (or wider), in gray green spotted with red. Leaf edges are notched; young plants sprout in the notches and can be removed and planted. Clusters of small, drooping, grayish purple flowers in winter.

K. fedtschenkoi. SOUTH AMERICAN AIR PLANT. Popular ground cover in south Florida. To 1–2 ft. tall, 10–12 in. wide, with smooth, scalloped blue-green leaves 1–2 in. long. Clusters of pendent reddish flowers in summer. Prostrate stems root where they touch soil. Often erroneously called gray sedum.

K. pinnata (Bryophyllum pinnatum). AIR PLANT. To 2–3 ft. tall and wide. First leaves to form are undivided and scallop edged; later ones divided into three to five leaflets, these also scalloped. Produces many plantlets in notches of scallops. Leaves can be removed and pinned to curtain, where they will produce plantlets until they dry up. Greenish white to reddish flowers in clusters to 3 in. long; not particularly attractive. Likes moisture.

K. tomentosa. PANDA PLANT. Branching plant eventually reaches 3 ft. high, 8 in. wide. Leaves 2 in. long, with dense, feltlike coating of white hairs. Leaf tips and shallow notches in leaves are strongly marked dark brown. Yellowish green flowers in spring.

K. uniflora. Trailing plant 6 in. high, 2 ft. wide; good in hanging pots. Thick, 1-in.-long leaves have a few scallops near rounded tips. Inch-long summer flowers; color ranges from red to purple.

KALE and COLLARDS

Brassicaceae (Cruciferae)

BIENNIALS GROWN AS COOL-SEASON ANNUALS

✺ US, MS, LS, CS, TS 🌣 7–1

☼ ◐ FULL SUN OR LIGHT SHADE

💧 REGULAR WATER

Kale

These cool-season cabbage relatives are grown for their leaves, which can be steamed, stir-fried, sautéed, or added to soups. Curly-leafed kales (such as 'Dwarf Blue Curled' and 'Dwarf Siberian') form compact clusters of tightly curled leaves. 'Toscano' is a noncurly green kale, 'Red Russian' a noncurly red kale (its leaves are actually gray green with purple veins). So-called flowering kale is similar to flowering cabbage, with brightly colored, decorative foliage; it too is edible and is sometimes sold in markets under the name "salad savoy." The type of kale known as collards is a large, smooth-leafed plant that does not form a head. Collard selections include 'Champion', 'Georgia', and 'Vates'.

Sow seeds in place; plant ¼ in. deep and thin seedlings to 15–18 in. apart (or set out transplants at same spacing). Space rows 2–3 ft. apart. Planted in early spring or late summer, collards and kale will yield edible leaves in fall, winter, and spring. Late summer planting is preferable for the Lower, Coastal, and Tropical South; plant in either season for the Upper and Middle South. Crops that mature in fall have fewer pest problems. Light frost sweetens flavor. For all types of kale and collards, harvest leaves for cooking by removing them from outside of clusters; or harvest entire plant. Both kale and collards are high in vitamins A and C and in calcium. Far fewer pest and disease problems than most other cabbage-family crops (see Cabbage).

KALIMERIS pinnatifida
(Asteromoea mongolica)

FALSE ASTER

Asteraceae (Compositae)

PERENNIAL

✺ US, MS, LS 🌣 8–1

☼ ◐ FULL SUN OR LIGHT SHADE

💧 REGULAR WATER

*Kalimeris
pinnatifida*

Native to east Asia. Perennial similar to *Boltonia asteroides*. White, 1-in. flowers resembling small chrysanthemums are borne by the hundreds all summer, forming a cloud over the foliage. Blossoms may be tinged pink or blue, have creamy yellow centers. The oval, pointed leaves are rich green. A basal rosette is formed by 3-in.-long leaves that are heavily serrated. Leaves on upper stems are only 1 in. long and usually have smooth edges. Grows to 2–4 ft. tall, 2 ft. wide; spreads slowly.

FOR INFORMATION ON YOUR CLIMATE ZONES
PLEASE SEE PAGES 28–38

KALMIA

Ericaceae

EVERGREEN SHRUBS

✺ ZONES VARY BY SPECIES

☼ ◐ FULL SUN OR PARTIAL SHADE

💧 REGULAR WATER

☣ LEAVES AND FLOWER NECTAR ARE POISONOUS IF INGESTED

Kalmia latifolia

Elegant shrubs related to rhododendron, with somewhat similar showy flower clusters. Each long flower stalk bears a small bud resembling a fluted turban; buds open to chalice-shaped blooms with five starlike points. Plants share rhododendron's need for moist air and rich, well-drained, acid soil, but they take more sun. Tolerate shade but bloom much better in sun (provided soil does not dry out).

K. angustifolia. SHEEP LAUREL, LAMBKILL. Zones US, MS. Native to eastern states from Georgia to Virginia, Michigan, and Canada. Ground cover or shrub, to 1–3 ft. (rarely 5 ft.) tall and 5 ft. wide. Spreads by self-layering (branches root where they touch the ground). Dark green leaves are leathery, oblong to pointed-oval, to 2½ in. long. Rose pink to purplish crimson flowers, ½ in. across, bloom in clusters in early summer. 'Candida' has white flowers, 'Rubra' dark purple blossoms.

K. latifolia. MOUNTAIN LAUREL. Zones US, MS, LS, CS; 9–4. Native to eastern North America from Canada to Florida, west across the Appalachians into states drained by the Ohio and Mississippi river systems. Southern forms of plant grow better in the Lower and Coastal South; those from more northerly seed sources grow better in the Upper and Middle South. Success also depends on plant source. Named selections are unlikely to perform well in all zones listed.

Slow growing to 6–8 ft. or taller, with equal spread. Glossy, leathery, oval leaves are 3–5 in. long, dark green above, yellowish green beneath. Blooms in late spring; typically bears 1-in.-wide light pink flowers opening from darker pink buds, but blossoms often have subtly different color in their throats and may have contrasting stamens. Flowers held in clusters to 5 in. across.

'Pristine' is a white-flowered selection. Red-budded selections include 'Nipmuck' and 'Olympic Fire', both with pink flowers; 'Ostbo Red', with blossoms that open pink and deepen in color with age; 'Raspberry Glow' and 'Richard Jaynes', deep pink blooms; and 'Sarah', reddish pink flowers.

Dwarf selections (to 3 ft. in 10 years) include 'Elf', with pink buds opening to white flowers; 'Little Linda', red buds opening to pink flowers; 'Minuet', light pink buds opening to white flowers with a maroon ring inside; and 'Tiddlywinks', pink buds opening to pink flowers.

KALOPANAX septemlobus
(K. pictus)

CASTOR ARALIA, TREE ARALIA

Araliaceae

DECIDUOUS TREE

✺ US, MS 🌣 8–4

☼ FULL SUN

💧 REGULAR WATER

Kalopanax septemlobus

Native to eastern Asia. Unusual in being the only cold-hardy large tree in its family. Also notable for the tropical look conferred by big (7- to 10-in.) leaves with five to seven lobes. On young trees, leaves may exceed 1 ft. in width. Tree is open and gaunt in youth but eventually develops an attractive, rounded habit; reaches 40–60 ft. tall and equally wide, with a spiny trunk and relatively few coarse, spiny branches. With age, spines eventually disappear from trunk and larger branches. Tiny white flowers appear in flattish, 1- to 2-ft. clusters at branch ends in summer. Tiny black fruits follow the blossoms; they are quickly consumed by birds.

K

KAPOK TREE. See CEIBA pentandra

KATSURA TREE. See CERCIDIPHYLLUM japonicum

KENTIA PALM. See HOWEA

KENTUCKY COFFEE TREE. See GYMNOCLADUS dioica

KENYA IVY. See SENECIO macroglossus

KERRIA japonica

JAPANESE KERRIA

Rosaceae

DECIDUOUS SHRUB

✔ US, MS, LS, CS H 9–1

◑ LIGHT SHADE

◗ MODERATE TO REGULAR WATER

Kerria japonica
'Pleniflora'

Though it hails from China and Japan, this shrub has become a true Southern passalong plant, often seen gracing older cottage and country gardens. Grows 3–6 ft. tall and somewhat wider, with an open, rounded habit. Bright green, 2- to 4-in.-long, tooth-edged leaves are oval and pointed, with prominent veining; they emerge early in spring and may turn soft lemon yellow in fall. Showy yellow flowers are single or double, 1¼–2 in. across; they appear mainly in spring but continue sporadically throughout the summer. Flowers are solitary and resemble small roses—in fact, Japanese kerria is sometimes mistakenly called "the yellow rose of Texas." In winter, the leafless bright green stems lend welcome color to the garden.

Give Japanese kerria room to display its naturally arching form. Use it in mixed borders and in combination with spring-blooming shrubs and bulbs; also striking when massed. Cut branches are easy to force into early bloom indoors. Flowers dry easily—just cut branches in full flower, place them in a vase of water, and let the stems gradually absorb the water.

Grows well in almost any reasonably well-drained soil. Best sited in some shade, as the flowers tend to fade in hot sun. Plants form colonies from spreading roots. Propagation by division is easy: use a sharp spade to separate a stem or two from the base of the mother plant in late winter. Or propagate by taking cuttings in summer. Prune heavily after bloom, cutting to the ground older stems that have bloomed. Also remove dead wood and spindly growth. Selections include the following.

'Albiflora'. Sometimes called white kerria, but single flowers are actually pale, creamy yellow with bright yellow stamens. Grows 3–5 ft. tall and a bit wider.

'Geisha'. Leaves variably flecked with white and yellow. Double yellow flowers. Grows 4–6 ft. tall, 6–8 ft. wide.

'Golden Guinea'. Single golden yellow flowers are especially large—to 2½ in. across. Plants reach 3–5 ft. tall and 6–8 ft. wide.

'Kin Kan'. Like the species but has soft yellow stems with thin, vertical green stripes.

'Picta' ('Variegata'). Gray-green leaves are attractively edged in white. Single bright yellow flowers are gaudy. Prune out any branches with leaves that revert to solid green. Grows 3–4 ft. tall, 5–6 ft. wide.

'Pleniflora'. Most popular form. Spreads more quickly than other types. Double golden blooms resemble tiny pompons. Upright grower; tends to be lanky. To 6–8 ft. tall and wide.

'Shannon'. Early bloomer, with large, deep yellow single flowers. Grows 5–6 ft. tall and a little wider.

KEY LIME. See CITRUS, Lime, Mexican

KING PALM. See ARCHONTOPHOENIX cunninghamiana

KINNIKINNICK. See ARCTOSTAPHYLOS uva-ursi

KIRENGESHOMA palmata

YELLOW WAXBELLS

Hydrangeaceae (Saxifragaceae)

PERENNIAL

✔ US, MS, LS H 8–5

◑ PARTIAL SHADE

● REGULAR WATER

Kirengeshoma palmata

Native to Japan, Korea. A perennial of great elegance. Reaches 2–4 ft. high, 1 ft. wide, with dark purplish stems carrying deeply lobed and toothed, pale green leaves to 8 in. across. Pale yellow flowers, borne in clusters of three, appear in joints of upper leaves and at tops of stalks in late summer and early autumn. Blossoms are drooping, narrowly bell shaped, 1½ in. long. Lovely in partially shaded border or woodland garden. Needs ample organic matter in soil.

KIWI

Actinidiaceae

DECIDUOUS VINES

✔ ZONES VARY BY SPECIES

☼◑ EXPOSURE NEEDS VARY BY SPECIES

● REGULAR WATER

Kiwi

From eastern Asia. Fast-growing, twining vines grown for fruit with flavor that is a combination of melon, strawberry, and banana. Fuzzy-skinned kiwifruit (the type sold in markets) has a delicious piquancy; the other kinds are sweeter. Unless you have a self-fruitful selection, you will need to grow a male plant nearby to pollinate the female (fruit-bearing) plant. Supply sturdy supports, such as a trellis, an arbor, or a patio overhead. You can also train kiwi vines to cover walls and fences; guide and tie vines to the support as necessary. These vines prefer good, well-drained soil and regular applications of nitrogen fertilizer. Plants are sensitive to salt burn in alkaline soils. In fall, harvest fruit while it is firm and let it ripen off the tree; fruit left on the vine too long will spoil or be eaten by birds. Start harvesting when the first fruits just start to soften or when fuzzy kiwis turn from greenish brown to fully brown.

During dormant season, prune for form and fruit production. Cut back to one or two main trunks and remove closely parallel or crossing branches. Fruit is borne on shoots from year-old or older wood; cut out shoots that have fruited for 3 years and shorten younger shoots, leaving three to seven buds beyond previous summer's fruit. In summer, shorten overlong shoots and unwind any shoots twining around main branches. Because male pollenizer's sole purpose is flower production, you can prune it back drastically after bloom.

Fuzzy-skinned kiwi (*Actinidia deliciosa* or *A. chinensis*) generally grows best in the Lower and Coastal South, where temperatures do not drop below 10°F; heat zones 9–8. Long, warm summers are needed to ripen the fruit. Give it full sun or partial shade. Note, however, that a vine can take up to 5 years from planting to flower or set fruit. Sometimes called Chinese gooseberry vine, it twines to 30 ft. if not curbed. Roundish, 5- to 8-in.-long leaves are rich dark green above, velvety white below. New growth often has rich red fuzz. Spring flowers are 1–1½ in. wide, opening cream colored and fading to buff. Fuzzy, brown-skinned, green-fleshed fruit is the size and roughly the shape of an egg. 'Hayward' is the most common fruiting selection. To pollinate it, use 'Chico Male', 'Matua', 'Tomuri', or plants simply sold as "male." 'Vincent' needs little winter chill and is a good choice for warmest-winter climates; use 'Chico Male' as its pollenizer. Male hardy kiwi selections (see below) can also supply pollen for female fuzzy-skinned kiwis.

Hardy kiwi (*A. arguta*) grows and produces well in the Lower, Middle, and Upper South; heat zones 8–4. It is much like fuzzy-skinned kiwi vine in appearance but has smaller leaves (which are smooth and fuzzless), flowers, and fruit. The 1- to 1½-in.-long, fuzzless fruit can be eaten skin and all. Best in partial shade in most of the South. Green-fruited female selections 'Ananasnaja', 'Hood River', and 'Jumbo', need a male plant (may be sold simply as "male") for pollen. 'Issai', also with green fruit, is self-fruitful. Female 'Ken's Red' is a hybrid with red fruit; it needs a pollenizer.

Ornamental or kolomikta kiwi (*A. kolomikta*) is suited to the Lower, Middle, and Upper South; heat zones 8–1. Male plants are ornamental vines grown for their splashy, heart-shaped foliage (see description under *A. kolomikta*). Female plants typically have somewhat less colorful leaves than males, but they produce small green fruit about the size of hardy kiwi fruit; a male vine must be planted nearby to supply pollen. Plants typically grow to 15 ft. or more. Prefers partial shade, especially in hotter climates. 'September Sun' has sweet fruit and the best foliage variegation among female selections.

KIWI, ORNAMENTAL or KOLOMIKTA. See ACTINIDIA kolomikta

KNAUTIA

Dipsacaceae

PERENNIALS

⚘ US, MS, LS ☰ 9–5

☼ FULL SUN

💧 REGULAR WATER

Knautia macedonica

R elated to pincushion flower (*Scabiosa*), with blossoms that are similar in structure—clustered in tight heads above ruffs of leafy bracts on bare stems. Basal leaves are barely lobed, but those on upper stems are deeply divided. These are meadow plants that make few demands on the gardener; they are at home in cottage gardens, wild gardens, perennial borders, roadside plantings. Cut flowers are good for fresh or dried arrangements.

K. arvensis. BLUE BUTTONS. From Europe, Caucasus, Mediterranean region. To 1–5 ft. tall, 1½ ft. wide. Blue, 1½-in. flower heads in summer.

K. macedonica. From central Europe. To 1½–3 ft. tall and as wide. Deep purplish, ½- to 1¼-in. red flower heads bloom from early summer to fall. Melton Pastels feature blooms in shades of blue, mauve, pink, rose, salmon pink, and crimson from late spring to fall.

KNIPHOFIA

RED-HOT POKER, TORCH LILY

Liliaceae

PERENNIALS

⚘ VARY BY SPECIES

☼ FULL SUN OR PARTIAL SHADE

💧💧 MODERATE TO REGULAR WATER

Kniphofia uvaria

D ense clumps of grasslike, finely toothed foliage send up bare stems topped by nodding, tubular flowers in tight, overlapping clusters. Flowering stems look like glowing pokers or torches, hence the common names. Blossoms open from bottom to top over the course of several days, changing color as they mature. Increasing numbers of species—mostly from South Africa—are now grown in gardens and hybridized. The old 3-ft.-high forms of *K. uvaria* in shades of coral orange and yellow have given way to kinds with blooms ranging from coral red through every conceivable shade of orange, peach, and yellow to near-white and light green, on plants varying in size from 1½-ft. dwarfs to 6-ft. giants. The flowers attract hummingbirds.

Red-hot pokers require adequate moisture when blooms are forming and will fail to flower if conditions are too dry then. In summer, they'll tolerate even marshy conditions—but for winter survival, well-drained soil is essential. Most of these plants flower in summer, but some start in late spring and repeat throughout the growing season. Where winter temperatures drop to 0°F or below, tie foliage over clumps in fall to protect growing points (or at least leave all foliage in place over winter). In milder climates, cut or pull out any ratty-looking leaves in fall; new leaves will replace them by spring. Crowns increase slowly, forming clumps 2–3 ft. wide (or wider) at base; you will get the best show if clumps are left in place for several years. Increase plantings by division in spring except for types still blooming then; for these, wait until summer to divide. New strains are available as seed (be aware that seedlings will vary in color and quality). Protect from slugs and snails. Not heavily browsed by deer.

K. caulescens. Zones US, MS, LS, CS; 9–4. Blue-green leaves (purple at base) are 3–4 ft. long, 2–3 in. wide; they are produced in rosettes on short, branching, woody stems like trunks. Stalks 2 ft. tall bear heads of coral red to terra-cotta buds that open to pale yellow flowers. Blooms from midsummer into fall.

K. citrina. Zones MS, LS, CS; 9–4. Smallish species with narrow, dark bluish green leaves and globular flower heads in various yellow shades on 2- to 2½-ft.-tall stems. Summer to fall bloom. 'Lime Select' has bright lime green buds that open chartreuse and fade to cream.

K. hybrids. Zones US, MS, LS, CS; 9–4. Although they involve several species, these hybrids generally share the narrow leaves and summer bloom season of *K. uvaria*. A distinct departure is 'Christmas Cheer', a hybrid of the vigorous species *K. rooperi*.

'Bees' Sunset'. Stems to 3 ft. high, with glowing yellow-orange buds opening light yellow.

'Border Ballet'. Buds are a soft, dusty coral pink opening to cream blooms. Stems reach 4–4½ ft.

'Christmas Cheer'. Zones LS, CS. Brilliant orange buds open to deep gold flowers on 4- to 5-ft. stems. Blooms fall through late spring in mild-winter areas, fall until frost elsewhere. Give it room; leaves (to 5 ft. long and 2 in. wide) become lax and collapse on the ground, smothering any plants in their way. Clump increases rapidly to 6–8 ft. or more across. Divide in early summer.

'Flamenco'. Seed-grown strain that blooms in early fall in its first year, in summer in subsequent years. Flower colors range from coral through orange and yellow to creamy white. Stems to 2½ ft. tall.

'Gold Mine'. Glowing orange-yellow buds opening golden amber on 3- to 3½-ft. stems.

'Little Maid'. Thin, grassy leaves and narrow flower stems to 2 ft. tall. Creamy white blossoms open from buds in buff-tinted pale yellow.

'Malibu Yellow'. Stems 5–6 ft. tall bear 8- to 10-in.-long heads of lime green buds that open primrose yellow.

'Peaches and Cream'. Stems about 4 ft. high bear peach-colored buds opening to cream blossoms.

'Percy's Pride'. To 4 ft. tall, with green-tinted yellow buds opening cream.

'Primrose Beauty'. To 3 ft. tall, with blossoms in clear light yellow.

'Shining Sceptre'. Plant sold in North America under this name is 3 ft. tall, with tangerine orange flowers; the English original is 4 ft. tall, with pale yellow buds opening ivory.

'Vanilla'. Stems 2–2½ ft. tall; buds are light yellow, opening cream.

K. uvaria. Zones US, MS, LS, CS; 9–4. Leaves to 1 in. wide, 2 ft. long. Oblong flower heads on stems 3–3½ ft. tall. Coral red buds open to orange or deep yellow blossoms in summer (in fall, in cold-winter climates). Most selections sold under this name are actually hybrids (see *K.* hybrids, above).

KNOTWEED. See PERSICARIA

FOR INFORMATION ON SELECTING PLANTS
PLEASE SEE PAGES 39–144

KOCHIA scoparia (Bassia scoparia)

SUMMER CYPRESS

Chenopodiaceae

ANNUAL

✔ US, MS, LS, CS, TS H 12–1

☼ FULL SUN

💧 REGULAR WATER

Kochia scoparia

Native to Eurasia. To 3 ft. high and 2 ft. wide. Branches are so thickly clothed in soft, narrow, light green leaves that plant is too dense to see through. Grow individually for its gently rounded form; or group plants for low, temporary hedge or edging. Can be sheared into any shape. Grow from seed sown in early spring or (in mild-winter climates) in fall. Seeds need light to germinate, so barely cover them with soil. Tolerates high heat.

K. s. trichophylla (Bassia scoparia trichophylla), known as Mexican fire bush or burning bush, is identical to the species, but its foliage turns bright red or purplish red in autumn. Can reseed profusely enough to become a pest; be sure to hoe out any unwanted seedlings when they're still small.

KOELREUTERIA

Sapindaceae

DECIDUOUS TREES

✔ ZONES VARY BY SPECIES

☼ FULL SUN

💧💧 MODERATE TO REGULAR WATER

Koelreuteria paniculata

Native to Asia, these small trees are admired for large, loose clusters of yellow flowers followed by fat, papery fruit capsules resembling little Japanese lanterns. Capsules are used in both fresh and dried arrangements. Good patio, lawn, or street trees. Very adaptable to different soils as long as drainage is fairly good. Control self-sown seedlings.

K. bipinnata (K. integrifoliola). CHINESE FLAME TREE. Zones MS, LS, CS, TS; 10–1. To 20–40 ft. tall and not quite as wide, eventually flat topped. Deep green leaves 1–2 ft. long, divided into 7 to 12 oval leaflets; turn yellow for a short time before dropping in fall. Blooms in mid- to late summer; flower clusters are like those of *K. paniculata,* but 2-in. capsules are more colorful, in shades of orange, red, or salmon. Capsules come quickly after flowers and persist into fall. Prune tree to develop high branching. Roots are deep but not invasive; good tree to plant under. Produces many seedlings.

K. elegans (K. formosana). FLAMEGOLD. Zones CS, TS; 11–6. Round-headed tree 20–30 ft. tall and equally broad. Dark green leaves about 1½ ft. long, with 9 to 16 leaflets. Bright yellow fall flowers in tall, erect clusters are followed by especially showy clusters of long-lasting, puffy orange-red to salmon fruits. Fall foliage is yellow but not consistent; show is often poor.

K. paniculata. GOLDENRAIN TREE. Zones US, MS, LS, CS; 9–1. To 20–35 ft. tall, 25–40 ft. wide. Open branching, giving slight shade. Leaves to 15 in. long, with 7 to 15 oval, toothed or lobed leaflets, each 1–3 in. long. New leaves are purplish, maturing to bright green in summer; may turn yellow to gold in fall. Very showy, 8- to 14-in.-long flower clusters in early to midsummer. Fruit capsules are red when young, maturing to buff and brown shades; last well into autumn. Tree takes cold, heat, drought, wind. Prune to shape; can be gawky without pruning. 'Fastigiata' is 25 ft. tall, only 3 ft. wide. 'Rose Lantern' (previously offered as 'September') blooms later than the basic species, at the end of summer; rose pink capsules persist for 5 to 6 weeks.

KOHLRABI

Brassicaceae (Cruciferae)

BIENNIAL GROWN AS COOL-SEASON ANNUAL

✔ US, MS, LS, CS, TS H 6–1

☼ FULL SUN

💧 REGULAR WATER

Kohlrabi

Cool-season cabbage relative and, like cabbage, a member of the genus *Brassica.* Leaves and leafstalks are edible, but edible part most commonly associated with kohlrabi is the enlarged, bulbous portion of the stem formed just above the soil surface. Standard selections are 'Early White Vienna' and 'Early Purple Vienna'—similar in size and flavor, differing only in skin color. Other white selections include 'Triumph' and early-maturing 'Grand Duke'. 'Kolibri' is a popular purple-skinned selection.

Plants are very fast growing, ready to harvest in 50 to 60 days from seed. Sow seed in rich soil about 2 weeks after average date of last frost. Before planting, work ½ cup of 10-10-10 fertilizer per 10 ft. of row into soil. Follow first planting with successive sowings 2 weeks apart. In areas with warm winters, plant again in late fall and early winter. Sow seed ½ in. deep, in rows spaced 1½ ft. apart; thin seedlings to 4–6 in. apart. Cabbageworms are the primary pests. For controls, see Cabbage.

Harvest bulbous part when 2–3 in. wide. Peel, slice, and serve raw; or steam or sauté slices or chunks. Steam young leaves and leafstalks.

KOLKWITZIA amabilis

BEAUTY BUSH

Caprifoliaceae

DECIDUOUS SHRUB

✔ US, MS, LS H 8–1

☼ ☼ FULL SUN OR PARTIAL SHADE

💧 REGULAR WATER

Kolkwitzia amabilis

Native to China. Graceful, upright growth to 10–12 ft. tall and about as wide. If grown in partial shade, it has an arching form; in full sun, it's denser and shorter. Gray-green leaves to 3 in. long sometimes turn reddish in fall. Blooms heavily in mid- to late spring, bearing clusters of 1-in.-long, yellow-throated pink flowers. Blossoms are followed by conspicuous pinkish brown, bristly fruits that prolong color display. Brown, flaky bark gradually peels from stems during winter. An old Southern favorite. 'Pink Cloud' is a particularly floriferous selection, bearing masses of pink blossoms.

Adapts to many soils and climates. Blooms on wood formed the previous year. Thin out oldest stems after blossoms have faded; or, to enjoy the fruit, wait until early spring to prune, then do so lightly. Plant can be renewed by cutting to ground after bloom.

KOREAN FORSYTHIA. See FORSYTHIA ovata

KOREAN GRASS. See ZOYSIA tenuifolia

KOSTELETZKYA virginica

SEASHORE MALLOW

Malvaceae

PERENNIAL

✔ US, MS, LS, CS, TS H 12–6

☼ FULL SUN

💧💧 REGULAR TO AMPLE WATER

Kosteletzkya virginica

Native to the coastal marshes of the Southeast, this upright, free-flowering mallow deserves much wider use in gardens. Breaking dormancy in late spring, it sends up thick stems in a cluster that may

K

reach 5 ft. tall and 2 ft. wide. Foliage is light green and fuzzy; lower leaves on stems are 6 in. long, with three to five lobes, while upper ones are smaller, either triangular or arrow shaped. Hundreds of pink, 2-in.-wide flowers resembling those of hibiscus smother the plant from midsummer to fall. Seashore mallow thrives in swampy soil and even standing water but adapts to regular garden soil as well. 'Immaculate' features large white blooms.

KUMQUAT. See CITRUS

Labiatae. See Lamiaceae

LABURNUM

GOLDENCHAIN TREE

Fabaceae (Leguminosae)

DECIDUOUS TREES OR SHRUBS

✎ US, MS ⊞ 7–3

☼ AFTERNOON SHADE

◐ MODERATE TO REGULAR WATER

☣ ALL PARTS, ESPECIALLY SEEDPODS, ARE HIGHLY POISONOUS IF INGESTED

Laburnum × watereri

Native to central and southern Europe, these are among the garden's prettiest flowering trees. They grow upright and are typically pruned to a single trunk, but can be shrubby if allowed to keep basal suckers and low branches. Olive green bark is a trademark; bright green leaves are divided into three leaflets (like clover leaves). Beautiful in bloom in mid- to late spring, when hanging clusters of bright yellow, fragrant flowers appear. Flexible branches make them easy to espalier; they can be trained on narrow arches to form spectacular flowering tunnels. They're also good as single specimens, in foundation plantings, and in groupings.

Plants need good drainage; will tolerate alkaline soil. Susceptibility to insects and disease can make them rather short lived. They don't do well in extended summer heat, so protect them from hot afternoon sun. Prune after bloom. Removing seedpods promptly may increase the next year's bloom.

L. alpina. SCOTCH LABURNUM. To 30–35 ft. tall, 20–25 ft. wide. Flower clusters are 10–15 in. long. 'Pendulum' has weeping branches.

L. anagyroides. COMMON GOLDENCHAIN. Bushy, spreading plant grows to 20–30 ft. tall and 15–20 ft. wide. Flower clusters 6–10 in. long. 'Pendulum' is a weeping form.

L. × watereri. Hybrid between species *L. anagyroides* and *L. alpina*. To 15–30 ft. tall, 10–20 ft. wide, with flower clusters 10–20 in. long. 'Vossii', with 20-in. blossom clusters, is the showiest, most widely grown selection.

LACE VINE. See FALLOPIA baldschuanica

LADY BELLS. See ADENOPHORA

LADY FERN. See ATHYRIUM filix-femina

LADY-OF-THE-NIGHT. See BRUNFELSIA americana

LADY PALM. See RHAPIS

LADY'S-MANTLE. See ALCHEMILLA

LADY'S SLIPPER. See PAPHIOPEDILUM

LAGENARIA. See GOURD

FOR GROWING SYMBOL EXPLANATIONS
PLEASE SEE PAGE 145

LAGERSTROEMIA

CREPE MYRTLE

Lythraceae

DECIDUOUS SHRUBS AND TREES

✎ US, MS, LS, CS ⊞ 10–6, EXCEPT AS NOTED

☼ FULL SUN

◐ MODERATE WATER

▸ SEE CHART PAGE 380

Lagerstroemia indica

The crepe myrtles are among the most satisfactory of plants for the South: showy summer flowers, attractive bark, and (in many cases) brilliant fall color make them year-round garden performers. Long, cool autumns yield the best leaf display; sudden frosts following warm, humid fall weather often freeze leaves while they're still green, ruining the show.

Most crepe myrtles in gardens are selections of *L. indica* or hybrids of that species with *L. fauriei*. The latter species has attracted much notice for its hardiness and exceptionally showy bark. Queen's crepe myrtle, *L. speciosa*, grows only in the Tropical South.

All crepe myrtles bloom on new wood and should be pruned in winter or early spring. On large shrubs and trees, remove basal suckers, twiggy growth, crossing branches, and branches growing toward the center of the plant. Also gradually remove side branches up to a height of 4–5 ft.; this exposes the handsome bark of the trunks. During the growing season, clip off spent flowers to promote a second, lighter bloom. Also prune dwarf forms periodically throughout the growing season, removing spent blossoms and thinning out small, twiggy growth.

Crepe myrtles are not usually browsed by deer.

L. fauriei. JAPANESE CREPE MYRTLE. Native to Japan. Tree to 20–30 ft. tall and wide, with erect habit and outward-arching branches. Light green leaves to 4 in. long and 2 in. wide turn yellow in fall. Especially handsome bark: the smooth gray outer bark flakes away to reveal glossy cinnamon brown bark beneath. Small white flowers are borne in 2- to 4-in.-long clusters in early summer; often blooms again in late summer. Resistant to mildew and best known as a parent of hardy, mildew-resistant hybrids with *L. indica*, though it is handsome in its own right. 'Fantasy', with even showier bark than the species, has a vase form—narrow below, spreading above. 'Kiowa' has outstanding cinnamon-colored bark.

L. indica. CREPE MYRTLE. The premier summer-flowering tree of the South. Tolerates heat, humidity, drought; does well in most soils as long as they are well drained. May be frozen to the ground in severe winters in the Upper South, but will resprout. Gardeners there should plant cold-hardy selections such as 'Acoma', 'Centennial Spirit', and 'Hopi'. Variable in size (some forms are dwarf shrubs, others large shrubs or small trees) and

▸ page 382

WHAT CREPE MYRTLES NEED

PLANTING SITE: A sunny location where the air moves freely will help limit powdery mildew and other diseases.

SOIL: Provide moist, moderately fertile, well-drained soil.

PRUNING: Crepe myrtles bloom on new wood, so prune them in late winter or early spring to increase next summer's flower production. Pruning off old flowers in summer before they set seed may produce a second wave of blooms. Except on dwarf types, remove side branches on trunks up to the 4- to 5-ft. level. To reveal attractive trunks, also remove branches growing inward toward center of plant.

Lagerstroemia 'Natchez'

LAGERSTROEMIA—CREPE MYRTLE

SELECTIONS AND HYBRIDS	FORM/HEIGHT	MILDEW RESISTANCE	FLOWERS/DAYS OF BLOOM	FALL FOLIAGE	COMMENTS
'Acoma'	Spreading, arching, nearly weeping shrub; to 10 ft. tall, 11 ft. wide	Good	White; 90	Reddish purple	Light gray bark. Cold-hardy hybrid
'Basham's Party Pink'	Broad tree to 40 ft. tall and wide	Good	Lavender pink; 80	Orange red	Very popular selection in South Texas. Not recommended for Upper and Middle South. Not very cold hardy
'Biloxi'	Upright, arching small tree; to 35 ft. tall, 12 ft. wide	High	Light pink; 80	Yellow orange to red	Mottled dark brown bark. Fast growing, cold-hardy hybrid
'Byers Wonderful White'	Upright small tree; to 30 ft. tall, 15 ft. wide	Good to fair	Clear white; 90	Yellow	Huge flower heads—larger than a basketball. Cold-hardy selection
'Catawba'	Upright small tree; to 12 ft. tall and wide	Good	Dark purple; 70	Orange red	Many consider it the best dark purple selection. Cold hardy
'Centennial'	Dwarf, round shrub; to 3–5 ft. tall and wide	Good	Bright purple; 70	Orange	Probably the best dwarf purple selection. Cold hardy
'Centennial Spirit'	Upright large shrub or small tree; to 20 ft. tall and nearly as wide	Good	Dark red; 110	Red orange	Extremely showy blooms. Cold-hardy selection
'Comanche'	Spreading large shrub or small tree; to 15 ft. tall and wide	High	Coral pink; 80	Orange red and purple red	Handsome tan to sandalwood bark. Cold-hardy hybrid
'Dynamite'	Upright small tree to 15–20 ft. tall and wide	Good	Vivid true red; 90	Red	Best true red to date; excellent heat and drought tolerance. Nearly seedless. Cold-hardy selection
'Hopi'	Spreading, semidwarf shrub; to 7 ft. tall, 10 ft. wide	High	Medium pink; 100	Orange red to dark red	Attractive gray-brown bark. Quite cold hardy. Hybrid
'Lipan'	Upright shrub or small tree; to 15 ft. tall and wide	High	Medium lavender; 80	Orange to red	Beautiful white to beige bark. Cold-hardy hybrid
'Miami'	Upright small tree; 20–25 ft. tall, 12–15 ft. wide	High	Medium pink; 100	Orange to dull russet	Chestnut brown bark. Very popular hybrid
'Muskogee'	Small, broad tree; to 25 ft. tall and wide	High	Light lavender; 120	Red	Tan-and-brown bark. Fast-growing, cold-hardy hybrid
'Natchez'	Small tree; to 30 ft. tall and wide	High	Pure white; 110	Orange red	Considered by many to be the best all-around crepe myrtle. Spectacular cinnamon brown bark. Fast-growing hybrid
'Near East'	Spreading small tree; to 18 ft. tall and wide	Fair	Soft, light pink; 90	Yellow orange	Beautiful blooms. Not recommended for Upper or Middle South. Not a very cold-hardy selection

Lagerstroemia indica 'Centennial Spirit'

Lagerstroemia 'Hopi'

Lagerstroemia 'Lipan'

Lagerstroemia 'Muskogee'

Lagerstroemia 'Natchez'

LAGERSTROEMIA—CREPE MYRTLE

SELECTIONS AND HYBRIDS	FORM/HEIGHT	MILDEW RESISTANCE	FLOWERS/DAYS OF BLOOM	FALL FOLIAGE	COMMENTS
'Osage'	Arching, open-branched shrub or small tree; to 15 ft. tall, 12 ft. wide	High	Clear light pink; 100	Red	Chestnut brown bark. Heavy bloomer. Hybrid
'Pink Velour'	Vase-shaped shrub or small tree; to 10 ft. tall and wide	Good	Neon pink; 80	Yellow orange	Selection with good heat and drought tolerance
'Pocomoke'	Dwarf, mounding shrub to 2–3 ft. high, 3–4 ft. wide	High	Rosy pink; 60	Bronzy red	Best dwarf for landscape use; terrific in borders and pots. No pruning needed. Hybrid
'Potomac'	Upright shrub or small tree; 10–20 ft. tall, 8–10 ft. wide	Fair	Clear pink; 90	Orange	Good for narrow spaces. Fast-growing hybrid. Early to leaf out; can be nipped by late frosts
'Prairie Lace'	Upright, semidwarf shrub; to 10 ft. tall, 6 ft. wide	Fair	Medium pink edged in white; 100	Red to red orange	Cold-hardy, nearly seedless selection
'Raspberry Sundae'	Upright, columnar, to 15–20 ft. tall, 10 ft. wide	Good to fair	Raspberry red with white petal edges; 90	Orange	Selection with excellent heat and drought tolerance. Nearly seedless. Flowers are fragrant
'Red Rocket'	Upright grower to 20 ft. tall, 15 ft. wide	High	Cherry red with occasional red flecks; 90	Orange	Selection with huge flower clusters, good heat and drought tolerance. Few seeds
'Regal Red'	Upright, rounded small tree; to 15 ft. tall and wide	Good	Vivid deep red; 70	Red orange	Probably the best deep red selection. Cold hardy
'Sioux'	Upright large shrub or small tree; 15–20 ft. tall, 10–15 ft. wide	High	Bright pink, slightly fragrant; 100	Red	Light gray-brown bark. Showy blooms. Summer foliage is dark green to burgundy green. Hybrid
'Tuskegee'	Small multitrunked tree with horizontal branching; to 20 ft. tall and wide	High	Deep pink to red; 100	Bright orange red	Beautiful gray-and-tan bark. Cold-hardy hybrid. Fine all-around performer
'Victor'	Dwarf round shrub; to 3 ft. tall and wide	Good	Dark red; 85	Reddish yellow	The best red-flowered dwarf. Cold-hardy selection
'Watermelon Red'	Upright, spreading tree to 25 ft. tall and wide	Fair to poor	Watermelon red; 90	Red orange	Despite susceptibility to mildew, still very popular. Several selections, including 'William Toovey', may be sold under this name
'Yuma'	Upright, multitrunked large shrub or small tree to 15 ft. tall, nearly as wide	Good	Medium lavender; 90	Yellowish to brownish red	Light gray bark. Cold-hardy hybrid
'Zuni'	Round, semidwarf shrub; 9 ft. tall, 8 ft. wide	High	Medium lavender; 100	Orange red to dark red	Light brown-and-gray bark; heavy bloomer. Cold-hardy hybrid

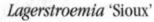

Lagerstroemia 'Sioux'

Lagerstroemia indica 'Red Rocket'

Lagerstroemia indica 'Watermelon Red'

Lagerstroemia 'Zuni'

habit (spreading or upright). Dark green leaves are 1–2½ in. long and somewhat narrower, usually tinted red when new; they often turn brilliant orange or red in fall. Crinkled, crepe-papery, 1- to 1½-in.-wide flowers in white or shades of pink, red, or purple are carried in dense clusters.

Trained as a tree, it develops an attractive trunk and branch pattern. Smooth gray or light brown bark peels off to reveal smooth, pinkish inner bark; winter trunk and branches seem polished.

Mildew can be a problem. Spray with triforine (Funginex) before plants bloom, or grow mildew-resistant hybrids of *L. indica* and *L. fauriei* (see chart on page 380 for those hybrids and selections with high mildew resistance). Almost all selections with names of Native American tribes, such as 'Hopi', 'Miami', and 'Zuni', are mildew resistant.

L. speciosa. QUEEN'S CREPE MYRTLE. Zones TS; 12–9. Tree to 25–30 ft. tall, 15–25 ft. wide. The showiest and most tender of the crepe myrtles, displaying huge clusters of white, pink, lavender, or purple flowers in June and July. Individual blossoms reach 3 in. across. Large leaves (8–12 in. long, 4 in. wide) turn red in fall. Smooth, mottled, exfoliating bark. Rank grower; annual pruning in winter is especially important to control size and form.

DON'T COMMIT "CREPE MURDER." *Don't chop your large crepe myrtles down to ugly stubs each spring just because your neighbors do. This ruins the natural form and encourages the growth of spindly, whiplike branches that are too weak to hold up the flowers. To reduce a crepe myrtle's height, use hand pruners or loppers to shorten the topmost branches by 2–3 ft. in late winter, always cutting back to a side branch or bud. For branches more than 2 in. thick, always cut back to the crotch or trunk. Don't leave big, ugly stubs.* ❖

LAMB'S EARS. See STACHYS byzantina

Lamiaceae. Members of the mint family of herbaceous plants and shrubs are easily recognized by their square stems, leaves in opposite pairs, and whorled flowers in spikelike, sometimes branched, clusters. Many of the group are aromatic; the family contains most of the familiar kitchen herbs, including basil *(Ocimum)*, mint *(Mentha)*, oregano *(Origanum)*, and sage *(Salvia)*. Many have attractive foliage or flowers (Coleus, sage). This family was previously called Labiatae.

LAMIASTRUM galeobdolon. See LAMIUM galeobdolon

LAMIUM

DEAD NETTLE

Lamiaceae (Labiatae)

PERENNIALS

✿ US, MS, LS ⬍ 8–1

◐ ● PARTIAL TO FULL SHADE

◖ REGULAR WATER

Native from Europe to western Asia. Heart-shaped, tooth-edged leaves, often marked with white or silver, are borne in opposite pairs; clustered flowers come in pink, white, yellow, lavender. Vigorous growers that thrive in shade; *L. maculatum* is used as a ground cover.

Lamium maculatum

L. galeobdolon (Galeobdolon luteum, Lamiastrum galeobdolon). YELLOW ARCHANGEL. Grows upright to 2 ft., spreading slowly to form tight clumps. Yellow flowers are inconspicuous. Best-known selection is 'Hermann's Pride', with leaves evenly streaked and spotted with white.

L. maculatum. SPOTTED DEAD NETTLE. Running or trailing plant used as a ground cover or in hanging baskets. To 6 in. tall, spreading 2–3 ft. wide, with grayish green leaves marked in silver. The species is very vigorous (even weedy) and is not planted as often as its selections. All of these nicely light up shady areas of the garden. Groom periodically to remove old, shabby growth.

'Anne Greenaway'. Lavender flowers. Unusual leaves have gold edges and a central silver streak surrounded by olive green.

'Beacon Silver'. Pink flowers and green-edged, silvery gray leaves.

'Beedham's White'. White blooms and yellow to chartreuse leaves with a white stripe in the center.

'Chequers'. Pink flowers and green leaves with a central white stripe.

'Orchid Frost'. Pink blossoms; silver leaves edged in bluish green.

'Pink Pewter'. Pink blooms and silvery leaves edged in greenish gray.

'White Nancy'. Like 'Beacon Silver' but with white flowers.

LANTANA

Verbenaceae

EVERGREEN SHRUBS

✿ LS, CS, TS; GROWN AS ANNUALS IN US, MS

☼ FULL SUN

◖ MODERATE WATER, EXCEPT AS NOTED

◈ FRUITS ARE POISONOUS IF INGESTED

Lantana montevidensis

Few plants supply as much long-lasting, dependable color as these tough-as-nails tropical American natives. Tiny flowers in tight clusters that resemble miniature nosegays appear continuously in warm weather. Foliage gives off a pungent odor when brushed against or crushed. Small fruits usually follow the flowers, maturing from green to bluish black; some selections are fruitless. Lantanas thrive in hot, dry weather and tolerate just about any well-drained soil, growing well even near the beach. They're a magnet for butterflies. Plant them in masses, let them cascade over a wall, or display them in window boxes, hanging baskets, or planters. Deer don't usually care for lantana species, but they may browse hybrid types.

Lantanas are treated as annuals in most of the Upper and Middle South, as perennials elsewhere. Where they overwinter, prune back hard in early spring to remove dead wood and encourage vigorous new growth. Unpruned plants may become large, woody shrubs. Feed and water lightly, as too much fertilizer and water will reduce bloom.

L. camara. COMMON LANTANA. Heat zones 12–1. The most popular species in the South, and one of two used in hybridizing (the other is *L. montevidensis*). Coarse, upright plant to 6 ft. tall and wide. Rough-textured dark green leaves are oval and pointed, to 4 in. long. Yellow, orange, or red flowers in 1- to 2-in. clusters.

L. horrida. TEXAS LANTANA. Heat zones 12–1. Native to southern Texas and Mexico. Prickly, coarse shrub, to 3 ft. (rarely 6 ft.) tall and wide. Broadly oval leaves to 3 in. long have pointed tips and coarsely toothed edges. Spreads by shoots that root where they touch the ground. Good ground cover on very dry sites in full sun. Flowers open yellow, age to orange.

L. montevidensis (L. sellowiana). TRAILING LANTANA. Heat zones 12–6. Along with *L. camara*, this species is used extensively in breeding. A little hardier than *L. camara*, it's a ground cover to about 2 ft. high, with branches trailing to 3 ft. or even 6 ft. Dark green, inch-long leaves have coarsely toothed edges; sometimes tinged red or purplish, especially in winter. Rosy lilac flowers in 1- to 1½-in.-wide clusters. 'Lavender Swirl' is a larger form that produces white, lavender, and white-and-lavender flower clusters. 'Sunny Daze' has leaves attractively edged in creamy yellow and grows more slowly than the species. 'White Lightnin' looks similar but has pure white flowers; it too is a slow grower.

L. selections and hybrids. In this list, some of the selections are forms of *L. camara* or hybrids between those forms; others are hybrids resulting from crosses between *L. camara* and *L. montevidensis*.

'Christine'. To 6 ft. by 5 ft. Cerise pink. Can be trained into a small patio tree.

'Confetti'. To 2–3 ft. by 6–8 ft. Blossoms in a mix of yellow, pink, purple.

'Cream Carpet'. To 2–3 ft. by 6–8 ft. Cream with bright yellow throat.

'Dallas Red'. To 3–4 ft. by 3–5 ft. Deep red.

'Gold Mound'. To 3 ft. by 3–5 ft. Golden yellow.

'Gold Rush'. To 1½–2 ft. by 4–6 ft. Rich golden yellow.

L

'Irene'. To 3 ft. by 4 ft. Compact. Clusters feature magenta and lemon yellow flowers.

Landmark Series. Dense, mounding plants to 1½ ft. tall, 2 ft. wide, in colors of orange, gold, white, peach, pink, and rose. Neat, uniform growth; great in borders.

'Lemon Swirl' ('Samantha'). Slow growing to 2 ft. tall, 3 ft. wide. Bright yellow band around each leaf; yellow flowers. Fruitless.

'Miss Huff'. To 3–5 ft. by 10 ft. Orange and pink. Hardier than other lantanas, surviving −3°F. Nearly fruitless.

'New Gold'. To 2–3 ft. by 6–8 ft. Golden yellow. Fruitless.

'Patriot Honeylove'. To 2 ft. by 3 ft. Honey gold and peach.

'Patriot Hot Country'. To 3 ft. tall and wide. Fuchsia pink.

'Patriot Rainbow'. To 1 ft. tall and wide. Flowers combine yellow, orange, and fuchsia pink.

'Pinkie'. To 1 ft. by 3 ft. Pink and cream. Fruitless.

'Radiation'. To 3–5 ft. high and wide. Rich orange red.

'Silver Mound'. To 2 ft. tall and wide. Cream blossoms with golden yellow centers.

'Spreading Sunset'. To 2–3 ft. by 6–8 ft. Vivid orange red.

'Spreading Sunshine'. To 2–3 ft. by 6–8 ft. Bright yellow.

'Sunburst'. To 2–3 ft. by 6–8 ft. Bright golden yellow.

'Tangerine'. To 2–3 ft. by 6–8 ft. Burnt orange.

L. trifolia. LAVENDER POPCORN. Heat zones 12–7. Somewhat rangy, sparsely branched shrub to 3–5 ft. tall and half as wide. Medium green leaves to 5 in. long, whorled around branches in groups of three. Dense clusters of pink, lavender, or purple blossoms appear in conjunction with showy spikes of lavender purple fruits that resemble those of beautyberry (*Callicarpa*).

LARCH. See LARIX

LARIX

LARCH

Pinaceae

DECIDUOUS TREES

☑ ZONES VARY BY SPECIES

☼ FULL SUN

🌢 REGULAR WATER

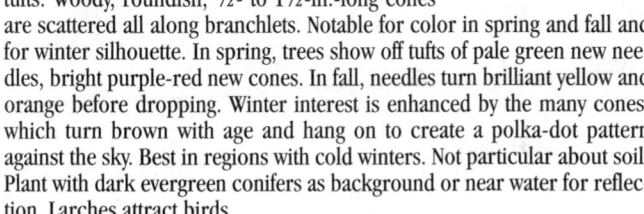

Larix decidua

These conifers form slender pyramids with horizontal branches and drooping branchlets. Needles are ½–1½ in. long, in soft, fluffy tufts. Woody, roundish, ½- to 1½-in.-long cones are scattered all along branchlets. Notable for color in spring and fall and for winter silhouette. In spring, trees show off tufts of pale green new needles, bright purple-red new cones. In fall, needles turn brilliant yellow and orange before dropping. Winter interest is enhanced by the many cones, which turn brown with age and hang on to create a polka-dot pattern against the sky. Best in regions with cold winters. Not particular about soil. Plant with dark evergreen conifers as background or near water for reflection. Larches attract birds.

L. decidua (L. europaea). EUROPEAN LARCH. Zones US; 6–1. From mountains of Europe. Moderate to fast growth to 30–60 ft. tall, 10–25 ft. wide. Summer foliage is grass green. Branches of 'Pendula' arch out and down, with branchlets hanging nearly straight down.

L. kaempferi. JAPANESE LARCH. Zones US, MS; 7–4. Native to Japan. Fast growing to 60 ft. or taller, 20–30 ft. wide, but can be dwarfed in containers. Summer foliage is a soft bluish green. 'Pendula' has long, weeping branches.

LARKSPUR. See CONSOLIDA ajacis

FOR INFORMATION ON YOUR CLIMATE ZONES
PLEASE SEE PAGES 28–38

LARREA tridentata

CREOSOTE BUSH

Zygophyllaceae

EVERGREEN SHRUB

☑ MS, LS, CS, TS ‖ 12–7

☼ FULL SUN

🌢 🌢 LITTLE TO MODERATE WATER

Larrea tridentata

One of the most common native shrubs in Texas and northern Mexico. Grows 4–8 ft. tall and about as wide, with many upright branches. Straggly and open in shallow, dry soil; with more constant moisture, becomes attractive and densely foliaged, with rounded, spreading form. Leathery, yellow-green to dark green leaves divided into two ³⁄₈-in.-long crescents. Gummy secretion makes leaves look varnished and yields distinctive creosote odor, especially noticeable after rain. Small yellow flowers bloom off and on all year, followed by small, roundish fruits covered with shiny white or rusty hairs.

This plant does not need fertilizer, but one or two feedings of balanced liquid fertilizer during the course of the growing season will produce shiny dark green leaves. Use as wind or privacy screen, foundation shrub, or small tree. Long taproot makes it very drought tolerant but also makes established plants difficult to transplant. Needs well-drained soil. Not a good choice for high-rainfall, high-humidity areas. Sometimes sold as *L. divaricata*.

LATHYRUS

SWEET PEA

Fabaceae (Leguminosae)

ANNUALS AND PERENNIALS

☑ ZONES VARY BY SPECIES

☼ FULL SUN

🌢 🌢 🌢 WATER NEEDS VARY BY SPECIES

Lathyrus odoratus

Few flowers are better suited to the cottage garden than beloved, old-fashioned sweet peas. Despite the name, not all are fragrant. But all have the classic pea-family bloom—one large, upright, roundish petal (called the banner or standard), two narrow side petals (the wings), and two lower petals that form a boat-shaped structure (the keel).

L. latifolius. EVERLASTING PEA. Perennial. Zones US, MS, LS; 9–5. Native to Europe. Strong-growing vine to 9 ft., with blue-green foliage. Plants usually bear unscented flowers in mixed colors (reddish purple, white, pink); single colors may be sold. Blooms all summer if not allowed to go to seed. Grows with little care, tolerates drought (best with moderate water). May escape and become naturalized, even weedy. Use as bank cover, as trailer over rocks, on trellis or fence.

L. odoratus. SWEET PEA. Annual. Zones US, MS, LS, CS, TS; 8–1, except as noted. Native to the Mediterranean region. Blooms in winter, spring, or summer, bearing many spikelike clusters of crisp-looking flowers with a clean, sweet perfume. Blossoms come in single and mixed colors. Mixes include deep rose, blue, purple, scarlet, white, cream, salmon, bicolors. Vining types grow to 5 ft. or more; bush kinds grow anywhere from 8 in. to 3 ft. tall. Sweet peas make magnificent cut flowers in quantity.

To hasten germination, soak seeds for a few hours before planting. Sow seeds 1 in. deep and 1–2 in. apart. When seedlings are 4–5 in. high, thin to at least 6 in. apart. Pinch out tops to encourage strong side branches. Where climate prevents early planting or soil is too wet to work, start three or four seeds in each small peat pot, indoors or in a protected place, and set out when weather has settled. Plant peat pots 1 ft. apart, thinning each to one strong plant. This method is ideal for bush types. Protect young seedlings from birds and control slugs and snails. Never let vines lack for water; soak heavily. To prolong bloom, cut flowers at least every other day and remove all seedpods. Regular monthly feeding with a general-purpose fertilizer will keep vines vigorous and productive.

For vining sweet peas, provide trellis, strings, or wire before planting. Seedlings need support as soon as tendrils form. A freestanding trellis running north and south is best. When planting against fence or wall, keep supports away from wall to ensure good air circulation.

TIPS FOR STARTING SWEET PEAS. *In less-than-perfect soil, prepare ground for sweet peas like this. Dig a trench 1–1½ ft. deep. Mix 1 part peat moss or other soil conditioner to 2 parts soil. As you mix, add in a complete fertilizer according to label directions. Backfill trench with mix; plant seeds in it.* ❖

The following entries describe vine-type sweet peas (heirloom types first, then in groups by time of bloom) and bush types.

Heirloom selections. Not as large and showy as modern hybrids, these old spring-blooming favorites (some dating back hundreds of years) are notable for powerful fragrance.

'America'. Crimson to scarlet with white stripes.

'Annie Gilroy'. Bright cerise standard with lighter wings.

'Blanche Ferry'. Carmine rose standard, pink wings. Similar to 'Painted Lady' but with more intense color.

'Cupani'. Deep blue standard, purple wings. More vigorous than 'Matucana'.

'Flora Norton'. Blossoms in bright, clear blue.

'Indigo King'. Purplish maroon standard, blue wings. Very prolific.

'Matucana'. Same coloring as 'Cupani'. This and 'Cupani' are very close to the original wild *L. odoratus*.

Old Spice Mix. A mixture of eight old-fashioned selections with flowers in white and in shades of pink, red, and purple.

'Painted Lady'. Dates from the 18th century; bears small rose-and-white flowers.

Early flowering (Early Flowering Multiflora, Early Multiflora, formerly called Early Spencers). Heat zones 6–1. The name "Spencer" once described a type of frilled flower (with wavy petals) that is now characteristic of almost all selections. "Multiflora" indicates that the plants carry more flowers per stem than the old Spencers did.

The value of early-flowering types is that they will bloom in midwinter when days are short; try them in the Coastal and Tropical South. (Spring-flowering types will not bloom until days have lengthened to 15 hours or more.) Sow seeds in late October and November for blooms in late winter and spring. If you want to force sweet peas in a greenhouse, use selections from this group. They are not heat resistant. Generally sold in mixtures of several colors.

Spring flowering (Spring-Flowering Heat-Resistant Cuthbertson Type, Cuthbertson's Floribunda, Floribunda-Zvolanek strain). Both mixtures and single-color named selections are available in seed packets. Wide color range: pink, lavender, purple, white, cream, rose, salmon, cerise, carmine, red, blue. Royal or Royal Family are somewhat larger flowered, more heat resistant than the others. Plant between October and early January.

Bush type. The so-called bush-type sweet peas are strong vines with predetermined growth, heights. Unlike vining kinds, these stop their upward growth at anywhere from 8 in. to 3 ft. high. Some kinds are completely self-supporting; others need support of a few sticks or pieces of brush (similar to what you would provide for many perennials). Suitable for all regions. Flowers come in full range of colors. Most are early or spring blooming, as noted on the seed packet; follow planting dates given for early- or spring-flowering vining types.

Bijou. To 1 ft. Available in single or mixed colors; four or five flowers appear on each 5- to 7-in. stem. Self-supporting plants are spectacular in borders, beds, window boxes, containers. Not as heat resistant or as long stemmed as Knee-Hi; performs better in containers.

Cupid. To 4–6 in. by 1 ft. Trails on ground or hangs from containers.

Jet Set. Bushy plants grow 2–3 ft. tall; need some support.

Knee-Hi. To 2½ ft.; need some support. Large, long-stemmed blooms are carried five or six to the stem. Has all the virtues and color range of Cuthbertson's Floribunda, but on bush-type plants. Good for mass display in beds, borders. Growth will exceed 2½ ft. where planting bed joins a fence or wall; keep in the open for uniform height.

Little Sweethearts are rounded bushes to about 8 in. tall; they need no support, bloom over a long season. Heat zones 6–1. Snoopea (12–15 in.) and Supersnoop (2 ft.) need no support.

Lauraceae. The laurel family contains evergreen and deciduous trees and shrubs with inconspicuous flowers and (usually) aromatic foliage. Fruits are fleshy, containing a single seed. Examples are avocado, camphor tree *(Cinnamomum camphora)*, and sweet bay *(Laurus nobilis)*.

LAUREL. See PRUNUS

LAURENTIA fluviatilis. See PRATIA pedunculata

LAURUS nobilis

BAY

Lauraceae

EVERGREEN SHRUB OR TREE

🌱 LS (PROTECTED), CS, TS ⊞ 12–8; OR GROW IN POTS

☼ ◗ FULL SUN OR PARTIAL SHADE

💧 MODERATE WATER

Laurus nobilis

This Mediterranean native grows slowly to 12–40 ft. tall and wide. Natural habit is compact and broad based—often that of a multistemmed, gradually tapering cone. Leathery, aromatic leaves are the traditional bay leaves of cookery—oval, 2–4 in. long, dark green. Clusters of small yellow flowers are followed by ½- to 1-in.-long, black or dark purple berries. 'Saratoga' has broader leaves and a more treelike habit.

Not fussy about soil but needs good drainage. Tends to sucker heavily. Dense habit makes it a good large background shrub, screen, or small tree. Takes well to clipping into standards, hedges, or topiary shapes such as globes and cones. A classic formal container plant and longtime favorite in the South. In the Upper and Middle South, grow in a container and move to greenhouse or cool, well-lighted room when temperatures reach about 20°F; water sparingly until spring.

LAURUSTINUS. See VIBURNUM tinus

LAVANDIN. See LAVANDULA ×intermedia

LAVANDULA

LAVENDER

Lamiaceae (Labiatae)

EVERGREEN SHRUBS

🌱 ZONES VARY BY SPECIES

☼ FULL SUN

💧 MODERATE WATER

Lavandula angustifolia

Native to the Mediterranean region, lavender is prized for its showy, fragrant lavender or purple flowers. The blossom spikes of some species are used for perfume, aromatic oil, soap, sachets, medicine, and flavoring. Narrow, aromatic blue-green or gray-green foliage is a hallmark.

Unfortunately, the South's hot, humid climate and heavy soils don't suit most lavenders at all. English lavender (*L. angustifolia*), considered by many the most desirable species, is also the most problematic in Southern gardens. Poor drainage, wet winters, and high humidity often lead to rot and quick demise. Success depends on planting in gravelly, fast-draining soil that contains few nutrients. Do not fertilize. To reduce humidity around plants, mulch with gravel. To keep plants neat and compact, shear back by one-third to one-half every year just after bloom. If they become woody and open in the center, remove a few of the oldest branches; take out more when new growth comes. Deer do not care for lavender.

To dry flowers for sachets and potpourri, cut the spikes or strip blossoms from stems just as they show color; dry in a cool, shady place. Dried flowers can also be used to add a fresh scent to water or soap. Dried spikes make fragrant wreaths, swags, and wands. To flavor ice cream, pastries, and salads, use fresh flowers of *L. angustifolia* and *L. ×intermedia* selections; other species contain toxic chemicals that should not be ingested.

Because lavenders have been cultivated for centuries and tend to interbreed, many selections and hybrids have arisen. Names are often confused, so some of the names that follow may not agree with those you see on nursery labels. Be aware that only cutting-grown plants are uniform; seed-grown strains vary in color and growth habit.

L. angustifolia (L. officinalis, L. spica, L. vera). ENGLISH LAVENDER. Zones US, MS, LS; 9–4. This is the sweetly fragrant lavender used for perfume and sachets. Common name notwithstanding, it is native to southern Europe. It's the hardiest, most widely planted species. Most selections are low growing, forming mounds of foliage from 8 in. to 2 ft. high and wide. Narrow, smooth-edged, gray-green or silvery gray leaves to 2 in. long. Unbranched flower stems rise 4–12 in. above foliage, topped with 1- to 4-in.-long spikes of flowers in white, pink, lavender blue, or various shades of purple. Blooms mainly from early to midsummer, but some selections repeat in late summer or fall. Named selections include the following.

'Alba'. To 1½–2 ft. high and wide. Pure white flowers, gray-green foliage.

'Blue Cushion'. To 1½ ft. tall, 2 ft. wide. Profuse bright violet-blue flowers above medium green foliage.

'Compacta'. To 1½ ft. high and wide; good dwarf hedge plant. Light violet flowers; gray-green leaves.

'England'. To 1 ft. high, 15 in. wide. Light violet-blue flowers; downy, silvery foliage.

'Gray Lady'. To 2 ft. tall and wide. Lavender-blue flowers; gray foliage.

'Hidcote'. The original had deep violet flowers and medium green leaves on a plant 1½–2 ft. tall. The plants sold under this name today are frequently grown from seed; they may bear gray foliage and/or vary in size from the original.

'Irene Doyle' ('Two Seasons Lavender'). To 1½–2 ft. high and wide, with gray-green leaves. Light violet flowers bloom in early summer and give a repeat performance in late summer.

'Jean Davis' ('Rosea'). To 1½–2 ft. high and wide. Pale lilac-pink flowers; gray-green foliage.

'Lavender Lady' ('Lady'). Seed-grown strain that blooms in 3 months from spring-sown seed. Gray-green foliage. Very short spikes of lavender-blue flowers on a plant 1–1½ ft. high and wide; some variation in flower color and growth habit.

'Martha Roderick'. Compact growth to 1½–2 ft. high and wide. Dense gray foliage. Bright violet-blue blossoms in great abundance from late spring to early summer.

'Melissa'. Dense, compact grower to 1½ ft. high and wide. Good pink flower color, fading to white in hottest sun. Gray-green leaves.

'Mitcham' ('Mitcham Grey'). Named for the former center of English perfume production. Semi-open habit to 2 ft. high and wide. Bright violet-blue flowers; gray foliage.

'Munstead'. The original is 1½ ft. tall, 2 ft. wide, with bright lavender-blue flowers and medium green foliage. Long bloomer; makes a good low hedge. Quite variable when grown from seed.

'Nana' ('Dwarf Blue'). Slow growing to 1 ft. high, 16 in. wide. Stiff lavender-blue flower spikes in midsummer; gray foliage. Ideal for rock garden or edging. Somewhat hardier than most other English lavenders.

'Nana Alba'. White-flowered version of 'Nana'.

'Sharon Roberts'. Semi-open growth a little over 2 ft. high and to 2 ft. wide. Profuse show of bright violet-blue flowers begins in late spring, often repeats in fall. Medium green to gray-green foliage.

'Skylark'. To 20 in. high and wide. Deep violet-blue spikes in profusion; gray-green foliage.

'Twickel Purple'. To 2–2½ ft. high, 3 ft. wide. Heavy, dense spikes of light violet flowers on long, wiry stems, fanning out around an open mound of gray-green foliage.

L. dentata. FRENCH LAVENDER, TOOTHED LAVENDER. Zones LS, CS; 9–4. To 3–4 ft. tall, 4–6 ft. wide. Narrow green or gray-green leaves are 1½ in. long, ½ in. wide, with square-toothed edges. Purple flowers in short, rounded spikes, each topped with a pair of flaglike bracts that look like rabbit ears. Long spring-into-summer flowering period; almost year-round in mild-winter areas. Takes humidity better than *L. angustifolia*. Should be treated as a tender perennial in Upper, Middle, and Lower South; pot up and bring indoors for winter. 'Linda Ligon' has smaller leaves with irregular creamy white variegation. *L. d. candicans* ('French Gray') has grayer, somewhat larger leaves than the species, with dense grayish white down on young foliage.

L. ×intermedia. LAVANDIN, HEDGE LAVENDER. Zones US, MS, LS; 9–4. This group of sterile hybrids between parents *L. angustifolia* and *L. latifolia* is distinguished from English lavender by larger growth and by branching stems topped with interrupted flower spikes; blooms from mid- to late summer. Long used in the perfume and soap industries, lavandins are vigorous, fragrant plants, almost as hardy as *L. angustifolia* and more tolerant of warm, humid summers. They include the following selections.

'Abrialii'. Once the mainstay of the French lavender oil industry. Grows to 2½ ft. high, 3 ft. wide, with gray-green foliage. Dark violet-blue blossoms in narrow, conical, 3½- to 5-in.-long spikes are excellent for drying.

'Alba' ('White Spikes'). To 2½ ft. high and wide, with silvery leaves. Spikes of white blossoms and sage green calyxes are 1½–2 in. long, bloom from early summer through fall. Becomes woody with age.

'Dutch' ('Hortensis'). To 3 ft. tall and 2–2½ ft. wide, with gray foliage. Few-branched stems topped with narrow, conical, 2- to 3-in. spikes of flowers in deep blue violet. Most common selection in U.S.

'Fred Boutin'. To 3–4 ft. tall and wide. Dense, silvery gray foliage topped in early to midsummer with 1½- to 3-in.-long spikes of violet-blue blossoms on unbranched stems.

'Grappenhall'. To 3 ft. tall and wide (or larger). Profuse, slightly fragrant, blue-violet flower spikes; green foliage.

'Grey Hedge'. To 3 ft. or more in height and width. Dense foliage in a very silvery gray; profuse lavender-blue flowers on few-branched stems. Makes an excellent rounded or square-sheared hedge; set plants 2 ft. apart.

'Grosso' ('Fat Spike'). Widely planted commercial variety in France and Italy; possibly the most fragrant lavandin of all. Compact growth to 2½ ft. high and wide. Silvery foliage; large (to 3½-in.-long), conical spikes of violet-blue flowers with darker calyxes. Often gives repeat bloom in late summer. Excellent flower for drying.

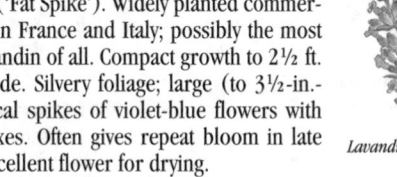

Lavandula × intermedia
'Grosso'

'Hidcote Giant'. To 2½ ft. high and 3 ft. wide, with gray-green foliage. Stout stems topped by fat spikes of vivid violet-blue flowers.

'Provence'. Though it is often described as a traditional perfume lavandin, this selection does not produce the kind of oil that is used in perfumery. Grows to 2 ft. high, 3 ft. wide, with fragrant light violet flower spikes that dry well. Good hedge plant.

'Super'. Superb, sweet perfume, close to that of *L. angustifolia*; yields high-quality essential oil. To 3 ft. high and wide, with gray-green foliage. Lavender-blue flower spikes on long, graceful, laterally branched stems.

L. latifolia (L. spica). SPIKE LAVENDER, BROADLEAF LAVENDER. Zones US, MS, LS; 8–1. Compact growth to 3 ft. tall and 1½–2 ft. wide, with gray-green leaves to 3 in. long, ¼ in. wide; resembles *L. angustifolia*. Slender, widely branching flower stems support interrupted spikes 1½–4 in. long; blossoms range from soft mauve to bright violet blue, with woolly gray calyxes tipped in violet. Blooms in late summer.

L. stoechas. SPANISH LAVENDER. Zones MS, LS, CS; 9–6. Includes several subspecies, all stocky plants 1½–3 ft. tall and wide, with narrow gray or gray-green, ½- to 1-in.-long leaves. Small flowers are typically blackish

L

maroon, borne on short, fat, 2-in. spikes topped by two to four flaglike bracts resembling rabbit ears; bracts come in assorted shades of purple and pink. Blossoms open first in four vertical rows, evenly spaced around the spike; then rest of spike fills in with flowers. Blooms from spring into summer; often repeats if sheared. Flower stem length varies from 1½ in. to 8 in. or more. Very drought resistant. Takes heat and humidity better than other species; best choice for Lower and Coastal South. Seeds profusely; can be invasive. Named forms include the following.

Lavandula stoechas
'Otto Quast'

L. s. leucantha (*L. s.* 'Snowman'). To 1½–2 ft. high and wide, with pale gray-green foliage and stems. White flowers and creamy white bracts with green veining.

'Otto Quast' ('Quasti'). To 2 ft. high or a bit more, 2½–3½ ft. wide. Flower stems 2–3 in. long, with maroon blossoms and red-purple bracts. Medium green to gray-green leaves. Plants sold under this name are usually grown from seed and often are shorter than the plant just described, with shorter flower stalks.

L. s. pedunculata. Taller than other forms, with longer flower stems. Green or gray-green foliage. Its selection 'Atlas' grows 2½–3 ft. tall, about as wide, with 7- to 14-in. flower stalks and vibrant red-violet bracts.

'Willow Vale'. Vigorous, upright, to 1½ ft. tall and wide. Wispy gray-green leaves; deep blue-violet flowers and bluish purple bracts. Short (1- to 2-in.) flower stems.

'Wings of Night'. Heavy bloomer resembles 'Otto Quast' but has a broader habit.

LAVATERA

TREE MALLOW

Malvaceae

ANNUALS AND EVERGREEN SHRUBS

✎ ZONES VARY BY SPECIES

☼ FULL SUN, EXCEPT AS NOTED

💧 REGULAR WATER

Lavatera trimestris
'Mont Rose'

Offering colorful single flowers throughout the summer, these easy-to-grow plants resemble their cousins, the hollyhocks (*Alcea*). Use them in the back of the border, in combination with other annuals and perennials.

L. maritima (**L. bicolor**). Evergreen shrub. Zones LS; 9–5. Native to western Mediterranean. Grows quickly to 6–8 ft. tall and 4 ft. wide, with gray-green, 2½-in. maplelike leaves and a summerlong show of light pink, 2- to 3-in. flowers with dark rose veining and a deep purple center. Open grower; cut back hard to keep it compact. Needs partial to full shade.

L. thuringiaca. Evergreen shrub. Zones US, MS, LS; 9–5. Native to central and southeastern Europe. Resembles *L. maritima* but has denser growth, greener leaves. Flowers are purplish pink, 3 in. across, nearly everblooming (except in colder-winter zones). 'Barnsley' has lighter pink flowers with deep pink centers. 'Rosea' has pink blossoms.

L. trimestris. ANNUAL MALLOW. Annual. Zones US, MS, LS, CS, TS; 12–1. Mediterranean native reaches 3–6 ft. tall and wide from spring-sown seed. Satiny flowers to 4 in. wide. Species is seldom seen in gardens; more commonly grown are named selections with blossoms in white, pink, or rosy carmine. Bloom extends from midsummer until frost if spent flowers are removed to halt seed production. Thin seedlings to allow each plant ample room to spread. Makes a colorful, fast-growing summer hedge or background planting. In mild-winter regions, can also be sown in autumn for winter-to-spring bloom. Compact (2- to 3-ft.) selections include white 'Mont Blanc', rose pink 'Mont Rose', and bright pink 'Silver Cup'. 'Ruby Regis', to 2 ft. high and wide, has 3½-in. flowers of deep rose veined in a deeper shade. 'Loveliness' has similar blossoms but grows 3–4 ft. tall and wide.

LEEK

Liliaceae

BIENNIAL GROWN AS COOL-SEASON ANNUAL

✎ US, MS, LS, CS, TS ⵜ 7–1

☼ ◐ PARTIAL SHADE IN HOTTEST CLIMATES

💧 REGULAR WATER

Leek

Botanically speaking, the leek is *Allium porrum*, an onion relative. Unlike onions, though, leeks don't form a distinct bulb. Plants grow 2–3 ft. tall; edible, mild-flavored stem resembles long, fat, green onion. Leeks need very rich soil. Plant them to grow and mature in cool weather. In most areas, fall planting is best. Sow seed or set out transplants. Leeks are quite cold hardy and can overwinter in ground; in fact, cold temperatures improve flavor. When plants have considerable top growth, mound up soil around fat, round stems to blanch them white. Harvest when stem bases are 1–2½ in. in diameter. Offsets may be detached and replanted. If leeks bloom, small bulbils may appear in flower clusters; plant these for later harvest. Leeks are free of many of the pests and diseases that attack onions.

LEONOTIS

LION'S TAIL, LION'S EAR

Lamiaceae (Labiatae)

ANNUALS AND TENDER SHRUBS

✎ ZONES VARY BY SPECIES

☼ FULL SUN

◊ LITTLE OR NO WATER

Leonotis leonurus

These showy members of the mint family include both annuals and tender shrubs. Most are native to South Africa. Fuzzy, square stems carry opposite pairs of narrow, pointed, toothed, 2- to 5-in.-long leaves. Bloom comes from summer through fall, when dense, ball-shaped, whorled flower clusters to 4 in. across appear at regular intervals up and down the stems. Each cluster is composed of deep orange, tubular, 2-in. flowers that are covered with fine hairs. The plants attract butterflies and hummingbirds; deer don't seem to care for them.

L. leonurus. LION'S TAIL. Zones CS, TS; 12–6. Semievergreen shrub, often grown as a tender perennial. One of the first South African plants brought back to Europe for cultivation. Grows 4–6 ft. tall and wide. Tolerates drought and salt spray. Needs good drainage; be careful not to overwater. Tends to get leggy and bare at the stem bases; to curb this tendency, prune back fairly hard in spring. Hardy in warmer parts of Lower South but loses its leaves after a frost. 'Harrismith White' has white flowers.

L. menthifolia. MINT-LEAFED LION'S TAIL. Zones LS, CS, TS; 12–8. Evergreen shrub, often grown as a tender perennial. To 3–5 ft. tall and wide. Resembles *L. leonurus* but is smaller and doesn't lose its foliage near the base.

L. nepetifolia. ANNUAL LION'S TAIL. Annual. Zones US, MS, LS, CS, TS; 12–6. Upright, gangly plant for the back of the border; may reach 8 ft. tall and 5 ft. wide in a single season. Rounded, spiny flower clusters are hummingbird magnets. Reseeds readily and has naturalized in warm-climate areas throughout the world, where it rapidly colonizes disturbed areas.

L. 'Staircase'. Annual. Zones US, MS, LS, CS, TS. Like *L. nepetifolia* but with larger leaves and flowers.

LEOPARD PLANT. See FARFUGIUM japonicum 'Aureomaculatum'

LEOPARD'S BANE. See DORONICUM

LEPTOSPERMUM scoparium

NEW ZEALAND TEA TREE

Myrtaceae

EVERGREEN SHRUB

☀ CS, TS ☵ 12–3

☼ FULL SUN

◊ ◖ LITTLE TO MODERATE WATER

Leptospermum scoparium
'Ruby Glow'

This is one of those choice plants that Southerners wish they could grow as well as folks do out West. A compact, rounded, evergreen shrub hailing from Australia and New Zealand, it features aromatic, needlelike leaves and a profusion of small summertime flowers that resemble little roses. Not browsed by deer.

Unfortunately, New Zealand tea tree's use in much of South is limited by poorly drained soils, high humidity, and summer downpours. Success depends on planting in fertile, fast-draining soil. Try mulching with gravel to reduce humidity around plant. Does better in containers than it does in the ground. Selections include 'Gaiety Girl' (double pink flowers and reddish foliage, 5 ft. tall and 4 ft. wide); 'Ruby Glow' (double red flowers and reddish foliage, 6–8 ft. tall and 4–5 ft. wide); and 'Snow White' (double white flowers and green foliage, 2–4 ft. high and 4–5 ft. wide).

LESPEDEZA thunbergii

SHRUB BUSH CLOVER

Fabaceae (Leguminosae)

DECIDUOUS PERENNIAL OR SHRUB

☀ US, MS, LS ☵ 8–5

☼ FULL SUN

◊ ◖ LITTLE TO MODERATE WATER

Lespedeza thunbergii
'Gibraltar'

Late summer flowers from a shrub are rare—but this one fills the void. It forms a spreading, fountain-shaped mass 6 ft. tall and 10 ft. wide, with arching branches clothed in blue-green leaves composed of three leaflets. Drooping, 6-in. clusters of showy, sweet pea–shaped flowers appear in late summer and fall. Tolerates hot, dry conditions and infertile soil. Good drainage is a must. Cut plant to within a few inches of the

ground in late winter; it will regrow rapidly and bear multitudes of blooms on the new growth. Recommended selections include white-flowered 'Avalanche', with cascading habit; purple-and-white 'Edo-Shibori'; rosy purple 'Gibraltar'; pink 'Pink Fountain', with cascading habit; and white-blossomed 'White Fountain', with weeping form.

LETTUCE

Asteraceae (Compositae)

COOL-SEASON ANNUAL

☀ US, MS, LS, CS, TS ☵ 7–1

☼ ◖ PARTIAL SHADE IN COASTAL AND TROPICAL SOUTH

◖ REGULAR WATER

Lettuce

Classified botanically as *Lactuca sativa*. A short browse through a seed catalog, seed display rack, or selection of nursery seedlings will reveal enough variety to keep your salad bowl crisp and colorful throughout the growing season. There are four principal types of lettuce: crisphead, butterhead or Boston, loose-leaf, and romaine.

Crisphead is the most exasperating for home gardeners to produce. Heads form best with monthly average temperatures of 55–60°F. Best selections include 'Great Lakes', 'Nevada', and 'Summertime'. 'Rosy' is a small crisphead with reddish burgundy leaves.

Butterhead or Boston type has a loose head with green, smooth outer leaves and yellow inner leaves. Good choices include 'Bibb' ('Limestone'), 'Buttercrunch', and 'Tom Thumb'. 'Mignonette' ('Manoa') stands heat without bolting to seed. 'Tennis Ball' is an heirloom Boston type with small, loose heads. 'Key Lime' is another heirloom that is larger than most butterheads and resists bolting.

Loose-leaf lettuce makes a rosette rather than a head. It stands heat better than other types. Choice selections are 'Black-seeded Simpson', 'Green Ice', and 'Oak Leaf' (all with green leaves); 'Salad Bowl' (with deeply cut green leaves); and 'Prizehead' and 'Ruby' (red-tinged leaves).

Romaine lettuce has an erect, cylindrical head of smooth leaves; outer leaves are green, inner ones yellowish. Stands heat moderately well. Try 'Medallion', 'Olga', or 'Parris Island'.

Lettuces with bronzy to pinkish red leaves add color to a salad. 'Freckles', 'Marveille des Quatre Saisons', and 'Perella Red' are butterheads; 'Lollo Rosso', 'Red Oak Leaf', 'Red Sails', and 'Ruby' are loose-leaf selections; 'Rouge d'Hiver' and 'Sierra' are romaines.

Various loose-leaf and romaine lettuces are typically included in mesclun mixes—mixtures of fast-growing, tender salad greens (usually some mild and some tangy) that may include mustards, arugula, cress, chicory, radicchio, and/or mizuna.

All lettuces need loose, well-drained soil. Sow in open ground; barely cover seeds. Loose-leaf lettuce can be grown as close as 4 in. apart; thin all other types to 1 ft. apart. Grow mesclun in blocks 4 in. wide and don't thin.

For prolonged harvest, sow at 2-week intervals. In Upper South, begin sowing seed for all types after frost, as soon as soil is workable. In the Coastal and Tropical South, plant in fall or winter for harvest in winter and early spring.

Feed plants lightly and frequently. Control snails, slugs, earwigs. Harvest when heads or leaves are of good size; once lettuce reaches maturity, it rapidly goes to seed, becoming quite bitter. Snip off young leaves of mesclun mix for salads.

LET US PICK LETTUCE. *With loose-leaf lettuce you get three opportunities to harvest over a long period. Use the thinnings for salads; clip off just the outer leaves as you need them; finally, when bloom stalks just begin to grow, pull up whole plants.* ❖

LEUCAENA retusa

GOLDEN BALL LEAD TREE

Fabaceae (Leguminosae)

EVERGREEN OR DECIDUOUS SHRUB OR TREE

✄ MS, LS, CS

☀ FULL SUN

◐ ⬖ LITTLE TO MODERATE WATER

Leucaena retusa

Native to Texas, northern Mexico. Grows 12–20 ft. tall and wide, with light green leaves twice divided into many tiny leaflets. Showy spring flowers are fluffy yellow balls 1 in. across; they are followed by flattened, beanlike pods 6–10 in. long. Useful tree for mini-oasis or transition between cultivated garden and native desert. Good choice for small patio tree. Evergreen in milder winters; deciduous otherwise.

LEUCANTHEMELLA serotina. SEE CHRYSANTHEMUM serotinum

LEUCANTHEMUM. See CHRYSANTHEMUM

LEUCOJUM

SNOWFLAKE

Amaryllidaceae

PERENNIALS FROM BULBS

✄ ZONES VARY BY SPECIES

☀ ◔ FULL SUN DURING BLOOM; LIGHT SHADE AFTER

⬖ REGULAR WATER DURING GROWTH AND BLOOM

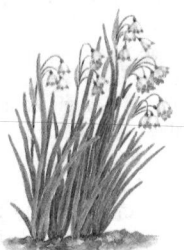

Leucojum aestivum

Native to Europe. Easy-to-grow perennial with dark green, strap-shaped leaves and nodding, bell-shaped, white flowers with segments tipped green. Naturalize under deciduous trees, in shrub borders or orchards, or on cool slopes. Plant bulbs in fall, setting them 4 in. deep and 3 in. apart. Do not disturb until really crowded; then dig, divide, and replant after foliage dies down.

L. aestivum. SUMMER SNOWFLAKE. Zones US, MS, LS, CS; 9–1. One of the classic passalong bulbs of the South, shared by gardeners for centuries. Often seen in cemeteries and on old home sites. Named "summer snowflake" by gardeners in Europe, where it blooms in summer and has been cultivated since 1594. Leaves are 1–1½ ft. long; stems grow 1½ ft. tall, each carrying three to five 1-in. flowers. 'Gravetye Giant' is a bit taller and larger flowered than the species; it has as many as nine flowers per stem.

Summer snowflake doesn't need much winter chill to bloom well; it even blooms dependably as far south as central Florida. In the Coastal South, flowers come from late fall through winter; elsewhere, expect bloom in late winter and early spring, with early daffodils.

L. vernum. SPRING SNOWFLAKE. Zones US, MS, LS; 8–3. Much less common than *L. aestivum* and less tolerant of mild winters. Leaves are 9 in. long. In earliest spring, each foot-long stem bears a single large white flower (occasionally two per stem).

LEUCOPHYLLUM

TEXAS RANGER, SILVERLEAF

Scrophulariaceae

EVERGREEN SHRUBS

✄ LS, CS, TS ⊞ 11–7

☀ FULL SUN

◐ ⬖ LITTLE TO MODERATE WATER

Leucophyllum frutescens

Native to the Southwest and northern Mexico, these compact, slow-growing shrubs are highly useful and attractive in desert gardens. Most have silvery foliage and a good show of ½- to

1-in.-wide flowers with an open bell shape. Flowering may occur at varying times of the year, often after summer showers. Need very good drainage. Tolerate heat, wind, and alkaline soil. Use as informal or clipped hedges, massed as tall ground cover, or in mixed dry-country gardens. Unless formally hedged, plants require little pruning. Old, leggy plants can be rejuvenated by cutting close to the ground.

L. candidum. VIOLET SILVERLEAF. To 5 ft. high and wide, with small (½-in.), silvery leaves and deep purple flowers. 'Silver Cloud' is a heavy bloomer with very white foliage. 'Thunder Cloud' is smaller than the species (to 3–4 ft. high and wide) and has deeper purple, more closely spaced blossoms.

L. frutescens. TEXAS RANGER, TEXAS SAGE, CENIZO. To 6–8 ft. tall and wide, with gray foliage and light purple flowers. 'Green Cloud' has bright green foliage and dark rose or magenta flowers; it may be deciduous in coldest winters. 'White Cloud' has gray foliage and white flowers. 'Compacta', with gray foliage and pink flowers, grows 5 ft. high and wide.

L. laevigatum. CHIHUAHUAN SAGE. Open, angular growth to 4 ft. tall, 5 ft. wide. Tiny dark green leaves; profuse lavender flowers.

L. langmaniae. Dense grower to 5 ft. high and wide, with bright green leaves and lavender flowers.

L. pruinosum. Open growth habit to 6 ft. tall and wide, with silvery foliage. Purple flowers have a strong fragrance of grape bubble gum.

L. 'Rain Cloud'. Hybrid derived from *L. frutescens*. Erect growth to 6 ft. tall, 3–4 ft. wide. Small, silvery leaves; violet-blue flowers.

L. revolutum. Slow growth to about 4 ft. tall, 4–5 ft. wide, with light green, somewhat succulent foliage. Bears purple flowers that appear in fall, later than for other leucophyllums. 'Houdini' has larger, showier blossoms than the species.

L. zygophyllum. To 3 ft. tall and wide, with gray-green, cupped leaves and light blue flowers.

LEUCOTHOE

Ericaceae

EVERGREEN AND DECIDUOUS SHRUBS

✄ ZONES VARY BY SPECIES

◔ ● PARTIAL TO FULL SHADE

⬖ ⬖ WATER NEEDS VARY BY SPECIES

☘ LEAVES AND NECTAR ARE POISONOUS IF INGESTED

Leucothoe fontanesiana

Related to *Pieris*. All have leathery leaves and clusters of small, urn-shaped white flowers reminiscent of lily-of-the-valley (*Convallaria*). They need acid, woodsy, deep soil; do best in woodland gardens. Best used in masses, since they are not especially attractive individually. Bronze-tinted winter foliage is a bonus.

L. axillaris. COASTAL LEUCOTHOE. Evergreen. Zones US, MS, LS; 9–5. Native to southeastern U.S. Spreading, arching growth to 2–4 ft. tall, 3–6 ft. wide. Leathery leaves to 4 in. long are bronzy when new. Flower clusters, 1–3 in. long, droop along stems in spring. Regular water.

L. fontanesiana (L. catesbaei, L. walteri). DROOPING LEUCOTHOE. Evergreen. Zones US, MS; 7–5. Native to southeastern U.S. Slow grower to 2–6 ft. high and wide; branches arch gracefully. Leathery, 3- to 6-in.-long leaves turn bronzy purple in fall (bronzy green in deep shade). Spreads from underground stems. Blooms in spring, bearing drooping clusters of slightly fragrant flowers. 'Rainbow' grows 3–4 ft. high, has leaves marked yellow, green, and pink. 'Lovita' is also smaller than the species (2 ft. tall, 4 ft. wide), with smaller, darker green leaves that turn mahogany red in winter. 'Scarletta' is similar in size to 'Lovita'; its leaves are brilliant red on expanding, deep green in summer, and deep red in late fall and winter.

The species and its selections take regular water. You can control the plants' height to make a 1½-ft. ground cover in shade; just cut older, taller stems to ground. Blooming branches make decorative cut flowers. Where summers are hot and humid, various leaf spot diseases can cause serious disfiguration or defoliation.

L

L. populifolia. See Agarista populifolia

L. racemosa. SWEETBELLS. Deciduous. Zones US, MS, LS, CS; 9–3. Native to southeastern U.S. Grows 3–8 ft. tall and wide, with 3-in. leaves that turn red before dropping from their red stems in autumn. Flowers in one-sided, 3-in. clusters at ends of branches in late spring or early summer. A pink-flowering form is available. Moderate water.

LEVISTICUM officinale

LOVAGE

Apiaceae (Umbelliferae)

PERENNIAL

US, MS, LS ⫶ 8–1

☼ ◑ LIGHT AFTERNOON SHADE IN HOTTEST CLIMATES

◐ REGULAR WATER

Levisticum officinale

From the eastern Mediterranean region. Ornamental herb with divided, glossy deep green leaves to 2½ ft. long. Hollow stems rise from the foliage clumps in summer, crowned by sprays of flat-topped, greenish yellow flower clusters. Flowering plants may reach 6 ft. tall under ideal conditions, but more usual size is 3 ft. high and wide. Plant has a history of culinary uses: seeds are valued for their celery flavor, leaves are added to salads and soups. Grow from seeds sown in place in fall; or start seeds in containers and transplant into garden in spring. You can also divide an established clump in early spring. Volunteer seedlings are another source of extra plants.

LEYLAND CYPRESS. See × CUPRESSOCYPARIS leylandii

LEYMUS arenarius

BLUE LYME GRASS

Poaceae (Gramineae)

PERENNIAL GRASS

US, MS, LS, CS ⫶ 10–1

☼ ◑ FULL SUN OR LIGHT SHADE

◊ ◐ LITTLE TO MODERATE WATER

Leymus arenarius

Formerly known as *Elymus arenarius* 'Glaucus', this Eurasian dune grass is the bluest ornamental grass of all. It is stunning as a 2- to 3-ft.-tall specimen in a flower border or when massed and used as a ground cover. Flowers are inconspicuous. Given moist, fertile soil, it spreads aggressively by rhizomes and can be invasive; better behaved in dry soils and heavy clay. Tolerates heat, drought, sandy soil, and salt spray. Good plant for the beach or in containers. Mow or cut back in late winter to stimulate fresh new blue growth. 'Findhorn' is a compact selection. 'Blue Dune' has especially bright blue foliage.

LIATRIS

BLAZING STAR, GAYFEATHER

Asteraceae (Compositae)

PERENNIALS

US, MS, LS, CS

☼ FULL SUN

◊ ◐ MODERATE TO REGULAR WATER

Liatris spicata

Showy plants native to the eastern and central U.S. Basal tufts of narrow, grassy leaves grow from thick, often tuberous rootstocks. In summer or early fall, the tufts lengthen into tall stems densely set with slender leaves and topped by a narrow plume of small, fluffy purple (sometimes white) flower heads. Flowers of most species are unusual in opening from top of spike downward. Choice cut flowers; attract butterflies. Not usually favored by browsing deer.

These plants endure heat, cold, drought, and poor soil. Fertilizing will give you larger flower spikes, but it also results in taller plants that need staking. Best used in mixed perennial borders, although the rosy purple color calls for careful placing to avoid color clashes.

L. callilepis. Plants grown and sold by Dutch bulb growers under this name are *L. spicata* (see below).

L. ligulistylis. ROCKY MOUNTAIN BLAZING STAR. Grows 3–5 ft. tall and 1½ ft. wide, with reddish purple flowers that open from dark red buds.

L. microcephala. Only 1–2 ft. tall and up to 1 ft. across, with rosy purple flowers. Try this small blazing star in rock gardens or as a ground cover in hot, dry areas.

L. mucronata. BOTTLEBRUSH BLAZING STAR. To 3 ft. tall and 1 ft. wide. Rosy purple spikes. Tolerates dry, limy soils, providing drainage is good.

L. pycnostachya. KANSAS BLAZING STAR. To 3–5 ft. tall, 1–2 ft. wide, with bright purple flowers. Likes some moisture but tolerates drought.

L. scariosa. TALL BLAZING STAR. To 2–3 ft. high, 1½ ft. wide. Reddish purple flowers. Differs from most other blazing stars in that its blossoms open nearly all at once; also prefers somewhat drier soil than most. 'September Glory' is taller than the species (to 4–5 ft.); 'White Spire' is similar but has white flowers.

L. spicata. SPIKE BLAZING STAR. Heat zones 9–1. To 5 ft. tall and 1½ ft. wide, with light purple blossoms tightly clustered in dense spikes. Lower-growing selections include white-flowered 'Alba' (3–4 ft. tall); 'Floristan White' (2–3 ft.), with profuse white blossom spikes that are good for cutting; 'Kobold' (2–2½ ft., needs no staking), with deeper purple blooms than the species; and 'Silvertips' (2½–3 ft.), bearing lavender flowers with a silvery finish.

L. squarrosa. SCALY BLAZING STAR. Heat zones 9–3. To 2–3 ft. tall and 1 ft. wide. Bears branched spikes of large red-purple flowers, with the top flower cluster larger than the lower ones.

LIBOCEDRUS. See CALOCEDRUS

LICORICE MINT. See AGASTACHE rupestris

LICORICE PLANT. See HELICHRYSUM petiolare

LIGULARIA

GOLDEN RAY

Asteraceae (Compositae)

PERENNIALS

US, MS, LS ⫶ 8–1, EXCEPT AS NOTED

◑ ● PARTIAL TO FULL SHADE

◖◗ AMPLE MOISTURE

Ligularia stenocephala
'The Rocket'

These stately perennials from China and Japan form 3-ft.-wide clumps of large leaves topped by daisy-type flowers in yellow to orange. All need rich soil, plenty of moisture, and some shade; they do not tolerate low humidity or hot afternoon sun. Good around pools, along streambeds, in bog gardens. Control slugs and snails. Clumps can remain undisturbed for years; if more plants are needed, divide clumps in early spring.

L. dentata. Grown primarily for big, attractive leaves (to more than a foot across), roundish with a heart-shaped base. In midsummer to early fall, sends up 3- to 5-ft. stems holding large, branching heads of orange-yellow, 4-in.-wide daisies. 'Othello' and 'Desdemona' have deep purple leafstalks, veins, and leaf undersides; upper surfaces of leaves are green.

L. 'Gregynog Gold'. Clump of 14-in.-wide, heart-shaped, tooth-edged leaves sends up stems to 6 ft. tall. In late summer and fall, stems bear conical clusters of 4-in. yellow flowers.

L. przewalskii. Deeply lobed and cut leaves grow to 1 ft. wide. Dark purplish blossom stalks rise to about 6 ft. and are loaded with dense, narrow spires of ¾-in. yellow flowers in summer.

L

▶

L. stenocephala. Especially stunning flower spikes. Usually represented by its selection 'The Rocket', which forms a large clump of footwide, irregularly toothed leaves topped by tall (up to 5-ft.), narrow, dark-stemmed spires bearing many 1½-in. yellow daisies in summer.

L. tussilaginea. See Farfugium japonicum

L. wilsoniana. GIANT GROUNDSEL. Heat zones 8–4. Bears kidney-shaped leaves that reach 20 in. wide. Stems grow to 6 ft. tall, carry spikes of inch-wide yellow daisies in summer.

LIGUSTRUM

PRIVET

Oleaceae

EVERGREEN, SEMIEVERGREEN, DECIDUOUS SHRUBS AND TREES

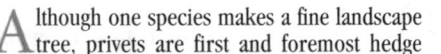 ZONES VARY BY SPECIES

☼ ◐ FULL SUN OR PARTIAL SHADE, EXCEPT AS NOTED

◖ REGULAR WATER

◊ LEAVES AND FRUITS CAUSE GASTRIC DISTRESS IF INGESTED

Ligustrum lucidum

Although one species makes a fine landscape tree, privets are first and foremost hedge plants. They take well to shearing and can be clipped into almost any shape. In spring or early summer, all bear abundant clusters of showy, white to creamy white flowers that are highly fragrant. Some people don't care for the cloyingly sweet scent—and the pollen may cause allergic reactions. Bees and wasps also swarm to the flowers. Clipped hedges produce fewer flowers, as shearing removes most of the flower buds. Blossoms are followed by small, berrylike blue-black fruits. Birds eat them and distribute the seeds everywhere—with the result that seedlings come up everywhere, too. Since most privets will grow well in any kind of soil, vigilance is required to keep them from taking over. Most make good container subjects. They are resistant to damage by browsing deer.

Privets are frequently mislabeled. The plant sold as *L. japonicum* often turns out to be the tree species *L. lucidum*. The true *L. japonicum* is available in two or more forms; the tall, shrubby kind is the plain species, while the lower-growing and more densely foliaged form is *L. japonicum* 'Texanum' (often sold as *L. texanum*). Smaller-leafed privets used for hedging are often confused as well. *L. amurense, L. ovalifolium, L. sinense,* and *L. vulgare* look much alike, and any of these is likely to be sold as "common privet"—a name that rightly belongs only to *L. vulgare*.

L. amurense. AMUR PRIVET. Deciduous shrub. Zone US, MS; 8–1. Native to northern China. To 15 ft. high and wide. Widely used for hedge and screen planting. Much like *L. ovalifolium* in appearance, but foliage is less glossy.

L. japonicum. JAPANESE PRIVET. Evergreen shrub. Zones MS, LS, CS, TS; 12–7. From northern China, Korea, Japan. Dense, compact growth to 10–12 ft. tall, 8 ft. wide, but can be kept smaller by trimming. Roundish oval leaves are 2–4 in. long, dark to medium green and glossy above, distinctly paler to almost whitish beneath; they have a thick, slightly spongy feel. Excellent plant for hedges or screens or for shaping into small trees. In caliche soil or where Texas root rot prevails, grow it in containers. Often confused with its selection 'Texanum'.

'Howard' ('Howardii Frazieri'). Two-tone shrub: leaves are yellow when new, aging to green. Both colors are usually present at once.

'Recurvifolium'. Leaves are wavy edged, twisted at the tip, and slightly smaller than those of the species. Somewhat open grower.

'Rotundifolium' ('Coriaceum'). ROUNDLEAF JAPANESE PRIVET. Grows 4–5 ft. high; has nearly round leaves to 2½ in. long. Partial shade.

'Silver Star'. Grows 6–8 ft. high. Deep green leaves have gray-green mottling and startling creamy white edges. Provides a good contrast to solid deep green foliage.

'Texanum'. Similar to the species but grows a little smaller (to 8–10 ft. tall, 4–6 ft. wide), with somewhat denser, lusher foliage. Useful as windbreak. Often sold as *L. texanum*.

'Variegatum'. Leaves have creamy white margins and blotches.

L. lucidum. GLOSSY PRIVET. Evergreen tree. Zones LS, CS, TS; 12–8. Native to China, Korea, Japan. Makes a round-headed tree that eventually reaches 35–40 ft. high and wide. Can be kept lower as a big shrub or may form multitrunked tree. Glossy, 4- to 6-in.-long leaves are tapered and pointed, dark to medium green on both sides. They feel leathery but lack the slightly spongy feel of *L. japonicum* leaves. Flowers in especially large, feathery clusters are followed by a profusion of fruit. Fine lawn tree. Can grow in narrow areas; good street tree if not planted near pavement or where fruit will drop on cars (see disadvantages noted below). Performs well in large containers. Or set 10 ft. apart for tall privacy screen. Useful as windbreak.

Before planting this tree, carefully weigh the advantages against the disadvantages. Eventual fruit crop is immense; never plant where fruits will fall on cars, walks, or other paved areas (they stain). Fallen seeds (and those dropped by birds) sprout profusely in ground cover and will need pulling. Fruiting clusters are bare and unattractive after fruit drop.

L. ovalifolium. CALIFORNIA PRIVET. Semievergreen shrub. Zones US, MS, LS; 8–6. Native to Japan. Dark green, oval, 2½-in.-long leaves. Grows rapidly to 15 ft. but can be kept to any height; reaches 10 ft. wide. For use as hedge, set plants 9–12 in. apart; clip early and frequently for low, dense branching. Be prepared for regular maintenance; you may need to shear every 3 weeks in hot, wet weather. Well-fed, well-watered plants hold their leaves the longest.

This species is a good choice for a fast-growing hedge or screen, but be aware of disadvantages: the plant has greedy roots, its seedlings come up everywhere, and once established, it is hard to eradicate.

'Aureum'. YELLOW-EDGE CALIFORNIA PRIVET, GOLDEN PRIVET. Leaves have broad yellow edges. Often sold as 'Variegatum'.

L. sinense. CHINESE PRIVET. Evergreen shrub. Zones MS, LS, CS, TS; 12–6. From China. To 10–15 ft. tall and wide. Avoid planting the plain species, which has become a horrible weed in the Southeast, conquering woodlands and stream banks. It tolerates just about any conditions and is known to pop up through cracks in the pavement. Hard to kill, but worth the effort required to annihilate it. The following two selections are better behaved.

'Pendulum'. WEEPING CHINESE PRIVET. To 10 ft. high and wide, with billowing, cascading branches that create a soft, cloudlike appearance. Branches occasionally revert to upright form; cut these out to maintain pleasing shape.

'Variegatum'. VARIEGATED CHINESE PRIVET. Heat zones 12–4. Grows quickly to 6 ft. tall and wide. One of the better-looking variegated plants, popular for its handsome matte green leaves with creamy white margins. Useful for brightening dull areas of the garden. Cut out any branches with leaves that revert to solid green.

L. 'Suwannee River'. Evergreen shrub. Zones MS, LS, CS, TS; 12–7. Reported to be a hybrid between *L. japonicum* 'Rotundifolium' and *L. lucidum*. Slow-growing, compact plant reaches 1½ ft. tall in 3 years, eventually grows 4–5 ft. high and wide. Leathery, somewhat twisted dark green leaves; no fruit. Use as low hedge, as foundation planting, in containers.

L. 'Vicaryi'. VICARY GOLDEN PRIVET. Deciduous shrub. Zones US, MS, LS, CS; 9–1. This one has yellow leaves; color is strongest on plants in full sun. To 4–6 ft. (possibly 12 ft.) high and 8–10 ft. wide. Best planted alone; color does not develop well under hedge shearing.

L. vulgare. COMMON PRIVET. Deciduous shrub. Zones US, MS, LS; 8–5. From northern Europe. Left unsheared, reaches 15 ft. tall, 12 ft. wide. Similar to *L. ovalifolium*, but roots are less greedy and leaves aren't as glossy. Conspicuous clusters of black fruit appear on unpruned or lightly pruned plants. 'Lodense' ('Nanum') is a densely foliaged dwarf that reaches only 4 ft. tall and wide.

LILAC. See SYRINGA

Liliaceae. The lily family contains hundreds of species of ornamental plants, as well as vegetables such as asparagus and the entire onion tribe. Most grow from bulbs, corms, or rhizomes. Flowers are often showy, usually with six petal-like segments of equal size.

LILIUM

LILY

Liliaceae

PERENNIALS FROM BULBS

US, MS, LS, CS **H** 9–1, EXCEPT AS NOTED

ROOTS COOL, TOPS IN SUN OR FILTERED LIGHT, EXCEPT AS NOTED

REGULAR WATER, EXCEPT AS NOTED

Lilium pumilum

Most stately and varied of bulbous plants. For many years, only the species—the same plants growing wild in parts of Asia, Europe, and North America—were available, and many of these were difficult and unpredictable. Around 1925, however, lily growers began a significant breeding program. They bred new hybrids from species with desirable qualities and also developed strains and selections that were healthier, hardier, and easier to grow than the original species. They produced new forms and new colors; what is more important, they developed the methods for growing healthy lilies in large quantities. Today, hybrids and strains are typically the best garden lilies, but it is still possible to get some desirable species.

Plant bulbs as soon as possible after you get them. If you must wait, keep them in a cool place until you plant. If bulbs are dry, place them in moist sand or peat moss until scales get plump and new roots begin to sprout.

Lilies need soil containing ample organic matter. If you want to plant in heavy clay or very sandy soil, add material such as peat moss, leaf mold, or composted ground bark. Spread a 3- to 4-in. layer of such material over the soil surface; broadcast a complete fertilizer (follow directions for pre-planting application) on top of it, then thoroughly till both into the soil to a depth of at least 1 ft.

Before planting bulbs, remove any injured portions; then dust cuts with sulfur or an antifungal seed and bulb disinfectant. For each bulb, dig a generous planting hole (6–12 in. deeper than height of the bulb). Place enough soil at bottom of hole to bring it up to proper level for bulb (see next paragraph). Set bulb with its roots spread; fill hole with soil, firming it around bulb to eliminate air pockets. If your area is infested with gophers, you may have to plant each bulb in a 6-in.-square wire basket made of ½-in. hardware cloth. (The depth of the basket will depend on the planting depth.)

Planting depths vary according to size and rooting habit of bulb. General rule is to cover smaller bulbs with 2–3 in. of soil, medium bulbs with 3–4 in., and larger bulbs with 4–6 in. (but never cover *L. candidum* bulbs with more than 1 in. of soil). Planting depth can be quite flexible. It's better to err on the side of too-shallow rather than too-deep planting, since lily bulbs have contractile roots that draw them down to the proper depth. Ideal spacing for lily bulbs is 1 ft. apart, but you can plant as close as 6 in. for densely massed effect.

Lilies need constant moisture; keep soil moist to about 6 in. deep. Reduce watering somewhat after tops turn yellow in fall, but never allow roots to dry out completely. (*L. candidum* is an exception to this rule.) Soaking is preferable to overhead watering, which may help to spread disease spores. Pull weeds by hand; hoeing may injure roots.

Wait until the stems and leaves turn yellow before you cut plants back. If clumps become too crowded, dig up, divide, and transplant them in spring or fall. If you're very careful, you can lift lily clumps at any time, even in bloom.

Lilies are fine container plants. Place one bulb in a deep 5- to 7-in. pot or five in a 14- to 16-in. pot. First, fill pot one-third full of potting mix. Then place bulb with roots spread and pointing downward; add about an inch of soil. Water thoroughly and place in greenhouse just warm enough to keep out frost. During root-forming period, keep soil moderately moist. When top growth appears, add more soil mixture and gradually fill pot as stems elongate. Leave 1-in. space between soil surface and pot rim for watering. Move pots onto partially shaded terrace or patio during blooming period. Later, you can repot bulbs in late fall or early spring.

Viral or mosaic infection is a problem. No cure exists. To avoid it, buy healthy bulbs from reliable sources. Dig and destroy any lilies that show

Lilium candidum

mottling in leaves or seriously stunted growth. Control aphids, which spread the infection. Control botrytis blight, a fungal disease, with chlorothalonil (Daconil).

Although the official classification of lilies lists eight divisions of hybrids and a ninth division of species, the following listings describe the lilies commonly available to Southern gardeners. Advances in breeding are producing lilies with forms, colors, and parentage hitherto considered unlikely, if not impossible. Consult specialists' catalogs to learn about these wonders, which are reaching the market faster than books can deal with them.

ASIATIC HYBRIDS

These are the easiest-to-grow, most reliable lilies for the average garden. Flowers are 6–8 in. long—upward facing in some types, horizontally held or drooping in others. Stems are strong, erect, and short (1½ ft.) to moderate (4½ ft.) in height. Colors range from white through yellow and orange to pink and red. Many have dark spots or contrasting "halos." They are the earliest to bloom (early summer). Examples are 'Enchantment', bearing orange-red blooms spotted with black; 'Impala', bright yellow; 'Lollipop', white with bright pink tips; 'Pink Floyd', creamy pink banded with rose pink; and 'Sancerre', unspotted pure white.

AURELIAN HYBRIDS

Derived from Asiatic species, excluding *L. auratum* and *L. speciosum*. They bear trumpet- or bowl-shaped, 6- to 8-in. flowers in midsummer. Flowers range from white and cream through yellow and pink; many show green, brown, or purple shading on their outer surfaces. Plants are 3–6 ft. tall, and each stem carries 12 to 20 flowers. Examples are 'Anaconda', coppery apricot; 'Black Dragon', white with maroon petal backs; 'Golden Splendour', yellow blooms from purple buds; and 'Thunderbolt', orange-apricot blossoms.

ORIENTAL HYBRIDS

The most exotic of the hybrids. Bloom from midsummer to early fall, with big (to 9-in.) fragrant flowers of white or pink, often spotted with gold and shaded or banded with red. Most are tall, with nodding flowers, but a few are dwarf and have upward-facing blooms. Examples are 'Casablanca', pure white; 'Le Rêve', soft lavender pink spotted with maroon; 'Pink Ribbons', light rose banded and spotted with deep rose; and 'Stargazer', rose red with white margins.

SPECIES AND VARIANTS

L. auratum. GOLD-BANDED LILY. Native to Japan. Sweetly fragrant white flowers to 5 in. long appear atop 4- to 6-ft. stems in summer. Petals feature reddish purple spots and a gold band along the midrib. ▶

TOP: Asiatic Hybrid Lily Mix
BOTTOM: *Lilium lancifolium*

TOP: Aurelian Hybrid Lily
'Golden Splendour'
BOTTOM: *Lilium longiflorum*

TOP: Oriental Hybrid Lily 'Casablanca'
BOTTOM: *Lilium martagon*

TOP: *Lilium philippinense*
BOTTOM: Asiatic Hybrid Lily
'Lollipop'

TOP: *Lilium henryi*
BOTTOM: *Lilium regale*

L. candidum. MADONNA LILY. Zones US, MS, LS, CS, TS; 10–6. Native to the Balkans and eastern Mediterranean. The lily of medieval romance, a sentimental choice for many gardeners. Pure white, fragrant, 4-in. blooms on 3- to 4-ft. stems in late spring, early summer. Unlike most lilies, it dies down soon after bloom, then makes new growth in fall; no summer water is needed. Plant while dormant in August. Choose a sunny location and set top of bulb only 1–2 in. deep (Madonna lilies do not have stem roots). Bulb quickly makes a foliage rosette that lives over winter, lengthens to become a blooming stem in spring. This species is subject to diseases that shorten its life. Seed-grown Cascade strain is more disease resistant than imported bulbs.

L. catesbaei. SOUTHERN RED LILY, PINE LILY. Zones LS, CS; 9–6. Native to moist sites from southeastern Virginia to Florida, Mississippi, and Louisiana. Blooms in late summer, early fall; each purple, 2- to 2½-ft.-tall stem bears a solitary 5-in.-long, 5- to 6-in.-wide red flower marked with purple spots and a patch of yellow near each petal base. Partial shade. Although native to bogs, it thrives in regular garden moisture.

L. cernuum. Zones US; 6–1. From Korea, Manchuria, Siberia. Summer bloomer reaches just 12–20 in. high, with fragrant lilac purple flowers often dotted in darker purple. Usually bears up to six 1½-in.-long blooms per stem.

L. formosanum. FORMOSA LILY. Zones MS, LS, CS, TS; 12–4. Native to Taiwan. An often-overlooked, easy-to-grow species that is worthy of wider use. Showy, fragrant flowers are narrow, pendent trumpets 8–12 in. long, appearing atop 5- to 7-ft. stems in late summer. Blooms are white, with a pinkish purple midrib on each petal back; stems are dark purple toward the base. Foliage is narrow and grasslike, and attractive, upright seedpods give rise to many seedlings. A delightful variant, *L. formosanum pricei*, reaches just 10 in. high and bears 6-in.-long white trumpets with plum-colored midribs. It blooms a month earlier than the species. Both are among the better lilies for the Coastal and Tropical South; bloom reliably throughout Florida.

Formosa lily is often confused with a similar but lower-growing lily that also grows well in the South, *L. philippinense.* The resulting hybrids, called Philippine lilies, retain the look and growth habit of *L. formosanum* but are more floriferous.

L. henryi. Zones US, MS, LS. From China. Slender stems reach 8–9 ft., each bearing 10 to 20 bright orange, 6-in.-long flowers with sharply recurved petals. Midsummer bloom. Best in light shade.

L. lancifolium (L. tigrinum). TIGER LILY. Heat zones 10–1. Native to China, Japan, Korea. Summer-blooming old Southern favorite to 4 ft. or taller, with pendulous, 7-in.-long orange flowers spotted in black. Very easy to grow. Newer tiger lilies are available in white, cream, yellow, pink, and red (all with the typical black spots).

L. langkongense. Heat zones 8–4. From China. To 3–5 ft. tall, spreading widely by stoloniferous stems. Blooms in mid- to late summer, when each flowering stem bears up to 15 small (3-in.-long), powerfully fragrant, recurved blossoms in pale to deep pink with purple spots. Tolerates alkaline soil.

L. leucanthemum centifolium. Zones US, MS, LS. Native to China. To 7–8 ft. tall. Blooms in midsummer; each stem carries as many as 18 fragrant, funnel-shaped, slightly pendulous blooms in white with external purple-red streaks. Blossoms are about 6 in. long.

L. longiflorum. EASTER LILY. Zones US, MS, LS, CS, TS; 12–1. Native to Japan and Taiwan. Short stems bear very fragrant, trumpet-shaped white blossoms to 7 in. long. Usually purchased in bloom at Easter. Set out in garden after flowers fade—but don't plant forced Easter lilies near other lilies, as they may transmit a virus. Stems will ripen and die down. Plant may rebloom in fall; in 1 or 2 years, it may flower in midsummer, its normal bloom time. Selections include 'Ace' (1½ ft. tall), 'Croft' (1 ft.), 'Estate' (to 3 ft.), and 'Nellie White' (2–2½ ft.; very popular). Hybridization has yielded pink, yellow, and red offspring. Does very well throughout Florida.

L. martagon. TURK'S CAP LILY. Zones US, MS, LS. Native from Europe to Mongolia. Purplish pink, recurved, pendent, 7-in.-long flowers bloom in early summer on 3- to 5-ft. stems. This old favorite is slow to establish, but it's long lived and eventually forms big clumps. Pure white *L. m. album* is one of the most appealing of lilies; it is a parent of the Paisley hybrids, a group with flowers in yellow, orange, and mahogany, most with maroon spots.

L. pumilum. CORAL LILY. Native to northern China, Mongolia, Siberia. Early summer bloomer to 1–1½ ft. high, with up to 20 fragrant red, recurved, 3-in.-long blossoms per stem. 'Yellow Bunting' has yellow flowers.

L. regale. REGAL LILY. From western China. Superseded in quality by modern hybrids but still popular and easy to grow. To 6 ft., with fragrant, trumpet-shaped, 6-in.-long white flowers in early to midsummer.

L. speciosum. SHOWY LILY. Native to China, Japan, Taiwan. Grows 2½–5 ft. tall. Wide, fragrant, 7-in.-long flowers with broad, deeply recurved segments bloom in late summer; they are white, heavily suffused with rose pink and sprinkled with raised crimson dots. Named forms are available, including pure white *L. s. album* and red *L. s. rubrum.* Does best in light shade (or at least afternoon shade); needs rich soil with plenty of leaf mold.

L. tigrinum. See L. lancifolium

L. tsingtauense. Zones US, MS; 7–1. From Korea, China. Stems 3 ft. tall carry unscented, upward-facing, 4-in.-long orange flowers with maroon spots. Flowers appear in summer, usually in clusters of up to 6 (sometimes as many as 15).

LILY. See LILIUM

LILY-OF-THE-NILE. See AGAPANTHUS

LILY-OF-THE-VALLEY. See CONVALLARIA majalis

LILY-OF-THE-VALLEY SHRUB. See PIERIS japonica

LILY TURF. See LIRIOPE

LIME. See CITRUS

LIMEQUAT. See CITRUS

LIMONIUM

STATICE, SEA LAVENDER

Plumbaginaceae

PERENNIALS AND ANNUALS

ZONES VARY BY SPECIES

FULL SUN

MODERATE WATER

Limonium perezii

Large, leathery, green basal leaves contrast with airy clusters of tiny, delicate flowers on nearly leafless, many-branched stems. The flowers consist of two parts: an outer, papery envelope (the calyx) and an inner part (the corolla). Calyx and corolla are often of different colors. Flowers are good for cutting and keep their color when dried. Plants tolerate heat and many kinds of soil but need good drainage. They often self-sow. For spring and summer bloom of annual kinds, sow indoors and move to garden when weather warms up. Or sow outdoors in early spring for later bloom. Resistant to damage by browsing deer.

L. gmelinii. Perennial. Zones US, MS, LS; 9–3. From eastern Europe, Siberia. Much like a slightly smaller *L. platyphyllum*, with 5-in. basal leaves and widely branching clusters of blue flowers in mid- to late summer.

L. perezii. Perennial. Zones TS; 12–1. Canary Island native. To 3 ft. tall, with flower clusters spreading nearly as wide. Calyx is rich purple, corolla white. Long spring and summer bloom. Leaves up to 1 ft. long, including stalks. First-rate beach plant. Well adapted to southern Rio Grande Valley. Damaged at 25°F but useful even where it freezes out occasionally; nursery-grown seedlings develop fast.

L. platyphyllum (L. latifolium). Perennial. Zones US, MS, LS, CS; 9–1. Native to central and southeastern Europe. Vigorous plant to 2½ ft. tall, covered in a 3-ft.-wide cloud of flowers in summer. Calyx is white, corolla bluish; pure white and pink kinds exist. Smooth-edged leaves to 10 in. long.

L. sinuatum. Annual. Zones US, MS, LS, CS, TS; 8–3. Mediterranean native widely grown for use as a cut flower in both fresh and dried arrangements. To 1½ ft. tall and 1 ft. wide, with basal leaves lobed nearly to midrib. Flower stems are distinctly "winged," with flattish extensions on their sides. Calyx is blue, lavender, or rose; corolla is white. Improved strains come in rose, yellow, apricot, orange, peach, light blue, deep blue, purple, and white. Plant in fall in Coastal and Tropical South.

L. tataricum. See Goniolimon tataricum

STATICE SYMBOLS. *Cut sprays of statice for fresh bouquets after most flowers in each cluster have opened. For dried arrangements, cut after blossoms are open but before sun has faded them. With a rubber band, join several bunches together by the stem bases; hang them upside down in a dry spot out of bright sun until flowers are dry.* ❖

Linaceae. The flax family of annuals, perennials, and shrubs displays cup- or disk-shaped flowers with four or five petals. Flowers are often showy; they are individually short lived but appear over a long season. A familiar example is flax *(Linum)*.

LINARIA

TOADFLAX

Scrophulariaceae

ANNUALS AND PERENNIALS

US, MS, LS, CS

FULL SUN OR LIGHT SHADE

MODERATE WATER

Linaria maroccana

Brightly colored flowers resemble small, spurred snapdragons *(Antirrhinum majus)*. Easy to grow; thrive in light or sandy soil. Look best when planted in masses, as individual plants are rather wispy. Toadflaxes are not usually browsed by deer.

L. maroccana. BABY SNAPDRAGON, TOADFLAX. Annual. Heat zones 8–1. From Morocco. To 1½–2 ft. high, 6 in. wide. Light green, narrow leaves to 1½ in. long. Summer flowers to ½ in. long, in rose, pink, mauve, chamois, blue, violet, purple, or a red-and-gold combination; all are blotched with a different shade on the lip. Spur is longer than flower. Fairy Bouquet strain is only 9 in. tall and has larger flowers in pastel colors. Northern Lights strain features shades of red, orange, and yellow as well as bicolors.

Seed baby snapdragon in quantity for a show. It performs best during cool weather. Where winters are cold, sow in early spring after danger of frost is past, then again in late summer; in mild-winter areas, sow in late summer for fall bloom, then again in autumn for winter flowers.

L. purpurea. PURPLE TOADFLAX. Perennial. Heat zones 8–5. From southern Europe. Narrow, bushy, erect plant to 2–4 ft. tall, 10 in. wide. Blue-green, very narrow leaves; violet-blue, ½-in. summer flowers. 'Canon Went' is a pink form. Short lived in hot, humid regions, but volunteer seedlings ensure a continuing supply.

L. vulgaris. COMMON TOADFLAX, BUTTER-AND-EGGS. Perennial. Heat zones 9–1. From Europe and Asia; naturalized in North America. Stiffly erect habit to 1–3 ft. high, 1 ft. wide. Narrow pale green leaves to 2½ in. long; pale yellow blossoms to 1¾ in. wide from spring into fall. Invasive, somewhat weedy plant; try it in a cottage garden, where you are more likely to appreciate its propensity to spread by rhizomes and self-sow.

LINDEN. See TILIA

LINDERA

SPICEBUSH

Lauraceae

DECIDUOUS SHRUBS OR TREES

US, MS, LS

FULL SUN OR PART SHADE

REGULAR WATER

Lindera obtusiloba

Spicebushes are grown principally for the beauty of their fall foliage; early spring clusters of small, greenish yellow flowers on leafless shoots are attractive but not conspicuous. On female plants, fruits will follow the blossoms if a male plant is nearby. Best used at woodland edge or as space fillers. Need good drainage; tolerate some drought. The common name refers to the spicy odor of the crushed leaves.

L. benzoin. SPICEBUSH. Heat zones 8–1. Native to woodlands of eastern U.S. Reaches 6–12 ft. tall and broad. Light green leaves are 3–5 in.

L

long, half as wide. Yellow fall color and plant form are best in full sun; if plants are grown in shade, foliage color isn't as pronounced and habit is loose and open. Fruits (noticeable after leaf fall) are bright red, up to ½ in. long.

L. obtusiloba. JAPANESE SPICEBUSH. Heat zones 9–6. Native to Japan, China, Korea. To 10–20 ft. tall, not quite as wide. Leaves are 5 in. long, 4 in. wide, occasionally lobed near the tip to give a mitten shape. Fall color is an exceptionally brilliant yellow that develops even in shade and holds for 2 weeks or more. Small (¼-in.-wide) red fruits eventually turn black.

LINDHEIMERA texana

TEXAS YELLOW STAR, STAR DAISY

Asteraceae (Compositae)

ANNUAL

☼ US, MS, LS, CS, TS H 12–1

☼ FULL SUN

◊ LITTLE WATER

Lindheimera texana

This rugged Texas native forms a basal rosette of coarse, tapered leaves that reach 2–3 in. long. Thick, hairy stems rise 1–2 ft. tall and are topped by star-shaped yellow flowers to 1½ in. across. Blooms profusely from March through May, providing early color for wildflower gardens. Spent petals drop cleanly. Does best in dryish, sandy or rocky soil. Space plants about 1 ft. apart.

LINUM

FLAX

Linaceae

PERENNIALS AND ANNUALS

☼ ZONES VARY BY SPECIES

☼ FULL SUN

◖ MODERATE WATER

Linum perenne

Plants with erect, branching stems and narrow leaves produce an abundance of shallow-cupped, five-petaled flowers over a long bloom period. Each bloom lasts only a day, but others keep coming. The flax of commerce—*L. usitatissimum*—is grown for its fiber and seeds, which yield linseed oil.

Use in borders; some naturalize freely in uncultivated areas. Do best in light, well-drained soil. Most perennial kinds live only 3 or 4 years and should be replaced regularly. Easy to grow from seed; perennials also can be propagated from cuttings. Difficult to divide.

L. flavum. GOLDEN FLAX. Perennial. Zones US, MS, LS, CS; 9–5. From central and southern Europe. To 12–15 in. high, 1 ft. wide, with somewhat woody base. Grooved branches, green leaves. Branched clusters of golden yellow, inch-wide flowers bloom in spring and summer. Often called yellow flax—a name correctly applied to the closely related *Reinwardtia indica* (a larger plant that is native to Pakistan and China). 'Compactum' is just 6 in. high and wide.

L. grandiflorum. FLOWERING FLAX. Annual. Zones US, MS, LS, CS, TS; 8–1. From North Africa. To 1½–2½ ft. tall and 6–12 in. wide, with narrow gray-green leaves. Summer flowers are rose pink, 1–1½ in. wide. Sow seed thickly in place in early spring or (in mild-winter climates) in fall. Self-sows without becoming a pest and is often included in wildflower mixes. Two selections are far more common than the species: 'Rubrum', scarlet flax, with bright red flowers; and 'Bright Eyes', bearing white flowers with a brownish red eye.

L. narbonense. Perennial. Zones US, MS, LS; 9–7. Wiry-stemmed Mediterranean native to 2 ft. tall, 1½ ft. wide. Narrow blue-green leaves. Open clusters of 1¾-in., azure blue flowers with white eye; blooms in late spring and early summer. 'Six Hills' has rich sky blue blossoms.

L. perenne. PERENNIAL BLUE FLAX. Perennial. Zones US, MS, LS; 8–5. Native from Europe to central Asia. Most vigorous blue-flowered flax, to 2 ft. tall, 1½ ft. wide. Narrow blue-green leaves; stems are usually leafless on lower part. Blooms profusely in late spring and summer, producing branching clusters of light blue flowers that close in shade or late in the day. Self-sows freely.

LION'S TAIL, LION'S EAR. See LEONOTIS

LIPPIA citriodora. See ALOYSIA triphylla

LIQUIDAMBAR

SWEET GUM

Hamamelidaceae

DECIDUOUS TREES

☼ ZONES VARY BY SPECIES

☼ FULL SUN

◖ MODERATE TO REGULAR WATER

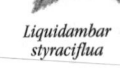

Liquidambar styraciflua

People often are of two minds when it comes to sweet gums: they praise them for their ravishing fall color but curse them for their copious gum balls. Distinguished by their maplelike leaves, they're upright, conical trees that spread with age. Inconspicuous flowers are followed by spiny seed balls that are a boon for fans of dried arrangements but a bane for those who like to walk barefoot. Seedless selections are becoming available, however, so the best of both worlds could be in sight.

Provide fertile, well-drained, slightly acid to neutral soil; alkaline soil often causes chlorosis (yellow leaves with green veins), and the problem can be hard to correct. Prune young trees to develop a strong central leader. Mature trees need little pruning.

Given ample room, sweet gums make fine street and shade trees, though their surface roots can be a problem in lawns or in the narrow space between sidewalk and curb. Fall foliage is brilliant in the Upper and Middle South, less so in the Lower, Coastal, and Tropical South. Young plants are somewhat resistant to browsing deer.

L. formosana. CHINESE SWEET GUM. Zones US, MS, LS, CS; 9–6. Native to China. To 40–60 ft. tall, 25 ft. wide. Free-form outline; sometimes pyramidal, especially when young. Three- to five-lobed leaves are 3–4½ in. across, violet red when expanding, deep green at maturity. Fall color ranges from red in northern part of range to yellow beige farther south. Leaves drop late, usually in early winter. 'Afterglow' has lavender-purple new growth, rosy red fall color.

L. orientalis. ORIENTAL SWEET GUM. Zones MS, LS, CS; 9–7. Native to Turkey. To 20–30 ft. tall and wide. Leaves 2–3 in. wide, deeply five lobed, each lobe again lobed to give a lacy effect. Leafs out early after short dormant period. Fall color varies from deep gold and bright red in cooler areas to dull brown purple farther south.

L. styraciflua. AMERICAN SWEET GUM. Zones US, MS, LS, CS; 10–5. Native to eastern U.S., and by far the most commonly planted sweet gum. To about 60 ft. tall in gardens; much taller in the wild. Narrow and erect in youth, with lower limbs eventually spreading to 20–25 ft. Tolerates damp soil. Good looking all year. Branching pattern, furrowed bark, and corky wings on twigs all provide winter interest, as do hanging seedpods—1½-in., spiky spheres reminiscent of tiny medieval maces. On mature trees, seedpods are profuse enough to cause a litter problem (especially on lawns, where they interfere with mowing).

Five- to seven-lobed, 3- to 7-in.-wide leaves are deep green in spring and summer, turning to purple, yellow, or red in fall. Even seedling trees usually give good fall color, though color may vary somewhat from year to year. To get desired and uniform color, purchase budded trees of a named variety, preferably while they are in fall leaf. Good selections include the following.

'Burgundy'. Deep purple-red fall color. Foliage hangs on late into winter—or even into early spring if storms are not heavy.

'Cherokee'. Produces very few or no seedpods. Fall color is burgundy red (yellow on trees grown in shade).

'Festival'. Narrow, columnar. Light green foliage turns a combination of yellow, peach, pink, orange, and red in fall.

'Golden Treasure'. Deep green leaves bordered in gold. In fall, gold rim lightens to pale yellow, then white; green center turns burgundy.

'Palo Alto'. Orange-red to bright red fall color.

'Rotundiloba'. Leaves have rounded rather than sharp-pointed lobes. Sets no seedpods. Fall color is yellow, red, burgundy, and purple.

'Silver King'. Leaves are edged in creamy white; may be flushed with rosy tones in late summer and fall.

'Variegata'. Green leaves with yellow streaks and splotches. In fall, the yellow variegation turns pink; green part of leaf becomes red.

'Worplesdon'. Narrow-lobed leaves turn orange red in fall.

LIRIODENDRON tulipifera

TULIP POPLAR

Magnoliaceae

DECIDUOUS TREE

US, MS, LS, CS **H** 10–1

FULL SUN

REGULAR WATER

Liriodendron tulipifera

Native to eastern U.S. Grows fast to 60–90 ft., with a spread of about 35–50 ft.; considerably larger in the wild. Straight, columnar trunk; spreading, rising branches that form a tall, pyramidal crown. The bright green, 5- to 6-in. leaves are variously described as lyre shaped, saddle shaped, or truncated; they're like blunt-tipped maple leaves missing the end lobe. They turn bright yellow green to bright yellow in fall.

Tulip-shaped, 2-in.-wide flowers in late spring are greenish yellow marked with orange at base. Handsome at close range but not showy on the tree, since they are carried high up and well concealed by leaves. Trees don't usually bloom until they are 10 to 12 years old.

This tree thrives in deep, rich, well-drained, neutral to slightly acid soil. Give it plenty of room to grow; it makes a good large shade or lawn tree. Wide-spreading network of shallow, fleshy roots, however, makes it difficult to garden under. Control scale insects and aphids as necessary.

Nurseries may carry two selections that are slower growing and somewhat smaller than the species. Columnar 'Arnold' ('Fastigiata') reaches 10–15 ft. wide; it will bloom just 2 to 3 years after planting. 'Aureomarginatum' ('Majestic Beauty') has yellow-edged leaves.

LIRIOPE

MONKEY GRASS, LILY TURF

Liliaceae

PERENNIALS

ZONES VARY BY SPECIES

PARTIAL TO FULL SHADE, EXCEPT AS NOTED

REGULAR WATER

Liriope muscari

Forming tufts of grasslike leaves, these popular, tough-as-nails ground covers from Asia are known by a number of names—but to most Southerners, they're plain old monkey grass. One species grows in clumps; the other spreads aggressively. Summer flowers, often quite showy, appear atop the foliage in spikes or branching clusters and come in lavender, blue, pink, purple, or white.

In addition to their use as a ground cover, these plants make excellent edgings for walks and planting beds. They're good beneath large trees, as they tolerate the shallow soil between surface roots. They also make nice additions to containers and mixed plantings. They generally prefer filtered sun to full shade, although some selections do well in full sun. Good drainage is important; regular fertilizing isn't necessary. To get more plants, divide in early spring, using a sharp spade to cut through the clumps. Deer don't usually eat the foliage.

Liriope's close cousin, *Ophiopogon japonicus,* is also called monkey grass. It has many of the same uses but is less cold hardy. See page 436.

L. muscari. BIG BLUE LIRIOPE, BIG BLUE LILY TURF. Zones US, MS, LS, CS, TS, 12–1, except as noted. Forms large clumps 1–2 ft. tall and eventually a bit wider—but does not spread by underground stems. Loose growth habit, with arching, typically dark green leaves to 2 ft. or longer, ½–¾ in. wide. Dense, spikelike, 6- to 8-in. blossom clusters reminiscent of grape hyacinth *(Muscari)* appear on 5- to 12-in. stems. Blooms are held above the foliage on young plants, partly hidden by leaves on older ones. Round, shiny black fruits follow flowers.

'Big Blue'. Stiffly arching plant to 12–15 in. high. Narrow leaves, dark violet flowers. Does well even in dry shade.

'Cleopatra'. To 2 ft. tall, with slightly twisted leaves. Dark purple flowers.

'Evergreen Giant'. Zones CS, TS. To 2 ft. tall, with straplike leaves and lavender flowers. Evergreen plant, best used as edging or border. Not cold hardy.

'John Burch'. To 12–15 in. high. Broad yellow-green leaves with wide green edging. Heavy flower spikes like lavender cockscombs stand well above the foliage. Performs best in full sun.

'Lilac Beauty'. Grows 12–15 in. tall. Pale violet flowers.

'Majestic'. To 15–18 in. high. Somewhat open clumps. Blooms heavily, bearing large (up to 10-in.-long) clusters of dark violet blossoms resembling cockscombs; flowers are held above the leaves. 'Royal Purple' and 'Webster Wideleaf' are similar.

'Monroe White'. To 12–15 in. high, with broad leaves and large white flower spikes that stand well above the foliage. Fruit is purple. Prefers more shade than most types.

'Samantha'. Dwarf form to only 10 in. high. Narrow leaves; lavender-pink blooms. For best flower color, give it a warm spot.

'Silvery Sunproof'. Open, strong growth to 12–15 in. high. Medium green foliage has gold stripes that age to white; whole leaf is whiter in sun, yellower or greener in shade. Lilac flowers are held well above foliage. One of the best for full sun and for flowers.

'Variegata'. To 10–15 in. high. Forms loose, soft clumps. Leaves are green with yellow edges when new, then turn solid dark green in second season. Violet flowers are held well above the leaves. May be sold as *Ophiopogon jaburan* 'Variegatus'.

L. spicata. CREEPING LIRIOPE, CREEPING LILY TURF. Zones US, MS, LS, CS, TS; 12–1. Dense ground cover that spreads widely by underground stems; can be invasive. Grows 8–9 in. high. Deep green, grasslike leaves are only ¼ in. wide. Foliage is not as upright as that of *L. muscari.* Pale lilac to white flowers appear in spikelike clusters barely taller than the leaves. Set plants 1 ft. apart for quick cover. For best effect, mow yearly in early spring, before new growth emerges. 'Silver Dragon' has a somewhat sparser habit, leaves striped in silvery white, and pale purple flowers held on short spikes. Fine ground cover for shade; slower growing than species.

MANICURING MONKEY GRASS. *Though liriope is evergreen in most of the South, its leaves look pretty ragged by late winter. Neaten it up by mowing plants or clipping all foliage back close to the ground in early spring, before new growth appears. Don't be late with this grooming, though—if you mow after new leaves emerge, those leaves will have unattractive cut tips the entire year.* ❖

LISIANTHUS. See EUSTOMA grandiflorum

LITCHI, LITCHI NUT. See LYCHEE

LIVERWORT. See HEPATICA

LIVISTONA

Arecaceae (Palmae)

PALMS

🗹 CS, TS ❙ H ❙ 12–10, EXCEPT AS NOTED

☼ FULL SUN

◖ REGULAR WATER, EXCEPT AS NOTED

Livistona australis

These slow-growing fan palms somewhat resemble *Washingtonia* but generally have shorter, darker, shinier leaves. They are generally hardy to about 22°F. All make good potted plants.

L. australis. AUSTRALIAN FAN PALM. From coastal forest of eastern Australia. To 40–50 ft. tall, 15 ft. wide. Trunk is clean and slender, marked with interesting-looking leaf scars. Dark green, 3- to 5-ft.-wide leaves.

L. chinensis. CHINESE FAN PALM, CHINESE FOUNTAIN PALM. Zones LS, CS, TS. From Japan, Taiwan. Very slow growing; eventually reaches 40 ft. tall, 15 ft. wide. Roundish, bright green, 3- to 6-ft.-wide leaves droop strongly at outer edges. Hardy to about 15°F.

L. decipiens. WEEPING FAN PALM. From northeastern Australia. To 30–40 ft. tall and 15 ft. wide in 20 years. Stiff, open head of leaves that are green on top, bluish beneath, 2–5 ft. across; leaves are carried on long, spiny stems.

L. mariae. BRONZE FAN PALM. Zone TS. From hot, dry, interior Australia. To 10–15 ft. tall and 15 ft. wide after many years (ultimately may reach 80 or even 100 ft. tall, 25 ft. wide). Leaves 3–4 ft. wide. Young plants and those grown in containers have attractive reddish leaves and leaf stems. Little to moderate water.

LOBELIA

Campanulaceae (Lobeliaceae)

PERENNIALS AND ANNUALS

🗹 ZONES VARY BY SPECIES

☼◑◖ PARTIAL TO FULL SHADE

◖◖ WATER NEEDS VARY BY SPECIES

✷ MOST CONTAIN POISONOUS ALKALOIDS

Lobelia erinus

All are grown for their tubular, lipped flowers, which resemble those of honeysuckle (*Lonicera*) or salvia. Annual kinds are low plants for edgings or hanging baskets; perennial sorts are larger, vertical-growing plants with flowering stalks that rise above the foliage clumps.

L. cardinalis. CARDINAL FLOWER. Perennial. Zones US, MS, LS, CS; 10–1. Native to eastern U.S. and to a few sites in mountains of the Southwest. Erect, single-stemmed plant to 2–4 ft. high, 1 ft. wide. Sawtooth-edged leaves are set directly on the stems. Spikes of flame red, inch-long flowers in summer. A bog plant in nature, it needs rich soil and ample moisture throughout the growing season. 'Summit Snow' is a white-flowering form.

L. erinus. EDGING LOBELIA. Annual. Zones US, MS, LS, CS, TS; 8–1. From South Africa. Popular and dependable edging plant to 3–6 in. high. Compact forms reach 5–9 in. wide; trailing types spread to 1½ ft. Leafy, branching stems with green or bronzy green foliage. Blooms from early summer to frost, bearing ¾-in.-wide flowers in light blue to violet (sometimes pink, reddish purple, or white) with white or yellowish throats. Lives over winter in mild climates. In the Coastal and Tropical South, grow it as a winter-to-spring annual. If started from seed sown in pots, takes about 2 months to reach planting-out size. Give rich soil, regular water. Self-sows where adapted.

Compact types include 'Cambridge Blue', with green leaves and flowers in a soft pure blue; and 'Crystal Palace', with rich deep blue blossoms and bronzy green leaves. Trailing, green-foliaged kinds include the Cascade series, with carmine red, violet-blue, blue, pink, or white blooms, and 'Sapphire', with bright blue flowers. Trailers are well suited to hanging baskets, wall plantings. They also make a graceful underplanting in containers, where the stems, loaded with flowers, can spill over the edges.

L. fulgens (L. splendens). Perennial. Zones US, MS, LS, CS; 9–5. Native to Mexico. Similar to *L. cardinalis* but with narrower leaves; both stems and leaves have deep red undertones. Give same growing conditions as *L. cardinalis*.

L. × gerardii. Perennial. Zones US, MS, LS; 9–5. Group of summer-blooming hybrids between *L. cardinalis* and *L. siphilitica*. All form clumps about 1 ft. wide, but heights vary. Most common is 4-ft.-tall 'Vedrariensis', with coppery green foliage and bright purple flowers. 'Cotton Candy', named for its bright pink blossoms, grows 2½ ft. tall. 'Grape Knee-Hi', 2 ft. high, has rich purple blooms; 'Monet Moment', to 3 ft. tall, bears big clusters of rich violet-pink blossoms. 'Ruby Queen' reaches 3 ft. high and has ruby red blooms; 'Ruby Slippers' grows to 3–4 ft. tall, with spikes of velvety, ruby red flowers and foliage that may take on purple tones. Provide rich soil and regular water.

L. siphilitica. BLUE CARDINAL FLOWER. Perennial. Zones US, MS, LS; 8–1. Native to eastern U.S. Leafy plant to 2–3 ft. tall, 1 ft. wide. Blue summer flowers. Give ample water. 'Alba' has white blossoms.

L. × speciosa. Perennial. Zones US, MS, LS, CS; 8–5. Group of hybrids of uncertain ancestry; probably crosses between *L. cardinalis* and *L. fulgens*. Can reach 5 ft. tall, 1 ft. wide; many combine red leaves and red flowers. Two 4- to 5-footers are 'Queen Victoria', with purple-red foliage and scarlet flowers; and 'Dark Crusader', with dark purple leaves and deep magenta flowers. Compliment series, to 2½ ft. high, has dark green leaves; blossoms may be scarlet, deep red, or blue purple. Ample water.

Lobeliaceae. See Campanulaceae

LOBSTER-CLAW. See HELICONIA

LOBULARIA maritima

SWEET ALYSSUM

Brassicaceae (Cruciferae)

ANNUAL

🗹 US, MS, LS, CS, TS ❙ H ❙ 12–1

☼◑ BEST IN SUN, TOLERATES LIGHT SHADE

◖ REGULAR WATER

Lobularia maritima
'Rosie O'Day'

Mediterranean native. Low, branching, trailing plant to 1 ft. high and wide, with narrow or lance-shaped leaves ½–2 in. long. Crowded clusters of tiny, four-petaled white flowers have a sweet honey fragrance, attract bees. In most areas, blooms from spring to frost. In the Coastal and Tropical South, it may go dormant during hottest period, but flowering will resume when weather cools. Seeds are sometimes included in wildflower mixes or erosion-control mixes for bare or disturbed earth.

Sweet alyssum is a dependable, easy-to-grow annual that takes almost any soil and blooms from seed in 6 weeks. Useful for carpeting, edging, bulb cover; temporary filler in rock garden or perennial border; between flagstones; in window boxes or containers. If you shear plants back by half about 4 weeks after they come into bloom, new growth will make another crop of flowers, and plants won't become rangy.

Garden selections are better known than the species. These self-sow too, but seedlings tend to revert to taller, looser growth and bear smaller, paler blossoms than the parent. 'Carpet of Snow' (2–4 in. tall), 'Little Gem' (4–6 in.), and 'Tiny Tim' (3 in.) are good compact whites. 'Tetra Snowdrift' (1 ft.) has long stems, large white flowers. 'Pink Heather' (6 in.) and 'Rosie O'Day' (2–4 in.) have lavender-pink blooms. 'Oriental Night' (4 in.) and 'Violet Queen' (5 in.) bear rich violet flowers.

LOCUST. See ROBINIA

FOR INFORMATION ON SELECTING PLANTS

PLEASE SEE PAGES 39–144

LOLIUM

RYEGRASS

Poaceae (Gramineae)

ANNUAL AND PERENNIAL LAWN GRASSES

ZONES VARY BY SPECIES

FULL SUN

REGULAR WATER

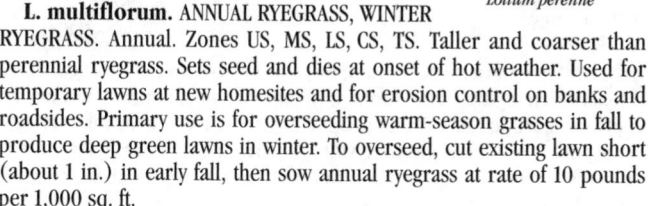

Lolium perenne

European clumping grasses that sprout quickly and are useful for winter lawns, pastures, soil reclamation. Perennial ryegrass is often used for year-round lawns in the Upper South.

L. multiflorum. ANNUAL RYEGRASS, WINTER RYEGRASS. Annual. Zones US, MS, LS, CS, TS. Taller and coarser than perennial ryegrass. Sets seed and dies at onset of hot weather. Used for temporary lawns at new homesites and for erosion control on banks and roadsides. Primary use is for overseeding warm-season grasses in fall to produce deep green lawns in winter. To overseed, cut existing lawn short (about 1 in.) in early fall, then sow annual ryegrass at rate of 10 pounds per 1,000 sq. ft.

L. perenne. PERENNIAL RYEGRASS. Perennial. Zones US; 7–1. Finer in texture than *L. multiflorum*, deep green with high gloss. Disadvantages are clumping tendency and tough flower and seed stems that lie down under mower blades. However, improved selections do produce a uniform lawn of fine appearance. These include 'Derby', 'Loretta', 'Manhattan', 'Pennfine', 'Yorktown'. Sow 8 to 10 pounds per 1,000 sq. ft. Mow at 1½–2 in., higher in summer.

LOLLIPOPS PLANT. See PACHYSTACHYS lutea

LONICERA

HONEYSUCKLE

Caprifoliaceae

EVERGREEN, SEMIEVERGREEN, DECIDUOUS SHRUBS AND VINES

ZONES VARY BY SPECIES

FULL SUN OR PARTIAL SHADE, EXCEPT AS NOTED

MODERATE TO REGULAR WATER, EXCEPT AS NOTED

Lonicera fragrantissima

Most honeysuckles are valued for their clustered or paired, often fragrant flowers. Blossoms are tubular in form. Some have two flaring, unequal lips; others are trumpets or straight tubes, sometimes flaring at the mouth into five equal lobes. Flowers attract hummingbirds, and the red or purple berries that follow provide food for many other kinds of birds. Blossoms typically deepen in color after opening, so clusters contain both pale and darker blooms. Vining species climb by twining and need staking until they are tall enough to reach a trellis or other support. As they grow, they may need to be tied to the support here and there to distribute the branches well.

Provide good drainage. Honeysuckles typically need some thinning; ideal time for the job is after bloom. Cut old, straggling honeysuckles to the ground before spring growth begins; they will regrow rapidly. Generally free of serious pests, though aphids sometimes infest them.

L. ×brownii. SCARLET TRUMPET HONEYSUCKLE. Deciduous vine. Zones US, MS, LS; 9–2. Represented in nurseries by its superior selection 'Dropmore Scarlet', which climbs to 9–10 ft. Unscented bright red flowers that look like trumpets bloom from late spring or early summer until frost. Pairs of triangular blue-green leaves to about 3 in. long appear to be joined at the bases.

L. fragrantissima. WINTER HONEYSUCKLE. Deciduous shrub, semievergreen in Lower South. Zones US, MS, LS; 8–3. From China. Longtime favorite of Southern gardeners, with arching, rather stiff growth to 8 ft. tall and at least as wide. Oval, 1- to 3-in.-long leaves are dull dark green above,

blue green beneath. Creamy white, ½-in.-long, two-lipped flowers bloom in late winter, early spring; they are sweetly fragrant but not showy. Berry-like red fruit. Can be used as a clipped hedge or a background plant; bring budded branches indoors to bloom.

L. ×heckrottii. GOLD FLAME HONEYSUCKLE. Deciduous vine or small shrub, semievergreen in Lower and Coastal South. Zones US, MS, LS, CS; 9–6. Vigorous grower to 12–15 ft., with oval, 2-in., blue-green leaves. Blooms profusely from spring to frost. Clusters of coral pink buds open to 1½-in.-long, two-lipped, slightly fragrant flowers that are bright coral pink outside, rich yellow within. Train as espalier or on wire along eaves.

L. japonica. JAPANESE HONEYSUCKLE. Evergreen to semievergreen vine. Zones US, MS, LS, CS, TS; 12–3. From eastern Asia. Beloved for its fragrant spring flowers, which yield drops of sweet nectar for children's tongues, but reviled for its invasive nature—if unchecked, it tangles its way through woodlands and throttles small trees.

Deep green, oval leaves to 3 in. long are held on reddish-brown stems. Two-lipped, 1½-in.-long blossoms age from white to yellow; they are followed by small black berries. Birds eat the berries and spread seeds everywhere. Grows very quickly, especially in the Southeast, and can twine its way to 30 ft.

Several selections are cultivated. 'Halliana', the most widely available, resembles the species and is every bit as weedy. It is sometimes used as a bank and ground cover in the Southwest, where it is somewhat less aggressive. 'Aureoreticulata' features green leaves netted with yellow. 'Purpurea' offers purple-tinged green foliage and flowers that are purple red on the outside, white inside.

Although Japanese honeysuckle does a great job of hiding chain link fences, it is seldom appropriate for home gardens. *L. ×heckrottii* and *L. periclymenum* are just as pretty and far better behaved.

L. korolkowii floribunda 'Blue Velvet'. Deciduous shrub. Zones US, MS; 7–1. Native to central Asia. To 12 ft. tall and 8 ft. wide. Tidy-looking, rounded, 2-in. leaves are light blue when young, maturing to gray green. Showy, fragrant, two-lipped light pink flowers open in mid- to late spring and are followed by bright red berries. Does best in full sun but tolerates part shade. Little to moderate water.

L. nitida. BOX HONEYSUCKLE. Evergreen shrub, deciduous in Upper South. Zones US, MS, LS, CS; 9–5. Native to southwestern China. To 4–6 ft. tall, with densely leafy branches. Tiny (½-in.), oval dark green leaves. Attractive bronze to plum-colored winter foliage. Late spring or early summer flowers are straight tubes—fragrant, creamy white, ½ in. long. Translucent blue-purple berries. Grows fast and tends to get untidy, but is easily pruned as hedge or single plant. Takes salt spray. 'Baggesen's Gold' has golden foliage in sun.

L. periclymenum. WOODBINE HONEYSUCKLE. Deciduous vine, semievergreen in Lower South. Zones US, MS, LS; 9–5. Native to Europe and the Mediterranean region. Grows 10–20 ft. tall; resembles *L. japonica* but is less rampant. Whorls of 2-in.-long, fragrant, two-lipped flowers in summer, fall. Blooms of 'Serotina' are purple outside, yellow inside. 'Berries Jubilee' has yellow flowers followed by a profusion of red berries. Heavy-blooming 'Belgica' is less vining, more bushy than most, with purple-flushed white flowers fading to yellow; flowers and red fruit come in large clusters. 'Graham Thomas' has white blossoms that age to copper-tinted yellow.

L. pileata. PRIVET HONEYSUCKLE. Evergreen to semievergreen shrub. Zones US, MS, LS; 9–5. Native to China. Low, spreading plant to 3 ft. tall, with stiff horizontal branches. Dark green, 1½-in. leaves resemble those of privet (*Ligustrum*). Small, fragrant, tubular white flowers in late spring; translucent violet purple berries. Good bank cover with low-growing euonymus or barberries (*Berberis*). Does well at the seashore. Give part or full shade in Lower South.

L. sempervirens. TRUMPET HONEYSUCKLE. Deciduous twining vine, semievergreen in Coastal South. Zones US, MS, LS, CS; 10–1. Old-time favorite, native to eastern and southern U.S.; can climb 10–20 ft. tall but is shrubby if not given support. From late spring into summer, bears showy, unscented, orange-yellow to scarlet flowers in whorls at branch ends. The trumpet-shaped, 1½- to 2-in.-long blooms are followed by scarlet berries. Oval, 1½- to 3-in.-long leaves are medium green above, bluish green beneath. 'Cedar Lane' (known by the name "coral honeysuckle" in Florida) is a vigorous selection with deep red flowers. 'Alabama Crimson' also has dark red blossoms; 'Magnifica' bears big scarlet flowers marked yellow inside. *L. s. sulphurea* (*L. s.* 'Flava') produces yellow flowers in late spring. For 'Dropmore Scarlet', see *L.* ×*brownii*.

Lonicera sempervirens

L. tatarica. TATARIAN HONEYSUCKLE. Deciduous shrub. Zones US, MS, LS; 9–1. Native from Russia to central Asia. Big, twiggy shrub to 10–12 ft. tall and wide, with dark green leaves up to 2½ in. long. Tubular white to pink flowers, widely flared at the tip, are borne in pairs in late spring. Red berries follow. Most widely grown selection is 'Arnold Red', with dark red flowers. Too large for most gardens; use for screening, bird shelter.

LOOSESTRIFE. See LYSIMACHIA, LYTHRUM virgatum

LOQUAT. See ERIOBOTRYA

LOROPETALUM chinense
CHINESE FRINGE, CHINESE WITCH HAZEL
Hamamelidaceae
EVERGREEN SHRUB
☒ MS, LS, CS ⊞ 9–3
☼ ◑ PARTIAL SHADE IN HOTTEST CLIMATES
◐ ◐ MODERATE TO REGULAR WATER

Loropetalum chinense 'Razzleberri'

Native to China and Japan. Large, rounded evergreen shrub to 8–15 ft. tall and wide. Neat, compact habit, with tiers of arching or drooping branches. Roundish light green leaves are 1–2 in. long; creamy white flowers consisting of four narrow, twisted, inch-long petals appear in clusters at the end of branch tips in late winter and early spring. Sporadic flowering may occur in fall.

This tough, pest-free plant tolerates heat and drought. Give it acid or neutral, well-drained soil; tends to suffer from chlorosis (yellow leaves with green veins) in alkaline soil. Once established, it grows fast; a transplant from a 1-gallon can will easily grow to 6 ft. in 3 years. Good in corner and understory plantings, as a screen, in mixed shrub borders, as a single specimen or espalier. You can also prune away lower branches to make a nice small tree.

Recently introduced burgundy-leafed, pink-flowered forms have taken garden centers by storm; they now share center stage with blue rug junipers (*Juniperus horizontalis* 'Wiltonii') and golden euonymus. To the untrained eye, most are identical and interchangeable. Use them judiciously—too much burgundy is not a good thing. Selections include the following.

'Burgundy'. Reddish purple new foliage matures to purple green. Very fast grower; young plants grow flat like cotoneasters the first year, then quickly shoot upward. Deep pink flowers.

'Fire Dance'. Ruby red new leaves mature to reddish purple. Deep pink flowers.

'Pipa's Red'. Like 'Fire Dance', but foliage is a more intense reddish purple and holds its color throughout summer. Hot pink flowers.

'Razzleberri'. Originally named 'Blush'. Leaves emerge bronze red and age to olive green. Fuchsia pink flowers.

'Sizzling Pink'. Similar to 'Burgundy' but with a growth habit that is more horizontal.

'Suzanne'. Compact, rounded shrub to 3–4 ft. tall and wide. Small, rounded, reddish maroon leaves. Pink flowers.

'Zhuzhou' ('Zhuzhou Fuchsia'). Upright, fast-growing plant with deep pink flowers. Narrow, elliptical leaves are nearly black.

LOVAGE. See LEVISTICUM officinale

LOVE GRASS. See ERAGROSTIS

LOVE-IN-A-MIST. See NIGELLA damascena

LOVE-LIES-BLEEDING. See AMARANTHUS caudatus

LUDISIA discolor
JEWEL ORCHID
Orchidaceae
TERRESTRIAL ORCHID
☒ TS OR HOUSEPLANT
☼ BRIGHT INDIRECT LIGHT
◐ REGULAR WATER

Ludisia discolor

If you think all orchids are hard to grow indoors, you haven't tried this one. Native to the forest floors of Indonesia and Malaysia, jewel orchid is prized more for its foliage than for its flowers. The handsome bronze leaves, up to 3 in. long and 1 in. wide, are streaked with parallel red veins. Creeping stems send up leafy rosettes, each of which produces a foot-tall spike of tiny white flowers in winter.

Jewel orchid is best sited in a north- or east-facing window. Shield it from direct midday or afternoon sunlight. Provide well-drained potting soil. Feed every 3 weeks with a general-purpose liquid houseplant fertilizer diluted to half-strength. Remove flower stalk after blossoms fade. Cut stems are easy to root in water.

LUFFA. See GOURD

LUNARIA annua
MONEY PLANT, HONESTY
Brassicaceae (Cruciferae)
BIENNIAL
☒ US, MS, LS, CS ⊞ 9–1
☼ ◑ AFTERNOON SHADE IN HOTTEST CLIMATES
◐ ◐ ◐ LITTLE TO REGULAR WATER

Lunaria annua

Native to Europe. Old-fashioned garden plant grown for the translucent, 1¼-in.-wide circles that hang onto flower stalks; these "coins" are all that remains of the ripened seedpods after the outer coverings have dropped with the seeds. Reaches 1½–3 ft. high, 1 ft. wide, with coarse, heart-shaped, tooth-edged leaves. Showy spring flowers resemble wild mustard blooms but are purple or white and larger in size. Plant in an out-of-the-way spot in poor soil, or use in a mixed flower bed where the shining pods can be admired before they are picked for dried arrangements. Tough and persistent; can reseed and become weedy.

LUNGWORT. See PULMONARIA

LUPINUS
LUPINE
Fabaceae (Leguminosae)
ANNUALS, PERENNIALS, AND EVERGREEN SHRUBS
☒ ZONES VARY BY SPECIES
☼ FULL SUN
◐ ◐ ◐ WATER NEEDS VARY BY SPECIES

Leaves are divided into many leaflets (like fingers of a hand). Sweet pea–shaped flowers are borne in dense spikes at stem ends. There are hundreds of species, many of them native to the

Lupinus Russell hybrids

southwestern U.S.; they're found in a wide range of habitats, from alpine rocks to beach sand. Most lupines take poor soil, but hybrids prefer rich, slightly acidic, well-drained soil.

L. hartwegii. Annual. Zones US, MS, LS, CS, TS; 12–1. Native to Mexico. Grows 1½–3 ft. tall, with flowers in shades of blue, white, and pink. Easy to grow from seed sown in place in spring for summer bloom. Moderate water.

L. havardii, L. subcarnosus, L. texensis. BLUEBONNET. Annuals. Zones MS, LS, CS; 12–1. All require poor, dry soil to survive; with regular flower border pampering, these Texas roadside flowers rot. For small areas, set out plants in fall to flower the following April. For meadows, scatter treated seeds (see "Help in the Nick of Time," below) onto moist ground in September and lightly rake the soil surface; keep soil moist only until seeds germinate. Replant or resow each fall for several years; seed from current year's flowers does not germinate reliably to produce next spring's floral display. Adequate fall and winter rains are necessary to produce spectacular spring show.

L. havardii, Big Bend bluebonnet, is the tallest bluebonnet, reaching 3–4 ft. high; its flowers are very deep blue. *L. subcarnosus,* the state flower of Texas, grows to 1 ft. tall, has sky blue flowers with a tinge of white. *L. texensis,* Texas bluebonnet, to 1 ft. tall, has dark blue flowers with a white eye that turns red after pollen is no longer viable, signaling bees not to visit plant.

L. hybrids. Perennials often treated as annuals. Zones US; 6–1. To 4–5 ft. tall, 2 ft. wide. These English-bred hybrid groups are descended from plants native to western America. Their dislike of summer heat and humidity makes them hard to grow in the South, even in the Upper South. Plant them in fall, be grateful for the flowers they produce the following year—and don't expect more than that. Self-sown seedlings won't resemble parents. Regular water.

Russell hybrids—the classic lupines—bloom during late spring or early summer, bearing tall flower spikes in white, cream, yellow, pink, red, orange, blue, purple, or bicolors. Little Lulu and Minarette are small strains—to 1½ ft. high and wide. All Russell hybrids tend to be short lived. They are prone to powdery mildew; provide good air circulation. Grow from seed or buy nursery plants.

New Generation hybrids have all the merits of the Russell hybrids (from which they were developed), but they are sturdier (needing no staking) and mildew resistant. They also come in a wider range of brighter, more intense colors, including interesting bicolors such as yellow-and-orange combinations. Bloom period is longer, too. Sold as seedling plants.

L. perennis. WILD LUPINE. Perennial. Zones US, MS, LS, CS; 9–1. Native to eastern U.S. To 2 ft. high, with purple flowers in late spring or early summer. Regular water.

HELP IN THE NICK OF TIME. *Lupine seeds are hard coated and often slow to sprout. They will germinate faster if you soak them in hot water or scratch or nick the seed coats with a file before planting.* ❖

LYCHEE

Sapindaceae

EVERGREEN TREE

CS (PROTECTED), TS 12–10

FULL SUN

REGULAR WATER

N ative to China and known botanically as *Litchi chinensis,* this is a round-topped tree with smooth gray bark. Grows slowly to 20–40 ft. tall and wide. Leaves consist of three to nine leathery, 3- to 6-in.-long, oval, pointed leaflets that emerge coppery red, then turn dark green.

Lychee

Inconspicuous flowers in late spring give rise to tasty, walnut-size fruits (variously known as lychees, litchis, or litchi nuts); they are ripe when the leathery rind covering them turns red (in summer and fall). The translucent white flesh surrounding the central pit is sweet, juicy, and delicious.

The fruit must ripen fully on the tree; after harvest, it can be frozen, dried, or stored fresh for up to 5 weeks in the refrigerator (if stored at room temperature, it will deteriorate within 3 days). The most widely grown selections are 'Brewster' (large fruit and seeds, midseason) and 'Mauritius' (medium-size fruit, small seeds, early).

Best grown in a frost-free site, although mature trees may withstand temperatures as low as 25°F for several hours. Provide acid, well-drained soil containing plenty of organic matter; mulch thoroughly with pine straw or ground bark after planting. Keep soil constantly moist during periods of active growth. Young trees need little fertilizer, but you should apply chelated iron and garden sulfur if planting in alkaline soil. Lychees do not tolerate salt spray.

LYCHNIS

Caryophyllaceae

PERENNIALS

US, MS, LS 8–1

FULL SUN OR LIGHT SHADE

WATER NEEDS VARY BY SPECIES

Lychnis coronaria

H ardy, old-fashioned garden flowers, all very tolerant of adverse soils. The different kinds vary in appearance, but all offer eye-catching colors in summer. Plants are generally short lived and need to be replaced every few years.

L. alpina. ALPINE CAMPION. From Europe and northeastern North America. Mounding, tufted plant, with narrow dark green leaves forming a rosette to 6–8 in. tall and wide. In summer, dense clusters of rosy purple flowers rise above the foliage. 'Alba' has white flowers; 'Rosea' bears soft pink blooms. Good edging or rock garden plant. Regular water.

L. × arkwrightii. ARKWRIGHT CAMPION. Hybrid of *L. chalcedonica* and *L. × haageana.* To 1½ ft. tall, 1 ft. wide, with brown-tinted dark green leaves. Clusters of 1½-in. orange-scarlet flowers. Remove faded blossoms for repeat bloom. 'Vesuvius' is taller (to 2 ft.), with large orange-red flowers; 'Orange Gnome' ('Orange Zwerg'), sporting bright orange flowers, grows only 5–7 in. tall and wide. Regular water.

L. chalcedonica. MALTESE CROSS. Native to Russia. Loose, open growth to 2–3 ft. high and 1 ft. wide, with hairy leaves and stems. Dense terminal clusters of scarlet, ½-in. flowers with deeply cut petals. Effective in large borders with white-blossomed or gray-foliaged plants. 'Alba' is a white-flowered form. Regular water.

L. cognata. ORANGE CATCHFLY. From Korea and northeast China. Grows 1½–3 ft. tall, 2 ft. wide. Upright stems carry deep green, oval, pointed leaves 2–3 in. long. Flowers in a lovely shade of salmon pink to apricot orange are 2–2½ in. wide, held singly or in clusters of three or more. Each petal has frilled edges, a deep central notch, and a long, slender "tooth" along one side. Easy to grow from seed, blooming in the first year. Pinch young plants to induce bushiness. Moderate to regular water.

L. coronaria. ROSE CAMPION. From southeastern Europe. Grows to 1½–2½ ft. tall, with attractive white, silky foliage and magenta to crimson flowers that are a little less than an inch across. Effective massed. 'Alba' has white flowers; 'Angel's Blush' bears white blossoms with a deep pink eye. Species and selections all self-sow freely if faded flowers are not removed. Moderate water.

L. × haageana. Red, orange, salmon, or white flowers carried in clusters of two or three throughout summer. Stems clothed in green leaves reach 1½–2 ft. high; plant grows 1 ft. wide. Dies down shortly after bloom. Mulch to protect against extreme heat or cold. Though a hybrid, it comes fairly true from seed. Regular water.

L. viscaria. GERMAN CATCHFLY. From Eurasia. Compact, low, evergreen clumps of grasslike leaves to 5 in. long. Pinkish purple, ½-in. flowers on 1½- to 2-ft. stalks. 'Alba' has white blooms. Foot-high 'Splendens' bears magenta blossoms; 'Splendens Plena' ('Flore Pleno') is similar but has double flowers. Two deep red bloomers are 1½-ft. 'Zulu' and 8-in. *L. v. atropurpurea.* Moderate to regular water.

L

LYCORIS

SPIDER LILY

Amaryllidaceae

PERENNIALS FROM BULBS

☒ US, MS, LS, CS, TS, EXCEPT AS NOTED;
  OR GROW IN POTS

☼ FULL SUN, EXCEPT AS NOTED

◐ REGULAR WATER DURING GROWTH AND BLOOM

Lycoris radiata

Most are native to China or Japan. Narrow, strap-shaped leaves appear in spring (or in fall, in mild-winter regions); they remain green until some point in summer, then die down completely. Leafless flower stalks emerge after the foliage disappears. In late summer or early fall, each stalk bears a cluster of blooms with narrow, pointed petal-like segments and—in some species—projecting, spidery-looking stamens. Blossoms may be funnel shaped or have segments splayed outward or reflexed.

Grow in a sunny site that can stay dry during summer dormancy. (In areas of summer rainfall, grow in pots that can be protected from moisture.) Plant in late summer, setting bulbs in well-drained soil about 1 ft. apart. Keep tops of bulb necks at or just above soil surface—except in coldest part of range, where tops of necks should be just under surface. Water regularly while plants are growing and again when flower stalks emerge. It's best to withhold water and let soil go dry in summer when foliage begins to wither, though plants can take some summer water if drainage is excellent. Disturb clumps (after bloom) only when you want to move them or divide them to increase a planting. Beyond hardiness range, grow spider lilies in containers and overwinter them indoors.

L. aurea (L. africana). GOLDEN SPIDER LILY, HURRICANE LILY. Zones CS, TS; or indoor/outdoor potted plant. Bright yellow blooms to 3–4 in. long.

L. chinensis. Heat zones 10–6. From China and Korea. To 2½ ft. tall, with flat-topped clusters of golden yellow, 3-in. blossoms.

L. ×haywardii. Heat zones 10–6. To 20 in. high. Magenta pink flowers resemble those of *L. squamigera*, but petals are more deeply divided. Easy to grow.

L. incarnata. Heat zones 10–6. To 20 in. high, with clusters of fragrant, 3-in. flowers that open white and then turn salmon to rose colored; each petal has a darker stripe running lengthwise down the center.

L. longituba. Heat zones 10–6. To 2½ ft. tall, bearing pure white, long-tubed (at least 2-in.) flowers.

L. radiata. SPIDER LILY. Heat zones 10–7. The best-known spider lily, and the easiest to grow. Coral red, 3- to 4-in. flowers with a golden sheen are borne on 1½-ft. stems. 'Alba', known as white spider lily, has white blossoms. Species and selections take light shade. In the Upper South, protect with mulch in winter.

L. sanguinea. Zones US, MS, LS, CS; 10–6. To 2 ft. tall, with 2- to 2½-in. bright red to orange-red flowers.

L. sprengeri. Zones US, MS, LS, CS; 12–6. Similar to *L. squamigera* but with slightly smaller purplish pink flowers.

L. squamigera (Amaryllis hallii). MAGIC LILY, SURPRISE LILY, NAKED LADY. Zones US, MS, LS, CS; 12–6. Clusters of funnel-shaped, 3-in., fragrant, pink or rosy lilac flowers on 2-ft. stems. Hardiest species, old favorite.

LYGODIUM japonicum

JAPANESE CLIMBING FERN

Schizaeaceae

PERENNIAL

☒ LS, CS, TS ⬥ 12–8; OR HOUSEPLANT

◑ PARTIAL SHADE; BRIGHT INDIRECT LIGHT

◐ REGULAR WATER

Lygodium japonicum

Lacy fern native to eastern Asia; naturalized in the Southeast. In the Lower South, twines daintily to 15 ft., climbing through shrubs and trees or up a trellis or slender post. In the Coastal and Tropical South, however, it may reach 100 ft. and become a pest. Grows fast in rich, moist, well-drained soil; particularly lush if air is humid. Evergreen in the Coastal and Tropical South; dies back to roots in winter in the Lower South. Long yellow-green fronds are triangular, 8–12 in. wide, on wiry stems. Fertile (spore-bearing) leaflets are much narrower than sterile ones. In spring, prune out old, tangled stems to make way for new growth.

Can be grown indoors in a hanging basket or on a trellis in bright indirect light. Make sure night temperatures do not drop below 40°F; mist to raise humidity. From spring through fall, feed monthly with a general-purpose liquid houseplant fertilizer; reduce watering and feeding somewhat during winter.

LYME GRASS, BLUE. See LEYMUS arenarius

LYONIA lucida

FETTERBUSH

Ericaceae

EVERGREEN SHRUB

☒ MS, LS, CS ⬥ 9–5

◑◐ PARTIAL TO FULL SHADE

◐ REGULAR WATER

Lyonia lucida

Native to moist woodlands from Virginia to Florida, west to Louisiana. Open, arching, suckering shrub to 3–5 ft. high and wide. Glossy bright green leaves to 3 in. long are broadly oval and pointed, reminiscent of *Leucothoe* foliage. Clusters of pale pink, urn-shaped, ¼-in. flowers emerge from leaf axils all along the stems in spring. Rather finicky—requires well-drained, acid soil and will not tolerate drought. Best used in a woodland garden or naturalized area. 'Morris Minor' is a compact, small-leafed selection.

LYSIMACHIA

Primulaceae

PERENNIALS

☒ US, MS, LS, EXCEPT AS NOTED

☼◑ FULL SUN OR PARTIAL SHADE,
  EXCEPT AS NOTED

◑◐ MODERATE TO REGULAR WATER

Lysimachia nummularia

Most of these perennials are vigorous spreaders with a penchant for conquering new territory, especially in moist, fertile soil. Keep them under surveillance to ensure they don't invade choicer plantings. Blossoms are yellow or white and appear in summer, except as noted.

L. barystachys. Heat zones 9–4. Native to eastern Russia and Asia. To 2 ft. high, 1½ ft. wide, with narrow green leaves to 3 in. long. Small white flowers come in foot-long spikes that start out horizontal and gradually turn upright.

L. ciliata. FRINGED LOOSESTRIFE. Zones US, MS, LS, CS; 9–3. Native to northeastern U.S. Erect clump to 4 ft. tall, 2 ft. wide, with narrow green leaves to 6 in. long. Nodding, 1-in. yellow flowers with red-brown centers appear singly or in loose clusters in upper leaf joints. 'Atropurpurea' ('Firecracker') is similar but has reddish leaves.

L. clethroides. GOOSENECK LOOSESTRIFE. Heat zones 9–1. Native to China, Korea, Japan. To 3 ft. tall, quickly spreading as wide or wider. Erect stems with pointed olive green leaves to 5 in. long. Flower spikes densely packed with tiny white blossoms are 6–8 in. long, arched like a goose's neck. 'Geisha' has leaves edged in creamy yellow.

L. congestiflora. GOLDEN GLOBES. Zones MS, LS, CS; 9–6. Native to China. Mat-forming plant grows to 4 in. high and 1 ft. or wider. Oval green leaves to 2 in. long; upturned yellow flowers, ½ in. across, in leafy terminal clusters. Blooms from spring to summer. Good in a rock garden or as ground cover in naturalized areas. 'Outback Sunset' has red-tinged leaves with yellow variegation and yellow flowers with red centers.

L

L. ephemerum. Heat zones 9–7. Native to southwestern Europe. Leathery gray-green leaves to 6 in. long form a neat clump to 3 ft. tall and 1 ft. wide. Slender clusters of white, ½-in.-wide, long-lasting flowers. Not invasive.

L. nummularia. CREEPING JENNY, MONEYWORT. Heat zones 8–1. Native to Europe; naturalized in eastern North America. Grows 4–8 in. high and spreads to 2 ft. or more, rooting as it goes. Forms an attractive mat of roundish, light green, 1-in. leaves. Yellow flowers about 1 in. across appear singly in leaf joints. Best use is in corners or containers where it need not be restrained. Also good in rock garden or as casual ground cover. Will spill from wall, hanging basket. 'Aurea' has bright yellow leaves that combine especially well with dark-foliaged plants such as black mondo grass (*Ophiopogon planiscapus* 'Nigrescens'); it requires a shady location.

L. punctata. YELLOW LOOSESTRIFE. Heat zones 8–1. Native to central Europe, Asia Minor. To 3 ft. tall, spreading to 2 ft. or more by underground stems. Narrow green leaves to 3 in. long are borne in whorls on erect stems; inch-wide yellow flowers, also in whorls, appear on top third of stems. Looks nice in masses or mixed borders. 'Alexander' has leaves with gold edges that fade to cream as the weather warms; it grows less vigorously than the basic species and reaches about 2 ft. tall.

Lythraceae. The loosestrife family is represented by such diverse plants as crepe myrtle (*Lagerstroemia*), wand loosestrife (*Lythrum*), and *Cuphea*. Some members of the genus *Lysimachia* are also commonly called loosestrife, but they belong to the primrose family (Primulaceae).

LYTHRUM virgatum

WAND LOOSESTRIFE

Lythraceae

PERENNIAL

✿ US, MS, LS ❙❙ 9–1

☼ FULL SUN

💧 REGULAR WATER; TOO MUCH MOISTURE ENCOURAGES INVASIVENESS

Lythrum virgatum

Native to Europe and Asia. Stems 2½–5 ft. tall form 2-ft.-wide clumps; lower portions of stems are clothed in narrow leaves, while the upper 8–18 in. are densely set with ¾-in. magenta flowers in late summer and fall.

Wand loosestrife is valued for cut flowers and showy at pond margins or in moist areas—but use it with caution, as it can be invasive. In fact, it has a bad reputation among lovers of native plants, thanks to the particularly invasive nature of its cousin, purple loosestrife (*L. salicaria*). Seedlings of *L. salicaria* often choke wetlands, crowding out native vegetation. Hybrids between the two species, including 'Dropmore Purple', 'Morden's Gleam', 'Morden's Pink', 'Pink Spires', 'Robert', 'Rose Queen', 'Roseum Superbum', and 'Rosy Spires', are said to be sterile, but they may interbreed with *L. salicaria* growing in the wild and set seed. In some states, it is illegal to plant purple loosestrife and its variants—and doing so is unwise, even if legal, wherever plants have ample moisture and may escape into unmanaged areas.

MACFADYENA unguis-cati

CAT'S CLAW, YELLOW TRUMPET VINE

Bignoniaceae

SEMIEVERGREEN VINE

✿ LS, CS, TS ❙❙ 12–8

☼ ◐ FULL SUN OR PARTIAL SHADE

💧 MODERATE WATER

Macfadyena unguis-cati

Formerly known as *Doxantha unguis-cati* and *Bignonia tweediana*. From Mexico, West Indies, Argentina. Climbs high (to 25–40 ft.) and fast by hooked, clawlike, forked tendrils. Leaves divided into two oval, glossy green leaflets to 2 in. long. Blooms in early spring, bearing yellow trumpets to 2 in. long. Vigorous; puts down roots where stems touch ground. Clings to any support—stone, wood, tree trunk. Good for covering chain-link fence. Tends to produce leaves and flowers at stem ends; after bloom, prune hard to stimulate new growth lower down. Loses all of its leaves in cold winters. May be invasive in the Coastal and Tropical South.

MACHILUS thunbergii. See PERSEA thunbergii

MACLEAYA

PLUME POPPY

Papaveraceae

PERENNIALS

✿ US, MS, LS ❙❙ 9–1

☼ ◐ FULL SUN OR LIGHT SHADE

💧 REGULAR WATER

Macleaya microcarpa

These tall perennials from China and Japan are often still listed as *Bocconia*, a name properly belonging to their shrubby tropical relatives. The two species described below resemble each other. Both have creeping rhizomes; tall, erect stems; large, deeply lobed leaves much like those of edible fig (*Ficus carica*); and small flowers in large, branching clusters. These plants have a tropical look, and their value lies in size and structure rather than flower color. Can be invasive if not controlled; plant among shrubs rather than amid delicate perennials.

M. cordata. PLUME POPPY. To 7–8 ft. tall, with 3-ft.-wide clumps of grayish green, 10-in. leaves and clouds of tiny white to beige flowers. Considered somewhat less invasive than *M. microcarpa*.

M. microcarpa. Resembles *M. cordata* but has pinkish beige flowers. Flowers of 'Kelway's Coral Plume' are more decidedly pink.

MACLURA pomifera

OSAGE ORANGE, BOIS D'ARC

Moraceae

DECIDUOUS TREE

✿ US, MS, LS ❙❙ 9–5

☼ FULL SUN

◑ 💧 LITTLE OR NO WATER TO REGULAR WATER

Maclura pomifera

An old Southern favorite, native from Arkansas to Oklahoma and Texas. Fast growth to 60 ft. tall and 40 ft. wide (though often smaller), with spreading, open habit. Orange-brown, fissured bark. Wood is very hard, orange in color, and highly resistant to rot. Glossy medium green leaves are oval and pointed, to 5 in. long. Young branches are thorny, mature ones less so. If a male tree is present, female trees may bear inedible, 4-in.-wide fruits that resemble bumpy yellow-green oranges and are prized for holiday decorations.

Withstands heat, cold, wind, and almost any kind of soil—acid or alkaline, wet or dry, fertile or terrible. Easy to transplant; easy to propagate by seed or cuttings. Makes a good windbreak or informal screen and is often planted in hedgerows. If people will be walking or sitting beneath the tree, always plant a male selection: a heavy, hard fruit falling from a high branch can knock a person silly. Two thornless male selections are worth seeking out. 'White Shield' features beautiful, lustrous dark green leaves and grows especially rapidly, up to 5 ft. per year. 'Wichita' forms an upright, spreading tree with a dense canopy.

MADAGASCAR JASMINE. See STEPHANOTIS floribunda

MADAGASCAR PALM. See PACHYPODIUM lamerei

MADAGASCAR PERIWINKLE. See CATHARANTHUS roseus

MADEIRA VINE. See ANREDERA cordifolia

M

MAGNOLIA

Magnoliaceae

DECIDUOUS AND EVERGREEN TREES AND SHRUBS

⚆ ZONES VARY BY SPECIES

☀ ☽ FULL SUN OR PARTIAL SHADE

● REGULAR WATER

▶ SEE CHART OPPOSITE

*Magnolia
×soulangeana*

Magnificent flowering plants featuring blossoms in white, pink, red, purple, or yellow. Magnolias are diverse in leaf shape and plant form, and they include both evergreen and deciduous sorts. They aren't usually munched by deer.

The following text classifies magnolias by general type; the chart lists species, hybrids, and selections alphabetically. New magnolias seem to appear almost hourly, but most garden centers carry only a few. To track down a prized selection, you'll probably need to hunt through mail-order catalogs.

MAGNOLIA TYPES

Whether evergreen or deciduous, most magnolias have large, striking blossoms composed of petal-like segments. A few are grown for use as foliage plants.

Evergreen magnolias. To many people, the word "magnolia" is synonymous with our native *Magnolia grandiflora*, the classic Southern magnolia with large, glossy leaves and huge, fragrant white blossoms—the state flower of Mississippi and Louisiana. Few trees can match it for year-round beauty. It does, however, have its drawbacks. Unnamed seedlings often take 10 years after planting before they come into bloom. Dense shade and shallow roots make it impossible to grow grass

Magnolia grandiflora

beneath the canopy, and the roots often crack and lift pavement if the tree is planted between sidewalk and curb. Leaves drop 365 days a year. And since the tree grows as wide as 40 ft., it takes up a lot of garden space.

Sweet bay (*M. virginiana*), a smaller tree, is easier to fit into most gardens. Though mostly deciduous in the Upper and Middle South, it's evergreen in the Lower and Coastal South and more cold hardy than *M. grandiflora*.

Deciduous magnolias with saucer flowers. This group includes the popular saucer magnolia (*M. ×soulangeana*) and its myriad selections, often called tulip trees because of the shape and bright color of their flowers. They prefer fertile, acid, well-drained soil. They do not tolerate heavy wind or salt spray. Early-flowering selections are prone to frost damage. Related to these, but less tolerant of winter cold and summer heat, are the spectacular magnolias from western China and the Himalayas—Sargent magnolia (*M. sargentiana*) and Sprenger magnolia (*M. sprengeri*). Though their early flowers may fall victim to late freezes, one spring season with good blooms will quickly make you forget the disappointments of years past.

Deciduous magnolias with star flowers. This group includes Kobus magnolia (*M. kobus*), Loebner magnolia (*M. ×loebneri*), and star magnolia (*M. stellata*). All are cold-hardy, heat-tolerant, adaptable plants. Late frosts sometimes damage their early blooms.

Other magnolias. Less widely planted—but deserving of greater attention—is a group of large-leafed native magnolias generally grown as bold accents or shade trees. Cucumber tree (*M. acuminata*) and its smaller sibling, yellow cucumber tree (*M. a. subcordata*), are the source of the yellow blossom color of many new hybrids. Bigleaf magnolia (*M. macrophylla*), umbrella magnolia (*M. tripetala*), Fraser magnolia (*M. fraseri*), and Ashe magnolia (*M. ashei*) are medium-size trees with huge leaves and large flowers that appear after the leaves unfurl.

WHAT MAGNOLIAS NEED

CAREFUL SITING: Pick a location where the shallow, fleshy roots won't be damaged by digging or by soil compaction from constant foot traffic.

SOIL: Magnolias appreciate fairly rich, well-drained, neutral to slightly acid soil amended with plenty of organic matter at planting time. They will grow in somewhat alkaline soil but may develop chlorosis (yellow leaves with green veins).

MULCHING: At least in the early years, keep a cooling mulch over the root area.

WATERING: Irrigate deeply and thoroughly, but don't waterlog the soil or the tree will drown. Only *M. virginiana* can take constantly wet soil.

FERTILIZING: Treat chlorosis with iron chelates. Feed trees if new growth is scanty or weak, or if you see significant dieback despite adequate watering and drainage. Use a controlled-release product; magnolias are very susceptible to salt damage from overfertilizing, resulting in burned leaf edges.

PRUNING: For deciduous magnolias, best time is after bloom; for evergreen kinds, do the job before the spring growth flush. Best method is to remove the entire twig or limb right to its base. Cuts on deciduous kinds are often slow to heal, so prune these only when necessary to correct plant's shape, eliminate or cut back wayward branches, or remove lower limbs from trunk as tree gains height.

Magnolia ×soulangeana

In its own category is Oyama magnolia (*M. sieboldii*), native to western China. It bears drooping, cup-shaped, fragrant blooms after leaves emerge.

MAGNOLIA CULTURE

For any magnolia, pick planting site carefully. Virtually all types are hard to move once established, and many grow quite large. The best soil for magnolias is fairly rich, well drained, and neutral to slightly acid; if necessary, add generous amounts of organic matter when planting. Southern magnolia (*M. grandiflora*) is good for planting at the beach, though not on dunes. Sweet bay (*M. virginiana*) tolerates wet soil. The species and selections listed in the chart are adapted to a wide range of growing conditions and are easy for most gardeners to grow.

Magnolias never look their best when crowded, and they may be severely damaged by digging around their roots. Larger deciduous sorts are most attractive standing alone against a background that will display their flowers at bloom time and show off their strongly patterned, usually gray limbs and big, fuzzy flower buds in winter. Small deciduous magnolias show up well in large flower or shrub borders and make choice ornaments in Asian-style gardens. Most magnolias are excellent lawn trees; try to provide a good-size grass-free area around the trunk, and don't plant under the tree.

Balled-and-burlapped plants are available in late winter and early spring; container plants are sold all year. Do not set plants lower than their original soil level. Stake single-trunked or very heavy plants to prevent them from being rocked by wind, which will tear the thick, fleshy, sensitive roots. To avoid damaging the roots, set stakes in planting hole before placing tree. Prevent soil compaction around root zone by keeping foot traffic to a minimum. Prune only when absolutely necessary. Magnolias seldom have serious pest or disease problems.

M

MAGNOLIA

NAME	ZONES	TYPE	HEIGHT	SPREAD	AGE AT BLOOM	FLOWERS	USES, CHARACTERISTICS, COMMENTS
Magnolia acuminata CUCUMBER TREE	US, MS, LS, CS; 9–2	Deciduous	60–80 ft.	25 ft.	12 yrs.	Greenish yellow, to 3½ in. wide; not conspicuous. Appear after leaves in late spring, summer. Handsome reddish seed capsules with red seeds	Shade or lawn tree. Canopy of glossy, 5- to 9-in. leaves provides dense shade. Hardy to cold; won't thrive in hot, dry winds
M. a. subcordata (M. cordata) YELLOW CUCUMBER TREE, YELLOW MAGNOLIA	US, MS, LS, CS; 9–2	Deciduous	25–35 ft.	20–35 ft.	12 yrs.	Yellow to yellow-green flowers larger than those of species (to 4 in.), with mild lemon scent. Blossoms appear as leaves start to expand	Slow-growing lawn or border tree for large properties. Showier, lower, and shrubbier than *M. acuminata*. Not ordinarily a tree you can walk or sit under. 'Miss Honeybee' has larger, pale yellow flowers
M. ashei ASHE MAGNOLIA	US, MS, LS, CS; 9–6	Deciduous	10–20 ft.	To 15 ft.	1–2 yrs.	To 6–10 in. wide, with creamy white, somewhat pointed segments that may be spotted with red. Late spring	Valuable for its tropical effect where space is limited. Multistemmed shrub with 2-ft.-long leaves. Very hardy. Like a shrubby version of *M. macrophylla*
M. × brooklynensis 'Black Beauty'	US, MS, LS, CS; 9–6	Deciduous	15–25 ft.	To 15 ft.	3–5 yrs.	Tulip-shaped flowers are dark purple outside, white inside. Blooms in late spring, escaping frost damage	Hybrid of *M. acuminata* and *M. liliiflora*
M. 'Butterflies'	US, MS, LS; 9–1	Deciduous	To 20 ft.	To 15 ft.	2 yrs. from grafts	Deep yellow, 3- to 5-in.-wide flowers with red stamens. Blooms in midspring, before leaves emerge	Hybrid of *M. acuminata* and *M. denudata*. Upright and pyramidal when young, spreading with age. Dark green leaves to 8 in. long. Hardy to –29°F without damage
M. 'Coral Lake'	US, MS, LS; 9–6	Deciduous	20–25 ft.	8–10 ft.	2–3 yrs.	Large (7-in.) blossoms in a blend of coral pink tones shading into vertical yellow stripes. Blooms late, but before leaves expand	Very upright growth habit. Unique flower color
M. 'Daybreak'	US, MS, LS; 9–5	Deciduous	To 18 ft.	To 4 ft.	3 yrs.	Huge (8- to 10-in.), very fragrant, bright rose pink blossoms in late spring, escaping frost damage	Columnar form. Useful in small lots, side yards
M. denudata (M. conspicua, M. heptapeta) YULAN MAGNOLIA	US, MS, LS, CS; 9–6	Deciduous	To 35 ft.	To 30 ft.	6–7 yrs.	Fragrant white flowers, sometimes tinged purple at base. Blossoms are erect, somewhat tulip shaped, 3–4 in. long, spreading to 6–7 in. Early bloom on base branches; often injured by late freezes	Tends toward irregular form; good in informal garden or at woodland edge. Choose a site where it can be shown off against dark background or sky. Leaves 4–7 in. long. Good cut flowers. 'Gere' blooms late, avoiding frosts
M. 'Elizabeth'	US, MS, LS, CS; 8–3	Deciduous	To 40 ft. or more	To 20 ft.	2–6 yrs. from grafts	Fragrant soft yellow flowers, 6–7 in. wide. Color is paler in mild-winter areas. Blossoms appear before or with the leaves	Hybrid between *M. acuminata* and *M. denudata*. Grow as single-trunked tree or multitrunked shrub-tree. Hardy to at least –20°F
M. fraseri (M. auriculata) FRASER MAGNOLIA	US, MS, LS, CS; 9–6	Deciduous	To 30 ft. or more	To 20 ft.	10–12 yrs.	Creamy to yellowish white, fragrant, 8–10 in. wide. Blooms in late spring, when leaves are full grown. Rose red, 5-in. seed capsules are showy in summer	Good lawn or woodland tree. Thin, stiff, brittle leaves 16–18 in. long, borne in whorls at branch ends. Handsome dark brown fall color
M. 'Galaxy'	US, MS, LS, CS; 9–6	Deciduous	To 40 ft.	To 25 ft.	5 yrs. from grafts	Abundant bright red-purple, slightly fragrant, goblet-shaped blossoms to 5 in. across. Blooms in midspring, before leaves emerge but usually after last frost	Fast-growing, broadly conical tree. Medium green leaves to 8 in. long. Cross between *M. liliiflora* and *M. sprengeri* 'Diva'

M

MAGNOLIA

NAME	ZONES	TYPE	HEIGHT	SPREAD	AGE AT BLOOM	FLOWERS	USES, CHARACTERISTICS, COMMENTS
M. grandiflora SOUTHERN MAGNOLIA, BULL BAY	US, MS, LS, CS; 10–6	Evergreen	To 80 ft.	40–60 ft.	15 yrs., sometimes much less; 2–3 yrs. from grafts or cuttings	Pure white, aging buff; large (8–10 in. across), powerfully fragrant. Usually have six segments. Species and its selections bloom throughout summer, fall	Classic Southern tree for street or lawn. Can grow as espalier or in big container. Unpredictable in form and age of bloom. Grafted plants more predictable; grow as multitrunked trees or prune to single trunk. Glossy, leathery leaves, 4–8 in. long. Tolerates salt spray, sandy soil
M. g. 'Alta'	US, MS, LS, CS; 10–6	Evergreen	40–50 ft.	15–25 ft.	2–3 yrs. from grafts	Like those of *M. grandiflora*	Grows quickly—to 20 ft. tall, 9 ft. wide in 10 years. Dark green leaves are brown on the undersides. Fibrous root system makes it easy to transplant. Dense, columnar form makes it an excellent screening plant
M. g. 'Bracken's Brown Beauty'	US, MS, LS, CS; 10–6	Evergreen	To 30 ft.	10–15 ft.	2–3 yrs. from grafts	Creamy white, lemon scented, 5–6 in. wide. Late spring	Leaves 5 in. long, with undulating edges, rust-colored felt beneath. Hardy. Dense, compact. Introduced by Ray Bracken, Easley, South Carolina
M. g. 'D. D. Blanchard'	US, MS, LS, CS; 10–6	Evergreen	To 50 ft. or more	25–35 ft.	2 yrs. from grafts	Like those of *M. grandiflora*	Handsome pyramidal tree. Lustrous dark green leaves are orange-toned brown on undersides
M. g. 'Edith Bogue'	US, MS, LS, CS; 10–6	Evergreen	To 35 ft.	To 20 ft.	2–3 yrs. from grafts	Like those of *M. grandiflora*. Young plants slower to come into heavy bloom than some other selections. Open habit; rather dull foliage	Shapely, vigorous tree. One of hardiest selections of *M. grandiflora*; has withstood −24°F. Excellent for Upper South but not a top choice elsewhere. Keep it out of strong winds
M. g. 'Little Gem'	US, MS, LS, CS; 10–6	Evergreen	Slow to 20–25 ft.	10–15 ft.	2 yrs. from grafts	To 5–6 in. wide; bloom from spring through late summer (fewer blossoms form during midsummer heat)	Narrow form. Good in container, as espalier, in confined area. Branches to ground. Half-size leaves are dark above, rusty beneath
M. g. 'Majestic Beauty'	US, MS, LS, CS; 10–6	Evergreen	35–50 ft.	To 20 ft.	2 yrs. from grafts	Very large (to 1 ft. across)	Vigorous, dense-branching street or shade tree. Broadly pyramidal form. Leaves are long, broad, and heavy. Most luxuriant of Southern magnolias
M. g. 'Samuel Sommer'	US, MS, LS, CS; 10–6	Evergreen	Fairly fast to 30–40 ft.	To 30 ft.	2–3 yrs. from grafts	Full and very large, ranging from 10 to 14 in. wide	Large, leathery, glossy leaves are very dark green above, with heavy, rusty red felt on undersides
M. g. 'St. Mary'	US, MS, LS, CS; 10–6	Evergreen	Usually 20 ft.; larger in old age	To 20 ft.	2–3 yrs. from grafts	Heavy production of 8- to 10-in. flowers on small tree	Left to its natural form, grows as a big, dense bush. Staked and pruned, it makes a small tree. Good plant for containers and espalier

Magnolia 'Butterflies'

Magnolia 'Elizabeth'

Magnolia 'Galaxy'

Magnolia 'Galaxy'

MAGNOLIA

NAME	ZONES	TYPE	HEIGHT	SPREAD	AGE AT BLOOM	FLOWERS	USES, CHARACTERISTICS, COMMENTS
M. grandiflora 'Symmes Select'	US, MS, LS, CS; 10–6	Evergreen	40–50 ft.	To 30 ft.	1–3 yrs. from grafts	Like those of *M. grandiflora*. Blooms at early age	Dark green, lustrous leaves backed with dark brown. Introduced by Cedar Lane Farm, Madison, Georgia
M. g. 'Victoria'	US, MS, LS, CS; 10–6	Evergreen	To 20 ft.	To 15 ft.	2–3 yrs. from grafts	Like those of *M. grandiflora*	Withstands –10°F with little damage, but locate out of wind. Dark green leaves are very broad and heavy
M. 'Iolanthe'	US, MS, LS; 9–6	Deciduous	To 25 ft.	To 25 ft.	3–5 yrs.	Abundant, bowl-shaped blossoms 10–12 in. across, in soft pink with paler pink interior; open from large, hairy, outward-facing buds. Blooms in late winter and early spring, before leaf-out	Small, wide-spreading tree has survived brief periods down to –12°F. Outward-facing blooms are more desirable than the more common upturned or downturned magnolia flowers
M. kobus KOBUS MAGNOLIA	US, MS, LS; 9–5	Deciduous	To 30 ft.	To 20 ft.	15 yrs.	White, slightly fragrant blossoms to 4 in. wide. Blooms in early to midspring, before leaves emerge	Cold-hardy, sturdy tree for planting singly in a lawn or in informal shrub and tree groupings
M. Kosar-De Vos Hybrids (the "Little Girl" series)	US, MS, LS; 9–5	Deciduous	To 12 ft.	To 15 ft.	4–5 yrs.	Flower color ranges from deep to pale purple (sometimes with pink or white interior), depending on selection. Trees bloom in spring before leaf-out; sporadic rebloom in summer	Hybrids between *M. liliiflora* 'Nigra' and *M. stellata* 'Rosea'; bred to bloom later than *M. stellata*, thus avoiding frost damage. Erect, shrubby growers bearing girls' names: 'Ann', 'Betty', 'Jane', 'Judy', 'Pinkie', 'Randy', 'Ricki', 'Susan'. Use in shrub border or singly in lawn
M. liliiflora (M. quinquepeta) LILY MAGNOLIA	US, MS, LS; 9–1	Deciduous	To 12 ft.	To 15 ft.	4–5 yrs.	White inside, purplish outside; about 4 in. across. Blooms in late spring	Good for shrub border; strong vertical effect in big flower border. Spreads slowly by suckering. Leaves 4–6 in. long. Blooms of 'Gracilis', 'Nigra', and 'O'Neill' are dark purplish red outside, pink inside
M. × loebneri LOEBNER MAGNOLIA	US, MS, LS, CS; 9–5	Deciduous	Slow to 12–15 ft.; can reach 50 ft.	12–15 ft.	3 yrs.	Narrow, strap-shaped flower segments similar to those of *M. stellata*, but generally fewer and somewhat longer and wider. Blooms appear before leaves in midspring. Some selections are fragrant	Hybrids between *M. kobus* and *M. stellata*. 'Ballerina', white with faint pink blush, and taller, pure white 'Spring Snow' are both fragrant. Very lightly scented are 'Leonard Messel', with pink blooms from darker buds, and 'Merrill' ('Dr. Merrill'), a vigorous, free-flowering, white-blossomed form. Use in lawn, shrub border, at woodland edge
M. macrophylla BIGLEAF MAGNOLIA	US, MS, LS, CS; 10–6	Deciduous	Slow to 30–50 ft.	To 20–30 ft.	12–15 yrs.	Fragrant white flowers to 16 in. across in late spring and early summer, after leaf-out	Showy tree with leaves 1–3 ft. long and 9–12 in. wide. Needs to stand alone. Be sure to give it some shade. Old Southern favorite

Magnolia grandiflora

Magnolia grandiflora

Magnolia grandiflora 'St. Mary'

Magnolia 'Iolanthe'

MAGNOLIA

NAME	ZONES	TYPE	HEIGHT	SPREAD	AGE AT BLOOM	FLOWERS	USES, CHARACTERISTICS, COMMENTS
M. quinquepeta (see **M. liliiflora**)							
M. sargentiana robusta	LS, CS; 9–7	Deciduous	To 35 ft.	To 35 ft.	10–12 yrs.; 8–10 yrs. from grafts	Huge (8- to 12-in.), fragrant mauve pink bowls open erect, then nod. Blooms in mid- to late spring, before leaves open	Among most spectacular of flowering plants. Leaves 6–8 in. long. Not for hot, dry areas. Give ample room. 'Blood Moon' has deep rose pink flowers
M. sieboldii OYAMA MAGNOLIA	US, MS, LS; 9–5	Deciduous	6–15 ft.	6–15 ft.	5 yrs.	Cup-shaped, fragrant white flowers centered with crimson stamens. Bloom begins in late spring, continues through late summer. Bright pink seedpods	Good for small gardens. Buds look like white Japanese lanterns. Nice planted upslope or at top of wall so people can look up into somewhat nodding flowers. Leaves 3–6 in. long. Best in part shade
M. × soulangeana SAUCER MAGNOLIA (often called TULIP TREE)	US, MS, LS, CS; 9–5	Deciduous	To 25 ft.	To 25 ft. or more	3–5 yrs.	White to pink or purplish red, fragrant, variable in form and size (from 3 to 6 in. wide). Blooms from late winter into spring, both before leaves emerge and as they open	Hybrid of *M. denudata* and *M. liliiflora*. Good lawn tree, anchor plant in big container plantings. Seedlings highly variable; look for named selections (especially later-blooming ones for frost-prone regions). Medium green, rather coarse-looking leaves 4–6 in. long or longer
M. × s. 'Alexandrina'	US, MS, LS, CS; 9–6	Deciduous	To 25 ft.	To 25 ft. or more	3–5 yrs.	Deep purplish pink outside, white inside, to 4 in. across. Midseason, before leaves emerge	Same uses as for *M. × soulangeana*. Large, rather heavy leaves. Subject to bloom damage in late freezes
M. × s. 'Brozzonii'	US, MS, LS, CS; 9–6	Deciduous	To 25 ft.	To 25 ft. or more	3–5 yrs.	White, 8-in. blossoms very slightly flushed purplish rose at base. Flowers come late in bloom season	One of the most handsome white-flowered forms. Vigorous tree. Often avoids bloom damage in late freezes
M. × s. 'Lennei' (M. lennei)	US, MS, LS, CS; 9–6	Deciduous	To 25 ft.	To 25 ft. or more	3–5 yrs.	Very large, globe-shaped blossoms are deep purple outside, white inside. Blooms late	Spreading, vigorous plant. Late bloom helps it escape frosts in cold areas
M. × s. 'Lennei Alba' (M. lennei 'Alba')	US, MS, LS, CS; 9–6	Deciduous	To 25 ft.	To 25 ft. or more	3–5 yrs.	Like those of 'Lennei', but white in color, slightly smaller, and earlier (midseason)	Spreading, vigorous plant; often avoids bloom damage in late frosts
M. × s. 'Rustica Rubra'	US, MS, LS, CS; 9–6	Deciduous	To 25 ft.	To 25 ft. or more	3–5 yrs.	Large, cup-shaped, deep reddish purple flowers. Blooms somewhat past midseason. Big (6-in.) dark rose seedpods	Vigorous grower for large areas. More treelike than many *M. × soulangeana* selections
M. × s. 'Verbanica'	US, MS, LS, CS; 9–6	Deciduous	To 20 ft.	To 15 ft.	2–3 yrs.	Segments soft purplish rose on outside, white on inside and at tips. Blooms late	One of the hardiest and most beautiful saucer magnolias. Not subject to bloom damage in late frosts

Magnolia kobus

Magnolia kobus

Magnolia 'Randy' (Kosar-De Vos Hybrid)

Magnolia liliiflora

M. × loebneri 'Spring Snow'

M

MAGNOLIA

NAME	ZONES	TYPE	HEIGHT	SPREAD	AGE AT BLOOM	FLOWERS	USES, CHARACTERISTICS, COMMENTS
M. sprengeri 'Diva'	MS, LS, CS; 9–7	Deciduous	To 40 ft.	To 30 ft.	3 yrs.	Spectacular, erect, sweet-scented blooms to 8 in. wide are bright rose pink outside, pink-suffused white with deeper pink lines inside. This selection blooms late winter to early spring, before leaves open	Big shrub that can be trained as tree. Young plants are broad, twiggy. 'Diva 711' is particularly cold hardy
M. stellata STAR MAGNOLIA	US, MS, LS, CS; 9–5	Deciduous	To 10 ft.	To 20 ft.	3 yrs.	White flowers to 3 in. across, with 12 to 18 narrow, strap-shaped segments. Profuse bloom comes very early—late winter to early spring, before leaves emerge. Some selections are fragrant	Slow growing, shrubby; fine for borders, entryway gardens, edge of woods. Quite hardy, but flowers often nipped by frost in colder part of range. Fine texture in leaf and twig. Fair yellow-and-brown autumn leaf color. Longtime favorite in Southern gardens
M. s. 'Centennial'	US, MS, LS, CS; 9–6	Deciduous	To 10 ft.	To 20 ft.	3 yrs.	White blossoms faintly marked pink, 5 in. across, with 40 to 50 segments. Midspring	Same uses as *M. stellata*. Like an improved *M. s.* 'Waterlily'
M. s. 'Dawn'	US, MS, LS, CS; 9–5	Deciduous	To 10 ft.	To 20 ft.	3 yrs.	White flowers have 25 or more segments, each with a longitudinal pink stripe	Same uses as *M. stellata*
M. s. 'Jane Platt'	US, MS, LS, CS; 9–5	Deciduous	12–15 ft.	10–12 ft.	3–5 yrs.	Rich pink, 4- to 5-in. blossoms with 40 to 50 segments. Blooms in early spring	Typical shrubby *M. stellata* plant form
M. s. 'Rosea' PINK STAR MAGNOLIA	US, MS, LS, CS; 9–5	Deciduous	12–15 ft.	15–20 ft.	3 yrs.	Pink buds open to light pink or white flowers	Same uses as for *M. stellata*. A very old selection, in cultivation in North America since the late 1800s. Probable parent of many pink-flowered selections of *M. stellata*
M. s. 'Royal Star'	US, MS, LS, CS; 9–5	Deciduous	10–15 ft.	15–20 ft.	3 yrs.	Fragrant white blooms with 25 to 30 segments. Blooms 2 weeks later than species	Same uses as for *M. stellata*. Faster growing
M. s. 'Two Stones'	US, MS, LS, CS; 9–5	Deciduous	15–20 ft.	15–20 ft.	3 yrs.	Thicker and more substantial than flowers of other *M. stellata* types. Fragrant	Bred with an extra set of chromosomes, giving it larger leaves and flowers than species. Dense, well-shaped plant
M. s. 'Waterlily'	US, MS, LS, CS; 9–6	Deciduous	To 10 ft.	To 20 ft.	3 yrs.	Pink buds open to very fragrant white blossoms to 5 in. across, with 40 to 50 segments. Blooms late, after most other *M. stellata* selections	Faster growing than most star magnolias. Leaves 2–4 in. long, with finer texture than those of other magnolias. Various plants are sold under this name

M

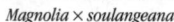

Magnolia × *soulangeana*

Magnolia × *soulangeana*

Magnolia sprengeri 'Diva'

Magnolia stellata 'Royal Star'

Magnolia virginiana

MAGNOLIA

NAME	ZONES	TYPE	HEIGHT	SPREAD	AGE AT BLOOM	FLOWERS	USES, CHARACTERISTICS, COMMENTS
M. tripetala UMBRELLA MAGNOLIA	US, MS, LS; 9–5	Deciduous	15–35 ft.	15–20 ft.	5 yrs.	Greenish white, to 10 in. across, with purple stamens; heavily fragrant	Huge leaves cluster at ends of branches. Vigorous and unkempt, with an open and irregular crown; difficult to site in a garden. Large red seedpods
M. virginiana (M. glauca) SWEET BAY	US, MS, LS, CS; 9–6	Semi-evergreen to deciduous	10–20 ft	To 20 ft.	8–10 yrs.	Creamy white, fragrant, nearly globular blossoms are 2–3 in. wide. Late spring to late summer	Prefers moist, acid soil. Grows in swamps in eastern U.S. Deciduous shrub in Upper South; semievergreen elsewhere. Multistemmed. Leaves bright green above, nearly white beneath, 2–5 in. long. Twigs and branches are bright green, adding winter interest if leaves fall. 'Plena' is a double-flowered form
M. v. australis SOUTHERN SWEET BAY	MS, LS, CS, TS; 12–6	Evergreen	45–50 ft	15–20 ft.	8–10 yrs.	White, lemon scented, 2–4 in. across	Single trunked with upright, open habit; glossy green, silver-backed leaves. Gets much larger in woodland setting, sometimes to 80 ft. tall
M. 'Vulcan'	MS, LS; 9–6	Deciduous	To 25 ft.	To 25 ft.	1 yr. from grafts	Showy, ruby red blossoms to 10–12 in. across. Flowers borne in tree's younger years may be smaller and paler than those on older trees. With good care, trees will produce mature flowers in 3–4 years. Blooms in spring, before leaves emerge	Open form when young, becoming more rounded with age
M. 'Wada's Memory'	US, MS, LS; 9–6	Deciduous	To 30 ft.	To 20 ft.	3–5 yrs. from grafts	White, slightly fragrant blossoms over 4 in. across. Blooms appear in early to midspring, before leaves emerge	Also sold as *M. × kewensis* 'Wada's Memory' or as *M. × proctoriana* 'Wada's Memory'. Same uses as *M. kobus*; grows faster than *M. kobus*. Coppery red new leaves
M. 'Yellow Bird'	US, MS, LS, CS; 9–2	Deciduous	To 40 ft.	To 20 ft.	2 yrs. from grafts	Deepest yellow of the yellow hybrids. Slight green tinge at base of erect, 3-in.-long flower segments. Blooms for 2–3 weeks in early to midspring, just as leaves emerge	Hybrid of *M. acuminata* and *M. × brooklynensis* 'Evamaria'. Upright and pyramidal when young, broadly oval when mature. Furrowed bark. Sometimes available as a multitrunked form

Magnoliaceae. The magnolia family contains evergreen and deciduous trees and shrubs with large, showy flowers, usually with a large number of petal-like segments (commonly called petals), sepals, and stamens. Tulip tree (*Liriodendron*), *Magnolia*, and *Michelia* are examples.

MAHONIA

Berberidaceae

EVERGREEN SHRUBS

🌿 ZONES VARY BY SPECIES

☀ ◐ ● EXPOSURE NEEDS VARY BY SPECIES

◗ ◖ ● WATER NEEDS VARY BY SPECIES

These useful and easy-to-grow plants remind many people of holly (*Ilex*), though they're closely related to barberry (*Berberis*). Handsome, typically spiny leaves are divided into leaflets. Showy yellow flowers are borne in dense,

Mahonia aquifolium

rounded or spikelike clusters in late winter or spring. Blooms are followed by berrylike blue, blue-black, or red fruits that attract birds. Prune to reduce size or lankiness, cutting selected stems to the ground or to a node. Avoid planting too close to walkways and sitting areas, where prickly foliage might snag passersby. Generally pest free and seldom browsed by deer. Provide well-drained soil.

M. aquifolium. OREGON GRAPE HOLLY. Zones US, MS, LS; 9–6. Native from British Columbia to Northern California. Erect growth to 6 ft. or taller; spreads by underground stems to 5 ft. wide. Leaves 4–10 in. long, with five to nine very spiny-toothed, oval, 1- to 2½-in. leaflets that are glossy green in some forms, dull green in others. Young growth is ruddy or bronzy; scattered mature red leaves. Purplish or bronzy leaves in winter, especially in Upper South or where plants are grown in full sun. Spring flowers in 2- to 3-in. clusters along stems; edible blue-black fruit with a powdery coating (makes good jelly).

'Compactum' grows 2–3 ft. tall and wide and spreads freely to make broad colonies. New leaves glossy, light to coppery green; mature leaves matte medium green. 'Orange Flame', 2 ft. tall and 3 ft. wide, has bronzy orange new growth and glossy green mature leaves that turn wine red in winter.

Oregon grape holly can take any exposure, though it does best with some shade in the Lower South and wind protection in the Upper South. Use in masses as foundation planting, in woodland garden, as low screen or garden barrier. Control height and form by pruning; if woody stems jut out, cut them down to ground (new growth fills in quickly). Unlike other mahonias, this one needs acid soil; develops chlorosis (yellow leaves with green veins) in alkaline soil. Regular water.

M. 'Arthur Menzies'. Zones LS, CS; 9–8. Probable hybrid between *M. lomariifolia* and *M. bealei*. Vigorous, upright grower to 15 ft. tall and at least half as wide; may be somewhat leggy. Toothed dark green leaves to 1½ ft. long, divided into many leaflets; foliage looks attractive year-round. Upright clusters of fragrant flowers appear in December and January, bringing a welcome splash of bright yellow to the winter garden. Blue berries with a powdery coating. Full sun or partial shade. Regular water.

M. bealei. LEATHERLEAF MAHONIA. Zones US, MS, LS, CS; 9–3. Native to China. Grows 10–12 ft. high and 10 ft. wide, with strong pattern of vertical stems, horizontal foliage. Leaves over 1 ft. long, divided into 7 to 15 broad, leathery leaflets to 5 in. long; leaflets grayish or bluish green above, olive green below, with spiny-toothed edges. Very fragrant flowers in erect, 3- to 6-in.-long, spikelike clusters at branch ends in earliest spring. Blue berries with a powdery sheen. Distinguished plant against stone, brick, wood, glass. Takes sun in Upper and Middle South; best in part shade elsewhere. Plant in rich soil with ample organic material. Regular water.

M. fortunei. CHINESE MAHONIA. Zones LS, CS; 9–4. Native to China. Grows to 6 ft. high, 3 ft. wide; stems bear 10-in., matte green leaves with 7 to 13 spiny-toothed leaflets. Undersurface of leaves is yellowish green, with heavily netted veins. Flowers in short clusters in late summer to early fall; purple-black berries seldom develop. Plant has an unusual stiff charm and is grown for form and foliage, not fruit. Full sun to light shade. Moderate water.

M. gracilis. Zones MS, LS, CS; 9–4. Native to Mexico. To 3 ft. high, 4 ft. wide. Glossy leaves have 5 to 13 overlapping leaflets, each about 1½ in. long. Foliage is most colorful in full sun: leaves are lime green when new, darker green in summer, and a lively mix of reds, oranges, yellows, and light green in winter. Bright yellow, very fragrant blossoms in winter. Blue fruit with a powdery sheen. Tolerates extreme heat and poor soils, even hard-packed clay. Needs little or no supplemental water.

M. 'King's Ransom'. Zones US, MS, LS; 9–1. Most likely a hybrid of *M. aquifolium* and *M. pinnata*. Upright grower to 5–6 ft. tall and 4–5 ft. wide. Dark bluish green leaves turn red purple in winter. Showy yellow flowers in spring; dark blue fruits. Give full or partial shade and moderate to regular water.

M. lomariifolia. BURMESE MAHONIA. Zones LS, CS; 9–5. Native to China. Showy plant to 6–12 ft. high and 6 ft. wide, with erect stems that branch only slightly. Young plants often have a single, vertical unbranched stem; with age, plants send up more near-vertical branches from near base. Clustered near ends of these branches are horizontally held leaves to 2 ft. long. In outline, leaves look like stiff, crinkly, barbed ferns; each has as many as 47 thick, spiny, glossy green leaflets arranged symmetrically along both sides of central stem. Flowers

Mahonia lomariifolia

in winter or earliest spring grow in foot-long, erect clusters at branch tips, just above uppermost cluster of leaves. Blue fruit has a powdery sheen. Prune stems at varying heights to induce branching. Needs shade at least in afternoon to keep deep green color. Regular water.

M. ×media. Zones MS, LS, CS; 9–7. Hybrids between *M. lomariifolia* and a Japanese species similar to *M. bealei*. Plants bear upright clusters of fragrant flowers in late fall and winter; generally resemble *M. lomariifolia* and require the same conditions. 'Buckland' and 'Charity' grow to 15 ft. high, 12 ft. wide; 'Faith' reaches 6–10 ft. high and 6 ft. wide; 'Hope' and 'Lionel Fortescue' grow to 6 ft. high and wide; 'Underway' and 'Winter Sun' reach 4–5 ft. high and as wide.

M. pinnata. CLUSTER MAHONIA. Zones MS, LS; 9–1. Native from southern Oregon to Southern California. Similar to *M. aquifolium*, but

leaves are blue gray and more crinkly and spiny, new growth often shows lots of red and orange, and plants may grow taller (to 10 ft.) in ideal conditions. Not always easy to find in nurseries. Takes heat and drought better than *M. aquifolium*. Also takes more sun, but in Lower South plant in light shade. Little water.

M. repens. CREEPING MAHONIA. Zones US, MS; 7–3. Native from British Columbia to Northern California, eastward to Rocky Mountains. To 1 ft. high and 3 ft. wide, spreading by underground stems when cold weather arrives. Leaves to 10 in. long, with three to seven spiny-toothed leaflets. One of the best mahonias for winter color: dull blue-green foliage turns bronzy or pinkish when cold weather arrives. Short clusters of flowers in mid- to late spring are followed by blue berries. Good ground cover. Full sun or partial shade. Little or no water.

M. swaseyi. TEXAS MAHONIA. Zones MS, LS, CS, TS; 10–7. Native to Texas and Mexico. Spiny growth to 3–5 ft. tall, 5 ft. wide. Leaves are rosy when young, light green in summer, reddish purple in fall and winter. Fragrant yellow spring flowers; bright red berries. Good barrier plant; can be sheared but looks most attractive when allowed to take its natural shape. Best in full sun; tolerates much heat. Provide well-drained soil. Needs little or no supplemental water.

M. trifoliolata (Berberis trifoliolata). AGARITA, TEXAS CURRANT. Zones MS, LS, CS, TS; 12–7. Native to Arizona, southern New Mexico, Texas. To 8 ft. tall, 6 ft. wide. Stiff, upright branches hold leathery, blue-green to gray-green leaves to 3 in. long, each consisting of three spiny-tipped leaflets. Fragrant yellow flowers in spring. Red berries ripen in summer; they make good jelly, are also favored by wildlife. Needs good drainage and full sun. Tolerates heat and drought, thriving on little or no supplemental water.

MAIDEN GRASS. See MISCANTHUS sinensis 'Gracillimus'

MAIDENHAIR FERN. See ADIANTUM

MAIDENHAIR SPLEENWORT. See ASPLENIUM trichomanes

MAIDENHAIR TREE. See GINKGO biloba

MAIDEN PINK. See DIANTHUS deltoides

MAJORANA hortensis. See ORIGANUM majorana

MALLOW. See MALVA

MALTESE CROSS. See LYCHNIS chalcedonica

MALUS

FLOWERING CRABAPPLE

Rosaceae

DECIDUOUS TREES

✦ ZONES VARY BY SELECTION

☼ FULL SUN

◐ ● MODERATE TO REGULAR WATER

▸ SEE CHART PAGE 410

Malus floribunda

From North America, Europe, Asia. These beloved ornamental trees have much to offer, including spectacular springtime flowers, ornamental (and occasionally edible) fruit, and adaptability to a wide range of soil types and growing conditions. More than 600 kinds are cultivated, and a new selection seems to appear every few days. The chart beginning on page 410 includes our top choices among widely available ornamental selections. For types used primarily for cooking and cider, see Crabapple.

Trees range in height from 6 to 40 ft., but most reach about 25 ft. high. Oval, pointed leaves may be solid deep green, burgundy tinged, or even purple; fall color is seldom rousing, but some types do turn yellow or even orange. Profuse single, semidouble, or double blossoms in white, pink, or red appear in spring, usually before the leaves unfurl; they sometimes have a sweet, musky fragrance. Small red, orange, or yellow apples

▸ page 412

MALUS

NAME AND ZONES	HABIT, SIZE	FLOWERS	FRUIT	COMMENTS
Malus 'Adams' US, MS, LS, CS; 9–1	Dense, round headed, to 20 ft. tall and wide	Red buds open to single pink flowers	Dull red, small, long lasting	Orange fall foliage. Low chill requirement for bloom; good disease resistance
M. 'Adirondack' US, MS, LS; 8–1	Columnar, to 12 ft. by 6 ft.	Red buds open to large, red-tinged, single, waxy white flowers	Red to orange red	Formal in appearance. High disease resistance
M. angustifolia SOUTHERN WILD CRAB US, MS, LS, CS; 9–1	Rounded tree 25–30 ft. by 25 ft.	Red buds open to single, very fragrant pink flowers that fade to white	Aromatic, yellowish green, to 1½ in. across	Susceptible to fireblight, rust, and scab. Attractive in natural settings
M. 'Brandywine' US, MS, LS; 8–1	Vigorous, shapely, to 15–20 ft. tall and wide	Double rose pink. Fragrant	Yellowish green	Leaves have a reddish cast. Fair disease resistance
M. 'Callaway' US, MS, LS, CS; 9–1	Attractive, round headed, to 15–25 ft. by 15–20 ft.	Pink buds open to single white flowers	Deep red, large, long lasting	Low chill requirement for bloom; good choice for warmer-winter climates. High disease resistance
M. 'Candied Apple' US, MS, LS; 8–1	Weeping form; to 10–15 ft. by 20 ft.	Reddish buds open to single blossoms with deep pink outer petals, whitish inner petals edged in pink	Bright red, small; persists all winter	Good disease resistance
M. 'Centurion' US, MS, LS; 8–1	Oval crowned, to 25 ft. by 15–20 ft.	Red buds open to single red flowers	Shiny, deep red, long lasting	Blooms young. High disease resistance
M. coronaria WILD SWEET CRABAPPLE US, MS, LS; 8–1	Broadly spreading, to 30 ft. by 35 ft.	Pink buds; single flowers in pure white or pink-tinged white	Yellowish green, large	Blooms late. Susceptible to rust and scab
M. 'Dolgo' US, MS, LS; 8–1	Willowy, spreading, to 40 ft. tall and wide	Pink buds open to single white flowers	Purple red, large. Good flavor; can be used for jelly	Moderate disease resistance
M. 'Donald Wyman' US, MS, LS, CS; 9–1	Broad, to 20 ft. by 25 ft.	Pink to red buds open to single white flowers	Shiny, bright red, small, long lasting	Lustrous foliage. Good disease resistance. An outstanding selection
M. floribunda JAPANESE FLOWERING CRABAPPLE US, MS, LS; 8–1	Broad, dense grower to 15–25 ft. tall and wide	Deep pink buds open to single white flowers. Fragrant, incredibly profuse blooms	Red-blushed yellow, small; does not last long	Moderate disease resistance
M. 'Harvest Gold' US, MS, LS; 8–1	Vigorous, narrow, to 30 ft. by 15 ft.	Pink buds open to single white flowers	Yellow, showy; hangs on until spring	Blooms late. High disease resistance
M. hupehensis (M. theifera) TEA CRABAPPLE US, MS, LS; 8–5	Broad form; moderate growth to 15 ft. by 25 ft.	Deep pink buds open to single white flowers. Fragrant	Greenish yellow to red, small, not showy	Picturesque form, with branches strongly angled from short trunk. Moderate disease resistance
M. 'Indian Magic' US, MS, LS; 8–5	Rounded, to 15–20 ft. tall and wide	Red buds open to single deep pink flowers	Shiny, red to orange, small, particularly long lasting	Moderate susceptibility to disease
M. 'Indian Summer' US, MS, LS; 8–1	Rounded, to 18 ft. tall and wide	Single rose red flowers	Bright red, long lasting	Good orange-red fall leaf color. High disease resistance
M. 'Jewelberry' US, MS, LS; 8–1	Dwarfish, dense, to 8 ft. by 12 ft.	Pink buds open to single white flowers	Shiny, red, small, long lasting	Blooms young. Moderate disease resistance

M

MALUS

NAME AND ZONES	HABIT, SIZE	FLOWERS	FRUIT	COMMENTS
M. 'Katherine' US, MS, LS; 9–1	Slow growing to 20 ft. tall and wide	Deep pink buds open to large, double pink flowers that quickly fade to white	Red-blushed yellow, very small	Fair disease resistance. Blooms more heavily in alternate years
M. 'Liset' US, MS, LS; 8–1	Roundish, dense growth to 15–20 ft. tall and wide	Crimson buds open to single flowers in deep red to crimson	Dark red to maroon; holds well on tree	Deep purplish green leaves. Fair disease resistance
M. 'Molten Lava' US, MS, LS; 8–5	Spreading, weeping tree to 12 ft. by 15 ft.	Deep red buds open to single white flowers	Red orange, small; lasts well on tree	Bark is yellow, looks especially attractive against snow in winter. Good disease resistance
M. 'Narragansett' US, MS, LS; 8–1	Broad, round headed, to 15 ft. tall and wide	Red buds open to single white flowers with faint touch of pink	Bright red, small, showy	High disease resistance
M. 'Pink Princess' US, MS, LS; 8–4	Low, broad, to 15 ft. by 12 ft.	Single rose pink flowers	Deep red, small; lasts well on tree	Reddish green foliage. Good disease resistance
M. 'Prairifire' US, MS, LS; 8–4	Round headed, to 20 ft. tall and wide	Red buds open to single flowers in deep pinkish red	Dark red, small; holds well on tree	Leaves emerge reddish maroon, turn dark green. High disease resistance
M. 'Professor Sprenger' US, MS, LS; 8–1	Dense and rounded, to 20 ft. by 20–25 ft.	Dark pink buds open to single white flowers. Fragrant	Orange red, long lasting	High disease resistance
M. 'Red Jade' US, MS; 7–1	Irregular, weeping form; to 15 ft. tall and wide	Small, single white flowers	Bright red, profuse; holds well into fall	Moderate disease resistance
M. 'Red Jewel' US, MS, LS; 8–1	Small, round headed, to 15 ft. by 12 ft.	Large, single white flowers	Bright red, small, long lasting	Fair disease resistance
M. 'Robinson' US, MS, LS; 8–1	Dense, upright, vase-shaped tree to 25 ft. by 15 ft.	Deep red buds open to single deep pink flowers	Dark red	Copper-tinged foliage. High disease resistance
M. sargentii SARGENT CRABAPPLE US, MS, LS; 8–1	Broad, densely branched, to 10 ft. by 20 ft.	Profuse show of small, single white flowers. Fragrant	Red, tiny, long lasting	Good disease resistance. 'Candymint' has pink flowers with petals outlined in red. 'Rosea', a pink-flowered form, may be more disease prone than the species
M. sieboldii 'Calocarpa' (M. ×zumi calocarpa) US, MS, LS; 8–1	Densely branched, rounded, to 15 ft. tall and wide	Single flowers open pale pink, then fade to white. Fragrant	Bright red, glossy, small; lasts well on tree	Moderate susceptibility to fireblight. Usually resistant to scab
M. 'Snowdrift' US, MS, LS; 8–5	Rounded, dense, to 20–25 ft. tall and wide	Red buds open to single white flowers. Has a long bloom season	Orange red, small, long lasting	Good disease resistance
M. 'Strawberry Parfait' US, MS, LS; 8–1	Open, vase shaped, to 20 ft. by 25 ft.	Red buds open to single pink flowers edged in red. Profuse bloomer	Red-blushed yellow	High disease resistance
M. 'Sugar Tyme' US, MS, LS; 8–1	Upright, oval form, to 18 ft. by 15 ft.	Delicate light pink buds open to single white flowers. Fragrant	Red, abundant, long lasting	High disease resistance
M. 'Thunderchild' US, MS, LS; 8–1	Erect, oval, to 20 ft. by 18 ft.	Single rose pink flowers	Dark red	Purple foliage. Good disease resistance

WHAT FLOWERING CRABAPPLES NEED

WINTER CHILL: For best growth and flowering, plants need at least 600 hours at 45°F or lower.

SOIL: They prefer good, well-drained, deep soils— but will grow in rocky or gravelly ones, can succeed even in clay, and tolerate acid to slightly alkaline conditions.

PROTECTION: Crabapples are often planted in lawns, where their bark can easily be nicked by mowers. To protect the trees, create a sod-free, mulched area around the trunk.

DISEASE CONTROL: Fireblight, scab, powdery mildew, and cedar-apple rust can be serious problems for crabapples. Prevention is the best control for all of these diseases—grow resistant selections.

PRUNING: Prune in winter to build a good framework, remove any suckers, and correct shape. Also remove watersprouts (unbranched shoots that grow straight up from main limbs). Crabapple trees can be trained as espaliers.

Malus 'Snowdrift'

M

(size varies from ¾ to 2 in. wide) ripen from midsummer into autumn and can be quite showy. In some types, the fruit persists well into winter and supplies food for robins, mockingbirds, cardinals, cedar waxwings, blue jays, and many other birds.

You can set out trees from nursery pots anytime, though spring and fall are preferred. Plant bare-root trees in late winter or early spring. All crabapples are terrifically cold hardy, but heat and humidity cause problems in the Coastal South. Gardeners there should select 'Adams', 'Callaway', or 'Donald Wyman', disease-resistant selections that need little winter chill.

Crabapples make fine lawn trees, informal screens, and espaliers. Small-fruited selections also make good street or patio trees, as fruits not consumed by birds will wither on the tree without causing a mess. Prune to shape in winter, removing basal suckers and watersprouts (unbranched shoots that grow straight up from the main limbs).

Many insects feast on crabapples, including aphids, Japanese beetles, tent caterpillars, and borers. But these pests are minor compared with several potentially serious diseases (see "What Flowering Crabapples Need," above). Disease resistance is noted in the chart. Unless you are fond of frequent spraying, avoid these disease-prone selections: 'Almey', 'Bechtel' (*M. ioensis* 'Plena'), 'Eleyi', 'Hopa', 'Radiant', 'Red Silver', 'Royal Ruby', and 'Royalty'.

MALVA

MALLOW

Malvaceae

PERENNIALS OR BIENNIALS

🌱 US, MS, LS ⊩ 8–1

☼ FULL SUN

💧 REGULAR WATER

Malva alcea

From Europe; naturalized in U.S. These plants are related to and somewhat resemble hollyhock (*Alcea*), but they are bushier, with smaller, roundish to heart-shaped leaves. They are easy to grow from seed and usually bloom the first year. Need good drainage, average soil. Use in perennial borders or for a quick tall edging. Not long lived.

M. alcea. Perennial. To 4 ft. tall, 2 ft. wide; upper leaves deeply divided. Saucer-shaped pink flowers to 2 in. wide appear from late spring to fall. Subject to root rot in hot, wet weather. The most widely available variety is *M. a. fastigiata*; it is narrower than the species.

M. moschata. MUSK MALLOW. Perennial. Erect, branching plant to 3 ft. tall, 2 ft. wide. Finely cut leaves; pink or white flowers to 1 in. wide or somewhat wider, summer to fall. Entire plant emits a mildly musky odor if brushed against or bruised. Named selections are more frequently grown than the species. 'Rosea' has pink blossoms; 'Alba' is shorter than the species (to 2 ft. tall) and bears white flowers.

M. sylvestris. FRENCH HOLLYHOCK. Perennial or biennial. Easy-to-grow plant with erect, bushy growth to 2–4 ft. tall, 2 ft. wide. Flowers are 2 in. across and appear throughout summer, often right up until frost. Reseeds; often seen in older gardens of the Lower South. Common selection 'Zebrina' (often sold as *M. zebrina*) has blossoms in pale lavender pink with pronounced deep purple veining. 'Marina' bears light blue blossoms; 'Mauritiana' has deep lavender-pink, often semidouble flowers with dark purple veining.

Malvaceae. The mallow family contains hundreds of species of mainly herbaceous plants and some shrubs and trees, often with lobed leaves and showy flowers. Ornamentals include flowering maple (*Abutilon*), hollyhock (*Alcea*), *Hibiscus*, mallow (*Malva*), and checkerbloom (*Sidalcea*). Commercially, the family is important as the source of cotton (*Gossypium*).

MALVAVISCUS arboreus drummondii

TURK'S CAP, TURK'S TURBAN

Malvaceae

PERENNIAL

🌱 LS, CS, TS ⊩ 12–8

◑ ● PARTIAL TO FULL SHADE

◊ 💧 ● LITTLE TO REGULAR WATER

Malvaviscus arboreus drummondii

Native from Florida west to Texas and Mexico. Spindly, shrubby perennial with semiwoody stems, almost evergreen in the Tropical South. Blooms from early summer right through fall, bearing nodding, bright red, twisted-looking, 1- to 1½-in.-long blossoms with long, prominent stamens similar to those of hibiscus. May reach 9 ft. tall if soil is fertile and growing season long and warm, but usually grows 3–5 ft. high and almost as wide. Dies back to the ground in winter in the Lower and Coastal South. Long-stalked yellow-green leaves are coarse textured, heart shaped, 2–3 in. wide. Blooms attract hummingbirds. Small, rounded, applelike fruits follow the flowers, changing from white to red as they ripen. Tough, easy plant; tolerates alkaline and rocky soils and drought. Not usually browsed by deer.

MANDARIN. See CITRUS

MANDEVILLA

Apocynaceae

EVERGREEN AND DECIDUOUS VINES OR VINING SHRUBS

🌱 ZONES VARY BY SPECIES; OR GROW IN POTS

☼ ◑ FULL SUN OR PARTIAL SHADE

💧 REGULAR WATER

Mandevilla 'Alice du Pont'

Widely grown for showy flowers, the genus *Mandevilla* includes plants formerly called *Dipladenia*. They thrive in warm, humid weather and bloom continuously from late spring to frost in most areas of the South. They are generally hardy outdoors in the Coastal and Tropical South; elsewhere, they can be overwintered indoors or treated as annuals.

Blossoms consist of five broad lobes that flare out from a tubular throat; except as noted, they are unscented. Plants climb by twining. Use them to cover arbors, trellises, fences, lampposts, even mailboxes. Excellent container plants. Plant in fertile, well-drained soil. Provide protection from hottest afternoon sun. Feed with a balanced water-soluble fertilizer every 2 to 3 weeks throughout the growing season. Growth may need thinning from time to time. Watch for spider mites.

M. boliviensis. Evergreen. Zones TS; 12–5. Native to Ecuador and Bolivia. Grows to 12 ft. as a vine; reaches 3 ft. tall and 5 ft. wide as a sprawling shrub. Glossy, oval, pointed leaves to 4 in. long; 2½-in.-wide white flowers with golden yellow throats.

M. hybrids. Evergreen. Zone TS; may grow as root-hardy perennials in Zone CS. The hybrid mandevillas described here are sometimes sold as selections of *M.* ×*amabilis* or *M.* ×*amoena.* Plants grow to 15–20 ft., with glossy dark green, oval leaves 3–8 in. long. Most widely grown is 'Alice du Pont', with clusters of glowing pink, 2- to 4-in. flowers appearing among the leaves; even very small plants in 4-in. pots will bloom. 'Moonlight Parfait' is a vigorous grower; pink buds open to large white blossoms with a double-petaled pink center. 'Summer Snow' ('Monte', 'Flora Snow') bears blush pink blossoms that eventually fade to white. 'White Delight' has pale pink buds opening to white blooms with a light yellow throat. 'Ruby Star' is a slightly more compact plant with narrower-lobed, 3-in.-wide flowers; blossoms open deep pink, then mature to magenta with a touch of yellow deep in the throat. 'Rita Marie Green' ('Pink Parfait') has long-lasting, hot pink double flowers; 'Tango Twirl' offers upright clusters of light pink double blooms. Plant all hybrids in rich soil and provide a frame, trellis, or stake for support. Pinch tips of young plants to induce bushiness.

M. laxa (M. suaveolens). CHILEAN JASMINE. Deciduous; evergreen in frost-free areas. Zones CS, TS; 12–2. Native to Chile and Argentina. Grows to 15 ft. or more, with heart-shaped, 2- to 6-in.-long leaves. Clustered flowers are white, 1½–2 in. across, with a powerful perfume like that of gardenia. Requires less heat to bloom than other mandevillas. Provide rich soil. If plant becomes badly tangled, cut to ground in winter; it will resprout and bloom on new growth. Roots are hardy to about 5°F.

M. splendens (Dipladenia splendens). Evergreen. Zones TS; 12–6; may grow as root-hardy perennial in Zone CS. Native to southeastern Brazil. Compact, shrubby plant to 2 ft. tall, 3 ft. wide; eventually starts to twine (to 15–20 ft. tall with support), but you can keep it bushy by pinching climbing shoots. Deep green leaves are 4–8 in. long, tinged with bronze when new. Flowers are 3–4 in. wide, rose pink with yellow throats; color fades as blossoms age. 'Red Riding Hood', with deep cherry red flowers; white-blossomed 'Faire Lady' ('My Fair Lady'); and scarlet 'Scarlet Pimpernel' are lower growing and shrubbier than the species (to 6–8 ft. as climbers) and superb in hanging baskets.

MANETTIA

Rubiaceae

EVERGREEN OR DECIDUOUS VINES

LS, CS, TS H 12-7

FULL SUN OR PARTIAL SHADE

REGULAR WATER

Manettia cordifolia

Twining vines from tropical parts of the world. In most locations, they offer abundant, colorful flowers from late spring through summer and on into fall; may bloom in winter in the Coastal and Tropical South. The tubular blooms attract hummingbirds and butterflies. In mild-winter regions, plants are evergreen; in colder areas, they die to the ground in winter and then resprout in spring. Provide fertile, well-drained soil. Train on trellises, fences, arbors, posts. Prune back hard in winter to remove tattered foliage and rejuvenate plants. Easily propagated by seed, cuttings, or division.

M. cordifolia. FIRECRACKER VINE. From Peru, Bolivia, Argentina. Lacy and thin stemmed, with bright green, oval or heart-shaped leaves to 3 in. long. Grows rapidly but is not usually invasive. Waxy red flowers, sometimes flushed yellow, are about 1½ in. long.

M. luteorubra (M. inflata). BRAZILIAN FIRECRACKER, CANDY CORN VINE. Native to Paraguay and Uruguay. Lush, much-branched vine with dark green, oval or lance-shaped leaves to 3 in. long. Bright red, 1- to 2-in.-long flowers have yellow tips and resemble candy corn.

MANFREDA

Agavaceae

SUCCULENT PERENNIALS

ZONES VARY BY SPECIES

FULL SUN OR PARTIAL SHADE

LITTLE TO REGULAR WATER

Manfreda maculosa

Bizarre yet attractive plants that look like crosses between century plant *(Agave)* and tuberose *(Polianthes)*. Long, spineless, succulent leaves grow in a rosette from a bulbous base. Flower spikes are tall and sturdy, requiring no staking. The blooms are real conversation pieces, good for cut flowers; they're appealing to hummingbirds, too.

The species described here are all easy to grow in well-drained soil. Good in rock gardens and containers.

M. maculosa. TEXAS TUBEROSE. Zones MS, LS, CS. Native to southern Texas, northern Mexico. Forms a 1-ft.-tall and 2-ft.-wide rosette of fleshy, narrow, 6- to 12-in.-long leaves in deep green blotched with purple. During summer, 2- to 3-ft.-tall flower stalks bear fragrant, tubular, 2-in.-long blossoms in creamy white aging to purple; long stamens give them a spidery look. Leaves die back in winter but reappear quickly in spring. Plants form new clumps by offsets.

M. variegata. Zones CS, TS. Native to southern Texas, eastern Mexico. Spreading ground cover for dry soil. Forms a mat to 1 ft. tall and 4 ft. wide. Slender, purple-mottled green leaves to 1½ ft. long. In summer, 4-ft.-tall blossom stalks bear exotic-looking flowers to 1½ in. long that resemble a green-and-maroon version of tuberose blooms.

M. virginica. FALSE ALOE, RATTLESNAKE MASTER. Zones US, MS, LS, CS; 10–5. Native from Maryland to Missouri, south to Texas and Florida. Spreads by rhizomes to form colonies. Dark green leaves may be mottled or striped with red; they grow 2 ft. long and only 2 in. wide. Greenish yellow, spicily fragrant flowers appear atop 6-ft. spikes in summer. Dry seedpods rattle with loose seeds.

MANGO

Anacardiaceae

EVERGREEN TREE

TS; OR GROW IN POTS

FULL SUN

REGULAR WATER

SAP AND JUICE FROM FRUIT CAUSE SKIN RASH IN SOME PEOPLE

Mango

Tropical Asian native known botanically as *Mangifera indica.* One of the easiest fruit trees to grow—but since it won't take frost, its cultivation in the South is limited to south Florida and South Texas. Trees range in size from 50-ft. giants with a 30-ft. spread to 6- to 10-ft. specimens better suited to the average backyard. Handsome, large (8- to 16-in.-long) leaves are often coppery red or purple when new, later turning dark green.

Mangoes are usually self-fruitful. Long clusters of yellow to reddish flowers appear at branch ends from spring into summer; these are followed by fleshy fruits that typically weigh from ¾ to 1 pound, though they can tip the scales at as much as 4 pounds. Most mangoes are more flavorful if allowed to ripen on the tree; they're usually ready to harvest 4 to 5 months after bloom. The trees can be incredibly productive—a 6-ft. tree can bear up to 60 pounds of fruit per year. Smaller plant selections make excellent container plants. ▶

Mangoes will grow in most well-drained soils. Water only to get them established; after that, they'll get by on rainfall. (However, trees grown in containers will need regular watering.) Spread ¼ pound of 6-6-6 fertilizer per inch of trunk diameter evenly at the drip line every 3 months and water it in well. Spraying for pests is seldom necessary, though scale, anthracnose, and powdery mildew cause occasional problems; for controls, consult your Cooperative Extension Office.

Mangoes typically have green to reddish or yellowish skin, a large seed, and very juicy pale yellow to deep orange flesh that tastes somewhat like a peach with flowery or perfumy overtones—but there's incredible diversity in size, shape, color, and flavor. Most groceries stock 'Tommy Atkins', a selection that is to mangoes what 'Red Delicious' is to apples; it looks pretty and ships well, but taste and texture are not exceptional. Choices offering better flavor and texture include the following.

'Cogshall'. Yellow-orange, red-blushed, aromatic, elongated oval fruit weighs up to 1 pound, has yellow flesh with rich, spicy flavor. Small, disease-resistant, very productive tree, easily kept pruned to about 6 ft. tall and wide.

'Fairchild'. Oblong, yellow, ½-pound fruit with sweet, fiberless deep orange flesh. Handsome, disease-resistant tree can be kept at 8 ft. tall and wide. Heavy producer.

'Glenn'. Oval, red-flushed yellow fruit to about ¾ pound; orange flesh has a mildly sweet, peachy flavor. Grows about 15 ft. tall and wide; heavy producer.

'Graham'. Oval yellow fruit to about ¾ pound, with sweet, fiberless deep orange flesh. Compact tree; easily kept to 8 ft. tall and wide with pruning.

'Ice Cream'. Flattened, greenish yellow, ½-pound fruit with sweet, rich, fiberless lemon yellow flesh. Disease-resistant, highly productive tree is easy to keep at 6 ft. tall and wide.

'Julie'. Somewhat flattened, greenish fruit is flushed pink and yellow, weighs about ¾ pound. Fiberless yellow flesh is delicious, with a slight pineapple flavor. Reaches about 10 ft. tall. Needs cross-pollination with another mango. Susceptible to fungal diseases, but superior flavor makes it worth growing.

'Keitt'. Oval fruit is very large, weighing up to 4 pounds. Yellowish green skin flushed reddish orange; firm yellow flesh has a resinous sweetness, few fibers. Bears late in the season, producing into fall. Dense-foliaged, disease-resistant tree to 6–10 ft. tall and not quite as wide.

'Kent'. Oval fruit to 1½ pounds, with greenish yellow skin flushed pink and red. Deep yellow, nearly fiberless flesh has excellent flavor. Large tree grows to 50 ft. high and wide; heavy producer.

'Lancetilla'. Oval fruit is very large, weighing 2 to 4 pounds or more. Bright red skin; fiberless lemon yellow flesh, intensely sweet and aromatic. With pruning, can be kept to about 10 ft. tall and wide.

'Mallika'. Bright yellow, potato-shaped fruit weighs about 1 pound; fiberless deep orange flesh has complex, honeylike flavor. For best flavor, harvest fruit before fully ripe and let stand at room temperature for a week or two. Keep trees pruned to 8–10 ft. tall and wide.

'Palmer'. Elongated oval fruit weighs 1 to 2 pounds, has purplish red skin and yellow, mild-flavored flesh with few fibers. Tree is best kept to 6–10 ft. high and wide.

'Rosigold'. Earlier than most mangoes—fruit may be ripe in March. Cylindrical fruits to ¾ pound are bright yellow with red highlights, have fiberless, juicy deep orange flesh with rich, sweet flavor. Small tree can be pruned to 8 ft. tall and wide.

'Vallenato'. Oval deep red fruit with firm, fiberless, delicious orange-red flesh. Large, disease-resistant, vigorous tree.

MAPLE. See ACER

FOR GROWING SYMBOL EXPLANATIONS
PLEASE SEE PAGE 145

MARANTA

Marantaceae

PERENNIALS

⚡ ZONES VARY BY SPECIES

◑ PARTIAL SHADE; BRIGHT INDIRECT LIGHT

💧 💧 AMPLE WATER DURING SUMMER

Maranta leuconeura erythroneura

Genus of about 20 species from tropical Central and South America. Densely spreading clumps of stems hold attractive leaves typically marked with colorful, interesting patterns.

M. arundinacea. ARROWROOT. Zones TS; 12–10. Slender branches grow 6 ft. tall, with small white flowers and tropical-looking dark green leaves to 10 in. long. Spreads by rhizomes, which are the source of the arrowroot starch used as a thickening agent for sauces, puddings, and fruit pie fillings. *M. a.* 'Variegata' has dark green leaves variegated with light green and yellowish green. A form with reddish purple leaves is sometimes offered.

M. leuconeura. PRAYER PLANT. Zones TS; 12–10; or houseplant. Satiny dark green leaves with light green and brownish black markings, silver or red veins. Spreads by rhizomes to make a striking ground cover in tropical gardens; soil must be rich and fast draining, air very warm and humid. The 5-in.-long leaves lie flat during the day, then fold toward the center of the plant at night—hence the common name "prayer plant."

Indoors, locate out of direct light. Keep soil moist during the growing season, and use a humidifier to keep moisture in the air; maintain night temperatures above 55°F. Indoors or out, feed monthly during summer with a general-purpose liquid houseplant fertilizer. Flowers are insignificant. *M. l. erythroneura* has red veins; *M. l. kerchoveana*, known as rabbit's foot, has light green leaves with dark blotches (like animal tracks) on either side of the midrib.

Marantaceae. The arrowroot family consists of tropical or subtropical herbaceous plants with fleshy rhizomes or tubers and highly asymmetrical flowers. Most are grown for handsome foliage, a few for flowers. Examples include *Calathea* and *Maranta*.

MARGUERITE. See CHRYSANTHEMUM frutescens

MARIGOLD. See TAGETES

MARJORAM. See ORIGANUM

MARLBERRY. See ARDISIA

MARRUBIUM vulgare

HOREHOUND

Lamiaceae (Labiatae)

PERENNIAL

⚡ US, MS, LS, CS, TS ◨ 12–1

☀ FULL SUN

◐ 💧 LITTLE TO MODERATE WATER

Marrubium vulgare

Native to Mediterranean region and western Asia; naturalized throughout Europe and the Americas. Coarse, upright plant to 1–3 ft. tall, 1–1½ ft. wide, with wrinkled, woolly, aromatic gray-green leaves to 2 in. long. Blooms in second year from seed, bearing rounded whorls of white flowers (similar to those of mint) on foot-long, branching stems in summer. As a garden plant, it is invasive and rather weedy looking, but it makes a serviceable edging in a garden of gray-leafed plants. Used for medicinal purposes and in candy. Foliage lasts well in bouquets. Requires little water but will take more if drainage is good; otherwise not fussy about soil. Give protection from cold and wind.

MARSH MARIGOLD. See CALTHA palustris

MASCAGNIA

ORCHID VINE

Malpighiaceae

DECIDUOUS VINES

🗡 ZONES VARY BY SPECIES

☼ FULL SUN

💧 MODERATE WATER

Mascagnia lilacina

Vines of Mexican origin that bloom during the hottest time of year. Bright green leaves in opposite pairs look like those of honeysuckle *(Lonicera)*. Clusters of five-petaled, 1-in. blooms centered with ten stamens; petals are shaped like Ping-Pong paddles. Oddly winged seedpods look something like butterflies and are sometimes used in dried arrangements.

M. lilacina. LAVENDER ORCHID VINE. Zones CS, TS. To 15–20 ft., with 1½-in. leaves and lilac flowers that are followed by inch-wide seedpods. Plant is hardy to 15–18°F; leaves drop off at 22°F.

M. macroptera. YELLOW ORCHID VINE. Zone TS. To 15 ft., with 3-in. leaves. Abundant bright yellow flowers are followed by conspicuous 2-in., yellow-green seedpods. Hardy to 22–24°F.

MASTERWORT. See ASTRANTIA

MATRICARIA recutita (M. chamomilla)

FALSE CHAMOMILE

Asteraceae (Compositae)

ANNUAL

🗡 US, MS, LS, CS, TS 12–1

☼ FULL SUN

💧 MODERATE WATER

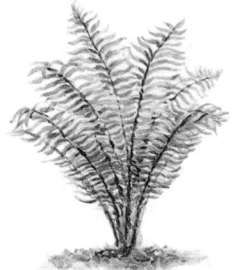

Matricaria recutita

Native to Europe, western Asia; naturalized in North America. Aromatic plant grows to 2 ft. tall and 1½ ft. wide, with finely cut, almost fernlike foliage. White-and-yellow daisy-type flowers to 1 in. wide bloom in summer. Grows easily in ordinary soil; sow seed in late winter or spring. Valued for its herbal use: dried flowers are used in making the familiar, fragrant chamomile tea.

Plants or seeds sold as *M.* 'White Stars', 'Golden Ball', and 'Snowball' are varieties of *Chrysanthemum parthenium*. Chamomile sold as a walk-on ground cover is *Chamaemelum nobile (Anthemis nobilis)*.

MATTEUCCIA struthiopteris

OSTRICH FERN

Polypodiaceae

FERN

🗡 US, MS 8–1

☼ LIGHT SHADE

💧 REGULAR TO AMPLE WATER

Matteuccia struthiopteris

Native to northern parts of North America, Europe, Asia. Tolerates extreme cold but cannot take long, hot, dry summers. Good choice for the Upper South and mountainous regions where summer nights cool off and there is ample moisture. Forms a clump that looks like a shuttlecock—narrow at the base, spreading out at the top. Can reach 6 ft. tall and 3 ft. wide in rich, moist soil; spreads by underground rhizomes. Attractive in woodland garden or growing beside a pond or stream. The unfolding young fronds (fiddleheads) are edible and can be served as a cooked vegetable.

MATTHIOLA

STOCK

Brassicaceae (Cruciferae)

BIENNIALS GROWN AS COOL-SEASON ANNUALS

🗡 US, MS, LS, CS, TS 6–1

☼ ◐ FULL SUN OR LIGHT SHADE

💧 REGULAR WATER

Matthiola incana

Old-fashioned plants native to the Mediterranean region, well suited to the cottage garden. All have long, narrow gray-green leaves and masses of delightfully scented flowers in erect, spikelike clusters. Need light, fertile soil and good drainage. Like pansies and violas, stocks bloom in cool weather. In the Upper South, choose early bloomers, and plant in earliest spring to get flowers before hot weather comes. Elsewhere, set out plants in fall for bloom in winter or early spring. Stocks take moderate frost but will not set flower buds if nights are too chilly, so late planting delays bloom until spring. In areas with heavy winter rainfall, plant in raised beds to ensure good drainage and prevent root rot.

M. incana. STOCK. Valued for fragrance, cut flowers. Oblong leaves to 4 in. long. Single or double, inch-wide flowers with spicy-sweet scent. Colors include white, pink, red, purple, lavender, blue, yellow, cream. Blues and reds are purple toned; yellows tend toward cream.

Many strains are available. Among branching types are Trysomic Seven Weeks, blooming in just 7 weeks from seed and growing to 12–15 in. tall; Ten Weeks, 15–18 in. high; Giant Imperial strain, 2–2½ ft. tall. Space all these branching sorts 1–1½ ft. apart. Upright, unbranched stocks can be planted in rows 6–8 in. apart and are ideal for cutting; two of the best are Cinderella Mix (8 in. tall) and Double Giant Flowering (2–3 ft.).

M. longipetala bicornis. EVENING SCENTED STOCK. To 1 ft. or a little taller, 9 in. wide, with lance-shaped leaves to 3½ in. long. Small purplish flowers are not showy but emit a powerful fragrance at night.

MAY APPLE. See PODOPHYLLUM

MAYHAW. See CRATAEGUS opaca

MAYPOP. See PASSIFLORA incarnata

MAZUS

Scrophulariaceae

PERENNIALS

🗡 US, MS, LS 8–5

☼ ◐ ● EXPOSURE NEEDS VARY BY SPECIES

💧 REGULAR WATER

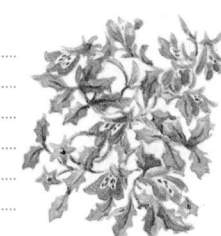

Mazus reptans

These low-growing plants form spreading mats of small, attractive leaves, with the bonus of colorful flowers in spring and early summer. Use in rock gardens, as small-scale ground cover, as filler between pavers (they take heavy foot traffic in this last role). Best in rich soil. They are evergreen in mild-winter climates; in colder areas, they freeze to the ground but usually recover quickly in spring if protected over winter by snow cover or light mulch.

M. radicans. From New Zealand. Grows 2–3 in. high, spreading to 1½–2 ft. Lime green, 1- to 2-in.-long leaves with bronzy purple spotting. Half-inch blossoms in white marked with purple and yellow. Can take some shade but blooms best with at least half a day of sunlight.

M. reptans. Himalayan native to 2 in. high; spreads 1 ft. or wider by slender stems that creep and root along the ground. Sparsely toothed, rather narrow leaves are bright green, about 1 in. long. Flowers are ¾ in. across, purplish blue with white and yellow markings. A white-blossomed form is available, sold by some nurseries as *M. reptans* 'Albus' and by others as *M. japonicus* 'Albiflorus'. Give full sun or partial shade in Upper and Middle South, partial to full shade in Lower South.

M

MEADOW RUE. See THALICTRUM

MEADOW SAFFRON. See COLCHICUM

MEADOW SWEET. See FILIPENDULA ulmaria

MEALYCUP SAGE. See SALVIA farinacea

MEDITERRANEAN FAN PALM. See CHAMAEROPS humilis

MELALEUCA quinquenervia

PAPERBARK TREE

Myrtaceae

EVERGREEN TREE

CS, TS ⫚ 12–9

☼ FULL SUN

◐ ◑ ● LITTLE TO REGULAR WATER

Melaleuca quinquenervia

What could possibly be wrong with a tree that looks attractive, is simple to grow, tolerates just about any soil, accepts salt spray, and suffers no serious pests or diseases? In the case of paperbark tree, just about everything.

Imported from Australia (and also known as cajeput tree), it quickly found favor among south Florida gardeners as an interesting choice for a lawn, shade, or street tree. Then intrepid land speculators decided to spread seeds of the thirsty tree throughout the south Florida swamplands to help drain them. Seedlings, which will grow on dry land or with their roots submerged, quickly invaded the wetlands to form impenetrable stands, virtually eliminating native vegetation. Hundreds of thousands of acres of the Florida Everglades have fallen victim.

Trees can reach 50–80 ft. tall and 30–50 ft. wide, with pendulous young branches. Thick, spongy, light brown to whitish bark peels off in sheets. Stiff, narrowly oval, shiny pale green leaves reach 2–4 in. long; spikes of yellowish white flowers resembling bottlebrushes crowd branch tips in summer and fall. Cylindrical or squarish, woody seed capsules contain many seeds.

Although paperbark tree can be a fine ornamental in the appropriate setting, its devastating impact on native ecosystems marks it as a tree that should never be planted. In fact, the state of Florida legally prohibits planting, growing, and selling it. It is included in this book as a warning, not a recommendation.

There is, however, one good, safe use for paperbark tree—cut and ground up, it makes an attractive, long-lasting, commercially available mulch that is a fine substitute for cypress mulch. Using this mulch helps reduce the cutting of cypresses, which are a vital component of many swampland ecosystems.

MELAMPODIUM

Asteraceae (Compositae)

ANNUALS AND PERENNIALS

ZONES VARY BY SPECIES

☼ FULL SUN, EXCEPT AS NOTED

● MODERATE WATER

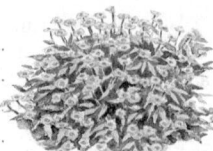

Melampodium paludosum 'Showstar'

These tough, drought-tolerant plants produce masses of small daisies over a long period. Provide well-drained soil.

M. cinereum. BLACKFOOT DAISY. Perennial. Zones LS, CS; 9–7. Native to limestone soils of Arkansas, Colorado, and Texas. To 4–12 in. tall and wide. Similar to *M. leucanthum* but not as hardy; blooms from spring until frost.

M. leucanthum. BLACKFOOT DAISY. Perennial. Zones US, MS, LS, CS, TS; 12–3. From Arizona, New Mexico, Texas, Mexico. Wiry stems set with narrow gray leaves form a clump to 1 ft. tall and wide. In spring, summer,

and (in mild climates) sporadically in winter, the foliage clump is topped by clouds of inch-wide, honey-scented white daisies with yellow centers.

M. paludosum. STAR DAISY. Annual. Zones US, MS, LS, CS, TS; 12–1. From Portugal and Spain. To 2–3 ft. tall and half as wide, with narrow dark green leaves and deep yellow daisies throughout summer and into fall (no deadheading required). Start seeds indoors for earliest bloom; or sow in ground after soil has warmed. Plants will also self-sow. 'Medallion' grows to 3 ft. tall and often becomes leggy by midsummer. 'Million Gold' is a lower-growing selection (1 ft. high) that blooms prolifically. Dense-growing 'Showstar' is also more compact than the species (to 1½–2 ft. tall), with showier blooms; 'Derby' is similar, but it's a little shorter and more compact still. All tolerate heat and humidity, perform well in full sun or light shade.

Melastomataceae. The melastoma family consists almost entirely of tropical shrubs and trees with strongly veined leaves and symmetrical flowers. An example is princess flower *(Tibouchina)*.

MELIA azedarach

CHINABERRY

Meliaceae

DECIDUOUS TREE

MS, LS, CS, TS ⫚ 12–7

☼ FULL SUN

● MODERATE WATER

◆ FRUIT IS POISONOUS IF INGESTED

Melia azedarach 'Umbraculiformis'

Native to China, northern India. To 30–50 ft. high and wide, with irregular habit. Shiny, rich green, 1- to 3-ft.-long leaves are cut into many toothed, narrow or oval leaflets 1–2 in. long. Blooms in spring or early summer, bearing loose clusters of lilac flowers that are fragrant in the evening. Blossoms are followed by hard, berrylike yellow fruits about ½ in. wide. Tough plant; tolerates heat, wind, poor alkaline soil, drought. In areas with year-round moisture, tends to self-sow and become a pest (birds eat the fruit and spread seedlings all over creation).

'Umbraculiformis', Texas umbrella tree, is less picturesque but far more common than the species. It reaches 25–30 ft. high, with a dense, dome-shaped crown and drooping leaves. Grows true from seed.

Meliaceae. The mahogany family, consisting largely of tropical trees and shrubs, includes two plants grown in the South: chinaberry *(Melia)* and West Indies mahogany *(Swietenia)*. Both of these have finely divided leaves and clustered flowers.

MELISSA officinalis

LEMON BALM, SWEET BALM

Lamiaceae (Labiatae)

PERENNIAL

US, MS, LS, CS, TS ⫚ 12–1

☼ ◐ FULL SUN OR PARTIAL SHADE

● REGULAR WATER

Melissa officinalis

From southern Europe. A single plant grows to about 2 ft. tall, 1½ ft. wide—but plants self-sow and spread rapidly, sometimes becoming pests. Leaves are used fresh in cold drinks, fruit cups, salads, fish dishes; dried leaves give lemon perfume to sachets, potpourris. Likes rich soil. Shear occasionally to keep compact. Lemon-scented, heavily veined foliage is light green in the species. Check catalogs to find 'Aurea' and 'All Gold', with solid yellow leaves, and 'Variegata', with green foliage variegated in yellow.

M

MELON

Cucurbitaceae

ANNUALS

✔ US, MS, LS, CS, TS ⊩ 12–3

☼ FULL SUN

💧 REGULAR WATER

Melon

Nothing says "summer" better than a sweet, juicy melon—and the South's long, warm growing season gives melons the time they need to develop their sweetest flavor. Known botanically as *Cucumis melo,* they probably originated in Africa. This entry covers cantaloupes (with orange flesh) and honeydews (with green flesh), and includes a list of selections recommended for the South. For information on watermelons, see Watermelon.

Melons should be planted after all danger of frost is past, and only in warm soil; seeds will rot in cold soil. Before planting, work ½ cup of 10-10-10 fertilizer per 10 ft. of row into the soil. Melons are usually planted in hills spaced 3–4 ft. apart. Sow four to six seeds per hill, planting them ½–1 in. deep; thin seedlings to the most vigorous one or two per hill. To space out the harvest, make two or three plantings 2 weeks apart; or plant selections with different maturity dates.

When vines begin to run, apply ¼ cup of 10-10-10 fertilizer per 10 ft. of row (or per hill) and water it in. Keep the soil moist throughout the growing season, but reduce watering as harvest approaches (too much water during the week or so before harvest can make the fruit less sweet).

Poor fruit set or misshapen fruit may be caused by poor pollination. Remove deformed melons from the vine to allow normal fruit to form. Some melons may shrivel instead of developing fully; this is a normal process by which the vine sheds fruit it cannot support.

It takes some practice to be able to tell when melons are ready to harvest. Fruit picked too early will not ripen further. To test cantaloupes, sniff the stem end for characteristic aroma, look for pronounced netting of the skin and a change in color from green or yellow to tan, and check for a crack between stem and fruit. This is called the "full slip" stage and is the best time to harvest. To test honeydews, look for a slightly soft or springy blossom end and a change in skin color from green to ivory or greenish white, depending on the selection. These melons do not typically have a "full slip" stage.

Powdery mildew and fusarium wilt sometimes plague melons. You can avoid them by planting disease-resistant selections such as 'Athena', 'Edisto 47', 'Hale's Best', and 'Honeymoon Hybrid'. It's also best not to get the foliage wet when you water.

Recommended cantaloupe selections for the South include 'Ambrosia' (86 days to maturity), 'Athena' (75 days), 'Burpee Hybrid' (82 days), 'Delicious 51' (77 days), 'Edisto 47' (88 days), 'Hale's Best' (86 days), 'Park's Whopper' (77 days), 'Saticoy' (90 days), and 'Sweet & Early' (75 days). Recommended honeydews include 'Earli-Dew Hybrid' (80 days), 'Honeymoon Hybrid' (90 days), 'Jenny Lind' (80 days), and 'Sweet Delight' (82 days).

MENTHA

MINT

Lamiaceae (Labiatae)

PERENNIALS

✔ US, MS, LS, CS, EXCEPT AS NOTED

☼ ◑ FULL SUN OR PARTIAL SHADE

💧 REGULAR WATER

Mentha spicata

These Mediterranean natives spread rapidly by underground stems and can be quite invasive; to keep them in bounds, grow them in pots or boxes. Tough and unfussy, they grow almost anywhere but perform best in light, moist, medium-rich soil. Not favored by deer. Plants disappear in winter in colder part of range. Replant about every 3 years; propagate from runners.

M. ×gracilis (M. ×gentilis). GOLDEN APPLE MINT. Heat zones 9–6. Grows to 2 ft. tall. Smooth deep green, 1½- to 3-in.-long leaves with yellow variegation have a spicy apple fragrance and flavor. Produces inconspicuous flowers. Use them for flavoring foods. Foliage is excellent in mixed bouquets.

M. ×piperita. PEPPERMINT. Heat zones 9–1. Grows to about 3 ft. tall. Strongly scented, tooth-edged leaves to 3 in. long, dark green often tinged with purple. Small purplish flowers come in 1- to 3-in. spikes. Leaves are good for flavoring tea.

M. ×p. citrata, known as orange mint or bergamot mint, grows to about 2 ft. high and produces small lavender flowers and broad, 2-in.-long leaves with a slight orange flavor. Orange mint is used in potpourris and for flavoring foods.

M. pulegium. PENNYROYAL. Zones MS, LS, CS; 9–1. Creeping plant 4–16 in. high, with inch-wide, bright green, nearly round leaves. Small lavender flowers in tight, short whorls. Strong mint fragrance and flavor. Poisonous if consumed in large quantities but safe as a flavoring. Needs a cool, moist site.

M. requienii. JEWEL MINT OF CORSICA. Zones LS, CS; 9–6. Creeping, mat-forming mint reaches only ½ in. high. Tiny, round bright green leaves give it a mossy appearance; leaves release a delightful minty or sagelike fragrance when bruised. Can be used as an aromatic filler between stepping-stones (but won't take heavy foot traffic). Bears tiny, tubular light purple flowers.

M. spicata. SPEARMINT. Heat zones 10–1. Grows to 1–3 ft. high. Dark green, toothed leaves are slightly smaller than those of *M. ×piperita.* Leafy spikes of flowers in pale lilac, pale blue, or white. Clip leaves and use them fresh from the garden or dry them and use to add flavor to foods, cold drinks, or jelly.

M. suaveolens (M. rotundifolia). APPLE MINT. Heat zones 9–6. Stiff stems reach to 1½–3 ft. tall, bearing rounded, somewhat hairy gray-green leaves 1–4 in. long. Produces purplish white flowers in 2- to 3-in. spikes. Aromatic foliage combines the fragrances of apple and mint. Good in container. 'Variegata', pineapple mint, has white-marked leaves with a faint pineapple scent.

MENTOR BARBERRY. See BERBERIS × mentorensis

MERRYBELLS. See UVULARIA

MERTENSIA pulmonarioides (M. virginica)

VIRGINIA BLUEBELLS

Boraginaceae

PERENNIAL

✔ US, MS, LS ⊩ 8–1

◑ ● PARTIAL TO FULL SHADE

💧 REGULAR WATER

Mertensia pulmonarioides

A relative of forget-me-not *(Myosotis);* native to eastern U.S. Bluish green, broadly oval leaves form loose clumps to 1½ ft. wide; from these clumps rise leafy, 1½- to 2-ft.-high stems bearing open clusters of nodding, 1-in. flowers. Buds usually range from pink to lavender, but they open to blue bells, sometimes with a pinkish cast. The plant rises from the ground and flowers early in spring; dies back soon after going to seed, usually by midsummer. Virginia bluebells are charming companion plants with naturalized daffodils *(Narcissus)* or with ferns, trillium, and bleeding heart *(Dicentra)* in woodland gardens.

Provide moist soil rich in organic matter. Use summer annuals to fill void after plants die back. Clumps can be left in place indefinitely; they will slowly spread. To get more plants, use volunteer seedlings or dig and divide clumps in early autumn.

MESCAL BEAN. See SOPHORA secundiflora

M

MESEMBRYANTHEMUM crystallinum

ICE PLANT

Aizoaceae

SUCCULENT ANNUAL OR BIENNIAL

US, MS, LS, CS, TS | 12–1

FULL SUN

LITTLE OR NO WATER TO MODERATE WATER

Mesembryanthemum crystallinum

The least ornamental of many plants commonly called *Mesembryanthemum* or ice plant, this native of South Africa is now considered the only true *Mesembryanthemum*. For other, showier kinds of ice plants, see *Carpobrotus*, *Delosperma*, and *Drosanthemum*.

M. crystallinum is a sprawling plant a few inches tall and several feet wide. Oval, flat, fleshy leaves grow to 4 in. long, turn red at dry times of year. Leaves are covered with tiny, transparent blisters that glisten like flecks of ice. Foliage is edible and resembles spinach in flavor. White to pinkish, 1-in. flowers bloom in summer. Easy to grow from seed; requires well-drained soil. Very drought-tolerant plant when grown in the ground. Best use in gardens, though, is in hanging baskets and window boxes—in which locations this plant will need at least moderate watering.

MESQUITE. See PROSOPIS

METASEQUOIA glyptostroboides

DAWN REDWOOD

Taxodiaceae

DECIDUOUS TREE

US, MS, LS, CS | 9–1

FULL SUN

REGULAR WATER

Metasequoia glyptostroboides

Thought to have been extinct for thousands of years, this plant was found growing in a few isolated sites in its native China during the 1940s. It is a pyramidal tree with small cones and soft, pale green needles that turn light bronze in autumn, then drop to reveal an attractive winter silhouette. Branchlets tend to turn upward. Young trees have reddish bark; older ones have darker, fissured bark and rugged, fluted trunk bases. Grows very fast when young—sometimes as much as 4–6 ft. a year. Reaches about 90 ft. tall and 20 ft. wide at the age of 40 or so (trees haven't been in cultivation long enough to determine the maximum garden size). Looks like bald cypress (*Taxodium distichum*), another deciduous conifer.

Grows best in good, well-drained soil with steady moisture. Good lawn tree, though in time surface roots may interrupt smooth flow of turf. Not suited to arid regions or seacoast, since dry heat and salty ocean winds will burn foliage.

MEXICAN BUCKEYE. See UNGNADIA speciosa

MEXICAN BUSH SAGE. See SALVIA leucantha

MEXICAN DAISY. See ERIGERON karvinskianus

MEXICAN FAN PALM. See WASHINGTONIA robusta

MEXICAN FEATHER GRASS. See NASSELLA tenuissima

MEXICAN FIRE BUSH. See KOCHIA scoparia trichophylla

MEXICAN FLAME VINE. See SENECIO confusus

MEXICAN GRASS TREE. See DASYLIRION quadrangulatum, NOLINA longifolia

MEXICAN HAT. See RATIBIDA columnifera

MEXICAN HEATHER. See CUPHEA hyssopifolia

MEXICAN MINT MARIGOLD. See TAGETES lucida

MEXICAN ORANGE. See CHOISYA ternata

MEXICAN OREGANO. See ALOYSIA wrightii

MEXICAN PALO VERDE. See PARKINSONIA aculeata

MEXICAN PETUNIA. See RUELLIA

MEXICAN PIÑON PINE. See PINUS cembroides

MEXICAN POPPY. See ARGEMONE mexicana

MEXICAN SUNFLOWER. See TITHONIA rotundifolia

MICHAELMAS DAISY. See ASTER novi-belgii

MICHELIA

Magnoliaceae

EVERGREEN SHRUBS OR TREES

ZONES VARY BY SPECIES

PARTIAL SHADE IN HOTTEST CLIMATES

REGULAR WATER

Michelia doltsopa

Magnolia relatives native to China and the Himalayas. When in flower, they might be mistaken for some kind of magnolia—but unlike magnolias, they bear their blossoms among the leaves rather than singly at branch ends.

M. figo has been in gardens for some 200 years, and *M. doltsopa* has been in cultivation in North America for perhaps half a century. The other species listed here, however, are newcomers about which we have much to learn; they have not yet had time to grow to maturity in North American gardens. All are attractive, with lush foliage and profuse, fragrant blossoms divided into petal-like segments. Not usually browsed by deer.

M. champaca. CHAMPACA. Shrub or tree. Zones CS, TS; 12–9. To 10–20 ft. tall and broad. Glossy bright green, 10-in. leaves. Orange-yellow, 3-in. flowers with up to 20 segments are borne intermittently throughout the year, most often in winter and summer; their perfume is legendary. 'Alba' (*M. alba*) has white flowers.

M. crassipes. Shrub or tree. Zones CS, TS; 12–9. Recently introduced. Rich green foliage. Plants have bloomed at a very young age, bearing a profusion of white flowers.

M. doltsopa. Tree. Zones CS, TS; 8–1. To 90 ft. tall in its native Himalayas. Varies from bushy (nearly as wide as high) to narrow and upright (about half as broad as tall); choose plants for desired form, then prune to shape. Thin-textured, leathery dark green leaves 3–8 in. long, 1–3 in. wide. In winter, furry brown buds open to blossoms ranging from cream colored to white, with a slight green tinge at the base; they are 5–7 in. across, with 12 to 16 segments, each 1 in. wide.

M. figo (M. fuscata). BANANA SHRUB. Shrub. Zones LS, CS, TS; 12–8. Slow growing to 6–8 ft. high (possibly to 15 ft. tall) and about two-thirds as wide. Densely clothed with glossy, leathery, 3-in. leaves. Plant blooms most heavily in spring but produces scattered flowers throughout summer. Blossoms are 1–1½ in. wide, creamy yellow with a thin brownish purple border on each segment. Notable feature is the powerful, fruity fragrance, like that of ripe bananas; the perfume is strongest in a warm, wind-free spot. Choice plant for entry or patio. 'Port Wine' has rose to maroon flowers.

Michelia figo

M. ×foggii. Shrub. Zones CS, TS; 12–8. Group of hybrids between *M. figo* and *M. doltsopa*. 'Allspice' grows 10–20 ft. tall, 6–15 ft. wide, with glossy dark green foliage; bears fruity-scented, 1½-in. light yellow flowers bordered in maroon from spring to early summer. 'Belle Durio', to 6–10 ft. tall and wide, is a spring bloomer bearing 3- to 4-in. white flowers with a purple style (reproductive structure) in the center. 'Jack Fogg' grows to 18 ft. tall, 6–8 ft. wide; spring flowers are white, with each segment bordered in purplish pink.

M. maudiae. Shrub or tree. Zones LS, CS, TS; 12–8. This newcomer is a large shrub or small tree, possibly to 25 ft. tall, with 6-in. leaves that are glossy medium green above, gray green beneath. White, 3- to 4-in. flowers bloom from late spring to midsummer.

M. sinensis (M. wilsonii). Tree. Zones CS, TS; 12–10. To 20 ft. tall, possibly much taller in time, with glossy green, 6-in. leaves. Blooms in early summer, bearing white flowers with 9 to 11 segments.

M. yunnanensis. Shrub or tree. Zones CS, TS; 12–10. Another newcomer. To 15 ft. tall. Blooms in early spring, when white flowers burst from dark, velvety buds.

WHAT'S IN A NAME? *Just when the gardening public gets comfortable with a botanical name, taxonomists feel compelled to change it. The banana shrub is a great example. Our grandparents knew it as* Magnolia fuscata. *Just to confuse everyone, experts changed the name to* Michelia fuscata *and then later changed it again to its present* Michelia figo. *Now they're about to change it to* Magnolia figo. *When they finally change it back to* Magnolia fuscata, *this old favorite will have come full circle.* ❖

MICROBIOTA decussata

SIBERIAN CARPET CYPRESS

Cupressaceae

EVERGREEN SHRUB

US, MS H 7–1

FULL SUN OR PARTIAL SHADE

MODERATE TO REGULAR WATER

Microbiota decussata

Native to Siberian mountains and hardy to any amount of cold. Neat, sprawling shrub that resembles a trailing arborvitae (*Thuja*). Grows 1½ ft. tall, 7–8 ft. wide, with many plumy, horizontal or trailing branches closely set with scalelike leaves. Foliage is green in summer, turning purplish or reddish brown in winter. More shade tolerant than junipers (*Juniperus*). Needs excellent drainage. Use as a bank cover.

MILFOIL. See ACHILLEA millefolium

MILIUM effusum 'Aureum'

BOWLES' GOLDEN GRASS

Poaceae (Gramineae)

PERENNIAL GRASS

US, MS, LS H 9–6

LIGHT SHADE

REGULAR TO AMPLE WATER

Milium effusum 'Aureum'

Species is native to eastern North America and Eurasia. Its colorful selection 'Aureum' forms a clump to 2 ft. high and wide. Bright greenish gold leaves first grow erect, then take on arching, weeping form. Foliage is brightest in spring, turns light green by summer. Effective for a spot of color in a woodland garden or shaded rock garden. Goes partially dormant in summer. Seedlings usually have yellow foliage, though color may vary.

MILK-AND-WINE LILY. See CRINUM

MILKBUSH. See EUPHORBIA tirucalli

MILKWEED. See ASCLEPIAS

MILKY BELLFLOWER. See CAMPANULA lactiflora

MILLETTIA reticulata

EVERGREEN WISTERIA

Fabaceae (Leguminosae)

EVERGREEN OR DECIDUOUS VINE

LS, CS, TS H 10–7

FULL SUN

REGULAR WATER

Millettia reticulata

From China. Vigorous, twining vine with leaves like those of wisteria: shiny, leathery, divided into many leaflets. In fall, bears tight clusters of dark purple-red flowers with odor of cedar and camphor; unlike those of true wisteria, they stand atop the foliage. Usually described as reaching 15 ft., but—like wisteria—can attain great size. Grows extremely fast; once established, can overwhelm trees if permitted to climb into them. Best used as cover for large arbor, pergola, or chain-link fence. Evergreen in the Tropical South, deciduous elsewhere.

MILLION BELLS. See CALIBRACHOA

MIMOSA. See ACACIA baileyana, ALBIZIA julibrissin

MIMULUS ×hybridus

MONKEY FLOWER

Scrophulariaceae

PERENNIAL GROWN AS COOL-SEASON ANNUAL

US, MS, LS, CS, TS H 7–1

LIGHT SHADE

REGULAR WATER

Mimulus ×hybridus

This uncommon annual gets its common name from its colorful, velvety flowers, which people with overactive imaginations liken to grinning monkey faces. Smooth, succulent medium green leaves form mounds about 1 ft. high and wide. Two-lipped, funnel-shaped blooms, 2–2½ in. long, range in color from cream to rose, orange, yellow, and scarlet, usually with brownish maroon spots. Magic Mix series features largely unspotted flowers in warm, vibrant colors. Monkey flower is among the better annuals for shade; use it in borders, hanging baskets, or window boxes.

This plant keels over in high temperatures, so in most places it's best used as a cool-weather annual. Sow seeds in fall for winter and spring bloom; or set out plants in early spring (or in winter, in Florida and South Texas). In the Upper South, sow in spring for summer bloom; the plant can take more sun there, too. Provide rich soil and feed with a balanced water-soluble fertilizer every 2 weeks. Pull up plants when heat causes them to decline.

MINA lobata. See IPOMOEA lobata

MING ARALIA. See POLYSCIAS fruticosa

MINT. See MENTHA

MINTLEAF. See PLECTRANTHUS madagascariensis

A PRACTICAL GUIDE TO GARDENING
PLEASE SEE PAGES 596–669

M

MIRABILIS

FOUR O'CLOCK
Nyctaginaceae
PERENNIALS (GROWN AS ANNUALS IN UPPER SOUTH)
US, MS, LS, CS, TS H 12-6
FULL SUN
LITTLE WATER, EXCEPT AS NOTED
SEEDS AND ROOTS ARE POISONOUS IF INGESTED

Mirabilis jalapa

Fragrant, trumpet-shaped summer flowers open in late afternoon—hence the common name "four o'clock." Frosts kill these bushy plants to the ground, but in mild-winter areas they'll resprout from large, tuberous roots the following spring. Sow seeds in fall or spring; plants also self-sow freely. Treat as annuals in the Upper South.

M. jalapa. FOUR O'CLOCK, MARVEL OF PERU. From Peru. Erect, many-branched shrub forms a mounding clump 3–4 ft. high and wide. Deep green, oval, 2- to 6-in.-long leaves; sweet-scented, 1- to 2-in. flowers in white, red, yellow, magenta, and many intermediate shades. The hard black seeds are often exchanged by gardeners seeking particular flower colors. 'Broken Colors' bears streaked and freckled blossoms of raspberry red, orange, lemon yellow, and white, all on a single plant. 'Golden Sparkles' has yellow flowers tipped with pink. 'Baywatch' is a giant reaching 6–9 ft. tall, with large blooms in palest yellow. Regular water.

M. longiflora. SWEET FOUR O'CLOCK. Native to western Texas, Arizona, and Mexico. Grows 3 ft. tall and wide. Medium green, oval, pointed leaves are about 2 in. long. Blossoms are very slender, 4- to 6-in.-long tubes that flare open at the end; they are white flushed with rose or violet and have prominent magenta stamens. The fragrance is particularly sweet, excellent for the night garden.

M. multiflora. DESERT FOUR O'CLOCK. Native to the southwestern U.S. Forms a bushy mound 1–3 ft. high and 3–5 ft. wide. Gray-green, roundish to heart-shaped leaves to 3 in. long. Rose pink or magenta, 2-in.-long flowers have a musky, sweet scent.

MISCANTHUS

SILVER GRASS
Poaceae (Gramineae)
PERENNIAL GRASSES
US, MS, LS, CS H 9–1, EXCEPT AS NOTED
FULL SUN OR PARTIAL SHADE, EXCEPT AS NOTED
MODERATE TO REGULAR WATER

Miscanthus sinensis 'Gracillimus'

Among the showiest and liveliest looking of ornamental grasses, these are clump-forming plants that range from very large kinds to dwarf types good for small gardens and containers. Attractive flower panicles appear atop tall stalks; they open as tassels and gradually expand into silvery to pinkish or bronze plumes that usually last well into winter. Leaves are broad or narrow, always graceful; they may be solid colored, striped lengthwise, or banded crosswise. In fall and winter, foliage of most species turns shades of yellow, orange, or reddish brown; it looks especially showy against snow or a background of dark evergreens. Stunning accent plants in large pots. Not favored by deer.

Need little care. Cut back old foliage nearly to the ground before new leaves sprout in early spring; in climates with a long growing season, you can cut back again in midsummer to keep compact and to freshen foliage. Some selections collapse at bloom time unless given support of four or five narrow stakes inserted inconspicuously at edge of clump, concealed by foliage; wind twine or wire around stakes and clump at two levels. Divide in early spring every 2 or 3 years to limit clump size and prevent decline in vigor. Variegated types and thin-leafed species don't do well in central and southern Florida.

M. 'Giganteus'. GIANT SILVER GRASS. Impressive upright grass to 10–14 ft. tall, 8–10 ft. wide; self-supporting on stems to 2 in. thick. Arching, drooping leaves to 3 ft. long, 1½ in. wide, dark green with white midrib. In cold-winter areas, plant does not bloom. In other regions, however, flower plumes to 1 ft. long rise 1–2 ft. above foliage during very late summer to fall; they emerge tan, open silver. Leaves turn purplish green in fall, then drop to leave tall, bare stalks over winter. Good summer screen or hedge; provides tropical effect. Takes seacoast conditions. Give partial shade in the Coastal South.

M. sinensis. JAPANESE SILVER GRASS. Native to Japan, Korea, China. Variable in size and foliage. Blooms in late summer or fall. Flowers are usually held well above foliage clumps; they may be cut for fresh or dried arrangements. Many selections are obtainable, and new ones arrive on the market every year. Here are some of the choicest.

'Adagio'. Very narrow green leaves form a clump 2–3 ft. high and wide. Pink plumes rise to 4–5 ft. Better flower production than similar 'Yaku Jima'. Yellow fall foliage. Good container plant.

M. s. condensatus 'Cabaret'. Heat zones 9–6. Boldest variegated miscanthus. Big, upright clump 6–7 ft. tall, 4–5 ft. across; wide (to 1¼-in.), ribbonlike leaves with a broad white center stripe and green edges. Pink-suffused stems to 8–9 ft. bear coppery pink plumes that age to cream. Seed-sterile.

M. s. condensatus 'Cosmopolitan'. Heat zones 9–6. Similar in growth and bloom to 'Cabaret', but foliage has the reverse pattern: leaves have a green center (with a white midrib) and white margins.

'Goldfeder' ('Gold Feather'). Clump grows 4–5 ft. high and wide, with ¾-in.-wide leaves edged light golden yellow. Silvery pink flower plumes on lax stems to 7 ft. tall. Stems tend to flop, but do so gracefully; can be staked to keep upright.

'Gracillimus'. MAIDEN GRASS. Narrow dark green leaves with silver midrib; graceful clump to 4–5 ft. high, 6–8 ft. wide. Stems 5–6 ft. tall bear coppery plumes that mature to cream. Tends to flop; divide in spring every year or two to keep compact. Bright orange fall foliage. Self-sows profusely and can become a pest.

'Graziella'. Narrow leaves form a clump 4–5 ft. tall, 5–8 ft. wide. Silvery "ostrich" plumes rise to 6–7 ft. Coppery red and orange fall foliage. More refined and upright than 'Gracillimus'.

'Kirk Alexander'. Clump to 3–4 ft. tall and wide, with green leaves horizontally banded in greenish yellow. Pinkish copper plumes on stems to 5 ft. tall.

'Malepartus'. Dark green leaves are broader than those of species, in a clump 3 ft. high and wide. Flower plumes on 6- to 7-ft. stalks open rose pink, fade to silvery white, finish tan. Orange fall foliage.

'Morning Light'. Sport of 'Gracillimus', with narrow band of white on leaf margins; less vigorous and more compact than 'Gracillimus'. Grows to 3–4 ft. high and wide; coppery flower plumes reach 5–6 ft. tall. Where the growing season is long, dig and divide clumps yearly to keep plants compact. Seedlings have leaves like those of 'Gracillimus'—deep green with silvery midrib.

'Purpurascens'. FLAME GRASS. Zones US, MS, LS. Best in Upper and Middle South, where summers are not so long and hot. Upright clump 3–4 ft. high and wide, with green leaves to ½ in. wide. Silvery flower plumes 5–6 ft. tall. Foliage turns orange red in fall, then fades to reddish brown. Short lived.

'Sarabande'. Resembles 'Gracillimus' but is finer textured overall, with narrower leaves that are held more erect.

'Strictus'. PORCUPINE GRASS. Narrow, erect clump 4–6 ft. tall, 3–4 ft. wide. Spiky, ½-in.-wide leaves are banded horizontally with creamy yellow, suggesting porcupine quills. Coppery plumes on 5- to 7-ft.-tall stems. Tends to flop with weight of blooms; should be staked.

'Variegatus'. A fountain of silver. Graceful, weeping clump 3–4 ft. high and wide, with ¾-in. green leaves edged and striped in white. Spikes 5–6 ft. tall, tend to flop, especially on older plants; need staking. Divide every year or two. Give partial shade in Coastal South.

'Yaku Jima'. Compact, fine-leafed selection similar in form to 'Adagio'. Tan flower plumes; reddish brown fall foliage.

'Zebrinus'. ZEBRA GRASS. Like 'Strictus' but lax and broadly arching; certain to flop in bloom unless staked. Most plants sold under this name are 'Strictus'.

M. transmorrisonensis. EVERGREEN MISCANTHUS. Native to Taiwan. Forms a compact clump 2½–3½ ft. high and 3–4 ft. wide, with leaves 2–3 ft. long, ½ in. wide. Foliage remains green into early winter (and is evergreen in mildest-winter areas). Slender, silvery flower plumes on stems 5–7 ft. tall.

Plant begins blooming in spring in Coastal South; cutting stems nearly to ground when plumes begin to fade will produce a second bloom flush—sometimes even a third one. Cutting back stems also keeps clump looking fresh. Where winters are cold, bloom time comes in mid- to late summer. Plumes age to tan and drop their seeds before winter, leaving bare stems. Makes a good large-scale ground cover if given regular moisture and yearly mowing.

MISTLETOE FIG. See FICUS deltoidea

MITCHELLA repens

PARTRIDGEBERRY, TWINBERRY

Rubiaceae

PERENNIAL

⚡ US, MS, LS, CS   ♨ 10–1

◐ ● PARTIAL TO FULL SHADE

💧💧 REGULAR TO AMPLE WATER

Mitchella repens

Attractive small, creeping evergreen plant native to much of eastern North America. Roundish leaves are less than 1 in. long, borne in pairs along trailing, somewhat woody stems that root where they touch the ground. Paired small white flowers appear in late spring or early summer; these are followed by bright red berries less than ¼ in. across. Small-scale ground cover best seen near eye level, such as on a shady bank or above a wall. Ideal for a woodland garden among shade-loving native plants such as ferns, mosses, may apple *(Podophyllum peltatum),* and galax. Provide steady moisture and acid soil containing plenty of leaf mold or other organic material.

MIZUNA. See ASIAN GREENS

MOCK ORANGE. See CHOISYA ternata, PHILADELPHUS

MOLE PLANT. See EUPHORBIA lathyris

MOLINIA caerulea

MOOR GRASS

Poaceae (Gramineae)

PERENNIAL GRASSES

⚡ US, MS, LS   ♨ 9–1

☼ ◐ FULL SUN OR PARTIAL SHADE

💧💧 REGULAR TO AMPLE WATER

Molinia caerulea

Native to moist places from the British Isles to Siberia, south to the Caucasus and Turkey; resents dry, alkaline conditions. Long lived but slow growing, taking several years to reach full size. Erect, narrow light green leaves form a neat, dense clump. In summer, spikelike clusters of yellowish to purplish flowers rise above clump; they age to tan and last well into fall. Wispy flowers give clump a see-through quality. Good cut flowers. In late fall, both leaves and flower clusters detach from plant's base, leaving nothing visible above ground. There are two forms of moor grass, each with several selections.

The typical form, often called purple moor grass, produces a leafy clump 1–2 ft. high and wide; flower stalks are 2–3 ft. tall. 'Moorflamme'

('Moor Flame') has airy flower heads held 2 ft. above the foliage, good red-orange autumn foliage color. 'Variegata' has leaves broadly edged in creamy white; yellowish flower stems arch out in all directions, giving a perfect fountain effect.

M. c. arundinacea, known as tall moor grass, has broader gray-green leaves that form a clump 2–3 ft. high and wide. Flowering stems are 5–8 ft. tall; they arch to the ground when wet, then straighten up as they dry. Give this one space so you can enjoy its form and motion in the wind. Among its forms are old favorite 'Karl Foerster', still one of the best; it has arching, 2½-ft.-long leaves and semierect flower stalks to 7 ft. tall. 'Skyracer' has erect, 3-ft.-tall leaves and 7- to 8-ft. stems bearing yellow flowers that sparkle with morning dew. The arching, 6-ft.-tall stems of 'Transparent' have a translucent section between highest leaf and beginning of flower spike; plant bears tiny, airy blossoms and has bright orange-yellow fall foliage. 'Windspiel' ('Windplay') has wiry, vertical, 7- to 8-ft.-tall stems that sway with the slightest breeze.

MOLUCCELLA laevis

BELLS-OF-IRELAND, SHELL FLOWER

Lamiaceae (Labiatae)

COOL-SEASON ANNUAL

⚡ US, MS, LS, CS, TS   ♨ 7–1

☼ FULL SUN

💧 REGULAR WATER

Though its common name implies Irish origin, this plant is in fact native to the Mideast. To 2–3 ft. high, 10 in. wide. Flowers are carried

Moluccella laevis

almost from base in whorls of six. Showy part of flower is its large, apple green, shell- or bell-shaped calyx, very veiny and crisp textured; small white tube of united petals in center is inconspicuous. Blossom spikes are quite attractive and long lasting in either fresh or dried arrangements; be sure to remove the leaves, which are not especially good looking. Deer don't usually bother it.

Not an easy plant to grow in the South, as it dislikes hot, humid weather. Sow seeds in an empty planting bed in loose, fertile, well-drained soil in fall. Do not cover them with soil—they need light to germinate. Sow where you want plants to grow, as seedlings do not transplant well. In most areas, seedlings appear in spring. For long flower spikes, fertilize with a balanced water-soluble fertilizer every 2 weeks. In Florida and South Texas, seeds will germinate in fall (refrigerate them for a week before sowing), and the plant can be grown as a winter annual.

MOMORDICA charantia. See BITTER MELON

MONARDA

Lamiaceae (Labiatae)

PERENNIALS

⚡ US, MS, LS   ♨ 8–1, EXCEPT AS NOTED

☼ ◐ AFTERNOON SHADE IN LOWER SOUTH

💧💧 REGULAR TO AMPLE WATER

Monarda didyma
'Marshall's Delight'

Native to eastern North America. Bushy, leafy clumps to 2–4 ft. high spread rapidly; can be invasive. Dark green leaves grow 4–6 in. long, have strong, pleasant odor like a blend of mint and basil. In summer, upright stems are topped by tight clusters of long-tubed flowers much visited by hummingbirds. Plant 10 in. apart. Divide every 3 or 4 years. Not long lived. Prone to mildew and other leaf diseases in humid weather. Deer don't care for them.

M. didyma. BEE BALM, OSWEGO TEA. An old Southern favorite. Basic species has scarlet flowers surrounded by reddish bracts. Garden selections and hybrids include scarlet 'Adam', pink 'Croftway Pink' and 'Granite Pink', 'Snow White', and dark red 'Mahogany'. 'Cambridge Scarlet' is an old selection still widely grown. Deep rosy red 'Jacob Cline' is reportedly the most mildew-resistant selection. Other resistant choices include violet purple 'Dark Ponticum' and 'Violet Queen', 'Gardenview Scarlet', and pink 'Marshall's Delight'. If spent flowers are removed, all selections bloom over a period of 2 months or more. Don't let soil dry out.

M. fistulosa. BERGAMOT. Lavender to light pink flowers encircled by whitish bracts are less showy than those of *M. didyma.* Best suited to wild gardens. This is not the source of the oil of bergamot used to flavor Earl Grey tea; that comes from the fruit of a type of citrus.

M. punctata. SPOTTED HORSEMINT, DOTTED MINT. Zones US, MS, LS, CS, TS; 11–1. Usually smaller than the other species listed here. Blooms in midsummer, bearing two or more whorled clusters of purple-spotted yellow or pink blossoms per stem. Good plant for wildflower meadows and naturalized areas.

MONDO GRASS. See OPHIOPOGON

MONEY PLANT. See LUNARIA annua

MONEYWORT. See LYSIMACHIA nummularia

MONKEY FLOWER. See MIMULUS ×hybridus

MONKEY GRASS. See LIRIOPE, OPHIOPOGON

MONKEY PUZZLE TREE. See ARAUCARIA araucana

MONKSHOOD. See ACONITUM

MONSTERA

Araceae

EVERGREEN VINES

🗡 TS 🌱 12–10; OR HOUSEPLANT

☼ FILTERED SUNLIGHT; BRIGHT LIGHT

💧 REGULAR WATER

Monstera deliciosa

Tropical American natives related to philodendrons and resembling them in the glossiness and texture of their foliage. Most have cut and perforated leaves. Need rich soil. They can be grown outdoors only in the Tropical South. Indoors, direct sun in winter and bright reflected light the rest of the year are ideal; in dim light, leaves will be small and widely spaced on long, droopy stalks. If a tall potted plant gets bare at the base, replant it in a larger container along with a younger, lower plant to fill in; or cut it back and let it regrow from new shoots. Plants benefit from frequent misting.

M. deliciosa. SPLIT-LEAF PHILODENDRON, CUT-LEAF PHILODENDRON. To 30–60 ft. if planted in open bed outdoors or in greenhouse. Protect from frost (recovers fairly quickly from frost damage, though). Long, cordlike roots hang from stems and root when they reach soil; they also help support plant on trees or on moss logs. Young foliage is uncut; mature leaves are heavy, leathery, dark green, deeply cut and perforated. Big plants may bear flowers like those of calla *(Zantedeschia),* with a thick, 10-in.-long spike surrounded by a boatlike white bract. If heat, light, and humidity are high, spike may ripen into edible fruit said to combine flavors of banana and pineapple. Eat only when fully ripe (green, caplike rind will knock off easily, exposing sticky fruit kernels); fruit can be painfully caustic before that stage. Allow plenty of room when growing this species as a houseplant; it may reach 15 ft. Often sold as *Philodendron pertusum.*

M. friedrichsthalii. SWISS CHEESE PLANT. Plant sold under this name is probably *M. obliqua.* Can reach 25 ft. outdoors but is more commonly used as an indoor plant. Smaller, thinner-textured leaves than those of *M. deliciosa,* with wavy rather than deeply cut edges. Common name comes from oval holes on either side of leaf midrib.

MONTBRETIA. See CROCOSMIA ×crocosmiiflora

MOONFLOWER, MOON VINE. See IPOMOEA alba

MOOR GRASS. See MOLINIA caerulea

Moraceae. The mulberry family includes deciduous and evergreen trees, shrubs, and vines. Individual fruits are tiny and single-seeded but often aggregated into clusters. Fig *(Ficus)* and mulberry *(Morus)* are examples.

MORAINE LOCUST. See GLEDITSIA triacanthos inermis 'Moraine'

MORNING GLORY. See CONVOLVULUS, IPOMOEA

MORNING-NOON-AND-NIGHT. See BRUNFELSIA australis

MORUS

MULBERRY

Moraceae

DECIDUOUS TREES

🗡 ZONES VARY BY SPECIES

☼ FULL SUN

💧 REGULAR WATER

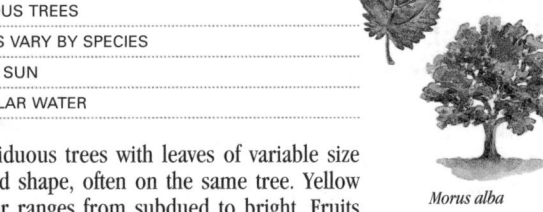

Morus alba

Deciduous trees with leaves of variable size and shape, often on the same tree. Yellow fall color ranges from subdued to bright. Fruits resemble miniature blackberries and are eagerly gobbled by birds.

M. alba. WHITE MULBERRY, SILKWORM MULBERRY. Zones US, MS, LS, CS; 9–4. Native to China, where its leaves are used as food for silkworms. Brought by European settlers to Jamestown, Virginia, where it escaped cultivation and quickly spread across the U.S., becoming a quite bothersome weed. Grows very fast, as much as 3 ft. per year. Takes rocky, alkaline soil; withstands just about any conditions, including heat, wind, salt spray, air pollution, and drought (but grows faster with regular water). Eventually reaches 30–50 ft. tall and wide. Leaves are 6 in. long, often lobed; flowers are inconspicuous.

Male trees produce prodigious amounts of pollen, which can be a problem for allergy sufferers. In summer, female trees bear sweet, insipid white, pink, or purple fruits that stain pavement where they fall—and birds flock to the fruit, gorge themselves, and then proceed to sully any deck, car, driveway, or passerby unlucky enough to be below. Seedlings come up everywhere, and surface roots make it difficult to garden beneath the tree. A weeping selection, 'Pendula', is sometimes used as an accent plant, but its form is rather awkward.

M. australis 'Unryu' (M. bombycis 'Unryu'). CONTORTED MULBERRY. Zones US, MS, LS, CS; 9–6. To 25 ft. tall and wide, with twisted, contorted branches useful in dried floral arrangements or for winter silhouette. Fast growth means that branches may be cut freely with no harm to the tree. Dark green, broadly oval, 6- to 7-in.-long leaves.

M. nigra. BLACK MULBERRY, PERSIAN MULBERRY. Zones US, MS, LS; 9–5. Likely a native of western Asia. To 30 ft. tall, 35 ft. wide, with short trunk and dense, spreading head. Heart-shaped leaves to 8 in. long. Large, juicy dark red to black fruit. 'Oscar' and 'Wellington' are heavy bearers. 'Black Beauty' is smaller (15 ft. tall).

M. papyrifera. See Broussonetia papyrifera

M. rubra. RED MULBERRY. Zones US, MS, LS, CS; 9–5. Native to eastern and central U.S. Well-behaved tree that resembles *M. alba* but is less weedy and produces less pollen and fewer fruits. Fruit—red when immature, ripening to black—is somewhat larger than that of *M. alba* and has a better flavor. Does best in rich soil. 'Illinois Everbearing' is a hybrid between this species and *M. alba;* its fruit ripens throughout summer.

MOSES-IN-THE-BOAT, MOSES-IN-THE-CRADLE. See TRADESCANTIA spathacea

MOSQUITO GRASS. See BOUTELOUA gracilis

MUHLENBERGIA

MUHLY GRASS

Poaceae (Gramineae)

PERENNIAL GRASSES

✄ MS, LS, CS, TS ⑂ 12–7, EXCEPT AS NOTED

☼ ☼ FULL SUN OR LIGHT SHADE

◌ ◍ LITTLE OR NO WATER TO MODERATE WATER

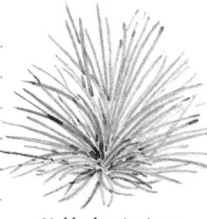

Muhlenbergia rigens

Showy and easy to grow, these native U.S. grasses combine handsome, slender leaves with eye-catching flower plumes that typically appear in late summer and fall. Foliage is semievergreen to evergreen in mild-winter areas, deciduous elsewhere. Plants tolerate heat and drought, but they look better and grow larger if given supplemental water. Good drainage is a must. Most are well adapted to Texas and the Southwest but will also succeed in many other areas, including Florida. Cut plants nearly to the ground in late winter to encourage fresh new growth.

M. capillaris. PINK MUHLY, HAIRY AWN MUHLY. Native to eastern U.S. Looks much like *M. filipes* but is taller and blooms earlier. Dark green foliage forms a mound to 3–4 ft. tall and at least as wide. Very showy flower plumes, like puffs of rosy red smoke, rise 2 ft. above the foliage in early fall. 'Regal Mist' ('Lenca') sports deep rosy pink flowers.

M. dumosa. BAMBOO MUHLY. Zone CS. Native to Arizona, Mexico. To 3–6 ft. high and wide. Resembles bamboo, with slender, pendulous, woody stems set with narrow bright green leaves up to 3 in. long. Inconspicuous flower clusters in spring. Endures heat, cold, and limy soil.

M. emersleyi. BULL GRASS. Native to Arizona, New Mexico, Texas. Gray-green leaves form a mound 1½–3 ft. tall, 3–4 ft. wide. From summer into fall, reddish or purplish flower spikes rise 2–3 ft. above the foliage; they fade to cream with age.

M. filipes. GULF MUHLY, SWEET GRASS. Native to the Southeast. Considered by some to be a variety of *M. capillaris,* this plant is shorter and blooms a little later in the year. Narrow dark green leaves form mounds 2–3 ft. tall and wide. Rosy purple, wispy plumes rise an additional 2 ft. in mid- to late fall. Young leaves are used by the Gullah people of South Carolina to make traditional baskets. Called sweet grass because of its pleasant fragrance, which some liken to the scent of freshly mown hay.

M. lindheimeri. LINDHEIMER'S MUHLY. Native to Texas, Mexico. Clump of soft, arching blue-green leaves grows to 5 ft. tall and wide, with amber flower spikes rising 2 ft. above foliage in autumn. Blooms of the species fade to gray; those of 'Amber Glow' turn yellow in fall. Tolerates moist conditions as well as dry, rocky, chalky soil.

M. rigens. DEER GRASS. Native from California to Texas and south into Mexico. Bright green leaves form a dense, tight clump to 4 ft. high and wide. Slender yellow or purplish flower spikes rise 2 ft. above the leaves in autumn; they are erect at first, then leaning. Good vertical accent.

M. rigida. PURPLE MUHLY. Native to Texas, New Mexico. Green clump to 2 ft. high and wide, producing 3-ft. spikes of brownish purple flowers in late summer and fall. Blossoms of 'Nashville' are an attractive true purple.

MURRAYA paniculata

ORANGE JESSAMINE

Rutaceae

EVERGREEN SHRUB

✄ TS ⑂ 12–9

☼ FILTERED SUNLIGHT

◍ REGULAR WATER

Murraya paniculata

Native to Southeast Asia. Open habit; fast grower to 6–15 ft. tall and wide. Good as hedge, filler, foundation plant. Sometimes grown as small single- or multi-trunked tree. Has graceful, pendulous branches with glossy dark green leaves divided into three to nine oval, 1- to 2-in. leaflets. Blooms in late summer and fall (sometimes in spring), with white, ¾-in., bell-shaped blossoms with a jasmine fragrance. On mature plants, small red fruits follow flowers. Closely related to citrus and subject to the same pests; also susceptible to nematodes. Needs rich soil, frequent feeding. Slowly recovers beauty after cold winters. Blooms attract bees. Reseeds and may become weedy.

A dwarf variety is usually sold as *M. exotica.* It is slower growing, more upright, and more compact than the species, reaching 6 ft. tall, 4 ft. wide. Its leaves are a lighter shade of green and have smaller, stiffer leaflets; bloom is usually less profuse.

MUSA

BANANA

Musaceae

PERENNIALS

✄ CS, TS, EXCEPT AS NOTED; OR GROW IN POTS

☼ ☼ FULL SUN OR PARTIAL SHADE

◍ AMPLE WATER

Musa × paradisiaca

For information on fruiting types, see Banana. The ornamental bananas described here include tall, medium-size, and dwarf plants; some of the tall sorts are the size of trees. All types are fast growing; all have soft, thickish stalks (called pseudostems) and spread by suckers or underground roots to form clumps that are often as wide as or wider than the plant is tall. Spectacular-looking long, typically broad leaves are easily tattered by strong winds, so choose protected planting sites. Will usually regrow from roots if cut down by frost; in frost-prone areas, locate plants where their absence won't be conspicuous. Attractive near swimming pools. Give rich soil; feed heavily. Can be grown in containers and overwintered indoors (cut tops off tall plants). No water or fertilizer needed until moved outdoors after last spring frost. To overwinter plants in the ground in northern parts of hardiness range, mulch heavily in early winter.

M. acuminata. Heat zones 12–6. From Southeast Asia. Many selections available. Plants are grown for fruit in warmest gardens, but they also make handsome ornamentals there as well as in cooler areas. Some have especially attractive foliage. Leaves of 6- to 10-ft.-tall 'Zebrina' ('Roja', 'Rojo', 'Sumatra', 'Sumatrana') are green with maroon stripes; the plant produces tiny, inedible dark maroon fruit.

M. basjoo. JAPANESE BANANA. Zones US, MS, LS, CS, TS; 12–1. From Japan. The hardiest of the banana clan. To 15 ft. tall, with narrow green leaves about 8 ft. long. Terminal spikes of yellow flowers may be followed by small, unpalatable fruit.

M. ensete. See Ensete ventricosum

M. lasiocarpa. See Musella lasiocarpa

M

M. ornata. FLOWERING BANANA. Heat zones 12–9. Grows to 9 ft. tall, with blue-green leaves 4–6 ft. long and 1–1½ ft. wide; each leaf has a red-purple midrib on the underside. Erect blossom stalks carry pale pink or pale purple bracts tipped with yellow; these are used as cut flowers. Small fruits (to 3 in. long) are decorative but inedible. 'African Red' has red bracts and yellow fruit. 'Bronze' features light green leaves and pink-tinged stems; it bears orange-bronze inflorescences. 'Milky Way' has white bracts and white fruit; 'Royal Purple' bears bluish purple bracts.

M. × paradisiaca (M. sapientum). Heat zones 12–6. The most common of the ornamental bananas. Makes a clump to 20 ft. tall and half as wide, with leaves to 9 ft. long. Flower stalks are pendent, bearing large, showy, powdery purple bracts; fruit (usually seedy and inedible) sometimes follows.

M. velutina. Heat zones 12–7. From India. Grows to 5–7 ft. tall, with 3-ft.-long leaves that are green above, bronzy beneath. Upright pink bracts, orange flowers, and small, velvety pink bananas that are inedible but highly decorative.

Musaceae. The banana family consists of giant herbaceous plants that resemble palm trees; the bases of the enormous leaves form a false trunk. *Ensete, Musa,* and *Musella* are grown in the South.

MUSCARI

GRAPE HYACINTH
Liliaceae
PERENNIALS FROM BULBS
US, MS, LS H 8–1, EXCEPT AS NOTED
FULL SUN OR LIGHT SHADE
REGULAR WATER DURING GROWTH AND BLOOM

Muscari armeniacum

Native to the Mediterranean and southwestern Asia. Clumps of grassy, fleshy leaves appear in fall and live through cold and snow. Spikes of small, typically urn-shaped blue or white flowers (fragrant, in some species) bloom in early spring. Plant in early fall, setting bulbs about 2 in. deep and 3 in. apart in well-drained soil. Plant in masses or drifts under flowering trees or shrubs; use in edgings and rock gardens; grow in containers. Very long lived. Dig and divide when clumps become crowded. Plants self-sow under favorable conditions. Naturalized grape hyacinths are often seen blooming in old cemeteries. Not usually favored by deer.

M. armeniacum. Bright blue, slightly fragrant flowers on 8-in. stems rise above a clump of floppy foliage. 'Blue Spike' has double blue flowers in a tight cluster at top of spike. 'Early Giant' blooms somewhat earlier than the species, has darker blue flowers edged in white. 'Cantab', with light blue blossoms, grows lower than the species and has neater foliage and a later bloom time.

M. aucheri (M. tubergenianum). Heat zones 9–5. Stems to 8 in. tall. Flowers on lower part of spike are bright blue; those on upper part are paler blue.

M. azureum (Hyacinthella azurea, Hyacinthus azureus). Heat zones 9–1. Blossom spikes are between those of hyacinth and grape hyacinth in appearance. Stalks to 8 in. high bear tight clusters of fragrant sky blue flowers that have a bell shape (rather than the usual urn shape).

M. botryoides. An old-time favorite. Medium blue, lightly scented flowers on stems to 1 ft. tall. 'Album' has white flowers.

M. comosum. FRINGE HYACINTH, TASSEL HYACINTH. Bears loose clusters of unusual, tattered-looking flowers on 1- to 1½-ft. stems. Blossoms are greenish brown on lower part of spike, bluish purple on upper part. 'Plumosum' ('Monstrosum'), feathered or plume hyacinth, produces violet-blue to reddish purple flowers that look like shredded coconut.

M. latifolium. Zones US, MS. Possibly the showiest of the grape hyacinths. Each bulb produces just one leaf and a flowering stem to 1 ft. tall. Flowers on lower part of spike are deepest violet, those on upper part vivid indigo blue.

M. neglectum. STARCH HYACINTH. Stems about 6 in. tall. Lower part of bloom spike holds tightly crowded, very dark blue blossoms edged in white, while upper part is set with pale blue blooms. Flowers are said to smell like laundry starch.

M. 'Valerie Finnis'. Probably a seedling of either *M. armeniacum* or *M. neglectum.* Foliage like that of *M. neglectum.* Lightly fragrant powder blue flowers are tightly packed onto 6- to 8-in.-tall stems in a roughly spiral pattern. Spreads more slowly than other types.

MUSELLA lasiocarpa

CHINESE YELLOW BANANA
Musaceae
PERENNIAL
MS, LS, CS, TS H 12–8
FULL SUN OR PARTIAL SHADE
REGULAR WATER

Musella lasiocarpa

Unusual ornamental banana from Yunnan Province in China. Very cold hardy, surviving temperatures into the teens. A single thick pseudostem, broad at the base and tapering toward the tip, grows 5–6 ft. tall and is topped with dark green, 3- to 4-ft.-long leaves. Prized by plant collectors for the exotic, waxy inflorescence that emerges at the plant's top and resembles a golden, 8-in.-wide artichoke; it can last all summer. Clusters of small true flowers peek out between the bracts. After flowering, the original pseudostem dies, but suckers sprout from the base. Best enjoyed as an oddity. During the course of flowering, it sometimes drops its foliage and looks like a big yellow starfish sitting atop a stump.

MUSTARD

Brassicaceae (Cruciferae)
COOL-SEASON ANNUAL
US, MS, LS, CS, TS H 8–1
FULL SUN
REGULAR WATER

Mustard

Eating mustard greens in spring and fall is a time-honored Southern tradition. Loaded with Vitamins A and C, the nutritious greens reach full size just 4 to 6 weeks after sowing.

Two types of mustard are widely grown. Curly-leafed mustard has leaves with crinkled edges; they take some time to clean, as grit tends to collect in the crinkles. Smooth-leafed mustard (also called tendergreen mustard or mustard spinach) has smooth dark green leaves. It matures earlier than the curly-leafed type and is more tolerant of warm, dry weather. Use young leaves of either as a salad green; older leaves can be cooked like spinach.

For spring harvests, sow seed 2 to 4 weeks before the expected last frost. A single spring planting will produce until plants bolt (go to seed) after the onset of warm weather. To extend the harvest, make a second planting 2 to 3 weeks after the first. For fall harvests, sow in late summer or early fall. A light frost will sweeten the greens' flavor.

Mustard is one of the easiest vegetables to grow. You can start from transplants, but direct seeding is easier. Before planting, work into the soil ¼ cup of 10-10-10 fertilizer per 10 ft. of row. Sow seeds thinly in rows spaced 2 ft. apart—or broadcast the seeds over a wide bed. Cover with ½ in. of soil. Thin seedlings to 4–8 in. apart (thinnings can be eaten cooked as a vegetable or fresh in salads). Keep the soil evenly moist throughout the growing season. Three to four weeks after planting, sprinkle 10-10-10 fertilizer around base of plants at the rate of ¼ cup per 10 ft. of row; water it in. To harvest, break off outer leaves when they are 4–5 in. long; let inner ones continue to grow. Once the plants flower, the leaves will develop a strong, peppery flavor.

Recommended curly-leafed selections include 'Green Wave' (heat tolerant; slow to bolt; 45 days), 'Old Fashioned Ragged Edge' (Southern heirloom with excellent flavor; early to bolt; 42 days), and 'Southern Giant

Curled' (large bright green leaves; slow to bolt; 45 days). Recommended smooth-leafed mustards include 'Florida Broadleaf' (very large leaves; slow to bolt; 47 days), 'Red Giant' (beautiful reddish purple leaves; can be used as an ornamental; slow to bolt; 43 days), and 'Savannah' (large deep green leaves; mild flavor; very early; slow to bolt; 20 days).

MYOSOTIS

FORGET-ME-NOT

Boraginaceae

PERENNIALS, BIENNIALS, AND COOL-SEASON ANNUALS

US, MS, LS

PARTIAL SHADE

REGULAR WATER

Myosotis sylvatica

Both species described feature exquisite, typically blue springtime flowers, tiny but profuse. Grow easily and densely as ground covers. Do best in cool, moist areas, as in woodland gardens, at pond edges, along stream banks. Not usually browsed by deer.

M. scorpioides. Perennial. Heat zones 9–5. Native to Europe, Asia, North America. This species is similar in most respects to *M. sylvatica*, but it grows a little lower, blooms even longer, and has roots that live over from year to year. Flowers are about ¼ in. wide; they come in blue, white, or pink, usually with a yellow or white eye. Shiny, oblong bright green leaves. Plant spreads by creeping roots.

M. sylvatica. Annual or biennial. Heat zones 7–1. Native to Europe. To 6–12 in. high, 2 ft. wide. Soft, hairy foliage; basal leaves reach 4 in. long, while those set higher on stems are ½–2 in. long. Pure blue flowers with a white eye are ⅓ in. wide, set loosely along top portions of stems. Blooms and seeds profusely for a long season, beginning in late winter or early spring. Self-sows and will persist for years unless weeded out. Often sold as *M. alpestris*. Improved selections include 'Blue Ball' and 'Royal Blue Improved'.

MYRICA

Myricaceae

EVERGREEN AND SEMIEVERGREEN OR DECIDUOUS SHRUBS OR TREES

ZONES VARY BY SPECIES

FULL SUN

WATER NEEDS VARY BY SPECIES

Myrica cerifera

These North American native plants may not be spectacular, but they are tough and adaptable and have no serious pests. Excellent as informal screens, as foundation plantings, and in naturalized areas; *M. cerifera* is attractive enough to serve as a specimen tree. Good plants for coastal gardens—tolerate wind, sandy soil, salt spray. Foliage is pleasantly aromatic, especially when bruised. Although neither of the two species described here is showy in flower, female plants bear great quantities of subtly attractive autumn fruits that are favored by birds. These plants are not usually browsed by deer.

M. cerifera. WAX MYRTLE. Evergreen shrub or small tree. Zones MS, LS, CS, TS; 12–6. Native to southeastern U.S. Grows quickly to at least 15–20 ft. tall and wide. Glossy olive green leaves are narrowly oval and pointed, to 3½ in. long. Small grayish white fruits, borne in dense clusters, are heavily coated with a wax valued in candle making. 'Luray' is a compact selection reaching just 4 ft. tall and wide. *M. c. pumila* is a dwarf, suckering form that grows to only 3 ft. tall but spreads widely. Tolerates dry or wet soil, but best with moderate to regular water.

M. pensylvanica. BAYBERRY. Deciduous to semievergreen shrub. Zones US, MS; 7–1. Native to coastal eastern North America. Dense and compact, to 9 ft. tall and 5–12 ft. wide. Narrowish glossy green leaves to about 4 in. long. Roundish fruit is covered with fragrant white wax—the bayberry wax used for candles. Regular water.

MYROBALAN. See PRUNUS cerasifera

Myrsinaceae. This family consists of evergreen shrubs and trees with attractive foliage and habit and (usually) inconspicuous flowers. Fruits are sometimes showy. One representative of the group is marlberry *(Ardisia)*.

Myrtaceae. The immense myrtle family of trees and shrubs is largely tropical and subtropical. Leaves are evergreen and often aromatic. Flowers are frequently showy, thanks to their large tufts of stamens. Fruits may be fleshy (as in *Feijoa*, the feijoa or pineapple guava) or dry and capsular (as in *Eucalyptus*). Other family members include bottlebrush *(Callistemon)*, myrtle *(Myrtus)*, and guava *(Psidium)*.

MYRTLE. See MYRTUS communis

MYRTUS communis

MYRTLE

Myrtaceae

EVERGREEN SHRUB

CS H 9–8

FULL SUN OR PARTIAL SHADE

LITTLE TO MODERATE WATER

Myrtus communis

Native to the Mediterranean, this venerable shrub has never quite made its mark in the South. It's a bulky, dense, rounded plant with fine-textured foliage: glossy bright green, oval, pointed leaves to 2 in. long, pleasantly aromatic when brushed or bruised. Typically reaches 5–6 ft. high and 4–5 ft. wide (though old plants may reach 15 ft. high, 20 ft. wide). White, sweet-scented, ¾-in. flowers with many stamens bloom in summer; they are followed by small, bluish black berries. Good for a foundation planting or informal hedge or screen; requires little or no pruning. Also takes well to shearing into a formal hedge or topiary; can be pruned like a small tree to reveal attractive branches. Best in fertile, well-drained soil. Fairly common in Florida but does not tolerate salt spray. Not usually bothered by deer.

Named selections vary in foliage character and overall size. 'Variegata' fits the basic description but has white-edged leaves. 'Boetica' is especially upright, with thick, twisted branches and larger, darker leaves. 'Buxifolia' has small leaves like those of boxwood *(Buxus)*. Dwarf forms include 'Compacta', a small-leafed selection popular for edgings and low formal hedges; 'Compacta Variegata', similar but with white-margined foliage; and 'Microphylla', with tiny, closely set leaves.

NAKED LADY. See AMARYLLIS belladonna, LYCORIS squamigera

NANDINA domestica

NANDINA, HEAVENLY BAMBOO

Berberidaceae

EVERGREEN OR SEMIEVERGREEN TO DECIDUOUS SHRUB

US, MS, LS, CS H 9–4

SUN OR SHADE; COLORS BETTER IN SUN

MODERATE TO REGULAR WATER

Nandina domestica

From China and Japan. A true survivor. Old plants are often seen growing in cemeteries, overgrown gardens, on abandoned homesites, where they fruit and flower for decades with absolutely no care. Nandina takes sun or shade and tolerates drought, though well-drained soil is essential. It has no serious pests and is hardy everywhere. Semievergreen or deciduous in the Upper South; leaves drop at 10°F and stems are damaged at 5°F, but plant usually recovers fast.

Nandina belongs to the barberry family but is reminiscent of bamboo in its lightly branched, canelike stems and delicate, fine-textured foliage. Slow to moderate growth to 6–8 ft. Spreads slowly by stolons to form large clumps. Can be divided in fall, winter, or spring. Leaves are intricately divided into many 1- to 2-in., pointed, oval leaflets, creating a lacy pattern. Foliage expands pinkish and bronzy red, then turns to soft light green. It picks up purple and bronze tints in fall and often turns fiery crimson in winter, especially in sun and with some frost. Pinkish white or creamy white blossoms in loose, erect, 6- to 12-in. clusters at branch ends in late spring or early summer. If plants are grouped, shiny red berries follow the flowers; single plants seldom fruit as heavily. Berries supply winter food for birds; clusters cut for holiday decorations last a long time. Resistant to damage by deer.

Does best in rich soil with regular water, but its roots can even compete with tree roots in dry shade. May suffer from chlorosis (yellow leaves with green veins) in alkaline soil. To reduce height, use hand pruners, never hedge shears. Maintain a natural look by pruning each stalk to a different height, cutting back to a tuft of foliage. Renew neglected clumps by cutting one-third of the main stalks to the ground each year for 3 years. Good for screen, containers. Selections include the following.

'Compacta'. To 4–5 ft. tall, 3 ft. wide. Very lacy looking, with more canes and narrower, more numerous leaflets than the species.

'Firepower'. To 2 ft. tall and wide. Red-tinged summer foliage turns bright red in winter.

'Gulf Stream'. Slow-growing, dense mound to 3–3½ ft. tall, 1½ ft. wide, with blue-green summer foliage and good red winter color. Does not sucker. No berries.

'Harbor Dwarf'. To 2–3 ft. tall. Rather than forming a discrete clump, it spreads by rhizomes to make a good ground cover. Foliage has orange-red to bronzy red winter color.

N. d. leucocarpa ('Alba'). To 4–6 ft. tall, 2–3 ft. wide, with creamy white berries and light yellow-green foliage that turns golden in fall. More subject to cold damage than the species.

'Moyers Red'. Standard-size plant with broad leaflets. Brilliant red winter color in regions that get frost. Flowers are pinker than those of the species, and berries ripen a month or two earlier.

'Nana' ('Nana Purpurea', 'Atropurpurea Nana'). To 2 ft. tall, 2–3 ft. wide. Coarse foliage is purplish green in summer, purplish red to bright red in winter. Leaves typically show cupping, curling, and color streaks. Much overused—and out of place in most gardens. A nice gas station plant. Not known to flower or fruit.

'Plum Passion'. Grows to 4–5 ft. tall and 3 ft. wide. Narrow leaves are deep purplish red when young, deep green during summer, and reddish purple in winter.

'Sienna Sunrise'. Slow grower to 3–4 ft. tall, 2½ ft. wide. Foliage is fiery red when new; it matures to medium green by summer, then picks up red highlights again in winter.

'Woods Dwarf'. Slow, dense grower to 1½ ft. high and wide. Foliage turns crimson-orange to scarlet in winter.

'Yellow Berries'. Similar to the species in size and shape, but berries of this selection are creamy yellow and the light green foliage lacks the typical reddish bronze tinge.

LOVE ME, LOVE ME NOT. *If familiarity really does breed contempt, there is no surer scorned than the ubiquitous nandina (Nandina domestica). Though it graces Southern homes in both countryside and city, many folks look down on it because it's just too easy to grow. It flourishes in sun as well as shade, laughs at drought, shrugs off pollution, couldn't care less about soil type, is virtually immune to most pests and diseases, and seems to live forever. If you want to immortalize yourself, forget about the statues and monuments and have a nandina planted in your name instead.* ❖

NANDING CHERRY. See PRUNUS tomentosa

NARCISSUS

DAFFODIL, NARCISSUS, JONQUIL

Amaryllidaceae

PERENNIALS FROM BULBS

✄ US, MS, LS, CS (NORTHERN THIRD)
⧗ 9–1, EXCEPT AS NOTED

☼ ◐ FULL SUN OR PARTIAL SHADE

🌢 REGULAR WATER DURING GROWTH AND BLOOM

Trumpet Daffodil

Native to Europe and North Africa, these are arguably the finest and most valuable spring bulbs for the South. They are long lived, increasing naturally from year to year; they stand up to cold and heat; they have many garden uses; and they offer a fascinating array of flower forms, sizes, and colors. Given minimal care at planting, all thrive with virtually no further attention. They do not require summer watering (although they'll accept it) and need only infrequent division. Finally, rodents and deer won't eat them.

Flowering commences in winter in the Lower and Coastal South, in early spring elsewhere. The basic colors are yellow and white, but you'll also find shades of orange, apricot, pink, cream, and even red.

SUREFIRE DAFFODILS FOR THE SOUTH. *These daffodils bloom dependably in most areas and increase with little care: 'Avalon', 'Carlton', 'February Gold', 'Geranium', 'Hawera', 'Ice Follies', 'Jack Snipe', 'Jetfire', 'Minnow', Narcissus × odorus, 'Quail', 'Saint Keverne', 'Salome', 'Tête-à-tête', 'Thalia', and 'Trevithian'.* ❖

Gardeners tend to use the names "daffodil" and "jonquil" interchangeably. Technically, however, "daffodil" refers to large-flowered kinds with flat, straplike leaves. "Jonquil" denotes *N. jonquilla* and its hybrids; they feature smaller, fragrant, clustered blooms and cylindrical leaves with pointed tips, reminiscent of quills. If you stick to calling them all "narcissus," you can't go wrong.

All have the same basic flower structure. Each bloom has a perianth (six outer petal-like segments) that surrounds (and is held at right angles to) a central corona (also called the trumpet or cup, depending on its length).

Tazetta Hybrid 'Falconet'

Most types reach 1–1½ ft. tall. Flowers usually face the sun; be sure to keep this in mind when choosing a planting spot. Use narcissus under high-branching trees and flowering shrubs, among ground cover plantings, in woodland and rock gardens, or in borders. Naturalize them in sweeping drifts. Grow them in containers. They make fine cut flowers, though they should have a vase of their own; freshly cut stems release a substance that causes other cut flowers to wilt.

Plant bulbs as soon as they are available in fall. They should feel solid and heavy and be free of discoloration. "Double-nose" bulbs will give you the most and largest flowers the first season after planting. For planting depth and spacing, see "What Daffodils Need" on facing page.

After the blossoms fade, let the leaves mature and yellow naturally—if you cut the foliage before it yellows, subsequent flowering may be reduced or eliminated. Lift and divide clumps when flowers get smaller and fewer. To make this job easier, dig clumps just after the foliage withers so you can tell where the bulbs are. Separate the bulbs and replant them in freshly amended soil.

Like other plants, narcissus bulbs need food. Bonemeal used to be the recommended fertilizer, but no more: it lacks the nitrogen that promotes healthy foliage. Special bulb fertilizers are much better; look for a 10-10-20 formulation with controlled-release nitrogen. Mix fertilizer into the soil at planting time. In subsequent years, sprinkle bulb fertilizer over the bulb bed each fall at the rate specified on the bag, then scratch or water it in.

The most serious pest is the narcissus bulb fly. An adult fly resembles a small bumblebee. The female lays eggs on leaves and on necks of bulbs; when eggs hatch, young grubs eat their way into bulbs. Check bulbs before planting and destroy any grubs. Planting at the recommended depth will reduce infestations.

Following are the 12 generally recognized divisions of daffodils and recommended selections in each division.

Trumpet daffodils. The trumpet is as long as or longer than the perianth segments; one flower per stem. The best known is yellow 'King Alfred', a top-selling old selection that is quickly giving way to better performers. Newer 'Arctic Gold', 'Dutch Master', and 'Marieke' are superior yellows. Pure white selections include 'Mount Hood' and 'Empress of Ireland'. Bicolors with white segments and a yellow trumpet include 'Bravoure', 'Holland Sensation', and 'Las Vegas'. Among selections with yellow segments and a white trumpet are 'Honeybird' and 'Spellbinder'.

Large-cupped daffodils. The cup is shorter than the perianth segments, but always more than one-third their length; one flower per stem. Solid yellow selections include 'Camelot', 'Carlton' (possibly the most popular daffodil of all), and 'Saint Keverne' (a great choice for the Lower South). Solid whites include 'Birthday Girl', 'Misty Glen', and 'Stainless'. Selections with white segments and a colored cup include 'Accent' (salmon pink cup), 'Ice Follies' (yellow cup), 'Pink Pride' (pink cup), 'Redhill' (red-orange cup), and 'Salome' (apricot-yellow cup that fades to salmon). Those with yellow segments and a colored cup include 'By George' (peachy pink cup), 'Ceylon' (red-orange cup), and 'Fortissimo' (orange cup). 'Avalon' has yellow segments and a white cup.

Small-cupped daffodils. The cup is no more than one-third the length of the perianth segments; one flower per stem. Selections include 'Audubon' (white segments and pale yellow cup banded with pink) and 'Barrett Browning' (white segments and orange-red cup).

Double daffodils. Doubling of the cup, perianth segments, or both; one or more flowers per stem. Flower looks more like a peony than a typical daffodil. Examples are 'Cheerfulness' (white with yellow flecks), 'Golden Ducat'

WHAT DAFFODILS NEED

EXPOSURE: Narcissus do best in full sun, though they'll tolerate the dappled shade beneath high-branching deciduous trees. They won't bloom well in shade.

SOIL: They are not fussy about soil as long as it is loose and well drained. To improve drainage in heavy soils, deeply dig in plenty of organic matter prior to planting.

PLANTING: Set bulbs about twice as deep as they are tall—typically 5–6 in. deep for large bulbs and 3–5 in. deep for smaller ones. Space bulbs approximately 6–8 in. apart.

WATERING: Water newly planted bulbs thoroughly. In many regions, fall and winter are wet or snowy enough to provide moisture. Keep plantings well watered if precipitation fails; continue until foliage begins to yellow. Plants don't need summer moisture.

DIVIDING: Clumps need dividing only when bloom quantity and/or quality declines. Wait until the leaves die back, then dig the clumps and replant.

Triandrus Hybrid 'Hawera'

(golden yellow), 'Replete' (white segments, pink cup), and 'White Lion' (white segments, yellow cup).

Triandrus hybrids. Cup at least two-thirds the length of perianth segments; several nodding flowers per stem. Diminutive 'Hawera' has four to six lemon yellow flowers per stem; it is good for naturalizing and will spread by seed. Old favorite 'Thalia' offers elegant white, fragrant blooms.

Cyclamineus hybrids. Early bloomers with one flower per stem. Perianth segments strongly swept back. Popular selections include 'February Gold' (solid yellow), 'Jack Snipe' (white segments, yellow cup), and 'Jetfire' (yellow segments, red-orange cup).

Jonquilla hybrids. Each stem bears one to five small, very fragrant flowers; leaves are dark green and very narrow. Choices include 'Baby Moon' (bright yellow); 'Intrigue' (lemon yellow segments, yellow cup fading to white); 'Pipit' (yellow segments, white cup); and 'Quail', 'Sun Disc', 'Sweetness', and 'Trevithian' (all solid yellow).

Tazetta and Tazetta hybrids. Heat zones 10–7. Early-blooming types bearing clusters of 3 to 20 flowers on each stout stem; many have a musky-sweet fragrance that can be overpowering indoors. The most heat-tolerant group, they do well in central Florida; hardy only to about 10°F. 'Avalanche' ('Seventeen Sisters') produces clusters of 15 to 20 blossoms with white segments and a yellow cup. 'Falconet' and 'Scarlet Gem' feature yellow segments and a red-orange cup. 'Geranium' has creamy white segments and an orange cup; 'Minnow' has a pale yellow cup and pale yellow segments that fade to cream.

This division also includes the popular paperwhite narcissus that are forced into early bloom indoors. Plant them in bowls of pebbles and give them cool temperatures (50–60°F) and bright light. 'Early Splendor' has white segments and an orange cup; 'Grand Soleil d'Or' has golden yellow segments and an orange cup. 'Nazareth' has soft yellow segments and a bright yellow cup; 'Paper White' is pure white. ▶

N

Daffodil Divisions

TOP: Trumpet Daffodil 'Bravoure'
BOTTOM: Double Daffodil 'Cheerfulness'

TOP: Large-Cupped Daffodil 'Ice Follies'
BOTTOM: Jonquilla Hybrid 'Sun Disc'

TOP: Small-Cupped Daffodil 'Barrett Browning'
BOTTOM: Tazetta Hybrid 'Early Splendor'

TOP: Cyclamineus Hybrid 'Jack Snipe'
BOTTOM: Poeticus Daffodil 'Actaea'

TOP: Triandrus Hybrid 'Thalia'
BOTTOM: Split-Corona Hybrid 'Colblanc'

Poeticus daffodils. Fragrant flowers with white perianth segments and a short, disk-shaped cup with a green or yellow center and a red rim; one blossom per stem. 'Actaea' has the largest flowers (up to 4 in. across) and is the best known. These daffodils are sometimes given the name "pheasant's eye," but this term is correctly applied to the heirloom *Narcissus poeticus recurvus*.

Split-corona hybrids. Cup is split for at least one-third its length into two or more segments. 'Cassata' (white perianth segments, yellow cup), 'Colblanc' (all white), and 'Palmares' (white perianth segments, peachy pink cup) are three of the more readily available selections in this small but growing class.

Heirloom species. These old favorites often can be seen blooming at old homesites and graveyards and along roadsides throughout the South.

N. bulbocodium. HOOP PETTICOAT DAFFODIL. Grows to 6 in. tall. Small, upward-facing flowers are mostly trumpet, with very narrow, pointed perianth segments. Deep and pale yellow selections are available. Spreads by seed; good choice for naturalizing.

N. 'Butter and Eggs' ('Golden Phoenix', 'Aurantius Plenus'). Double yellow flowers. An old Southern favorite similar to *N. pseudonarcissus* 'Telemonius Plenus', but flowers open dependably throughout climate range and are softer in color, without streaks. Grows 16–18 in. tall.

Narcissus bulbocodium

N. cyclamineus. Backward-curved lemon yellow segments and narrow, tubular golden cup; 6 in. high.

N. jonquilla. JONQUIL. Semicylindrical, erect to spreading, rushlike leaves. Clusters of early, very fragrant, golden yellow flowers with short cups. To 1 ft. tall.

N. × *medioluteus.* TWIN SISTERS. Grows to 14 in. tall, bearing two flowers per stem; white segments, small yellow cup. Very late; last daffodil of the season.

N. × *odorus.* CAMPERNELLE JONQUIL. A sweet-scented, old-fashioned favorite. Often found in older gardens and cemeteries in Texas, Louisiana, and Arkansas. Grows to 1 ft. tall. Early in the season bears golden yellow, bell-like cups with recurved round segments; two to four flowers per stem. Rushlike leaves. Tolerates heavy clay and limy soils. 'Plenus' has double flowers.

N. poeticus recurvus. PHEASANT'S EYE. Old favorite. To 1 ft. tall. Small yellow cup with green central "eye" and red rim; pure white, reflexed segments.

N. pseudonarcissus. LENT LILY. One of the oldest daffodils—in cultivation since 1200 A.D. Grows to 12–14 in. tall. Long yellow cup; twisted yellow perianth segments that are swept forward, giving the blossoms a dog-eared look. Blooms early. 'Telemonius Plenus' (considered by many to be identical to 'Van Sion') has double yellow flowers with green streaks. Flowers of this selection often fail to open properly in the warm, humid springs of the Lower and Coastal South.

N. triandrus. ANGEL'S TEARS. Clusters of small white or pale yellow flowers on stems to 10 in. Rushlike foliage.

Miscellaneous. This category contains all types that don't fit the other divisions. 'Tête-à-tête' and 'Jumblie' (both yellow) have flowers like those of the Cyclamineus hybrids, but they're dwarf plants that reach a height of only 6 in.

FORCING DAFFODILS FOR EARLY BLOOM. *For early bloom indoors, set bulbs close together in a pot with their tips level with the soil surface. Place the pot in a well-drained trench or a cold frame and cover with 6–8 in. of sand, chopped leaves, or pine straw. Look for roots in 8 to 10 weeks (carefully remove the soil mass from the pot). Then move the pot to a cool room or greenhouse and watch for blooms. Keep well watered. After the blooms fade and the last frost is past, transfer the bulbs to your garden.* ❖

NASSELLA tenuissima

MEXICAN FEATHER GRASS, TEXAS NEEDLE GRASS

Poaceae (Gramineae)

PERENNIAL GRASS

🌿 MS, LS, CS, TS H 12–7

☀ FULL SUN

💧 LITTLE OR NO WATER

Nassella tenuissima

Native to Texas and Mexico, this is one of the finest-textured, softest-looking ornamental grasses. Threadlike bright green leaves form a clump to 2 ft. tall, 2–3 ft. wide. In summer, produces very thin flowering stems that arch outward and downward, ending in a cloud of silvery green inflorescences that age to a light straw color and remain attractive into winter. Especially effective when massed toward the front of a border, on slopes, and beside walkways or pools. This plant was formerly known as *Stipa tenuissima*.

NASTURTIUM. See TROPAEOLUM

NATAL IVY. See SENECIO macroglossus

NATAL PLUM. See CARISSA macrocarpa

NEANTHE bella. See CHAMAEDOREA elegans

NECTARINE. See PEACH and NECTARINE

NEEDLE PALM. See RHAPIDOPHYLLUM hystrix

NELUMBO (Nelumbium)

LOTUS

Nymphaeaceae

AQUATIC PLANTS

🌿 US, MS, LS, CS, TS H 12–1, EXCEPT AS NOTED

☀◐ FULL SUN OR PARTIAL SHADE

🌊 LOCATE IN PONDS, WATER GARDENS

Nelumbo nucifera

Huge, round leaves attached at their centers to leafstalks rise above the water. Large, fragrant summer flowers form above or below leaves. Ornamental, woody fruit is perforated like a saltshaker and looks attractive in dried arrangements.

If you buy started plants in containers, put them in a pond, positioned so soil in pots is 8–10 in. below surface of water. If you acquire roots, plant them in spring, setting them horizontally and about 4 in. deep in a 1- to 1½-ft.-deep container of fairly rich soil; then place container at the recommended depth in pond, as described above for started plants. Do not let roots freeze; where freezes are possible, cover the pond or fill it deeper with water. Beware of introducing lotus plants or roots into earth-bottomed ponds 3–4 ft. or shallower; plants will eventually fill in pond, and rhizomes are difficult to remove.

N. lutea (Nelumbium luteum). AMERICAN LOTUS. Native to North America. Similar to *N. nucifera* but somewhat smaller in leaf and flower. Flowers are pale yellow.

N. nucifera (Nelumbium nelumbo). INDIAN or CHINESE LOTUS. Heat zones 12–3. Native to Asia, Australia. Round leaves to 2 ft. or wider are carried 3–6 ft. above the water's surface. Pink, 4- to 10-in.-wide flowers are borne singly on stems. Both the tubers and the seeds are esteemed in Chinese cookery, and entire plant has great religious significance for Buddhists: it represents the human soul rising from the mud and aspiring to light and purity. White, rose-colored, and double-blossomed selections exist. 'Speciosum' is the classic, single light pink lotus of Oriental art. 'Alba Grandiflora' bears large, very fragrant white flowers. 'Empress' has single white blooms with deep pink edges. Dwarf forms (1–2 ft. tall) suitable for tubs and small ponds include 'Tulip' ('Shirokunshi'), single white; and 'Momo Botan', with double blooms in deep rose, fading to white.

N

NEMOPHILA

Hydrophyllaceae

COOL-SEASON ANNUALS

✎ US, MS, LS, CS, TS ◫ 6–1

☼ ◑ FULL SUN OR PARTIAL SHADE

◕ REGULAR WATER

Nemophila menziesii

Cool-weather annuals to 6–12 in. high and trailing to 1 ft. wide, with saucer-shaped flowers to 1 in. across. Pale green, hairy, ferny leaves give plants a delicate appearance. Often used as bulb cover. Sow seed in place in fall; plants will bloom in winter in the Coastal and Tropical South, in spring in the Upper, Middle, and Lower South.

N. maculata. FIVE-SPOT NEMOPHILA. Native to California. Flowers are white, marked with fine purple lines and dots; a large purple dot appears at the tip of each of the five lobes.

N. menziesii (N. insignis). BABY BLUE EYES. From California, southern Oregon. Plant blooms freely, bearing sky blue blossoms with a white or near-white center. 'Snowstorm' has white flowers dotted with black. 'Pennie Black' bears blackish purple flowers rimmed in white.

NEOMARICA

Iridaceae

PERENNIALS

✎ CS, TS ◫ 12–7; OR GROW IN POTS

☼ ◑ FULL SUN OR LIGHT SHADE; BRIGHT LIGHT

◕ REGULAR WATER

Neomarica caerulea

Like iris, these old favorites produce fans of lance-shaped leaves that arise from rhizomes. Foliage and flowering stems grow to about the same height. Flowers are intricate, with three large, rounded outer segments around three smaller, curled inner segments banded in contrasting colors. Each flower lasts only a day, but others follow over an extended period. Indoors, give bright light but protect from hot sun. During active growth, feed monthly with a balanced fertilizer; let soil go fairly dry between soakings. In winter, stop feeding and give little water.

N. caerulea. BRAZILIAN WALKING IRIS. From Brazil. To 5–5½ ft. tall, 2–3 ft. wide, with stiffly erect leaves. As plant grows, lower leaves fan out to the side. Branching flower stems carry a succession of 3- to 4-in. blue blossoms, their centers intricately banded in yellow, white, and brown. Blooms in early summer. Offsets are produced at flowering points on the stems; they detach easily for additional plants.

N. gracilis. WALKING IRIS. Native from Mexico to Brazil. To 2–2½ ft. tall, 1–1½ ft. wide. Blooms in late spring and summer; flower stems resemble the leaves so closely that blossoms appear to emerge directly from the foliage. Flowers are 2½ in. wide, with white outer segments and inner ones in a combination of blue, brown, and yellow. As flowers fade, the blossom stalk bends downward and produces plantlets that take root—hence the common name.

N. longifolia. YELLOW WALKING IRIS. From Brazil. Upright growth to 2 ft. tall, 1–1½ ft. wide. Blooms all summer, bearing 2-in. yellow flowers banded with brown. "Walks" the same way *N. gracilis* does.

NEOREGELIA

Bromeliaceae

PERENNIALS

✎ TS ◫ 12–10; OR HOUSEPLANTS

◐ LIGHT SHADE; BRIGHT INDIRECT LIGHT

◕ SEE TEXT FOR WATERING INSTRUCTIONS

Neoregelia carolinae 'Tricolor'

Native to South America, these bromeliads consist of rosettes of leathery, often strikingly banded or marbled leaves. Inconspicuous flowers appear in a cup at the center of the rosette; the cup turns red when the plant is ready to bloom. In the rain forest, this central cup serves to collect rain, which quickly evaporates. For neoregelias grown outdoors, you can keep the cup filled with water from spring to fall. For indoor plants, though, be sure to let the cup dry completely before refilling—otherwise, the water can become stagnant and the plant may rot.

Give loose, fast-draining soil, and let it go dry to the touch between waterings. From spring through summer, feed monthly with a general-purpose liquid houseplant fertilizer diluted to half-strength; to apply, sprinkle the liquid over the entire plant.

N. carolinae. To 1 ft. tall, 2½ ft. wide. Many medium green, shiny leaves about 1 ft. long, 1½ in. wide. 'Tricolor' is identical but sports lengthwise white stripes on its leaves.

N. spectabilis. PAINTED FINGERNAIL PLANT. To 1½ ft. tall, 3 ft. wide. Leaves are about 1 ft. long, 2 in. wide, olive green with bright red tips. Foliage takes on a bronzy color in strong light.

NEPETA

Lamiaceae (Labiatae)

PERENNIALS

✎ ZONES VARY BY SPECIES

☼ ◑ FULL SUN OR PARTIAL SHADE

◔ ◕ MODERATE TO REGULAR WATER

Nepeta cataria

Vigorous, spreading members of the mint family with aromatic foliage. With the exception of catnip (*N. cataria*), these plants are valuable for their spikes of two-lipped blue or blue-violet (or sometimes pink, white, or yellow) flowers. As soon as blossoms fade, shear plants back by half or cut faded flower stems to the ground to encourage rebloom. (Most species seed freely and can become invasive if spent flowers are not removed.) Plants make attractive, informal low hedges or edgings. Deer don't usually eat them.

In winter or early spring, cut out last year's growth to make way for new stems. At that time, you can also divide clumps for increase, though it's easy to start new plants from cuttings (take them before flower buds form). When buying named selections, be sure to obtain cutting-grown plants; seedlings vary in flower color and habit. Flowering is spotty in the Tropical South. Provide good drainage.

N. cataria. CATNIP. Zones US, MS; 7–1. From the Mediterranean and western Asia. To 2–3 ft. high and wide, with downy, heart-shaped, tooth-edged gray-green leaves. Spikes of small (¼- to ½-in.) whitish or pinkish flowers in late spring, early summer. Not very ornamental but worthy of a place in the herb garden. Grows easily in light soil and self-sows readily. Common name refers to stimulant effect on cats. Their susceptibility to the herb varies, though: some felines fall into a rapturous frenzy, rolling wildly on the plant, but others ignore it. If necessary, protect crown of plant with an inverted wire basket; stems will grow through. The same tactic also helps preserve potted plants grown outdoors and brought indoors occasionally for cats to enjoy. You can also sprinkle dried leaves over your cat's food or use them to stuff cloth toys. Some people use catnip to flavor tea. 'Citriodora' has lemon-scented foliage.

N. ×faassenii. CATMINT. Zones US, MS, LS, CS; 9–1. Sterile hybrid of *N. racemosa* and a European species; often sold as *N. mussinii*. Soft, silvery gray-green, spreading mound grows to 1 ft. high, 1½–2 ft. wide. Scallop-edged, heart-shaped leaves to 1 in. long. Attractive to some cats, who enjoy nibbling on and rolling in plantings; insert short, blunt-tipped sticks in the ground among the leaves to discourage cats and prevent destruction. Loose, lax spikes of ½-in. lavender-blue flowers in late spring, early summer. Set plants 1–1½ ft. apart for ground cover. 'Select Blue' has darker flowers than the species; 'Snowflake' has pure white blooms. 'Dropmore' grows to 1½ ft. high and 3 ft. wide; it may be a hybrid involving another species.

N. grandiflora. GIANT CATMINT. Zones US, MS, LS; 8–1. Native to Europe, Caucasus. Open clump to 2½ ft. tall, 1½ ft. wide. Gray-green, hairless or sparsely hairy, scallop-edged, egg-shaped leaves to 4 in. long. Violet-blue, ¾-in. flowers in late spring, early summer. 'Bramdean' has lavender-blue blossoms with purple calyxes; 'Dawn to Dusk' has lilac-pink blooms, smoky violet calyxes. Calyxes of both these selections persist after flowers have faded.

N. nervosa. Zones US, MS; 7–5. Native to Kashmir. Bushy habit to 1–2 ft. tall, 1 ft. wide. Bright green, conspicuously veined, tooth-edged leaves are lance shaped, 2–4 in. long. Brilliant violet-blue (rarely yellow), ½-in. flowers bloom from midsummer to early fall.

N. racemosa (N. mussinii). Zones US, MS, LS; 8–1. Native to the Caucasus, Turkey, Iran. Sprawling plant grows from 6 in. to 1 ft. tall and about 2 ft. or more wide. Roundish, scallop-edged, ½- to 1¼-in.-long leaves range in color from medium green to gray green; they are covered with fine hairs. The typical form produces ⅓-in.-long lavender flowers for a short period in midsummer; may rebloom if sheared. Reseeds wildly. Inferior to its hybrid N. ×faassenii, but there are several worthwhile selections that are more compact than the species and bloom over a longer period. 'Blue Ice' has dense gray-green foliage and pale blue flowers that fade to near-white. 'Superba' has a dense, matlike habit and gray-green leaves that are smaller than those of the species; it bears lavender-blue blossoms from spring through fall. Violet-blue flowers of 'Walker's Low' appear over an equally long season.

N. sibirica (N. macrantha, Dracocephalum sibiricum). SIBERIAN CATNIP. Zones US, MS, LS; 8–1. Native to Siberia. Sturdy, upright habit to 2–3 ft. tall and 1½–2 ft. wide. Dark green, oblong to lance-shaped, 3-in.-long leaves are softly hairy beneath. Spikes of large (1½-in.) violet-blue blossoms appear for about a month, beginning in early summer.

N. 'Six Hills Giant'. Zones US, MS, LS; 8–1. Possibly a hybrid of N. ×faassenii and similar to it—but grows taller (reaches 2½–3 ft. high and as wide), has greener foliage, and bears deeper blue flowers. More tolerant of damp climates than other nepetas.

N. 'Souvenir d'André Chaudron' ('Blue Beauty'). Zones US, MS, LS; 8–1. Probably a hybrid of N. sibirica. Quite similar to parent but grows only 1½ ft. high and blooms for a longer period, with season extending into late summer.

NEPHROLEPIS

SWORD FERN

Polypodiaceae

· FERNS

✎ TS H 12–10; OR HOUSEPLANT

☼ ◐ SOME SHADE; BRIGHT INDIRECT LIGHT

▲ REGULAR WATER

Nephrolepis exaltata 'Bostoniensis'

Tough and easy to grow, these are the most widely used of all ferns. Where winters are cold, they're popular houseplants, benefiting from well-drained soil, frequent misting, and monthly applications of a general-purpose liquid houseplant fertilizer from spring through fall. In frost-free areas, they make splendid ground covers for shady areas. Not usually browsed by deer.

N. cordifolia. SOUTHERN SWORD FERN. Native to many tropical regions of the world. To 2–3 ft. tall, 5 ft. wide. Tufts of bright green, narrow (2-in.-wide), upright fronds with closely spaced, finely toothed leaflets. Roots often have small, roundish tubers. Plant spreads by thin, fuzzy runners and can be invasive. Will not take hard frosts but is otherwise adaptable, tolerating poor soil and erratic watering. Good in narrow, shaded beds; can thrive in full sun with adequate water. Good in pots and hanging baskets. Often sold as *N. exaltata*.

N. exaltata. SWORD FERN. Like *N. cordifolia*, this is a tropical species, but it grows larger (to 7 ft. high and as wide) and has broader fronds (to 6 in. wide). Most common are named selections grown as houseplants. Best known is 'Bostoniensis', Boston fern. Growing about 3 ft. high, it is the classic parlor fern, with spreading, arching habit and graceful, eventually drooping fronds broader than those of the species. Among the many forms

with more finely cut and feathery fronds are 'Fluffy Ruffles', 'Rooseveltii', and 'Whitmanii'.

N. obliterata. From northwestern Australia. Grows to 3–4½ ft. high and wide. Similar to *N. cordifolia* but has darker green, somewhat narrower fronds. Used mainly as a houseplant. Habit is stiffer and more erect than that of *N. exaltata* 'Bostoniensis', and plant is more tolerant of low humidity and both high and low light conditions. Selections include 'Kimberley Queen' and 'Western Queen'.

OVERWINTERING YOUR BOSTON FERN. *There seems to be an unwritten law in the South that any house with a spacious front porch is required to display two or more Boston ferns in pots or hanging baskets. When cold weather arrives, many folks simply let the plants die, then start over with new ones the following spring. But if you can't bear the thought of your fern's demise, take heart: you can help it survive the winter. In fall, use sharp scissors to cut back all side fronds to the rim of the pot, leaving the top growth about 10 in. high. Place the pot indoors next to your brightest window, and keep the soil fairly moist. By spring, your plant should be bushy again and ready for its return to the porch.* ❖

NERINE

Amaryllidaceae

PERENNIALS FROM BULBS

✎ LS, CS, TS H 10–8; OR GROW IN POTS

☼ ◐ PARTIAL SHADE IN HOTTEST CLIMATES

▲ REGULAR WATER DURING GROWTH AND BLOOM

Nerine sarniensis curvifolia fothergillii

South African relatives of spider lily *(Lycoris)*, which they closely resemble. Most have strap-shaped leaves to about 1 ft. long; these usually die back well before bloom time in late summer or early autumn, then reappear later in the year (typically around bloom time or shortly afterward). Some types are essentially evergreen. All have attractive broad, funnel- or trumpet-shaped flowers carried in clusters atop leafless stems; each blossom has six spreading segments, recurved at their tips. Good plants for containers.

Same planting instructions, cultural conditions as for *Lycoris*. Withhold summer water for species that experience summer dormancy, but keep watering the essentially evergreen kinds. As is true for *Lycoris*, these plants can be grown in pots in areas beyond their hardiness range or where soil cannot be kept dry for summer-dormant types.

N. bowdenii. Bears flowers to 3 in. long that are soft pink marked with deeper pink, in clusters of 8 to 12 on 2-ft. stems. Forms with taller stems and larger flower clusters are available in deeper pink, crimson, and red. One example is 'Pink Triumph', with large blossoms in dark pink. Goes dormant in summer.

N. filifolia. Essentially evergreen or nearly so, since new leaves—narrow, grassy, and reaching 6–8 in. long—are produced as old ones fade. Inch-wide, rose red flowers with narrow, crinkled segments are carried in clusters of 8 to 12 on each 1-ft. stem. Plant spreads rapidly. Mulch in late fall in Lower South.

N. masoniorum. Virtually evergreen species like *N. filifolia*, but it bears its flowers in clusters of 4 to 12 on 9-in. stems. Mulch in late fall in Lower South.

N. sarniensis. GUERNSEY LILY. Large clusters of 1½-in., iridescent crimson flowers with prominent stamens, borne on stalks to 2 ft. tall. Pink, orange, scarlet, and pure white selections are available. *N. s. curvifolia fothergillii* has scarlet flowers overlaid with shimmering gold. Goes dormant in summer.

FOR INFORMATION ON YOUR CLIMATE ZONES

PLEASE SEE PAGES 28–38

NERIUM oleander

OLEANDER

Apocynaceae

EVERGREEN SHRUB

✿ LS, CS, TS ⊩ 12–7; OR GROW IN POT

☼ FULL SUN

◐ ◑ ● LITTLE TO REGULAR WATER

⬧ ALL PARTS ARE POISONOUS IF INGESTED.
DON'T BURN PRUNINGS; SMOKE CAN CAUSE
SEVERE IRRITATION

Nerium oleander

Selections of this species are superb landscape plants wherever they are winter hardy. These Mediterranean natives are tough as nails and combine spectacular flowers with handsome foliage. Growing quickly to 3–20 ft. tall and 4–12 ft. wide (depending on the selection), they naturally form billowing shrubs but are easy to train into single-trunked trees. They make outstanding windbreaks and tall screens and also do well in containers. Narrow, 4- to 12-in.-long leaves are dark green, leathery, and attractive in all seasons. Clusters of single or double, sometimes fragrant flowers in red, pink, salmon, yellow, or white appear at branch tips from spring to fall, depending on the climate.

Few plants are as adaptable to challenging growing conditions as oleanders. They are ubiquitous along Southern coasts, because they tolerate wind, salt spray, and sandy soil. Once established, they need little water; they'll also grow in poorly drained soil, be it acid or alkaline. Their only limitation is susceptibility to cold. Most selections will weather brief periods of 10°F or a bit colder, but they may be killed to the ground. They will, however, usually resprout the following spring and bloom at the usual time. Older, established plants are hardier than young ones. In the Upper and Middle South, grow oleanders in containers and bring them indoors for the winter.

Regular pruning isn't necessary, but if you need to shape the plant or reduce its size, do so immediately after flowering. Avoid pruning within 3 months of the first expected fall frost. To renew old, unattractive, leggy plants, lop them nearly to the ground before new growth begins in spring.

Oleanders are usually pest free, but infestations of bright orange oleander caterpillars can defoliate entire plants; the damage typically isn't fatal. A new scourge called oleander leaf scorch has recently appeared in Texas. Caused by a bacterium spread by a sucking insect, this disease causes leaves to turn brown, then drop; eventually, the plant succumbs. There is no cure, quickly remove and dispose of infected plants.

All parts of oleander plants are poisonous; deer don't browse them. Caution children against eating oleander leaves or flowers, and make sure that pets do not do so; keep prunings and dead leaves away from hay or animal feed, and don't use branches for barbecue fires or skewers. Smoke from burning oleander branches can cause severe irritation to mucous membranes.

Dozens of named selections exist, some of which are described below. They typically grow about half as wide as tall. For the plant called yellow oleander, see *Thevetia.*

'Algiers'. Single dark red flowers. To 10–12 ft. tall.

'Casablanca'. Profuse show of single white flowers. To 4–6 ft. tall.

'Franklin D. Roosevelt'. Single deep salmon flowers with yellow throat. Very hardy. To 10 ft. tall.

'Hardy Pink'. Single salmon pink flowers. The hardiest oleander, tolerating temperatures into the low teens without damage. Reaches 10 ft. tall.

'Isle of Capri'. Single light yellow blossoms. To 5–7 ft. tall.

'Lane Taylor Sealy'. Single, fragrant light salmon blooms with a yellow throat. To 8 ft. tall.

'Little Red'. Single dark red flowers. Hardier than most. Compact grower to 3–4 ft. tall.

'Morocco'. Single white blossoms. To 5–7 ft. tall and wide.

'Mrs. George Roeding' ('Carneum Plenum'). Double, fragrant salmon pink flowers; fine-textured foliage. Slightly weeping form. Grows to about 6 ft. tall.

'Petite Pink'. Single shell pink blooms. To 3–4 ft. tall.

'Petite Salmon'. Single salmon pink flowers. To 3–4 ft. tall.

'Ruby Lace'. Single, large ruby red blossoms. Grows to 8 ft. tall.

'Sister Agnes' ('Soeur Agnès'). Single white flowers. Vigorous grower reaches 15–20 ft. tall.

'Sue Hawley Oakes'. Creamy yellow flowers with a yellow throat. Grows to 8 ft. tall.

'Sugarland' ('Hardy Red'). Single red flowers. Hardier selection than most. Reaches 10 ft. tall.

NERVE PLANT. See FITTONIA simplex

NEVIUSIA alabamensis

ALABAMA SNOW-WREATH

Rosaceae

DECIDUOUS SHRUB

✿ US, MS, LS ⊩ 8–1

☼ ◐ FULL SUN OR PARTIAL SHADE

● ◐ REGULAR TO AMPLE WATER

Neviusia alabamensis

Native to Alabama. Ornamental multistemmed shrub 3–6 ft. tall and wide, with arching, delicate branches and clouds of feathery white flowers in spring. Grows rather slowly. Medium green, pointed, oval leaves to 3 in. long. Unusual, showy flowers: spreading, inch-wide bunches of white stamens, without petals. Easy to grow if given well-drained soil and plenty of water during summer.

NEW JERSEY TEA. See CEANOTHUS americanus

NEW ZEALAND FLAX. See PHORMIUM tenax

NEW ZEALAND TEA TREE. See LEPTOSPERMUM scoparium

NICOLAIA elatior. See ETLINGERA elatior

NICOTIANA

Solanaceae

PERENNIALS USUALLY GROWN AS ANNUALS

✿ US, MS, LS, CS, TS ⊩ 12–1

☼ ◐ FULL SUN OR PARTIAL SHADE

● REGULAR WATER

⬧ ALL PARTS ARE EXTREMELY POISONOUS IF
INGESTED

Nicotiana alata

Tender perennials from South America. All but *N. glauca* are grown as annuals, but they may live over in the Coastal and Tropical South. Upright-growing plants with soft, oval, often quite large leaves; both foliage and stems are slightly sticky. Flowers—very fragrant, in some species— are tubular, typically flaring at the mouth into five pointed lobes; they appear near tops of branching stems in summer. They usually open at night or on cloudy days, though some kinds open during the day. Some nicotianas reseed readily.

N. alata (N. affinis). FLOWERING TOBACCO. Wild species (for which seed is available) grows 2–4 ft. tall (possibly to 6 ft. under ideal conditions), 1 ft. wide. Leaves to 10 in. long. Bears large, intensely fragrant white flowers that open toward evening. Selection and hybridization with other species have produced many garden strains that stay open day and night and come in colors including white, pink shades, red, and lime green, but their perfume is not as strong as that of the "unimproved" species.

Domino strain grows 12–15 in. high and has upward-facing flowers that take heat and sun better than taller kinds. Nicki strain is taller, to 15–18 in. The older Sensation strain is taller still (to 4 ft.) and looks more at home

N

in informal mixed borders than as a bedding plant. Fragrance in these strains is erratic. If scent (especially during evening) is important to you, plant 3-ft.-tall 'Grandiflora'.

N. 'Avalon Bright Pink'. Compact hybrid to 10 in. high, 1 ft. wide. Inch-long leaves are virtually hidden by a profusion of star-shaped, 1½-in. flowers in bright pink. Quite heat tolerant; good in containers.

N. glauca. TREE TOBACCO. Naturalized from California to Texas and Mexico. Shrubby or treelike habit to 10–25 ft. tall, 10 ft. wide. Bluish green leaves to 6 in. long; small, unscented yellow-green flowers. Be especially careful with the leaves—they can be deadly if eaten.

N. langsdorffii. To 5 ft. tall, 1½ ft. wide. Leaves to 10 in. long. Branching stems are hung with drooping sprays of bell-shaped bright green flowers about 2 in. long. Unusual blossom color blends well with blues, yellows in flower border. No noticeable scent.

N. sylvestris. FLOWERING TOBACCO. To 5 ft. tall, 2 ft. wide, with leaves that can reach 1–2 ft. long. Intensely fragrant, 3½-in.-long, tubular white flowers are borne in tiers atop a statuesque plant. Striking in a night garden.

NIEREMBERGIA

CUP FLOWER

Solanaceae

PERENNIALS OFTEN GROWN AS ANNUALS

US, MS, LS, CS, TS 12–1

LIGHT SHADE IN HOTTEST CLIMATES

REGULAR WATER

Nierembergia repens

These plants bear tubular flowers that flare into saucerlike or bell-like cups. The first species listed here grows as a spreading mound; the other is a ground-covering mat. Both are covered with blooms during summer. Can be grown as perennials in the Lower South, cool-weather annuals in the Coastal and Tropical South, summer annuals elsewhere.

N. caerulea (N. hippomanica). DWARF CUP FLOWER. To 6–12 in. high and wide. Much-branched, mounding plant with very small, stiff leaves. Flowers are blue to violet. Trimming back plant after bloom to induce new growth seems to lengthen its life. 'Purple Robe' is a common variety; 'Mont Blanc' bears white flowers.

N. repens (N. rivularis). WHITE CUP. Bright green foliage forms a mat to 4–6 in. high, 2 ft. wide. White blossoms. For best performance, don't crowd it with more aggressive plants. Not as heat tolerant as *N. caerulea.*

NIGELLA damascena

LOVE-IN-A-MIST

Ranunculaceae

ANNUAL

US, MS, LS, CS, TS 12–1

FULL SUN OR PARTIAL SHADE

REGULAR WATER

Nigella damascena
Persian Jewels

Mediterranean native. Old-fashioned favorite to 1–1½ ft. high, 10 in. wide. All leaves, even those that form under collar beneath each flower, are finely cut into threadlike divisions. Blue, white, or rose-colored blooms, 1–1½ in. wide, appear singly at branch ends in spring. Curious papery-textured, horned seed capsules lend an airy effect to bouquets and mixed borders, look decorative in dried arrangements. Miss Jekyll Series, to 1½ ft. tall, has semidouble blossoms in sky blue, deep blue, rose, and white. Persian Jewels, to 15 in. tall, is a superior strain in mixed colors.

Love-in-a-mist comes into bloom quickly in spring, dries up in summer heat. Sow seed in fall on open ground where plants are to grow, since long taproot makes transplanting unsatisfactory. Self-sows freely.

NIGHT-BLOOMING CEREUS. See HYLOCEREUS undatus

NIGHT-BLOOMING JESSAMINE. See CESTRUM nocturnum

NINEBARK, COMMON. See PHYSOCARPUS opulifolius

NOBLE FIR. See ABIES procera

NOLANA paradoxa

Nolanaceae

PERENNIAL GROWN AS ANNUAL

US, MS, LS, CS, TS 12–1

FULL SUN OR LIGHT SHADE

MODERATE WATER

Nolana paradoxa

Unusual plant from Chile that looks like a trailing blue-flowered petunia to 6–8 in. high and 2 ft. wide, with trailing stems bearing oval, pointed, 2-in.-long leaves. In summer, plant is covered with 2-in., funnel-shaped blooms in bright blue with a white or yellow throat. 'Blue Bird' has deep sky blue blossoms with a white throat. Use as edging or in hanging basket. Withstands a wide range of temperatures. Needs good drainage.

NOLINA

Agavaceae

PERENNIALS

ZONES VARY BY SPECIES

FULL SUN

LITTLE OR NO WATER TO MODERATE WATER

Nolina longifolia

Yucca and agave relatives with tough, narrow, grassy leaves, typically carried atop a thick trunk. Mature plants bear flowers; the blossoms are tiny, but they're usually borne on tall stalks that make for a good show. Good for dry areas; tolerate poor, alkaline soil. Not suited to areas with high rainfall and high humidity.

N. erumpens. BEAR GRASS. Zones LS, CS, TS; 12–1. Native to Mexico and western Texas. Sharp-edged, thick leaves to 3 ft. long form a mound 3–4 ft. tall, 6 ft. wide. Showy spikes of creamy white flowers flushed with rose pink rise several feet above the foliage, spring into summer.

N. lindheimeri. DEVIL'S SHOESTRING. Zones MS, LS, CS, TS; 12–1. Native to central Mexico. Wiry, narrow, 2- to 3-ft.-long leaves; foliage mounds reach 6 ft. across. Wands of white flowers rise to 3–4 ft. in late spring.

N. longifolia. MEXICAN GRASS TREE. Zones CS, TS; 12–1. Native to central Mexico. In youth, forms a fountain (to about 6 ft. wide) of grasslike, 3-ft.-long, 1-in.-wide leaves. In time, the foliage fountain is carried atop a 6- to 10-ft. trunk, sometimes with a few branches. White flowers come in late spring, on stalks up to 6 ft. tall.

N. nelsoni. BLUE BEAR GRASS TREE. Zones MS, LS, CS, TS; 12–1. Slow-growing plant native to the deserts of northern Mexico. Forms a foliage rosette 3–5 ft. tall and twice as wide; narrow (1- to 1½-in.-wide), finely tooth-edged leaves are gray green and flexible when young, silvery blue gray and stiff when mature. In time, foliage is carried atop a 5- to 12-ft. trunk. Dead leaves hang on to the trunk; remove them for a neater look. Blooms in summer, bearing creamy blossoms on a 7- to 10-ft. spike. Dramatic and sculptural.

N. recurvata. See Beaucarnea recurvata

N. texana. SACAHUISTA, BASKET GRASS. Zones MS, LS, CS, TS; 12–1. Native to Texas, the Southwest, and Mexico. Very grasslike foliage forms a mound 1½–2 ft. tall and twice as wide. Stalks of creamy white blossoms are 1–1½ ft. tall; they don't rise above the leaves. Blooms from spring into summer. Especially hardy.

NORFOLK ISLAND PINE. See ARAUCARIA heterophylla

NUN'S ORCHID. See PHAIUS tankervilliae

N

Nyctaginaceae. The four-o'clock family contains annuals, perennials, shrubs, and vines with showy flowers or bracts. Two familiar members are *Bougainvillea* and four o'clock (*Mirabilis*).

NYMPHAEA

WATER LILY

Nymphaeaceae

AQUATIC PLANTS

🗡 US, MS, LS, CS, TS ⊩ 12–1

☼ FULL SUN

💧 LOCATE IN PONDS, WATER GARDENS

Nymphaea

Floating leaves are rounded, with deep notch at one side where leafstalk is attached. Showy flowers either float on surface or stand above it on stiff stalks. There are hardy and tropical kinds. Hardy types come in white, yellow, copper, pink, and red. Tropical types add blue and purple to the color range, as well as an unusual greenish blue. Some tropicals in the white-pink-red color range are night bloomers; all others close at night. Many are fragrant.

Hardy kinds are easiest for beginners. Plant them from February to October in mild-winter areas, from April to July in cold-winter regions. Set 6-in.-long pieces of rhizome on soil at pool bottom or in boxes (not redwood ones, since these can discolor the water), placing rhizome in a nearly horizontal position with its bud end up. In either case, top of soil should be 8–12 in. below surface of water. Feed at planting time and monthly thereafter, using a controlled-release product. Groom plants by removing spent leaves and blossoms. They usually bloom throughout warm weather and go dormant in fall, reappearing in spring.

Tropical kinds begin to grow and bloom later in summer but last longer, often until the first frost. Buy started tropical plants and set them at the same depth as hardy rhizomes. Tropical types go dormant but do not survive really low winter temperatures. Their best chance of long-term survival is in the Tropical South. Where winters are colder, store dormant tubers in damp sand indoors over winter or buy new plants each year.

Nymphaeaceae. The water lily family consists of aquatic plants, usually with floating leaves and flowers. Two examples are lotus (*Nelumbo*) and water lily (*Nymphaea*).

Nyssaceae. Deciduous trees from Asia and North America. Two grown in the South are dove tree (*Davidia*) and black gum (*Nyssa*).

NYSSA sylvatica

BLACK GUM, SOUR GUM, TUPELO

Nyssaceae

DECIDUOUS TREE

🗡 US, MS, LS, CS ⊩ 10–2

☼ ◐ FULL SUN OR PARTIAL SHADE

💧 💧 MODERATE TO REGULAR WATER

Nyssa sylvatica

Native to the eastern U.S., this is one of our finest large trees for fall color—and one of the first to color up in autumn, with leaves turning yellow, orange, burgundy, crimson, or bright scarlet before they drop. Display is best in the Upper and Middle South, where foliage turns color all at once; in the Lower and Coastal South, individual leaves tend to color and drop over a period of weeks, diminishing the show.

Grows at a slow to moderate rate, reaching 30–60 ft. tall, 20–30 ft. wide; pyramidal when young, rounded or flat-topped when mature. Horizontal branches and rugged, nearly black bark create a dramatic picture

against the winter sky. Plants are usually entirely male or entirely female, but some are a little of both. Flowers of all are inconspicuous. If pollinated by a nearby male, females bear bluish black fruits resembling small olives that ripen in late summer and autumn. Birds relish them, but fruit drop can make a mess on decks and driveways. Lustrous dark green leaves are oval and pointed, 3–6 in. long.

Because cuttings are hard to root and seedlings tend to grow slowly, few named selections exist. Two choices, both with red fall color, are fast-growing 'Forum', with conical form, and the weeping selection 'Autumn Cascade'.

Black gum prefers moist, acid, well-drained soil containing lots of organic matter, but it takes poorly drained clay soil. It doesn't tolerate pollution, though, so it's not a good choice for city gardens. Superb shade or lawn tree; excellent for naturalized areas. Select a permanent location, as taproot makes it difficult to move later on. Trees that are cut down seem to produce suckers forever.

Two other American species, native to Southern swamps, are best appreciated in their natural settings. *N. aquatica*, water tupelo, is similar to *N. sylvatica* but has larger leaves and fruits and a trunk that is swollen at the base. *N. ogeche*, Ogeechee tupelo, is smaller (to 30–40 ft. high) and has only negligible fall color. Its edible, ¾-in., reddish fruits are pickled to make "Ogeechee limes."

OAK. See QUERCUS

OAT GRASS, BLUE. See HELICTOTRICHON sempervirens

OAT GRASS, BULBOUS. See ARRHENATHERUM elatius bulbosum 'Variegatum'

OCIMUM basilicum

BASIL

Lamiaceae (Labiatae)

ANNUAL

🗡 US, MS, LS, CS, TS ⊩ 12–1

☼ FULL SUN

💧 REGULAR WATER

Ocimum basilicum

Native to tropical and subtropical Asia, basil is so simple to grow that even first-time gardeners can plant it with confidence. It thrives in hot, humid weather and grows well throughout the South from spring until frost. The plant produces spikes of small white or pinkish flowers, but it's prized for its shiny green leaves—oval, 1–2 in. long, with a clovelike fragrance and spicy-sweet flavor that make them indispensable in the kitchen. Fresh basil leaves are a must for summer salads, especially with tomatoes.

For best results, plant in full sun in loose, well-drained soil. You can start with transplants, but basil grows quite easily from seed. Sow directly in the garden in spring, after the danger of frost is past and the soil has warmed. Plant seeds ¼ in. deep. When seedlings are 2–3 in. tall, thin them to 1½–2 ft. apart. Fertilize once or twice during the growing season with an all-purpose fertilizer; be sure to keep the soil moist. To extend the life of the plants, pinch out the flowers.

For fresh use, simply pluck the leaves when you need them. For drying or using in pesto or basil vinegar, harvest just before the flower buds open, clipping the plant back to one-third its original size. You should get several harvests in one season.

The plain species, often called sweet basil, is used both fresh and dried to flavor sauces and dishes of all types. It grows 2 ft. tall, about 1 ft. wide. Larger 'Genovese', to 2½ ft. tall, is intensely aromatic and spicy, highly favored for pesto. 'Siam Queen', to 2 ft. tall, is a licorice-flavored basil that's good for Thai and Vietnamese dishes. 'Magical Michael' forms a neat mound to 1½ ft. tall and wide and has both culinary and ornamental value. Dwarf sweet basils form dense, compact plants under 1 ft. tall; they're good for edging and also do well in containers. Recommended selections include 'Minette' and 'Spicy Bush'.

▶

'Citriodorum', lemon basil (also known as *O. ×citriodorum*), about 2 ft. tall and 1 ft. wide, produces small light green leaves with a pungent, lemony-sweet flavor. It doesn't transplant well, so start it from seed sown in place. 'Sweet Dani' grows 2–2½ ft. tall and has larger leaves.

'Purpurascens', purple basil, is similar to the species, but it has purplish red foliage with a tealike scent and pinkish or purplish blooms. It isn't as pungent or sweet as the green-leafed kind and is best used fresh. Other purple-foliaged selections include 'Dark Opal' (2 ft. tall, good for vinegars), 'Purple Ruffles' (1½ ft. tall, with crinkled leaves), and 'Red Rubin' (1½–2 ft. tall, with uniform, bronzy purple leaves); all are useful as ornamentals in mixed plantings as well as for cooking.

OCONEE BELLS. See SHORTIA galacifolia

OCTOPUS TREE. See SCHEFFLERA actinophylla

ODONTONEMA strictum

FIRESPIKE

Acanthaceae

EVERGREEN SHRUB

✿ CS, TS ⊩ 12–8; OR GROW IN POT

☼ FULL SUN

💧 REGULAR WATER

Odontonema strictum

This Central American native is one of autumn's showiest plants. It forms a multistemmed mound to 6 ft. tall and about half as wide, with shiny deep green leaves that are oval, pointed, and up to 6 in. long. Stunning, foot-long spikes of small, tubular, fiery red flowers crown the foliage for weeks, beginning in late summer and continuing through the fall. Hummingbirds and butterflies frequent the blossoms. If given moderately fertile, well-drained soil, the plant needs little care. It is very tender to cold—stems and leaves blacken with the first touch of frost. Often comes back from the roots in the Coastal and Tropical South; elsewhere, treat it as an annual or overwinter indoors. Easily propagated by cuttings.

OENOTHERA

EVENING PRIMROSE, SUNDROPS

Onagraceae

PERENNIALS, ANNUALS, OR BIENNIALS

✿ ZONES VARY BY SPECIES

☼ ◑ FULL SUN OR PARTIAL SHADE, EXCEPT AS NOTED

💧 LITTLE TO MODERATE WATER, EXCEPT AS NOTED

Oenothera speciosa 'Rosea'

Valued for showy, four-petaled, silky flowers in bright yellow, pink, or white. Some types display their blossoms during the day, but others open in late afternoon and close the following morning. Flowers of some are fragrant. Plants succeed in tough, rough places.

O. berlandieri. See O. speciosa 'Rosea'

O. biennis. EVENING PRIMROSE. Annual or biennial. Zones US, MS, LS, CS; 10–1. Variable in size, ranging from 1 ft. to 4 ft. or even as much as 6 ft. tall. Best grown in meadows, as it is usually weedy, reseeds, and can be invasive. Fragrant yellow blossoms open in the evening; they are yellow at first, then fade to gold. Japanese beetles are particularly fond of this species.

O. elata hookeri (O. hookeri). Perennial or biennial. Zones MS, LS; 9–7. Native to moist places in many parts of western U.S. To 3 ft. high and wide. Basal rosette of medium green, lance-shaped, 2- to 5-in.-long leaves; branching flower stems are hairy and are set with smaller leaves. Blooms all summer, bearing upright spikes of 2- to 3-in. flowers that open in the evening; they unfurl pale yellow, later turn orange red. Reseeds heavily. Grow in moist areas. Tolerates both drought and flooding.

O. fremontii 'Lemon Silver'. Perennial. Zones US, MS, LS; 8–1. Selection of a species native to Kansas and Nebraska. Forms a loose,

spreading clump to 6 in. high, 1 ft. wide; not invasive. Narrow, silvery leaves to 2 in. long; lemon yellow, 2-in. flowers all summer long. Good rock garden or edging plant.

O. fruticosa. SUNDROPS. Perennial or biennial. Zones US, MS, LS, CS; 9–1. Native to eastern U.S. Erect growth to 2 ft. high and wide. Branching reddish stems are set with medium green, lance-shaped leaves to 4½ in. long; leaves turn dull red with frost. From late spring through summer, bears clusters of 1- to 2-in.-wide, deep yellow flowers that open in daytime. 'Fireworks' ('Fyrverkeri') has red flower buds and leaves tinted purplish brown. Foliage of 'Summer Solstice' ('Sonnenwende') turns bright red in summer, darkens to burgundy in fall. *O. f. glauca* (O. tetragona) has light yellow flowers and red stems; its leaves (red-tinted when young) are broader than those of the species.

O. macrocarpa (O. missouriensis). OZARK SUNDROPS. Perennial. Zones US, MS, LS; 8–3. Native to south-central U.S. To 6 in. tall and 2 ft. wide, with narrow, medium green, lance-shaped leaves to 3 in. long. Late spring to early fall, bears pure yellow, 4-in. flowers that remain open all day. Large winged seedpods follow the flowers. Good in rock gardens. Give partial shade in hottest climates. *O. m. incana* 'Silver Blade' has silvery blue leaves.

O. speciosa. SHOWY EVENING PRIMROSE. Perennial. Zones US, MS, LS, CS, TS; 11–1. Native to southwestern U.S. and Mexico. An old favorite in the South. To 1 ft. high and 3 ft. or more wide, spreading by rhizomes. Forms rosettes of medium green, narrow, 1- to 3-in.-long leaves. Fragrant, 2-in. flowers are white to pinkish, aging to pink; despite plant's common name, they open during the day. Blooms from spring or early summer into fall, then stems die back. Good ground cover for dry slopes or parking strips, but can be aggressive and is potentially invasive. Selections include pure white form 'Alba', light pink 'Rosea' (O. berlandieri, O. speciosa childsii), pink 'Siskiyou', and 'Woodside White' (white blossoms with a chartreuse eye).

O. stubbei. SALTILLO EVENING PRIMROSE. Perennial. Zones LS, CS; 10–5. Native to Mexico. Evening-blooming plant that forms a foliage mat 5 in. high and 4 ft. wide; prostrate stems root along the ground, forming offset plants. Narrow dark green leaves to 2½ in. long. Yellow, 2½-in. flowers rise on individual stems 6–8 in. above foliage. Blooms most heavily in spring, sporadically throughout the rest of the year. Endures heat and drought but does better with occasional water. Often sold as *O. drummondii*.

O. tetragona. See O. fruticosa glauca

OKRA

Malvaceae

ANNUAL

✿ US, MS, LS, CS, TS ⊩ 12–6

☼ FULL SUN

💧 REGULAR WATER

Okra

Vegetable gardeners can't claim to be truly Southern unless they've grown okra. Native to tropical Asia, this vegetable (known botanically as *Abelmoschus esculentus*) arrived aboard slave ships from Africa in the 1600s and quickly became a regional staple. It's a large, erect, bushy plant to 6 ft. or taller, with big, bold, deeply lobed leaves. The edible seedpods are produced in leaf joints and can be pickled, fried in batter, or used in stews, gumbos, and soups.

Okra loves hot weather, so don't plant it until the soil has warmed to at least 75°F. To speed germination, soak the hard seeds in water overnight before planting; use only those that are swollen. Work ½ cup of 10-10-10 fertilizer per 10 ft. of row into the soil. Sow seeds ½–1 in. deep and about 2 in. apart in rows 3–4 ft. apart. When seedlings reach 2 in. tall, thin them to 6–12 in. apart. After the first pods set, apply ¼ cup of 10-10-10 fertilizer per 10 ft. of row; repeat 3 to 4 weeks later.

Allow 48 to 60 days from planting to harvest. Developing pods grow quickly, as much as an inch per day in hot weather; begin harvesting them when they are 2–4 in. long, and be sure to pick every couple of days (plants

O

stop producing if pods are left to mature fully). Pods longer than 4 in. are typically too tough to eat. Use a sharp knife or pruners to remove the pods from the stems—and wear gloves, since okra pods are usually prickly.

For small gardens, try a dwarf form that reaches only 3–4 ft. tall, such as 'Annie Oakley II' (48 days), 'Cajun Delight' (50 days), or 'Lee' (50 days). Despite their smaller size, these are heavy producers. 'Clemson Spineless' (56 days), the old standby, grows 5–6 ft. tall; its pods lack prickles.

Some selections have pods that remain tender even when they reach large size. 'Burgundy' (49 days) features maroon red pods (green when cooked) that stay tender to 8 in. long. 'Cow Horn' (55 days), a Southern heirloom, grows 7–8 ft. tall and produces tender pods 10 in. long. 'Jade' (55 days) grows to 4½ ft. tall, bears tender pods to 6 in. long.

Oleaceae. The olive family encompasses about 900 species of trees and shrubs with opposite leaves and flower parts that are usually in fours. Members include privet (*Ligustrum*) and lilac (*Syringa*).

OLEANDER. See NERIUM oleander

OMPHALODES verna

BLUE-EYED MARY

Boraginaceae

PERENNIAL

🌿 US, MS, LS H 9–6

◐ PARTIAL SHADE

💧 REGULAR WATER

Omphalodes verna

Native to the mountains of Europe. Attractive creeping perennial, nice for ground cover in shaded rock garden or woodland planting; evergreen in mild-winter areas. Medium green leaves are oval, pointed, 2–4 in. long; form a mat about 3 in. high, spreading to 3 ft. or more. Half-inch-wide spring flowers are an intense pure blue with a tiny white eye. Tolerates drought but looks better with regular water.

Onagraceae. Most members of the evening primrose family have flower parts in fours, but otherwise they are diverse in appearance and structure. They include *Fuchsia*, *Gaura*, and *Oenothera*.

ONCIDIUM

Orchidaceae

EPIPHYTIC ORCHIDS

🌿 TS H 12–10; OR GROW IN POTS

◐ PARTIAL SHADE; BRIGHT INDIRECT LIGHT

💧 REGULAR WATER

Oncidium crispum

Orchids native from Florida and Mexico through South America. The several hundred species and countless hybrids range from tiny plants just 1 in. tall to giants with branching flower spikes to 6 ft. or more, bearing dozens of blooms. Most produce long spikes of yellow or brown-and-yellow flowers; a few come in white or rose. Some (including the plants described here) have compressed pseudobulbs, while others are almost without pseudobulbs; some have just one or two large leaves, others cylindrical, pencil-like leaves. Plants typically produce a few large blossoms or many small ones, but some have numerous large flowers and a few bear their blooms singly. In many, flowers have a large, flaring lip reminiscent of a flamenco dancer's skirt; these are sometimes called dancing ladies. Blossoms of some are scented.

As outdoor plants, oncidiums are usually grown on tree trunks or in pots on the patio; indoor plants can be brought outdoors during warm weather. Take same houseplant culture as cattleya. Also see Orchidaceae.

O. crispum. Pseudobulbs 4 in. high are topped by 8-in. leaves. In fall, produces a branching, 3-ft.-tall spike carrying many 4-in. flowers in chestnut brown spotted with yellow. Each bloom has a brown lip with a large bright yellow spot.

O. ornithorhynchum. Pseudobulbs 2½ in. tall are topped by leaves to 1 ft. long. In summer, many branching, 8- to 12-in.-tall spikes carry a cloud of inch-wide pink or purplish pink flowers with yellow markings.

O. Sharry Baby. A series of powerfully fragrant hybrids with 4-in.-high pseudobulbs topped by 8-in.-long leaves. Spikes to 2–3 ft. long bear many inch-wide blossoms in summer and fall; some liken the flowers' perfume to chocolate, others to vanilla. 'Oshima' has ivory flowers with maroon markings and a white lip; 'Red Fantasy' bears deep red blooms with a fuchsia pink lip; 'Sweet Fragrance' has reddish purple blossoms with a white lip.

ONION

Amaryllidaceae

BIENNIAL GROWN AS ANNUAL

🌿 US, MS, LS, CS, TS H 12–1

☀ FULL SUN

💧 REGULAR WATER

Onion

People who love onions (*Allium cepa*) may be used to weeping for joy—but tears don't have to be part of the affair. "Sweet" onions contain little pyruvate, the chemical that causes tears and hot flavor. Unfortunately, these types don't keep as well as their stronger-tasting brethren, so choosing the right onion depends on your needs.

In addition to flavor and shelf life, onions vary in size, shape, and color. More important, different types form bulbs in response to varying day lengths. If you choose a type inappropriate for your area, it may go to seed before bulbing up, form small bulbs, or not form bulbs at all.

Short-day selections need 10 to 12 hours of daylight and are well adapted to most areas of the South. These tend to be sweet, but they are poor keepers. They typically begin to form bulbs in spring. Examples are 'Burgundy', 'Crystal White Wax', 'Granex 33' ('Vidalia'), 'Southern Belle', 'Sweet Georgia Brown', 'Texas Grano 502', 'Texas Grano 1015' ('1015 Supersweet'), and 'Yellow Bermuda'.

Intermediate-day onions, requiring 12 to 14 hours of daylight, also grow well in the South. They have a stronger flavor than short-day types and keep longer. Examples include 'Candy Hybrid', 'Stockton Sweet Red', and 'Super Star Hybrid'. They usually form bulbs in summer.

Long-day onions, which need 14 to 16 hours of sunlight, are the most pungent and keep the best. They form bulbs in summer. They're suited only to the Upper South and parts north. Examples include 'Ebenezer', 'Sweet Spanish', 'Walla Walla', and 'Yellow Globe'.

So-called bunching onions do not form large bulbs but have slightly swollen white stalks. Depending on where you're from, you may know them as green onions, scallions, or spring onions. They can be planted in fall or spring. 'Evergreen White Bunching' is a favorite selection. Egyptian walking onion (*A. cepa proliferum*) gets its name from the bulbils that cluster near the tops of the leaves; the foliage bends to the ground, and the bulbils take root. Shallots and potato onions (*A. cepa aggregatum*) are smaller, milder-flavored regular onions; see Shallots.

You can grow onions from seeds, sets (small bulbs), or transplants. Sets and transplants are quicker and easier for beginners; starting from seed gives a larger crop for a smaller investment and offers a wider choice of selections.

In the Lower, Coastal, and Tropical South, onions grow well from seeds sown in fall. Sets and transplants can be planted from late fall throughout the winter. In the Upper and Middle South, sow seeds outdoors 6 to 8 weeks before the last frost in spring; plant sets and transplants 4 weeks before the last frost.

Soil should be loose, fertile, and well drained. Space sets and transplants 4–5 in. apart (closer if you want to harvest some early as green onions). When planting sets, push them just under the soil surface, so the

O

point of the bulb remains visible; when planting transplants, trim foliage back by about half after planting. Sow seeds ¼ in. deep in rows spaced 15–18 in. apart. Thin seedlings to 4–5 in. apart; thinnings can be eaten as green onions or transplanted.

To produce large bulbs, onions need moist soil and repeated applications of fertilizer. Scratch in ¼ cup of 10-10-10 fertilizer per 10 ft. of row before planting. Sprinkle this same amount around plants 4 to 6 weeks later and again when bulbs begin to form; water it in. Carefully eliminate weeds, being sure you don't damage the onion bulbs or their shallow roots. When most of the tops have begun to yellow and fall over, dig the bulbs, leaving the tops on; spread them out (tops and all) in a dry, dark place for 10 to 14 days to cure. When tops and necks are completely dry, pull off the tops and brush dirt from the bulbs. Store in a dark, cool, airy place; use mesh or cloth bags, not plastic ones.

ALL HAIL THE VIDALIA! *The Vidalia onion, often touted as "the world's sweetest onion," got its start as a Bermuda onion imported into South Texas in 1898. Breeders worked to produce a sweet onion that matured early and enjoyed the Southern heat. In 1952, their hard work paid off with the introduction of 'Granex 33', a somewhat flattened-looking yellow onion with a sweet, mild flavor. Before long, the new onion made its way to Toombs County in Georgia, where the favorable climate and low-sulfur soil produced an especially sweet flavor. The state of Georgia built a farmer's market in the town of Vidalia and began promoting "Vidalia onions." Today, this crop enjoys legal protection—no onion grown outside the official 20-county production area in Georgia can be called a "Vidalia." But Texans don't mind—they'll tell you their 'Texas Grano 1015' ('1015 Supersweet') is even sweeter.*

ONOCLEA sensibilis

SENSITIVE FERN

Polypodiaceae

FERN

✿ US, MS, LS, CS ◫ 9–1

☼ ◐ ● SUN OR SHADE

◖◗ REGULAR TO AMPLE WATER

Onoclea sensibilis

Native to the eastern U.S. This bold-textured, easy-to-grow fern gets its name because it turns brown with the very first kiss of frost in fall. It produces two types of fronds. The sterile ones are large (2–4 ft. long) and lance-shaped to triangular; the fertile ones are smaller, holding erect clusters of beadlike leaflets that turn brown at maturity. Fronds grow from creeping rhizomes that spread quickly in moist, fertile soil. Plant is a good choice for pond and streamside plantings and naturalized areas. Be sure plants grown in sun are kept well watered. Dies to the ground in winter.

OPHIOPOGON

Liliaceae

PERENNIALS

✿ MS, LS, CS, TS

◐ ● PARTIAL TO FULL SHADE

◖◗ MODERATE TO REGULAR WATER

Ophiopogon japonicus 'Nana'

It's hard to imagine more serviceable ground covers for shade than these Asian natives. Though slightly less cold hardy than their *Liriope* cousins (see page 395), they're just as care-free, needing little more than well-drained soil and shelter from hot sun. Deer don't generally bother them. Plant them in large sweeps in areas where you don't want to mow or under large trees where grass won't grow. They also do well in containers. Use them for their lush evergreen foliage; the summer flowers, borne on short spikes, are largely hidden by the leaves.

It's easy to obtain more plants by division. Use a sharp spade to divide clumps in early spring; or use a knife to divide clumps sold in flats or cell-packs at garden centers. To get divisions of mondo grass (*O. japonicus, O. planiscapus* 'Nigrescens') off to a fast start, trim the roots back by half before replanting. This encourages rapid root growth.

O. intermedius 'Argenteomarginatus'. AZTEC GRASS. Forms foot-tall clumps with a cascading look and spreads widely and aggressively. Thin dark green leaves with yellowish white margins grow 1½ ft. long, ½ in. wide; white flowers are followed by bright blue fruits. Sometimes sold as *Liriope muscari* 'Variegata'.

O. jaburan. GIANT LILY TURF. Heat zones 10–7. Sometimes sold as *Liriope gigantea*. Grows 2–3 ft. tall, 1½ ft. wide, with dark green leaves to 1½–3 ft. long, ½ in. wide. Clump forming; does not spread. Nodding clusters of small white flowers are followed by showy fruits in metallic violet blue (attractive in arrangements). 'Vittatus' (sometimes sold as *Liriope muscari* 'Variegata') has leaves edged in creamy white.

O. japonicus. MONDO GRASS, MONKEY GRASS. Heat zones 12–1. Dark green, grasslike leaves grow 8–12 in. long, ⅛ in. wide. Forms dense, 6- to 8-in.-tall clumps that steadily spread by underground stems to form an evergreen mat at least 1 ft. across. Short spikes of lilac flowers are followed by metallic blue fruits. Makes an excellent, shade-tolerant lawn that never needs mowing, though it takes several years to fill in. Great for filling cracks between pavers and stepping-stones. A number of dwarf selections spread much more slowly than the species; these include 'Gyoku Ryu' (1–2 in. tall), 'Kyoto Dwarf' (2–4 in.), and 'Nana' (3 in.). 'Little Tabby' (also sold as *O. planiscapus* 'Little Tabby') and 'Shiroshima Ryu' (also sold as *O. japonicus* 'Variegatus') have green-and-white striped leaves and grow 4–6 in. tall.

O. planiscapus 'Nigrescens' ('Arabicus'). BLACK MONDO GRASS. Nearly black, grasslike leaves grow to 14 in. long, ⅛–¼ in. wide. New leaves are green, but they soon darken. Spreads slowly, forming tufts to 8 in. high; clumps can reach 1 ft. across, but they don't form a thick carpet. Flowers are white or (sometimes) light pink. Looks great in mixed containers; striking when combined with yellow or chartreuse foliage, such as yellow creeping Jenny (*Lysimachia nummularia* 'Aurea').

OPUNTIA

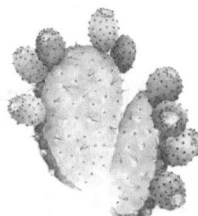

Cactaceae

CACTI

✿ ZONES VARY BY SPECIES

☼ FULL SUN

◊ LITTLE OR NO WATER, EXCEPT AS NOTED

Opuntia ficus-indica

Some of the species described here originate in the desert Southwest and Mexico; others are native to those areas and/or to other parts of the western U.S., the Great Plains, Canada, and Florida. Many kinds, with varied appearance. Most species fall into one of two sorts: those having flat, broad joints (pads) or those having cylindrical joints. Members of the first group are often called prickly pear; those in the second group are frequently known as cholla. Hardiness is variable, but all require excellent drainage. Flowers are generally large and showy. The fruit is a berry, often edible.

O. compressa (O. humifusa). PRICKLY PEAR. Zones US, MS, LS, CS, TS; 12–1. An old Southern favorite, native from Canada south to Florida and eastern Texas. Spreading clump grows to 2–3 ft. tall, with few-spined, 3- to 6-in.-long pads. Bears yellow, 3- to 4-in.-wide flowers in early summer; 2-in.-long fruits, purple when ripe. Takes moister soil than most cacti. Very cold hardy; good choice for the beach.

O. ficus-indica. PRICKLY PEAR. Zones CS, TS; 12–1. From Mexico. Big, shrubby or treelike cactus to 15 ft. tall, 10 ft. wide, with woody trunks and smooth, flat green joints with clusters of bristles; few or no spines. Bears yellow to orange, 3- to 5-in.-wide flowers in late spring, early summer. Blossoms are followed by roundish, 2- to 3½-in.-long fruits that ripen from yellow to red; these are the prickly pears you may see sold in grocery stores. Handle them carefully; the bristles break off easily and irritate the skin. Wear rubber gloves when peeling the fruit, or impale it on a fork and carefully strip off skin, avoiding bristly areas. This species is very drought tolerant, but in the hottest regions it will need regular moisture for best fruit.

O. imbricata. CHAIN-LINK CACTUS, WALKING-STICK CHOLLA. Zones US, MS, LS, CS, TS; 12–1. Native from Colorado to Mexico. Treelike cactus with short trunk and branching, cylindrical stems; very slow growing, eventually reaching 3–6 ft. (sometimes as much as 10 ft.) tall. Never plant it near walkways or in gardens where children play; it has many sharp, inch-long spines as well as small, hairlike prickles that are more painful when they stick you (and harder to remove). Magenta, 2- to 3-in. blossoms in early summer; yellow, 1½-in.-long fruits. Very cold hardy.

O. lindheimeri. TEXAS PRICKLY PEAR. Zones LS, CS, TS; 12–1. Native to southern Texas. Large, clumping cactus with pads that grow to 1 ft. long and carry 1- to 2-in. spines. Typically 2–5 ft. tall, but it can reach 12 ft. high and spread even wider. Yellow, 3- to 4-in.-wide summer flowers; red-purple, 2- to 3-in. fruits.

O. microdasys. BUNNY EARS. Zones TS; 12–1; or houseplant. Native to northern and central Mexico. Grows fast to 2 ft. high, 4–5 ft. wide (much smaller in pots). Flat, thin, nearly round, velvety green pads reach 6 in. wide; they are set with neatly spaced tufts of short golden bristles, giving a polka-dot effect. 'Albispina' has white bristles. Small, round new pads grow atop larger old ones, giving the plant a silhouette reminiscent of an animal's head. A great favorite with children.

Opuntia microdasys

Indoors, site in bright light. In spring through fall, let soil become dry between soakings; every 2 to 3 months, apply a general-purpose liquid houseplant fertilizer diluted to half-strength. In winter, water sparingly and stop fertilizing.

O. phaeacantha. Zones MS, LS, CS, TS; 12–7. Native from northern Texas to California. Low, spreading clump, with 4- to 6-in. pads and thick, 2-in. spines. Yellow flowers, 2–3 in. across, in spring; inch-long red fruit.

ORANGE. See CITRUS

ORANGE CLOCK VINE. See THUNBERGIA gregorii

ORANGE JESSAMINE. See MURRAYA paniculata

ORANGEQUAT. See CITRUS, Kumquat Hybrids

Orchidaceae. The orchid family is probably the largest in the plant kingdom, with nearly 800 genera and over 17,000 species. Among the best known are *Bletilla, Cattleya, Cymbidium, Dendrobium, Oncidium,* and *Phalaenopsis.*

Orchid growers' terms. Here are definitions of the orchid growers' terms you will encounter in this book.

Epiphytic. In nature, epiphytic orchids cling to high branches of trees in tropical or subtropical jungles, deriving their nourishment from air, rain, and whatever decaying vegetable matter they can trap in their root systems.

Pseudobulb. Epiphytic orchids have thickened stems called pseudobulbs that store food and water and allow the plants to survive drought. These may be short and fat (like typical true bulbs) or erect and slender. They vary from green to brown in color. The leaves may grow along the pseudobulbs or from their tips.

Terrestrial. Some orchids (including most native North American orchids) are terrestrial and must grow in loose, moist soil rich in humus. They are found in wooded areas but sometimes grow in open meadows as well. These orchids require constant moisture and food.

Sepals, petals, and other flower parts. Segments of an orchid flower include three sepals and three petals; stamens, style, and stigma are united into a single organ, the column. One of the petals, usually the lowest one, is called the lip. The lip is usually larger and more brightly colored than the other segments and may be marked with stripes, spots, or streaks. In some orchids, it is unusually shaped (having various appendages) or folded into a slipperlike "pouch."

Rafts, bark. Nearly all orchids, terrestrial or epiphytic, are grown in pots. A few are grown on "rafts" (slabs of bark or wood) or in baskets of wood slats; a few natives are grown in open ground.

Potting and growing. Osmunda fiber or ground bark, the potting materials used for cattleyas (the most commonly grown orchids), will work for most epiphytic orchids. Most popular is bark; it's readily available, easy to handle, and fairly inexpensive. Use fine grade for pots 3 in. or smaller, medium grade for pots 4 in. or larger. You can use ready-made mixes, blended for proper texture and acidity and sold by orchid growers.

Water plants once a week, or when mix dries out and becomes lightweight. Feed with a commercial water-soluble houseplant fertilizer once every 2 weeks during the growing season (you can find products formulated especially for orchids). To provide humidity for houseplants, fill a metal or plastic tray with gravel to within an inch of the top (the space is necessary for air circulation), then add just enough water to reach almost to top of gravel. Stretch hardware cloth over the tray. Set pots on top of hardware cloth; check water level periodically, and add more water to tray as needed.

Temperature requirements. This list classifies orchids according to temperature requirements. Some cool-growing orchids are hardy enough to grow outdoors in most places.

Temperate-climate orchids can be grown in pots on a windowsill with other houseplants, but they will perform best if given additional humidity. (An excellent method of supplying humidity is described in "Potting and growing," above.) Most temperate-climate orchids can be moved outdoors in summer; locate them in the shade of high-branching trees, on a patio, or in a lathhouse. Examples are *Cattleya, Dendrobium* (some), *Oncidium,* and *Paphiopedilum* (mottled-leaf forms).

Warm-climate orchids need greenhouse conditions to provide the uniform warm temperatures and high humidity they require. An example is *Phalaenopsis.*

Cool-climate orchids take colder temperatures than other types. The group includes *Bletilla* (*Bletilla striata,* Chinese ground orchid, is hardy as far north as the Upper South), *Cymbidium, Dendrobium* (some), *Paphiopedilum* (green-leafed forms), and *Spiranthes* (hardy in the Upper South too).

ORCHID CACTUS. See EPIPHYLLUM

ORCHID TREE. See BAUHINIA

ORCHID VINE. See MASCAGNIA, STIGMAPHYLLON

OREGANO. See ORIGANUM

OREGON GRAPE HOLLY. See MAHONIA aquifolium

ORIENTAL ARBORVITAE. See THUJA orientalis

ORIENTAL POPPY. See PAPAVER orientale

ORIGANUM

OREGANO, MARJORAM

Lamiaceae (Labiatae)

PERENNIALS SOMETIMES GROWN AS ANNUALS

☀ ZONES VARY BY SPECIES

☼ FULL SUN

◌ ◑ LITTLE TO MODERATE WATER

Origanum majorana

What would spaghetti sauce be without oregano? As all fans of "The Andy Griffith Show" know, it's the secret ingredient. But the dried leaves of this pungent herb are also used in Mexican, French, Greek, and Mideastern cooking— cuisines sorely lacking in Mayberry.

▶

These mint relatives have tight clusters of small flowers. Each blossom has a collar of bracts—large, colorful, and quite decorative in some species—that can overlap to give the look of a small pinecone. Flowers are especially attractive to bees and butterflies. Most oreganos have pleasantly aromatic foliage. Though several kinds are valued for cooking, others are chiefly ornamentals, used as ground covers or to cascade over rocks and retaining walls. Some are hardy and evergreen; others are tender and killed by frost. None is seriously damaged by browsing deer.

Oreganos aren't fussy about soil as long as it is well drained. They'll tolerate light shade, but most do better in full sun (culinary types need full sun to develop best flavor). In milder areas, many species become woody and less productive with age; to restore vigor, cut the previous year's stems to the ground in winter or early spring. You can start plants from seed, but because oreganos cross-pollinate freely, you may not get the plant you want. It's a better bet to purchase potted plants whose identities are certain.

To keep plants producing, cut sprigs often. For a large harvest for drying, wait until just before plants bloom and cut the stems above the lowest set of leaves; new foliage will sprout, and you can cut again in late summer. Don't harvest within a month before the first expected frost, however, as the plants need time to reestablish themselves before cold weather. Strip leaves from stems after they dry.

WITH THIS WREATH, I THEE WED. *You've probably heard of people using wreaths of garlic to ward off vampires. But did you know that in ancient Greece, newlywed couples wore wreaths of oregano to symbolize their happiness? Sadly, history fails to record whether they also stood in vats filled with pasta and marinara sauce.*

O. dictamnus (Amaracus dictamnus). DITTANY OF CRETE, HOP MARJORAM. Zones LS, CS; 12–8. Native to Crete. Aromatic herb to 8 in. high, 1½–2 ft. wide, with slender, arching stems to 1 ft. long. Thick, roundish, woolly white leaves to ¾ in. long. Pink to purplish flowers emerge from rose-tinted light green bracts; blooms summer to fall. Shows up best when planted individually in rock garden or in hanging basket.

O. ×hybridum. Zones LS, CS. Resembles parent *O. dictamnus*, but its leaves are gray green and downy rather than woolly.

O. laevigatum. Zones US, MS, LS, CS; 12–1. Native to Turkey, Cyprus. Sprawling plant with grayish green leaves about 1¼ in. long; reaches 2 ft. tall in bloom. It spreads by rhizomes and arching stems that root at the joints to form a dense clump 2–3 ft. wide. Branching, airy clusters of ½-in., tubular pink or purple flowers and small purplish bracts appear from late spring to fall. Useful as bank or ground cover. 'Herrenhausen' has larger bracts and more compact heads of lilac-pink flowers. 'Hopleys', probably a hybrid with *O. vulgare*, blooms from mid- to late summer, bearing denser heads of purplish pink flowers and purplish bracts; it self-sows freely, producing seedlings with variable foliage and flower color. Both 'Herrenhausen' and 'Hopleys' have purple leaves in cool weather.

O. majorana (Majorana hortensis). SWEET MARJORAM. Zones CS, TS; 10–2. Native to the Mediterranean and Turkey. To 1–2 ft. tall and wide. Oval gray-green leaves to ¾ in. long. In summer, inconspicuous white flowers emerge from clusters of knotlike heads at top of plant. Keep blossoms cut off and plant trimmed to encourage fresh growth. Fresh or dried leaves are used for seasoning meats, scrambled eggs, salads, vinegars, casseroles, and tomato dishes. Often grown in pots indoors on sunny windowsill in cold-winter areas. Leaves of 'White Anniversary' have a distinct cream margin.

O. ×majoricum. ITALIAN MARJORAM, SICILIAN MARJORAM. Zones US, MS, LS, CS; 9–4. Similar to *O. majorana* but with wider, greener leaves. Some gourmet cooks consider this the best marjoram for seasoning.

O. microphyllum. Zones MS, LS, CS; 9–8. Native to Crete. Grows to 10 in. high and 1 ft. wide, with domelike form. Reddish branches bear tiny gray-green leaves to ¼ in. long. Clusters of small pale pink to purple flowers bloom in summer. Thrives in dry rock crevices.

O. onites. POT MARJORAM, RHIGANI. Zones US, MS, LS, CS; 12–6. Eastern Mediterranean native. To 2 ft. tall and wide, with bright green, inch-long leaves and 2-in.-wide, flattish heads of white or purplish flowers

in late summer. Sometimes called Cretan oregano. Has a strong, musky fragrance.

O. syriacum. BIBLICAL HYSSOP, SYRIAN MARJORAM. Zones CS, TS. From Syria, Turkey, Cyprus. With its strong, sweet, pungent flavor, this plant is a favorite herb for flavoring Mideastern dishes. To 1½ ft. tall and wide. Soft gray-green leaves to 1½ in. long. Blooms in late spring and early summer, with pale pink, ¼-in. flowers in branching, 2- to 3-in. clusters.

O. vulgare. OREGANO, WILD MARJORAM. Zones US, MS, LS, CS; 10–2. Native to most of Europe and temperate Asia. Upright growth to 2½ ft. tall, 2–3 ft. wide. Oval dark green leaves to 1½ in. long and ¾ in. wide; white or purplish pink blossoms from midsummer to early fall. Fresh or dried leaves are used in many dishes, especially Spanish and Italian ones.

Most wild forms have scentless leaves and are useless for cooking; be sure to choose a selected form with a good aroma and a flavor that you like. For best flavor, keep this plant trimmed to prevent flowering—but let some clumps bloom for bees and butterflies to enjoy.

'Aureum' has pinkish flowers and foliage that is bright golden in spring (if the plant gets morning sun), green by late summer and fall; 'Thumble's Variety' is similar but has white blossoms. 'Aureum Crispum' has curly golden leaves. 'Compactum' ('Humile') is a wide-spreading plant just a few inches tall, suitable for a ground cover or a filler between paving stones; it seldom flowers, but leaves turn purple in winter. 'Country Cream' (with white flowers) and 'Polyphant' (lilac-pink blooms) are compact growers to 4–6 in. and have leaves with a distinct creamy white edge; they are often confused in commerce (and both are sometimes sold as 'Variegatum'). 'Roseum' has bright rose pink flowers, green leaves.

O. v. hirtum (O. heracleoticum). GREEK OREGANO. Native to Greece, Turkey, the Aegean islands. Like the species, but with broader, slightly fuzzy gray-green leaves. Spicy and pungent; considered by many to have the best true oregano flavor.

ORNITHOGALUM

Liliaceae

PERENNIALS FROM BULBS

⚹ ZONES VARY BY SPECIES; OR HOUSEPLANTS

☼ ◑ FULL SUN OR PARTIAL SHADE; BRIGHT LIGHT

◐ REGULAR WATER, EXCEPT AS NOTED

☣ ALL PARTS, ESPECIALLY BULBS, ARE POISONOUS IF INGESTED

Ornithogalum dubium

Clusters of typically star-shaped flowers appear in spring; *O. dubium* may start blooming in late winter. Leaves vary from narrow to broad and tend to droop. In areas where they are hardy, ornithogalums can fill many different roles. Set them in open woodlands, wild gardens, or rock gardens, where many kinds will naturalize; plant them in containers or mass them in borders. Where winters are too cold for in-ground growing, plant the bulbs in pots and force them into early bloom indoors or in a greenhouse.

Plant bulbs in early fall in well-drained soil amended with plenty of organic matter, setting them 3 in. deep and 3–4 in. apart. Provide regular moisture during growth and bloom. Dig and divide plantings of all species only when plant vigor and bloom quality decline. Indoors, grow in bright light but protect from hottest summer sun. Let soil dry slightly between thorough soakings, and feed every 2 weeks with a general-purpose liquid houseplant fertilizer. After flowering has ended and leaves begin to yellow, withhold water and fertilizer; don't resume watering and feeding until new growth appears in fall.

O. arabicum. STAR OF BETHLEHEM. Zones LS, CS, TS; 12–8. From the eastern Mediterranean. Stems to 2 ft. tall carry clusters of 2-in., waxy-looking white flowers, each centered with a shiny, beadlike black eye. Bluish green, strap-shaped, inch-wide leaves may reach same length as stems, but they're usually floppy. Requires a dry dormant period from midsummer through winter, so best grown in pots. Water from spring through early summer, then let foliage dry out. Store indoors over winter.

O

O. balansae. Zones US, MS, LS; 10 – 4. From the eastern Mediterranean. Stems grow 3–5 in. high, bearing thick clusters of white, green-centered, 1¼-in. blossoms with bright yellow stamens and a faint green stripe on the outside of each petal. Medium green leaves to 6 in. long. This species naturalizes but is not an aggressive spreader.

O. dubium. Zones CS, TS; 10 – 7. From South Africa. Stems 8–12 in. high bear blooms resembling those of *O. arabicum*, but petals surrounding the beady black eye come in shades of yellow orange. Dark green to yellowish green, lance-shaped leaves are about 4 in. long, nearly prostrate. Same cultural requirements as *O. arabicum*.

O. longibracteatum (O. caudatum). PREGNANT ONION, FALSE SEA ONION. Zones TS; 12 – 8. From South Africa. Grown for bulb and foliage rather than its tall wands of small green-and-white flowers. To 3 ft. tall in leaf; flowers increase height to 5 ft. Long, drooping, strap-shaped light green leaves. Gray-green, smooth-skinned bulb is 3 – 4 in. wide and grows on top of, not in, the soil. Bulblets form under skin and grow quite large before they drop out and root. Hardy to 25°F. Moderate water.

Ornithogalum longibracteatum

O. nutans. NODDING STAR OF BETHLEHEM. Zones US, MS, LS, CS; 9 – 5. From the eastern Mediterranean. To 1½ – 2 ft. tall. Starlike to nearly bell-shaped, 1¼-in. flowers are white striped with green on the outside; they have pronounced central clusters of stamens. Up to 15 blooms are spaced along upper part of each stalk. Narrow, floppy bright green leaves. Spreads rapidly and may become weedy. Sometimes called silver bells.

O. thyrsoides. CHINCHERINCHEE. Zone TS. Flower stems to 2 ft. high carry tapering, compact clusters of 2-in. white blossoms with a brownish green center; they are excellent for cutting. Bright green, upright leaves grow 1 ft. long, 2 in. wide. May survive cooler winters along the Gulf Coast if given a sheltered southern or southwestern location and protected with mulch. Moderate water.

O. umbellatum. STAR OF BETHLEHEM. Zones US, MS, LS, CS; 12 – 2. Native to the eastern Mediterranean. Erect stems to 1 ft. tall produce clusters of inch-wide white flowers striped green on the outside. Semierect, grassy-looking leaves are about as long as the flower stems. Cut flowers last well but close at night. Once this species is established, it may naturalize and become weedy.

ORTHOSIPHON aristatus (O. stamineus)

CAT'S WHISKERS
Lamiaceae (Labiatae)
PERENNIAL OFTEN GROWN AS ANNUAL
☀ TS
☀ FULL SUN
◖ ◖◖ REGULAR TO AMPLE WATER

Orthosiphon aristatus

Native to tropical and subtropical regions from India to Australia, this tender perennial gets its common name from the long white stamens that protrude from its white or pale blue flowers. In frost-free areas, the plant can grow to 5 ft. tall and 3 ft. wide; in cold-winter areas, where it's treated as an annual and must be replanted each spring, it reaches only half that size. Purple stems hold deep green, shiny, toothed leaves that are 1–3 in. long. Upright clusters of many flowers appear continuously in warm weather and attract bees, butterflies, and hummingbirds. Requires fertile, well-drained soil that is not allowed to dry out; it will not tolerate frost. Makes an excellent addition to the mixed border, never failing to elicit comment, questions, and admiration. Also good grown in containers.

OSAGE ORANGE. See MACLURA pomifera

OSMANTHUS

Oleaceae
EVERGREEN SHRUBS
☀ ZONES VARY BY SPECIES
☀ ◖ FULL SUN OR PARTIAL SHADE, EXCEPT AS NOTED
◖ ◖◖ LITTLE TO REGULAR WATER

Osmanthus fragrans

This versatile group of easy-to-grow broad-leafed evergreens combines handsome foliage with fragrant—though inconspicuous—flowers (white, in most cases). Most are large shrubs that can eventually reach the size of a small tree. Use them as tall screens, hedges, or foundation plantings. They tolerate many soils (including heavy clay), accept heavy pruning, and do well with little moisture or regular garden watering. Somewhat resistant to damage by browsing deer.

O. americanus. DEVILWOOD. Zones US, MS, LS, CS; 10 – 6. Native to Mexico, and from North Carolina to Florida and Mississippi. Grows rather slowly to 15 – 25 ft. tall and 15 – 20 ft. wide, though it may eventually become much larger. Neat, upright, oval form. Handsome leathery, shiny olive-green foliage: smooth-margined leaves to 7 in. long, 2½ in. wide. Creamy flowers in spring; dark blue, ½-in. fruit in early fall. Very cold hardy. Tolerates wet soil.

O. ×burkwoodii (×Osmarea burkwoodii). Zones US, MS, LS; 9 – 7. Slow growing to 6 – 10 ft. tall, 8 – 12 ft. wide. Densely clothed in 1- to 2-in., glossy bright green, tooth-edged leaves. Spring bloom. Useful as hedge.

O. delavayi (Siphonosmanthus delavayi). DELAVAY OSMANTHUS. Zones LS, CS, TS; 9 – 7. From China. Slow-growing, graceful plant with arching branches; reaches 4 – 6 ft. tall, 6 – 8 ft. wide. Dark green, oval, tooth-edged leaves to 1 in. long. Blooms profusely in spring, bearing clusters of four to eight blossoms (blooms are ½ in. wide—the largest of any osmanthus). Attractive all year. Good choice for foundation plantings, massing. Handsome on retaining walls where branches can hang down. Does best in partial shade.

O. ×fortunei. FORTUNE'S OSMANTHUS. Zones MS, LS, CS; 9 – 7. Hybrid between *O. heterophyllus* and *O. fragrans*. Slow, dense growth to an eventual 15 – 20 ft. tall, 6 – 8 ft. wide; usually seen at about 6 ft. tall. Oval, 4-in.-long leaves resemble those of holly (*Ilex*). Extremely fragrant flowers in autumn. Selection 'San Jose' bears flowers ranging in color from cream to orange.

O. fragrans. SWEET OLIVE, TEA OLIVE. Zones LS, CS, TS; 12 – 8. Native to China, Japan, Himalayas. Long a favorite of Southern gardeners. Broad, dense, compact. Grows at a moderate rate to 15 ft. tall, 8 – 10 ft. wide (though older plants may reach 30 ft. tall, 12 – 15 ft. wide). Oval, glossy medium green leaves to 4 in. long, toothed or smooth edged. Flowers are powerfully fragrant, with a scent like that of ripe apricots. Bloom is heaviest in spring, but plants flower sporadically through-out year. Can be pruned to upright growth where space is limited; can be trained as a small tree, hedge, screen, background, espalier, or container plant. Pinch out growing tips of young plants to induce bushiness. Give afternoon shade. *O. f. aurantiacus* has narrower, less glossy leaves than the species; its crop of wonderfully fragrant orange flowers is concentrated in early fall. 'Butter Yellow' produces lots of butter yellow flowers. 'Orange Supreme' is a well-shaped plant with bright orange blossoms.

Osmanthus fragrans

O. heterophyllus (O. ilicifolius). HOLLY OSMANTHUS. Zones US, MS, LS, CS; 9 – 4. From Japan. Grows to 8 – 10 ft. (possibly 20 ft.) tall and slightly wider, with 2½-in., spiny-edged, glossy green leaves. Resembles English holly (*Ilex aquifolium*), but leaves are opposite one another on stems rather than alternate. Fragrant white flowers in late fall and winter are followed by berrylike blue-black fruit. Useful as hedge.

'Goshiki'. Erect growth to 3½ ft. tall, 5 ft. wide. New leaves have pinkish orange markings; in mature foliage, the variegations are creamy yellow (on a deep green background). Few flowers. ▶

'Gulftide'. Dense grower to 8–10 ft. tall and 10 ft. wide (may eventually reach 20 ft. high), with deep green, very glossy foliage. More cold hardy than the species. Probably the most popular selection.

'Purpureus'. Same growth habit as species. Leaves are dark purple when new, maturing to purple-toned deep green.

'Rotundifolius'. Slow growing to 5 ft. tall and wide. Small, roundish leaves are lightly spined.

'Variegatus'. Slow growing to an eventual 8–10 ft. tall and wide, with densely set leaves edged in creamy white. Useful for lighting up shady areas. A bit less cold tolerant than the species.

OSMUNDA

Osmundaceae

FERNS

⚘ US, MS, LS, CS, TS ◫ 12–1, EXCEPT AS NOTED

☼ ◐ ● EXPOSURE NEEDS VARY BY SPECIES

💧 AMPLE WATER

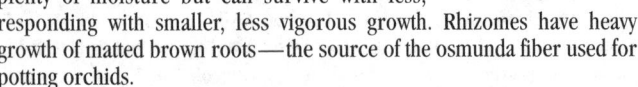

Osmunda regalis

Three species of graceful, imposing deciduous ferns useful in naturalistic plantings. All like plenty of moisture but can survive with less, responding with smaller, less vigorous growth. Rhizomes have heavy growth of matted brown roots—the source of the osmunda fiber used for potting orchids.

O. cinnamomea. CINNAMON FERN. To 5 ft. tall, 2 ft. wide. Plant has erect sterile fronds that arch out toward top. Fertile fronds are also erect but are narrower and much shorter, turning cinnamon brown as spores ripen. Unfolding young fronds (fiddleheads) are edible; they are usually served as a cooked vegetable, steamed and lightly buttered. Fronds turn showy yellow to orange in fall. Full or light shade.

O. claytoniana. INTERRUPTED FERN. Zones US, MS, LS, CS; 10–1. Grows as tall as 5 ft., more typically to 3 ft. tall, 2 ft. wide. Shorter in dryish soils. Each frond is "interrupted" in the middle by several short brown spore-bearing segments. Full or light shade.

O. regalis. ROYAL FERN. Heat zones 9–1. Large fern (to 6 ft. tall, 3 ft. wide) with twice-cut fronds, each leaflet quite large. Coarser in texture than most ferns. Tips of fronds have modified segments that somewhat resemble flower buds; these produce the spores. One of the better ferns for fall color; fronds may turn bright yellow. 'Cristata' has crested fronds; 'Purpurascens' has purplish red new growth and stems that remain purple throughout the season. Likes light shade, but will thrive in sun in wet soil, even in mud. Especially attractive beside streams or ponds.

OSTEOSPERMUM

AFRICAN DAISY

Asteraceae (Compositae)

PERENNIALS

⚘ CS, TS; ANYWHERE AS ANNUALS ◫ 12–1

☼ FULL SUN

💧💧 MODERATE TO REGULAR WATER

Osteospermum fruticosum

Native to South Africa, these woody perennials are closely related to *Dimorphotheca* and often sold as such. Mounded or trailing in habit, they bear a profusion of daisylike flowers during mild weather; flowering decreases or halts altogether during long, hot stretches. Tend to be short lived in the South. Used as winter annuals in Florida. Narrow, oval leaves are 2–4 in. long. Flowers of most open only in sunlight.

Tolerate heat and drought but look better with moderate water. Give loose, fertile soil; good drainage is a must. Pinch out growing tips of young plants to induce bushiness; cut back old, sprawling branches to young side growth in late summer to midautumn. Mass along driveways and paths; or

use in borders, rock gardens, containers. Types that spread by rooting stems are good on slopes. Not usually browsed by deer.

O. ecklonis (Dimorphotheca ecklonis). To 2–5 ft. tall, 2–4 ft. wide. Long stems bear 3-in. flowers centered in dark blue, with rays that are white above, lavender blue beneath. Blooms in spring.

'Lavender Mist'. To 1 ft. tall, 15 in. wide; 3-in. flowers open white, age to soft pale purple. Blooms from midspring until fall.

Passion Mix. Compact growth to 1–1½ ft. high and about as wide, with 2- to 2½-in. flowers in a variety of colors (pink, rose, purple, white), all with sky blue centers. Blooms throughout the year, more heavily in spring and fall. Blossoms stay open in low light better than those of many nonhybrid selections.

O. fruticosum (Dimorphotheca fruticosa). TRAILING AFRICAN DAISY. To 6–12 in. tall, spreading rapidly by trailing, rooting stems; will cover a 2- to 4-ft.-wide circle in a year. Deep lilac buds open to 2-in.-wide flowers with a dark purple center; rays are lilac above (fading nearly to white by second day), deeper lilac beneath. Blooms during the cool weather of spring, autumn, and (in mild-winter areas) winter. Essentially dormant in summer. Requires well-drained soil. Does well near the ocean. Use as ground cover or bank cover; if it gets too tall or weedy, mow or cut back in midsummer. Also a good choice planted at the top of a wall or in a hanging basket.

The following hybrids reach 18–20 in. high. 'African Queen' and 'Burgundy' have purple blooms. 'Whirlygig' ('Pinwheel') bears unusual white-and-blue flowers with rays that are white on upper surface, blue on back; each ray is pinched in the middle to reveal its blue underside, giving it the look of a spoon with a blue handle and a white bowl. 'Silver Sparkler' has green leaves edged in creamy white; blossoms have a dark blue eye and rays that are silvery white above, pale blue beneath. 'Gold Sparkler' has similar flowers, but its leaves are yellowish green with golden yellow margins. Blossoms of Side Series stay open on overcast days and at night; selections include 'Brightside' (white with a blue eye), 'Highside' (bicolor blooms in white and dark pink), 'Riverside' (butter yellow), 'Seaside' (bicolor in white and light pink), and 'Wildside' (dark purple).

O. Symphony Series. Mounding habit to 8–12 in. high, 3 ft. wide (1 ft. wide as annual). Among the most heat tolerant of osteospermums, flowering throughout moderately hot summers as well as during cool weather. Flowers are 2–2½ in. wide, with dark blue centers. Choices include 'Cream Symphony' (pale yellow rays), 'Lemon Symphony' (medium yellow), 'Orange Symphony' (light orange). Particularly attractive in window boxes and hanging baskets.

OSTRICH FERN. See MATTEUCCIA struthiopteris

OSTRYA

HOP HORNBEAM

Betulaceae

DECIDUOUS TREES

⚘ US, MS, LS, CS

☼ ◐ FULL SUN OR LIGHT SHADE

💧💧 MODERATE TO REGULAR WATER

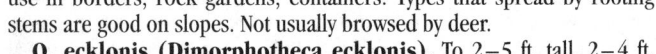

Ostrya virginiana

Slow-growing, small to medium-size trees (seldom more than 40 ft. high and wide), hop hornbeams get their common name from the female flowers and fruit, which are enclosed in bractlike husks that form 1½- to 2½-in. clusters resembling those of hop (*Humulus*). Oval, pointed, 4- to 5-in.-long leaves turn from dark green to yellow in fall. Inch-long male catkins are attractive in winter. Wood is hard, heavy, and dense. Grow best in well-drained, slightly acid soil; perform well in city plantings.

Hop hornbeams are attractive trees, but they're little used because of their slow growth—a fault to nurseryfolk, perhaps, but a possible advantage from the gardener's point of view.

O. carpinifolia. EUROPEAN HOP HORNBEAM. Heat zones 9–6. Scarcely differs from the more common American species, *O. virginiana*.

O. virginiana. AMERICAN HOP HORNBEAM, IRONWOOD. Heat zones 9–2. Native to eastern North America, where it is typically planted as an understory tree.

OSWEGO TEA. See MONARDA didyma

OXALIS

Oxalidaceae

PERENNIALS

ZONES VARY BY SPECIES

FULL SUN OR LIGHT SHADE

REGULAR WATER

Oxalis tetraphylla 'Iron Cross'

Leaves typically divided into three leaflets, giving them the look of clover leaves. Flowers may be pink, white, rose, or yellow.

O. acetosella. WOOD SORREL, SHAMROCK. Zones US, MS, LS; 8–1. From many northern temperate regions of the world. To 5 in. high, spreading widely by rhizomes. Typical clover-type leaves with three heart-shaped leaflets. Blooms in late spring, bearing ¾-in.-wide white flowers with purple to pink veins; blossoms rise just above the foliage. Can be somewhat invasive in its favored woodland conditions (moist, rich soil and partial shade). See also Shamrock.

O. adenophylla. Zones US, MS, LS; 8–6. Native to South America. Dense, compact, leafy tuft to 4 in. high, 6 in. wide. Each leaf has 9 to 22 crinkly gray-green leaflets. In late spring, 4- to 6-in. stalks bear 1-in., bell-shaped flowers in lilac pink with deeper veins. Good rock garden plant or companion to bulbs such as species tulips or smaller kinds of narcissus, either in pots or in the ground. Needs good drainage. Plant tubers in fall, setting 1 in. deep, 3–5 in. apart.

O. brasiliensis. Zones TS; 10–8. Native to Brazil. To 6 in. high and wide, with purplish leaves to 1 in. long. Blooms in spring and summer, bearing inch-wide reddish purple flowers with a yellow throat. Plant bulbs in fall, setting them 1 in. deep, 3–5 in. apart.

O. crassipes. PINK WOOD SORREL. Zones MS, LS, CS, TS; 10–6. Probably to be from South America. Similar to but slightly less hardy than the species *O. rubra*. Like that species, it often becomes a weed in lawns in the Lower and Coastal South and is highly susceptible to rust. Selection 'Alba' has white flowers.

O. purpurea (O. variabilis). Zones LS, CS, TS; 10–8. Native to South Africa. Grows to 4 in. tall and 6 in. wide; dark green leaves have large (up to 1½-in.-wide) leaflets. Bears 1- to 2-in., rose red flowers over a long period in fall and winter. Spreads by bulbs and rhizomelike roots but is not aggressive or weedy. Plant bulbs in fall, setting them 1 in. deep, 3–5 in. apart. Improved kinds, sold under the name "Grand Duchess," have larger flowers in rose pink, white, or lavender.

O. regnellii. Zones LS, CS, TS. Native to South America. To 8–10 in. high, 1 ft. wide. Grows from rhizomes. Green leaves 1–3 in. across; tiny white blossoms in spring and summer. 'Triangularis' (*O. r. atropurpurea*), called purple shamrock, features large, velvety purple leaves and pinkish lilac blossoms.

O. rubra. OXALIS, WOOD SORREL. Zones US, MS, LS, CS, TS. Native of Brazil and Argentina. Forms low mounds, 6–12 in. tall and wide. Clover-like leaves with three notched leaflets. Showy flowers in pink, rose, or lavender with darker veins, late winter or early spring. Pretty as ground cover or in rock garden or front of border. In fertile, moist soil in the Lower and Coastal South, it may spread and become hard to eradicate. Very susceptible to rust.

O. tetraphylla (O. deppei). GOOD LUCK PLANT. Zones LS, CS; 10–8. From Mexico. Forms a clump to 6–10 in. high and wide. Medium green leaves to 3 in. across have four leaflets instead of the usual three, each one

banded purple toward the base. In 'Iron Cross', the purple markings are more extensive splotches that form a cross shape. Both species and selection are usually grown as foliage plants, but they bear attractive clusters of 1-in. reddish flowers with greenish yellow throats in spring and summer. Plant bulbs in fall—1 in. deep, 3–5 in. apart.

O. versicolor. CANDY CANE SORREL. Zones LS, CS, TS; 10–8. Native to South Africa. To 3–6 in. high and 8 in. wide. Medium green leaves have deeply notched leaflets smaller than ½ in. wide. Funnel-shaped flowers are white, over 1 in. wide, with a crimson margin on the petal backs; buds also show striping. Plant bulbs in fall for spring flowers (set them 1 in. deep, 3–5 in. apart); bloom lasts for months.

OXBLOOD LILY. See RHODOPHIALA bifida

OXLIP. See PRIMULA elatior

OXYDENDRUM arboreum

SOURWOOD, SORREL TREE

Ericaceae

DECIDUOUS TREE

US, MS, LS, CS **H** 9–3

FULL SUN OR LIGHT SHADE

REGULAR WATER

Oxydendrum arboreum

Native from Pennsylvania and Ohio south to Florida, Mississippi, and Louisiana. Beautiful flowering tree that offers year-round interest. Very slow growth (often less than 1 ft. a year) to 25–30 ft. tall and wide, though 50 ft. is possible. Pyramidal shape with slender trunk, rounded top, slightly pendulous branches; handsome winter silhouette. Narrow, 5- to 8-in.-long leaves somewhat resemble peach leaves; they are bronze tinted in early spring, rich green in summer, orange and scarlet to blackish purple in autumn. Bark of new stems is bright red. Blooms in summer, bearing fragrant, bell-shaped, creamy white flowers in 10-in.-long, drooping clusters at branch tips. Flowers are used to make a prized honey. In fall, when foliage is brilliantly colored, branching clusters of greenish seed capsules extend outward and downward like fingers; capsules turn light silver gray, hang on late into winter.

Grow in well-drained, acid soil. Tolerates some drought but not urban pollution. Will grow in partial shade, but for best bloom and fall color plant in full sun. Excellent specimen, patio, or lawn tree (remove grass from beneath canopy and mulch well). Also good in naturalized areas or in large containers.

'Chameleon' is a bit more upright and offers reliably brilliant fall colors, including lime green, yellow, rosy red, and purple. 'Mt. Charm' is symmetrical and gives a bright show of autumn color a little earlier than the species.

PACHISTIMA canbyi. See PAXISTIMA canbyi

PACHYPODIUM lamerei

MADAGASCAR PALM

Apocynaceae

SUCCULENT SHRUB

TS **H** 12–10; OR HOUSEPLANT

FULL SUN OR PARTIAL SHADE; BRIGHT LIGHT

REGULAR WATER

Pachypodium lamerei

Native to Madagascar. Not a palm, though it looks something like one. Attractive, easy-to-grow shrub with impressive silhouette: spiny, succulent, unbranched trunk topped with a circle of strap-shaped leaves to 1 ft. long and 1–4 in.

P

wide. Usually seen at 2–4 ft. high and 2 ft. wide, though it can grow to 18 ft. tall and 8 ft. wide under ideal conditions. Large, old plants may bloom in summer, bearing fragrant, saucer-shaped white flowers to 4 in. across; smaller, younger plants seldom bloom. May take up to 10 years or more to fully mature.

Madagascar palm can be grown outdoors year-round in south Florida. Elsewhere, it can be raised in a container (use a clay pot, not a plastic one) and summered outside or grown exclusively as a houseplant. Indoors, place it in maximum light before a south- or west-facing window. In spring and summer, let the soil go dry between waterings, and fertilize at every other watering with a general-purpose liquid houseplant fertilizer diluted to half-strength. Good drainage is critical. Leaves usually drop in winter (though specimens grown in south Florida and houseplants may hold their foliage). Whether grown indoors or out, the plant requires no water or fertilizer in fall and winter; resume watering and feeding when new growth begins.

PACHYRHIZUS erosus. See JICAMA

PACHYSANDRA

PACHYSANDRA, SPURGE

Buxaceae

PERENNIALS

◩ ZONES VARY BY SPECIES

◐ ● PARTIAL TO FULL SHADE

◐ REGULAR WATER

Pachysandra terminalis

Spreading slowly but surely from underground runners, these low-growing evergreen perennials are invaluable ground covers for shady places. They are hardy to cold and well able to compete with tree roots. Compact growth and clean, attractive foliage are their chief virtues. Small spring flowers aren't showy when viewed casually, but they're attractive at close range.

For best growth, give well-drained soil amended with plenty of organic matter. Set 6 in. apart for reasonably quick cover; apply a mulch and keep soil moist until plants are established. Give them light to full shade; too much sun causes foliage to turn yellow. Deer don't usually bother pachysandra.

P. procumbens. ALLEGHENY PACHYSANDRA, ALLEGHENY SPURGE. Zones US, MS; 8–3. From the southeastern U.S. Not as widely available or as quick to spread as *P. terminalis*. Grows 6–12 in. high, with grayish green leaves (2–4 in. long, 2–3 in. wide) clustered near stem tips; leaves are often mottled with gray or brown. Fragrant white or pinkish flowers. Prefers neutral soil.

P. terminalis. JAPANESE PACHYSANDRA, JAPANESE SPURGE. Zones US, MS, LS; 8–1. Native to Japan and northern China. Grows to 8–12 in. high. Shiny, leathery dark green leaves, clustered at ends of stems, are 2–4 in. long and ½–1½ in. wide; upper half of leaf has shallowly toothed edges. White flowers are borne in 1- to 2-in. spikes. Popular selections include 'Green Carpet', shorter and denser in growth than the species, with shinier, deeper green leaves; 'Green Sheen', with especially glossy leaves; 'Silver Edge' ('Variegata'), with creamy-edged foliage; and fast-spreading 'Cut Leaf', with deeply dissected leaves.

Japanese pachysandra can stand very heavy shade and is widely used under trees; it is also an excellent filler for these difficult spots where lawn grass won't grow. Luxuriant-looking, top-choice ground cover for shade in the Upper and Middle South. In the Lower South, it sulks during long, dry summers. Prefers slightly acid soil. Seldom bothered by pests, but a leaf blight can cause serious damage if it gets out of hand; control with fungicides and, if possible, by limiting overhead watering.

FOR INFORMATION ON SELECTING PLANTS
PLEASE SEE PAGES 39–144

PACHYSTACHYS

Acanthaceae

EVERGREEN SHRUBS

◩ CS, TS ⯁ 12–8; OR GROW IN POTS

◑ ◐ EXPOSURE NEEDS VARY BY SPECIES

◐ ◑ WATER NEEDS VARY BY SPECIES

Pachystachys lutea

Large-foliaged plants with showy terminal blossom spikes that attract hummingbirds. Stems are soft wooded, more herbaceous than shrubby. Similar to *Justicia*, another member of the same family.

P. coccinea. CARDINAL'S-GUARD. Native to the West Indies and South America. Lanky-looking plant to 5 ft. or taller, 2–3 ft. wide; for a tidier look, cut back established plants in late winter. Oval, prominently veined leaves to 8 in. long. Summertime flower spikes reach about 6 in. long, with green bracts and tubular, 2-in.-long blossoms in blazing scarlet. Give light shade, well-drained soil, regular water.

P. lutea. YELLOW SHRIMP PLANT, LOLLIPOPS PLANT. Native to Peru. To 3–6 ft. tall, 1½–2½ ft. wide, with narrow dark green leaves to 5 in. long. Pinch tips during growing season and cut plant back in winter to reduce lankiness. Blooms constantly in warm weather, bearing 3- to 6-in.-long spikes of neatly overlapping golden yellow bracts; flowers are slender white tubes that emerge from between the bracts. Good for massing and in mixed borders. Give full sun or light shade, moderate water.

PAEONIA

PEONY

Paeoniaceae

PERENNIALS AND DECIDUOUS SHRUBS

◩ US, MS, LS ⯁ 8–1

◑ ◐ AFTERNOON SHADE IN HOTTEST CLIMATES

◐ REGULAR WATER

Herbaceous Peony,
Single

True royalty among garden plants, peonies feature blossoms that can take your breath away. Most types flourish in areas with long, cold winters, leading folks to the mistaken conclusion that they're not suitable for the South. But while it's true that peonies do generally perform best in the Upper and Middle South, quite a few tolerate the mild winters and hot summers of the Lower South, blooming as far south as Jackson, Mississippi; Montgomery, Alabama; and Columbus, Georgia.

The two basic types are herbaceous peonies, which die to the ground in late fall, and tree peonies (really shrubs), which form woody trunks. Both are from Chinese species: herbaceous peonies are chiefly from *P. lactiflora*, tree types from *P. suffruticosa*. Most garden peonies are hybrids.

Peonies dominate many a flower border in late spring—they're great companions for iris, old roses, poppies (*Papaver*), dianthus, and early daylilies (*Hemerocallis*). Just remember that they grow to a good size over time and may get too big for a small border. When given proper care, with special attention to site preparation, all are extremely long lived, bringing spectacular beauty to your garden for as long as you live.

Herbaceous peonies are best planted in fall or earliest spring, as bare-root plants consisting of compact rhizomes with thick, fleshy roots and several "eyes" (growth buds). Tree peonies, nearly all of which are grafted onto herbaceous peony roots, may also be purchased bare-root and planted in fall or spring. However, many growers offer container-grown tree peonies that can be set out at any time the ground isn't frozen.

Proper site preparation prior to planting is crucial for success. Choose a sunny, well-drained spot free from competing roots of nearby trees and shrubs. For each rhizome, dig an area 1½–2 ft. wide, loosening and turning the soil to a depth of at least 1 ft. Work in copious amounts of organic matter—such as garden compost, composted manure, sphagnum peat moss, or chopped leaves—to which you've added a cup of superphosphate. Let the soil settle for a couple of days before planting. Position herbaceous peony roots so that the eyes are exactly 1 in. below the soil surface; deeper

WHAT PEONIES NEED

EXPOSURE: Choose a site in full sun (light afternoon shade in the Lower South), free from competing roots from trees and shrubs.

SOIL: Dig the planting site deeply, working in plenty of organic material and a high-phosphate fertilizer. Good drainage is essential

PLANTING: Set herbaceous peony roots with their growth buds 1 in. deep, no deeper. Plant tree peonies so that the graft line is 3–4 in. below the soil surface.

FERTILIZING: Peonies are unlikely to bloom the first year, but they should bloom every year from then on if fertilized twice annually—once following bloom, a second time in autumn. The American Peony Society recommends a balanced 8-8-8 fertilizer and bonemeal; apply according to package directions.

DISEASE CONTROL: To discourage fungal diseases, be sure to provide good air circulation and dispose of fallen and withered foliage each autumn.

Paeonia 'Kansas'

planting may reduce flowering. Make sure each rhizome has at least three eyes; rhizomes with fewer eyes take a long time to bloom. Set tree peonies so that the graft line is 3–4 in. below the soil surface (the object is to get the shrubby top to root on its own). Mulch peonies in spring to cool the roots and retain soil moisture. Plants usually don't bloom the first year, so be patient.

To gather peony flowers for bouquets, cut them just as the buds begin to open. Leave at least three leaves behind on every stem you cut, and don't remove more than half the blooms from any clump. This preserves sufficient leaf surface to build up food reserves for the following year. Promptly removing spent flowers before they set seed also aids future flowering.

A fungal disease called botrytis sometimes appears during cool, damp weather. Flower buds blacken and fail to develop, and stems wilt and collapse. To prevent the problem, make sure there's adequate air circulation around the plants, and clean up the garden in autumn, disposing of all fallen peony leaves. As new growth emerges in spring, spray it with a copper fungicide. Peonies are resistant to damage by browsing deer.

Herbaceous peonies. Perennials. Need varying degrees of winter chill to bloom well. Established plants need no dividing and resent disturbance. If you must transplant them, move them during their dormancy in fall, and be aware that transplants may take a year or two to begin blooming again.

Plants grow 3–4 ft. tall and wide. Large, deep green, attractively divided leaves are an effective background for the spectacular spring or early summer flowers and look good throughout the summer. Depending on the selection, blossoms can be anywhere from 2 in. to 10 in. across; colors range from pure white through cream and rose to red. Many have a perfume reminiscent of old-fashioned roses.

Herbaceous peonies are classified by flower form. Depending on which expert you consult, there are anywhere from three to eight categories; here, we'll list four.

Single peonies have one row of broad petals surrounding a central cluster of yellow stamens.

Semidouble types are similar, but with an additional row or two of broad central petals.

Double types have very full flowers bursting with broad petals; stamens are absent or inconspicuous.

Japanese peonies have a single row of petals surrounding a central mass of thin, petal-like segments called staminodes.

In the South, early-blooming peonies tend to outperform those that flower late—but all the selections listed below are proven performers in our region. If you have room for only one peony, choose 'Festiva Maxima' (double white flowers with red flecks), a Southern heirloom plant that blooms dependably throughout our region. Other recommended selections include the following.

'Big Ben'. Early double. Fragrant dark red blooms. To 38 in. tall and wide.

'Do Tell'. Midseason Japanese type. Pink outer petals surround rose pink and red staminodes. To 34 in.

'Edulis Superba'. Very early double. Fragrant rose pink blossoms. Very floriferous; good cut flower. To 36 in.

'Elsa Sass'. Late double. Large, very fragrant white flowers with creamy yellow centers. Strong stems make it excellent for cut flowers. Vigorous grower to 26 in.

'Félix Crousse'. Late double. Fragrant ruby red blossoms. Very floriferous; superb cut flower. To 34 in.

'Festiva Maxima'. Early double. Fragrant pure white flowers flecked with red. Very floriferous. Long-lived, dependable bloomer, even in the Lower South. To 34 in.

'Kansas'. Midseason double. Long-lasting red blossoms on strong, upright stems. Very reliable bloomer. To 36 in.

'Karl Rosenfield'. Midseason double. Mildly fragrant, velvety crimson flowers. Floriferous; great cut flower. To 36 in.

'Kelway's Glorious'. Midseason double. Huge, very fragrant white flowers with creamy centers. Strong stems; very floriferous. To 34 in.

'Minnie Shaylor'. Midseason semidouble. Light pink blossoms fade to pure white. Blooms over a long period. To 36 in.

'Monsieur Jules Elie'. Midseason double. Giant-size, moderately fragrant blossoms in light pink shading to deeper rose. Good cut flower. To 36 in.

'Mrs. Franklin D. Roosevelt'. Midseason double. Fragrant blossoms with shell pink outer petals surrounding a peach-colored center. Floriferous; excellent cut flower. Vigorous grower to 34 in.

'Nippon Beauty'. Late Japanese type. Deep garnet blooms with gold-tipped staminodes. Floriferous and vigorous. To 38 in.

'Philippe Rivoire'. Midseason double. Fragrant deep crimson blossoms. Good cut flower. To 30 in.

'Sarah Bernhardt'. Midseason double. Fragrant rose pink blossoms with silver-edged petals. Very reliable. Excellent cut flower. To 34 in.

'Sea Shell'. Midseason single. Lightly fragrant pink blossoms. Excellent cut flower. To 3 ft.

'Shirley Temple'. Very early double. Very fragrant pale pink blossoms age to blush white. Floriferous and vigorous. To 34 in.

Three species are also recommended for the South. *P. tenuifolia,* called fernleaf peony, hails from southeastern Europe. It reaches 1½–2½ ft. high and wide and has dark green, exceedingly finely cut leaves. Deep red, single flowers on short stems seem to be sitting on the foliage. From Asia come *P. obovata* and *P. japonica,* both only 1½–2 ft. high and wide. *P. obovata* has deep green foliage that is pale gray green and slightly hairy beneath. It produces cup-shaped, single white to purplish red blossoms with yellow stamens; the seed heads that follow split open to reveal red receptacles holding metallic blue seeds. *P. japonica* is similar but with hairier leaf undersides and yellow-centered white flowers that appear a little earlier than those of *P. obovata.*

Tree peonies. Deciduous shrubs. Slow growth to 3–5 ft. tall and eventually as wide, with handsome, blue-green to bronzy green, divided leaves. Single to double, typically very large flowers (to 10–12 in.) appear in spring. These peonies seldom show their full potential until they have spent several years in your garden, but the spectacular results are worth the wait. Small, recently grafted packaged plants are sometimes available, usually sold only by color (red, pink, white, yellow, purple). These are a good buy if you are patient—they'll take longer to reach flowering size than older, container-grown or field-grown plants costing much more. Count on 2 or 3 years before they come into flower for the first time.

Tree Peony, Double

P

Catalogs offer named selections of Japanese origin in white and shades of pink, red, and purple; blossoms are generally semidouble. More recent and more expensive are orange, yellow, and copper-colored hybrids resulting from crosses of *P. suffruticosa* with *P. delavayi* and *P. lutea;* these bear semidouble blooms that face outward and upward.

Tree peonies require less winter chill than herbaceous peonies. The large flowers are fragile and should be sheltered from strong winds. Prune only to remove faded flowers and any dead wood.

WHY DIDN'T MY PEONY PUT ON A SHOW? *Poor flowering has many possible causes, including these: the plant is too young (wait awhile); planting depth is too deep or too shallow (lift during dormant season and plant at proper depth); flower buds were killed by a late freeze (wait until next year); location is too shady (move to a sunnier spot during dormancy); weather was too hot too soon (plant early-flowering types); plant has nutrient deficiency (apply fertilizer); clump has been moved or divided too often (leave it alone).* ❖

PAINTED DAISY. See CHRYSANTHEMUM coccineum

PAINTED FINGERNAIL PLANT. See NEOREGELIA spectabilis

PAINTED TONGUE. See SALPIGLOSSIS sinuata

Palmae. See Arecaceae

PALMETTO. See SABAL

PALMS. Most palms are tropical or subtropical; a few are surprisingly hardy (specimens are seen in northern locales such as Edinburgh, London, and southern Russia, as well as in Montgomery, Augusta, and Raleigh). These trees offer great opportunity for imaginative planting; in nature, they grow not only in solid stands but also with other plants, notably broad-leafed evergreen trees and shrubs. They are effective near swimming pools.

Most young palms prefer shade, and all tolerate it; this fact makes them good house or patio plants when they are small. As they grow, they can be moved into full sun or partial shade, depending on the species. Growth rates vary, but keeping plants in pots usually slows down the faster-growing kinds. If temperatures are 60°F or higher, fertilize potted palms often; also wash them off frequently to provide some humidity and clean the foliage. Washing also dislodges insects, which (indoors, at any rate) are protected from their natural enemies and can increase extremely rapidly.

To pot a palm, supply good potting soil, adequate drainage, and not too big a container. As with all potted plants, pot or repot a palm in a container just slightly larger than the one in which it is already growing.

Some shade-tolerant palms such as *Rhapis, Chamaedorea,* and *Howea* may spend decades in pots indoors. Others that later may reach great size—*Phoenix, Washingtonia, Chamaerops*—make charming temporary indoor plants but eventually must be moved.

Planting holes for palms should generally be the same depth as and 1–2 ft. wider than the root ball, and you can use unamended native soil for backfill. If you are planting in very poor, alkaline, or clay soil, however, some experts suggest a different procedure. For a 5-gal.-size palm, dig a 3-ft.-wide hole that is 8 in. deeper than root ball. Place 1–2 cu. ft. of well-rotted manure, nitrogen-fortified sawdust, or other organic amendment in the hole, then mix in a handful or two of blood meal and top with a 6-in. layer of soil. Set in the palm and fill in around it with a mixture of half native soil and half nitrogen-fortified sawdust, ground bark, or peat moss. Water newly planted palms faithfully until established.

Most palms, even big ones, transplant easily in late spring or early summer. Since new roots form from the base of the trunk, the root ball need not be large; a new root system will form and produce lush new growth. When transplanting large palms, contractors usually tie leaves together over the center "bud" or heart, then secure the leaf mass to a length of 2-by-4 tied to the trunk.

Established palms need little maintenance; they thrive in reasonably fertile soil, with the appropriate amount of moisture (see individual entries

for recommendations). All tropical palms do their growing during warm times of year. Winter rains wash the foliage down (and, in areas with salty soil, leach out accumulated salts). Palms growing in dry or dusty areas or beyond the reach of rain or dew should be hosed off periodically; this helps control populations of spider mites and sucking insects that find refuge in the long leaf stems. Beach plantings should also be washed off occasionally to keep salt from accumulating on the leaves. Most palms are not heavily browsed by deer.

Feather palms and many fan palms look neater when old leaves are removed after they have turned brown. Make neat cuts close to trunk, leaving leaf bases. Some palms shed old leaf bases on their own. Others, including *Syagrus* and *Chamaedorea,* may hold old bases. You can remove them by slicing them off at the very bottom of base (be careful not to cut into trunk).

Many palm admirers say that dead leaves of *Washingtonia* should remain on the tree, the thatch being part of the palm's character. If you agree but prefer a neater look, you can cut lower fronds uniformly close to trunk but leave leaf bases, which present a rather attractive lattice surface.

Most palms are frost sensitive. Frost becomes more damaging to them as it extends its stay and is repeated. A light frost that lasts for half an hour may not harm plants at all, but if the same degree of frost persists for 4 hours, it may injure some palms, kill others. Hardiness is also a matter of plant size; larger palms may survive severe frosts without harm while smaller ones perish. At its least serious, frost damage consists simply of burned leaf edges—but frost may affect whole leaves, parts of trunk, or crown. Damage to the crown is usually fatal (though some trees have recovered from it).

Following are eight roles that the right kinds of palms can fill. Palms in each listing are described under their own entries elsewhere in this book.

Sturdy palms for street trees and vertical effects in large gardens. *Archontophoenix, Brahea, Cocos nucifera, Jubaea chilensis, Livistona, Phoenix canariensis, P. dactylifera, P. loureirii, P. rupicola, Ptychosperma elegans, Roystonea, Sabal causiarum, S. palmetto, S. uresana, Syagrus romanzoffianum, Washingtonia.*

Small to medium-size palms for frost-free gardens. *Archontophoenix, Caryota, Chamaedorea, Chamaerops humilis, Chrysalidocarpus lutescens, Howea.*

Small to medium-size palms that will tolerate light, brief frost. *Acoelorrhaphe wrightii, Brahea armata, B. dulcis, Butia capitata, Chamaedorea, Chamaerops humilis, Livistona, Phoenix canariensis, P. dactylifera, P. loureirii, P. roebelenii, Ptychosperma macarthuri.*

Hardiest palms that tolerate temperatures below freezing. *Brahea armata, Chamaerops humilis, Jubaea chilensis, Livistona, Rhapidophyllum histrix, Rhapis, Sabal causiarum, S. etonia, S. mexicana, S. minor, S. palmetto, S. × texensis, Serenoa repens, Trachycarpus fortunei, Washingtonia.*

Salt-tolerant palms for seaside planting. *Butia capitata, Chamaerops humilis, Cocos nucifera, Phoenix canariensis, P. dactylifera, P. reclinata, Roystonea, Sabal, Washingtonia robusta.*

Palms for hot, dry climates. *Brahea armata, Butia capitata, Chamaerops humilis, Jubaea chilensis, Livistona chinensis, L. mariae, Phoenix canariensis, P. dactylifera, P. loureirii, P. sylvestris, Sabal mexicana, S. minor, Washingtonia.*

Palms to grow under overhangs or indoors. *Archontophoenix, Caryota mitis, C. ochlandra, C. urens, Chamaedorea, Howea, Livistona* (when young), *Phoenix reclinata* (when young), *P. roebelenii, Rhapis.* Indoor palms should occasionally be brought outdoors into mild light.

Palms as underplantings. Young palms, especially slow growers such as *Livistona chinensis* and *Chamaerops humilis,* stay low for 5 to 10 years and can be used effectively as plantings under tall trees. *Sabal × texensis* takes many years to reach its ultimate height of 15 ft. Or choose among these shrubby palms that rarely exceed 6 ft. tall: *Sabal etonia, S. minor, Serenoa repens, Rhapidophyllum histrix.*

LIGHT UP YOUR PALMS. *Thanks to their stateliness and spectacular leaves, practically all palms are excellent subjects for night lighting. You can backlight them, illuminate them from below, side-light them, or use directed light to project dramatic silhouettes against a light-colored wall.* ❖

PAMPAS GRASS. See CORTADERIA selloana

PANDANUS utilis

SCREWPINE

Pandanaceae

EVERGREEN TREE

✂ TS H 12–10; OR GROW IN POT

☼ FULL SUN; DIRECT OR BRIGHT FILTERED LIGHT

💧 REGULAR WATER

Pandanus utilis

Native to many Pacific islands, including Hawaii. Palmlike, round-headed tree 20–30 ft. high, 20–40 ft. wide. Striking appearance; sends down aerial roots and bears spirals of stiff, spiny, 3-ft.-long leaves at the ends of stubby branches. Female plants develop large fruits that resemble pineapples.

Screwpine can be grown outdoors only in south Florida. It has good wind and salt tolerance; thrives in any well-drained soil, even beach sand. Excellent shade or windbreak tree for the beach garden. Produces litter; needs maintenance to remove old leaves.

Outside of south Florida, grow this tree in pots. Young plants make picturesque container subjects; bring them indoors during winter and maintain night temperatures above 55°F. They need high humidity (mist frequently), direct or bright filtered light, and ample water (less in winter). Fertilize frequently with a general-purpose liquid houseplant fertilizer during the growing season.

PANDA PLANT. See KALANCHOE tomentosa

PANDOREA

Bignoniaceae

EVERGREEN VINES

✂ CS, TS

☼ PARTIAL SHADE

💧 WATER NEEDS VARY BY SPECIES

Pandorea jasminoides

Twining vines noted for clusters of trumpet-shaped flowers and for rich green, glossy, divided leaves; the foliage is so attractive that the plants look lovely even when out of bloom. Perform best in good, organically enriched soil. Blooms are borne on previous year's growth; prune to shape or thin vines after flowering.

P. jasminoides (Bignonia jasminoides, Tecoma jasminoides). BOWER VINE. Heat zones 12–8. Native to Australia. Fast growth to about 20–30 ft. Each leaf has five to seven oval, 1- to 2-in.-long leaflets with pointed tips. Typically unscented flowers are white with pink throats, 1½–2 in. long; bloom from late spring to early fall. 'Alba' and the stronger-growing 'Lady Di' have pure white flowers; 'Rosea' produces soft pink blooms with nearly red throats. 'Rosea Superba' and a selection known simply as 'Deep Pink Form' are fragrant. There is a form with variegated leaves. Plant in lee of prevailing wind. Prolonged freezes will kill this species and its selections. Regular water.

P. pandorana (Bignonia australis, Tecoma australis). WONGA-WONGA VINE. Heat zones 12–9. Native to Australia, Pacific islands. More vigorous than *P. jasminoides,* covering twice the space; give it plenty of room. Leaves are divided into 8 to 17 leaflets that are 1–3 in. long and somewhat narrower than those of *P. jasminoides.* Small (to ¾-in.-long), unscented spring flowers are typically creamy white, often spotted brownish purple in the throat. 'Golden Showers' has golden yellow blossoms. Tougher, more wind resistant, and less susceptible to freeze damage than *P. jasminoides.* Moderate water.

PANICUM virgatum

SWITCH GRASS

Poaceae (Gramineae)

PERENNIAL GRASS

✂ US, MS, LS H 9–1, EXCEPT AS NOTED

☼ ☼ FULL SUN OR LIGHT SHADE

💧 💧 💧 💧 ANY AMOUNT OF WATER

Panicum virgatum

Bold ornamental grass native to many parts of the U.S.; a major component of the tall-grass prairies of the Great Plains. Upright, 2- to 4-ft.-wide clump of narrow deep green or gray-green leaves grows 3–5 ft. tall; it is topped in summer by slender flower clusters that increase the plant's height to 4–7 ft. The loose, airy sprays of tiny pinkish blossoms gradually age to white; foliage turns yellow or red in fall, then slowly fades to beige. Flowers and leaves persist all winter, making for an attractive silhouette in the cold-season garden. Switch grass tolerates many soils, takes little or regular water, even endures salt spray. Use in masses, sweeps, or mixed borders, or as an accent. Selections include the following.

'Cloud Nine'. Metallic blue foliage turns gold in autumn. Billowing clouds of reddish brown flowers. Reaches 6 ft. tall in bloom. Best selection for Florida.

'Dallas Blues'. Powder blue foliage fades to attractive rust and tan tones. Large, layered clusters of reddish purple flowers. Plant reaches height of 5 ft. in bloom.

'Haense Herms'. Delicate light green leaves turn bright red by early fall, then deepen to burgundy. To 4–5 ft. tall in bloom.

'Heavy Metal'. Heat zones 9–4. Silvery blue, sturdy leaves turn bright yellow in fall. To 4–5 ft. in bloom.

'Northwind'. Strongly vertical olive green foliage turns yellow in autumn. Narrow, erect flower plumes increase plant height to 5 ft.

'Shenandoah'. Heat zones 9–5. Foliage emerges blue green, turns maroon red by midsummer to early fall. Airy red flower clusters. To 3–4 ft. tall in bloom.

PANSY. See VIOLA

PAPAVER

POPPY

Papaveraceae

PERENNIALS AND COOL-SEASON ANNUALS

✂ ZONES VARY BY SPECIES

☼ FULL SUN

💧 💧 MODERATE TO REGULAR WATER

Papaver orientale

Poppies provide bright spring and summer color for borders and cutting. Give ordinary, well-drained soil (note exception for *P. alpinum*); feed lightly until established. Perennial species tend to be short lived. When using poppies as cut flowers, sear cut stem ends in a flame before placing them in water.

P. alpinum. ALPINE POPPY. Perennial. Zones US, MS; 7–3; best adapted to Upper South. From the Pyrenees, Alps, and Carpathians. Rock garden plant; needs gritty, very fast draining soil. Produces a 4-in.-wide basal rosette of divided, 2- to 6-in.-long leaves; foliage is blue green, nearly hairless. In spring or summer, leafless flower stems to 5–8 in. tall

P

bear 1½- to 2-in. blossoms in white, orange, yellow, or salmon. Blooms first year from seed sown in autumn or early spring. Where adapted, self-sows freely.

P. atlanticum. Perennial. Zones US, MS; 7–4. Native to Morocco. Grows to 1½–2 ft. tall, with downy gray-green leaves in a basal rosette to 6 in. across. Flowers are soft orange to red, 2–4 in. across, opening in late spring and early summer. Sow seed in fall. To prolong bloom period, remove spent flowers.

P. bracteatum. Perennial. Zones US, MS, LS; 8–5. Native to northern Iran. Forms a bushy clump (to 4 ft. tall, 3 ft. wide) of deeply lobed and toothed green leaves. Rather stiff stems hold solitary, 4- to 7-in. bright red flowers with a black spot at each petal base. Early summer bloom.

P. commutatum 'Lady Bird'. Annual. Zones US, MS, LS, CS, TS; 6–1. Selection of a species native to Greece, Turkey, the Caucasus, Iran. To 1½ ft. tall and nearly as wide. Downy, coarsely lobed medium green leaves to 6 in. long. Blooms profusely for several weeks in midsummer, producing 3-in., bright red flowers with a black blotch in the middle of each petal; flower stems are softly hairy. Sow in late winter or early spring; or set out plants in midspring.

P. nudicaule. ICELAND POPPY. Short-lived perennial in Zones US, MS; 5–1. Grown as annual in most places. Native to subarctic regions. Blue-green, coarsely hairy, divided leaves make basal rosettes 6 in. wide. Hairy, 1- to 2-ft. stalks bear cup-shaped, slightly fragrant flowers to 3 in. across, in yellow, orange, salmon, rose, pink, cream, white. For winter or spring bloom, sow seed or set out transplants in fall. Gardeners in colder parts of the Upper South should set out transplants in spring. To prolong flowering, pick flowers freely. Deer don't seem to care for Iceland poppies.

Champagne Bubbles (to 1 ft.) and wind-resistant Wonderland (to 10 in.) are widely grown strains. Oregon Rainbows (to 15–20 in.) produces large (to 8-in.-wide) blooms in pastel colors, including bicolors and picotees, but in the South many buds fail to open. Misato Carnival strain has 6-in. flowers on 2- to 3-ft. stems.

P. orientale. ORIENTAL POPPY. Perennial. Zones US, MS, LS; 9–1. Native to the Caucasus, northeastern Turkey, northern Iran. Needs winter chill for best performance. In mild-winter areas, flowers tend to form without stalks, so they are partly or completely hidden among the leaves. Height is variable; some types are just 16 in. tall, others reach 4 ft. Plants spread by offsets to 2 ft. or more. These are among the leafiest of poppies, forming bushy clumps of hairy, medium green, coarsely cut leaves to 1 ft. long. Blooms are 4–6 in. across; deeply crinkled petals often have a black blotch at the base. Many named varieties are sold, offering single or double flowers in orange, scarlet, red, pink, salmon, or white.

A great many named selections are sold; they bloom in late spring and early summer, then die back in midsummer. The sterile Minicap Hybrids were bred for greater heat tolerance and for profuse bloom over a longer period (2 to 4 months). In all types, new leafy growth appears in fall, lasts over winter, and develops rapidly in spring.

Set sprawling plants such as baby's breath (*Gypsophila*) nearby to cover bare areas after poppies die down. Plant dormant roots in fall with tops 3 in. deep; set container-grown plants flush with soil line. Give well-drained soil and make sure air circulation is good. Divide crowded clumps in August, after foliage has died down.

P. rhoeas. SHIRLEY POPPY, FLANDERS FIELD POPPY. Annual. Zones US, MS, LS, CS, TS; 5–1. Native to Eurasia, North Africa. Slender, branching, hairy-stemmed plant to 3 ft. tall, 1 ft. wide, with short, irregularly divided leaves. Single or double flowers are 2 in. or wider, in white, pink, red, orange, salmon, scarlet, lilac, soft blue, bicolors. Selections bearing single scarlet flowers with black petal bases are sold as 'American Legion' or 'Flanders Field'. Angels' Choir strain

Papaver rhoeas

offers double flowers in a wide range of colors on 2- to 2½-ft. stems.

Mix seed with an equal amount of fine sand, then broadcast it in fall where plants are to grow. For cut flowers, pick when buds first show color. Remove seed capsules (old flower bases) weekly to prolong the bloom season. Notorious self-sower. Not usually browsed by deer.

P. rupifragum. Perennial. Zones US, MS, LS; 9–6. From Spain. Grows 1½ ft. high and 8 in. wide, with lobed or toothed green leaves. Light brick red flowers to 3 in. across in summer. May self-sow. 'Double Tangerine Gem' has bluish green leaves and double blossoms in soft orange.

P. somniferum. OPIUM POPPY. Annual. Zones US, MS, LS, CS, TS; 8–1. Believed to have originated in southeastern Europe and western Asia. To 4 ft. tall, 1 ft. wide. Virtually hairless gray-green leaves have jagged edges. Late spring flowers are 4–5 in. across, in white, pink, red, purple, deep plum; they are typically double (sometimes with fringed petals), though there are also single-blossomed forms. Blooms are followed by large, decorative seed capsules used in dried arrangements. Opium is derived from the sap of the green capsules; ripe pods yield large quantities of the poppy seed used in baking. Shake pods over a tray to collect the seeds. Because of its narcotic properties, this species is not as widely offered as many other types—but since the flowers are exceedingly beautiful, the seed is often shared among gardeners. Sow in fall; barely cover seed with soil.

Papaveraceae. The poppy family of annuals, perennials, and shrubs displays showy flowers, usually borne one per stem. In addition to *Papaver*, members include bloodroot (*Sanguinaria*), *Eschscholzia*, greater celandine (*Chelidonium*), plume poppy (*Macleaya*), and prickly poppy (*Argemone*).

PAPAYA

Caricaceae

PERENNIALS

✿ TS ⏱ 12–10

☼ FULL SUN, EXCEPT AS NOTED

💧 REGULAR WATER

Papaya

It may look like a tree, but papaya (*Carica papaya*) is actually a big perennial with a hollow stem. Native to lowland regions of the tropical Americas, it forms an erect, unbranched trunk 6–20 ft. tall, with a palmlike, 3- to 6-ft.-wide head of foliage. Leafstalks about 2 ft. long carry deeply lobed leaves to 2 ft. across. Plants flower and fruit simultaneously throughout the year. Most have either all male or all female flowers, so you'll usually need at least one plant of each sex to get fruit. Male flowers are yellowish and held on stalks; female flowers are larger, white or cream colored, and sprout directly from the trunk. Plants usually begin blooming 6 to 12 months after germination. Some selections have both male and female flowers or self-fertile flowers.

Papayas are easily started from the soft black seeds found inside the fruit; just be sure that the seeds are fresh. Germination takes 2 to 5 weeks. Sow the seeds in pots indoors in winter, then set out plants in the garden in spring. Give full sun and fertile, well-drained soil. These plants will survive light frosts—but because such cold greatly reduces fruit production, they are best grown in south Florida and the Rio Grande Valley of Texas. In other areas, they make attractive houseplants or container plants but don't bear fruit. Give them lots of water from spring to fall and little to none during the winter. Shield from strong wind. Papayas are short lived, and young trees produce better fruit than older ones, so it's a good idea always to keep a few plants coming along.

Major pests are fruit flies and nematodes. Consult your local Cooperative Extension Office for controls. Papaya ringspot virus, for which there is no chemical control, can be a serious disease. Symptoms include sunken green rings on the leaves, bumpy fruit, and poor fruit production. Hawaiian selections are particularly susceptible. A few selections, however, do tolerate the disease, and 'Rainbow' resists it.

Two types of papaya are grown in the South—Hawaiian and Mexican. Hawaiian types (the kinds found in grocery stores) bear oblong, pear-shaped, or rounded fruits that typically weigh 1 to 2 pounds and have orange, red, or pinkish flesh. The fruits of Mexican types weigh up to 10 pounds and have yellow, orange, or pink flesh. Though you can pick papayas slightly green and let them ripen at room temperature (do not chill unripe fruit), they'll have the sweetest flavor if allowed to ripen on the tree. Harvest when the fruit feels slightly soft and its skin is almost completely yellow. Avoid touching the stem's milky sap, which can cause dermatitis. Selections include these eight.

'Mexican Yellow'. Mexican type. Yellow-fleshed fruit up to 10 pounds.

'Rainbow'. Hawaiian. Pear-shaped, 1- to 2-pound fruit is similar to 'Solo'. Genetically modified to resist ringspot.

'Solo'. Hawaiian type. Pear-shaped to rounded fruit has reddish orange flesh, weighs 1 to 2 pounds. Plant may be either female or bisexual.

'Sunrise'. Hawaiian type. Pear-shaped, 1- to 2-pound fruit with reddish orange flesh. Tree bears fruit when only 3 ft. tall.

'Tainung No. 1'. Hawaiian type developed in Taiwan. Roundish, red-fleshed fruits weigh about 2 pounds. Good keeper. Tolerates ringspot.

'Tainung No. 2'. Hawaiian type developed in Taiwan. Tree is more productive than 'Tainung No. 1'; fruits are similar but are slightly smaller and have reddish orange flesh. Tolerates ringspot.

'Tainung No. 3'. Hawaiian type developed in Taiwan. Smaller plant than the preceding two but produces the largest fruits—up to 3 pounds. Fruits are roundish to oblong; flesh is yellowish orange. Tolerates ringspot.

'Waimanalo'. Hawaiian type. Rounded, 1- to 2-pound fruit. Orange-yellow flesh. Bears fruit when only 3 ft. tall.

PAPERBARK MAPLE. See ACER griseum

PAPER BUSH. See EDGEWORTHIA chrysantha

PAPER MULBERRY. See BROUSSONETIA papyrifera

PAPHIOPEDILUM

TROPICAL LADY'S SLIPPER

Orchidaceae

TERRESTRIAL ORCHIDS

✿ INDOOR OR GREENHOUSE PLANTS, EXCEPT AS NOTED

◑ PARTIAL SHADE; BRIGHT INDIRECT LIGHT

● REGULAR WATER

Paphiopedilum insigne

Sometimes sold as *Cypripedium,* these terrestrial orchids are native to tropical regions of Asia. The group includes large-flowered hybrids grown commercially for cut flowers. The perky blooms often shine as if lacquered; they are usually carried one to a stem but may appear in clusters of two or more. Colors include white, yellow, green with white stripes, pure green, or a combination of background colors and markings in tan, mahogany, brown, maroon, green, and white.

Plants have graceful, arching leaves and no pseudobulbs. Green-leafed types usually flower in winter, mottled-leafed kinds in summer. Most of the plants obtained from orchid dealers are hybrids.

In general, mottled-leafed forms do best with temperatures of 60–65°F at night, 70–85°F during the day. Plain-leafed forms require temperatures of 50–55°F at night, 65–75°F during the day. For a good potting medium, combine equal parts ground bark and sandy loam. Don't plant in oversize pots, as these orchids thrive when crowded. The hardiest kinds can be grown in pots indoors in indirect, fairly bright light (they flourish in less light than most orchids require). Paphiopedilums never go dormant; keep them at their preferred temperatures in steadily moist soil year-round.

A noteworthy species is *P. insigne.* Among the hardiest of the green-leafed types, it withstands brief exposure to 28°F and can remain outdoors year-round in south Florida and South Texas; grows in heat zones 12–10. Lacquered-looking flowers on stiff, brown, hairy stems appear at any time from October to March. Sepals and petals are a combination of green and white, with brown spots and stripes; pouch is reddish brown.

PAPYRUS. See CYPERUS papyrus, C. prolifer

PARADISE PALM. See HOWEA forsteriana

PARAGUAY NIGHTSHADE. See SOLANUM rantonnetii

✕ PARDANCANDA norrisii

CANDY LILY

Iridaceae

PERENNIAL FROM RHIZOME

✿ US, MS, LS, CS, TS

☼ ◑ FULL SUN OR LIGHT SHADE

● REGULAR WATER

✕Pardancanda norrisii

Group of garden hybrids resulting from a cross between *Belamcanda* (blackberry lily) and *Pardanthopsis,* an iris relative. To 3 ft. tall, 2 ft. wide. Foliage fans are like those of iris. From midsummer to fall, plants produce six-segmented, 3- to 4-in.-wide flowers in a great range of colors, including yellow, blue, red, purple, pink, white, orange, and bicolors. Each bloom lasts only a day, but new flowers keep the show going. Good cut flowers. Plants are short lived, often blooming themselves to death, but they do self-sow. Grow from seed; in areas where the growing season is long, early sowing results in flowers the first year. Provide good drainage. Drought tolerant.

PARKINSONIA aculeata

JERUSALEM THORN, MEXICAN PALO VERDE

Fabaceae (Leguminosae)

DECIDUOUS TREE

✿ CS, TS ⊞ 12–9

☼ FULL SUN

◐◐● LITTLE TO REGULAR WATER

Parkinsonia aculeata

Native to southwestern U.S. and Mexico. Rapid growth at first, then slowing; eventually reaches 15–30 ft. high and wide. Yellow-green bark, spiny twigs, picturesque form. Sparse foliage; leaves 6–9 in. long, with many tiny leaflets that quickly fall in drought or cold. Numerous yellow flowers in loose, 3- to 7-in.-long clusters. Blooms over a long season in spring, intermittently throughout the rest of the year. Flowers are followed by 2- to 6-in.-long seedpods that mature in summer.

Good choice for water-conserving gardens, since it grows in dry soil; also performs well in moist soil as long as drainage is good. Tolerates alkaline soil. Requires minimal care once established. Stake young trees and train for high or low branching. As a shade tree, it filters sun rather than blocking it. Thorns and sparse foliage rule it out for tailored gardens, and litter drop can be a problem. Flowering branches are attractive in arrangements.

PARROTIA persica

PERSIAN PARROTIA

Hamamelidaceae

DECIDUOUS TREE OR SHRUB

✿ US, MS, LS ⊞ 8–1

☼ ◑ FULL SUN OR LIGHT SHADE

◐● MODERATE TO REGULAR WATER

Parrotia persica

Native to Iran. Slow growing to 15–35 ft. tall and wide, but more often seen as a 15-ft. shrub or small multitrunked tree. Young trees are fairly upright; older ones have a wide-spreading, rounded form. Oval, 3- to 6-in.-long leaves have wavy margins; upper half

P

is shallowly toothed. Choice, colorful tree, attractive in all seasons. Most dramatic display comes in autumn: leaves usually turn golden yellow, then orange or rosy pink, and finally scarlet. Smooth gray bark flakes off to reveal white patches and looks especially showy when on display in winter. Dense clusters of tiny flowers with red stamens and woolly brown bracts appear in late winter or early spring before leaves open; they give the plant an overall reddish haze. New foliage unfurls reddish purple, matures to a lustrous dark green. Prefers slightly acid soil but tolerates alkaline soil. Plant is pest resistant.

PARSLEY. See PETROSELINUM crispum

PARSNIP

Apiaceae (Umbelliferae)

BIENNIAL GROWN AS ANNUAL

US, MS ⫽ 7–1

☼ FULL SUN

◗ REGULAR WATER

Parsnip

If growing okra marks you as Southern, growing parsnips surely signals that you're from the North. Known botanically as *Pastinaca sativa,* this carrot relative from Siberia and Europe is among the most cold hardy of vegetables. It's grown for its delicately sweet, creamy white to yellowish root, most often used in stews. To develop long roots, parsnips need well-prepared, loose, deep soil (roots of some selections grow to 15 in. long). Sow seeds in late summer or fall, planting them ¼–½ in. deep in rows spaced 2 ft. apart. Thin seedlings to 3 in. apart. Leave plants in the ground over winter, as cold weather sweetens the roots. Harvest in spring; twist off the leaves to keep moisture in the roots. Parsnips left in the ground will continue to grow and become tough and woody. Interplanting them with onions or garlic is said to help keep pests away. Avoid planting parsnips near carrots, as the two will compete for nutrients.

PARTHENOCISSUS

Vitaceae

DECIDUOUS VINES

ZONES VARY BY SPECIES

☼ ◑ ● SUN OR SHADE

◗ MODERATE WATER

*Parthenocissus
quinquefolia*

Valued for handsome foliage—green in summer, reliably turning to superb orange or red shades in fall. Blossoms are insignificant; more noticeable are clusters of small blue-black fruits that form in late summer or fall and hang on into winter if not consumed by birds. Vines typically cling to walls by suction disks at ends of tendrils. All but the fairly restrained *P. henryana* are said to grow to 50–60 ft., but they are really limited only by the size of the support.

These vines thrive in organically enriched soil. Think twice before letting them attach to shingles, clapboard, or mortared brick or stone. At repainting time, the clinging tendrils are hard to remove, and the stems can creep under siding. They also hasten deterioration of wood and mortar. When vines reach desired size, prune each dormant season to restrain spread and—for those trained on buildings—to keep them away from doors, windows, and eaves. Cut out any wayward branches; likewise cut out any that have pulled away from their support, since disks will not reattach. Trim as needed during the growing season.

P. henryana. SILVERVEIN CREEPER. Zones US, MS, LS; 9–1. Native to China. Grows to 20 ft.; less aggressive growth than the other species listed here. Leaves have five leaflets to 2 in. long; they open purplish, then turn an attractive dark bronzy green with pronounced silver veining and purple undersides. Color is best in partial or full shade; in strong light, leaves fade

to plain green. Foliage turns rich red in autumn. This vine clings to walls, but it needs some support to get started. Also a good choice for spilling over walls or as a small-scale ground cover.

P. quinquefolia. VIRGINIA CREEPER. Zones US, MS, LS, CS; 9–1. Native to eastern U.S. Big, vigorous vine that clings or runs over ground, fences, trellises, arbors, trees. Looser growth than *P. tricuspidata;* has a see-through quality. Leaves divided into five 6-in. leaflets with saw-toothed edges. Foliage is bronze-tinted when new, matures to semiglossy dark green, turns crimson and burgundy in early fall. Good ground cover on slopes; can control erosion. 'Engelmannii' is a denser, smaller-leafed selection; 'Star Showers' has white-splashed leaves that in fall first take on pink tones, then turn red.

P. tricuspidata. BOSTON IVY. Zones US, MS, LS; 8–1. Native to China, Japan. Semievergreen in mild-winter areas. This species is even more vigorous than *P. quinquefolia.* Foliage color is similar to that of *P. quinquefolia* in spring and summer but covers a broader spectrum in fall, varying from orange to wine red. Leaves are glossy, to 8 in. wide, variable in shape; usually three lobed or divided into three leaflets. Clings tightly, grows fast to make a dense, uniform wall cover. This is the "ivy" of the Ivy League; covers brick or stone in areas where English ivy (*Hedera helix*) freezes. Grows best on walls with northern or eastern exposure. 'Green Showers' has large (10-in.) leaves that turn burgundy in fall. 'Lowii' and 'Veitchii' produce half-size leaves on less rampant vines.

*Parthenocissus
tricuspidata*

PARTRIDGEBERRY. See MITCHELLA repens

PARTRIDGE-BREAST ALOE. See ALOE variegata

PASPALUM

Poaceae (Gramineae)

PERENNIAL GRASSES

CS, TS ⫽ 12–9, EXCEPT AS NOTED

☼ FULL SUN

◔ ● MODERATE TO REGULAR WATER

*Paspalum
notatum*

Large group of grasses that includes several species used for pasture or hay. Of the three described here, two are lawn grasses, while the third is an ornamental. None needs much fertilizer.

P. notatum. BAHIA GRASS. From Brazil. Tough, rather coarse grass used for lawns in Florida. Green blades turn brown with the first frost. Tolerates drought and takes heavy wear. Tall seed heads are produced continuously from May through November, so frequent mowing is needed to keep lawn looking tidy. Mow at 3–4 in. Establish from seed or sod. Prefers acid soil; does not tolerate shade or salt spray.

P. quadrifolium. CROWN GRASS. Evergreen ornamental grass native to Uruguay, now used extensively in Florida. Dark blue-green leaves form a soft mound 3–4 ft. tall and wide. Attractive when used in masses and sweeps. Adapts to most soils.

P. vaginatum. SEASHORE PASPALUM. Zones LS, CS, TS; 12–7. Native to sandy soils along the coast from North Carolina to Texas. Finer textured and more cold hardy than *P. notatum.* Spreads by stolons and rhizomes. Establish from sod or sprigs. Tolerates salt spray better than any other lawn grass and is used for lawns and fairways along the coast. Withstands drought once established, but be sure to water sod or sprigs thoroughly for 3 weeks after planting, until roots are well settled. 'Sea Isle 2000', released by the University of Georgia, is similar in texture to hybrid Bermuda grass (*Cynodon dactylon),* but it is more cold tolerant—it doesn't go dormant and turn brown until temperatures reach 28°F. Mow at 1–2 in.

PASSIFLORA

PASSION VINE

Passifloraceae

EVERGREEN, SEMIEVERGREEN, DECIDUOUS VINES

⚘ ZONES VARY BY SPECIES

☼ ◐ FULL SUN OR PARTIAL SHADE

💧 💧 MODERATE TO REGULAR WATER

*Passiflora
×alatocaerulea*

You'd be hard pressed to find flowers more exotically beautiful than those of a passion vine. To many, the flower parts symbolize the passion of Christ—the circle of whiskerlike filaments represents the crown of thorns; the five stamens, the five wounds; the five petals and five sepals, the ten steadfast apostles.

With the exception of *P. incarnata*, all the passion vines listed here are native to South America. All have rich green leaves, will tolerate most well-drained soils, and can climb by tendrils to 20–30 ft. in a rather short time. Flowers are often fragrant and usually appear during warm weather. Many species produce edible fruit; for the species cultivated specifically for their fruit, see Passion Fruit.

Train passion vines on trellises, arbors, or walls. They tend to be rampant, so be prepared to prune and thin unwanted growth. Chemicals in the leaves forestall attack by most insects—but *Passiflora* foliage attracts and is the favorite food for caterpillars of several butterflies, including the Julia longwing, zebra longwing, and Gulf fritillary. Most passion vines are quite tender to cold and suitable for outdoor culture only in the Coastal and Tropical South. You can grow them as houseplants, but this requires a very sunny window, a sizable support, and frequent misting. Feed indoor plants with a general-purpose liquid houseplant fertilizer weekly from spring through fall.

P. ×alatocaerulea. Evergreen or semievergreen. Zones TS; 12–7. Among the best-known, most widely planted passion vines—and probably the least subject to caterpillar damage. Three-lobed leaves are 3 in. long; fragrant pink-and-white flowers are 4 in. wide, with deep blue or purple crowns. No fruit. Excellent for indoors.

P. 'Amethyst' ('Lavender Lady'). Evergreen. Zones TS; 12–7. Profuse show of 4-in.-wide lavender flowers with deep violet crowns. No fragrance; no fruit.

P. caerulea. BLUE PASSION FLOWER. Evergreen or semievergreen. Zones LS, CS, TS; 12–6; dies to the ground in the Lower South, but comes back if roots are mulched in late fall. Leaves to 4 in. long, with three to nine lobes; flowers to 4 in. wide, with white sepals and petals and a blue-and-white crown. Egg-shaped, bright orange, 2½-in. fruits are edible but not very tasty. 'Constance Elliott' has pure white blooms.

P. coccinea. RED PASSION FLOWER. Evergreen or semievergreen. Zones CS, TS; 12–10. Bright scarlet, 3- to 5-in.-wide flowers with white, purple, and yellow crowns. Oblong leaves to 5 in. long and 2½ in. wide. Mottled orange or yellow, 2-in.-long fruits are quite tasty. Not a good houseplant.

P. 'Coral Glow'. Evergreen. Zones CS, TS; 12–6. Pendent coral pink flowers up to 4 in. across have very short crowns. Broad, three-lobed, lustrous leaves to 6 in. wide. Unlike most passion vines, blooms most heavily in winter. No fruit.

P. 'Elizabeth'. Evergreen. Zones CS, TS; 12–6. Spectacular flowers up to 5 in. across, in a combination of mauve and deep purple. Crown contains dozens of long, crinkled, purple-and-white filaments. Sweet, edible purple fruit.

P. incarnata. MAYPOP. Deciduous. Zones US, MS, LS, CS, TS; 12–10. Native to southeastern U.S. This old Southern favorite is the hardiest of the passion vines, surviving temperatures as low as −10°F. Dies to the ground in winter in most areas. Three-lobed leaves are 4–6 in. wide. Blooms profusely, bearing fragrant, 3-in. flowers in pale lavender with showy crowns banded in purple and pink. Egg-shaped, yellow, 2-in. fruits are edible, though not exactly luscious. Spreads vigorously from seeds and

underground roots and can become an attractive pest. 'Alba' has pure white flowers.

P. 'Incense'. Deciduous. Zones US, MS, LS, CS, TS; 12–6. Dies back to ground in cold weather but will survive −8°F. Fragrant flowers are 5 in. wide, royal purple, with wavy purple crowns. Egg-shaped, 2-in., olive green to yellow-green fruit has fragrant, tasty pulp.

P. 'Jeanette'. Evergreen. Zones TS; 12–6. Very free flowering. Large mauve-and-white blossoms with deep purple, curly crowns. No fruit.

P. 'Pura Vida'. Evergreen. Zones TS; 12–7. Very free flowering. Fragrant, 4-in.-wide lavender blue flowers with deep blue crowns. No fruit. Good for indoors.

P. vitifolia. GRAPE LEAF PASSION FLOWER. Evergreen. Zones TS; 12–10. Dazzling bright red flowers to 3 in. wide. Deep green, three-lobed leaves resemble those of grapevines. Very free flowering; widely considered the best red passion flower. A good choice for beginners. Good for indoors.

PASSION FRUIT

Passifloraceae

EVERGREEN OR SEMIEVERGREEN VINE

⚘ TS ⥊ 12–10

☼ FULL SUN

💧 REGULAR WATER

Passion Fruit

Passion fruit is prized for the exotic, citruslike flavor of its orange pulp. Use the fruit for juice; or cut it in half and eat it from the skin, seeds and all, with a spoon. Most of the commercially produced passion fruit in the U.S. comes from California and Hawaii, but three types are grown in Florida: purple passion fruit (*Passiflora edulis*), yellow passion fruit (*P. edulis flavicarpa*), and giant granadilla (*P. quadrangularis*). Purple passion fruit is hardy as far north as Tampa; the others are restricted to south Florida.

Purple passion fruit has light yellow-green, tooth-edged leaves with three lobes. White, 2- to 3-in. flowers with white-and-purple crowns bloom in warm weather; rounded or egg-shaped, dark purple fruit to 2 in. long follows in spring and early summer. Plant is self-pollinating. Due to its susceptibility to nematodes, purple passion fruit grown in south Florida must be grafted onto rootstocks of yellow passion fruit or other resistant species.

Yellow passion fruit has leaves and flowers similar to those of purple passion fruit, but its fruits are deep yellow and slightly longer. Giant granadilla has four-sided stems set with oval leaves to 10 in. long, 6 in. wide. From midsummer to fall, bears fragrant, 5-in., pink to brick red flowers with prominent bluish purple crowns banded with pink, purple, and white. Oblong golden fruits are ready for harvest 2 to 3 months later; each one may weigh a pound or more. Both yellow passion fruit and giant granadilla need cross-pollination from another passion vine.

Grow passion fruit in well-drained soil, in a spot protected from wind. All types are easy to start from seed sown in flats or pots (be sure seed is fresh). Germination takes 10 to 20 days. From early spring until fall, feed lightly at 4- to 6-week intervals with a balanced low-nitrogen fertilizer (such as 6-6-6 or 8-8-8) that contains micronutrients. Train plants on a trellis, fence, or wall. Harvest purple and yellow passion fruits when fruit turns color and drops to the ground; giant granadilla is ready to pick when it turns deep golden. Prune vines in late winter when they're not actively growing, removing dead and weak wood. Withhold water during winter. Plants are naturally short lived, generally lasting only 3 to 5 years.

PASSION VINE. See PASSIFLORA

FOR GROWING SYMBOL EXPLANATIONS
PLEASE SEE PAGE 145

P

PATRINIA

Valerianaceae

PERENNIALS

US, MS, LS H 8–4

EXPOSURE NEEDS VARY BY SPECIES

REGULAR WATER

Patrinia scabiosifolia

Native to eastern Asia, these easy-to-grow, long-blooming perennials have yet to be discovered by many gardeners. The plants form mounds of deeply cut or lobed leaves that are typically medium green, up to 6 in. long. Nearly leafless blossom stalks rise from the foliage from mid- to late summer; these carry flat-topped clusters of tiny yellow or white flowers that attract butterflies and make a nice addition to both fresh and dried bouquets. Excellent in perennial borders. All appreciate rich, well-drained soil. Fans of daylilies (*Hemerocallis*) should avoid patrinias, however, as they are alternate hosts of daylily rust.

P. gibbosa. GREATER PATRINIA. Compact, clump-forming plant to 1–1½ ft. tall and about 1 ft. wide, with coarsely toothed leaves and loose clusters of tiny yellow flowers. Full sun or partial shade.

P. scabiosifolia. PATRINIA, GOLDEN LACE. The showiest and most popular species. Grows 5–6 ft. tall and 2 ft. wide; may require staking. Finely divided leaves. Sparsely foliaged stalks and open clusters of lemon yellow flowers give plant a see-through quality that makes it useful for either the front or back of the border. Looks nice in combination with asters, ironweed (*Vernonia*), Joe-pye weed (*Eupatorium purpureum*), and 'Indigo Spires' salvia. 'Nagoya' grows only 2–3 ft. tall. Full sun.

P. triloba. Grows 1–1½ ft. tall and spreads slowly to make a small-scale ground cover. Glossy deep green leaves are 2–4 in. long and deeply divided into three to five lobes. Bears fragrant yellow flowers. Grows best in light shade.

P. villosa. WHITE PATRINIA. To 2–3 ft. tall, 2 ft. wide, with leaves that may or may not be divided. Showers of white blossoms over a long period. Spreads steadily but is not invasive. Full sun.

PAULOWNIA tomentosa

EMPRESS TREE

Bignoniaceae

DECIDUOUS TREE

US, MS, LS H 8–5

FULL SUN OR PARTIAL SHADE

MODERATE TO REGULAR WATER

Paulownia tomentosa

Native to China. Somewhat similar to catalpa in growth habit and leaves. Fast growth to 40–50 ft., with nearly equal spread. Can grow 8–10 ft. a year in youth. Often touted as "miracle shade tree" in advertising supplements. Heavy trunk and heavy, nearly horizontal branches. Foliage gives tropical effect: light green, roughly heart-shaped leaves are 5–12 in. long, 4–7 in. wide. No significant fall color. Brown flower buds the size of small olives form in fall and persist through winter; they open before leaf-out in early spring, unfurling into 6- to 12-in.-long clusters of trumpet-shaped, 2-in.-long, fragrant flowers of lilac blue with darker spotting and yellow stripes on inside. Flowers are followed by 1½- to 2-in. seed capsules shaped like tops; these remain on tree with flower buds. Does not bloom well where winters are very cold (buds freeze) or very mild (buds may drop off).

Performs best in deep, moist, well-drained soil, though it will grow in many soils—and even in cracks in the pavement and in mine spoil. Tolerates air pollution. Protect from strong winds. Plant where falling flowers and leaves are not objectionable. Not a tree to garden under because of dense shade, surface roots. If tree is cut back annually or every other year,

it will grow as billowy foliage mass with giant-size leaves up to 2 ft. long; however, such pruning will reduce or eliminate flower production. The wood is lightweight but strong, highly prized in Japan for making bowls, pots, spoons, furniture, and sandals. A mature tree commands a high market price—and, unfortunately, this has led to "tree rustling" in the South. A happy tree owner retires at night, only to discover a stump the next morning.

PAUROTIS wrightii. See ACOELORRHAPHE wrightii

PAVONIA

Malvaceae

SHRUBS

LS, CS, TS H 12–8, EXCEPT AS NOTED

FULL SUN OR PARTIAL SHADE

LITTLE WATER, EXCEPT AS NOTED

Pavonia lasiopetala

Native to North and South America, this group includes both hardy and tender shrubs. All are grown chiefly for their attractive, mallow-like flowers in shades of pink and purple.

P. cymbalaria. ARGENTINE MALLOW. Low, spreading shrub to about 8 in. tall, 2½–3 ft. wide. Gray-green leaves to 1 in. long and ¾ in. wide; pink, dark-centered, 2½-in. flowers over a long period in summer.

P. hastata. SPEARLEAF PAVONIA. Gangly, hardy shrub to 3–5 ft. tall and 2–3 ft. wide. Narrow evergreen leaves; pink, dark-centered flowers up to 3–4 in. across from spring to fall. Self-seeds readily and can become a pest. Responds well to shearing.

P. lasiopetala. ROCK ROSE. Most popular species. Grows in the dry, rugged limestone soils of Texas; nearly evergreen except in coldest parts of range, where it dies back to the roots each winter. Bears many showy, 2-in.-wide rose pink flowers from June to first frost. Light green leaves are slightly lobed, coarsely toothed, to 1½ in. long and wide. The plant naturally grows as a spindly, open-structured bush to 5 ft. tall and almost as wide, but it can be cut back in winter for a neater appearance. Useful for dry, shady areas. Tends to be short lived but self-seeds freely; let a few seedlings survive each year to replace the original plant.

P. multiflora (P. ×gledhillii, Triploclamys multiflora). Zones TS; 12–10. Tender evergreen shrub grows to 6 ft. tall and 3 ft. wide. Deep green, lobed leaves to 10 in. long. Spidery bright red bracts enclose tubular purple flowers (they never fully open) with protruding blue stamens. Needs regular water.

PAWPAW

Annonaceae

DECIDUOUS TREE

US, MS, LS, CS H 10–6

FULL SUN OR PARTIAL SHADE

REGULAR WATER

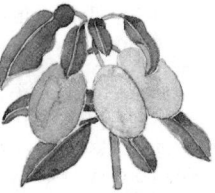

Pawpaw

Native to eastern North America, the pawpaw (*Asimina triloba*), sometimes called Indian banana, is a hardy member of a family of tropical fruits that includes cherimoya (*Annona cherimola*). The tree grows to 30 ft.; it generally spreads as wide as tall when grown alone, but you'll often see thickets of narrow, erect plants that arise from suckering. Large, tropical-looking medium green leaves are oval, somewhat drooping, 4–10 in. long; they turn bright yellow in fall. Purplish or brownish (sometimes green) flowers with three prominent petals are large but not showy. Fruits are roughly oval, 3–5 in. long, yellowish green ripening to brown. Soft, custardlike flesh has a flavor between that of banana and mango and contains numerous large brown seeds.

Pawpaw is a pest-resistant plant and needs no spraying. It fruits well in sun or shade but grows better if given light shade in its early years. The only major drawback is the perishability of the fruit, which won't keep for more than a week unless frozen. If possible, purchase grafted plants of named selections such as 'Mango', 'Mitchell', 'Overleese', 'Prolific', 'Rebecca's Gold', 'Sunflower', 'Taylor', and 'Wilson'. Plant two or more selections for cross-pollination.

Dwarf pawpaw (*A. parviflora*) resembles *A. triloba* but is smaller in all respects. It grows 6–8 ft. tall and 4–6 ft. wide, bearing small brownish purple to greenish purple flowers in early spring. Fruits are ½–2 in. long. Often found in dry woods. Better used for naturalizing than for fruit.

PAXISTIMA canbyi (Pachistima canbyi)

Celastraceae

EVERGREEN SHRUB

US, MS H 7–1

FULL SUN OR PARTIAL SHADE

REGULAR WATER

Paxistima canbyi

Native to mountains of Virginia and West Virginia. Slowly forms a mat 9–12 in. tall and 3–5 ft. wide. Leathery leaves, ¼–1 in. long, ¼ in. wide, are shiny dark green, turning bronzy in fall and winter. Good as edging and ground cover. Best in well-drained soil. Tolerates alkaline soil.

PEA

Fabaceae (Leguminosae)

COOL-SEASON ANNUAL

US, MS, LS, CS, TS H 7–1

FULL SUN

REGULAR WATER

Pea

In the South, you can't simply say "peas" and be done with it. You might be talking about black-eyed peas, cowpeas, purple hulls, or crowder peas—all of which are lumped into the category of Southern peas (see Southern Pea). Or you might mean garden peas, *Pisum sativum*, the subject of the following discussion.

Though native to southern Europe, garden peas are often called English peas to distinguish them from Southern peas. They come in three basic types: shelling, snow, and snap peas. *Shelling peas* form large, sweet peas inside tough pods that are not good for eating. Recommended selections include 'Mr. Big' (60 days from sowing to harvest), 'Maestro' (60 days), and 'Green Arrow' (70 days). *Snow peas,* popular in Asian cooking, feature edible pods as well as peas. 'Oregon Giant' (60 days) is a good bush type. 'Dwarf White Sugar' (50 days) grows only 2½ ft. tall. 'Snow Wind' (70 days) has few leaves on its upper stems, putting most of its energy into producing peas. *Snap peas* combine the best qualities of shelling and snow peas. You can eat the immature pods; eat pods whole with peas inside, as you would string beans (the most popular way); or wait for the peas to mature and harvest them for shelling. Try 'Super Sugar Snap' (64 days), 'Sugar Sprint' (62 days), and the semileafless 'Sugar Lace' (68 days).

All peas are easy to grow when conditions are right. They need coolness and moisture at planting time. In the Upper South, plant shelling and snow peas as soon as the ground can be worked in spring. Snap peas like slightly warmer soil, so plant them 2 weeks later. In the Middle and Lower South, plant all types in late summer for a fall crop (snap peas are especially good for this, as they take some heat) and late winter for a spring crop. In the Coastal and Tropical South, plant around late December. Successive plantings made several days apart will extend the harvest.

Grow peas in slightly acid to slightly alkaline soil that retains moisture but drains well. If you have the space and don't mind the bother, grow tall vining peas on trellises, strings, or chicken wire; they climb by tendrils to 6 ft. or more and bear heavily. Bush types are better for small gardens; they

require no support, though they can be grown on short trellises for easy picking. Soak seeds in water overnight before planting. Sow 2 in. deep in sandy soil, ½–1 in. deep in heavy soil. Leave 2 ft. between rows for bush types, 5 ft. for tall vines. Water thoroughly after planting; then don't water again until seedlings sprout. Thin seedlings to 2–4 in. apart. Plants need little fertilizer, but if soil is very sandy, give one application of a complete fertilizer (such as 5-10-5) about 6 weeks after planting. Don't wet the foliage when watering; wet leaves encourage mildew. Provide support for tall vining types, such as 'Super Sugar Snap', as soon as the tendrils form. Compact vining selections, such as 'Snow Wind' and 'Sugar Lace', are self-supporting.

When peas reach harvesting size, pick all the pods that are ready; if seeds are allowed to ripen, the plants will stop producing. Harvest shelling peas when the pods swell to an almost cylindrical shape but before they lose their bright green color. Harvest snow and snap peas when the pods are 2–3 in. long, before the seeds begin to swell (unless you are growing your snap peas for the peas). Vines are brittle; steady them with one hand while picking with the other. Refrigerate peas without washing them; then rinse and use them as soon as possible.

PEACH and NECTARINE

Rosaceae

DECIDUOUS FRUIT TREES

ZONES VARY BY SELECTION

FULL SUN

REGULAR WATER DURING FRUIT DEVELOPMENT

SEE CHART NEXT PAGE

Peach

Which came first—the peach or the nectarine? At first glance, the nectarine (*Prunus persica nucipersica*) looks like a peach (*P. persica*) that has lost its fuzz. Recent evidence suggests, however, that the nectarine evolved first. No matter—peaches and nectarines, while native to Asia, do just fine throughout the South. In most areas, crops ripen between May and September, depending on the selection. A standard-size fruiting peach or nectarine grows rapidly to 15 ft. high and wide, though properly pruned trees are usually kept to a height of 10–12 ft. They start bearing at 3 to 4 years old and reach peak production at 6 to 8 years of age. Genetic dwarf trees, most of which grow to 5–6 ft. tall and produce medium-size fruit, are good for containers and small gardens. With a few exceptions (see comments in chart), most peaches and nectarines are self-pollinating. For ornamental peaches grown for their flowers, see *Prunus*.

If you're considering planting a peach or nectarine, keep several things in mind. First, these are not low-maintenance plants. They require good drainage, heavier pruning than other fruit trees, and regular spraying if you expect to get fruit. Second, it is essential to consider the chill hours a particular selection needs in order to bloom and set fruit (see care box). Once a tree's chill requirement has been satisfied, the onset of mild weather will bring it into bloom within 3 weeks. A subsequent sudden freeze may doom the crop. Therefore, growers in the Upper, Middle, and Lower South are safer planting selections that require at least 750 chill hours and bloom later in spring. On the other hand, growers in Florida and along the Gulf and South Atlantic Coasts, where winters are mild, need to plant low-chill selections that require less than 650 hours of winter chill. Third, remember that cold air is heavier than warm air, so it collects in low spots. Air temperatures of 28°F and lower can kill peach and nectarine flowers. Plant these trees on slopes and hilltops to avoid frost pockets. A mere 10 ft. of elevation can mean the difference between saving and losing a crop.

Although you can buy peach and nectarine trees in containers, most people purchase and plant them as dormant bare-root plants in late winter. Soak the roots in water for 24 hours before planting.

▶ page 455

P

PEACH AND NECTARINE

NAME	ZONES	FRUIT	COMMENTS
PEACHES			
'Belle of Georgia'	US, MS, LS; 8–1	Large. Freestone. Skin is creamy white blushed red; flesh is white. Fine flavor. Midseason	Vigorous tree; heavy bearer. Old favorite. Originated in Georgia around 1810. Bruises easily. Needs 850 hours of winter chill. Not a good keeper
'Bonanza II'	CS; 9–1	Large. Freestone. Attractive red-and-yellow skin; deep yellow to orange flesh. Good flavor. Midseason	Genetic dwarf. Showy flowers. Improvement on 'Bonanza', the original dwarf selection for home gardens. Needs 400 chill hours
'Carolina Belle'	US, MS, LS; 8–1	Large. Freestone. White skin blushed red. Rich flavor. Midseason	Thought to be an improved form of 'Belle of Georgia' but bears earlier in season. Needs 750 hours of winter chill
'Contender'	US, MS, LS; 8–1	Large. Freestone with good-quality yellow flesh. Resists browning. Blooms late, so fruit often survives late freezes. Ripens about 9 days before 'Elberta'	Consistent producer. Needs 1,050 hours of winter chill. Introduced by North Carolina State University
'Cresthaven'	US, MS, LS; 8–1	Medium to large. Freestone. Golden skin with red blush; yellow flesh. High-quality, firm fruit. Midseason to late	Blooms late. Fruit holds well on tree. Good fresh, frozen, or canned. Needs 850 hours of winter chill
'Dixiland'	US, MS, LS; 8–1	Large. Freestone. Yellow skin blushed red; little fuzz. Firm yellow flesh. Good quality. Late midseason	From Georgia. Vigorous, productive. Showy flowers. Needs 750 hours of winter chill
'Dixired'	US, MS, LS; 8–1	Yellow-fleshed clingstone. Round, deep red fruit, sweet and juicy. Early, 41 days before 'Elberta'. Thin fruit	Good quality. Requires 1,000 hours of winter chill. Bears young. Self-fertile. Tends to over-bear; thin out fruit. Fruit holds well on the tree
'Elberta'	US, MS, LS (northern half); 8–1	Medium to large. Freestone. Yellow skin blushed red; yellow flesh. Good quality. Midseason	From Georgia. The classic peach by which all others are measured. Needs 850 hours of winter chill
'Flordaglo'	CS, TS; 10–1	Medium to large. Semifreestone. Yellow skin; white flesh. Fine flavor	Low chill requirement (only 225 hours)
'Flordaking'	CS; 9–1	Medium to large. Semifreestone. Firm yellow fruit. Early	Very vigorous. Good fruit if thinned well. Low chill requirement (400 hours)
'Flordaprince'	TS; 10–1	Small. Semifreestone. Yellow skin speckled with red. Good flavor. Early	Good peach for central Florida. Needs only 150 hours of winter chill. Susceptible to bacterial spot
'Garnet Beauty'	US, MS, LS; 8–1	Medium to large. Semifreestone. Red-blushed yellow skin; yellow flesh streaked with red. Early	Earlier-ripening mutation of 'Redhaven', originating in Canada. Vigorous tree, heavy bearer. Needs 850 hours of winter chill

'Belle of Georgia' Peach

'Elberta' Peach

'Flordaprince' Peach

'Indian Cling' Peach

'July Elberta' Peach

PEACH AND NECTARINE

NAME	ZONES	FRUIT	COMMENTS
'Halehaven'	US, MS, LS; 8–1	Medium to large. Freestone. Highly colored yellow fruit is firm, very sweet. Midseason	Flower and leaf buds are winter hardy. Fruit is good fresh or canned. Needs 900 chill hours
'Harvester'	US, MS, LS; 8–1	Medium-size. Freestone. Yellow fruit of excellent quality. Early	Good producer, but needs 4 or 5 years to produce heavy crops. Needs 750 chill hours
'Indian Cling'	US, MS, LS; 8–1	Large. Clingstone. Dark crimson skin and flesh. Midseason	Old-fashioned, disease-resistant peach. Heavy, dependable bearer. Needs 800 chill hours
'J. H. Hale'	US, MS, LS; 8–1	Very large. Freestone. Yellow skin overlaid with deep red; little fuzz. Yellow flesh. High quality; fine keeper. Midseason	Use any other peach except 'Indian Cling' as pollenizer. Needs 800 hours of winter chill
'July Elberta'	US, MS, LS; 8–1	Medium to large. Freestone. Yellow skin blushed red; yellow flesh. High quality. Early, 3 weeks before 'Elberta'	Prolific bearer. Needs 500 chill hours
'La Feliciana'	LS, CS; 9–1	Medium-size. Freestone. Yellow fruit of high quality. Early midseason	Originated in Louisiana. Needs only 550 hours of winter chill. Disease resistant
'Loring'	US, MS, LS; 8–1	Large. Freestone. Attractive yellow skin imbued with red; little fuzz. Good-quality fruit with great flavor, moderately juicy yellow flesh. Midseason	Vigorous. Showy flowers appear early; susceptible to frost. Needs 750 hours of winter chill
'Madison'	US, MS, LS; 8–1	Medium-size. Freestone. Golden yellow skin blushed bright red. Firm golden flesh. Very good flavor. Midseason	Seedling of 'Redhaven' from Virginia. Good frost tolerance during bloom period. Heavy bearer. Needs 850 chill hours
'Ranger'	US, MS, LS; 8–1	Medium to large. Freestone. Red-blushed fruit with firm, yellow, good-tasting flesh. Ripens 24 days before 'Elberta'	Vigorous, productive tree; requires 900 hours of winter chill. Good for areas with late spring frosts. Can or freeze the fruit
'Redhaven'	US, MS, LS; 8–1	Medium-size. Semifreestone. Yellow skin blushed bright red. Firm yellow flesh. Good flavor. Early	Among best of early peaches. Productive. Thin out fruit. Colors up early, so test for ripeness. Good fresh; freezes well. Needs 950 hours of winter chill
'Redskin'	US, MS, LS; 8–1	Large. Freestone. Yellow skin with good red coloring; yellow flesh. High quality. Midseason	'Elberta' seedling from Maryland. Showy flowers. Fruit is good for eating fresh, canning, or freezing. Needs 750 chill hours
'Reliance'	US, MS; 8–1	Medium to large. Freestone. Yellow skin blushed dull medium red; yellow flesh can be fairly soft. Fair flavor. Midseason	Very hardy; has produced crops after temperatures of −25°F. Showy flowers. Needs heavy thinning. Needs 950 hours of winter chill
'Rio Grande'	CS; 9–1	Medium to large. Freestone. Red-blushed yellow skin. Firm yellow flesh with mild flavor. Early	Low-chill selection from Florida. Productive. Showy flowers. Fruit has irregular surface and varies in size. Needs 450 chill hours

P

'Redhaven' Peach

'Rio Oso Gem' Peach

Genetic Dwarf Peach Tree

'Sunglo' Nectarine

'Fantasia' Nectarine

PEACH AND NECTARINE

NAME	ZONES	FRUIT	COMMENTS
'Rio Oso Gem'	US, MS, LS; 8–1	Large. Freestone. Red-blushed yellow skin; firm yellow flesh with excellent flavor. Late midseason	Small tree. Large, showy blossoms. Needs 850 chill hours. Fruit freezes well
'Southern Rose'	CS; 9–1	Medium-size. Freestone. Yellow skin with red blush; yellow flesh. Fair flavor. Midseason	Genetic dwarf. Requires only 300 hours of winter chill. 'Southern Flame' and 'Southern Sweet' are two other selections available in the series
'Springold'	US, MS, LS; 8–1	Small. Clingstone. Yellow skin and flesh. Early	Needs 850 hours of winter chill
'Surecrop'	US, MS; 8–1	Medium-size. Semifreestone. Yellow flesh. Ripens 6 weeks before 'Elberta'. Late bloomer; fruit often survives spring freezes	Cold hardy. Needs 1,000 hours of winter chill
'Texstar'	CS; 9–1	Semifreestone. Red-blushed yellow skin; yellow flesh. Early	Needs 500 hours of winter chill
'Tropic Beauty'	TS; 10–1	Large. Semiclingstone. Round, firm fruit with yellow flesh. Midseason	Needs only 150 hours of winter chill
'Tropic Snow'	TS; 10–1	Medium-size. Freestone. Red skin; white flesh. Superb flavor. Early	Best low-chill white peach; needs only 200 chill hours
'Tropic Sweet'	CS, TS; 9–1	Large. Semifreestone. Red-blushed skin. Very sweet and tasty. Midseason	Excellent choice for central Florida. Needs only 175 hours of winter chill
NECTARINES			
'Fantasia'	CS; 8–1	Large. Freestone. Bright yellow-and-red skin. Firm yellow flesh. Midseason	Vigorous. Showy flowers. Needs 650 hours of winter chill
'Flavortop'	US, MS, LS; 8–1	Large. Freestone. Yellow skin heavily blushed red; yellow flesh. Good flavor. Midseason	Vigorous, productive. Showy flowers. Needs 850 hours of winter chill
'Karla Rose'	LS, CS; 8–1	Medium-size. Freestone. Red skin; white flesh. Ripens 5 weeks before 'Elberta'	Needs 750 hours of winter chill. Good choice for cooler parts of the Gulf Coast region and for areas farther north
'Mayfire'	CS; 9–1	Small to medium. Clingstone. Firm, flavorful yellow flesh. Ripens 9 weeks before 'Elberta'	Very productive. Requires 650 chill hours
'Redgold'	US, MS, LS; 8–1	Large. Freestone. Deep red skin; golden yellow flesh. Good flavor. Midseason	Vigorous, productive. Excellent flavor. Has fair disease resistance. Requires 850 hours of winter chill
'Rose Princess'	US, MS, LS; 8–1	Medium-size. Freestone. Attractive round to elongated fruit. Ivory skin flushed rose; white, slightly tart flesh of good quality. Ripens 3 weeks before 'Elberta'	Requires 850 hours of winter chill. Productive tree. Introduced by USDA
'Southern Belle'	MS, LS, CS; 9–1	Large. Freestone. Yellow skin with red blush; yellow flesh. Good flavor. Early	Genetic dwarf. Needs only 300 chill hours
'Sunglo'	US, MS, LS; 8–1	Large. Semiclingstone. Red-and-yellow skin; firm, sweet deep yellow flesh of high quality. Ripens 24 days before 'Elberta'	Developed in California. Requires 850 hours of winter chill. Very sweet
'Sunmist'	CS; 9–1	Medium. Semifreestone. Red-blushed white skin; white flesh with excellent flavor. Early	Needs 350 hours of winter chill. Resists bacterial leaf spot
'Sunraycer'	CS, TS; 10–1	Large. Semifreestone. Beautiful red-and-yellow fruit with good flavor. Midseason	Needs only 250 hours of winter chill. Good choice for central Florida

P

If you buy a bare-root tree that is an unbranched "whip," cut it back to 24–28 in. high. New branches will form below the cut. Select three of these branches to become scaffold limbs, making sure they are evenly spaced and between 18 and 32 in. above the ground. Remove all other branches. During the first winter, cut back these scaffold branches by a third, to an outward-facing lateral branch or bud; this encourages a spreading growth habit. Repeat this procedure during the second and third winters. Thereafter, prune in winter to remove overcrowded branches, suckers from the base, and watersprouts (unbranched shoots that grow straight up from main branches). Prune to open up the center of the tree so that sunlight can reach all of the leaves. Genetic dwarfs need much less pruning than standard trees.

Peaches and nectarines are plagued by a host of diseases and insects. If you're philosophically opposed to spraying, you may want to reconsider growing them. Among the most serious ailments these trees suffer are peach leaf curl, brown rot, and peach scab. Peach leaf curl causes emerging leaves to thicken, pucker, and fall by midsummer. Brown rot causes fruit to rot on the tree. Peach scab covers the fruit with small, circular, greenish to black spots. To control these diseases, practice good sanitation, getting rid of diseased parts to avoid reinfection the next year. Also give two dormant season sprayings of chlorothalonil (Daconil), fixed copper, or lime sulfur; spray once after autumn leaf drop, then again in spring just before leaf-out.

Peach tree borer is the most serious insect pest, causing defoliation, dieback, and even death. It tends to attack trees stressed by wounds or poor growing conditions. Jellylike material exuding from holes near the base of the trunk is the first indication of the insect's presence. To control borers, insert a wire into the holes to kill the wormlike larvae or spray the trunk with an appropriate pesticide (consult your Cooperative Extension Office for advice). Nematodes are another problem for peaches and nectarines. In Florida, trees must be budded onto nematode-resistant rootstocks such as 'Flordaguard', 'Nemaguard', and 'Okinawa'. For more detailed information on pest control, see the *Southern Living Garden Problem Solver.*

The peach and nectarine selections listed in the chart are the most widely available and recommended. For information on those likely to perform best in your area, check with your Cooperative Extension Office or a local nursery.

WHAT PEACHES AND NECTARINES NEED

WINTER CHILL: Most selections need 600 to 900 hours of winter chill (45°F or lower). Low-chill selections are the best bet for mild-winter regions.

PRUNING: They need more pruning than other fruit trees, since they produce fruit on 1-year-old branches. Severe annual pruning (see text) not only renews fruiting wood—it encourages fruiting throughout the tree rather than at the ends of sagging branches that can easily break.

FRUIT THINNING: Even with good pruning, peaches and nectarines form too much fruit. When fruits are 1 in. wide, thin them out so remaining fruits are at least 6 in. apart.

DISEASE CONTROL: Where peach leaf curl, peach scab, and brown rot of stone fruit are troublesome, apply dormant sprays annually (see text).

'J. H. Hale' Peach

PEACOCK GINGER. See KAEMPFERIA

PEANUT

Fabaceae (Leguminosae)

ANNUAL

⚲ US, MS, LS, CS, TS ⊬ 12–6

☀ FULL SUN

💧 REGULAR WATER

Peanut

Known botanically as *Arachis hypogaea,* the peanut originated in South America and bears best where summers are long and warm. It is tender to frost but worth growing even in the Upper South. Plants resemble bush sweet peas *(Lathyrus)* 10–20 in. tall. After the bright yellow flowers fade, a "peg" (shootlike structure) develops at each flower's base and grows down into soil; peanuts develop underground. For best performance, give fertile, well-drained soil; sandy or other light-textured soil is ideal for penetration by pegs.

The four basic classes of peanuts are Virginia and Runner types, with two large seeds per pod; Spanish, with two or three small seeds per pod; and Valencia, with three to six small seeds per pod. Buy seeds (unroasted peanuts) from mail-order suppliers. Plant just as soon as soil has warmed in spring, setting seeds (with shells removed but skins intact) 1½–2 in. deep. Sow seeds of Virginia and Runner peanuts 6–8 in. apart; sow Spanish and Valencia peanuts 4–6 in. apart. Fertilize at planting time. In 110 to 120 days after planting, foliage yellows and plants are ready to dig; loosen soil, then pull up plants. Let peanuts dry on vines in a warm, airy, shaded place for 2 to 3 weeks; then strip them from plants.

PEAR, ASIAN

Rosaceae

DECIDUOUS FRUIT TREES

⚲ US, MS, LS, EXCEPT AS NOTED

☀ FULL SUN

💧 REGULAR WATER

Asian Pear

These pears are descendants of two Asian species: *Pyrus pyrifolia* (*P. serotina*) and *P. ussuriensis.* Unlike the more familiar European pears, they have crisp, firm flesh. Asian pears of Japanese origin are roundish in shape and are often called "apple pears" (even though they are not hybrids between apples and pears, as some folks mistakenly believe); those of Chinese origin have a traditional pear shape. To produce heavy crops, Asian pears need cross-pollination with another selection that flowers at the same time; European pears are not reliable pollenizers, because they generally bloom later. When fruit appears, thin it to one pear per fruiting spur. Unlike European kinds, Asian pears should be left to ripen on the tree before picking. They're excellent combined with other fruits and vegetables in salads. Store in refrigerator or cool, dark place.

Trees grow 25–30 ft. tall and wide but are easily kept to half that size by pruning. They thrive in the same general growing conditions as European pears but typically have a lower winter chill requirement (as few as 500 chill hours). This would seem to indicate suitability for South Texas, the Gulf and South Atlantic Coasts, and Florida—but because most Asian pears are susceptible to fireblight (a devastating disease in warm, humid areas), growing them in the Deep South is problematic. Spraying with streptomycin (Agri-Strep) or fixed copper at bloom time and again a week later may help. Selections include the following; all will keep for months if stored in the refrigerator.

'Chojuro'. Heat zones 9–4. Orange-brown, russeted, medium-size fruit has mildly sweet flesh. Ripens in mid- to late August. Stores for 4 to 5 months. Pollinate with 'Hosui' or 'Twentieth Century'.

'Hosui'. Heat zones 9–4. Excellent golden brown, russeted, medium to large fruit. Juicy, crisp, very sweet flesh. Ripens from late July to mid-August. Stores for 3 months. Pollinate with 'Chojuro', 'Shinko', or 'Twentieth Century'.

▸

P

'Korean Giant' ('Dan Bae'). Heat zones 9–4. Olive green, russeted, very large fruit (can weigh up to a pound). Very juicy, sweet, and crisp. Ripens later than other selections—in mid- to late September. Stores for up 6 months. Resists fireblight. Pollinate with 'Shinseiki'.

'Shinseiki'. Heat zones 9–4. Medium-large, yellow-green to pale yellow fruit. Tender, juicy, sweet flesh. Ripens from late July to mid-August. Excellent keeper; stores for 7 to 8 months. Pollinate with 'Hosui', 'Korean Giant', or 'Twentieth Century'.

'Shinko'. Large brownish green fruit with some russeting. Crisp texture and sweet flavor. Ripens early to mid-August. Stores for 4 to 5 months. Resists fireblight. Pollinate with 'Hosui'.

'Twentieth Century' ('Nijisseiki'). Zones US, MS; 8–3. Most popular and best-tasting selection. Round, pale yellow, medium-size fruit. Crisp, juicy, sweet flesh with a hint of tartness. Ripens in mid- to late August. Stores for 5 months. Pollinate with 'Shinseiki', 'Hosui', or 'Chojuro'.

PEAR, EUROPEAN

European Pear

Rosaceae

DECIDUOUS FRUIT TREES

ZONES VARY BY SELECTION

FULL SUN

REGULAR WATER

SEE CHART NEXT PAGE

Most pears sold in markets and grown in gardens are derived from *Pyrus communis,* a European species. Some selections are of pure European stock; these are noted for their soft, juicy, sweet flesh and are good for fresh eating. Others are European hybrids; they share many of the qualities of purely European pears, but tolerate more heat and need less winter chill. A few, classified as "hard pears," are hybrids of European and Asian species; these have coarse or gritty flesh and are usually used for canning or baking.

Trees are pyramidal in form, with strongly vertical branching, and grow 30–40 ft. tall (or taller) and 15–25 ft. wide. Pears on dwarfing understocks are good for small gardens; they range from one-half to three-fourths the size of standard trees. All types have leathery, glossy bright green leaves and bear handsome clusters of white flowers in early spring. Pears also make excellent espaliers. For ornamental pears grown for flowers and foliage, see *Pyrus.*

European pears are long lived and among the easiest of fruit trees to grow. They adapt to most soils, even poorly drained ones. Some selections are said to be self-pollinating, but the vast majority need cross-pollination with a different selection to bear fruit. They don't bloom quite as early as peaches, so late frosts don't damage them as often. Nevertheless, it's a good idea to plant them on slopes or higher ground to avoid low-lying frost pockets. Plant dormant trees in fall, winter, or early spring. Soak the roots of bare-root trees in water overnight before planting. Dig a hole wide enough to spread the roots easily and set the tree at the same depth it had been growing previously.

To help a bare-root tree develop a strong framework of branches, cut back the trunk to 24–28 in. tall at planting time. New shoots will sprout below the cut. When they reach a foot long, select three to five well-spaced ones to become the ascending main stems or "leaders." Leave three or four shoots below the leaders to become side branches. During the first winter, cut back the leaders to 1½–2 ft. long. During the second and third winters, cut back the leaders to 20–30 in. of new growth. Thereafter, prune in winter to remove crowded, crossing, or inward-growing branches. Also promptly remove suckers growing from the base. For both bare-root trees and those transplanted from containers, prune to promote strong, spreading branches. Open up the tree's center so that sunlight can reach all of the branches.

Thinning the fruit isn't usually necessary. Harvest season is July through October, depending on the selection. Fruit doesn't ripen properly on the

WHAT EUROPEAN PEARS NEED

WINTER CHILL: Pears need at least 600 hours of winter chill (45°F or lower), and most do better with 900 hours. In the Coastal South, choose a low-chill selection such as 'Baldwin', 'Hood', 'Pineapple', and 'Warren'.

POLLINATION: They normally need cross-pollination for good fruit set; plant two or more selections.

PRUNING AND TRAINING: Best done when trees are young to establish a good framework of main branches. Prune lightly each year during the dormant season to maintain good form, eliminate crowding branches.

HARVESTING: Don't wait for pears to ripen on the tree—they'll be ruined. Pick them unripe, when they're green and firm. If a pear is ready to harvest, the stem will snap free from the branch when you lift the fruit so that it is horizontal. If stem remains connected, check again in a few days.

'Bartlett'

tree, so pick when it is full size but unripe (firm and green), then store in a cool, dark place until ripe.

Fireblight, a bacterial disease that blackens leaves and twigs, can demolish pears in the South. Spraying trees with streptomycin (Agri-Strep) or fixed copper at bloom time and again a week later may prevent the disease, but it's preferable to plant resistant trees whenever possible.

PEARL BUSH. See EXOCHORDA

PEARLY EVERLASTING. See ANAPHALIS

PECAN

Juglandaceae

DECIDUOUS TREE

US, MS, LS, CS H 9–5

FULL SUN

REGULAR WATER

Pecan

Native to the southern and central U.S. While commercial production of pecans (*Carya illinoensis*) is largely limited to the Lower and Coastal South, hardy selections do quite well in the Upper and Middle South. Graceful, shapely tree to 70 ft. tall and equally wide. Foliage like that of English walnut (*Juglans regia*) but prettier, with more (11 to 17) leaflets that are narrower and longer (4–7 in.); foliage has a finer-textured look and casts less shade. Inconspicuous flowers are followed by nuts enclosed in husks. In autumn, husks split and mature nuts drop. To harvest, gather fallen nuts and remove any husks right away; then dry and store the nuts.

Papershell pecans have thin shells and are easy to harvest, making them good choices for home gardens. They need a 210-day growing season to ripen. 'Caddo', 'Elliot', 'Houma', 'Melrose', 'Stuart', and 'Sumner' resist scab (a common fungal disease) and are suitable for the Southeast. Western papershells, recommended for drier areas of West Texas, include 'Western Schley' and 'Wichita'. Hardy northern types suitable for the southern Midwest include the prevalent 'Major' as well as 'Fritz', 'Greenriver', and 'Peruque'. Most selections need a pollenizer (consult a local nursery about the best combination for your area). ▶ page 458

PEAR, EUROPEAN

NAME	ZONES	FRUIT	COMMENTS
'Anjou' ('d'Anjou', 'Beurre d'Anjou')	US, MS; 9–1	Medium to large fruit may be round or have a short neck. Yellow to russeted yellow skin. Fine flavor. Late	Upright, vigorous tree. Tie down limbs for more consistent bearing. Susceptible to fireblight. 'Red d'Anjou' is a red-skinned form
'Ayers'	MS, LS, CS; 9–1	Small to medium size; yellow flushed with red. Excellent for fresh eating. Midseason	Needs a pollenizer; 'Moonglow' is a good choice. Resists fireblight. One of the best for Lower and Coastal South; requires little winter chill
'Baldwin'	LS, CS; 9–1	Medium to large oblong fruits, light green and russeted. good fresh or canned. Late	Moderately resistant to fireblight and leaf spot. Requires little winter chill. Good selection for Lower and Coastal South
'Bartlett'	US, MS; 9–5	Medium to large, with short but definite neck. Thin skinned, yellow or slightly blushed, very sweet and tender. Midseason	Standard summer pear of fruit markets. Use any selection listed here except 'Seckel' to pollinate. Tree does not have the best form, is susceptible to fireblight; nevertheless a good choice for home gardens. 'Sensation Red Bartlett' is bright red over most of skin, less vigorous than 'Bartlett'
'Bosc' ('Beurre Bosc', 'Golden Russet')	US, MS; 9–1	Medium to large, quite long necked, interesting and attractive in form. Heavy russeting on green or yellow skin. Fine flavor; firm, juicy flesh. Holds shape when cooked. Midseason	Large, upright, vigorous tree. Needs pruning in youth. Highly susceptible to fireblight
'Clapp Favorite'	US, MS; 9–1	Resembles 'Bartlett'. Soft, sweet flesh. Early	Productive, shapely tree; attractive foliage. Highly prone to fireblight
'Flordahome'	LS, CS; 9–1	Small to medium, light green fruit with short pear shape. Juicy flesh. Early	Resistant to fireblight. Requires little winter chill. Pollinate with 'Hood'. Tends to overbear; thin well
'Harrow Delight'	US, MS; 9–1	Resembles 'Bartlett' but is smaller. Smooth texture, very good flavor. Early	Cold-hardy selection developed in Canada. Excellent resistance to fireblight
'Harvest Queen'	US, MS, LS; 9–1	Medium to large pear with red-flushed yellow skin; similar to its parent 'Bartlett'. Good for fresh eating, preserves, and canning. Midseason (a week before 'Bartlett')	Can be pollinated by most selections (but not 'Bartlett' and its strains). Resists fireblight. Hardy
'Honeysweet'	US, MS, LS; 9–1	Medium size. Yellow-green skin with red blush; sweet flesh. Midseason	Moderately resistant to fireblight
'Hood'	LS, CS; 9–1	Large yellow-green fruit with typical pear shape. A little later than 'Flordahome'	Vigorous tree. Resistant to fireblight. Needs very little winter chill. Pollinate with 'Flordahome'
'Kieffer'	US, MS, LS, CS; 9–1	Medium to large, oval; greenish yellow skin blushed red. Gritty texture. Fair flavor; best used for canning, baking. Late	European-Asian pear hybrid. Low-chill selection. Good for hot or cold climates. Most widely grown hybrid pear in the South. Quite resistant to fireblight

'Anjou'

'Sensation Red Bartlett'

'Bartlett'

'Bosc'

'Seckel'

P

PEAR, EUROPEAN

NAME	ZONES	FRUIT	COMMENTS
'Louisiana Beauty'	MS, LS, CS; 9–1	Yellow-green skin; sweet, crisp, tender flesh. Great for fresh eating. Midseason	Consistent bearer. Low winter-chill requirement. Very resistant to fireblight. An excellent selection for Louisiana and the Gulf Coast
'Magness'	US, MS, LS; 9–1	Medium to large, russeted fruit; sweet, juicy, and aromatic. Midseason	Does not produce good pollen; pollinate with two other selections for good fruit set
'Maxine'	US, MS, LS, CS; 9–1	Large, yellow, smooth-textured fruit. Good for eating fresh and canning. Midseason	Moderately resistant to fireblight
'Moonglow'	US, MS, LS; 8–3	Somewhat like 'Bartlett' in looks. Juicy, soft fruit with good flavor. Ripens 2 weeks before 'Bartlett'	Upright, vigorous tree; very heavy bearer. Moderately resistant to fireblight
'Orient'	US, MS, LS, CS; 9–1	Large, bell-shaped fruit with russeting on yellow skin. Firm, juicy, and somewhat sweet; good for canning, baking. Late	European-Asian pear hybrid. Heavy producer. Highly resistant to fireblight. A good selection for Lower and Coastal South; needs little winter chill
'Pineapple'	LS, CS; 9–1	Yellow fruit with red blush and pineapple flavor. Good for preserves. Coarse texture. Early	European-Asian pear hybrid. Self-pollinating. Good resistance to fireblight. Needs only 150 hours of winter chill. Good choice for north-central Florida
'Seckel' ('Sugar')	US, MS, LS; 9–1	Quite small, aromatic fruit with roundish to pear shape. Yellow-brown skin; very sweet, granular flesh. A favorite for home gardens; good for preserves. Early midseason	Highly productive. Moderately resistant to fireblight. Self-fruitful but bears more heavily with pollenizer (any except 'Bartlett' and its strains will do)
'Tyson'	US, MS, LS, CS; 9–1	Medium-size yellow fruit with spicy-sweet flavor. Great for fresh eating. Early to midseason	Resists fireblight
'Warren'	MS, LS, CS; 9–1	Medium to large fruit with teardrop shape; pale green skin, often with a red blush. Buttery, juicy flesh with excellent flavor. Good keeper. Late	Discovered in Mississippi. Cold-hardy, heavy-bearing tree with low chill requirement. Resistant to fireblight

Pecan trees need well-drained, deep soils (6–10 ft. deep); they won't stand salinity. To plant, set out bare-root trees in winter. Dig planting hole deep to accommodate the long taproot; position bud union above soil level. Firm soil around roots; then water thoroughly. If you're counting on a quality nut crop, don't let soil dry out. Prevent or cure pecan rosette (abnormal clumps of twigs caused by zinc deficiency) with zinc sulfate sprays or soil treatment. Pecan is prone to aphid infestations. Pruning is needed only to remove suckers from below graft union and to clear out dead, broken, or poorly placed limbs.

PEDILANTHUS
tithymaloides smallii

DEVIL'S BACKBONE
Euphorbiaceae

EVERGREEN SHRUB

TS 12–1; OR HOUSEPLANT

FULL SUN OR PARTIAL SHADE; BRIGHT INDIRECT LIGHT

MODERATE WATER

MILKY SAP CAN CAUSE STOMACH UPSET

Pedilanthus tithymaloides smallii

Native to the Caribbean, this bizarre plant is passed from gardener to gardener as a curiosity. It grows 3 ft. tall and about half as wide, featuring succulent, zigzagging stems set with 3- to 6-in.-long, medium green, diamond-shaped leaves. If growing conditions are good, it may produce small red flowers in summer. Commonly grown on windowsills, where it thrives in bright indirect light. Fertilize houseplants monthly from spring through summer with a general-purpose liquid houseplant fertilizer; let soil go fairly dry between thorough waterings and provide excellent drainage. Ease up on watering in winter. Easy to propagate by cuttings. 'Variegatus', the most popular form, has leaves variegated with pink and creamy white.

PELARGONIUM

GERANIUM
Geraniaceae

SHRUBBY PERENNIALS

CS, TS 12–1, EXCEPT AS NOTED; AS ANNUALS ANYWHERE; OR GROW IN POTS

SOME SHADE IN HOTTEST CLIMATES; BRIGHT SUNNY WINDOW

MODERATE TO REGULAR WATER

Pelargonium ×domesticum

The common name "geranium" is widely used for *Pelargonium*—but botanically speaking, it is not really accurate. To the botanist, pelargoniums are woody-based perennials (most of them native to South Africa) that endure light frosts but not hard freezes and have slightly asymmetrical flowers in clusters. True geraniums, on the other hand, are members of the genus *Geranium*—annuals and perennials (some woody-based) native mainly to the Northern Hemisphere, bearing symmetrical flowers either singly or in clusters. Some are weeds, while others are valued border or rock garden plants.

In the past, the commonly grown pelargoniums were *P. ×domesticum*, Lady Washington pelargonium; *P. ×hortorum*, common geranium (this group also includes variegated forms usually referred to as fancy-leafed or color-leafed geraniums); and *P. peltatum*, ivy geranium. Today, other kinds are increasingly available, including many with scented leaves.

Plant in any good, fast-draining soil. Amend poor soil with plenty of organic matter. Geraniums growing in good garden soil need little fertilizer; those in light, sandy soil should receive two or three feedings during active growth. Remove faded flowers regularly to encourage new bloom. Pinch growing tips of young, small plants to force side branches. All geraniums do well in pots; they bloom best when somewhat pot-bound. Common pests include aphids, whiteflies, and spider mites. Geranium (tobacco) budworm may be a problem in some areas; affected flowers look tattered or fail to open at all.

P. cordifolium (P. cordatum). HEARTLEAF GERANIUM. Rounded plant to 4 ft. tall and wide, with 2½-in., dull green, toothed and lobed leaves. Loose clusters of reddish purple, 1-in. flowers. Good for borders.

P. ×domesticum. LADY WASHINGTON PELARGONIUM, MARTHA WASHINGTON PELARGONIUM, REGAL GERANIUM. Heat zones 9–1. Erect or somewhat spreading, to 3 ft. tall and wide. Rangier than *P. ×hortorum*. Heart-shaped to kidney-shaped leaves are dark green, 2–4 in. wide, with crinkled margins and unequal sharp teeth. Loose, rounded clusters of large (2-in. or wider), showy flowers; colors include white and many shades of pink, red, lavender, purple, with brilliant blotches and markings of darker colors. Can be planted in beds if pruned hard after flowering to prevent lanky, rangy growth. First-class potted plant. Some selections are used in hanging baskets.

P. ×hortorum. COMMON GERANIUM, GARDEN GERANIUM. Succulent stemmed; grows to 3 ft. or more high and wide. In mild climates, older plants grown in the open become woody. Round or kidney-shaped leaves are velvety and hairy, soft to the touch, aromatic, edges indistinctly lobed and scallop toothed; most selections show a zone of deeper color just inside edge of leaf, though some have plain green foliage. Flowers are single or double; they are flatter and

Pelargonium ×hortorum

smaller than those of *P. ×domesticum*, but clusters bear many more blossoms. Many selections are sold, in white and shades of pink, rose, red, orange, and violet; flowers are usually solid colored.

Tough, attractive geraniums for outdoor bedding can be grown from seed; will flower the first summer. Available strains include Americana (bright green foliage, compact); Eclipse (dark green foliage, compact); Elite (quick to reach blooming stage, compact, needs no pinching); Maverick (open habit with many flowering stems); Multibloom (compact, early blooming); and Orbit (distinct leaf zoning; broad, rounded flower clusters). 'Orange Appeal', a seed-grown selection, has blooms in

pure bright orange. There are also dwarf, cactus-flowered, and other novelty types.

Fancy-leafed or color-leafed selections have zones, borders, or splashes of brown, gold, red, white, and green in various combinations. Some also have highly attractive flowers. 'Golden Ears', 1 ft. high and wide, has small, deeply cut, almost star-shaped leaves of deep bronzy red with a wide border of chartreuse; flowers are bright coral. 'Vancouver Centennial' is very similar if not identical. 'Mrs. Pollock' has green leaves with a red zone and a creamy yellow margin; it bears vermilion blooms.

Common geraniums sometimes stop blooming during extended periods of high summer heat—a condition known as "heat check." (They'll resume blooming when cooler weather arrives.) To avoid this condition, give plants light afternoon shade; or grow heat-tolerant types, such as the Americana, Eclipse, Maverick, or Orbit series.

P. peltatum. IVY GERANIUM. To 1½ ft. tall, trailing to 3 ft. wide. Rather succulent, 2- to 3-in.-wide, glossy bright green leaves with pointed lobes resemble foliage of ivy *(Hedera)*. Spectacular summer show of single or double, inch-wide flowers in rounded clusters of five to ten; colors include white, pink, rose, red, salmon, and lavender. Upper petals may be blotched or striped. Many named selections are available. Most types cannot tolerate extended heat and are grown as summer annuals only in the Upper and Middle South (though they perform well as winter annuals in the Coastal and Tropical South). However, heat-tolerant Blizzard and Cascade series perform well throughout summer in much of the Lower South, as well as farther north. Use ivy geraniums in hanging baskets, window boxes, and tall planters.

Scented geraniums. Many aromatic species, hybrids, and selections are available. Most grow 1–3 ft. tall, spreading as wide as high. Foliage scent is the main draw; clusters of small, typically white or rosy flowers are secondary in appeal. Leaves vary in shape from nearly round to finely cut and almost ferny; they range in size from minute to 4 in. across. Plants' common names usually refer to the fragrance of their leaves:

Pelargonium tomentosum

almond geranium *(P. quercifolium)*, apple geranium *(P. odoratissimum)*, lime geranium *(P. nervosum)*, nutmeg geranium *(P. ×fragrans* 'Nutmeg'), peppermint geranium *(P. tomentosum)*. There are several rose geraniums, including *P. capitatum, P. graveolens,* and *P.* 'Lady Plymouth'. Various types offer lemon fragrance, including *P. crispum* and *P.* 'Prince Rupert'. All scented geraniums are good for herb gardens, edgings, front of borders, window boxes, hanging baskets; peppermint geranium makes a good ground cover in frost-free gardens. Use fresh leaves of all types for flavoring jelly and iced drinks; use dried leaves in sachets and potpourri.

Pelargonium graveolens

PELICAN FLOWER. See ARISTOLOCHIA grandiflora

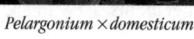
Pelargonium ×domesticum

Pelargonium peltatum

Pelargonium ×hortorum 'Mrs. Pollock'

Scented Geranium *Pelargonium graveolens*

Scented Geranium *Pelargonium ×fragrans*

PELLAEA

CLIFF-BRAKE

Polypodiaceae

FERNS

🌿 ZONES VARY BY SPECIES H 10–8 OR HOUSEPLANTS

☼ FILTERED SUNLIGHT; BRIGHT INDIRECT LIGHT

◖ WATER NEEDS VARY BY SPECIES

Pellaea rotundifolia

The appeal of these small plants lies in subtle beauty, not overwhelming show. They sport charmingly detailed foliage, with thin-stemmed leaves divided into numerous narrow to rounded leaflets. Where hardy (down to 24°F), they make nice rock garden plants, but they are most popular as houseplants. Indoors, give them good light but protect from midday sun; feed monthly with a general-purpose liquid houseplant fertilizer diluted to half-strength.

P. mucronata. BIRD'S FOOT FERN. Zones US, MS, LS, CS, TS. Native from California to Texas. To 6–12 in. high and wide, with gray-green, airy-looking fronds and narrow leaflets arranged in groups of three. Little water. Good tucked into rock walls.

P. rotundifolia. ROUNDLEAF FERN. Zone TS. Native to Australia, New Zealand. Neat little plant grows to 1 ft. high and 2 ft. wide, with spreading fronds divided into nearly round, evenly spaced leaflets. Pretty fern for contrast with finer-textured ferns or to show off in pots, baskets, or raised beds. Regular water.

P. viridis (P. adiantoides). Zone TS. Native to Africa. Grows to 1 ft. high and about as wide, with fronds consisting of fresh green, oval to lance-shaped leaflets. Good as ground cover, in rock garden, in containers. Regular water.

PELTIPHYLLUM peltatum. See DARMERA peltata

PELTOPHORUM
pterocarpum

YELLOW POINCIANA

Fabaceae (Leguminosae)

EVERGREEN TREE

🌿 TS H 12–1

☼ FULL SUN

◖ REGULAR WATER

Peltophorum pterocarpum

Native to Australia and Malaysia, this fast-growing, highly ornamental tree is popular in central and south Florida. It reaches 50 ft. tall and 25–30 ft. wide and features large, feathery leaves that resemble those of mimosa (*Albizia julibrissin*). Handsome smooth, gray bark. Erect flower spikes, 1–1½ ft. long, carry fragrant, 1½-in. yellow flowers over a long period in summer. Flowers give rise to flattened, winged, wine red seedpods up to 4 in. long.

Yellow poinciana is easy to grow; tolerates most well-drained soils and has no serious pests. It naturally forms a multitrunked, wide-spreading tree but is easily pruned to a single trunk. Good choice for a lawn, shade, or street tree. Roots can lift pavement, so allow 8–10 ft. between tree and sidewalk or other paved area.

PENCILBUSH, PENCIL TREE. See EUPHORBIA tirucalli

A PRACTICAL GUIDE TO GARDENING
PLEASE SEE PAGES 596–669

PENNISETUM

FOUNTAIN GRASS

Poaceae (Gramineae)

ANNUAL AND PERENNIAL GRASSES

🌿 ZONES VARY BY SPECIES

☼ ☽ FULL SUN OR PARTIAL SHADE, EXCEPT AS NOTED

◖ ◖ MODERATE TO REGULAR WATER, EXCEPT AS NOTED

Pennisetum setaceum
'Rubrum'

Growing in graceful, fountainlike mounds, these are among the most foolproof grasses for the South. They have long, narrow leaves and arching stems that bear fuzzy flower plumes resembling foxtails. Bloom begins in summer and often extends into fall. Cut back perennial types to within a few inches of the ground in late winter for fresh new growth in spring. Excellent in containers, in mixed borders, as dramatic sweeps, and for bank covers.

P. alopecuroides. CHINESE PENNISETUM. Perennial. Zones US, MS, LS, CS; 9–6. From eastern Asia. To 5 ft. high and wide. Foliage clump is topped by silvery pink, tan, or whitish flower plumes. Bright green leaves turn yellow in fall, then brown in winter. Will self-sow. Recommended selections include 'Cassian' (2 ft. high and wide, with creamy tan plumes), 'Hameln' (2–2½ ft. tall and wide; silvery plumes), 'Little Bunny' (dwarf form to only 1 ft. tall and wide; pinkish plumes), and 'Moudry' (3 ft. high and wide; striking black plumes).

P. 'Burgundy Giant'. Perennial in Zones CS, TS; 10–6; annual elsewhere. Bold, tropical-looking, very tender grass resembles a reddish purple corn plant. Grows 4–5 ft. tall and 2 ft. across, with broad alternate leaves to 1 in. wide and 1 ft. long on strong, upright burgundy stems. Red-purple, 8- to 12-in.-long flower plumes appear on nodding stems above the foliage in midsummer; fade to cream in fall. Needs full sun and regular water. Not to be confused with purple fountain grass (*P. setaceum* 'Rubrum'), a shorter, more graceful plant that is a better choice for most gardens.

P. glaucum (P. americanum). INDIAN MILLET, ORNAMENTAL MILLET. Annual. Zones TS; 10–3. From Asia and Africa; widely cultivated for its edible seeds. To 7 ft. tall and 3 ft. wide, with spear-shaped leaves to 3 ft. long, 2 in. wide. Stiff, cylindrical flower spikes to 20 in. long appear atop foliage in summer. 'Purple Majesty' is a popular ornamental selection to 3–5 ft. tall, 2–3 ft. wide; it boasts purple blossom spikes and leaves that turn dark purple in full sun. Cut the flower spikes before they mature and use them in dried arrangements; or leave them to mature on the plant, where they'll attract birds. Easy to start from seed. Best in full sun, with regular water.

P. orientale. ORIENTAL FOUNTAIN GRASS. Perennial. Zones US, MS, LS, CS; 10–4. From central and western Asia. To 2 ft. high, 2½ ft. wide, with green to gray-green foliage. Pinkish plumes are held above the leaves and mature to light brown; foliage turns straw colored in winter. Seldom self-sows. Recommended selections include 3-ft.-tall 'Karley Rose', an upright grower sporting dark green foliage and deep pink plumes; and 'Tall Tails', a very heat-tolerant 6-footer with tan plumes that does well in Florida.

P. setaceum. FOUNTAIN GRASS. Perennial in Zones CS, TS; 12–7; annual elsewhere. From tropical Africa, southwestern Asia, Arabian Peninsula. Dense, rounded, medium green foliage clump to 4 ft. high and wide. Coppery pink or purplish plumes are held within the clump or just above it. Tolerates drought once established. Particularly prone to self-sowing. Less likely to set seed is its selection 'Rubrum', purple fountain grass, with reddish purple leaves and showy rose-colored plumes; it's among the most popular of ornamental grasses, outstanding in containers and mixed borders.

P. villosum. FEATHERTOP. Perennial in Zones TS; 12–1; annual elsewhere. From Africa. Thin, cascading, medium green leaves form a mound to 3 ft. tall and wide. Foliage is topped in summer by soft, feathery, creamy white plumes that look great in fresh or dried arrangements. Easy to start from seed. Will self-sow. Best in full sun, with regular water.

PENNYROYAL. See MENTHA pulegium

PENSTEMON

PENSTEMON, BEARD TONGUE

Scrophulariaceae

PERENNIALS

🌱 ZONES VARY BY SPECIES

☼ ◐ AFTERNOON SHADE, EXCEPT AS NOTED

🌢 ● MODERATE TO REGULAR WATER, EXCEPT AS NOTED

Penstemon digitalis

Penstemons are beloved for their colorful flowers, but in most areas of the South, they're difficult to grow. Of the more than 250 species, the majority are native to the West, ranging from Canada to Mexico—and they prefer dry air, cool night temperatures, and excellent drainage, which doesn't sound much like Dixie. Fortunately, there are native Southern species that thrive here naturally; and the hybrids and selections presented here also accept Southern conditions.

Most species have narrow, pointed leaves. Narrow, tubular or bell-shaped flowers are typically ¾–1½ in. long and are held in erect clusters. Bright reds and blues are the common colors, but you'll also find blooms in shades of soft pink through salmon and peach to deep rose, lilac, dark purple, white, and yellow. Blossoms attract hummingbirds. Plants are generally short lived (3 to 4 years). All need fast-draining soil.

P. australis. Zones MS, LS, CS; 10–8. Native from southeastern Virginia to Florida and west to Mississippi. Grows to 3 ft. tall, 1½ ft. wide. Creamy white flowers marked with shades of reddish purple bloom in summer.

P. baccharifolius. ROCK PENSTEMON. Zones LS, CS, TS; 12–9. Native to southern Texas. Woody-based growth to 1½ ft. high and wide. Small, broad, glossy dark green leaves with toothed edges have a thick, leathery feel. Coral pink, inch-long flowers bloom all summer long. Grows on limestone; prefers dry conditions.

P. barbatus. BEARDLIP PENSTEMON. Zones US, MS, LS; 9–1. Native to mountain regions from Colorado and Utah south to Mexico; needs some winter chill for best performance. Open, somewhat sprawling plant to 3 ft. tall, 1½ ft. wide. Inch-wide red flowers bloom in tall, loose spikes from midsummer to early fall. Selections include bright pink 'Elfin Pink', with 1-ft. flower spikes; pink 'Pink Beauty', 2–2½ ft.; deep purple 'Prairie Dusk', to 2 ft.; scarlet 'Prairie Fire', 2–2½ ft.; coral pink 'Rose Elf', with 2-ft. spikes and some rebloom later in fall; and lemon yellow 'Schooley's Yellow', 2 ft.

P. canescens. PINK BEARD TONGUE. Zones US, MS, LS; 9–1. Native to dry slopes and woods of the Appalachian Mountains. Green leaves (often densely covered with gray hairs) form a clump 1–3 ft. high, 1–1½ ft. wide. Blooms in late spring and early summer, when upright, hairy gray stems hold pale to dark violet flowers to 1½ in. long.

P. cardinalis. CARDINAL PENSTEMON. Zones LS, CS; 9–2. Native to New Mexico. Good for borders; takes irrigation well and also tolerates some drought. To 2–3 ft. tall, 1½–2 ft. wide, with thick dark green leaves. Spikes of brilliant red, 1-in. flowers bloom in summer.

P. cobaea. WILD FOXGLOVE. Zones US, MS, LS, CS; 12–6. Native from Nebraska to Texas. To 1–2 ft. tall, 1–1½ ft. wide. Blooms in mid- to late spring, bearing showy clusters of large (2-in.), foxglovelike blossoms in white or lavender with deeper-colored throat markings. Leathery, glossy green leaves form a basal rosette. Takes little to regular water; tolerates limy soil and clay.

P. digitalis. SMOOTH PENSTEMON. Zones US, MS, LS; 8–1. Native to eastern and central U.S. To 5 ft. tall, 3 ft. wide. Medium green leaves to 7 in. long; flowers to 1½ in. long in white or pink shades, often with faint purple lines. Spring to early summer bloom. 'Husker Red', 2½–3 ft. tall, has maroon leaves and pink-tinted white flowers.

P. dissectus. FEATHERLEAF PENSTEMON. Zones US, MS, LS, CS; 9–5. Native to sandstone outcrops in Georgia's coastal plain. To 2 ft. high, 1½ ft.

wide. Finely cut leaves; stiff stems topped with inch-long purple flowers in late spring, early summer.

P. havardii. HAVARD PENSTEMON. Zones MS, LS, CS, TS; 9–5. Native to Texas. In spring, several upright, 2- to 4-ft. stems clad in rounded light green leaves rise from a low foliage rosette to about 2 ft. wide. Scarlet, 2-in.-long flowers bloom from late spring until June. Tolerates a wide range of soils, including limestone and clay. Cut back after bloom.

P. smallii. SMALL'S PENSTEMON. Zones MS, LS, CS; 9–1. Native to North Carolina and Tennessee. Grows 1–3 ft. tall and 1–2 ft. wide. Pink-purple or lavender flowers, 1 in. long, in late spring. Tolerates moist woodland soils as well as dry soils.

P. tenuis. GULF COAST PENSTEMON. Zones MS, LS, CS; 9–7. This native of the wet prairies of Louisiana, Texas, and Arkansas blooms heavily in spring, bearing ¾-in. pink or purple flowers. To 2 ft. tall and wide, with large medium green leaves. Tolerates wet soils and partially shaded areas. Self-sows to produce plenty of new plants.

PENTAS lanceolata

PENTAS, EGYPTIAN STAR CLUSTERS

Rubiaceae

PERENNIAL OFTEN GROWN AS ANNUAL; OR HOUSEPLANT

🌱 US, MS, LS, CS, TS 🌡 12–6

☼ FULL SUN; BRIGHT LIGHT

● REGULAR WATER

Pentas lanceolata

It's hard to beat this tropical African native for continuous, eye-catching color. Spreading, multistemmed plants reach 2–3 ft. tall and wide, thickly foliaged in deep green, lance-shaped leaves to 6 in. long. During warm weather, 4-in.-wide clusters of red, pink, lavender, or white starlike flowers appear above the leaves. The blooms attract a host of butterflies and hummingbirds; cut flowers can last for 2 weeks.

Thrives in fertile soil with good drainage; will not tolerate drought. Feed monthly in summer with water-soluble 20-20-20 fertilizer; remove spent flowers to encourage more blooms. Pentas can be grown as a perennial in the Coastal and Tropical South; prune it heavily each year (before spring growth begins) to keep it compact and encourage flowering. It can also be used as a houseplant: set in bright west- or south-facing window, keep soil moist (barely moist in winter), and feed monthly from spring through fall with a general-purpose liquid houseplant fertilizer.

The hybrid Butterfly series, to 12–20 in. tall and a little wider, is a better performer offering larger flowers on denser-foliaged, rounder plants. The New Look series offers compact plants to only 8–10 in. tall and wide. Star series plants grow 2–3 ft. tall and not quite as wide, with an open, casual look. 'Stars and Stripes' is about the same size and combines showy red flowers with green-and-white variegated foliage.

PEONY. See PAEONIA

PEPEROMIA

Piperaceae

PERENNIALS

🌱 HOUSEPLANTS

◐ BRIGHT LIGHT

🌢 MODERATE WATER

Peperomia caperata

Native to Central and South America, these perennials belong to the same family as *Piper nigrum*—the source of black pepper. Small and compact, they rarely exceed 1 ft. in height and are grown for their highly ornamental foliage. Some are trailing, others upright; most feature stout, fleshy stems and leaves. Tiny flowers are borne on erect, cordlike spikes, usually in late summer.

▶

Peperomias are very tender to cold, with 55°F being the minimum temperature they'll tolerate. Place in a bright window, but protect from hot afternoon sun, which will burn the leaves. Excellent drainage is essential, so make sure pots have adequate drainage holes. Let the soil go nearly dry between thorough waterings; feed twice a month with a general-purpose liquid houseplant fertilizer diluted to half-strength. Reduce watering and feeding in winter. Propagate by division or by taking leaf or stem cuttings in spring or summer. Frequent repotting isn't necessary—peperomias prefer to be slightly pot-bound.

P. argyreia (P. sandersii). WATERMELON PEPEROMIA. To 6–12 in. tall, not quite as wide. Rounded to oval leaves to 5 in. long and 4 in. wide; they are shiny green above and pale green beneath, with silver blotches between the veins. Leaves are held on short red stems. Green flowers appear on spikes 2–3 in. tall.

P. caperata. EMERALD RIPPLE PEPEROMIA. Compact plant to 6 in. tall and wide. Short, pinkish red stems hold tufts of heart-shaped, rich green, waxy leaves to 2 in. long. White flowers are borne on 2- to 3-in.-tall spikes.

P. obtusifolia. BABY RUBBER PLANT. Bushy plant to 6–12 in. tall and wide, noted for its smooth, glossy deep green foliage. Leaves reach 4 in. long and 2½ in. wide, rounded to oval, notched at the tip. The leaves of 'Variegata' have wide, irregular margins of creamy white.

PEPPER

Solanaceae

ANNUAL

US, MS, LS, CS, TS **H** 12–1

FULL SUN, EXCEPT AS NOTED

REGULAR WATER

Hot Pepper
'Long Red Cayenne'

Among the treasures Christopher Columbus brought back from the New World was a bushy plant whose fiery fruits tasted to him like black pepper. These fruits became wildly popular in Spain—and before long, people were calling them "peppers," though in fact they're not related to the source of black pepper, *Piper nigrum* (a vining plant native to India). Most New World peppers are varieties and selections of *Capsicum annuum* (the Tabasco pepper derives from *C. frutescens*).

Attractive, shrubby plants range from less than a foot high to 4 ft. tall, depending on selection; some are attractive enough to be used as ornamentals. Edible peppers are divided into two basic categories, sweet and hot, according to the amount of capsaicin (the substance that causes the heat) they contain. One way to measure a pepper's heat level is by Scoville units (SU), which were developed through extensive taste tests. Sweet bell peppers, for example, are rated at 0 SU and can easily be eaten whole—but do the same with a volcanic 'Habanero', rated at up to 600,000 SU, and your hair will catch fire. Keep in mind: the hotter the climate, the hotter the pepper.

Sweet peppers are ready to pick when they have reached good size (like those you see in markets). Pimientos should be picked only when red-ripe, but you can pick other sweet types green or ripe (the flavor typically sweetens as the fruit ripens). Pick hot peppers when they are fully ripe. Possible pests include aphids, whiteflies, cutworms, hornworms, and Colorado potato beetles. For controls, consult the *Southern Living Garden Problem Solver.*

Sweet peppers. These peppers are mild in flavor, even when they ripen and change color. The group includes bell peppers, commonly used for stuffing and salads. Outstanding selections are 'California Wonder' (75 days from planting to harvest), 'Big Bertha' (72 days), and 'Peto Wonder' (75 days); all change from green to red as they mature (red fruits are very high in vitamin C). You can also buy selections that ripen to yellow ('Early Sunsation', 70 days), orange ('Valencia', 70 days), purple ('Purple Beauty', 70 days), and even brown ('Choco Hybrid', 70 days). These hybrids are bred for high yield and disease resistance.

Many other sweet peppers are popular. Banana peppers (65 to 75 days), shaped like the namesake fruit, are heavy bearers, with fruits

---

CLIMATE: Peppers need a long, warm growing season. As soon as weather warms up in spring and nighttime temperatures remain consistently above 55°F, set out transplants 1½–2 ft. apart.

WATER: Keep soil moist, particularly during flowering and fruiting.

FERTILIZER: Apply a balanced liquid fertilizer once or twice after plants become established, but before blossoms set. Too much fertilizer produces lots of leaves but few fruits.

HARVEST: Snip the stem with pruning shears or scissors. Be careful when handling hot peppers, as oils on the outside of the fruit can irritate the skin and burn the eyes.

'Purple Beauty' Pepper

ripening from green through yellow and orange to red; use them for frying and in salads. Bell-shaped pimientos (75 to 85 days) are very sweet—perfect for salads, cooking, and canning. Sweet cherry peppers are good for pickling. Long, cylindrical Italian peppers, such as 'Giant Marconi' (63 days), are great for grilling and roasting.

Hot peppers. Hot peppers range from pea-size firebombs to fingerlike types reaching 6–7 in. long. All are pungent, ranging from mildly hot Italian pepperoncini (73 days; 500 to 800 SU) to the aforementioned, nearly incandescent 'Habanero' (85 to 95 days; up to 600,000 SU). 'Anaheim' (74 days; 800 to 1,400 SU) is a mildly spicy pepper used for making canned green chiles. Mexican cooking employs a wide variety of hot peppers, including 'Pasilla Bajio' (75 days; 100 to 250 SU), 'Ancho' (76 days; 1,200 to 3,000 SU), 'Jalapeño' (73 days; 2,500 to 5,000 SU), and 'Serrano' (75 days; 5,000 to 15,000 SU). 'Long Red Cayenne' (70 days; 30,000 to 50,000 SU) is used both for cooking and for decoration; often dried for use in wreaths and arrangements. 'Tabasco' (80 days; 30,000 to 50,000 SU) is a foundation for hot sauces (as are 'Habanero' and 'Jalapeño'). Thai cuisine also uses very hot peppers; one example is 'Thai Dragon' (70 days; 35,000 to 45,000 SU).

Ornamental peppers. These small, bushy plants, usually 10–15 in. tall and wide, are often used for bedding and in pots. Rounded or conical, ½- to 2-in.-long fruits may be yellow, red, orange, or purple. Showy enough to take the place of flowers, they're typically quite hot and seldom used for cooking.

An exceptional plant with both ornamental and culinary uses is chili pequin (*Capsicum annuum glabrisculum*). Native to Texas, Mexico, and Central America, it forms a mounding shrub 2–5 ft. tall and wide and bears small white flowers continuously from spring to fall. Jewel-like, rounded fruits, about ½ in. in diameter and orange red when ripe, decorate the plant in summer and fall, lending welcome color to the lightly shaded areas it favors. Fruits are quite hot (30,000 to 50,000 SU) and are widely used in salsas, sauces, soups, and vinegars.

Pepper
Chile Pequin

PEPPERMINT. See MENTHA × piperita

PEREGRINA. See JATROPHA integerrima

PERICALLIS ×hybrida. See SENECIO ×hybridus

PERILLA frutescens

PERILLA, WILD BASIL

Lamiaceae (Labiatae)

ANNUAL

☀ US, MS, LS, CS, TS 🌡 12–1

☼ ◐ FULL SUN OR LIGHT SHADE

💧 REGULAR WATER

Perilla frutescens

This longtime Southern favorite is native from the Himalayas to eastern Asia. It's a sturdy, leafy, warm-weather plant that grows quickly to 2–3 ft. tall, 1 ft. wide. Leaves are broadly oval, pointed, and deeply toothed, reaching about 5 in. long. The kinds most commonly seen have bronzy or purple leaves resembling those of purple-foliaged forms of basil (*Ocimum basilicum*). Extremely easy to grow. Self-sows freely, winding up in all sorts of unlikely places. Tiny white flowers appear in spikes to 6 in. long; seedheads of dead plants are prominent in winter. 'Magilla' offers striking plum red foliage with a bright red streak down the center of each leaf. Dense and shrubby, it reaches 3 ft. tall and wide and looks like a coleus on steroids.

Perilla makes an attractive addition to summer borders, and various parts of the plant are also edible. Use leaves as a vegetable or flavoring (they taste something like mint, something like cinnamon); fry the long, thin clusters of flower buds in tempura batter and serve as a vegetable. In Asia, the seeds are pressed for edible oil.

PERIWINKLE. See CATHARANTHUS roseus, VINCA

PEROVSKIA atriplicifolia

RUSSIAN SAGE

Lamiaceae (Labiatae)

SHRUBBY PERENNIAL

☀ US, MS, LS, CS 🌡 9–6

☼ FULL SUN

◐ 💧 LITTLE TO MODERATE WATER

Perovskia atriplicifolia
'Blue Spire'

Native to western and central Asia, this clumping perennial combines handsome foliage with colorful summer flowers. Mature plants stand 3–4 ft. tall and wide, with graceful, upright, whitish stems holding finely cut, aromatic, gray-green leaves. Sprays of small lavender-blue flowers appear continuously from late spring through summer, forming a soft haze above the foliage. 'Blue Spire' has deep violet-blue blossoms; 'Filagran' sports silvery foliage and a distinctive upright form. 'Little Spire' grows only 2 ft. tall.

Russian sage can be used in the garden in many ways. Its cool-colored flowers and foliage combine well with reds, oranges, and yellows; its fine-textured foliage is a good foil for plants with coarser leaves, such as coneflower (*Echinacea, Rudbeckia*), iris, aster, and sedum. Mass plantings are very effective.

Even though it is scarcely bothered by pests (not even deer have much interest in it) and withstands heat, drought, and infertile soils, Russian sage is difficult for some Southerners to grow. The most common problem is heavy, poorly drained soil. If you have clay, try planting in raised beds and mixing gravel with the soil. Water infrequently, and don't fertilize or crowd plants. Instead of pruning in fall, wait until new growth begins in spring, then cut old stems nearly to the ground.

FOR INFORMATION ON YOUR CLIMATE ZONES
PLEASE SEE PAGES 28–38

PERSEA

Lauraceae

EVERGREEN TREES AND SHRUBS

☀ ZONES VARY BY SPECIES

☼ ◐ EXPOSURE NEEDS VARY BY SPECIES

💧 💧 💧 WATER NEEDS VARY BY SPECIES

Persea borbonia

Group of about 150 species of trees and large shrubs grown chiefly for their handsome evergreen foliage. Related to avocado (*Persea americana*) and camphor tree (*Cinnamomum*). None is very common, but all are well worth seeking out.

P. borbonia. RED BAY. Tree. Zones MS, LS, CS, TS; 12–7. Native to swamps from Delaware to Florida. Grows 20–40 ft. tall and 20 ft. wide, with a dense crown of aromatic, shiny dark green leaves to 6 in. long and 2 in. wide. Often multitrunked and shrubby. Creamy flowers in May or June are inconspicuous. Small dark blue to black fruits appear in early fall, borne on attractive red stalks. Needs regular to ample water; tolerates very wet soil and salt spray. Full sun or light shade.

P. humilis. SILK BAY. Shrub or small tree. Zones LS, CS, TS; 12–8. Native to Florida scrub. Handsome plant to 10 ft. tall, 6–10 ft. wide. Leaves are shiny green above and covered with silky, chestnut brown hairs beneath; they grow 1–3 in. long and ½–1¼ in. wide. When crushed, foliage smells like that of culinary bay (*Laurus nobilis*). Small, yellowish spring flowers are followed by small purplish black fruits in fall. Very drought tolerant; needs good drainage and full sun.

P. thunbergii (Machilus thunbergii). JAPANESE PERSEA. Zones LS, CS, TS; 12–5. Tree. Native to Japan, China, Korea. Fast grower to 60–80 ft. tall, 40–60 ft. wide. Thick, glossy leaves are deep green above, paler beneath, to 6 in. long and 2½ in. wide. Tiny, yellowish spring flowers; blackish purple fruits in summer. A nice lawn, shade, or street tree. Provide regular water and full sun.

Persea thunbergii

PERSIAN SHIELD. See STROBILANTHES dyeranus

PERSIAN VIOLET. See EXACUM affine

PERSICARIA

KNOTWEED

Polygonaceae

PERENNIALS

☀ ZONES VARY BY SPECIES

☼ ◐ FULL SUN OR PARTIAL SHADE

💧 REGULAR WATER, EXCEPT AS NOTED

Persicaria virginiana
'Painter's Palette'

Sturdy plants with jointed stems and small white or pink flowers. Some kinds tend to get out of hand and need to be controlled.

P. affinis (Polygonum affine). Zones US, MS, LS; 8–1. Himalayan native. Spreading plant to 1 ft. high, 2 ft. or more wide. Deep green, lance-shaped, finely tooth-edged leaves are mostly basal; they grow 2–4½ in. long, turn bronze in winter. Dense, erect, 2- to 3-in. spikes of bright rosy red flowers bloom in summer, early fall. Informal border or ground cover. 'Darjeeling Red' forms 3-in.-high foliage mats, has 10-in. spikes of deep pink flowers that age to red; its foliage turns red in fall. 'Dimity' sports pale pink flowers and larger leaves than the species.

P. amplexicaulis (Polygonum amplexicaule). Zones US, MS; 8–1. Himalayan native. Forms a big clump—to 4 ft. tall and wide when plants are in flower. Medium green leaves are pointed ovals up to 10 in. long. Blooms profusely from midsummer to fall, bearing narrow, 4-in. blossom spikes similar to those of lavender *(Lavandula)* but in a wider range of colors—pink, purple, red, white. 'Firetail' has bright scarlet flowers.

P. bistorta (Polygonum bistorta). Zones US, MS; 8–1. Native to Eurasia. Makes a clump to 2½ ft. tall, 3 ft. wide, with broadly oval, medium green, 4- to 12-in.-long leaves. Tight, 2- to 3-in. spikes of pale pink or white flowers bloom from late spring until well into summer. 'Superba' is a good pink selection.

P. capitata (Polygonum capitatum). Perennial in Zones TS; 9–8; annual elsewhere. Himalayan native. Tough, trailing ground cover grows 3–6 in. high, spreading indefinitely both by rooting stems and by self-seeding. Oval, 1½-in.-long leaves are dark green when new, take on pink-ish overtones when mature. Leaves of all ages have a bronzy cast that deepens in cooler weather; they discolor and die below 28°F. Stems and small, round flower heads are pink. Blooms almost all year in mild climates. Best in confined spots (where it won't be able to spread) or in uncultivated areas. No watering needed.

P. polymorpha (Polygonum polymorphum). Zones US, MS, LS, CS; 9–1. Native to China, Japan. To 4–6 ft. tall, 4 ft. wide. Forms a bushy clump of rough-textured, lance-shaped dark green leaves to 8 in. long. In summer, sturdy stems are topped by big, fluffy, creamy white flower plumes reminiscent of astilbe. Not invasive. Tolerates heat and humidity.

P. vacciniifolia (Polygonum vacciniifolium). Zones US, MS, LS; 9–7. Himalayan native. Prostrate plant forms a foliage mat to 3 in. high, trailing to 2 ft. or wider. Slender, branching, reddish stems are clothed in oval, ½-in.-long, shiny green leaves that turn red in fall. In late summer, 6- to 9-in. flower stalks bear dense, upright, foxtail-like, 2- to 3-in. spikes of rose pink blossoms. Excellent as a bank cover or for draping over a boulder in a large rock garden.

P. virginiana (Polygonum virginianum, Tovara virginiana). Zones US, MS, LS; 9–5. Native to eastern North America, eastern Asia. To 2–4 ft. tall, spreading indefinitely by creeping rhizomes. Oval green leaves 3–10 in. long; insignificant flowers. The species is rarely found in gardens. More commonly seen is 'Painter's Palette', valued for its flashy foliage: leaves are marbled in green, pale gray green, and ivory, with a ragged chocolate maroon V in the center. On new growth, the ivory patches are closer to yellow, and the central V-shaped mark has a pink cast.

PERSIMMON

Ebenaceae

DECIDUOUS FRUIT TREES

🌊 ZONES VARY BY SPECIES

☼ FULL SUN

◐ ◑ WATER NEEDS VARY BY SPECIES

Persimmon

Two types of fruiting persimmons are grown in the South. The native American species is a bigger, more cold-tolerant tree than its Asian counterpart, but the Asian type bears larger fruit. Neither species is fussy about soil, as long as it is well drained. For the ornamental Texas persimmon, see *Diospyros texana.*

American persimmon *(Diospyros virginiana)* is native from Connecticut to Kansas and southward to Texas and Florida. Grows well in Zones US, MS, LS, CS; 9–1. Can grow to 35–60 ft. tall, 20–35 ft. wide. As a landscape tree, it is not as ornamental as the Asian species and is probably best used in woodland gardens, where its tendency to form thickets from root suckers can be tolerated. Attractive gray-brown bark is fissured in a checkered pattern. Glossy green, broadly oval leaves to 6 in. long turn yellow, pink, or reddish purple in fall. Round, 1½- to 2-in.-wide fruit is yellow to orange (often blushed red); very astringent until soft-ripe, then very sweet. On wild species, fruit ripens in early fall after frost; some selections do not require winter chill. Both male and female trees are usually needed to get fruit. 'Meader' is self-fruitful; its fruit is seedless if not pollinated. 'Early

Golden' has more flavorful fruit; it needs cross-pollination for best crop. Trees usually need pruning only to remove broken or dead branches. Does best with regular moisture but will also perform well with moderate water.

Japanese or Oriental persimmon *(Diospyros kaki)* grows and fruits best in Zones MS, LS, CS; 10–1. It reaches 30 ft. tall (or more) and at least as wide. Has a handsome branch pattern and is one of the best fruit trees for ornamental use; makes a good small shade tree and is suitable for espalier. Leaves are leathery ovals 6–7 in. long—light green when new, maturing to dark green. They turn vivid yellow, orange, or red in fall (even in mild climates). After leaves drop, brilliant orange-scarlet, 3- to 4-in. fruits brighten the tree for weeks and persist until winter unless harvested. Without pollination, sets seedless fruit; pollinated trees often produce more abundant crops.

Prune trees when they are young to establish a good framework; thereafter, prune only to remove dead wood, shape the tree, or open up a too-dense interior. Remove any suckers that shoot up from below the graft line.

Fruit drop is a common problem in young trees. To avoid it, water regularly and feed once in late winter or early spring; too little or inconsistent moisture causes fruit drop, as does overfertilizing (too much fertilizer also causes excessive growth). Excessive fruit drop can also be reduced by providing a pollenizer (such as 'Gailey'), but fruit will be seedy.

Some Japanese persimmon selections are astringent until soft-ripe—at which stage they become very sweet. To save the crop from birds, pick fruit when fully colored but still hard, then let it ripen off the tree. Eat when the flesh is mushy and puddinglike. Nonastringent types are hard (like apples) when ripe, with a mildly sweet flavor; they can be eaten hard, but their flavor improves when they are allowed to soften slightly off the tree.

'Chocolate'. Nonastringent. Medium-size, acorn-shaped fruit. When pollinated, has seeded flesh with dark streaks; when unpollinated, has seedless yellow-orange flesh. Fruit from pollinated trees has best flavor.

'Fuyu'. Nonastringent. Firm fleshed; about the size of a baseball but flattened like a tomato. Similar but larger is 'Gosho', widely offered as 'Giant Fuyu'.

'Gailey'. Astringent. Roundish to conical fruit. Bears many male flowers and is often used as a pollenizer.

'Hachiya'. Astringent. Big, slightly pointed fruit. Very shapely tree for ornamental use.

'Izu'. Nonastringent. Medium-size, round fruit borne on a tree about half the standard size. Ripens early.

'Matsumoto Wase Fuyu'. Nonastringent. An early-ripening form of 'Fuyu'. Thin fruit to prevent limb breakage.

'Tamopan'. Astringent. Large, acorn-shaped fruit.

TRY DRYING SOME PERSIMMONS. *To dry persimmon fruit, pick it when hard-ripe with some stem remaining. Peel and hang by string in sun until it shrivels. Dried fruit tastes something like dates or very high-quality prunes.* ❖

PETASITES japonicus

JAPANESE COLTSFOOT, FUKI

Asteraceae (Compositae)

PERENNIAL

🌊 US, MS, LS, CS   ⌶ 9–5

◐ ● PARTIAL TO FULL SHADE

💧 AMPLE WATER

Petasites japonicus

Giant perennial for constantly moist locales near ponds, streams. Creeping rhizomes give rise to big (2½-ft.-wide), round leaves on edible, 3-ft.-long stalks that are used by the Japanese as a vegetable (called *fuki*). Short, thick spikes of fragrant white daisies appear in early spring before the leaves emerge. Locate this plant with care; it has thick, invasive rhizomes and can be difficult to eradicate. *P. j. giganteus* has leaves to 4 ft. wide on 5-ft. stalks. Its selection 'Variegatus', with 3- to 4-ft. stalks, has 2- to 3-ft.-wide leaves with bold white markings.

PETREA volubilis

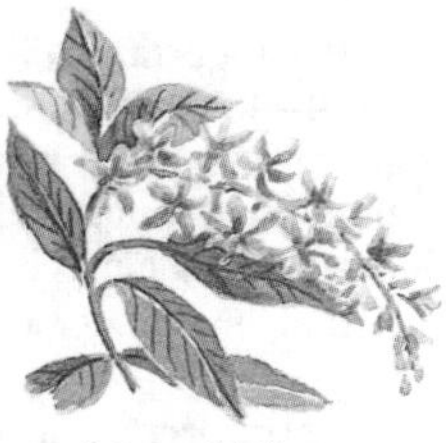

Petrea volubilis

QUEEN'S WREATH

Verbenaceae

EVERGREEN VINE

TS H 12–6

FULL SUN

REGULAR WATER

Woody vine native to Mexico, Central America, and the West Indies. Twines to 20–40 ft. but can easily be kept smaller. Elliptical deep green leaves to 8 in. long have a sandpapery surface. Stunning floral display several times a year during warm weather: pendent, foot-long clusters of star-shaped, blue-purple, 1½-in.-wide blossoms. Blue calyxes hang on after the petals drop.

Beautiful plant trained on arbor or pergola, along eaves, on a high wall. Grow in organically enriched, well-drained soil. Provide support for climbing stems. Prune and thin growth as needed in winter. Wind resistant. Frost sensitive.

PETROSELINUM crispum

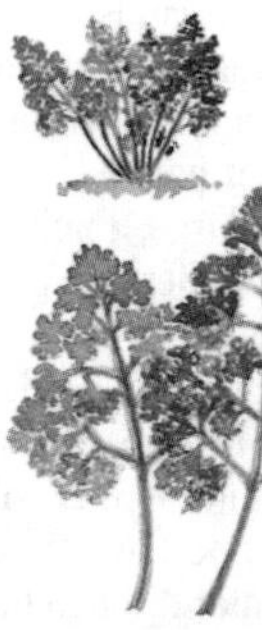

Petroselinum crispum

PARSLEY

Apiaceae (Umbelliferae)

BIENNIAL GROWN AS ANNUAL

US, MS, LS, CS, TS H 9–1

AFTERNOON SHADE

REGULAR WATER

This popular and ubiquitous herb is native to southern Europe. Two kinds are grown, both with finely cut dark green foliage: curly-leafed and Italian flat-leafed. Leaves of both are used as a seasoning (both fresh and dried), and fresh sprigs and minced leaves are classic garnishes. Curly-leafed parsley is more often grown for its good looks; it makes a lush, deep green, 6- to 12-in.-high border or edging and also looks great when combined with other plants in containers. Italian flat-leafed parsley grows 2–3 ft. tall and is considered more flavorful.

Buy plants at garden centers or sow seeds directly in the garden—in spring in the Upper South, in fall or spring elsewhere. To speed germination, soak seeds in warm water for 24 hours before planting. (Even after soaking, they may not sprout for several weeks; according to an old story, they must first go to the devil and back.) Thin seedlings to 1–1½ ft. apart for flat-leafed parsley, 6–8 in. apart for curly-leafed parsley—or space plants at these distances. Pick fresh leaves as needed or dry them on a wire rack. Where plants are left to overwinter, they'll flower at the beginning of their second year, then set seed and die. Most gardeners simply set out new plants each year.

Be merciful if you spot large caterpillars with black, green, and yellow stripes munching on the leaves; these are the larvae of the stunning black swallowtail butterfly.

PETUNIA × hybrida

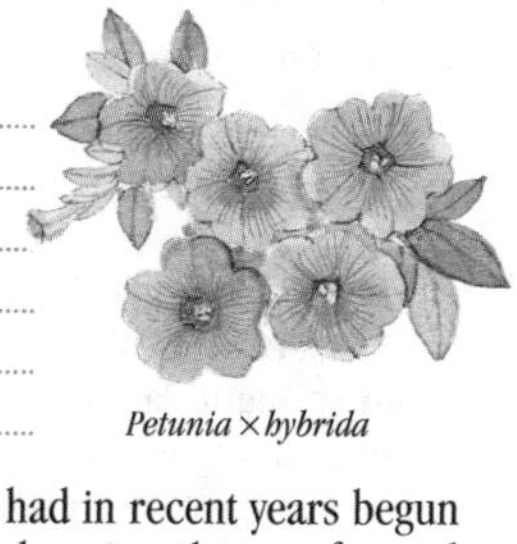

Petunia × hybrida

Solanaceae

PERENNIAL GROWN AS ANNUAL

US, MS, LS, CS, TS H 12–1

FULL SUN

MODERATE TO REGULAR WATER

Long a mainstay in flower borders, petunias had in recent years begun to lose popularity in the South, probably because they performed poorly in our hot, humid climate. But thanks to several new heat-tolerant types, such as the Multiflora Plum strain and the trailing Wave series, Surfinias, and Supertunias, petunias have made a comeback. For information on parents of these hybrids—valuable in their own right—see "Species petunias," page 466.

Hybrid petunias are low-growing, bushy to spreading plants with thick, broad leaves that are slightly sticky to the touch. Flowers vary from funnel-shaped single blooms to very double, heavily ruffled ones reminiscent of carnations *(Dianthus)*. The color range is phenomenal—pure white, cream, yellow, and the whole gamut of reds and blues—from soft pink to velvety red, and light blue to inky purple. Bicolors and picotees are also available, as are types with contrasting veins on the petals and kinds with fluted or fringed edges. In the Upper, Middle, and Lower South, these hybrids bloom from summer until frost. In the Lower South, you can also set out transplants in late summer or early fall for bright color all the way to the first hard freeze. In the Coastal and Tropical South, hybrid petunias are done in by summer heat and humidity, so grow them there for fall, winter, and spring color. Botrytis (gray mold) disease can damage blossoms and foliage of most petunias when the weather is humid, though Multifloras are somewhat resistant to this malady.

Listed below are the various kinds of petunias sold. Grandiflora and Multiflora are older hybrid classes that have been popular for a number of years. Great advances in petunia breeding have produced new types and strains, some strikingly different from the older sorts. (A small-flowered plant sold under the name "million bells" is closely related to petunia and is even considered a petunia by some botanists; see *Calibrachoa.*) Petunias labeled F_1 are first-generation hybrids; they are more vigorous and uniform in color, height, and growth habit than their offspring, F_2 hybrids. Single-flowered types tend to outperform doubles in the South.

Hybrid Grandiflora. These bear the largest flowers of all petunia classes but bloom the least profusely. Sturdy plants grow 15–27 in. high, 2–3 ft. across. Flowers are usually single, to 4½ in. across, with ruffled or fringed edges; colors include pink, rose, salmon, red, scarlet, blue, white, pale yellow, and striped combinations.

'Fluffy Ruffles' has the largest blossoms, to 6 in. across. Cascade, Countdown, and Supercascade series plants have a trailing habit that makes them good selections for hanging baskets. Magic and Supermagic are compact, heavy-blooming plants bearing large (4- to 5-in.) single flowers in white, pink, red, blue. Newer strains include durable Storm, compact Ultra, cascading Cloud, and Hula Hoop and Frost (both with white-rimmed blossoms). 'Prism Sunshine' is a much-improved yellow. Double Hybrid Grandifloras have heavily ruffled flowers that come in all petunia colors except yellow.

Hybrid Multiflora. This hybrid group is sometimes called Floribunda. Plants are about the same size as Grandifloras, but flowers are single or

WHAT PETUNIAS NEED

EXPOSURE: Choose a spot in full sun, and make sure air circulation is good.

SOIL: Provide loose, fertile, well-drained soil.

FERTILIZING: For best growth and bloom, feed monthly with a balanced water-soluble fertilizer.

PINCHING: Once plants are established, pinch back by half to encourage compact growth. Pinch them back by half again after a period of heavy bloom; they tend to get leggy then, and pinching forces new growth and more flowers. (Hybrid Millifloras are an exception; they need no pinching.)

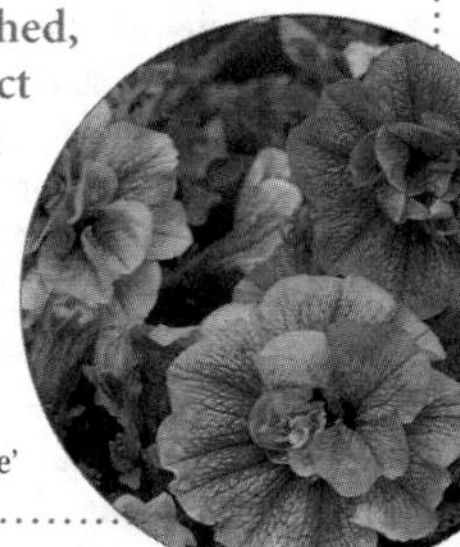

Petunia 'Purple Pirouette'

P

double, generally smooth edged, and smaller (to 2 in. wide). Neat, compact growth makes them ideal for bedding, massing. Many named selections in pink, rose, salmon, yellow, white, blue. Joy and Plum strains have single, satiny-textured flowers in white, cream, pink, coral, red, blue. 'Summer Sun' has single bright yellow blossoms. Celebrity and Prime Time are newer strains with single flowers somewhat larger than those of the typical Hybrid Multiflora. 'Laura Bush', a cross involving *P. violacea* 'VIP' and an old-fashioned petunia, grows 2 ft. tall and 3 ft. wide, bearing a profusion of rosy purple, 2-in. flowers. It reseeds readily, blooms nonstop in summer heat, and takes temperatures down to 22°F. There is also a pink form.

Hybrid Milliflora. These dwarf petunias form mounds 6–8 in. high and wide; they need no pinching or pruning. Plants cover themselves with small (1- to 1½-in.) flowers that come in all petunia colors except yellow. Effective planted in groups of a single color; highly attractive in containers, hanging baskets, window boxes.

Trailing hybrid petunias. These low, wide-spreading plants are used as ground covers and in tubs, window boxes, hanging baskets. There are seed-grown and cutting-grown types. Plants in the seed-grown Wave series cover themselves with 2½- to 3-in. flowers in pink, lilac, rose, or purple; among purple choices is the remarkably vigorous 'Purple Wave', the first member of the series. All color selections are fast growers to 6 in. high, spreading to more than 5 ft. across. The cold-hardy, heat-tolerant Tidal Wave series features blossoms in pink, purple, or white. When set out in masses, the plants form dense mounds up to 2½ ft. high that are smothered in flowers.

The following cutting-grown types grow lower than the Wave and Tidal Wave series and spread to 4 ft. wide. Surfinias have 1½-in. flowers in pink, violet, purple, blue, or white. Cascadias are very similar to Surfinias but come in more than a dozen colors, including white and various pink, blue, and purple shades. Supertunias have 2½-in. flowers in shades of pink, violet, and purple. Petitunias bear profuse ¾-in. blossoms in colors including pink, purple, and white with darker veins.

Species petunias. In addition to hybrids, several species have considerable merit. Violet petunia (*P. violacea*, also listed as *P. integrifolia*), a parent of modern hybrids, still garners rave reviews. This trailing plant boasts multitudes of rosy purple, 1-in. flowers with dark throats. It blooms nonstop from spring to fall and is outstanding in window boxes, pots, hanging baskets, and planters. It is very heat tolerant and is usually winter hardy as far north as the Lower South. 'VIP' is an especially strong-growing selection, touted for its outstanding performance in Texas. White petunia (*P. axillaris*), another parent of modern hybrids, sports 2-in., white to blush pink flowers that are fragrant at night. It reseeds readily and sometimes naturalizes in fields and country gardens.

PHACELIA

Hydrophyllaceae

ANNUALS AND BIENNIALS

✷ ZONES VARY BY SPECIES

☼ ◐ ● EXPOSURE NEEDS VARY BY SPECIES

● REGULAR WATER

Phacelia bipinnatifida

Large genus of flowering plants native mostly to western U.S. and Mexico. One of the species listed here is native to the Texas prairie; the other is a wildflower from shady, moist areas of the Southeast.

P. bipinnatifida. SCORPION WEED, FERNLEAF PHACELIA. Biennial. Zones US, MS, LS; 9–3. Native from West Virginia and Illinois to Arkansas and Georgia. Deeply divided, dark green leaves to 4 in. long and wide. Overwinters as an attractive low foliage mound to 1 ft. wide; in late spring, flower stalks to 2 ft. tall bear sprays of white-eyed lavender-blue blossoms. Showy as a mass planting. Dies after flowering; self-sows reliably. Grow in partial or full shade, in soil with lots of organic matter.

P. congesta. BLUE CURLS. Annual or biennial. Zones US, MS, LS, CS, TS; 9–3. Native to Texas and New Mexico. Grows 3 ft. tall, 1½ ft. wide. Deeply cut, bright green, soft leaves to 4 in. long, 1½ in. wide. Blooms throughout spring; buds form on a curled spike, which uncoils as the buds open into blue-purple flowers. Easy to grow from seed. For a long bloom period, be sure to water during dry spells. Full sun.

PHAEDRANTHUS buccinatorius. See DISTICTIS buccinatoria

PHAEOMERIA speciosa. See ETLINGERA elatior

PHAIUS

Orchidaceae

TERRESTRIAL ORCHIDS

✷ CS, TS; OR HOUSEPLANTS

◐ LIGHT SHADE; BRIGHT LIGHT

● REGULAR WATER

Phaius tankervilliae

These orchids owe their popularity to their attractive foliage, striking flowers, and ease of cultivation. Large, broad, rich green leaves somewhat resemble those of cast-iron plant (*Aspidistra*); they are marked with prominent parallel veins. Erect flower spikes to 3 ft. tall arise from the bases of large, thick pseudobulbs. In the Coastal and Tropical South, *Phaius* species are perennials; elsewhere, they're quite easy to grow as houseplants.

Although they'll take full sun for short periods, these orchids prefer light shade. Those grown indoors will bloom just fine if placed next to a bright window (they will, however, need protection from hot, direct sun). Give them fertile, well-drained soil that contains plenty of organic matter. From winter through the end of summer, keep the soil evenly moist (never use cold water); then let it go slightly dry for 3 to 4 weeks in fall. From spring through summer, feed every other week with water-soluble 20-20-20 fertilizer diluted to half-strength. Be careful with the leaves, which break easily. Plants are easy to divide. Scale can be a serious pest, especially on indoor plants; control it by spraying with horticultural oil.

P. flavus. Heat zones 12–1. From India, Thailand, Malaysia, and Indonesia. Leaves to 2 ft. long are attractively marked with yellow blotches and spots. In spring, blossom spikes carry many fragrant, 3-in.-wide flowers in sulphur yellow with a reddish brown band on the lip. 'Punctata' has yellow-spotted foliage.

P. tankervilliae. NUN'S ORCHID. Heat zones 12–6. Native to China, India, Sri Lanka, Southeast Asia, and Australia. May well be the easiest of all orchids to grow. Handsome, oblong to oval and pointed leaves 2–3 ft. long. Fragrant, 2- to 3-in.-wide blooms appear from late winter into spring; they are dusty rose inside and creamy white outside, with a rosy purple lip.

PHALAENOPSIS

MOTH ORCHID

Orchidaceae

EPIPHYTIC ORCHIDS

✷ TS ⊞ 9–3 OR HOUSEPLANTS

◐ FILTERED SUN; BRIGHT INDIRECT LIGHT

● REGULAR WATER

Phalaenopsis

These are tropical orchids with thick, broad, leathery leaves and no pseudobulbs. Leaves are rather flat, to 1 ft. long. From spring to fall, plants bear long (to 3-ft.) sprays of 3- to 6-in.-wide flowers in white, cream, pale yellow, or light lavender pink; some are spotted or barred or have lips in a contrasting color. Many lovely hybrids are sold. Very popular orchid commercially.

If you've never grown orchids before, moth orchids are good ones to start with. They are usually greenhouse plants, since they need fairly high

P

humidity and warmer growing conditions than most orchids (minimum of 60–65°F at night, 70–85°F during the day). In the house, a good location is near a bathroom or kitchen window with light coming through a gauze or other sheer curtain (foliage burns easily in direct sun). Some smaller-flowered new hybrids give promise of being easier to grow, tolerating somewhat lower night temperatures. Give moth orchids same potting medium as cattleya (see Orchidaceae). When cutting flowers, cut back to just above one of the tiny bracts on the stem; secondary sprays may form. To promote stronger new growth, many growers prefer to cut out the entire stem after blossoms fade.

PHALARIS arundinacea picta

RIBBON GRASS

Poaceae (Gramineae)

PERENNIAL GRASS

US, MS, LS, CS H 9–1

FULL SUN OR PARTIAL SHADE

REGULAR WATER

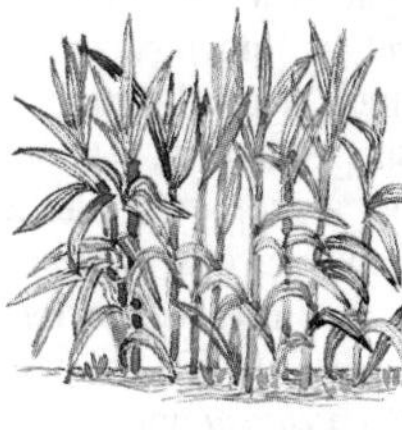

Phalaris arundinacea picta

Native to North America, Eurasia. This tough, tenacious grass is an old Southern favorite; it forms a 2- to 3-ft.-high clump that spreads aggressively—and indefinitely—by underground runners. Deep green leaves with longitudinal white stripes turn buff colored in autumn; airy white flower clusters age to pale brown. To keep this plant in bounds, grow it in large containers or use same control methods as for running kinds of bamboo (see Bamboo). Less invasive selections are 'Woods Dwarf' ('Dwarf's Garters'), which grows about half as tall as the species and has brighter white stripes; and 'Feesey' ('Strawberries and Cream'), to 1½–2 ft. tall, with white stripes that usually take on pink tints during cool weather.

PHASEOLUS. See BEAN

PHASEOLUS caracalla. See VIGNA caracalla

PHEASANT'S EYE. See NARCISSUS poeticus recurvus

PHILADELPHUS

MOCK ORANGE

Hydrangeaceae (Philadelphaceae)

DECIDUOUS, SEMIEVERGREEN, EVERGREEN SHRUBS

ZONES VARY BY SPECIES

PARTIAL SHADE IN HOTTEST CLIMATES

MODERATE TO REGULAR WATER

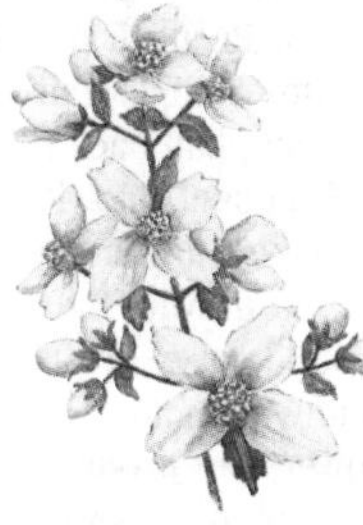

Philadelphus × lemoinei

Grown for white or cream-colored, usually fragrant flowers that bloom in late spring or early summer. Blossoms are four petaled, typically 1–2 in. wide; they range from single to fully double and may be borne singly or in clusters, depending on species. Mock oranges are generally large and vigorous, with fountainlike form. Oval, 2- to 4-in.-long leaves (typically medium green in color) are arranged in pairs along the stems.

Prune every year just after bloom, cutting out oldest wood and surplus shoots at base. To rejuvenate, cut to the ground after bloom. Taller types are striking planted in lawns and as background and corner plantings; smaller kinds can be planted near foundations or used as low screens or informal hedges. Buy plants in bloom to check for best fragrance. Not fussy about soil type but must have good drainage.

P. coronarius. SWEET MOCK ORANGE, ENGLISH DOGWOOD. Deciduous. Zones US, MS, LS, CS; 9–4. Native to southern Europe, Caucasus. Strong-growing old favorite to 10–12 ft. tall and wide. Clusters of fragrant, 1½-in. flowers. 'Aureus', to 8 ft. high, has bright golden foliage that turns yellow green in summer.

P. × lemoinei. Deciduous. Zones US, MS, LS; 8–5. Group of hybrids, most to 5–6 ft. high and wide. All bear clusters of particularly fragrant, 1-in. flowers. Single-flowered 'Avalanche' and 'Mont Blanc' and double-flowered 'Enchantment' are well-known selections.

P. mexicanus. EVERGREEN MOCK ORANGE. Zones CS, TS; 12–9. From Mexico. Vining shrub has long, supple stems clothed with evergreen leaves. Creamy white, highly fragrant, 1½-in. flowers in small clusters may bloom sporadically throughout year. Can be kept to 6 ft. high and wide as a free-standing shrub. It is best used, however, as a vine or bank cover; can climb 15–20 ft. if given support.

P. microphyllus. Deciduous. Zones US, MS, LS, CS; 9–6. From southwestern U.S., Mexico. To 4–5 ft. tall and wide (often smaller), with small (¾- to 1½-in.-long) leaves. Extremely fragrant, inch-wide flowers are borne singly or in pairs. Endures some drought.

P. × purpureomaculatus. Deciduous. Zones US, MS, LS; 9–6. This group of hybrids includes the ever-popular 'Belle Etoile', a compact shrub that grows to 5 ft. tall and 8 ft. wide; it bears fringed, purple-centered single flowers to 2½ in. across. Sometimes sold as *P. × lemoinei* 'Belle Etoile'.

P. texensis. TEXAS MOCK ORANGE. Semievergreen. Zones LS, CS; 10–8. Texas native to 3 ft. tall and wide. Small, shiny dark green leaves. Fragrant spring flowers are 1–3 in. across. Grows in virtually any well-drained soil—limestone, clay, sand, or loam.

P. × virginalis. VIRGINAL MOCK ORANGE. Deciduous. Zones US, MS, LS; 8–1. This hybrid has produced several garden selections, most with fragrant double flowers. Low-growing kinds include 'Dwarf Minnesota Snowflake' (2–3 ft. high and wide, with 1- to 1½-in. double flowers) and 'Glacier' (3–4 ft. tall and about as wide, with 1½-in. double blossoms). Larger selections, 6–8 ft. high and wide, include 'Minnesota Snowflake' (reputedly hardy to –30°F) and 'Virginal', both with 2-in. double flowers. 'Natchez' (to 8–10 ft.) is the showiest selection of all, with profuse, unscented single white blooms up to 2 in. across.

PHILODENDRON

Araceae

EVERGREEN VINES AND SHRUBS

ZONES VARY BY TYPE; OR HOUSEPLANTS

EXPOSURE NEEDS VARY BY TYPE; BRIGHT INDIRECT LIGHT

REGULAR WATER

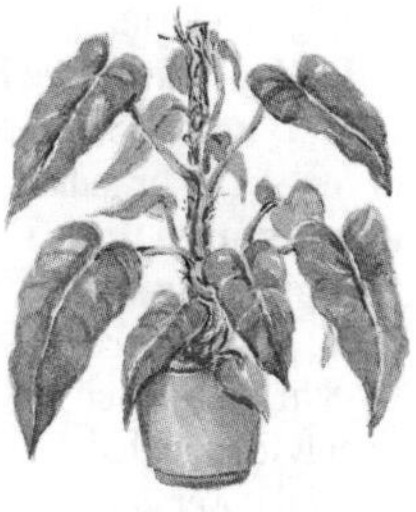

Philodendron erubescens

From the tropical Americas. Fast-growing plants that are nearly indestructible—can be grown well even by those who manage to kill everything else. Plants are favored for attractive, leathery, usually glossy leaves. In good conditions, old plants may bloom; flowers resemble those of calla *(Zantedeschia)*, with a boatlike bract surrounding a club-shaped structure. Bracts are usually greenish, white, or reddish. Browsing deer don't seem to care for these plants.

Whether grown in containers or open ground, all philodendrons need rich, loose, well-drained soil. Feed lightly and frequently for good growth and color. Clean dust from leaves of indoor plants. Most philodendrons—especially those grown in containers—tend to drop their lower leaves, leaving a bare stem. Once a plant gets gangly and overgrown, the best course is often simply to discard it and replace it with a new plant. However, you can also cut the plant back to short stub, then let it regrow; or you can air-layer the leafy top, then plant the layer once it roots (and discard the parent). Some philodendrons send down aerial roots. Push these into soil or cut them off (removing them won't hurt plant).

Philodendrons fall into two main classes.

Arborescent; relatively hardy. These are large, shrub-size plants with big leaves and sturdy, self-supporting trunks. They can be grown indoors but need much more space than most houseplants. They grow outdoors in the Coastal and Tropical South (and in heat zones 12–9). As landscape plants, they do best in sun (some shade at midday where light is intense) but can take considerable shade. Use them for tropical effects or as massive silhouettes against walls or glass. Excellent in large containers; very effective near swimming pools.

Vining and self-heading; tender. This class includes tender plants of two different habits. They can grow outdoors only in the Tropical South (and in heat zones 12–9), where they require partial or full shade; elsewhere, they are houseplants. Many kinds are sold, with many different leaf shapes and sizes. *Self-heading* types form short, broad plants with leaves radiating out from a central point. *Vining* types do not really climb and must be tied to or leaned against a support until they eventually shape themselves to it. The support can be almost anything, but certain water-absorbent columns (sections of tree fern stem, wire and sphagnum "totem poles," slabs of bark) serve especially well, since they can be kept moist.

The following list indicates the class of each species and selection. Note that one popular "philodendron"—the so-called split-leaf philodendron—belongs to another genus, *Monstera.*

P. bipinnatifidum (P. selloum). Arborescent. Treelike shrub to 6–15 ft. high and wide, typically with a single upright trunk that leans with age. Deeply cut leaves to 3 ft. long, on equally long stalks.

P. cordatum. See P. scandens oxycardium

P. domesticum. Vining. Often sold as *P.* 'Hastatum'. Grows to 10–20 ft. high, with arrow-shaped bright green leaves to 2 ft. long and 1 ft. wide.

P. erubescens. Vining. Often sold as *P.* 'Hastatum'. To 10–20 ft. high, with foot-long, arrow-shaped deep green leaves with coppery undersides. Subject to leaf spot in overly warm, moist conditions. A number of selections and hybrids are available; they are more resistant to leaf spot and tend to be more compact. Some, possibly hybrids, have much red in new foliage and in leafstalks. 'Royal Queen' has bright red new growth; mature leaves are dark green heavily tinged with red. 'Emerald Queen' is a choice deep green form.

P. 'Hastatum'. See P. domesticum, P. erubescens

P. 'Lynette'. Self-heading. To 1 ft. high, 2 ft. wide. Makes a tight cluster of foot-long, broadish, bright green leaves that are strongly patterned by deeply sunken veins. Good tabletop plant.

P. martianum (P. cannifolium). Self-heading. To 2 ft. tall, 3–4 ft. wide. Leathery, lance-shaped dark green leaves grow to 1½ ft. long and 6–8 in. wide; each leaf has a broad midrib and a swollen-looking, spongy, deeply channeled leafstalk to 15 in. long. Makes a nice coarse-leafed ground cover.

P. melanochrysum (P. andreanum). BLACK-GOLD PHILODENDRON. Vining. To 10–20 ft. high, with velvety, lance-shaped greenish black leaves to 3 ft. long, 1 ft. wide. Midribs and lateral veins are pale green. The new leaves are heart shaped and have a coppery tinge.

P. oxycardium. See P. scandens oxycardium

P. pertusum. See Monstera deliciosa

P. scandens. HEART-LEAF PHILODENDRON. Vining. Among the most common philodendrons. Can reach 50 ft. Deep green, heart-shaped leaves; juvenile leaves are 4–6 in. long, while mature ones can grow to 1 ft. long. *P. s. micans* has velvety young leaves; mature leaves are smooth. *P. s. oxycardium* (often sold as *P. oxycardium* or *P. cordatum*) has glossy leaves throughout its life. Juvenile forms of both are most popular; they are grown on tree trunks, in hanging baskets and window boxes, as houseplants. Indoors, train them on string or wire for a variety of decorative effects; or grow on moisture-retentive columns.

Philodendron scandens oxycardium

P. wendlandii. Self-heading. To 1 ft. high, 2 ft. wide. Compact clusters of 12 or more deep green, foot-long, broadly lance-shaped leaves on short, broad stalks. Indoors, this species is useful where a tough, compact foliage plant is needed. *P.* 'Lynette' is similar.

P. williamsii. Arborescent. Arrow-shaped, glossy deep green leaves to 2½ ft. long and 1 ft. wide. Leafstalks almost as long as leaves.

PHLOMIS

Lamiaceae (Labiatae)

PERENNIALS AND EVERGREEN SHRUBS

◪ ZONES VARY BY SPECIES

☼ FULL SUN, EXCEPT AS NOTED

◐◓ LITTLE TO MODERATE WATER

Mediterranean natives related to sage *(Salvia)*. Erect stems are set with widely spaced whorls of hooded, two-lipped flowers in yellow, purple, or lilac. Moisture-conserving thick, typically furry or hairy leaves are lance shaped to oval, set opposite each other on stems. Not particular about soil but must have good drainage. Not usually damaged by browsing deer. Cut flowers are striking in arrangements.

Phlomis fruticosa

P. 'Edward Bowles' ('Grande Verde', 'Lemon Swirl'). Shrub. Zones US, MS, LS, CS; 9–6. Grows to 3–4 ft. tall, 5–6 ft. wide. Hybrid between *P. fruticosa* and *P. russeliana.* Resembles a bulkier *P. fruticosa* and has broader leaves (to 6 in. long, 3 in. wide) and larger, pure yellow flowers. Often sold as *P. fruticosa* and takes the same care.

P. fruticosa. JERUSALEM SAGE. Shrub. Zones US, MS, LS; 9–6. To 4 ft. tall and wide, with woolly gray-green leaves to 6–8 in. long, 1¼ in. wide. Deep golden yellow, 1-in. flowers in ball-shaped whorls along upper half of stems. Cut plants back by half in fall to keep them compact. With watering, will produce several waves of bloom in spring and summer if cut back lightly after each flowering. Can tolerate light shade for part of day.

P. italica. Shrub. Zones LS, CS, TS; 12–8. Arching, suckering habit to 3–4 ft. tall, 5–6 ft. or more wide. Gray-green, 2- to 3-in.-long leaves are covered with silvery wool. Lilac-pink flowers in 1-in. whorls from early to midsummer. To keep plant neat, remove faded flowering stems; cut out basal branches that are more than 3 years old.

P. lanata. Shrub. Zones CS; 9–1. Dense, compact plant to 2½ ft. tall, 4–6 ft. wide. Woolly, wrinkled sage green leaves to about 1 in. long. Stems and leaf undersides have brownish scales. Whorls of deep yellow, 1-in. flowers bloom from spring to fall if faded stems are cut out.

P. purpurea. Shrub. Zones CS; 10–9. Rather lax habit to 4–6 ft. high and wide. Lance-shaped leaves to 4 in. long are gray green and sparsely hairy above, white and woolly beneath; new shoots are also white and woolly. Purplish pink flowers bloom mainly in late spring, but scattered blossoms appear all year long where winters are mild. After each flowering, cut plant back by one-third to keep it neat and compact.

P. russeliana. Perennial. Zones US, MS, LS; 9–1. Spreads by rhizomes to make a low clump of furry olive green foliage. Leaves are large (to 8 in. long, 6 in. wide) and heart shaped. Creates an effective weed-suppressing ground cover. Sends up 2- to 3-ft.-tall stems bearing flowers in soft yellow fading to cream. The main bloom period comes in early summer, but some flowers are produced later as well. Flower spikes are attractive even after blooms fade; they dry out and remain upright throughout winter. Tolerates partial shade.

P. samia. Perennial. Zones US, MS, LS; 9–3. Similar in habit and size to *P. russeliana*, forming a low mat of oval, scallop-edged, 4- to 8-in.-long leaves that are medium green above, white and woolly below. Blooms all summer, sending up 2- to 3-ft.-tall stems of flowers in purple or purplish pink (greenish or white in some forms).

P. tuberosa. Zones US, MS, LS; 8–5. Perennial from tuberous roots. Basal rosette of deep green foliage covered with fine hairs; deeply toothed, arrow-shaped leaves to 10 in. long. From late spring into summer, sends up 3- to 6-ft. stems with purple or pinkish mauve blossoms along upper third; upper lip of each flower is straight rather than hooded. Blooming plants resemble foxgloves *(Digitalis).* Disappears in winter.

FOR INFORMATION ON SELECTING PLANTS

PLEASE SEE PAGES 39–144

P

PHLOX

Polemoniaceae

PERENNIALS AND ANNUALS

ZONES VARY BY SPECIES

FULL SUN OR LIGHT SHADE, EXCEPT AS NOTED

REGULAR WATER, EXCEPT AS NOTED

Phlox divaricata

M ost are from North America. With the exception of *P. drummondii* (annual phlox), the species described here are perennial. The many types show wide variation in form, but all have showy flower clusters. Tall kinds are excellent border plants; dwarf ones are mainstays of the rock garden. Unless otherwise noted, grow in ordinary garden soil and provide regular moisture. Two major problems affect phlox: red spider mites (attack almost all species) and powdery mildew (*P. paniculata* is especially susceptible).

P. × arendsii. Zones US, MS, LS, CS; 8–1. Hybrid between *P. divaricata* and *P. paniculata*. To 1½ ft. high, not quite as wide, with 1-in.-wide blossoms in clusters to 6 in. across, early summer. Cut off faded flowers for later rebloom. Selections include reddish purple 'Anja'; lavender 'Hilda'; and 'Suzanne', bearing white blooms with a red eye. 'Ping Pong' is a mildew-resistant variety with soft rose flowers, reddish green leaves, and reddish stems.

P. bifida. SAND PHLOX. Zones US, MS, LS; 8–1. From the central U.S. Clumps to 8–10 in. tall, 6–8 in. wide, with narrow light green leaves. Blooms spring through early summer, bearing profuse, ½-in. lavender to white flowers with deeply notched petals. Likes full sun and excellent drainage; tolerates drought.

P. buckleyi. Zones US, MS, LS; 8–5. Native to Virginia and West Virginia. Trailing stems, set with willowlike evergreen leaves to 5 in. long, form a clump to 6 in. tall, 2 ft. wide. Upright stems to 1½ ft. high hold clusters of rosy purple flowers in late spring and summer. Makes a good ground cover.

P. 'Chattahoochee'. Zones US, MS, LS, CS; 9–3. Semievergreen. Cross between *P. divaricata laphamii* and *P. pilosa*. Low grower to 6–12 in. tall and 1 ft. wide; can spread by rooting stems to form colonies. Shiny dark green, lance-shaped leaves to 2 in. long. Profuse clusters of lightly fragrant, lavender-blue flowers with maroon centers appear over a long period in spring. Sometimes sold as *P. pilosa* 'Moody Blue'.

P. divaricata. BLUE PHLOX. Zones US, MS, LS, CS; 8–1. Native to eastern North America. To 1 ft. high, 2 ft. wide, with creeping underground shoots. Slender stems are clothed in oblong, 1½- to 2-in.-long leaves. Blooms in spring, bearing open clusters of ¾- to 1½-in.-wide, somewhat fragrant blossoms; color varies from pale blue (sometimes with pinkish tones) to white. Flowers of 'Dirigo Ice' are palest blue, those of *P. d. laphamii* bright blue. 'Blue Moon' has deep violet-blue blooms; flowers of 'Louisiana Purple' are an intense blue purple. 'Montrose Tricolor' has lavender-blue blossoms and leaves variegated in pink, white, and green. Use in rock garden or as bulb cover. Grow in good, deep soil. Light shade.

P. drummondii. ANNUAL PHLOX, DRUMMOND PHLOX. Zones US, MS, LS, CS, TS; 12–1. Native to Texas. To 6–18 in. high, 10–12 in. wide, with erect, leafy stems more or less covered with rather sticky hairs. Lance-shaped to oval, nearly stalkless leaves are 1–3 in. long. Profuse blossoms in tight clusters at tops of stems. Comes in bright and pastel colors (no blue or orange), some with contrasting eye. Tall strains (about 1½ ft. high) in mixed colors include Finest and Fordhook Finest. Dwarf (6- to 8-in.) strains include Beauty and Globe, both with roundish flowers; and starry-blossomed Petticoat and Twinkle. Bloom period lasts from early summer until frost if faded flowers are removed. Plant in spring in Upper South, in fall elsewhere. Grow in light, rich soil well amended with organic matter. Full sun.

P. glaberrima triflora. SMOOTH PHLOX. Zones US, MS, LS, CS; 9–1. From the eastern U.S. Grows to 1½–2 ft. tall, 1–1½ ft. wide, with smooth, narrow, 3-in.-long leaves. Lavender-pink flowers in late spring. This species is mildew-free.

P. maculata. CAROLINA PHLOX, THICK-LEAF PHLOX. Zones US, MS, LS; 8–1. Native to eastern North America. To 3–4 ft. tall, 1½ ft. wide, with thick, narrow, pointed leaves 2–4 in. long. Early summer flowers about ¾ in. wide in 15-in.-long clusters; colors range from white (often with a colored eye) through pink shades to magenta. Shiny, mildew-resistant foliage. Selections include 'Alpha', rose pink; 'Delta', white with pink eye; 'Natascha', pink and white bicolor; 'Omega', white with purplish pink eye; and 'Rosalinde', deep rose pink. 'Miss Lingard', with pure white flowers, may be a hybrid between *P. maculata* and another eastern species, *P. carolina*.

P. nivalis. TRAILING PHLOX. Zones US, MS, LS; 8–6. Native to central U.S. Trailing plant to 4–6 in. high, 1 ft. wide. Forms a loose mat of narrow, inch-long leaves. Pink or white, 1-in. flowers in fairly large clusters, late spring or early summer. Excellent in rock gardens; needs good drainage. 'Camla' is a good pale salmon pink selection. 'Snowdrift' has pure white blooms.

P. ovata. MOUNTAIN PHLOX. Zones US, MS, LS; 8–5. From the eastern U.S. To 15–20 in. tall, 1 ft. wide, with smooth, green, oval, mildew-free leaves to 6 in. long. Deep pink flowers in late spring.

P. paniculata. SUMMER PHLOX. Zones US, MS, LS, CS; 9–1. From eastern North America. To 3–5 ft. tall, 2 ft. wide, with narrow, 2- to 5-in.-long leaves tapering to a slender point. Fragrant, 1-in. flowers in large, dome-shaped clusters throughout summer. Colors include white and shades of lavender, pink, rose, and red; blooms of some selections have a contrasting eye. Plants do not come true from seed—most seedlings tend toward an uncertain purplish pink, though some may be attractive.

Summer phlox thrives in full sun, but flower color may bleach in hottest areas. After setting out young plants, pinch stem tips to induce branching. Mulch to keep roots cool. Divide every few years, replanting young shoots from outside of clump.

Very susceptible to mildew at end of bloom season. To minimize the problem, provide good air circulation: don't crowd plants, and thin mature plants to leave only six to eight stems. Among mildew-resistant selections are white-flowered 'David' and 'Mt. Fuji' ('Fujiyama'); 'Delta Snow', white with purple eye; 'Eva Cullum', pink with red eye; 'Franz Schubert', lilac pink; 'Laura', purple with white eye; 'Nicky', deep magenta; and 'Robert Poore', violet pink.

P. stolonifera. CREEPING PHLOX. Zones US, MS, LS; 8–1. Old favorite from eastern North America. Creeping, mounding plant to 6–8 in. high, 1 ft. wide, with narrow evergreen leaves to 1½ in. long. Profuse springtime show of 1-in. lavender flowers. Selections include lavender-blue 'Blue Ridge', white 'Bruce's White', and deep lavender 'Sherwood Purple'. Light shade.

P. subulata. MOSS PINK. Zones US, MS, LS; 8–1. From eastern U.S. Forms a mat to 6 in. high, 1½ ft. or wider, with creeping stems clothed in ½-in., needlelike evergreen to semievergreen leaves. Blooms in late spring or early summer, bearing ¾-in. flowers in colors including white, pale to deep shades of pink, and lavender blue. Makes sheets of brilliant color in rock gardens. Plant in loose, not-too-rich soil; give moderate water. After flowering, cut back halfway. Specialists offer two dozen or more selections of this old Southern favorite; many are actually selections of other low-growing species, or hybrids between those species and *P. subulata*. 'Tamaongalei' ('Candy Stripe') has rose pink blossoms edged in white; it is somewhat drought tolerant and has good fall rebloom.

PHOENIX

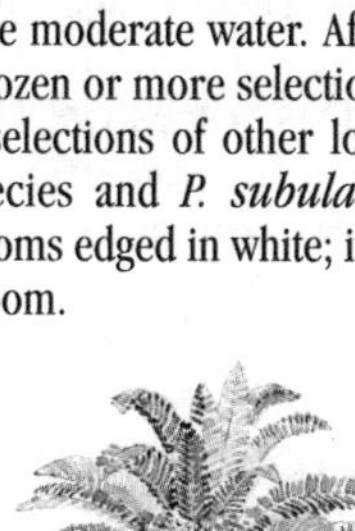

DATE PALM

Arecaceae (Palmae)

PALMS

CS (MILDER PARTS), TS 12–9

FULL SUN, EXCEPT AS NOTED

REGULAR WATER

Phoenix canariensis

T hese feather palms are mostly large trees, though the following list includes two that grow less than 20 ft. tall. Trunks are patterned with bases of old leafstalks. Small yellowish flowers in large, hanging sprays. On female trees, blossoms are followed by clusters of dates—but only if the tree has been in the ground for at least several years and if a male tree is nearby. Dates of *P. dactylifera* and *P. sylvestris* are used commercially; those of other species don't have as much edible flesh. Date palms hybridize freely, so buy these trees from a reliable nursery that knows the seed or plant source. Deer seldom bother date palms.

P. canariensis. CANARY ISLAND DATE PALM. Hardy to 20°F; slow to develop new head of foliage after damage from hard frosts. Canary Island native. Big, heavy-trunked palm to 60 ft. tall, with a great many bright green to deep green, gracefully arching fronds that form a crown to 50 ft. wide. Grows slowly until it forms a trunk, then speeds up a little. Young plants do well in pots for many years, looking something like pineapples. Best planted in parks, along wide streets, or in other large spaces; not for small city lots. Takes seacoast conditions.

P. dactylifera. DATE PALM. Leaves killed at 20°F, but plants have survived 4°F. Native to the Mideast. Classic palm of desert oases. Slender-trunked tree to 80 ft., with a crown 20–40 ft. wide; gray-green, waxy leaves have stiff, sharp-pointed leaflets. Sends up suckers from base; its natural habit is a clump of several trunks. Bears the dates you find in markets; principal variety is 'Deglet Noor'. Too large and stiff for most home gardens. Does well at seaside, in desert.

Phoenix dactylifera

P. loureirii (P. humilis). Hardy to 20°F. Native from India to China. Resembles a smaller, slimmer, more refined *P. canariensis*. Slow grower to 10–18 ft. tall and wide, with dark green leaves. Thrives in containers.

P. reclinata. SENEGAL DATE PALM. Damaged below 25°F. Native to tropical Africa. To 20–30 ft. high and wide. Produces offshoots, forming picturesque clumps with several curving trunks; if you want a single-trunked tree, remove offshoots. Fertilize for fast growth. Good seaside plant.

P. roebelenii. PYGMY DATE PALM. Foliage browns at around 26°F but recovers rapidly in spring. From Laos. Small, slow-growing, single-trunked palm to 6–10 ft. high. Fine-textured, curving leaves form a dense crown 6–8 ft. across. Good in groves or as a potted plant. Full sun or partial shade.

Phoenix roebelenii

P. rupicola. CLIFF DATE PALM. Hardy to 26°F. Native to India. As stately as *P. canariensis,* but it has a slender trunk and is a much smaller tree, reaching only 25 ft. high, 15–20 ft. wide. Lower leaves droop gracefully.

P. sylvestris. SILVER DATE PALM. Hardy to 22°F. Native to India. Beautiful single-trunked palm to 30 ft. tall, 20–25 ft. wide. Tapering trunk is wide at base, narrow at top. Dense, rounded crown of gray-green leaves. Fruit is used commercially for making date sugar.

PALMS FOR MANY USES. *The various species of* Phoenix *can fill a number of roles. Some are good as stately sentinels along an avenue. Several are surprisingly cold hardy, taking temperatures well below freezing. Some are salt-tolerant plants for seashore gardens; others flourish in hot, dry climates. See Palms for more information.*

PHORADENDRON
serotinum

AMERICAN MISTLETOE

Loranthaceae

EVERGREEN SHRUB

✂ MS, LS, CS, TS ⚑ 10–7

☼ ◑ FULL SUN TO LIGHT SHADE

● REGULAR WATER

Phoradendron serotinum

Native from New Jersey to Florida, west to southern Illinois and Texas. The deep green boughs of mistletoe are familiar sights in the South in winter, when they festoon the leafless branches of deciduous trees.

Growing 1–3 ft. tall and wide, this plant begins its life as a seed dropped by a bird onto the branch of a host tree. The seed quickly sprouts rootlike structures which penetrate the bark and tap into the flow of water and nutrients. Leathery, oval leaves, about 1 in. long, line mistletoe's crowded, forked branches. Small whitish flowers appear in late spring to early summer and are followed by clusters of single-seeded white berries. Although commonly thought to be highly poisonous, the berries are only moderately toxic; one would have to consume a large quantity to become seriously ill. In ancient times, people associated the berries with fertility; this may explain the custom of kissing under the mistletoe.

Mistletoe infests more than 100 species of hardwood trees; oaks, particularly water oak (*Quercus nigra*), are its favorite hosts. Others include hickory and pecan (*Carya*), honey locust (*Gleditsia triacanthos*), apple, hawthorn (*Crataegus*), and linden (*Tilia*). In most cases, the host tree is not seriously harmed. Pruning mistletoe removes it only temporarily; it will grow back from the point of attachment. For permanent removal, the infested branch must be removed at least 1 ft. below the point of attachment. But since this process may disfigure the tree—and reinfestation from nearby trees is likely—it's usually best to leave the tree alone. Mistletoe is the state flower of Oklahoma.

PHORMIUM tenax

NEW ZEALAND FLAX

Agavaceae

PERENNIAL

✂ LS, CS, TS ⚑ 12–6; OR GROW IN POTS

☼ ◑ FULL SUN OR PARTIAL SHADE

◐ ◗ ● LITTLE TO REGULAR WATER

Native to New Zealand. Large, bold plant with rigid, upright, swordlike leaves that grow in a fan pattern. Leaves are bronzy green, up to 6 ft. long and 2 in. wide. Mature clumps are about as wide as or a little wider than high. Vertical flower spikes held well above the foliage carry numerous dull red or reddish orange blossoms in late spring or early summer; twisted seedpods are held erect.

Phormium tenax

New Zealand flax makes a great focal point. The many colored-leaf and variegated selections provide year-round color in perennial and shrub borders, on hillsides, in seaside plantings, and near swimming pools. Outstanding in pots. Cool weather intensifies foliage color.

While most phormiums dislike humid summers and cold winters, New Zealand flax accepts the Southern climate. It takes almost any soil and tolerates drought and coastal conditions; good drainage, however, is essential to success. Selections include the following.

'Atropurpureum', 'Bronze', 'Purpureum', 'Rubrum'. These names are used interchangeably in the trade for plants with purplish or brownish red foliage that grow 6–8 ft. tall and wide. Usually grown from seed and somewhat variable; if you want a particular color, make sure you see the actual plant before buying.

'Atropurpureum Compactum' ('Monrovia Red'). To 5 ft. tall and wide, with burgundy-bronze foliage. Uniform; propagated by tissue culture.

'Bronze Baby'. To 3 ft. tall and wide, with 1½-in.-wide leaves. Foliage is deep reddish brown aging to deep bronze; narrow orange leaf edges and midrib (on underside) glow in sunlight.

'Chocolate'. To 4–5 ft. high and wide. Rich brown leaves have reddish undertones.

'Dusky Chief'. Dense clump to 6 ft. high and wide. Wine red leaves are 2–3 in. wide and have coral edges that glow when backlit.

'Jack Spratt'. To 1½ ft. high and wide, with ½-in.-wide, twisting, reddish brown leaves. 'Thumbelina' is similar but a little darker.

'Morticia'. To 3–4 ft. high and wide, with stiff, 1½-in.-wide, purple-black leaves.

'Pink Stripe' ('Pink Edge'). To 4–5 ft. high and wide. Gray-green foliage has a purplish tinge. Each leaf has a bright pink margin that is broader at base, gradually narrowing to almost nothing at tip.

'Tiny Tiger' ('Aurea Nana'). Miniature of 'Variegatum', reaching barely 1 ft. high and wide. Leaves are flushed pink in cool weather. 'Toney Tiger' is a 2-ft. version.

'Tom Thumb'. Upright clump to 2–3 ft. high and wide. Green, wavy-edged, ½-in.-wide leaves have red-bronze margins.

'Variegatum'. To 6–8 ft. tall and wide, with ¾-in.-wide, grayish green leaves that have creamy yellow stripes along edges.

'Veitchianum' ('Radiance', 'Williamsii Variegatum'). To 5–6 ft. tall, 7 ft. wide. Green leaves have a central yellow stripe and lime green margins with a thin orange edge.

PHOTINIA

Rosaceae

EVERGREEN AND DECIDUOUS SHRUBS AND TREES

☀ ZONES VARY BY SPECIES

☼ FULL SUN

◗◗ MODERATE TO REGULAR WATER

Photinia × fraseri 'Birmingham'

Densely foliaged plants with oval, pointed leaves and bright-colored new growth that matures to dark green. In early spring, all bear flattish clusters of small white flowers. In most types, blossoms are followed in fall by red or black berries that may last into winter. Evergreen species may suffer considerable damage if temperatures remain below 10°F for prolonged periods. Good for screen and background plantings. Tip-pinch plants to encourage colorful new growth. Prune to shape before spring growth begins or after bloom; don't allow new growth to get away from you and make long, bare switches. Many photinias can be converted to small trees by limbing up; or they can be trained as trees from the beginning. Berries are attractive to birds. All photinias are susceptible to fireblight, and all but *P. × fraseri* are subject to powdery mildew.

P. × fraseri. FRASER PHOTINIA, REDTIP. Evergreen shrub or small tree. Zones US (protected), MS, LS, CS; 9–7. Moderate to fast growth to 10–15 ft., spreading wider. Leaves to 5 in. long are bright, showy bronzy red when new. The flower clusters resemble those of *P. glabra* but are not followed by berries. Good as espalier or small single-stemmed tree, or hedge or tall screen. Cut branches are excellent in arrangements. Resists mildew. A fungus-induced leaf spot can be a serious problem; control by spraying new, healthy foliage with chlorothalonil (Daconil). Aphids may be a problem. The original Fraser photinia, officially named 'Birmingham' (a name that is hardly ever used), was born at Fraser Nursery in Birmingham, Alabama, around 1940. Because of the shrub's fast growth and appealing red-tipped evergreen foliage, it quickly became overplanted in the South; susceptibility to disease hasn't dimmed its popularity. Superior selections now exist, including 'Indian Princess', which has smaller leaves than those of species, and 'Red Robin', a compact grower resistant to leaf spot. Japanese cleyera *(Ternstroemia gymnanthera)* is a good substitute where leaf spot is a problem.

P. glabra. JAPANESE PHOTINIA. Evergreen shrub. Zones LS, CS; 9–7. From Japan. Broad, dense growth to at least 6–10 ft. high and wide. Leaves oval, broadest toward tip, to 3 in. long. Coppery new growth; scattered bright red leaves give a touch of color through fall and winter. Summer pruning will restrict size of plant to a neat 5 ft. and give continuing show of new foliage. Flowers in 4-in.-wide clusters have a fragrance similar to that of hawthorn *(Crataegus)*. Red berries age to black.

P. serratifolia (P. serrulata). CHINESE PHOTINIA. Evergreen shrub or small tree. Zones US, MS, LS, CS; 9–7. Broad, dense-growing Chinese native to 35 ft., though it can easily be held to 10 ft. high and wide. Stiff, crisp-textured, prickly-edged deep green leaves to 8 in. long. Bright copper new growth; scattered crimson leaves in fall and winter. Profuse 6-in. flower clusters (with rather unpleasant odor) are followed by bright red berries that often last into the winter; birds eat the fruit and spread seedlings far and wide. 'Aculeata' (often sold as 'Nova' or 'Nova Lineata') is more compact; its leaves have ivory yellow midribs and main veins.

P. villosa. ORIENTAL PHOTINIA. Deciduous shrub or small tree. Zones US, MS, LS; 9–1. From China, Korea, Japan. Usually multistemmed, to 15 ft. tall and 10 ft. wide. Leaves are 1½–3 in. long—pale gold with rosy tints when expanding, dark green at maturity, and bright red or yellow in fall. Flower clusters 1–2 in. across. Bright red fruit. Susceptibility to fireblight limits its use in the Lower South. Do not feed with high-nitrogen fertilizer in spring, as that will make it more susceptible to fireblight.

PHYGELIUS

CAPE FUCHSIA

Scrophulariaceae

PERENNIALS

☀ US, MS, LS ╫ 9–6

☼ ☽ FULL SUN OR LIGHT SHADE

◗ REGULAR WATER

Phygelius capensis

While true fuchsias sulk in hot Southern summers, these South African natives like the weather just fine. They die to the ground in winter in the Upper and Middle South but remain shrubby in the Lower South. Plants grow 3–4 ft. high, spreading about as wide by underground stems or rooting prostrate branches. From summer into fall, plants bear tubular, curved flowers resembling fuchsias in loosely branched clusters. After bloom, cut out old flower stalks to neaten plants. In the Upper South, mulch heavily in late fall. Species can be started from seed, but named selections should be grown from cuttings or by layering bottom branches.

P. aequalis. Pyramidal clusters of dusty rose flowers. 'Yellow Trumpet' has pale yellow blooms.

P. capensis. More open and sprawling than *P. aequalis,* with loose clusters of orange to red flowers.

P. × rectus. Hybrids between the previous two species. 'African Queen' has deep salmon orange flowers with a yellow throat; 'Devil's Tears', scarlet with yellow throat; 'Moonraker', solid pale yellow; 'Salmon Leap', orange; 'Tommy Knockers', peach with yellow throat; 'Winchester Fanfare', deep rose with yellow throat. 'Pink Elf' bears pink flowers on a smaller plant than the usual (2 ft. high, 3 ft. wide).

PHYLLITIS scolopendrium. See ASPLENIUM scolopendrium

PHYLLOSTACHYS. See BAMBOO

PHYSALIS alkekengi

CHINESE LANTERN PLANT

Solanaceae

PERENNIAL OFTEN GROWN AS ANNUAL

☀ US, MS, LS ╫ 8–1

☼ ☽ FULL SUN OR LIGHT SHADE

◗ REGULAR WATER

Physalis alkekengi

From Europe, Asia. Grown for the flowers' decorative, papery, 2-in. calyxes, which look like lanterns and mature to a striking orange red in late summer and fall. Plant grows 1½–3 ft. high and wide, with angular branches and light green, oval, 2- to 3-in.-long leaves. Small white flowers appear in leaf joints in summer; these are followed by inedible berries, each enclosed in a colorful inflated husk. Dry, leafless stalks hung with these "lanterns" make choice winter arrangements.

Sow seeds in light soil in spring. Plant is clump forming, spreading widely by long, creeping, whitish underground stems; can become invasive. Increase established plantings by digging and dividing the roots. 'Pygmy' is a dwarf selection just 8 in. high; it makes a good potted plant.

A *Physalis* species that produces edible fruit within a papery husk is *P. ixocarpa;* see Tomatillo.

P

PHYSIC NUT. See JATROPHA curcas

PHYSOCARPUS opulifolius

COMMON NINEBARK

Rosaceae

DECIDUOUS SHRUB

✿ US, MS ⑂ 7–1

☼ ◑ ● SUN OR SHADE

◗ ◗ MODERATE TO REGULAR WATER

Physocarpus opulifolius

Native to eastern and central North America. The common name refers to the plant's peeling bark, which strips off to reveal several layers. Graceful, arching growth to 9 ft. tall, 10 ft. wide; looks something like a larger version of spiraea, to which it is closely related. Medium green leaves to 3 in. long are broadly oval, with lobed edges. Rounded clusters of many tiny white or pinkish blossoms appear in spring or early summer. Prune as needed after bloom; rejuvenate by cutting old stems to the ground.

Selections are more attractive than the species. 'Diabolo', to 9–12 ft. high and wide, has intense reddish purple leaves (foliage color can tend toward dark green in very hot summers or when plant is grown in partial shade). Leaves of 'Luteus' are yellow when plant is grown in sunlight, yellow green in shade. Compact types to 4–6 ft. tall and broad include 'Dart's Gold', similar to 'Luteus' but brighter; 'Nanus', with small, shallowly lobed dark green leaves; and 'Nugget', with leaves that unfold golden yellow, gradually mature to lime green, and then turn gold again in fall.

PHYSOSTEGIA

OBEDIENT PLANT, FALSE DRAGONHEAD

Lamiaceae (Labiatae)

PERENNIAL

✿ US, MS, LS, CS

☼ ◑ FULL SUN OR PARTIAL SHADE

◗ REGULAR WATER

Physostegia virginiana
'Vivid'

These North America native plants have many fine qualities—but common name notwithstanding, obedience isn't one of them: they are notoriously invasive when growing in moist, fertile soil. Keep that in mind when choosing a site, and don't let them spread into wild areas. Slender, upright stems carry medium green, oblong, 3- to 5-in. leaves with toothed edges and pointed tips. Dense spikes of funnel-shaped, 1-in. flowers in pink, rose, white, or lavender top the stems. Blossoms resemble snapdragons (hence the name "false dragonhead") and remain in place if pushed or twisted out of position (hence "obedient plant"). Long-lasting cut flowers.

Spiky form makes these plants useful in composing borders. Combine with summer phlox (*Phlox paniculata*), asters, patrinia, Japanese anemone (*Anemone ×hybrida*), false aster (*Boltonia*). Tall bloom stalks may need staking. Cut to ground after bloom; divide every 2 years to keep plants in bounds.

P. angustifolia. Heat zones 9–1. Native to Texas, Illinois, Mississippi. Grows 2–6 ft. tall, 2–3 ft. wide; tallest in swampy conditions, where plant forms thick colonies. Pink-purple flowers on 4- to 6-in. spikes in spring and summer.

P. pulchella. Heat zones 9–4. Native to eastern Texas. Grows to 2 ft. tall (taller if kept moist), 1½ ft. wide. Bears spikes of rosy purple flowers in spring and summer.

P. virginiana. Heat zones 9–1. Native to the eastern U.S. To 4 ft. or taller, 2 ft. wide. Flowers are borne on 10-in. spikes from mid- or late summer into autumn. Rose pink 'Bouquet Rose' grows 3 ft. tall. 'Miss Manners' has pure white blooms and forms a neat clump 2–2½ ft. high; it spreads to 3 ft. or a little wider rather than running aggressively. Selections to about 2 ft. tall include white 'Summer Snow'; bluish pink 'Variegata', with white-edged leaves; and rose pink 'Vivid'.

PICEA

SPRUCE

Pinaceae

EVERGREEN TREES

✿ US, MS, EXCEPT AS NOTED

☼ ◑ FULL SUN OR LIGHT SHADE

◗ ◗ MODERATE TO REGULAR WATER, EXCEPT AS NOTED

Picea pungens

Like firs, spruces are pyramidal and have stiff needles, with branches arranged in neat tiers. But unlike firs, they have pendent cones, and their needles are attached to branches by small pegs that remain after needles drop. Most spruces are tall timber trees that lose their lower branches fairly early in life as they head upward; their canopies thin out noticeably as they age. Many species have dwarf forms useful as foundation plantings, for rock gardens, in containers. Spruces grow best in the Upper South.

Check spruces for aphids in late winter; if the pests are present, take prompt control measures to avoid spring defoliation. Other common pests are bagworms, spruce budworms, pine needle scale, and spider mites.

Prune only to shape. If a branch grows too long, cut it back to a well-placed side branch. For slower growth and denser form, trim part of each year's growth to force side branches. When planting larger spruces, don't place them too close to buildings, fences, or walks; they need space.

P. abies (P. excelsa). NORWAY SPRUCE. Heat zones 8–1. Native to northern Europe. Fast growth to 100–150 ft. tall, 20 ft. wide. Stiff, deep green, attractive pyramid in youth; ragged in age, as branchlets droop and oldest branchlets (those nearest trunk) die back. Extremely hardy and wind resistant; valued for windbreaks. Tolerates heat and humidity better than most spruces. Resists damage by browsing deer.

P. glauca. WHITE SPRUCE. Heat zones 8–2. Native to Canada and northern U.S. Narrowly cone-shaped tree grows 60–70 ft. tall, 10–12 ft. wide. Dense when young, with pendulous twigs and silvery green foliage. Crushed needles have an unpleasant odor. Not usually browsed by deer. The following two types are widely grown.

P. g. albertiana 'Conica'. DWARF ALBERTA SPRUCE, DWARF WHITE SPRUCE. Compact, pyramidal tree, slowly reaching 6–8 ft. tall, 4–5 ft. wide in 35 years. Short, soft needles are bright grass green when new, gray green when mature. Needs shelter from drying winds (whether hot or cold) and from strong reflected sunlight. Popular container plant.

P. g. densata. BLACK HILLS SPRUCE. Heat zones 6–1. Slow-growing, dense pyramid; can reach 20 ft. tall, 10–12 ft. wide in 35 years.

P. omorika. SERBIAN SPRUCE. Heat zones 8–1. Native to southeastern Europe. Narrow, conical, slow-growing tree to 50–60 ft. tall, 6–10 ft. wide. Shiny dark green needles with silvery undersides. Retains branches to the ground for many years. Considered by some to be the most attractive spruce; one of the best for hot, humid climates. 'Nana' is a dwarf to 3–4 ft. tall and wide (possibly to 10 ft. high), with short, closely packed needles.

P. orientalis. ORIENTAL SPRUCE. Heat zones 8–5. Native to the Caucasus, Asia Minor. Dense, compact, cone-shaped tree with very short needles; grows slowly to 50–60 ft. high, 20 ft. wide. Can tolerate poor soils if they are well drained, but may suffer leaf burn in very cold, dry winds.

P. pungens. COLORADO BLUE SPRUCE. Zones US, MS, LS (cooler parts); 8–1. Native to the Rocky Mountains, from Colorado and Wyoming to New Mexico. The many blue-needled forms have made this the most popular spruce for home gardens; it does well in dry soil and is not usually browsed by deer. Stiff, dense, horizontal branches form a narrow to broad pyramid with a very formal look. Grows at a slow to moderate rate; in the wild, it can reach 100 ft. tall, 25–35 ft. across, but typically grows 30–60 ft. tall, 10–20 ft. wide in gardens. Will grow in the Lower South but definitely prefers the shorter summers and longer winters farther north. Foliage of seedlings varies in color from dark green through blue-green shades to steely blue. The following selections have consistent blue color.

'Fat Albert'. Broad, formal-looking tree to 10–15 ft. tall, 10–12 ft. wide. Good as living Christmas tree. Particularly handsome blue foliage.

'Foxtail' ('Iseli Foxtail'). Vigorous, heat-tolerant selection that has performed well in cooler parts of the Lower South. Grows faster than the species, with upright, symmetrical habit. Young plants are bushy, with bluish, slightly twisted needles.

'Hoopsii'. Beautiful plant with striking silver-blue color. Fast growing; train early to ensure pyramidal shape. Many consider this the finest selection.

'Koster'. KOSTER BLUE SPRUCE. Forms a blue-gray cone, though growth habit may be irregular.

'Moerheimii'. Same blue-gray color as 'Koster', but shape is more compact and symmetrical. Needles are longer than those of other selections.

'Montgomery'. Slow-growing dwarf forms a broad silver-blue mound to 3–5 ft. high, 3 ft. wide.

'Thompsen'. Similar to 'Hoopsii' in color, but needles are twice as thick. Vigorous, symmetrical habit.

PICKEREL WEED. See PONTEDERIA cordata

PIERIS

Ericaceae

EVERGREEN SHRUBS

US, MS

FILTERED SUN OR PARTIAL SHADE

REGULAR WATER

LEAVES AND NECTAR ARE POISONOUS IF INGESTED

Pieris japonica

Elegant in foliage and form the year around, these plants make good companions for rhododendron and azalea, to which they are related. They have whorls of leathery, narrowly oval, glossy leaves in medium to dark green. Most plants form flower buds by autumn; these resemble strings of tiny beads in greenish pink, red, or white and provide a subtle decorative feature during winter. Clusters of small, urn-shaped, typically white flowers open from late winter to midspring. New spring growth is often brightly colored (pink to red or bronze).

Same cultural requirements as rhododendron and azalea. Need acid, well-drained but moisture-retentive soil; do not thrive in hot, dry conditions. Choose a planting location sheltered from wind, where plants will get high shade or dappled sunlight at least during the warmest afternoon hours. Prune by removing spent flowers. Thin older specimens by taking out whole branches; or limb them up to reveal attractive, peeling bark. Splendid in containers, in woodland and Japanese gardens, in entryways where year-round quality is essential. Deer usually avoid these shrubs.

P. floribunda (Andromeda floribunda). MOUNTAIN PIERIS. Zones US, MS; 8–5. Native to southeastern U.S. Compact, rounded shrub to 6 ft. tall, 10 ft. wide. Differs from the other species—new growth is pale green, mature leaves dull dark green, 1½–3 in. long. Blossoms in upright clusters. Cold hardy. Tolerates sun, heat, and low humidity better than the others, but does not thrive in hot, humid regions.

P. japonica (Andromeda japonica). JAPANESE ANDROMEDA, LILY-OF-THE-VALLEY SHRUB. Heat zones 8–6. Upright, dense, tiered growth to 9–10 ft. high and wide. Leaves are 3 in. long, bronzy pink to red when new. Drooping clusters of white, pink, or nearly red flowers; flower buds are often dark red. Many selections, some rare. The superior choices below are divided into two groups—the first grown for form or foliage, the second for flowers.

Selections grown for smaller-than-usual size or unusual leaves:

'Bert Chandler'. Salmon pink new foliage ages to cream, then white; then matures to pale green.

'Compacta'. Grows 4–6 ft. high and wide. Heavy bloomer.

'Crispa'. To 6–7 ft. high and wide, with handsome wavy-edged leaves.

'Karenoma'. Compact grower to 3–6 ft. high and wide, with upright flower clusters.

'Mountain Fire'. Fiery red new growth.

'Prelude'. To 2–3 ft. high and wide; pink new growth.

'Pygmaea'. Tiny dwarf to 1 ft. high and wide, with very few flowers and narrow leaves to 1 in. long.

'Spring Snow'. Similar to 'Karenoma'.

'Valley Fire'. Brilliant red new growth.

'Variegata'. Slow growing to 6 ft. high and wide. Creamy white leaf variegation; the white markings are tinged pink in spring. Prune out any green-leafed shoots.

Selections grown principally for flowers:

'Christmas Cheer'. Early bloomer with bicolor flowers in white and deep rose red; flower stalks are rose red.

'Coleman'. Pink flowers open from red buds.

'Daisen'. Bears flowers like 'Christmas Cheer' but has broader leaves.

'Dorothy Wyckoff'. White flowers open from deep red buds.

'Pink'. Shell pink flowers age to white.

'Purity'. To 3–4 ft. high and wide. Late bloomer with unusually large white flowers.

'Snowdrift'. Dense, slow growth to 4–6 ft. tall and a little wider. Pure white flowers come in large, upright clusters—the largest among selections listed here.

'Temple Bells'. Compact, tiered habit; slow grower to 3–5 ft. high and wide. A bit less cold tolerant than the species. Ivory flowers.

'Valley Rose'. Light pink flowers.

'Valley Valentine'. To 5–7 ft. tall and wide. Deep red buds and flowers.

'White Cascade'. Extremely heavy show of pure white blooms.

PIGEON BERRY. See DURANTA erecta

PIGEON PLUM. See COCCOLOBA diversifolia

PIGGYBACK PLANT. See TOLMIEA menziesii

PILEA

Urticaceae

ANNUALS AND PERENNIALS

TS H 12–10; OR HOUSEPLANTS

PARTIAL TO FULL SHADE; BRIGHT INDIRECT LIGHT

REGULAR WATER

Pilea cadierei

Plants in this large group are grown for their colorful, often interestingly patterned and textured leaves; flowers of most are inconspicuous. Many are popular houseplants—but where hardy, they also make nice outdoor potted plants or even ground covers for shady areas. Outdoors, they'll grow in moist soil in dappled morning sun to full shade. Indoors, they like bright indirect light and high humidity. Make sure soil is well drained, and let it go somewhat dry between thorough soakings. Feed every other week in spring and summer and once a month in fall and winter with liquid houseplant fertilizer. Mealybugs are common pests; dispatch them by dabbing with a cotton swab dipped in alcohol.

P. cadierei. ALUMINUM PLANT. Perennial. Native to Vietnam. Prominent silver markings on the oval, quilted-looking dark green leaves explain the common name. Leaves are 3 in. long; plant grows erect to 12–15 in. tall, 6–9 in. wide. Pinch periodically to induce bushiness. Dwarf 'Minima' is less than half the size of the species.

P. involucrata. FRIENDSHIP PLANT. Perennial. Native to Central and South America. Grows just 1¼ in. tall, spreading to 1 ft. wide. Broadly oval, tooth-edged, heavily quilted leaves to 1½ in. long are bronzy green above, purplish beneath. Pinch periodically to induce bushiness. 'Moon Valley' is more upright, to 1 ft. tall and wide, with larger green leaves featuring prominent bronze veins.

P. microphylla. ARTILLERY PLANT. Annual or short-lived perennial. From Florida, Mexico, West Indies, South America. Trailing, succulent stems form a mound to 1 ft. tall and somewhat wider. Bright green oval, tiny leaves (¼–½ in. long) are crowded along the wandering stems. Tiny flowers eject pollen forcefully, hence the common name. Outdoors, can spread widely and become a pest. ▶

P. nummulariifolia. CREEPING CHARLIE. Perennial. Native to West Indies and Panama, south to northern South America. Fast-growing, trailing plant to 6 in. tall and 2 ft. wide; perfect for hanging baskets. Roots at the nodes and spreads to make a good ground cover where hardy. Rounded light green leaves to about ¾ in. wide are deeply quilted, with prominent veins and scalloped edges.

PIMPINELLA anisum

ANISE
Apiaceae (Umbelliferae)
ANNUAL
✿ US, MS, LS, CS, TS ❙❙ 7–5
☼ FULL SUN
● REGULAR WATER

Pimpinella anisum

Mediterranean native to 2 ft. tall, 1½ ft. wide. First growth produces a clump of bright green, roundish to heart-shaped, tooth-edged leaves. Foliage clumps send up stems set with feathery leaves; in summer, stems bear umbrellalike clusters of tiny white flowers at their tips. Use fresh leaves in salads; use seeds for flavoring baked goods, confections.

Grow in light, well-drained soil. Plants are fairly wispy and look better when grouped. They develop taproots and do not transplant easily once they pass the seedling stage. Not usually browsed by deer.

Intolerance for heat and humidity makes this herb difficult to grow in much of the South. In the Upper and Middle South, sow seeds ½ in. deep in the garden after the last spring frost—or get a head start by sowing seeds indoors in peat pots 4 weeks before the last frost, then planting outdoors once the weather has warmed. Plants take about 4 months to mature. In the Lower, Coastal, and Tropical South, sow seeds in the garden in autumn; plants will grow through the winter and flower in spring. Seed production in these areas is iffy.

Pinaceae. Members of the pine family are evergreen trees with narrow, usually needlelike leaves and seeds borne on the scales of woody cones. Cedar (*Cedrus*), larch (*Larix*), spruce (*Picea*), pine (*Pinus*), Douglas fir (*Pseudotsuga*), and hemlock (*Tsuga*) are examples.

PINCUSHION FLOWER. See SCABIOSA

PINDO PALM. See BUTIA capitata

PINE. See PINUS

PINEAPPLE

Bromeliaceae
PERENNIAL
✿ TS ❙❙ 12–8; OR GROW IN POTS
☼ ◑ FULL SUN FOR FRUIT; BRIGHT LIGHT
● REGULAR WATER

Native to South America, this familiar bromeliad is known botanically as *Ananas comosus*. Reaches 2–3 ft. tall, 1½–2 ft. wide, with a short, thick stem topped by a rosette of long (1½- to 6-ft.), narrow dark green leaves with saw-toothed edges. At bloom time, the stem lengthens and produces a head of small red or purple flowers, which eventually develops into the pineapple fruit. Fruits are typically borne one per stem.

Pineapple

To grow pineapple, cut the leafy top from a market pineapple (cut about an inch below the leaves). Root in water or fast-draining but moisture-retentive potting mix. When roots have formed, move pineapple to an 8-in. pot of rich soil. Plant will overwinter only in the Tropical South; elsewhere, grow it as a full-time houseplant or move it indoors in winter. Water when soil goes dry; feed every 3 or 4 weeks with a general-purpose liquid houseplant fertilizer. If you're lucky, fruit will form in about 2 years, but it will be much smaller than a typical market pineapple.

A selection with leaves variegated in pink, white, and olive green is sometimes sold as a houseplant; it can take reduced light, since it is grown for foliage rather than fruit.

PINEAPPLE GUAVA. See FEIJOA

PINEAPPLE LILY. See EUCOMIS

PINK. See DIANTHUS

PINKROOT. See SPIGELIA marilandica

PINK SHOWER. See CASSIA grandis

PINK TRUMPET VINE. See PODRANEA ricasoliana

PIÑON. See PINUS cembroides, P. edulis

PINUS

PINE
Pinaceae
EVERGREEN TREES, RARELY SHRUBS
✿ ZONES VARY BY SPECIES
☼ FULL SUN
◐ ● LITTLE TO MODERATE WATER, EXCEPT AS NOTED
▶ SEE CHART NEXT PAGE

Pines are the great individualists of the garden, each species differing not only in its characteristics but also in the ways it responds to wind, heat, and other growing conditions. Differences in cone size and shape offer one way to tell these trees apart; another identifying characteristic is the number of needles in a bundle (pines bear their needles in clusters, or "bundles," on the

Pinus thunbergii

WHAT PINES NEED

DRAINAGE: Well-drained soil is crucial to a pine's good health. In nature, many pines grow on rocky slopes or sandy barrens, where drainage is very fast. Symptoms of excessive moisture are yellowing needles (seen first in older growth) and a generally unhealthy appearance.

WATERING: Most pines are quite drought tolerant; exceptions are noted in the chart.

FERTILIZING: Pines need little if any fertilizer; heavy feeding encourages too rapid, rank growth.

PRUNING: To fatten up a rangy pine or to keep a young one chubby, cut back the spires of new growth (the candles) when they begin to emerge in spring. Cutting back partway will promote bushiness and allow some overall increase in size; cutting out candles entirely will limit size without distorting the natural shape. This kind of careful pruning can even allow you to maintain pines as screens or hedges.

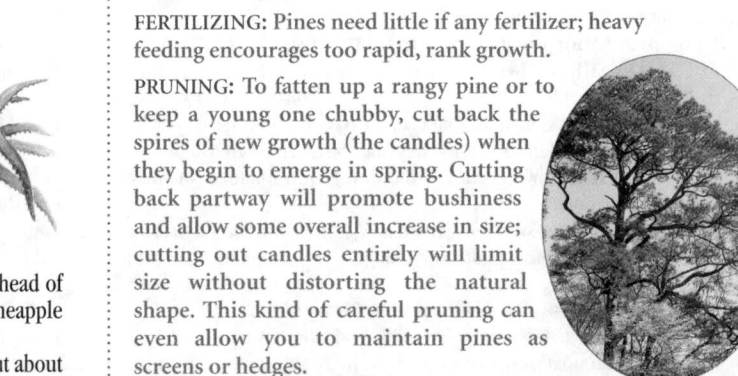

Pinus taeda

PINUS

NAME, NATIVE HABITAT	ZONES	GROWTH RATE, SIZE	GROWTH HABIT	NEEDLES AND CONES	COMMENTS
P. bungeana LACEBARK PINE Northern and central China	US, MS; 7–1. Hardy to –20°F	Slow to 50–75 ft. tall, 30–50 ft. wide	Starts out pyramidal to rounded, then becomes more open, spreading, picturesque. Often multitrunked; sometimes shrubby	Needles: in 3s, 2–4 in., bright green. Cones: 2–2½ in., oval, yellowish brown	Smooth, dull gray bark on main branches and trunk flakes off like that of sycamore *(Platanus)* to show smooth, creamy white patches. Brittle limbs can break under heavy snow loads
P. cembroides MEXICAN PIÑON PINE Arizona to Baja California and northern Mexico	US, MS, LS, CS; 9–1	Slow to 10–25 ft. tall, nearly as wide	Rather rangy in youth; in older trees, stout, spreading branches form a round-topped head	Needles: in 3s or 2s, 1–2 in., dark green. Cones: 1–2 in., rounded, yellowish or reddish brown	Very drought tolerant; adapted to poor, rocky, limy soils. Good choice for drier areas of Texas and Oklahoma. Cones contain edible seeds (pine nuts)
P. clausa SAND PINE Gulf Coast and coastal areas of Florida	LS, CS, TS; 12–8	Moderate to 30–40 ft. tall, 15–20 ft. wide	Slender and upright, with irregular crown	Needles: in 2s, 2–3½ in., dark green. Cones: 2–3 in., ovoid-conic	Good in sandy soils along the coast
P. echinata SHORTLEAF PINE Dry upland soils of Georgia, Oklahoma, and Texas	US, MS, LS, CS; 9–5	Fast to 50–80 ft. tall, 30–45 ft. wide	Open pyramidal habit when mature, with sinuous branches	Needles: in 2s or 3s, 3–5 in., dark bluish green. Cones: 1½–2½ in., pale brown, ovoid-oblong	Important timber species. Adaptable, but deep rooted and difficult to move once established. Good lawn tree. Resistant to most diseases and insects that affect most other pines
P. edulis **(P. cembroides edulis)** PIÑON, NUT PINE California's desert mountains; east to Arizona, New Mexico, and Texas; north to Wyoming	US, MS, LS; 8–3	Slow to 10–20 ft. tall, 8–16 ft. wide	Horizontally branching tree is bushy and symmetrical in youth. In age, a spreading tree with a gnarled trunk, rounded or flat crown	Needles: usually in 2s, ¾–1½ in., dark green, stiff. Cones: 2 in., roundish, light brown	Beautiful, densely foliaged small pine for container, rock garden. Cones contain edible seeds— the pine nuts sold commercially in markets. Well adapted to dry, rocky soils of Southwest
P. eldarica AFGHAN PINE Southwestern Asia	US, MS, LS, CS; 9–1	Fast to 30–80 ft. tall, 15–30 ft. wide	Denser, more erect than *P. halapensis,* with more classic pine tree shape	Needles: in 2s, 5–6½ in., dark green. Cones: like those of *P. halapensis,* but not stalked or bent back	Tolerates drought, alkaline soil. Well adapted to Southwest. Often grown there for Christmas trees
P. elliottii SLASH PINE Coastal Plains, South Carolina to Louisiana	LS, CS, TS; 12–8	Fast to possible 80 ft. high, 35 ft. wide	Dense, rounded crown	Needles: in 2s or 3s, to 1 ft., dark green, stiff. Cones: 3½–6 in., shiny brown	Usually planted for quick shade, erosion control. Adapted to acid-soil areas of East Texas. *P. e. densa* thrives in southern Florida
P. glabra SPRUCE PINE From South Carolina to Louisiana	LS, CS; 9–8	Moderate to 40–60 ft. high, 30 ft. wide	Horizontal branching at top of trunk; rounded crown. Branches low; casts heavy shade; difficult to grow grass under	Needles: in 2s, 2–3½ in., dark green, twisted. Cones: 2–2½ in., buff colored, ovoid	Likes fertile, moist acid soil; tolerates heavy clay. Widely planted in Lower South gardens east of Mississippi River

branches). Most species carry their long, slender needles in groups of two, three, or five. Those with two needles tend to tolerate unfavorable soil and climate better than three-needle species, and three-needle pines more so than five-needle ones. As a group, pines are much more adaptable to Southern growing conditions than spruce *(Picea)* or fir *(Abies)*. The chart describes pines that are well adapted to Southern climate zones.

Young trees tend to be pyramidal, while older ones are more open or round topped. The chart gives typical dimensions for pines in cultivation, but trees often grow much larger in the wild. Seeds of all pines attract birds; some species produce the pine nuts enjoyed by people and sold commercially.

All pines can be shaped, and often improved, by some pruning. The best time to prune is in spring, when new growth emerges. Cut the candles to promote bushiness or limit the plant's size. You can remove unwanted limbs to accent a pine's branching pattern—but before you cut out a branch, remember that a new one won't sprout to take its place. Avoid cutting back branches to bare stubs, as those will not produce new foliage. In time, lower limbs of most pines will die naturally; when this happens, cut them off.

Pines are vulnerable to air pollution, which causes abnormal needle drop and poor growth and may even kill the tree. Numerous pests can attack them, including aphids, spider mites, pine tip moths, pine sawflies, spittlebugs, and scale. A healthy tree can usually cope; those weakened by drought, air pollution, compacted soil, or cut roots are at greater risk. Tip blight has ravaged Austrian pines *(P. nigra)* in the Upper South. Most

▶ page 478

PINUS

NAME, NATIVE HABITAT	ZONES	GROWTH RATE, SIZE	GROWTH HABIT	NEEDLES AND CONES	COMMENTS
P. halepensis ALEPPO PINE Mediterranean region	LS, CS; 10–9	Moderate to fast, to 30–60 ft. tall, 20–40 ft. wide	Already shows rugged character at 5 years; in age, has open, irregular crown of many short, ascending branches	Needles: usually in 2s, 2½–4 in., light green. Cones: 3 in., oval to oblong, reddish brown; stalked and bent backward	Takes poor soils, trying conditions (desert heat, seacoast). Better-looking trees can be found for milder climates. In Southwest, Aleppo blight causes temporary dieback in winter
P. mugo mugo MUGHO PINE Eastern Alps and Balkan states	US, MS; 7–1	Slow to 4–8 ft. high, 8–15 ft. wide	From the start, a shrubby, symmetrical little pine. Often spreads in old age	Needles: in 2s, 2 in. or less, dark green, crowded on branches. Cones: to 1½ in., oval, tawny to dark brown	Widely used in rock gardens, containers. Not usually browsed by deer. Pick plants with dense form. Pumilio Group includes several compact selections
P. nigra (P. austriaca) AUSTRIAN PINE, AUSTRIAN BLACK PINE Europe, western Asia	US, MS; 8–4	Slow to moderate, to 40–60 ft. tall, 20–30 ft. wide	Dense, stout, pyramidal tree with uniform crown. Branches grow in regular whorls. In old age, broad and flat topped	Needles: in 2s, 3–6½ in., very dark green, stiff. Cones: to 2–3½ in., oval, brown	Tolerant of urban environment and seacoast conditions. Problem of tip blight has caused severe dieback in Upper South. Regular water
P. palustris LONGLEAF PINE Virginia to Florida and west to Mississippi, southeastern coast	MS, LS, CS, TS; 11–7	Slow for 5–10 years, then fast to 55–80 ft. tall, 25–30 ft. wide	Young plants look like fountains of grass. With age, gaunt, sparse branches ascend to form open, oblong head	Needles: in 3s, dark green; 1½ ft. in youth (called grass stage), replaced by 9-in. needles when mature. Cones: 6–10 in., dull brown	Prefers deep soils (grows on sandy ridges in its native range). The classic, graceful pine of the South
P. parviflora JAPANESE WHITE PINE Japan and Taiwan	US, MS; 8–6. Will survive –20°F	Slow to moderate, to 20–50 ft. tall and wide (or larger)	In youth, a dense pyramid; in age, wide spreading and flat topped	Needles: in 5s, 1½–2½ in., bluish or gray to green. Cones: 2–3 in., oval to oblong, reddish brown	Popular. Good bonsai subject, container tree. Dwarf forms include gray-green 'Adcock's Dwarf'. Regular water
P. resinosa RED PINE Newfoundland to Manitoba, south to the mountains of Pennsylvania and west to Michigan	US, MS; 7–1	Moderate to 50–60 ft. tall, 20–25 ft. wide	Short trunked and densely branched, eventually a dense oval	Needles: in 2s, 5–6 in., dark green. Cones: 3–6 in., light brown	Orange-red bark in youth, reddish brown plates in maturity. Attractive tree for difficult situations, poor soils. Use for windbreak, shelter belt, erosion control
P. strobus WHITE PINE, EASTERN WHITE PINE Newfoundland to Manitoba, south to Georgia, west to Illinois and Iowa	US, MS; 7–1	Slow in seedling stage, then fast to 50–80 ft. tall (or taller), 20–40 ft. wide	Symmetrical pyramid; horizontal branches in regular whorls. Becomes broad, open, irregular with age. Fine textured, handsome	Needles: in 5s, 3–5½ in., blue green, soft. Cones: 3–8 in., slender, often curved, light brown	Intolerant of strong winds, pollution, salt. Subject to white pine blister rust, white pine weevil. Popular Christmas tree. Selections include 'Contorta', with twisted branches and needles; 'Fastigiata', among most beautiful of upright pines; 'Pendula', with weeping, trailing branches; 'Prostrata', low and trailing

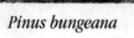
Pinus bungeana

Pinus edulis

Pinus balepensis

Pinus mugo mugo

Pinus palustris

PINUS

NAME, NATIVE HABITAT	ZONES	GROWTH RATE, SIZE	GROWTH HABIT	NEEDLES AND CONES	COMMENTS
P. strobus Nana Group DWARF WHITE PINE	US, MS; 7–1	Very slow to 3–7 ft. tall, 6–12 ft. wide	Broad shrub	Same as for *P. strobus*, but needles are shorter	Useful in rock garden or container, though plants sold under this name have been known to grow into small trees. 'Blue Shag' is a blue-needled form. Regular water
P. sylvestris SCOTCH PINE Northern Europe, western Asia, northeastern Siberia	US, MS; 7–1	Fast first, then moderate to 30–70 ft. (possibly to 100 ft.) tall, 25–30 ft. wide	In youth, a narrow, well-branched pyramid. In age, irregular, open, and picturesque, with drooping branches	Needles: in 2s, 1½–3 in., blue green, stiff; often turn yellow green in winter. Cones: 2 in., egg shaped, gray to reddish brown	Popular as a Christmas tree and in gardens. Showy red bark, sparse foliage in maturity. Wind and deer resistant. 'French Blue' keeps its blue color in winter. Other forms include columnar 'Fastigiata' (to 25 ft. tall, 3–10 ft. wide) and dwarfs 'Nana' and 'Watereri' (both to 12 ft.). Regular water in hottest areas
P. taeda LOBLOLLY PINE Southern New Jersey to Florida, East Texas, and Oklahoma	US, MS, LS, CS; 10–6	Fast to 50–90 ft. tall, 30–40 ft. wide	Loose cone shape in youth; as it matures, loses lower branches to become a rather open-crowned tree	Needles: in 3s (rarely 2s), 6–10 in., dark yellowish green. Cones: 3–6 in., oval to narrowly conical, rust brown, in clusters of 2–5	Tough tree; withstands poor soils. Useful in Lower South for quick screening and shade. Adapted to acid-soil areas of East Texas. Widely planted for pulp, lumber. Provides light shade; good to garden under. Old favorite in the South
P. thunbergii **(P. thunbergiana)** JAPANESE BLACK PINE Japan	US, MS, LS, CS; 8–5	Moderate to 20–40 ft. tall, 15–20 ft. wide	Spreading branches form broad, conical tree; irregular and spreading in age, often with leaning trunk	Needles: in 2s, 3–4½ in., bright green, stiff; new growth (candles) nearly white. Cones: 3 in., oval, brown	Handsome tree that can be sheared as a Christmas tree or pruned as a cascade or giant bonsai. Not browsed by deer. Very salt tolerant. 'Majestic Beauty' tolerates smog. Dwarf selection 'Thunderhead' (6 ft. tall, 5 ft. wide in 10 years) has dark foliage. Subject to nematodes. Needs regular water in hottest areas
P. virginiana VIRGINIA PINE, SCRUB PINE New York to Georgia and Alabama	US, MS, LS; 8–1	Slow to 45–55 ft. tall, 30–40 ft. wide	Broad, open, sparsely branched habit with wide, stiff top	Needles: in 2s, 1¼–4 in., yellow green to dark green, twisted. Cones: To 3 in., in clusters of 2–4, conical to ovoid, persistent	Seldom used as an ornamental, but valuable in clay or poor soils. Popular cut Christmas tree in Lower South. Adapts to most well-drained soils
P. wallichiana **(P. griffithii)** HIMALAYAN WHITE PINE Himalayas	US, MS; 7–5	Slow to moderate, to 30–50 ft. tall, 15–30 ft. wide. To 150 ft. high in the wild	Broad, conical. Often retains branches to the ground in age	Needles: in 5s, 6–8 in., blue green, drooping. Cones: 6–10 in., slender, elongated oval, light brown	Good form and color make it a fine choice for featured pine in a big lawn or garden. Resistant to white pine blister rust

P

Pinus parviflora

Pinus parviflora

Pinus strobus

Pinus thunbergii 'Thunderhead'

Pinus wallichiana

Pinus parviflora 'Adcock's Dwarf'

five-needle pines are susceptible to white pine blister rust, a disease that can kill the tree. Pine bark beetles have devastated stands of loblolly (*P. taeda*), slash (*P. elliottii*), and shortleaf (*P. echinata*) pines in the Southeast: needles turn brown, trunks ooze sap, and trees die. Infested trees cannot be saved; promptly removing and burning them is the best control. For more information about pests and diseases of pines, see the *Southern Living Garden Problem Solver.* Your Cooperative Extension Office can also offer advice concerning each species' adaptability to your area and any local environmental or pest problems.

PISTACHE. See PISTACIA

PISTACHIO, PISTACHIO NUT. See PISTACIA vera

PISTACIA

PISTACHE

Anacardiaceae

LARGE SEMIEVERGREEN TO DECIDUOUS TREES, SHRUBS

🌿 ZONES VARY BY SPECIES

☼ ◑ EXPOSURE NEEDS VARY BY SPECIES

◔ ◔ ● WATER NEEDS VARY BY SPECIES

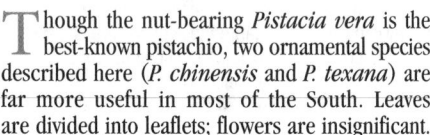

Pistacia chinensis

Though the nut-bearing *Pistacia vera* is the best-known pistachio, two ornamental species described here (*P. chinensis* and *P. texana*) are far more useful in most of the South. Leaves are divided into leaflets; flowers are insignificant. Trees may be either male or female; if a male is nearby, females bear clusters of tiny fruits in fall. Young trees tend to be irregular in form and benefit from early training and pruning.

P. chinensis. CHINESE PISTACHE. Deciduous tree. Zones US, MS, LS, CS. Native to China. Slow to moderate growth to 30–60 ft. tall, with nearly equal spread. Young trees are often gawky and lopsided; older ones become dense and shapely with reasonable care. Foot-long leaves consist of 10 to 16 dark green leaflets, each 2–4 in. long, ¾ in. wide. Good fall color of luminous orange to red (sometimes yellow), even in mild climates. Female trees bear fruits that ripen from red to blue black.

Tolerates many soils, including alkaline types. Where verticillium wilt is present, provide good drainage and water as little as possible during dry spells. Best with moderate water but tolerates considerable drought. Stake young tree and prune for the first few years to develop a head high enough to walk under. Good tree for street, lawn, or courtyard. Full sun.

P. texana. TEXAS PISTACHIO. Large semievergreen to deciduous shrub or small multitrunked tree. Zones LS, CS, TS; 12–8. Native to Texas. Grows 20–30 ft. tall, rarely to 40 ft.; eventually a bit wider than tall. Makes a feathery screen or, if cut back annually when young to promote dense habit, a fine-textured hedge. Female plants bear attractive red berries. Leaves have 7 to 21 oval, pointed leaflets; they have a reddish cast when new, then mature to glossy dark green. Foliage persists late into winter (plant is semievergreen where temperatures stay above 15°F). Does well with moderate water but grows faster with regular water. Thrives in regular garden soil but is well adapted to a range of conditions, including limestone and caliche, provided drainage is good. Partial shade or full sun.

P. vera. PISTACHIO, PISTACHIO NUT. Deciduous tree. Zones CS, TS; 12–9. From Iran. Broad, bushy tree to 30 ft. tall and at least as wide. Gray-green leaves have three to five roundish, 2- to 4-in.-long leaflets. Reddish, wrinkled fruit in heavy clusters. Needs cold winters and long, hot, dry summers to perform well. This limits pistachio production in the South to parts of West Texas and western Oklahoma. To get nuts, include a male tree in your planting; 'Peters' is the most widely planted male selection. 'Kerman' is the principal fruiting (female) type.

When planting, avoid rough handling; budded tops are easily broken away from rootstock. Pistachios are inclined to spread and droop; stake them and train branches to good framework of four or five limbs beginning at 4 ft. above ground. Established trees need little watering. Full sun.

PISTIA stratiotes

WATER LETTUCE

Araceae

AQUATIC PERENNIAL, USUALLY TREATED AS ANNUAL

🌿 CS, TS ╟ 12–4

☼ ◑ FULL SUN OR LIGHT SHADE

💧 LOCATE IN PONDS, WATER GARDENS

Pistia stratiotes

Native to tropical regions. Attractive plant that resembles a floating, grayish green loose-leaf lettuce; each foliage rosette grows to about 4 in. high and wide. The trailing roots provide a refuge for small fish. Inconspicuous flowers. Reproduces rapidly by offsets and seeds and is now considered a serious pest in many lakes, rivers, and coastal waters of Florida, Georgia, South Carolina, Mississippi, and Texas. Can survive temperatures as low as 15°F. Be careful not to let it escape into the wild.

PITANGA. See EUGENIA uniflora

PITCHER PLANT. See SARRACENIA

Pittosporaceae. This family consists of evergreen shrubs, trees, and vines from Australia, New Zealand, and eastern Asia. Many have attractive flowers, foliage, or fruit. *Pittosporum* is the only representative in this book.

PITTOSPORUM

Pittosporaceae

EVERGREEN SHRUBS OR SMALL TREES

🌿 ZONES VARY BY SPECIES

☼ ◑ FULL SUN OR PARTIAL SHADE

◔ ● MODERATE TO REGULAR WATER

Pittosporum undulatum

These plants are valued primarily for their foliage and form, though they also bear clusters of small, bell-shaped, sweetly fragrant flowers in early spring, followed by fairly conspicuous fruits the size of large peas. These are basic, dependable plants with pleasing outlines when allowed to branch naturally. Prune periodically to enhance form, thinning out weak branches and wayward shoots. They make good clipped hedges. Excellent for screens, windbreaks. Susceptible to aphids and scale; sooty mold on leaves is a sign of infestation. Ripe fruits (yellowish or orange) split open to reveal sticky seeds; fallen fruit can be a nuisance on lawns and paving.

P. tobira. JAPANESE PITTOSPORUM. Zones LS (protected), CS, TS; 11–8. From Japan. Dense, rounded shrub, eventually reaching 10–15 ft. tall and wide if not restricted by pruning. Lower limbs can be removed from older plants to make small trees. Whorls of leathery, narrowly elliptical, shiny dark green leaves to 5 in. long. Creamy white flowers, borne at branch tips, smell like orange blossoms. Very tolerant of seacoast conditions. One of the few plants that will thrive on dunes. 'Variegatum', whitespot Japanese pittosporum, grows 5–10 ft. high and wide, with gray-green leaves edged in white; 'Turner's Variegated Dwarf' has the same leaf color but reaches only 2–3 ft. high and wide. 'Cream de Mint' forms a compact mound 2–2½ ft. high and wide, with mint green leaves that are edged in creamy white. 'Wheeler's Dwarf' grows 3–4 ft. high and a little wider; it is not as hardy as the species (may die at 10°F), but it (and other dwarf types) can be moved indoors where winters are cold (site in bright light and water sparingly while indoors).

P. undulatum. VICTORIAN BOX. Zone TS; 12–10. From Australia. Moderately fast growth to 15 ft., then slow to 30–40 ft. high and wide. Planted 5–8 ft. apart, can be kept to dense, 10- to 15-ft. screen by pruning (not shearing). Glossy green, lance-shaped, wavy-edged leaves to 6 in. long. Very fragrant creamy white flowers. Strong roots become invasive with age. Susceptible to insects and disease in Florida.

P

PLANE TREE. See PLATANUS

PLANTAIN LILY. See HOSTA

PLATANUS

SYCAMORE, PLANE TREE

Platanaceae

DECIDUOUS TREES

ZONES VARY BY SPECIES

FULL SUN

REGULAR WATER

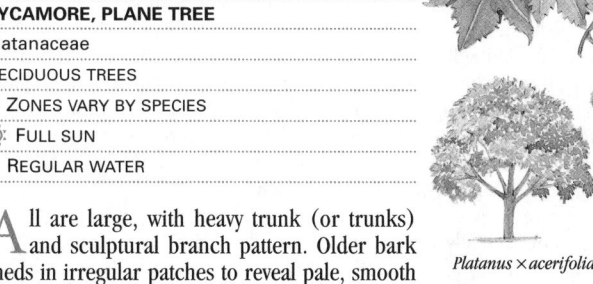

Platanus × acerifolia

All are large, with heavy trunk (or trunks) and sculptural branch pattern. Older bark sheds in irregular patches to reveal pale, smooth new bark beneath. Big, rough-surfaced bright green leaves (to 10 in. across) have three to five lobes, resemble maple *(Acer)* leaves. Fall foliage color is yellowish to brown, not striking. Ball-shaped brown seed clusters, usually on threadlike stalks, hang on the bare branches through winter; these are prized for winter arrangements. Plane trees do best in rich, deep, moist, well-drained soil. All are subject to anthracnose, which causes early leaf drop and twig dieback. Rake up and dispose of dead leaves, since fungus spores can overwinter on them. Chlorosis (yellow leaves with green veins) may be a problem in the desert.

P. × acerifolia (P. × hispanica). LONDON PLANE TREE. Zones US, MS, LS; 8–3. Hybrid between *P. occidentalis* and *P. orientalis,* and often sold under the latter name. Grows 30–40 ft. tall in 20 years; it may reach 70–100 ft. tall, 65–80 ft. wide in gardens. Smooth, cream-colored upper trunk and limbs. Handsome in winter. Tolerates many soils, city smog, soot, dust, reflected heat. Susceptible to powdery mildew. Good avenue, street tree. Can fit smaller spaces when pollarded to create a low, dense canopy. 'Columbia' and 'Liberty' are resistant to both anthracnose and powdery mildew and somewhat resistant to cankerstain disease, which can kill branches or the entire tree. 'Bloodgood' resists anthracnose; 'Yarwood' is mildew resistant.

P. mexicana. MEXICAN SYCAMORE. Zones MS, LS, CS, TS; 9–3. Native to northeastern Mexico. To 60 ft. tall, not quite as wide. Five-lobed, smooth-edged leaves are about 8 in. wide, with felty white undersides. Well adapted to dry, rocky, alkaline soils of the Southwest.

P. occidentalis. AMERICAN SYCAMORE, AMERICAN PLANE TREE. Zones US, MS, LS, CS; 9–3. Very hardy. Native to the South and north to Maine and Minnesota. Similar to *P. × acerifolia* but has whiter new bark and a longer leafless period. Irregular habit, contorted branches. Occasionally grows with multiple or leaning trunks; good climbing tree. Old trees near streams sometimes reach 100 ft. or more in height and spread. Because of its size and habit of dropping bark, seedballs, and leaves year-round, it's not a good choice for small properties.

P. orientalis. See P. × acerifolia

PLATYCERIUM

STAGHORN FERN

Polypodiaceae

FERNS

TS 12–10, EXCEPT AS NOTED

PARTIAL SHADE

REGULAR WATER

Platycerium bifurcatum

Native to tropical regions, where they grow on trees; gardeners grow them on slabs of bark or tree fern stem, occasionally in hanging baskets or attached to trees. They do best with regular moisture, though they can dry out briefly without suffering damage.

These ferns have two kinds of fronds. Sterile ones are pale green in color, aging to tan and brown; they support the plant and accumulate organic matter to help feed it. Fertile fronds vary in color from gray green to deep green; they are forked, resembling spreading antlers held either erect or pendent. For plants growing on slabs, be sure to water behind the sterile frond that attaches it to the slab.

P. bifurcatum. STAGHORN FERN. Zones CS (protected), TS. From Australia and New Guinea. Surprisingly hardy; survives 20°F with only lath structures for shelter. Clustered gray-green fertile fronds to 3 ft. long. Makes numerous offsets, which can be used in propagation. Often sold as *P. alcicorne.*

P. coronarium. From Southeast Asia. Sterile fronds are thick and deeply lobed at top. Deep green, deeply forked fertile fronds droop in a mass; some are 3 ft. long, and on older plants they may reach 6 or even 9 ft. long. Particularly sensitive to cold; needs nighttime temperatures above 60°F.

P. grande. From Australia. Erect, fan-shaped sterile fronds; pendulous, forked gray-green fertile fronds to 6 ft. long. Very similar to *P. superbum* but more cold sensitive; needs minimum temperature of 50°F.

P. hillii. ELK'S-HORN FERN. From Australia. Similar to *P. bifurcatum.* Kidney-shaped sterile fronds grow like plaques behind the fertile fronds, which fan out almost horizontally; they resemble deep green fingers to 3 ft. long, with forked tips.

P. superbum. Heat zones 12–3. From Australia. Grayish green fertile fronds may reach 6 ft. long. Both fertile and sterile fronds are forked; fertile ones are broad but divided somewhat like moose antlers. Protect plants from frosts.

PLATYCLADUS orientalis. See THUJA orientalis

PLATYCODON grandiflorus

BALLOON FLOWER

Campanulaceae (Lobeliaceae)

PERENNIAL

US, MS, LS, CS 9–1

AFTERNOON SHADE

REGULAR WATER

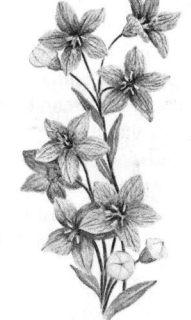

Platycodon grandiflorus

Attractive, easy-to-grow, pest-free plant from Siberia, Japan, and northern China. To 3 ft. tall and 2 ft. wide. Inflated, balloonlike buds are carried on slender stalks at the ends of upright stems clad in broadly oval, 1- to 3-in. leaves. Buds open into 2-in., star-shaped blue-violet flowers with purple veins. Bloom begins in early summer and will continue for 2 months or more if spent blossoms (but not entire stems) are removed. Double-flowered types are available, as well as pink- and white-flowered types. *P. g. albus* has white flowers, often veined in blue. Blooms of 'Shell Pink' and 'Mother of Pearl' ('Perlmutterschale') are soft pink. 'Komachi' bears clear blue blossoms that maintain their balloon shape, never opening fully. 'Park's Double Blue' grows 2 ft. tall and has intense blue flowers; *P. g. mariesii* (often sold as *P. g.* 'Mariesii'), a dwarf to only 1–1½ ft., also bears rich blue blossoms. 'Misato Purple' has deep purple flowers and grows just 8 in. tall.

Plant is deep rooted and takes 2 or 3 years to get well established. Dies back completely in fall, and new growth appears quite late in spring; mark position to avoid digging up fleshy roots. If you do unearth a root, replant it—or the pieces—right away. Protect roots from gophers by planting in buried wire cages.

BALLOON FLOWER IN BORDERS. *With its round buds, graceful star-shaped blossoms, and long bloom season, balloon flower is a nice choice for a summer border. Companion plants in shades of pink, yellow, deep to light blue, and white make for a lovely color combination; try astilbe, various kinds of yarrow (Achillea), phlox, coral bells (Heuchera), and mallow (Malva). Lush foliage plants such as hosta are good partners, too.* ❖

PLECOSTACHYS serpyllifolia

DWARF LICORICE PLANT

Asteraceae (Compositae)

PERENNIAL

CS, TS; ANYWHERE AS ANNUAL

FULL SUN

MODERATE WATER

Plecostachys serpyllifolia

South African native to 1½ ft. tall, spreading to twice as wide or more. Tiny, furry, whitish leaves are closely packed along sprawling, woody-based stems. Grown for its foliage rather than its clusters of small pinkish flowers. This plant has been sold as a dwarf form of *Helichrysum petiolare,* which it resembles in miniature. Attractive gray plant for ground or bank cover, large rock garden, or border.

PLECTRANTHUS

Lamiaceae (Labiatae)

PERENNIALS AND EVERGREEN SHRUBS; OFTEN GROWN AS ANNUALS

TS H 12–10; OR HOUSEPLANTS

PARTIAL SHADE, EXCEPT AS NOTED; BRIGHT INDIRECT LIGHT

REGULAR WATER

Plectranthus oertendahlii

Close relatives of coleus; native to many tropical regions of the world. They have square stems, opposite pairs of fleshy, tooth-edged or scalloped leaves, and whorls of tubular, two-lipped blossoms. Some are highly aromatic, used as seasonings or home remedies. Others are grown for their attractive foliage, yet others for their striking floral displays. Some are good bedding plants for summer color; some make dense, weed-suppressing ground covers for frost-protected areas. Several are trailing plants that drape gracefully from hanging baskets or wall pots. All are superb in containers, either alone or in combination with other plants.

Easy to grow. Stems take root wherever they touch the ground, and cuttings root quickly in soil or water. Remove flower spikes after they fade. Site houseplants in a bright window, but protect from hottest sun; keep moist and apply a general-purpose liquid houseplant fertilizer monthly in spring and summer. Stop fertilizing and reduce watering in fall and winter.

P. argentatus and *P. fruticosus* are the shrubbiest of the species listed here, but the others get somewhat woody at the base after a year or more. Pinch all types to induce branching; discard old plants when they become leggy or too woody, and start new ones.

Confusion reigns in *Plectranthus* nomenclature, with different nurseries selling the same plant under different names. Here are some of the most interesting species.

P. amboinicus (Coleus amboinicus). CUBAN OREGANO, SPANISH THYME, INDIAN MINT. From Africa. Summer-blooming trailer to 1 ft. high, 3 ft. wide, with white, lilac-pink, or light purple flowers in 6-in. spikes. Velvety, ovate gray-green leaves are 3 in. long, with broadly toothed edges. Popular in Cuban cooking, with a fragrance that falls midway between oregano and thyme but has a sweet note not present in either. Leaves of 'Variegatus' are bordered in cream, with the very edge often tinged bright pink; excellent flavor. 'Well-Sweep' ('Wedgwood'), with extra-sweet flavor, has Wedgwood blue flowers and leaves in chartreuse and gray green with a dark green margin.

P. argentatus. From Australia. Erect to spreading plant to 3 ft. tall, 6 ft. or wider. Densely hairy, scallop-edged, oval leaves to 7 in. long are silvery gray green, with a light purplish flush on growing tips and stems. Pink-tinged white flowers in foot-long spikes in late summer, fall. Best in at least half-day direct sun; will take hot afternoon sun if adequately watered.

P. australis. See P. verticillatus

P. ciliatus. From southern Africa. Handsome, burgundy-stemmed trailer to 6–12 in. high, 3–5 ft. wide. Excellent dense ground cover. Blooms in late summer and fall, with white or purplish flowers in 8- to 12-in. spikes. Oval leaves to 3½ in. long, with finely toothed edges and pointed tips; leaves have deep green upper surfaces, burgundy undersides and veins. 'Old Gold' leaves are yellow or chartreuse above, burgundy beneath; new leaves are flushed with burgundy. 'Tricolor' is similar, but tops of leaves also have dark green splotches. Both selections have white blooms.

P. coleoides 'Marginata'. See P. forsteri 'Marginatus'

P. cylindraceus (P. marrubioides). VICK'S PLANT, MENTHOLATO. From Africa. Mounding growth to 1½–3 ft. high, 2–4 ft. wide. Sometimes blooms, bearing blue or lavender flowers in dense, narrow, pointed spikes 12–15 in. long (there may be a pair of shorter spikes near base). Velvety, triangular gray-green leaves 1½–3 in. long, with three to five broad teeth on each side of leaf. Foliage smells like a combination of camphor and menthol and is used medicinally in Mexico.

P. forsteri. From Australia, Fiji, New Caledonia. To 10 in. high, 3 ft. wide; stems actually grow 3 ft. tall, but they arch over from weight of foliage. Tip-pinch early to induce branching; repeat to keep compact. Medium green, ovate, irregularly toothed leaves to 4 in. long. White or pale mauve flowers in 6- to 8-in. spikes are produced intermittently throughout the year. Leaves of 'Marginatus' (*P. coleoides* 'Marginata') are irregularly edged in creamy white. 'Green and Gold' has lime green leaves with a neat gold margin.

P. fruticosus. From South Africa. Upright growth to 3–5 ft. tall, 2–4 ft. wide. Lance-shaped, coarsely toothed leaves to 4 in. long are olive green above, purplish beneath. Blooms in autumn, bearing mauve pink or bluish blossoms in very showy clusters to 1 ft. long, half as wide.

P. madagascariensis. MINTLEAF. From southern Africa. Vigorous trailer reaches 1 ft. high; spreads 3–4 ft. wide initially, eventually much wider by rooting at leaf joints. Medium green leaves to 2 in. long are hairy, roundish, scallop edged; they smell like mint when crushed. Lavender blue or white flower spikes in late spring, early summer. 'Variegated Mintleaf', the most commonly grown form, has irregular white leaf margins. Good ground cover to brighten shady areas. Often mistakenly sold as *Iboza,* another genus in the same family.

P. 'Mona Lavender'. Hybrid developed in South Africa. Multistemmed plant to 2–3 ft. tall and wide, with deep purple stems holding glossy deep green, coarsely toothed leaves with purple-bronze veins and undersides. Leaves reach 2 in. long, 1 in. wide. Lavender blue flowers with darker flecks, borne in 6-in. spikes, appear continuously in warm weather. Great as a bedding plant or grown in containers.

P. nummularis. See P. verticillatus

P. oertendahlii. MOSAIC SWEDISH IVY, ROYAL CHARLIE, CANDLE PLANT. From South Africa. Easy-care specimen for hanging basket or pot; most often grown as houseplant. To 8–12 in. high, with branches trailing to 1½–2 ft. long. Roundish, irregularly toothed, velvety dark green leaves up to 2½ in. long, with purple undersides and intricate network of silver veins. In autumn, white or light blue flowers bloom in loose, 8- to 12-in.-long spikes. Foliage of 'Uvongo' is more heavily netted with silver than that of the species; leaves of 'Variegatus' are irregularly edged in creamy white.

P. saccatus. From South Africa. Woody-based plant to 1½–3 ft. high and wide. Green, almost canelike stems are set with fragrant, nearly triangular bright green leaves with prominently toothed edges. Large blue to lilac (sometimes white) flowers bloom in midsummer.

P. verticillatus. SWEDISH IVY, CREEPING CHARLIE. From southern Africa. Typically grown in hanging basket or pot in the house or outdoors; also makes a good ground cover in a warm, protected spot. To 4–8 in. high, 4–6 ft. wide, with trailing branches. Waxy, shiny dark green, scallop-edged leaves are roundish, up to 1½ in. across. White or pale purplish blossoms in 8-in. spikes bloom intermittently all year. To grow as a ground cover, plant cuttings 1–2 ft. apart for quick coverage. Often incorrectly sold as *P. australis* or *P. nummularis.* 'Marmoratus' produces leaves irregularly marked with ivory.

PLEIOBLASTUS. See BAMBOO

PLUM (including Prune)

Rosaceae

DECIDUOUS FRUIT TREES

🗡 ZONES VARY BY SELECTION

☼ FULL SUN

💧💧 MODERATE TO REGULAR WATER

▶ SEE CHART PAGE 482

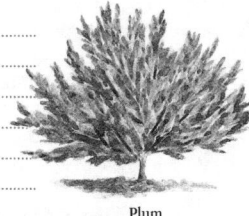
Plum

Like their cherry, peach, and apricot relatives, these are stone fruits belonging to the genus *Prunus;* for flowering plums, see pages 494–495. Three categories of edible plums and prunes are grown in the diverse climates of North America: European, Japanese, and native species. Plants bloom in late winter or early spring. Harvest season is from June into September, depending on type and variety.

The two most widely grown groups in the South are European plums (*P. × domestica*) and Japanese plums (*P. salicina*). Prunes are European plum selections with a high sugar content, a trait that allows them to be sun-dried without fermenting at the pit.

In general, European types are better plums for the South. They live longer than Japanese types, and they are more cold hardy and bloom later, making them less susceptible to late freezes. Japanese types, on the other hand, need less winter chill and tolerate heat and humidity better, making them good choices for the Lower and Coastal South—but greater susceptibility to diseases and insects makes them short lived in most areas. Plant disease-resistant selections, if possible.

Native species include wild plum (*P. americana*), Chickasaw plum (*P. angustifolia*), and Mexican plum (*P. mexicana*). These tough, hardy trees are easy to grow; their fruits are used to make jelly and preserves.

Most plum types are grafted onto another rootstock. Standard trees grow about 15 ft. high and wide, dwarf trees about half that size. There is also an intermediate, semidwarf category.

Plums come in many colors—both inside and out. The skin may be yellow, red, purple, green, blue, or almost black; the flesh may be yellow, red, orange, or green. Japanese plums are the largest and juiciest of the lot, with a pleasant blend of acid and sugar; they are typically eaten fresh. European kinds are firmer fleshed and can be eaten fresh or cooked; prune types are used for drying or canning, but they can also be eaten out of hand if you like the very sweet flavor.

Train young trees to a vase shape. After selecting framework branches, cut back to lateral branches. If tree tends to grow upright, cut to outside branches; if it is spreading, cut to inside branches. Prune to avoid formation of V-shaped crotches. On types that produce excessive upright growth (mainly Japanese plums), shorten shoots to outside branchlets. Mature European plum trees require limited pruning, mainly to thin out annual shoot growth. Do any pruning of plum trees in late winter, before bloom.

Most European plums don't require a pollenizer, though they set fruit better when grown near other European selections. Japanese plums produce better crops when cross-pollinated, so plant two Japanese selections.

Certain insects and diseases plague most plums. Black knot (black, warty growths caused by a fungus) is a common problem. To control it, prune off infected branches, cutting at least 4 in. below signs of disease. Or plant resistant selections 'Damson', 'Methley', 'Shiro', and 'Stanley'. Peach tree borer may also cause trouble; see Peach and Nectarine for controls.

The more humid the climate, the more troublesome are plum curculio (a weevil that infests the fruit) and the diseases bacterial canker (which causes open wounds on trunk and branches) and brown rot of stone fruit. If you only have a few fruit trees, you may be able to control the curculio with traps. Dormant-season applications of sprays combining horticultural oil with lime sulfur will control brown rot and various insect pests such as scale; also prune trees to provide good air circulation. To reduce risk of bacterial canker, prevalent in the South, don't leave stubs when pruning, and remove dead or broken branches right away. AU hybrid plums,

Plum

developed by Auburn University in Alabama, have excellent resistance to disease; several of these are listed in the chart.

Most plum trees will not succeed in areas where nematodes are prevalent, though rootstocks 'Nemaguard' and 'Guardian' are resistant to root-knot nematodes. 'Guardian' also resists bacterial canker.

SOME PLUMS NEED TO BE THINNED. *Japanese selections bear very heavily, producing lots of small fruit. If the entire crop were allowed to ripen, its weight might damage the tree—so thin fruits to 4–6 in. apart as soon as they are large enough to be seen. European plums usually don't need thinning unless the tree sets a particularly large amount of fruit.* ❖

PLUM, FLOWERING. See PRUNUS

Plumbaginaceae. The leadwort family consists of shrubs and perennials with clusters of funnel-shaped flowers. Members include thrift (*Armeria*) and two genera commonly called plumbago (*Ceratostigma, Plumbago*).

PLUMBAGO

Plumbaginaceae

EVERGREEN OR SEMIEVERGREEN SHRUBS

🗡 ZONES VARY BY SPECIES

☼ ☼ FULL SUN OR LIGHT SHADE

💧💧💧 LITTLE TO REGULAR WATER

Plumbago auriculata

Sprawling plants that bloom over a long season, bearing phloxlike clusters of blue or white flowers at branch ends. Prune these shrubs back hard in late winter to control their growth and keep them compact. For other plants that are called plumbago, see *Ceratostigma.*

P. auriculata (P. capensis). CAPE PLUMBAGO. Evergreen or semievergreen. Zones CS, TS; 12–7. Native to South Africa. Makes a mounding shrub to 6 ft. tall, 8–10 ft. wide; or, if tied to a support, grows as a vine to 12 ft. or more. Oblong, 1- to 2-in., light to medium green leaves. Inch-wide flowers. In seedling plants, blossom color varies from white through pure

▶ page 484

WHAT PLUMS NEED

LOCATION: Trees should be planted on slopes or hilltops to avoid frost damage to flowers.

WINTER CHILL: Most Japanese plums require 500 to 900 hours at 45°F or lower; European plums demand 700 to 1,000 hours of chill.

SOIL: Plants tolerate many soil types but do best in fertile, well-drained soil.

FERTILIZING: In March, broadcast 10-10-10 fertilizer in a circle around the tree, starting 6 in. from the trunk and continuing out to 3 ft. Apply 1 cup of fertilizer for each year of the tree's age, up to a maximum of 12 cups. Water in thoroughly. Repeat the application in July.

PRUNING: Japanese selections require heavy annual pruning to ensure fruit set and healthy growth throughout the tree. European plums need much less attention.

'Green Gage'

PLUM

NAME	ZONES	FRUIT	COMMENTS
EUROPEAN SELECTIONS			
'Damson'	US, MS, LS; 8–3	Small. Purple or blue-black skin; green flesh. Very tart flavor. Late	Old favorite. Fruit makes fine jam and jelly. Strains of this selection are sold as 'French Danson', 'Shropshire'
'Earliblue'	MS, LS; 8–3	Medium. Blue skin; tender green-yellow flesh. Early	Light to moderate producer. Slow to begin bearing
'Green Gage' ('Reine Claude')	US, MS, LS; 8–3	Small to medium. Greenish yellow skin; amber flesh. Good flavor. Midseason	Very old selection; still a favorite for eating fresh, cooking, canning, or jam. Selected strain sold as 'Jefferson'
'Stanley'	US, MS, LS; 8–3	Large. Purplish black skin; yellow flesh. Sweet and juicy. Midseason	Good prune plum; good for canning. Old Southern favorite. Tends to overbear; best if fruit is thinned
'Sugar'	US, MS, LS; 8–3	Medium to large. Dark blue skin; yellow flesh. Very sweet, highly flavored. Early midseason	Good for eating fresh, drying, and canning. Tends to bear heavily in alternate years
JAPANESE SELECTIONS			
'AU-Cherry'	US, MS, LS, CS; 9–3	Small. Red skin and flesh. Good flavor. Midseason	Very disease resistant. Auburn University introduction
'AU-Producer'	US, MS, LS, CS; 9–3	Small to medium. Dark red skin; red flesh. Good quality. Midseason	Very disease resistant. Good yields. Auburn University introduction
'AU-Roadside'	US, MS, LS, CS; 9–3	Medium to large. Red skin and flesh. Very good quality. Midseason	Very disease resistant. Auburn University introduction
'AU-Rosa'	US, MS, LS, CS; 9–3	Small to medium. Dark red skin; yellow flesh of excellent quality. Midseason, a few days after 'Santa Rosa'	Very disease resistant. Auburn University introduction
'Beauty'	US, MS, LS; 8–3	Medium. Bright red skin; amber flesh with scarlet streaks. Good flavor. Very early	Consistent heavy bearer. Fruit softens quickly
'Black Ruby'	US, MS, LS, CS; 9–3	Medium. Purple-black skin; sweet yellow flesh. Midseason to late	Developed by USDA in Byron, Georgia
'Bruce'	US, MS, LS; 8–3	Large. Green to red skin; red flesh. Early	Disease resistant. Self-fruitful. Good for jams, preserves. Blooms often escape damage from late spring frosts
'Byrongold'	US, MS, LS; 8–3	Medium to large. Yellow skin, sometimes blushed red; yellow flesh with mild to slightly tart flavor. Aromatic. Midseason to late	Excellent quality. Disease resistant. Developed by USDA in Byron, Georgia
'Crimson'	US, MS, LS; 8–3	Small. Crimson skin and flesh. Excellent flavor and texture. Early to midseason	Productive tree; excellent fruit set. Good for eating fresh and for jams, jellies. Disease resistant

'Damson'   'Earliblue'   'Green Gage'   'Stanley'   'AU-Producer'   'Beauty'

P

PLUM

NAME	ZONES	FRUIT	COMMENTS
'Elephant Heart'	US, MS, LS, CS; 9–3	Very large. Dark red skin; rich red, highly flavored flesh. Midseason to late	Tart skin; some prefer to peel fruit. Long harvest season. Use 'Santa Rosa' as pollenizer
'Explorer'	US, MS, LS; 8–3	Large. Reddish black skin; sweet, juicy yellow flesh. Midseason	Developed at the Georgia Agricultural Experiment Station
'Homeside'	US, MS, LS, CS; 9–3	Medium to large. Orange to light red skin; orange flesh. Very good texture; excellent flavor. Early	Tree is quite vigorous and spreading
'Howard Miracle'	US, MS, LS, CS; 9–3	Medium. Yellow skin with red blush; juicy yellow flesh with distinctive spicy, sweet flavor reminiscent of pineapple. Midseason	Very vigorous. Fruit is more acid than most Japanese plums, but truly distinctive in flavor
'Methley'	US, MS, LS, CS; 9–3	Medium. Reddish purple skin; dark red flesh. Sweet, mild flavor. Early	Bud-hardy, with early bloom. Self-pollinating; good pollenizer for other Japanese plum selections
'Morris'	US, MS, LS; 8–5	Large. Purple skin; deep red flesh. Good, sweet flavor. Midseason	Productive, reliable, disease resistant. Texas A&M introduction
'Ozark Premier'	US, MS, LS; 8–3	Very large. Red to purple skin; juicy yellow flesh. Very good flavor. Late midseason	Vigorous, productive. Good for eating fresh, canning, cooking, jelly. Can be short lived
'Red Heart'	US, MS, LS, CS; 9–3	Medium to large. Dark red fruit of good quality, but with rather tough skin. Late midseason	One of best pollenizers for other Japanese selections. Vigorous, productive. Fruit holds well
'Robusto'	US, MS, LS; 8–3	Medium. Bright red skin; red flesh. Midseason	Vigorous and productive. Blossoms often escape damage from late spring frosts
'Rubysweet'	US, MS, LS; 8–3	Medium. Red skin; orange-red flesh. Sweet and juicy	Disease resistant. Developed by USDA in Byron, Georgia
'Santa Rosa'	US, MS, LS, CS; 9–3	Medium to large. Purplish red skin with heavy blue bloom; yellow flesh (dark red near skin). Rich, pleasing, tart flavor. Early	Important commercial type for fresh eating. Good canned if skin is removed. Very prone to disease in Southeast; grows and produces best in drier climates. 'Late Santa Rosa' follows by a month
'Satsuma'	US, MS, LS; 8–3	Small to medium. Dull deep red skin; dark red, solid, meaty flesh. Mild, sweet flavor. Small pit. Early midseason	Preferred for jams and jellies. Sometimes called blood plum because of red juice. Tends to overbear; thin fruit for best size
'Segundo'	US, MS, LS, CS; 9–3	Medium. Red skin; orange-red flesh. Midseason	Blossoms often escape damage from late spring frosts
'Shiro'	US, MS; 8–3	Medium to large. Flavorful fruit with yellow skin and flesh. Early midseason	Heavy producer. Fruit is good for eating fresh or cooking
'Wade'	MS, LS, CS; 8–3	Large. Dark red skin; juicy, sweet yellow flesh streaked red. Flattish shape. Very early	Low winter-chill requirement. Good choice for Florida, Coastal South

'Elephant Heart'   'Explorer'   'Howard Miracle'   'Ozark Premier'   'Santa Rosa'   'Satsuma'

light blue to sky blue; best way to get good blue color is to buy cutting-grown selections such as 'Royal Cape' or 'Imperial Blue'. 'Alba' and 'White Cape' are white-flowering forms. Blooms from spring through summer—or nearly all year in warm, frost-free locations.

Evergreen where frosts are absent or light; heavy frost can burn new growth and blacken leaves, but recovery is fast. Prune out any damaged parts when frost danger is past. Not fussy about soil type but must have good drainage. Good cover for bank, fence, wall; good background and filler plant. Does very well in pots. Tolerates light salt spray. Not browsed by deer.

P. indica. SCARLET LEADWORT. Evergreen. Zones LS, CS, TS; 12–8. From Asia. Thin-stemmed plant to 6 ft. high, 3 ft. wide, with smooth, oval, medium to deep green leaves to 4 in. long. Blooms from winter to spring, bearing long-tubed, deep rose pink to red flowers in clusters to 1 ft. long.

P. scandens. DOCTOR BUSH. Evergreen. Zones CS, TS; 12–9. Native from Florida to Arizona, south to Central America. To 4 ft. or more high and wide. Oblong leaves to 4 in. long are deep red when new, maturing to medium green; nearly all foliage turns red in late fall and winter. Blooms year-round (with a short break during hottest part of summer), bearing typically white (sometimes blue-tinged) flowers nearly 1 in. wide. Particularly striking when white blooms appear in combination with red leaves. With this species, hard pruning both controls size and encourages the growth of colorful new foliage. Accepts most soils. Can get powdery mildew in late summer but doesn't seem to be greatly harmed by it. Attractive ground cover. 'Summer Snow' has pure white blooms.

PLUMBAGO larpentae. See **CERATOSTIGMA plumbaginoides**

PLUME CEDAR, PLUME CRYPTOMERIA. See **CRYPTOMERIA japonica 'Elegans'**

PLUME HYACINTH. See **MUSCARI comosum 'Plumosum'**

PLUME POPPY. See **MACLEAYA**

PLUMERIA

FRANGIPANI
Apocynaceae
DECIDUOUS SHRUBS OR TREES

🌿 TS ⬡ 12–8; OR GROW IN POTS

☼ ◑ PARTIAL SHADE IN HOTTEST CLIMATES

💧 MODERATE WATER

🔹 SAP IS POISONOUS AND MAY CAUSE SKIN RASH

Plumeria rubra

Handsome additions to the landscape in the warmest climates, these natives of tropical regions have a spreading to round-headed form, with leathery leaves clustered near the tips of thick, succulent branches (branches exude caustic sap when injured). Large clusters of showy, waxy, typically fragrant, five-petaled flowers are produced at branch tips during warm weather. The flowers are used in making Hawaiian leis.

Plumerias are somewhat tolerant of salt and wind; not fussy about soil type but cannot take cold, wet soils. Prune them at any time of year to maintain desired size and shape; they will withstand severe pruning (do it at warm times of year). Tender to frost. Beyond hardiness range, may be grown in a container and overwintered indoors. Stop watering when nights begin to turn cool; leaves will soon yellow and drop. Move plants into a dark room or a heated garage; they will go dormant and need no water or light until the following spring.

P. alba. WHITE FRANGIPANI. From Puerto Rico, Lesser Antilles. Slow growth to 20 ft. tall, 12–15 ft. wide. Rich green leaves to 1 ft. long are narrow, lance shaped, and somewhat puckered. Fragrant, 2½-in.-wide white flowers with a yellow center.

P. obtusa. SINGAPORE PLUMERIA, BLUNT-NOSE FRANGIPANI. From Cuba, Hispaniola, Yucatán Peninsula. Fast growing to 30–35 ft. high, 15 ft. wide. Dark green leaves are retained most of the year; they grow to 6 in. or longer, have blunt or rounded tips. Sweet-scented, 3-in.-wide white

TOP: *Plumeria rubra* 'Aztec Gold'
BOTTOM: *Plumeria rubra* 'Daisy Wilcox'

TOP: *Plumeria rubra* 'Candystripe'
BOTTOM: *Plumeria rubra* 'Celadine'

flowers with a yellow center bloom from spring through fall. More difficult to grow than *P. rubra*.

P. rubra. PLUMERIA, TEMPLE TREE, NOSEGAY FRANGIPANI. Native from Mexico south to Panama. Grows at a moderate rate to 25–35 ft. tall, 15–20 ft. wide. Medium green leaves are 8–16 in. long, with pointed tips. Bloom begins in spring, often before foliage emerges, and continues for more than 6 months. Well over 100 selections have been developed; flowers are typically 2–4½ in. wide, in colors ranging from white through yellow, gold, and orange to shades of pink and red. Fragrance varies. Dwarf types and forms with semidouble flowers are sometimes available. The following are full-size selections with large, very fragrant single flowers.

'Aztec Gold'. Buttercup yellow shading to white at petal edges.

'Candystripe'. Vibrant blooms suffused with white and pink; petals are marked with bright yellow on upper surfaces, striped red and white beneath. 'Smith's Candystripe' is similar but more fragrant.

'Celadine' ('Hawaiian Yellow'). Yellow with white petal margins. Especially sturdy plant.

'Daisy Wilcox'. Extra-large blossoms with yellow centers and pale pink petals aging to white.

'Dean Conklin'. Salmon with orange center.

'Guillot Sunset'. Pink-and-white bicolor with orange center.

'Intense Rainbow'. Yellow blending to pink.

'Kauka Wilder'. Combination of reds and yellows gives blossoms an overall rich orange color. Very sweet fragrance.

'Pink Parfait'. Large reddish pink blooms.

PLUM YEW. See **CEPHALOTAXUS**

POA

BLUEGRASS
Poaceae (Gramineae)
PERENNIAL AND ANNUAL GRASSES

🌿 ZONES VARY BY SPECIES

☼ FULL SUN, EXCEPT AS NOTED

💧 REGULAR WATER

Native to Europe but naturalized in North America. One is the best-known cool-season lawn grass; the others sometimes turn up in lawns, either intentionally or as an annual weed. Leaves of all types have the characteristic boat-prow tip.

Poa pratensis

P. annua. ANNUAL BLUEGRASS. Zones US, MS, LS, CS, TS. Cool-season weed of lawns. Bright green, soft-textured grass that germinates in fall, then goes to seed and dies when weather warms in spring. To discourage it, maintain thick turf of good grasses or apply a pre-emergence herbicide to lawn in fall.

P. pratensis. KENTUCKY BLUEGRASS. Zones US, MS; 7–1. Rich blue-green perennial lawn grass best adapted to Upper South and southern Midwest. Forms the most lush and beautiful of lawns—an utter delight to stroll upon in bare feet. Unfortunately, it demands much maintenance, including regular watering and fertilizing. Susceptible to disease during warm, humid weather. Mow at 2 in. high in spring and fall, at 3 in. in summer. Use Kentucky bluegrass alone or in mixture with other grasses. Many selections are available as seed or sod, including the following.

'Adelphi'. Darkest green, medium texture; good disease resistance.
'Bonnieblue'. Medium dark green, medium texture; establishes quickly.
'Glade'. Dark green, fine texture, dense; tolerates shade better than most.
'Majestic'. Dark green, medium texture; establishes fast.
'Parade'. Medium green, fine texture; good disease resistance.
'Touchdown'. Medium dark green, fine texture; tolerates shade well.
'Victa'. Dark green, medium texture; establishes fast.

P. trivialis. ROUGH-STALKED BLUEGRASS. Zones US; 6–1. Fine-textured, bright green perennial meadow and pasture grass. Occasionally used in shady lawn mixtures for its tolerance of shade and damp soil.

Poaceae. The grass family is undoubtedly the most important plant family in terms of usefulness to humans. All the world's important grain crops are grasses; the bamboos (giant grasses) are useful in building and crafts. Many grasses are used in lawns or as ornamental annual or perennial plants. Some botanists still use Gramineae as the family name for grasses.

PODOCARPUS

Podocarpaceae

EVERGREEN SHRUBS OR TREES

✘ ZONES VARY BY SPECIES

☼ ◑ FULL SUN OR PARTIAL SHADE

💧 REGULAR WATER

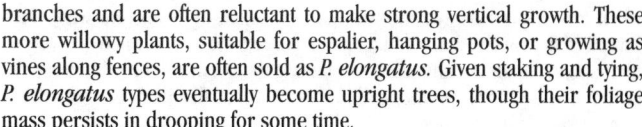

Versatile plants grown for their good-looking foliage and interesting form. They are adaptable to many climates and have many uses. Make good screens and background plants. Foliage generally resembles that of related yews *(Taxus),* but leaves of the better-known species are longer, broader, and lighter in color. If a male plant is growing nearby, female plants bear fruit after many years, producing small, fleshy fruits rather than cones. Grow well (if slowly) in most soils, but may develop chlorosis (yellow leaves with green veins) where soil is alkaline or heavy and damp. Tolerate salt spray and resist pests. Deer don't seem to care for them.

Podocarpus gracilior

Some botanists now divide these plants into three genera *(Afrocarpus, Nageia, Podocarpus);* where they apply, new names are given in parentheses.

P. elongatus. For plants sold under this name, see P. gracilior

P. gracilior (Afrocarpus elongatus). FERN PINE. Tree, often grown as espaliered vine or even in hanging baskets. Zones TS; 12–7. From eastern Africa. To 20–60 ft. tall, 10–20 ft. wide. Among the cleanest, most pest-free trees for street, lawn, patio, garden; good as big shrub, as hedge, in container.

Method of propagation determines growth habit. If grown from seed, plants are upright even when young (and stay that way); these plants are usually sold as *P. gracilior.* In youth, they have branches set somewhat sparsely with glossy dark green leaves 2–4 in. long, ½ in. wide. With age, they produce 1- to 2-in., soft grayish green to bluish green leaves that are more closely spaced on branches. Stake seedling plants until a strong trunk develops.

If grown from cuttings or grafts of a mature tree, plants have the smaller, more closely set leaves just described, but they have very limber branches and are often reluctant to make strong vertical growth. These more willowy plants, suitable for espalier, hanging pots, or growing as vines along fences, are often sold as *P. elongatus.* Given staking and tying, *P. elongatus* types eventually become upright trees, though their foliage mass persists in drooping for some time.

P. macrophyllus. SOUTHERN YEW. Shrub or tree. Zones LS, CS, TS; 12–7. Native to eastern China, Japan. Generally narrow and upright; to 15–50 ft. tall, 6–15 ft. wide. Bright green leaves 4 in. long, ½ in. wide. Good as a street or lawn tree, screen, or large shrub; limber enough to espalier. Easily pruned as clipped hedge or topiary. Does well in containers. Very heat tolerant.

P. m. 'Maki'. SHRUBBY YEW PINE. Slower growing and smaller than the species, reaching just 8–15 ft. tall, 2–4 ft. wide. Dense and upright, with leaves to 3 in. long, ¼ in. wide. A choice shrub; one of the best container plants for outdoor or indoor use.

P. nagi (Nageia nagi). BROADLEAF PODOCARPUS. Tree. Zones CS, TS; 12–7. From Japan, where it reaches 80–90 ft. tall. In the South, more commonly seen at 15–20 ft. tall, 6–8 ft. wide. Pendulous branchlets; leathery, smooth, dark green, sharp-pointed leaves to 1–3 in. long, ½–1½ in. wide. Grows upright in youth without staking; plant in groves for slender sapling effect. Makes a decorative foliage pattern against wood or masonry background. Excellent container plant.

PODOPHYLLUM

Berberidaceae

PERENNIALS

✘ ZONES VARY BY SPECIES

☼ ● PARTIAL TO FULL SHADE

💧 💧 REGULAR TO AMPLE WATER

💧 ALL PARTS (EXCEPT RIPE FRUIT) ARE POISONOUS IF INGESTED

Podophyllum peltatum

Odd-looking yet striking plants, these herbaceous barberry *(Berberis)* relatives grow from thick underground rhizomes that send up stalks crowned with large, shield-shaped, deeply lobed leaves. Shoots with a single leaf are barren; those with two leaves bear a single 2-in.-wide flower (set between the leaves) in mid- to late spring. Blossoms are followed by juicy, 2-in. berries; these are edible when fully ripe (poisonous until that stage) but can have a powerful laxative effect. Make attractive, slowly spreading deciduous ground covers for shady areas with rich, moist, woodsy soil.

P. hexandrum. HIMALAYAN MAYAPPLE. Zones US, MS, LS; 8–4. From Himalayas, western China. To 1–1½ ft. tall and wide. Dark green, brown-mottled leaves to 10 in. wide are divided into three or five lobes; each lobe is further divided. White or pink flowers are followed by bright red berries.

P. peltatum. MAYAPPLE, WILD MANDRAKE. Zones US, MS, LS, CS; 8–2. From eastern North America. To 1–1½ ft. high, 1 ft. wide. New growth pushing up through leaf litter is one of the earliest signs of spring in woodlands. Foliage is bronze when new; mature leaves are shiny dark green, to 1 ft. wide, divided into five to nine lobes. White flowers are followed by bright yellow berries. Spreads fairly fast in its preferred rich, moist soil. Dies back completely in late summer.

PODRANEA ricasoliana

PINK TRUMPET VINE

Bignoniaceae

EVERGREEN VINE

✘ CS (PROTECTED), TS ⋈ 12–9; OR GROW IN POTS

☼ ◑ FULL SUN OR PARTIAL SHADE

💧 💧 MODERATE TO REGULAR WATER

Podranea ricasoliana

Native to South Africa. Sprawling growth to 20 ft.; must be fastened to its support. Glossy dark green leaves consist of two to five opposite pairs of 2-in. leaflets plus one terminal leaflet. Blooms in spring or summer, when tips of new growth produce loose clusters of 2- to 3-in.-wide, red-veined pink flowers shaped like open trumpets. Grows slowly when young, then speeds up as it matures. Likes heat, good drainage. Planting in sterilized, fertile soil is recommended in Florida, since this plant is very subject to nematode damage there.

Use pink trumpet vine on posts, arbors, trellises, walls, trunks of high-branching trees. It also does well in large pots. Thin out any tangling growth in winter. Light frosts may cause leaves to drop; heavier frosts may kill vine to the ground, but regrowth is almost certain as long as soil doesn't freeze.

POINCIANA. See CAESALPINIA, DELONIX regia

POINSETTIA. See EUPHORBIA pulcherrima

Polemoniaceae. The phlox family consists mostly of annuals and perennials, including many wildflowers; examples are *Ipomopsis* and *Phlox.* Cup-and-saucer vine *(Cobaea)* is another member.

POLEMONIUM

JACOB'S LADDER

Polemoniaceae

PERENNIALS

US, MS, LS

PARTIAL TO FULL SHADE

REGULAR WATER

Polemonium caeruleum

These shade-loving perennials form lush rosettes of finely divided, ferny, typically light to medium green foliage; clusters of bell-shaped flowers appear in spring or early summer. Good under trees. Lovely in combination with bellflower *(Campanula)*, bleeding heart *(Dicentra)*, ferns, hellebore, hosta, lilies. Grow from seed or from divisions made after bloom or in spring; give well-drained soil. The following species and hybrids are among those most commonly available in nurseries.

P. boreale. NORTHERN JACOB'S LADDER. Heat zones 8–3. Native to far northern regions. Dainty-looking yet tough species to 9 in. high, 1 ft. wide. Half-inch-wide, yellow-eyed blue to violet flowers are held above ferny foliage. 'Heavenly Habit' has larger blue flowers with a white eye surrounded by a yellow halo.

P. caeruleum. JACOB'S LADDER. Heat zones 9–1. Native to Europe and Asia. Fairly upright-growing plant to 1–3 ft. high, 1–1½ ft. wide. Lavender blue, pendulous, inch-wide flowers. 'Brise d'Anjou', with each leaflet neatly outlined in white, is one of the most striking of variegated-foliage plants.

P. 'Firmament'. Heat zones 8–3. Hybrid between *P. caeruleum* and *P. reptans.* To 20 in. high, 1 ft. wide, with bright blue flowers. Use in borders.

P. foliosissimum. Heat zones 8–1. Native from Idaho and Wyoming south to Arizona and New Mexico. To 2½ ft. high, 2 ft. wide, with stems clothed in dark green leaves. Lavender blue, ½-in. flowers are enhanced by bright orange stamens. Tends to be short lived where summers are hot and humid.

P. 'Lambrook Mauve'. Heat zones 8–1. Nonseeding hybrid to 1 ft. high and wide. Forms a mound of deeply cut pale green leaves. Blooms in late spring or early summer (and usually again in early fall), bearing lilac-blue flowers to ¾ in. wide.

P. reptans. CREEPING JACOB'S LADDER. Heat zones 8–1. Native from New Hampshire to Georgia, west to Minnesota, Oklahoma, and Alabama. Weak-stemmed plant to 1–1½ ft. high, 1 ft. wide; light blue, ¾-in. flowers. Better known than the species is heavy-blooming 'Blue Pearl'; it grows 10 in. high, 1½ ft. wide and bears bright blue blossoms. Good in shaded rock gardens.

POLIANTHES tuberosa

TUBEROSE

Agavaceae

PERENNIAL FROM RHIZOME

MS, LS, CS, TS 11–7; OR GROW IN POTS

FULL SUN

REGULAR WATER DURING GROWTH AND BLOOM

Polianthes tuberosa

Native to Mexico; longtime favorite in Southern gardens. Noted for powerful, heady fragrance. Blooms in late summer or fall, with glistening white, tubular, 2½-in.-long flowers loosely arranged in spikelike clusters on stems to 3 ft. tall. Long, narrow, grasslike basal leaves. Double-flowered selection 'The Pearl' is most widely available; it's a good garden plant but not as long lasting a cut flower as the single type. 'Mexican Single' is a more dependable bloomer in the Lower, Coastal, and Tropical South. 'Marginata' has white-edged leaves.

To bloom year after year, tuberoses require a warm season of at least 4 months before flowering. Start indoors or plant outside after soil is warm. Set rhizomes 2 in. deep, 4–6 in. apart. If soil or water is alkaline, apply acid fertilizer when growth begins. Where winter temperatures remain above 20°F, rhizomes may stay in ground all year; divide clumps about every 4 years. Even in those mild areas, however, most gardeners dig and store them over winter. Dig plants in fall after leaves have yellowed; cut off dead foliage. Allow rhizomes to dry for 2 weeks, then store them in a cool (40–50°F), dry place. Tuberoses can also be grown in pots and moved to a protected area during cold weather.

P. howardii, another Mexican native, grows in alkaline soil and has red-and-green blooms that attract hummingbirds. Hybrids between it and other species are good choices for the Southwest.

POLKA-DOT PLANT. See HYPOESTES phyllostachya

POLYANTHUS PRIMROSE. See PRIMULA × polyantha

Polygonaceae. The buckwheat family consists of annuals, perennials, shrubs, trees, and vines. Flowers lack petals, but sepals are often showy. Stems are jointed. Fruit is small, dry, single seeded. Best-known Southern examples are coral vine *(Antigonon)* and sea grape *(Coccoloba).* Other family members include knotweed *(Persicaria)* and rhubarb *(Rheum).* True buckwheat—the pancake-flour kind—is *Fagopyrum,* a crop plant of no ornamental value.

POLYGONATUM

SOLOMON'S SEAL

Liliaceae

PERENNIALS

US, MS, LS, EXCEPT AS NOTED

PARTIAL TO FULL SHADE

REGULAR WATER

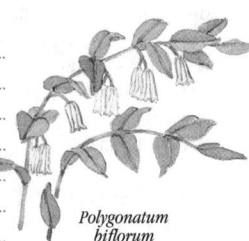

Polygonatum biflorum

Slowly spreading rhizomes send up arching stems clothed in broadly oval leaves arranged in nearly horizontal planes. Where leaves join stems, pairs or clusters of small, bell-shaped greenish white flowers appear in spring, hanging beneath the stems on threadlike stalks. Small blue-black berries may follow flowers. Leaves and stems turn bright yellow in fall before plant dies to the ground. Attractive for form and flowers in woodland garden; good with astilbe, ferns, hellebore, hosta, wild ginger *(Asarum).* Grow in loose, woodsy soil. Can remain in place for years; to increase your plantings, dig rhizomes from clump edges in early spring and replant. Good in containers. For false Solomon's seal, see *Smilacina.*

P. biflorum. SOLOMON'S SEAL. Zones US, MS, LS, CS; 9–1. Native to eastern North America. To 1–3 ft. tall, 2 ft. wide, with bright green leaves to 4 in. long and flowers usually in pairs or threes. A form sometimes sold as *P. commutatum* or *P. canaliculatum* is much more vigorous, growing 3–7 ft. tall, 3–4 ft. wide. It has leaves to 7 in. long and flowers in groups of two to ten.

P. humile. DWARF SOLOMON'S SEAL. Heat zones 8–4. Native to eastern Europe, western Asia. Dwarf species to just 4–6 in. tall, spreading to 20 in. wide. Erect, upright stems carry dark green, 1½- to 3-in.-long leaves. In spring, diminutive white flowers are produced singly or in pairs along the length of the stems.

P. odoratum (P. japonicum, P. officinale). Heat zones 8–1. Native to Europe, Asia. To 1½–3½ ft. tall, 2 ft. wide, with bright green, 4- to 6-in. leaves. Flowers are fragrant, usually borne in pairs but sometimes borne singly. 'Variegatum' has white-edged leaves; its stems are dark red until fully mature.

POLYGONUM. See FALLOPIA, PERSICARIA

Polypodiaceae. The polypody family contains the vast majority of ferns. Ferns in other families differ only in technical details concerning spore-bearing bodies (sporangia).

POLYPODIUM

POLYPODY FERN

Polypodiaceae

FERNS

⬥ ZONES VARY BY SPECIES; OR HOUSEPLANTS

☼ ◑ PARTIAL TO FULL SHADE; BRIGHT INDIRECT LIGHT

◑ REGULAR WATER

Polypodium aureum 'Mandaianum'

Widespread and quite variable group. Types described here are most commonly used in hanging baskets, often in the house or greenhouse. Indoors, best spot is near an east-facing window. Water regularly with room-temperature water in spring and summer, letting soil become fairly dry between soakings; reduce watering in fall and winter. Needs high humidity and benefits from frequent misting with room-temperature water. Feed monthly with a general-purpose liquid houseplant fertilizer diluted to quarter-strength.

As with many ferns, reclassification has added new names, which are given below in parentheses.

P. aureum (Phlebodium aureum). GOLDEN POLYPODY FERN, HARE'S FOOT FERN. Zones TS; 12–9. Native from Florida south to Argentina. To 2½ ft. high and 5 ft. wide, with heavy, brown, creeping rhizomes. Coarse blue-green fronds drop if hit by frost, but plants recover fast. 'Mandaianum', sometimes called crisped blue fern or lettuce fern, has frilled and wavy frond edges. Both it and the species are showy.

P. polypodioides. RESURRECTION FERN. Zones US, MS, LS, CS, TS; 12–6. Native from Delaware to southern Illinois, south to Florida, Texas, and Central and South America. An old Southern favorite that grows about 1 ft. high and spreads widely by slender, creeping rhizomes. Often found on massive limbs of live oaks. Fronds are deeply cut and leathery, with scaly undersides; they reach 7 in. long, 2 in. wide. Fronds curl up and "play dead" in dry weather but quickly come back to life when it rains (hence the plant's common name).

P. subauriculatum 'Knightiae' (Goniophlebium subauriculatum 'Knightiae'). LACY PINE FERN, KNIGHT'S POLYPODY. Zones TS; 12–10. Native to tropical Asia. Gracefully drooping, fringe-edged fronds to 3 ft. or longer. Spectacular when well grown. Outdoor plants shed old fronds in spring, then quickly produce new ones.

FOR GROWING SYMBOL EXPLANATIONS
PLEASE SEE PAGE 145

POLYSCIAS

Araliaceae

EVERGREEN SHRUBS OR TREES

⬥ TS ⬥ 12–10; OR HOUSEPLANTS

☼ ◑ FULL SUN OR PARTIAL SHADE; BRIGHT INDIRECT LIGHT

◑ ◑ MODERATE TO REGULAR WATER

Polyscias fruticosa

Like many other aralia relatives, these natives of Polynesia are grown for their handsomely divided leaves; flowers are unimportant and seldom produced outside the tropics. Plants appreciate warmth, humidity, and good drainage. Outdoors, they need protection from frost and mites. Often grown as hedges in south Florida. As houseplants, they are considered fussy: they need fresh, fairly still air (they cannot tolerate drafts), good light but no direct sun, and enough water but not too much. Overwatering and mite damage are the two main causes of failure. Misting is useful, along with light feeding. If plants are doing well, don't move them. They will grow slowly, maintaining their shapeliness for years.

P. balfouriana (P. scutellaria 'Balfourii'). To 15 ft. tall, 4–8 ft. wide. The species has green foliage, but more commonly sold is its selection 'Marginata', with white-edged leaflets. 'Pennockii' has white to pale green leaflets with irregular green spots.

P. fruticosa. MING ARALIA, PARSLEY PANAX. Grows 6–10 ft. tall, 4–6 ft. wide. Leaves finely divided and redivided into a multitude of narrow, toothed segments. 'Elegans' is a small selection with extremely dense foliage.

P. guilfoylei 'Victoriae'. Grows to 15 ft. tall, 4–6 ft. wide. Has white-edged leaflets that are deeply slashed and cut.

POLYSTICHUM

Polypodiaceae

FERNS

⬥ ZONES VARY BY SPECIES

☼ ◑ PARTIAL TO FULL SHADE

◑ REGULAR WATER, EXCEPT AS NOTED

Polystichum munitum

Hardy, symmetrical plants with medium-size, evergreen (except on *P. braunii*) fronds. Among the most useful and widely planted ferns, they combine well with other plants and are easy to grow. Do best in rich, organic, well-drained soil. Use in shady beds, along house walls, in mixed woodland plantings.

P. acrostichoides. CHRISTMAS FERN. Zones US, MS, LS, CS; 9–1. Native to eastern North America. Grows to 1–1½ ft. tall, about 3 ft. wide, with dark green leaves that make a fine contrast to snow or to the brown of dead leaves during the winter holiday season. The easiest evergreen fern to grow in the Upper, Middle, and Lower South. Stiff fronds stay upright until pushed over by heavy snow or hard frost.

P. aculeatum. PRICKLY SHIELD FERN, HARD SHIELD FERN. Zones US, MS, LS; 8–1. Native to Europe. Grows 2–4 ft. tall, 3 ft. wide. Glossy, firm, fairly upright, once- or twice-cut fronds; final segments are tipped by soft prickles. Pale green young fronds make an attractive show against the dark green mature ones.

P. braunii. BRAUN'S HOLLY FERN. Zones US, MS; 8–1. Semievergreen to deciduous. Native to northern latitudes of America and Asia. Grows 1–3 ft. tall and wide, with twice-divided fronds. Silvery green new growth.

P. munitum. SWORD FERN. Zones US; 8–1. Native to western North America. To 2–4 ft. high and wide, with leathery, shiny dark green fronds that emerge erect, then spread at the top to give plant a wide vase shape. Old plants may have 75 to 100 fronds. Once established, needs little water.

P. polyblepharum. TASSEL FERN, JAPANESE LACE FERN. Zones US, MS, LS, CS; 9–5. Native to Asia. Handsome, dense, lacy plant to 2–3 ft. tall, 3 ft. wide. Resembles *P. setiferum* but is taller, darker green, and

P

487

somewhat coarser; shiny fronds are a little more upright (to 2 ft. high). Usually sold as *P. setosum* (a name of no botanical standing).

P. setiferum. SOFT SHIELD FERN. Zones US, MS, LS; 9–6. Native to Europe. Finely cut fronds give effect of dark green lace, spread out in flattened vase shape. Many forms, 2–4½ ft. tall and wide. 'Proliferum' makes plantlets on midribs of older fronds; these can be detached and planted. Other fancy selections are sometimes sold under the name "English fern."

P. setosum. See *P. polyblepharum*

POMEGRANATE

Punicaceae

DECIDUOUS SHRUB OR TREE

🌱 MS, LS, CS ⬧ 12–5

☼ FULL SUN

💧 REGULAR WATER

Pomegranate

Native from Iran to the Himalayan region of northern India; naturalized throughout the Mediterranean. Naturally grows as a rounded plant to 15–20 ft. tall and broad, though it is often kept pruned to about 10 ft. high and wide. Showy red flowers at branch tips in spring; thick calyx persists as a projection at base of fruit. Roundish fruit to 5 in. wide is yellow overlaid with pink or red; it contains sacs of seedy, sweet-tart, juicy pulp. Self-fruitful.

Pomegranate is known botanically as *Punica granatum;* for ornamental selections, see that entry. The best-known selection grown for fruit is 'Wonderful', with orange-red flowers and burnished red fruit with red pulp. Other selections are sometimes available, including 'Sweet' (yellow flowers, pink pulp) and 'Fleishman', 'Granada', 'King' (all with pink flowers, pink pulp). 'Eversweet' ripens very early and bears virtually seedless fruit with transparent red pulp and clear, nonstaining juice. 'Utah Sweet' has very sweet, light pinkish pulp and nonstaining pink juice.

Pomegranates ripen in fall; harvest them when they reach full color. Fruit left on the tree is likely to split and rot, especially if weather is rainy. Can be stored for up to 7 months in the refrigerator. To eat fresh, cut into quarters or eighths and pull rind back (starting from the ends) to expose the juicy sacs; eat them, seeds and all. To remove juice for drinking fresh or for use in jams, jellies, or sauces, cut fruit in half and ream with a juicer. Or roll fruit firmly on hard surface; then cut a hole in stem end and squeeze juice into a container.

In the Middle South, where pomegranate grows and blooms but may not fruit, locate against south or west wall. Tolerates a wide variety of soils, growing well even in alkaline soil. Can take considerable drought but produces better fruit with regular moisture. Do any pruning late in dormant season. Not well adapted to Florida.

PONCIRUS trifoliata

HARDY ORANGE, TRIFOLIATE ORANGE

Rutaceae

DECIDUOUS SHRUB OR SMALL TREE

🌱 US, MS, LS, CS ⬧ 9–5

☼ FULL SUN

💧 MODERATE TO REGULAR WATER

Poncirus trifoliata

Native to China and Korea, this is the hardiest member of the citrus family, tolerating temperatures as low as −20°F. It is also a formidable barrier plant: stout, needle-sharp spines, 1–2 in. long, arm the length of its glossy green stems. Anyone planning to penetrate a hedge of hardy orange should line up blood donors first.

Dense, low-branched plant reaches 20 ft. tall and 12 ft. wide. Takes pruning and shearing into hedges very well; also good as espalier. Used as a dwarfing rootstock for many types of citrus. Glossy dark green, 2½-in.-long leaves are composed of three oblong leaflets; foliage turns yellow or yellow-green in autumn. Fragrant, 1- to 2-in.-wide white blossoms appear in spring. Sticky, aromatic (but inedible) fruits follow the flowers; they are green at first, ripening to yellowish orange in fall. Seeds from fallen fruits sprout prolifically. Easy to grow in just about any well-drained soil. 'Flying Dragon', to about one-third the size of the species, is a rather bizarre dwarf selection with twisted branches and curving, clawlike thorns.

Pontederiaceae. The pickerel weed family contains aquatic or marsh plants with showy, usually blue flowers. Members include water hyacinth (*Eichhornia*) and pickerel weed (*Pontederia*).

PONTEDERIA cordata

PICKEREL WEED

Pontederiaceae

AQUATIC PERENNIAL

🌱 US, MS, LS, CS, TS ⬧ 12–1

☼ ◐ FULL SUN OR LIGHT SHADE

💧 LOCATE IN PONDS, WATER GARDENS

Pontederia cordata

From eastern North America. To 3–4 ft. high, 2–2½ ft. wide. Long-stalked, glossy green leaves stand well above surface of water; they are heart shaped, to 10 in. long, 6 in. wide. From late spring to fall, bears short spikes of blue flowers. Blooms attract bees and butterflies; dragonflies use the flower spikes as landing pads. Good companion to water lilies (*Nymphaea*); plant in pots of rich soil placed in 1 ft. of water. Gives an informal garden pool the look of a wild pond. To use in natural ponds, set plants at shoreline—underwater, directly in the soil. Dormant in winter.

PONYTAIL PALM. See BEAUCARNEA recurvata

POOR MAN'S RHODODENDRON. See IMPATIENS sodenii

POPCORN. See CORN

POPLAR. See POPULUS

POPPY. See PAPAVER

POPPY, MEXICAN. See ARGEMONE mexicana

POPPY MALLOW. See CALLIRHOE

POPULUS

POPLAR, COTTONWOOD, ASPEN

Salicaceae

DECIDUOUS TREES

🌱 ZONES VARY BY SPECIES

☼ FULL SUN

💧 MODERATE TO REGULAR WATER

Populus nigra 'Italica'

Fast-growing, tough trees, best suited to rural areas and fringes of large properties. They are almost signature trees in semiarid plains regions and westward into desert and intermountain territory. If they are planted in smaller gardens, their aggressive surface roots crowd out other plants; most will sucker profusely if their roots are cut or disturbed. These trees are also subject to many pest and disease problems. Nonetheless, some poplars are beautiful or distinctive enough to be widely sold despite their liabilities. Several have good fall color. Leaves of most poplars are roughly triangular, sometimes toothed or lobed. Pendulous catkins appear before spring leaf-out; those on male trees are denser textured. Female trees later bear masses of cottony seeds that blow about and become a nuisance; for that reason, male (seedless) selections are offered in garden centers. Deer don't usually browse poplars.

P. alba. WHITE POPLAR. Zones US, MS, LS; 9–1. Native to Europe, Asia. Broad, wide-spreading tree to 40–60 ft. tall and wide. Leaves are dark green above, white and woolly beneath, 2–5 in. long, usually with three to five lobes. A "lively" tree even in light breezes, with flickering white and green highlights. Poor fall color. Tolerates a wide range of soils. Suckers profusely. A seedless selection, 'Pyramidalis', called Bolleana poplar (and often sold as *P. bolleana*), forms a narrow column; it has a white trunk like that of birch (*Betula*).

P. deltoides. EASTERN COTTONWOOD. Zones US, MS, LS, CS; 9–1. Native from Quebec to Florida and Texas. Grows very fast in moist soils, quickly reaching 30 ft. tall; eventually attains 75–100 ft. tall, up to 70 ft. wide. Provides fast shade and tolerates wet sites, drought, salt spray, acid and alkaline soils, and winter cold, but not good in gardens because of its huge size, short life, and tendency to break up in storms.

P. fremontii. WESTERN COTTONWOOD, FREMONT COTTONWOOD. Zones US, MS, LS, CS, TS; 12–1. From California and Arizona. The cottonwood of desert water holes and watercourses. To 40–60 ft. or taller, about 30 ft. wide, with 2- to 4-in.-wide, thick, coarsely toothed, glossy yellow-green leaves that turn bright lemon yellow in fall. Does well in West Texas. 'Nevada' is a male selection. *P. f. wislizenii*, Rio Grande cottonwood, is similar but has slightly larger leaves. It is well adapted to arid regions; its native range is from southern Colorado to northern Mexico.

P. nigra 'Italica'. LOMBARDY POPLAR. Zones US, MS, LS, CS; 9–1. Male selection of a European species. Lovely columnar tree to 40–100 ft. tall, 15–30 ft. wide, with upward-reaching branches. Bright green, 4-in. leaves turn a beautiful golden yellow in autumn. In dry, cold-winter climates, this tree has few problems; elsewhere, however, it's subject to a canker disease that will soon kill it. In these areas, it's best used as a quick, temporary screen. Upright English oak (*Quercus robur* 'Fastigiata'), a more permanent tree, is a good substitute. Another possibility with a similar columnar habit is *P. tremula* 'Erecta', also less subject to canker.

P. tremula. EUROPEAN ASPEN. Zones US; 6–1. From Europe, North Africa, Asia. Similar to *P. tremuloides*, but its bark is somewhat darker and its leaves more coarsely toothed. Seedless 'Erecta', sometimes called Swedish columnar aspen, is a narrow grower with red fall color.

P. tremuloides. QUAKING ASPEN. Zones US, MS; 7–1. Widely distributed in North America; native to northern latitudes and mountains. Takes poor soil; generally performs poorly or grows slowly at low elevations. To 40–50 ft. tall, 20–30 ft. wide; often grows with several trunks or in a clump. Smooth, pale gray-green to whitish bark. Dainty, round, 2- to 4-in. light green leaves flutter and quake with even the slightest movement of air. Brilliant golden yellow autumn foliage. Apt to suffer from sudden dieback or borers.

STAY OUT OF ROOT TROUBLE. *Do not plant any kind of* Populus *near pavement or close to sewer lines, septic tanks, or their leach lines. Also keep these trees out of lawns and small gardens. Their roots are invasive, and they form suckers.* ❖

PORCELAIN BERRY. See AMPELOPSIS brevipedunculata

PORCUPINE GRASS. See MISCANTHUS sinensis 'Strictus'

PORTERWEED. See STACHYTARPHETA

PORTUGAL LAUREL. See PRUNUS lusitanica

PORTULACA

Portulacaceae

ANNUALS

☘ US, MS, LS, CS, TS ⏏ 12–1

☼ FULL SUN

◐ ● MODERATE TO REGULAR WATER

Portulaca grandiflora

Low-growing, fleshy plants. One is called a weed but can be used in cooking and salads. The others are grown for their brilliant flowers, on display from late spring until frost; generally, the blossoms open fully in bright light and close by midafternoon in hot weather. The various plants described here thrive in high temperatures and intense sunlight. Not fussy about soil. Bright-flowered types are attractive in rock gardens, parking strips, hanging baskets, or as edgings and bank covers; they don't require deadheading to prolong bloom.

P. grandiflora. MOSS ROSE, PORTULACA. From South America. To 6 in. high, 1½ ft. across. Trailing, branching reddish stems are set with narrow, cylindrical, pointed leaves to 1 in. long. Inch-wide, lustrous-petaled flowers shaped like tiny roses, in white and many bright and pastel shades of red, cerise, rose pink, orange, yellow. Available as single colors or mixes, in either single- or double-flowered strains; Prize, Magic Carpet, Sunglo, Sunkiss are popular. Afternoon Delight and Sundance strains stay open longer in the afternoon. The newer Sundial strain also resists closing and has larger (2-in.), double blossoms; 'Sundial Peach' is especially attractive. 'Margarita Rosita' is a hybrid with masses of deep pink semi-double flowers. All self-sow, but they often fail to come true from seed.

P. oleracea. PURSLANE. Unimproved form is thought to have originated in India; it's an edible weed with tiny yellow flowers and plump, oval leaves to 1¼ in. long. Warm weather and moisture encourage its growth. Control by hoeing or pulling before it goes to seed; don't let pulled plants lie about, since they can reroot or ripen seed.

P. Wildfire hybrids. Sometimes offered as *P. oleracea*, sometimes as *P. grandiflora*, but actually a strain of *P. umbraticola*. Best in hot-summer areas; popular in the Lower South and Texas. Plants grow a few inches tall and spread to 2 ft.; they have the broad leaves of *P. oleracea* but bear brightly colored, 1½-in. single flowers in red, pink, lavender, yellow, orange, peach, white, or bicolors. Each flower lasts only a day, but new ones keep the show going. Plants live over in the absence of frost.

PURSLANE FOR DINNER? *The French call it* pourpier, *the Mexicans call it* verdolaga, *and both cultures use it in cooking. You can use purslane to add an interesting, peppery flavor to salads, soups, pork stews, tomato sauce, and scrambled eggs.* ❖

Portulacaceae. The portulaca family contains annuals, perennials, and a few shrubs, usually with succulent foliage and frequently with showy flowers. Examples are *Lewisia* and *Portulaca*.

POSSUMHAW. See ILEX decidua

POTATO

Solanaceae

PERENNIAL TREATED AS ANNUAL

☘ US, MS, LS, CS, TS ⏏ 12–1

☼ FULL SUN

● REGULAR WATER

◆ GREEN SKIN AND RAW SHOOTS ARE POISONOUS IF INGESTED

Potato

Andean native, botanically known as *Solanum tuberosum*. For ornamental relatives, see *Solanum*. Though other vegetables are more common in home gardens, growing potatoes can be very satisfying: 2 pounds of seed potatoes can yield 50 pounds of potatoes for eating. The many pests and diseases that beleaguer commercial growers are not likely to plague home gardeners. Colorado potato beetles can be controlled by dusting plants with *Bacillus thuringiensis* San Diego (*Bt*; sold as Dipel) or Neem (azadirachtin). To avoid disease problems, plant certified disease-free starter potatoes or disease-resistant selections.

Potatoes can be grown from seed potatoes that you cut into 1½-in. cubes (each with at least two eyes) or from minitubers, which are planted whole and are less likely to rot in the ground. Home gardeners have access to a number of selections, including types with red, yellow, or bluish purple skin; yellow-fleshed sorts; and even potatoes with blue skin and flesh. Shapes vary from round to fingerlike. Some selections mature faster than others, but most reach harvesting size about 3 months after planting. Most dislike the South's summer heat, preferring instead temperatures that are cool to moderate. For best success, plant heat-tolerant selections such as 'Anoka', 'Caribe', 'Irish Cobbler', 'Kennebec', 'Red La Soda', 'Red Pontiac', and 'Yukon Gold'.

Potatoes need sandy, fast-draining, fertile soil; tubers become deformed in heavy, poorly drained soil. In the Upper, Middle, and Lower South, plant as soon as soil can be worked in early spring. Elsewhere, plant in fall or winter. Let seed potato pieces dry for a day or two before planting. Then set minitubers or potato pieces 2 in. deep, 1–1½ ft. apart. As plants grow, mound loose soil around their bases (taking care not to cover stems completely); developing tubers should always be covered with soil to keep skin from turning green.

The aboveground potato plant is sprawling and bushy, with much-divided dark green leaves somewhat like those of a tomato plant. Clustered, inch-wide flowers are pale blue.

Dig early potatoes (so-called new potatoes) when the plants begin to bloom; dig mature potatoes when plants die down. Dig carefully to avoid bruising or cutting the tubers. Well-matured potatoes free of defects are the best keepers; store them in a cool (40°F), dark, dry place. Where ground doesn't freeze, late potatoes can remain in ground until needed. Dig before warmer temperatures start them growing again.

Another method of growing potatoes is to prepare soil so surface is loose, plant potato pieces or minitubers ½–2 in. deep, and water well. Mound loose soil over plants as directed above; then cover soil with a 1- to 1½-ft.-thick layer of straw, hay, or dead leaves. Surround the planting with chicken wire to keep loose material from blowing away. Potatoes will form on the soil surface or just beneath it, requiring little digging; you can probe through the mulch with your fingers to harvest them.

POTATO VINE. See **SOLANUM jasminoides**

POTENTILLA

CINQUEFOIL

Rosaceae

PERENNIALS AND DECIDUOUS SHRUBS

ZONES VARY BY SPECIES

PARTIAL SHADE IN HOTTEST CLIMATES

MODERATE WATER

Potentilla fruticosa
'Tangerine'

Hardy plants useful for ground covers and borders, with bright green or gray-green leaves divided into small leaflets. Small, roselike, typically single flowers come in white, cream, and soft to bright shades of pink, red, yellow, and orange. Cinquefoils typically prefer cool nights and cool soils. Deer don't usually bother them.

EVERGREEN PERENNIALS

These include creeping plants used as ground covers as well as sturdy, clumping types for rock gardens or perennial borders. Leaves are divided fanwise into leaflets and are reminiscent of strawberry foliage; flowers are generally about 1 in. wide.

P. alba. WHITE CINQUEFOIL. Zones US, MS; 7–3. From central and southern Europe. To 4 in. high, spreading to about 1 ft., with bright green, 2½-in. leaves divided into five leaflets. Bears white flowers in early spring; occasionally reblooms.

P. atrosanguinea. RUBY CINQUEFOIL. Zones US, MS, LS; 8–5. Sprawling, mounding Himalayan native to 1½ ft. high, 2 ft. wide, with furry, three-leafleted, 2- to 3-in.-long leaves and red blossoms in summer. A parent of superior hybrids such as 1- to 2-ft. 'Flamenco', bearing blood red flowers with a dark center; 1½-ft. 'Gibson's Scarlet', bright red with dark center; and 'William Rollison', semidouble bright orange with yellow center.

P. nepalensis. NEPAL CINQUEFOIL. Zones US, MS, LS, CS; 9–4. From the Himalayas. To 1–2 ft. high, 2 ft. wide. Leaves are 3–4 in. long, divided into five roundish leaflets; branching clusters of purplish red blossoms in

summer. Selections are superior to the species for borders, cut flowers. 'Melton Fire', 12–15 in. high, bears bright red blooms marked with yellow and blending to a deep red center. 'Miss Willmott', 10–12 in. high, has salmon pink flowers.

P. neumanniana 'Nana' (P. verna 'Nana'). DWARF SPRING CINQUEFOIL. Zones US, MS, LS; 8–5. Selection of a European species. May be sold as *P. tabernaemontani*. Dainty-looking yet tough and persistent creeping ground cover. Grows quickly to 3–6 in. high and about 1 ft. wide. Bright green leaves divided into five leaflets; butter yellow, ¼-in. flowers in spring and summer. Takes more water than other cinquefoils, but also tolerates heat and drought. May turn brown in cold winters. Foliage blankets the ground completely yet is permeable enough to be a good bulb cover. Good lawn substitute for no-traffic areas; mow annually before spring growth begins. Subject to a disfiguring rust in some areas.

P. recta 'Warrenii'. WARREN'S SULFUR CINQUEFOIL. Zones US, MS, LS; 8–1. Selection of a European species. Grows 2 ft. tall, 1½ ft. wide, with 4-in. leaves divided into five to seven leaflets. Profuse show of bright yellow flowers in late spring. Tolerates a wide range of soils. Longer blooming and less weedy than *P. recta* itself; sometimes sold as *P. warrenii*. 'Macrantha' (which may be listed as *P. warrenii* 'Macrantha') is the same or a very similar plant.

P. ×tonguei. STAGHORN CINQUEFOIL. Zones US, MS, LS; 8–3. Hybrid between *P. nepalensis* and another species. Creeping plant to just 4 in. tall, with foot-long stems and 2-in. leaves divided into three to five leaflets. Blooms in late spring or summer, bearing ½-in.-wide apricot flowers with a red center.

P. tridentata 'Minima'. MINIMA WINELEAF CINQUEFOIL. Zones US, MS, LS; 8–1. Selection of a species native to Greenland and North America (from Wisconsin south to Georgia and Iowa). Creeping ground cover with shiny, 1-in., three-leafleted leaves that turn red in fall. Small white flowers resembling strawberry blossoms appear in spring and summer. Space plants 15–18 in. apart.

P. warrenii. See *P. recta* 'Warrenii'

DECIDUOUS SHRUBS

The shrubby potentillas, most often sold as named forms of bush cinquefoil (*P. fruticosa*), are native to northern latitudes everywhere. They perform well in Zones US, MS; 6–1. All have leaves divided into three to seven leaflets; some are distinctly green on top, gray beneath, while others look more gray green all over. All bloom cheerfully from late spring to early fall.

Fairly trouble-free. Best in well-drained soil with moderate water, but tolerate poor soils, limestone, drought, heat. Selections with red or orange tinting should be grown in light shade, since they tend to fade quickly in hot sun. After bloom period ends, cut out older stems from time to time to make room for new growth. Here are some of the selections found in garden centers.

'Abbotswood'. To 3 ft. high and wide, with dark blue-green leaves, 2-in. white flowers.

'Goldfinger'. Dense-foliaged dark green plant to 3 ft. tall, 4 ft. wide, with golden yellow, 1½-in. blooms.

'Gold Star'. To 2 ft. tall, 2½ ft. wide, with large, deep green leaves and 2-in. bright yellow flowers.

'Jackman's Variety'. To 4 ft. tall and 5 ft. wide, with 1½-in. bright yellow blossoms.

'Katherine Dykes'. Can reach 5 ft. but usually stays much lower; spreads at least as wide as high. Pale yellow, 1-in. flowers.

'Klondike'. Dense grower to 2 ft. high and wide; 1½- to 2-in. yellow blossoms.

'Mount Everest'. Bushy, upright grower to 4½ ft. high and wide; 1½-in. pure white blooms.

'Primrose Beauty'. Silvery gray-green foliage on a plant 2–3 ft. high and wide. Pale yellow, 1½-in. flowers.

'Red Ace'. To 2 ft. high, 3–4 ft. wide. Flowers are 1½ in. wide, bright red with yellow center and yellow petal backs. Blooms fade to yellow as they age (fading is rapid in hot summer weather or poor growing conditions).

'Sunset'. To 2–2½ ft. tall, 3 ft. wide, with bright green foliage, 1½-in. yellow flowers shaded orange.

P

'Sutter's Gold'. To 1 ft. high, spreading to 3 ft. Clear yellow flowers about 1 in. across.

'Tangerine'. To 2½ ft. high and wide, with bright yellow-orange, 1½-in. blooms.

POTERIUM. See SANGUISORBA

POTHOS. See EPIPREMNUM aureum

POT MARIGOLD. See CALENDULA officinalis

POWDER PUFF. See CALLIANDRA haematocephala

PRAIRIE DROPSEED. See SPOROBOLUS heterolepis

PRATIA pedunculata

BLUE STAR CREEPER

Campanulaceae (Lobeliaceae)

PERENNIAL

✿ US, MS, LS ⊞ 8–5

◐ PARTIAL SHADE

◆ REGULAR WATER

Pratia pedunculata

Native to Australia, this dainty creeper is excellent for growing between stepping-stones, filling in niches in rock walls, or forming a prostrate ground cover. It produces an inch-tall mat of tiny (½-in.-long), oval leaves. Equally tiny light blue flowers appear atop the foliage in spring. Can take light foot traffic. Provide moist, well-drained soil. Feed lightly once a month from spring until fall. Formerly known as *Laurentia fluviatilis*.

PRAYER PLANT. See MARANTA leuconeura

PRICKLY PEAR. See OPUNTIA

PRICKLY POPPY. See ARGEMONE

PRIMROSE. See PRIMULA

PRIMULA

PRIMROSE

Primulaceae

PERENNIALS, MOST GROWN AS COOL-SEASON ANNUALS

✿ ZONES VARY BY SPECIES OR TYPE

◐ LIGHT SHADE

◆ REGULAR WATER, EXCEPT AS NOTED

Primula malacoides

Primroses form tufts of foliage, above which rise flowering stems carrying showy, circular, five-petaled blossoms. The blooms may come on individual stems, in clusters at stem ends, or in tiered clusters like candelabra up the stem. Most are spring blooming, but some start flowering in late winter and a few bloom in early summer.

Specialists have organized the hundreds of species, selections, named hybrids, and hybrid strains into 34 divisions, but only a few are fairly easy to grow in home gardens. Most primroses are native to the Himalayas and cool regions of southeast Asia and Europe, so they thrive with a combination of moist, rich soil and cool, humid air. Few areas in the South supply these conditions. Most kinds that winter over do so only in the Upper and Middle South; a few tolerate warmer climates. Most of the primroses listed below will grow as perennials in the zones indicated, but almost all of them are best treated as cool-weather annuals.

Specialty nurseries offer seeds and plants of many kinds of primroses; fanciers exchange seeds and plants through primrose societies.

P. acaulis. See P. vulgaris

P. auricula. AURICULA. Zones US, MS, LS; 8–1. To 6–8 in. high, with broad, leathery gray-green leaves to 5 in. long forming rosettes to 1 ft. wide. Blooms in early spring, bearing clusters of fragrant, yellow- or white-eyed flowers in colors including orange, pink, rose, red, purple, blue, white, cream, and brownish. Usually grown in pots.

P. elatior. OXLIP. Zones US, MS, LS; 8–1. Leaves to 8 in. long, hairy on undersides, form foliage clumps to 10 in. wide. Sulfur yellow spring blossoms appear in many-flowered clusters on 8- to 12-in. stems.

P. japonica. JAPANESE PRIMROSE. Zones US, MS, LS; 8–1. From Japan. Stout, 2½-ft. stems bear whorls of up to five yellow-eyed purple flowers. Leaves are 6–9 in. long, 3 in. wide; clumps grow about 1½ ft. wide. 'Miller's Crimson' is a choice red selection; white and pink forms are also available. Blooms from late spring to early summer. Ample water; will even grow in shallow water.

P. juliae hybrids (Pruhonicensis hybrids). JULIANA PRIMROSE. Zones US, MS, LS; 8–6. Parentage involves a native of rocky forests in mountainous regions of the eastern Caucasus. Rounded, scallop-edged, bright green leaves to 2½ in. long form a 10-in.-wide rosette. In early spring, flowers are borne singly or in clusters on 3- to 4-in. stalks; colors include white, blue, yellow, orange, red, pink, purple. Excellent for edging, woodland, rock gardens. Best with regular water but will accept drier soil than most primroses.

P. malacoides. FAIRY PRIMROSE, BABY PRIMROSE. Zones US, MS, LS, CS, TS; 12–1. Usually grown as annual (indoor potted plant). Foot-wide evergreen rosettes of soft, pale green, long-stalked leaves, oval with lobed and cut edges, 1½–3 in. long. White, pink, rose, red, or lavender blooms in lacy whorls along upright, 8- to 15-in. stems. Available from greenhouses in late winter and early spring.

P. obconica. Zones US, MS, LS, CS, TS; 12–1. Usually grown as annual (indoor potted plant). White, pink, salmon, lavender, or reddish purple flowers, 1½–2 in. wide, in broad clusters on 1-ft. stems. Plants reach 1 ft. wide. Evergreen, roundish, hairy leaves on long stems. Hairs on stems (except those of Freedom strain) may irritate skin. Available from greenhouses in late winter and early spring.

P. × polyantha. POLYANTHUS PRIMROSE. Zones US, MS; 7–3. Often called English primrose. Foliage clumps to 9 in. wide; the 8-in.-long green leaves resemble romaine lettuce. Bloom season runs from winter to early or midspring; 1- to 2-in.-wide flowers in many brilliant colors come in large, full clusters on 1-ft.-tall stems.

Primula × polyantha

Miniature Polyanthus types have smaller flowers on shorter stalks. Fine large-flowered strains include Barnhaven, Clarke's, Concorde, Pacific, Santa Barbara. Novelties include Gold Laced, with gold-edged mahogany petals. All good for massing, bulb companions, or pots.

P. veris. COWSLIP. Zones US, MS; 7–1. Leaves to 8 in. long, slightly hairy on undersides, form a clump to 10 in. wide. Large clusters of fragrant, bright yellow (sometimes red or apricot) flowers are held on 8- to 12-in. stems. Blossoms of 'Sunset Shades' feature yellow throats and petals in a blend of orange to deep red.

P. vulgaris (P. acaulis). ENGLISH PRIMROSE, PRIMROSE. Zones US, MS, LS; 8–1. Tufts of leaves much like those of *P. × polyantha*; clumps grow about 1 ft. wide. Spring flowers are typically borne singly on 8-in. stalks, though some garden strains have two or three blossoms per stalk; colors include white, yellow, red, blue, bronze, brown, and wine. A double-flowered form is sold. Nosegay and Biedermeier strains are very heavy blooming. Use as edging, in woodland garden.

Primulaceae. The primrose family of annuals and perennials has single or clustered flowers with five-lobed calyxes and corollas. Examples are *Cyclamen* and primrose (*Primula*).

PRINCE'S FEATHER. See AMARANTHUS hypochondriacus

PRINCESS FLOWER. See TIBOUCHINA urvilleana

PRIVET. See LIGUSTRUM

P

PROSOPIS glandulosa

MESQUITE, HONEY MESQUITE

Fabaceae (Leguminosae)

DECIDUOUS TREE

MS, LS, CS, TS (DRY AREAS) H 12–7

FULL SUN

LITTLE TO NO WATER

Native to Mexico and a common sight on dry grasslands and hills of West, Southwest, and Central Texas. Seeds believed to have entered Texas in the stomachs of cattle driven across the Rio Grande. The plant quickly spread and is now considered a nuisance by ranchers, because its greedy, wide-spreading roots compete with pasture grasses for water.

Prosopis glandulosa

Mesquite's gnarled, sculptural trunks and wispy, light green foliage make it a picturesque lawn tree. Its light shade allows grass to grow right up to the trunk. Reaches 30 ft. tall and about as wide. Deep taproot makes it nearly impossible to transplant. Does not need watering. Tolerates lawn irrigation better if soil is sandy. Little pruning is needed; just cut out dead or broken limbs. Thorniness is variable. Some selections have branches set with very long, sharp, almost needlelike thorns, but thornless selections, such as cutting-grown 'Maverick', are available.

Many prize mesquite for its wood, which is used in flavoring smoked and grilled meats. But its long seedpods, which change from red to mottled purple and tan as they dry, do just as good a job.

Two other forms of mesquite are found in Texas—screw bean *(P. pubescens)* and Arizona mesquite *(P. velutina)*. Both are smaller and shrubbier than *P. glandulosa*. Screw bean is named for its spirally twisted pods, which are popular in dried arrangements. All three species hybridize freely, making exact identification of individual plants difficult.

Proteaceae. The protea family of evergreen shrubs and trees is characterized by leathery leaves and irregular, somewhat tubular flowers in spikelike clusters or heads often surrounded by showy colored bracts. The sole representative in this book is *Grevillea*.

PRUNE. See PLUM

PRUNELLA

SELF-HEAL, HEAL-ALL

Lamiaceae (Labiatae)

PERENNIALS

US, MS, LS

FULL SUN OR LIGHT SHADE

REGULAR WATER

Prunella vulgaris

Native to Europe, these creeping perennials spread by surface and underground runners to form low, dense foliage mats. Upright spikes of hooded flowers rise above the leaves in summer. Though names are much confused, all species are tough, tolerant, and deep rooted. They are useful for small-scale ground covers and can endure the occasional footstep; set 1 ft. apart. Choose location carefully, though: these plants are too invasive to risk near choice, delicate rock garden plants. After bloom, shear off spent flower spikes to keep the planting neat and prevent seed formation.

P. grandiflora. Heat zones 8–5. Leaves to 4 in. long; stems to 1½ ft. tall, bearing spikes of 1- to 1½-in. purple blossoms. Selections include 'Pink Loveliness', 'Purple Loveliness' (lilac purple touched with white), and 'White Loveliness'.

P. vulgaris. Heat zones 8–1. This is the common species. Smaller in all its parts than *P. grandiflora*, with leaves to 2 in. long, 1-ft. stems, and purple or pink flowers just ⅓ in. long. *P. v. incisa* has deeply cut leaves.

PRUNUS

Rosaceae

EVERGREEN AND DECIDUOUS SHRUBS AND TREES

ZONES VARY BY SPECIES

FULL SUN, EXCEPT AS NOTED

MODERATE TO REGULAR WATER, EXCEPT AS NOTED

SEE CHARTS ON FOLLOWING PAGES

Prunus 'Okame' Flowering Cherry

Discussed here are the ornamental members of the genus *Prunus*. Fruit trees belonging to *Prunus*—collectively called the stone fruits—can be found under their common names. See Almond, Apricot, Cherry, Peach and Nectarine, and Plum.

Ornamentals are divided into two classes: evergreen and deciduous. Evergreens are used chiefly as shade trees, street trees, hedges, and screens. Deciduous flowering trees and shrubs, closely related to the fruit trees mentioned above, are valued for their floral display as well as for attractive form and for foliage shape and texture. Many of these also bear edible fruit.

EVERGREEN FORMS

The following evergreen species are all large shrubs or small trees.

P. caroliniana. CAROLINA CHERRY LAUREL. Zones US, MS, LS, CS; 10–1. Native from North Carolina to Texas. As an upright shrub, it can be well branched from the base and used as clipped hedge or tall screen to 20 ft. high; can also be sheared into formal shapes. Trained as a tree, it is a broad-topped plant reaching 35–40 ft. high and nearly as wide; looks attractive with multiple trunks. Densely foliaged in glossy green, smooth-edged, 2- to 4-in.-long leaves. Small, creamy white flowers in 1-in. spikes appear in late winter or spring, followed by black fruit to ½ in. wide. Flower and fruit litter can be a problem in paved areas. Very tolerant of heat, wind, drought. 'Bright 'n Tight' and 'Compacta' are denser than the species, reach only 8–10 ft. tall and 6–8 ft. wide, and take well to pruning.

P. laurocerasus. CHERRY LAUREL. Zones US, MS, LS; 9–6. Hardy to 5°F; selections listed below are hardier. Native from southeastern Europe to Iran. To 20 ft. tall and wide, though generally seen as a lower clipped hedge. Leathery, glossy dark green leaves are 3–7 in. long, 1½–2 in. wide. Blooms in summer, bearing 3- to 5-in. spikes of creamy white flowers that are often hidden by leaves. Small purple to black fruit appears in late summer and fall.

Where adapted, a fast-growing, greedy plant that's difficult to garden under or around. Regular water and nutrients will speed growth and keep top dense. Needs reasonably good drainage. Give partial shade in hottest areas. Tolerates salt spray. Stands heavy shearing but with considerable mutilation of leaves; best pruned by one cut at a time, using hand pruners, to remove overlong twigs just above a leaf. Leaf spot can be a serious problem in the Lower South.

The compact selections listed below are good garden plants, better behaved than the species.

'Otto Luyken'. Zones US, MS, LS. To 4 ft. tall, 5–6 ft. wide. Deep green, glossy leaves 2–4 in. long.

'Schipkaensis'. SCHIPKA LAUREL. Zones US, MS, LS. Usually 4–5 ft. high (possibly 10 ft. tall), 7 ft. wide. Narrow leaves are 2–4½ in. long.

'Zabeliana'. ZABEL LAUREL. Zones US, MS, LS. Narrow, 2- to 4½-in.-long leaves; branches angle upward and outward from plant base. Eventually reaches 6 ft., with equal or greater spread. More tolerant of full sun than species. Versatile plant; good for low screen, big foundation plant, bank cover (with branches pegged down), espalier.

P. lusitanica. PORTUGAL LAUREL. Zones MS, LS, CS; 9–4. Native to Spain, Portugal. Densely branched shrub 10–20 ft. high and wide; or multitrunked, spreading tree to at least 30 ft. tall and wide. Trained to a single trunk, it is used as formal street tree. Glossy dark green leaves to 5 in. long, 2 in. wide. Small, creamy white flowers in 5- to

Prunus laurocerasus 'Zabeliana'

P

PRUNUS—FLOWERING CHERRY

NAME	ZONES	GROWTH HABIT, FOLIAGE	HEIGHT, SPREAD	FLOWERS, SEASON, COMMENTS
P. campanulata TAIWAN FLOWERING CHERRY	MS, LS, CS; 9–7	Graceful, slender, upright-growing small tree; densely branched	To 20–25 ft. high and wide	Single, bell shaped, drooping, ¾ in. wide, in clusters of two to five. Striking shade of bright purplish pink. Early. Red fruit about ½ in. long. Good choice for Coastal South
P. 'Okame'	US, MS, LS, CS; 9–4	Upright, oval habit. Fast growing. Dark green, fine-textured foliage. Good yellow-orange to orange-red fall color	To 25 ft. by 20 ft.	Single carmine pink, 1 in. wide. Very early. Hybrid between *P. campanulata* and another species. Blooms well even in Coastal South
P. serrulata 'Amanogawa' (species *P. serrulata*, JAPANESE FLOWERING CHERRY)	US, MS; 8–5	Columnar in youth, becoming vase shaped with age	To 20–25 ft. tall, 4–8 ft. wide	Semidouble light pink with deep pink petal margins; 1 in. wide. Early midseason
P. s. 'Kwanzan' ('Kanzan', 'Sekiyama')	US, MS, LS; 8–5	Stiffly upright branches form a narrow, inverted cone that spreads with age. Orange fall foliage	To 30 ft. by 20 ft.	Large (2½ in. wide), double, deep rosy pink, in pendent clusters. Blossoms appear before or with red young leaves. Midseason. Tolerates heat and humidity well
P. s. 'Shirofugen'	US, MS; 8–6	Wide horizontal branching	To 25 ft. high and wide	Long-stalked double blooms to 2 in. wide, in pink fading to white. Flowers appear at same time as coppery red new leaves. Latest to bloom among *P. serrulata* selections
P. s. 'Shirotae' ('Mt. Fuji')	US, MS, LS; 8–6	Strong horizontal branching	To 20 ft. by 25 ft.	Semidouble, to 2 in. wide. Pink in bud; white when fully open, aging to purplish pink. Early
P. s. 'Shogetsu' ('Shimidsu Sakura')	US, MS, LS; 8–6	Spreading growth, arching branches	To 15 ft. by 25 ft.	Semidouble and fully double, to 2 in. wide. Pale pink, often with white center. Late
P. × subhirtella 'Autumnalis'	US, MS, LS; 8–6	Loose-branching, bushy tree with flattened crown	To 25–30 ft. high and wide	Double white or pinkish white, ½ in. wide. Often blooms during mild autumn or winter weather as well as in early spring
P. × s. 'Pendula' SINGLE WEEPING CHERRY, WEEPING HIGAN CHERRY	US, MS, LS; 8–6	Usually sold grafted at 5–6 ft. high on upright-growing understock. Graceful branches hang down, often to ground	To 15–25 ft. high and wide	Profuse show of ½-in., pale pink single flowers. Trees grown on own roots are rare but more graceful than those grown from grafts. Early
P. × yedoensis YOSHINO FLOWERING CHERRY	US, MS, LS; 8–3	Horizontal branches; graceful, open pattern. Fast growing. Leaves may turn orange or red in fall	To 40 ft. by 30 ft.	Single light pink to nearly white, to 1½ in. wide. Early. This is the cherry planted around the Tidal Basin in Washington, D.C. Tolerates heat and humidity
P. × y. 'Akebono' (sometimes called 'Daybreak')	US, MS, LS; 8–6	Same as *P. × yedoensis*	To 25 ft. high and wide	Flowers pinker than those of *P. × yedoensis*

10-in. spikes in spring and early summer, followed by clusters of tiny bright red to dark purple fruit. Slower growing than *P. laurocerasus* and more tolerant of heat, sun, and wind. Drought tolerant.

DECIDUOUS FLOWERING FRUIT TREES

Flowering cherry. Zones vary by type; see chart. Cultural needs of all are identical. They require full sun and fast-draining, well-aerated soil; if your soil is substandard, plant in raised beds. Prune only to remove awkward or crossing branches; pinch back the occasional overly ambitious shoot to force branching. You can cut during bloom time and use branches in arrangements. Trees bloom in early to midspring, depending on type.

All are good to garden under. Use them as their growth habit indicates: large, spreading kinds make good shade trees, while smaller ones are indispensable in Japanese gardens. Foliage may sustain damage from insect pests. Plants growing in heavy soil are sometimes subject to root rot (for which there is no cure); an afflicted tree will usually bloom, then send out new leaves that suddenly collapse.

Flowering peach. Zones US, MS, LS, CS; 9–1. Most are more widely adapted than fruiting peach but otherwise identical in size, growth habit, cultural needs, and potential problems. Place trees where they will be striking when in bloom yet fairly unobtrusive out of bloom. Bloom period runs from late winter to early spring. The following selections are strictly "flowering" in that the 2- to 2½-in. blooms are showy and fruit is either absent or inferior. In areas with late frosts, choose late bloomers; early bloomers are best in areas with hot, early springs. ▶

PRUNUS—FLOWERING PLUM

NAME	ZONES	GROWTH HABIT, FOLIAGE	HEIGHT, SPREAD	FLOWERS, FRUIT, COMMENTS
Prunus × blireiana	US, MS, LS; 8–5	Graceful form. New leaves reddish purple; turn greenish bronze by summer	To 25 ft. by 20 ft.	Double, fragrant pink to rose flowers to 1¼ in. wide. Little or no fruit. Hybrid of *P. cerasifera* 'Pissardii' and *P. mume*
P. cerasifera MYROBALAN, CHERRY PLUM	US, MS, LS; 8–1	Most often used as rootstock for various stone fruits. Dark green leaves	To 30 ft. high and wide	Pure white flowers to 1 in. wide. Red, 1- to 1¼-in.-wide fruit is sweet but bland. Self-sows freely; some seedlings bear yellow fruit. Purple- and red-leafed selections are more popular than species
P. c. 'Allred'	US, MS, LS; 8–1	Upright, slightly spreading. Red leaves	To 20 ft. by 12–15 ft.	Single white flowers. Red, 1½-in., tart fruit good for preserves, jelly
P. c. 'Krauter's Vesuvius'	US, MS, LS; 8–1	Upright, oval form. Darkest foliage (blackish purple) of any flowering plum	To 18 ft. by 12 ft.	Single light pink flowers. Little or no fruit
P. c. 'Mt. St. Helens'	US, MS, LS; 8–1	Upright, spreading, with rounded crown. A sport of *P. c.* 'Newport' but more robust, with larger leaves of a richer purple color	Faster growing than 'Newport', to 20 ft. high and wide	Same as 'Newport'
P. c. 'Newport'	US, MS, LS; 8–1	Upright and spreading, with rounded crown. Foliage is dark purple all summer, attractively reddish in autumn	To 15–20 ft. by 20 ft.	Fragrant, single white to pale pink flowers. Will bear a little fruit
P. c. 'Pissardii' ('Atropurpurea') PURPLE-LEAF PLUM	US, MS, LS; 8–1	Rounded habit. Leaves are coppery red when new, later deepen to dark purple; turn red in autumn	Fast to 25–35 ft. high and wide	Single white flowers. Heavy crop of red, 1- to 1½-in. fruit
P. c. 'Thundercloud'	US, MS, LS; 8–1	Rounded in habit (more so than *P. c.* 'Pissardii'). Dark coppery leaves	To 20 ft. high and wide	Fragrant, single light pink to white flowers. Sometimes sets good crop of 1-in. red fruit

P

'Bonfire'. Dwarf form to only 5–6 ft. tall, 7 ft. wide. Red leaves; double pink flowers. Midseason.

'Early Double Pink'. Very early.

'Early Double Red'. Deep purplish red or rose red. Very early. Brilliant color is beautiful but likely to clash with other pinks and reds.

'Early Double White'. Blooms with 'Early Double Pink'.

'Helen Borchers'. Semidouble clear pink flowers. Late.

'Icicle'. Double white flowers. Late.

'Late Double Red'. Later than 'Early Double Red' by 3 to 4 weeks.

'Peppermint Stick'. Double flowers striped red and white; may also bear all-white and all-red flowers on same branch. Midseason.

'Weeping Double Pink'. Smaller than other flowering peaches, with weeping branches. Requires careful staking and tying to develop main stem of suitable height. Midseason.

'Weeping Double Red'. Like 'Weeping Double Pink', but with deep rose red flowers. Midseason.

'Weeping Double White'. White version of weeping forms listed above.

Flowering plum. Zones vary by type; see chart. Flowers appear before leaves, from late winter to early spring. Less particular about soil than flowering cherries, nectarines, and peaches, but will fail if soil is water-logged for long periods. If soil is boggy, plant in raised beds. Little pruning is needed. Potential pests include aphids, borers, scale, tent caterpillars. Possible diseases include canker and leaf spot. The most ornamental flowering plums are described in the chart above. Note that purple-foliaged types have a dominating color that makes them difficult to work into a landscape successfully—so use them sparingly (and never plant them in front of red brick). For more flowering plums, see listings for *P. americana*, *P. angustifolia*, *P.* × *cistena*, *P. maritima*, and *P. mexicana*.

ADDITIONAL DECIDUOUS TYPES

P. americana. WILD PLUM, GOOSE PLUM. Shrub or small tree. Zones US, MS, LS; 9–1. Native from Manitoba to Massachusetts, south to Utah, New Mexico, and Georgia. Tough, hardy plant grows to 15–20 ft. high and 10–15 ft. wide, spreading to form thickets. Blooms profusely before the dark green leaves emerge, bearing clusters of white, inch-wide blossoms. Yellow to red, 1-in. fruit is sour but good for jelly.

P. angustifolia. CHICKASAW PLUM. Large shrub. Zones US, MS, LS, CS; 9–1. Native from New Jersey to Missouri, south to Florida and Texas. Grows to 12–16 ft. tall and wide, forming a somewhat thorny, shiny dark green thicket; spreads by root suckers. Clouds of ½-in. white blossoms in early spring; ¾-in. red or yellow fruits are prized by wildlife. Likes sandy soils; takes sun or partial shade.

P. besseyi. WESTERN SAND CHERRY. Shrub. Zones US; 6–1. Native from Manitoba to Wyoming, south to Kansas and Colorado. To 3–6 ft. tall and wide. Good show of ½-in. white flowers in spring, followed by sweet black cherries used for pies, jams, jellies. Withstands heat, cold, wind, drought.

P. × **cistena.** PURPLE-LEAF SAND CHERRY, DWARF RED-LEAF PLUM. Shrub. Zones US, MS; 7–4. Dainty, multibranched hybrid to 6–10 ft. high. Can be trained as single-stemmed tree; good for small patios. Bears white to light pink flowers as leaves emerge, then covers itself in red-purple foliage. May offer a summer crop of small blackish purple fruit.

P. glandulosa. DWARF FLOWERING ALMOND. Shrub. Zones US, MS, LS; 8–3. Native to China and Japan. An old Southern favorite. To 4–6 ft. high, with clumps of upright, spreading branches and light green, willowlike, 4-in. leaves. In early spring, before leaf-out, the slender stems are transformed into wands of blossoms. Double-flowered 'Alba Plena' (white) and 'Sinensis' (pink) are commonly sold; both have fluffy, 1- to 1¼-in. blooms. A rare single-blossomed type known in some areas as Easter cherry is the only one that fruits. Prune heavily during or after flowering to promote new growth for next year's bloom. Suckers freely. Fireblight can be a problem.

P. maackii. AMUR CHOKECHERRY. Tree. Zones US; 6–1. Native to Manchuria and Siberia; extremely hardy to cold and wind. To 25–30 ft. tall, 25 ft. wide. Main feature is handsome yellowish trunk bark, which peels like that of birch *(Betula)*. Strongly veined, rather narrow, pointed leaves to 4 in. long. Small white flowers in 2- to 3-in.-long clusters come after leaf-out in midspring. Black, ¼-in. fruits.

P. maritima. BEACH PLUM. Shrub. Zones US, MS; 7–1. Native to Atlantic coast from Maine to Virginia. Suckering shrub to 6 ft. or taller, spreading to form large colonies. Dull green leaves grow 1½–3 in. long, half as wide. White, ½-in. flowers in spring are followed by ½- to 2-in., dark red or purple fruits that are highly valued for preserves. Tolerates strong winds and salt spray.

P. mexicana. MEXICAN PLUM. Tree. Zones US, MS, LS, CS; 9–6. Native from Kentucky to Texas and northeast Mexico. Beautiful native plum with delicate, spreading form and handsome, peeling bark. Usually single trunked; grows 15–25 ft. (occasionally to 35 ft.) tall, not quite as wide. Yellow-green, oval, pointed leaves to 4 in. long turn orange in autumn. Not a suckering species. Very fragrant, ½-in. white blossoms (fading to pink) bloom in early spring; purplish red fruit, good for jellies and preserves, follows in late summer. Foliage turns orange before dropping in fall. Tolerates drought but grows fast with regular water; takes many soils, including limestone and sand, but must have good drainage. Full sun or partial shade.

P. mume. JAPANESE FLOWERING APRICOT. Tree. Zones US, MS, LS, CS; 9–6. From China, Korea. Not a true apricot. Longer lived, tougher, and more trouble-free than many other flowering fruit trees. Eventually develops into a gnarled-looking, picturesque tree to 20 ft. tall and wide. Broadly oval, pointed leaves to 4½ in. long; profuse, inch-wide winter blossoms with a clean, spicy perfume. In the Lower and Coastal South, sudden freezes following warm spells will kill just-opened blossoms. Fruit is small and inedible. 'Bonita' has semidouble rose red blooms. 'Dawn' has large, ruffled double pink flowers. 'Peggy Clarke' sports double deep rose flowers with extremely long stamens and red calyxes; most widely planted selection. 'Rosemary Clarke' has double white flowers with red calyxes; very early. 'W. B. Clarke' has double pink flowers on weeping plant; effective large bonsai, container plant, or focal point in winter garden.

P. padus. EUROPEAN BIRD CHERRY. Tree. Zones US; 6–1. Very cold-hardy species native from Europe and northern Asia to central Japan. Moderate growth to 15–20 ft. tall and wide, occasionally taller. Rather thin and open in habit while young. Dull dark green, oval leaves, 3–5 in. long, are among the first to unfold in spring. Big midspring show of small white flowers in slender, drooping, 3- to 6-in. clusters that nearly hide foliage. Small black fruit follows; it is bitter but loved by birds.

P. serotina. BLACK CHERRY, WILD CHERRY. Large tree. Zones US, MS, LS, CS; 10–1. Native from Canada to Florida and Texas. Fast growing to 50–60 ft. tall, 30 ft. wide; possibly much taller. Leaves to 5 in. long, oval and pointed; dark green above, light green below. Yellow to red fall foliage. Fragrant white spring flowers in drooping clusters; red to purple-black, bittersweet cherries, used in jellies and wines. Wood is prized for furniture. Tolerates many soils, but not extremely wet or very dry sites. Not good for planting near the house; dropping fruits are messy, and nests of eastern tent caterpillars in branches are unsightly in spring. Reseeds.

P. tomentosa. NANKING CHERRY. Shrub. Zones US, MS; 7–1. From Tibet, China. Like *P. besseyi*, extremely tough and cold hardy. To 6–8 ft. tall, 10 ft. wide. Small, fragrant white flowers open from pinkish buds in spring; ½-in. scarlet fruit follows.

P. triloba. DOUBLE FLOWERING PLUM, FLOWERING ALMOND. Small tree or large treelike shrub. Zones US, MS; 7–3. From China. Slow to 8–10 ft. (possibly to 15 ft.) tall, with equal spread. The rather broad leaves are 1–2½ in. long. Double pink flowers about 1 in. wide appear in early spring before leaf-out. A white form is sometimes available.

P. virginiana. CHOKECHERRY. Shrub or small tree. Zones US, MS; 7–1. Native from Newfoundland to Saskatchewan, south to Kansas, east to North Carolina. To 20–30 ft. high, 18–25 ft. wide, with suckering habit. Oval, pointed leaves are 2–4 in. long; they are dark green above, grayish green beneath. In late spring, small, very fragrant white flowers appear in slender, 3- to 6-in. clusters among the leaves; these are followed by astringent, dark red to black fruit to ½ in. wide. 'Canada Red' ('Shubert') has leaves that open green, turn red as they mature.

FLOWERING PLUM FOR INDOOR BLOOM. *Branches of flowering plum (or flowering cherry, peach, or almond) are beautiful for indoor decoration. For the longest-lasting bloom, cut branches when buds first begin to show color or when they have just opened. Follow proper pruning procedures when you cut branches: prune to thin or shape; always cut back to a side branch; and never leave stubs. Place branches in a deep container of water, not in florist's foam; strip off any buds or flowers that will be below water level.* ❖

PSEUDERANTHEMUM

Acanthaceae

EVERGREEN SHRUBS

TS 12–10; OR GROW IN POTS

PARTIAL SHADE; BRIGHT LIGHT

REGULAR WATER

Pseuderanthemum laxiflorum 'Shooting Stars'

Group of about 60 species from tropical woodlands in many parts of the world. Of the two discussed here, one is grown for its colorful leaves, the other for its showy flowers. Plants thrive in fertile, well-drained soil free from nematodes. In areas where they aren't hardy, they make excellent container plants for deck, porch, or greenhouse. If you grow them in pots, give bright light (with protection from hot afternoon sun); let soil dry out somewhat between soakings, and feed monthly during active growth with a general-purpose liquid houseplant fertilizer.

P. atropurpureum. From Polynesia. Upright, open-growing plant to 3–5 ft. tall, 1–2½ ft. wide. Shiny blackish purple leaves, sometimes spotted with pink, yellow, green, or white, are 4–6 in. long, broadly oval and pointed. Tubular, inch-long white flowers appear occasionally in summer. Dark foliage is perfect for contrast with yellow or orange flowers or yellow or chartreuse leaves. Pinch back in youth to encourage bushiness. 'Variegatum' ('Tricolor') has bronzy purple leaves heavily marked with pink and creamy yellow; flowers are pink.

P. laxiflorum 'Shooting Stars'. SHOOTING STARS, AMETHYST STARS. Probably a selection of a Polynesian species. Upright and spreading, to 3–4 ft. tall, 2–3 ft. wide. Bright green, narrowly oval, pointed leaves to 3 in. long are good looking, but the inch-long, star-shaped purple blossoms provide the real show: they bloom profusely and almost continuously in warm weather and are attractive to hummingbirds.

PSEUDOCYDONIA sinensis

CHINESE QUINCE

Rosaceae

DECIDUOUS SHRUB OR SMALL TREE

US, MS, LS

FULL SUN

REGULAR WATER

Pseudocydonia sinensis

Seldom seen, curious tree, usually 15–20 ft. high (sometimes taller) and about as wide. Trunk is attractive, with bark that flakes off to reveal shades of brown, green, and gray. Trunks on old trees are often fluted. Roundish oval, dark green leaves to 4½ in. long turn yellow and red in fall. Spring bloom produces a scattering of flowers rather than a show—the pale pink, 1- to 1½-in. blossoms are borne singly at ends of year-old twigs. Blossoms are followed by extraordinary fruits: fragrant, yellow, egg-shaped quinces to 7 in. long, weighing over a pound apiece. The fruits can be made into jam. Very susceptible to fireblight in warm, humid areas; control by pruning out damaged wood. Needs acid soil and good drainage.

P

PSEUDOSASA. See BAMBOO

PSEUDOTSUGA menziesii (P. taxifolia)

DOUGLAS FIR

Pinaceae

EVERGREEN TREE

ZONES US, MS 7–4

FULL SUN; TAKES PART SHADE IN YOUTH

MODERATE TO REGULAR WATER

Pseudotsuga menziesii

Of the five (possibly eight) species of genus *Pseudotsuga*, only this one is widely grown. Popular Christmas tree. Reaches 70–200 ft. tall in Western forests, but in gardens it is more likely to grow 40–80 ft. tall and 12–20 ft. wide. Trees are cone shaped and foliaged to the ground when young, but lose lower limbs as they age. Soft, densely set, green or blue-green needles to 1½ in. long radiate in all directions from the branches; they give off a lemon scent when crushed. Pointed, wine red buds form at branch tips in winter, then open to apple green new growth in spring. Reddish brown, oval cones are about 3 in. long, with three-pronged bracts. Unlike upright cones of true firs (*Abies*), these hang down.

Native from Alaska through Northern California, eastward into the Rocky Mountains, and southward into northern Mexico. In the Upper South, tree is fast growing, dark green, with slightly drooping branchlets. Rocky Mountain form, *P. m. glauca*, is blue green and slower growing, more cold tolerant, more compact, and stiffer than the species. Compact, weeping, and other forms are grown mostly in arboretums and botanical gardens. All tolerate wind; will grow in most soils except boggy ones. Deer don't care for them.

PTELEA trifoliata

HOP TREE

Rutaceae

DECIDUOUS SHRUB OR SMALL TREE

US, MS, LS, CS 10–5

FULL SUN OR PARTIAL SHADE

MODERATE TO REGULAR WATER

Ptelea trifoliata

Native to the eastern U.S. Gets its name from its late-summer fruits, once used as a substitute for hops. Bushy plant grows slowly to 15–20 ft. tall and wide. Dark green, 2½- to 5-in.-long leaves are divided into three oval, pointed leaflets; they turn yellow in fall. Greenish white flowers appear in late spring; they aren't showy, but the fruits that follow are conspicuous—roundish and flattened, to 1 in. across, pale green aging to brown. Easy to grow, very adaptable, and free from serious pests, hop tree is a good candidate for a woodland garden, naturalized area, or even a shrub border. Stems and leaves emit a somewhat unpleasant odor when bruised. Leaves of 'Aurea' emerge bright yellow in spring, then fade to lime green by late summer.

PTERIDIUM aquilinum

BRACKEN

Polypodiaceae

FERN

US, MS, LS, CS, TS

FULL SUN OR PARTIAL SHADE

LITTLE TO REGULAR WATER

FRONDS ARE POISONOUS IF INGESTED

Pteridium aquilinum

Found all over the world, bracken is represented by various subspecies that differ in minor details. Coarse, much-divided fronds rise directly from deep, running rootstocks; plant grows from as low as 2 ft.

high to as tall as 7 ft. under good conditions. Occurs naturally in many places and can be tolerated in untamed gardens, but beware of planting it: deep rootstocks can make it a tough, invasive weed. Do not gather fronds to cook as fiddleheads, since they contain a slow poison. Deer avoid these ferns.

PTERIS

BRAKE

Polypodiaceae

FERNS

TS 12–9; OR HOUSEPLANTS

PARTIAL TO FULL SHADE; BRIGHT LIGHT

REGULAR WATER

Pteris cretica

Small evergreen ferns of tropical origin. They are mostly used as houseplants, but some will grow outdoors in the Tropical South. Indoors, they should be sited in bright light but shielded from hot sun; an east-facing window is ideal. They benefit from frequent misting. Provide good drainage; keep the soil evenly moist. Fertilize every 2 weeks during spring and summer and once monthly in fall and winter with a general-purpose liquid houseplant fertilizer.

P. cretica. CRETAN BRAKE. To 2½ ft. high, 2 ft. wide, with comparatively few long, narrow leaflets. Numerous selections exist; some have forked or crested fronds, others are variegated. Light green 'Wimsettii' has fronds that are forked at the tip on mature plants; it is so dense and frilly that it does not even look like a fern.

P. 'Ouvrardii'. To 1–2½ ft. high and wide. Dark green fronds have extremely long, narrow, ribbonlike divisions.

P. quadriaurita 'Argyraea'. SILVER FERN. To 2–4 ft. tall and wide, with rather coarsely divided fronds that are heavily marked in white. Showy, unusual coloring for a fern. Protect from frost; watch for slugs and snails.

P. tremula. AUSTRALIAN BRAKE. To 5 ft. tall and 3 ft. wide. Extremely graceful fronds on slender, upright stalks. Good landscape fern with excellent silhouette. Fast growing but tends to be rather short lived.

PTEROSTYRAX hispida

EPAULETTE TREE

Styracaceae

DECIDUOUS TREE

US, MS, LS 8–5

FULL SUN

REGULAR WATER

Pterostyrax hispida

Native to Japan. Single- or multitrunked tree grows to 20–30 ft. (possibly 40 ft.) tall and equally wide. Somewhat coarse, 3- to 8-in.-long leaves are light green above, gray green beneath; they may be oblong in shape, or oval and pointed. Blooms in late spring or early summer, bearing creamy white, lightly fragrant flowers with fringed petal edges in drooping clusters 4–9 in. long, 2–3 in. wide. Pendent clusters of small, furry gray fruits hang on well into winter and are attractive on bare branches.

Plant this tree where you can look up into it—on a bank beside a path, above a bench, in a raised bed. Rare in gardens and not easy to find in garden centers, but nonetheless a choice selection for woodland edge or as a focal point in large shrub border. Established trees need little pruning.

A PRACTICAL GUIDE TO GARDENING
PLEASE SEE PAGES 596–669

PTYCHOSPERMA

Arecaceae (Palmae)

PALMS

TS 12–10; OR GROW IN POTS

LIGHT SHADE

REGULAR WATER

Ptychosperma macarthuri

Native to Australia and the South Pacific. Small feather palms with slender, ringed trunks and well-defined crown shafts (the smooth, usually green upper portion of the trunk, formed by overlapping bases of newer leaves). Frond segments are toothed at the tip. Small, fragrant flowers come in 1- to 2-ft.-long clusters in summer; these are followed by bright red fruit. Grow in well-drained soil.

P. elegans. ALEXANDER PALM, SOLITAIRE PALM. From Australia. Erect, single-trunked palm to 25 ft. tall, 15 ft. wide. Fronds to 8 ft. long.

P. macarthuri. MACARTHUR PALM. Native to New Guinea. To 10–25 ft. tall, 12–15 ft. wide, with several clustered trunks. Fronds to 6½ ft. long. Good large understory plant. Often grown in containers.

PUERARIA lobata

KUDZU

Fabaceae (Leguminosae)

DECIDUOUS VINE OR GROUND COVER

MS, LS, CS, TS 11–3

FULL SUN

REGULAR WATER

Pueraria lobata

Native to Japan but now known as "the vine that ate the South," kudzu has covered millions of acres since it was introduced in 1876. Smothers arbors, telephone poles, houses, and fields—and any plant in its path—at the rate of up to 1 ft. per day. Thrives under almost any conditions. Medium green, 3- to 6-in.-long leaves are broadly oval, with three leaflets. Leaves and stems are somewhat hairy and coarse. Fragrant red-purple flowers in clusters 8–12 in. long, July through September. Too invasive for garden use unless you're hiding from the government and need something to cover your tracks. Its good points: tubers and leaves are edible, and you can make a tasty jelly from the flowers.

PULMONARIA

LUNGWORT

Boraginaceae

PERENNIALS

US, MS, LS

PARTIAL TO FULL SHADE

REGULAR WATER

Pulmonaria saccharata
'Mrs. Moon'

Low-growing shade lovers with quiet charm. In many kinds, foliage is attractively dappled with gray or silver. The long-stalked leaves are mostly in basal clumps, though there are a few on the flower stalks. Plants bloom in spring (just before leaves appear or as they emerge), bearing drooping clusters of funnel-shaped, typically blue or purplish flowers. After flowering finishes, more leaves arise from the base of the clump. If plants are well watered, foliage will remain ornamental through the growing season. All have creeping roots and can be used as small-scale ground covers or edgings for beds or woodland paths. Look good beneath spring-flowering trees, in combination with ferns, azaleas, rhododendrons, blue scillas, pink tulips. Need moist, well-drained, organically enriched soil. Clumps may become crowded after a few years; divide them in early fall.

P. angustifolia. COWSLIP LUNGWORT. Heat zones 8–1. Native to Europe. To 8–12 in. high, 1½ ft. wide, with narrowish dark green leaves and bright blue flowers that open from pink buds. *P. a. azurea* has sky blue blossoms.

P. longifolia. Heat zones 8–4. Native to the British Isles, western Europe. To 8–12 in. high, 1½ ft. wide. Slender leaves to 20 in. long are deep green spotted with silver. Blooms a little later than other species; flowers are purplish blue. 'Bertram Anderson' has deep blue blossoms.

P. 'Raspberry Splash'. To 1 ft. high, 2 ft. wide. Stiffly upright, narrow green leaves spotted with silver. Bright raspberry purple flowers open from burgundy buds.

P. 'Roy Davidson'. Hybrid between *P. saccharata* and *P. longifolia*. Resembles *P. longifolia* 'Bertram Anderson' but has slightly wider leaves and flowers that open pink before deepening to blue.

P. rubra. RED LUNGWORT. Heat zones 8–3. Hairy, unspotted, light green leaves to 2 ft. long, 5 in. wide; clumps can reach 3 ft. across. Blooms very early in spring, sending up flowering stems to 16 in. tall; blossoms are typically red, but there are also selections with blue or white blooms. The following reach 1 ft. high: 'Bowles Red', with deep red to rosy coral flowers and leaves spotted in lime green; 'David Ward', brick red blossoms and white-edged leaves; and 'Redstart', bearing blossoms in an interesting shade between salmon and brick red.

P. saccharata. BETHLEHEM SAGE. Heat zones 8–1. To 1–1½ ft. high, 2 ft. wide, with broadly oval, pointed leaves in medium green spotted with silver. Blue flowers open from pink buds. Specialists usually offer named selections, including the following compact, foot-high plants. 'Janet Fisk' has leaves that are silvery almost all over, while old favorite 'Mrs. Moon' has larger foliage than the species; both these selections bear pink flowers aging to blue. 'Pierre's Pure Pink' features shiny leaves and pink blossoms; 'Sissinghurst White' has large white flowers.

PUMPKIN

Cucurbitaceae

ANNUAL

US, MS, LS, CS, TS 12–3

FULL SUN

REGULAR WATER

Pumpkin

Member of the genus *Cucurbita*. Thought to have originated in South America; related to squash, gourd, melon. Fruit varies greatly in size, depending on selection. One of the best for a jumbo Halloween pumpkin is 'Atlantic Giant' (which can weigh upwards of 500 pounds!). A great choice for pies is 'Small Sugar', a smaller pumpkin with finer-grained, sweeter flesh. 'Jack Be Little' and 'Wee-B-Little' are miniature (3- to 4-in.) types used for decoration. Novelties with white skin and orange flesh include miniature 'Baby Boo' and 8- to 10-in. 'Lumina'. Seeds of all are edible, but the easiest to eat are those of hull-less selections like 'Trick or Treat'.

GROW A GIANT PUMPKIN. *Plant 'Atlantic Giant' seeds in spring as soon as soil warms. Grow one plant per hill, spacing hills 40 ft. apart. (Yes, we do mean 40 ft.—one hill and plant could cover most of a small garden!) As plant develops, cut off all but one main stem; after fruits have formed, remove all but one fruit. Along the length of the stem, mound a 4-in.-wide hill of soil every 2 ft.; roots will form there. Feed every few weeks. Keep soil moist, but don't overdo it—too much water causes pumpkins to split. To avoid damaging the stem, don't move pumpkins until harvest. Good luck!* ❖

Pumpkins are available in vining and bush types. Both need lots of room: a single vine can cover 500 sq. ft., and even bush sorts can spread over 20 sq. ft. Where the growing season is short, start plants indoors and use floating row covers early in the season. In most areas, sow seeds outdoors in late spring after soil has warmed; plant in rich soil. For vining pumpkins, sow five or six seeds 1 in. deep in hills 6–8 ft. apart; thin seedlings to two per hill. Plant bush pumpkins in rows spaced 3 ft. apart; plant seeds 1 in. deep in clusters of three or four, spacing clusters 2 ft. apart along the row. Thin seedlings to one or two plants per cluster.

P

Before planting, work ¼ cup of 10-10-10 fertilizer into each hill. Then feed periodically with a balanced water-soluble fertilizer. Water during rainless periods, but keep foliage dry to prevent leaf diseases. Plants do not do well in high heat and humidity. In late summer, slide wooden shingles under fruit to protect it from wet soil and rot. Pumpkins are ready to harvest about 90 to 120 days after sowing, when the shell has hardened. Pick after first frost kills the plant. Use a sharp knife or hand pruners to harvest fruit, leaving 1–2 in. of stem. Subject to same pests and diseases as squash.

PUNICA granatum

ORNAMENTAL POMEGRANATE

Punicaceae

DECIDUOUS SHRUB OR TREE

🌿 MS, LS, CS, TS ⊞ 11–7

☼ FULL SUN

◐ ◐ MODERATE TO REGULAR WATER

Punica granatum

Native from Iran to the Himalayas. For fruiting types, see Pomegranate. Plants described here either fail to fruit at all or bear red fruit that is more decorative than tasty. Good landscape plants. Use taller types as foundation plants, in shrub borders, as tall hedges or small trees; lower-growing kinds are excellent for edgings, in containers. All bear showy single or double summer flowers with ruffled petals surrounding a central cluster of stamens. Narrow leaves are bronzy when new, maturing to glossy bright green or golden green; they turn brilliant yellow in fall except where winters are very mild. Take many soil types, including alkaline soil. In the Middle South, plant against south or west wall. In late dormant season, prune as needed to shape. On shrubby types, remove oldest stems occasionally to encourage strong new growth. Resistant to damage by deer.

'Chico'. DWARF CARNATION-FLOWERED POMEGRANATE. Compact shrub to 3 ft. high and wide. Easily kept to 1½ ft. high with occasional pruning. Double orange-red flowers. No fruit.

'Legrellei' ('California Sunset'). To 8–10 ft. high and wide. Creamy white double flowers heavily striped coral red. No fruit.

'Nana'. DWARF POMEGRANATE. Dense grower to 3 ft. high, 6 ft. wide. Blooms when a foot tall or less. Orange-red single flowers followed by small fruit. Nearly evergreen in mild winters.

'Nochi Shibari'. Grows to 8–10 ft. high and wide. Bears double dark red flowers. No fruit.

'Toyosho'. To 8–10 ft. high and wide. Double light apricot flowers. May produce small fruits.

PURPLE CONEFLOWER. See ECHINACEA purpurea

PURPLE HEART. See TRADESCANTIA pallida 'Purpurea'

PURPLE-LEAF PLUM. See PRUNUS cerasifera 'Pissardii'

PURPLE VELVET PLANT. See GYNURA aurantiaca

PURSLANE. See PORTULACA oleracea

PUSSY TOES. See ANTENNARIA dioica

PYCNANTHEMUM incanum

MOUNTAIN MINT

Lamiaceae (Labiatae)

PERENNIAL

🌿 US, MS, LS ⊞ 8–1

☼ ◐ FULL SUN OR PARTIAL SHADE

◐ ◐ LITTLE TO MODERATE WATER

Pycnanthemum incanum

Native to the eastern U.S. This is one of those subtly attractive plants you see growing by the roadside—and then ask yourself, "I wonder what that is?" Grows 2–3 ft. tall and 3–4 ft. wide, with multiple upright stems. Dense clusters of silvery white flowers resembling those of bee balm (*Monarda didyma*) appear atop the stems by midsummer. Blooms are often spotted with green and pale pink. The silvery coloring extends down from the flowers to include the top 6–12 in. of the stems and leaves. Foliage has a pleasant minty fragrance; flowers attract bees and butterflies. Carefree plant for sun or dappled shade, moist or dry soils. Good candidate for meadows, naturalized areas, woodland edges, even mixed borders.

PYRACANTHA

FIRETHORN

Rosaceae

EVERGREEN SHRUBS

🌿 ZONES VARY BY SPECIES

☼ FULL SUN

◐ MODERATE WATER

Pyracantha coccinea

Grown for bright fruit, evergreen foliage (may be semievergreen in cold climates), versatility in the landscape, ease of culture. All grow fast and vigorously, varying in habit from upright to sprawling. All have glossy green, 1- to 4-in.-long, ½- to 1-in.-wide leaves that are generally oval or rounded at ends; all bear flowers and fruit on spurs along wood of last year's growth. Small, spring blooms are dull creamy white, carried in flattish clusters; they're effective thanks to their profusion. Nearly all species have needlelike thorns.

The real glory of firethorns is in their thick clusters of pea-size, orange-red berries, which light up the garden for months. Selections with red, orange, or yellow berries are available; if color is important to you, buy plants when they are in fruit. Depending on selection, berries color up from late summer to midautumn; some types hang on until late winter, when they're cleared out by birds, storms, or decay. Dislodge old, withered or rotted berries with a jet of water or an old broom.

As shrubs and ground covers, firethorns look better and fruit more heavily if allowed to follow their natural growth habit. Prune to check wayward branches. Plants can also be espaliered or sheared as hedges (though shearing comes at the expense of much fruit). Firethorns tolerate most soils but should not be overwatered. Two serious problems are fireblight (which can kill the plant) and scab (which causes defoliation and sooty-looking fruit); for best success, choose disease-resistant selections.

P. angustifolia 'Yukon Belle'. Zones US, MS, LS, CS; 10–1. Selection of a Chinese native. To 8–10 ft. tall, 6–8 ft. wide. Bright orange berries.

P. coccinea. SCARLET FIRETHORN. Zones US, MS, LS, CS; 9–6. From the eastern Mediterranean. Rounded growth to 8–10 ft. high (20 ft. trained against wall). Red-orange fruit. Best known for its cold-hardy selections, which include the following.

'Kasan'. Long-lasting orange-red berries. Spreading growth habit. Susceptible to scab.

'Lalandei' and 'Lalandei Monrovia'. Similar selections with orange berries. Susceptible to scab. Among the hardiest.

'Wyattii'. Orange-red berries color early. Very prone to fireblight and scab.

P. crenatoserrata (P. fortuneana, P. yunnanensis). CHINESE FIRETHORN. Zones MS, LS, CS; 10–3. From China. Vase-shaped plant to 15 ft. tall, 10 ft. wide. Limber branches make it a good choice for espalier. Orange to coral berries last through winter.

'Cherri Berri'. To 10 ft. tall and 8 ft. wide; deep red berries.

'Graberi'. More upright than the species, with huge clusters of dark red fruit.

P. hybrids. This category includes some of the most desirable firethorns. Plants vary in size, habit, and cold hardiness.

'Apache'. Zones US, MS, LS, CS. To 5 ft. high and 6 ft. wide. Large bright red berries last well into winter. Resistant to fireblight and scab.

'Fiery Cascade'. Zones US, MS, LS, CS. To 8 ft. tall, 9 ft. wide; berries turn from orange to red. Good disease resistance.

'Gnome'. Zones US, MS, LS. Very cold hardy. Densely branched shrub to 6 ft. high, 8 ft. wide. Orange berries. Highly susceptible to scab.

P

'Lowboy'. Zones US, MS, LS, CS. Spreading plant to 2–3 ft. high. Orange fruit. Very prone to scab.

'Mohave'. MOHAVE PYRACANTHA. Zones US, MS, LS, CS. To 12 ft. tall and wide. Heavy producer of big orange-red fruit that colors in late summer and lasts well into winter. Resistant to fireblight and scab.

'Red Elf'. Zones MS, LS, CS. Densely branched plant to 2 ft. high and wide—good in containers. Long-lasting bright red fruit. Some disease resistance. Apparently the same as the plant sold as 'Leprechaun'.

'Ruby Mound'. Zones MS, LS, CS. Among the most graceful of ground cover firethorns. Long, arching, drooping branches make broad mounds 2½ ft. high, spreading to about 10 ft. Bright red fruit.

'Teton'. TETON PYRACANTHA. Zones US, MS, LS, CS. Very cold hardy. Columnar growth to 12 ft. tall, 4 ft. wide. Golden yellow fruit. Resistant to fireblight and scab.

'Tiny Tim'. Zones US, MS, LS, CS. Compact, small-leafed plant to 3 ft. high. Few or no thorns. Red berries. Informal low hedge, barrier, tub plant.

'Watereri'. Zones US, MS, LS, CS. To 8 ft. tall and wide. Very heavy producer of long-lasting bright red fruit.

P. koidzumii. FORMOSA FIRETHORN. Zones LS, CS; 10–8. Unruly grower to 8–12 ft. tall and wide. Selections are better known than the species and include the following.

'Santa Cruz' ('Santa Cruz Prostrata'). Low-growing, spreading plant, branching from base. To 6 ft. tall but easily kept below 3 ft. by pinching out the occasional upright branch. Red fruit. Plant 4–5 ft. apart for ground or bank cover. Very resistant to scab.

'Victory'. Vigorous growth to 10 ft. tall, 8 ft. wide. Dark red berries color late in the year but hold on well. Resistant to scab.

'Walderi' ('Walderi Prostrata'). Wide-spreading, low-growing ground cover (to 1½ ft. high, with a few upright shoots that should be cut out). Red berries. Plant 4–5 ft. apart for fast cover.

PYRETHRUM. See CHRYSANTHEMUM coccineum, C. pacificum

PYROSTEGIA venusta
(P. ignea, Bignonia venusta)

FLAME VINE

Bignoniaceae

EVERGREEN VINE

✿ CS (MILDER PARTS), TS ⊪ 12–9

☼ ◑ FULL SUN OR PARTIAL SHADE

◐ MODERATE WATER

Pyrostegia venusta

Native to South America. Fast growth to 20 ft. or more, climbing by tendrils; where well adapted, grows rampantly. Leaves consist of oval, 2- to 3-in. leaflets. Impressive show of tubular, 3-in. orange flowers in clusters of 15 to 20 at branch ends; main bloom comes in winter. Plants growing in Florida sometimes form slender, foot-long fruit capsules. In central Florida, this is the most popular vine for covering fences and other structures. Tolerates many soils. Prune right after bloom to restrain growth.

PYRROSIA lingua

JAPANESE FELT FERN

Polypodiaceae

FERN

✿ CS, TS ⊪ 12–8

☼ PARTIAL SHADE

◐ MODERATE WATER

Pyrrosia lingua

Native to China, Japan. To 1½ ft. high, spreading slowly to 1 ft. wide by creeping rootstocks. Dense clusters of broad, lance-shaped, dark green fronds with a felty texture. Most often used in hanging baskets but makes a choice ground cover for small areas. Crested and sawtooth-edged forms are collectors' items. Hardy to 20°F.

PYRUS calleryana

CALLERY PEAR

Rosaceae

DECIDUOUS TREE

✿ US, MS, LS, CS ⊪ 9–3

☼ FULL SUN

◐ ◐ MODERATE TO REGULAR WATER

Pyrus calleryana
'Chanticleer'

Fruiting pear is described under Pear. The following ornamental pears, all selections of *Pyrus calleryana*, are grown for the profuse pure white flowers they bear in late winter or early spring and for their glossy, leathery deep green leaves, which turn yellow, orange, scarlet, or burgundy in late fall. Leaves are oval, scallop edged, 1½–3 in. long. The blossoms appear before leaf-out; late freezes sometimes spoil the show. Fruits are inedible and very small.

The species can grow to 50 ft. tall and nearly as wide, with a strong, horizontal branching pattern and generally pyramidal shape. Its limbs are savagely thorny, but the improved selections listed below are thornless. All of these trees tolerate pollution, drought, and most soils (as long as drainage is good); make good city, street, or lawn trees. If planted in rows, they're also useful for tall screens. Species and most selections are susceptible to fireblight, with the extent of the disease varying from year to year; it's usually more of an aesthetic problem than a life-threatening one.

'Aristocrat'. ARISTOCRAT PEAR. Grows to 40 ft. tall, 20 ft. wide. Pyramidal, with well-spaced branches that are more horizontal than those of 'Bradford' and less prone to storm damage. Fall color ranges from yellow to red. Somewhat subject to fireblight.

'Bradford'. BRADFORD PEAR. Fast growing, easy to transplant, easy to grow, with showy spring flowers and spectacular red fall foliage. These attributes have led it to become one of the South's most overplanted trees. Lacks a central leader; main branches emerge from a common point on trunk, often causing tree to split in storms. Bradford pear grows much bigger than people usually envision: in 20 years, it can reach 50 ft. high, 40 ft. wide. Newer pears, such as 'Chanticleer' and 'Trinity', are better choices for most gardens.

'Capital'. Narrowly columnar growth; 35–40 ft. tall and 15 ft. wide. Coppery fall color.

'Chanticleer' ('Cleveland Select', 'Stone Hill'). Narrow but not columnar; about 40 ft. tall, 15 ft. wide. Fall color varies from orange to reddish purple. Resistant to fireblight.

'Redspire'. Shorter, narrower pyramid than 'Aristocrat'; reaches 40 ft. tall and wide. Large blossom clusters; yellow to red fall color. Quite prone to fireblight.

'Trinity'. Round-headed form; grows to 30 ft. tall. Attractive orange-red fall color.

'White House'. Narrowly columnar; 35–40 ft. tall, 15 ft. wide. Red to reddish purple fall color. Often gets a disfiguring leaf spot.

QUAKER LADIES. See HOUSTONIA caerulea

QUAKING ASPEN. See POPULUS tremuloides

QUAKING GRASS. See BRIZA maxima

QUAMOCLIT pennata. See IPOMOEA quamoclit

QUEEN ANNE'S LACE. See DAUCUS carota carota

QUEEN OF THE NIGHT. See HYLOCEREUS undatus

QUEEN OF THE PRAIRIE. See FILIPENDULA rubra

QUEEN PALM. See SYAGRUS romanzoffiana

QUEEN SAGO. See CYCAS circinalis

QUEEN'S TEARS. See BILLBERGIA nutans

QUEEN'S WREATH. See ANTIGONON leptopus, PETREA volubilis

QUERCUS

OAK

Fagaceae

DECIDUOUS AND EVERGREEN TREES

ZONES VARY BY SPECIES

FULL SUN

REGULAR WATER, EXCEPT AS NOTED

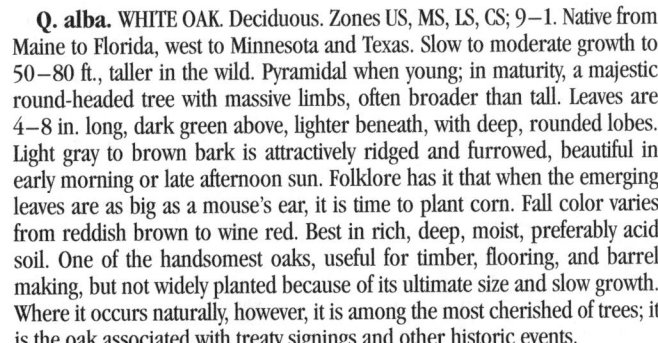

Quercus alba

The oaks comprise 600 or so species, almost all native to the Northern Hemisphere. Their appearance and hardiness vary widely, but all produce acorns—single nuts more or less enclosed in a cup. Some oaks are widely planted, while others have a limited range.

Homeowners acquire oaks either by planting them or by inheriting trees that were present before the land was developed. Oaks that have been planted usually thrive without difficulty, but inherited types often require special attention; they are very sensitive to any disturbance of the soil. Protect trunks from earth-moving machinery with cribs of 2-by-4s or heavier timbers. Avoid piling excavated soil around trunks or above root systems (which extend somewhat beyond the branch spread); or provide drains for aeration and removal of excess water. Do not excavate or pave above the root zone without consulting a tree expert. Do not cut roots. Avoid compacting soil.

Caterpillars are the most serious potential pest of oaks. Gypsy moth caterpillars are most common in the Upper South. Heavy infestation can cause defoliation; serious attacks for 2 or more years in a row can weaken or even kill a tree. However, these pests tend to attack cyclically, striking perhaps every 7 to 10 years. If control becomes necessary, consult a professional arborist or tree service; oak trees are too large for the limited spray equipment available to the home gardener.

Oak wilt, a fungal disease, has killed millions of oaks, especially in Texas. It is spread by oak bark beetles and by contact between healthy and infected roots. Starting from the top of the tree and moving down, leaves wilt, turn dull, curl, dry, and drop. Avoid pruning in spring, when bark beetles are most active. Don't plant a new oak within the root zone of a tree that has died.

When choosing an oak for your yard, it is essential to consider your soil. A common mistake is to plant acid-loving oaks, such as pin oak (*Q. palustris*) and red oak (*Q. rubra*), in alkaline soil. Trees quickly begin to suffer from chlorosis (yellow leaves with green veins) and eventually die. Good oaks for alkaline soil include chinkapin oak (*Q. muehlenbergii*), Chisos red oak (*Q. gravesii*), live oak (*Q. virginiana*), Shumard red oak (*Q. shumardii*), and Texas red oak (*Q. texana*).

Q. acutissima. SAWTOOTH OAK. Deciduous. Zones US, MS, LS, CS; 9–3. Native to China, Korea, Japan. Moderate to fast growth to 35–45 ft. tall and wide, usually with open, spreading habit. Deeply furrowed bark. Bristle-toothed, shiny dark green leaves are 3½–7½ in. long, a third as wide; they look like chestnut (*Castanea*) leaves. Foliage is yellowish on expanding, yellow to yellowish brown in fall; it may hang on late into winter. Fairly tolerant of various soils, though it prefers well-drained acid soil. Stands up well to heat and humidity. No serious problems. Good shade, lawn, or street tree.

Q. alba. WHITE OAK. Deciduous. Zones US, MS, LS, CS; 9–1. Native from Maine to Florida, west to Minnesota and Texas. Slow to moderate growth to 50–80 ft., taller in the wild. Pyramidal when young; in maturity, a majestic round-headed tree with massive limbs, often broader than tall. Leaves are 4–8 in. long, dark green above, lighter beneath, with deep, rounded lobes. Light gray to brown bark is attractively ridged and furrowed, beautiful in early morning or late afternoon sun. Folklore has it that when the emerging leaves are as big as a mouse's ear, it is time to plant corn. Fall color varies from reddish brown to wine red. Best in rich, deep, moist, preferably acid soil. One of the handsomest oaks, useful for timber, flooring, and barrel making, but not widely planted because of its ultimate size and slow growth. Where it occurs naturally, however, it is among the most cherished of trees; it is the oak associated with treaty signings and other historic events.

Q. bicolor. SWAMP WHITE OAK. Deciduous. Zones US, MS, LS; 8–1. Native from Quebec to Georgia, west to Michigan and Arkansas. Slow to moderate growth to 50–60 ft., rarely taller, with equal or greater spread. Shallowly lobed or scalloped leaves are 3–7 in. long, a little more than half as wide, shiny dark green above, silvery white beneath. Fall color usually yellow, sometimes reddish purple. Bark of trunk and branches flakes off in scales. Needs acid soil. Tolerates drought but will also take wet conditions.

Q. coccinea. SCARLET OAK. Deciduous. Zones US, MS, LS, CS; 9–4. Native from Maine to Florida, west to Minnesota and Missouri. In deep, rich, acidic soil, grows at a moderate to rapid rate, reaching a possible 60–80 ft. tall, 40–60 ft. wide. High, light, open-branching habit. Bright green leaves are 3–6 in. long, a little more than half as wide, with deeply cut, pointed lobes. Foliage turns scarlet where fall nights are cold. Scaly gray-brown bark. Deep roots. Good street or lawn tree. Fine to garden under.

Q. falcata. SOUTHERN RED OAK, SPANISH OAK. Deciduous. Zones US, MS, LS, CS; 10–5. Native from Virginia to Florida, westward to southern Illinois and Arkansas. Moderate growth to 70–80 ft., eventually with rounded crown as wide or wider than tree is tall. Dark green leaves 5–9 in. long, sometimes longer, with sharp-pointed lobes varying in number from three to nine. Fall color not significant. Dark gray bark has deep, narrow furrows. Best in acidic soils, but tolerates relatively poor and dry soils as well as occasionally flooded ones.

Q. glauca. BLUE JAPANESE OAK, EVERGREEN OAK. Evergreen. Zones LS, CS; 10–8. Native to Japan, China, Taiwan. Moderately slow growth to 20–30 ft. (rarely 40 ft.) tall and about half that wide; upright, oval form. Foliage grows in a dense mass, making this tree an excellent choice for a screen. Leathery, wavy-margined leaves to 5½ in. long, 2½ in. wide; dark green above, silky gray beneath. New leaves are especially handsome, often bronzy or purplish green. Smooth bark. Prefers well-drained, fertile, slightly acid soil but tolerates heavy clay.

Q. glaucoides (Q. laceyi). LACEY OAK. Zones MS, LS, CS; 10–7. Evergreen. Native to the Texas Hill Country and central and southern Mexico. Rounded form to 20–25 ft. tall, 20–30 ft. wide. Bluish green leaves to 6 in. long, half as wide, smooth edged or very subtly toothed; new growth is pinkish. Textured gray bark. Tolerates heat, drought, alkaline soil. Moderate water.

Q. gravesii. CHISOS RED OAK. Deciduous. Zones US, MS, LS, CS; 10–6. Texas native to 40 ft. tall, 35 ft. wide. Lobed leaves are smaller and

Quercus acutissima

Quercus alba

Quercus alba

Quercus coccinea

Quercus muehlenbergii

Q

less deeply indented than those of *Q. texana*. Dark green leaves; blackish bark. Foliage often turns bright yellow and red in fall. Tolerates drought and limy soils.

Q. hemisphaerica. See Q. laurifolia

Q. laurifolia. LAUREL OAK. Zones MS, LS, CS, TS; 12–7. Evergreen in Coastal and Tropical South, deciduous elsewhere. Native to Coastal Plains and piedmont from southern New Jersey to Florida, eastward to East Texas and southeast Arkansas. To 40 ft. or more in height, somewhat less in spread. Narrowly oval, smoth-edged, leathery leaves are shiny dark green, 1–4 in. long, ½–1¼ in. wide. Needs acid soil. *Q. hemisphaerica,* also called laurel oak, is similar but takes both acid and alkaline soil. Both are useful street trees, being smaller and less spreading than *Q. virginiana.*

Q. macrocarpa. BUR OAK, MOSSY CUP OAK. Deciduous. Zones US, MS, LS; 9–1. Native from Nova Scotia to Pennsylvania, westward to Manitoba and Texas. Rugged-looking tree growing slowly to 60–80 ft. high and at least as wide. Deeply furrowed dark gray bark. Leaves are glossy green above, whitish beneath, 4–10 in. long and half as wide, broad at tip, tapered at base. Yellowish fall color. Large acorns form in mossy cups. Similar to *Q. bicolor* but faster growing, more tolerant of adverse conditions. Needs lots of room. Acid or alkaline soil.

Quercus macrocarpa

Q. muehlenbergii. CHINKAPIN OAK. Deciduous. Zones US, MS, LS, CS; 9–2. Native from New England, west to Minnesota and Texas. Moderate growth during early years, slowing with age. Reaches 80 ft. or more in the wild, with an even greater spread; usually smaller in cultivation, and slender until middle-aged. Leaves are 6½ in. long and 3 in. wide, with coarse, sawtoothed margins; dark glossy green above, silvery beneath. Fall color varies from yellow brown to rust brown. Scaly gray bark. Grows in a wide range of soils, including clay and dry, rocky limestone.

Q. myrsinifolia. JAPANESE LIVE OAK. Evergreen. Zones MS, LS, CS; 9–6. Native to Japan, China. To 20–30 ft. tall and nearly as wide; usually round headed in age. Narrow, glossy dark green leaves 2½–4 in. long, toothed toward tip; purplish when new. Smooth dark gray bark. Grows well in almost all soils. Unlike most oaks, it is graceful rather than sturdy; typically identified as an oak by its acorns. No serious problems. Most cold-hardy evergreen oak.

Q. nigra. WATER OAK. Deciduous. Zones US, MS, LS, CS; 12–6. Native to lowland stream banks throughout southeastern U.S. Moderate to fast growth to 50–80 ft. tall and not quite as wide, with conical or rounded canopy. Dark green, fairly narrow leaves, 1½–4 in. long, are narrowly oval and pointed, variably lobed; turn yellow to brown in fall, hang on late. Dark gray bark is smooth in youth, rougher with age. Limbs subject to breakage by wind, snow, ice. Tolerates many types of soil, but not alkaline soil. Provide moist to wet conditions. Used as shade and street tree. A favorite host for mistletoe *(Phoradendron serotinum).*

Q. palustris. PIN OAK. Deciduous. Zones US, MS, LS; 8–5. Native from Massachusetts to Delaware, westward to Wisconsin and Arkansas. Moderate to fairly rapid growth to 50–80 ft. tall, 25–40 ft. wide. Slender and pyramidal when young, open and round headed at maturity. Smooth brownish gray bark becomes shallowly ridged with age. Lower branches tend to droop almost to the ground; if the lowest whorl is cut away, branches above will adopt same habit. Only when fairly tall will it have good clearance beneath lowest branches. Glossy dark green leaves, 3–6 in. long and nearly as wide, are deeply cut into bristle-pointed lobes. In fall, leaves turn yellow, red, and then russet brown; may hang on in winter. Needs plenty of water; tolerates poorly drained soils. Widely used as a lawn and street tree. Needs acid soil.

Q. phellos. WILLOW OAK. Deciduous. Zones US, MS, LS, CS; 10–3. Native from New York to Florida, westward to Missouri and Texas. Fast to moderate growth to 50–90 ft. tall, 30–50 ft. wide. Superior lawn or street tree. Somewhat like *Q. palustris* in growth habit 0and spreading form. Smooth gray bark becomes shallowly ridged in

Quercus phellos

age. Smooth-edged leaves are bright rich green, 2½–5 in. long, ⅓–1 in. wide; they look more like willow *(Salix)* leaves than oak leaves. Foliage turns yellowish or russet red before falling. Most delicate foliage pattern of all oaks. No serious problems. Tolerates poor drainage. Needs acid soil.

Q. prinus. CHESTNUT OAK, BASKET OAK. Deciduous. Zones US, MS, LS; 8–3. Native from southern parts of Maine and Ontario southward to South Carolina and Alabama. Moderate growth to an eventual dense, rounded form, 60–70 ft. tall, 50 ft. wide. Large, edible acorns are prized by wildlife. Bark often quite dark, even nearly black, becoming deeply furrowed with age. Unlobed leaves with coarse, rounded teeth are 4–6 in. long, 1½–3½ in. wide; in fall, they change from deep yellowish green to yellow or orange. This tree needs acid soil; it tolerates poor, dry, rocky soil but looks better and grows faster with good soil and adequate water. Does not tolerate poor drainage.

Q. robur. ENGLISH OAK. Deciduous. Zones US, MS, LS; 8–3. Native to Europe, northern Africa, western Asia. Moderate growth rate; reaches 90 ft. tall in the wild, but in gardens typically grows 40–60 ft. tall, 30 ft. wide. Rather short trunk and very wide, open head in maturity. Grayish black, deeply furrowed bark. Dark green leaves grow 3–4½ in. long and half as wide, with rounded lobes; they hold until late fall, then drop without much color change. Takes acid or alkaline soil.

'Fastigiata', upright English oak, is narrow and columnar (much like Lombardy poplar, *Populus nigra* 'Italica') when young, then branches out to a broad, pyramidal form at maturity. Both 'Fastigiata' and the species are prone to mildew. Mildew-resistant selections include 'Crimson Spire', a columnar form to 45 ft. tall and only 15 ft. wide, with red fall color; 'Rose Hill', with particularly attractive glossy foliage; and 'Skyrocket', an excellent performer with the same form as 'Crimson Spire' but with yellow-brown fall foliage.

Q. rubra (Q. r. maxima, Q. borealis). RED OAK, NORTHERN RED OAK. Deciduous. Zones US, MS, LS; 9–5. Native from Nova Scotia to Pennsylvania, westward to Minnesota and Iowa. Fast growth to 60–75 ft. tall, 50 ft. wide in gardens (over 100 ft. tall in wild), with broad, spreading branches and round-topped crown. With maturity, bark becomes quite dark and fissured. Dark green leaves to 5–8 in. long, 3–5 in. wide, with

Quercus palustris

Quercus phellos

Quercus phellos

Quercus rubra

Quercus virginiana

sharp-pointed lobes. New leaves and leafstalks are red in spring, turning dark red, ruddy brown, or orange in fall. Smooth gray bark. Needs fertile soil and plenty of water. Stake young plants. High-branching habit and reasonably open shade make it a good tree for big lawns, parks, broad avenues. Deep roots make it good to garden under. Usually fairly trouble free. Needs acid soil.

Q. shumardii. SHUMARD RED OAK. Deciduous. Zones US, MS, LS, CS; 10–1. Native from Kansas to southern Michigan, southward to North Carolina and Florida, westward to Texas. Similar to *Q. coccinea* but slightly less hardy. Smooth gray bark. Dark green leaves turn yellow to red in autumn. Tolerates drought and a wide range of soils, including both acid and alkaline types.

Q. stellata. POST OAK. Deciduous. Zones US, MS, LS, CS; 9–5. Native from Florida to Massachusetts, west to Kansas and Texas. Slow growing to 40–50 ft. tall and wide (may reach 100 ft. tall). Forms dense, round canopy and stout, picturesque branches. Leathery dark green leaves are large (to 8 in. long), with straplike lobes that give them a cruciform appearance. Fall color is not usually bright—it varies from yellow to brown—but leaves hang from branches through winter. Distinctive gray bark with scales, ridges, furrows, cracks. Tolerates dry, rocky, and sandy soils; takes acid or alkaline soil.

Q. texana (Q. nuttallii). TEXAS RED OAK. Deciduous. Zones US, MS, LS, CS; 9–5. Native to Texas. To 15–30 ft. with nearly equal spread; makes either a low-branching, multitrunked small tree or a multistemmed shrubby clump. Yellow-green leaves, to 4 in. long, are deeply cut into five to seven sharp-pointed lobes; turn maroon and scarlet in fall. Gray-brown bark is smooth in youth, develops narrow ridges and shallow fissures with age. Adapts to various soils; tolerates drought.

Q. virginiana. LIVE OAK. Evergreen. Zones LS, CS, TS; 12–8. Native from Virginia to Florida, westward to Texas. Signature tree of the South. Moderate growth to 40–80 ft. tall, with spreading, heavy-limbed crown up to twice as wide. Very long lived; with age, bark becomes very dark and checked. Smooth-edged, quite narrow leaves, 1½–5 in. long, shiny dark green above, whitish beneath. Old leaves are all shed in spring before new growth emerges. Tree is often draped with Spanish moss *(Tillandsia usneoides)*. Thrives on moisture and does best in deep, rich soil, though it tolerates most soils, including alkaline ones. Also tolerates salt spray; makes an excellent tree for the beach when planted in groups back from the dunes. Not usually browsed by deer. Widely used as street tree in native range. Needs lots of space. A gall insect causes unsightly damage to leaves. Loss of trees to oak wilt has been severe in Central Texas. Termites have killed many live oaks in New Orleans.

QUINCE

Rosaceae

DECIDUOUS OR SEMIEVERGREEN SHRUBS OR TREES

US, MS, LS ⟋ 9–3

☼ FULL SUN

◖ MODERATE WATER

Quince

For flowering quince, see *Chaenomeles*. Discussed here is the closely related *Cydonia oblonga,* a native of western Asia grown for fruit rather than flowers (it is often confused with flowering quince). Fruiting quince is a multistemmed shrub to 15–20 ft. tall and wide. White or blush pink flowers bloom in midspring; these are followed in autumn by fragrant, yellow, round to pear-shaped or oblong fruits traditionally used in the South for jelly and preserves. Fruits reach 3½–4½ in. long and remain as hard as a golf ball even after ripening.

Quince

Quince is easy to grow in a sunny spot with slightly acid, well-drained soil; once established, it is incredibly tenacious and nearly impossible to kill, deliberately or otherwise. Named selections are usually available only through mail-order catalogs. Some selections need a pollenizer; planting at least two different ones ensures cross-pollination and larger crops.

'Cooke's Jumbo'. Pear-shaped fruit with white flesh. Very large; can weigh more than a pound.

'Orange'. Medium-size, rounded fruit with orange-yellow flesh.

'Pineapple'. Large, roundish, golden yellow fruit. White flesh has a pineapple flavor.

'Portugal'. Oblong fruit with pinkish flesh that turns red when cooked. Ripens early.

'Smyrna'. Large, round to oblong fruit with lemon yellow skin and white flesh. Good flavor.

QUISQUALIS indica

RANGOON CREEPER

Combretaceae

DECIDUOUS VINE

⟋ TS ⫘ 12–8

☼ ◖ FULL SUN OR PARTIAL SHADE

◖ REGULAR WATER

Quisqualis indica

This plant had early botanists scratching their heads for some time. Translated from the Latin, its name means "Who?" and "What?" The confusion stems from the fact that the plant is shrubby in youth, then becomes a scrambling vine. Its flowers also change color with age.

Native to Burma, Malaysia, New Guinea, and the Philippines. In south Florida and South Texas, where it is hardy, it climbs to an eventual 30 ft.; elsewhere, it may reach half this size in a season. Rich green, oval, pointed leaves with prominent veins grow to 5 in. long; new growth is covered with brownish fuzz. Fragrant, long-tubed flowers up to 3 in. long are borne at stem ends during summer. Blossoms are white at first, then change to pink and, finally, to red. Rangoon creeper is easy to grow and tolerates most soils. Prune to shape after flowering.

RABBIT'S FOOT FERN. See DAVALLIA fejeensis

RADERMACHERA sinica

CHINA DOLL

Bignoniaceae

EVERGREEN TREE

⟋ TS ⫘ 12–10; OR HOUSEPLANT

☼ ◖ FULL SUN OR PARTIAL SHADE; BRIGHT LIGHT

◖ REGULAR WATER

Radermachera sinica

This beautiful native of China is most often grown as a houseplant, but when planted outdoors in South Texas or central or southern Florida, it grows quickly into a small, graceful tree about 25 ft. tall and 10–12 ft. wide. Prized for its handsome, glossy, rich green leaves, which are divided into many 2-in. leaflets. Hardy to about 20°F. Airy, layered branches and symmetrical, upright form are reminiscent of chinaberry *(Melia)*. Mature plants bloom in summer, bearing at their branch tips clusters of powerfully fragrant, 3-in. blossoms in pure white to sulphur yellow. The flowers open at night and drop from the branches the next day. 'Crystal Doll' is a slower-growing selection with striking yellow-and-green variegated leaves.

Indoors, place in a very bright window (but be sure to protect from hottest afternoon sun). Insufficient light results in leggy growth. Provide evenly moist, well-drained soil; do not let soil dry out or plant will drop leaves. Fertilize every other week in spring and summer and once a month in fall and winter with a general-purpose liquid houseplant fertilizer. Spider mites and aphids are frequent pests; control them with insecticidal soap or horticultural oil. Plants grown outdoors have fewer problems; they thrive in fertile, well-drained soil.

RADICCHIO. See CHICORY and RADICCHIO

RADISH

'French Breakfast' Radish

Brassicaceae (Cruciferae)

COOL-SEASON ANNUAL

US, MS, LS, CS, TS H 7–1

LIGHT SHADE IN HOTTEST CLIMATES

REGULAR WATER

Known botanically as *Raphanus sativus,* the radish is a fast-maturing, easy-to-grow vegetable that prefers cool weather. It is also surprisingly varied. The edible roots may be short and rounded or long and slender; flavor may be sweet, mild, or hot; and colors include red, pink, rose, lavender, purple, black, and white.

Radishes are divided into spring, summer, and winter types. Spring radishes mature in just 3 to 4 weeks from seed. Their crisp texture and mildly pungent flavor result from growing in cool weather. Begin planting 2 to 6 weeks before the last frost and continue until 4 weeks after it; quality declines with warm weather in late spring. You can also plant them for a fall crop by sowing seed in early fall, 4 to 6 weeks before the first frost. And in the Coastal and Tropical South, radishes can be grown in winter. Recommended selections include 'Burpee White' (25 days from sowing to harvest; round white roots), 'Cherry Belle' (22 days; round red), 'Cherriette' (24 days; round red), 'Easter Egg II' (25 days; oval roots in mix of lavender, pink, rose, red, white), and 'Sparkler White Tip' (24 days; round red-and-white).

Summer radishes tolerate heat better than spring types. Plant for harvest in spring, early summer, or fall. The group includes 'French Breakfast' (23 days; oblong red roots with white tip) and 'Icicle' (25 days; long, slender white roots).

Winter radishes, which require 50 to 60 days to mature, are larger and firmer than spring and summer radishes. Some are rounded; others, including the oriental daikon types, are long and carrot shaped. Roots are crisp and mildly pungent and keep well in storage. They require cool weather at the end of their growing season, so plant them as a fall crop (or as a winter crop in the Coastal and Tropical South). Sow seeds at least 4 weeks before the first fall frost. If you plant them in spring, they may flower before forming roots. Selections include 'April Cross' (60 days; white daikon type), 'Miyashige' (50 days; white daikon type), 'Red Meat' (50 days; pink flesh, green skin), 'Round Black Spanish' (55 days; round black roots with white flesh), and 'Summer Cross' (50 days; white daikon type).

Like other root crops, radishes need soft, loose soil. If your soil is heavy clay, till in plenty of organic matter or plant in raised beds. Sow spring and summer radishes ½ in. deep in rows spaced 6–12 in. apart. Sow winter radishes ¾ in. deep; space rows 18–20 in. apart. Thin plants soon after they emerge, leaving 2–3 in. between spring and summer radishes and 6 in. between winter radishes. When first true leaves emerge, apply ¼ cup of 10-10-10 fertilizer per 10 ft. of row. Keep soil evenly moist; excessive or uneven moisture may cause radishes to split or become tough and hot in flavor. Floating row covers placed over developing plants will protect them against flea beetles (which eat the foliage) and root maggots (which eat the roots).

Harvest spring and summer radishes as soon as they reach ¾–1½ in. in diameter. ('Icicle' pushes up out of the ground when it is ready.) Leaving them in longer than this can result in hot-tasting, woody roots. Winter radishes can stay in the ground longer, especially in cool weather. Daikon types can grow 1–1½ ft. long with no loss in quality.

RAINBOW SHOWER. See CASSIA × nealiae

RAIN LILY. See HABRANTHUS, ZEPHYRANTHES

RANGOON CREEPER. See QUISQUALIS indica

RANGPUR LIME. See CITRUS, Sour-Acid Mandarin

Ranunculaceae. The immense buttercup family numbers nearly 2,000 species, among them numerous ornamental annuals and perennials. Members include *Anemone,* columbine *(Aquilegia), Clematis, Delphinium,* hellebore *(Helleborus),* and *Ranunculus.* Many are poisonous if eaten.

RANUNCULUS

Ranunculus asiaticus

Ranunculaceae

PERENNIALS

ZONES VARY BY SPECIES

EXPOSURE NEEDS VARY BY SPECIES

REGULAR WATER

This very large genus comprises about 250 species of widely differing habit and appearance, but the two listed here are the ones most commonly grown in gardens.

R. asiaticus. PERSIAN RANUNCULUS, TURBAN RANUNCULUS. Zones LS, CS, TS; 12–6 (see below). Native to Asia Minor. Tuberous-rooted plant to 1½–2 ft. tall and wide, with fresh green, almost fernlike leaves. Blooms profusely in spring, when each flowering stalk bears one to four 3- to 5-in.-wide, semidouble to fully double blossoms that some say resemble small peony blooms. Flowers come in white, cream, and many shades of yellow, orange, red, pink. Popular Tecolote Giant strain is available in single colors, mixed colors, and picotees. Bloomingdale strain offers the same range of colors on dwarf plants 8–10 in. high. All types are good in the ground or in pots.

Tuberous roots are hardy to 10°F. In the Coastal and Tropical South, plant in fall for bloom in winter, early spring; treat plants as annuals there. Beyond hardiness range, plant in spring as soon as ground is workable; or start roots indoors 4 to 6 weeks before the usual last-frost date. Nurseries sell tuberous roots of various sizes; all produce equally large blossoms, but bigger roots yield a greater number of flowers.

Grow in full sun, in organically enriched, very well-drained soil (if necessary, plant in raised beds). Set roots with prongs down, 2 in. deep (1 in. deep in heavier soils) and 6–8 in. apart. Water thoroughly, then withhold water until leaves emerge. Birds are fond of ranunculus shoots, so protect sprouting plants with netting or wire. Or start plants in pots or flats, then set them in the garden when they're 4–6 in. tall—too mature to appeal to birds. (You can also start with nursery-grown seedlings.) Remove faded flowers to encourage more bloom.

When flowering tapers off and leaves start to yellow, stop watering the plants and allow the foliage to die back. Where tuberous roots are hardy in the ground, they can be left undisturbed—as long as soil can be kept dry during summer. Some gardeners dig plants when foliage turns yellow, cut off the tops, let roots dry for a week or two, and store them in a cool, dry place until planting time. But most people find it simpler to discard the plants and set out new roots when the time comes.

R. repens pleniflorus. CREEPING BUTTERCUP. Zones US, MS, LS; 8–1. From Eurasia; naturalized in North America. Vigorous plant with thick, fibrous roots and runners that root at the joints. Forms a lush, glossy green mat to 1 ft. high, 6 ft. wide; leaves are roundish, deeply cut into three tooth-edged, 2-in.-long leaflets. Fully double, 1-in., button-shaped, bright yellow flowers are held above foliage on 1- to 2-ft. stems in spring. Can be invasive in constantly moist soil. Attractive deciduous ground cover for full sun to deep shade. Basic species is single flowered, as aggressive as *R. r. pleniflorus.*

RAPHIOLEPIS. See RHAPHIOLEPIS

RASPBERRY

Red Raspberry

Rosaceae

DECIDUOUS SHRUBS

US, MS H 8–1, EXCEPT AS NOTED

FULL SUN

REGULAR WATER

Savoring a mouthful of sweet, juicy raspberries is one of life's heady experiences. Several different species are found in Southern gardens. Red and yellow raspberries are derived from *Rubus idaeus,* native to North America, Europe, and

R

Asia. Black raspberries are selections of *R. occidentalis,* a North American species. Purple raspberries are hybrids between red and black types. Gardeners in the Tropical South grow Mysore raspberry (*R. niveus),* which, unlike other species, needs no winter chill to flower and fruit. For species grown as ornamentals, see *Rubus.*

Raspberries grow from shallow perennial roots that produce thorny biennial stems called canes. The canes of *summer-bearing* types grow to full size in the first year, then bear fruit the following summer. Red and yellow raspberries known as *everbearing* (or fall-bearing) produce two crops on the same canes—one in fall of the first year, the second in summer of the next year. In either case, the canes die after fruiting in the second year. New canes sprout to replace the old. Mysore raspberries bloom and fruit throughout the year, but the best crop comes from February to June.

Most raspberries generally have a high winter-chill requirement (more than 1,000 hours below 45°F per year), a demand not often met in the South. Without sufficient chill, bloom and fruit are poor. In addition, most raspberries don't like high summer heat. Thus, the most dependable areas for growing raspberries are the Upper and Middle South. For exceptions, see "Raspberries That Take the Heat," this page.

Raspberries prefer deep, slightly acid, moist but well-drained soil that contains plenty of organic matter. Choose a sunny, slightly sloping site with good air movement; avoid low-lying frost pockets. Do not plant where tomatoes, potatoes, eggplants, or peppers have been recently grown, as this increases the danger of soil-borne wilt disease. Also, remove any nearby wild raspberry or blackberry plants, which may harbor viral diseases.

Plant bare-root plants during the dormant season (soak the roots in water overnight before planting). Set red and yellow raspberries and Mysore types 2½–3 ft. apart, in rows spaced 6–10 ft. apart; plant black and purple raspberries in slightly raised mounds 2–3 ft. apart, in rows 6–8 ft. apart. Cut back all canes to 6 in. at this time. Mulch plantings to discourage weeds and keep soil moist. Feed by sprinkling a handful of 10-10-10 fertilizer around each plant in spring and watering it in. Give plants extra water during blooming and fruiting.

Red, yellow, and Mysore raspberries are produced on erect plants with long, straight canes; they can be grown as freestanding shrubs and staked, but they are tidier and easier to manage if trained on a trellis or confined to a hedgerow (pairs of parallel wires strung at 3 ft. and 5 ft. above ground along either side of a row of plants).

Summer-bearing raspberries should produce three to five canes in the first year. Tie these to a trellis or confine them to a hedgerow. Dig or pull out any canes that grow more than 1 ft. away from trellis or outside of hedgerow. In late dormant season, cut canes on trellis to 5–5½ ft. high, those in hedgerow to 4 ft. When growth recommences, new canes will appear all around the parent plant and between rows. After the original canes bear fruit, cut them to the ground. Then select the best 5 to 12 new canes and train these (they will bear the following summer); cut remaining new canes to ground.

Everbearing red and yellow raspberries fruit in first autumn on top third of cane, then again in second summer on lower two-thirds of cane. Cut off upper portion of cane after first harvest; cut out cane entirely after second harvest. As an alternative, you can follow the example of growers who cut everbearing canes to the ground yearly in fall after fruiting has finished (wait until late dormant season in cold-winter regions). You'll sacrifice one of the annual crops but get an extended harvest from late summer into fall, since the energy that would have gone into a summer crop is available for a bang-up fall harvest. Use a power mower in a large berry patch.

Canes of Mysore raspberries should be pruned heavily in late fall of the first year. This forces new growth that will produce berries the following year, from late winter to late spring. After canes have fruited, cut them to the ground.

Black and purple raspberries are produced on clump-forming plants with arching canes. No support is needed. In the first summer, force branching by heading back new canes of black selections to 2 ft., those of purple kinds to 2½ ft. If you prefer trellising, cut black selections to 2–2½ ft., purple ones to 2½–3 ft. In late dormant season, remove all weak or broken canes. Leave six to eight canes in a hill or spaced 6–8 in. apart in a row. Shorten side branches to 8–10 in. for black raspberries, to

12–14 in. for purple types. The side branches will bear fruit in summer. After harvest, cut to the ground all canes that have fruited and cut back all new canes as described for first summer's growth.

To control anthracnose and other fungal diseases on all raspberries, spray with lime sulfur during dormancy and again as leaf buds begin to open; this also helps control many insect pests, including spider mites and cane borer. If borers attack, prune out and destroy damaged canes below entry points (pinhead-size holes at or near ground level).

Red and yellow raspberries. Red selections are the most common; yellow types are mutations of red raspberries.

'Autumn Bliss'. Zones US, MS, LS. Everbearing. Very large red berries with fine flavor. Resists root rot.

'Boyne'. Summer-bearing. Very hardy red raspberry bred in Manitoba. Medium-size fruit. Early ripening. Subject to anthracnose.

'Dorman Red'. Zones US, MS, LS, CS. Summer-bearing. Large, firm red fruit ripens late. Widely adapted selection with low winter-chill requirement. Vigorous, blackberry-like habit; must be trellised.

'Fallgold'. Everbearing. Large yellow fruit with good flavor. Very productive; very cold hardy.

'Goldie'. Everbearing. A sport of 'Heritage'. Produces deep yellow, high-quality fruit.

'Heritage'. Zones US, MS, LS. Everbearing. Firm, tasty red berries. Very popular selection.

'Indian Summer'. Everbearing. Small crops of large, tasty red berries. Fall crop is often larger.

'Killarney'. Summer-bearing. Medium-size, firm red fruit with sweet-tart flavor. Good all-purpose raspberry that can be harvested over a long period. Vigorous, hardy.

'Kiwigold'. Everbearing. Yellow sport of 'Heritage' with excellent flavor. Vigorous and erect.

'Latham'. Summer-bearing. Older, very hardy type; for coldest regions. Mildews in humid summers. Ripens late. Large red berries often crumbly.

'Newburgh'. Summer-bearing. Large red berries. Late-ripening selection. Takes heavy soil fairly well.

'Redwing'. Zones US, MS, LS, CS. Everbearing. Larger, softer, and earlier than 'Heritage'. Heat tolerant.

'Reveille'. Summer-bearing. Very large, choice, bright red berries. Early. Vigorous, upright, and productive.

'Ruby'. Everbearing. Very large, mild-flavored red berries.

'Southland'. Everbearing. Medium-size, juicy red fruit with excellent flavor. Early. Vigorous and hardy.

'Summit'. Everbearing. Large red berries with good flavor. Very productive. Resistant to root rot.

Black and purple raspberries. Black selections have blue-black fruit that is firmer and seedier than the fruit of red and yellow types, with a more pronounced flavor. Purple raspberries are crosses between black and red kinds.

'Black Hawk'. Large, glossy black berries. Sweet to mildly acid. Vigorous and productive.

'Brandywine'. Large purple berries. Tart flavor; good for jams and jellies. Ripens late.

'Cumberland'. Large black berries. Old, heavy-bearing selection.

'Jewel'. Large black berries. Vigorous, disease-resistant plant.

'Royalty'. Dusty purple, very large berries with excellent flavor. Vigorous and very productive.

RASPBERRIES THAT TAKE THE HEAT. *Though most raspberries dislike hot summers and need extended winter cold, there are some that take heat and thrive with little or no chill. 'Heritage' and 'Autumn Bliss' grow well in the Lower South. In the Coastal South, try 'Dorman Red' or 'Redwing'. In the Tropical South, plant Mysore raspberry (R. niveus), which has fruit that is black when ripe but is grown like red or yellow raspberry. Gardeners in the Tropical South can also grow everbearing raspberries such as 'Autumn Bliss' and 'Heritage' as annuals: plant in spring and harvest in fall.* ❖

RATIBIDA

Asteraceae (Compositae)

PERENNIALS

US, MS, LS, CS

FULL SUN

REGULAR WATER

*Ratibida
columnifera*

Stiffly erect, branched, roughly hairy plants with deeply cut leaves. Flower heads like those of black-eyed Susan (*Rudbeckia hirta*) but have fewer ray flowers and a taller, more prominent central cone. Plant with other easy-care perennials.

R. columnifera. MEXICAN HAT. Heat zones 10–1. From the Great Plains. To 2½ ft. tall, 1 ft. wide. Flowers have drooping yellow or brownish purple rays and a tall, columnar brown cone; look like sombreros.

R. pinnata. PRAIRIE or YELLOW CONEFLOWER. Heat zones 9–1. Native to central North America. To 4 ft. tall, 1½ ft. wide, with yellow rays and a nearly globular brown cone.

RATTLESNAKE GRASS. See BRIZA maxima

RATTLESNAKE MASTER. See ERYNGIUM yuccifolium

RATTLESNAKE PLANT. See CALATHEA lancifolia

RAVENALA madagascariensis

TRAVELER'S TREE, TRAVELER'S PALM

Strelitziaceae

EVERGREEN TREE

TS 12–10; OR GROW IN POT

FULL SUN

REGULAR WATER

*Ravenala
madagascariensis*

Native to Madagascar. Upright clump to 30–40 ft. tall, 25–30 ft. wide, with numerous large leaves held in the shape of a gigantic fan atop an unbranched trunk. Foliage resembles that of banana (*Musa*). Spectacular accent in the garden or displayed against a large building. Protect from strong winds, which will shred the leaves. Small plants have some shade tolerance, can be used as potted specimens.

RED BAY. See PERSEA borbonia

REDBUD. See CERCIS

RED GINGER. See ALPINIA purpurata

RED-HOT POKER. See KNIPHOFIA

RED IVY. See HEMIGRAPHIS alternata

RED TOWER GINGER. See COSTUS barbatus

REED GRASS. See CALAMAGROSTIS

REHMANNIA elata

CHINESE FOXGLOVE

Gesneriaceae

PERENNIAL

MS (PROTECTED), LS, CS 12–7

PARTIAL SHADE

REGULAR WATER

Rehmannia elata

Native to China. To 3 ft. tall, 1½–2 ft. wide. Clump of coarse, deeply toothed leaves (evergreen in mild-winter climates) sends up stalks loosely set with tubular, 3-in.-long flowers that look something like big, gaping foxgloves (*Digitalis*). Common form bears rosy purple blossoms with a yellow throat dotted in red; there is also a fine white form with cream throat (this one must be grown from cuttings or divisions). Where winters are mild, blooms from midspring well into fall; in colder climates, bloom comes in summer. Long lasting as a cut flower. Provide rich soil. Easy to grow from seed, root cuttings, divisions. Spreads quickly in moist, fertile soil and can be invasive.

Rhamnaceae. The buckthorn family of shrubs and trees has small, usually clustered flowers and fruits that are either drupes (single seeded, juicy) or capsules. Examples include *Ceanothus*, jujube, and *Rhamnus*.

RHAMNUS caroliniana

CAROLINA BUCKTHORN, INDIAN CHERRY

Rhamnaceae

DECIDUOUS SHRUB OR SMALL TREE

US, MS, LS, CS 9–4

FULL SUN OR PARTIAL SHADE

MODERATE WATER

Rhamnus caroliniana

Native from New York to Florida and Texas. Grows moderately fast to 15–20 ft. tall and about as wide; may reach 30 ft. Grown for its form, foliage, and color. Coarse dark green leaves to 6 in. long turn yellow, orange, or red in fall. Small flowers are inconspicuous; they are followed by clusters of showy, sweet berries that ripen from red to black in fall (both colors are often present at the same time). Good understory tree.

RHAPHIOLEPIS

Rosaceae

EVERGREEN SHRUBS

LS, CS

FULL SUN OR LIGHT SHADE

LITTLE TO REGULAR WATER

Rhaphiolepis indica
'Dancer'

These dependable shrubs are among the best plants for the beach (they tolerate wind and salt spray), but they have many other uses as well. Their glossy, leathery leaves and compact form make them good subjects for foundation plantings, berms, low hedges, and containers. They bloom profusely from fall or midwinter until late spring, with flowers ranging in color from white through pink to nearly red. Berrylike dark blue fruits (not especially showy) follow the blossoms. Emerging leaves are tinged bronze and red.

Most stay low. The taller kinds seldom reach more than 5–6 ft., and pruning can keep them at 3 ft. almost indefinitely. For bushy, compact plants, pinch back branch tips at least once yearly, after flowering. Tolerate drought; need good drainage. Plants growing in partial shade are less compact and have fewer flowers than those growing in full sun.

R. ×delacourii. Heat zones 10–8. Pink-flowered hybrid of *R. indica* and *R. umbellata*. To 6 ft. tall, 8 ft. wide. Small pink flowers in upright clusters. Leaves are 1¼–2¾ in. long.

R. indica. INDIAN HAWTHORN. Heat zones 9–3. Native to China. To 4–5 ft. high, 5–6 ft. wide, with 1½- to 3-in.-long pointed leaves and ½-in. flowers in white tinged with pink. The species is seldom seen in gardens, but its selections are widely grown and sold. They differ mainly in flower color and in plant size and form; there is variation even within a selection. Flower color is especially inconsistent: in warmer climates and exposures, blossoms are usually lighter, and in general blooms are paler in fall than in spring. In high-rainfall, high-humidity areas such as Florida and Gulf Coast, the same fungal leaf spot disease that defoliates photinia can ravage this species. In these regions, choose resistant selections such as 'Eskimo', 'Indian Princess', 'Olivia', 'Snow Pink', and 'Snow White'; avoid susceptible ones like 'Enchantress', 'Fascination', 'Harbinger of Spring', 'Heather', 'Spring Rapture', 'Springtime', and 'White Enchantress'. ▶

R

Selections include the following.

'Ballerina'. To 2 ft. tall, 4 ft. wide. Deep rosy pink flowers. Leaves take on a reddish tinge in winter.

'Clara'. To 3–5 ft. tall and wide. White flowers. Red new growth.

'Dancer'. Reaches 4 ft. tall, 5 ft. wide. Pure pink flowers.

'Enchantress' ('Pinkie'). To 3 ft. tall, 5 ft. wide, with rose pink blooms. 'White Enchantress' has white blossoms.

'Eskimo'. To 6 ft. tall, 8 ft. wide. Highly resistant to leaf spot; hardy to 5°F.

'Indian Princess'. Up to 3 ft. high, 5 ft. wide. Light pink flowers. Resists leaf spot.

'Jack Evans'. To 4–5 ft. high, 4 ft. wide. Bright pink flowers. Leaves sometimes have a purplish tinge.

'Olivia'. To 4 ft. high, 2 ft. wide. Pure white flowers. Resistant to leaf spot.

'Snow Pink'. Compact grower to 3 ft. high and wide. Pink flowers. Resists leaf spot.

'Snow White'. To 3–4 ft. high, 5 ft. wide. White flowers. Spreading habit. Resistant to leaf spot.

'Spring Rapture'. To 3–4 ft. high and wide. Rose red blossoms.

'Springtime'. Vigorous, upright; 4–6 ft. tall and wide. Deep pink flowers.

R. 'Majestic Beauty'. Heat zones 10–7. Larger in every detail than the others. Can be trained as a single- or multitrunked tree to 20–25 ft. tall, 8–10 ft. wide; as a shrub, easily kept at 10–12 ft. tall, 6–8 ft. wide. Fragrant light pink flowers in clusters to 10 in. wide. Leaves are 4 in. long. Thought by some to be a hybrid between *Rhaphiolepis* and loquat *(Eriobotrya).*

R. umbellata (R. japonica, R. ovata). Heat zones 10–8. Native to Japan, Korea. Vigorous grower to 4–6 ft. (sometimes to 10 ft.) high and wide. Distinguished from *R. indica* by its leathery dark green, 1- to 3-in.-long, roundish leaves. White, about ¾-in.-wide flowers. Thick and bushy in full sun. Sometimes called Yeddo hawthorn. 'Minor' ('Gulf Green') is a compact, slow-growing form to 3–4 ft. high and wide.

RHAPIDOPHYLLUM hystrix

NEEDLE PALM

Arecaceae (Palmae)

PALM

US, MS, LS, CS, TS H 10–4

SUN OR SHADE

MODERATE TO AMPLE WATER

Rhapidophyllum hystrix

Perhaps the hardiest palm in the world, taking temperatures well below 0°F; has reportedly survived winters as far north as Massachusetts. Native to the Coastal Plains from South Carolina to Florida and Mississippi. Shrubby and very slow growing, eventually reaching 6–8 ft. tall and wide; does not have a distinct trunk. The common name refers to the sharp black needles that protect the plant's crown and seeds. Dramatic-looking leaf fans are carried at the ends of smooth stems—they are lustrous dark green, to 3 ft. across, deeply cut into 6 to 12 segments.

Needle palm tolerates a wide range of soils and resists damage by browsing deer. Makes a good accent or understory plant. It's hard to find in garden centers and is usually purchased by mail. Buy only nursery-propagated plants, not those collected from the wild.

RHAPIS

LADY PALM

Arecaceae (Palmae)

PALMS

CS, TS H 12–8, EXCEPT AS NOTED; OR HOUSEPLANTS

SOME SHADE; BRIGHT INDIRECT LIGHT

REGULAR WATER

Rhapis excelsa

These choice, slow-growing fan palms are beautiful, extremely versatile, and easy to grow. Cultivated in China since the 17th century, they achieved star status in Japan, where the samurai collected multitudes of prized forms. The two species described here, both hardy to 18°F, feature large deep green leaves on sturdy canes like those of bamboo. In the Tropical South and milder parts of the Coastal South, they may be grown outdoors in the shade, where they make excellent additions to foundation and understory plantings. Perfect for a large container in a Florida room. Elsewhere, they're wonderful, low-maintenance houseplants and patio plants (bring them indoors during cold weather). Because they take many years to reach a large size, lady palms command a premium price.

These palms do best with light shade and fertile, well-drained soil. Outdoors, site in the shadow of the house or the shade of tall trees. Indoors, place in bright indirect light and let soil go dry between waterings (but when you do water, soak the entire root system). Feed monthly from spring through fall with a general-purpose liquid houseplant fertilizer diluted to quarter-strength. Yellowing leaves are typically a sign that more fertilizer is needed. Regular repotting isn't necessary, as lady palms prefer to be slightly rootbound. To get more plants, divide in spring or early summer.

R. excelsa. LADY PALM. The only ornamental palms to have named selections in both green-leafed and variegated forms. Coarse dark brown fiber covers the canes. Well adapted to summer heat.

Divided into three classes by size; most grow about as wide as tall. Standard forms grow to 14 ft. high; dwarf types to 5–8 ft.; mini-dwarfs to 4 ft. tall after 30 to 40 years. Selections include the following.

'Daruma'. Dwarf. Upright form. Resembles a small version of a standard lady palm.

'Gyokuho'. Mini-dwarf. Small, oval leaves and short, bushy habit. Grows only a few inches per year.

'Heiseinishiki'. Dwarf. Leaves are heavily variegated with broad, creamy yellow stripes.

'Koban'. Dwarf. Most popular selection. Full, spreading plant with large, wide leaves.

'Kodaruma'. Mini-dwarf. The shortest of all *R. excelsa* selections, often wider than tall. Good subject for bonsai.

'Tenzan'. Dwarf. Tallest of the dwarfs. Large, drooping leaves and slender canes.

'Zuikonishiki'. Dwarf. Leaves are elegantly striped in white and green.

R. humilis. SLENDER LADY PALM. Heat zones 12–10. The tallest of lady palms, sometimes exceeding 18 ft. high—but it grows only 3 ft. wide. Common name refers to slender canes. Large leaves are divided into many narrow segments. Not as heat tolerant as *R. excelsa;* does better in South Texas and Southern California than south Florida.

RHIPSALIDOPSIS gaertneri (Schlumbergera gaertneri)

EASTER CACTUS

Cactaceae

CACTUS

TS; OR HOUSEPLANT

PARTIAL SHADE; BRIGHT LIGHT

REGULAR WATER

Rhipsalidopsis gaertneri

Native to Brazil. For culture and description, see *Schlumbergera.* Much like *S.* ×*buckleyi* but initially more upright, then semipendent to 6 in. high, 1 ft. wide (*S.* ×*buckleyi* is completely pendent). Blooms in spring, often again in late summer or early fall. There are many selections, with blossoms in various shades of pink and red. In marginal climates, give protection of lathhouse or covered terrace. Good houseplant; bring outdoors during warm times of year, if desired. Suffers in temperatures above 100°F. Plant has been renamed *Hatiora gaertneri* but is not generally offered as such.

FOR INFORMATION ON YOUR CLIMATE ZONES
PLEASE SEE PAGES 28–38

RHODODENDRON
(includes Azalea)

Ericaceae

EVERGREEN AND DECIDUOUS SHRUBS

FOR ZONES, SEE BELOW

FILTERED SUNLIGHT

REGULAR TO AMPLE WATER

LEAVES ARE POISONOUS IF INGESTED

Rhododendron
'Trude Webster'

Rhododendrons and azaleas are arguably the South's favorite shrubs. Many people think of them as entirely different plants, but they both belong to the genus *Rhododendron*, which comprises more than 800 species and 10,000 named selections. Even to the untrained eye, one difference between the two groups is obvious: rhododendrons generally have much larger leaves. From a technical standpoint, rhododendron flowers are bell shaped and have ten or more stamens, while azalea blooms are typically funnel shaped and have five stamens.

By making their choices carefully, gardeners in almost every part of the South can enjoy some of these plants, even if that means growing them in containers. Rhododendrons generally do better in the Upper and Middle South, though a number of selections thrive in the Lower South (see "Heat-tolerant hybrids," this page). Azaleas, however, are more accommodating; with the necessary attention to soil, light, and proper selection, they can be grown throughout the South.

Rhododendrons and azaleas have much the same basic requirements for soil and water. They need acid, well-drained, organically enriched soil that should neither get too dry nor remain soggy. Planting in heavy clay is a no-no: root rot often ensues, indicated by yellowing, wilting foliage and collapse of the plant. Planting in limy, alkaline soil is another mistake; lack of iron quickly results in chlorosis (yellow leaves with green veins). Alkaline soil has not, however, discouraged azalea lovers in Texas and Oklahoma. The recommended practice there is to build raised beds 15–18 in. deep and fill them with a half-and-half mixture of finely milled bark and coarse sphagnum peat moss (be sure to mix the two thoroughly with water before filling the beds). Irrigating with alkaline water will slowly raise the pH; to keep it in the desired range of 5.0–6.0, prepare a mixture of 3 parts garden sulfur to 1 part iron sulfate, then apply it at the rate of 1 pound per 100 sq. ft. of garden bed. This should lower the pH by one point.

Plant azaleas and rhododendrons with the top of the root ball slightly above soil level. Don't cultivate around these plants, as they have shallow roots. Because they absorb water through their foliage, wet both the leaves and root zone when you water. Overhead watering with sprinklers works well, but to prevent fungal diseases do this in morning so that leaves dry by afternoon. Avoid drip irrigation—it doesn't wet the root system uniformly.

In spring, just after the blooms fade, apply a mulch and fertilize with a controlled-release, acid-forming fertilizer such as cottonseed meal or commercial azalea/camellia food. Do not mulch in fall; this will hold heat in the soil and delay the onset of dormancy, increasing the chances of winter damage. And don't fertilize *before* bloom—you'll encourage leafy growth at the wrong time.

The sun tolerance of azaleas and rhododendrons varies by species and selection. In general, most types prefer the partial sun or filtered shade beneath tall trees. The east and north sides of the house are better locations than the west and south. Too much sun bleaches or burns the leaves; too little results in lanky plants that don't bloom.

Insects and diseases seldom bother healthy, vigorous plants. However, rhododendrons growing in heavy clay often fall victim to *Phytophthora*, a deadly soil-borne fungus that causes dieback. Azaleas growing in full sun are often plagued by sucking insects called lace bugs. For solutions to both problems, see the *Southern Living Garden Problem Solver*.

The rhododendrons listed here are all evergreen; azalea species and hybrids may be evergreen or deciduous. Plant sizes vary somewhat within groups, but most individual plants are roughly equal in height and width.

Pruning rhododendrons is simple—just follow these general guidelines. Tip-pinch young plants to make them bushy; prune older, leggy plants to restore shape by cutting back to a side branch, leaf whorl, or cluster of latent buds. Do any extensive pruning in late winter or early spring. Pruning at this time will sacrifice some flower buds, but the plant's energies will be diverted to latent growth buds, which will then be ready to push out their new growth early in the growing season. You can do some shaping while plants are in bloom; use cut branches in arrangements. To prevent seed formation, which can reduce next year's bloom, clip or break off spent flower trusses, taking care not to damage growth buds at base of each truss.

Evergreen azaleas are dense, usually shapely plants; heading back the occasional wayward branch restores symmetry. To keep bushes compact, tip-pinch frequently, starting after flowering ends and continuing until mid-June. Prune deciduous azaleas while they are dormant and leafless. You don't have to prune azaleas as carefully as you do rhododendrons—the leaves are fairly evenly spaced along the branches, with a bud at base of each leaf, so new growth will sprout from almost anywhere you cut (in either bare or leafy wood).

KINDS OF RHODODENDRONS

Most people know rhododendrons as big, leathery-leafed shrubs with rounded clusters ("trusses") of stunning white, pink, red, or purple blossoms. These are primarily hybrids of catawba rhododendron, *R. catawbiense*, which is native to the Appalachians. But there are also dwarfs just a few inches tall, giants that reach 40 ft. or even 80 ft. in their native Southeast Asia, and a host of species and hybrids of intermediate size. Hybrids with Asian parentage may display exotic colors of yellow, apricot, and salmon; unfortunately, plants with these colors are often less tolerant of the South's summer heat.

The following sections place named selections in categories to help you decide whether they're suited to your garden and how to employ them.

Heat-tolerant hybrids. These are some of the selections that accept the long, hot summers of the Lower South: 'A. Bedford', 'Album Elegans', 'Anah Kruschke', 'Anna Rose Whitney', 'Belle Heller', 'Caroline', 'Cheer', 'Chionoides', 'Cynthia', 'English Roseum', 'Fastuosum Flore Pleno', 'Ginny

---

WHAT RHODODENDRONS AND AZALEAS NEED

EXPOSURE: Generally, they fare best in filtered sunlight. They can take more sun in the Upper and Middle South, but full sun will be too much for them in the Lower, Coastal, and Tropical South. Shield them from strong winds. Choose species and selections well adapted to your climate.

SOIL: Provide moist, acid, well-drained soil rich in organic matter such as sphagnum peat moss, ground bark, chopped leaves, and compost. Avoid clay as well as limy, alkaline soils.

FERTILIZING: Plants growing in fertile, acid soil need only infrequent fertilizing. When you do feed, use a controlled-release, acid-forming fertilizer such as cottonseed meal or commercial azalea/camellia food. Feed in spring, right after bloom. If chlorosis (yellow leaves with green veins) is a problem, apply garden sulfur or iron sulfate.

PINCHING: This is necessary for shaping plants and encouraging thick, bushy growth. For specifics on this and other pruning, see text.

WATERING: Be sure to thoroughly water the entire plant—both the foliage and the whole root zone (not just one side of the plant). Water in the morning, so that leaves dry by afternoon.

Rhododendron 'Mrs. Furnivall'

Gee', 'Holden', 'Janet Blair', 'Jean Marie de Montague', 'Lee's Dark Purple', 'Nova Zembla', 'Purple Splendour', 'Roseum Elegans', 'Scintillation', 'Trude Webster', 'Vulcan'.

Cold-hardy hybrids. Most of the hybrids listed here are quite cold hardy. The following can take temperatures to at least −20°F: 'Album Elegans', 'America', 'Boule de Neige', 'Catawbiense Album', 'Catawbiense Boursault', 'English Roseum', 'Nova Zembla', 'PJM', 'President Lincoln', 'Ramapo', 'Roseum Elegans'.

Vireyas for indoors and frost-free areas. The Vireya rhododendrons, from the tropics of Southeast Asia, manage nicely in frost-free and nearly frostless zones. They are also fine container plants (even indoors), so they can be grown in colder zones if brought inside for the winter. They need an especially fast-draining potting mix (many species are epiphytes in the wild); a combination of equal parts peat moss, ground bark, and perlite works well. Typically, plants flower on and off throughout the year rather than in one blooming season. They bear waxy-textured blossoms in exciting shades of yellow, gold, orange, vermilion, salmon, and pink, plus cream, white, and bicolors. Species, named hybrids, and unnamed seedlings are offered by some specialty growers.

Among the best ones you are likely to find are *R. aurigeranum* (a hybrid of *R. brookeanum* commonly listed as 'Gracile'), *R. javanicum*, *R. konori*, *R. laetum*, *R. lochae*, *R. macgregoriae*, and the hybrids 'George Budgen' (orange yellow), 'Ne Plus Ultra' (a red-flowering hybrid between *R. laetum* and *R. zoelleri*), and 'Taylori' (pink).

Low-growing rhododendrons. These selections grow to 3 ft. tall or less: 'Blue Diamond', 'Bow Bells', 'Dora Amateis', 'Elizabeth', 'Ginny Gee', 'Molly Ann', 'Patty Bee', 'Ramapo', 'Sapphire', 'Scarlet Wonder'.

RHODODENDRONS IN CLAY OR ALKALINE SOIL? *They don't like it. Planting in raised beds that are 1–2 ft. above the original soil level is the simplest way to give these plants the conditions they need. Liberally mix organic material into top foot of native soil, then fill bed above it with a mixture of 50 percent organic material, 30 percent soil, 20 percent builder's sand. This mixture will hold air and moisture while allowing excess water to drain.* ❖

RHODODENDRON HYBRIDS AND SPECIES

Dozens of recommended rhododendrons are described in the lists that follow. Hybrids are listed first, then species. As a general rule, hybrids prefer the Upper and Middle South, but those noted as being heat tolerant also grow well in the Lower South. Many are available at garden centers; you'll have to order others by mail. All are evergreen unless otherwise noted. While most people concentrate on hybrids, rhododendron species have plenty to offer, especially in woodland gardens and naturalized areas. Four of the species we list are native to the Southeast.

The lists include cold hardiness for each plant—the minimum temperature a mature plant can tolerate without serious injury. We also state typical height for each; most grow at least as wide as tall. Bloom times given are approximate and vary with weather and location. In the descriptions, "very early" corresponds to late winter, "early" to early spring, "midseason" to midspring, "late" to late spring, and "very late" to early summer.

'A. Bedford'. −5°F. To 6 ft. Large trusses of lavender-blue blooms with darker flare. Late. Heat tolerant.

'Album Elegans'. −20°F. To 6 ft. Flowers open pale mauve and fade to white. Vigorous, open form. Late. Heat tolerant.

'America'. −20°F. To 5 ft. Dark red. Late. Heat tolerant.

'Anah Kruschke'. −15°F. To 6 ft. Lavender blue to reddish purple. Flower color not the best, but plant has good foliage and is very tolerant of heat and sun. Can be sensitive to root rot in warm, wet soils. Midseason to late. Heat tolerant.

'Anna Rose Whitney'. −5°F. To 6 ft., with excellent foliage. Big trusses of blossoms in rich, deep pink. Late midseason. Heat tolerant.

'Antoon Van Welie'. −5°F. To 6 ft. Tall trusses of carmine pink blooms. Late midseason.

'Autumn Gold'. −5°F. To 5 ft. Well-branched plant with rather upright growth. Salmon blossoms in flat-topped trusses; blooms from an early age. Very late.

'Belle Heller'. −10°F. To 5 ft. Pure white with gold blotch. Midseason. Takes sun and heat.

'Blue Diamond'. −5°F. To 3 ft.; compact, erect. Small leaves. Small lavender-blue flowers cover plant in early midseason. Takes considerable sun.

'Blue Ensign'. −15°F. To 4 ft.; compact, well-branched, rounded growth. Leaves tend to spot. Lilac-blue flowers have a striking dark blotch. Midseason. Tolerates sun and heat.

'Blue Peter'. −10°F. To 4–5 ft. Broad, sprawling growth; needs regular pruning. Large trusses of lavender-blue flowers with purple blotch. Midseason. Tolerates heat and sun.

'Boule de Neige'. −25°F. To 5 ft. Rounded plant with bright green leaves and snowball-like clusters of white flowers. Midseason.

'Bow Bells'. −5°F. Forms a 3-ft. mound. Rounded leaves; bronzy new growth. Loose clusters of bright pink, cup-shaped flowers open from deeper pink buds. Early midseason.

Rhododendron 'Blue Ensign'

'Caroline'. −15°F. To 6 ft. Lightly fragrant flowers in orchid pink. Light green, twisted leaves. Midseason to late. Heat tolerant.

'Catawbiense Album'. −25°F. To 6 ft. Pink buds; white flowers with greenish blotch. Midseason to late. Takes cold and heat.

'Catawbiense Boursault'. −20°F. Like 'Catawbiense Album' but with pinkish lavender flowers. Takes cold and heat.

'Cheer'. −10°F. Mound-shaped, glossy-leafed plant to 4 ft. Pink flowers. Early. Heat tolerant.

'Chionoides'. −15°F. To 4 ft.; dense, compact, rounded form. White flowers with light yellow spotting. Late midseason. Takes sun and heat.

'Cunningham's White'. −15°F. To 4 ft. An old-timer bearing blooms in white with greenish yellow blotch. Late midseason.

Rhododendron 'Autumn Gold'

Rhododendron 'Blue Peter'

Rhododendron 'Catawbiense Album'

Rhododendron 'Fastuosum Flore Pleno'

R

'Cynthia'. −15°F. To 6 ft. Rosy crimson blooms with blackish markings. Midseason. Old favorite for background. Heat tolerant.

'Dora Amateis'. −15°F. To 3 ft. Compact, rather small-foliaged plant; good for foreground. Profuse bloomer with green-spotted white flowers. Spicy fragrance. Early midseason.

'Elizabeth'. 0°F. To 3 ft. One of the most popular low-growing red rhododendrons, very widely planted. Attractive foliage sets off large, bright red, waxy, trumpet-shaped flowers that are carried in clusters of three to six at branch ends and in upper leaf joints. Blooms very young. Early midseason; often reblooms in early fall. Very susceptible to fertilizer burn, salts in water or soil.

'English Roseum' ('Roseum Pink'). −25°F. Erect habit to 6 ft. Lavender-pink blooms. Midseason. Tough and undemanding. Heat tolerant.

'Fastuosum Flore Pleno'. −15°F. Open, rounded habit to 6 ft. Lavender-blue double flowers marked with gold blotch. Flower center is filled with small, lavender, petal-like structures. Midseason. Dependable old-timer. Tolerates heat and sun.

'Furnivall's Daughter'. −10°F. To 5 ft. Tall trusses of bright pink flowers with cherry red blotch. Midseason.

'Ginny Gee.' −10°F. Striking 2-ft. dwarf with small leaves, dense growth. Small pink bells are dotted inside and out with white. Profuse bloom in early midseason. Heat tolerant.

'Gomer Waterer'. −15°F. To 5 ft. Pink buds open to white flowers with yellowish green blotch. Late midseason. Old-timer. Tolerates sun; endures heat and drought better than most.

'Holden'. −15°F. To 4 ft. Compact plant. Rose red flowers marked with deeper red. Midseason. Heat tolerant.

'Janet Blair'. −15°F. To 5 ft.; vigorous and spreading. Large, ruffled flowers blend pastel pink, cream, white, and gold; rounded trusses. Midseason to late. Heat tolerant.

'Jean Marie de Montague'. −5°F. To 5 ft., with brilliant scarlet flowers and attractive foliage. Midseason. Heat tolerant.

'Johnny Bender'. −5°F. To 4−5 ft. Glossy dark green leaves set off blood red flowers. Midseason.

'Kluis Sensation'. −5°F. Compact grower to 5 ft. Small, tight trusses of dark red, faintly spotted flowers. Midseason.

'Lee's Dark Purple'. −15°F. To 6 ft. Dark purple blossoms with greenish blotch. Wavy-edged dark green leaves. Early midseason.

'Lem's Stormcloud'. −15°F. To 5 ft. Large, erect trusses of bright red flowers; blossoms flare out flat when fully open. Late midseason.

'Leo'. −5°F. To 5 ft., well clothed in large dark green leaves. Rounded to dome-shaped trusses packed with rich cranberry red blooms. Midseason to late.

'Loder's White'. 0°F. Shapely growth to 5 ft. Tall trusses of white flowers with faint yellow throat and light pink picotee edge; blooms turn pure white as they age. Midseason. Blooms freely even when young. Best white for most regions. Heat tolerant.

'Lord Roberts'. −15°F. To 5 ft. Handsome dark green foliage and rounded trusses of red flowers spotted in black. Midseason. Plants grown in sun are more compact, bloom more profusely.

'Marchioness of Lansdowne'. −15°F. Spreading, open growth to 5−6 ft. Rosy violet flowers with a dark blotch and white stamens. Midseason to late.

'Mars'. −15°F. To 4 ft. Dark red. Late midseason. Handsome form, foliage, flowers.

'Molly Ann'. −10°F. To 3 ft. Compact grower with roundish leaves. Rose pink flowers in upright trusses. Early midseason. Heat tolerant.

'Mrs. Furnivall'. −15°F. To 4 ft. Compact-growing plant. Tight, round trusses of light pink flowers with deep red blotch. Late midseason.

'Nova Zembla'. −25°F. To 5 ft. Bears profuse red flowers in midseason. Takes heat.

'Patty Bee'. −10°F. To 1½ ft. Small plant, well clothed with small (1-in.-wide) leaves that turn dark red in winter. Loose trusses of lemon yellow flowers cover even young plants. Early midseason.

'Pink Pearl'. −5°F. To 6 ft.; open and rangy if not pruned. Tall trusses of rose pink flowers. Midseason. Grows and blooms dependably.

'PJM'. −25°F. Dense, bushy plant to 4 ft. Exceptional purplish pink flowers; profuse bloom. Flowers early, when foliage still has its mahogany winter color. Takes heat as well as cold. Can be sheared into a hedge.

'President Lincoln'. −25°F. To 6 ft. Lilac-toned lavender pink with bronze blotch. Midseason to late.

'Purple Splendour'. −5°F. To 5 ft. Informal habit. Ruffled-looking deep purple blossoms with black-purple blotch. Late midseason. Tolerates sun and heat.

'Ramapo'. −20°F. Dense, spreading growth to 2 ft. in sun, taller in shade. New growth is dusty blue green, maturing to dark green. Pinkish violet flowers cover plant in early midseason. Useful rock garden or low border plant.

'Roseum Elegans'. −25°F. To 6 ft. Olive green foliage. Lilac-pink flowers. Midseason to late. Tolerates both heat and cold. Very tough.

'Sapphire'. −5°F. To 2½ ft. Twiggy, rounded, and dense, with tiny, narrow gray-green leaves. Small, azalealike light blue flowers. Early midseason.

'Sappho'. −15°F. To 6 ft. Easy to grow; gangly without pruning. Use at back of border. White blossoms with a dark purple eye. Midseason. Heat tolerant.

'Scarlet Wonder'. −15°F. Outstanding, compact dwarf to 2 ft. Shiny, quilted-looking foliage forms backdrop for many bright scarlet blossoms. Midseason.

'Scintillation'. −15°F. To 5 ft. Compact plant covered in lustrous dark green leaves. Blossoms come in rounded trusses; they open pastel pink with deep pink markings in throat, then age to brownish pink. Midseason. Heat tolerant.

'Trilby'. −15°F. To 5 ft. Deep burgundy flowers with black markings. Matte green leaves; red stems. Midseason.

'Trude Webster'. −10°F. To 5 ft. Strong-growing plant with large leaves. Huge trusses of pure pink flowers in midseason. One of the best pinks. Heat tolerant.

'Unique'. −5°F. To 4 ft.; oustanding neat, rounded, compact habit. Bright pink buds open to tight, rounded trusses of creamy pale yellow blossoms. Early midseason. Heat tolerant. ▶

Rhododendron 'Janet Blair'   *Rhododendron* 'Nova Zembla'   *Rhododendron mucronulatum*   *Rhododendron* 'Patty Bee'   *Rhododendron* 'Pink Pearl'

'Van Nes Sensation'. −5°F. To 5 ft. Strong grower. Large trusses of pale lilac flowers. Midseason.

'Virginia Richards'. 0°F. Upright, compact habit to 4 ft. Flowers open unspotted pink, then turn yellow with a dark red blotch. Big, deep green, strongly veined leaves. Early to midseason.

'Vulcan'. −15°F. To 5 ft. Bright brick red flowers. Late midseason. New leaves often grow past flower buds, partially hiding them. Heat tolerant.

R. carolinianum. CAROLINA RHODODENDRON. Zones US, MS, LS; 8–5. Hardy to −25°F. Native to mountains of the Carolinas and Tennessee. To 3–6 ft. tall and as broad or broader, with tight clusters of pink flowers in midseason. Leaves turn purplish in cold winters. 'Carolina Gold' is an upright grower with yellowish white blossoms. 'White Perfection' has light pink buds that open to white flowers; it is more compact than the basic species (to 4 ft. high and wide) and bears younger and more profusely.

R. catawbiense. CATAWBA RHODODENDRON. Zones US, MS, LS; 8–1. Hardy to −25°F. Native to mountains from West Virginia to Alabama. To 5 ft. tall and wide, eventually much larger. Lavender (or sometimes reddish purple) flowers in midseason. An ancestor of many heat-tolerant selections.

R. chapmanii. CHAPMAN'S RHODODENDRON. Zones US, MS, LS, CS; 9–5. Hardy to −5°F. Native to pine woods in northwest Florida. Very upright grower to 4 ft. (eventually 6 ft.) tall. Round clusters (up to 4 in. across) of spotted or flecked, rose pink blossoms with distinctive dark anthers. Shiny, oblong leaves to just 3 in. long. Endangered species; be careful to buy only nursery-propagated plants. Heat tolerant. Midseason.

R. maximum. ROSEBAY RHODODENDRON. Zones US, MS; 8–1. Hardy to −25°F. Native from New England to Georgia and Alabama; the state flower of West Virginia. Large, handsome, densely foliaged shrub or small tree with open habit. Usually 10–15 ft. tall, but may reach 30 ft. Striking, satiny dark green leaves to 4–10 in. long. Small clusters of many rose or purplish pink, 1½-in. flowers with white centers and green freckles. Tolerates full shade. Late to very late.

R. mucronulatum. Zones US, MS. Hardy to −15°F. From China, Mongolia, Korea, Japan. Deciduous, azalealike rhododendron. Open, thin growth to 5 ft.; very early bloom makes up for bare, leggy branches. Small clusters of bright purple flowers. Form 'Cornell Pink' also available.

R. yakushimanum. Zones US, MS, LS; 8–5. Hardy to −25°F. From Japan. Forms a tight mound to 1–4 ft. high. New growth has a feltlike coating of white hairs; older leaves are glossy dark green above, brown and felted beneath. Clear pink bell-like flowers age to white. Late midseason. Selections include 'Ken Janeck', a large (to 4-ft.) form with intense pink flowers, and smaller-growing 'Yaku Angel', with pink-tinged buds opening to pure white flowers. There are also a number of hybrids that perform as well in cold climates as they do in milder ones. Among them are 'Mardi Gras', 'Yaku Sunrise', and 'Yaku Princess' (this last selection is part of a good series of hybrids, all with names including royal titles). The three hybrids just mentioned all have blooms in white or pink-tinged white.

KINDS OF AZALEAS

Azaleas are divided into evergreen and deciduous categories. The following describes evergreen hybrids first, then deciduous hybrids and species.

Evergreen azaleas fall into more than a dozen groups, though an increasing number of hybrids have such mixed parentage that they don't fit conveniently into any category. The following list includes some of the most popular groups. Except as noted, bloom season is late winter or spring. Plants grown in greenhouses can be forced for winter bloom. Size varies considerably, but most of these slow-growing plants reach 2–5 ft. high and at least as wide.

Belgian Indica Hybrids. Zones TS; 12–9. These hybrids were originally developed for greenhouse forcing. Where winter lows don't dip below 20°F, many of them serve well as landscape plants. They are profuse bloomers with lush, thick foliage and typically semidouble or double, 2- to 3-in. blossoms. Among the most widely sold are 'Albert and Elizabeth', white with pink edges; 'California Sunset', salmon pink with white border; 'Chimes', dark red; 'Mardi Gras', salmon with white border; 'Mission Bells', red semidouble; 'Mme Alfred Sanders', cherry red; 'Orange Sanders', salmon orange; 'Orchidiflora', orchid pink; 'Paul Schame', salmon. Three choices with pendent growth are 'Red Poppy', deep purple 'Violetta', and orange-red 'William Van Orange'; all are suitable for hanging baskets.

Beltsville Hybrids. Zones US, MS, LS, CS; 9–6. Hardy to 0°F. Similar to the Glenn Dale Hybrids. 'Casablanca Improved' is a large white single; 'Eureka' and 'Guy Yerkes' have pink flowers. Selection 'H. H. Hume' has single white blossoms with a yellowish throat; 'Polar Bear' is an exceptionally hardy white.

Carla Hybrids. Zones MS, LS, CS; 9–7. Probably hardy to 0°F. Bred at North Carolina State University for resistance to *Phytophthora*. These midseason bloomers include deep rose pink 'Adelaide Pope', double light pink 'Elaine', deep rose red 'Emily', deep rose pink 'Sunglow', and bright red 'Wolfpack Red'.

Encore Hybrids. Zones LS, CS; 9–5. Probably hardy to 5–10°F. Introduced by Flowerwood Nursery in Mobile, Alabama, these azaleas promise flowers in both fall and spring. They include soft purple 'Autumn Amethyst', deep pink 'Autumn Cheer', salmon pink 'Autumn Coral', orange-red 'Autumn Embers', vivid pink 'Autumn Rouge', and purple 'Autumn Royalty'. They are still too new to have been evaluated conclusively, but questions do exist about their cold hardiness, and they may not be well suited to the Upper and Middle South.

Gable Hybrids. Zones US, MS, LS, CS; 9–5. Bred to produce azaleas of Kurume type that take 0 to −5°F temperatures. In the Upper South, they may lose some leaves during winter. Bloom heavily in midseason. Frequently sold pink selections include 'Caroline Gable' (bright pink), 'Louise Gable', 'Pioneer', and 'Rosebud'. Among purple choices are 'Herbert', 'Purple Splendor', and the less rangy 'Purple Splendor Compacta'. 'Rose Greeley' has white blossoms.

Girard Hybrids. Zones US, MS, LS, CS; 9–5. Hardy to −5°F or somewhat lower. Handsome-foliaged plants bred for extra cold hardiness; originated from Gable crosses. Selections include 'Girard's Crimson', with bright

Rhododendron 'Unique'

Rhododendron yakushimanum 'Yaku Angel'

Kurume Hybrid Azalea 'Coral Bells'

Kurume Hybrid Azalea 'Sherwood Red'

Southern Indica Hybrid Azalea 'George Lindley Taber'

crimson red blooms and maroon fall foliage; 'Girard's Fuchsia', reddish purple flowers; 'Girard's Hot Shot', with orange-red blossoms as well as orange-red fall and winter foliage; 'Girard's National Beauty', rose pink blooms; and 'Girard's Roberta', double pink, 3-in. blooms.

Glenn Dale Hybrids. Zones US, MS, LS, CS; 9–6. Hardy to 0°F. Developed primarily for hardiness, though they do drop some leaves in cold winters. Some are tall and rangy, others low and compact. Growth rate varies from slow to rapid. Some have small leaves like Kurume Hybrids; others have large leaves. Some familiar selections include orange 'Anchorite'; pale pink 'Aphrodite'; orange-red 'Buccaneer', 'Copperman', and 'Fashion'; white 'Everest' and 'Glacier'; 'Geisha', white with red stripes; 'Martha Hitchcock', white edged with magenta; and 'Treasure', white edged with pink.

Greenwood Hybrids. Zones US, MS, LS, CS; 9–6. Bred in Canby, Oregon. Most of these are compact, hardy plants bearing large double flowers. They were developed to take lows of about 0°F but will succeed in colder climates if you keep them from drying out—it is desiccation, not freezing, that does them in. Some of the most popular selections are 'Greenwood Orange'; 'Greenwood Rosebud', pink with a slight purple blush; 'Sherry', very deep red flowers and maroon winter foliage; 'Silver Streak', reddish purple flowers and white-edged leaves; and 'Sleigh Bells', single white flowers.

Kaempferi Hybrids. Zones US, MS, LS, CS; 9–6. From *R. kaempferi*, the torch azalea, a cold-hardy plant with orange-red flowers. These are hardier than Kurume Hybrids (to −15°F), with a taller, more open habit. Nearly leafless below 0°F. Profuse bloom. Available choices are salmon rose 'Fedora'; 'Holland', a late-season bloomer with large red flowers; and orange-red 'John Cairns'.

Kurume Hybrids. Zones US, MS, LS, CS; 9–5. Hardy to near 0°F. Compact, twiggy plants densely clothed in small, glossy leaves. Small flowers are borne in incredible profusion. Plants have mounded or tiered form, look handsome even out of bloom. Widely used in foundation plantings—to the point of cliché. Of the many available selections, these are among the most widely sold: pink 'Coral Bells', crimson 'Hexe', bright red 'Hershey's Red' and 'Hino-crimson', cerise red 'Hinodegiri', red-violet 'Sherwood Orchid', orange-red 'Sherwood Red', and white 'Snow'.

Kurume Hybrid Azalea 'Sherwood Orchid'

Monrovia Hybrids. Zones LS, CS; 10–8. Hardy to 10°F. Developed by Monrovia Nursery in Southern California, using Belgian Indica and Southern Indica azaleas as parents. They resemble Southern Indicas, with especially handsome, rich green foliage; form dense, 4- to 6-ft. mounds. Sun tolerant; thrive in warm, dry areas. 'Imperial Princess' has single pink flowers; 'Imperial Countess' bears deep salmon pink flowers; 'Imperial Queen' has double pink blooms. Midseason.

North Tisbury Hybrids. Zones US, MS, LS; 9–6. Hardy to −9°F. Most of these hybrids reflect the characteristics of a common prostrate-growing ancestor, *R. nakaharai*. Their dwarf, spreading habit and very late bloom (into midsummer) make them naturals for hanging baskets and ground covers. Some of the best selections are 'Alexander', with red-orange flowers and bronze fall foliage; pink-blossomed 'Pink Cascade'; and 'Red Fountain', with dark red-orange blooms that appear around the Fourth of July.

Pericat Hybrids. Zones US, MS, LS; 9–6. These were originally developed for greenhouse forcing but are about as hardy as Kurume Hybrids and look much the same, though flowers tend to be somewhat larger. Selections include light pink 'Mme Pericat', blush pink 'Sweetheart Supreme', and rose pink 'Twenty Grand'.

Robin Hill Hybrids. Zones US, MS, LS, CS; 9–6. Hardy to 0°F, probably lower. A large group with typically large flowers. Most are 2- to 4-ft. plants; some are more dwarf. Late bloom. There are so many good ones—several with "Robin Hill" in their names—that it's difficult to single out only a few. Try pink 'Betty Ann Voss'; 'Conversation Piece', pink with light center; 'Nancy of Robin Hill', pink with red blotch; red-orange 'Robin Hill Gillie'; and 'Hilda Niblett', with blossoms in a combination of light pink, deep pink, and white.

Rutherfordiana Hybrids. Zones CS, TS; 12–9. Greenhouse plants; also good in gardens where temperatures don't go below 20°F and midday shade can be provided. Bushy plants with handsome foliage. Medium-size blossoms may be single, semidouble, or double. Available selections include 'Alaska', white with chartreuse blotch; light orchid pink 'Constance'; brick red 'Dorothy Gish'; rosy red 'Firelight'; orchid pink 'L. J. Bobbink'; white 'Purity'; deep pink 'Rose Queen'; and 'White Gish', very pale pink fading to white.

Satsuki Hybrids. Zones MS, LS, CS; 9–7. Includes azaleas referred to as Gumpo and Macrantha Hybrids. Hardy to 5°F. Low-growing plants; some make nice ground covers. Bloom late, bearing large flowers. Popular selections include blush pink 'Bunkwa'; orange-red 'Flame Creeper'; white 'Gumpo'; rose pink 'Gumpo Pink' and 'Rosaeflora'; bright pink 'Hi Gasa' and 'Macrantha Pink'; salmon red 'Macrantha Red'; violet-red, white-centered 'Shinnyo-No-Tsuki'; and salmon pink 'Wakebisu'.

Southern Indica Hybrids. Zones MS, LS, CS; 9–7. Selected from Belgian Indica Hybrids for vigor and sun tolerance. Most take temperatures of 10–20°F, but some are damaged even at the upper end of that range. They generally grow faster, more vigorously, and taller than other kinds of evergreen azaleas. Used for massing and as specimens—as shrubs, standards, espaliers. Popular choices include carmine red 'Brilliant'; salmon pink 'Duc de Rohan'; 'Fielder's White';

Southern Indica Hybrid Azalea 'Formosa'

R

Mucronatum Hybrid 'Delaware Valley White'

Rhododendron austrinum

Rhododendron periclymenoides

Rhododendron prinophyllum

Rhododendron prunifolium

brilliant rose purple 'Formosa' (also sold as 'Coccinea', 'Phoenicia', 'Vanessa'); light pink 'George Lindley Taber'; deep salmon pink 'Imperial Countess'; rich pink 'Imperial Princess'; pink 'Imperial Queen'; 'Iveryana', white with orchid streaks; white 'Mrs. G. G. Gerbing' and 'White April'; bright orange 'Orange Pride'; orange-red 'President Claeys'; brilliant red 'Pride of Dorking'; deep rose pink 'Pride of Mobile'; and watermelon pink 'Southern Charm' (sometimes sold as 'Judge Solomon'). A selection grown largely for foliage color is 'Little John', a dense, rounded 6-ft. bush with burgundy leaves; its red flowers are borne only sparsely.

Other hybrids of note. These popular azaleas (all about 3–5 ft. high and wide) belong to other hybrid categories. 'Delaware Valley White' (heat zones 8–6) is a cold-hardy Mucronatum Hybrid; 'Elsie Lee' (heat zones 9–6) is a lovely semidouble lavender Shammarello Hybrid. Two double white selections (both suitable for heat zones 8–5) are 'Hardy Gardenia', a Linwood Hybrid, and 'Helen Curtis', a Shammarello Hybrid. 'Marian Lee' is a white-and-purple Back Acres Hybrid, 'Palestrina' (heat zones 8–3) a Vuykiana Hybrid featuring large white flowers with a yellow blotch.

DECIDUOUS AZALEA HYBRIDS AND SPECIES
Few deciduous shrubs can equal azaleas for showiness and range of color, and this has fueled the development of many excellent hybrids over the years. They offer the yellow, gold, peach, orange, and flaming red colors that are missing or rare among evergreen azaleas—and fall foliage is often brilliant orange red to maroon. Flowers of some are highly fragrant. Deciduous species (typically with blossoms 1–1½ in. across) are listed after the hybrids below. Many of these species are native to the South and are less fussy about soil and watering than evergreen types; they need a good amount of sun, however, and won't bloom well in full shade.

Aromi Hybrids. Zones MS, LS, CS; 8–6. Hardy to 10°F. Bred by Dr. Eugene Aromi of Mobile, Alabama, who wanted azaleas of Knap Hill–Exbury type that would tolerate long, hot summers. Crossing Exburys with Southern native species *R. austrinum*, *R. canescens*, *R. oblongifolium*, and *R. viscosum* produced azaleas with large trusses of striking, almost incandescent blooms. All are very heat tolerant. They are upright growers to 12–15 ft. (though they may reach only half that height in the Upper South). Most have fragrant flowers. Selections include 'Aromi Sunny Side Up', golden yellow with a darker, egg yolk–yellow blotch; 'Aromi Sunrise', orange-red buds opening to light orange blossoms with a deep orange center; 'Carousel', pale pink with prominent gold blotch; 'Centerpiece', white with yellow blotch; and 'Sunstruck', pale yellow buds opening to lemon yellow blooms with a dark yellow blotch. Midseason.

Choptank River Hybrids. Zones US, MS, LS; 8–5. Hardy to −20°F. Natural hybrids of *R. atlanticum* and *R. periclymenoides* found near the Choptank River in Maryland by Mr. and Mrs. Julian Hill. Grow 3–6 ft. tall. Fragrant flowers in midseason. Selections include: 'C-1', white, spreads by rooting stems; 'Choptank River Belle', white flushed with pink; 'Choptank Rose', rose-and-white blooms with golden blotch; 'Choptank Yellow', yellow with golden blotch; and 'Nacoochee', white and pale pink.

Confederate Series Hybrids. Zones US, MS, LS, CS; 9–6. Hardy to −10°F. Similar to Aromi Hybrids. Bred for heat tolerance by Bob Schwindt, Tom Dodd, Jr., and Tom Dodd III of Semmes, Alabama. Crossing the Knap Hill–Exbury Hybrid 'Hotspur Yellow' with *R. austrinum* produced (among others) the following, all with fragrant blossoms: 'Admiral Semmes', large yellow flowers with a deep yellow blotch; 'Colonel Mosby', frilly salmon pink blooms with a yellow flare; 'J.E.B. Stuart', rose pink with yellow blotch. Midseason.

Ghent Hybrids. Zones US, MS; 8–5. Many are hardy to −25°F. Upright growers, variable in height. Flowers are generally 1½–2¼ in. wide. Colors include shades of yellow, orange, umber, red, and pink. Two double-flowered selections are soft pink 'Corneille' and light yellow 'Narcissiflora'. Midseason.

Knap Hill–Exbury Hybrids. Zones US, MS, some in LS; most in 7–5. Hardy to −25°F. These extraordinary hybrids come from crosses made in England, first at Knap Hill, then at Lionel de Rothschild's estate at Exbury.

Plants are spreading to upright, reaching 4–6 ft. tall. Midseason to late bloom. Huge trusses of large (3- to 5-in.-wide) flowers stand atop the foliage; blossoms are sometimes ruffled or fragrant. Colors include white, pink, orange, yellow, salmon, and red, often with contrasting blotches. Among the best are pink 'Cannon's Double'; orange 'Gibraltar' and 'Hotspur Orange'; double deep pink 'Homebush'; yellow 'Hotspur Yellow'; golden tangerine 'Klondyke'; and 'Oxydol', white with yellow markings. 'Gibraltar' and 'Homebush' accept the heat of the Lower South; most of the others do not.

Knap Hill–
Exbury Hybrid
Azalea 'Klondyke'

Mollis Hybrids. Zones US, MS; 7–6. Hardy to −25°F. Hybrids of *R. molle* and *R. japonicum*. Upright growth to 4–5 ft. Flowers 2½–4 in. wide, in clusters of 7 to 13. Colors range from chrome yellow through bright red. Very heavy bloom in midseason. Leaves have a light skunky fragrance when new, but they turn a lovely yellow to orange in autumn. Blooms of 'Hamlet' are yellowish pink with a reddish orange blotch; 'Koster's Brilliant Red' has bright orange-red flowers; 'Radiant' is deep red.

Viscosum Hybrids. Zones US, MS. Hardy to −15°F. Hybrids of Mollis azaleas and *R. viscosum*. Size varies from 3 to 8 ft. Flowers have colors of Mollis types but wonderful clove fragrance of *R. viscosum*. Late.

R. alabamense. ALABAMA AZALEA. Zones MS, LS; 9–7. Hardy to −5°F. Native to Alabama and Georgia. Grows 5–6 ft. tall and spreads by suckering to form colonies. Highly fragrant white flowers, usually blotched with yellow. Early.

R. arborescens. SWEET AZALEA. Zones US, MS, LS; 9–4. Hardy to −10°F. Native to mountains from Pennsylvania to Alabama. Erect, open shrub to 8 ft. (possibly 20 ft.) tall. Fragrant white to pale pink, 1½- to 2-in. flowers appear late, after leaves have expanded.

R. atlanticum. COAST AZALEA. Zones US, MS, LS, CS; 9–4. Hardy to −15°F. Native from Delaware to South Carolina. Suckering shrub to 3–6 ft. tall. Fragrant, somewhat sticky, white to pink flowers bloom early, before or as leaves expand.

R. austrinum. FLORIDA FLAME AZALEA. Zones MS, LS, CS; 10–6. Hardy to 5°F. Native to northern and western Florida and southern parts of Georgia, Alabama, Mississippi. To 8–10 ft. tall, with fragrant flowers that may be pale yellow, cream, pink, orange, or red in color. One of the easiest native azaleas to grow. Tolerates heat, humidity, drought. Early bloom. 'Millie Mac' has reddish orange buds opening to bright yellow flowers edged in white; 'My Mary' bears pure yellow blooms; 'Pretty One' has salmon red flowers blotched yellow.

R. bakeri (R. cumberlandense). CUMBERLAND AZALEA. Zones US, MS; 8–5. Hardy to −15°F. Native to mountains of Kentucky, Virginia, Tennessee, Georgia, Alabama. Grows 3–8 ft. tall. Flowers about 1¾ in. wide; typically red, sometimes yellow or orange. Late midseason. Does not like long, hot summers. Flowers of 'Camp's Red' are a strong red in the mountains, a lighter red at lower elevations. Blossoms of 'Sunlight' blend deep orange-red and gold; its leaves turn bright plum red in fall.

R. calendulaceum. FLAME AZALEA. Zones US, MS, LS; 8–4. Hardy to −25°F. Native to mountain regions from southern Pennsylvania to Georgia and Florida. Grows to 4–8 ft. or taller. Clusters of 2-in.-wide flowers in yellow, red, orange, or scarlet. Late. A very important parent of many hybrid deciduous azaleas. Dislikes extended summer heat and drought. 'Cherokee' bears soft apricot blossoms with red stamens; 'Currahee' has striped red-and-yellow buds that open to orange blooms bordered with rosy pink. 'Soquee River' produces big trusses of orange, red, and yellow blooms. Hybrid 'Chattooga' has ruffled pink flowers with a yellow blotch.

R. canescens. PIEDMONT AZALEA. Zones US, MS, LS, CS; 9–4. Hardy to −5°F. Native from North Carolina to Texas. Large (to 10-ft.), suckering shrub with fragrant white to pink or rose flowers. Early. Sun or shade.

R. eastmanii. Zones MS, LS. Possibly hardy to −10°F. Recently identified azalea native to South Carolina. Looks much like *R. alabamense* but blooms later—in midseason, after the leaves have expanded. Stems are noticeably hairy. Intensely sweet-scented flowers are white (sometimes tinged pink) with a yellow blotch. In the wild, this rare species has been found in both dry and wet sites, on bluffs and lowlands, and in shady as well as sunnier spots. Do not disturb native populations.

R. flammeum. OCONEE AZALEA. Zones US, MS, LS; 9–5. Hardy to −15°F. Native to South Carolina, Georgia. Fairly compact to 6 ft., with clusters of 1¾-in. flowers in midseason. Colors range from red and pink to yellow or orange. Resembles *R. calendulaceum* but is more tolerant of heat and drought.

R. oblongifolium. TEXAS AZALEA. Zones US, MS, LS; 9–6. Hardy to −5°F. Native to East Texas, Oklahoma, and Arkansas. To 6 ft. tall. Small (¾- to 1-in.), slightly fragrant white flowers appear in midseason, after leaves emerge. Tolerates drought better than most other deciduous azalea species.

R. occidentale. WESTERN AZALEA. Zones US, MS; 8–6. Hardy to −5°F. Native to mountains and foothills of California and Oregon. Erect growth to 6–8 ft. high. Clusters of fragrant, funnel-shaped flowers, midseason to late. Color varies from white to pinkish white, with a yellow blotch; blossoms of some kinds are heavily marked with carmine rose. This species doesn't like extended summer heat and does best in the Upper South. Hybrids between *R. occidentale* and Mollis Hybrids are more heat tolerant and have a wider color range. Among these are 'Jock Brydon', bearing fragrant white flowers with a striking orange flare; 'Lawrence Olson', with soft pink, very fragrant blooms with a golden orange flare; and 'Washington State Centennial', sporting big, sweet-scented, frilly flowers in light orange yellow marked with a large yellow flare.

R. periclymenoides (R. nudiflorum). PINXTERBLOOM AZALEA. Zones US, MS, LS; 8–5. Hardy to −15°F. Native from Massachusetts to Ohio and North Carolina. Suckering shrub grows 2–3 ft. high, sometimes much taller. Pale pink to deep pink, fragrant, 1½-in. flowers appear in midseason, as leaves expand. 'Paxton's Blue' has showy lavender-blue flowers.

R. prinophyllum (R. roseum). ROSESHELL AZALEA. Zones US, MS, LS; 8–3. Hardy to −25°F. Native from southern Quebec to Virginia, west to Missouri and Oklahoma. To 4–8 ft. tall, occasionally much taller; bright pink (sometimes white), 1½-in. flowers with strong clove fragrance. Blooms in midseason, before or as leaves emerge. 'Marie Hoffman' has clear pink blossoms.

R. prunifolium. PLUMLEAF AZALEA. Zones US, MS, LS, CS; 9–5. Hardy to −15°F. Native to Georgia and Alabama. To 10 ft., with orange-red to bright red, 1½- to 1¾-in. flowers. This is the signature plant of Callaway Gardens in Pine Mountain, Georgia. One of the latest azaleas, blooming in July and August. 'Apricot Glow' has orange flowers, 'Pine Prunifolium' bright red ones. Hybrid 'Summer Lyric' bears pink blossoms with a yellow throat.

R. schlippenbachii. ROYAL AZALEA. Zones US, MS; 7–5. Hardy to −20°F. Native to Korea and Manchuria. Densely branched shrub to 6–8 ft. Leaves in whorls of five at tips of branches. Blooms in early midseason as leaves are expanding, producing large (2- to 4-in.), highly fragrant, pure light pink flowers in clusters of three to six. A white form is also available. Good fall color: yellow, orange, scarlet, crimson. Protect from full sun.

R. serrulatum. SWEET AZALEA, SOUTHERN SWAMP AZALEA. Zones US, MS, LS, CS; 9–1. Native from Georgia and Florida to Louisiana. Tall shrub (to 12–20 ft.) with reddish branches. Extremely fragrant white flowers, sometimes tinged cream, pale pink, or pale violet, bloom among new foliage. Small (to 3-in.-long), distinctly toothed leaves. Blooms very late—from July into September.

R. vaseyi. PINKSHELL AZALEA. Zones US, MS, LS; 8–4. Hardy to −20°F. Native to mountains of North Carolina. Upright plant with irregular, spreading form. To 10–15 ft. Blooms before leaf-out, bearing light pink, 1½- to

2-in. flowers in clusters of five to eight. Midseason. 'Pinkerbell' has deep pink blossoms, 'White Find' fragrant white blooms with a greenish yellow blotch.

R. viscosum. SWAMP AZALEA. Zones US, MS, LS, CS; 10–1. Hardy to −25°F. Native to damp or wet ground, Maine to Alabama. To 5–8 ft. tall. Flowers are white (sometimes pink), 2 in. long, sticky on the outside, with a powerful clove scent. Blooms late, often in June. Hybrids include 'Jolie Madame', fragrant rosy pink flowers with a gold blotch; 'Lemon Drop', peach buds opening to lemon-scented pale yellow blooms; and 'Peaches and Cream', yellowish white flowers with a purplish pink margin and yellow blotch.

NATIVE WILD HONEYSUCKLES. *The South is home to almost all of the deciduous azaleas indigenous to North America. Many are intensely fragrant (hence their common name, wild honeysuckle); their leaves may have brilliant fall colors. Purchase only nursery-propagated plants, and plant them in small groves or drifts in filtered light below native trees. Native wild honeysuckles include* Rhododendron alabamense, R. arborescens, R. atlanticum, R. austrinum, R. bakeri, R. calendulaceum, R. canescens, R. flammeum, R. oblongifolium, R. periclymenoides, R. prinophyllum, R. prunifolium, R. serrulatum, R. vaseyi, *and* R. viscosum. ❖

RHODOPHIALA bifida

OXBLOOD LILY

Amaryllidaceae

PERENNIAL FROM BULB

🌿 MS, LS, CS, TS H 12–7

☀️ FULL SUN

💧 REGULAR WATER DURING GROWTH AND BLOOM

Rhodophiala bifida

Native to Argentina, this tough-as-nails amaryllis relative was introduced into the Texas Hill Country by German settlers in the 1850s. Narrow, foot-long leaves emerge in fall, persist through winter and spring, and then die down. In August or September, following a rain, clusters of blood red, 2-in.-long flowers appear atop leafless foot-tall stalks.

Set bulbs out in spring, planting them 4 in. deep, 1½ ft. apart. The plant multiplies naturally in just about any well-drained soil. It likes moisture during winter and spring, but needs no water in summer. An old Southern favorite and a popular passalong plant.

RHODOTYPOS scandens

BLACK JETBEAD

Rosaceae

DECIDUOUS SHRUB

🌿 US, MS, LS H 8–5

☀️◐ FULL SUN OR LIGHT SHADE

💧 REGULAR WATER

☠️ FRUITS ARE POISONOUS IF INGESTED

Rhodotypos scandens

Native to Japan and China; longtime favorite in Southern gardens. Trouble-free shrub for light shade or tough soil conditions, with interesting, showy flowers and fruits. Grows moderately fast to 6 ft. tall and wide (often much more in the wild), with spreading branches that leaf out early in spring. Leaves are bright green, oval, prominently veined and toothed, to about 4 in. long and 2 in. wide. Single white flowers, 2 in. across, appear in late spring and early summer, followed by pea-size, jet black, shiny berries, four per cluster, in fall and persisting through winter. Fruits are quite toxic.

Thin out overcrowded mature plants by cutting back old branches to base after flowering.

RHOEO spathacea. See TRADESCANTIA spathacea

R

RHUBARB

Polygonaceae

PERENNIAL

US, MS 8–1, EXCEPT AS NOTED

PARTIAL SHADE IN HOTTEST CLIMATES

REGULAR WATER

LEAVES ARE POISONOUS IF INGESTED; USE LEAF STEMS ONLY

Rhubarb

Just as many Northerners have never tried black-eyed peas, many Southerners have never partaken of rhubarb *(Rheum × cultorum)*. There are a couple of good reasons for this. First, the plant grows best where winters are long and cold—a condition met only in the Upper South and cooler parts of the Middle South. Second, most garden centers here don't carry rhubarb, so Southerners usually have to start with divisions ordered through the mail.

Rhubarb bears big, crinkled leaves borne on thick, typically reddish stalks. Leaves are toxic if eaten, but the stalks have a delicious, sweet-tart flavor and are used for sauces, pies, and preserves (strawberry-rhubarb pie is a real treat). Flowers are insignificant, held in spikelike clusters. Preferred selections include 'Cherry' ('Crimson Cherry'), 'MacDonald', and 'Strawberry', all producing red stalks; and 'Victoria', which produces green stalks.

Plant divisions (each containing at least one bud) in late winter or early spring. Loosen the soil to a depth of 1 ft. and work in lots of organic matter. Set the divisions 1–2 in. deep and 3–4 ft. apart. After the plants come up, sprinkle ⅛ cup of 10-10-10 fertilizer around each plant and water it in. Keep plants well watered and mulch them to keep the soil cool.

Let plants grow for two full seasons before you begin harvesting stalks. After that, harvest stalks for 4 to 5 weeks in spring; older, huskier plants can be harvested for up to 8 weeks. To harvest stalks, grasp them near the base of the plant and pull sideways and then outward; do not cut stalks, as this leaves a stub that will decay. Never remove all the leaves from a single plant; stop harvesting when slender stalks appear. After the final harvest, feed and water freely. Cut out any blossom stalks that appear.

In the Lower South, treat rhubarb as an annual. Set out divisions in fall for winter-to-spring harvest. 'Victoria' is the recommended selection for this treatment.

RHUS

SUMAC

Anacardiaceae

EVERGREEN AND DECIDUOUS SHRUBS AND TREES

ZONES VARY BY SPECIES

FULL SUN, EXCEPT AS NOTED

LITTLE TO MODERATE WATER

Rhus typhina

Though gardeners frequently dismiss them as weeds, sumacs can make fine ornamentals. Most display brilliant fall color and (on female plants) showy clusters of berries that attract birds. All species thrive in almost any well-drained soil and tolerate drought with ease. On the down side, most sumacs sucker freely—especially if their roots have been disturbed by cultivation—and they can be quite invasive. They are best used in naturalized areas.

R. aromatica. FRAGRANT SUMAC. Deciduous shrub. Zones US, MS, LS, CS; 9–1. Native to eastern North America. Fast-growing plant to 3–5 ft. tall, sprawling 5 ft. or wider. Three-leafleted leaves to 3 in. long are fragrant when brushed against or crushed. Foliage turns red in fall. Tiny yellowish flowers in spring; small red fruit. Coarse bank cover, ground cover for poor or dry soils. 'Gro-Low' grows 2–3 ft. high, 6–8 ft. wide. 'Green Globe' is dense and rounded, to 6 ft. high and wide.

R. copallina. SHINING SUMAC. Deciduous shrub or small tree. Zones US, MS, LS, CS, TS; 12–1. Native to the eastern U.S. Grows quite fast to 10–25 ft. tall, becoming very broad as it matures, with a picturesque flat top. Highly ornamental—but unsuitable for small gardens, as it produces suckers and self-sows freely, forming large colonies. Shiny dark green leaves are divided featherwise into 9 to 21 leaflets. Fall color varies from plant to plant, so purchase in autumn for a reliable display of rich crimson, red-purple, or scarlet. Bears showy chartreuse flower spikes in summer, followed by fuzzy clusters of crimson fruits that persist into winter. Particularly well adapted to dry, poor, rocky soils.

R. glabra. SMOOTH SUMAC. Deciduous shrub or tree. Zones US, MS, LS, CS; 9–1. Native to much of North America. Upright grower to 10 ft., sometimes treelike to 20 ft. Spreads widely by suckers; in the wild, forms large patches. Looks much like *R. typhina* and has the same garden uses, but usually grows lower and does not have velvety branches. Leaves divided into 11 to 23 tooth-edged, rather narrow, 2- to 5-in.-long leaflets that are deep green above, whitish beneath; foliage turns scarlet in fall. Inconspicuous flowers in early summer are followed by showy clusters of scarlet fruits that remain on the bare branches well into winter. Leaves of 'Laciniata' are deeply cut and slashed, giving the plant an almost fernlike appearance.

R. trilobata. SQUAWBUSH, SKUNKBUSH. Deciduous shrub. Zones US, MS, LS; 9–6. Native from Illinois westward to Texas and California, north to Washington. Similar in most details to *R. aromatica*, but most people find the scent of the bruised leaves unpleasant. Clumping habit makes it a natural low hedge. Brilliant yellow to red fall color.

R. typhina. STAGHORN SUMAC. Deciduous shrub or tree. Zones US, MS, LS; 8–1. Native to eastern North America. Upright to 15 ft. (sometimes 30 ft.) tall, spreading much wider by suckers. Very similar to *R. glabra*, but the branches have a velvety coat of short brown hairs—much like antlers of a deer "in velvet." Leaves are divided into 11 to 31 toothed leaflets, to 5 in. long; they are deep green above, grayish beneath, turns yellow-orange to rich red in fall. About 4- to 8-in.-long clusters of tiny greenish blooms show in early summer, followed by clusters of fuzzy crimson fruits that hang on all winter, gradually turning brown. 'Laciniata', known as cutleaf staghorn sumac, is a female selection with deeply cut leaflets; it grows 10–12 ft. tall. 'Dissecta' is similar. 'Tiger Eyes', to 6 ft. tall and wide, has deeply cut golden leaves with pink leafstalks; foliage turns orange and scarlet in autumn.

Both *R. typhina* and *R. glabra* take extreme heat and cold. Big, divided leaves give tropical effect; fall show is brilliant (for best effect, plant among evergreens). Bare branches make a fine silhouette in winter; fruit is decorative. Both species colonize aggressively by root suckers—a potential problem, especially in small gardens. They grow well when confined to large containers.

R. virens. EVERGREEN SUMAC. Evergreen shrub. Zones LS, CS, TS; 12–8. Native to southeastern Arizona, New Mexico, Texas, Mexico. Generally makes a mounding clump about 6 ft. tall and wide, with lowest branches close to or touching ground, but can reach 12 ft. high and wide. Relatively slow growing. New leaves are often reddish; mature leaves (to 6 in. long, with five to nine leaflets) are glistening dark green, with purple winter tints. Honey-scented white flowers in late summer attract bees and butterflies and are followed by plump, fuzzy clusters of red fruits. Highly tolerant of dry, rocky, or chalky soils. Sun or light shade.

A RASH STATEMENT ABOUT SUMACS. *Contrary to popular belief, touching the leaves and stems of sumacs does not cause dermatitis. The real culprit is a similar-looking tree or shrub (native to swamps and other moist areas) called poison sumac (Toxicodendron vernix). This itchy villain can be easily identified by its greenish white berries (good sumacs have red berries) and the reddish stripe down the center of the compound leaf. Poison sumac and its dastardly cousins, poison ivy (T. radicans) and poison oak (T. diversilobum), were once considered members of the genus Rhus, but they have now been reclassified.* ❖

FOR INFORMATION ON YOUR CLIMATE ZONES

PLEASE SEE PAGES 28–38

RHYNCHELYTRUM
(Melinis)
NATAL RUBY GRASS

Poaceae (Gramineae)

PERENNIAL GRASSES

✿ TS ⊩ 12–6; ANYWHERE AS ANNUALS

☼ FULL SUN

💧 💧 MODERATE TO REGULAR WATER

Rhynchelytrum nerviglume 'Pink Crystals'

These tropical African grasses are just the ticket if you want lots of show in a sweltering site. They're easy to grow, adapt to any well-drained soil, tolerate drought once established, and are impervious to heat. Bloom in summer, when nodding, pinkish, 3- to 4-in.-long plumes rise above the clumps of slender, arching blue-green leaves. Excellent complements to agaves, yuccas, and salvias. Great in drifts; also make good container subjects. Though short lived, they're easy to start from seed and are often grown as annuals. They reseed rampantly.

R. nerviglume. RUBY GRASS. To 2–2½ ft. tall, up to 1½ ft. wide. Coral pink plumes appear in June and fade to silvery pink by September. 'Pink Crystals' has bright ruby plumes.

R. repens. NATAL GRASS. Similar to above but shorter (to just 1–2 ft. tall). Billowy clouds of soft pink plumes fade to cream and tan.

RIBBON GRASS. See PHALARIS arundinacea picta

RIBES
FLOWERING CURRANT

Grossulariaceae (Saxifragaceae)

EVERGREEN SHRUBS

✿ ZONES VARY BY SPECIES

☼ ◐ FULL SUN OR PARTIAL SHADE

💧 💧 MODERATE TO REGULAR WATER

Ribes sanguineum

Fruiting currants aren't grown commercially in the South, as they don't care for our climate. The following ornamental species, however, are definitely worth a try; all offer a nice flower show, and female plants of some species bear attractive fruits. Note that all are alternate hosts of white pine blister rust and may be banned in some areas; rust-resistant selections are being introduced. Mildew may also be a problem.

R. aureum. GOLDEN CURRANT. Zones US, MS, LS; 8–3. Native to the West, Midwest, and High Plains down to Texas and Oklahoma. Upright growth to 3–6 ft. tall and wide. Broad light green leaves to 3 in. long have lobed, toothed edges. Blooms in spring, with small, typically spicy-scented, bright yellow flowers in pendent, 1- to 2½-in. clusters. Blossoms are followed by berries that ripen from yellow to red to black. Tolerates most soils.

R. odoratum. CLOVE CURRANT. Zones US, MS, LS; 8–5. Native from South Dakota to western Texas, east to Minnesota and Arkansas. Similar in culture and appearance to *R. aureum,* but grows 6–8 ft. high and wide. Yellow spring flowers have a powerful, clovelike fragrance; black fruit is edible. 'Crandall' has large, shiny black fruit with a sweet-tart flavor; it resists rust and mildew.

R. sanguineum. RED FLOWERING CURRANT. Zones US, MS; 8–6. Native to the Coast Ranges from California to British Columbia. Rarely seen in the eastern U.S. Grows 5–12 ft. tall and wide. Maplelike dark green leaves to 2½ in. wide; very showy pink, red, or white flowers in spring, borne in drooping clusters of 10 to 30. Small, edible blue-black fruit. Doesn't thrive in extended summer heat. Prefers moist, well-drained soil but tolerates drought. 'Barrie Coate', 'Elk River Red', and 'King Edward VII' are red-flowering selections. Pink selections include 'Claremont', with two-tone blossoms aging to red, and 'Spring Showers'. 'Album', 'Inverness White', and 'White Icicle' have white flowers.

RICE PAPER PLANT. See TETRAPANAX papyriferus

RICINUS communis
CASTOR BEAN

Euphorbiaceae

TENDER SHRUB USUALLY GROWN AS ANNUAL

✿ CS, TS ⊩ 12–1

☼ FULL SUN

💧 REGULAR WATER

🔸 SEEDS (OR BEANS) ARE POISONOUS IF INGESTED

Ricinus communis 'Dwarf Red Spire'

Long a fixture in old Southern gardens, this bold, striking plant from Africa and Asia remains a source of dread for children with digestive problems: mothers still prescribe a spoonful of foul-tasting castor oil, pressed from the plant's seeds, to "clean you out." Enemies of the former Soviet Union had even more to fear. Ricin, a poison extracted from the seeds, was used by the KGB to dispatch selected targets (it is deadlier than cyanide). Fortunately, castor oil doesn't contain ricin—but ingesting just one of the beautifully marbled beans can cause serious illness, so do not plant this shrub where small children play.

Soak seeds in water overnight before planting in warm soil. Castor bean can provide a tall screen or accent in a hurry; it grows 6–15 ft. tall and half as wide in a single season. The plant overwinters in the Coastal and Tropical South and can become woody and treelike there. Large, coarsely lobed leaves are 1–3 ft. across on young, vigorous plants, smaller on older plants. Small white flowers are borne on foot-high stalks in summer; they're unimpressive but are followed by attractive, prickly seedpods. To prevent the toxic seeds from forming, pinch off the seedpods while they are still young. Selections include 'Carmencita', with deep purple leaves and leafstalks and coral red seedpods; 'Dwarf Red Spire', a lower grower (to 6 ft.) with red leaves and seedpods; 'Sanguineus', with blood red leaves and stems; and 'Zanzibarensis', sporting huge green leaves with white veins.

ROBINIA
LOCUST

Fabaceae (Leguminosae)

DECIDUOUS TREES AND SHRUBS

✿ US, MS, LS, CS ⊩ 9–1

☼ FULL SUN

💧 💧 LITTLE OR NO WATER TO MODERATE WATER

🔸 BARK, LEAVES, AND SEEDS ARE POISONOUS IF INGESTED

Robinia pseudoacacia

Fairly fast-growing plants, well adapted to hot, dry regions. Leaves are divided like feathers into many roundish leaflets. Clusters of white or pink, sweet pea–shaped flowers bloom from midspring to early summer, followed by beanlike pods about 4 in. long. Locust trees tolerate poor soil and can get by on little or no water, but they do have some drawbacks: wood is brittle, roots are aggressive, and plants often spread by suckers.

R. ×ambigua. Tree. Hybrid between *R. pseudoacacia* and *R. viscosa,* a seldom-grown pink-flowering locust. The following are the best-known selections.

'Decaisneana'. To 40–50 ft. tall, 20 ft. wide. Flowers are like those of *R. pseudoacacia,* but color is pale pink.

'Idaho' ('Idahoensis'). Shapely tree 25–40 ft. tall and 15–30 ft. wide. Reddish bronze new growth and bright rose pink flowers in 8-in. clusters make it one of the showiest locusts. Bears no seedpods. Thrives under arid conditions; good choice for western parts of Texas and Oklahoma.

'Purple Robe'. Resembles 'Idaho' but is more rounded, to 30–40 ft. tall and wide, with darker, purple-pink flowers, reddish bronze new growth. Blooms 2 weeks earlier and over a longer period.

R. hispida. ROSE ACACIA, BRISTLY LOCUST. Shrub. Native from Virginia and Kentucky to Georgia and Alabama. Small, showy shrub that will form colonies from root suckers. Extremely invasive in good soil. Grows to

7 ft. (sometimes 10 ft. tall), 8 ft. wide. Bristly stems; blue-green leaves to 10 in. long, with 7 to 15 leaflets. Rose or pale purplish pink flowers in dangling, 4-in. clusters in late spring. Tolerates dry, poor soils. Use on dry banks, in naturalized settings.

R. ×margaretta (R. ×slavinii). Tree. Hybrid between *R. hispida* and *R. pseudoacacia*. Grows at a moderate rate into an open, rounded tree 15–30 ft. high and wide. Bristly stems; leaves to 8 in. long, with up to 19 leaflets. Fragrant, ¾-in. pink flowers hang in clusters to 7 in. long. 'Flowering Globe' reaches 18 ft. tall and wide, with 8- to 10-in. clusters of dark pink flowers. 'Pink Cascade' ('Casque Rouge') reaches 15 ft. tall and wide, has purplish pink flowers and pinkish new growth.

R. pseudoacacia. BLACK LOCUST. Tree. Native to eastern and central U.S. Fast growth up to 40–75 ft. tall, 30–60 ft. wide, with rather sparse, open branching habit. Deeply furrowed brown bark. Thorny branches. Leaves divided into 7 to 19 leaflets, each 1–2 in. long. White, fragrant, ½- to ¾-in.-long flowers are held in dense, pendent clusters 4–8 in. long.

Robinia pseudoacacia

Black locust is little valued in its native territory, but it is a favorite in Europe. Rot-resistant wood is sought after for fence posts. Bees make delicious honey from the nectar of its flowers. The tree manufactures its own fertilizer through nitrogen-fixing root nodule bacteria and can colonize the poorest soil. Given some pruning and training in its early years, it can be a truly handsome flowering tree, but locust borer limits its usefulness in many regions; locust leaf miner is also a damaging pest, especially in the Upper and Middle South.

Often used as street tree, but not good in space between sidewalk and curb or under power lines. Wood is extremely hard; suckers are difficult to prune out where not wanted.

Recommended selections include the following.

'Frisia'. To 50 ft. tall, 25 ft. wide. New growth is nearly orange; mature leaves are yellow, turning greener in summer heat. Thorns and young wood are red.

'Pyramidalis' ('Fastigiata'). Narrow, columnar, to 50 ft. tall, 10 ft. wide.

'Tortuosa'. Slow grower to 50 ft. tall, 30 ft. wide, with twisted branches. Few flowers.

'Umbraculifera'. Dense and round headed, to 20 ft. tall and wide. Usually grafted 6–8 ft. high on another locust to create a living green lollipop. Very few flowers.

R. viscosa. CLAMMY LOCUST. Tree. To 40 ft. tall, 20 ft. wide. Rare. Native to eastern U.S., from North Carolina to Alabama. Leaves are divided into 12 to 24 leaflets. Deep pink flowers in 3-in. clusters appear in late spring. Common name refers to sticky glands on the stems, leafstalks, and seedpods.

ROCKCRESS. See ARABIS

ROCKET. See ARUGULA

ROCK ROSE. See PAVONIA lasiopetala

ROCKROSE. See CISTUS

ROCK SPIRAEA. See HOLODISCUS dumosus

RODGERSIA

Saxifragaceae

PERENNIALS

✿ US, MS, LS ⊩ 8–5, EXCEPT AS NOTED

◐ PARTIAL SHADE

💧 AMPLE WATER

Rodgersia aesculifolia

Native to China, Japan. Large plants with imposing leaves and clustered tiny flowers in plumes somewhat like those of astilbe; bloom in early to midsummer. Primary feature is handsome foliage, which often takes on bronze tones in

late summer. Plants spread by thick rhizomes, need rich soil. The various species hybridize freely. Dormant in winter; provide winter mulch in cold climates. Showy in moist woodland or bog gardens.

R. aesculifolia. To 6 ft. tall, 3 ft. wide. Leaves are divided like fingers of a hand into five to seven tooth-edged, 10-in. leaflets; they are similar to those of horsechestnut *(Aesculus)*. Shaggy brown hairs on flower stalks, leaf stems, major leaf veins. White flowers.

R. pinnata. Zones US, MS; 7–1. To 4 ft. tall, 2½ ft. wide. Leaves have five to nine 8-in. leaflets. Red flowers.

R. podophylla. To 5 ft. tall, 6 ft. wide. Coppery green leaves divided into five 10-in.-long leaflets. Creamy flowers.

R. sambucifolia. To 3 ft. high and wide. Leaves have up to 11 leaflets. Flat-topped clusters of white or pink flowers.

R. tabularis. See Astilboides tabularis

ROHDEA japonica

LILY OF CHINA, SACRED LILY

Liliaceae

PERENNIAL

✿ MS, LS, CS ⊩ 9–7

◐ PARTIAL OR LIGHT SHADE

◗ ● MODERATE TO REGULAR WATER

Rohdea japonica
'Miyako No Jo'

Native to Japan and China. Useful, low-maintenance plant for massing in a shade garden. Thick, arching or erect tufts of evergreen, leathery leaves, each to 2 ft. long, 2–3 in. wide. Pale yellow flowers bloom on small spikes in early spring; they're barely noticeable amid the foliage but are followed by showy red berries. Grows slowly; space plants about 1 ft. apart. Withstands neglect and is not fussy about soils. Combines well with ferns, hostas, hellebores. Several selections with leaves variegated in cream or white are available, including white-streaked 'Gunjaku'; white-edged 'Miyako No Jo'; 'Mure Suzume', with white streaking that intensifies toward leaf edges; and 'Suncrest', with a raised white area running down the center of each leaf.

ROSA

ROSE

Rosaceae

DECIDUOUS AND EVERGREEN SHRUBS AND VINES

✿ US, MS, LS, CS, TS, EXCEPT AS NOTED

☀ ◐ FULL SUN OR LIGHT SHADE

● REGULAR WATER, EXCEPT AS NOTED

Grandiflora Rose
'Queen Elizabeth'

The rose is undoubtedly the best-loved flower and most widely planted shrub in the South and all other temperate parts of the world. Although mostly deciduous, roses can be evergreen in mild climates. Centuries of hybridizing have brought us the broadest possible range of forms and colors. There are foot-high miniatures, tree-smothering climbers, flowers as tiny as a thumbnail or as large as a salad plate, and all possible variations in between. Red, pink, and white are the traditional colors, but you'll also find flowers in cream, yellow, orange, blends, and bicolors, as well as magenta, purple, lavender, and even tan and brown.

Despite the delicate appearance of their blooms, roses are often quite resilient plants. Growing them is not difficult, provided you choose types suited to your climate, buy healthy plants, locate and plant them properly, and attend to their basic needs—water, nutrients, pest and disease control, and pruning.

CLIMATE

When you're selecting the best roses for your garden, the American Rose Society rating of each plant is one factor to consider. Every year, the ARS rates modern roses (and an increasing number of old roses) on a scale of

1 to 10. The higher the rating, based on a national average of scores, the better the rose. The highest-rated roses are likely to do well in most climates and so are good choices for novice growers. But a rating does not tell the entire story: a rose with a low rating may flourish in certain regions but fail in others. The following tips will help guide your selection.

In areas with cool, wet springs, try to avoid roses having a great number of petals. Many of these tend to "ball," opening poorly or not at all. Also keep in mind that warm, humid summers of the South encourage foliage diseases—primarily mildew and black spot. Choose selections noted for disease resistance; then be sure to plant them in open areas where air circulation is good.

Our warm summers encourage vigorous growth, but flowers open rapidly—selections with few petals (under 30) may go from bud to flat-open blossom in several hours. Flowers with more petals take longer to open and stay attractive longer. Roses need at least 6 hours of direct sun per day, and 8 hours is even better. Light shade during the hottest part of the afternoon will keep colors from fading in the Lower, Coastal, and Tropical South. However, avoid planting roses where they will receive reflected heat from light-colored walls or fences—especially in southern or western exposures. Best flowering is always in spring and fall (and in winter, in the Coastal and Tropical South); plants approach dormancy during intensely hot weather, so summer flower production may drop markedly.

In any region, the best place to see roses suitable for your climate is a municipal or private rose garden. The types and selections that are performing well there are obviously good choices for you.

BUYING PLANTS

All roses are available as bare-root plants from late fall through early spring. In the Lower, Coastal, and Tropical South, you can plant bare-root roses throughout winter. Where the soil freezes, plant either in fall before ground freezes (then protect plants over winter) or in early spring after soil has thawed.

Most modern roses are sold as budded plants: growth eyes of the desired selections are budded onto rootstock plants that are carefully selected to promote rapid top growth of the desired roses and to produce root systems capable of thriving in a wide range of soils and climates. In Florida, for example, hybrid roses should be budded onto nematode-resistant rootstocks of *Rosa × fortuniana*. However, many old roses, species and their hybrids, and virtually all miniatures are "own-root" plants raised from cuttings.

Both budded and own-root roses can grow well and produce fine flowers, though budded plants offer more uniform root quality and (often) larger size at the time of purchase than own-root plants. And hybrid teas—the most popular group of roses—perform better when grown on rootstocks. Own-root roses have several advantages, however. They tend to live longer. Their original characteristics are not altered by the vigor and hardiness of the rootstock. And if the plant is killed to the ground by cold (or mowed down by accident), it will regrow as the rose you want. Regrowth from the roots of a budded plant, on the other hand, will be the rootstock rose rather than the selection you purchased—and many growers still use rootstocks of *Rosa multiflora,* which has become an invasive pest in many areas.

Bare-root plants are the best buy, and they are graded 1, 1½, or 2 according to strict standards. Plants graded 1 and 1½ are the most satisfactory; number 1 is the best. Number 2 plants may take longer to develop into decent bushes than the huskier numbers 1 and 1½. Retail nurseries and mail-order suppliers of modern roses usually offer only number 1 plants, and they will often replace plants that fail to grow. Old roses, shrub roses, and species roses (most commonly available by mail order) are typically offered as own-root plants that may or may not be up to number 1 size, though some growers sell them as budded plants that conform to the numbered grading standards. Catalogs usually state what size plant to expect.

During bare-root planting time, retail nurseries and other stores also may offer a selection of "boxed" roses with root systems encased in cartons. Markets, discount stores, and some garden centers sell dormant roses with roots packed in moist material and enclosed in cartons or long,

---

WHAT ROSES NEED

LOCATION: Choose a spot in full sun (light afternoon shade in hottest regions). An open area with good air circulation helps discourage foliage diseases. Don't plant where roots of trees or other shrubs will compete with rose roots.

DRAINAGE: Be sure the soil is reasonably well drained.

WATERING: Regular moisture is essential for good growth and bloom of most popular garden roses. Mulch soil beneath plants to help conserve moisture.

FERTILIZING: Repeat-flowering roses do best with repeated feedings throughout the growing season. Once-flowering roses need less fertilizer: feed them once as growth begins, a second time after blooming stops.

PRUNING: All roses will be more productive and attractive with some pruning. Thin out dead, weak, and old growth; reduce plant size according to type of rose and the demands of your climate.

PEST AND DISEASE CONTROL: It may be necessary to thwart various trouble-makers (see text), especially if you are growing modern roses.

Shrub Rose 'Sally Holmes'
(Miscellaneous Group)

---

narrow bags. These packaged roses may be a good value, but you should buy them as soon as they appear for sale. Those that are displayed indoors on store shelves may dry out or begin growing prematurely due to the indoor heating. These bargain roses also tend to be mislabeled.

If you wish to plant roses during the growing season, you can buy container-grown plants. These are costlier than bare-root roses, but they let you see unfamiliar selections before purchase and quickly fill in gaps in your garden. The best time to buy container-grown roses is in mid- to late spring—when plants are fairly well rooted and can be set out before summer heat arrives. For standard bush and climbing roses, look for robust plants growing in large (preferably 2-, 3-, or 5-gallon) containers; this guarantees that root systems were not severely cut back to fit the container. Also try to buy only roses planted in containers toward the end of the most recent dormant season; they generally will be in better condition than plants that have been in containers for a year or more. Avoid plants showing considerable dead or twiggy growth. Miniature roses usually are sold in containers that range from 4-in. pots to 2-gallon cans. Healthy new growth and foliage are signs of a good miniature plant, regardless of container size.

The presence of a patent number on a rose plant's label is no assurance of quality. It simply means that for that selection's first 17 years in commerce, the patent holder receives a royalty on each plant sold. Many fine roses that bear no patent number on name tags once were patented but have been in commerce for longer than the 17-year patent life span.

LOCATION AND PLANTING

For best results, plant roses where they will receive full sun all day (exceptions are noted under "Climate," facing page). Avoid planting where roots of trees or shrubs will steal water and nutrients intended for roses. To lessen any problem with foliage diseases, plant roses where air circulates freely (but not in the path of regular, strong winds). Generous spacing between plants will also aid air circulation. How far apart to plant depends on the growth habit of the roses and the climate. The colder the winter and the shorter the growing season, the smaller the bushes will be; where the growing season is long and winters are mild, plants can attain greater size. But some selections are naturally small, others tall and massive—and those relative size differences will hold in any climate. In the Upper South, you might plant the most vigorous sorts 3 ft. apart, whereas the same selections could require 6-ft. spacing in the Coastal South.

Soil for roses should drain reasonably well; if it does not, the best alternative is to plant in raised beds. Dig soil deeply, incorporating organic matter such as ground bark, peat moss, or compost to help aerate dense clay soils and improve moisture retention in sandy soils. Add a complete fertilizer to soil and dig supplemental phosphorus and potassium into planting holes; this puts nutrients at the level where roots can use them. A soil test can tell you which nutrients are needed.

Healthy, ready-to-plant bare-root roses have plump, fresh-looking canes (branches) and roots. Plants that have dried out slightly can be revived by burying them, tops and all, for a few days in moist soil, sand, or sawdust. Before planting any bare-root rose, immerse the entire plant in water for several hours to be certain all canes and roots are plumped up. Plant according to directions for bare-root planting (see "A Practical Guide to Gardening," page 596), making sure that holes are large enough to let you spread out roots without bending them or cutting them back. Set a budded rose in hole so that the bud union (the "knob" from which canes grow) is just above soil level. Plant own-root roses so that the crown (the point where roots and shoots meet) is at soil level. Water the newly planted rose well; then mound soil, damp peat moss, ground bark, or sawdust over bud union and around canes to conserve moisture. Gradually (and carefully) remove soil or other material when leaves begin to expand.

If you plan to plant new roses in ground where existing bushes have been growing for 5 or more years, dig generous planting holes (at least 1½ ft. wide, 1½ ft. deep), and replace old soil with fresh soil from another part of the garden. A condition known as specific replant disease inhibits growth of new roses planted directly in soil of established rose gardens.

ROUTINE CARE

All roses require water, nutrients, pruning, and, at some point, pest and disease control.

Water. For best performance, the most popular garden roses need watering at all times during the growing season. (Exceptions are certain old and species roses that thrive on little water once established.) Inadequate water slows or halts growth and bloom. Water deeply enough to moisten the entire root system. How often to water depends on soil type and weather. Big, well-established plants need more water than newly set plants, but

Hybrid Tea Rose 'Mr. Lincoln'

you will need to water new plants more frequently to get them established.

Soaking the soil around the base is a simple way to water individual rose bushes. If you have a drip irrigation system, you will be able to water many plants at one time. Overhead sprinkling helps freshen foliage and provides partial control for aphids and spider mites; on the minus side, it washes off spray residues, may leave mineral deposits on foliage if water is hard, and encourages foliage diseases. If you sprinkle, do it early in the day to be sure foliage dries off during the daytime.

A 2- to 3-in.-thick layer of mulch around the bushes conserves moisture, prevents the soil surface from baking hard, deters weed growth, and contributes to healthy soil structure (well aerated, permeable by water and roots). It also helps keep soil cool.

Nutrients. Regular fertilizing produces the most gratifying results. In the Coastal and Tropical South, begin feeding established plants with a complete fertilizer in February. Elsewhere, give first feeding just as growth begins. Thereafter, time fertilizer applications according to bloom periods. For roses that flower repeatedly throughout the growing season, the ideal time to fertilize is after each blooming cycle has ended and new growth is just beginning for the next round of flowers. For roses that bloom only in spring, one additional feeding just after flowering ends will encourage vigorous new growth that will bear the next year's flowers. Depending on expected arrival of freezing temperatures, stop feeding in late summer or autumn, at least 8 weeks before the earliest usual hard-frost date. In mild-winter zones experiencing virtually no subfreezing weather, you may continue fertilizing until mid-October for a crop of late-fall flowers.

Dry fertilizer, applied to soil, is most frequently used. A variation on this type is controlled-release fertilizer; follow package directions for amount and frequency of applications. Don't use controlled-release fertilizers for late-summer or fall feedings, however; instead, use those that release their nitrogen fairly quickly. This ensures that plants won't delay hardening off for winter due to late uptake of nitrogen. Liquid fertilizers are useful for applying around plants in smaller gardens. Most liquids can also be sprayed on foliage, which absorbs some nutrients immediately.

Pest and disease control. Roses require certain controls during the growing season. Principal rose pests are aphids, spider mites, and (in some areas) Japanese beetles, rose midges, and thrips. If you don't want to rely on natural predators, start controlling aphids and spider mites when they first appear in spring, and repeat as needed until they are gone or their numbers are severely reduced. Spray with insecticidal soap or horticultural oil. To control Japanese beetles, apply carbaryl (Sevin). Rose midge larvae in the soil are susceptible to applications of imidacloprid (Merit) in granular or liquid drench form. Thrips do their damage inside flower buds, disfiguring petals so badly that buds may not open—and if they do, flowers look discolored or appear scorched at the edges. Contact insecticide sprays can't reach most thrips hidden in petals; systemic insecticides are more successful.

Black spot and powdery mildew are the most common foliage diseases. First line of defense is thorough cleanup of all dead leaves and other debris during the dormant season; this is simplest right after you have pruned plants. Then, before new growth begins, spray plants and soil with a dormant-season spray of horticultural oil or lime sulfur (calcium polysulfide). This will destroy many disease organisms (as well as insect eggs) that might live over winter to reinfect plants in spring. During the growing season, apply triforine (Funginex), chlorothalonil (Daconil), myclobutanil (Immunox), or azadirachtin (Neem) to control these diseases. Preventive measures usually are recommended for disease control; unchecked infections can weaken plants, especially if defoliation occurs from black spot.

Chlorosis—evidenced by leaves turning light green to yellow while veins remain dark green—is not a disease but a symptom, usually of iron deficiency. This occurs in strongly alkaline soil. Adding iron chelate to the soil corrects chlorosis most quickly; iron sulfate is also effective, but slower to act.

Leaves that show irregular yellow or cream patterning indicate the presence of a mosaic virus. Some plants show symptoms consistently, others just occasionally. Although plants may appear to grow with vigor, the virus does impair overall strength and productivity, and it can make foliage unsightly. Fortunately, it is not transferred from plant to plant by insects or by pruning; it is transmitted in propagation—from infected rootstock or budwood. Commercial rose producers are diligently working to eliminate virus-infected stock. If you have an infected plant that is growing poorly or is unattractive, remove it from the garden.

LAZY ROSES. *The following roses flourish with little or no spraying: China roses 'Louis Philippe' and 'Old Blush'; climbing Noisette rose 'Lamarque'; tea roses 'Duchesse de Brabant', 'Marie van Houtte', and 'Mrs. B. R. Cant'. Also try Lady Banks's rose (R. banksiae); polyanthas 'Perle d'Or' and 'The Fairy'; David Austin English roses 'Abraham Darby' and 'Mary Rose'; shrub roses 'Ballerina', 'Bonica', 'Carefree Beauty', 'Carefree Wonder', and 'Knock Out'; and Bourbon roses 'Souvenir de la Malmaison' and 'Zépherine Drouhin'.* ❖

Pruning. Done properly each year, pruning will contribute to the health and longevity of your rose plants. Sensible pruning is based on several facts about the growth of roses. First, blooms are produced on new growth. Unless pruning promotes strong new growth, flowers will come on spindly outer twigs and be of poor quality. Second, the more healthy wood you retain, the bigger the plant will be; and the bigger the plant, the more flowers it can produce. Nutrients are stored in woody canes, so a larger plant is a stronger plant. Therefore, prune conservatively; never chop down a vigorous, 6-ft. bush to 1½-ft. stubs unless you want only a few huge blooms for exhibition. Third, the best pruning time for most roses (certain climbers and shrub types excepted) is at end of dormant season when growth buds begin to swell. Exact time will vary according to locality.

General pruning guidelines. The following pruning practices apply to all roses except certain shrub and species roses. Special instructions for pruning those roses are included later in this section.

Use sharp pruners. Remove wood that is obviously dead and wood that has no healthy growth coming from it, branches that cross through plant's center and any that rub against larger canes, branches that make the bush appear lopsided, and any old and unproductive canes that strong new ones have replaced during past season. Cut back growth produced during the previous year, making cuts above outward-facing buds (except for very spreading selections: some cuts to inside buds will promote more height without producing many crossing branches). As a general rule, remove from one-third to no more than one-half the length of previous season's growth. Ideal result is a V-shaped bush with a relatively open center.

If any suckers (growth produced from rootstock) are present, completely remove them. Dig down to where suckers grow from rootstock and pull them off with a downward motion; that removes growth buds that would have produced additional suckers in subsequent years. Let the wound air-dry before you replace soil around it.

Be certain you are removing a sucker rather than a new cane growing from the bud union of the budded selection. Usually you can note a distinct difference in foliage size, shape, and color and in size of thorns on sucker growth. If in doubt, let the presumed sucker grow until you can establish that it is growth from the rootstock, not the budded rose. A sucker's flowers will be different; a flowerless, climbing cane from a bush rose is almost certainly a sucker.

Consider cutting flowers as a form of pruning. Cut off enough stem to support the flower in the vase, but don't deprive the plant of too much foliage; leave a stem with at least two sets of five-leaflet leaves. Prune to an outward-growing bud or to a five-leaflet leaf.

The most widely planted modern roses—hybrid teas and grandifloras—can be pruned successfully according to the preceding guidelines. A few additional tips apply to the following popular rose types.

Floribunda, polyantha, and many shrub roses. These are grown for amount of bloom rather than quality of individual flowers. Cut back previous season's growth by only one-fourth, and leave as many strong new canes and stems as the plant produced. Most produce more canes per bush than do hybrid teas and grandifloras. If you have a hedge of one selection, cut back all plants to uniform height.

Modern Climbing Rose
'Golden Showers'

Climbing roses. For pruning purposes, climbers fall into two groups: those that bloom in spring only (including a large category known as natural climbers, discussed in "Modern climbing roses," page 521) and those that bloom off and on in other seasons as well as in spring (including climbing versions of hybrid tea roses). All climbers should be left unpruned for the first 2 or 3 years after planting; remove only dead, weak, and twiggy wood, allowing plants to get established and produce their long, flexible canes. Most bloom comes from lateral branches that grow from long canes, and most of those flowering branches develop when long canes are spread out horizontally (as along a fence). Types that bloom only in spring produce strong new growth after they flower, and that new growth bears flowers the following spring. Prune these climbers just after they bloom, removing oldest canes that show no signs of strong new growth. Repeat-flowering climbers (many are climbing versions of bush selections) are pruned at the same time you'd prune bush roses in your area. Remove oldest, unproductive canes and any weak, twiggy growth; cut back lateral branches on remaining canes to within two or three buds from main canes.

Pillar roses. Not quite bush or climber, these produce tall, somewhat flexible canes that bloom profusely without having to be trained horizontally. Prune them according to general guidelines for bush roses.

Standards. Often called tree roses, standards are an artificial creation: a bush rose budded onto a 2- to 3-ft.-high rootstock stem. Be sure to stake trunk securely to keep it from breaking under the weight of the bush it supports. A ½-in. metal pipe makes a good permanent stake; use a tie between stake and trunk to hold them securely. General pruning guidelines apply, with particular attention to maintaining a symmetrical plant.

Miniature Rose 'Starina'

Miniature roses. Prune these back to at least half the height they attained during the previous year; remove all weak and twiggy stems. Some rose growers prune miniatures severely—all the way back to the lowest outward-facing growth buds on the previous year's new stems.

Winter protection. Where winter temperatures regularly drop to 10°F or lower, some cold protection is needed for almost all modern roses. Prolonged low temperatures can kill exposed canes, as can repeated freezing and thawing (by rupturing cells). And winter winds can fatally desiccate exposed canes, because plants are unable to draw moisture from frozen soil to replace that lost through transpiration.

A healthy plant that is hardened off before the first hard frost withstands harsh winters better than a weak or actively growing one. Prepare plants for winter by timing your last fertilizer application of the growing season so that bushes will have ceased putting on new growth by expected date of first sharp frost. Leave the last crop of blooms on plants to form hips (fruits), which will aid the ripening process by stopping growth. Keep plants well watered until soil freezes.

After a couple of hard freezes have occurred and nighttime temperatures remain consistently below freezing, mound soil over base of each bush to a height of 1 ft. Collect soil from another part of garden; do not scoop soil from around roses, exposing their surface roots. Cut excessively long canes back to 2–4 ft. (the lower figure applies in the Upper South); then, with soft twine, tie canes together to keep them from whipping around in wind. When the mound has frozen, cover it with evergreen boughs, straw, or other fairly lightweight material that will act as insulation to keep the mound frozen. Your objective is to prevent alternate freezing and thawing of mound (and canes it covers), maintaining plant at a constant temperature of 15–20°F. A 3- to 4-ft.-high wire-mesh cylinder filled with noncompacting insulating material (such as straw, hay, oak leaves, or pine needles) may preserve much of the cane growth it encloses.

Remove protection in spring after frost danger is past. Gradually remove soil mounds as they thaw, working carefully to avoid breaking new growth that may have begun sprouting under the soil.

Standards (tree roses) may be insulated in the same manner as climbers, but they still may not survive severe winters, since the head of the tree is the most exposed. Some rosarians wrap the entire plant with straw and burlap, then construct a plywood box to cover it. Others dig their standards each year, pack the roots loosely in soil or another medium, and store plants in a cool garage, basement, or shed until replanting time in spring. A simpler technique is to grow standards in large containers and move them in fall to a cool shed or garage where temperatures won't drop below 10°F.

HOW TO BE HAPPY WITH ROSES. *Recognize that roses take more care than most other plants, and don't plant more than you can easily maintain. Choose roses that do well in your area, and select the right rose for the right spot. (Don't plant a vigorous rambler where you have to prune it constantly.) Give your roses good soil, regular feeding, and plenty of water and sun. Favor plants that are disease resistant or need little spraying; see "Lazy Roses," facing page.* ❖

TYPES OF ROSES

A renewed interest in old and species roses, continued development of new hybrids, and breeding programs directed toward producing landscape shrubs have led to a greatly expanded offering of roses to the gardening public. For convenience, the following sections describe three broad categories: modern roses, old roses, and species and species hybrids. ▶

Modern roses. Types described below constitute the majority of roses offered for sale and planted by hundreds of thousands each year. Those that have been All-America Rose Selections, recognized on the basis of their performance in nationwide test gardens, are indicated by the letters AARS; those with an asterisk (*) before their names have been rated 8.0 or higher by the American Rose Society.

Hybrid teas. This, the most popular class of rose, outsells all other types combined. Flowers are large and shapely, generally produced one to a stem on plants that range from 2 ft. to 6 ft. or more, depending on the selection and climate zone. Thousands of selections have been produced since the first rose in the class, 'La France', appeared in 1867; hundreds are cataloged, and new ones appear each year. The most popular ones are listed in the following color groups.

Red: 'Chrysler Imperial' (AARS), *'Mr. Lincoln' (AARS), *'Olympiad' (AARS).

Pink: 'Bewitched' (AARS), 'Brigadoon' (AARS), *'Century Two', *'Color Magic' (AARS), *'Dainty Bess' (single), 'Duet' (AARS), *'First Prize' (AARS), *'Miss All-American Beauty' (AARS), 'Perfume Delight' (AARS), *'Royal Highness' (AARS), 'Secret' (AARS), 'Sheer Bliss' (AARS), *'Tiffany' (AARS), *'Touch of Class' (AARS).

Multicolors, blends: 'Broadway' (AARS), 'Chicago Peace', *'Double Delight' (AARS), *'Granada' (AARS), 'Just Joey', 'Medallion' (AARS), 'Rio Samba' (AARS), 'Seashell' (AARS), 'Voodoo' (AARS).

Orange, orange tones: 'Brandy' (AARS), *'Folklore', *'Fragrant Cloud', 'Tropicana' (AARS).

Yellow: *'Elina', 'Graceland', 'King's Ransom' (AARS), 'Midas Touch' (AARS), 'Oregold' (AARS), *'Peace' (AARS), 'Saint Patrick', 'Summer Sunshine', 'Sunbright'.

White: *'Garden Party' (AARS), 'Honor' (AARS), 'John F. Kennedy', *'Pascali' (AARS), *'Pristine'.

Lavender: 'Blue Girl', 'Blue Ribbon', 'Heirloom', *'Lady X', *'Paradise' (AARS).

Grandifloras. Vigorous plants, sometimes 8–10 ft. tall, with hybrid tea–type flowers borne singly or in long-stemmed clusters. Some are derived from crosses between hybrid teas and floribundas; others are just extra-vigorous, cluster-flowering plants with hybrid tea ancestry. They're good for mass color effect, for number of cuttable flowers produced per plant, and as background or barrier plants.

Red: 'Love' (AARS), 'Olé'.

Pink, blends: *'Aquarius' (AARS), 'Camelot' (AARS), *'Earth Song', *'Pink Parfait' (AARS), *'Queen Elizabeth' (AARS), *'Sonia', *'Tournament of Roses' (AARS).

Orange, blends: 'Arizona' (AARS), 'Montezuma', 'Solitude' (AARS).

Yellow: *'Gold Medal'.

White: 'White Lightnin'' (AARS).

Lavender: 'Lagerfeld'.

Floribundas. Originally developed from hybrid teas and polyanthas, these produce quantities of flowers in clusters on vigorous and bushy plants. Plant and flower sizes are smaller than those of most hybrid teas. Some have flowers of elegant hybrid tea shape; others are softer and looser. Use for informal hedges, low borders, barriers, or as container plants.

Red: *'Europeana' (AARS), 'Impatient', *'Sarabande' (AARS), 'Scentimental', *'Showbiz' (AARS), *'Trumpeter'.

Pink: *'Betty Prior', *'Bridal Pink', 'Cherish' (AARS), 'Else Poulson', 'Gene Boerner' (AARS), 'Pleasure' (AARS), *'Sexy Rexy', 'Sweet Inspiration' (AARS), *'Sweet Vivien'.

Orange, blends: *'Apricot Nectar' (AARS), 'Cathedral', *'First Edition' (AARS), 'Gingersnap', 'Marina', *'Orangeade', 'Redgold' (AARS), *'Summer Fashion'.

Yellow: *'Sun Flare' (AARS), *'Sunsprite'.

White: *'Evening Star', *'French Lace' (AARS), *'Iceberg', *'Ivory Fashion' (AARS).

Lavender: *'Angel Face' (AARS), 'Intrigue' (AARS).

Polyanthas. The original members of this class appeared in the late 19th century, the result of crosses involving *R. multiflora*. Small flowers (under 2 in. across) come in large sprays; plants are vigorous, usually low growing, nearly everblooming, and quite disease resistant. 'Margo Koster' (1½–2 ft. tall) has coral orange, double flowers that resemble ranunculus; it has sported to produce white, pink, orange-scarlet, and red variants. 'The Fairy' has huge clusters of light pink flowers on a plant that can reach 4 ft. high. 'China Doll' is a knee-high plant with larger, deeper pink flowers in smaller clusters. Vigorous, bushy 'Marie Daly' reaches 3–4 ft. tall and sports double soft pink flowers. With light pruning, two 19th-century classics make sizable bushes that resemble bushy Noisettes (see under "Old roses," page 522).

Polyantha Rose
'Margo Koster'

'Cécile Brunner' (often called 'Sweetheart Rose') has light pink flowers of perfect hybrid tea form; 'Perle d'Or' (sometimes called 'Yellow Cécile Brunner') is similar but has apricot orange flowers.

Miniature roses. These plants are perfect replicas of modern hybrid teas and floribundas, but plant size is reduced to about 1–1½ ft. tall (grown in the ground) with flowers and foliage in the same reduced proportion. Derived in part from *R. chinensis minima*, they come in all the modern hybrid tea colors. Plants are everblooming. Grow them outdoors in containers, window boxes, or as border and bedding plants. To grow them indoors, pot in rich soil in 6-in. (or larger) containers and locate in a cool, bright window. Miniatures are hardier than hybrid teas but may still need winter protection in the Upper South. They also require a good amount of care. The shallow roots demand regular water, regular feeding, and mulching; powdery mildew, black spot, and spider mites are common problems. On the plus side, nearly all are own-root, cutting-grown plants.

Many new miniature selections are introduced on the market each year. Among the best available are the following, all rated 8.5 or higher.

Red, orange: 'Jean Kenneally', 'Loving Touch', 'Orange Sunblaze', 'Peggy T', 'Starina'.

Hybrid Tea Rose 'Double Delight'

Grandiflora Rose 'Gold Medal'

Modern Climbing Rose 'New Dawn'

Miniature Rose 'Little Artist'

Pink: 'Coral Sprite', 'Cupcake', 'Millie Walters', 'Pierrine', and 'Pink Meillandina'.

Blends: 'Dreamglo', 'Earthquake', 'Little Artist', 'Little Jackie', 'Magic Carrousel', 'Minnie Pearl', 'Party Girl', 'Rainbow's End', 'Shortcake'.

Yellow: 'Morain', 'My Sunshine', 'Rise 'n' Shine'.

White: 'Pacesetter', 'Snowbride'.

Lavender, purple: 'Ruby Pendant', 'Winsome'.

Climbing roses. Modern climbing roses may be divided into two general categories: natural climbers (large flowered, except for miniatures) and climbing versions of bush roses (hybrid teas, grandifloras, floribundas, polyanthas, miniatures).

The following are popular natural climbers.

Red: *'Altissimo' (single), 'Blaze', *'Don Juan', *'Dortmund', *'Dublin Bay', 'Solo', 'Tempo'.

Pink: 'Blossomtime', *'Clair Matin', 'Dr. W. van Fleet', *'Galway Bay', *'Hi Ho' (miniature), *'Jeanne Lajoie' (miniature), 'New Dawn', *'Pink Perpétué', *'Rhonda'.

Orange, blends: *'America' (AARS), *'Compassion', *'Handel', 'Joseph's Coat', *'Royal Sunset', 'Spectra'.

Yellow: 'Golden Showers' (AARS), 'Royal Gold'.

White: *'City of York', 'Lace Cascade', 'White Dawn'.

Popular selections of climbing bush roses include the following.

Red: 'Cl. Chrysler Imperial', 'Cl. Crimson Glory' (both hybrid teas).

Pink: 'Cl. Cécile Brunner' (polyantha), 'Cl. China Doll' (polyantha), 'Cl. Dainty Bess' (hybrid tea), 'Cl. First Prize' (hybrid tea), 'Cl. Pinkie' (polyantha), 'Cl. Queen Elizabeth' (grandiflora).

Orange, blends: 'Cl. Double Delight', 'Cl. Granada', 'Cl. Mrs. Sam McGredy', 'Cl. Peace' (all hybrid teas).

White: *'Cl. Iceberg' (floribunda).

Shrub roses. Significant breeding is under way to develop roses for general landscape use. These are collectively known as shrub roses. The goal is to create plants that combine showy flowers, disease-resistant foliage, and increased cold hardiness. Mail-order rose specialists lead the way in offering these plants, but retail nurseries have begun to carry them ever more often. Here is an overview of the types available.

Hybrid musk roses. The hybrid musks are large (6- to 8-ft.) shrubs or small climbers that perform well in dappled or partial shade or in sun. Most are nearly everblooming, with fragrant, clustered flowers in white, yellow, buff, pink shades, red. Popular selections include buff apricot 'Buff Beauty', coral 'Cornelia', pink 'Felicia', pink 'Kathleen' (with single flowers reminiscent of apple blossoms), salmon 'Penelope', and red 'Will Scarlet'.

English roses. England's David Austin has crossed various old roses (albas, centifolias, gallicas) with modern roses in order to combine the forms and fragrances of old roses with the colors and repeat flowering of modern hybrids. The group is extremely varied and includes low shrubs as well as plants that are determined to be climbers regardless of pruning. Popular selections include 'Abraham Darby', an upright to climbing plant with flowers in a blend of pink, yellow, and apricot; 'Charles Austin', a bushy grower with apricot blossoms; 'Fair Bianca', spreading plant with creamy white blooms; 'Gertrude Jekyll', tall, upright grower bearing deep

pink flowers; 'Graham Thomas', tall bush with rich yellow blooms; 'Mary Rose', tall and upright, with rose pink flowers; and 'Othello', featuring dusky dark red blooms on a tall bush or climber.

Ground cover roses. European and American breeders are producing roses that spread widely but grow to no more than 2 ft. tall—perfect for covering slopes, cascading over walls, or container culture. Vigor, disease resistance, and profusion of bloom are the hallmarks of these roses. Examples are 'Essex', 'Flower Carpet' (the original deep pink selection as well as its color variants), 'Nozomi', 'Pink Bells', 'Rosy Carpet'.

Miscellaneous shrub roses. Many modern shrub roses of complex ancestry can't be pigeonholed into categories according to species affiliation or specific characteristics. The plants may be spreading or upright; they

are usually 3 ft. or greater in height, and their flowers come in small to large clusters. These include such gems as 'Alchymist'; 'Ballerina' (classed as hybrid musk but more like a giant polyantha); 'Caldwell Pink'; 'Carefree Beauty' and 'Carefree Wonder' (like large floribundas); 'Erfurt'; 'Knock Out'; 'Martha's Vineyard'; the various Meidiland roses, such as 'Bonica', 'Pink Meidiland', 'Red Meidiland', 'White Meidiland'; 'Pearl Drift'; 'Sally Holmes'; and 'Sea Foam'. Check individual descriptions of catalog offerings to find appealing candidates that meet your specific landscape needs and conditions.

Shrub Rose 'Bonica' (Miscellaneous Group)

Old roses. Old roses belong to the various rose classes that existed prior to 1867 (even though some in these classes were introduced as late as the early 20th century). These roses fall into two categories. The old European roses comprise albas, centifolias, damasks, gallicas, and moss roses—the oldest hybrid groups derived from species native to Europe and western Asia. Most flower only in spring; many are hardy throughout the South with little or no winter protection. The second group contains classes derived entirely or in part from east Asian roses: Chinas, Bourbons, damask perpetuals, hybrid perpetuals, Noisettes, and teas. The original China and tea roses were brought to Europe from eastern Asia; 19th-century hybridizers greatly increased their numbers and also developed the other classes from crosses with European roses. Repeat flowering is a characteristic of these classes; hardiness varies, but nearly all need winter protection in cold-winter areas. In the Tropical South, try China roses, Noisettes, teas, and Bourbons.

Alba roses. Developed from *R. alba,* the White Rose of York; associated with England's Wars of the Roses. Spring flowers range from single to very double, white to delicate pink. Upright plants are vigorous and long lived, with green wood and handsome, disease-tolerant gray-green foliage. Garden forms include white 'Alba Semiplena' and these in shades of pink: 'Celestial', 'Félicité Parmentier', 'Great Maiden's Blush', 'Königin von Dänemark'.

Centifolia roses. The roses often portrayed by Dutch painters; developed from *R. centifolia,* the cabbage rose. Open-structured plants have prickly stems that can reach 6 ft. tall but arch with the weight of the blossoms. ►

R

Polyantha Rose 'Cécile Brunner'

Floribunda Rose 'Iceberg'

Floribunda Rose 'Angel Face'

Shrub Rose 'Ballerina' (Miscellaneous Group)

Intensely fragrant spring flowers typically are packed with petals, often with large outer petals that cradle a multitude of smaller petals within. Colors include white and pink shades. 'Paul Ricault' produces silken deep pink flowers on an upright plant; 'Rose des Peintres' is a typical rich pink cabbage rose; 'Tour de Malakoff' is a tall, rangy plant with peony-like blossoms of pink fading to grayish mauve. Dwarf forms (to 3 ft. or less) are 'Petite de Hollande', 'Pompon de Bourgogne', and 'Rose de Meaux'.

Damask roses. Originating with *R. damascena*. Plants reach 6 ft. or taller, typically with long, arching, thorny canes and light green or grayish green, downy leaves. The summer damasks flower only in spring; forms of these are cultivated to make attar of roses (used in the perfume industry). Available selections include blush pink 'Celsiana'; white 'Mme Hardy'; 'Leda', white with crimson markings; and 'Versicolor'('York and Lancaster'), with petals that may be pink, white, or a blend of pink and white. The autumn damask rose, *R. d.* 'Semperflorens' *(R. d. bifera),* flowers more than once in a year; slender buds open to loosely double, clear pink blossoms. This is the Rose of Castile of the Spanish missions.

Gallica roses. Heat zones 9–1. Cultivated forms of *R. gallica,* also known as French Rose. Fragrant spring flowers range in color from pink through red to maroon and purple shades. Plants reach 3–4 ft. tall, with upright to arching canes bearing prickles (but few thorns) and dark green, often rough-textured leaves. Grown on their own roots, these plants will spread into clumps from creeping rootstocks. Historic 'Officinalis', known as the Apothecary Rose, is presumed to be the Red Rose of Lancaster from Wars of the Roses; it is a dense, medium-size plant with semidouble cherry red flowers. A mutation, 'Versicolor'—known as 'Rosa Mundi'—has pink petals boldly striped and stippled red. Other gallicas include 'Belle de Crécy', pink aging to violet; 'Cardinal de Richelieu', slate purple; 'Charles de Mills', crimson to purple; and 'Tuscany', dark crimson with gold stamens.

Moss roses. Two old rose classes—centifolia and damask—include variant types that feature mosslike, balsam-scented glands covering unopened buds, flower stems, and sometimes even leaflets. The "moss" of centifolias is soft to the touch; that of damasks is stiffer and pricklier. Flowers are white, pink, or red, often intensely fragrant. 'Centifolia Muscosa' ('Muscosa') and 'Communis' are typical pink centifolias with moss added; 'White Bath' is 'Centifolia Muscosa' in white. Other available selections are pale pink to white 'Comtesse de Murinais', deep pink 'Gloire des Mousseux', salmon pink 'Mme Louis Lévêque', dark red 'Nuits de Young', and dark red to purple 'William Lobb'. Repeat-flowering mosses include creamy pink 'Alfred de Dalmas', apricot 'Gabriel Noyelle', red 'Henri Martin', and bright pink 'Salet'.

China roses. Heat zones 10–5. The first two China roses to reach Europe (around 1800) were cultivated forms of *R. chinensis* that had been selected and maintained by Chinese horticulturists. Flowers were pink or red, less than 3 in. across, borne in small clusters on 2- to 4-ft.-high plants. 'Old Blush' ('Parson's Pink China'), one of the original two, is still sold. Other available selections include 'Archduke Charles', with pink blossoms aging to crimson; red 'Cramoisi Supérieur' ('Agrippina'); white 'Ducher';

crimson 'Louis Philippe'; and 'Mutabilis', with flowers that open soft yellow buff and age to pink, then crimson. Also sold is the bizarre-looking Green Rose, *R. c. viridiflora,* with blossoms resembling clusters of bright green leaves. China rose ancestry is the primary source of repeat flowering in roses developed in the late 19th and early 20th centuries.

Bourbon roses. Heat zones 10–5. The original Bourbon rose was a hybrid between *R. chinensis* and the autumn damask rose (*R. damascena* 'Semperflorens'). Later developments were shrubs, semiclimbers, and climbers with flowers in white, pink shades, and red, mostly quite fragrant. Best known today are 'La Reine Victoria', 'Mme Ernst Calvat', 'Mme Pierre Oger', 'Souvenir de la Malmaison' (all pink); and 'Zéphirine Drouhin' and the supremely fragrant 'Madame Isaac Pereire' (both magenta red). A famous Bourbon-China hybrid, 'Gloire des Rosomanes', gained widespread distribution as a rootstock (called Ragged Robin) in commercial production. Occasionally it is offered as a hedge rose; growth is upright to fountainlike, with coarse foliage and semidouble cherry red flowers throughout the growing season.

Damask perpetuals. This was the first distinct hybrid group to emerge, beginning around 1800, combining the China roses with old European rose types. Ancestries vary, but all appear to include China roses and the autumn damask rose (*R. damascena* 'Semperflorens'); generally they were known as Portland roses after the first representative, 'Duchess of Portland'. All are fairly short, bushy, repeat-flowering plants with centifolia- and gallica-like flowers. Among those sold are 'Comte de Chambord', cool pink;

Damask Perpetual Rose 'Rose du Roi'

'Duchess of Portland', crimson; 'Jacques Cartier', bright pink; and 'Rose du Roi', crimson with purple shadings.

Hybrid perpetuals. In the 19th and early 20th centuries, before hybrid teas dominated the catalogs, these were *the* garden roses. They are big, vigorous, and hardy to about −30°F with minimal winter protection. Plants need more water and fertilizer than hybrid teas to produce repeated bursts of bloom. Prune high, thin out oldest canes, and arch over remaining canes to encourage many blooms. Flowers are full, often large (to 6–7 in. wide), and strongly fragrant; buds usually are shorter and plumper than those of hybrid teas. Colors range from white through pink shades to red and maroon. Selections still sold include white 'Frau Karl Druschki'; cherry red 'Général Jacqueminot'; rose pink 'Mrs. John Laing'; deep pink, peony-like 'Paul Neyron'; and carmine red 'Ulrich Brünner Fils'.

Noisette roses. Not reliably hardy in the Upper and Middle South. Heat zones 10–5. In Charleston, South Carolina, in the early 1800s, the union of a China rose and the musk rose (*R. moschata*) produced the first Noisette rose: 'Champneys' Pink Cluster', a shrubby, repeat-flowering climber with small pink flowers in medium-size clusters. Crossed with itself and China roses, it led to a race of similar fragrant roses in white, pink shades, and red; crossed with tea roses, it yielded the large-flowered, climbing tea-Noisettes. Small-flowered Noisettes include white 'Aimée Vibert Scandens', light pink 'Blush Noisette', and cherry red 'Fellenberg'. Among

Alba Rose 'Alba Semiplena'

Rosa centifolia

Gallica Rose 'Rosa Mundi'

Moss Rose 'Mme Louis Lévêque'

tea-Noisettes are yellow 'Alister Stella Gray' and 'Maréchal Niel'; orange 'Crépuscule'; white 'Lamarque' and 'Mme Alfred Carrière'; and buff apricot 'Rêve d'Or'.

Tea roses. This race of elegant, virtually everblooming, relatively tender roses does best in the Lower, Coastal, and Tropical South, in heat zones 10–5. Plants are long-lived, building on old wood and disliking heavy pruning. Flowers are in pastel shades—white, soft cream, light yellow, apricot, buff, pink, and rosy red; flower character varies, but many resemble hybrid teas. In crosses with hybrid perpetuals, tea roses were parents of the first hybrid teas. Available selections include 'Duchesse de Brabant', warm pink, tuliplike; 'Lady Hillingdon', saffron; 'Maman Cochet', creamy rose pink; 'Marie van Houtte', soft yellow and pink; 'Mlle Franziska Krüger', pink and cream to orange; 'Monsieur Tillier', warm dark pink with gold and rosy red; 'Mrs. B. R. Cant', silvery pink; 'Sombreuil', creamy white; and 'White Maman Cochet', creamy white shaded pink. The cross of a tea rose and the tea ancestor *R. gigantea* produced 'Belle Portugaise' ('Belle of Portugal'), a rampant climber bearing large pale pink blossoms in spring.

TEN SWEET ROSES. *For those who love fragrant roses most of all, here are ten of our favorites: 'Blanc Double de Coubert', white rugosa; 'Blush Noisette', light pink Noisette; 'Chrysler Imperial', deep red hybrid tea; 'Double Delight', creamy white and dark pink hybrid tea; 'Fragrant Cloud', coral red hybrid tea; 'Gertrude Jekyll', deep pink English rose; 'Mme Hardy', white damask; 'Madame Isaac Pereire', magenta red Bourbon; 'Mr. Lincoln', dark red hybrid tea; 'Sombreuil', creamy white tea.* ❖

Species and species hybrids. Among this assemblage of wild species roses and their hybrids are excellent shrub and climbing roses, useful for mass floral effect and for attractiveness of plant and foliage.

R. banksiae. LADY BANKS'S ROSE. Evergreen climber. Zones LS, CS, TS; 10–8. From China. An old-time favorite. Vigorous grower to 20 feet or more. Aphid resistant, almost immune to disease. Stems have almost no prickles; glossy, leathery leaves have three to five leaflets to 2½ in. long. Large clusters of small yellow or white flowers bloom in spring. Good for covering banks, ground, fence, or arbor. The two forms sold are

Rosa banksiae 'Lutea'

'Lutea', with scentless, double yellow flowers, and *R. b. banksiae* ('Alba Plena' or 'White Banksia'), with violet-scented, double white flowers. The fragrant 'Fortuniana' (*R. ×fortuniana*) is sometimes sold as the double white banksia; it differs in having thorny canes, larger leaves, and larger flowers that come individually rather than in clusters.

R. bracteata. MACARTNEY ROSE. Evergreen climbing shrub with large, creamy white single blossoms. Zones LS, CS, TS; 10–1. From southeastern China; naturalized in the Southeast. Its celebrated offspring is 'Mermaid', an evergreen or semievergreen climber hardy in the Coastal and Tropical South. Vigorous (to 30 ft.) and thorny, it has glossy, leathery dark green leaves and many single, creamy yellow, lightly fragrant flowers to 5 in. across. Bloom comes in spring, summer, fall, and intermittently through winter. Tough and disease resistant; thrives in sun or partial shade. Plant 8 ft. apart for quick ground cover; or use to climb walls (will need tying), run along fences, or climb trees.

R. eglanteria. See R. rubiginosa

R. foetida (R. lutea). AUSTRIAN BRIER. Deciduous shrub. Zones US, MS, LS; 9–1. From central and western Asia. Slender, prickly, erect or arching green stems to 5–10 ft. long. Dark green, smooth or slightly hairy leaves are especially susceptible to black spot and may drop in early fall. Single bright yellow, 2- to 3-in. flowers with an odd scent bloom in mid- to late spring. This species and its well-known selection 'Bicolor', often called Austrian Copper, are the source of orange and yellow color in modern roses. 'Bicolor' is a 4- to 5-ft. shrub with brilliant coppery red flowers, their petals backed in yellow. Its form 'Persiana', called Persian Yellow, has fully double yellow blooms.

Species and selections do best in warm, fairly dry, well-drained soil and in full sun. Prune only to remove dead wood.

R. glauca (R. rubrifolia). REDLEAF ROSE. Deciduous shrub. Zones US, MS, LS; 8–1. From mountains of central and southern Europe. Foliage, not blossoms, is the main feature of this rose: the 6-ft. plant is clothed in leaves that combine gray green and coppery purple. Small, single pink flowers bloom in spring; they are followed by small, oval hips that turn red in autumn.

R. ×harisonii. HARISON'S YELLOW ROSE. Deciduous shrub. Zones US, MS, LS; 9–1. Hybrid between *R. foetida* and *R. pimpinellifolia*. Very old rose that was taken westward to Texas by pioneers. Vigorous, disease free, cold hardy, and drought tolerant, with fine-textured foliage on thickets of thorny stems to 6–8 ft. tall. Profuse show of semidouble, fragrant bright yellow flowers in late spring, with occasional rebloom in fall. Blackish red, showy hips. Useful deciduous landscape shrub; also called the Yellow Rose of Texas.

R. hugonis. See R. xanthina hugonis

R. laevigata. CHEROKEE ROSE. Evergreen climber. Zones LS, CS, TS; 10–7. Native to Southeast Asia, but highly naturalized in the southern U.S.; the state flower of Georgia. Green stems to 10 ft. long hold sharp, hooked thorns and lacquered-looking dark green leaves, each with three leaflets. Single white flowers to 3½ in. wide appear only in spring. Crossed with a tea rose, this species produced 'Anemone', a mostly spring-flowering climber bearing single, soft silvery pink flowers reminiscent of Japanese anemone (*Anemone ×hybrida*). 'Ramona' is a magenta pink variation.

R. moschata. MUSK ROSE. Deciduous shrub. Zones MS, LS, CS, TS; 9–7. Probably from western Asia; an old Southern favorite. Vigorous, arching plant to 10 ft. high and wide, densely clothed in matte medium green leaves that turn butter yellow in late fall. Clusters of ivory white single flowers with a delicious, somewhat honeylike perfume appear in late spring and bloom through the summer. *R. m. plena* has double blossoms, though their effect is lessened because the inner petals wither before the outer ones.

R. moyesii. Deciduous shrub. Zones US, MS, LS; 9–3. From western China. Large, loose shrub to 10 ft. high, 8 ft. wide; best as background

Bourbon Rose 'Mme Pierre Oger'

Hybrid Perpetual Rose 'Général Jacqueminot'

Rosa foetida 'Bicolor'

Rosa × harisonii

Rosa rugosa 'White Grootendorst'

plant or featured shrub-tree specimen. Spring bloom is a glorious display of bright red single flowers to 2½ in. across, carried singly or in groups of two. A second show comes in fall, when the large, bottle-shaped hips ripen to brilliant scarlet. 'Geranium' is a somewhat shorter, more compact selection with red flowers in clusters of up to five. The hybrid 'Sealing Wax' offers pink flowers, also on a smaller and more compact bush.

R. multiflora. JAPANESE ROSE. Deciduous shrub. Zones US, MS, LS, CS; 9–4. From Japan. Arching growth on dense, vigorous plant to 8–10 ft. tall and wide. Susceptible to mildew, spider mites. Profuse clusters of small white flowers (like blackberry blossoms) in mid- to late spring; sweet fragrance akin to that of honeysuckle (*Lonicera*). Heavy fall crop of ¼-in. red hips, much loved by birds. One of the most widely used rootstocks in commercial rose production.

R. multiflora is promoted as a hedge, but it's truly useful for this purpose only on the largest acreages; it is far too big and vigorous for most gardens. Furthermore, profuse volunteer seedlings can put it in the "pest" category. It has become so invasive in some areas that it has been declared a noxious weed, and people have been forbidden to sell or plant it. A number of distinctive climbing roses, however, are noninvasive hybrids of this species. Known as multiflora ramblers, they include several well-known "blue ramblers": 'Bleu Magenta', with crimson purple blooms fading to grayish violet; 'Rose-Marie Viaud', crimson purple aging to violet and lilac; 'Veilchenblau', maroon purple turning grayish lilac with age; and 'Violette', with maroon purple blooms that turn grayish plum.

R. m. platyphylla, also known as 'Seven Sisters', is an heirloom rose often seen in old Southern gardens. It is not invasive and sports larger flowers than species, in shades of deep reddish purple to palest mauve.

R. pimpinellifolia (R. spinosissima). SCOTCH ROSE, BURNET ROSE. Deciduous shrub. Zones US, MS, LS; 9–1. From western Europe east to Korea. Spreading shrub to 3–4 ft. tall; initially as wide as high, then spreading wider by suckers. Upright, spiny, bristly stems are closely set with small, ferny leaves. Handsome bank cover in good soil; helps prevent erosion. White to pink, 1½- to 2-in. spring flowers; dark brown to blackish hips. Its form 'Altaica', with larger leaves and garlands of 3-in. white flowers, can reach 6 ft. high. Several hybrids are noteworthy. 'Stanwell Perpetual' bears blush pink double blooms from spring to fall on a mounding, twiggy plant with small gray-green leaves. 'Frühlingsmorgen' is the best known of several German hybrids; it's a tall, arching plant that bears large, single yellow flowers edged in cherry pink and centered with maroon stamens. 'Golden Wings', to 6 ft., blooms throughout the growing season; its 4-in., single blossoms have light yellow petals and red stamens.

R. roxburghii. CHESTNUT ROSE. Deciduous shrub. Zones US, MS, LS, CS; 9–5. Native to western China. Spreading plant with prickly, 8- to 10-ft.-long stems and peeling gray bark. Light green, ferny, very fine-textured foliage is tipped in bronze and gold when new. Immune to mildew and black spot. Buds and hips are spiny, like chestnut burrs. Unscented, soft rose pink, typically double flowers appear in mid- to late spring. Normally a big shrub for screen or border, but if stems are pegged down, it makes a good bank cover, useful in preventing erosion.

R. rubiginosa (R. eglanteria). SWEET BRIAR ROSE, EGLANTINE. Deciduous shrub or climber. Zones US, MS, LS; 9–1. From Europe, western Asia, North Africa. Vigorous grower to 8–12 ft. tall, 6–8 ft. wide. Prickly stems bear dark green leaves that smell like green apples, especially after a rain. Pink, 1½-in. single flowers appear singly or in clusters in late spring. Red-orange hips. Used as hedge, barrier, or screen, can be held to 3–4 ft.; plant 3–4 ft. apart and prune annually in early spring. Good hybrid forms are 'Lady Penzance' and 'Lord Penzance'.

R. rugosa. RUGOSA ROSE. Deciduous shrub. Zones US, MS, LS, CS; 9–1. From northern China, Siberia, Korea, Japan. Vigorous, hardy shrub with prickly stems. To 3–8 ft. tall and wide. Bright glossy green leaves have distinctive heavy veining that gives them a crinkled look. Wonderfully fragrant flowers are 3–4 in. across and range from single to double and from pure white and creamy yellow through pink to deep purplish red. Blooms spring, summer, early fall. Bright red, tomato-shaped fruit, an inch or more across, is seedy but edible, sometimes used in preserves.

All rugosas are extremely tough, withstanding hard freezes, wind, drought, salt spray. They make fine hedges; plants grown on their own roots make sizable colonies and help prevent erosion. Foliage remains free of diseases and insects, except possibly aphids. Among the most widely sold rugosas and rugosa hybrids are 'Blanc Double de Coubert', double white; 'Frau Dagmar Hartopp' ('Fru Dagmar Hastrup'), single pink; 'Hansa', double purplish red; 'Will Alderman', double pink. Four unusual rugosa hybrids are cherry red 'F. J. Grootendorst', crimson red 'Grootendorst Supreme', 'Pink Grootendorst', and 'White Grootendorst'; their semidouble to double flowers with deeply fringed petals resemble carnations (*Dianthus*) more than roses.

Rosa rugosa
'Frau Dagmar Hartopp'

R. wichuraiana. MEMORIAL ROSE. Evergreen or partially evergreen vine. Zones US, MS, LS, CS; 9–3. From Japan, Korea, eastern China. Trailing stems grow 10–12 ft. long in one season, root in contact with moist soil. Leaves 2–4 in. long, with five to nine smooth, shiny, ¼- to 1-in. leaflets. Midsummer flowers are white, to 2 in. across, in clusters of six to ten. Good ground cover, even in relatively poor soil. Wichuraiana ramblers, produced in the first 20 years of the 20th century, are hybrids between the species and various garden roses. Pink 'Dorothy Perkins' and red 'Excelsa' produce lavish spring displays of small blooms that obscure the often-mildewed leaves. Larger, shapelier flowers and glossy, healthier leaves are found in creamy white 'Albéric Barbier', coral pink 'Francois Juranville', light yellow 'Gardenia', coppery salmon 'Paul Transon', and white 'Sander's White Rambler'.

R. xanthina hugonis (R. hugonis). FATHER HUGO'S ROSE, GOLDEN ROSE OF CHINA. Deciduous shrub. Zones US, MS, LS; 9–5. From northern China. Dense growth to 8 ft. tall, 5 ft. wide. Arching or straight stems with bristles near base. Handsome deep green, 1- to 4-in.-long leaves; each has 5 to 11 leaflets. Blooms profusely in mid- to late spring, when branches become garlands of 2-in.-wide, bright yellow, faintly fragrant flowers. Good in borders, for screen or barrier plantings, against a fence, trained fanwise on a trellis. Takes high, filtered afternoon shade. Prune oldest wood to ground each year to shape the plant and get maximum bloom.

Rosaceae. The rose family contains an immense number of plants of horticultural importance. Beyond roses, family members include strawberry, bramble fruits (blackberry, raspberry), many flowering and fruiting trees (apple, crabapple, pear, plum), *Photinia*, firethorn (*Pyracantha*), *Spiraea*, and other ornamental trees, shrubs, and perennials.

ROSA DE MONTANA. See ANTIGONON leptopus

ROSE. See ROSA

ROSE-MALLOW. See HIBISCUS moscheutos

ROSE OF SHARON. See HIBISCUS syriacus

ROSINWEED. See SILPHIUM

ROSMARINUS officinalis

ROSEMARY

Lamiaceae (Labiatae)

EVERGREEN SHRUB

US (SOME), MS (SOME), LS, CS, TS H 12–7; OR GROW IN POTS

FULL SUN

LITTLE TO MODERATE WATER

Rosmarinus officinalis
'Prostratus'

The genus name means "dew of the sea," reflecting the plant's native habitat on seaside cliffs in the Mediterranean region. Tough and versatile, rosemary grows most luxuriantly just above the tide line, braving wind and salt spray—but it will thrive inland, even enduring blistering sun and poor alkaline soil, if given moderate water and infrequent light feeding.

The many forms of rosemary vary in habit from stiff, erect types through rounded shrubs and squat, dense tufts to rock-hugging creepers. Height ranges from as low as 1 ft. to as tall as 6 ft. or more. Plants are thickly clothed in narrow, typically 1- to 1½-in.-long, resinous, aromatic leaves that are usually glossy dark green above, grayish white beneath. Small clusters of ¼- to ½-in. blossoms in various shades of blue (rarely pink or white) bloom through winter and spring; bloom occasionally repeats in fall. Leaves are widely used as a seasoning. Flowers also are edible; add them to salads or use as a garnish. Blossoms attract birds, butterflies, and bees and are the source of excellent honey. Deer leave rosemary alone.

Good drainage is essential; lighten heavy soils with plenty of organic matter. Heavy feeding and too much water result in rank growth, subsequent woodiness. Control growth by frequent tip-pinching when plants are small. Prune older plants frequently but lightly; cut to side branch or shear. If plants become woody and bare in center, cut back selected branches by half so plant will fill in with new growth (be sure to cut into leafy wood; plants will not regrow from bare wood). Or discard plant and start over with a new one. Branches root wherever they touch the ground; creeping types will spread indefinitely, forming extensive colonies. To get new plants, root tip cuttings or dig and replant layered branches.

Cold hardiness varies considerably, depending on selection. In general, upright types are hardier, while prostrate ones (native to Majorca and Corsica) are more tender, suffering damage at 20°F or even higher. In the Upper and Middle South, choose the hardiest types and shelter them from winter winds. Note that even the hardiest types can succumb to cold if they have wet feet. Beyond hardiness range, grow rosemary in pots and winter indoors on a sunny windowsill; or treat as an annual.

Use taller types of rosemary as clipped or informal hedges or in dry borders with native and gray-leafed plants. Lower kinds are good ground or bank covers, useful in erosion control. Set container-grown plants or rooted cuttings 2 ft. apart for moderately quick cover. Foliage of most types has culinary uses, but flavor and fragrance vary; the best have a mildly pungent flavor and a complex aroma with sweet as well as resinous notes. Rosemary is also an ingredient in medicines, cosmetics, potpourri, and moth repellents.

Rosemary plants sold without names are frequently seedlings, which lack the uniformity of cutting-grown, named selections. Unfortunately, variety names are often confused, and many have synonyms; but named plants are still a better bet than nameless ones.

'Albus' ('Albiflorus'). Semi-upright grower, eventually reaching 6 ft. tall and wide. White flowers veined in pale lavender. Hardy to 0°F.

'Arp'. One of the hardiest selections, taking temperatures as low as −10°F. Discovered in Arp, Texas. Open grower to 4 ft. tall and wide; best with frequent pruning. Dark green foliage has a grayish tinge. Bright medium blue flowers.

Rosmarinus officinalis 'Albus'

'Benenden Blue' ('Balsam'; also called pine-scented rosemary). Semi-upright plant to 3 ft. high, 4 ft. or more wide. Especially narrow leaves with strong pine fragrance; light blue flowers. Bitter flavor with turpentine overtones. Tender.

'Blue Boy'. Young plant makes a dense, symmetrical mound 8–12 in. high, 14–18 in. across, reminiscent of a dwarf spruce *(Picea)*. Leaves are just ½ in. long; flowers are light blue. Plant creeps with age, but habit becomes irregular; shear to maintain domed appearance. Good in rock gardens, pots. Pleasant fragrance and flavor. Tender.

'Blue Spires'. Strong vertical grower, to 5–6 ft. tall and as wide or wider with age; can be pruned for narrower form. Deep blue flowers. Superb landscape plant; makes tight sheared hedge. Excellent for seasoning.

'Collingwood Ingram' ('Ingramii', 'Rex #4'). To 2–2½ ft. high, sprawling to 4 ft. or wider; narrower and more upright with pruning. Branches curve gracefully. Flowers in rich, bright deep blue with violet veining. Tallish bank or ground cover that provides excellent color. Not good for seasoning; flavor is too piny. Tender.

'Hill's Hardy'. Compact, bushy plant grows semi-upright to 5 ft. high and wide. Stiff foliage. Light blue flowers; repeat bloom in fall. Pleasant, light fragrance. Discovered by Madalene Hill of Round Top, Texas. Hardy to −10°F.

'Huntington Carpet' ('Huntington Blue'). To 1½ ft. high; spreads quickly yet maintains a dense center. Pale blue flowers. Best selection for ground or bank cover.

'Irene' ('Renzel's', 'Renzel's Irene'). Vigorous spreader that covers 2–3 ft. or more per year, mounding to 1–1½ ft. high. Deep lavender-blue flowers. Reputedly one of the most cold-hardy prostrate selections.

'Majorca Pink'. Initially erect to 2–4 ft. tall and 1½–2 ft. wide; eventually twists into picturesque shape under the weight of its heavy seed crop, flopping to 3–4 ft. wide. Lilac-pink flowers. Slightly fruity fragrance.

'Prostratus'. To 2 ft. tall, with 4- to 8-ft. spread. Will trail straight down over wall or edge of raised bed to make a green curtain. Pale lavender-blue flowers come in waves from fall into spring. With age, tends to mound up and become woody and bare in center (except at seashore, where it remains lush throughout). Effective in hanging containers. Tender.

'Salem'. Dependable old selection with dense, erect growth to 3 ft. high and wide; lavender-blue flowers. Fairly cold hardy.

'Tuscan Blue'. Vita Sackville-West's original, brought to England from Tuscany, had relatively broad (to ¼-in.-wide), 1- to 1½-in.-long leaves, deep violet-blue flowers, and upright habit to 6–7 ft. tall and 1½–2 ft. wide. A plant long sold as 'Tuscan Blue' in the U.S. fits this general description but has light blue flowers; with age, it becomes woody and bare at the base. Some nurseries sell 'Blue Spires' under this name.

'Very Oily'. To 3 ft. high and wide. Selected for its high essential-oil content. Bluish white flowers.

ROYAL CHARLIE. See PLECTRANTHUS oertendahlii

ROYAL FERN. See OSMUNDA regalis

ROYAL PALM. See ROYSTONEA

ROYAL POINCIANA. See DELONIX regia

ROYAL TRUMPET VINE. See DISTICTIS 'Rivers'

ROYSTONEA

ROYAL PALM

Arecaceae (Palmae)

PALMS

✂ TS H 12–10

☼ FULL SUN

● REGULAR WATER

Roystonea regia

Stately, symmetrical, fast-growing feather palms. Tall, smooth gray trunk is marked with rings and topped by a green crown shaft formed by the overlapping frond bases. Hardy to 28°F. Do best in moist, well-drained soil. If grown in alkaline soil, they are subject to a disfiguring disease called frizzle top, caused by a deficiency of manganese or potassium. To prevent this, feed regularly with an 8-4-12 palm fertilizer containing manganese. Has good wind and salt resistance. Resist damage by browsing deer. Can be used as street or avenue trees, to frame large buildings, in groups with other palms. Look especially majestic planted in rows.

R. elata. FLORIDA ROYAL PALM. Native to southern Florida. May grow taller than the species *R. regia* but otherwise differs from it only in minor botanical details.

R. regia. CUBAN ROYAL PALM. Native to Cuba. To 50–75 ft. high, 30 ft. wide. Trunk is swollen at base, tapering toward top, sometimes swollen toward middle. Bright green, 10- to 20-ft.-long fronds arch gracefully in all directions. Segments stand out from midrib at many angles.

RUBBER PLANT. See FICUS elastica

Rubiaceae. The madder family contains herbs, shrubs, and trees with opposite or whorled leaves, usually clustered flowers. Its members include *Bouvardia*, coffee *(Coffea)*, sweet woodruff *(Galium)*, and *Gardenia*.

R

RUBUS

BRAMBLE

Rosaceae

EVERGREEN AND DECIDUOUS SHRUBS

ZONES VARY BY SPECIES

EXPOSURE NEEDS VARY BY SPECIES

MODERATE TO REGULAR WATER

Rubus odoratus

Though best known for blackberry and rasp-berry (see separate entries), the brambles include many ornamental plants, most of them thornless. Those listed here differ from blackberry and raspberry not only in their lack of prickles but also in having perennial rather than biennial stems. Spring flowers are followed by small, edible berries that attract birds. Need good drainage; spread widely by rhizomes. Plant ground cover types about 2 ft. apart. Deer seldom bother these plants.

R. odoratus. FLOWERING RASPBERRY. Zones US, MS; 8–6. Decidu-ous. Native to northeastern U.S. and Appalachians. Loose, rambling shrub to 5–8 ft. tall and wide. Handsome, rich green, maplelike leaves grow 5–10 in. long, with three to five lobes. Clusters of showy, rosy purple, 1- to 2-in.-wide flowers appear in early summer; these are followed by mealy reddish berries (edible but tasteless) that ripen in July or August. Good for woodland gardens, naturalized areas. Grow in moist, organically enriched soil and filtered shade.

R. pentalobus (R. calycinoides, R. fockeanus). CREEPING BRAM-BLE. Evergreen. Zones MS, LS; 9–7. Native to mountains of Taiwan. Thickly foliaged stems spread at a moderate rate to form a dense carpet to 1 ft. high. Rounded, 1- to 1½-in. leaves have three to five broad, ruffled-edged lobes; upper surfaces are lustrous dark green and rough textured, under-sides are grayish white and felted. Small white flowers resemble those of strawberry; berries are salmon colored. Full sun or light shade. 'Emerald Carpet' is a commonly sold selection with superior foliage.

R. rosifolius. ROSELEAF RASPBERRY. Evergreen. Zones US, MS, LS; 9–1. Native to Asia and Australia. Rambling shrub to 6 ft. tall; spreads to form large thickets. Dark green, corrugated-looking leaves, 4–6 in. long, have three to seven leaflets and resemble rose foliage. Single, inch-wide white flowers bloom in early summer and again in fall; tasteless red berries ripen in summer and late fall. 'Coronarius' is a spectacular 4- to 5-ft.-tall selection with double white, 4-in.-wide blossoms that strongly resemble old roses; they appear from March through June on last year's growth, from August through September on the current year's growth. Blooms at an early age; produces no berries. Tolerates most soils and prefers light shade. Sometimes listed as *R. coronarius*.

RUDBECKIA

CONEFLOWER, RUDBECKIA

Asteraceae (Compositae)

PERENNIALS AND BIENNIALS

US, MS, LS, CS, EXCEPT AS NOTED

FULL SUN

MODERATE TO REGULAR WATER

Rudbeckia hirta

The showy garden rudbeckias that brighten summer and fall borders are descended from wild plants native mainly to the eastern U.S. All are tough and easy to grow. Blossoms have yellow or orange rays and a raised central cone. Choice cut flowers; cutting also encourages rebloom late in season. Divide perennials when crowded, usually every few years.

R. fulgida. YELLOW CONEFLOWER. Perennial. Heat zones 9–1. Initially 3 ft. tall, 2 ft. wide; after a few years, spreads by rhizomes to form a larger clump. Branching stems; broadly lance-shaped, 5-in.-long, hairy dark green leaves. Yellow, 2- to 2½-in.-wide flowers with a black to brown central cone bloom in summer. Selections are more often grown than the species. Among the most popular is *R. f. sullivantii* 'Goldsturm', bearing 3-in., black-eyed yellow flowers on 2- to 2½-ft. stems. Some nurseries offer the taller, more variable seed-grown Goldsturm strain.

R. f. speciosa (R. speciosa), to 2½ ft. high and 2 ft. wide, is native from New Jersey to Alabama and Georgia; it has bright orange-yellow petals sur-rounding a black cone. Its selection 'Viette's Little Suzy' is a dwarf to about 14 in. high and wide, with dark-eyed yellow blooms.

R. hirta. BLACK-EYED SUSAN, GLORIOSA DAISY. Biennial or short-lived perennial; often grown as annual because it blooms the first summer from seed sown in early spring. Zones US, MS, LS, CS, TS; 12–1. To 3–4 ft. tall, 1½ ft. wide, with upright, branching habit. Stems and lance-shaped leaves to 4 in. long are rough and hairy. Daisylike, 2- to 4-in.-wide flowers have orange-yellow rays and a prominent purplish black cone. Not usually browsed by deer.

Gloriosa Daisy strain has 5- to 7-in.-wide daisies in yellow, orange, rus-set, or mahogany, often zoned or banded. Gloriosa Double Daisy strain has somewhat smaller (to 4½-in.) double flowers, nearly all in lighter yellow and orange shades. 'Indian Summer' produces 6- to 9-in., single to semidouble flowers in golden yellow. 'Irish Eyes' ('Green Eyes') has 2- to 3-in., golden yellow flowers with a light green central cone that ages to brown. 'Prairie Sun' has golden petals with light yellow tips surrounding a pale green cone. For front of border, try lower-growing selections 'Goldilocks' (double flowers) and 'Toto', both 8–10 in. high; Becky Mix (12–15 in.); 'Sonora' (15 in.); and 'Marmalade' (2 ft.).

R. laciniata. CUTLEAF CONEFLOWER. Perennial. Heat zones 9–1. The species grows 10 ft. tall, 4 ft. wide; it has light green, deeply lobed leaves to 4 in. long and blooms from summer to fall, bearing 2- to 3½-in.-wide flowers with drooping yellow rays and a green cone. Very heat tolerant. More widely grown in gardens are the following two selections. 'Golden Glow' ('Hortensia'), to 6–7 ft. tall, is an old favorite that bears bright yellow double flowers 2–3½ in. wide. Good summer screen or tall plant for back of borders. Does not seed, but spreads rapidly (sometimes aggressively) by underground stems. Seems to attract aphids. 'Goldquelle', with double blooms in lemon yellow, is a less aggressive form growing 3 ft. tall, 1½ ft. wide.

R. maxima. GREAT CONEFLOWER. Perennial. Heat zones 9–1. Large (to 5-in.) bluish gray leaves form a mound to 2–3 ft. tall and wide. In mid-summer, 5- to 6-ft. stems bear flowers to 3 in. across, with a prominent brown central cone and drooping yellow rays.

R. nitida. Perennial. Heat zones 10–1. Similar to *R. laciniata* but shorter (to 6 ft. tall). More widely grown than the species is 'Herbstsonne' ('Autumn Sun'), which may be a hybrid between *R. laciniata* and *R. nitida*. It grows to 6 ft. tall, 2 ft. wide; bears single, 4- to 5-in.-wide flowers with yellow rays and a bright green cone that ages to yellow.

R. triloba. BROWN-EYED SUSAN. Biennial or perennial. Heat zones 10–1. To about 4 ft. tall and as wide, with stiff, much-branched stems and 5-in.-long leaves, some deeply lobed. Blossoms to 3 in. wide, with yellow-orange rays and dark brown-purple centers. Can be weedy looking.

RUE. See RUTA graveolens

RUE ANEMONE. See ANEMONELLA thalictroides

RUELLIA

Acanthaceae

EVERGREEN SHRUBS AND SHRUBBY PERENNIALS

US, MS, LS, CS, TS 12–1, EXCEPT AS NOTED

FULL SUN OR LIGHT SHADE

MODERATE TO REGULAR WATER

Ruellia brittoniana

Thanks to their pretty blooms and easy culture, ruellias have come into their own in recent years. Though most common in Texas, they're quickly making inroads into the rest of the South, especially among gardeners who want lots of bloom with little fuss. The flowers resemble small, thin-textured petunias. These plants resist damage by browsing deer.

R. brittoniana. WILLOWLEAF MEXICAN PETUNIA. Shrubby perennial. Mexican native naturalized in many areas of the southern and southwestern U.S. To 3 ft. high; initially 1–1½ ft. wide, but can be invasive and should be contained (by an edging, for example). Narrow dark green leaves to 3 in. long, ¾ in. wide; 2-in.-long, lavender-blue flowers throughout warm times of year. 'Chi-Chi' bears soft pink blossoms. 'Katie' is a noninvasive dwarf (10- to 12-in.-tall) selection. Other dwarfs include 'Colobe Pink', pink flowers; 'Strawberries and Cream', lavender blossoms and white-speckled leaves; and 'White Katie', similar to 'Katie' but with white blooms.

R. humilis. WILD PETUNIA. Shrubby perennial. Native to central U.S. Grows 1–2 ft. tall and wide, with oval to lance-shaped leaves 1½–4 in. long. Bears 2-in.-long lavender flowers from early summer into fall. 'Blue Shade' is a low-growing (6- to 10-in.), wide-spreading form with lavender-blue flowers; roots by creeping stems. Selection is popular in Central Texas as a ground cover for light shade.

R. macrantha. PINK WILD PETUNIA. Shrub. Zones CS, TS; 12–10. Native to Brazil. To 3 ft. high and wide, with oval dark green leaves to 6 in. long. Clusters of rose pink, 3- to 4-in. flowers with deeper pink veining. Blooms in late fall in most areas, through winter in the Tropical South. Best grown as a container plant and given shelter during frosty weather.

R. malacosperma. MEXICAN PETUNIA. Shrubby perennial native to Mexico. Often confused with *R. brittoniana,* but its leaves are a bit shorter and wider. Tough plant that takes dry or wet soil. Grows 3 ft. tall, 1 ft. wide, with lavender flowers in summer. 'Alba' (sometimes sold as White Flower Form) produces hundreds of pure white blooms from June through September.

RUMOHRA adiantiformis

LEATHERLEAF FERN

Polypodiaceae

FERN

🗡 CS, TS **H** 12–8

☼ ◐ FULL SUN OR PARTIAL SHADE

◍ ◍ MODERATE TO REGULAR WATER

Rumohra adiantiformis

From many tropical and subtropical areas of the Southern Hemisphere. To 3 ft. high and wide, spreading wider by rhizomes. Deep glossy green, triangular, finely cut fronds are firm textured, last well in arrangements. Hardy to 24°F. Often sold as *Aspidium capense.*

RUPTURE WORT. See HERNIARIA glabra

RUSCUS

BUTCHER'S BROOM

Liliaceae

EVERGREEN SHRUBS

🗡 MS, LS, CS, TS **H** 10–7

◐ ● BEST IN SHADE, TOLERATE SOME SUN

◌ ◍ ● LITTLE TO REGULAR WATER

Ruscus hypoglossum

Native to Mediterranean region. Unusual leafless plants with some value as small-scale ground cover, curiosity, or source of material for dried arrangements. These old favorites are usually not sold by garden centers, but rather passed around by gardeners. Flattened, leaflike branches do the work of leaves and bear tiny greenish white flowers in centers of upper surfaces. If male and female plants are present, or if you have a plant with male and female flowers, bright red (sometimes yellow) fruit follows the flowers. Plants spread widely by rhizomes. Tolerate competition from tree roots. Subject to chlorosis (yellow leaves with green veins) in alkaline soil.

R. aculeatus. To 1–4 ft. tall, with branched stems. Spine-tipped "leaves" are 1–3 in. long, one-third as wide, leathery dull dark green. Fruit is ½ in. across. 'Wheeler's Variety' is a self-fruiting form.

R. hypoglossum. To 1½ ft., with unbranched stems. "Leaves" to 4 in. long, 1½ in. wide, glossy green, not spine tipped. Fruit is ¼–½ in. across. Spreads faster than *R. aculeatus.* Superior as small-scale ground cover.

RUSSELIA

Scrophulariaceae

SHRUBBY PERENNIALS

🗡 CS (MILDER PARTS), TS **H** 12–8; OR HOUSEPLANTS

☼ ◐ FULL SUN OR PART SHADE; BRIGHT LIGHT

◍ ● MODERATE TO REGULAR WATER

Russelia equisetiformis

Group of about 50 plants native to Cuba, Mexico, and Central America. Prized for colorful flowers produced nearly continuously in warm weather. The two species listed below are the most common; both look great billowing over the top of a retaining wall, massed on a slope, or used in raised planters and hanging baskets. Provide well-drained soil. Propagate by taking cuttings, layering branches that touch the ground, or dividing. Can be grown indoors in a sunny window. During active growth, water moderately and feed monthly with a general-purpose liquid houseplant fertilizer; then reduce water and fertilizer in winter.

R. equisetiformis. FIRECRACKER PLANT. Suckering shrub to 3–4 ft. tall and wide, with cascading, wiry, nearly leafless bright green stems. Blooms all summer, with side branches bearing a profusion of tubular bright red flowers resembling 1¼-in.-long firecrackers. Hardy to about 24°F; comes back quickly if cut down by mild frost. A yellow-flowered form is available.

R. sarmentosa. CORAL PLANT. Often confused with *R. equisetiformis,* but stems are leafy and floral display is even showier. Grows about 4 ft. tall and 6 ft. wide. Abundant clusters of small bright red flowers nearly hide the oval, 3-in.-long leaves. Not as hardy as *R. equisetiformis.*

RUSSIAN OLIVE. See ELAEAGNUS angustifolia

RUSSIAN SAGE. See PEROVSKIA atriplicifolia

RUTABAGA. See TURNIP and RUTABAGA

Rutaceae. Besides rue *(Ruta),* the rue family includes many perennials, shrubs, and trees, the most important of which are those in the citrus clan. Gas plant *(Dictamnus),* Mexican orange *(Choisya),* and *Skimmia* are other notable members. Most are aromatic, thanks to oil glands in leaves or other plant parts.

RUTA graveolens

RUE, HERB-OF-GRACE

Rutaceae

PERENNIAL

🗡 US, MS, LS, CS **H** 9–5

☼ FULL SUN

◍ ◍ MODERATE TO REGULAR WATER

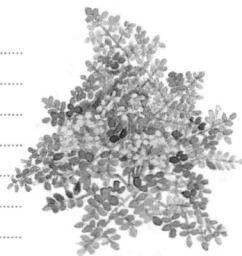

Ruta graveolens 'Jackman's Blue'

To 2–3 ft. high and wide, with aromatic, fernlike blue-green leaves. Small, greenish yellow flowers are followed by decorative brown seed capsules. Sow seeds in flats; transplant to 1 ft. apart. Needs good garden soil; add lime to strongly acid soil. Cut back in early spring to encourage bushiness. Seed clusters can be dried for use in wreaths or swags. 'Blue Beauty' and 'Jackman's Blue' are dense, compact selections with fine blue-gray color; 'Blue Mound' and 'Curly Girl' are even more compact.

Rue owes its status as an herb to history and legend rather than to any medicinal or culinary use. It was once thought to ward off disease, guard against poisons, and aid eyesight. It was also used to make brushes for sprinkling holy water. The sap causes dermatitis in some people.

RYEGRASS. See LOLIUM

SABAL

PALMETTO

Arecaceae (Palmae)

PALMS

ZONES VARY BY SPECIES

FULL SUN OR PARTIAL SHADE

MODERATE WATER

Sabal palmetto

Sterling group of cold-hardy fan palms, unsurpassed for their versatility, adaptability, and ease of culture. They tolerate almost any soil and thrive in sun or light shade; they'll even take salt spray. Some have trunks, while others do not; all grow rather slowly. Tree types make excellent street, lawn, and shade trees; shrubby sorts are useful in understory plantings and naturalized areas. Mature plants bear large clusters of tiny flowers among the leaves, typically in summer.

S. blackburniana (S. domingensis, S. umbraculifera). HISPANIOLAN PALMETTO. Zones LS, CS, TS; 12–8. From the Caribbean. Ultimately reaches 80 ft. or taller, 20 ft. wide, with immense green fans 9 ft. across. Hardy to 10°F.

S. causiarum. PUERTO RICAN HAT PALM. Zones CS, TS; 12–9. Native to Puerto Rico. Young leaves are collected and woven into hats, hence the plant's common name. This is a stout, columnar tree that grows to 60 ft. tall and about 12 ft. wide. Distinguished from other species by its smooth, massive gray trunk, which can reach 4 ft. in diameter. Leaves to 6 ft. long, divided into 50 to 60 segments. Unlike other palmettos, this one drops its dead leaves quickly, and the bases of old leaves shed from the trunk. Hardy to 16°F.

S. etonia. SCRUB PALM. Zones MS, LS, CS, TS; 12–8. Shrubby palm native to the dry, sandy Florida scrub. Usually trunkless; grows to 6 ft. tall, 8 ft. wide. Resembles *S. minor,* but leaves are smaller, with more and thinner segments. Hardy to 0°F.

S. mexicana (S. texana). TEXAS PALMETTO, OAXACA PALMETTO. Zones CS, TS; 12–9. Native from Texas to Guatemala. Leaf stems hang on trunk in early life, then drop to show attractive, slender trunk. Grows 30–50 ft. high, 12 ft. wide. Established trees are hard to transplant. Hardy to 18°F.

S. minor. DWARF PALMETTO. Zones MS, LS, CS, TS; 12–7. Shrubby palm native to the forest understory, scrublands, and alluvial floodplains of the Southeast. Slow growing to 6 ft. tall, 10 ft. wide. Usually trunkless; older specimens have a short, thick trunk. Blue-green, fan-shaped leaves to 3 ft. long; old leaves fold at base, hang down like closed umbrellas. Tolerates wet or dry soils and salt spray. One of the hardiest palms. Seedlings collected in McCurtain County, Oklahoma, have survived temperatures of −24°F.

S. palmetto. CABBAGE PALM. Zones LS, CS, TS; 12–9. Native to the hammocks, marshes, and Coastal Plains of the Southeast, from North Carolina to Florida. Grows slowly to 90 ft., with a dense, globular, 12- to 18-ft.-wide head formed by leaves 5–8 ft. across. Together with live oak *(Quercus virginiana),* cabbage palm helps define the urban character of Charleston, Savannah, and other coastal cities of the Old South. Excellent street or lawn tree; best tree for the beach. Tolerates wind, salt spray, and sand; can be planted right on dunes. Very easy to transplant. Huge, dormant specimens are often stacked up like cordwood, then trucked to new locations and plopped like telephone poles into deep, narrow holes. Hardy to 10°F.

S. × texensis. Zones LS, CS, TS; 12–8. Naturally occurring hybrid between *S. minor* and *S. mexicana.* Usually found as an understory plant. Slowly grows to 15 ft. tall and 10 ft. wide, forming a stout trunk after many years. Hardy to 10°F.

S. uresana. SONORAN PALMETTO. Zones LS, CS, TS; 12–8. Highly ornamental, surprisingly hardy Mexican species, deserving of a spot in more gardens. Straight-trunked tree grows to about 40 ft. tall and reaches 10 ft. across. Impressive leaves to 6 ft. long, in a striking silvery blue. Hardy to 10°F.

SACAHUISTA. See NOLINA texana

SACCHARUM (Erianthus)

PLUME GRASS, SUGAR CANE

Poaceae (Gramineae)

PERENNIAL GRASSES

ZONES VARY BY SPECIES

FULL SUN, EXCEPT AS NOTED

REGULAR WATER, EXCEPT AS NOTED

Saccharum ravennae

These very large grasses include the species known as sugar cane. They are spectacular in the garden—but be sure to give them plenty of room. Use in masses, group as tall screens, or plant as specimens and accents where you want a dramatic vertical element in the garden. Easy to grow in moist, well-drained, fertile soil. No serious pests.

S. arundinaceum. HARDY SUGAR CANE. Zones US, MS, LS, CS, TS; 10–6. Native to China, India, and Southeast Asia. Its pulp has been used in the making of paper. The grass forms a huge clump—up to 10 ft. tall (in bloom) and quite nearly as wide. Long, narrow gray-green leaves have white midribs. Blooms in early autumn, holding its upright flower plumes well above the foliage; plumes emerge purplish pink, then fade to silver by late fall. Hardy even in the Upper South.

S. contortum. BENT-AWN PLUME GRASS. Zones US, MS, LS, CS; 9–7. Native to the eastern U.S., from Delaware south to Florida and Texas. Forms a 3- to 4-ft.-tall, narrowly upright clump of slender bluish green leaves that turn purple, bronze, and red in fall and hold their color in winter. Erect, reddish to purple-brown plumes rise 2–4 ft. above the foliage in late summer and fall. Self-sows. Full sun or light shade. Formerly listed as *Erianthus contortus.*

S. officinarum. SUGAR CANE. Zones CS, TS; 12–8. Probably native to India and Southeast Asia. This giant grass has been grown for centuries—the sweet juice contained in its thick canes is the commercial source of sugar. Only recently, however, has it been more broadly appreciated for its ornamental potential. Forms an imposing clump (eventually expands to 6–8 ft. wide) of upright, long, slender, green to bluish green leaves; clump can reach 15 ft. tall, growing 8–10 ft. in just 1 year. Fluffy, whitish, nodding flower plumes are slender and arching, appear in early fall (though they are rarely seen in nontropical areas). Hardy to 20°F. Tolerates wet soils. In most gardens, it's treated as an annual and used as a vertical accent; sometimes grown as an edible novelty or a substitute for bamboo. Selections with colored canes and leaves are becoming available and popular; one of these is 'Pele's Smoke', featuring showy bronze purple leaves with pink midribs growing from dusky purple canes.

S. ravennae. RAVENNA GRASS. Zones US, MS, LS, CS, TS; 10–2. Native to southern Europe. The slender gray-green leaves form a dense, 4- to 6-ft.-wide and 6-ft.-tall fountain that bears giant plumes of silvery gray flowers in late summer. Mature plants may produce 40 plumes—each 15 ft. high—that cast a spectacular silhouette when backlit by the sun. Similar to pampas grass *(Cortaderia)* but less symmetrical and much hardier; good substitute for pampas grass in the Upper South and Midwest. Vigorous grower. Does well in average to poor soils but must have good drainage. Little to moderate water once established. Formerly listed as *Erianthus ravennae.*

SACRED LILY. See ROHDEA japonica

SAFFLOWER. See CARTHAMUS tinctorius

SAFFRON CROCUS. See CROCUS sativus

SAGE. See SALVIA

SAGE, RUSSIAN. See PEROVSKIA atriplicifolia

FOR INFORMATION ON SELECTING PLANTS
PLEASE SEE PAGES 39–144

S

SAGINA subulata

IRISH MOSS, SCOTCH MOSS

Caryophyllaceae

PERENNIAL

US, MS, LS, CS 9–6

Full sun or partial shade

Regular water

Sagina subulata

Of two different prostrate plants of similar appearance, *Sagina subulata* is the more common. The other is *Arenaria verna*, usually called *A. v. caespitosa*. Both of these European natives make dense, compact, mosslike masses of slender leaves on slender stems. But *A. verna* has tiny white flowers in few-flowered clusters, while *S. subulata* bears flowers singly and differs in other details. In common usage, however, green forms of the two plants are called Irish moss, and golden green forms (*A. v.* 'Aurea' and *S. s.* 'Aurea') are called Scotch moss.

Both *Sagina* and *Arenaria* are grown primarily as ground covers for limited areas; they're also useful for filling gaps between paving blocks. They won't grow well under conditions that suit true mosses. They need good soil, good drainage, and occasional feeding with controlled-release fertilizer. They take some foot traffic and tend to hump up over time; control this by occasionally cutting out narrow strips, then pressing or rolling lightly. Control snails, slugs, and cutworms. Set out plants 6 in. apart for fast cover.

SAGO PALM. See CYCAS revoluta

ST. AUGUSTINE GRASS. See STENOTAPHRUM secundatum

SAINTPAULIA

AFRICAN VIOLET

Gesneriaceae

PERENNIALS GROWN AS HOUSEPLANTS

FILTERED EARLY SUN, BRIGHT INDIRECT LIGHT

Watering is an art; see below

Saintpaulia

Most popular of all flowering houseplants; given proper care, they bloom almost continuously. Most of the African violets grown are hybrids derived from several species native to east Africa. They form rosettes of velvety green (sometimes variegated) leaves that may be roundish or pointed, with a smooth or quilted surface and scalloped or smooth margins. The original species bear pale blue to lavender and purple blossoms that are typically five petaled—with two smaller petals at the top of the flower, three larger ones below. Hybrids also include flowers in bell, cup, and star shapes, in colors including not only blues and purples but also white, various pink shades, burgundy, and crimson. Creamy yellows exist, but they tend to revert to pink or purple. Some hybrids have bands of color, contrasting veining, or dark accents on paler petals. All have bright yellow centers. Flowers may be single, semidouble, or fully double, sometimes with fringed or ruffled petals.

African violets need a moisture-retentive yet fast-draining potting mix. You can buy packaged mixes; if you prefer to make your own, use 3 parts peat moss to 1 part perlite and 1 part compost or sterilized loam. Don't use too large a pot; plants bloom best when roots are crowded. Choose a location where temperatures average 60–70°F. Humidity should be high; if house air is quite dry, increase humidity around plant by setting each plant on a saucer filled with wet gravel. Water plants from above or below, but avoid watering root crown or leaves. Wick-irrigated pots work well. Use room-temperature or slightly warmer water; wet potting mix thoroughly, then wait to water again until mix is dry to the touch. After watering, don't let bottom of pot sit in water in saucer for more than 2 hours. Feed well-established plants (only when soil is moist) with slightly acid fertilizer once every 2 to 4 weeks. Pick off spent leaves and flowers regularly. Propagate from seeds, leaf cuttings, or divisions. Common pests are aphids, cyclamen mites, thrips, and mealybugs.

Salicaceae. The willow family consists of deciduous trees or shrubs with flowers in catkins and (generally) with silk-tufted seeds that blow about. Besides willow (*Salix*), examples are cottonwood and poplar (*Populus*).

SALIX

WILLOW

Salicaceae

DECIDUOUS TREES AND SHRUBS

US, MS, LS, EXCEPT AS NOTED

Full sun, except as noted

Regular to ample water

Salix babylonica

It's easy to see what people like about willows. They're fast growing and tolerate just about any type of soil. They're also the easiest of trees and shrubs to propagate: just take cuttings at any time of year and stick them into moist soil (no rooting powder required). On the other hand, they are weak-wooded, short-lived trees, and their shallow, greedy roots make them hard to garden under and can invade water lines. Most are attacked by a host of pests (tent caterpillars, aphids, borers, spider mites) and diseases. Weeping willows do best near lakes and streams, although they can, with training, make satisfactory shade trees. Shrubby willows are grown chiefly for their showy catkins (this group is known as "pussy willows") or colorful twigs, or to control erosion on riverbanks. Branches of pussy willows can be cut in bud in late winter and brought indoors to bloom. Willow species hybridize freely, resulting in much confusion of names in the nursery trade.

S. alba. WHITE WILLOW. Tree. Heat zones 9–1. Native to Europe, North Africa. Upright to 75–100 ft. tall, 50–100 ft. wide. Yellowish brown bark. Narrow, 1½- to 4-in., bright green leaves are silvery beneath, may turn golden in fall. The following forms are valued for colorful twigs.

S. a. 'Tristis' (*S. ×sepulcralis* 'Chrysocoma'). GOLDEN WEEPING WILLOW. Pendulous form, to 50–70 ft. tall and wide (or wider). Young stems are bright yellow. Among the most attractive of weeping willows; may be sold as *S. alba* 'Niobe', *S. babylonica* 'Aurea', or *S. vitellina* 'Pendula'.

S. a. vitellina. Upright, with brilliant yellow twigs in winter. Can grow to tree size, but cutting back gives best color display: lop to 1 ft. high yearly, just before spring growth begins. Stems may grow 8 ft. in a season. 'Britzensis' and 'Chermesina' have red or orange-red winter stems and are often confused with each other.

S. babylonica. WEEPING WILLOW. Tree. Heat zones 9–1. From China. To 30–50 ft. tall and wide (or wider). Longer (3- to 6-in.) leaves, more pronounced weeping habit than *S. alba* 'Tristis'. Greenish or brown branchlets. This is a popular lawn tree, but keep its size in mind; planting anywhere near the house or a driveway, walk, or patio is usually a mistake. Be sure to give it moist soil, as it quickly becomes disconsolate and ratty looking in dry soil. 'Crispa' ('Annularis'), ringleaf or corkscrew willow, has leaves curled into rings or circles; it is somewhat narrower than the species.

S. caprea. GOAT WILLOW, FLORIST WILLOW. Shrub or tree. Heat zones 8–6. Native from Europe to northeastern Asia. Grows to 15–25 ft. tall, 12–15 ft. wide. Broad, 3- to 6-in.-long leaves are dark green above, gray and hairy beneath. Before leaf-out, male plants produce fat, woolly, pinkish gray catkins about 1 in. long. Can be kept to shrub size by cutting to ground every few years. 'Pendula' (a male plant known as Kilmarnock willow) and 'Weeping Sally' (its female counterpart) are two selections that will naturally sprawl on the ground; they are more effective grafted or staked to form small weeping trees 6–8 ft. tall, 6 ft. wide.

S. discolor. PUSSY WILLOW. Shrub or tree. Heat zones 8–2. Native to eastern U.S.; an old favorite in the South. To 15–25 ft. tall, 12–15 ft. wide. Slender red-brown stems; bright green, 2- to 4-in. leaves with bluish undersides. Catkins of male plants are main draw—soft, silky, pearl gray, to 1½ in. long.

S. gracilistyla. ROSE-GOLD PUSSY WILLOW. Shrub. Heat zones 8–5. To 6–10 ft. tall, 12 ft. wide. Narrowly oval, 2- to 4-in.-long leaves are gray green above, bluish green beneath. Male plants produce plump, gray, furry,

S

1½-in.-long catkins with numerous stamens sporting rose-and-gold anthers. Cut branches for arrangements to curb plant's size. Every 3 or 4 years, cut plant back to short stubs; you'll get very vigorous shoots with large catkins. *S. g. melanostachys* has black catkins with red anthers.

S. matsudana. HANKOW WILLOW. Tree. Heat zones 9–4. Upright, pyramidal growth to 40–50 ft. tall, 30–40 ft. wide. Bright green, narrow, 2- to 4-in.-long leaves. Can thrive on less water than most willows.

'Navajo'. GLOBE NAVAJO WILLOW. Large, spreading, round-topped tree to 70 ft. tall and wide.

'Tortuosa'. CORKSCREW WILLOW. To 30 ft. tall, 20 ft. wide; branches fantastically twisted into upright, spiraling patterns. Valued for winter silhouette and cut branches for arrangements.

'Umbraculifera'. GLOBE WILLOW. To 35 ft. high and wide. Umbrella-shaped crown with upright branches, drooping branchlets.

S. nigra. BLACK WILLOW. Tree. Zones US, MS, LS, CS; 9–5. Native to central and eastern North America, where it is common along streamsides and riverbanks. To 30–60 ft. tall, 30 ft. wide. Narrow, finely toothed leaves to 7 in. long are shiny dark green above, light green beneath. Tree bark is scaly, furrowed, and dark brown to black. The soft wood is used for making baskets and wicker furniture. Tolerates flooding; often used for wetland reclamation. Will take full sun but does best in partial shade.

SALPIGLOSSIS sinuata

PAINTED TONGUE

Solanaceae

COOL-SEASON ANNUAL

🌿 US, MS, LS, CS, TS H 6–1

☼ FULL SUN

💧 REGULAR WATER

Salpiglossis sinuata

Native to South America. Upright, open habit to 2–3 ft. tall, 1 ft. wide. Stems and narrow, 4-in.-long leaves are sticky. Flowers are 2–2½ in. wide; resemble petunias in shape but offer more unusual colors—mahogany red, reddish orange, yellow, purple, and pink shades, marbled and penciled with contrasting colors. Plants bloom most heavily in late spring and early summer. Good background plant for border; handsome cut flower. Bolero (to 2 ft. tall) and Royale (12–16 in.) are compact strains.

Seeds are rather difficult to start, especially when sown directly in garden. A better way to start them is to plant in potting mix in peat pots, several seeds to a pot. Keep pots in a warm, protected location; thin seedlings to one per pot. In most areas, plant seeds in late winter, then set out young plants once they're well established and all danger of frost is past. In Florida and South Texas, sow seeds in early fall and grow plants for winter and spring bloom. Performs best in rich soil. Stake tall types. Tip-pinch growing plants to induce branching.

SALTBUSH. See BACCHARIS halimifolia

SALT CEDAR. See TAMARIX gallica

SALVIA

SAGE

Lamiaceae (Labiatae)

EVERGREEN AND DECIDUOUS SHRUBS, PERENNIALS, AND BIENNIALS (SOME GROWN AS ANNUALS)

🌿 ZONES VARY BY SPECIES

☼ FULL SUN, EXCEPT AS NOTED

💧 REGULAR WATER, EXCEPT AS NOTED

Salvia nemorosa 'Ostfriesland'

Planting sages proves a wise move for many a Southern gardener. *Salvia* is the largest genus of the mint family, including as many as 900 species from around the world. Some serve as annual bedding plants, others are border perennials, and still others are shrubs, culinary herbs, or ground covers. Where winters are cold, tender perennials and shrubs are grown as annuals.

All sages have square stems and whorls of two-lipped flowers, either neatly spaced along the flower stalks or so tightly crowded that they look like one dense spike; some species have branched inflorescences. Flower colors range from white and yellow through salmon and pink to scarlet, red, lavender, blue, and darkest purple. A few sages have fragrant blossoms; many have aromatic foliage. They attract hummingbirds, bees, and butterflies.

Sages are for the most part pest free, though aphids, whiteflies, slugs, and snails may favor some species. Give plants good air circulation to deter fungal diseases. Deer may nibble flowers, but they usually don't browse plants heavily. Remove spent blossoms to encourage continued bloom. You can tip-pinch shoots to maintain form. To succeed with a species that is marginally hardy in your area, provide excellent drainage, let the soil go somewhat dry in fall (to encourage dormancy), delay mulching until after the first hard frost, and wait until late winter to do any heavy pruning.

S. ambigens. See *S. guaranitica*

S. 'Anthony Parker'. Evergreen shrub. Zones LS, CS, TS. Hybrid between *S. leucantha* and *S. elegans*. To 5 ft. high and wide. Leaves are similar to those of *S. elegans*. Wands of blossoms appear at stem ends throughout the year where winters are mild; in colder climates, they come from spring to frost. The flowers are like those of *S. leucantha*, but the color is an intense dark blue violet.

S. argentea. SILVER SAGE. Biennial or short-lived perennial. Zones US, MS, LS, CS; 9–5. From southern Europe, northwestern Africa. Soft, scalloped-edged, silky-haired gray-green leaves grow 6–10 in. long, form a low foliage rosette to 2 ft. wide. In summer, many-branched, 3- to 4-ft. flowering stems bear 1¼-in.-long, hooded white flowers (sometimes tinged pink or yellow) with silvery calyxes. Cut to ground when flowers fade. Handsome focal point for front of border. Protect from slugs, snails.

S. azurea grandiflora (S. pitcheri). PRAIRIE SAGE, PITCHER SAGE. Shrubby perennial. Zones US, MS, LS, CS, TS; 10–5. Native from Colorado and Texas east to Michigan and Georgia. Slender, vertical, usually unbranched stems to 5 ft. form a 2- to 3-ft.-wide clump. Plant is lax, needs support. Smooth or hairy, medium green to deep green, narrow leaves to 4 in. long. Pure azure blue flowers with white-blotched lower lip on spikes to 1 ft. long; blooms summer to frost. Tolerates heat and humidity.

S. blepharophylla. EYELASH SAGE. Shrubby perennial. Zones LS, CS, TS; 10–8. From northeastern Mexico. To 1½–2 ft. tall, spreading indefinitely by creeping rhizomes. Thin, hairy, purplish stems; oval, glossy dark green leaves to 1½ in. long, edged with fine hairs resembling eyelashes. Blooms nearly all year in mild-winter climates, from spring to frost elsewhere; inch-long scarlet flowers are carried on stems that lengthen to about 1 ft. as season goes on. If confined, makes a good ground cover in partial shade. 'Diablo' is more upright, and its vivid red flowers have two upright anthers that could be said to look like horns. 'Painted Lady' grows 1 ft. high and 4 ft. wide, bearing vivid red flowers that sport a velvety hood; it remains evergreen where temperatures stay above 20°F.

S. 'Blue Chiquita'. Shrubby perennial. Zones CS, TS. From Mexico. To 3 ft. high and wide. Heavily quilted leaves are blue green above, silvery beneath. From spring until frost, the foliage clump is topped by upright, 15- to 20-in. spires of rich blue, widely spaced flowers.

S. chamaedryoides. GERMANDER SAGE. Perennial. Zones LS, CS, TS; 12–7. From eastern Mexico. Rounded plant to 1–2 ft. tall, spreading to 2–3 ft. or more by underground runners. Silvery, ¾-in.-long leaves; brilliant true blue, 1-in. flowers on stems to 8 in. long. Heaviest bloom comes in late spring and fall, with intermittent flowering during rest of growing season. Deadhead to encourage rebloom. Elegant front-of-border plant. Drought tolerant but blooms longer and better with more water.

S. coccinea. TEXAS SAGE. Perennial in Zones CS, TS; annual anywhere; 12–1. From Mexico. Bushy, upright grower to 2–3 ft. tall, 2½ ft. wide. Dark green, hairy, oval to heart-shaped leaves to 2½ in. long. In summer, slender stems to 1 ft. long carry many ¾- to 1-in. flowers with broad lower lip. Colors range from bright red through orange red to pink and white, including many bicolors. Widely used as bedding plant, border filler. Stems are brittle; shelter from wind. Deadhead to encourage rebloom.

If plant lives over, cut back to 4–6 in. when new spring growth begins, then fertilize. By end of second season, plant will be woody and in decline. Reseeds copiously. Several good seed-grown selections are offered, including salmon pink 'Brenthurst' ('Lady in Pink'); 'Coral Nymph', near white with coral lip; and white 'Snow Nymph' ('White Nymph'). 'Lady in Red', with scarlet blooms, is a compact plant (to about 16 in.), excellent in the foreground of a colorful border.

S. elegans. PINEAPPLE SAGE. Perennial. Zones CS, TS; 12–1. Native to southern Mexico, Guatemala. In the wild, this species is variable in habit, bloom time, and leaf fragrance. The most commonly grown form, 'Scarlet Pineapple' *(S. rutilans),* grows upright to 3–4 ft. high and wide, with branching, brittle stems; in part shade, growth is lush and needs support. Densely hairy, bright green leaves to 4 in. long, broadly oval with pointed tip. Foliage has fragrance of ripe pineapple; use it in cool drinks, fruit salads. Slender, 1½-in., bright red flowers in loose clusters of 8 to 12 are carried on 6- to 8-in. stems. In mild-winter areas, blooms from late fall through spring; elsewhere, flowers come from late summer into fall. 'Sonora Red' is more compact than the species (to 2 ft. tall and wide) and hardier to cold.

S. farinacea. MEALYCUP SAGE. Perennial usually grown as annual in all zones. Native to southern New Mexico, Texas, Mexico. Upright growth to 3–4 ft. tall, half as wide. Narrowly lance-shaped leaves to 3 in. long are smooth above, woolly white below. Tall, densely packed spikes of ¾- to 1-in. flowers on stems 6–12 in. long, late spring to frost. Blossom color varies from deep violet blue to white; cuplike calyxes are covered with white hairs that often have a blue or violet tinge. Many strains are sold for bedding and container use; typically have heavier bloom, better branching, more compact than species. 'Cirrus', 14 in. high, has silvery white blossoms, calyxes, stems. 'Rhea', 14–16 in. high, has deep blue flowers, bluish calyxes; starts blooming earlier in spring. 'Strata', 12–14 in. high, has blue flowers and large, woolly, silvery white calyxes. 'Victoria', to 18–20 in. high, has violet-blue flowers and calyxes; 'Victoria White' is a white form.

S. greggii. AUTUMN SAGE. Evergreen or deciduous shrub. Zones MS, LS, CS, TS; 9–4. Native to southwestern Texas, north-central Mexico. Rounded plant, branching from base; typically grows 1–4 ft. high and wide. Slender, hairy stems are closely set with glossy green, ¾- to 1¼-in.-long leaves that vary in shape from rounded to linear. Blooms throughout summer and fall, bearing ¼- to 1-in. flowers on 3- to 6-in. stems, in colors ranging from deep purplish red through true red to various rose and pink shades to white. To keep plants tidy and free blooming, prune and remove dead flower stems frequently. Before new spring growth begins, shorten and shape plants, removing dead wood. Good low hedge. Replace plants every 4 or 5 years, when they become woody and unproductive. Drought tolerant but does best with moderate water. Grows best in the Southwest. Full sun or partial shade (be sure to give some shade in hottest climates). A few of the best selections are pure white 'Alba'; hot pink 'Big Pink', with extra-large lower lip; raspberry red 'Dark Dancer'; 'Desert Blaze', with brilliant true red flowers and gold-edged leaves; and deep red 'Furman's Red'. (Selections sold as *S. greggii* with flowers in shades of orange, orange red, or yellow actually belong with *S. ×jamensis.*)

S. guaranitica (S. ambigens). ANISE-SCENTED SAGE. Shrubby perennial. Zones MS, LS, CS, TS; 12–6. From South America. Upright, branching plant to 4–5 ft. high and nearly as wide. Spreads by short underground runners; roots form tubers resembling small sausages. Narrowly heart-shaped, sparsely hairy, mint green leaves to 5 in. long. Blooms from early summer to frost. Most common form bears 2-in. cobalt blue blossoms, carried several to each foot-long stem; calyxes are bright green, turning purplish on sunny side. Needs support. Gets woody by season's end—but that wood dies during winter and must be cut back to ground. Elegant container plant. Can be demolished by Mexican giant whitefly. Tolerates partial shade, especially in hottest climates. 'Argentine Skies' has light blue flowers. 'Black and Blue' produces deep blue blossoms with dark purplish blue calyxes. 'Costa Rica Blue' is similar but grows 6 ft. high, with larger flowers.

S. 'Indigo Spires'. Shrubby perennial. Zones LS (protected), CS, TS; 12–6. Can build up to a sprawling 6–7 ft. by 10 ft. but is easily kept to 3–4 ft. high, 2–3 ft. wide with support and selective pruning. Soft, silky, oval to oblong leaves (to 6 in. long near base of plant, shorter higher up) have a grayish sheen above, are white and woolly beneath. Narrow, twisted spikes of closely spaced, ½-in., violet-blue flowers can reach 3 ft. or longer. Blooms from early summer to frost (almost all year in mildest climates). Indigo calyxes are colorful long after blossoms fall. Excellent cut flowers. Top growth damaged by frost. Full sun or partial shade.

S. koyamae. JAPANESE YELLOW SAGE. Perennial. Zones US, MS, LS, CS, TS; 10–4. From Japan. Loose-growing ground cover to about 1 ft. tall, with lax stems up to 2 ft. long. Very attractive, heart-shaped yellow-green leaves to 6 in. long, 5 in. wide. Whorls of pale yellow flowers on 6- to 12-in. spikes in summer and fall. Does best in a shady spot, in rich, moisture-retentive, well-drained soil; looks great weaving among other shade-loving plants.

S. leucantha. MEXICAN BUSH SAGE. Evergreen shrub. Zones LS (protected), CS, TS; 12–4. From central and eastern Mexico. Vigorous, upright, velvety plant 3–4 ft. tall, 3–6 ft. or more wide; sprawls in bloom. Lance-shaped to linear, 5- to 6-in.-long leaves are dark grayish green above, whitish below. Stems to 1 ft. long bear whorls of ¾- to 1¼-in. white flowers with purple calyxes. Bloom period runs from fall through spring in the Tropical South, throughout the fall elsewhere. To limit plant size and renew flowering stems, cut back close to ground before spring growth begins or at end of bloom cycle; where growing season is especially long, cut back again in early to midsummer. Also limit watering to every 2 or 3 weeks and remove blossoms as soon as they fade. 'Eder' has leaves with creamy white edges. 'Midnight' ('Purple Velvet'), considered by many to be the best-looking form, has purple flowers and calyxes. Dwarf form 'Santa Barbara' reaches only 2 ft. high and 3 ft. wide.

S. lyrata. LYRE-LEAF SAGE. Perennial. Zones US, MS, LS, CS, TS; 12–6. Woodland wildflower native to the Southeast. To 1–2 ft. high, spreading widely by rhizomes and seeds. The main attraction is the foliage: rosettes of 3-in., lyre-shaped leaves with reddish purple markings. Spikes of little lavender-blue flowers in winter and spring are secondary. Takes sun or shade. Prefers drier, well-drained soils; good for hillsides. A seed strain with solid burgundy foliage is available.

S. madrensis. FORSYTHIA SAGE. Perennial. Zones MS, LS, CS, TS; 10–5. From west-central Mexico. Strong grower, building up to 5–8 ft. tall and wide. Spreads by rhizomes to make a broad thicket (but stems are easily pulled out). Square stems are very thick—to 2 in. on a side at base. Bright green, rough-textured leaves with an elongated heart shape reach 6 in. long at bottom of plant, become smaller toward top. Butter yellow,

Salvia argentea

Salvia chamaedryoides

Salvia coccinea 'Coral Nymph'

Salvia farinacea

Salvia 'Maraschino' (*S. microphylla* hybrid)

1-in. flowers on 1- to 2-ft. stems; good for cutting. Blooms from fall until frost (through spring in the Tropical South). Top growth damaged by frost. Plant in sun or light shade, in moist, well-drained soil. Propagate by division or cuttings. Cold-hardy selection 'Dunham', from the garden of Rachel Dunham in Cary, North Carolina, has survived −9°F. 'Red Neck Girl' has deep reddish purple stems.

S. microphylla. BABY SAGE. Evergreen shrub. Zones MS, LS, CS, TS; 12–7. Native from southeastern Arizona through southern Mexico. This species grows wild over an enormous geographical area and has many local variants. Drought tolerant but performs best with moderate water. Full sun or partial shade.

S. m. microphylla (S. grahamii). The form most often found in nurseries. Tough, dense, wiry-looking plant to 3–4 ft. high, 3–6 ft. wide. Stems marked with fuzzy white stripes. Triangular to oval, tooth-edged leaves are dark green, ½–1 in. long. Short stems bear pairs of rosy red, 1-in. flowers with small, hooded upper lip, three-lobed lower lip. Blooms most heavily in late spring and fall, sporadically at other times of year.

Forms of *S. m. microphylla* bear flowers in many shades of red, pink, orange, magenta, and violet. 'Alba' is a white-blooming form. 'Belize Form', to 5 ft. tall and 8 ft. wide, is a more tender plant with brighter green leaves; puts on a continuous show of brilliant red flowers. 'Berzerkeley' is more compact (2 ft. tall, 3–4 ft. wide), bears glowing pinkish red blossoms. 'Orange Door' reaches 3 ft. tall and wide, bears coral orange flowers. 'San Carlos Festival', 2–3 ft. tall, 4–6 ft. wide, is a nonstop bloomer bearing raspberry pink flowers. Hybrids with *S. greggii* include vigorous 'Maraschino', 3–4 ft. high, 6 ft. wide, bearing bright cherry red flowers; purplish pink 'Plum Wine', 3–4 ft. high and 2½–3½ ft. wide; 'Raspberry Royale', to 2½ ft. high and 3–4 ft. wide, with purplish red upper lip, dark red lower lip; and 'Wild Watermelon', which resembles 'Maraschino' but bears fuchsia-colored blooms.

S. m. neurepia. 'Kew Red' is the name given to the originally introduced form. To 3–5 ft. tall, 4–6 ft. wide. More open-branched plant than *S. m. microphylla,* with yellowish green leaves, brilliant red flowers.

S. miniata. Evergreen shrub treated as tender perennial or annual in all but the Tropical South. Zones TS; 12–1. Native to moist regions of Mexico and Belize. Tropical-looking plant to about 3 ft. tall and wide, with arching stems carrying toothed, glossy dark green leaves that reach 5 in. long, 2 in. across. Small bright red flowers held in dark bracts bloom year-round in the Tropical South, from spring until frost in colder climates. Good container plant. Best in partial shade.

S. nemorosa. VIOLET SAGE. Perennial. Zones US, MS. LS; 9–1. From eastern Europe, eastward to central Asia. To 1½–3 ft. tall, spreading 2–3 ft. wide by rhizomes. Forms a tight foliage rosette from which rise erect, branching flower stems. Wrinkled, dull green, finely toothed leaves are oval or lance shaped. Lower leaves are stalked, to 4 in. long; upper ones are smaller, virtually stalkless, and clasp flower stem. Sprawls if not supported. Stems 3–6 in. long hold ¼- to ½-in. flowers in violet, purple, pink, or white, with persistent violet, purple, or green bracts. Blooms for several weeks in late spring and early summer; may rebloom if deadheaded. 'Lubecca' has grayish green leaves, violet flowers with reddish purple bracts; 'Ostfriesland' ('East Friesland') has intense violet-blue flowers, pink to purple bracts. Both selections grow 1½ ft. high.

S. officinalis. COMMON SAGE. Shrubby perennial. Zones US, MS, LS, CS, TS; 10–5. From the Mediterranean region. The traditional culinary and medicinal sage. To 1–3 ft. tall, 1–2½ ft. wide; stems often root where they touch soil. Aromatic, oval to oblong, wrinkled, 2- to 3-in. leaves are gray green above, white and hairy beneath. Branching, 8- to 12-in. stems bear loose, spikelike clusters of ½-in. flowers in late spring, summer. Usual color is lavender blue, but violet, red-violet, pink, and white forms exist. Delay pruning until new leaves begin to unfurl, then cut just above fresh growth; cutting into bare wood usually causes dieback. Replace plants when they become woody or leggy (about every 3 or 4 years). Subject to root rot where drainage is less than perfect. Give afternoon shade in hottest climates.

Salvia officinalis 'Icterina'

'Berggarten' ('Mountain Garden'). Compact; to 16 in. high. Denser growth, rounder leaves, fewer flowers than species; may be longer lived.

'Compacta' ('Nana', 'Minimus'). A half-size (or even smaller) version of the species, with narrower, closer-set leaves.

'Holt's Mammoth'. Leaves are large, 4–5 in. long, used in making condiments.

'Icterina'. Gray-green leaves with golden border. Does not bloom.

'Purpurascens' ('Red Sage'). Leaves are flushed with red violet when new, slowly mature to gray green.

'Tricolor'. Gray-green leaves with irregular cream border; new foliage is flushed with purplish pink.

S. pratensis. MEADOW SAGE. Perennial. Zones US, MS, LS; 9–1. Native to Europe, Morocco. To 3 ft. tall, 1 ft. wide, with broadly oval, pointed, dark green basal leaves to 8 in. long. Spikes of small lavender blue blooms (less than 1 in. long) on branching, foot-tall stems put on a very showy (but short) springtime display. Needs a warm, well-drained site. Reseeds.

S. 'Purple Majesty'. Shrubby perennial. Zones CS, TS; 12–7. To 3 ft. tall, 4 ft. wide. Hybrid of *S. guaranitica,* with leaves of a yellower green; brilliant royal purple flowers with violet-black calyxes. Blooms from summer until frost in most of the Coastal South, nearly all year in the Tropical South (where it is evergreen).

S. regla. ROYAL SAGE. Evergreen or deciduous shrub. Zones LS, CS, TS; 10–6. Native to western Texas, central Mexico. Upright stems to 4–6 ft. high; these arch and branch out to form an almost equally wide mass. Scalloped, puckered, fan-shaped leaves (drawn out to sharp points in some forms) are 1 in. across. Orange-scarlet, 1-in. flowers with flaring calyxes appear in short clusters at branch ends; calyxes persist for several weeks after flowers drop. Profuse bloom from fall until frost (through early spring—though less profusely—in the Tropical South). Prune this plant (if ever) only when it is growing strongly in summer; winter-pruned plants recover slowly, may even die. Loses leaves at 28°F. Excellent nectar source for hummingbirds. 'Huntington' has larger flowers, spreading habit (4–5 ft. tall, to 6 ft. wide); 'Royal' is an upright grower to 6–8 ft.

S. reptans. Perennial. Zones LS, CS, TS; 10–7. From the high mountains of Mexico. Light green, almost needlelike leaves on thin stems form a dense mound to 2 ft. high and 3 ft. wide; masses of light blue, ½-in. flowers

Salvia guaranitica

Salvia officinalis 'Tricolor'

Salvia splendens

Salvia nemorosa 'Ostfriesland'

Salvia uliginosa

S

held in dark calyxes bloom from late spring through fall. Plant disappears in winter. Although native to dry, gravelly washes, it thrives in the humid Southeast. Hardy to 20°F. A West Texas form discovered in the Trans-Pecos region is more upright, to 3 ft. high and about 2 ft. wide.

S. splendens. SCARLET SAGE. Perennial grown as annual. Zones US, MS, LS, CS, TS; 12–1. Native to Brazil. The traditional bright scarlet bedding sage now comes in a range of colors, from vivid true red through salmon and pink to purple shades. White forms are also available. Plants vary in size from compact 1-ft. dwarfs to 3- to 4-ft. kinds. Leaves are bright green, heart shaped, 2–4 in. long. Blooms from late spring or summer

Salvia splendens

through fall (all year in the Tropical South); 4- to 12-in. stems bear 2-in. flowers that emerge from 1-in. calyxes of same color. Can be ravaged by Mexican giant whitefly. Give afternoon shade in hottest climates. Seed-grown strains include Firecracker, to 1 ft. high and wide, in many single colors and bicolors; and Sizzler, an early bloomer offering mixed colors that grows a little taller. 'Van Houttei' is a vigorous old cutting-grown selection to 3 ft. tall, 4 ft. wide (even larger in mild-winter climates); it bears maroon flowers with an orange-scarlet tinge from early fall through spring where temperatures remain above 28°F. Similar to 'Van Houttei' are 'Louie's Orange Delight' (with orange-toned red blooms and bracts) and 'Paul' (with reddish purple flowers and bracts).

S. ×superba. Perennial. Zones US, MS, LS; 9–5. Form generally available is 'Superba'. However, many plants sold under this name are seedlings or selections of *S. ×sylvestris* or *S. nemorosa*. The real 'Superba' forms a tight foliage clump that spreads 2–3 ft. by rhizomes and sends up erect, much-branched, 3-ft.-tall flowering stems. Smooth, scallop-edged green leaves are lance shaped; basal ones are stalked and 3–4 in. long, upper ones stalkless and smaller. At bloom time, top 6–8 in. of stems bear clusters of ½-in. violet-blue flowers with reddish purple bracts that persist long after flowers fall. (Bracts on most seedlings are green, sometimes with a purple tinge.) Blooms for several weeks in early to midsummer; may rebloom if deadheaded. Blooming plant will sprawl 5–6 ft. wide unless staked.

S. ×sylvestris (S. deserta). Perennial. Zones US, MS, LS; 9–3. Like its parent *S. nemorosa* but more compact, with stems that are less leafy. Oblong to lance-shaped, medium green, scalloped leaves are wrinkled, softly hairy, to 3 in. long. Typically unbranched or few-branched flowering stems to 6–8 in. long, set with pinkish violet, ½-in. blossoms. Blooms for several weeks in early to midsummer; may rebloom if deadheaded. 'Blauhügel' ('Blue Hill'), to 2 ft., has medium blue flowers. 'Mainacht' ('May Night'), 2–2½ ft., bears ¾-in. indigo flowers with green bracts (purplish at base), begins blooming in midspring. Two 1½- to 2-ft. forms are 'Rosakönigen' ('Rose Queen'), with purplish pink flowers and crimson bracts, and 'Schneehügel' ('Snow Hill'), bearing pure white blossoms with green bracts.

S. texana. BLUE TEXAS SAGE. Perennial. Zones MS, LS, CS, TS; 10–5. From Central and West Texas. Well-branched, bushy plant to 15 in. tall and about half as wide. Densely hairy stems; narrow, tapering, 2-in.-long leaves, also hairy, toothed along the upper margins. Produces spikes of inch-long flowers in purplish blue with a white throat that appear in spring. Takes moderate water.

S. uliginosa. BOG SAGE. Perennial. Zones US, MS, LS, CS, TS; 12–6. From moist lowlands in South America. Upright, dense; to 4–6 ft. tall, 3–4 ft. wide, spreading aggressively by rhizomes. Smooth green leaves are lance shaped, toothed; they reach 3½ in. long near plant's base, decrease in size toward top. Branched inflorescence with 5- to 6-in. stems carries whorls of ½-in., intense sky blue flowers with white throat, wide lower lip. Plant produces blooms from summer through fall. To restrain its spread, give only moderate water or confine roots by planting it in 15-gallon nursery can sunk in ground to its rim.

S. verticillata. WHORLED CLARY. Perennial. Zones US, MS, LS; 8–6. From central Europe, western Asia. Foliage clump to 2½ ft. wide sends up branching, 2½- to 3-ft.-tall flower stems. Wavy-margined, medium green, softly hairy leaves to 5–6 in. long; shape varies from oval to elliptical or

oblong. Basal leaves often divided into one or two pairs of smaller leaflets. Widely spaced whorls of 20 to 40 buds open to violet or lavender-blue flowers nearly ½ in. long, with purple-tinged, persistent calyxes. Blooms in summer; may rebloom if deadheaded. Protect from slugs, snails. 'Alba' has pure white flowers and calyxes. 'Purple Rain' is 1–2 ft. high, with profuse, showy deep purple blossoms and calyxes.

SAMBUCUS canadensis

AMERICAN ELDERBERRY

Caprifoliaceae

DECIDUOUS SHRUB

US, MS, LS, CS H 12–1

FULL SUN OR LIGHT SHADE

REGULAR WATER

Sambucus canadensis

Native to central and eastern North America. Spreading, suckering shrub to 8–12 ft. tall and wide; to keep plant dense, prune hard during dormant season. Almost tropical-looking light green leaves, each with seven 2- to 6-in.-long leaflets. Blooms in early summer, bearing flat, creamy white flower clusters to 10 in. wide; these are followed by tasty purple-black berries. The ripe fruit is good in pies, jams, jellies; both flowers and fruit are used for wine. Strictly fruiting selections include 'Adams', 'Johns', and many more; plant any two for cross-pollination. Ornamental selections include 'Aurea', with golden green foliage (golden in full sun) and red berries; 'Laciniata', cutleaf or fernleaf elder, with finely cut foliage, near-black berries; and 'Maxima', with leaves to 1–1½ ft. long, flower clusters 10–18 in. wide, black fruit.

SAND CHERRY. See PRUNUS besseyi, P. ×cistena

SANDWORT. See ARENARIA montana

SANGUINARIA canadensis

BLOODROOT

Papaveraceae

PERENNIAL

US, MS, LS H 8–1

PARTIAL TO FULL SHADE

REGULAR TO AMPLE WATER

Sanguinaria canadensis

Native to North America. This low-growing member of the poppy family gets its common name from the orange-red juice that seeps from cut roots and stems. Deeply lobed gray-green leaves reach 6–12 in. across. Blooms in spring, bearing lovely (but ephemeral) white or pink-tinged, 1½- to 2-in. flowers carried singly on 8-in. stalks. Spreads slowly by rhizomes; good choice for damp, shaded rock gardens or woodland plantings. Combines well with ferns. Mulch in spring. 'Multiplex' has double flowers.

SANGUISORBA

BURNET

Rosaceae

PERENNIALS

US, MS, LS H 8–1, EXCEPT AS NOTED

LIGHT SHADE IN HOTTEST CLIMATES

REGULAR WATER

Sanguisorba minor

These plants grow from creeping rhizomes. Leaves divided featherwise into toothed, oval or roundish leaflets. Small flowers carried in dense, feathery spikes much like small bottlebrush (*Callistemon*) blossoms. Often sold as *Poterium*.

S. canadensis. GREAT BURNET, CANADIAN BURNET. Native to eastern North America. To 3–6 ft. tall, 3 ft. wide, with bright green foliage and

S

8-in. spikes of white flowers in late autumn. Dies to the ground in winter even in mild climates.

S. minor. GARDEN BURNET, SALAD BURNET. Zones US, MS, LS, CS; 9–1. Native to Europe, western Asia. Can reach 1½ ft. high and wide but is usually kept clipped to a few inches to maintain a fresh supply of new foliage. Leaves have a mild cucumber flavor and are used in salads, soups, cool drinks. Can be used as an edging for border or herb garden. If not sheared too low, bears roundish, inch-long clusters of red flowers from late spring to midsummer. Self-sows prolifically if allowed to go to seed. Evergreen in all but the Upper South.

S. obtusa. Native to Japan. To 4 ft. tall, 2 ft. wide, with grayish green leaves and pink flower spikes 4 in. tall in summer. Evergreen in all but the coldest winters.

SANSEVIERIA

Agavaceae

PERENNIALS

🗡 TS ⊩ 12–7; OR HOUSEPLANTS

☼ ◐ SUN OR LIGHT SHADE; BRIGHT LIGHT

💧 MODERATE WATER

Sansevieria trifasciata 'Laurentii'

Group of approximately 60 species native to Africa and India. Admired for their stiff, attractive leaves, which grow from rhizomes. Very popular as houseplants; can also be grown outdoors in mild-winter areas. Outdoors, they accept sun or light shade and just about any well-drained soil, tolerating drought and even salt spray. Indoors, they do best in bright light but will accept dim light. Allow soil to go dry between soakings. For best growth, feed monthly in spring and summer with a general-purpose liquid houseplant fertilizer diluted to half-strength. Easy to propagate from leaf cuttings. Mature, pot-bound plants may occasionally bear spikelike clusters of fragrant flowers in spring or summer.

S. cylindrica. SPEAR SANSEVIERIA. Forms a rosette of three or four rigidly upright, unusual-looking leaves, each 2–4 ft. long and only about 1 in. wide; they are cylindrical, in dark green with lighter green horizontal bands. White or pinkish, 1½-in.-long flowers.

S. parva. KENYA HYACINTH. Rosette of 6 to 12 narrow leaves that grow upward, then arch outward; each leaf is 8–16 in. long and ½–1 in. wide. Leaves are medium green with dark green horizontal bands; flowers are pinkish white.

S. trifasciata. SNAKE PLANT, MOTHER-IN-LAW'S TONGUE, BOW-STRING HEMP. The original brown-thumb houseplant, supremely tolerant of neglect. If you kill this one, better give up gardening and turn to macramé. Dark green leaves with gray-green horizontal bands can reach 4 ft. tall, 2 in. wide; they are rigidly upright or slightly spreading at the top. Tiny greenish white flowers.

Few plants boast such colorful common names. The first one listed refers to the banded or mottled foliage, resembling the skin of some snakes; the second name comes from the long leaves, which are always fully extended. The third comes from the tough leaf fibers, which were used for bowstrings. Selections include the following six.

'Bantel's Sensation'. Narrow, upright dark green leaves heavily marked with irregular vertical stripes of creamy white.

'Hahnii'. BIRD'S-NEST SANSEVIERIA. Dwarf to just 1 ft. tall, forming a vase-shaped rosette of short, broad dark green leaves with horizontal silver bands. Good tabletop houseplant.

'Laurentii'. GOLDBAND SANSEVIERIA. Similar to the species, but leaves have golden yellow margins. The most popular snake plant.

'Robusta'. Like the species, but leaves are shorter and nearly twice as wide.

'Silver Hahnii'. Same shape and size as 'Hahnii', but leaves are silvery gray green with faint horizontal dark green bands.

'Silver Queen'. New leaves are silvery gray green, edged with a thin dark green margin; older leaves turn solid dark green.

SANTA BARBARA DAISY. See ERIGERON karvinskianus

SANTOLINA

Asteraceae (Compositae)

EVERGREEN SHRUBS

🗡 US, MS, LS, CS ⊩ 9–6, EXCEPT AS NOTED

☼ FULL SUN

◐ 💧 LITTLE OR NO WATER TO MODERATE WATER

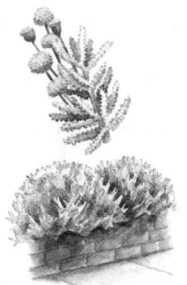

Santolina chamaecyparissus

These Mediterranean natives are notable for their attractive foliage, profuse summer show of small, round, buttonlike flower heads, and stout constitutions. All are aromatic if bruised. Unpruned plants tend to become sparse and woody in the center. Cut back yearly, before spring growth begins; you can simply trim as needed around the edges (as if giving the plant a haircut) or cut the whole plant back to a few inches high. After blossoms fade, shear or clip off flowering shoots. Remove and replace plants if they become too woody. In coldest part of range, plants may die to the ground, but they should grow back from roots. Good as ground covers, bank covers, edgings for walks or borders, low informal or sheared hedges. Grow in any well-drained soil. Not usually browsed by deer.

S. chamaecyparissus (S. incana). LAVENDER COTTON. To 2 ft. tall, 3 ft. wide. Brittle, woody stems are densely clothed with rough, finely divided, whitish gray leaves. Bright yellow flower heads. Smaller versions of the species include 'Nana', to 1 ft. tall and 2–3 ft. wide; and 'Pretty Carol', to 16 in. high and wide. 'Lemon Queen', to 2 ft. tall and wide, has creamy yellow flowers.

S. pinnata (S. ericoides). Heat zones 12–7. Grows to 2–2½ ft. tall, 3 ft. wide; narrow, tooth-edged dark green leaves, cream-colored flowers. Variety *S. p. neapolitana* grows to 12–15 in. tall, has silvery foliage and bright yellow flowers.

S. rosmarinifolia (S. virens). GREEN SANTOLINA. To 2 ft. tall, 3 ft. wide, with narrow green leaves like those of rosemary *(Rosmarinus)*. Leaves may have tiny teeth or none at all. Bright yellow flowers. 'Morning Mist' is similar but more compact.

SANVITALIA procumbens

CREEPING ZINNIA

Asteraceae (Compositae)

ANNUAL

🗡 US, MS, LS, CS, TS ⊩ 12–1

☼ FULL SUN

◐ 💧 MODERATE TO REGULAR WATER

Sanvitalia procumbens

This bright-blossomed, heat-resistant Mexican native is not really a zinnia, but it looks enough like one to fool most people. Grows only 4–6 in. high but spreads or trails to 1½ ft. or wider. Leaves are like miniature (to 2-in.-long) zinnia leaves. Flowers are nearly 1 in. wide, with vivid yellow or orange rays around a dark purple-brown center. Blooms from midsummer until frost. Selections include 'Mandarin Orange' and double-flowered 'Gold Braid'.

Needs good drainage. Sow seeds or set out nursery transplants in spring (creeping zinnia resents transplanting, so sow where plants are to grow). Use in borders or edgings, as annual cover for slope or bank; or plant in hanging baskets or pots.

Sapindaceae. Members of the soapberry family are trees and shrubs with (usually) divided leaves, clustered small flowers (sometimes showy), and fruit that is berrylike, often showy. Some have edible fruit. Examples are *Koelreuteria*, lychee, and soapberry *(Sapindus)*.

S

SAPINDUS

SOAPBERRY

Sapindaceae

DECIDUOUS AND EVERGREEN TREES

✿ ZONES VARY BY SPECIES

☼ FULL SUN

�○ ◑ LITTLE TO MODERATE WATER

Sapindus drummondii

Group of about 12 species of deciduous or evergreen trees and shrubs from tropical and subtropical parts of the world; the two described here are both U.S. natives. All of these plants are tough and easy to grow. Saponin, a substance contained in the berries, lathers when mixed with water—hence the common name.

S. drummondii. WESTERN SOAPBERRY. Deciduous. Zones US, MS, LS, CS; 10–2. Native to south-central U.S. Attractive round-headed, spreading tree to 25–30 ft. tall and eventually as wide, with yellowish green, 10- to 15-in.-long leaves divided into many leaflets. In early summer, tiny yellowish white flowers bloom in 8- to 10-in.-long clusters; these are followed by beadlike, ½-in., orange-yellow fruits that turn black by winter. More common in Texas and Oklahoma than elsewhere in the South. Makes a good shade or street tree, thanks to its tolerance for adverse conditions: poor, dry, rocky, alkaline soil; polluted air; wind; occasional drought. Fruit drop and self-sown seedlings can cause problems. 'Narrow Leaf' has narrower leaves than the species.

S. marginatus. FLORIDA SOAPBERRY. Evergreen. Zones LS, CS; 10–8. Native to the South Atlantic coast, from South Carolina to Florida. Grows 40 ft. tall and 30 ft. wide. Bright green leaves to 14 in. long, each with 7 to 13 lance-shaped leaflets; turn golden in fall. Clusters of small white flowers in spring.

SAPIUM sebiferum

CHINESE TALLOW, POPCORN TREE

Euphorbiaceae

DECIDUOUS TREE

✿ LS, CS, TS H 12–8

☼ FULL SUN

◑ MODERATE TO REGULAR WATER

❦ MILKY SAP IS POISONOUS IF INGESTED

Sapium sebiferum

Native to China and Japan. Fast-growing tree to 40 ft. tall, 30 ft. wide, with a rounded or conical crown. Its names come from its unusual seeds: the Chinese once extracted wax from the seed capsules to make soap and candles, and the ripened, whitish seeds resemble popcorn. Decorating wreaths with this "popcorn" is a popular tradition in Charleston and other southeastern cities. The tree has long been prized in the South for its spectacular scarlet, orange, burgundy, and yellow fall display; it's one of the few trees with brilliant fall color in the Deep South. In the northern end of the Lower South, young trees may be killed to the ground in winter, and branches of established trees may be frozen back several feet.

Medium green leaves to 3 in. long and wide are rounded, tapering to a slender point; they flutter in the slightest breeze. Tree has an airy look and casts moderate shade, making it a good choice for lawns and terraces. Blooms in summer; flowers are yellowish green, stringlike catkins 2–4 in. long. The seed capsules that follow open by October, revealing the white, waxy seeds.

Chinese tallow tolerates almost any soil. Seedlings can easily grow 5 ft. tall the first year. Unfortunately, almost every seed produced germinates somewhere; the tree has spread so prolifically in Florida and along the South Atlantic coast that in those areas it is considered a noxious weed. Japanese tallow, *S. japonicum,* is similar, but its seeds are borne singly instead of in clusters.

SAPONARIA

Caryophyllaceae

PERENNIALS

✿ US, MS H 8–1, EXCEPT AS NOTED

☼ FULL SUN

◑ ◑ MODERATE TO REGULAR WATER

Saponaria ocymoides

These European natives are generally low, spreading plants that are useful as ground covers or in rock gardens. Best in lean, very well-drained soil.

S. ×lempergii. GIANT-FLOWERED SOAPWORT. Heat zones 8–4. Handsome blue-green leaves to ½ in. long form a mat 8 in. tall, 1½ ft. wide. Large clusters of bright pink, inch-wide flowers virtually smother the foliage for weeks in midsummer. 'Max Frei' has soft pink blooms.

S. ocymoides. ROCK SOAPWORT. Trailing habit to 1 ft. high and 3 ft. across. Dark green, oval, ½-in.-long leaves. In spring, plants are covered with ¼-in. pink flowers in loose bunches shaped much like those of phlox. Looks especially nice cascading over a wall. Selections include white 'Alba' and deep pink 'Rubra Compacta'.

S. officinalis. SOAPWORT, BOUNCING BET. Zones US, MS, LS, CS; 9–1. Grows to 2 ft. tall, spreading wider by underground runners. Can be invasive in rich, moist soil. Dark green, oval, pointed leaves to 4 in. long; loose clusters of inch-wide red, pink, or white flowers in midsummer. When crushed in water, roots produce a sudsy, detergent-like lather. This is one tough plant; before the days of herbicides, it could be seen growing in the cinders along railroad rights-of-way. The selection 'Rosea Plena', with double light pink flowers, is the common garden form. 'Rubra Plena' has crimson blooms that turn paler as they age.

S. ×olivana. Tiny dark green leaves form a compact cushion spreading to 2–4 in. tall, 8 in. wide. In early summer, the foliage mound is covered with short-stemmed pink blooms to ¾ in. across.

S. pumilio (S. pumila). Linear, bright green, inch-long leaves form a tight cushion to 2 ft. high and 1 ft. wide. Inch-wide purplish pink flowers are borne singly at branch ends in spring, making a ring of blossoms around the plant's base.

SARCOCOCCA

SWEET BOX

Buxaceae

EVERGREEN SHRUBS

✿ US, MS, LS, CS H 9–5

◐ ● PARTIAL TO FULL SHADE

◑ ● MODERATE TO REGULAR WATER

Sarcococca ruscifolia

Native to the Himalayas, China. Grown for handsome, waxy dark green leaves and tiny, powerfully fragrant white blossoms that come in late winter or early spring, hidden in the foliage. Small, berrylike fruit follows the flowers. Useful in shaded areas—under overhangs, in entryways, beneath low-branching evergreen trees. Plants maintain slow, orderly growth and polished appearance in deepest shade. Grow best in organically enriched soil. Scale insects are the only pests.

S. confusa. Quite similar to the species *S. ruscifolia* and generally sold as such. However, *S. ruscifolia* produces red fruit, while that of *S. confusa* is black.

S. hookeriana humilis (S. humilis). Low growing, seldom more than 1½ ft. high; spreads to 8 ft. or more by underground runners. Branches are thickly set with pointed leaves 1–3 in. long, ½–¾ in. wide. Glossy blue-black fruit. Good ground cover.

S. ruscifolia. FRAGRANT SARCOCOCCA. Slow growth to 4–6 ft. high, 3–7 ft. wide. If grown against a wall, it will form a natural espalier, with branches fanning out to create patterns. Oval to elliptical leaves to 2 in. long, densely set on branches. Red fruit.

SARRACENIA

PITCHER PLANT

Sarraceniaceae

CARNIVOROUS PERENNIALS

US, MS, LS, CS

FULL SUN

AMPLE WATER

Sarracenia flava

Famed for having insects for dinner, pitcher plants can also make excellent garden plants. Ten or so species inhabit bogs from Maryland south to Florida. They are found where soils are constantly moist but only briefly flooded, and where periodic wildfires remove encroaching trees and shrubs, providing full sun. The soil in such sites is usually nutrient starved and acidic, lacking nitrogen and other elements. Pitcher plants compensate by obtaining these nutrients from the creatures they consume, including insects, spiders, and the occasional small frog.

Growing from fleshy roots, plants form whorls of hollow, modified leaves—the "pitchers" of the common name—that both carry out photosynthesis and trap insects. Attracted by nectar, victims fall into pools of digestive fluid at the bottom of the pitchers. Depending on the species, the pitchers range from a few inches to over 3 ft. tall; they may be upright and shaped like tubes or trumpets, or they may look like jugs and lie on the ground. Some have "lids" above the opening, giving the plant a hooded appearance. Colors include green, yellow green, burgundy, and bright red, and some pitchers also sport dramatic red veining—apparently a ploy to attract more prey. Showy, solitary spring blossoms in red, pink, or yellow, typically 2–3 in. across, rise on stalks alongside or above the pitchers. Complex crosses have produced many interesting hybrids.

Pitcher plants need a dormant period in winter, so they're not suited to indoors or the Tropical South. They grow best in sunny bogs. To create a bog garden, dig out a large depression about 1½ ft. deep, line it with a plastic pond liner, then fill it with a mixture of 2 parts sphagnum peat moss, 1 part perlite, and 1 part builder's sand. Keep the soil constantly moist but not flooded. Do not fertilize. Never feed meat to pitcher plants; propagate them by seed or division. Most species and a number of fancy new hybrids are available from mail-order specialists.

S. alata. PALE PITCHER PLANT. Heat zones 9–5. Native to the Gulf Coast from Alabama west to Texas. Upright, trumpet-shaped, green to yellow-green pitchers to 2½ ft. tall; lid is held nearly erect. Pale yellow flowers in early spring. Some variants have reddish bronze pitchers.

S. ×catesbaei. CATESBY'S PITCHER PLANT. Naturally occurring hybrid of *S. flava* and *S. purpurea*. Found along the Coastal Plains from Virginia to South Carolina. Upright brick red pitchers to 15 in. tall; brick red flowers in late spring.

S. 'Dixie Lace'. Heat zones 9–4. Complex hybrid. Butterscotch yellow pitchers with dramatic red veining grow 1½ ft. tall and are held at a 45° angle. Showy maroon red flowers.

S. flava. YELLOW PITCHER PLANT. Heat zones 10–7. Native to Coastal Plains from Virginia to Florida. Erect pitchers to 3 ft. or taller, in yellowish green with striking crimson veining. Pendulous bright yellow flowers to 4 in. across appear on tall stalks. The showiest pitcher plant in bloom.

S. 'Flies Demise'. Heat zones 10–6. Complex hybrid. Upright, hooded pitchers to 10 in. tall are dusty orange with dramatic red veining near the top. Maroon flowers.

S. 'Judith Hindle'. Heat zones 10–6. Complex hybrid. Upright pitchers to 3 ft. tall are brilliant ruby maroon, with ruffled lids veined in ruby and pink. Maroon flowers.

S. 'Ladies in Waiting'. Heat zones 9–4. Complex hybrid. Vigorous plant with upright pitchers to 2 ft. tall; they are bright red with white speckles on the upper part, fading to bright green near the base. Fluted lids. Showy maroon red flowers.

S. leucophylla. WHITE PITCHER PLANT. Heat zones 10–6. Native to southern Georgia, southern Alabama, southern Mississippi, Florida Panhandle. Considered by many to be the most beautiful species—and it catches more insects than any other. Upright pitchers to nearly 3½ ft. tall sport open lids. Pitchers are green on the lower half; the upper half and lid are white laced with reddish purple veins. Large (to 4-in.-wide) purplish red flowers.

S. minor. HOODED PITCHER PLANT. Heat zones 10–6. Native to Coastal Plains from North Carolina to Florida. Unusual pitchers to 1 ft. tall resemble the hooded robes of monks, with the lid forming a domed canopy over the mouth; they are green with coppery red shading on the upper quarter. Yellow flowers.

S. oreophila. GREEN PITCHER PLANT. Heat zones 9–1. Very rare species; native to northeastern Alabama and mountainous juncture of Georgia and the Carolinas. Upright light green pitchers with red veining grow 2½ ft. tall. Yellowish green flowers bloom in late spring.

S. psittacina. PARROT PITCHER PLANT. Heat zones 9–1. Native to Coastal Plains from south Georgia to Mississippi. Jug-shaped, red-veined green pitchers to 8 in. long lie on the ground and form a rosette; their interiors are lined with needlelike hairs. Small, sweet-smelling, purplish red blooms appear over a long period. In its native grassy swamps, periodic flooding allows this one to feed on tadpoles and small fish.

S. purpurea. PURPLE PITCHER PLANT. Heat zones 9–1. Native to bogs of the eastern U.S. and Canada. A variable and widespread species. Jug-shaped pitchers to 1 ft. long lie on the ground; they may be green with red veining or solid maroon or red. Flower colors include purple, red, pink, and purplish red.

Sarracenia purpurea

S. rubra. SWEET PITCHER PLANT. Heat zones 9–5. A highly variable species divided into five subspecies; found in the Carolinas, Florida, and Alabama. Upright, trumpetlike pitchers with open lids range from 10 in. to 2 ft. tall; they may be green with red veining or solid red. Bright red to dark red flowers, sometimes fragrant.

SASA. See BAMBOO

SASSAFRAS albidum

SASSAFRAS

Lauraceae

DECIDUOUS TREE

US, MS, LS, CS 10–3

FULL SUN OR PARTIAL SHADE

REGULAR WATER

Sassafras albidum

Native to eastern U.S. Grows fast to 20–25 ft. high, then more slowly to reach an eventual 50–60 ft. Often shrubby in youth; with maturity, it becomes dense and pyramidal, to 40 ft. across, with heavy trunk and rather short branches. Interesting winter silhouette. Dark reddish brown, furrowed bark. Leaves 3–7 in. long, 2–4 in. wide; they may be oval, mitten shaped, or lobed on both sides. Excellent fall color—shades of yellow, orange, scarlet, and purple. Yellow flowers aren't usually showy, but clusters outline the bare branches in early spring. Male and female flowers are borne on separate trees; when the two sexes are grown near each other, the female tree bears dark blue, ½-in. berries on bright red stalks.

Sassafras is a pleasantly aromatic tree; the bark of roots is sometimes used for making tea, which has a flavor like that of root beer. The tree's volatile oil contains safrole, which is carcinogenic in animals, but extracts sold in markets for making sassafras tea are safrole free.

Performs best in well-drained, nonalkaline soil; won't take prolonged drought. Hard to transplant. Tends to produce suckers, especially if roots are cut during cultivation. No noteworthy diseases, but Japanese beetles can be a serious problem in the Upper and Middle South. Deer don't seem to care for the taste of sassafras.

SATIN POTHOS. See SCINDAPSUS pictus

SATUREJA

Lamiaceae (Labiatae)

ANNUALS AND PERENNIALS

ZONES VARY BY SPECIES

FULL SUN

WATER NEEDS VARY BY SPECIES

Satureja montana

These aromatic plants serve many culinary purposes. They're used to flavor sauces, vinegars, stews, soups, meat stuffings, and vegetables. Summer savory has a mild, delicate flavor; winter savory has a strong, pungent taste and retains its intensity when dried.

S. hortensis. SUMMER SAVORY. Annual. Zones US, MS, LS, CS, TS; 12–1. From southeastern Europe. Upright to 1½ ft., with loose, open habit. Aromatic, rather narrow leaves to 1½ in. long; use fresh or dried as a seasoning. Whorls of tiny, delicate, pinkish white to rose flowers in summer. Grow in light, well-drained, organically enriched soil. Sow seeds in place; thin to 1–1½ ft. apart. Good potted plant. Regular water.

S. montana. WINTER SAVORY. Shrubby perennial. Zones US, MS, LS, CS. From southern Europe. To 15 in. high, 2 ft. wide. Stiff, narrow to roundish leaves to 1 in. long. Use leaves fresh or dried; clip at start of flowering season for drying. Blooms profusely in summer, bearing whorls of small white to lilac flowers that attract bees. Use in rock garden, as dwarf clipped hedge in herb garden (space plants 1½ ft. apart). Grow in light, well-drained soil. Prune as needed to keep compact. Moderate water.

SAVORY. See SATUREJA

SAWBRIER. See SMILAX glauca

SAW PALMETTO. See SERENOA repens

Saxifragaceae. The saxifrage family once included a number of shrubs, but these now occupy their own families—Grossulariaceae (currants and gooseberries) and Hydrangeaceae. Saxifragaceae now includes herbaceous plants, such as *Astilbe, Bergenia,* coral bells *(Heuchera),* and *Saxifraga.*

SAXIFRAGA stolonifera

STRAWBERRY GERANIUM,
STRAWBERRY BEGONIA

Saxifragaceae

PERENNIAL

MS, LS, CS 9–5; OR HOUSEPLANT

PARTIAL TO FULL SHADE;
BRIGHT INDIRECT LIGHT

REGULAR WATER

Saxifraga stolonifera

Native to Asia, this pretty, old-timey plant is neither strawberry, geranium, nor begonia. It forms rosettes of nearly round, silver-veined leaves to 4 in. across; leaves are olive green above, purplish underneath. Spreads like strawberries do, by sending out threadlike runners with baby plants attached. Clusters of white or pink, dovelike, inch-long flowers appear on 1- to 2-ft. spikes in late summer and fall. Where hardy, grows beautifully outdoors—as a ground cover or in rock gardens, strawberry pots, hanging baskets. Give it a mostly shady spot and moist, well-drained soil containing lots of organic matter.

Indoors, it makes a nice houseplant for pots and hanging baskets. Give it morning sun or day-long bright indirect light. Allow soil to dry only slightly before watering. Feed monthly with a general-purpose liquid houseplant fertilizer; stop feeding and reduce watering slightly in fall and winter. Colorful selections include the following three.

'Harvest Moon'. Sulphur yellow to golden foliage and pink flowers.

'Maroon Beauty'. Vigorous spreader with silver-veined leaves that are dark green above, deep purple beneath. White flowers.

'Tricolor' ('Magic Carpet'). Hardier than species. Cupped leaves are rich green with white-and-pink edging above, raspberry red beneath. White flowers.

SCABIOSA

PINCUSHION FLOWER

Dipsacaceae

ANNUALS AND PERENNIALS

US, MS, LS, CS, TS, EXCEPT AS NOTED

FULL SUN, EXCEPT AS NOTED

MODERATE TO REGULAR WATER

Scabiosa columbaria

Stamens protrude beyond curved surface of flower head, giving illusion of pins stuck into a cushion. Bloom begins in midsummer, continues until frost if flowers are deadheaded or cut regularly. Good in mixed or mass plantings. Excellent cut flowers.

S. atropurpurea. PINCUSHION FLOWER, MOURNING BRIDE. Annual. Heat zones 8–3. May also be sold as *S. grandiflora.* From southern Europe. To 2½–3 ft. tall, 1 ft. wide. Oblong, coarsely toothed leaves. Many carry flowers to 2 in. or more wide, in colors ranging from blackish purple to salmon pink, rose, white. Double Mixed strain and 'Salmon Queen' reach 3 ft. tall; Dwarf Double Mixed grows to 1½ ft. high.

S. caucasica. PINCUSHION FLOWER. Perennial. Zones US, MS, LS; 9–1. From the Caucasus, Turkey, Iran. To 1½–2½ ft. high, 1–2 ft. wide. Leaves vary from finely cut to uncut. Flowers 2½–3 in. across, in blue to bluish lavender or white, depending on selection. Needs partial shade in hottest climates. 'Alba' has white blossoms. 'Fama' has branching stalks carrying blue, 3-in. flowers with broad rays; 'Blue Perfection' bears lavender-blue flowers with fringed rays. House's Mix (House's Novelty Mix) contains a mixture of blue shades and white.

S. columbaria. Perennial. Heat zones 8–1. From Europe, Africa, Asia. To 2 ft. high and wide, with finely cut gray-green leaves. Flowers to 3 in., in lavender blue, pink, or white; bloom almost all year in the Tropical South. 'Butterfly Blue' (deep lavender blue) and 'Pink Mist' (bright pink) are superior selections.

SCAEVOLA aemula

FANFLOWER

Goodeniaceae

PERENNIAL

CS, TS; ANYWHERE AS ANNUAL; 12–1

FULL SUN

MODERATE TO REGULAR WATER

Scaevola aemula

This Australian native gets its common name from the shape of its flowers—they do indeed resemble little fans, with all the petals on one side. Some forms are prostrate, others upright to 2½ ft.; fleshy stems of some spread to 3 ft. wide, while those of others trail or sprawl to twice that width. Bright green, 1½- to 2-in.-long leaves; lavender-blue, 1½-in. flowers all along the leafy branches. The plant is evergreen and nearly everblooming in the Coastal and Tropical South; elsewhere, it blooms continuously from spring until frost.

Excellent in hanging baskets, as a ground cover, or spilling over walls. Good drainage is a must. Not favored by browsing deer. Selections feature blue, lavender-blue, purple, or white blossoms. Popular 'Blue Wonder' and 'New Wonder' are lavender blue; 'Jacob's White' and 'White Charm' have snowy white blooms. Flowers of 'Zig Zag' sport blue and white stripes.

SCARLET WISTERIA TREE. See SESBANIA grandiflora

S

SCHEFFLERA

Araliaceae

EVERGREEN SHRUBS OR TREES

TS H 12–10, EXCEPT AS NOTED;
OR HOUSEPLANTS

SOME SHADE IN HOTTEST CLIMATES;
BRIGHT INDIRECT LIGHT

REGULAR WATER

Schefflera actinophylla

The hallmark of these fast-growing plants is their exotic leaves, which are divided into leaflets that spread out like the fingers of a hand. In most of the South, they are popular houseplants. They prefer bright light but need protection from direct sun, which may burn leaves. Give good drainage; let the soil go fairly dry between soakings. Feed once a month with a general-purpose liquid houseplant fertilizer; stop feeding and reduce watering in fall and winter. Watch for mealybugs, red spider mites, aphids, and scale; apply insecticidal soap or horticultural oil to control these pests. Dust-free, well-humidified plants suffer the fewest problems, so frequent misting is a good idea.

Outdoors, plant scheffleras in fertile, well-drained soil, either in the ground or in large pots. In central and south Florida, they grow into small trees. Bold texture makes them useful accents for patios and Florida rooms. Summer flowers (showy in some species) are followed by tiny dark fruits; houseplants are unlikely to bloom.

S. actinophylla (Brassaia actinophylla). QUEENSLAND UMBRELLA TREE, OCTOPUS TREE, SCHEFFLERA. Zones CS (milder parts), TS. Native to Australia. Fast growth to 20–40 ft. tall and eventually as wide. The "umbrella" of the common name comes from the foliage form: the long-stalked, glossy green leaves are divided into 7 to 16 large (1-ft.-long) leaflets that radiate outward like ribs of an umbrella. Foliage grows in tiers. "Octopus" refers to showy flower heads: narrow, raylike structures to 3 ft. long, set all along their length with little blossoms, radiate from a central point. Flowers age from greenish yellow to pink to dark red. Good for striking tropical effects, silhouette, contrast with fern-type foliage plants. Cut out tips occasionally to keep plant from becoming leggy. Cut back overgrown plants nearly to ground level; they will grow back with a better form.

S. arboricola (Heptapleurum arboricolum). DWARF SCHEFFLERA. Native to Taiwan. To 20 ft. tall with equal or greater spread, but easily kept smaller with pruning. The dark green leaves are much smaller than those of *S. actinophylla*, with 3-in. leaflets that broaden toward rounded tips. If plants are set into the ground with stems at an angle, they'll continue to grow at that angle—which can give attractive multistemmed effects. Yellowish flowers are clustered in flattened, foot-wide spheres; they turn bronze with age. Overall, this species produces a denser, darker, less tree-like effect than *S. actinophylla*. Less prone to pests than *S. actinophylla*—a far better houseplant. 'Worthii' has variegated green-and-yellow leaves; low light causes variegation to fade.

Schefflera arboricola

S. elegantissima (Dizygotheca elegantissima). FALSE ARALIA. Native to New Caledonia. Airy and elegant. As a juvenile, it is a houseplant; when mature, it's a garden plant to 25 ft. tall and wide. Leaves are divided like fans into leaflets with notched edges. Young plants are unbranched, with narrow (1-in.), lacy-looking leaflets to 9 in. long; foliage is shiny dark green above, reddish beneath. The plant branches as it matures, and leaflets grow slightly longer, broaden to 3 in., and become less glossy. Greenish yellow flowers in clusters to 1 ft. long. Be warned that false aralia bears a striking resemblance to marijuana, and be prepared to explain its presence in your garden to local authorities and nosy neighbors.

S. pueckleri (Tupidanthus calyptratus). Native to southern Asia. Resembles *S. actinophylla* but is a denser plant that branches from the base. May be trained to single trunk. Leaves to nearly 2 ft. wide are divided into seven to nine stalked, glossy bright green leaflets, each to 7 in. long, 2½ in. wide. Flowers are greenish, borne on shorter, fewer "rays" than those of *S. actinophylla*.

SCHIZACHYRIUM
scoparium

LITTLE BLUESTEM

Poaceae (Gramineae)

PERENNIAL GRASS

US, MS, LS, CS H 9–1

FULL SUN

MODERATE TO REGULAR WATER

Schizachyrium scoparium

Native to much of North America; an important grass in the native tall-grass prairie. Formerly known as *Andropogon scoparius*. Clump-forming grass 2–4 ft. tall, 1–2 ft. wide, with narrow leaves that may be erect or arching. Late summer flowers are inconspicuous but age to an attractive silvery shade. Leaf color varies from bright green to distinctly bluish in summer, from light brown to dark red in fall and winter. Types that are bluer in summer take on the deeper cold-weather colors: blue-green leaves of 'Blaze' turn a strong red in fall, while 'The Blues' has striking light blue leaves that turn burgundy red. All are pest-free plants that look especially nice in meadow plantings and thrive in just about any well-drained soil.

SCHIZOPHRAGMA
hydrangeoides

JAPANESE HYDRANGEA VINE

Hydrangeaceae

DECIDUOUS VINE

US, MS, LS H 9–6

PARTIAL SHADE

REGULAR WATER

Schizophragma hydrangeoides

Native to Korea, Japan. Resembling climbing hydrangea (*Hydrangea anomala petiolaris*), vine climbs to 30 ft. or more by holdfasts. Pointed, tooth-edged dark green leaves are 3–5 in. long. Blooms in summer, producing flat, 8- to 10-in.-wide clusters of white flowers. Like the bloom clusters of lace-cap hydrangeas, these feature tiny fertile flowers surrounded by a ring of sterile ones—but the sterile blossoms of this plant have only a single "petal." Use to climb shaded walls or trees. Needs good, well-drained soil. Prune only errant growth. 'Moonlight' has blue-green foliage with a silvery cast. 'Roseum' bears pink flowers.

SCHIZOSTYLIS coccinea

CRIMSON FLAG

Iridaceae

PERENNIAL FROM RHIZOME

LS, CS, TS H 10–7; OR GROW IN POTS

FULL SUN OR LIGHT SHADE

REGULAR TO AMPLE WATER

Schizostylis coccinea

Virtually evergreen South African native. Like gladiolus, it has upright, swordlike leaves and a spike of closely set flowers, but the blossoms themselves—star shaped, bright colored, 2 in. wide—recall another relative, watsonia. Crimson flowers are carried on slender, 1½- to 2-ft.-tall stems; other forms include white 'Alba', watermelon red 'Oregon Sunset', and several pink types ('Mrs. Hegarty', 'Sunrise', 'Viscountess Byng'). All bloom in fall; may also bloom late winter and spring in Coastal and Tropical South. Excellent cut flowers. Plant in spring, in humusy, well-drained soil. Set rhizomes ½–1 in. deep, 1 ft. apart. Water generously from planting until autumn flowering ends, then sparingly until growth resumes in spring. If clumps become crowded, divide them in early spring; each division should have at least five shoots. In the Lower South, mulch heavily in fall. In colder regions, grow in pots and protect in winter.

S

SCHLUMBERGERA

Cactaceae

CACTI

✂ TS ⬆ 12–10; OR GROW IN POTS

◑ PARTIAL SHADE; BRIGHT INDIRECT LIGHT

💧 REGULAR WATER

Schlumbergera truncata

In nature, these cacti live on trees, as epiphytic orchids do. Need rich, porous soil, such as a mix of equal parts coarse sand, peat moss, and leaf mold. Feed with liquid fertilizer every 7 to 10 days during growth and bloom. Plants are often confused with *Zygocactus*. The many kinds differ principally in flower color.

S. ×buckleyi. CHRISTMAS CACTUS. May be labeled *S. bridgesii.* Old favorite to 2 ft. high, 3 ft. wide. Arching, drooping bright green branches of flattened, scallop-edged, smooth, spineless, 1½-in. joints. Can bear hundreds of many-petaled, long-tubed, 3-in.-long, rosy purplish red flowers at Christmastime. For late December bloom, give plant cool night temperatures (50–55°F), 12 to 14 hours of darkness per day during November.

S. gaertneri. See Rhipsalidopsis gaertneri

S. truncata. THANKSGIVING CACTUS. Native to Brazil. To 1 ft. high and wide. Bright green, 1- to 2-in., toothed joints; two large teeth at tip of last joint on each branch. Short-tubed, 3-in.-long, scarlet flowers with spreading, pointed petals from late fall through winter. Tends to bloom earlier than *S. × buckleyi,* though bloom periods may overlap. Many selections are sold, with blooms in white, pink, salmon, orange.

SCIADOPITYS verticillata

UMBRELLA PINE

Sciadopityaceae

EVERGREEN TREE

✂ US, MS, LS ⬆ 9–4

☼ ◑ FULL SUN OR PARTIAL SHADE

💧 REGULAR WATER

Sciadopitys verticillata

In its native Japan, this tree reaches 100–120 ft. tall, but in Southern gardens it is not likely to exceed 25–40 ft. tall, 25–30 ft. wide. Very slow grower. In youth, it is symmetrical, dense, and rather narrow; with age, it is more open, and limbs tend to droop. Small, scalelike leaves are scattered along branches and bunched at branch ends. Glossy dark green needles grow in whorls of 20 to 30 at branch and twig ends, radiating out like spokes of an umbrella; they are flattened, firm, fleshy, 3–6 in. long. Woody, 3- to 5-in. cones may appear on older trees.

Choice decorative tree for open ground or containers. Plant in rich, well-drained, neutral or slightly acid soil. Watch for mites in hot, dry weather. Leave unpruned; or thin to create Japanese effect. Boughs are beautiful and long lasting in arrangements.

SCILLA

SQUILL, BLUEBELL

Liliaceae

PERENNIALS FROM BULBS

✂ US, MS, LS, EXCEPT AS NOTED

☼ ◑ FULL SUN DURING BLOOM,
    PARTIAL SHADE AFTER

💧 REGULAR WATER DURING GROWTH AND BLOOM

⬥ ALL PARTS ARE POISONOUS IF INGESTED

Scilla peruviana

The three hardier species are native to cold-winter regions of Europe and Asia and need some winter chill. Gardeners in cold-winter climates know them as harbingers of spring; the earliest ones come into flower with winter aconite (*Eranthis*) and snowdrop (*Galanthus*). Less hardy to cold is Peruvian scilla *(S. peruviana);* despite its name, it is native to the Mediterranean region. All squills have bell-shaped or starlike flowers borne on leafless stems that rise from clumps of strap-shaped leaves.

Cold-hardy species look best when naturalized; grow them in small patches or larger drifts. *S. peruviana* is most attractive in clumps along pathways, at edges of mixed plantings, in pots. Plant all types in fall, in well-drained, organically enriched soil. Set bulbs of cold-hardy species 2–3 in. deep, 4 in. apart; set those of *S. peruviana* 3–4 in. deep, 6 in. apart. Reduce watering when foliage yellows after bloom. Hardy kinds will tolerate less moisture during summer dormancy, but don't let soil dry out completely. *S. peruviana* will accept summer moisture but doesn't need any. Divide clumps (during dormancy) when vigor and bloom quality decline. Deer seem to avoid all species.

S. bifolia. Zones US, MS, LS; 8–1. Each 8-in. stem carries three to eight star-shaped, inch-wide flowers in turquoise blue. White, pale purplish pink, and violet-blue varieties are available. Each bulb produces only two leaves.

S. campanulata. See Hyacinthoides hispanica

S. hispanica. See Hyacinthoides hispanica

S. mischtschenkoana (S. tubergeniana). Heat zones 9–6. Each 6-in. stem bears nodding clusters of three or four starlike flowers in pale blue with darker blue stripes.

S. non-scripta. See Hyacinthoides non-scripta

S. peruviana. PERUVIAN SCILLA. Zones LS, CS; 9–8. Large bulb produces numerous floppy leaves; in late spring, 10- to 12-in. stems appear, each topped with dome-shaped cluster of 50 or more starlike flowers. Most forms have bluish purple blooms, but there is a white form.

S. siberica. SIBERIAN SQUILL. Heat zones 8–5. Each 3- to 6-in. stem bears several flowers shaped like flaring bells. Typical color is intense medium blue, but there are selections in white, lilac pink, and light to dark shades of violet blue, often with darker stripes. 'Spring Beauty' has brilliant violet-blue blooms that are larger than those of the species.

SCINDAPSUS pictus

SATIN POTHOS

Araceae

EVERGREEN VINE

✂ TS ⬆ 12–10; OR HOUSEPLANT

◑ DAPPLED SHADE; BRIGHT INDIRECT LIGHT

💧 REGULAR WATER

⬥ ALL PLANT PARTS ARE POISONOUS IF INGESTED

Scindapsus pictus

Resembles more familiar green-and-yellow pothos (*Epipremnum aureum;* also sold as *Scindapsus aureus*) but has dark green leaves with gray-green mottling. Leaves are also thinner in texture and usually somewhat larger (to 6 in., compared with the 2- to 4-in. leaves of pot-grown pothos). Flowers are insignificant. All plant parts are poisonous, and the sap can cause a skin rash. The most frequently grown selection is 'Argyraeus', with silky-sheened leaves carrying almost silvery markings that are more prominent and larger than those of the species.

Satin pothos is fussier than pothos: needs perfect drainage, high humidity, and good light but no direct sun. Water as soon as soil becomes dry to the touch; feed every other week with a general-purpose liquid fertilizer. In winter, reduce watering and cease fertilizing.

SCORPION WEED. See PHACELIA bipinnatifida

SCOTCH HEATHER. See CALLUNA vulgaris

SCOTCH MOSS. See SAGINA subulata, SELAGINELLA kraussiana

SCREWPINE. See PANDANUS utilis

Scrophulariaceae. The figwort family consists principally of annuals and perennials. Most have irregular flowers, with four or five lobes often arranged as two lips. Some examples are snapdragon (*Antirrhinum*), pocketbook plant (*Calceolaria*), foxglove (*Digitalis*), *Penstemon*, and wishbone flower (*Torenia*).

S

SCUTELLARIA

SKULLCAP
Lamiaceae (Labiatae)
PERENNIALS AND ANNUALS
US, MS, LS
FULL SUN OR LIGHT SHADE
REGULAR WATER

Scutellaria wrightii

Clump-forming mint relatives, with the family's typical square stems and paired leaves. Long, tubular flowers flare out into two lips, the upper one narrow and hooded, the lower one broad. The shrubby species presented here are native to the Southwest. They are easy to grow if given good drainage; tolerate drought and alkaline soil.

S. drummondii. DRUMMOND SKULLCAP. Annual. Heat zones 8–1. Native to Texas, New Mexico, Oklahoma, Mexico. Upright, branching plant forms a mound 1 ft. tall and wide. Oval gray-green leaves to 1 in. long; lavender spring flowers about ½ in. across.

S. resinosa. RESINOUS SKULLCAP. Perennial. Heat zones 9–1. Native from Kansas and Colorado south to Texas and Arizona. Mounding plant 6–8 in. tall, 1 ft. wide, with roundish, resinous, grayish green leaves less than ½ in. long. One-sided, elongated clusters of deep purple-blue, 1-in. flowers in late spring. Deadhead to encourage intermittent bloom through autumn.

S. suffrutescens. PINK SKULLCAP. Perennial. Heat zones 9–7. From Mexico. Forms a dense mound to 1 ft. tall, 1½ ft. wide, with oval bright green leaves just ½ in. long. Deep rosy pink flowers to 1 in. long bloom from late spring until frost. 'Texas Rose' is a superior selection.

S. wrightii. SHRUBBY SKULLCAP. Perennial. Heat zones 8–5. Native to Texas and Oklahoma. Mounding plant 6–10 in. high and a bit wider, with small, rounded green leaves. Deep violet-blue, ½- to 1-in.-long flowers have prominent white anthers that give them a striped appearance. Blooms heavily in June, then off and on until frost. Good for massing and rock gardens. Evergreen in mild-winter areas.

SEA BUCKTHORN. See **HIPPOPHAE** rhamnoides

SEAFORTHIA elegans. See **ARCHONTOPHOENIX** cunninghamiana

SEA GRAPE. See **COCCOLOBA**

SEA HOLLY. See **ERYNGIUM**

SEA LAVENDER. See **LIMONIUM**

SEA PINK. See **ARMERIA**

SEASHORE MALLOW. See **KOSTELETZKYA** virginica

SEDGE. See **CAREX**

SEDUM

SEDUM, STONECROP
Crassulaceae
SUCCULENT PERENNIALS
US, MS, LS, EXCEPT AS NOTED
FULL SUN OR PARTIAL SHADE, EXCEPT AS NOTED
LITTLE TO MODERATE WATER, EXCEPT AS NOTED

Sedum spathulifolium
'Purpureum'

Native to many parts of the world. Some are quite hardy to cold, others fairly tender; some are tiny and trailing, others much larger and upright. Fleshy leaves are evergreen (unless otherwise noted) but highly variable in size, shape, and color. Typically small, star-shaped flowers, sometimes brightly colored, are usually borne in fairly large clusters.

Smaller sedums are useful in rock gardens, as ground or bank covers, in small areas where unusual texture is needed. Some are prized by collectors of succulents, who grow them in pots, dish gardens, or miniature gardens.

Larger types are good in borders or containers. Most sedums are easy to propagate by stem cuttings; even detached leaves will root and form new plants. Soft and easily crushed, they will not take foot traffic, but they are otherwise tough, low-maintenance plants. Low-growing types often escape damage by browsing deer. Some plants sold as *Sedum* have been reassigned by botanists to the genus *Hylotelephium;* these are noted in the descriptions.

S. acre. GOLDMOSS SEDUM. Zones US, MS, LS, CS; 8–1. Native to Europe, North Africa, Turkey. To 2–5 in. high, with upright branchlets rising from trailing, rooting stems. Light green leaves only ¼ in. long; clustered yellow flowers in spring. This old favorite is extremely hardy but can get out of bounds and become a weed. Use as ground cover (set plants 1–1½ ft. apart), between stepping-stones, or in chinks of dry walls.

S. album. Heat zones 9–4. Often sold as *S. brevifolium.* From Europe, Siberia, western Asia, North Africa. Creeping plant to 2–6 in. high, with ½-in.-long, light to medium green, sometimes red-tinted leaves. White or pinkish summer flowers. Plant 1–1½ ft. apart for ground cover. This species will root from the smallest fragment, so beware of planting it near choice, delicate rock garden plants. 'Coral Carpet' has coral pink new growth and turns reddish bronze in winter.

S. altissimum. See S. reflexum

S. anglicum. Zones US, MS, LS, CS; 9–1. From western Europe. Low, spreading plant 2–4 in. high. Dark green leaves are tiny, to just ⅛ in. long. Pinkish or white flowers appear in spring. For ground cover, set plants 9–12 in. apart.

S. 'Autumn Joy' (*Hylotelephium* 'Autumn Joy', *H.* 'Herbstfreude'). Zones US, MS, LS, CS; 9–1. Hybrid of *S. telephium* and *S. spectabile.* To 1–2 ft. tall, 2 ft. wide, with green leaves to 2–3 in. long and about as wide. Rounded clusters of blossoms are pink when they open in late summer or autumn, age later to coppery pink and finally to rust. Dies down in winter.

S. bithynicum (*S. pallidum bithynicum*). TURKISH SEDUM. Zones US, MS, LS, CS. From Turkey and the Caucasus. Prostrate, very low spreader to 1 in. high and 2 ft. wide or wider. Stems are crowded with cylindrical blue-gray leaves only ¼ in. long; they take on russet tones in cold weather. Tiny, starry white flowers are held 3 in. above the foliage on brownish stems in summer.

S. cauticolum (*Hylotelephium cauticolum*). Heat zones 9–4. Native to Japan. Slowly forms a mound 4–6 in. high, 1–1½ ft. wide. Blue-gray, slightly toothed, 1-in. leaves. Clusters of rose red flowers top stems in late summer or early fall. Dies to ground in winter.

S. dasyphyllum. Native to the Mediterranean region. Forms a low (1½- to 4½-in.-high) mat that spreads to 1 ft. or wider. Gray-green, ⅛- to ¼-in. leaves are densely packed on stems. Blooms in summer, bearing white flowers with pink streaks. Pink-blossomed 'Riffense' has silver gray leaves that are especially plump and succulent. Partial shade.

S. 'Frosty Morn'. Zones US, MS, LS, CS. Resembles *S.* 'Autumn Joy', but the light blue-green leaves are boldly outlined in creamy white. Blooms in late summer, bearing large clusters of flowers that are white in hot climates, pale pink in cooler ones. Dies down in winter. Excellent for rock gardens, edgings.

S. kamtschaticum. Heat zones 8–1. Native to Korea, Japan. Variable species to 4–12 in. high, 2 ft. wide, with trailing stems set with thick, somewhat triangular, 1- to 1½-in. medium green leaves, toothed on the upper third. Summer flowers open yellow, age to red. Useful in colder climates as a rock garden plant or small-space ground cover (set plants 1 ft. apart). 'Variegatum' has cream-edged leaves. *S. k. ellacombianum* (sometimes sold as *S. ellacombianum*) is a shorter plant (4–6 in. high) with more compact growth, unbranched stems, and brighter green leaves. *S. k. floriferum* (sometimes sold as *S. floriferum*) is a more profuse bloomer with smaller flowers in a lighter yellow; its selection 'Weihenstephaner Gold' has abundant golden yellow blossoms that turn orange with age.

S. lineare. Zones MS, LS, CS; 9–5. Often sold as *S. sarmentosum.* Native to China, Japan. To 4 in. high. Trailing, rooting stems to 1 ft. long are closely set with narrow, inch-long light green leaves. Loads of yellow flowers in late spring, early summer. For ground cover, set plants 1–1½ ft. apart. 'Variegatum', with white-edged leaves, is often grown in containers.

S. morganianum. DONKEY TAIL, BURRO TAIL. Zone TS; or houseplant. Thought to have originated in Mexico. Produces long, trailing stems

S

that reach 3–4 ft. in 6 to 8 years. Thick, ¾-in.-long, light gray-green leaves overlap each other along stems to form braided-looking "tails" less than 1 in. thick. Pink to deep red flowers may appear from spring to summer but are only rarely seen. Because of its long stems, this species is best grown in a hanging basket or wall pot; or try it spilling from the top of a wall or in a rock garden. Provide rich, fast-draining soil (such as a half-and-half mixture of sand and potting soil). Protect from wind and give partial shade. Indoors, site in a south-facing window. Allow soil to become quite dry between thorough

Sedum morganianum

waterings, and feed in spring and summer with a general-purpose liquid houseplant fertilizer diluted to half-strength. Reduce watering and cease feeding in winter.

S. 'Purple Emperor'. Upright habit to 1½ ft. high and wide. Purple stems hold lance-shaped leaves in a rich red purple. Dusty rose flowers bloom in late summer, carried in clusters to 6 in. across. Flowers and foliage contrast beautifully.

S. reflexum (S. rupestre). Zones US, MS, LS, CS; 9–6. Native to Europe. Often sold as *S. altissimum*. Creeping plant to 4 in. high, with cylindrical gray-green leaves to ¾ in. long. Yellow summer flowers. Spreads freely; plant 9–12 in. apart for ground cover.

S. sarmentosum. See S. lineare

S. sieboldii (Hylotelephium sieboldii). Heat zones 9–6. Native to Japan. Low-growing plant just 4 in. high, 8–12 in. wide, with spreading, trailing, unbranched stems to 8–9 in. long. Blue-gray leaves with red edges are carried in threes; they are nearly round, stalkless, toothed along upper half. Plant turns coppery red in fall, dies to ground in winter. Each stem bears a broad, dense, flat cluster of dusty pink flowers in

Sedum sieboldii

autumn. Leaves of 'Variegatum' have yellowish white markings. Species and selection are beautiful in rock gardens, hanging baskets. Light shade.

S. spathulifolium. Zones US, MS, LS, CS; 9–5. Native from California's Coast Ranges and Sierra Nevada north to British Columbia. Spoon-shaped, ½- to 1-in. blue-green leaves tinged with reddish purple are packed into rosettes on short, trailing stems. Light yellow flowers bloom in spring and summer. Use as ground cover (set plants 1–1½ ft. apart), in rock garden. Very drought tolerant. 'Cape Blanco' is a selected form with good leaf color; 'Purpureum' has deep purple foliage.

S. spectabile (Hylotelephium spectabile). SHOWY SEDUM. Zones US, MS, LS, CS; 9–1. Native to China, Korea. Long a favorite in Southern gardens. To 1½ ft. tall and wide, with upright or slightly spreading stems thickly clothed in blue-green, roundish, 3-in. leaves. Dense, 6-in.-wide, dome-shaped flower clusters appear atop stems in late summer and fall; they open pink, mature to dark brown seed heads that put on a long-lasting show. Dies to ground in winter. Full sun. Moderate to regular water. 'Brilliant' has deep rose red blossoms; its sport 'Neon' has bubble-gum pink flowers in thicker, more rounded clusters. Other selections include 'Carmen', soft rose; 'Indian Chief', coppery red; 'Meteor', carmine red; and 'Ruby Jewel', deep maroon.

S. spurium. TWO-ROW SEDUM. Zones US, MS, LS, CS; 9–1. From the Caucasus. Low-growing plant with trailing stems and dark green or bronze-tinted leaves just an inch or so long; spreads to 2 ft. or wider. In summer, pink flowers appear in dense clusters at ends of 4- to 5-in. stems. For rock garden, pattern planting, ground cover. 'Bronze Carpet' has bronze leaves and pink flowers; 'Dragon's Blood' ('Schorbuser Blut') bears purplish bronze leaves, dark red blooms. 'John Creech' has purplish pink blossoms and small leaves. 'Red Carpet' has red leaves and blossoms. Leaves of 'Tricolor' are variegated in green, creamy white, and pink; flowers are pink.

S. telephium (Hylotelephium telephium). LIVE-FOREVER SEDUM. Zones US, MS, LS, CS; 9–1. Native from eastern Europe eastward to Japan. Old favorite. To 2 ft. high, 1–2 ft. wide. Resembles *S. spectabile* but has gray-green, somewhat narrower leaves. Long-lasting floral display begins in late summer and fall; blossom clusters open purplish pink, age to

brownish maroon. Plant dies to ground in winter. Leaves of 'Matrona' are gray green with dark pink edges; they age to grayish brown (retaining the pink edge). Large heads of pink flowers are borne on red stems. 'Mohrchen' has purple new growth and rosy pink flowers. *S. t. maximum* 'Atropurpureum' has attractive burgundy foliage all season; flowers are dusty pink. Plant in full sun (stems tend to flop in shaded sites). Moderate to regular water.

S. ternatum. MOUNTAIN SEDUM. Heat zones 9–1. Native to moist, open woodlands in eastern U.S. Spreads by creeping stems to form large, low (3- to 6-in.-tall) mats of pretty foliage. The small, roundish, ½- to 1-in.-long leaves grow in whorls of three; they are pale green when new, aging to dark green. Blooms profusely in late spring and early summer, when ½-in. white flowers with purple-red stamens open along the stems. Thrives in moist soil with plenty of organic matter. Partial to full shade.

S. tetractinum. CHINESE SEDUM. Zones US, MS, LS, CS; 9–1. From China. Cascading stems, loaded with flat, nearly round leaves ½–¾ in. across, form a clump 2–3 in. tall and 1–2 ft. wide. Leaves are bright glossy green, often with reddish margins; they turn a rich reddish bronze in fall. In early summer, clusters of bright yellow flowers are held just above the foliage.

S. 'Vera Jameson' (Hylotelephium 'Vera Jameson'). Heat zones 8–1. Cross between *S. telephium maximum* 'Atropurpureum' and *S.* 'Ruby Glow' (a low-growing hybrid with purple-gray leaves and ruby red flowers). To 8–12 in. high and 1½ ft. wide, with spreading purple stems clothed in pinkish purple leaves. Rose pink flowers in late summer, fall. Dies to ground in winter.

SELAGINELLA

Selaginellaceae

PERENNIALS

🌿 MS, LS, CS, TS ⊩ 12–8, EXCEPT AS NOTED

◑ ● PARTIAL TO FULL SHADE

● REGULAR WATER

Selaginella kraussiana

Evergreen or semievergreen ground covers—mosslike, beautiful, and easy to grow in humid, moist shade and slightly acid soils with lots of organic matter. Some of the many species form erect tufts of green often mistaken for ferns, but most spread very low to the ground, the sprawling stems rooting as they grow. One has electric blue leaves.

S. braunii. ARBORVITAE FERN. From China. Easy-to-grow, erect plant to 1½ ft. high, spreading widely. Lower stems are undivided; upper, much-branched stems carry lacy dark green leaves.

S. involvens. From Indonesia, China, Japan. Grows 6–12 in. tall, 2 ft. wide. Erect, tufty habit. Much-branched stems are crowded with bright green leaves.

S. kraussiana. IRISH MOSS, SCOTCH MOSS, CLUB MOSS. Heat zones 9–5. Native to tropical and southern Africa. Creeping, trailing habit; grows 1 in. tall and spreads widely by rooting stems. Bright green leaves. Useful for hanging baskets. 'Aurea' has bright golden green foliage; 'Brownii' is especially dwarf, forming a 2-in.-tall cushion on the soil.

S. lepidophylla. RESURRECTION PLANT. Heat zones 10–8. Native from Arizona and Texas southward to Peru. To 3 in. high, 6 in. wide; branched to base. Dense tufts of dark green leaves. Gets its common name from the fact that it curls into a ball when dry but opens flat when soaked in water.

S. pallescens. DWARF CEDAR FERN. Native to North and Central America. To 6 in. high, 1 ft. wide; branched nearly to base. Leaves are light yellow green above, white beneath.

S. uncinata. PEACOCK MOSS. Heat zones 9–5. From China. Creeping, trailing habit; 1–2 in. tall, spreading to 2 ft. across by rooting stems. In filtered light, leaves are bright metallic blue green.

SELF-HEAL. See PRUNELLA

SEMIARUNDINARIA. See BAMBOO

SEMPERVIVUM

HOUSELEEK

Crassulaceae

SUCCULENT PERENNIALS

US, MS, LS, CS

LIGHT SHADE IN HOTTEST CLIMATES

LITTLE TO MODERATE WATER

Sempervivum tectorum

Native to mountains of Europe. Form tightly packed rosettes of fleshy, evergreen leaves; spread by little offsets that cluster around parent rosette. Clustered, star-shaped summer flowers in white, yellowish, pink, red, or greenish; pretty in detail but not showy. Blooming rosettes die after setting seed, but offsets (easily detached and replanted) carry on. There are many species; all are good in rock gardens, pots, even in pockets in boulders or pieces of porous rock. Need excellent drainage. Water only to prevent shriveling.

S. arachnoideum. COBWEB HOUSELEEK. Heat zones 8–5. Gray-green rosettes of many leaves are joined by fine hairs for a cobweb-covered look. Larger rosettes (to 2 in. wide) are surrounded by a host of smaller ones. Spreads slowly to make a dense mat to 1 ft. or wider. Bright red flowers on 4- to 6-in. stems.

S. tectorum. HEN AND CHICKENS. Heat zones 8–1. Gray-green, 2- to 5-in.-wide rosettes spread quickly to form clumps to 2 ft. or wider. Leaves have red-brown, bristly tips. Red or reddish blossoms are borne on stems to 2 ft. tall. An old-time passalong plant.

SENECIO

Asteraceae (Compositae)

ANNUALS, PERENNIALS, AND EVERGREEN OR DECIDUOUS VINES

ZONES VARY BY SPECIES

EXPOSURE NEEDS VARY BY SPECIES

WATER NEEDS VARY BY SPECIES

Senecio cineraria

Daisy relatives that range from garden cineraria and dusty miller to vines, shrubs, perennials, succulents, even a few weeds. Succulents are often sold as *Kleinia,* an earlier name.

S. aureus (Packera aurea). GOLDEN GROUNDSEL. Perennial. Zones US, MS, LS; 8–4. Native to eastern North America. To 2 ft. high, 6 in. wide. Clump of bright green, toothed leaves is topped in spring by flat clusters of deep yellow, ½- to 1-in.-wide daisies. Full sun or part shade. Ample water; good bog garden plant.

S. cineraria. DUSTY MILLER. Shrubby perennial in Zones MS, LS, CS; 8–4. Annual in the Upper South. To 2–2½ ft. tall and wide. Woolly white leaves cut into many blunt-tipped lobes; clustered heads of yellow or creamy yellow flowers in summer. Gets leggy unless sheared occasionally. Full sun. Needs good drainage, little to moderate water. Striking in night garden. Deer don't seem to care for it.

S. confusus. MEXICAN FLAME VINE. Evergreen or deciduous vine. Zones CS, TS; 12–8; dies to ground in mild frost but comes back fast from roots. Native from Mexico to Honduras. Twines to 8–10 ft. Light green, rather fleshy leaves are 1–4 in. long, ½–1 in. wide, coarsely toothed. Large clusters of ¾- to 1-in., startling orange-red blooms with golden centers appear at branch ends; 'São Paulo' is deeper orange, almost brick red. Plants bloom all year where winters are mild. Provide light soil, regular water. Full sun or light shade. Use on trellis or column, let cascade over bank or wall, or plant in hanging basket.

S. glabellus (Packera glabella). BUTTER-WEED. Annual. Zones US, MS, LS, CS, TS. Native to the southeastern U.S. Fast-growing, prolifically self-seeding, easy-to-grow plant that makes a bright swath of yellow in wet soils from very early spring to the beginning of summer. Medium green, broadly toothed leaves to 10 in. long form a basal rosette, from which rises a 1- to 3-ft.-tall stem topped by clusters of golden yellow, inch-wide, daisy-like flowers. Regular to ample water. Full sun or partial shade.

S. × hybridus (S. cruentus, Pericallis × hybrida). CINERARIA. Annual. Zones US, MS, LS, CS, TS; 6–1. Most common are large-flowered dwarf kinds, usually sold as Multiflora Nana or Hybrida Grandiflora. These are compact growers (to 12–15 in. high and wide) bearing broad clusters of 3- to 5-in. daisies; colors range from white through pink and purplish red to blue and purple, often with contrasting eyes or bands. You'll usually find plants for sale in garden centers and supermarkets between Valentine's Day and Easter. Give them moist, cool, loose, rich soil. Once they finish blooming, throw them away. Partial to full shade; regular water.

Senecio × hybridus

S. leucostachys. See S. viravira

S. macroglossus. KENYA IVY, NATAL IVY, WAX VINE. Evergreen vine in the Tropical South; heat zones 12–10; houseplant anywhere. From Africa. Twining or trailing vine to 6½ ft., with thin, succulent stems and thick, 2- to 3-in.-wide, waxy or rubbery leaves shaped like ivy leaves, with three, five, or seven shallow lobes. Tiny yellow daisies in summer. Leaves of 'Variegatus' are boldly splashed with creamy white. Give part shade and moderate water. As houseplant, grow in sunny window and water only when soil is dry. Feed monthly with a general-purpose liquid houseplant fertilizer; in winter, stop fertilizing and reduce water.

S. viravira (S. leucostachys). DUSTY MILLER. Shrubby perennial. Zones MS, LS. Native to Argentina. To 4 ft. tall and wide, with sprawling habit. Leaves like those of *S. cineraria* but more strikingly white, more finely cut into much narrower, pointed segments. Creamy white summer flowers are not showy. In full sun, it is brilliantly white and densely leafy; in part shade, it is looser and more sparsely foliaged, with larger, greener leaves. Tip-pinch young plants to keep them compact. Moderate water.

WILL THE REAL DUSTY MILLER PLEASE STAND UP? *Many plants answer to the name; all have whitish, silvery, or grayish foliage, grow best in full sun, and tolerate some drought. A number of plants are sold by this common name; the best known is* Senecio cineraria. *Others include* S. viravira, Artemisia stellerana, Centaurea cineraria, *and* C. gymnocarpa.

SENNA

Fabaceae (Leguminosae)

PERENNIALS AND EVERGREEN AND DECIDUOUS SHRUBS

ZONES VARY BY SPECIES

FULL SUN OR LIGHT SHADE

MODERATE TO REGULAR WATER, EXCEPT AS NOTED

Senna artemisioides

Previously included in *Cassia* and still often sold as such, these species have been reclassified as *Senna*—a move not accepted by all botanists. Grown for their lavish show of yellow, five-petaled flowers that look something like those of potentilla. Blossoms are followed by seedpods that may create litter; to reduce pod production, prune lightly after bloom. Rangy, rank growers should also be cut back periodically to encourage more compact growth. Good for screens, massing, background plantings. Prefer well-drained soil.

S. alata (Cassia alata). CANDLESTICK SENNA. Evergreen shrub. Zones TS; 12–8. Native to many tropical regions of the world. May reach 30 ft. tall and half as wide, but more likely to be 6–10 ft. tall and 3–4 ft. wide in gardens. Bright green leaves divided into 14 to 28 oblong leaflets, each 2½ in. long. Golden yellow, inch-wide flowers in big, spikelike clusters appear from fall into winter. Prune hard after bloom.

S. artemisioides (Cassia artemisioides). FEATHERY CASSIA. Evergreen shrub. Zones CS, TS. Native to Australia. To 3–5 ft. tall and wide, with attractive light, airy structure. Gray leaves divided into six to eight needlelike, 1-in.-long leaflets. Bears bright yellow, ¾-in. flowers in clusters of five to eight in winter and spring, with bloom often continuing

S

into summer. Heavy seed production. Very drought tolerant but looks better with moderate to regular water.

S. bicapsularis (Cassia bicapsularis). Evergreen shrub. Zones CS, TS; 12–10. Native to tropical Central and South America. Recovers after being killed to ground by frost. To 10 ft. tall and wide. Bright green leaves with six to ten roundish, rather thick leaflets, each to ¾ in. long. Bright yellow, ½-in.-wide flowers in spikelike clusters from midautumn to midwinter or until cut down by frost. Prune severely after flowering.

S. corymbosa (Cassia corymbosa). FLOWERY SENNA. Evergreen shrub. Zones CS, TS; 12–8. Native to South America. Rangy growth to 10 ft. tall, 10–12 ft. wide. Dark green leaves with six narrow, oblong, 1- to 2-in. leaflets. Rounded clusters of 1½-in. bright yellow flowers, spring to fall. Self-sowing can be a problem.

S. lindheimeriana (Cassia lindheimeriana). VELVET-LEAF SENNA. Perennial. Zones LS, CS, TS; 12–8. Native to Texas, Arizona, Mexico. Usually slender and upright to 2–3 ft. tall, but may reach 6 ft. tall, 2 ft. wide. Velvety gray leaves are divided into 8 to 16 narrowly oval, pointed leaflets, each 1–2 in. long. Rich yellow, 1½-in.-wide flowers in late summer and fall. Grows well in caliche soils. Not a good choice for high-rainfall areas or heavily watered gardens; it will rot if soil is too wet.

S. marilandica (Cassia marilandica). WILD SENNA. Perennial. Zones US, MS, LS, CS; 9–1. Native from Pennsylvania to Florida, west to Iowa, Kansas, and Texas. Slender and usually unbranched; grows 4–6 ft. tall, 2–3 ft. wide. Feathery bright green leaves are divided into 8 to 16 oval, inch-long leaflets. Tall clusters of brownish yellow flowers top the stems in summer. Dies to ground in winter.

S. splendida (Cassia splendida). GOLDEN WONDER SENNA. Evergreen shrub. Zones CS, TS; 12–10. Native to Brazil. To 9–12 ft. high and 6–10 ft. wide, with bright green leaves divided into four oval, pointed leaflets to 3 in. long. Deep golden yellow, 1½-in.-wide flowers come in loose clusters at branch ends from autumn into winter. This common name has been applied to a number of sennas of varying growth habits; other "golden wonder sennas" have bright yellow flowers and are strongly horizontal in branch pattern, growing 5–8 ft. high and spreading to 12 ft. wide. All sennas known by this name produce many seeds and should be severely pruned after flowering.

S. wislizenii (Cassia wislizenii). CANYON SENNA. Deciduous shrub. Zones LS, CS, TS; 12–8. Native to West Texas, New Mexico, Arizona, and Mexico. To 5–8 ft. tall and 5–10 ft. wide. Attractive upright branches hold small green leaves divided into four to six leaflets, each 1¼ in. long. Clusters of bright yellow, inch-wide flowers appear all summer. Little water.

SENTRY PALM. See HOWEA

SERENOA repens

SAW PALMETTO

Arecaceae (Palmae)

PALM

✿ LS, CS, TS ♓ 12–8

☼ ◑ FULL SUN OR PARTIAL SHADE

◐ ● MODERATE TO REGULAR WATER

Serenoa repens

Native to the Coastal Plains from South Carolina to Florida, and west to Texas. This charming and trouble-free fan palm grows into a clump only 4–7 ft. tall and wide. It adapts to a wide range of habitats, from sand dunes and dry scrub to moist woods and wetlands. The short trunk may be entirely underground or run parallel to the ground. Green to bluish green, palmate leaves are 2–3 ft. across, held on saw-toothed leaf stems to 2 ft. long; teeth are quite sharp, so take care when handling. Clusters of small white flowers give rise to berries that age from yellowish green to blue black. An extract from the berries is used to treat enlarged prostate in men.

Saw palmetto looks good in foundation plantings, in naturalized areas, or massed under tall trees. Plant in its permanent location, as established plants don't transplant well. Hardy to 15°F. 'Silver Form' sports attractive silvery foliage.

SERVICEBERRY. See AMELANCHIER

SESBANIA

Fabaceae (Leguminosae)

DECIDUOUS SHRUBS AND TREES

✿ CS, TS

☼ FULL SUN

● REGULAR WATER

✧ SEEDS ARE POISONOUS IF INGESTED

Sesbania punicea

Fast-growing but short-lived plants with broad, open canopies of feathery foliage. Pretty, pendent clusters of summer flowers, reminiscent of wisteria, are followed by beanlike seedpods that dry and then rattle in the wind. Need well-drained soil. Some drought tolerance.

S. drummondii. RATTLEBUSH. Shrub. Heat zones 10–9. Native from Florida to Arkansas and Texas. To 20 ft. tall, 15 ft. wide; usually smaller in colder part of range, where branches often die back. Leaves to 8 in. long, with 10 to 25 pairs of oblong, 1-in. leaflets. Small (½-in.) flowers are yellow, sometimes marked with red; 2-in.-long seedpods.

S. grandiflora. SCARLET WISTERIA TREE. Tree. Heat zones 11–9. Native to tropical Asia; almost evergreen in warmest parts of the South. To 30–40 ft. tall, 15–20 ft. wide, with foot-long leaves made up of 10 to 30 pairs of 1- to 2-in. leaflets. Pendent clusters of sweet pea–shaped blossoms to 4 in. long, in rusty red, pink, or white. Pods can reach over 1 ft. long.

S. punicea. RATTLE BOX. Shrub. Heat zones 12–9. Native to North America; naturalized in the Coastal South. Sometimes sold as *Daubentonia*. Usually grows to 6 ft. tall, though it can reach up to 12 ft.; 5–8 ft. wide. Self-seeds, forming colonies (sometimes rather rangy looking) with broad, flat crowns of delicate foliage. Leaves are variable in length, with 6 to 20 pairs of ½- to 1-in. leaflets. Small vermilion flowers in 4-in. clusters appear over an especially long season, from early summer into early fall. Seedpods are 3–4 in. long.

SETARIA palmifolia

PALM GRASS

Poaceae (Gramineae)

PERENNIAL

✿ CS, TS ♓ 12–9; OR GROW IN POTS

☼ ◑ FULL SUN OR LIGHT SHADE

● REGULAR WATER

Setaria palmifolia

To most people, this native of India doesn't look like a grass at all—its deeply pleated, swordlike leaves, 1–3 ft. long and 2–5 in. wide, more closely resemble the foliage of cast-iron plant (*Aspidistra*) or the expanding young fronds of a palm. The leaves arch gracefully from a central crown to form a large mound. In south Florida, clumps can grow 8–10 ft. tall and wide; where frosts occur (but the ground doesn't freeze), they reach about 3 ft. tall and wide. Cylindrical greenish flower spikes appear above the foliage in summer but are not particularly showy. Leaves of 'Rubra' have purplish midribs; 'Variegata' features white-edged foliage, burgundy stems, and reddish flower spikes.

In the garden, the coarse foliage of palm grass is an excellent foil for smaller or thinner leaves. The plant makes a fine container subject and also looks good as an understory plant in woodland gardens. Tolerates drought but looks better with regular moisture. Be careful where you plant it; palm grass self-sows aggressively and can become a pest.

SETCREASEA pallida 'Purple Heart'. See TRADESCANTIA pallida 'Purpurea'

SEVEN SONS FLOWER. See HEPTACODIUM miconioides

SHADBLOW. See AMELANCHIER

SHALLOT

Liliaceae

PERENNIAL OFTEN GROWN AS ANNUAL

US, MS, LS, CS, TS H 12–1

FULL SUN

REGULAR WATER

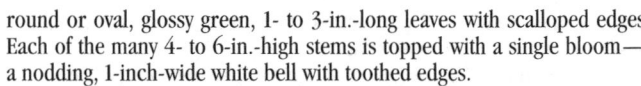
Shallot

Closely related to onion and, like it, a member of the genus *Allium*. Thought to have originated in western or central Asia. The bulb is divided into cloves that grow on a common base; it is prized in cooking for its distinctive flavor, a combination of mild onion and pungent garlic. Young green shoots are also edible. Dutch shallots have golden brown skin and white cloves; red shallots have coppery skin, purple cloves.

In the Lower, Coastal, and Tropical South, you can plant shallots in fall to harvest green tops through winter and early spring, bulbs in late spring and summer. In the Upper and Middle South, plant them in early spring for green shoots in summer, bulbs in autumn.

Shallots are usually grown from cloves (sections of bulbs). You can purchase these from a seed company or simply buy shallots in the grocery store and separate them into cloves. Plant cloves pointed end up, 4–8 in. apart; cover with ½ in. of soil. You'll have green shoots in about 60 days, new bulbs in 90 to 120 days. Some seed companies sell seeds of selections such as 'Bonilla', 'Matador', and 'Prima'; plant 12 seeds per foot. Bulbs will be ready to harvest in about 100 days. Nurseries with stocks of herbs may sell growing plants.

When bulbs are mature, shoots turn yellow and die. To harvest, pull up clumps and separate the bulbs; before using them, let dry for about a month in a cool, dry place. If stored properly, shallots will keep for up to 8 months.

SHAMROCKS. Around St. Patrick's Day, nurseries and florists sell "shamrocks." These are small potted plants of *Medicago lupulina* (hop clover, yellow trefoil, black medick), an annual plant; *Oxalis acetosella* (wood sorrel), a perennial; or *Trifolium repens* (white clover), also a perennial. The last is the most commonly sold. All of these have leaves divided into three leaflets, symbolic of the Trinity. They can be kept on a sunny windowsill or planted out, but they have little ornamental value and are likely to become weeds.

SHASTA DAISY. See CHRYSANTHEMUM maximum

SHEEP LAUREL. See KALMIA angustifolia

SHELL FLOWER. See ALPINIA zerumbet, MOLUCCELLA laevis

SHELL GINGER. See ALPINIA zerumbet

SHE-OAK. See CASUARINA

SHOOTING STAR. See DODECATHEON meadia

SHORTIA

Diapensiaceae

PERENNIALS

US, MS H 8–5, EXCEPT AS NOTED

PARTIAL TO FULL SHADE

REGULAR TO AMPLE WATER

Shortia galacifolia

Beautiful, small, spring-blooming evergreen plants that spread slowly by underground stems. *S. galacifolia* is native to the southeastern U.S.; the other two species are native to Japan. Intolerant of extended summer heat. Need acid, organically enriched soil. Grow with azaleas and rhododendrons.

S. galacifolia. OCONEE BELLS. Heat zones 9–6. From the mountains of Georgia and North and South Carolina. Forms a foot-wide clump of round or oval, glossy green, 1- to 3-in.-long leaves with scalloped edges. Each of the many 4- to 6-in.-high stems is topped with a single bloom— a nodding, 1-inch-wide white bell with toothed edges.

S. soldanelloides. FRINGE BELLS. Similar to *S. galacifolia* but has round, coarsely toothed leaves and pink to rose-colored blossoms with deeply fringed edges.

S. uniflora 'Grandiflora'. Like *S. galacifolia* but with somewhat heart-shaped, wavy-edged leaves. Flowers are large, fringed bells in pure soft pink.

SHOWER OF GOLD. See CASSIA fistula, GALPHIMIA glauca

SHRIMP PLANT. See JUSTICIA brandegeeana

SHRUB BUSH CLOVER. See LESPEDEZA thunbergii

SIAM TULIP. See CURCUMA alismatifolia

SIDALCEA

CHECKERBLOOM, MINIATURE HOLLYHOCK

Malvaceae

PERENNIALS

US, MS H 8–2, EXCEPT AS NOTED

FULL SUN

REGULAR WATER, EXCEPT AS NOTED

Sidalcea malviflora

All are grown for clusters of five-petaled flowers like little hollyhocks (*Alcea*). Plants described here range from erect to sprawling; leaves are typically dark green, roundish to kidney-shaped, about 3 in. across. Basal leaves are shallowly lobed, stem leaves more deeply cut. Provide good drainage. Divide clumps every few years in spring or fall.

S. candida. Heat zones 8–3. Native to High Plains. To 2–3 ft. high, spreading by rhizomes to 1½ ft. wide. Unbranched stems bear bluish green leaves to 8 in. across. Crowded spikes of white, 1-in. flowers in midsummer.

S. hybrids. Most sidalceas grown in gardens are hybrids between *S. candida* and *S. malviflora*. They form clumps to about 2 ft. wide and bear 1½- to 2-in. flowers; bloom all summer if deadheaded. Popular choices include 3-ft. 'Elsie Heugh', with fringed pale pink flowers; 2½-ft. 'Loveliness' (shell pink); and 2- to 3-ft. 'Party Girl' (deep pink).

S. malviflora. CHECKERBLOOM. Native to Oregon, California, Baja California. May grow erect to 2 ft. high and wide; or may sprawl and spread more widely by rooting at the nodes. Pink or purplish pink, 2-in. flowers in early spring. Moderate water.

S. neomexicana. SALTSPRING CHECKERBLOOM. Native from eastern Oregon to Wyoming, south to Mexico. To 3 ft. tall, 1 to 1½ ft. wide; branched or unbranched spikes of white or pinkish, ¾-in. flowers appear in summer.

SILENE

Caryophyllaceae

PERENNIALS

ZONES VARY BY SPECIES

FULL SUN OR PARTIAL SHADE, EXCEPT AS NOTED

WATER NEEDS VARY BY SPECIES

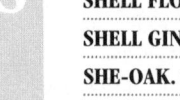
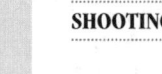
Silene virginica

The plants listed here are North American wildflowers with showy white, pink, or bright red blossoms. Some grow upright; others form low mats. Excellent for use in naturalized areas, in woodland and rock gardens, and at the front of the border. Provide fertile, well-drained soil.

S. caroliniana. WILD PINK. Zones US, MS, LS, CS; 9–3. Native from Florida to New Hampshire, west to Missouri. Low-growing (4- to 8-in.-tall) mound to 1 ft. across. Bluish green leaves to 5 in. long; clusters of upward-facing, inch-wide, white to deep pink flowers with notched petals in late spring, early summer. Best in sandy or gravelly soil. Little to moderate water.

S. laciniata. INDIAN PINK, MEXICAN CAMPION. Zones LS, CS; 9–5. Native to mountains of Mexico, New Mexico, and California. Somewhat sprawling, 2- to 3-ft. stems carry leaves 1–5 in. long. Blooms in summer, bearing showy bright red, inch-wide flowers with deeply fringed petals. Likes full sun and lean soil. Little to moderate water.

S. polypetala. FRINGED CAMPION. Zones US, MS, LS; 8–6. Native to the southern Appalachians. Rare and endangered; be careful to buy only nursery-propagated plants. Dark green, spoon-shaped leaves to 4 in. long form a mat to 1½ ft. across, 4–6 in. high. Blooms in late spring, bearing lovely soft pink flowers to 1½ in. across; petal tips are deeply fringed, the fringes fading to white with age. Lovely plant for a woodland garden; needs partial shade and moist, well-drained soil loaded with organic matter.

S. regia. ROYAL CATCHFLY. Zones US, MS, LS, CS; 9–1. Native to eastern U.S. To 3–4 ft. high, 1½–2 ft. wide. Slender, often reclining stems carry thick, lance-shaped leaves to 5 in. long. Small clusters of 2-in.-wide scarlet blossoms appear in summer. The common name "catchfly" comes from the sticky calyxes—they can trap small insects. Best in partial shade. Little to moderate water.

S. virginica (Melandrium virginicum). FIRE PINK. Zones US, MS, LS; 9–3. Native to eastern and central U.S. Narrow, lance-shaped leaves to 4 in. long in a clump 1–2 ft. tall and 1 ft. wide. Clusters of inch-wide crimson flowers with deeply notched petals in late spring or early summer. 'Longwood', a hybrid between *S. virginica* and *S. polypetala*, has fringed deep pink flowers and forms an evergreen mound to 8 in. high. Unlike *S. polypetala*, this one is easily obtained through mail-order nurseries. Regular water.

SILK BAY. See PERSEA humilis

SILK-COTTON TREE. See CEIBA pentandra

SILK OAK. See GREVILLEA robusta

SILPHIUM

Asteraceae (Compositae)

PERENNIALS

✴ US, MS, LS, CS ◷ 9–5, EXCEPT AS NOTED

☼ ◐ FULL SUN OR LIGHT SHADE

💧 💧 MODERATE TO REGULAR WATER, EXCEPT AS NOTED

Silphium laciniatum

Native to the Midwestern prairies as well as the scrublands of the Southeast, these tough, pest-free, underappreciated perennials feature tall spikes of showy, sunflower-like blooms in mid- to late summer. Broken stems exude a gummy sap that smells like pine or turpentine—hence the common name "rosinweed." Erect stalks holding loose, branching clusters of blooms rise from a clump of large basal leaves; stalk leaves are smaller. In most species, the foliage is rough and hairy. Plants tolerate wet or dry conditions, grow particularly well in heavy soil. Easily started from seed or grown from young transplants. Good additions to wildflower meadows, naturalized areas, and (if staked) the back of the border.

S. dentatum. STARRY ROSINWEED. To 6 ft. tall, 2–3 ft. wide. Dark green, shallowly toothed leaves reach 1 ft. long. Star-shaped light yellow flowers with greenish yellow centers reach 4 in. across.

S. laciniatum. COMPASS PLANT. Common name refers to the basal leaves' tendency to orient themselves on a north-south axis. Foliage is green with pink veins; deeply cut basal leaves reach 1½ ft. long, form a clump 2 ft. across. Blossom stalks rise 6–9 ft. high, carrying showy yellow flowers up to 5 in. across.

S. perfoliatum. CUP PLANT. Paired basal leaves are fused at the squarish stems, forming a "cup" that catches water; birds and butterflies will stop by for a sip. Dark green, nearly hairless, coarsely toothed leaves

reach 14 in. long, may be triangular or pointed-oval; plant grows about 3 ft. wide. Stalks rising 4–8 ft. bear bright yellow, daisylike flowers up to 3 in. wide. Grows naturally in moist soils; provide regular water.

S. terebinthinaceum. PRAIRIE DOCK. Heat zones 9–1. Light green, spade-shaped basal leaves with coarsely toothed edges can reach 2 ft. long. Almost leafless flower stalks range from 3 to 10 ft. tall, may be red or green; blossoms are bright yellow, 2–3 in. wide. Plants reach 4–6 ft. wide. Once the stout taproot is established, prairie dock tolerates considerable drought.

SILVER BELL. See HALESIA

SILVERBERRY. See ELAEAGNUS pungens

SILVER DOLLAR TREE. See EUCALYPTUS cinerea

SILVER FERN. See PTERIS quadriaurita 'Argyraea'

SILVER GRASS. See MISCANTHUS

SILVER LACE VINE. See FALLOPIA baldschuanica

SILVERLEAF. See LEUCOPHYLLUM

SINNINGIA

Gesneriaceae

PERENNIALS

✴ ZONES VARY BY SPECIES

☼ ◐ FULL SUN OR LIGHT SHADE; BRIGHT INDIRECT LIGHT

💧 💧 WATER NEEDS VARY BY SPECIES

Sinningia speciosa

This group includes a number of perennials and shrubs, mostly native to South America. Only a few are cultivated in the South. Of the two species described here, the first is the familiar florist's gloxinia, the second a surprisingly hardy newcomer.

S. speciosa (Gloxinia speciosa). GLOXINIA. Indoor plant. Native to Brazil. Squat, full-foliaged plant to 1 ft. high and wide. Broad, oval leaves reach 6 in. or longer, look like quilted green velvet. Blooms in summer, producing showy, velvety-sheened, ruffled bells up to 4 in. wide in a cluster near top of plant. Colors include white, red, pink, blue, and light to dark shades of purple. Some flowers have dark dots or blotches, others contrasting bands at edges.

Gloxinias need constant warmth and are most often grown in a greenhouse or as houseplants, though they can be taken outdoors in warm weather. Tubers are usually available in winter or spring. For each tuber, choose a container big enough to leave 2 in. between all sides of tuber and container edges. Fill with a mix of equal parts peat moss, perlite, and leaf mold or compost; set tuber ½ in. deep. Place in a warm spot (about 72°F during day, no cooler than 65°F at night) with plenty of bright light but no direct sun. Water sparingly until first leaves appear, then increase watering as roots and leaves grow. Apply water to soil only, or pour it into drip saucer to be absorbed through pot's drainage holes (pour off any water left unabsorbed after an hour). Feed with a general-purpose liquid houseplant fertilizer diluted to half-strength; start feeding when leaves emerge, then feed every 2 weeks until flowers fade. After bloom has finished, gradually dry off plants. When leaves have died down completely, move container to dark place where temperatures remain around 60°F. Mist soil just enough to keep tubers from shriveling. When tubers show signs of resuming growth in midwinter, repot in fresh soil mix. If roots have filled container, move tuber to a larger pot.

S. tubiflora. HARDY GLOXINIA. Zones LS, CS, TS; 12–1. From Argentina, Paraguay, Uruguay. As its name suggests, this is a hardy perennial in much of the South. Growing from tubers, it forms 1- to 2-ft.-wide clumps of velvety green leaves to 5 in. long, 1½ in. wide. Fragrant, tubular white flowers, 2–3 in. long, appear on spikes to 2 ft. tall throughout the summer. Needs moderate water and fertile, very well-drained soil. Excellent in a rock garden or large container.

S

SISYRINCHIUM

Iridaceae

PERENNIALS

ZONES VARY BY SPECIES

FULL SUN OR LIGHT SHADE

WATER NEEDS VARY BY SPECIES

Sisyrinchium bellum

Iris relatives with narrow, grasslike leaves and small, six-segmented flowers that open in sunshine. The blossoms are pretty up close but not showy from a distance. Best suited for informal gardens or naturalizing; small types are good in rock gardens. Easy to start from seed; will self-sow. Not usually browsed by deer.

S. angustifolium (S. graminoides). COMMON BLUE-EYED GRASS. Zones US, MS, LS, CS, TS; 12–5. Native to North America. Grows 6–18 in. tall, 6 in. wide, with dark green leaves and clusters of ½-in. blue blossoms in summer. 'Lucerne' is 8–10 in. tall and bears large bright blue flowers over a long period; 'Mrs. Spivey', with pure white blooms, may reach 2½ ft. tall. Moderate to regular water.

S. atlanticum. ATLANTIC BLUE-EYED GRASS. Zones US, MS, LS; 8–4. Native to eastern U.S. Violet-blue flowers with yellow centers are carried on slender, wiry, branched stems that range in height from 4 in. to 2½ ft. tall. Plants reach 6–8 in. wide. Pale grayish green leaves. Blooms from late spring into early summer. Regular water.

S. bellum (S. idahoense bellum). WESTERN BLUE-EYED GRASS. Zones MS, LS; 8–3. Native to coasts of California and Oregon. To 4 in.–2 ft. high, 6 in.–2 ft. wide. Green or bluish green leaves. Purple to bluish purple, ½-in. flowers in spring. Several named forms, many of them dwarf, are available. Among these are 'California Skies', to 8 in. tall, with light blue flowers, and 6- to 8-in.-tall 'Marion', with large blooms in deep purplish blue. Plants sold as *S. macounii* (purple blooms) or *S. m.* 'Album' (white flowers) are probably forms of *S. bellum.* Moderate to regular water.

S. bermudianum. BERMUDIANA. Zones US, MS, LS, CS; 9–5. Native to Bermuda. Branched, flattened, stout stems to 2 ft. tall. Blooms from spring through early summer, bearing yellow-eyed violet-blue flowers to ¾ in. across. Plants reach 6–8 in. wide. Some authorities consider this to be the same plant as *S. angustifolium.* Moderate to regular water.

S. californicum. YELLOW-EYED GRASS. Zones MS, LS; 9–7. From California and British Columbia. To 8–10 in. wide, 6 in. to 2 ft. tall. Dull green leaves are broader than those of *S. bellum*. Yellow flowers in late spring or early summer. Succeeds in wet or low spots. Ample water.

S. striatum. ARGENTINE YELLOW-EYED GRASS. Zones MS, LS, CS; 9–7. Recently reclassified as *Phaiophleps nigricans* but seldom sold under that name. Native to Chile, Argentina. To 3 ft. tall, 1 ft. wide, with attractive gray-green leaves. In spring, produces spikelike clusters of many ½-in. flowers in pale yellow streaked with brown; blooms well into summer if old flower clusters are removed (if you don't remove them, you may have hordes of unwanted seedlings the next year). Leaves of 'Aunt May' ('Variegatum') are striped with creamy yellow. Moderate water.

S. tinctorium. MEXICAN YELLOW-EYED GRASS. Zones US, MS, LS, CS; 8–7. From Mexico and South America. To 1 ft. high and wide. Narrow blue-green leaves; light yellow, ¾-in. flowers from early spring into summer. 'Puerto Yellow' has bright yellow blossoms. Moderate to regular water.

SKIMMIA

Rutaceae

EVERGREEN SHRUBS

US, MS, LS H 12–7

PARTIAL TO FULL SHADE

REGULAR WATER

Skimmia japonica

Slow growing and compact, with glossy, rich green leaves neatly arranged along the branches. In spring, tiny, fragrant white flowers open from clusters of pinkish buds held well above foliage. Red fruit resembling holly *(Ilex)* berries appears in fall and winter. Individual plants are dense mounds; when massed, they form a solid foliage cover. Good under windows, beside shaded walks, flanking entryways, in containers.

Prefer moist, highly organic, acid soils; must have good drainage. Mites are the main pests; they give foliage a sunburned look. Thrips may also attack. Water mold can be a problem. Shield from cold, sweeping winds.

S. japonica. JAPANESE SKIMMIA. From Japan. Slow-growing plant of variable size; typically to 2–5 ft. or taller, 3–6 ft. wide. Oval and pointed leaves to 3–4 in. long and 1 in. wide, most often clustered near the twig ends. Flowers are borne in 2- to 3-in. clusters; they are larger and more fragrant on male plants. If a male plant is present, female plants produce bright red berries—attractive enough to make planting both sexes worth the effort. A form with ivory white berries is available. Male selection 'Macrophylla' is a rounded, spreading shrub to 5–6 ft. tall, with large leaves and flowers.

S. reevesiana (S. japonica reevesiana). REEVES SKIMMIA. From China. Similar in leaf and flower to *S. japonica*, but looser and more open in habit, growing slowly to 1½–3 ft. high, 2–3 ft. wide. Self-fertile; produces crimson berries.

SKULLCAP. See SCUTELLARIA

SKUNKBUSH. See RHUS trilobata

SKY FLOWER. See DURANTA, THUNBERGIA grandiflora

SMILACINA

Liliaceae

PERENNIALS

US, MS, LS

LIGHT SHADE

REGULAR WATER

Smilacina racemosa

These perennials spread by creeping rhizomes to form dense colonies. Need rich, loose, moist, slightly acid soil. Good for naturalizing in wild garden; commonly seen in moist woods and roadside ditches. The fruit is favored by wildlife.

S. racemosa. FALSE SOLOMON'S SEAL, FALSE SPIKENARD. Heat zones 9–1. Native to woods throughout much of North America. Grows 1–3 ft. tall. Each arching stalk has several 3- to 6-in.-long leaves with hairy undersides; foliage is medium green, turning golden yellow in autumn. In spring, stalks are topped by fluffy, conical clusters of small, fragrant, creamy white flowers. Red autumn berries have purple spots. Resembles true Solomon's seal *(Polygonatum)*.

S. stellata. STARFLOWER, STARRY SOLOMON'S SEAL. Heat zones 8–1. Native to Virginia, north to Newfoundland and west to Kansas and California. Grows 1–2½ ft. tall. Stems erect or somewhat spreading. Light green, 6-in. leaves are folded lengthwise, or channeled, and clasp the stem. Creamy white spring flowers smaller than those of *S. racemosa.* Berries are green with black stripes, maturing to deep red or dark blue.

SMILAX

GREENBRIER, CATBRIER

Liliaceae

EVERGREEN, SEMIEVERGREEN, DECIDUOUS VINES

MS, LS, CS H 12–9

FULL SUN OR PARTIAL SHADE, EXCEPT AS NOTED

LITTLE TO REGULAR WATER

Smilax smallii

Native to the Americas, this is a large group of tough, moderately fast-growing, evergreen to deciduous vines that grow from rhizomes or large tubers. Some species are valuable ornamentals, others flat-out weeds; some are viciously thorny, others nearly thornless. All climb by tendrils. Greenish or yellowish flowers in spring or early summer are small and insignificant, but the berries that follow are often showy and are relished by birds. Because many species look similar, this is a difficult group to sort out; the common names can be as tangled as the vines.

S. bona-nox. CATBRIER, BULLBRIER. Semievergreen to deciduous. May scramble to 20 ft., but usually forms large thickets close to the ground. The prickly, squarish green stems are set with glossy green, 2- to 5-in.-long leaves shaped like fiddles or arrowheads; leaves may have lighter green blotches. Blue-black berries. Best use for this weedy plant is as wildlife cover. Partial shade.

S. glauca. SAWBRIER. Deciduous. To 8–12 ft., with thin stems armed with short prickles. Oval to kidney-shaped green leaves with silvery undersides reach 6 in. long, turn orange red in fall. Blue-black berries. Worth leaving in a naturalized area to attract birds.

S. pumila. DWARF SMILAX, WILD SARSAPARILLA. Evergreen in the southern part of its range, deciduous farther north. Low-growing vine trails to 10 ft., with oval to lance-shaped, glossy green leaves to 4 in. long. Thornless, fuzzy stems. Clustered, showy berries change from golden to red in fall. Can be used as a casual ground cover. Best in sandy soil and partial to full shade.

S. rotundifolia. COMMON GREENBRIER, HORSE BRIER. Deciduous. Vigorous, high-climbing (to 20-ft.) scrambler with thorny, squarish stems. Green leaves with lighter green markings are round to heart shaped, up to 6 in. long. Blue-black berries. Grows from a huge tuber. Good choice for a wildlife garden.

S. smallii. JACKSON VINE. Evergreen. The most important ornamental species, this old favorite is prized for its glossy deep green foliage; leaves and stems are popular for holiday decorations, as they retain their color long after cutting. The plant climbs to 10 ft.; it's a favorite for training over doorways, windows, and arbors in the Lower South. Stems near the plant's base are thorny, but thinner stems higher up are essentially thornless. Oval, pointed leaves are 6 in. long. Clustered berries are large and colorful, maturing from green through red to blackish blue. Jackson vine is usually started from enormous tubers dug from the wild but can be easily started from seed.

S. walteri. CORAL GREENBRIER. Deciduous. Thin-stemmed species to a possible 20 ft.; noted for bright orange-red berries. Leathery, rounded to oval, bright green leaves to 5 in. long; they turn orange red in fall. Stems near the plant's base are prickly, but upper stems are thornless. Tolerates wet soil and just about any exposure. Good for bringing fall color to naturalized areas.

SMOKE TREE. See COTINUS

SNAIL VINE. See VIGNA caracalla

SNAKE PLANT. See SANSEVIERIA trifasciata

SNAKESHEAD. See FRITILLARIA meleagris

SNAPDRAGON. See ANTIRRHINUM majus

SNEEZEWEED. See HELENIUM autumnale

SNOWBALL, FRAGRANT. See VIBURNUM × carlcephalum

SNOWBELL. See STYRAX

SNOWBERRY. See SYMPHORICARPOS

SNOW BUSH. See BREYNIA nivosa

SNOWDROP. See GALANTHUS

SNOWFLAKE. See LEUCOJUM

SNOW GUM. See EUCALYPTUS pauciflora niphophila

SNOW-IN-SUMMER. See CERASTIUM tomentosum

SNOW-ON-THE-MOUNTAIN. See EUPHORBIA marginata

SOCIETY GARLIC. See TULBAGHIA violacea

Solanaceae. Members of the potato family bear flowers that are nearly always star or saucer shaped and five petaled; fruits are berries or capsules. Plants are frequently rank smelling or even poisonous, but many are important food crops—eggplant, pepper, potato, tomato. Others are garden annuals, perennials, shrubs, and vines—amethyst flower (*Browallia*), *Cestrum, Nicotiana,* and *Petunia,* to name a few.

SOLANDRA maxima

CUP-OF-GOLD VINE, CHALICE VINE

Solanaceae

EVERGREEN VINE

⚡ TS **H** 12–6

☀ FULL SUN

💧 REGULAR WATER

Solandra maxima

Native from Mexico to Venezuela and Colombia. Fast-growing, sprawling, rampant vine to 40 ft.; must be tied to its support. Heavy stems bear highly polished, broadly oval, rich green leaves to 6 in. long. Inflated-looking buds open to big (6- to 8-in.), leathery, bowl-shaped, five-lobed flowers that release a coconut fragrance at night; blooms are golden yellow, with a red-brown stripe running down the inside of each lobe. Main bloom period is summer, but scattered flowering can occur at any time.

Give good, well-drained soil for best growth. Use on big walls and pergolas, along eaves, as bank cover. Spectacular along fence near swimming pool. Cut back long, vigorous shoots to induce branching and more flowers. To make it easy to see inside the big flowers, encourage growth low on plant by tip-pinching. Can be trimmed back to make a rough hedge. Pruning is best done in late winter or early spring. Provide shade for roots in hottest climates. Light frost blackens the leaves, but plants usually recover to produce new growth. Often sold as *S. guttata.*

SOLANUM

Solanaceae

EVERGREEN, SEMIEVERGREEN, AND DECIDUOUS SHRUBS AND VINES

⚡ ZONES VARY BY SPECIES

☀ ◑ FULL SUN OR PARTIAL SHADE

💧 MODERATE TO REGULAR WATER, EXCEPT AS NOTED

⚠ MANY SPECIES ARE POISONOUS IF INGESTED; MOST ARE SUSPECT

Solanum pseudocapsicum

In addition to eggplant and potato (described under those names), *Solanum* includes a number of ornamental plants. All have small, star-shaped, five-petaled blue or white flowers with reproductive parts that form a pointed yellow structure in the blossom's center. A few of the species described here produce decorative fruit.

S. crispum. Evergreen vine. Zones CS, TS; 12−1. From Chile, Peru. Modest (even shrubby) climber to 12 ft., with ovate to lance-shaped, soft green, often wavy-edged leaves to 5 in. long. In summer, bears 4-in. clusters of fragrant lilac-blue flowers with yellow centers. Small, inedible yellowish fruit. Must be fastened to its support; well suited to trellises, walls, posts. May lose leaves in hard frost. Selection 'Glasnevin' has deeper blue flowers in larger clusters.

S. jasminoides. POTATO VINE. Evergreen or semievergreen vine. Zones CS, TS; 12−3. From Brazil. Twines rapidly to 30 ft. Purplish-tinged, arrow-shaped, 1½- to 3-in.-long leaves. Bluish white, 1-in. flowers are carried on threadlike stalks in clusters of up to 12; bloom is almost continuous all year, heaviest in spring. Grown for flowers or to provide light overhead shade. Cut back severely at any time to prevent tangling, promote vigorous new growth. Control rampant runners that grow along ground. 'Album' bears pure white flowers; 'Variegatum' has leaves edged with creamy yellow.

▶

S

S. pseudocapsicum. JERUSALEM CHERRY. Evergreen shrub. Zones CS, TS; 12–6; annual or indoor/outdoor plant anywhere. From Madeira; widely naturalized in tropics and subtropics. To 3–4 ft. high and wide (about half that size if grown as an annual). Shiny deep green, smooth, elliptical leaves to 4 in. long. White, ½-in. summer flowers are followed in autumn by a fine show of scarlet (rarely yellow), ½-in. fruits that look like cherry tomatoes but are poisonous. In mildest-winter areas, plant bears flowers and fruit (and self-sows) year-round. More popular than taller kinds are the many dwarf strains, which grow to 1 ft. high and bear larger fruit (to 1 in. across). Leaves and developing fruit of 'Variegatum' are striped in green and white; fruit matures to orange.

S. rantonnetii (Lycianthes rantonnetii). Evergreen shrub. Zones TS; 12–6. From Paraguay, Argentina. As freestanding plant, it makes a shrub 8–12 ft. tall and 6–10 ft. wide, but it can be staked into tree form or, with support, grown as a vine to 12–15 ft. or more. Can also be allowed to sprawl and used as a ground cover. Bright green, oval leaves to 4 in. long; violet-blue, ½- to 1½-in. flowers throughout warm weather, often nearly year-round. Informal, fast growing, not easy to use in tailored landscape; prune hard to keep it neat. Where winters are cold, plants can be brought indoors to a cool room next to a sunny window; water sparingly. The species is seldom seen; common plant in the nursery trade is 'Grandiflorum'. 'Royal Robe' is more compact (to 6–8 ft. high and wide), bears darker purple flowers over a longer season.

Solanum rantonnetii

S. seaforthianum. BRAZILIAN NIGHTSHADE. Evergreen or semievergreen vine. Zones TS; 12–6. Slender-stemmed plant to 15 ft.; must be fastened to its support. Oval, 4- to 8-in.-long, medium green leaves are either undivided or quite deeply cleft into three or more lobes. Clusters of violet-blue, 1-in.-wide flowers bloom in summer. Pea-size red fruits are enjoyed by birds but should not be eaten by people.

S. wendlandii. COSTA RICAN NIGHTSHADE. Deciduous vine. Zones TS; 12–10. From Costa Rica. To 15–20 ft., climbing by twining stems and hooked spines. Glossy green, ovate or (sometimes) lobed leaves 4–10 in. long are corrugated in texture. Foliage forms a lush backdrop for dense, domed clusters of lavender blue, 2½-in. summer flowers. Somewhat reminiscent of bougainvillea. Let it clamber into tall trees, cover a pergola, decorate eaves of large house. Loses leaves in low temperatures, even without frost; slow to leaf out in spring.

SOLEIROLIA soleirolii (Helxine soleirolii)

BABY'S TEARS

Urticaceae

PERENNIAL

CS, TS | 12–1; OR HOUSEPLANT

PARTIAL TO FULL SHADE; BRIGHT INDIRECT LIGHT

REGULAR TO AMPLE WATER

Soleirolia soleirolii

You practically have to accept on faith that baby's tears has leaves, because even from a short distance they're almost too tiny to see. Native to the Mediterranean region, this tender perennial grows 2–4 in. high, spreading indefinitely by creeping stems to form a lush green mat. Gardeners in the Coastal and Tropical South can grow it outside in a moist, shady spot—but most people treat it as a favored houseplant. Indoors, give it bright indirect light; be sure to shield it from hot sun. Keep the soil evenly moist, but water a bit less in winter. Feed every other week in spring

and summer and monthly in fall and winter with a general-purpose liquid houseplant fertilizer diluted to half-strength. Makes an excellent tabletop or windowsill houseplant and also does well in terrariums. Easily propagated by division or cuttings. Selections with golden green and silver leaves are sometimes offered.

SOLENOSTEMON scutellarioides. See COLEUS ×hybridus

SOLIDAGO

GOLDENROD

Asteraceae (Compositae)

PERENNIALS

US, MS, LS, CS | 9–1, EXCEPT AS NOTED

FULL SUN OR LIGHT SHADE

MODERATE WATER, EXCEPT AS NOTED

Solidago 'Goldenmosa'

These North American natives are not as widely grown as they deserve, largely due to the mistaken belief that their pollen causes hay fever (in fact, other plants are responsible). Although a few of the hundred-plus species are weeds in many regions, many are choice garden plants. All have leafy stems rising from tough, woody, spreading rootstocks; all bear small yellow flowers in large, branching, typically one-sided clusters from mid- or late summer into fall. These are tough plants that thrive in not-too-rich soil. Use in borders with black-eyed Susan (*Rudbeckia hirta*) or Michaelmas daisy (*Aster novi-belgii*), or naturalize in meadows.

S. altissima. TALL GOLDENROD. Heat zones 10–3. The state flower of Kentucky, this species is a stiff, erect, much-branched plant to 3–7 ft. tall, 1½ ft. wide. Every part of it is bristly. Bears large, branched, pyramidal flower heads.

S. canadensis. CANADA GOLDENROD. Stands 3–5 ft. tall, 3 ft. wide. Large, showy flower panicles, densely packed with blossoms. Robust and vigorous, spreading widely by underground runners; can be invasive.

S. hybrids. The following are among the best garden selections.

'Cloth of Gold'. To 1½ ft. tall, 1 ft. wide, with a long bloom season beginning in midsummer.

'Crown of Rays'. To 2–3 ft. tall, 1–2 ft. wide. Stiff and erect, with flattish flower clusters.

'Golden Baby'. To 2 ft. high, 1½ ft. wide, with plumelike flower clusters.

'Goldenmosa'. To 2½–3 ft. tall, 1½ ft. wide, with very large flower clusters reminiscent of florist's mimosa (*Acacia baileyana*).

'Gold Spangles'. Heat zones 9–5. To 2–2½ ft. high, 1–1½ ft. wide. Leaves are splashed with gold and green. Showy plumes of fragrant bright yellow flowers.

'Laurin'. Vigorous dwarf selection to 1 ft. high, 9 in. wide.

S. nemoralis. GRAY GOLDENROD. Heat zones 9–5. Tidy-looking plant ranging from 6 in. to 2 ft. tall and wide. Soft gray-green basal leaves; curved flower plumes in rich yellow. Blooms over a longer period than most species. Likes dryish soil. Short lived; best treated as a biennial.

S. odora. SWEET GOLDENROD. Tall grower to 6½ ft. high, 3 ft. wide. Unbranched stems are set with anise-scented leaves. Large, long-lasting flower heads. Particularly tolerant of poor, dry soils.

S. rigida. STIFF GOLDENROD. Heat zones 10–4. To 1½–2½ ft. wide, with stems 2–5 ft. high. Dense golden blossom heads. Very adaptable to garden conditions; takes average or rich soil, much or little moisture.

S. rugosa. ROUGH-LEAFED GOLDENROD. Hairy-stemmed plant to 5 ft. tall, 3 ft. wide, with arching, widely branching stems. 'Fireworks' makes a more compact clump (3 ft. tall, 2 ft. wide).

S. sempervirens. SEASIDE GOLDENROD. Stately species to 8 ft. tall, 1½ ft. wide. Tolerates dry soil, heat, salt, wind. May topple in rich soil. Spoon-shaped basal leaves.

S. sphacelata 'Golden Fleece'. Stands just 1½–2 ft. high when in bloom. Low foliage mound makes it a good ground cover; if you set plants 15 in. apart, you'll have a solid mat in just a year.

S

×SOLIDASTER luteus

Asteraceae (Compositae)

PERENNIAL

🌾 US, MS, LS 🌱 8–5

☼ FULL SUN

💧 MODERATE WATER

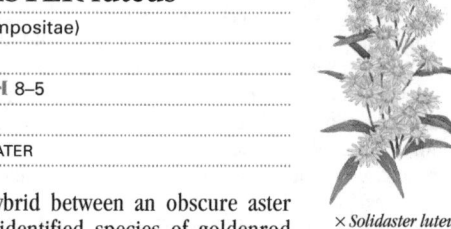

× *Solidaster luteus*

Bigeneric hybrid between an obscure aster and an unidentified species of goldenrod (*Solidago*). Grows erect to 2–3 ft. tall and 1–2 ft. wide, with sturdy stems holding medium green, lance-shaped leaves to 6 in. long. In late summer or early autumn, sprays of ½-in., daisylike yellow flowers (wonderful for cutting) appear atop the foliage. Impressively trouble-free in well-drained soil. An excellent companion for fall-blooming asters, perennial salvias, and ironweed (*Vernonia noveboracensis*). 'Lemore' features larger blooms in creamy yellow.

SOLOMON'S SEAL. See POLYGONATUM

SOPHORA

Fabaceae (Leguminosae)

EVERGREEN AND DECIDUOUS TREES AND SHRUBS

🌾 ZONES VARY BY SPECIES

☼ ☀ FULL SUN OR PARTIAL SHADE

💧 MODERATE WATER

☣ SEEDS OF S. AFFINIS AND S. SECUNDIFLORA ARE POISONOUS IF INGESTED

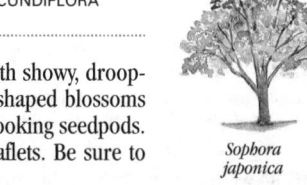

Sophora japonica

Attractive flowering plants with showy, drooping clusters of sweet pea–shaped blossoms that are followed by interesting-looking seedpods. Leaves are divided into many leaflets. Be sure to provide good drainage.

S. affinis. EVE'S NECKLACE. Small deciduous tree. Zones MS, LS, CS. Native to the Southwest. Fast growth to 15–20 ft. (rarely 30 ft.) tall, with a round canopy to about 15 ft. across. Dark green, 3- to 10-in.-long leaves with 13 to 19 leaflets, each 1½ in. long. Blooms in late spring, bearing pink to white, lightly scented flowers in pendent, 4- to 6-in. clusters; choose trees when they're in bloom, as flower color varies and can be disappointing. Lovely, slender, twisted black seedpods grow 3–6 in. long and look like strings of beads; they hang on through fall and winter. Tolerates thin, dry, limy soils.

S. davidii (S. viciifolia). Deciduous shrub. Zones US, MS, LS. From China. Bushy, rounded plant to 8–12 ft. tall and a little wider. Gray-green, 3½-in. leaves divided into 13 to 19 oval leaflets, each under ½ in. long. In late spring or early summer, produces 6-in.-long clusters of small white flowers marked with purplish blue. Long (to 2-in.), narrow pods are constricted between the two to four seeds held inside.

S. japonica. JAPANESE PAGODA TREE, CHINESE SCHOLAR TREE. Deciduous tree. Zones US, MS, LS; 9–1. To 50–75 ft. high and wide. Young wood is smooth, dark gray green. Old branches and trunk gradually take on rugged look of oak. Dark green, 6- to 10-in. leaves divided into 7 to 17 oval leaflets, each 1–2 in. long; undistinguished yellow fall color. Small, yellowish white flowers carried in branched, foot-long sprays in summer. Pods 2–3½ in. long, narrowed between big seeds for a bead necklace effect. Takes heat, drought, city conditions. 'Regent' is an exceptionally vigorous, uniform grower; 'Princeton Upright' is similar but more erect. 'Pendula', to 15–25 ft. high and wide, has weeping branches. Spreading forms are good shade trees, though stains from flowers and pods may be a problem on paved surfaces and parked cars.

S. secundiflora. TEXAS MOUNTAIN LAUREL, MESCAL BEAN. Evergreen shrub or tree. Zones LS, CS; 12–7. Shrubby, but can be trained into 25-ft. tree with short, slender trunk or multiple trunks, narrow crown, upright branches. To 15–20 ft. wide. Leaves are 4–6 in. long, divided into 7 to 11 oval, glossy dark green leaflets, each up to 2 in. long. Sweet-scented violet-blue flowers in drooping, 4- to 8-in. clusters reminiscent of wisteria; midwinter to early spring bloom. Silvery gray, woody, 1- to 8-in.-long seedpods open when ripe to show poisonous, bright red, ½-in. seeds. If possible, remove pods before they mature. Thrives in heat and alkaline soil with good drainage. Choice small tree for street, lawn, courtyard. Old-time favorite in Southern gardens, though its floral display may be eliminated or sharply reduced if late freezes hit when the plants are in bud. 'Alba' is a white-flowered form. 'Silver Peso' has silvery foliage.

SORBARIA

FALSE SPIRAEA

Rosaceae

DECIDUOUS SHRUBS

🌾 ZONES VARY BY SPECIES

☼ ☀ FULL SUN OR LIGHT SHADE

💧 REGULAR WATER

Sorbaria sorbifolia

These good-size shrubs bloom from mid- to late summer, producing big, plumelike clusters of tiny white or creamy flowers at branch ends. Flowers mature into brown seed clusters, so cut off faded blossoms unless you like the look of brown plumes. Green, ferny-looking leaves are finely divided into many narrow, toothed leaflets. Use in large shrub borders or at edge of woodland, near water; effect is almost tropical. Spread by suckering and will cover large areas if not curbed.

S. sorbifolia. Zones US, MS, LS; 8–1. Native to eastern Asia. To 3–8 ft. tall, 10 ft. wide. Leaves 6–12 in. long; flower plumes to 1 ft. long.

S. tomentosa angustifolia (S. aitchisonii). Zones US, MS; 7–5. Native to Afghanistan, Pakistan. To 10 ft. tall and wide. Leaves to 1½ ft. long; flower plumes to 16 in. long.

SORBUS

MOUNTAIN ASH

Rosaceae

DECIDUOUS TREES AND SHRUBS

🌾 ZONES VARY BY SPECIES

☼ ☀ FULL SUN OR LIGHT SHADE

💧💧 MODERATE TO REGULAR WATER

Sorbus aucuparia

Natives of mountainous areas, valued for showy flowers and showier fruit. Blossoms are grouped in broad, flat clusters that are scattered over the foliage canopy in spring; they develop into hanging clusters of small, berrylike fruit that colors up in late summer or early fall. Most species have red or orange-red fruit, but white, pink, and golden forms are occasionally available. Birds feed on the fruit, but usually not until after leaves have fallen. Foliage is typically finely cut and somewhat fernlike, though some less widely planted species have undivided leaves.

Mountain ashes need some winter chill, and their dislike of extended summer heat makes them poor choices for most of the South. Provide good, well-drained soil. Like other members of the rose family, they are subject to fireblight. Borers and cankers are problems for plants under stress. Where adapted, they are good small garden trees or street trees, though fruit can make a mess on paved surfaces.

S. alnifolia. KOREAN MOUNTAIN ASH. Tree. Zones US, MS, LS; 8–1. From China, Korea, Japan. Dense growth to 40–50 ft. tall, 20–30 ft. wide. The specific name *alnifolia* refers to the leaves, which are undivided (like those of alder, *Alnus*); they are 2–4 in. long, toothed, dark green, turning yellow to orange in fall. Reddish pink to orange-red fruit. Grayish bark is mottled with white. Tolerates heat, drought, and humidity better than other mountain ashes. Takes acid or alkaline soils and is less susceptible than its kin to borers. A superior tree for Southern gardens; should be planted more often for its beautiful foliage, flowers, fruit, and bark. ▸

S

S. americana. Tree or shrub. Zones US, MS; 8–1. From eastern North America. Grows 10–30 ft. tall and wide. Dark green leaves with paler undersides are 10 in. long and consist of 11 to 17 leaflets; turn yellow in fall. Orange-red fruit. This species is very hardy and tolerates damp soil, but it is not the choicest of mountain ashes. Attractive in its native environment.

S. aucuparia. EUROPEAN MOUNTAIN ASH. Tree. Zones US, MS; 7–1. Native from Europe to western Asia and Siberia; naturalized in North America. To 20–40 ft. tall (or taller), 15–25 ft. wide. Sharply rising branches form a dense, oval to round crown. Leaves are 5–9 in. long, with 9 to 15 leaflets; they are dull green above, gray green below, turning tawny yellow to reddish in autumn. Orange-red fruit. 'Cardinal Royal' has especially large bright red berries. 'Black Hawk' and 'Fastigiata' are slightly narrower, upright forms.

S. tianshanica. TURKESTAN MOUNTAIN ASH. Shrub or tree. Zones US, MS; 7–5. From central Asia. To 16 ft. tall and wide. Leaves are 5–6 in. long, with 9 to 15 leaflets; shiny dark green above, grayish beneath. Bright red fruit. Tidy-looking, slow-growing plant, excellent for a small garden. 'Red Cascade' is compact, oval crowned.

SORREL, GARDEN

Polygonaceae

PERENNIAL OFTEN GROWN AS ANNUAL

☘ US, MS, LS, CS, TS

☼ FULL SUN

💧 REGULAR WATER

Garden Sorrel

Two similar species are grown for their edible leaves, which can be used raw in salads or cooked in soups, sauces, egg dishes. Flavor is like that of a sharp, sprightly spinach, but sorrel is more heat tolerant and produces throughout the growing season. Common sorrel (*Rumex acetosa*) is the larger plant (to 3 ft. tall), with leaves to 6 in. long, many shaped like elongated arrowheads. It is native to northern climates. French sorrel (*R. scutatus*) is a more sprawling plant to 1½ ft. high, with shorter, broader leaves and a milder, more lemony flavor than *R. acetosa.* Native to Europe, western Asia, and North Africa.

Grow sorrel in reasonably good soil. Sow seeds in early spring; thin seedlings to 8 in. apart. Or set out transplants at any time, spacing them 8 in. apart. Pick tender leaves when they are big enough to use; cut out flowering stems to encourage leaf production. Replace (or dig and divide) plants after 3 or 4 years.

SORREL, WOOD or CANDY CANE. See OXALIS

SOTOL. See DASYLIRION

SOUR GUM. See NYSSA sylvatica

SOURWOOD. See OXYDENDRUM arboreum

SOUTHERN PEA

Fabaceae (Leguminosae)

ANNUAL

☘ US, MS, LS, CS, TS ⊩ 12–1

☼ FULL SUN

💧 REGULAR WATER

Long a staple of Southern cuisine, Southern peas grow somewhat like ordinary green peas ("garden" or "English" peas), but their pods look more like lumpy string beans. Unlike green peas, Southern peas thrive in the long, hot summers of the South, where they are ready for harvest about 65 days after sowing.

"Southern pea" is a collective term; there are many different types. Field peas (also called cowpeas) are planted primarily for animal feed and for

Southern Pea
(Purple Hull Type)

loosening and improving the soil. Some, however, do make good table peas. For example, 'Red Ripper' is very popular in Texas because it tolerates very hot, dry summers and bears as many as 18 tasty peas per pod.

The best-known Southern pea is the black-eyed pea, named for the dark spot on the notch of its tan or white seeds. Ironically, it grows better in the West than in the South—but if you want to try it, plant the selections 'Queen Anne' or 'California Blackeye #5'.

By far the largest group is crowder peas, named for the blocky, square-edged seeds that "crowd" into the pod. Crowders do a great job of fixing atmospheric nitrogen, thereby enriching the soil, and they are very productive. Recommended selections include 'Mississippi Silverbrown', 'Calico', and 'Colossus'.

Two other types of Southern peas, purple hulls and cream peas, are quite popular. The pods of purple hulls turn purple at maturity. Folks like them because they're highly productive and make a dark, flavorful "pot liquor" (the liquid left in the cooking pot). Favorite selections include 'Mississippi Pinkeye', 'Pinkeye Purple Hull', and 'Purple Hull 49'. Cream peas are named for their white or cream-colored seeds. Try 'Zipper Cream' (its pods have a "zipper" for easy shelling), 'Lady Cream', 'Mississippi Cream', 'Texas Cream 40', and 'White Acre'.

All Southern peas tolerate drought and poor soil, need little fertilizer, and fend off pests. If nematodes plague your soil, plant resistant selections such as 'Mississippi Cream' and 'Mississippi Pinkeye'. All types need warm soil to germinate. Sow seeds for summer crops about 2 weeks after your last spring frost. For fall crops, sow in early July. To speed germination, soak seeds overnight before planting.

Sow in rows 2 ft. apart, planting seeds 1 in. deep in clay soils and 2 in. deep in sandy soils. When seedlings have reached 3 in. tall, thin them to 6–12 in. apart. Don't feed with nitrogen fertilizer or you'll get all leaves and no peas. Peas are almost ready for picking when the green pods start to change color; purple hulls turn purple, other types turn tan or yellow. Pick when they're halfway turned. Shell and cook the peas right away or freeze them for later. Frozen fresh peas keep up to a year. Or let the peas dry in the pod until they rattle, then shell and store them in a bag or jar.

SOUTHERNWOOD. See ARTEMISIA abrotanum

SOUTHERN YEW. See PODOCARPUS macrophyllus

SPANISH BAYONET. See YUCCA aloifolia

SPANISH BLUEBELL. See HYACINTHOIDES hispanica

SPANISH DAGGER. See YUCCA gloriosa, Y. treculeana

SPANISH THYME. See PLECTRANTHUS amboinicus

SPATHIPHYLLUM

PEACE LILY

Araceae

PERENNIALS

☘ TS ⊩ 12–10; OR HOUSEPLANTS

◐ ● SOME SHADE; LOW TO BRIGHT INDIRECT LIGHT

💧 💧 REGULAR TO AMPLE WATER

Spathiphyllum 'Mauna Loa'

From the tropics, mainly in the Americas. The various types range from dwarf forms a few inches high to 8-footers; foliage color varies from light to dark green. Leaves are carried on slender stalks that rise directly from the soil; they are generally large for the plant size, oval or elliptical, narrowed to a point. Flowers—fragrant in some species and selections—resemble those of calla (*Zantedeschia*) or anthurium, consisting of a leaflike white or greenish white bract surrounding a central club-shaped structure of closely set tiny flowers. Outdoors, use as border plants or accents, for ground cover, in containers on shaded lanai or patio. Provide rich soil, wind protection. Deer aren't fond of them.

Peace lilies are among the few flowering plants that grow and bloom readily indoors; grow them in loose, fibrous potting mix and feed weekly with dilute liquid fertilizer. Mist frequently. If plants refuse to bloom, move them to a brighter spot, but avoid hot, direct sun. Good choices include *S. wallisii* 'Clevelandii', to 2 ft. high, 20 in. wide; *S.* 'Mauna Loa', 3½ ft. high, 2 ft. wide; and *S.* 'Sensation', 4–6 ft. tall, 3 ft. wide.

SPATHODEA campanulata

AFRICAN TULIP TREE

Bignoniaceae

EVERGREEN TREE

⚡ TS ╫ 12–10

☀ FULL SUN

💧 MODERATE WATER

Spathodea campanulata

From tropical Africa. Very showy, fast-growing tree to 40–75 ft. tall, 20–50 ft. wide. Glossy deep green leaves to 1½ ft. long, divided featherwise into 9 to 19 oblong to ovate leaflets. Clusters of spectacular, tulip-shaped, 4-in. flowers in scarlet, blood red, or yellowish orange appear at branch ends. Blooms mainly in spring and summer, but flowers may appear in any season. Give good drainage and a warm site. This tree grows rapidly and blooms young, but it can be devastated by frosts. Best suited to south Florida.

SPEARMINT. See MENTHA spicata

SPEEDWELL. See VERONICA

SPHAERALCEA

GLOBE MALLOW

Malvaceae

PERENNIALS

⚡ ZONES VARY BY SPECIES

☀ FULL SUN

💧 LITTLE WATER

Sphaeralcea coccinea

Grown for attractive downy leaves and bright flowers shaped like miniature hollyhocks *(Alcea)*, these upright to trailing plants have a persistent woody base with softer stems above. Need well-drained soil. Any more than a little water causes weedy growth and rust. Cut old stems almost to ground before spring growth begins. Colorful accent plants for hot, dry locations.

S. coccinea. PRAIRIE MALLOW. Zones US, MS, LS, CS, TS; 12–5. Native from Manitoba south to Texas, Arizona. Spreading plant with branching stems and rounded olive green leaves that are deeply lobed, to 1½ in. long. Usually grows 2–3 ft. tall and wide but can spread wider if given summer moisture. Produces short wands of cup-shaped, orange to red flowers to 1½ in. across throughout summer.

S. incana. ORANGE MALLOW. Zones US, MS, LS, CS; 9–5. Native to Arizona, New Mexico, and Texas. Forms slowly spreading clump to 2–4 ft. high, 2 ft. wide, with many upright stems clothed in rounded, 2-in. long, yellowish green leaves. In summer (spring in hottest regions), bears a succession of clustered 1-in., light to deep orange blossoms.

SPHAEROPTERIS cooperi. See CYATHEA cooperi

SPICE BUSH. See CALYCANTHUS occidentalis

SPICEBUSH. See LINDERA

SPIDER FLOWER. See CLEOME hasslerana

SPIDER LILY. See LYCORIS

SPIDER PLANT. See CHLOROPHYTUM comosum

SPIDERWORT. See TRADESCANTIA virginiana

SPIGELIA marilandica

INDIAN PINK, PINKROOT

Loganiaceae

PERENNIAL

⚡ US, MS, LS, CS ╫ 9–2

☀ LIGHT SHADE

💧 REGULAR WATER

☠ ALL PARTS ARE POISONOUS IF INGESTED

Spigelia marilandica

Woodland plant native to the Southeast. Grows 1–2 ft. high, with stiff, erect stems bearing pairs of glossy green, 4-in., broadly lance-shaped leaves. Clusters of 2-in., trumpetlike flowers; blossoms are red on the outside and yellow inside, facing upward to show a yellow five-pointed star at the mouth. Early summer bloom. Easy to grow if given light shade and moist, acid soil. With enough moisture, will tolerate much sun. Although once used medicinally, the plant is actually poisonous.

SPINACH

Chenopodiaceae, Aizoaceae, Basellaceae

ANNUALS AND PERENNIALS

⚡ ZONES VARY BY TYPE

☀ FULL SUN

💧 REGULAR WATER

True Spinach

One of the three plants described here is true spinach *(Spinacia);* the other two are warm-season vegetables used as substitutes for the real thing, which needs cool weather to succeed. All are grown for their edible leaves, used raw or cooked. All do best in rich, well-drained soil.

True spinach. This is the cool-season annual *Spinacia oleracea,* a member of the goosefoot family (Chenopodiaceae). It probably originated in southwestern Asia. Zones US, MS, LS, CS, TS; 7–1. Spinach matures slowly during fall, winter, and spring; long days of late spring and heat of summer make it bolt (go to seed) quickly. For a spring harvest, sow seeds in earliest spring. Choose heat-tolerant selections that are slow to bolt, such as 'Avon' (44 days from seed to harvest), 'Bloomsdale Long Standing' (48 days), 'Indian Summer' (39 days), 'Space' (39 days), or 'Tyee' (38 days). For fall and winter harvests, sow seeds 4 to 8 weeks before the first expected fall frost. Plants will survive freezing temperatures and can be harvested through the winter. Look for disease-resistant, cold-hardy selections, such as 'Bloomsdale Long Standing', 'Dixie Market' (45 days), 'Melody' (42 days), and 'Winter Bloomsdale' (47 days).

Before planting, work into the soil ¼ cup of 10-10-10 fertilizer per 10 ft. of row or bed. Sow seeds thinly in rows spaced 1½ ft. apart, or scatter them over a wide bed; cover with ½ in. of soil. Thin seedlings to 4–6 in. apart. When seedlings have four or five leaves, sprinkle ¼ cup of 10-10-10 fertilizer per 10 ft. of row (or bed) around the plants and water in.

There are two ways to harvest. You can pinch off only the large outer leaves when they are 3–6 in. long, allowing the plant to produce new foliage from its center. Or you can cut the entire plant at soil level when it reaches 4–6 in. wide.

New Zealand spinach. Native to New Zealand and Australia, *Tetragonia tetragonioides* belongs to Aizoaceae, a family of succulent plants. It is an evergreen perennial in the Coastal and Tropical South but goes dormant after a frost. Elsewhere it can be grown as a summer annual. Sow seeds in early spring after danger of frost is past; thin established seedlings to 1–1½ ft. apart. Plants

New Zealand Spinach

S

reach maturity about 50 days after sowing; they are 1–2 ft. tall, with spreading form. Harvest greens by plucking off top few inches of tender stems and attached leaves; a month later, new shoots will have grown up for another harvest. New Zealand spinach tolerates heat and drought but also thrives in cool, damp conditions.

Malabar spinach. *Basella alba* is a native of India; it belongs to the family Basellaceae. Perennial vine in the Tropical South; grown as an annual elsewhere. It needs night temperatures above 58°F and will not survive frost. There is an especially attractive red-stemmed form. Sow seeds in early summer; thin established seedlings to 1 ft. apart. When young plants are about 1 ft. high, train them on wires or a trellis. At 2 ft. high, pinch out a few inches of stem tip (harvesting any young, tender leaves) to encourage the plants to branch and form more stems. Vine grows about 4 ft. tall. As leaves reach full, succulent size (about 4 in. long; 50 to 60 days after sowing), pick them individually. They are bigger and thicker than leaves of true spinach, so you'll need fewer per serving.

SPINDLE TREE. See EUONYMUS europaeus

SPIRAEA

Rosaceae

DECIDUOUS SHRUBS

⚡ ZONES VARY BY SPECIES

☼ ◑ FULL SUN OR LIGHT SHADE

💧 ◐ REGULAR TO MODERATE WATER

Spiraea japonica
'Anthony Waterer'

Unless your garden sits in a cave or the middle of the ocean, you probably have room for a spiraea. They are a varied lot, offering a number of sizes, forms, and flowering seasons—but they can be broken down into two basic groups according to bloom time. Spring bloomers feature clusters of white flowers cascading down from arching branches; summer bloomers are compact and shrubby, with pink, red, or white flowers clustered at the branch ends. Both types look more effective when massed in sweeps and borders than when used singly. White-flowered spiraeas look better against a dark background. The cut branches of spring-flowering types are great for forcing into bloom for indoor arrangements.

Spiraeas are tough and easy to grow; with few exceptions, they are not fussy about soil. Deer don't seem to favor them. Prune spring bloomers yearly in late spring after flowering, cutting one-third of the oldest branches to the ground. Prune summer bloomers in winter or earliest spring, before new growth begins; they generally need less pruning than spring bloomers. If you remove spent flower clusters in summer, plants will produce a second (but less lavish) bloom.

S. ×bumalda. See S. japonica 'Bumalda'

S. cantoniensis 'Lanceata' ('Flore-Pleno'). DOUBLE REEVES SPIRAEA. Zones US, MS, LS, CS. From China, Japan. To 5–6 ft. tall, 10 ft. wide, with arching branches. Double white flowers wreathe the leafy branches in late spring to early summer. Lance-shaped blue-green leaves to 2½ in. long; they drop late, show no fall color. Plant is nearly evergreen in mildest climates. Prune as for spring bloomers.

S. japonica. Zones US, MS, LS; 9–1. Native to Japan, China. Upright and shrubby to 4–6 ft. tall and wide, with flat, 8-in.-wide clusters of pink flowers carried above oval, toothed, 1- to 4-in.-long green leaves. Best known through its selections, which are typically lower than the species and bloom between summer and fall. They include plants formerly classified as hybrids of *S. ×bumalda,* itself now considered merely a selection.

S. j. albiflora. To 2 ft. tall, 3 ft. wide. Pale green leaves; white flowers.

'Anthony Waterer'. To 3–5 ft. tall and wide. Carmine pink blossoms. Leaves are reddish purple when new, maturing to bright green.

'Bumalda'. To 3 ft. high and wide. Dark pink flowers; bronzy new growth.

'Coccinea'. To 2–3 ft. tall and wide. Maroon-tinged foliage; red flowers.

'Dart's Red'. To 2 ft. high and wide. A compact sport of 'Anthony Waterer', with redder flowers.

'Fire Light'. To 2–3 ft. high, 4 ft. wide. Leaves emerge reddish orange and retain their color into summer, then turn fiery red in fall. Pink flowers.

'Golden Elf'. Dwarf to 6–9 in. high, 1–2 ft. wide. Golden leaves usually hold their color into autumn. Tiny pink blossoms.

'Goldflame'. To 2½ ft. high and wide. Bronze new growth matures to yellowish green, turns dark reddish orange in fall. Red flowers.

'Limemound'. To 3 ft. tall, 6 ft. wide. Lemon yellow new leaves mature to lime green, then turn orange red in fall. Light pink flowers.

'Little Princess'. To 3 ft. tall, 6 ft. wide. Rose pink blossoms.

'Magic Carpet'. To 1½–2½ ft. tall, slightly wider. Reddish bronze new leaves turn chartreuse to yellow as they mature. Pink flowers.

'Nana' ('Alpina'). ALPINE SPIRAEA. To 2 ft. tall, 5 ft. wide. Pink flowers. Good red fall foliage in some years.

'Neon Flash'. To 3–4 ft. tall, 4–5 ft. wide. Purple-tinted foliage; bright rose pink flowers.

'Shirobana'. To 2–3 ft. high and wide. Red buds open to bicolored blossoms in white and deep pink.

S. nipponica 'Snowmound'. Zones US, MS, LS; 8–1. From Japan. Compact, spreading plant to 2–3 ft. tall, 3–5 ft. wide. Profusion of white flowers in late spring or early summer. Ovate to roundish, dark green leaves to 1¼ in. long; little autumn color. Prune as for spring bloomers.

S. prunifolia (S. p. 'Plena'). BRIDAL WREATH SPIRAEA. Zones US, MS, LS; 8–2. From China, Taiwan. Graceful, arching branches on a suckering, clump-forming plant to 6–7 ft. tall and wide. In early to midspring, bare branches are lined with small, double white flowers resembling tiny roses. Small dark green leaves turn bright shades of red, orange, and yellow in autumn. An old Southern favorite.

S. thunbergii. BABY'S BREATH SPIRAEA. Zones US, MS, LS; 8–5. From China, Japan. Showy, billowy, graceful species 3–6 ft. or taller, 6 ft. wide, with many slender, arching branches. Round clusters of small white flowers appear all along the bare branches in early spring. Blue-green, extremely narrow leaves to 1½ in. long turn soft reddish brown in fall. An old-time favorite in the South, with several outstanding selections. 'Fujino Pink' has dark pink buds that open to light pink flowers. 'Mount Fuji' bears the typical white blooms, but its leaves (some of them twisted and curled) are green striped with white. White-flowered 'Ogon' has foliage that emerges yellow but gradually turns green in summer.

S. trilobata 'Swan Lake'. Zones US, MS; 7–1. Selection of a species from Siberia and northern China. Like a small version of *S. prunifolia.* Grows 3–4 ft. tall and wide, with a massive show of tiny white flowers in mid- to late spring. Leaves are just 1 in. long, often three lobed. 'Fairy Queen' is similar but more compact, seldom exceeding 3 ft.

S. ×vanhouttei. Zones US, MS, LS; 8–1. Hybrid between *S. cantoniensis* and *S. trilobata.* The classic spring-blooming spiraea for Southern gardens. Arching branches form a fountain to about 6 ft. high by 8 ft. or wider. Leafy branches are covered with circular, flattened clusters of white blossoms in mid- to late spring. Dark green, diamond-shaped leaves to 1½ in. long may turn purplish in fall.

SPIRANTHES cernua odorata

NODDING LADIES' TRESSES

Orchidaceae

TERRESTRIAL ORCHID

⚡ US, MS, LS, CS ❄ 10–1

☼ ◑ FULL SUN OR PARTIAL SHADE

💧 ◐◐ REGULAR TO AMPLE WATER

Spiranthes cernua odorata

Native to swamps of southeastern U.S. Forms low rosettes of dark green, 2- to 10-in.-long leaves; spreads slowly by underground rhizomes to form small colonies. In late summer and early fall, gorgeous, 1- to 2-ft.-tall spikes appear atop the foliage, with small, bell-shaped white flowers arranged spirally up and down their length. Blooms are very fragrant, like a blend of vanilla and jasmine. Easy to grow in constantly moist soil that is highly enriched with organic matter. Excellent addition to bog or streamside garden; lovely at the edge of a pond.

S

SPLIT-LEAF PHILODENDRON. See MONSTERA deliciosa

SPOROBOLUS
DROPSEED

Poaceae (Gramineae)

PERENNIAL GRASSES

US, MS, LS, CS

FULL SUN

LITTLE TO MODERATE WATER

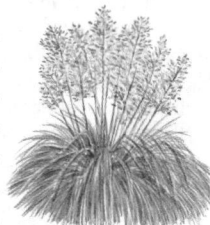

Sporobolus heterolepis

Don't let the graceful appearance and fine texture of these clumping grasses fool you—they're as tough as they come. Deep rooted and drought tolerant; excellent for massing in hot, dry areas and effective in meadow gardens, mixed borders, naturalized areas, rock gardens, even by swimming pools. Plumelike flower heads appear in summer or fall; after they fade, tiny seeds drop to the ground, hence the common name.

S. airoides. ALKALI SACATON, ALKALI DROPSEED. Heat zones 10–4. Native from Arkansas and Missouri northwest to Washington and south to Mexico. Foliage clump grows 3 ft. high and wide; leaves are grayish green during growing season, yellow in fall, beige in winter. In summer or fall, showy, erect or arching flower plumes increase plant height to 5 ft.; plumes are pinkish, eventually fading to pale straw color. Takes a wide range of soils; good for alkaline conditions. Noninvasive.

S. heterolepis. PRAIRIE DROPSEED. Heat zones 10–2. Native to the Midwest, High Plains, and much of the eastern U.S. Emerald green, hairlike leaves form a billowing mass to 15 in. tall and 1½ ft. wide. Foliage turns golden to orange in fall, then fades to light bronze in winter. Slender-stemmed panicles of flowers rise to 3 ft. tall, soaring above the foliage in late summer. Blossoms are pink to light brown and smell faintly of coriander. The seeds are highly nutritious and were ground into flour by Plains Indians. Plant tolerates almost any soil but likes it on the dry side. It can be started from seed but is rather slow to establish. Unlike many other grasses, this one doesn't self-sow extravagantly, so volunteer seedlings are seldom a problem.

SPOTTED HORSEMINT. See MONARDA punctata

SPREKELIA formosissima
AZTEC LILY, JACOBEAN LILY, ST. JAMES LILY

Amaryllidaceae

PERENNIAL FROM BULB

LS (PROTECTED), CS, TS 12–10;
OR DIG AND STORE; OR GROW IN POTS

FULL SUN

REGULAR WATER DURING GROWTH AND BLOOM

Sprekelia formosissima

Mexican native often sold as *Amaryllis formosissima*. Foliage looks like that of daffodil *(Narcissus)*, but each 1-ft.-tall stem is topped with a dark red, 6-in.-wide bloom resembling an orchid, with three erect upper segments and three drooping lower ones that are united at their bases (near the flower's center) to form a tube. Bloom comes primarily in early summer. In mild climates, foliage may be evergreen and plant may bloom several times a year if you can give it a dry period after flowering, then resume regular watering to trigger a new growth cycle.

Where bulbs are hardy, plant them in fall, setting them 3–4 in. deep and 8 in. apart in good, well-drained soil. Look most effective in groups. Display increases if plants are left undisturbed for several years. Where winters are cold, set out bulbs in spring; lift plants in fall when foliage yellows and store in a cool, dark, dry place over winter (leave dry tops on). Or grow in pots as directed for amaryllis *(Hippeastrum)*; repot every 3 or 4 years.

SPRING STAR FLOWER. See IPHEION uniflorum

SPRUCE. See PICEA

SPURGE. See PACHYSANDRA

SQUASH
Cucurbitaceae

ANNUAL

US, MS, LS, CS, TS 12–1

FULL SUN

REGULAR WATER

Summer Squash

Few vegetables give you as big a return on your investment of time and energy as squash. There are two main forms. Summer squash is harvested all summer long, while still soft skinned and immature. It's served steamed, sautéed, or fried. Winter squash is harvested in late summer and fall after it has matured and developed a tough skin; it stores very well and is used for baking, stuffing, and pies. A special kind of winter squash, called spaghetti squash, can substitute for pasta; its nutty-tasting flesh consists of long, spaghetti-like strands. Squash plants produce both male and female flowers, with the female flowers forming fruit after bees transfer pollen from male blossoms. The first flowers are typically male, so if your vine doesn't start fruiting right away, be patient.

Summer squash yields prodigious crops from just a few plants and continues to bear for many weeks. The three most popular types are yellow (both straightneck and crookneck), zucchini, and pattypan (also called scallop). Plant immediately after the last spring frost, then again 3 weeks later for an extended harvest. Summer squash is usually planted in hills (mounds) spaced 3–4 ft. apart. For better pollination and fruiting, plant two rows of hills side by side instead of one long row. Vines are large (up to 5 ft. at maturity) and need plenty of room; if space is limited, plant bush types such as 'Peter Pan' and 'Sweet Zuke'.

Sow five to seven seeds per hill, planting them 1 in. deep. Thin seedlings to the strongest two plants per hill. Four weeks after planting, fertilize each hill with ¼ cup of 10-10-10 fertilizer. Fruits reach harvest size quickly, usually within 5 to 7 days after the flowers open. Pick yellow squash when they're 4–6 in. long, zucchini when 6–8 in. long, and pattypans when 3–5 in. wide. Don't allow fruit to reach full maturity on the vines, as this may halt fruit production.

Good yellow straightneck selections include 'Early Prolific Straightneck' (48 days from sowing to harvest), 'Seneca Prolific' (50 days), and 'Park's

S

WHAT SQUASH NEEDS

LOCATION: Choose a spot with full sun and good air circulation. Most selections need plenty of room.

SOIL: Provide fertile, well-drained soil containing plenty of organic matter, such as composted manure, chopped leaves, or garden compost. If your soil is strongly acid (pH 5.5 or lower), add lime.

WATERING: Water often enough to keep soil moist and prevent the plants from wilting, especially when fruit is forming.

PEST CONTROL: To control squash vine borers and squash bugs, plant under floating row covers; or dust or spray with rotenone or carbaryl (Sevin) according to label instructions. Plant squash in a different place each year to avoid a buildup of pests.

'Sunburst' Summer Squash

Super Creamy' (55 days). For yellow crookneck, try 'Yellow Crookneck' (58 days), 'Early Golden Summer' (53 days), and 'Sunglo' (40 days). Recommended zucchini selections include 'Embassy' (45 days), 'Gold Rush' (45 days), and 'Burpee Hybrid' (50 days). Among the best pattypans are 'Sunburst' (52 days), 'Scallopini' (50 days), and 'White Pattypan' (60 days). Novelties include 'Eight Ball' (40 days), a round zucchini; 'Magda' (50 days), a white-fleshed, nutty-tasting squash shaped like a thick zucchini to 4 in. long; and 'Kuta' (48 days), a light green squash that can be eaten like summer squash at 6 in. long or allowed to mature into a 1-ft. winter squash.

Winter squash typically needs more room than summer squash. It doesn't perform well in the Coastal and Tropical South. Plant smaller types, such as acorn, buttercup, butternut, and spaghetti squash, in hills spaced 4–5 ft. apart. These produce fruit weighing 2 to 5 pounds. Large types, such as banana and Hubbard, bear fruit weighing 12 to 15 pounds or more; they require 5–7 ft. between hills and 6–10 ft. between rows. Planting and care are the same as for summer squash. Fruit is ready to harvest when you can't pierce the skin with your thumbnail. Cut the squash from the vine, leaving 1–2 in. of stem attached; store in a cool, dry place.

Recommended winter squash selections include acorn types 'Table Ace' (70 days), 'Jersey Golden' (70 days), and 'Cream of the Crop' (85 days); buttercup type 'Sweet Mama' (85 days); butternut types 'Waltham Butternut' (105 days) and 'Nicklow's Delight' (78 days); spaghetti type 'Pasta Hybrid' (85 days); banana type 'Pink Banana Jumbo' (120 days); and Hubbard type 'Blue Hubbard' (100 days).

For all types of squash, the most serious pest is squash vine borer, a large white caterpillar that tunnels through stems, causing vines to wilt and die. Squash bugs are another possible pest; they suck plant juices, causing stems to blacken and wilt. To control both pests, plant under floating row covers, or dust or spray the base of the plants with rotenone or carbaryl (Sevin) every 7 to 10 days during the growing season. Squash bugs lay yellowish to brown egg clusters on the undersides of leaves; look for these and destroy them. You can also spray the undersides of leaves with rotenone or insecticidal soap.

The most common disease affecting squash is powdery mildew on the foliage; to discourage it, plant in full sun, maintain good air circulation around plants, avoid wetting the foliage, and remove infected leaves as soon as you see them. Neem oil and antitranspirants can also be effective. For more information, consult the *Southern Living Garden Problem Solver*.

SQUAWBUSH. See RHUS trilobata

SQUILL. See SCILLA

SQUIRREL'S FOOT FERN. See DAVALLIA trichomanoides

STACHYS

Lamiaceae (Labiatae)

PERENNIALS

⚡ US, MS, LS ⌶ 8–1, EXCEPT AS NOTED

☼ ◑ FULL SUN OR LIGHT SHADE

💧 MODERATE WATER

Stachys byzantina

These mint-family members have the typical square stems and leaves in opposite pairs; foliage ranges from rough textured to furry. Most of the species described here have short-stalked or stalkless leaves. Spikelike clusters of small, usually two-lipped flowers bloom in late spring and summer; blossoms are attractive to bees. All are fairly unfussy about soil type, needing only good drainage. Green-leafed species need some shade where summers are hot. Clumps often die out in center; divide and replant outer sections. Deer usually leave these plants alone.

S. albotomentosa. HIDALGO. Native to Mexico. To 2½ ft. tall, sprawling to 5–6 ft. wide. Green, heavily veined leaves have a felty texture and an elongated heart shape. Stems and leaf undersides are woolly. Flowers are peach to salmon pink when they open, then age to brick red. Sometimes listed as *S. coccinea* 'Hidalgo'.

S. byzantina (S. lanata, S. olympica). LAMB'S EARS. Native to the Caucasus, Iran. To 1½ ft. high, spreading freely by surface runners. Dense, ground-hugging rosettes of soft, thick, rather tongue-shaped, woolly white leaves to 4–6 in. long. Blossom stalks 1–1½ ft. high bear small purplish flowers; many gardeners feel that these flowering stems detract from the foliage and so cut them off or pull them out. Continued rains can mash plants down and make them mushy, and frost can damage foliage, but recovery is usually strong.

'Silver Carpet' does not produce flower spikes and is somewhat less vigorous than the species. 'Big Ears' ('Countess Helen von Stein') has larger leaves. Flowers of 'Cotton Boll' are like little balls of fluff spaced along the stem. Furry leaves of 'Primrose Heron' are yellow when new, maturing to chartreuse, then gray green.

Use all forms for contrast with dark green foliage and with leaves of different shapes, such as those of strawberry or some sedums. Good edging for paths, flower beds. Excellent ground cover in high, open shade, such as under tall oaks; space plants 2 ft. apart.

S. coccinea. SCARLET HEDGE NETTLE. Native to southern Texas, New Mexico, Arizona. Forms a clump to 1½ ft. high and wide, with wrinkled, heavily veined, medium green foliage. Leaves are elongated ovals to 3 in. long. Bears short spikes of scarlet flowers. For the form sometimes sold as 'Hidalgo', see *S. albotomentosa*.

S. macrantha (S. grandiflora). BIG BETONY. Heat zones 9–7. Native to the Caucasus, Turkey, Iran. Dense foliage clump to 1 ft. high and wide, with long-stalked, heart-shaped, scallop-edged dark green leaves to 3 in. across; they are wrinkled and roughly hairy. Showy purplish pink blossoms are held on 1½- to 2-ft.-tall stems. 'Robusta' and 'Superba' offer larger flowers; 'Alba' has white blooms.

S. officinalis. BETONY. Heat zones 8–4. Similar to *S. macrantha*, but leaves are elongated (to 5 in. long) and may be hairy or nearly smooth. The purplish or dark red flowers are densely packed into short spikes atop leafy stems. Little grown except by herb fanciers, but white-blooming 'Alba' and pink-blooming 'Rosea Superba' are attractive 2-ft. plants for perennial border or woodland edge.

STACHYTARPHETA

PORTERWEED

Verbenaceae

PERENNIALS OFTEN GROWN AS ANNUALS

⚡ TS ⌶ 12–7

☼ ◑ EXPOSURE NEEDS VARY BY SPECIES

💧 REGULAR WATER

Stachytarpheta jamaicensis

Group of shrubby perennials native to New and Old World tropics and treasured for their flowers. Bloom continuously in warm weather, with long, whiplike spikes bearing clusters of small, showy blossoms that attract butterflies and hummingbirds. Effective in naturalized areas, in mixed herbaceous borders, and when massed. Plants self-sow readily and can be weedy.

S. jamaicensis. PORTERWEED. Native to south Florida, where it is widely sold and planted. Mounding plant to 2–4 ft. tall and wide, with dull green, coarsely toothed, pointed-oval leaves to 3 in. long. Slender flower spikes resembling a rat's tail rise at least a foot above the foliage. Blue, ¼-in. flowers appear singly or in clusters, starting at bottom of spike and proceeding upward. Individual flowers last just 1 day. Best in partial shade.

S. mutabilis. PINK PORTERWEED. Native to South America. Shrubby, sprawling growth to 7 ft. tall and wide. Fuzzy light green leaves to 4 in. long are oval and pointed. Thick flower spikes rise a foot above the foliage, bearing clusters of ½-in. pink flowers that last for several days. 'Coral' is very showy, flaunting masses of coral pink blossoms. Full sun.

S. urticifolia. BLUE PORTERWEED. Native to Asia. Similar to and often confused with *S. jamaicensis*, but leaves are darker green and noticeably quilted on upper surface. Flowers are also slightly smaller and darker blue and have white centers. Upright, shrubby growth to 5 ft. high, not quite as wide. Individual flowers last for only a day. Full sun.

STACHYURUS praecox

Stachyuraceae

DECIDUOUS SHRUB

✿ US, MS, LS ⊞ 8–6

☼ ◑ FULL SUN OR LIGHT SHADE

💧 REGULAR WATER

Stachyurus praecox

Native to Japan. Slow grower to 10 ft. tall and about as wide, with slender, polished-looking, chestnut brown branches. Pendulous, 3- to 4-in.-long flower stalks, each carrying 12 to 20 buds, hang from branches in fall and winter. In late winter, buds open into bell-shaped, pale yellow or greenish yellow flowers ⅓ in. wide. Greenish yellow, berrylike fruit follows in late summer. Bright green, toothed leaves are 3–7 in. long and oval, tapering to sharp tip; foliage is often somewhat sparse. Rosy red and yellowish fall color is pleasant but not spectacular. Grow this plant under a deciduous tree to shelter its winter buds from heavy freezes.

STAGHORN FERN. See PLATYCERIUM

STANDING CYPRESS. See IPOMOPSIS rubra

STAPELIA

STARFISH FLOWER, CARRION FLOWER

Asclepiadaceae

SUCCULENT PERENNIALS

✿ CS (WARMER PARTS), TS ⊞ 12–9; BEST IN POTS

☼ FULL SUN

💧 MODERATE WATER

Stapelia variegata

From Africa. Plants resemble cacti, with clumps of four-sided, spineless stems. Summer flowers are large, fleshy, shaped like five-pointed stars; they usually have an elaborate circular fleshy disk in the center. Blossoms of most smell like carrion, but odor is not usually pervasive enough to be offensive. They need a cool, dry rest period in winter. Best managed in pots. Tolerate extreme heat.

S. gigantea. Grow this plant as a remarkable novelty. Stems grow about 9 in. tall, bearing wrinkled, fringy-edged, brown-purple flowers marked in creamy white or yellow; each bloom reaches 10–16 in. wide. Protect plants where frosts can occur.

S. variegata (Orbea variegata). Most common. Stems to 6 in. Yellow flowers to 3 in. across, spotted and barred in dark purple brown, not strongly scented. There are many hybrids and color variants. Plant can take light frost.

STAR CLUSTERS, EGYPTIAN. See PENTAS lanceolata

STAR DAISY. See LINDHEIMERA texana, MELAMPODIUM paludosum

STARFISH FLOWER. See STAPELIA

STARFLOWER. See SMILACINA stellata

STARFRUIT. See CARAMBOLA

STAR GRASS. See HYPOXIS

STAR JASMINE. See TRACHELOSPERMUM

STAR OF BETHLEHEM. See ORNITHOGALUM arabicum, O. umbellatum

STAR OF THE ARGENTINE. See TWEEDIA caerulea

STARRY ROSINWEED. See SILPHIUM dentatum

STATICE. See LIMONIUM

STENOLOBIUM stans. See TECOMA stans

STENOTAPHRUM
secundatum

ST. AUGUSTINE GRASS

Poaceae (Gramineae)

PERENNIAL GRASS

✿ LS, CS, TS ⊞ 12–8

☼ ◑ BEST IN SUN, TOLERATES LIGHT SHADE

💧 REGULAR WATER

Stenotaphrum secundatum

Native to the Gulf Coast and other tropical and subtropical regions, St. Augustine is a coarse-textured warm-season grass, spreading rapidly by surface runners that root at the joints. In warm, rainy weather, runners can completely hide a sidewalk in a few weeks. It turns brown in winter but never goes completely dormant, and it greens up early in spring. It can be difficult to mow, especially when tall and wet, and it's not very tolerant of drought or severe cold. On the plus side, it establishes rapidly, recovers quickly from wear, and accepts more shade than other warm-season lawn grasses. It also grows in almost any soil and tolerates salt spray, making it the best choice for beach areas. A variegated form is sometimes offered; it's an interesting subject for hanging baskets.

St. Augustine grass is very popular in Florida, South Texas, and along the Gulf and South Atlantic coasts. It can be started from sod or plugs. Mow standard selections at 2½–4 in. tall; mow semidwarf selections at 1½–2 in. tall. Chinch bugs, which suck the juices from leaf blades, can be a major pest. They can be controlled with insecticides, but planting a resistant selection is the best defense.

Selections include the following.

'Bitterblue'. Standard type, blue green. This is the most shade-tolerant selection.

'Delmar'. Semidwarf, dark green. Fine-textured, cold-hardy selection with good shade tolerance.

'Floralawn'. Standard type, dark green. Very coarse textured. Not particularly tolerant of shade or cold, but resists chinch bugs.

'Floratam'. Similar to 'Floralawn'.

'Jade'. Semidwarf, dark green. Very fine textured. Cold-hardy selection with good shade tolerance.

'Palmetto'. Semidwarf, dark green. Quite cold hardy. Good shade and drought tolerance.

'Raleigh'. Standard type, medium green. Very cold-hardy selection with good shade tolerance.

'Seville'. Semidwarf, dark green. Fine textured. Cold-hardy selection with excellent shade tolerance. Some resistance to chinch bugs.

STEPHANOTIS floribunda

MADAGASCAR JASMINE

Asclepiadaceae

EVERGREEN VINE

✿ TS ⊞ 12–10; OR HOUSEPLANT

◑ ROOTS COOL, TOPS IN FILTERED SUN; BRIGHT LIGHT

💧 REGULAR WATER

Stephanotis floribunda

Native to Madagascar. Twines to 15–30 ft. Waxy, glossy green, oval leaves to 4 in. long. Valued for the intense fragrance of its funnel-shaped, 1- to 2-in.-long, waxy white blossoms. Borne in open clusters, the flowers are a favorite for bridal bouquets and are also used in leis. Blooms from June until summer's end. Needs warmth. Provide support; train on trellis or fence or along eaves. Give good drainage.

As houseplant, will bloom if given ample light; better suited to greenhouse. Feed liberally from spring through fall with a general-purpose liquid houseplant fertilizer. Watch for scale and mealybugs; both pests can be dispatched with a cotton swab dipped in alcohol. Give indoor plants a rest period by letting them dry out in winter. Can be brought outdoors during warm times of year. May be sold as *Marsdenia floribunda*.

Sterculiaceae. The sterculia family of shrubs and trees has flowers in which the calyx (usually bowl shaped and five lobed) replaces the corolla as the conspicuous element. The only example in this book is Chinese parasol tree *(Firmiana)*.

STERNBERGIA lutea

Amaryllidaceae

PERENNIAL FROM BULB

US, MS, LS H 9–6; OR GROW IN POTS

FULL SUN

REGULAR WATER DURING GROWTH AND BLOOM

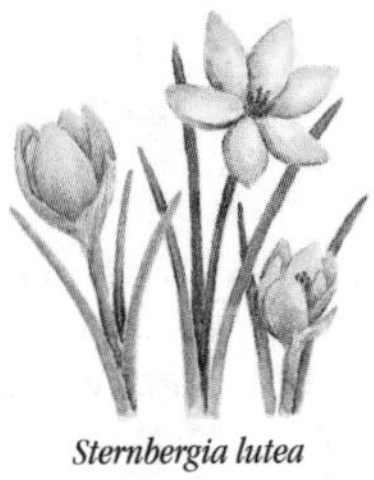

Sternbergia lutea

Native to the western Mediterranean region and central Asia, these bulbs bear golden yellow flowers that provide a pleasant autumn surprise in borders, rock gardens, and along paths. In early fall, the 1½-in. blooms appear singly on 6- to 9-in. stems; they are chalice shaped at first, then open out to a star. Narrow, 6- to 12-in.-long leaves appear in fall along with the flowers; they remain green all winter, then die to the ground in spring.

Plant bulbs as soon as they become available in garden centers (usually in August and September). Set them 4 in. deep and about 6 in. apart in well-drained soil. Where winter temperatures drop to 20°F or lower, cover them with a thick layer of mulch. Try to keep planting bed dry in summer when bulbs are dormant. After planting, the bulbs often take 2 or 3 years to settle in and begin blooming well. Divide clumps only when vigor and flowering decline.

If you can't keep the planting area dry during summer dormancy, grow sternbergia in pots and move them to a dry spot in summer. It blooms better when pot-bound, so don't be in a hurry to repot. Also, don't fret if this temperamental bulb fails to bloom in any one year, as it is sensitive to annual variations in the weather. There's nothing the gardener can do about this but sigh.

STEVIA rebaudiana

PARAGUAYAN SWEET HERB, HONEYLEAF, STEVIA

Asteraceae (Compositae)

PERENNIAL

TS H 12–7; OR GROW IN POTS

FULL SUN

REGULAR WATER

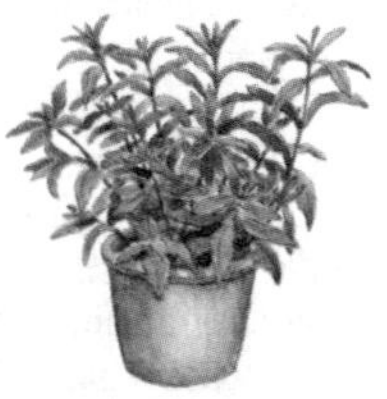

Stevia rebaudiana

Native to Paraguay, Colombia, Venezuela, and Brazil. For growers of this herb, life is sweet indeed: extracts from the leaves contain a noncaloric compound called stevioside, a substance that is 100 to 300 times sweeter than sugar. In China, Japan, Korea, Brazil, Paraguay, and Israel, stevia is used to sweeten a variety of foods and drinks. In the U.S., however, government regulations forbid its sale as a sweetener, and it can be sold only as a "dietary supplement." The leaves are extremely sweet, with a slight hint of licorice—apparently too sweet for most insects, which refuse to eat them.

Stevia is a shrubby plant to 1½ ft. tall and about 1 ft. wide, with toothed, oblong to lance-shaped, papery-textured leaves to about 2 in. long. Clusters of small white flowers with purple throats appear in summer atop wandlike stems.

Start with plants purchased at a garden center or from a mail-order nursery. Choose a site with full sun and moist, fertile, well-drained soil. Stevia does equally well in the ground or in pots, but it will not tolerate frost. Propagate by cuttings taken in summer. Wait until late fall to harvest leaves, as cool temperatures and short days intensify the sweetness. Cut stems near the base of the plant and place them on a net or screen to dry. When stems and leaves have dried completely, strip and crush the leaves. Foliage retains its bright green color even when dry.

STEWARTIA

Theaceae

DECIDUOUS SHRUBS OR TREES

ZONES VARY BY SPECIES

LIGHT SHADE

REGULAR WATER

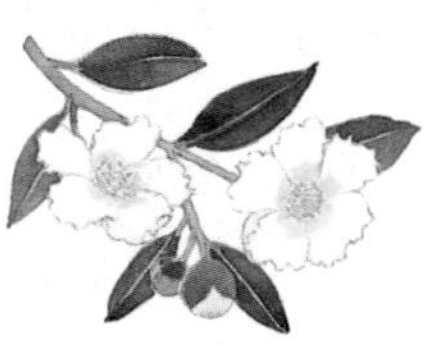

Stewartia koreana

These little-known plants are all-season performers. They show off fresh green leaves in spring, white flowers like single camellias in summer, and colorful foliage in fall; winter reveals a distinctive pattern of bare branches and smooth bark that flakes off in varying degrees, depending on species. *S. koreana* and *S. pseudocamellia* have the showiest bark; it sheds to reveal a patchwork of green, gray, brown, rust, terra-cotta, and cream.

Best in well-drained, acid soil with lots of organic matter. Good in woodland gardens and as foreground specimens against dark backdrop.

S. koreana. KOREAN STEWARTIA. Tree. Zones US, MS; 8–4. From Korea. Pyramidal growth to 20–25 ft. tall, 10–15 ft. wide. May eventually reach 50 ft. tall. Leaves are 1–4 in. long, turn orange to red orange in fall. Flowers, carried on short stalks among leaves, reach 3 in. wide and have yellow-orange stamens. Very similar to *S. pseudocamellia;* in fact, some authorities consider it to be a variant of that species. Two good selections of *S. koreana* are 'Ballet', with flowers nearly 4 in. wide, and 'Milk and Honey', an especially profuse bloomer with brighter-colored bark.

S. malacodendron. SILKY STEWARTIA. Shrub or small tree. Zones MS, LS, CS; 9–6. Native to the Southeast. Heat-tolerant plant to 10–15 ft. tall and wide. Young shoots and leaf undersides are downy textured. Leaves grow 2–4 in. long; flowers are 3½ in. wide and feature purple stamens with blue anthers. Bark is not as showy as that of other species.

S. monadelpha. TALL STEWARTIA. Tree. Zones US, MS, LS; 9–6. From Korea, Japan. To 25 ft. tall, 20 ft. wide, with slender, upward-angled branches. Leaves are 1½–3 in. long; brilliant red in fall. Flowers to 1½ in. wide. Smooth, cinnamon brown bark. Heat tolerant.

S. ovata. MOUNTAIN CAMELLIA. Shrub or small tree. Zones US, MS, LS; 8–1. From the Southeast. To 10–15 ft. tall and wide. Leaves grow 2–5 in. long, turn orange to scarlet in fall; 3-in.-wide flowers have frilled petals. Bark is not as handsome as that of other species. *S. o. grandiflora* has 4-in. flowers with lavender anthers; it will bloom even as a young plant.

S. pseudocamellia. JAPANESE STEWARTIA. Tree. Zones US, MS; 8–4. Native to Japan. Forms a pyramid that may reach 30–40 ft. tall, 20–25 ft. wide after many years. Leaves to 2½–3 in. long; bronze to purple fall color. Flowers are more cup shaped than those of *S. koreana;* they reach 2½ in. wide, have orange anthers. Needs cool, moist soil. Suffers badly from leaf scorch if planted in hot, dry areas.

STIGMAPHYLLON

ORCHID VINE

Malpighiaceae

EVERGREEN OR SEMIEVERGREEN VINES

ZONES VARY BY SPECIES

ROOTS COOL, TOPS IN SUN

REGULAR WATER

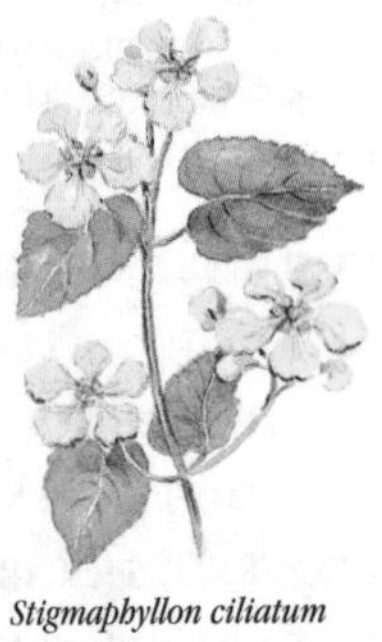

Stigmaphyllon ciliatum

From tropical Central and South America. Woody, fairly fast-growing twiners with paired leaves and bright yellow, irregularly shaped flowers somewhat like oncidium orchids; blossoms rise in long-stalked clusters from upper portions of stems. Plants bloom most heavily in summer, but they may produce some flowers all year in the Tropical South. Grow in organically enriched, well-drained soil. Provide support; prune out dead or straggling growth.

S. ciliatum. FRINGED AMAZON VINE. Zones CS, TS; 12–9; or greenhouse plant. To 15 ft. Delicate, open foliage cover of heart-shaped, medium green, 1- to 3-in.-long leaves with a few long, bristly teeth on edges. Clusters of three to seven flowers, each 1½ in. across. Easy to keep small; good on posts, trellises, walls.

S. littorale. BRAZILIAN GOLDEN VINE. Zones TS; 12–9. Larger vine than *S. ciliatum* (to 20–30 ft. or even higher), with a coarser texture. Oval dark green leaves to 5 in. long; inch-wide flowers in clusters of 10 to 20. Extremely vigorous; can climb to tops of tall trees. Good for covering arbors, pergolas, heavy wire fencing.

STIPA

FEATHER GRASS

Poaceae (Gramineae)

PERENNIAL GRASSES

US, MS, LS, CS H 10–1, EXCEPT AS NOTED

FULL SUN

REGULAR WATER, EXCEPT AS NOTED

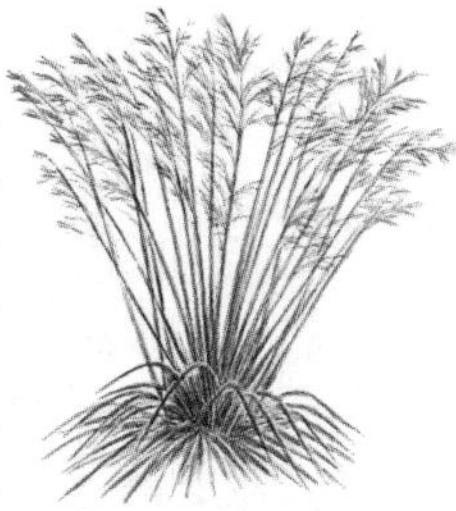

Stipa gigantea

These clump-forming grasses produce large, open, airy inflorescences that can add lightness and motion to the garden. The genus has undergone much revision by botanists, and some of its former members are now known by other names; for one example, see *Nassella tenuissima,* the highly ornamental Mexican feather grass. Deer don't seem to care for these grasses.

S. arundinacea. PHEASANT'S-TAIL GRASS. From New Zealand. Arching, semievergreen foliage in clump to 2 ft. tall and wide. Medium green leaves have a coppery tinge (strongest in fall, winter). Feathery green flowers with purple tints appear in early summer, rising barely higher than leaves. Tolerates light shade.

S. gigantea. GIANT FEATHER GRASS. From Spain, Portugal, Morocco. Narrow, arching, evergreen leaves in a clump to 2–3 ft. tall and slightly wider. Open, airy sheaves of yellowish flowers bloom in summer, forming a broad, shimmering cloud that rises 6 ft. tall and as wide or slightly wider. Little to moderate water.

S. ramosissima (Austrostipa ramosissima). PILLAR OF SMOKE. Heat zones 10–6. From Australia. To 6–7 ft. tall, 3 ft. wide. The erect column of evergreen foliage and blossoms does somewhat resemble a pillar of smoke. Flowering is almost continuous; the airy, light tan inflorescences make up half (or a little more) of the plant's total height.

STOCK. See MATTHIOLA

STOKESIA laevis

STOKESIA, STOKES' ASTER

Asteraceae (Compositae)

PERENNIAL

US, MS, LS, CS H 9–5

FULL SUN

REGULAR WATER

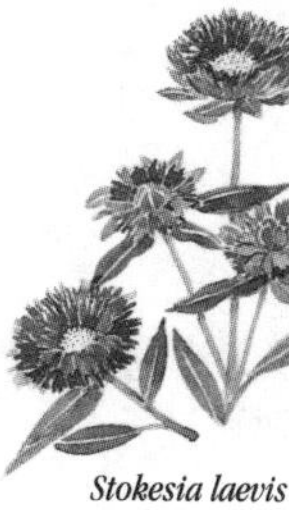

Stokesia laevis 'Bluestone'

Native to the Southeast. Rugged and very adaptable; one of the best perennials for Florida. Semievergreen in the Upper South, evergreen elsewhere. Grows 1½–2 ft. high, 1½ ft. wide, with stiff, erect, much-branched stems. Smooth, firm-textured, medium green leaves are 2–8 in. long, sometimes toothed at the base. Blooms from May to September. Leafy, curved, finely toothed bracts surround the tight flower buds, which open to 3- to 4-in.-wide, asterlike blossoms in blue, purple, white, or yellow. Each flower consists of a central button of small florets surrounded by a ring of larger rays. Choices include these favorite selections, all of which grow a little taller than wide.

'Blue Danube'. Large flowers in medium blue. Grows 12–15 in. tall.

'Bluestone'. Heavy bloomer with medium blue blossoms. To 10 in. tall.

'Mary Gregory'. Striking lemon yellow blooms on a 1½-ft.-tall plant.

'Purple Parasols'. Flowers change from powder blue through purple to magenta with age. To 1½ ft. tall.

'Silver Moon'. Pure white flowers. Grows to 1½ ft. tall.

'Wyoming'. Deep purple blooms. To 1½ ft. tall.

STONECROP. See SEDUM

STRAWBERRY

Rosaceae

PERENNIAL

ZONES VARY BY SELECTION

FULL SUN

REGULAR WATER, EXCEPT AS NOTED

SEE CHART PAGE 558

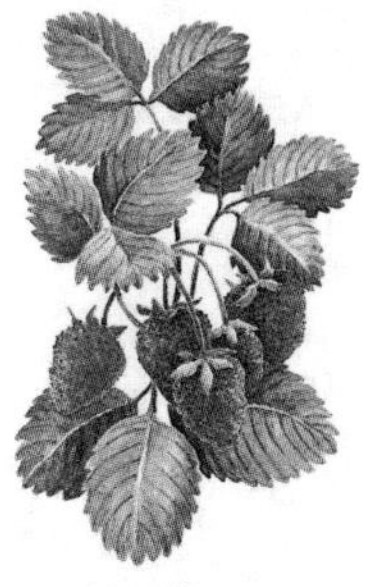

Strawberry

Strawberries of one type or another can be grown pretty much throughout the South. Known botanically as *Fragaria* × *ananassa,* they are easily accommodated in most any garden. Plants have toothed, roundish, medium green leaves and white flowers. They grow 6–8 in. tall and spread by long runners to about 1 ft. across. For descriptions of ornamental strawberries, see *Fragaria.*

Strawberries are grouped into three main categories. *June-bearing* types produce one crop per year in late spring or early summer; they are generally the highest-quality, most dependable strawberries Southerners can grow. *Everbearing* types (a rather misleading term in the South) bear one crop in late spring or early summer and a second, smaller crop in fall. With a few exceptions, they're better performers in the Upper and Middle South than they are farther south, where long, hot summers do them in. *Day-neutral* strawberries (so-called because day length doesn't determine when they fruit) are similar to everbearing types in that they bear both spring and fall crops—but they produce more fruit in fall over a longer period, and the fruit quality is better. Everbearing and day-neutral types produce few runners and are great for small gardens.

How many strawberries should you plant? For a small harvest, grow a dozen or so plants in a sunny patch in a flower or vegetable garden, or put them in containers on the patio. For a big crop, set out as many plants as you can handle, spacing them 14–18 in. apart in rows 2–2½ ft. apart. Strawberries reproduce by making new plants (offsets) on the ends of runners, although some make few or no offsets. To get bigger berries (but smaller yields), pinch off all runners. For heavy crops of smaller berries, let runners and offsets fill in the space between rows. ▸ page 559

WHAT STRAWBERRIES NEED

LOCATION: Open, sunny area with little root competition. Avoid low spots, where frosts might damage flowers in spring. Don't plant where tomatoes, potatoes, peppers, and eggplants have previously grown, as the soil may harbor wilt disease.

SOIL: Well drained, fertile, slightly acid with pH of 6–6.5. If your soil is alkaline, plant in raised beds or containers such as strawberry pots.

WATERING: Plants need constant moisture during bearing season. Water in early morning so that foliage can dry out before nightfall.

FERTILIZING: Feed twice a year—once when spring growth begins, then again after the spring crop is harvested. Apply ¼–½ cup of 10-10-10 fertilizer per 10 ft. of row. Don't use more than this, or you'll get all leaves and few berries.

THINNING AND RENEWING: Crowding leads to diseases and small crops of poor fruit. If planting gets too dense, remove runners as needed. Get rid of older "mother" plants every few years and leave the "daughter" plants (offsets).

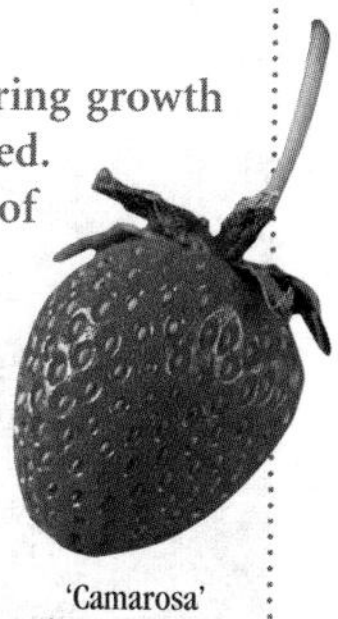

'Camarosa' (June Bearing)

STRAWBERRY

SELECTION	ZONES	DESCRIPTION AND COMMENTS	RESISTANCE
JUNE-BEARING TYPES			
'Allstar'	US, MS, LS, CS; 10–1	Large, tasty light red berries. Consistent producer. Great all-around performer	Resists most diseases; susceptible to anthracnose
'Apollo'	US, MS, LS, CS; 10–1	Big crop of large, tasty berries. Reliable. Fairly late	Disease resistant
'Camarosa'	US, MS, LS, CS; 10–1	Huge, conical berries of excellent quality. Needs little winter chill; not very cold hardy. Introduced in California, now popular in Florida	Susceptible to powdery mildew
'Chandler'	US, MS, LS, CS, TS; 11–1	Very large, bright red berries with good flavor. Does well in all areas	Resists most diseases; susceptible to anthracnose
'Florida Belle'	CS, TS; 11–1	Large, conical, firm, deep red fruit. Needs little winter chill; popular in Florida	Disease resistant
'Rosa Linda'	CS, TS; 11–1	Early, good-size crop of large, bright red, aromatic fruit with good flavor. Needs little winter chill; popular in Florida	Resists most diseases and pests
'Sunrise'	US, MS, LS; 10–1	Bright red, medium to large berries of good flavor and aroma. Doesn't freeze well	Resists most diseases
'Surecrop'	US, MS, LS; 10–1	Large crop of medium to large berries with excellent flavor. Very productive. Tolerates drought and poor soil	Resists most diseases
'Sweet Charlie'	CS, TS; 11–1	Large, very sweet orange-red berries. Needs little winter chill; does well in Florida	Resists anthracnose; susceptible to botrytis (gray mold)
'Tennessee Beauty'	US, MS, LS; 10–1	Late crop of dark red, medium to large berries with slightly tart flavor. Vigorous and productive	Resists most diseases; susceptible to red stele
EVERBEARING TYPES			
'Ozark Beauty'	US, MS, LS; 10–1	Large, long-necked fruit with mild, sweet flavor. Produces many runners. Very cold hardy	Resists most diseases
'Quinault'	US, MS; 10–1	Large, attractive berries are tasty but rather soft	Resists most diseases; susceptible to botrytis (gray mold)
DAY-NEUTRAL TYPES			
'Aromas'	US, MS, LS, CS; 10–1	Excellent vigor; produces large, sweet, high-quality berries. Developed in California; popular in Florida	Resists mites and mildew
'Tribute'	US, MS, LS; 10–1	Medium to large fruit with great flavor. Widely adapted	Disease resistant
'Tristar'	US, MS, LS; 10–1	Large berries with excellent flavor. Bears well the first year. Widely adapted	Disease resistant

'Allstar' (June Bearing)   'Chandler' (June Bearing)   'Surecrop' (June Bearing)   'Ozark Beauty' (Everbearing)   'Tribute' (Day Neutral)   'Tristar' (Day Neutral)

S

Planting time often depends on when plants are available from local garden centers. In the Coastal and Tropical South, set out June-bearing sorts in October for a spring crop; elsewhere, plant in early spring for a harvest the following year. Set out everbearing and day-neutral plants in spring for summer and fall berries. (In the Coastal and Tropical South, day-neutrals may be available for fall planting; everbearing types aren't recommended there.) Mulch to deter weeds, conserve soil moisture, and keep berries clean. Pinch off the first set of blooms to increase plant vigor. Don't let plants dry out. Drip irrigation is ideal, because it keeps foliage dry and reduces disease problems.

Strawberries grown as perennials benefit greatly from annual renovation. After harvest, use a lawn mower set at 2½ in. to cut off the foliage without injuring the crowns. Rake up and dispose of the foliage. Water and fertilize to encourage new growth. Some home gardeners follow the example of commercial growers, who treat strawberries as annuals. Plants are set out in summer or fall with the ground between them covered with black plastic. They're not allowed to make offsets. After harvest, the plants are yanked out and new ones put in. This results in healthier plants, fewer weeds, and bigger berries. June-bearing 'Chandler' is especially well adapted to this technique, but almost any selection can be grown this way.

Where winter temperatures dip below 20°F, plants need a winter mulch. Cover with a 4- to 6-in. layer of straw or other light, weed-free, organic material. When weather warms in spring, rake the mulch between plants.

Strawberry plants are subject to many diseases: fruit rots such as anthracnose and botrytis (gray mold); leaf diseases (leaf spot, leaf scorch, leaf blight); crown diseases (anthracnose, Southern blight); and root diseases (verticillium wilt, red stele, black root rot). Powdery mildew can be a problem. Anthracnose is of particular concern in Florida. Strawberry weevils, aphids, mites, slugs, thrips, leafrollers, and nematodes are potential pests. To reduce problems, purchase only certified disease-free, disease-resistant plants; also remove and destroy diseased foliage and fruit. Replace plants with new ones as they begin to decline, usually after 3 years; or start a whole new bed with new plants every few years.

Strawberries are sensitive to local conditions, so a selection that does well in one area may perform poorly in another. Consult with local experts (nursery personnel, Cooperative Extension agents) about the best selections for your garden.

STRAWBERRY, ORNAMENTAL. See FRAGARIA hybrids

STRAWBERRY BUSH. See EUONYMUS americanus

STRAWBERRY CACTUS. See ECHINOCEREUS enneacanthus

STRAWBERRY GERANIUM. See SAXIFRAGA stolonifera

STRAWBERRY GUAVA. See GUAVA

STRAWBERRY TREE. See ARBUTUS unedo

STRAWFLOWER. See HELICHRYSUM bracteatum

STRELITZIA

BIRD OF PARADISE

Strelitziaceae

PERENNIALS

✺ ZONES VARY BY SPECIES

☼ ◑ LIGHT SHADE IN HOTTEST CLIMATES

◐ REGULAR WATER

Strelitzia reginae

From South Africa. Evergreen plants with long-stalked, leathery leaves. Remarkable blossoms are produced intermittently throughout year; they are long lasting on plant and as cut flowers. Good for poolside; plants produce no litter and withstand some splashing. Resist deer damage. Hardy to about 28°F.

S. nicolai. GIANT BIRD OF PARADISE. Zones TS; 12–10. Clumping, treelike plant to 30 ft. tall and wide. Grown mainly for its dramatic foliage, similar to that of banana *(Musa):* gray-green, 5- to 10-ft.-long leaves arranged fanwise on erect or curving trunks. Flowers are larger than those of *S. reginae* but not as colorful. Floral envelope is purplish gray; flower is white with dark blue "tongue." Feed young plants frequently until they reach full dramatic size; then give little or no fertilizer. The goal is to achieve and maintain maximum size without lush growth and need for dividing. Cut off dead leaves and thin out any surplus growth.

S. reginae. BIRD OF PARADISE. Zones CS (protected), TS; 12–1. This old favorite is grown for its spectacular flowers, which bear a startling resemblance to the heads of crested tropical birds. Blooms combining orange, blue, and white are borne on long, stiff stems. Flowering is best in cooler seasons (though blooms appear year-round). This species is trunkless, growing 5–6 ft. high and about as wide; blue-green leaves are 1½ ft. long. Benefits greatly from frequent, heavy feeding. Divide infrequently, since large, crowded clumps bloom best. Good in containers. Recovers slowly from frost damage.

STREPTOCARPUS

CAPE PRIMROSE

Gesneriaceae

PERENNIALS

✺ TS ╟ 12–10; OR HOUSEPLANTS

◐ ● SOME SHADE; BRIGHT INDIRECT LIGHT

◐ ◑ REGULAR TO AMPLE WATER

Streptocarpus 'Constant Nymph'

These tender plants are related to gloxinia *(Sinningia)* and African violet *(Saintpaulia)* and look something like a cross between the two. Fleshy, sometimes velvety leaves; trumpet-shaped flowers with a long tube and spreading mouth. They bloom over a long season, and some kinds flower intermittently all year. Many species and hybrids of interest to fanciers; most widely available kinds are hybrids. All types are typically grown in containers. When grown as houseplants, take same care as African violets.

Large-flowered hybrids. Form a 2-ft.-wide clump of long, narrow leaves. Foot-tall stems carry 1½- to 2-in. flowers in white, blue, pink, rose, red, purple, often with blotches in a contrasting color. Medium blue 'Constant Nymph' is the best known of the cutting-grown Nymph series.

S. saxorum (Streptocarpella saxorum). Native to eastern Africa. Unlike others, this species forms a shrubby, much-branched, spreading mound to 6 in. high, 2 ft. wide. Furry, fleshy gray-green leaves to 1½ in. long. Bloom comes in waves over much of the year; the two-tone flowers are pale blue and white, 1½ in. wide, carried on long, slender stems. Splendid in hanging baskets. Hybrids developed from *S. saxorum* include 'Concord Blue', a nonstop bloomer with medium blue flowers.

STROBILANTHES dyeranus

PERSIAN SHIELD

Acanthaceae

TENDER SHRUB

✺ LS (PROTECTED), CS, TS ╟ 12–7; OR GROW IN POTS

◐ PARTIAL SHADE

◐ REGULAR WATER

Strobilanthes dyeranus

Native to Burma. Beautiful foliage plant for warm, humid gardens. Grows to 4 ft. tall and 3 ft. wide; soft stemmed and more like a perennial than a shrub. Broadly oval, pointed leaves are 6–8 in. long, somewhat puckered, dark green but richly variegated with purple and iridescent silver-blue tints. Leaf undersides are bright purple. Pale violet, tubular flowers come in summer in 1½-in. spikes; less showy than foliage. Needs rich soil and regular watering. Becomes straggly with age; replace or start over from cuttings. May survive freezing in Lower South if mulched heavily in late fall; or grow in container, move to shelter over winter. Can also be overwintered indoors in a sunny window.

STYLOPHORUM diphyllum

CELANDINE POPPY, WOOD POPPY

Papaveraceae

PERENNIAL

✿ US, MS, LS ⬒ 8–1

◑ ● PARTIAL TO FULL SHADE

◆ REGULAR WATER

Stylophorum diphyllum

Native to eastern U.S. Forms a 1- to 2-ft.-wide basal rosette of downy, gray-green, 8- to 12-in.-long leaves that are deeply lobed into five or seven scallop-edged segments. Golden yellow, quite showy flowers are 1–2 in. wide; they appear singly or in loose, few-flowered clusters on branched stems 1–2 ft. tall. Resembles greater celandine (*Chelidonium majus*) but is shorter and blooms in spring rather than summer. Easy to grow in acid or alkaline soil; reseeds and forms colonies if soil is rich and moist. Stems leak yellow sap when cut. Excellent in woodland gardens as companion to blue phlox, foamflower (*Tiarella*), Virginia bluebells (*Mertensia pulmonarioides*), and mayapple (*Podophyllum*).

Styracaceae. The storax family includes trees and shrubs with bell-shaped, usually white flowers. Members include silver bell (*Halesia*), epaulette tree (*Pterostyrax*), and snowbell (*Styrax*).

STYRAX

SNOWBELL

Styracaceae

DECIDUOUS TREES AND SHRUBS

✿ ZONES VARY BY SPECIES

☼ ◑ FULL SUN OR PARTIAL SHADE, EXCEPT AS NOTED

◆ REGULAR WATER

Styrax japonicus

Neat, well-behaved flowering trees of modest size for patios or lawns; make a nice contrast in front of larger, darker-leafed trees. The species described below put on a spring or early summer show of white, bell-shaped flowers in hanging clusters. Leaves of most are oval and pointed. Easy to garden under, since roots are deep and nonaggressive. Provide good, well-drained, acid soil, except as noted.

S. americanus. AMERICAN SNOWBELL. Zones US, MS, LS, CS, TS; 11–6. Native from Florida to Virginia, west to Missouri, Arkansas, and Louisiana. Round-topped shrub, 6–9 ft. tall and not quite as wide, with zigzagging stems carrying bright green leaves to 3½ in. long. Fragrant, ¾-in. flowers, solitary or in clusters of four. Some tolerance of poor drainage. Performs better in light shade.

S. grandifolius. BIGLEAF SNOWBELL. Zones US, MS, LS, CS; 9–7. Native from Virginia to Florida. To 12 ft. tall and 6 ft. wide, but often smaller. Dark green leaves up to 7 in. long. Fragrant, ½- to 1-in. flowers in 8-in.-long, drooping clusters. Best in light shade and cool, moist soil.

S. japonicus. JAPANESE SNOWBELL, JAPANESE SNOWDROP TREE. Zones US, MS, LS; 8–6. To 30 ft. tall and 25 ft. wide, with slender, graceful trunk; branches often strongly horizontal, giving tree a broad, flat top. Scallop-edged leaves to 3 in. long turn from dark green to red or yellow in fall. Faintly fragrant, white, ¾-in. flowers hang in small clusters on short side branches. Leaves angle upward from branches while flowers hang down, giving the effect of parallel green and white tiers. Prune to control shape; tends to be shrubby unless lower side branches are suppressed. Splendid tree to look up into; plant it in raised beds near outdoor entertainment areas, or on a high bank above a path. 'Pendula' ('Carillon') is a shrubby selection with weeping branches; 'Pink Chimes', also shrubby, has a more upright form and bears pink flowers.

S. obassia. FRAGRANT SNOWBELL. Zones US, MS, LS; 8–6. Grows to 20–30 ft. tall, about two-thirds as wide. Oval to round, deep green leaves

to 3–8 in. long. Where frosts come very late, leaves may color yellow in autumn. Foliage may partly obscure fragrant, 1-in. flowers carried in drooping, 6- to 8-in. clusters at branch ends. Blooms earlier in spring than *S. japonicus*. Newly planted trees often take a few years to start blooming. Good against background of evergreens, or for height and contrast above border of rhododendrons and azaleas.

SUCCULENTS. Strictly speaking, a succulent is any plant that stores water in juicy leaves, stems, or roots to withstand periodic drought. Practically speaking, fanciers of succulents exclude such fleshy plants as epiphytic orchids and include in their collections many desert natives that are not fleshy, such as yuccas and puyas. Although cacti are succulents, common consent sets them up as a separate category (see Cactaceae).

Most succulents come from desert or semidesert areas in warmer parts of the world. Mexico and South Africa are two very important sources. Some (notably sedums and sempervivums) come from colder climates, where they grow on sunny, rocky slopes and ledges.

Succulents are grown everywhere as houseplants; many are useful and decorative as landscaping plants, either in open ground or in containers. When well grown and well groomed, they are attractive all year, in bloom or out. Although considered low-maintenance plants, they look shabby if neglected; they may live through extended drought but will drop leaves, shrivel, or lose color. Amount of irrigation needed depends on summer heat, humidity, and rainfall level. Give plants just enough water to keep them plump leafed and attractive.

One light feeding at start of growing season should be enough for plants in open ground. Larger and later-blooming kinds may benefit from additional fertilizing.

Some succulents make good ground covers. Some are sturdy and quick growing enough for erosion control on large banks. Other, smaller kinds are useful between stepping-stones or for creating patterns in small gardens. Most of these are easily started from stem or leaf cuttings, and a stock can quickly be grown from a few plants. See *Echeveria*, Ice Plants, *Sedum*, *Senecio*.

The larger succulents have great decorative value. See *Agave*, *Aloe*, *Crassula*, *Echeveria*, *Kalanchoe*. Some smaller succulents are primarily collectors' items, grown for odd form or flowers. See smaller species of *Aloe*, *Crassula*, *Echeveria*, *Euphorbia*, *Stapelia*.

Many succulents have showy flowers. For some of the best, see *Aloe*, some species of *Crassula* and *Sedum*, *Hoya*, Ice Plants, *Kalanchoe*.

A few words of caution to growers of succulents—variety of forms, colors, textures offers many possibilities for handsome combinations, but be sure you don't end up with a jumbled medley. Don't use too many kinds in one planting; mass a few species instead of putting in one of each.

You can combine succulents with other types of plants, but plan combinations carefully. Not all plants look right with them. Consider also their different cultural requirements. For example, not all succulents like hot sun; read species descriptions carefully. Some do not thrive in hottest-summer areas, even if given some shade.

SUGARBERRY. See CELTIS laevigata

SUGAR BUSH. See RHUS ovata

SUGAR CANE. See SACCHARUM

SUMAC. See RHUS

SUMMER CYPRESS. See KOCHIA scoparia

SUMMER HYACINTH. See GALTONIA candicans

SUMMER LILAC. See BUDDLEIA davidii

SUMMERSWEET. See CLETHRA alnifolia

SUNDEW. See DROSERA

SUNDROPS. See CALYLOPHUS, OENOTHERA

S

SUNFLOWER. See HELIANTHUS

SUNROSE. See HELIANTHEMUM nummularium

SURINAM CHERRY. See EUGENIA uniflora

SUTERA cordata

BACOPA

Scrophulariaceae

PERENNIAL

☑ TS ▯ 12–6; ANYWHERE AS ANNUAL

☼ ◑ AFTERNOON SHADE IN HOTTEST CLIMATES

◉ REGULAR WATER

Sutera cordata

From moist regions of South Africa. Wiry-stemmed creeper with green, roughly heart-shaped, toothed leaves less than 1 in. long. Sold by the name "bacopa"—the botanical name of water hyssop, another member of the same family. To 3–8 in. tall, 12–20 in. wide. Blooms continuously and profusely in temperate weather, bearing small, five-petaled, golden-throated flowers in white, pink, mauve, lavender blue, or red—but in most of the South it gives out once the dog days of summer arrive. Perhaps best employed as a cool-season annual for spring or fall, or as a winter annual in Florida. Hardy to 28°F.

Excellent in hanging baskets. If used at the front of a border, plant in masses for greater impact. Needs good drainage and air circulation, fertile soil, and regular feeding. Pinch branches often to keep plant shapely, but avoid severe pruning. A form with leaves variegated in golden yellow is available.

SWAN RIVER DAISY. See BRACHYSCOME iberidifolia

SWEDISH IVY. See PLECTRANTHUS verticillatus

SWEET ALYSSUM. See LOBULARIA maritima

SWEET BALM. See MELISSA officinalis

SWEET BAY. See MAGNOLIA virginiana

SWEETBELLS. See LEUCOTHOE racemosa

SWEET BOX. See SARCOCOCCA

SWEET BRIAR ROSE. See ROSA rubiginosa

SWEET DRAGON. See ALPINIA henryi

SWEET GUM. See LIQUIDAMBAR

SWEETLEAF. See SYMPLOCOS paniculata

SWEET OLIVE. See OSMANTHUS fragrans

SWEET PEA. See LATHYRUS

SWEET POTATO

Convolvulaceae

PERENNIAL GROWN AS ANNUAL

☑ US, MS, LS ▯ 12–1

☼ FULL SUN

◉ REGULAR WATER

Sweet Potato

Not a true potato but the thickened root of a trailing tropical American vine closely related to morning glory (*Convolvulus, Ipomoea*). Sweet potato's botanical name is *Ipomoea batatas* (see that entry for ornamental selections of sweet potato). Thrives in the South's long, hot summers. Requires well-drained soil (preferably sandy loam) and plenty of room. Start with certified, disease-free "slips" (rooted cuttings) bought at a nursery or by mail-order.

There are two classes of edible sweet potatoes. The first has soft, sugary yellow-orange flesh; examples are 'Beauregard', 'Centennial', 'Gold Rush', 'Jewel', 'Nemagold', 'Puerto Rico', 'Topaz', and 'Vardaman'. (People sometimes incorrectly refer to this class as "yams"; the true yam is *Dioscorea batatas*.) The second class of sweet potato has firm, dry whitish flesh; an example is the misnamed 'Yellow Jersey'.

Plant in late spring when the soil has warmed to 70°F. Before planting, work in a controlled-release, low-nitrogen fertilizer such as cottonseed meal or composted manure; too much nitrogen produces lots of leaves and small roots. Set slips so that only stem tips and leaves show above the ground. Space them 1 ft. apart, in rows 3 ft. apart. To ensure good drainage, dig shallow ditches between rows. If you don't have much room, plant a bush type that doesn't run, such as 'Puerto Rico' or 'Vardaman'. Most types are ready to harvest 90 to 120 days after planting.

Sweet potato weevil is a common pest; its larvae tunnel into stems and roots. Hiding plants under floating row covers during the growing season provides good control. Common diseases include fusarium wilt, internal cork, and soil rot. Look for resistant selections such as 'Beauregard' and 'Topaz'; if nematodes are present, plant 'Jewel', 'Nemagold', or 'Topaz'. To prevent a buildup of disease organisms in the soil, don't grow sweet potatoes in the same location 2 years in a row.

Harvest before first frost; if tops are killed by sudden frost, harvest immediately. Dig carefully to avoid cutting or bruising roots. Flavor improves in storage (starch is converted to sugar). Let roots dry in the sun until soil can be brushed off; then cure by storing 10 to 14 days in a warm (about 85°F), humid place. Store in a cool, dry environment (not below 55°F).

SWEET ROCKET. See HESPERIS matronalis

SWEET SULTAN. See CENTAUREA moschata

SWEET WILLIAM. See DIANTHUS barbatus

SWEET WOODRUFF. See GALIUM odoratum

SWISS CHARD

Chenopodiaceae

BIENNIAL GROWN AS ANNUAL

☑ US, MS, LS, CS, TS ▯ 12–1

☼ FULL SUN

◉ REGULAR WATER

Swiss Chard

A form of beet (*Beta vulgaris*) grown for its tasty leaves and stalks, this is one of the easiest vegetables for the home garden. It probably originated in the Mediterranean area. For a summer crop, sow the big, crinkly, tan seeds ½ to ¾ in. deep, at any time from early spring to early summer. For a fall crop, sow in early August. For a winter crop in the Coastal and Tropical South, sow in October. Sow about six seeds per foot in rows 1½–2 ft. apart. Thin seedlings to 1 ft. apart. About 2 months after sowing (when plants are generally 1–1½ ft. tall), you can begin to harvest leaves from the base by cutting or breaking them off. New leaves grow up from the center of plants, continue for months, and seldom bolt (go to seed). They're delicious eaten fresh in salads or steamed.

'Fordhook', with white stalks and crinkled green leaves, is the standard Swiss chard. For something more colorful, try 'Rhubarb' or 'Vulcan'; both sport blood red stalks. 'Bright Lights', with stalks of yellow, orange, pink, purple, white, and red, is as good an ornamental as it is a vegetable. All Swiss chards take about 60 days from sowing to harvest.

SWISS CHEESE PLANT. See MONSTERA friedrichsthalii

SWITCH GRASS. See PANICUM virgatum

SWORD FERN. See NEPHROLEPIS, POLYSTICHUM munitum

S

SYAGRUS romanzoffiana (Arecastrum romanzoffianum)

QUEEN PALM

Arecaceae (Palmae)

PALM

CS (PROTECTED), TS **H** 12–10

FULL SUN

REGULAR WATER

Syagrus romanzoffiana

This South American palm grows 40–50 ft. tall, 20–25 ft. wide, with an arrow-straight trunk. A common lawn and street tree throughout south Florida, though it is weak wooded and prone to breaking or toppling in storms. Arching, feathery, glossy green fronds are 10–15 ft. long. White summer flowers come in drooping spikes to 3 ft. long; these are followed in winter by copious quantities of decorative (though messy) yellow-orange fruits. Prefers slightly acid, well-drained soil. If grown in alkaline soil, subject to a disfiguring disease called frizzle top, caused by a deficiency of manganese or potassium. To prevent it, feed regularly with 8-4-12 palm fertilizer containing manganese. Hardy to about 26°F. Sometimes sold as *Cocos plumosa*.

SYCAMORE. See PLATANUS

SYMPHORICARPOS

SNOWBERRY, CORALBERRY

Caprifoliaceae

DECIDUOUS SHRUBS

US, MS **H** 7–1

EXPOSURE NEEDS VARY BY SPECIES

LITTLE TO MODERATE WATER

Symphoricarpos albus

North American natives. The various plants described here are upright or arching, typically 2–6 ft. high and wide, often spreading by root suckers. Most are best used as informal hedges or as wild thickets for erosion control on steep banks. Clusters of small pink or white flowers in spring or early summer. Attractive round, berrylike fruit remains on stems after leaves drop in autumn; looks nice in winter arrangements, attracts birds. Plants are not usually damaged by browsing deer.

S. albus (S. racemosus). COMMON SNOWBERRY. Native from California to Alaska, east to Montana. Roundish, dull green, ¾- to 2-in.-long leaves (to 4 in. and often lobed on sucker shoots). Pink flowers are followed by white fruit from late summer to winter. Produces most fruit in full sun but takes shade. Not a first-rate shrub but useful for its tolerance of poor soil, lower light, general neglect.

S. ×chenaultii. Hybrid between *S. orbiculatus* and a species from Mexico. Bears inch-long blue-green leaves, greenish white flowers, and red fruit lightly spotted with white. Can take full sun in cooler climates; needs partial or full shade in hot areas. 'Hancock' is foot-high dwarf valued as woodland ground or bank cover.

S. ×doorenbosii. This hybrid was developed from *S. orbiculatus*, *S. ×chenaultii*, and a selection of *S. albus*. Rounded habit to about 5 ft. high, spreading at least as wide by runners. Broadly oval, pointed leaves to 1½ in. long are dark green above, lighter green beneath. Greenish white flowers are followed by clusters of ½-in., pink-tinged white fruits. Sun or shade. 'Magic Berry' is a compact, spreading plant with rosy pink fruit; 'Mother of Pearl' has a somewhat drooping habit and pink-cheeked white fruit. Stiffly upright 'White Hedge' bears white fruit in clusters that are held mainly above the foliage.

S. orbiculatus (S. vulgaris). CORALBERRY, INDIAN CURRANT. From eastern U.S. Resembles *S. albus* but bears white or pink-tinged flowers followed by small purplish red fruit. Fruit is bright and plentiful enough to provide a good fall-into-winter show. Full sun.

SYMPHYTUM officinale

COMFREY

Boraginaceae

PERENNIAL

US, MS, LS, CS **H** 9–1

PARTIAL SHADE IN HOTTEST CLIMATES

REGULAR WATER

LEAVES CAN BE HARMFUL IF INGESTED

Symphytum officinale

From Eurasia. Deep-rooted plant forms a clump to 3–4 ft. high, 2 ft. wide. Furry leaves are set with stiff hairs. Basal leaves grow to 8 in. or longer; upper leaves are smaller. Small (½-in.-long), unshowy flowers are usually dull rose in color but sometimes white, cream, or purple. In frost-free climates, plant remains leafy through winter; elsewhere, it dies to the ground in fall.

Comfrey has a long history as a folk remedy. The leaves can be dried and brewed to make a medicinal tea, though this use is no longer recommended (leaves have been found to contain potentially carcinogenic substances). Herb enthusiasts claim that the plant adds minerals to compost, but think hard before establishing it in your garden: it spreads freely from roots and is difficult to eradicate.

SYMPLOCOS paniculata

SAPPHIREBERRY, SWEETLEAF

Symplocaceae

DECIDUOUS SHRUB

US, MS, LS **H** 8–4

FULL SUN

REGULAR WATER

Symplocos paniculata

To 10–20 ft. tall; wider than tall in maturity. Can be trained as a low-branching or multitrunked small tree. Dark green leaves to 3½ in. long and half as wide. In late spring or early summer, 2- to 3-in. clusters of small, fragrant white flowers bloom on previous year's wood—but the main draw is the autumn show of sapphire blue, ⅓-in. fruits that garland the branches. Berries are much appreciated by birds. Single plants set little or no fruit, so it's best to plant groups of seedlings; groups of cutting-grown plants from the same parent will not produce well. Some growers always sell plants in groups of three seedlings to ensure fruiting. Use for screening or as a feature in a large shrub border.

SYNGONIUM

ARROWHEAD VINE

Araceae

EVERGREEN VINES

TS **H** 12–10; OR HOUSEPLANTS

PARTIAL SHADE; BRIGHT INDIRECT LIGHT

REGULAR WATER

Syngonium podophyllum

Outdoors in the Tropical South, these vines trail over the ground or loop around palm trees, their stems wrist thick and their leaves huge, green, and multifingered. They are hardly recognizable compared to the juvenile forms, which are common houseplants. Young leaves have an arrowhead shape and range in color from solid green to shades of green with white, pink, or yellow markings that usually fade on adult leaves. Grow fast in moderately moist soil with lots of organic matter; reduce watering in winter. Indoors, maintain a minimum temperature of 60°F, place in bright indirect light, and mist to keep leaves looking lush. Feed with a general-purpose liquid houseplant fertilizer monthly, spring through fall. For a compact, clumping plant that keeps producing young leaves, pinch stem tips and cut back runaway vining stems.

In the following entries, leaf descriptions apply to juvenile leaves.

S

S. podophyllum. Native from Mexico to Panama. Dark green, glossy leaves, 6–12 in. long, on slender, 1- to 2-ft.-long leafstalks. Many selections are available, including 'Emerald Gem', quilted green leaves with a varnished luster; 'Maya Red', pink young leaves; and 'White Butterfly', green-and-white marbled leaves on stout stems.

S. wendlandii. Native to Costa Rica. Velvety, thin-textured green leaves, 4–8 in. long, with silver-gray veins.

SYRINGA

LILAC

Oleaceae

DECIDUOUS SHRUBS, RARELY TREES

☀ ZONES VARY BY SPECIES

☀ ◑ LIGHT SHADE IN HOTTEST CLIMATES

◐ REGULAR WATER

Syringa × laciniata

If there is one shrub Northerners wish they could bring with them to the South, this is it. No plant is more cherished than lilac for big, flamboyant, fragrant flowers. Most popular are the common lilac (*S. vulgaris*) and its scads of selections, but many other species and hybrids merit attention. Most are medium-size to large shrubs with no particular appeal when out of bloom. Leaves are typically oval and pointed or rounded, with smooth edges. Floral show (always after leaf-out) comes from numerous small flowers packed into dense clusters shaped like pyramids or cones. Depending on where you live, flowering may occur anywhere from earliest spring to early summer—that is, *if* flowering occurs. Like the Green Bay Packers, most lilacs are used to long, cold winters, and without that chill they are likely to perform poorly. This disappoints folks who are looking for the same spectacle in Atlanta that they enjoyed in Bangor. Some types, however, such as *S. × laciniata* and others described here, bloom well with only light winter chill and put on a good show even in the Lower South. Most lilacs won't bloom in the Coastal South—and certainly not in the Tropical South.

Provide well-drained, neutral to slightly alkaline soil. These plants typically bloom on wood formed the previous year, so prune just after flowers fade. Remove spent blossom clusters, cutting back to a pair of leaves; growth buds at that point will make flowering stems for next year. Renovate old, overgrown plants by cutting a few of the oldest stems to the ground each year. For the few types that bloom on new growth, prune in late winter, before new growth starts. Major insect and disease problems include borers, scale, and powdery mildew. For information on controlling them, see the *Southern Living Garden Problem Solver*.

S. × chinensis. CHINESE LILAC. Zones US, MS; 8–1. Hybrid between *S. vulgaris* and *S. × persica*. To 15 ft. high and wide, usually much less. More graceful than *S. vulgaris*, with finer-textured leaves to 3 in. long. Profuse, open clusters of fragrant, rosy purple flowers. Does well in mild-winter, hot-summer climates. 'Alba' has white blossoms. 'Lilac Sunday' is a vigorous, disease-resistant selection with light purple blossoms.

S. × hyacinthiflora. Zones US; 7–1. Group of fragrant hybrids between *S. vulgaris* and *S. oblata*, a Chinese species. Resemble *S. vulgaris* but generally bloom 7 to 10 days earlier. 'Assessippi' (lavender) and 'Mount Baker' (white) are earliest. Other selections include 'Alice Eastwood' (double

magenta), 'Blue Hyacinth' (lavender), 'Clarke's Giant' (lavender; larger flowers than others), 'Esther Staley' (magenta), 'Excel' (light lavender), 'Gertrude Leslie' (double white), 'Grace McKenzie' (lilac blue), 'Pocahontas' (purple), 'Purple Heart' (purple), and 'White Hyacinth' (white).

S. × laciniata (S. × persica laciniata). Zones US, MS, LS, CS; 8–1. Open-structured plant to 8 ft. tall, 10 ft. wide. Leaves to 2½ in. long, divided nearly to midrib into three to nine segments; good rich green color. Many small clusters of fragrant, lilac-colored blooms. Highly mildew resistant. Blooms well even in Lower and Coastal South.

S. meyeri 'Palibin'. Zones US, MS, LS; 7–1. Selection of a Chinese species. Dense, twiggy growth to 3–5 ft. tall and wide. Fine-textured, mildew-resistant leaves to 1¾ in. long. Blooms when only 1 ft. high. Profusion of reddish purple buds that open to fragrant, single bright pink flowers in 5-in. clusters. Sometimes sold as *S. palibiniana* or *S. velutina*.

S. microphylla 'Superba' (S. pubescens microphylla 'Superba'). Zones US, MS, LS; 8–5. Selection of a Chinese native. Compact grower to 7 ft. tall, twice as wide. Mildew-resistant leaves to 2 in. long, with bronze fall color. Deep red buds open to fragrant, single bright pink flowers. May rebloom in early autumn. Heat tolerant.

S. patula 'Miss Kim' (S. pubescens patula 'Miss Kim'). Zones US, MS, LS; 8–1. Selection of a lilac from northern China and Korea. Dense, twiggy, rounded; eventually to 8–9 ft. high and wide, but stays small for many years. Sometimes grafted high to make a standard tree. Purple buds open to very fragrant ice blue flowers. Leaves are 2–4½ in. long; may turn burgundy in fall. Heat tolerant.

S. × persica. PERSIAN LILAC. Zones US, MS; 7–1. Graceful, loose form to 6 ft. high and wide; leaves 2½ in. long. Many clusters of fragrant, pale violet flowers appear all along arching branches.

S. × prestoniae. Zones US; 7–1. Group of extra-hardy hybrids bred in Canada. To 6–12 ft. tall and wide, with leaves to 6 in. long. Flowers come on new growth at the end of the lilac season, after *S. vulgaris* has bloomed. Bulky, dense plants resemble *S. vulgaris*, but individual flowers are smaller and are not particularly fragrant. Good selections include 'Donald Wyman' (dark rosy purple), 'Isabella' (lilac), 'Jessica' (violet), 'Minuet' (pale lilac), 'Miss Canada' (bright pink), 'Nocturne' (bluish lilac),

S

Syringa × chinensis

Syringa × hyacinthiflora 'Excel'

Syringa meyeri 'Palibin'

Syringa × prestoniae

Syringa reticulata

Syringa vulgaris 'Primrose'

and 'Royalty' (purple to violet). For 'James MacFarlane', sometimes sold as a member of this group, see *S. ×swegiflexa*.

S. reticulata. JAPANESE TREE LILAC. Zones US, MS; 7–3. From Japan. To 30 ft. tall, 20 ft. wide; can be grown as large shrub or easily trained as single-stemmed tree. Smooth, glossy red-brown bark. Leaves to 5 in. long. Blooms on new growth late in the lilac season, bearing white, musky-scented flowers in showy clusters to 1 ft. long. This is the most problem-free lilac. It makes a good lawn tree, street tree, or informal screen. 'Ivory Silk' is a compact grower to 20 ft. tall, with cream-colored flowers borne in profusion even at a young age. *S. r. mandshurica*, from Manchuria and Korea, tends to be shrubby, growing about 6–8 ft. tall and wide. It has smaller foliage and flowers than the basic species.

S. ×swegiflexa. Zones US, MS; 7–6. Hybrid between two Chinese species, *S. reflexa* and *S. sweginzowii*; sometimes called pink pear lilac. To 12 ft. tall, 8 ft. wide; leaves are 2–5 in. long. Deep reddish buds; pink flowers in clusters to 8 in. on new growth, about 3 weeks after *S. vulgaris*. 'James MacFarlane' is the best-known selection; it blooms well as far south as Atlanta.

S. 'Tinkerbelle'. Zones US, MS; 7–1. Hybrid between *S. meyeri* 'Palibin' and *S. microphylla* 'Superba'. Compact, rounded shrub to 5–6 ft. tall and wide. Wine red, spicily fragrant flowers in 4- to 5-in. panicles; handsome, mildew-resistant dark green leaves about 1½ in. long. Makes a nice specimen shrub or informal hedge.

S. vulgaris. COMMON LILAC. Zones US, MS, LS (some); 8–1. From eastern Europe. Can eventually reach 20 ft. tall, with nearly equal spread. Suckers strongly. Prune out suckers on grafted plants (no need to do so on own-root plants). Dark green leaves to 5 in. long. Blooms in mid-spring, bearing pinkish or bluish lavender flowers in clusters to 10 in. long or longer ('Alba' has pure white flowers). Fragrance is legendary; lilac fanciers swear that the species and its older selections are more fragrant than newer types. Excellent cut flowers.

Syringa vulgaris

Selections, often called French hybrids, number in the hundreds. They generally flower a little later than the species and have larger clusters of single or double flowers in a wide range of colors. Singles are often as showy as doubles, sometimes more so. All of these lilacs require 2 to 5 years to settle down and produce flowers of full size and true color. Here are just a few of the many choice selections: 'Andenken an Ludwig Spaeth' (reddish purple to dark purple), 'Charles Joly' (double dark purplish red), 'Miss Ellen Willmott' (double pure white), 'President Grevy' (double medium blue), 'President Lincoln' (Wedgwood blue), 'President Poincaré' (double two-tone purple), 'Sensation' (wine red with white picotee edge), and 'William Robinson' (double pink).

Newer hybrids include 'Krasavitsa Moskvy' ('Beauty of Moscow'), with large clusters of pink buds opening into white double flowers; 'Nadezhda' ('Hope'), with deep purple buds opening into lilac-blue double flowers; and 'Primrose', with pale yellow blooms.

The Descanso Hybrids, developed to accept mild winters, perform exceptionally well in the Lower South. Best known is 'Lavender Lady'; others include 'Blue Boy', 'Blue Skies', 'Chiffon' (lavender), 'Forrest K. Smith' (light lavender), 'Sylvan Beauty' (rose lavender), and 'White Angel' ('Angel White').

FRESH-CUT LILACS. *To enjoy the fragrance and beauty of lilacs indoors, cut the flowers in early morning, using sharp pruners. For the longest-lasting bouquet, choose stems on which at least half the buds are still tightly closed. Take a container of water with you into the garden and completely submerge both stems and flowers as soon as you cut them. Back indoors, fill a tall glass or ceramic vase with cold water, then add a floral preservative according to label directions (don't use a metal container, or the flowers will quickly wilt). Keeping stems underwater, cut each one again at a 45° angle, about an inch above the previous cut. Quickly transfer the stems to the vase. Be sure to remove any leaves or buds below the waterline.* ❖

TABEBUIA
TRUMPET TREE

Bignoniaceae

DECIDUOUS, EVERGREEN, SEMIEVERGREEN TREES

TS ⊬ 12–10, EXCEPT AS NOTED

☼ ◑ FULL SUN OR LIGHT SHADE

💧 REGULAR WATER

Tabebuia heterophylla

Native to the tropical Americas. Showy, trumpet-shaped flowers are borne in rounded clusters that become larger and more profuse as trees mature. Leaves are typically green; may be simple (undivided) or divided into as many as seven leaflets arranged like fingers of hand. Number of leaflets is often variable within a species.

Tend to be gangly or irregular when young; benefit from training in early years. Need well-drained soil; respond well to regular fertilizing. All are useful as color accents and as stand-alone flowering trees for display. Larger types are excellent as street or park plantings; smaller species make beautiful patio trees or container plants.

T. chrysotricha. GOLDEN TRUMPET TREE. Briefly deciduous. To 25–50 ft. high and wide. Young twigs, leaf undersides covered with tawny fuzz. Golden yellow flowers are 3–4 in. long, often with maroon stripes in throat. Blooms most heavily in spring, when tree loses leaves for brief period. May also bloom lightly at other times, when in leaf. Sometimes sold as *T. pulcherrima*.

T. heterophylla. PINK TECOMA, PINK TRUMPET TREE. Evergreen to semievergreen. Slender habit to 40 ft. tall, 20 ft. wide; sometimes grown as a large shrub. Flowers 2–3 in. long, in colors ranging from pinkish purple through pink shades to white. Blossoms appear abundantly in spring but may also be seen occasionally throughout the rest of the year.

T. impetiginosa (T. ipe). PURPLE or PINK TRUMPET TREE. Semievergreen. Heat zones 12–9. Slow to 25–50 ft. high and wide. In late winter or spring, bears 2- to 3-in. flowers in white to light pink and purple. May rebloom in late summer or fall. Does not bloom as a young tree.

T. pallida (T. heterophylla pallida). CUBAN PINK TRUMPET TREE. Evergreen. From the West Indies. To about 30 ft. tall and wide. Attractive leaves with one to three leaflets. Yellow-throated, 2-in. flowers in palest lilac pink appear sometimes singly, sometimes in small clusters.

TAGETES
MARIGOLD

Asteraceae (Compositae)

ANNUALS AND PERENNIALS

ZONES VARY BY SPECIES

☼ FULL SUN

💧 REGULAR WATER, EXCEPT AS NOTED

Tagetes erecta

Native to Mexico, Central America. Robust, free-branching, nearly trouble-free plants ranging from 6 in. to 6 ft. tall, with flowers in colors ranging from pale yellow through gold to orange and brownish maroon. Finely divided, ferny, usually strongly scented leaves. Annuals will bloom from early summer to frost if old flowers are picked off. Handsome, long-lasting cut flowers; strong aroma from leaves, stems, and blossoms permeates a room. Easy to grow from seed, which sprouts in a few days in warm soil; to get earlier bloom, start seeds in containers indoors or buy nursery plants. Watch out for snails and slugs, which often devour young plants. Spider mites are common pests, too.

T. erecta. AFRICAN MARIGOLD. Annual. Zones US, MS, LS, CS, TS; 12–1. Original strains were single-flowered plants to 3–4 ft. tall, 2 ft. wide. Modern strains are more varied; most have fully double flowers. They range from dwarf Guys and Dolls and Inca series (12–14 in.) through Galore, Lady, and Perfection (16–20 in.) to Climax (2½–3 ft.). Novelty tall strains include Odorless (2½ ft.). Sweet Cream has creamy white flowers on 16-in. stems. Triploid hybrids, crosses between *T. erecta* and *T. patula,* have exceptional vigor and bear profuse 2-in. flowers over a long bloom season; they are generally shorter than other *T. erecta* strains. Examples are Trinity Mix and Nugget, both 10–12 in. high. Avoid overhead sprinkling on taller kinds; stems will sag and even break under weight of water.

T. filifolia. IRISH LACE. Annual. Zones US, MS, LS, CS, TS; 12–1. Forms a mound of bright green, finely divided foliage to 6 in. high and wide; resembles an unusually fluffy, rounded fern. Used primarily as an edging plant for its foliage effect, but tiny white flowers are attractive.

T. lemmonii (T. palmeri). COPPER CANYON DAISY. Shrubby perennial. Zones LS, CS; 12–1. Grows 3–6 ft. tall and wide. Finely divided, 2- to 4-in.-long leaves are strongly fragrant when brushed against or rubbed—they smell like a blend of marigold, mint, and lemon. Golden yellow flowers with orange cones are carried at branch ends late summer through fall; may bloom sporadically at other times. Cut back before new spring growth begins. Damaged by frost in open situations; cut back to remove damaged growth or to correct shape. Tends to be short lived. Moderate to regular water.

T. lucida. MEXICAN MINT MARIGOLD, MEXICAN TARRAGON. Perennial in Zones MS, LS, CS, TS; 12–1; often grown as an annual in all zones. To 3 ft. high and wide, typically with unbranched stems. Narrow, uncut, smooth dark green leaves have strong scent and flavor of tarragon or licorice (stems and roots are similarly fragrant). Unimpressive yellow flowers, produced in fall and spring, are less than ½ in. wide. Moderate to regular water.

T. patula. FRENCH MARIGOLD. Annual. Zones US, MS, LS, CS, TS; 12–1. Selections from 6 in. to 1½ ft. high and wide, in flower colors from yellow to rich maroon brown. Blossoms may be fully double or single; many are strongly bicolored. Excellent for edging are dwarf, very double strains such as Janie (8 in.), Bonanza (10 in.), and Hero (10–12 in.), with 2-in. flowers in a range of colors from yellow through orange to red and brownish red. Aurora and Sophia strains have flowers that are larger (to 2½ in. wide) but not as double.

T. tenuifolia (T. signata). SIGNET MARIGOLD. Annual. Zones US, MS, LS, CS, TS; 12–1. Infrequently grown species. Flowers are small (just 1 in. wide) and single, but bloom is incredibly profuse. Finely cut foliage. Gem strain offers golden yellow, lemon yellow, and tangerine orange blossoms on 10- to 12-in.-tall plants.

MAKE A TALL MARIGOLD PLANT STAND STRAIGHT. *To help tall marigold plants stand firm (perhaps stoutly enough to not need staking), dig planting holes extra deep, strip any leaves off lower 1–3 in. of stem, and plant with stripped portion below soil line.* ❖

TALINUM

Portulacaceae

PERENNIALS OFTEN GROWN AS ANNUALS

CS, TS H 12–7

FULL SUN

MODERATE WATER

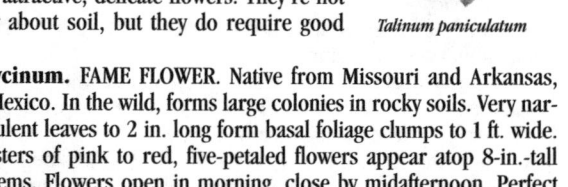

Talinum paniculatum

These easy-to-grow perennials are prized for their attractive, delicate flowers. They're not particular about soil, but they do require good drainage.

T. calycinum. FAME FLOWER. Native from Missouri and Arkansas, south to Mexico. In the wild, forms large colonies in rocky soils. Very narrow, succulent leaves to 2 in. long form basal foliage clumps to 1 ft. wide. Open clusters of pink to red, five-petaled flowers appear atop 8-in.-tall leafless stems. Flowers open in morning, close by midafternoon. Perfect for a rock garden.

T. paniculatum. JEWELS-OF-OPAR. Tender perennial, native from southern U.S. to Central America. A true Southern passalong plant, rarely purchased at garden centers but frequently showing up as an unannounced but welcome guest in gardens. Forms a low, 1- to 2-ft.-wide rosette of oval, pointed, bright green leaves to 3 in. long. In summer, thin

stalks to 2 ft. tall carry large clusters of tiny pink flowers; these are followed by beadlike yellow seedpods that mature to a rich burgundy red. Good in containers or at the front of the border. Reseeds readily. 'Variegatum' has grayish green leaves with white margins.

TAM. See JUNIPERUS sabina 'Tamariscifolia'

TAMARIX

TAMARISK

Tamaricaceae

DECIDUOUS SHRUBS OR TREES

ZONES VARY BY SPECIES

FULL SUN

LITTLE OR NO WATER TO MODERATE WATER

Tamarix ramosissima

Native to Europe and Asia. These large shrubs or small trees are useful in areas where wind, salt, and poor soil are challenges, as in coastal gardens. Their only demands are sun and good drainage. Tiny, scalelike, light green or bluish leaves are held on airy, arching, reddish branches; in spring or summer, narrow plumes of small pink or rose blooms appear at branch ends. Prune regularly to maintain graceful effect. Locate where plant won't be prominent while out of leaf. These plants have become pests in the arid Southwest, where their greedy roots compete with those of native plants for water. *T. gallica* is abundant along stream banks in western Oklahoma and Texas. There is much confusion in labeling of tamarisks in nurseries and among botanists.

T. gallica. FRENCH TAMARISK, SALT CEDAR. Zones US, MS, LS, CS; 9–2. Variable in size, but typically 15–20 ft. tall and wide. Reddish brown to dark purple bark and blue-green foliage. Blooms in summer, mostly on new season's growth, so prune in late winter; flowers are white to pink, in 2-in.-long clusters. Thrives in sandy, alkaline soil. Tolerates drought and salt spray. Good plant for beach areas. Excellent drainage is essential.

T. parviflora. Zones US, MS, LS; 8–3. To 12–15 ft. tall, not as wide. Pink blossoms in late spring. Blooms on old wood; prune right after bloom.

T. ramosissima (T. pentandra). Zones US, MS, LS; 8–1. Grows 10–15 ft. tall, usually not as wide. Bears rosy pink flowers in spring or early summer. Blooms on new wood; prune in late dormant season. Selection 'Cheyenne Red' has deeper pink blooms than the species; 'Rosea' bears rich pink flowers later in summer; 'Summer Glow' has bright pink flowers and blue-tinged foliage.

TAMBOOKIE THORN. See ERYTHRINA acanthocarpa

TANACETUM

Asteraceae (Compositae)

PERENNIALS

ZONES VARY BY SPECIES

FULL SUN

MODERATE TO REGULAR WATER

Tanacetum vulgare

Most species have finely divided leaves (often highly aromatic) and clusters of daisylike flower heads. Some have gray to nearly white foliage.

T. balsamita. See Chrysanthemum balsamita

T. coccineum. See Chrysanthemum coccineum

T. densum amani. Zones US, MS, LS; 8–6. Native to Turkey. Sometimes sold as *Chrysanthemum haradjanii.* Low-growing (6- to 8-in.-high) plant, spreading slowly to make a mat about 1½ ft. wide. Leaves are finely cut, silvery white, featherlike in appearance. Small yellow flower heads appear a few inches above foliage in late spring. Use in rock garden or as small-scale ground cover in bright, sunny area with good drainage. Can withstand some dry spells when established. One of the whitest-looking plants. ▸

T. parthenium. See Chrysanthemum parthenium

T. vulgare. TANSY. Zones US, MS, LS, CS; 8–1. Native to Europe. Coarse, rather weedy garden plant to 3 ft. tall, 2 ft. wide, with finely divided, bright green, aromatic (some say smelly) leaves. Small, buttonlike yellow flowers appear in late summer. Thin clumps yearly to keep in bounds. This plant is no longer used medicinally, though it is still grown in herb gardens. *T. v. crispum*, fern-leaf tansy, grows 2½ ft. tall; it has finely cut foliage and is more decorative than the species.

TANGELO, TANGOR. See CITRUS, Mandarin Hybrids

TANGERINE. See CITRUS, Mandarin

TANSY. See TANACETUM vulgare

TARO. See COLOCASIA esculenta

TARRAGON, FRENCH or TRUE. See ARTEMISIA dracunculus

TARRAGON, MEXICAN. See TAGETES lucida

TASMANIAN TREE FERN. See DICKSONIA antarctica

TASSEL FERN. See POLYSTICHUM polyblepharum

TASSEL FLOWER. See AMARANTHUS caudatus

TATER VINE. See DIOSCOREA bulbifera

Taxodiaceae. The taxodium family includes evergreen (and some deciduous) coniferous trees, usually with small cones containing two to six seeds on each scale. Members include *Cryptomeria*, dawn redwood (*Metasequoia*), and *Taxodium*.

TAXODIUM

Taxodiaceae

DECIDUOUS TREES

✗ US, MS, LS, CS ⊩ 12–5

☼ FULL SUN

◐ ◐ ◔ MODERATE TO AMPLE WATER

Taxodium distichum

Conifers of great size with shaggy, cinnamon-colored bark and graceful sprays of short, narrow, flat, needlelike leaves. Female flowers are followed by round, fragrant cones about 1 in. across. All are very tough, tolerant trees. Need acid soil. Both of the following species are native to the southeastern U.S.

T. ascendens (T. distichum imbricarium). POND CYPRESS. Somewhat narrower, more erect than *T. distichum*; trunk not as strongly buttressed. Awl-shaped leaves stand erect on branchlets; those of *T. distichum* are spirally arranged. Can grow 70–80 ft. tall, 20 ft. wide. Leafs out late in spring. In the wild, found on higher ground around ponds, but will grow in standing water, as *T. distichum* does. 'Nutans' is widely grown; it has somewhat pendent branchlets. 'Prairie Sentinel' is very narrow, reaching only about 10 ft. wide.

T. distichum. BALD CYPRESS. From southeastern U.S. Can grow into 100-ft.-tall, broad-topped tree in the wild, but young and middle-aged garden trees are pyramidal to 50–70 ft. high, 20–30 ft. wide. Feathery foliage sprays with narrow, ½-in.-long leaves in a pale, delicate, yellow-tinged green. Foliage turns orange-toned brown before dropping. Interesting winter silhouette.

Takes any except strongly alkaline soils. Takes extremely wet conditions (even grows in swamps) but also tolerates rather dry soil. Trunk is buttressed near base. When growing in waterlogged soil, develops knobby growths called knees. Bagworms may be troublesome in some years, but otherwise this tree is not much bothered by pests or diseases. Requires only corrective pruning to remove dead wood and unwanted branches. An outstanding tree for stream bank or edge of lake or pond.

TAXUS

YEW

Taxaceae

EVERGREEN SHRUBS OR TREES

✗ US, MS, EXCEPT AS NOTED

☼ ◐ ● SUN OR SHADE, EXCEPT AS NOTED

◐ ◔ MODERATE TO REGULAR WATER

◈ FRUIT (SEEDS) AND FOLIAGE ARE POISONOUS IF INGESTED

Taxus baccata 'Stricta'

Yews are conifers, but they do not bear cones. Instead, they produce fleshy, scarlet (rarely yellow), cup-shaped, single-seeded, berrylike fruit. In general, yews are darker green, more formal looking, and more tolerant of shade and moisture than most cultivated conifers. Long lived; take much shearing and pruning, since they sprout from bare wood. Excellent for hedges, screens; low-growing types make good foundation plants or bank covers.

Yews can be moved without harm even when large, but since they grow at a slow to moderate rate, big plants are luxury items. They tolerate many soils but do not thrive in strongly alkaline or strongly acid conditions. These plants will not take extreme heat, and reflected heat from a hot south or west wall will burn their foliage. Only female plants produce berries, and many do so without male plants nearby. Subject to vine weevils, scale, spider mites. During prolonged spells of hot, dry weather, hose off plants every 2 weeks.

T. baccata. ENGLISH YEW. Tree or shrub. Heat zones 7–5. From Europe, North Africa, western Asia. To 25–40 ft. or taller, 15–25 ft. wide, with broad, low crown. Needles ½–1½ in. long, dark green and glossy above, pale beneath; spirally arranged. Far more common than the species are garden selections, including the following.

'Adpressa'. Usually sold as *T. brevifolia*. Wide-spreading, dense shrub to 4–5 ft. high, 6–8 ft. wide.

'Aurea'. Broad pyramid to 25 ft. tall, 12 ft. wide after many years. New foliage is golden yellow from spring to fall, then turns green.

'Repandens'. SPREADING ENGLISH YEW. Long, horizontal, spreading branches make 2- to 4-ft.-high ground cover; extend to 8–10 ft. after many years. Useful low foundation plant. Will arch over wall.

'Stricta' ('Fastigiata'). IRISH YEW. Dark green column to 15–30 ft. tall, 3–10 ft. wide. Has larger needles and more crowded, upright branches than the species. Branches tend to spread near top, especially in snowy regions or where moisture is plentiful. Branches can be tied together with wire. Plants that outgrow their space can be reduced by heading back and thinning; old wood sprouts freely. There is a form with yellowish white variegation.

T. cuspidata. JAPANESE YEW. Tree or shrub. Heat zones 7–1. In its native Japan, reaches 50 ft. tall; in North America, usually seen as a compact, pyramidal tree to 10–25 ft. (possibly taller), half as wide. Can be kept lower by pinching new growth. Fruits heavily. Needles ½–1 in. long, dark green above, tinged yellowish beneath; usually arranged in two rows along twigs to make a flat or V-shaped spray. The following selections are commonly sold.

'Capitata'. PYRAMIDAL YEW. Plants sold under this name are probably ordinary *T. cuspidata*.

'Emerald Spreader'. Flat-topped form to 2½ ft. high, 8–10 ft. wide. Good ground cover for large areas.

'Nana'. Often sold as *T. brevifolia*. Very slow growing—just 1–4 in. a year. Can reach 3 ft. tall, 6 ft. wide in 20 years. Serves as a good low barrier or foundation plant for many years.

T. floridana. FLORIDA YEW. Zones LS, CS; 9–8. Extremely rare tree found only on the banks of the Apalachicola River in northern Florida. Bushy evergreen shrub to 15 ft. tall, spreading a bit wider. Flat, inch-long needles are arranged in two ranks on stems. Female plants bear red berries in fall. Prefers shade and slightly acid soil. Do not disturb wild populations of this endangered plant.

T. ×media. Shrubs. Heat zones 7–5. Hybrids between *T. baccata* and *T. cuspidata*; intermediate between the two in color and texture. Of the dozens of selections available, the following (all with dark green foliage) are among the most widely offered.

'Brownii'. Compact, rounded plant to 6–8 ft. tall, 8–10 ft. wide. Good dense hedge.

'Densiformis'. Dense, flat-topped; grows 2–3 ft. tall, 4–6 ft. across.

'Hatfieldii'. Broad column or pyramid. Reaches 12 ft. tall, 10 ft. wide after 20 years.

'Hicksii'. Upright-growing selection to 10–12 ft. tall, 3–4 ft. wide; slightly broader at center than at top or bottom, widening with age. Good hedge, foundation plant.

'Wardii'. Wide-spreading, flat-topped shrub to 6 ft. tall, 15 ft. wide.

TEA PLANT. See CAMELLIA sinensis

TECOMA

Bignoniaceae
EVERGREEN SHRUBS, TREES, VINES
ZONES VARY BY SPECIES
FULL SUN OR LIGHT SHADE
MODERATE WATER, EXCEPT AS NOTED

Tecoma stans

Various trumpet vines once lumped together as *Tecoma* now have different names. Remaining in this genus are several showy shrubs, one of which can be grown as a vine, another as a tree. All have 2-in.-long, trumpet-shaped flowers in the yellow-orange-red range and leaves divided featherwise into many leaflets. Heat tolerant. Take drought but look best with periodic soakings. Tip-pinch young growth to induce branching, reduce tendency toward legginess. Cut faded flowers to prolong bloom and lessen production of seedpods. Prune to remove unwanted seedpods and freeze-damaged wood.

T. ×alata (T. ×smithii). ORANGE BELLS. Shrub. Zones CS, TS; 12–8. Grows to 8 ft. tall, 4–5 ft. wide, with bright green foliage and orange flowers throughout warm weather. Tolerates light frost; may die to ground in a hard freeze but recovers quickly in warm weather. Some consider 'Orange Jubilee' to be a selection of this plant; others identify it as a hybrid between *T. capensis* and *T. stans*.

T. australis. See Pandorea pandorana

T. capensis (Tecomaria capensis). CAPE HONEYSUCKLE. Shrub or vine. Zones CS (warmer parts), TS; 12–8. From South Africa. If tied to a support, can scramble to 15–30 ft.; with hard pruning, makes an upright shrub 6–8 ft. tall, 4–5 ft. wide. Shiny dark green leaflets give it a fine-textured look. Brilliant orange-red flowers in compact clusters appear from fall into spring. Takes wind, salt air. Use as espalier, bank cover (good on hot, steep slopes), coarse barrier hedge. Resists deer damage. Little water. 'Aurea' has lighter green foliage and yellow flowers; somewhat less vigorous than the species. 'Buff Gold' has golden orange blooms.

T. garrocha. ARGENTINE TECOMA. Shrub. Zones CS, TS; 12–8. From Argentina. To 5 ft. (possibly 10 ft.) tall and wide. Clusters of salmon to orange blossoms throughout warm weather. Reacts to freezes like *T. ×alata*.

T. jasminoides. See Pandorea jasminoides

T. stans (Stenolobium stans). YELLOW BELLS, YELLOW TRUMPET FLOWER, YELLOW ELDER, ESPERANZA. Shrub or tree. Zones CS, TS; 12–8. Native from southern U.S. to Guatemala. In Tropical South, can be trained as a tree. Usually a large shrub in the Coastal South. Wood may die back in hard freezes, but new growth comes on quickly. Can reach 25 ft. tall, 10–20 ft. wide. Large clusters of lightly fragrant bright yellow flowers from late spring to early winter. Good for boundary planting, big shrub border, screening. Needs heat, deep soil, fairly heavy feeding.

Tecoma stans

T. s. angusta. Zones LS, CS, TS; 12–7. Native from Arizona to Texas and adjoining Mexico. To 4–10 ft. tall, 3–8 ft. wide. Narrow leaflets. Blooms from midspring to late fall. Needs less water and fertilizer than the species. Hardy to 10°F.

TERNSTROEMIA gymnanthera (T. japonica)

JAPANESE CLEYERA
Theaceae
EVERGREEN SHRUB
MS, LS, CS, TS 10–8
SUN OR LIGHT SHADE
REGULAR WATER

Ternstroemia gymnanthera

Large, slow-growing, carefree shrub to 10 ft. tall, 6 ft. wide (easily kept smaller through pruning). Good substitute for the overused and disease-prone Fraser photinia (*Photinia ×fraseri*). In the Southeast, plants are usually sold as *Cleyera japonica*.

Glossy, leathery, rounded oval to narrowly oval leaves are 1½–3 in. long, borne on red leafstalks; they are bronzy red when new, maturing to deep green, bronzy green, or purplish red depending on season, exposure, and the particular plant. Red tints are deeper in cold weather. Summer flowers are ½ in. wide, creamy yellow, fragrant but not showy. Fruit resembles little yellow to red-orange holly berries or cherries.

Grow in moist, well-drained acid soil. Tip-pinch to encourage compact growth. Use as basic landscaping shrub, informal hedge, foundation plant, poolside plant. Good companion for camellias (to which it is related), azaleas, nandina, pieris, ferns. Cut foliage keeps well.

Several interesting selections are available. 'Bigfoot' has large, glossy light green leaves and a notably upright habit; it grows quickly to 12–14 ft. tall and only 5–6 ft. wide. 'Burnished Gold' produces bright golden new growth that gradually fades to bronzy green. 'Variegata' has dark green leaves with a creamy white edge that turns pink in winter.

TETRADIUM daniellii (Evodia daniellii)

KOREAN EVODIA
Rutaceae
DECIDUOUS TREE
US, MS, LS 8–5
FULL SUN
MODERATE TO REGULAR WATER

Tetradium daniellii

From northern China and Korea. Distantly related to citrus, but the shiny dark green leaves leaves are more reminiscent of walnut (*Juglans*): 12–16 in. long, each with five pairs of 2- to 5-in.-long, pointed-oval leaflets plus a single leaflet at the end. Quickly grows to 30–50 ft. tall and wide. Foliage is handsome throughout summer and early fall; in autumn, it may turn yellow or simply drop from the branches while still green. Blooms in early summer, bearing showy, 4- to 6-in.-long, rather flat clusters of small white flowers that are very popular with bees. Fruits are small but eye catching because of their numbers; they age from red to black. Although the plant was introduced nearly a century ago, it remains little known despite its good looks, soil tolerance, and freedom from pests. Casts light shade, making it a good specimen tree for a lawn.

TETRANEURIS (Hymenoxys)

Asteraceae (Compositae)
PERENNIALS
US, MS, LS, CS 9–1
FULL SUN
LITTLE TO MODERATE WATER

Tetraneuris acaulis

Taprooted plants with narrow, grassy, aromatic leaves that form small, evergreen foliage tufts about 8 in. high, 1 ft. wide. Somewhat reminiscent of thrift (*Armeria*). Blooms during warm months (nearly all year in mild-winter climates). Yellow daisies to 1½ in.

wide have rays with notched edges; blossoms are usually carried singly on stems. Give well-drained soil. Cut off faded flower spikes to neaten plants and prolong bloom. Tolerant of heat, cold, drought. With some moisture, will reseed. Attractive in containers.

T. acaulis. ANGELITA DAISY. Native to plains from Canada to Texas. Golden yellow flowers on stems to 1 ft. high.

T. scaposa. CLUSTERED GOLDFLOWER. Native from Colorado to Kansas, south to New Mexico, Texas. Leaves are sometimes lobed. Bright yellow flowers on 16-in. stems; rays may have red-brown veins on undersides.

TETRAPANAX papyriferus (Aralia papyrifera)

RICE PAPER PLANT

Araliaceae

EVERGREEN SHRUB

LS (PROTECTED), CS, TS ⧓ 12–6

☼ ◑ AFTERNOON SHADE IN HOTTEST CLIMATES

● REGULAR WATER

Tetrapanax papyriferus

From China. Fast growing to 10–15 ft. tall and wide; often multitrunked. Big, bold, long-stalked leaves are 1–2 ft. wide, deeply lobed, gray green above, white and felted beneath, carried in clusters at ends of stems. Fuzz on new growth can irritate eyes or skin. Tan trunks often curve or lean. Big, branched clusters of creamy white flowers on furry tan stems appear in winter.

Young plants sunburn easily; older ones adapt. Seems to suffer only from high winds, which break or tatter leaves, and from frost—foliage is severely damaged at 22°F (however, it recovers fast and often puts up suckers to form thickets). Digging around roots stimulates sucker formation; suckers may arise 20 ft. from parent plant. Use this old Southern favorite for silhouette against walls, on patios; combines well with other sturdy, bold-leafed plants for a tropical effect. Name comes from the thick pith of the stems, which is used to make Chinese rice paper.

TEUCRIUM

GERMANDER

Lamiaceae (Labiatae)

SHRUBBY PERENNIALS

US, MS, LS, CS

☼ FULL SUN, EXCEPT AS NOTED

● MODERATE WATER, EXCEPT AS NOTED

Teucrium chamaedrys

Most germanders are from the Mediterranean, though one listed here (*T. canadense*) is native to eastern North America. All have aromatic evergreen foliage and whorls of little flowers. These are tough plants that endure poor, rocky soils; most can't stand wet or poorly drained soils but will tolerate regular watering where drainage is good. Not usually browsed by deer.

T. canadense. AMERICAN GERMANDER, WOOD SAGE. Heat zones 9–3. From prairies and meadows of eastern North America. Erect grower to 3 ft. tall, 6 in. wide, usually with a single stem. Spreads by creeping rhizomes to form colonies. Narrowly oval, pointed dark green leaves are large for a germander—up to 4 in. long. Rosy pink flowers appear on 8- to 12-in.-tall spikes in mid- to late summer. Full sun or partial shade. Regular to ample water.

T. chamaedrys. GERMANDER. Heat zones 12–4. To 1 ft. tall and 2 ft. wide, with many upright, woody-based stems densely clothed in toothed, dark green, ¾-in.-long leaves. Red-purple or white summer flowers in loose spikes (white-flowered form is looser). Attracts bees. Use as edging, foreground, low clipped hedge, or small-scale ground cover. Shear back once or twice a year to keep neat and force side branching. 'Prostratum' is 4–6 in. high, spreading to 3 ft. or more.

T. fruticans. BUSH GERMANDER, TUTTI-FRUTTI. Heat zones 9–8. Loose, silvery-stemmed plant to 4–8 ft. tall and wide (or wider). Gray-green, 1¼-in.-long leaves have silvery white undersides, giving plant an overall silvery gray appearance. Blooms almost year-round, bearing lavender-blue flower spikes at branch ends. Thin and cut back before spring growth begins. 'Azureum' has deeper blue flowers than the species; 'Compactum', also with dark blue blooms, grows just 3 ft. high and wide.

T. marum. CAT THYME. To 1½ ft. high and wide. Upright, densely clustered stems are closely set with tiny gray-green leaves. Blooms profusely in summer, when stems are covered with many deep pink or purplish flowers in 2-in. spikes. Attracts cats.

TEXAS CURRANT. See MAHONIA trifoliolata

TEXAS MADRONE. See ARBUTUS xalapensis

TEXAS MOUNTAIN LAUREL. See SOPHORA secundiflora

TEXAS RANGER, TEXAS SAGE. See LEUCOPHYLLUM

TEXAS STAR. See HIBISCUS coccineus

TEXAS TUBEROSE. See MANFREDA maculosa

TEXAS YELLOW STAR. See LINDHEIMERA texana

THALICTRUM

MEADOW RUE

Ranunculaceae

PERENNIALS

ZONES VARY BY SPECIES

◑ LIGHT SHADE

● REGULAR WATER

Thalictrum aquilegiifolium

Foliage clumps resemble those of columbine (*Aquilegia*). Plants typically bloom in late spring or summer, sending up sparsely leafed stems topped by puffs of small flowers, each consisting of four sepals and a prominent cluster of stamens. Superb for airy effect; offer a pleasing contrast to sturdier perennials. Delicate tracery of leaves and flowers is particularly effective against dark green background. Foliage is good in arrangements. Most meadow rues need some winter chill; all thrive in dappled sunlight at woodland edges. Protect from wind. Divide clumps every 4 or 5 years.

T. aquilegiifolium. COLUMBINE MEADOW RUE. Zones US, MS, LS; 9–5. From Europe, northern Asia. To 2–3 ft. tall, 1 ft. wide, with bluish green foliage. Earliest of the meadow rues to bloom: clouds of fluffy stamens (the white or greenish sepals drop off) appear for a couple of weeks in mid- to late spring. Rosy lilac is the usual color, but white and purple selections are available. If left in place, spent flowers are followed by attractive, long-lasting seed heads. Heat tolerant. 'Purpureum' has pinkish purple flowers.

T. delavayi (T. dipterocarpum). CHINESE MEADOW RUE. Zones US, MS, LS; 8–1. From western China. To 3–4 ft. (even 6 ft.) tall, 1½–2 ft. wide, with thin, dark purple stems that need support. Green foliage. Violet to lavender sepals, yellow stamens. 'Hewitt's Double' sports double lilac-colored flowers (one row of sepals, another of modified stamens that resemble petals); bloom continues for 2 months or longer. Heat tolerant.

T. flavum. YELLOW MEADOW RUE. Zones US, MS, LS, CS; 9–1. Native from Europe to the Caucasus and Siberia. Heat-tolerant, green-foliaged species to 3–5 ft. tall, 1½–2 ft. wide; stems need staking. Blooms in summer, bearing flowers like those of *T. aquilegiifolium*, but in lemon yellow. Leaves of 'Illuminator' emerge yellow green, then turn bright green. *T. f. glaucum (T. speciosissimum)* has blue-green leaves and stems. 'True Blue' is an improved, sturdier selection.

T. kiusianum. DWARF MEADOW RUE. Zones US, MS, LS; 8–1. From Japan. Bluish green leaves; plant spreads to form mats of tidy rosettes, each to 6 in. high and wide. Light purple, ½-in. blooms rise just above the foliage in late spring or early summer. Excellent in rock gardens or along paths.

T. rochebrunianum. Zones US, MS, LS, CS; 9–5. From Japan. To 4–6 ft. tall, 1½–2 ft. wide, with sturdy stems that don't need staking. Flowers consist of white or lavender sepals and pale yellow stamens. 'Lavender Mist', with violet sepals, is a superior selection.

THANKSGIVING CACTUS. See SCHLUMBERGERA truncata

Theaceae. The tea family consists of evergreen or deciduous trees and shrubs with leathery leaves and five-petaled flowers that have a large number of stamens. *Camellia, Franklinia,* and *Stewartia* are important representatives.

THELYPTERIS

Thelypteridaceae (Polypodiaceae)

FERNS

ZONES VARY BY SPECIES

PARTIAL TO FULL SHADE, EXCEPT AS NOTED

REGULAR TO AMPLE WATER

Thelypteris palustris

Among the easier ferns to grow. Deciduous in most areas, they thrive in moist, organic soil but will tolerate some drought if soil is rich. They take more sun than most ferns, provided moisture is plentiful. Effective in masses or combined with plants having coarser leaves. All spread by rhizomes to form colonies.

T. hexagonoptera (Phegopteris hexagonoptera). BROAD BEECH FERN. Zones US, MS, LS; 8–1. From eastern North America. Medium green, triangular fronds to 1½–2 ft. long and wide. Fronds are once divided, each division deeply toothed.

T. kunthii (T. normalis). SOUTHERN SHIELD FERN, WOOD FERN. Zones MS, LS, CS; 9–5. Native from the southeastern U.S. to South America; an old-time Southern favorite. Triangular fronds to 3 ft. (sometimes 5 ft.) long, with leaflets widely spaced along the stem; the light green color contrasts well with dark green–foliaged plants. Spreads quickly to form a tall, soft, pretty mass. Takes poor soils and considerable sun. Brown winter fronds are quite attractive, but cut them back before new spring growth begins.

T. noveboracensis. NEW YORK FERN. Zones US, MS, LS; 8–1. Native from Newfoundland to Georgia, Alabama, and Tennessee. Pale green, 1- to 2-ft.-long fronds are once divided, with the segments deeply lobed. A vigorous colonizer, it can be used as a ground cover in shade—or even in full sun if kept moist.

T. palustris. MARSH FERN. Zones US, MS, LS; 8–5. From Europe, Asia. The bluish green fronds, which occur singly or in tufts, are of two kinds: sterile and fertile. Sterile fronds are 6–24 in. long and half as wide, tapered at both ends, once divided, with segments deeply lobed. Fertile fronds are 1–3 ft. long, sturdier and stiffer than the sterile ones. Spreads rapidly.

THERMOPSIS

BUSH PEA, FALSE LUPINE

Fabaceae (Leguminosae)

PERENNIALS

ZONES VARY BY SPECIES

FULL SUN OR LIGHT SHADE

REGULAR WATER

Thermopsis villosa

These easy-to-grow perennials resemble lupines *(Lupinus)*. Silvery leaves are divided into leaflets that spread like fingers on a hand; erect, spikelike clusters of sweet pea–shaped yellow flowers appear in spring. Because of their tendency to spread by underground rhizomes, they are best in informal or wild gardens. Need little care. Somewhat drought tolerant.

T. chinensis. Zones US, MS, LS; 8–6. Native to China. Grows 2 ft. high, 1½ ft. wide, with 8-in. flower spikes.

T. rhombifolia (T. montana). MOUNTAIN BUSH PEA. Zones US; 9–1. Native to western North America. To 2–4 ft. tall, 2 ft. wide, with 8-in. flower clusters.

T. villosa (T. caroliniana). CAROLINA BUSH PEA. Zones US, MS, LS; 9–1. Native to the Carolinas and Georgia. To 3–4 ft. tall, 2 ft. wide, with 10-in. flower clusters. More heat tolerant than the other species.

THEVETIA

Apocynaceae

EVERGREEN SHRUBS OR TREES

ZONES VARY BY SPECIES

FULL SUN

REGULAR WATER

ALL PARTS ARE POISONOUS IF INGESTED

Thevetia peruviana

Fast-growing plants with narrow, glossy deep green leaves and clusters of showy, funnel-shaped flowers at branch ends. Thrive in heat; extremely sensitive to frost.

T. peruviana (T. neriifolia). YELLOW OLEANDER, LUCKY NUT. Zones CS (protected), TS; 12–10. From the tropical Americas. In frostless areas, it can be trained as a tree to 20–30 ft. tall and wide. Where frosts are light or rare, it's an 8-ft. (or larger) shrub; makes a good hedge, screen, or background plant. Leaves 3–6 in. long, with edges rolled under. Fragrant, 2- to 3-in., yellow to apricot flowers bloom from early summer into fall (all year where winters are warm). Small (1-in.), squat, four-angled fruits are red at first, then age to black. Provide good drainage, wind protection. In colder part of range, mound sand 6–12 in. deep around base of stem in late autumn. Dies back in freezes but recovers quickly; new growth will bloom same year.

T. thevetioides. GIANT THEVETIA. Zones TS; 12–10. From Mexico. Open growth to 12 ft. or more tall and wide. Leaves are darker green than those of *T. peruviana;* they resemble oleander *(Nerium)* leaves but are corrugated and have heavily veined undersides. Large clusters of brilliant yellow, 4-in. flowers bloom from late spring through fall; these are followed by 2½-in.-wide fruits that ripen from green to black. Makes an attractive patio tree, but fruit can be a litter problem.

THRIFT. See ARMERIA

THRYALLIS glauca. See GALPHIMIA glauca

THUJA

ARBORVITAE

Cupressaceae

EVERGREEN TREES OR SHRUBS

ZONES VARY BY SPECIES

PARTIAL SHADE IN HOTTEST CLIMATES

MODERATE TO REGULAR WATER

Thuja orientalis
'Aurea Nana'

Neat, symmetrical plants often trimmed into geometrical forms—globes, cones, cylinders. Juvenile foliage is feathery, with small, needlelike leaves; mature foliage is scalelike, carried in flat sprays. Foliage in better-known selections is often yellow green or bright golden yellow. Small (½- to ¾-in.-long) cones are green or bluish green, turning to brownish. Although arborvitaes will take both damp and fairly dry soils, they grow best in well-drained soil. Bagworms and spider mites are common pests on all species. Generic name is sometimes spelled *Thuya.*

T. occidentalis. AMERICAN ARBORVITAE. Zones US, MS; 7–1. Native to eastern U.S. Upright, open growth to 30–60 ft. tall, 10–15 ft. wide, with branches that tend to turn up at ends. Bright green to yellowish green leaf sprays. Foliage turns brown in severe cold. Needs moist air to look its best. Basic species is seldom seen, but smaller garden selections are common. Among these, the taller ones make good informal or clipped screens, while lower kinds are often used around foundations, along walks or walls, as hedges. Be sure to check on the ultimate height of selections used for foundation plantings; plants are too often seen wedged under an overhang at the corner of a house. The following are some good choices.

'Brandon'. Fast growth to 12−15 ft. tall, 6−8 ft wide. Useful as screen.

'Douglasii Pyramidalis'. Vigorous-growing pyramid to 15 ft. tall (or taller), 10 ft. wide.

'Fastigiata' ('Pyramidalis', 'Columnaris'). Dense, columnar growth to 25 ft. tall, 5 ft. wide. Tends to get a bit unruly as it puts on size, with branches spreading out; they can be tied together for a neater look. Set 4 ft. apart for screen. Especially valuable in damp soils and cold regions, where few other columnar choices are available.

'Globosa' ('Little Gem', 'Little Giant', and 'Nana' are similar selections). GLOBE ARBORVITAE, TOM THUMB ARBORVITAE. Dense and rounded, with bright green foliage. To about 4 ft. high and wide in 10 years; eventually larger.

'Hetz Midget'. Globe-shaped plant with rich green foliage. Not likely to exceed 3−4 ft. tall and wide.

'Nigra'. Dense dark green cone to 20−30 ft. tall, 4−5 ft. wide.

'Rheingold'. Cone-shaped, slow-growing, bright golden plant with a mixture of scale and needle foliage. Even very old plants seldom exceed 6 ft. tall and wide.

'Smaragd' ('Emerald', 'Emerald Green'). Neat, dense-growing, narrow cone to 10−15 ft. tall, 3−4 ft. wide. Holds its color throughout winter.

'Woodwardii'. Widely grown dense, globe-shaped shrub with rich green color. May attain considerable size with age but stays small over a reasonably long period; to 4 ft. high and wide in 10 years.

'Yellow Ribbon'. To 8−10 ft. tall, 2−3 ft. wide, with bright yellow foliage throughout the year.

T. orientalis (Platycladus orientalis). ORIENTAL ARBORVITAE. Zones US, MS, LS, CS, TS; 9−6. Native to northern China, Manchuria, Korea. Species (to 25 ft. tall, 15 ft. wide) is rarely grown; nurseries offer more attractive, shrubbier selections. Widely used around foundations, by doorways or gates, in formal rows. Less hardy to cold than *T. occidentalis* but tolerates heat and low humidity better. Has survived well in nematode-infested soils. Give good drainage; protect from reflected heat of light-colored walls or pavement.

'Aurea Nana'. DWARF GOLDEN ARBORVITAE, BERCKMAN DWARF ARBORVITAE. Golden-foliaged, compact globe. Usually 3 ft. tall and 2 ft. wide but can grow as high as 5 ft. Sometimes sold as *T. o.* 'Berckmanii'.

'Bakeri'. Compact, cone shaped, bright green. To 5−8 ft. high, 4 ft. wide.

'Beverleyensis'. BEVERLY HILLS ARBORVITAE, GOLDEN PYRAMID ARBORVITAE. Upright, globe-shaped to conical plant with somewhat open habit. Golden yellow branchlet tips. Eventually reaches 10 ft. tall and wide.

'Blue Cone'. Dense, upright, conical; good blue-green color. To 8 ft. tall, 4 ft. wide.

'Bonita' ('Bonita Upright', 'Bonita Erecta'). Rounded, full, dense cone to 3 ft. tall, 2 ft. wide. Dark green with slight golden tinting at branch tips.

'Fruitlandii'. FRUITLAND ARBORVITAE. Compact, upright, cone shaped, with deep green foliage.

'Minima Glauca'. DWARF BLUE ARBORVITAE. To 3−4 ft. tall and wide. Blue-green foliage.

'Raffles'. Resembles 'Aurea Nana' but is smaller, with denser growth and brighter color.

'Westmount'. To 3 ft. tall, 2 ft. wide. Green foliage has yellow tips throughout the growing season.

T. plicata. WESTERN RED CEDAR. Zones US, MS; 8−6. Native from coastal Northern California north to Alaska and inland to Montana. One of the West's most beautiful and imposing native trees. Can reach 200 ft. tall in the temperate rain forests of coastal Washington. Does surprisingly well in the lower Midwest and Upper and Middle South if planted in moist, fertile, well-drained soil; it can grow at least 2−3 ft. per year. Makes a magnificent lawn tree, but give it plenty of room—in gardens, it may reach 75 ft. tall and 25 ft. wide. Selections include the following.

Thuja plicata

'Atrovirens'. Narrow pyramid to 70 ft. tall, 25 ft. wide, with gracefully drooping limbs.

'Clemson #2'. Selected for good tolerance of heat and cold. To 30 ft. tall, 8 ft. wide. New growth has creamy highlights.

'Fastigiata'. Narrow, erect growth to 80−90 ft. tall, 20−25 ft. wide. Very dense foliage; fine for tall screen.

'Green Giant'. Hybrid between *T. plicata* and *T. standishii*, a Japanese species. Can grow 3−5 ft. a year, ultimately reaching 30−50 ft. tall, 10−20 ft. wide. Shear as a tall hedge or use as a tall screen.

'Hillieri'. Irregularly shaped, dense plant to 6−10 ft. high and wide, eventually larger.

'Spring Grove'. To 8−10 ft. high in 5 years; ultimately reaches 40−60 ft. tall, 10−15 ft. wide. Can be sheared as a hedge.

'Stoneham Gold'. Dense, slow-growing dwarf to 6 ft. tall, 2 ft. wide. Orange-yellow new growth.

'Zebrina'. Slow grower; same size as species. Foliage is banded in green and golden yellow. Often sold as 'Aurea', a less commonly seen selection with green foliage tinted golden.

THUNBERGIA

Acanthaceae

PERENNIAL VINES AND SHRUBS, SOME GROWN AS ANNUALS

🌿 TS ❚ 12–10, EXCEPT AS NOTED

☼ ◑ PARTIAL SHADE IN HOTTEST CLIMATES

💧 REGULAR WATER

Thunbergia alata

Tropical, typically twining plants noted for showy flowers. Some grow fast enough to bloom the first season and can be treated as annuals. Those grown as perennials are evergreen in the Tropical South. Provide rich, well-drained soil. Good greenhouse plants.

T. alata. BLACK-EYED SUSAN VINE. Perennial vine grown as annual. May live over in Zones CS, TS. From Africa. To 10 ft., with triangular, 3-in., medium green leaves. Blooms all summer long; tubular flowers flare out to 1 in. wide, come in orange, yellow, or white, all with purple-black throat. Start seed indoors; set plants out in good soil in a sunny spot as soon as weather warms. Display in hanging basket or window box, use as ground cover, or train on strings or low trellis.

T. battiscombei. Vining shrub. From Africa. Unless given support, it forms a mound 4−6 ft. high, 6−8 ft. wide. Scrambling stems bear broadly oval, glossy bright green leaves to 7 in. long. Fuzzy greenish white buds appear in leaf joints; from spring into fall, these open to 2- to 3-in.-long, yellow-throated flowers in an intense blue purple. Top dies back in cold weather, but roots are hardy to 20°F.

T. erecta. KING'S MANTLE. Vining shrub to 6 ft. tall and wide. Heat zones 12−1. Native to Africa. Erect, sometimes twining, with dark green, ovate to oblong leaves to 3 in. long. Velvety dark blue, 3-in.-long flowers with orange or cream throats resemble those of gloxinia *(Sinningia)*; they appear in joints of upper leaves throughout summer and fall. 'Alba' is a white-flowered form.

T. fragrans. SWEET CLOCK VINE, WHITE LADY. Perennial vine. Heat zones 12−1. Native to India. Woody, twining stems reach 8−10 ft. high, set with notched, oval green leaves to 3 in. long. Lightly scented summer flowers to 3 in. across appear singly or in clusters; white is the usual color, but blossoms may be blue, lavender, or even yellow. Prune this vine regularly, or it may get away from you.

T. grandiflora. SKY FLOWER. Perennial vine. From India. Vigorous growth to 20 ft. or more, with 8-in., heart-shaped, medium to dark green leaves. Slightly drooping clusters of tubular, flaring, sky blue flowers to 3 in. across appear through summer and into fall. Use on arbor, large trellis, or wire fence; casts dense shade. There is a white selection.

T. gregorii (T. gibsonii). ORANGE CLOCK VINE. Perennial vine; grow as summer annual outside Tropical South. Native to Africa. Showy and easy to grow; twines to 6 ft. high or sprawls over ground to cover a 12-ft. circle.

Gray-green, triangular, tooth-edged leaves to 3 in. long. Tubular, flaring, bright orange, 3-in. flowers are borne singly on 4-in. stems. Blooms nearly all year long in the Tropical South, in summer elsewhere. Set plants 3–4 ft. apart to cover a wire fence, about 6 ft. apart as ground cover. Plant above a wall and let stems cascade down; or grow in hanging baskets.

T. mysorensis. Perennial vine. From India. Climbs to 15–35 ft., with narrow, elliptical dark green leaves up to 6 in. long. Spectacular, pendent, 1- to 1½-ft.-long clusters of gaping, 2-in.-long flowers that are red on the outside, yellow within. Blooms much of the year, most heavily in spring. Train on pergola, arbor, or other overhead structure to permit flowers to dangle. Protect from frost.

THYME. See THYMUS

THYMOPHYLLA (Dyssodia)

Asteraceae (Compositae)

PERENNIALS, SOME GROWN AS ANNUALS

✿ CS, TS ⑂ 12–6

☼ FULL SUN

⬤ MODERATE WATER

Thymophylla tenuiloba

Low-growing plants with little yellow daisies; quick and easy to start from seed planted in flats or sown in place. Not particular about soil type but must have good drainage.

T. acerosa. PRICKLY-LEAF DOGWEED. Shrubby perennial. Native from Nevada and Utah to Texas and Mexico. Much-branched, mounding plant to 6–8 in. high, 1 ft. wide; covered with daisies from late spring to fall. Sharp-pointed, needle-thin, medium green leaves to ½ in. long. Good in beds, in cactus gardens, as edging, as informal ground cover. Especially useful for erosion control on slopes.

T. pentachaeta. GOLDEN DYSSODIA, FIVE-NEEDLE DOGWEED. Perennial. Native from California and Nevada to southern Texas, Mexico. To 4–6 in. high and wide, with open, sparse appearance. Needlelike dark green leaves are ½–1 in. long; stems are covered with fine, silky hairs. Blooms most profusely in late spring, sporadically later in the year. Short lived. Use like *T. acerosa*.

T. tenuiloba. DAHLBERG DAISY, GOLDEN FLEECE. Short-lived perennial usually grown as annual. Heat-loving plant native from Texas to Florida and Mexico. Mounding growth to 1 ft. high, 1½ ft. wide. Divided, thread-like leaves make a dark green background for flowers that look like tiny golden marguerites *(Anthemis)*. Blooms from early summer to fall. Use for mass display or pockets of color. When plants become ragged with age, pull them out. In warm-winter areas, can be planted in fall for winter-to-spring bloom.

THYMUS

THYME

Lamiaceae (Labiatae)

SHRUBBY PERENNIALS

✿ ZONES VARY BY SPECIES

☼ ◐ LIGHT SHADE IN HOTTEST CLIMATES

⬤ MODERATE WATER

Thymus vulgaris

Diminutive Mediterranean members of the mint family with tiny, usually heavily scented leaves and masses of little flowers in whorls. Well suited to herb garden, rock garden; prostrate, mat-forming types make good small-space ground covers. Attractive to bees but not to deer. Provide light, well-drained soil. Shear or cut back established plants to keep them compact. Easy to propagate from cuttings taken in early summer. Botanical names are constantly undergoing revision.

T. camphoratus. CAMPHOR THYME. Zones US, MS, LS, CS; 9–1. To 1½ ft. high and wide, with narrow gray-green leaves that smell like camphor. Blooms in late spring, early summer; flower clusters consist of woolly, rosy purplish bracts and tiny white flowers.

T. ×citriodorus. LEMON THYME. Zones US, MS, LS, CS; 9–6. Variable hybrid with erect or spreading growth to 1 ft. high, 2 ft. wide. Ovate to lance-shaped, medium green leaves with lemon fragrance. Pale lilac flowers in summer. Leaves of 'Argenteus' are splashed with silver, those of 'Aureus' with gold. 'Lime' has lime green foliage. 'Doone Valley', with yellow-spotted leaves, reaches only 5 in. high.

T. herba-barona. CARAWAY-SCENTED THYME. Zones US, MS, LS, CS; 9–6. Fast growing to 2–4 in. high, 2 ft. or more wide; stems root as they spread. Forms a dense mat of wiry stems set with widely spaced dark green, ovate to lance-shaped leaves with caraway fragrance. Clusters of rose pink flowers in midsummer.

T. lanuginosus. See T. pseudolanuginosus

T. mastichina. MASTIC THYME. Zones MS, LS; 8–7. Upright and spreading plant to 1 ft. tall, 16 in. wide, with oval, pointed, medium green leaves to ½ in. long. Foliage smells something like eucalyptus leaves. Tiny white flowers in summer.

T. praecox arcticus (T. drucei). MOTHER-OF-THYME, CREEPING THYME. Zones US, MS, LS, CS; 9–4. Variable species to 3 in. high, 3 ft. wide, with roundish dark green leaves and purplish summer flowers. Good for small areas or as filler between stepping-stones where foot traffic is light. Soft and fragrant underfoot. Leaves can be used as seasoning and in potpourris. Often incorrectly sold as *T. serpyllum*.

The many selections include the following. 'Album' ('Albus') has light green leaves and white flowers; 'Coccineum' produces purplish red flowers. Nonblooming 'Elfin' grows 2 in. high and 5 in. wide. 'Minus' is extremely fine textured, forming a carpet to ½ in. high, 1 ft. wide. 'Pink Chintz' (may actually be a variety of *T. polytrichus*) grows 1 in. high and 1½ ft. wide, bears salmon pink flowers; 'Pink Ripple' has lemon-scented leaves and pink flowers; 'Reiter's', with lavender blooms, is a tough, vigorous ground cover for sun or shade; it grows 3 in. high and 2½ ft. wide. 'Reiter's Red', to 1 in. high and 1½ ft. wide, has red flowers; its leaves are smaller than those of 'Reiter's'.

T. pseudolanuginosus (T. lanuginosus). WOOLLY THYME, SILVER THYME. Zones US, MS, LS, CS; 9–1. Forms a flat to undulating mat 2–3 in. high, 3 ft. wide. Stems are densely clothed with elliptical, woolly gray leaves. Blooms seldom and sparsely; when it does, produces pinkish flowers in leaf joints in midsummer. Becomes slightly rangy in winter. Use in rock crevices, between stepping-stones, spilling over bank or raised bed, covering small patches of ground. 'Hall's Woolly' is a profuse bloomer.

T. pulegioides. PENNSYLVANIA DUTCH TEA THYME. Zones US, MS, LS. Fast grower to 3 in. high, 1 ft. wide, with shiny green, oval, lemon-scented leaves. Purplish pink flowers in summer. Sometimes sold as *T. serpyllum*.

T. serpyllum. See T. praecox arcticus, T. pulegioides

T. vulgaris. COMMON THYME. Zones US, MS, LS, CS; 9–1. Variable plant to 1 ft. high, 2 ft. wide, with gray-green, narrow to oval leaves. White to lilac flowers in late spring, early summer. Low edging for flower, vegetable, or herb garden. Good container plant. Use leaves fresh or dried for seasoning fish, shellfish, poultry stuffing, soups, vegetables. 'Argenteus', called silver thyme, has leaves variegated with silver. 'Orange Balsam' has narrow, orange-scented leaves.

TIARELLA

FOAMFLOWER, SUGAR-SCOOP

Saxifragaceae

PERENNIALS

✿ US, MS, LS

◐ ⬤ PARTIAL TO FULL SHADE

⬤ REGULAR WATER

Tiarella wherryi

Clump-forming plants to about 1½ ft. tall (in bloom) and 1½–2 ft. wide; spread by rhizomes (and by aboveground runners, in the case of *T. cordifolia*). Leaves arise directly from rhizomes; they are evergreen but may change color in autumn. Selections with year-round colorful foliage are becoming popular; look for new introductions in addition to those described below. Narrow, erect flower stems carry many small white or pink flowers. Useful in shady rock gardens; make pretty ground covers but will not bear foot traffic.

T. cordifolia. FOAMFLOWER. Heat zones 8–1. Rapid spreader from eastern North America. Light green, lobed, 4-in. leaves show red and yellow fall color. Creamy white flowers on foot-tall stalks. Leaves of 'Eco Red Heart' have dark red centers and veins; those of 'Oakleaf' are deeply lobed. Both selections have pink blossoms.

T. selections and hybrids. Many of the choicest foamflowers are of uncertain origin.

'Butterfly Wings'. Light green leaves have centers heavily splashed with purplish black. Light pink flowers.

'Cygnet'. Star-shaped leaves with purple markings along the veins. White flowers open from pink buds.

'Mint Chocolate'. Deeply lobed leaves have a central zone of deep brownish purple. Pinkish white flowers.

'Ninja'. Leaves marbled with blackish purple, turning almost entirely purple in winter. Pinkish white blooms.

'Skeleton Key'. Very deeply cut leaves with deep purple midrib. White blossoms.

'Spring Symphony'. Green leaves with a central black blotch; pink flowers. Tolerates heat and humidity.

T. wherryi (T. cordifolia collina). Heat zones 7–1. From southeastern U.S. Like *T. cordifolia* but lacks aboveground runners, is slower to spread. Flower clusters are somewhat more slender, often tinged pink. 'Heronswood Mist' has leaves heavily marbled and blotched with creamy white; pink stems hold light pink flowers.

TIBOUCHINA

Melastomataceae

EVERGREEN SHRUBS AND TREES

TS 12–10; OR GROW IN POTS

PARTIAL SHADE IN HOTTEST CLIMATES

REGULAR WATER

Tibouchina urvilleana

Brazilian natives with deeply veined, oval, pointed leaves and big, showy, five-petaled flowers in various shades of purple. Bloom is intermittent over a long period. These plants prefer rich, well-drained, slightly acid soil. They have a tendency to legginess and should be pruned lightly after every bloom cycle, somewhat more heavily in spring; resprout quickly after heavy pruning. Pinch tips of young plants to encourage bushiness. Resistant to deer damage.

T. elegans. Shrub. To 6 ft. tall and wide, with glossy green, 2-in. leaves and purple flowers 1½–2½ in. across.

T. grandifolia. Shrub. To 4–6 ft. tall, 6–8 ft. wide, with very large (to 9-in.-long), fuzzy, silvery green leaves. Inch-wide violet flowers are held above the foliage in upright, 8- to 16-in.-tall spikes.

T. granulosa. PURPLE GLORY TREE. Tree. To 40 ft. in its native setting, but more likely to reach 20 ft. tall and at least as wide in gardens. Broad, spreading habit. Glossy dark green, 5- to 8-in.-long leaves with fuzzy undersides. Deep rose to violet flowers are 2 in. across, held in clusters up to 1 ft. long.

T. urvilleana (T. semidecandra). PRINCESS FLOWER. Shrub. Open growth to 5–18 ft. high, 3–10 ft. wide. Branch tips, buds, and new growth are shaded with velvety hairs in orange and bronze red. Velvety, 3- to 6-in.-long, rich green leaves are often edged red; older leaves add spots of red, orange, or yellow, especially in winter. Clusters of brilliant royal purple, 3- to 5-in.-wide flowers. Protect from strong winds.

TICKSEED. See BIDENS, COREOPSIS

TIGER LILY. See LILIUM lancifolium

TILIA

LINDEN

Tiliaceae

DECIDUOUS TREES

ZONES VARY BY SPECIES

FULL SUN

REGULAR WATER

Tilia cordata

Stately, attractive, densely foliaged trees that grow at a moderate rate. All have irregularly heart-shaped leaves and small, fragrant, yellowish white flowers in drooping clusters in late spring, early summer. Flowers develop into nutlets, each with an attached papery bract. Best in deep, rich, moist soil. In cold-winter areas, fall color varies from negligible to a good yellow. Young trees need shaping, older ones only corrective pruning. Aphids can cause honeydew, which drips disagreeably and encourages sooty mold.

T. americana. AMERICAN LINDEN, BASSWOOD. Zones US, MS, LS, CS; 10–1. Native to eastern North America. To 40–60 ft. tall, 20–25 ft. wide. Straight-trunked tree with a narrow crown. Dull dark green leaves to 4–6 in. long, nearly as wide. 'Redmond' is a pyramidal form with glossy foliage.

T. cordata. LITTLE-LEAF LINDEN. Zones US, MS; 7–1. Native to Europe. Dense pyramid to 30–50 ft. tall, 15–30 ft. wide. Leaves 1½–3 in. long and as wide (or wider), dark green above, silvery beneath. Excellent lawn or street tree. Given room to develop its crown, it can be a fine patio shade tree (but expect bees in flowering season). Can be sheared into hedges. Very tolerant of city conditions. Selected forms include 'Chancellor', 'Glenleven', 'Greenspire', 'June Bride' (especially heavy bloomer), and 'Olympic'.

T. ×euchlora. CRIMEAN LINDEN. Zones US, MS; 7–1. Hybrid derived from *T. cordata*. To 25–35 ft. (perhaps eventually to 50 ft.) tall, almost as wide. Slightly pendulous branches. Rich green, glossy leaves have paler undersides, reach 2–4 in. long and wide. Casts more open shade than *T. cordata*.

T. tomentosa. SILVER LINDEN. Zones US, MS, LS; 8–1. From Europe, western Asia. To 40–50 ft. tall, 20–30 ft. wide. Leaves are 3–5 in. long and wide, light green above, silvery beneath; they turn and ripple in the slightest breeze. Take more heat and drought than other species. 'Sterling' has silvery young leaves and an especially handsome winter silhouette.

Tiliaceae. Only one member of the linden family of trees and shrubs is commonly grown in the South: linden (*Tilia*).

TILLANDSIA

Bromeliaceae

PERENNIALS

TS, EXCEPT AS NOTED; OR HOUSEPLANTS

EXPOSURE NEEDS VARY BY SPECIES

WATER NEEDS VARY BY SPECIES

Tillandsia cyanea

This large family of bromeliads is commonly found throughout Texas, Mexico, and Central and South America. Most are epiphytes (tree dwellers) that depend on rain, dew, and fog for moisture. A few grow in soil. Plants vary greatly in size and appearance. Leaves may be wide, narrow (even hairlike), or sword shaped; they may be twisted or curled. Those with green leaves generally need regular water and filtered light; types with gray-green to bluish foliage need less water and tolerate more sun. Often seen mounted on plaques of wood that are hung on walls, indoors or out; also look good in containers filled with loose, fast-draining potting mix. Let the mix go dry between waterings.

T. caput-medusae. From Mexico and Central America. Mass of curling, channeled, gray-green leaves to 1 ft. long resembles the head of Medusa. Blooms in late spring, producing a foot-long spike with red bracts and blue flowers. Prefers bright filtered light.

T. cyanea. From Ecuador. Rosette of bright green, arching, 1-ft. leaves produces a showy flower cluster in spring or autumn: a flattened plume of

T

deep red or pink bracts, from which violet-blue flowers emerge one or two at a time over a long season.

T. ionantha. From Mexico and Nicaragua. Rosettes of 2-in.-long leaves covered with silvery gray fuzz. Small, tubular spring flowers are violet; at bloom time, center of rosette turns red. Tough and undemanding plant.

T. juncea. Native from southern Florida to northern South America. Forms a rosette of upright, very narrow, 12- to 16-in.-long leaves in olive green tinged with copper. Short, erect inflorescence appears in summer, consists of bright red bracts and bluish purple petals.

T. latifolia. From Ecuador and Peru. Bayonet-shaped gray-green leaves to 8 in. long. Blossom spike reaches 15 in. tall, with yellow-orange bracts and flowers ranging in color from fuchsia to blue. Spring bloom.

T. recurvata. BALL MOSS. Zones LS, CS, TS. From southern U.S. and South America. Ball-like clusters of gray-green leaves to 6 in. across grow on the branches; blue-violet flowers bloom in summer.

T. usneoides. SPANISH MOSS. Zones LS, CS, TS. Native from Florida and Texas south to Argentina. Drapes itself on live oaks *(Quercus virginiana)*, cypresses *(Cupressus)*, and telephone lines, hanging as long as 15 ft.; a live oak draped with Spanish moss is a classic image of the South. Greenish gray stems and leaves are wiry, threadlike. Has no roots. Inconspicuous green flowers in late spring or fall. Thrives in shade and high humidity; very sensitive to air pollution.

TITHONIA rotundifolia (T. speciosa)

MEXICAN SUNFLOWER

Asteraceae (Compositae)

PERENNIAL GROWN AS ANNUAL

☀ US, MS, LS, CS, TS ⊞ 12–1

☼ FULL SUN

◐ REGULAR WATER

Tithonia rotundifolia

Native from Mexico to Central America. Husky, rather coarse plant with velvety green leaves, spectacular gaudy flowers. Grows rapidly to 6 ft. tall, 4 ft. wide. Blooms from summer to frost, bearing 3- to 4-in.-wide blossoms with orange-scarlet rays and tufted yellow centers. Use taller selections for temporary screens or hedges. All have hollow stems, so cut carefully for bouquets to avoid bending stalks. Sow seed in place in spring, in well-drained soil that's not too rich. Tolerates intense heat and some drought; attractive to butterflies and hummingbirds. Will self-sow.

Available choices on the smaller side include 2- to 2½-ft.-tall Arcadian Blend, with gold, orange, and yellow flowers; 2½-ft. 'Fiesta del Sol', bearing 2- to 3-in. orange flowers earlier in the season than other selections. Taller selections (to 4 ft.) are 'Aztec Sun', bearing apricot gold blooms; bushy 'Goldfinger', with deep orange flowers; and 'Torch', another bushy grower bearing orange-red to vivid red blooms.

TITI. See CYRILLA raciflora

TOADFLAX. See LINARIA

TOLMIEA menziesii

PIGGYBACK PLANT

Saxifragaceae

PERENNIAL

☀ TS ⊞ 10–6; OR HOUSEPLANT

◑● PARTIAL TO FULL SHADE; BRIGHT INDIRECT LIGHT

◐◖ REGULAR TO AMPLE WATER

Tolmiea menziesii

Native to the Coast Ranges from California to Alaska, this plant gets its common name from the little plantlets that appear atop its hairy leaves once they've matured. Attractive, triangular to heart-shaped, shallowly lobed leaves are of variable size (to 5 in. long), borne on leafstalks that also vary in length. Leaves are usually solid medium green, but there is a form irregularly mottled in yellow to chartreuse. Flowers are small and inconspicuous.

Where it's winter hardy, piggyback plant makes a nice, spreading, foot-tall ground cover for moist shade; plantlets formed at the junction of leafstalks and leaf blades root where they touch soil. Most people, however, grow it as a houseplant, usually in a hanging basket. Indoors, it prefers bright indirect light (no hot sun). Let the soil surface go dry to the touch between waterings. Fertilize every other week in spring and summer and monthly in fall and winter with a general-purpose liquid houseplant fertilizer. Easy to propagate: just detach a leaf carrying a plantlet and place on top of moist potting mix so that the juncture between stem and leaf is in contact with soil. Pins or a U-shaped wire will help keep the leaf in position. Keep the soil evenly moist. The leaf will gradually die, but the plantlet will root.

TOMATILLO

Solanaceae

ANNUAL

☀ US, MS, LS, CS, TS ⊞ 12–6

☼ FULL SUN

◐ REGULAR WATER

Tomatillo

From Mexico. Easy-to-grow, summer-fruiting tomato relative known botanically as *Physalis ixocarpa*. Bushy, sprawling growth to 4 ft. high and at least as wide. Fruit swells to fill—and eventually split—the loose, papery husk (calyx) that surrounds it. When fully ripe, fruit is yellow to purple, about 2 in. wide, and very sweet, but it is usually picked when green and tart and used in sauces and other dishes.

Sow seeds directly in fertile soil 4 to 6 weeks after last frost, when soil has warmed; in moist, warm soil, seeds will germinate in 5 days. Thin seedlings to 10 in. apart. Or start plants indoors and set out in the garden; plant deep, as for tomatoes. Tomatillos can be trained to a trellis like tomatoes but are usually left to sprawl. Once fruiting begins, cut back on water but don't let plants become stressed. Harvest fruit when walnut size (or smaller, if it seems fully developed) and deep green. Don't remove the papery husk until you are ready to use the fruit.

TOMATO

Solanaceae

PERENNIAL GROWN AS ANNUAL

☀ US, MS, LS, CS, TS ⊞ 12–1

☼ FULL SUN

◐ REGULAR WATER

Tomato

There are two kinds of gardeners in the South—those who have grown tomatoes and those who will grow them. No other crop produces so much for so many for so little expense. Just about everyone swears by his or her own favorite method of growing tomatoes. If yours works, stick with it—but if you're a beginner or dissatisfied with the results you've achieved thus far, the following information should help.

First, choose selections adapted to your area. Those listed on the following pages perform well in most of the South. Fine-tune these recommendations by checking with local garden centers and your Cooperative Extension Service. Next, decide whether you want big tomatoes for slicing, meaty ones for canning and sauce, or small ones for popping into your mouth.

Factor into the equation when you expect to plant and how long you want to wait for harvest. It's hard to go wrong with midseason types; they ripen fruit anywhere from 60 to 75 days after transplants are set out. But if it's midsummer and you're trying to squeeze in a fall crop before frost, you'll need to plant an early tomato that ripens in 50 to 60 days. Late tomatoes that ripen in 80 to 95 days are best planted in spring. ▶

Also consider how much fruit you want and how much space you can devote to your plants. Tomato plants (*Lycopersicon esculentum*, native to the Andes) are classified as either determinate or indeterminate. Determinate tomatoes are bushy and ripen all of their fruit over several weeks; they need less space and support than indeterminate types. Indeterminate tomatoes are vinelike and ripen their fruit over a period of months; they give more total fruit, but need more space and support.

Good soil is crucial for great tomatoes. Plants like fertile, moist, well-drained soil loaded with organic matter. Work in lots of composted manure, garden compost, or chopped leaves before planting. The soil should be slightly acid to neutral (pH 6.5–7.0). If the pH drops below 6.5, add lime to prevent blossom-end rot (a sunken brown or black spot on the end of the tomato opposite the stem). In Florida, where nematodes are prevalent, gardeners should consider treating their soil with a soil sterilant before planting, even if they're planting nematode-resistant selections. 'Better Boy' has shown resistance to root-knot nematodes.

You can plant tomatoes in spring for summer crops, in summer for fall crops, and (if you live in the Tropical South) in fall for winter crops. Just remember that tomatoes can't take frost and don't like cold soil. Most people start with purchased transplants, but the choice of selections is often limited. To grow heirloom or novelty types, you'll probably be starting from seed. About 5 to 7 weeks before you plan to set out plants, sow seeds in flats or pots filled with light, seed-starting

Heirloom Tomato
'Cherokee Purple'

soil mix (available at garden centers); cover seeds with ½ in. of mix. Place containers in a warm, sunny spot with a temperature of at least 65–70°F; keep the soil moist. When seedlings are 2 in. tall, transplant them to individual 3- or 4-in. pots. If you opt to buy transplants, look for sturdy plants that haven't begun flowering or fruiting.

Don't worry if tomato plants get a bit leggy before you plant. Because of the way they're planted, this can actually be an advantage. Most folks use either the hole-planting or trench-planting method. With the first, you use a shovel or posthole digger to dig a fairly deep hole, fill the bottom of the hole with a few inches of compost, place the plant vertically in the hole, then fill in with soil so that only the top pair of leaves shows above ground level. With the second, you dig a trench about 4 in. deep and 15 in. long, place the plant horizontally in the trench, bend the top end of the plant upward, and then fill in the trench so that, again, only the top pair of leaves shows. Both methods accomplish the same thing: they encourage the plant to form roots all along the buried stem, producing a larger, more vigorous, and more drought-tolerant plant. After planting, give each plant a drink of liquid 20-20-20 fertilizer.

Tomato plants, particularly indeterminate types, tend to sprawl along the ground—but if you allow this, you'll end up with fruit that's rotten or half-eaten by insects. Instead, stake or cage your plants. To stake, drive a sturdy, 6-ft. stake (at least 1 by 1 in.) into the ground a foot away from the plant. Use soft ties to secure the plant to the stake as it grows. You'll need to prune staked plants to one or two main stems to make them manageable. To cage, grow each plant inside a cylinder made from iron reinforcing wire (6-in. mesh). Use iron reinforcing bars on opposite sides to anchor

the cage to the ground. As the vine grows, poke protruding branches back inside the cage. No pruning is required.

Space staked plants 1–2 ft. apart and caged plants 3 ft. apart. Allow 3 ft. between rows. After the first fruit has set, sprinkle ¼ cup of 10-10-10 fertilizer per 10 ft. of row around plants and water in well. Repeat every 4 weeks. Mulch plants generously to keep soil evenly moist and discourage weeds. Don't wet leaves when watering plants.

Harvest when fruit is fully colored and juicy. When frost is predicted, harvest all fruit, even if it is green. Store in a dry place away from direct sunlight at 60–70°F. Unripe tomatoes that have turned a whitish green and formed a corky ring where the fruit joins the stem will ripen slowly indoors.

Hornworms (large green caterpillars with diagonal white stripes) are major pests. Handpick them or spray in early evening with *Bt* (*Bacillus thuringiensis;* sold as Dipel). Other pests include whiteflies (spray with horticultural oil) and nematodes (sterilize soil and plant resistant selections). Tomatoes are also prone to a host of diseases. Early blight (also called alternaria blight) shows up on leaves as dark spots with concentric rings and on fruit as sunken lesions with the same ring pattern. Spraying with copper fungicide is an effective control. If plants are growing strongly, then suddenly wilt and die, the cause is probably verticillium wilt, fusarium wilt, or both. Pull up and discard affected plants. Diseases and pests often live over in soil, so plant in a different location each year.

You can minimize fussing, cussing, and spraying by planting selections that resist one or more problems. Keys to resistance to look for on seed packets, on plant labels, or in catalog descriptions include V (verticillium wilt), F (fusarium wilt), FF or F2 (fusarium wilt races 1 and 2), T (tobacco mosaic virus), N (nematodes), A (early or alternaria blight), S (septoria leaf spot), and St or L (stemphylium gray leaf spot). For example, a plant labeled VFFNT resists verticillium wilt, two races of fusarium, nematodes, and tobacco mosaic virus.

Some tomato problems—leaf roll, blossom-end rot, cracked fruit—are caused by growing conditions. These can usually be prevented or corrected by maintaining uniform soil moisture and proper pH. For more solutions to tomato problems, see the *Southern Living Garden Problem Solver.*

TOMATO SELECTIONS

The following lists offer just a sampling of the incredible number of different tomatoes you can buy as seeds or started plants.

Main crop or midseason tomatoes. 'Atkinson', 'Better Boy', 'Big Boy', 'Celebrity', 'Creole', 'Floramerica', 'Rutgers', and 'Supersonic' are among the most widely grown.

Early tomatoes. When you want the first tomato on the block or aim to get a fall crop in just under the wire, try 'Burpee's Early Pick', 'Early Girl', 'First Lady', and 'Park's Early Challenge'.

Late tomatoes. These generally taste better than early types, because plants have more time to develop flavor. 'Abraham Lincoln', 'Arkansas Traveler', 'Homestead 24', 'Mule Team', and 'Tropic' are delicious examples.

Heat-tolerant tomatoes. Tomato plants often fail to set fruit once daytime temperatures rise above 95°F and night temperatures exceed 78°F. Those that bear up under the heat include midseason 'Atkinson', 'Creole',

Heirloom Tomato
'Arkansas Traveler'

Main-crop Tomato
'Better Boy'

Early Tomato
'Early Girl'

Heirloom Tomato
'Eva Purple Ball'

Novelty Tomatoes
'Evergreen', 'Green Zebra'

Paste Tomato
'Viva Italia'

T

Cherry Tomato 'Sun Gold'

'Heatwave', 'Neptune', 'Ozark Pink', 'Solar Set', 'Sun Chaser', 'Sun Leaper', and 'Sunmaster'; paste tomato 'Viva Italia'; cherry tomato 'Sun Gold'; and heirloom 'Arkansas Traveler'.

Large-fruited tomatoes. These grow to full size where the growing season is warm and long. Fruits can weigh more than a pound. 'Beefsteak', 'Beefmaster', 'Big Boy', 'Brandywine', 'German Johnson', and 'Mortgage Lifter' are typical. 'Burpee Supersteak' can produce 2-pound fruits; 'Goliath' weighs in at 3 pounds; 'Giant Belgium' has tipped the scales at 5 pounds; and 'Delicious' has produced a tomato weighing 7 pounds, 12 ounces for Gordon Graham of Edmond, Oklahoma.

Small-fruited tomatoes. Plants bear large clusters of round, oblong, or pear-shaped fruits that range from grape size to cherry size. Grape types include 'Juliet' and 'Summer Sweet'. Among standard cherry types are 'Gardener's Delight', 'Jolly', 'Sun Gold', 'Sweet 100', and 'Sweet Million'. 'Yellow Pear' and 'Red Pear' are pear-shaped novelties. Small-fruited types that grow on dwarf plants suitable for pots or hanging baskets include 'Florida Basket', 'Florida Petite', 'Micro-Tom', 'Patio', 'Small Fry', and 'Tiny Tim'.

Paste tomatoes. These bear prodigious quantities of meaty, oval fruits. Often called plum tomatoes, they're favorites for canning, sauces, and tomato paste. Look for 'La Roma', 'Plum Dandy', 'Roma', 'San Marzano', and 'Viva Italia'.

Novelty tomatoes. Among these are selections of various colors: yellow ('Lemon Boy', 'Yellow Brandywine'), orange ('Orange Banana', 'Sun Gold'), white ('White Beauty'), green ('Evergreen'), and even striped ('Green Zebra', 'Mr. Stripey'). 'Health Kick' contains 50% more of the antioxidant lycopene than other tomatoes. 'Long Keeper' stays fresh in storage (at 60–70°F) for 3 months. 'Red Stuffer' and 'Yellow Stuffer' produce large, hollow fruits that resemble bell peppers.

Heirloom tomatoes. Varying in size, appearance, and growth habit, these represent old types lovingly maintained by tomato growers all over the country. 'Brandywine', thought to have been developed by the Pennsylvania Amish, is considered by many to be the best-tasting tomato of all. Unfortunately, it doesn't like our Southern summers. Better bets for the South include 'Arkansas Traveler', 'Cherokee Purple', 'Eva Purple Ball', 'German Johnson', 'Giant Belgium', 'Mule Team', and 'Mortgage Lifter'.

Determinate tomatoes. Examples of these bushy types include 'Celebrity', 'Floramerica', 'Health Kick', 'Heatwave', 'La Roma', 'Long Keeper', 'Patio', 'Rutgers', 'Sunmaster', and 'Viva Italia'.

Indeterminate tomatoes. 'Arkansas Traveler', 'Atkinson', 'Beefmaster', 'Better Boy', 'Big Boy', 'Creole', 'Delicious', 'Early Girl', 'First Lady', 'German Johnson', 'Juliet', 'Mortgage Lifter', 'Supersonic', and 'Sweet Million' are just a few of the plants in the vinelike category.

TORCH GINGER. See ETLINGERA elatior

TORCH LILY. See KNIPHOFIA

TORENIA fournieri

WISHBONE FLOWER

Scrophulariaceae

ANNUAL

🌿 US, MS, LS, CS, TS ⊩ 12–1

☼ PARTIAL SHADE

💧 REGULAR WATER

Torenia fournieri

From tropical Asia. Compact, bushy, to 1 ft. high and wide. Blooms from summer into autumn; the flowers look like miniature gloxinias

(*Sinningia*), have stamens arranged in wishbone shape. Species has pale lavender blossoms with deeper purple markings and bright yellow throat; a white-flowered form is also sold. Sow seeds in pots and transplant to garden after frost danger is past; or buy nursery plants. Use as edging or in pots and window boxes. Keep roots cool with a mulch. Summer Wave hybrids thrive in heat and take more sun; their spreading habit makes them a good choice for hanging baskets. Duchess strain prefers more shade, is more compact (6–8 in. tall and wide), and offers blooms in four color combinations: light blue with blue throat, blue with white throat, deep blue with blue throat, and pink with white throat.

TOVARA virginiana. See PERSICARIA virginiana

TRACHELOSPERMUM

STAR JASMINE

Apocynaceae

EVERGREEN SHRUBS OR VINES

🌿 LS, CS, TS ⊩ 11–8

☼ ☼ FULL SUN OR PARTIAL SHADE

💧 💧 MODERATE TO REGULAR WATER

Trachelospermum jasminoides

These old favorites are among the most versatile and useful of plants, serving as ground covers, trailers, or climbers. They bear delightfully fragrant, pinwheel-shaped blossoms in spring and early summer. Plant in well-drained soil; for lush growth, fertilize once before spring growth begins, again after flowering. Prune back as needed to shape. Cut stems exude a milky sap.

T. asiaticum. ASIAN STAR JASMINE. From Japan, Korea. Excellent, tough, fast-growing ground cover. Hardier than *T. jasminoides,* with smaller, darker, duller green leaves; flowers are also smaller, in creamy yellow or yellowish white. Selections grown for attractive foliage include 'Bronze Beauty', with bronzy new growth maturing to dark green, and 'Elegant' ('Asia Minor'), featuring small, very dark green leaves.

T. jasminoides. CONFEDERATE JASMINE, STAR JASMINE. From China. Given support, a twining vine to 20–30 ft.; without support and with some tip-pinching, a spreading shrub or ground cover to 1½–2 ft. tall, 4–5 ft. wide. Oval leaves to 3 in. long are glossy light green when new, mature to lustrous dark green. Profusion of white, inch-wide flowers in small clusters on short side branches. Attractive to bees. If grown as a shrubby plant, it is good in raised beds or entry gardens, for edging a walk or drive, as extension of lawn, spilling over walls, as ground cover under trees and shrubs. Set plants 5 ft. apart for ground cover. As a vine, good for training on a wall, pergola, trellis, or over a doorway. Leaves of 'Variegatum' are bordered and blotched in white.

TRACHYCARPUS fortunei

WINDMILL PALM

Arecaceae (Palmae)

PALM

🌿 LS, CS, TS ⊩ 12–7; OR HOUSEPLANT

☼ ☼ FULL SUN OR LIGHT SHADE; BRIGHT INDIRECT LIGHT

💧 💧 MODERATE TO REGULAR WATER

Trachycarpus fortunei

From China. Medium-size, very hardy fan palm (to 10°F or lower). Moderate to fast growth to 30 ft. high, 10 ft. wide. Trunk is usually thicker at top than at bottom and is covered with dense, blackish fiber; as trunk elongates, fiber falls off its lower portion. Toothed, 1½-ft. stalks carry 3-ft.-wide leaves. Tolerates some drought and is quite easy to grow. May look untidy in high winds. Sometimes sold as *Chamaerops excelsa.* Young plants can be grown indoors in good light (but with protection from hot sun); plant them outdoors when they become too big. Selection 'Charlotte' is especially hardy—down to 5°F.

T

TRACHYMENE coerulea

BLUE LACE FLOWER

Apiaceae (Umbelliferae)

COOL-SEASON ANNUAL

US, MS, LS, CS, TS **H** 6–1

FULL SUN

REGULAR WATER

Trachymene coerulea

From Australia. Upright plant to 2 ft. tall, 10 in. wide, with finely divided leaves and numerous small lavender-blue flowers in 2- to 3-in.-wide, flat-topped clusters. Blossoms have a lacy look, make good cut flowers. Grow in light, rich, well-drained soil. Sow seeds in place, as taproot makes transplanting difficult. Does not perform well in heat. Sow in fall for winter and spring bloom. Once sold as *Didiscus coeruleus*.

TRADESCANTIA

Commelinaceae

PERENNIALS

ZONES VARY BY SPECIES

EXPOSURE NEEDS VARY BY SPECIES

WATER NEEDS VARY BY SPECIES

Tradescantia pallida 'Purpurea'

Most are virtually indestructible plants with long, trailing stems. Usually seen in pots or hanging baskets, but can be used as ground covers—though the most vigorous, rambling types are likely to be invasive. On variegated forms, pinch out any growth that reverts to solid green. Deer don't normally browse these plants. Types grown as houseplants should be given bright indirect light and kept fairly moist; feed them with a general-purpose liquid houseplant fertilizer twice a month from spring through fall, once a month in winter.

T. ×andersoniana. See T. virginiana

T. fluminensis. WANDERING JEW. Zones CS, TS; 12–1; or houseplant. From South America. Rapid grower to 2 in. high, with indefinite spread. Succulent stems have swollen joints where dark green, oval or oblong, 2½-in.-long leaves are attached. Tiny, unshowy white flowers. Easy to grow. Excellent for window boxes and dish gardens. If plants are overgrown, renovate by cutting back severely; or discard them and start new plants with fresh tip growth. Stems will live a long time in water, rooting quickly and easily. Partial to full shade; regular to ample water. Variegated forms include 'Albovittata', leaves finely and evenly streaked with white; 'Aurea', bright yellow-green foliage; 'Laekenensis Rainbow', leaves banded in white and pale lavender; and 'Variegata', yellow- or white-striped foliage.

T. pallida 'Purpurea' (Setcreasea pallida 'Purple Heart'). PURPLE HEART, PURPLE QUEEN. Zones MS, LS, CS, TS; 12–1; or houseplant. From Mexico. Creeping plant to 1–1½ ft. high, 1 ft. wide; stems tend to flop. Pointed, rather narrowly oval leaves are strongly shaded with purple, particularly on undersides. Pale or deep purple flowers (not showy). *T. p.* 'Variegata' is similar, but leaves are striped lengthwise in pink and red. Pinch back after bloom. Generally unattractive in winter. Frost may kill tops, but recovery is fast in warm weather. Use as ground cover, for bedding, in pots. Full sun or light shade. Moderate water.

T. spathacea (Rhoeo spathacea). MOSES-IN-THE-CRADLE, OYSTER PLANT. From Mexico, Central America. Zones TS; 12–1; or houseplant. Grows 2 ft. tall and 1 ft. wide. Each plant has a dozen or so broad, sword-shaped, rather erect leaves that are dark green above, deep purple beneath. Small, three-petaled white blooms are interesting rather than beautiful, crowded into boat-shaped bracts borne down among leaves. There is also a dwarf form. 'Variegata' has leaves striped in red and yellowish green. Most often used as a potted plant or in hanging baskets. Tough plant; takes heat, low humidity, sun or

Tradescantia spathacea

shade. Best with regular moisture but withstands inconsistent watering. Try to keep water out of leaf joints when irrigating.

T. virginiana. SPIDERWORT. Zones US, MS, LS, CS; 9–5. From the eastern U.S., but long a favorite in Southern gardens. Clump-forming border plant to 1½ ft. high and wide. Long, grassy-looking, deep green, erect or arching leaves. Three-petaled flowers last for only a day, but buds come in large clusters, and plants are seldom out of bloom in summer. May self-sow and become somewhat invasive. Divide clumps when crowded. Sun or shade; regular to ample water. Named garden selections offer flowers in white, blue shades, lavender, purple, shades of pink from pale to near-red; these plants are often sold as *T. ×andersoniana*.

T. zebrina (Zebrina pendula). WANDERING JEW. Zone TS; or houseplant. From southern Mexico. Similar to *T. fluminensis* but not as hardy; bears pinkish or bluish flowers. Most widely grown are forms with colorful leaves, including 'Quadricolor', purplish green leaves with longitudinal bands of silver, pink, and red; and 'Purpusii', dark red or greenish red foliage. Attractive ground covers for shady, frost-free sites. Partial to full shade. Regular water.

TRANSVAAL DAISY. See GERBERA jamesonii

TREE FERN. See CIBOTIUM, CYATHEA cooperi, DICKSONIA

TREE MALLOW. See LAVATERA

TREE-OF-HEAVEN. See AILANTHUS altissima

TRICYRTIS

TOAD LILY

Liliaceae

PERENNIALS

US, MS, LS, CS **H** 9–1, EXCEPT AS NOTED

PARTIAL TO FULL SHADE

REGULAR TO AMPLE WATER

Tricyrtis hirta

Woodland plants that resemble false Solomon's seal (*Smilacina*) in foliage. Interesting, heavily spotted, inch-long flowers appear at leaf joints and in terminal clusters in late summer and fall. They are complex in structure, somewhat orchidlike: each blossom has three petals and three sepals, with a column of decorative stamens and styles rising from the center. Need soil enriched with plenty of organic matter. Excellent companions to ferns, foamflower (*Tiarella*), and hostas. Unfortunately (like hostas), they are a favorite snack for voles.

T. formosana (T. stolonifera). Heat zones 9–6. From Taiwan. To 2½ ft. tall. Spreads by aboveground runners to form a clump 1½ ft. or wider, but is not invasive. More erect than *T. hirta*, with flowers mostly in terminal clusters. Leaves are green, mottled with deeper green; brown or maroon buds open to white to pale lilac flowers spotted with purple. 'Amethystina' blooms several weeks earlier than species, bears lavender-blue blossoms with red-spotted white throat. 'Gates of Heaven' has bright golden foliage and purple flowers. Late-blooming 'Variegata' has lavender blossoms and gold-edged leaves.

T. hirta. From Japan. To 3 ft. tall, 2 ft. wide; it lacks runners. Arching stems bear pale green, softly hairy foliage. White to pale lilac blossoms are peppered with purple; they appear in leaf joints all along the stems. 'Miyazaki' bears pink to white flowers with crimson spots; 'Miyazaki Gold' is similar but has gold-edged leaves. 'White Towers' has pure white blossoms with purple stamens.

T. hybrids. The following two hybrids feature extra-large blooms. 'Empress', to 2 ft. high and 1 ft. wide, bears spidery-petaled blossoms in white heavily spotted with purple. 'Togen', to 3 ft. high and 2 ft. wide, has flowers that are lavender purple at the tips, fading to white in the center.

T. macropoda (T. dilatata). Heat zones 9–8. From China. Upright growth to 2 ft. high, 16 in. wide. Rounded gray leaves are unspotted. Profuse show of white flowers with purple spots and backward-pointing petals. 'Tricolor' has gray leaves striped with pink and white.

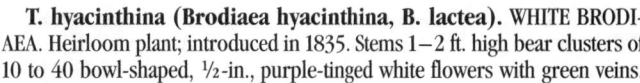

TRILLIUM

WAKE ROBIN

Liliaceae

PERENNIALS

⚡ US, MS, LS, EXCEPT AS NOTED

◐ ● PARTIAL TO FULL SHADE

💧 REGULAR WATER

Trillium grandiflorum

If you asked folks to name their favorite wildflowers, these charming woodland plants would rank high on many lists. They bloom in early spring and need some winter chill. Each stem is topped with a whorl of three leaves; from center of these rises a single flower with three petals. Plant the thick, deep-growing, fleshy rhizomes in a shady, woodsy site. Left undisturbed, they will gradually increase. Plants die to the ground in mid- to late summer. In addition to species listed below, many others are offered by specialists in native plants. Browsing deer often pass trilliums by.

T. catesbaei (T. stylosum). CATESBY TRILLIUM. From the southeastern U.S. Resembles *T. grandiflorum* but has pink flowers.

T. decipiens. Zones LS, CS; 9–8. From Alabama, Georgia, and Florida. To 6–18 in. high, 4 in. wide. Mottled green leaves with pale centers, to 7 in. long. Greenish flowers, sometimes with purplish tints. Takes limy soils.

T. erectum. PURPLE TRILLIUM. Heat zones 9–1. From eastern North America. Grows to 2 ft. high, 1 ft. wide, with 7-in. leaves and 2-in., erect, brownish purple flowers. Sometimes known by the name "stinking Benjamin" due to the odd odor of its flowers.

T. grandiflorum. WHITE TRILLIUM. Heat zones 8–3. From eastern North America. The showiest trillium. To 1½ ft. tall, 1 ft. wide, with stout stems and 2½- to 6-in.-long leaves. Nearly stalkless flowers are nodding, to 3 in. across, white aging to rose. Several choice double-flowered forms are available, including 'Flore Pleno'.

T. recurvatum. PRAIRIE TRILLIUM, BLOODY BUTCHER. Heat zones 8–3. Native to eastern U.S. To 15 in. high, 1 ft. wide. Leaves to 3 in. long, spotted in reddish purple; purple-brown flowers.

T. sessile. TOADSHADE. Heat zones 8–1. From northeastern U.S. Grows 1 ft. high, 8 in. wide, with purple-spotted, 5-in.-long leaves and dark purplish red flowers.

T. underwoodii. UNDERWOOD'S TRILLIUM. Zones LS, CS; 9–5. Native to southeast U.S. To 8 in. tall, not quite as wide. Dark purple flowers contrast nicely with the beautiful foliage: 2- to 4-in.-long leaves mottled in light and dark green, with an irregular silver streak running down the center.

T. undulatum. PAINTED TRILLIUM. Heat zones 8–1. From eastern U.S. To 1½ ft. high, 6 in. wide, with 6-in. leaves and upright, somewhat nodding, 1½-in. white flowers marked reddish purple near petal bases. Not easy to grow; needs cool conditions and acid soil.

TRITELEIA

Liliaceae

PERENNIALS FROM CORMS

⚡ US, MS, LS, CS H 10–6

☀ FULL SUN

◇ NO IRRIGATION NEEDED

Triteleia laxa

Many are native to the West Coast, where they bloom in sunny fields and meadows in spring and early summer, but they also adapt to Midwestern prairies and the Texas Hill Country. Plants sport a few grasslike leaves topped by a cluster of funnel-shaped or tubular, ½- to 2-in.-long blossoms; they die to the ground after blooming. Good cut flowers.

These plants grow naturally in heavy adobe soil in areas that are rainy in winter and early spring, then dry the rest of the year. If you can't provide a long dry period, be sure to plant in sandy or gritty soil. Set corms 2–3 in. deep and 2–4 in. apart. Many *Triteleia* species were previously listed as *Brodiaea*.

T. hyacinthina (Brodiaea hyacinthina, B. lactea). WHITE BRODIAEA. Heirloom plant; introduced in 1835. Stems 1–2 ft. high bear clusters of 10 to 40 bowl-shaped, ½-in., purple-tinged white flowers with green veins.

T. ixioides (Brodiaea ixioides, B. lutea). PRETTY FACE, GOLDEN BRODIAEA. Flower stalk to 2 ft.; inch-long, golden yellow flowers with purple-black midrib and veins. 'Starlight' has soft yellow buds that open to creamy white, star-shaped flowers.

T. laxa (Brodiaea laxa). GRASS NUT, ITHURIEL'S SPEAR. Stalks to 2 ft. tall are topped with trumpet-shaped, ¾- to 1½-in.-long purple-blue flowers. 'Königin Fabiola' ('Queen Fabiola') sports large, upward-facing dark blue flowers.

T. ×tubergenii. Blossom stalk 1½–2½ ft. tall; 1-in. lavender-blue flowers with petals edged in darker blue.

TROLLIUS

GLOBEFLOWER

Ranunculaceae

PERENNIALS

⚡ US, MS H 8–5, EXCEPT AS NOTED

☀ ◐ FULL SUN OR PARTIAL SHADE

💧💧 REGULAR TO AMPLE WATER

Trollius chinensis

Clumps of finely cut, shiny dark green leaves put up 2- to 3-ft.-tall stems bearing yellow to orange flowers typically shaped like globes or rounded cups. Remove faded flowers to prolong bloom. Excellent cut flowers. Cannot take drought or extreme heat; constantly damp area near a pond or stream is an ideal planting site. If you are growing globeflowers in a regular garden bed, liberally amend soil with organic matter and keep well watered. Divide clumps only when they thin out in center.

T. chinensis (T. ledebourii). Heat zones 8–1. From China, Siberia. To 3 ft. tall, 1½ ft. wide. Light orange-yellow, 2-in. flowers with open bowl shape; summer bloom.

T. ×cultorum. Group of hybrids between *T. europaeus* and two Asian species. Plants grow to 2–3 ft. tall and resemble *T. europaeus* in most details. Bloom comes at some time from spring into summer, depending on hybrid. Choices include 2-ft. 'Earliest of All', with pale orange-yellow blooms; 2-ft. 'Golden Queen', deep orange; and 2½-ft. 'Lemon Queen', soft yellow.

T. europaeus. COMMON GLOBEFLOWER. To 1½–2 ft. tall, 1½ ft. wide. Globular, lemon yellow or orange flowers, 1–2 in. across, in spring. Somewhat more tolerant of dry soil than other species.

TROPAEOLUM majus

NASTURTIUM

Tropaeolaceae

COOL-SEASON ANNUAL

⚡ US, MS, LS, CS, TS H 6–1

☀ ◐ FULL SUN OR LIGHT SHADE

💧 REGULAR WATER

Tropaeolum majus

Few flowers capture the carefree feeling of a cottage garden better than nasturtiums, whether they're poking through a wire fence, spilling from a window box, or tumbling over rocks. These easy-to-grow plants fall into two main groups. Mounding types are bushy; they grow to 15 in. tall and stay put. Climbing types trail over the ground or use coiling leafstalks to climb as high as 6 ft. Both sport distinctive, long-stemmed, rounded leaves with prominent veins and a fresh bright green color. Broad, showy blossoms (to 2½ in. across) have a pleasant fragrance and come in many colors, including orange, yellow, maroon, red, and creamy white; you can get mixed or single colors in seed packs. Both single- and double-flowered forms are available. Young leaves, flowers, and unripe seedpods add a peppery flavor to salads. ▶

T

Nasturtiums need well-drained, preferably sandy soil. They give out in hot weather, so grow them as a cool-season annual. To speed germination, soak the large seeds in water overnight before planting. In the Upper, Middle, and Lower South, plant immediately after the last spring frost for spring and early summer flowers. In the Coastal and Tropical South, sow in fall for autumn and winter blooms. Fertilize sparingly or you'll get all leaves and no flowers. Use nasturtiums in hanging baskets, pots, or window boxes, as bedding plants or flowering ground covers.

Popular selections include Alaska series (mounding type with variegated leaves speckled in cream and flowers in yellow, coral, or dark red); 'Empress of India' (mounding, with blue-green leaves and dark scarlet blossoms); 'Moonlight' (climbing, with pale yellow blooms); Out of Africa series (climbing, with cream-variegated leaves and red, yellow, peach, or cream flowers); 'Vesuvius' (mounding, with blue-green leaves and salmon blooms); and Whirlybird Mix (mounding, with yellow, orange, rose, and red blooms).

TROUT LILY. See ERYTHRONIUM americanum

TRUMPET CREEPER, TRUMPET VINE. See CAMPSIS, DISTICTIS

TSUGA

HEMLOCK
Pinaceae
EVERGREEN TREES
⚡ ZONES VARY BY SPECIES
☀️◐ FULL SUN OR PARTIAL SHADE, EXCEPT AS NOTED
💧 REGULAR WATER

These are mostly big trees with horizontal to drooping branches and an unusually graceful appearance. Needlelike leaves are banded with white beneath, flattened and narrowed at the base to form distinct, short stalks. Small, oval, medium brown cones hang down from branches. Bark is deeply furrowed, cinnamon colored to brown.

Tsuga canadensis

All hemlocks need some winter chill; all are shallow rooted. They do best in acid soil and high summer humidity, with protection from hot sun and wind. Take well to heavy pruning; make excellent clipped hedges, screens. Easily damaged by salt and drought. Subject to various pests and diseases, but damage is not always serious if plants are well grown. Recently, a woolly adelgid (a type of aphid) has caused the decline and even death of many hemlocks stressed by drought and improper cultural practices.

T. canadensis. CANADIAN HEMLOCK. Zones US, MS, LS (cooler parts); 8–1. Native from Nova Scotia to Minnesota, southward along mountain ranges to Alabama and Georgia. Dense, pyramidal tree grows 40–70 ft. or taller, half as wide. Tends to be multitrunked. Outer branchlets droop gracefully. Dark green, about ½-in.-long needles are mostly arranged in opposite rows on branchlets. Fine specimen tree, tall screen, or clipped hedge. Needs afternoon shade in the Lower South. 'Pendula', Sargent weeping hemlock, grows slowly to 10–15 ft. tall and twice as wide, with pendulous branches; with careful pruning, it can easily be kept to handsome, 2- to 3-ft., cascading mound suitable for a large rock garden. 'Cole's Prostrate' is 1 ft. tall (usually less) and spreads to 3 ft. or more. 'Gentsch White', to 2 ft. high and 1½ ft. wide, has white-tipped new growth. Many other dwarf, weeping, and variegated selections are sold.

T. caroliniana. CAROLINA HEMLOCK. Zones US, MS; 7–3. Native to mountains in the southeastern U.S. Resembles *T. canadensis* but is somewhat slower growing, a little stiffer in habit, and darker green in color. Longer needles are arranged all around the twigs instead of in opposite rows. More tolerant of polluted air and city conditions than *T. canadensis*, but not as well adapted to lowlands of the eastern seaboard.

TUBEROSE. See POLIANTHES tuberosa

TULBAGHIA

Amaryllidaceae
PERENNIALS FROM RHIZOMES
⚡ LS, CS, TS ❘❘ 11–7
☀️ FULL SUN
💧 REGULAR WATER

Tulbaghia violacea

From South Africa. Dense clumps of straight, narrow, evergreen leaves send up slim, 1- to 2-ft. stems topped by clusters of small, trumpet-shaped, pinkish lavender flowers. Suffer frost damage at 20–25°F but recover quickly. Start plants from containers or divisions in early spring or early fall. Give well-drained, organically enriched soil. Divide clumps to increase plantings; set divisions 1½ ft. apart.

T. simmleri (T. fragrans). Gray-green, 1-in.-wide leaves. Lightly fragrant flowers in clusters of 20 to 30 in winter or early spring. Good cut flower. 'Alba' has white blossoms.

T. violacea. SOCIETY GARLIC. Bluish green, very narrow leaves. Clusters of 8 to 20 flowers; bloom is heaviest in spring and summer. Leaves and flower stems have an onion or garlic odor if cut or crushed; leaves can be used in cooking. Deer don't browse these plants. 'Variegata' has a creamy stripe down the middle of each leaf; in 'Silver Lace', leaves are edged in white. Foliage of 'Tricolor' has white edges with a pinkish cast that intensifies in cool weather.

TULIPA

TULIP
Liliaceae
PERENNIALS FROM BULBS
⚡ US, MS ❘❘ 8–1; TREAT MOST AS ANNUALS IN LS, CS, TS
☀️◐ FULL SUN DURING BLOOM, PART SHADE AFTER IN HOT CLIMATES
💧 REGULAR WATER DURING GROWTH AND BLOOM

Darwin Hybrid Tulip

No other spring bulb matches the tulip for sheer spectacle. Tulips come in just about every color; their imposing flowers atop strong stems form the backbone of many a spring garden display. If you've only tried the big-flowered sorts, though, you're missing out on a lot. Many kinds are available, from the tall and stately to the dainty and whimsical—and even to the decidedly bizarre. In fact, many of the smaller, lesser-known species perform better in the South than their aristocratic cousins.

Nearly all hybrid tulips and most species types need an extended period of winter chill to bloom well. This poses a problem for gardeners in the Lower, Coastal, and Tropical South, where winters are short and mild. To ensure sufficient chilling, gardeners in these areas should refrigerate bulbs for 8 to 10 weeks prior to planting in fall (don't put them in the freezer). Bloom comes at some time from March to May, depending on type.

Even with proper care, hybrid tulips (categorized below as early, midseason, and late types) are not a long-term investment. The bulbs form offsets that take a few years to reach blooming size, but as these mature, they draw energy from the mother bulb. The result is a gradual decline in flowering. For this reason, most hybrid tulips are best treated as annuals or short-lived perennials. You can encourage repeat flowering by fertilizing with a 9-9-6 bulb fertilizer just as shoots break the soil in spring and also by allowing foliage to yellow and wither before removing it. In areas with warm, wet summer soil, bulbs are prone to rot and shouldn't be counted on for more than a year or two. A number of species tulips, however, perform quite well under these conditions.

Large-flowered tulips, such as the Darwin Hybrids, are ideal for sweeps and borders; mass at least 50 of a single color for impact. Plant them behind low, spring-blooming perennials such as candytuft (*Iberis*) or pinks (*Dianthus*), or with annuals such as forget-me-nots (*Myosotis*), sweet alyssum (*Lobularia*), or pansies and violas (*Viola*). Plant smaller, lower-growing species in rock gardens, raised beds, and alongside paths. Tulips are superb container plants; especially lovely in this role are the more unusual kinds, such as the Double Early, Parrot, and Rembrandt types.

Buy tulips as soon as you see them offered in garden centers. Choose the biggest bulbs you can find; bigger bulbs produce bigger flowers. Look for firm, fat bulbs; avoid those that are soft, shriveled, or moldy.

Squirrels, chipmunks, and gophers like tulips as much as you do, but for a different reason. To keep these pesky rodents from gobbling up your bulbs, plant the bulbs inside baskets made from ¼-in. wire mesh. See care box for additional cultural information.

Tulips have been classified into many divisions, defined mainly by flower type. For the convenience of gardeners, we have arranged the divisions into additional groupings; the first three are by bloom season, while the fourth contains species and their hybrids. For most divisions, we've also included "best bets"—selections that perform especially well in the South.

EARLY TULIPS

Single Early tulips. Single flowers on 10- to 16-in. stems. Colors include white, yellow, salmon, pink, red, dark purple. Popular for forcing and growing indoors in pots. Best bets include 'Apricot Beauty' (soft salmon pink), 'Christmas Marvel' (cherry red), and 'Flair' (yellow heavily marked with red).

Double Early tulips. Peonylike double flowers, often measuring 4 in. across, on 6- to 12-in. stems. Same color range as Single Early tulips. Effective massed in borders. In rainy areas, mulch around plants or surround with ground cover to keep mud from splashing the short-stemmed flowers. Look for 'Monsella' (yellow with red streaks) and 'Monte Carlo' (bright yellow).

MIDSEASON TULIPS

Triumph tulips. Single flowers on sturdy stems to 20 in. tall. Wide range of solid colors, including red, white, and yellow, and bicolors. Try 'Arabian Mystery' (purple fringed with white) and 'Hibernia' (white).

Darwin hybrids. Spectacular group with brightly colored flowers on 24- to 28-in. stems. Most are in scarlet-orange to red range; some have contrasting eyes or penciling. Some reach 7 in. across. Pink, yellow, and white selections exist. Best bets include 'Daydream' (apricot orange), 'General Eisenhower' (scarlet red), 'Golden Apeldoorn' (golden yellow), 'Golden Oxford' (golden yellow), 'Gudoshnik' (yellow heavily marked with red), 'Ivory Floradale' (ivory white), 'Jewel of Spring' (soft yellow with thin red margins), 'Oxford' (scarlet red), and 'Pink Impression' (soft pink marked with deep rose).

LATE TULIPS

Single Late. Graceful plants with large, oval or egg-shaped blooms on 1½- to 3-ft. stems. Clear, beautiful colors: white, yellow, orange, pink, red, mauve, lilac, purple, maroon. May have contrasting margins. Includes old Darwin and Cottage groups. Good choices are 'Maureen' (white), 'Queen of Night' (blackish maroon), and 'Temple of Beauty' (salmon rose).

Lily-flowered tulips. Graceful, lilylike flowers with recurved, pointed segments; come in white and shades of yellow, pink, red, and magenta, often with contrasting markings. Stems 20–26 in. high. Look for the elegant 'White Triumphator' (ivory white).

Fringed tulips. Flowers have finely fringed edges. Colors include white, yellow, pink, red, and violet; fringing is often in a different color than rest of flower. Stems 16–24 in. high. Recommended are 'Fringed Elegance' (yellow), 'Burgundy Lace' (wine red), and 'Swan Wings' (white).

Viridiflora tulips. Flowers edged in green or colored in blends of green with other hues—white, yellow, rose, red, buff. Stems 10–20 in. high. Try 'Spring Green' (white and soft green), 'Groenland' ('Greenland'; rose pink and green), and 'Formosa' (yellow and green).

Rembrandt tulips. Streaks and variegation on the original Rembrandts were caused by a transmittable virus; these infected bulbs can no longer be imported and should not be planted. Tulips now sold as Rembrandts have

patterning of genetic, not viral, origin. The division now includes other variegated types and the old Bizarre and Bybloem groups.

Parrot tulips. Large, long, deeply fringed and ruffled flowers atop 16- to 20-in. stems are striped, feathered, and flamed in various colors, including green. They once had weak, floppy stems, but modern types are stouter. Best bets include 'Blue Parrot' (deep violet) and 'Orange Favorite' (deep orange).

Double Late tulips. Often called peony-flowered tulips, these have very large (to 5-in.-wide), heavy-textured double blossoms on 14- to 20-in. stems. Colors include orange, rose, red to purple shades, yellow, and white. Recommendations include 'Angelique' (pink and white), 'Mount Tacoma' (white), 'Orange Princess' (orange marked with purple), and 'Uncle Tom' (deep maroon).

SPECIES TULIPS

Kaufmanniana tulips. Often called waterlily tulip, *T. kaufmanniana* is a very early bloomer with 3-in., creamy yellow flowers (marked red on petal backs) with dark yellow centers; the flowers open flat in sun. Stems reach 6–8 in. high. Hybrids come in various colors, usually with flower centers in a contrasting color; many have mottled leaves like Greigii tulips.

Fosteriana tulips. Early-blooming *T. fosteriana* has the largest flowers—to 8 in. wide—of any tulip. The huge red blossoms appear atop 8- to 10-in. stems. Hybrids include selections with flowers in red, orange, yellow, pink, and white. The 16-in.-high 'Red Emperor' ('Mme Lefeber') has fiery red flowers.

Greigii tulips. Midseason-blooming *T. greigii* has big (6-in.) flowers borne on 10-in. stems; leaves are heavily spotted and streaked with brown. Hybrids have flowers in white, pink, orange, red; many feature several colors in a single blossom.

Other species. Sold mainly by bulb specialists. Most are from western and central Asia. Simpler looking than large hybrid tulips, with a wildflower charm. Generally best in rock gardens or wild gardens, where plantings can remain undisturbed for many years; plant 4 in. apart. Also good in pots. Species that will persist from year to year in mild-winter areas are noted.

T

TOP: Fringed Tulips
BOTTOM: *Tulipa kaufmanniana*

TOP: Darwin Hybrid Tulip 'Ivory Floradale'
BOTTOM: *Tulipa greigii*

TOP: *Tulipa fosteriana* Hybrids
BOTTOM: Darwin Hybrid Tulip 'Daydream'

TOP: Lily-flowered Tulips
BOTTOM: Double Late Tulip 'Angelique'

TOP: *Tulipa tarda*
BOTTOM: Parrot Tulip 'Orange Favorite'

T. acuminata. Flowers have long, twisted, spidery segments of red and yellow on 1½-ft.-tall stems. Late.

T. bakeri. Similar to and often listed as *T. saxatilis*. Lilac to purple flowers with a yellow base open to a wide, flat star; they are borne in clusters of three or four on stems to 1 ft. high. 'Lilac Wonder', to 6–7 in. high, has rosy purple flowers with a large, circular lemon yellow base. Midseason. Good in mild-winter areas.

T. batalinii. Soft yellow flowers on 6- to 10-in. stems. Very narrow leaves. 'Red Jewel' has scarlet red blossoms; 'Yellow Jewel' has lemon yellow blossoms tinged with rose. Midseason.

T. clusiana. LADY or CANDY TULIP. Slender flowers on 9-in. stems are rosy red outside, white inside. Midseason bloom; good permanent tulips in mild-winter areas. Segments of 'Cynthia' are red with a green margin on the outside, solid green on the inside. Blossoms of 6-in.-high *T. c. chrysantha (T. stellata chrysantha)* are star shaped when fully open; they have rose carmine outer segments (shading to buff at base), bright yellow inner segments.

T. daystemon. See T. tarda

T. eichleri. Foot-tall stems bear shining scarlet flowers with jet black centers outlined in yellow. Early.

T. humilis (T. pulchella). One to three pale pink or purplish pink flowers with a yellow center atop each 4- to 6-in. stem. Early. 'Violacea' has deep violet flowers, usually with a yellow base.

T. praestans. Up to six orange-red flowers on each 2-ft. stem. Midseason. 'Fusilier' is an improved selection growing 10–14 in. high.

T. pulchella. See T. humilis

T. saxatilis. Fragrant, yellow-based pale lilac flowers open nearly flat, are carried one to three to each 1-ft. stem. Early. Good choice for areas with mild winters.

T. stellata chrysantha. See T. clusiana chrysantha

T. sylvestris. Yellow, 2-in. flowers, one or two to each 1-ft. stem. Late. Good in mild-winter areas.

T. tarda (T. dasystemon). Each 3- to 5-in. stem has three to six upward-facing, starlike flowers with golden centers, white-tipped segments. Early.

TULIP POPLAR. See LIRIODENDRON tulipifera

TULIP TREE. See MAGNOLIA ×soulangeana

TUNG-OIL TREE. See ALEURITES fordii

A PRACTICAL GUIDE TO GARDENING
PLEASE SEE PAGES 596–669

TUPELO. See NYSSA

TURKEYFOOT. See ANDROPOGON gerardii

TURK'S CAP, TURK'S TURBAN. See MALVAVISCUS arboreus drummondii

TURNIP and RUTABAGA

Brassicaceae (Cruciferae)

BIENNIALS GROWN AS COOL-SEASON ANNUALS

✐ US, MS, LS, CS, TS ☰ 7–1

☼ FULL SUN

◗ REGULAR WATER

Turnip

These Mediterranean natives are cabbage relatives and, like cabbage, belong to the genus *Brassica*. Although turnips are best known in other parts of the country for their roots, in the South their leaves are also enjoyed as a green vegetable and some selections are grown for leaves only. Turnip roots come in various colors (white, white topped with purple, creamy yellow) and shapes (globe, flattened globe). Rutabaga is a tasty turnip relative with large yellowish roots; its leaves are palatable only when very young (they turn coarse as they mature). Turnip roots are quick growing and should be harvested and used as soon as big enough to eat; rutabaga is a late-maturing crop that stores well in the ground. Flavor of rutabaga improves with light frost.

Grow both in rich, loose, well-drained soil. In the Upper and Middle South, plant in early spring for early summer harvest, or in summer for fall harvest. Elsewhere, plant in August to October for fall and winter crops. Before planting, apply ½ cup of 10-10-10 fertilizer per 10 ft. of row to the soil and water in. Sow seeds ½ in. deep, 1 in. apart. Thin turnips to 2–6 in. apart if growing for roots, 1–4 in. apart for greens. Thin rutabagas to 5–8 in. apart; they need ample space for roots to reach full weight of 3 to 5 pounds.

Roots of both turnip and rutabaga are milder flavored if soil is kept moist; they become more pungent under drier conditions. Turnip roots are ready to harvest 40–70 days after sowing, rutabaga in 90 to 120 days. Cabbage root maggot is a pest of turnip (it is less likely to infest rutabaga); see Cabbage for control. For a quick crop of greens only, try 'Seven Top' (45 days). For both turnip greens and tasty roots, plant 'Purple-Top White Globe' (50–60 days), 'Royal Crown' (45–55 days), or 'White Lady' (35–45 days). A widely recommended rutabaga is 'American Purple Top' (90 days).

TURTLEHEAD. See CHELONE

TWEEDIA caerulea

Tweedia caerulea

SOUTHERN STAR, STAR OF THE ARGENTINE

Asclepiadaceae

PERENNIAL

CS, TS H 12–6

FULL SUN

MODERATE WATER

Native to southern Brazil and Uruguay, this shrubby, scrambling plant produces some of the garden's bluest blues. Where winter hardy, it can grow 3 ft. tall and wide; where grown as an annual, reaches 1½–2 ft. Give its vining stems something to climb, or pinch them back in youth to encourage bushy growth. In summer, bears small clusters of star-shaped, 1-in., sky blue flowers among and atop narrow, fuzzy gray-green leaves to 4 in. long. Flowering continues throughout summer if spent blooms are promptly removed. Blossoms give rise to elongated seedpods, which break open to release fluffy seeds that sail away on the breeze. Easily started from seed sown indoors 6 to 8 weeks before the last expected frost, then transplanted to the garden when danger of frost is past. Will overwinter where temperatures remain above 20°F. Needs well-drained soil; tolerates extended summer heat and drought. Formerly known as *Oxypetalum caeruleum.*

TWINBERRY. See MITCHELLA repens

TWINLEAF. See JEFFERSONIA diphylla

TWINSPUR. See DIASCIA

Ulmaceae. The elm family contains trees and shrubs, usually deciduous, with inconspicuous flowers and fruit that may be nutlike, single-seeded and fleshy, or winged. Hackberry *(Celtis),* elm *(Ulmus),* and *Zelkova* are representatives.

ULMUS

Ulmus parvifolia

ELM

Ulmaceae

DECIDUOUS OR SEMIEVERGREEN TREES

ZONES VARY BY SPECIES

FULL SUN

REGULAR WATER, EXCEPT AS NOTED

Once highly prized shade trees, elms have fallen on hard times. Dutch elm disease (spread by a bark beetle) has killed millions of American elms throughout North America and can attack most other elm species. Many of the larger elms are appealing fare for various beetles, leafhoppers, aphids, and scale, making them time consuming to care for, messy, or both. Elms have other problems not related to pests. They have aggressive, shallow root systems, so you'll have trouble growing other plants beneath them. Many types produce suckers; branch crotches are often narrow, splitting easily in storms. Still, elms are widely planted, valued for their fast growth, moderate shade, and environmental toughness. Researchers continue to devote much effort to finding disease-resistant selections. All elms are fairly soil tolerant, have handsome oval leaves.

U. alata. WINGED ELM. Deciduous. Zones US, MS, LS, CS; 10–5. Native to the Southeast. To 20–40 ft. tall, not quite as wide. Open, airy canopy. Leaves 1–2½ in. long, finely toothed, dark green turning pale yellow in fall. Common name derives from corky outgrowths ("wings") on twigs and young branches. Degree of winging varies among seedlings—the wings stand out on some, while on others they're almost nonexistent. Your best bet is to get a cutting-grown tree from a parent with good bark characteristics. Small red spring flowers are followed by small reddish seeds. 'Lace Parasol' is a weeping form (to 8 ft. tall, 12 ft. wide after 45 years).

U. americana. AMERICAN ELM. Deciduous. Zones US, MS, LS, CS, TS; 12–1. Native to eastern North America. This majestic tree once graced lawns and streets throughout its range, but its ranks have been decimated by Dutch elm disease. Grows fast to 100 ft. tall, with equal or greater spread. Prized for its high, arching branches, which create a beautiful, symmetrical canopy. Dark green, tooth-edged, pointed-oval leaves are 3–6 in. long and rough to the touch; they turn yellow in fall, with the intensity of the color varying from tree to tree. Small red flowers in early spring. Easily transplanted. Tolerates wet, alkaline, and saline soils.

A long search for American elms resistant to Dutch elm disease has culminated in a number of improved selections. 'Liberty', a series of six genetically different trees released by the Elm Research Institute in 1983, shows good resistance and classic elm form. To date, approximately 300,000 'Liberty' elms have been planted around the country, and only 1% have been lost to Dutch elm disease. One tree, planted at the State House in Annapolis, Maryland, in 1991, is more than 60 ft. tall. More recent introductions, including 'Delaware #2' and 'Valley Forge', have also shown resistance.

U. crassifolia. CEDAR ELM. Deciduous; semievergreen in extreme South Texas. Zones US, MS, LS, CS, TS; 10–6. Native from Texas to Mississippi and northern Mexico. Fairly fast growth to 50–75 ft. tall and 40–60 ft. wide. Stiff, shiny dark green leaves to 2 in. long, rough to the touch; they turn burnt yellow or gold in autumn. Twigs and branches (like those of *U. alata*) have corky wings. Tiny flowers in late summer. Well adapted to alkaline soils. Little to moderate water.

U. parvifolia. CHINESE ELM, LACEBARK ELM. Semievergreen or deciduous, depending on winter temperature and particular selection. Zones US, MS, LS, CS; 10–5. The best elm for home gardens and an excellent shade or lawn tree. Fast growth to 40–60 ft. tall, 25–40 ft. wide. Extremely variable in form, but generally rounded, with long, arching, pendulous branchlets. On older trees, bark flakes off in patches, creating a beautifully mottled combination of gray, green, orange, and brown. Leathery dark green leaves are ¾ to 2½ in. long, broadly oval and pointed, evenly toothed; may turn yellow to reddish orange in fall. Tiny red flowers from late summer to autumn. Resistant to Dutch elm disease, elm leaf beetle, and Japanese beetle.

Forms that hold their leaves are often sold as 'Sempervirens', but that is not a valid name. Two more or less evergreen selections popular in the Coastal South are 'Drake' and 'True Green'; they are not as cold hardy as others and are not recommended for the Upper or Middle South. Newer selections with particularly showy exfoliating bark include 'Allee', a vase-shaped tree to 70 ft. tall, 60 ft. wide; 'Athena', a lower, wide-spreading tree to 40 ft. tall, 55 ft. wide; and 'Burgundy', a rounded tree to 18 ft. tall, 20 ft. wide after 8 years, with burgundy fall color. Numerous dwarf and compact selections, such as 'Hokkaido', are popular for bonsai.

A word of caution: A vastly inferior species, *U. pumila,* Siberian elm, is sometimes sold as Chinese elm.

UMBRELLA PINE. See SCIADOPITYS verticillata

UMBRELLA PLANT. See CYPERUS alternifolius

UMBRELLA TREE, QUEENSLAND. See SCHEFFLERA actinophylla

UNGNADIA speciosa

Ungnadia speciosa

MEXICAN BUCKEYE

Sapindaceae

DECIDUOUS SHRUB OR SMALL TREE

MS, LS, CS H 10–4

FULL SUN OR PARTIAL SHADE

LITTLE TO REGULAR WATER

SEEDS ARE POISONOUS IF INGESTED

Native to Texas, New Mexico, and northern Mexico. Shrub or small, multitrunked tree, usually 12–15 ft. (occasionally 30 ft.) tall and not quite as wide as high. Easy-to-grow plant with appealing flowers, interesting seedpods, and lush foliage. Clusters of showy, fragrant blossoms with purplish pink petals and red anthers appear in early spring, before or with the new leaves. Flowers are followed in fall by leathery dark brown, buckeye-like seed capsules that split and drop black, shiny, ½-in. seeds. Dark green, 5- to 12-in.-long leaves with three to seven leaflets turn golden yellow in fall. Tolerates a wide range of soils, including dry, limy ones.

UVULARIA

MERRYBELLS, BELLWORT

Liliaceae

PERENNIALS

⚡ US, MS, LS H 9–1

◐ ● PARTIAL TO FULL SHADE

💧 REGULAR WATER

Uvularia grandiflora

Delightful wildflowers native to eastern and central North America. Grown for their handsome foliage and bell-shaped yellow blooms. Easy to grow in shady places with rich, moist, acid soil. Plants grow about 1 ft. wide and spread by rhizomes to form colonies; propagate by division. Good companions to hostas and ferns.

U. grandiflora. BIG MERRYBELLS. To 2½ ft. tall. Upright, leafy stems, somewhat reminiscent of Solomon's seal (*Polygonatum*), hold downward-pointing, medium green, narrowly oval and pointed leaves to 5 in. long. In spring, bright yellow, 2-in.-long, narrowly bell-shaped flowers with twisted petals hang from upper leaf axils.

U. perfoliata. WOOD MERRYBELLS. To 2 ft. tall, with narrow, oval, pointed blue-green leaves to 4 in. long. Leaf bases encircle the stems. Pale yellow bells are 1½ in. long.

U. sessilifolia. LITTLE MERRYBELLS. Dainty, charming plant to 1½ ft. tall. Wiry stems carry stalkless, lance-shaped leaves to 3 in. long. Nodding yellow flowers to 1½ in. long appear at stem ends in spring. 'Cobblewood Gold' has gold-edged green leaves; 'Variegata' has foliage edged in white.

VACCINIUM

Ericaceae

EVERGREEN AND DECIDUOUS SHRUBS

⚡ ZONES VARY BY SPECIES

☼ ◐ ● EXPOSURE NEEDS VARY BY SPECIES

◌ ◌ ● ●◦ WATER NEEDS VARY BY SPECIES

Vaccinium arboreum

Excellent ornamental shrubs with clusters of small, bell-shaped spring flowers and colorful, edible fruit that attracts birds. Species described here are shrubs—ranging from ground covers to the height of a small tree—that are grown for decorative, landscaping use; see Blueberry for relatives grown primarily for their edible fruits. All require rich, organic, acid soil. Good for woodland gardens.

V. arboreum. FARKLEBERRY. Evergreen or deciduous, depending on winter cold. Zones MS, LS, CS; 9–7. Native to the South and to southeastern and eastern Texas. Spreading plant to 10–25 ft. tall and about as wide, with shiny dark green leaves to 2 in. long; leaves turn rich red and crimson in fall and persist through most of the winter. Fragrant white flowers; unpalatable, ¼-in. black berries. Older shrubs have beautiful, exfoliating cinnamon brown to gray-orange bark. Full sun or partial shade. Needs only moderate water.

V. ashei. See Blueberry

V. corymbosum. See Blueberry

V. crassifolium. CREEPING BLUEBERRY. Evergreen. Zones MS, LS; 8–7. Native from southeast Virginia to South Carolina. Sprawling ground cover to 6 in. tall and 6 ft. across, with leathery dark green leaves just ½ in. long. Rosy red flowers in late spring; sweet black berries to ½ in. across. 'Bloodstone' has reddish new and mature leaves, red stems in winter. 'Wells Delight' is particularly broad spreading and disease tolerant. Full sun or partial shade; regular water.

V. darrowii. Evergreen. Zones LS, CS; 9–7. Native to Florida, Georgia, Alabama. Grows to 2 ft. tall in the wild, but can reach 5 ft. tall and 3 ft. wide in garden conditions. Very small blue-green leaves; pinkish new growth. White flowers are followed by small, sweet black berries with a bluish bloom. Two named selections are 'John Blue' and 'Sebring'. Full sun; little to regular water.

V. elliottii. ELLIOTT'S BLUEBERRY. Deciduous. Zones US, MS, LS, CS; 9–6. Native from Florida to Virginia, west to Arkansas and Louisiana. Clump-forming, straggly shrub of variable size; grows from 6 to 13 ft. tall and about 6 ft. wide. Shiny, thin-textured green leaves to 1½ in. long. Pink to white flowers often appear before leaf-out; dark purple-blue or black berries are less than ½ in. wide. Full sun or partial shade; moderate to regular water.

V. macrocarpon. CRANBERRY. Evergreen. Zones US, MS; 7–1. Native from Newfoundland to Minnesota, south to North Carolina. Creeping plant 2–6 in. high, spreading indefinitely by rooting stems. Narrow, ¾-in.-long leaves are dark green in summer, turning coppery or purplish red in winter. Tiny pinkish flowers are followed by tart red fruits to ¾ in. across in autumn. Commercial producers grow cranberries in bogs—beds that can be flooded to control weeds and pests, provide winter protection, and make harvesting easier. Gardeners can use cranberry as an attractive small-scale ground cover in full sun, with regular to ample water.

V. myrsinites. GROUND BLUEBERRY. Evergreen. Zones MS, LS, CS, TS; 12–4. Native from Virginia to Florida and Louisiana. To 2 ft. tall, more sprawling than erect. White to pink flowers; tiny blue-black or black berries. Full sun; moderate to ample water.

V. stamineum. DEERBERRY. Deciduous. Zones US, MS, LS, CS; 9–5. Native to eastern North America. Open, airy growth to a possible 10–15 ft. high and wide, although many mature specimens are half that size or even smaller. Twisted trunks and branches; peeling reddish brown bark. Oval leaves to 3 in. long are green above, whitish underneath; they turn red and orange in autumn. Clustered white flowers have prominent yellow stamens and flaring petals. Purplish berries less than ½ in. across are edible but not always sweet. Full sun or partial shade; moderate to regular water.

V. vitis-idaea. COWBERRY, FOXBERRY. Evergreen. Zones US; 6–1. Native to Europe. Slow growth to 1 ft. high, spreading to 3 ft. wide by underground stems. Glossy dark green leaves to 1 in. long; new growth often tinged bright red or orange. Clustered white or pinkish flowers are followed by sour red berries similar to tiny cranberries and valued for preserves, syrups. Handsome plant for small-scale ground cover, informal edging for larger plantings. Needs regular to ample water and partial to full shade.

VALERIAN. See CENTRANTHUS ruber, VALERIANA officinalis

Valerianaceae. The valerian family of perennial herbs (rarely shrubs) has clustered small flowers. In addition to *Valeriana*, members include valerian (*Centranthus*) and *Patrinia*.

VALERIANA officinalis

VALERIAN, GARDEN HELIOTROPE

Valerianaceae

PERENNIAL

⚡ US, MS, LS, CS H 9–1

☼ ◐ FULL SUN OR PARTIAL SHADE

💧 REGULAR WATER

Valeriana officinalis

From Europe and western Asia. To 5 ft. tall in bloom, spreading to 4 ft. wide. Most of the foliage remains fairly close to ground. Light green leaves, each with eight to ten pairs of narrow, jagged-edged leaflets. Tall, straight flowering stems carry tiny, fragrant pink blossoms in rounded clusters at stem ends in summer; useful for cut flowers. White- and red-flowered forms exist. Strong-smelling roots are widely

V

used in herbal preparations with sedative qualities. Roots also attract cats. Start new plants from seed or divisions. Grow in mixed herb or flower borders, but be aware that it can become invasive; don't let it crowd other plants. For the plant sold as *V. rubra*, see *Centranthus ruber.*

VALLOTA speciosa. See CYRTANTHUS elatus

VELVET PLANT. See GYNURA

VENUS'S FLYTRAP. See DIONAEA muscipula

VERBASCUM

MULLEIN

Scrophulariaceae

BIENNIALS AND PERENNIALS

☘ US, MS, LS, EXCEPT AS NOTED

☼ FULL SUN

💧 MODERATE WATER

Verbascum bombyciferum
'Arctic Summer'

Large group of rosette-forming, summer-blooming plants that send up spikes closely set with nearly flat, five-petaled, circular flowers about an inch across. Both foliage and stems are often covered in woolly hairs. Taller mulleins make striking vertical accents. Grow all in well-drained soil. Cut off spent flowers to encourage a second round of blooming. Leave spikes of biennial species in place if you want plants to spread by reseeding. All mulleins self-sow freely—and some are downright weedy, such as the attractive roadside wild-flower *V. thapsus*. Perennial species are short lived in hot, humid climates.

V. blattaria. MOTH MULLEIN. Biennial. Zones US, MS, LS, CS; 10–2. Native from Europe to central Asia. To 2–4 ft. tall, 1–1½ ft. wide, with smooth-textured, dark green, cut or toothed leaves to 10 in. long. Pale yellow or white flowers have purple centers. 'Pink Form' has rose pink flowers that open from red buds.

V. bombyciferum 'Arctic Summer'. Biennial. Heat zones 8–1. Selection of a species native to Turkey. To 6 ft. tall, 2 ft. wide, with furry gray-green leaves to 1½ ft. long. Yellow flowers on powdery white stems.

V. chaixii. CHAIX MULLEIN. Perennial. Heat zones 8–5. From Europe. To 3 ft. tall and 2 ft. wide, with hairy green leaves to 6 in. long. Red-eyed, pale yellow flowers in narrow, often branching spikes. 'Album' has white flowers with purple centers.

V. hybrids. Many hybrids are obtainable, either as blends or in single colors. Most must be grown from seed.

'Banana Custard'. Biennial. To 5–6 ft. tall, 2 ft. wide. Bright yellow flowers.

'Copper Rose'. Perennial. To 4–6 ft. tall, 2 ft. wide, with blossoms in buff, apricot, rose, or tan. Blooms the first year from seed sown in late winter or earliest spring.

Cotswold Hybrids. Perennials. These resemble *V. phoenicium* but come in white, cream, yellow, pink, and purple. Named selections are sometimes offered, including creamy yellow 'Gainsborough' and bright pink 'Pink Domino'.

'Helen Johnson'. Perennial. To 3–4 ft. tall, 2 ft. wide. Apricot flowers with purple centers; large, silvery green leaves. To propagate this sterile hybrid, take root cuttings in early spring.

'Jackie'. Short-lived perennial. To 1½–2 ft. high, 1½ ft. wide. Purple-eyed blossoms are a soft orange, similar to the color of cantaloupe flesh. To propagate this sterile hybrid, take root cuttings in early spring.

'Southern Charm'. Perennial. To 2–3 ft. high, 1½–2 ft. wide. Seed strain in mixed colors, including cream, buff, lavender, rose.

V. olympicum. OLYMPIC MULLEIN. Perennial. Heat zones 9–5. From Greece. To 5 ft. high, 3 ft. wide, with soft, downy white leaves to over 2 ft. long. Bright yellow flowers are very showy; many flowering stems.

V. phoeniceum. PURPLE MULLEIN. Perennial. Heat zones 8–1. To 2–4 ft. high, 1½ ft. wide. Dark green leaves to 6 in. long are smooth on top, hairy beneath. Slender spikes of purple flowers.

VERBENA

Verbenaceae

PERENNIALS, SOME GROWN AS ANNUALS

☘ ZONES VARY BY SPECIES

☼ FULL SUN

💧 MODERATE WATER, EXCEPT AS NOTED

Verbena peruviana
Hybrid

This large group includes some of the garden's most colorful, useful, and easy-to-grow plants. Most bear clusters of small, five-petaled, tubular blossoms from late spring until frost. Low verbenas make good ground covers and edging plants; they're also great in hanging baskets and containers or tumbling over rock walls. Use taller types in borders. Most thrive in heat and tolerate drought. Provide good air circulation and well-drained soil.

V. bipinnatifida. DAKOTA VERBENA. Perennial. Zones US, MS, LS; 8–1. Native from Great Plains to Mexico. Grows 8–15 in. high, 1½ ft. wide or wider, with blue flowers and finely divided leaves. Spreads by self-sowing in most areas.

V. bonariensis. Perennial in Zones MS, LS, CS, TS; 12–6; annual in Upper South. Native to South America, but naturalized in the southeastern U.S. Airy, branching stems to 3–6 ft. carry purple flowers. Leaves are mostly in a basal clump to 1½ ft. high and 1½–3 ft. wide. This plant has a see-through quality that makes it suited for foreground or back of border. Self-sows freely.

V. canadensis. ROSE VERBENA. Perennial in Zones US, MS, LS, CS, 10–1, but usually treated as annual. Native from Virginia to Florida, west to Colorado and Mexico. To 1½ ft. high, 1½–3 ft. wide, with rosy purple flowers. There is a compact (6-in.-high) form suitable for rock gardens; white- and pink-flowering forms are also offered. 'Greystone Daphne', to 6–8 in. tall and up to 1½ ft. wide, has dark green leaves and lavender-pink flowers; it thrives in Southern gardens. When growing the species or its selections as perennials, provide good winter drainage; in the Upper South, cover with light winter mulch.

V. gooddingii. Short-lived perennial. Zones LS, CS, TS; 12–8. Native to the Southwest. Grows to 1½ ft. high, spreading to about 3 ft. wide. Oval, deeply cut leaves. Pinkish lavender flowers at ends of short spikes. Will bloom first summer from seed sown in spring. Can reseed where moisture is adequate. Tolerates dry heat.

V. ×hybrida (V. ×hortensis). GARDEN VERBENA. Short-lived perennial grown as annual. Zones US, MS, LS, CS, TS; 12–1. Much-branched plant to 6–12 in. high, spreading 1½–3 ft. wide. Oblong, 2- to 4-in., bright green or gray-green leaves with toothed margins. Flowers come in flat, compact clusters to 3 in. wide; colors include white, pink, bright red, purple, blue, and combinations. Superior strains include Romance (to 6 in. tall) and Showtime (to 10 in.). All are colorful but prone to insect damage.

V. hybrids. Perennials. Zones LS, CS, TS; 12–1. Grow as annuals where not hardy. Group of mostly low-growing, wide-spreading plants that love hot, dry weather and bloom all summer.

'Batesville Rose'. To 1–2 ft. high, 3 ft. wide. Magenta flowers.

'Blue Princess'. To 1 ft. high, 2–3 ft. wide. Fragrant lavender-blue blossoms; mildew-resistant leaves.

'Homestead Purple'. To 1 ft. high, 4 ft. wide. Rich deep purple blooms; mildew-resistant foliage. Thrives in the South.

'Hot Lips'. To 6–10 in. high, 2–3 ft. wide. Bright red-violet flower heads, with each tiny blossom shading to a darker color toward the center.

'Mystic'. To 6–10 in. high, 2–3 ft. wide. Light lavender-blue flowers.

'Pinwheel Princess'. To 1–2 ft. high, 2–3 ft. wide. Sport of 'Blue Princess'. Lightly scented blossoms are striped in lavender and white; they look like little pinwheels.

'Sissinghurst'. To 8 in. high, 3–4 ft. wide. Coral pink flowers.

'Texas Appleblossom'. To 6 in. high, 2–3 ft. wide. Flowers open cotton candy pink, then gradually fade to white.

V. peruviana (V. chamaedrifolia). Perennial in Zones CS, TS, 12–6, but usually treated as an annual everywhere. Native to South America. Spreads rapidly, forming a flat mat to 2 ft. wide. Small, closely set leaves; flat-topped clusters of scarlet-and-white flowers on stems to 3 in. tall cover the

V

foliage. Hybrids feature blossoms in white, pink, or red; they spread more slowly than the species and have slightly larger leaves and stouter stems.

V. rigida (V. venosa). Perennial in Zones MS, LS, CS, 9–5, or grow as annual anywhere. Native to South America, but naturalized in Southeast. To 1–2 ft. high, spreading to 3–4 ft. wide. Rough, strongly toothed, dark green leaves to 2–4 in. long. Lilac to purple-blue flowers in cylindrical clusters on tall, stiff stems. Blooms in 4 months from seed. 'Flame', to 4 in. high, is a cutting-grown selection with bright scarlet flowers.

V. Tapien hybrids. Perennials in Zones CS, TS, 12–1, annuals anywhere. Prostrate plants to 4 in. high, 1–1½ ft. wide, with finely cut dark green leaves. Wide range of colors, including pink, lavender, pale blue, deep purple, red. Resistant to mildew. Regular water.

V. Temari hybrids. Perennials in Zones CS, TS, 12–1, annuals anywhere. Low, spreading plants to 3 in. high, 2½ ft. wide. Broad dark green leaves. Bright pink, burgundy, or violet flowers. Regular water.

V. tenuisecta (V. pulchella gracilior). MOSS VERBENA. Short-lived perennial in Zones MS, LS, CS, TS, 12–6, annual in Upper South. Native to South America, but naturalized in the Lower South. To 8–12 in. high, with finely cut leaves. Rose violet to pink flowers. Short lived. Selections include white 'Alba', lavender-pink 'Edith', and violet 'Michelle'.

VERBENA, LEMON. See ALOYSIA triphylla

Verbenaceae. This immense family contains annuals, perennials, shrubs, and a few trees and vines. Leaves are usually opposite or in whorls, flowers in spikes or spiky clusters. Fruits may be berries or nutlets. Glorybower *(Clerodendrum), Lantana, Verbena,* and chaste tree *(Vitex)* are examples.

VERNONIA noveboracensis

IRONWEED

Asteraceae (Compositae)

PERENNIAL

US, MS, LS H 8–1

FULL SUN OR LIGHT SHADE

MODERATE TO AMPLE WATER

Vernonia noveboracensis

Native from Massachusetts to Mississippi and Georgia. This meadow plant is a handsome choice for the back of a border or for a contrasting color scheme with goldenrod *(Solidago)* and black-eyed Susan *(Rudbeckia hirta)*. Clumps of leafy stems to 6–8 ft. tall, 2 ft. wide are topped in late summer by broad, flat clusters of fluffy, bright purple, ½-in. flower heads. These should be clipped off before they develop into the rust-colored seed clusters that give the plant its name (unless you want plants to naturalize). Grows in wet or fairly dry soils and needs no coddling.

V. altissima is a similar species, somewhat taller and with longer leaves. Its selection 'Purple Pillar' produces 10-ft.-tall stalks topped with large clusters of clear purple flowers in midsummer.

VERONICA

SPEEDWELL

Scrophulariaceae

PERENNIALS

US, MS, LS H 8–1, EXCEPT AS NOTED

FULL SUN, EXCEPT AS NOTED

WATER NEEDS VARY BY SPECIES

Veronica
'Sunny Border Blue'

Handsome plants ranging from less than an inch tall to 2 ft. in height. Masses of small (¼- to ½-in.-wide) flowers in white, rose, pink, or pale to deep blue make an effective display. Use in borders and rock gardens. Prostrate kinds are good between stepping-stones, as bulb covers. Named selections are not easily assigned to a species; authorities differ.

V. alpina. From Europe, Eurasia, North America. Creeping rootstock forms a low foliage rosette 4–8 in. high, 1 ft. wide; narrowly oval to roundish leaves to 1 in. long, ½ in. wide. Spikelike clusters of blue flowers in spring or early summer; in warmer parts of range, often reblooms in fall. White-flowered 'Alba' grows 10 in. high. Regular water.

V. austriaca teucrium 'Crater Lake Blue'. Selection of a species native to Europe. To 12–15 in. high and wide, with tooth-edged, 1½-in.-long leaves. Short spikes of intensely blue flowers in midsummer. Regular water.

V. gentianoides. GENTIAN SPEEDWELL. Zones US, MS; 7–1. From the Caucasus. Creeping rootstock forms a dense mat to 1–2 ft. high and wide. Oblong, glossy dark green, 2- to 3-in.-long leaves. In spring, foliage is topped by leafy stems carrying 10-in. spikes of ice blue flowers with darker veining. 'Variegata' has leaves marked with white. Regular water.

V. hybrids. The following are among the best selections. Regular water, except as noted.

'Blue Reflection'. Forms a gray-green foliage mat to 3–4 in. high and 1–1½ ft. wide, covered with blue flowers in midspring. Little to moderate water.

'Goodness Grows'. Bushy growth to 1 ft. tall and wide, with medium green, lance-shaped leaves. Violet-blue blossoms over long bloom period—from late spring to frost, if old flowers are removed.

'Sunny Border Blue'. Compact, clump-forming plant to 1½–2 ft. tall, 1 ft. wide, with crinkled dark green leaves. Spires of dark violet-blue flowers appear in late spring or early summer; deadheading prolongs the show until frost.

'Waterperry Blue' ('Waterperry'). Low, trailing plant to 4–6 in. high and 1½ ft. or more wide; roots as it spreads. Small, rounded, bronze-tinted leaves. Loose clusters of pale blue flowers veined in deeper blue; main bloom in spring, with sporadic flowering throughout summer and fall.

V. pectinata. Western Mediterranean native. Forms prostrate mat of foliage to 3 in. high and 1 ft. wide; spreads by creeping stems that root at joints. Small grayish leaves have scalloped or deeply cut edges. Profuse spring or early summer show of deep blue flowers with white centers; blossoms are borne on 5- to 6-in. spikes among the leaves. Little to moderate water.

V. peduncularis 'Georgia Blue'. From Georgia, in the former Soviet Union. Forms a 6- to 8-in.-high mat that spreads to several feet wide; small dark green leaves turn bronze in cool weather. Profuse, white-eyed cobalt blue flowers in spring, with a few flowers appearing throughout summer and fall. Regular water.

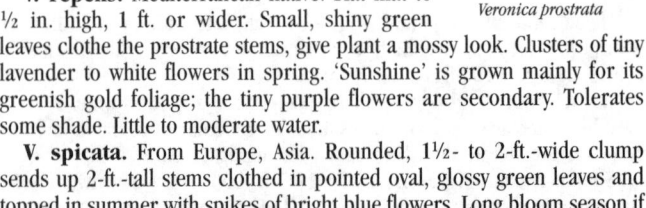

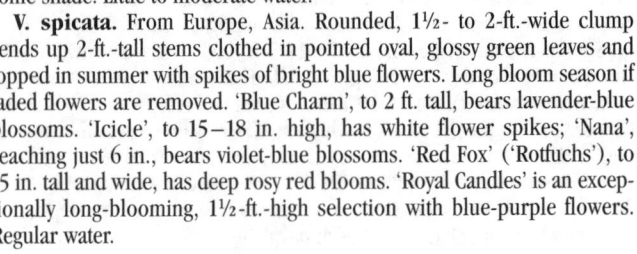

Veronica prostrata

V. prostrata (V. rupestris). From Europe. Stems are hairy and tufted. Some are prostrate and form a 1- to 1½-ft.-wide foliage mat; others grow erect to 8 in. high and are topped by short clusters of pale blue flowers in late spring or early summer. 'Heavenly Blue' is almost entirely prostrate, with flower stems reaching 6 in. high. 'Mrs. Holt' has pale pink flowers. 'Aztec Gold' and 'Trehane' have golden yellow leaves, bright blue flowers. Little to moderate water.

V. repens. Mediterranean native. Flat mat to ½ in. high, 1 ft. or wider. Small, shiny green leaves clothe the prostrate stems, give plant a mossy look. Clusters of tiny lavender to white flowers in spring. 'Sunshine' is grown mainly for its greenish gold foliage; the tiny purple flowers are secondary. Tolerates some shade. Little to moderate water.

V. spicata. From Europe, Asia. Rounded, 1½- to 2-ft.-wide clump sends up 2-ft.-tall stems clothed in pointed oval, glossy green leaves and topped in summer with spikes of bright blue flowers. Long bloom season if faded flowers are removed. 'Blue Charm', to 2 ft. tall, bears lavender-blue blossoms. 'Icicle', to 15–18 in. high, has white flower spikes; 'Nana', reaching just 6 in., bears violet-blue blossoms. 'Red Fox' ('Rotfuchs'), to 15 in. tall and wide, has deep rosy red blooms. 'Royal Candles' is an exceptionally long-blooming, 1½-ft.-high selection with blue-purple flowers. Regular water.

V. s. incana (V. incana). SILVER SPEEDWELL. Furry, silvery white foliage forms a 1- to 1½-ft.-wide mat. Blooms in summer, producing deep blue blossoms on stems to about 1 ft. high. Little to moderate water.

V. virginica. See Veronicastrum virginicum

VERONICASTRUM virginicum (Veronica virginica)

CULVER'S ROOT

Scrophulariaceae

PERENNIAL

US, MS, LS ⊢ 8–3

☼ ◐ FULL SUN OR LIGHT SHADE

● REGULAR WATER

Veronicastrum virginicum

From eastern U.S. Erect grower to 5–7 ft. tall, 1½ ft. wide; resembles a very tall *Veronica*. Stems are clothed with whorls of toothed, 6-in., lance-shaped dark green leaves. Stems branch in the upper portions and are topped by slender, spikelike clusters (to 9 in. long) of tiny pale blue or white flowers. Useful plant for background in large borders. Makes a striking pattern against dark background, such as tall hedge or woodland edge, but too much shade makes it floppy. Likes fertile, well-drained, slightly acid soil. Selections with flowers in specific colors include white 'Album', reddish purple 'Apollo', light lavender 'Lavendelturm', and rosy pink 'Pink Glow'.

VIBURNUM

Caprifoliaceae

DECIDUOUS, EVERGREEN, SEMIEVERGREEN SHRUBS OR TREES

ZONES VARY BY SPECIES

☼ ◐ FULL SUN OR PARTIAL SHADE, EXCEPT AS NOTED

● REGULAR WATER, EXCEPT AS NOTED

Viburnum opulus 'Roseum'

Large, diverse group of plants with generally oval, often handsome leaves and clusters of typically white, sometimes fragrant flowers. Blossoms are usually followed by single-seeded, often brilliantly colored fruit much appreciated by birds. Many viburnums are grown for their flower display, a few for their showy fruit. In general, heaviest fruit set occurs when several different named selections of seedlings that bloom at the same time are planted together. Many evergreen types are valuable as foliage plants. Several species (noted below) can be grown as small trees.

V. davidii needs acid soil, but the other viburnums are very soil tolerant, accepting even heavy or limy soils. Many have a wide range of climate adaptability. Where summers are long and hot, most evergreen viburnums look better with some shade. Prune to prevent legginess; some evergreen kinds can be sheared. Nematodes can be a problem, and aphids, thrips, spider mites, scale, and root weevil are potential pests in many areas, but plants are not usually seriously troubled by them. Powdery mildew sometimes afflicts viburnums, but don't treat it with sulfur sprays, which will damage the leaves; see the *Southern Living Garden Problem Solver* for alternative treatments. Viburnums are somewhat resistant to deer damage.

V. ×bodnantense. BODNANT VIBURNUM. Deciduous. Zones US, MS, LS. To 10 ft. (or more) tall, 6 ft. wide. Dark green, 1½- to 4-in.-long leaves are deeply veined, turn dark scarlet in fall. Loose clusters of very fragrant deep pink flowers age to paler pink; blooms in winter, but buds often freeze. Red fruit is not showy. Best known is 'Dawn' ('Pink Dawn').

V. ×burkwoodii. BURKWOOD VIBURNUM. Deciduous in cold areas, nearly evergreen elsewhere. Zones US, MS, LS. To 6–12 ft. tall, 4–8 ft. wide. Glossy leaves to 3½ in. long are dark green above, white and hairy beneath; turn purplish red in cold weather. Dense, 4-in. clusters of pink buds open to very fragrant white flowers in late winter or early spring.

Blue-black fruit is not showy. Early growth is straggly, but mature plants are dense. Can be espaliered.

'Chenaultii' *(V. ×chenaultii).* Denser, more compact, slightly later blooming, more deciduous in mild climates than the species.

'Mohawk'. To 7 ft. tall, 5 ft. wide. Red buds are showy long before they open into white flowers. Orange-red fall color.

V. ×carlcephalum. FRAGRANT SNOWBALL. Deciduous. Zones US, MS, LS. To 6–10 ft. tall and wide. Dull grayish green, 2- to 3½-in.-long leaves are downy beneath; turn reddish purple in autumn. Long-lasting, waxy, sweetly perfumed spring flowers in dense, 4- to 5-in. clusters. No fruit. As showy as *V. opulus* 'Roseum' but has the bonus of fragrance.

V. carlesii. KOREAN SPICE VIBURNUM. Deciduous. Zones US, MS, LS; 8–5. Native to Korea, Japan. Old Southern favorite. Loose, open habit to 4–8 ft. tall and wide. Leaves like those of *V. ×carlcephalum;* inconsistent reddish fall color. Pink buds in 2- to 3-in. clusters open to sweetly fragrant white flowers in spring. Blue-black fruit is not showy. Does best with part shade during hottest months.

V. davidii. DAVID VIBURNUM. Evergreen. Zones US, MS, LS. Native to China. This species undoubtedly has the most handsome foliage of all viburnums: glossy dark green, deeply veined leaves 3–6 in. long. Forms a compact mound to 3–4 ft. high and wide. White spring flowers aren't especially showy, but the display of metallic turquoise blue fruit that follows is definitely eye catching. Unfortunately, David viburnum seldom sets fruit unless growing conditions are perfect and several genetically distinct plants (not "sibling" seedlings, but individuals from different parents) are grouped together for cross-pollination. It's better suited to the mild climate of the Pacific Northwest than the extremes of the South. Here, it requires very well drained, moist, acid soil and afternoon shade.

V. dentatum. ARROWWOOD. Deciduous. Zones US, MS, LS, CS; 10–1. Native from New Brunswick to Minnesota, south to Georgia. To 6–10 ft. or taller, equally wide. Cream-colored flowers in late spring are followed by blue-black fruit. Dark green, oval to rounded, 4-in. leaves turn yellow, orange, or deep red in fall. Plants tolerate heat, cold, and alkaline soil. Use as screen or tall hedge. 'Cardinal' has reliable brilliant red fall color. 'Blue Muffin' is a compact variety reaching only 5–7 ft. high and 4 ft. wide.

V. dilatatum. LINDEN VIBURNUM. Deciduous. Zones US, MS, LS; 8–5. From China, Japan. Grows to 8–10 ft. tall and not quite as wide. Nearly round, 2- to 5-in. gray-green leaves; inconsistent rusty red fall color. Tiny, creamy white, somewhat unpleasant-smelling flowers in 5-in. clusters, late spring or early summer. Showy bright red fruits ripen in early fall, hang on into winter. Outstanding named selections include the following.

'Cardinal Candy'. To 4–5 ft. high and wide. Extra-hardy selection; has survived −25°F. Bright red fruit. Leaves turn bronze and burgundy in fall.

'Catskill'. Compact growth to 5–8 ft. tall, 8–10 ft. wide, with smaller leaves than species. Dark red fruit. Fall color is a combination of yellow, orange, and red.

'Erie'. Rounded habit to 6 ft. tall, 10 ft. wide. Coral fruit. Leaves turn yellow, orange, and red in autumn. Highly disease resistant.

'Iroquois'. To 9 ft. tall, 12 ft. wide. Selected for heavy production of larger, darker red fruit. Orange-red to maroon fall foliage.

V. hybrids. Zones US, MS, LS. These spring-blooming viburnums all have complex ancestries.

'Cayuga'. Deciduous. To 5 ft. tall and wide. Dark green, 1- to 3-in.-long leaves. White flowers open from pink buds. Small black fruit.

'Chesapeake'. Semievergreen. To 8 ft. tall, 10 ft. wide, with glossy, wavy-edged, 3½-in. dark green leaves. Two-inch clusters of fragrant white flowers open from pink buds; dull red fruit matures to black.

'Chippewa'. Semievergreen to deciduous. To 8–9 ft. tall, 9 ft. wide. Dense plant with glossy dark green leaves that turn maroon and red in fall. Big show of creamy white flowers; glossy deep red fruit. Cold hardy.

'Conoy'. Evergreen. Dense growth to 5 ft. high and wide. Lustrous, 2- to 2½-in. leaves are dark green above, whitish beneath; take on a maroon tinge in cold winters. Slightly fragrant flowers are followed by long-lasting red berries. Tolerates shearing.

'Eskimo'. Semievergreen. Dense, compact habit to 5 ft. tall and wide. Shiny dark green leaves to 4 in. long. Unscented flowers in 3- to 4-in., snowball-like clusters; dull red fruit. ▶

V

'Huron'. Semievergreen to deciduous. Dense grower to 8–9 ft. tall, 9–10 ft. wide. Glossy dark green leaves with good fall color in rich red and maroon tones. Flowers virtually cover the plant at bloom time. Dark red fruit. Cold hardy.

V. japonicum. Evergreen. Zones CS, TS; 11–8. From Japan. Grows 10–15 ft. tall, 8–12 ft. wide; can be trained as a small tree. Leathery, glossy dark green leaves to 6 in. long. Sparse spring show of fragrant flowers in 4-in. clusters. Red fruit is likewise sparse—but very attractive. Best with some shade.

V. × juddii. Deciduous. Zones US, MS, LS. To 4–8 ft. tall, 6–10 ft. wide. Bushier and more spreading than *V. carlesii* but similar to it in other respects, including fragrance.

V. macrocephalum (V. m. 'Sterile'). CHINESE SNOWBALL. Deciduous in coldest areas, nearly evergreen elsewhere. Zones US, MS, LS, CS; 9–6. Rounded habit to 12–20 ft. tall and wide. Dull green, oval to oblong, 2- to 4-in.-long leaves. Spectacular big, rounded, 6- to 8-in. flower clusters bloom in spring (or any time during warm weather); they are composed of sterile flowers that start out lime green, change to white. No fruit. Can be espaliered.

V. opulus. EUROPEAN CRANBERRY BUSH. Deciduous. Zones US, MS, LS; 8–1. From Europe, North Africa, central Asia. To 8–15 ft. tall and wide, with arching branches. Lobed, maplelike dark green leaves to 2–4 in. long and as wide or wider. Fall foliage color may be yellow, bright red, or reddish purple. Blooms in spring; flower heads have a lace-cap look, with a 2- to 4-in. cluster of small fertile blossoms ringed with larger sterile blossoms. Large, showy red fruit persists from fall into winter. Takes moist to boggy soils. Control aphids. Selections include the following.

'Aureum'. Golden yellow foliage. Give some shade to prevent sunburn.

'Compactum'. To 4–5 ft. high and wide.

'Nanum'. To 2 ft. high and wide. Needs no trimming as low, informal hedge. Cannot take poorly drained, wet soils. No flowers or fruit.

'Roseum' ('Sterile'). COMMON SNOWBALL. Resembles the species but has snowball-like flower clusters 2–2½ in. across, composed entirely of sterile flowers (so bears no fruit). Aphids are especially troublesome.

V. plicatum plicatum. JAPANESE SNOWBALL. Deciduous. Zones US, MS, LS; 8–1. From China, Japan. To 8–15 ft. tall and wide. Horizontal branching pattern gives plant a tiered look, especially when in bloom; flower clusters are held above the branches, while leaves hang down. Strongly veined, 3- to 6-in.-long, dull dark green leaves turn purplish red in autumn. Showy, 3-in., snowball-like clusters of sterile flowers look like those of *V. opulus* 'Roseum', but this plant is less bothered by aphids. Midspring bloom. No fruit. Tolerates occasionally wet soils. 'Newport' is compact and dense, to 5 ft. tall and wide.

V. plicatum tomentosum. DOUBLEFILE VIBURNUM. Deciduous. Zones US, MS, LS; 8–1. This truly beautiful viburnum is native to China and Japan. It resembles *V. plicatum plicatum,* but midspring flower display consists of small fertile flowers in flat, 2- to 4-in. clusters edged with 1- to 1½-in. sterile flowers in lace-cap effect. Fruit is red aging to black, showy, not always profuse. Needs good drainage and moist soil. Excessive summer heat and drought often result in leaf scorch.

Selections include the following.

'Cascade'. To 10 ft. tall, 12 ft. wide. Wide-spreading branches bear large sterile flowers.

'Mariesii'. Grows to 10 ft. tall and 12 ft. wide. Has large flower clusters, large sterile flowers.

'Pink Beauty'. To 9 ft. tall, 12 ft. wide, with white flowers that age to pink.

'Shasta'. Horizontal habit (to 10 ft. tall, 15 ft. wide), with large sterile flowers. Considered by many to be the finest selection.

'Shoshoni'. To 5 ft. tall, 8 ft. wide.

'Summer Snowflake'. Reaches 5–8 ft. tall and wide. Blooms from spring to autumn.

V. × pragense (V. 'Pragense'). PRAGUE VIBURNUM. Evergreen. Zones US, MS, LS. Fast-growing, rounded plant to 10 ft. tall and broad. Shiny dark green, 2- to 4-in.-long leaves. Faintly fragrant white flowers in 3- to 6-in. clusters open from pink buds in early spring.

V. prunifolium. BLACK HAW. Deciduous. Zones US, MS, LS, CS; 9–1. Native from Michigan and Connecticut south to Texas and Florida. Upright to 15 ft., spreading as wide. Can be trained as a small tree. Common name comes from dark fruit and from plant's resemblance to hawthorn (*Crataegus*). Oval, finely toothed leaves to 3 in. long turn purplish to reddish purple in fall. Many clusters of creamy white flowers in spring; edible blue-black fruit in fall and winter. Use as dense screen or barrier, attractive specimen shrub. Best in full sun. Tolerates drought.

V. × rhytidophylloides. Zones US, MS, LS, CS; 9–6. These are hybrids between *V. rhytidophyllum* and *V. lantana,* a deciduous species from Europe and Asia Minor. Among the best is 'Allegheny', a dense, rounded plant 6–8 ft. tall and broad; it is evergreen in most winters. Leaves resemble those of *V. rhytidophyllum* but are broader and less wrinkled. Flowers and fruit are also similar. 'Willowwood' resembles 'Allegheny' but has a more arching habit.

Viburnum rhytidophyllum

V. rhytidophyllum. LEATHERLEAF VIBURNUM. Evergreen. Zones US, MS, LS. From central and western China. Upright grower to 8–15 ft. tall, 6–12 ft. wide. Narrow, 4- to 10-in.-long leaves are deep green and wrinkled above, fuzzy beneath. Yellowish white spring flowers come in 4- to 8-in. clusters; scarlet fruit ages to black. Leaves droop in cold weather, and plant looks tattered where cold winds blow. Tolerates deep shade. Some find this plant striking; others consider it coarse.

V. rufidulum. SOUTHERN BLACK HAW. Deciduous. Zones US, MS, LS, CS; 9–5. Native from Texas to Florida and north to Virginia. Large shrub or small tree growing 12–20 ft. tall and spreading a little wider. Blossoms come in 5-in.-wide clusters in late spring; they're followed by handsome dark blue berries. Oval, 2- to 4-in., glossy dark green leaves; young shoots, leafstalks, and leaf undersides are covered with rust-colored hairs. Fall foliage color ranges from orange and yellow through red and purple shades.

V. setigerum. TEA VIBURNUM. Deciduous. Zones US, MS, LS; 7–5. From China. To 8–12 ft. tall, 6–8 ft. wide. Multistemmed, rather erect; often bare at base (plant lower-growing shrubs around it for concealment). Leaves were once used for making tea; they are 3–6 in. long, dark green or blue green turning to purplish in fall. Spring flowers in 1- to 2-in. clusters are not striking, but heavy production of scarlet fruit makes this the showiest of fruiting viburnums.

V. suspensum. SANDANKWA VIBURNUM. Evergreen. Zones CS, TS. From Japan. To 8–10 ft. tall and broad. Leathery, 2- to 4-in.-long leaves are glossy deep green above, paler beneath. Blooms in early spring, bearing flowers in loose, 2- to 4-in. clusters; some people find the scent objectionable. Red fruit ages to black, is not long lasting. Serviceable screen or hedge; very popular in Florida. Watch for thrips, spider mites, aphids. Little to moderate water.

V. tinus. LAURUSTINUS. Evergreen. Zones CS, 10–8, except as noted. Mediterranean native. To 6–12 ft. tall, half as wide. Leathery dark green, 2- to 3-in.-long leaves with edges slightly rolled under. Wine red new stems. Blooms in winter; tight clusters of pink buds open to lightly fragrant white flowers. Bright metallic blue fruits last through summer. Dense foliage right to ground makes it good for screens, hedges, clipped topiary shapes. Can be trained as a small tree. Susceptible to mildew, mites. Selections include the following.

'Bewley's Variegated'. Upright grower to 3–5 ft. tall and wide. Deep green leaves edged in creamy white.

'Lucidum'. SHINING LAURUSTINUS. Zone TS. Less hardy than the species, with larger leaves. Less prone to mildew.

'Spring Bouquet' ('Compactum'). Upright to 4–6 ft. high and wide; good for hedges. Leaves are deeper green, slightly smaller than those of the species.

V. trilobum. AMERICAN CRANBERRY BUSH. Deciduous. Zones US, MS; 7–1. Native to Canada, northern U.S. To 15 ft. tall, 12 ft. wide. Leaves look much like those of *V. opulus;* they emerge reddish tinged, mature to dark green, turn yellow to red-purple in fall. Blooms midspring, bearing lacecap flowers to 4 in. across. Fruit is similar to that of *V. opulus* but is used for preserves and jellies. Less susceptible to aphid damage than *V. opulus*. 'Wentworth' has larger berries and bright red fall foliage. 'Compactum' is a smaller form, to 6 ft. high and wide.

V. wrightii. WRIGHT VIBURNUM. Deciduous. Zones US, MS, LS; 8–4. From Japan. Similar to *V. dilatatum* except for its larger leaves, which may turn a good red in fall. Useful tall hedge.

VICK'S PLANT. See PLECTRANTHUS cylindraceus

VICTORIAN BOX. See PITTOSPORUM undulatum

VIGNA caracalla
(Phaseolus caracalla)

SNAIL VINE

Fabaceae (Leguminosae)

PERENNIAL VINE SOMETIMES GROWN AS ANNUAL

✿ TS H 12–6; OR GROW IN POTS

☼ FULL SUN

💧 REGULAR WATER

Vigna caracalla

Tropical American native that generally resembles pole bean in form and foliage. The spring-to-summer flowers are different, though: fragrant, cream to pale purple, with lilac or purple markings and twisted keel petals that are coiled like a snail shell—odd and pretty. Twines rapidly to 10–20 ft.; good summer screen or bank cover. Evergreen in Tropical South; in colder regions, treat as annual or bring indoors for winter. Sometimes sold as *Phaseolus gigantea*.

VINCA

PERIWINKLE

Apocynaceae

PERENNIALS

✿ ZONES VARY BY SPECIES

◑ ● PARTIAL TO FULL SHADE

💧💧 MODERATE TO REGULAR WATER

Vinca minor

With trailing, arching stems that root where they touch soil, these plants are useful as ground and bank covers. Shiny dark green, oval to oblong leaves. Lavender-blue, five-petaled, pinwheel-shaped flowers appear in leaf joints in early spring. Plant the larger species and its selections 2–2½ ft. apart, dwarf kinds 1½ ft. apart. When plantings mound up or are layered with old stems, shear or mow before new spring growth begins. Very soil tolerant. Compete successfully with surface tree roots. Deer don't seem to care for periwinkles.

V. major. GREATER PERIWINKLE. Zones MS, LS, CS; 9–7. The larger, more aggressive species. Leaves to 3 in. long, flowers to 2 in. across; mounds to 1–2 ft. high. Spreads rapidly and can be extremely invasive in sheltered, forested areas. 'Variegata', probably as common as the green form, has leaves strongly edged in white.

V. minor. COMMON PERIWINKLE, DWARF PERIWINKLE. Zones US, MS, LS, CS; 9–1. Miniature version of *V. major*, with ¾- to 1¾-in.-long leaves, flowers to 1 in. wide, and a height of just 4–6 in. More restrained, less likely to invade adjacent plantings. Selections include *V. m. alba*, with white flowers; 'Atropurpurea', deep purple flowers, small leaves; 'Gertrude Jekyll' ('Miss Jekyll'), smaller grower with white flowers; 'Green Carpet', with dense foliage and few flowers; 'La Grave' ('Bowles' Variety'), deeper blue flowers, larger leaves; 'Ralph Shugert', white-edged leaves, blue flowers, repeat autumn bloom; and 'Sterling Silver', blue flowers, white-edged leaves speckled with pale green.

V. rosea. See Catharanthus roseus

VIOLA

VIOLA, VIOLET, PANSY

Violaceae

PERENNIALS, SOME GROWN AS ANNUALS

✿ ZONES VARY BY SPECIES

☼ ◑ ● EXPOSURE NEEDS VARY BY SPECIES

💧 REGULAR WATER

Viola × wittrockiana

Botanically speaking, violas, pansies, and almost all violets are perennials belonging to the genus *Viola*. However, violas and pansies are usually treated as annuals, invaluable for winter and spring bloom in mild-winter areas, for spring-through-early-summer color in colder climates. Typically used for mass color in borders and edgings, as covers for spring-flowering bulbs, in containers. Violets are more often used as woodland or rock garden plants.

Violas and pansies take sun or partial shade, though pansies will bloom longer into spring if given afternoon shade. Violets grow in part or full shade, but most are natives of deciduous forests and bloom best with at least some sun during the flowering season. Violas are tougher than pansies, more tolerant of both heat and cold.

Almost all violets have two kinds of flowers: normal, conspicuous ones that are held above the foliage and may be pollinated and set seed, and short-stemmed, inconspicuous cleistogamous (Greek for "closed mouth") flowers that set copious seed without pollination and produce offspring identical to the parent. Many violets also spread by aboveground runners. Some reproduce so freely they can crowd out other small plants.

In the Upper South, set out nursery plants of pansies and violas in spring for summer bloom; elsewhere, plant in autumn for winter-to-spring (or longer) bloom. Or start from seed: in the Upper South, sow in mid- to late summer and overwinter seedlings in cold frame until spring; or sow indoors in winter, plant in spring. Elsewhere, sow in mid- to late summer, plant out in fall. To prolong bloom, pick flowers (with some foliage) regularly and remove faded blooms before they set seed. In hot areas, plants get ragged by mid- to late spring and should be removed.

Violas and pansies have such complex ancestries that many botanists are unwilling to assign them to species, preferring to list them by selection name. However, we believe it will avoid confusion if we retain these plants under their former names, invalid though they now may be.

V. affinis. LECONTE VIOLET. Zones US, MS, LS; 8–4. Native from New England south to Georgia and Alabama, west to Wisconsin. To 3 in. tall, spreading wider, with small, triangular, wavy-toothed leaves. Dark-veined violet flowers, white at petal bases and centered with a lighter eye, open above the foliage in spring.

V. blanda. SWEET WHITE VIOLET. Zones US, MS, LS; 9–5. From eastern North America. To 2–3 in. high, spreading indefinitely by runners. Fragrant white flowers with purple veining have sharply reflexed petals. Likes moist soil with lots of organic material.

V. cornuta. VIOLA. Perennials grown as cool-season annuals. Zones US, MS, LS, CS, TS; 6–1. Native to Spain. To 6–8 in. high and 8 in. wide, with smooth, wavy-edged leaves. Purple, pansylike, slender-spurred flowers about 1½ in. across. Modern strains and selections are complex hybrids with larger, shorter-spurred flowers; they come in solid colors (purple, blue, yellow, apricot, ruby red, white) or with elaborate markings ("faces"). Crystal strain has extra-large flowers in pure, unshaded colors. Sorbet strain, which comes in pastel bicolors, is especially hardy to cold.

Some nurseries offer English violas—named selections propagated by cuttings or division. These form 2-ft.-wide clumps. Selections include 'Better Times', 2-in. yellow flowers; 'Columbine', creamy white liberally splashed in purple; 'Etain', pale yellow with purple border; 'Mt. Spokane', white with a shading of palest blue; and 'Whiskers', cream marked with thin purple lines.

V. obliqua (V. cucullata). MARSH BLUE VIOLET. Zones US, MS, LS; 9–7. From eastern and central North America. To 6 in. high, 10 in. wide. Toothed, heart-shaped leaves to 4 in. across. Blue, ¾-in.-wide flowers are held well above the leaves in early spring. Good ground cover; no runners,

V

but self-sows liberally and can become a pest. The violet often sold as 'White Czar'—white, with yellow throat veined in black—is a selection of this species; the name correctly belongs to an old variety of *V. odorata*, however.

V. odorata. SWEET VIOLET. Zones US, MS, LS; 8−6. The violet of song and story. To 8 in. high, 1½ ft. wide. Probably native to Europe. Dark green, heart-shaped, 2½-in.-long leaves with toothed margins. Fragrant, short-spurred flowers to ¾ in. wide or wider in deep violet, bluish rose, or white. Selections include 'Rosina' (pink), 'Royal Elk' (violet), and 'Royal Robe' (deep violet). Clump-forming 'Charm' has small white flowers. For better spring display, remove runners and shear rank growth in late fall, then apply a complete fertilizer in earliest spring.

V. Parma Violets. Zones MS, LS. Hybrids with small, usually double, intensely fragrant flowers. They resemble *V. odorata,* but are far less vigorous and less inclined to spread; they advance slowly by runners. Give them rich soil and a cool location. 'Duchesse de Parme' (lavender), 'Marie Louise' (deep violet), and 'Swanley White' are sometimes available. Beyond hardiness range, grow as houseplants.

V. pedata. BIRD'S-FOOT VIOLET. Zones US, MS, LS; 8−1. From eastern North America. So named because its finely divided leaves resemble a bird's foot. Forms a clump to 2 in. high, 4 in. wide; does not spread by runners. Blooms early spring to early summer; 4-in. stems bear inch-wide, typically two-tone violet-blue flowers with darker veining. Not as easy to grow as other violets; likes excellent drainage, filtered sun or high shade, and acidic soil.

V. riviniana. Zones US, MS, LS; 8−5. From southern Europe, North Africa. Tiny violet to 3 in. high or less, spreading (sometimes aggressively) by runners and seed. Heart- or kidney-shaped, 1-in. leaves; tiny lavender-blue flowers in spring (fall through late spring in mild-winter areas). Useful for small-scale ground cover in partial shade or morning sun (away from choice small perennials) or as filler between stepping-stones or paving blocks. Most often seen is 'Purpurea', with leaves that emerge deep maroon and eventually mature to dusky green. Succeeds with moderate water if shaded from summer heat.

V. sororia. DOORYARD VIOLET. Zones US, MS, LS, TS; 11−1. From eastern and central North America. To 4−6 in. high, 8 in. wide; does not spread by runners but self-sows freely. Roughly heart-shaped leaves to 5 in. wide vary from densely hairy to almost smooth. Good ground cover under woodland shrubs. Nearly scentless, ½- to ¾-in. flowers in spring to early summer are held close to leaves; colors range from white to red-violet to blue-violet. Most commonly seen are the following smooth-leafed selections (all come true from seed): 'Albiflora', pure white with yellow in throat; 'Freckles', white liberally spotted with blue; 'Priceana' (popularly known as Confederate violet), white with blue-violet veining in throat.

V. tricolor. JOHNNY-JUMP-UP. Perennial grown as cool-season annual. Zones US, MS, LS, CS, TS; 6−1. From Europe, Asia. Spring bloomer to 6−12 tall and broad; spreads widely by profuse self-sowing. Oval, deeply lobed leaves to 1¼ in. long. Pert, ½- to ¾-in., velvety purple-and-yellow or blue-and-yellow flowers are the original wild pansies. Same planting and care as pansy. Crosses with closely related small-flowered species have produced forms with flowers in violet, blue, white, yellow, lavender, mauve, apricot, orange, red—with or without markings ("faces"). Flowers of 'Molly Sanderson' are very dark purple—almost black.

V. walteri. WALTER'S VIOLET. Zones MS, LS, CS; 9−7. Native from South Carolina to Florida and west to Texas, Ohio. To 6−8 in. tall, wide spreading, with mottled, dark green foliage, often tinged purple beneath. Stems root where they touch the ground, producing new plants. In spring, bears blue-violet flowers with dark veins and white petal bases, paler eye.

V. × wittrockiana. PANSY. Perennial grown as cool-season annual. Zones US, MS, LS, CS, TS; 5−1. To 6−10 in. high, 9−12 in. wide. Many strains with 2- to 4-in. flowers in white, blue, mahogany red, rose, yellow, apricot, purple; also bicolors. Most have dark blotches on the lower three petals; such flowers are often said to resemble faces. Shiny green leaves are oval to nearly heart shaped, slightly lobed, 1½ in. or longer.

Strains are almost too numerous to mention; here are just a few. Accord/Banner and Universal Plus produce 2- to 2½-in. flowers in a wide range of solid and blotched colors. Clear Sky, Crystal Bowl (Clear Crystal), and Delta strains bear flowers without blotches or other markings. Contessa has ruffled, 2-in. blooms. Flowers of Ghost Mix are 2½ in. wide,

carried on long stems good for cutting. Imperial Hybrids and Majestic Giants offer extra-large (to 4-in.-wide) flowers. Unlike the others, Sprite Mix is a ground cover pansy, growing 4−5 in. high, 1½ ft. wide, with 2-in. blossoms. A few named selections deserve mention. Flowers of 'Jolly Joker' show striking contrast between bright orange lower petals and deep purple upper petals; 'Padparadja' has flowers of pure reddish orange; 'Springtime Black' has 2-in., velvety black blooms.

VIOLET. See VIOLA

VIOLET TRUMPET VINE. See CLYTOSTOMA callistegioides

VIRGINIA BLUEBELLS. See MERTENSIA pulmonarioides

VIRGINIA CREEPER. See PARTHENOCISSUS quinquefolia

Vitaceae. The grape family contains vines that climb by tendrils and produce berries. Besides grape, best-known representatives are Boston ivy and Virginia creeper (both species of *Parthenocissus*).

VITEX

CHASTE TREE

Verbeneaceae

DECIDUOUS AND EVERGREEN SHRUBS OR TREES

✂ US, MS, LS, CS, EXCEPT AS NOTED

☼ FULL SUN

◐ ◖ MODERATE TO REGULAR WATER

Vitex agnus-castus

Given the paucity of blue-flowered summer-blooming trees and shrubs, it's a wonder more people aren't planting chaste trees. These drought-tolerant, pest-free plants combine striking blue, tubular summer blossoms with handsome leaves shaped like an open hand. They grow in almost any well-drained soil, will take coastal conditions, and are not usually browsed by deer.

V. agnus-castus. LILAC CHASTE TREE. Deciduous shrub or small tree. Native to southern Europe, central Asia. In most areas, grows fast to make a multitrunked tree with a broad, spreading habit—about 15−20 ft. high and wide. In the Upper South, growth is slower and mature size is 8−10 ft. high and wide. Aromatic leaves are divided into five to seven narrowly oval, pointed leaflets that are grayish green above, green beneath; each leaflet is 2−6 in. long. No real fall color.

Small, lightly fragrant, lilac to dark blue flowers in 6- to 12-in. spikes appear at branch ends and leaf joints in summer. Blooms come on new growth, so prune in late winter, removing twiggy growth and crowded branches. If you remove spent flowers before seeds form, plant will send out a second flush of blooms.

Unnamed seedlings vary in showiness of flowers, so buy a plant in bloom to see what you're getting. Or choose one of the following superior named selections. For blue or violet flowers, look for 'Abbeville Blue', with very showy deep blue spikes; 'Montrose Purple', a strong grower with rich violet flowers; and 'Shoal Creek', with blue-violet blossoms on spikes up to 1½ ft. long. Pink-flowered choices include 'Fletcher Pink', a fast grower with lavender-pink flowers, and 'Rosea', with mauve-pink blooms. White-flowered selections include 'Alba', with particularly large flower spikes, and fast-growing 'Silver Spire'.

V. negundo. Deciduous shrub or small tree. Native to southeast Africa, eastern Asia. Similar to *V. agnus-castus* but a little larger and more cold hardy. The 5- to 8-in. flower spikes aren't as showy. 'Heterophylla' has delicate-looking, finely lobed leaflets.

V. rotundifolia. BEACH VITEX. Evergreen shrub. Native to coastal areas of Hawaii, Australia, Asia. Sprawls to 1½−4 ft. high, 6−8 ft. wide; roots as it spreads to make a dense ground cover. Aromatic, medium green, broadly oblong to roundish leaves to 2½ in. long. Short spikes of bluish purple, ½-in. flowers (popular in leis) appear all year in warmest areas, in summer in colder part of range. Tiny bluish black fruits.

V. trifolia. Evergreen shrub or small shrubby tree. Zones US, MS, LS, CS, TS. Native to Asia and Australia. Fast growth to 12–20 ft. high and wide. Leaves are sometimes simple but are usually divided into three 4-in.-long leaflets with felted gray undersides. Lavender-blue flowers with a white spot on the lip open in summer on 4- to 10-in.-long spikes. Makes a fine-textured hedge; clip regularly. 'Variegata' has white-variegated foliage; cut out shoots that revert to plain green.

VOODOO LILY. See AMORPHOPHALLUS

VRIESEA

Bromeliaceae

PERENNIALS

✿ TS H 12–10; OR HOUSEPLANTS

◐ PARTIAL SHADE; BRIGHT INDIRECT LIGHT

● REGULAR WATER

Vriesea hieroglyphica

Vrieseas combine spectacular, long-lasting flower spikes with the most handsome foliage of any bromeliad. Rosettes of long, leathery leaves may be banded, mottled, or plain. Spear-shaped flower spikes rising from the plant's center may hold their color for months.

Vrieseas are epiphytes, naturally growing in the crotches of trees. In the Tropical South, you can grow them that way, too—just wrap the plant's base in coarse sphagnum moss and secure it to a tree branch. Mist the moss daily. Elsewhere, grow these bromeliads as a potted plants you take in for the winter. Plant in loose, fast-draining potting mix; let the mix go slightly dry between waterings, and mist plants frequently. You can fill the central cup with water occasionally during the warmer months, but do not keep it continuously filled or the plant may rot. Feed with a general-purpose liquid houseplant fertilizer diluted to half-strength once a month in spring and summer; don't feed in fall and winter. Indoors or out, place vrieseas where they'll get good light but not hot, direct sun.

There are dozens of vrieseas from which to choose, offering a wide range of colors, shapes, and sizes. Hybridization has produced many plants of complex parentage.

V. carinata. LOBSTER CLAW. Pale green foliage in a small rosette—just 8 in. high and wide. Colorful inflorescence with red bracts and green-tipped yellow flowers increases plant height to 1 ft.

V. fosteriana. Rosette to 2½ ft. tall, 3 ft. wide. Yellowish to deep green leaves sport crosswise bands of purple or maroon. Yellow inflorescence increases height to 5 ft. 'Red Chestnut' has light green to whitish leaves with red and maroon bands; 'Vista' produces white foliage with reddish brown markings.

V. gigantea 'Nova'. Rosette to 2½ ft. high, 3–4 ft. wide. Bluish green leaves have light green markings that fade to near-white as the plant ages. Spike to 1½ ft. tall holds yellow-and-white flowers in green bracts.

V. hieroglyphica. Rosette to 3 ft. tall and wide. Leaves are yellowish green with pronounced cross-banding; bands are dark green on upper surface of leaf, dark purplish brown on underside. Greenish flower spike to 2½ ft. tall holds yellow flowers in greenish yellow bracts.

V. imperialis. GIANT VRIESEA. Light green leaves with reddish purple undersides form a rosette to 5 ft. high and wide. Inflorescence features red bracts and yellow or white flowers; it increases plant height dramatically—to 10–15 ft.

V. splendens. FLAMING SWORD. Rosettes to 3 ft. tall, 1 ft. wide. Bluish-green leaves sport blackish purple cross-banding. Flower stalk resembles a 1½- to 2-ft.-long feather of bright red bracts from which small yellow flowers emerge. 'Chantrierei' has particularly bright colors.

WAKE ROBIN. See TRILLIUM

WALLFLOWER. See ERYSIMUM

WALNUT. See JUGLANS

WANDERING JEW. See TRADESCANTIA fluminensis, T. zebrina

WAND LOOSESTRIFE. See LYTHRUM virgatum

WASHINGTONIA

Arecaceae (Palmae)

PALMS

✿ CS, TS

☼ FULL SUN

◊◐● LITTLE TO REGULAR WATER

Washingtonia filifera

These fast-growing fan palms are too tall for most suburban gardens; they are best suited to large properties, avenues, parkways. The two species often hybridize if growing near each other. Widely grown in Florida.

W. filifera. DESERT FAN PALM. Heat zones 12–8. From California, Arizona. Hardy to 18°F. To 60 ft. tall, 20 ft. wide, with thicker trunk than *W. robusta*. Long-stalked, 3- to 6-ft., light green leaves stand well apart in open crown. As leaves mature, they bend down to form a "skirt" of thatch.

W. robusta. THREAD PALM, MEXICAN FAN PALM. Heat zones 12–10. From Mexico. Hardy to 20°F. To 100 ft. tall, 10 ft. wide; trunk is slightly curved or bent, slimmer than that of *W. filifera*. Head of bright green foliage is more compact; leafstalks are shorter, with a red streak on the undersides. Good plant for the beach.

WASHINGTON HAWTHORN. See CRATAEGUS phaenopyrum

WATER AVENS. See GEUM rivale

WATER LILY. See NYMPHAEA

WATERMELON

Cucurbitaceae

ANNUAL

✿ US, MS, LS, CS, TS H 12–2

☼ FULL SUN

● REGULAR WATER, ESPECIALLY WHEN PLANTS ARE YOUNG

Watermelon

One of the South's favorite late-summer treats. World records for size of melons have been held by families in Arkansas and Tennessee. Needs a long growing season, more heat than most other melons, and more space than other vine crops—about 8 ft. by 8 ft. for each hill (circle of seed). Other than that, culture is as described under Melon. Large selections such as 'Charleston Gray', 'Congo', and 'Crimson Sweet' may need as many as 85 to 95 days of hot, sunny weather to mature. If your summers are shorter, choose a smaller, earlier-ripening "icebox" type that will produce in 70 to 75 days, such as 'Minilee', 'Sugar Baby', or yellow-skinned 'Golden Crown'. 'New Queen' is an icebox type with orange flesh. Seed companies also offer yellow-fleshed kinds ('Golden Honey', 'Yellow Doll'), seedless types ('Honey Red Seedless Hybrid', 'Redball Seedless'), and heirlooms ('Amish Moon and Stars', 'Sugar Lump White'). Dwarf-fruited types are also available. Unlike other melons, watermelon does not grow sweeter after harvest—it must be picked ripe. Three tests for ripeness: thumping the melon produces a "thunk"; underside has turned from white to pale yellow; and tendril opposite stem has withered.

WATER-WILLOW. See JUSTICIA americana, J. runyonii

WAX FLOWER, WAX PLANT. See HOYA

WAX MYRTLE. See MYRICA cerifera

WAX VINE. See SENECIO macroglossus

W

WEDELIA trilobata

Asteraceae (Compositae)

PERENNIAL

⚟ CS (WARMER PARTS), TS ⦚ 12–9

☼ ◐ FULL SUN OR LIGHT SHADE

▲ REGULAR WATER

Wedelia trilobata

Native to Central and South America. Trailing evergreen plant to 1½–2 ft. high, spreading to 6 ft. or more by stems that root where they touch damp earth. Fleshy, glossy dark green leaves to 4 in. long, half as wide, with a few coarse teeth or shallow lobes toward tips. Inch-wide flowers resembling tiny yellow zinnias or marigolds *(Tagetes)* bloom almost year-round. Spreads fast; easily propagated by lifting rooted pieces or placing tip cuttings in moist soil. Best in sandy, fast-draining soils but takes heavier soils if drainage is good. If killed to ground by frost, it makes a fast comeback. Tolerates high heat, seaside conditions. Can take lower light but blooms more sparsely in shady conditions. Good for erosion control on slopes: plant 1½ ft. apart, feed lightly. Shear close to ground if planting mounds up or becomes stemmy. Can become invasive.

WEEPING MARY. See BUDDLEIA lindleyana

WEIGELA

Caprifoliaceae

DECIDUOUS SHRUBS

⚟ US, MS, LS ⦚ 8–1

☼ ◐ FULL SUN OR LIGHT SHADE

▲ REGULAR WATER

Weigela florida

From China, Korea, Japan. Weigelas have long been valued in the South for their lavish springtime display of funnel-shaped, 1-in.-long flowers. They aren't attractive out of bloom, have no real fall color. Most are rather coarse leafed and stiff, becoming rangy unless pruned. After flowering, cut back stems that have bloomed to side shoots that have not flowered; leave only one or two of these to each stem. Cut some of the oldest stems to the ground, and thin new suckers to a few of the most vigorous. Another method is to cut back entire plant about halfway just after blooms fade; do this every other year. Resulting dense new growth will provide plenty of flowers the next spring. Use as background plants, as summer screens, in mixed borders.

W. coraeensis. WHITE WEIGELA. To 12–15 ft. tall and wide, with leaves to 6 in. long. Flowers are 1½ in. long, white or light pink aging to red.

W. florida (W. rosea). Fast growth to 6–10 ft. tall, 9–12 ft. wide, with branches often arching to the ground. Leaves 2–4½ in. long. Pink to rose red flowers. The following selections grow about 6 ft. high and wide: 'Bristol Snowflake', white flowers opening from pinkish buds; 'Java Red', red-tinted foliage, red buds opening to deep pink flowers; 'Pink Princess', lilac-pink flowers.

W. hybrids. These are hybrids involving *W. florida*, the early-flowering species *W. praecox*, and other species.

'Briant Rubidor' ('Rubidor', 'Olympiade'). A sport of 'Bristol Ruby' with yellow foliage. To 6 ft. high and wide.

'Bristol Ruby'. To 6–7 ft. tall and nearly as wide, with ruby red flowers. Some repeat bloom in midsummer and fall.

'Candida'. To 5 ft. tall and wide; white flowers that are tinged with green.

'Lucifer' ('Courtared'). Compact growth to 3–5 ft. high and wide. Dark green leaves and extra-large deep red flowers.

'Minuet'. Dwarf selection to 3 ft. tall, 5 ft. wide. Purplish leaves. Flowers blend red, purple, and yellow.

'Newport Red' ('Vanicek'). To 6 ft. tall and wide, with bright red flowers. Young stems are bright green in winter.

'Red Prince'. To 5–6 ft. tall and wide, with red flowers, some summer rebloom.

'Variegata'. Compact growth to 4–6 ft. tall and wide, with leaves edged in creamy yellow to white. Deep rosy red flowers. 'Variegata Nana' is 3 ft. tall and wide.

'Wine and Roses' ('Alexandra'). To 5 ft. tall and wide. Deep purple new leaves are highlighted by bright pink flowers. Foliage matures to purplish green, turns blackish purple in autumn.

WESTERN RED CEDAR. See THUJA plicata

WHITE CEDAR. See CHAMAECYPARIS thyoides

WILD BASIL. See PERILLA frutescens

WILD FOXGLOVE. See PENSTEMON cobaea

WILD GINGER. See ASARUM

WILD INDIGO. See BAPTISIA

WILD LILAC. See CEANOTHUS

WILD MANDRAKE. See PODOPHYLLUM peltatum

WILD OLIVE. See COCCULUS laurifolius

WILD PINK. See SILENE caroliniana

WILD SARSAPARILLA. See SMILAX pumila

WILLOW. See SALIX

WILLOW-LEAFED JESSAMINE. See CESTRUM parqui

WINDFLOWER. See ANEMONE

WINDMILL PALM. See TRACHYCARPUS fortunei

WINTER ACONITE. See ERANTHIS hyemalis

WINTERCREEPER EUONYMUS. See EUONYMUS fortunei

WINTERGREEN. See GAULTHERIA procumbens

WINTER HAZEL. See CORYLOPSIS

WINTERSWEET. See CHIMONANTHUS praecox

WISHBONE FLOWER. See TORENIA fournieri

WISTERIA

Fabaceae (Leguminosae)

DECIDUOUS VINES

⚟ US, MS, LS, CS

☼ FULL SUN

◗ ▲ LITTLE TO MODERATE WATER

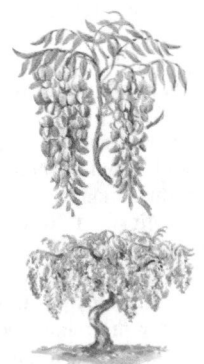

Wisteria sinensis

Twining, woody vines of great size, long life, and exceptional beauty in flower. So adaptable they can be grown as trees, shrubs, or vines. All have large bright green leaves divided into many leaflets, spectacular clusters of blue, violet, pinkish, or white blossoms, and velvety, pealike pods to about 6 in. long. Fall color in subdued shades of yellow. To get off to a good start, buy a cutting-grown, budded, or grafted wisteria; seedlings may not bloom for many years. If you start with budded or grafted plants, keep suckers removed for the first few years, or they may take over. Plants are not fussy about soil, but need good drainage; in alkaline soil, watch for chlorosis (yellow leaves with green veins) and treat with iron chelates or iron sulfate. Wisterias resist damage by browsing deer.

Often considered aggressive pests in the South, but such "nuisance" wisterias are usually untamed. Pruning and training are important for control of size and shape and for bloom production. Let newly planted wisteria grow to establish framework you desire, either single trunked or multi-trunked. Remove stems that interfere with desired framework and pinch back side stems and long streamers. For single-trunked form, rub off buds that develop on trunk. For multiple trunks, select as many vigorous stems

W

as you wish and let them develop; if plant has only one stem, pinch it back to encourage others to develop. The main stem will become a good-sized trunk, and the weight of a mature vine is considerable. Support structures should be sturdy and durable. Do not allow Asian species to twine around and thereby damage railings, trellises, gutters, or small trees.

Tree wisterias can be bought already trained; or you can train your own. Remove all but one main stem and stake this one securely. Tie stem to stake at frequent intervals, using plastic tape to prevent girdling. When plant has reached height at which you wish head to form, pinch or prune out tip to force branching. Shorten branches to beef them up. Pinch back long streamers and rub off all buds that form below head.

In general, wisterias do not need fertilizer. Prune blooming plants every winter: cut back or thin out side shoots from main or structural stems, and shorten back to two or three buds the flower-producing spurs that grow from these shoots. It's easy to recognize fat flower buds on these spurs.

In summer, cut back long streamers before they tangle up in main body of vine; save those you want to use to extend height or length of vine and tie them to support—eaves, wall, trellis, arbor. If old plants grow rampantly but fail to bloom, withhold all nitrogen fertilizers for an entire growing season (buds for the next season's bloom are started in early summer). If that fails to produce bloom the next year, you can try pruning roots in spring—after you're sure no flowers will be produced—by cutting vertically with a spade into plant's root zone.

Using an herbicide is the most effective way to eradicate an unwanted wisteria. First, fill a large bucket with glyphosate (Roundup) solution mixed to the strength specified on the label. Then push as much of the vine's leaves and green stems into the bucket as you can (choose young, flexible shoots). Leave the stems there for several days; leaves and stems will absorb the chemical and carry it down to the roots. Be sure to keep children and pets away from the bucket of herbicide.

W. brachybotrys (W. venusta). SILKY WISTERIA. Heat zones 9–6. Native to Japan. Silky-haired, 8- to 14-in.-long leaves divided into 9 to 13 leaflets. White, very large, long-stalked, highly fragrant flowers in short (4- to 6-in.) clusters that open all at once during leaf-out. 'Violacea' has purple-blue flowers. Older plants (especially in tree form) have remarkably profuse bloom. 'Shiro Kapitan', sometimes sold as 'Alba', is the most commonly cultivated form; it bears pure white (sometimes double) flowers with yellow markings. Other selections include 'Murasaki Kapitan' (also sold as *W. venusta* 'Violacea'), bearing blue-violet flowers with white markings; and 'Okayama', with faintly scented deep mauve blossoms.

W. floribunda. JAPANESE WISTERIA. Heat zones 9–3. From Japan. Leaves are 12–16 in. long, divided into 15 to 19 leaflets. Fragrant, 1½-ft. clusters of violet or violet-blue flowers appear during leaf-out. Clusters open gradually, starting from the base; this prolongs bloom season but makes for a less spectacular burst of color than that provided by *W. sinensis.* Many selections are sold in white, pink, and shades of blue, purple, and lavender, usually marked with yellow and white. 'Macrobotrys' ('Longissima') has long (1½- to 3-ft.) clusters of violet flowers. 'Longissima Alba' bears 2-ft. clusters of white blossoms; 'Ivory Tower' is similar. 'Rosea' has lavender-pink blooms; 'Violacea Plena' sports very full clusters of double, deep violet-blue flowers. 'Texas Purple' blooms at an early age.

W. frutescens. AMERICAN WISTERIA. Heat zones 9–6. Native from Virginia to Florida and Texas. Leaves 7–12 in. long, divided into 9 to 15 leaflets. Later blooming and less vigorous than *W. floribunda* and *W. sinensis,* with thinner stems; not as potentially destructive. Fragrant pale lilac flowers with yellow blotch appear in dense, 4- to 6-in.-long clusters in late spring after leaf-out; blossoms are followed by 2- to 4-in. pods. White-flowered 'Nivea' blooms earlier than species.

W. macrostachya. KENTUCKY WISTERIA. Heat zones 9–6. Native from Illinois to Texas. A good choice for smaller gardens. Like *W. frutescens,* blooms among new leaves in late spring, after the Asian species bloom. Flowers are light blue to violet or blue-purple, in 8- to 12-in.-long, fragrant, pendulous clusters. Shiny leaves usually divided into nine leaflets, each to 3 in. long. The 4-in. pods are smooth, sometimes twisted. Less vigorous and better behaved than Asian species. 'Clara Mack' has white flowers. 'Bayou Two o' Clock' has blue-violet flowers held in long, pointed racemes. 'Pondside Blue' bears pale blue-violet blossoms.

W. sinensis. CHINESE WISTERIA. Heat zones 9–5. Native to China; the classic wisteria of the South. Leaves are 10–12 in. long, divided into 7 to 13 leaflets. Violet-blue, slightly fragrant flowers appear before leaf-out; they come in shorter clusters (to 1 ft.) than those of *W. floribunda* but make quite a show by opening all at once, nearly all along the cluster. In the Lower South, Chinese wisteria has escaped cultivation and smothers entire hillsides and woodlands with blue blossoms in spring. 'Alba' has white flowers; 'Caroline' and 'Cooke's Special' are grafted forms.

WITCH HAZEL. See HAMAMELIS

WOADWAXEN. See GENISTA

WONGA-WONGA VINE. See PANDOREA pandorana

WOODBINE HONEYSUCKLE. See LONICERA periclymenum

WOOD FERN. See DRYOPTERIS, THELYPTERIS kunthii

WOOD HYACINTH. See HYACINTHOIDES

WOOD POPPY. See STYLOPHORUM diphyllum

WOODRUFF, SWEET. See GALIUM odoratum

WOOD VAMP. See DECUMARIA barbara

WOODSIA obtusa

BLUNT-LOBED WOODSIA, COMMON WOODSIA

Dryopteridaceae (Polypodiaceae)

FERN

US, MS, LS, CS | 9–1

FULL SUN OR LIGHT SHADE

REGULAR WATER

Woodsia obtusa

Native from Quebec to Florida. Small deciduous fern to 2 ft. tall, 1½ ft. wide. Fronds 12–15 in. long, 4 in. wide, bright green in shade, gray green in sun. May be once cut into deeply lobed segments or twice cut. Fronds produced throughout growing season. Likes well-drained soil that is neutral or even slightly alkaline. Use in woodland or rock garden.

WOODWARDIA

CHAIN FERN

Blechnaceae (Polypodiaceae)

FERNS

US, MS, LS, CS | 10–1

PART SHADE

AMPLE WATER

Woodwardia areolata

Medium to large, upright, usually coarse-textured, deciduous ferns with rich green fronds. Common name comes from the chainlike pattern of spore cases beneath frond segments. Shade beneath canopy of tall trees is an ideal site. Deer aren't fond of these ferns.

W. areolata. NETTED CHAIN FERN. Native to eastern, southeastern U.S. To 2 ft. high and wider than tall, with deeply lobed fronds, the lobes finely toothed. Spore-bearing fronds are narrower. Can take considerable sun if roots are kept wet.

W. virginica. Native to eastern, southern U.S. To 1–2 ft. tall, 1 ft. wide, with twice-cut fronds that are bronzy green when they emerge. Likes wet soil and can even grow with roots submerged.

WORMWOOD. See ARTEMISIA

FOR INFORMATION ON YOUR CLIMATE ZONES
PLEASE SEE PAGES 28–38

W

XANTHOSOMA

Araceae

PERENNIALS

TS | 12–10; OR HOUSEPLANTS

FILTERED SUNLIGHT; BRIGHT INDIRECT LIGHT

AMPLE WATER

*Xanthosoma
sagittifolium*

Tropical plants related to *Alocasia*. Both species are stemless, grow to 6 ft. tall and wide, produce big, arrow-shaped leaves on long stalks. Bloom intermittently throughout the year. Flowers are more curious than attractive, resembling those of calla (*Zantedeschia*), with a central spike surrounded by a usually greenish or yellowish bract. These plants need moist, rich soil for best performance. They can grow in standing water or in pots submerged in a pond or pool. Protect from hard frosts.

X. sagittifolium. Dark green, 3-ft.-long leaves on 3-ft. stalks. Greenish white, 7- to 9-in.-long bracts. 'Lanceolatum' has lance-shaped blackish green leaves. Leaves and leafstalks of 'Yellow Leaf' have a golden cast.

X. violaceum (X. nigrum). Grows from edible tubers. Dark green leaves to 2 ft. long have paler undersides, purplish veins and margins, powdery appearance. Purple, 2½-ft. leafstalks have a heavy, waxy, bluish or grayish coating. Yellowish white bracts to 1 ft. long.

YARROW. See ACHILLEA

YAUPON. See ILEX vomitoria

YELLOW ARCHANGEL. See LAMIUM galeobdolon

YELLOW BELLS, YELLOW ELDER. See TECOMA stans

YELLOW-EYED GRASS. See SISYRINCHIUM

YELLOW OLEANDER. See THEVETIA peruviana

YELLOW POINCIANA. See PELTOPHORUM pterocarpum

YELLOW SHRIMP PLANT. See PACHYSTACHYS lutea

YELLOW TRUMPET FLOWER. See TECOMA stans

YELLOW TRUMPET VINE. See MACFADYENA unguis-cati

YELLOW WAXBELLS. See KIRENGESHOMA palmata

YELLOW WOOD. See CLADRASTIS kentukea

YESTERDAY-TODAY-AND-TOMORROW. See BRUNFELSIA pauciflora

YEW. See TAXUS

YUCCA

Agavaceae

EVERGREEN PERENNIALS, SHRUBS, TREES

ZONES VARY BY SPECIES; OR HOUSEPLANTS

FULL SUN; BRIGHT LIGHT

WATER NEEDS VARY BY SPECIES

Yucca aloifolia

Yuccas grow over much of North America; hardiness depends on species. All have tough, sword-shaped leaves and large clusters of white or whitish, rounded to bell-shaped flowers. Some are stemless, while others reach tree size. Best in well-drained soil.

Taller kinds make striking silhouettes, and even stemless species provide important vertical effects when in bloom. Some have stiff, sharp-pointed leaves; keep these away from walks, terraces, and other well-traveled areas. Yuccas are not usually browsed by deer.

Young plants of some species can be used as indoor plants; they withstand the dry indoor atmosphere and will grow well near hot, sunny windows. Buy 1-gallon size or smaller; set out in ground when plants become too large for indoors. Successful indoors are *Y. aloifolia* (but beware of sharp-pointed leaves), *Y. elephantipes*, *Y. filamentosa*, *Y. gloriosa*, and *Y. recurvifolia*.

Y. aloifolia. SPANISH BAYONET. Zones LS, CS, TS; 12–1. Native to the South. Slow growth to 10 ft. by 5 ft. or larger; trunk may be single or branched, sometimes sprawling in picturesque effect. Stems densely clothed in dark green, sharp-pointed leaves to 2½ ft. long and 2 in. wide. White flowers (sometimes tinged purple) to 4 in. across, in dense, erect clusters to 2 ft. tall in summer. 'Variegata' has foliage marked in yellowish white. Moderate water.

Y. baccata. DACTIL YUCCA. Zones US, MS, LS, CS, TS; 12–5. Native to the Southwest. Slow growth to 3 ft. high, 5 ft. wide. Foliage clump may have no stem or a short, prostrate one. Leaves to 2 ft. long, 2 in. wide, with fibers along the edges. Large, fleshy flowers in late spring are red brown outside, white inside, in dense, 2-ft.-long clusters. Fleshy, edible, bananalike fruits to 6 in. long. Little water.

Y. elata. SOAPTREE YUCCA. Zones LS, CS, TS; 12–8. Native to the Southwest, northern Mexico. Slow growth to 6–20 ft. tall, 8–10 ft. wide, with single or branched trunk. Leaves to 4 ft. long, ½ in. wide. Tall spikes of white flowers in summer. Little water.

Y. elephantipes (Y. gigantea). GIANT YUCCA. Zones CS, TS; 12–9. Native to Mexico. Fast growing (to 2 ft. per year), eventually 15–30 ft. tall, 8 ft. wide, usually with several trunks. Leaves 4 ft. long, 3 in. wide, dark rich green. Striking silhouette alone or combined with other big-scale foliage plants; out of scale in smaller gardens. Large spikes of creamy white flowers in spring. Does best in good, well-drained soil with regular water.

Y. filamentosa. ADAM'S NEEDLE. Zones US, MS, LS, CS, TS; 12–5. Native to the Southeast. Stemless plant to 2½ ft. tall, 5 ft. wide. Stiff dark green leaves 2½ ft. long, 1 in. wide, with long, loose fibers at edges. Blooms in late spring and summer, with lightly fragrant, yellowish white flowers, 2–3 in. wide, carried in tall, narrow clusters to 4–7 ft. or taller. Looks similar to *Y. flaccida* and *Y. smalliana*. One of the most cold-hardy and widely planted yuccas. 'Bright Edge' has leaves edged in yellow; 'Concava Variegata' has cream-edged leaves tinted pink in cold weather; 'Garland Gold' leaves have gold center stripe; 'Golden Sword' has yellow leaves edged in dark green; 'Ivory Tower' has out-facing rather than drooping flowers. Moderate water.

Y. flaccida. Zones US, MS, LS, CS; 9–5. Native to the Southeast. Stemless. Differs from *Y. filamentosa* in having less rigid leaves, straight fibers on leaf edges, and somewhat shorter flower clusters. Moderate water.

Y. glauca. SOAPWEED. Zones US, MS, LS, CS; 10–5. Native to central and southwestern U.S. To 3–4 ft. high and wide or larger, with short or prostrate trunk. Stiff, narrow, 1- to 2½-ft.-long leaves form a clump 3–4 ft. wide. Leaves are grayish green, edged with a hairline of white and a few thin threads. White summer flowers bloom on a spike 4–5 ft. tall. Moderate water.

Y. gloriosa. MOUND-LILY YUCCA, SPANISH DAGGER, SOFT-TIP YUCCA. Zones MS, LS, CS, TS; 12–7. Native to the Southeast. Much like *Y. aloifolia*; generally multitrunked to 10 ft. tall and 8 ft. wide. Plant is usually stemless in youth. Leaf points are soft and will not penetrate skin. Summer bloom. Good green color blends well with tropical-looking, lush plants. Leaves of 'Variegata' are edged in creamy white. Needs moderate water; too much moisture may produce black areas on leaf margins.

Y. pallida. PALE-LEAF YUCCA. Zones MS, LS, CS, TS; 12–7. Native to Texas. To 1½ ft. tall, 2½ ft. wide. Compact rosette of 1- to 2-ft.-long, pale blue-green leaves with thin yellow or brownish margins and a spine at the tip. Branched spikes to 7 ft. high hold many pale green to creamy white flowers in spring. Little to moderate water.

Y. recurvifolia (Y. pendula). CURVE-LEAF YUCCA. Zones MS, LS, CS; 9–7. Native to the Southeast. Single trunk to 6–10 ft. tall; it is unbranched in younger plants but may be lightly branched in age. You can cut plant back to keep it single trunked. Reaches 6–8 ft. wide; spreads by offsets to form large groups. Beautiful blue-gray leaves are 2–3 ft. long, 2 in. wide, sharply bent downward; leaf tips are spined but bend to the touch (they aren't dangerously sharp). Less stiff and metallic looking than most yuccas. Loose, open, 3- to 5-ft.-tall clusters of large white flowers in late spring or

Y

early summer. Easy to grow in all garden conditions; give moderate water. 'Banana Split' has golden yellow leaves edged in gray green.

Y. rostrata. Zones US, MS, LS, CS, TS; 12–6. Native to Mexico, extreme southwestern Texas. To 12 ft. tall, 9 ft. wide. The most notable feature is the trunk: up to 8 in. thick, covered with soft gray fuzz (fibers remaining from old leaf bases). Needle-pointed leaves to 2 ft. long, ½ in. wide. Blooms in autumn, bearing 2-ft. clusters of white flowers on a 2-ft. stalk. Little to moderate water.

Y. rupicola. TWISTED-LEAF YUCCA. Zones MS, LS, CS, TS; 12–7. Clump-forming Texas native to 3 ft. high and wide. Sharp-pointed green leaves reach 2 ft. long; they are straight when young, then twist with age. In spring, stalks to 3–8 ft. tall bear bell-shaped, creamy white flowers with a yellow-green tinge. Little to moderate water.

Y. smalliana. ADAM'S NEEDLE, BEAR'S GRASS. Zones US, MS, LS, CS, TS; 12–6. Native to southeastern and south-central U.S. Like *Y. filamentosa* but has narrower, flatter leaves and smaller flowers. Moderate water.

Y. thompsoniana. THOMPSON'S YUCCA. Zones MS, LS, CS, TS; 12–7. Native to Texas. Tree to 6–10 ft. tall, 5 ft. wide. Trunk (sometimes branched) is topped with an asymmetrical rosette of narrow, foot-long blue-green leaves; old brown leaves hang from its sides. Blooms in late spring, when white to cream flowers with green-tinged petal bases appear on a 4- to 5-ft. spike. Moderate water.

Y. torreyi. TORREY YUCCA. Zones CS, TS; 12–9. Native from New Mexico and Texas into Mexico. Eventually forms a tree to 15 ft. tall, 9 ft. wide. Begins as a rosette of rigid, sharp-tipped, blue-green leaves on short trunks that slowly elongate. White flowers are borne in late spring on a 4-ft. spike. Needs very little water but tolerates wetter conditions.

Y. treculeana. SPANISH DAGGER. Zones LS, CS, TS; 12–8. Native to Texas and Mexico. Single-trunked or branching tree to 25 ft. tall, 12 ft. wide, topped with symmetrical rosettes of sharp-pointed, thick, stiff dark green to blue-green leaves to 2½–4 ft. long. White or purple-tinged white flowers bloom on a 3-ft. spike in late winter or early spring. Little to moderate water.

ZABEL LAUREL. See PRUNUS laurocerasus 'Zabeliana'

Zamiaceae. This family is closely related to Cycadaceae, differing only in technical details; both families are generally considered to be cycads. Representatives include *Ceratozamia, Dioon,* and *Zamia.*

ZAMIA

Zamiaceae (Cycadaceae)

CYCADS

✿ CS, TS **H** 12–9; OR HOUSEPLANTS

◐ PARTIAL SHADE; BRIGHT LIGHT

💧 REGULAR WATER

Zamia pumila

Of 100 or so species, only the following two are generally seen. Slow growing and costly, but with good care will last for many years, both indoors and out. Short trunks (may be completely or partially beneath soil level) are usually marked with scars from old leaf bases. Trunks are topped with circular crowns of leaves that resemble stiff fern fronds or small palm fronds. Give organically enriched, fast-draining soil. Grown as houseplants, they need bright light (with protection from hottest sun), occasional misting, and monthly feeding in spring and summer with a general-purpose liquid houseplant fertilizer. Water when soil becomes dry to the touch; reduce watering in winter.

Z. furfuracea. CARDBOARD PALM. From southeastern coastal Mexico. To 3 ft. high, 6 ft. wide. Short, sometimes subterranean stem. Fronds to 3 ft. long, usually much less; have as many as 12 pairs (usually fewer) of extremely stiff, leathery, dark green segments to 4½ in. long, 1½ in. wide. Segments may have a few teeth toward the tip. Best in a fairly sunny spot, but with protection from hottest midday sun.

Z. pumila (Z. integrifolia). COONTIE. From Florida, Cuba, West Indies. To 4 ft. high, 6 ft. wide. Short trunk is largely below soil level. Fronds to 3 ft. long, with as many as 30 pairs of dark green segments to 5 in. long, 1¼ in. wide. Good seaside plant; tolerates salt spray.

ZANTEDESCHIA

CALLA

Araceae

RHIZOMES

✿ CS, TS **H** 12–4; OR DIG AND STORE; OR GROW IN POTS

☼ ◐ FULL SUN OR PARTIAL SHADE

💧 REGULAR WATER DURING GROWTH AND BLOOM

Zantedeschia aethiopica

Native to South Africa. Basal clumps of long-stalked, shiny, rich green, arrow- or lance-shaped leaves, sometimes spotted white. Flower bract (spathe) surrounds central spike (spadix) that is tightly covered with tiny true flowers.

Common calla (*Z. aethiopica*) is basically evergreen, but goes partly dormant even in the Tropical South. It is soil tolerant and will thrive in moist, even boggy, soil all year. It cannot withstand storage and so should be grown as a container plant where winter temperatures fall below 10°F.

The other callas described here die to the ground yearly in fall and reappear in spring. They need slightly acid soil and regular water during growth and bloom, followed by a resting period in which, ideally, water is withheld. In rainy climates, rhizomes will tolerate moisture if soil is well drained. Store potted rhizomes dry in their containers. Beyond their hardiness range, rhizomes of deciduous species can be dug and stored over winter, then replanted in spring.

Where callas are hardy, plant all types in fall, setting rhizomes of *Z. aethiopica* 4–6 in. deep, those of other species 2 in. deep. Space rhizomes 8–12 in. apart. Leave undisturbed until overcrowding causes a decline in vigor and bloom quality. Elsewhere, plant rhizomes in spring and lift them in fall. Deer usually leave callas alone.

Z. aethiopica. COMMON CALLA. To 2–4 ft. tall. Forms a large clump of unspotted deep green leaves that are 1½ ft. long, 10 in. wide. Pure white or creamy white, 8-in.-long spathes on 3-ft. stems appear mostly in spring and early summer. 'Green Goddess' is a robust selection with large spathes that are white at the base, green toward the tip. 'Hercules' is larger than species, with big spathes that open flat and curve backward. Dwarf types include 'Childsiana', to 1 ft. tall, and 'Little Gem' ('Minor'), to 1½ ft. tall.

Z. albomaculata. SPOTTED CALLA. Grows to 2 ft. high, with bright green, white-spotted leaves 1–1½ ft. long, 10 in. wide. Creamy yellow or white, 4- to 5-in.-long spathes have a purplish crimson blotch at base. Blooms from early spring into summer.

Z. elliottiana. GOLDEN CALLA. To 1½–2 ft. tall, with bright green, white-spotted leaves 10 in. long, 6 in. wide. Spathes 4–5 in. long, changing from greenish yellow to rich golden yellow. Blooms in late spring or early summer. Tolerates full sun.

Z. hybrids. Plants are usually about the size of *Z. rehmanii* and bloom in late spring and summer. Leaves are typically unspotted, though some selections have spots on foliage. Spathe colors include cream, buff, orange, pink shades, lavender, purple.

Z. pentlandii. Resembles *Z. albomaculata,* but leaves are usually unspotted and 5-in.-long spathes are deep golden yellow with a purple blotch at the base.

Z. rehmanii. RED or PINK CALLA. To 1½–2 ft., with narrow, lance-shaped, unspotted green leaves to 1 ft. long, 2½ in. wide. Pink or rosy pink spathes to 5 in. long in midspring. 'Superba' has dark pink spathes.

ZEBRA GRASS. See MISCANTHUS sinensis 'Zebrinus'

ZEBRA PLANT. See APHELANDRA squarrosa, CALATHEA zebrina

ZEBRINA pendula. See TRADESCANTIA zebrina

ZELKOVA serrata

SAWLEAF ZELKOVA

Ulmaceae

DECIDUOUS TREE

US, MS, LS 9–5

FULL SUN

MODERATE TO REGULAR WATER

East Asian relative of elm *(Ulmus)*. Good shade tree; sometimes used as a substitute for American elm *(U. americana)*, which is highly prone to Dutch elm disease (zelkova is also susceptible but rarely succumbs). Grows at moderate to fast rate to 60 ft. or higher, equally wide. Silhouette ranges from vase shaped to quite spreading. Has smooth gray bark. Narrowly oval, sawtoothed, 2- to 3½-in.-long leaves are dark green and similar to those of elm but rougher in texture. Fall color varies from yellow to dark red to orange-red. Among vase-shaped selections, 'Halka' is the fastest growing and the best American elm mimic; 'Green Vase' has a narrower vase shape than vigorous 'Village Green'.

Zelkova serrata

Excellent shade, lawn, or street tree. Takes wide range of soils. Fairly tolerant of drought, wind. You may need to train and prune young trees to establish a good framework; thin out crowded ascending branches.

ZEPHYRANTHES

RAIN LILY, ZEPHYR FLOWER, FAIRY LILY

Amaryllidaceae

PERENNIALS FROM BULBS

ZONES VARY BY SPECIES; OR GROW IN POTS

FULL SUN, EXCEPT AS NOTED

REGULAR WATER DURING GROWTH AND BLOOM

Zephyranthes candida

Clumps of grassy, 1- to 1½-ft.-long leaves give rise to slender, hollow stems, each bearing a single funnel-shaped flower with six segments. Flowers of some kinds resemble lilies; those of other types look like crocuses. In the wild, flowers bloom after a rain (hence the common name "rain lily"), and they may appear in the garden after a good soaking. These are old-timey passalong plants.

Need little care. Pretty in rock garden or foreground of border. Excellent pot plant for patio or greenhouse. Plant in late summer or early fall; set bulbs 1–2 in. deep, 3 in. apart. In the Upper South, mulch hardier species heavily over winter. Container plants bloom better when somewhat pot-bound.

Z. atamasco. ATAMASCO LILY. Semievergreen. Zones MS, LS, CS, TS; 12–7. Native to the Southeast. Blooms in midspring, with pink-striped buds opening to fragrant, crocuslike, pure white flowers to 3 in. long.

Z. candida. WHITE RAIN LILY. Evergreen. Zones MS, LS, CS, TS; 12–7. From Argentina and Uruguay. Glossy, crocuslike flowers are 2 in. long, pure white outside, tinged with rose inside, borne on stems as long as the leaves. Blooms in late summer, early fall.

Z. citrina. YELLOW RAIN LILY. Deciduous. Zones MS, LS, CS, TS; 10–7. From tropical South America. About the same size as *Z. candida* and blooms at the same time, but the fragrant blossoms are yellow.

Z. drummondii. GIANT PRAIRIE LILY. Deciduous. Zones LS, CS, TS; 12–8. Native to the Texas Hill Country and Mexico. Large (4-in.), fragrant, lilylike pure white flowers open in the evening. Blooms most heavily in early spring, then sporadically through late summer, fall. 'San Carlos Form' is a Mexican selection.

Z. grandiflora. PINK RAIN LILY. Deciduous. Zones MS, LS, CS, TS; 12–7. From Central America. Lilylike, rose pink, 4-in.-wide flowers bloom on 8-in. stems in summer. Blossoms open out flat at midday, close by afternoon.

Z. hybrids. Deciduous. Zones MS, LS, CS, TS. Most widely offered is *Z. ×ajax* (a cross between *Z. candida* and *Z. citrina*), a free-flowering plant with light yellow blossoms. Other hybrids available from mail-order specialists include 'Alamo', with deep rose pink flowers flushed yellow;

'Apricot Queen', yellow blossoms stained pink; 'Big Dude', large white flowers blushed pink at the tips; 'Prairie Sunset', large light yellow blooms suffused with pink; 'Ruth Page', rich pink blooms; and 'Tenexico Apricot', rich apricot flowers that turn pale pink on their second day of bloom.

Z. macrosiphon. Evergreen in warmer part of range. Zones MS, LS, CS, TS; 12–7. From Mexico. Similar to *Z. grandiflora* but produces smaller (nearly 3-in.), rich pink flowers, comes into flower a little earlier, and continues blooming over a longer period. Full sun or partial shade.

Z. reginae. Deciduous. Zones MS, LS, CS, TS; 12–7. From Mexico. Bears 2½-in., crocuslike yellow flowers in midsummer; blossoms open bright yellow, then fade to cream on the second day. Originally sold as 'Valles Yellow'.

Z. treatiae (Z. atamasco treatiae). Semievergreen. Zones CS, TS; 12–9. Native to Florida. Pure white, crocuslike flowers open from red buds. Blooms 2 to 4 weeks before *Z. atamasco*. Gray-green, extremely slender foliage.

Zingiberaceae. The ginger family contains tropical or subtropical perennials with fleshy rhizomes, canelike stems, and (usually) large leaves. Flowers are irregular in form, in spikes or heads, often showy or with showy bracts. Many are aromatic or have fragrant flowers. Members that grow well in Southern gardens include *Alpinia*, spiral flag *(Costus)*, *Curcuma*, torch ginger *(Etlingera)*, dancing girl ginger *(Globba)*, ginger lily *(Hedychium)*, peacock ginger *(Kaempferia)*, and ginger *(Zingiber)*.

ZINGIBER

GINGER

Zingiberaceae

PERENNIALS FROM RHIZOMES

LS, CS, TS 12–8

PARTIAL SHADE

REGULAR TO AMPLE WATER

Zingiber officinale

Growing gingers is a snap. Plants thrive in Southern heat and humidity, spreading slowly but widely by rhizomes. Most folks' knowledge of this genus begins and ends with one species, *Z. officinale*, the source of culinary ginger—but there are also dozens of highly ornamental species, of which a small sampling is presented here. Plant in rich, moist, well-drained soil, placing rhizomes just below the soil surface. Propagate by division in early spring. Plants go dormant in winter, and rhizomes may rot in cold, wet soil. You can grow gingers in pots and move them to shelter in winter; feed once a month during active growth with a general-purpose liquid fertilizer.

Z. hybrids. The following hybrids are grown for their spectacular flowers or foliage.

'Chiang Mai Princess' *(Z. citriodorum)*. To 3–4 ft. tall, with glossy green leaves. Large (8-in.) flowering cone with sharp-pointed bracts starts out dark green, turns blood red. Blooms appear 1–1½ ft. above the ground. Good cut flower.

'Midnight' *(Z. malaysianum)*. To 2–3 ft. high. Grown primarily for dark purplish brown foliage, borne on dark stems. Ground-level flowers open yellow, then age to pink.

'Milky Way'. Grows 2½–3 ft. high, with light green foliage. Ground-level, 4- to 6-in. flowering cones are yellow, with pink flowers.

'Thai Giant'. To 4½–5½ ft. tall, with dark green foliage. Grown for cone-shaped red inflorescences (each as large as 9 in. high and 5 in. wide) that appear at the ends of 3½-ft. stalks. Long-lasting cut flower.

Z. mioga. MIOGA GINGER. Native to China. To 2 ft. high, with dark green leaves. Small yellow flowers with white edges are borne at ground level. Commonly cultivated in Japan for edible shoots in spring, flower buds in summer or fall. In hot climates, goes dormant in summer. Highly attractive foliage of 'Dancing Crane' is green, with white streaks reminiscent of lightning bolts running vertically through each leaf. This selection spreads slowly and is noninvasive; it looks great massed in a shade garden.

Z. officinale. COMMON GINGER. Native to Southeast Asia. This is the ginger used in cooking. Stems 2–4 ft. tall, with narrow, glossy bright green leaves to 1 ft. long. Summer flowers (rarely seen) are yellowish green, with purple lip marked yellow; not especially showy. Buy roots (fresh, not dried) at the grocery store in early spring; cut into 1- to 2-in.-long sections with well-developed growth buds. Let cut ends dry before planting. Allow several months for roots to reach some size, then harvest at any time.

Z. rubens. BENGAL GINGER. From India. To 4 ft. tall. Green foliage. Bright red flowering cones about 1½ in. across bloom at ground level or even partially below the soil. Each scale of the cone produces a single inch-wide red flower with a cream lip marked in red; blossoms emerge one after the other, over the course of several weeks.

Z. spectabile. BEEHIVE GINGER. From Malaysia. To 6 ft. tall. Deep green, slender-pointed leaves to 1–1½ ft. long, with long, slender, pointed tips. Stem about 3 ft. tall bears a showy, foot-long inflorescence; overlapping bracts are yellow, aging to scarlet, and flowers are yellowish with black tips. Good cut flower.

Z. zerumbet. PINE CONE GINGER, SHAMPOO GINGER. Native to India and Malaysia. To 6 ft. tall. Dark green leaves to 1 ft. long and 3 in. wide (broader than those of *Z. officinale*). Inflorescence is a 3- to 5-in. green cone that appears on a separate, short stalk in late summer, then turns brilliant red for 2 to 3 weeks. Small yellow flowers open between the bracts. 'Darcyi' (*Z. darceyi*) has cream-striped leaves. Good cut flower.

ZINNIA

Asteraceae (Compositae)

ANNUALS AND PERENNIALS

US, MS, LS, CS, TS ‖ 12–1, EXCEPT AS NOTED

FULL SUN

REGULAR WATER, EXCEPT AS NOTED

Zinnia elegans

Longtime favorites for colorful, round flowers, typically in summer and early fall. These hot-weather plants don't gain from being planted early; they stand still until weather warms up. Subject to mildew in humid places, if given overhead water, and when autumn brings longer nights, more dew and shade. Sow seeds where plants are to grow (or set out nursery plants) from late spring to early summer. Give good garden soil, feed generously. Most garden zinnias belong to *Z. elegans*.

Z. acerosa. DESERT ZINNIA. Perennial. Zones MS, LS, CS. From southern Arizona, Texas, Mexico. To 6–10 in. high, 2 ft. wide, with hairy, needlelike, ¾-in.-long leaves. Flowers are 1½ in. wide, with fairly large, creamy white rays veined in green on underside. Blooms sporadically from spring through fall, whenever moisture is present; goes dormant during extended periods of drought.

Z. angustifolia. NARROW-LEAF ZINNIA. One of the best annuals for the South; does not get mildew. Compact growth to 16 in. high and wide, with very narrow leaves to 2½ in. long. Orange, 1-in. flowers; each ray has a paler stripe. Blooms in 6 weeks from seed, continues late into fall. 'Classic' grows to 1 ft. high and 2 ft. wide, has 1½-in. flowers. 'Crystal White', 8–10 in. high and 1 ft. wide, bears 1-in. single flowers in pure white. The Star series, also to 1 by 2 ft., has 2-in. blooms in orange, yellow, and white. 'Golden Eye' is much like 'Star White': both have white rays, yellow centers.

Hybrids between *Z. angustifolia* and *Z. elegans* include 'Profusion Cherry Pink', 'Profusion Orange', and 'Profusion White'. All grow 1–1½ ft. high and wide, with 2½-in. flowers with more than one row of rays.

Z. elegans. COMMON ZINNIA. Annual. From Mexico. Sold in strains ranging from less than a foot high and wide to 4 ft. tall, half as wide. Oval to lance-shaped leaves to 5 in. long; summer flowers from less than 1 in. to as much as 5–7 in. across. Forms include full double, cactus flowered (with quilled rays), and crested (cushionlike center surrounded by rows of broad rays); the many colors available include white, pink, salmon, rose, red, yellow, orange, lavender, and purple. 'Envy' is a novelty type with lime green flowers.

Among smaller strains (to 1 ft.) for edging or foreground are Dasher Hybrid Mixed, very quick to bloom; bushy Dreamland; Peter Pan Hybrid Improved; and mildew-resistant Small World. All have 3-in. blooms.

Intermediate types include 1½- to 2 ft.-tall Lilliput mix, with 2-in. pompons in red, pink, yellow, lavender, and white; 2-ft.-tall 'Candy Stripe', with 4-in. white flowers striped with pink, rose, or red; 2½-ft. Ruffles Hybrids, 3½-in. blossoms with ruffled rays; and 18- to 20-in. Sun Bow, with fully double, 1½-in. flowers. Sun Hybrids, 2–2½ ft., have 5-in. flowers; Giant Cactus-flowered Mix, to 3 ft., has 4- to 5-in. semidouble blooms.

Tall plants for cutting and back-of-border planting include 4-ft. Benary's Giants (also sold as Park's Picks, Blue Point) and 3-ft., double-blossomed Dahlia-flowered Mix; both have 4- to 5-in. blooms. 'Big Red Hybrid', to 3 ft., has bright red, 5- to 6-in. flowers.

Z. grandiflora. ROCKY MOUNTAIN ZINNIA. Perennial in Zones CS, TS; annual elsewhere. Native to Rocky Mountains, south into Mexico. To 1 ft. high and wide. Bright green leaves to 1 in. long, ⅛ in. wide. Spring-into-fall flowers are 1½ in. wide, bright yellow with orange eye. Survives with no supplemental moisture but needs regular water to bloom satisfactorily.

Z. haageana. ORANGE ZINNIA. Annual. From southeastern U.S., Mexico. To 2 ft. tall, 1 ft. wide. Narrow, 3-in. leaves. Persian Carpet (1 ft. tall) and Old Mexico (16 in. tall) have double blossoms in yellow, orange, and mahogany red, with all three colors usually mixed in the same flower. Long summer bloom season.

Z. peruviana. PERUVIAN ZINNIA. Annual. Native from southern U.S. to Argentina. Grows to 3 ft. tall and as wide; leaves to 3 in. long, 1¼ in. wide. In summer, bears profuse, 1½-in. flowers in brick red or soft gold. Blossoms dry well for arrangements, either in a vase or on the plant. Also called Bonita zinnia or *Z. pauciflora*.

ZIZIPHUS jujuba. See JUJUBE

ZOYSIA

Poaceae (Gramineae)

PERENNIAL LAWN GRASSES

ZONES VARY BY SPECIES

THRIVE IN SUN, TOLERATE SOME SHADE

REGULAR TO MODERATE WATER

Zoysia tenuifolia

Among the South's best and most popular lawn grasses. These tough Asian natives resist pests, tolerate drought, and withstand much wear. Green in summer, straw colored in winter. Started from sod or plugs. Spread more slowly and are more expensive than other warm-season grasses. Form a dense carpet of turf that chokes out weeds. Mow at 1–2 in. Susceptibility to nematodes limits use in Florida.

Z. 'Cashmere'. Zones LS, CS, TS; 12–8. Dark green, fine, dense turf; similar to 'Emerald' but softer. Not cold hardy.

Z. 'Emerald'. EMERALD ZOYSIA. Zones MS, LS, CS, TS; 12–8. Hybrid between *Z. japonica*, *Z. tenuifolia*. Dense, fine-textured, medium green grass; turns a beautiful beige in winter. Somewhat prickly to bare feet.

Z. japonica. Zones US, MS, LS, CS, TS; 12–6. Several selections: 'Meyer' ('Z-52'), called Meyer zoysia, is coarser than Z. 'Emerald' and even tougher, and it's the preferred selection for the Upper South. Turns brown earliest in winter, turns green latest in spring. 'Belaire' is medium green, particularly cold hardy, coarser textured than 'Meyer', and faster to establish. 'El Toro' resembles 'Meyer' but has a faster establishment rate, better color in cool season, and less thatch buildup.

Z. matrella. MANILA GRASS. Zones LS, CS, TS; 12–8. Like Bermuda grass (*Cynodon dactylon*) in color, texture. Holds color a little better than Meyer zoysia but is not as cold hardy. Susceptible to nematodes.

Z. tenuifolia. KOREAN GRASS. Zones CS, TS; 12–8. The finest-textured zoysia grass but also the least cold hardy. Makes a beautiful grassy meadow or gives mossy effect in areas impossible to mow or water often. Can develop excessive thatch.

ZUCCHINI. See SQUASH

ZYGOCACTUS. See SCHLUMBERGERA

A Practical Guide to
Gardening

Success in gardening, as in any other endeavor, involves a good understanding of certain basic principles and procedures. In these pages, you'll find the fundamental information and step-by-step instructions you need to plant and care for your garden. Arranged in an easy-to-use alphabetical format, this guide offers advice on topics such as making compost, choosing and using fertilizers, plant propagation and planting techniques, pruning, soil management, watering and water conservation, and buying and caring for tools. You'll also find help in dealing with garden problems—plant diseases, insects, animal pests, and weeds—based on the principles of Integrated Pest Management, with emphasis on the least toxic means of control. You can also look to these pages for information on selecting and growing the major categories of plants, from annuals and biennials through grasses and perennials to shrubs, trees, vegetables, and vines.

Annuals

Annuals are plants that germinate, grow shoots and leaves, flower, set seed, and die within a period of less than a year. Biennials (page 597), in contrast, take two growing seasons to complete their life cycle, while perennials (page 615) live for more than 2 (and sometimes for many) years. Though the annual-biennial-perennial distinction seems clear on paper, in the garden it is somewhat blurred. For example, some tender perennials (those that cannot survive freezing temperatures), such as coleus and some kinds of salvia and verbena, are year-round staples in the Tropical South but are grown as annuals where winters are cold. A few of the hardier perennials, such as snapdragon (*Antirrhinum majus*), are grown as annuals because older plants do not grow as well as young ones.

Favorite annuals are listed in "Annuals for Seasonal Color" in A Guide to Plant Selection, beginning on page 39.

Annual Shirley poppies *(Papaver rhoeas)* and corn cockles *(Agrostemma githago)*

PLANTING ANNUALS. The best planting time for annuals depends on your climate and the specific plant. *Cool-season annuals,* such as calendula, sweet pea *(Lathyrus odoratus)*, and pansies *(Viola)*, grow best in the cool soil and mild temperatures of fall and early spring. Also called hardy annuals, these plants can withstand fairly heavy frosts. Indeed, if they are to bloom vigorously, they must develop roots and foliage during cool weather. Gardeners in the Upper South should plant them in very early spring, as soon as the soil can be worked. Elsewhere, they can be planted in fall for bloom in winter and early spring. To ensure winter flowers, timing is important: plant while the days are still warm enough to encourage growth but when day length is decreasing. If you plant too soon, the plants will rush into bloom before they have become established; if you plant too late, you probably won't get flowers until spring. In the Lower, Coastal, and Tropical South, cool-season annuals can also be planted in late winter for spring bloom.

Warm-season annuals are a large group of plants that includes cosmos, impatiens, and zinnia. These plants grow and flower best in the warm months of late spring, summer, and early fall. They are cold tender and may perish in a late frost if planted too early. Set them out in spring after all danger of frost has passed; in the Lower, Coastal, and Tropical South, plant in midspring. (In the Coastal and Tropical South, you can also plant some warm-season annuals, such as petunias, in early fall for winter bloom.)

You can start annuals from seed sown in containers or, in many cases, directly in the garden (see page 632 for more on starting seeds). Many annuals are also sold in pots at nurseries; for best results, choose those that are relatively small, with healthy foliage and few or no flowers. Plants with yellowing leaves and those that are leggy, root-bound, too big for their pots, or already in full bloom will establish very slowly in the garden, and they'll usually flower poorly. (See page 629 for directions on planting from containers.)

To get your annuals off to a good start, prepare the garden soil carefully before setting out transplants or sowing seed. You'll find information on preparing planting beds on page 628.

CARING FOR ANNUALS. The key to success with annuals is to keep them growing steadily, through attention to watering, fertilizing, and deadheading (that is, removing dead flowers and any seedpods).

Water the bed thoroughly after you plant; thereafter, water enough to keep soil moist, but not soggy. Young seedlings or transplants may need water once a day in warm weather, but as they become established they will be able to get by with less. Apply a 1- to 2-inch-thick layer of mulch (such as compost, ground bark, or pine needles) to conserve water and discourage weeds from establishing.

Mixing a complete fertilizer into the soil before planting will generally supply annuals with nutrients sufficient for at least half the growing season. Give supplemental feedings both after flowering starts and again in late summer.

As their flowers fade, annuals focus their energy into ripening seeds. If you regularly deadhead a plant, it will usually bear more flowers in a continued effort to produce seeds. Deadheading also keeps the garden tidy. To do the job, just pinch or cut off individual, spent flowers or shear the flower heads with pruning or hedge shears, being careful not to remove any more than one-third of the plant.

Deadheading

WATER JUNKIES. *Many annuals sold at garden centers are water junkies. They receive all the water and fertilizer they can handle—and as a result, they grow more leaves, stems, and flower buds than their roots can normally support. They expect the same care to continue when you plant them at home, and they wilt and die unless you water them every day. To help these junkies break their thirsty habit, trim them back by a third before planting. This gives them time to adjust to a new home with less water; soon they'll be blooming profusely.* ❖

Biennials

Biennials typically complete their life cycle in 2 years—in contrast to annuals (opposite page), which live for less than a year, and perennials (page 615), which live for more than 2 years. During their first year, biennials grow from seed into leafy but nonblooming plants. They live through the winter (experiencing the period of cold temperatures that most require for bloom); then, in the following year, they flower, set seed, and die. This is the life cycle you'll observe if you start seeds yourself. Biennials sold in nurseries, though, usually bloom the year you buy them, since the grower has taken the plants through their first phase of growth for you.

Familiar biennials include common foxglove (*Digitalis purpurea*), hollyhock (*Alcea rosea*), and sweet William (*Dianthus barbatus*), as well as vegetables such as carrot and onion. Breeders have developed strains of some biennials (including hollyhock and foxglove) that grow as annuals; these bloom the first year from seed, assuming the seed is sown early in spring. You'll also find hollyhock and foxglove strains that grow as short-lived perennials.

To grow biennials, sow seeds in containers or directly in the garden at the time indicated on the seed packet, typically mid- to late spring or summer. (For more on starting seeds, see page 632.) Transplant young plants into the garden in early fall, setting them in well-prepared soil; water as needed. Where the ground freezes, place a protective mulch of straw or chopped leaves around the plants, taking care not to smother the foliage rosettes. In spring, feed with a complete fertilizer as soon as new growth begins.

HOW DEEP?

This illustration shows the depth for planting some common spring- and summer-blooming bulbs. Spacing is also noted.

1″ **Anemone**
(4 in. apart)

2″ **Grape hyacinth**
(*Muscari*; 3 in. apart)
Freesia
(2–3 in. apart)
Ranunculus
(6–8 in. apart)

Grape hyacinth bulb

3″ **Crocus**
(2–3 in. apart)

4″ **Dutch iris**
(3–4 in. apart)
Gladiolus
(4–6 in. apart)

Gladiolus corm

5″ **Daffodil**
(*Narcissus*, large; 6–8 in. apart)
Calla
(*Zantedeschia*;
1–2 ft. apart)
Tulip
(*Tulipa*, large;
4–8 in. apart)

6″ **Hyacinth**
(*Hyacinthus*, large;
4–6 in. apart)

Tulip and hyacinth bulbs

Bulbs

Commonly grouped together as "bulbs" are a multitude of plants with underground structures (specialized roots or stem bases) that serve as storage organs, accumulating nutrient reserves that will ensure the plant's survival through dormancy and supply energy for its growth and bloom in the year to come. The five bulb types recognized by botanists—true bulbs, corms, tubers, rhizomes, and tuberous roots—are described on pages 598–599.

SELECTING AND PLANTING BULBS. Choose plump, firm bulbs that feel heavy for their size; reject any that are soft, squashy, or shriveled. Many bulbs are graded by size. Larger bulbs generally yield more flowers, but they are also the

AVOID WILD BULBS

Certain bulbs have been dug so extensively in the wild that they are fast vanishing from their native habitats; many of these are considered endangered species. Wild-dug types that have been offered for sale in the United States include species anemones and narcissus (rather than named varieties or selections) as well as various species of cyclamen, fritillary (*Fritillaria*), snowdrop (*Galanthus*), snowflake (*Leucojum*), sternbergia, and winter aconite (*Eranthis hyemalis*). To avoid contributing to the disappearance of such plants from the wild, buy only bulbs labeled "commercially propagated" or "from cultivated stock." If the bulbs are not labeled, ask about their origin before purchasing.

THE FIVE BULB TYPES AND WAYS TO DIVIDE THEM

The characteristics of each bulb type are summarized below, with advice on how to divide each type. For information on the best time to divide and replant specific bulbs, consult the Plant Encyclopedia. The photos show bulbs oriented as they should be planted.

True bulb. A true bulb is an underground stem base containing an embryonic plant surrounded by scales—modified leaves that overlap each other. A basal plate at the bottom of the bulb holds the scales together and produces roots. Most true bulbs have a protective papery outer skin called a tunic. Lilies, however, lack a tunic, making them more susceptible to drying and damage than other true bulbs; be sure to handle them with care. Most true bulbs produce offsets (also called *increases*). To divide, simply separate these from the mother bulb.

Grape hyacinth
(Muscari)

Iris (bulbous)

Snowflake *(Leucojum)*

Daffodil
(Narcissus)

Lily *(Lilium)*, Oriental hybrid

Corm. A corm is a swollen underground stem base, but unlike a true bulb, it's composed of solid tissue rather than scales. Roots grow from a basal plate at the corm's bottom; the growth point is at the top. Many corms have a tunic formed from the dried bases of the previous season's leaves. Each corm lasts for a single year; as it shrinks away, a new corm and, in many species, small increases *(cormels)* form on top of it. To divide, separate healthy new corms and any cormels from the old corms (cormels may take as long as 2 to 3 years to reach flowering size).

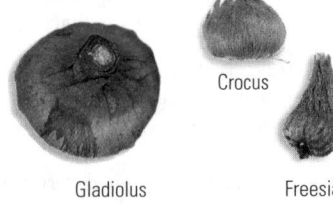

Crocus

Gladiolus

Freesia

priciest. If you're planting a large quantity, buy midsize specimens; they'll build up after a year or two to bloom as lavishly as larger bulbs.

Like most plants, bulbs need good drainage. If your soil drains very poorly, plant on a slope or in raised beds.

You can put bulbs in a separate bed or set them among other plants, digging an individual hole for each bulb. (See page 628 for information on preparing a planting bed.) Work a complete fertilizer into the soil in the bed; or, if you are planting bulbs in individual holes, dig up to a tablespoon of bulb fertilizer into the bottom of each hole, add about 2 inches of compost or soil over that, then plant the bulb.

In most soils, true bulbs and most corms should be planted about three times as deep as the bulb is wide. In hot climates or sandy soils, plant slightly deeper; in heavy soils, plant a bit shallower. The illustration on page 597 shows how deep and how far apart to plant some widely grown spring- and summer-blooming bulbs; for depth and spacing for other bulbs, check the entries in the Plant Encyclopedia.

CARING FOR BULBS. Bulbs need water while they're growing actively. For most sorts, this period begins after planting and continues until the foliage dies back, until flowering is finished, or—for some types—until autumn. If you must supplement rainfall, water deeply enough to penetrate the root zone; the roots grow beneath the bulb.

When leaves first appear in spring, apply a water-soluble 20-20-20 fertilizer to enhance the quality of the current season's flowers. After bloom ends, much or all of a bulb's stored nutrients are depleted; to ensure a good show next year, those nutrients must be replenished.

NATURALIZING BULBS

A number of bulbous plants can be planted in meadows, fields, or light woodlands, where they'll form a carpet of wildflower-like blooms year after year. Consult the Plant Encyclopedia to see if the bulbs you want to naturalize are good candidates for this treatment and to check their climate, exposure, and moisture needs. If they aren't likely to receive enough water naturally, be prepared to supply it through irrigation.

The traditional naturalizing method is to broadcast a handful of bulbs over the desired planting area, then plant them where they fall. To achieve the most realistic effect, you may need to adjust the pattern slightly: the drift should be denser at one end or toward the center, as if the bulbs began to grow in one spot and gradually spread to colonize outlying territory. Once you have the pattern you want, use a trowel or bulb planter to set the bulbs at their preferred depths.

Following bloom, fertilize the bulbs and allow the foliage to remain until it withers. After a number of years, overcrowding may cause a decrease in the number of flowers; when this happens, it's time to dig, divide, and replant.

Naturalized daffodils

Rhizome. A rhizome is a thickened stem growing partially or entirely below-ground. Its roots grow directly from the under-side. The primary growing point is at one end of the rhizome; additional grow-ing points form along the sides. To divide, cut into sections that have visible growing points.

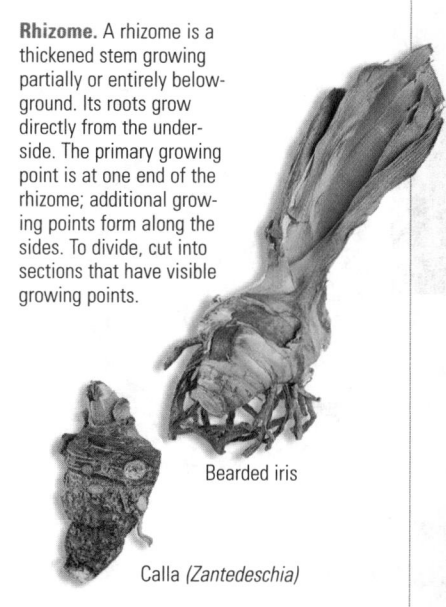

Bearded iris

Calla *(Zantedeschia)*

Tuber. Tubers, like corms, are swollen under-ground stem bases, but they lack the corm's distinct organization. There is no basal plate; roots can grow from all sides. Instead of just one (or a few) growing points, a tuber has mul-tiple growth points scattered over its surface; each is a scalelike leaf with a growth bud *(eye)* in its axil. Some tubers, such as cyclamen and caladium, are perennial; they increase in size each year. Others (the potato is the best-known example) are annual; as new tubers grow, the old ones disintegrate. To divide either kind of tuber, cut it into sections, making sure each has one or more growing points.

Cyclamen

Caladium

Tuberous roots. While the other four bulb types are specialized stems, a tuberous root is a true root, thickened to store nutrients. Fibrous roots for the uptake of water and nutrients develop from its sides and tip. Tuberous roots grow in a cluster, with the swollen portions radiating out from a central point. The growth buds are at the bases of old stems rather than on the roots themselves. To divide, cut the root cluster apart so each division contains both roots and part of a stem base with one or more growth buds.

Dahlia

As long as the leaves are green and growing, they will continue to manufacture food for the coming year, so it's vital to leave them on the plant—bedraggled and weary though they may appear!—until they yellow and pull away easily. (If you want to hide the dying foliage, try over-planting with annuals or a ground cover.) After flowering is finished, it's also important to apply some complete fertilizer such as a 9-9-6 for-mula or a "bulb food" high in phosphorus and potassium. For these last two nutrients to be effective, they must reach the root zone (see "Fertilizers," page 606); scratch the fertilizer into the soil or apply it in narrow trenches dug near the bulbs, then water thoroughly.

FOILING LITTLE ALVIN. *If chipmunks and other rodents keep eating your crocuses and similar small bulbs and corms, start saving those plastic mesh baskets when you buy strawberries or blueberries at the super-market. When you plant, put the bulbs at the bottom of the hole, then place a basket upside down on top of them and fill in the hole. The plants will come right up through the holes in the mesh, but rodents won't be able to find their way in.* ❖

Composting

Composting is a natural process that converts raw organic materials into a soil conditioner that improves a soil's texture, boosts its nutrient content, and makes it more water retentive. As well as being good for your garden, composting lightens the landfill: you recycle garden debris at home rather than consigning it to the dump.

A pile of leaves, branches, and other garden trimmings will eventually decompose with no intervention on your part. This type of compost-ing is called *slow* or *cold composting.* With a little effort, however, you can speed up the process. If you create optimum conditions for the organisms responsible for decay—by giving them the mixture of air, water, and the carbon- and nitrogen-rich nutrients they need—the compost pile will heat up quickly and decompose in a few months. Such *hot composting* also destroys many (though not all) weeds and disease pathogens.

You can make compost in a freestanding pile or use some sort of enclosure (see page 600). Regardless of the method, though, the funda-mentals of composting are the same.

GATHER MATERIALS. You'll need approxi-mately equal amounts by volume of brown mat-ter and green matter. *Brown matter* is high in carbon and includes dry leaves, hay, sawdust, straw, and wood chips. *Green matter* is high in nitrogen; it includes grass clippings, fruit and vegetable scraps, coffee grounds, tea bags, and manure from cows, horses, goats, sheep, poul-try, and rabbits. The compost will heat up faster if you collect all the ingredients in advance and assemble the pile all at once. Don't use bones, cat or dog waste, dairy products, meat scraps, badly diseased or insect-infested plants, or per-nicious weeds that might survive composting (such as annual bluegrass, quack grass, and kudzu).

CHOP MATERIALS. Shredding or chopping large, rough materials into smaller pieces (ideally no larger than ¾ inch to 2 inches) allows decay-producing organisms to reach more surfaces

C

COMPOSTING SYSTEMS

You can make compost in a freestanding pile or in a homemade structure, or use a purchased manufactured composter.

Freestanding pile

◗ **Freestanding compost piles.** These piles should be at least 3 feet high and wide; at this size, their mass is great enough to generate the microbial activity needed for heating the materials. The upper size limit is about 5 feet high and wide; a pile larger than that may not receive enough air at its center. When siting the pile, allow space alongside for turning.

◗ **Wire cylinders or hoops.** For these, use welded wire, chicken wire, or snow fencing, supporting it with stakes if necessary. The cylinder or hoop should be about 4 feet in diameter and 3 to 4 feet tall. To turn the pile, lift the cylinder and move it to one side; then fork the materials back into it.

Wire cylinder

◗ **Three-bin systems.** Bin systems are more complex than freestanding piles or those corralled with wire, but they also offer a more flexible way to make compost. The left bin holds new green and brown material; the center one contains partly decomposed material, while the right bin holds finished or nearly finished compost. Turn the material in each bin weekly, moving decomposed material to the right. (The right bin will be empty for a few weeks at the start.)

Static bin

◗ **Manufactured composters.** These include various sorts of tumblers, systems that make it easier to turn materials and produce finished compost quickly. Most are turned with a crank, but some roll on the ground or are turned with foot treads. Such devices provide a tidy way to make compost, especially in small gardens.

Another manufactured composter is the static compost bin, in which the contents sit without turning (though occasional aerating with a spading fork is helpful). You add new materials at the top; the finished compost is removed through a door at the base. Though tidy, these units produce fairly small amounts of compost—and they do so rather slowly.

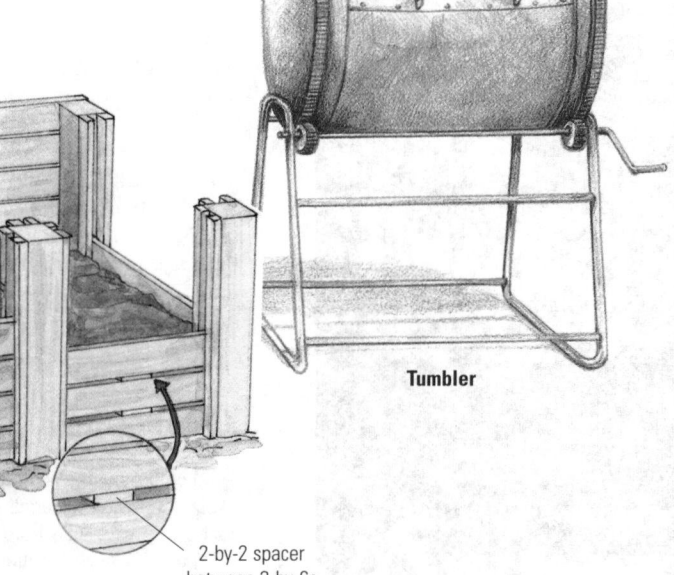

Tumbler

Three-bin system

4-by-4   1-by-1   2-by-6

2-by-2 spacer between 2-by-6s

and thus speeds up the entire composting process. Shredder-chippers and lawn mowers are good tools to use for this purpose. Shredding dry leaves is a good idea too; rake leaves into an open area and just run a lawn mower over them.

BUILD THE PILE. Building the pile like a layer cake makes it easier to judge the ratio of brown to green materials. Start by spreading a 4- to 8-inch layer of brown material over an area at least 3 feet square; then add a layer of green material about 2 to 8 inches deep. (Layers of grass clippings should be only 2 inches deep; less-dense green materials can be layered more thickly.) Add another layer of brown material and sprinkle the pile with water. Mix these first three layers with a spading fork. Continue adding layers, watering, and mixing. To heat up efficiently, the pile should be about 3 feet tall, giving it a volume of one cubic yard.

TURN THE PILE. In just a few days, the pile should have heated up dramatically. In time, it will decompose on its own, but you can hurry things along by turning the contents to introduce more oxygen—which is needed by the organisms responsible for decomposition. Using a spading fork or pitchfork, restack the pile, redistributing it so that the materials originally on the outside are moved to the pile's center, where they'll be exposed to higher heat. If necessary, add water; the pile should be as moist as a wrung-out sponge. Turn the pile weekly, if possible, until it is no longer generating internal heat and most of the materials have decomposed.

USE THE COMPOST. Finished compost is dark and crumbly, with a pleasant, earthy aroma. Mix it into your planting beds or use it as a mulch. If some of the material from the compost pile's exterior is still coarser than you prefer for either a soil amendment or mulch, simply incorporate it into your next compost pile. To obtain a finer-textured compost to use as potting soil for containers or for starting seeds, sift the finished compost through a screen with ½-inch mesh.

Container Gardening

Growing plants in containers lets you have a garden even when the space for one is limited. You can install a planter box below a window or use containers to turn a tiny balcony or patio into a leafy haven. Gardeners with plenty of room appreciate containers, too, valuing the versatility they offer. Blooming pot plants bring seasonal color to garden beds, a porch, or the front steps and are easily replaced with new ones when their flowers fade. In addition, containers give you the chance to experiment with new plant combinations and with kinds not suited to the native conditions. For instance, if your soil is alkaline or claylike but you are longing to raise acid-loving plants or those that

COMPOST TROUBLESHOOTING

PROBLEM	POSSIBLE CAUSES	SOLUTIONS
Rotten odor	Too wet Lacks oxygen	Turn pile to aerate; add layers of dry material such as sawdust, dry leaves.
Ammonia odor	Excess nitrogen (green material)	Turn pile; add layers of dry material such as sawdust, dry leaves.
Pile not heating up	Too dry Too much dry or woody material	Turn pile, adding water. Add fresh green material such as grass clippings, fruit or vegetable scraps; bury scraps in pile.
Pile is attracting rodents and flies	Fruit or vegetable scraps are on the surface Meat or dairy scraps have been added	Always bury kitchen scraps inside the pile. Don't add meat or dairy products. Turn pile to increase temperature. If a rodent problem continues, use a covered bin made of fine-mesh wire.

demand fast drainage, just fill their pots with the sort of soil they need. Plants too tender for your winters can be moved to shelter when cold weather hits.

PREPARING CONTAINERS. Choose containers with at least one drainage hole, so water won't accumulate around plant roots. Submerge terra-cotta pots in clean water and let them soak thoroughly; if the pots are too dry, they can initially draw water away from the potting mix. Scrub used containers with a solution of 1 part household bleach to 9 parts hot water. Cover the drainage hole(s) with a small piece of fine wire screen to keep soil from washing out.

CHOOSING A POTTING MIX. A good potting soil allows roots to grow easily; it should be fast draining yet moisture retentive. Quick drainage means roots won't suffocate in soggy soil, while good water retention saves you from having to water too often. Regular garden soil, even good loam, is too dense for container use. For best success, most gardeners turn to packaged potting mixes—soilless mixtures of organic materials (such as ground bark, sphagnum peat moss, and/or compost) plus mineral matter such as perlite or sand. Lime may be added to balance the acidity of peat moss; fertilizers and

GONE TO POTS. When selecting trees to grow in containers, choose those that either stay small or grow slowly. That way, you'll be able to enjoy them for a long time in the container you've chosen. The best candidate for most gardens is laceleaf Japanese maple. Other good choices include bay, calamondin, dogwood, dwarf crepe myrtle, edible fig, loblolly bay, Sargent crabapple, Sasanqua camellia, sourwood, star magnolia, and weeping yaupon. In the Upper and Middle South, you can also grow many different dwarf and slow-growing conifers, such as dwarf Alberta spruce and dwarf Japanese white pine. See page 103 for a Guide to Trees and Shrubs for Containers. ❖

wetting agents (see "Soil Polymers," page 647) may also be included. Before planting, slowly stir water into the mix to wet it thoroughly; dry potting soil won't absorb water that's simply poured on the top.

A 2-cubic-foot bag of potting mix holds enough to transplant 8 to 10 plants from 1-gallon nursery pots into individual 10- to 12-inch containers or to fill a 36- by 8- by 10-inch planter box. For large planting projects, though, you may want to make your own mix. For a basic no-soil mix, combine ⅔ cubic yard nitrogen-stabilized ground bark or sphagnum peat moss; ⅓ cubic yard washed 20-grit sand; 6 pounds 0-10-10 granular fertilizer; and 10 pounds dolomite or dolomite limestone. Mix all ingredients in a wheelbarrow.

WATERING. Because they have only a limited area from which to draw moisture, container plants must be watered more often than those grown in the ground. In hot or windy weather, some (especially those in hanging baskets) may need watering several times a day; in cool weather, it may be sufficient to water weekly or even less often. Test with your finger: if the soil is dry beneath the surface, it's time to water.

Apply water over the entire soil surface until it flows from the pot's drainage holes. This moistens the entire soil mass and prevents any potentially harmful salts from accumulating in the mix. If the water drains out too fast—virtually the instant you pour it in—there's probably air space between the soil and the container walls. In this case, completely submerge the container in a tub of water for about half an hour; or, for large pots, set a hose on the soil surface near plant's base and let water trickle slowly into the mix.

A drip irrigation system (see page 661) can make watering container plants almost effortless. Kits designed for this purpose are widely available.

FERTILIZING. Container plants need regular feeding, because the necessary frequent watering leaches nutrients from the potting mix. Apply a liquid fertilizer every 2 weeks during the growing season, following the directions on the label. Or mix a controlled-release type (see page 606) into the potting mix before planting.

REPOTTING. If roots are crowded and protruding from the drainage holes, the plant has outgrown its container and needs a roomier home. Because you want to keep the soil mass fairly well filled with roots, it's best to shift the plant to a slightly larger container rather than a much bigger one. If the pot is too large, the ratio of soil to roots will be too great for the roots to absorb all the moisture after watering—a situation that often leads to root rot. Select a new container that allows just an inch or two of fresh mix on all sides of the root mass. If the root ball is compacted (with tightly twined roots), make four shallow vertical cuts down its sides with a sharp knife to encourage the roots to move out into the new soil.

If you want to keep an older plant in the same large pot indefinitely, you can root-prune the plant periodically. Gently turn it out of its container and use a sharp knife to shave off an inch or two from all four sides and the bottom of the root ball. Place fresh potting mix in the bottom of the container, put in the plant, and add fresh mix around the sides.

Cover Crops

Also known as green manure, cover crops are legumes or grasses planted expressly to improve garden soil. They also help prevent erosion and effectively loosen soil compacted by heavy equipment during the construction of new homes. Most cover crops are planted in fall and dug into the soil in spring. As they decay, they form humus, which improves the soil's structure and increases its ability to hold moisture. Legumes such as fava beans, alfalfa, field peas, clovers, and vetch also add extra nitrogen, thanks to their association with so-called nitrogen-fixing bacteria (genus *Rhizobium*). These bacteria draw nitrogen from air in the soil and "fix" it in nodules on a legume's roots; when the plants eventually decompose, the nitrogen is released back into the soil and made available to plants.

Grass or cereal cover crops such as rye, barley, buckwheat, and mustard don't contribute extra nitrogen to the soil, but they do produce plenty of organic matter. Gardeners often combine legumes and grasses as cover crops to enjoy the benefits of both.

Before planting, till or dig the area and rake it smooth. Treat legume seeds with an inoculant powder (available from seed companies selling cover-crop seeds) to be certain that *Rhizobium* bacteria are present. Broadcast seeds at the rate recommended by the supplier and rake again to cover them. In spring, dig in the cover crop by hand (for small areas) or with a tiller, then wait until most of the stems and leaves have decayed before planting the garden. You can also cut the stems and leaves and add them to your compost pile, then dig just the lower stems and roots into the soil.

TOP: Buckwheat is a fast-growing cover crop that needs warm weather to grow well; its flowers attract beneficial insects. BOTTOM: Nitrogen-containing nodules on fava bean roots.

Diseases

Although few gardens escape diseases entirely, the advice in this section will help you prevent the most common plant diseases and, if problems do occur, assist you in identifying them and taking action. For a more detailed discussion of specific diseases, including diagnosis, control, and prevention, see the *Southern Living Garden Problem Solver.*

The Integrated Pest Management (IPM) approach discussed on page 616 applies to dealing with diseases as well as pests. The goal of IPM is to maintain an attractive, productive garden with only minimal use of synthetic (chemical) controls; it is intended to reduce diseases and pest populations to tolerable levels, not to eradicate them entirely (which is rarely possible in any case).

PLANT PATHOGENS. Covered here are plant diseases caused by several kinds of organisms. Bacteria, fungi, and viruses are responsible for most leaf, stem, and flower diseases; fungi cause the most widespread soilborne diseases. Plant problems brought on by other factors are sometimes mistaken for diseases; this is true of iron-deficiency chlorosis, sunburn, and sunscald.

Fungi are microscopic, typically multicellular organisms. Some obtain their food parasitically from green plants, causing diseases in the process. Many produce multitudinous tiny reproductive bodies called spores, which can be disseminated in numerous ways—by wind, insects, splashing water from rain or irrigation, garden equipment, and handling. Given the right conditions, each spore will germinate and grow, producing a new infection.

A number of diseases resulting from fungal infection are described on the following pages.

Bacteria are single-celled organisms. Like fungi, they cannot create their own food supply, so they feed on organic matter, including plants. Unlike fungi, however, the bacteria that afflict plants must remain inside their host or in plant debris to survive. They do not produce spores but multiply rapidly by cell division. Since they require both moisture and warmth for reproduction, the diseases they cause are generally less prevalent in dry-summer areas than in rainy or humid regions. Nonetheless, garden watering can provide the moisture they need to flourish. Bacteria are spread by insects, splashing water, garden equipment, and handling.

The bacterial disease fireblight is described on the facing page.

Viruses are ultramicroscopic parasites capable of invading plant tissue and reproducing in it, usually at the expense of the host plant. They produce a variety of symptoms, including stunting and other abnormalities in growth, spots or discoloration on leaves, and damaged fruit. (Some attractive plants, such as variegated-leaf abutilon and certain tulips with bizarrely striped flowers, owe their variegation to a virus.) Most garden plants are susceptible to at least one viral disease; especially prone to attack are a number of vegetables, including beans, cucumbers, squash, tomatoes, and peppers.

Viral diseases are commonly spread by plant-eating insects such as aphids, leafhoppers, and whiteflies. Some viruses can spread via infected seeds and pollen; through pruning, grafting, budding, and other forms of vegetative propagation; and even by contaminated hands, clothing, and tools.

To prevent viral diseases, plant resistant selections (if available) and buy certified virus-free stock. Control virus-spreading insects and remove weeds, which are hosts for some viruses. If you find a virus-infected plant, the best course of action is to destroy it, as there are no chemical controls for viruses at this time.

D

PREVENTING DISEASES. Because many diseases cannot effectively be controlled once their symptoms become apparent, prevention is of prime importance. Whenever possible, plant resistant selections; many are noted in the entries in the Plant Encyclopedia, and your Cooperative Extension Office (see page 694) can also give you recommendations. Choose certified and disease-free plants and seeds to avoid introducing pathogens into your garden.

Give your plants the climate, exposure, and amount of moisture they prefer. A sun-loving plant sited in the shade may be more susceptible to fungal diseases, and one that does best in dry conditions may succumb to certain root and foliage diseases if overwatered. Allow good air circulation between plants. Also fertilize according to each plant's needs; too much or too little can increase susceptibility to some diseases.

Use soil solarization (see page 664) to help destroy soil-dwelling pathogens. Control weeds, since they may harbor pathogens; control insects that spread diseases. Clean up the garden each fall so disease organisms can't overwinter in plant debris.

MANAGEMENT OPTIONS. If diseases do appear in your garden, immediately remove diseased annuals and vegetables to keep the problem from spreading. On larger plants (including perennials), remove diseased flowers, leaves, and, if possible, branches. Discard all infected material in the trash, not the compost heap. Disinfecting tools used on afflicted plants may help prevent the spread of some diseases; dip them between cuts in a solution of 1 part household bleach to 9 parts water.

PLANT DISEASES. Discussed on the following three pages are some of the plant diseases you're most likely to encounter in your garden. Many diseases that affect only one kind of plant—such as peach, rose, or elm *(Ulmus)*, for example—are covered in the appropriate entry in the Plant Encyclopedia. For lawn diseases, see page 611.

Anthracnose. Caused by a number of fungi, anthracnose appears early in the growing season. It affects many different plants but seldom kills them. Dogwood *(Cornus)*, English ivy *(Hedera helix)*, maple *(Acer)*, sycamore *(Platanus)*, grapes, peppers, and tomatoes are frequent targets. Symptoms depend on the particular plant, but you'll typically see sunken, gray or tan to dark brown spots on leaves, stems, fruit, or twigs. Leaves may turn brown along the veins, wither, and drop.

The spores that cause anthracnose are spread by rain and garden sprinkling. To discourage the disease, avoid overhead watering and use a mulch to decrease splashing of rain or sprinkler water. Give plants sufficient space for good air circulation; grow vining plants on trellises to keep them dry. Whenever possible, plant resistant selections. Remove infected leaves, fruit, twigs, and branches; then destroy them to prevent reinfection.

To prevent anthracnose, you may use fungicides containing lime sulfur (during the dormant season), copper compounds, or chlorothalonil (Daconil). Consult your Cooperative Extension Office or a commercial sprayer for information on the best chemical spray for your area and the appropriate time to apply it.

Black spot. No problem creates more headaches for rose lovers than this one. Caused by the fungus *Diplocarpon rosae*, it spreads by spores splashed onto healthy foliage. Small black spots soon appear on the leaves and grow to about ½ inch wide; they may be surrounded by a yellow halo. Leaves eventually turn yellow and drop; in severe cases, the rose may defoliate, weakening the plant and reducing bloom.

Several strategies can be used against black spot. First, make it harder for the disease to spread. Plant roses where they get lots of sun (at least 6 hours a day) and good air circulation; avoid wetting the foliage when watering; and pick off and destroy all infected leaves. Every spring, spread fresh mulch under plants.

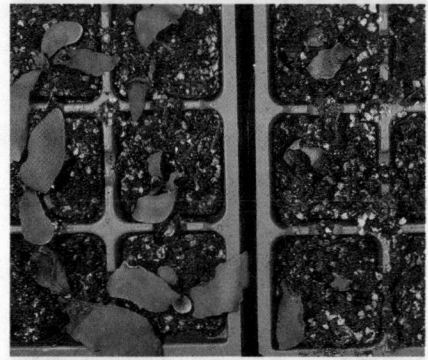

TOP TO BOTTOM: Anthracnose, Damping off, Fireblight

Second, spray plants according to label directions with an appropriate fungicide, such as triforine (Funginex), myclobutanil (Immunox), azadirachtin (neem oil), Rose Defense, or chlorothalonil (Daconil). Third, plant rose selections that resist black spot, such as 'Bonica', Carefree Beauty', 'Carefree Wonder', 'Flower Carpet', and 'Knock Out'.

Citrus canker. Citrus canker is a highly contagious bacterial disease that is spreading among citrus trees in Florida (see page 247). To control the canker's spread, the Florida Department of Agriculture and Consumer Services prohibits the movement of citrus trees into or out of certain areas of Florida. In addition, it can remove all citrus trees within 1,900 ft. of an infected tree. To date, the state has removed more than 2 million trees from both commercial groves and private residences. Florida gardeners can get more information by calling the Citrus Canker Helplines, or visiting the Web site at *http://www.doacs.state.fl.us/canker/*. In Miami-Dade, Broward, Palm Beach, and Monroe counties, the helpline is (800) 850-3781; in all other counties call (800) 282-5153.

Damping off. A type of fungus is usually responsible for this disease, which affects young seedlings, causing them to collapse at or near the soil surface. In some cases, seeds rot before they can sprout.

To prevent damping off, use sterilized potting soil or seed-starting mix for containers; also, thoroughly clean and disinfect used containers before planting in them (scrub them with a solution of 1 part household bleach to 9 parts hot water). Provide good air circulation around seedlings, thinning them if necessary to eliminate crowding, and do not overwater. You can buy some seeds pretreated with fungicides.

Fireblight. Resulting from infection by a bacterium, this disease attacks only those members of the rose family that produce pomes (apple-like fruits), including apple, cotoneaster, crabapple, hawthorn *(Crataegus)*, pear, pyracantha, and quince. Fireblight causes shoots (and sometimes the entire plant) to blacken and die suddenly; affected parts look as though they have been scorched by fire.

In moist weather, especially in early spring when temperatures are above 60°F, the bacteria are carried to blossoms by splashing water and by flies and other insects. Once in the blossoms, they're transported to other flowers by honeybees; the infection then spreads to the shoots and limbs. The bacteria survive in infected twigs and cankers, ready to infect blossoms again the following spring.

Whenever possible, plant resistant selections. To protect blossoms from infection, spray at 3- or 5-day intervals during the bloom season with copper compounds. You can also spray with the antibiotic streptomycin (Agri-Strep).

To control the pathogen once it has appeared, prune out and discard diseased branches, making pruning cuts at least 6 to 8 inches below blighted tissue. Disinfecting tools between cuts with a solution of 1 part household bleach to 9 parts water may help stop the disease from spreading.

Powdery mildews. These diseases are caused by fungi that can infect leaves, buds, flowers, or stems, depending on the host plant and the particular fungus. The disease first appears as small, white or gray circular patches on plant tissue, then spreads rapidly to form powdery areas of fungal filaments and spores. New growth may be stunted; blossoms may fail to set fruit or may produce fruit covered with powdery fungus. Most powdery mildews thrive in humid air, but the spores—unlike those of other fungi—need dry surfaces, such as leaves, stems, and flowers, to become established.

To prevent powdery mildews, plant resistant selections; many are noted in the entries in the Plant Encyclopedia. Be sure to give plants sufficient light and air circulation.

To control the fungi, first spray infected plants with jets of water; this washes spores from the plant and kills some of them. (To avoid encouraging other fungal diseases, spray plants with water early in the day, so they can dry before nightfall.) Pick off and destroy infected leaves and flowers. If necessary, spray with copper soap fungicide, myclobutanil (Immunox), neem oil, sulfur, triadimefon (Bayleton), or triforine (Funginex). Rose growers have had some success controlling powdery mildews with baking soda mixtures or antitranspirants such as Cloud Cover or Wilt-Pruf.

Root rots, water molds. Certain fungi (notably *Pythium* and *Phytophthora*) produce mobile spores that can swim short distances through water in the soil and attack plant roots. The fungi kill roots and also invade the crowns of plants, sometimes girdling them. Diseased plants wilt, and their leaves discolor, become stunted, and drop prematurely. Branches or even the entire plant may die. Root rot and water mold fungi are most active in warm soils (55 to 80°F), but they can survive in dry, cold ones, becoming active when favorable conditions arise. Many plants are susceptible, especially if they are overwatered or planted in heavy, poorly drained soils.

To prevent the problem, improve drainage (see page 645) or plant in raised beds. Do not overwater. Select disease-resistant plants.

Rust. Most strains of the 4,000 or so types of these fungi are specific to particular plants; rose rust will not infect hollyhocks, for example, nor will hollyhock rust infect roses. The first sign of infection is the appearance of powdery pustules on leaf undersides; these are usually yellow to rusty brown but may be purple or another color. As the disease progresses, leaf undersides become covered with powdery masses of spores, and the upper surfaces may be spotted with yellow; eventually, the whole leaf may turn yellow, then drop.

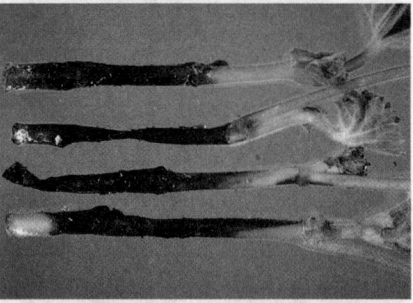

TOP TO BOTTOM: Black spot, Powdery mildew, Pythium root rot, Rust

Prevent rust by planting resistant selections. Give plants the best possible air circulation. Remove infected leaves immediately; in winter, clean up all fallen leaves and debris. If watering from overhead, be sure plants have time to dry off before dusk.

Sprays that may be effective (depending on the kind of rust and the infected plant) include copper soap fungicide, myclobutanil (Immunox), Rose Defense, sulfur, triadimefon (Bayleton), and triforine (Funginex).

Sooty mold. Commonly seen on the leaves and twigs of many trees and shrubs, sooty mold is caused by a fungus that grows on honeydew produced by sap-sucking insects such as aphids, mealybugs, scale, and whiteflies. Sooty mold is considered fairly harmless (since it does not feed on plants), but extremely heavy infestations can block sun from reaching leaves, which may then turn yellow and drop prematurely. To prevent the problem, control honeydew-excreting insects. Wash or wipe the fungus from leaves.

Texas root rot. Also known as cotton root rot, this fungal disease is found in the arid Southwest. The fungus destroys the outer portion of the roots, thus cutting off the water supply to the upper part of the plant. Leaves become slightly yellow or bronzed and soon wilt, yet they remain firmly attached to the plant. Small plants may die within a few days; trees and shrubs may be stunted but survive for several years.

Avoid infestation by buying disease-free plants. Replace diseased plants with resistant types. Incorporate organic matter and acidify the soil (see page 645).

Verticillium wilt. A widespread and destructive disease, verticillium wilt results from infection by a fungus that invades and plugs the water-conducting tissues in the roots and stems of plants. It can affect crops such as tomatoes and strawberries as well as roses and some trees. A common symptom is wilting or death of one side of the plant. Leaves turn yellow or brown, then die; as the disease progresses, entire branches die. Small plants may be destroyed in one season, but mature trees may live on (though in compromised health) for long periods. The fungus can survive in the soil for years, even in the absence of host plants.

Plant resistant selections when these are available. In areas where verticillium wilt is present, grow susceptible crops in containers filled with pasteurized potting mix. Soil solarization can be effective in destroying the fungus.

Mildly affected trees or shrubs may recover from an attack. You can aid recovery by deep but infrequent irrigation. If a plant has been neglected, apply fertilizer; do not, however, fertilize infected trees and shrubs that show lush growth, since excess nitrogen may encourage the disease's development. Prune out dead branches. Clean soil off tools after using them, as infected soil can carry the fungus to other parts of the garden.

Sooty mold

Texas root rot

Verticillium wilt

PRODUCTS FOR DISEASE PREVENTION AND CONTROL

You'll find a number of products aimed at disease prevention or control. These include *preventatives,* products that prevent diseases from occurring but cannot control them once they become established; *eradicants,* which help control diseases once they have appeared (many simply protect new growth); and *systemics,* materials that are taken up by plant roots and act as preventatives, eradicants, or both. Controls described here are the most useful and commonly available ones; other, generally less widely sold products are mentioned in the descriptions of specific diseases beginning on page 603.

Synthetic fungicides are manufactured compounds that do not normally occur in nature. *Natural fungicides and bactericides* are products whose active ingredients originate in a plant, animal, or mineral. "Natural," however, does not mean "harmless"; some of these products can harm people or plants if not used properly.

When using any product, *read label directions carefully and follow them exactly.* The package will clearly state the plants and diseases for which the control product is registered for use. It is illegal to use it on a plant or to control a disease not so listed.

The following products are listed by the accepted common name of the *active ingredient*—the actual chemical that prevents or controls the disease or diseases listed on the package label. Some widely used trade names, if they differ from the common name, are noted in parentheses. Before you buy, read the label to make sure you're getting the active ingredient you want. (For more on understanding pesticide labels, see page 622.) Always dispose of pesticides safely (see page 624).

NATURAL FUNGICIDES AND BACTERICIDES

▶ **Baking soda, sodium bicarbonate.** You can buy baking soda sprays, but it's easy to make your own by mixing 2 teaspoons each of baking soda and fine-grade horticultural oil with 1 gallon of water. This solution helps to control powdery mildew on roses. Commercial versions contain a "sticker" ingredient to help keep the spray on the plant.

▶ **Copper compounds (Bordeaux mixture).** General-purpose fungicides and bactericides used to prevent fireblight, peach leaf curl, shot hole, brown rot, and other foliar diseases. Toxic to fish.

▶ **Copper soap fungicide.** Broad-spectrum fungicide used to control many plant diseases, including rust, black spot, brown rot, fireblight, and powdery mildews.

▶ **Lime sulfur, calcium polysulfide.** Used as a spray in winter (when plants are dormant) to prevent various leaf spots and peach leaf curl. Very caustic; wear goggles and plastic gloves when applying.

▶ **Neem oil (Rose Defense, others).** Used to prevent and control black spot, powdery mildews, and some other foliar diseases. (Also used as an insecticide and miticide.) Toxic to fish.

▶ **Sulfur (Sulfur Dust, others).** Controls black spot, powdery mildews, rust, and other diseases. Do not use in conjunction with horticultural oil sprays or when the outdoor temperature is above 85°F.

SYNTHETIC FUNGICIDES

▶ **Chlorothalonil (Daconil, others).** Broad-spectrum liquid fungicide used to prevent powdery mildews, leaf spots, gray mold, scab, and a variety of lawn and other diseases. Toxic to fish.

▶ **Myclobutanil (Immunox).** Liquid systemic for prevention and eradication of black spot, powdery mildews, rust, and some lawn diseases.

▶ **Triadimefon (Bayleton, Fungi-Fighter).** Wettable powder; systemic used for the prevention or eradication of powdery mildews, rust, and some lawn diseases. Toxic to fish.

▶ **Triforine (Funginex).** Liquid systemic for prevention and eradication of powdery mildews, rust, black spot, and a variety of other diseases. You must wear goggles and a face mask during application. Keep animals out of treated areas.

Fertilizers

When plants are actively growing, they need a steady supply of nutrients. Though many of these are present in soil, water, and air, the gardener may need to supply others. Most likely to require supplemental feeding are fast-growing annuals (such as vegetables and flowering plants), lawns, perennials, fruit trees, and immature plants of numerous kinds. Mature trees and shrubs, on the other hand, may need little or no fertilizing. The entries in the Plant Encyclopedia cover fertilizing needs and schedules for many plants. General guidelines are also given in the listings for specific plant types. A soil test (see page 646) is a good way to determine any nutrient deficiencies in your soil; test results will also give advice on correcting problems. Your Cooperative Extension Office is another excellent source of information on nutrient needs specific to your region's soil.

FERTILIZER TYPES AND FORMS. Visit almost any nursery and you'll encounter a bewildering array of fertilizers in different forms and formulas. To decide which ones to buy, start by reading the labels. Every fertilizer label states the percentage by weight that the product contains of the three macronutrients used in mineral form: nitrogen (N), phosphorus (P), and potassium (K). These nutrients are always listed in the order N-P-K. For example, a fertilizer labeled 10-8-6 contains 10 percent nitrogen, 8 percent phosphorus, and 6 percent potassium. The label also tells you the source of each nutrient.

Nitrogen is often listed on fertilizer labels as nitrate or some form of ammonium (many products contain both forms). Fertilizers containing nitrogen in the nitrate form are water soluble and fast acting, especially in cool soils, but are easily leached away by rain or irrigation (thus requiring fairly frequent replenishment) and can pollute surface and ground water if used to excess. Fertilizers in the form of ammonium, those from organic sources (such as blood meal), and IBDU (isobutylidene diurea, a synthetic organic fertilizer) are released more slowly and last longer in the soil.

Phosphorus is expressed on product labels as phosphate, P_2O_5, and listed as "available phosphoric acid." Potassium is expressed as potash, K_2O, and may be described in various ways, including "available phosphate" and "water-soluble potash." It is important to note that, unlike nitrogen, phosphorus and potassium do not move readily through the soil in solution. They must therefore be applied near plant roots to do the most good. Dig these nutrients into the soil when planting or scratch them into the soil around existing plants.

Complete fertilizers contain the three macronutrients N, P, and K; some may also include secondary and/or micronutrients (which will be listed on the label). *Simple fertilizers* supply just one macronutrient. Most familiar are the nitrogen-only types, such as ammonium sulfate (21-0-0), and phosphorus-only superphosphate (0-20-0). Falling between complete and simple types are *incomplete fertilizers,* which contain two of the three major

elements; an example is 0-10-10, providing phosphorus and potassium but no nitrogen.

Natural and chemical fertilizers. You can buy fertilizers in either natural (organic) or synthetic (chemical) form.

Natural fertilizers, derived from dead or living organisms, include fish emulsion, all kinds of animal manures including bat and seabird guano, and meals made from blood, bone, fish, alfalfa, cottonseed, and soybeans. Most contain lower levels of nutrients than do chemical products. They release their nutrients more slowly, as well: rather than dissolving in water, they are broken down by microorganisms in the soil, providing nutrients as they decay (decomposition proceeds more quickly in warm, moist soils than in cold or dry ones). Thanks to this slow nutrient release, natural fertilizers are much less likely to burn roots than are chemical types.

Many natural fertilizers are high in just one major nutrient. Blood meal, for example, supplies only nitrogen (N-P-K ratio 12-0-0), while steamed bonemeal (0-10-0) provides only phosphorus. Some manufacturers combine several natural fertilizers in a single package to produce a complete fertilizer.

Chemical fertilizers are derived from the chemical sources listed on the product label. Compared with natural fertilizers, they usually provide higher levels of nutrients and are faster acting, especially in cold soils; they typically cost less too. They're a good choice for greening up lawns in spring and giving plants suffering from nutrient deficiencies a quick tonic. Keep in mind that chemical products can burn roots if applied too heavily.

Liquids or solids? Both natural and chemical fertilizers are sold in liquid and solid forms.

Liquid fertilizers, including fish emulsion and water-soluble crystals, deliver nutrients to the roots immediately. They're easy to use, especially on container plants, and if you follow label directions for dilution you'll run no risk of burning roots. Liquid fertilizers must be reapplied frequently, since their nutrients leach through the root zone rapidly.

Solid fertilizers are usually sold as powders, granules, or pellets. Solid fertilizers can be broadcast or spread over lawns and ground covers, scratched or dug into the soil around other plants, and dug into the soil when preparing new planting beds.

Other solids include *controlled-release fertilizers,* sold as spikes, tablets, or beadlike granules that release nutrients gradually over a fairly long period—typically 3 to 9 months—if the soil receives regular moisture. Dig granules into soil at planting time (they're useful for fertilizing container plants) or scratch them into the soil surface. Use a mallet to pound spikes into the ground; dig holes for tablets.

General- and special-purpose fertilizers. The various fertilizers labeled "general-purpose" or "all-purpose" contain equal or

Fertilizer forms, clockwise from bottom left: Soluble crystals (dry and dissolved), Dry granules, Organic fish meal, and Controlled-release granules

nearly equal amounts of the macronutrients N, P, and K (a 10-10-10 formula, for example). They are intended to meet most plants' requirements throughout the growing season.

Other fertilizers are formulated for specific needs. High-nitrogen blends (such as 29-3-4) help keep lawns green and growing quickly, while higher-phosphorus mixes (6-10-4, for example) are intended to promote flowering and fruiting. Some packaged fertilizers are formulated for particular types of plants. Those designed for acid lovers such as camellias, rhododendrons, and azaleas are especially useful, as are fertilizers for citrus.

Another special kind of fertilizer is *foliar fertilizer*. These liquids are applied to leaves, which can absorb nutrients through small openings in leaves. Some solutions are high in the macronutrients, while others offer an effective way to apply micronutrients. To avoid burning leaves, water plants thoroughly before spraying them, follow dilution directions, and don't apply the fertilizer at all if outdoor temperatures will rise above 85°F.

You can also buy formulas that combine fertilizers with insecticides (chiefly for roses) or with weed killers, fungicides, or moss killers (all for lawns). These products are appropriate if you need the extra ingredient every time you fertilize; if not, it's more economical to buy it separately. Before using any such products, read the label carefully, as you would for any pesticide. The herbicides included in some combination products, for example, can damage plants with roots growing into the application area, such as a lawn.

PLANT NUTRIENTS

The nutrients plants need are divided into three groups: macronutrients, secondary nutrients, and micronutrients.

Macronutrients. These are nutrients that plants need in fairly large quantities. Three—carbon, oxygen, and hydrogen—are found in air and water; plants use the others in mineral form.

Nitrogen (chemical symbol N) is used in the synthesis of proteins, chlorophyll, and enzymes—all substances that plant cells require to live and reproduce. Nitrogen is the nutrient most often lacking in garden soils. When it's in short supply, the plant yellows from the bottom upward, with its leaves yellowing from the tips toward the stem, and growth is stunted (see photograph above).

Phosphorus (P) promotes flowering and fruiting, strong root growth, and the transfer of energy within the plant. Plants deficient in phosphorus show stunted growth and reduced yield of fruit; in some, you may see purplish areas on the leaf undersides.

Potassium (K) is important for regulating the synthesis of proteins and starches that make sturdy plants. It also helps increase resistance to diseases, heat, and cold. Symptoms of deficiency include reduced flowering and fruiting, spotted or curled older leaves, and weak stems and roots.

Secondary nutrients. Plants need these in about the same amounts as they do the macronutrients, but they're less likely to be deficient in most soils.

Calcium (Ca) plays a fundamental role in cell formation and growth, and most roots require some calcium right at the growing tips.

Magnesium (Mg) forms the core of the chlorophyll molecules in the cells of green leaves.

Sulfur (S) acts with nitrogen in the manufacture of protoplasm for plant cells.

Micronutrients. Also known as trace elements, micronutrients are required in very small quantities; in fact, excess amounts can be toxic. Among them are zinc (Zn) and manganese (Mn), both thought to function as catalysts in the utilization of other nutrients. Iron (Fe) is essential for chlorophyll formation (see page 627 for information on iron-deficiency chlorosis).

METHODS OF APPLYING FERTILIZERS

Before planting a new bed, work in a general-purpose fertilizer. This puts these essential nutrients at the level in the soil where they are readily available to plant roots. (Some soils don't need extra phosphorus—a soil test will tell you for sure.)

Sprinkle granular fertilizer on the soil beneath plants and water thoroughly. Roots of larger plants may extend several feet beyond the spread of the foliage, so be sure to distribute fertilizer widely enough to reach all the roots.

Liquid fertilizers can be applied with a watering can. You can also use an injector device to run the fertilizer through a drip watering system. A simple siphon attachment (above) draws a measured amount of fertilizer from concentrate in a pail and dilutes it as it is mixed with water from a hose.

Frost and Cold Protection

F

Wherever you garden, the best defense against cold damage is to choose trees, shrubs, and screen and hedge plants that are hardy in your climate zone. Use tender plants for summer display in borders, or plant them in containers that can be moved to shelter when the weather turns frigid.

It's also helpful to know your garden's microclimates—that is, to learn which areas tend to be warmer, which colder. For marginally hardy plants, the riskiest spots are stretches of open ground exposed to air from all sides (particularly from the north). Other high-risk locations include hollows and low, enclosed areas that catch cold air as it sinks, then hold onto it. The warmest part of any garden—and the one offering maximum frost protection—is usually the area beside a south-facing wall with an overhang. Lath structures and evergreen trees also provide shelter from frost.

To some extent, you can condition plants and soil for cold weather. Water and fertilize as needed in late spring and early summer, while plants are growing the fastest. In late summer, taper off nitrogen feeding: actively growing plants are more susceptible to frost than dormant and semidormant ones, so you don't want to stimulate new growth that won't have time to mature (harden off) before cold weather arrives. Reducing water also helps harden growth—but keep soil moist through the onset of the frost season, since moist soil holds and releases more heat than dry soil.

A frost that hits in early fall (before the growing season ends) or in spring (after growth is under way) is much more damaging than one striking when plants are semidormant or dormant. At these dangerous times of year, be alert for signs of an impending freeze: still air, clear skies, low humidity, and, of course, low temper-

PROTECTING BROAD-LEAFED EVERGREENS

To protect plants in exposed locations, spray them with an antitranspirant (such as Cloud Cover or Wilt-Pruf) shortly before the first hard freeze. These products form a thin film on the leaves, sealing in moisture and helping prevent desiccation. Or, make a protective structure by driving three or four stakes into the ground around the plants, then nailing or stapling burlap to the stakes. Don't use plastic film for the structure, since it hinders proper air circulation.

atures. You can also check TV and radio weather bulletins and Web sites. If you notice danger signals late in the afternoon, move at-risk container plants under a porch roof or into the garage. Give in-ground plants temporary shelter; two types of shelters are shown above. Remove coverings during the day unless the threat of frost continues. (For ways to protect vegetables from frost and extend their productivity, see page 653.)

Broad-leafed evergreens suffer in winter because the leaves continue to transpire and thus lose moisture (particularly on relatively warm, windy days). And if the soil is frozen, the roots cannot take up water to replace what has been lost, and the plant becomes desiccated. To minimize damage to these plants, water thoroughly before the ground freezes, then apply a thick mulch of oak leaves, pine needles, wood chips, or ground bark. The mulch layer limits the penetration of frost into the ground and protects surface roots from alternate freezing and thawing. When you plant broad-leafed evergreens, avoid locations where bright sun—especially in early morning—will strike frozen plants. To avoid rupturing plant tissues, thawing should be gradual.

Don't hurry to prune frost-damaged plants. Cutting them back too soon can stimulate tender new growth that will be nipped by later frosts, and you may mistake leafless but living stems for dead ones. When new growth begins in spring, remove wood that is clearly dead.

BEAT THE FROST. *When a sudden frost threatens tender plants, there's an easy way to save them. Fill plastic milk jugs with water and place them between your plants; then drape spunbonded polyester row cover (you can get this at garden centers) over the plants. As the water freezes, it gives off heat; the row cover holds the heat inside, protecting the plants.* ❖

PROTECTING PLANTS FROM OCCASIONAL FROST

1 Make a frame of four strong stakes around the plant. Lay plastic or burlap over tops of stakes; make sure it does not touch the leaves, since this would cause them to freeze. If you need more heat, place one or two small spotlights or a string of holiday lights in the shelter. Plug the lights into an extension cord or outlet intended for outdoor use; do not let them contact the plastic or burlap.

2 For a quick cover for smaller plants, use a large cardboard box. Cut the bottom on three sides to make a lid you can open and close as needed.

Grasses. See Lawns; Ornamental Grasses   pp. 610, 615

Greenhouses

For avid gardeners, a greenhouse is an essential outdoor room for plants, where temperature, humidity, and day length are all under human control. Greenhouses are useful for a number of purposes:

Providing winter shelter for tender plants. Potted citrus, for example, often spend the winter in a greenhouse.

Starting seeds of annuals and vegetables in early spring so that plants will be growing vigorously and ready to set out in the garden as soon as weather permits.

Starting cuttings that need a protected, moist location.

Raising vegetables and flowers to mature out of season, particularly when outdoor conditions are too cold for them to develop fully.

Growing specialty crops (such as orchids and tropical plants) that require controlled temperatures and humidity.

Greenhouses vary in size and complexity, from small bay windows attached to the house to simple lean-tos to more elaborate freestanding structures. Greenhouse frame materials include wood, aluminum, and PVC pipe. The glazing used for the walls and roof may be single- or double-walled glass, fiberglass, double-walled polycarbonate plastic, double-walled polyethylene, or acrylic. Double-walled glazing holds heat more efficiently. Shade covers, automatic vents, and heaters—activated by temperature sensors—help to keep greenhouse temperatures at the desired levels. If you garden where heavy snowfalls are common, be sure the greenhouse can stand up to the weight of the snow.

Mow No More. *Steep slopes planted with turf can be difficult and dangerous to mow. To make life easier, kill the grass with a herbicide such as glyphosate (Roundup); then plant a ground cover. To prevent erosion from washing away the growing plants, do some preparation before you plant. First lay 3 to 4 inches of pine straw; next, cover the straw with biodegradable jute netting, available at some garden centers and home supply stores. Cut holes in the jute and plant the starts through the holes. By the time the jute rots away, the plants will have covered the slope.* ❖

Ground Covers

Gardeners rely on ground covers to blanket the soil with dense foliage, adding beauty and variety to the garden and suppressing weeds at the same time. Though lawn grasses (see page 610) are doubtless the best-known cover for bare ground, the term "ground cover" typically refers to other kinds of plants, among them shrubs, vines, and many perennials. If chosen carefully, they require considerably less maintenance and water than lawns do. Ground cover plants usually create a relatively even surface, though heights range from a few inches to knee-high or even taller.

CHOOSING GROUND COVERS. When selecting ground covers, start by considering your site. Is it level or sloping, sunny or shady? How much water will be available for the plants? Also decide if you want a ground cover you can walk across or one that will serve as a traffic barrier.

PLANTING GROUND COVERS ON A SLOPE

When setting plants on a steep slope where erosion may occur, arrange them in staggered rows. Make an individual terrace for each plant and create a basin or low spot behind each one to catch water. Set the crowns of the plants high, so they won't become saturated and rot after watering.

Japanese pachysandra *(Pachysandra terminalis)* is an invaluable ground cover for shady places.

Settle on a deciduous cover or an evergreen one; decide if you want flowers or prefer just foliage. Ask yourself how the ground cover will fit in with the garden's other plants and hardscape. As you consider these questions and issues, you'll zero in on the right plants for your situation. For ideas on plant choices, consult "Ground Covers" in A Guide to Plant Selection, beginning on page 39.

PLANTING AND CARING FOR GROUND COVERS. In most of the South, fall planting is preferred because it gives plants time to establish their roots over winter. Most ground covers grow best in well-prepared soil; for these, ready the planting area as directed on page 628, adding plenty of organic matter. Some kinds of ground covers, however, can be planted directly in native soil with little or no amendment. This group includes juniper *(Juniperus)*, liriope, and wintercreeper euonymus.

When planting ground covers purchased in small pots or flats, set them in holes the same depth as and slightly wider than the root ball. For directions on setting out plants from gallon-size containers, see page 630. The required spacing varies with the plant; check entries in the Plant Encyclopedia for details.

Water thoroughly after planting, then keep soil moist (but not soggy) as the plants settle in. Apply a mulch to help conserve moisture and to prevent weeds from sprouting.

Once ground covers are established, their water needs vary depending on the particular plant and the soil in which it is growing. Fertilizer requirements differ too. As a rule of thumb, though, most woody, shrubby ground covers (especially drought-tolerant sorts) have fairly low nutrient needs; many get along with little or no fertilizing. Perennial ground covers with softer, lusher growth generally have higher nutrient requirements and should receive an annual feeding in spring.

Herbs

The word "herb" applies to any plant that, at some time in history, has been valued for seasoning, medicine, fragrance, or general household use. Within this broad category, you will find tall, willowy plants like dill as well as low, fine-textured creepers (some kinds of thyme, for example) that spread along the ground to form a fragrant carpet. Many herbs are annuals and biennials grown for their leaves and seeds; others, such as French tarragon and oregano, are perennials; still others are tough shrubs like rosemary, as useful in the landscape as in the kitchen.

Herbs have numerous garden uses. They can, of course, be grouped in an all-herb garden, be it a sunny corner of the vegetable plot, a special raised bed, or a traditional circular planting around a birdbath or sundial. They are excellent container plants—and pot culture is a good way to grow them near the kitchen door, handy for snipping. And many herbs add interest to the perennial or shrub border.

PLANTING AND CARING FOR HERBS. Choose a planting spot that receives 6 to 8 hours of full sun each day. Well-drained soil is essential; if drainage is poor, dig in plenty of organic matter or plant in raised beds. Work in a complete fertilizer before planting. Herbs aren't heavy feeders, so this should suffice for the entire season.

Most perennial and shrubby herbs are easier to start from transplants than from seed. Nurseries offer many kinds, typically in 2- or 4-inch pots; some are also sold in gallon containers. Annual and biennial herbs (such as basil, dill, and parsley), on the other hand, can easily be started from seed; see page 632.

After planting herbs from containers, water regularly until the plants are growing steadily; thereafter, most will need only occasional irrigation. Exceptions are basil, chives, mint, and parsley, which prefer evenly moist soil. (Keep a close eye on mint—it's naturally invasive.)

15 CULINARY HERBS

Many cooks consider these herbs essential: basil *(Ocimum basilicum)*, bay *(Laurus nobilis)*, chives *(Allium schoenoprasum)*, cilantro *(Coriandrum sativum)*, dill *(Anethum graveolens)*, fennel *(Foeniculum vulgare)*, French tarragon *(Artemisia dracunculus)*, mint *(Mentha)*, oregano *(Origanum vulgare)*, parsley *(Petroselinum crispum)*, rosemary *(Rosmarinus officinalis)*, sage *(Salvia officinalis)*, sweet marjoram *(Origanum majorana)*, thyme *(Thymus vulgaris)*, and winter savory *(Satureja montana)*.

'Dark Opal' basil

H

DRYING HERBS

Harvest herbs for drying just as the first flower buds begin to open. The oils in the leaves are most concentrated at this time, and the herbs will maintain their flavor when preserved. Cut sprigs or branches in the morning, after dew has evaporated. Tie them together at the cut ends and hang them upside down in a warm, dry, well-ventilated place out of direct sunlight. When the leaves are crisp and crumble readily, strip them from the stems and store them whole in airtight jars. Another way to dry herbs is to remove the leaves from the stems and spread them on screens placed in a warm, dry, airy place out of direct sun; stir them with your fingers every few days as they dry. Once they feel crisp, they're ready to store in airtight containers.

For herbs grown for their seeds, harvest seed heads or pods when they turn brown. Dry them in paper bags until you can shake the seeds loose; then store seeds in airtight containers.

When perennial herbs resume growth in early spring, feed them lightly with a complete fertilizer or spread compost around the base of each plant, taking care not to cover the crown (in order to avoid suffocating it).

Lawns

The classic lawn—lush, green, and crisply mowed—became a basic landscaping element in the South early in the 20th century, when dams, pipelines, and electric pumps made water easily available to homeowners. Today, however, a burgeoning population is straining the water supply in much of the region. Conservation is an important issue, and attention has naturally focused on the huge amount of water needed to keep lawns lush and green. Research has shown that many lawn grasses require more water per square foot than almost any other kind of garden plant. Moreover, up to half the water used by a typical single-family household is applied outdoors, primarily to lawns—and most homeowners give the lawn more water than it really needs.

Responding to these findings, some communities now restrict the amount of lawn that can be planted around new homes. Many gardeners, too, have reconsidered the value of a lawn. Some have eliminated it entirely, replacing it with one of the alternatives discussed under "Water Conservation" (page 658); others have sharply reduced its size. Besides demanding less water than a large expanse does, a small lawn requires less labor, time, and money to maintain.

If you plan to include a lawn in your landscape, you can do more to save on time and water than just keep it small. Opt for a simple geometric shape; it will allow you to irrigate without overspray, and it's easier to mow. Keeping the lawn fairly level makes good sense, too, since it minimizes runoff and makes mowing safer. Finally, be sure you choose the right grass for your climate, prepare and plant the site carefully, and maintain the lawn properly.

PLANTING A NEW LAWN. When you plant a new lawn—whether you start it from seed, sod, sprigs, or plugs—proper site preparation is essential. Remove any existing sod with a sod cutter (available from rental yards); for easier removal, you can kill the sod with an herbicide such as glyphosate (Roundup) before using the cutter. It's wise to have the soil's pH tested (see 646) before you plant. Most lawn grasses prefer slightly acid to slightly alkaline soil; centipede grass needs acid soil.

Till the site to a depth of about 8 inches and spread a 3- to 4-inch layer of topsoil or commercial compost over it. Also apply a complete fertilizer and any materials recommended by the soil test lab to adjust the pH. Till again; rake the area smooth and water it thoroughly. Let the soil settle for a few days; then sow seed, lay sod, or set out plugs or sprigs as shown on page 612.

CARING FOR LAWNS. To look their best, lawns require consistent watering and fertilizing as well as regular mowing.

Watering. To encourage deep rooting and conserve water, irrigate lawns deeply yet infrequently. Once or twice a week should be adequate in moderately warm weather; during hotter spells, you'll probably have to water more often. During cooler times of year, you can cut back on watering. Check with local water agencies or your Cooperative Extension Office for guidelines, which are often based on evapotranspiration (ET)—a localized, weather-based measurement of how much water a plant uses and how much evaporates from the soil.

To determine how thirsty the lawn really is, you can also perform a few informal tests. First, just step on the grass: if the blades don't spring back from your footprint, it's time to water. Or push a screwdriver into the soil; if it doesn't penetrate easily, the lawn probably needs water. A soil sampling tube (see page 659) will give you a more accurate indication of the soil's moisture content.

Many sprinklers apply water faster than the soil can absorb it. To prevent runoff, water in cycles; sprinkle until just before runoff or puddling occurs (typically 10 to 15 minutes), then repeat the cycle in an hour. Adjust sprinklers so they don't overshoot onto paving.

To improve water penetration and reduce runoff, aerate and dethatch your lawn once a year. Local nurseries offer information and equipment to help you with these tasks.

Fertilizing. Most lawns are heavy feeders, requiring regular applications of high-nitrogen fertilizer. In regions with alkaline soil, iron may also be beneficial. Give cool-season lawns two applications of fertilizer in spring and two in fall. Fertilize warm-season lawns monthly in late spring and summer. Numerous bagged lawn fertilizers, both synthetic and natural, are sold; check the packages for recommended application rates.

If you cut back on watering because of drought, hold back on fertilizer as well.

Mowing. To keep a lawn healthy, mow it regularly; grass is weakened if allowed to grow too long between mowings. When the blades are about one-third taller than the recommended growing height (see the descriptions of lawn grasses on the facing page), it's time to mow. Unless the clippings are quite long, leave them on the lawn to decompose and add nutrients to the soil (long clippings might smother the grass).

THREE STEPS TO FEWER WEEDS. *Lawn weeds are opportunists: they grow wherever grass doesn't. You'll have far fewer weeds if you observe the following dos and don'ts. First, don't park your car on the lawn. Weeds like compacted soil; grass doesn't. Second, don't scalp your lawn. This weakens grass more than it does weeds. Cut your grass no lower than the recommended mowing height; taller grass shades the soil surface and keeps weed seeds from sprouting. Finally, do water and fertilize regularly. Thick, healthy grass allows fewer openings for weeds.* ❖

LAWN PROBLEMS. To avoid lawn problems, plant grass that's well adapted to your area and care for it properly. If you do encounter problems, the following information will help you identify and correct them. (For a discussion of weeds that grow in lawns, see page 664.)

Brown patch. Caused by the fungus *Rhizoctonia solani,* this is a very common lawn disease. High fertility and warm, rainy weather favor its development. Initially, small, irregular brown patches or circular spots appear in the lawn; a ring of darker grass may surround each patch. Eventually, the patches merge and the affected grass dies.

To prevent brown patch, avoid excessive fertilizing, especially with quick-release nitrogen. Water only in early morning, so grass blades dry quickly. Control the disease with a lawn fungicide containing triadimefon (Bayleton), myclobutanil (Immunox), or chlorothalonil (Daconil).

Chinch bugs. These small (⅙-inch-long), grayish black insects suck sap from grass blades (particularly in hot weather), attacking St. Augustine and sometimes Bermuda, buffalo, and zoysia grasses. Symptoms are brown or yellow patches, especially in dry locations; these patches eventually die. To identify these pests, push a can with both ends removed into the soil where grass is discolored and fill it with water; if present, chinch bugs will float to the surface.

To control, eliminate thatch. Plant resistant selections. Keep lawn moist to promote beneficial fungi that attack chinch bugs. For chemical control, use diazinon.

Dollar spot. This common disease, caused by the fungus *Sclerotinia homeocarpa,* frequently attacks malnourished lawns during periods of warm, wet weather. Small brown spots appear in the lawn, later becoming straw colored. Spots may coalesce. Walking or mowing across infected spots spreads the disease.

CHOOSING THE RIGHT LAWN GRASS FOR YOUR AREA

Lawn grasses fall into two basic categories: *cool-season* and *warm-season* (subtropical). Each group comprises a variety of plants with varying water needs. For more information on specific grasses, consult the individual listings in the Plant Encyclopedia.

COOL-SEASON GRASSES withstand winter cold but typically languish in hot, dry summers. They do better in the Upper and Middle South; when planted elsewhere, they require extensive summer watering. Cool-season grasses are often sold as mixes of several kinds; even if one of them is not adapted to the soil or sun

Buffalo grass lawn

and shade conditions in your garden, chances are that others in the package will do well.

Kentucky bluegrass. Zones US, MS (cooler parts). Beautiful but high-maintenance turf; requires average feeding and plenty of water. Will tolerate some foot traffic and some shade, but not too much of either. Establish by seed or sod; mow at 2 to 3 inches.

Tall fescue. Zones US, MS, LS (upper half). Can grow in shade; fairly drought tolerant and able to resist wear. Needs average feeding. Good alternative to bluegrass or ryegrass. Establish by seed only; mow at 2 to 3 inches.

Perennial ryegrass. Zones US, MS (cooler parts). Fair to good wear resistance; moderate tolerance of drought and shade. Requires average feeding. Establish by seed. Good for overseeding dormant grass in Lower and Coastal South. Mow at 1½ to 2½ inches.

WARM-SEASON GRASSES thrive in hot weather but turn brown in cold winter weather. Gardeners who want a year-round green lawn sometimes overseed these warm-season grasses with some types of cool-season grasses for the colder months.

Bahia grass. Zones CS, TS. Drought-tolerant, durable turf grass that thrives in sun but does poorly in shade. Good for dry, sandy, acid soil; requires only light feeding. Produces numerous seed heads. Establish by seed or sod; mow at 3 to 4 inches.

Bermuda (common). Zones MS, LS, CS, TS. Tolerant of drought and most soil types, Bermuda spreads rapidly and is highly resistant to wear. Requires full sun, moderate feeding. Establish by seed, sod, or plugs. Mow at ½ to 1½ inches. Will invade planting beds.

Bermuda (hybrid). Zones MS, LS, CS, TS. Though less tolerant of drought than common Bermuda, the improved type is just as wear resistant and has a finer texture. It requires more maintenance, including heavy fertilizing, and it does poorly in shade. Establish by seed, sod, or plugs. Mow Bermuda grass at ½ to 1½ inches.

Buffalo grass. Zones US, MS, LS. Low-maintenance, drought-tolerant grass with good wear resistance. Requires little feeding. Will not thrive in shade. Establish by seed, sod, sprigs, or plugs. Mow at 1 to 6 inches, depending on season and preference.

Carpet grass. Zones CS, TS. Though it requires little feeding and is fairly shade tolerant, this is the lawn grass of last resort; it is fragile, needs lots of water, and does best in wet, acid soil. Establish by seed or sprigs; mow at 1 to 2 inches.

Centipede grass. Zones LS, CS. This grass is fairly tolerant of shade, prefers poor, acid soil, and needs little fertilizing—but it cannot tolerate much wear. Establish by seed, sod, sprigs, or plugs; mow at 1 to 2 inches.

St. Augustine grass. Zones LS, CS, TS. Tolerates shade and can withstand salt spray near the coast; moderately drought resistant. Requires average feeding. Spreads quickly. Establish by sod, sprigs, or plugs; mow at 2 to 4 inches.

Zoysia grass. Zones MS, LS, CS, TS. Extremely drought tolerant and tough, this dense, slow-spreading turf can be established by sod, sprigs, or plugs. Tolerates light shade and a great deal of wear; chokes out weeds. Mow at 1 to 2 inches.

SEED, SOD, SPRIGS, OR PLUGS?

Lawn grass is sold in several forms. All except sod require diligent weed control after planting.

Seed is the least expensive way to start a lawn, and it's offered for a wide variety of grasses. Read the package label carefully. It should list the named selections of the grass or grasses included and indicate a high rate of germination for those grasses; it should also show a low percentage of crop or weed seeds in relation to the percentage of lawn grass seeds.

Fall seeding is recommended for cool-season grasses, because fall and winter rains help establish the lawn. Seed warm-season grasses in spring and summer.

Sod is the most expensive way to start a lawn, but it does give instant coverage with almost no weed problems. Local suppliers offer selections adapted to your area. Sod cool-season grasses in fall or spring; sod warm-season grasses in spring or summer.

Plugs are small rooted plants. Usually sold in trays, they're used for warm-season grasses that spread as they grow, such as buffalo, hybrid Bermuda, St. Augustine, and zoysia. Plant them in spring, following the supplier's directions.

Sprigs are pieces of grass stem and root; like plugs, they're used to plant warm-season spreading grasses. Plant in spring, following the supplier's directions.

SOWING GRASS SEED

1 After preparing the area, scatter seed. A mechanical spreader helps sow seed evenly.

2 Lightly rake the seed into the soil.

3 Spread a 1/16-inch layer of soil over the area; roll with an empty roller to press down seed. Water thoroughly. Keep the seedbed moist with frequent, light watering until the seed sprouts.

LAYING SOD

1 After preparing the site, moisten the soil. Unroll the strips and lay them out with their ends staggered, pressing the edges together firmly.

2 Use a knife to trim sod so it fits snugly around paving and other obstacles.

3 To press roots firmly into the soil, roll the lawn with a roller half-filled with water. Water the new lawn once daily (more often in hot weather) for 6 weeks.

PLANTING PLUGS AND SPRIGS

Two-inch plugs of buffalo grass and some other warm-season spreading grasses are sold in trays. Planted at 8-inch intervals, they'll grow together in a year.

Sprigs of hybrid Bermuda grass root and spread quickly in well-prepared soil. Be sure to water plugs or sprigs often until roots take hold.

Bermuda grass sprig

Buffalo grass plug

If grass is properly fertilized with nitrogen, lawns usually overcome dollar spot on their own. Water only in the morning. For serious infestations, apply a lawn fungicide containing triadimefon (Bayleton), myclobutanil (Immunox), or chlorothalonil (Daconil).

Fairy ring. This fungal disease is common in lawns growing in soil high in organic matter or containing wood debris (such as boards or old roots). Symptoms include small circular patches of dark green grass surrounding areas of dead or light-colored grass. Mushrooms may or may not be present.

To control, apply a nitrogen fertilizer and keep the lawn wet for 3 to 5 days. Also aerate the lawn. There are no chemical controls.

TOP TO BOTTOM: Chinch bug, Fairy ring, Rust, Sod webworms, White grubs

Mole crickets. Three species of mole cricket *(Scapteriscus)* inhabit the South; all can devastate a lawn in short order. These 1½-inch-long pests use the big claws on their forelegs to dig through patches of warm-season grass.

To control them, avoid heavy watering and fertilizing, which results in thatch that mole crickets like. Apply a lawn insecticide containing imidacloprid (Merit).

Rust. Rust fungi can afflict Kentucky bluegrass, perennial ryegrass, tall fescue, and zoysia lawns. Infected lawns have an overall yellowish to reddish color; small, reddish pustules form in circular or elongated patches on older leaf blades and stems. Blades eventually shrivel and die.

To control, apply adequate (but not excessive) nitrogen fertilizer. For rust spores to germinate, leaf surfaces must be wet for 4 hours; water in the morning so that grass will dry out during the day. The fungicides triadimefon (Bayleton) and chlorothalonil (Daconil) may be effective.

Sod webworms. The larvae of several kinds of moths, these pests attack all turf grasses. Small dead patches appear in spring and gradually enlarge during summer. Pale moths fly close to the lawn in a zigzag pattern at dusk. To confirm the presence of sod webworms, drench an affected patch of lawn with a solution of 1 tablespoon dishwashing soap to 1 gallon water. Larvae will float to the surface; if you find 15 or more per square yard, treat the lawn.

To control these pests, try beneficial nematodes (see page 618). For chemical control, use a granular lawn insecticide.

White grubs. These 1- to 1½-inch grubs are the larvae of several species of beetles; they have three pairs of legs and curl into a C shape when exposed. White grubs feed on the roots of all turf grasses. Distinct, irregularly shaped brown patches appear in afflicted lawns; symptoms are most severe in late summer. Sections of dead turf pull up easily.

To control, apply beneficial nematodes (see page 618), first checking to be sure the species you buy is recommended for use against white grubs. For chemical control, use a granular lawn insecticide containing imidacloprid (Merit, GrubEx). This works best if you first dethatch the lawn.

Mulching

Mulching is the practice of applying organic or inorganic materials to the surface of the soil around plants. Mulches help hold moisture in the soil, and they insulate it from extreme or rapid changes of temperature. They prevent most weed seedlings from becoming established (and make it easier to remove any that do grow); keep mud from splashing up onto foliage, flowers, fruit, and surfaces such as house walls; help prevent erosion; and make your garden beds look tidy. Before applying any mulch, clear away existing weeds.

LAYING LANDSCAPE FABRIC

Unroll fabric, then use scissors or a knife to cut X-shaped slits for plants. Tuck the flaps back in around the plants' bases.

INORGANIC MULCHES. Inorganic mulches include gravel and other kinds of rock; plastic sheeting; and landscape fabrics. Stones make permanent mulches that can discourage weeds effectively; check with your supplier for the amount you need. Plastic warms the soil, and black plastic suppresses weeds.

Landscape fabrics—unlike plastic—are porous, allowing air, water, and dissolved nutrients to reach the soil. Sold in nurseries and garden supply centers, these fabrics are best used in permanent plantings around trees and

M

HOW MUCH ORGANIC MULCH SHOULD YOU BUY?

Bulk quantities of organic mulch are sold by the cubic yard. Determine how many square feet you want to cover (multiply the area's length by its width), then consult the chart below to determine the approximate amount of mulch you need.

HOW MUCH MULCH TO USE

To cover this area	2 inches deep	3 inches deep	4 inches deep
100 square feet	⅔ cubic yard	1 cubic yard	1⅓ cubic yards
250	1⅔	2½	3⅓
500	3⅓	5	6⅓
1,000	6⅔	10	13⅓

shrubs; they aren't really suited for beds of vegetables or annuals, where you change plants often. Install them as shown on the previous page (you can lay them around existing plants or cut slits in them to accommodate new ones). After installation, cover the fabric with a 2- to 3-inch layer of a weed-free organic mulch. Replenish the mulch as often as necessary.

ORGANIC MULCHES. Derived from once-living matter, organic mulches break down slowly, improving the soil and adding nutrients as they decompose. Choices include chopped leaves, compost, grass clippings (be sure to apply clippings in thin layers, letting each layer dry before applying another), pine needles, shredded bark, ground bark, wood chips, and straw.

Apply organic mulches in a 2- to 4-inch-thick layer on paths and around plants, but don't pile mulch against tree trunks or over a plant's crown, as this can encourage insects and rot.

Native Plants

Native plants are a hot topic among Southern gardeners today, and for good reason. They give your garden a sense of place, establishing it as an integral part of the area where you live. They're part of what makes Austin look different from Raleigh, and Raleigh look different from Jackson or Orlando. And because they're adapted to the climate, they're generally easy to grow and need little care once established.

That said, it's tempting to conclude that native plants are always better choices than exotic ones. This isn't true. For one thing, some native plants are difficult to grow in the home garden, requiring very special conditions. For another, just because a plant is native to "the South" doesn't mean it likes your part of the South. Finally, many non-native plants make excellent, beautiful, and trouble-free additions to the garden. Your primary goal should simply be to choose the right plant for the right spot—and if that plant is native, all the better. In fact, so many native plants are available that you're almost certain to find suitable places for them in your garden. A hot, dry, gravelly bed may be a perfect spot for plants of the Texas Hill Country.

A cool, moist, shady area sounds right for ferns and many woodland wildflowers. Dry woods are ideal for oakleaf hydrangea *(Hydrangea quercifolia),* while Eastern red cedar *(Juniperus virginiana)* thrives in limy soil in sunny fields and hillsides.

CARING FOR NATIVE PLANTS. Native plants will thrive in your garden if you take care getting them established. When setting out container-grown plants, start with young ones that are not root-bound—they may not be much to look at when first planted, but they'll adapt more successfully than larger plants. Water immediately after planting, being sure to saturate the soil. Then water carefully and steadily for the first summer or two: don't inundate the plants, but don't let them dry out, either. Once you've established your natives through their first 2 years (and assuming you have planted them where the natural conditions suit them), they should do well with little or no supplemental watering. In general, Southern natives don't require fertilizing (and some are actually weakened by it). A light mulch is beneficial, but to avoid rot, keep it a few inches away from the plants' crowns.

Organic Gardening

Also known as chemical-free or natural gardening, organic gardening is often associated with raising crops that are safer to eat, but its principles apply to any sort of garden, not just the vegetable plot and the fruit orchard. Organic gardeners (and farmers) strive to produce the healthiest plants possible with minimal impact on the environment and minimal risk to all creatures—human and otherwise—who enjoy the garden. They avoid using chemical fertilizers and pesticides, focusing instead on creating healthy soil, which in turn promotes healthy plants that are less susceptible to diseases and insects. Organic gardeners aim for biological diversity in their gardens, choosing plants that will attract a wide variety of organisms, including the beneficial creatures that help keep damaging pests under control. The result is often a healthier, more productive garden.

ELEMENTS OF AN ORGANIC GARDEN. As noted below, many aspects of organic gardening are covered in greater detail elsewhere in this guide to gardening.

Building healthy soil. Healthy garden soil is home to earthworms and numerous other beneficial creatures. Its structure is hospitable to plant roots—neither too dense nor too loose, fast draining yet moisture retentive. To achieve this kind of soil, enrich your planting beds with organic amendments such as compost and manure (see pages 599 and 646 for more on composting and soil amendments). Cover crops (page 602) offer an easy way to add large amounts of organic material into the soil. Fertilizers, too, can increase the soil's store of organic matter. Organic gardeners prefer natural fertilizers (page 606), which, though slower acting than chemical ones, provide a more sustained release of nutrients and encourage beneficial soil-dwelling organisms.

Controlling pests and diseases. Be diligent about monitoring the garden, so you know which problems are present and what natural controls (beneficial insects, for example) may already be at work. Physical controls such as barriers, handpicking, and spraying with jets of water (page 617) can curtail insect damage. Choosing plants that are resistant to specific diseases and pests is important; you will find many such selections listed in the Plant Encyclopedia. Crop rotation (page 653) prevents diseases and insects that are specific to certain plants from building up in any one part of the garden.

For more specific information on disease control, see page 603. The topic of pest control, including a discussion of beneficial insects and biological controls, begins on page 617.

Controlling weeds. To keep weeds down, use mulches (see page 646; organic mulches also help improve the soil). Physical management techniques such as pulling and hoeing (page 663) are also effective.

Organic gardening practices are designed to protect beneficial insects such as bees, the primary pollinators of many flowering plants.

N

Ornamental Grasses

Grown for their graceful form and varying textures, ornamental grasses provide a handsome foil to shrubs and perennials. Many are excellent container plants too. Like lawn grasses, ornamental sorts can be divided into warm- and cool-season types. *Warm-season grasses* include most species of *Miscanthus, Molinia, Panicum,* and *Pennisetum;* they grow from spring through summer, bloom in fall, and then go dormant. Their foliage and flowering plumes remain attractive—albeit dry and brown—through the winter.

Cool-season grasses are typically evergreen, though some may die back. They begin new growth in fall, then flower in spring and summer. This group includes *Calamagrostis, Deschampsia, Festuca,* and *Helictotrichon sempervirens,* as well as the sedges (*Carex*).

For help in choosing these plants, see "Ornamental Grasses" in A Guide to Plant Selection, on page 87. Be aware that a few ornamental grasses can be invasive, spreading too extensively in the garden or into wild lands; these are noted in the entries in the Plant Encyclopedia.

PLANTING AND CARING FOR ORNAMENTAL GRASSES. Ornamental grasses need more or less the same care you'd give perennials. Most should be planted in spring, though cool-season sorts can also be set out in autumn. Before planting, work organic matter (such as compost) and a complete fertilizer into the soil. Don't bury the plants' crowns when you set them in, as this can lead to rot. A mulch will help keep down weeds and conserve soil moisture, but again, be careful not to let it pile up around the grasses' crowns.

Ornamental grasses vary greatly in their moisture requirements—some need water regularly, others only rarely. Check the listings in the Plant Encyclopedia for details. If planted in well-prepared beds and mulched, most ornamental grasses can do without feeding, but if they're growing poorly, give them an application of general-purpose fertilizer in early spring.

Most grasses benefit from an annual cleanup in late winter. Cut back warm-season grasses just as you see new growth emerging at the plants' bases, using pruning shears to trim dead foliage and flowering stems to within a few inches of the ground. (If you have a number of large clumps, electric hedge shears or a mechanical weed trimmer will make quick work of this project.) Evergreen cool-season grasses needn't be cut back every year. Instead, clean them up by removing dead foliage; you can often simply "comb" out old growth by running your (gloved) fingers through the clumps. After a few years, however, the grasses may develop a great deal of unattractive or dead leaves; at this point, cut them back by two-thirds in fall or early spring to encourage fresh new growth.

TOP: Oriental fountain grass
BOTTOM: A mechanical weed trimmer with a blade can be used to cut back ornamental grasses.

Divide ornamental grasses every few years or so, when the clump's center dies out. Divide warm-season kinds in spring. For cool-season sorts, do the job in fall or early spring. To divide, dig up the clump; if it's very large, you may first need to cut it into sections with a sharp spade or an ax. Then cut off and replant the vigorous sections from the outside of the clump.

Perennials

The general category of perennials encompasses plants with widely varying habits of growth, but all have at least one thing in common: they live for more than 2 years, in contrast to annuals and biennials (pages 596 and 597), which complete their life cycles within 1 and 2 years, respectively. Some perennials die down to the ground at the end of each growing season, then reappear at the start of the next. These include hosta and peony (*Paeonia*) and are often called "herbaceous" plants. Others, such as Shasta daisy (*Chrysanthemum maximum*) and coral bells (*Heuchera*), go through winter as low tufts of leaves, ready to grow when spring arrives. A third type of perennial is truly evergreen, its foliage persisting almost unchanged throughout the winter months. Candytuft (*Iberis sempervirens*) and yucca are two examples.

PLANTING PERENNIALS. Perennials are sold both bare-root and in containers. Nurseries and garden centers offer them in containers ranging from cell-packs to 5-gallon pots; for information on planting these, see page 629.

Nurseries and mail-order catalogs also sell some perennials bare-root during their dormant period. As the name implies, bare-root plants have had most or all of the soil removed from around their roots, which are then surrounded with packing material and enclosed in plastic bags. If you'll be planting bare-root perennials within a day or two after purchase or receipt, open the bags slightly, add a little water, and hold them in a cool place. If planting must be delayed by more than a few days, however, pot up the plants in small containers or heel them in—plant them temporarily in a shallow trench in the garden. Before setting out bare-root perennials in their permanent location, prepare the soil as described on page 628. Then plant as shown on page 631.

CARING FOR PERENNIALS. Routine watering during growth and bloom will satisfy most perennials. There are, of course, exceptions—some plants prefer drier soil, while others demand lots of moisture. These are noted in the Plant Encyclopedia. Keep in mind that young plants require more frequent watering than older ones, which have deeper, more extensive root systems. A layer of mulch helps conserve water, suppresses weeds, and improves the soil as it decomposes. Once perennials are established in the garden, feed them annually in late winter or early spring, using a complete fertilizer, or as recommended for specific plants in the Plant Encyclopedia.

Throughout the bloom season, deadhead your perennials (that is, remove the spent flowers), both to keep the plants tidy and to prevent them from diverting energy to seed production. Of course, you may not want to deadhead in all cases. Certain perennials, for example, have attractive seedheads that you can leave in place

P

until winter or early spring, both for decoration and to provide food for seed-eating birds.

Later in the year (in fall or winter), it's a good idea to clean up most perennials by removing old, dead, and fallen foliage, flowers, and stems. Besides neatening up the garden, this deprives pests (especially snails and slugs) of hiding places and helps eliminate disease organisms.

Over time, many perennials form such thick clumps that the plants are too crowded to bloom. This is especially true of perennials with fibrous roots—such as hostas, Shasta daisies, yarrow, or dianthus—and of grasses and grasslike plants, which tend to die out in the center of the clump. The best time to divide perennials is in fall or early spring, but in the Upper South, make divisions at least a month before any hard freezes. For more on dividing perennials, see page 638.

Many gardeners in the Upper and Middle South mulch perennials over the winter to protect them from alternate freezing and thawing. As soon as the ground freezes, apply a light-weight mulch that won't pack down into an airtight mass; evergreen boughs, chopped leaves, and pine needles are all good choices.

MORE FLOWERS IN A PINCH. *There's a simple way to get two or three times as many flowers from perennials—pinching. As the plants grows, pinch the top of each stem back to a node (the point at which leaf and stem meet). Two stems will then grow from this spot. After a while, pinch those back too. You'll then have four stems—each with as many flowers as the original would have had. This technique works on many common plants, including balloon flower, butterfly weed, fall asters, ironweed, Joe-pye weed, perennial phlox, purple coneflower, salvia, speedwell, and toad lily. ❖*

STAKING PERENNIALS

Some perennials are naturally inclined to sprawl or flop over. To display their blooms most effectively and to keep them from smothering neighboring plants, you'll need to prop them up. These illustrations show three useful staking techniques.

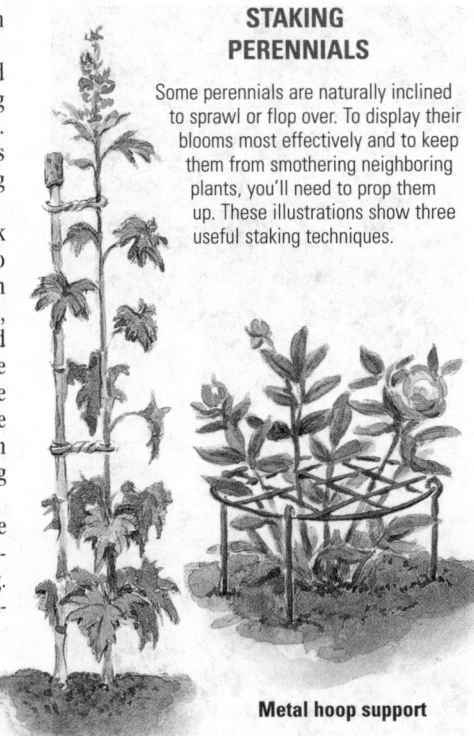

Metal hoop support

Bamboo stake and tie; cork at tip of stake protects eyes from injury

Stakes and string

Pest Management

Chemical-based pesticides were popularized in the 1940s, ushering in a long era of pest control through attempted eradication. Beyond being generally unsuccessful, this approach has been actively harmful to a wide range of nontarget organisms, including humans and other animals, birds, and beneficial insects. In recent years, recognizing that gardens are complex and interdependent systems, more and more gardeners have rejected the "elimination" method: far from solving a problem, wiping out a particular pest simply upsets the garden's natural balance. The focus today has shifted to maintaining a diversified garden, where pests are largely kept in check by natural forces. If one or more pests do cause unacceptable damage, gardeners first attempt to manage the situation by using physical or biological controls. Chemicals are employed only as a last resort.

The balanced, safety-conscious approach described above reflects the goals and methods of Integrated Pest Management (IPM), first developed for commercial agriculture but just as appropriate for the home garden. Its primary aim is to *prevent* problems. When diseases or pest infestations do arise, a number of integrated techniques are brought into play to reduce them to tolerable levels—not to eliminate them completely.

PREVENTING AND IDENTIFYING PROBLEMS. To thwart problems before they start, IPM begins with good cultural practices. Choose healthy plants adapted to your climate and garden conditions; whenever possible, select those resistant to diseases and pests prevalent in your area. Plant carefully and follow up with proper watering, fertilizing, garden cleanup, and other care as needed. Use soil solarization (page 664) to reduce or eliminate soil-dwelling pests

PLANTING BARE-ROOT PERENNIALS

1 Remove packing material and soak the roots in water for about 30 minutes.

2 Dig a hole about twice as wide as the root system. Then make a cone of soil in the center to support the roots. Set the plant on the cone of soil and spread the roots evenly.

3 Fill with soil so that the crown of the plant is level with or slightly above the soil, then water well.

P

and weed seeds. In the vegetable garden, rotate crops to prevent the buildup of specific pests (page 653).

Another basic practice of IPM is regular garden monitoring. If you check your plants frequently, you're more likely to spot problems before they get out of hand. Note the general condition of each plant; then look for fungal growth, holes in leaves or fruit, sap oozing from bark, and wilted branches. Check for insects hiding on leaf undersides, in bark fissures, or beneath fallen leaves. A hand lens is useful for spotting tiny pests like spider mites.

Because beneficial or harmless creatures sometimes resemble damaging pests, it's important to identify any organisms you find accurately. For help with identification, check the photos and descriptions beginning on page 618 or consult your Cooperative Extension Office.

MANAGEMENT OPTIONS. Even if your garden inspection reveals a few pest problems, you may not need or want to employ controls. Keep in mind that a truly pest-free garden does not exist, and learn to accept some marred fruit, flowers, or foliage. More extensive damage doesn't automatically require control, either. Sometimes it may be better simply to remove and replace an afflicted plant.

If you decide that a problem is serious enough to warrant action on your part, begin with physical and biological controls, turning to chemicals only when all else fails.

Physical controls. These nontoxic controls include a number of techniques.

Handpicking. Remove and destroy slugs, snails, caterpillars, and other pests. To get rid of some pests, you may need to pluck and destroy entire leaves (a tactic that can also help control some foliage diseases).

Pruning. Prune and destroy entire branches infested with a pest or disease.

Spraying with water. A jet of water can knock pests from plants and often kill them.

Erecting barriers. These can prevent pests from reaching susceptible plants and include row covers (page 653); plant cages made by fastening screening to frames of wood or PVC pipe; and plant collars (paper cups, plastic cartons, or empty cans with the ends cut out) to protect seedlings from insects such as cutworms. Other barriers are discussed in the descriptions of individual pests.

Using traps. You can trap pests in various ways. Colored sticky traps are designed to catch specific insects; some are attracted to the color red, others to white or yellow, for example. Pheromone traps contain chemicals involved in communication between insects of the same species; a sticky material in the trap prevents the insect from escaping. Some pheromone traps are used to control pest caterpillars (notably codling moth) by mass trapping of males.

Biological controls. When you use biological controls, you're relying on living organisms to

TOP: Plant collars made from plastic cartons prevent cutworms from reaching vegetable seedlings.
BOTTOM: Yellow sticky cards attract and trap whiteflies.

destroy garden pests—the sort of control that occurs naturally in the garden all the time. To draw beneficials to your garden and encourage them to remain, provide food in the form of nectar-producing flowering plants and avoid chemical sprays that destroy both helpful and harmful creatures. See the following page for more information on beneficials and plants that attract them.

Certain microorganisms are also classed as biological controls. The best known of these is *Bacillus thuringiensis* (*Bt;* sold as Dipel), a bacterium that, once ingested by susceptible pest larvae, causes them to stop feeding and eventually die. Many different strains have been identified, each effective against specific types of larvae. *Bt* does not affect nontarget creatures.

Chemical controls. As a last resort, IPM turns to various sorts of pesticides, first selecting the least toxic ones (products such as insecticidal soap, for example). If these are not successful, the use of stronger chemicals (synthetics) may be warranted. For lists of both natural and synthetic pesticides, see page 623.

PLANTS THAT ATTRACT BENEFICIAL INSECTS

Certain flowering plants provide sources of food that many beneficials need at various times during their life cycle. Integrate these plants into a border or plant them in swaths around the garden. Mix many kinds: the wider the range of food and shelter you provide, the more varieties of insects you'll attract (and the more likely they are to stay).

Angelica
Basket-of-gold (*Aurinia saxatilis*)
Buckwheat (*Eriogonum*)
Butterfly weed (*Asclepias tuberosa*)
Carpet bugleweed (*Ajuga reptans*)
Clovers (*Trifolium* and other species)
Coriander (*Coriandrum sativum*)
Coreopsis
Corn cockle (*Agrostemma githago*)
Cosmos (*Cosmos bipinnatus*)
Dill (*Anethum graveolens*)
Fennel (*Foeniculum vulgare*)
Feverfew (*Chrysanthemum parthenium*)
Golden marguerite (*Anthemis tinctoria*)
Mustard (*Brassica*)
Queen Anne's lace (*Daucus carota*)
Sweet alyssum (*Lobularia maritima*)
Tansy (*Tanacetum vulgare*)
Tidytips (*Layia platyglossa*)
Wine cups (*Callirhoe involucrata*)
Yarrow (*Achillea*)

Plant a wide variety of flowers to attract beneficials.

P

BENEFICIALS

Some of the beneficial creatures described here are naturally present in Southern gardens; others, as noted, can be introduced to reduce various pest populations. Spiders and centipedes are also important predators, as are toads, frogs, and birds.

Assassin bugs. These slim, ½- to ¾-inch-long insects have long legs and even longer angled antennae. Some species are a brilliant red or black; others are brown or gray. They prey on many insects, stabbing their victims with a long, curved beak.

Beneficial nematodes. Beneficial nematodes include several species of microscopic worms. Also known as parasitic or predatory nematodes, they're effective against hundreds of pests that spend part of their lives in the ground, including cucumber beetles, cutworms, fire ants, flea beetles, grubs, root weevils, and sod webworms. (They do not harm earthworms.) They attack the larvae, releasing a toxic bacterium that kills the host. Read directions carefully, as effectiveness depends on proper soil conditions and release techniques.

Damsel bugs are dull gray or brown, about ½ inch long, and very slender, with a long, narrow head. Nymphs resemble the adults, but they're smaller and have no wings. Both adults and nymphs feed on aphids, leafhoppers, and small caterpillars.

Ground beetles. Ranging from ½ to 1 inch long, most ground beetles are shiny black, though some are also marked with bright colors. The smaller species eat other insects, caterpillars, cutworms, and soil-dwelling maggots and grubs. Some larger species eat slugs and snails and their eggs.

Lacewings. An adult lacewing is an inch-long, flying insect with lacy, netted wings and long antennae. The immature or larval form looks something like a ½-inch-long alligator; it has visible legs and is equipped with pincers at the mouth end. Lacewing larvae devour aphids, leafhoppers, mealybugs, mites, psyllids, thrips, whiteflies, and other insects; adults of most species feed only on nectar, pollen, and honeydew from garden plants. Larvae are commercially available.

Lady beetles. Also known as ladybugs, these familiar garden helpers and their larvae (which look like ¼-inch-long, six-legged alligators with orange and black spots or stripes) feed on aphids, mealybugs, and the eggs of many insects. Mail-order and garden centers sell lady beetles, but once released, they often fly away rather than staying in your garden. Freeing them at night or keeping them in cages for the first few days may encourage them to remain.

Minute pirate bugs. Both the adults (⅛-inch-long, black-and-white bugs) and pale orange nymphs feed on thrips, spider mites, and insect eggs. Also called flower bugs, they occur naturally in gardens; they can also be purchased for release.

Parasitic wasps. Many species of naturally occurring parasitic wasps lay their eggs in the larvae, pupae, or eggs of other insects, thus destroying them. These tiny wasps are not harmful to humans. One type offered in many garden catalogs is the trichogramma wasp, which lays its eggs within the eggs of many moths and butterflies. Several species are sold; check with the seller to get the one best adapted to your situation.

Soldier beetles. These narrow, ¾-inch-long, typically red or orange insects have leathery-looking black, gray, or brown wing covers. The adults eat aphids and other soft-bodied insects; the tiny soil-dwelling larvae attack smaller insects. Adults also feed on pollen and nectar.

Syrphid flies. Also known as flower or hover flies, these insects are important naturally occurring beneficials. Adults have bodies banded with yellow; they look a bit like bees but have only one set of wings. While adults feed only on nectar and pollen, the larvae (tapered green or gray maggots with small fangs) consume dozens of aphids each day.

Tachinid flies. The gray, bristled adults look something like houseflies. They feed only on nectar, but their tiny, spined, green larvae parasitize pests such as armyworms, cutworms, stinkbugs, and smaller beetle larvae. There are many species, each attacking specific insects.

P

TOP: Assassin bug
BOTTOM: Parasitic wasp

TOP: Damsel bug
BOTTOM: Soldier beetle

TOP: Ground beetle
BOTTOM: Syrphid fly

TOP: Lacewing
BOTTOM: Tachinid fly

PLANT PESTS. Some of the pests most commonly encountered in Southern gardens are discussed here. A number of pests that afflict only one kind of plant—ash trees *(Fraxinus)*, apples, or tomatoes, for example—are treated in the appropriate entry in the Plant Encyclopedia. The controls mentioned for each pest are discussed in order of toxicity, from least to most toxic.

Ants. Most ants aren't harmful to plants, but they can cause problems in the garden. Certain species, however, nurture and protect sap-sucking insects such as aphids and mealybugs, soft scales, and whiteflies. These sap-sucking insects in turn produce sticky honeydew, and sooty mold often grows on the honeydew. To prevent ants from crawling onto plants to tend these insects, place sticky barriers (such as Tanglefoot) around the trunks and stems.

Of course, the major problem ant in the South is the fire ant. Fire ants build large mounds in lawns and gardens; when disturbed, they boil out of the mound to inflict painful stings on whomever has disturbed them. Beneficial nematodes applied to the lawn can provide good long-lasting control. For one-season control, use a spreader to apply fibroril (Over 'n Out). To destroy individual mounds and kill the queens, use slow-acting poisons such as hydramethylnon (Amdro) or abamectin (Affirm). For quicker results, treat the mound with acephate (Orthene) or cyfluthrin.

ANTS IN YOUR PANTS? *With the exception of fire ants, ants are mostly beneficial; they're relentless predators that dispatch a host of harmful insects. But when ants invade your home, how do you give them the heave-ho without using chemical controls? One way is to mix boric acid, a natural insecticide, with sugar, then place small amounts in ant trails and problem areas. The ants will carry the mixture back to their nest and share it with others, thus eventually decimating their own colony.* ❖

Aphids. These soft, oval insects range from pinhead to matchhead size and may be black, white, pink, or pale green. They cluster together on young shoots, buds, and leaves. Both adult and immature aphids (nymphs) damage a wide variety of plants by piercing the leaves and stems and sucking out plant juices. Some aphids also transmit viral diseases.

Prevent aphids from damaging vegetables by planting under row covers (page 653). Reflective aluminum mulches (available from nurseries and mail-order sources) deter flying adult aphids from laying eggs.

Because numerous creatures keep aphid populations in check, the best tactic is often to do nothing and leave the pests to natural controls: lady beetles, lacewing larvae, soldier beetles, syrphid flies, predatory midges, parasitic wasps, and even lizards and some small

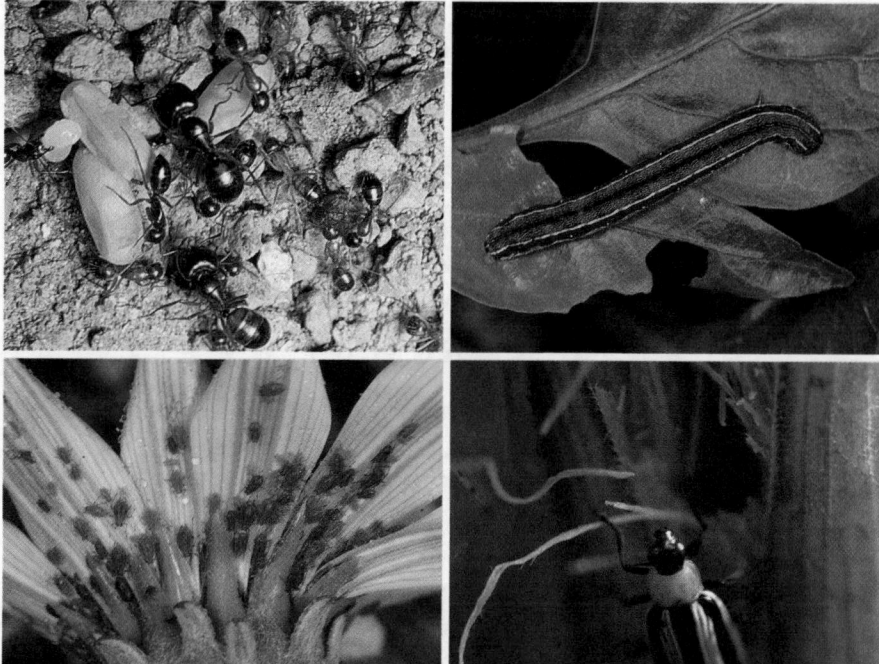

TOP: Ants
BOTTOM: Aphids

TOP: Armyworm
BOTTOM: Striped cucumber beetle

birds. Encourage beneficials by growing plants that attract them (see list on page 617).

You can blast aphids from plants with strong jets of water; they can also be killed by spraying with insecticidal soap or horticultural oil. Used as a dormant spray in winter, oil will also kill the overwintering eggs of aphids on deciduous trees and shrubs.

Pesticides containing *pyrethrins* can be used to control severe infestations. Other pesticides are also effective in controlling aphids, but call upon them only when all other methods have failed. These include malathion and (on nonedible plants) acephate (Orthene).

Armyworms. Armyworms are large caterpillars named for their unsettling habit of marching in troops, devouring all vegetation in their path. Most operate at night; the fall armyworm, however, eats at any time. Armyworms relish beans, beets, cabbage, corn, cucumber, lettuce, and tomato. Fall armyworms are also fond of turf grasses and can polish off a small lawn in a single night.

To control armyworms, apply *Bacillus thuringiensis* (*Bt;* sold as Dipel) against caterpillars less than an inch long. For larger caterpillars, spray the foliage of vegetables with azadirachtin (Neem) or carbaryl (Sevin). To kill fall armyworms in lawns use carbaryl or a granular insecticide containing cyfluthrin.

Cucumber beetles. Two kinds of cucumber beetles—both about ¼ inch long—cause trouble in Southern gardens. The spotted

cucumber beetle looks a bit like a lady beetle with about a dozen black spots on its back; the more common striped cucumber beetle is yellowish orange and marked with three black stripes. Adult beetles chew holes in leaves and flowers and damage stems of cucumbers, melons, squash, and other vegetables; the spotted cucumber beetle also feeds on roses and other garden plants. Both kinds can spread diseases. The larvae, which live underground, may damage roots.

Protect young plants by using row covers (page 653). Natural controls include birds and tachinid flies. You can also handpick the beetles, dropping them into a bucket of soapy water. Beneficial nematodes applied to the soil will reduce larval populations. For major infestations, spray with a natural insecticide containing pyrethrins. Chemical controls include malathion and carbaryl (Sevin).

Cutworms. A large variety of hairless larvae of night-flying moths make up the diverse group called cutworms. They feed at night and on overcast days; during the daylight hours, they hide underground, curled up in a C shape. Most cut off young plants at ground level—hence their name.

To help prevent cutworm damage, clear and till garden beds to destroy the eggs, larvae, and pupae before you sow seeds. To protect transplants, encircle each with a can (with both ends removed) or a paper cup or plastic carton with the bottom cut out; it should extend 1 to 2 inches both into the soil and aboveground.

P

TOP: Cutworm
BOTTOM: Flea beetle

TOP: Grasshopper
BOTTOM: Japanese beetles

TOP: Leaf miner trails
BOTTOM: Mealybugs

Encourage or introduce natural predators such as ground beetles and beneficial nematodes. Spread diatomaceous earth around young seedlings to deter cutworms.

Flea beetles. These tiny ($\frac{1}{10}$-inch-long), oval, shiny beetles may be blue black, brown, or bronze; they jump like fleas when disturbed. Adult flea beetles riddle leaves with small holes. They feed on many vegetable crops and are especially damaging to seedlings; they also spread diseases. Dichondra lawns are attacked by flea beetle larvae.

Adult flea beetles overwinter in weeds and garden debris; a fall cleanup will remove these havens. Protect seedlings with row covers. To control flea beetles, use azadirachtin (neem extract), Rose Defense, or carbaryl (Sevin).

Grasshoppers. During their periodic outbreaks, grasshoppers can cause severe damage, especially in areas with hot, dry summers. They generally lay their eggs in dry, undisturbed areas—along roadsides, in empty lots, on rangeland—but they will also do so in gardens. Eggs hatch from late winter to early summer, depending on temperature and climate. Newly hatched nymphs resemble adults, but they are wingless and smaller in size, and they feed voraciously. Once mature, they fly out to find new feeding areas.

Cultivating the soil in fall, winter, and early spring destroys grasshopper egg clusters. Keep the garden clear of weeds, which can harbor grasshoppers. Row covers (page 653) can be effective, though in severe outbreaks grasshoppers will chew through them.

Grasshoppers are most vulnerable to control in spring and early summer, while they are still young and wingless. Diatomaceous earth deters them. A biological control, *Nosema locustae* (sold as Grasshopper Attack) targets only grasshoppers. It works best when used over large areas, such as ranchland or a weedy field bordering several gardens. For chemical control, use a bran-and-carbaryl bait or acephate (Orthene; on nonedibles).

Japanese beetles. Japanese beetles ambush the garden in two ways. The grubs live underground and chew plant roots. During serious infestations, they can eat so many grass roots that large patches of lawn die. Adult beetles, distinguished by metallic green bodies and copper-colored wings, ravenously devour the foliage, stems, and flowers of hundreds of different plants, including roses, fruit trees, grapes, hollyhocks, and many others.

To control grubs in lawns, apply imidacloprid (Merit) or beneficial nematodes. To control adults, spray plants with azadirachtin (neem extract), Rose Defense, carbaryl (Sevin), or acephate (Orthene). If possible, avoid spraying flowers to prevent harm to bees.

Leaf miners are the larvae of certain moths, beetles, and flies. They tunnel within foliage, leaving twisting trails on the surface. Adult leaf miners are rarely seen. Various species attack vegetables, ornamental and fruit trees, annuals, and perennials. The damage is mostly cosmetic, although yield of some crops may be reduced.

Protect vegetables by planting under row covers (page 653). Remove infested leaves.

Parasitic wasps are natural enemies of leaf miners and lay their eggs on larvae or near leaf miner egg sites. Azadirachtin (neem extract) may discourage adults from laying eggs on leaf surfaces. Once the insect is inside the leaf, chemical control is difficult; the systemic insecticides acephate (Orthene) and dimethoate (Cygon) can be used on nonedibles.

Mealybugs have an oval body with overlapping soft plates and a white, cottony covering. They are closely related to scale insects—but unlike scales, most mealybugs can move around (slowly). They suck plant juices, causing stunting and, in some cases, killing the plant. Sooty mold (page 604) may grow on the honeydew they excrete. Mealybugs are houseplant pests and they also plague outdoor plants.

For any infestation inside and for minor infestations outside, daub the pests with a cotton swab dipped in rubbing alcohol. Outdoors, hose plants with water jets (or insecticidal soap sprays) every 2 to 4 weeks to remove adult and immature mealybugs and their eggs as well as sooty mold. Control ants (page 619), which nurture mealybugs for their honeydew.

Beneficial insects, including lacewings, lady beetles, and syrphid flies, help control these pests. You can release the mealybug destroyer (*Cryptolaemus montrouzieri*), a lady beetle relative whose adults and larvae both consume mealybugs; it needs warm temperatures, so it's most effective in greenhouses and during the warmer months outdoors. For severe infestations, spray with horticultural oil, azadirachtin (neem extract), pyrethrins, acephate (Orthene; on nonedibles), or malathion.

P

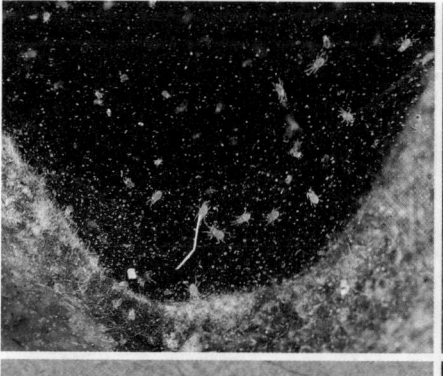

TOP: Mites
BOTTOM: Pillbug (left), Sowbug (right)

TOP: Black vine weevil (a root weevil)
BOTTOM: Scales

Mites. To the naked eye, these tiny spider relatives look like flecks of red, yellow, or green. Signs of mite infestation include yellow-stippled leaves (where the pests have sucked plant juices) and a tan or bronze cast to the foliage. Heavily infested plants are weakened and may eventually die.

To check plants for the presence of mites, hold a piece of white paper under the affected foliage and briskly tap the plant: the disturbed pests will drop down onto the paper, looking much like specks of pepper, then try to crawl away. Of the many kinds of mites, some are host specific (such as clover and citrus bud mites), but others—notably spider mites—attack a variety of outdoor and indoor plants.

Dust that settles on leaves encourages mites, so hose off plants frequently to keep the pest population down. Increased humidity also helps. Drought-stressed plants are more susceptible to mites.

Many natural predators help keep mites in check. You can purchase lacewing larvae and several species of predatory mites that prey on spider mites.

Wash mites from foliage with jets of water or spray with insecticidal soap. Spraying with horticultural oil in late winter smothers mites and eggs (it can be applied in summer as well). On some plants (check the product label for listings), you can control mites with sulfur dusted on leaf undersides. (Do not use sulfur in combination with oil sprays or when the temperature is above 85°F.) Azadirachtin (neem extract) and Rose Defense kill mites. Chemical miticides are also available in some areas.

Pillbugs and sowbugs. These familiar creatures are soil-dwelling crustaceans, not insects. When disturbed pillbugs roll up into black balls about the size of a large pea; sowbugs are usually gray and don't roll up. Both pests' principal food is decaying vegetation (which they help break down into humus), but they also eat very young seedlings, the skins of melons and cucumbers, and berries.

To limit these pests' populations, remove hiding places, such as boards lying on the ground and weedy areas with decaying foliage. Lift ripening fruit off the ground with pebbles or strawberry baskets. Plastic mulch is helpful, because the soil under it gets too hot for the pests' comfort. Chemical control is generally not required, but slug baits are effective.

Root weevils. A number of root weevils and their larvae can harm plants. In some species, such as the black vine weevil, both adults and larvae are harmful; the adults feed on the leaves, flowers, and bark of rhododendron, yew, grape, and other plants, while the larvae consume roots, especially those of young plants. Billbugs are root weevil larvae that damage lawns.

Beneficial nematodes or imidacloprid (Merit) help control root weevil larvae. Azadirachtin (neem extract) and some pyrethroids are effective against adults. Acephate (Orthene) can be used to control adults on nonedible plants.

Scales can cause garden problems throughout the South. Though related to mealybugs and aphids, they differ in having a waxy, shell-like covering that camouflages them and protects them from some natural enemies (and insecticides). Scales are classified as "armored" (hard) or soft; soft scales are more mobile and excrete a sticky honeydew.

An adult scale lives under its waxy shell, which sticks to the host plant. Running from the underside of the insect into the plant tissue is a tiny filamentous mouth part, through which the scale sucks plant juices. Scale eggs hatch beneath the shell; in spring or summer, the young scales ("crawlers") leave the protective cover to seek their own feeding sites.

Many naturally occurring parasites and predators, including several species of small, dark lady beetles, control or limit scale populations; a few of these are sold for release in the garden or greenhouse. Get rid of ants (page 619), which tend and protect soft scales.

You can control light infestations by picking scales off the plant or scraping them off with a plastic scouring pad. On deciduous plants, you can kill some adult scales in winter with horticultural oil. Scales are vulnerable to insecticides when they are in the crawler stage. To check for crawlers, wrap double-sided sticky tape around branches; if you find trapped crawlers, apply controls. Horticultural oil, insecticidal soap, and insecticides such as or malathion may be effective against crawlers.

Slugs and snails. Slugs and snails are similar creatures: a slug is simply a snail without a shell. These mollusks have toothlike jaws that rasp large, ragged holes in leaves and flowers. Seedlings and new transplants may be eaten entirely. For the most part, they hide by day and feed at night, though they may be active on gray or rainy days.

Try to eliminate these pests' favorite daytime hiding places—weedy areas, boards, stones, unused flower pots. You can protect newly planted seedlings by encircling them with a 3- to 4-inch-high "fence" made from copper strips; such strips can also be stapled to raised beds and wrapped around tree trunks and containers. Wood ashes and diatomaceous earth also make good barriers.

If done regularly, handpicking is effective. Go hunting after dark (with a flashlight) or early in the morning. You can also trap these creatures. A wide plank elevated about an inch off the ground offers a daytime hiding place from which you can collect and dispatch the pests. Shallow containers filled with beer or a simple solution of 1 teaspoon each active baking yeast and sugar in 1 cup water may lure slugs and snails to their deaths.

Commercial baits containing iron phosphate (Sluggo) are fairly effective,

P

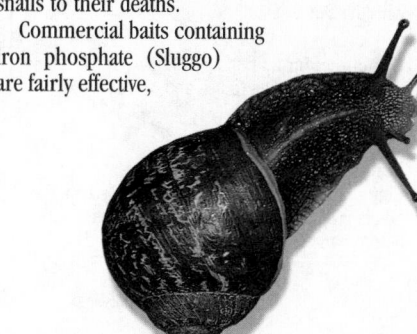

Spittlebugs

Damage from thrips

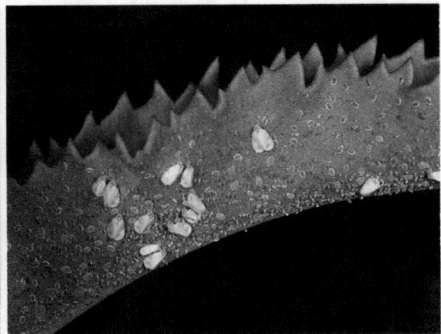

Whiteflies

causing the mollusks to stop feeding and die within a few days. These baits are considered nonhazardous to humans, pets, and wildlife. Commercial baits containing metaldehyde are sold as pellets, meal, or emulsion. Set them out in late evening and clear them away (along with dead pests) in the morning, as they can be toxic to birds and pets.

Spittlebugs. It's easy to spot a spittlebug—just look for a gob of foamy froth oozing over a leaf or stem. Hiding under the foam is a gray or brown insect that sucks plant juices. Spittlebugs attack a wide range of annuals, perennials, and herbs; rosemary and strawberries are favorite targets. Two-lined spittlebug can be a serious pest of centipede and Bermuda grass lawns.

Regular dethatching decreases the number of spittlebugs in lawns. Applying granular lawn insect controls such as cyfluthrin (Tempo) also helps. To control spittlebugs on ornamentals and fruits, blast the foam off the foliage with jets of water.

Thrips are almost microscopic. The light or dark brown adults are less than $1/20$ inch long, with narrow, feathery wings; the wingless, light green or pale yellow nymphs are even smaller. Both adults and nymphs feed by rasping soft flower and leaf tissue, then sucking plant juices. Besides damaging foliage and blossoms, they may spread plant diseases.

In heavy infestations, both flowers and leaves are discolored and fail to open normally, looking twisted or stuck together. If you look closely, you will see stippled, puckered areas on flowers and foliage. Leaves may take on a silvery or tan cast similar to that caused by mites—but if thrips are present, you'll see numerous small, black, varnishlike fecal pellets on leaf undersides.

Natural enemies include lacewing larvae, minute pirate bugs, predaceous thrips and mites, and spiders. Insecticidal soaps and horticultural oil help control thrips. For chemical control, acephate (Orthene; on nonedibles) and malathion can be effective.

Whiteflies are small (about $1/8$-inch-long) winged insects that fly up in clouds when you brush or touch an infested plant. The immature form is a nearly transparent wingless nymph; it excretes honeydew as it feeds, attracting ants and promoting the growth of sooty mold (page 604). Both adults and nymphs suck plant juices. Affected foliage may first show yellow stippling, then curl and turn brown.

Whiteflies thrive in the warm, still air of greenhouses. Outside, they flourish year-round in the Coastal and Tropical South, but cause trouble mainly during the summer elsewhere. In chilly-winter zones, they do not overwinter outside; garden infestations originate from indoor plants or purchased transplants. To protect your garden, inspect greenhouse and indoor plants and eliminate any whiteflies you find. And no matter what your climate, when you buy new garden plants—particularly bedding plants—carefully examine leaf undersides for adults and nymphs.

P

READING A PESTICIDE LABEL

Precautionary statements: This section may start with the headline "Precautionary statements" or with a repeat of the signal word found on the front of the label. Information is customized for product type and its associated toxicity-level category. It tells you of known hazards to humans, domestic animals, and the environment.

First aid instructions: Indicates the immediate action required if the product is ingested or inhaled or comes into contact with the skin or eyes.

Directions for use: Indicates how much of the product to use and how to mix and apply it.

Plants: Lists the plants that can safely be treated by the pesticide. If it can be used on edible crops, also tells you how many days before harvest the product can be applied.

Note to physicians: Specifies the action a physician should take in the event the product is ingested or inhaled or comes into contact with the skin or eyes.

Controls: Lists the pests that the product is formulated to control.

Storage & disposal: Specifies how to safely store and dispose of the product.

Product code identification: Provides the number assigned to the product by the manufacturer and the Environmental Protection Agency (EPA) to identify it. Use this number when contacting the manufacturer or EPA about the pesticide.

Product name: Provides the pesticide's trade name, often includes marketing information that positions the product against its competitors and attracts the eye of potential buyer. Sometimes the accepted common name of the active ingredient is included as part of the brand name, especially if that name has become familiar to the public.

Active ingredients: Lists the accepted common name of the pesticide's active ingredient. Learn to identify pesticides by their common names and look here first to find out exactly what is in the pesticide before purchasing it. The chemical name of the pesticide may also be included in this section.

Signal word: Look for words such as *Caution, Warning, Danger,* or *Poison.* These words signal the toxicity-level category associated with the pesticide. Additional information will be found on the back of the container, under the section "Precautionary statements."

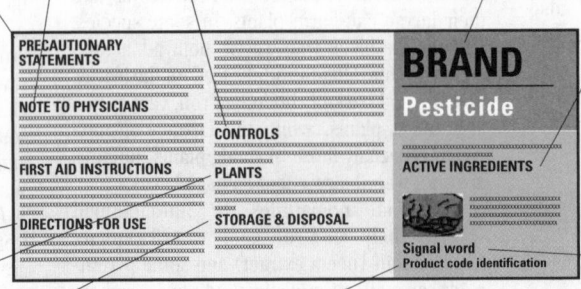

PRECAUTIONARY STATEMENTS

NOTE TO PHYSICIANS

FIRST AID INSTRUCTIONS

DIRECTIONS FOR USE

CONTROLS

PLANTS

STORAGE & DISPOSAL

BRAND

Pesticide

ACTIVE INGREDIENTS

Signal word
Product code identification

PRODUCTS FOR PEST CONTROL

Sold in liquid, powder, or granular form, pesticides contain one or more active ingredients—the chemical that controls the pest listed on the package label. Pesticides' availability is constantly shifting: new products continue to arrive on the market, while older ones may be withdrawn if research reveals them to be health or environmental hazards.

The lists below cover the most useful and widely available natural and synthetic pesticides for the Southern gardener. Others, generally targeting only one kind of pest, are mentioned in the individual pest descriptions beginning on page 619. *Synthetic pesticides* are manufactured compounds that do not normally occur in nature. *Natural pesticides*, in contrast, are products whose active ingredients originate in a plant, animal, or mineral, or whose action results from a biological process (as in the case of *Bacillus thuringiensis*; see page 617). Be aware that "natural" does not mean "harmless"; some natural products can still harm people or plants if they are used incorrectly.

When using any pesticide, *read the label directions carefully and follow them exactly.* The package will clearly state the plants and pests on which the control is registered for use, and it is illegal to apply it to a plant or pest not so listed.

The following products are listed by the accepted common name of the active ingredient. Some widely used trade names, if they differ from the common name, are noted in parentheses. Check with your state EPA or local Cooperative Extension Office to find out if a product is registered in your area. For more on reading and understanding pesticide labels, see the facing page. Always dispose of pesticides in a safe manner (see following page).

NATURAL PESTICIDES

▶ **Azadirachtin, neem oil (Bioneem; Fruit, Nut, and Vegetable Spray; others).** Neem extract is derived from a tropical tree (*Azadirachta indica*). Most neem products contain azadirachtin. It repels pests and, once ingested, interrupts their growth cycle, killing larvae as well as adults. Effective against aphids, beetles, caterpillars, grasshoppers, leaf miners, mealybugs, root weevils, whiteflies, others. Neem oil (primarily the oil of the neem seed) controls insects in egg, larval, and adult stages; it also controls mites and some plant diseases. Rose Defense contains a formula of neem oil and sulphur to control beetles, mites, and some plant diseases. Both azadirachtin and neem oil can kill nontarget insects such as honeybees and lady beetles. Toxic to fish.

▶ *Bacillus thuringiensis*, *Bt* **(Dipel, Thuricide).** A bacterium that controls many pest larvae. *Bt kurstaki* is lethal to certain caterpillars, including cabbageworm, geranium budworm, and tomato hornworm; other *Bt* strains are effective against the larvae of mosquitoes, fungus gnats, Colorado potato beetles, and elm leaf beetles.

▶ **Diatomaceous earth.** A powdery substance made from the skeletons of microscopic marine organisms. Effective against pests such as ants, aphids, cutworms, slugs, and snails. Works by damaging the insect's protective coat. Be sure to use the insecticidal product, not the one intended for swimming pool filters. Wear a breathing mask during application to avoid inhaling the dust. Must be reapplied after rain.

▶ **Horticultural oils.** These are highly refined petroleum oils that smother pests, pest eggs, and disease spores. In winter,

during the dormant season, they are applied to control insect eggs, some overwintering insects, and certain diseases. In summer, these oils are used at a lower rate, sprayed on the foliage of many plants to combat insects such as aphids, mealybugs, mites, scales, thrips, and whiteflies. Before using these products on plants in leaf, test-spray a small portion of the plant to be sure foliage will not be damaged.

▶ **Insecticidal soap.** Made not from detergent, but from potassium salts of fatty acids found in plants and animals. Effective against pests such as aphids, mealybugs, mites, scales, thrips, and whiteflies. Hard water may inactivate it, so mix the concentrate with soft water, distilled water, or rainwater. Toxic to earthworms.

▶ **Orange oil.** Orange oil (d-Limonene), found in orange peels, is a safe, biodegradable solvent and degreaser. Popular as a cleaner, it also kills ants (including fire ants), termites, roaches, and many other insects on contact, breaking down the insects' exoskeletons and causing them to die from desiccation. Orange oil shows considerable promise as a contact herbicide as well, though the EPA has not yet approved it for that use.

▶ **Pyrethrins.** Derived from compounds found in the dried flowers of *Tanacetum cinerariifolium.* Both a contact and a stomach poison; lethal to many pests. Breaks down quickly in sunlight; to give it more time to act, apply after sundown. Some products combine pyrethrins with other pesticides. Toxic to fish. The dried flowers, known as pyrethrum, are also sold as an insecticide.

▶ **Sulfur.** Dusted or sprayed over plants to control mites and psyllids as well as some plant diseases. Do not use sulfur in conjunction with horticultural oil spray or when air temperature is above 85°F. Can irritate the eyes.

SYNTHETIC PESTICIDES

▶ **Acephate (Orthene).** A systemic poison (one absorbed by the plant and incorporated into its tissues), this broad-spectrum product is used against aphids, beetles, caterpillars, grasshoppers, leaf miners, mealybugs, thrips, root weevils, whiteflies, other pests. Do not use on edible crops. Toxic to honeybees and birds.

▶ **Carbaryl (Sevin).** Broad-spectrum contact insecticide. Controls most chewing insects but is not effective against many sucking types—in fact, it often increases problems with the latter by destroying natural predators. Registered for use on edible crops. Highly toxic to honeybees, fish, and earthworms.

▶ **Imidacloprid (Merit, GrubEx).** Controls a variety of pests of lawns and ornamentals. Toxic to fish.

▶ **Malathion.** Broad-spectrum contact insecticide that controls aphids, beetles, caterpillars, mealybugs, scales, thrips, whiteflies, other pests. Registered for use on edible crops. Toxic to honeybees, birds, and fish. Future registration limitations are possible.

▶ **Pyrethroids.** Synthetic versions of plant-based pyrethrins (see above), pyrethroids are increasingly being used in pesticides and are effective against many garden and household pests. Formulations may include the pyrethroids permethrin, cyfluthrin, and others. Less hazardous to humans, birds, and mammals than many other pesticides; toxic to honeybees and fish.

Natural enemies, which can be attracted to or introduced into the garden, include lacewing larvae and *Delphastus pusillus,* a species of lady beetle known as a whitefly predator. Two species of tiny parasitic wasps, *Encarsia formosa* and *Eretmocerus californicus,* can be released to help control whiteflies in greenhouses.

Handpicking heavily infested leaves helps reduce whitefly populations. Yellow sticky traps can capture significant numbers of the pests. Hose off infested plants every few days, hitting both sides of all leaves. Insecticidal soap can be more effective than water and is less hazardous to natural enemies than other insecticides. Other controls include azadirachtin (neem extract), horticultural oil, and pyrethrins.

BIRDS AND MAMMALS. Most gardeners welcome some—though not all—wildlife into their gardens. (See page 668 for ways to draw wildlife to your yard.) Certain birds and animals, however, can cause significant damage to plants. Some of the worst troublemakers are discussed below, along with suggestions for controlling them.

Birds. For the most part, gardeners see birds as friends who can play a significant role in controlling pests such as caterpillars (including cutworms and sod webworms), grasshoppers, and scales. Some kinds of birds, however, can be a nuisance at certain times, eating newly planted seeds (including lawn seed), tender seedlings, transplants, fruits, nuts, or berries.

Providing alternative foods can sometimes reduce damage to the fruits and berries you want to harvest; try planting elderberries *(Sambucus),* fruiting mulberries *(Morus),* or hawthorns *(Crataegus).* Reflectors, fluttering objects, and scarecrows may reduce damage briefly, but birds soon become accustomed to them. The best solution to protect fruiting trees and other plants is to use netting or screen. Broad-mesh (¾-inch) nylon or plastic netting is popular for fruit trees, since it readily admits air, water, and sunlight. Enclose trees with netting 2 to 3 weeks before fruit ripens, tying it around the trunk beneath the lowest branches or securing it to the ground so birds can't find an opening.

Row covers (page 653) are the easiest way to protect sprouting seedlings and maturing vegetables, because they require no support. You can also make wooden or plastic pipe frames with screen, aviary wire, or netting attached to cover the top and all sides. Such frames are mobile and reusable, and they can be designed to make harvesting easy.

Deer. As development reduces their territory, deer move into gardens to forage. They develop feeding patterns, visiting tasty gardens regularly (most often in the evening). Fond of many flowering plants, especially roses, they'll also eat the foliage or fruit of nearly anything you grow for the table. For a list of plants that deer usually ignore, see "Deer-Resistant Plants" in A Guide to Plant Selection, on page 138.

DISPOSING OF PESTICIDES

You may need to dispose of pesticides (insecticides, fungicides, and herbicides) if you have mixed up more solution than you need or if you have a product that is no longer considered safe due to changes in its registration status. Until you can dispose of such pesticides properly, keep them—and all others—secured in a locked cabinet.

Never pour pesticide down any type of drain, including a storm drain; it could pollute the water supply. Instead, contact your city or county public works department, garbage company, or Cooperative Extension Office to find out where you can discard such products. Many communities sponsor hazardous waste disposal sites, which typically accept used motor oil and leftover paint as well as undiluted pesticides in their original containers and diluted solutions that you have mixed. Since federal law requires that products containing hazardous ingredients be labeled, carefully pour leftover solutions into a glass or plastic container with a tight-fitting lid; write the product name (name of active ingredient and trade name) and its dilution ratio on the container. Empty any powdered or granular pesticide (such as a lawn-care product applied with a spreader) into a heavy-duty garbage bag; then seal and label the bag.

Fencing is the most certain protection. On level ground, an 8-foot woven wire fence will usually keep deer out; on slopes, you may need to erect a 10- to 12-foot barrier to guard against the animals jumping from higher ground. A horizontal extension on a fence makes it harder for deer to clear. Because deer cannot high-jump and broad-jump at the same time, double fencing has worked for many gardeners: construct a pair of parallel 4- to 5-foot fences spaced 4 to 5 feet apart. Low-growing plants can be set out in the area between the fences.

If fencing your entire garden is impractical, put chicken-wire cages around young plants and cylinders of wire fencing around larger

TOP: Starling
BOTTOM: Netting over strawberries

specimens. Cover raised beds with mesh or row covers (page 653).

Commercial deer repellents can work if sprayed often enough to keep new growth covered with repellent and to replace what rain and irrigation wash away. Changing the type of repellent may be helpful, since deer get used to smells. Do not apply repellents to edible plants unless the label indicates you can do so.

KEEPING BAMBI AT BAY. *Hungry deer will eat almost anything. But one way to decrease the amount of destruction they cause is to use plants they normally don't like. These include barberry, boxwood, cedar, daffodil, daphne, daylily, English ivy, flowering quince, most grasses, hellebore, juniper, Lenten rose, mahonia, oak, oleander, persimmon, petunia, pink, star jasmine, tulip, yarrow, yaupon, yucca, and zinnia. For more information, see pages 138–141.* ❖

Moles. Notorious pests in good soils throughout the South, moles are primarily insectivorous; they subsist largely on earthworms, soil insects, and grubs, only occasionally (if at all) nibbling greens and roots. Irrigation and rain keep them near the soil surface, where they do the most damage as they tunnel—heaving plants from the ground, severing tender roots, and disfiguring lawns. A mole's main runways, which are used repeatedly, are usually 6 to 10 inches underground and are frequently punctuated with volcano-shaped mounds of excavated soil, plugged in the center.

Trapping is the most efficient way to control moles. The spear- or harpoon-type trap is the easiest to set, since you simply position it above the soil. A scissor-jaw trap must be carefully positioned in a main runway (probe with a sharp stick to find it), and if it's improperly set, a wily mole will spring it, heave it out, or walk around it.

Due to their feeding habits, moles are very difficult to control with poison baits. Like pocket gophers, they are also hard to kill with toxic gas (fumigants). To be successful with the latter, place gas "mole bombs" directly in the main runways and block all holes. Be persistent with follow-up treatments.

MOLES OR VOLES? *Moles are often blamed when plants are chewed off at the ground, but in fact voles are the likely culprits. These mouselike rodents burrow under leaf litter or just below the soil surface, eating roots and stems as they go. And they're very difficult to discourage. One useful strategy is to remove mulch and leaf litter from around their favorite plants, such as hostas. Placing a few shovelfuls of sharp gravel in the hole around the roots when you plant can also be helpful.* ❖

Pocket gophers, named for the external, fur-lined cheek pouches they use to carry food to storage areas, are serious pests in parts of the South. They use their strong, long-clawed forefeet to dig out a network of tunnels, usually 6 to 18 inches below the surface. They eat roots, bulbs, and sometimes entire plants by pulling them down into their burrows.

The first sign of gophers is often a fan-shaped mound of fresh, finely pulverized earth in a lawn or flower bed; a plug of earth is used to close the hole, which is off to one side. (Mole mounds, in contrast, are conical and plugged in the center.)

Trapping is the most efficient method of control. Avoid the temptation to place a single trap down a hole; your chances of catching a gopher are much greater when you dig down to the main horizontal runway connecting with the surface hole and place two traps in it, one on either side of your excavation. Use chain or wire to attach each trap to a stake on the surface (this prevents a trapped gopher from dragging the trap farther into a burrow). A two-pronged pincer trap (such as the Macabee) is the most effective. Box-type traps also work and are easier to set, but they require a larger hole for insertion.

When the traps are in place, plug the hole with a ball of carrot tops, fresh grass, or other tender greens; their scent attracts gophers. Next, place a board or soil over the greens to block all light. Check the traps frequently; clear the tunnels if the gopher has pushed soil into the traps. Be persistent: a clever gopher may avoid your first traps.

Poison baits are effective for the control of trap-wise gophers. Probe for the deep burrows with a rod or sharp stick, insert the bait, and close the hole. Be aware that these baits are hazardous to other animals; take care not to spill any on the ground. Also keep in mind that dogs and cats can be poisoned by eating poisoned gophers, though incidences are rare.

If your garden is subject to ongoing invasion by gophers from neighboring fields—or if all your trapping efforts fail—you can protect the roots of young plants by lining the sides and bottom of planting holes with hardware cloth or chicken wire. Raised beds lined on the bottom

TOP TO BOTTOM: Mole, Pocket gopher, Ground squirrel, Tree squirrel, Vole

with hardware cloth offer a secure way to grow vegetables in gopher country.

Squirrels. Both ground and tree squirrels can cause trouble in gardens.

Ground squirrels (chipmunks). Most troublesome in areas that border fields or wild lands, ground squirrels live in underground burrows, where they store food, raise their young, and hide from predators such as foxes, cats, and hawks. They are most active in midmorning or late afternoon (except in very hot weather); most of them hibernate in winter. When they're up and about, they feed on fruits, nuts, and vegetables as well as eating roots and bark.

Keep ground squirrels out of trees by placing metal rodent guards around the trunks. Poison baits and traps can be effective; check with your local Cooperative Extension Office for methods available in your area, or hire a pest-control professional.

Tree squirrels. Familiar pests in much of the South, tree squirrels include several native and introduced species. They behave differently from ground squirrels when alarmed, heading for the safety of a tree rather than retreating to a burrow. And unlike ground squirrels, they do not hibernate in winter. Tree squirrels eat fruits, nuts, vegetables, and some kinds of bulbs; they raid bird feeders and birds' nests; and they also invade attics in winter.

To control tree squirrels, clean up fallen fruits and nuts to eliminate some of their food sources. Use squirrel-proof bird feeders. To protect vulnerable trees, use metal rodent guards; prune low branches (if practical) and try to place the guards a minimum of 6 feet from the ground because the squirrels can leap at least that high. (Bear in mind, however, that if there are structures or other trees nearby, the agile pests will still be able to jump into trees you wish to protect.) Cover bulb beds with fine-mesh chicken wire or line planting holes with hardware cloth or fine-mesh chicken wire. Before resorting to traps or poison baits, check with your local Cooperative Extension Office, since some squirrel species are protected by law.

Voles. Also known as meadow mice, voles are small rodents (just 5 to 8 inches long when mature) with short ears and tails. They feed on a wide variety of vegetables, grasses, bulbs, and tubers and gnaw on the bark of trees, sometimes girdling them; damage to bark may occur just above or below ground. Voles travel in aboveground runways, usually hidden beneath tall grasses or ground covers, that connect the openings to their short, shallow burrows.

You can control voles by managing the vegetation they use for cover: mow weeds, remove heavy mulches and leaf litter, and cut back ground covers. When planting, add a few shovelfuls of sharp gravel around plant roots. Also mow or use herbicides to clear the edges of fields near gardens. Protect the lower trunks of shrubs and young trees by encircling them with hardware cloth, being sure to bury the bottom edges so voles can't dig beneath them.

Trapping can be an effective control. Use simple wooden mousetraps, baited with peanut butter or apple slices. Place these along the runways and check them daily. Keep small children and pets away from areas where you have set traps. Baits are sometimes used; check with your Cooperative Extension Office for types available in your area.

P

Plant Anatomy and Growth

Understanding a plant's basic structure and the role each of its parts plays in growth and reproduction can help you garden more successfully. The box below describes the functions of flowers, leaves, roots, and stems.

Though we often think of these elements as separate, their functions are interrelated—and all must work as they should if the plant is to thrive.

Integrally involved in the function of every plant part is the surrounding environment—air, water, light, and soil. A good knowledge of the relationship between a plant's growth and its environment will help you provide the best possible conditions for each plant and help you to choose the best plants for your garden's conditions.

For illustration and more about flowers, see the Glossary (page 689). Seed germination is illustrated on page 632.

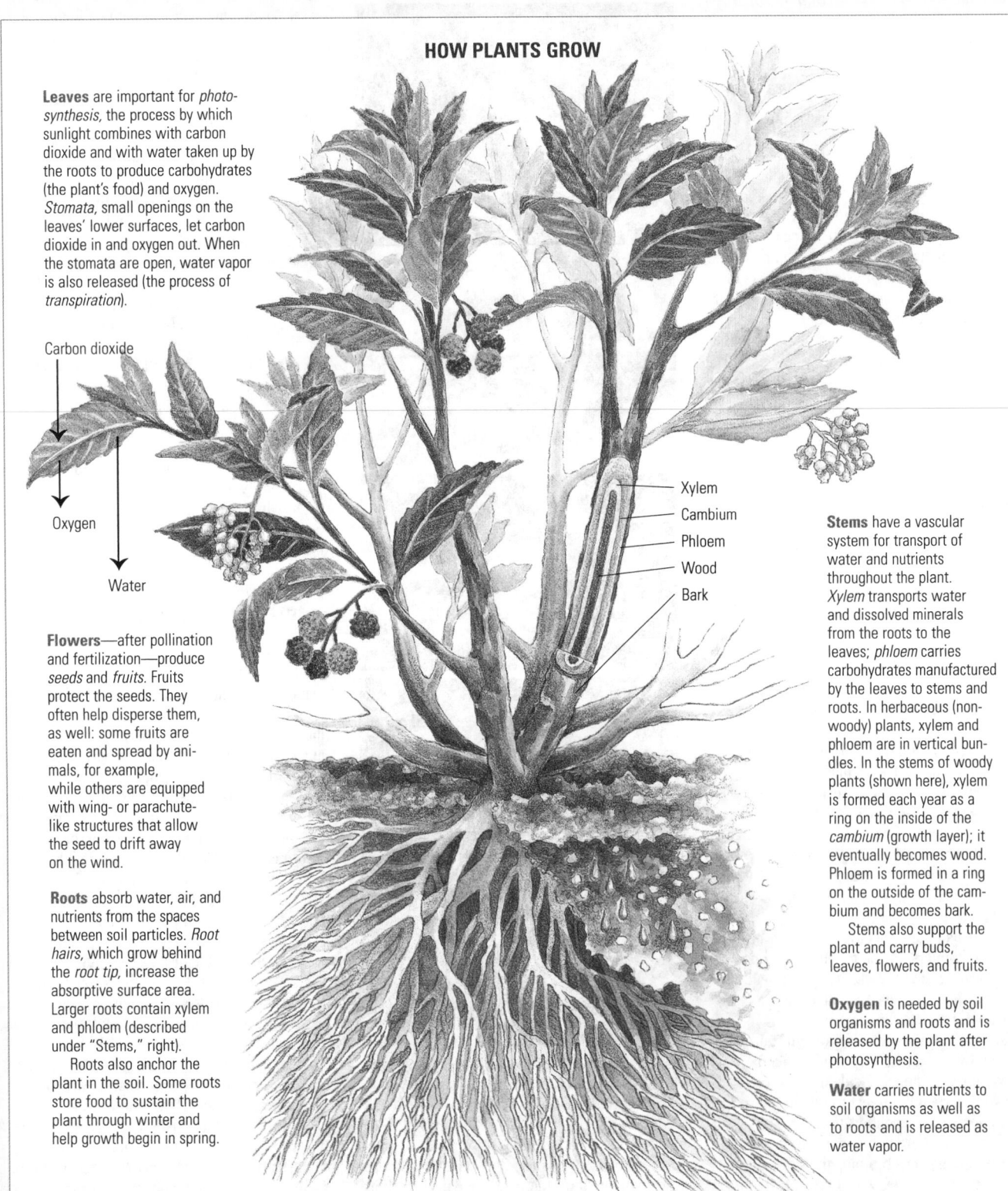

HOW PLANTS GROW

Leaves are important for *photosynthesis*, the process by which sunlight combines with carbon dioxide and with water taken up by the roots to produce carbohydrates (the plant's food) and oxygen. *Stomata*, small openings on the leaves' lower surfaces, let carbon dioxide in and oxygen out. When the stomata are open, water vapor is also released (the process of *transpiration*).

Carbon dioxide

Oxygen

Water

Flowers—after pollination and fertilization—produce *seeds* and *fruits*. Fruits protect the seeds. They often help disperse them, as well: some fruits are eaten and spread by animals, for example, while others are equipped with wing- or parachute-like structures that allow the seed to drift away on the wind.

Roots absorb water, air, and nutrients from the spaces between soil particles. *Root hairs*, which grow behind the *root tip*, increase the absorptive surface area. Larger roots contain xylem and phloem (described under "Stems," right).

Roots also anchor the plant in the soil. Some roots store food to sustain the plant through winter and help growth begin in spring.

Xylem
Cambium
Phloem
Wood
Bark

Stems have a vascular system for transport of water and nutrients throughout the plant. *Xylem* transports water and dissolved minerals from the roots to the leaves; *phloem* carries carbohydrates manufactured by the leaves to stems and roots. In herbaceous (nonwoody) plants, xylem and phloem are in vertical bundles. In the stems of woody plants (shown here), xylem is formed each year as a ring on the inside of the *cambium* (growth layer); it eventually becomes wood. Phloem is formed in a ring on the outside of the cambium and becomes bark.

Stems also support the plant and carry buds, leaves, flowers, and fruits.

Oxygen is needed by soil organisms and roots and is released by the plant after photosynthesis.

Water carries nutrients to soil organisms as well as to roots and is released as water vapor.

P

Plant Conservation

Plants, both wild and cultivated, supply food for humans and other creatures; habitats for insects and wildlife; and medicines, timber, and other essential products. However, it is estimated that more than 34,000 species—some 12.5 percent of all known higher plants (ferns, conifers, and flowering plants)—are either extinct in the wild or threatened with extinction. Concerned gardeners can take some steps to help preserve such plants.

Avoid buying plants dug from their native habitat. Though most plants available to gardeners are commercially propagated, some rare species are still routinely dug in the wild, especially those that are slow growing or difficult to propagate. Bulbs falling into this group are listed on page 597. Other plants threatened by wild collection include some cacti and succulents, trilliums, orchids, Jack-in-the-pulpit (*Arisaema* species), several kinds of carnivorous plants, and various palms and ferns.

Don't include invasive plants in your garden if you live near wild lands. Such plants may escape and take over the habitat of natives, crowding them out. For more on invasive plants, see page 663.

Support the conservation of plants in their natural habitats, botanical gardens, and seed banks. Various preserves and other protected areas in the U.S. and abroad practice *in situ* (on-site) conservation: they maintain plants along with the insects, birds, animals, and soil and disease organisms normally associated with them in the wild, preserving the natural diversity of the ecosystem. Such sanctuaries include nature preserves, wildlife refuges, and state and national parks.

Native pitcher plants and wildflowers in an Alabama preserve.

Botanical gardens feature *ex situ* (off-site) conservation. They are important repositories of samples of rare and endangered plants and also maintain some that have already become extinct in the wild.

Seeds, especially those of crop plants and their wild relatives, are conserved in special seed banks. They are first dried, then stored at low temperatures, remaining viable for many years.

TRAVELERS' ALERT: BRINGING PLANTS HOME

Think twice before packing those plants. The U.S. government regulates the importation of plants, seeds, fruits, and vegetables from foreign countries to America, as well as from Hawaii, Puerto Rico, and the U.S. Virgin Islands to the mainland. The regulations are intended to prevent the introduction of insects, diseases, and potentially invasive plants. Thus, plants must be free of leaf mold and of sand or other soil, and seeds must be cleaned. For more information on bringing home plants or seeds, contact the Animal and Plant Health Inspection Service of the U.S. Department of Agriculture: USDA APHIS, Plant Protection and Quarantine, 4700 River Road, Unit 136, Riverdale, MD 20737-1236, Attn: Permit Unit. You can also call (301) 734-8645 or visit the service's Web site (*www. aphis.usda.gov*).

In addition, the Convention on International Trade in Endangered Species (CITES) of Wild Fauna and Flora regulates international trade in species deemed threatened or likely to be threatened by commercial exploitation. If you want to bring back any plant listed under CITES, you will need permits from the country of origin as well as from the U.S. Department of Interior's Fish and Wildlife Service (FWS), which regulates CITES in the United States. For more information, including a list of threatened and endangered species, contact the U.S. Fish and Wildlife Service, Office of Management Authority, 4401 North Fairfax Drive, Arlington, VA 22203. Or call (703) 358-2095 or visit the Web site at *www.fws.gov.*

Plant Disorders

Some plant problems are caused by environmental or cultural factors rather than by disease organisms or pests. Drying winds and extremes of temperature may hinder plant growth, for example. Other plant problems may be related to soil conditions such as hardpan (see page 645), under- or overfertilizing (see page 607 for information on nitrogen deficiency), and too much or too little water (see page 659). Besides damaging plants directly, such cultural and environmental problems can stress plants, making them more vulnerable to insects and diseases.

If you aren't certain why a plant is languishing, get help before you act. Simply assuming that a pest or disease is the culprit can result in the needless—and useless—application of pesticides. Regular garden monitoring and, when necessary, consultation with nursery personnel or your Cooperative Extension Office can assist you in identifying the precise causes of problems in your garden.

CHLOROSIS. This disorder affects many types of trees and shrubs as well as some vegetables and annuals. Leaves lose their green color from the edges inward; leaf veins usually remain green. The newest leaves are the most noticeably affected; they may be unusually small and either white or bright yellow in color. Chlorosis is usually caused by a deficiency of iron (though it occasionally results from lack of another mineral, such as zinc or manganese). When plants are chlorotic, the soil itself is not necessarily iron poor; it may simply be alkaline, a condition under which iron becomes unavailable to roots. Soggy, poorly aerated soils also delay or hinder the release of iron to plant roots.

Adjusting soil pH by adding organic matter or, if necessary, sulfur, is the best long-term solution to chlorosis. Improving drainage is

Chlorosis

P

also helpful. Chelated iron, applied according to the directions on the label, can temporarily correct the problem.

SUNBURN, SUNSCALD. Overexposure to sunlight can harm leaves, fruits, or bark. Symptoms include bleached-out, yellowish, or brown foliage; pale, sunken, often wrinkled areas on fruits; and bark that turns dark brown, splits, and dies. Damaged tissue may be invaded by disease-causing organisms.

Plants most likely to experience sunburn or sunscald are those moved into the sun from shaded locations (for example, from a nursery to a home garden) and those that have been heavily pruned, reducing the leafy cover that shades and protects bark and fruits.

To prevent sunburn and sunscald, transplant in cool weather, if possible. If conditions are warm, shade new transplants with shade cloth, burlap stapled to wooden frames, or broad, flat pieces of wood placed on end in the ground on the sunny side of the plants. Use burlap or tree-wrapping paper (available at nurseries) to wrap trunks of newly planted or heavily pruned trees. Or protect exposed tree trunks by painting them with water-based interior white latex paint, diluted by half with water. Finally, note that plants adapted to shaded conditions will continue to suffer from sunburn if planted in a bright location and the only solution is to replant them elsewhere. Check the Plant Encyclopedia listings for plants suited to the conditions—whether sun or shade—in your garden.

These raised beds contain a mix of flowering plants, vegetables, and herbs.

Planting Beds, Raised Beds

Before sowing seeds or setting out annuals, perennials, or vegetables, you will want to prepare a planting bed. In most gardens, the simple sort of bed described here will suffice. In some cases, however—notably when soil or drainage is poor—constructing raised beds may be a better choice.

MAKING A PLANTING BED. Good soil preparation is the first step toward success with seeds sown directly in the garden as well as with small plants set out from pots or flats. Begin by eliminating weeds (see page 663). Then loosen the soil with a spading fork or tiller; it should be slightly damp when you work it, neither wet nor bone-dry. Dig down 10 to 12 inches if you can, breaking up clods and removing stones as you go. Spread a 3- to 4-inch-thick layer of organic matter (such as compost, sphagnum peat moss, or chopped leaves) over the area. As noted in "Fertilizers" (page 606), both phosphorus and potassium benefit plants most when placed near the roots; work a fertilizer high in these nutrients (such as a 5-10-10 or similar formula) into the soil before planting, rather than applying it to the surface afterward. A soil test will tell you how much fertilizer to use. Also add any amendments needed to alter soil pH at this time.

Incorporate all the amendments evenly with spading fork or tiller, then level out the planting bed with a rake.

MAKING RAISED BEDS. Besides solving problems involving poor soil and poor drainage, raised beds have other advantages. Their soil warms earlier in spring, and because it is typically not walked upon, it remains loose and easier for roots to penetrate. You can also fill beds with particular types of soil to suit specific plants—acid soil for blueberries, for example. The simplest raised beds are made by piling amended soil, either purchased or dug from pathways or other parts of your garden, on the area you want to plant. It's a good idea to loosen the area's existing soil as much as possible first, to ease penetration by water and roots.

Many gardeners enclose their raised beds with a low border. Two-inch-thick, rot-resistant wood is most common, but rocks, cinder blocks, or any other sturdy barrier can also be used. Plan to make enclosed beds at least 8 inches high and any length that fits the space and available building materials, but it's usually best to limit its width to about 4 feet, so that you can reach the center from either side. Ensure that the bed is well-drained. If pocket gophers are a problem, line the bottom of the bed with hardware cloth, fastening it to the sides. Fill the raised beds with good topsoil amended with plenty of organic matter, such as compost.

Planting Techniques

Proper planting techniques depend on the plant and how it is sold. Many plants—annuals, vegetables, and some perennials and ground covers—are sold as seedlings in small containers or flats during the growing season. Larger plants, such as shrubs, trees, and certain vines and more mature perennials, may be offered in several ways: in containers of various sizes during the growing season; as bare-root plants in the dormant season; or with the root ball enclosed in burlap, typically from late fall to early spring. The following pages discuss planting all of the above types. For information on planting seeds and bulbs, see pages 632 and 597.

PLANTING ANNUALS AND PERENNIALS. Nurseries offer seedlings of both annuals and perennials, saving you from raising the plants from seed yourself. Many of these, as well as vegetables and some ground covers, are sold in plastic cell-packs, individual plastic pots, peat pots, and flats. (Some perennials, perennial vegetables, and strawberries may also be sold bare-root during their dormant season; for planting instructions, see page 631.) Before planting annuals and perennials, make a planting bed as described at left.

At the nursery, choose stocky young plants with good leaf color and a root ball that holds together but is not tangled or matted. Root-

P

bound plants won't grow as well as younger ones, even if you cut or loosen coiled roots.

PLANTING BARE-ROOT SHRUBS AND TREES. Bare-root plants are sold in late winter and early spring by retail nurseries and mail-order companies. Many deciduous plants are available this way, including fruit and shade trees, flowering shrubs, roses, grapes, and cane fruits.

Though venturing out in the cold and wet of winter to set out bare-root plants takes a certain amount of determination, the effort is worthwhile. Such plants typically cost only 40 to 70 percent as much as the same types purchased in containers later in the year; beyond that, they usually establish more quickly and grow better initially than container plants. This faster growth is in part due to the fact that when you set out a bare-root plant, you refill the planting hole with soil dug from that hole—and the plant's roots thus grow in just one kind of soil. When you plant a containerized or balled-and-burlapped plant, on the other hand, you put two soils, usually with different textures, in contact with each other. The combination of two different soils can make it difficult for water to penetrate uniformly into the rooting area.

When buying from a local nursery, select bare-root plants with strong stems and fresh-looking, well-formed roots. Avoid any with slimy roots or dry, withered ones; also reject any that have already leafed out.

It's always best to plant bare-root plants as soon as possible after purchase. If bad weather

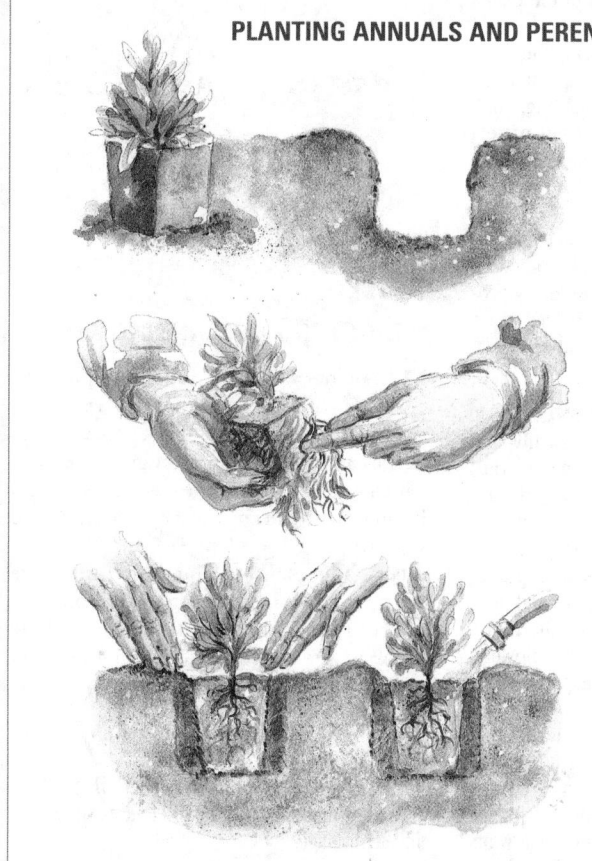

PLANTING ANNUALS AND PERENNIALS

1 Dig a hole for each plant, making it the same depth as the container and an inch or two wider.

2 With your fingers, lightly separate matted roots. If there is a mat of coiled roots at the bottom of the pot, cut or pull it off so that new roots will form and grow into the soil.

3 Place each plant in its hole so that the top of the root ball is even with the soil surface. Firm soil around the roots; then water each plant with a gentle flow that won't disturb soil or roots.

REMOVING PLANTS FROM CONTAINERS

Small pots. To remove plants from small pots, turn pot upside down, holding plant in place with your fingers. The plant should slip out easily.

Flats. Separate the plants in a flat by cutting straight down around each one with a putty knife or spatula. Or gently separate the plants from each other with your fingers.

Cell-packs. Plants in plastic cell-packs are easy to remove from the container, because each plant is in an individual cube of soil. Turn the cell-pack over and push down on the bottom of each cell with your thumbs.

Peat pots. These plants are not removed from their pots, but go into the ground pot and all; the roots then grow through the pot into the soil, while the pot eventually decomposes. Make sure the pots are moist before planting by letting them stand in a shallow container of water for several minutes. If they're dry, they'll absorb moisture too slowly from the soil and the roots may have trouble breaking through them, resulting in a stunted plant. It's also important to cover the tops of the pots with soil, since exposed peat acts as a wick, drawing moisture from the soil. If covering the peat would bury the plant too deeply, break off the pot's rim to slightly below the soil level inside it.

Small pot

Flat

Cell-pack

Peat pots

P

629

prevents immediate planting, heel in the plants by laying them temporarily in a trench dug in a shady spot in the garden and covering the roots with moist soil or potting mix; it's important not to let the roots dry out. Before planting, soak the roots for a minimum of 4 hours (or preferably overnight) in a bucket of water. Just before planting, be sure to cut any broken or damaged roots back to healthy tissue.

Dig a planting hole as shown at right. In heavy clay or hardpan, make the hole somewhat wider; this lets the plant establish faster by providing a larger area of loosened soil that's easier for roots to penetrate. Set in the plant as shown on the facing page.

SETTING OUT PLANTS FROM CONTAINERS. Most of the broad-leafed evergreen shrubs and trees that are the South's landscaping favorites are only offered in containers. But container plants are popular for many other reasons. You can buy them throughout the growing season, choosing from a variety of sizes and prices; they're relatively easy to transport; and they needn't be planted immediately. Furthermore, because you can buy these plants with flowers, fruit, or autumn leaf color on display, you're able to see exactly what you are getting.

When selecting container-grown plants, look for healthy foliage and strong shoots. Check the leaves and stems to be sure no insects are present. Do your best to avoid root-bound plants. Two common signs of this condition are roots protruding above the container's soil level and husky roots growing through the drainage holes; additional indicators are plants that are large for the size of the container, leggy plants, and dead twigs or branches. If you do end up with a root-bound plant, loosen the roots as shown below.

To remove plants from 1-gallon or larger plastic containers, tap sharply on the bottom and sides to loosen the root ball. With fiber or pulp

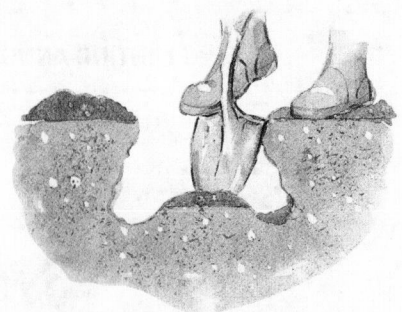

DIGGING THE PLANTING HOLE

To plant trees and shrubs, dig a planting hole with sides that taper outward into the soil. Make the hole at least twice as wide as the roots of the plant. Roughen the sides with a spading fork; if the sides are smooth, it can be difficult for roots to penetrate the soil. To keep the plant from settling too much after planting and watering, make the hole a bit shallower than the root ball or root system, then dig deeper around the edges of the hole's bottom. This leaves a firm plateau of undug soil to support the plant at the proper depth.

pots, tear the pot away from the root ball, taking care not to damage the roots. Plant as shown on the facing page.

PLANTING BALLED-AND-BURLAPPED SHRUBS AND TREES. Some kinds of woody plants have root systems that won't survive bare-root transplanting; others are evergreen and cannot be sold bare-root. Instead, such plants are dug from the field with a ball of soil around their roots, and the soil ball is then wrapped in burlap or a synthetic material and tied with

twine or wire. These are called balled-and-burlapped (B-and-B) plants. Some deciduous trees and shrubs (large specimens, in particular), evergreen shrubs such as holly *(Ilex)* and boxwood *(Buxus),* and various conifers are sold this way from late fall to early spring.

When buying B-and-B plants, look for healthy foliage and an even branching structure. The covering should be intact (so that the roots are not exposed), and the root ball should feel firm and moist.

B-and-B plants can be damaged if handled roughly. Always support the bottom of the root ball when moving the plant; don't pick the plant up by the trunk or drop it, which might shatter the root ball. Because a B-and-B plant is usually quite heavy, it's a good idea to have the nursery deliver it or have a friend help you move it in a sling of stout canvas. Once home, you can move the plant by sliding it onto a piece of plywood and pulling it to the planting spot. For planting directions, see the facing page.

Note: Most shrubs and trees grow best if planted in the soil native to your garden rather than in amended soil, but B-and-B plants are sometimes an exception. They are generally grown in clay or heavy soil that holds together well when the plants are dug up and wrapped. If you have medium- to heavy-textured garden soil (such as fairly heavy loam or clay), there's no need to amend the soil you return to the planting hole. If the B-and-B soil is denser than your garden's soil, however, the plant may have a hard time getting established. The heavy soil around its roots will absorb water more slowly than the surrounding garden soil—so the B-and-B's soil can be dry even if the garden soil is kept moist. To avoid this problem, mix an organic amendment such as compost into the soil removed from the planting hole, using about one shovelful of amendment for every three shovelfuls of soil. Use this blend to fill in around the roots.

DEALING WITH ROOT-BOUND PLANTS

1 It is important to loosen coiled roots before planting so they will grow into the soil. With your hands, tease the roots apart. Then cut off any extra-long roots with clippers.

2 Another method is to spray the soil away from the root ball with a strong jet of water and then loosen and uncoil the roots.

3 A third—and more drastic—method is to make several vertical slits in the root ball with a knife to stimulate the growth of new roots.

PLANTING BARE-ROOT PLANTS

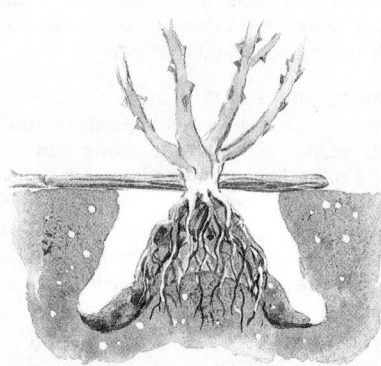

1 Make a firm cone of soil in the planting hole. Spread the roots over the cone, positioning the plant at the same depth as (or slightly higher than) it was in the growing field. Use a shovel handle or yardstick to check the depth.

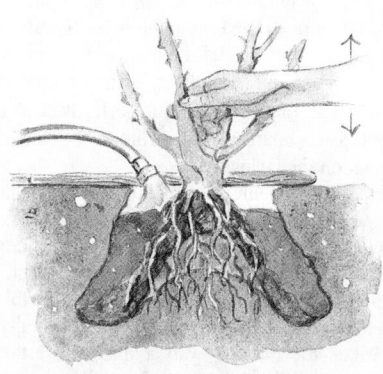

2 Hold the plant upright as you firm soil around its roots. When backfilling is almost complete, add water. This settles the soil around the roots, eliminating any air pockets. If the plant settles below the level of the surrounding soil, pump it up and down while soil is saturated to raise it to the proper level.

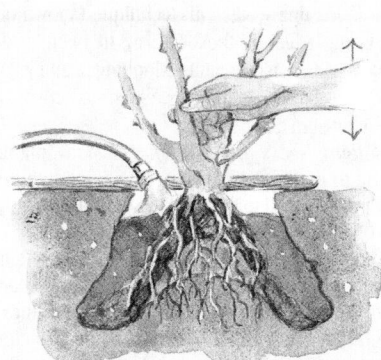

3 Finish filling the hole with soil; then water again. Take care not to overwater while the plant is still dormant, since soggy soil may inhibit the formation of new roots. When the growing season begins, make a ridge of soil around the planting site to form a watering basin; water when the top 2 inches of soil are dry.

PLANTING BALLED-AND-BURLAPPED PLANTS

1 Measure the root ball from top to bottom. The planting hole should be a bit shallower than this distance, so that the top of the root ball is about 2 inches above the surrounding soil. Adjust the hole to the proper depth; then set in the plant.

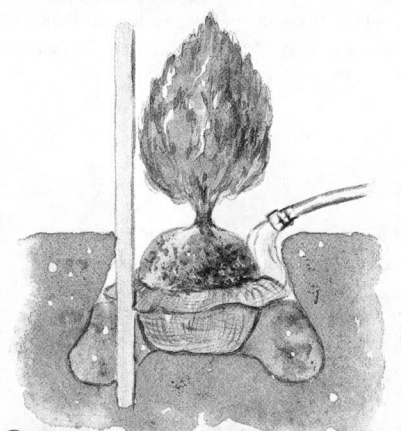

2 Untie the covering. If it's burlap, it will eventually rot; spread it out to uncover about half the root ball. If it's synthetic, however, remove it entirely. Drive a stake in alongside the root ball. Fill the hole with soil to within 4 inches of the top and water gently.

3 Firm the soil as you fill the hole. Make a berm of soil to form a watering basin; then water the plant. Cover the root ball with mulch but don't pile it up against the trunk. If you staked the plant, loosely tie it to the stake. As the plant becomes established, keep the soil moist but not soggy. Remove the stake after the first growing season.

PLANTING FROM A CONTAINER

1 Dig a hole as shown at top of facing page. Spread roots out over the central plateau of firm soil. The top of the root ball should be 1 to 2 inches above the surrounding soil.

2 Backfill with the unamended soil you dug from the hole, adding the soil in stages and firming it around the roots with your hands as you work.

3 Make a berm of soil to form a watering basin. Irrigate gently. Spread a layer of mulch on top of the root ball, but take care not to mound it up against the trunk.

P

Plant Propagation

In gardening lingo, "propagation" refers to the various ways of starting new plants. Plants can be propagated either sexually or asexually. *Sexual propagation* involves the union of male and female parts of a flower to produce seed. Plants grown from seed reflect the characteristics of both their parents. In *asexual (vegetative) propagation,* the new plant is produced from a vegetative part (root, stem, bud, or leaf) of just one plant. This new plant is a *clone,* in most cases genetically identical to its single parent. Asexual propagation maintains uniformity—assuring, for example, that each plant of the rose 'Queen Elizabeth' is like every other. Methods of asexual propagation include taking cuttings, dividing plants, layering, budding, and grafting.

SOWING SEEDS. Starting plants from seed is an economical way to get lots of plants. It also gives you many choices, since most seed catalogs offer more varieties of flowering plants and vegetables than you're likely to find at the local nursery. Increase your chances of success by making sure you understand what seeds need in order to germinate.

How seeds germinate. To sprout, all seeds require the favorable environmental conditions described under "Seed Germination" (below). Beyond these needs, the seeds of some plants have specialized requirements. For example, seeds of plants native to areas with cold winters normally need a period of low temperatures before they will sprout. In the wild, this happens naturally: the seeds mature in late summer or autumn, are moistened by rain in fall and chilled throughout the winter, then sprout in spring. Gardeners can mimic this cold period by *stratifying* the seeds—either sowing them in containers that are set outdoors for the winter, or placing them between layers of moist paper towels enclosed in a plastic bag, then refrigerating them for a month or two.

Some seeds—including those of diverse plants such as acacia, false indigo (*Baptisia*), morning glory (*Ipomoea*), and locust (*Robinia*)—have a hard seed coat that does not allow water to penetrate. Before they can germinate, they must be *scarified*. In nature, scarification may be accomplished by soil fungi and bacteria that partially decompose the seed coat; it also occurs when birds or animals consume and then excrete the seeds. Gardeners can scarify seeds by nicking the seed coat with a file or scratching it with sandpaper.

Planting the seeds. Many annuals, wildflowers, and vegetables can be seeded directly in the garden, either broadcast over a bed to give a planted-by-nature look or in the traditional rows of a vegetable or cutting garden. Many other kinds of plants, however, are best raised from seed sown in containers. These include slow-growing types as well as warm-season vegetables and annuals that may need to be started when the soil is still too cold and wet for in-ground planting.

Sowing seeds outdoors. Whether you are planting rows of vegetables, broadcasting a wildflower mixture, or sowing several kinds of annuals for a showy border, start by preparing a planting bed (see page 628).

❱ Planting seeds in rows. Make furrows following seed packet instructions for their depth and spacing. If possible, lay out the rows in a north-south direction, so that both sides will receive an equal amount of sunlight. Form the furrows with a hoe, rake, or stick; for perfectly straight rows, use a board or taut string as a guide, as shown on the facing page.

Sow seeds evenly, spacing them as the packet directs. You can tear off a small corner of the packet and tap the seeds out as you move along, or pour a small quantity into your palm and scatter pinches of seed as evenly as possible. Place larger seeds, such as beans, individually.

Water the furrows with a fine spray; then keep the soil surface moist but not dripping wet until seeds sprout. After the seedlings are up and growing, gradually cut back on watering, being sure to keep the root zone moist. Thin seedlings once they've developed two sets of true leaves. Thinned plants can be transplanted into any empty spaces in the rows.

❱ Broadcasting seeds. This technique (shown on the facing page) is the best way to plant wildflowers. It also makes natural-looking plantings of other easy-to-grow annuals, such as cosmos, sweet alyssum, and zinnia.

Sowing seeds in containers. Many plants get off to a better start when sown in containers and transplanted to garden beds later in the season. It's easier to provide plants in containers with the warm temperatures and bright light they need for quick growth; it's easier to protect them from insects and birds as well. The information on the seed packet will help you decide when to plant. Most annual flowers and vegetables should be sown 4 to 8 weeks before it's time to transplant them outdoors.

❱ Container choices. Convenience, cost, and reusability all determine which containers you select. If you're reusing old containers, scrub

---

P

SEED GERMINATION

Seeds cannot germinate until certain favorable environmental conditions are met. These include adequate moisture, a preferred temperature, and a loose-textured soil that provides oxygen to the sprouting seed. Seeds of some species also require light, meaning that no newspaper or other covering should be placed over the planted seeds; seed packets note these requirements.

Once the necessary conditions are met, the radicle—the embryonic root—emerges from the seed and begins growing downward, with root hairs and lateral roots developing from it. The lower part of the stem (the hypocotyl) pulls the seed leaves or cotyledons upward and into the light. Food stored in the cotyledons nourishes the seedling until first true leaves begin photosynthesis (see page 626). (In some species, like peas, the cotyledons remain underground during germination.)

Some plants—corn, grasses, lilies, onions—have only one cotyledon and are called monocots. Plants with two cotyledons, such as beans, are called dicots.

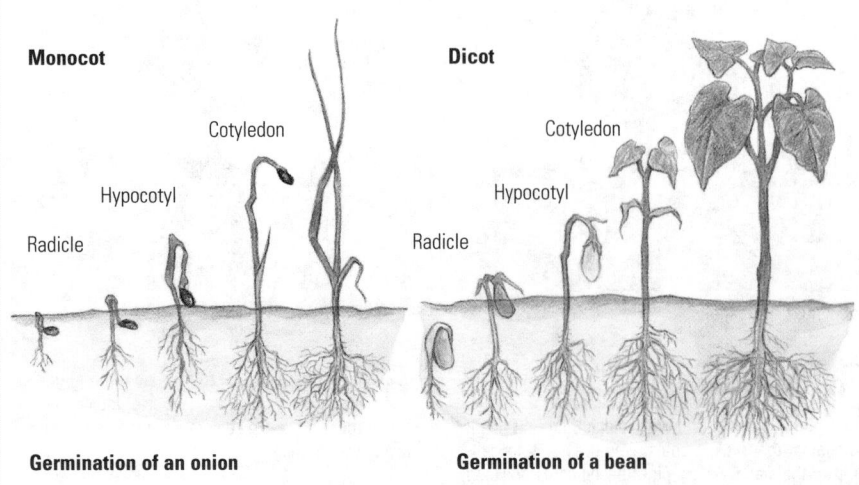

Monocot

Cotyledon

Hypocotyl

Radicle

Germination of an onion

Dicot

Cotyledon

Hypocotyl

Radicle

Germination of a bean

For straight rows, stretch a string between two stakes and plant beneath it. Or lay a board on the surface of the soil, then plant along its edge.

BUYING AND STORING SEEDS

Be sure the seeds you buy are fresh; they should be dated for the current year. For many plants, seed may be sold in three different forms: loose, pelletized, and in tapes. Loose seeds, traditionally sold in packets, are familiar to all gardeners. Pelletized seeds, also sold in packets, are individually coated (like small pills) to make handling and proper spacing easier. Seed tapes are strips of biodegradable paper with seeds embedded in them, properly spaced for growing to maturity (which makes thinning unnecessary). You just unroll the tape in a prepared furrow and cover it with soil.

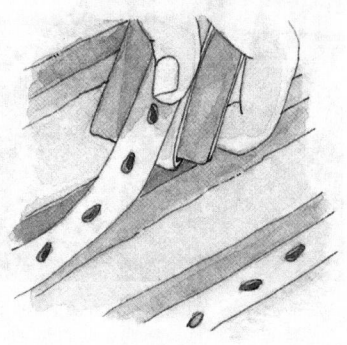

Store extra seeds in an airtight jar or other container in a cool, dry place. With proper storage, many kinds of seeds remain viable for a year, and some stay good for several years.

them out and soak them for 30 minutes in a solution of 1 part household bleach to 9 parts hot water to prevent infection by damping-off fungi (page 603), which destroy seedlings.

Plastic flats with no dividers are an old favorite. They are readily available from garden supply stores and mail-order catalogs, and free when you buy seedlings at nurseries.

Plastic cell-packs and 2- to 4-inch plastic pots (recycled from nursery purchases) are easy to obtain and use.

Peat pots are inexpensive but not reusable. However, because you plant seedlings pot and all, such pots minimize disturbance to roots. Keep them moist after seeding (so roots can penetrate them easily) as shown on page 634.

Plastic foam flats with tapered individual cells are sold by nurseries and through mail-order catalogs. They come in several cell sizes; some have capillary matting that draws water from a reservoir, making seedling care easier.

Recycled household items—plastic cups, cut-down milk cartons, foil baking pans—are also good choices. Be sure to punch several drainage holes in any container that lacks them, since seedlings will die if water collects around their roots.

Growing medium. Buy a seed-starting mix or potting soil at the nursery, or make your own by combining 1 part peat moss or finely shredded bark with 1 part perlite. Before using purchased mixes, flush them with water to eliminate excess salts. The mix should be moist but not soggy when you plant seeds.

BROADCASTING SEEDS IN A PREPARED BED

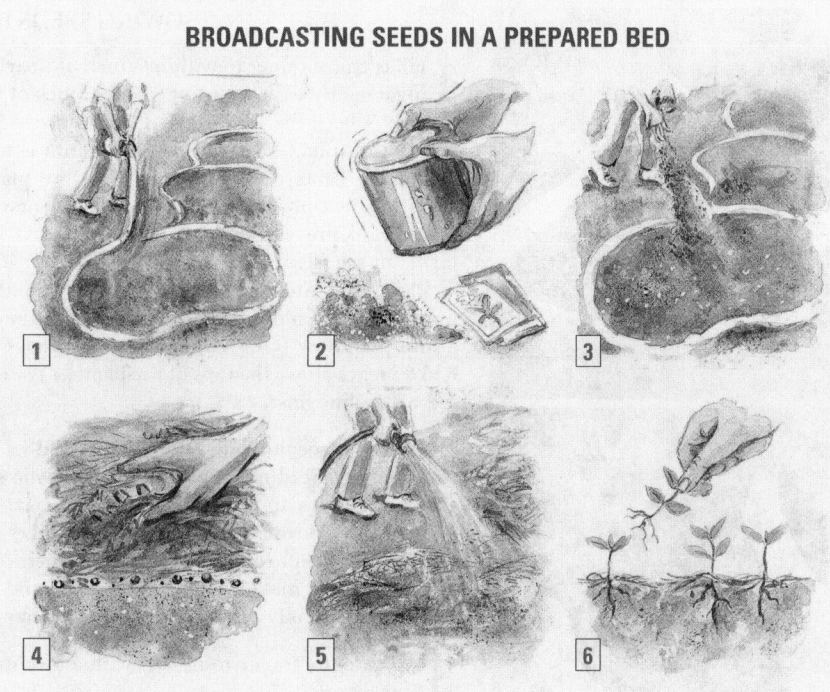

1 For a patterned planting, outline the areas for each kind of seed with gypsum, flour, or stakes and string. You may want to put a label in each area.

2 To achieve a more even distribution, shake each kind of seed (or an entire seed mixture) in a covered can with several times its bulk of sand.

3 Scatter the seed-sand mixture as evenly as possible over the bed or individual planting areas; then rake lightly, barely covering the seeds with soil. Take care not to bury them too deeply.

4 Spread a very thin layer of mulch (such as sifted compost) over the bed to help retain moisture, keep the surface from crusting, and protect the seeds from birds.

5 Water with a fine spray. Keep the soil surface barely damp until the seeds sprout; once seedlings are up, gradually decrease watering frequency.

6 When seedlings have two sets of true leaves, thin seedlings that are too closely spaced. Transplant the thinned seedlings to fill empty spaces in the bed.

P

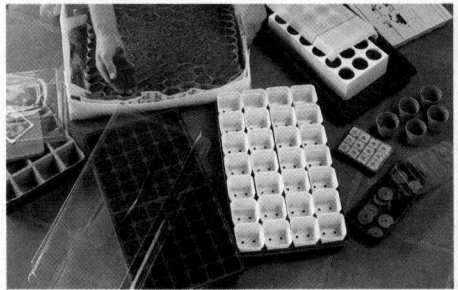

ABOVE: Various seed-starting trays and pots are available at nurseries and through mail-order catalogs.

MIDDLE: Plant two seeds in each cell of a plastic foam flat; later thin seedlings to one in each cell.

RIGHT: To help peat pots retain moisture after seeding, set them in a flat filled with 1½ inches of moist potting mix.

SOWING SEEDS IN CONTAINERS

1 Fill each container to within ½ inch of the rim with damp, sterile seed-starting mix, firming it gently with your fingers or a block of wood. Scatter seeds thinly over the surface of the mix. Check the seed packet for recommended planting depth and cover with the proper amount of mix. (A general rule of thumb is to cover seeds to a depth equal to twice their diameter.) Label each container with the plant name and sowing date. Moisten lightly. Covering the containers loosely with damp newspaper will help keep soil moist but still allow air to get in, preventing the growth of fungi. (Don't cover if the seeds need light to germinate, however; see page 632.)

Place the containers in a warm spot. When the seeds germinate, uncover the containers, if necessary; then move them to a spot where they'll be in bright light, such as a greenhouse or a sunny window. (Or give them 12 to 14 hours of fluorescent light each day, setting the light 6 to 8 inches above the tops of the plants.) Water when the surface of the soil feels dry, spraying with a fine mist.

2 When the seedlings develop their second set of true leaves, it's time to transplant them. (If you don't need many plants, just thin the seedlings to one plant per pot—or thin flat-grown seedlings to a distance of 2 inches apart—and skip transplanting them to larger containers.) To transplant, fill new containers (such as 4-inch plastic pots) with dampened potting mix. Remove the seedlings from their original pot by squeezing its sides and turning it upside down, making sure to keep one hand around the soil ball. Once the soil ball is out of the pot, carefully pull it apart with both hands and set it down on a flat surface.

3 Separate the fragile root balls with a toothpick or pencil point, or tease them apart with your fingers.

4 Poke a hole in each new container's planting mix. Handle each seedling by the leaves to avoid damaging the tender stem; support the root ball with your finger. Place each seedling in its new container and firm the mix around it. Water immediately, then set pots in bright light; keep them out of direct sunlight for a few days to let the seedlings recover from transplanting. Fertilize weekly with a fertilizer sold for starting seeds or a liquid type diluted to half-strength. About 10 days before the seedlings are ready to plant outdoors, they'll need to harden off as follows so they can withstand the bright outdoor sun and cooler temperatures. Stop fertilizing them and set them outside for several hours each day in a wind-sheltered spot receiving filtered light. Over the next week or so, gradually increase exposure until the plants are in full sun all day (shade lovers are an exception; they should not be exposed to daylong sun). Then set the young plants out in the garden, as illustrated on page 629.

P

CUTTINGS. Plants can be propagated from cuttings in several ways, depending on the plant part used for propagation. Any plant that produces sprouts from its roots will grow from root cuttings. Some kinds of plants will root successfully from a leaf or a portion of a leaf. Stem cuttings—in which roots are induced to grow from stem sections—are described as softwood, semihardwood, or hardwood, depending on the maturity of the stems; see pages 636 and 637 for details.

Root cuttings. Numerous perennials and other plants can be propagated by root cuttings. A few examples are globe thistle *(Echinops)*, Japanese anemone, Oriental poppy *(Papaver orientale)*, trumpet vine *(Campsis)*, blackberry, and raspberry.

Make root cuttings when the plant is dormant—in late fall or early winter, for most species. You can dig up an entire plant or just a section of its roots. With a sharp knife, remove vigorous, healthy pieces of root 2 to 4 inches long; those growing close to the crown will form new plants most quickly. (Note that rooting hormone is not needed and may actually delay rooting.) If you have only a few cuttings, place them upright in a container filled with damp potting mix, with the top cut ends (those that were closest to the crown on the parent plant) at soil level (see above). For larger numbers of cuttings, fill a flat to within an inch of the top with potting mix; lay the cuttings flat on top of the mix, then cover them with ½ inch more mix.

ROOT CUTTINGS

To start a few root cuttings, insert them upright in a pot. For a larger number, lay the cuttings in a flat.

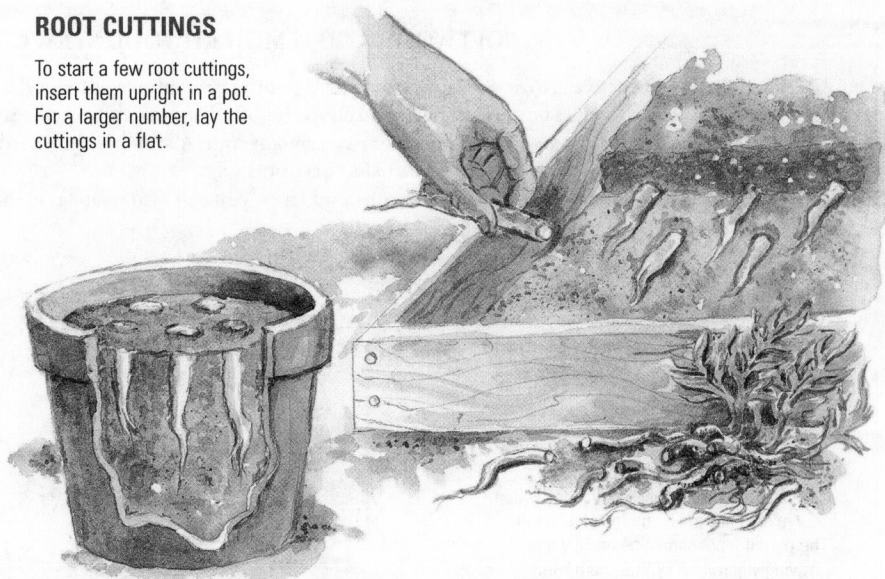

Water the planted containers well. Then place them in a growing area such as a greenhouse or cold frame; protect from direct sun. Once stems and leaves have formed, move the containers into full light and water as needed. When the young shoots are several inches tall and new roots have formed (check by gently digging up a cutting), transplant them to individual pots and feed with liquid fertilizer.

Leaf cuttings. Some plants can form roots from a leaf or a portion of one. Three examples are shown at left. For rooting medium, use a mix of 1 part peat moss and 1 part perlite or coarse builder's sand.

DIVIDE AND MULTIPLY. *A single pot of lily turf* (Liriope) *or mondo grass* (Ophiopogon japonicus) *bought at a garden center can easily yield a half-dozen or more plants. Just slip the root ball out of the pot and use a knife, trowel, or pruning shears to divide it into smaller pieces. Ensure that each piece of root has a tuft of leaves. Trim back the roots by about half to encourage the plants to spread and fill in faster. Then set out the new plants about 6 inches apart in a grid pattern. Keep the young divisions well watered. The ground cover will fill in completely within a few years.* ❖

DIVISION. Division is the easiest way to propagate many perennials, grasses, bulbs, and shrubs that form suckers or clumps of stems with rooted bases. In essence, dividing a plant involves separating it into several rooted, self-supporting plants. Besides giving you new plants, division rejuvenates overgrown plants, improving bloom and overall appearance.

Most plants can be divided in either fall or early spring. Avoid dividing plants in the heat of summer, since it is difficult for divisions to become established then. If you plan to divide in fall and you live in a cold-winter climate, do the job early enough in the season to let roots get established before freezing weather arrives (generally 6 to 8 weeks before the first hard frost).

A day or two before dividing, thoroughly moisten the soil around the clump to be divided. To make the plants easier to handle, cut back

THREE TYPES OF LEAF CUTTINGS

Rex begonias are propagated by making cuts in the large veins on the underside of a mature leaf. Lay the leaf flat, cut side down, on a rooting medium; then enclose the container in a plastic bag. In time, new plants will grow at the point where each vein was cut.

To root leaf cuttings of African violet *(Saintpaulia ionantha)*, insert a young leaf with an inch or two of stem into a rooting medium. Enclose the container in a plastic bag to retain humidity. New plants form at the base of the stem.

To root leaf cuttings of mother-in-law's tongue *(Sansevieria)*, cut a leaf into 3- to 4-inch-long sections. Insert these into a rooting medium, covering as much as three-fourths of their length. A new plant will eventually form at the base of each cutting.

Rex begonia

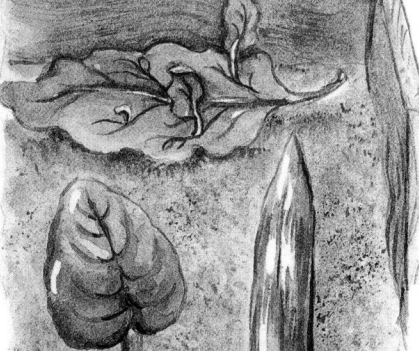

African violet   Mother-in-law's tongue

▶ page 638

SOFTWOOD AND SEMIHARDWOOD STEM CUTTINGS

Taken during the active growing season, from spring until late summer, softwood cuttings are the easiest stem cuttings to take and the fastest to root. They are made from relatively soft, flexible new growth. Semihardwood cuttings are taken somewhat later in the growing season, usually in summer or early autumn. A suitable semihardwood stem is firm enough to snap if bent sharply; if it just bends, it's too mature for satisfactory rooting.

In addition to deciduous and evergreen shrubs and trees, you can also propagate many perennials by semihardwood and softwood cuttings.

ROOTING THE CUTTINGS

1 Prepare containers first. Use clean pots or flats with drainage holes. Fill them with a half-and-half mixture of perlite and peat moss, or with perlite alone. Dampen the mixture.

2 Gather cuttings early in the day, when plants are fresh and full of moisture. The parent plant should be healthy and growing vigorously. With a sharp knife or bypass pruners, cut off an 8- to 12-inch length of stem.

Prepare the cuttings by removing and discarding any flower buds, flowers, and side shoots. Then slice the stem into 3- to 4-inch pieces, each with at least two nodes (points at which leaves are attached). Make each cut just below a node, since new roots will form at this point. Strip the lower leaves from each cutting.

3 Dip the lower cut ends of the cuttings in liquid or powdered rooting hormone; shake off any excess. (Many plants will root without the use of hormones.)

Using a pencil or thin dowel, make holes in the rooting medium an inch or two apart; then insert the cuttings. Firm the medium around the cuttings and water with a fine spray. Label each container with the name of the plant and the date. Set containers in a warm spot that's shaded but not dark.

Enclose each container in a plastic bag; fasten the bag closed to maintain humidity. Open the bag for a few minutes every day to provide ventilation.

4 Once the cuttings have taken hold and are growing roots, they will begin to send out new leaves. To test for rooting, gently pull on a cutting; if you feel resistance, roots are forming. At this point, expose the cuttings to drier air by opening the bags; if the cuttings wilt, close the bags again for a few days.

When the plants seem acclimated to open air, transplant each to its own pot of lightweight potting soil. By the next planting season, the new plants should be ready to go out in the garden.

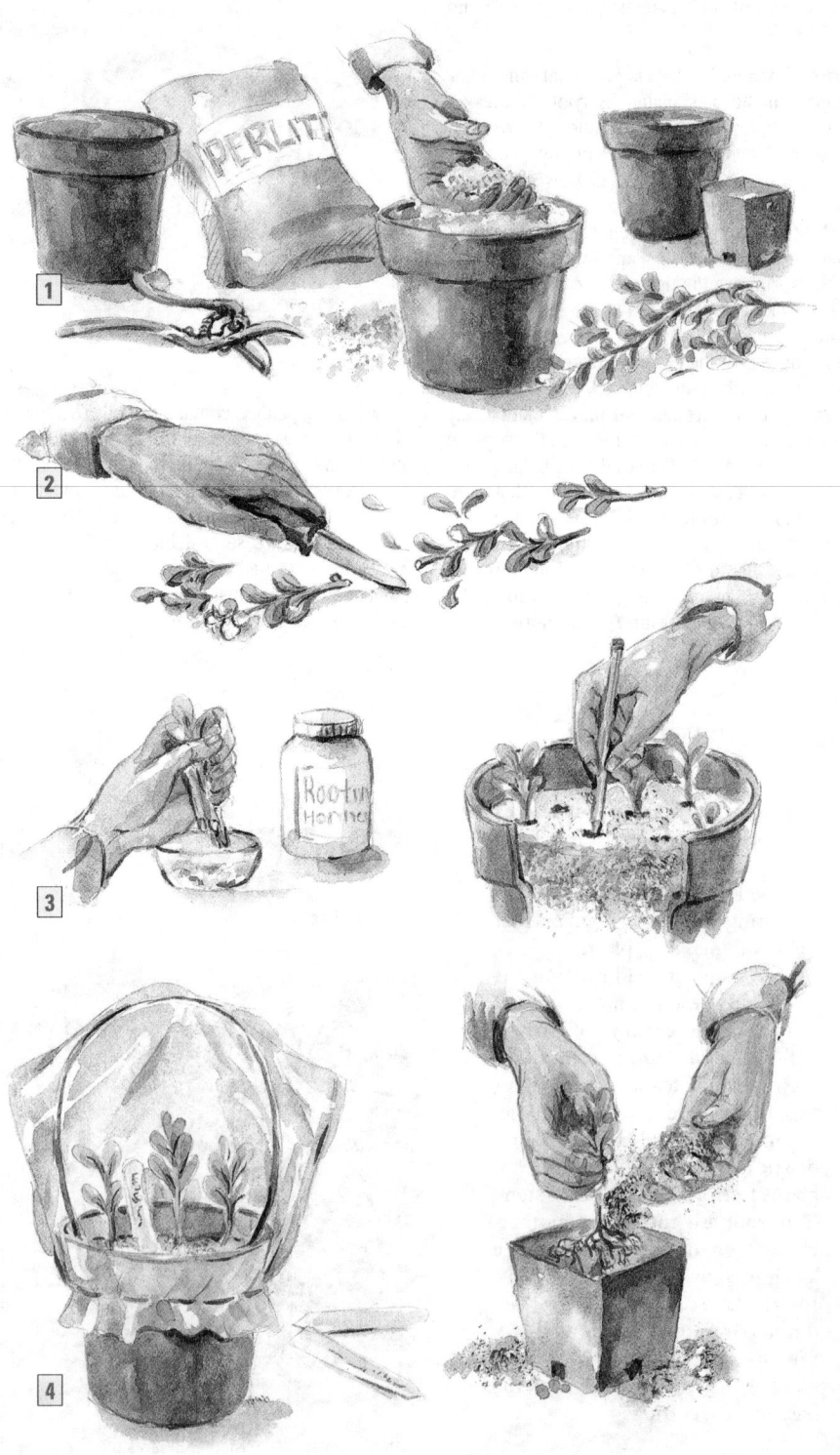

P

HARDWOOD CUTTINGS

Take hardwood cuttings during the dormant season (when plants are leafless), from late fall to early spring. Most deciduous shrubs and trees can be propagated by this method. Candidates include crepe myrtle *(Lagerstroemia)*, dogwood *(Cornus)*, elderberry *(Sambucus)*, forsythia, honeysuckle *(Lonicera)*, privet *(Ligustrum)*, spiraea, and willow *(Salix)*. Some fruit species, such as fig, grape, mulberry *(Morus)*, and some plums, are easily propagated by hardwood cuttings.

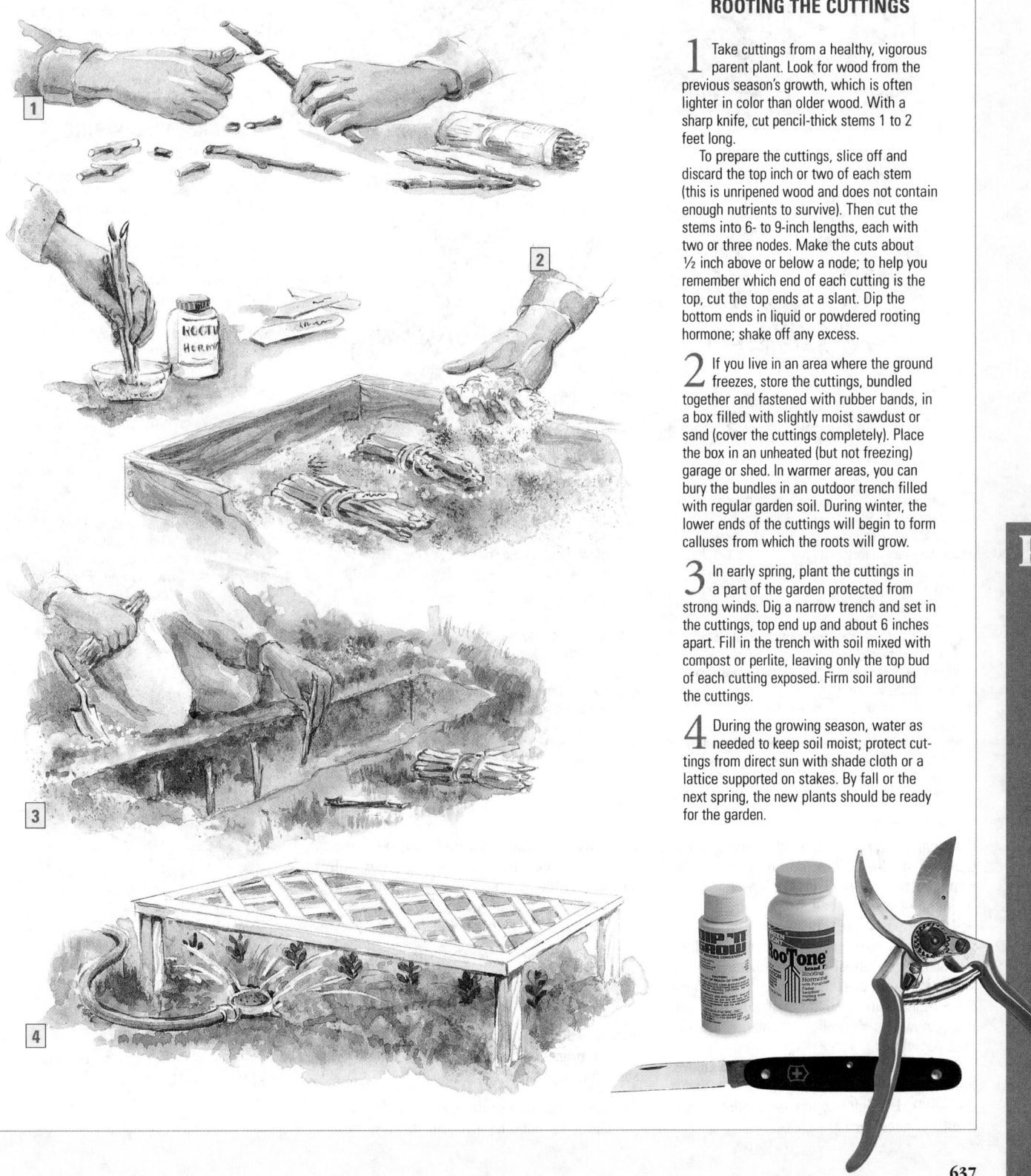

ROOTING THE CUTTINGS

1 Take cuttings from a healthy, vigorous parent plant. Look for wood from the previous season's growth, which is often lighter in color than older wood. With a sharp knife, cut pencil-thick stems 1 to 2 feet long.

To prepare the cuttings, slice off and discard the top inch or two of each stem (this is unripened wood and does not contain enough nutrients to survive). Then cut the stems into 6- to 9-inch lengths, each with two or three nodes. Make the cuts about ½ inch above or below a node; to help you remember which end of each cutting is the top, cut the top ends at a slant. Dip the bottom ends in liquid or powdered rooting hormone; shake off any excess.

2 If you live in an area where the ground freezes, store the cuttings, bundled together and fastened with rubber bands, in a box filled with slightly moist sawdust or sand (cover the cuttings completely). Place the box in an unheated (but not freezing) garage or shed. In warmer areas, you can bury the bundles in an outdoor trench filled with regular garden soil. During winter, the lower ends of the cuttings will begin to form calluses from which the roots will grow.

3 In early spring, plant the cuttings in a part of the garden protected from strong winds. Dig a narrow trench and set in the cuttings, top end up and about 6 inches apart. Fill in the trench with soil mixed with compost or perlite, leaving only the top bud of each cutting exposed. Firm soil around the cuttings.

4 During the growing season, water as needed to keep soil moist; protect cuttings from direct sun with shade cloth or a lattice supported on stakes. By fall or the next spring, the new plants should be ready for the garden.

P

DIVIDING PERENNIALS

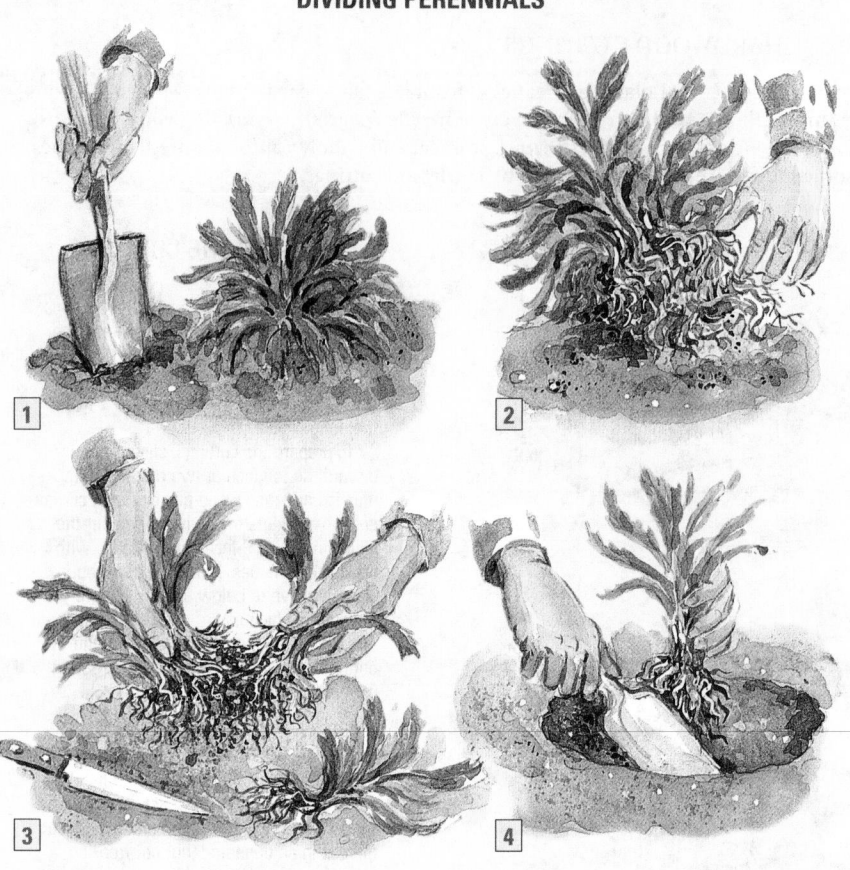

1 Loosen the soil in a circle around the clump, cutting 6 to 12 inches beyond the plant's perimeter with a shovel or spading fork. Then dig under the roots to free them from the soil. Lift the whole clump out of the ground; if it's too heavy to lift, cut it into sections. Set the clump (or sections) in a convenient working spot such as a path.

3 Now make the divisions. Note natural dividing points between stems or sections. You can divide some perennials by pulling the clumps apart by hand. Those with mats of small, fibrous roots can be cut with a knife, small pruning saw, or trowel; types with thick, tough roots may require a sharp-bladed shovel or an ax. Divide clumps into good-sized sections. Trim any damaged roots, stems, or leaves.

2 Gently tease some soil from the root ball so you can see what you are doing. For larger, fibrous-rooted perennials such as daylilies *(Hemerocallis)*, hose off as much of the soil as possible.

4 Replant the divisions as soon as possible, then keep them well watered while they get established. You can also plant divisions in containers (a good idea if they're very small) to set out later or share with other gardeners.

the stems of larger perennials, leaving about 6 inches of foliage. (When dividing shrubs, cut stems back to 6 to 12 inches long.) If you'll be planting in a new bed, prepare the planting bed (see page 628) before you divide, so the divisions won't have to spend too long out of the ground. If you're replanting in the same location as the parent clump, keep the divisions in a shady spot covered with damp newspapers while you amend the soil (see page 646).

Division of perennials is illustrated above. For division of bulbous plants, see pages 598–599. For information on dividing ornamental grasses, turn to page 615.

LAYERING. Layering is a technique that encourages new roots to form on branches still attached to the parent plant. The parent plant supplies the layer—the new plant—with water and nutrients during the rooting process.

Ground layering. Also called simple layering, ground layering is an easy way to produce a few new plants, though it may take as long as a year. This technique can be used to propagate many shrubs and perennials that have low-growing or trailing branches. To ground layer, follow the steps shown at right.

Air layering. This process involves the same principle as ground layering, but air layering is used for branches higher on a plant. It is often employed to propagate large houseplants—overgrown rubber plants *(Ficus elastica)*, for example—but it's also successful in some outdoor trees and shrubs, including citrus, witch hazel *(Hamamelis)*, magnolia, and rhododendron. To air layer, follow the steps at right.

BUDDING AND GRAFTING. These methods involve joining parts of two different—but closely related—plants so that they will grow as one. With a steady hand and a little practice, you can learn to use budding and grafting to propa-

GROUND LAYERING

1 In spring, select a young, healthy, pliable shoot growing low on the plant to be layered. Loosen the soil where the shoot will be buried and work in a shovelful of compost. Dig a shallow hole in the prepared area.

With a sharp knife, make a cut where the shoot will touch the soil; cut about halfway through the shoot, starting from the underside. Dust the cut with rooting hormone powder and insert a pebble or wooden matchstick to hold it open.

Lay the shoot (the layer) in the hole and fasten it down with a piece of wire or a forked stick. Some gardeners tie the layer's tip to a stake to help it grow upward.

2 Fill in the hole, firming the soil around the layer. A rock or brick can be placed on top to help hold the layer in place.

During the growing season, keep the soil around the layer moist. Adding a few inches of mulch will help retain moisture.

When you are sure roots have formed (this may take anywhere from a few months to possibly more than a year; gently dig into the soil to check), cut the new plant free from the parent. Dig it up, keeping plenty of soil around the roots, and move it to its intended location.

P

AIR LAYERING

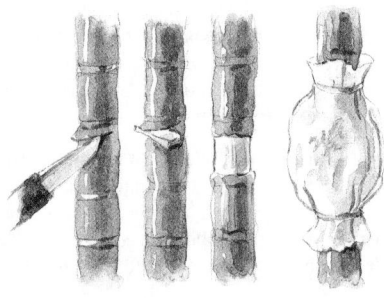

Air layering is most successful if done while a plant is growing actively. To encourage such growth in houseplants, fertilize the plant to be layered, then place it in a sunny window. When new leaves appear, proceed with layering.

Begin below a node. Make a slanting cut (insert a wooden matchstick to keep it open) in the bark or remove a ring of bark. Dust the cut with rooting hormone, encase it in damp sphagnum peat moss, and then cover it with plastic wrap.

If layering succeeds, roots will appear in the moss after a few months; you can then sever the rooted stem from the parent and pot it. At this point, it's usually a good idea to remove about half of the new plant's leaves to prevent excessive moisture loss through transpiration while it gets established.

If no roots form, the cut you made will form a callus, and new bark will eventually grow over it.

gate roses, grapes, and fruit and ornamental trees or to add one or more new selections to an existing fruit or nut tree. The part that becomes the upper or aboveground portion of the plant is known as the *scion;* it may be a piece of a branch or a single bud. The scion gives the new plant the desired qualities of flowering, fruiting, or form. The part that provides the roots is called the *stock, rootstock,* or *understock.* In some cases, the stock is a young plant chosen because it causes the new plant to be hardier, more disease resistant, or smaller in size (as in dwarf fruit trees, for instance). In other cases, the stock may be a mature tree that you want to graft over to a new variety.

Successful budding and grafting depend upon uniting the *cambium* layers of scion and stock—the thin green layer of growing cells just inside the bark. When these layers join with each other, new growth can occur. Use a very sharp knife to make all cuts: the cleaner the cut, the better the chance for a successful union.

T-budding and cleft grafting are illustrated below and on page 640. Other methods include chip budding, patch budding, whip grafting, and side grafting; consult a plant propagation manual for details on these.

Budding. Also called bud-grafting, this operation is carried out in summer or early fall when plants are actively growing. Roses and some other flowering shrubs, as well as grapes and fruit trees, are propagated by this method. Budding involves inserting a growth bud (the scion) from one plant beneath the bark of a related plant (the stock). The stock is either a pencil-thick rooted cutting of a sort known to produce a strong root system or a seedling plant of such a species. Usually, buds are inserted just a few inches above the soil. (They are also occasionally placed in small branches in the upper portion of a tree.) If the plants are compatible and budding is successful, the bud will unite with the stem into which it was inserted. It will stay plump but dormant through fall and

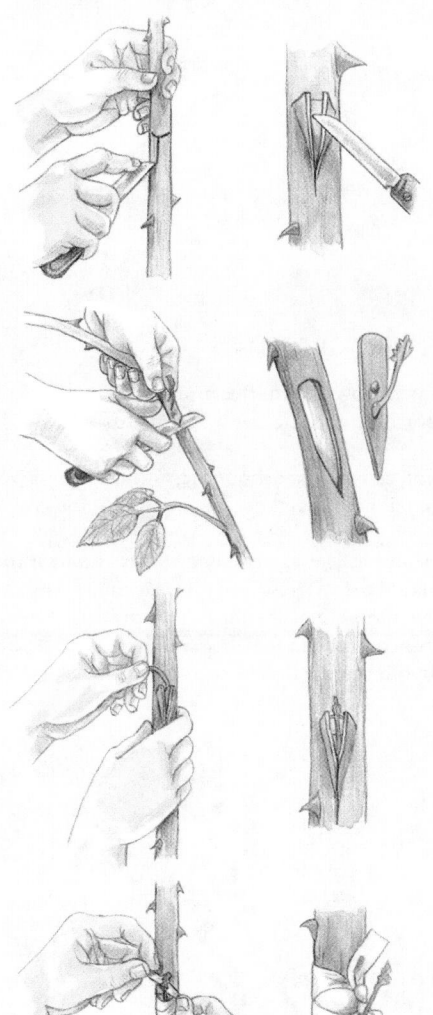

winter, then begin to grow in spring, when all the plant's buds burst into growth. At this point, the stem is cut back to just above the new, growing bud. The flowers, fruit, and leaves arising from the implanted bud will have the characteristics of the plant from which it was taken.

Grafting. This technique unites a short length of stem—the scion—with a stock. The stock plant may be a slim seedling to be grafted near ground level or an old fruit tree to be grafted on its major limbs. Cleft grafting (illustrated on the following page) is popular for converting fruit and nut trees to new selections. Cleft grafts are made in early spring, when the growth buds of the stock swell. However, the scion wood should be dormant when the graft is made—so gather it in late fall or winter. Cut ¼- to ½-inch-thick tip growth, making sure each piece has three or four buds. Bundle the stems together, label them, and place them in a sealed plastic bag in the refrigerator. Some mail-order companies offer scion wood in winter.

T-BUDDING

1 Choose a stock stem ¼ to ½ inch in diameter. Make a T-shaped cut in the bark; the top of the T should extend about a third of the way around the stem. Gently pry up the corners of the T. If the bark does not pull away easily, it may be too early in the season; try again in a week or two.

2 Select a bud (located at the base of a leaf) from the budwood plant; remove the leaf but retain its stalk to use as a handle. Be sure to take a vegetative bud, which is usually small and pointed, rather than a larger, plumper flower bud. Cut a shield-shaped patch containing the bud, starting about ½ inch below the bud and finishing about 1 inch above it; leave a bit of wood attached to the back of the bud shield.

3 Push the bud shield down between the flaps of the T-cut, being careful not to damage the bud. Cut off the top of the shield to make it even with the horizontal cut of the T. All of the shield should fit between the bark flaps.

4 Bind the budding site snugly with plastic grafting tape or rubber budding strips, starting beneath the bud and finishing above it. Cover the top of the T, but leave the bud exposed.

P

CLEFT GRAFTING

1 Prepare the stock by splitting it several inches down into a smooth, straight-grained section (so the split will be even). Shape the bottom end of the scion into a long, gradually tapering wedge; the outside edge of the wedge should be slightly thicker than the inside (as shown in the cross-section diagram).

2 Use a wedge or large screwdriver to hold open the split stock while you work. Insert the scion (or two, as illustrated) into the stock, carefully placing them so that the cambium layers of stock and scion match. After the scion is properly placed, remove the wedge and cover the entire union with grafting wax. Also coat the top of the scion so it won't dry out. If the graft is successful, buds on the scion wood will show growth during spring.

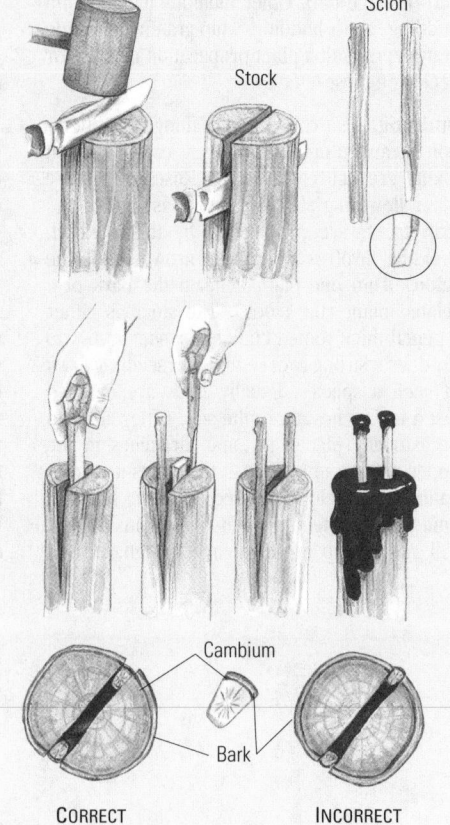

Scion

Stock

Cambium

Bark

CORRECT   INCORRECT

Pruning

Pruning tasks vary in scope—from removing large tree limbs to pinching out new growth on perennials—and your goals in pruning will differ too. Here are a few reasons why you may need or want to prune.

To maintain the health of your plants. Trees and shrubs will be healthier and more attractive if you remove branches that are badly diseased, dead, or rubbing together. Plants that have become too densely branched should be thinned to allow air and sunlight to reach their inner leaves and stems, helping to discourage some diseases.

To direct growth. Each time you make a pruning cut, you stop growth in one direction and encourage it in another, since growth continues in the buds and branches left behind.

To remove undesirable growth. Prune out wayward branches and remove suckers (stems growing up from the roots) and water sprouts (upright shoots growing from the trunk and branches). It should not, however, be necessary to cut back a plant continually to keep it in bounds. If it requires such treatment, it was probably a poor choice for its location and should be replaced with a plant that will naturally remain smaller.

To increase quality or yield of flowers or fruit. Most fruit trees and many flowering trees and shrubs need regular pruning to produce a good annual crop of fruit or blossoms. Specifics of pruning these plants are given in the Plant Encyclopedia.

To maintain safety. Remove split or broken branches that threaten to fall, injuring people or damaging buildings or cars. Also prune away any branches that obscure oncoming traffic from view.

To create hedges, topiary, or espalier. Suitable plants can be shaped into topiary or maintained as hedges through regular shearing. Others can be pruned and carefully trained as espalier (see illustration on page 643).

FOUR TYPES OF PRUNING CUTS. Most pruning involves four basic techniques: thinning, heading, shearing, and pinching. What sets these methods apart is where you cut in relation to growth buds and side branches.

Thinning. Most of the cuts you make when pruning should be thinning cuts. Such cuts can direct growth, eliminate competing or old stems, reduce overall size, and open up a plant's structure.

To thin, you remove an entire stem or branch, taking it back to its point of origin or to its junction with another branch. You might cut a branch back to the trunk, to the parent branch from which it arose, or (in the case of plants that send up stems directly from the roots) all the way to the ground. When removing one

PRUNING AND PLANT GROWTH

Some kinds of pruning cuts are made near a growth bud. Because subsequent growth varies depending on the bud's location, learning about growth buds (shown below, far left) will help you decide where to make cuts.

The *terminal bud* grows at the tip of a shoot, causing that shoot to grow longer. Actively growing terminal buds produce hormones that move down the stem and inhibit the growth of other buds on that stem.

Lateral buds grow along the sides of the shoot at leaf attachment points (nodes); they produce the sideways growth that makes a plant bushy. These buds stay dormant until the shoot has grown long enough to diminish the influence of the hormones produced by the terminal bud, or until the terminal bud is pruned off; then they begin to grow.

Latent buds lie dormant beneath the bark. If a branch breaks or is cut off near a latent bud, that bud may develop into a new shoot.

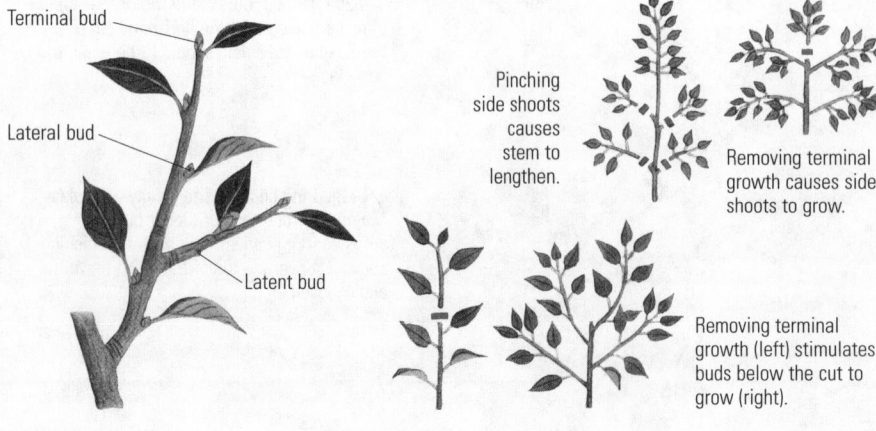

Terminal bud

Lateral bud

Latent bud

Pinching side shoots causes stem to lengthen.

Removing terminal growth causes side shoots to grow.

Removing terminal growth (left) stimulates buds below the cut to grow (right).

branch at a branch junction, be sure the remaining branch is at least one-third the diameter of the one being removed. If it's any smaller than that, it will be unable to assume the terminal role, and the effect will be more like that resulting from a heading cut.

When you remove a branch, you of course also remove the buds on that branch. Thinning cuts can cause bud growth elsewhere on the plant, but they're much less likely than heading cuts to stimulate clusters of shoots. Thus, thinning lets you reduce the bulk of a plant with minimal regrowth.

Heading. Heading cuts remove just part of a stem or branch—not the whole thing, as thinning cuts do. Such cuts can be made back to a bud or to a twig or branch too small to take over the terminal role (less than one-third the diameter of the branch you're removing). Heading stimulates the growth of lateral buds just below the cut. (Shearing and pinching, discussed below, are also forms of heading.)

For maintenance pruning of most woody plants, heading is less desirable than thinning. Though it may initially make a plant smaller and more compact, this situation won't last for long: once headed, the plant will produce vigorous new growth from lateral buds. If you head a wayward shoot instead of thinning it out, you can expect a candelabra of shoots to grow in its place. Continual heading thus ruins the natural shape of most woody plants. It is, however, useful when your goal is precisely to induce vigorous growth beneath a cut—when you want to force branching at a particular point on a branch or stem to train young fruit trees; fill a hole in the tree's crown; increase bloom production in roses or other flowering shrubs; or rejuvenate old or neglected shrubs.

Shearing. An indiscriminate form of heading, shearing does not involve careful, precise cutting just above a growing point. Instead, you simply clip a plant's outer foliage to create an even surface, as in hedges or topiary. However, because the plants best suited to shearing have main and lateral branches bearing closely spaced buds, almost every cut ends up near a growing point.

Pinching. This is the simplest, most basic type of pruning. Using your thumb and forefinger or a pair of hand shears, you nip off the tips of new growth, removing the terminal bud. This stops the shoot from growing longer and stimulates branching. Pinching is used primarily on annuals and perennials to make them bushy and encourage the production of more flowers.

MAKING PRUNING CUTS. When pruning, always cut back to a part that will continue to grow—to the trunk, another branch, a bud, or even to the plant's base, if it sends up stems from the roots. At these points of active growth, callus tissue will start to grow inward from cells at the end of the cut; in time, the wound will seal off. Clean cuts callus over faster than ragged

ones, so it's important to use an appropriate, well-sharpened pruning tool (for more on tools, see page 649). Forcing a tool to cut a branch bigger than it is designed to handle can can damage the tool and the branch.

The precise placement of a cut is usually also important. If you cut too close to a bud, the bud is likely to die. If you cut too far away from it, on the other hand, you'll leave a stub that, though still attached to the plant, is no longer

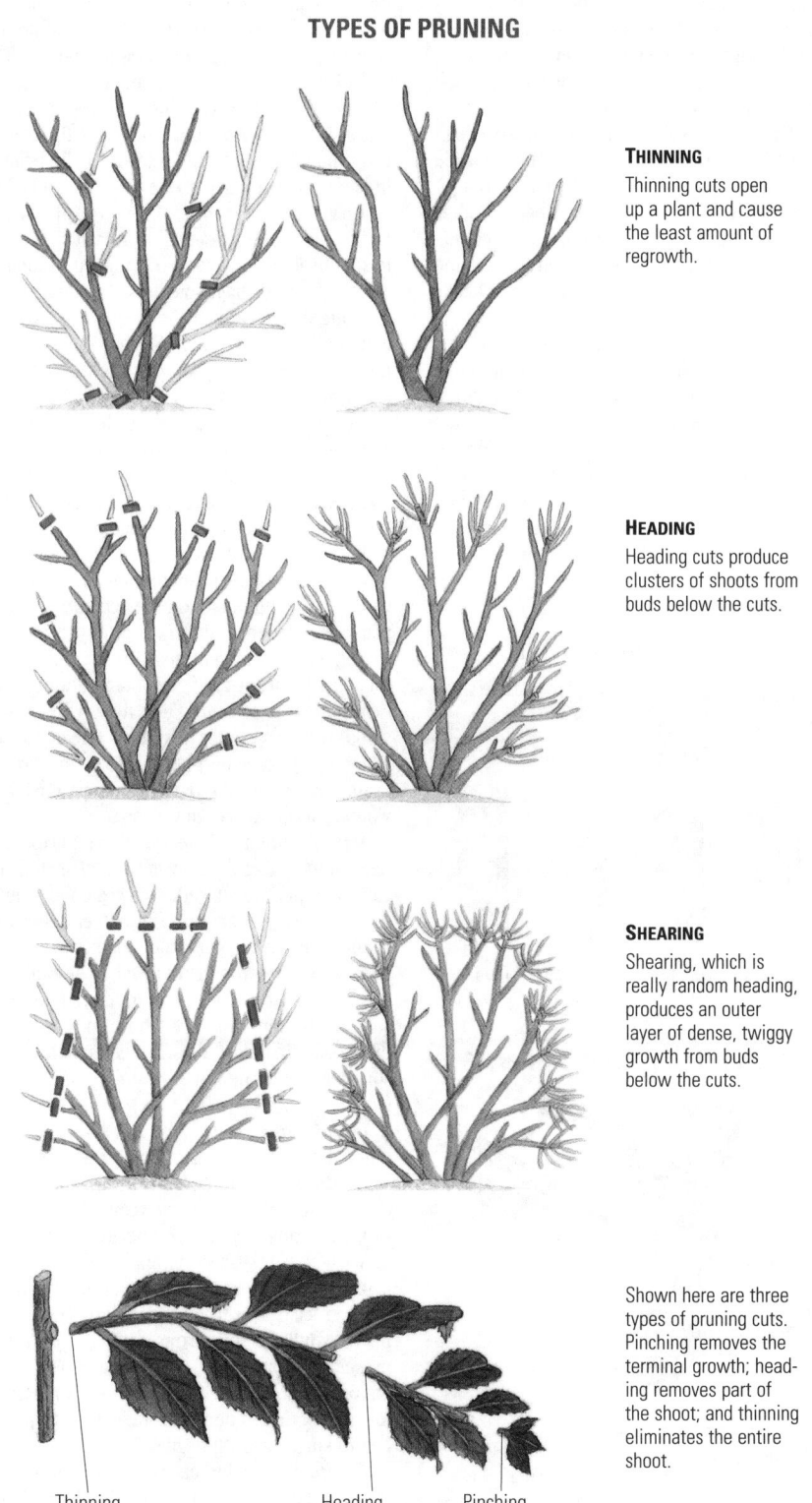

TYPES OF PRUNING

THINNING
Thinning cuts open up a plant and cause the least amount of regrowth.

HEADING
Heading cuts produce clusters of shoots from buds below the cuts.

SHEARING
Shearing, which is really random heading, produces an outer layer of dense, twiggy growth from buds below the cuts.

Shown here are three types of pruning cuts. Pinching removes the terminal growth; heading removes part of the shoot; and thinning eliminates the entire shoot.

Thinning   Heading   Pinching

P

involved in its active metabolism. In time, the stub will wither and die, then decay and drop off to leave an open patch of dead tissue—an invitation to disease or insect infestation.

When cutting back to a bud, look for a healthy specimen pointing in the direction you want the new shoot to grow. A proper cut will be about ¼ inch away from the bud, sloping away at approximately a 45° angle. Its lowest point should be opposite the bud and even with it, and it should slant upward in the direction to which the bud points (see illustration below).

When removing a branch, don't make a flush cut. Position your shears or saw just outside the *branch collar,* the wrinkled area (or bulge) at the branch's base where it meets another branch or the trunk. Also refrain from cutting into the *branch bark ridge* (raised bark in the branch crotch). Leaving these areas intact keeps decay to a minimum.

If you need to remove larger branches (any that are too big to support in one hand while sawing with the other), make the cut in three steps to avoid ripping the bark and tearing the tissue around the collar, as shown at right. If the limb in question is very heavy or high in a tree, however, it's wisest to hire a professional arborist. This is also the best course for repairing storm-damaged trees and for pruning around power lines.

CUTTING ABOVE A BUD

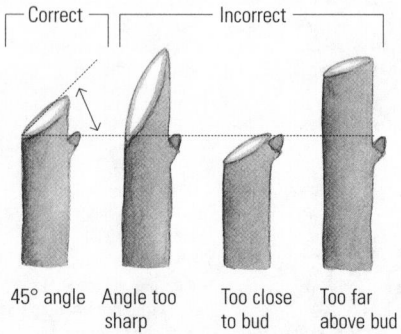

Correct — Incorrect

45° angle   Angle too sharp   Too close to bud   Too far above bud

POSITIONING PRUNING SHEARS

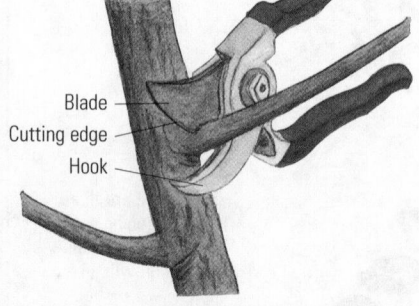

Blade
Cutting edge
Hook

To make a proper close pruning cut, hold shears so that the blade is closer than the hook to the growth that will remain on the plant. A stub results when you reverse the position and place the hook closer to the plant.

WHEN TO PRUNE. In general, pruning is best done in late winter (when plants are dormant) or during mid- to late summer; specific pruning times are given for many plants described in the Plant Encyclopedia. Dead or badly diseased wood is an exception: it should be removed as soon as you notice it. (Be sure, however, that dead-looking wood truly is dead. For example, freeze-damaged tissue that looks beyond help is sometimes in fact still alive; see page 608.) The best time to prune also depends in part on whether the plant is deciduous or evergreen.

Deciduous trees and shrubs—those that drop their leaves in fall—are typically pruned in late winter or early spring, just before or just as they resume growth. When the plants are leafless, it's easier to see their overall shape and to spot broken and awkwardly placed branches. To avoid cold damage to exposed tissues, prune after the danger of heavy frost is past. (Maples and birches—*Acer* and *Betula*—are exceptions; prune these in summer, as they "bleed" sap if pruned in winter or spring.)

Flowering trees and shrubs demand a little extra attention to timing—you'll need to know whether they bloom on old or new wood before you decide just when to prune. Plants that bear flowers in spring on wood that grew the preceding year should be pruned only after the flowering season is finished; if you prune in late winter, you'll eliminate the flower buds. Woody plants that produce flowers later in the growing season on the current season's growth, however, can be pruned in late winter without sacrificing blossoms, since the new (flowering) wood will grow after pruning. Check to see which category your plants belong to—older branches are usually darker, less pliable, and woodier looking than new growth.

Many deciduous plants can also be pruned in midsummer, after the growth flush of spring and early summer has slowed. This is a good time to thin out excess growth; moreover, vigorous shoots such as suckers and water sprouts are less likely to regrow if removed in summer. In cold-winter areas, be sure to complete such summer pruning no later than a month before the usual first-frost date, since pruning may stimulate tender new growth susceptible to cold damage.

Broad-leafed evergreen trees and shrubs don't drop their foliage, but growth of most slows down to a level approaching dormancy during the coldest time of year. Most can be pruned during this dormant period (late winter or early spring) or in summer. For flowering broad-leafed evergreens, however, timing is more precise; as is true for deciduous flowering plants, you'll need to prune with an eye toward preserving flower buds. For evergreens flowering on last season's growth, prune after bloom; for those that bloom on new wood, prune before spring growth begins.

Conifers, in many cases, don't require any pruning. For those that do, timing depends on the growth habit of the conifer in question.

REMOVING A BRANCH

When removing larger branches, avoid ripping the bark by shortening the branch to a stub before cutting it off just outside the branch collar. Using a sharp pruning saw, make three cuts, as shown below.

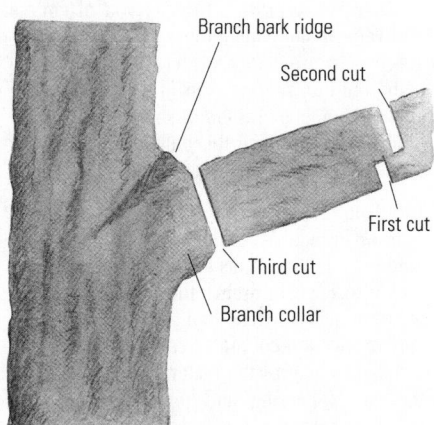

Branch bark ridge
Second cut
First cut
Third cut
Branch collar

1. About a foot from the branch base, make a cut from the underside approximately a third of the way through.

2. About an inch farther out on the branch, cut through the top until the branch rips off. The branch should split cleanly between the two cuts.

3. Make the final cut by placing your saw just outside the branch bark ridge and cutting downward and just outside of the branch collar. (If the crotch is very narrow, cut upward from the bottom to avoid cutting into the branch collar.)

These typically evergreen plants (which bear needles or scalelike leaves) fall into two broad classes: those with branches radiating out from the trunk in whorls and those that sprout branches in a random fashion.

Fir *(Abies),* spruce *(Picea),* and most pines *(Pinus)* are examples of whorl-type conifers. They produce all their new growth in spring, with buds appearing at the tips of new shoots as well as along their length and at their bases. (On pines, the new shoots are called candles, since that's what they look like until the needles grow.) Prune these conifers in early spring. You can cut new shoots back about halfway to induce more branching, making sure to cut above growth buds; or you can cut them out entirely to force branching from buds at their bases. Cutting back into an old stem—even one that bears foliage—won't necessarily force branching unless you happen to cut back to a latent bud.

Random-branching conifers, including cedar *(Cedrus),* cypress *(Cupressus),* juniper *(Juniperus),* arborvitae *(Thuja),* yew *(Taxus),* and hemlock *(Tsuga),* grow in spurts throughout the growing season rather than just in spring. They can be pruned much as deciduous plants and broad-leafed evergreens are. New growth will sprout from the branches below your cuts as long as the remaining part of the branch bears some foliage; most won't develop new growth from bare branches (hemlock and yew are exceptions). You usually have more leeway in timing for pruning random-branching conifers than you do for whorl-branching types, though the best time for the job is usually right before spring growth begins.

Shrubs

Shrubs are woody plants that live for many years. They are typically planted to provide long-lasting features in a landscape, forming a framework to help unite the garden's various elements. Many establish a permanent woody structure in their youth, then increase in size by growing new branches from older ones. Others produce shorter-lived woody stems (canes) each year from the roots, with a few to many new stems emerging as the older ones decline.

In form, shrubs may be rounded, vase shaped, conical, or columnar; in size, they range from ankle-high dwarfs to plants as tall as small trees. In contrast to trees, though, most have foliage all the way to the ground, rather than only at the top of a bare trunk.

SELECTING SHRUBS. So many different shrubs are available that you may have some difficulty choosing the best ones for your garden. Start by considering adaptability: select plants that will thrive in your climate and soil conditions. (Check the Plant Encyclopedia for specific information on the shrubs you're considering.) It's also important to think about mature size. That little tuft of greenery from a gallon can may look cute in a 4- by 4-foot space for a while, but if it ultimately will reach 12 feet in all directions, it's the wrong plant for the spot. In the same vein, bear in mind that the most attractive shrubs are those allowed to grow according to their natural inclinations, without excessive pruning. (Shrubs intended for hedges are an exception; in this case you can control size by pruning. For a list of good shrubs for hedges as well as those that can serve as privacy screens, see "Plants for Hedges and Screens" in A Guide to Plant Selection, on pages 77–78). You will also want to decide whether a deciduous or an evergreen shrub best suits your purposes.

Weigela *(Weigela florida)* is a fast-growing shrub that bears pink to rosy red flowers in late spring.

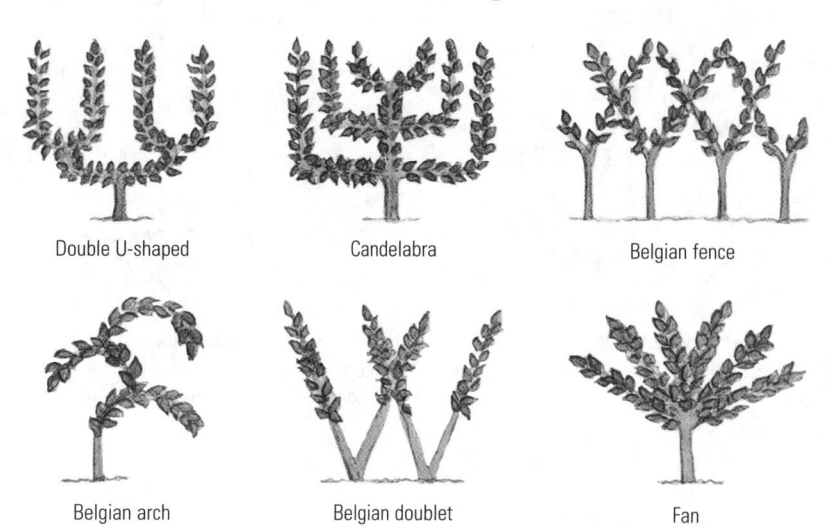

ESPALIER

This is a method of training a tree or shrub so that its branches grow in a flat pattern against a wall or fence. The branches are tied to a support—usually a trellis made of wire. The illustration shows several espalier forms.

Double U-shaped   Candelabra   Belgian fence

Belgian arch   Belgian doublet   Fan

Finally, consider ornamental features such as foliage texture, variegated or unusually colored leaves, attractive flowers, and colorful fruits.

PLANTING AND CARING FOR SHRUBS. Shrubs may be sold bare-root, in containers, or balled-and-burlapped (B-and-B). See pages 630–631 for planting directions for each type. How the plant is sold also affects the best time of year for planting. Bare-root plants must be set out soon after you purchase them; this is also true of B-and-B shrubs, available from late fall to early spring. You can plant container-grown shrubs at any time during the growing season, but to avoid stressing them, it's best to plant in spring or fall rather than in the heat of summer.

Water newly planted shrubs immediately, then keep the soil moist but not soggy as the plants settle in. Mulching will help conserve water and prevent weed growth around shrubs. Future watering needs depend on the particular shrub. Once established (after a year or two in the garden), many native shrubs and others well adapted to Southern climates may survive on rainfall alone or require watering only during summer dry spells.

Fertilizer needs vary too. Some shrubs (notably roses) do best with regular fertilizing, and other flowering sorts may also benefit from at least an annual application of fertilizer. But many shrubs grow well with no supplemental nutrients. If the shrub puts out strong new growth with good color each year, it's doing well without feeding—but if new growth is scant, pale, or weak, it should be fertilized.

To prune shrubs, follow the principles outlined on pages 640–642. Shrubs that have become overgrown—with long, straggling, tangled branches—may require rejuvenation, a rather severe form of pruning (illustrated on page 644). This method works best on shrubs that send up stems (canes) from the roots. Some can even take drastic rejuvenation, which involves cutting back all stems almost to the ground before new spring growth begins. Shrubs so pruned may need several seasons to recover fully, but in the long run they will be more compact and attractive. Plants amenable to this treatment include glossy abelia *(Abelia ×grandiflora)*, barberry *(Berberis)*, common butterfly bush *(Buddleia davidii)*, forsythia, mock orange *(Philadelphus)*, rose of Sharon *(Hibiscus syriacus)*, spiraea, and weigela.

On most other cane-producing shrubs, it's safest to proceed much more gradually with rejuvenation, spreading the pruning over a period of 3 years. In any case, once you have gotten rid of the old stems, keep the shrub under control by continuing to remove just a few of the oldest stems each spring.

GOOD TREES FOR TRAINING. *It's easier to espalier trees that have weeping forms or wide-spreading limbs, because they'll naturally follow horizontal lines and not keep putting up vertical leaders. Good selections include blue Atlas cedar (great year-round foliage color), crabapple or apple (spring flowers plus fall fruit), 'Little Gem' Southern magnolia (glossy evergreen leaves), pyracantha (orange, red, or yellow fall and winter berries), and weeping yaupon (red fall and winter berries).* ❖

S

REJUVENATING SHRUBS THAT GROW FROM THE BASE

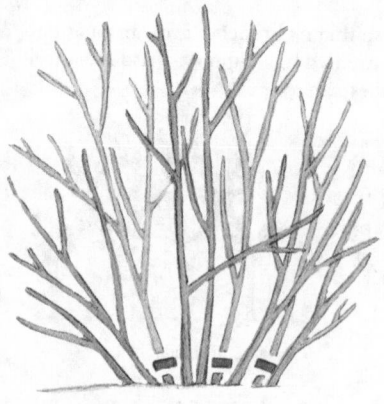

GRADUALLY

Remove about a third of the oldest growth annually for 3 years.

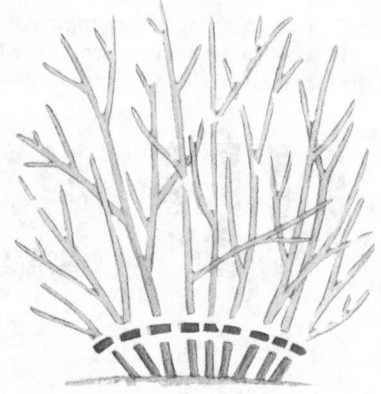

DRASTICALLY

If the shrub can withstand severe pruning, cut back the whole plant before new spring growth begins.

Soils and Soil Management

Understanding your soil and learning how to improve it will help make the garden more productive. Soil types affect plants' watering and fertilizing needs, and in some cases, it determines the kinds of plants you'll be able to grow.

Soil supports roots and gives them access to nutrients, water, and air. Most roots grow in the uppermost soil layer, called *topsoil,* which is relatively active biologically and is most directly affected by weather. Below the topsoil is the *subsoil.* It is less affected by microorganisms and weather, and while it may contain plant nutrients, it is not as hospitable to roots as topsoil. Discussions of soil quality and improvement generally focus on topsoil.

Soil is composed of mineral particles, living and dead organic matter, and pore spaces containing water and air. Good garden soil is approximately 45 percent minerals, 5 percent (or more) organic matter, and 50 percent pore spaces. The *mineral* portion is composed of rock broken down into tiny particles, while *organic matter* includes roots, decaying leaves and stems, materials added by gardeners, and myriad soil-dwelling organisms.

The network of *pore spaces* determines the permeability of the soil to water and air, as well as its water-holding capacity. This network includes large pores *(macropores)* and small ones *(micropores).* Macropores permit water and air to enter the soil easily and allow excess water to drain away. Micropores are responsible for a soil's water-holding capacity: they hold water against the force of gravity, making it available when needed by plants. The proportion of macro- to micropores affects soil quality. Soils that contain a preponderance of large pores are loose in texture; they are well aerated but cannot retain water for long and need more frequent irrigation. Soils with many small pores, on the other hand, are dense types that can hold a lot of water but not much air.

SOIL TEXTURE. Texture describes the size of a soil's mineral particles. These include large, coarse sand particles; smaller silt particles; and tiny particles of clay.

Clay soils. Also called adobe, gumbo, or simply "heavy" soils, clay soils are composed of flattened, platelike, microscopic particles that pack closely together, leaving little pore space for either water or air. But because these particles offer the largest surface area per volume of all soil particles, clay soils can hold the greatest volume of nutrients in soluble form. They also hold water for a longer time after getting wet. Drainage (the downward movement of water) is slow in clay soils, so the loss of soluble nutrients through leaching is slow as well. Due to their high density, clay soils are the slowest to warm in spring.

Sandy soils. Sand particles are comparatively large, and they're irregularly rounded rather than flattened. Their size and shape allow for much larger pore spaces between particles than in clay soils; consequently, sandy soils contain lots of air and drain well. In a given volume of sandy soil, the surface area of the particles is less than in the same volume of clay—so that the volume of soluble nutrients in sandy soil is correspondingly lower. And because sandy soil drains quickly and thus loses nutrients faster than clay, plants in sand need watering and feeding more often than those growing in clay. Sandy soils warm more quickly in spring than do clay soils.

Loam. Loam is considered the ideal garden soil. It contains a mix of all three particle types—clay, silt, and sand—but none pre-dominates. With a combination of large and small pore spaces, it drains well (but doesn't dry out too fast), loses nutrients at only a moderate rate, and contains enough air for healthy root growth.

Determining soil texture. To identify the texture of your garden soil, thoroughly wet a patch of soil, then let it dry out for a day. Now pick up a handful of soil and squeeze it firmly in your fist. If it forms a tight ball and has a slippery feel, it's predominantly clay. If it feels gritty and doesn't hold its shape at all but simply crumbles apart when you open your hand, it's sandy. If it is slightly crumbly but still holds a loose ball, it's closer to loam.

SOIL STRUCTURE. A soil's *texture* is defined by the size of its primary particles; its *structure* is determined by the way those particles bind together to form small clumps, called *aggregates.* In soil with a good structure, the pores between and within the aggregates are large enough to contain air and allow water to drain through easily, yet small enough to retain some water for roots to use.

Though you can't change a soil's basic texture, you *can* improve its structure by adding

---

SOIL TEXTURE AND TYPE

The size of a soil's mineral particles determines its texture and designates its type: clay, sand, or loam. Clay has the smallest particles, sand the largest; silt particles are intermediate in size. Loam, the ideal garden soil, contains a mix of all three types of particles.

SOIL PARTICLES

Clay
Less than 1/12,500 in.

Silt
Up to 1/500 in.

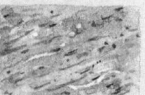

Fine sand
Up to 1/250 in.

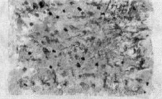

Medium sand
Up to 1/50 in.

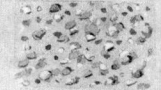

Coarsest sand
1/12 in.

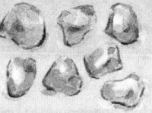

organic matter. Such improvement is especially important in fine-textured (clay) soils, since it increases porosity: organic matter helps bind the small particles together into larger aggregates. Gypsum and lime, both inorganic amendments, are sometimes used to improve structure in clay soils; for advice on using them, consult soil professionals or your Cooperative Extension Office.

In sandy soils, organic matter lodges in the pore spaces and acts like a sponge, holding water and nutrients.

Be aware that soil structure can be damaged, especially in soils high in clay. Running heavy machinery over the soil or even walking on planting areas compresses the pore spaces, as does tilling soil when it's too wet. Always let soil dry out until it's barely moist before working it.

SOIL PROBLEMS. Some of the soil problems that result in poor plant growth may be due to factors other than basic soil texture or structure. Here are a few of the most common such problems—and practical ways to deal with them.

Poor drainage. For most plants, good drainage is essential for healthy growth. If the soil drains poorly, water remains in the pore spaces rather than draining away, and air, necessary both to roots and beneficial soil-dwelling organisms, is thus unable to enter the soil. Soil texture, a low-lying location, and hardpan (see below) can all contribute to poor drainage.

As noted earlier, clay soils often drain poorly. To improve the situation, work in plenty of organic matter. Planting in raised beds filled with good, well-drained soil is another option.

Poor drainage may also occur naturally in the garden's low spots. Solving the problem may require installing drainage tiles to carry away excess water. If this is impractical, consider adapting your garden to the site and growing plants suited to moist areas.

A simple way to check drainage in various parts of your garden is shown above.

Hardpan is an impervious layer of soil that can cause trouble when it lies near the surface. Hardpan is found naturally in some regions—in the Southwest, for example, where the most common natural hardpan layer is called *caliche*. Hardpan can also be created, as when builders spread excavated subsoil over the soil surface and then repeatedly drive heavy equipment over it. In either case, though a thin layer of topsoil may conceal the hardpan, roots cannot penetrate it nor water drain through it.

If the hardpan layer is thin and close to the surface, it may be possible to break it up by having the soil plowed to a depth of 1 foot or more. If the hardpan is thicker, you may be able to drill through the hardpan with a soil auger when planting, creating a drainage chimney as shown at right. Thick hardpan, however, may require the installation of a subsurface drainage system, a project that usually requires hiring a contractor. Growing plants in raised beds filled with good soil is another alternative.

To check drainage, dig a 2-foot-deep hole and fill it with water. After it drains, fill it again. If this second amount of water drains away quickly (in an hour or less), the drainage is good. If it remains for several hours or longer, the soil drains poorly.

Soil pH. Soil ranges from acid through neutral to alkaline. This characteristic is stated as a pH number. Soil with a pH of 7 is neutral—neither acid nor alkaline. A pH below 7 indicates acidity, while one above 7 indicates alkalinity. The soil's degree of acidity or alkalinity primarily affects the availability of certain nutrients. If the pH is extreme in either direction, key nutrients are chemically "tied up" in the soil and not available to plant roots. The best way to determine your soil's pH is to have the soil tested (see "Testing Your Soil," page 646).

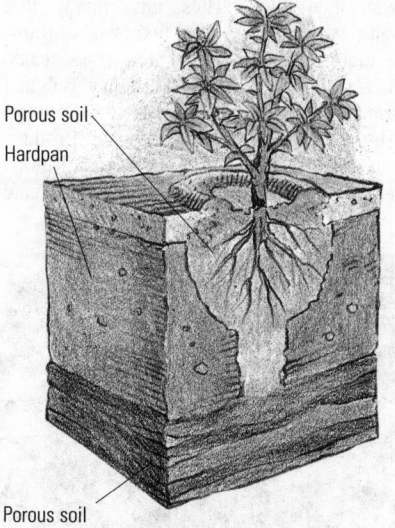

Porous soil
Hardpan
Porous soil

If hardpan is close enough to the soil surface to interfere with root growth and impede drainage, you can form a "chimney"—a narrow passage to the more porous soil beneath—when planting trees and shrubs. Drill through the hardpan with a soil auger; in severe cases, a jackhammer may be needed.

Acid soil is most common in regions where rainfall is heavy and is often associated with sandy soils and those high in organic matter. In the South, acid soil typically is found east of the Mississippi River, though limestone deposits cause pockets of alkaline soil in many places. Most plants grow well in mildly acid soil, but highly acid soils are inhospitable. Adding calcium carbonate (lime) is often suggested to raise pH. Follow the recommendations of your soil test lab for amounts to apply.

THE pH SCALE

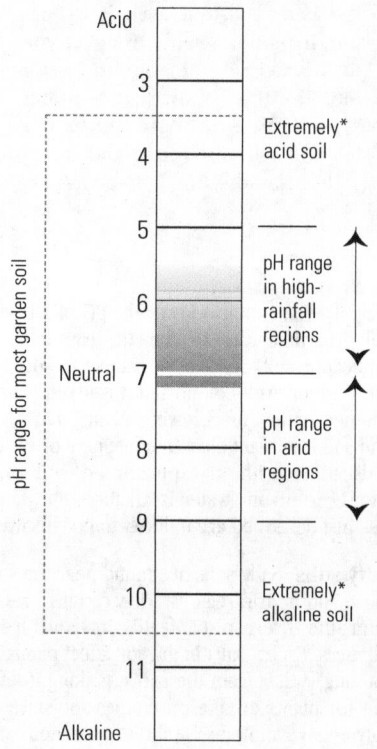

pH range for most garden soil

Acid	3		Extremely* acid soil
4		
5		pH range in high-rainfall regions
6		
Neutral 7		
8		pH range in arid regions
9		
10		Extremely* alkaline soil
11		
Alkaline		

pH range preferred by acid-loving plants

pH range preferred by most garden plants

*Soils nearing extremes require professional intervention to modify pH.

Alkaline soil is usually found west of the Mississippi River, in much of Texas and Oklahoma. In these areas, rainfall is typically light, and the result is a soil high in calcium carbonate (lime). Many plants grow well in moderately alkaline soil; others, notably camellias, rhododendrons, and azaleas, do not, because the alkalinity reduces the availability of certain elements (including iron and zinc) necessary for their growth.

Sulfur can be used to lower soil pH; follow the testing lab's recommendation for amounts

S

TESTING YOUR SOIL

A soil test and analysis will determine your soil's pH (acidity or alkalinity) and can also reveal nutrient deficiencies. The simple test kits sold at nurseries can give you a general indication of your soil's condition; for a more precise reading, have the test done at a laboratory. In some states, the Cooperative Extension Office will test your soil, but even if it does not, it should be able to direct you to commercial soil laboratories. Or look in the Yellow Pages under "Laboratories—Analytical." The lab will tell you where and how to collect the soil sample to be tested.

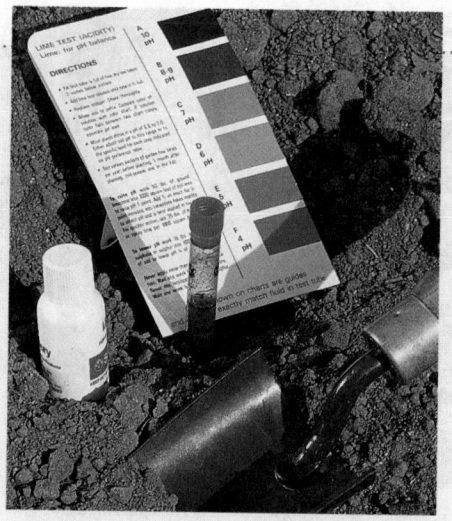

To use this pH soil test kit, you mix the provided solution with a bit of soil; the resulting color is compared with the color chart that indicates pH.

to apply. You can also lower the pH of alkaline soil over time with regular (at least annual) applications of organic amendments such as compost or well-composted (aged) manure. Another option for growing plants that need acid soil is to plant them in containers or raised beds filled with an appropriate soil mix. (However, if your water is alkaline, the remedies just described are unlikely to be effective.)

Salty soils. Salty soils are found near the seashore and in arid regions. They can also result from the overuse of fertilizers and fresh manures. Excess salts in the soil affect plants by "pulling" water from the roots, making it difficult for plants to take up enough moisture or nutrients; symptoms include scorched and yellowed leaves or browned and withered leaf margins. Seed germination is also inhibited. Salty soils include *saline* and *sodic* types.

Saline soils contain unusually large quantities of any of several soluble salts, such as compounds of calcium, sulfate, chloride, or sodium. To correct the condition, you can improve drainage by adding organic matter and leach the soil periodically with water to wash the salts below the plants' root zones.

Sodic soils, on the other hand, are specifically high in insoluble sodium, which bonds to soil particles; such soils are alkaline and poorly drained (they're also known as black alkali). To correct the problem, you must displace the sodium. In many areas, it's effective to incorporate calcium sulfate (gypsum), then leach the soil to wash away the sodium. However, if the calcium level of your soil is already high, a better course is to lower the alkalinity by incorporating organic amendments or through the use of sulfur. Check with a soil-testing laboratory or with your Cooperative Extension Office for advice specific to your area's soils.

ORGANIC SOIL AMENDMENTS. The decaying remains of plants and animals, organic matter is vital to maintaining the fertility of all soils and is especially necessary in soils high in clay and sand. Gardeners incorporate organic soil amendments to improve or maintain a soil's structure and to encourage healthy populations of beneficial soil-dwelling microorganisms.

As organic matter decomposes, it releases nutrients that increase fertility. However, the nitrogen released by decaying organic matter isn't immediately available to plants. It must first be converted by various microorganisms (such as bacteria, fungi, and actinomycetes) into ammonia, then into nitrites, and, finally, into nitrates, which can be absorbed by plant roots. The final product of the breakdown of organic matter is humus, a soft, sticky material that decomposes slowly and improves soil structure.

The microorganisms that ultimately produce humus require a certain amount of soil moisture, air, and warmth. Soils high in organic matter tend to contain relatively high populations of these organisms. Earthworms are also plentiful in soils rich in organic matter; as they tunnel along, they improve drainage and aeration, while their castings add nutrients.

Many types of organic amendments are available in the South, either commercially packaged or sold in bulk. One choice is manure, which contains more nutrients than most other amendments (manures should be aged well to avoid adding excess salts to the soil). Compost is an excellent amendment; see page 599 for more on homemade compost. Municipal compost is made from grass clippings, leaves, and tree prunings gathered and composted by municipal agencies, then sold or given to local residents. Mushroom compost, a by-product of mushroom farming, is available in some areas; it tends to be high in salts, so use it in smaller quantities than other composts. Sphagnum peat moss increases acidity and is thus often used to amend soils around acid-loving plants.

If you add raw (green or uncomposted) organic matter to your soil as an amendment, it may be proportionally higher in carbon than in nitrogen. During the time soil organisms are breaking down high-carbon materials, they require nitrogen and may temporarily compete with plants for nitrogen available in the soil. (Of course, once the organic material has had time to decompose, it will release extra nitrogen into the soil.) For this reason, high-carbon soil amendments such as sawdust, wood shavings, and ground bark should be bolstered with nitrogen before use. Some materials can be purchased already fortified with nitrogen. If you use unfortified amendments, mix a little nitrogen fertilizer into them.

Using organic amendments. Be generous when adding organic amendments. When preparing a new planting bed, spread a 3- to 4-inch layer of amendment over the soil and dig or till it into the top 9 to 12 inches.

Around established plantings, you can add organic material to the soil by spreading it over the soil surface as a mulch; earthworms, microorganisms, and water will help mix it into

Pine needles, straw, chopped hay, and wood chips all make good mulches.

S

the top layer of soil. Good mulches include straw, wood chips, chopped leaves, hay, and pine needles. (Note that peat moss is not very effective as a mulch; once it dries out, it's hard to moisten again, and it may blow away. To use peat as an amendment, always mix it into the top few inches of soil.) If the established plants are deep rooted—as are most mature trees and shrubs, for example—you can gently work the amendment into the top inch or so of soil, using a three-pronged cultivator.

SOIL POLYMERS

When added to soil, tiny gel-like soil polymers absorb hundreds of times their weight in rain or irrigation water that would otherwise drain away—holding it (and the dissolved nutrients it contains) for plants to use. The gel's ability to retain water means that plants still have a steady source of moisture when the soil itself is dry. This helps them grow better—since they don't suffer from wide fluctuations in moisture—and lets you stretch the time between waterings. Soil polymers are most often used in potting mixes; in fact, some kinds come with a polymer already incorporated. However, they're also useful in outdoor planting beds in areas with limited rainfall.

Various brands of polymers are available. Sorts containing polyacrylamide are the longest lasting, staying effective for up to 10 years. To do their job, polymers must be mixed into the soil, since root hairs have to grow into the particles to extract water. Mix the dry gel with water to expand the particles, then blend them evenly into the soil at the rate recommended by the manufacturer. Note that if you add too great an amount of gel, the particles will ooze to the surface when the soil is moistened by rain or irrigation. Too much gel can also result in overly wet soil, leading to root rot.

Tools, Hand

Stores, nurseries, and specialized mail-order catalogs offer gardening tools in bewildering array. This section describes a number of useful tools—many of them quite versatile—and offers tips for selecting them and using them comfortably and efficiently.

SHOVELS. With their wide, dished heads, *round-point shovels* are efficient soil movers. Use them to loosen soil, pick it up, and transfer it to a pile or wheelbarrow; they're also a good choice for digging planting holes. Select a larger round-point shovel (such as one with a 9-inch-long, 12-inch-wide head) for general digging. If you're working in a confined space, you may find it more convenient to use a smaller model

(a *floral shovel*), which has a 6- by 8-inch head and a shorter handle.

Round-point shovels vary in lift—the angle formed between the ground and the shovel handle when the shovel head is laid flat on the ground. To make digging easier by minimizing the amount of bending you'll have to do, choose a tool with generous lift.

Square-nose shovels and *scoops* are not meant for digging. They're used to scoop up loose material such as compost or gravel from a flat surface and move it to a different spot. They come in various sizes; choose one that will pick up the greatest amount of material you can lift repeatedly without tiring.

SPADES. In contrast to shovels, spades have longer, narrower, relatively flat heads. They're used to prepare soil for planting, to dig narrow, straight-sided trenches, and (sometimes) to prune roots.

Most familiar and most generally useful is the *English garden spade*, which has an almost flat blade (about 7 inches wide by 11 inches long) and forward-turned steps (the ledge at the top of the blade where you place your foot when you dig). The handle—often a short D-shaped type—extends almost straight up from the blade with little or no lift.

Border spades are smaller, with blades about 6 inches wide and 8 inches long. As the name indicates, they're handy in confined spaces such as flower beds and borders. At the opposite extreme in size are various spades with long, narrow blades, such as *transplanting spades,* which have slightly dished blades about 5 inches wide and 14 or 16 inches long.

SPADING FORKS. Substitutes for spades in clay or rocky soils, spading forks (also called digging forks) help fracture large clods of soil, breaking them into smaller clumps. They're useful for turning the soil prior to planting and for lifting perennials from the ground without cutting the roots. Like spades, they come with shorter D handles or longer straight handles.

When you shop for a spading fork, look for one that has four tines that are square or rectangular in cross-section and about ½ inch wide. Tines this thick help concentrate your pulling strength, and they don't bend easily.

PITCHFORKS. These tools (as well as manure forks and compost forks) aren't for spading. Instead, they're used to move manure or piles of prunings or to turn compost. Various styles in a range of sizes and weights are available; their long, curved tines are thinner than those of a spading fork. For a long-lasting fork, look for one with forged tines rather than welded ones. A T-shaped handle makes turning compost easier.

HOES. You'll find hoes designed for a variety of jobs, including cultivating, moving soil, digging furrows, and removing weeds. *Conventional* or *American-style garden hoes* have flat front edges to cut weeds off at ground level and sharp

corners that work like small picks. The most common kind has a 6-inch-wide blade. Narrower (2½-inch-wide) blades are useful for light jobs in tight spots; a wider (8-inch) blade is ideal for paths and driveways.

V-shaped hoes come in blade sizes varying from 1 by 3 inches to 4 by 6 inches. The most common is the *Warren hoe,* which is especially useful in vegetable gardens. Use the point to make small furrows, and the sides—well sharpened—to slice weeds.

Eye hoes and *grape hoes* are heavy-duty hoes with wide, deep blades set perpendicular to the handle. They are used for breaking ground, chopping tough weeds, scraping away dense growth, and moving soil.

A number of hoes are intended specifically for weeding. These hoes have little or no blade surface and are used with the blade parallel to the ground (or nearly so). They come in a variety of sizes and shapes, such as circle, diamond, stirrup, rectangle, arrowhead, and scuffle. However, there are only three variables in the way they function: they may be push hoes, draw hoes, or scuffle hoes (which cut on both the push and draw strokes). When using any of these hoes, the idea is to run the blade just under the soil surface to cut off weeds at ground level. Disturb the soil as little as possible to avoid bringing more weed seeds to the surface, where they will be able to germinate.

RAKES. *Garden* or *hard rakes* have thick steel tines, either straight or curved. The tines may be attached to the handle directly by a tang or socket, or indirectly by a curving bow. The bow type has more spring or resilience. These types of rakes are used to break up clods of dirt, level the soil, tamp seedbeds to make them firm, and work amendments into the top few inches of a planting bed.

Hard rakes are available with 6, 8, 14, or 16 tines. Select a rake with some weight in its head; if it's too light, you'll have to work harder to provide the downward force needed to break clods or move soil.

Leaf rakes have wide, thin, flat, springy tines. The best models have closely spaced tines that curve downward and slightly inward at the tip; they're arranged in a curving fan with a stabilizing brace about 8 inches up from the tip of the tines. Metal tines will last longer than those made of bamboo or polypropylene. In addition to raking leaves, these rakes are useful for gathering grass clippings and other lightweight materials into piles.

A leaf rake should be light but sturdy, allowing you to apply firm pressure to the ground with a minimum of effort. Widths may be as great as 4 feet—ideal for large properties with lots of deciduous trees. Smaller versions (only 8 or 10 inches wide) are useful for raking between shrubs and perennials.

T

GARDEN TOOLS

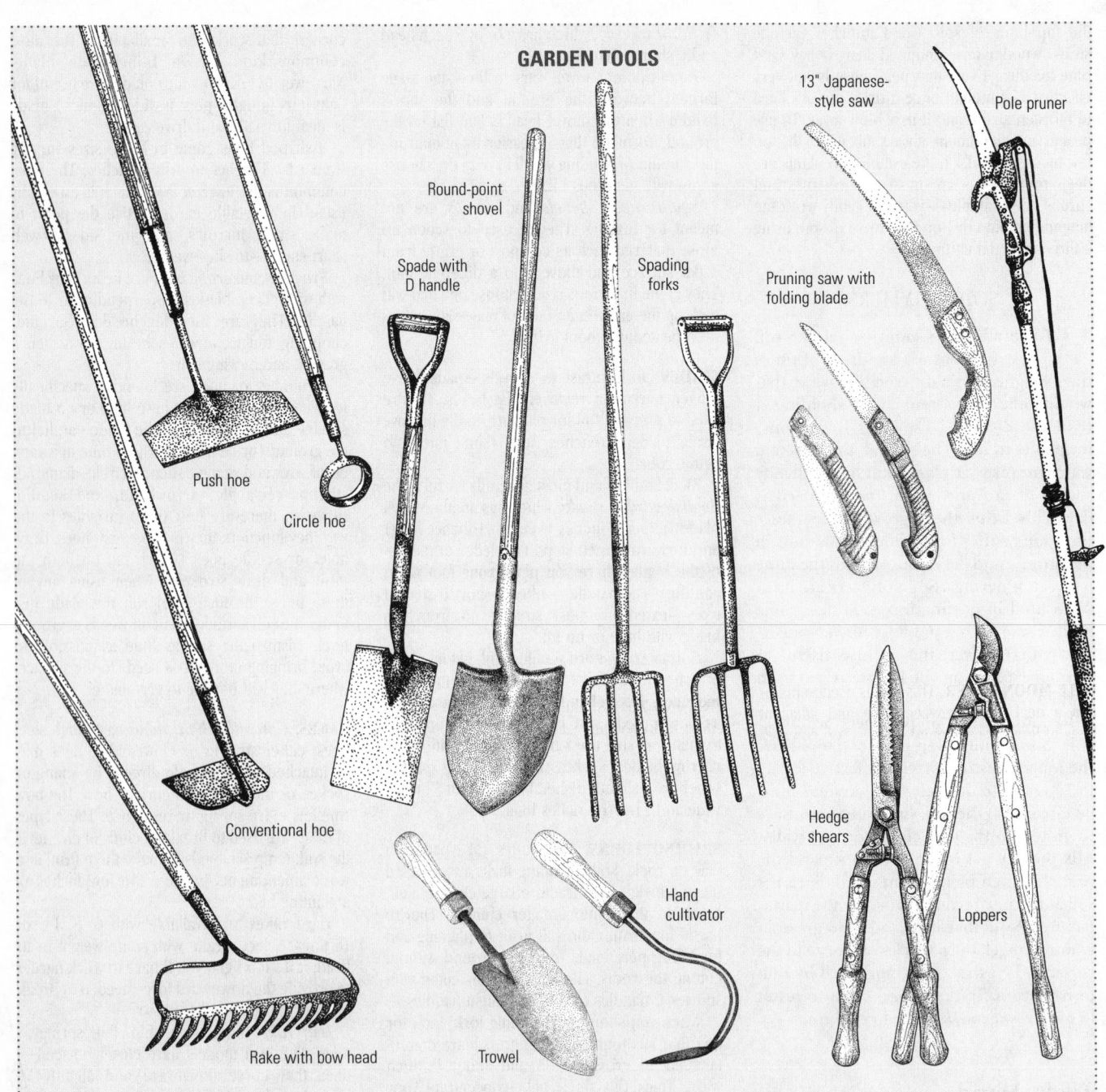

Push hoe

Circle hoe

Spade with D handle

Round-point shovel

Spading forks

13" Japanese-style saw

Pole pruner

Pruning saw with folding blade

Conventional hoe

Hedge shears

Loppers

Hand cultivator

Rake with bow head

Trowel

SELECTING TOOLS: HANDLES AND HEADS

When choosing tools for your garden, look for high-quality tools that fit your body type. For example, shovels, spades, and spading forks are available with either shorter D-type handles or long handles. D handles are best for shorter, smaller gardeners (though they're also useful in confined spaces); tall people are usually more comfortable using long-handled tools. If possible, buy hoes, cultivators, and rakes that are at least as tall (preferably an inch taller) than you are; this allows you to use them in a standing rather than a stooping position.

Handles made of straight-grained, knot-free wood are generally the best choice for most garden tools (make sure handle and head are attached with a rivet that passes all the way through the handle).

Tubular aluminum handles are easily bent, while tubular fiberglass ones can be shattered, especially on heavily used digging tools. What's more, these handles are usually narrower in diameter than wooden ones and thus more tiring to grasp for long periods.

Forging—heating metal until it is almost molten, then pounding it into shape—produces a denser tool head that is less likely to bend or break and takes an edge better than less expensive stamped steel. Highly polished, forged stainless steel tools are preferred by some gardeners because they don't rust, and they slide easily into the soil. However, they're somewhat more brittle than tools made of conventional carbon steel, which makes them more difficult to sharpen and more likely to fracture if they are used improperly.

T

A *thatching rake* is used to clear thatch out of lawn grasses. It has semicircular metal tines that are attached with the rounded edge facing forward. When you use this rake, you keep the head on the ground. Pulled through dense grass, the tines rip out thatch; the push or forward stroke clears material from the tines.

CULTIVATORS. These tools may have only one tine or two to five tines, spaced 1½ to 2 inches apart. The tines may be long or short, curved or straight; the tine ends are pointed in some models, flattened to form a lozenge-shaped tooth in others. Use cultivators to break up compacted soil around plants, keeping it loose and friable, and to work amendments into the upper few inches of soil; they are also effective for weeding.

Select a narrow cultivator if you plan to cultivate between closely spaced plants or if your soil is heavy; the fewer the tines, the more concentrated your pulling force will be. A cultivator with tines arranged in a V shape rather than lined up in a row is also easier to pull through heavy soils. If plants are widely spaced, a four- or five-tine cultivator is more practical; it also works best in sandy or well-amended soils.

A single-tine cultivator is known as a *finger hoe.* If you sharpen the sides of its tooth or tine, you can use it both for nicking weeds out of small spaces and for cultivating.

HALF-MOON EDGER. This tool is used to maintain a neat edge between lawn and adjacent beds of flowers or ground covers. You can also use it to edge between lawn and paving.

SMALLER TOOLS. In addition to scaled-down versions of hoes and cultivators, hand tools include knives, dibbles, specialized weeders— and, of course, the indispensable trowel.

Trowels. Though principally planting tools, trowels are also useful for cultivating, weeding, and scooping out fertilizers and soil amendments.

A trowel should be both strong and sharp; the best ones are made of forged steel and have a wooden handle pinned into a socket at the base of the blade. For general use, select one with a shallowly dished blade about 4 inches wide and 6 inches long. *Transplanting trowels* are narrower (about 3 inches wide), tapered, and deeply dished; they may have marks on the blade to help you gauge planting depth. *Potting trowels* are even narrower—about 2½ inches wide—and only shallowly dished. *Crevice* or *rockery trowels* are just 1 inch wide; they are invaluable for weeding as well as for planting a rock garden.

Knives. A sturdy knife comes in handy for diverse tasks: dividing roots of plants, opening bags of soil or soil amendments, carving points on the ends of wooden stakes. The *Japanese farmer's knife* (Hori Hori) features a slightly dished blade that can be used as a trowel; one side of the blade is saw-toothed, while the other has a sharp edge that can cut roots and burlap.

DIGGING AND HOEING

Learning to dig and hoe properly can literally save your back. When digging with a shovel, don't drive the tool into the ground at a low angle, bend over to lever the soil loose, and then lift with your back bent. Instead, drive the shovel blade straight down, as close to your body as you can manage comfortably. (The shovel handle will be angled away from you.) When you've driven the blade in as far as possible, step back with the foot that is not on the shovel's step or tread and pull the handle toward the center of your chest. Then, grasping the handle at the top with one hand and sliding the other hand toward the bottom, bend your knees and lower your body, keeping your back straight. Lift the shovelful of soil, using the strength of your legs, not your back.

Using a spade involves the same techniques, except that you'll usually be turning the soil over in a bed instead of lifting and moving it.

When using a hoe, rake, or cultivator, stand sideways to the work—as if you were using a kitchen broom. Grasp the handle with your thumbs wrapped around it near the top. As you work, flex your knees slightly and pull the tool across the front of your body. This position keeps your back straight and, if you hit a buried rock or large root, you'll naturally pull with the strong muscles in your upper legs instead of straining your lower back.

Dibbles. These poke holes in prepared soil to plant bulbs, bedding plants, and vegetables. They are usually carrot shaped, with a metal point and a rounded or T-shaped handle.

Weeders. Look for a hand weeder with a bent shaft or with a ball attached to the shaft to serve as a fulcrum, giving you leverage to pop weeds out of the ground. The weeder's head should be small and forked.

PRUNING TOOLS. Shears and saws for pruning come in many different forms and sizes—not surprising, when you consider that pruning cuts and techniques (not to mention the plants being pruned) vary, too (see "Pruning," page 640).

Hand pruners. Many gardeners take this tool with them whenever they go into the garden, carrying it in a leather case that clips to a belt or pants pocket. There are two basic types. *Bypass pruners* have a curved hook and a curved blade. The branch to be cut rests against the hook; the blade cuts it, passing the hook as it slices through the branch. In some models, the cutting blade bends away from the handle at an angle up to 45°; this gives you more cutting power and minimizes strain on your wrists.

HAND PRUNERS

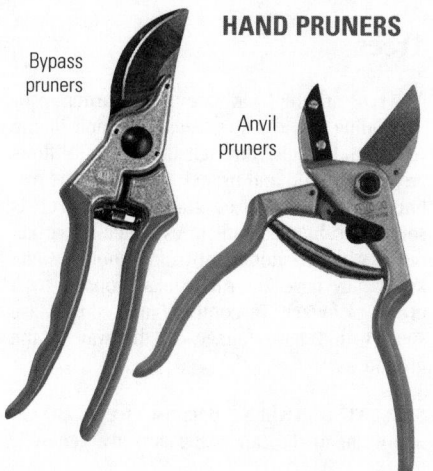

Bypass pruners

Anvil pruners

Anvil pruners have a flat anvil (instead of a hook) and a straight blade; the blade cuts through the branch until it hits the anvil.

Hand pruners should not be used on any branch thicker than your little finger; doing so risks damaging the plant, the tool, or both. Use a lopper or a saw instead.

Loppers. These powerful branch cutters have long handles that give you much more leverage than the short handles of hand pruners. They range from 1 to 3 feet in length and may have either bypass or anvil blades. Smaller loppers can substitute for hand pruners if you lack the hand strength needed to operate the latter; they're also good for cutting among thorny branches without scratching your hands and arms. The cutting capacity of loppers (that is, the diameter of branch they can cut) is the distance between the center of the blade and the center of the hook or anvil when the blades are opened at right angles to each other. The largest loppers will cut 3-inch-thick branches. A good in-between size for most garden jobs, capable of cutting branches up to 2 inches thick, is a 26-inch model. Be sure to select loppers with strong handles, preferably bolted on. A shock absorber, located below the pivot point, saves wear on your arms.

Pruning saws. If a branch is too large to cut with hand pruners or loppers, use a pruning saw. In contrast to carpenter's saws, most modern pruning types cut on the pull rather than the push stroke. They may have straight or curved blades; a curved one fits more easily into tight spots between branches. They may also have fixed or folding blades. Some models come with gullets—deep slots about every fourth tooth that accumulate and release sticky sawdust, so cutting teeth don't get gummed up.

Older-style saws have teeth bent slightly to right and left. When used, such a saw makes a wide kerf (slot), preventing binding. Newer types omit this feature; instead, each tooth is ground on three edges. These models (some-

T

CARING FOR GARDEN TOOLS

Given proper care, well-made tools not only make gardening easier but will last for generations. All tools need cleaning after use, and any tool with an edge—be it a shovel, spade, hoe, or pruning tool—should be kept sharp. When blades eventually become dull, it's easiest to have a professional restore them; many garden supply and hardware stores can recommend a reliable sharpening service.

Cleaning tools. To remove accumulated sap and rust from pruning shears, use a little oil and steel wool; you can also buy special oil/solvent mixtures (such as CLP Shear Oil) to clean sap and dirt from pruning tools and to lubricate them. To maintain the smoothest operation, occasionally disassemble the tool and work a dab of synthetic white lithium grease onto the pivot bolt and into the area around the bolt hole.

Clean the sawdust from pruning saws after each use and remove any sap and rust with steel wool and oil. Thinly coat the blade with paraffin before using.

A metal barbecue brush (with scraper) is handy for cleaning digging tools. Use the scraper to remove layers of dirt and mud as you work in the garden. The bristles give a final cleanup before you store the tool.

Give tool heads a thorough cleaning annually. Remove rust with medium steel wool and a little oil; then use paint thinner to clean off the oily residue. Finally, apply a rust-proofing paint.

Maintaining wooden handles. Wooden handles on all types of garden tools last for many years if kept clean and oiled. Wipe them off after every use. Once a year or so, sand them lightly and apply a coat of boiled linseed oil with a cloth; if the oil soaks in completely, apply another coat. Then buff the handles.

---

times referred to as *Japanese-style saws*) cut much more rapidly and give a smoother cut. They can snap if you apply too much force or try to cut on the push stroke, and they cannot be resharpened, but most gardeners feel that their ease of use and cutting speed more than make up for any drawbacks. A 13-inch Japanese-style saw with a fixed blade is a good choice for most gardens; it easily cuts branches 1 to 5 inches in diameter. Call an arborist if you need to cut larger branches.

Pole pruning tools. Look to these when you need extra reach for cutting high branches. They typically come with both shears and a saw, which attach to a pole. To make the shears work, you pull a cord or press a lever to draw the blade through the branch; most will cut through branches ¾ to 1 inch thick. The saw is usually a standard pull-cut curved saw. The poles are available in various lengths; some are telescoping, while others fit together in sections. In either case, the pruners will be easiest to use if the poles are fairly stiff.

Hedge shears. In addition to trimming hedges, these are useful for shearing flowering shrubs and cutting back perennials. For heavy-duty pruning of dense, woody hedges, select shears with a short (7-inch) blade. One blade will often be serrated and notched; the notch helps hold the bigger twigs in place while you cut. Hedge shears with longer blades (up to 11 inches) are meant for light-duty shearing of leafy tip growth; the longer blades shear a larger area with each stroke. Be sure any hedge

shears you buy are equipped with shock absorbers, which reduce strain to the wrist.

SPRAYERS. Garden sprayers are used to apply fungicides, pesticides, herbicides, and foliar fertilizers. Many styles and sizes are available. If you don't do much spraying, a 1-quart, hand-pumped compression sprayer is a good choice; it allows you to mix small amounts of chemicals, avoiding waste. Select one with a brass spray nozzle and sturdy innards. For more extensive spraying, choose a 2-gallon-capacity hand pump model. It should have a polyethylene tank and a brass valve wand, adjustable brass nozzle, and pump. An extra-long hose allows you to leave the sprayer on the ground and move around as you spray.

Trees

Trees are the backbone of the garden, providing shade and shelter and contributing year-round beauty through their foliage, flowers, fruits, bark, and branch structure. The distinction between a tree and a large shrub is sometimes blurred, but trees typically are tall plants with one dominant trunk (though some kinds may have several trunks) topped by a crown of foliage. In contrast, most shrubs are smaller and have foliage all the way to the ground.

SELECTING TREES. Because trees are so important to the landscape and are generally

slow growing, it's worth taking the time to choose them carefully. Start by considering the points below; also consult local nursery personnel and look at the trees in your neighborhood to see which ones perform particularly well. "Garden Trees" in A Guide to Plant Selection (on pages 73–76) lists trees suitable for many situations.

Landscape function. What role should the tree play in your garden? If you need a source of shade, choose a tree with a wide canopy. Deciduous trees give you shade (and can significantly reduce air-conditioning expenses) in summer, then admit sun to warm the house after their leaves drop in fall. If you want to block views into your home or garden, choose relatively tall, dense trees. If you're looking for a specimen tree to serve as a garden focal point, search for interesting foliage or a striking display of blossoms or berries. Fruit trees have special appeal, providing delicious fruit as well as lovely form and flowers.

Climate adaptability. Be sure that any tree you consider planting is well adapted to your climate zone.

Cultural preferences. Match the needs of each tree to the conditions in your garden. Select those that will grow well in the soil you have, with the amount of water they'll receive naturally or that you can provide.

Deciduous versus evergreen. Deciduous trees start their growth with a burst of new leaves (and often flowers) in early spring, then remain in leaf through summer. In autumn, the foliage drops to reveal bare limbs, often changing color before it falls.

Evergreen trees include both broad-leafed evergreens and conifers (though there are a few deciduous conifers); both kinds serve well as screens and windbreaks. Broad-leafed evergreens have the same sort of foliage as deciduous plants, but they keep their leaves all year. Older leaves may fall intermittently throughout the year or in one season, but there's always enough foliage on the branches to give the tree a well-clothed look. Most conifers have leaves that are narrow and needlelike or tiny and scalelike; they, too, may drop some of their leaves year-round.

Growth rate and size. Trees grow at very different rates. If you need a tree to shade a south-facing window or provide privacy, select a fast-growing sort for quick results—but not one that will outgrow its site. In fact, it's important to visualize the ultimate height and spread of a tree you consider for any role: not only is an overly large one out of scale in most gardens, but it will eventually crowd structures and other plants and may ultimately have to be removed.

Root system. A tree with a network of greedy surface roots is a poor candidate for planting in a lawn or garden, as it will soon hog most of the available water and nutrients. The same tree

T

STAKING YOUNG TREES

A young tree will develop a sturdier trunk if it grows unsupported and can sway in the breeze. Stake it only if it is planted in an extremely windy location or if the main trunk is too weak to stay upright on its own. Use ties that won't bind or cut into the bark, such as wide strips of canvas or rubber; fasten each tie around the tree and both stakes in a figure-8 pattern, as shown at right. The tree should be able to move an inch in either direction.

Run your hand up the trunk, holding it firmly, to the point where the top of the tree begins to flop over. This is where you will attach the ties. Cut off the stakes an inch or so above the ties.

In a windswept site, a young tree's roots may need anchoring to keep them in firm contact with the soil; use stakes and ties only a foot above ground level for this kind of staking. In both cases, sink stakes at right angles to the prevailing wind. Remove them after a year or as soon as the tree appears to be self-supporting.

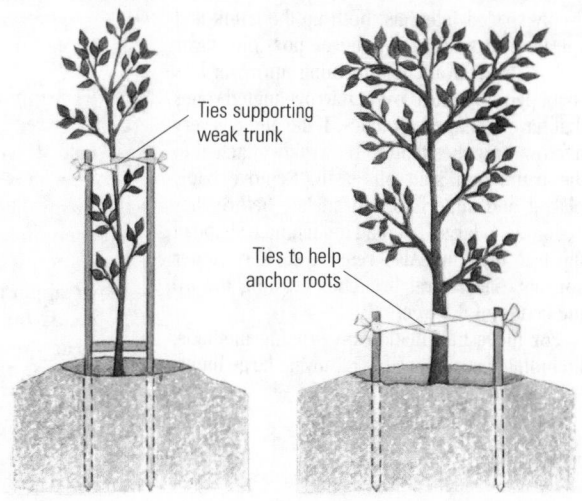

Ties supporting weak trunk

Ties to help anchor roots

may be just right, however, at the garden's fringes or along a country drive. Some trees have surface roots that can lift and crack nearby pavement, making them less-than-ideal choices for a patio, entryway, or parking strip.

Maintenance. Trees that produce a fair amount of litter from falling leaves, flowers, or fruits shouldn't be planted beside a patio, in a lawn, or near a swimming pool—you'd be spending far too much time cleaning up. Such trees are better candidates for background areas, where the litter can remain where it falls. In regions with regular high winds or heavy annual snowfall, avoid trees with weak or brittle wood: they can be hazardous to people and property, and removing broken limbs can both ruin the tree's beauty and cost you a tidy sum.

Pest and disease problems. Make sure the trees you're considering aren't overly susceptible to pests or diseases. Keep in mind that a particular tree may be trouble free in one climate but plagued with problems in another.

Longevity. Some trees can be planted for future generations to enjoy; others grow quickly but also decline quickly. Trees that are planted for screening or shade should be long lived, but for specimen planting, shorter-lived kinds may be an excellent choice. Plant the latter, however, only where removal will be relatively easy and won't compromise your overall landscape. Many attractive flowering trees, for example, run their course in about 20 years, but when they die you can fill the resulting gap with another tree of the same sort.

PLANTING AND CARING FOR TREES. Many deciduous trees are sold bare-root during the dormant season, from late fall through early spring. Deciduous trees as well as conifers and broad-leafed evergreens may also be sold balled-and-burlapped from early fall into the following spring, or in containers throughout the year. For instructions on planting all types, see pages 630–631.

The exposed trunk of a newly planted tree needs protection from drying winds, hot sun, freezing temperatures, gnawing animals (such as rabbits, deer, and rodents), and damage from lawn mowers or string trimmers. To keep a trunk free from harm, wrap it loosely in burlap or a manufactured trunk-wrapping material. Remove the wrapping after a year, when the bark has become thicker and tougher (don't leave wrapping in place longer than this, since it can eventually girdle the tree).

All trees, even drought-tolerant kinds, need regular water during the first several years after planting, until their roots have grown deep enough to carry them through dry periods. Once established, however, many kinds require only infrequent irrigation.

Regular fertilizing, too, is needed for a few years after planting. By ensuring a good supply of nitrogen for the springtime growth surge, you'll encourage young trees to get established quickly. Once a tree is well settled in, though, it may grow satisfactorily with no further feeding—and in fact, fertilizing a tree that continues to put out healthy, vigorous new growth is a waste of both time and fertilizer. Feeding may be in order, however, if a tree's new growth is weak, sparse, or unusually pale, or if it has a fair amount of dieback that cannot be ascribed to over- or underwatering.

TRAINING AND PRUNING. Most young trees benefit from some early training or pruning. The idea is to encourage the development of a sturdy trunk from which radiate strong, well-placed main limbs (scaffold branches). Conifers are an exception: they seldom need training unless they develop more than one leader (central upward-growing stem). If that occurs, remove the weaker of the two stems. Deciduous and broad-leafed evergreen trees, on the other hand, are more likely to require training, but don't rush the job. Prune newly planted trees as little as possible: just remove dead, broken, or rubbing branches and the weaker limb of a double leader (if present). Wait a full year—until the tree's roots are growing well—before doing more than this. Prune the tree gradually over the next 3 to 5 years, but don't remove too much wood in any one year.

Though you may be tempted to begin training a tree by removing lower limbs, it's best to leave these in place for the first few years, as shown below. Never remove the lower limbs of conifers such as spruce (*Picea*), fir (*Abies*), and others with a strongly pyramidal shape. They look most natural when allowed to branch all the way to the ground.

As the tree grows, encourage well-placed scaffold branches by selecting shoots at fairly

FORMING A STRONG TREE TRUNK

Young trees develop a strong trunk more quickly if their lower branches are left in place for the first few years after planting; these branches also help shade the trunk. During this time, shorten the side branches only if they become too long or vigorous, pruning during the dormant season or just before spring growth begins. Once the trunk is at least 2 inches thick, begin removing the lower branches gradually, over a period of several years.

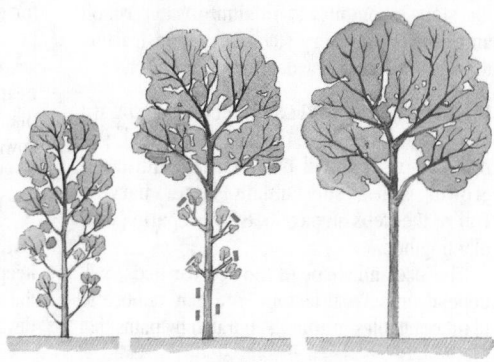

T

evenly spaced intervals, both up the trunk and spiraling around it. Whenever possible, favor wide-angled branches forming more-or-less U-shaped crotches over narrow-angled ones that have V-shaped crotches. If the angle is very narrow, branches tend to be weakly attached to the trunk and split off easily. Remove badly placed and superfluous branches before they become too large, keeping the ultimate shape of the tree in mind. Also remove suckers, water sprouts, and lateral branches growing toward the center of the tree.

For more information on pruning methods, including instructions for removing large limbs, see page 642.

Vegetable Gardening

Growing your own vegetables is rewarding and enjoyable. In return for your efforts, you'll harvest food that's fresh and bursting with flavor. To make your vegetable patch a success, plan before you plant. If you're new to vegetable gardening, start small: an area of just 100 to 130 square feet can provide a substantial harvest. As you gain experience, you may elect to expand the plot.

To decide which vegetables to plant, first list the kinds your family really enjoys. Then consider how much room each type requires. If space is limited, raise those that give a good yield for the area they occupy. Beans, tomatoes, and cabbage, for example, can overwhelm you with produce from a postage stamp–size plot. At the other extreme are melon and squash selections that grow on long vines; these, as well as corn, require a great deal of space relative to their yield.

Because vegetables grow best with at least 6 hours of full sun each day, be sure to choose a sunny planting area. To avoid both shade and root competition, locate the garden away from trees and large shrubs. It's also important to choose a spot protected from cold winds in spring and hot, dry winds in summer. Steer clear of "frost pockets"—low-lying areas that may experience frosts later in spring and earlier in fall than other parts of the garden. To make watering and other routine tasks easier, aim for a level site; if only sloping land is available, try to find a south- or southeast-facing slope to take full advantage of the sun. Lay out rows along the slope's contours to minimize water runoff and erosion. On very steep sites, constructing terraces will make gardening much easier.

PLANTING VEGETABLES. The first step toward a satisfying vegetable garden is careful soil preparation: you will be rewarded with faster growth and a substantially larger harvest. Follow the steps on page 628 for preparing your planting bed.

The size and shape of the bed (or beds) will depend on several factors. You may choose to plant vegetables in *rows,* separated by paths that give you access to the plants and let you easily till or hoe the soil. This layout works well for tall-growing plants like corn and for those that need support, such as tomatoes and pole beans. Other plants, however, grow best in *hills*—that is, grouped in a cluster (though not necessarily on a mound). This method is useful for sprawling plants such as most types of melons and winter squash. Smaller-growing vegetables, such as beets, carrots, spinach, and lettuce, can be grown efficiently in *wide beds.* In this arrangement, you prepare a bed about 3 feet wide, then broadcast the seeds over it rather than sowing them in rows. Paths on either side allow access to the plants.

If your soil is very poor or does not drain well, you may elect to grow your vegetables in raised beds (see page 628) filled with a mixture of compost and good topsoil.

You can start vegetables by planting seeds outdoors in the garden or by setting out transplants you have either started yourself or purchased from a nursery. Vegetables requiring a long growing season—peppers and tomatoes, for example—need many weeks of warm temperatures before they produce fruit and are best set out as transplants. But other types, including beans, carrots, corn, and peas, do not transplant well and grow best if started from seed sown directly in the garden. For more on sowing seeds and on starting and setting out transplants, see pages 632 and 634.

CARING FOR VEGETABLES. For the best harvest, keep your vegetables growing steadily throughout the season, trying to avoid any checks in their development. Those started from seed sown in the ground usually require thinning, so that each plant will have enough space to develop properly. Thin plants when they're a few inches tall, making sure that you space them as indicated in descriptions provided in the Plant Encyclopedia or on the seed packet.

Provide a steady supply of moisture from planting until harvest. Until they're well established, transplants will need frequent watering—enough to keep the soil moist but not soggy. Rows or beds of seeds and young seedlings likewise need steady moisture, sometimes requiring sprinkling as often as two or three times a day in hot weather. As transplants and seedlings grow and their roots reach deeper, you can water less often—but when you do, be sure to moisten the entire root zone thoroughly. To water the garden, use sprinklers, furrows, or a drip system (see "Watering Methods," page 660).

Mulching the garden is important: it conserves moisture and suppresses weed growth. An organic mulch such as straw or compost also improves soil structure as it decomposes, making the top few inches looser and more crumbly. However, because organic mulches also keep the soil cool, it's best not to apply them until warm weather arrives; don't put them down too early in spring. A mulch of plastic sheeting, on the other hand, helps warm the soil quickly—making it especially useful for growing heat-loving crops such as melons and eggplant. After preparing the soil, cover it with black plastic; then cut small holes where you want to sow seeds or set out plants.

For many vegetables, the fertilizer applied when you prepare the bed at planting time will be sufficient for the entire season. However,

WHAT'S WRONG WITH TOPPING?

Topping—reducing the height of a mature tree by sawing off its top limbs—is the fastest way to ruin a tree's appearance. It doesn't reduce height for long, either. Unlike a bushy hedge that soon sprouts new growth even after severe shearing, an older tree does not grow back in a natural-looking way when its upper limbs are pruned to stubs. Instead, it sends out scores of weak shoots from buds near the cutoff points, and these shoots are often taller, coarser, denser, and more weakly attached than the natural top was. Topping may also shorten a tree's life, both because the resultant large wounds are exposed to decay and insect attack and because the process removes much of the leafy growth needed to manufacture food for the plant.

Though some topped trees can eventually recover their form, it may take decades. A good professional arborist will not top a tree that has grown too large for its space, but instead will gradually scale it back by making thinning cuts to groups of branches in the upper part of the canopy.

heavy feeders (such as corn) and those requiring a long growing season, including tomatoes and some selections of cabbage and broccoli, may need one or two follow-up feedings. Lightly scratch dry granular fertilizer into the soil (keep it off plant foliage), then water it in thoroughly; or use a water-soluble fertilizer.

As is true for the garden as a whole, caring for a vegetable plot involves preventing pest and disease damage. You'll find information on many diseases and pests as well as advice for controlling them on pages 602–605, 616–628, and in the entries for specific vegetables in the Plant Encyclopedia. The following measures will also help keep your garden productive and healthy.

Keep the garden clean. Composting or discarding spent plants and tilling the soil (especially in fall) can help you avoid trouble, since some insects and diseases overwinter or spend certain developmental stages on plant debris.

Plant resistant selections when available. Seed packets and plant tags may bear code letters noting inbred resistance to certain serious problems. Tomatoes, for example, may be designated V, F, N, and/or T, indicating resistance to verticillium wilt, fusarium wilt, harmful nematodes (which cause root knots), and tobacco mosaic virus, respectively.

Mix different kinds of plants. Expanses of just one sort can result in large populations of pests fond of that particular plant. Mixed plantings of ornamental and edible plants encourage more kinds of insects, including beneficial species that prey on the troublemakers, so consider adding some flowers to your vegetable beds, and vice versa.

Encourage natural controls. Toads, lizards, many birds, and beneficial insects (see page 618) all prey on pests. Avoid chemical sprays, if possible—and be aware that even sprays made from natural ingredients can harm helpful creatures as well as pests, leaving the garden vulnerable to new attack.

Rotate crops from season to season. This tactic prevents the buildup of diseases and insects specific to certain kinds of vegetables in any one part of the garden.

TOMATOES TILL CHRISTMAS. *You can enjoy ripe tomatoes well after a killing frost destroys your plants. How? First, pick the healthy tomatoes (green ones too) from the vine before the first frost. Leave a piece of stem attached to each fruit. Dip each green tomato in a solution of 4 tablespoons bleach to one gallon water (this kills rot-causing fungi). Dry the fruit, then wrap it in newspaper. Place all the wrapped tomatoes in a basket—greenest ones on the bottom—and set the basket in a cool, dark, place. Check the fruit occasionally for ripeness or rot.* ❖

WARM-SEASON AND COOL-SEASON VEGETABLES

Depending on the weather they need for best growth, vegetables are classed as warm-season or cool-season. *Cool-season* crops grow best at temperatures an average of 10 to 15°F below those needed by warm-season types. Most will endure short spells of frost. Many familiar cool-season vegetables have edible leaves or roots (carrots, lettuce, radishes, and spinach, for example), while others (such as broccoli and cauliflower) are grown for their immature flowers. A few—such as peas—produce edible seeds. Success depends on bringing plants to maturity in cool weather; in hot conditions, many become bitter tasting and may bolt to seed rather than producing edible parts. Plant them in very early spring—so the crop will mature before summer heat settles in—or in the late part of summer, for a crop in fall or winter. In the Coastal and Tropical South, cool-season vegetables can be planted from late summer to early fall to provide harvests in late fall, winter, and early spring.

For planting schedules for cool-season crops by frost dates, see pages 654–657.

Warm-season vegetables require both warm soil and high temperatures (with little cooling at night) to grow steadily and produce a harvest. They include traditional summer crops such as corn, cucumbers, melons, peppers, snap beans, squash, and tomatoes. So-called winter squashes such as acorn, banana, and hubbard are warm-season crops; their name refers not to the planting season, but to the fact that they can be stored for winter consumption. For almost all of these vegetables, the fruit (rather than the leaves or roots) is the edible part. Warm-season vegetables are killed by frost, so don't plant them until after the last frost in spring unless you give them cold protection; see box at left. For planting schedules for warm-season crops by frost dates, see pages 654–657.

ROW COVERS AND OTHER SEASON EXTENDERS

Warm-season vegetables may need protection from frost when they are first planted in spring, then again as temperatures begin to dip in fall. In spring, protect individual plants by covering them temporarily with flower pots or with 2-liter clear plastic soda bottles with the bottoms cut out.

Floating row covers made of polyethylene, polyester, or polypropylene are one of the most useful tools for protecting plants from cold temperatures (and from certain insect pests and birds, as well). Sold in rolls, these fabric-type covers can be laid directly over seeded beds or plants or propped on stakes; they serve as miniature greenhouses. They are extremely lightweight, transmit 80 to 95 percent of the sunlight that strikes them, and allow both water and air to pass through. Burying the cover's edges in the soil will seal out insect pests, though any pests already on the plants may proliferate (remove covers when plants begin to bloom, to admit pollinating insects).

V

The chart that begins at right gives approximate planting times for both cool-season and warm-season vegetables, along with other information, such as the length of time from planting until the crop matures and the best way to plant (whether from seed, transplants, or a method particular to a certain plant).

There are several ways to determine when to plant. The most common is based on your region's first frost date in fall or last frost date in spring. These dates are averages and vary from year to year; you can find out the average frost dates in your area by contacting your local Cooperative Extension Office or a knowledgeable garden center. Keeping year-to-year records of specific planting dates will help you pinpoint the best dates for your garden.

The soil temperature is another indication that conditions are right for planting crops. Many plants will simply sulk if put into ground that is too cold for them—or, worse, they will rot before germination occurs. To take your soil temperature, you'll need a probe thermometer (available through garden-supply stores). To avoid breaking the thermometer, make a pilot hole at least 2 to 4 inches deep before inserting it. Take the soil temperature at midday over several days and then average out the results.

Remember that not all vegetables are suited to growing in all areas. Some, such as rhubarb, require a prolonged period of winter chill and will not grow well in the Lower, Coastal, or Tropical South. Choose carefully; selections of many vegetables have been bred to ripen early, resist bolting in hot weather, or tolerate short days. More detailed information for each vegetable, along with recommended selections, is given in the Plant Encyclopedia.

PLANTING VEGETABLES

VEGETABLE	COOL/WARM SEASON	DAYS TO MATURITY	TRANSPLANT/ SEED	SOIL TEMP. RANGE
Asparagus (p. 184)	cool	2–3 years	dormant crowns	60–85°F
Beans, lima (p. 195)	cool	65–95 days	seed	65–85°F
Beans, pole and bush (p. 195)	warm	50–70 days	seed	60–85°F
Beets (p. 196)	cool	50–80 days	seed or transplants	50–85°F
Broccoli (p. 208)	cool	50–85 days	transplants	58–68°F
Brussels sprouts (p. 210)	cool	80–100 days	transplants	58–68°F
Cabbage (p. 213)	cool	55–88 days	seed or transplants	58–68°F
Carrots (p. 228)	cool	60–70 days	seed	45–85°F
Cauliflower (p. 231)	cool	50–78 days	transplants	58–68°F
Celery (p. 233)	cool	85–130 days	seed or transplants	60–70°F
Chayote (p. 238)	warm	3–5 months	seeds or sprouted fruit	60–95°F
Chinese Cabbage (p. 241)	cool	45–80 days	seed or transplants	58–68°F
Corn (p. 260)	warm	62–95 days	seed	65–95°F
Cucumbers (p. 271)	warm	45–60 days	seed	60–95°F
Eggplant (p. 294)	warm	50–100 days	transplants	75–90°F
Garlic (p. 319)	cool	6–10 months	cloves	50–95°F
Gourd (p. 327)	warm	85–120 days	seed	70–95°F
Jerusalem artichoke (p. 339) (*Helianthus tuberosa*)	cool/warm	120–150 days	tubers	65–95°F
Jicama (p. 369)	warm	4–8 months	seed	60–95°F
Kale and Collards (p. 375)	cool	50–80 days	seed or transplants	58–68°F
Kohlrabi (p. 378)	cool	50–60 days	seed	58–68°F
Leek (p. 386)	cool	4 months	seed or transplants	55–80°F
Melons (p. 417)	warm	75–90 days	seed	75–95°F

Asparagus

Broccoli 'Green Goliath'

'Blue Lake' snap beans

Cucumber

| | FALL PLANTING
AVERAGE FIRST FROST DATE | | | | SPRING PLANTING
AVERAGE LAST FROST DATE | | |
SEP 30	OCT 30	NOV 30	DEC 20	JAN 30	FEB 28	MAR 30	APR 30 AND LATER
n/a	n/a	n/a	n/a	n/a	Jan 1–Feb 18	Feb 1–Mar 20	Mar 20–Apr 15
June 1–July 15	July 1–30	Aug 1–Sep 15	Sep 1–30	Feb 10–Apr 15	Mar 15–June 1	Apr 15–May 15	May 15–June 15
June 1–July 15	July 1–Aug 15	Aug 15–Sep 20	Sep 1–Nov 1	Feb 1–Apr 1	Mar 1–May 15	Apr 1–June 1	May 1–June 30
July 1–30	July 25–Sep 1	Aug 15–Sep 25	Sep 5–Oct 15	Jan 1–Mar 15	Feb 1–Apr 15	Mar 1–June 1	Apr 1–June 15
June 1–30	July 1–Aug 15	Aug 1–Oct 1	Sep 1–Nov 1	Jan 1–30	Feb 1–28	Mar 1–20	Apr 1–30
July 1–25	July 25–Aug 20	Aug 20–Sep 20	Sep 10–Oct 10	n/a	n/a	Mar 1–20	Apr 1–30
June 25–Aug 5	July 25–Sep 5	Aug 20–Oct 1	Sep 10–Oct 20	Dec 15–Jan 30	Jan 15–Feb 25	Feb 15–Mar 20	Mar 20–Apr 10
June 5–July 10	July 5–Aug 10	Aug 15–Oct 10	Sep 5–Nov 1	Dec 20–Mar 1	Jan 15–Mar 1	Feb 20–Apr 10	Mar 20–June 1
July 25–Aug 5	Aug 20–Sep 5	Sep 20–30	Oct–25	Jan 1–30	Feb 1–28	Mar 1–30	Mar 30–Apr 30
n/a	June 15–Aug 1	July 15–Aug 30	Aug 5–Sep 20	Jan 1–30	Feb 1–28	Mar 1–Apr 15	Mar 30–May 1
n/a	n/a	n/a	n/a	Jan 30–Feb 15	Feb 28–Mar 15	Mar 30–Apr 15	Apr 30–May 15
June 25–Aug 5	July 25–Sep 5	Aug 20–Oct 1	Sep 10–Oct 20	Dec 15–Jan 30	Jan 15–Feb 25	Feb 15–Mar 10	Mar 20–Apr 10
June 1–30	June 1–Aug 1	Aug 1–30	n/a	Feb 1–May 15	Mar 1–June 1	Mar 30–July 15	Apr 30–July 15
July 1–25	Aug 1–20	Aug 30–Sep 20	Sep 20–Oct 10	Feb 15–Mar 15	Mar 10–Apr 15	Apr 15–May 15	May 15–June 15
n/a	n/a	n/a	n/a	Feb 10–Mar 10	Mar 10–Apr 10	Apr 15–May 15	May 15–June 15
July 15–30	Aug 1–Sep 15	Oct 1–30	Oct 1–30	n/a	n/a	Feb 15–Mar 5	Mar 20–Apr 1
n/a	n/a	n/a	n/a	Feb 15–Apr 15	Mar 15–May 1	Apr 15–May 15	May 15–June 15
Aug 1–Sep 30	Aug 30–Oct 30	Sep 30–Nov 30	Nov 20–Dec 20	Jan 1–30	Feb 1–28	Feb 10–Mar 30	Mar 20–Apr 20
n/a	n/a	n/a	n/a	Feb 15–Apr 15	Mar 1–May 1	Mar 30–May 30	May 1–May 15
July 10–Aug 20	Aug 5–Sep 15	Sep 1–Oct 15	Sep 25–Nov 5	Dec 15–Jan 30	Jan 15–Feb 25	Feb 15–Mar 10	Mar 15–Apr 10
July 1–30	Aug 1–30	Oct 1–Nov 1	Nov 1–Dec 10	Jan 1–30	Feb 1–20	Mar 1–30	Mar 30–May 10
n/a	Sep 1–15	Oct 1–15	Oct 25–Nov 5	Jan 1–Feb 1	Jan 15–Feb 15	Feb 15–Mar 15	Apr 1–May 1
n/a	n/a	July 1–Aug 30	Aug 1–30	Feb 10–Mar 15	Mar 10–Apr 10	Apr 15–May 15	May 15–June 15

Eggplant

'Green Arrow' peas

'Yellow Banana' sweet pepper

Pink new potatoes

Red and white radishes

Romaine lettuce

V

PLANTING VEGETABLES (CONTINUED)

VEGETABLE	COOL/WARM SEASON	DAYS TO MATURITY	TRANSPLANT/ SEED	SOIL TEMP. RANGE
Okra (p. 434)	warm	48–60 days	seed	75–95°F
Onion (p. 435)	cool	30–60 days	sets, seeds, or transplants	50–95°F
Parsnip (p. 448)	cool	100–130 days	seed	50–70°F
Peas, English (p. 451)	cool	50–70 days	seed	40–75°F
Peppers (p. 462)	warm	65–78 days	transplants	65–95°F
Potatoes (p. 489)	cool	75–100 days	"seed" potatoes	55–90°F
Pumpkins (p. 497)	warm	90–120 days	seed	70–90°F
Radishes (p. 503)	cool	22–60 days	seed	45–90°F
Rhubarb (p. 514)	cool/warm	2nd year	crowns	45–75°F
Southern Peas (p. 550)	warm	60–90 days	seed	70–90°F
Spinach (p. 551)	cool	38–60 days	seeds	45–75°F
Squash, summer (p. 553)	warm	48–60 days	seed	70–95°F
Squash, winter (p. 553)	warm	70–120 days	seed	70–95°F
Sweet potatoes (p. 561)	warm	90–120 days	slips	70–90°F
Tomatillos (p. 573)	warm	90 days	seed	70–95°F
Tomatoes (p. 573)	warm	60–95 days	seed or transplants	70–95°F
Turnip and Rutabaga (p. 580)	cool	40–120 days	seeds	60–105°F
Watermelon (p. 589)	warm	70–95 days	seeds or transplants	70–95°F

Missouri Botanical Garden

Vines

Versatile additions to almost any landscape, vines can be used to frame entryways, decorate bare walls and fences, and cover arbors with foliage and flowers. Defined in the most basic terms, a vine is simply a flexible shrub that doesn't stop extending its growth—it just keeps getting taller or longer, depending on whether you train it vertically or horizontally. If unsupported, it won't climb at all; it will sprawl across the ground (some vines are grown in this manner for use as ground covers).

SELECTING VINES. Like trees and shrubs, vines vary widely. They may be deciduous, semievergreen, or evergreen. Some provide greenery alone; others bear decorative fruits or blossoms.

Ultimate size and weight vary, too: some vines are lightweight enough to adorn a flimsy trellis without damaging it, but others eventually become weighty enough to pull down all but the sturdiest supports. As noted below, the vine's method of attachment will also determine the kind of support needed.

Once you have a good idea of what you're looking for—an evergreen flowering vine for a delicate trellis, say—narrow the list to just those plants suited to your climate zone. For ideas, see "Vines" in A Guide to Plant Selection, on pages 79–80.

METHODS OF ATTACHMENT. Some vines twine around their supports with stems, others with tendrils; some cling with special growths such as suction disks, while others need to be tied to their support to climb along it.

Twining vines. New growth twists or spirals as it elongates, coiling around a support or even around growth on the same or nearby plants. Nearly all twiners make too tight a spiral to encircle a post; support them with cord or wire.

Vines with tendrils. Specialized growths along stems or at leaf tips reach out and wrap around anything within reach—a wire, another stem of the same vine, an adjoining plant. The tendrils grow out straight until they make contact, then contract into a spiral; supply narrow supports that they can easily grasp.

Clinging vines. Special growths along the stems of these vines attach to flat surfaces. Some clingers have tendrils equipped at their tips with suction disks that grip the support; others have "claws" that hook into small irregularities or

FALL PLANTING AVERAGE FIRST FROST DATE					SPRING PLANTING AVERAGE LAST FROST DATE		
SEP 30	OCT 30	NOV 30	DEC 20	JAN 30	FEB 28	MAR 30	APR 30 AND LATER
n/a	n/a	n/a	n/a	Feb 5–Apr 1	Mar 5–June 1	Apr 10–July 15	May 1–30
n/a	Sep 1–15	Oct 1–15	Oct 25–Nov 5	Jan 1–15	Jan 1–30	Mar 1–15	Apr 1–30
June 1–July 1	June 1–July 15	Aug 1–Sep 15	Aug 15–Sept 30	n/a	n/a	n/a	n/a
July 10–25	Aug 1–15	Sep 5–20	Sep 25–Oct 10	Dec 5–Feb 15	Jan 1–Feb 28	Feb 5–Mar 20	Mar 5–May 1
n/a	n/a	July 15–Aug 30	Aug 1–30	Feb 10–Mar 15	Mar 10–Apr 10	Apr 15–May 15	May 15–June 15
n/a	n/a	Aug 1–Sep 5	Aug 20–Sep 25	Jan 1–Feb 15	Jan 15–Mar 1	Feb 20–Mar 20	Mar 20–May10
n/a	July 1–30	Aug 1–30	Aug 20–Sep 20	Feb 15–Mar 15	Mar 10–July 1	Apr 15–May 15	May 15–25
July 21–Sep 5	Aug 20–Oct 1	Sep 20–Nov 1	Oct 10–Nov 20	Dec 20–Feb 28	Jan 15–Mar 25	Feb 20–Apr 30	Mar 20–May 30
Sep 25–Oct 30	Oct 25–Nov 30	Nov 1–30	Nov 1–30	n/a	n/a	Mar 1–15	Apr 1–15
June 1–15	July 1–20	July 1–Aug 10	July 1–Sep 30	Feb 15–May 1	Mar 10–June 20	Apr 15–July 1	May 10–June 1
Sep 1–30	Oct 1–30	Nov 1–30	Dec 1–20	Nov 30–Jan 20	Dec 30–Feb 20	Jan 30–Mar 20	Feb 28–Apr 20
June 25–July 20	July 25–Aug 15	Aug 20–Sep 10	Sep 10–30	Feb 1–Apr 15	Mar 1– May 15	Apr 1–June 1	May 1–30
n/a	July 1–30	Aug 1–30	Sep 10–30	Feb 15–Mar 30	Mar 10–July 1	Apr 1–May 15	May 1–25
n/a	n/a	n/a	n/a	Feb 20–May 15	Mar 20–June 15	Apr 25–June 1	May 20–June 10
June 5–25	July 1–30	Aug 1–20	Aug 20–Sep 10	Feb 1–Apr 1	Mar 1–May 1	Apr 1–June 1	May 1–June 15
June 5–25	July 1–30	Aug 1–20	Aug 20–Sep 10	Feb 1–Apr 1	Mar 1–May 1	Apr 1–June 1	May 1–June 15
June 25–Aug 20	July 25–Sep20	Aug 20–Oct 15	Sep 10–Nov 5	Jan 1–Feb 15	Feb 1–Mar 10	Mar 1–Apr 10	Mar 15–Apr 10
June 1–15	July 1–Aug 1	Aug 1–Sep 1	Sep 1–Oct 1	Feb 10–Mar 15	Mar 10–Apr 10	Apr 15–May 15	May 15–Jun 15

VINE ATTACHMENTS

Twining stems   Tendrils   Suction (holdfast) disks   Aerial rootlets   Scrambles; no means of attachment

V

crevices of a flat surface. Another type of clinger has aerial rootlets along its stems that tenaciously grip all but absolutely smooth, slick surfaces. Bear in mind that all of these clinging devices—known collectively as holdfasts—can damage brick, wood, concrete, and other building materials.

Vines that require tying. Some vines have no means of attachment. They simply thread their way through and over other plants, depending on this living support to hold their stems in place. A few (climbing roses, for example) have thorns on their stems; these help secure the stems in place as they scramble but offer no permanent support. In the garden, these sorts of plants must be tied to their supports.

PLANTING AND CARING FOR VINES. Most vines are sold in containers; a few deciduous kinds (roses and grapes, for example) are available bare-root. See pages 630 and 631 for container and bare-root planting guidelines.

Many vines grow well in ordinary soil with an annual feeding in spring; likewise, many require only average amounts of water. To look their best, almost all require yearly pruning. Check the Plant Encyclopedia for comments on the specific needs of each vine.

Water Conservation

In an average year, most of the South receives plenty of rain. In fact, the Southeast is the rainiest region in the continental U.S., with a number of cities recording more than 50 inches a year (Mobile, Alabama, heads the list with 64 inches). With water, water everywhere, why do we need to conserve? For one thing, you never know when a severe drought will occur or how long it will last. A second—and more important—reason is that the South's population is exploding. And that means more houses, more lawns, more sprinkler systems, and an ever-increasing strain on existing water resources. There's no question that in the future, wise management of water will be critical to your garden. Here are some ways to meet the challenge.

LOCATE PLANTS WISELY. If you mix plants that require little or no irrigation with those that require regular moisture, you'll be wasting water on the undemanding plants (and may even harm them). To avoid this situation, organize your garden into *hydrozones*—groups of plants with similar water needs. This simplifies irrigation while giving each plant the right amount of moisture. High-water-use plants are typically located nearest the house, while those needing less water are planted progressively farther away. This frees you from dragging hoses to the far reaches of the garden or extending an irrigation system farther than necessary. (For a list of drought-tolerant plants, see "Plants that Tolerate Drought" in A Guide to Plant Selection, on pages 130–134.)

CONSERVING WATER ON SLOPES

Plants on slopes are often challenging to irrigate, since water can run downhill faster than it can seep into the root zone. To prevent wasteful runoff, make basins or terracing to channel water directly to plant roots, as shown below.

Individual basin. Make a wide basin. Build up on the low side to increase water-holding capacity.

Terracing. Headers help control runoff. Because surface reservoir is small, water must be applied slowly.

RECONSIDER YOUR LAWN. Most conventional lawn grasses use water at a rate disproportionate to other plants, largely because they have a shallow root system that dries out quickly (especially in sandy soil). Consider reducing the size of your lawn or choosing a lawn alternative such as a ground cover, permeable paved surface (unmortared brick or stone), wooden deck, or simple mulch. If you feel that a lawn is a necessary component of your garden, select a grass requiring less water than the more familiar types; see page 611 for less-thirsty turf types adapted to your climate.

MULCH YOUR PLANTINGS. An organic mulch spread several inches thick over planting beds acts as an insulating blanket, slowing evaporation from the soil and keeping it cooler than it would be if unprotected. Black plastic sheeting, sold in rolls, conserves moisture and suppresses weeds. You can also buy rolls of various plastic materials, known collectively as landscape fabrics. For more information on all these mulches, see page 613.

ELIMINATE RUNOFF. Don't waste water by irrigating paved surfaces. If your sprinkler system showers water over a sidewalk, patio, or driveway, replace the heads with models that deliver water only where it is needed; or, if necessary, redesign the system.

Sloping land and heavy clay soils invite runoff—due to gravity in the first case, slow water penetration in the second. To avoid runoff in such sites, adjust the rate at which water is applied. If you use sprinklers, you can improve penetration by watering in successive short intervals, giving the water time to soak in between each spell of sprinkling. On slopes, terraces and basins can also help prevent runoff (see illustrations above), as can ground cover plantings.

USE LOW-VOLUME WATERING DEVICES. Soaker hoses are effective and easy to install. Drip irrigation (see page 661) offers an excellent way to reduce water use. You can also upgrade an existing underground sprinkler system: install low-volume sprinkler heads or convert the system to a drip setup, using the parts and kits available at hardware stores.

USE TIMERS. With the simplest timers, you set the dial for the length of time you want the water to run; then you turn on the water. The timer turns off the faucet for you.

More sophisticated timers operate on batteries or household current. You set them to a schedule; they turn the water on and off as programmed. Such timers ensure that your garden will be watered whether you're at home or away. What's more, you can select a schedule that will give your plants the precise amount of water they need to thrive.

The flaw of automatic controllers is that they follow your schedule regardless of weather: they'll turn on the water during a deluge or apply amounts of water appropriate for hot summer temperatures on a cool fall day. To solve this problem, reset the controller so that it takes seasonal rainfall and weather conditions into account. Or use electronic attachments that function as weather sensors. By linking a soil moisture sensor to the controller, for example, you can trigger the sprinklers to switch on only when the sensor indicates that soil moisture has dropped to the point where water is needed. Another useful attachment is a rain shutoff device; it accumulates rainwater in a special collector pan, turning off the controller when the pan is filled to a prescribed depth and triggering it to resume watering when the collected water has evaporated. Before installing either of these sensors, be sure that they are compatible with the automatic controller.

Watering

Plants, like animals, need water to live. A seed must absorb water before it can germinate. Roots can take up nutrients only when water is present in the soil, and water transports nutrients throughout plants. Water is also essential for photosynthesis.

WATERING GUIDELINES. A number of interrelated factors—including soil texture, the particular plants and their ages and root depths, and the weather—determine how much water your plants need and how often they need it.

A soil's ability to absorb and retain water is closely related to its composition. Clay soils absorb water slowly and drain slowly too, retaining water longer than other soils. Sandy soils, in contrast, absorb water quickly and drain just as rapidly. Loamy soils absorb water fairly quickly and drain well, but not too fast. Absorption patterns vary too: though water moves primarily downward, it also moves laterally to some extent. Lateral movement is greatest in clay soils; in sandy ones, most water seeps straight down and there is little horizontal movement.

To improve absorption and drainage in clay and to make sandy soils more moisture retentive, work in organic amendments. (For more on soil texture and organic amendments, see pages 644–647.)

Once their roots are established, different plants have widely differing water needs. Those native to semiarid and arid climates, called *xerophytes,* have evolved features that allow them to survive with little water and low relative humidity. They may have deep root systems, for example, or water-retaining leaves that are small, hairy, or waxy. Many familiar garden plants, however, are adapted to moist soil and high relative humidity. Called *mesophytes,* they

COMPARATIVE ROOT DEPTHS

Lawn grasses | Annuals and other nonwoody plants | Small and medium-size shrubs | Trees and large shrubs

6 in.
12 in.
18 in.
24 in.

The rooting depths illustrated here will help you determine the amount of water needed to supply moisture to your plants' root zones. Even in the case of large trees, most of the feeder roots are within the top 2 feet of soil, though taproots (which serve to anchor the tree) may penetrate farther. It's also important to note that the feeder roots of trees and shrubs extend well beyond the plant's leafy top or canopy; be sure to apply water to all of the root area.

SOIL TEXTURE AND WATER PENETRATION

Applied to sand (left), 1 inch of water penetrates about 12 inches. Applied to loam (center), 1 inch of water reaches about 7 inches. Applied to clay (right), 1 inch of water soaks only 4 to 5 inches.

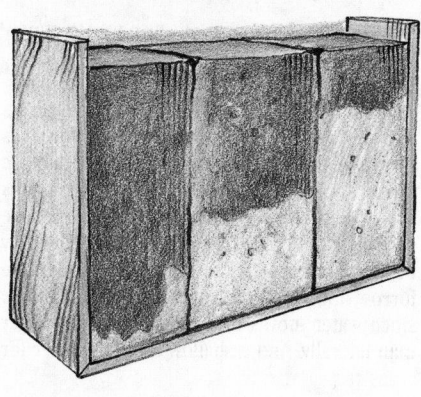

usually have broad, thin leaves that lose moisture readily.

Keep in mind that *all* young plants, including xerophytes, need more frequent watering than mature ones until their root systems become well established. And many annuals and vegetables require regular moisture throughout the growing season if they are to bloom well or produce a good crop.

The depth of a plant's root zone also influences watering practices; typical root depths of trees, shrubs, and other plants are shown above. Applying enough water to moisten the entire root zone encourages roots to grow throughout that area, whereas shallow watering keeps them near the soil surface. Deeper roots have access to more moisture, thus letting the plant go longer between waterings. They're also less subject to stress from heat and drying winds than shallow roots are.

Root hairs of underwatered plants will dry out and die, causing the plant to slow its growth, wilt, and eventually die. But you don't want to overdo it, either. It's important to learn how often you must water to keep the root zone moist. Watering below the root zone is wasteful, since the water is not used—and beyond that, keeping the soil too moist can cause as many problems as letting it get too dry. Roots need air as well as water, and they absorb both from the pore spaces between soil particles. When water penetrates the soil, it displaces the air in the pores; then, as it drains away, evaporates, and is taken up by roots, the pore spaces fill with air again. If water is applied too often, the pore spaces never have a chance to drain. They remain filled with water, cutting off the roots' air supply. This lack of oxygen makes roots susceptible to various water-mold fungi, which in turn can lead to rot.

To check how far water penetrates your soil, water for a set amount of time (say, 30 minutes). Wait for 24 hours, then use a soil sampling tube (shown below) or dig a hole to check for moisture. Sampling tubes are especially useful in lawns or around established trees and shrubs; they let you test moisture at deeper levels without digging a hole that might disturb roots. A metal rod or a long screwdriver pushed into the ground can also serve as a soil probe. It will move easily through moist soil but slow down or stop when it reaches dry soil, allowing you to estimate how deeply the moist area extends. You'll soon learn to judge how long to water each plant or group of plants to soak the root zone thoroughly.

USING A SOIL SAMPLING TUBE

This device allows you to check soil moisture at deeper levels than you can reach with a trowel, without disturbing plant roots too much. Push the tube into the ground, pull it out, and examine the soil in the sample. If it is dry or only slightly moist, it's time to water. If the top layer is damp and the rest is dry, you need to water for a longer time to ensure deeper penetration. A soil sampling tube is also useful for detecting compacted layers of soil, checking depth of root penetration, and taking samples for soil tests.

W

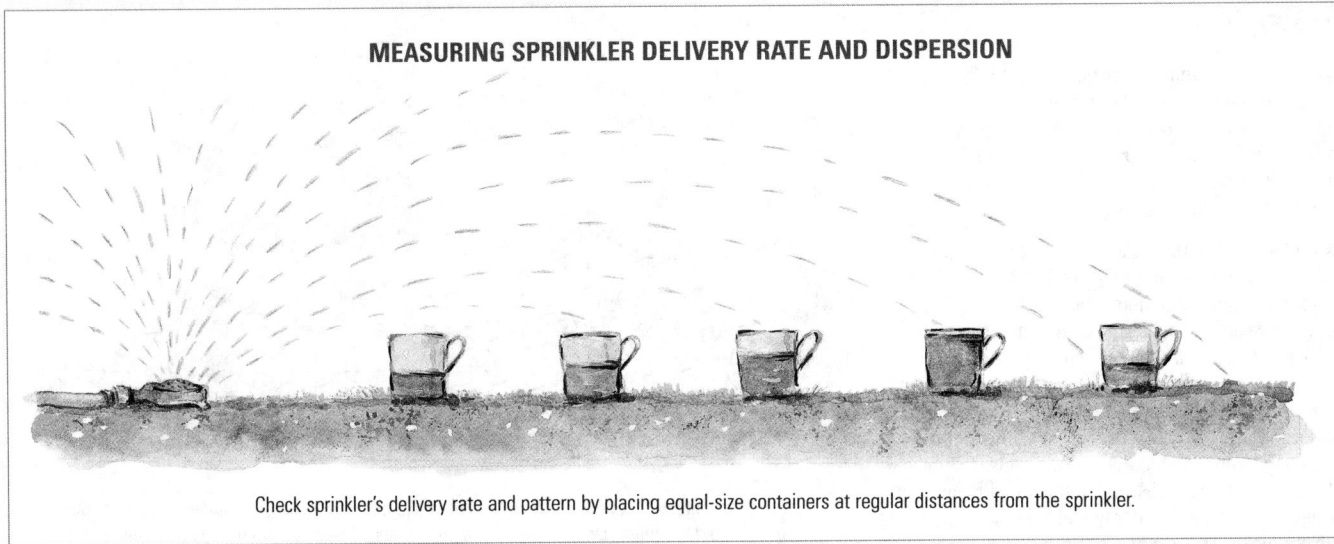

MEASURING SPRINKLER DELIVERY RATE AND DISPERSION

Check sprinkler's delivery rate and pattern by placing equal-size containers at regular distances from the sprinkler.

Weather affects water needs as well. When it's hot, dry, and windy, plants use water quickly, and young or shallow-rooted ones sometimes cannot absorb it fast enough to keep foliage from wilting. Such plants need frequent watering to keep moisture around their roots. During cool, damp weather, on the other hand, plants require much less water.

Because the factors just discussed—soil texture, plant characteristics and age, and weather—are variable, following a fixed watering schedule year-round (or even all summer) isn't the most efficient way to meet your plants' needs. Before you water, always test the soil for moisture content (see page 659) and examine plants for signs of wilting.

WATERING METHODS. Methods for applying water range from simple handheld sprayers to hose-end sprinklers to more complex underground rigid-pipe systems and drip systems. The method or methods appropriate for your garden depend on how often you need to water, the size of your garden, and how much equipment you want to buy.

Hand watering. Watering with a handheld nozzle may be a relaxing pastime, but it's usually inadequate for plants; it takes too long to truly soak the soil. Hand watering is, however, useful for new transplants, seedlings, and container plants, since you can apply the water gently and put it exactly where it's needed.

Sprinklers. Water can be applied through sprinklers attached to the end of a hose or via an in-ground sprinkler system. In either case, the sprinklers apply a high volume of water over a large surface. Many plants, particularly those that like a cool, humid atmosphere, thrive with overhead sprinkling. This method also rinses dust from foliage and discourages certain pests (especially spider mites). But sprinkling has some negative aspects as well. It can be wasteful: wind may carry off some water

before it even reaches the ground, and water that falls on or runs off onto pavement is lost too. In humid climates, sprinkling encourages foliage diseases such as black spot and powdery mildew—though you can minimize this risk by sprinkling early in the morning, so that leaves dry as the day warms. Another potential drawback is that plants with weak stems and/or heavy flowers may collapse under a heavy load of water.

The wide assortment of portable, hose-end sprinklers includes stationary models that resemble salt shakers or rings; oscillating, rotating, and impulse sprinklers; and "walking" types that slowly roll through the area to be watered. When selecting a sprinkler, look for one with a coverage pattern that most closely matches the area to be irrigated; the shape and size of the space the sprinkler covers should be listed on the package.

Permanent underground sprinkler systems—fixtures in many suburban neighborhoods—offer some advantages over hose-end watering. They free you from moving hoses and sprinklers and can be automated to operate even if you're away from home for an extended period. And recent refinements in the design of the sprinklers have improved such systems' efficiency: the newer sprinklers produce less runoff and overspray onto buildings, walkways, and fences and distribute water more evenly. For such a system to work properly, though, it must be well designed; consult with a licensed landscape contractor or a company specializing in irrigation systems. And if your water bills are already high, consider this—the more convenient watering becomes, the more water you may end up applying.

Sprinkler application rates. To sprinkle effectively with a portable or an underground system, you need to know how fast water penetrates your soil and the delivery rate of your sprinklers. As the illustration on page 659 shows, 1 inch of water (from sprinkling or rain-

fall) moistens about 12 inches in sandy soil, 7 inches in loam, and 4 to 5 inches in clay. Thus, if you want to water to a depth of 12 inches, you'll need to apply about an inch of water to sandy soil, 2½ to 3 inches to clay soil.

To determine delivery rate, place a number of equal-size containers (straight-sided coffee cups, for example) at regular intervals outward from the sprinkler, as shown above. (If you are testing an underground system, place the containers among the sprinkler heads.) Then turn on the water and note how long it takes to fill a container with an inch of water. This test will also show you the delivery pattern. If the containers fill unevenly, move portable sprinklers to achieve more even coverage, or check the sprinkler heads of underground systems to see if they need adjusting or replacing.

Root irrigators. These devices—which resemble giant hypodermic needles—are useful for getting water to root zones of trees growing near sidewalks, patios, or other areas with a minimum of open soil. They also help get water deep into the soil on sloping land, where deep penetration without runoff can be hard to achieve. Attach the tool to the end of a garden hose; then insert it into the ground as you turn the water on. Water travels down a hollow probe and shoots out of holes at the tip. Some models also supply fertilizer as they water.

Soaking. Soaking is an effective way to supply sufficient water to the roots of plants.

For vegetables or flowers growing in rows, you can build adjoining basins for large plants like squash or make furrows between rows (as shown on the facing page). To minimize damage to roots, construct the furrows when the plants are young, before their root systems have spread. Broad, shallow furrows are generally better than deep, narrow ones: the wider the furrow, the wider the root area you can soak, since water moves primarily downward rather than laterally. And a shallow furrow is safer for plants—nearby roots are less likely to be disturbed when you scoop out the furrow.

Soil soaker hoses. Soaker hoses, the forerunners of drip irrigation systems, are still useful for slow, steady delivery of water. They are long tubes made of perforated or porous plastic or rubber, with hose fittings at one or both ends. When you attach a soaker to a regular hose and turn on the water supply, water seeps or sprinkles from the soaker along its entire length. You can also water wide beds by snaking soakers back and forth around the plants; trees and shrubs can be watered with a soaker coiled over the outermost edges of the root zone. You'll probably need to leave soakers on longer than you would sprinklers; to determine timing, check water penetration with a trowel or soil sampling tube.

Drip irrigation. The term "drip irrigation" describes the application of water by drip emitters and microsprays. Both devices operate at low pressure, and both deliver a low volume of water compared to standard sprinklers. Because the water is applied slowly on or near the ground, there should be no waste from runoff and little or no loss to evaporation. You position the emitters to deliver water just where plants need it; you control penetration by varying the time the system runs and/or the emitters' delivery capacity (rated in gallons per hour—or gph). You can also regulate the volume of water delivered to each plant by varying the type and number of emitters you set up for each.

In addition to water conservation, drip systems offer the advantage of flexibility. You can tailor them to water individual plants by provid-

WATERING IN FURROWS AND BASINS

Furrows 3 to 6 inches deep help irrigate straight rows on level ground. Bubbler on hose end softens flow of water. Note that furrows don't work well in very sandy soils, since in sand—even more so than in other soils—water moves primarily downward and has little horizontal movement.

Basins with sides 3 inches high hold water around large plants such as tomatoes and peppers. On level ground, you can link basins as shown to make watering easier.

ing each with its own emitter(s), or distribute water over larger areas with microsprays. A standard layout might include hookups to two or more valves and several kinds of parts. Because the lines are aboveground (they are easily concealed with mulch) and are made of flexible plastic, modifying the system is simple: just add or subtract lines or emitters as needed.

A drip system can be attached to a hose end or provided with fittings to allow it to be screwed into a hose bibb. Or you can connect it permanently to your main water source. Like underground irrigation systems, drip systems should be equipped with a backflow preventer. In addition, a filter is necessary (even when

you're using municipal supplies of clean water) to keep the small openings on drip emitters and microsprays from becoming clogged. A pressure regulator is also needed—drip systems are designed to run best at a much lower pressure than is found in most household water supplies. The regulator protects the fittings from blowing apart under excess force and allows the watering devices to work properly.

Emitters for drip systems. Emitters vary in shape, size, and internal mechanism, but all operate on the principle of dispensing water slowly; flow rates of most range from ½ to 2 gallons per hour (gph). Insert the emitters directly into ½- or ⅜-inch drip irrigation

DRIP IRRIGATION COMPONENTS

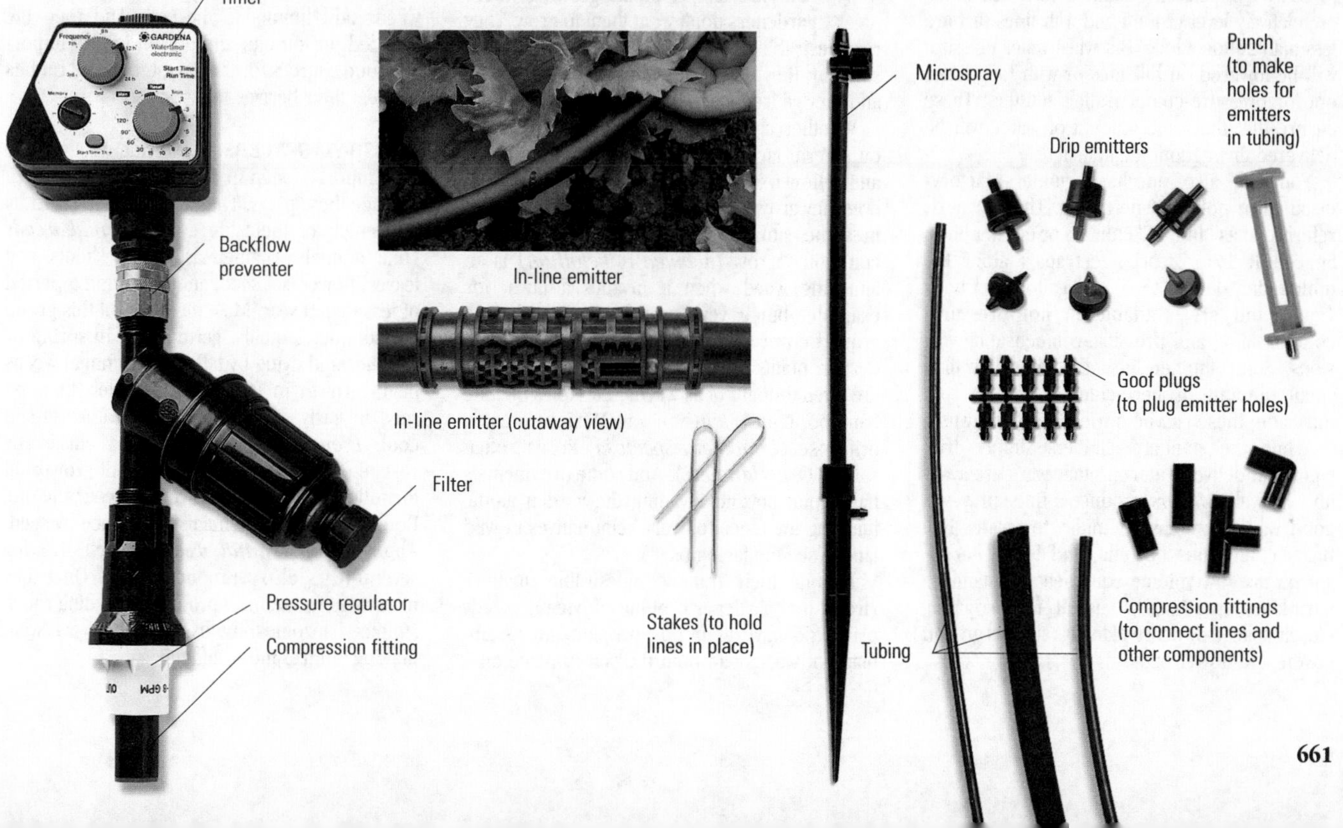

Timer

Backflow preventer

Filter

Pressure regulator

Compression fitting

In-line emitter

In-line emitter (cutaway view)

Stakes (to hold lines in place)

Microspray

Tubing

Drip emitters

Goof plugs (to plug emitter holes)

Compression fittings (to connect lines and other components)

Punch (to make holes for emitters in tubing)

W

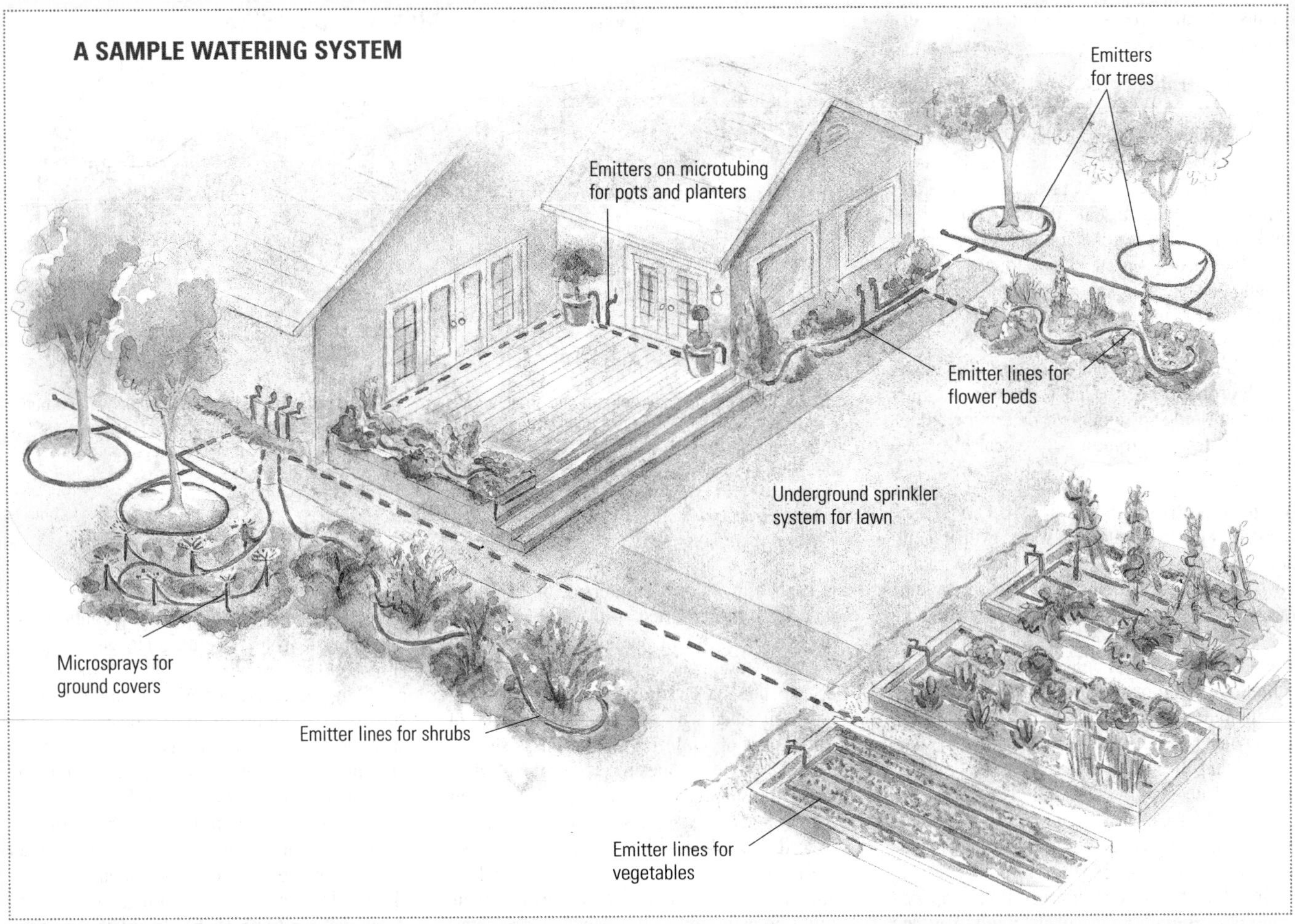

A SAMPLE WATERING SYSTEM

Emitters for trees

Emitters on microtubing for pots and planters

Emitter lines for flower beds

Underground sprinkler system for lawn

Microsprays for ground covers

Emitter lines for shrubs

Emitter lines for vegetables

tubing or thinner microtubing positioned to run from the larger tubing to each plant. Non-pressure-compensating emitters work well on flat or relatively level ground and with lines that are less than 200 feet long. But when water pressure will be lowered on hillsides or with long lines, opt for pressure-compensating emitters. These ensure that the same amount of water will be delivered throughout the system.

You can also purchase emitters factory-installed in polyethylene tubing. These may be referred to as "in-line" emitters or emitter lines. Spaced 1, 1½, 2, or 3 feet apart along the tubing, they deliver ½, 1, or 2 gallons per hour (gph) and are available in non-pressure-compensating and pressure-compensating versions. Some emitter lines are infused with a small amount of herbicide to prevent root intrusion; these can be buried to water lawns.

While the standard emitters simply drip, types that deliver water in other ways are available as well. *Misters* produce a fine spray—a good way to increase humidity for plants like fuchsia, tuberous begonia, and ferns. *Microsprays* are low-volume equivalents of standard sprinklers, particularly useful for irrigating closely spaced or dense plantings such as ground covers and flower beds.

Weeds

Weeds are simply plants growing where gardeners don't want them to grow. They rob desirable plants of water, nutrients, and sunlight; they may harbor insects and diseases, and they're frequently unattractive.

Whether a plant is labeled a weed depends on several factors. Some plants, like bindweed and yellow oxalis, are regarded as weeds wherever they grow. Others may be considered weeds in some situations, garden plants in others: common yarrow *(Achillea millefolium)* is an annoying weed when it invades a lawn, for example, but a very useful ornamental as a ground cover in a hot, dry part of the garden. Certain plants spread so aggressively that they are often thought of as weeds; examples include bamboo, mint *(Mentha),* and Mexican evening primrose *(Oenothera speciosa* 'Rosea', often sold as *O. berlandieri).* And some ornamentals have gone beyond invading the garden alone, jumping the fence to overwhelm natives in wild lands (see the facing page).

Despite their frankly undesirable qualities (from the gardener's point of view), weedy plants do have their positive side. An assemblage of weeds can hold the soil in place on a steep bank, preventing erosion. Some weeds provide nectar and shelter for beneficial insects and butterflies. When they die and decompose, weeds add humus to the soil. And even the dreaded poison oak and poison ivy are important food sources for the deer, birds, and rabbits who eat their berries.

CLASSIFYING WEEDS. Identifying weeds is the first important step in choosing the best way to manage these pests. They are often classified by the length of their life cycle. *Annual weeds* (like annual ornamentals) grow shoots and leaves, flower, set seed, and die within a period of less than a year. Most members of this group are summer annuals, germinating in spring or summer and dying by fall. Winter annual weeds begin growth in fall or early winter, then set seed in early spring while the weather is still cool. *Biennial weeds* produce a cluster or rosette of leaves in their first year of growth; in the following year, they flower, set seed, and die. Both annuals and biennials reproduce by seed. Almost all *perennial weeds,* which live for several years, also reproduce by seed. Once they mature, however, most produce spreading roots, stolons, rhizomes, bulbs, or tubers as well, making control more difficult.

You'll find descriptions of some of the most common Southern weeds in each of these groups on pages 664–668, along with suggestions for controlling them. You can also consult your Cooperative Extension Office or the *Southern Living Garden Problem Solver* for advice on identifying and controlling troublesome weeds in your area.

MANAGEMENT OPTIONS. As is true of other kinds of pests, it is rarely possible to eradicate weeds entirely. You can, however, substantially reduce infestations and prevent further problems through physical controls—employing methods that range from hand pulling through mowing, flaming, and mulching—as well as soil solarization (see page 664). If these measures are unsuccessful, chemical management may be needed.

Physical controls. When you're confronted with a weed problem, turn to these methods first.

Hand pulling or hoeing is your first line of defense against most weeds. If you're diligent for several consecutive years about pulling or hoeing out annual and biennial weeds before they set seed, their numbers will decline significantly. These methods will also help control perennial weeds, as long as you catch the plants while they're young. Once perennials have passed the seedling stage, though, it's usually necessary to dig out their roots; if you just pull up or cut off the tops, the pests can resprout from fragments left behind. Even with assiduous digging, you'll probably need to repeat the process several times to manage perennial weeds. Some useful tools for weeding are discussed on page 649.

Don't leave pulled or hoed-out weeds on bare ground, since they may take root again.

Leafy annual or biennial types that do not yet have flowers or seeds can safely be relegated to the compost pile, as can the top growth of perennial weeds (before seeding). But roots of perennials (dandelions and quack grass, for example) should be tossed in the trash rather than composted—as should any weeds that have set seed.

Rototilling or disking will do the job on annual and biennial weeds in larger areas, such as orchards, vacant lots, roadsides, and plots intended for future gardens. These methods not only knock down weeds but also incorporate them into the soil, where they eventually decay to form humus. However, perennial weeds usually sprout again from the roots or crowns—and some kinds even grow more abundantly after tilling.

Using rotary mowers or string trimmers is another good choice for seasonal weed control in larger areas. Both tools cut the weeds: string trimmers leave the severed tops behind, while mowers grind them up as they cut them. These methods are also effective for reducing weeds in fire-prone areas.

Smothering effectively kills weeds in areas earmarked for future planting. After mowing or cutting off the top growth, put down a layer of heavy cardboard, newspapers (in a layer at least three dozen sheets thick), or black plastic. Overlap these materials so weeds can't grow through the cracks. Anchor the covering with a layer of bark chips or other organic mulch. Leave these smothering materials in place for at least a full growing season; allow a year or more for tough or perennial weeds.

Flaming offers another way to knock down weeds. Powered by propane or a mixture of propane and butane, flamers are not meant to

burn weeds; instead, they heat them to the point at which their cell walls burst. Though this damage is drastic enough to kill many young weeds, types with deep perennial roots usually regrow; destroying these requires several treatments. Take care when using flamers around mulches, wooden fences, or wood-bordered raised beds, and never use them in dry, fire-prone areas.

Presprouting is a useful technique for preparing planting areas for vegetables, perennial beds, or new lawns in parts of the garden plagued by weeds. Add needed amendments, till the soil, water, and then wait a week or two for weed seeds to germinate. When they're only a few inches high, scrape them away. Then sow or transplant your vegetables, flowers, or lawn, disturbing the soil as little as possible to avoid bringing more weed seeds to the surface.

Soil solarization (see page 664) controls many kinds of weed seeds as well as harmful fungi, bacteria, and some nematodes.

Once you've destroyed weeds in a garden area, take steps to prevent their reappearance. Mulching bare soil is an effective deterrent to weed growth; see page 613 for information on choosing and using mulches, including landscape fabrics. Ground covers, sometimes called living mulches, are effective in preventing weed growth: like organic and inorganic mulches, they keep sunlight from reaching weeds and their seeds. You'll usually have to do some hand weeding or apply a mulch for the first few seasons after you plant a ground cover, but as it grows and spreads to form a tight carpet, weed growth is much reduced. For more on ground covers, see page 609.

Chemical controls. Synthetic herbicides are not recommended for food gardens. In home ornamental gardens, use them only when all

WHO LET 'EM IN?

The vast majority of plants brought to the South from other parts of the world have been good guests. What would the South look like without azalea, camellia, crepe myrtle, gardenia, hydrangea, and nandina, all of which came from Japan or China?

Yet many other imported plants have quickly worn out their welcome. Unchecked by the natural forces (insects, diseases, animals, or climate) that control them in their native lands, they run rampant in their new home, displacing native plants, altering ecosystems, and destroying wildlife habitats. Here are a few of the worst offenders.

Ever since highway departments innocently planted it to control erosion in the early 20th century, kudzu *(Pueraria lobata)* has greedily devoured millions of acres and swallowed entire forests. Japanese honeysuckle *(Lonicera*

Kudzu *(Pueraria lobata)*

japonica) and Chinese privet *(Ligustrum sinense)*, both introduced as ornamentals, choke our woodlands. Water hyacinth *(Eichhornia crassipes)*, a lovely flower for a backyard pond, reproduces with lightning speed, quickly smothering lakes, ponds, and rivers. In the Lower South, wisteria vines climb to the top of 100-foot trees and strangle their hosts. Running bamboo, escaped from gardens, forms impenetrable thickets. In Florida, millions of paperbark trees *(Melaleuca quinquenervia)* are consuming wetlands, pushing out native plants upon which wildlife depends.

While many invasive plants are banned from commerce and horticulture, many others are not. Controlling their spread is up to individual gardeners. Native plant societies maintain lists of problem plants in each state. Learn what they are and do not plant them.

W

other methods have failed. Beyond the risks they may pose to health and the environment, many of these chemicals can damage desirable plants if they drift through the air or run off in irrigation or rainwater. Some persist in the soil for long periods, injuring later plantings. And often the entire process of herbicide use—selecting a product, mixing and applying it, cleaning up—takes more effort than pulling or digging out the weeds.

If you use herbicides, always make sure the product is safe for the desirable plants growing in and near the areas to be treated. Also keep in mind that you can be held responsible for any damage to neighboring properties resulting from herbicides you use (do not apply them on windy days). See page 667 for lists of natural and synthetic herbicides as well as explanations of terms used in describing herbicides, such as pre-emergence and postemergence.

ANNUAL WEEDS. Most of these weeds can be controlled by diligent hand weeding and hoeing. This should be carried out before the weeds go to seed, since most annual weeds produce prodigious amounts of seed. To discourage the growth of these weeds in lawns, maintain a thick turf (for more on lawns, see pages 610–613). Mulches are effective in reducing the germination of annual weeds in garden areas; most such weeds can also be destroyed by soil solarization. If chemical control is required, use a pre-emergence herbicide labeled for the weed in question. Apply it in late summer or fall for winter annual weeds, in early spring for summer annuals. For postemergence treatment, spot-treat annual weeds with herbicidal soaps or products containing glufosinate-ammonium (Finale) or glyphosate (Roundup); don't get these chemicals on desirable plants. Selective postemergence herbicides effective on particu-larly troublesome annual weeds are included in the following descriptions.

Control biennial weeds such as mallows in the same way as you would annual ones.

Annual bluegrass *(Poa annua).* A winter annual that forms a bright light green tuft of soft-textured grass. It is troublesome in brown winter lawns, flower borders, and winter vegetable beds. To prevent bluegrass, apply a pre-emergence herbicide, such as pendimethalin (Halts) or trifluralin (Treflan).

Burclover *(Medicago polymorpha).* Winter annual in most areas. Low, spreading, broad-leafed weed with yellow flowers and spiny burs. Common in lawns and garden beds that lack nitrogen (high phosphorus). It is also troublesome in gravel paths and driveways. To help control burclover, increase nitrogen fertilizing. To kill it, spray with 2,4-D.

SOIL SOLARIZATION

Soil solarization takes advantage of the sun's heat, trapped under clear plastic sheeting, to control many kinds of weed seeds as well as harmful fungi, bacteria, and some nematodes. The process works best in hot, sunny weather; daytime temperatures above 80°F are ideal. Solarization isn't very effective in windy areas.

Plan to solarize areas you intend to use for fall vegetables, ornamental beds, or lawn. Follow these steps.

1 Cultivate soil, clearing it of weeds, debris, and large clods of earth. It is important to get rid of growing weeds, because clear plastic—unlike black plastic—doesn't halt growth of plants in the soil beneath it.

2 Make a bed at least 2½ feet wide (narrower beds make it difficult to build up enough heat to have much effect). Carve a small ditch around perimeter and rake to level surface. Soak soil to a depth of 1 foot: moist soil conducts heat better than dry soil and initiates germination of weed seeds. Both seeds and any seedlings will then be killed by heat.

3 Cover soil with 1- to 4-mil clear plastic; use UV-resistant plastic if it's available, since it won't break down during solarization. Stretch plastic tightly so that it is in contact with the soil. Bury the edges in the perimeter ditch. An optional second layer of plastic increases heat and makes solarization more effective; use soda cans as spacers between the two sheets (see inset at right). Leave plastic in place for 4 to 6 weeks (8 weeks for really persistent weeds); then remove it. Don't leave it down longer than 8 weeks, or soil structure may suffer. You can now plant and mulch. Don't dig in the mulch or cultivate more than the upper 2 inches of soil, since weed seeds at deeper levels may still be viable.

W

TOP: Annual bluegrass; BOTTOM: Burclover

TOP: Crabgrass; BOTTOM: Henbit

TOP: Purslane; BOTTOM: Sowthistle

Chickweed *(Stellaria media)*. Winter annual usually found in lawns. Germinates in late fall, forming a spreading green mat with star-shaped white flowers. Sets seed in spring, then dies with the arrival of hot weather. Prevention is the best control: apply a pre-emergence herbicide containing pendimethalin (Halts) to the lawn. Existing chickweed can be killed with a postemergence herbicide such as 2,4-D.

Crabgrass *(Digitaria* species). Summer annual. This shallow-rooted weed thrives in hot, moist areas. Seeds germinate in early spring in warmer climates, later in colder areas. As the plant grows, it branches out at the base; stems can root where they touch the soil. It is typically found in lawns and flower beds that receive frequent surface watering; infrequent deep watering can dry out crabgrass roots, killing the weeds or diminishing their vigor.

To prevent crabgrass from germinating, apply pendimethalin (Halts), dithiopyr (Dimension), or trifluralion (Preen) in early spring. Corn gluten meal is a natural alternative. For postemergence treatment around ornamental plants, use herbicides that kill grasses, such as fluazifop-P-butyl (Grass-B-Gon) or 2,4-D.

Henbit *(Lamium aplexicaule)*. Winter annual in lawns and gardens. Distinguished by stacked pairs of coarsely toothed leaves that crowd the tops of 12- to 16-inch-tall, square-sided stems. Small pinkish purple flowers appear atop the foliage in spring. Plants germinate in fall and grow over the winter; they bloom and set seed in spring, then die. Control is fairly easy. Individual plants are easy to pull; you can also treat them with 2,4-D, or imazaquin (Image). To prevent germination in the first place, apply a pre-emergence product containing pendimethalin (Halts), dithiopyr (Dimension), or trifluralin (Preen).

Mallows *(Malva* species). Winter or summer annual or biennial, depending on climate. Also known as cheeseweed (thanks to the fruits, which resemble a round of cheese), these broad-leafed weeds have rounded, lobed leaves and pinkish white flowers. They grow quickly, ranging in height from a few inches to 4 feet tall, and are found in lawns, in gardens, and on roadsides. They're easiest to pull when young; older plants develop a deep taproot that can resprout if broken. Spray established plants with glyphosate (Roundup).

Purslane *(Portulaca oleracea)*. Summer annual. A prostrate broad-leafed weed with small yellow flowers and fleshy stems and leaves (which are edible, with a tart, lemony flavor), purslane thrives in moist conditions but can withstand considerable drought. Though it's easy to pull or hoe, pieces of stem reroot readily, so be sure to remove them from the garden. Do not compost these weeds. Related to the bright-blossomed garden flowers rose moss *(Portulaca grandiflora)* and ornamental purslane *(P.* Wildfire hybrids).

Sowthistles *(Sonchus* species). Summer annual. These upright, 1- to 4-foot-tall weeds have stout taproots, hollow stems, and milky sap that oozes out when a leaf or stem is broken. The yellow flowers look like those of dandelions. Common in gardens, they may grow in lawns as well. Easy to control with 2,4-D.

Spotted spurge *(Chamaesyce maculata;* also listed as *Euphorbia maculata)*. Summer annual, though seeds can germinate as early in the year as February in warm regions. This weed is particularly aggressive: not only does it produce large quantities of seed, it also sets seed just a few weeks after germination— and the seeds may germinate immediately. It grows from a shallow taproot and forms a low mat of branching stems that exude a milky juice when cut or broken. Spot-treat with 2,4-D or apply a weed-and-feed combination herbicide/fertilizer.

W

Chickweed

Mallow

Spotted spurge

665

PERENNIAL WEEDS. Described below are some of the South's most troublesome perennial weeds. Management options are described from least to most toxic—physical controls first, then chemical ones. In general, growth of perennial weeds can be controlled with landscape fabrics installed so that no light reaches the soil (note that these must be applied *after* clearing the area of weeds; see pages 613 and 663). Organic mulches are not as effective, since seeds or plants sprouting from roots left in the ground often grow through them.

Bamboos. These giant perennial grasses develop woody, jointed stems and spread by rhizomes. Clumping bamboos (*Bambusa* and other genera) are safe for most home gardens, because their rhizomes extend only a short distance from the main clump. However, running bamboos (*Phyllostachys* and other genera) are invasive, form large thickets, and are difficult to control. To eradicate existing bamboo, cut off all shoots at ground level—and keep on doing so whenever they start to grow back. This ultimately starves the roots, but it does take time. For quicker results, cut the stems nearly to the ground, chop vertical gashes in the stumps, and spray or paint the cut stumps with glyphosate (Roundup). Repeated treatments may be necessary. For more information on well-behaved bamboo, see pages 190–193.

Bermuda grass (*Cynodon dactylon*). A fine-textured and fast-growing perennial, Bermuda grass is frequently planted as a lawn grass. It spreads by underground stems (rhizomes), aboveground runners (stolons), and, in the case of common Bermuda grass, by seed—and easily becomes a difficult-to-control weed in shrub borders, flower beds, and lawns planted with other kinds of grasses. If you have a Bermuda lawn, use 8-inch-deep barriers or edging to prevent it from advancing into other parts of the garden.

Dig up stray clumps before they form sod, being sure to remove all the underground stems; any left behind can start new shoots. Repeated pulling and digging are usually necessary to eliminate this weed. Seeds and shallow-growing rhizomes of Bermuda grass are destroyed by soil solarization, but deeply buried rhizomes will survive.

For chemical control, you can use a pre-emergence herbicide containing pendimethalin (Halts) or dithiopyr (Dimension) to prevent seeds from germinating. Postemergence products include herbicides that kill grasses, such as fluazifop-P-butyl (Grass-B-Gon); these are effective against most grasses and can be sprayed over some broad-leafed ornamentals without harming them (check the product label). Spot-treat actively growing Bermuda grass with glyphosate (Roundup), taking care not to get it on desirable plants.

Dandelion (*Taraxacum officinale*). Familiar as a lawn weed throughout the South, dan-

TOP TO BOTTOM: Bamboo, Dandelion, Johnsongrass, Yellow nutsedge, Oxalis

delions form a deep, fleshy taproot. They spread by windborne seeds that appear in fluffy heads after the familiar yellow blossoms fade.

If dandelions are growing in your lawn, the turf is probably thin and undernourished. A healthy lawn can outcompete this weed, so thicken the turf by overseeding and proper fertilizing, watering, and mowing. Pull dandelions from lawns and gardens while they're small, before they produce a deep taproot and set seed. Once the taproot has formed, it's necessary to remove all of it to get rid of the plant, since new plants can sprout from even a small piece. A dandelion weeder with a forked blade is helpful. A hand weeder with a bent shaft (or a ball attached to the shaft) to serve as a fulcrum increases leverage, helping to pop dandelions out of the ground.

For chemical control in lawns, use a post-emergence product labeled for dandelions in turf or a weed-and-feed combination herbicide/fertilizer. Spot-treating with glyphosate (Roundup) will partially control dandelions in gardens, but take care not to get the chemical on desirable plants.

Johnsongrass (*Sorghum halapense*). Tough, spreading, bright green perennial grass that invades lawns and vegetable and flower gardens. Grows 2 to 8 feet tall, with conspicuous purplish pink flower spikes. Spreads by both seed and thick, underground rhizomes. Frequent mowing will control it in lawns. Do not rototill infested gardens, as this breaks the rhizomes into many pieces that then root and grow. Instead, treat the weed with glyphosate (Roundup) or fluazifop-P-butyl (Grass-B-Gon), or dig out entire plants. To prevent Johnsongrass from germinating, apply a pre-emergence herbicide in early spring; use one containing pendimethalin (Halts) on lawns, use one containing trifluralin (Preen) in garden beds.

Kudzu (*Pueraria lobata*). Reputed to grow as much as a foot a day during the summer, kudzu is one of the South's most feared weeds. It blankets entire woods and fields and engulfs abandoned houses, utility poles, and anything else that gets in its way. Vines grow from enormous underground tubers, sprouting large leaves consisting of three-lobed leaflets. Fragrant reddish purple flowers appear in summer. To kill kudzu on the ground, spray it with glyphosate (Roundup) when vines are actively growing. To kill it in trees, cut the stems near ground level and paint the cut ends with glyphosate or triclopyr (Brush-B-Gon).

Nutsedge, yellow (*Cyperus esculentus*). Yellow nutsedge resembles a grass, but its stems are solid and triangular in cross-section, and its leaves grow from the base in groups of three. True grasses, in contrast, have hollow stems that are oval or flat in cross-section, and their leaves grow in sets of two. Yellow nutsedge forms small, roundish tubers (nutlets) at tips of roots; it spreads by these tubers as well as by seed.

W

PRODUCTS FOR WEED CONTROL

Herbicides are classified according to what stage of weed growth they affect, as well as by how they damage weeds. *Pre-emergence herbicides* work by inhibiting the growth of germinating weed seeds and very young seedlings; they do not affect established plants. To be effective, they must thus be applied before the seeds sprout. Before applying these chemicals in ornamental gardens, remove any existing weeds. Some pre-emergence products are formulated to kill germinating weeds in lawns; these may be sold in combination with fertilizers, which increase the vigor of the lawn and improve its ability to compete against weeds. (Such dual-purpose products should not, however, be treated solely as fertilizers and reapplied whenever the lawn needs feeding—for that purpose, use a regular lawn fertilizer.) Some pre-emergence products must be watered into the soil, while others must be dug into the planting bed. Some may also harm seeds you sow later in the season. Check the label to learn how long the product remains active in the soil.

Postemergence herbicides act on growing weeds rather than on seeds. They damage plants in different ways. Those that are translocated must be absorbed by the plant through its leaves or stems; they then kill it by interfering with its metabolism. Contact herbicides kill only the plant parts on which they are sprayed; regrowth can still occur from roots or unsprayed buds.

The natural and synthetic herbicides listed here are widely available to Southern gardeners. *Synthetic herbicides* are manufactured compounds that do not normally occur in nature. *Natural herbicides,* in contrast, are products whose active ingredients originate in a plant or mineral.

When using any herbicide, *read the label directions carefully and follow them exactly.* The package will clearly state the weeds the product controls and the other plants, if any, around which it can be safely used; it is illegal to apply it to any plant not designated as a target. Always dispose of pesticides in a safe manner (see page 624).

The following products are listed alphabetically by the accepted common name of the *active ingredient*—the actual chemical that controls the weed or weeds listed on the package label. Some widely used trade names, if they differ from the common name, are noted in parentheses. Before you buy, read the label to make sure you're getting the active ingredient you want. (For more on reading and understanding pesticide labels, see page 622.)

NATURAL HERBICIDES

▶ **Corn gluten meal (Suppressa, others).** Pre-emergence. Used to control some germinating weed seeds in lawns. This product is also a fertilizer, serving to thicken lawns and thus suppress weed growth (some research shows that this may be its primary contribution to weed control).

▶ **Herbicidal soap (Superfast, others).** Postemergence. Contact herbicides that degrade quickly. Kills top growth of young, actively growing weeds; works most effectively on annual weeds. Made from fatty acids (as is insecticidal soap).

SYNTHETIC HERBICIDES

▶ **2,4-D.** Postemergence. Controls many broad-leaf weeds. Available as liquid and granules; often mixed with other herbicides. Toxic to fish.

▶ **Dithiopyr.** Pre-emergence. Controls grassy and broad-leafed lawn weeds. Highly toxic to fish. Do not apply more than once per year. Apply only to healthy, established lawns.

▶ **Fluazifop-P-butyl (Grass-B-Gon).** Postemergence. A translocated herbicide that controls actively growing grasses. Can be sprayed over many broad-leafed ornamentals without damaging them; check the label.

▶ **Glufosinate-ammonium (Finale).** Postemergence. Contact herbicide that damages or kills many kinds of weeds. Take care not to apply to desirable plants.

▶ **Glyphosate (Roundup).** Postemergence. Translocated herbicide. Effective on a broad range of troublesome weeds, but must be used with care to avoid contacting desirable plants.

▶ **Imazaquin (Image).** Postemergence. Used for many hard-to-control lawn weeds, such as nutsedge, dollar weed, and wild onion. Toxic to fish.

▶ **Pendimethalin (Halts).** Pre-emergence. Used to control many grasses and broad-leafed weeds in turf and in ornamental plantings. Toxic to fish.

▶ **Triclopyr (Brush-B-Gon).** Postemergence. Translocated herbicide. Used to control hard-to-kill woody plants such as vines, shrubs, and trees. Use with care to avoid damaging desirable plants.

▶ **Trifluralin (Preen, Treflan).** Pre-emergence. Controls many grasses and broad-leafed weeds in turf and ornamental plantings. Toxic to fish.

Remove plants when they are young and still small. Older, taller plants are mature enough to produce tubers; when you dig or pull the plant, the tubers remain in the soil to sprout. Repeatedly removing top growth eventually weakens tubers. Soil solarization provides only partial control.

For postemergence chemical control, try glyphosate (Roundup), being careful not to get the chemical on desirable plants. It is most effective on young plants; it will not kill mature tubers or those that have become detached from the treated plant. Imazaquin (Image) is also effective.

Oxalis, yellow *(Oxalis corniculata).* Also called yellow wood sorrel, this aggressive weed is happy in sun or shade and spreads quickly by seed. Seedlings start from a single taproot, which soon develops into a shallow, spreading, knitted root system. Tiny, five-petaled yellow flowers are followed by elongated seed capsules that can propel seed as far as 6 feet.

Dig out small plants before they have a chance to set seed. Keep lawns vigorous to provide tough competition; water deeply but infrequently, since frequent shallow watering encourages this shallow-rooted weed.

For chemical control, use a pre-emergence herbicide containing trifluralin (Preen) or pendimethalin (Halts) on the turf grasses and around the ornamental plants listed on the label. For post-emergent control in lawns, use a weed-and-feed product containing 2,4-D. Spot-treat oxalis in gardens with glyphosate (Roundup), taking care to keep the chemical from contacting desirable plants.

Poison ivy

Poison ivy, poison oak *(Toxicodendron radicans, T. diversilobum)*. Poison ivy is common in shady areas and along the edges of woodlands. It sprawls along the ground until it finds something to climb; then it becomes a clinging vine. Established plants bear clusters of pale green flowers in spring; these are followed by small white berries. Poison oak grows as a dense, leafy shrub in open or filtered sun; in shade, it becomes a tall, climbing vine. Its leaves are divided into three leaflets with scalloped, toothed, or lobed edges.

A resin on the leaves, stems, fruits, and roots of both plants causes severe contact dermatitis in most people. Leaves turn red in fall, then drop—but plants are just as poisonous in winter as when in leaf. Never burn poison oak or ivy; the smoke is toxic.

Poison oak and poison ivy are most effectively controlled with an appropriately labeled herbicide, such as triclopyr (Brush-B-Gon) or glyphosate (Roundup); avoid getting these chemicals on desirable plants. Repeated applications are needed as new leaves grow.

TOP: Quack grass, BOTTOM: Wild onion

DIE, IVY, DIE. *Here's an easy way to kill established poison ivy, roots and all. Wearing gloves and long sleeves, pull a long stem of poison ivy from a tree, making sure the stem remains attached to the ground. Then fill a bucket with water and add the amount of glyphosate (Roundup) recommended on the label. Place as much of the poison ivy stem as you can in the solution and leave it there for several days (be sure that the bucket is not accessible to children and pets). The stem will gradually take the chemical down to the roots, where it will kill the plant. This technique also works for wisteria and other hard-to-kill vines.* ❖

Quack grass *(Elytrigia repens)*. Also known as couch grass or devil's grass, this aggressive weed invades both lawns and gardens. It can reach 3 feet tall but stays much lower in mowed areas. It produces an extensive network of long, slender, branching, yellowish white rhizomes that can spread laterally 3 to 5 feet.

Because it reproduces readily from even small pieces of rhizome left in the soil, quack grass is difficult to manage. Before planting, thoroughly dig the area and remove all visible pieces of rhizome; this will slow the weed's growth for a few years.

For chemical control, use an herbicide that controls grassy weeds, such as fluazifop-P-butyl (Grass-B-Gon). Or spot-treat with an herbicide containing glyphosate (Roundup), taking care to avoid contact with desirable plants.

Wild onion and wild garlic *(Allium canadense, A. vineale)*. These are some of the worst and hardest-to-control winter lawn weeds. The clumps of dark green, narrow leaves are especially noticeable when growing in warm-season lawns that have turned brown for the winter. The weeds spread by seed and also by *bulbils,* small bulblike organs that fall from a flowering stem to the ground and take root. Digging is an effective control if you have just a few clumps. To control widespread infestations, spray with a product containing 2,4-D; or apply imazaquin (Image).

Wildlife-Friendly Gardening

Making your garden attractive to wildlife—songbirds, hummingbirds, butterflies, toads, lizards, frogs, and other creatures—is primarily a matter of providing shelter, water, and food. It's also important to avoid using pesticides. Try to emphasize native plants, since they're familiar to the local wildlife and adapted to your climate. Also remember that a garden teeming with wildlife is not overly tidy; parts of it are left to grow naturally, providing safe havens for creatures of all sorts. See A Guide to Plant Selection (beginning on page 39) for lists of plants attractive to butterflies and hummingbirds, including kinds that provide food for butterfly larvae (caterpillars).

A GARDEN FOR WILDLIFE

Tall trees. Provide shelter, food (seeds or fruits), and nesting places; also protect the garden from strong winds.

Hummingbird feeder. To prepare feeder solution, combine 1 part granulated sugar and 4 parts water and bring to a boil; let cool. Keep feeder clean; hummers can develop a deadly infection from dirty feeders.

Birdbath. To provide some protection from cats and other predators, place in an open area; a location 10 to 20 feet from shrubs offers a safety zone. In freezing weather, thaw water with boiling water or use a birdbath heater.

W

Hedgerow. Provides food, shelter, and nesting sites for birds. Plant a selection of small trees and low to medium-size shrubs; include fruit-bearing types as well as kinds that feed butterfly larvae.

Brush pile. Instead of hauling away or shredding tree prunings and brush, make piles to shelter birds and other wildlife. But, keep the piles away from the house.

Flower borders. Include a wide selection of plants that provide nectar for butterflies, beneficial insects, and hummingbirds; also plant species whose foliage feeds butterfly larvae. Let plants go to seed to furnish food for songbirds.

Bird houses. Install them away from the activity around feeders and facing away from prevailing weather. Mount on metal poles to keep cats and raccoons at bay.

Meadow. Plant native grasses, wildflowers, and low shrubs for food, shelter, and nest-building materials.

Pond. Ensures a source of water for birds and a habitat for frogs and turtles. Birds are especially attracted to the splashing water of a small fountain. Make a "beach" at one side to provide shallow water. An "island" (a large rock) in the center can be a refuge for turtles and frogs. Water plants add more shelter, and protect fish in the pond.

Vines. Flowering vines offer shelter, nesting sites, and nectar; many also bear berries and foliage that are sources of food for birds and butterfly larvae.

Rocky area. Shelters lizards and toads.

Bird feeders. Locate feeders near trees or shrubs so birds can fly to cover; keep them off the ground to protect the clientele from cats. Set up feeders in fall and maintain them through winter when natural foods are scarce. Keep feeders clean. Besides seeds (sunflower, millet, safflower, thistle, and so on), birds enjoy suet, offered in mesh bags or special feeders.

W

Resource Directory

No book can answer every gardening question. A dozen new plants are introduced practically every day. This section is for those whose thirst for knowledge still hasn't been quenched.

Botanical Display Gardens

The outstanding public gardens described on pages 671–680 range in scale from modest backyards to estates that cover hundreds of acres. Some emulate nature, while others present carefully tailored or even formal designs. But the best gardens share one trait: they teach you how to grow, display, and appreciate plants. Whether you're planning your very first garden or renovating an existing one, you'll benefit from visiting public gardens and exploring what they have to offer.

Mail-Order Suppliers

Local garden centers, far too numerous to list here, usually sell a reasonable variety of plants and supplies. But they tend to stock mass-marketed items that everyone and their neighbor have. If you're looking for the new, rare, slightly offbeat, or just plain weird, mail-order catalogs are usually your best bet. True, mail-order plants are often smaller than what you could get locally, and you have to carefully check prices, guarantees, shipping dates, and return policies. But the incredible selection of items and wealth of gardening advice offered in catalogs more than compensate. Turn to page 681 for an extensive list of mail-order nurseries and suppliers.

Glossary

If you think "chlorotic" has something to do with bleach or that a "corolla" is simply a Japanese car, you need the glossary on pages 689–693. All sorts of gardening terms are explained in language every person can understand. You need never again be intimidated at a flower show or garden club meeting.

Cooperative Extension Offices

No one knows better how plants grow and the problems they face in your area than someone who lives there. On pages 694–697 we've listed the telephone numbers of Cooperative Extension offices in the most populous counties of each Southern state. If you can't find the information you seek in this book, give these local horticultural experts a call.

Botanical Names, Index

Latin isn't a dead language when it comes to gardening. Knowing the Latin (botanical) names of plants can be very helpful. To see how Latin names provide interesting clues to a plant's characteristics and origin, turn to "Solving the Mystery of Botanical Names" on pages 698–699. The index that follows contains both botanical and common names for every plant species in this book.

Botanical Gardens, Display Gardens,
and Other Gardens of Note

B otanical gardens, estate gardens, and arboretums display plants from around the world, along with native species, often in landscape settings. Some feature demonstration gardens filled with flowers, fruits, and vegetables; others include greenhouses and conservatories, interesting garden structures, or water features. Many offer classes in gardening techniques, operate horticultural libraries, and sell hard-to-find plants. Some are living laboratories, overseeing the propagation and preservation of endangered plants. The gardens described here, listed alphabetically by state and including the District of Columbia, are some of the major establishments (and a few lesser-known ones) that we have visited across the South. Call or look at Web sites for directions and times of operation, as well as upcoming educational programs, classes, and opportunities to volunteer.

The lake at Aldridge Gardens, Hoover, Alabama

ALABAMA

Aldridge Gardens

3530 Lorna Road

Hoover, AL 35216

(205) 682-8019

www.aldridgegardens.com

This 30-acre botanical garden is home to the South's largest collection of hydrangeas, along with woodland gardens, native plants, walking trails, and a 7-acre lake.

Bellingrath Gardens and Home

12401 Bellingrath Road

Theodore, AL 36582

(251) 973-2217

www.bellingrath.org

In its 906 acres, this property encompasses a variety of habitats, including an Oriental-American garden, a conservatory, and a boardwalk that winds through a wetland preserve of indigenous plants and animals.

Birmingham Botanical Gardens

2612 Lane Park Road

Birmingham, AL 35223

(205) 414-3900

www.bbgardens.org

These gardens contain many features, including an herb garden, a bog garden, a natural woodlands garden, an All-America Selections display garden, a Japanese garden, a fern glade, a tropical conservatory, and even a *Southern Living* garden. Check out their large horticultural lending library under Botanical Gardens in the Libraries' Information section of *www.jclc.org*.

Dothan Area Botanical Gardens

5130 Headland Avenue

Dothan, AL 36301

(334) 793-3224

www.dabg.com

Currently, the property includes rose, herb, camellia, azalea, heirloom, butterfly, and meditation gardens, in addition to a pond and a greenhouse.

Huntsville-Madison County Botanical Garden

4747 Bob Wallace Avenue

Huntsville, AL 35805

(256) 830-4447

www.hsvbg.org

Features annual, herb, perennial, and vegetable gardens, as well as a fern glade, an aquatic garden, a butterfly garden, and a wildflower walk and dogwood trail. Seasonal events, such as the Spring Festival of Flowers, are held throughout the year.

Minamac Wildflower Bog

13199 MacCartee Lane

Silverhill, AL 36576

(251) 945-6157

A hillside meadow here stretches along a five-acre lake and is smothered in bog-loving pitcher plants, rare orchids, and lilies. Blooms April through September; tours are by reservation only.

Mobile Botanical Gardens

5151 Museum Drive

Mobile, AL 36608

(251) 342-0555

www.mobilebotanicalgardens.org

Features native azaleas, camellias, ferns, magnolias, hollies, perennial displays, an herb garden, and a fragrance and texture garden for the physically challenged.

ARKANSAS

Arkansas State Capitol Rose Garden

Office of Secretary of State

State Capitol, Room 256

Little Rock, AR 72201-1094

(501) 682-1010

www.sosweb.state.ar.us

The grounds of the capitol building contain an All-America Rose Selections trial garden with over 1,800 roses.

Eureka Springs Gardens

1537 Carroll County Road 210

Eureka Springs, AR 72632

(479) 253-9244

www.eurekagardens.com

Thirty-three acres of developed grounds with daffodils, tulips, anemones, dogwoods, redbuds, crabapples, azaleas, annuals, perennials, and wildflowers. Included in the National Register of Historic Places.

DELAWARE

Mount Cuba Center for the Study of Piedmont Flora

P.O. Box 3570

Greenville, DE 19807-0570

(302) 239-4244

This nonprofit institution on a 630-acre estate seeks to increase the appreciation and use of native eastern-Piedmont plants. The beautiful woodland gardens have extensive plantings of wildflowers. Gardens open in the spring and fall; tours are by reservation only.

Winterthur Museum, Garden, and Library

Route 52

Winterthur, DE 19735

(800) 448-3883; (302) 888-4600

www.winterthur.org

The former mansion of Henry Francis du Pont is surrounded by acres of mature and rare azaleas, rhododendrons, magnolias, and oaks. Highlights include a mature pinetum, a peony garden, a winterhazel walk,

Magnificent woodlands at Winterthur, Delaware

and ponds—all designed for a succession of bloom throughout the year. Children of all ages are invited to explore the three-acre Enchanted Woods Garden.

DISTRICT OF COLUMBIA

Dumbarton Oaks

1703 32nd Street, NW

Washington, DC 20007

(202) 339-6401; fax (202) 339-6419

www.doaks.org

This beautiful garden was designed by Beatrix Farrand and boasts majestic trees, perennial borders, and formal features such as an orangery, terraces, fountains, and a highly original pebble garden.

Hillwood Museum and Gardens

4155 Linnean Avenue, NW

Washington, DC 20008

(202) 686-5807

www.hillwoodmuseum.org

The former mansion of Marjorie Merriweather Post is surrounded by 13 acres of rose, parterre, cutting, and Japanese gardens and 12 acres of woodlands. A highlight is the greenhouse orchid collection.

U.S. Botanic Garden

245 First Street, SW

Washington, DC 20024

(202) 225-8333;

plant hotline (202) 226-4785

www.usbg.gov

Contains a conservatory and two gardens: Bartoldi Park and the National Garden. Noteworthy collections include economic and medicinal plants, orchids, cacti and succulents, bromeliads, cycads, and ferns. The new three-acre National Garden will feature unusual, useful, and ornamental plants for the mid-Atlantic region.

U.S. National Arboretum

3501 New York Avenue, NE

Washington, DC 20002

(202) 245-2726

www.usna.usda.gov

Contains outstanding collections of bonsai, flowering trees, azaleas, dwarf and slow-growing conifers, hollies, roses, native plants, an Asian collection, perennials, and the National Herb Garden—the largest of its kind in the United States.

U.S. Botanic Garden conservatory, Washington, D.C.

FLORIDA

Edison & Ford Winter Estates

2350 McGregor Boulevard

Fort Myers, FL 33901

(239) 334-7419

www.edison-ford-estate.com

The former winter estates of neighbors Thomas Edison and Henry Ford. Edison's tropical botanical garden contains one of the most extensive collections of tropical plants in America, including bromeliads, orchids, and exotic specimens such as sausage, banyan, and candle trees.

Fairchild Tropical Garden

10901 Old Cutler Road

Coral Gables (Miami), FL 33156

(305) 667-1651; fax (305) 661-8953

www.fairchildgarden.org

An extensive collection of rare tropical plants including flowering trees, palms, cycads, and vines. The Web site features a Botanical Resource Center with a virtual herbarium, a garden plantings database, and a gallery of Floridian flora.

Historic Bok Sanctuary

1151 Tower Boulevard

Lake Wales, FL 33853

(863) 676-1408

www.boktower.org

Designed by landscape architect Frederick Law Olmsted, Jr., the Sanctuary consists of 157 acres surrounding a stunningly beautiful bell tower. Plants include azaleas, camellias, magnolias, ferns, palms, other tropicals, oaks, and pines.

Harry P. Leu Gardens

1920 North Forest Avenue
Orlando, FL 32803-1537

(407) 246-2620

www.leugardens.org

One of the most beautiful botanical gardens in the U.S., Leu Gardens has the largest camellia collection in the South, the biggest formal rose garden in Florida, a butterfly garden, and extensive collections of gingers, palms, bananas, bromeliads, flowering vines, and other semitropical plants.

Alfred B. Maclay State Gardens

3540 Thomasville Road
Tallahassee, FL 32309

(850) 487-4556

www.ssnow.com/maclay

Features both native and exotic plants, including oaks, dogwoods, redbuds, camellias, and azaleas. The Web site contains a virtual tour of the garden.

Marie Selby Botanical Gardens

811 South Palm Avenue
Sarasota, FL 34236-7726

(941) 366-5731

www.selby.org

At this world-renowned orchid and bromeliad center, you'll find cactus, orchid, succulent, and cycad collections; a fernery, a hibiscus garden, a palm grove, a tropical food garden, a butterfly garden, and a perennial wildflower garden.

GEORGIA

Atlanta Botanical Garden

1345 Piedmont Avenue NE
Atlanta, GA 30309

(404) 876-5859

www.atlantabotanicalgarden.org

The many display gardens include five acres of shade-loving ornamentals from around the world, the walking trails and natural undergrowth of the Storza Woods, a children's "wellness" garden, the Dorothy Chapman Fuqua Conservatory of rare and endangered plants, and the Fuqua Orchid Center.

The Gardens at Callaway

U.S. Highway 27
Pine Mountain, GA 31822

**(800) CALLAWAY or (800) 225-5292;
(706) 663-2281**

www.callawayonline.com

The world's largest public display of azaleas, with over 40 acres of native and exotic selections. Six walking trails—Wildflower, Rhododendron, Azalea, Holly, Laurel Springs, and Mountain Creek—as well as a 10-mile bicycle trail, wander through a woodland garden. The Cecil B. Day Butterfly Center is home to more than 100 species of tropical butterflies, and its outdoor gardens are planted to attract native butterflies. The John A. Sibley Horticultural Center features temperate and tropical plants.

Beautiful flower displays are standard at Callaway Gardens, Georgia.

Lockerly Arboretum

1534 Irwinton Road
Milledgeville, GA 31061

(478) 452-2112

www.lockerlyarboretum.org

This 50-acre arboretum is planted with perennial, herb, and daylily beds; has a rhododendron collection, a butterfly garden, and a vineyard; and contains both tropical and desert greenhouses. Click on the interactive garden map at the Web site to see photos of the gardens.

The State Botanical Garden of Georgia

2450 South Milledge Avenue
Athens, GA 30605

(706) 542-1244

www.uga.edu/~botgarden

Even though this botanical garden is a relative newcomer, it has much to offer in its 313 acres. In the International Garden you can learn about the geographic origins of plants and those who collected them. Elsewhere, there are shade, rose, annual, perennial, dahlia, rhododendron, ground cover, and azalea gardens. The Trial Garden features a unique collection of non-native shrubs and trees, planted to test their adaptability to the Southeast.

Exotic foliage bursting out of a garden bed at the Leu Gardens in Orlando, Florida

Winter brings a quiet beauty to the forest at Bernheim Arboretum in Clermont, Kentucky.

KENTUCKY

Ashland, the Henry Clay Estate

120 Sycamore Road

Lexington, KY 40502

(859) 266-8581

www.henryclay.org

The 19th-century home of Henry Clay has grounds designed by Henry Fletcher Kenney. They include parterre and herb gardens, herbaceous borders, boxwoods, hollies, hornbeams, peonies, roses, and a wide variety of perennials. Maintained by the Garden Club of Lexington.

Bernheim Arboretum and Research Forest

State Highway 245

Clermont, KY 40110

(502) 955-8512

www.bernheim.org

Among its 1,900 different plants, the arboretum contains an extensive collection of hollies, along with beech, ginkgo, and nut sections. Ongoing research projects include restoring American chestnut trees and native grassland areas. The extensive grounds include a Nature Center Museum and 35 miles of hiking trails through six different types of forest.

LOUISIANA

American Rose Society

8877 Jefferson Paige Road

Shreveport, LA 71130-0030

(318) 938-5402

www.ars.org

The headquarters of the largest single-plant society in the United States are here in Shreveport, as is its rose garden, which has over 20,000 bushes—400 selections of old and modern roses.

Briarwood, Caroline Dormon Nature Preserve

216 Caroline Dormon Road

Saline, LA 71070

(318) 576-3379

www.cp-tel.net/dormon

This wild garden contains native shrubs, trees, perennials, and wildflowers in a largely untouched setting. Of special interest is the large collection of Louisiana irises in a natural bog setting.

Hodges Gardens, Park, and Wilderness Area

U.S. Route 171

Florien, LA 71429

(800) 354-3523

www.hodgesgardens.com

Miles of trails lead past a fishing lake and acres of seasonal gardens, including old

roses, herbs, annuals, and perennials. The Web site gives details of seasonal highlights, activities, and special events.

Longue Vue House and Gardens

7 Bamboo Road

New Orleans, LA 70124-1065

(504) 488-5488

www.longuevue.com

Listed on the National Register of Historic Places, this classically beautiful Greek Revival mansion is surrounded by eight acres of gardens, designed by Ellen Biddle Shipman, with later modifications by William Platt. Some of the many theme gardens include the magnificent Spanish Court, the Oak Alley, the Walled Garden (which features roses), and the Wild Garden, with natural forest walks.

Rosedown Plantation and Historic Gardens

12501 LA Highway 10

St. Francisville, LA 70775

(888) 376-1867; (225) 635-3332

www.crt.state.la.us/crt/parks/rosedown/rosedown.htm

This 19th-century mansion is surrounded by 28 acres of grounds that include kitchen, herb, medicinal, and formal gardens. Contains many Southern favorites such as azaleas, camellias, hydrangeas, cryptomerias, gardenias, crape myrtles, deutzias, and magnolias.

MARYLAND

Brookside Gardens

1800 Glenallan Avenue

Wheaton, MD 20902

(301) 962-1400

www.brooksidegardens.org

Fifty acres of flowering trees and shrubs in formal and informal settings, a fragrance garden, a Japanese-style garden, and two conservatories.

Cylburn Arboretum

4915 Greenspring Avenue

Baltimore, MD 21209

(410) 367-2217

www.cylburnassociation.org

This urban garden contains trails that lead through woodlands of rare trees, native plants, wildflowers, and a bog, along with gardens ranging from formal to kid-friendly.

Hampton National Historic Site

535 Hampton Lane
Towson, MD 21286

(410) 823-1309 x226

www.nps.gov/hamp

This Georgian mansion has formal gardens and 18th-century English-style landscaping, including exotic trees and an herb garden.

Ladew Topiary Gardens

3535 Jarrettsville Pike
Monkton, MD 21111

(410) 557-9466

www.ladewgardens.com

Self-taught gardener Harvey S. Ladew left a 22-acre legacy of topiaries and 15 thematic garden rooms at his 250-acre estate

Lilypons Water Gardens

6800 Lilypons Road
Buckeystown, MD 21717-0010

(800) 999-5459

www.lilypons.com

The display ponds on this 300-acre aquatic farm are stocked with water-loving plants, such as lilies and lotus, and plenty of goldfish. Open Memorial Day to Labor Day.

London Town House and Gardens

839 Londontown Road
Edgewater, MD 21037

(410) 222-1919

www.historiclondontown.com

Eight acres of gardens surround this 18-century inn and tavern. The Winter Garden highlights evergreens, while the Spring Walk shows off spring-flowering plants and collections of hollies, magnolias, daffodils, and both herbaceous and tree peonies.

William Paca House and Garden

186 Prince George Street
Annapolis, MD 21401

(800) 603-4020; (410) 267-7619

www.annapolis.org

A restored 18th-century house and garden (part of the Historic Annapolis Foundation), this "pleasure" garden has formal terraces and parterres, a fish-shaped pond, and a wilderness garden.

MISSISSIPPI

The Crosby Arboretum

P.O. Box 1639
Picayune, MS 39466-1639

(601) 799-2311, ext. 22

www.msstate.edu/dept/crec/camain.html

As a native plant conservatory representing the southeastern United States, the arboretum is home to the Piney Woods Lake display of native water plants, several lovely pitcher-plant bogs, as well as rare, threatened, or endangered plants and wildlife.

Mynelle Gardens

4736 Clinton Boulevard
Jackson, MS 39209-2402

(601) 960-1894

www.lnstar.com/mynelle

You'll find azalea and camellia trails, an all-white garden, an Oriental Island, and colorful swathes of naturalized bulbs, daylilies, perennials, and annuals.

MISSOURI

Missouri Botanical Garden

4344 Shaw Boulevard
St. Louis, MO 63110

(800) 642-8842; (314) 577-9400

www.mobot.org

Arguably the finest botanical garden in the United States. Gardens include English woodlands, Chinese and Japanese styles, a Victorian-era garden, and scented, rock, and succulent collections. Many flowering trees and shrubs enhance the grounds.

The Climatron at the Missouri Botanical Garden

Home to the Kemper Center for Home Gardening, as well as the Climatron®, the world's first geodesic dome conservatory.

Powell Gardens

1609 N.W. U.S. Highway 50
Kingsville, MO 64061

(816) 697-2600

www.powellgardens.org/

This 915-acre botanical garden east of Kansas City features more than 6,000 different plants. Highlights include a three-acre perennial garden, a woodland garden, rock and waterfall gardens, wildflower and prairie grass meadows, and a conservatory.

NORTH CAROLINA

Biltmore Estate

1 Approach Road
Asheville, NC 28803

800 624-1575; (828) 225-1333

www.biltmore.com

The gardens and grounds of Biltmore remain one of the premier achievements of Frederick Law Olmsted. His design style and love of nature are visible today in the four-acre Walled Garden, the Conservatory, the Shrub Garden, the Italian Garden, and other areas, where many of his original plantings have been preserved.

Botanical Gardens at Asheville

151 W. T. Weaver Boulevard
Asheville, NC 28804-3414

(828) 252-5190

www.ashevillebotanicalgardens.org

Plants native to the Southern Appalachian Mountains area are featured here, including trees, shrubs, vines, wildflowers, herbs, grasses, sedges, aquatic plants, ferns, mosses, and lichens—approximately 700 species altogether.

Sarah P. Duke Gardens

418 Anderson Street
Duke University
Durham, NC 27708-0341

(919) 684-3698

www.hr.duke.edu/dukegardens

Terraces designed by Ellen Biddle Shipman are just one of the highlights here; there's also an Asiatic arboretum, a native-plant garden, a reflecting pond, and beautiful displays of bulbs and perennials.

The terraces at the Sarah P. Duke Gardens

North Carolina Botanical Garden

The University of North Carolina at Chapel Hill
CB 3375 Totten Center
Chapel Hill, NC 27599-3375
(919) 962-0522
www.ncbg.unc.edu

Fifteen collections and display gardens are found here, including carnivorous and endangered plants, an herb garden, a medicinal garden, the Native American Garden, and a poison garden. Holder of the largest National Rosemary Collection of the Herb Society of America.

Old Salem

P.O. Box F, Salem Station
Winston-Salem, NC 27108-0346
(888) 653-7253
www.oldsalem.org

This inspired collection of restored vegetable, fruit, and flower gardens was originally tended by the Moravians, who settled in North Carolina from 1766 to 1850. Most plants grown are authentic to the period and include many heirlooms. Small family gardens offer ideas to modern visitors.

Orton Plantation Gardens

9149 Orton Road SE
Winnabow, NC 28479
(910) 371-6851
www.ortongardens.com

Twenty acres of gardens are dominated by flowering annuals and perennials, with countless azaleas and camellias bordering the pathways. There are also mixed pines, deciduous hardwoods, ponds, lakes, lagoons, and the Cape Fear River.

J. C. Raulston Arboretum at North Carolina State University

4415 Beryl Road
Raleigh, NC 27606
(919) 515-3132
www.ncsu.edu/jcraulstonarboretum

Features a fine collection of cold-hardy, temperate-zone plants adapted to Piedmont North Carolina conditions. Extensive collections of annuals, perennials, bulbs, vines, ground covers, shrubs, and trees from over 50 different countries.

Reynolda Gardens of Wake Forest University

100 Reynolda Village
Winston-Salem, NC 27106
(336) 758-5593
www.wfu.edu/gardens

The original 1917 four-acre formal gardens here have been restored to reflect their English, Italian, and Japanese influences. Most of the remaining 129 acres are woodlands, fields, and wetlands.

Sandhills Horticultural Gardens

Sandhills Community College
3395 Airport Road
Pinehurst, NC 28374
(910) 695-3882
www.sandhills.cc.nc.us/lsg/hort.html

Features the Ebersole Holly Garden, conifer and rose gardens, the Sir Walter Raleigh English Garden, a hillside garden, a fruit and vegetable garden, as well as a native wetland trail.

Daniel Stowe Botanical Garden

6500 New Hope Road
Belmont, NC 28012
(704) 825-4490
www.dsbg.org

Examples of some of the many garden displays here include the Four Seasons Garden (with year-round interest using regionally adapted plants). The Cottage Garden contains pre-1920 "pass-along" trees, perennials, and shrubs. The Canal Garden has a tropical flavor with flowers, grasses, and fountains, and the Perennial Garden contains four separate garden rooms.

Tryon Palace Historic Sites and Gardens

P.O. Box 1007
610 Pollock Street
New Bern, NC 28563
(800) 767-1560; (252) 514-4900
www.tryonpalace.org

These re-created 18th-century gardens feature both native and exotic plants of the period. The historic homes around the palace are also worth exploring.

University of North Carolina at Charlotte Botanical Gardens

9201 University City Boulevard
Charlotte, NC 28223-0007
(704) 687-2364
http://gardens.uncc.edu

The woodland garden features native plants of the Carolinas mixed with hybrid rhododendrons. The Harwood Garden contains

Lush vegetable gardens at Old Salem, North Carolina

hardy ornamentals in a semi-Oriental style. There are also greenhouses of orchids, rainforest plants, desert succulents, and tropicals, separated by a courtyard bog garden with carnivorous plants.

Winghaven Gardens and Bird Sanctuary

248 Ridgewood Avenue

Charlotte, NC 28209

(704) 331-0664

www.winghavengardens.com

This three-acre organic garden combines formal gardens with natural woodlands. Pools, birdbaths, and fountains attract birds of all kinds. Environmental education programs on horticulture, ornithology, and ecology are offered.

OKLAHOMA

Myriad Botanical Gardens

301 West Reno

Oklahoma City, OK 73102

(405) 297-3995

www.myriadgardens.com

This 17-acre botanical garden houses the Crystal Bridge Tropical Conservatory collections of exotic plants.

Oklahoma Botanical Garden and Arboretum

360 Agriculture Hall

Stillwater, OK 74078-6027

(405) 744-5414

www.okstate.edu/ag/asnr/hortla

This 100-acre site features over 1,000 species of herbaceous and woody plants. Display gardens include annuals and perennials, a water garden, a rock garden, a miniature railroad garden, a wildscape garden, a Japanese tea garden, and yearly theme gardens.

Tulsa Garden Center

2435 South Peoria Avenue

Tulsa, OK 74114

(918) 746-5125

www.tulsagardencenter.com

Tulsa Garden Center, located in the Snedden Mansion at Woodward Park, offers educational programs. The 45-acre Woodward Park includes rock gardens, an English herb garden, an arboretum, a terraced Italian Renaissance rose garden, a Victorian conservatory, and an azalea garden.

Spring trees and shrubs in bloom at Brookgreen Gardens in South Carolina

Will Rogers Horticultural Gardens

3400 NW 36th Street

Oklahoma City, OK 73112

(405) 943-0827

www.okc.gov

Includes the Ed Lycan conservatory, with its extensive collection of cacti and succulents, as well as an arboretum with both native and exotic species.

SOUTH CAROLINA

Boone Hall

1235 Long Point Road

Mt. Pleasant, SC 29464

(800) 468-8060 ; (843) 856-5361

www.boonehallplantation.com

Huge live oaks line the half-mile entrance to this restored plantation. The gardens feature antique roses and displays of bulbs, annuals, perennials, camellias, and azaleas.

Brookgreen Gardens

1931 Brookgreen Drive

Murrells Inlet, SC 29576

(800) 849-1931; (843) 235-6000

www.brookgreen.org

Over 2,000 kinds of plants are found here, including a replicated rice field and a Lowcountry center with wildflowers. Hundreds of magnificent American sculptures are located throughout the gardens.

Cypress Gardens

3030 Cypress Gardens Road

Moncks Corner, SC 29461

(843) 553-0515

www.cypressgardens.org

Here you can explore a swamp on a flatbottom boat, hike a nature trail, and visit a butterfly house, a freshwater aquarium and reptile center, or an antique rose garden.

Magnolia Plantation and Its Gardens

3550 Ashley River Road

Charleston, SC 29414

(800) 367-3517; (843) 571-1266

www.magnoliaplantation.com

The wide range of displays here includes the Biblical Garden, the Barbados Tropical Garden, the Audubon Swamp Garden, and a holly and camellia maze.

Middleton Place

4300 Ashley River Road

Charleston, SC 29414

(800) 782-3608; (843) 556-6020

www.middletonplace.org

The oldest landscaped garden in the United States, Middleton Place has 65 acres of terraces, ornamental ponds, shady allées, and garden rooms. Among the many featured plants are camellias, rhododendrons, crepe myrtles, hydrangeas, and magnolias.

Riverbanks Zoo and Garden

500 Wildlife Parkway
Columbia, SC 29210
(803) 779-8717
www.riverbanks.org

This 70-acre zoo gives plants equal billing with the animals. Features include a shade garden, a bog garden, a dry garden, a knot garden, and displays of annuals, perennials, roses, fruits, and berries.

The South Carolina Botanical Garden

102 Garden Trail
Clemson University
Clemson, SC 29634-0174
(864) 656-3405
www.clemson.edu/scbg

Camellia, conifer, hosta, rhododendron, wildflower, butterfly, and turf gardens are on display here, along with wildlife habitat and low-water-use gardens. Also houses the Bob Gamble Geology Museum.

TENNESSEE

Cheekwood: Nashville's Home of Art and Gardens

1200 Forrest Park Drive
Nashville, TN 37205
(615) 356-8000
www.cheekwood.org/garden

This 55-acre site includes pools, fountains, statuary, and extensive boxwood plantings. Among its gardens are a Japanese garden, an herb garden, two perennial gardens, a color garden, a water garden, a four-seasons garden, and an award-winning wildflower garden. There's also the Central American Cloud Forest Greenhouse.

The Hermitage

4580 Rachel's Lane
Nashville, TN 37076-1344
(615) 889-2941
www.thehermitage.com

The former home of President Andrew Jackson features a one-acre formal garden with old roses, irises, peonies, pinks, jonquils, herbs, crepe myrtles, and old trees, including eastern red cedar and other trees planted by Jackson himself.

A glimpse of one of Chandor Gardens' fountains

Memphis Botanic Garden

750 Cherry Road
Memphis, TN 38111
(901) 685-1566
www.memphisbotanicgarden.com

Home of the Goldsmith Civic Garden Center and a world-class Japanese garden. Twenty different plant collections include the Tennessee bicentennial iris garden, wildflower and sensory gardens, azalea and dogwood trails, a magnolia grove, and a daffodil hill.

TEXAS

Bayou Bend Collection and Gardens

1 Westcott Street
Houston, TX 77007
(713) 639-7750
www.mfah.org/bayoubend

The gardens feature a variety of regional plants, including camellias, azaleas, crepe myrtles, and magnolias. Eight formal gardens border the property's 1927 mansion, filled with statues, a butterfly-shaped parterre, and topiaries of Texas animals.

Chandor Gardens

711 W. Lee Street
Weatherford, TX 76086-4024
(817) 613-1700
www.chandorgardens.com

The estate of the late painter Douglas Chandor combines ornate Chinese architecture with formal English gardens. Recently restored and now in the hands of the city of

Weatherford, the gardens contain pathways bordered by hedges and walls leading to garden rooms, fountains, grottos, and a 30-foot waterfall.

The Dallas Arboretum

8525 Garland Road
Dallas, TX 75218
(214) 515-6500
www.dallasarboretum.org

Near downtown Dallas, the arboretum and botanical garden feature a color garden showcasing over 2,000 azalea selections, along with a fern dell and a Woman's Garden (a formal garden with sculpture, water features, and a poetry section).

Fort Worth Botanic Garden

3220 Botanic Garden Boulevard
Fort Worth, TX 76107
(817) 871-7686
www.fwbg.com

This is the oldest botanic garden in Texas, with more than 2,500 native and exotic

Seasonal color at the Fort Worth Botanic Garden

plants. Highlights include several rose gardens, the Japanese Garden, a fragrance garden, and a 10,000-square-foot tropical conservatory. The Entrance Garden features native, low-water-use plants.

Lady Bird Johnson Wildflower Center

4801 La Crosse Avenue
Austin, TX 78739
(512) 292-4100
www.wildflower.org
The 284-acre center showcases native plants of the Texas Hill Country and has a rooftop rainwater collection system, theme gardens, wheelchair-accessible nature trails, and a wildflower meadow, as well as ongoing research projects.

Lilypons Water Gardens

839 FM 1489
Brookshire, TX 77423
(800) 999-5459
www.lilypons.com
The front 2 acres of this 13-acre property contain a store and aquatic display gardens.

Behind this are dozens of propagating ponds and five cold frames for overwintering tender plants.

Mercer Arboretum and Botanic Gardens

22306 Aldine Westfield Road
Humble, TX 77338-1071
(281) 443-8731
www.cp4.hctx.net/mercer
The botanic gardens here include varied plantings of herbs, gingers, ferns, daylilies, bamboo, and other tropicals, along with endangered-species collections. Winding through the arboretum are three miles of woodland walking trails. The Web site features an interactive map with details of the paths and garden areas.

San Antonio Botanical Gardens

555 Funston
San Antonio, TX 78209
(210) 207-3250
www.sabot.org
There are 33 acres of gardens here, including those with formal and old-fashioned garden designs. The Lucile Halsell Conservatory is dominated by dramatic glass pyramids. The Watersaver Garden demonstrates ways that home gardeners can use efficient irrigation, mulch, and other techniques, along with plantings that perform well in hot, dry climates.

Tyler Municipal Rose Garden

Tyler Parks Department
420 South Rose Park Drive
Tyler, TX 75702
(903) 597-3130
www.texasrosefestival.com/museum/garden.htm
This All-America Rose Selections display and test garden has thousands of rose bushes representing approximately 500 selections. One of the many garden highlights is the one-acre Heritage Rose and Sensory Garden, with mid-19th-century roses and companion perennial borders.

The Lady Bird Johnson Wildflower Center

VIRGINIA

Agecroft Hall Museum and Gardens

4305 Sulgrave Road
Richmond, VA 23221
(804) 353-4241
www.agecrofthall.com
These thematic gardens reflect the style of early-17th-century England, including such features as a crepe myrtle walk, a woodland walk, sunken gardens, knot gardens, terraces, and gardens designed for herbs and fragrance. The hall itself is an original Tudor estate, reassembled after being shipped over from Lancashire, England.

The Colonial Williamsburg Foundation

P.O. Box 1776
Williamsburg, VA 23187
(757) 229-1000
www.history.org
This extensive 18th-century restoration has 500 buildings and 100 gardens spread over more than 90 acres. Kitchen, herb, formal, fruit, and parterre gardens of the Colonial period are featured, and both European and Asian plant species, imported by the colonists, are combined with native plants.

Lewis Ginter Botanical Garden

1800 Lakeside Avenue

Richmond, VA 23228-4700

(80 -9887

www.lewisginter.org

Among the seasonally changing floral displays are perennial gardens, a conifer collection, a children's garden, an island garden, as well as the Tea House and Asian Valley garden. There is also a conservatory of exotic and unusual subtropical and tropical plants.

Gunston Hall Plantation

10709 Gunston Road

Mason Neck, VA 22079

(703) 550-9220

www.gunstonhall.org

The formal 250-year-old boxwood garden and allée here were planted by the 18th-century American patriot George Mason. The ongoing garden archaeology project is excavating various 18th-century features from the garden and grounds.

Maymont

1700 Hampton Street

Richmond, VA 23220

(804) 358-7166

www.maymont.org

This 100-acre Victorian estate has an arboretum stocked with thousands of trees and shrubs, both native and exotic. There are Italian and Japanese gardens, along with a variety of other specialty gardens.

Monticello

P.O. Box 316

Charlottesville, VA 22902

(434) 984-9800

www.monticello.org

The renowned estate where Thomas Jefferson lived from 1770 to 1826 has restored flower and vegetable gardens, orchards, vineyards, and an ornamental grove of trees carefully pruned to showcase their contrasting foliage textures.

Norfolk Botanical Garden

6700 Azalea Garden Road

Norfolk, VA 23518-5337

(757) 441-5830

www.virginiagarden.org

You can tour this multifaceted garden by foot, tram, or boat. Highlights include an

Colorful displays command attention at the Lewis Ginter Botanical Garden in Richmond, Virginia.

All-America Rose Selections display and test garden, the Bicentennial Rose Garden (with more than 4,000 plants representing over 250 selections), an award-winning camellia collection, and a rhododendron collection. The Garden also offers many educational programs, summer camps, and family activities and events.

George Washington's Mount Vernon Estate and Gardens

3200 George Washington Memorial Parkway

Mount Vernon, VA 22121

(703) 780-2000

www.mountvernon.org

The 500-acre estate of George Washington reflects his practical nature, with a kitchen garden, a botanical garden, and the George Washington fruit garden and nursery. But he also delighted in flowers, and visitors were then, as now, invited to stroll through the pleasure gardens as well.

Woodlawn

9000 Richmond Highway

Alexandria, VA 22309

(703) 780-4000

www.nationaltrust.org/national_trust_ sites/woodlawn.html

This Federal-style estate—originally part of the Mount Vernon property—has 19th-century-style gardens, parterres, and a heritage rose garden.

WEST VIRGINIA

Core Arboretum

West Virginia University

Morgantown, WV 26506-6057

(304) 293-5201

www.as.wvu.edu/biology/facility/ arboretum.html

Ninety-one acres of mostly old-growth forest here include hiking trails, a steep hillside, the Monongahela River flood plain, and three acres of lawn dotted with specimen trees.

Mail-Order Suppliers

In an era where gigantic home centers sell everything from groceries to plants to plumbing supplies, it's nice to know that there are still plenty of specialty nurseries and garden retailers who maintain the personal touch. Whether you leaf through a mail-order catalog or browse their products online, you'll find practically every garden item your heart desires, including seeds, roses, bulbs, trees, perennials, shrubs, trees, herbs, houseplants, tropicals, tools, natural pest controls, and more.

The following pages list a sampling of the many reputable firms that ship quality seeds, plants, and garden accessories. (We're sorry if we've left somebody out, but we only have room for so many.) Many of these companies reside in the South. Regardless of their geographic location, however, all ship far and wide. Some charge a modest price for a printed catalog, but once you're on their mailing list, future catalogs usually come free. Keep in mind that street addresses, telephone numbers, and website addresses are subject to change.

The Terra Ceia Farms, North Carolina

SEED SUPPLIERS

Baker Creek Heirloom Seeds
2278 Baker Creek Road
Mansfield, MO 65704
(417) 924-8917 phone and fax
www.rareseeds.com
In addition to many American favorites, boasts the largest selection of Asian and European heirloom vegetable and flower seeds in the United States.

The Cook's Garden
P. O. Box 535
Londonderry, VT 05148
(800) 457-9703; fax (800) 457-9705
www.cooksgarden.com
The Cook's Garden tests and saves seeds collected from all over the world. You can order organic vegetable seeds and seedlings, as well as herbs, flowers, books, and garden supplies.

J. L. Hudson, Seedsman
Star Route 2, Box 337
La Honda, CA 94020
www.jlhudsonseeds.net
Carries rare seeds and native plants from every continent, including flowers, vines, trees, cacti, herbs, heirloom vegetables, ornamentals, hardy perennials, medicinal plants, and tropicals.

Johnny's Selected Seeds
955 Benton Avenue
Winslow, ME 04901-2601
(207) 861-3901; fax (800) 738-6314
www.johnnyseeds.com
This certified organic farm carries flower, vegetable, culinary, medicinal, and aromatic herb seeds, as well as gardening tools, accessories, and supplies. All seeds are tested on-site.

Park Seed Company
1 Parkton Avenue
Greenwood, SC 29647
(800) 213-0076; fax (800) 275-9941
www.parkseed.com
More than 1,500 selections of vegetable and flower seed available here, as well as a variety of bulbs for indoor and outdoor use. Also includes perennials suited for planting while bulbs are dormant.

Pinetree Garden Seeds
P. O. Box 300
New Gloucester, ME 04260
(207) 926-3400; fax (888) 527-3337
www.superseeds.com
Extensive selection of vegetable, herb, and flower seeds. Also sells fruits, bulbs, tools, garden books, soil conditioners, and organic fertilizers, and pesticides.

Ronniger's Potato Farm
Star Route RD. 73
Moyie Springs, ID 83845
(208) 267-7938; fax (208) 267-3265
www.ronnigers.com
This large selection of seed potatoes is sorted by color, heat tolerance, keeping quality, and scab resistance. Also offered are cover crops, garlic, shallots, and onions—all certified organic.

Seeds of Change
P. O. Box 15700
Santa Fe, NM 87593-1500
(888) 762-7333
www.seedsofchange.com
Grows certified organic flower, herb, and vegetable seeds, as well as gourmet greens and theme collections, such as heirloom tomatoes, chiles, and sunflowers. Very complete and informative catalog with many photos.

Seeds of Change Research Farm, New Mexico

Seed Savers Exchange

3076 North Winn Road
Decorah, IA 52101
(563) 382-5990; fax (563) 382-5872
www.seedsavers.org
This extensive listing of heirloom vegetables, fruits, and grains has excellent descriptions and color photos.

Select Seeds Antique Flowers

180 Stickney Hill Road
Union, CT 06076-4617
(860) 684-9310; fax (800) 653-3304
www.selectseeds.com
Specializes in heirloom seeds, annuals, fragrant plants, flowering vines, and wildflowers. The catalog is beautifully photographed and illustrated.

Shepherd's Garden Seeds

See White Flower Farms in Perennials.

Southern Exposure Seed Exchange

P. O. Box 460
Mineral, VA 23117
(540) 894-9480; fax (540) 894-9481
www.southernexposure.com
Produces seed for flowers, herbs, peppers, spinach, tomatoes, and many Southern heirloom vegetables. All seeds are guaranteed free of chemical treatment and genetic modification.

Thompson & Morgan Seedsmen, Inc.

P. O. Box 1308
Jackson, NJ 08527-0308
(800) 274-7333; (888) 466-4769
www.thompson-morgan.com
This established company offers an extensive selection of seeds for flowers, vegetables, herbs, trees, and shrubs.

Tomato Growers Supply Company

P. O. Box 2237
Fort Myers, FL 33902
(888) 478-7333; fax (888) 768-3476
www.tomatogrowers.com
Hundreds of selections of tomato seed, from beefsteaks to cherry tomatoes. They also feature seeds for sweet and hot chili peppers, tomatillos, and eggplants.

Wildseed Farms

425 Wildflower Hills
P. O. Box 3000
Fredericksburg, TX 78624-3000
(800) 848-0078; fax (830) 990-8090
www.wildseedfarms.com
Regional wildflower mixes, native grasses, and exotic garden species and selections are pictured and described in the catalog.

Willhite Seed, Inc.

P. O. Box 23
Poolville, TX 76487-0023
**(800) 828-1840; (817) 599-8656;
fax (817) 599-5843**
www.willhiteseed.com
Specializes in vegetables suited to the South, including melons, corn, tomatoes, peas, peppers, gourds, and squash.

ROSES

Antique Rose Emporium

9300 Lueckemeyer Road
Brenham, TX 77833-6453
**(800) 441-0002; (979) 836-9051;
fax (979) 836-0928**
www.weareroses.com
Old garden roses selected for Southern climates and grown on their own roots. Handy reference chart allows you to choose roses by light needs, type, color, and zone.

Carroll Gardens

444 East Main Street
Westminster, MD 21157-5540
(800) 638-6334; fax (410) 857-4112
www.carrollgardens.com
Roses are a specialty here, but also carries over 2,300 perennials, herbs, vines, bulbs, evergreen and deciduous shrubs, unusual and dwarf conifers, and shade and flowering trees. Catalog provides great descriptions and cultural information.

Heirloom Roses

24062 N.E. Riverside Drive
St. Paul, OR 97137
**(800) 820-0465; (503) 538-1576;
fax (503) 538-5902**
www.heirloomroses.com
Specializes in a wide variety of rose types and selections, especially old, fragrant, and disease-resistant roses. Stock is grown both in the greenhouse and outside, so that plants can be shipped year round.

Jackson & Perkins

1 Rose Lane
Medford, OR 97501
(877) 322-2300; fax (800) 242-0329
www.jacksonandperkins.com
Carries roses of every kind and color, in addition to perennials, gifts, and various garden and home accessories.

Nor'East Miniature Roses, Inc.

P. O. Box 307

Rowley, MA 01969

(800) 426-6485; fax (978) 948-7964

www.noreast-miniroses.com

A large selection of hardy miniature roses. Catalog organized by color and category; company ships year-round.

Wayside Gardens

1 Garden Lane

Hodges, SC 29695-0001

(800) 213-0379; fax (800) 817-1124

www.waysidegardens.com

A varied collection of roses, including climbers, hybrid teas, grandifloras, floribundas, and David Austin English roses. Each plant is at least two years old and field-grown. Also sells perennials for sun and shade, grasses, bulbs, shrubs, trees, vines, and garden supplies and accessories.

Witherspoon Rose Culture

P. O. Box 52489

Durham, NC 27717-2489

(800) 643-0315; (919) 489-4446; fax (919) 490-0623

www.witherspoonrose.com

Selections include hybrids, grandifloras, David Austin English roses, floribundas, Ol' Country Garden roses, climbers, miniatures, and tree roses.

'Alba' Lady Banks's rose

BULBS, CORMS, AND TUBERS

Brent and Becky's Bulbs

7900 Daffodil Lane

Gloucester, VA 23061

(804) 693-3966; fax (804) 693-9436

www.brentandbeckysbulbs.com

Huge selection of fall and spring-flowering bulbs, including daffodils, tulips, hyacinths, iris, lilies, alliums, dahlias, and gladiolus. Also offered are gardening tools, books, bulb fertilizer, and other accessories.

Dutch Gardens

144 Intervale Road

Burlington, VT 05401

(800) 944-2250; (888) 821-0448; fax (800) 551-6712

www.dutchgardens.com

Many types of bulbs, including begonias, dahlias, gladiolus, tulips, daffodils, and specialty bulbs shipped directly from the Netherlands. Also sells field-grown perennials, roses, and shrubs.

Louisiana Nursery

1908 Parkview Drive

Opelousas, LA 70570

(337) 948-3696; fax (337) 942-6404

www.durionursery.com

A huge assortment of daylilies, irises, and rare bulbs such as crinums. A separate catalog offers fruit trees (like apricots, plums, and figs), shrubs, vines, bamboo, and ornamental grasses.

'Too Sweet' tall bearded iris

McClure & Zimmerman

108 Winnebago Street

P. O. Box 368

Friesland, WI 53935-0368

(800) 883-6998; fax (800) 374-6120

www.mzbulb.com

This extensive list of bulbs includes many rare and hard-to-find selections. Catalog also contains valuable planting information.

Old House Gardens Heirloom Bulbs

536 Third Street

Ann Arbor, MI 48103-4957

(734) 995-1486; fax (734) 995-1687

www.oldhousegardens.com

Specialty catalog lists antique bulbs such as daffodils, crocus, hyacinths, and tulips, many native to the United States, including the South; Southern heirloom bulbs are a specialty. Catalog also offers a great selection of reference books.

John Scheepers, Inc.

23 Tulip Drive

P. O. Box 638

Bantam, CT 06750

(860) 567-0838; fax (860) 567-5323

www.johnscheepers.com

More than 700 selections of tulips, daffodils, scilla, alliums, fritillaries, lilies, and hard-to-find bulbs, along with amaryllis and paperwhites for indoor culture.

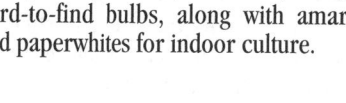

Swan Island Dahlias

P. O. Box 700, Dept. 1
Canby, OR 97013-0700
(800) 410-6540; (503) 266-7711;
fax (503) 266-8768
www.dahlias.com
Both dahlia collections and individual tubers are available. Catalog lists various dahlia types ranging from ten inches or greater to miniatures and novelties.

The Terra Ceia Farms

3810 Terra Ceia Road
Pantego, NC 27860-9312
(800) 858-2852; fax (252) 943-3382
www.terraceiafarms.com
Catalog specializes in bulk bulb orders for the spring and fall seasons including lilies, daffodils, alliums, tulips, hyacinths, and irises. Also look for peonies and hostas.

Van Bourgondien

245 Farmingdale Road
P. O. Box 1000
Babylon, NY 11702-9004
(800) 622-9997; (800) 327-4268
www.dutchbulbs.com
Home of many kinds of bulbs, including amaryllis, daffodils, begonias, peonies, tulips, dahlias, and Asiatic and Oriental hybrid lilies; also carries a large selection of perennials.

FRUITS AND NUTS

Acorn Springs Farms

2488 Hickey Road
Hallsville, TX 75650
(866) 4Citrus; (866) 424-8787;
fax (903) 668-1623
www.acornsprings.com
Offers dwarf lemon, lime, orange, calamondin, citron, Mandarin, and grapefruit trees, many suited to growing in containers.

Bass Pecan Company

400 Hwy. 13
925 East Main
Lumberton, MS 39455-0042
(800) 732-2671; fax (601) 796-3630
www.basspecanco.com
This company sells trees and in-shell or shelled pecans. Gift items such as wood grain buckets and tins are also available.

Cider Mill from 1929

Big Horse Creek Farm

P. O. Box 70
Lansing, NC 28643
(336) 384-1134
www.bighorsecreekfarm.com
Specializes in custom-grafting of antique and heirloom apple trees, including Appalachian mountain apple trees.

Century Farm Orchards

David C. Vernon
1614 Rice Road
Reidsville, NC 27320
(336) 349-5709
dcvernon@netpath.net
Specializes in apples grown in the South from the 1600s to the early 1900s. These old selections are grafted to hardy, disease- and drought-resistant modern rootstocks.

Classical Fruits

8831 AL Highway 157
Moulton, AL 35650
(256) 974-8813; fax (256) 974-4060
www.classicalfruits.com
Unique selection of fruit trees include heirloom apples (including disease-resistant types), pears, peaches, nectarines, cherries, plums, and figs. Other fruits available are strawberries, grapes, raspberries, blackberries, and muscadines.

Edible Landscaping

361 Spirit Ridge Lane
P. O. Box 77
Afton, VA 22920
(800) 524-4156; fax (434) 361-1916
www.eat-it.com
Extensive variety of fruit trees and shrubs ranges from hardy kiwi to black currants and pawpaw. Catalog has concise plant descriptions.

Hidden Springs Nursery

170 Hidden Springs Lane
Cookeville, TN 38501
(931) 268-2592
Bare-root trees and bushes include apple, blueberry, grape, kiwi, pawpaw, pear, quince, and raspberry. Look for plants marked as a "surefire success."

Ison's Nursery and Vineyards

P. O. Box 190
Brooks, GA 30205
(770) 599-6970; (800) 733-0324;
fax (770) 599-1727
www.isons.com
Features muscadine and other berries. Trees include apple, peach, pear, plum nectarine, fig, cherry, pecan, walnut, persimmon, and pomegranate; also sell selections of flowering trees.

Johnson Nursery

1352 Big Creek Road
Ellijay, GA 30540
(888) 276-3187; fax (706) 276-3186
www.johnsonnursery.com
Grows hardy fruit trees and small fruit for the home orchard, including heirloom and disease-resistant selections. Books and orchard supplies available.

Just Fruits and Exotics

30 St. Francis Street
Crawfordville, FL 32327
(888) 926-7441; (850)926-5644;
(850) 926-9885
www.justfruitsandexotics.com
Specializes in low-chill and other fruits including figs, kiwis, peaches, grapes, pears, mayhaw, apples, plums, hardy citrus. Also sells exotic fruits like bananas, pawpaw, jujuba, and pineapple guava.

Louisiana Nursery

See listing in Bulbs, Corms, and Tubers.

Raintree Nursery

391 Butts Road

Morton, WA 98356

(360) 496-6400; fax (888) 770-8358

www.raintreenursery.com

Specializes in fruit and nut trees of all kinds and unusual edible plants from around the world. Also offers roses, vines and other ornamental plants.

Simmons Berry Farm

11542 North Highway 71

Mountainburg, AR 72946

(479) 369-2345

www.alcasoft.com/simmons

Has a good selection of strawberries, blackberries, blueberries, raspberries, grapes, and muscadines.

Stark Bro's Nurseries & Orchards

Highway 54 West

Louisiana, MO 63353

(800) 325-4180; (573) 754-5111;

fax (573) 754-8880

www.starkbros.com

Offers berries and fruit trees of all kinds; specializes in 'Delicious' apples. Also look for its expanding list of ornamentals and roses. All plants are shipped bare-root.

PERENNIALS

Asiatica

P. O. Box 270

Lewisberry, PA 17339

(717) 938-8677; fax (717) 938-0771

www.asiaticanursery.com

This micronursery specializes in rare Asian plants, mostly for shade gardens. Stocks a large selection of wild gingers, Asian Jack-in-the-pulpits, and orchids.

Bluestone Perennials

7211 Middle Ridge Road

Madison, OH 44057-3096

(800) 852-5243 phone and fax

www.bluestoneperennials.com

Offers 1,000 types of perennials and shrubs, presented in a nicely photographed catalog. Includes preplanned perennial garden collections.

Carroll Gardens

See listing in Roses.

Crownsville Nursery

P. O. Box 797

Crownsville, MD 21032

(410) 849-3143; fax (410) 849-3427

www.crownsvillenursery.com

Offers more than 200 selections of hostas; other specialties include cannas and coleus. Perennials, ferns, shrubs, and vines are also available.

Peonies in full bloom

Earthly Pursuits

2901 Kuntz Road

Windsor Mill, MD 21244

(410) 496-2523; fax (410) 496-5894

www.earthlypursuits.net

Sells a variety of ornamental grasses, bamboos, ferns, and aquatic plants.

Eco-Gardens

P. O. Box 1227

Decatur, GA 30031

(404) 294-6468; fax (404) 294-8173

Features native and exotic plants hardy in the eastern Piedmont region, including hellebores, trilliums, sedums, asarums, and more than 100 different ferns.

ForestFarm

990 Tetherow Road

Williams, OR 97544-9599

(541) 846-7269; fax (541) 846-6963

www.forestfarm.com

Extensive listings including native plants, ferns, grasses, common and uncommon perennials, shrubs, and trees. Detailed print catalog and searchable online catalog help you choose among the wealth of plant material offered.

Goodness Grows, Inc.

P. O. Box 311

332 Elberton Road

Lexington, GA 30648-0311

(706) 743-5055; fax (706) 743-5112

Catalog lists perennials, annuals, roses, and shrubs with excellent descriptions.

Heronswood Nursery

7530 N.E. 288th Street

Kingston, WA 98346-9502

(360) 297-4172; fax (360) 297-8321

www.heronswood.com

This astonishing selection includes many new and unusual perennials, a huge collection of conifers and shrubs, as well as rare to common trees. Informative, lively catalog has detailed descriptions and horticultural information.

**Klehm's Song Sparrow
Perennial Farm**

13101 E. Rye Road

Avalon, WI 53505

(800) 553-3715; fax (608) 883-2257

www.songsparrow.com

This nursery sells hostas, daylilies, irises, herbaceous and tree peonies, ornamental shrubs, and trees.

Niche Gardens

1111 Dawson Road

Chapel Hill, NC 27516

(919) 967-0078; fax (919) 967-4026

www.nichegdn.com

Specializes in perennials, ornamental grasses, wildflowers, southeastern natives, and underused trees and shrubs.

Park's Countryside Garden

See Park Seed Company in Seed Suppliers.

Pine Ridge Gardens

P. O. Box 200

832 Sycamore Road

London, AR 72847

(479) 293-4359; fax (479) 293-4659

www.pineridgegardens.com

Stocks native plants of the south-central region as well as other perennials, hostas, Japanese and Siberian irises, and shrubs.

Plant Delights Nursery, Inc.

9241 Sauls Road

Raleigh, NC 27603

(919) 772-4794; fax (919) 662-0370

www.plantdelights.com

An extensive breeding program has produced such hostas as 'White Wall Tire', 'Tattoo', and 'Elvis Lives', but more traditional hostas are also included. Impressive selection of perennials and native and exotic plants. Price of amusingly written catalog is 10 stamps or a box of chocolates (preferred payment).

Shooting Star Nursery

444 Bates Road

Frankfort, KY 40601

(502) 223-1679; fax (502) 227-5700

www.shootingstarnursery.com

Specializes in nursery-propagated plants and seeds native to the eastern United States. Includes perennials, seeds, seed mixes, prairie plants, and trees and shrubs.

Shade-loving poolside plants

Singing Springs Nursery

8802 Wilkerson Road

Cedar Grove, NC 27231

(919) 732-9403; fax (919) 732-6336

www.singingspringsnursery.com

Tender tropicals and hardy perennials, including many unique selections of coleus, are offered. Catalog provides good descriptions and photos.

Sunlight Gardens

174 Golden Lane

Andersonville, TN 37705

(800) 272-7396; (865) 494-8237;

fax (865) 494-7086

www.sunlightgardens.com

This nursery propagates wildflowers, ferns, perennials, vines, trees, and shrubs that are native or naturalized to the eastern United States. Catalog addresses common questions and provides background material.

The Viette Farm and Nursery

P. O. Box 1109

Fisherville, VA 22939

(800) 575-5538; fax (540) 943-0782

www.inthegardenradio.com

More than 3,000 kinds of daylilies, hostas, peonies, iris, poppies, and many unusual plants are listed, for both sun and shade gardens. Website contains articles and discussions of interest to gardeners.

Wayside Gardens

See listing in Roses.

Weird Dude's Plant Zoo

1164 Frog Pond Road

Staunton, VA 24401

(540) 886-6364; fax (540) 885-8223

www.weirddudesplantzoo.com

Just as you'd expect, the Weird Dude carries a good selection of rare and unusual perennials, alpines, trees, shrubs, and tropical plants.

White Flower Farm

P. O. Box 50

Litchfield, CT 06759-0050

(800) 503-9624; fax (860) 496-1418

www.whiteflowerfarm.com

Well-written, detailed catalog shows a selected range of perennials, shrubs, vines, bulbs, and houseplants. Also offers Shepherd's Garden Seeds for vegetables, herbs, and flowers.

TREES AND SHRUBS

Camellia Forest Nursery

9701 Carrie Road

Chapel Hill, NC 27516

(919) 968-0504; fax (919) 960-7690

www.camforest.com

Wide variation of camellias—from small, simple-flowered plants to large, many-petaled hybrids—is sold here. Also offered are trees and herbaceous plants.

Carroll Gardens

See listing in Roses.

Fairweather Gardens

P. O. Box 330
Greenwich, NJ 08323
(856) 451-6261; fax (856) 451-0303
www.fairweathergardens.com
Grows unusual trees, shrubs, and perennials. Catalog provides complete descriptions of all plants available.

Girard Nurseries

P. O. Box 428
6839 North Ridge East
Geneva, OH 44041-0428
(440) 466-2881; fax (440) 466-3999
www.girardnurseries.com
Full-color catalog provides lengthy descriptions of flowering trees and shrubs, ground covers, perennials, grasses, and conifers.

Greer Gardens, Inc.

1280 Goodpasture Island Road
Eugene, OR 97401
(800) 548-0111; (541) 686-8266; fax (541) 686-0910
www.greergardens.com
The catalog photographs show the large variety of plants available. Look for conifers, bonsai, ferns, magnolias, maples, and of course rhododendrons and azaleas.

Heronswood Nursery

See listing in Perennials.

Louisiana Nursery

See listing in Bulbs, Corms, and Tubers.

Rare Find Nursery

957 Patterson Road
Jackson, NJ 08527
(732) 833-0613; fax (732) 833-1965
www.rarefindnursery.com
Carry thousands of rhododendron species and selections, including favorite 'oldtimers' and new selections.

Roslyn Nursery

211 Burrs Lane
Dix Hills, NY 11746
(631) 643-9347; fax (631) 427-0894
www.roslynnursery.com
Stocks exotic and rare trees, shrubs, rhododendrons, azaleas, camellias, perennials, ground covers, and other ornamentals.

Wilkerson Mill Gardens

9595 Wilkerson Mill Road
Palmetto, GA 30268
(770) 463-2400; fax (770) 463-9717
www.hydrangea.com
In addition to 150 different hydrangeas, this specialist nursery also offers hard-to-find shrubs, perennials, and vines.

Woodlanders Inc.

1128 Colleton Avenue
Aiken, SC 29801
(803) 648-7522 phone and fax
www.woodlanders.net
Specializes in ornamentals for warm climates that have been overlooked and underused. Look for trees, shrubs, vines, perennials, ferns, subtropicals, and an extensive selection of reference books.

'Snow Queen' oak-leaf hydrangea

HERBS

Dabney Herbs

P. O. Box 22061
Louisville, KY 40252
(502) 893-5198 phone and fax
www.dabneyherbs.com
Herbs and native Midwestern plants, essential oils, books, and related gardening products. Website features herb lore, tips, and recipes.

Garden Medicinals and Culinaries

P. O. Box 320
Earlysville, VA 22936
(434) 964-9113; fax (434) 973-8717
www.gardenmedicinals.com
Offers a good selection of seeds and plants for the home herbalist, along with related books, supplies, and equipment.

Richters Herb Specialists

#357 Highway 47
Goodwood, ON
Canada L0C 1A0
(905) 640-6677; fax (905) 640-6641
www.richters.com
Colorful catalog shows numerous selections of herb and vegetable plants and seeds. Books, dried herbs, and gardening tools are also available.

Sandy Mush Herb Nursery

316 Surrett Cove Road
Leicester, NC 28748-5517
(828) 683-2014 phone and fax
www.brwm.org/sandymushherbs
Carries a selection of herbs for culinary use, teas, and decorative and medicinal purposes, as well as flowering perennials, scented geraniums, ivies, dye and fiber plants, and native plants.

TROPICAL PLANTS

Aloha Tropicals

1247 Browning Court
Vista, CA 92083
(760) 941-0920 phone and fax
www.alohatropicals.com
A wide assortment of tropical plants, vines, and shrubs, including gingers, plumerias, heliconias, and bananas.

Cala's Tropicals

2209 Clinton Highway
Powell, TN 37849
(865) 945-5584
www.calastropicals.com
An extensive list of Brugmansia seeds as well as exotic vines, such as passionflower, and perennials such as gingers, elephant's ears, and many others.

Gardino Nursery

P. O. Box 83-2024
Delray Beach, FL 33483
(888) 323-1333; fax (561) 495-7383
www.rareflora.com
Rare and unusual plants, including houseplants, vines, ferns, bromeliads, flowering trees, and bonsai starter plants.

Ivies of the World
P. O. Box 408
Weirsdale, FL 32195
(352) 821-2201
Specializes in exotic and common ivies for the enthusiast market; many plants with unique variegation or unusual leaf shapes.

Logee's Greenhouses
141 North Street
Danielson, CT 06239
(888) 330-8038; (860) 774-8038;
fax (888) 774-993
www.logees.com
An enormous collection of tropical and subtropical plants for indoor and outdoor culture. Many rare and exotic plants.

Steve Ray's Bamboo Garden
250 Cedar Cliff Road
Springdale, AL 35146
(205) 594-3438
www.thebamboogardens.com
The catalog lists over 50 bamboos that can be ordered and shipped. In addition, the 50-acre nursery displays and sells over 100 selections on-site.

Yucca Do Nursery Inc.
P. O. Box 907
Hempstead, TX 77445
(979) 826-4580; fax (979) 826-4571
www.yuccado.com
Outstanding collection of hardy, rare and unusual warm-season plants. They offer bromeliads, bulbs, cacti, cycads, grasses, palms, perennials, subtropicals, and trees.

Weird Dude's Plant Zoo
See listing in Perennials.

ORGANIC SUPPLIES

The Beneficial Insect Company
P. O. Box 119
Glendale Springs, NC 28629
(336) 973-8490
www.thebeneficialinsectco.com
Specializes in beneficial insects and other natural and biological pest controls for gardens, farms, orchards and greenhouses.

Angel's trumpet at Weird Dude's Plant Zoo, Virginia

Gardens Alive!
5100 Schenley Place
Lawrenceburg, IN 47025
(812) 537-8650; fax (812) 537-8660
www.gardensalive.com
Catalog describes products and techniques to help control pests and disease, as well as selling fertilizers and soil amendments.

Home Harvest Garden Supply, Inc.
3807 Bank Street
Baltimore, MD 21224
(800) 348-4769; (410) 327-8403;
fax (410) 327-8411
www.homeharvest.com
Beneficial insects, natural and biological pest controls, organic fertilizers and soil amendments, hydroponics supplies, and grow lights.

The Natural Gardening Company
P. O. Box 750776
Petaluma, CA 94975-0776
(707) 766-9303; fax (707) 766-9747
www.naturalgardening.com
Specializes in certified organic seeds and seedlings for vegetables (especially tomatoes), culinary herbs and flowers, drip irrigation supplies, and organic pest controls, including pheromone traps and beneficial insects.

Peaceful Valley Farm Supply
P. O. Box 2209
Grass Valley, CA 95945
(888) 784-1722; (530) 272-4769
www.groworganic.com
Catalog features books and products for and information about propagation, seed-starting, cover crops, irrigation, season extenders, composting, fertilizers, tools, and weed and pest management.

TOOLS AND SUPPLIES

Duncraft
102 Fisherville Road
Concord, NH 03303
(800) 593-5656; fax (603) 226-3735
www.duncraft.com
Features bird-feeding supplies—feeders, baths, seed, houses, hardware accessories, squirrel baffles, as well as garden décor and field guides.

Gardener's Supply Company
128 Intervale Road
Burlington, VT 05401
(888) 833-1412; fax (800) 551-6712
www.gardeners.com
Here you'll find garden-tested tools, plant labels, watering supplies, floating row covers, seed germination kits, plant supports, garden ornaments, composters, containers, garden furniture, greenhouses, and more.

Kinsman Company
P. O. Box 428
Pipersville, PA 18947
(800) 733-4146; (800) 733-4129;
fax (215) 766-5624
www.kinsmangarden.com
An extensive collection of gardening supplies, including planters, plant supports, pruners, tools, and terra-cotta items, as well as products to attract birds and butterflies.

Smith & Hawken
P. O. Box 8690
Pueblo, CO 81008-9998
(800) 776-3336
www.smithandhawken.com
Company specializes in gifts, plants and flowers, containers, garden ornaments, high-quality tools, garden furniture (especially teak), clothing, footwear, and books.

Glossary
Gardening Terms

Acid soil. A soil with a pH of less than 7. See "Soil pH" (page 645).

Aerial roots. Roots produced above the ground—for instance, by a vine, to help it cling to a surface. English ivy *(Hedera helix)* is an example.

Alkaline soil. A soil with a pH of more than 7. See "Soil pH" (page 645).

Alternate leaves. See Opposite leaves.

Annual. A plant that completes its life cycle in a year or less. For information on planting and caring for annuals, see page 596.

Anther. See illustration for Flower.

Axil. The inner angle between a leaf (or other organ of a plant) and the stem from which it springs. Organs in the axil, such as flowers and buds, are called "axillary."

Balled-and-burlapped (B-and-B). Refers to specimen shrubs and trees sold for planting with a large ball of soil around the roots, wrapped in burlap or a synthetic material to hold the soil together. Usually available from late fall to early spring. For planting instructions, see page 630.

Bare-root. Refers to deciduous shrubs and trees and some perennials sold for planting with the soil removed from their roots. Usually sold in winter and early spring. For information on planting bare-root shrubs and trees, see page 631; for perennials, see page 616.

Bedding plant. Any colorful plant suitable for massing in beds. Most bedding plants are annuals, or perennials that are grown as annuals.

Biennial. A plant that germinates and produces foliage and roots during its first growing season, then blooms, produces seed, and dies during its second growing season. For information on planting and caring for biennials, see page 597.

Blanching. The process of blocking light from parts of vegetables to keep them paler in color or milder in flavor (or both). For cauliflower, endive, or cardoon (an artichoke relative), the outer leaves are tied over the inner head or leaves. Asparagus is blanched by mounding soil over the emerging spears.

Bolt. To produce seeds or flowers prematurely; the term usually refers to annual flowers and vegetables. Bolting most frequently occurs when plants that prefer cool weather (lettuce, for example) are set out too late in the year or when unseasonably hot weather rushes growth.

Bonsai. Bonsai (the word is Japanese for "tray planting") is the fine art of growing and carefully training dwarfed plants in containers selected to harmonize with them. The objective is to create a tree or landscape in miniature; often the dwarfed trees take on the appearance of very old, gnarled specimens.

Bracts. Modified leaves growing just below a flower or flower cluster; not all plants have them. Bracts are usually green, but in some cases they are conspicuous and colorful, so much so that people often mistake them for flowers or petals. Bougainvillea, dogwood *(Cornus)*, and poinsettia *(Euphorbia pulcherrima)* all have showy bracts.

Broad-leafed. Used to describe evergreen shrubs or trees, this term refers to plants that have foliage year-round—boxwood *(Buxus)* and camellia, for example—but are not conifers (such as juniper), which have needle-like or scalelike leaves. When used to categorize weeds, "broad-leafed" refers to any weed that is not a grass.

Bud. An undeveloped or rudimentary organ or shoot of a plant. A flower bud develops into a blossom, whereas a growth bud produces shoots of leafy growth. Terminal buds (also called apical buds) are produced at the end of a shoot. Lateral buds (also called axillary buds) are produced in the axil of a plant. Latent buds lie dormant beneath the bark; if a branch breaks or is cut off near a latent bud, that bud may develop into a new shoot. For an illustration of growth buds, see page 640.

Budding. A method of propagation in which a bud (the scion) from one plant is inserted beneath the bark of another related plant. See "Budding and Grafting" (page 639).

Bud union. The point at which a shoot or bud (scion) unites with the rootstock. See "Budding and Grafting" (page 639).

Bulb. In layman's terms, any plant that grows from a thickened underground structure is a bulb. Botanically speaking, however, that's not accurate. A true bulb consists of an underground stem base that contains an embryonic plant surrounded by scales—modified leaves that overlap each other. Bulblike structures include corms, rhizomes, tubers, and tuberous roots. See "The Five Bulb Types" (page 598).

Calyx. Collectively, the sepals of a flower.

Cambium. The green layer of growing cells between the xylem and phloem. See "Plant Anatomy and Growth" (page 626).

Cane. An elongated flowering or fruiting stem, usually arising directly from the roots. Examples of cane-producing plants include barberry *(Berberis)*, forsythia, rose, raspberry, and grape.

Catkin. A slender, spikelike, often drooping flower cluster. Birch *(Betula)*, chestnut *(Castanea)*, and oak *(Quercus)* are three familiar trees that produce catkins.

Chill requirement. Many bulbs, perennials, and deciduous shrubs and trees (fruit trees in particular) need a certain amount of cold weather—measured in hours required at temperatures below 45°F—in order to grow and bloom well in the following year. In mild-winter areas where these plants do not receive the necessary winter chill, their performance is often disappointing: they leaf out late, fail to flower or fruit well, and often decline in health and vigor. For some of these plants—apples and lilacs *(Syringa)*, for example—selections have been developed that require less winter chill. In milder-winter areas, bulbs that require winter chilling can be stored in the vegetable bin of the refrigerator prior to planting; chill them for as long as the supplier recommends.

Chlorosis. A disorder affecting the foliage of trees, shrubs, and other plants, in which leaves turn yellowish while veins remain green. See page 627.

Clone. A vegetatively reproduced plant that is genetically identical to its parent plant. See "Plant Propagation" (page 632).

Composite head. See Inflorescence.

Compound leaf. See Leaf.

Conifer. A more precise term for some of the plants many people call evergreens, such as cedar *(Cedrus)*, juniper *(Juniperus)*, and pine *(Pinus)*. Leaves are usually narrow and needle-like or tiny and scalelike. A few conifers, including larch *(Larix)* and dawn redwood *(Metasequoia)*, are deciduous. All conifers bear seeds in cones or in conelike structures (juniper berries, for example). Yew *(Taxus)* and *Podocarpus* bear single seeds on fleshy bases, but because of their needlelike foliage, they are sometimes grouped with conifers.

Corm. A swollen underground stem base composed of solid tissue (unlike the scales of a true bulb). See "The Five Bulb Types" (page 598).

Corolla. Collectively, the petals of a flower.

Crown. This word has two meanings. A tree's crown is its entire branch structure, including foliage. "Crown" also refers to the point at which a plant's roots and top structure join, usually at or near the soil line.

Deadhead. To remove spent flowers. By preventing a plant from setting seed, deadheading both prolongs the bloom season and eliminates unwanted seedlings. It also keeps the garden looking tidy.

Deciduous. This term describes any plant that naturally sheds all of its leaves at any one time (usually in fall).

Defoliation. Refers to the unnatural loss of foliage, usually to the detriment of the plant's health. Defoliation may result from high winds that strip away foliage; intense heat (especially if accompanied by wind) that critically wilts leaves; drought; unusually early or late frosts that strike a plant while it is actively growing; or severe damage caused by chemicals, insects, or diseases.

Dieback. This occurs when a plant's stems die for part of their length, beginning at the tips. Causes of dieback include inadequate moisture, nutrient deficiency, poor climate adaptation, and severe injury from pests or diseases.

Division. A plant propagation method in which a plant is separated into several smaller, rooted plants. See page 635.

Dormancy. The annual period when a plant's growth processes greatly slow down. For many plants, dormancy commences with the onset of winter, when the days grow shorter and the temperatures colder.

Double flower. See Flower forms.

Drainage. The downward movement of water through the soil. When this process happens quickly, the soil is well drained; when it occurs slowly, it is poorly drained. See "Soils and Soil Management" (page 644) for more information on soils and drainage.

Drip line. The circle you would draw on the soil around a tree directly under its outermost branch tips is called the drip line; rainwater tends to drip from the tree at this point. The roots of established trees usually extend beyond the drip line.

Epiphyte. Epiphytes grow on another plant for support but take no nourishment from the host plant. Examples include Spanish moss *(Tillandsia usneoides)* and staghorn ferns *(Platycerium)*. Epiphytes are sometimes mistakenly considered parasites, but true parasites draw nourishment from the host, while epiphytes live on nutrients drawn from the air, rainwater, and organic debris on the supporting plant.

Espalier. A tree or shrub trained so that its branches grow in a flat pattern—against a wall or fence, on a trellis, along horizontal wires. For espalier patterns, see page 643.

Established plant. A plant that is firmly rooted and producing good foliage growth.

Evergreen. Unlike deciduous plants, evergreens never lose all their leaves at one time, although they may shed their foliage regularly. See also Broad-leafed; Conifer.

Exotic plant. A plant that is not indigenous to the region in which it is grown.

BASIC FLOWER FORMS

Single

Semidouble

Double

Family. Every plant belongs to a family whose members share certain broad characteristics that set them apart from plants in other families. Family names are in Latin and typically end in "aceae"; examples include *Rosaceae* (the rose family) and *Iridaceae* (the iris family). A few family names formerly ended simply in "ae": for instance, *Compositae,* the daisy family; *Palmae,* the palm family; and *Leguminosae,* the pea family. Botanists have renamed these, giving them the "-aceae" ending: *Asteraceae* (formerly *Compositae*), *Arecaceae* (formerly *Palmae*), *Fabaceae* (formerly *Leguminosae*). However, some reference works still use the earlier names.

Fertilization. The fusion of male and female gametes (fertile reproductive cells) following pollination.

Fertilize. To apply nutrients (fertilizer) to a plant; see "Fertilizers" (page 607).

Flower. The part of a seed-bearing plant that contains the reproductive organs.

Flower forms: single, semidouble, double. The basic flower forms are single, with one row of petals containing the minimum number of petals for the blossoms of that particular species (usually four, five, or six); semidouble, with two or three times the minimum number of

COMPLETE FLOWER

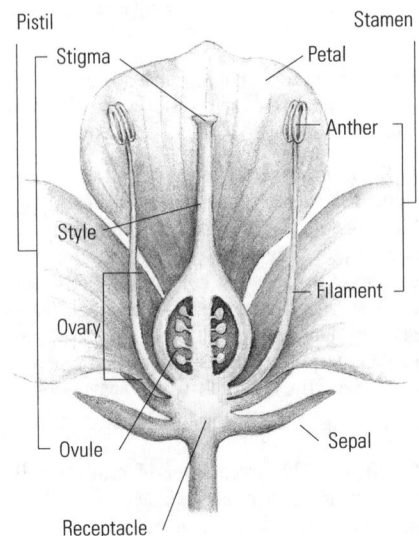

Pistil

Stamen

- Stigma
- Petal
- Anther
Style
- Filament
Ovary
- Sepal
- Ovule
Receptacle

petals, usually in two or three rows; and double, with multitudinous densely packed petals that typically produce a rounded blossom shape. See also Inflorescence.

Forcing. The process of hastening a plant to maturity or a marketable state, or of growing it to the flowering or fruiting stage out of its normal season. Forcing often occurs in a greenhouse, where temperature, light, and humidity can be controlled.

Foundation plant. This term originally described a plant used to hide the foundation of a house. Since many of today's homes lack high or even visible foundations, the term now suggests any shrub planted near house walls.

Frond. In the strictest sense, fronds are the foliage of ferns. Often, however, the word is applied to the leaves of palms or used to describe any foliage that looks fernlike.

Fruit. A general term used to describe the mature ovary of a plant, containing one to many seeds. Fruits may be soft and fleshy, as in the case of peaches or apples, or dry, like an acorn or dried pea pod.

Genus (plural: Genera). Plant families are subdivided into groups of more closely related plants known as genera. Some families contain only a single genus: for example, the family *Ginkgoaceae* includes only the genus *Ginkgo.* Others contain hundreds of genera; *Asteraceae* (the daisy family), for instance, comprises around 950 genera. The first word in a plant's botanical name is its genus—such as *Rosa,* which comprises all the roses, and *Hemerocallis,* which includes all the daylilies. The second word is the species (see also Species). Both genus and species are written in italics, with just the name of the genus capitalized—as in *Rosa moschata,* musk rose; and *Hemerocallis lilioasphodelus,* lemon daylily.

Girdling. The removal of bark all around a stem or branch, cutting off the flow of water and nutrients. Girdling often occurs when a woody plant has been tied tightly to a stake or support; as the plant grows, the tie constricts the stem. If girdling goes unnoticed, the part of the plant above the constriction will die. Carelessly used string trimmers can also girdle plants, as can damage from insects or gnawing rodents. Girdling is done deliberately in some cases;

a gardener may remove a narrow ring of bark to reduce overly vigorous growth or to kill an unwanted plant.

Growing season. In technical terms, "growing season" refers to the number of days between the average dates of the last killing frost in spring and the first killing frost in fall. The term is also used to describe the period of time a plant is actively growing and not dormant. For information on the growing season in each Southern climate zone, see pages 28–38.

Harden off. To adapt for the outdoors a plant that has been grown indoors or in a greenhouse or other shelter. Over a week or more, the plant is exposed to increasing periods of time outside, so that when it is planted in the garden it can make the transition with a minimum of shock.

Hardy. In horticultural terms, a plant's hardiness is its resistance to, or tolerance of, frosts or freezing temperatures. For example, a plant hardy to −20°F will survive undamaged to a temperature that low. The word does not mean tough, pest resistant, or disease resistant.

Herbaceous. The opposite of "woody," the word "herbaceous" describes a plant with soft or fleshy (nonwoody) tissue. In the strictest sense, the term refers to plants that die to the ground each year and regrow stems the following growing season. In common parlance, it refers to any nonwoody plant—annual, perennial, or bulb.

Humus. The soft brown or black substance formed in the last stages of decomposition of animal or vegetable matter. Common usage, however, incorrectly applies the term to almost all organic materials that will eventually decompose into humus—sawdust, ground bark, leaf mold, and animal manures, for example.

Hybrid. A distinct plant resulting from a cross between two species, subspecies, varieties, selections, strains, or any combination of the above; or, less commonly, between two plants from different genera. Hybrids sometimes occur in the wild, but more often they are produced by plant breeders. Hybrids are indicated with the symbol ×, as in *Erythrina × bidwillii*, a hybrid of *E. crista-galli* and *E. herbacea*.

Hydroponics. A method of gardening without soil. Nutrients are provided in a water-based solution; in some systems, an inert medium is used to anchor plant roots. One such medium is rockwool, a material made from fibers spun from molten mineral rock and formed into planting blocks.

Inflorescence. A group of individual flowers borne on a single stem. Inflorescences can take many forms. For example, a spike has flowers attached to the main stem without stalks, as in bottlebrush *(Callistemon)* or montbretia *(Crocosmia)*. In an umbel, all the individual flowers spring from approximately the same point, as in the blossoms of dill *(Anethum*

INFLORESCENCES

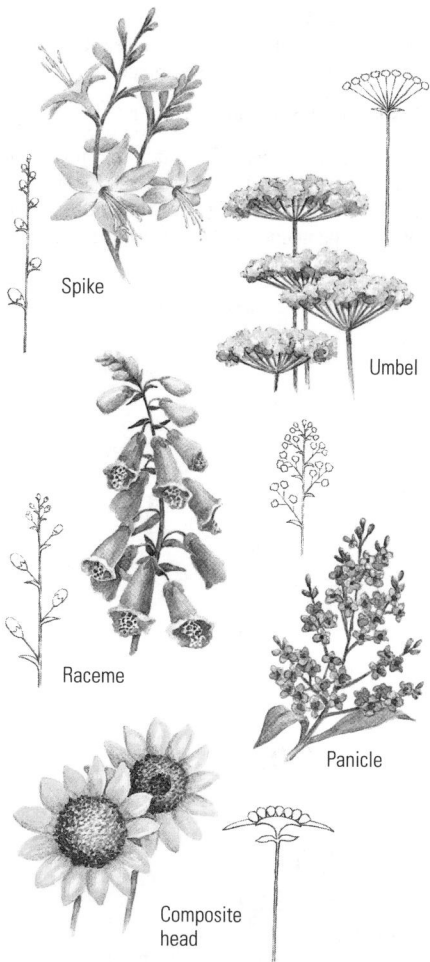

Spike

Umbel

Raceme

Panicle

Composite head

LEAF TYPES

Simple

Palmate

Pinnate

Bipinnate

graveolens). In a raceme, flowers are formed on stalks arising from the main stem, as in foxglove *(Digitalis)*. A panicle has groups of flowers borne on stalks (racemes) arising from the main stem; the flowers of lilac *(Syringa)* and privet *(Ligustrum)* are panicles. A composite head refers to small, closely packed, stalkless flowers of the sort found in the daisy family; these may include central disk flowers and outer ray flowers, as in sunflower *(Helianthus)*. See also Flower forms.

Internode. See Node.

Lath. Any overhead structure (originally a roof of spaced laths) that reduces the amount of sunlight reaching plants beneath its cover and protects them from frost.

Leader. The central upward-growing stem of a single-trunked tree or shrub.

Leaf. The main photosynthetic organ of most plants. A simple leaf is a single unit, while a compound leaf is divided into separate segments called leaflets. In a palmately compound leaf, the leaflets grow from one point at the end of a stem. In a pinnately compound (once-divided) leaf, the leaflets are arranged along a central axis; a bipinnately compound leaf is twice pinnate or twice-divided.

Leaflet. A division or segment of a compound leaf. See also Leaf.

Leaf mold. Partially decomposed leaves used as an organic amendment or in potting soil mixes.

Leaf scar. A rounded or crescent-shaped mark on a branch where a leafstalk was once attached.

Leaf scorch. Results from damage to or destruction of a leaf's tissues from sunlight, chemicals (in the soil or on the leaves), strong wind, or lack of water. Leaf scorch usually starts as brownish, dried-out tissue around the edges of the leaves. In bad cases, the whole leaf can dry out. Leaf scroch often occurs in Japanese maples *(Acer palmatum)* and flowering dogwood *(Cornus florida)*.

Limbing up. A form of pruning in which the lower limbs are removed to produce more headroom beneath a tree and to increase the amount of sunlight reaching the ground.

Lip. Irregular flowers (those in which the segments are not equal in size and arrangement) often show two divisions, an upper and a lower, each bearing one or more segments. Each division is known as a lip. Examples are honeysuckle *(Lonicera)* and snapdragon *(Antirrhinum majus)*.

Microclimate. The climate of a small area or locality (such as a backyard or even just a portion of it). Microclimates are determined by such factors as hills, hollows, and the location of houses and other structures. They influence which plants you choose for a particular area and how well they grow there. See "Frost and Cold Protection" (page 608).

Native plant. A plant that is indigenous to the region in which it is grown.

Naturalize. To set out plants or bulbs randomly, without a precise pattern, and leave them in place to spread at will, as they would in the wild (see "Naturalizing Bulbs," page 598). The term also refers to a plant's becoming established in an area to which it is not native. Queen Anne's Lace *(Daucus carota carota)*, for example, has naturalized in parts of the South.

Node. The joint in a stem where a bud, branch, or leaf starts to grow. The area of stem between nodes is the internode.

Offset. A young plant that develops by natural vegetative reproduction, usually at or near the base of the parent plant. Hen and chicks *(Echeveria)* and strawberry readily produce offsets. The word also refers to the increases of bulbs and corms.

Open-pollinated plants. Varieties or selections of plants produced from natural, random pollination. These are in contrast to hybrids, which are the result of deliberate crosses (controlled pollination).

Opposite leaves; alternate leaves. Leaves are opposite when they spring from the same node on a stem, but on opposite sides. Alternate leaves arise from different nodes on opposite sides of the stem.

Organic matter. Any material originating from a living organism—peat moss, ground bark, compost, or manure, for example—that can be dug into soil to improve its condition. See "Organic Soil Amendments" (page 646).

Ovary. See illustration for Flower; Fruit.

Overseeding. An operation—usually undertaken in fall or spring—in which grass seed is spread on an existing lawn, either to provide green color in winter or to thicken the turf.

Panicle. See Inflorescence.

Parasite. A plant that attaches itself to a host plant to obtain necessary nutrients and water. Mistletoe *(Phoradendron)* is a good example.

Peat moss. A highly water-retentive, spongy, organic soil amendment, peat moss is the partially decomposed remains of any of several mosses. It increases soil acidity. Sphagnum peat moss is generally considered the highest quality.

Perennial. A perennial is a nonwoody plant that lives for more than 2 years. For information on perennials, see page 615.

Petal. See illustration for Flower.

Pinching. A form of pruning in which the growing point of a stem is removed, usually to delay flowering and induce branching.

Pistil. See illustration for Flower.

Pleaching. A method of training plants in which branches are interwoven and plaited together to form a hedge or arbor. Subsequent pruning maintains a neat, rather formal pattern.

STEM NODES

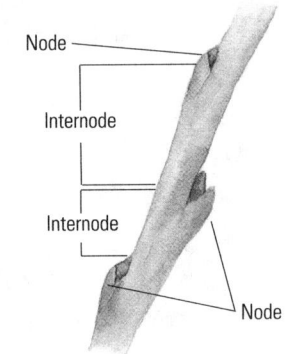

Node

Internode

Internode

Node

OPPOSITE/ALTERNATE LEAVES

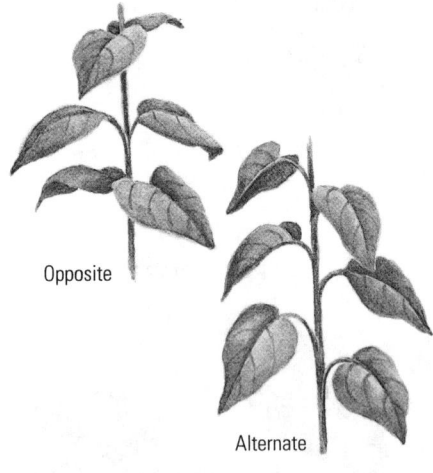

Opposite

Alternate

Pollenizer. A plant used to provide pollen for another plant. An example is an apple selection planted to provide pollen for a nearby selection that does not produce fertile pollen.

Pollination. The transfer of pollen from the male reproductive organs to the female ones, which leads to fertilization and seed production.

Pollinator. An insect or animal that transfers pollen from one part of a flower to another or from flowers on one plant to flowers on another.

Pseudobulb. A modified aboveground stem that serves as a storage organ; variable in size and shape. Some orchids have pseudobulbs; see *Orchidaceae* (page 437) in the Southern Plant Encyclopedia.

Raceme. See Inflorescence.

Rhizome. A modified stem growing horizontally under or at the soil surface. It may be long and slender, as in some perennials (and in perennial weeds like blackberry), or thick and fleshy, as in many irises. See "The Five Bulb Types"(page 598).

Root-bound. Plants suffer from this condition when they grow in the same container for too long. The roots become tangled and matted and grow in circles. See "Dealing with Root-bound Plants" (page 630).

Rootstock. The part of a budded or grafted plant that furnishes the root system and sometimes part of the branch structure. "Understock" is another word for rootstock. See "Budding and Grafting" (page 638).

Rosette. Leaves closely set around a crown or center, usually at or close to ground level. Hen and chicks *(Echeveria)* and dandelion *(Taraxacum officinale)* both grow in rosettes.

Runner. See Stolon.

Scion. A shoot or bud cut from one plant to be grafted or budded onto the rootstock of another. See "Budding and Grafting" (page 638).

Selection. A genetically distinct plant maintained in cultivation by human effort. It may be either a hybrid or a selected form of a plant found in the wild. Selections are propagated by divisions, cuttings, or (in some cases) seed. Selection names are enclosed in single quotes and are not italicized, as in *Lagerstroemia indica* 'Watermelon Red'. Gardeners often (incorrectly) use the terms "selection" and "variety" interchangeably.

Self-seed, self-sow. Refers to a plant shedding fertile seeds that produce seedlings, usually near the parent plant.

Semidouble flower. See Flower forms.

Sepal. See illustration for Flower.

Shrub. A woody plant, usually less than 10 feet tall, that branches close to the ground and has multiple stems.

Simple leaf. See Leaf.

Single flower. See Flower forms.

Species. Each genus is subdivided into groups of individuals called species. Each species is generally a distinct entity (though it may closely resemble other species in the genus), with each generation reproducing from seed with only a small amount of variation from the previous one. The second word in a plant's botanical name designates the species; the first word designates the genus. Both genus and species are italicized; the name of the species is not capitalized. For example, French marigold is, in botanical terms, *Tagetes patula*—genus *Tagetes*, species *patula*. See also Genus.

Specimen. A tree or shrub large or striking enough to make an immediate, significant impact in a planting. The term may also refer to a single large plant in a conspicuous location in the garden.

Sphagnum. Various mosses native to bogs. Much of the peat moss sold in the South is composed partly or entirely of decomposed sphagnum. These mosses are also collected live and packaged in whole pieces, fresh or dried. In this form, they are used for lining hanging baskets and for air layering (page 639).

Spike. See Inflorescence.

Spore. A simple type of reproductive cell that is capable of producing a new plant. Certain kinds of plants, including algae, fungi, mosses, and ferns, reproduce by spores.

Sport. A mutation, or spontaneous variation from the normal pattern. In horticulture, a sport is usually seen as a branch that differs noticeably from the rest of the plant. Examples include the spurred apple selections that occur as limb sports on standard apple selections, and camellias and azaleas propagated from branches that have shown changes in flower color or form.

Spur. This term has two meanings. Used in relation to grapevines and fruit trees (particularly apples and cherries), it refers to a specialized short twig that bears the plant's blossoms and, later, its fruit. Used to describe flowers, "spur" refers to short and saclike or long and tubular projections from a blossom's petals or sepals; most species of columbine *(Aquilegia),* for example, have flowers with pronounced spurs.

Stamen. See illustration for Flower.

Standard. A plant trained to resemble a small tree, with a single, upright trunk topped by a rounded crown of foliage. In some standards, the trunk and top are joined by grafting. The "tree rose" is a familiar example of a standard.

Stolon. A stem that creeps along the soil surface, taking root at intervals and forming new plants where it roots. Bermuda and St. Augustine grasses spread by stolons.

Strain. Many popular annuals and some perennials are sold as strains (sometimes referred to as series). Examples include State Fair zinnias, Super Elfin impatiens, and Pacific delphiniums. Plants in a strain generally share similar growth characteristics but are variable in some respect—usually in flower color.

Subshrub. This term can refer to a low-growing plant with woody stems—a small shrub. It also describes a plant, usually classified as a perennial, with a woody base but soft, herbaceous stems in its upper part.

Subspecies. A simple botanical name consists of two words in italics, denoting genus and species. When a third name in italics appears, it may denote a subspecies—a major division within a species, indicating geographical or other variations. An example is thornless honey locust *(Gleditsia triacanthos inermis).* (The name of the subspecies may be preceded by the abbreviation "ssp.") A third italicized name may also denote a variety (see Variety).

Sucker. In a grafted or budded plant, sucker growth originates from the rootstock rather than from the desired grafted or budded part of the plant. See also Water sprout.

Taproot. A thick central root that may penetrate deeply into the ground. In some plants, such as carrots and parsnips, taproots are storage organs.

Tender. The opposite of hardy. Tender plants cannot survive frost or freezing temperatures.

Tendrils. Specialized growths along the stems or at the ends of leaves on some vines. Tendrils

SUCKER VS. WATER SPROUT

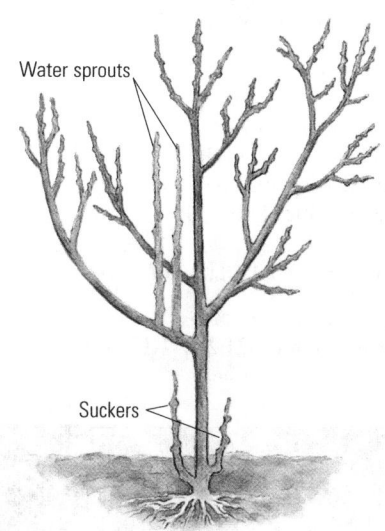

Water sprouts

Suckers

WHORL

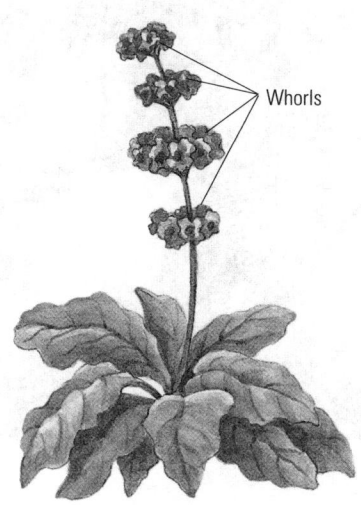

Whorls

wrap around supports, enabling the vine to climb. See "Vines" (page 656).

Thin. With regard to pruning, to thin is to remove entire branches, large or small, cutting back to the main trunk, a side branch, or the ground; see "Pruning" (page 640). Seedlings or developing fruits may also be thinned; in this case, the term refers to removing excess plants or fruits so that the remaining ones are spaced far enough apart to grow well.

Topiary. The technique of pruning and training shrubs and trees into formal shapes. Some topiary plants are shaped to resemble animals; others are trained to geometric forms such as cones, spheres, pyramids, and rectangles.

Tree. A woody plant that usually has one main stem and few branches close to the ground.

Tuber. A swollen underground stem with multiple growth points scattered over its surface. The potato is a familiar example. See "The Five Bulb Types" (page 598).

Tuberous root. A true root, thickened to store nutrients. Unlike tubers, tuberous roots carry their growth buds at the bases of old stems rather than on the roots themselves. See "The Five Bulb Types" (page 598).

Umbel. See Inflorescence.

Underplanting. Planting one plant beneath another, such as setting out a ground cover under a tree.

Understock. See Rootstock.

Variegation. Striping, edging, or other markings in a color different from the primary color of a leaf or petal.

Variety. Like a subspecies (see Subspecies), a botanical variety is a variant of the basic species as it occurs in nature. For example, it may be a type whose leaves are narrow rather than broad. Like a subspecies name, a botanical variety name is written in italics as the third word in a plant's botanical name; it may be preceded by the abbreviation "var." The word "variety" is also used frequently (but incorrectly) by gardeners to indicate a named selection. See also "Selection."

Vine. A plant of indeterminate growth that uses flexible stems to climb up a support. If a support is lacking, it scrambles along the ground.

Water sprout. In trees, any strong vertical shoot growing from the main framework of trunk and branches is properly called a water sprout, though the word "sucker" may also be used.

Whorl. Three or more leaves, branches, or flowers growing in a circle from a node on a stem or trunk.

Woody. This word describes a plant with hardened (woody) stems or trunks. A herbaceous plant, in contrast, has soft stems.

University of Arkansas, Cooperative Extension Service

Cooperative Extension Services

A re you looking for a local Master Gardener program, local weather and climate information, or classes for children? Do you have a baffling gardening problem? If so, check with university-linked horticultural specialists for help. Websites contain a wealth of information, and most Extension offices have a hotline or Master Gardener program you can call with specific questions. Phone numbers are subject to change, so check with your state Website for the most up-to-date contact information.

U. S. Department of Agriculture
www.reeusda.gov

ALABAMA

www.aces.edu
Baldwin (251) 937-7176
Bibb (205) 926-3117
Blount (205) 274-2129
Butler (334) 382-5111
Calhoun (256) 237-1621
Chilton (205) 280-6268
Colbert (256) 386-8570
DeKalb (256) 845-8595
Etowah (256) 547-7936
Hale (334) 624-8710
Houston (334) 794-4108
Jefferson (205) 325-5342
Lee (334) 749-3353
Limestone (256) 232-5510
Madison (256) 532-1578
Marion (205) 921-3551
Mobile (251) 690-8445
Montgomery (334) 265-0233
St. Clair (205) 338-9416
Shelby (205) 669-6763
Talladega (256) 362-6187
Tallapoosa (256) 825-1050
Tuscaloosa (205) 349-4630
Walker (205) 221-3392

ARKANSAS

www.uaex.edu
Benton (479) 271-1060
Cleburne (501) 362-2524
Craighead (870) 933-4565
Crittenden (870)739-3239
Faulkner (501) 329-8344
Grant (870) 942-2231
Hot Spring (501) 332-5267
Jefferson (870) 534-1033

Miller (870) 779-3609
Ouachita (870) 231-1160
Perry (501) 889-2661
Sebastian (479) 484-7737
Washington (479) 444-1755

DELAWARE

ag.udel.edu/extension
Kent (302) 730-4000
New Castle (302) 831-2667
Sussex (302) 856-7303

DISTRICT OF COLUMBIA

www.udc.edu/coes/ces/
Washington (202) 274-7115

FLORIDA

extension.ifas.ufl.edu/
Alachua (352) 955-2402
Brevard (321) 633-1702
Broward (954) 370-3725
Charlotte (941) 764-4340
Duval (904) 387-8850
Flagler (386) 437-7464
Hillsborough (813) 744-5519, ext 7
Jackson (850) 482-9620
Lake (352) 343-4101
Lee (239) 461-7501
Leon (850) 487-3003
Manatee (941) 721-6608
Marion (352) 620-3440
Miami-Dade (305) 248-3311

University of Arkansas, Cooperative Extension Service

Nassau (904) 879-1019
Okeechobee (803) 763-6469
Orange (407) 836-7570
Palm Beach (561) 233-1700
Pasco (352) 521-4288
Pinellas (727) 582-2100
Polk (863) 519-8677
Saint Johns (904) 824-4564
Santa Rosa Co, Milton (850) 623-3868
Santa Rosa Co, Jay (850) 675-3107
Sarasota (941) 861-9800
Seminole (407) 665-5551
Volusia (386) 257-6012

GEORGIA

www.ces.uga.edu
Bibb (478) 751-6338
Bleckley (478) 934-3220
Bulloch (912) 764-0370
Chatham (912) 652-7981
Chattooga (706) 857-0744
Clarke (706) 613-3640
Cobb (770) 528-2464
Coweta (770) 254-2620
Decatur (229) 248-3033
DeKalb (404) 298-4080
Dougherty (229) 436-7216
Douglas (770) 920-7224
Fayette (770) 460-5730, ext. 5412
Fulton (404) 730-7000
Glynn (912) 267-5655
Gwinnett (678) 377-4010
Habersham (706) 754-2318
Hall (770) 531-6988
Harris (706) 628-4824
Lowndes (229) 333-5185
Monroe (478) 994-7014
Montgomery (912) 583-2240
Muscogee (706) 653-4200
Pierce (912) 449-2034
Pike (770) 567-2010
Thomas (229) 225-4130
Tift (229) 391-7980
Walker (706) 638-2548

KENTUCKY

www.ca.uky.edu/ces
Boone (859) 586-6101
Bourbon (859) 987-1895
Boyle (859) 236-4484
Bullitt (502) 543-2257
Butler (270) 526-3767
Calloway (270) 753-1452
Christian (270) 886-6328
Daviess (270) 685-8480
Fayette (859) 257-5582
Franklin (502) 695-9035
Graves (270) 247-2334
Hardin (270) 765-4121

University of Georgia Cooperative Extension Service

Harlan (606) 573-4464
Jefferson (502) 425-4482
Jessamine (859) 885-4811
Madison (859) 623-4072
Simpson (270) 586-4484
Warren (270) 842-1681
Woodford (859) 873-4601

LOUSIANA

*www.lsuagcenter.com/nav/extension/
extension.asp*
Bossier (318) 965-2326
Caddo (318) 226-6805
DeSoto (318) 872-0533
East Baton Rouge (225) 389-3055
Lincoln (318) 251-5134
Morehouse (318) 281-5742
Natchitoches (318) 357-2224
Orleans (504) 278-7495
Ouachita (318) 323-2251
Plaquemines (504) 433-3664
Rapides (318) 473-6605
St. Charles (504) 783-6231
St. James (225) 562-2320
St. John (985) 497-3261
St. Landry (337) 948-0561
St. Martin (337) 332-2181
St. Mary (337) 828-4100, ext 300
St. Tammany (985) 875-2635
West Baton Rouge (225) 336-2416
Winn (318) 628-4528

MARYLAND

www.agnr.umd.edu/MCE
Allegany (301) 724-3320
Anne Arundel (410) 222-6755
Baltimore City (410) 396-1753
Calvert (301) 855-1150
Caroline (410) 479-4030
Carroll (410) 386-2760
Cecil (410) 996-5280
Charles (301) 934-5403
Dorchester (410) 228-8800
Frederick (301) 694-1594
Garrett (301) 334-6960
Harford (410) 638-3255
Howard (410) 313-2707
Kent (410) 778-1661
Montgomery (301) 590-9638
Prince George (301) 868-9366
Queen Anne's (410) 758-0166
St. Mary's (301) 475-4482
Somerset (410) 651-1350
Talbot (410) 822-1244
Washington (301) 791-1304
Wicomico (410) 749-6141
Worcester (410) 632-1972

MISSISSIPPI

msucares.com
Adams (601) 445-8201
Attala (662) 289-5431

4-H volunteers, Ag Extension, James Newburn, U. of Tennessee, Institute of Agriculture

Choctaw (662) 285-6337
DeSoto (662) 429-1343
Forrest (601) 545-6083
Harrison (228) 865-4227
Hinds (601) 372-4651
Holmes (662) 834-2795
Jackson (228) 769-3047
Lafayette (662) 234-4451
Lamar (601) 794-3910
Lauderdale (601) 482-9764
Lee (662) 841-9000
Leflore (662) 453-6803
Lowndes (662) 328-2111
Oktibbeha (662) 323-5916
Pike (601) 783-5321
Rankin (601) 825-1462
Tallahatchie (662) 647-8746
Tate (662) 562-4274
Warren (601) 636-5391
Washington (662) 334-2670
Yazoo (662) 746-2453

MISSOURI

www.outreach.missouri.edu
Boone (573) 445-9792
Butler (573) 686-8064
Cape Girardeau (573) 243-3581
Clay (816) 792-7760
Clinton (816) 539-3765
Cole (573) 634-2824
Greene (417) 862-8284
Jackson Co, Independence (816) 252-5051
Jackson Co, Kansas City (816) 482-5850
Jefferson (636) 797-5391
Newton (417) 455-9500
St. Charles (636) 970-3000
St. Louis (314) 615-2911

NORTH CAROLINA

www.ces.ncsu.edu
Alamance (336) 570-6740
Alleghany (336) 372-5597
Ashe (336) 219-2650
Brunswick (910) 253-2610
Buncombe (828) 255-5522
Carteret (252) 222-6352
Catawba (828) 465-8240
Columbus (910) 640-6605
Cumberland (910) 321-6860
Davidson (336) 242-2080
Durham (919) 560-0525
Edgecombe (252) 641-7815
Forsyth (336) 767-8213
Gaston (704) 922-2130
Guilford (336) 375-5876
Henderson (828) 697-4891
Lenoir (252) 527-2191
Mecklenburg (704) 336-2561
Moore (910) 947-3188
Onslow (910) 455-5873
Orange (919) 245-2050
Pamlico (252) 745-4121
Pasquotank (252) 338-3954
Pitt (252) 757-2801
Randolph (336) 318-6000
Transylvania (828) 884-3109
Wake (919) 250-1100
Wayne (919) 731-1520

OKLAHOMA

www1.dasnr.okstate.edu/oces
Canadian (405) 262-0155
Choctaw (580) 326-3359
Cleveland (405) 321-4774

Comanche (580) 355-1176
Creek (918) 224-2192
Garfield (580) 237-1228
Kay (580) 362-3194
McClain (405) 527-2174
Muskogee (918) 687-2458
Oklahoma (405) 713-1125
Oklahoma Panhandle (580) 349-5440
Okmulgee (918) 756-1958
Osage (918) 287-4170
Payne (405) 747-8320
Rogers (918) 341-2736
Sequoyah (918) 775-4838
Tulsa (918) 746-3700
Wagoner (918) 486-4589
Washington (918) 534-2216

SOUTH CAROLINA

www.clemson.edu/extension
Aiken (803) 649-6297
Anderson (864) 226-1581
Beaufort (843) 470-3655
Charleston (843) 722-5940
Cherokee (864) 489-3141
Florence (843) 661-4800
Georgetown (843) 546-6421
Greenville (864) 232-4431
Greenwood (864) 942-8590
Kershaw (803) 432-9071
Lexington (803) 359-8515
Marion (843) 423-8285
Marlboro (843) 479-6851
Oconee (864) 638-5889
Orangeburg (803) 534-6280
Pickens (864) 878-1394
Richland (803) 929-6030
Spartanburg (864) 596-2993
Sumter (803) 773-5561
Williamsburg (843) 355-6106
York (803) 684-9919

TENNESSEE

www.tnstate.edu/cep/
Anderson (865) 457-6246
Bradley (423) 476-4552
Campbell (423) 562-9474
Coffee (931) 723-5141
Davidson (615) 862-5995
Fayette (901) 465-5233
Fentress (931) 879-9117
Franklin (931) 967-2741
Henry (731) 642-2941
Lawrence (931) 762-5506
Madison (731) 668-8543
Maury (931) 388-9557
Montgomery (931) 648-5725
Obion (731) 885-3742
Putnam (931) 526-4561
Rhea (423) 775-7807
Roane (865) 376-5558

Rutherford (615) 898-7710
Sequatchie (423) 949-2611
Sevier (865) 453-3695
Shelby (901) 544-0243
Warren (931) 473-8484
Washington (423) 753-1680
Williamson (615) 790-5721

TEXAS

agextension.tamu.edu
Austin (979) 865-5911
Bastrop (512) 332-7286
Bell (254) 933-5306
Bexar (210) 467-6575
Brazoria (979) 864-1558
Brazos (979) 823-0129
Cameron (956) 361-8236
Chambers (409) 267-8347
Comal (830) 620-3440
Comanche (915) 356-2539
Dallas (214) 904-3050
Denton (940) 434-8812
El Paso (915) 859-7723
Galveston (281) 534-3413
Harris (281) 855-5600
Harrison (903) 935-8413
Houston (936) 544-3255
Jones (915) 823-4242
Lubbock (806) 767-1190
McLennan (254) 757-5180
McMullen (361) 274-3323
Midland (915) 686-4700
Milam (254) 697-7045
Nacogdoches (936) 560-7711

Nueces (361) 767-5223
Parker (817) 599-6591
Potter (806) 373-0713
San Patricio (361) 364-6234
Smith (903) 535-0885
Tarrant (817) 884-1553
Taylor (915) 672-6048
Tom Green (915) 659-6528
Travis (512) 854-9600
Tyler (409) 283-8284
Upshur (903) 843-4019
Val Verde (830) 774-7591
Victoria (361) 575-4581
Wichita (940) 716-5580

VIRGINIA

www.ext.vt.edu
Albemarle (434) 984-0727
Alexandria (703) 519-3325
Alleghany (540) 862-0369
Appomattox (434) 352-8244
Arlington (703) 228-6400
Chesapeake (757) 382-6348
Chesterfield (804) 751-4401
Culpeper (540) 727-3435
Essex (804) 443-3551
Fairfax (703) 324-5369
Fauquier (540) 341-7950
Frederick (540) 665-5699
Giles (540) 921-3455
Gloucester (804) 693-2602
Hanover (804) 752-4310
Henrico (804) 501-5160
Henry Co/Martinsville (276) 634-4650

Lynchburg (434) 847-1585
Madison (540) 948-6881
Middlesex (804) 758-4120
Newport News (757) 591-4838
Norfolk (757) 683-2816
Northampton (757) 414-0731
Northumberland (804) 580-5694
Orange (540) 672-1361
Portsmouth (757) 393-5197
Prince William (703) 792-6289
Richmond (804) 333-3420
Richmond City (804) 786-4150
Roanoke (540) 772-7524
Shenandoah (540) 459-6140
Virginia Beach (757) 427-4769
Warren (540) 635-4549

WEST VIRGINIA

www.wvu.edu/~exten
Berkeley (304) 264-1936
Cabell (304) 743-7151
Calhoun (304) 354-6332
Clay (304) 587-4267
Greenbrier (304) 647-7408
Harrison (304) 624-8650
Jackson (304) 372-8199
Jefferson (304) 728-7413
Kanawha (304) 768-1202
Monroe (304) 722-3003
Morgan (304) 258-8400
Ohio (304) 234-3673
Preston (304) 329-1391
Putnam (304) 586-0217
Raleigh (304) 255-9321

University of Tennessee, Institute of Agriculture/volunteers

Solving the Mystery of
Botanical Names

Although Southerners feel comfortable with common names, botanical names are often intimidating. So why do we need botanical names at all? For a very good reason—common names for plants vary from region to region and even from town to town. One plant may live under several common names. Or a single common name may refer to several plants that don't look anything alike.

Are Common Names Precise?

A common name may refer to several different plants. A good example of this is the plant commonly known as "dusty miller." This name actually applies to four similar plants that have silvery foliage—*Senecio viravira, Senecio cineraria, Centaurea cineraria,* and *Artemisia stellerana.* Only the first of these plants is frequently sold at garden centers.

Rudbeckia hirta

And some plants that share a common name aren't the least bit similar. "Black-eyed Susan" applies to a golden-flowered perennial *(Rudbeckia hirta),* as well as to a vine that is usually planted and grown as a summer annual *(Thunbergia alata).* "Texas sage" is a shrub with silvery leaves and purple flowers *(Leucophyllum frutescens)* and also a perennial with purple-blue flowers *(Salvia texana).*

Thunbergia alata

Having multiple common names for the same plant also causes confusion. For instance, if you call a shrub with brilliant-red autumn foliage "burning bush" and someone else knows it as "winged euonymus," you may not realize that you're both talking about the same plant—in this case, *Euonymus alata.*

So there are practical reasons for using botanical names. They provide the most accurate means we have for identifying a plant. And they're still the best way to ensure that the plants you buy are ones you really want.

Keep an Eye Out for Clues

Botanical names, once you break them down, reveal important clues to the natures of plants. The first word of a botanical name is the genus, which tells you the group of plants to which this one belongs. The second word is the species name, which is usually descriptive and easy to decipher once you know how to look for clues.

Descriptive words used often in species names are listed at right. When you know the meanings of these words, many plant names become easy to understand and can help you identify plants. For example, the species name for twinleaf *(Jeffersonia diphylla)* combines *di* (double or two) with *phylla* (leaves) to mean "two leaves."

The easiest botanical names to remember are those directly translated into common names. For instance, bigleaf magnolia *(Magnolia macrophylla)* does have huge leaves. And *macro* means large, *phylla* means leaves.

Some botanical names are so much like English words that they offer immediate clues to that plant's appearance. We can easily gather the meaning of words like *compacta, contorta, canadensis, deliciosa, fragrans,* and *micro*.

A GUIDE TO BOTANICAL NAMES

Color of Flowers or Foliage

alba—white

argentea—silvery

aurantiaca—orange

aurea—golden

azurea—azure, sky blue

caerulea—dark blue

caesia—blue-gray

candida—pure white, shiny

cana—ashy gray, hoary

cereus—waxy

citrina—yellow

coccinea—scarlet

concolor—one color

cruenta—bloody

discolor—two colors, separate colors

glauca—blue-gray, blue-green

incana—gray, hoary

lutea—yellow

pallida—pale

purpurea—purple

ruber, rubra—red, ruddy

rufa—ruddy

viridis, virens—green

Form of Leaf (*folia*—leaves or foliage)

acerifolia—maplelike

angustifolia—narrow

aquifolia—spiny

buxifolia—boxwoodlike

ilicifolia—hollylike

laurifolia—laurel-like

parvifolia—small

populifolia—poplarlike

salicifolia—willowlike

Lavandula angustifolia 'Hidcote'

Shape of Plant

adpressa—pressing against, hugging

alta—tall

arborea—treelike

capitata—headlike

compacta—compact, dense

conferta—crowded, pressed together

contorta—twisted

decumbens—lying down

depressa—pressed down

elegans—elegant, slender, willowy

fastigiata—branches erect and close together

humifusa—sprawling on the ground

humilis—low, small, humble

impressa—impressed upon

nana—dwarf

procumbens—trailing

prostrata—prostrate

pumila—dwarf, small

pusilla—puny, insignificant

repens—creeping

reptans—creeping

scandens—climbing

Where It Came From

A number of suffixes are added to place names to specify the habitat where the plant was discovered or the place where it is usually found.

africana—of Africa

alpina—from the mountains

australis—southern

borealis—northern

campestris—of the field or plains

canadensis—of Canada

canariensis—of the Canary Islands

capensis—of the Cape of Good Hope area

caroliniana—of the Carolinas

chinensis—of China

hispanica—of Spain

hortensis—of gardens

indica—of India

insularis—of the island

japonica—of Japan

montana—of the mountains

riparia—of riverbanks

Calocedrus decurrens

saxatilis—inhabiting rocks

texana—of Texas

virginiana—of Virginia

Plant Parts

dendron—tree

flora, florum, flori, florus—flowers

phyllus, phylla—leaf or leaves

Cestrum elegans

Zephyranthes grandiflora

Elaeagnus pungens

Ligustrum japonicum

Passiflora caerulea

Rosa rugosa

Plant Peculiarities

armata—armed

baccata—berried, berrylike

barbata—barbed or bearded

campanulata—bell or cup shaped

ciliaris—fringed

cordata—heart shaped

cornuta—horned

crassa—thick, fleshy

decurrens—running down the stem

densi—dense

diversi—varying

edulis—edible

florida—free flowering

Hydrangea macrophylla

fruticosa—shrubby

fulgens—shiny

gracilis—slender, thin, small

grandi—large, showy

-ifer, -ifera—bearing or having; e.g., *stoloniferus,* having stolons

imperialis—showy

laciniata—fringed or with torn edges

laevigata—smooth

lobata—lobed

longa—long

macro—large

maculata—spotted

micro—small

mollis—soft, soft-haired

mucronata—pointed

nutans—nodding, swaying

obtusa—blunt or flattened

officinalis—medicinal

-oides—like or resembling; e.g., *jasminoides,* like a jasmine

patens—open, spreading growth

pinnata—constructed like a feather

platy—broad

plena—double, full

plumosa—feathery

praecox—precocious, early

pungens—piercing

radicans—rooting, especially along the stem

reticulata—net-veined

retusa—notched at blunt apex

rugosa—wrinkled, rough

saccharata—sweet, sugary

sagittalis—arrowlike

scabra—rough feeling

scoparia—broomlike

Gardenia jasminoides

Index
Gardening Terms and Topics

Index
Scientific and Common Names

Italic page numbers indicate pictures. **Bold** page numbers refer to the plant's encyclopedia entry. Common names of ornamentals are followed by the scientific name, which can be used to find more page references to the plant.

Acknowledgments

Our thanks to the following for their contributions to this book:

Carl Campbell, Tropical Fruits; Brent Heath, Bulbs; Joe Kemble, Vegetables; Brent Pemberton, Roses; and Arlie Powell, Fruits. We would also like to thank H. Marc Cathey and Arabella S. Dane for providing the American Horticultural Society Heat Zone ratings.

Our thanks also to Parker Andes, Director of Horticulture, Biltmore Gardens; Robert E. Bowdon, Executive Director, Harry P.,Leu Gardens; Carrie Dodson; William A. Dozier, Department of Horticulture, Auburn University; David G. Himelrick, Department of horticulture, Louisiana State University; Michael Janis, University of South Carolina; Danielle Javier; W. Terry Kelley, University of Georgia Cooperative Extension Service; Ed Laivo, Dave Wilson Nursery; Ron Ludekens, L. E. Cooke Co.; Jim McCausland; Audrey Mak; Sharon Omahen, University of Georgia Cooperative Extension Service; Buffy Summer, University of South Carolina; Mike Tomlinson, Dave Wilson Nursery; and Douglas F. Welsh, Texas Cooperative Extension.

A special thanks to those consultants who contributed to the development of previous editions of the Southern Living Garden Book. Much of their work lives on in this edition.

Photography Credits

Photographs are listed sequentially either in horizontal or vertical order. For additional clarification, the following position indicators may be used: Left (L), Center (C), Right (R); Top (T), Middle (M), Bottom (B).

William D. Adams: 331 4; 482 5; 483 2; 500 5. **William H. Allen, Jr.:** 244 T1. **Curtis Anderson:** 171; 175 BC; 175 BR. **Scott Atkinson:** 101 L2; 646 T. **Max Badgley:** 613 L3; 613 L7; 618 T4. **BIOS (W. Lapinski)/Peter Arnold, Inc.:** 63 R3. **Noel Barnhurst:** 89 L3. **Paul Black:** 363 1. **Marion Brenner:** 42 R3; 49 R4; 52 R4; 61 L3; 65 R2; 67 L5; 71 L5; 72 R4; 73 L4, R5; 85 L2; 99 L5; 104 L1; 109 L3; 110 R4; 112 R4; 113 R4; 115 L1; 125 R5; 128 L2, R2; 134 L3; 139 R1, R2; 140 L3; 141 L4, R3; 699 LC1, RC2. **Kathleen Norris Brenzel:** 90 L4. **Ralph S. Byther:** 603 C. **James Carrier:** 70 R1; 71 R4; 101 R2. **David Cavagnaro:** 34 BL, BC; 38 BC; 45 R6; 48 L2; 59 R1; 64 L1; 80 L3, R1; 87 L5, R1; 88 L6; 89 R1; 90 L1; 91 L1; 100 L1; 105 L2; 107 R1; 117 R1; 125 R1; 144 R4; 200; 331 1; 362 3; 391; 392 T5, B2; 476 3; 523 5; 553; 563 B6; 574 T, B2, B3; 628; 653; 699 RC3; 719. **Van Chaplin/Sylvia Martin/Mary-Gray Hunter:** 144 R3. **Van Chaplin/Mary-Gray Hunter:** 92 L3. **Peter Christiansen:** 175 TR; 597 BR; 613 TR. **Gary Clark:** 43 L2; 109 R5; 120 L3. **Philip Clayton-Thompson:** 58 R2. **Albert Cohen:** 484 BL. **Richard Cowles:** 613 L8; 665 B3. **Crandall & Crandall:** 102 L5; 114 L1; 124 L2; 132 L4; 248; 405 2; 452 3; 482 6; 483 6; 613 L5, L6; 617 T. **Rosalind Creasy:** 89 R4; 655 R1. **Claire Curran:** 40 L4; 48 R2; 49 R3; 51 R3; 53 L3; 54 L3; 56 L2, L4; 57 L1, R2; 60 L6, R5; 63 L4; 64 L2; 67 R5; 78 R5; 79 L5, R4; 83 R3; 91 R2; 94 L5; 98 R2; 99 L4; 101 R3; 104 L2, L6, R1; 105 R1; 106 L1, R3, R4; 109 L4; 110 L4; 123 R4; 130 L4, L5; 131 L1, R3; 132 R1; 133 L1, L2; 134 L1; 143 L3; 392 T3; 520 3; 615 B; 698 TL, BL; 699 LC3, RC1. **Robin B. Cushman:** 53 R1; 57 R4; 68 R5; 91 L5; 94 L4. R. **Todd Davis:** 58 L3; 69 L3, L4; 72 R1; 109 R2; 135 L2, L5; 349 2; 509 1. **Alex Demyan:** 37 BL, MR. **Arnaud Descat/M.A.P.:** 101 R1; 116 R4; 125 L4. **Alan & Linda Detrick:** 42 L3; 45 R2, R3; 47 L1; 63 L2; 66 L1; 70 L2; 77 R4; 81 L5; 84 L3; 85 R5; 92 R4; 93 L4, R1, R4, R5; 94 L1, L2, R1, R2, R4, R6; 95 L1, L2, R4, R6; 98 L3; 116 L4, L5; 119 R1; 120 R1; 121 L2; 122 L4, L5, R1; 123 L3; 124 L1, R4; 127 R1, R4; 128 L1; 131 L3; 133 R5; 136 R3; 139 L2; 140 R3; 141 L1, L2, L3; 257 2; 574 B5. **William B. Dewey:** 39; 40 R2; 45 L3; 51 L4; 97 R3; 99 R2; 107 L1; 532 3. **William Dickey:** 28. **Frédéric Didillon/M.A.P.:** 114 R1. **Ken Druse:** 58 R1. **Colleen Duffley:** 175 MR.

Philip Edinger: 362 4. **Clyde Elmore:** 665 C3, B2. **Thomas E. Eltzroth:** 89 L1; 90 R5; 331 3; 558 2; 604 UM, B. **Craig Engle:** 108 R2. **Tina Evans:** 50 L5; 52 L4; 59 R3; 74 R2; 91 R5; 99 R3; 118 R1; 137 R3; 139 L1. **Derek Fell:** 29 TM; 60 R1, R3; 63 L1, R4; 70 R4; 83 R6; 84 L5; 86 L3; 95 R5; 96 L5; 101 R5; 102 L4; 104 L4; 106 R5; 108 R5; 109 R3; 112 L1; 114 L3; 118 R4; 132 L3; 135 L4; 137 L3; 138 R3; 175 BL; 176; 193 TR, BR; 196; 204; 213; 225; 243; 249 T2, T5, B2; 261; 263 2, 4; 283; 294; 342; 348; 349 4; 370; 380 1; 381 3; 392 T1, B4; 407 5; 452 2; 455; 465; 474; 476 5; 477 4, 6; 482 2; 501 5; 511 3; 521 1; 523 3; 558 1, 3, 5, 6; 574 B1, B4; 580 T3; 663; 683 B; 687. **William E. Ferguson:** 625 T. **Roger Foley:** 29 TL; 34 T; 35 TL; 38 TR; 676 B. **Gardener's Supply Company:** 637. **Debbie Gartzke:** 688. **Adam Gibbs:** 42 R1. **Fiona Gilsenan:** 60 R4; 125 L1; 127 L2; 453 2. **Nicholas Gitts/Swan Island Dahlias:** 277 T4, M1. **John Glover/The Garden Picture Library:** 482 1; 580 B1. **David Goldberg:** 42 L1; 49 R1, R5; 85 L3; 93 R2; 101 L3; 102 R5; 103 R1; 138 L1; 142 L1; 362 1; 666 LC; 668 CL. **Harold E. Greer:** 105 R2; 453 3; 508 1, 2, 3; 509 2, 5; 510 2; 563 B5. **Todd Gustafson/Natural Selection:** 625 C. **Paul Hammond:** 107 L3. **Jessie M. Harris:** 68 L1. **Lynne Harrison:** 129 L2; 365 2; 510 1; 522 3; 580 B5. **Philip Harvey:** 645. **Walter H. Hodge/Peter Arnold, Inc.:** 97 R2. **Neil Holmes/The Garden Picture Library:** 481. **Gary Holscher/AG Stock USA, Inc.:** 330 2. **Gary Holscher Photography:** 453 4. **Saxon Holt:** 38 BL; 41 L3; 46 L2; 50 L4, R3; 51 R2; 55 R1; 62 R2; 68 R3; 70 L3; 72 L1, L5; 76 R2; 77 L4; 86 R2; 90 L5; 93 L3; 100 L2, R3, R5; 103 L3; 113 L1; 123 L5; 126 L4; 130 L2, R3; 131 R4; 133 R3; 135 R2; 139 R5; 142 L5, R5; 220; 244 T2, T4, B2, B3; 249 B5; 371 4; 459 2; 500 4; 522 2; 523 1; 532 4; 607 **BL. Horticultural Photography:** 483 4. **Mary-Gray Hunter:** 27 BCL; 41 R3; 45 R1; 48 L1; 51 L5; 53 R2, R4; 54 R2; 61 L2; 80 R4; 82 R2; 84 L1, L2; 85 R4; 86 R4; 87 L4; 88 L4; 98 R4; 114 R4; 121 R2; 126 L5; 132 R2; 143 R5; 144 L1, R2; 604 T; 615 T; 665 B1. **Dan Isakeit:** 605 C. **Emily Jenkins:** 328. **Dency Kane:** 29 BL, TR; 36 M; 68 R6; 121 L3; 244 B5; 263 6; 364 2; 412; 427 M5, B1, B5; 443; 459 5; 580 B2. **Ted King/King's Mums:** 244 B4. **Dwight Kuhn:** 602 T. **Mayer/LeScanff/The Garden Picture Library:** 501 1. Kirsten **Leitner/Friends of the Urban Forest:** 652. **A.M. Leonard:** 649 BR. **George Lepp/AG Stock USA, Inc.:** 483 5. **Janet Loughrey:** 64 R1; 70 R3; 96 R1; 125 L2; 206 B4. **Raymond R. Maleike:** 607 T. **Allan Mandell:** 104 R4; 134 R3; 483 1. **Charles Mann:** 45 R5; 51 L2; 57 R3; 62 L5; 64 R3, R5; 68 R4; 70 L4; 71 L2; 73 R3; 74 L2; 75 L1, L3; 85 R2; 111 L4, R2,

Illustration Credits
A Practical Guide to Gardening; Glossary